HANDBOOK OF AUTISM AND
PERVASIVE DEVELOPMENTAL DISORDERS

Handbook of Autism and Pervasive Developmental Disorders

Second Edition

Edited by
Donald J. Cohen, M.D.
Fred R. Volkmar, M.D.

JOHN WILEY & SONS, INC.

New York • Chichester • Weinheim • Brisbane • Singapore • Toronto

Copyright © 1997 by John Wiley & Sons, Inc.

Library of Congress Cataloging-in-Publication Data:

Handbook of autism and pervasive developmental disorders / edited by
    Donald J. Cohen, Fred R. Volkmar. — 2nd ed.
       p.   cm.
    Includes bibliographical references and index.
    ISBN 0-471-53242-8 (cloth : alk. paper)
    1. Autism in children. 2. Developmental disabilities.
  3. Autistic children—Services for. 4. Developmentally disabled
children—Services for. I. Cohen, Donald J. II. Volkmar, Fred R.
    [DNLM: 1. Autism. 2. Child Development Disorders, Pervasive. WM
203.5 H236 1997]
RJ506.A9H26   1997
618.92'89—dc20
DNLM/DLC
for Library of Congress   96-34955

To
Lucy, Emily, and Lisa
and
Matthew, Rebecca, Rachel, Joseph, Allan, Andres, Aviva, Max, and Phyllis

Contributors

DR. MIGUEL CHERRO AGUERRE
Centro Pediatrico
Montevideo, Uruguay

GEORGE M. ANDERSON
Child Study Center and the Department of
    Laboratory Medicine
Yale University
New Haven, Connecticut

SHOSHANA ARBELLE, M.D.
Department of Psychiatry
Ben Gurion University Medical School
Beer-Sheva, Israel

ANTHONY BAILEY
MRC Psychiatry Unit
Institute of Psychiatry
London, England

SIMON BARON-COHEN, PH.D.
Departments of Experimental Psychology
    and Psychiatry
University of Cambridge
Cambridge, England

MARGARET L. BAUMAN, M.D.
Harvard Medical School
Massachusetts Hospital
Boston, Massachusetts

MIRIAM BERKMAN, J.D. M.S.W.
Yale Child Study Center
New Haven, Connecticut

PAOLA BERNABEI, M.D.
Departimento di Neurologische e Psychiatrische
dell'eta Evolutina
Via de Sabelli 108
Rome, Italy

JOEL BREGMAN, M.D.
Department of Psychiatry
University of Connecticut
Storrs, Connecticut

AVRIL V. BRERETON
Monash University
Monash Medical Centre
Clayton, Australia

SUSAN E. BRYSON, PH.D.
Department of Psychology
York University
North York, Ontario

JACOB BURACK, PH.D.
Department of Educational Psychology
McGill University
Montreal, Quebec
and
Department of Psychology
Hebrew University
Jerusalem, Israel

ALICE CARTER, PH.D.
Department of Psychology
Yale University
New Haven, Connecticut

SOO CHURL CHO, M.D.
Division of Child & Adolescent Psychiatry
Seoul National University Hospital
Seoul, South Korea

DONALD J. COHEN, M.D.
Yale Child Study Center
New Haven, Connecticut

CHERYL DISSANAYAKE, PH.D.
School of Psychology LaTrobe University
Bundoora, Victoria, Australia

ELISABETH M. DYKENS, PH.D.
University of California, Los Angeles
Neuropsychiatric Institute
Los Angeles, California

JAMES T. ENNS, PH.D.
Department of Psychology
The University of British Columbia
Vancouver, British Columbia

DEBORAH FEIN, PH.D.
Psychology Department
University of Connecticut
Storrs, Connecticut

PROFESSEUR PIERRE FERRARI
Centre Hospitalier Public de Psychiatre de
    l'Enfant et de l'Adolescent
Gentilly, France

JOAQUIN FUENTES, M.D.
Gautena
San Sebastian, Spain

JOHN GERDTZ, PH.D.
Spectrum Center
Berkley, California

PETER F. GERHARDT, A.B.D.
Eden W.E.R.C.S.
Princeton, New Jersey

TEMPLE GRANDIN, PH.D.
Department of Animal Sciences
Colorado State University
Fort Collins, Colorado

GERALD GRODEN, PH.D.
The Groden Center, Inc.
Providence, Rhode Island
and
Psychology Department
University of Rhode Island

JUNE GRODEN, PH.D.
Groden Center for Autism
Providence, Rhode Island

JAMES GROSSMAN
Department of Psychology
Yale University
New Haven, Connecticut

SARA HANDLAN, PH.D.
Chapel Hill TEACCH Center
The University of North Carolina at
    Chapel Hill
Chapel Hill, North Carolina

JAN S. HANDLEMAN, ED.D.
Douglass Developmental Disabilities Center
Rutgers University
New Brunswick, New Jersey

SANDRA L. HARRIS, PH.D.
Graduate School of Applied and Professional
    Psychology
Rutgers University
Piscataway, New Jersey

DAVID L. HOLMES, ED.D.
Eden Family of Services
Princeton, New Jersey

YOSHIHIKO HOSHINO, M.D.
Department of Neuropsychiatry
Fukushima Medical College
Fukushima City, Japan

AMI KLIN, PH.D.
Yale Child Study Center
New Haven, Connecticut

JASON B. KONIDARIS, B.A.
Norwalk, Connecticut

LINDA J. KUNCE, PH.D.
Illinois Wesleyan University
Bloomington, Illinois

ANN COBB LA CAMERA, BSN
Department of Human Resources
Yale-New Haven Hospital
New Haven, Connecticut

ROBERT G. LA CAMERA, M.D.
Yale School of Medicine
New Haven, Connecticut

JUDITH M. LeBLANC, PH.D.
Life Span Institute
Department of Human Development
University of Kansas
Lawrence, Kansas

PROFESSOR GABRIEL LEVI, M.D.
Departimento di Neurologische e Psichiatrische
dell'eta Evolutina
Via de Sabelli 108
Rome, Italy

CATHERINE LORD, PH.D.
Department of Psychiatry
University of Chicago
Chicago, Illinois

KATHERINE A. LOVELAND, PH.D.
Center for Human Development Research
Department of Psychiatry & Behavioral
    Sciences
University of Texas Medical School, Houston
University of Texas Health Science Center
    at Houston
Houston, Texas

WENDY MARANS, M.A.
Yale Child Study Center
New Haven, Connecticut

LEE M. MARCUS, PH.D.
Division TEACCH
The University of North Carolina at
    Chapel Hill
Chapel Hill, North Carolina

LILIANA MAYO, PH.D.
Department of Human Development
University of Kansas
Lawrence, Kansas

CHRISTOPHER J. McDOUGLE, M.D.
Yale Child Study Center
New Haven, Connecticut

GARY B. MESIBOV, PH.D.
Chapel Hill TEACCH Center
The University of North Carolina at
    Chapel Hill
Chapel Hill, North Carolina

RICHARD MILLS
The National Autistic Society
Filton, England

NANCY J. MINSHEW, M.D.
University of Pittsburgh
Western Psychiatric Institute and Clinic
Pittsburgh, Pennsylvania

TAMAR MOSES, M.D.
The Gehah Psychiatric Hospital
Tel Aviv, Israel

LAURENT MOTTRON, PH.D.
Département de Psychiatrie
Université de Montréal
Montreal, Quebec

SHIN-CHI NIWA, M.D.
Department of Neuropsychiatry
Fukushima Medical College
Fukushima City, Japan

J. GREGORY OLLEY, PH.D.
Clinical Center for the Study of Development
    and Learning
Development of Medical Allied Health
    Professions
The University of North Carolina at
    Chapel Hill
Chapel Hill, North Carolina

SALLY OZONOFF, PH.D.
Department of Psychology
The University of Utah
Salt Lake City, Utah

RHEA PAUL, PH.D.
Portland State University
Portland, Oregon

ANDREW PICKLES
MRC Psychiatry Unit
Institute of Psychiatry
London, England

MICHAEL D. POWERS, PSY.D.
Center for Children with Special Needs
Tolland, Connecticut

BARRY M. PRIZANT, PH.D.
Division of Communication Disorders
Emerson College
Boston, Massachusetts

BETH RANDOLPH
Department of Educational Psychology
McGill University
Montreal, Quebec

ISABELLE RAPIN, M.D.
Albert Einstein College of Medicine
Bronx, New York

CHRISTINE E. REEVE, PH.D.
Murdoch Center
Butner, North Carolina

NANCY C. REICHLE, PH.D.
Division TEACCH
The University of North Carolina at
    Chapel Hill
Chapel Hill, North Carolina

RHODA ROOT, PH.D.
West Island Readaptation Center
Pointe-Claire, Quebec

ELLEN RUSKIN, PH.D.
Department of Psychiatry
UCLA School of Medicine
Los Angeles, California

MICHAEL RUTTER, C.B.E., M.D., F.R.C.P.,
    F.R.C.PSYCH, F.R.S.
MRC Psychiatry Unit
Institute of Psychiatry
London, England

PER-ANDERS RYDELIUS
Department of Woman and Child Health
Child and Adolescent Psychiatry Unit
Karolinska Instituet
St. Goran Children's Hospital
Stockholm, Sweden

PATRICK J. RYDELL, ED.D.
Autism Communication Services
Lakewood, Colorado

MARTIN SCHMIDT, M.D.
Kinder-Jungenpsychiatrische Klinik
Zentralinstitute fur Seelische Genundheit
Mannheim, Germany

ERIC SCHOPLER, PH.D.
Division TEACCH
The University of North Carolina at
    Chapel Hill
Chapel Hill, North Carolina

LAURA SCHREIBMAN, PH.D.
Department of Psychology
University of California at San Diego
La Jolla, California

STEPHEN R. SCHROEDER, PH.D.
University of Kansas
Lawrence, Kansas

ADRIANA L. SCHULER, PH.D.
Department of Special Education
San Francisco State University
San Francisco, California

BRYNA SIEGEL, PH.D.
Langley Porter Psychiatric Institute
University of California, San Francisco
San Francisco, California

MARIAN SIGMAN, PH.D.
Department of Psychiatry
UCLA School of Medicine
Los Angeles, California

EMILY SIMONOFF
MRC Psychiatry Unit
Institute of Psychiatry
London, England

SARA SPARROW, PH.D.
Child Study Center
Yale University
New Haven, Connecticut

VIRGINIA WALKER SPERRY, M.A.
Yale Child Study Center
New Haven, Connecticut

JOHANNES E. A. STAUDER, PH.D.
Département de Psychiatrie
Université de Montréal
Montreal, Quebec

WENDY STONE, PH.D.
Child Development Center
Vanderbilt University Medical Center
Nashville, Tennessee

RUTH C. SULLIVAN, PH.D.
Autism Services Center
Huntington, West Virginia

JOHN A. SWEENEY, PH.D.
University of Pittsburgh
Western Psychiatric Institute and Clinic
Pittsburgh, Pennsylvania

JOHN SWETTENHAM, PH.D.
Department of Psychology
Goldsmith College
University of London
London, England

PETER SZATMARI, M.D.
Department of Psychiatry
McMaster University
Hamilton, Ontario

HELEN TAGER-FLUSBERG, PH.D.
Department of Psychology
University of Massachusetts-Boston
Boston, Massachusetts

KUO-TAI TAO, M.D.
Nanjing Child Mental Health Research Center
Nanjing, China

BRUCE TONGE, M.D.
Centre for Developmental Psychiatry
Monash Medical Centre
Clayton, Australia

KENNETH E. TOWBIN, M.D.
Department of Psychiatry
Children's National Medical Center
and
The George Washington University School
    of Medicine
Washington, D.C.

NATALIA TRENCHI, M.D.
Centro Pediatrico
Montevideo, Uruguay

BELGIN TUNALI-KOTOSKI, PH.D.
Center for Human Development Research
Department of Psychiatry & Behavioral
    Sciences
University of Texas Medical School, Houston
University of Texas Health Science Center
    at Houston
Houston, Texas

SAMUEL TYANO, M.D.
The Gehah Psychiatric Hospital
Tel Aviv, Israel

RICHARD VAN ACKER
University of Illinois at Chicago
Chicago, Illinois

MARY E. VAN BOURGONDIEN, PH.D.
Division TEACCH
The University of North Carolina at
    Chapel Hill
Chapel Hill, North Carolina

HERMAN VAN ENGELAND
Divise Psychiatrie Kiner en Jeugdpsychiatrie
Academiesch Ziekenhuis Utrecht
Utrecht, The Netherlands

FRED R. VOLKMAR, M.D.
Yale Child Study Center
New Haven, Connecticut

LYNN WATERHOUSE, PH.D.
Child Behavior Study
The College of New Jersey
Trenton, New Jersey

AMY WETHERBY, PH.D.
Department of Communication Disorders
Florida State University
Tallahassee, Florida

LORNA WING, M.D.
The Centre for Social & Communication
    Disorders
Bromley, Kent, England

EDWARD ZIGLER, PH.D.
Department of Psychology
Yale University
New Haven, Connecticut

Editorial Board

Preface

A comprehensive handbook devoted to autism and pervasive developmental disorders testifies to the volume of research, services, theory, and advocacy related to children and adults with the most severe disorders of development. Indeed, this volume is a two-hands book. Its expansion in size and sophistication reflects substantial advances in knowledge during the one decade that separates it from its predecessor (Cohen & Donnellan, 1987).

Autism has attracted, to a remarkable degree, the interest and concern of clinicians and researchers, from the time of its first scientific description 50 years ago by Leo Kanner (1943). As a disorder that afflicts the core of socialization, it has posed scientific challenges to theories of developmental psychology and neurobiology as well as therapy and education. Virtually every type of theory relating to child development—cognitive, social, behavioral, affective, neurobiological—has been applied to understanding the enigmatic impairments and competencies of autistic individuals. And the results of empirical studies inspired by these diverse theoretical perspectives have enriched not only the field of autism but also the broad field of developmental psychopathology. Indeed, autism has served as a paradigmatic disorder for theory testing and for research on the essential preconditions for normal social-cognitive maturation—expression and recognition of emotions, intersubjectivity, sharing a focus of interest with other people, the meaning and uses of language, forming first attachments and falling in love, empathy, the nuanced understanding of the mind of others—indeed, the whole set of competencies and motivations that allow a child to become a family member and social being.

This edition of the *Handbook* is guided by a developmental psychopathological orientation (Cicchetti & Cohen, 1995). Within this framework, principles and findings about normal development are used to illuminate how development may become derailed and lead to pathological conditions; conversely, studies of disorders such as autism are used to cast light on normal developmental processes. Autism and other developmental disorders may serve as "experiments of nature." Their underlying biology and psychology, as well as the types of adaptations that individuals can use to compensate for their difficulties, may reveal mechanisms and processes that are otherwise concealed from awareness or scientific scrutiny.

As a profound, lifelong condition, autism has generated important challenges to the systems that relate to individuals with disabilities, including educational, vocational, medical, and psychiatric systems, as well as to social policy, legislation, and the legal system. Because of its multifaceted impact on development, autism also has focused the attention of all the professions concerned with children and adults with difficulties, including psychology, education, psychiatry, physical rehabilitation, recreational therapy, speech and language, nursing, pediatrics, neurology, occupational therapy, genetics, social work, law, neuroradiology, pharmacology—indeed, virtually every caring profession. By drawing these disciplines together in the clinic and laboratory, autism has helped forge the multidisciplinary approach to developmental disabilities. One goal of this *Handbook* is to provide an orientation of shared concepts and knowledge to facilitate future collaboration among the disciplines and professionals who work with autistic individuals and their families.

Nothing strikes more at the core of a family's functioning than the birth of a child with a severe disability. Kanner recognized the central involvement of families in his first reports when he described the peculiarities of social relations in families who came for his consultation and care. In his first accounts, he misread the data presented to him and postulated an etiologic role of parental behavior in the pathogenesis of autism. This mistake haunted the field, and pained families, for many years; it still may arise in certain places, as ghosts tend to do. However, Kanner soon righted his theory and emphasized the central message of his initial report: Autism is essentially a reflection of an inborn dysfunction underlying affective engagement. Because social interaction is a two-way street, parents and others who spend time with an autistic child will no doubt relate differently than with his or her socially engaged, ebullient, linguistically gifted siblings. Of interest, more recent genetic information about autism and Asperger's Syndrome, discussed in the *Handbook,* returns us to Kanner's observations about social variations and impairments running within families. New findings of aggregation of autism, cognitive problems, and social difficulties within families suggest that an underlying vulnerability may be transmitted from one generation to the next. If so, explicating the interaction between genetic and environmental factors in the course of these disorders will bring us back to questions not too far from where Kanner started his speculations.

The impact of autistic individuals on family life has changed with the creation of more adequate services. Burdens on families have been eased by early identification, initiation of educational and other treatments during the first years of life, suitable family guidance and support, high-quality educational and other programs, respite care, supportive living and other arrangements for adults with autism, effective pharmacological treatments, and knowledge that can guide lifetime planning. Yet, with perhaps rare exception, an autistic child in the family is experienced by parents, siblings, and extended family as profoundly painful. There can, of course, be consolations in dealing well with adversity; yet, however well a family and an individual may cope, a lifetime with autism brings with it more than a fair share of disappointment, sadness, and emotional scarring for all involved. Only with scientific advances that will prevent, greatly ameliorate, or even cure these conditions will this pain be fully eased. Clinicians and researchers have been drawn to autism in the hope of achieving this result, and their remarkable commitments are also reflected in this *Handbook* and in services throughout the world.

At times, however, therapeutic zeal has exceeded the knowledge available. The *Handbook* aims at providing authentic knowledge that is broadly accepted by experts. Yet, we recognize that there are sometimes sharp differences of opinion and theoretical perspective, and that today's wisdom may be tomorrow's delusion. Thus, it is important to foster diversity while encouraging the pursuit of rigorous empirical research that will improve future treatments. Scientific progress oddly leads, for a long time, to many divergent ideas and findings before a deeper level of clarity is achieved. When there are real breakthroughs in understanding autism, as there have been in infectious and metabolic diseases, they will bring new consensus about cause and treatment. At that time, this volume will become far slimmer: indeed, it may shrink to a chapter in a general textbook.

We encourage tolerance of differing views, but we do not think that "anything goes." Virtually every month or two, parents and others who care for autistic children and adults are likely to hear announcements of new, miraculous treatments. They may be confused by the options and feel guilty for not making the sacrifices necessary to try still another approach. Today, within a stone's throw of our own university, parents are engaged in a medley of divergent treatments—hugging, vitamin supplementation, allergic desensitization, diets, aversive controls, music therapies, pharmacological combinations, intensive marathon encounters, and other modalities. These "alternative therapies" compete with more traditional educational, behavioral, and medical treatment plans of the types described in this volume, in an effort to gain parental and societal allegiance and resources.

At times, differences between advocates and skeptics in relation to treatment ethics and efficacy arouse passions—or result in legal proceedings and splits between professionals and among families. These tensions emotionally burden families and clinicians. Examples of such conflicts include disagreements concerning the forceful use of aversive methods to manage self-injurious behavior; the value of patterning and similar movement treatments to accelerate social development; and the validity of so-called facilitative communication to reveal the untapped language gifts, insight, and knowledge of autistic individuals who otherwise appear very retarded and nonverbal.

On all three, we are among the skeptics. We believe that the field of autism will advance like other scientific fields that accept the standards of scientific research and the results of studies, wherever they may lead. Individuals with autism and their parents deserve no less than those with other serious neurobiological and behavioral disorders. Thus, in the *Handbook,* we have attempted to provide a comprehensive account of current scientific thinking and findings, and to mark out speculation and theory for what these are. We also have eschewed accounts of ideas and treatments, however fascinating they might be, that are too far from the mainstream of scientific research and empirically guided practice. Our decisions may leave some advocates feeling shortchanged or even angry; they retain their right to free speech and, who knows, may yet be vindicated.

In underlining the importance of data in guiding decisions about treatment, we also recognize that clinical care always occurs within a social context and is shaped by beliefs, values, and other historical and cultural values. Prevailing views about the rights of individuals with disabilities and their role in society have changed dramatically over the past decades. Embodied in legislation and judicial decision, the emergent viewpoint about rights to education, services, access, job opportunities—and to basic human respect—has shaped services and improved the quality of the lives of individuals who, only decades ago, would have been subject to abuses of various

types that limited freedom, stigmatized, or dehumanized.

Parents and individuals with disabilities have been effective advocates. Communities and professionals have been sensitized to the subtle ways in which individuals with disabilities may be deprived of autonomy and are made to be more handicapped by lack of provision for their special needs. This has had a major impact on the care and treatment of individuals with autism, as well. Far more than most experts believed possible 20 or even 10 years ago, many individuals with autism have not only the right, but the capacities, to participate within their communities—to study, work, live, recreate, and share in family life. The *Handbook* reflects this judicial, educational, and cultural evolution that emphasizes community-based, normalizing, mainstreaming opportunities.

We also appreciate that there are enormous differences among individuals with autism, in their abilities and needs; among families, in their strengths and resources; and among communities and nations, in their own viewpoints and histories. These differences should be respected, and policy and discussion should recognize that "autistic people" do not form a homogeneous class. Clinicians and practitioners, of course, generally are able to keep the individual at the focus of concern, as we do when we think, together with families, about their unique child, or with an adult with autism, about his or her own special life situation. At such times, broader issues of social policy recede into the background, and the fullness of the individual's needs and interests is paramount. In shaping social policy and planning regional and national systems, however, there is a clear consensus for the approach to treatment and lifetime planning that is captured by the ideology of autonomy and community-based living and working. This orientation is conveyed by this *Handbook*. At the same time, we believe that there is no single, right formula for every child or adult with autism. A community and a nation should strive to have available a spectrum of services to satisfy the varied and changing needs and values of individuals with autism and their families.

Clearly defined concepts are essential for communication among scientists, especially for interdisciplinary and international collaboration. In the field of autism and other behavioral disorders, there has been substantial progress in nosology and diagnosis. Collaboration has enhanced discussion and research.

The 1980 *Diagnostic and Statistical Manual of Mental Disorders (DSM)* of the American Psychiatric Association introduced the concept of Pervasive Developmental Disorder (PDD) as the broad category in which autism was the sole exemplar. PDD was a step toward creating a language that could be used for cross-disciplinary exchange. It had the merit of underlining the concept of developmental disorder and the breadth of dysfunctions in social, cognitive, language, and other domains. Similarly, the introduction of multiaxial diagnosis underscored that patients have to be seen from varied points of view and that "categorical disorders" (such as autism) need to be supplemented by knowledge about other aspects of functioning, including medical status and adaptive abilities.

The revisions of the *Diagnostic and Statistical Manual* improved the nosological system and generated new research on diagnosis. The most recent version, *DSM-IV,* published in 1994, embodies this new knowledge and represents a major step forward in relation to autism and pervasive developmental disorders. *DSM-IV* provides the diagnostic framework for this *Handbook.* For the first time, diagnostic criteria are provided by *DSM-IV* not only for Autistic Disorder, but for other conditions included among the pervasive developmental disorders: Rett's Disorder, Childhood Disintegrative Disorder, and Asperger's Disorder. This expansion of coverage is a useful advance in the taxonomy of PDD.

Previous versions of the *Diagnostic and Statistical Manual (DSM)* used the available empirical studies about autism to define the core diagnostic features. The process of revising *DSM-III-R* (1987) provided a special opportunity for international field testing of diagnostic criteria. The final criteria in *DSM-IV* are based on this empirical, large-scale, multinational investigation. The findings from this process provide evidence that clinicians and researchers throughout the world are able to reliably use the same diagnostic approach in relation to autism and other

pervasive developmental disorders. (Volkmar, Klin, Siegel, et al., 1994). At least at the level of diagnosis, they can speak the same language. Many of the participants in the international field trial are contributors to this *Handbook.*

Internationally, *DSM* has achieved recognition within the field of child and adolescent psychiatry as well as general psychiatry. Alongside the *DSM* taxonomy in these fields, the internationally recognized system of medical diagnosis, and the one that has legal status in many nations, is the *International Classification of Diseases (ICD).* Concurrent with the process of revising *DSM-III-R,* which led to *DSM-IV,* the World Health Organization engaged in the process of revising the ninth edition of the *ICD (ICD-9,* 1977) to create *ICD-10* (1992, 1993). This coincidence provided an opportunity to bring consistency to the two systems, where possible. A dedicated committee worked to integrate *DSM* and *ICD* based on the empirical data. Their efforts were successful, and today the two internationally recognized systems provide a consistent approach to the diagnosis of the most severe disorders of early onset. There are still some regional or national diagnostic alternatives, particularly in the French-speaking world, but there is general acceptance of the value of *DSM-IV* and *ICD-10.* This *Handbook* rests firmly on the foundations of *DSM-IV* and *ICD-10.*

The universal acceptance of a standard meter and of Greenwich time do not ensure great science or lack of debate. They are essential tools to help avoid babble. The same is true of diagnostic criteria: they provide a shared metric for describing clinical reality. With an adequate system in place, taxonomy, we hope, now can recede into the background and allow researchers to concentrate on the really tough problems.

The thousands of publications—scientific papers, monographs, chapters, books—about autism and PDD are evidence of their intrinsic interest to researchers and clinicians, and of the human importance of these disorders for those who suffer from them and for families who must cope with them. At times, more papers seem to be published about autism than there are children with this condition. A pundit commented, in a chastening review of another book on this subject, that researchers and writers seem to succumb to a major symptom—the need to preserve sameness. We acknowledge a stereotypy in the literature, and we feel that adding still another publication needs to be justified. A defense is especially in order because the archival responsibility of a *Handbook* to be a repository of what is known will make us, to some degree at least, guilty of the sin of the repetition compulsion.

There are compelling reasons, we believe, to persevere.

This *Handbook* is based on the *Handbook of Autism and Pervasive Developmental Disorders* that appeared in 1987, edited by Donald J. Cohen and Anne M. Donnellan. The 1987 edition of the *Handbook* served a useful function as a source of information for many disciplines; its frequent citation established its acceptance as a scholarly resource. Much has changed during these past years, including the diagnostic systems, as noted above. Conditions that were of marginal interest in the first edition of the *Handbook,* such as Asperger's Disorder, are now hot areas of clinical concern and research. Disintegrative Disorder a decade ago was a rarely discussed entity; it now has a well-earned place in the formal nosology. With the filling in of the map of pervasive developmental disorders, this *Handbook* has a broader scope.

A decade of rapid scientific progress also has fundamentally changed a number of domains of clinical and research importance, including biomedical, behavioral, and educational advances such as the following:

- Genetic research provides new information about the transmission of the vulnerability to autism and the nature of the autistic phenotype, and may help guide genetic counselling.
- Pharmacological treatments are available to ameliorate classes of symptoms.
- Cognitive research and studies on children's theory of mental activity provide a fresh view of the psychological processes that underlie the dysfunctions in autism and Asperger's Syndrome.
- Educational and treatment methods are enhancing adaptive functioning in the community and helping autistic individuals assume more fulfilling roles.

- Formalized methods of assessment provide reliable and sensitive data to guide research and clinical work.

In a real sense, this *Handbook* is not a revision of the 1987 volume. An index of the progress in the field is that more than 70% of the material in this *Handbook* is new. The *Handbook* is also reshaped by Fred Volkmar's joining the process; as the chair of the committee that created the *DSM-IV* system for autism and PDD, he brings special expertise in nosology as well as more than 15 years of research and clinical experience with autism, Asperger's, Disintegrative, and other disorders.

The *Handbook* is organized in nine sections that reflect the nature and breadth of work within the field. The sections convey major theories and findings about mechanisms and processes, as well as about approaches to intervention and treatment.

A new section of the *Handbook* provides international perspectives. Individuals with autism are diagnosed and treated throughout the world, and there is much to learn from cross-national collaboration. Authentic communication requires understanding each other's histories, systems of health care and education, what we read, and styles of thinking, investigating, and treating. The International Perspectives section contains chapter units by leaders in their nation who describe the history of autism and the status of research and services in more than 20 countries.

In creating this *Handbook,* we invited chapters from recognized scholars. The responses to our invitation were gratifying. Each completed chapter was reviewed by the editors and by two members of a distinguished editorial committee. The use of peer review is not typical for volumes such as this, and we are grateful that all authors of chapters welcomed this process. The reviewers wrote careful critiques, sometimes many pages in length; these reviews were provided to the authors for their consideration during revision. The interactive process of revising chapters has helped to ensure that the contributions are as good as the field allows.

The state of the field, however, is not all that it could potentially be. By any metric, too little is invested in basic research, the only hope for eventually fundamentally changing the incidence and altering the natural history of autistic and other pervasive disorders. The cost of caring for one autistic individual over a lifetime may be more than any single investigator will ever have to spend during a career of research. Many hundreds of millions of dollars are spent internationally on direct services; only a tiny percentage of this expenditure is devoted to any type of formal research. It is as if the United States committed all of its funding to building iron lungs and considered virology to be a secondary concern in relation to polio. To fully exploit the many new methods for studying brain development and brain–behavior relations, and to attempt to translate biological and behavioral research findings into treatments, will require substantial investment of research funds. The payoff, we believe, will not only be reduction in suffering and in costs for those with autism, but also important knowledge that will benefit a far larger group of children and adults with other serious neuropsychiatric and developmental disorders. We hope that one contribution of the *Handbook* will be to suggest the potential gains from systematic research and the importance of sustained support for multidisciplinary clinical research groups.

We wish to recognize the support that has been provided, over the decades, to our own clinical and research program by the National Institute of Child Health and Human Development and the National Institute of Mental Health, as well as by the Korczak Foundation, the W.T. Grant Foundation, the Merck Foundation, and private donors.

We thank the members of our editorial board for their excellent contributions to this process. We also thank Mr. Mark Romoser, who helped us to coordinate this effort. We have been very fortunate in being able to work within the scholarly environment provided by the Yale School of Medicine and the Child Study Center. The unique qualities of the Child Study Center reflect the contributions of generations of faculty who have committed themselves to clinical scholarship, teaching, and service. We particularly wish to acknowledge the guidance and support of senior mentors— Albert J. Solnit, Sally Provence, and Edward Zigler—as well as our many colleagues and collaborators in this work, including George Anderson, James Leckman, Ami Klin, Wendy Marans, and Christopher McDougle. Rhea Paul was the managing editor of the first edition of the *Handbook* as well as a collaborator in research. She has had enduring influence on our thinking. The Harris Program in Child Psychiatry, Child Development, and Social Policy has provided a sustaining source of support. We are grateful to Mr. Irving Harris and his family for their continuing trust, embodied in the Program and the new Harris Building of the Child Study Center.

A *Handbook* portrays what is known and reveals what is poorly understood. Although many studies have been conducted and areas explored, there is no hard biological or behavioral finding that can serve as a reliable compass point to guide research; in spite of great efforts and decades of commitment by researchers and clinicians, the fate of most autistic individuals remains cloudy; and even with new knowledge, there are still too many areas of controversy. That investigators and clinicians, working alongside families and advocates, have learned so much, often with very tight resources, testifies to their commitment to understanding and caring for autistic children and adults. The goal of this *Handbook* is to document their achievements and inspire their future efforts.

Donald J. Cohen, M.D.
Fred R. Volkmar, M.D.

Yale Child Study Center
New Haven, Connecticut
April 1997

REFERENCES

American Psychiatric Association. (1980). *Diagnostic and statistical manual of mental disorders* (3rd ed.). Washington, DC: Author.

American Psychiatric Association. (1994). *Diagnostic and statistical manual of mental disorders* (4th ed.). Washington, DC: Author.

Cicchetti, D., & Cohen, D.J. (1995). *Developmental psychopathology* (Vols. 1 and 2). New York: John Wiley & Sons.

Cohen, D.J., & Donnellan, A.M. (1987). *Handbook of autism and pervasive developmental disorders.* New York: John Wiley & Sons.

Kanner, L. (1943). Autistic disturbances of affective contact. *Nervous Child, 2,* 217–250.

Volkmar, F., Klin, A., Siegel, B., et al. (1994). Field trial for Autistic Disorder in *DSM-IV. American Journal of Psychiatry, 151,* 1361–1367.

World Health Organization. (1977). *Manual of the international statistical classification of diseases, injuries and causes of death* (9th ed., Vol. 1). Geneva: Author.

World Health Organization. (1992). *The ICD-10 classification of mental and behavioral disorders. Clinical descriptions and diagnostic guidelines.* Geneva: Author.

World Health Organization. (1993). *The ICD-10 classification of mental and behavioral disorders. Diagnostic criteria for research.* Geneva: Author.

Contents

SECTION SIX
PUBLIC POLICY PERSPECTIVES

SECTION SEVEN
THEORETICAL PERSPECTIVES

SECTION EIGHT
INTERNATIONAL PERSPECTIVES

SECTION NINE
PERSONAL PERSPECTIVES

SECTION ONE

Diagnosis and Classification

The paired processes of diagnosis and classification are fundamental to research and intervention.

The *diagnostic process* includes all of a clinician's activities when he or she is trying to understand the nature of the patient's difficulty. The result of this process is often a narrative account—a portrait of the individual's past, the current problems, and the ways in which these problems can be related to each other and to possible underlying causes. A useful diagnostic process suggests methods for being helpful, including specific treatments. In the course of the diagnostic process, a clinician will learn about the patient's history, talk to others about the patient, observe the patient, engage in specialized examinations, and use laboratory and other methods to arrive at a definition of the patient's problems and their causes. The clinician will integrate the findings from these activities with whatever specialized scientific knowledge is available. Some patients will have several types of problems. The diagnostic process may lead to a narrative that links them to an underlying common cause, or it may separate the problems on the basis of their differing causes or treatments. More than one clinician may be involved in the diagnostic process, but the final, clinical, diagnostic formulation should integrate the pooled information into a coherent and consensual narrative that reflects the entire extent of the research.

One component of the diagnostic process is the assignment of the patient's difficulties—his or her signs, symptoms, pains, troubles, worries, dysfunctions, abnormal tests—to a specific class or category of illness or disorder. Through classification, the patient's unique and individual signs and symptoms are given a context and a more general meaning. For example, the clinician may assign the patient's coughing and fever to the category "pneumonia." This categorical diagnosis is placed within the narrative of the patient's life and current problems. It may be related to the patient's family or genetic background, experiences, exposures, or vulnerabilities, and it will be used to explain why the patient has come for help and what type of treatment may be useful.

The diagnostic process is based on current knowledge, technologies, and skills; it can sometimes be quite brief (as in the evaluation for an earache) or remarkably extensive (as in the diagnostic process for autism). Diagnostic classifications are based on available knowledge and laboratory methods; they also embody conventions—clinicians' and experts' consensus about a *useful* way of sorting illnesses and troubles.

New knowledge and methodologies change the diagnostic and classification processes. The advent of methods such as molecular genetic testing, magnetic resonance imaging of the brain, and structured, formal assessment of cognitive processes has changed the diagnostic and classification processes.

A skillful diagnostic process, and the resultant account about the patient and his or her illness, often is broad-based, nuanced, and individualized. The clinical formulation, the full statement of findings, may capture the many dimensions of a person's life, including his or her competencies as well as any specific impairments and difficulties. A diagnostic categorization—a label or classification of specific troubles and their designation as a *syndrome,* a *disorder,* or a *disease*—is delimited. Providing the label of a specific disease delimits individuality for the sake of being able to utilize general knowledge gained from scientific study and experience with other persons who have similar problems. In this respect, it is important to remember that *individuals* are engaged in the process of diagnosis and *symptoms and signs* are classified and labeled. A diagnostic label is not able or intended to capture the fullness of an individual. Diagnostic classification systems and specific assignments to a disease or disorder category are tools for crafting a helpful understanding and correct treatment.

In the *process of classification,* the newer methods of identifying developmental, psychiatric, behavioral, or mental disorders respect the distinction between diagnosing an individual and classifying his or her problems. The methods are multidimensional: they elicit information about other domains of the patient's life, beyond the areas of impairment. This approach shapes and has been shaped by the two international systems of classification in which autism and pervasive developmental disorders are included: the *Diagnostic and Statistical Manual of Mental Disorders* of the American Psychiatric Association, and the *International Classification of Diseases and Related Health Problems* of the World Health Organization. The introductions to the most recent editions of these two systems (*DSM-IV,* 1994; *ICD-10,* 1992) provide helpful overviews of the goals of classification and the roles of diagnostic categories in clinical understanding.

A new diagnostic term was introduced in the American Psychiatric Association's *Manual (DSM-III)* in 1980: Pervasive Developmental Disorder (PDD). The umbrella term PDD gained broad popularity among professionals from various disciplines, as well as parents and advocates. With no previous history in psychiatry, psychology, or neurology, PDD was free of any excessive theoretical baggage or controversy. It had a broad interdisciplinary appeal and a recognizable emphasis on *development* and *disorders of development.* No specific diagnostic criteria were provided for PDD, but the clinical description conveyed a sense of the contours of its clinical territory. To have a disorder in this territory, a child had to exhibit, from the first several years of life, difficulties involving several domains (social, language, emotional, cognitive) and significant impairment of functioning. In 1980, and again when *DSM-III* was revised in 1987 (*DSM-III-R),* autism was the most specifically defined example of PDD. Indeed, autism remains the paradigm or model form of PDD.

The 1994 edition of the American Psychiatric Association's *Manual (DSM-IV),* which benefited from new evidence and international field testing, refined the diagnostic criteria for autism and formalized three new categories or types of pervasive developmental disorders: Childhood Disintegrative Disorder, Asperger's Disorder, and Rett's Disorder. A term for "subthreshold" PDD, for example, for a disorder which appeared best grouped with autism but which did not specifically fit recognized categories was also included—PDD-NOS (Pervasive Developmental Disorder—Not Otherwise Specified). A consensus on classification and specific diagnostic criteria was reached between the two major systems, *DSM* and *ICD.* Thus, for the first time, there is an internationally accepted, field-tested, diagnostic system for the most severe disorders of development. The *DSM-IV* and *ICD-10* system form the epistemological backbone of this *Handbook.*

The chapters in this section describe current frameworks for classification, the four forms of pervasive developmental disorders for which specific criteria are provided in *DSM-IV,* and the kinds of disturbances that remain within the pervasive developmental disorders that are not yet further classified.

In the future, advances in understanding the pathogenesis of pervasive developmental disorders will, no doubt, have major impact on the diagnostic and classification processes. Thus, in any discussions about diagnosis and nosology, it is important to recognize their provisional nature. And, when using categories to describe the conditions affecting individuals, it is important to balance categorical approaches to diagnosis with a full understanding of the many dimensions of individual children, adolescents, and adults as whole people.

REFERENCES

American Psychiatric Association. (1980). *Diagnostic and statistical manual of mental disorders, DSM-III* (3rd ed.). Washington, DC: Author.

American Psychiatric Association. (1987). *Diagnostic and statistical manual of mental disorders, DSM-III-R* (3rd ed., rev.). Washington, DC: Author.

American Psychiatric Association. (1994). *Diagnostic and statistical manual of mental disorders, DSM-IV* (4th ed.). Washington, DC: Author.

World Health Organization (WIIO). (1992). *The ICD-10 classification of mental and behavioural disorders: Clinical descriptions and diagnostic guideline.* Geneva: Author.

World Health Organization (WHO). (1993). *The ICD-10 classification of mental and behavioural disorder: Diagnostic criteria for research.* Geneva: Author.

CHAPTER 1

Diagnosis and Classification of Autism and Related Conditions: Consensus and Issues

FRED R. VOLKMAR, AMI KLIN, AND DONALD J. COHEN

Clinicians and researchers have achieved consensus on the validity of autism as a diagnostic category and on the many features central to its definition (Rutter, 1996). This consensus has made possible the convergence of the two major diagnostic systems: the 4th edition of the American Psychiatric Association (APA) *Diagnostic and Statistical Manual of Mental Disorders* (*DSM-IV;* 1994) and the 10th edition of the World Health Organization (WHO) *International Classification of Diseases* (*ICD-10;* 1992, 1993). (See Table 1.1.) Although some differences remain, these major diagnostic systems have become much more alike than different—an achievement that has allowed the development of diagnostic assessments keyed to broadly accepted, internationally recognized guidelines (Lord, Rutter, & Le Couteur, 1994; see also Chapter 20). Today, among the complex psychiatric or developmental disorders, autism probably has the best empirical basis for its cross-national diagnostic criteria. The availability of a shared clinical concept and language for differential diagnosis is a great asset for clear communication among clinicians, researchers, advocates, and social policy formulators worldwide. In the future, the discovery of biological correlates, causes, and pathogenetic pathways will, no doubt, change the ways in which autism is diagnosed and lead to a new nosology. The availability of the current, solid nosological foundation is likely to facilitate just such scientific advancements.

In contrast with autism, the definitions of autistic-like conditions remain in need of more clarification (Rutter & Schopler, 1992).

TABLE 1.1 Conditions Currently Classified as Pervasive Developmental Disorders: Correspondence of *ICD-10* and *DSM-IV* Categories

ICD-10	DSM-IV
Childhood Autism	Autistic Disorder
Atypical Autism	Pervasive Developmental Disorder Not Otherwise Specified (PDD-NOS)
Rett's Syndrome	Rett Disorder
Other Childhood Disintegrative Disorder	Childhood Disintegrative Disorder
Overactive disorder with mental retardation with stereotyped movements	No corresponding category
Asperger's Syndrome	Asperger's Disorder
Other Pervasive Developmental Disorder	PDD-NOS
Pervasive developmental disorder, unspecified	PDD-NOS

Note: ICD-10 and *DSM-IV* terms are used interchangeably in the text discussion.

Although the available research is less extensive than that on autism, several of these autistic-like conditions are broadly recognized and clinically important, and have been well enough studied to be included in *DSM-IV* and *ICD-10*. We anticipate that further studies will improve the definition of these conditions and that "new" disorders may be delineated within the broad and heterogeneous class of Pervasive Developmental Disorder (PDD).

In addition to the international and cross-disciplinary agreement about diagnostic criteria for autism, a consensus has emerged about issues that previously were the subject of debate. Today, there is broad agreement that autism is a developmental disorder; that autism and associated disorders represent the behavioral manifestations of underlying dysfunctions, of generally undetermined etiology, in the neurobiological maturation and functioning of the central nervous system; and that sustained educational and behavioral interventions are useful and constitute the core of treatment (Bristol et al., 1996).

In this chapter, we summarize the development of current diagnostic concepts, with particular focus on the paradigmatic PDD—autism—and the empirical basis for the current official definition. We summarize the rationale for inclusion of other nonautistic pervasive developmental disorders that are discussed in detail in other chapters within this section. We also note areas in which knowledge is lacking, such as the relationship of autism to other comorbid conditions, and the ongoing efforts to provide alternative approaches to subtyping these conditions.

ISSUES IN CLASSIFICATION

Systems for classification exist for many reasons, but their fundamental purpose is to enhance communication. For researchers, such communication is essential for achieving reliability and validity in the findings of research studies, sharing knowledge among investigators, and encouraging a gradual buildup of knowledge. For clinicians and educators, classification helps guide the selection of treatments for an individual and the evaluation of the benefits of an intervention for groups of individuals with shared problems (Cantwell, 1996). For the legal system, government regulation, insurance programs, and advocates, classification systems define individuals who have special entitlements. To be effective in these varied domains, a diagnostic classification system must be clear, broadly accepted, and relatively easy to use. In general, reasonably diagnostic stability is important. (This goal was not met for autism until quite recently.) A classification system should provide

descriptions that allow disorders to be differentiated in significant ways—for example, in course or associated features (Rutter, 1996). Official classification systems must be applicable to conditions that afflict individuals of different ages, developmental levels, and from different ethnic, social, and geographical backgrounds. Finally, a system must be logically consistent and comprehensive (Rutter & Gould, 1985). Achieving these divergent goals is not easy (Volkmar & Schwab-Stone, 1996).

The clinical provision of a diagnosis, or of multiple diagnoses, is only one part of the *diagnostic process* (Cohen, 1976). This process provides a rich description of a child or adult as a full person; it includes a historical account of the origins of difficulties and changes over time, along with other relevant information about the individual's development, life course, and social situation. The diagnostic process highlights areas of competence as well as difficulties and symptoms. It notes the ways in which the individual has adapted, and it describes previous treatments, available resources, and other information that will allow the individual, the family, and the clinician to understand the problems involved. The diagnostic process may also suggest or delineate biological, psychological, and social factors that may have placed the individual at risk, led to the disorder, changed its severity, or modified the symptoms and course. The result of the diagnostic process should be an increasingly rich formulation—an account that will be elaborated with new knowledge, including the response of the individual to intervention. A diagnostic formulation, based on an extended diagnostic process, is provisional and subject to change with new information and experience. Because individuals with autism have varied and changing needs, the diagnostic process is a continuing activity involving the individual and his or her family, clinicians, and educators.

As a clinical activity, the diagnostic process depends on a body of scientific knowledge; thus, the process is enriched when a common diagnostic language is used for both clinical and research purposes. Information provided by this process is useful at the level of the individual case as an aid to understanding general aspects of natural history, intervention, and prognosis (Rutter, 1978). At a broader level, information on diagnosis has important public health and social policy implications—for example, in formulating intervention strategies and allocating resources.

Diagnostic systems lose their value if they are either overly broad or overly narrow. They must provide sufficient detail to be used consistently and reliably by clinicians and researchers in varied settings. When they achieve "official" status by appearing in *ICD* or *DSM,* classification schemes have important regulatory and policy implications. Sometimes, conflicts may arise between scientific and clinical needs versus the impact of definitions on policy. For example, there may be good scientific reasons for a narrowly defined categorical diagnosis that includes only individuals who *definitely and clearly have* a specifically defined condition and excludes individuals who *may have* the condition. From the point of view of service provision, broader diagnostic concepts may be most appropriate. Unfortunately, there has often been a failure to recognize the validity of these two tensions. Classification schemes of an official nature may have unintended, but nevertheless important, implications in terms of legal mandates for services; this is particularly true in the United States, where federal regulations may be tied to specific diagnostic categories (Rutter & Schopler, 1992). Such an approach tends, unfortunately, to emphasize the diagnostic label rather than the diagnostic process. Conversely, if a governmental body adopts a broad diagnostic concept, available resources may be diluted; individuals most in need of intensive treatment may be deprived of programs (Rutter & Schopler, 1992). The change from *DSM-III* to *DSM-III-R* is an example of the broadening of the concept of autism; from *DSM-III-R* to *DSM-IV,* a corrective narrowing occurred.

There are common misconceptions about diagnosis and classification (see Rutter, 1996; Volkmar, 1996). For example, *DSM-IV* and similar systems of classification are organized around dichotomous categories; in these systems, an individual either has or does not have a disorder. Yet, classification can also be dimensional: an individual may have a problem, a group of problems, or a dysfunction to a certain degree. Dimensional approaches offer

many advantages, as exemplified by the use of standard tests of intelligence, adaptive behavior, or communication. Dimensional and categorical classification systems are not incompatible. It is possible to set a boundary point along a dimension that can be used to define when a disorder is diagnosed. This boundary can be determined by empirical studies that indicate when crossing an important threshold will influence a child's or an adult's functioning or life course; or, the boundary can be defined by a convention stated by clinicians, researchers, policy makers, or some combination of sources. For example, disorders such as depression are amenable to dimensional definitions. To some extent, all of us have experienced the symptoms of depression (depressed mood, diminished interest or pleasure, sleep problems, and so on). Yet, for the clinical syndrome of depression, a threshold must be surpassed: there must be a sufficient number and range of symptoms that cause suffering, interfere with daily functioning, and persist. For studies of autism and associated conditions, a dimensional metrification of socialization (social competence) using the Vineland Adaptive Behavior Scales has been proposed (Volkmar et al., 1987). Using this approach, a marked disparity between socialization and intelligence is typical of autism. This social dimension can be used to characterize other types of disorders in which social impairment is salient.

Another misunderstanding is that classification systems must be based on a theory. All accounts of an event, process, clinical set of findings, or disorder relate, to some degree, to a theory of what is most important to convey (salience or relevance), a sense of orderliness or narrative coherence, and the like. There is no truly naive form of description, let alone a naive description of what clinicians and researchers mean by symptoms of a disorder. Even the decision about what to consider a disorder of an individual presupposes a theory of what should be considered a personal disorder or dysfunction. The boundaries of the nosology for *DSM-IV* and *ICD-10* of mental, behavioral, and developmental disorders also reflect a history of the professions of neurology, psychiatry, and general medicine as well as preconceptions of where the current lines should be drawn. For example, the inclusion of Rett's Disorder in *DSM-IV* raised the question of why a clearly neurological condition (with similarities to hundreds of other organically based syndromes that are not specifically included, such as William's syndrome) should be classified within the pervasive developmental disorders (PDDs). The decision to do so related, in part, to the educational function of *DSM-IV* in teaching about differential diagnosis for conditions that may resemble autism. No nosology, including *DSM-IV* or *ICD-10*, can be totally free of theory, although there are good reasons for current psychiatric systems to aspire to be as atheoretical and descriptive as possible.

DSM-IV and *ICD-10* attempt to avoid all-encompassing, grand theories of pathogenesis or concepts that require adherence to a particular viewpoint about the functioning of the mind or the origins of psychopathology. In this sense, they attempt to provide a relatively common language and framework that can be used by adherents of different theoretical points of view.

Theoretically oriented classification systems often are difficult to use because there are divergent theories for the same domain of clinical disorder. Theories change, and the practical applications of the theoretical concepts may lead to differences even among those who share a theoretical perspective. Since 1980, the trend in psychiatry has been toward descriptive, operational definitions that emphasize observable behaviors and discrete clinical findings. This approach to diagnosis is often called *phenomenological,* although this term introduces some confusion. Phenomenology is a branch of philosophy that is concerned with the underlying structures of experience and the modes of learning about mental and psychological phenomena (including the use of introspection and dense description). Phenomenology represents a theoretical approach to diagnosis that has an important history in psychology and psychiatry. When contemporary researchers and clinicians speak of phenomenological systems, they usually mean something quite different: descriptions of the surface (signs and symptoms), or accounts of observable phenomena.

Another misunderstanding is that classification systems require etiologies and causes. Here, too, the trend within psychiatry has been toward systems that recognize that the causes of most psychiatric, developmental, and emotional disorders remain uncertain. Also, there is a realization that many different causes may lead to one apparently very similar clinical condition, and that one specific cause may be associated with various conditions. Scientific studies will reveal new causes for old diseases and different underlying factors for what has appeared to be a simple, homogeneous clinical condition. The increasing knowledge and the disparity between *genotype* (underlying cause) and *phenotype* (clinical presentation) indicate the importance of not basing a classification system only on purported causes. However, as etiologies are elucidated, it makes sense to consider including them within a diagnostic framework. In *DSM-IV,* a causal framework is very clear in the definition of Posttraumatic Stress Disorder (PTSD), a condition in which a clear precipitant (a traumatic experience) is related to a range of persistent symptoms. For autism, a causal nosology is not yet available, although genetic, neuroimaging, behavioral, or other findings during the next few years may make a nosology more feasible in diagnosing and subtyping autism (as they have for hundreds of types of syndromes of mental retardation or intellectual disability).

Like other human constructions, classification systems can be misused (Hobbs, 1975). One misuse is to confuse the person with the diagnostic label. A person with a disorder is a person first; an individual with autism is not an "autist." A label does not capture the fullness or the humanity of the person. There is a risk that categorical terms may minimize the tremendous differences among persons who have a particular condition. The very broad range of syndrome expression in autism requires multiple kinds of information in addition to the categorical diagnosis. Does the individual have communicative speech? Does she or he have associated intellectual handicap? What are his or her interests and sources of pleasure? What can she or he do or not do?

Another misuse of a categorical diagnosis is its elevation to an *explanation* or its use to obscure a lack of knowledge. In Molière's plays, the physician would mystify and impress the patients with long Latin terms that were offered as explanations but merely redescribed the patient's symptoms. Many diagnoses still imitate Molière. For example, parents may be told that their three-year-old son is not talking because he has a disorder. However, it is quite different when this disorder is deafness—which may *explain* the muteness, at some interesting level of understanding—rather than autism. A diagnosis of autism clarifies some aspects of the nature of an individual child's muteness by placing this child within a class of individuals about whom a great deal of valuable information about treatment and course has been learned. But the classification does not really *explain* the language disorder, any more than the diagnosis of Attention Deficit Hyperactivity Disorder (ADHD) explains a child's overactivity and frustration intolerance. When a label is mistaken for an explanation, areas of ignorance may be covered over, and the search for underlying causes may end prematurely.

The final misuse of classification is the potential for stigmatization. Parents and advocates are understandably anxious about the ways in which classification may negatively skew how the child or adult is seen by others, or the limitations and adversities that may follow upon being labeled. Unfortunately, this danger is real. When a child has been classified as mentally retarded, this has sometimes meant removal from the mainstream of education and a lifelong reduction of opportunity. A diagnosis of schizophrenia has negative connotations associated with madness and danger. Autism, too, has had its social disadvantages; at one time, it may have implied a particular view of etiology in which parents were placed at fault. A diagnostic label may exclude individuals from programs or reduce their chances of purchasing insurance. For these reasons, parents and advocates have sometimes balked at having a child with autism diagnosed as also being intellectually disabled or retarded, because these terms were felt to be pejorative. Indeed, some advocates have objected to the very inclusion of autism in *DSM-IV* or the placement of autism among child psychiatric

conditions in *ICD-10*. They have felt that inclusion of autism as a mental disorder may imply that autism is the result of an emotional upset within the child or family—when it clearly isn't—and stigmatize the child. Dealing with these issues is a continuing process, and there have been major advances in destigmatization during recent years. Public education and professional awareness of the potential abuse of diagnostic labels are important in reducing prejudice against individuals with handicaps and disabilities.

In summary, categorical diagnoses organize professional experience and data, promote communication, and facilitate the provision of suitable treatments and interventions. They are, however, always open to improvement. They derive their full meaning within the context of a continuing diagnostic process, and they may be misused. They can be helpful in clarifying the nature of an individual's difficulties and thus suggesting care and indicating course. They can, in contrast, stigmatize an individual or limit the search for greater understanding of the individual's problems. For autism, as for other developmental and psychiatric disorders, the diagnostic categorization also represents a convention. It summarizes the current agreements among researchers and clinicians and the current state of knowledge. New experience will no doubt lead to changes.

THE ROLE OF EMPIRICAL RESEARCH

Initial descriptions of disorders such as autism, and related conditions, were invariably made by a clinician-investigator who noticed some seeming element(s) of commonality among children with very complex and severe developmental difficulties. Although modifications in early descriptions of these conditions have, not surprisingly, often been made over time, there usually has been a fundamental continuity of basic aspects of definitions with the historical definition. Over the past several decades, empirical research has assumed a progressively greater role in refining diagnostic criteria and categories. In this regard, even when empirical research suggests that some feature or features are central to the definition, these need not, necessarily, have a similarly central etiological role. Conversely, features less critical for purposes of definition may have major importance for intervention. In autism, the unusual pattern of social deficit originally described by Kanner (1943) remains the central defining core of the condition (Siegel, Vukicevic, Elliott, & Kraemer, 1989); stereotyped motor mannerisms, on the other hand, do not as clearly separate autism from other conditions with severe and profound mental handicap. Similarly, unusual sensory experiences are commonly observed in individuals with autism; they, too, may be a focus of intervention, but they are not robust, defining features of the condition. Other symptoms may be highly predictive of the presence of autism, but they are of such low frequency that they are not included in the usual definitions. For example, a child's unusual attachment to a physical object—such as a piece of string or a frying pan—is highly suggestive of the diagnosis of autism, but this preoccupation is not included in the official diagnostic criteria because the behavior is not invariably present and, when present, tends to be observed only in younger individuals.

Developmental aspects of syndrome expression are particularly important in autism and related conditions. A developmental approach to classification views specific behaviors within the context of normative development. For example, the echolalia of autistic individuals is similar in some respects to the repetitions observed in the speech of normally developing two- and three-year-olds. From this perspective, echolalia is not simply a symptom of a disorder but is also seen among normal children at a particular phase of development. When an older, mute, autistic child begins to use echolalia, it may be a sign of progress in language development. On the other hand, as originally noted by Kanner, some aspects of the functioning of individuals with autism are not developmentally appropriate at any age (see Chapters 12 through 14). This is specifically true of the social dysfunction and lack of engagement. Even infants are engaged socially. The social problems of autistic persons are distinctly abnormal at any age and appear out of proportion to these individuals' functioning in other domains.

Behavioral deviance, exhibited as a lack of social reciprocity or as abnormal preoccupations, is often the focus of the criteria and of the rating scales and other assessment instruments used in relation to autism. This diagnostic approach may be combined with an assessment of how the individual compares with normal children and adults, for example, in relation to language use. The multiaxial system of *DSM-IV* is an attempt to convey systematically the value of considering an individual from multiple perspectives. Assessment includes the individual's personality, educational and social resources, ongoing stresses, medical problems and diseases, adaptive functioning, and impairment (Cohen, Paul, & Volkmar, 1986; Rutter & Schopler, 1992). Multiaxial diagnostic approaches are especially helpful in understanding individuals who have disorders, such as autism, that start during childhood and persist into adulthood. Chronic, serious disorders have a major impact on all spheres of development and increase a child's vulnerability to other difficulties (Rutter, Shaffer, & Shepherd, 1975). Multiaxial systems help to ensure that, in the search for a single, encompassing, categorical diagnosis, the rich and multifaceted diagnostic process is not undervalued.

DEVELOPMENT OF AUTISM AS A DIAGNOSTIC CONCEPT

Kanner's Description—Early Controversies

Kanner's (1943) beautiful clinical description of eleven children with "autistic disturbances of affective contact" has proven to be remarkably enduring in many ways. His description of the children was grounded in data and theory of child development, particularly the work on normal social development of infants and young children of Gesell, who demonstrated that normal infants, early in life, exhibit marked interest in social interaction. Kanner suggested that early infantile autism was an inborn, constitutional disorder; children were born lacking this usual motivation for social interaction. Using the model of inborn errors of metabolism, Kanner felt that individuals with autism were born without the biological preconditions—the enzymes—for psychologically metabolizing the social world and making it a part of themselves. His use of the word *autism* to convey this self-contained quality was, in a sense, unfortunate. The term was borrowed from the field of schizophrenia, where Bleuler (1991/1950) used *autism* to describe idiosyncratic, self-centered thinking that led to autistic withdrawal into a private fantasy world. Autism, for Kanner, was intended to suggest that autistic children, too, live in their own world, cut off from normal social intercourse. Yet, the autism of individuals with autism is distinct from that of schizophrenia: it represents a failure of development, not a regression, and fantasy is impoverished if present at all. The sharing of the term increased early confusion about a relationship between the two conditions.

In addition to the remarkable social failure of autistic individuals, Kanner observed, in the clinical histories of the children, additional unusual features that revealed the broad base of the children's difficulties with symbolization, abstraction, and understanding of meanings. Kanner described the profound disturbances in communication among the original cohort. Three of the children were mute. The language of the others was marked by echolalia and literalness, as well as a fascinating difficulty with acquiring the use of the first-person pronoun "I" and a reference to oneself in the third person ("he," or by first name). Another intriguing feature was the children's unusual response to the inanimate environment; for example, a child might be unresponsive to parents yet overly sensitive to sounds or to small changes in daily routine. This selective insensitivity suggested that autistic individuals actively withdrew from the social world.

Although Kanner's brilliant clinical accounts of the unusual social isolation, resistance to change, and dysfunction in communication have stood the test of time, other aspects of the original report have been refined or refuted by later research.

A contentious issue raised by Kanner in his first papers, and then clarified by him and by others, concerns the role of parents in pathogenesis. Kanner observed that the parents of the initial cases were often remarkably successful educationally or professionally; he also appreciated that there were major problems in the relations between these parents and their respective children. He believed that the condition was congenital, but, as a clinician, he also felt, for a time, that strains in parenting played a role in the origin of the autistic disorder, as they did in other conditions. The question of the importance of experiential factors, especially parent–child relations, in the pathogenesis of autism plagued the history of the field for many years and tended to pit clinicians against parents. Since the 1960s, however, it has been recognized that parental behavior as such plays no role in pathogenesis. Yet, the pain of parents' being blamed for a child's devastating disorder tended to linger in the memories of families, even those whose children were born long after the theory was dead.

Two types of information went against Kanner's first formulation. First, it is now known that, if one controls for possible factors that might bias case ascertainment (Wing, 1980), children with autism are found in families from *all* social classes, and not from only those who are well-educated or professional. Second, children with autism have problems interacting with other people, as well as with their parents. The interactional problems of autistic individuals arise from the child, not the parents (Mundy, Sigman, Ungerer, & Sherman, 1986).

Regarding the role of parents in the onset of autism, it is of interest to note that more recent research on the genetics of autism has reopened the role of familial (genetic) factors in pathogenesis (for more detail see Chapter 17). Today, the data appear to support the concept that biological and genetic factors may convey a vulnerability to autism. This underlying vulnerability may be expressed in a range of social and cognitive problems, evident to varying degrees in a child's parents, siblings, and other relatives. This familiality may be most apparent in Asperger's Disorder, where father–son transmission of the vulnerability seems to be relatively common. Thus, it is not rare to find autistic children in families burdened by other types of social, linguistic, and cognitive problems. The autistic individuals are victims of a genetic and biological vulnerability that interferes with normal brain maturation, and they are burdened by social communicative difficulties.

Kanner speculated that autism was not related to other medical conditions. Subsequent research has shown that various medical conditions can be associated with autism (see Chapter 18) and, most importantly, that approximately 25% of persons with autism develop a seizure disorder (Rapin, 1991; Rutter, 1970; Volkmar & Nelson, 1990; see also Chapter 16). When the prevalence of medical problems was recognized, some investigators proposed a distinction between primary and secondary autism, depending on whether associated medical conditions, such as congenital rubella (Chess et al., 1974), could be demonstrated.

Kanner also misconstrued the relation between autism and intellectual disability. His first cases were attractive youngsters without unusual physical features, such as those of children with Down syndrome; they also performed well on *some parts* of IQ tests (particularly those that test rote memory and copying, such as block design, rather than comprehension of abstract, verbal concepts). Kanner thus felt that autistic children were not mentally retarded, and he, and many psychologists after him, invoked motivational factors to explain poor performance on the full battery of an intelligence test. Autistic individuals were called "functionally retarded." The "functional" designation suggested that, although they performed on the level of other retarded individuals who had severe intellectual disability, they had some innate capacity or underlying competence that was not being fully tapped by the tests or exhibited in real life. This view held out an optimism about these children's potential for intellectual functioning that has been refuted by decades of research and clinical experience. Considerable research has now shown that when developmentally appropriate tests are given in their entirety, full-scale intelligence (IQ) and developmental (DQ) scores are in the mentally retarded range for the majority of individuals with autism (Rutter, Bailey, Bolton, & Le Couteur, 1994) and have

some stability over time. Kanner's impression of potentially normal intelligence, even in the face of apparent retardation, was based on what has proven to be a consistent finding on psychological testing. Children with autism often have unusually scattered abilities; their nonverbal skills may be significantly advanced over more verbally mediated ones (see Chapter 19). Indeed, many of the behaviors commonly observed in autism—for example, stereotypies—are seen in other mentally retarded, nonautistic individuals.

The severity of the autistic syndrome, the assumed psychosis of afflicted children, and the confusion entailed by the use of the word *autism* led some clinicians in the 1950s to speculate that autism was the earliest form of schizophrenia (Bender, 1947). Working from this point of view, clinicians during the first decades of study of autism tended to attribute such complex mental phenomena as hallucinations and delusions to children who were, and remained, entirely mute (see Volkmar & Cohen, 1991a). Subsequent research has dismissed the concept that autism and schizophrenia are related etiologically. Although the question of possible continuity of autism with schizophrenia was a major source of diagnostic confusion in the 1950s and 1960s, issues of continuity with other syndromes proved problematic.

Other Diagnostic Concepts

Diagnostic concepts with similarities to autism were proposed before and after Kanner's clinical research. Shortly after the turn of the century, Theodor Heller, a special educator in Vienna, described an unusual condition in which children appeared normal for a few years and then suffered a profound regression in their functioning and a derailment of future development (Rutter et al., 1994). This condition was originally known as dementia infantilis or disintegrative psychosis; it now has official status in *DSM-IV* as Childhood Disintegrative Disorder (see Chapter 3). Similarly, the year after publication of Kanner's original paper, Hans Asperger, a medical student working in Vienna on his medical school thesis, proposed the concept of autistic psychopathy or, as it is now known in *DSM-IV,*

Asperger's Disorder (Asperger, 1944; see Chapter 5). Although Asperger apparently was not aware of Kanner's paper or his use of the word autism, Asperger used the same term in his description of the marked social problems in a group of boys he had worked with. Asperger's concept was not widely recognized for many years, but it has recently received much greater attention and is now included in both *DSM-IV* and *ICD-10* (Asperger's Syndrome). Another clinician, A. Rett, observed in girls an unusual developmental disorder characterized by a short period of normal development and then a multifaceted form of intellectual and motor deterioration (Rett, 1966). Rett's Disorder is now officially included in the Pervasive Developmental Disorder (PDD) class (see Chapter 5).

In contrast with the observations of Heller, Asperger, and Rett, the descriptions proposed by some other clinicians have not fared as well. For example, Margaret Mahler, a child psychoanalyst, proposed the concept of symbiotic psychosis (Mahler, 1952) for children who seemed to fail in the task of separating their psychological selves from the hypothesized, early fusion with their mothers. This concept now has only historical interest, as does Mahler's view of a "normal autistic phase" of development. In contrast, Rank (1949), also working from the framework of psychoanalysis, suggested that, in early development, a spectrum of dysfunctions affects children's social relations and their modulation of anxiety. Her detailed descriptions of atypical personality development are of continuing interest in relation to the large number of children who are not autistic but exhibit multiple, serious, early-onset disturbances in development. These ideas were developed by Sally Provence in her studies of young children with atypical development (Provence & Dahl, 1987) and in the elaboration of the concept of multiplex developmental disorder (Cohen, Paul, & Volkmar, 1986; Cohen, Towbin, Mayes, & Volkmar, 1994; Dahl, Cohen, & Provence, 1986; Towbin, Dykens, Pearson, & Cohen, 1993; see also Chapter 6).

Rigorous research is still required to fill in the varieties of developmental disorders that appear in the first years of life; these conditions probably reflect a host of pathogenetic pathways that lead to dysharmonies and interferences in the orchestration of biologically programmed maturational capacities. The importance and scope of this research are reflected in the presence, in the official *DSM-IV* nosology, of the concept of Pervasive Developmental Disorder Not Otherwise Specified (PDD-NOS). This "subthreshold" category of PDD provides a diagnostic holding place for a very large number of children whose conditions are not well captured by the available, categorically designated disorders, such as autism (see Chapter 6).

In the first and second editions of the *DSM* (APA, 1952, 1968), only the term *childhood schizophrenia* was officially available to describe autistic children. Much of the early work on autism and related conditions is difficult to interpret because it is unclear exactly what disorders are being studied. As information on life course and family history became available (Kolvin, 1971; Rutter, 1970), it became clear that: autism could not simply be considered an early form of schizophrenia; most autistic individuals were retarded; the final behavioral expression of the autistic syndrome was potentially the result of several factors not the result of deviant parent–child interaction (Cantwell, Baker, & Rutter, 1980; DeMyer, Hingtgen, & Jackson, 1981). These findings greatly influenced the inclusion of autism in the third edition of *DSM* (APA, 1980), to which we will return.

APPROACHES TO CATEGORICAL DEFINITIONS OF AUTISM

In contrast to many conditions in child psychiatry, autism does not "shade off" into normalcy (Rutter & Garmezy, 1983), and it represents one of the more robust disorders for purposes of categorical diagnosis. Unfortunately, even for autism, there are problems in the development of explicit definitions. A tremendous range exists in the expression of the syndrome, which includes some individuals with profound degrees of intellectual disability and others with normal levels of intelligence. In addition, aspects of the syndrome typically change over the course of development. Because the person with autism often cannot provide a direct verbal report of his or her current experience or history, the reports of parents or caregivers must be relied on, as with very young children. However, this reliance may obscure some aspects of the autistic individuals' full range of experiences, and it raises issues of reliability and validity of reports. Some methods proposed for diagnosis focus on very early development. These methods, which sometimes use dimensional ratings scales (see Chapter 21), may be problematic in relation to providing a categorical diagnosis for an adolescent or adult with autism. One would wish to consider both the historical information and the course and current functioning before conferring a diagnosis of a severe developmental or psychiatric disorder. Yet, the use of development and history raises practical problems for categorical diagnostic systems. In general, history has been overlooked in the current nosologies (with the exception of noting the age of onset; see Chapter 7 for a discussion). Interesting and relevant questions also arise when determining what should be included in a categorical diagnostic set of criteria. Should such a set emphasize only those symptoms and signs that most clearly differentiate one condition from another, or should the set of criteria include important symptoms (such as rushes of panic and anxiety, or overactivity and impulsiveness) that are also found among other conditions? Should the criteria capture the largest number of children who may have the condition, or be more selective? What about symptoms that may be infrequent but are of great clinical importance when they occur, such as self-injurious behavior? To what degree should diagnostic criteria be fuller descriptions of the condition?

Investigators began to propose more explicit categorical definitions of autism in the 1970s, when a consensus on the validity of autism as a diagnostic category emerged. The proposals were parallel to attempts in adult psychiatry to provide better definitions of psychiatric disorders for research purposes (Spitzer, Endicott, & Robins, 1978). The importance of a multiaxial or multidimensional approach to diagnosis was also increasingly appreciated (Rutter et al., 1975). Rutter (1978) synthesized Kanner's original report and subsequent research into a highly influential

definition of autism as having four essential features:

1. Early onset by age $2\frac{1}{2}$ years.
2. Impaired and distinctive social development.
3. Impaired and distinctive communication.
4. Unusual behaviors consistent in many ways with Kanner's concept of "insistence on sameness" (resistance to change, idiosyncratic responses to the environment, motor mannerisms and stereotypies, and so on).

Rutter specified that the social and communication impairments were distinctive and not just a function of any associated mental retardation.

It is of interest to contrast the simplified Rutter criteria—which shaped the official systems—with the more elaborate definition devised by Edward Ritvo for the National Society for Autistic Children (NSAC, 1978) in the United States. The Ritvo definition included disturbances in:

1. Rates and sequences of development.
2. Responses to sensory stimuli.
3. Speech, language-cognition, and nonverbal communication.
4. Capacity to relate appropriately to people, events, and objects.

This definition emphasized the neurobiological basis of autism. Although it provided more clinical detail, the Ritvo–NSAC definition proved less influential than the Rutter synthesis, probably because the latter seemed conceptually clearer and closer to Kanner's original description. Many of these definitional developments were incorporated into *DSM-III* (APA, 1980).

DSM-III

Infantile Autism in *DSM-III*

DSM-III (APA, 1980) was a landmark in developing psychiatric taxonomy based on research findings, and emphasizing valid, reliable descriptions of complex clinical phenomena. Autism was included along with several other disorders in Pervasive Developmental Disorder (PDD), a newly designated **class** of childhood onset disorders. Other disorders included

Residual Infantile Autism, Childhood Onset Pervasive Developmental Disorder (COPDD), and Residual COPDD. A "subthreshold" condition, Atypical PDD, was included as well. The newly coined class name, Pervasive Developmental Disorder, was meant to convey that individuals with these conditions suffered from impairment in the development and unfolding of multiple areas of functioning. The term also was intended to avoid a theoretical presupposition about etiology. It quickly achieved broad acceptance, in large part because it did not emphasize any specific professional discipline or theory. Subsequently, the choice of the term PDD has been debated (see Gillberg, 1991; Volkmar & Cohen, 1991b) but has remained broadly accepted in the field. French-speaking clinicians and researchers have raised special issue with the concept for its apparent merging of autism among other forms of developmental disabilities with clear organic bases, and for their sense that this conceptualization may reduce clinical attention to emotional features and therapy (e.g., see Golse, 1995; Klin & Cohen, 1995).

DSM was a major advance in the classification of autism and other severe developmental disorders of childhood. For autism, *DSM* extended official recognition and provided a useful definition, based on Rutter's (1978). The use of a multiaxial approach and the elaboration of criteria that could be used for research and clinical work were major accomplishments. At the same time, shortcomings with this system were relatively quickly apparent (Rutter et al., 1975; Volkmar, Cohen, & Paul, 1986), especially for the other disorders proposed within PDD.

Critique of *DSM-III*

A considerable body of data supported including autism in *DSM-III,* but much less data supported the inclusion of other diagnostic concepts. The rationale for the inclusion of Childhood Onset Pervasive Developmental Disorder related to a desire to be comprehensive in coverage and to an awareness that a small number of children developed an autistic-like disorder after age 30 months (Kolvin, 1971). This disorder was not, however, meant to be analogous with the concept of Heller's

syndrome (disintegrative psychosis) because it was assumed (incorrectly) that the latter was invariably a function of some related general medical condition (Volkmar, 1992). The COPDD diagnostic concept was provided with a very detailed definition which, somewhat paradoxically, was more flexibly formulated than the definition for autism. However, there was essentially no empirical research on which to base this definition and the COPDD diagnostic concept essentially languished into obscurity.

The term Atypical PDD was used for subthreshold conditions, a constellation of difficulties that appeared to most appropriately be placed within the PDD class but did not actually meet criteria for infantile autism or another explicitly defined condition. The term *atypical* was used throughout *DSM-III* in this fashion; the use of the term in the PDD category was complicated by Rank's earlier use of the same word in her description of atypical personality development (1949). The similarity of terms suggested an unintended, although probably relatively substantial and actual, overlap with the older diagnostic concept.

The definition of autism in *DSM-III* was not particularly developmental; even the term Infantile Autism indicates that the definition was most applicable to younger children and more impaired individuals. For example, the definition emphasized that pervasive deficits in social interaction had to be present. The problem of developmental change in the expression of the syndrome was acknowledged by including a "residual" category for individuals whose disorder had once met the criteria for Infantile Autism but no longer did so. This approach, however, did not directly address the manner in which the syndrome changed over time; it suggested that children with autism somehow grow out of the condition, which unfortunately is not the case (Rumsey, Rapoport, & Sceery, 1985; Rutter, 1970; Volkmar & Cohen, 1985; see also Chapters 14 and 49). The criteria for COPDD were more flexible and could have been used to address aspects of syndrome change in autism.

Another set of problems with *DSM-III* related to the emphasis on gross deficits in language development. Many autistic individuals are mute and others have profound disturbances in language, but the central impairment is one of communication.

Childhood schizophrenia had previously been the *only* available *DSM* category for describing children with very major psychiatric disturbance; in contrast, *DSM-III* no longer included childhood schizophrenia as a separate diagnostic category. This change reflected the large body of work suggesting that childhood-onset schizophrenia is very rare and generally can be diagnosed using adult criteria (see Werry, 1996, for a review). In correctly taking note of the research that separates autism from schizophrenia, *DSM-III* took an unwarranted further step. Individuals with hallucinations and delusions were specifically excluded from the PDD diagnoses. It is unlikely that many persons with autism will develop schizophrenia, but there is no reason why they should somehow be protected against ever developing this condition which afflicts about 1% of all individuals. Thus, it might be anticipated that individuals with autism would develop schizophrenia at least as often as other individuals in the general population, a hypothesis that seems to be sustained by available evidence (Volkmar & Cohen, 1991a).

The multiaxial placement of disorders in *DSM-III* also was a source of controversy. Autism and the other PDDs were placed on Axis I, as was mental retardation. However, six "specific developmental disorders" were listed on Axis II of the multiaxial system. The arrangement was intended to increase clinicians' awareness of developmental problems in patients with other Axis I disorders; this argument, however, could be made for all developmental disorders and could not be justified on the basis of severity because such disorders can, potentially, have a serious impact on the child's development.

Problems also arose in the use of the remaining diagnostic axes. Axis III allowed clinicians to note medical conditions; however, there was no convention for indicating the association between these medical problems and autism or the other disorders on Axis I. The proposed scheme for psychosocial stressors (Axis IV) and adaptive functioning (Axis V) was not sufficiently oriented to development (Rutter et al., 1975), nor was there a method for noting protective factors or the potentially important "buffering" effects on severity of autism or other conditions by educational placement (Cohen, Volkmar, & Paul, 1986). The problems with *DSM-III* were widely recognized, and a major effort at improvement was undertaken as part of the process of revision for *DSM-III-R* (APA, 1987).

DSM-III-R

Autistic Disorder in *DSM-III-R*

Preparations for the revision of *DSM-III* were undertaken quite soon after it appeared. What started as a revision soon became a major renovation. Radical changes were introduced into the concept of autism in *DSM-III-R* (APA, 1987; see Siegel, Vukicevic, & Spitzer, 1990; Spitzer & Siegel, 1990; Waterhouse, Wing, Spitzer, & Siegel, 1992, 1993, for discussion of these changes). The rapid revision of the official nosology posed problems for researchers who were required to rediagnose their patients if they wished to remain au courant. In practice, the diagnostic conventions remained rather unclear for a few years, and the literature was burdened by the rapid changes in official nosology.

The definition of autistic disorder in *DSM-III-R* was more consistent with that of Wing (Wing & Gould, 1979) and others who advocated a somewhat broader view of the diagnostic concept (see Chapter 7 for a discussion). Three major domains of dysfunction were included, and specific criteria were provided for each domain: (a) qualitative impairment in reciprocal social interaction; (b) qualitative impairment in verbal and nonverbal communication and in imagination; and (c) restricted repertoire of activities and interests. These domains parallel and extend the broad categories of the triad—social, communicative, and perseverative symptoms—of Kanner, Rutter, and others.

A national field trial was conducted to finalize scoring rules for the *DSM-III-R* definition of autism (Spitzer & Siegel, 1990). Sixteen proposed criteria for autistic disorder were grouped into the three broad categories. Cases in this field trial were rated, often on the basis of chart review, and alternate diagnostic rules were then examined. The field trial led to the conclusion that the diagnosis of autism required that an individual child or adult had to exhibit at least eight of these sixteen criteria, in total, with a specified distribution over the three areas of disturbance (at least two symptoms from the social domain and one each from the communication and restricted activities categories).

DSM-III-R also introduced other changes to the definition. In *DSM-III,* the diagnosis of autism required an early age of onset—specifically, before age 30 months. This requirement was dropped in *DSM-III-R* partly because of a wish to provide a generally applicable set of criteria, regardless of age, and partly for the philosophical reason that the age of onset should not be considered a diagnostic feature; that is, clinicians should rely on present examination rather than past history in making the diagnosis. In *DSM-III-R,* the clinician was able to specify whether the syndrome started before or after age 3 years. Changes in the definition meant that the diagnosis of autism could be made on the basis of current examination regardless of knowledge of early history.

DSM-III-R was attentive to changes in the expression of autism with age and developmental level. This represented a clear improvement over *DSM-III* (Volkmar, Cicchetti, Cohen, & Bregman, 1992b), where the concept of Residual Autism was used to characterize individuals who once had all the findings necessary for the diagnosis of autism but who, with development, no longer did. In *DSM-III-R,* Residual Autism was dropped, and the criteria offered for Autistic Disorder were applicable to the entire range of the expression of the syndrome. Thus, an individual could retain the diagnosis of autism even if he or she was functioning at a higher developmental level or had experienced an amelioration of symptoms with age, perhaps as a result of educational intervention or maturation. The name of the condition was changed from Infantile Autism to Autistic Disorder, to emphasize the persistence of the condition throughout the life span.

In *DSM-III-R,* the problematic COPDD category was dropped, leaving those children who had carried this diagnosis either in the autistic disorder or the Pervasive Developmental Disorder-Not Otherwise Specified (PDD-NOS) category. Indeed, the term for all subthreshold categories was changed to Not Otherwise Specified (NOS) rather than Atypical PDD, which was replaced with PDD-NOS. Individuals with autism were no longer, by definition, excluded from also exhibiting schizophrenia.

Critique of *DSM-III-R*

The ambitious goal of a heuristic definition in *DSM-III-R* was a conceptual advance over *DSM-III,* but it carried an unforeseen empirical consequence. *DSM-III-R* criteria included more children as autistic than either *DSM-III* or the usual "gold standard" for diagnosis, the judgments of experienced clinicians (Factor, Freeman, & Kardash, 1989; Hertzig, Snow, New, & Shapiro, 1990; Szatmari, 1992a; Volkmar et al., 1992b). The rate of false positive cases (if clinician judgment is taken as the standard) diagnosed according to *DSM-III-R* was nearly 40% (see Rutter & Schopler, 1992, and Spitzer & Siegel, 1990, for a discussion of some of these issues).

Several other problems arose. First, the criteria set was more complex and detailed as a result of the attempt to address the entire spectrum of autism. Second, the inclusion of specific examples within the actual criteria seemed to limit the operational definition to these examples. Third, the elimination of age of onset as a central diagnostic feature was not consistent with Kanner's original report (1943) nor with subsequent studies that firmly established that the great majority of cases had an onset during the first and second years of life (e.g., Harper & Williams, 1975; Kolvin, 1971; Short & Schopler, 1988; Volkmar, Cohen, Hoshino, Rende, & Paul, 1988; Volkmar, Stier, & Cohen, 1985). Thus, age of onset was not accidentally related to the concept of autism; it was intrinsic to current understanding. Probably the main issue with *DSM-III-R,* however, was the major changes introduced in the diagnostic concept relative to the earlier *DSM-III* definition. As a practical matter, these changes severely complicated the interpretation of studies that used different diagnostic criteria. This issue was particularly acute relative to the pending changes in the classification of autism and similar conditions in the draft version of the 10th edition of the *International Classification of Diseases (ICD-10)* (WHO, 1990), because it appeared that *DSM-III-R* markedly overdiagnosed autism relative to the *ICD-10* draft definition (Volkmar, Cicchetti, Bregman, & Cohen, 1992a).

ICD-10

The process of revision in the *International Classification of Diseases,* 10th edition *(ICD-10),* was closely related to the development of the *DSM-IV* (APA, 1994). The International *(ICD)* and American *(DSM)* systems are fundamentally related and, by formal agreement, they must share, to some degree, a common approach to diagnostic coding. At the same time, important general and specific differences persist between the two major diagnostic systems (Volkmar & Schwab-Stone, 1996). For example, the *ICD-10* system highlighted the importance of knowing an individual's history when making a diagnosis, whereas *DSM-III-R* relied on contemporaneous examination.

The framers of *DSM* have adopted the principle of having one definition that is applicable to both research and clinical approaches. The findings from research can then be more easily translated into practice, and clinical experience can enrich formal investigation. In contrast, *ICD-10* was specifically designed to have one set of research diagnostic criteria (WHO, 1993) and a separate set of clinical guidelines (WHO, 1992), which allows *ICD-10* research definitions to be much more detailed than those employed in *DSM-IV.* In the initial (draft) version, the *ICD-10* research definition of autism included 20 criteria. In addition, there were important specific differences between *DSM-III-R* and *ICD-10* in the PDD category. *ICD-10* (WHO, 1990) included a much larger set of disorders within the overarching PDD class than did *DSM-III-R* (see Table 1.1). For example, Asperger's Syndrome, Rett's Syndrome, Childhood Disintegrative Disorder, and Atypical Autism were included in *ICD-10,* along with Childhood Autism. The ability to correlate the two systems—to "crosswalk" between them—was compromised by these disparities; if left unchanged, the *DSM* and *ICD* approaches would probably have resulted in very different patterns of diagnosis.

Moreover, initial work with the *ICD-10* system for autism (e.g., Volkmar et al., 1992a) suggested that it did not correlate well with *DSM-III-R* but agreed quite well with the diagnoses of experienced clinicians and with those generated by application of *DSM-III* criteria. This very unsatisfactory state of affairs set some goals for the production of *DSM-IV.*

DSM-IV

Preparations for the creation of the fourth edition of *DSM* began very shortly after *DSM-III-R* appeared. Almost before the ink was dry on *DSM-III-R,* committee work started on still another edition. This haste reflected, in part, the pending changes in the *ICD-10,* because these two systems are, by legal convention, fundamentally related. *DSM-III-R* was supposed to be a revision of *DSM-III.* From the start, *DSM-IV* was conceptualized as a more sweeping update of the nosology, based on detailed evaluation of current data. Work groups reviewed current classification systems in light of existing research, and they identified areas both of consensus and controversy. They considered issues involving clinical utility, reliability, and descriptive validity of categories and criteria. Changes from *DSM-III-R* had to be based on reasonable evidence. Coordination with the *ICD-10* revision was an important part of the *DSM* process, even when a decision was made that the *DSM* criteria should differ from *ICD* in important respects (Frances, Davis, Kline, Pincus, & First, 1991).

As part of the process of creating *DSM-IV,* clinical investigators conducted literature reviews for each of the potential diagnostic categories. These reviews critically examined evidence regarding the validity and definition of each category and identified areas in which knowledge was lacking. (The reviews were published in the *Journal of Autism and Developmental Disorders,* in December 1992.) For example, although Childhood Disintegrative Disorder (Heller's Syndrome) is apparently much less common than autism, the data supported the view that it differed from autism in a number of important ways (Volkmar, 1992). Asperger's Syndrome was included in *ICD-10,* but the text indicated that the validity of the syndrome as a distinct disorder, separable from autism, was not yet fully established (Rutter & Schopler, 1992; Szatmari, 1992a, 1992b). The absence of "official" or other generally agreed-on definitions for Asperger's Syndrome had contributed to markedly different uses of the term in clinical and research work: (a) as a highly specific diagnostic concept, close to Asperger's original (1944) description as modified by Wing (1981); (b) for individuals with disorders that would otherwise be classified as PDD-NOS in *DSM-III-R;* (c) for individuals with "higher functioning" autism; and (d) for adults with autism whose difficulties were less severe in childhood, or who had more language and a higher IQ, or whose problems were ameliorated with time (see Chapter 5). A further complication was that the condition was generally not familiar to clinicians in the United States. With Rett's Syndrome, the issues revealed by the review process had less to do with the validity of the diagnostic concept— girls with Rett's Syndrome had a characteristic history and set of findings. The central question was whether Rett's Syndrome should be included in the PDD class rather than as a neurological disorder (Gillberg, 1994; Rutter, 1994; Tsai, 1992). Rett himself felt that there was no overlap with autism; for example, clinically, girls with the condition are remarkably more socially attentive even when they are otherwise quite impaired.

Although the literature identified major gaps in knowledge and persistent issues, the consensus of opinion favored the inclusion of additional diagnostic categories within the PDD class. There was also agreement about the desirability of compatibility between *DSM-IV* and *ICD-10* (Rutter & Schopler, 1992).

A series of data reanalyses was undertaken by the *DSM-IV* working group to address the issues relating to autism, the best studied of the PDDs by far. These reanalyses used data that were previously collected at several different clinics and institutions and were generally consistent with the previous findings that the *DSM-III-R* definition of Autistic Disorder was overly broad compared with *DSM-III, ICD-10,* and expert opinion (Volkmar et al., 1992a). The analyses provided evidence that *DSM-III-R* was indeed more developmentally oriented (Volkmar et al., 1992b) but that a

price had been paid in terms of specificity. False positive cases of autism, based on the *DSM-III-R* criteria, included individuals with a range of other clinical diagnoses in addition to individuals who would have been termed Atypical PDD in *DSM-III.* Both the review of the literature and the data analyses supported the rationale of *DSM-III* and *ICD-10* for a criterion that specified an early age of onset; at the same time, the issues intrinsic to the use of such a criterion were noted. As a practical matter, this finding required that information about an individual's early history was required for the diagnosis of autism. The *DSM-III-R* convention for the diagnosis of schizophrenia in the presence of autism was supported; a review of a large series of autistic adolescents and adults revealed a rate of schizophrenia consistent with that observed in the general population (Volkmar & Cohen, 1991a).

Several issues were identified that needed clarification for *DSM-IV,* including: (a) the extent, nature, and source of the discrepancy among *DSM-III-R, DSM-III,* and expert clinicians' diagnoses of autism; (b) how to ensure a developmental orientation for the definition that would be sensitive to the natural history of autism, (c) the rationale for including aspects of history in the diagnosis, (d) patterns of convergence and divergence with the definition proposed by the draft of *ICD-10,* and (e) the validity and definition of other conditions that were included within the PDD class in *ICD-10.* Consistent with the empirical principles guiding the creation of *DSM-IV,* the working group decided that the clarification of these and other issues would be based on the findings from a large, multinational field trial (Volkmar et al., 1994).

DSM-IV Field Trial

The *DSM-IV* field trial for autism represents a model of international collaboration among clinicians and researchers. The goal was to establish a conceptual framework that could be used across nations, languages, and local histories and theoretical orientations. Twenty-one sites and 125 raters participated from the United States and other countries. All the sites had clinical programs for individuals with autism. By design, the raters had a range of experience in the diagnosis of autism (about half had evaluated more than 25 patients) and a range of professional backgrounds.

The field trial included information on nearly 1,000 cases; many of the individuals were evaluated by multiple raters. Where the same case was rated by multiple raters to assess reliability, the rating by one clinician was chosen at random to be included in the main database. The preference for the entire field trial was for cases to be rated on the basis of contemporaneous examination, and not just on review of records, by examiners who had a range of experience in the diagnosis and assessment of autism. By design, five contributing sites provided ratings on approximately 100 consecutive cases of individuals with either autism or other disorders in which the diagnosis of autism would reasonably be included in the differential diagnosis. These sites contributed the bulk of the cases in the field trial. The other 16 sites provided ratings of a minimum of about 20 cases. Cases were also included to address likely gaps in coverage in a consecutive case sample—for example, to ensure that uncommon disorders were included in the field trials. In contrast to the *DSM-III-R* field trial, cases were included only if they seemed to exhibit difficulties that would reasonably include autism in the differential diagnosis. The availability of clinical ratings of cases seen at clinical centers around the world was of interest in terms of issues of compatibility between *DSM-IV* and *ICD-10*. Characteristics of the field trial sample are presented in Table 1.2. The sample might be termed a consecutive case series that has been enriched: Consecutive cases constituted the bulk of the sample, but some cases with special features or certain disorders were specifically recruited. In about 50% of the cases, previous contact had been made with the rater. Typically, multiple sources of information were available to the rater, and the quality of the available information was judged to be excellent or good for about 75% of the cases. Individuals from a variety of ethnic backgrounds and in various educational settings were included.

A standard system of coding was created for the field trial, and the same information was obtained about each case. The rating system elicited information on basic case characteristics (age, IQ, communicative ability, educational placement), the quality of information available to the rater, and the experience of the rater (to address issues of clinical applicability by raters with different levels of experience). The rater's clinical diagnosis was recorded along with estimates of the rater's confidence in the clinical diagnosis. In addition, *DSM-III, DSM-III-R,* and *ICD-10* diagnostic criteria were rated, as were new criteria that were being considered for inclusion in the definition of the disorders. Raters could indicate whether a criterion applied to an individual case, whether the criterion could or could not be rated, or whether the criterion did not apply for the particular individual (e.g., items that concerned language functioning were scored "Does not apply" in situations where the individual was mute). The coding form also provided criteria for Asperger's Syndrome, Rett's Syndrome, and Childhood Disintegrative Disorder, based on the *ICD-10* draft definitions.

As expected, there were more males than females in the autistic group, and many individuals were entirely or largely mute. The diagnostic subgroups were similar in terms of age distribution, and the autistic group had a significantly lower full-scale IQ. The primary *clinical* diagnoses, given on the basis of the clinician's best judgment for the children in the group of PDD other than autism, included Rett's Syndrome (13 cases), Childhood Disintegrative Disorder (Heller's Syndrome; 16 cases); Asperger's Syndrome (48 cases), PDD-NOS (116 cases), and Atypical Autism (47

TABLE 1.2   *DSM-IV* Autistic Disorder Field Trial Group Characteristics

	Clinically Autistic (N = 454)	Other PDDs (N = 240)	Non-PDD (N = 283)
Sex ratio (M:F)	4.49:1	3.71:1	2.29:1
% Mute	54%	35%	33%
$\overline{X}$ Age	8.99	9.68	9.72
$\overline{X}$ IQ	58.1	77.2	66.9

Note: Cases grouped by clinical diagnosis. See text for numbers of cases in each group.

TABLE 1.3   Sensitivity/Specificity by IQ Level

| | | DSM-III* | | DSM-III-R | | ICD-10[†] | |
| | | Se | Sp | Se | Sp | Se | Sp |
Overall	N	0.82	0.80	0.86	0.83	0.79	0.89
By IQ level:							
<25	64	.90	.76	.84	.39	.74	.88
25–39	148	.88	.76	.90	.60	.88	.92
40–54	191	.79	.76	.93	.74	.84	.83
55–69	167	.86	.78	.84	.77	.78	.89
70–85	152	.79	.81	.88	.81	.74	.96
>85	218	.78	.83	.78	.78	.78	.91

*"Lifetime" diagnosis (current IA or residual IA).
[†]Original *ICD-10* criteria and scoring.

Adapted, with permission, from "Field Trial for Autistic Disorder in *DSM-IV*," by F. R. Volkmar, A. Klin, B. Siegel, P. Szatmari, and C. Lord, 1994, *American Journal of Psychiatry, 151*(9), 1361–1367.

cases). In the group of cases that were not suffering from PDD, the primary clinical diagnoses included Mental Retardation (132 cases), Language Disorder (88 cases), Schizophrenia of Childhood Onset (9 cases), and other or mixed developmental disorders (54 cases).

The field trial provided rich data for studying the patterns of agreement among raters based on their clinical diagnosis, as well as relations among *DSM-III, DSM-III-R,* and *ICD-10* definitions. These results are presented in Table 1.3. The *DSM-III* diagnoses of Infantile Autism and Residual Autism had a reasonable balance of sensitivity and specificity; the use of the Residual Autism category in *DSM-III* was associated with other problems. In contrast, *DSM-III-R* criteria had a higher sensitivity (but lower specificity) and a relatively high rate of false positive cases, especially among individuals with very low IQ, where the rate reached 60%. The *ICD-10* draft definition, designed to be a research diagnostic system, had, as expected, higher specificity.

As mentioned earlier, one of the major differences between *DSM-III-R* and both *DSM-III* and *ICD-10* was the failure to include age of onset as an explicit diagnostic criterion. Reported age of onset of autism was thus examined carefully in the field trial. In addition to rating the explicit diagnostic criteria associated with age of onset, clinicians were asked to estimate the apparent age of onset of autism based on the historical information and the reports of parents. The mean reported age at onset for autism was quite early: there were only two individuals whom a clinician diagnosed as having autism with an apparent onset after 36 months. One of these would have been given a diagnosis of autism in the more liberal *DSM-III-R* definition (although not in the *DSM-III* or *ICD-10* definitions), and the other case did not meet criteria for autism in any diagnostic system. The data on reported age of onset are presented in Figure 1.1. Consistent with Kanner's report and subsequent research, the onset of autism was usually in the first 18 months of life. Age at onset had a modest, positive relationship with measured intelligence.

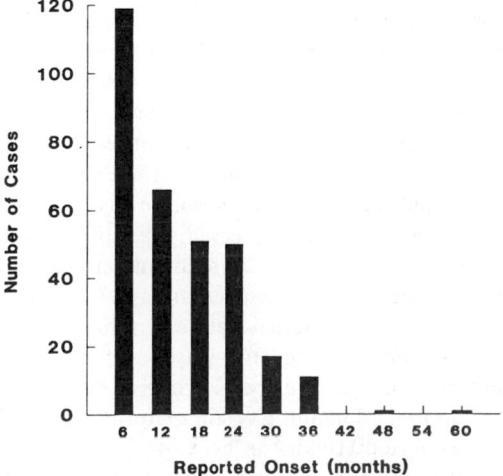

Figure 1.1 Age of onset: Cases with clinical diagnosis of autism.

Individuals with slightly later onset were more likely to have higher IQ scores. If onset by 36 months was added as an essential feature to *DSM-III-R,* the sensitivity of that system was increased. Thus, inclusion of age of onset as an essential diagnostic feature for autism was supported by the field trial data and also had the further advantage of being consistent with the *ICD-10* draft criteria.

Aspects of the reliability of criteria and of diagnoses made by the various diagnostic systems were examined in approximately 125 cases that had been evaluated independently by two or more raters. Interrater reliability was assessed using chance corrected statistics such as kappa (Cohen, 1960; Fleiss, 1981). Because raters with a range of experience had participated in the field trial, it was possible to address rater experience in relation to reliability. In general, the interrater reliability of individual diagnostic criteria was in the good-to-excellent range. Only one criterion had poor interrater reliability: the criterion in *DSM-III* concerning whether the patient had once met criteria for autism but no longer did so. Typically, the more detailed *ICD-10* criteria had greater reliability. Also, as expected, experienced evaluators usually had excellent agreement among themselves and were more likely to agree with each other than with less experienced raters. The experience of the raters, rather than their professional discipline, had the greatest impact on reliability.

Reliability coefficients were also obtained for the primary clinical diagnosis offered by the clinical raters. Overall, agreement was quite high, especially among the more experienced raters; most disagreements occurred over finer-grained distinctions between autism and other possible disorders in the PDD class. The same pattern, with lower levels of overall agreement, was observed for pairs of expert–nonexpert raters. Agreement was highest for distinctions between autism and Non-PDD conditions, and somewhat less robust when raters were making fine-grained distinctions between autism and the alternative categories in the PDD domain. Certain criteria appeared to be more difficult for less experienced clinicians to rate; there was a higher-than-expected rate of missing values or "Can't rate" responses for items involving peer relationships

and imaginative play. Unfortunately, these criteria are among those most helpful in making a diagnosis of autism (Stone & Hogan, 1993). Internal consistency of the criteria was generally high.

The temporal stability of ratings was assessed in two ways. A small number of cases for test-retest reliability were collected as part of the field trial; in addition, follow-up information was available on the cohort of 114 cases originally reported by Volkmar et al. (1988). Criteria and diagnostic assignments were highly stable over relatively short periods of time (in the range of less than one year). Findings with the cases followed up by Volkmar et al. (1988) suggested more diagnostic instability for individuals who were assigned a diagnosis of autism only by *DSM-III-R.* This instability of diagnostic classification was most apparent for younger children.

The field trial data were analyzed via signal detection methods and principal components analyses. The various approaches to the data suggested that certain items, particularly those with low base rates or strong developmental associations, could be eliminated from the *ICD-10* definition. For example, the criterion of being attached to an unusual object was highly specific but of very low frequency and not very sensitive. Before final decisions could be made on the *DSM-IV* definition, a broader issue had to be addressed: whether other explicitly defined disorders would be included in the PDD class in *DSM-IV.*

As part of the field trial, an attempt was made to solicit contributions of cases of non-autistic PDD to assess their distinctiveness, apart from autism. The definition of these disorders and their validity apart from autism raised complex questions (see Szatmari, 1992a, 1992b; Tsai, 1992; Volkmar, 1992). Although the *DSM-IV* autism field trial was not primarily focused on the definition (and even less on the validity) of these conditions, the issues of their definition and validity were relevant to the *DSM-IV* and *ICD-10* definitions of autism. For example, aspects of early development and history were used in the *ICD-10* definitions of these disorders; if any of these disorders were to be included in *DSM-IV,* the patient's history would, of necessity, be included. The boundaries for autism and the

nonautistic PDD were mutually related: a narrow definition of autism would force some
cases into the nonautistic PDD group. The
broad definition of autism in *DSM-III-R* had
certain advantages—for example, in ensuring
access to services—but a narrower definition
might be important for research studies that
require greater homogeneity. (To some extent,
this tension was paralleled in the different approaches to clinical and research definitions in
the *ICD-10* and *DSM-IV* systems.)

A second set of issues about nonautistic
PDDs arose as a result of the absence of a generally accepted definition of Asperger's Syndrome (Asperger, 1944; see Chapter 5). The
text in *ICD-10* flagged the possibility that Asperger's Syndrome might be a variant of
autism. But the draft conceptualized the syndrome as a specific kind of disorder potentially separable from autism on a basis
generally consistent with Asperger's original
concept (Wing, 1981). In addition to the conceptual difficulties concerning the boundary
with the concept of autism, other conditions
had been described as being similar to Asperger's Syndrome (see Chapter 5). Given the
current limitations of knowledge, what was the
best approach to defining Asperger's Syndrome and should it be included in the official
nosology?

The diagnostic issues with Rett's Syndrome
and Childhood Disintegrative Disorder were
different. There were few concerns about the
validity of the entity explicated by Rett; also,
the transient, autistic-like phase of social withdrawal clearly occurred early in the child's development. The question in relation to Rett's
Syndrome was whether, as a neurological syndrome, it should be grouped with autism or
placed within *DSM-IV* at all. Gillberg (1994)
and Rutter (1994) were among the experts who
had contrasting views. The framers of *DSM-IV*
knew that Rett's Syndrome was to be included
in *ICD-10* within the PDD class; by convention, if Rett's Syndrome were included in *DSM-
IV*, it would also be within that class.

The presumption of *DSM-III-R* was that individuals with Childhood Disintegrative Disorder (also known as Heller's Syndrome or
Disintegrative Psychosis) usually suffered
from a neurological or other progressive process that accounted for their marked behavioral

and developmental deterioration. The literature, however, did not support this notion
(Volkmar, 1992). Although rare, Childhood
Disintegrative Disorder appeared to be a disorder that could be distinguished from autism
and had a different course but that was, like
autism, of generally unknown etiology.

The issues surrounding the *ICD-10* concept
of Atypical Autism and the *DSM-III-R* concept
of PDD-NOS were very complex. *DSM-III-R*
provided for coding of the onset of autism but
otherwise provided no other explicitly defined
PDD disorders. In *ICD-10*, a case was considered atypical if its age of onset was unusual or
if there were atypical behavioral features, similar to the PDD-NOS concept in *DSM-III-R*.
The *ICD-10* approach had certain advantages
in that it suggested that children other than
those with strictly defined autism might benefit from the same kinds of intensive and sustained services; from a scientific point of view,
"atypicalities" may be informative in differentiating individuals with "classical" autism
from those with other conditions.

A substantial number of cases with nonautistic forms of PDD were studied in the
international field trial. The overarching diagnostic constructs and specific criteria may
have been somewhat unfamiliar to some raters,
particularly those with less experience. Yet,
certain proposed conditions, as defined in
ICD-10, shared essential features with autism.
Once it is established, Childhood Disintegrative Disorder resembles autism; also, individuals with Asperger's Syndrome, according to
ICD-10, do not have major delay in language
and communication but exhibit the same types
of social deficits found in autistic persons.

Rett's Disorder

In the field trial, 13 female cases were clinically diagnosed with Rett's Syndrome. For
these individuals, the *DSM-IV* and *ICD-10*
draft definitions were satisfactory. As expected (Tsai, 1992), the individuals with
Rett's Syndrome differed from the autistic
cases. Only individuals with Rett's Syndrome
exhibited the combination of characteristic
hand-washing stereotypies, loss of purposeful
hand movement, and development of various
aberrant motor behaviors (see Chapter 4).
Given that the Rett's Syndrome cases were (as

expected) all female, a series of comparisons was made with females with a clinical diagnosis of autism or, for some analyses, with females with a clinical diagnosis of autism who also were mute. Individuals with Rett's Syndrome were significantly more likely than autistic females to be mute and more likely than mute autistic females to be profoundly mentally retarded. Relative to females with autism who were mute, those girls with Rett's Syndrome satisfied significantly fewer criteria for autism. As expected, the two groups did not significantly differ in reported age of onset, although the pattern of onset in Rett's was quite distinctive. Of the cases that received a clinical diagnosis of Rett's Syndrome, one individual would have received a *DSM-III* diagnosis of Infantile Autism (i.e., she met all the *DSM-III* criteria), and 10 of the 13 would have been given a diagnosis of Autistic Disorder by *DSM-III-R.* (In *ICD-10* and now in *DSM-IV*, Rett's Syndrome and Childhood Autism are mutually exclusive diagnoses.)

Childhood Disintegrative Disorder (CDD)

CDD is an uncommon condition. Approximately 100 cases have been reported in the literature since Heller's original (1908) description (Volkmar, 1992; see Chapter 3). Accordingly, efforts were made in the *DSM* field trial to identify known cases of CDD. In addition, several new cases were reported during the field trial. In addition, small handful of additional cases was discovered in which it appeared that the individual satisfied the criteria for CDD even though the clinical diagnosis was not made.

Sixteen individuals in the field trial were clinically diagnosed as having Childhood Disintegrative Disorder. These included the 10 cases reported by Volkmar and Cohen (1989), which had all originally met *ICD-10* draft criteria for CDD and were rerated for the field trial. Four additional cases with a clinical diagnosis of CDD were identified at the Yale Child Study Center site, and two cases were diagnosed at the Maudsley Hospital in London. Every case in the field trial was reviewed for features suggestive of the diagnosis of CDD, such as an apparent late onset of autism or a period of clear deterioration and persistent regression. On this basis, an additional 15 cases

were identified as exhibiting some features of CDD (Volkmar & Rutter, 1995). Of these 15 cases, 13 had received clinical diagnoses of autism; one individual was clinically diagnosed as PDD-NOS and another as Atypical Autism.

Regardless of whether a clinical diagnosis of CDD had been given at the time of the initial clinical rating, the individuals who exhibited the features of Childhood Disintegrative Disorder were generally remarkably similar. Comparing individuals with CDD and autism was informative. Individuals with CDD on the basis of clinician diagnosis or application of *ICD-10* criteria were more likely than autistic individuals to be mute and to be in residential placement. Consistent with Volkmar and Cohen's (1989) report, the mean IQ of the CDD cases was also lower than that for cases with late-onset autism.

Asperger's Syndrome

The absence of fully accepted definitions of Asperger's Syndrome contributed to the confusion surrounding the validity of this diagnostic concept (see Chapter 5). In *ICD-10,* the condition differs from autism in that, by definition, there is a "lack of any clinically significant general delay in language or cognitive development." By definition, single words develop by age 2, phrases are used by age 3, and self-help and adaptive behavior are consistent with normal development in the first 3 years of life, although motor development may be delayed. In *ICD-10,* by definition, individuals with Asperger's Syndrome meet the same criteria for qualitative impairments in social interactions as for autism, and the criteria for restricted, repetitive, and stereotyped patterns of behavior, interests, and activities are also of the type exhibited in autism. The *ICD-10* research criteria state that early motor delays and motor clumsiness are usual (although not a necessary feature for diagnosis), that isolated special skills (often related to abnormal preoccupations) may be present (but are not required for diagnosis), and that it would be less typical for stereotyped behaviors or preoccupation with part-objects to be exhibited. By *ICD* definition, Asperger's Syndrome cannot be attributed to other varieties of PDD, nor to schizotypal disorder, reactive attachment disorder, simple schizophrenia, obsessional personality disorder, or obsessive-compulsive disorder.

In the field trial, the primary clinical diagnosis of Asperger's Syndrome was made for 48 cases. Issues were noted in the application of the *ICD-10* criteria (see Chapter 5). Individuals with clinician assigned diagnoses of Asperger's Syndrome almost invariably exhibited an encompassing preoccupation or circumscribed interest, consistent with Asperger's original description (see also Wing, 1981), and serious difficulties in negotiating social relations. Stereotyped behaviors and motor mannerisms were significantly less common than in autism.

Could individuals with Asperger's Syndrome be distinguished from those with higher-functioning autism? A series of analyses addressed this issue. The cases rated as having Asperger's Syndrome, either by clinical diagnosis or on the basis of the criteria proposed in *ICD-10,* were indeed unlikely to exhibit delays in the development of spoken language. When individuals with Asperger's Syndrome were compared with brighter (IQ > 85) individuals with autism (based on either clinical or *ICD* criteria), the Asperger's Syndrome cases had fewer symptoms of deviance in language and communication. Another interesting contrast emerged in profiles of functioning on intelligence tests. Individuals with Asperger's Syndrome were more likely to score higher on verbal IQ than on performance IQ; the opposite result was obtained for higher-functioning individuals with autism. Also, compared to those with autism, the individuals with Asperger's Syndrome had fewer symptoms of social deviance.

A series of analyses compared Asperger's Syndrome cases to those with clinical diagnoses of either Atypical Autism or PDD-NOS. Compared to individuals with Atypical Autism, those with Asperger's Syndrome had greater disability and exhibited more symptoms of social deviance and resistance to change.

PDD-NOS/Atypical Autism

The draft version of *ICD-10* provided for this diagnosis in three somewhat disparate contexts: (a) when a case fails to meet the age-of-onset criterion for autism; (b) when an individual meets the onset criterion but fails to satisfy the criteria for social or communicative impairments or the restricted range of interests; or (c) when individuals fail to meet both the onset and the behavioral criteria. The first sense of the term *atypical in age of onset* is probably the most consistent with the *DSM-III-R* definition (which provided for coding of onset after 36 months) and the least controversial. The vast majority of cases of autism, as in the field trial, meet the age-of-onset criterion of 3 years. Cases that otherwise meet the behavioral criteria could then be coded as being atypical in onset; this distinction would have potentially greater implications for research than for clinical service (see Chapter 7).

In the field trial, 46 cases were given a clinical diagnosis of Atypical Autism, and 117 were diagnosed as PDD-NOS. In about one-fourth of the cases, the individual met the criteria for autism according to one diagnostic system but not the others. Generally, the other cases were subthreshold in the sense that they did not meet specific criteria for autism but exhibited difficulties in multiple areas of functioning, consistent with being in the PDD category.

Definition of Autism in DSM-IV and ICD-10

The field trial data provided an important empirical basis for constructing the definition of autism for *DSM-IV.* The data showed that the *DSM-III-R* definition could be substantially improved by adding a criterion related to age of onset and by raising the diagnostic threshold. Similarly, various combinations of *DSM-III, DSM-III-R,* and new criteria all could have been used to provide a reasonably balanced diagnostic system. Given the concern about compatibility with *ICD-10* and the implications for research of a universally accepted definition, the working group of *DSM-IV* considered the benefits of the *ICD-10* system and some possible modifications. The goal was to establish a definition for *DSM-IV* that balanced clinical and research needs, was reasonably concise and easy to use, provided reasonable coverage over the range of syndrome expression in autism, and was applicable over the full life span, from early childhood through adulthood.

TABLE 1.4   *ICD-10* Criteria for Autism

F84.0 Childhood Autism

A. Abnormal or impaired development is evident before the age of 3 years in at least one of the following areas:
    (1) receptive or expressive language as used in social communication;
    (2) the development of selective social attachments or of reciprocal social interaction;
    (3) functional or symbolic play.

B. A total of at least six symptoms from (1), (2), and (3) must be present, with at least two from (1) and at least one from each of (2) and (3):
    (1) Qualitative impairments in social interaction are manifest in at least two of the following areas:
        (a) failure adequately to use eye-to-eye gaze, facial expression, body postures, and gestures to regulate social interaction;
        (b) failure to develop (in a manner appropriate to mental age, and despite ample opportunities) peer relationships that involve a mutual sharing of interests, activities, and emotions;
        (c) lack of socioemotional reciprocity as shown by an impaired or deviant response to other people's emotions; or lack of modulation of behavior according to social context; or a weak integration of social, emotional, and communicative behaviors;
        (d) lack of spontaneous seeking to share enjoyment, interests, or achievements with other people (e.g., a lack of showing, bringing, or pointing out to other people objects of interest to the individual).
    (2) Qualitative abnormalities communication as manifest in at least one of the following areas:
        (a) delay in, or total lack of, development of spoken language that is *not* accompanied by an attempt to compensate through the use of gestures or mime as an alternative mode of communication (often preceded by a lack of communicative babbling);
        (b) relative failure to initiate or sustain conversational interchange (at whatever level of language skill is present), in which there is reciprocal responsiveness to the communications of the other person;
        (c) stereotyped and repetitive use of language or idiosyncratic use of words or phrases;
        (d) lack of varied spontaneous make-believe play or (when young) social imitative play.
    (3) Restricted, repetitive, and stereotyped patterns of behavior, interests, and activities are manifested in at least one of the following:
        (a) an encompassing preoccupation with one or more stereotyped and restricted patterns of interest that are abnormal in content or focus; or one or more interests that are abnormal in their intensity and circumscribed nature though not in their content or focus;
        (b) apparently compulsive adherence to specific nonfunctional routines or rituals;
        (c) stereotyped and repetitive motor mannerisms that involve either hand or finger flapping or twisting, or complex whole-body movements:
        (d) preoccupations with part-objects or nonfunctional elements of play materials (such as their odor, the feel of their surface, or the noise or vibration they generate).

C. The clinical picture is not attributable to the other varieties of pervasive developmental disorders; specific development disorder of receptive language (F80.2) with secondary socioemotional problems' reactive attachment disorder (F94.1) or disinhibited attachment disorder (F94.2); mental retardation (F70-F72) with some associated emotional or behavioral disorders; schizophrenia (F20.-) of unusually early onset; and Rett's Syndrome (F84.12).

F84.1 Atypical Autism

A. Abnormal or impaired development is evident at or after the age of 3 years (criteria as for autism except for age of manifestation).

B. There are qualitative abnormalities in reciprocal social interaction or in communication, or restricted, repetitive, and stereotyped patterns of behavior, interests, and activities. (Criteria as for autism except that it is unnecessary to meet the criteria for number of areas of abnormality.)

C. The disorder does not meet the diagnostic criteria for autism (F84.0).

Autism may be atypical in either age of onset (F84.10) or symptomatology (F84.11); the two types are differentiated with a fifth character for research purposes. Syndromes that are typical in both respects should be coded F84.12.

F84.10 Atypicality in age of onset

A. The disorder does not meet criterion A for autism (F84.0); that is, abnormal or impaired development is evident only at or after age 3 years.

B. The disorder meets criteria B and C for autism (F84.0).

TABLE 1.4   *(Continued)*

F84.11 Atypicality in symptomatology

A. The disorder meets criterion A for autism (F84.0); that is, abnormal or impaired development is evident before age 3 years.

B. There are qualitative abnormalities in reciprocal social interactions or in communication, or restricted, repetitive, and stereotyped patterns of behavior, interests, and activities. (Criteria as for autism except that it is unnecessary to meet the criteria for number of areas of abnormality.)

C. The disorder meets criterion C for autism (F84.0).

D. The disorder does not fully meet criterion B for autism (F84.0).

F84.12 Atypicality in both age of onset and symptomatology

A. The disorder does not meet criterion A for autism (F84.0); that is, abnormal or impaired development is evident only at or after age 3 years.

B. There are qualitative abnormalities in reciprocal social interactions or in communication, or restricted, repetitive, and stereotyped patterns of behavior, interests, and activities. (Criteria as for autism except that it is unnecessary to meet the criteria for number of areas of abnormality.)

C. The disorder meets criterion C for autism (F84.0).

D. The disorder does not fully meet criterion B for autism (F84.0).

Reprinted, with permission, from the *ICD-10 Classification of Mental and Behavioural Disorders—Diagnostic criteria for research,* (1993). Geneva: World Health Organization, pp. 147–150.

Of the original 20 *ICD-10* criteria, 4 were identified for possible elimination. Alternatives to specific criteria were examined, and a modified definition was developed. This modified definition worked well both overall and across different levels of age and associated mental retardation; it was also readily utilized by less experienced examiners.

Diagnostic criteria for autism in *ICD-10* and *DSM-IV* are presented in Tables 1.4 and 1.5, respectively. For the diagnosis of autism, at least six criteria must be exhibited, including at least two criteria relating to social abnormalities (group 1) and one each relating to impaired communication (group 2) and range of interests and activities (group 3). In addition, the onset of the condition must have been prior to age 3 years, as evidenced by delay or abnormal functioning in social interaction, language as used in social interaction, and symbolic/imaginative play. In addition, *DSM-IV* accepted the diagnostic convention that the disorder could not better be accounted for by the diagnosis of Rett's Disorder or Childhood Disintegrative Disorder.

Qualitative impairment in social interaction can take the form of markedly impaired nonverbal behaviors, failure in developmentally expectable peer relationships, lack of shared enjoyment or pleasure, or lack of socioemotional reciprocity. During the field trial, the stronger weighting of the impairments in socialization was noted to be important in avoiding overdiagnosis of autism in more intellectually handicapped persons. This is also consistent with extensive clinical work, from the time of Kanner onward (e.g., Caparulo & Cohen, 1977; Cohen, 1980; Cohen, Caparulo, & Shaywitz, 1976; Siegel et al., 1989), that highlighted social dysfunction as the critical domain of impairment in autism.

Impairments in communication can take the form of delay or lack of spoken language, impairment in conversational ability, stereotyped language use, and deficits in imaginative play. For persons with autism, the delay or lack of spoken language must not be accompanied by compensations through other communicative means, such as gestures.

The domain of restricted patterns of behavior, interests, and activities includes encompassing preoccupations that are abnormal in either focus or intensity, adherence to nonfunctional routines or rituals, stereotyped motor movements, and persistent preoccupation with parts of objects.

Although *DSM-IV* and *ICD-10* are the most recent and most extensively evaluated diagnostic approaches for autism, they are undoubtedly not the last word on diagnosis. The

TABLE 1.5 *DSM-IV* Criteria for Autistic Disorder (299.0)

A. A total of at least six items from (1), (2), and (3), with at least two from (1), and one each from (2) and (3):
  (1) Qualitative impairment in social interaction, as manifested by at least two of the following:
    (a) Marked impairment in the use of multiple nonverbal behaviors such as eye-to-eye gaze, facial expression, body postures, and gestures to regulate social interaction;
    (b) Failure to develop peer relationships appropriate to developmental level;
    (c) Markedly impaired expression of pleasure in other people's happiness;
    (d) lack of social or emotional reciprocity.
  (2) Qualitative impairments in communication as manifested by at least one of the following:
    (a) Delay in, or total lack of, the development of spoken language (not accompanied by an attempt to compensate through alternative modes of communication such as gestures or mime);
    (b) In individuals with adequate speech, marked impairment in the ability to initiate or sustain a conversation with others;
    (c) Stereotyped and repetitive use of language or idiosyncratic language;
    (d) Lack of varied spontaneous make-believe play or social imitative play appropriate to developmental level.
  (3) Restricted repetitive and *stereotyped patterns of behavior, interests, and activities,* as manifested by at least one of the following:
    (a) Encompassing preoccupation with one or more stereotyped and restricted patterns of interest that is abnormal either in intensity or focus;
    (b) Apparently compulsive adherence to specific nonfunctional routines or rituals;
    (c) Stereotyped and repetitive motor mannerisms (e.g., hand or finger flapping or twisting, or complex whole-body movements);
    (d) Persistent preoccupation with parts of objects.
B. Delays or abnormal functioning in at least one of the following areas, with onset prior to age 3 years: (1) social interaction, (2) language as used in social communication, or (3) symbolic or imaginative play.
C. Not better accounted for by Rett's Disorder or Childhood Disintegrative Disorder.

Reprinted, with permission, from the *Diagnostic and Statistical Manual of Mental Disorders,* 4th Edition, (1994). Washington, DC: American Psychiatric Association, pp. 70–71.

present *DSM-IV* and *ICD-10* systems have the considerable advantage of being based on a relatively extensive set of data analyses. The "dual use" constraints on *DSM* (the use of the same criteria for both research and service) made brevity and ease of use important considerations. The *ICD-10* system does not, at least for the research definitions, have this constraint. It remains to be seen whether the more detailed *ICD-10* research definitions will, in the end, predominate. From the point of view of research, the attempt to link diagnostic instruments to specific diagnostic criteria is a considerable advantage and may mean that, for research purposes, the more detailed research definitions will dominate.

The definitions of other disorders in the PDD class in *DSM-IV* are much less detailed than those for autism. There are some relatively minor differences from *ICD-10* (see Volkmar & Rutter, 1995). Two categories deserve particular mention. Far more work will be needed to define Asperger's Disorder and separate it from autism, with which it shares so many features (e.g., Klin et al., 1995). Whether Asperger's Disorder will remain a distinct category or will be reintegrated in the spectrum of autism remains to be seen (see Chapter 5). Neither the *ICD-10* nor the *DSM-IV* definition explicitly requires a highly circumscribed interest or a motor delay, both of which would appear more typical of cases that correspond most closely to Asperger's original definition.

The disorder(s) presently encompassed within the overarching category of Atypical Autism and PDD-NOS also deserve considerably more study (Sponheim, 1996). This category has received increasing clinical use; unfortunately, the essentially negative definition provided by *DSM-IV* may compound diagnostic inconsistency. During the final editing of *DSM-IV,* what appeared to be a minor change was introduced relative to *DSM-III-R.* It is worthwhile to comment on this change to avoid future confusion. In *DSM-III-R,* for a diagnosis of PDD-NOS, an individual had to have problems in social interaction **and** in communication or restricted interests. In *DSM-IV,* this **and** has been changed to **or.** The specificity of the diagnostic concept has suffered markedly, and the overbroadening of the concept raises a number of other problems. It is hoped that this change will be reconsidered.

CURRENT CONTROVERSIES IN DIAGNOSIS

Comorbid Conditions and Autism

The issue of comorbidity with autism has become increasingly important in recent years; it is intimately related to the search for subgroups of autism. Any serious disability, such as autism or intellectual disability, appears to increase the risk for other problems. Indeed, autism has now been reported to co-occur with various other developmental, psychiatric, and medical conditions. Some of the associations appear to be very common; others are occasional or rare. The real issue is not whether any such associations are observed but the nature of their relationship—whether they occur together at greater-than-chance levels and are related to the same underlying cause, or whether one leads to the other (Tsai, 1996).

Evolving diagnostic concepts and research findings have sometimes clarified such associations. For example, Kanner's original impression (1943) that persons with autism had normal intellectual potential has been shown to be incorrect. The pattern of cognitive and adaptive abilities in autism is unusual, but, for the majority of children with autism, overall scores on cognitive testing are stable within the mentally retarded range (see Chapter 19). Yet, a substantial minority of persons with autism have cognitive abilities in the average or above-average range. Similarly, it is now well recognized that seizure disorders of various types are associated with autism in about 25% of cases (see Chapter 16). A much smaller proportion of autistic individuals exhibit Fragile X Syndrome or tuberous sclerosis (see Chapter 18). Apart from these well-recognized links, the association of autism with other medical and behavioral conditions is much less convincing.

Issues relating to comorbidity arise from several sources. Perhaps most important is a basic philosophical difference between the approaches to diagnosis in *DSM-IV* and *ICD-10*. Both systems are meant to be comprehensive in coverage. However, any system that attempts to move past the level of symptom description must deal with complicated problems or ensuring clinical utility, reliability, and validity. As a practical matter, this leads to decisions—some fairly obvious and others much less so—about relationships between categories, including whether one condition takes precedence over another in a diagnostic hierarchy. The *ICD-10* system reflects a nosological tradition of searching for a single, parsimonious diagnostic label to explain a patient's problems. This top-down approach tends to be concerned with broader heuristic diagnoses and is less focused on symptoms as such. *DSM-IV* and its immediate predecessors have tended to be more bottom-up in orientation. They start with symptoms and move toward broader categories. No single diagnosis is expected to convey the entire range of a patient's major problems, and there is more comfort with multiple categorical diagnoses, each covering a smaller domain of difficulties. *ICD* may miss some trees and *DSM* may not capture the forest, but each approach has inherent advantages and limitations (see Volkmar & Schwab-Stone, 1996). The *DSM-IV* approach has some advantages for clinical utility: important symptoms are less likely to be overlooked, and the issue of comorbid relationships is not prejudged. The *ICD-10* approach has the advantage of providing a robust "big picture" that is less focused on single symptoms and that minimizes what are often spurious or meaningless associations.

The issue of comorbidity in relation to autism is further complicated by the nature of the syndrome. Autism is a lifelong disorder and probably one of the "best" examples of a disorder in psychiatry, but symptoms change with age and developmental level. If the approach to diagnosis focuses on symptoms, an individual with autism will receive a large number of additional diagnoses over the course of the life span, including diagnoses that focus on anxiety, language, social problems, and the like. Such a list of additional diagnoses might serve a useful function by cataloging behaviors that need clinical attention. But the list does not change the fundamental diagnosis that the person has autism.

Given the wide range and the severity of the disabilities experienced by individuals with autism, it is not surprising that they are vulnerable to many types of behavioral difficulties: hyperactivity, obsessive-compulsive phenomena, self-injury and stereotypy, tics, and affective symptoms (Brasic et al., 1994; Ghaziuddin, Alessi, & Greden, 1995; Ghaziuddin, Tsai, & Ghaziuddin, 1992; Jaselskis, Cook, & Fletcher, 1992; McDougle et al., 1995; Nelson & Pribor, 1993; Poustka & Lisch, 1993; Quintana et al., 1995; Realmuto & Main, 1982). Interpretations of the available data are more complex when one moves past the level of behavioral observation and tries to consider these associations within a causal framework. For example, the diagnosis of Tourette's Syndrome requires only a history of motor and vocal tics for a year or more. Do the compulsive behaviors, unusual movements, and vocalizations emitted by many individuals with autism and intellectual disability warrant a second diagnosis of Tourette's Syndrome? When should obsessive-compulsive disorder be diagnosed in a retarded, autistic individual who has many perseverative behaviors?

As noted previously, diagnostic systems like *DSM-IV* and *ICD-10* strive for logical consistency in their approach to diagnosis; this usually means that some degree of hierarchical decision must be employed when, for example, features that are part of the definition of autism are observed in other disorders. Thus, because stereotyped behaviors are common in autism and are included as a diagnostic feature in both *DSM-IV* and *ICD-10,* persons with autism cannot also receive a diagnosis of stereotyped movement disorder. Similarly, diagnostic problems arise with difficulties such as unusual affective responses, which are commonly observed to be "associated features" of autism. Mental Retardation is not an essential diagnostic feature of autism, and it is thus possible (and important) for this diagnosis *and* one of autism to be made, when both sets of criteria are satisfied.

The task of moving from the level of behavioral problems and symptoms to formal psychiatric/developmental diagnosis is complicated by the nature of autism itself. Half of autistic persons are largely or entirely mute, and, for some disorders, this presents a profound diagnostic problem (Tsai, Tsai, & August, 1985). For example, early investigators (Bender,

1947) incorrectly assumed a continuity between autism and schizophrenia. Subsequently, it became apparent that the two conditions were not related, although persons with autism may also develop schizophrenia (Petty, Ornitz, Michelman, & Zimmerman, 1984). There is, however, an understandable bias for such positive single-case associations to be reported when negative associations are not; as a result, more large-scale studies are usually needed to clarify whether any observed comorbid associations are higher than expected, given chance alone. One study of autistic adolescents and adults revealed that the rate of schizophrenia in autism is not increased over the general population (Volkmar & Cohen, 1991a).

The issue of comorbid obsessive-compulsive disorder and autism has generated great interest, especially because of the availability of effective pharmacological treatment. Phenomena very suggestive of obsessions or compulsions are often observed in adults with autism. Rumsey et al. (1985) noted that over 80% of their sample of autistic individuals demonstrated stereotyped compulsive behaviors that included ordering and reordering of objects. Other studies have noted varying levels of such phenomena; the variations in levels presumably reflect differences in sample and method (Brasic et al., 1994; Fombonne, 1992; McDougle et al., 1995). Obsessive-compulsive symptoms of autistic individuals may respond to medications that are useful in the treatment of a more "classic" obsessive-compulsive disorder (Gordon, Rapoport, Hamburger, State, & Mannheim, 1992; Gordon, State, Nelson, Hamburger, & Rapoport, 1993; McDougle et al., 1992; see Chapter 32). However, the response to medication may be a function of many factors; various disorders may be ameliorated with the same medication; for example, tricyclic antidepressants are helpful in the treatment of depression and enuresis, and both hyperactive and normal children may respond to stimulant medication with improved attention. In this context, investigators have noted that the ritualistic phenomena of autism cannot simply be equated with typical obsessions and compulsions (Baron-Cohen, 1989).

Stereotyped motor movements, verbal stereotypies such as the repetition of words or phrases, and other mannerisms are very common in autism and are ordinarily included among the diagnostic features. Levels of such behavior vary over time and developmental level. Stereotyped movements that are specifically intrinsic to autism do not qualify a case for the additional diagnosis of stereotyped movement disorder. However, a number of case reports and some limited case series have suggested a potentially more interesting association between autism and Tourette's Syndrome. In the latter condition, the child exhibits persistent motor *and* vocal tics (Burd, Fisher, Kerbeshian, & Arnold, 1987; Nelson & Pribor, 1993; Realmuto & Main, 1982). Differentiation of tics and stereotyped motor mannerisms can be confusing but usually can be accomplished by an experienced examiner. It remains to be seen whether such an association is more frequent than would be expected by chance alone. A genetic vulnerability to Tourette's Syndrome has been defined for individuals without autism (Leckman et al., 1997), but no information is available in relation to the potential role of genetic factors in the transmission of tic disorders in autistic individuals. Possibly, the pathogenetic pathway for a tic disorder in autism differs from that in children without PDD; in this case, the comorbid tic + autism cases may be highly informative about alternate biological factors for Tourette's and other tic syndromes.

Affective symptoms are frequently observed in persons with autism. These include affective lability, inappropriate affective responses, anxiety, and depression. For higher-functioning autistic persons, an awareness of their difficulties may result in overt clinical depression; bipolar disorders have also been reported and may respond to lithium treatment (Gillberg, 1985; Kerbeshian, Burd, & Fisher, 1987; Komoto, Usui, & Hirata, 1984; Lainhart & Folstein, 1994; Steingard & Biederman, 1987).

Given the characteristic difficulties in social interaction and communication, as well as the frequent association of autism with mental retardation, it is not surprising that deployment and sustaining of attention would be problematic for individuals with autism (see Chapter 10). In *DSM-III-R,* the convention was established that autism and Attention Deficit Disorder (ADD) were made mutually exclusive. This

was based on the clinical belief that attentional problems in autism were better viewed as an aspect of the autistic condition and the individual's developmental level. Also, there was a clinical impression that stimulant medications used in the treatment of ADD often led to deterioration in the behavior of individuals with autism (see also Chapter 32). A few investigators have suggested that Attention Deficit Hyperactivity Disorder (ADHD) should be considered an additional diagnosis and a target of treatment in persons with autism (Ghaziuddin, Tsai, & Ghaziuddin, 1992). Firm empirical data on this issue are lacking. In *DSM-IV,* the diagnostic hierarchy has been removed and ADHD may be diagnosed for autistic individuals; but the more basic issue of their relationship remains.

Barkely (1990) has noted that the issue of an attentional problem is of much greater interest in children with PDD-NOS, particularly those who exhibit what Cohen and colleagues (1986) have referred to as Multiplex Developmental Disorder (see Chapter 6). Such children do not exhibit classical autism but have persistent problems in social interaction and the regulation of affective responses and behavior, which may suggest disorders of attention. As Barkely notes, the response to stimulant medications is sometimes dramatically negative in this group of patients. Gillberg and colleagues (Hellgren, Gillberg, & Gillberg, 1994) have described a putative condition characterized by deficits in attention, motor control, and perception (DAMP); on the basis of the follow-up data, they hypothesize that this disorder may be composed of at least two subtypes.

Autistic individuals are not immune to any other known medical conditions (Chapters 16 and 18). Yet, specific associations between autism and general medical conditions generally have not been sustained by formal research. Although some investigators (e.g., Gillberg, 1990) suggest that many different associations are common, studies that employ stringent diagnostic criteria have not supported this view (e.g., Rutter, Bailey, Bolton, & Le Couteur, 1994). In one sense, this issue is simply definitional. If one takes a very broad view of autism, a large number of persons with profound intellectual disability will be included in samples of autistic individuals;

this population has a marked increase in the number of medical conditions that may be significantly involved in these persons' developmental difficulties. The difficulties inherent in including such cases among those with more strictly defined autism are exemplified in the early reports about the association of autism with congenital rubella. Children with congenital rubella initially were reported to have many autistic-like features and to be very low functioning; over time, however, the "autism" of these cases have proven questionable.

SUBTYPES OF AUTISM

Investigators have used various approaches to subtype autism and the broader PDD class of conditions. Essentially, these attempts have fallen into two broad categories. The more common approach rests on clinical experience and the ability of clinician-investigators to notice features that are then used to delineate a specific diagnostic concept. Kanner's description of autism, or the work of Asperger, Rett, or Heller, exemplifies this approach. More recent examples include the proposed typology based on social characteristics proposed by Wing and colleagues (see Chapter 7). The major alternative is to utilize more complex statistical procedures to derive subgroups or subtypes empirically. The latter approach might seem to be more productive, but, somewhat surprisingly, this really has not been the case.

Statistical Approaches to Subtyping

Complex statistical approaches have been helpful in developing and validating screening and assessment instruments, as well as in developing criteria to operationalize diagnostic concepts. Their value in developing *new* diagnostic categories has been limited by several factors. Approaches such as cluster and factor analysis are very dependent on the characteristic of the sample being studied and on the information originally provided; one cannot identify relevant variables or combinations of variables if they are not measured in the sample. Because our knowledge regarding the underlying neuropathological basis of autism and its relationship to development and behavior

remains limited, the exact measures that would best be included in such analyses are not clear. Another set of issues surrounds a set of interrelated problems: the marked range in syndrome expression associated with age and developmental level, and the issues related to sample selection and sample size. Nosological research using complex statistical models generally requires large and representative samples of patients. Unfortunately, the samples used in most studies are small and not representative. Results may be highly dependent on the original sample and may not generalize to other samples. This problem is compounded by the fact that the meaning of behaviors may change with age and with developmental level. The diagnosis of autism may be particularly difficult to make in very young children (below age 3 years). One might assume that the "purest" form of autism is exhibited at this young age. However, as Lord (1995) has shown, some characteristic symptoms of autism, such as repetitive behaviors, often do not clearly develop before age 3 years, and significant social deficits, suggestive of autism, may markedly improve after the first 2 years of life.

Because of the strong developmental nature of changes in syndrome expression, variables such as age, developmental level, or IQ become important variables in statistical analyses. It is a testament to the creativity of engaged clinicians and to the human capacity to notice regularities that, to date, the diagnostic concepts we are presently familiar with have emerged from clinical work and not from complex statistical analyses. Such analyses may be helpful, however, in examining current diagnostic concepts and alternative ways to conceptualize syndrome boundaries. Perhaps, in the future, better diagnostic concepts will be derived, for example, within the broad category of PDD-NOS.

Despite these problems, cluster and factor-analytic approaches have been used with some frequency. For example, in an early study, Prior and colleagues (1975) observed two clusters of cases. One cluster was more similar to Kanner's syndrome in terms of early onset and clinical features; the other cluster exhibited later onset and more complex features. Siegel, Anders, Ciaranell, Bienenstock, and Kraemer (1986) identified four possible subgroups in a larger group of children with PDDs. Two groups appeared to correspond roughly to low- and higher-functioning autism; the other two groups were characterized by either schizotypal features or affective symptoms and behavior problems. Dahl, Cohen, and Provence (1986) identified two clusters of children in the PDD spectrum who had similar behavior problems but somewhat different patterns of language functioning and onset. Depending on the sample and the range of variables included in the analyses, various numbers of clusters have been derived. The less robust clusters— those with fewer cases and very complex clinical features—are less likely to be observed in subsequent studies. Eaves and colleagues (Eaves, Eaves, & Ho, 1994) used data from over 150 children with "autism spectrum" disorders. In their sample, four meaningful subtypes emerged with different behavioral and cognitive profiles. Over half the sample fell into the subtype described as typically autistic, and approximately 20% were also autistic but were cognitively functioning at a lower level. The remaining cases formed two subtypes: one was a higher-functioning group with similarities to Asperger's Syndrome, and the other had less severe difficulties. Fein, Waterhouse, Lucci, and Snyder (1985) identified eight cognitive profiles that could be related to handedness but not to more usual autistic features. More recently, Waterhouse and colleagues (1996), after studying a relatively large group of children with some form of PDD not associated with an overt medical condition, suggested that at least two overlapping continua were present, corresponding roughly to lower- and higher-functioning autism.

Methods other than cluster and factor analysis have been employed in the search for subgroups. For example, Cohen, Sudhalter, Landon-Jimenez, and Keogh (1993) utilized a novel system of pattern recognition (neural networks) as well as discriminant analyses; they argued that the neural network procedure was superior in correctly identifying whether autism was or was not present. In a well-controlled study by Cicchetti and colleagues (Cicchetti, Volkmar, Klin, & Showalter, 1995), however, the neural networks procedure was not as effective as the simple diagnostic algorithm proposed in *ICD-10* and *DSM-IV*.

Multivariate methods have also been utilized to validate existing diagnostic groupings and new possible subgroups, for example, within the broad PDD-NOS category (see also Chapter 6). Van der Gaag, Buitelar et al. (1995) utilized a multivariate cluster analysis and demonstrated differences between cases with autistic disorder and a specific subtype of PDD-NOS (multiplex or multiple complex developmental disorder) on the basis of clinical and developmental features.

Clinical Approaches to Subtyping

The issue of subtypes has also been approached from a clinical standpoint. Wing and Gould (1979) proposed a classification scheme based on the nature of observed patterns of social interaction (aloof, passive, active but odd) (see also Chapter 7). Other classifications have focused on cognitive profiles (Fein et al., 1985), language problems (Allen & Rapin, 1992), presence of signs of overt central nervous system dysfunction (Tsai, Tsai, & August, 1985), and so forth. A decade ago, it appeared that possible associations of autism with various medical conditions would have major implications for understanding subtypes and etiology. At present, however, distinctions based on the presence of a strictly defined etiology or associated medical condition simply do not correspond to obvious behavioral subtypes (Rutter, 1996).

As with the more statistically based approaches, clinically inspired approaches also must deal with the major confounding problem of intellectual level. For example, the three-group subtyping (aloof, passive, active but odd) proposed by Wing and Gould (1979) appears to sort children into relatively reliable groups; the typology has some measure of validity as well as potential benefits for planning interventions (Borden & Ollendick, 1994; Castelloe & Dawson, 1993; Volkmar & Cohen, 1989). However, differences between the subgroups appear to be largely a function of associated IQ. When IQ is controlled for, differences among the groups largely vanish (Volkmar et al., 1989).

Individuals with profound mental retardation exhibit a number of autistic-like features (Wing & Gould, 1979) without, however, meeting the full criteria for autism. These cases have many of the same service needs as those with more strictly defined autism. Various investigators have, accordingly, proposed a distinction between primary (higher) and lower-functioning autism, given the very different patterns of educational need, associated medical problems, outcome, family history, and so forth associated with lower and higher IQ (Cohen et al., 1987; Piven, Berthier, Starkstein, & Nehme, 1990; Rutter, 1996; Tsai, 1992; Waterhouse et al., 1996). This important issue remains unresolved.

SUMMARY

Leo Kanner's description (1943) of the syndrome of early infantile autism has proven to be robust and enduring. To a remarkable degree, his observations and intuitions remain fresh and inspiring. False leads in the original work have been clarified by research, and, fifty years later, we remain aware of how much work remains to be done.

Studies have clarified that the "disintegrative" PDDs (Rett's Disorder and Childhood Disintegrative Disorder) differ from strictly defined autism in various ways (Tsai, 1992; Volkmar & Rutter, 1995). The study of these unusual conditions may be helpful in clarifying mechanisms of pathogenesis relevant to autism (see Chapters 2 and 3). The validity of the newest PDD—Asperger's Disorder—apart from higher-functioning autism is less clearly established, but recent research tends to support the usefulness of distinguishing the conditions (Frith, 1991; Klin, Volkmar, Sparrow, Cicchetti, & Rourke, 1995; Ozonoff, Rogers, & Pennington, 1991). The boundaries of Asperger's Syndrome with autism and other disorders, such as schizoid disorder of childhood (Wolff, 1995) and semantic-pragmatic disorder (Bishop, 1989), remain to be firmly established (Rutter, 1996; see Chapter 5).

Probably the greatest nosological need, at present, is the classification of conditions that appear to fall within the broad class of Pervasive Developmental Disorder but do not meet criteria for presently recognized disorders. This group of conditions, referred to as either Atypical Autism or Pervasive Developmental Disorder—Not Otherwise Specified, includes a larger number of children than those who are stringently defined as autistic, and their nosological status is much less well-defined (see Chapter 6). Concepts such as multiplex developmental disorder have been proposed for some of these individuals. A large subgroup of such cases is associated with severe mental handicap. These conditions require special services similar to those required for autism (Wing & Gould, 1979; see also Chapter 7); their relationship to strictly defined autism remains an area of considerable interest and may have particular importance for genetic studies of families (Rutter, 1996). Biological and behavioral research depends on well-defined groups of patients and rigorous application of diagnostic methodologies. For example, genetic studies require clear definition of affected individuals and exclusion of false positive cases. In turn, we can hope that future nosologies will be enriched by the inclusion of other types of data, including genetic, neuroimaging, neurochemical, and other behavioral and biological markers. A critical dialectic exists between research in nosology and research of other types. Advances in both fields are mutually dependent and have the same goal: enhancing the understanding and care of individuals.

Cross-References

Other syndromes presently included as PDDs are discussed in Chapters 2 through 6; Chapter 7 provides an alternative view of issues of diagnosis and classification; changes in syndrome expression with age are discussed in Chapters 12–14.

REFERENCES

Allen, D., & Rapin, I. (1992). Autistic children are also dysphasic. In H. Naruse & E. Ornitz (Eds.), *Neurobiology of infantile autism* (pp. 157–168). Amsterdam: Exerpta Medica.

American Psychiatric Association. (1980). *Diagnostic and statistical manual of mental disorders* (3rd. ed.). Washington, DC: Author.

American Psychiatric Association. (1987). *Diagnostic and statistical manual of Mental Disorders* (3rd. ed. rev.). Washington, DC: Author.

American Psychiatric Association. (1994). *Diagnostic and statistical manual* (4th. ed.). Washington, DC: Author.

Asperger, H. (1944). Die "autistichen Psychopathen" im Kindersalter ["Autistic Psychopathy" in childhood]. *Archive fur Psychiatrie und Nervenkrankheiten, 117,* 76–136.

Barkely, R.A. (1990). *Attention Deficit Hyperactivity Disorder: A handbook for diagnosis and treatment.* New York: Guilford Press.

Baron-Cohen, S. (1989). Do autistic children have obsessions and compulsions? *British Journal of Clinical Psychology, 28*(3), 193–200.

Bender, L. (1947). Childhood schizophrenia: Clinical study of one hundred schizophrenic children. *American Journal of Orthopsychiatry, 17,* 40–56.

Bishop, D.V. (1989). Autism, Asperger's Syndrome and semantic-pragmatic disorder: Where are the boundaries? Autism [Special Issue]. *British Journal of Disorders of Communication, 24*(2), 107–121.

Bleuler, E. (1950). *Dementia praecox oder Gruppe der Schizophrenien* [Dementia Praecox or the Group of Schizophrenia] (J. Zinkin, Trans.). New York: International Universities Press.

Borden, M.C., & Ollendick, T.H. (1994). An examination of the validity of social subtypes in autism. *Journal of Autism and Developmental Disorders, 24*(1), 23–37.

Brasic, J.R., Barnett, J.Y., Kaplan, D., Sheitman, B.B., Aisemberg, P., Lafargue, R.T., Kowalik, S., Clark, A., Tsaltas, M.O., & Young, J.G. (1994). Clomipramine ameliorates adventitious movements and compulsions in prepubertal boys with autistic disorder and severe mental retardation. *Neurology, 44*(7), 1309–1312.

Bristol, M.M., Cohen, D.J., Costello, E.J., Denkla, M., Eckberg, T.J., Kallen, R., Kraemer, H.C., Lord, C., Mawer, R., McIllvane, W.I., Minshew, N., Sigman, M., & Spence, A.M. (1996). State of the science in autism: Report to the National Institute of Health. *Journal of Autism and Developmental Disorders, 26,* 121–154.

Burd, L., Fisher, W.W., Kerbeshian, J., & Arnold, M.E. (1987). Is development of Tourette disorder a marker for improvement in patients with autism and other pervasive developmental disorders? *Journal of the American Academy of Child and Adolescent Psychiatry, 26*(2), 162–165.

Cantwell, D. (1996). Classification of child and adolescent psychopathology. *Journal of Child Psychiatry and Psychology, 37,* 3–12.

Cantwell, D.P., Baker, L., & Rutter, M. (1980). Families of autistic children and dysphasic children: Family life and interaction patterns. *Advances in Family Psychiatry, 2,* 295–312.

Caparulo, B.K., & Cohen, D.J. (1977). Cognitive structures, language, and emerging social competence in autistic and aphasic children. *Journal of the American Academy of Child Psychiatry, 16*(4), 620–645.

Castelloe, P., & Dawson, J. (1993). Subclassification of children with autism and pervasive developmental disorders: A questionnaire based on Wing's subgrouping scheme. *Journal of Autism and Developmental Disorders, 23*(2), 229–241.

Chess, S., Fernandez, P., & Korn. S. (1974). Behavioral consequences of congenital rubella. *Journal of Pediatrics, 93,* 699–712.

Cicchetti, D.V., Volkmar, F.R., Klin, A., & Showalter, D. (1995). Diagnosing autism using *ICD-10* criteria: A comparison of neural networks and standard multivariate procedures. *Journal of Child Neuropsychology, 1,* 26–37.

Cohen, D.J. (1976, September). The diagnostic process in child psychiatry. *Psychiatric Annals, 6*(9), 29–56.

Cohen, D.J. (1980). The pathology of the self in primary childhood autism and Gilles de la Tourette syndrome. In B. Blinder (Ed.), *Psychiatric Clinics of North America, 3*(3), 383–402. Philadelphia, PA: W.B. Saunders.

Cohen, D.J., Caparulo, B., & Shaywitz, B. (1976). Primary childhood aphasia and childhood autism: Clinical, biological, and conceptual observations. *Journal of the American Academy of Child Psychiatry, 15*(4), 604–645.

Cohen, D.J., Paul, R., & Volkmar, F.R. (1986). Issues in the classification of pervasive and other developmental disorders: Toward *DSM-IV. Journal of the American Academy of Child Psychiatry, 25*(2), 213–220.

Cohen, D.J., Towbin, K.E., Mayes, L., & Volkmar, F.R. (1994). Developmental psychopathology of multiplex developmental disorder. In S.L. Freidman & H.C. Haywood (Eds.), *Developmental follow-up: Concepts, genres, domains and methods* (pp. 155–179). New York: Academic Press.

Cohen, D.J., Volkmar, F.R., & Paul, R. (1986). Issues in the classification of pervasive developmental disorders: History and current status of nosology. *Journal of the American Academy of Child Psychiatry, 25*(2), 158–161.

Cohen, D.J., Volkmar, F.R., & Paul, R. (1987). Issues in the classification of pervasive developmental disorders and associated conditions. In

D. Cohen & A. Donnellan (Eds.), *Handbook of Autism and Pervasive Developmental Disorders* (pp. 20–40). New York: Wiley.

Cohen, I.L., Sudhalter, V., Landon-Jimenez, D., & Keogh, M. (1993). A neural network approach to the classification of autism. *Journal of Autism and Developmental Disorders, 23*(3), 443–466.

Cohen, J. (1960). A coefficient of agreement for nominal scales. *Educational and Psychological Measurement, 20,* 37–46.

Dahl, K., Cohen, D.J., & Provence, S. (1986). Clinical and multivariate approaches to nosology of pervasive developmental disorders. *Journal of the American Academy of Child Psychiatry, 25,* 170–180.

DeMyer, M.K., Hingtgen, J.N., & Jackson, R.K. (1981). Infantile Autism reviewed: A decade of research. *Schizophrenia Bulletin, 7*(3), 388–451.

Eaves, L.C., Eaves, D.M., & Ho, H.H. (1994). Subtypes of autism by cluster analysis. *Journal of Autism and Developmental Disorders, 24*(1), 3–22.

Factor, D.C., Freeman, N.L., & Kardash, A. (1989, December). A comparison of *DSM-III* and *DSM-III-R* criteria for autism. *Journal of Autism and Developmental Disorders, 19*(4), 637–640.

Fein, D., Waterhouse, L., Lucci, D., & Snyder, D. (1985). Cognitive subtypes in developmentally disabled children: A pilot study. *Journal of Autism and Developmental Disorders, 15*(1), 77–95.

Fleiss, J.L. (1981). *Statistical methods for rates and proportions* (2nd ed.). New York: Wiley.

Fombonne, E. (1992). Diagnostic assessment in a sample of autistic and developmentally impaired adolescents. Classification and diagnosis [Special Issue]. *Journal of Autism and Developmental Disorders, 22*(4), 563–581.

Frances, A., Davis, W.W., Kline, M., Pincus, H., & First, M. (1991). The *DSM-IV* field trials: Moving towards an empirically derived classification. *European Psychiatry, 6*(6), 307–314.

Frith, U. (Ed.). (1991). *Autism and Asperger Syndrome.* Cambridge, MA: Cambridge University Press.

Ghaziuddin, M., Alessi, N., & Greden, J.F. (1995). Life events and depression in children with pervasive disorders. *Journal of Autism and Developmental Disorders, 25*(5), 495–502.

Ghaziuddin, M., Tsai, L., & Ghaziuddin, N. (1992). Comorbidity of autistic disorder in children and adolescents. *European Child & Adolescent Psychiatry, 1*(4), 209–213.

Gillberg, C. (1985). Asperger's Syndrome and recurrent psychosis: A case study. *Journal of Autism and Developmental Disorders, 15*(4), 389–397.

Gillberg, C. (1990). Medical work-up in children with autism and Asperger's Syndrome. *Brain Dysfunction, 3*(5–6), 249–260.

Gillberg, C. (1991). Debate and argument: Is autism a Pervasive Developmental Disorder? *Journal of Child Psychology & Psychiatry & Allied Disciplines, 32*(7), 1169–1170.

Gillberg, C. (1994). Debate and argument: Having Rett's Syndrome in the *ICD-10* PDD category does not make sense. *Journal of Child Psychology & Psychiatry & Allied Disciplines, 35*(2), 377–378.

Golse, B. (1995). L'autisme infantile en France en 1994. [Infantile autism in France in 1994]. *Psychiatrie de l'enfant, 38*(2), 463–476.

Gordon, C.T., Rapoport, J.L., Hamburger, S.D., State, R.C., & Mannheim, G.B. (1992). Differential response of seven subjects with autistic disorder to clomipramine and desipramine. *American Journal of Psychiatry, 149*(3), 363–366.

Gordon, C.T., State, R.C., Nelson, J.E., Hamburger, S.D., & Rapoport, J.L. (1993). A double-blind comparison of clomipramine, desipramine, and placebo in the treatment of autistic disorder. *Archives of General Psychiatry, 50*(6), 441–447.

Harper, J., & Williams, S. (1975). Age and type of onset as critical variables in early Infantile Autism. *Journal of Autism and Childhood Schizophrenia, 5,* 25–35.

Heller, T. (1908). Dementia infantilis. *Zeitschrift fur die Erforschung und Behandlung des Jugenlichen Schwachsinns, 2,* 141–165.

Hellgren, L., Gillberg, C., & Gillberg, I.C. (1994). Children with deficits in attention, motor control and perception (damp) almost grown up: The contribution of various background to outcome at age 16 years. *European Child and Adolescent Psychiatry, 3*(1), 1–15.

Hertzig, M.E., Snow, M.E., New, E., & Shapiro, T. (1990, January). *DSM-III* and *DSM-III-R* diagnosis of autism and pervasive developmental disorders in nursery school children. *Journal of the American Academy of Child and Adolescent Psychiatry, 29*(1), 123–126.

Hobbs, N. (1975). *Issues in the classification of children.* San Francisco: Jossey-Bass.

Jaselskis, C.A., Cook, E.H., & Fletcher, K.E. (1992). Clonidine treatment of hyperactive and impulsive children with Autistic Disorder. *Journal of Clinical Psychopharmacology, 12*(5), 322–327.

Kanner, L. (1943). Autistic disturbances of affective contact. *Nervous Child, 2,* 217–250.

Kerbeshian, J., Burd, L., & Fisher, W. (1987). Lithium carbonate in the treatment of two patients with Infantile Autism and atypical bipolar symptomatology. *Journal of Clinical Psychopharmacology, 7*(6), 401–405.

Klin, A., & Cohen, D.J. (1995). Perspectives theoriques sur l'autisme. [Theoretical perspectives of autism]. *Psychiatrie de l'enfant, 38*(2), 477–494.

Klin, A., Volkmar, F.R., Sparrow, S.S., Cicchetti, D.V., & Rourke, B. P. (1995). Validity and neuropsychological characterization of Asperger Syndrome: Convergence with nonverbal learning disabilities syndrome. *Journal of Child Psychology and Psychiatry, 36*(7), 1127–1140.

Kolvin, I. (1971). Studies in childhood psychoses, I: Diagnostic criteria and classification. *British Journal of Psychiatry, 118,* 381–384.

Komoto, J., Usui, S., & Hirata, J. (1984). Infantile Autism and affective disorder. *Journal of Autism and Developmental Disorders, 14*(1), 81–84.

Lainhart, J.E., & Folstein, S.E. (1994). Affective disorders in people with autism: A review of published cases. *Journal of Autism and Developmental Disorders, 24*(5), 587–601.

Leckman, J., Peterson, B., Anderson, G., Arnsten, A., Pauls, D., & Cohen, D.J. (1997). Pathogenesis of Tourette's Syndrome. *Journal of Child Psychology & Psychiatry & Allied Disciplines.*

Lord, C. (1995). Follow-up of two-year-olds referred for possible autism. *Journal of Child Psychology and Psychiatry, 36,* 1365–1382.

Lord, C., Rutter, M., & Le Couteur, A. (1994). Autism Diagnostic Interview—Revised: A revised version of a diagnostic interview for caregivers of individuals with possible pervasive developmental disorders. *Journal of Autism and Developmental Disorders, 24*(5), 659–685.

Mahler, M. (1952). On child psychoses and schizophrenia: Autistic and symbiotic infantile psychoses. *Psychoanalytic Study of the Child, 7,* 286–305.

McDougle, C.J., Kresch, L.E., Goodman, W.K., Naylor, S.T., Volkmar, F.R., Cohen, D.J., & Price, L.H. (1992, July). Clomipramine in autism: Preliminary evidence of efficacy. *Journal of the American Academy of Child and Adolescent Psychiatry, 31*(4), 746–750.

McDougle, C.J., Kresch, L.E., Goodman, W.K., Naylor, S.T., Volkmar, F.R., Cohen, D.J., & Price, L.H. (1995). A case-controlled study of repetitive thoughts and behavior in adults with Autistic Disorder and Obsessive-Compulsive Disorder. *American Journal of Psychiatry, 152*(5), 772–777.

Mundy, P., Sigman, M.D., Ungerer, J., & Sherman, T. (1986). Defining the social deficits of autism: The contribution of non-verbal communication measures. *Journal of Child Psychology & Psychiatry & Allied Disciplines, 27*(5), 657–669.

National Society for Autistic Children (NSAC). (1978). National Society for Autistic Children definition of the syndrome of autism. *Journal of Autism and Developmental Disorders, 8,* 162–167.

Nelson, E.C., & Pribor, E.F. (1993). A calendar savant with autism and Tourette syndrome: Response to treatment and thoughts on the interrelationships of these conditions. *Annals of Clinical Psychiatry, 5*(2), 135–140.

Ozonoff, S., Rogers, S.J., & Pennington, B.F. (1991). Asperger's Syndrome: Evidence of an empirical distinction from high-functioning autism. *Journal of Child Psychology and Psychiatry and Allied Disciplines, 32*(7), 1107–1122.

Petty, L.K., Ornitz, E.M., Michelman, J.D., & Zimmerman, E.G. (1984). Autistic children who become schizophrenic. *Archives of General Psychiatry, 41,* 129–135.

Piven, J., Berthier, M.L., Starkstein, S.E., & Nehme, E. (1990). Magnetic resonance imaging evidence for a defect of cerebral cortical. *American Journal of Psychiatry, 147*(6), 734–739.

Poustka, F., & Lisch, S. (1993). Autistic behaviour domains and their relation to self-injurious behaviour. *Acta Paedopsychiatrica: International Journal of Child and Adolescent Psychiatry, 56*(2), 69–73.

Provence, S., & Dahl, K. (1987). Disorders of atypical development: Diagnostic issues raised by a spectrum disorder. In D. Cohen & A. Donnellan (Eds.), *Handbook of autism and pervasive developmental disorders* (pp. 677–689). New York: V.H. Winston and John Wiley & Sons.

Quintana, H., Birmaher, B., Stedge, D., Lennon, S., Freed, J., Bridge, J., & Greenhill, L. (1995). Use of methylphenidate in the treatment of children with autistic disorder. *Journal of Autism and Developmental Disorders, 25*(3), 283–294.

Rank, B. (1949). Adaptation of the psychoanalytic technique for the treatment of young children with atypical development. *American Journal of Orthopsychiatry, 19,* 130–139.

Rapin, I. (1991). Autistic children: Diagnosis and clinical features. *Pediatrics, 87*(5, Pt. 2), 751–760.

Realmuto, G.M., & Main, B. (1982). Coincidence of Tourette's disorder and Infantile Autism. *Journal of Autism and Developmental Disorders, 12*(4), 367–372.

Rett, A. (1966). Uber ein eigenartiges hirntophisces Syndroem bei hyperammonie im Kindersalter, [Studies on the ammonia content in the serum of children with brain damage with special reference to hyperammonemia]. *Wein Medizinische Wochenschrift, 118,* 723–726.

Rumsey, J.M., Rapoport, J.L., & Sceery, W.R. (1985, July). Autistic children as adults: Psychiatric, social, and behavioral outcomes. *Journal of the American Academy of Child Psychiatry, 24*(4), 465–473.

Rutter, M. (1970). Autistic children: Infancy to adulthood. *Seminars in Psychiatry, 2,* 435–450.

Rutter, M. (1978). Diagnostic validity in child psychiatry. *Advances in Biological Psychiatry, 2,* 2–22.

Rutter, M. (1994). Debate and argument: There are connections between brain and mind and it is important that Rett syndrome be classified somewhere. *Journal of Child Psychology & Psychiatry & Allied Disciplines, 35*(2), 379–381.

Rutter, M. (1996). Autism research: Prospects and priorities. *Journal of Autism and Developmental Disorders, 26,* 257–276.

Rutter, M., Bailey, A., Bolton, P., & Le Couteur, A. (1994). Autism and known medical conditions: Myth and substance. *Journal of Child Psychology & Psychiatry & Allied Disciplines, 35*(2), 311–322.

Rutter, M., & Garmezy, N. (1983). Developmental psychopathology. In E.M. Hetherington (Ed.), *Handbook of child psychology* (Vol. 4). New York: Wiley.

Rutter, M., & Gould, M. (1985). In M. Rutter & L. Hersov (Eds.), *Child and adolescent psychiatry: Modern approaches* (2nd ed., pp. 304–321). Oxford: Blackwell Scientific Publications.

Rutter, M., & Schopler, E. (1992). Classification of pervasive developmental disorders: Some concepts and practical considerations. Classification and diagnosis [Special Issue]. *Journal of Autism and Developmental Disorders, 22*(4), 459–482.

Rutter, M., Shaffer, D., & Shepherd, M. (1975). *A multiaxial classification of child psychiatric disorders.* Geneva: World Health Organization.

Short, A., & Schopler, E. (1988). Factors relating to age of onset in autism. *Journal of Autism and Developmental Disorders, 18,* 207–216.

Siegel, B., Anders, T.F., Ciaranello, R., Bienenstock, B., & Kraemer, H.C. (1986). Empirically derived subclassification of the autistic syndrome. *Journal of Autism and Developmental Disorders, 16*(3), 275–293.

Siegel, B., Vukicevic, J., Elliott, G.R., & Kraemer, H.C. (1989, July). The use of signal detection theory to assess *DSM-III-R* criteria for autistic disorder. *Journal of the American Academy of Child and Adolescent Psychiatry, 28*(4), 542–548.

Siegel, B., Vukicevic, J., & Spitzer, R.L. (1990). Using signal detection methodology to revise *DSM-III-R:* Re-analysis of the *DSM-III-R* national field trials for autistic disorder. *Journal of Psychiatric Research, 24*(4), 293–311.

Spitzer, R. L., Endicott, J.E., & Robins, E. (1978). Research diagnostic criteria. *Archives of General Psychiatry, 35,* 773–782.

Spitzer, R.L., & Siegel, B. (1990). The *DSM-III-R* field trial of pervasive developmental disorders. *Journal of the American Academy of Child and Adolescent Psychiatry, 29*(6), 855–862.

Sponheim, E. (1996). Changing criteria of autistic disorders: A comparison of the ICD-10 research criteria and DSM-IV with DSM-III-R, CARS, and ABC. *Journal of Autism and Developmental Disorders, 26,* 513–526.

Steingard, R., & Biederman, J. (1987). Lithium responsive manic-like symptoms in two individuals with autism. *Journal of the American Academy of Child and Adolescent Psychiatry 26*(6), 932–935.

Stone, W.L., & Hogan, K.L. (1993). A structured parent interview for identifying young children with autism. *Journal of Autism and Developmental Disorders, 23*(4), 639–652.

Szatmari, P. (1992a). A review of the *DSM-III-R* criteria for Autistic Disorder. Classification and diagnosis [Special Issue]. *Journal of Autism and Developmental Disorders, 22*(4), 507–523.

Szatmari, P. (1992b). The validity of autistic spectrum disorders: A literature review. Classification and diagnosis [Special Issue]. *Journal of Autism and Developmental Disorders, 22*(4), 583–600.

Towbin, K.E., Dykens, E.M., Pearson, G.S., & Cohen, D.J. (1993). Conceptualizing "borderline syndrome of childhood" and "childhood schizophrenia" as a developmental disorder. *Journal of the American Academy of Child and Adolescent Psychiatry, 32*(4), 775–782.

Tsai, L. (1992). Is Rett Syndrome a subtype of Pervasive Developmental Disorder? *Journal of Autism and Developmental Disorders, 22,* 551–561.

Tsai, L. (1996). Brief report: Comorbid psychiatric disorders in autistic disorders. *Journal of Autism and Developmental Disorders, 26,* 159–164.

Tsai, L.Y., Tsai, M.C., & August, G.J. (1985). Brief report: Implication of EEG diagnoses in the subclassification of infantile autism. *Journal of Autism and Developmental Disorders, 15*(3), 339–344.

Van der Gaag, R.J., Buitelaar, J., Van den Ban, E., Bezemer, M., Njio, L., & Van Engeland, H. (1995). A controlled multivariate chart review of multiple complex developmental disorder. *Journal of the American Academy of Child and Adolescent Psychiatry, 34*(8), 1096–1106.

Volkmar, F.R. (1992). Childhood disintegrative disorder: Issues for *DSM-IV. Journal of Autism and Developmental Disorders, 22*(4), 625–642.

Volkmar, F.R. (1996). Brief report: Diagnostic issues in autism. *Journal of Autism and Developmental Disorders, 26,* 155–158.

Volkmar, F.R., Bregman, J., Cohen, D.J., Hooks, M., & Stevenson, J. (1989). An examination of social typologies in autism. *Journal of the American Academy of Child and Adolescent Psychiatry, 28*(1), 82–86.

Volkmar, F.R., Cicchetti, D.V., Bregman, J., & Cohen, D.J. (1992a). Three diagnostic systems for autism: *DSM-III, DSM-III-R,* and *ICD-10.* Classification and diagnosis [Special Issue]. *Journal of Autism and Developmental Disorders, 22*(4), 483–492.

Volkmar, F.R., Cicchetti, D.V., Cohen, D.J., & Bregman, J. (1992b). Brief report: Developmental aspects of *DSM-III-R* criteria for autism. Classification and diagnosis [Special Issue]. *Journal of Autism and Developmental Disorders, 22*(4), 657–662.

Volkmar, F.R., & Cohen, D.J. (1985). The experience of Infantile Autism: A first-person account by Tony W. *Journal of Autism and Developmental Disorders, 15*(1), 47–54.

Volkmar, F.R., & Cohen, D.J. (1989). Disintegrative disorder of "late onset" autism. *Journal of Child Psychology & Psychiatry & Allied Disciplines, 30*(5), 717–724.

Volkmar, F.R., & Cohen, D.J. (1991a). Comorbid association of autism and schizophrenia. *American Journal of Psychiatry, 148*(12), 1705–1707.

Volkmar, F.R., & Cohen, D.J. (1991b). Debate and argument: The utility of the term Pervasive Developmental Disorder. *Journal of Child Psychology & Psychiatry & Allied Disciplines, 32*(7), 1171–1172.

Volkmar, F.R., Cohen, D.J., Hoshino, Y., Rende, R.D., & Paul, R. (1988, February).

Phenomenology and classification of the childhood psychoses. *Psychological Medicine, 18*(1), 191–201.

Volkmar, F.R., Cohen, D.J., & Paul, R. (1986). An evaluation of DSM-III criteria for infantile autism. *Journal of the American Academy of Child Psychiatry, 25,* 190–197.

Volkmar, F.R., Klin, A., Siegel, B., Szatmari, P., Lord, C., Campbell, M., Freeman, B.J., Cicchetti, V., Rutter, M., Kline, W., Buitelaar, J., Hattab, Y., Fombonne, E., Fuentes, J., Werry, J., Stone, W., Kerbeshian, J., Hoshino, Y., Bregman, J., Loveland, K., Szymanski, L., & Towbin, K. (1994). Field trial for Autistic Disorder in *DSM-IV. American Journal of Psychiatry, 151*(9), 1361–1367.

Volkmar, F.R., & Nelson, D.S. (1990). Seizure disorders in autism. *Journal of the American Academy of Child and Adolescent Psychiatry, 29*(1), 127–129.

Volkmar, F.R., & Rutter, M. (1995). Childhood Disintegrative Disorder: Results of the *DSM-IV* autism field trial. *Journal of the American Academy of Child and Adolescent Psychiatry, 34*(8), 1092–1095.

Volkmar, F.R., & Schwab-Stone, M. (1996). Annotation: *DSM-IV. Journal of Child Psychology and Psychiatry, 37*(7), 779–784.

Volkmar, F.R., Sparrow, S.A., Goudreau, D., Cicchetti, D.V., Paul, R., & Cohen, D.J. (1987). Social deficits in autism: An operational approach using the Vineland Adaptive Behavior Scales. *Journal of the American Academy of Child and Adolescent Psychiatry, 26*(2), 156–161.

Volkmar, F.R., Stier, D.M., & Cohen, D.J. (1985). Age of recognition of Pervasive Developmental Disorder. *American Journal of Psychiatry, 142*(12), 1450–1452.

Waterhouse, L., Morris, R., Allen, D., Dunn, M., Fein, D., Feinstein, C., Rapin, I., & Wing, L. (1996). Diagnosis and classification in autism. *Journal of Autism and Developmental Disorders, 26,* 59–86.

Waterhouse, L., Wing, L., Spitzer, R., & Siegel, B. (1992). Pervasive developmental disorders: From *DSM-III* to *DSM-III-R.* Classification and diagnosis [Special Issue]. *Journal of Autism and Developmental Disorders, 22*(4), 525–549.

Waterhouse, L., Wing, L., Spitzer, R.L., & Siegel, B. (1993). Diagnosis by *DSM-III-R* versus *ICD-10* criteria. *Journal of Autism and Developmental Disorders, 23*(3), 572–573.

Werry, J.S. (1996). Childhood schizophrenia. In F.R. Volkmar (Ed.), *Psychoses and pervasive developmental disorders in childhood and adolescence* (pp. 1–48). Washington, DC: American Psychiatric Press.

Wing, L. (1980, November). Childhood autism and social class: A question of selection? *British Journal of Psychiatry, 137,* 410–417.

Wing, L. (1981). Asperger's Syndrome: A clinical account. *Psychological Medicine, 11*(1), 115–129.

Wing, L., & Gould, J. (1979, March). Severe impairments of social interaction and associated abnormalities. *Journal of Autism and Developmental Disorders, 9*(1), 11–29.

Wolff, S. (1995). *Loners: The life path of unusual children.* London: Routledge.

World Health Organization. (1990). *International classification of diseases.* (10th ed., Draft version). Geneva: Author.

World Health Organization (WHO). (1990). *The ICD-10 classification of mental and behavioural disorders: Diagnostic criteria for research* [Draft of 2/90]. Geneva: Author.

World Health Organization (WHO). (1992). *The ICD-10 classification of mental and behavioural disorders: Clinical descriptions and diagnostic guidelines.* Geneva: Author.

World Health Organization (WHO). (1993). *The ICD-10 classification of mental and behavioural disorders: Diagnostic criteria for research.* Geneva: Author.

CHAPTER 2

Epidemiology of Autism: Overview and Issues Outstanding

SUSAN E. BRYSON

Epidemiological research serves both theoretical and practical purposes. It has the potential to reveal not only the prevalence of disorders, but also their course and outcomes, and their underlying neuropsychopathology and etiology. Epidemiological research can also tell us about affected persons' needs and responsiveness to treatment. Ultimately, we seek understanding so that prevention and more effective treatment are possible.

This chapter provides an overview of prevalence data on autism. For a comprehensive review of studies conducted over a 30-year period, the reader is referred to Wing (1993). The consistent patterns that emerged from Wing's review are outlined here, with particular attention to recent reports of a higher prevalence of autism than was previously documented. Data on outcomes in autism are summarized. Discussion then turns to issues outstanding, including those of both theoretical and practical importance. The concluding section suggests that future epidemiological research on autism needs to be more analytical (than descriptive) and should be grounded within a comprehensive developmental framework.

OVERVIEW OF FINDINGS

Wing's (1993) review highlights at least three important issues in existing epidemiological

research on autism. First, recent studies generally have yielded prevalence estimates at least twice as high as those reported earlier. Wing concludes that there is no clear evidence for real increases across time or place, although escalation on either dimension is possible. Second, evidence of a higher prevalence among first-generation immigrants may be contributory (Gillberg, Steffenburg, Borjesson, & Andersson, 1987; Wing, 1979, 1980), but both the reliability and the theoretical significance of this evidence remain to be established. Third, Wing attributes the higher estimates to changes in diagnostic criteria, and to an increasing awareness of the expression of autism in individuals who are either severely cognitively impaired or cognitively more capable (for similar conclusions, see Bryson, 1996; and Gillberg, Steffenburg, & Schaumann, 1991).

In the initial surveys, the prevalence of autism was estimated at 4 to 5 per 10,000 persons (see, c.g., the exemplary work of Lotter, 1966). Recent studies, notably those with the most rigorous methods of ascertainment, have consistently yielded rates of about 1 per 1,000 persons (e.g., Bryson, Clark, & Smith, 1988; Sugiyama & Abe, 1989). Only one study has provided prevalence data on the broader Pervasive Developmental Disorder (PDD) category, of which autism is the most extreme form. Wing and Gould (1979) report that about 2 per

This work was supported by funds from the National Health Research Development Program. I thank Isabel Smith and Ann Wainwright for their helpful comments on an earlier draft. Address correspondence to: Susan Bryson, Department of Psychology, York University, 4700 Keele Street, North York, Ontario, Canada M3J 1P3.

1,000 persons show the triad of social, communicative, and imaginative impairment—including autism and related PDDs, but not those defined by two rather than three domains of impairment (see, e.g., American Psychiatric Association, 1994).

What do we make of these data, which, at first glance, appear discrepant? The method of ascertainment is clearly important (see Wing, Yeates, Brierley, & Gould, 1976, for a relevant discussion). Studies based on an exhaustive screening of an entire geographically defined population or an entire birth cohort tend to yield higher prevalence estimates. Even more fundamental, Wing (1993) argues, are the criteria used for inclusion. Autism continues to be defined behaviorally, and, over time, our conceptualization of autism, and hence the way we define it, has changed.

In the early epidemiological studies, autism was defined by a set of behaviors operationalized by Lotter (1966) and in conformance to Kanner's (1943) rich original description of the syndrome. Kanner emphasized two main features: (a) affective aloofness and (b) elaborate rituals. These features capture the essence and uniqueness of autism; they define a prototype referred to as "classic" autism, which is generally considered to be the most extreme expression of the disorder.

More recently, diagnostic criteria have focused on the coexistence of domains of impairment (in socialization, communication, and imagination), expressed in various but related ways (see, e.g., Denckla, 1986; Waterhouse, Wing, Spitzer, & Siegel, 1992; for a comparison of recent diagnostic criteria, see Volkmar, Cicchetti, Bregman, & Cohen, 1992). This broader conceptualization of autism owes much to the landmark work of Wing and her colleagues. Wing and Gould (1979) have argued for the primacy of severe social impairment (notably, a lack of social reciprocity) and have shown that this invariably coexists with communicative and imaginative impairment and a tendency to engage in various repetitive behaviors. In their study, like that of Lotter (1966), 0.05% conformed to the prototype of autism (classic or classiclike autism); an additional 0.16% showed less severe but clinically significant impairment in the same triad of functions (see Ehlers & Gillberg, 1993, for

even higher estimates for the most intellectually capable PDD persons).

Wing and Gould (1979) emphasize that no clear (behavioral) boundaries exist between classic autism and less severe variant forms (socially passive or "active-but-odd" vs. aloof, as elaborated by Wing & Attwood, 1987). By the same token, Bryson et al. (1988) acknowledge that their estimate of 0.10% for autism no doubt overlaps Wing and Gould's larger socially impaired group. The main point is that a spectrum of similarly impaired children exists (Wing, 1981, 1988), and, in the absence of a biological marker specific to autism, lines of demarcation remain arbitrary. A sizable number of children show the triad of "autistic" impairments; their health and the social significance of their impairments need to be evaluated against the burden of suffering and care incurred (see below).

Two additional and related findings bear emphasizing. First, broader definitions of autism have yielded somewhat different distributions in measured intelligence (IQ). As Wing (1993) has noted, there is a higher proportion of both severely cognitively impaired and more cognitively capable individuals than is the case with more classic autism, which tends to predominate in the 50-to-70 IQ range. By implication, individuals at either end of the IQ distribution should, on average, be less severely autistic. Systematic research has failed to show a linear relationship between IQ and severity of autism (McLennan, Lord, & Schopler, 1993; Volkmar, Szatmari, & Sparrow, 1993).

Second, there is evidence that the ratio of males to females varies with how autism is defined. The ratio of males to females is 3:1 or 4:1 for more classic autism (e.g., Lotter, 1966; Wing & Gould, 1979). In studies using broader definitions, the ratio appears to vary in a linear fashion with IQ. It approaches 2:1 in those with severe cognitive impairment and appears considerably greater than 3:1 or 4:1 in the cognitively most capable (Ehlers & Gillberg, 1993; Wing & Gould, 1979), although cognitively capable females may be less likely to be diagnosed PDD by virtue of being less socially impaired than their male counterparts (McLennan et al., 1993; Volkmar et al., 1993). In any event, with broader definitions of autism, the IQ distribution for females may be either skewed toward the lower end or bimodal; for males, IQ appears to be more normally distributed (with a lower-than-normal mean), or skewed toward the upper (autistic) end. As others have suggested (e.g., Lord & Schopler, 1987), sex-related differences in phenotype may index differences in etiology, genetic or otherwise.

A final comment is warranted about outcomes in autism. Comprehensive reviews of existing research are provided by Lotter (1978), Gillberg (1991), and Venter, Lord, and Schopler (1992). Very briefly, results from the earlier studies indicated that outcome was generally poor. Few individuals (10% to 15%) had gainful employment; most required some degree of ongoing care or supervision; and as many as 50% required a great deal of assistance. Recent studies are scarce but, where they do exist, the results are more promising. Measures of educational attainment, employment status, self-sufficiency, and social adaptation suggest the outcomes are better. Evidence of improved outcomes over the past decade has been linked to upgraded diagnostic, psychoeducational, and social services (Bryson, 1996; Gillberg, 1991; Kobayashi, Murata, & Yoshinga, 1992; Szatmari et al., 1989; Venter, Lord, & Schopler, 1992).

An overriding finding is that higher IQs and functional language prior to age 5 are associated with better outcomes in autism (e.g., Lotter, 1974; Rutter, Greenfield, & Lockyer, 1967; Venter et al., 1992), although a significant proportion of the variance remains unexplained. For example, a subset of linguistically and cognitively more capable individuals fares relatively poorly; yet, some cognitively capable but linguistically weak individuals, despite their more flagrant autism, do remarkably well. The presence of an additional psychiatric disturbance may contribute to the variability in outcome. In addition, systematic study of the effects of treatment on outcome is needed.

A sizable number of individuals with autism appear at considerable risk. During adolescence, approximately 30%, most of whom are lower-functioning (IQ < 50), show evidence of behavioral regression or aggravation, which may persist well into adulthood (e.g., Gillberg, 1984; Kanner, Rodriquez, & Ashenden, 1972;

Kobayashi et al., 1992). This regression or aggravation has been associated with the concurrent development of seizures (in 25% to 30% of the total population) and may reflect the presence of an additional psychiatric disturbance, notably depression (Gillberg & Steffenburg, 1987; Wing & Attwood, 1987; for a relevant review, see Lainhart & Folstein, 1994). This group bears further investigation. They serve to underscore the need for longitudinal data aimed at identifying the nature of, and possible differences in, the developmental pathways characteristic of autism or PDD.

ISSUES OUTSTANDING

To date, little is known about borderline autistic conditions, namely, the broader PDD category and Asperger's Syndrome. Individuals so affected are assumed to be less impaired, although even among the more classically autistic, improvement is most striking in the social domain (Kanner et al., 1972; Rutter, 1970). Some autistic persons are described as resembling those with PDD or Asperger's Syndrome later in life (i.e., some change from being predominantly aloof to being more socially passive or active but odd; Wing & Attwood, 1987). In an ongoing longitudinal study, preliminary evidence has been provided for parallel developmental trajectories that differ in rate or timing rather than in kind (Szatmari, Archer, & Fisman, 1992). At age 4 to 6 years, high-functioning autistic children were distinguished from those with Asperger's Syndrome by virtue of their inferior language (both receptive and expressive) and social competence. These differences were stable 2 years later, but the gap decreased considerably in a subgroup of autistic children who developed better language in the interim.

These data are consistent with and extend Wing's (1981, 1988) claim of a continuum of autistic conditions. They also underscore the potential usefulness of a broader definition of autism, as does evidence that milder variants coexist with more classic autism in the same (extended) families (Pickles et al., 1995). Among the outstanding questions are whether the developmental trajectories of lower-functioning autistic children are similar to or different from those of higher-functioning children, and whether phenotypic differences in development serve as markers for differences in etiology. It is also possible that heterogeneity in the expression of autism reflects the same causal factors operating at different points in fetal or postnatal development.

In any event, there is a pressing need for longitudinal outcome data on the entire spectrum of autistic conditions. Patterns of development in the same children over time (on multiple occasions) need to be identified, taking into account the overlap between PDDs and other phenotypically similar disorders of development (see, e.g., Dykens, Hodapp, Ort, & Leckman, 1993, for relevant data on Fragile X Syndrome). Longitudinal research can address basic theoretical questions while informing our approach to diagnosis and treatment. Is it possible, for example, to reliably and accurately identify autism and related PDDs prior to age 3 years (see, e.g., Baron-Cohen et al., 1996; Lord, Rutter, & Le Couteur, 1994)? What pathways or trajectories of development are specific to autism and PDD? Which ones are associated with better outcomes, and why? And to what extent does method, intensity, and/or duration of treatment, or age of treatment onset, explain the variability in outcome?

Bradley and Bryson (in preparation) are currently conducting an epidemiological study of a geographically defined population of 14- to 21-year-olds who have developmental disorders. This study will provide data on the prevalence of individuals who exhibit the triad of social, communicative, and imaginative impairment (both autism and the broader PDD category). For this purpose, we are using the Autism Diagnostic Interview—Revised (Lord, Rutter, & Le Couteur, 1994), which will allow comparison to the estimates reported by Wing and Gould (1979; approximately 2 per 1,000 persons and roughly 30% of the developmentally disabled population). Among the questions of interest are whether additional behavioral or psychiatric disturbances are more prevalent in those with autism or PDD, and whether these disturbances are associated with poorer outcomes, as defined by functional status. The study is also designed to identify factors that might contribute to the development of behavioral and psychiatric disturbances in developmentally disabled individuals with and without autism or PDD.

Epidemiological research has played an important role in advancing our understanding and treatment of individuals with autism. It originally served to underscore the rejection of a psychogenic account of the disorder, and it continues to generate ideas about the underlying pathology and etiology (see, e.g., Rodier, Ingram, Tisdale, Nelson, & Romano, 1996). Data on prevalence, course, outcome, and associated disorders have also been useful in planning appropriate services. Future epidemiological research needs to be more analytic—that is, designed to test specific hypotheses about causality and prevention, and about how we can best identify and treat those affected even earlier in life. Future research also needs to be grounded in developmental theory (psychosocial or neurobiological) and sensitive to both the heterogeneity in autism and the overlap with other similar developmental disorders.

CONCLUSION

Recent estimates of the prevalence of autism are generally at least twice as high as those reported earlier. The higher rates have been attributed to changes in how we define and thus diagnose autism, and to an increasing awareness of its expression in both severely cognitively impaired and more cognitively capable individuals. Autism continues to be defined behaviorally, and lines of demarcation between classic or classiclike autism and the broader PDD category appear arbitrary. There is evidence for continuity within the population of those affected, although a better understanding of the nature of differences in developmental course and outcomes is needed. Heterogeneity in the expression of autism also needs to be evaluated relative to phenotypically similar disorders of development.

Studies conducted during the previous two decades indicated that outcomes in autism are generally poor. Recent reports of more positive outcomes are attributed to improvements in the availability and appropriateness of treatment. Issues outstanding include the need for: earlier identification and treatment; research aimed at identifying pathways or trajectories of development; and systematic studies of the effects of treatment on outcome. Future epidemiological research needs to be both driven by specific hypotheses and embedded within a comprehensive developmental framework. It is to be hoped that the momentum achieved in all fronts—basic and applied research, and clinical service—will be adequately fostered. Research on autism is a health issue that has social priority in its own right and by virtue of its very real potential to advance our understanding of normal psychosocial and neurobiological development.

Cross-References

Issues in diagnosis of autism and other pervasive developmental disorders are discussed in Chapter 1 and Chapters 3 through 7. Diagnostic instruments specific to autism are reviewed in Chapter 21.

REFERENCES

American Psychiatric Association. (1994). *Diagnostic and statistical manual of mental disorders, DSM-IV* (4th ed.). Washington, DC: Author.

Baron-Cohen, S., Cox, A., Baird, G., Swettenham, J., Nightingale, N., Morgan, K., Drew, A., & Charman, T. (1996). Psychological markers in the detection of autism in infancy in a large population. *British Journal of Psychiatry, 168,* 1–6.

Bradley, E., & Bryson, S.E. (in preparation). *Epidemiological study of triad of impairment among young people.* Bradley-University of Toronto.

Bryson, S.E. (1996). Epidemiology of autism. *Journal of Autism and Developmental Disorders, 26,* 165–167.

Bryson, S.E., Clark, B.S., & Smith, I.M. (1988). First report of a Canadian epidemiological study of autistic syndromes. *Journal of Child Psychology and Psychiatry, 29,* 433–446.

Denckla, M.B. (1986). Editorial: New diagnostic criteria for autism and related behavioral disorders—guidelines for research protocols. *Journal of the American Academy of Child Psychiatry, 25,* 221–224.

Dykens, E.M., Hodapp, R.M., Ort, S.I., & Leckman, J.F. (1993). Trajectory of adaptive behavior in males with Fragile X Syndrome. *Journal of Autism and Developmental Disorders, 23,* 135–145.

Ehlers, S., & Gillberg, C. (1993). The epidemiology of Asperger Syndrome: A total population study. *Journal of Child Psychology and Psychiatry, 34,* 1327–1350.

Gillberg, C. (1984). Autistic children growing up: Problems during puberty and adolescence. *Developmental Medicine and Child Neurology, 26,* 122–129.

Gillberg, C. (1991). Outcome in autism and autistic-like conditions. *Journal of the American Academy of Child and Adolescent Psychiatry, 30,* 375–382.

Gillberg, C., & Steffenburg, S. (1987). Outcome and prognostic factors in Infantile Autism and similar conditions: A population-based study of 46 cases followed through puberty. *Journal of Autism and Developmental Disorders, 17,* 273–287.

Gillberg, C., Steffenburg, S., Borjesson, B., & Andersson, L. (1987). Infantile Autism in children of immigrant parents: A population-based study from Göteborg, Sweden. *British Journal of Psychiatry, 150,* 856–857.

Gillberg, C., Steffenburg, S., & Schaumann, H. (1991). Is autism more common now than ten years ago? *British Journal of Psychiatry, 158,* 403–409.

Kanner, L. (1943). Autistic disturbances of affective contact. *Nervous Child, 2,* 217–250.

Kanner, L., Rodriquez, A., & Ashenden, B. (1972). How far can autistic children go in matters of social adaptation? *Journal of Autism and Childhood Schizophrenia, 2,* 9–33.

Kobayashi, R., Murata, T., & Yoshinga, K. (1992). A follow-up study of 201 children with autism in Kyushu and Yamaguchi areas, Japan. *Journal of Autism and Developmental Disorders, 22,* 395–411.

Lainhart, J.E., & Folstein, S.E. (1994). Affective disorders in people with autism: A review of published cases. *Journal of Autism and Developmental Disorders, 24,* 587–601.

Lord, C., Rutter, M., & Le Couteur, A. (1994). Autism Diagnostic Interview—Revised: A revised version of a diagnostic interview for caregivers of individuals with possible pervasive developmental disorders. *Journal of Autism and Developmental Disorders, 24,* 659–685.

Lord, C., & Schopler, E. (1987). Neurobiological implications of sex differences in autism. In E. Schopler & G. Mesibov (Eds.), *Neurobiological issues in autism* (pp. 191–211). New York: Plenum Press.

Lotter, V. (1966). Epidemiology of autistic conditions in young children, I. Prevalence. *Social Psychiatry, 1,* 124–137.

Lotter, V. (1974). Factors related to outcome in autistic children. *Journal of Autism and Childhood Schizophrenia, 4,* 263–277.

Lotter, V. (1978). Follow-up studies. In M. Rutter & E. Schopler (Eds.), *Autism: A reappraisal of concepts and treatment* (pp. 475–495). New York: Plenum Press.

McLennan, J.D., Lord, C., & Schopler, E. (1993). Sex differences in higher-functioning people with autism. *Journal of Autism and Developmental Disorders, 23,* 217–227.

Pickles, A., Bolton, P., MacDonald, H., Bailey, A., Le Couteur, A., Sim, C.H., & Rutter, M. (1995). Latent-class analysis of recurrence risks for complex phenotypes with selection and measurement error: A twin and family history study of autism. *American Journal of Human Genetics, 57,* 717–726.

Rodier, P.M., Ingram, J.L., Tisdale, B., Nelson, S., & Romano, J. (1996). Embryological origin for autism: Developmental anomalies of the cranial nerve motor nuclei. *Journal of Comparative Neurology, 370,* 247–261.

Rutter, M. (1970). Autistic children: Infancy to adulthood. *Seminars in Psychiatry, 2,* 435–450.

Rutter, M., Greenfield, D., & Lockyer, L. (1967). A five- to fifteen-year follow-up study of infantile psychoses, II. Social and behavioral outcome. *British Journal of Psychiatry, 113,* 1183–1199.

Sugiyama, T., & Abe, T. (1989). The prevalence of autism in Nagoya, Japan: A total population study. *Journal of Autism and Developmental Disorders, 19,* 87–96.

Szatmari, P., Archer, L., & Fisman, S. (1992, October). *A two-year follow-up study of high-functioning preschool children with pervasive developmental disorders.* Presented at annual meeting of the American Academy of Child and Adolescent Psychiatry, Washington, DC.

Szatmari, P., Bartolucci, G., Bremner, R., Bond, S., & Rich, S. (1989). A follow-up study of high-functioning autistic children. *Journal of Autism and Developmental Disorders, 19,* 213–225.

Venter, A., Lord, C., & Schopler, E. (1992). A follow-up study of high-functioning autistic children. *Journal of Child Psychology and Psychiatry, 33,* 489–507.

Volkmar, F.R., Cicchetti, D.V., Bregman, J., & Cohen, D.J. (1992). Three diagnostic systems for autism: *DSM-III, DSM-III-R,* and *ICD-10. Journal of Autism and Developmental Disorders, 22,* 483–492.

Volkmar, F.R., Szatmari, P., & Sparrow, S.S. (1993). Sex differences in pervasive developmental disorders. *Journal of Autism and Developmental Disorders, 23,* 579–591.

Waterhouse, L., Wing, L., Spitzer, R., & Siegel, B. (1992). Pervasive developmental disorders: From *DSM-III* to *DSM-III-R. Journal of Autism and Developmental Disorders, 22,* 525–549.

Wing, L. (1979). Mentally retarded children in Camberwell (London). In H. Hafner (Ed.), *Estimating needs for mental health care* (pp. 107–112). Berlin: Springer-Verlag.

Wing, L. (1980). Childhood autism and social class: A question of selection. *British Journal of Psychiatry, 137,* 410–417.

Wing, L. (1981). Asperger's Syndrome: A clinical account. *Psychological Medicine, 11,* 115–130.

Wing, L. (1988). The continuum of autistic disorders. In E. Schopler & G.M. Mesibov (Eds.), *Diagnosis and assessment in autism* (pp. 91–110). New York: Plenum Press.

Wing, L. (1993). The definition and prevalence of autism: A review. *European Child and Adolescent Psychiatry, 2,* 61–74.

Wing, L., & Attwood, T. (1987). Syndromes of autism and atypical development. In D.J. Cohen & A.M. Donnellan (Eds.), *Handbook of autism and pervasive developmental disorders* (pp. 3–19). New York: Wiley.

Wing, L., & Gould, J. (1979). Severe impairments of social interaction and associated abnormalities in children: Epidemiology and classification. *Journal of Autism and Childhood Schizophrenia, 9,* 11–29.

Wing, L., Yeates, S.R., Brierley, L.M., & Gould, J. (1976). The prevalence of early childhood autism: A comparison of administrative and epidemiological studies. *Psychological Medicine, 6,* 89–100.

CHAPTER 3

Childhood Disintegrative Disorder

FRED R. VOLKMAR, AMI KLIN, WENDY MARANS, AND DONALD J. COHEN

Nearly 90 years ago, Theodore Heller, a Viennese educator, reported on six children who had exhibited severe developmental regression at ages 3 to 4 years, following a period of apparently normal development. Once the condition had its onset, developmental recovery was quite limited. Initially, Heller (1908) termed this condition dementia infantilis. Over the subsequent years, the concept has been variously named, and perhaps 100 cases have been reported in the world literature (Volkmar, 1992). Information on the condition is much more limited as compared, for example, to autism. This chapter reviews the development of the diagnostic concept, current definitions, information on clinical features, and evidence for the validity of this condition apart from autism. Available information on the course, epidemiology, associated conditions, and differential diagnosis of the condition is summarized, although this information must be regarded as somewhat tentative and limited. Given the relatively small number of reported cases, a lack of familiarity with the condition and a lack of official recognition and formal diagnostic guidelines may have caused many cases to have been overlooked or misdiagnosed.

DEVELOPMENT OF THE DIAGNOSTIC CONCEPT

Historical Background

Although Heller's work occurred early in the 20th century, many decades were to pass before his diagnostic concept was widely recognized. Diagnostic debate initially centered around issues of continuity with schizophrenia and, more recently, with autism. This debate has reflected other developments in diagnostic terminology. The closing years of the 19th century had been a time of major developments in psychiatric taxonomy. Psychiatric disturbances such as manic-depressive illness and schizophrenia had been identified in adults. Subsequent attempts were made to extend the concept of schizophrenia, or, as it was then known, dementia praecox, to children (see, e.g., de Sanctis's 1906 work on dementia praecossima).

Until recently, researchers and clinicians commonly assumed a continuity of phenotypic expression of all childhood "psychotic" conditions with schizophrenia. This tendency to lump cases together posed a substantial impediment to research studies. Various lines of evidence began to suggest the importance of making distinctions; for example, it became clear that autism differed from schizophrenia of childhood onset in terms of clinical features, course, outcome, and family history. The pioneering studies of Kolvin (1971) were particularly important because they demonstrated that, within a large group of "psychotic" children, there was a bimodal pattern of onset. The early-onset group had begun to have troubles at birth or within a year or so after birth; the later-onset group apparently developed normally for many years. Clinical features of the early-onset group included

The authors acknowledge the support of NICHD Grant 5P01-HD-03008-28.

marked impairments in social, cognitive, and language development similar to those dscribed by Kanner for autism, whereas the later-onset group exhibited delusions, hallucinations, and other features more similar to schizophrenia. There was no higher-than-expected frequency of schizophrenia among family members of the early-onset group, but there was such an increase among first-degree relatives of the late-onset group. This observation has been replicated at several centers (e.g., Makita, 1966; Volkmar, Cohen, Hoshino, Rende, & Paul, 1988). In these studies, a handful of cases did not seem to fall easily into the early- or the late-onset group; for example, 3 of the 83 cases in Kolvin's series exhibited an intermediate age of onset between the autistic and schizophrenic groups.

These and other data on the validity of autism led to its official recognition in the *Diagnostic and Statistical Manual of Mental Disorders* (*DSM-III;* American Psychiatric Association [APA], 1980), where it was placed in a new class, Pervasive Developmental Disorder. Infantile Autism was defined on the basis of marked social, language, and other problems that were evident by 30 months of age. Partly in recognition of the fact that a few children seemed to develop an autistic-like condition after 30 months, *DSM-III* included a category termed Childhood Onset Pervasive Developmental Disorder (COPDD). This category was not meant to be analogous to Heller's diagnostic concept; the implicit presumption in *DSM-III* was that such cases invariably reflected some progressive neuropathological process. However, the ninth revision of the *International Classification of Diseases* (*ICD-9;* World Health Organization [WHO], 1987) had included a category for disintegrative psychosis or Heller's Syndrome, defined on the basis of "normal or near normal development in the first years of life, followed by a loss of social skills and of speech together with a severe disorder of emotion, behavior, and relationships." *ICD-9* did not, however, prove as influential as *DSM-III,* primarily because the latter system included explicit guidelines for diagnosis.

Although a very detailed definition of COPDD was included in *DSM-III,* it quickly became clear that this diagnostic concept was problematic in many respects (Volkmar, 1987), and only a handful of reports appeared in the literature (Burd, Fisher, & Kerbeshian, 1988). When *DSM-III* was revised (*DSM-III-R;* APA, 1987) the COPDD concept was dropped. Diagnostic criteria for autism were expanded in number and in concept, and early onset of autism was dropped as an essential diagnostic feature; Autistic Disorder was the only operationally defined disorder within the PDD class. These changes meant that historical information, such as the pattern and time of onset, was not particularly relevant to the diagnosis of autism. Children who would have been described as having Disintegrative Psychosis in *ICD-9* were usually said to have Autistic Disorder in *DSM-III-R*. This unfortunate state of affairs became even more complex when the drafts of the *ICD-10* revision began to appear.

Childhood Disintegrative Disorder in *ICD-10* and *DSM-IV*

In contrast to *DSM-III-R, ICD-10* (WHO, 1990) included a draft definition of Childhood Disintegrative Disorder. This definition was largely consistent with earlier work (e.g., Heller, 1930; Zappert, 1921) that had generally suggested the following diagnostic features:

1. A distinctive pattern of syndrome onset (a period of several years of normal development before a marked deterioration).
2. Progressive deterioration (either gradual or abrupt) and loss of skills in multiple areas once the syndrome had its onset.
3. Behavioral and affective symptoms.
4. An absence of features of gross neurological dysfunction.

In the draft version of *ICD-10,* criteria for the condition included apparently normal development *for at least 2 years* with age-appropriate social, communicative, and other skills; a *definite loss* of skills in more than one area; development of problems in social interaction, communication, and restricted patterns of interest or behavior of the type observed in autism; and a loss of interest in the environment. By definition, the disorder could not coexist with autism or with any other explicitly defined Pervasive Developmental Disorder—schizophrenia, elective mutism, or the syndrome of acquired aphasia with epilepsy.

Using the *ICD-10* draft version's criteria, Volkmar and Cohen (1989) identified a series of 10 cases of apparent CDD from within a larger sample. Clinical characteristics were then contrasted to cases of autism that had been identified before or after age 24 months. This comparison was particularly appropriate to the issue of whether CDD simply represented late-onset autism, because differences between the groups on some external measure(s) would tend to support the validity of CDD apart from late-onset autism. This was indeed the case. Cases with late-onset autism tended to be higher functioning, and the CDD cases were more likely to be mute, to be in residential placement, and so forth. Rather than being simply late-onset autism, CDD appeared to have distinctive features, a clinical course, and an even worse outcome.

The inclusion of CDD in *ICD-10* represented a marked divergence from *DSM-III-R* and had clear implications for the definition of autism in *DSM-IV* (APA, 1994). As part of the *DSM-IV* revision process, Volkmar (1992) conducted a review of the available data on autism. Issues of concern in this review were: (a) use of the diagnostic concept in clinical practice; (b) evidence supporting the validity of the diagnostic relative to autism on the one hand and a host of neurological conditions on the other; (c) definition of the disorder; and (d) whether the condition would be appropriately grouped with autism in the PDD class. Seventy-seven cases were reviewed, and the results suggested that, although the condition was apparently relatively rare, it did appear to merit inclusion in *DSM-IV* because it differed significantly from autism in several respects, and the condition was not always or even usually associated with an identifiable neurological condition that might account for the deterioration.

Inclusion of CDD in *DSM-IV* was also suggested by the results of the *DSM-IV* field trial for autism and related conditions (Volkmar, Klin, et al., 1994; Volkmar & Rutter, 1995). Although the field trial was primarily concerned with the development and validation of the *DSM-IV* diagnosis of autism, 16 cases of CDD that had been previously evaluated at participating centers were included. Of even more interest, 15 additional cases that met *ICD-10* criteria for CDD were identified in the field trial. In these cases, the clinician had not given CDD as the clinical diagnosis but had noted the presence of various diagnostic features of the condition. This is not surprising. Particularly in the United States, clinicians have been much less familiar with the diagnostic concept. Relative to cases with autism in the field trial, cases with CDD were more likely to be mute and had greater degrees of associated mental handicap. As a result of these various lines of data, CDD was included in *DSM-IV*.

As noted by Volkmar and Rutter (1995), the *DSM-IV* and *ICD-10* (WHO, 1993) criteria for the condition are conceptually very similar. However, for the sake of brevity, the *DSM-IV* system is somewhat less detailed and less truly operationalized. In addition, *ICD-10* includes loss of interest in the objects and the environment as a diagnostic criterion. *ICD-10* also gives a more explicit indication that the actual behavioral criteria for autism must be met. As a practical matter, it would appear that the diagnosis should probably *not* be made if this is not in fact the case. In both *DSM-IV* and *ICD-10,* the age and pattern of onset are particularly important for the definition of the condition; that is, after a period of prolonged normal development, there must be a marked regression associated with the acquisition of behaviors commonly seen in autism. It is hoped that increased awareness of CDD will stimulate identification and research of cases, and that increasingly better guidelines for diagnosis will be developed (Kurita, 1989). *ICD-10* criteria are listed in Table 3.1.

CLINICAL FEATURES

Onset of CDD

Age of Onset

As noted previously, the onset of CDD is a highly distinctive and essential diagnostic feature. Development prior to the regression is relatively prolonged (several years) and should

TABLE 3.1   ICD-10 Diagnostic Criteria for Childhood Disintegrative Disorder

Childhood Disintegrative Disorder

A. Development is apparently normal up to the age of at least 2 years. The presence of normal age-appropriate skills in communication, social relationships, play, and adaptive behavior at age 2 years or later is required for diagnosis.

B. There is a definite loss of previously acquired skills at about the time of onset of the disorder. The diagnosis requires a clinically significant loss of skills (not just a failure to use them in certain situations) in at least two of the following areas:

  (1) expressive or receptive language;

  (2) play;

  (3) social skills or adaptive behavior;

  (4) bowel or bladder control;

  (5) motor skills.

C. Qualitatively abnormal social functioning is manifest in at least two of the following areas:

  (1) qualitative abnormalities in reciprocal social interaction (of the type defined for autism);

  (2) qualitative abnormalities in communication (of the type defined for autism);

  (3) restricted, repetitive, and stereotyped patterns of behavior, interests, and activities, including motor stereotypies and mannerisms;

  (4) a general loss of interest in objects and in the environment.

D. The disorder is not attributable to the other varieties of pervasive developmental disorder; acquired aphasia with epilepsy (F80.6); elective mutism (F94.0); Rett's syndrome (F84.2); or schizophrenia (F20.-).

Reprinted with permission from the International Classification of Diseases, 10th edition: Diagnostic Criteria for Research, WHO, Geneva, 1993, pages 151–152.

be reasonably normal; for example, the child has the capacity to speak in sentences by age 2 (WHO, 1990). Interestingly, Heller's impression (1930) was that onset was often between ages 3 and 5 years, and this continues to be the case; Volkmar (1992), in a review of 77 cases, reported a mean age at onset of 3.4 years. The issue of the time of onset is particularly relevant in distinguishing CDD from autism because it is clear that, in some cases, autism is recognized after 24 months of age (although almost invariably before age 3; Volkmar, Stier, & Cohen, 1985). For example, in the case series collected at Division TEACCH in North Carolina, over 75% of children with autism had been identified by their parents as having difficulties by 2 years of age (Short & Schopler, 1988). Diagnosis of autism is also sometimes delayed by primary clinicians' lack of familiarity with the condition (Siegel, Pliner, Eschler, & Elliott, 1989).

Children with late-onset autism (difficulties are apparent after age 2 but before age 3) tend to be higher-functioning, and it seemed likely that case detection might be delayed by the relative preservation of cognitive abilities (Volkmar & Cohen, 1989). Wolgemuth, Klin, Cohen, and Volkmar (1994) compared aspects of deterioration in autism and in CDD. When deterioration in autism was reported, it typically involved loss of the ability to speak in single words, or failure of this ability to progress. In contrast, in CDD, the previously acquired level of language was much higher, and deterioration was always observed in multiple areas, not merely in speech.

Occasional ambiguities will sometimes be observed; for example, a child with recurrent ear infections and delayed speech may then go on to develop a more typical CDD presentation at age 3. Kurita (1988a) has suggested that early development (prior to age 2) may not always be perfectly normal, and there may be a history of mild delay (see also Kurita, Kita, & Miyake, 1992). Despite current diagnostic criteria, some cases of CDD may develop before age 2, although the diagnosis of such cases is problematic and may be a source of some confusion of CDD with autism or Rett's Syndrome, although the regression in the latter usually occurs relatively early in life. Similarly, in Landau-Kleffner Syndrome (acquired aphasia with epilepsy), there may be occasional confusion with CDD or autism, but it appears that the clinical features and course of this syndrome are relatively distinctive (Bishop, 1985, 1994). The use of "historical" information always calls for some degree of judgment on the part of clinicians. When considering a diagnosis of CDD in older children and adolescents, the use of movies, videotapes, baby books, and other external validating sources of information may be helpful. When information on early development is lacking, or when the timing or pattern of developmental

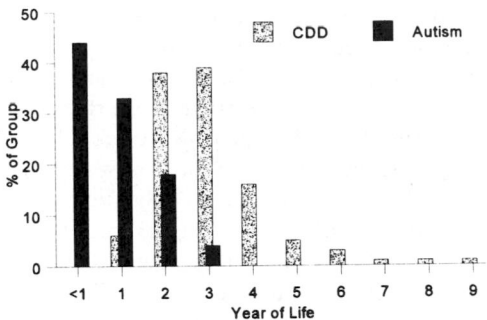

Figure 3.1 Age of onset in 104 cases with clinical diagnoses of CDD and 316 cases with clinical diagnoses of autism.

regression differs from that specified in the criteria for the condition, a diagnosis of Atypical Autism may be most appropriate.

Data related to age of onset of autism and Childhood Disintegrative Disorder, as abstracted from the *DSM-IV* field trial results, are summarized in Figure 3.1. The difference in the two distributions of onset of the two conditions is clear and significant.

Characteristics of the Onset

Several different patterns of onset of CDD have been observed. Occasionally, the condition has a relatively abrupt onset (days to weeks); more frequently, it develops more gradually (weeks to months). Prior to the marked deterioration,

there may be a premonitory phase during which the child may be nonspecifically agitated, anxious, or dysphoric.

In several case series, the onset of CDD has been noted to be associated with some psychosocial stress or medical event (Evans-Jones & Rosenblum, 1978; Kurita, 1988a; Volkmar, 1992). However, the significance of stressful events in syndrome pathogenesis is unclear. The group of stressors reported has been diverse, but all share the feature of being relatively common to preschool children: birth of a sibling, death of a grandparent, hospitalization for elective surgery, immunizations, and so on. Such associations do not appear to have etiological significance (Rutter, 1985).

BEHAVIORAL AND CLINICAL FEATURES

Table 3.2 summarizes the clinical features in cases reported by Kurita (1988a), Volkmar (1992), Malhotra and Singh (1993), and Volkmar and Rutter (1995), and in several others not previously reported.

Once Childhood Disintegrative Disorder is established, it resembles autism in its phenomenological manifestations. Typically, social skills are markedly impaired, but there is some suggestion that the degree of impairment may be slightly less than that observed in autism (Kanner, 1973; Kurita, 1988a; Makita,

TABLE 3.2   Characteristics of Childhood Disintegrative Disorder (CDD) Cases*

Variable	Cases, 1908–1975: N = 48		Cases, 1977–1995: N = 58		Entire Sample: N = 106	
Sex ratio	Male/Female: 35/12		Male/Female: 49/9		Male/Female: 84/21	
Average age at onset (years)	3.42 (SD: 1.12)		3.32 (SD: 1.42)		3.36 (SD: 1.30)	
Average age at follow-up (years)	8.67 (SD: 4.14)		10.88 (SD: 5.98)		10.10 (SD: 5.38)	
Symptoms:	% of	Cases	% of	Cases	% of	Cases
Speech deterioration/loss	100	47	100	58	100	105
Social disturbance	100	43	98	57	99	100
Stereotypy/Resistance to change	100	38	85	54	91	92
Overactivity	100	42	77	37	90	79
Affective symptoms/Anxiety	100	17	78	38	74	58
Deterioration of self-help skills	94	33	82	49	87	82

* Results based on available data. Adapted, with permission, from "Childhood Disintegrative Disorders: Issues for *DSM-IV*," by F. R. Volkmar, 1992, *Journal of Autism and Developmental Disorders, 22*, pp. 625–642. Includes cases from Malhorta and Singh (1993), Volkmar and Rutter (1995), and Wolgemuth et al. (1994).

Nakamura, & Takahashi, 1960). Parents usually report that the loss of social interaction skill is quite dramatic and of great concern to them.

When a child has been speaking quite well, in full sentences, the development of either total mutism or marked deterioration in verbal language at the onset of CDD is quite frequent and very striking. Even when speech is subsequently regained, it does not typically return to previous levels of communicative ability. Rather, communicative abilities are more similar to those observed in autism: a sparsity of communicative acts, limited expressive vocabulary, and markedly impaired pragmatic skills.

Unusual behaviors, including stereotyped behaviors, problems with transitions and change, and nonspecific overactivity, are typically observed. As noted previously, various affective responses that appear inexplicable are often observed at the time of syndrome onset. *ICD-10* suggests that a general loss of interest in the personal environment also occurs. Deterioration in self-help skills such as toileting is striking (Kurita, 1988a; Volkmar, 1992). In contrast, such skills are often acquired somewhat late in autism but are not dramatically lost.

EPIDEMIOLOGY

Epidemiological data on CDD are quite limited, reflecting both (a) the true relative frequency of the condition apart from autism and (b) the likelihood that cases have been markedly underdiagnosed. In the series of consecutive cases reported by Volkmar and Cohen (1989), the disorder appeared to be one-tenth as common as autism; however, these data were not based on a truly epidemiological sample. Interestingly, a similar rate was observed in children with autism who had regressed after age 3 (Rogers & DiLalla, 1990). A different study, using a somewhat more epidemiologically based sample, suggested a prevalence rate of 1 in 100,000 persons (Burd, Fisher, & Kerbeshian, 1989). This rate would be roughly comparable to the rate suggested by Volkmar and Cohen's (1989) data. It must be emphasized that clinicians' relative lack of familiarity with this concept makes interpretation of the available data very suspect.

Initially, the condition seemed to equally affect males and females. However, in a recent review, Volkmar (1992) noted that the preponderance of males was similar to the ratio seen in autism (Lord, Schopler, & Revicki, 1982). Some instances of Rett's Syndrome were originally misdiagnosed as Heller's Syndrome; that is, Rett's condition was described only in 1966, and the degree of the deterioration in Rett's cases may be suggestive of Childhood Disintegrative Disorder (Burd et al., 1989; Hill & Rosenbloom, 1986; Millichap, 1987; Volkmar, 1992). In cases of Childhood Disintegrative Disorder observed in the past 20 years, there is a high male predominance.

COURSE AND PROGNOSIS

Information on course and outcome is an important factor for evaluating the validity of psychiatric conditions. In the literature on CDD, information on course and follow-up has sometimes been available. In approximately 75% of cases, the child's behavior and development deteriorate to a much lower level of functioning and remain there. No further deterioration occurs, but subsequent developmental gains appear to be minimal (Volkmar & Cohen, 1989). In other cases, the marked developmental regression seems to be followed by a partial recovery—for example, a child regains the capacity to speak, although usually only in a limited way (Volkmar & Cohen, 1989). In a small number of cases, the developmental deterioration is identifiable as a progressive neuropathological process that does not plateau. Death may then be the eventual result (Corbett, 1987). Aside from those few cases, life expectancy appears to be normal. In a handful of cases, the children have been observed to make a noteworthy recovery.

NEUROBIOLOGICAL FINDINGS AND ETIOLOGY

Heller's (and others') first impression was that CDD, which he termed dementia infantilis, was not associated with apparent organic disease. This was originally Kanner's impression (1943) about autism. In both cases, the initial impressions had to be modified. About 25% of individuals with autism have seizures, often with an onset later than is typical in children, and another 25% have various other EEG abnormalities. In the Volkmar (1992) review, EEGs had been obtained in 45 cases of apparent CDD. These data have been supplemented by additional, more recent, reports of CDD cases (Malhotra & Singh, 1993; Volkmar & Rutter, 1995; Wolgemuth et al., 1994), but in about half of the cases studied, the EEG was reported to be either probably or definitely abnormal. Seizures have been noted in various case reports, for example, Hill and Rosenbloom (1986; 2 of 9 cases), Volkmar and Cohen (1989; 2 of 10 cases), and Malhotra and Singh (1993; 1 case). In the Malhotra and Singh report (1993), the onset of developmental deterioration was associated with seizures. Although these data are limited, the rates of seizure disorder and EEG abnormality appear to be similar to those observed in autism (e.g., Deykin & MacMahon, 1979; Rutter, 1985; Volkmar & Nelson, 1990).

In another parallel with Kanner's original work, Heller's impression that CDD was not associated with other specific medical conditions has had to be modified. CDD has been associated with various conditions: tuberose sclerosis (Creak, 1963); neurolipidoses (Malmud, 1959); metachromatic leukodystrophy and Addison-Schilder's disease (Corbett, Harris, Taylor, & Trimble, 1977); and subacute sclerosing panencephalitis (Rivinus, Jamison, & Graham, 1975). As noted previously, the impression given in *DSM-III* and *DSM-III-R* was that such associated conditions were generally found. In fact, this is not the case.

In Volkmar's (1992) review of published cases, specific neuropathological conditions were only occasionally identified. Late onset (after age 6) of CDD appears more likely to be associated with some specific neuropathological process. Given the child's marked regression, parents typically consult with many different specialists who conduct various tests, laboratory studies, and diagnostic procedures. Beyond revealing EEG abnormalities and occasional seizure disorder, such tests usually are not particularly productive, although they should be undertaken. Even very extensive medical investigations will not always identify a specific general medical condition that accounts for the child's deterioration (Volkmar, 1992). When such an etiology can be identified, the diagnosis of Childhood Disintegrative Disorder is made, and the presence of the associated medical condition is noted. This approach is similar to the association of autism with various general medical conditions (Rutter, Bailey, Bolton, Le Couteur, 1994).

Except for the EEG results, there is essentially a total absence of information regarding the neurochemistry, neuropsychology, neurophysiology, or neuroanatomy of CDD. Information on the genetics of this condition is also extremely limited. This limitation is particularly unfortunate because there is some indication that the etiology (or etiologies) in CDD may be somewhat more homogeneous than those more typically seen in autism—that is, given the pattern of onset and the relative infrequency of such cases.

Although the cause (or causes) of CDD remains unknown, the course of the disorder, the association with EEG abnormalities and seizure disorder, and the occasional link to known medical conditions suggest that neurobiological factors are likely central in pathogenesis. As with autism, multiple pathogenic pathways may possibly act to produce the condition, and the absence of clearly identified neuropathological mechanisms likely reflects more on current research techniques than on the absence of such factors (Rivinus et al., 1975; Wilson, 1974). Despite the progress in our understanding of the central nervous system, much remains to be discovered, and the absence, to date, of specific neurobiological mechanisms is probably an indication of the present state of science.

DIFFERENTIAL DIAGNOSIS

The differential diagnosis of CDD includes the entire Pervasive Developmental Disorder class and other conditions. Because of the very distinctive pattern of onset of CDD, historical information is critical in making the diagnosis.

Autism

Once established, CDD shares the same essential features as autism on current clinical examination. Historical information is particularly important in distinguishing the two conditions. In about 75% of cases of autism, parents do not report an unequivocally normal period of development; usually, social development is markedly delayed and deviant, and language fails to develop in expected ways. In a smaller group of cases, the parents report that the child seemed to develop normally up to about 18 to 24 months of age, and that single words developed but the child did not go on to develop more complex speech. These cases should *not* be diagnosed with CDD. Complexities may arise: if historical information is absent, if the report of a truly prolonged period of normal development is questionable, if the clinician fails to obtain an adequate history, or if the autistic child is somewhat higher-functioning. In the latter case, early language may seem to develop in a near normal fashion, but the parent becomes concerned when more complex social and communicative difficulties become apparent. Careful history will usually reveal that no actual period of regression of the type seen in CDD occurred. As noted previously, the use of baby books, videotapes, or home movies may be helpful. In CDD, it is essential that the early development should be essentially unequivocally normal, with the child able to speak in sentences prior to the onset of the condition. If such a history cannot be documented, a diagnosis of CDD should not be made and a diagnosis of atypical autism may be appropriate. Some exceptions tend to prove the rule, for example, children who were reared in a bilingual context and whose language was slightly delayed but who otherwise appeared to be developing appropriately prior to the onset of the regression.

Rett's Disorder

Rett's Disorder (see Chapter 5) is occasionally confused with CDD because some degree of regression is observed in both conditions, and the more autistic-like phase of Rett's Disorder may be most prominent in the preschool years, which is when diagnostic evaluations are first conducted. For practitioners familiar with both conditions, misdiagnosis is relatively unlikely, given their very different histories and clinical features.

Asperger's Disorder

In this condition, early language and cognitive development may seem to have been normal or near normal; some parents become aware of the social and other difficulties when the child enters a preschool program. The delayed recognition may, incorrectly, lead some care providers to suspect that there was a marked regression in functioning. However, in Asperger's Disorder, cognitive functions are relatively preserved and a truly marked and severe regression, of the kind seen in CDD, does not occur.

Childhood Schizophrenia

In rare instances, CDD may be confused with other psychiatric disorders such as schizophrenia. Although very early onset schizophrenia (VERS) is very rare, the degree of regression and deterioration may suggest CDD (see Werry, 1996). Usually, the characteristic findings of schizophrenia on clinical examination will clarify the diagnosis.

Landau-Kleffner Syndrome

This syndrome (acquired aphasia with epilepsy) has its onset in children and is characterized by acquired aphasia in association with multifocal spike and spike or wave discharges on EEG (Beaumonanoir, 1992). The condition is relatively well described but remains poorly understood (Rapin, in press). Children with Landau-Kleffner Syndrome usually exhibit marked interest in communication using nonverbal modalities, and the regression is largely confined to the area of language. Nonverbal abilities tend to be spared, and recovery is often considerable (Bishop, 1985). In contrast to CDD, where later onset of the disorder is usually associated with a worse prognosis, later onset of Landau-Kleffner Syndrome is associated with better outcome (Bishop, 1985). Other epileptic conditions may also mimic autism or CDD (Deonna, Ziegler, Malin-Ingvar, Ansermet, & Roulet, 1995).

Other Associated Medical Conditions

A thorough search for any associated neurological or other general medical condition is indicated in CDD. Specific findings on examination or in the history may help guide the process of evaluation. If any such condition is identified, it is then specified on Axis III. Disorders that have their onset after some period of normal development include gangliosidosis, metachromatic leukodystrophy, Niemman-Pick Disease, and so forth. Developmental deterioration and the development of an autistic-like clinical picture can follow central nervous system infection or other insult, as indicated by Weir and Salisbury (1980). Very rarely clinically significant regression occurs in the context of overt seizures (Rapin, 1995).

EVALUATION AND MANAGEMENT

Assessment of a child with CDD may be most effectively accomplished by a group of professionals who work together as a team or in close collaboration. Referrals will usually come from primary care providers, although mental health workers, educators, and others may occasionally question a diagnosis (e.g., of autism), because they know that some features of the case are unusual. Because of the potential that multiple assessments might be conducted, the professionals involved in the child's care— child psychiatrists, psychologists, speech pathologists, pediatric neurologists, occupational and physical therapists, orthopedists, and so forth—must work effectively to avoid fragmentation and duplication of effort. It is appropriate and desirable to engage parents actively in the assessment process.

Given the unusual onset of CDD, a careful history of the pregnancy and neonatal period, the early developmental stages, and the general medical and family health problems is particularly critical. Again, videotapes may clearly document the child's early normal development. Information on the pattern and age of onset of the condition is essential.

Although extensive medical investigations usually fail to reveal the presence of another specific medical condition or specific neurodegenerative disorder, a careful search for such conditions is indicated, particularly if aspects of the case are unusual (e.g., onset after age 6 or deterioration that is progressive and does not plateau). Initial consultation with a pediatric neurologist is always indicated, and an EEG plus a CT or MRI scan will usually be ordered.

Tests of communication and cognitive ability should be chosen according to the child's current levels of functioning. The goal is to obtain estimates of functioning that will be useful in documenting subsequent developmental change as well as in educational and rehabilitative programming. The developmental and other tests typically given to younger children may be appropriate (e.g., Bayley, 1969; Dunst, 1980; Uzgiris & Hunt, 1975). For somewhat higher-functioning but nonverbal children, the Leiter International Performance Scale (Leiter, 1948) may be useful. Some modifications in the usual assessment procedures may have to be made. Communication scales that may be appropriate include the Receptive-Expressive Emergent Language (REEL) Scale (Bzoch & League, 1971); the Sequenced Inventory of Communicative Development (SICD; Hedrick, Prather, & Tobin, 1975); and the Reynell Developmental Language Scales (Reynell, 1990).

The Vineland Adaptive Behavior Scales (expanded form; Sparrow, Balla, & Cicchetti, 1984) should be administered to document the level of adaptive behaviors. This instrument provides useful information for both diagnostic and programming purposes.

As part of the psychiatric or psychological assessment, the child should be observed in more structured and less structured activities, for example, during developmental assessment or while interacting with parents. As part of the history, the examiner should specifically inquire about the child's current and past social skills (differential attachments, interest in parents and peers, use of gaze), communication (receptive and expressive, articulation problems, typical utterances, level of language organization prior to the regression, unusual features such as echolalia, and nature of language loss), and responses to the environment and motor behaviors (self-stimulatory behaviors, difficulties with change or transition, and so on). Acquisition or loss of any adaptive skills, such as toileting, self-care, or related activities, should also be reviewed. Observation of the child's play is helpful in documenting levels of language, cognitive and social organization, and gross and fine motor skills. Problematic or unusual behaviors that are relevant to the diagnosis or are likely to present obstacles for intervention should be noted.

Treatment of CDD is essentially the same as for autism. Behavior modification and special education methods should be used to help encourage the acquisition, or reacquisition, of basic adaptive skills. There are no specific pharmacological treatments for CDD, although many of the same agents used, with some benefit, in autism will sometimes be helpful. The decision to use any pharmacological agent should be preceded by a careful assessment of the potential risks and benefits.

Patients' families (parents, siblings, and extended family members) should be given supportive consideration via appropriate information about the diagnosed condition, the availability of local and other resources, and the existence and meeting times of support groups. Because the prognosis of CDD appears, in general, to be somewhat worse than that of autism, proportionally greater stresses may be experienced by parents and siblings.

CASE REPORT*

Donald was the youngest of three children born to college-educated parents. The pregnancy, labor, delivery, and early development were unremarkable. Donald appeared to be a normally active and sociable baby. He was smiling at 6 weeks, sitting at 7 months, crawling at 9 months, and walking without support at 15 months. He had several ear infections in the first year of life, but said his first words by 12 months and was speaking in full sentences shortly after his second birthday. Videotapes provided by his parents confirmed his apparently normal developmental status at that time.

Shortly after his third birthday, Donald's parents became concerned about his development. Over the course of several weeks, he lost both receptive and expressive language and became progressively less interested in interaction and the inanimate environment. He developed various self-stimulatory behaviors and lost the ability to use the toilet independently. No apparent reason for the regression was identified.

Extensive medical investigations were undertaken. Although Donald was noted to have a borderline abnormal EEG, no specific medical condition that might account for his developmental deterioration was identified. Subsequent evaluations at other centers and by other specialists (including pediatric neurologists and geneticists) similarly failed to identify a specific medical condition. There was no history of similar problems or developmental difficulties among members of the immediate or extended family.

Although Donald had previously attended a nursery school, his changed behavior and developmental deterioration warranted his placement in a special educational setting. At age 4 years, comprehensive evaluation revealed that his cognitive skills were at about the 18-month level, and his language and social skills were at an even lower level. Over the course of many months, some highly limited expressive language skills returned; he was able to say an occasional single word. His social unrelatedness, lack of interest in the environment, and unusual behaviors continued. At age 6, he continues to be severely impaired.

SUMMARY AND DIRECTIONS FOR FUTURE RESEARCH

Although described nearly 100 years ago, CDD is still infrequently reported and very uncommonly studied. As noted by Rapin (1995), the classification of children who take on an appearance of autism after they have had several years of normal development remains very poorly understood. Once the condition is established, it is, behaviorally, very similar to autism, but is differs from autism in the nature and pattern of its onset and course, and in certain clinical features. Very likely, some underlying neurobiological basis (or bases) of the condition exists, but precise etiological mechanisms have not yet been identified. Beyond their obvious importance for affected children and their families, studies of such mechanisms may be important in providing a better under-

* Reprinted, with permission, from *Psychoses and Pervasive Developmental Disorders in Childhood and Adolescence,* Fred R. Volkmar (Ed.), Washington, DC: American Psychiatric Association Press, 1996. The authors are grateful to Drs. Kurita, Malhotra, and Deonna for their kind provision of additional information.

standing of a pathogenesis that may have relevance to autism (Darby & Clark, 1992).

Cross-References

Issues of diagnosis and classification are discussed in Chapters 1 and 7, Rett's Disorder is reviewed in Chapter 4. Medical and neurological conditions potentially relevant to Childhood Disintegrative Disorder are reviewed in Chapters 16, 18, and 39.

REFERENCES

American Psychiatric Association. (1980). *Diagnostic and statistical manual of mental disorders* (3rd ed.). Washington, DC: Author.

American Psychiatric Association. (1987). *Diagnostic and statistical manual of mental disorders* (3rd ed., rev.). Washington, DC: Author.

American Psychiatric Association. (1994). *Diagnostic and statistical manual of mental disorders* (4th ed.). Washington, DC: Author.

Bayley, N. (1969). *Bayley Scales of Infant Development.* New York: Psychological Corporation.

Beaumonanoir, A. (1992). The Landau-Kleffner Syndrome. In J. Roger, M. Bureau, D.A. Dreifuss, A. Perret, & P. Wolf (Eds.), *Epileptic seizures in infancy, childhood, and adolescence* (2nd ed., pp. 231–243). London: John Libbey.

Bishop, D.V.M. (1985). Age of onset and outcome in "acquired aphasia with convulsive disorder" (Landau-Kleffner Syndrome). *Developmental Medicine and Child Neurology, 27,* 705–712.

Bishop, D.V.M. (1994). Developmental disorders of speech and language. In M. Rutter, E. Taylor, & L. Hersov (Eds.), *Child and adolescent psychiatry: Modern approaches* (3rd ed., pp. 546–568). London: Blackwell.

Burd, L., Fisher, W., & Kerbeshian, J. (1988). Childhood Onset Pervasive Developmental Disorder. *Journal of Child Psychology & Psychiatry & Allied Disciplines, 29*(2), 155–163.

Burd, L., Fisher, W., & Kerbeshian, J. (1989). Pervasive developmental disorder: Are Rett Syndrome and Heller dementia infantilis subtypes? *Developmental Medicine and Child Neurology, 31*(5), 609–616.

Bzoch, K., & League, R. (1971). *Receptive-Expressive Emergent Language Scale.* Gainesville, FL: Computer Management Corporation, Language Educational Division.

Corbett, J. (1987). Development, disintegration and dementia. *Journal of Mental Deficiency Research, 31*(4), 349–356.

Corbett, J., Harris, R., Taylor, E., & Trimble, M. (1977, August). Progressive disintegrative psychosis of childhood. *Journal of Child Psychology & Psychiatry & Allied Disciplines, 18*(3), 211–219.

Creak, E.M. (1963). Childhood psychosis: A review of 100 cases. *British Journal of Psychiatry, 109,* 84–89.

Darby, J.K. (1976). Neuropathologic aspects of psychosis in children. *Journal of Autism and Childhood Schizophrenia, 6,* 339–351.

Darby, J.K., & Clark, L. (1992). Autism syndrome as a final common pathway for behavioral expression for many organic disorders. *American Journal of Psychiatry, 149*(1), 146.

Deonna, T., Ziegler, A., Malin-Ingvar, M., Ansermet, F., & Roulet, E. (1995). Reversible behavioural autistic-like regression: A manifestation of a special (new?) epileptic syndrome in a 28-month-old child: A 2-year longitudinal study. *Neurocase, 1,* 1–9.

de Sanctis, S. (1906). On some variations of dementia praecox. *Revista Sperimentali di Frenciatria, 32,* 141–165.

Deykin, E.Y., & MacMahon, B. (1979). The incidence of seizures among children with autistic symptoms. *American Journal of Psychiatry, 126,* 1310–1312.

Dunst, C. (1980). *A clinical and educational manual for use with the Uzgiris and Hunt scales.* Baltimore: University Park Press.

Evans-Jones, L.G., & Rosenbloom, L. (1978, August). Disintegrative psychosis of childhood. *Developmental Medicine and Child Neurology, 20*(4), 462–470.

Fitzpatrick, C. (1987). Rett syndrome and Heller dementia [letter]. *Developmental Medicine and Child Neurology, 29,* 834.

Harper, J., & Williams, S. (1975). Age and type of onset as critical variables in early infantile autism. *Journal of Autism and Childhood Schizophrenia, 5,* 25–35.

Harrison, D.J., & Webb, P.J. (1990). Scoliosis in Rett syndrome: Natural history and treatment. *Brain Development, 12,* 154–156.

Hedrick, D., Prather, F., & Tobin, A. (1975). *Sequenced inventory of communicative development.* Seattle: University of Washington Press.

Heller, T. (1908). Dementia infantilis. *Zeitschrift für die Erforschung und Behandlung des Jugenlichen Schwachsinns, 2,* 141–165.

Heller, T. (1930). Uber Dementia infantilis. *Zeitschrift für Kinderforschung, 37,* 661–667.

Hill, A.E., & Rosenbloom, L. (1986, February). Disintegrative psychosis of childhood: Teenage follow-up. *Developmental Medicine and Child Neurology, 28*(1), 34–40.

Kanner, L. (1943). Autistic disturbances of affective contact. *Nervous Child, 2,* 217–250.

Kanner, L. (1973). Dementia infantilis. In L. Kanner (Ed.), *Childhood psychosis* (pp. 279–281). Washington, DC: V. Winston & Sons.

Kolvin, I. (1971). Studies in childhood psychoses: 1. Diagnostic criteria and classification. *British Journal of Psychiatry, 118,* 381–384.

Kurita, H. (1985). Infantile autism with speech loss before the age of thirty months. *Journal of the American Academy of Child Psychiatry, 24*(2), 191–196.

Kurita, H. (1988a, June). Brief report: A case of Heller's Syndrome with school refusal. *Journal of Autism and Developmental Disorders, 18*(2), 315–319.

Kurita, H. (1988b). The concept and nosology of Heller's Syndrome: Review of articles and report of two cases. *Japanese Journal of Psychiatry and Neurology, 42,* 785–793.

Kurita, H. (1989). Heller's Syndrome as a type of Pervasive Developmental Disorder. *Journal of Mental Health, 35,* 71–81.

Kurita, H., Kita, M., & Miyake, Y. (1992). A comparative study of development and symptoms among disintegrative psychosis and infantile autism with and without speech loss. *Journal of Autism and Developmental Disorders, 22*(2), 175–188.

Leiter, R.G. (1948). *Leiter International Performance Scale.* Chicago: Stoelting.

Lord, C., Schopler, E., & Revicki, D. (1982). Sex differences in autism. *Journal of Autism and Developmental Disorders, 12,* 317–330.

Makita, K. (1966). The age of onset of childhood schizophrenia. *Folia Psychiatric Neurologica Japonica, 20,* 111–112.

Makita, K., Nakamura, M., & Takahashi, T. (1960). A case report of Heller's disease. *Japanese Journal of Psychiatry, 1,* 377–386.

Malamud, N. (1959). Heller's disease and childhood schizophrenia. *American Journal of Psychiatry, 116,* 215–218.

Malhotra, S., & Singh, S. (1993). Disintegrative psychosis of childhood: An appraisal and case study. *Acta Paedopsychiatrica, 56,* 37–40.

Millichap, J.G. (1987). Rett's Syndrome: A variant of Heller's dementia [letter]? *Lancet, 1,* 440.

Rapin, I. (1995). Autistic regression and disintegrative disorder: How important the role of epilepsy? *Seminars in Pediatric Neurology, 2,* 278–285.

Rett, A. (1966). Uber ein eigenartiges hirntophisces Syndroem bei hyperammonie im Kindersalter. *Wein Medizinische Wochenschrift, 118,* 723–726.

Reynell, J., & Gruber, C. (1990). *Reynell developmental language scales—U.S. edition.* Western Psychological Services: Los Angeles, CA.

Rivinus, T.M., Jamison, D.L., & Graham, P.J. (1975). Childhood organic neurological disease presenting as a psychiatric disorder. *Archives of Disease in Childhood, 50,* 115–119.

Rogers, S.J., & DiLalla, D.L. (1990). Age of symptom onset in young children with Pervasive Developmental Disorder. *Journal of the American Academy of Child and Adolescent Psychiatry, 29,* 863–872.

Rutter, M. (1972, October). Childhood schizophrenia reconsidered. *Journal of Autism and Childhood Schizophrenia, 2*(4), 315–337.

Rutter, M. (1985). Infantile autism and other pervasive developmental disorders. In M. Rutter & L. Hersov (Eds.), *Child and adolescent psychiatry—Modern approaches* (pp. 545–566). London: Blackwell.

Rutter, M., Bailey, A., Bolton, P., & Le Couteur, A. (1994). Autism and known medical conditions: Myth and substance. *Journal of Child Psychology & Psychiatry & Allied Disciplines, 35*(2), 311–322.

Rutter, M., & Schopler, E. (1992). Classification of pervasive developmental disorders: Some concepts and practical considerations. *Journal of Autism and Developmental Disorders, 22,* 459–482.

Short, A., & Schopler, E. (1988). Factors relating to age of onset in autism. *Journal of Autism and Developmental Disorders, 18,* 207–216.

Siegel, B., Pliner, C., Eschler, J., & Elliott, G.R. (1989). How children with autism are diagnosed: Difficulties in identification of children with multiple developmental delays. *Developmental and Behavioral Pediatrics, 9,* 199–204.

Sparrow, S.S., Balla, D., & Cicchetti, D.V. (1984). *Vineland Adaptive Behavior Scales (expanded form).* Circle Pines, MN: American Guidance Service.

Stutsman, R. (1948). *Merrill-Palmer Scale.* Los Angeles: Western Psychological Services.

Uzgiris, I.C., & Hunt, J. McV. (1975). *Assessment in infancy: Ordinal scales of psychological development.* Urbana: University of Illinois Press.

Volkmar, F.R. (1987). Diagnostic issues in the pervasive developmental disorders. *Journal of Child Psychology & Psychiatry & Allied Disciplines, 28*(3), 365–369.

Volkmar, F.R. (1992). Childhood Disintegrative Disorder: Issues for *DSM-IV. Journal of Autism and Developmental Disorders, 22,* 625–642.

Volkmar, F.R. (1994). Childhood Disintegrative Disorder. *Child and Adolescent Psychiatry Clinics of North America, 4,* 119–130.

Volkmar, F.R., & Cohen, D.J. (1989). Disintegrative disorder of "late onset" autism. *Journal of Child Psychology & Psychiatry & Allied Disciplines, 30*(5), 717–724.

Volkmar, F.R., Cohen, D.J., Hoshino, Y., Rende, R.D., & Paul, R. (1988). Phenomenology and classification of the childhood psychoses. *Psychological Medicine, 18*(1), 191–201.

Volkmar, F.R., Klin, A., Siegel, B., Szatmari, P., Lord, C., Campbell, M., Freeman, B.J., Cicchetti, D.V., Rutter, M., Kline, W., Buitelaar, J., Hattab, Y., Fombonne, E., Fuentes, J., Werry, J., Stone, W., Kerbeshian, J., Hoshino, Y., Bregman, J., Loveland, K., Szymanski, L., & Towbin, K. (1994). Field trial for Autistic Disorder in *DSM-IV. American Journal of Psychiatry, 151*(9), 1361–1367.

Volkmar, F.R., & Nelson, D.S. (1990). Seizure disorders in autism. *Journal of the American Academy of Child & Adolescent Psychiatry, 29*(1), 127–129.

Volkmar, F.R., & Rutter, M. (1995). Childhood Disintegrative Disorder: Results of the *DSM-IV* autism field trial. *Journal of the American Academy of Child and Adolescent Psychiatry, 34,* 1092–1095.

Volkmar, F.R., Stier, D.M., & Cohen, D.J. (1985). Age of recognition of Pervasive Developmental Disorder. *American Journal of Psychiatry, 142*(12), 1450–1452.

Weir, K., & Salisbury, D.M. (1980). Acute onset of autistic features following brain damage in a ten-year-old. *Journal of Autism and Developmental Disorders, 10*(2), 185–191.

Werry, J. (1996). Childhood schizophrenia. In F. Volkmar (Ed.), *Psychoses and pervasive developmental disorders in childhood and adolescence* (pp. 1–48). Washington, DC: American Psychiatric Press.

Wilson, J. (1974). Investigation of degenerative disease of the central nervous system. *Archives of Disease in Childhood, 47,* 163–170.

Wolgemuth, D., Klin, A., Cohen, D.J., & Volkmar, F.R. (1994, October). *Childhood Disintegrative Disorder: Diagnosis and phenomenology.* Paper presented at the annual meeting of the American Academy of Child and Adolescent Psychiatry, New York.

World Health Organization (WHO). (1987). *Mental disorders: Glossary and guide to their classification in accordance with the ninth revision of the International Classification of Diseases.* Geneva: Author.

World Health Organization (WHO). (1990). *International classification of mental and behavioural disorders—diagnostic criteria for research* (10th ed., draft version). Geneva: Author.

World Health Organization (WHO). (1993). *International classification of mental and behavioural disorders—diagnostic criteria for research* (10th ed., pp. 151–152). Geneva: Author.

Zappert, J. (1921). Dementia infantilis Heller. *Monatsschrift für Kinderheilkunde, 22,* 389–391.

CHAPTER 4

Rett's Syndrome: A Pervasive Developmental Disorder

RICHARD VAN ACKER

Few disorders have generated a level of interest or controversy equal to that of Rett's Syndrome. At least in its classical form, Rett's Syndrome is a phenotypically distinct, progressive developmental disorder that has a characteristic pattern of cognitive and functional stagnation and subsequent deterioration. The disorder was first described by Andreas Rett, an Austrian physician, following his serendipitous discovery that two preadolescent girls seated in his waiting room were displaying strikingly similar hand-wringing mannerisms. Upon discussing this observation and enlisting his receptionist's help in reviewing patients' records, six additional patients with similar behavioral characteristics and developmental histories were identified. Unable to find a known classification for the disorder, Rett (1966) published a report (in German) describing 22 girls with a syndrome consisting of stereotyped hand movements, dementia, autistic behavior, ataxia, cortical atrophy, and hyperammonemia (increased levels of blood ammonia). Unfortunately, the reported hyperammonemia was subsequently found to be associated only rarely with this disorder. This false lead, coupled with very limited exposure (Rett, 1977) of this information in English-language medical literature, resulted in a general failure to recognize Rett's Syndrome, previously termed cerebroatrophic hyperammonemia, as a nosologic entity.

Unaware of Rett's work, Bengt Hagberg was working, in Sweden, with patients who displayed similar symptoms. In 1980, in a paper presented to the European Federation of Child Neurology Societies, Hagberg described 16 girls he had observed. Later, he and a number of colleagues (Hagberg, Aicardi, Dias, & Ramos, 1983) published in the *Annals of Neurology* their report on 35 girls, from France, Portugal, and Sweden, who had Rett's Syndrome. This landmark account awakened recognition and interest among clinicians and researchers, and credited Rett for his pioneering efforts on the disorder that bears his name.

CLINICAL PRESENTATION AND NATURAL HISTORY

Individuals with Rett's Syndrome exhibit a unique and characteristic course of development (Naidu, Murphy, Moser, & Rett, 1986). Prenatal and perinatal histories of these persons are generally unremarkable. Although minor pre- and perinatal problems (e.g., mild hypotonia, tremulous neck movements, a low intensity of interpersonal contact, and abnormal hand use and language development) can be identified retrospectively in as many as 80% of girls with Rett's Syndrome (Hanefeld, 1985; Nomura & Segawa, 1990; Opitz & Lewin, 1987; Sekul & Percy, 1992) these mild symptoms are unlikely to be detected as relevant even with detailed neurologic or developmental assessment. Excess levels of hand patting, waving, and involuntary movements,

Editors' note: As indicated in Chapter 1, *ICD-10* and *DSM-IV* terms are used interchangeably in this work. Rett's Syndrome, used in *ICD-10,* appears as Rett's Disorder in *DSM-IV.*

including alternate opening and closing of the fingers; twisting of the wrists and arms; or nonspecific circulating hand–mouth movements appear to be the most characteristic early warning signals for the syndrome (Holm, 1985; Kerr, Montague, & Stephenson, 1987; Witt-Engerstrom, 1987). Given the wide range of functioning in the first 12 months, such "soft signs" would generally be dismissed. Thus, parents report normal physical and mental development for the first 6 to 8 months of life, as evidenced by physical growth and psychomotor and verbal behavior (Gillberg, 1987; Sekul & Percy, 1992). This apparently normal period of development is followed by a slowing or cessation of the acquisition of developmental milestones and by significant deviations in the acquisition of skills requiring balance (e.g., walking). By 15 months, approximately half of the girls with Rett's Syndrome demonstrate serious developmental delays and abnormal neurologic signs or symptoms. By age 3 years, the children experience a rapid deterioration of behavior as evidenced by loss of acquired speech, voluntary grasping, and purposeful use of the hands. The girls begin to exhibit a lack of sustained interest in persons or objects and demonstrate limited interpersonal contact; however, eye contact is maintained (Holm, 1985; Trevathan & Naidu, 1988; Witt-Engerstrom, 1987). This deterioration occurs very quickly (typically, within 1 year or less) and results in severe to profound disabilities and stereotyped behaviors. Deceleration of head growth (acquired microcephaly); coarse, jerky movements of the trunk and limbs; a stiff-legged, broad-based gait with rather short steps; and swaying movements of the shoulders when ambulating accompany the developmental deterioration (Coleman & Gillberg, 1985; Hanefeld, 1985; Kerr & Stephenson, 1986; Naidu et al., 1986; Percy, Zoghbi, & Riccardi, 1985). With the loss of purposeful hand movements, the most prominent symptom of the syndrome appears (Figure 4.1): stereotypic hand clasping, hand "washing," and hand-to-mouth movements (Ishikawa et al., 1978; Leiber, 1985).

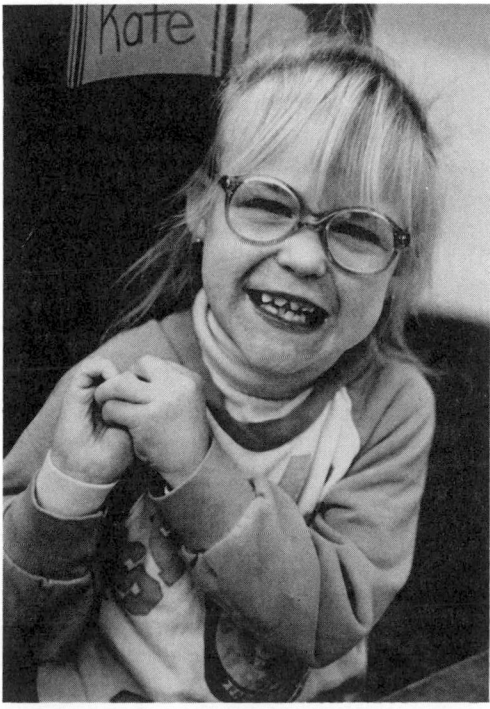

Figure 4.1   Stereotypic hand movements in Rett's syndrome.

The developmental regression seems to plateau during the early school years. Some parents report that their daughters attempt to increase their functional use of retained skills and become more responsive to their environment. As individuals with Rett's Syndrome approach adolescence, they are frequently subject to increased spasticity and vasomotor disturbances of the lower limbs, possible loss of existing ambulation, scoliosis, and a diminished rate of growth. Facial grimacing, bruxism (teeth grinding), hyperventilation, apnea (breath holding), aerophagia (air swallowing), constipation, and seizure activity sometimes accompany the syndrome (Trevathan & Naidu, 1988).

Hagberg and Witt-Engerstrom (1986) proposed a staging system to facilitate the characterization of the disorder patterns and profiles from infancy through adolescence. Their system of four clinical stages was derived from a synthesis of clinical observations in 50 cases of Rett's Syndrome in Sweden. The purpose of the staging system is to provide average guidelines for stage patterns thought to be of use when confronted with the diagnostic problems resulting from the complex symptomatology and longitudinal profile of the condition. The four stages are:

1. Early Onset Stagnation Phase.
2. Rapid Destructive Stage.
3. Pseudostationary Stage.
4. Late Motor Degeneration Stage.

This staging system has gained general acceptance; however, because the names assigned to each stage have been criticized (Opitz, 1986, Trevathan & Naidu, 1988), the stages are simply referred to by number. Descriptions of the symptoms and features of each of the four stages follow.

Stage 1 (Onset 6 to 18 Months)

The clinical profile at this stage suggests a deterioration, or at least a general slowing down or stagnation, of motor development. Hypotonia is typically noted. Deviation from normal development is often compensated for, or hidden, in part, by the rapid development that occurs during infancy. For example, most of the affected children can sit independently prior to the initiation of Stage 1, but many fail to develop the subsequent postural skills needed for balance when crawling, standing, and walking. Sekul and Percy (1992) report that as many as 60% of the girls appear to compensate for this delay by using alternative means of locomotion (e.g., rolling, creeping, or shuffling). Approximately 80% of persons with Rett's Syndrome will attain independent ambulation. Additional gross motor abilities often are learned during this stage but are delayed in their appearance. The symptoms of Stage 1 are nonspecific and are not predictive of subsequent deterioration.

Stage 2 (Onset 1 to 3 Years)

During this stage, the syndrome becomes significantly more pronounced as previously acquired abilities are lost. Most affected girls exhibit a relatively well-demarcated period of rapidly declining social interaction; stagnation or loss of acquired cognitive abilities; and loss of purposeful hand use and speech. Stereotyped movements, often virtually continuous during waking hours, become a prominent symptom. Intellectual functioning is generally reported to fall to within the severe to profound range of mental retardation. Ataxic/apraxic gait abnormalities are observed in ambulatory girls. While a child is awake, she may display aberrant breathing patterns. Hyperventilation and respiratory pauses (generally lasting 30 to 40 seconds) are common.

This deterioration frequently has been sufficiently dramatic to simulate a toxic or encephalitic state (Hagberg & Witt-Engerstrom, 1986). Parents frequently report that their children seem irritable. Unprovoked episodes of screaming and "spontaneous tantrums" are common (Coleman, Brubaker, Hunter, & Smith, 1988). Seizure activity is present in approximately one-fourth of the girls during this stage. Sleep abnormalities, including delayed sleep onset and increased night awakenings, are manifested by more than three fourths of the girls (Piazza, Fisher, Kiesewetter, Bowman, & Moser, 1990).

Stage 3 (Onset 2 to 10 Years)

Persons with Rett's Syndrome generally demonstrate diminishing autistic symptomatology and improved social interaction during this period. They appear to be more aware of their surroundings and seem to be attempting to use residual functional skills. Communication skills are reported to improve, producing better interaction. Some girls employ eye pointing, babbling, or even word pieces to signal communicative intent (Sekul & Percy, 1992). Seizures occur in up to 80% of the girls with Rett's Syndrome (Coleman et al., 1988). Spasticity or rigidity and scoliosis tend to progress, and "jerky" truncal ataxia and apraxia become prominent.

Stage 4 (Onset 10+ Years)

Progressive muscle wasting, scoliosis, spasticity, and rigidity are displayed frequently during this late stage. Decreasing mobility and a number of late-stage second-neuron abnormalities (e.g., drop foot abnormalities, remarkably plantar-flexed feet) may require the use of a wheelchair. Spinal cord dysfunction appears to act in conjunction with extrapyramidal features to lessen mobility (Witt-Engerstrom & Hagberg, 1990). Interestingly, this stage is marked by increased motor deterioration, but the individuals' cognitive functioning remains stable, and social interaction (eye contact) and attentiveness improve. Seizure activity often becomes less problematic, allowing a decrease in the anticonvulsant regimen for some girls.

Although persons over the age of 25 have received initial diagnoses of Rett's Syndrome, the oldest being 65 years of age (International Rett Syndrome Association, 1990), little systematic research has been conducted on the course of the disorder past adolescence. Some evidence suggests that the life expectancy of persons with Rett's Syndrome may be diminished; however, precise information is not available at this time. Failure to keep accurate developmental histories, infrequent diagnostic evaluations of adults, and the probability that secondary contractures mask the more classic signs of the disorder—all these factors impede the identification of older persons with Rett's Syndrome. Malnutrition and health problems secondary to immobility increase the risk for a shortened life span; however, premature deaths have been reported among ambulatory girls who were thought to be healthy, outside of demonstrating Rett's Syndrome, and whose seizures were under control (Hagberg, 1989;

Iyama, 1993). These deaths are reported throughout the first three decades of the life span; their peak occurrence is within the second decade of life. Cardiac disturbances (Percy, 1992; Sekul, Moak, Schultz, & Percy, 1991), breathing dysfunctions, and seizures (Hagberg, 1989) have been suggested as possible causes for these premature deaths.

The four-stage clinical pattern or profile for Rett's Syndrome has been reported to be "a sometimes crude and a somewhat simplistic frame" for specifically characterizing and covering the whole profile in all cases (Hagberg & Witt-Engerstrom, 1986, p. 58). Transitions between stages are commonly indistinct and may be difficult to discern precisely for research purposes (Philippart, 1986). Even so, the four-stage system has been found to be a useful instrument for a more systematic approach to the complex clinical manifestations of Rett's Syndrome as individuals progress through the disorder.

DIAGNOSTIC CRITERIA

Diagnostic criteria for inclusion and exclusion of Rett's Syndrome have been delineated (Hagberg, Goutieres, Hanefeld, Rett, & Wilson, 1985; Rett Syndrome Diagnostic Criteria Work Group, 1988). *The ICD-10 Classification of Mental and Behavioural Disorders: Diagnostic Criteria for Research* (World Health Organization, 1992) has included Rett's Syndrome as a subcategory (F84.2) of Disorders of Psychological Development. The fourth edition of the *Diagnostic and Statistical Manual of Mental Disorders* (*DSM-IV;* American Psychiatric Association, 1994) presents criteria for Rett's Syndrome (termed Rett's Disorder) as a subcategory (299.80) of Pervasive Developmental Disorder. The *ICD-10* and the *DSM-IV* diagnostic criteria for Rett's Syndrome and Rett's Disorder, respectively, generally coincide with those proposed by the Rett Syndrome Diagnostic Work Group. Both *ICD-10* and *DSM-IV* have adopted 5 months as the upper age level for normal psychomotor development and the lower age limit for purposeful hand skills. This criterion, in both systems, coincides with setting 5 months as the lower limit for the appearance of decelerated head growth, but, unfortunately, the adoption of the 5-month upper age limit for normal development may prove too restrictive. The Rett Syndrome Diagnostic Work Group in a footnote to their criteria indicated that "Apparently normal development may appear for up to 18 months" (1988, p. 426). No such notation is provided within the current *ICD-10* or *DSM-IV* criteria. The greatest differences in the various diagnostic criteria is found in the identification of exclusionary criteria and associated features. *ICD-10* and *DSM-IV* criteria fail to indicate exclusionary criteria that are critical for differential diagnosis. *DSM-IV* includes EEG abnormalities, seizure disorder, nonspecific brain-imaging abnormalities, and severe or profound mental retardation (Axis II) as associated features and disorders. Table 4.1 compares the diagnostic criteria specified by the Rett Syndrome Diagnostic Criteria Work Group and those provided in *ICD-10* (which are virtually identical to those found in *DSM-IV*).

Rett's Syndrome, to date, has been exclusively described in female patients. Some researchers (Coleman, 1990; Eeg-Olofsson et al., 1990; Philippart, 1990; Topcu, Topaloglu, Renda, Berker, & Turanli, 1991), however, have presented case study reports of males displaying similar behavioral symptoms and developmental histories. Twenty-one males have been registered with the International Rett Syndrome Association, but, in each case, the strict criteria necessary to be included as a confirmed case have not been met. The male sex is not included in the exclusionary criteria at this time.

VARIANTS OF RETT'S SYNDROME

Because no specific cause or marker variable has yet been identified for Rett's Syndrome, clinical homogeneity is essential for epidemiological and research purposes. The strict diagnostic criteria discussed above, however, may result in a failure to recognize the entire spectrum of phenotypic manifestations that might be included under the Rett's Syndrome classification. Two clinical variants of children with similar clinical courses who do not fulfill all the current diagnostic criteria have been recognized in the literature: (a) atypical form and (b) forme fruste.

The atypical form includes girls who have developmental delays prior to regression or lack regression; girls who have maintained purposeful hand use or lack stereotypies, or fail to exhibit both symptoms; and girls whose initial manifestation is a severe seizure disorder (Goutieres & Aicardi, 1986; Hagberg & Witt-Engerstrom, 1987). The group with early seizure activity is being recognized more frequently (Sekul & Percy, 1992). These girls display infantile spasms and later develop the features of typical Rett's Syndrome, which may suggest that the lowered seizure threshold distorts the classical presentation of the disorder (Goutieres & Aicardi, 1986).

Girls classified as forme fruste display more subtle initial symptoms and have a more protracted clinical course. They often retain some language, lack classical hand stereotypies, and manifest less prominent developmental deviations. As these girls approach adolescence and adulthood, additional signs and symptoms develop that conform to the clinical picture of older individuals with Rett's Syndrome.

Support for the assumption that forme fruste are true variants of Rett's Syndrome recently has been presented. In a study by Akesson, Hagberg, and Wahlstrom (1996), females 10 years of age and older fulfilling the criteria for the forme fruste type of Rett's Syndrome (Hagberg, 1995) were selected from the Swedish National Register. For 32 forme fruste cases, a complete genealogical analyses on 61 parental lines was completed. Details for approximately 3200 ancestors were uncovered. Eleven of the forme fruste females could be traced to a previously defined geographical area known to display high numbers of females with classical Rett's Syndrome. In fact, six of the cases had their origin in the same homestead as a female with classical Rett's Syndrome. Four of the pedigrees contained females with both classical and forme fruste types of Rett's Syndrome; two each contained one forme fruste and two classical types and two each contained one forme fruste and one classical type. All of the 10 cases in these four pedigrees were descendants of the same four couples who had lived several generations ago. The data suggest strong common genealogical origins for both classical and forme fruste types of Rett's Syndrome.

TABLE 4.1   Comparison of Diagnostic Criteria

Rett Syndrome Diagnostic Criteria Work Group[a]	ICD-10[b]

Necessary Criteria

1. Apparently normal prenatal and perinatal period.
2. Apparently normal psychomotor development through the first 6 months.[c]
3. Normal head circumference at birth.
4. Deceleration of head growth between ages 5 months and 4 years.
5. Loss of acquired purposeful hand skills between ages 6 and 30 months, temporally associated with communication dysfunction and social withdrawal.
6. Development of severely impaired expressive and receptive language, and presence of apparent severe psychomotor retardation.
7. Stereotypic hand movements such as hand wringing/squeezing.

Necessary Criteria

1. There is an apparently normal prenatal and perinatal period *and* apparently normal psychomotor development through the first 5 months *and* normal head circumference at birth.
2. There is deceleration of head growth between 5 months and 4 years *and* loss of acquired purposeful hand skills between 5 and 30 months of age that is associated with concurrent communication dysfunction and impaired social interactions *and* the appearance of poorly coordinated/unstable gait and/or trunk movements.
3. There is severe impairment of expressive and receptive language, together with severe psychomotor retardation.
4. There are stereotyped midline hand movements (such as hand-wringing or "hand-washing") with an onset at or after the time when purposeful hand movements are lost.

Supportive Criteria

1. Breathing dysfunction
   a. Periodic apnea during wakefulness.
   b. Intermittent hyperventilation.
   c. Breath-holding spells.
   d. Forced expulsion of air or saliva.
2. Electroencephalographic (EEG) abnormalities:
   a. Slow waking background and intermittent rhythmic slowing (3–5 Hz).
   b. Epileptiform discharges, with or without clinical seizures.
3. Seizures.
4. Spasticity, often with associated development of muscle wasting and dystonia.
5. Peripheral vasomotor disturbances.
6. Scoliosis.
7. Growth retardation.
8. Hypotrophic small feet.

Exclusionary Criteria

1. Evidence of intrauterine growth retardation.
2. Organomegaly, or other signs of storage disease.
3. Retinopathy or optic atrophy.
4. Microcephaly at birth.
5. Evidence of perinatally acquired brain damage.
6. Existence of identifiable metabolic or other progressive neurologic disorder.
7. Acquired neurologic disorders resulting from severe infections or head trauma.

[a] Reproduced with permission from "The Clinical Recognition and Differential Diagnosis of Rett Syndrome," by E. Trevathan & S. Naidu, 1988, *Journal of Child Neurology, 3*(Suppl.), S6–S16.
[b] Reproduced with permission from World Health Organization, *The ICD-10 Classification of Mental and Behavioral Disorders: Diagnostic Criteria for Research,* 1992, Geneva, Switzerland: World Health Organization.
[c] Development may appear to be normal for up to 18 months.

DIFFERENTIAL DIAGNOSIS

The presentation of Rett's Syndrome differs considerably, depending on the stage and age of observation. For example, a child of 4 or 5 years of age with classical Rett's Syndrome can be correctly diagnosed with relative ease, but because of vague symptomatology, diagnosis during infancy frequently misinterprets the condition. Likewise, the late stage in adolescence, which displays a complex picture of severe multiple disabilities with secondary contractures resembling any number of disorders, is often misdiagnosed. To fully understand this condition, the entire disease process must be recognized and considered (Trevathan & Naidu, 1988).

Only 22% to 28% of the estimated 8,000 to 10,000 girls in the United States who are afflicted with Rett's Syndrome (Moser, 1986) have been identified thus far (K. Hunter, personal communication, November 22, 1996). Physicians' and clinicians' lack of awareness of this disorder is undoubtedly a major contributing factor to this low rate of diagnosis. Even when physicians are aware of Rett's Syndrome, an accurate diagnosis is not always forthcoming. Table 4.2 lists, by stage and differential diagnoses, some of the clinical characteristics often assigned to persons with Rett's Syndrome.

The most common nonspecific diagnosis for children with Rett's Syndrome above age 1 is reported to be the early infantile autism (*DSM-IV*, 299.00 Autistic Disorder; Olsson, 1987). In fact, many children with Rett's Syndrome seem to fulfill the criteria necessary to establish the diagnosis of infantile autism (Gillberg, 1987; Olsson, 1987; Olsson & Rett, 1985). Thus, some researchers (Allen, 1988; Gillberg, 1989) argue that Rett's Syndrome might best be thought of as a subtype of autism or overlapping diagnostic entities. *DSM-IV* includes Autistic Disorder and Rett's Disorder as subcategories of Pervasive Developmental Disorder. The behavioral patterns, progression, and prognosis of these two conditions, nevertheless, vary significantly. A number of clinically important differences have been identified between Rett's Syndrome (especially during the latter two stages) and other conditions with

autism or autistic traits (Naidu et al., 1990; Olsson, 1987; Olsson & Rett, 1985, 1990; Percy, Zoghbi, Lewis, & Jankovic, 1988). A basic distinction between the two disorders can be made on the basis of motor behavioral analysis (Olsson & Rett, 1985, 1987; Percy, Zoghbi et al., 1988). "Whereas autism represents a regression of verbal but not motor skills, Rett syndrome involves the apparently simultaneous regression of both skills" (Percy, Zoghbi et al., 1988, p. S67). Stereotypic behavior associated with infantile autism is generally more complex, and, unlike the behavior in Rett's Syndrome, often involves the manipulation of an object with preservation of the pincer grasp. Children with Rett's Syndrome reportedly differ from children with infantile autism with respect to the respiratory pattern they display (breath holding, hyperventilation, and air or saliva expulsion); the presence of ataxia, apraxia, bruxism, hypoactivity, and a general slowness of movements; and an absence of purposeful hand movement (Gillberg, 1986; Olsson, 1987; Percy, Zoghbi et al., 1988; Sekul & Percy, 1992). Persons with Rett's Syndrome demonstrate a very restricted repertoire of movements that appear monotonous in both form and speed (Olsson & Rett, 1985). Van Acker (1987) reported that the stereotypic behaviors of persons with Rett's Syndrome were displayed in patterned sequences with significant conditional probabilities, and those of persons with infantile autism were displayed in a random fashion. Another critical feature that may help in the differential diagnosis of Rett's Syndrome and infantile autism has been presented by Budden (1986): Persons with Rett's Syndrome frequently develop appropriate speech before the onset of symptoms. On the other hand, children with autism differed from those with Rett's Syndrome in their display of overactivity and inappropriate vocalizations, and their tendency to replicate simple motor activities or complex movements within a rich repertoire of motor behavior (Percy, Zoghbi et al., 1988). Table 4.3 compares the clinical manifestations that differentiate Rett's Syndrome from infantile autism.

One must acknowledge that, considering the present concept of infantile autism as a behavioral syndrome, the initial differential

TABLE 4.2   Rett's Syndrome: Clinical Characteristics and Differential Diagnosis, by Stage*

Stage	Clinical Characteristics	Differential Diagnosis
Early onset stagnation stage Onset: 6 to 18 months Duration: Months	Developmental stagnation Deceleration of head/brain growth Disinterest in play activity Hypotonia	Benign congenital hypotonia Prader-Willi syndrome Cerebral palsy

Rapid destructive stage
Onset: 1 to 3 years
Duration: Weeks to months
	Rapid developmental regression
	  with irritability
	Loss of hand use
	Seizures
	Hand stereotypies: wringing,
	  clapping, tapping, mouthing
	Autistic manifestations
	Loss of expressive language
	Insomnia
	Self-abusive behavior (e.g.,
	  chewing fingers, slapping face)
		Autism
		Psychosis
		Hearing or visual disturbance
		Encephalitis
		Infantile spasms (West syndrome)
		Tuberous sclerosis
		Ornithine carbamoyl transferase
		  deficiency
		Phenylketonuria
		Infantile neuronal ceroid
		  lipofuscinosis (INCL)

Pseudostationary stage
Onset: 2 to 10 years
Duration: Months to years
	Severe mental retardation/apparent
	  dementia
	Amelioration of autistic features
	Seizures
	Typical hand stereotypies:
	  wringing, tapping, mouthing
	Prominent ataxia and apraxia
	Spasticity
	Hyperventilation, breath holding,
	  aerophagia
	Apnea during wakefulness
	Weight loss with excellent appetite
	Early scoliosis
	Bruxism
		Spastic ataxic cerebral palsy
		Spinocerebral degeneration
		Leukodystrophies or other storage
		  disorders
		Neuroaxonal dystrophy
		Lennox-Gastaut Syndrome
		Angelman Syndrome

Late motor deterioration
Onset: 10+ years
Duration: Years
	Combined upper and lower motor
	  neuron signs
	Progressive scoliosis, muscle
	  wasting, and rigidity
	Decreasing mobility; wheelchair-
	  bound
	Growth retardation
	Improved eye contact
	Staring, unfathomable gaze
	Virtual absence of expressive and
	  receptive language
	Trophic disturbance of feet
	Reduced seizure frequency
		Unknown degenerative disorder

*Reproduced with permission from "Diagnostic Criteria for Rett Syndrome," by Rett Syndrome Diagnostic Criteria Work Group, 1988, *Annals of Neurology, 23,* 125–128.

diagnosis of Rett's Syndrome for some children may prove somewhat problematic. Infantile autism, however, is more rare in females, which means that the mere presence of severe autistic symptomatology in a girl under the age of 2 years should prompt the consideration of Rett's Syndrome in the differential diagnosis. One must also be aware that "a large percentage of children with Rett syndrome age 0–6 months or older than 3–5 years are not autistic"

**TABLE 4.3 Comparison of Rett's Syndrome and Infantile Autism*

Rett's Syndrome

1. Normal development, for 6 to 18 months.
2. Progressive loss of speech and hand function.
3. Profound mental retardation in all functional areas.
4. Acquired microcephaly, growth retardation, decreased weight gain.
5. Stereotypic hand movements always present.
6. Progressive gait difficulties, with gait and truncal apraxia and ataxia; may become nonambulatory.
7. Language always absent.
8. Eye contact present, sometimes very intense.
9. Little interest in manipulating objects.
10. Seizures in at least 70% in early childhood (various seizure types).
11. Bruxism, hyperventilation with air swallowing and breath holding common.
12. Choreoathetoid movements and dystonia may be present.

Infantile Autism

1. Onset from early infancy.
2. Loss of previously acquired skills does not occur.
3. More scatter of intellectual function; visual-spatial and manipulative skills often better than apparent verbal skills.
4. Physical development normal in the majority.
5. Stereotypic behavior more varied in manifestation and always more complex; midline manifestations rare.
6. Gait and other gross motor functions normal in first decade of life.
7. Language sometimes absent; if present, speech patterns are always peculiar; markedly impaired nonverbal communication.
8. Eye contact with others typically avoided or inappropriate.
9. Stereotypic ritualistic behavior, usually involving skillful but odd manipulation of objects or sensory self-stimulation.
10. Seizures (usually temporal-limbic complex partial) in 25%, in late adolescence and adulthood.
11. Bruxism, hyperventilation, and breath holding not typical.
12. Dystonia and chorea not present.[a]

*Reproduced with permission from "The Clinical Recognition and Differential Diagnosis of Rett Syndrome," by E. Trevathan & S. Naidu 1988, *Journal of Child Neurology, 3*(Suppl.), pp. S6–S16.
[a] Extrapyramidal signs may appear after puberty in some patients with autism.

(Olsson & Rett, 1987). Thus, physicians and clinicians must realize that the presence of an autistic behavioral syndrome is not an obligatory condition for a diagnosis of Rett's Syndrome (Olsson & Rett, 1987).

Millichap (1987) has suggested that Rett's Syndrome might represent a variant of Childhood Disintegrative Disorder (CDD; Heller's Syndrome). Compared to girls with Rett's Syndrome, children with CDD develop their symptoms later (e.g., at age 2 years, or, more typically, age 3 or 4 years), and normal neurologic findings are reported in persons with CDD. In a comparison of 2 boys with CDD and 6 girls with Rett's Syndrome, Burd, Fisher, and Kerbeshian (1989) reported that persons afflicted with these disorders differed from children with classic autism. Children with CDD and children with Rett's Syndrome displayed normal prenatal and perinatal periods, followed by marked developmental regression after which they acquired few or no new skills. The authors have suggested that these children should be distinguished from those with classic autism, and should be classified as "Pervasive Disintegrative Disorder, Heller Type" and "Pervasive Disintegrative Disorder, Rett Type." *DSM-IV* has included both Rett's Disorder (Rett's Syndrome) and Childhood Disintegrative Disorder (Heller's Syndrome) as subcategories of Pervasive Developmental Disorder.

The developmental regressions in Stage 2 often suggest neurodegenerative diseases. For example, the earliest stages of Rett's Syndrome are difficult to distinguish from infantile neuronal ceroid lipofuscinosis (INCL), an autosomal recessive disease especially frequent in the Finnish population. Both disorders cause a rapid regression of psychomotor development and the manifestation of hand and finger stereotypies at approximately the same age. As INCL progresses, however, myoclonus and retinal degeneration becomes apparent and differentiates the disease from Rett's Syndrome (Sekul & Percy, 1992). The failure to designate retinopathy or optic atrophy as an exclusionary criterion for Rett's Disorder within *DSM-IV* may complicate the differential diagnosis of this disorder.

A recent report (Philippart, 1993) links Rett's Syndrome with tuberous sclerosis, a neurocutaneous disorder. Although this disorder may show initial similarities to Rett's Syndrome, close examination of the skin with a Wood's lamp, revealing the presence of serial computed tomography abnormalities, will distinguish this disorder (Sekul & Percy, 1992). Chromosomal disorders, such as Angelman Syndrome ("happy puppet syndrome"), can display features similar to those of Rett's Syndrome. Children with Angelman Syndrome, however, fail to display a period of normal development and subsequent rapid regression. Acute and chronic encephalitis may be distinguished by examination of the cerebrospinal fluid (CSF) and by characteristic electroencephalography. The loss of language and the development of seizures in preschool-age children are similar in both Rett's Syndrome and the Landau-Kleffner Syndrome. Head circumference growth and motor skills are preserved in the Landau-Kleffner Syndrome.

In summary, the diagnosis of Rett's Syndrome rests on careful exploration of clinical manifestations and a specific pattern of symptom progression. A diagnosis of Rett's Syndrome should remain tentative until after 3 to 5 years of age, to allow the evolution of symptoms that might rule out Rett's Syndrome. Differential diagnosis, although frequently difficult at presentation (especially during the earliest stages), becomes much easier when follow-up extends over several months or a few years.

EPIDEMIOLOGY

Rett's Syndrome has been reported on all of the populated continents and in most countries of the world (e.g., Budden, 1986; Goutieres & Aicardi, 1985; Hanaoka, Ishikawa, & Kamoshita, 1985; Kerr & Stephenson, 1986; Moodley, 1992). Thus, the literature supports the view that Rett's Syndrome, rather than being a rare disorder, is more or less universal; additionally, fewer than 2 per 100 persons with Rett's Syndrome display familial relationships (Zoghbi, 1988). Thus, the pattern of occurrence of Rett's Syndrome is quite dissimilar to that of traditional inborn errors of metabolism (e.g., glactosemia, Hartnup's disease, ketoaciduria, phenylketonuria), which often display strong geographic, ethnic, and familial accumulation.

In 1996, a total of 2,660 cases of Rett's Syndrome were registered with the International Rett Syndrome Association, with the following distribution: United States 2,212; Canada 115; Australia 34; Sweden 32; England 24; Italy 23; Israel 12; Chile 12; Scotland 11; Mexico 11, and another 54 countries registering ten or fewer each (K. Hunter, personal communication, November 22, 1996). The prevalence of Rett's Syndrome has been studied, based on the Swedish registry for mental retardation and surveys of neuropediatricians, in a part of southwestern Sweden comprising five counties and the city of Gothenburg (Hagberg, 1985). In a population of 315,469 children and adolescents (6 to 17 years of age), 13 cases were detected, all girls. The corresponding prevalence was about 1 per 15,000 live female births. In their study of 5,400 consecutive referrals to the pediatric neurology center in western Scotland, Kerr and Stephenson (1985) identified 19 cases of Rett's Syndrome. The resulting prevalence rate was similar to that reported by Hagberg (1985): 1 per 12,000–13,000 females (Kerr & Stephenson, 1986).

A recent prevalence study was conducted within several areas of the State of Texas, in the Southern United States, by a number of researchers at the Baylor University College of Medicine (Kozinetz et al., 1993). The study employed the Texas Rett Syndrome Registry and explored females aged 2 through 18 years. Interestingly, this was the first study with a large ethnic mix, which allowed an exploration of racial and ethnic group-specific prevalence of Rett's Syndrome. An estimate of approximately 1 per 22,800 live female births was reported, with no significant differences in prevalence estimates by race or ethnicity. This estimate is lower than those reported in earlier studies, suggesting that the prevalence of Rett's Syndrome may have been overestimated.

Regardless of which estimate is employed, Rett's Syndrome seems to be significantly more prevalent among girls than phenylketonuria (PKU), a condition for which all neonates are screened in the majority of developed countries (Hagberg, 1985). Because progressive brain disorders and metabolic diseases together constitute only 5% to 6% (1.5 to 2.0 per 10,000 children) of the etiologies in persons with severe or profound mental retardation, Rett's Syndrome should be considered an important etiologic factor in females. In fact, this syndrome might well be responsible for one-fourth to one-third of progressive developmental disabilities among females (Hagberg, 1985).

ETIOLOGY

Although it has been systematically researched, the genesis of Rett's Syndrome has eluded explanation. However, several aspects of the disorder suggest a genetic origin. Confirmed diagnosis of Rett's Syndrome has, to date, been described only in females. A number of familial cases (represented in Table 4.4) have indicated a prominent pattern of commonality along maternal lines (Zoghbi, 1988).

Several investigators (Anvret & Wahlstrom, 1992; Gillberg, Wahlstrom, & Hagberg, 1984, 1985; Hanefeld, Hanefeld, Wilichowski, &

TABLE 4.4   Familial Cases in Rett's Syndrome*

	Number of Pairs
Monozygotic twins:	
Both females afflicted	11 (plus 2 provisional)
Only one female afflicted	1
Dizygotic twins (female/female):	
Both females afflicted	2
Only one female afflicted	5
Dizygotic twins (female/male):	
Female afflicted	8 (plus 1 provisional)
Full sisters	8 (plus 2 provisional)
Half-sisters	2
Full cousins	1
Second cousins	2
Second half-cousins	1
Aunt–niece	2
Great-grandaunt–niece	1
Sister and half-brother, both of whom have children with Rett's Syndrome	1
Mother–daughter	1

*Modified from "Genetic Aspects of Rett Syndrome," by H. Y. Zoghbi, 1988, *Journal of Child Neurology,* *3*(Suppl.), pp. 576–577, with information provided through the International Rett Syndrome Association (November 22, 1996).

Schmidtke, 1986; Killian, 1986; Riccardi, 1986) have sought a genetic basis for the disorder, but their efforts have been inconclusive.

The leading hypothesis proposes dominant X-linked new mutations that might cause early abortions of hemizygous male fetuses and a dominant phenotype in heterozygous females (Comings, 1986; Riccardi, 1986). A few males have been described as demonstrating symptoms phenotypically similar to Rett's Syndrome, but none has satisfied the established criteria (Sekul & Percy, 1992). Zoghbi (1988) suggests that a familial pattern in which more than one daughter has Rett's Syndrome but the mother is apparently not affected could best be explained by the possibility of a nonrandom X-chromosome inactivation in the mother. The typical X-chromosome inactivation process, however, is random and occurs in every somatic cell during embryogenesis in females. As these cells divide, the same X-chromosome inactivation pattern is observed in subsequent cells. (Lyon, 1972). The process of a nonrandom pattern of X-chromosome inactivation, as has been proposed for Rett's Syndrome, is not well understood but has been demonstrated in female carriers in other X-linked diseases such as Lesch-Nyhan Syndrome and Wiskott-Aldrich disease (Greer, Lwong, Peacocke, Ip, Rubin, & Siminovitch, 1989; Nyhan, Bakay, & Conner, 1970). Support for skewing of X-chromosome inactivation, causing a nonrandom pattern to evolve, has been reported for Rett's Syndrome. A nonrandom-pattern X-chromosome inactivation was reported in the peripheral leukocytes for 38% of the girls with Rett's Syndrome compared to 8% of the control group (Zoghbi, Percy, Schultz, & Fill, 1990). Brain tissue from three of the girls with Rett's Syndrome who manifested the peripheral leukocyte skewing failed to demonstrate a similar pattern of skewing. One might conclude, therefore, that the selection process in the central nervous system may be less severe, allowing the survival of cells carrying the allele for Rett's Syndrome on the active X chromosome.

Recent generational chromosomal studies of females with Rett's Syndrome and their family members failed to support the X-chromosome inactivation hypothesis. In a study of two generations of a family in Sweden, Anvret and Wahlstrom (1992) reported that none of the females in the family demonstrated a specific nonrandom inactivation pattern that could explain the inheritance of Rett's Syndrome. In a study of 8 families, Webb, Watkiss, and Woods (1993) found that all 8 mothers and 2 nonaffected sisters of girls with Rett's Syndrome demonstrated random X-chromosome inactivation.

Wahlstrom and his associates (Gillberg et al., 1985; Wahlstrom, 1985; Wahlstrom & Anvret, 1986) have suggested a convincing argument for a two-step mutation that might explain the epidemiological findings in Rett's Syndrome. This hypothesis postulates that girls with Rett's Syndrome would have an inherited mutated gene in one of the X chromosomes, in addition to a somatic mutation at the same locus in the other X chromosome. An inherited mutated gene or a somatic cell mutation in a male zygote would result in an early abortion. Mitochondrial inheritance (Eeg-Olofsson, Al-Zuhair, Teebi, & Al-Essa, 1989) also has been suggested to explain the maternal transmission displayed by Rett's Syndrome. Unfortunately, this hypothesis would not easily explain inheritance of Rett's Syndrome only in females.

Buhler, Malik, and Alkan (1990) present yet another model for the inheritance of Rett's Syndrome. This model, based on Johnson's (1980) hypothesis of metabolic interference of X-linked alleles, proposes the action of an autosomal modifying gene in addition to the X-chromosomal "Rett" gene. The presence of a locus on an autosomal chromosome interferes with a locus on the X chromosome. A carrier state in the female is the result of a mutation at the automsomal locus, but when it is not mutated, the girl develops Rett's Syndrome. This last model has some support in the Carlin, Arena, and Ing (1989) study that presented two cases of females with Rett's Syndrome who manifested abnormalities of autosomes only.

Cytogenetic analyses have been undertaken in hopes of identifying a DNA marker for Rett's Syndrome. Evidence supporting a contributory role of the X chromosome in the development of Rett's Syndrome includes various translocations involving the short arm of the X chromosome: one is a t(X;3) (p22.11;q13.31) (Zoghbi, Ledbetter, Schultz, Percy, & Glaze, 1990), and another is a t(X;22) (p11.22;p11) (Journel,

Melki, Turleau, Munnich, & deGrouchy, 1990). Interestingly, the latter translocation was found in sisters; one was affected with classical Rett's Syndrome and the other exhibited a forme fruste. Their nonaffected mother, however, has the same translocation, which could be explained by different X-inactivation patterns in the mother and daughters. Journel et al. (1990) postulate that the gene for Rett's Syndrome may be located distally to the breakpoint.

Decreased ornitine carbamoyltransferase (OCT) loci activity noted in girls with Rett's Syndrome (Thomas, Hjelm, Oberholzer, Brett, & Wilson, 1987) also increased interest in X-chromosome research. The OCT gene locus was considered a strong possibility for the marker because many girls with Rett's Syndrome demonstrate laboratory abnormalities similar to female carriers of OCT deficiency (Sekul & Percy, 1992). The OCT locus, however, has recently been excluded as a possible site for the Rett's Syndrome marker on the basis of multiloci linkage analysis (Clarke et al., 1990; Ellison et al., 1992) and analysis of restriction fragment length polymorphisms and microsatellite markers (Curtis et al., 1993). Two additional candidate genes on the short arm of the X chromosome—the synapsin I gene and the synaptophysin gene (DeGennaro, McCaffery, Kirchgessner, Yang-Feng, & Francke, 1987; Yang-Feng, DeGennaro, & Francke, 1986)—are thought to code for synaptic vesicle protein (important for neurotransmitter release) and have been implicated in Rett's Syndrome. The analyses of Ellison et al. (1992) and Curtis et al. (1993) have eliminated these genes from serious consideration as well.

The existence of Fragile X sites has been explored in Rett's Syndrome research because Fragile X has been reported in a number of autistic syndromes. The Fragile X sites Xp22 and Xq27 have been associated with Rett's Syndrome (Wahlstrom, Witt-Engerstrom, Mellquist, Anvret, & Oden, 1990), but this association holds little diagnostic value because both sites can be found in phenotypically normal females (Barbi, Steinbach, & Vogel, 1984; Sekul & Percy, 1992).

The evidence for a genetic etiology for Rett's Syndrome seems promising but is inconclusive at the present time. Recent reports

(MacLeod, 1994; Naidu, 1994) of a pair of monozygotic twins who are discordant for Rett's Syndrome are puzzling and complicate the genetic origin hypothesis. Additional research is needed to determine whether any of the present hypotheses is indeed valid. Future cytogenetic investigations are clearly needed "to find a common breakpoint in some girls with Rett syndrome or to find a structural chromosome aberration co-segregating with the Rett syndrome in a family" (Anvret & Wahlstrom, 1992, p. S102). Ultimately, the female-limited nature of Rett's Syndrome may prove misleading as regards the importance of the X chromosome.

NEUROPATHOLOGY

A limited number of neuropathological studies have been conducted in the research of Rett's Syndrome. One brain autopsy from England (Harding, Tudmay, & Wilson, 1985), a forensic report from Vienna (Missliwetz & Depastas, 1985), a summary of eight autopsies done in Vienna by Jellinger and Seiteberger (1986), and a later single autopsy from Vienna (Brucke, Sofic, Killian, Rett, & Riederer, 1988) indicated that malnutrition was common before death, and that diffuse brain atrophy, with a decrease in brain weight by 13.8% to 33.8% compared to that of age-matched controls, is a common nonspecific finding. The degree of atrophy appeared to be related to the duration of the disorder. Mild nonselective neuronal loss and gliosis also were noted. No evidence of active degenerative disease had been seen, however, and the whole brain seemed to be affected by the atrophy. The most conspicuous specific finding was deficient pigmentation of the substantia nigra (especially the zona compacta), which contained notably fewer (53% to 73%) well-pigmented neurons in relation to the age of the person, and fewer pigmented granules per neuron. The total number of nigral neurons and the triphasic substructure of neuromelanin were within the normal range. The basal ganglia of some patients showed mild gliosis. These findings were supported in a study of 38 patients with Rett's Syndrome, conducted in Sweden by Lekman et al. (1989). Brucke et al. (1988) also reported low melanin content in the locus coeruleus. Because the melanin pigmentation in the substantia nigra

normally increases with age, this lack of pigmentation serves as "evidence of a retardation in maturation of these neurons [in the substantia nigra and locus coeruleus] which possibly leads to a decreased synthesis rate of dopamine and a compensatory enhancement in its turnover rate" (Brucke et al., 1988, p. 323). Increased levels of dopamine and serotonin metabolites in the subject supported the hypothesis. The abnormalities of the substantia nigra and the related changes in dopamine synthesis could account for the prominent movement disorder associated with Rett's Syndrome.

Jellinger, Armstrong, Zoghbi, and Percy (1988) presented evidence, from electron microscopic studies, of abnormal neurites in the frontal cortex and caudate nucleus with greatly reduced axonal or dendritic connections. In a study of two females with Rett's Syndrome (Armstrong, 1992), the cortical neurons appeared to be less mature and demonstrated significantly decreased dendritic arborization that did not appear to be age-related. This could be the result of the general growth arrest manifested in Rett's Syndrome and may, in part, explain the acquired microcephaly witnessed in Stage 1 of the disorder.

Using the technique of gapless serial section, Bauman, Kemper, and Arin (1995) conducted microscopic analysis of the brains from three girls with classical Rett's Syndrome and those of identically processed age-matched controls. Throughout the brain in all three cases of Rett's Syndrome significantly smaller neuronal cell size and increased cell packing density were reported, without evidence of gliosis or active degeneration. These data suggest a curtailment of brain development which may begin before birth.

A study of the role of neurotrophic factors in Rett's Syndrome has provided additional support for a neurological growth arrest hypothesis. Lappalainen, Lindholm, and Riikonen (1996) employing a sensitive two-site enzyme-linked immunoassay, examined the content of nerve growth factor in the cerebrospinal fluid of 11 children with Rett's Syndrome and of 24 control subjects with various neurologic diagnoses or suffering from other diseases. The levels of nerve growth factor for the subjects with Rett's Syndrome were significantly lower than those of the control subjects. The authors suggest that this reduction in the level of nerve growth factor may be involved in the pathogenesis of this disorder or reflect the underlying brain damage present.

A recent study (Cornford, Philippart, Jacobs, Scheibel, & Vinters, 1994) reports on the neuronal changes in the brain of a girl with Rett's Syndrome, observed in a frontal lobe biopsy performed at age 3 years and in the postmortem brain at age 15 years. Widespread neuronal mitochondrial inclusions and the appearance of dendritic retraction in Golgi-stained cortical pyramidal and Purkinji neurons were the most significant neuropathological features. Interestingly, the Golgi preparations of the frontal cortex and cerebellar folia (autopsy brain) manifested truncation and thickening of the dendrites and a degenerate appearance of cortical pyramidal neurons similar to that of an aged brain. Thus, neuronal and mitochondrial deterioration appeared to continue after stabilization of the neurologic deterioration (at 3 years) in Rett's Syndrome. This discovery has led these authors to speculate that "Rett syndrome could result from inadequate maintenance of a full array of neuronal contacts, similar to the aging process, in which such dendritic regression apparently occurs over the span of many years" (p. 430).

The pathogenic mechanisms of the morphologic brain lesions, and their relations to clinical and neurochemical findings in Rett's Syndrome, remain unknown. Neuropathological studies at autopsy serve a critical role in furthering an understanding of Rett's Syndrome. The International Rett Syndrome Association (IRSA) urges parents of persons with this disorder to consider the gift of autopsy should their children die prematurely. To this end, a uniform procedure has been developed for the postmortem examination (Percy, Hass, Kolodny, Moser, & Naidu, 1988) and is available from IRSA. Advance arrangements must be made with a pathologist so that tissues can be frozen, optimally within 4 to 6 hours following death.

NEUROANATOMY

The development of sophisticated methods for visualization of the human central nervous system in vivo has provided a means to quantify brain structure and function in persons with brain dysfunction. Routine neuroimaging studies in persons with Rett's Syndrome, however, have revealed only occasional nonspecific changes. Serial CT and MRI studies have shown evidence of a progressive brain atrophy in some girls, particularly in the frontal and temporal regions, after age 2 years (Krageloh-Mann, Schroth, Niemann, & Michaelis, 1989; Nihei & Naitoh, 1990; Nomura, Segawa, & Hasegawa, 1984; Yano, Yamashita, Matsuishi, Abe, Yamata, Shinohara, 1991). These findings are consistent with the pathologic findings of Jellinger et al. (1988), reported above.

Decreased cerebral blood flow (88% of the flow noted in age-matched controls) was reported in seven persons with Rett's Syndrome (Nielsen, Friberg, Lou, Lassen & Sam, 1990). Single photon emission CT demonstrated significantly decreased cerebral blood flow to the prefrontal and temporal regions, although the flow to the primary sensorimotor cortex remained unaffected. Because a similar pattern of cerebral blood flow is observed in infants (Chugani, Phelps, & Mazziotta, 1987), this finding may reflect the growth arrest noted in Rett's Syndrome. Further evidence of abnormal cerebral blood flow in Rett's Syndrome was reported by Yoshikawa, Fueki, Suzuki, Sakuragawa, and Masaaki (1991). The developmental increase of the frontal-to-temporal cerebral blood flow ratio demonstrated in age-matched controls was not observed in 6 females with Rett's Syndrome.

Employing quantitative methods of analysis in neuroimaging, Casanova and associates (1991) reported smaller cerebral hemispheres in 8 persons with Rett's Syndrome, when compared to controls. A decreased area of caudate nucleus, even when the overall smaller brain area was taken into account, also was noted in the girls with Rett's Syndrome. Smaller cerebral hemispheres, basal ganglia, corpus callosum, cerebellar hemispheres, inferior olive, and anterior vermis were reported in 13 females with Rett's Syndrome compared to 10 female control subjects (Murakami, Courchesne, Haas, Press, & Yeung-Courchesne, 1992). Reiss et al. (1993) completed a quantitative neuroimaging study that provided in vivo neuroanatomical correlates of the neurologic and developmental features of Rett's Syndrome. This group reported reduced cerebral volume; a disproportionate reduction in brain tissue volumes, with a greater decrease in the ratio of gray matter to white; regional variation in the percentage of cortical gray matter (with frontal regions showing the greatest decrease); reduced volume of subcortical gray matter (with the caudate nucleus showing significant volume reduction); and increased CSF volume when controlling for brain volume differences in the females with Rett's Syndrome. These findings, especially those related to the caudate nucleus, are of interest from a clinical standpoint because they may help to explain the significant motor and cognitive-developmental symptoms present in Rett's Syndrome.

The consistency of data obtained through neuroimaging research with results from neuropathological investigations supports the need for continued neuroimaging studies in Rett's Syndrome. Longitudinal studies from the time the children manifest the earliest signs of the syndrome would be especially enlightening. Information gained from neuroimaging studies could make a significant contribution to our understanding of the etiology, homogeneity, and pathogenesis of this disorder.

NEUROCHEMICAL ALTERATIONS

The progressive nature of Rett's Syndrome following an apparently normal pre- and neonatal period is highly suggestive of a metabolic disorder similar to PKU. The pathogenesis of the disorder, however, remains a mystery. Extensive research is exploring biogenic amines and endorphins through analysis of serum amino acids, urine amino and organic acids, lysosomal enzymes, and routine chemistries. One hypothesis is that symptoms result from an abnormality in the dopamine system, a neurotransmitter system that regulates the control of voluntary movements in the extrapyramidal system. This hypothesis, based on the decreased pigmentation of the substantia nigra and the prominent movement disorders suggestive of extrapyramidal dysfunction (Zoghbi, Percy, Glaze, Butler, & Riccardi, 1985), led Nomura and associates (Nomura et al., 1984; Nomura, Segawa, & Higurashi, 1985) to speculate that, as the disease progresses, the dopamine system becomes hyperactive as a result of postsynaptic supersensitivity caused by

hypoactive dopamine neurons. Abnormality in the dopamine system is supported by the finding of a decrease of biogenic amine metabolites in CSF in 6 children with Rett's Syndrome. The most significant reductions were in homovanillic acid (HVA), the major dopamine metabolite (Zoghbi et al., 1985). These findings were extended to 32 girls found to have significant reductions in HVA and in 4-hydroxy-3-methoxyphenylethylene glycol (HMPG), the metabolites of dopamine and norepinephrine (Zoghbi et al., 1989; Zoghbi et al., 1985). An abnormality in this system is further supported by demonstration of decreasing binding of 3H spiperone (a ligand with high affinity for dopamine D2 receptors) in the putamen in an autopsy study (Riederer et al., 1985). Hand–mouth stereotypies, hypotonia, and ataxia similar to that seen in Rett's Syndrome are demonstrated in boys with the Lesch-Hyhan Syndrome, a disorder in which all biochemical aspects of the function of dopamine neuron terminals in the corpus striatum have been found to be decreased (10% to 30% of control values) in autopsy studies of three affected cases (Lloyd et al., 1981).

A number of studies, however, have failed to replicate the findings that seemed to indicate that Rett's Syndrome is characterized by abnormal neurotransmitter levels. Unlike the 6 cases reported by Zoghbi et al. (1985), where norepinephrine and dopamine metabolites were reduced in comparison to controls, subjects in a later investigation (Harris et al., 1986) did not demonstrate a reduction in the metabolites of either of these neurotransmitter substances. Reduction of dopamine D2 receptor binding in the putamen was not demonstrated in living subjects by in vivo positron emission tomography (PET) scanning as found by Riederer et al. (1985) with 3H spiperone in an autopsy study. Additionally, low normal receptor binding, rather than dopamine receptor supersensitivity, was reported (in direct opposition to the results reported by Nomura et al., 1985). Similar findings were described in a second study (Riederer et al., 1986), where preliminary biochemical analyses on plasma, urine, CSF, and postmortem brain areas indicated no disturbance of neurotransmitter function. These researchers suggested that various drug therapies administered to the girls prior to sample testing, plus undernutrition (a common problem among girls with Rett's Syndrome) might have influenced the synthesis and turnover of these biogenic amines. An alternative hypothesis might suggest, however, that such a deficit was triggered as a primary consequence of the disease process. Efforts to understand the often contradictory results are complicated further by the differing laboratory procedures employed by investigators throughout the world.

Rett's Syndrome appears to share a number of neurochemical features (without the associated neuropathological features) with a number of age-related neurodegenerative diseases such as Alzheimer's disease and Parkinson's disease. Decreased cortical and subcortical levels of choline acetyltransferase (ChAT) activity has been reported by Wenk and his associates (Wenk, Naidu, Casanova, Kitt, & Moser, 1991; Wenk et al., 1993) in a series of postmortem brain studies. The decreased ChAT activity may be related to loss of cholinergic cells, a condition qualitatively similar to the loss in Alzheimer's disease. These studies (Wenk et al., 1991; Wenk et al., 1993) also report decreased ChAT activity in the hippocampus and thalamus, which is consistent with a loss of cholinergic cells in the medial septum and vertical limb of the Broca and the pedunculopontine tegmental nucleus. This loss of cholinergic cells throughout the basal forebrain might be responsible for the cognitive stagnation and memory loss that are characteristic of Rett's Syndrome, as has been suggested for the dementia associated with Alzheimer's disease and Parkinson's disease (Collerton, 1986; Whitehouse, Price, Clark, Coyle, & DeLong, 1981).

Persons with Rett's Syndrome have been reported to display a remarkable tolerance for pain, a high rate of stereotyped behavior, seizure activity, and respiratory disturbances. These symptoms have been induced in laboratory animals by exposing them to elevated endorphin levels. Several research groups have therefore studied the β-endorphin system in females with Rett's Syndrome. Budden, Myer, and Butler (1990) found elevated β-endorphin immunoreactivity in the CSF of 11 out of the 12 girls studied. These findings were extended when elevated CSF β-endorphins were reported in 90% of over 150 persons with Rett's Syndrome (Myer, Tripathi, Brase, & Dewey, 1992). The degree of elevation of the β-endorphins, however, did not correlate to the severity of the symptoms (e.g., stereotypy, breathing disturbance) or the stage of the disorder. Contradictory results have been reported among researchers (Genazzani, Zappella, Nalin, Hayek, & Facchinetti, 1989; Gillberg, Terenius, Hagberg, Witt-Ingerstrom, & Eriksson, 1990) who found significantly lower levels of β-endorphins in girls with Rett's Syndrome, when compared with age-matched controls. As in the biogeneic amine studies reported above, the basis for these contradictory findings remains unknown.

Perhaps the most promising lead for a neurochemical marker for Rett's Syndrome has developed recently from a study that explored brain and CSF glycolipids in 5 autopsied cases (Lekman, Hagberg, & Svennerholm, 1991). The concentrations of two major brain gangliosides—GD1a in frontal gray matter and GD1b in temporal gray matter—appear to be lowered selectively in the cerebral cortex and cerebellum in girls with Rett's Syndrome. The ganglioside GD1a is thought to play an important role in synaptogenesis because it is prominent in synaptic membranes, and high concentrations are reported during the time when nerve-ending growth and synapse formation are most intense (from the 25th fetal week until age 2 years). Ganglioside GD1b is rich in axons and accrues more slowly, reaching maximum concentration at age 20 years. The reduction of GD1a would help explain the pathogenic findings of decreased dendritic arborization reported by Armstrong (1992). These findings appear to be specific for Rett's Syndrome; however, replication of a larger series is required to validate the results.

DRUG THERAPY

Treatment of Underlying Causes

To date, there is no cure for Rett's Syndrome, and therapeutic interventions directed at its fundamental mechanisms have failed to demonstrate any lasting or substantive improvements. Based on the biochemical findings in the research, the effect of bromocriptine, a dopamine agonist, has been explored in 12 girls with Rett's Syndrome (Zappella, 1990; Zappella & Genazzani, 1986; Zappella, Genazzani, Facchinetti, & Hayek, 1990). Improvements in communication and a decreased frequency of agitation episodes were initially reported; however, these improvements failed to recur following the "washout" phase of the study. A number of uncontrolled studies have explored the effects of other anti-Parkinsonian drugs aimed at the monoamine system (e.g., L-dopa, pergolide, deprenyl), but they have failed to provide evidence of improvement on a consistent basis. L-dopa and Sinemet (DuPont) have been reported to show benefit for a limited number of patients in the later stages of the disorder, when increasing rigidity has appeared (Percy, Schultz, Glaze, Skender, del Junco, Waring, & Zoghbi, 1991). Tetrabenazine, a monoamine depleter and blocker, resulted in an exacerbation of symptoms in one patient (Sekul & Percy, 1992). Egger, Hofacker, Schiel, and Holthausen (1992) reported that magnesium orotate or citrate (4 to 10 mg/kg/day), initially given as an anticonvulsant (after more traditional anticonvulsants had failed), resulted in a decrease in hyperventilation in a girl with Rett's Syndrome. When they extended their findings to 6 additional patients with Rett's Syndrome, a decrease in hyperventilation was reported in all girls, and the parents reported a decrease in their daughters' hand stereotypies and episodes of agitation. Convulsions were reduced in 4 of the girls. Serum magnesium levels were normal for all patients prior to the start of the treatment, suggesting that magnesium was acting pharmacologically rather than correcting a deficit. These researchers suggest that the magnesium is counteracting intracellular lactic acidosis and serving as a N-methyl-D-asparate channel blocker, thus reducing excitotoxic neuronal damage.

Following two months of treatment with L-carnitine (50/mg/kg/day), Plioplys and Kasnicka (1993) reported that a 17-year-old girl with Rett's Syndrome demonstrated improved alertness and eye contact. She also displayed an improved interest in her environment and would reach for objects and began to answer simple questions with one or two words. When the L-carnitine was discontinued she lapsed into her pretreatment state of lethargy, poor eye contact, disinterest in her environment,

and failure to employ speech. One week after the L-carnitine was resumed, she again displayed improved alertness, interest in her environment, and simple one or two word speech. These preliminary findings of L-carnitine treatment with a single subject are encouraging, however, replication of these results are needed.

Neurotransmitter precursor therapy with amino acids has been attempted, using tyrosine (the precursor for dopamine and norepinephrine) and tryptophan (precursor for serotonin) in 9 girls (Nielsen, Lou, & Andresen, 1990). No clinical performance or EEG pattern changes as a result of treatment were observed.

Naltrexone, an opiate antagonist, was employed in a double-blind crossover trial (Percy et al., 1991). The use of an opiate antagonist was attempted when elevated levels of β-endorphins were reported in girls with Rett's Syndrome. The motor behavior and other symptoms of the disorder displayed no improvement during the naltrexone treatment phase. In fact, the girls' performance on the Bayley Scales of Infant Development worsened during the phase of naltrexone treatment. A more recent study, Matsuihi et al., (1994) reported that naltrexone had a positive effect upon the abnormal respiratory characteristics of Rett's Syndrome. The study goes on to report, however, that naltrexone treatment led to a decline in the motor functioning and a more rapid progression of the disorder in 40% of the subjects. Given the lack of a biochemical marker and a rather limited understanding of the biological basis of Rett's Syndrome, the ineffectiveness of drug therapy is not particularly surprising.

EEG Profile and Seizure Control

At this time, we must be satisfied to provide suitable medication aimed at symptomatic relief (e.g., of seizure activity). The EEG has been demonstrated to be significantly abnormal for persons with Rett's Syndrome throughout all but the earliest stage of the disorder. A study based on the EEG records of 44 persons with Rett's Syndrome found abnormal EEG tracings to be almost universal (Niedermeyer, Rett, Renner, Murphy, & Naidu, 1986). Abnormal sleep patterns have also been noted.

For example, Haas, Rice, Trauner, and Merritt (1986) report the "presence of intermittent episodes of high amplitude bursts of spike wave or slow wave discharges followed by a brief period of relative suppression of background activity" (p. 238) during sleep. Robb, Harden, and Boyd (1989) report that, in their study of 52 girls with Rett's Syndrome, discharges, consisting of short waves or spikes, were a common feature. These discharges could be infrequent or almost continuous, and they were most prominent around the middle third of the head.

Pronounced EEG abnormalities were most often found between the ages of 3 and 10 years, and they tended to become less severe during the second decade of life (Niedermeyer et al., 1986; Rett, 1986). Glaze, Frost, Zoghbi, and Percy (1987) described the progressive changes in the EEG and correlated them with the clinical staging system. Their work is summarized in Table 4.5. The EEG changes generally appear at the beginning of Stage 2 and then follow a stepwise progression, with slowing, loss of normal sleep characteristics, multifocal abnormalities, and, finally, generalized slow spike and wave activity (Verma, Chheda, & Nigro, 1986).

All girls with Rett's Syndrome demonstrate abnormal EEG tracings, but seizure activity is not universal. Naidu et al. (1986) reported that approximately 84% of the girls in their study demonstrated seizures. The most common types of clinical seizures are generalized tonic-clonic and partial complex seizures. Infantile spasms with hypsaarrythmia may be an early symptom (Iyama, 1993). Selection of a specific medication should be based on clinical seizure type and EEG pattern. Several clinicians (Adkins, 1986; Budden, 1986; Naidu et al., 1986; Philippart, 1986) agree that standard dosages of Tegretol (carbamazepine) constitute the best seizure management program. Adrenocorticotrophic hormone or prednisone has been helpful in treating infantile spasms (Sekul & Percy, 1992). Hagberg (1985) warns, however, that many girls with Rett's Syndrome overreact and must therefore be taken off the medication. Haas et al. (1986) has employed the ketogenic diet to reduce seizures in girls. As the girls enter late adolescence, seizure activity may decrease; this allows modification

of their medication regimen. Staring spells, eye rolling, and other episodic behavior may be observed in girls with Rett's Syndrome, but these are not always indications of seizure activity (Garofalo, Drury, & Goldstein, 1988). Therefore, these behaviors should not be treated as seizures without EEG documentation.

GROWTH PATTERNS AND NUTRITION

Following the first 6 months of life, a pattern of deceleration across all growth measurements is witnessed in most persons with Rett's Syndrome (Schultz, Glaze, & Motil, 1993). The exact cause is unknown. A systemic deficiency in mitochondrial energy production, as reported from muscle biopsy tissue, has been suggested (Coker & Melnyk, 1991; Schultz et al., 1993). The best evidence to date, however, suggests that nutritional—rather than chromosomal, neurologic, or hormonal—factors underlie this failure to grow. Some evidence suggests defects in carbohydrate (Clark et al., 1990; Haas & Rice, 1985; Haas et al., 1986), ascorbic acid, and glutathione (Sofic, Riederer, Killian, & Rett, 1987) metabolism. Malabsorption of critical nutrients and failure to benefit from adequate caloric intake must be considered when examining the malnutrition displayed in some persons with Rett's Syndrome (Missliwetz & Depastas, 1985). Motil, Schultz, Brown, Glaze, and Percy (1994) report that energy expenditure associated with involuntary motor movement places these girls in a situation of lower energy balance (energy intake vs. expenditure) than controls. The lowered energy balance in girls with Rett's Syndrome has paralleled their degree of height and weight deficits, despite similar dietary energy intakes between groups. Haas and his associates (Haas & Rice, 1985; Haas et al., 1986) have reported improved weight gain in conjunction with diminished stereotyped behavior and better seizure control when a high-calorie, high-fat ketogenic diet was implemented. If weight gain is a problem, a nutritionist should be available to consult with parents and program staff relative to diet.

Constipation is commonly experienced by persons with Rett's Syndrome. Many of the

TABLE 4.5 Correlation of EEG Characteristics with Clinical Stages

State	EEG Characteristics*			
	Stage 1	Stage 2	Stage 3	Stage 4
Awake	Normal or minimal slowing of occipital-dominant rhythm and background activity.	Marked slowing of occipital-dominant rhythm and background activity; rare focal spike or sharp-wave discharges.	Further, gradual slowing of occipital-dominant rhythm, with its subsequent disappearance; moderate-to-marked slowing of background activity; appearance of multifocal spike and sharp-wave discharges; during latter part of this stage; appearance of generalized slow spike-wave pattern.	Absence of occipital-dominant rhythm; marked slowing of background activity (delta frequencies); multifocal spike and/or sharp wave discharges or generalized slow spike-wave pattern.
Asleep	Normal, with well-defined vertex transients and sleep spindles.	Less well-defined vertex transients and spindles, and subsequent loss of these sleep characteristics; appearance of focal or multifocal spike and/or sharp-wave discharges.	Absent vertex transients and spindles during NREM sleep; multifocal spike and/or sharp-wave discharges, with later development of generalized slow spike-wave pattern during NREM sleep.	Almost continuous generalized slow spike-wave activity.

*Modified from Glaze et al. (1987). "Rett's Syndrome: Correlation of Electroencephalographic Characteristic with Clinical Staging," by D. G. Glaze, J. D. Frost, H. Y. Zoghbi et al., 1987, *Archives of Neurology, 44*, pp. 1053–1056.

girls fail to consume adequate fluids and fiber, which may result in an impacted bowel (Hunter, 1987). Dietary measures (ingestion of high-liquid-content fruit, fiber, mineral oil, etc.) may prove adequate, although the use of artificial laxatives, enemas, or suppositories is often required (Naidu et al., 1990).

COGNITIVE AND ADAPTIVE FUNCTIONING

Rett's Syndrome is characterized by an especially debilitating combination of an extrapyramidal movement disorder, delayed response latencies, and the loss of acquired speech. The combination of disabilities significantly limits a researcher's ability to estimate the cognitive functioning of persons with this disorder. Traditional methods of cognitive assessment require unimpaired motor or verbal responses from the individual to generate valid estimates. If the person is required to employ a means of responding that is itself impaired, it can never be determined whether the assessed functioning is a measure of cognitive ability or of a motor and verbal disability. Thus, the assessment of cognitive functioning in persons with Rett's Syndrome is particularly problematic.

Much of the research on Rett's Syndrome suggests that the girls function within the severe-to-profound range of mental retardation. For example, Perry, Sarlo-McGarvey, and Haddad (1991) employed the Cattell Infant Intelligence Scale (Cattell, 1940) to assess the cognitive functioning of 15 girls with Rett's Syndrome. Each of the girls tested below the 8-month cognitive functioning level (average = 3 months), suggesting profound cognitive deficits. Considerable debate, however, centers on whether children with Rett's Syndrome experience a true dementia involving cognitive degeneration that results in severe or profound mental retardation (e.g., Budden, Meek, & Henighan, 1990; Charnov, Stach, & Didonato, 1989; Rolando, 1985) or a cognitive arrest or stagnation at the point of the initial motor and language regression (e.g., Fontanesi & Haas, 1988; Kerr et al., 1987; Naidu et al., 1986). Charnov and her associates (Charnov et al., 1989) evaluated the developmental histories of 16 girls with Rett's

Syndrome through parent interview (regarding preregression development) and current functioning assessment employing the Birth to Three Developmental Scale (Bangs & Dodson, 1979). In all developmental areas, the current functioning of each subject was substantially below that which the children were attributed to have achieved prior to the onset of the disorder. Interestingly, the developmental skills profile at the time of testing mirrored that of the preregression skills, although at a lower level of functioning.

There is some support, however, for a hypothesis that Rett's Syndrome results in cognitive arrest or stagnation at the developmental level achieved at the age of onset of the condition, in combination with a severe extrapyramidal movement and expressive language disorder as opposed to cognitive dementia (Hagberg & Witt-Engerstrom, 1986; Kerr & Stephenson, 1986; Stephenson & Kerr, 1987). Fontanesi and Haas (1988) evaluated the cognitive functioning of 18 girls with Rett's Syndrome. They administered the Vineland Adaptive Behavior Scales and the Bayley Scales of Adaptive Abilities, in addition to examining medical and developmental histories and interviewing parents regarding the age at which their daughters attained developmental milestones. Their results indicated that "skills not dependent on either language or fine motor function are retained at a developmental level equivalent to the age of onset" (p. S23). Gross motor functioning, daily living skills, and object permanence were found to be relatively preserved, but fine motor control and language functioning displayed substantial degeneration from preregression developmental levels.

In a longitudinal study of the cognitive skills in 6 girls with Rett's Syndrome, Woodyatt and Ozanne (1993) reported patterns of similarity across the group as well as individual variations across subjects and within subjects over a period of 3 years. Using the Uzgiris and Hunt (1975) Scales of Infant Psychological Development, they found the girls resembled one another and remained relatively stable, over the 3 years, in the sensorimotor domains of Object Permanence (Piagetian Stages I and II), Vocal Imitation (Piagetian Stages 0 and I), Gestural Imitation (Piagetian Stages 0 and I), and Scheme Actions (Piagetian Stages

II and III). There was considerable individual variation among the girls in relation to the sensorimotor domain of Means–Ends Abilities, ranging from Piagetian Stages I to IV. The girls also demonstrated the greatest level of individual improvement in this area over the 3-year study (from Piagetian Stage I to Stages II and IV for 3 of the girls).

Current best estimates suggest that persons with Rett's Syndrome function within the severe-to-profound range of mental retardation following the regression in Stage II of the disorder. The areas of gross motor activity and daily living skills appear to be more advanced than other adaptive functions, and the girls are capable of some cognitive improvement over time. Further research is needed to gain a fuller understanding of the cognitive abilities of girls with Rett's Syndrome. Multidisciplinary assessments of children with Rett's Syndrome are required to gather information on factors that may influence cognitive development and performance. Inconsistency of response in the test situation is a common report across the studies. Standardized testing is difficult, and care should be taken not only to provide standardized administrations of cognitive tests, but also to look across the daily functioning of the girls and identify actions that indicate target abilities. For example, in one study (Van Acker & Grant, 1995), one of the girls failed to demonstrate awareness of a covered object during testing, suggesting a lack of object permanence. Later in the testing situation, however, she dropped a toy and it rolled under a table. She repeatedly looked under the table for the missing item.

COMMUNICATION

Communication abilities and subsequent programming for persons with Rett's Syndrome have been the topic of very limited empirical research. Prior to regression, most of the girls with this disorder are reported to have developed single spoken words, word combinations, or both. Comprehension skills appropriate to the child's age also are typically noted (Budden, Meek, & Henighan, 1990; Woodyatt & Ozanne, 1992). The loss of language skills during regression is sufficiently rapid to be mistaken for hearing loss. Following the regression

phase of the disorder, speech and language skills are observed to be severely impaired. Verbalizations are typically nonexistent or limited to "nonfunctional" consonant–vowel combinations (Budden, Meek, & Henighan, 1990). As the girls approach adolescence, improved eye contact, social interaction, and communicative intentionality are reported (Woodyatt & Ozanne, 1993).

Individuals with Rett's Syndrome become a part of the estimated 1 million children and adults in the United States who are unable to communicate orally (Diggs, 1981). Most successful communication programs for these girls take advantage of the limited communicative behaviors they display (e.g., Donnellan, Mirenda, Mesaros, & Fassbender, 1984). Vocalizations, facial expressions, gestures, walking toward a desired item or activity, and eye gaze are common communicative behaviors displayed by persons with Rett's Syndrome. Parents and educators must attune themselves to their child's communicative behavior and respond contingently to these signals. As with any child, the critical element in the development of a meaningful communication system depends on the contingent interaction of the person and her environment (Lewis, Alessandri, & Sullivan, 1990). When others learn to detect the communicative behaviors and to respond to them in a systematic fashion, a formal and effective system of communication can be developed. Parents have taken photographs of their daughters' facial and gestural communicative behaviors and developed a "dictionary" for those who interact frequently with their children (International Rett Syndrome Association, 1990).

Until recently, persons with multiple disabilities, such as those displayed in Rett's Syndrome, would have been deemed unlikely candidates to benefit from formal communication intervention. In the past, a powerful relationship between cognition and language development was asserted in the literature. Intentional communication was thought to require performance at Piaget's (1929) sensorimotor development Stage V (Bates, Benigni, Bretherton, Camaioni, & Volterra, 1979; Bates, Camaioni, & Volterra, 1975; Kahn, 1977, 1981, 1984). Formal testing suggests that girls with Rett's Syndrome are at a presymbolic language level (Woodyatt & Ozanne, 1992, 1993), although, again, one cannot determine whether these results relate primarily to cognitive deficits or to an expressive language, a motor disorder, or both. Numerous anecdotal reports suggest, however, that these girls may well understand more than they can express (Weisz, 1987). Moreover, the assumption that Stage V functioning is required for intentional communication has been called into question (Reichle & Keogh, 1986; Rice, 1983).

Persons with Rett's Syndrome can be taught to employ augmentative communication systems that involve eye pointing, communication boards (pictures), facial expressions, gestures, and the activation of switches or computers. Van Acker and Grant (1995) employed, with 3 girls, a dynamic computer graphic presentation contingent on touch-screen activation to signal a desired food item selection. Two of the 3 girls demonstrated a reduction in stereotypic hand use and significantly increased their requests for items when they received computer-based requesting instruction. Interestingly, cognitive assessment of all 3 girls indicated a functioning level below the Piagetian Sensorimotor Stage V, yet benefit from instruction was obvious.

Speech and language services appear to be warranted for persons with Rett's Syndrome. Programming should emphasize functional receptive and expressive language skills, as well as cognitive, social, pragmatic, and affective communication skills. Early intervention could target eye contact and attending to the environment. Cause-and-effect relationships that allow the child to gain an understanding of her ability to impact her environment are essential for communication training. An awareness of cause-and-effect relationships may be enhanced through the use of simple switches to activate toys or computer monitors. Musical instruments also have been shown to promote the child's desire to interact with her environment (Wesecky, 1986; Zappella, 1986). Given the importance of communication skills, further research is needed to identify the range of communication functioning in Rett's Syndrome, and to implement effective methods for teaching improved communication skills to persons with the disorder.

ORTHOPEDIC ASPECTS AND INTERVENTION

Persons with Rett's Syndrome exhibit multiple orthopedic and motor movement disorders. The exact nature of these disorders can vary significantly across the different phases of the syndrome. Physical and occupational therapists, therefore, must play an important role in the care of girls with Rett's Syndrome (Braddock, Braddock, & Graham, 1993; Hanks, 1986, 1990). Intensive therapy, while failing to alter the actual course of the disease, has been successful in addressing symptoms by maintaining or improving functional movement or mobility; preventing deformities; and keeping the girls in contingent contact with their environments. Therapeutic intervention is especially important, and should be more frequent during the periods of regression associated with the disorder, when transition skills are at risk (Hanks, 1990). Although persons with Rett's Syndrome display numerous similarities, their specific therapeutic problems and responses to treatment vary dramatically (Hanks, 1986, 1990; Lieb-Lundell, 1988; Sponseller, 1989). A therapeutic intervention program must be highly individualized.

Apraxia and ataxia are frequently the earliest manifestations of motor problems in Rett's Syndrome. Hypotonia interferes with postural stability. Fitzgerald, Jankovic, Glaze, Schultz, and Percy (1990) suggest that the typical "jerky truncal tremors" may reflect a derangement of postural reflexes rather than cerebellar pathology. The girls develop compensatory increased tone to achieve stability, but abnormal movement patterns result. A marked fixing or locking of their joints, to counter disruption in balance, is typical, but it inhibits the ability to shift positions. Thus, the legs are often kept in wide abduction while sitting and standing (see Figure 4.2), and weight shift is absent (Hanks, 1986).

The girls will often express agitation and fear in response to any movements that are not self-initiated. Similar voluntary movements, however, are not related to these stress reactions. Lieb-Lundell (1988) reports that "no amount of practice or exposure alters this response of fear to extrinsically initiated movement" (p. 533).

Figure 4.2 Example of legs in wide abduction to counter disruption in balance.

A number of therapeutic interventions have been successful in the treatment of apraxia/ataxia. Tone reduction techniques similar to those used with patients afflicted with cerebral palsy or impaired through a stroke are appropriate. Interventions might include: (a) use of the therapy ball; (b) balance-stimulating floor activities, (c) segmental rolling, and (d) rotation and weight-shift activities (Hanks, 1986, 1990). Vestibular movement activities (e.g., carousels, swings) have also been reported as helpful if the child can tolerate this intervention (Havlak & Covington, 1989).

Efforts to facilitate normal movement while maintaining reduced tone are usually not successful, however (Hanks, 1990). Because the girls often resist being moved, close physical contact and a slow, firm approach aimed to reduce the child's anxiety during physical assistance are suggested. Girls with Rett's Syndrome often have very long response latency. Therapists must provide verbal directions and encouragement and allow the time needed for a response.

Stereotyped hand movements represent one of the most distinguishing characteristics of Rett's Syndrome. Hand wringing, hand washing, hand tapping, and hand-to-mouth movements are common stereotypes resulting in the loss of purposeful hand function. These movements appear to evolve with age; they proceed from simple, rapid movements to a slower, more complex form, and, ultimately, to slow, less complicated repetitive movements (Clare, 1986). Most researchers consider the stereotypic hand movements to represent primary circular reactions resulting from an underlying extrapyramidal disorder. Thus, they represent nonvoluntary movements. Persons with Rett's Syndrome appear to require a great deal of concentration and effort to "break out" of the stereotypic movements, even for brief attempts at purposeful hand use.

The behavior is more remarkable under stressful situations, and it diminishes or disappears momentarily when changing posture or eating. In some girls, stereotypic movements are exacerbated during periods of respiratory dysrhythmia (hyperventilation and apnea) (Kerr et al., 1990). Increased stereotypic hand movements in Rett's Syndrome have been reported to coincide with improved EEG tracings. Niedermeyer and Naidu (1990) have suggested that this passive finger movement may serve to block focal and multifocal spike activity. This phenomenon has been reported previously in Rolandic epilepsy (Sekul & Percy, 1992). Despite their neurological origin, the stereotypic behaviors of persons with Rett's Syndrome appear to be influenced, at least minimally, by environmental stimuli. Recently, an analog study of the stereotypic behavior of 2 young women with Rett's Syndrome demonstrated that their moment-to-moment expression appeared to be influenced by environmental contingencies (Wehmeyer, Bourland, & Ingram, 1993). Each of the participants increased or decreased the level of stereotypic responding as a result of various consequences within the social setting. For example, one of the girls would demonstrate a significant increase in stereotypy when placed into a task demand situation. The authors speculated that her stereotypy was being negatively reinforced through escape, avoidance of task engagement, or both. Van Acker (1987) reported a 40% reduction in the stereotypic hand movements displayed by one girl when she became involved in computer-assisted instruction. These findings were extended in a later study in which the stereotypic behavior of 2 additional girls displayed a significant decrease during computer-assisted requesting.

The suspected neurophysiological etiology of stereotypy in Rett's Syndrome has led researchers to caution practitioners who attempt to modify these behaviors. Because these behaviors appear to represent basically involuntary movements, attempts to change them, especially through the use of aversive consequences, appear ill-advised (Hanks, 1990). Moreover, previous attempts to use operant conditioning procedures to alter symptomatic behaviors of persons with Rett's Syndrome have not proven particularly promising. For example, differential reinforcement, response interruption, and contingent hand restraint have been used to decrease self-injurious behavior (Iwata, Pace, Willis, Gamache, & Hyman, 1986). The hand biting of these girls, though moderately reduced through intervention, appeared to "be related to organic predisposition rather than being shaped inadvertently by the environment" (p. 164). Facial screening has been attempted, without success, to decrease breathing irregularities (Lugaresi, Cirignotta, & Montagna, 1985). Recently, however, operant approaches employing prompting, backward chaining, shaping, and positive reinforcement have shown success (Bat-Haee, 1994; Piazza, Anderson, & Fisher, 1993; Van Acker & Grant, 1995). For example, Piazza and associates (1993), through the use of graduated prompting and positive reinforcement, were able to reestablish functional self-feeding in 3 girls with Rett's Syndrome. These researchers suggest that feeding may represent a good first step in developing improved hand use. The girls generally enjoy eating, and the food serves as a natural positive reinforcer. Parents and practitioners must be aware that the period needed for skill acquisition may be longer than that displayed in other children with severe or profound disabilities. Moreover, because the girls display variable progress from day to day, data collection is suggested, to plot change over the course of the training and to counteract discouragement.

Thus, operant procedures, especially nonaversive approaches, may prove effective in the treatment of some of the behavioral characteristics of Rett's Syndrome; however, maintenance of treatment effects has not been documented. Treatment with various medications such as L-dopa, haloperidol, 5-HTP, and various anticonvulsants, has proved unrewarding thus far (Percy et al., 1985).

Splinting has been found to be successful in interrupting hand-to-mouth movements (Hanks, 1986) and hand wringing (Aron, 1990; Naganuma, 1988). The girls can then direct their attention to tasks and persons in their environment, and the risk of skin breakdown related to these high-rate behaviors is reduced. In fact, some persons with Rett's Syndrome have demonstrated improved functional hand use while splints were in use (Naganuma, 1988). Tuten and Miedaner (1989), however, were unable to replicate the effectiveness of hand splints. The two subjects involved in their study displayed no decrease in stereotyped hand wringing, nor any subsequent increase in functional hand use as a result of hand-splint application. In a recent study, Sharpe (1992) employed an alternating-treatments design to compare the effectiveness of bilateral hand splints and an elbow orthosis for 2 girls with Rett's Syndrome. Both girls demonstrated a decrease in stereotypic hand movements and a corresponding increase in toy play with the use of the elbow orthosis. The bilateral hand splints had no obvious treatment effect. To date, no studies have demonstrated any maintenance effects of hand splints over time, once the splints have been removed. In addition, many persons with Rett's Syndrome are unable to tolerate the application of hand or arm splints for even short periods of time.

Instructional strategies that reinforce behaviors incompatible with stereotypic movements are recommended. Many of the girls accept having the stereotypic behavior interrupted. In fact, they often seem to relax when their stereotypic behavior is stopped for short periods of time. This can be accomplished by having the girls placed in the prone position or by simply holding one hand while assisting functional hand use (see Figure 4.3). Hanks (1986) reports "toys that combine bright colors

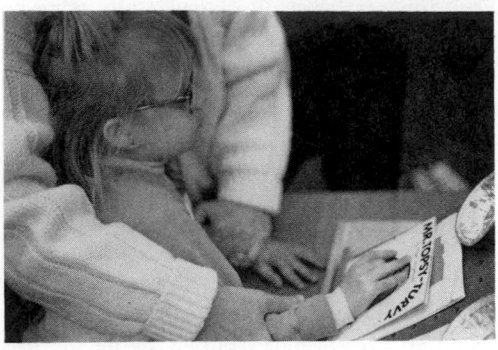

Figure 4.3 Interruption of stereotypic behavior to promote functional hand use.

and sound and require input from the child are helpful in keeping the child involved with the environment and making attempts to use her hands" (p. 250). Music therapy has also proved useful in the promotion of functional hand use. The music appears to increase the level of awareness, and the instruments motivate efforts to reach out and interact (Wesecky, 1986). Battery-operated toys and computers that have been modified to respond to an easily activated switch provide an almost limitless array of possibilities not only for decreasing stereotyped behavior (Van Acker, 1987; Van Acker & Grant, 1995) but also for increasing functional hand use, communication, and cognitive development (Hanks, 1986; Sponseller, 1989; Zappella, 1986).

Spasticity has been reported as a typical development during Stage II of the disorder. The spasticity may "vary from a mild increase in tone in the gastroc-soleus complex, resulting in toe walking, to severe involvement throughout the body affecting even respiration and swallowing" (Hanks, 1986, p. 248). The resulting muscle imbalance may lead to severe contractures, especially distally (e.g., a downward pointing of the foot). This spasticity may also be responsible, at least in part, for the high incidence of scoliosis in girls with Rett's Syndrome (Hanks, 1986; Sponseller, 1989).

Hydrotherapy that emphasizes movement in the water, range of motion, and basic water skills has been helpful in the improvement of range of motion and the reduction of discomfort (Hanks, 1986; Lieb-Lundell, 1988; Schleichkorn, 1987). Tone reduction activities

such as rotation, weight shift, and vibration have been reported to result in a temporary reduction of spasticity (Hanks, 1986, 1990).

Ambulation remains one of the critical skills to develop and maintain in persons with Rett's Syndrome. Many of the girls fail to develop this skill prior to Stage II; others lose this ability as part of the rapid motor degeneration. As spasticity and apraxia increase, the girls often lose many of the functional gross motor skills they had previously achieved, and may manifest spatial disorientation. Their perception of an upright posture results in a forward, backward, or lateral leaning. Ambulation may be lost, especially for girls with a backward lean orientation, because they are unable to initiate their forward weight shift. They fear falling when attempting weight shift in a forward direction. The typical gait pattern displayed in this syndrome results from a combination of spasticity, ataxia, apraxia, compensatory spinal rigidity, and spatial disorientation. Asymmetries may develop as one leg becomes stiffer or weaker. Weight shift is accomplished through lateral rocking, and trunk rotation is lost.

Independent standing and ambulation represent realistic therapy goals, especially in the early years. Many girls, although unable to walk independently, can do so with assistance. Such aided ambulation should be encouraged. Weight-bearing exercises, walking, and gait training have been successful (Hanks, 1986, 1989, 1990). If appropriate, activities designed to elicit righting and equilibrium responses might include use of the large therapy ball (prone position, and then standing, leaning forward), weight shifting (seating the child on a bench and then tipping the bench slightly backward), and, ultimately, an active shift forward to come from sitting to standing (Hanks, 1990).

Frequently, foot deformities (e.g., ankle pronation, plantar flexion inversion, and toe curling) must be corrected through the use of polypropylene ankle-foot orthosis, hinged to allow dorsiflexion. Attempts to correct pronation foot deformities with below-ankle orthosis have not proven effective; they destabilize the child's gait. Gentle manual stretching, night splints, and weight shifting in controlled standing with the heels down have all proven useful if started prior to signs of actual contractures (Hanks, 1990).

Girls who have the ability to ambulate must engage in activities that will maintain this skill and promote stimulation of the joints and muscles (Kjoerholt & Salthammer, 1989). Walking and stair climbing should be a regular part of the daily routine to maximize these skills. Kjoerholt and Salthammer (1989) caution that therapists must be patient as the girls walk "very slowly and will often stop without any noticeable reason, probably due to apraxia" (p. 84). Many of the commonly utilized assisting devices for ambulation (e.g., a push-type walker) are of limited usefulness because of the loss of purposeful hand function.

Scoliosis (a side-to-side curvature of the spine) in Rett's Syndrome is well documented (Hagberg et al., 1983; Hanks, 1986, 1989; Harrison & Webb, 1990; Loder, Lee, & Richards, 1989; Sponseller, 1989) and kyphosis ("hunchback") is common (Rett, 1977; Sponseller, 1989). Together, these deformities represent the primary musculoskeletal concern in Rett's Syndrome. Unfortunately, there are no rigid guidelines to predict deformity or to recommend treatment. Standard criteria (e.g., sex of patient, curve pattern, onset of menarche, Risser sign) typically useful in the determination of an appropriate intervention strategy do not appear to be effective with this syndrome (Hennessy & Haas, 1988). Scoliosis results in a muscle imbalance in the area around the curve. The muscles on one side of the spinal column will be spastic and hypertonic. One the other side, atrophic or hypotonic musculature may be noticed. The person often will tend to lean toward the hypotonic side. Initially, tone reduction activities, such as gentle lengthening of the concave side and activation of the convex side through elicitation of equilibrium reactions, are recommended (Hanks, 1990). Placing the child on her side, lying with the apex of the curve down, may prove helpful. Exercises designed to maximize use of the muscles the girl avoids using are in order (e.g., feed and lead the child by the hand on her hypotonic side). Good positioning is vital, and strollers, wheelchairs, and high chairs should be fitted properly to produce a symmetrical sitting posture and an erect spine (Hanks, 1986; Kjoerholt & Salthammer, 1989).

SUMMARY

Only a small percentage of the estimated 10,000 girls in the United States afflicted with Rett's Syndrome have been identified thus far (Moser, 1986). Lack of awareness of this disorder on the part of physicians and clinicians is undoubtedly a major contributing factor. Even when physicians are aware of Rett's Syndrome, however, an accurate diagnosis is not always forthcoming. There is often a hesitation to accept, as a specific entity, a disorder for which there is no laboratory marker. In the absence of a specific chromosomal or biochemical marker, as was true of Down syndrome for the first 90 years after that disorder was recognized (Hutt & Gibby, 1976), the diagnosis of Rett's Syndrome depends on careful analysis of signs and symptoms. Despite the lack of a known biological marker, researchers have made considerable progress in understanding this disorder. Rett's Syndrome does not appear to be a degenerative disease, as first suspected; rather, it is a disorder characterized by arrested neurodevelopment of unknown cause. Further research into the cause, pathogenesis, effective treatment, and, ultimately, the prevention of this disorder, is ongoing. Future research could lead to the discovery of a genetic or a biochemical marker. When this happens, there will be increased hope for the development of an effective prenatal screening procedure, treatment (e.g., medication), and, perhaps, a cure (e.g., gene therapy). As one of the slogans of the International Rett Syndrome Association states, "If we care today, we can cure tomorrow."

Cross-References

Issues of diagnosis are discussed in Chapters 1 and 7, and childhood disintegrative disorder in Chapter 3.

REFERENCES

Adkins, W.N. (1986). Rett syndrome at an institution for the developmentally disabled. *American Journal of Medical Genetics, 24*(Suppl. 1), 85–97.

Akesson, H.O., Hagberg, B., & Wahlstrom, J. (1996). Rett syndrome: Classical and atypical: Genealogical support for a common origin. *Journal of Medical Genetics, 33,* 764–766.

Allen, D.A. (1988). Autistic spectrum disorders: Clinical presentation in preschool children. *Journal of Child Neurology, 3*(Suppl.), S48–S56.

American Psychiatric Association. (1994). *Diagnostic and statistical manual of mental disorders* (4th ed.). Washington, DC: Author.

Anvret, M., & Wahlstrom, J. (1992). Genetics of the Rett Syndrome. *Brain and Development, 14*(Suppl.), S101–S103.

Armstrong, D.D. (1992). The neuropathology of the Rett Syndrome. *Brain and Development, 14*(Suppl.), S89–S100.

Aron, M. (1990). The use and effectiveness of elbow splints in the Rett Syndrome. *Brain and Development, 12,* 162–163.

Bangs, T., & Dodson, S. (1979). *Birth to Three Developmental Scale.* Hingham, MA: Teaching Resources Corp.

Barbi, G., Steinbach, P., & Vogel, W. (1984). Nonrandom distribution of methotrexate-induced aberrations of human chromosomes: Detection of further folic acid fragile sites. *Human Genetics, 68,* 290–294.

Bates, E., Benigni, L., Bretherton, I., Camaioni, L., & Volterra, V. (1979). *The emergence of symbols: Cognitive communication in infancy.* New York: Academic Press.

Bates, E., Camaioni, L., & Volterra, V. (1975). The acquisition of performatives prior to speech. *Merrill-Palmer Quarterly, 26,* 407–423.

Bat-Haee, M.A. (1994). Behavioral training of a young woman with Rett Syndrome. *Perceptual and Motor Skills, 78,* 314.

Bauman, M.L., Kemper, T.L., & Arin, D.M. (1995). Microscopic observations of the brain in Rett syndrome. *Neuropediatrics, 26,* 105–108.

Braddock, S.R., Braddock, B.A., & Graham, J.M. (1993, October). Rett Syndrome: An update and review for the primary pediatrician. *Clinical Pediatrics, 43,* 613–625.

Brucke, T., Sofic, E., Killian, W., Rett, A., & Riederer, P. (1988). Reduced concentrations and increased metabolism of biogenic amines in a single case of Rett Syndrome: A postmortem brain study. *Journal of Neural Transmission, 68,* 315–324.

Budden, S.S. (1986). Rett Syndrome: Studies of 13 affected girls. *American Journal of Medical Genetics, 24*(Suppl. 1), 99–109.

Budden, S.S. (1987). The role of the physician in the care of the child with Rett Syndrome. *Brain and Development, 9*(5), 532–534.

Budden, S.S., Meek, M., & Henighan, C. (1990). Communication and oral-motor function in Rett Syndrome. *Developmental Medicine and Child Neurology, 32,* 51–55.

Budden, S.S., Myer, E., & Butler, I. (1990). Cerebrospinal fluid studies in the Rett Syndrome: Biogenic amines and β-endorphins. *Brain and Development, 12,* 81–84.

Buhler, E.M., Malik, N.J., & Alkan, M. (1990). Another model for the inheritance of Rett Syndrome. *American Journal of Medical Genetics, 36,* 126–131.

Burd, L., Fisher, W., & Kerbeshian, J. (1989). Pervasive Disintegrative Disorder: Are Rett Syndrome and Heller dementia infantilis subtypes? *Developmental Medical Child Neurology, 31*(5), 609–616.

Carlin, M.E., Arena, J.F.P., & Ing, P.S. (1989). Rett Syndrome seen in association with a complex chromosomal translocation: Possible mapping to the short arm of the chromosome X. *American Journal of Human Genetics, 45,* A73.

Casanova, M.F., Naidu, S., Goldberg, T.E., Khoromi, S., Kumr, A., Kleinman, J.E., & Weinberger, D.R. (1991). Quantitative magnetic resonance imaging in Rett Syndrome. *Journal of Neuropsychiatry, 3,* 66–72.

Cattell, P. (1940). *Infant Intelligence Scale.* New York: Psychological Corp.

Charnov, E.K., Stach, B.A., & Didonato, R.M. (1989, November). *Pre and post onset developmental levels in Rett Syndrome.* Paper presented at the American Speech-Language-Hearing Association Convention.

Chugani, H.T., Phelps, M.E., & Mazziotta, J.C. (1987). Positron emission tomography study of human brain functional development. *Annals of Neurology, 22,* 487–497.

Clare, A.J. (1986). *Rett syndrome: Behind their eyes is more than they can show us.* Unpublished dissertation, Thames Polytechnic Incorporating Avery Hill College, Kent, United Kingdom.

Clark, A., Gardner-Medwin, D., Richardson, J., McGann, A., Bonham, J.R., Carpenter, K.H., Bhattacharya, S., Haggerty, D., Fleetwood, J.A., & Aynsley-Green, A. (1990). Abnormalities of carbohydrate metabolism and of OCT gene function in the Rett Syndrome. *Brain and Development, 12,* 119–124.

Coker, S.B., & Melnyk, A.R. (1991). Rett Syndrome and mitochondrial enzyme deficiencies. *Journal of Child Neurology, 6,* 164–166.

Coleman, M. (1990). Is classical Rett Syndrome ever present in males? *Brain and Development, 12,* 31–32.

Coleman, M., Brubaker, J., Hunter, K., & Smith, G. (1988). Rett Syndrome: A survey of North American patients. *Journal of Mental Deficiency Research, 32,* 117–124.

Coleman, M., & Gillberg, C. (1985). *The biology of autistic syndromes* (pp. 45–50). New York: Praeger.

Collerton, D. (1986). Cholinergic function and intellectual decline in Alzheimer's disease. *Neuroscience, 19,* 1–28.

Comings, D.E. (1986). The genetics of Rett Syndrome: The consequences of a disorder where every case is a new mutation. *American Journal of Medical Genetics, 24*(Suppl. 1), 383–388.

Cornford, M.E., Philippart, M., Jacobs, B., Scheibel, A.B., & Vinters, H.V. (1994). Neuropathology of Rett Syndrome: Case report with neuronal and mitochondrial abnormalities in the brain. *Journal of Child Neurology, 9*(4), 424–431.

Curtis, A.R.J., Headland, S., Lindsay, S., Thomas, N.S.T., Boye, E., Kamakari, S., Roustan, P., Anvret, M., Wahlstrom, J., McCarthy, G., Clarke, A.J., & Bhattacharya, S. (1993). X chromosome linkage studies in familial Rett Syndrome. *Human Genetics, 90,* 551–555.

DeGennaro, J.L., McCaffery, C.A., Kirchgessner, C.U., Yang-Feng, T.L., & Francke, U. (1987). Molecular analysis of synapsin I, a candidate gene for Rett Syndrome. *Brain and Development, 9,* 469–474.

Diggs, C.C. (1981). School services. *Language, Speech, and Hearing Services in Schools, 4,* 269–271.

Donnellan, A.M., Mirenda, P.L., Mesaros, R.A., & Fassbender, L.L. (1984). Analyzing the communicative functions of aberrant behavior. *Journal of the Association for Persons with Severe Handicaps, 9*(3), 201–212.

Eeg-Olofsson, O., Al-Zuhair, A.G.H., Teebi, A.S., & Al-Essa, M.M.N. (1989). Rett Syndrome: Genetic clues based on mitochondrial changes in muscle. *American Journal of Medical Genetics, 32,* 142–144.

Eeg-Olofsson, O., Al-Zuhair, A.G.H., Teebi, A.S., Daoud, A.S., Zaki, M., Besisso, M.S., & Al-Essa, M.M.N. (1990). The Rett Syndrome: A mitochondrial disease? *Journal of Child Neurology, 5,* 210–214.

Egger, J., Hofacker, N., Schiel, W., & Holthausen, H. (1992). Magnesium for hyperventilation in Rett's Syndrome. *Lancet, 340,* 621–622.

Ellison, K.A., Fill, C.P., Terwilliger, J., DeGennaro, L.J., Martin-Gallardo, A., Anvret, M., Percy, A.K., Ott, J., & Zoghbi, H. (1992). Examination of X chromosome markers in Rett Syndrome: Exclusion mapping with novel variation in multilocus linkage analysis. *American Journal of Human Genetics, 50,* 278–287.

Fitzgerald, P.M., Jankovic, J., Glaze, D.G., Schultz, R., & Percy, A.K. (1990). Extrapyramidal involvement in Rett's Syndrome. *Neurology, 40,* 293–295.

Fontanesi, J., & Haas, R.H. (1988). Cognitive profile of Rett Syndrome. *Journal of Child Neurology, 3*(Suppl.), S20–S24.

Garofalo, E., Drury, I., & Goldstein, G. (1988). EEG abnormalities aid diagnosis of Rett Syndrome. *Pediatric Neurology, 4,* 350–353.

Genazzani, A., Zappella, M., Nalin, A., Hayek, Y., & Facchinetti, F. (1989). Reduced cerebrospinal fluid β-endorphin levels in Rett Syndrome. *Child Nervous System, 5,* 111–113.

Gillberg, C. (1986). Autism and Rett Syndrome: Some notes on differential diagnosis. *American Journal of Medical Genetics, 24*(Suppl. 1), 127–131.

Gillberg, C. (1987). Autistic symptoms in Rett Syndrome: The first two years according to mother reports. *Brain and Development, 9*(5), 499–501.

Gillberg, C. (1989). The borderland of autism and Rett Syndrome: Five case histories to highlight diagnostic difficulties. *Journal of Autism and Developmental Disorders, 19*(4), 545–559.

Gillberg, C., Terenius, L., Hagberg, B., Witt-Ingerstrom, I., & Eriksson, I. (1990). CSF β-endorphins in childhood neuropsychiatric disorders. *Brain and Development, 12,* 88–92.

Gillberg, C., Wahlstrom, J., & Hagberg, B. (1984). Infantile autism and Rett's Syndrome: Common chromosomal denominator. *Lancet, 2,* 1094–1095.

Gillberg, C., Wahlstrom, J., & Hagberg, B. (1985). A "new" chromosome marker common to the Rett Syndrome and infantile autism? The frequency of fragile sites at X P22 in 81 children with infantile autism, childhood psychosis and the Rett Syndrome. *Brain and Development, 7*(3), 365–367.

Glaze, D.G., Frost, J.D., Zoghbi, H.Y., & Percy, A.K. (1987). Rett Syndrome: Correlation of the electroencephalographic characteristics with clinical staging. *Archives of Neurology, 44*(10), 1053–1056.

Goutieres, F., & Aicardi, J. (1985). Rett Syndrome: Clinical presentation and laboratory investigations in 12 further French patients. *Brain and Development, 7*(3), 305–306.

Goutieres, F., & Aicardi, J. (1986). Atypical forms of Rett Syndrome. *American Journal of Medical Genetics, 24,* 183–194.

Greer, W.L., Lwong, P.C., Peacocke, M., Ip, P., Rubin, L.A., & Siminovitch, K.A. (1989). X-chromosome inactivation in the Wiskott-Aldrich syndrome: A marker for detection of the carrier state and identification of cell lineages expressing the gene defect. *Genomics, 4,* 60–67.

Haas, R., & Rice, M.L.A. (1985). Is Rett's Syndrome a disorder of carbohydrate metabolism? Hyperpyruvic acidemia and treatment by ketogenic diet. *Annals of Neurology, 18,* 418.

Haas, R.H., Rice, M.A., Trauner, D.A., & Merritt, A. (1986). Therapeutic effects of a ketogenic diet in Rett Syndrome. *American Journal of Medical Genetics, 24*(Suppl. 1), 225–246.

Hagberg, B. (1980, June). *Infantile autistic dementia and loss of hand use: A report of 16 Swedish girl patients.* Paper presented at the research session of the European Federation of Child Neurology Societies, Manchester, England.

Hagberg, B. (1985). Rett Syndrome: Swedish approach to analysis of prevalence and cause. *Brain and Development, 7*(3), 277–280.

Hagberg, B. (1989). Rett Syndrome: Clinical peculiarities, diagnostic approach, and possible cause. *Pediatric Neurology, 5,* 75–83.

Hagberg, B. (1995). Clinical delineation of Rett syndrome variants. *Neuropediatrics, 26,* 62.

Hagberg, B., Aicardi, J., Dias, K., & Ramos, O. (1983). A progressive syndrome of autism, dementia, ataxia, and loss of purposeful hand use in girls: Rett Syndrome: Report of 35 cases. *Annals of Neurology, 14*(4), 471–479.

Hagberg, B., Goutieres, F., Hanefeld, F., Rett, A., & Wilson, J. (1985). Rett Syndrome: Criteria for inclusion and exclusion. *Brain and Development, 7*(3), 372–373.

Hagberg, B., & Witt-Engerstrom, I. (1986). Rett Syndrome: A suggested staging system for describing impairment profile with increasing age towards adolescence. *American Journal of Medical Genetics, 24*(Suppl. 1), 47–59.

Hagberg, B., & Witt-Engerstrom, I. (1987). Rett Syndrome: Epidemiology and nosology—Progress in knowledge 1986—A conference communication. *Brain and Development, 9*(5), 451–457.

Hanaoka, S., Ishikawa, N., & Kamoshita, S. (1985). Three cases of Rett Syndrome. In S. Kamoshita (Ed.), *Abstracts for the workshop on Aicardi Syndrome and Rett Syndrome* (20) (Abstract 9). Tokyo: Dainippon Tosho.

Hanefeld, F. (1985). The clinical pattern of the Rett Syndrome. *Brain and Development, 7*(3), 320–325.

Hanefeld, F., Hanefeld, U., Wilichowski, E., & Schmidtke, J. (1986). Rett Syndrome—Search for genetic markers. *American Journal of Medical Genetics, 24*(Suppl. 1), 377–382.

Hanks, S.B. (1986). The role of therapy in Rett Syndrome. *American Journal of Medical Genetics, 24*(Suppl. 1), 247–252.

Hanks, S.B. (1989, May). *Motor disabilities and physical therapy strategies in Rett Syndrome.* Paper presented at the Fifth Annual Conference of the International Rett Syndrome Association, Washington, DC.

Hanks, S.B. (1990). Motor disabilities in the Rett Syndrome and physical therapy strategies. *Brain and Development, 12,* 157–161.

Harding, B.N., Tudmay, A.J., & Wilson, J. (1985). Neuropathological studies in a child showing some features of the Rett Syndrome. *Brain and Development, 7*(3), 342–344.

Harris, J.C., Wong, D.F., Wagner, H.N., Rett, A., Naidu, S., Dannals, R.F., Links, J.M., Batshaw, M.L., & Moser, H.W. (1986). Positron emission tomographic study of D2 dopamine receptor binding and CSF biogenic amine metabolites in Rett Syndrome. *American Journal of Medical Genetics, 24*(Suppl. 1), 201–210.

Harrison, D.J., & Webb, P.J. (1990). Scoliosis in the Rett Syndrome: Natural history and treatment. *Brain and Development, 12,* 154–156.

Havlak, C., & Covington, C. (1989). Motor function: Physical and occupational therapy strategies. *Education and Therapeutic Intervention in Rett Syndrome* (pp. 71–79). Ft. Washington, MD: International Rett Syndrome Association.

Hennessy, M.J., & Haas, R.H. (1988). The orthopedic management of Rett Syndrome. *Journal of Child Neurology, 3*(Suppl.), S43–S47.

Hillig, U. (1985). On the genetics of the Rett Syndrome. *Brain and Development, 7*(3), 368–371.

Holm, V.A. (1985). Rett Syndrome: A case report from an audiovisual program. *Brain and Development, 7*(3), 297–299.

Hunter, K. (1987). Rett Syndrome: Parents' views about specific symptoms. *Brain and Development, 9*(5), 535–538.

Hutt, M.L., & Gibby, P.G. (1976). *The mentally retarded child: Development, education, and treatment.* New York: Allyn & Bacon.

International Rett Syndrome Association. (1990). *Parent idea book: Managing Rett Syndrome.* Ft. Washington, MD: Author.

Ishikawa, A., Goto, T., Narasaki, M., Yokochi, K., Kitahara, H., & Fukuyama, Y. (1978). A new syndrome (?) of progressive psychomotor deterioration with peculiar stereotyped movement and autistic tendency: A report of three cases. *Brain and Development, 3,* 258.

Iwata, B.A., Pace, G.M., Willis, K.D., Gamache, T.B., & Hyman, S.L. (1986). Operant studies of self-injurious hand biting in the Rett

Syndrome. *American Journal of Medical Genetics, 24,* 157–166.

Iyama, C.M. (1993). Rett Syndrome. *Advances in Pediatrics, 40,* 217–245.

Jellinger, K., Armstrong, D., Zoghbi, H.Y., & Percy, A.K. (1988). Neuropathology of Rett Syndrome. *Acta Neuropathologica, 76,* 142–158.

Jellinger, K., & Seiteberger, F. (1986). Neuropathology of Rett Syndrome. *American Journal of Medical Genetics, 24*(Suppl. 1), 259–288.

Johnson, W.F. (1980). Metabolic interference and the +/− heterozygote. A hypothetical form of simple inheritance which is neither dominant nor recessive. *American Journal of Human Genetics, 32,* 374–386.

Journel, H., Melki, J., Turleau, C., Munnich, A., & deGrouchy, J. (1990). Rett phenotype with X/autosome translocation: Possible mapping to the short arm of chromosome X. *American Journal of Medical Genetics, 35,* 142–147.

Kahn, J.V. (1977). Comparison of manual and oral language training. *Mental Retardation, 12,* 3–5.

Kahn, J.V. (1981). A comparison of sign and verbal language training with nonverbal retarded children. *Journal of Speech and Hearing Sciences, 47,* 113–119.

Kahn, J.V. (1984). Cognitive training and initial use of referential speech. *Topics in Language Disorders, 5,* 14–28.

Kerr, A.M., Montague, J., & Stephenson, J.B.P. (1987). The hands, and the mind, pre- and post-regression, in Rett Syndrome. *Brain and Development, 9*(5), 487–490.

Kerr, A.M., Southall, D., Amos, P., Cooper, R., Samuels, M., Mitchell, J., & Stephenson, J. (1990). Correlation of electroencephalogram, respiration, and movement in the Rett Syndrome. *Brain and Development, 12,* 61–68.

Kerr, A.M., & Stephenson, J.B.P. (1985). Rett's Syndrome in the west of Scotland. *British Medical Journal, 291,* 579–582.

Kerr, A.M., & Stephenson, J.B.P. (1986). A study of the natural history of Rett Syndrome in 23 girls. *American Journal of Medical Genetics, 24,* 77–83.

Killian, W. (1986). On the genetics of Rett Syndrome: Analysis of family and pedigree data. *American Journal of Medical Genetics, 24*(Suppl. 1), 369–376.

Kjoerholt, K., & Salthammer, E. (1989). *Kjoerholt Salthammer Fysioterapi. Educational and therapeutic intervention in Rett Syndrome.* Ft. Washington, MD: International Rett Syndrome Association.

Kozinetz, C.A., Skender, M.L., MacNaughton, N., Almes, M.J., Schultz, R.J., Percy, A.K., & Glaze, D.G. (1993). Epidemiology of Rett Syndrome: A population-based registry. *Pediatrics, 91,* 445–450.

Krageloh-Mann, I., Schroth, G., Niemann, G., & Michaelis, R. (1989). The Rett Syndrome: Magnetic resonance imaging and clinical findings in four girls. *Brain and Development, 11,* 175–178.

Lappalainen, R., Lindholm, D., & Riikonen, R. (1996). Low levels of nerve growth factor in cerebrospinal fluid of children with Rett syndrome. *Journal of Child Neurology, 11,* 296–300.

Leiber, B. (1985). Rett Syndrome: A nosological entity. *Brain and Development, 7*(3), 275–276.

Lekman, A., Hagberg, B., & Svennerholm, B.A. (1991). Membrane cerebral lipids in Rett Syndrome. *Pediatric Neurologist, 7,* 186–190.

Lekman, A., Witt-Engerstrom, I., Gottfries, J., Hagberg, B.A., Percy, A.K., & Svennerholm, L. (1989). Rett Syndrome: Biogenic amines and metabolites in postmortem brain. *Pediatric Neurology, 5*(6), 357–362.

Lewis, M., Alessandri, S.M., & Sullivan, M.W. (1990). *Expectancy, loss of control, and anger expression in young infants.* Report of the Institute for the Study of Child Development, Robert Wood Johnson Medical School Department of Pediatrics, New Brunswick, NJ.

Lieb-Lundell, C. (1988). The therapist's role in the management of girls with Rett Syndrome. *Journal of Child Neurology, 3*(Suppl.), S31–S34.

Lloyd, K.G., Hornykiewicz, O., Davidson, L., Shannak, K., Farley, I., Goldstein, M., Shibuya, M., Kelly, W.N., & Fox, I.H. (1981). Biochemical evidence of dysfunction of brain neurotransmitters in the Lesch-Nyhan Syndrome. *New England Journal of Medicine, 305,* 1106–1111.

Loder, R.T., Lee, C.L., & Richards, B.S. (1989). Orthopedic aspects of Rett Syndrome: A multicenter review. *Journal of Pediatric Orthopedics, 9*(5), 557–562.

Lugaresi, E., Cirignotta, F., & Montagna, P. (1985). Abnormal breathing in the Rett Syndrome. *Brain and Development, 7,* 328–333.

Lyon, M.F. (1972). X chromosome inactivation and developmental patterns in mammals. *Biological Review, 47,* 1–35.

MacLeod, P. (1994, October). *Genetics and Rett Syndrome.* Paper presented at the annual meeting of the Canadian Rett Syndrome Association, Kitchner, Ontario, Canada.

Matsuishi, T., Urabe, F., Percy, A.K., Komori, H., Yamashita, Y., Schultz, R.S., Ohtani, Y., Kuriya, N., & Kato, H. (1994). Abnormal carbohydrate metabolism in cerebrospinal fluid in Rett syndrome. *Journal of Child Neurology, 9,* 26–30.

Millichap, J.G. (1987). Rett's Syndrome: A variant of Heller's dementia? *Lancet, 1,* 440.

Missliwetz, J., & Depastas, G. (1985). Forensic problems in Rett Syndrome. *Brain and Development, 7*(3), 326–328.

Moodley, M. (1992). Rett Syndrome in South Africa. *Annals of Tropical Paediatrics, 12,* 409–415.

Moser, H.W. (1986). Preamble to the workshop on Rett Syndrome. *American Journal of Medical Genetics, 24*(Suppl. 1), 1–20.

Motil, K.J., Schultz, R., Brown, B., Glaze, D.G., & Percy, A.K. (1994). Altered energy balance may account for growth failure in Rett Syndrome. *Journal of Child Neurology, 9*(3), 315–319.

Murakami, J.W., Courchesne, E., Haas, R.H., Press, G.A., & Yeung-Courchesne, R. (1992). Cerebellar and cerebral abnormalities in Rett Syndrome: A quantitative MR analysis. *American Journal of Roentgenology, 159,* 177–183.

Myer, E.C., Tripathi, H.L., Brase, D.A., & Dewey, W.L. (1992). Elevated CSF beta-endorphin immunoreactivity in Rett's Syndrome: Report of 158 cases and comparison with leukemic children. *Neurology, 42,* 357–360.

Naganuma, G. (1988). Motor function: Physical therapy strategies. *Educational and Therapeutic Intervention in Rett Syndrome* (pp. 80–92). Ft. Washington, MD: International Rett Syndrome Association.

Naidu, S. (1994, October). *Rett Syndrome: Syndrome overview.* Paper presented at the annual meeting of the Canadian Rett Syndrome Association, Kitchner, Ontario, Canada.

Naidu, S., Hyman, S., Piazza, K., Savedra, J., Perman, J., Wenk, G., Kitt, C., Troncoso, J., Price, D., Cassanova, M., Miller, D., Thomas, G., Niedermeyer, E., & Moser, H. (1990). The Rett Syndrome: Progress report on studies at the Kennedy Institute. *Brain and Development, 12,* 5–7.

Naidu, S., Murphy, M., Moser, H.W., & Rett, A. (1986). Rett Syndrome: Natural history in 70 cases. *American Journal of Medical Genetics, 24*(Suppl. 1), 61–72.

Niedermeyer, E., & Naidu, S. (1990). Further EEG observations in children with Rett Syndrome. *Brain and Development, 12,* 53–54.

Niedermeyer, E., Rett, A., Renner, H., Murphy, M., & Naidu, S. (1986). Rett Syndrome and the electroencephalogram. *American Journal of Medical Genetics, 24*(Suppl. 1), 195–200.

Nielsen, J.B., Friberg, L., Lou, H., Lassen, N.A., & Sam, I.L. (1990). Immature pattern of brain activity in Rett Syndrome. *Archives of Neurology, 47,* 982–986.

Nielsen, J.B., Lou, H.C., & Andresen, J. (1990). Biochemical and clinical effects of tyrosine and tryptophan in the Rett Syndrome. *Brain and Development, 12,* 143–148.

Nihei, K., & Naitoh, H. (1990). Cranial computed tomographic and magnetic resonance imaging studies on the Rett Syndrome. *Brain and Development, 12,* 101–105.

Nomura, Y., & Segawa, M. (1990). Clinical features of the early stage of the Rett Syndrome. *Brain and Development, 12,* 16–19.

Nomura, Y., Segawa, M., & Hasegawa, M. (1984). Rett Syndrome—Clinical studies and pathophysiological consideration. *Brain and Development, 6,* 475–486.

Nomura, Y., Segawa, M., & Higurashi, M. (1985). Rett Syndrome—An early catecholamine and indolamine deficient disorder? *Brain and Development, 7*(3), 334–341.

Nyhan, W.L., Bakay, B., & Conner, J.D., (1970). Hemizygous expression of glucose 6-phosphate dehydrogenase in erythrocytes of heterozygotes for Lesh-Nyhan Syndrome. *Proceedings of the National Academy of the Sciences (USA), 65,* 214–218.

Olsson, B. (1987). Autistic traits in the Rett Syndrome. *Brain and Development, 9*(5), 491–498.

Olsson, B., & Rett, A. (1985). Behavioral observations concerning differential diagnosis between the Rett Syndrome and autism. *Brain and Development, 7*(3), 281–289.

Olsson, B., & Rett, A. (1987). Autism and Rett Syndrome: Behavioral investigations and differential diagnosis. *Developmental Medicine and Child Neurology, 29,* 429–441.

Olsson, B., & Rett, A. (1990). A review of the Rett Syndrome with a theory of autism. *Brain and Development, 12,* 11–15.

Opitz, J.M. (1986). Rett Syndrome: Some comments on terminology and diagnosis. *American Journal of Medical Genetics, 24,* 27–37.

Opitz, J.M., & Lewin, S. (1987). Rett Syndrome—A review and discussion of syndrome delineation. *Brain and Development, 9*(5), 445–450.

Owen, V.E. (1990). *The use of a total communication intervention to examine the communication skills in girls with Rett Syndrome.* Unpublished doctoral dissertation, University of Illinois at Chicago.

Percy, A.K. (1992, May). *Medical updates and overviews.* Paper presented at the meeting of the International Rett Syndrome Association, San Diego, CA.

Percy, A.K., Glaze, D.G., Schultz, R.J., Zoghbi, H.Y., Williamson, D., Frost, J.D., Jankovic, J.J., Deljunco, D., Skender, M., Waring, S., & Myer, E.C. (1994). Rett syndrome:

Controlled study of an oral opiate antagonist, Naltrexone. *Annals of Neurology, 35,* 464–470.

Percy, A.K., Hass, R., Kolodny, E., Moser, H., & Naidu, S. (1988). Recommendations regarding handling of the necropsy in Rett Syndrome. *Journal of Child Neurology, 3*(Suppl.), 91–93.

Percy, A.K., Schultz, R., Glaze, D.G., Skender, M., del Junco, D., Waring, S.C., Zoghbi, H.Y., Jankovic, J.J., Williamson, W.D., & Stach, B.S. (1991). Trial of the opiate antagonist, naltrexone, in children with Rett Syndrome. *Annals of Neurology, 30,* 486.

Percy, A.K., Zoghbi, H.Y., Lewis, K.R., & Jankovic, J. (1988). Rett Syndrome: Qualitative and quantitative differentiation from autism. *Journal of Child Neurology, 3*(Suppl.), S65–S67.

Percy, A.K., Zoghbi, H.Y., & Riccardi, V.M. (1985). Rett Syndrome: Initial experience with an emerging clinical entity. *Brain and Development, 7*(3), 300–304.

Perry, A. (1991). Rett Syndrome: A comprehensive review of the literature. *American Journal on Mental Retardation, 96,* 275–289.

Perry, A.K., Sarlo-McGarvey, N., & Haddad, C. (1991). Brief report: Cognitive and adaptive functioning in 28 girls with Rett Syndrome. *Journal of Autism and Developmental Disorders, 21*(4), 551–556.

Philippart, M. (1986). Clinical recognition of Rett Syndrome. *American Journal of Medical Genetics, 24*(Suppl. 1), 111–118.

Philippart, M. (1990). The Rett Syndrome in males. *Brain and Development, 12,* 33–36.

Philippart, M. (1993). Rett Syndrome associated with tuberous sclerosis in a male and in a female: Evidence for arrested motor and mental development. *American Journal of Medical Genetics, 48,* 229–230.

Piaget, J. (1929). *The child's conception of the world.* New York: Harcourt Brace Jovanovich.

Piazza, C.C., Anderson, C., & Fisher, W. (1993). Teaching self-feeding skills to patients with Rett Syndrome. *Developmental Medicine and Child Neurology, 35,* 991–996.

Piazza, C.C., Fisher, W., Kiesewetter, K., Bowman, L., & Moser, H. (1990). Aberrant sleep patterns in children with Rett Syndrome. *Brain and Development, 12,* 488–493.

Plioplys, A.V., & Kasnicka, I. (1993). L-carnitine as a treatment for Rett syndrome. *Southern Medical Journal, 86*(12), 1411–1413.

Reichle, J., & Keogh, W. (1986). Communication instruction for learners with severe handicaps: Some unresolved issues. In R. Horner, L. Meyer, & B. Fredricks (Eds.), *Education of learners with severe handicaps: Exemplary services* (pp. 189–220). Baltimore: Paul H. Brookes.

Reiss, A.L., Faruque, F., Naidu, S., Abrams, M., Beaty, T., Bryan, R.N., & Moser, H. (1993). Neuroanatomy of Rett Syndrome: A volumetric imaging study. *Annals of Neurology, 34*(2), 227–234.

Rett, A. (1966). Ueber ein eigenartiges hirnatrophisches syndrom bei hyperammonamie im kindesalter. *Wien Med Wochenschr, 116,* 723–738.

Rett, A. (1969). Ein zerebral-atrophisches syndrom bei hyperammonamie im kindesalter. *Forschr Med, 87,* 507–509.

Rett, A. (1977). A cerebral atrophy associated with hyperammonaemia. In P.J. Vinken & G.W. Bruyn (Eds.), *Handbook of clinical neurology, 29,* 305–329. Amsterdam, North Holland.

Rett, A. (1986). History and general overview. *American Journal of Medical Genetics, 24*(Suppl. 1), 21–26.

Rett Syndrome Diagnostic Criteria Work Group. (1988). Diagnostic criteria for Rett Syndrome. *Annals of Neurology, 23,* 125–128.

Riccardi, V.M. (1986). The Rett Syndrome: Genetics and the future. *American Journal of Medical Genetics, 24*(Suppl. 1), 389–402.

Rice, M. (1983). Contemporary accounts of the cognitive/language relationship: Implications for speech-language clinicians. *Journal of Speech and Hearing Disorders, 48,* 347–359.

Riederer, P., Brucke, T., Sofic, E., Kienzl, E., Schnecker, K., Eng, D., Schay, V., Kryzik, P., Killian, W., & Rett, A. (1985). Neurochemical aspects of the Rett Syndrome. *Brain and Development, 7*(3), 351–360.

Riederer, P., Wieser, M., Wichart, I., Schmidt, B., Killian, W., & Rett, A. (1986). Preliminary brain autopsy findings in progredient Rett Syndrome. *American Journal of Medical Genetics, 24*(Suppl. 1), 305–315.

Robb, S.A., Harden, A., & Boyd, S.G. (1989). Rett Syndrome: An EEG study in 52 girls. *Neuropediatrics, 20*(4), 192–195.

Rolando, S. (1985). Rett Syndrome: Report of eight cases. *Brain and Development, 7*(3), 290–296.

Schleichkorn, J. (1987). Rett Syndrome: A neurological disease largely undiagnosed here. *Physical Therapy Bulletin, 2,* 16–18.

Sekul, E.A., Moak, J.P., Schultz, R.J., & Percy, A.K. (1991). Electrocardiographic changes in Rett Syndrome. *Annals of Neurology, 30,* 496.

Sekul, E.A., & Percy, A.K. (1992). Rett Syndrome: Clinical features, genetic considerations, and the search for a biological marker. *Current Neurology, 12,* 173–198.

Sharpe, P.A. (1992). Comparative effects of bilateral hand splints and an elbow orthosis on stereotypic hand movements and toy play in two children with Rett Syndrome. *The American Journal of Occupational Therapy, 46,* 134–140.

Sofic, E., Riederer, P., Killian, W., & Rett, A. (1987). Reduced concentrations of ascorbic acid and glutathione in a single case of Rett Syndrome: A postmortem brain study. *Brain and Development, 9*(5), 529–531.

Sponseller, P.D. (1989). *Orthopaedic problems in Rett Syndrome.* Ft. Washington, MD: International Rett Syndrome Association.

Stephenson, J.B., & Kerr, A.M. (1987). Rett Syndrome: Disintegration not dementia. *Lancet, 1,* 741.

Thomas, S., Hjelm, M., Oberholzer, V., Brett, E.M., & Wilson, J. (1987). Rett's Syndrome and ornitine carbamoyltransferase deficiency. *Lancet, 2,* 1330–1331.

Topcu, M., Topaloglu, H., Renda, Y., Berker, M., & Turanli, G. (1991). The Rett Syndrome in males. *Brain and Development, 13*(1), 62.

Trevathan, E., & Naidu, S. (1988). The clinical recognition and differential diagnosis of Rett Syndrome. *Journal of Child Neurology, 3*(Suppl.), S6–S16.

Tuten, H., & Miedaner, J. (1989). Effect of hand splints on stereotypic hand behavior of girls with Rett Syndrome: A replication study. *Physical Therapy, 69*(12), 1099–1103.

Uzgiris, I.C., & Hunt, J.M. (1975). *Assessment in infancy: Ordinal scales of psychological development.* Urbana: University of Illinois Press.

Van Acker, R. (1987). *Stereotypic responding associated with Rett Syndrome: A comparison of girls with this disorder and matched subject controls without the Rett Syndrome.* Unpublished doctoral dissertation, DeKalb: Northern Illinois University.

Van Acker, R., & Grant, S.B. (1995). An effective computer-based requesting system for persons with Rett Syndrome. *Journal of Childhood Communication Disorders, 16,* 31–38.

Verma, N.P., Chheda, R.L., & Nigro, M.A. (1986). Electroencephalographic findings in Rett Syndrome. *Electroencephalography and Clinical Neurophysiology, 64,* 394–401.

Wahlstrom, J. (1985). Genetic implications of Rett's Syndrome. *Brain and Development, 7,* 573–574.

Wahlstrom, J., & Anvret, M. (1986). Chromosome findings in the Rett Syndrome and a test of a two-step mutation theory. *American Journal of Medical Genetics, 24*(Suppl. 1), 361–368.

Wahlstrom, J., Witt-Engerstrom, I., Mellquist, L., Anvret, M., & Oden, A. (1990). The Rett Syndrome related to fragile X (P22) in caffeine-induced lympocyte culture. *Brain and Development, 12,* 128–130.

Webb, T., Watkiss, E., & Woods, C.G. (1993). Neither uniparental disomy nor skewed X-inactivation explains Rett Syndrome. *Clinical Genetics, 44,* 236–240.

Wehmeyer, M., Bourland, G., & Ingram, D. (1993). An analogue assessment of hand stereotypies in two cases of Rett Syndrome. *Journal of Intellectual Disability Research, 37,* 95–102.

Weisz, C.L. (1987). Range of emotion. *Brain and Development, 9*(5), 543–545.

Wenk, G.L., Naidu, S., Casanova, M.F., Kitt, C.A., & Moser, H. (1991). Altered neurochemical markers in Rett Syndrome. *Neurology, 41,* 1753–1756.

Wenk, G.L., O'Leary, M., Nemeroff, C.B., Bissette, G., Moser, H., & Naidu, S. (1993). Neurochemical alterations in Rett Syndrome. *Developmental Brain Research, 74,* 67–72.

Wesecky, A. (1986). Music therapy for children with Rett Syndrome. *American Journal of Medical Genetics, 24*(Suppl. 1), 253–257.

Whitehouse, P.J., Price, D.L., Clark, A.W., Coyle, J.T., & DeLong, M.R. (1981). Alzheimer disease: Evidence for selective loss of cholinergic neurons in the nucleus basalis. *Annals of Neurology, 10,* 122–126.

Witt-Engerstrom, I. (1987). Rett Syndrome: A retrospective pilot study on potential early predictive symptomatology. *Brain and Development, 9*(5), 481–486.

Witt-Engerstrom, I., & Hagberg, B. (1990). The Rett Syndrome: Gross motor disability and neural impairment in adults. *Brain and Development, 12,* 23–26.

Woodyatt, G.C., & Ozanne, A.E. (1992). Communication abilities and Rett Syndrome. *Journal of Autism and Developmental Disorders, 22,* 155–173.

Woodyatt, G.C., & Ozanne, A.E. (1993). A longitudinal study of cognitive skills and communication behaviors in children with Rett Syndrome. *Journal of Intellectual Disability Research, 37,* 419–435.

World Health Organization (WHO). (1992). *The ICD-10 classification of mental and behavioral disorders: Diagnostic criteria for research.* Geneva: Author.

Yang-Feng, T.L., DeGennaro, J.L., & Francke, U. (1986). Genes for synapsin I, a neuro phosphoprotein map to conserved regions of human and marine X chromosome. *Proceedings of the*

National Academy of the Sciences (USA), 83, 8679–8683.

Yano, S., Yamashita, Y., Matsuishi, T., Abe, T., Yamata, S., & Shinohara, M. (1991). Four adult Rett patients at an institution for the handicapped. *Pediatric Neurology, 7,* 289–292.

Yoshikawa, H., Fueki, N., Suzuki, H., Sakuragawa, N., & Masaaki, I. (1991). Cerebral blood flow and oxygen metabolism in Rett Syndrome. *Journal of Child Neurology, 6*(3), 237–242.

Zappella, M. (1986). Motivational conflicts in Rett Syndrome. *American Journal of Medical Genetics, 24*(Suppl. 1), 143–151.

Zappella, M. (1990). A double-blind trial of bromocriptine in the Rett Syndrome. *Brain and Development, 12,* 148–150.

Zappella, M., & Genazzani, A. (1986). Girls with Rett Syndrome tested with bromocriptine. *Wiener klinische Wochenschrift, 98,* 780.

Zappella, M., Genazzani, A., Facchinetti, F., & Hayek, G. (1990). Bromocriptine in the Rett Syndrome. *Brain and Development, 12,* 221–225.

Zoghbi, H.Y. (1988). Genetic aspects of Rett Syndrome. *Journal of Child Neurology, 3*(Suppl.), S76–S78.

Zoghbi, H.Y., Ledbetter, D.H., Schultz, R.J., Percy, A.K., & Glaze, D.G. (1990). A *de novo* X;3 translocation in Rett Syndrome. *American Journal of Medical Genetics, 35*(1), 148–151.

Zoghbi, H.Y., Milstien, S., Butler, I.J., Smith, E.O., Kaufman, S., Glaze, D.G., & Percy, A.K. (1989). Cerebrospinal fluid biogenic amines and biopterin in Rett Syndrome. *Annals of Neurology, 25,* 56–60.

Zoghbi, H.Y., Percy, A.K., Glaze, D.G., Butler, I.J., & Riccardi, V.M. (1985). Reduction of biogenic amine levels in the Rett Syndrome. *New England Journal of Medicine, 313,* 921–924.

Zoghbi, H.Y., Percy, A.K., Schultz, R.J., & Fill, C. (1990). Patterns of X chromosome inactivation in the Rett Syndrome. *Brain and Development, 12,* 131–135.

CHAPTER 5

Asperger's Syndrome

AMI KLIN AND FRED R. VOLKMAR

Asperger's Syndrome (AS) is a severe developmental disorder characterized primarily by marked and sustained difficulties in social interaction and emotional relatedness, and by unusual patterns of circumscribed interests and behavioral peculiarities. The relation of this condition to other early-onset disorders—particularly autism unaccompanied by mental retardation, or higher-functioning autism—has been the subject of considerable research and discussion. This chapter describes the historical background and current diagnostic issues of this disorder, reviews the published clinical and research experience with individuals whose lives are captured by the designation AS, and provides a current appraisal of nosological validity and future research directions.

BACKGROUND

Asperger's "Autistic Psychopathy"

Hans Asperger (1906–1980), an Austrian physician with training in pediatrics and psychiatry, had a special interest in the integration of psychiatry and remedial education. His writings reflect a deep concern with the special education teaching strategies used in the clinical work of Asperger and his colleagues. In his original paper, Asperger (1944) described 4 children, aged 6 to 11 years, who represented a group of patients with a disability marked by difficulties in social integration despite seemingly adequate cognitive and verbal skills. (Frith, 1991, has provided an English translation and an account of Asperger's professional background.)

Asperger originally termed the condition *Autistischen Psychopathen im Kindesalter,* or autistic personality disorders in childhood, echoing Bleuler's (1916–1951) use of the term autism to signify extreme egocentrism or a shutting-off of relations between the affected person and other people. Asperger distinguished this condition from schizophrenia by emphasizing that, in contrast to schizophrenic patients who showed a progressive loss of contact with the outside social world, his patients exhibited this rift between themselves and others from the outset. Where Asperger chose the label *autism,* he was unaware, because of World War II, of the work of Leo Kanner (1943) on early infantile autism.

Asperger emphasized the difficulties in social integration as the defining feature of the condition, but he also provided a detailed description of the various clusters of behavioral symptoms and clinical features that were associated with and, in some cases, led to the social isolation. These features, which continue to be commonly observed, are:

- *Impairment in nonverbal communication.* This cluster includes a paucity of facial and gestural expressions as well as a pervasive

---

Editors' note: As indicated in Chapter 1, *ICD-10* and *DSM-IV* terms are used interchangeably. Asperger's Syndrome, used in *ICD-10,* appears as Asperger's Disorder in *DSM-IV.*

inability to modulate and intonate the voice in a way that is appropriate to social context.

- *Idiosyncracies in verbal communication.* Spontaneous communication is characterized by highly circumstantial utterances (e.g., failing to distinguish abstractions from autobiographical narration), long-winded and incoherent verbal accounts that fail to convey a clear thought (e.g., tangential speech prompted by a series of associations), and one-sidedness (e.g., failing to demarcate changes of topic or to introduce new material).

- *Social adaptation and special interests.* Asperger emphasized an egocentric preoccupation with unusual and circumscribed interests that absorb most of the person's attention and energy, thus precluding the acquisition of practical skills necessary for self-help and social integration. Some of these interests (e.g., in letters and numbers) are quite precocious. Later in life, special interests often tend to evolve into specific subject-related bodies of factual knowledge, such as astronomy or geography.

- *Intellectualization of affect.* Emotional presentation was marked by poor empathy, a tendency to intellectualize feelings, and an accompanying absence of intuitive understanding of other people's affective communication.

- *Clumsiness and poor body awareness.* Motoric presentation is characterized by odd posture and gait, poor body awareness, and extreme clumsiness. Asperger emphasized his patients' inability to participate in group sports or other activities involving motor coordination and integration, and described in detail their extremely poor graphomotor skills.

- *Conduct problems.* The most common reason for referral of Asperger's patients involved behavioral problems, especially aggressiveness, noncompliance, and negativism, which were accounted for in terms of marked egocentrism and extreme pursuit of the highly circumscribed interests. Asperger was particularly concerned about his patients' poor adjustment at school, and how they were mercilessly bullied and teased by peers.

- *Onset.* Asperger thought that the condition could not be recognized in infancy or, usually, before the third year of life. Speech and language skills, as well as curiosity about the general (including social) environment, are not conspicuously deviant.

- *Familial and gender patterns.* Asperger highlighted the familial nature of the condition affecting his patients (who were almost exclusively boys), suggesting that similar traits in parents or relatives could be found in almost every case.

The year before Asperger's article on autistic psychopathy was published, Leo Kanner (1943) had published his classic description of 11 children whom he thought had "autistic disturbances of affective contact." Asperger and Kanner were unaware of each other's work, but their patients shared many commonalities, such as problems with social interaction, affect, and communication, and unusual and idiosyncratic patterns of interest. Asperger observed that his patients' speech and language acquisition was less commonly delayed, their motor deficits were more common, the onset appeared to be later, and all the initial cases occurred in boys. More importantly, there were significant differences in severity of symptomatology in the areas of social-emotional functioning, speech and language skills, motor mannerisms, and circumscribed interests, which, at least in part, may have been a function of the specific patients described by Kanner (primarily preschoolers who were less verbal and more mentally handicapped) and by Asperger (primarily school-age children who were highly verbal, and brighter). Consequently, Kanner's description became associated with the "classically" lower-functioning autistic child, and Asperger's description has lent itself more readily to an association with the nonretarded and highly verbal older children with autism.

Discussions of Asperger's work were not available in English until the 1970s. Prior to their translation, a handful of related publications had touched on the subject. For example, Robinson and Vitale (1954) described three cases of children, aged 8 to 11 years, who showed a pattern of circumscribed interests reminiscent of Asperger's description. The children were interested in topics such as chemistry, transportation systems, astronomy, electricity, and mortgages, about which they talked incessantly in one-sided conversations with adults and peers, without ever participating more meaningfully with their listeners or considering their needs and interests.

The concept of "autistic psychopathy" was introduced to a wider English-speaking readership by Van Krevelen (1963), who attempted to distinguish it from Kanner's autism. In Van Krevelen's view (1971), the conditions are sharply different. Kanner's autism is manifested from the first months of life: the child walks before he or she talks, speech is delayed or absent, language never attains the function of communication, there is a lack of interest in others, and prognosis is poor. In contrast, Asperger's condition is manifested from the third year of life or later: the child talks before he or she walks, language aims at communication but remains one-sided, the child seeks interaction but in an awkward fashion, and prognosis is rather good.

Asperger's work remained essentially unknown in the English-language literature until an influential review and series of case reports by Lorna Wing in 1981. She reported 34 cases, aged 5 to 35 years, of whom 19 had a clinical presentation similar to Asperger's account, and 15 had a consistent current presentation but did not have the characteristic onset patterns and early history. Concerned that the term *psychopathy* might be associated with sociopathic behavior (rather than the intended personality disorder), she proposed the eponymous label *Asperger's Syndrome* (AS). Wing summarized Asperger's description and proposed some modifications for the syndrome, based on her case series. These modifications concerned primarily the onset patterns of the syndrome. In contrast to Asperger, who thought the condition could not be recognized before age 3 years, Wing suggested that the following delays and deviances are present in *the first 2 years of life:*

1. A lack of normal interest and pleasure in other people is evident from babyhood.
2. Babbling may be limited in quantity and quality.
3. Sharing of interests and activities may be very reduced.

4. There may be a lack of intense drive to communicate verbally and nonverbally with others.
5. Speech acquisition may be delayed, and speech content may be very impoverished, reflecting primarily utterances copied inappropriately from other people or learned by rote from books.
6. Asperger's talking-before-walking assertion does not apply to a great number of cases.
7. Imaginative pretend play does not occur or is confined to one or two rigid themes enacted repetitively without variation.

Wing also suggested that AS can be found in individuals with mild mental retardation, and that, although males outnumbered females in her sample, around 20% of those afflicted were girls.

These modifications blurred the distinctions originally suggested by Van Krevelen (1971) and reiterated by Asperger (1979), clearly bringing the syndrome into the autistic spectrum of disorders defined by Wing in terms of a triad of impairments involving social, communicative, and imaginative activities (see Chapter 7).

Wing's (1981) publication sparked a great deal of interest. The number of case reports and research studies increased yearly, and the literature has exceeded 100 publications since 1981. Many of these contributions concern attempts to delineate the boundaries (or show the lack thereof) between autism and Asperger's Syndrome. Until recently, there was considerable variability in different researchers' use of the label; liberties were taken in modifying or emphasizing different elements of the syndrome, depending on individual's clinical experience and beliefs. With the subject of inquiry defined in different ways, comparison of findings became impossible. Some progress has been achieved with the advent of studies comparing the different definitions of Asperger's Syndrome (e.g., Ghaziuddin, Tsai, & Ghaziuddin, 1992a), and the establishment of the consensual and "official," though still tentative, definitions now incorporated in the *International Classification of Diseases* (*ICD-10;* World Health Organization [WHO], 1992) and the *Diagnostic and Statistical Manual of Mental Disorders* (*DSM-IV;* American Psychiatric Association [APA], 1994).

Related Diagnostic Concepts

Several diagnostic concepts—originating from adult psychiatry, neuropsychology, neurology, and other disciplines—share, to some degree, phenomenological similarity with AS.

Schizoid Personality

From psychiatry, the term *Schizoid Personality in Childhood* has been employed by Wolff and colleagues (Wolff & Barlow, 1979; Wolff & Chick, 1980), who described a group of individuals with an abnormal pattern of behavior characterized by social isolation, rigidity of thought and habits, and an unusual style of communication. In agreement with Van Krevelen's (1971) discussion of Asperger's work, they characterized the condition as a personality (rather than a developmental) disorder, extending Kretschmer's (1925) original concept of "schizothymia" from adulthood into childhood. Follow-up studies (e.g., Wolff, 1991, 1995; Wolff, Townsend, McGuire, & Weeks, 1991) suggested the persistence of symptoms into adulthood, when 75% of the children fulfilled criteria for schizoid personality disorder and showed increased risk for schizophrenia. Wolff (e.g., Wolff & Barlow, 1979) considered Asperger's Syndrome (AS) to be a manifestation of schizoid personality disorder. Tantam (1988b) and Nagy and Szatmari (1986) made attempts to directly compare the two diagnostic concepts. Consistent with Wolff and colleagues' equation of schizoid personality and AS, they found an increase of abnormal nonverbal behaviors in their sample of individuals with schizoid personality disorder. In contrast, Tantam reported an association between abnormal nonverbal expression, but not of a schizoid measure, and other autistic-like characteristics such as unusual interests and several indexes of clumsiness. There were significant correlations between the autistic-like features (but not the schizoid measure) and developmental abnormalities, which suggested important differences between the two diagnostic concepts. More importantly, the conceptualization of AS as an unchanging personality trait fails to fully appreciate the developmental aspects of the disorder, which may prove to be of great importance for differential diagnosis as well as for a better understanding of the pathogenesis of AS.

Nonverbal Learning Disability

In neuropsychology, the concept of *Nonverbal Learning Disabilities* (NLD), originally proposed by Johnson and Myklebust (Myklebust, 1975) and studied by Rourke (1989), conveys a profile of neuropsychological assets and deficits that have a deleterious impact on the person's capacity for socialization as well as on interactive and communicative styles. The neuropsychological characteristics of individuals with the NLD profile include deficits in tactile perception, psychomotor coordination, visual-spatial organization, nonverbal problem solving, and appreciation of incongruities and humor. Persons with NLD also exhibit well-developed rote verbal capacities and verbal memory skills; difficulty in adapting to novel and complex situations, and overreliance on rote behaviors in such situations; relative deficits in mechanical arithmetic as compared to proficiencies in single-word reading; poor pragmatics and prosody in speech; and significant deficits in social perception, social judgment, and social interaction skills. The marked deficits in the appreciation of subtle and even fairly obvious nonverbal aspects of communication often result in other people's social disdain and rejection. As a result, NLD individuals show a marked tendency toward social withdrawal and are at risk for development of serious mood disorders (Rourke, Young, & Leenaars, 1989).

The NLD profile can be seen as a neurocognitive model of AS but not of autism, suggesting some overlap between the concepts of NLD and AS (e.g., Klin, Volkmar, Sparrow, Cicchetti, & Roarke, 1995). A surprisingly large number of individuals with AS appear to show the NLD profile, but the converse does not appear to hold true: the NLD profile is associated with many different conditions (Klin, Sparrow, Volkmar, Cicchetti, & Roarke, 1995). Rourke's emphasis on the *developmental* changes in expression of NLD adds an important perspective to studies of AS.

Developmental Learning Disability of the Right Hemisphere

Many of the clinical features clustered together in NLD have also been described in the neurological literature as a form of *Developmental Learning Disability of the Right Hemisphere* or *Social-Emotional Learning Disabilities* (SELD; Denckla, 1983; Weintraub & Mesulam, 1983). Children presenting with this condition exhibit profound disturbances in interpretation and expression of affect and other basic interpersonal skills (Voeller, 1986). A familial link has also been suggested (Weintraub & Mesulam, 1983). The core deficit of these related diagnostic concepts lies in an inability to process information of a social-emotional nature, which is postulated to be a result of underlying right-hemisphere dysfunction. This hypothesis is based on the special role played by the right hemisphere in processing social-emotional information as well as on the other associated cognitive deficits and learning problems documented in children with these characteristics (Voeller, 1986). A possible overlap with AS has been suggested (Voeller, 1991).

The importance of these concepts (NLD and SELD) lies in the hypothesis that a right-hemisphere dysfunction may account for the phenotypic presentation of AS, which contrasts to the typical left-hemisphere hypothesis in autism (e.g., Dawson, Finley, Phillips, & Galpert, 1986). Thus, an empirical distinction unrelated to the definition of AS and autism—namely, the neuropsychological characterization of individuals with these conditions—may eventually be possible (Klin, Volkmar, et al., 1995).

Semantic-Pragmatic Processing Disorder

The literature on language disorders has included descriptions of children whose communication patterns were very similar to those described by Asperger (1944). For example, Blank, Gessner, and Esposito (1979) considered speech and language patterns that were particularly impoverished in terms of their communicative value. Rapin and Allen (1983) coined the term *Semantic-Pragmatic Disorder* to describe speech and language patterns that were characterized as competent in terms of form and impoverished in terms of content and function. Bishop (1989, 1995) has thoroughly researched this concept by carefully characterizing the language and communication peculiarities of a group of children, some of whom had a behavioral presentation consistent with AS.

It is currently unclear whether these concepts describe different entities or, more probably, provide different perspectives on a heterogeneous group of individuals who share at least some common phenomenological aspects. These overlapping concepts have been proposed to account for a condition that manifests itself in ways that involve members of various disciplines: neuropsychology, psychiatry, language-communication, and neurology. The disability affecting individuals with AS may quite legitimately be discussed at different levels of analysis—behavioral, neuropsychological, neurological, and linguistic. The various disciplines can make important contributions toward a transdisciplinary coordination, thereby minimizing confusion and furthering a more integrated and comprehensive understanding of individuals with AS. This is particularly important for patients and their families, who may be given different "diagnoses," depending on the discipline that is their point of entry into the mental health, medical, or educational system.

ISSUES IN DEFINITION OF ASPERGER'S SYNDROME

Toward a Consensual Definition of Asperger's Syndrome

Although Wing (1981) did not provide a specific set of categorical diagnostic criteria, many case reports and research studies derived such criteria from her publication and used these to characterize their respective patient or subject population. However, accounts often included different sets of criteria, reflecting each author's decision as to which behaviors were necessary, or only suggestive, or altogether irrelevant. Such variability in diagnostic assignment suggested that comparisons among studies would be difficult, and pointed to the need for a uniform nosology of AS (Rutter & Gould, 1985).

The search for a definition of AS that could provide the basis for validity studies, particularly in contrast to high-functioning autism (HFA), was fueled by several forces:

1. The need for a *consensual diagnosis* that would be universally adopted.
2. The need to extract a core set of criteria that would provide a *categorical definition* of the disorder, capturing areas of consensus amid highly variable accounts. These criteria were to encompass not only Asperger's (1944) description but also the empirical work of authors who published on this subject after Wing (1981).
3. The need to define AS in terms that would contrast it, at least in some areas, to autism. This task, which was necessary for a *mutually exclusive diagnostic assignment of AS and autism,* was complicated by the fact that Wing's (1981) account, from which most subsequent definitions were derived (Gillberg & Gillberg, 1989; Szatmari, Bremmer, & Nagy, 1989; Tantam, 1988a), implied that the two conditions could not be separated and that AS was a subtype of autism.

Many case reports and some research studies avoided the latter issue altogether. Their subjects were diagnosed as having AS, and authors did not consider diagnostic validity more carefully—for example: To what extent did subjects also fulfill criteria for autism? Designation of Asperger's Syndrome as a "variant" or "subtype" of autism (e.g., HFA, or adults with autism) would be acceptable, but it would not add to a categorical classification system. Accordingly, the central issue in recent years has been whether AS' and HFA are distinctive in ways that *are independent of the definition used to assign group membership.* The end result of this process was the inclusion of AS in *ICD-10* (WHO, 1992) and in the *DSM-IV* autism/PDD field trials (Volkmar et al., 1994).

The *ICD-10* (WHO, 1992) definition attempted to bridge the differences among the previous definitions and to contrast AS with autism. It focused primarily on the number of overall symptoms (greater in autism and lower in AS, reflecting degrees of severity), the exclusion of the language cluster included in the diagnosis of autism (indicating the absence of severe language impairment in AS while sidestepping an attempt to define the peculiarities typical of verbal communication in AS), and the inclusion of onset criteria that contrasted, to some extent, with those for autism (the absence, in AS, of clinically significant delays in speech and language and in cognitive development). In many respects, this definition was both stricter than some (particularly in regard to the onset criteria) and less specific than others (it subsumed the more unique symptoms of AS under the autism clusters of social impairment and restricted areas of interest).

More importantly, AS was defined in terms of the criteria for autism (either present or absent). The process itself has highlighted the differences among some influential definitions. Table 5.1 compares key diagnostic features among the most widely known definitions: Asperger's (1944) original account and later emphases and changes (Asperger, 1979; Van Krevelen, 1971), as well as those of Wing (1981), Gillberg and Gillberg (1989), Tantam (1988a), and Szatmari, Bremmer, and Nagy (1989). These definitions are compared with the formalized definition in *DSM-IV* (APA, 1994), which is conceptually equivalent to the one included in *ICD-10* (WHO, 1992; Volkmar et al., 1994). Bold type (**Yes**) in Table 5.1 indicates the features deemed *necessary* for the diagnosis of AS, according to the given diagnostic system.

Table 5.1 shows that a direct comparison among the various diagnostic systems is not a straightforward task. Ghaziuddin and colleagues (1992a) attempted to compare these various systems. Having simplified the criteria for comparison, they compared Asperger's (1944) definition with Wing's (1981)—which was made equivalent to Gillberg and Gillberg's (1989) and Tantam's (1988a)—and the definitions of Szatmari, Bremmer, and Nagy (1989) and *ICD-10* (WHO, 1992). Of 15 patients identified as having AS according to Wing's criteria, only 10 patients met Szatmari et al.'s criteria, and only 8 patients met the description by Asperger as well as the *ICD-10* criteria. The primary reason why 7 patients

TABLE 5.1   Comparison of Six Sets of Clinical Criteria Defining AS*

Clinical Feature	Asperger (1944, 1979)	Wing (1981)	Gillberg & Gillberg (1989)	Tantam (1988a)	Szatmari, Bremmer, & Nagy (1989)	DSM-IV (APA, 1994)
Social impairment	**Yes**	**Yes**	**Yes**	**Yes**	**Yes**	**Yes**
Poor nonverbal communication	**Yes**	**Yes**	**Yes**	**Yes**	**Yes**	Yes
Poor empathy	**Yes**	**Yes**	**Yes**	Yes (Implied)	**Yes**	Yes
Failure to develop friendship	**Yes**	**Yes**	**Yes**	**Yes**	**Yes**	Yes
Language/Communication						
Poor prosody and pragmatics	**Yes**	**Yes**	**Yes**	**Yes**	**Yes**	Not stated
Idiosyncratic language	**Yes**	**Yes**	Not stated	Not stated	**Yes**	Not stated
Impoverished imaginative play	Yes	**Yes**	Not stated	Not stated	Not stated	Not stated
All-Absorbing interest	**Yes**	**Yes**	**Yes**	**Yes**	Not stated	Often
Motor clumsiness	**Yes**	**Yes**	**Yes**	**Yes**	Not stated	Often
Onset (0–3 years)						
Speech delays/ deviance	**No**	May be present	May be present	Not stated	Not stated	**No**
Cognitive delays	**No**	May be present	Not stated	Not stated	Not stated	**No**
Motor delays	Yes	Sometimes	Not stated	Not stated	Not stated	May be present
Exclusion of autism	Yes (1979)	**No**	**No**	**No**	**Yes**	**Yes**
Mental retardation	**No**	May be present	Not stated	Not stated	Not stated	Not stated

*Symptoms that are defined, by the respective sources, as necessary for the presence of the condition, have **Yes** printed in bold type.

did not fulfill *ICD-10* (and Asperger's) criteria was their failure to meet the onset criteria—specifically, the lack of clinically significant delay in speech and language acquisition. Therefore, despite the lack of required specific social, language/communication, and absorbing interests criteria (which differs from Asperger's account), the *ICD-10* definition is, in practice, more restrictive than other systems because of its emphasis on specific onset patterns (which is consistent with Asperger's account). This state of affairs raises several issues for future research on nosology:

1. By simultaneously emphasizing the lack of speech and cognitive delays in the first years of life and failing to specify required social, communication, motor, and absorbing-interest features that are thought to be typical in AS, the *ICD-10* definition may be differentiating autism from AS solely on the basis of onset criteria—in fact, irrespective of the nature of the patient's social impairment later in life. Whether individuals diagnosed in this manner will have a later presentation consistent with Asperger's description remains to be documented.

Various authors (Gillberg & Gillberg, 1989; Wing, 1981) have reported on persons who would not meet the *ICD-10* onset criteria and yet presented with what they thought was AS. On the other hand, even high-functioning autistic subjects appear to have the onset of their condition before age 3 years (Volkmar & Cohen, 1989).

2. By failing to include specific social, communicative, or restricted interest patterns by subsuming them under general clusters that are identical for the diagnosis of autism, the *ICD-10* definition of AS disregards features that could serve as discriminative factors and that may be unique among AS patients. For example, Tantam (1988a) suggests that, in contrast to the prevailing view of autistic patients, individuals with AS may wish to be sociable and yet fail to establish relationships. This may also be true for older autistic adolescents and adults, but it would be unusual for a younger autistic child. This important point was raised by Van Krevelen (1971), who thought children with autism disregarded others, and children with AS approached others in an eccentric fashion. Both were socially impaired, but in a qualitatively different way.

3. Just as autistic social dysfunction can be defined only in the context of the child's overall developmental level (Rutter, 1978), there may be a host of developmental factors that should be considered in any attempt to contrast the social/affective/communicative presentation of HFA with that of AS. These factors include chronological age (e.g., more difficult in older adolescents and adults), IQ and language level (e.g., more difficult for lower IQ and lower language capacities), and the presence of any medical condition that might disrupt speech and language acquisition (e.g., cleft palate, ear infection, and fluctuating hearing loss).

The different diagnostic systems provide different sets of criteria and fail to address key issues; some also bring the definition of AS closer to that of autism (by trying to make a case for continuity or to directly contrast them), perhaps taking the diagnosis of AS

further away from what Asperger had in mind. A strict exegetic analysis of Asperger's writing does not necessarily clarify the issue, and it is probably good that it does not. Despite the remarkably enduring quality of Kanner's (1943) description of autism, many key issues have been modified as a result of subsequent research. The fact that Rutter's (1978) codification of Kanner's prose proved to be an effective and reliable diagnostic tool is partially creditable to Kanner's brilliance, but it is also a function of the severity of the condition he described. Given that the syndrome described by Asperger is more equivocal than Kanner's autism—overlapping with autism to some extent, but also shading into eccentric normalcy—it is appropriate to direct additional work to the creation of an effective and reliable definition.

In addition to the conflictual writings on AS, various other diagnostic concepts derived from neurology, neuropsychology, and adult psychiatry quite likely overlap with AS. Interdisciplinary synthesis is needed to avoid duplication of effort and confusion among researchers working in different disciplines. Although the current definitions of AS may become obsolete, the disability conveyed by the available definitions will not disappear. Research on the severe social disability of individuals whose intelligence and verbal abilities are high should provide unique opportunities for study of the course of abnormal sociability when the clinical situation is not confounded by mental retardation and severe language impairment.

The *ICD-10* Definition of Asperger's Syndrome

As defined in *ICD-10* (WHO, 1992), the criteria for AS follow the same format as (and, in some cases, overlap) the criteria for autism. The required symptomatology is clustered in terms of onset, social/emotional, and restricted-interests criteria. Two common but not necessary characteristics are added: (a) motor deficits and (b) isolated special skills. A final criterion is the necessary exclusion of other conditions—most importantly, autism or a "subthreshold" form of autism (atypical autism/PDD). As previously noted, the *ICD-10* definition of AS has autism as its point of reference; hence, some of the criteria actually involve the *absence* of abnormalities in some areas of functioning that are affected in autism. Table 5.2 reproduces the proposed *ICD-10* criteria for AS.

The *DSM-IV* (APA, 1994) definition of AS is conceptually equivalent to the definition in *ICD-10,* with some minor modifications. The impact of slightly different definitions of AS on research studies utilizing *ICD-10* or *DSM-IV* diagnostic systems remains unclear. As a practical matter, *ICD-10* diagnostic guidelines for research are more detailed.

TABLE 5.2   Proposed *ICD-10* (WHO, 1993) Research Diagnostic Guidelines for Asperger's Syndrome

A. There is no clinically significant general delay in spoken or receptive language or cognitive development. Diagnosis requires that single words should have developed by 2 years of age or earlier and that communicative phrases be used by 3 years of age or earlier. Self-help skills, adaptive behavior, and curiosity about the environment during the first 3 years should be at a level consistent with normal intellectual development. However, motor milestones may be somewhat delayed and motor clumsiness is usual (although not a necessary diagnostic feature). Isolated special skills, often related to abnormal preoccupations, are common, but are not required for the diagnosis.

B. There are qualitative abnormalities in reciprocal social interaction (criteria as for autism).

C. The individual exhibits an unusual intense, circumscribed interest or restricted, repetitive, and stereotyped patterns of behaviour, interests, and activities (criteria as for autism; however, it would be less usual for these to include either motor mannerisms or preoccupations with part-objects or nonfunctional elements of play materials).

D. The disorder is not attributable to other varieties of pervasive developmental disorder; simple schizophrenia schizotypal disorder; obsessive-compulsive disorder; anakastic personality disorder; reactive and disinhibited attachment disorders of childhood.

Reprinted with permission from the *ICD-10 Classification of Mental and Behavioural Disorders—Diagnostic Criteria for Research,* (1993). Geneva: World Health Organization, pp. 154–155.

CLINICAL FEATURES OF ASPERGER'S SYNDROME

Social Functioning

In contrast to the social presentation in autism, AS usually involves fewer symptoms and has a different presentation (Volkmar et al., 1994). Individuals with AS are often socially isolated but are not unaware of the presence of others, even though their approaches may be inappropriate and peculiar. For example, they may engage the interlocutor, usually an adult, in one-sided conversation characterized by long-winded, pedantic speech about a favorite and often unusual and narrow topic. Also, although individuals with AS are often self-described "loners," they express interest in friendships and in meeting people. These wishes are invariably thwarted by their awkward approaches and their insensitivity to other people's feelings, intentions, and nonliteral and implied communications (e.g., signs of boredom, haste to leave, and need for privacy). Chronically frustrated by their repeated failures to engage others and form friendships, some individuals with AS develop symptoms of a mood disorder that may require treatment, including medication.

Individuals with AS may react inappropriately to, or fail to interpret the valence of the context of the affective interaction. Often, they convey insensitivity, formality, or disregard for the other person's emotional expressions. They may be able to describe correctly, in a cognitive and often formalistic fashion, other people's emotions, expected intentions, and social conventions; yet, they are unable to act on this knowledge in an intuitive and spontaneous fashion, and they lose the tempo of the interaction. Their deficient intuition and lack of spontaneous adaptation are accompanied by marked reliance on formalistic rules of behavior and rigid social conventions. This presentation is largely responsible for the impression of social naïveté and behavioral rigidity that is so forcefully conveyed by these individuals.

At least some of these characteristics are also exhibited by individuals with HFA. More typically, however, autistic persons are withdrawn and may seem to be unaware of, and disinterested in, other persons. Individuals with AS, in contrast, are often keen (sometimes painfully so) to relate to others, but lack the skills to engage others successfully.

Communication Patterns

Although significant abnormalities of speech are not typical of AS, at least three aspects of these individuals' communication patterns are of clinical interest (Klin, 1994). First, speech may be marked by poor prosody, although inflection and intonation may not be as rigid and monotonic as in autism. Individuals with AS often exhibit a constricted range of intonation patterns that is used with little regard to the communicative functioning of the utterance (assertion of fact, humorous remark, and so on). Rate of speech may be unusual (e.g., too fast) or fluency may be lacking (e.g., jerky phrasing). Often, modulation of volume is poor (e.g., voice is too loud despite physical proximity to the conversational partner). The latter feature may be particularly noticeable in the context of a lack of adjustment to the given social setting (e.g., in a library, in a noisy crowd).

Second, speech may often be tangential and circumstantial, conveying a sense of loose associations and incoherence. Even though, in some cases, this symptom may indicate a possible thought disorder (Caplan, 1994; Dykens, Volkmar, & Glick, 1991), the lack of contingency in speech is a result of the one-sided, egocentric conversational style (e.g., unrelenting monologues about the names, codes, and attributes of innumerable TV stations in the country), failure to provide the background for comments and to clearly demarcate changes in topic, and failure to suppress the vocal output accompanying internal thoughts.

Third, the communication style of individuals with AS is often characterized by marked verbosity. The child or adult may talk incessantly, usually about a favorite subject, and often with complete disregard for whether the listener might be interested, engaged, or attempting to interject a comment or change the subject of the conversation. Despite such long-winded monologues, the individual may never "come to the point" or reach a conclusion. Attempts by the interlocutor to elaborate on issues

of content or logic, or to shift the interchange to related topics, are often unsuccessful.

These symptoms may result from significant deficits in pragmatic skills and/or lack of insight into, and awareness of, other people's expectations. Yet, the challenge is to understand these communication problems developmentally as strategies of social adaptation.

Isolated Special Skills and Circumscribed Interests

An array of "splinter skills" is evident in individuals with Pervasive Developmental Disorder (PDD)—from proficiency at assembling puzzles, drawing, and musical abilities, to amassing vast amounts of factual knowledge about unusual subjects such as meteorology. However, although skills that involve object manipulation, visual-spatial abilities, or musical skills, as well as "savant talents," are more commonly described in autism, the amassing of factual information about an all-absorbing, circumscribed topic appears to be more typical of AS. Consistent with Asperger's original description (1944), such abilities may be pursued so intensively that skills in other areas suffer. Potentially, a distinction between such skills and those seen more commonly in autism may be helpful diagnostically.

The actual topic of particular interest to the child with AS may change from time to time (e.g., every year or every 2 years), but it often dominates the content of social interchange as well as the child's activities. Frequently, the entire family may be immersed in the subject for long periods of time. This symptom may not always be easily recognizable in childhood because strong interests in certain topics, such as dinosaurs or fashionable fictional characters, are ubiquitous. However, in both younger and older AS children, the special interests typically become more unusual and more narrowly focused. This behavior is peculiar in the sense that extraordinary amounts of factual information may be learned about very circumscribed topics (e.g., snakes, names of TV stars, deep fryers, weather information, personal information on members of Congress) without a genuine understanding of the broader phenomena involved.

Motor Functioning

Individuals with AS may have a history of delayed acquisition of motor skills such as pedaling a bike, catching a ball, opening jars, and climbing outdoor play equipment. They are often visibly awkward and poorly coordinated, and they may exhibit odd gait patterns and posture, poor manipulative skills, and significant deficits in visual-motor skills (Gillberg, 1990; Tantam, 1988a).

Although this presentation contrasts with the pattern of motor development in autistic children, for whom the area of motor skills is, at least early on, often a relative strength (Volkmar et al., 1987), it is similar in some respects to the pattern observed in older autistic individuals. Nevertheless, the commonality in later life may result from different underlying factors—for example, psychomotor deficits in the case of AS, and poor body image and sense of self in the case of autism. This possibility highlights the importance of describing this symptom in developmental terms.

Associated Features

Conduct Problems

Many publications, primarily case reports, have associated AS with violent and criminal behavior (e.g., Baron-Cohen, 1988; Everall & LeCouteur, 1990; Mawson, Grounds, & Tantam, 1985; Tantam, 1988b). In a letter justifying the revival of the term Asperger's Syndrome, Wing (1986) mentioned that a number of forensic cases had come to her attention since the publication of the 1981 paper. An impression had been formed that violent and even criminal behavior may result from the unique AS profile, which combines high intelligence and verbal skills with poor empathy and social cognition.

Although clinical attention and impressions were intended to protect patients with AS rather than to vilify them, there was parental mobilization against this negative characterization. The limited available clinical data also questioned the underlying assumptions. Ghaziuddin, Tsai, and Ghaziuddin (1991) reviewed the literature on the incidence of violence among AS persons and concluded that there was no support for speculation that increased violent and criminal behavior was typical of patients with AS. In contrast, Scragg and Shah (1994) reported a prevalence of 1.5% of individuals with AS in a secure hospital, a prevalence that is greater than the number reported so far for the general population. Thus, this debate has been rekindled.

In our experience, individuals with AS—children and adults alike—are much more often victimized, not victimizers; more often still, they are in the periphery of social situations as children and are loners in adulthood. Their poor empathy frequently yields emotional insensitivity and leads to their isolation and alienation from others rather than to acts of violence and criminal behavior. In fact, many individuals with AS adhere to rigid rules of behavior that are excessively moralistic or literal (e.g., Dewey, 1991). Paradoxically, their inflexible adherence to "the rules" seems to cause them trouble. Wing (1981) opted for the eponymous label *Asperger's Syndrome* rather than Asperger's own *Autistic Psychopathy,* in order to characterize the syndrome as a developmental disorder and differentiate it from sociopathic behavior. Increased attention to violence and criminal behavior may blur this distinction once again.

Scragg and Shah's (1994) study awaits replication. If their findings are corroborated, they would carry many implications for the management of and educational intervention with individuals with AS. Studies in this area, however, must be performed with utmost care, particularly in regard to developmental and behavioral history and current diagnostic characterization.

Comorbid Psychiatric Conditions

A number of case reports have suggested that individuals with AS may be at increased risk for various other psychiatric conditions: psychosis in general and/or schizophrenia in particular (e.g., Clarke, Littlejohns, Corbett, & Joseph, 1989; Taiminen, 1994; Tantam, 1988a), Tourette's Syndrome (Gillberg & Rastam, 1992; Kerbeshian & Burd, 1986; Littlejohns, Clarke, & Corbett, 1990), affective disorders (Berthier, 1995; Fujikawa, Kobayashi, Koga, & Murata, 1987), and obsessivecompulsive disorder (Thomsen, 1994).

Early interest in AS stemmed, in part, from reports of the association of the condition with schizophrenia. It appeared that AS might be, in some sense, a "bridging" condition between autism and schizophrenia (see Wolff, 1995, for a discussion). Although reports of associations with psychosis and AS have typically focused on depression, relationships to other psychotic conditions (e.g., manic depressive psychosis) have also been reported (Gillberg, 1985).

Given the diagnostic ambiguities and other issues surrounding interpretation of single cases, case series would provide somewhat better evidence regarding the co-occurence of psychosis with AS. Tantam (1991) reported a rate of 3.5 for schizophrenia in his series of adults with AS; Nagy and Szatmari (1986), in their review of 20 children with schizotypal disorders, noted that 2 children had developed schizophrenia. Ghaziuddin, Leininger, and Tsai (1995) noted that although patients with AS had greater levels of disorganized thinking than an HFA comparison group, overall differences on measure of thought disorder were not significant. When the problem has been addressed from the point of view of schizoid personality features as premorbid antecedents of schizophrenia, there is some evidence that schizoid personality, although not clearly AS, may appear more frequently in children who develop early-onset schizophrenia (Werry, 1992).

Several factors suggest considerable caution in interpreting the available information on this issue. First, it is important to remember the initial, incorrect assumption of continuity between infantile autism and childhood schizophrenia. This assumption, made on the basis of both an appreciation of the severity of the conditions and a very broad view of the concept of schizophrenia, proved unfounded (Rutter, 1972). Even after this issue was clarified, reports of occasional associations of autism and schizophrenia appeared, although reviews of larger series of cases revealed that schizophrenia was no more common than would be expected, given its prevalence in the population (i.e., based on chance alone, some

cases where both conditions are observed can be expected; Volkmar & Cohen, 1991).

Second, as a result of the combination of excessive verbalization and poor social judgment, persons with AS often say what is on their mind. They have little capacity for self-monitoring or censorship. One adolescent boy with AS was initially evaluated for psychotic thinking after he responded to a polite offer from a female classmate ("Is there anything I can do to help you") with a very explicit sexual request. At times, the tendency of persons with AS to verbalize about their special interest(s) may seem highly inappropriate and lends a bizarre quality to their social interactions.

Ryan (1992) reported three cases of men with apparent AS who were originally thought to have various episodes of chronic, treatment-resistant mental illness. As Ryan points out, the emotional liability, social peculiarity, unusual interests and eccentricities, anxiety, and unusual behaviors associated with AS may lead to misdiagnosis—a most unfortunate outcome because a treatment plan that concentrates on a patient's strengths in order to address his or her areas of weakness may be particularly helpful in vocational and rehabilitative interventions. The difficulties of differential diagnosis of AS and schizophrenia have been echoed by various other investigators (e.g., Bejerot & Duvner, 1995; Taiminen, 1994).

Much of the literature on AS has focused on the comorbidity of the condition with psychosis or violence. Other reports have suggested an increased risk for mood disorders of various types (Ellis, Ellis, Fraser, & Deb, 1994; Fujikawa et al., 1987; Ghaziuddin, Tsai, & Ghaziuddin, 1992b; Grandin, 1990). This observation is consistent with that of Rourke and colleagues (1989), which suggests high rates of depression and suicidality in individuals with the NLD profile.

Onset Patterns

Typically, individuals with AS do not present with clinically significant delays in language acquisition, cognitive development, or self-help skills. In contrast, typical developmental accounts of autistic children show pervasive deficits and deviance in these areas prior to the age of 3 years. As noted previously, even in high-functioning children with autism, the onset is before age 3, although there is some potential for overlap on this point and various factors may bias case detection.

Two common features of early development of individuals with AS are noteworthy. First, there is often a fascination with letters and numbers and a certain precociousness in learning to talk—in fact, the young child may even be able to decode words, although often with little or no understanding ("hyperlexia"). Second, patterns of attachment to family members are typically established, although approaches to peers and other persons may be highly inappropriate or awkward (e.g., the child may attempt to initiate contact with other children by hugging them or screaming at them and is then puzzled by their responses). These features contrast with autism, in which attachment to family members is often limited, and early social presentation is typically marked by withdrawal or aloofness (see Chapter 1).

Outcome

Asperger's *initial* description (1944) predicted a positive outcome for many of his patients, especially those who were able to utilize their special talents for the purpose of obtaining employment and leading self-supporting lives. His observation of similar traits in family members (i.e., fathers) may have made him more optimistic about ultimate outcomes. Although his account was tempered somewhat by the time he had seen 200 patients with the syndrome (Asperger, 1979), he continued to believe that a more positive outcome was a central criterion that differentiated individuals with AS from those with Kanner's autism. Although some clinicians have concurred informally with this statement, no studies specifically addressing the outcome for individuals with AS are currently available. However, in terms of gainful employment, independence, and establishment of a family, it is thought that individuals with AS have, generally, a better outcome than those with HFA. The social impairment (particularly the eccentricities and social insensitivity) is thought to be lifelong (e.g., Tantam, 1988a).

Outcome studies will depend on a more solid nosologic basis for the syndrome. This is an extremely important area for future research. Differences in outcome may be one of the strongest justifications for a differentiation between AS and autism—provided, of course, that differences in outcome measures are not shown to be solely a function of developmental skills such as IQ and language levels.

Prevalence

Of all the various areas of clinical research, studies of prevalence are probably most affected by different definitions of a given disorder. This is not unique to AS (cf. Schwartz Gould, Wunsch-Hitzig, & Dohrenwend, 1981), but it is certainly quite complex in the context of AS (Ehlers & Gillberg, 1993), given the wide use of different diagnostic definitions. A few studies have attempted to explore epidemiological issues in the context of AS.

Based on an epidemiological study in one area of London (Wing & Gould, 1979), Wing (1981) reported mild mental retardation in 0.6 to 1.1 per 10,000 children under the age of 15. This was almost certainly an underestimate because the sample included only children with a mild degree of mental retardation, and they are a minority among individuals with AS. The male:female ratio reported was 9:1 in the epidemiological study, but was closer to 3:1 in Wing's (1981) series of cases. Gillberg and Gillberg (1989) reported rates of 10 to 26 per 10,000 children as the minimal figures among children with normal intelligence, and another 0.4 per 10,000 children showing the combination of AS and mental retardation. In a more recent study by the Swedish group cited above (Ehlers & Gillberg, 1993), a minimum prevalence of 3.6 per 1,000 children (7 to 16 years of age) was reported, and a male:female ratio of 4:1. When cases for whom the diagnosis of AS was suspected were included in the computation, the prevalence rose to 7.1 per 1,000 children and the male:female ratio dropped to 2.3:1.

These findings contrast with current prevalence data on autism (see Chapter 2). If these numbers are confirmed in future studies, the prevalence of AS will emerge as several times higher than the prevalence of autism (i.e., AS could be considered a much more common disorder than autism) and the male:female ratio in AS would be much lower than in autism—that is, there would be many more girls with AS than girls with autism (given the very low number of females who are autistic but not mentally retarded; Volkmar, Szatmari, & Sparrow, 1993), despite Asperger's belief that the condition was primarily present in boys. If AS is as common as these findings indicate, the implications for service provision, allocation of resources, and training of clinicians are very serious and far-reaching. There is an urgent need for careful replications of prevalence studies of AS.

The lack of generally accepted diagnostic guidelines for AS means that, at present, it is impossible to provide more than an estimate of its prevalence. In our clinical experience, the condition is very frequently misdiagnosed and, if a strict definition of AS is adopted, it is certainly less common than autism (see Chapter 1).

VALIDITY OF ASPERGER'S SYNDROME

The validity of Asperger's Syndrome (AS) as distinct from other conditions, notably the other pervasive developmental disorders, remains controversial (Rutter & Schopler, 1992; Wing, 1991). Disagreements about the validity of the category and the absence, until recently, of "official" definitions of AS have meant that the concept has often been used inconsistently. Clinicians have employed it to refer to autistic persons with higher levels of intelligence, adults with autism, or even all "atypical" children who do not fulfill criteria for autism (Volkmar & Cohen, 1991). A lack of uniformity in usage of the term also characterizes definitions adopted for the purpose of research. Different sets of diagnostic criteria have been used by different researchers, with resulting complications for interpretation of findings (Ghaziuddin et al., 1992a).

Of the various pervasive developmental disorders, the validity of AS as distinct from autism unaccompanied by mental retardation, or HFA, has generated the greatest debate (Rutter, 1989). The *ICD-10* (WHO, 1993) diagnostic system specifically notes this issue in the description of AS. There is little disagreement about the fact that AS is on a phenomenological continuum with autism, particularly in relation to problems in the areas of social and communicative functioning (Wing, 1991). For example, within the *DSM-III-R* (APA, 1987) diagnostic system, persons with AS either would meet criteria for autistic disorder or would be said to exhibit Pervasive Developmental Disorder Not Otherwise Specified (PDD-NOS; Tsai, 1992). What is less clear is whether the condition is qualitatively different from autism rather than just a milder form of it.

Several studies have investigated different aspects of the disorder in an attempt to identify the criteria that discriminate the two conditions. Results to date are mixed. Two factors appear to have contributed to this state of affairs: first, a lack of operationalization of diagnostic assignment in a way that is systematic and is broadly accepted by researchers; and second, the great degree of circularity that has characterized validation studies, where findings often reflect the criteria adopted in the assignment of a diagnosis of AS or HFA in the first place (Klin, 1994). These studies have involved primarily the neuropsychological, social cognitive, and neurobiological aspects of the disorders.

Neuropsychological Studies

At least three studies of neurocognitive profiles have been conducted to differentiate individuals with AS from those with HFA (Klin, Volkmar, et al., 1995; Ozonoff, Pennington, & Rogers, 1991; Ozonoff, Rogers, & Pennington, 1991; Szatmari, Tuff, Finlayson, & Bartolucci, 1990). Results are mixed and are difficult to reconcile. The first study was conducted by Szatmari and colleagues, who administered a comprehensive test battery, including intelligence, achievement, and neuropsychological measures, to 26 AS and 17 HFA subjects who differed in chronological age but not in Mean IQ. Very few differences were found. The AS group had a significantly higher score on one of the WISC-R subtests (Similarities). The HFA group showed higher performance on a test of motor speed and coordination (Grooved Pegboard, nondominant hand) and differed from the AS group on one measure of executive function (WCST, perseverative errors). On several other measures, there were no significant differences between the groups. The authors concluded that the lack of differentiation on the neurocognitive battery suggested that the AS and HFA groups could be combined into a more general PDD category.

The second study was conducted by Ozonoff, Pennington, and Rogers (1991) and Ozonoff, Rogers, and Pennington (1991), who administered a neuropsychological battery to 13 HFA subjects and 10 AS subjects who differed in verbal IQ but not in full-scale or performance IQs, or in chronological age. Besides intelligence, the battery included measures of executive function, verbal learning and memory, and visual-spatial abilities. Although both groups differed on some measures from their controls, they differed from each other only in regard to verbal memory, which was very likely a function of the significantly higher verbal skills (the correlation between Verbal IQ and verbal memory was $r = .73$, $p < .001$; Ozonoff, Pennington, & Rogers, 1991; Ozonoff, Rogers, & Pennington, 1991). There was little evidence, therefore, that the two groups could be differentiated in terms of their neuropsychological profiles. The only deficit that was present in both groups relative to controls was in executive function, which suggests that the primacy of deficits in this area is a neuropsychological feature underlying a more broadly defined PDD group.

In contrast to Ozonoff, Pennington, and Rogers (1991), Ozonoff, Rogers, and Pennington (1991), and Szatmari et al.'s (1990) results, which revealed very few differences between the neurocognitive profiles of AS and HFA subjects, the third study (Klin, Volkmar, et al., 1995) reported major differences between the two groups. In this study, a group of AS and HFA individuals of comparable chronological age and Full Scale IQ were compared in terms of their functioning in a variety of neuropsychological areas. Eleven of these areas discriminated between the two groups. Interestingly, some neuropsychological skills represented areas of strength in AS and weakness in HFA; for other skills, the reverse pattern was obtained. Six areas of psychological deficits were predictive of a diagnosis of AS:

(a) fine motor skills, (b) gross motor skills, (c) visual-motor integration, (d) visual-spatial perception, (e) nonverbal concept formation, and (f) visual memory. Five areas of psychological deficits were predictive of a diagnosis of "not-AS" (i.e., they were negatively correlated with a diagnosis of AS): (a) articulation, (b) verbal output, (c) auditory perception, (d) vocabulary, and (e) verbal memory. This study also revealed a different pattern of Verbal-Performance IQ for the two groups: VIQ > PIQ in the AS group, and VIQ ≈ PIQ in the HFA group. Finally, 18 of 21 subjects with AS had a neuropsychological profile that was consistent with a nonverbal learning disability (NLD; Rourke, 1989). In the HFA group, only 1 of 19 was consistent. This study indicated an overlap between AS (but not HFA) and NLD, suggesting an empirical distinction between AS and HFA based on neurocognitive profiles.

Quite likely, the differences in results and conclusions reported in these three studies of neurocognitive functioning in AS and HFA are a function of the different diagnostic characterization procedures adopted by the various groups of investigators. In other words, it is very likely that the groups of AS subjects differed markedly from study to study. Klin and colleagues adopted what they thought would be the most stringent diagnostic procedure, in order to select the most phenomenologically prototypical cases of HFA and AS, with a view to maximizing differences in developmental history and presentation. This strategy was based on the assumption that if neuropsychological differences could not be found with the most prototypic cases, there would be little reason to pursue this line of research. Operationally, the authors adopted the *ICD-10* (WHO, 1993) definition of AS, but they added a requirement for the presence of motor clumsiness and restricted interest. This approach yielded results consistent with those obtained in the *DSM-IV* Autism/PDD field trial (Volkmar et al., 1994). In contrast, Szatmari and colleagues adopted a much broader definition. Ozonoff and colleagues used the *ICD-10* definition of AS, but modified it by excluding the onset criteria. Although the exclusion was justified because of the current debate regarding the validity of the AS onset criteria (see above), it made the AS definition broader than the one adopted by Klin and colleagues (for example, 4 of the 10 AS subjects also met *DSM-III-R* [APA, 1987] criteria for autism).

In conclusion, although there are some exciting findings in this area of research, a comparison of the available studies underscores the need to adopt a consensual nosology in future investigations, so that findings can be compared and research groups can build on the work of colleagues who share the same interest.

Social Cognitive Studies

In the past 10 years, several research studies have explored autistic children's ability to impute mental states such as beliefs, desires, and intentions to others and to themselves, or to have a theory of other people's (and their own) subjectivity—a "theory of mind" (Baron-Cohen, Tager-Flusberg, & Cohen, 1993). The major hypothesis emerging from this work is that individuals with autism lack this capacity, and that this fundamental deficit may explain Wing's (Wing & Gould, 1979) triad of symptoms defining autism: impairment of social and communicative functioning and imaginative activities (see Chapter 41 for a review).

To date, two studies (Bowler, 1992; Ozonoff, Pennington, & Rogers, 1991; Ozonoff, Rogers, & Pennington, 1991) have explored theory-of-mind capacities in individuals with AS. Ozonoff and colleagues compared the performance of 13 autistic persons with that of 10 AS children and young adults on five tasks of "first-order theory of mind" and one task of "second-order theory of mind." "First-order attributions" refer to a situation in which a subject must attribute a mental state (e.g., a false belief) to another person. "Second-order attributions" require recursive thinking about mental states. A subject is required to predict one person's thoughts about another person's thoughts. First-order tasks begin to be mastered by age 4 in normally developing children, and the ability to make second-order (e.g., belief) attributions develops at around the age of 7 (Perner & Wimmer, 1985). Group comparisons revealed significant differences for first-order and second-order theory-of-mind tasks between the two groups. The autistic group exhibited significant impairment in relation to both the AS and an age- and IQ-matched control group.

The AS group exhibited no impairment in relation to the control group. The suggestion was raised, therefore, that AS and HFA could be distinguished in terms of theory-of-mind abilities. These results are consistent with those of Bowler (1992), who tested 15 young adults with AS on both first-order and second-order theory-of-mind tasks. The great majority of the subjects (93% on the first-order task, and 73% on the second-order task) showed no impairment in theory-of-mind abilities relative to an IQ-matched control group of schizophrenic patients and a normative group.

The conclusion that theory-of-mind deficits might discriminate between groups of AS and autistic individuals is, however, not straightforward. In both studies, performance on theory-of-mind tasks was significantly correlated with verbal IQ. Several studies of theory-of-mind abilities have highlighted the important role played by verbal skills in the subject's performance of such tasks (e.g., Happe, 1995; Sparrevohn & Howie, 1995). In the study by Ozonoff and colleagues, the AS subjects had significantly higher verbal IQ. The possibility remained that the discrepancy in verbal skills could account for the difference in performance between the groups. In fact, when verbal IQ was covaried, the initial differences were no longer significant.

Although deficits in theory-of-mind tasks are not typical of individuals with AS, their ability to take the perspective of other persons and adequately evaluate their interests, beliefs, intentions, and feelings, is typically impaired. This observation, originally made by Asperger (1944), was reiterated by Van Krevelen (1971). He captured this phenomenon as a lack of an intuitive understanding of other people's social behavior, which precludes empathic feelings and negotiation of social interaction by means of quick-paced nonverbal communication. In this context, individuals with AS were said to mediate their social and emotional exchange, through explicit verbal and logical means, cognitively, rigidly, and in a rule-governed fashion, rather than affectively, intuitively, and in a self-adjusting fashion. It is not surprising, therefore, that individuals with AS may succeed in perspective-taking tasks that are highly correlated with verbal skills and can be performed in a logical, rule-governed fashion. A future challenge for investigators interested in theory-of-mind capacities will be to devise experimental situations that are less amenable to logical and verbal solutions. Optimally, these should involve processing of more visual than verbal stimuli, and more naturalistic and socially contextualized rather than abstract and logical situations. Processing time (i.e., latency of response) should be considered an important parameter, given that, clinically, individuals with AS typically cannot avail themselves of their formal social knowledge in quick-paced, simultaneously shifting, social situations. They often miss the *tempo* of the interaction and lose any possibility of rapidly adjusting themselves to the forever shifting social and communicative demands of others.

Neurobiological Studies

Several reports of neurobiological abnormalities associated with AS have appeared, but they have been limited by the small number of cases studied. Wing (1981) was impressed with the frequency of perinatal problems (reported for nearly half of her original sample). However, Gillberg and Gillberg (1989) actually concluded that reduced obstetric optimality was more common in autism than in AS. Other reports have associated certain medical conditions—for example, aminoaciduria (Miles & Capelle, 1987) and ligamentous laxity (Tantam, Evered, & Hersov, 1990)—to single cases of AS. Specific genetic abnormalities have been similarly reported: one case with a balanced de novo translocation (Anneren, Dahl, Uddenfeldt, & Janols, 1995), one case with an autosomal fragile site (Saliba & Griffiths, 1990), and a possible association with Fragile X syndrome (Bartolucci & Szatmari, 1987).

There have been at least five neuroimaging studies of AS. The various findings cannot, at this point, be collectively analyzed and compared with similar research in autism, given the small number of patients involved and the discrepancy in the diagnostic characterization employed by the various research groups. Berthier and colleagues (Berthier, Starkstein, & Leiguarda, 1990; Berthier, Bayes, & Tolosa, 1993) have reported MRI results for 9 patients with AS. In their first study, one patient had

left frontal macrogyria, and another patient had bilateral opercular polymicrogyria. A CT scan performed on one of the patients' first-degree relatives (who presented with a bipolar disorder) also showed cortical migration anomalies. Their second study compared 7 individuals with AS and Tourette's Syndrome (TS) with 6 individuals with TS only. MRI findings revealed cortical and subcortical abnormalities in 5 of the 7 patients with AS and TS, but in only 1 of the 9 patients with TS only. These findings are intriguing not only because of the positive findings in the AS group, but also because of the stated comorbidity of AS and TS, which, in fact, appears to occur much less frequently than with other disorders such as obsessive-compulsive disorder or affective disorders (see the section on comorbidity, later in this chapter). Other case studies have revealed left temporal lobe damage (CT scan; Jones & Kerwin, 1990) and left occipital hypoperfusion (SPECT; Ozbayrak, Kapucu, Erdem, & Aras, 1991). McKelvey, Lambert, Mottron, and Shevell (1995) reported on three patients with abnormal right hemisphere functioning on SPECT and MRI imaging. In a case study by Volkmar and colleagues (1996), a father and son with AS showed virtually identical abnormalities on their MRIs. The father's images showed a large, bilateral, V-shaped wedge of missing tissue just superior to the ascending ramus of the Sylvian fissure, at about the level where the middle frontal gyrus normally intersects with the precentral sulcus. The son's images showed similar dysmorphology in the same area, although it was larger on the right side; his images also showed decreased tissue in the anterior-inferior right temporal lobe, suggesting an atrophic process or a regional neurodevelopmental growth failure. The similarity of abnormalities suggested potential familial transmission. Both father and son exhibited a similar neuropsychological profile.

Although it is not possible at present to derive conclusions from this preliminary body of data, this area of research may hold a great deal of promise. Increasingly, neuroimaging work is being done in autism (e.g., Zilbovicius et al., 1995) and would be available for comparison with the work on AS. It will be interesting to see whether any of the neuropsychological models proposed (e.g., involving executive function abnormalities, or nonverbal learning disability) receive any support from neuroimaging work, and whether any abnormalities found reflect a convergence with or a divergence from autism.

Summary of Validation Studies

A review of validation studies of AS has highlighted the fact that progress in this area hinges on the definition of the disorder adopted by the various investigators in the field. Accordingly, future research should attempt to:

1. Avoid the circularity that has characterized past studies, in which findings may have been a function of the criteria used for diagnostic assignment. Dependent variables should be independent of (i.e., not a function of, not highly correlated with, not associated with, and not a result of) diagnostic criteria.
2. Adopt an agreed-on definition, such as the one provided in *ICD-10* or *DSM-IV*, and use it to make progress toward better definitions. In this regard, investigators should define their diagnostic process explicitly and thoroughly.
3. Develop standard diagnostic procedures that may eventually evolve into quantified methodologies such as the ones currently available for autism (Lord et al., 1989; Lord, Rutter, & LeCouteur, 1994).
4. Embrace the complexity involved in key clinical phenomena such as absorbing interests, clumsiness, social awkwardness, rigid patterns of prosody, and so forth. Investigate these symptoms systematically and in detail while avoiding premature simplifications and generalizations.

Investigators might choose to depart from the prevalent model of validation research in which two clinical groups are formed based on certain criteria for diagnostic assignment, a procedure is performed, and the groups are then compared on their results on the procedure. Given the rather precarious nosologic status of some of the pervasive developmental disorders (Klin & Volkmar, 1995a), notably AS and PDD-NOS, it would be worthwhile to reverse this process, beginning with meaningful and interesting regularities (e.g., specific neuropsychological profiles, onset patterns) and then carefully charting the range of phenotypic expressions associated with such regularities. This approach would redefine phenotype as a dependent variable, thus necessitating the development of sophisticated methodologies designed to accomplish this goal.

ASSESSMENT OF ASPERGER'S SYNDROME

Clinical assessment in pervasive developmental disorders (PDDs) in general is discussed in detail elsewhere in this volume (see Chapter 19). In this section, discussion is limited to a summary of assessment procedures, with special attention to individuals with AS.

Like other PDDs, AS involves delays and deviant patterns of behavior in multiple areas of functioning. The behavior often requires input from professionals who have different areas of expertise, particularly overall developmental functioning, neuropsychological features, and behavioral status. Hence, the clinical assessment of individuals with this disorder is most effectively conducted by an experienced interdisciplinary team. A few principles should be made explicit, prior to a discussion of the various areas of assessment. First, given the complexity of the condition, the importance of developmental history, and the common difficulties in securing adequate services for children and individuals with AS, it is very important to encourage parents to observe and participate in the evaluation (Morgan, 1988). This guideline helps to demystify assessment procedures, avails the parents of shared observations that can then be clarified by the clinician, and fosters parental understanding of the child's condition. All of these contribute to the parents' evaluation of the programs of intervention offered in their community. Second, evaluation findings should be translated into a single coherent view of the child; easily understood, detailed, concrete, and realistic recommendations should be provided. When writing their reports, professionals should strive to express the implications of their findings for the patient's day-to-day adaptation, learning, and vocational training. Third, the lack of awareness, among many mental health and educational professionals, of the disorder's features and associated disabilities often necessitates direct and continuous contact, on the part of the evaluators, with the various agencies that are securing and implementing the recommended interventions. This is particularly important for AS individuals, most of whom have average levels of Full Scale IQ and are often not thought of as needing special programming. Conversely, as AS becomes a more well-known, almost fashionable diagnostic label, there is danger that it will be used by practitioners who intend to convey only that their client is currently experiencing difficulties in social interaction and in peer relationships. The disorder is a serious and debilitating developmental syndrome that impairs a person's capacity for socialization. It is not a transient or mild condition. Parents should be briefed about the present unsatisfactory state of knowledge about AS and the current confusion in the mental health community regarding use and abuse of the disorder. Ample opportunity should be given to clarify misconceptions and establish a consensus about the patient's abilities and disabilities. They should not be simply assumed under the use of the diagnostic label.

In the majority of cases, a comprehensive assessment will involve the following components: history, psychological assessment, communication assessment, psychiatric evaluation, further consultation (if needed), parental conferences, and recommendations.

History

A careful history should be obtained, beginning with pregnancy and the neonatal period, continuing with early development and the characteristics of the present stage of development, and concluding with a medical record and family health history. A review of records, including previous evaluations, should be performed; the information and results can be compared periodically to obtain a sense of a course of development. Several other specific areas should be directly examined because of

their importance in the diagnosis of AS: a careful history of the onset or recognition of the problems, past and current development of motor skills, language patterns, and areas of special interest (e.g., favorite occupations, unusual skills, collections). Particular emphasis should be placed on social development, including past and present problems in social interaction, patterns of attachment of family members, development of friendships, self-concept, emotional development, and mood presentation.

Psychological Assessment

This component aims at establishing the overall level of intellectual functioning, profiles of strengths and weaknesses, and style of learning. The specific areas to be examined and measured include neuropsychological functioning (e.g., motor and psychomotor skills, problem solving, concept formation, memory, and executive functions), adaptive functioning (degree of self-sufficiency in real-life situations), academic achievement (performance in school-like subjects), and personality assessment (e.g., common preoccupations, compensatory strategies of adaptation, and mood presentation).

The neuropsychological assessment of individuals with AS involves procedures that are of specific interest to this population. Regardless of whether a Verbal-Performance IQ discrepancy is obtained in intelligence testing, it is advisable to conduct a fairly comprehensive neuropsychological assessment that includes measures of motor skills (coordination of the large muscles, visual-motor coordination, and grapho-motor skills), visual-perceptual skills and gestalt perception, spatial orientation, visual memory, facial recognition, concept formation (both verbal and nonverbal), and executive functions. A recommended protocol would include the measures used in the assessment of children with NLD (Rourke, 1989). Particular attention should be given to demonstrated or potential compensatory strategies; for example, individuals with significant visual-spatial deficits may translate the task or mediate their responses by means of verbal strategies or verbal guidance. Hence, if a response is not clear, the patient should be asked to explain the strategy used to perform the task.

Communication Assessment

The communication assessment aims to obtain both quantitative and qualitative information regarding the various aspects of the child's communication skills. It should go beyond the testing of speech and formal language (e.g., articulation, vocabulary, and sentence construction and comprehension). The assessment should examine nonverbal forms of communication (e.g., gaze and gestures), nonliteral language (e.g., metaphor, irony, absurdities, and humor), suprasegmental aspects of speech (e.g., patterns of inflection, stress, and pitch), pragmatics (e.g., turn taking, and sensitivity to cues provided by the interlocutor), and content, coherence, and contingency of conversation. Particular attention should be given to perseveration on circumscribed topics, metalinguistic skills (Tager-Flusberg, 1993), reciprocity, and rules of conversation (Grice, 1975). Even if a child meets the formal diagnostic criteria for the relative preservation of *early* language, this does not guarantee that subsequent communication skills will be spared. Indeed, the verbosity of patients with AS sometimes misleads clinicians about actual communication skills, which may be significantly impaired.

Psychiatric Examination

The psychiatric examination should include observations of the child during more and less structured periods—for example, while interacting with parents or engaged in assessment by other members of the evaluation team. Specific areas for observation and inquiry include the patient's patterns of special interest and leisure time, social and affective presentation, quality of attachment to family members, development of peer relationships and friendships, capacities for self-awareness, perspective on and level of insight into social and behavioral problems, typical reactions in novel situations, and ability to intuit other people's feelings and infer their intentions and beliefs. Problem behaviors that are likely to interfere with remedial programming (e.g., anxiety and temper tantrums) should be noted. The patient's ability to understand ambiguous nonliteral communications (particularly teasing and sarcasm) should be examined (misunderstandings of such communications may elicit aggressive behaviors). Other areas of observation involve obsessions or compulsions, depression and panic attacks, integrity of thought, and reality testing.

Differential Diagnosis

The differential diagnosis of AS involves primarily autism without associated retardation (i.e., HFA and PDD-NOS in *DSM-IV,* or Atypical Autism in *ICD-10*). Some authors might include personality disorders characterized by significant deficits in social-emotional functioning (e.g., Schizoid Personality Disorder), but such diagnoses do not take into account the developmental factors of AS that may greatly aid understanding of its pathogenesis and course.

AS differs from HFA in that the onset is usually later and the outcome is more positive. In addition, social and communication deficits are less severe, motor mannerisms are usually absent, and circumscribed interest is more conspicuous. Motor "clumsiness" is more frequently seen in AS, and family history of similar problems is more frequently ascertained in AS than in HFA.

The distinction between AS and PDD-NOS is problematic. Essentially, the latter is a residual category with no defining criteria (see Chapters 1 and 6). PDD-NOS is used to describe a rather large and heterogeneous group of children who do not meet strict criteria for autism but who exhibit a pattern of developmental and behavioral dysfunction similar to that observed in autism. These children typically reveal unusual sensitivities and affective responses in the presence of more differentiated social relatedness, and their cognitive and communicative skills are better than those of most autistic children (Klin & Volkmar, 1995a). The *ICD-10* definition of Atypical Autism, despite its attempt to operationally identify the areas of "atypicality" (e.g., in age of onset and symptomatology), is also, essentially, a negative or subthreshold definition (i.e., not, or not quite, autism). From the information revealed in the very few attempts to study this population (e.g., Cohen, Paul, & Volkmar, 1986; Dahl, Cohen, & Provence, 1986), we can draw some acceptable conclusions:

1. If AS is strictly defined, it differs from the much more common PDD-NOS in that social, emotional, and communicative deficits are more severe and outcome is poorer in AS.
2. Circumscribed interests and motor "clumsiness" are more pronounced in AS.
3. IQ range is probably more variable in PDD-NOS.

Empirical evidence substantiating some of these observations was obtained in the Autism/PDD *DSM-IV* field trials (Volkmar et al., 1994).

Comorbidity

Discussion of co-occurrence of two or more separate child psychiatric conditions are complex and depend on a series of factors (Caron & Rutter, 1991). Discussions of comorbidity are particularly problematic in the context of AS, where the use of the diagnostic label has probably been less strict than for most other developmental disorders. Additionally, given that the literature is still very much based on case studies or small series, some anomalies may occur. For example, at least four studies have reported the association between AS and Tourette's Syndrome (TS; Berthier et al., 1993; Kerbeshian & Burd, 1986; Littlejohns et al., 1990; Marriage, Miles, Stokes, & Davey, 1993), conveying the impression that AS and TS may occur together frequently. Preliminary data on 99 subjects with AS (Klin & Volkmar, 1995b), however, suggest that the co-occurrence is much less frequent than was implied by these publications (only 2 of 99 patients with AS also had TS). Other disorders appear to be much more prominent. The same set of preliminary data documented the copresence, in the 99 patients with AS, of obsessive-compulsive disorder (19%), depression (15%), and ADHD (28%). The co-occurrence of some disorders appears to be developmentally dependent; for example, ADHD is more often observed in younger children, and depression

is more often observed in older children, adolescents, and adults.

TREATMENT AND INTERVENTION

As in autism, treatment of AS is essentially supportive and symptomatic; to a great extent, treatment overlaps with the guidelines that are applicable to individuals with autism unaccompanied by mental retardation (Mesibov, 1992). Special educational services are sometimes helpful, although there is, as yet, very little reported experience on the effectiveness of specific interventions. Acquisition of basic skills in social interaction, as well as in other areas of adaptive functioning, should be encouraged. Supportive psychotherapy focused on problems of empathy, social difficulties, and depressive symptoms may be helpful, although it is usually very difficult for individuals with AS to engage in more intensive, insight-oriented psychotherapy.

Despite the paucity of published information on intervention strategies and issues, a few guidelines may be offered, based on (a) informal observations made by experienced clinicians and (b) intervention strategies used with individuals with HFA (Mesibov, 1992; Van Bourgondien & Woods, 1992) and individuals with learning disabilities associated with severe social dysfunction (Minskoff, 1980a, 1980b; Rourke, 1989).

Securing Services

The authorities who decide on entitlement to services are usually unaware of the extent and significance of the disabilities in AS. Proficient verbal skills, overall IQ (usually within the normal range), and a solitary lifestyle often mask outstanding deficiencies observed primarily in novel or otherwise socially demanding situations. The very salient needs for supportive intervention are not perceived. Active participation is needed on the part of the clinician, together with parents and possibly an advocate, to foreecfully pursue the patient's eligibility for services. The formalization of the diagnosis in *ICD-10* and *DSM-IV* will certainly help this effort. In the past, many individuals with AS were diagnosed as learning disabled with eccentric features

(Klin & Volkmar, 1995b), a nonpsychiatric diagnostic label that is much less effective in securing services. Others, who were given the diagnosis of autism or PDD-NOS, often had to contend with educational programs designed for much lower-functioning children; thus, their own relative strengths and unique disabilities were not properly addressed. Yet another group of individuals with AS is sometimes characterized as exhibiting "Social-Emotional Maladjustment" (SEM), an educational label associated with conduct problems and volitional maladaptive behaviors. These individuals are often placed in educational settings for individuals with conduct disorders, creating the worst mismatch possible: individuals with a very naïve understanding of social situations become foils for those who can and do manipulate social situations to their advantage without the benefit of self-restraint.

Learning

Skills, concepts, appropriate procedures, cognitive strategies, and behavioral norms may be effectively taught in an explicit and rote fashion using a parts-to-whole verbal instructional approach, where the verbal steps are in the correct sequence for the behavior to be effective. Additional guidelines should be derived from the individual's neuropsychological profile of assets and deficits; specific intervention techniques should be similar to those usually employed for many subtypes of learning disabilities, and an effort should be made to circumvent the identified difficulties by means of compensatory strategies, usually of a verbal nature. If significant motor and visual-motor deficits are corroborated during the evaluation, the individual should receive physical and occupational therapies. The latter should not only focus on traditional techniques designed to remediate motor deficits, but should also reflect an effort to integrate these activities with learning of visual-spatial concepts, visual-spatial orientation, and body awareness.

Adaptive Functioning

The acquisition of self-sufficiency skills in all areas of functioning should be a priority in any plan of intervention. The tendency of individuals with AS to rely on rigid rules and routines can be used to foster positive habits and enhance the quality of life of the person and the family. The teaching approach should follow closely the guidelines for learning, and should be practiced routinely in naturally occurring situations and across different settings, in order to maximize generalization of the acquired skills.

Maladaptive Behaviors

Specific problem-solving strategies, usually following a verbal algorithm, may be taught for handling frequently occurring, troublesome situations (e.g., involving novelty, intense social demands, or frustration). Training is usually necessary for recognizing situations as troublesome and for selecting the best available learned strategy to use in such situations.

Social and Communication Skills

These skills are possibly best taught by a communication specialist who has an interest in pragmatics in speech. Alternatively, social skills training groups may be used, if they allow enough opportunities for individual contact with the instructor and for practicing of specific skills. Teaching may include: (a) appropriate nonverbal behavior (e.g., the use of gaze for social interaction, and the need to monitor and pattern verbal inflection), which may involve imitative drills, working with a mirror, and so forth; (b) verbal decoding of the nonverbal behaviors of others; (c) processing of visual information simultaneously with auditory information (in order to foster integration of competing stimuli and to facilitate the creation of the appropriate social context of the interaction); and (d) cultivation and practice of social awareness, perspective-taking skills, and correct interpretation of ambiguous communications (e.g., nonliteral language).

Strategies for teaching nonverbal communication skills and effective intervention activities have been extensively described in the learning disabilities literature. Excellent guidelines are offered for learning body language cues (Minskoff, 1980a) and proxemic and prosodic cues (Minskoff, 1980b).

Vocational Training

Adults with AS often fail to meet entry requirements (e.g., a college degree) for jobs in their area of training, or they are unable to maintain a job because of their poor interview skills, social disabilities, eccentricities, or anxiety attacks. Having failed to secure skilled employment, these individuals may be helped by well-meaning friends or relatives to find a manual job. Their typically poor visual-motor skills may cause them to fail again, which leads to devastating emotional implications. Individuals with AS must be trained for and placed in jobs for which they are not neuropsychologically impaired, and in which they will enjoy a certain degree of support and shelter. Preferably, the job should not involve intensive social demands. Many vocational possibilities are available for individuals with AS (Van Bourgondien & Woods, 1992), and, as initially suggested by Asperger (1944), when a special talent is available and can be utilized for the purpose of remunerated employment, the prospects for success are very favorable. The individual will still need help and support in coping with the social demands associated with regular employment—contact with coworkers and with clients, and the give-and-take of less structured situations, such as recess periods.

Self-Support

Because individuals with AS are usually self-described as loners despite an often intense wish to make friends and have a more active social life, social contact within the context of activity-oriented groups (e.g., church communities, hobby clubs, and self-support groups) should be facilitated. The little experience available with self-support groups suggests that individuals with AS enjoy the opportunity to meet others with similar problems and may develop relationships around an activity or subject of shared interest. The Internet is an area of great promise. It opens opportunities for individuals to correspond or interact with others on subjects of special interest.

Pharmacotherapy

Little information about pharmacological interventions with individuals with AS is available. A conservative approach based on the evidence from autism should probably be adopted (McDougle, Price, & Volkmar, 1994). Pharmacological interventions are discussed in detail in Chapter 32.

Pharmacological interventions in AS have not yet been well studied. This is paradoxical, in a sense, because persons with AS commonly receive multiple medication trials with single agents and even with combinations of drugs. Often conducted before a definitive diagnosis of AS has been reached, these drug trials are undertaken essentially on an empiric basis. In a sample of over 100 individuals who likely had AS and were awaiting screening in the authors' clinic, over three-fourths had received stimulant medications, over one-third had received serotonin reuptake inhibitors, and nearly one-fifth had received antidepressants. In contrast to autism, neuroleptics (major tranquilizers) had been used much less frequently. As testimony to the multiple problems that these patients had exhibited (and the eager response of their physicians and/or family members), a total of nearly 50 different behavior-modifying agents (alone or in combination) had been used in this group.

The absence of rigorous, controlled studies is unfortunate. In general, pharmacological interventions with young children are probably best avoided. Emergence of what appear to be comorbid conditions, such as depression, may suggest very specific, and sometimes highly effective, drug treatments. As with all drugs, it is important to weigh the potential risks and benefits of the agent and to discuss potential side effects with the child and parents. The presence of severe obsessions and compulsions or severe anxiety may suggest specific pharmacological interventions (McDougle, Price, & Volkmar, 1994).

CONCLUSION

The study of Asperger's Syndrome is really just beginning. Little can be stated that is firmly established. The disability severely debilitates individuals' capacity for socialization, despite their desire to establish relationships; AS is developmental in nature and lifelong in course. The inclusion of AS in *DSM-IV* (APA, 1994) and *ICD-10* (WHO, 1992) may have had positive effect in giving increased and more detailed attention to a large number of individuals whose needs have often been neglected in the past. Parents may have obtained some comfort from a clinical "address" that appears to answer their questions more directly and appropriately. Much work toward an increased awareness of the condition remains to be done. In a preliminary survey of 99 families with an individual with AS (Klin & Volkmar, 1995b), 88% reported that educational professionals were unaware of the disorder and could not, therefore, plan a regimen for their afflicted child, and 70% reported that mental health professionals from whom advice was sought were equally at a loss. Research is ongoing, and it is hoped that validation efforts will be boosted by the recent advent of consensual diagnostic criteria and by the ever-increasing interest in this disorder among the clinical and scientific community.

Cross-References

Issues in diagnosis are discussed in Chapter 1, and PDD-NOS is described in Chapter 6. Alternative views on the Autism/PDD Spectrum appear in Chapters 7 and 39. Assessment issues are discussed in Chapters 19 to 21, psychopharmacology in Chapter 32, and executive function deficits and theory of mind in Chapters 40 and 41, respectively.

REFERENCES

American Psychiatric Association. (1987). *Diagnostic and statistical manual of mental disorders* (3rd ed., rev.). Washington, DC: Author.

American Psychiatric Association. (1994). *Diagnostic and statistical manual of mental disorders* (4th ed.). Washington, DC: Author.

Anneren, G., Dahl, N., Uddenfeldt, U., & Janols, L.O. (1995). Asperger Syndrome in a boy with a balanced *de novo* translocation: t(17;19)(p13.3;p11) [Letter]. *American Journal of Medical Genetics, 56*(3), 330–331.

Asperger, H. (1944). Die "Autistischen Psychopathen" im Kindesalter. *Archiv für Psychiatrie und Nervenkrankheiten, 117,* 76–136.

Asperger, H. (1979). Problems of infantile autism. *Communication, 13,* 45–52.

Bailey, A., Le Couteur, A., Gottesman, I., Bolton, P., Simonoff, E., Yuzda, E., & Rutter, M. (1995). Autism as a strongly genetic disorder: Evidence from a British twin study. *Psychological Medicine, 25,* 63–77.

Baron-Cohen, S. (1988). An assessment of violence in a young man with Asperger's Syndrome. *Journal of Child Psychology and Psychiatry, 29,* 351–360.

Baron-Cohen, S., Tager-Flusberg, H., & Cohen, D.J. (Eds.). (1993). *Understanding other minds: Perspectives from autism.* Oxford, England: Oxford University Press.

Bartolucci, G., & Szatmari, P. (1987). Possible similarities between the Fragile X and Asperger's Syndrome [Letter]. *American Journal of Disorders of Childhood, 141*(6), 601–602.

Bejerot, S., & Duvner, T. (1995). Asperger's Syndrome or schizophrenia? *Nordic Journal of Psychiatry, 49*(2), 145.

Berthier, M. (1995). Hypomania following bereavement in Asperger's Syndrome: A case study. *Neuropsychiatry, Neuropsychology, & Behavioral Neurology, 8*(3), 222–228.

Berthier, M.L., Bayes, A., & Tolosa, E.S. (1993). Magnetic resonance imaging in patients with concurrent Tourette's Disorder and Asperger's Syndrome. *Journal of the American Academy of Child and Adolescent Psychiatry, 32*(3), 633–639.

Berthier, M.L., Starkstein, S.E., & Leiguarda, R. (1990). Developmental cortical anomalies in Asperger's Syndrome: Neuroradiological findings in two patients. *Journal of Neuropsychiatry and Clinical Neurosciences, 2*(2), 197–201.

Bishop, D.V.M. (1989). Autism, Asperger's Syndrome and Semantic-Pragmatic Disorder: Where are the boundaries? *British Journal of Disorders of Communications, 24,* 107–121.

Bishop, D.V.M. (1995, October). *Semantic-Pragmatic Disorder and Asperger Syndrome.* Paper presented at the 42nd annual meeting of the American Academy of Child and Adolescent Psychiatry, New Orleans, LA.

Blank, M., Gessner, M., & Esposito, A. (1979). Language without communication: A case study. *Journal of Child Language, 6,* 329–352.

Bleuler, E. (1951). *Lehrbuch der Psychiatrie* [Textbook of Psychiatry] (A. A. Brill, Trans.). New York: Dover. (Original work published 1916)

Bolton, P., MacDonald, H., Pickles, A., Rios, P., Goode, S., Crowson, M., Bailey, A., & Rutter, M. (1994). A case-control family history study of autism. *Journal of Child Psychology and Psychiatry, 35*(5), 877–900.

Bowler, D.M. (1992). "Theory of Mind" in Asperger's Syndrome. *Journal of Child Psychology and Psychiatry, 33*(5), 877–893.

Burgoine, E., & Wing, L. (1983). Identical triplets with Asperger's Syndrome. *British Journal of Psychiatry, 143,* 261–265.

Cantwell, D.P., Baker, L., Rutter, M., & Mawhood, L. (1989). Infantile autism and developmental receptive dysphasia: A comparative follow-up into middle childhood. *Journal of Autism and Developmental Disorders, 19,* 19–32.

Caplan, R. (1994). Thought disorder in childhood. *Journal of the American Academy of Child and Adolescent Psychiatry, 33*(5), 605–615.

Caron, C., & Rutter, M. (1991). Comorbidity in child psychopathology: Concepts, issues, and research strategies. *Journal of Child Psychology and Psychiatry, 32*(7), 1063–1080.

Clarke, D.J., Littlejohns, C.S., Corbett, J.A., & Joseph, S. (1989). Pervasive developmental disorders and psychoses in adult life. *British Journal of Psychiatry, 155,* 692–699.

Cohen, D.J., Paul, R., & Volkmar, F.R. (1986). Issues in the classification of pervasive developmental disorders: Toward *DSM-IV. Journal of the American Academy of Child and Adolescent Psychiatry, 25,* 213–220.

Dahl, K., Cohen, D.J., & Provence, S. (1986). Clinical and multivariate approaches to nosology of the pervasive developmental disorders. *Journal of the American Academy of Child and Adolescent Psychiatry, 25,* 170–180.

Dawson, G., Finley, C., Phillips, S., & Galpert, L. (1986). Hemispheric specialization and the language abilities of autistic children. *Child Development, 57*(6), 1440–1453.

DeLong, G.R., & Dwyer, J.T. (1988). Correlation of family history with specific autistic subgroups: Asperger's Syndrome and bipolar affective disease. *Journal of Autism and Developmental Disorders, 18*(4), 593–600.

Denckla, M.B. (1983). The neuropsychology of social-emotional learning disabilities. *Archives of Neurology, 40,* 461–462.

Dewey, M. (1991). Living with Asperger's Syndrome. In U. Frith (Ed.), *Autism and Asperger Syndrome* (pp. 184–206). Cambridge, England: Cambridge University Press.

Dykens, E., Volkmar, F.R., & Glick, M. (1991). Thought disorder in high-functioning autistic adults. *Journal of Autism and Developmental Disorders, 21,* 291–321.

Ehlers, S., & Gillberg, C. (1993). The epidemiology of Asperger Syndrome: A total population study. *Journal of Child Psychology and Psychiatry, 34*(8), 1327–1350.

Ellis, H.D., Ellis, D.M., Fraser, W., & Deb, S. (1994). A preliminary study of right-hemisphere cognitive deficits and impaired social judgments among young people with Asperger Syndrome. *European Child & Adolescent Psychiatry, 3*(4), 255–266.

Everall, I.P., & LeCouteur, A. (1990). Firesetting in an adolescent with Asperger's Syndrome. *British Journal of Psychiatry, 157,* 284–287.

Frith, U. (Ed.). (1991). *Autism and Asperger Syndrome.* Cambridge, England: Cambridge University Press.

Fujikawa, H., Kobayashi, R., Koga, Y., & Murata, T. (1987). A case of Asperger's Syndrome in a nineteen-year-old who showed psychotic breakdown with depressive state and attempted suicide after entering university. *Japanese Journal of Child and Adolescent Psychiatry, 28*(4), 217–225.

Ghaziuddin, M., Butler, E., Tsai, L.Y., & Ghaziuddin, N. (1994). Is clumsiness a marker for Asperger Syndrome? *Journal of Intellectual Disabilities Research, 38*(5), 519–527.

Ghaziuddin, M., Leininger, L., & Tsai, L.Y. (1995). Brief report: thought disorder in Asperger Syndrome: Comparison with high-functioning autism. *Journal of Autism and Developmental Disorders, 25*(3), 311–317.

Ghaziuddin, M., Tsai, L.Y., & Ghaziuddin, N. (1991). Brief report: Violence in Asperger Syndrome, a critique. *Journal of Autism and Developmental Disorders, 21*(3), 349–354.

Ghaziuddin, M., Tsai, L.Y., & Ghaziuddin, N. (1992a). Brief report: A comparison of the diagnostic criteria for Asperger Syndrome. *Journal of Autism and Developmental Disorders, 22*(4), 643–649.

Ghaziuddin, M., Tsai, L.Y., & Ghaziuddin, N. (1992b). Comorbidity of autistic disorder in children and adolescents. *European Child and Adolescent Psychiatry, 1*(4), 209–213.

Ghaziuddin, M., Tsai, L.Y., & Ghaziuddin, N. (1992c). A reappraisal of clumsiness as a diagnostic feature of Asperger Syndrome. *Journal of Autism and Developmental Disorders, 22,* 651–656.

Gillberg, C. (1985). Asperger's Syndrome and recurrent psychosis: A case study. *Journal of Autism and Developmental Disorders, 15*(4), 389–397.

Gillberg, C. (1989). Asperger Syndrome in 23 Swedish children. *Developmental Medicine and Child Neurology, 31,* 520–531.

Gillberg, C. (1990). Autism and the pervasive developmental disorders. *Journal of Child Psychology and Psychiatry, 31*(1), 99–119.

Gillberg, C. (1991). Outcome in autism and autistic-like conditions. *Journal of the American Academy of Child and Adolescent Psychiatry, 30*(3), 375–382.

Gillberg, C., & Rastam, M. (1992, March). Do some cases of anorexia nervosa reflect underlying autistic-like symptomtology? *Behavioural Neurology, 5*(1), 27–32.

Gillberg, I.C., & Gillberg, C. (1989). Asperger Syndrome—Some epidemiological considerations.

Journal of Child Psychology and Psychiatry, 30, 631–638.

Grandin, T. (1990). Needs of high-functioning teenagers and adults with autism: Tips from a recovered autistic. *Focus on Autistic Behavior, 5*(1), 16.

Grice, H.P. (1975). Logic and conversation. In R. Cole & J. Morgan (Eds.), *Syntax and semantics: Speech acts* (pp. 85–102). New York: Academic Press.

Hallett, M., Lebiedowska, M.K., Thomas, S.L., Stanhope, S.J., Denckla, M.B., & Rumsey, J. (1993). Locomotion of autistic adults. *Archives of Neurology, 50,* 1304–1308.

Happe, F.G. (1995). The role of age and verbal ability in the theory-of-mind task performance of subjects with autism. *Child Development, 66*(3), 843–855.

Jones, P.B., & Kerwin, R.W. (1990). Left temporal lobe damage in Asperger's Syndrome. *British Journal of Psychiatry, 156,* 570–572.

Kanner, L. (1943). Autistic disturbances of affective contact. *Nervous Child, 2,* 217–253.

Kanner, L. (1954). Discussion of Robinson & Vitale's paper on "Children with circumscribed interests." *American Journal of Orthopsychiatry, 24,* 764–766.

Kanner, L. (1971). Follow-up study of eleven children originally reported in 1943. *Journal of Autism and Childhood Schizophrenia, 1,* 119–145.

Kerbeshian, J., & Burd, L. (1986). Asperger's Syndrome and Tourette Syndrome: The case of the pinball wizard. *British Journal of Psychiatry, 148,* 731–736.

Klin, A. (1994). Asperger Syndrome. *Child and Adolescent Psychiatry Clinic of North America, 3,* 131–148.

Klin, A., Carter, A., & Sparrow, S.S. (1997, this volume).

Klin, A., Sparrow, S.S., Volkmar, F.R., Cicchetti, D.V., & Rourke, B.P. (1995). Asperger Syndrome. In B.P. Rourke (Ed.), *Syndrome of nonverbal learning disabilities: Neurodevelopmental manifestations* (pp. 93–118). New York: Guilford Press.

Klin, A., & Volkmar, F.R. (1995a). Autism and the pervasive developmental disorders. *Child and Adolescent Psychiatric Clinics of North America, 4*(3), 617–630.

Klin, A., & Volkmar, F.R. (1995b, October). *Preliminary data of the Yale-LDA Social Learning Disabilities Project.* Paper presented at the 42nd annual meeting of the American Academy of Child and Adolescent Psychiatry, New Orleans, LA.

Klin, A., & Volkmar, F.R. (1996). The pervasive developmental disorders: Nosology and profiles of development. In S. Luthar, J. Burack, D. Cicchetti, & J. Wiesz (Eds.), *Developmental perspectives on risk and psychopathology.* New York: Cambridge University Press.

Klin, A., Volkmar, F.R., Sparrow, S.S., Cicchetti, D.V., & Rourke, B.P. (1995). Validity and neuropsychological characterization of Asperger Syndrome. *Journal of Child Psychology and Psychiatry, 36*(7), 1127–1140.

Kretschmer, E. (1925). *Physique and character.* London: Kegan-Paul, Trench & Trubner.

Littlejohns, C.S., Clarke, D.J., & Corbett, J.A. (1990, March). Tourette-like disorder in Asperger's Syndrome [Special Issue]. *British Journal of Psychiatry, 156,* 430–403.

Lord, C., Rutter, M., Goode, S., Heemsbergen, J., Jordan, H., Mawhood, L., & Schopler, E. (1989). Autism diagnostic observation schedule: A standardized observation of communicative and social behavior. *Journal of Autism and Developmental Disorders, 19*(2), 185–212.

Lord, C., Rutter, M., & LeCouteur, A. (1994). Autism Diagnostic Interview—Revised: A revised version of a diagnostic interview for caregivers of individuals with possible pervasive developmental disorders. *Journal of Autism and Developmental Disorders, 24*(5), 659–685.

Lord, C., & Venter, A. (1992). Outcome and follow-up studies of high-functioning autistic individuals. In E. Schopler & G.B. Mesibov (Eds.), *High-functioning individuals with autism* (pp. 187–199). New York: Plenum Press.

Lotter, V. (1978). Follow-up studies. In M. Rutter & E. Schopler (Eds.), *Autism: A reappraisal of concepts and treatment* (pp. 142–167). New York: Plenum Press.

Manjiviona, J., & Prior, M. (1995). Comparison of Asperger Syndrome and high-functioning autistic children on a test of motor impairment. *Journal of Autism and Developmental Disorders, 25*(1), 23–39.

Marriage, K., Miles, T., Stokes, D., & Davey, M. (1993). Clinical and research implications of the co-occurrence of Asperger's and Tourette Syndrome. *Australian and New Zealander Journal of Psychiatry, 27*(4), 666–672.

Mawson, D., Grounds, A., & Tantam, D. (1985). Violence and Asperger's Syndrome: A case study. *British Journal of Psychiatry, 147,* 566–569.

McDougle, C.J., Price, L.H., & Volkmar, F.R. (1994). Recent advances in the pharmacotherapy of autism and related conditions. *Child and Adolescent Psychiatry Clinics of North America, 3,* 71–90.

McKelvey, J.R., Lambert, R., Mottron, L., & Shevell, M.I. (1995). Right-hemisphere dysfunction in Asperger's Syndrome. *Journal of Child Neurology, 10*(4), 310–314.

Mesibov, G.B. (1992). Treatment issues with high-functioning adolescents and adults with autism. In E. Schopler & G.B. Mesibov (Eds.), *High-functioning individuals with autism* (pp. 143–156). New York: Plenum Press.

Miles, S.W., & Capelle, P. (1987). Asperger's Syndrome and aminoaciduria: A case example. *British Journal of Psychiatry, 150,* 397–400.

Minskoff, E.H. (1980a). Teaching approach for developing nonverbal communication skills in students with social perception deficits: Part I. The basic approach and body language clues. *Journal of Learning Disabilities, 13*(3), 118–124.

Minskoff, E.H. (1980b). Teaching approach for developing nonverbal communication skills in students with social perception deficits: Part II. Proxemic, vocalic, and artifactual cues. *Journal of Learning Disabilities, 13*(4), 203–208.

Morgan, S. (1988). The autistic child and family functioning: A developmental-family systems perspective. *Journal of Autism and Developmental Disorders, 18,* 263–278.

Myklebust, H.R. (1975). Nonverbal learning disabilities: Assessment and intervention. In H.R. Myklebust (Ed.), *Progress in learning disabilities* (Vol. 3, pp. 281–301). New York: Grune & Stratton.

Nagy, J., & Szatmari, P. (1986). A chart review of schizotypal personality disorders in children. *Journal of Autism and Developmental Disorders, 16*(3), 351–367.

Ozbayrak, K.R., Kapucu, O., Erdem, E., & Aras, T. (1991). Left occipital hypoperfusion in a case with Asperger Syndrome. *Brain Development, 13*(6), 454–456.

Ozonoff, S., Pennington, B.F., & Rogers, S.J. (1991). Executive function deficits in high-functioning autistic individuals: Relationship to theory of mind. *Journal of Child Psychology and Psychiatry, 32*(7), 1081–1105.

Ozonoff, S., Rogers, S.J., & Pennington, B.F. (1991). Asperger's Syndrome: Evidence of an empirical distinction from high-functioning autism. *Journal of Child Psychology and Psychiatry, 32*(7), 1107–1122.

Perner, J., & Wimmer, H. (1985). "John thinks that Mary thinks that . . .": Attribution of second-order beliefs by 5–10 year old children. *Journal of Experimental Child Psychology, 39,* 437–471.

Rapin, I., & Allen, D. (1983). Developmental language disorders. In U. Kirk (Ed.), *Neuropsychology of language, reading and spelling* (pp. 96–112). New York: Academic Press.

Robinson, J.F., & Vitale, L.J. (1954). Children with circumscribed interests. *American Journal of Orthopsychiatry, 24,* 755–764.

Rourke, B. (1989). *Nonverbal learning disabilities: The syndrome and the model.* New York: Guilford Press.

Rourke, B., Young, G.C., & Leenaars, A.A. (1989). A childhood learning disability that predisposes those afflicted to adolescent and adult depression and suicide risk. *Journal of Learning Disabilities, 22,* 169–185.

Roy, E.A., Elliott, D., Dewey, D., & Square-Storer, P. (1990). Impairments to praxis and sequencing in adult and developmental disorders. In C. Bard, M. Fleury, & L. Hay (Eds.), *Development of eye–hand coordination across the life span* (pp. 358–384). Columbia: University of South Carolina Press.

Rutter, M. (1972, October). Childhood schizophrenia reconsidered. *Journal of Autism and Childhood Schizophrenia, 2*(4), 315–337.

Rutter, M. (1978). Diagnosis and definition of childhood autism. *Journal of Autism and Childhood Schizophrenia, 8*(2), 139–161.

Rutter, M. (1985). Infantile autism and other pervasive developmental disorders. In M. Rutter & L. Hersov (Eds.), *Child and adolescent psychiatry: Modern approaches* (2nd ed., pp. 367–379). Oxford, England: Blackwell.

Rutter, M. (1989). Annotation: Child psychiatric disorders in *ICD-10. Journal of Child Psychology and Psychiatry, 30,* 499–513.

Rutter, M., & Gould, M. (1985). Classification. In M. Rutter & L. Herson (Eds.), *Child and adolescent psychiatry: Modern approaches* (2nd ed., pp. 304–321). Oxford, England: Blackwell.

Rutter, M., & Schopler, E. (1992). Classification of pervasive developmental disorders: Some concepts and practical considerations. *Journal of Autism and Developmental Disorders, 22*(4), 459–482.

Ryan, R.M. (1992). Treatment-resistant chronic mental illness: Is it Asperger's Syndrome? *Hospital and Community Psychiatry, 43*(8), 807–811.

Saliba, J.R., & Griffiths, M. (1990). Brief report: Autism of the Asperger type associated with an autosomal fragile site. *Journal of Autism and Developmental Disorders, 20*(4), 569–575.

Schwartz Gould, M., Wunsch-Hitzig, M.A., & Dohrenwend, B. (1981). Estimating the prevalence of childhood psychopathology. *Journal of the American Academy of Child and Adolescent Psychiatry, 20,* 462–476.

Scragg, P., & Shah, A. (1994). Prevalence of Asperger's Syndrome in a secure hospital. *British Journal of Psychiatry, 165*(5), 679–682.

Smith, I.S., & Bryson, S.E. (1994). Imitation and action in autism: A critical review. *Psychological Bulletin, 116*(2), 259–273.

Sparrevohn, R., & Howie, P.M. (1995). Theory of mind in children with autistic disorder: Evidence of developmental progression and the role of verbal ability. *Journal of Child Psychology and Psychiatry, 36*(2), 249–263.

Sparrow, S.S., Balla, D.A., & Cicchetti, D.V. (1984). *Vineland Adaptive Behavior Scales.* Circle Pines, MI: American Guidance Service.

Szatmari, P., Bartolucci, G., Brenner, R., Bond, S., & Rich, S. (1989). A follow-up study of high-functioning autistic children. *Journal of Autism and Developmental Disorders, 19,* 213–225.

Szatmari, P., Bremmer, R., & Nagy, J.N. (1989). Asperger's Syndrome: A review of clinical features. *Canadian Journal of Psychiatry, 34*(6), 554–560.

Szatmari, P., Tuff, L., Finlayson, M.A.J., & Bartolucci, G. (1990). Asperger's Syndrome and autism: Neurocognitive aspects. *Journal of the American Academy of Child and Adolescent Psychiatry, 29,* 130–136.

Tager-Flusberg, H. (1993). What language reveals about the understanding of minds in children with autism. In S. Baron-Cohen, H. Tager-Flusberg, & D.J. Cohen (Eds.), *Understanding other minds: Perspectives from autism* (pp. 138–157). Oxford, England: Oxford University Press.

Taiminen, T. (1994). Asperger's Syndrome or schizophrenia: Is differential diagnosis necessary for adult patients? *Nordic Journal of Psychiatry, 48*(5), 325–328.

Tantam, D. (1988a). Annotation: Asperger's Syndrome. *Journal of Child Psychology and Psychiatry, 29*(3), 245–255.

Tantam, D. (1988b). Lifelong eccentricity and social isolation: 2. Asperger's Syndrome or schizoid personality disorder? *British Journal of Psychiatry, 153,* 783–791.

Tantam, D. (1991). Asperger's Syndrome in adulthood. In U. Frith (Ed.), *Autism and Asperger Syndrome* (pp. 147–183). Cambridge, England: Cambridge University Press.

Tantam, D., Evered, C., & Hersov, L. (1990). Asperger's Syndrome and ligamentous laxity. *Journal of the American Academy of Child and Adolescent Psychiatry, 29*(6), 892–896.

Thomsen, P.H. (1994). Obsessive-compulsive disorder in children and adolescents: A 6–22-year follow-up study: Clinical descriptions of the course and continuity of obsessive-compulsive symptomatology. *European Child and Adolescent Psychiatry, 3*(2), 82–96.

Tsai, L.Y. (1992). Diagnostic issues in high-functioning autism. In E. Schopler & G.B. Mesibov (Eds.), *High-functioning individuals with autism* (pp. 11–40). New York: Plenum Press.

Van Bourgondien, M.E., & Woods, A.V. (1992). Vocational possibilities for high-functioning adults with autism. In E. Schopler & G.B. Mesibov (Eds.), *High-functioning individuals with autism* (pp. 227–239). New York: Plenum Press.

Van Krevelen, D.A. (1963). On the relationship between early infantile autism and autistic psychopathy. *Acta Paedopsychiatrica, 30,* 303–323.

Van Krevelen, D.A. (1971). Early infantile autism and autistic psychopathy. *Journal of Autism and Child Schizophrenia, 1*(1), 82–86.

Venter, A., Lord, C., & Schopler, E. (1992). A follow-up study of high-functioning autistic children. *Journal of Child Psychology and Psychiatry, 33*(3), 489–507.

Vilensky, J.A., Damasion, A.R., & Maurer, R.G. (1981). Gait disturbances in patients with autistic behavior. *Archives of Neurology, 38,* 646–649.

Voeller, K.K.S. (1986). Right-hemisphere deficit syndrome in children. *American Journal of Psychiatry, 143,* 1004–1009.

Voeller, K.K.S. (1991). Social-emotional learning disabilities. *Psychiatric Annals, 21*(12), 735–741.

Volkmar, F.R., Bregman, J., Cohen, D.J., & Cicchetti, D.V. (1988). *DSM-III* and *DSM-III-R* diagnoses of autism. *American Journal of Psychiatry, 145*(11), 1404–1408.

Volkmar, F.R., & Cohen, D.J. (1989). Disintegrative disorder or "late onset" autism. *Journal of Child Psychology and Psychiatry, 30*(5), 717–724.

Volkmar, F.R., & Cohen, D.J. (1991). Nonautistic pervasive developmental disorders. In R. Michels (Ed.), *Psychiatry* (Vol. 2, pp. 1–6). Philadelphia: Lippincott.

Volkmar, F.R., Klin, A., Schultz, R.B., Bronen, R., Marans, W.D., Sparrow, S.S., & Cohen, D.J. (1996). Grand rounds in child psychiatry: Asperger Syndrome. *Journal of the American Academy of Child and Adolescent Psychiatry, 35,* 118–123.

Volkmar, F.R., Klin, A., Siegel, B., Szatmari, P., Lord, C., Campbell, M., Freeman, B.J., Cicchetti, D.V., Rutter, M., Kline, W., Buitelaar, J., Hattab, Y., Fombonne, E., Fuentes, J., Werry, J., Stone, W., Kerbeshian, J., Hoshino, Y., Bregman, J., Loveland, K., Szymanski, L., & Towbin, K. (1994). *DSM-IV* autism/Pervasive Developmental Disorder field trial. *American Journal of Psychiatry, 151,* 1361–1367.

Volkmar, F.R., Sparrow, S.S., Goudreau, D., Cicchetti, D.V., Paul, R., & Cohen, D.J. (1987).

Social deficits in autism: An operational approach using the Vineland Adaptive Behavior Scales. *Journal of the American Academy of Child and Adolescent Psychiatry, 26,* 156–161.

Volkmar, F.R., Stier, D.M., & Cohen, D.J. (1985). Age of recognition of Pervasive Developmental Disorder. *American Journal of Psychiatry, 142*(12), 1450–1452.

Volkmar, F.R., Szatmari, P., & Sparrow, S.S. (1993). Sex differences in pervasive developmental disorders. *Journal of Autism and Developmental Disorders, 23*(4), 579–591.

Weintraub, S., & Mesulam, M.M. (1983). Developmental learning disabilities of the right hemisphere: Emotional, interpersonal, and cognitive components. *Archives of Neurology, 40,* 463–468.

Werry, J.S. (1992). Child and adolescent (early onset) schizophrenia: A review in light of *DSM-III-R. Journal of Autism and Developmental Disorders, 22,* 601–624.

Wing, L. (1981). Asperger's Syndrome: A clinical account. *Psychological Medicine, 11,* 115–129.

Wing, L. (1986). Clarification on Asperger's Syndrome [Letter]. *Journal of Autism and Developmental Disorders, 16*(4), 513–515.

Wing, L. (1991). The relationship between Asperger's Syndrome and Kanner's autism. In U. Frith (Ed.), *Autism and Asperger Syndrome* (pp. 93–121). Cambridge, England: Cambridge University Press.

Wing, L., & Gould, J. (1979). Severe impairments of social interaction and associated abnormalities in children: Epidemiology and classification. *Journal of Autism and Childhood Schizophrenia, 9,* 11–29.

Wolff, S. (1991). "Schizoid" personality in childhood and adult life: 3. The childhood picture. *British Journal of Psychiatry, 159,* 629–635.

Wolff, S. (1995). *Loners: The life path of unusual children.* London: Routledge.

Wolff, S., & Barlow, A. (1979). Schizoid personality in childhood: A comparative study of schizoid, autistic and normal children. *Journal of Child Psychology and Psychiatry, 20,* 19–46.

Wolff, S., & Chick, J. (1980). Schizoid personality in childhood: A controlled follow-up study. *Psychological Medicine, 10,* 85–100.

Wolff, S., Townsend, R., McGuire, R.J., & Weeks, D.J. (1991). "Schizoid" personality in childhood and adult life: 2. Adult adjustment and the continuity with Schizotypal Personality Disorder. *British Journal of Psychiatry, 159,* 620–629, 634–635.

World Health Organization. (1993). *International classification of mental and behavioural disorders—diagnostic criteria for research* (10th ed., pp. 124–125). Geneva: Author.

Zilbovicius, M., Garreau, B., Samson, Y., Remy, P., Barthélémy, C., Syrota, A., & Lelord, G. (1995). Delayed maturation of the frontal cortex in childhood autism. *American Journal of Psychiatry, 152*(2), 248–252.

Pervasive Developmental Disorder Not Otherwise Specified

KENNETH E. TOWBIN

Pervasive Developmental Disorder Not Otherwise Specified (PDD-NOS) is a diagnostic term derived from a conceptual model of pervasive developmental disorders (PDDs). This model regards all the conditions under PDD, including autism, as a set of related maladies that exist along a hypothetical spectrum bounded by severe autism at one end and by a condition of being nearly normal, save for a distinctive lifelong social or empathetic "blindness," at the other (Wing, 1992). Although PDD-NOS is a single diagnosis in *DSM-IV* (American Psychiatric Association, 1994) it is not a uniform clinical entity. The conditions encompassed by PDD-NOS do not share a specific etiology, like Rett's Syndrome, nor a particular phenomenologic pattern, like autism or Childhood Disintegrative Disorder. However, the majority of the maladies on the PDD spectrum is subsumed under the concept of PDD-NOS.

Within this chapter, PDD will be the term for the full spectrum of the pervasive developmental disorders: Autistic Disorder, PDD-NOS, Asperger's Syndrome, and so on. PDD-NOS will be used as a diagnostic convention to indicate individuals with pervasive developmental disorders whose clinical features are not better described by one of the several operationally defined categorical diagnoses of *DSM-IV* or *ICD-10* (World Health Organization, 1993). These individuals have disturbances in many areas of functioning (social, linguistic, emotional, behavioral, cognitive). Symptoms appear during the first years of life but do not definitively earn a diagnosis of Autistic Disorder, Asperger's Syndrome, Rett's Syndrome, or other specific conditions. In certain respects, individuals with PDD-NOS occupy a domain of developmental psychopathology that is closely related to autism and these other conditions, but deserves further specification and research.

This chapter offers a comprehensive overview of PDD-NOS as a conceptual and clinical entity. It begins by laying out a conceptual view and reviewing the representation of PDD-NOS in *DSM-IV* and *ICD-10*. Because PDD-NOS is synonymous with "not anything else in PDD," it cannot be understood without competent knowledge of the alternative diagnoses and conditions defined under PDD. For this reason, a detailed account of the differential diagnoses is included. Explication of descriptive elements such as epidemiology, etiology, and natural history follows, and the chapter ends with a condensed discussion of treatments and future research directions.

NOSOLOGY: *DSM-III, DSM-III-R, AND ICD-10*

The most recent official diagnostic schemes, *DSM-IV* and *ICD-10*, introduced several new subgroups to represent individuals who previously would have been diagnosed PDD-NOS under *DSM-III-R* or *ICD-9*. Each of these subgroups now has a separate designation: Asperger's Syndrome (*ICD-10;* Asperger's Disorder in *DSM-IV*), Atypical Autism *(ICD-10)*, Other Childhood Disintegrative Disorder (*ICD-10;* Childhood Disintegrative Disorder in *DSM-IV*), and Rett's Syndrome (*ICD-10;* Rett's Disorder in *DSM-IV*).

The diagnostic terms and guidelines that encompass the concept of PDD-NOS are not identical in *DSM-IV* and *ICD-10*. *ICD-10* includes a category of PDD-unspecified (F84.9). However, the *ICD-10* clinical guidelines and descriptions reveal that a more precise analog to *DSM-IV*'s PDD-NOS is a combination of PDD-unspecified and Atypical Autism (F84.1). *DSM-IV* states literally that "atypical autism" is included in *DSM-IV*'s meaning of PDD-NOS (p. 78), and that prototypical individuals in this category fail to meet age criteria or do not display key elements of autism or the other subtypes of PDD; or, when these other elements are present, they are not always of sufficient severity to meet the full criteria for autism or the other subtypes of PDD.

The guidelines for PDD-NOS in *DSM-IV* are too vague to be readily translated into clear definitions that have explicit operational criteria. PDD-NOS does not evidence positive criteria that depend on the presence of a sign or symptom. As a subgroup of PDD, PDD-NOS represents a heterogeneous collection of disorders that share core features of delays in social relatedness and/or deficits in the capacity to reciprocate and understand social interactions, but these can be much milder than those seen in autism. Like other individuals with PDD, persons with PDD-NOS *can* have restricted interests, limitations in imaginative play, and stereotyped activities but these may be quite mild—or absent. In contrast with other PDDs, PDD-NOS *may not* exhibit deficits in language. However, by definition, these individuals differ in important ways from those who would be considered autistic, or those who meet criteria for Rett's Syndrome, Asperger's Syndrome, or Childhood Disintegrative Disorder.

CONCEPTUAL BACKGROUND

Although the terminology is new, the concept of an intermediate or mild PDD condition is not. Individuals with autistic-like developmental disorders have been recognized for over 100 years (Itard, 1962). After Leo Kanner identified the features of autism (1943), a series of reports appeared describing individuals who were nearly but not quite like those characterized by Kanner (Bender, 1946; Despert,

1986). The individuals in these new reports all exhibited, in early life, profound deficits in relating; yet they displayed other features that were different from autism.

Wing and co-workers introduced the concept of a continuum of autistic conditions that could be differentiated by the degree of impairment in social reciprocity (Wing & Gould, 1979). In their view, the most severe end of the spectrum was represented by individuals who were aloof and resisted interactions with others. Next, in order of decreasing severity, were individuals who were passive but accepting of interactions if forced to participate. The least severe group was "active but odd"; they approached others but behaved in idiosyncratic and egocentric ways. During childhood, individuals in this group had displayed a failure to comprehend ordinary social rules, but as adults their deficits were relatively mild and more subtle. Investigation suggested that a longer time and repeated interaction might be needed to recognize their deficits (Wing & Gould, 1979). Further differentiation of this social continuum could be accomplished by considering language deficits, which could also be stratified by severity.

However accurate Wing's vision may have been, the continuum models it advanced cannot be accommodated to fit standard diagnostic systems. Systems of nosology demand that conditions be compiled into relatively homogeneous phenotypic subgroups. A consequence of this subtyping is that important details and data are sacrificed when one imposes categorical diagnostic boundaries on dimensional characteristics. Defining a boundary in the spectrum of a dimensional variable is a Procrustean Bed. It risks producing, on the one hand, blurry definitions that cause confusion or, on the other, false dichotomies that canonize nonexistent differences. Nevertheless, as Cantwell and Rutter (1994) have discussed, categorical systems offer the benefits of efficient communication and conceptual clarity, and they may facilitate treatment. In addition, historically, science has condoned imposing categorical distinctions on known dimensional variables. Two examples are: (a) dividing the electromagnetic wave spectrum into colors, and (b) dividing dimensional characteristics like IQ into subdivisions such as mild, moderate, and severe mental retardation (Cantwell & Rutter, 1994). Yet nowhere is there more uncertainty about the validity and significance of the distinctions among the current various subtypes than in the spectrum of PDD.

It follows logically that when the diagnosis of PDD-NOS is extended clinically, it generates ambiguity and confusion. The label alone cannot convey where a patient's condition is positioned on this extensive spectrum. *DSM-IV* reflects this nebulous quality by, on the one hand, designating PDD-NOS as a diagnosis, but, on the other, offering only a description without specific operationalized criteria. The diagnosis PDD-NOS is a sort of tautology. The *DSM* description restates a logically fundamental criterion of any valid diagnosis—a collection of disorders that are not other disorders (Rutter & Gould, 1985). Were this criterion not met, the resulting category would be unnecessary and redundant. The term PDD-NOS accurately conveys the paradox of this chapter; in describing PDD-NOS, one attempts to specify the common characteristics of a group of disorders that are "not otherwise specified."

Despite its inherent *diagnostic* vagueness, the concept underlying PDD-NOS is indispensable. It encompasses relatively unique points on the spectrum of PDD and conveys important clinical information about persons who are so diagnosed. PDD-NOS exists for a collection of conditions that (a) share important features resembling but distinguishable from other PDD subtypes or (b) cannot be accommodated by a complete diagnostic appraisal that relies on these other diagnoses. There may be a relationship between this one important group of disorders and the other more defined PDD subtypes. Whether the relationship is valid must be confirmed by future longitudinal, pathophysiologic, cognitive, etiologic, and genetic studies. One way to understand PDD-NOS is as a set of conditions that are "works in progress" and need further investigation. Without a definition and nosological location, however, the nature of any relationship among these disorders cannot be explored.

The three major developmental domains that define impairment in autistic conditions are largely independent of one another and can be understood as continuous variables. These complex features have thwarted attempts to impose demarcations within the spectrum of PDD conditions. Diagnostic guidelines for any of the PDD diagnoses do not declare how much impairment or competence is necessary in each domain in order to justify one or another PDD diagnosis. Imagine a multiaxial system for PDD in which each component—social relatedness, language development, and circumscribed interests/resistance to change—had its own independent quantitative axis. What might result? This mental experiment allows a view of the conditions under which PDD-NOS might be applied in preference to another PDD diagnosis. However, these conditions can hardly be understood as a set of diagnostic rules. Table 6.1 suggests the diagnoses that might result from mapping these axes on one another. For graphic simplicity, the table dichotomizes (as absent or present) language impairment; a more faithful depiction would present this impairment as a continuous variable.

Close scrutiny reveals that PDD-NOS has multiple meanings, each of which is supported by official diagnostic guidelines. Because of its four different definitions or concepts, PDD-NOS is employed under the following different circumstances:

1. PDD-NOS is not actually a clinical entity; it is a label to use under unfavorable diagnostic conditions. For some authorities, PDD-NOS is a "default" diagnosis to be used when information is inadequate or as a last resort when the developmental history is unreliable. In this view, PDD-NOS may be a temporary or deferral category that should be offered when the absence of sources prevents the assertion of a more specific PDD diagnosis or until the clinician can acquire a complete history.

2. Within the continuum of PDD, PDD-NOS is a collection of entities that reside on the border of relatively more normal functioning. PDD-NOS describes conditions in which the impairment in one of the three core features is quite mild or perhaps is absent. In this view, PDD-NOS is a group of disorders in which, according to stringent criteria, the impairment in one or more domains is too moderate to permit assignment

TABLE 6.1   Diagnostic Categories Resulting from the Mapping of Three Developmental Axes: Relatedness, Language, and Circumscribed Interests/Resistance to Change

	No Impairment or Almost No Impairment in Social Interaction		Mild to Moderate Impairment in Social Interaction		Moderate to Severe Impairment in Social Interaction	
	Developmental Language Disorder		Developmental Language Disorder		Developmental Language Disorder	
	Absent	Present	Absent	Present	Absent	Present
No evidence of CI/RRSB[a]	Normal	DLD[b]	"Normal" or "Schizoid"	PDD-NOS	Asperger's Syndrome	PDD-NOS
Mild to moderate CI/RRSB[a]	"Normal," "odd," "rigid"	DLD[b] and possibly SPD[c]	Asperger's Syndrome	PDD-NOS	Asperger's Syndrome	Autism
Moderate to severe CI/RRSB[a,d]	possible OCD or OCPD[e]	DLD[b] possibly SPD[c]	PDD-NOS	PDD-NOS	PDD-NOS	Autism

[a] Circumscribed interests/restrictive, repetitive, and stereotyped behaviors (includes resistance to change).
[b] Developmental Language Disorder (*DSM-IV*), including expressive, receptive, and mixed subtypes.
[c] Semantic-Pragmatic Disorder.
[d] Circumscribed interests, adherence to rituals, or restrictive, repetitive, and stereotyped behaviors of such severity as to result in impairment of daily living/functioning, adaptive behavior, or curiosity about the environment.
[e] Obsessive-Compulsive Disorder or Obsessive-Compulsive Personality Disorder.

of the severe diagnosis, yet the severity of impairment and the limitations are too great to warrant the condition's being considered a mere variant of normality. This view is congruent with *ICD-10*'s Atypical Autism, and it advances the idea that PDD-NOS is "mild" autism. The boundaries separating high-functioning autism (HFA) and this kind of PDD-NOS are exceedingly uncertain. This definition of PDD-NOS has evolved from an acceptance of an autistic spectrum of disorders, and it relies on factors such as prognosis and range of disturbance to define its points.

3. PDD-NOS is the diagnosis for individuals who have a late age of onset of autistic symptoms. Rutter and Schopler (1988) suggest that the positive criteria for autism include the three core features plus early age of onset. Seen this way, PDD-NOS is the diagnosis when this fourth feature is absent (as in item 2 above). Volkmar and coworkers (Volkmar, Steir, & Cohen, 1985) have described how age of onset and age of clinical diagnosis may be widely discrepant. However, there have been rare reports of individuals in whom onset occurs after age 30 months and who do not meet the criteria for Childhood Disintegrative Disorder (Volkmar & Cohen, 1989).

4. The heterogeneous clinical entities that comprise PDD-NOS share two critical features: (a) early onset of symptoms and (b) impairment in relatedness. Such a definition implies that the "autistic spectrum," which theoretically spans a range from autism to normality, actually may exhibit discontinuities. It serves to focus on the existence of conditions other than autism in which there is prominent impairment of relatedness. However, these other conditions display additional symptoms that are not part of the spectrum of autism per se— for example, impairments in understanding affect, in affective modulation, and in patterns of attachment. From this perspective, PDD-NOS is the best placement within the current official nosology for conditions in which there are impairments in both reciprocal social interactions and the capacity to develop empathy. These impairments are related to PDD but, with further study, may be determined to be clinically distinct from autism (Volkmar & Cohen, 1988).

This last view proposes that other disorders of relatedness exist that are not well characterized currently and might be temporarily placed under PDD-NOS. The evolution of Asperger's Syndrome (AS) as a clinical diagnosis illustrates this idea. The relationship between AS and autism remains uncertain; some believe AS is a variant of autism (Frith, 1991) or of HFA (Szatmari, Bartolucci, Bremner, Bond, & Rich, 1989); others, Asperger among them (1979), assert that AS is a condition quite separate from autism. PDD-NOS may be the best temporary location for disorders that need to be characterized more fully but may not be readily located on a spectrum from autistic to normal. Some candidates for inclusion in this perspective are: schizoid disorders in children (Wolff & Chick, 1980), Multiple Complex Developmental Disorder (Towbin, Dykens, Pearson, & Cohen, 1993; Cohen, Paul, & Volkmar, 1986), Multiple Developmental Impairment (MDI; McKenna et al., 1994), Semantic-Pragmatic Disorder (Bishop, 1989), some infant regulatory disorders, and some reactive attachment disorders (Richters & Volkmar, 1994).

DIFFERENTIAL DIAGNOSIS

Any discussion of PDD-NOS would be incomplete if it did not convey the complexity of the diagnosis. Because PDD-NOS is defined in relation to other PDD subtypes, it is dependent on their definitions and boundaries. Ordinarily, PDD-NOS implies that the clinical presentation is "nearly" some other PDD subtype, although invariably this is not the case. Therefore, beginning students must "back into" PDD-NOS by looking toward the disorders with which it shares a boundary.

This section begins with general comments about complications in the diagnostic process related to PDD-NOS. Subsequently, there is a discussion of the relationship between PDD-NOS and three other major categories of disorders: (a) specific diagnoses within PDD, (b) other developmental disorders outside PDD, and (c) other psychiatric disorders that may arise in infancy and early childhood.

Table 6.2 lists diagnoses that may overlap or be confused with PDD-NOS. Confusion usually arises because the patient's presentation

TABLE 6.2   Conditions to Be Considered in the Differential Diagnosis of PDD-NOS

A. Conditions within PDD
  Asperger's Syndrome
  Autism
  Childhood Disintegrative Disorder

B. Other Developmental Disorders
  Developmental Language Disorder
  Mental Retardation
  Semantic-Pragmatic Disorder

C. Disorders That May Have Onset in Early Childhood
  Attention Deficit Hyperactivity Disorder
  Avoidant Disorder
  Generalized Anxiety Disorder (childhood type)
  Obsessive-Compulsive Disorder
  Overanxious Disorder
  Reactive Attachment Disorder
  Schizophrenia (childhood onset type)
  Schizotypal Disorder
  Social Phobia

shares one or more features of impairment in socialization, language, and restricted patterns of behavior. PDD-NOS may be overlooked when emphasis on one prominent feature eclipses a more complete assessment—one that would consider current and historical features in *each* of these three domains.

The vagueness of PDD-NOS is most evident when clinicians must devine the boundaries that separate it from other PDD spectrum conditions and from a number of other syndromes. One source of uncertainty is that the domains of impairment that define autism—impairment in social relatedness; communication disorder and/or restriction in imaginative play; and repetitive patterns of behavior or restricted interests—are highly qualitative and lack precise definitions. Consequently, each domain introduces a measure of uncertainty into any deliberation. The experience, training, and opinions of the diagnostician influence whether an individual with an atypical presentation will be declared to have PDD-NOS, autism, or some other condition.

Even if the domains could be defined clearly, there would be uncertainty over how much (or how little) impairment is consistent with the diagnosis of PDD-NOS. Attempts to clarify the boundaries for PDD-NOS, other PDDs, and comorbid or related conditions have not proved successful. In the diagnosis of mental retardation clinicians face a similar task. Yet their relatively arbitrary definitions have been established by consensus to determine the "cut points" for borderline, mild, moderate, and severe retardation. Furthermore, there is a consensus on what instruments are appropriate for making these categorical determinations. Autism research has not yet reached the point where one can define the instruments or the performance criteria. Until our knowledge and capacity for reliable measurement permit a better definition of how high-functioning or low-functioning an individual can be in each of these three domains and still warrant the diagnosis of PDD-NOS, the boundaries will be vague. The implications of how much these differences in functioning contribute to the prognosis or treatment also have yet to be spelled out. As long as this uncertainty persists, cautious consideration of the differential diagnosis will be critical to every evaluation.

PDD-NOS and Other PDD Entities

Asperger's Syndrome (AS)

Current criteria offer little direction or guidance for separating PDD-NOS from AS. Past editions of diagnostic guidelines did not force clinicians to make distinctions between PDD-NOS and AS or to worry much about whether a patient might have one or the other. The creation of specific diagnoses for AS and PDD-NOS (in *ICD-10* and *DSM-IV*) has made it incumbent on practitioners (and researchers) to distinguish and choose among these diagnoses, although the choice usually presents a clinical challenge. Furthermore, it is not yet clear which features, if any, represent valid differences among these entities, and no evidence points to different etiologies or identifies features that influence prognosis, treatment, or genetic recurrence risk. There is some evidence to suggest that social dysfunction of the type shown in AS may be more common in first-degree relatives of autistic individuals, although the criteria

employed in these studies did not make specific diagnoses of PDD-NOS or AS (Piven et al., 1990). However, two features of the natural history of AS may be distinctive: (a) language development and (b) motor coordination (Klin, 1994). Individuals with PDD-NOS would be expected to show delays in language development and may or may not be clumsy; those with AS, it has been proposed, show quite normal language development, normal adaptive functioning aside from socialization, and awkwardness in motor tasks (see Table 6.2). There is reason to question whether motor clumsiness reliably discriminates between these two conditions (Manjiviona & Prior, 1995). Further studies will clarify the relevance of motor clumsiness; for many experts, AS is still considered a PDD-NOS variant (Szatmari, Tuff, Finlayson, & Bartolucci, 1990). *ICD-10* declares that the validity of the AS construct remains in doubt *(ICD-10)*. Furthermore, there are disagreements about whether "language development" can be termed "normal" in AS when pragmatic functions, prosody, or intonations are disturbed. A great deal must be learned about AS before its unique features can be specified. The ambivalence over whether AS and PDD-NOS are separate can be seen in the decisions by the Task Force on Nomenclature for *DSM-IV*. A new and unique category has been created for AS. In initial printings of *DSM-IV*, AS and PDD-NOS share the same code; this will change as *ICD-10* becomes official.

Autism

Determining whether an individual has autism or PDD-NOS can be most perplexing—and only partly because of the need to attempt to subdivide a continuum into discrete parts. The absence of measurable standards and of specific cut points that define the levels of impairment within domains is particularly problematic. The confusion over which diagnosis is most appropriate may be greatest for individuals nearest the border: high-functioning autistic individuals and low-functioning PDD-NOS individuals. This was borne out in the *DSM-IV* field trials (Volkmar et al., 1994), where 977 patients who were thought to have autism, or for whom autism was a reasonable question in the differential diagnosis, were reviewed by 125 raters half of whom had considerable experience in the diagnosis of autism. The field trial results suggested that clinicians could make reliable distinctions among autism, AS, and PDD-NOS. However, for PDD-NOS more than the other PDD subtypes, there was greater disagreement about how individuals would be diagnosed under the different diagnostic systems. Within the group of individuals given PDD-NOS diagnoses, 71 of 153 cases (46%) met criteria for autism in one of the three diagnostic systems *(DSM-III, DSM-III-R, ICD-10)* but were beneath criteria for autism in one or more of the other systems. In only 55 of 153 cases (36%) was there agreement that individuals did not meet criteria for autism according to any of the diagnostic schemes.

Uncertainty over the definition and quantification of relatedness compounds this difficulty. Clinicians frequently must face the dilemma of how much relatedness is compatible with autism or PDD-NOS. Experienced clinicians know that autistic children may enjoy cuddling, seek comfort when injured, or make eye contact, but may also exhibit features of aberrant and delayed social interaction. However, less knowledgeable clinicians may hold to the idea that certain behaviors—such as proximity seeking of caretakers during times of stress, ability to follow simple commands, or eye contact—preclude the diagnosis of autism. How much relatedness or reciprocity is necessary to place one into PDD-NOS or out of autism remains obscure.

Another source of diagnostic confusion arises as individuals with autism grow up and gain skills in domains that previously were severely delayed. In some clinicians' views, improvement itself is an argument against a diagnosis of autism. However, there is growing consensus that autistic individuals do improve and can develop greater skill, including in social domains. Consequently, the clinician might be uncertain about whether to diagnose Autistic Disorder (high functioning) or PDD-NOS when confronted by a child who displays many social skills now but had previously exhibited profound typical delays and deviance. If the developmental history is

not obtainable or is unreliable, the likelihood that such an individual would be diagnosed PDD-NOS rises dramatically. However, the diagnostic guides are inconsistent in the handling of improvement in developmental conditions. When there is no longer any impairment, it is reasonable to consider the condition resolved. However, when impairment persists, though with less severity, the usual convention is to consider the condition in partial remission or improved, rather than to depart from the previous diagnosis altogether.

Childhood Disintegrative Disorder

Childhood Disintegrative Disorder (CDD) is a rare condition (Volkmar, 1992; Volkmar et al., 1994; Volkmar & Rutter, 1995). Typically, as in Heller's original descriptions (Heller, 1908), patients with CDD have a 3- to 4-year history of early unequivocally normal development followed by intellectual decline (particularly in language skill) that leads to profound impairment, including social impairment and unrelatedness. This sequence is distinctive in comparison with PDD-NOS and is not likely to lead to confusion. However, such a clear-cut history is rare; a decline in function between 18 and 24 months occurs for many autistic and PDD-NOS patients who also display a plateau or mild decline in social development (Volkmar, Steir, & Cohen, 1985). Consequently, a history of onset after 30 months, language delay, and milder declines in function points many clinicians toward PDD-NOS rather than CDD (Volkmar et al., 1994). However, such a history should raise the possibility of CDD, including, among others, Rett's Syndrome, Landau-Kleffner Syndrome, inborn errors of metabolism, glycogen storage disorders, and mitochondrial disorders. Landau-Kleffner Syndrome (acquired aphasia; Beaumanoir, 1992) has recently received particularly wide attention (Volkmar, personal communication, 1995). Concomitant medical conditions should not preclude the diagnosis of autism or PDD-NOS; when both are displayed, the medical and PDD diagnoses should be submitted. There are no phenomenologic guidelines that specifically distinguish between PDD-NOS and CDD or spell out the conditions under which a decline in function warrants diagnosing one rather than the other. In practice, patients with later onset routinely receive diagnosis of PDD-NOS in preference to CDD, although, in the *DSM-IV* field trials, a period of normal development up to age 2 years, current mutism, and placement in residential facilities were salient features that led clinicians to diagnose CDD (Volkmar et al., 1994; Volkmar & Rutter, 1995).

PDD-NOS and Other Developmental Disorders

Developmental Language Disorders

Developmental language disorders and Semantic-Pragmatic Disorder are conditions that may be misrepresented as the primary malady of individuals with PDD-NOS. As defined by Rapin and Allen (1983), Semantic-Pragmatic Disorder is a condition in which complex language is intact, but use, content, and understanding of language are impaired. It is uncertain whether Semantic-Pragmatic Disorder represents a separate condition or is synonymous with PDD-NOS (Bishop, 1989). It is likely that other conditions described by neuropsychology or speech and language pathology, such as auditory processing disorders, overlap with PDD.

The primary source of confusion regarding these disorders is rooted in reliance on the separate, parallel, autonomous diagnostic systems used by communication pathology or child and adolescent psychiatry. There is a relative absence of correspondence between speech and language diagnoses and those employed by child and adolescent psychiatrists. Speech and language pathologists who are unfamiliar with recent research and diagnostic developments in autism may be relying on outdated criteria or information. Because they do not use psychiatric diagnoses, they may have no requirement to remain current on these matters. Instead of considering autism, they substitute conditions that are more explicitly detailed in communication pathology but may have only a very weak correspondence with medical nosology. Conversely, psychiatric nosology has collapsed the wide variety of expressive and receptive language problems into three mutually exclusive categories. Thus, communication pathologists, who are capable of producing assessments that exhibit considerable breadth and precision, find themselves held to a system that dilutes their observations and conclusions. The characterization of communication disorders in current psychiatric nosology does not reflect the precision of modern speech pathology, and most speech and language experts shun it.

In addition, the diagnostic objectives of the two fields are dissimilar. The conclusions offered by communication pathology focus predominantly on elements of language and seek to provide a clear description of that "piece" of the disorder. Psychiatry aims to furnish a comprehensive, parsimonious diagnostic formulation for the entire panoply of symptoms. For example, a communication pathologist may recognize syntactic, prosodic, and linguistic impairments but may view information regarding circumscribed interests or restricted patterns of behavior to be outside his or her discipline. Should this occur, the PDD-NOS patient will be viewed as suffering from a language disorder—a description that is accurate as far as it goes, but insufficient as a complete diagnostic formulation.

Mental Retardation

Young children who exhibit mental retardation, language delay or impairment, and delays in social reciprocity occupy a position at another border with PDD-NOS. There is general agreement that language delays, deficient social skills, and stereotyped mannerisms are very common among retarded persons (Fraser & Rao, 1991; Bregman, 1991), and that abilities decline as IQ level descends. When social delays are severe, autism becomes a serious consideration; but the presence of milder impairments in social reciprocity or language, or the absence of imaginative play, creates a dilemma. When are these delays or deficits consonant with mental retardation, and when is an additional diagnosis of PDD-NOS appropriate? The impairments must be considered in the context of the child's general level of retardation. Even when standardized screening devices such as the Vineland Adaptive Behavior Scales are employed (Volkmar et al., 1993), they provide little help in determining whether delays are commensurate with the level of retardation or represent manifestations of a developmental disorder. Standardized measures alone cannot answer the question of how much lower social performance must be, compared to communication or daily living skills, in order for PDD-NOS to be a legitimate consideration. There is considerable uncertainty over how a discrepancy in specific domains of socialization, language, and stereotyped interests compares with the general level of retardation among retarded individuals with PDD-NOS. The uncertainty surfaces in studies of prevalence rates of PDD among retarded persons. Some researchers have reported that as many as 30% of mentally retarded individuals also have PDD spectrum disorders (Gillberg, Persson, Grufman, & Themner, 1986). This estimate is to be contrasted with the report of 5 to 10 per 10,000 persons among the general population. Considerable work is necessary to understand the distribution of these features among the general population of retarded persons. We still do not know how much impairment must be exhibited before a retarded or nonretarded patient is appropriately considered to have PDD-NOS.

PDD-NOS and Conditions with Possible Childhood Onset

Attention Deficit Hyperactivity Disorder

It may not be intuitive that Attention Deficit Hyperactivity Disorder (ADHD) and PDD-NOS would be confused with one another. The typical child with ADHD does not display extensive problems in relating to others, although impulsivity can discourage social relationships and make a child appear unempathic (Whalen & Henker, 1992). Moreover, a highly distractible child can seem to be in his or her "own world" and unrelated. Consequently, it is not unusual for children with higher-functioning PDD to be diagnosed with ADHD exclusively. Often, a careful developmental history is not obtained when a child is a candidate for a PDD-NOS diagnosis. The child may be described as "the worst case ever" of ADHD, or as having "treatment refractory ADHD" or "schizotypal ADHD." Even greater puzzlement arises when trying to distinguish between PDD spectrum disorders and ADHD in individuals who have either moderate to severe mental retardation (MR) or developmental language disorder. When hyperactivity is severe (as in *ICD-10* hyperkinesis), diagnosis can be very difficult. The uncertainty stems from (a) impairment of and delays in social relationships, which individuals with ADHD plus MR or developmental language disorders may display, and (b) the relatively high frequency of symptoms of impulsivity or inattention in higher-functioning individuals with PDD. Under *DSM-III-R* and *DSM-IV,* hierarchical rules prevent the diagnosis of both conditions. Autism or PDD-NOS is understood to be primary, and symptoms of inattention or distractibility are viewed in the context of the larger syndrome. In the absence of a detailed developmental history, ADHD can be a common preliminary diagnosis or a presenting complaint.

Obsessive-Compulsive Disorder

A nebulous line separates obsessions and compulsions from stereotyped movements and restricted interests. When developmentally delayed or retarded persons display habits and repetitive behaviors, the dividing line can become very vague. In individuals who possess some language but whose developmental age is very low, one cannot expect a capacity for self-reflection or an ability to formulate concepts of anxiety, senselessness, or resistance to performing the acts. Thus, some clinicians will diagnose comorbid Obsessive-Compulsive Disorder (OCD) and mental retardation without eliciting information about early development of relatedness, language, unusual interests, and patterns of behavior. The confusion can be further compounded when reverse logic is injected—for example, by citing a favorable response to serotonin reuptake inhibitors as justification of the diagnosis of OCD. Obviously, retarded persons can develop habit disorders or OCD. However, the most complete diagnostic explanation may emerge from opening a wider scope of inquiry that encompasses a detailed developmental history (including language development) and antecedents of the phenomena that are the current objects of attention.

Overanxious Disorder

The *DSM-III-R* definition of Overanxious Disorder was ambiguous and of uncertain validity

(Werry, 1991). It was merged with Generalized Anxiety Disorder in *DSM-IV* (APA, 1994). Excessive concern about past events, a need for constant reassurance, feelings of tension or an inability to relax, and self-consciousness may be vaguely formulated as Overanxious Disorder in children with PDD-NOS. Within the symptoms of Generalized Anxiety Disorder is constant worry, which can result in sleep disturbance or excessive fatigue. Higher-functioning individuals with PDD-NOS will commonly exhibit these symptoms, but neither Overanxious Disorder nor Generalized Anxiety Disorder calls attention to the primary impairments in social functioning and the restricted interests that often prove so disabling to these individuals. Nor do these diagnoses underscore the causal role of these deficits in relation to the anxiety symptoms. Underscoring this primacy of PDD symptoms in persons with anxiety, hierarchical rules in *DSM-IV* prohibit the diagnosis of Generalized Anxiety Disorder in persons with PDD conditions. Nevertheless, these anxiety disorders occasionally surface as presenting diagnoses in children with lifelong social delays, restricted patterns of behavior, and narrow interests.

Personality Disorders and Schizophrenia

Several personality disorder diagnoses may be ascribed to persons with developmental histories and childhood-onset features of PDD-NOS. When older children, adolescents, or young adults with PDD-NOS exhibit avoidance of social contact but possess more developed language skills, they might be viewed as having either schizoid or avoidant personality disorder. Some practitioners have argued that the desire for social relationships precludes the diagnosis, but it has been recognized that many higher-functioning AS and PDD-NOS individuals do wish for social contact and are aware that they are different from others—an awareness that can be a source of distress to individuals with PDD-NOS (Wing, 1992). Their inability to enter social situations successfully can make them appear shy, and their need for considerable reassurance before venturing into novel social situations suggests avoidant personality disorder. Somewhat lower-functioning individuals with PDD-NOS may harbor more wariness or prefer to avoid social interaction altogether. This more aloof group resembles the schizoid children described by Wolff and Chick (1980). When language disorder, featuring poor pragmatic behaviors and unrelated or circumstantial utterances, is also displayed, these individuals may be erroneously considered to have schizotypal personality disorder (or even schizophrenia, when circumscribed interests and preoccupations are prominent; Rumsey, Andreasen, & Rapoport, 1986). Tantum (1988b) advocates making AS a subtype of schizoid personality disorder. When a reliable developmental history cannot be obtained, clinicians might be led to estimate that an adolescent or young adult with these features has a personality disorder.

Experience in diagnosing autistic spectrum disorders may be important in differentiating between developmental disorders and personality disorders. Very early onset, enduring impairments in imaginary play and socialization, and restricted patterns of behavior throughout childhood, would point toward developmental disorder diagnoses. A present, assistance in interpreting developmental histories is lacking because there are too few investigations of the developmental history of adults with unequivocal avoidant, schizoid, or schizotypal personality disorder. Consequently, we do not know whether features characteristic of PDD are displayed during childhood or adolescence in persons with avoidant, schizoid, or schizotypal personality disorder. One study suggests that differences do exist. According to Tantum (1988b), elevated measures of abnormal nonverbal expression were correlated with early developmental disturbances, whereas schizoid features were not. Features of developmental delays and abnormal nonverbal expression appeared to be clustered together, but schizotypal features did not correlate with developmental abnormalities. Watkins, Asarnow, and Tanguay (1988) reviewed 18 children diagnosed with schizophrenia and reported that 7 subjects (39%) had symptoms that would have been sufficient to meet the criteria for autism before 30 months. It is unclear whether other typical features in the childhood course or natural history of schizoid, schizotypal, or avoidant personality disorder might permit differentiation of these conditions from PDD-NOS. *DSM-IV* points to the complexity of differentiating HFA and AS from schizoid personality disorder *(DSM-IV)*.

Consider a hypothetical individual who presents with mild to moderate impairment in socialization and a history of significant progress in social reciprocity following profound delays in early childhood. This person's developmental achievements introduce a diagnostic problem resembling the one for autistic persons (see above). The clinician must decide whether this person suffers from one or more of these personality disorders or from PDD-NOS. Many clinicians, given such a history, will favor a personality diagnosis. If a history of language development, restricted patterns of behavior, and narrow interests is not pursued, the assessment may favor a personality disorder diagnosis. However, if the decision to reject the diagnosis of PDD-NOS or autism is based on gains in language, social skill, or relatedness, this seems inappropriate.

Discarding the diagnosis of PDD-NOS because of improvements promotes two perplexing concepts. The first concept is that the patient has recovered from PDD-NOS and has gone on to develop a new, separate disorder affecting personality. The idea of complete recovery in PDD-NOS is very questionable, but it is more tenuous when the same symptoms, present continuously, are being viewed as resulting from one disorder in childhood and a different disorder in later years. The second concept is that the individual has displayed, throughout his or her lifetime, a personality disorder with features of language delay, social impairment, and restricted interests or patterns of behavior. If this is factual, then these personality disorders must be hierarchically related to, continuous with, or a muted forme fruste of PDD-NOS or autism. Empirically, longitudinal studies of these personality disorders fail to confirm this formulation (Kolvin, 1971). Conceptually, this view takes a regressive step by reverting to the pre-Kolvin era in which the disorders in the PDD spectrum and the schizophrenia spectrum, and conditions exhibiting social isolation, were all presumed to be related and, nosologically, warranted being "lumped" into a single entity. Wolff and Chick (1980) have favored a view

that autism and schizophrenia are on a continuum, although this dismisses findings suggesting that the two are distinct (Kolvin, 1971; Volkmar & Cohen, 1991; Werry, 1992).

Reactive Attachment Disorder

When a child has a verified history of psychosocial adversity (termed "pathogenic care" in *DSM-IV*) during his or her first years of life, and displays disinhibited or inhibited responses in social situations, he or she may receive a diagnosis of Reactive Attachment Disorder (RAD). Closer scrutiny reveals that many children who undergo profound neglect or abuse subsequently show vigorous physical and emotional improvement when they receive compassionate and nurturing care. Others in this group show a relatively protracted or intractable course and present a clinical conundrum. Because the social dysfunction of persistent RAD may resemble PDD-NOS, it may be difficult to decide which is the more suitable diagnosis. As suggested by Richters and Volkmar (1994), there are several reasons to reflect carefully on the relationship between PDD-NOS and RAD. The first reason is clinical. For children who receive profoundly detrimental parenting in early life, it is most difficult to obtain a reliable developmental history or to conclude whether the care they received has been pathogenic. In the absence of an accurate and reliable developmental history, clinicians prematurely or hastily may decide that the symptom picture is exclusively the result of adversity during the child's early years. The key consequence of a hasty decision is that the plan for educating such a child and the expectations of his or her care providers are very different when RAD, as opposed to PDD-NOS, is the working diagnosis. Second, although most abused and neglected children are not developmentally delayed, a developmentally delayed child is more likely to receive abuse. Children who have impairments in language and relatedness and who display inflexibility in patterns and routines are more likely to be mistreated or neglected by an angry parent who does not understand why the child is so exhausting and unrewarding. An aloof child who does not become calm or go to sleep when held, or who does not eat well, comply with rules and limits, or reciprocate a smile or greeting, may further inflame abusive or neglectful handling. An uninformed parent may believe the child is oppositional or willfully disobedient. Thus, a child's developmental delays could aggravate and incite, as readily as emanate from, profound mistreatment. Third, RAD may require reconsideration in light of a broader concept of PDD. The biological determinants of protracted RAD are poorly understood; the acute and chronic course of RAD could be explained on the basis of constitutional vulnerability to impairment in social relatedness. It seems possible that the children who display a protracted course could be biologically susceptible to disorders of social reciprocity. In this model, abuse and neglect become another impediment to suboptimal adjustment but are not its exclusive cause. Under ordinary circumstances, these children might have appeared only mildly peculiar and idiosyncratic, but the harshness of their early experiences may have produced the worst set of results.

Social Phobias

Social phobias are the least common anxiety disorders of childhood and they form a very uncommon early-childhood-onset disorder (Beidel, 1991). Patients typically begin having symptoms in their teen years, although childhood-onset cases have been described and, of the group with "generalized" social phobias, nearly half will have their onset prior to age 10 years (Mannuzza et al., 1995). As with several of the conditions discussed above, a clinician who narrows the range of possibilities too quickly risks making a diagnostic error. It is critical to recognize the difference between the social aloofness of HFA individuals and the extreme shyness, or avoidance accompanied by anxiety, that is characteristic of social phobias or avoidant disorders. Under the impediment of PDD-NOS or social phobia, a patient may display anxiety and may attempt to refrain from social interactions. However, the concept of social phobia has traditionally been reserved for individuals who exhibit normal development in other domains of their lives and have socially appropriate relationships within a small circle of family and friends (Beidel, 1991). The typical individual with social phobia enjoys the company of others and

will experience loneliness. It is less clear whether the loneliness of HFA or PDD-NOS persons has these same qualities, although they certainly may wish to participate and "fit in" with their peer group. Individuals with social phobias ought to display empathy and a strong capacity for understanding complex emotional situations. A history of normal language, imaginative play, flexibility in facing novel situations, and ordinary social development is crucial. Comorbid depressive, anxiety, or substance abuse disorders were found to be common in adults with social phobia (Mannuzza et al., 1995), but these subjects did not have the pervasive impairment in relationships and restricted interests that are characteristic of HFA or AS individuals.

Although the terminology for describing PDD-NOS children is contemporary, individuals with features of PDD-NOS have been recognized for more than 60 years. A variety of widely divergent labels, both official and personal, have been applied to children who currently comprise the modern concept of PDD-NOS. This proliferation of labels reflects the divergent ways in which clinicians have understood these children and conceptualized PDD-NOS in relation to adult-onset and other childhood-onset syndromes.

A Subgroup within PDD-NOS: Multiplex Developmental Disorder

Multiple Complex (or Multiplex) Developmental Disorder (MCDD) is a descriptive term for an early-onset syndrome in which there are basic deficits in affective modulation, capacity for relating, and stability of thinking. Characteristics of onset in infancy, sustained limitations in the capacity to form reciprocal relationships, and impoverished affective regulation suggest that MCDD might be appropriately placed in the category of PDD. MCDD has specific criteria and can be reliably diagnosed and differentiated from other childhood-onset disorders of behavior or affect (Towbin et al., 1993). Impairments in social relating are reflected in the diminished amounts and the primitive quality of peer relationships, as well as the fundamental impairments in the child's manner of relating to primary caretakers. Children with MCDD syndrome exhibit consistent avoidance and detachment, and high degrees of ambivalence, clinging, or intense irritability. Deficits in affective regulation result in peculiar fears, chronic anxiety, frequent incidents of intense anger, and extreme behavioral reactions. These demonstrate limitations in modulation of internal affective states and affective expression. Recurrent episodes of disorganization in thinking or perceptual distortions are also characteristic (Cohen et al., 1986; Towbin et al., 1993). Disorganization may be more consistent; however, problems in thinking reach neither the proportions nor the sustained intensity that would qualify for delusional or chronic psychotic conditions. Disorganization is often precipitated by changes in routine or structure, a vulnerability that is reminiscent of the patterned behavior and inflexibility typical of PDD. However, as the condition is characterized and its boundaries are explored, it is appropriate to place it under the wider umbrella of PDD-NOS (Cohen et al., 1986).

Interest in MCDD emerged when children such as these presented in large numbers for developmental evaluation at a clinic for preschool-age patients (Dahl, Cohen, & Provence, 1986). In addition to significant impairment in their capacity to interact successfully with peers and adults, these children were found to show profound impairments in their capacity for empathy and their ability to tolerate negative affects, such as frustration or anxiety, without becoming highly disorganized in their behavior and thinking (Dahl et al., 1986). The patients who demonstrated these cardinal features had sufficient language to permit clinicians to evaluate the quality of their thinking under emotional stress. Standardized evaluations suggested that these children were an "intermediate group" between autistic children and so-called "reactive" children who appeared anxious and depressed (Rescorla, 1986). The MCDD group showed high scores on a factor of "bizarre" features such as confusion, having strange ideas, exhibiting strange behaviors, and being lost in thoughts. This bizarre factor was more common among this group and a group of autistic children who were high functioning enough to have language than among the reactive group (Rescorla, 1986). However, unlike the autistic group and

like the reactive group, the MCDD individuals also scored highly on a factor for being anxious and depressed, which included items like worrying, being tense and anxious, and demanding attention (Rescorla, 1986).

The impairments of MCDD children have led other investigators to consider this syndrome an early-onset analog of a variety of adult disorders, such as bipolar illness, borderline personality disorder, schizotypal personality disorder, and schizophrenia. Indeed, the affective dysregulation and impairment in thinking and interpersonal relationships in MCDD are reminiscent of these conditions. However, it is not clear whether MCDD is continuous with the adult conditions or whether linking it to these other disorders is an appropriate model for their etiology, pathophysiology, and treatment (Towbin et al., 1993). Reading descriptions of these conditions, one is struck by how much their clinical presentations resemble one another (Caplan, 1994; Tantum, 1988b; Watkins et al., 1988). Investigators have commented on the persistent confusion between so-called "childhood-onset schizophrenia" and HFA or schizophrenia (Szatmari et al., 1990; Tantum, 1988; Watkins et al., 1988b).

Progress in other areas of investigation has promoted greater interest in this early-onset condition. In one of those areas, advances in neurodevelopmental perspectives of schizophrenia (Bloom, 1993; Fish, Marcus, Hans, Auerbach, & Perdue, 1992), this concept proposes that early-onset neural defects associated with stable cognitive impairments set the stage for an increased risk of schizophrenia. What is not clear is whether these developmental adversities routinely generate schizophrenia or are nonspecific risk factors that produce unsatisfactory adjustment in adulthood. There is insufficient longitudinal investigation to determine whether MCDD presages schizophrenia. Sparrow et al. (1986) reported that measures of social immaturity and dysfunction had stability and persistence, but that deterioration in function overall was not seen at a 7-year follow-up. Similarly, Kestenbaum (1983) reported a variety of outcomes, with psychosis only rarely ensuing in a similar, albeit small, cohort. Lofgren and coworkers (1991) also found no specific outcome in children identified as having a "borderline" syndrome. It can be difficult to distinguish MCDD children from the so-called schizoid conditions of Wolff and Chick (1980) and from some individuals with AS (Tantum, 1988b). A syndrome of poor interpersonal relatedness, odd language, and idiosyncratic thinking seems to be stable and constant.

EPIDEMIOLOGY

The reported prevalence rates of PDD-NOS have been heavily influenced by changes in the diagnostic criteria of the official classification systems. Definitions of Autistic Disorder (AD) are particularly relevant; a broader or narrower definition will influence the size of the population that is ascertained, and may inversely affect the size of the nonautistic PDD population. Consequently, the interpretation of epidemiologic studies must consider the diagnostic system that has been employed.

For example, in *DSM-III,* the alternatives to AD were Childhood-Onset PDD and Atypical PDD. Under *DSM-III-R,* the latter two categories were collapsed into PDD-NOS. A simple comparison of the prevalence rates of Atypical PDD *(DSM-III)* and PDD-NOS *(DSM-III-R)* does not draw from equivalent populations. In *DSM-III-R,* the criteria were broader than those in *DSM-III* (Spitzer & Siegel, 1990; Volkmar et al., 1994). Compared to *DSM-III, DSM-III-R* increased the proportion of PDD spectrum children who received the diagnosis of AD (Hertzig, Snow, New, & Shapiro, 1990; Spitzer & Siegel, 1990). In addition, the revised *DSM-III-R* criteria may have transferred into the PDD spectrum some individuals who could not have met the *DSM-III* criteria (Spitzer & Siegel, 1990).

Studies aimed toward finding the prevalence of autism have produced wide-ranging results, depending on the methods used. The discrepancies in results can be explained on the basis of diagnostic criteria, methods of ascertainment, and diagnostic procedures. Wider-scope or more inclusive definitions for autism produce higher rates (Bryson, Clark, & Smith, 1988; Zahner & Pauls, 1987). Investigators who combined infantile autism and other, more broadly defined PDD subtypes in their cohort have reported estimates of AD

ranging from 1.9 to 4.9 per 10,000 persons (Burd, Fisher, & Kerbeshian, 1987; Ritvo, Freeman, & Pingree, 1989; Steinhausen, Gobel, Bereinlinger, & Wohlleben, 1986; Wing & Gould, 1979; Zahner & Pauls, 1987). Studies that limited their ascertainment to narrow or strict definitions of infantile (or Kanner's) autism ("nuclear autism") gave fairly consistent estimates of 2.0 to 2.2 per 10,000 persons (Steffenberg & Gillberg, 1986; Steinhausen et al., 1986; Gillberg & Coleman, 1992). Gillberg (1992) posited that rising prevalence rates of AD over the past 10 years could be a consequence of broadened definitions. Ritvo and coworkers (1989) suggested that, in their study, recognition may have increased as information about the disorder became more widely disseminated. The Canadian study by Bryson et al. (1988), the first to employ a broad definition and research criteria, reported the highest prevalence in the literature, 10 per 10,000 persons.

Only a few studies have reported the prevalence of PDD-NOS specifically or have enabled the researchers to obtain an estimate (Zahner & Pauls, 1987). Wing and Gould (1979) reported an overall estimate of 21 per 10,000 persons for disorders akin to PDD. Their data suggest that approximately 16 per 10,000 children have disorders of "reciprocal social interaction" other than "typical autism." Burd and coworkers (1987) studied the prevalence of *DSM-III*-defined PDD in North Dakota. Rates of 1.99 per 10,000 persons were reported for "atypical PDD" and .11 per 10,000 children for childhood-onset PDD. The available studies report prevalence rates for nonautistic PDD that are equal to or greater than those for autism. However, *these studies have been conducted using a variety of diagnostic methods.* Current *ICD-10* or *DSM-IV* criteria have not been applied in prevalence studies; because the population ascertained using these criteria is apparently smaller than the pre-*DSM-IV* PDD-NOS population, these data have become outmoded. Taken together, they suggest that all other forms of nonautistic PDD are more common than autism, but until specific criteria are applied to large community-based populations, the prevalence of PDD-NOS will remain speculative.

ETIOLOGY

No single disorder gives rise to Autistic Disorder (AD). Similarly, multiple pathways ultimately may give rise to PDD-NOS. The genetic, neurochemical, and cognitive abnormalities that have been proposed for AD are likely to produce clinical pictures in the range of PDD-NOS. The current models suggest that no single contribution is unique and that combinations of genetic, congenital, and life events are important. The neurochemical findings in autism are equally applicable in PDD-NOS and have not provided any means of subtyping AD or PDD-NOS successfully. It therefore follows that any genetic or metabolic disorder that has been reported in conjunction with AD could equally result in an expression consistent with PDD-NOS. All the genetic conditions that have been reported in AD individuals also give rise to affected children who do not exhibit AD features. Each genetic or metabolic condition seems to confer a risk (but less than a certainty) for AD or PDD-NOS. Consequently, it would not be surprising to discover that a disorder such as Fragile X Syndrome could yield a range of social impairments from nuclear autism to PDD-NOS to nearly developmentally appropriate social reciprocity (Reiss et al., 1986).

Genetic hypotheses have long been promoted to account for autism, although early assessments suggested that this was a weak contribution (DeMyer, Hingtgen, & Jackson, 1981). Many specific genetic disorders have been observed with more than chance frequency in cohorts of autistic children (Gillberg & Coleman, 1992). The most common is Fragile X Syndrome, but a long list of other disorders of probable genetic etiology, including Cornelia de Lang Syndrome, tuberous sclerosis (Gillberg, Gillberg, & Ahlsen, 1994), and PKU, have also been identified in association with autism (Gillberg & Coleman, 1992). Twin studies (Folstein & Rutter, 1977) have reported high rates of concordance among monozygotic twins when compared to dizygotic pairs.

An etiologic relationship between autism and PDD-NOS disorders surfaces from genetic studies. In Folstein and Rutter's twin study (1977), the reported concordance for monozygotic twins was 38% for narrowly defined autism. However, when the data analysis considered concordance with high-functioning but oddly related relatives, the rate increased to 82% (Folstein & Rutter, 1987). These results parallel a study cited by Wing (1981) in her report on family members of AS patients. Nearly 30% of fathers and 10% of mothers of those with AS appeared to have a disorder resembling AS themselves, although no family members were reported to have autism. Wolff, Narayan, and Moyes (1988) examined family members of 21 autistic children and reported elevated rates of schizoid features among parents. Schizoid features were strikingly absent, however, in Piven's (1991) study of parents of autistic children. Using rigorous family study methodology, Piven and coworkers (1990) lent further support for a genetic connection between autism and PDD-NOS disorders in their report of higher rates of "severe social dysfunction and isolation" among adult siblings of autistic children.

The search for biologic mechanisms has resulted in the cataloging of a large number of the genetic and medical conditions and anomalies that arise in autistic individuals. However, no condition has been identified that might be considered a principal or specific cause of autism or PDD-NOS. There is no evidence that any etiology of autism is unique, and the mechanisms that lead to autism seem just as likely to produce PDD. Study cohorts typically have pooled individuals diagnosed as having PDD-NOS or Autistic Disorder into a single group (e.g., "autistic syndromes"; Gillberg, 1992).

Prior (1979) and Gillberg (1992) reviewed the mechanisms considered to be active in autism. Taken together, studies suggest that combinations of genetic, infectious, and perinatal complications contribute to the etiology of PDD-NOS as readily as autism. One SPECT study compares individuals with "high-functioning autism" (perhaps AS) with normals (Gillberg & Coleman, 1992). The results suggest that the affected individuals displayed temporal lobe hypoperfusion. Comparison of epileptic and nonepileptic autistic individuals revealed equivalent temporal-lobe perfusion patterns, implying that seizures were an unlikely cause of hypoperfusion. Similarly, a large cohort (N = 112) of children, adolescents, and adults with autism was examined using magnetic resonance imaging (MRI) and age-matched controls (Hashimoto et al., 1995). Of the autistic cohort, 15% was considered high-functioning (e.g., IQ > 80). Results suggested the autistic individuals had diminished volumes in the cerebellar vermian lobes VI and VII as well as hypoplasia of the brain stem itself. These findings are in agreement with many previous studies of autistic individuals that have reported vermian hypoplasia, although none heretofore has used controls or a cohort size as convincing as the Hashimoto study (Courchesne, 1995).

There has been a sustained effort to better characterize the cognitive features of autistic children (Prior, 1979; Sigman, Ungerer, Mundy, & Sherman, 1987). During the past decade, investigation has resulted in a more precise characterization of one aspect of the complex cognitive deficits found in autistic individuals (Baron-Cohen, Tager-Flusberg, & Cohen, 1993). Limitations in the autistic person's attention to emotional expression (Hobson, 1986), capacity for affective imitation (Rogers & Pennington, 1991), and abilities in visual-spatial perspective (Wainwright-Sharpe & Bryson, 1993) have been reported. Until recently, the connection between these impairments and the profound social impediments of autism was obscure. However, more detailed study has suggested that autistic persons display consistent, profound limitations in their capacity to understand that other persons have thoughts, desires, and intentions, or that a mental apparatus can influence other persons' actions (Baron-Cohen, Leslie, & Frith, 1985; Perner, Frith, Leslie, & Leekam, 1989). This capacity for recognition of others' thoughts and mental apparatus has been termed "theory of mind." It is the cognitive function that permits a child to perceive and relate to the mental state of another.

Klin, Volkmar, and Sparrow (1992) have suggested that autistic subjects may be an unsuitable choice for investigation of theory-of-mind problems. They reason that, because autistic individuals have an early onset of extreme social impairment, it is only logical to expect that their primary abilities to recognize subtle social signals would be severely impaired as well. It is inappropriate, they surmise, to make generalizations about defects in theory-of-mind functions being central to autism by relying on conditions that display such extreme social impairment. They propose that studying persons with higher-functioning autism, MCDD, or AS would be more appropriate. These groups generally possess better language skills and higher intellect, which permits more detailed examination of the individual's thinking. Klin et al. have also suggested that impairment in theory of mind is more likely to be a consequence, as opposed to a cause, of the impairment that produces autism.

Severely impaired PDD or HFA individuals could be particularly suitable subjects for an evaluation of theory-of-mind hypotheses. Higher-functioning subjects do not appear to possess the same very early impairments, but may exhibit deficits equal to autistic individuals as measured by theory-of-mind tasks. This has recently been addressed by Bowler (1992) and by Rutter and Bailey (1993). Bowler (1992) reported that HFA individuals were able to correctly identify the mental state of another in an experimental paradigm, but could not explain their success by applying an understanding of mental state. Of additional interest, successful performance under experimental conditions did not correlate with adaptive social function. Possessing a theory of mind did not engender social competence among these subjects (this was further supported in a study by Ozonoff & Miller, 1995). Further exploration of theory-of-mind tasks in higher-functioning PDD individuals could yield a deeper understanding of these functions and the disorders.

NATURAL HISTORY

There have been few longitudinal studies of the disorders comprising PDD-NOS, particularly when compared to numerous studies of individuals with autism. Narrowly defined autism exhibits a wide range of outcomes (Gillberg & Steffenberg, 1987). A very small number of autistic persons are able to attend college and live independently. Although many more make obvious strides in achieving greater social awareness, they remain socially odd, and they require lifelong supervision and educational support. The largest portion, perhaps 60%, makes modest gains or remains severely impaired (Gillberg, 1992). The outcome of autism has been directly correlated with overall IQ, language development, and appearance of seizures. Seizures occur in as many as 30% of cases and are more frequent among individuals with lower IQ scores.

Most studies of nonautistic PDD assemble cohorts of persons with AS. Relative to lower-functioning autistic children, the prognosis for those with AS can be fairly good, although findings of most studies favor restrained optimism. Szatmari and co-workers (1989) reported a high overall adaptive level on follow-up, but methodologic flaws in selection and diagnoses may have compromised the generalizability of these findings. Most others give disappointing results, though better outcomes are reported among those with higher IQ and verbal skills (Venter, Lord, & Schopler, 1991). Asperger believed that the disorder that bears his name remained stable throughout adolescence and adulthood (1944). Although a majority of the individuals in his cohort made good academic adjustments, they sustained, throughout life, the social deficits first displayed in childhood. Deficits in social impairment improve but do not keep pace with gains in IQ among these higher-functioning individuals (Schatz & Hamdan-Allen, 1995).

There are many opinions on whether AS increases the risk of developing other disorders. Schizophrenia occurred in only 1 of 200 cases in Asperger's original cohort (1979). One individual in Wing's cohort (1981) was thought to have schizophrenia. Wolff and Chick (1980) conducted a controlled follow-up study of individuals with schizoid personality who were ascertained using operational criteria. This has generally been regarded as a longitudinal study of AS. In this sample, 2 of 22 persons developed schizophrenia, and nearly half had suicidal ideation. However, "mystical or psychotic symptoms" were evident in nearly half the cohort (Wolff & Chick, 1980). Szatmari and coworkers (1989) reported that anxiety, obsessive-compulsive symptoms, conduct symptoms, and schizotypal symptoms were more common in those with AS, as compared

to autistic persons. This compares more closely to Wolff et al.'s reports on "schizoid" children who have been followed into adult life (Wolff, Townsend, & Moyes, 1991). Both studies suggest that bizarre ideation was more common in AS than in autism. Wing (1981) found anxiety symptoms to be prominent in her AS sample. Gillberg (1992) cautioned that clinicians unfamiliar with the disorder may misinterpret the bizarre, concrete, and idiosyncratic thoughts and behaviors of adolescents or adults with AS as signs of schizophrenia. This possibility has been further supported in studies that employed standardized measures to assess HFA individuals who have language. A high frequency of thought disorder in this populations was reported by two separate teams (Dykens, Volkmar, & Glick, 1991; Ghaziuddin, Leininger, & Tsai, 1995).

These studies suggest that individuals with PDD-NOS appear to have a better prognosis than persons with autism, but they do not fare as well as persons with AS. These graded outcomes appear to be directly correlated with the degree of language impairment. Until the boundaries separating the subtypes of PDD are clearer, it will be difficult to determine whether differences in outcome are related to diagnoses or are simply related to functional abilities. Lower-functioning autistic persons have the most limited prognosis. Estimating the prognosis of persons with high-functioning autism, compared to those with PDD-NOS, cannot be reliably accomplished at this point. Overall IQ, social skills (measured by standardized means), and language abilities are the most reliable factors to be considered.

Only one investigation has been published on the outcome of individuals diagnosed with MCDD. Van der Gaag (1993) reported a variety of outcomes, ascertained with a standardized diagnostic assessment of 43 adolescents and 12 adults previously identified as MCDD. Seven adolescents (16%) were free of any Axis I or II diagnoses. The most common adolescent Axis I diagnoses were anxiety disorders (17%) and mood disorders (10%). Axis II diagnoses of the adolescents identified PDD-NOS (37%), schizoid (12%), and schizotypal (2%) personality disorders. Of the 12 adults, 17% (2 persons) developed schizophrenia, 30% had schizoid personality, and 17% had schizotypal personality disorder. Apparently, MCDD may produce a variety of outcomes; however, it is equally evident that it is associated with a great risk of chronic mental disorder.

TREATMENT

No single treatment, method, or approach has been shown to be effective for all individuals with PDD-NOS. Any decision to implement a treatment is based on the symptoms, setting, strengths, and limitations that exist at the time. This approach reflects the polymorphic symptoms, diverse deficits, and wide range of impairment exhibited by children with PDD-NOS.

For every patient, treatment begins with a thoughtful and comprehensive evaluation. It cannot be completed in a single session. The objectives of the evaluation are to detect: the predominant symptoms that are impeding the patient's development; the capacities, talents, and resources that can be recruited in support of the patient's care; and the principal limitations under which the patient operates (Towbin, 1994). The evaluation must include direct interviews with primary caretakers and others who are knowledgeable about the patient's early development. Information from persons familiar with the patient, including pediatricians, teachers, and extended family, can be valuable. Standardized measures can be extremely helpful (Klin & Shepard, 1994); they are discussed in Chapter 19. Laboratory studies, including electroencephalogram, karyotype, Fragile X testing, blood analysis to identify quantitative amino acids, and urinalysis for organic acids may be needed. In older children, for whom general anesthesia is no longer needed, there may be some value in obtaining MRI scans, but the therapeutic value of these studies is questionable.

Compilation of a history must include family members' participation. It may be constructive to include siblings in separate meetings. When the history has been collected and a formulation has been prepared, the interpretation must be conducted in a manner that permits parents and family members to raise concerns about the findings and discuss their implications. This is a process that unfolds

over time and requires supplemental meetings to reiterate the formulation, correct misunderstandings, and refine the prognosis and plans for the patient. Attempts to understand the cause and treatment of PDD-NOS are beset with misconceptions and distortions. Parents and family members should have the opportunity to discuss their fears and doubts in an atmosphere of candor and compassion. Approaches to treatment can then be consistent with the child's optimal requirements and the families basic values, beliefs, and capacities. A treatment plan rooted in the parent's values and capacities is critical. When the clinician and family have this kind of consensus it offers the best chance for the child to benefit from the wider milieu—the extended family, school system, and community—in which he or she lives.

The foundation of treatment is appropriate educational instruction that conforms to the patient's capacities and limitations. The educational curriculum should ensure an adequate emphasis on objectives related to language and social skills development. However, each child is different; each possesses particular skills and requires interventions aimed toward specific maladaptive behaviors. This individuality demands a tailored program conducted by teachers who are experienced in the education of students with developmental delays. Ordinarily, language and social skills training are integrated into a unitary program of instruction that includes achievement of academic skills. Such an integrated approach facilitates the child's ability to generalize language and social skills across settings, persons, and situations. In contrast to the traditional "resource room" or "pull-out" methods used to assist children with specific learning or speech and language disorders, the integrated classroom model provides opportunities for children with PDD to practice skills across a variety of domains in the same setting with the same people. This reduces the number of novel persons, experiences, and settings to which the child must become accustomed.

There are no generalizable guidelines on classroom assignments and classmate mixtures. Some children benefit most from being placed in classrooms with ordinary children. Others cannot manage without the consistent specialized instruction that comes from full-time assignment to small classes dedicated to special programs conducted in contained classrooms. Others learn best from a mix of mainstream and specialized classroom placements. The tendency to assign a child based on his or her highest or lowest functional domain tends to obscure specific needs. A child with good academic progress may still require the support and skills of a specialized classroom setting; a lower-functioning child might do well in a mainstream remedial class for academic topics and a mainstream class in nonacademic areas.

Cognitive and behavioral methods are the most investigated and commonly used interventions in the treatment of autistic individuals, and they are likely to be applicable across the spectrum of PDD conditions. They have been administered to decrease self-injury, perseveration, and behaviors that impede social interaction. They have also been implemented to promote social competence and relating (Mesibov, 1984). An example of the application of these methods is the Treatment and Education of Autistic and Related Communication Handicapped CHildren (TEACCH) program in North Carolina (Schopler, 1994). As defined by Schopler, a primary aim of the program is to improve skills in socialization and communication through manipulation of the environment in an effort to accommodate the child's deficit. The program can be integrated successfully into a school curriculum and reinforced at home and in other social settings. Alternative approaches attempt to amplify social interaction indirectly by increasing language learning (Lovaas, 1987). The child's behavior is modified by using parents or hired assistants as therapists in intensive one-on-one teaching sessions (Lovaas, 1987). Cognitive techniques have been applied to teaching imaginative play and making an effort to have children understand "other minds" in false belief paradigms. The development of prosocial behaviors may have enduring effects that will influence adaptation in adulthood (Mesibov, 1983). However, whether these interventions can improve social functioning in spontaneous interaction or increase motivation for social interaction remains to be demonstrated (Bowler, 1992; Rutter & Bailey, 1993).

Pharmacotherapy can play a useful role in the treatment of PDD-NOS. No specific agent or class of agents appears to be helpful for whatever "core" deficit produces PDD-NOS nor for every symptom that may arise. However, specific symptoms may be responsive to particular agents. Assessment of the *symptoms* rather than the *diagnosis* presented by a patient becomes much more critical in making decisions about pharmacologic intervention (Towbin, 1995). Symptoms that frequently lead patients or their families to consider pharmacologic interventions include: aggressive or self-injurious behaviors; repetitive stereotypic behaviors; hyperkinesis, inattention, and distractibility; emotional lability; withdrawal; or extreme tantrums.

Perhaps the most troubling symptoms that are displayed by patients are self-injurious behaviors. These may be closely allied to compulsive or repetitive stereotypical patterns of behavior (Zubieta & Alessi, 1993). A variety of agents have been employed for the treatment of self-injurious behaviors. Although case reports and small studies have suggested that naltrexone might be useful in some patients (Leboyer, Bouvard, & Dugas, 1988; Sandman, Barron, & Colman, 1990), attempts to demonstrate its efficacy in controlled trials have been unsuccessful, even to the point of suggesting harm (Campbell et al., 1993; Willemsen-Swinkels, Buitelaar, Nijhof, & van Engeland, 1995). There is no simple formula for the management of this class of symptoms, but there is some evidence that selective serotonergic reuptake inhibitors (SSRI) agents, such as clorimipramine, fluvoxamine, and sertraline, may be useful (Cook, Rowlett, Jaselskis, & Leventhal, 1992; McDougle, Price, & Volkmar, 1994; McDougle et al., 1996). These agents may also aid in treating the extremes of inflexible behavior in individuals with PDD. Tantrums subsequent to changes in routine or in the presence of novel stimuli are examples of possible other indications for these agents. These agents might be helpful in the treatment of aggressive episodes as well (Zubieta & Alessi, 1993).

Symptoms of hyperactivity, inattention, and distractibility may respond to stimulant agents that have been useful for these symptoms in non-PDD populations (Birmaher,

Quintana, & Greenhill, 1988; Quintana et al., 1995). Although clinicians have been taught that there may be a great risk of adverse reactions to stimulants in PDD patients, the actual studies on which this warning is based may have been poorly designed (Quintana et al., 1995). More study of this phenomenon is warranted.

Children with PDD-NOS who are aggressive may benefit from agents such as lithium (Steingard & Biederman, 1987), valproate, carbamazepine, or propranolol (Ratey et al., 1987). Trazodone may be useful as well (Zubieta & Alessi, 1992). Disorganization, agitation, and aggression may respond to neuroleptics, although the dose and total duration of treatment with agents like haloperidol and pimozide should be minimal (Perry et al., 1989).

Pharmacologic treatment for PDD-NOS requires exceptional care and thoroughness. Individuals with PDD-NOS are a particularly vulnerable patient population; often they have difficulty reporting side effects and identifying their fears and worries about medication. As a group, they are susceptible to misapplication of medications for extended periods. Safeguarding their care requires thoughtful consideration and painstaking technique. The process of pharmacologic treatment must move forward patiently, steadily, and planfully, with attention to symptom targets, vigilant tracking of responses, administration of sufficient doses over an adequate duration for each agent, and minimization of polypharmacy as much as possible (Towbin, 1995).

Reassessment and measurement of areas of strength form a keystone of responsible care. Although the deficits of PDD-NOS are longitudinally stable, persons who have PDD-NOS do grow and develop. As they do, the nature and severity of their symptoms and limitations change. Educational regulations require periodic re-evaluation of the child's academic progress. These should also serve as reminders for reevaluating the patient's overall development and symptom profile. Reassessment of developmental and adaptive functioning is important for correcting unwanted side effects of therapeutic interventions or symptomatic misinterpretations that have become clearer since initial diagnosis and planning. This is particularly important if plans were laid when the child was young or had very limited verbal capacities. Repeated psychological and developmental assessments should be conducted routinely, perhaps at 2- to 3-year intervals.

SUMMARY

A myriad of questions, many of them absolutely basic, remain to be answered by careful research into PDD-NOS. Important lines of investigation include exploration of the continuity and demarcations within the wider spectrum of PDD. There is a benefit to understanding more of the relationship between symptoms and physiology. Genetic studies hold out the hope of learning how "core" autism might be related to high-functioning autism, Asperger's Syndrome, and milder PDD conditions. The relationships among Multiple Complex Developmental Disorder, other PDD conditions, and schizophrenia are an equally crucial area of research that has broad implications for the understanding of "very early onset" schizophrenia (McClellan & Werry, 1994). Carefully crafted epidemiologic investigations will bring us closer to understanding the prevalence of these conditions and will highlight the breadth of treatment and educational needs. Effective treatments such as cognitive approaches, social skills training, pharmacologic agents, and educational modifications continue to be indispensable for higher-functioning individuals in this group.

Overall, clinicians are in a better position to diagnose and treat PDD-NOS conditions than ever before. For patients previously viewed as being merely idiosyncratic, new treatments and clearer definitions have provided opportunities to be understood in a more useful way. Kanner's articulation promoted sensitivity toward persons with autism. Individuals with PDD-NOS now have a similar opportunity to receive the benefits of thoughtful multidisciplinary approaches. The benefits of modern educational models, cognitive strategies, pharmacotherapies, and social skills training, which have been offered to those with autism, can be extended to others who may have even better prognoses. Instead of being seen as treatment refractory, psychotic, conduct-disordered, or "oppositional," those with PDD-NOS now have opportunities to place their symptoms into a developmental and social-emotional context in which each individual's potential is considered. This process highlights treatments that are most likely to be helpful, and it focuses the efforts of those who teach or treat these individuals. It promotes understanding and compassion for the complex social, emotional, and cognitive symptoms experienced by those with PDD-NOS. For those closest to individuals with PDD-NOS, those seeking help for their loved ones, such knowledge provides a coherent framework and opens opportunities for collaboration.

Cross-References

Issues of diagnosis and atypical autism are discussed in Chapters 1–5 and 7.

REFERENCES

American Psychiatric Association. (1994). *Diagnostic and statistical manual of mental disorders* (4th ed.). Washington, DC: Author.

Asperger, H. (1944). "Autistic psychopathy" in childhood. (trans. U. Frith) In U. Frith (Ed.) *Autism and Asperger Syndrome* (pp. 37–92). Cambridge, England: Cambridge University Press.

Asperger, H. (1979). Problems of infantile autism. *Communication, 13,* 45–52.

Baron-Cohen, S., Leslie, A.M., & Frith, U. (1985). Does the autistic child have a "theory of mind"? *Cognition, 21,* 37–46.

Baron-Cohen, S., Tager-Flusberg, H., & Cohen, D.J. (1993). *Understanding other minds: Perspectives from autism.* Oxford, England: Oxford Medical.

Beaumanoir, A. (1992). The Landau Kleffner Syndrome. In J. Roger, M. Bureau, F.E. Dravet, A. Dreyfus, A. Perret, & P. Wolf (Eds.), *Epileptic syndromes in infancy, childhood, and adolescence* (2nd ed., pp. 231–243). London: John Libbey & Co.

Beidel, D.C. (1991). Social phobia and overanxious disorder in school age children. *Journal of the American Academy of Child and Adolescent Psychiatry, 30,* 545–552.

Bender, L. (1946). Childhood schizophrenia. *American Journal of Orthopsychiatry, 17,* 40–56.

Birmaher, B., Quintana, H., & Greenhill, L. (1988). Methylphenidate treatment of hyperactive autistic children. *Journal of the American Academy of Child Psychiatry, 27,* 248–251.

Bishop, D. (1989). Autism, Asperger's Syndrome, and pragmatic semantic disorder: Where are the boundaries? *British Journal of Disorders of Communication, 24,* 107–121.

Bloom, F.E. (1993). Advancing a neurodevelopmental etiology for schizophrenia. *Archives General Psychiatry, 50,* 224–227.

Bowler, D.M. (1992). "Theory of mind" in Asperger's Syndrome. *Journal of Child Psychology and Psychiatry, 33*(5), 877–893.

Bregman, J. (1991). Current developments in the understanding of mental retardation, part II. *Journal of the American Academy of Child and Adolescent Psychiatry, 30,* 861–872.

Bryson, S.E., Clark, B.S., & Smith, I.M. (1988). First report of a Canadian epidemiological study of autistic syndromes. *Journal of Child Psychology and Psychiatry, 29,* 433–445.

Burd, L., Fisher, W., & Kerbeshian, J. (1987). A prevalence study of pervasive developmental disorders in North Dakota. *Journal of the American Academy of Child and Adolescent Psychiatry, 26*(5), 700–703.

Campbell, M., Anderson, L.T., Small, A.M., Adams, P., Gonzalez, N.M., & Ernst, M. (1993). Naltrexone in autistic children: Behavioral symptoms and attentional learning. *Journal of the American Academy of Child and Adolescent Psychiatry, 32,* 1283–1291.

Cantwell, D.P., & Rutter, M. (1994). Classification: Conceptual issues and substantive findings. In M. Rutter, E. Taylor, & L. Hersov (Eds.), *Child and adolescent psychiatry: A modern approach.* (3rd ed., pp. 3–21). London: Blackwell Scientific.

Caplan, R. (1994). Childhood schizophrenia assessment and treatment: A developmental approach. *Child and Adolescent Psychiatry Clinics of North America, 3*(1), 15–30.

Cohen, D.J., Paul, R., & Volkmar, F.R. (1986). Issues in the classification of pervasive developmental disorders: Toward *DSM-IV. Journal of the American Academy of Child Psychiatry, 25,* 213–229.

Cook, E.H., Rowlett, R., Jaselskis, C., & Leventhal, B.C. (1992). Fluoxetine treatment of children and adults with autistic disorder and mental retardation. *Journal of the American Academy of Child and Adolescent Psychiatry, 31,* 739–745.

Courchesne, E. (1995). New evidence of cerebellar and brain stem hypoplasia in autistic infants, children and adolescents: The MR imaging study by Hashimoto and colleagues. *Journal of Autism and Developmental Disorders, 25*(1), 19–22.

Dahl, E.K., Cohen, D.J., & Provence, S. (1986). Clinical and multivariate approaches to the nosology of pervasive developmental disorders, *Journal of the American Academy of Child Psychiatry, 25*(2), 170–180.

DeMyer, M.K., Hingtgen, J.N., & Jackson, R.K. (1981). Infantile autism reviewed: A decade of research. *Schizophrenia Bulletin, 7*(3), 388–451.

Despert, L. (1986). *Schizophrenia in children.* New York: Robert Brunner.

Dykens, E., Volkmar, F., & Glick, M. (1991). Thought disorder in high-functioning autistic adults. *Journal of Autism and Developmental Disorders, 21*(3), 291–301.

Fish, B., Marcus, J., Hans, S.L., Auerbach, J.G., & Perdue, S. (1992). Infants at risk for schizophrenia: sequelae of a genetic neurointegrative defect. *Archives of General Psychiatry, 49,* 221–235.

Folstein, S., & Rutter, M. (1977). Infantile autism: A genetic study of 21 twin pairs. *Journal of Child Psychology and Psychiatry, 18,* 297–321.

Folstein, S., & Rutter, M. (1987). Autism: Familial aggregation and genetic implications. *Journal of Autism and Developmental Disorders, 18,* 3–29.

Fraser, W.I., & Rao, J.M. (1991). Recent studies of mentally handicapped young people's behavior. *Journal of Child Psychology and Psychiatry, 32,* 79–108.

Frith, U. (1991). *Autism and Asperger Syndrome.* Cambridge, England: Cambridge University Press.

Ghaziuddin, M., Leininger, L., & Tsai, L. (1995). Brief report: Thought disorder in Asperger's Syndrome: Comparison with high-functioning autism. *Journal of Autism and Developmental Disorders, 25*(3), 311–318.

Gillberg, C. (1992). The Emanuel Miller Memorial Lecture 1991: Autism and autistic-like conditions: Subclasses among disorders of empathy. *Journal of Child Psychology and Psychiatry, 33,* 813–842.

Gillberg, C., & Coleman, M. (1992). *The biology of autistic syndromes* (2nd ed.). Oxford, England: Blackwell.

Gillberg, C., Persson, E., Grufman, M., & Themner, U. (1986). Psychiatric disorder in mildly and severely mentally retarded urban children and adolescents: Epidemiologic aspects. *British Journal of Psychiatry, 149,* 68–74.

Gillberg, C., & Steffenberg, S. (1987). Outcome and prognostic factors in infantile autism and similar conditions: A population-based study of 46 cases followed through puberty. *Journal of Autism and Development Disorders, 17,* 273–287.

Gillberg, I.C., Gillberg, C., & Ahlsen, G. (1994). Autistic behavior and attention deficits in tuberous sclerosis: A population based survey. *Developmental Medicine and Child Neurology, 36,* 50–56.

Hashimoto, T., Tayama, M., Murakawa, K., Yoshimoto, T., Miyazaki, M., Harada, M., & Kuroda, Y. (1995). Development of the brain stem and cerebellum in autistic patients. *Journal of Autism and Developmental Disorders, 25*(1), 1–18.

Heller, T. (1908). Dementia infantilis. *Zeitschrift fur die Erforschung und Behandlung des Jugenlichen Schwachsinns, 2,* 141–165.

Hertzig, M., Snow, M.E., New, E., & Shapiro, T. (1990). *DSM-III* and *DSM-III-R* diagnosis of autism and pervasive developmental disorder in nursery school children. *Journal of the American Academy of Child and Adolescent Psychiatry, 29,* 123–126.

Hobson, R.P. (1986). The autistic child's appraisal of expressions of emotion. *Journal of Child Psychology and Psychiatry, 27,* 321–342.

Itard, J. (1962). *The wild boy of Aveyron.* New York: Appleton-Century-Crofts.

Kanner, L. (1943). Autistic disturbances of affective contact. *Nervous Child, 2,* 217–250.

Kestenbaum, C. (1983). The borderline child at risk for major psychiatric disorder in adult life: Seven case reports with follow-up. In K. Robson (Ed.), *The borderline child: Approaches to etiology, diagnosis, and treatment* (pp. 49–81). New York: McGraw-Hill.

Klin, A. (1994). Asperger Syndrome. *Child and Adolescent Psychiatry Clinics of North America, 3*(1), 131–148.

Klin, A., & Shepard, B.A. (1994). Psychological assessment of autistic children. *Child and Adolescent Psychiatry Clinics of North America, 3*(1), 53–70.

Klin, A., Volkmar, F.V., & Sparrow, S.S. (1992). Autistic social dysfunction: Some limitations of the theory-of-mind hypothesis. *Journal of Child Psychology and Psychiatry, 33,* 861–876.

Kolvin, I. (1971). Studies in the childhood psychoses: I. Diagnostic criteria and classification. *British Journal of Psychiatry, 118,* 381–384.

Leboyer, M., Bouvard, M.P., & Dugas, M. (1988). Effects of naltrexone on infantile autism. *Lancet, 26,* 715.

Lofgren, D.P., Bemporad, J., King, J., Lindem, K., & O'Driscoll, G. (1991). A prospective follow-up study of so-called borderline children. *American Journal of Psychiatry, 148*(11), 1541–1547.

Lovaas, O.I. (1987). Behavioral treatment and normal intellectual and educational functioning in young autistic children. *Journal of Consulting and Clinical Psychology, 55,* 3–9.

Manjiviona, J., & Prior, M. (1995). Comparison of Asperger's Syndrome and high-functioning autistic children on a test of motor impairment. *Journal of Autism and Developmental Disorders, 25*(1), 23–40.

Mannuzza, S., Schneier, F.R., Chapman, T.F., Liebowitz, M.R., Klein, D.F., & Fyer, A.J. (1995). Generalized social phobia. *Archives of General Psychiatry, 52,* 230–237.

McClellan, J., & Werry, J. (1994). Practice parameters for the assessment and treatment of children and adolescents with schizophrenia. *Journal of the American Academy of Child and Adolescent Psychiatry, 33*(5), 616–635.

McDougle, C.J., Naylor, S.T., Cohen, D.J., Volkmar, F.R., Heninger, G.R., & Price, L.H. (1996). A double-blind placebo controlled study of fluvoxamine in adults with autistic disorder. *Archives of General Psychiatry, 53,* 1001–1008.

McDougle, C.J., Price, L.H., & Volkmar, F.R. (1994). Recent advances in the pharmacotherapy of autism and related conditions. *Child and Adolescent Psychiatry Clinics of North America, 3*(1), 71–89.

McKenna, K., Gordon, C.T., Lenane, M., Kaysen, D., Fahey, K., & Rapoport, J.L. (1994). Looking for childhood onset schizophrenia: The first 71 cases screened. *Journal of the American Academy of Child and Adolescent Psychiatry, 33,* 636–644.

Mesibov, G. (1983). Current perspectives and issues in autism and adolescence. In E. Schopler & G.B. Mesibov (Eds.), *Autism in adolescents and adults* (pp. 37–53). New York: Plenum Press.

Mesibov, G. (1984). Social skills training with verbal autistic adolescents and adults: A program model. *Journal of Autism and Developmental Disorders, 14,* 395–404.

Ozonoff, S., & Miller, J.N. (1995). Teaching theory of mind: A new approach to social skills training for individuals with autism. *Journal of Autism and Developmental Disorders, 25,* 415–434.

Perner, J., Frith, U., Leslie, A.M., & Leekam, S. (1989). Exploration of the autistic child's theory of mind: Knowledge, belief and communication. *Child Development, 60,* 689–700.

Perry, R., Campbell, M., Adams, P., Lynch, N., Spencer, E.K., Curen, E.L., & Overall, J.E. (1989). Long-term efficacy of haloperidol in autistic children: Continuous versus discontinuous drug administration. *Journal of the American Academy of Child and Adolescent Psychiatry, 28,* 87–92.

Piven, J., Gayle, J., Chase, G.A., Fink, B., Landa, R., Wzorek, M.M., & Folstein, S.E. (1990). A family study of neuropsychiatric disorders in the adult siblings of autistic individuals. *Journal of the American Academy of Child and Adolescent Psychiatry, 29,* 177–189.

Piven, J., Chase, G., Landa, R., Wzorek, M., Gayle, J., Cloud, D., & Folstein, S. (1991). Psychiatric disorders in parents of autistic individuals. *Journal of the American Academy of Child and Adolescent Psychiatry, 30*(3), 471–478.

Prior, M. (1979). Cognitive abilities and disabilities in infantile autism: A review. *Journal of Abnormal Child Psychology, 7,* 357–380.

Quintana, H., Birmaher, B., Stedge, D., Lennon, S., Freed, J., Bridge, J., & Greenhill, L. (1995). Use of methylphenidate in treatment of children with autistic disorder. *Journal of Autism and Developmental Disorders, 25*(3), 283–295.

Rapin, I., & Allen, D. (1983). Developmental language disorders: Nosological considerations. In U. Kirk (Ed.), *Neuropsychology of language, reading and spelling* (pp. 155–184). New York: Academic Press.

Ratey, J.J., Bemporad, J., Sorgi, P., Bick, P., Polatkoff, S., O'Driscoll, G., & Mikkelsen, E. (1987). Brief report: Open trial effects of beta-blockers on speech and social behaviors in 8 autistic adults. *Journal of Autism and Developmental Disorders, 17,* 439–446.

Reiss, A.L., Feinstein, C., Toomey, K.E., Goldsmith, B., Rosenbaum, K., & Caruso, M.A. (1986). Psychiatric disability associated with the Fragile X chromosome. *American Journal of Medical Genetics, 23,* 393–402.

Rescorla, L.A. (1986). Preschool psychiatric disorders: Diagnostic classification and symptom patterns. *Journal of the American Academy of Child Psychiatry, 25*(2), 162–169.

Richters, M.M., & Volkmar, F.R. (1994). Case study: Reactive attachment disorder of infancy or early childhood. *Journal of the American Academy of Child and Adolescent Psychiatry, 33,* 328–332.

Ritvo, E.R., Freeman, B.J., & Pingree, C. (1989). University of Utah epidemiological survey of autism: Prevalence. *American Journal of Psychiatry, 146,* 194–199.

Rogers, S.J., & Pennington, B.F. (1991). A theoretical approach to the deficits in infantile autism. *Development and Psychopathology, 3,* 137–162.

Rumsey, J.M., Andreasen, N., & Rapoport, J.L. (1986). Thought, language, communication, and affective flattening in autistic adults. *Archives of General Psychiatry, 43,* 771–777.

Rutter, M., & Bailey, A. (1993). Thinking and relationships: Mind and brain (some reflections on theory of mind and autism). In S. Baron-Cohen, H. Tager-Flusberg, & D.J. Cohen (Eds.), *Understanding other minds: Perspectives from autism* (pp. 481–504). Oxford, England: Oxford Medical Publications.

Rutter, M., & Gould, M. (1985). Classification. In M. Rutter & L. Hersov (Eds.), *Child and adolescent psychiatry: Modern approaches* (pp. 304–321). Oxford, England: Blackwell Scientific.

Rutter M., & Schopler, E. (1988). Autism and pervasive developmental disorders. In M. Rutter, A.H. Tuma, & I.S. Lann (Eds.), *Assessment and diagnosis in child psychopathology* (pp. 408–434). New York: Guilford Press.

Sandman, C.A., Barron, J.L., & Colman, H. (1990). An orally administered opiate blocker, naltrexone, attenuates self-injurious behavior. *American Journal Mental Retardation, 95,* 93–102.

Schatz, J., & Hamdan-Allen, G. (1995). Effects of age and IQ on adaptive behavior domains for children with autism. *Journal of Autism and Developmental Disorders, 25,* 51–60.

Schopler, E. (1994). A statewide program for treatment and education of autistic and related communication handicapped children (TEACCH). *Child and Adolescent Psychiatry Clinics of North America, 3*(1), 91–103.

Sigman, M., Ungerer, J.A., Mundy, P., & Sherman, T. (1987). Cognition in autistic children. In D.J. Cohen & A.M. Donnellan (Eds.), *Handbook of autism and pervasive developmental disorders* (pp. 103–120). New York: John Wiley & Sons.

Sparrow, S.S., Rescorla, L.A., Provence, S., Condon, S.O., Goudreau, D., & Cicchetti, D. (1986). Follow-up of "atypical" children. *Journal of the American Academy of Child Psychiatry, 25,* 181–186.

Spitzer, R., & Siegel, B. (1990). The *DSM-III-R* field trials of pervasive developmental disorders. *Journal of the American Academy of Child and Adolescent Psychiatry, 29,* 855–862.

Steffenberg, S., & Gillberg, C. (1986). Autism and autistic-like conditions in Swedish rural and urban areas: A population study. *British Journal of Psychiatry, 149,* 81–87.

Steingard, R., & Biederman, J. (1987). Lithium responsive maniclike symptoms in two individuals with autism and mental retardation: Case Report. *Journal of the American Acad-emy of Child and Adolescent Psychiatry, 26,* 932–935.

Steinhausen, H., Gobel, D., Bereinlinger, M., & Wohlleben, B. (1986). A community survey of infantile autism. *Journal of the American Academy of Child Psychiatry, 25*(2), 186–189.

Szatmari, P., Bartolucci, G., Bremner, R., Bond, S., & Rich, S. (1989). A follow-up study of high-functioning autistic children. *Journal of Autism and Developmental Disorders, 19,* 213–225.

Szatmari, P., Tuff, L., Finlayson, A.J., & Bartolucci, G. (1990). Asperger's Syndrome and autism: Neurocognitive aspects. *Journal of the American Academy of Child and Adolescent Psychiatry, 29*(1), 130–136.

Tantum, D. (1988a). Asperger's Syndrome: Annotation. *Journal of Child Psychology and Psychiatry, 29,* 245–255.

Tantum, D. (1988b). Lifelong eccentricity and social isolation: II. Asperger's Syndrome or schizoid personality disorder? *British Journal of Psychiatry, 153,* 783–791.

Towbin, K.E. (1994). Pervasive Developmental Disorder Not Otherwise Specified: A review and guidelines for clinical care. *Child and Adolescent Psychiatry Clinics of North America, 3*(1), 149–161.

Towbin, K.E. (1995). Evaluation, establishing the treatment alliance, and informed consent in child and adolescent psychopharmacotherapy. *Child and Adolescent Psychiatric Clinics of North America, 4*(1), 1–15.

Towbin, K.E., Dykens, E.D., Pearson, G.S., & Cohen, D.J. (1993). Conceptualizing "Borderline syndrome of childhood" and "Childhood schizophrenia" as a developmental disorder. *Journal of the American Academy of Child and Adolescent Psychiatry, 32*(4), 775–782.

Van der Gaag, R. (1993). *Multiplex Development Disorder: An exploration of the borderlines on the autistic spectrum.* Unpublished thesis, University of Utrecht, The Netherlands.

Venter, A., Lord, C., & Schopler, E. (1991). A follow-up study of high-functioning autistic children. *Journal of Child Psychology and Psychiatry, 32*(7), 489–507.

Volkmar, F.R. (1992). Childhood disintegrative disorder: Issues for *DSM-IV. Journal of Autism and Developmental Disorders, 22,* 625–642.

Volkmar, F.R., Carter, A., Sparrow, S.S., & Cicchetti, D.V. (1993). Quantifying social development in autism. *Journal of the American Academy of Child and Adolescent Psychiatry, 32,* 627–632.

Volkmar, F.R., & Cohen, D.J. (1988). Classification and diagnosis of childhood autism. In

E. Schopler & G.B. Mesibov (Eds.), *Diagnosis and assessment in autism* (pp. 71–76). New York: Plenum Press.

Volkmar, F.R., & Cohen, D.J. (1989). Disintegrative disorder or "late onset" autism. *Journal of Child Psychology and Psychiatry, 30,* 717–724.

Volkmar, F.R., & Cohen, D.J. (1991). Comorbid association of autism and schizophrenia. *American Journal of Psychiatry, 148,* 1705–1707.

Volkmar, F.R., Klin, A., Siegel, B., Szatmari, P., Lord, C., Campbell, M., Freeman, B.J., Cicchetti, D.V., Rutter, M., Kline, W., Buitelaar, J., Hattab, Y., Fombonne, E., Fuentes, J., Werry, J., Stone, W., Kerbeshian, J., Hoshino, Y., Bregman, J., Loveland, K., Szymanski, L., & Towbin, K.E. (1994). Field trial for autistic disorder in *DSM-IV. American Journal of Psychiatry, 151,* 1361–1367.

Volkmar, F.R., & Rutter, M. (1995). Childhood Disintegrative Disorder: Results from the field trials for *DSM-IV. Journal of the American Academy of Child and Adolescent Psychiatry, 34,* 1092–1097.

Volkmar, F.R., Sparrow, S.S., Goudreau, D., Cicchetti, D.V., Paul, R., & Cohen, D.J. (1987). Social deficits in autism: An operational approach using the Vineland Adaptive Behavior Scales. *Journal of the American Academy of Child Psychiatry, 26,* 156–161.

Volkmar, F.R., Steir, D., & Cohen, D.J. (1985). Age of onset of Pervasive Developmental Disorder. *American Journal of Psychiatry, 142,* 1450–1452.

Wainwright-Sharpe, J.A., & Bryson, S.E. (1993). Visual orienting deficits in high functioning people with autism. *Journal of Autism and Developmental Disorders, 23,* 1–13.

Watkins, J.M., Asarnow, R.F., & Tanguay, P. (1988). Symptom development in childhood-onset schizophrenia. *Journal of Child Psychology and Psychiatry, 29,* 865–878.

Werry, J. (1992). Child and adolescent (early onset) schizophrenia: A review in light of *DSM-III-R. Journal of Autism and Developmental Disorders, 22*(4), 601–624.

Werry, J.S. (1991). Overanxious disorder: A review of its taxonomic properties. *Journal of the American Academy of Child and Adolescent Psychiatry, 30,* 533–544.

Whalen, C.K., & Henker, B. (1992). The social profile of attention-deficit hyperactivity disorder: Five fundamental facets. *Child and Adolescent Psychiatric Clinics of North America, 1,* 395–410.

Willemsen-Swinkels, S.H.N., Buitelaar, J.K., Nijhof, G.J., & van Engeland, H. (1995). Failure of naltrexone hydrochloride to reduce self-injurious and autistic behavior in mentally retarded adults. *Archives of General Psychiatry, 52,* 766–773.

Wing, L. (1981). Asperger's syndrome: A clinical account. *Psychological Medicine, 11,* 115–129.

Wing, L. (1992). Manifestations of social problems in high-functioning autistic people. In E. Schopler & G. Mesibov (Eds.), *High functioning individuals with autism* (pp. 129–142). New York: Plenum Press.

Wing, L., & Gould, J. (1979). Severe impairments in social interaction and associated abnormalities in children: Epidemiology and classification. *Journal of Autism and Developmental Disorders, 9,* 11–29.

Wolff, S., & Chick, J. (1980). Schizoid personality in childhood: A controlled follow-up study. *Psychological Medicine, 10,* 85–100.

Wolff, S., Narayan, S., & Moyes, B. (1988). Personality characteristics of parents of autistic children: A controlled study. *Journal of Child Psychology and Psychiatry, 29,* 143–153.

Wolff, S., Townshend, R., & Moyes, B. (1991). "Schizoid" personality in childhood and adult life II: Adult adjustment and the continuity with schizotypal personality disorders. *British Journal of Psychiatry, 159,* 620–629.

World Health Organization. (1993). *International classification of mental and behavioural disorders—diagnostic criteria for research* (10th ed.). Geneva: Author.

Zahner, G.E.P., & Pauls, D.L. (1987). Epidemiological surveys of infantile autism. In D.J. Cohen & A.M. Donnellan (Eds.), *Handbook of autism and pervasive developmental disorders* (pp. 199–207). New York: Wiley-Interscience.

Zubieta, J.K., & Alessi, N.E. (1992). Acute and chronic administration of trazodone in the treatment of disruptive behavior disorders in children. *Journal of Clinical Psychopharmacology, 12,* 346–351.

Zubieta, J.K., & Alessi, N.E. (1993). Is there a role of serotonin in the disruptive behavior disorders? A literature review. *Journal of Child and Adolescent Psychopharmacology, 3,* 11–35.

CHAPTER 7

Syndromes of Autism and Atypical Development

LORNA WING

Kanner (1943) deserves great credit for his work in delineating the behavior pattern he named early infantile autism. However, the excellence of his account drew attention away from other work describing children with behavioral abnormalities that overlap with but are not identical to Kanner's Syndrome. As research on autism has expanded, advances in development of theory and in provision of services can clearly be seen to depend on recognition of the whole spectrum of autistic disorders.

PROBLEMS OF CLASSIFICATION

The abnormalities of behavior and impairments of function that occur in autism and related conditions are so numerous and so varied that they can be described clearly only with the use of a system of subclassification. The problem besetting all attempts to produce a reliable and valid subgrouping is the continuing lack of any independent biological or psychological marker. The difficulties are illustrated in the developmental history of the two international systems of classification.

International Systems of Classification

Successive editions of the World Health Organization's *International Classification of Diseases (ICD)* and the American Psychiatric Association's *Diagnostic and Statistical Manual of Mental Disorders (DSM)* have reflected changing ideas of autism and related disorders. The evolution of these systems illustrates both

the advances in understanding that have occurred in the past three decades and the confusions and conflicts of the concepts that remain.

The chapter on mental disorders in the eighth edition of the *ICD* (World Health Organization [WHO], 1967) mentioned only *infantile autism*—and this only as an atypical form of schizophrenia. Ten years later, this same chapter in *ICD-9* (WHO, 1977) included a section titled "Psychoses with Origins Specific to Childhood." In a notable change from the eighth edition, schizophrenia of adult type occurring in childhood was specifically excluded from the list of so-called childhood psychoses.

Three years after ICD-9 came the third edition of the *DSM*, referred to as *DSM-III* (American Psychiatric Association [APA], 1980), which introduced the term *pervasive developmental disorders* to cover autism and related conditions. This edition was later revised *(DSM-III-R;* APA, 1987). The diagnostic categories were changed from those in *DSM-III,* but the classification as disorders of development and not as psychoses remained secure.

New editions of both classification systems, namely, *ICD-10* (WHO, 1992a) and *DSM-IV* (APA, 1994), have recently been published. The mental and behavioral disorder chapter of *ICD-10* has appeared in much expanded form in two other volumes that give, respectively, clinical descriptions and diagnostic guidelines (WHO, 1992b) and diagnostic criteria for research (WHO, 1993). Clinical descriptions and diagnostic criteria are all included in the one volume of *DSM-IV*. Both

---

Editors' note: As indicated in Chapter 1, *ICD-10* and *DSM-IV* terms are used interchangeably in this work.

systems classify autism and related conditions as pervasive developmental disorders. Four of the diagnostic categories, termed *Autistic Disorder, Rett's Disorder, Childhood Disintegrative Disorder,* and *Asperger's Disorder,* in *DSM-IV,* and given similar though not identical labels in *ICD-10,* have diagnostic criteria that are almost the same in both systems, although the *ICD-10* research criteria are presented in more detail (WHO, 1993). *ICD-10* includes two other diagnostic categories, *Atypical Autism* and *Overactive Disorder Associated with Mental Retardation and Stereotyped Movements,* that are not given separate entries in *DSM-IV.* Both systems allow for other and unspecified categories.

The above brief history indicates that the authors of the two international classification systems have responded to research findings that differentiate autism from schizophrenia (Anthony, 1958; Kolvin, 1971; Kolvin, Ounsted, Humphrey, & McNay, 1971; Rutter, 1972) and have recognized the appropriateness of regarding autism as one of a wider range of developmental disorders. It is less clear whether the changes between editions have represented advances in the specifying of diagnostic categories within the pervasive developmental disorders. The bases for distinguishing categories have included age of onset, etiology, level of ability, and current clinical picture. The advantages and disadvantages of grouping for each of these are considered in the following sections.

Age of Onset

Following Kanner, age of onset has been used as one of the criteria for typical autism in the *ICD* and *DSM* systems, with a cutoff point of 30 months in earlier editions and 36 months in the latest. The category of Childhood Disintegrative Disorder, included in *DSM-IV* and *ICD-10,* is defined as loss of certain skills after the age of 24 months, although the clinical description overlaps with Autistic Disorder and Atypical Autism. *DSM-III-R* differed from other editions in that age of onset was not used as a criterion for any category, although it was mentioned in the clinical descriptions.

Kolvin (1971) noted that the age of onset of childhood psychoses was, with only a few ex-

ceptions, before 3 years. Volkmar, Stier, and Cohen (1985), in a study of 118 children with pervasive developmental disorders, whose apparent age of onset could be identified, found only 5 children (4%) with onset said to be between 31 and 48 months of age. In two of these children, the evidence of onset was equivocal and may have been earlier. Clinically, the 5 children could not be distinguished from those with onset before 30 months. The authors pointed out that the term *age of recognition* was more appropriate than age of onset because the early signs of abnormal development may not be detected by parents. Wing and Gould (1979), in their epidemiological study, found 3 children out of 74 (4%) with pervasive developmental disorders; whose reported age of onset was between 37 and 60 months. These children could not be differentiated from the rest on any aspect of the clinical picture.

The criteria for Asperger's Disorder demand normal development of various skills, including language and curiosity, up to 3 years of age. However, some older children, adolescents, and adults with the behavior pattern described by Asperger (1944, 1991) have histories dating from infancy that are identical to those with typical Autistic Disorder (Wing, 1981a, 1991). The conclusion is that age of onset is not a useful basis for delineating syndromes among persons with pervasive developmental disorders.

Etiology

There is strong evidence for a genetic factor in the etiology of autistic disorders (Bolton, et al., 1994) but various conditions affecting brain function can be associated with these disorders—for example, maternal rubella (Chess, 1971, 1977), tuberous sclerosis (Hunt & Dennis, 1987; Hunt & Shepherd, 1993), herpex simplex encephalitis (Ghaziuddin, Tsai, Eilers, & Ghaziuddin, 1992; Gillberg, 1986;), infantile spasms (Taft & Cohen, 1971), and untreated phenylketonuria (PKU) (Jervis, 1963). Such conditions are found in a minority of children with autism and other pervasive developmental disorders (Gillberg, 1992; Wing & Gould; 1979), but the size of this minority is disputed (Rutter, Bailey, Bolton, & Le Couteur, 1994), perhaps at least partly because of the differences between clinic-based samples and populations identified by using epidemiological techniques. The latter tend to contain more cases with identifiable medical conditions (Wing, Yeates, Brierley, & Gould, 1976). Epidemics of viral infections (such as rubella) that cause encephalitis before birth or early in life could, in theory, cause a temporary relative increase in the percentage of children with autism due to a medical condition.

Certain syndromes are of interest because (a) the behavioral phenotypes associated with them have some features that resemble aspects of autism, and (b) a small minority of persons suffering from such syndromes meet the full diagnostic criteria for an autistic condition. These syndromes include, among others, the Fragile X anomaly (Bailey et al., 1993; Meryash, Szymanski, & Park, 1982) and Williams Syndrome (Gillberg & Rasmussen, 1994; Udwin, Yule, & Martin, 1987). Rett's Syndrome (Hagberg, Aicardi, Dias, & Ramos, 1983) presents a particular problem of classification because the children with this neurological condition go through a stage in early childhood when they may meet diagnostic criteria for autism (Gillberg, 1989; Tsai, 1992), but, after a few years, some (but not all) of these children become sociable and affectionate. Among the conditions that overlap in various ways with autism, only Rett's Syndrome appears as a diagnostic category under pervasive developmental disorders in *DSM-IV* and *ICD-10*.

Progressive intellectual and behavioral deterioration due to conditions affecting the brain, such as lipoidosis or demyelinizing disorders, can follow a period of normal development in childhood. The neurological diagnosis depends on the neurological signs, but these may be delayed in onset and preceded by behavior disorders that can take different forms, including autistic spectrum disorders (Corbett, Harris, Taylor, & Trimble, 1977). If the autistic disorder, together with loss of skills, begins after 2 years of age, the diagnostic category of Childhood Disintegrative Disorder (CDD) would be applicable. If a progressive neurological disorder is manifest, there is no problem in using this diagnosis. However, the behavioral criteria overlap with those of other pervasive developmental disorders, and evidence of a progressive neurological condition is not required by the rules in *DSM-IV* or *ICD-10*. A child given this diagnosis could, after the initial setback in development and the loss of skills (and as long as these occur between 2 and 3 years of age), be indistinguishable from others with typical or atypical autistic disorders and could remain so for the rest of his or her life

Volkmar (1992) concluded from a case review that there was some support for the validity of this diagnostic concept on grounds of clinical features, onset, course, and prognosis, but he noted that there could be problems of differential diagnosis. From the parents' point of view, the term *disintegrative* suggests a continuing deterioration, with all that implies for the child's future care, although this deterioration did not occur in most of the children who had been given this diagnosis and were reviewed by Volkmar. It might be more logical, informative, and helpful to parents to use a multiaxial system, describing the nature of the organic condition separately from the overt behavioral syndrome, and not using the term *disintegrative disorder* unless there is unequivocal evidence for a continuing deterioration.

Work on behavioral phenotypes characteristic of specific biological syndromes is advancing. However, comparisons of the clinical pictures in autistic spectrum disorders occurring with and without associated biological syndromes have not, as yet, reliably identified any specific differences (Wing, 1988; Wing & Gould, 1979), apart from the fact that individuals with an associated biological syndrome tend more often to be severely or profoundly mentally retarded (Rutter et al., 1994; Wing & Gould, 1979). Subgrouping on etiology is of no help when the overt behavior pattern is the main focus of attention, although it is important to identify any associated conditions for other reasons.

Variations in the overt behavior pattern in pervasive developmental disorders will probably prove to be closely related to the details of the neuropathogenesis, which can vary widely even in conditions with the same gross etiology (Rapin, 1994). A system of classification based on neuropathogenesis may be the eventual outcome of work in this field (Bauman & Kemper, 1994a).

Level of Ability

Bartak and Rutter (1976) compared children with autism who had intelligence quotients (IQs) of 69 and below (low-functioning) with those who had IQs of 70 and above (high-functioning). Before the *ICD* and *DSM* definitions were available, autism was defined as onset, before 30 months of age, of a severe or profound failure to develop normal social relationships; delayed and deviant language development; and ritualistic or compulsive phenomena. Bartak and Rutter found significant differences between the two IQ groups, but these differences were more marked in phenomena that are less central to the criteria considered to be diagnostic of autism, although social relationships and language development were more severely affected in the low-functioning group. The greatest difference was in prognosis in adult life, which was significantly better for the high-functioning group. Other differences included more socially disruptive behavior, a higher incidence of epilepsy, a wider range of perceptual deficits, and more neurodevelopmental abnormalities in the low-functioning group. The authors discussed the possibility of differences in etiology between these two groups, but the question is still unresolved.

Wing and Gould (1979) and Wing (1981b) also found that the severity of the impairment of social interaction was related to IQ. Level of intelligence is an important variable in any system of classification of the pervasive developmental disorders.

Current Clinical Picture

The earliest attempts to introduce order into confusion were made by authors (including Asperger, 1944, 1991; De Sanctis, 1906, 1908; Earl, 1943; Heller, 1954; Kanner, 1943; Mahler, 1952) who tried to detect "syndromes" among the wide variety of clinical features found in children regarded as "psychotic." As Anthony (1958) pointed out, these syndromes, named after their authors, overlapped to such an extent that, in practice, they could not be properly differentiated. This historical system of subgrouping also left unclassified a substantial proportion of children who have marked autistic features but do not fit any particular author's description. The only one of these early syndrome authors whose name survives in *ICD-10* and *DSM-IV* is Asperger.

Wing (1993) compared epidemiologically based prevalence studies of typical autism, conducted in Europe, the United States, Canada, and Japan, and published between 1966 and 1991. The diagnostic criteria used were: Kanner and Eisenberg's (1956; 5 studies), Rutter's (1978; 2 studies), *DSM-III* (APA, 1980; 7 studies), *DSM-III-R* (APA, 1987; 2 studies) and other sources (1 study). The age-specific rates reported varied from 3.3 to 16.0 per 10,000 children. The most consistent findings (4.3–5.0 per 10,000 children) were in the studies using Kanner and Eisenberg's two criteria: (a) profound lack of affective contact and (b) repetitive, ritualistic behavior of an *elaborate* kind. Wide variations in prevalence could possibly exist over space and time, but differences also could result, at least in part, from problems of applying the available diagnostic criteria reliably. The researchers found it difficult to define the cutoff points separating diagnostic groups.

All the diagnostic systems used in these studies that were carried out in different countries, and those in the latest editions of *DSM* and *ICD,* are identical in their selection of impairments of social interaction and a repetitive pattern of behavior as the key features for typical autism. All except the system of Kanner and Eisenberg also specify impairments in language development. (Kanner and Eisenberg assumed that these impairments would be found whenever their two key features were present.) The differences among the systems lie in the details of the definitions of these features and, for the *ICD* and *DSM* systems, the division of the pervasive development disorders into different diagnostic categories.

A working group chaired by Denckla (1986) emphasized that these generally accepted criteria for autism and related disorders could occur in widely varying degrees of severity, and recommended that the subtlest forms of social and communication impairments and verbal and abstract repetitive routines be recognized as part of the range of pervasive development disorders. Age of onset was excluded as a defining feature. The final version of *DSM-III-R* was influenced by these views (Waterhouse, Wing, Spitzer, & Siegal, 1992). *DSM-IV* and *ICD-10* have retained some aspects of these ideas but age of onset has been reinstated as a criterion for typical autism.

A MULTIAXIAL SYSTEM

The use of the mixture of etiology, past history (as represented by age of onset), level of ability, and current clinical picture—as the basis for classification over the years—has produced numerous problems, as shown by the changes in successive editions of the international systems. A multiaxial approach to diagnosis and classification could overcome many of those problems (Ferrari, 1982; Rutter et al., 1969; Wing, 1970). *DSM-IV* contains recommendations for such a system, but a further modification would be helpful for autism and related disorders. The diagnostic formulation should include at least three dimensions (axes): (a) the overt behavior pattern (the psychiatric syndrome), (b) the gross etiology (if known), and (c) the level of intelligence on standardized tests. A fourth axis, concerning coexisting disorders, would also be useful in clinical practice, because autistic and related disorders can occur along with any other mental or physical condition (Wing & Gould, 1979). Epileptic seizures, for example, occur in about one-third of autistic people by the time they reach adult age (Rutter, 1970).

Expression of intelligence level presents some problems because autism and related conditions are characterized by large discrepancies between different types of cognitive skills. Ideally, results of testing verbal and visuospatial skills should be given separately.

The major difficulty in classifying an overt behavior pattern remains unresolved. Without knowledge of the precise relationship between the clinical picture and the underlying neuropathology, there is no certainty of how the many clinical features relate to each other or where the boundaries with other (nonautistic) conditions should be drawn. In the following section, a possible behavioral classification is described. This classification is suggested on grounds of practical utility in the absence of any system proven to have external validity.

THE AUTISTIC SPECTRUM

As mentioned, no objective criteria are available as a basis for judging the validity of the various diagnostic categories that have been used in the existing classification systems. Rett's Syndrome can be identified because of its physical signs, but these do not indicate whether the child has autistic behavior at the time of assessment. The categories have not proved helpful in prescribing type of education, behavior management, medication, or other treatment. They are useful in comparative research only if their reliability is enhanced by increasing the details of the specifications, thereby narrowing the categories, and by training the workers involved (Le Couteur et al., 1989; Wing & Gould, 1978).

Wing and Gould (1979), in an epidemiological study of children with special educational needs in one area of London, found that the features listed above as appearing in all diagnostic systems did cluster together very significantly. They formulated these features as impairments of reciprocal social interaction, verbal and nonverbal communication, and imagination (identified as being closely related to the narrow, rigid, repetitive pattern of behavior). They referred to this cluster as the triad of impairments. Impairments of two-way social interaction and nonverbal communication can be detected even in the first year of a child's life, if the condition is present at that stage (Klin, Volkmar, & Sparrow, 1992; Osterling & Dawson, 1994; Ricks, 1975, 1979; Ricks & Wing, 1975).

Among the children with the triad in Wing and Gould's epidemiological study, those with very typical autism could be recognized by applying Kanner and Eisenberg's (1956) two criteria. Children with the syndrome described by Asperger could also be identified, although the concentration on the population with special educational needs meant that only a small number of cases were found. A study conducted in Gothenburg, Sweden by Ehlers and Gillberg (1993) showed that most children with Asperger's Syndrome were likely to be in mainstream schools. However, the borderlines between the named syndromes and other manifestations of the triad were hard to define and were continuous rather than discrete.

Furthermore, in some children, the clinical pictures changed as they grew older (Wing, 1988); for example, some children with Kanner's Syndrome in early childhood developed the behavior described by Asperger in adolescence. In addition to those with the named syndromes, a larger number with the triad of impairments did not fit into either of the named diagnostic categories but had various admixtures of features. The whole range of conditions of which the triad was a part was referred to as the autistic continuum; the term *autistic spectrum* is now more generally accepted and is used here.

The concept of the autistic spectrum includes all or almost all of the pervasive developmental disorders, as defined in the *DSM* and *ICD* systems. The spectrum is wider, however, because it includes the most subtle manifestations of the triad. On the other hand, *ICD-10,* under pervasive developmental disorders, includes a new diagnostic category termed Overactive Disorder Associated with Mental Retardation and Stereotyped Movements. Children in this category are described as having no social impairment of the autistic type; they would not be included in the autistic spectrum. Support for the concept of a wide spectrum of autistic disorders can be found, for example, in a genetic study of families by Rutter and his colleagues (Bolton et al., 1994), who provided evidence for broadening the phenotypic definition beyond the criteria for autism and other pervasive developmental disorders. Gillberg (1992) has suggested that autism be regarded as a subclass among a very wide group of disorders of empathy, claiming that this approach would have value for both research and clinical work.

Classification by Types of Social Interaction

Wing and Gould (1979) examined the relevance of the named syndrome diagnoses and confirmed that they were by no means the best indicators of the types of services needed by the children. One fact was clear: the quality of social interaction was closely related to the children's practical needs. This aspect of the autistic spectrum was used as the main criterion and as the basis for a system of subclassification. A legitimate question

arises: Why should this one feature be selected as the key, when so many other features can be found in autistic spectrum disorders and none has been independently validated as the fundamental impairment? It would be possible to select groups of individuals that have in common, for example, particular language abnormalities, or oversensitivity to sound, or poor motor coordination, or any other aspect or combination that can be defined. These groups would overlap in their clinical features but would not be identical, and any of them might be of interest for research. The quality of social interaction was chosen for a purely pragmatic reason: impairment in this aspect of behavior has particularly marked effects on the whole life of the individuals concerned. No claim is made that this subgrouping has validity in terms of the neuropathology or that it is the only or best system possible. In the author's experience, however, it has proved useful in planning education, management, and the provision of services. As Szatmari (1992) has pointed out, at this stage, the major issue regarding classification within the autistic spectrum may be usefulness for clinical practice, education, and research rather than any absolute concept of validity. The grouping on social interaction is used here to give some structure to the clinical description of disorders in the autistic spectrum.

In recent years, the impairment of social interaction has moved to center stage in one area of psychological research. Frith and her colleagues (Frith, 1989) found evidence that a theory of mind was absent in children with typical autism and that this ability was impaired in high-functioning adolescents and adults (Bowler, 1992; Fombonne, Siddons, Achard, Frith, & Happé, 1994). Such children do not understand, or are impaired in understanding, that other people have thoughts and feelings—knowledge that normally develops during the early years of life and is crucial for coping in the social world. Absence of a theory of mind may be the basic impairment underlying autism and other autistic spectrum disorders. A more fundamental hypothesis is that people with autistic spectrum disorders cannot make connections among their experiences and therefore fail to comprehend the meaning of these experiences in the context of the past, present, and future. Simple connections are less affected, but the subtleties of social interaction and the complexities of understanding other people become particularly difficult, or impossible for these individuals to comprehend (Rimland, 1965; Shah & Wing, 1986; Wing, 1982). Frith (1989) expressed this condition as a lack of drive for central coherence. The strange behavior seen in the autistic spectrum disorders is more understandable in the light of this hypothesis, which fits well with the report by Bauman and Kemper (1994b) on their neuropathological findings in the limbic system and cerebellar circuits.

Wing and Gould (1979) divided the abnormal social interactions occurring in the spectrum of autistic disorders into three types: (a) aloof, (b) passive, and (c) active but odd. The validity of these subtypes has received some support from studies by Castelloe and Dawson (1993), Borden and Ollendick (1994), Eaves, Ho, and Eaves (1994), Gillberg (1992), and Volkmar, Cohen, Bregman, Hooks, and Stevenson (1989), even though the studies varied in the degree to which each of the three groups differed from the others. Each subtype tends to be associated with particular kinds of clinical pictures. These are described below, along with the variations produced by different levels of cognitive ability and the relationships to other systems of classification.

The Aloof Group

This group corresponds most closely to the popular image of autism. Most of the phenomena associated with autism and related conditions are likely to be seen in the aloof group and are therefore described in this section. The group comprises, by definition, children and adults who are most cut off from social contact. They may become agitated when in close proximity to others, and they usually reject unsolicited physical or social contact, although, for a brief time, they may enjoy rough physical play. Some individuals in this group approach other persons to obtain food or other needs, or they seek the physical comfort of sitting on a lap or being cuddled; but once satisfied, they move away abruptly and without a backward glance. Their social aloofness, which is particularly marked with age peers, tends to be less obvious with well-known

people, especially parents. However, at least in the first years, the signs of normal attachment behavior are minimal or absent (Churchill & Bryson, 1972; Wing, 1969; Wolff & Chess, 1964). Unlike normal toddlers, autistic children tend not to follow their parents around the house, to run to greet them if they have been away, or to seek comfort when in pain or upset. The lack of these overt signs of affection is, to parents, one of the most puzzling and distressing aspects of autism.

Understanding and use of verbal and nonverbal communication are severely impaired; in the most handicapped members of this group, they can be virtually absent. In the early years, a lack of response to speech often leads to a suspicion of deafness, but parents usually reject this possibility because of the children's ability to react to sounds that have meaning for them, such as the rustle of a chocolate wrapper or the jangle of car keys.

Many persons in this group remain mute all their lives. If they do develop speech, certain abnormalities are typical: echolalia, reversal of pronouns, repetitiveness, literalness of meaning, idiosyncratic use of words and phrases, and abbreviation of phrases to the minimum required to convey basic needs (Kanner, 1943, 1946). Most characteristic of all, these children do not use speech as a means of social interaction, to get to know another person, or to exchange ideas for mutual pleasure and profit. Speech is simply a medium for getting what the autistic person wants, or, in later years, for indulging in talk about his or her circumscribed interests, as described below.

Impairments of nonverbal communication affect many aspects of behavior. If the complete triad of impairment (in social interaction, communication, and imagination) is present from infancy, parents may notice that these babies make few demands for social attention, show little or no attempt to engage in two-way communication, have limited babble, and, unlike sociable babies, do not make themselves ready to be picked up when they are around 6 months of age. At 10 to 12 months, autistic children do not develop joint referencing—sharing their interests and pleasures with their parents by pointing things out and wanting the parents to look. When the children begin to walk, they do not bring things to show the parents just for the fun of sharing (Wing, 1971). Later, these children have poor eye contact (even actual visual avoidance), poverty of facial expression, and a lack of social gestures such as waving, nodding the head, and touching other people in an appropriate way to attract their attention or to show sympathy. Some of the children, especially girls, tend to have a fixed smile; this trait can be misleading until its unchanging quality and lack of relevance to an ongoing social situation are observed. Prespeech sounds are peculiar and idiosyncratic to the individual concerned (Ricks, 1975, 1979). If the child does develop speech, his or her vocal intonation is monotonous or inappropriate for the meaning of the utterance (Ricks & Wing, 1975).

Some autistic persons, especially those in the aloof group, have problems copying other people's actions (DeMyer, 1976). They may learn simple actions—such as clapping, if their hands are passively moved for them—but they do not have the capacity for spontaneous copying, which is a prerequisite for learning many skills. There is evidence that children with Autistic Disorder have difficulty recognizing faces (Boucher & Lewis, 1992; Langdell, 1978) and age-related features in humans (Hobson, 1983).

As children, most of the aloof group have no symbolic pretend play, either on their own or with their parents. They may be able to manipulate objects, or even to dismantle and rebuild them, but they show no signs of pretending that toys represent real things. They do not build up an inner world of imagination for themselves (Wing, Gould, Yeates, & Brierley, 1977). Instead, they fill their time with repetitive, stereotyped activities. Such children may engage for several hours in one pursuit, which totally absorbs them. They do not share this activity with others, and they are not distracted by events going on around them. In contrast, their attention span is poor when others attempt to engage them in social interaction or practical tasks. The same repetitive routine may occur many times a day and may continue for months or even years before it is replaced by another. The stereotypies of persons who are severely or profoundly retarded are usually simple and tend to be self-directed, such as finger flicking, arm flapping, or body

rocking (Rutter & Lockyer, 1967; Shah, Holmes, & Wing, 1982). Some individuals dexterously spin objects or twirl a piece of string. To the observer, such children appear transfixed by the object's movement.

As the more able aloof children grow older, simple stereotypies tend to diminish (Gillberg & Schaumann, 1981), only to be replaced by more complex repetitive behavior—collecting certain types of objects (tin cans, animal bones, building bricks, and so on); organizing objects into lines or patterns; insisting on a lengthy bedtime ritual; taking exactly the same route to shops or to school every day (Kanner, 1943; Wing, 1985). Boucher (1977) described how children with typical autism impose their own rigid routine when introduced to new play situations. Once the routine is established, they may display strong resistance and temper tantrums if it is disturbed. This type of behavior is remarkably persistent over time, even if other aspects of the clinical picture change (Gould, 1982).

Young children in the aloof group are often agile climbers. Because they are unaware of danger, this skill can lead them into perilous situations if they are not closely supervised. Paradoxically, they may show intense fear of some harmless things or situations, such as a particular color, entering a bus, getting into a bathtub, or meeting specific people. The fears may later turn into a special fascination, or vice versa.

Aloof children can experience inexplicable changes of mood, giggling and laughing, or weeping for no apparent reason, although the explanation may become apparent later if the child develops expressive language. Sometimes, young children with autistic conditions will stand in a dejected posture, with tears streaming down their faces, as if they suddenly feel their helplessness in a world they cannot understand. This is a painful sight for parents because they can offer only physical comfort, which the children may reject.

In their early years, their tendency to walk on tiptoe, their springy gait, and their rapid movements may make the aloof children appear graceful. They tend to have large, somewhat widely-spaced eyes with long, curved eyelashes; symmetrical facial features; and an appearance of innocence and remoteness that adds to their attractiveness. The odd flapping movements of the arms, the jumping, and the facial grimaces that accompany any excitement or distress are acceptable in a small child. As adolescence approaches, however, their posture and gait tend to become more obviously ill-coordinated and abnormal, and the absence of facial expression becomes more noticeably strange and less appealing.

Unusual reactions to sensory stimuli may also be observed, especially in the early years. These include ignoring, being distressed by, or becoming unusually fascinated with sound, light, heat, cold, touch, pain, vibration, or kinesthetic sensations, including self-spinning or watching things that spin.

Lack of response to pain can lead to diagnostic problems in physical illness. The author knows of autistic children with acute appendicitis or broken bones who made no complaint and showed no outward sign of discomfort. Responses to sensory stimuli may be paradoxical—for example, covering the eyes upon hearing a loud sound.

Some features of autistic spectrum disorders appear to be related to physiological abnormalities. These include excessive drinking of fluids, irregular patterns of sleeping and eating, and marked fluctuations of body weight. Signs of autonomic disturbance—sweating, irregular breathing, and rapid pulse, for example—may be noticed at times.

Inappropriate or socially embarrassing behavior is very common. Temper tantrums, aggression, destructiveness, restlessness, screaming, grabbing objects from shop counters, removing clothes in public, running away, and entering the homes of strangers to collect particular objects are all-too-familiar behaviors to parents of autistic children. They may be responses to interference with repetitive routines. The underlying problem is a lack of understanding of instructions and of the rules of social behavior. Those who can speak may repeatedly make inappropriate, even obscene, remarks in a loud voice in public as well as at home. Some, whether or not they have speech, may grunt, bellow, or otherwise vocalize in socially unacceptable ways.

Aloofness and indifference to others are most likely to persist throughout childhood and into adult life in individuals who are severely or profoundly mentally retarded. On standardized psychological tests, the visuospatial skills of such individuals tend to be better than their verbal skills, but the most severely retarded aloof autistic people lack any real islets of ability (Wing, 1981b).

Among the minority of aloof people whose intelligence quotient (IQ) is in the moderately retarded, mildly retarded, or normal range, some individuals may demonstrate special skill in drawing, fitting and assembling tasks, or arithmetic calculations, or they may show surprisingly good rote memory for visual or verbal material or music. As noted previously, these are the people who have elaborate repetitive routines, presumably because a certain minimum level of visuospatial skill and rote memory is needed to carry out and remember a complicated ritual. A small minority, the "autistic savants," have very high levels of ability in one or more of the skills mentioned above (Rimland, 1965; Treffert, 1989). O'Connor and Hermelin (1988) estimated that about 6% of people with Autistic Disorder had such special talents, in contrast to their retardation in other areas.

An identifiable gross etiology is more often found in the history or present state of severely or profoundly retarded aloof people (Wing & Gould, 1979), but this etiology is much less common in those who have higher levels of visuospatial skills.

Those in the aloof group who have an IQ in the mildly to moderately retarded range are most likely to fit Kanner's (1943, 1946, 1971, 1973) descriptions of his syndrome (Gillberg, 1992; Wing, 1993). They may be found in any of the diagnostic categories of *DSM-IV* and *ICD-10,* including Childhood Disintegrative Disorder but excluding Asperger's Disorder and Overactive Disorder Associated with Mental Retardation and Stereotyped Movements. (The criteria for the latter specify absence of social impairment of the autistic type.)

The Passive Group

Children and adults in the passive group do not make spontaneous social approaches, except to obtain their needs, but they accept others' approaches without protest and even with some appearance of enjoyment. They can be led to join in games and activities organized by others, although they typically take a passive role, such as that of the baby in the game of mothers and fathers. They are able to copy other people's actions, although without full understanding. Occasionally, a passive person will show echopraxia of gestures equivalent to echolalia of speech (Attwood, 1984).

Speech among passive individuals tends to be better developed than in the aloof group, but it shows the characteristic autistic abnormalities and a lack of interpersonal communication for pleasure. Some of these people have large vocabularies and even good grammar. They may show a fascination with long words and a tendency to use pedantic turns of phrase: "I wish to thank you for the hospitality you have extended to me this afternoon," meaning "Thanks for the cup of tea." However, the content is mostly repetitive and confined within a narrow range of subjects. Imaginative play may be absent; they may simply copy other children's activities—for example, bathing and feeding dolls. Their play lacks spontaneity and inventiveness and remains repetitive and limited in form.

Other characteristics of the aloof group are found in passive children, but the traits tend to be less marked, especially after the early years. The stereotyped movements and odd responses to sensory stimuli may be minimal or absent. Passive individuals have repetitive routines, but, compared to the aloof group, they show less intense resistance to interference. In the most able passive persons, routines may take the form of circumscribed interests that require rote memorization of masses of facts about a chosen subject, though with little understanding of the real meaning. (Examples are given below, in the section on the active-but-odd group.) Passive individuals have little appreciation of subtle verbal jokes, but they often enjoy slapstick humor and simple word-meaning games. For instance, one young man was very amused when he saw that the proprietor of a grocer shop was named Butcher.

Passive children and adults are likely to be the best behaved and the most easily managed of all the autistic groups. They tend to have higher levels of ability than the aloof group. Most perform better on visuospatial than on verbal tasks, though some have poorly coordinated gross motor skills. Paradoxically, this last problem is more likely to occur in the more able people (DeMyer, 1976). The high-functioning passive children, because of their amiability and their useful skills, may manage fairly well in mainstream schools. Those who are more severely retarded can often fit into schools for sociable children with mental retardation. They are less likely than the aloof group to have an identifiable gross etiology for their impairments (Wing & Gould, 1979). Despite their generally more amenable behavior, those in the passive group can become difficult in periods of stress or pressure, especially in adolescence. They may not be diagnosed in their early years because the main signs of impairment are (a) absence of spontaneous social interaction and (b) poor nonverbal communication, rather than indifference to others and overtly strange and difficult behavior, which are noticeable in the aloof group.

Some children who have classic Kanner's Syndrome early in life become passively sociable as they grow older (Kanner, 1971, 1973; Wing, 1988). Those who are poorly coordinated in movement and who have circumscribed intellectual interests may fit the picture of Asperger's Syndrome (Asperger, 1944; Ehlers & Gillberg, 1993; Wing, 1981a, 1988). Among the *DSM-IV* and *ICD-10* diagnostic categories, they are unlikely to fit the criteria for Childhood Disintegrative Disorder or Retts and would be excluded, by definition, from Overactive Disorder Associated with Mental Retardation and Stereotyped Movements. However, any of the other categories (Autistic Disorder, Asperger's Disorder, other PDD, PDD unspecified) could be validly assigned.

The Active-but-Odd Group

Autistic people who make spontaneous approaches to others, but in a peculiar, naïve, and one-sided fashion, comprise the active-but-odd group. These individuals seek to indulge their circumscribed interests by talking *at* another person or by asking questions, but not for the pleasure of reciprocal social interaction. Their active approaches may be so persistent—perhaps accompanied by physical clinging—that these people are boring, unwelcome, or even distressing to their unwilling listeners.

Compared to the aloof and passive groups, their speech tends to be better but is characterized by delay in talking and by the same abnormalities as previously described. Some individuals, however, can use correct grammar and can employ large vocabularies even at a young age. Stories are told of children in this group who spoke late, but whose first utterance was a long, coherent sentence. Repetitiveness, long-windedness, and lack of ease with colloquial turns of phrase are characteristic of even the best speakers in the group. Much of their speech is comprised of phrases they originally heard someone else say; they store these phrases and bring them out as whole chunks that have varying degrees of appropriateness. Their literal interpretation of words can produce strange usages. One young man thought that the adjective *independent* was used to describe people who could jump in at the deep end of a swimming pool (Wing, 1981a). Hurtig, Ensrud, and Tomblin (1982), examining the conversations of active-but-odd children with normal adults, describe how the children use direct questions as conversational openers without prefacing their inquiries with social conventions such as a greeting. This behavior generally seems very odd to the conversational partner.

Active-but-odd individuals also have impairments in the nonverbal aspects of their communication. Vocal intonation is monotonous or has strange inflections; they have poor breath and volume control. They may not use gestures, especially those indicating feeling and emotions (Attwood, 1984), but some in this group make exaggerated and inappropriate movements of face and limbs when speaking. Their eye contact is also inappropriate, being too fixed at some times and averted when it would be socially correct to look at their conversational partner.

As children, many in this group have repetitive, stereotyped, pseudo-pretend play. They build and rebuild the same imaginary system of roads and bridges, or they pretend to be the same animal or the same inanimate object, such as a train (Wing et al., 1977). In recent years, with increased availability of technology in the home, all three groups, especially the active-but-odd children, have frequently taken special interest in playing computer games and watching videos. Some children act out scenes from their favorite videos, which they watch over and over. Their reenactment is remarkable for the accuracy with which they copy the fragments chosen, for their repetitiveness without adding any imaginative embroidery, and for their lack of comprehension of (or even interest in) the meaning. This activity can be misinterpreted by the unsophisticated watcher as imaginative play, but careful observation reveals its true nature as a repetitive routine.

As in the aloof group, repetitive routines involving objects may occur in some active-but-odd children. Others may have more abstract circumscribed interests, like some in the passive group. This list of possible interests is extremely wide, including timetables, calendars, genealogy of royal families, physics, astronomy, particular birds or animals, or specific people. The interests in themselves are not necessarily abnormal; the problem is that they are pursued relentlessly, to the exclusion of virtually everything else and with little grasp of the meaning of the acquired knowledge or its applicability to everyday life. Some, especially those who are severely retarded, have repetitive activities of a less abstract nature. Their odd social approaches tend to consist of repeating the same questions ("What's your name?" "How old are you?" "What color is your car?") or pestering people for things they want. They may display motor stereotypies and unusual responses to sensory stimuli in their early years, but these may fade as the children grow older.

Individuals in the active-but-odd group frequently have problems of motor coordination. Unlike children in the aloof group, those who are active but odd in social interaction tend to be clumsy. They are wary of balancing and climbing, and they have an odd, immature gait and posture. Some have been described as puppetlike in their movements.

Most but not all members of this group have higher levels of skill than those who are aloof. Some active-but-odd people have verbal scores that are equal to or higher than their performance scores on Wechsler IQ batteries, but the subtests on which they do well depend on rote memory, not on reasoning ability.

Behavior problems are common. Irrelevant remarks and repetitive questioning can include socially inappropriate themes such as physical abnormalities, details of other people's personal lives, or sex and violence. Odd approaches to others might easily turn to pestering and then to temper tantrums and physical aggression. Oversensitivity to criticism can be expected.

A small minority get into trouble with the law (Wing, 1981a), partly because they may lack understanding of social rules—for example, they may make inappropriate approaches in public to strangers of the opposite sex. As a consequence of misinterpretation, they may assault someone thought to have made a disparaging remark. Or, immersed in their circumscribed interests, they may act illegally— for example, taking books on special subjects without paying for them. Asperger (1944) described small subgroups of people who would fit the active-but-odd category. One group appeared to take delight in malicious acts against others; another group's detached curiosity in their special field of interest led them to do experiments with dangerous results. Such actions may include starting fires or testing the effects of chemicals on unsuspecting relatives or acquaintances. Mawson, Grounds, and Tantam (1985) described a man with active-but-odd social interaction and Asperger's Syndrome who was preoccupied with poisons but who also attacked individuals, such as babies, who were making high-pitched sounds that he intensely disliked. Ghaziuddin, Tsai, and Ghaziuddin (1991) have argued that violence is not more common in people with Asperger's Syndrome than in the general population, but in this author's observation, when it does occur, it tends to be bizarre and initiated by someone who does not come from a violent or criminal background. To date, no study has been done of the incidence of such behavior in the active-but-odd group as a whole.

As with the passive group, parents may not be aware of their children's abnormalities until the children approach school age, although careful history taking usually reveals the characteristic impairments of social interaction, nonverbal communication and imagination, and absorption in repetitive activities from early in life. Diagnosis and classification may continue to present problems, even when the child is referred for psychiatric assessment. In some cases, the autistic features are fairly obvious, despite the active social approaches. In other cases, different aspects of the person's behavior capture attention, and the autistic characteristics are overlooked. A child or an adult may show very high levels of anxiety. As mentioned above, he or she may have a circumscribed interest in particularly bizarre or frightening themes, perhaps involving violence, sex, or imaginary monsters. A repetitive fantasy could be mistaken for a delusional belief. Such fantasies are often equivalent to those found in some normal preschool children, who may act out being, for example, a horse, an owl, a robot, or a railway train. Irrelevant remarks and repetitions of conversations heard in the past may make the person's speech seem rambling and incoherent. Literal interpretations of words and phrases may produce dramatic responses, as with the child who exhibited acute terror when someone said, "You are always losing things; you will lose your head one day." All kinds of inappropriate behavior can be expected in active-but-odd children and adults who have enough language and symbolic development to take in something of the environment, but not enough to make a coherent whole of their experience. Identifiable gross etiologies may be present, but less often than in the aloof group.

Some active-but-odd people who have circumscribed interests fit Asperger's description of his syndrome. Mahler's (1952) symbiotic psychosis would probably include some of the children, although her accounts are hard to follow. Newson's (1983) pathological demand-avoidance syndrome can also be found in some children in the active-but-odd group. Wing (1988) found one child (out of a group of 17) with typical Kanner's Syndrome who became active-but-odd in later childhood after having been aloof as a young child. Among the diagnostic categories in *DSM-IV* and *ICD-10,* the active-but-odd group would be most likely to show the criteria for Asperger's Disorder or Atypical Autistic Disorder. Some might possibly meet the criteria for Autistic Disorder.

CHANGES WITH AGE

The above classification of the behavioral abnormalities found in the spectrum of autistic disorders should not be regarded as rigid. The borderlines between the groups are ill defined, lending weight to the view that they are part of a spectrum of related conditions. One person can show the behavior of different groups in different environments (Lord, 1984).

In general, autistic behavior is seen in its most typical form when the affected individuals are between 2 and 5 years of age, although the abnormalities in some passive and some active-but-odd children are not detected until the children are school age. Wing (1988) found that one-fifth of the children with autistic spectrum disorders in an epidemiological study had changed their type of social interaction by later childhood or adolescence. Such changes were mainly from aloof to passive or from aloof to active-but-odd, but a small number of children became more aloof as they grew older. Nevertheless, by the time they reach school age, children can usually be assigned to one or another of the categories on the basis of their most characteristic behavior. This behavior is best observed in their reaction to age peers in unstructured play time and to adults who are strangers.

The major behavior problems tend to lessen during middle and later childhood. A small minority make steady progress, becoming semi- or fully independent as adults, though often retaining the basic impairments in a mild form (Rutter, 1970; Wing, 1988). For others, many difficulties may emerge in adolescence and early adult life (Gillberg & Schaumann, 1981). Aggression and temper tantrums may return. Psychiatric conditions may be superimposed on the autism (see the next section on differential diagnosis).

Prognosis for individuals in the three groups is closely related to their levels of intelligence (DeMyer et al., 1973; Lotter, 1974; Rutter, 1970), but, given equal levels of ability, the passive group is likely to do best. The aloof group would come in next, and the active-but-odd group would do least well. The active-but-odd group is particularly prone to psychiatric complications in response to stress, including brief episodes of very disturbed behavior that may be referred to as undifferentiated psychosis, for want of a better term (Wing, 1981a; Wolff & Chick, 1980). These episodes usually clear up when the stressful circumstance is identified and removed, but they can occasionally become chronic.

In any of the three groups, individuals with high levels of ability, who make the most progress and become independent in adult life, tend to develop a stilted and over-polite form of social interaction (Wing, 1992). As models of conventionality who stick rigidly to the rules, they may do very well in their occupations. Problems tend to occur in more intimate relationships within the family, where empathy and give-and-take are required rather than a rigid demand for an unchanging routine. An individual may have childish temper tantrums at home, in contrast to his or her even demeanor at work. However, many of these people do find a way of life in which they manage well, even if they are regarded as eccentric by others (Carpenter, 1992; Grandin, 1992; Lissner, 1992; Ronan, 1992; Sinclair, 1992).

DIFFERENTIAL DIAGNOSIS

The borderlines that separate the autistic spectrum, and other disorders that begin in childhood and affect development, from some psychiatric conditions and even from eccentric normality are not clearly demarcated. It has been well said that nature never draws a straight line without smudging it.

Disorders Beginning in Childhood

All the disorders that begin in childhood can coexist with each other and with an autistic spectrum disorder. When a clinician is making a diagnostic formulation, the question to ask is not which one of these conditions is present but how many can be identified. Diagnosis of a disorder in the autistic spectrum depends on detection of the pattern of impairments and repetitive behavior described in this chapter as well as recognition that the manifestations of these problems vary with different mental and chronological ages.

The disorders likely to cause diagnostic problems, and the reasons for confusion among these disorders, are discussed below. The list is not exhaustive, but it includes those that frequently cause diagnostic difficulties. Where relevant, the terms used are from *DSM-IV;* the *ICD-10* diagnostic categories are similar but vary somewhat in their labeling.

Mental Retardation

Retardation of cognitive, language, and motor skills from any cause can occur with or without autism. Down syndrome is usually associated with appropriate sociability and good nonverbal communication, but autistic behavior can occur with this condition (Howlin, Wing, & Gould, 1995; Wakabayashi, 1979; Wing & Gould, 1979).

Accurate diagnosis may be a problem if a person's mental age is too low for pretend play to have developed—that is, below 20 months (Wing et al., 1977). People at this mental level often display simple stereotypies such as body rocking or finger flicking, but when their social responsiveness is observed, a differential diagnosis can be made even at this low level of function. Some simple stereotypies can occur in young retarded children whose mental age is above 20 months, but, if the children are not autistic, the behaviors do not dominate their activity pattern, and social responses and pretend play that are appropriate to their mental age will be evidenced.

Developmental Language Disorders

Disorders that affect receptive and/or expressive language can occur alone or with other disorders, including the autistic spectrum conditions. To differentiate a diagnosis of developmental language disorders from one for autism and related conditions, clinicians must observe the individual's social relationships, imaginative activities, and desire to communicate, as shown in the use of gesture and other nonverbal methods (Wing, 1969). Rutter and his colleagues (Bartak, Rutter, & Cox, 1975, 1977; Cox, Rutter, Newman, & Bartak, 1975) studied young children with severe developmental language disorders (including impairment of receptive language) and compared them with children with autism; members of both groups had nonverbal IQs of 70 or above. The researchers found clear differences between the groups on the variables mentioned above, and they noted the presence of deviant as well as delayed language in the group with autism. There was, however, some overlapping of the clinical symptoms, especially in a small number of children who exhibited features of both groups. Cantwell, Baker, Rutter, and Mawhood (1989) followed the children into middle childhood, and Rutter, Mawhood, and Howlin (1992) extended the study into the individual's early adult life.

In both follow-up studies, marked differences between the groups remained. Those with SDLD (Severe Developmental Language Disorder), however, tended to have limited social relationships, and these limitations lasted into early adult life despite improvement in the individual's conversational language.

Rapin and Allen (1983) introduced the term *semantic pragmatic* syndrome to refer to children who have fluent expressive language but do not use this skill for reciprocal communication. Because pragmatic impairment is an essential feature of autistic spectrum conditions, Rapin and Allen made clear that they were referring to a semantic-pragmatic syndrome *without* the underlying social impairment found in autism. Difficulties arise in diagnosing children with autistic spectrum disorders who have active-but-odd social interactions and fluent speech. This grouping includes many children diagnosed as having Asperger's Syndrome. A number of authors have studied semantic-pragmatic problems in children, though not all have used this label. Lister Brook and Bowler (1992) reviewed 10 such studies and noted that, although the language problem was the primary focus, the authors in each case noted the presence of one, two, or all three components of the triad of impairments (Wing & Gould, 1979) in the children they described. Yet, despite evidence of these impairments, the authors implicitly or explicitly rejected the diagnosis of autism. Whatever the theoretical arguments, in practice it is important to recognize when social impairment is present. When therapeutic efforts are concentrated solely on the language disorder, the more fundamental impairments are not addressed.

Developmental Coordination Disorder

Some children are particularly clumsy in gross or fine motor movements, or in both. This problem is characteristic of the subgroup of autistic people described by Asperger, which overlaps with the passive and the active-but-odd groups. However, such clumsiness can occur in children who do not have the autistic pattern of behavior. Because of their difficulty in participating in the physical activities of their peer group, they may become diffident, shy, or socially awkward.

Attention Deficit Hyperactivity Disorder

Many children with autistic spectrum disorders are restless and distractible, although typically they are able to concentrate on the repetitive activities of their own choosing. Gillberg, Rasmussen, Carlström, Svenson, and Waldenström (1982), in an epidemiological study of 6-year-old children in Gothenburg, Sweden, identified a group of 14 children (1.2% of the population not mentally retarded) who had a combination of severe motor clumsiness and attention deficit disorder. (In later papers, this condition was referred to as deficits of attention, motor control, and perception—the DAMP syndrome.) Gillberg and Gillberg (1989) found that 8 of the 14 children had autistic-like traits. One had Autistic Disorder (*DSM-III-R* definition); 3 met the criteria for Asperger's Syndrome as defined by the authors, based on Asperger's (1944, 1991) original description; and 4 had many of the features of this syndrome.

Autistic spectrum disorders can be associated with deficits of attention, motor control, and perception. When these deficits are present, they can mask the autistic spectrum disorder, allowing it to be overlooked. Therefore, careful assessment of the total behavior pattern is essential so that all the impairments are detected.

Tourette's Disorder

The tics, compulsive shouting and swearing, and echoing of words, sounds, and actions that can occur in Tourette's Disorder (Shapiro, Shapiro, Brown, & Sweet, 1978) resemble the same phenomena occurring in autism. This disorder can also occur along with autistic spectrum disorders (Kerbeshian & Burd, 1986; Realmuto & Main, 1982).

Hearing Impairments

Hearing loss is often suspected in young children who exhibit the speech delay associated with autistic spectrum disorders. Rutter and Lockyer (1967) noted that this concern had been expressed for one-third of their sample of children with autism. The presence of the triad of impairments (Wing & Gould, 1979), especially the lack of nonspoken methods of communication, points to a diagnosis of an autistic spectrum disorder. However, hearing impairments can occur with autistic disorders and can be difficult to diagnose because autistic individuals commonly ignore some sounds. Careful investigation is important because poor hearing can exacerbate the children's social and communication problems.

Visual Impairments

Impairments of social interaction, communication, and imagination, and stereotypies such as eye poking, body rocking, and hand flapping have been described in a substantial minority of children who have severe congenital visual impairments. Cass, Sonksen, and McConachie (1994) noted that this pattern of behavior sometimes occurs as part of a developmental setback in the second or third year of life in some children with severe visual impairments, even though the children were initially thought to have normal cognitive potential. These authors observed that the developmental impairments were strongly associated with the severity of the visual loss. Because the most severe congenital visual impairments are known to be associated with central nervous system disorders, diagnosticians often have difficulty estimating how much of the developmental problem is due to the visual impairment and how much to the neuropathology.

Wing (1969) studied 15 children with severe congenital visual problems as well as hearing impairments, comparing them with 20 children who had autistic spectrum disorders. She found marked similarities in the behavioral profiles of the two groups. Twelve of the former group had been affected by maternal rubella; possible causes for impairments in the other 3 children were not known. Again, the contribution of brain pathology to the behavior pattern (as compared with the effect of the sensory impairments) could not be determined. A follow-up study of children with congenital rubella, by Chess (1977), suggested that the autistic behavior followed from the effects of the virus on the central nervous system rather than from the sensory impairments. The relationship of such impairments to autistic conditions is of considerable interest, especially because some visually impaired children experience a period of apparent normality before a setback, and the timing of this setback is similar to that in autistic spectrum disorders.

Psychiatric Conditions

Any of the psychiatric conditions that usually begin in adult life can occur along with autistic spectrum disorders. The commonest of these are the affective disorders, especially anxiety and depression (Wright, 1982). Because some clinical features found in certain psychiatric conditions resemble those found in autism, these conditions pose problems of differential diagnosis.

Schizophrenia

The relationship between autism and schizophrenia has long been the subject of controversy. Some workers (for example, Bender, 1947; Despert, 1938; Goldfarb, 1974) have hypothesized that autism is the childhood form of schizophrenia, but more recent research has shown that the autistic spectrum can be differentiated on genetic and demographic grounds from adult schizophrenia beginning in childhood (Kolvin, 1971; Kolvin, Ounsted, Humphrey, & McNay, 1971). People with autism and related conditions do not have a raised prevalence of schizophrenia in their families (Kolvin, Ounsted, Richardson, & Yarside, 1971). The higher male:female ratio, the frequency of mental retardation, and the almost invariable onset before the individual is 5 years of age also differentiate autistic conditions from schizophrenia.

The clinical symptoms seen in some people with autistic spectrum disorders, especially adolescents and adults in the passive or active-but-odd groups, may cause confusion. The symptoms of schizophrenia can be divided into two types: (a) negative features comprising slowness, lack of motivation, social withdrawal, and emotional flattening; and (b) florid features, comprising delusions and hallucinations (Schneider, 1971; J. Wing, 1978, 1995). The social impairments characterizing the autistic spectrum may resemble the social withdrawal in schizophrenia. People with autistic conditions may be slow and lacking in motivation if asked to perform a task that has no meaning for them. However, many show great speed and determination when pursuing their own special interests. In individuals with autism, lack of use of nonverbal communication and inappropriate laughing or weeping due to their difficulty in comprehending the meaning of events can be interpreted as emotional flattening.

Some aspects of autistic behavior can suggest the presence of the florid symptoms. It is quite common for people with autistic spectrum disorders to answer yes to questions they do not understand, and an inexperienced interviewer may then record the presence of delusions and hallucinations. Some individuals may have ideas of reference or of persecution, but these are based on reality: people with autistic spectrum disorders do attract adverse comments, teasing, and mockery because of their odd behavior. Concrete, literal interpretations of the meanings of words can cause problems, as with the young man who said he could hear voices when no one was in the room with him but failed to explain that this was because he could hear, through the wall, real people conversing in the next room. The more talkative people in the autistic spectrum tend to make irrelevant remarks and to ramble on about their special interests; this behavior can be interpreted as thought disorder. The tendency for autistic individuals to repeat things they have heard in the past can suggest the presence of delusions or hallucinations; this possibility can arise especially if they have been in contact with people with psychiatric disorders or with psychiatrists who have tried to establish a diagnosis of schizophrenia and the autistic individuals repeat what they have heard these people say. Occasionally, people with autistic conditions do report experiences suggesting perceptual disorders; one such boy said that he sometimes saw colored shapes in the air when he was alone in his room at night. Those with little or no speech may laugh to themselves while looking at something the observer cannot identify. This behavior tends to be misinterpreted as responding to hallucinations, but those who know such people well recognize that they are looking at or listening to some simple sensory stimulus that holds their attention and gives them pleasure. Childish fantasies of being an animal or an inanimate object such as a train or robot can be mistaken for delusions by someone who is unfamiliar with the autistic spectrum of disorders.

A correct diagnosis has to be made on the basis of a detailed developmental history from an informant who has known the person well from early childhood, and from a clear description of the current behavior pattern. An interview with the individual is not sufficient basis for identifying the nature of the problems; an interview alone can be highly misleading because of the communication problems that are an essential part of the autistic spectrum disorders.

Psychiatric conditions can be superimposed on the original autistic disorder. Some authors have reported the development of schizophrenia in children with autistic spectrum disorders (Petty, Ornitz, Michelman, & Zimmerman, 1984; Watkins, Asarnow, & Tanguay, 1988; Wolff & Chick, 1980), although the clinical descriptions are not detailed enough for a reader to be sure of the diagnoses. When precise knowledge of the neuropathology of either group of conditions is lacking, the hypothesis of a relationship between autistic and schizophrenic disorders remains unproven. Both involve disorders of empathy, to use the concept suggested by Gillberg (1992). Both affect social interaction, verbal and nonverbal communication, and imaginative symbolic activities, so both possibly involve similar aspects of brain function. However, the history and clinical pictures of the two conditions differ considerably in their details, and it would seem sensible to classify them separately. Nothing can be gained from putting them in the same category and much can be lost by obscuring their real differences, especially for management and treatment.

Catatonia

The phenomena of catatonia, including odd hand postures, interruption and freezing of ongoing movements, difficulty in completing actions, and catatonic excitement, can be seen in minor or marked form in association with the autistic spectrum (Realmuto & August, 1991). In the author's observation, these phenomena tend to become more marked during adolescent exacerbations of behavior problems, and, in a very few individuals, the features have increased in number and severity almost to the point of catatonic stupor. Sometimes, the symptoms improve over time; in other cases, they show no signs of remitting.

The occurrence of catatonic phenomena has probably added to the confusion between autistic spectrum disorders and schizophrenia. Although it can occur in schizophrenia, catatonia can also be associated with a variety of neurological and psychiatric conditions (Rogers, 1992) and is particularly characteristic of postencephalitis states, as described in considerable detail by Sacks (1982). The diagnosis of associated autistic spectrum disorder has to be made on the full history from early childhood and on the complete clinical picture.

Obsessive-Compulsive Disorder

Some of the phenomena seen in Obsessive-Compulsive Disorder (OCD) or Obsessive-Compulsive Personality Disorder—including the urge to count and manipulate numbers, to carry out the same action over and over, or to fearfully avoid particular situations—have obvious similarities to the repetitive routines of autistic people. Baron-Cohen (1989) discussed use of the term *obsessions* to describe the repetitive behaviors typical of autistic disorders. He considered the term inappropriate because the subjective phenomena of resistance to the repetitive activities could not be discerned in autism. Overlap of the features of OCD and autistic spectrum disorders, especially in high-functioning individuals with autism, can obscure the diagnosis of an autistic spectrum disorder unless a detailed developmental history of the person is obtained (Szatmari, 1991; Szatmari, Bartolucci, Bremner, Bond, & Rich, 1989; Thomsen, 1994).

The similarities and differences among autism, catatonia, obsessional disorders, Parkinson's disease, Tourette's Syndrome, and encephalitic encephalopathy raise interesting questions concerning the possible site and nature of their neuropathology and neurochemistry (Damasio & Maurer, 1978).

Schizoid Personality Disorder

All the criteria given in *DSM-IV* and *ICD-10* for diagnosis of *schizoid personality disorder* in adults (such as, almost always chooses solitary activities, lacks close friends or confidants other than first degree relatives; emotional coldness, detachment or flattened affectivity) can occur in people with high-functioning autism or in Asperger's Syndrome. In the author's clinical experience, some high-functioning individuals with autistic spectrum conditions are misdiagnosed as having schizoid personality disorders because the details of their development throughout childhood have not been considered. The relationship between the autistic spectrum and schizoid personality disorder in adults has never been systematically examined. However, for over 30 years, Wolff has studied a group of children whom she originally described as having *schizoid personality disorder of childhood.* In her book summarizing the results of her work in this field (Wolff, 1995), she acknowledged the large degree of overlap of her group with Asperger's Syndrome. She considered that the children she studied were at the most able end of the autistic spectrum. The majority became independent as adults although, throughout their lives, they had unusual patterns of social interaction and communication.

Unlike the label of schizoid personality, the diagnosis of autistic spectrum disorder is useful because it helps the individual, the parents, and others involved to understand the underlying impairments, it has implications for education and treatment, and the Autism Societies provide reference groups.

Schizotypal Personality Disorder

DSM-IV, but not *ICD-10,* includes the category of *schizotypal personality disorder.* All the criteria listed for this diagnosis (such as, ideas of reference: unusual perceptual experiences: behavior or appearance that is odd, eccentric or peculiar) can occur in high-functioning autism and in Asperger's Syndrome but the points raised in the discussion of schizoid personality disorder apply also to this diagnosis.

Psychosocial Deprivation

Children deprived, from their earliest years, of social interaction and opportunities for learning can appear withdrawn, may be delayed in developing speech, and may even show stereotyped movements. If the deprivation is gross and prolonged, they may function as severely retarded. If they are of potentially normal cognitive ability, recovery tends to be rapid once the environment is improved (Clarke & Clarke, 1976; Koluchova, 1972, 1976). A child who is autistic may have the added disadvantage of a poor environment, but the coincidence should not be taken to imply a causal connection.

Borderlines of Normality

The normal variation of human behavior encompasses people who collect objects, people who have circumscribed interests, and people who are not particularly sociable or adept in social interaction. As pointed out by Asperger (1944, 1991), artists and scientists need a capacity to lose themselves at times in their own special fields, to the exclusion of all else. The borderlines of normality and the autistic spectrum overlap, sometimes blurring the edge where normal variation ends and pathology begins (Newson, Dawson, & Everard, 1982). The theoretical issues are of great interest, but, in practice, differential diagnosis is of importance only when the individuals concerned, or their families, experience problems and need help.

Consideration of classification problems shows clearly that syndromes of autism and atypical development are most easily understood when seen in the context of the full range of developmental and psychiatric disorders and the borderlines of normality, and not as unique and separate conditions.

Cross-References

Aspects of diagnosis are discussed in Chapters 1, 3 through 7, and 39. Life span and developmental issues are addressed in Chapters 12 through 14 and 45. Social development in autism is discussed in Chapters 8 and 43. Alternative approaches to diagnosis are discussed in Chapters 1 and 21.

REFERENCES

American Psychiatric Association. (1980). *Diagnostic and statistical manual of mental disorders* (3rd ed.). Washington, DC: Author.

American Psychiatric Association. (1987). *Diagnostic and statistical manual of mental disorders* (3rd ed., rev.). Washington, DC: Author.

American Psychiatric Association. (1994). *Diagnostic and statistical manual of mental disorders* (4th ed.). Washington, DC: Author.

Anthony, E.J. (1958). An experimental approach to the psychopathology of childhood autism. *British Journal of Medical Psychology, 21,* 211–225.

Asperger, H. (1944). Die "autistischen psychopathen" im kindersalter. *Archives fur Psychiatrie und Nervenkrankheiten, 117,* 76–136.

Asperger, H. (1991). "Autistic psychopathy" in childhood (U. Frith, trans.). In U. Frith (Ed.), *Autism and Asperger Syndrome* (pp. 37–92). Cambridge, England: Cambridge University Press.

Attwood, A. (1984). *The gestures of autistic children.* Unpublished doctoral dissertation, University of London.

Bailey, A., Bolton, P., Butler, L., Le Couteur, A., Murphy, M., Scott, S., Webb, T., & Rutter, M. (1993). Prevalence of the Fragile X anomaly amongst autistic twins and singletons. *Journal of Child Psychology and Psychiatry, 34,* 673–688.

Baron-Cohen, S. (1989). Do autistic children have obsessions and compulsions? *British Journal of Clinical Psychology, 28,* 193–200.

Bartak, L., & Rutter, M. (1976). Differences between mentally retarded and normally intelligent autistic children. *Journal of Autism and Childhood Schizophrenia, 6,* 109–120.

Bartak, L., Rutter, M., & Cox, A. (1975). A comparative study of infantile autism and specific developmental receptive language disorder: 1. The children. *British Journal of Psychiatry, 126,* 127–145.

Bartak, L., Rutter, M., & Cox, A. (1977). A comparative study of infantile autism and specific developmental receptive language disorder: III. Discriminant function analysis. *Journal of Autism and Childhood Schizophrenia, 7,* 297–302.

Bauman, M., & Kemper, T. (Eds.). (1994a). *The neurobiology of autism.* Baltimore: Johns Hopkins University Press.

Bauman, M., & Kemper, T. (1994b). Neuroanatomic observations of the brain in autism. In M. Bauman & T. Kemper (Eds.), *The neurobiology of autism* (pp. 119–145). Baltimore: Johns Hopkins University Press.

Bender, L. (1947). Childhood schizophrenia: A clinical study of 100 schizophrenic children. *American Journal of Orthopsychiatry, 17,* 40–56.

Bolton, P., MacDonald, H., Pickles, A., Rios, P., Goode, S., Crowson, M., Bailey, A., & Rutter, M. (1994). A case-control family history study of autism. *Journal of Child Psychology and Psychiatry, 35,* 877–900.

Borden, M., & Ollendick, T. (1994). An examination of the validity of social subtypes in autism. *Journal of Autism and Developmental Disorders, 24,* 23–38.

Boucher, J. (1977). Alternating and sequencing behavior, and response to novelty in autistic children. *Journal of Child Psychology and Psychiatry, 18,* 67–72.

Boucher, J., & Lewis, V. (1992). Unfamiliar face recognition in relatively able autistic children. *Journal of Child Psychology and Psychiatry, 33,* 843–860.

Bowler, B. (1992). "Theory of mind" in Asperger's Syndrome. *Journal of Child Psychology and Psychiatry, 33,* 877–894.

Cantwell, D., Baker, L., Rutter, M., & Mawhood, L. (1989). Infantile autism and developmental receptive dysphasia: A comparative follow-up into middle childhood. *Journal of Autism and Developmental Disorders, 19,* 19–32.

Carpenter, A. (1992). Autistic adulthood: A challenging journey. In E. Schopler & G. Mesibov (Eds.), *High functioning individuals with autism* (pp. 289–293). New York: Plenum Press.

Cass, H., Sonksen, P., & McConachie, H. (1994). Developmental setback in severe visual impairment. *Archives of Diseases of Childhood, 70,* 192–196.

Castelloe, P., & Dawson, G. (1993). Subclassification of children with autism and pervasive developmental disorder: A questionnaire based on Wing's subgrouping scheme. *Journal of Autism and Developmental Disorders, 23,* 229–242.

Chess, S. (1971). Autism in children with congenital rubella. *Journal of Autism and Childhood Schizophrenia, 1,* 33–47.

Chess, S. (1977). Follow-up report on autism in congenital rubella. *Journal of Autism and Childhood Schizophrenia, 7,* 69–81.

Churchill, D.W., & Bryson, C.Q. (1972). Looking and approach behavior of psychotic and normal children as a function of adult attention or preoccupation. *Comprehensive Psychiatry, 13,* 171–177.

Clarke, A.M., & Clarke, A.D.B. (1976). *Early experience: Myth and evidence.* London: Open Books.

Corbett, J., Harris, R., Taylor, E., & Trimble, M. (1977). Progressive disintegrative psychosis of childhood. *Journal of Child Psychology and Psychiatry, 17,* 211–219.

Cox, A., Rutter, M., Newman, S., & Bartak, L. (1975). A comparative study of infantile autism and specific developmental receptive language disorder: II. Parental characteristics. *British Journal of Psychiatry, 126,* 146–159.

Damasio, A.R., & Maurer, R.G. (1978). A neurological model for childhood autism. *Archives of Neurology, 35,* 777–786.

DeMyer, M. (1976). Motor, perceptual-motor and intellectual disabilities of autistic children. In L. Wing (Ed.), *Early childhood autism* (2nd ed., pp. 169–196). Oxford, England: Pergamon.

DeMyer, M.K., Barton, S., DeMyer, W.E., Norton, J.A., Allen, J., & Steel, R. (1973). Prognosis in autism: A follow-up study. *Journal of Autism and Childhood Schizophrenia, 3,* 199–246.

Denckla, M.B. (1986). New diagnostic criteria for autism and related behavior disorders: Guidelines for research protocols (Editorial). *Journal of the American Academy of Child and Adolescent Psychiatry, 25,* 221–224.

De Sanctis, S. (1906). Sopra alcune varieta della demenza precoce. *Rivista Sperimentale di Freniatria e di Medicina Legale, 32,* 141–165.

De Sanctis, S. (1908). Dementia praecocissima catatonica oder katatonie des fruheren kindersalters? *Folia Neurobiologica, 2,* 9–12.

Despert, J.C. (1938). Schizophrenia in children. *Psychiatric Quarterly, 12,* 366–371.

Earl, C.J.C. (1943). The primitive catatonic psychosis of idiocy. *British Journal of Medical Psychology, 14,* 230–253.

Eaves, L., Ho, H., & Eaves, D. (1994). Subtypes of autism by cluster analysis. *Journal of Autism and Developmental Disorders, 24,* 3–22.

Ehlers, S., & Gillberg, C. (1993). The epidemiology of Asperger Syndrome. A total population study. *Journal of Child Psychology and Psychiatry, 34,* 1327–1350.

Ferrari, M. (1982). Can differences in diagnostic criteria be stopped? *Journal of Autism and Developmental Disorders, 12,* 85–88.

Fombonne, E., Siddons, F., Achard, S., Frith, U., & Happé, F. (1994). Adaptive behavior and theory of mind in autism. *European Child and Adolescent Psychiatry, 3,* 176–186.

Frith, U. (1989). *Autism: Explaining the enigma.* Oxford, England: Blackwell.

Ghaziuddin, M., Tsai, L., Eilers, L., & Ghaziuddin, N. (1992). Autism and herpes simplex encephalitis. *Journal of Autism and Developmental Disorders, 22,* 107–114.

Ghaziuddin, M., Tsai, L., & Ghaziuddin, N. (1991). Violence in Asperger's Syndrome: A critique. *Journal of Autism and Developmental Disorders, 21,* 349–354.

Gillberg, C. (1986). Onset at age 14 of a typical autistic syndrome: A case report of a girl with herpes simplex encephalitis. *Journal of Autism and Developmental Disorders, 16,* 369–376.

Gillberg, C. (1989). The borderland of autism and Rett Syndrome: Five case histories to highlight diagnostic difficulties. *Journal of Autism and Developmental Disorders, 19,* 545–560.

Gillberg, C. (1992). The Emmanuel Miller Memorial Lecture 1991. Autism and autistic-like conditions: Subclasses among disorders of empathy. *Journal of Child Psychology and Psychiatry, 33,* 813–842.

Gillberg, I.C., & Gillberg, C. (1989). Asperger Syndrome: Some epidemiological considerations. *Journal of Child Psychology and Psychiatry, 30,* 631–638.

Gillberg, C., & Rasmussen, P. (1994). Four case histories and a literature review of Williams syndrome and autistic behavior. *Journal of Autism and Developmental Disorders, 24,* 381–393.

Gillberg, C., Rasmussen, P., Carlström, G., Svenson, B., & Waldenström, E. (1982). Perceptual, motor and attentional deficits in six-year-old children. *Journal of Child Psychology and Psychiatry, 23,* 131–144.

Gillberg, C., & Schaumann, H. (1981). Infantile autism and puberty. *Journal of Autism and Developmental Disorders, 11,* 365–371.

Goldfarb, W. (1974). *Growth and change of schizophrenic children.* New York: John Wiley & Sons.

Gould, J. (1982). *Social communication and imagination in children with cognitive and language impairments.* Unpublished doctoral dissertation, University of London.

Grandin, T. (1992). An inside view of autism. In E. Schopler & G. Mesibov (Eds.), *High functioning individuals with autism* (pp. 105–128). New York: Plenum Press.

Hagberg, B., Aicardi, J., Dias, K., & Ramos, O. (1983). A progressive syndrome of autism, dementia, ataxia, and loss of purposeful hand use in girls: Rett's Syndrome. A report of 35 cases. *Annals of Neurology, 14,* 471–479.

Heller, T.T. (1954). Dementia infantilis (W. C. Hulse, trans.). *Journal of Nervous and Mental Diseases, 119,* 471–477.

Hobson, R.P. (1983). The autistic child's recognition of age-related features of people, animals and things. *British Journal of Developmental Psychology, 1,* 343–352.

Howlin, P., Wing, L., & Gould, J. (1995). The recognition of autism in children with Down syndrome: Implications for intervention and some speculations about pathology. *Developmental Medicine and Child Neurology, 37,* 406–414.

Hunt, A., & Dennis, J. (1987). Psychiatric disorder among children with tuberous sclerosis. *Developmental Medicine and Child Neurology, 29,* 190–198.

Hunt, A., & Shepherd, C. (1993). A prevalence study of autism in tuberous sclerosis. *Journal of Autism and Developmental Disorders, 23,* 323–340.

Hurtig, R., Ensrud, S., & Tomblin, J.B. (1982). The communicative function of question production in autistic children. *Journal of Autism and Developmental Disorders, 12,* 57–69.

Jervis, G.A. (1963). The clinical picture. In F.L. Lyman (Ed.), *Phenylketonuria* (pp. 52–61). Springfield, IL: Thomas.

Kanner, L. (1943). Autistic disturbances of affective contact. *Nervous Child, 2,* 217–250.

Kanner, L. (1946). Irrelevant and metaphorical language in early childhood autism. *American Journal of Psychiatry, 103,* 242–246.

Kanner, L. (1971). Follow-up study of eleven autistic children originally reported in 1943. *Journal of Autism and Childhood Schizophrenia, 1,* 119–145.

Kanner, L. (1973). *Childhood psychosis: Initial studies and new insights.* Washington, DC: Winston & Sons.

Kanner, L., & Eisenberg, L. (1956). Early infantile autism, 1943–1955. *American Journal of Orthopsychiatry, 26,* 55–65.

Kerbeshian, J., & Burd, L. (1986). Asperger's Syndrome and Tourette Syndrome. *British Journal of Psychiatry, 148,* 731–735.

Klin, A., Volkmar, F., & Sparrow, S. (1992). Autistic social dysfunction: Some limitations of the theory of mind hypothesis. *Journal of Child Psychology and Psychiatry, 33,* 861–876.

Koluchova, J. (1972). Severe deprivation in twins: A case study. *Journal of Child Psychology and Psychiatry, 13,* 107–114.

Koluchova, J. (1976). A report on the further development of twins after severe and prolonged deprivation. In A.M. Clarke & A.D.B. Clarke (Eds.), *Early experience: Myth and evidence* (pp. 56–66). London: Open Books.

Kolvin, I. (1971). Studies in the childhood psychoses: 1. Diagnostic criteria and classification. *British Journal of Psychiatry, 118,* 381–384.

Kolvin, I., Ounsted, C., Humphrey, M., & McNay, A. (1971). Studies in the childhood psychoses: II. The phenomenology of childhood psychoses. *British Journal of Psychiatry, 118,* 385–395.

Kolvin, I., Ounsted, C., Richardson, L., & Yarside, R.F. (1971). The family and social background in childhood psychoses. *British Journal of Psychiatry, 118,* 396–402.

Langdell, T. (1978). Recognition of faces: An approach to the study of autism. *Journal of Child Psychology and Psychiatry, 19,* 255–268.

Le Couteur, A., Rutter, M., Lord, C., Rios, P., Robertson, S., Holdgrafer, M., & McLennan, J. (1989). Autism diagnostic interview: A standardized investigator instrument. *Journal of Autism and Developmental Disorders, 19,* 363–387.

Lissner, K. (1992). Insider's point of view. In E. Schopler & G. Mesibov (Eds.), *High functioning individuals with autism* (pp. 303–306). New York: Plenum Press.

Lister, Brook, S., & Bowler, D. (1992). Autism by another name? Semantic and pragmatic impairments in children. *Journal of Autism and Developmental Disorders, 22,* 61–82.

Lord, C. (1984). The development of peer relations in children with autism. In F.J. Morrison, C. Lord, & D.P. Keating (Eds.), *Applied developmental psychology* (pp. 165–229). New York: Academic Press.

Lotter, V. (1974). Factors related to outcome in autistic children. *Journal of Autism and Childhood Schizophrenia, 4,* 263–277.

Mahler, M.S. (1952). On child psychoses and schizophrenia: Autistic and symbiotic infantile psychoses. *Psychoanalytic Study of the Child, 7,* 286–305.

Mawson, D., Grounds, A., & Tantam, D. (1985). Violence and Asperger's Syndrome: A case study. *British Journal of Psychiatry, 147,* 566–569.

Meryash, D.L., Szymanski, L.S., & Park, G.S. (1982). Infantile autism associated with the Fragile-X syndrome. *Journal of Autism and Developmental Disorders, 12,* 295–302.

Newson, E. (1983). Pathological demand-avoidance syndrome. *Communication, 17,* 3–8.

Newson, E., Dawson, M., & Everard, M.P. (1982). *The natural history of able autistic people: Their management and functioning in social context.* Unpublished manuscript, University of Nottingham, Child Development Research Unit, Nottingham, England.

O'Connor, N., & Hermelin, B. (1988). Low intelligence and special abilities. *Journal of Child Psychology and Psychiatry, 29,* 391–396.

Osterling, J., & Dawson, G. (1994). Early recognition of children with autism: A study of first birthday home videotapes. *Journal of Autism and Developmental Disorders, 24,* 247–258.

Petty, L., Ornitz, E., Michelman, J., & Zimmerman, E. (1984). Autistic children who become schizophrenic. *Archives of General Psychiatry, 41,* 129–135.

Rapin, I. (1994). Introduction and overview. In M.L. Bauman & T.L. Kemper (Eds.), *The neurobiology of autism* (pp. 1–17). Baltimore: Johns Hopkins University Press.

Rapin, I., & Allen, D. (1983). Developmental language disorders: Nosologic considerations. In U. Kirk (Ed.), *Neuropsychology of language, reading and spelling* (pp. 155–183). London: Academic Press.

Realmuto, G., & August, G. (1991). Catatonia in autistic disorder: A sign of co-morbidity or variable expression? *Journal of Autism and Developmental Disorders, 21,* 517–528.

Realmuto, G.M., & Main, B. (1982). Coincidence of Tourette's Disorder and infantile autism. *Journal of Autism and Developmental Disorders, 12,* 367–372.

Ricks, D.M. (1975). Vocal communication in pre-verbal normal and autistic children. In N. O'Connor (Ed.), *Language, cognitive deficits and retardation* (pp. 75–80). London: Butterworths.

Ricks, D.M. (1979). Making sense of experience to make sensible sounds. In M. Bullowa (Ed.), *Before speech: The beginning of interpersonal communication* (pp. 245–268). Cambridge, England: Cambridge University Press.

Ricks, D.M., & Wing, L. (1975). Language, communication and the use of symbols in normal and autistic children. *Journal of Autism and Childhood Schizophrenia, 5,* 191–221.

Rimland, B. (1965). *Infantile autism.* London: Methuen.

Rogers, D. (1992). *Motor disorder in psychiatry: Towards a neurological psychiatry.* Chichester: John Wiley & Sons.

Ronan, T. (1992). My essay. In E. Schopler & G. Mesibov (Eds.), *High-functioning individuals with autism* (pp. 302–303). New York: Plenum Press.

Rutter, M. (1970). Autistic children: Infancy to adulthood. *Seminars in Psychiatry, 2,* 435–450.

Rutter, M. (1972). Childhood schizophrenia reconsidered. *Journal of Autism and Childhood Schizophrenia, 2,* 315–337.

Rutter, M. (1978). Diagnosis and definition. In M. Rutter & E. Schopler (Eds.), *Autism: A reappraisal of concepts and treatment* (pp. 1–25). New York: Plenum Press.

Rutter, M., Bailey, A., Bolton, P., & Le Couteur, A. (1994). Autism and known medical conditions: Myth and substance. *Journal of Child Psychology and Psychiatry, 35,* 311–322.

Rutter, M., Lebovici, S., Eisenberg, L., Sneznevskij, A.V., Sadoun, R., Brooke, E., & Tsung-Yi, Lin. (1969). A tri-axial classification of mental disorders in childhood: An international study. *Journal of Child Psychology and Psychiatry, 10,* 41–61.

Rutter, M., & Lockyer, L. (1967). A five- to fifteen-year follow-up study of infantile psychosis: 1. Description of the sample. *British Journal of Psychiatry, 113,* 1169–1182.

Rutter, M., Mawhood, L., & Howlin, P. (1992). Language delay and social development. In P. Fletcher & D. Hall (Eds.), *Specific speech and language disorders in children* (pp. 63–78). London: Whurr.

Sacks, O. (1982). *Awakenings* (Rev. ed.). London: Pan Books.

Schneider, K. (1971). *Klinische psychopathologie* (9th ed.). Stuttgart, Germany: Thieme.

Shah, A., & Wing, L. (1986). Cognitive impairments affecting social behavior in autism. In E. Schopler & G. Mesibov (Eds.), *Social behavior in autism* (pp. 153–170). New York: Plenum Press.

Shah, A., Holmes, N., & Wing, L. (1982). Prevalence of autism and related conditions in adults in a mental handicap hospital. *Applied Research in Mental Retardation, 3,* 303–317.

Shapiro, A.K., Shapiro, E.S., Brown, R.D., & Sweet, R.D. (1978). *Gilles de la Tourette Syndrome.* New York: Raven Press.

Sinclair, J. (1992). Bridging the gaps: An inside-out view of autism. In E. Schopler & G. Mesibov (Eds.), *High functioning individuals with autism* (pp. 294–302). New York: Plenum Press.

Szatmari, P. (1991). Asperger's Syndrome: Diagnosis, treatment, and outcome. *Psychiatric Clinics of North America, 14,* 81–93.

Szatmari, P. (1992). The validity of autistic spectrum disorders: A literature review. *Journal of Autism and Developmental Disorders, 22,* 583–600.

Szatmari, P., Bartolucci, G., Bremner, R., Bond, S., & Rich, S. (1989). A follow-up study of high-functioning autistic children. *Journal of Autism and Developmental Disorders, 19,* 213–226.

Taft, L.T., & Cohen, H.J. (1971). Hypsarrhythmia and childhood autism: A clinical report. *Journal of Autism and Childhood Schizophrenia, 1,* 327–336.

Thomsen, P. (1994). Obsessive-Compulsive Disorder in children and adolescents. A review of the literature. *European Child and Adolescent Psychiatry, 3,* 138–158.

Treffert, D. (1989). *Extraordinary people.* New York: Bantam.

Tsai, L. (1992). Is Rett Syndrome a subtype of pervasive developmental disorders? *Journal of Autism and Developmental Disorders, 22,* 551–562.

Udwin, O., Yule, W., & Martin, N. (1987). Cognitive abilities and behavioral characteristics of children with idiopathic infantile hypercalcemia. *Journal of Child Psychology and Psychiatry, 28,* 297–310.

Volkmar, F. (1992). Childhood Disintegrative Disorder: Issues for *DSM-IV. Journal of Autism and Developmental Disorders, 22,* 625–642.

Volkmar, F., Cohen, D., Bregman, J., Hooks, M., & Stevenson, J. (1989). An examination of social subtypologies in autism. *Journal of the American Academy of Child and Adolescent Psychology, 28,* 82–86.

Volkmar, F., Stier, D., & Cohen, D. (1985). Age of recognition of Pervasive Developmental Disorder. *American Journal of Psychiatry, 142,* 1450–1452.

Wakabayashi, S. (1979). A case of infantile autism associated with Down's syndrome. *Journal of Autism and Developmental Disorders, 9,* 31–36.

Waterhouse, L., Wing, L., Spitzer, R., & Siegal, B. (1992). Pervasive developmental disorders: From *DSM-III* to *DSM-III-R*. *Journal of Autism and Developmental Disorders, 22,* 525–550.

Watkins, J., Asarnow, R., & Tanguay, P. (1988). Symptom development in childhood onset schizophrenia. *Journal of Child Psychology and Psychiatry, 29,* 865–878.

Wing, J. (1978). Clinical concepts of schizophrenia. In J. Wing (Ed.), *Schizophrenia: Towards a new synthesis* (pp. 1–30). London: Academic Press.

Wing, J. (1995). Concepts of schizophrenia. In S. Hirsch & D. Weinberger (Eds.), *Schizophrenia* (pp. 3–16). Oxford, England: Blackwell.

Wing, L. (1969). The handicaps of autistic children—A comparative study. *Journal of Child Psychology and Psychiatry, 10,* 1–40.

Wing, L. (1970). Observations on the psychiatric section of the *International Classification of Diseases* and the British *Glossary of Mental Disorders. Psychological Medicine, 1,* 78–85.

Wing, L. (1971). Perceptual and language development in autistic children: A comparative study. In M. Rutter (Ed.), *Infantile autism: Concepts, characteristics and treatment* (pp. 173–197). London: Churchill.

Wing, L. (1981a). Asperger's Syndrome: A clinical account. *Psychological Medicine, 11,* 115–129.

Wing, L. (1981b). Language, social and cognitive impairments in autism and severe mental retardation. *Journal of Autism and Developmental Disorders, 11,* 31–44.

Wing, L. (1982). Development of concepts, classification and relationship to mental retardation. In J.K. Wing & L. Wing (Eds.), *Handbook of psychiatry* (pp. 185–190). Cambridge, England: Cambridge University Press.

Wing, L. (1985). *Autistic children: A guide for parents.* New York: Brunner/Mazel.

Wing, L. (1988). The continuum of autistic characteristics. In E. Schopler & G. Mesibov (Eds.), *Diagnosis and assessment in autism* (pp. 91–110). New York: Plenum Press.

Wing, L. (1991). Asperger Syndrome and Kanner's autism. In U. Frith (Ed.), *Autism and Asperger syndrome* (pp. 93–121). Cambridge, England: Cambridge University Press.

Wing, L. (1992). Manifestations of social problems in high-functioning autistic people. In E. Schopler & G.B. Mesibov (Eds.), *High functioning individuals with autism* (pp. 129–142). New York: Plenum Press.

Wing, L. (1993) The definition and prevalence of autism: A review. *European Child and Adolescent Psychiatry, 2,* 61–74.

Wing, L., & Gould, J. (1978). Systematic recording of behaviors and skills of retarded and psychotic children. *Journal of Autism and Childhood Schizophrenia, 8,* 79–97.

Wing, L., & Gould, J. (1979). Severe impairments of social interaction and associated abnormalities in children: Epidemiology and classification. *Journal of Autism and Developmental Disorders, 9,* 11–29.

Wing, L., Gould, J., Yeates, S., & Brierley, L. (1977). Symbolic play in severely mentally retarded and in autistic children. *Journal of Child Psychology and Psychiatry, 18,* 167–178.

Wing, L., Yeates, S., Brierley, L., & Gould, J. (1976). The prevalence of early childhood autism: A comparison of administrative and epidemiological studies. *Psychological Medicine, 6,* 89–100.

Wolff, S. (1995) *Loners: The life path of unusual children.* London: Routledge.

Wolff, S., & Chess, S. (1964). A behavioral study of schizophrenic children. *Acta Psychiatrica Scandinavica, 40,* 438–466.

Wolff, S., & Chick, J. (1980). Schizoid personality in childhood: A controlled follow-up study. *Psychological Medicine, 10,* 85–100.

World Health Organization. (1967). *Manual of the international statistical classification of diseases, injuries and causes of death* (8th ed., Vol. 1). Geneva: Author.

World Health Organization. (1977). *Manual of the international statistical classification of diseases, injuries and causes of death* (9th ed., Vol. 1). Geneva: Author.

World Health Organization. (1992a). *Manual of the international statistical classification of diseases, and related health problems* (10th ed., Vol. 1). Geneva: Author.

World Health Organization. (1992b). *The ICD-10 classification of mental and behavioral disorders. Clinical descriptions and diagnostic guidelines.* Geneva: Author.

World Health Organization. (1993). *The ICD-10 classification of mental and behavioral disorders. Diagnostic criteria for research.* Geneva: Author.

Wright, E.C. (1982). The presentation of mental illness in mentally retarded adults. *British Journal of Psychiatry, 141,* 496–502.

SECTION TWO

Development and Behavior

The concept of pervasive developmental disorders implies that individuals with these conditions—autism, Rett's Disorder, Childhood Disintegrative Disorder, Asperger's Disorder, and other, less well specified disorders—display difficulties across a range of developmental domains, rather than simply in one or another sector. The unfolding and maturation of basic competencies are affected to a greater or lesser degree, and there are varied downstream behavioral consequences of earlier difficulties. The patterns of dysfunction, the extent of impairment, and the areas of relatively better or even normal functioning differ among individuals within one category of disorder and across the range of disorders. Although the pathways of development—socialization, communication, perception and attention, and cognition—are separated in theoretical discussion and research, the minds of children are not so neatly divisible by chapter headings or disciplinary designations. Thus, the complex interactions among the domains, and the changing relations among them at different phases of development, also need to be considered.

The scientific study of the development and behavior of individuals with autism and other disorders aims at defining the nature of the underlying dysfunctions. What specific types of social dysfunctions are exhibited by individuals with autism, and how do these differ from those seen in Asperger's Disorder, Rett's Disorder, or other forms of mental retardation? In autism, what accounts for the relatively better performance on some cognitive tasks (e.g., those that call on rote memory) in contrast with others (e.g., those that require particular

types of social judgment)? What is the meaning of the disparity between verbal and performance skills in Asperger's Disorder, and how does this pattern relate to social difficulties?

To understand the behavioral and developmental findings among individuals with pervasive developmental disorders, it is necessary to carefully study individuals with different levels of cognitive ability (from profoundly retarded through normal intelligence), at different chronological ages (from early childhood through adulthood), and with various observational, laboratory, interview, and other approaches that have demonstrated reliability and validity. The interpretation of findings requires thoughtful consideration of possible methodological problems, including whether the sample is representative of the full population of individuals with the disorder; the adequacy of control and contrast groups; how well the behavioral measure captures the function that is to be studied; and the validity of the measures as well as other issues concerning the design of instruments and studies. Research in developmental psychopathology can be as rigorous and replicable as in any other area of psychological study.

The developmental psychopathological perspective on autism and similar conditions explains the empirical findings concerning atypical behavior and development within the context of normal principles of development. From this perspective, the concepts of normal development highlight the specific types of deviations, abnormalities, rates, and patterns of development of individuals and groups with pervasive disorders. In turn, the study of individuals with autism and other conditions is used to test and expand hypotheses about preconditions of normal development and the unfolding of basic competencies—for example, the relations among cognitive, social, and affective development.

Autism and the other pervasive disorders almost always are lifelong, but the functioning of individuals is not static. Although intellectual abilities tend to remain relatively stable, individuals with autism and other pervasive disorders mature and change during their lives, as do normal children and adolescents. For example, autistic individuals tend to become increasingly social during their later childhood and adolescent years; occasionally, other children with pervasive disorders show dramatic improvement in social and adaptive functioning, and may seem only odd or eccentric in

adulthood. On the other hand, for some autistic and pervasively disordered individuals, new types of difficulties emerge with maturation. Adolescence may be quite difficult as these children experience an upsurge of sexual and aggressive behavior; for higher-functioning individuals, young adulthood may be a time of heightened loneliness and depression as they recognize the profound nature of their difficulties, their differences from others, and their lost and limited opportunities. The study of development during the life span is important for practical as well as theoretical reasons.

The chapters in this section describe the major domains in which individuals with pervasive disorders manifest their cardinal problems and the various phases of life in which these manifestations occur.

CHAPTER 8

Social Development in Autism

FRED VOLKMAR, ALICE CARTER, JAMES GROSSMAN, AND AMI KLIN

The syndrome of early infantile autism was first described in 1943 by Leo Kanner. In a remarkably enduring paper, he reported on 11 children who exhibited what Kanner identified as a congenital lack of interest in other people. He named the condition autism, from the Greek autos, meaning self. In contrast to these children's very limited interest in the social environment, they often were highly interested in aspects of the inanimate environment; for example, a child might appear not to recognize his or her parents but would become panicked if the furniture were rearranged. Kanner regarded the social dysfunction and the unusual responses to the environment as the two essential features of the syndrome. Given the broad range of autism's expression, it is remarkable that, 50 years later, the social disability of persons with autism remains probably the most striking and least understood aspect of the condition (Lord, 1993).

Social deficits have been repeatedly described in persons with autism (e.g., Rimland, 1964; Rutter, 1978; Wing, 1976). Although some social skills emerge over time, even higher-functioning adults with autism have major problems in social relationships (Volkmar & Cohen, 1985). Subsequent work has modified Kanner's original description in important ways, but social deviance continues to be recognized as a significant phenomenological aspect of the syndrome. Diagnostic and assessment instruments developed for autism typically emphasize social factors (Parks, 1983; see also Chapter 21, this volume), as do current diagnostic criteria for the disorder (see Chapter 1).

Social encounters with persons with autism illustrate the severity of their social deficit; social interactions with persons with autism who vary in chronological age and developmental level highlights the complex issues posed by developmental changes and syndrome heterogeneity. A young autistic child may prefer to spend most of his or her time engaged in solitary activities and may fail to respond differentially to a strange person. Very young and severely impaired children may have relatively little interest in social interaction, even with their parents. In contrast to normally developing infants, for whom the social environment is of greatest interest, autistic infants may be exquisitely sensitive to the nonsocial environment and may become profoundly distressed in response to minute changes in the arrangement of furniture in the home. Older children with autism may exhibit some specific attachments to their parents and may passively accept bids for social interaction but will rarely initiate it. The highest-functioning individuals with autism may be very interested in social interaction, but, because of their odd and eccentric social style, they have great difficulty in negotiating the nuances of social interaction. Higher-functioning persons with autism may evidence the following social deficits: (a) failure to establish a joint

Portions of this chapter were presented at a conference, "The Integrative Neurobiology of Affiliation," sponsored by the New York Academy of Sciences and held in Washington, DC, March 14, 1996.

frame of reference for an interaction (e.g., they may begin a discussion without providing the listener with adequate background information); (b) failure to observe social norms or take a listener's feelings into account (e.g., they may approach an unfamiliar adult and remark, "You're very fat"), (c) exclusive reliance on limited or conventional conversational stratagems or stereotyped expressions (e.g., "Do you know about prime numbers?"), followed by elaboration of some idiosyncratic interest or echoing of a previous statement. Failure to use the nonverbal cues that modulate social interaction is common among autistic individuals who never speak; mute persons with autism may not use eye contact appropriately or respond to extralexical social signals, and they may seem to avoid interaction. As their social relationships develop, the richness and intimacy seen even among young normally developing children are typically lacking.

Over the past decade, a substantial body of research on social functioning in autism has emerged. This literature stands in marked contrast to that available a decade ago (e.g., Volkmar, 1987), when a relatively comprehensive review could readily be undertaken in a single chapter. Progress has been made in understanding the developmental aspects of autism; the nature of the social dysfunction, as reflected in specific developmental processes; and the formulation of broader theoretical views of autistic social dysfunction. Unfortunately, disagreements over definition and diagnosis, methodological problems, and theoretical issues still impede research, and, as in the past, a "cognitive primacy hypothesis" (Cairns, 1979) has often been assumed implicitly.

This chapter selectively reviews the topic of social development in autism. It is organized around several broad areas of interest: social dysfunction as a diagnostic feature of autism; the course of social development in normally developing children and in children with autism; selected research findings; and theoretical models for understanding autistic social dysfunction. To the extent possible, research findings are presented within a developmental context. This approach helps to emphasize the distinctiveness of the course of social development in autism.

SOCIAL DYSFUNCTION AS A DIAGNOSTIC FEATURE OF AUTISM

Although certain aspects of Kanner's original description proved to be false leads for research, his phenomenological report of autism has been remarkably enduring. Several aspects of his initial report deserve particular mention. Kanner emphasized that social deviance and delay was a hallmark, if not *the* hallmark, of autism. He was careful to contrast the social interest displayed by children with autism with that of normally developing infants and to emphasize that the autistic social dysfunction was distinctive. This emphasis has continued to be reflected in the various official and unofficial guidelines for diagnosing autism that have appeared since Kanner's original report. The need for diagnostic guidelines became more critical during the late 1970s as the validity of autism as a diagnostic category became more clearly established. Various attempts, both categorical and dimensional, have been made to specify the nature of the social deficit.

Rutter (1978) emphasized that the unusual social development observed in autism was one of the essential features for definition; it was distinctive and was not just a function of associated mental retardation. Early epidemiological studies (e.g., Wing & Gould, 1979) also highlighted some of the difficulties in assessing social development relative to overall cognitive ability, particularly among the more severely handicapped. By 1980, there was general agreement on the need to include autism in official diagnostic systems such as the American Psychiatric Association's (APA) third edition of the *Diagnostic and Statistical Manual of Mental Disorders* (*DSM-III;* APA, 1980). The *DSM-III* definition of infantile autism defined the social deficit as *pervasive;* the use of this term was most appropriate for the youngest and most impaired children—that is, it was consistent with the name of the category. The term *residual autism* was available for persons who had once exhibited the *pervasive* social deficit but no longer did so. Over time, these individuals did manifest some social skills, and the imprecision related to describing the nature of the social deficit was clearly problematic (Cohen, Paul, & Volkmar,

1986). The revision of *DSM-III* was undertaken relatively quickly after its publication, and changes in the definition of autism were made. In *DSM-III-R* (APA, 1987), qualitative impairment in social interaction was retained as one of three essential diagnostic features for autistic disorder (along with qualitative impairments in communication and a restricted range of interests and activities). In contrast to *DSM-III*, the revised manual defined the social deficit much more carefully. To be considered as exhibiting the social deficit, a person had to manifest at least two behaviors from a list of five criteria (see Table 8.1). The *DSM-III-R* criteria for the social deficit also included many examples within the criteria themselves. The *DSM-III-R* approach to defining the autistic social dysfunction reflected an awareness among clinicians that developmental changes do occur in syndrome expression among individuals with autism; they develop some social skills, but these are unusual in quality and/or quantity. This realization was also reflected in

TABLE 8.1   Evolution of the Definition of Social Dysfunction in Autism

Rutter (1978)	Social delays/deviance but not just secondary to Mental Retardation
DSM-III (APA, 1980)	Pervasive social problems
DSM-III-R (APA, 1987)	Qualitative impairment in social interaction: evidence of at least two of the following: 1. Lack of awareness of others. 2. Absent/Abnormal comfort seeking. 3. Absent/Impaired imitation. 4. Absent/Abnormal social play. 5. Gross deficits in ability to make peer friendships.
DSM-IV (APA, 1994) and *ICD-10* (WHO, 1993)	Qualitative impairment in social interaction: evidence of at least two of the following: 1. Marked deficits in nonverbal behaviors used in social interaction. 2. Absent peer relations relative to developmental level. 3. Lack of shared enjoyment/pleasure. 4. Problems in social-emotional reciprocity.

the name of the disorder, which was changed from infantile autism to autistic disorder.

Certain aspects of the revision in the *DSM-III-R* system for autism were major improvements, and others were problematic. One important advantage of the increased number and specification of criteria was that these allowed the system to be better evaluated statistically (see Chapter 1). For example, Siegel, Vukicevic, Elliott, and Kraemer (1989) reanalyzed data about ratings of *DSM-III-R* criteria for autism using an interesting statistical procedure–signal detection analysis. This approach identifies the most robust single criterion or combination of the fewest criteria that can be used to assign a diagnosis. Consistent with Kanner's original impression and subsequent research, social criteria were found to be the most potent predictors of diagnosis. Unfortunately, the broader orientation of *DSM-III-R* also led to many problems with misdiagnosis; as a result, major revisions were made in *DSM-IV* (APA, 1994), which, in the end, paralleled the major changes in the International Classification System (*ICD-10;* World Health Organization [WHO], 1993; see Chapter 1). In both *DSM-IV* and *ICD-10,* qualitative impairment in social interaction has been maintained as one of the essential diagnostic features (see Table 8.1). In contrast to *DSM-III-R, DSM-IV* reduced the number and the detail of these criteria. Problems in at least two of the four areas listed in Table 8.1 must be manifested for the autistic social dysfunction to be considered present in an individual.

In addition to categorical approaches to the definition of social dysfunction, various rating scales, interviews, and checklists have been used to provide dimensional definitions of autism. These are particularly important in the area of social skills where, in contrast to measures of cognitive or language ability, well-developed, norm-referenced tests of ability have not generally been available. Several different approaches have been used to deal with this problem. Some instruments attempt to assess highly unusual features—for example, problems in attachment, reciprocal interaction, and so on, based either on parent report (usually of the child's behavior early in life) or on contemporaneous observation or examination (see Chapter 21 for a review).

Another approach has utilized a widely available, norm-referenced test—the Vineland Adaptive Behavior Scales (Sparrow, Balla, & Cicchetti, 1984)—to provide metrics of social dysfunction in autism. The Vineland is a semi-structured interview that assesses adaptive (real-life) skills in communication, daily living, and socialization. Volkmar and colleagues (1987) reported that, relative to overall cognitive abilities, children with autism exhibited much lower than expected social skills, compared to a mentally handicapped group (see Figure 8.1). Subsequently, this group of researchers used information from the Vineland and signal detection methodology (see also Kraemer, 1988) to demonstrate that delays in social skills are robust predictors of the diagnosis of autism, even when compared to delays in communication (Volkmar, Carter, Sparrow, & Cicchetti, 1993). A series of studies using this instrument has now been conducted and generally supports the notion that deficits in social skills among individuals with autism are greater than expected relative to overall developmental level (e.g., Freeman et al.,

1991; Loveland & Kelley, 1991; Rodrigue, Morgan, & Geffken, 1991; Rumsey, Rapoport, & Sceery, 1985).

Supplementary norms for the Vineland are presently being developed for use in persons with autism; this instrument may also have potential utility in screening for autism because, in contrast with many of the instruments focused specifically on autism, the Vineland assesses more familiar and normative developmentally appropriate skills. As part of their study of the nature of social dysfunction in autism, it is appropriate for clinicians to consider the course of social development in typical children. Kanner (1943) emphasized that discussion of development must begin with an examination of social skills from the very beginning of life.

THE COURSE OF SOCIAL DEVELOPMENT

Social Skills in Normal Development

Normal infants come into the world with the motivation and capacity to begin establishing an immediate social relationship with their caregivers. The earliest evidence of this social drive is the newborn's preference for the human voice (especially its mother's) over other sounds (DeCasper & Fifer, 1980; Mills & Melhuish, 1974). Very young infants also show a preference for the human face over other patterns (Olson & Sherman, 1983; Spitz, 1965), and normal newborns will orient themselves perceptually and motorically toward their parents (Mayes, Cohen, & Klin, 1993).

In the normally developing child, social development follows a predictable course. Selective attention to social stimuli is typically evident in the first months of life, when infants show preferential attention to human faces, which appear to acquire substantial visual meaning for them. Faces, as opposed to representative masks, begin to function differentially as "social releasers" when infants are around 3 months of age (Spitz, 1965)—the approximate time when caregivers assume a more active role in play with infants and show an increased interest in the infants' actions. This is also the time when infants begin vocalizing when spoken to, temporal regularities appear

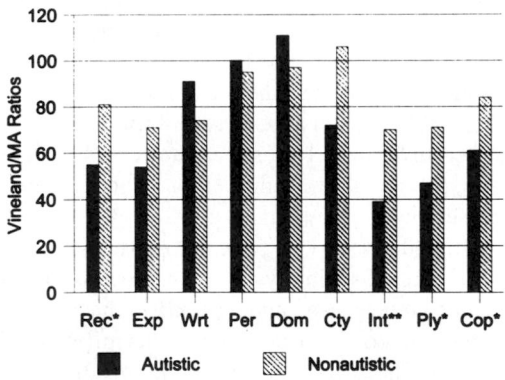

Figure 8.1 Ratios of Vineland age equivalent scores to mental age (MA).

Rec = Receptive communication, Exp = Expressive communication, Wrt = Written communication, Per = Personal skills, Dom = Domestic, Cty = Community, Int = Interpersonal Relationships, Ply = Play and leisure time, Cop = Coping.

* p < .05, ** p < .01. Adapted, with permission from F. R. Volkmar, S. Sparrow, D. Goudreau, D. Cicchetti, R. Paul, & D. J. Cohen. Social deficits in autism: An operational approach using the Vineland Adaptive Behavior Scales. *Journal of the American Academy of Child and Adolescent Psychiatry, 26,* pp. 156–161.

in the pattern of mother–infant gaze (Jaffe, Stern, & Perry, 1973), and infants are capable of distinguishing emotions in caregivers' facial expressions (Charlesworth, 1992). Head turning and gaze aversion, observed early in life, provide infants with a measure of control over their environment. Facial expressions and eye contact are the most frequent modes of communication between the preverbal infant and his or her mother (Ling & Ling, 1974), and initial socialization occurs primarily in the facial dialogue between the infant and caregivers. Children deprived of early social interaction exhibit a variety of deficits, but these are different from the deficits seen in children with autism (Provence & Lipton, 1962).

Vocal communications are an important part of social interchange even before the child acquires speech. Vocal expressions are observed from the first days of life, and long before an infant can respond differentially to the verbal content of speech, he or she can respond with great accuracy to tone and pitch of the voice (Lewis, 1963). The precise mechanisms by which early reciprocal social interactions facilitate the emergence of lexical-communicative speech remain unclear, but Bruner (1983) and other theorists have emphasized the role of such transactions for subsequent linguistic development. For example, in Bruner's view (1975, p. 2), language is "a specialized and conventionalized extension of cooperative action" and the infant actively participates in this process (Bell & Harper, 1977).

During the first year of life, infants learn to respond differentially to their caregivers and other individuals. By the end of the first year of life, typically developing infants have established a coherent pattern of social behaviors, referred to as attachment, that serves to maintain proximity to the caregivers and facilitates exploration (Bowlby, 1969). The complex processes underlying attachment are among the evolved characteristics on which infant survival is based (Freedman, 1974; see also Chapter 43). Attachment behaviors are characterized by a child's concern for maintaining proximity with its caregiver and by extreme distress in that caregiver's absence (Bowlby, 1969; Rutter, 1981). In normal attachment, the caregiver acts as a kind of home

base from which the child may engage in exploration of the world. Early patterns of infant–caregiver interaction can be related to the quality of later attachment, which is, in turn, related to subsequent cognitive and social skills (see Seifer & Schiller, 1996). The strength of these processes is suggested by the observation that even neglected or abused infants typically form attachments, as do infants with mental handicaps not associated with autism (Moser-Richters & Volkmar, 1996; Thompson, 1996). Over the course of development, social skills become increasingly differentiated as children develop peer relations, prosocial skills, and an increasing capacity for self-regulation (Schaffer, 1984; Singer, 1996).

Play skills normally develop within the first 2 years of life. At first, infants simply manipulate objects—that is, they mouth or visually regard them. Later, children move from simple manipulations and inspection to combining objects in play (e.g., stacking blocks) as spatial relationships are explored. Functional use of play objects, such as using a cup to give a doll an imaginary drink, typically develops toward the end of the first year of life. True symbolic play typically develops from 18 to 24 months of age; play objects become completely independent of action, and play is no longer constrained by an object's physical properties (see Singer, 1996). The development of play skills parallels other aspects to cognitive development as the child acquires the capacity for symbolic thought (Piaget, 1951).

Social Skills in Autism

Early Development

Initial studies of the social development of children with autism (e.g., Ornitz, Guthrie, & Farley, 1977; Volkmar, Cohen, & Paul, 1986) were often based on retrospective parent report rather than direct observation. Social deficits, however, have been shown, during various experimental procedures and clinical observations, to be present in very young children with autism (Loveland & Landry, 1986; Trad, Bernstein, Shapiro, & Hertzig, 1993). Although failures or delays in speech acquisition, or concern about possible deafness, are common reasons for initial referral, the manifestations of social deviance in autism are striking and apparently arise in the first months of life, when infants fail to develop reciprocal eye contact and do not acquire the social smile. Young children with autism may be highly responsive to even minute environmental changes, yet the human face and social interaction may hold much less interest for them. Their disinterest is in striking contrast to the behavior of normally developing or of retarded but nonautistic children (see Table 8.2). For autistic children, the powerful influence of social motivational factors does not appear on schedule, and specific social attachments are delayed or deviant in their development, although such behaviors do eventually develop. As reflected in current criteria for autism, infants and young children may not be as likely to seek physical comfort from their parents, to share interesting or pleasurable events, or to take pleasure in interaction with their parents (DeMyer, 1979).

Consistent with Kanner's original impression that the social deviance associated with autism is present from birth, most research studies suggest that, at least in retrospect, parents become concerned about the child's development during the first year of life. In a minority (perhaps 25%) of cases, the child's early development is reported to be normal or near normal, but the parents become concerned when the child is 18 to 36 months of age (see Chapter 1). Given that autism does indeed appear to be an early-onset disorder, it is somewhat paradoxical that actual observational data on extremely young children with autism are highly limited. This scarcity of data reflects the fact that diagnosis is very difficult in this age group (Lord, 1993); even when parents are concerned about their child's development, a considerable period of time often elapses before a diagnosis is given (Siegel, Pliner, Eschler, & Elliott, 1988; Stone & Rosenbaum, 1988; see also Chapter 12).

A handful of studies have attempted to deal with this problem by retrospectively reviewing home movies or videos made of children with autism when they were infants. Osterling and Dawson (1994), for example, reviewed videotapes of first birthday parties of 22 children (11 who were autistic and 11 who were developing normally). Data were collected on social, affective, communicative, and joint-attention behaviors as well as symptoms suggestive of

TABLE 8.2   Vineland Socialization Items of Behavior Differentiating Autistic Children from Controls Matched for Age and Mental Age

Item of Behavior	Expected Age (years–months)	Significance (p <)
Shows interest in new objects/people	<0–2	.05
Anticipates being picked up by caregiver	<0–2	.01
Shows affection to familiar persons	0–4	.001
Shows interest in children/peers other than siblings	0–4	.001
Reaches for familiar person	0–5	.001
Plays simple interaction games	0–6	.001
Uses household objects for play	0–7	.05
Shows interest in activities of others	0–8	.01
Imitates simple adult movements	0–7	.01
Laughs/smiles in response to positive statements	0–11	.01
Calls at least two familiar people by name	0–11	.01
Participates in at least one activity/game with others	1–7	.05
Imitates adult phrases heard previously	1–11	.05

Items drawn from the Vineland Adaptive Behavior Scales (Sparrow et al., 1984); data abstracted from Klin, Volkmar, & Sparrow (1992). Expected age is the median age at which the behavior is present in the general population; cases were matched on age and mental age and were included in comparison only if mental age of the pair was equal to that typically associated with the behavior in the general population.

autism. The children with autism exhibited fewer social and joint-attention behaviors and more autistic symptoms. Behaviors such as pointing, showing objects, looking at others, and orienting in response to name could be used to differentiate the groups. Prospective studies are uncommon, but, in one study, Gillberg et al. (1990) reported that various social behaviors (isolation, problems in eye contact and gaze, indifference to others, and problems in imitation) were more frequent in children who subsequently were identified as autistic than in normally developing children. The results of these studies are consistent with direct observational studies of preschool children with autism. For example, Adrien (1991, 1992) reported that behaviors differentiating young children with autism from those with developmental delay and those developing normally included imitation, eye contact, and social interest.

During early childhood, the overall impression is often one of social aloofness in the affected child (Wing & Attwood, 1987). Difficulties in gaining the child's attention may be prominent, and attempts to disrupt routines or to engage the child may lead to major behavioral upset. Affective responses may seem only minimally related to the ongoing interactional context. At the same time, some important social skills do begin to emerge—that is, the difficulties in social interaction are both quantitative and qualitative in nature, but they do not reflect a total absence of social interest. Evidence of differential relatedness includes the development of some form of attachment to parents (Shapiro, Sherman, Calamari, & Koch, 1987; Sigman & Mundy, 1989; Sigman & Ungerer, 1984a) and differential responsiveness to familiar and unfamiliar individuals (Landry & Loveland, 1988; Sigman & Ungerer, 1984b). The beginnings of capacities for self-observation and self-monitoring can also be observed (e.g., Dawson & McKissick, 1984).

School Age

Although social functioning improves after age 5 years (Rutter & Garmezy, 1983), even the small proportion who markedly improve will rarely achieve normalcy, and they may become more passive or odd in their style of interaction (Wing & Gould, 1979). Many children with autism remain apparently content to be left alone to engage in self-stimulatory and other unusual activities. In older children, the social failures in communication are most evident; they fail to engage in usual forms of social interchange and have difficulties taking another person's point of view into account (Volkmar & Cohen, 1985). Social relationships that develop tend to be with adults; other children seem to hold little interest for the child with autism. Mutual or cooperative play of the type usually expected in children of this age is typically absent.

The nature of the processes underlying social gains during middle childhood remains relatively unstudied. Some controversy exists as to whether gains are made steadily and progressively, or whether, for the individual child, gains (and sometimes losses) in skill levels follow a more unpredictable course. In addition, discrepancies between skill levels in various areas (Burack & Volkmar, 1992) and rates of advance in different areas may not directly correlate with age (Loveland & Kelley, 1991). This issue remains controversial (Ando, Yoshimura, & Wakabayashi, 1980; Loveland & Kelley, 1991).

Adolescence and Adulthood

Eventual social outcome appears to be the result of many factors. For some individuals with autism, social interest expands significantly during adolescence (Rutter, 1970; Schopler & Mesibov, 1983; see also Chapter 14). Unfortunately, even when social interest increases, marked problems usually remain. The individual has difficulty dealing with social rules and conventions and with the reciprocal give-and-take inherent in social situations (Rutter, 1983). People with autism often have difficulties learning, and then generalizing, the rules of social interchange (Schopler & Mesibov, 1983). Even though gradual improvement is common, some individuals unfortunately lose skills during adolescence.

In adults, a range of social outcomes is observed. Higher-functioning individuals often have marked problems in developing friendships and relating to others. Their desire to make social contact may be strong, but their practical ability to carry on the complex tasks

related to intense social interaction is deficient, and feelings of inadequacy and isolation
are common (Bemporad, 1979; Kanner, Rodriguez, & Ashden, 1972; Volkmar & Cohen,
1985). Kanner et al. (1972) suggested that
those individuals with good outcome at follow-
up had learned, by adolescence, to perceive
themselves as unusual and, to develop strategies for coping with their disability. Unfortunately, only a few intervention programs
targeting social skills have been systematically implemented and studied (see Chapter 14
for a review of adolescent development in
autism).

SPECIFIC SOCIAL PROCESSES
IN AUTISM

Social Orientation

Gaze

Normally developing infants spend a significant proportion of their waking time in eye
contact with their caregivers; persons with
autism, however, fail to establish this pattern of
mutual gaze (Volkmar & Mayes, 1990). In the
normal child, facial expressions and eye contact represent an initial "dialogue" between infant and caregiver (Ling & Ling, 1974; Stern,
1985), a basic, nonverbal communication that is
centered on the sharing of affective states.
Data on very young children with autism are
limited, but studies with preschool-age and
older children reveal that the human face holds
little interest for children with autism (Volkmar, 1987); similarly, they appear to lack a
preference for speech sounds (Klin, 1991,
1992). If present from birth, this lack of attrac-
tion to social stimuli may result in a failure to
initiate and integrate the basic interpersonal
patterns that are believed to be the foundation
for later communication.

Eye gaze is frequently reported to be abnormal by parents of children with autism; in one
retrospective study, 90% of parents reported
that their child often, very often, or almost always avoided eye contact (Volkmar et al.,
1986). These data are based on global parental
impression; systematic studies suggest important situational effects—for example, eye
contact increases with adult structure (i.e.,

when adults set the agenda for the interaction)
(Dawson, Hill, Spencer, Galpert, & Watson,
1990; Sigman, Mundy, Sherman, & Ungerer,
1986) and changes, depending on the situation
(Kasari, Sigman, & Yirmiya, 1993). Similarly,
the nature of task demands may influence
amounts of eye contact (Dawson & Adams,
1984; Dawson & Galpert, 1990). Gaze behavior also varies as a function of developmental
level: more developmentally advanced children exhibit an increased frequency of eye
contact (Dawson & Galpert, 1990; Kasari
et al., 1993; Mundy, Sigman, & Kasari, 1994).

Joint Attention

The absence or deviance of gaze behaviors
and other forms of early nonverbal interchange in children with autism also interferes
with the emergence of intersubjectivity, the
co-construction of shared emotional meaning
between child and caregiver (Stern, 1987; Trevarthen, 1979). When children with autism
fail to achieve intersubjectivity, they often
fail to develop a series of behaviors known as
joint attention, which typically emerge when
the child is 8 to 12 months old (Bakeman &
Adamson, 1984; Hannan, 1987). Joint attention refers to those preverbal social communicative skills that allow a child to share with
another person the experience of a third object
or event (Bruner, 1983; Schaffer, 1984); they
are sometimes known as triadic exchanges. A
typically developing infant will, for instance,
smile and point at a toy he or she finds interesting, alternately looking at the toy and at
mother. However, such triadic exchanges are
consistently impoverished in children of similar mental age who have autism (Mundy, Sigman, & Kasari, 1990). With autism, a child
may fail to show or point to objects or to gaze
alternately at the interactive partner and a desired or interesting object/activity. Deficits in
joint attention are among the most striking
and persistent problems in younger children
with autism (Lewy & Dawson, 1992; Mundy
et al., 1994; Sigman et al., 1986). Even when
joint attention is observed, its quality is unusual. Children with autism may also show
less positive affect (Kasari, Sigman, Mundy,
& Yirmiya, 1990).

As with other aspects of gaze behavior,
developmental relationships and correlates of

joint attention have been observed. Lower developmentally functioning children usually show lower levels of joint attention (Mundy et al., 1994), and levels of joint attention can be related to language abilities (Mundy, Sigman, Ungerer, & Sherman, 1987) and to aspects of executive functioning (McEvoy, Rogers, & Pennington, 1993). Environmental correlates of joint attention have also been reported (Lewy & Dawson, 1992).

A specific pattern of joint-attention skills is usually apparent in children with autism; they may, for example, display *protoimperative* gesturing. *Protodeclarative* gesturing is usually completely absent (Baron-Cohen, 1989a; Curcio, 1978; Gomez, Sarria, & Tamarit, 1993; Kasari et al., 1990). Protoimperatives involve the use of gaze and/or gestures to gain another person's aid in obtaining a particular object or outcome (such as pointing to a box of cookies on a high shelf); protodeclaratives involve similar combinations of eye contact and gesturing, but solely with the aim of calling another person's attention to an object or experience—that is, without any instrumental purpose (such as showing a parent that one has found an interesting toy; Bates, 1976). Autistic preverbal communication appears to be almost entirely *requestive;* even those children with autism who do coordinate eye contact with gestures and actions appear rarely to use the coordination merely to share an awareness or an experience of an object or event, as do normal children and developmentally matched children with mental retardation. Before any true verbal language exists, typically developing children have already established an important means of sharing with their caregivers their affective experiences involving objects and events in the world; because children with autism lack crucial joint-attention skills, their ability to engage others and forge social relations is greatly diminished.

Difficulties in integrating gaze with other nonverbal communicative behaviors are frequent (e.g., Buitelaar, Van Engeland, de Kogel, de Vries, & van Hooff, 1991). For example, younger children with autism are less likely to use gaze to augment other sources of information about ambiguous interactions (Phillips, Baron-Cohen, & Rutter, 1992).

Imitation and Play

Imitation

Deficits in the areas of imitation and play have important consequences for other aspects of development. The ability of an infant to share with its caregiver its experience of an object of reference is an important context for symbolic development (Werner & Kaplan, 1963). The capacity to imitate also appears to be a prerequisite for subsequent symbolic activities; here, too, children with autism display serious deficits (Prior, 1979). Various studies have documented deficits in this area (see Smith & Bryson, 1994, for a review).

Studies have revealed that younger children with autism consistently have problems in imitating simple body movements and those that involve objects (e.g., DeMyer et al., 1972; Stone, Lemanek, Fishel, Fernandez, & Altemeier, 1990; Stone, Ousley, & Littleford, 1995). Infants and children with autism seldom spontaneously imitate the actions of their parents (Dawson & Adams, 1984; Meltzoff & Gopnik, 1993), and they are less adept at elicited imitation (Charman & Baron-Cohen, 1994; Stone & Caro-Martinez, 1990). They show little ability for reciprocal social play, such as "peek-a-boo" and "patt-a-cake" games, which integrate imitation and social dialogue (Klin, 1992). However, as with other social behaviors, important effects of developmental level and context are observed (Dawson & Adams, 1984; Sigman & Ungerer, 1984b).

Play

Lack of symbolic play in autism may emerge from social difficulties or may be part of a more general problem in achieving symbolic thought and language. An autistic child's play stands in stark contrast to the richness of play in a normally developing child. Parents reporting on the play of children with autism say that it lacks social engagement and is characterized by repetitive and stereotyped object manipulation and nonfunctional use of objects (Black, Freeman, & Montgomery, 1975; Mundy et al., 1987; Sigman & Ungerer, 1984b; Stone et al., 1990). For example, a toy truck may interest the child only to the extent that parts of it may be spun or whirled. Compared to children with mental retardation, comparatively less symbolic play is observed in children with autism (DeMyer et al., 1967; Stone et al., 1990; Wing et al., 1977). They are more interested in the smell, taste, or feel of play materials than in their function; in addition, play in younger children with autism is highly repetitive in nature (Sherman, Shapiro, & Glassman, 1983; Stone et al., 1990). Thus, deficits are observed in both functional and symbolic play (e.g., Sigman & Ungerer, 1984b; Stone et al., 1990).

To develop functional and symbolic play skills, a child must be able to differentiate objects and actions, and to separate thought processes from concrete reality (Piaget, 1951). Symbolic play skills also relate to broader symbolic development, including the emergence of differential attachment (Sigman & Ungerer, 1984b) and of symbolic language (see Chapter 9). Although available research suggests that the immature and impoverished play observed in children with autism is part of a more general deficiency of symbolic thought and language, many aspects of their play— e.g., the extent to which play skills may be fostered and fantasy can be differentiated from reality, and the relationship of observed individual differences in cognitive and social factors—remain to be studied.

Attachment

The relative absence or oddness of attachment behaviors in children with autism indicates their failure to forge basic social-affective connections with the important figures in their lives (Lord, 1993). For example, these children may not develop social attachments when expected, but they often form idiosyncratic attachments to objects (Volkmar, 1987).

Some researchers, employing the attachment paradigm known as the "strange situation," have argued that children with autism do display some attachment behaviors during the departure and return of a parent, and may be securely attached to their caregivers (Capps, Sigman, & Mundy, 1994; Rogers, Ozonoff, & Maslin-Cole, 1991, 1993; Shapiro et al., 1987; Sigman & Mundy, 1989; Sigman & Ungerer, 1984a). Younger children with autism seek proximity to their mother more than to a stranger, and they increase their proximity to their mother following a reunion with her (Sigman & Mundy, 1989; Sigman & Ungerer, 1984a). The quality of these behaviors may, however, be unusual (Rogers et al., 1993). Various developmental correlates of these behaviors have also been noted (Capps et al., 1994; Rogers et al., 1991, 1993; Sigman & Ungerer, 1984a).

Two lines of work related to attachment behavior in autism deserve further explanation. Even though behavioral research has clearly documented the observation of attachment behaviors, the perception of parents is very different (Volkmar et al., 1986). This discrepancy likely demonstrates that certain aspects of these behaviors are unusual. Young children who are developing normally will often (but not always) form attachments to transitional objects—typically, soft and cuddly materials that aid them with various transitions. When younger children with autism have attachments to objects, these attachments are often odd: the objects are hard (favorites include cereal boxes, metal cars, or magazines) or the class of object is more important than a specific choice (a magazine of a certain type, but not a specific magazine). In the *DSM-IV* field trials (Volkmar et al., 1994), attachments to unusual objects were noted, of low frequency but when they were present, they were relatively specific to the diagnosis of autism. The significance of such objects and their relation to the more typical transitional objects preferred by normally developing children remain to be understood.

Affective Development

Like their attachment behaviors, social behaviors of children with autism in general are impoverished or atypical (Klin & Volkmar, 1993). The children may not seek physical comfort from their parents and may be difficult to hold (DeMyer, 1979; Volkmar, 1987). They may ignore friendly greeters and show no or little response to the speech of their parents, leading some parents to believe their child is deaf (Ornitz, Guthrie, & Farley, 1977). Older children with autism typically fail to engage in social interchange with peers or in cooperative play; compared with normal children, they make far fewer approaches to peers, respond far less often to the approaches of others, and frequently appear more content when left alone (Attwood, Frith, & Hermelin, 1988; Volkmar, 1987). Although not all persons with autism are uninterested in all other people (Lord, 1993), and some social functioning may improve over time, autistic social behavior can rarely be called normal, and even the highest-functioning individuals show obvious signs of social deviance (Wing & Gould, 1979; Volkmar, 1987).

In the second or third year of life, typically developing children begin to recognize and label their own and others' emotional states (Bretherton & Beeghly, 1982). In contrast, children with autism appear to have difficulty recognizing emotions in others. Opinions differ on whether they have a truly perceptual difficulty in recognizing facial affect, rather than a more cognitive-affective inability to infer others' mental states (De Gelder, 1991; Hobson, 1986; Ozonoff, Pennington, & Rogers, 1990).

Specific difficulties in processing information provided by human faces have been noted. Langdell (1978) observed age-related changes in the level of facial recognition among autistic persons; other studies have suggested problems in recognizing faces and producing facial displays of emotion. Related problems include the recognition of unfamiliar faces relative to nonsocial objects (Boucher & Lewis, 1992) and difficulties in utilizing contextual cues (Teunisse & DeGelder, 1994). On the other hand, children with autism can use some aspects of the face, at least as depicted in photographs, as sources of information (Volkmar, Sparrow, Rende, & Cohen, 1989).

Difficulties have been observed in both expressing and producing affective responses. The range, frequency, and integration of autistic children's affective displays are unusual (Ricks & Wing, 1975; Snow, Hertzig, & Shapiro, 1987; Yirmiya, Kasari, Sigman, & Mundy, 1989). These children have particular difficulty integrating appropriate affective displays into an ongoing interaction (Dawson et al., 1990; Kasari, Sigman, & Yirmiya, 1993; McGee, Feldman, & Chernin, 1991). Similar differences have been observed with regard to displays of negative affects; children with

autism may less frequently look at an adult who is demonstrating distress (Sigman, Kasari, Kwon, & Yirmiya, 1992). Persons with autism also find it difficult to imitate facial displays of emotion; relative to Down syndrome subjects, those with autism were more likely to produce unusual facial displays (Loveland, Tunali-Kotoski, Pearson, Brelsford, Ortegon, & Chen, 1994).

These deficits in the recognition and imitation of emotion have implications for the development of empathy. Experiments designed to elicit empathic response from autistic participants have yielded an absence of expressed concern in response to a display of distress by an adult (Sigman et al., 1992). Children with autism are also often totally devoid of prosocial behaviors, such as giving, sharing, helping, or offering comfort or affection (Lord, 1993; Ohta, Nagai, Hara, & Sasaki, 1987).

Pragmatic Skills

The use of expressive language is a landmark in child development. Between 9 and 30 months, normally developing children embark on a whirlwind of language acquisition; they progress from babbling to expression of short but meaningful utterances and then to employment of true syntactical sentence construction (Clark, 1993). Delays in language acquisition, however, are probably the most common reason for the initial referral of children with autism; grossly apparent disturbances in language development, particularly the social aspects of language, form one of the hallmarks of the syndrome. Approximately 50% of children with autism never develop expressive language (Paul, 1987); in those who do, speech is often characterized by echolalia, abnormal speech tone and rhythm, and general lack of speech for communication (DeMyer, 1981; Volkmar, 1987). In persons with autism who do speak, one of the greatest areas of deficit is *pragmatics*—the use of language within a social context (Tager-Flusberg, 1981, 1989). An individual employs pragmatic knowledge to organize and express language in a manner that a listener can understand; similarly, he or she uses that knowledge to comprehend another speaker's meaning. The problematic use of pragmatics has led some to view language deficits in autism as a lack of a *theory of mind*—an inability, when speaking, to take into account what a listener knows, and, when listening to others, to infer their intent (Sperber & Wilson, 1986; Tager-Flusberg, 1993).

THEORETICAL MODELS OF AUTISTIC SOCIAL DYSFUNCTION

Since Kanner first identified the disorder, many different theories have been advanced to explain the pattern of deficits apparent in autism. Initial theories tended to emphasize psychogenic etiologies, and social deficits were viewed as attempts to avoid painful or distressing life experience. As longitudinal studies became available, such notions were largely discarded and neuroanatomic or neurophysiological models of the disorder became common. Sites of the disorder were hypothesized at various points in the central nervous system from the brain stem and vestibular nuclei to the cortex. A plethora of psychological models have also posited the origins of autism in various processes—cognitive functioning, language, arousal, perception, and so forth. Although social deficits have been viewed as essential aspects of syndrome definition, there has been a tendency to see social difficulties as secondary to other problems. This tendency has, in turn, impeded the attempts to develop more robust theoretical models that focus on the social deficit per se. Research on the social dysfunction associated with autism has also been impeded by: (a) difficulties in syndrome definition, (b) the broad range of syndrome expression, (c) a tendency to view different sources of information about the disorder (such as parental report and behavioral observation) in isolation from each other, and (d) a failure to view processes in a truly developmental fashion. Although the importance of developmental factors such as cognitive or communicative ability has been increasingly appreciated, sufficient attention has still not been given to constructing a truly developmental model for autistic social dysfunction. Such a developmental model must address mechanisms by which initial deficits become entrained in compensatory strategies.

In recent years, much excitement and empirical work have been generated by the theory of mind hypothesis, which has attempted to define the autistic condition as a failure to perceive and understand mental states (Astington, Harris, & Olson, 1988; Baron-Cohen, 1989a; Happe, 1994; Perner, 1991). The theory of mind model first emerged in studies with nonhuman primates that explored whether chimpanzees could use deception to obtain a reward (Premack & Woodruff, 1978). The researchers hoped to ascertain whether chimpanzees possess a theory of mind—an ability to impute mental states to others and thereby predict their behavior. Soon thereafter, developmental psychologists began investigating theory of mind ability in human children. Employing a suggestion by Dennett (1978), Wimmer and Perner (1983) tested what is now known as the classic *false belief* task, which involves asking subjects where young Maxi will look for his chocolate, given that Maxi does not know his mother has moved it to another location from where he had left it. It is called a false belief task because, in order to answer the question correctly, the subject, who has access to the correct location of the chocolate, must recognize that Maxi holds an incorrect belief about its location and will act on that mistaken knowledge. Through Wimmer and Perner's study (and scores of replications and modifications), a robust finding has emerged that normally developing 4-year-olds generally display the ability to master false belief tasks, whereas 3-year-olds and younger children usually fail (Astington & Gopnik, 1991; Gopnik & Astington, 1988; Moses & Flavell, 1990).

Researchers soon adapted Wimmer and Perner's task for subjects with autism (Baron-Cohen, Leslie, & Frith, 1985). In this task, the subject sees Sally put a marble in a certain place, and, after Sally leaves, sees Anne put the marble someplace else. The test question is: "Where will Sally look for her marble?" To answer correctly, subjects must realize that because Sally was absent when her marble was moved, she will still look for her marble in its original location. Among 20 verbal children with autism and mental ages well above 4 years, 80% failed the Sally–Anne task (i.e., they failed to comprehend Sally's false belief). In comparison, 86% of Down syndrome children tested in the same study had a lower average mental age than the autistic group who *passed* the Sally–Anne task, suggesting that the autistic group's failure was due to autism-specific deficits and not merely to general developmental delay.

The general failure of autistic subjects on a host of false belief tasks (see Happe & Frith, 1995, for a review) has led Baron-Cohen and others to argue that the core deficit in autism is lack of a theory of mind. According to Baron-Cohen, autism is a condition of *mindblindness;* just as blind children cannot see, children with autism are unable to recognize mental states (Baron-Cohen, 1989a, 1995). Because they cannot understand beliefs, they cannot realize that Sally will look for her marble anywhere other than where it actually is. Similarly, in real-life settings, a range of autistic social behaviors can be explained by a deficit in *metarepresentation—* an inability to develop mental representations for the contents of other people's minds. Pretend play is also absent in children with autism because it requires a similar metarepresentational ability to mark one's own thoughts as imaginary versus real (Leslie, 1987).

According to the theory of mind hypothesis, this deficit in metarepresentation has very serious consequences for the autistic child. Without the ability to think about thoughts, individuals with autism can understand little of the social world around them. They cannot predict the actions of others based on an understanding of those others' beliefs, desires, and intentions, because they don't comprehend that people have beliefs, desires, and intentions. Consequently, they are able to interpret what people do only on the level of actions; they are unable to make use of cognitions or emotions. The commonly observed autistic behavior of treating other people like objects (for instance, climbing on a person to reach things, putting the person's hand on the doorknob and attempting to turn it) speaks to the child with autism inability to understand people as autonomous objects with minds rather than as merely complicated objects themselves. In the theory of mind view, all the autistic individual's serious deficiencies in social interaction and communication stem from this basic cognitive inability to understand other minds.

The *mindblindness* hypothesis of autism argues that the underlying disorder is a discrete one; that is, only certain social skills that suppose theory of mind or metapresentational capacity should be affected. Thus, we do see in autistic individuals the use of protoimperatives, which require only remembering that a parent is likely to initiate the action of bringing over a cookie if one points to the cookie box on the shelf. Children with autism do not employ protodeclaratives, however; to use these, the children would have to understand that other people have minds (for instance, in showing a parent a new toy the child had found, the child would want the parent to understand that he or she is excited because of finding this new toy). Similarly, cognitive functions that do not involve metarepresentation should be unimpaired in individuals with autism who do not also exhibit mental retardation, thus explaining the good rote memory and average or even high IQ possessed by some autistic people (Frith, 1989).

Because a minority of subjects with autism *do* pass basic false belief tasks, theory of mind proponents interpret this to mean there are different levels of developmental delay (Baron-Cohen, 1989b). At the lowest end may be those individuals who never acquire language and are utterly aloof from human interaction (perhaps because they never grasp the basic insight that language has meaning and that people are about something). At the highest end are those individuals who acquire language in some measure of fluency and display a desire for social contact, but who still demonstrate a deficit in language pragmatics (i.e., being able to understand the conventions and expectations of social discourse) and a persistent oddness in day-to-day interaction because of their lack of comprehension of others' internal states. The latter group may grasp basic false belief tasks but fail at more complicated theory of mind tasks testing second-order false beliefs—others' beliefs about beliefs (Baron-Cohen, 1989b; Perner & Wimmer, 1985).

The theory of mind hypothesis has offered a powerful new paradigm for viewing the cognitive deficits in autism, but it has its detractors among those who feel it does not fully explain the early social deviance displayed by persons with autism. Some take issue with the construct of theory of mind from a cognitive/information-processing standpoint (Frye,

Zelazo, & Falfai, 1995); others argue, alternatively, that the social deficits found in autism are primary, and the deficits in social cognition described by theory of mind result from a basic disability in social relatedness (Hobson, 1990, 1993; Klin & Volkmar, 1993; see also Chapter 40).

In Kanner's original report (1943), the inability to relate to others was viewed as primary in autism, present from birth, and affecting such early social contacts as babies' anticipatory posture just before they were picked up and their body-molding to caregivers. To Kanner, children with autism lacked the "constitutional components of emotional reactivity" that were necessary for normal interpersonal relatedness; they had "come into the world with an innate inability to form the usual, biologically provided affective contact with people" (p. 250). Detractors of the theory of mind hypothesis target the theory's holding that social deficits should not be observable in children with autism before an age when metarepresentational capacities normally develop (and can thus be observably impaired).

Theorists differ as to when metarepresentational capacities first emerge. Some argue that a theory of mind is first observable with the emergence of pretend play during the second year of life (Leslie, 1987); others claim that it appears earlier, with the development of joint-attention behaviors when the child is 8 to 12 months old (Baron-Cohen, 1989a, 1989b). The implication of this timetable is that, according to a theory of mind deficit, abnormalities in autistic children's social functioning should not be apparent before the age of 8 to 12 months (Klin et al., 1992). Certain retrospective data have indicated that a minority of parents of children with autism recollect having thought that their children seemed to be developing normally in their first year or so of life (Newson, Dawson, & Everard, 1984; Ornitz et al., 1977). Yet there is emerging evidence that children with autism do display deficits in basic social-affective processes from very early infancy (Adrien, 1991, 1992; Osterling & Dawson, 1994). Klin et al. (1992) noted that various social behaviors that normally occur in children in the first year of life discriminate children with autism from age-

and mental-age-matched control subjects—that is, impairments are evident in some social behaviors that emerge prior to the age predicted by the theory of mind (see Table 8.2).

The members of the neo-Kanner school do not necessarily deny that most children with autism ultimately lack the social cognitive skills described within the rubric of a theory of mind. They assert, however, that the failure to acquire a theory of mind may be the result of a deficit in basic ("prewired") capacities for social relatedness; this deficit may be as simple as a lack of *desire to be with others* (Mayes et al., 1993). Proponents of the theory of mind hypothesis interpret deficits in joint-attention skill as evidence of an inability to read other minds; those who posit a primary social affective problem would see a *motivational* deficit in the failure of children with autism to share their experiences with their caregivers (Gomez et al., 1993). If this motivational deficit is indeed present from birth, then the primary failure of an infant to develop intersubjectivity leads to a cascade of deficiencies across development, including impairments in social behavior, language, and cognition. The influence of this motivational deficit does not rule out the existence of other cognitive or linguistic deficits, but, in a developmental model, it is sufficient to account for a majority of deficits observed across domains.

CONCLUSION

If autism represents a fundamental failure in relatedness, then the challenge facing researchers is to explain the relatedness that is present and to account for the complex interplay observed among cognitive, communicative, and social deficits. For example, some researchers have found what they see as evidence of attachment behaviors in autistic infants and toddlers. They argue that the reactions of children with autism to separation from and reunion with their caregivers are similar to those of normal children of the same mental age (Shapiro et al., 1987; Sigman & Mundy, 1989; Sigman & Ungerer, 1984a).

One hypothesis that might explain this seeming contradiction in autistic social behavior involves a distinction made by Waterhouse and Fein (in press) between *strategic* and *affiliative* social behaviors (see also Chapter 43). Within a social-affective framework that posits a primary deficit in social relations, social behavior may be further divided into strategic behaviors that involve basic food and safety reinforcers, and affiliative behaviors that reflect a related, but not identical, need for closeness and human contact. Following Bowlby's (1969) model of attachment as an adaptive evolutionary mechanism, the most fundamental attachment behaviors would include proximity seeking and distress calls required to maintain safety through physical closeness to the caregiver. These mechanisms do appear to be intact (albeit utilized less frequently, compared to controls) in infants with autism (Rogers et al., 1991; Sigman & Mundy, 1989). However, maintaining contact, or seeking comfort or affective feedback from the caregiver, is not evident; similarly, there is no sharing of explorative competence, a subset of behaviors called *mastery motivation.* In other words, infants with autism may display social behaviors in the sense of adaptive mechanisms involving recognition of the caregiver as a source of sustenance and protection, but they do not appear to display social behaviors that are primarily affective or relational for their own sake, rather than goal-directed or instrumental. (This demarcation between strategic and affiliative behavior may also be seen in persons with autism employment of protoimperatives ("Get me that cookie") versus their lack of use of protodeclaratives ("I've found a toy").)

This hypothesis, that individuals with autism may display strategic but not affiliative social behavior, is testable and may have neurobiological implications. Waterhouse and Fein (in press) note that *affiliativeness* is likely to represent a discrete, innate system that is distinct from strategic interaction skill. Consequently, if the hypothesis about autistic social behavior appears to be supported by experimental data, one may hypothesize that the neurobiological mechanisms involved in the disorder primarily involve damage to regions of motivational and emotional behavior, such as the limbic system. Candidates for further exploration include the oxytocin system,

which is hypothesized to represent the neurochemical basis for social attachment and "affiliativeness" across mammalian species (Insel, 1992); the amygdala, which is proposed as the source of empathy and "hot" theories of mind (Brothers, 1989; Brothers & Ring, 1992); and the orbitofrontal cortex, which is involved in emotion regulation and may be implicated in various psychopathologies linked to attachment experience (Schore, 1996).

A further challenge for autism researchers is the need for new evolutionary models. Currently, the theory of mind hypothesis has been touted as the first evolutionary model of autism that has been developed in the context of the emerging subfield known as evolutionary psychology—that is, psychology informed by the belief that the "organization of the mind is the result of evolutionary processes" (Baron-Cohen, 1995; Cosmides & Tooby, 1992). The progenitors of evolutionary psychology argue that natural selection has produced specific and discrete brain modules for various aspects of social interchange, including several modules regulating language ability, one for recognition of the faces of others, and one involved in the computation of others' mental states (Cosmides & Tooby, 1992). This last module, the theory of mind module, is hypothesized to be damaged or absent in the brains of individuals with autism (Baron-Cohen, 1995).

The theory of mind hypothesis is evolutionary by fiat only—not by content. All the acquired wisdom of evolutionary biology can do little to illuminate the enigma of autism when an evolutionary perspective is adopted only so far as proclaiming that the *absence* of autism is an evolutionarily adaptive trait. The possession of a theory of mind is adaptive for survival, but it does not help us to further explain the development and range of deficits in autism by suggesting only that individuals with autism lack some kind of naturally selected black box.

The assumption that some kind of theory of mind module is lacking in autistic persons has led researchers to advocate a model for autism in nonhuman primates who lack our advanced metacognitive abilities (Gomez et al., 1993; Whiten, 1993). The evidence is so far equivocal, but it appears likely that even chimpanzees and gorillas, our closest evolutionary relatives, lack a full human theory of mind, by the measure of various adapted tasks of purported mind reading (Povinelli, 1993). This research is fascinating for its own sake and will no doubt add much to our understanding of cognitive ethology. However, those who seek an evolutionary parallel for autism by comparing the state of persons with autism with the state of primates, because both lack a theory of mind, are perhaps largely misdirected, if indeed theory of mind deficits emerge from a more primary deficit in affiliative motivation and behavior. The great apes may lack certain higher cognitive functions, theory of mind included, but they are nevertheless hugely social beings and occupy diverse but highly complex social habitats. The level of social skills evident in a typical autistic individual is not adequate for survival in the sophisticated social networks of our relative higher primates. Thus, primates probably cannot be considered good models for autism in any sense of the term as we employ it with humans.

We are left with a need, then, for new and more efficacious animal and evolutionary models that may shed light on the deficits apparent in autism. One direction worth pursuing might be indicated by the hypothesis that individuals with autism demonstrate strategic but not affiliative social behavior. Nonhuman primates, although lacking our own metacognitive skills, are both strategic and affiliative in their behavior (the latter is evidenced by how closely the original studies on monkey attachment appeared to generalize to the emotional bonding of human parents and children (Bowlby, 1969; Harlow & Zimmerman, 1959)). Collaboration with colleagues in biology and zoology will be necessary to develop appropriate animal models that address the social and affiliative as well as the cognitive and communicative deficits evident in autism. This will be an important path to pursue if we hope to develop a true evolutionary theory of autism.

The attempt to understand observed deficits within a truly developmental framework will be important in this regard. Finally, although social deficits are pervasive in autism, it is important to recognize a tremendous variability in phenotypic expression of the social relatedness that is present. The possibility exists that there are multiple etiologies, with varying developmental trajectories, which might all lead to rather similar phenotypes.

Cross-References

Aspects of communication, attention, and cognition are discussed in Chapters 9 to 11; Chapters 12–14 provide a summary of aspects of natural history. Diagnostic features of autism are discussed in Chapter 1 and Chapter 7. Theory of mind in autism is discussed in Chapter 41; a theoretical perspective on social development is provided in Chapter 43.

REFERENCES

Adrien, J. (1991). Autism and family home movies: Preliminary findings. *Journal of Autism and Developmental Disorders, 21,* 43–49.

Adrien, J. (1992). Early symptoms in autism from family home movies: Evaluation and comparison between 1st and 2nd year of life using IBSE Scale. *Acta, 55,* 71–75.

American Psychiatric Association. (1980). *Diagnostic and statistical manual of mental disorders* (3rd ed.). Washington, DC: Author.

American Psychiatric Association. (1987). *Diagnostic and statistical manual of mental disorders* (3rd ed., rev.). Washington, DC: Author.

American Psychiatric Association. (1994). *Diagnostic and statistical manual of mental disorders* (4th ed.). Washington, DC: Author.

Ando, H., Yoshimura, I., & Wakabayashi, S. (1980). Effects of age on adaptive behavior levels and academic skill levels in autistic and mentally retarded children. *Journal of Autism and Developmental Disorders, 10,* 173–184.

Astington, J., & Gopnik, A. (1991). Theoretical explanations of children's understanding of the mind. *British Journal of Developmental Psychology, 9,* 7–31.

Astington, J., Harris, P., & Olson, D. (Eds.). (1988). *Developing theories of mind.* Cambridge, England: Cambridge University Press.

Attwood, A., Frith, J., & Hermelin, B. (1988). The understanding and use of interpersonal gestures by autistic and Down syndrome children. *Journal of Autism and Developmental Disorders, 18,* 241–258.

Bakeman, R., & Adamson, L. (1984). Coordinating attention to people and objects in mother-infant and peer–infant interaction. *Child Development, 55,* 1278–1289.

Baron-Cohen, S. (1989a). Perceptual role-taking and protodeclarative pointing in autism. *British Journal of Developmental Psychology, 7,* 113–127.

Baron-Cohen, S. (1989b). The autistic child's theory of mind: A case of specific developmental delay. *Journal of Child Psychology and Psychiatry, 30,* 285–297.

Baron-Cohen, S. (1995). *Mindblindness: An essay on autism and theory.* Cambridge: MIT Press.

Baron-Cohen, S., Leslie, A., & Frith, U. (1985). Does the autistic child have a "theory of mind"? *Cognition, 21,* 3746.

Bates, E. (1976). *Language and context: The acquisition of pragmatics.* New York. Academic Press.

Bell, R.Q., & Harper, L.V. (1977). *Child effects on adults.* Hillsdale, NJ: Erlbaum.

Bemporad, J.R. (1979). Adult recollections of a formerly autistic child. *Journal of Autism and Developmental Disorders, 9,* 179–197.

Boucher, J., & Lewis, V. (1992). Unfamiliar face recognition in relatively able autistic children. *Journal of Child Psychology & Psychiatry & Allied Disciplines, 33*(5), 843–859.

Bowlby, J. (1969). *Attachment and loss: Vol 1. Attachment.* New York: Basic Books.

Bretherton, I., & Beeghly, M. (1982). Talking about internal states: The acquisition of an explicit theory of mind. *Developmental Psychology, 19,* 906–921.

Brothers, L. (1989). A biological perspective on empathy. *American Journal of Psychiatry, 146,* 10–19.

Brothers, L., & Ring, B. (1992). A neuroethological framework for the representation of minds. *Journal of Cognitive Neuroscience, 4,* 107–118.

Bruner, J. (1975). The ontogenesis of speech acts. *Journal of Child Language, 1,* 1–20.

Bruner, J. (1983). *Child's talk: Learning to use language.* New York: Norton.

Buitelaar, J.K., Van Engeland, H., de Kogel, K.H., de Vries, H., & van Hooff, H. (1991). Differences in the structure of social behaviour of autistic children and non-autistic retarded controls. *Journal of Child Psychology & Psychiatry & Allied Disciplines, 32*(6), 995–1015.

Burack, J.A., & Volkmar, F.R. (1992). Development of low- and high-functioning autistic children. *Journal of Child Psychology & Psychiatry & Allied Disciplines, 33*(3), 607–616.

Cairns, R.B. (1979). *Social development: The origins and plasticity of interchanges.* San Francisco: Freeman.

Capps, L., Sigman, M., & Mundy, P. (1994). Attachment security in children with autism. *Development and Psychopathology, 6,* 249–261.

Charlesworth, W.R. (1992). Facial expressions of infants and children. In P. Ekman (Ed.), Darwin and developmental psychology: Past and present. *Developmental Psychology, 28*(1), 5–12.

Charman, T., & Baron-Cohen, S. (1994). Another look at imitation in autism. *Development and Psychopathology, 6,* 403–413.

Clark, E. (1993). *The lexicon in acquisition.* Cambridge, England: Cambridge University Press.

Cohen, D.J., Paul, R., & Volkmar, F.R. (1986). Issues in the classification of pervasive and other developmental disorders: Toward *DSM-IV. Journal of the American Academy of Child Psychiatry, 25*(2), 213–220.

Cosmides, L., & Tooby, J. (1992). Cognitive adaptations for social exchange. In J. Barkow, L. Cosmides, & J. Tooby (Eds.), *The adapted mind* (pp. 163–228). Oxford, England: Oxford University Press.

Curcio, F. (1978). Sensorimotor functioning and communication in mute autistic children. *Journal of Autism and Childhood Schizophrenia, 8,* 282–292.

Dawson, G., & Adams, A. (1984). Imitation and social responsiveness in autistic children. *Journal of Abnormal Child Psychology, 12,* 209–226.

Dawson, G., & Galpert, L. (1990). Mothers' use of imitative play for facilitating social responsiveness and toy play in young autistic children. *Development and Psychopathology, 2*(2), 151–162.

Dawson, G., Hill, D., Spencer, A., Galpert, L., & Watson, L. (1990). Affective exchanges between young autistic children and their mothers. *Journal of Abnormal Child Psychology, 18,* 335–345.

Dawson, G., & McKissick, F.C. (1984). Self-recognition in autistic children. *Journal of Autism and Developmental Disabilities, 14,* 383–395.

DeCasper, A., & Fifer, W. (1980). Of human bonding: Newborns prefer their mothers' voices. *Science, 171,* 1174–1176.

De Gelder, B. (1991). Face recognition and lip-reading in autism. *European Journal of Cognitive Psychology, 3,* 69–86.

DeMyer, M. (1979). *Parents and children in autism.* Washington, DC: Victor H. Winston.

DeMyer, M.K., Hingtgen, J.N., & Jackson, R.K. (1981). Infantile autism reviewed: A decade of research. *Schizophrenia Bulletin, 7*(3), 388–451.

Dennett, D. (1978). Beliefs about beliefs. *Behavioral and Brain Sciences, 4,* 568–570.

Freedman, D.G. (1974). *Human infancy: An evolutionary perspective.* Hillsdale, NJ: Erlbaum.

Freeman, B.J., Rahbar, B., Ritvo, E.R., Bice, T.L., Yokota, A., & Ritvo, R. (1991). The stability of cognitive and behavioral parameters in autism: A twelve-year prospective study. *Journal of the American Academy of Child and Adolescent Psychiatry, 30,* 479–482.

Frith, U. (1989). *Autism: Explaining the enigma.* Oxford, England: Blackwell.

Frye, D., Zelazo, P., & Falfai, T. (1995). Theory of mind and rule-based reasoning. *Cognitive Development, 10,* 483–527.

Gillberg, C., Ehlers, S., Schaumann, H., Jakobsson, G., Dahlgren, S.O., Lindbolm, R., Bagenholm, A., Tjuus, T., & Blidner, E. (1990). Autism under age 3 years: A clinical study of 28 cases referred for autistic symptoms in infancy. *Journal of Child Psychology and Psychiatry, 31,* 921–934.

Gomez, J., Sarria, E., & Tamarit, J. (1993). The comparative study of early communication and theories of mind: Ontogeny, phylogeny, and pathology. In S. Baron-Cohen, H. Tager-Flusberg, & D. Cohen (Eds.), *Understanding other minds: Perspectives from autism* (pp. 397–426). Oxford, England: Oxford University Press.

Gopnik, A., & Astington, J. (1988). Children's understanding of representational change and its relation to the understanding of false belief and the appearance/reality distinction. *Child Development, 59,* 26–37.

Hannan, T. (1987). A cross-sequential assessment of the occurrences of pointing in 3- to 12-month-old human infants. *Infant Behavior and Development, 10,* 11–22.

Happe, F. (1994). *Autism: An introduction to psychological theory.* Cambridge, MA: Harvard University Press.

Happe, F., & Frith, U. (1995). Theory of mind in autism. In E. Schopler & G. Mesibov (Eds.), *Learning and cognition in autism* (pp. 177–197). New York: Plenum Press.

Harlow, H., & Zimmerman, R. (1959). Affectional responses in the infant monkey. *Science, 130,* 421–432.

Hobson, P. (1986). The autistic child's appraisal of expressions of emotion. *Journal of Child Psychology and Psychiatry, 27,* 321–342.

Hobson, P. (1990). On acquiring knowledge about people and the capacity to pretend: Response to Leslie (1987). *Psychological Review, 97,* 114–121.

Hobson, P. (1993). Understanding persons: The role of affect. In S. Baron-Cohen, H. Tager-Flusberg, & D. Cohen (Eds.), *Understanding other minds: Perspectives from autism* (pp. 204–227). Oxford, England: Oxford University Press.

Insel, T. (1992). Oxytocin—a neuropeptide for affiliation: Evidence from behavioral, receptor autoradiographic, and comparative studies. *Psychoneuroendocrinology, 17,* 3–35.

Jaffe, J., Stern, M., & Perry, M. (1973). Conversational coupling and gaze behavior in prelinguistic human development. *Journal of Psycholinguistic Research, 2,* 321–329.

Kanner, L. (1943). Autistic disturbances of affective contact. *Nervous Child, 2,* 227–250.

Kanner, L., Rodriguez, A., & Ashden, B. (1972). How far can autistic children go in matters of social adaptation? *Journal of Autism and Childhood Schizophrenia, 2*(1), 9–33.

Kasari, C., Sigman, M., Mundy, P., & Yirmiya, N. (1990). Affective sharing in the context of joint attention interactions of normal, autistic and mentally retarded children. *Journal of Autism and Developmental Disorders, 20,* 87–100.

Kasari, C., Sigman, M., & Yirmiya, N. (1993). Focused and social attention of autistic children in interactions with familiar and unfamiliar adults: A comparison of autistic, mentally retarded, and normal children. *Development and Psychopathology, 5*(3), 403–414.

Klin, A. (1991). Young autistic children's listening preferences in regard to speech: A possible characterization of the symptom of social withdrawal. *Journal of Autism and Developmental Disorders, 21,* 29, 217–250.

Klin, A. (1992). Listening preferences in regard to speech in four children with developmental disabilities. *Journal of Child Psychology and Psychiatry, 33,* 763–769.

Klin, A., & Volkmar, F.R. (1993). The development of individuals with autism: Implications for the theory of mind hypothesis. In S. Baron-Cohen, H. Tager-Flusberg, & D. Cohen (Eds.), *Understanding other minds: Perspectives from autism* (pp. 317–331). Oxford, England: Oxford University Press.

Klin, A., Volkmar, F.R., & Sparrow, S. (1992). Autistic social dysfunction: Some limitations of the theory of mind hypothesis. *Journal of Child Psychology and Psychiatry, 33,* 861–876.

Kraemer, H.C. (1988). Assessment of 2×2 associations: Generalization of signal detection methodology. *American Statistician, 42,* 37–49.

Landry, S.H., & Loveland, K.A. (1988). Communication behaviors in autism and developmental language delay. *Journal of Child Psychology and Psychiatry, 29*(5), 621–534.

Langdell, T. (1978). Recognition of faces: An approach to the study of autism. *Journal of Child Psychology & Psychiatry, 19,* 255–268.

Leslie, A. (1987). Pretence and representation: The origins of "theory of mind." *Psychological Review, 94,* 412–426.

Lewis, M. (1963). *Language, thought and personality in infancy and childhood.* London: G. Harapth.

Lewy, A.L., & Dawson, G. (1992). Social stimulation and joint attention in young autistic children. *Journal of Abnormal Child Psychology, 20*(6), 555–566.

Ling, D., & Ling, A.H. (1974). Communication development in the first three years of life. *Journal of Speech and Hearing Research, 17*(1), 146–159.

Lord, C. (1993). The complexity of social behavior in autism. In S. Baron-Cohen, H. Tager-Flusberg, & D. Cohen (Eds.), *Understanding other minds: Perspectives from autism* (pp. 292–316). Oxford, England: Oxford University Press.

Loveland, K., & Kelley, M. (1988). Development of adaptive behavior in adolescents and young adults with autism and Down syndrome. *American Journal on Mental Retardation, 93,* 84–92.

Loveland, K., & Kelley, M. (1991). Development of adaptive behavior in preschoolers with autism or Down syndrome. *American Journal on Mental Retardation, 96*(1), 13–20.

Loveland, K., & Landry, S. (1986). Joint attention and communication in autism and language delay. *Journal of Autism and Developmental Disorders, 16,* 335–349.

Loveland, K.A., Tunali-Kotoski, B., Pearson, D.A., Brelsford, K.A., Ortegon, J., & Chen, R. (1994). Imitation and expression of facial affect in autism. *Development and Psychopathology, 6*(3), 433–444.

Mayes, L., Cohen, D., & Klin, A. (1993). Desire and fantasy: A psychoanalytic perspective on theory of mind and autism. In S. Baron-Cohen, H. Tager-Flusberg, & D. Cohen (Eds.), *Understanding other minds: Perspectives from autism* (pp. 450–464). Oxford, England: Oxford University Press.

McEvoy, R.E., Rogers, S.J., & Pennington, B.F. (1993). Executive function and social communication deficits in young autistic children. *Journal of Child Psychology and Psychiatry, 34,* 563–578.

McGee, G.G., Feldman, R.S., & Chernin, L. (1991). A comparison of emotional facial

display by children with autism and typical preschoolers. *Journal of Early Intervention, 15*(3), 237–245.

Meltzoff, A., & Gopnik, A. (1993). The role of imitation in understanding persons and developing a theory of mind. In S. Baron-Cohen, H. Tager-Flusberg, & D. Cohen (Eds.), *Understanding other minds:* Perspectives from autism (pp. 333–366). Oxford, England: Oxford University Press.

Mills, M., & Melhuish, E. (1974). Recognition of mother's voice in early infancy. *Nature, 252,* 123–124.

Moser-Richters, M., & Volkmar, F.R. (1996). Reactive Attachment Disorder. In M. Lewis (Ed.), *Child and adolescent psychiatry: A comprehensive textbook* (2nd ed., pp. 498–501). Baltimore: Williams & Wilkins.

Moses, L., & Flavell, J. (1990). Inferring false beliefs from actions and reactions. *Child Development, 61,* 929–945.

Mundy, P., Sigman, M., & Kasari, C. (1990). A longitudinal study of joint attention and language disorders in autistic children. *Journal of Autism and Developmental Disorders, 20,* 115–123.

Mundy, P., Sigman, M., & Kasari, C. (1994). Joint attention, developmental level, and symptom presentation in autism. *Development and Psychopathology, 6,* 389–401.

Mundy, P., Sigman, M., Ungerer, J., & Sherman, T. (1987). Nonverbal communication and play correlates of language development in autistic children. *Journal of Autism and Developmental Disorders, 17,* 349–364.

Newson, E., Dawson, G., & Everard, P. (1984). The natural history of able autistic people. *Communication, 18,* 16–22.

Ohta, M., Nagai, Y., Hara, H., & Sasaki, M. (1987). Parental perception of behavioral symptoms in Japanese autistic children. *Journal of Autism and Developmental Disorders, 17,* 549–564.

Olson, G., & Sherman, T. (1983). Attention, learning, and memory in infants. In M. Mussend (Ed.), *Handbook of Child Psychology,* (4th ed., Vol. 2, pp. 1001–1080) and in M.M. Haith & J.J. Campos (Eds.), *Infancy and developmental psychology* (Vol. 2, pp. 117–134). New York: John Wiley & Sons.

Ornitz, E.M., Guthrie, D., & Farley, A.H. (1977). Early development of autistic children. *Journal of Autism and Childhood Schizophrenia, 7,* 207–229.

Osterling, J., & Dawson, G. (1994). Early recognition of children with autism: A study of first birthday home videotapes. *Journal of Autism and Developmental Disorders, 24,* 247–257.

Ozonoff, S., Pennington, B., & Rogers, S. (1990). Are there specific emotion perception deficits in young autistic children? *Journal of Child Psychology and Psychiatry, 31,* 343–361.

Parks, S.L. (1983). The assessment of autistic children: A selective review of available instruments. *Journal of Autism & Developmental Disorders, 13,* 255–267.

Paul, R. (1987). Communication. In D. Cohen & A. Donnellan (Eds.), *Handbook of autism and pervasive developmental disorders* (pp. 61–84). New York: John Wiley & Sons.

Perner, J. (1991). *Understanding the representational mind.* Cambridge, MA: MIT Press.

Perner, J., & Wimmer, H. (1985). "John thinks that Mary thinks that . . .": Attribution of second-order beliefs by 5–10-year-old children. *Journal of Experimental Child Psychology, 39,* 437–471.

Phillips, W., Baron-Cohen, S., & Rutter, M. (1992). The role of eye contact in goal detection: Evidence from normal infants and children with autism or mental handicap. *Development and Psychopathology, 4*(3), 375–383.

Piaget, J. (1951). *Play, dreams and imitation in childhood.* New York: Norton.

Povinelli, D. (1993). Reconstructing the evolution of mind. *American Psychologist, 48,* 493–509.

Premack, D., & Woodruff, G. (1978). Does the chimpanzee have a theory of mind? *Behavioral and Brain Sciences, 4,* 515–526.

Prior, M.R. (1979). Cognitive abilities and disabilities in infantile autism: A review. *Journal of Abnormal Child Psychology, 7,* 357–380.

Provence, S., & Lipton, R. (1962). *Infants in institutions.* New York: International Universities Press.

Ricks, D.M., & Wing, L. (1975). Language, communication, and the use of symbols in normal and autistic children. *Journal of Autism and Childhood Schizophrenia, 5,* 191–221.

Rimland, B. (1964). *Infantile autism.* New York: Appleton-Century-Crofts.

Rodrigue, J.R., Morgan, S.B., & Geffken, G.R. (1991). A comparative evaluation of adaptive behavior in children and adolescents with autism, Down syndrome, and normal development. *Journal of Autism and Developmental Disabilities, 21,* 187–196.

Rogers, S., Ozonoff, S., & Maslin-Cole, C. (1991), A comparative study of attachment behavior in young children with autism or other psychiatric disorders. *Journal of Child and Adolescent Psychiatry, 30,* 483–488.

Rogers, S., Ozonoff, S., & Maslin-Cole, C. (1993). Developmental aspects of attachment behavior in young children with Pervasive Developmental Disorder. *Journal of Child and Adolescent Psychiatry, 32,* 1274–1282.

Rumsey, J.M., Rapoport, J.L., & Sceery, W.R. (1985). Autistic children as adults: Psychiatric, social, and behavioral outcomes. *Journal of the American Academy of Child Psychiatry, 24,* 465–473.

Rutter, M. (1970). Autistic children: Infancy to adulthood. *Seminars in Psychiatry, 2,* 435–450.

Rutter, M. (1978). Diagnosis and definition. In M. Rutter & E. Schopler (Eds.), *Autism: A reappraisal of concepts and treatment* (pp. 1–25). New York: Plenum.

Rutter, M. (1981). *Maternal deprivation reassessed* (2nd ed.). New York: Penguin.

Rutter, M. (1983). Cognitive deficits in the pathogenesis of autism. *Journal of Child Psychology and Psychiatry, 24,* 513–531.

Rutter, M., & Garmezy, N. (1983). Developmental psychopathology. In E.M. Hetherington (Ed.), *Handbook of child psychology,* (Vol. 4., pp. 775–991). New York: John Wiley & Sons.

Schaffer, R. (1984). *The child's entry into a social world.* London: Academic Press.

Schopler, E., & Mesibov, G. (Eds.). (1983). *Autism in adolescents and adults.* New York: Plenum Press.

Schore, A. (1996). The experience-dependent maturation of a regulatory system in the orbital prefrontal cortex and the origin of developmental psychopathology. *Development and Psychopathology, 8,* 59–87.

Seifer, R., & Schiller, M. (1996). The role of parenting sensitivity, infant temperament, and dyadic interaction in attachment theory and assessment. In E. Waters et al. (Eds.), *Caregiving, cultural and cognitive perspectives on behavior and working models* (pp. 146–174). Monographs of the Society for Research in Child Development.

Shapiro, T., Sherman, M., Calamari, G., & Koch, D. (1987). Attachment in autism and other developmental disorders. *Journal of Child and Adolescent Psychiatry, 226,* 485–590.

Sherman, M., Shapiro, T., & Glassman, M. (1983). Play and language in developmentally disordered preschoolers: A new approach to classification. *Journal of the American Academy of Child Psychiatry, 22,* 511–524.

Siegel, B., Pliner, C., Eschler, J., & Elliott, G.R. (1988). How children with autism are diagnosed: Difficulties in identification of children with multiple developmental delays.

Developmental and Behavioral Pediatrics, 9, 199–204.

Siegel, B., Vukicevic, J., Elliott, G.R., & Kraemer, H.C. (1989). The use of signal detection theory to assess *DSM-III-R* criteria for autistic disorder. *Journal of the American Academy of Child & Adolescent Psychiatry, 28,* 542–548.

Sigman, M., Kasari, C., Kwon, J.H., & Yirmiya, N. (1992). Responses to the negative emotions of others by autistic, mentally retarded, and normal children. *Child Development, 63,* 796–807.

Sigman, M., & Mundy, P. (1989). Social attachments in autistic children. *Journal of Child Psychiatry, 28,* 74–81.

Sigman, M., Mundy, P., Sherman, T., & Ungerer, J. (1986). Social interactions of autistic, mentally retarded, and normal children and their caregivers. *Journal of Child Psychology and Psychiatry, 27,* 647–656.

Sigman, M., & Ungerer, J. (1984a). Attachment behaviors in autistic children. *Journal of Autism and Developmental Disorders, 14,* 231–244.

Sigman, M., & Ungerer, J. (1984b). Cognitive and language skills in autistic, mentally retarded, and normal children. *Developmental Psychology, 20,* 293–302.

Singer, J. (1996). Cognitive and affective implications of imaginative play in childhood. In M. Lewis (Ed.), *Child and adolescent psychiatry: A comprehensive textbook* (2nd ed., pp. 202–210). Baltimore: Williams & Wilkins.

Smith, I.M., & Bryson, S.E. (1994). Imitation and action in autism: A critical review. *Psychological Bulletin, 116*(2), 259–273.

Snow, M.E., Hertzig, M.E., & Shapiro, T. (1987). Expression of emotion in young autistic children. *Journal of the American Academy of Child and Adolescent Psychiatry, 26*(6), 836–838.

Sparrow, S., Balla, D., & Ciccheti, D. (1984). *Vineland Adaptive Behavior Scales.* Circle Pines, MN: American Guidance Service.

Sperber, D., & Wilson, D. (1986). *Relevance: Communication and cognition.* Cambridge, MA: Harvard University Press.

Spitz, R. (1965). *The first year of life.* New York: International Universities Press.

Stern, D. (1985). *The interpersonal world of the human infant.* New York: Basic Books.

Stone, W., & Caro-Martinez, L. (1990). Naturalistic observations of spontaneous communication in autistic children. *Journal of Autism and Developmental Disorders, 20,* 437–454.

Stone, W.L., Lemanek, K.L., Fishel, P.T., Fernandez, M.C., & Altemeier, W.A. (1990). Play and imitation skills in the diagnosis of autism in young children. *Pediatrics, 86,* 267–272.

Stone, W.L., Ousley, O.Y., & Littleford, C. (1995, March). *A comparison of elicited imitation in young children with autism and developmental delay.* Poster session presented at the annual Gatlinburg Conference on Research and Theory in Mental Retardation and Developmental Disabilities, Gatlinburg, TN.

Stone, W.L., & Rosenbaum, J.L. (1988). A comparison of teacher and parent views of autism. *Journal of Autism and Developmental Disorders, 18,* 403–414.

Tager-Flusberg, H. (1981). On the nature of linguistic functioning in early infantile autism. *Journal of Autism and Developmental Disorders, 11,* 45–56.

Tager-Flusberg, H. (1989). A psycholinguistic perspective on language development in the autistic child. In G. Dawson (Ed.), *Autism: New directions in diagnosis, nature, and treatment* (pp. 92–118). New York: Guilford Press.

Tager-Flusberg, H. (1993). What language reveals about the understanding of minds in children with autism. In S. Baron-Cohen, H. Tager-Flusberg, & D. Cohen (Eds.), *Understanding other minds: Perspectives from autism* (pp. 138–157). Oxford, England: Oxford University Press.

Teunisse, J.-P., & de Gelder, B. (1994). Do autistics have a generalized face processing deficit? *International Journal of Neuroscience, 77*(1/2), 1–10.

Thompson, R.A. (1996). Attachment theory and research. In M. Lewis (Ed.), *Child and adolescent psychiatry: A comprehensive textbook* (2nd ed., pp. 126–133). Baltimore: Williams & Wilkins.

Trad, P.V., Bernstein, D., Shapiro, T., & Hertzig, M. (1993). Assessing the relationship between affective responsivity and social interaction in children with Pervasive Developmental Disorder. *Journal of Autism and Developmental Disorders, 23,* 361–377.

Trevarthen, C. (1979). Communication and cooperation in early infancy: A description of primary intersubjectivity. In M. Bullowa (Ed.), *Before speech: The beginning of interpersonal communication* (pp. 321–347). New York: Cambridge University Press.

Volkmar, F.R. (1987). Social development. In D. Cohen & A. Donnellan (Eds.), *Handbook of autism and pervasive developmental disorders* (pp. 41–60). New York: John Wiley & Sons.

Volkmar, F.R., Carter, A., Sparrow, S.S., & Cicchetti, D.V. (1993). Quantifying social development in autism. *Journal of Child and Adolescent Psychiatry, 32,* 627–632.

Volkmar, F.R., & Cohen, D.J. (1985). A first-person account of the experience of infantile autism by Tony W. *Journal of Autism and Developmental Disorders, 15,* 47–54.

Volkmar, F.R., Cohen, D.J., & Paul, R. (1986). An evaluation of *DSM-III* criteria for infantile autism. *Journal of the American Academy of Child Psychiatry, 25,* 190–197.

Volkmar, F.R., Klin, A., Siegel, B., Szatmari, P., et al. (1994). Field trial for Autistic Disorder in *DSM-IV. American Journal of Psychiatry, 151*(9), 1361–1367.

Volkmar, F.R., Sparrow, S.A., Goudreau, D., Cicchetti, D.V., Paul, R., & Cohen, D.J. (1987). Social deficits in autism: An operational approach using the Vineland Adaptive Behavior Scales. *Journal of the American Academy of Child and Adolescent Psychiatry, 26,* 156–161.

Volkmar, F.R., Sparrow, S.S., Rende, R.D., & Cohen, D.J. (1989). Facial perception in autism. *Journal of Child Psychology & Psychiatry & Allied Disciplines, 30*(4), 591–598.

Waterhouse, L., & Fein, D. (In press). Autism and the evolution of human social skills. In F.R. Volkmar (Ed.), *Autism and the Pervasive Developmental Disorders.* Cambridge: Cambridge University Press.

Werner, H., & Kaplan, B. (1963). *Symbol formation.* New York: John Wiley & Sons.

Whiten, A. (1993). Evolving a theory of mind: The nature of non-verbal mentalism in other primates. In S. Baron-Cohen, H. Tager-Flusberg, & D. Cohen (Eds.), *Understanding other minds: Perspectives from autism* (pp. 367–396). Oxford, England: Oxford University Press.

Wimmer, H., & Perner, J. (1983). Beliefs about beliefs: Representation and the constraining function of wrong beliefs in young children's understanding of deception. *Cognition, 13,* 103–128.

Wing, L. (1976). *Early childhood autism.* New York: Pergamon Press.

Wing, L., & Attwood, A. (1987). Syndromes of autism and atypical development. In D. Cohen & A. Donnellan (Eds.), *Handbook of Autism and Pervasive Developmental Disorders* (pp. 3–19). New York: John Wiley & Sons.

Wing, L., & Gould, J. (1979). Severe impairments of social interaction and associated abnormalities in children: Epidemiology and classification. *Journal of Autism and Developmental Disorders, 9,* 11–29.

World Health Organization. (1993). *International classification of diseases: Diagnostic criteria for research* (10th ed.). Geneva: Author.

Yirmiya, N., Kasari, C., Sigman, M., & Mundy, P. (1989). Facial expressions of affect in autistic, mentally retarded, and normal children. *Journal of Child Psychology and Psychiatry, 30,* 725–735.

CHAPTER 9

Language and Communication in Autism

CATHERINE LORD AND RHEA PAUL

Knowledge about human communication is central to theoretical principles and clinical practice in the field of autism. Milestones in language and communication play a major role in evaluating development and understanding autism. Most parents of autistic children first begin to be concerned that something is not quite right in their child's development when early delay or regression occurs in the development of speech (Short & Schopler, 1988). Achievement of useful expressive language by the age of 5 years has been perhaps the most powerful predictor of behavioral and vocational outcome in autism (Rutter, 1970). Fluency and flexibility of expressive language underlie the distinction between high-functioning and low-functioning autism in school-age or adolescent children. A history of language delay can be particularly crucial in differentiating autism from other psychiatric disorders in high-functioning adults (Lord & Venter, 1992).

A strong relationship exists between social nonverbal communication and the level of language development in autism. Preschool-age autistic children who are flexible and skilled in the use of nonverbal modes of communication (e.g., gesture and gaze) develop more receptive language, at an earlier age, than children who have greater deficits in nonverbal communication (Lord & Schopler, 1989; Mundy, Sigman, & Kasari, 1994). Mentally handicapped nonautistic children who have particularly severe language delays are similar to autistic children in many aspects of social interaction, including some components of

nonverbal communication that one might expect them to use to compensate for their language problems (Lord & Pickles, 1996).

On the other hand, even though autism is often first recognized because of slow or unusual patterns of speech development, many early aspects of the language deficit associated with autism overlap with other disorders (Beitchman & Inglis, 1991; Bishop & Adams, 1989). Thus, skill in language is important to the functioning of autistic individuals, but delays in expressive language during the early preschool years are not specific to autism (Cantwell, Baker, & Mattison, 1980). When there is a good description of a child's early social history and use of objects, the diagnosis of autism can often be made without any reference to language delay (Cohen, Sudhalter, Landon-Jimenez, & Koegh, 1993; Lord, Storoschuk, Rutter, & Pickles, 1993; Siegel, Vukicevic, Elliott, & Kraemer, 1989). Asperger's Syndrome (see Chapter 5) is an autism spectrum disorder characterized by lack of general delay in language and cognition, but marked social deficits. Its existence suggests that, even though abnormalities in communication are a core feature of pervasive developmental disorders, slower language acquisition is not necessary or sufficient for a diagnosis within the spectrum of disorders associated with autism (see Chapters 1 to 6).

Furthermore, even when language level is equated in autistic and nonautistic children, significant differences in social behaviors (e.g., initiation of joint attention) characterize

The authors acknowledge the contributions of Terri Rossi in the preparation of this chapter.

children with autism (Mundy et al., 1994). Some aspects of deviant language in autism, such as delayed echolalia or inability to carry on a conversation, may be better represented as part of more general cognitive or social deficits than as pure language difficulties (Fein, Humes, Kaplan, Lucci, & Waterhouse, 1984; Frith, 1989; Paul, 1987). By itself, language delay does not account for most of the features of autism, though parents of young autistic children often feel that their child would be like other children if he or she could just talk. There is evidence that rather subtle abnormalities in the use of language may affect some parents and siblings of autistic individuals (Landa et al., 1992). In a recent family study, a severity score assessed deficits in social, communicative, and/or repetitive behaviors, separately for families with verbal and nonverbal children with autism. In the families with verbal children, the severity score predicted the number of affected relatives in families of autistic children and adults (Bolton et al., 1994). These findings suggest that there may be separable contributions of specific qualitative forms of deviance (social, communicative, repetitive) and general language delay, and that both have strong associations with autism.

In addition, evidence from numerous sources suggests that the social and linguistic environments of autistic children and adolescents, most of whom have active, loving, and determined parents and teachers, are quite different from those of other students. Thus, initial deficits in language acquisition and in social or cognitive factors affecting language may be compounded by experiential differences (Konstantareas, Zajdemann, Homatidis, & McCabe, 1988). The root of these differences is thought to be the limited nature of the social and linguistic demands that these youngsters place on others (Lord, Merrin, Vest, & Kelly, 1983). Approaches to intervention that emphasize functional communication are aimed in part at remediating or preventing the secondary effects of limited communicative experience on the development of individuals with autism (see Chapters 23 to 25). The question of priorities in this area has no simple answer. The choices might include providing a typical environment for language learning (even if the child could benefit from more structure and stimulation); creating a specialized environment for enhanced language learning (even if others are then behaving in atypical ways); or focusing on clearly measurable communication goals for an individual child or adult (even if the environment that elicits them is atypical and results in less generalizable progress). Recognition that different deficits, including delay in language acquisition and deviance in social communication, may require somewhat different strategies, is a start.

The history of autism has included waxing and waning interest in language and communication. The initial interpretation of language abnormalities as indicative of social-emotional dysfunction (Kanner, 1943) evolved into a focus on primary language deficits in the 1970s (Rutter, 1970) and then into recent interest in using language to study other behaviors, particularly higher-order cognitive abilities such as theory of mind (Baron-Cohen, 1993). For investigators of such topics, who are interested in proving that particular cognitive explanations account for autism-specific differences, the goal generally has been to ensure that language was *not* a factor that differentiated autistic participants from others. In most cases, relatively high-functioning populations of school-age and adolescent students with autism have been matched with more severely mentally handicapped youngsters of equivalent language level. The findings, which compared these matched populations, have consistently shown that some cognitive abnormalities are not solely attributable to language level. However, in studies of very young autistic children, for whom such matching is much more difficult, nonhandicapped 12-month-olds scored higher on tests of language comprehension than most 3-year-olds referred for possible autism (DiLavore, Lord, & Opsahl, 1994). Mentally handicapped 4-year-olds who are ambulatory, do not have sensory handicaps (such as hearing impairments), and are equivalent in language level to severely retarded autistic children of the same age but do not have significant social deficits, are rare (Wing & Gould, 1979). Thus, although language delay itself is not specific (and perhaps is not even necessary) to a diagnosis of autism, very severe delays in comprehension do character-ize most young autistic children. The practical and theoretical significance of language deficits to autism is unarguable, if not simple.

THE STUDY OF LANGUAGE DEVELOPMENT IN TYPICAL POPULATIONS

Early Communicative Intent

Often, parents acknowledge the absence of early communication in their young autistic children when they realize that the majority of children the same age have acquired vocabu-laries of numerous words (Short & Schopler, 1988). Nonhandicapped children actually show communicative behaviors from the first weeks of life (Figure 9.1). Children with typi-cal development exhibit, by the end of their first year, a variety of communicative behav-iors that a knowing observer will not usually see in young autistic children. These nonverbal

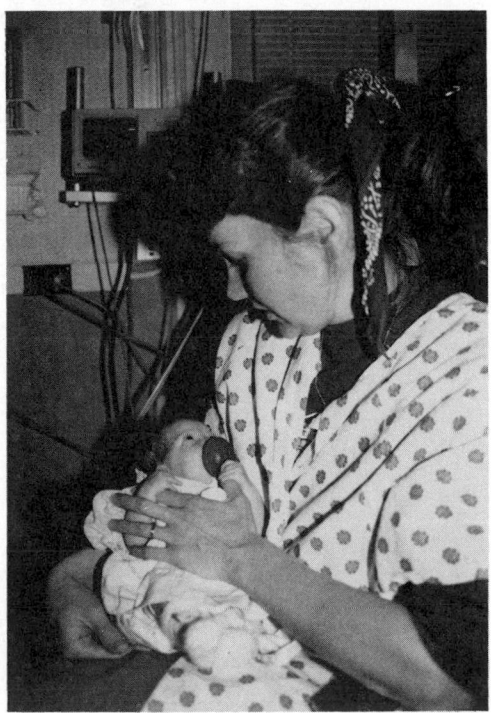

Figure 9.1 Children with typical development com-municate with gaze from the first weeks of life.

communications express messages for which words will be used in the ensuing months—re-questing objects and actions, rejecting offered objects or actions, and calling attention to or reacting to the appearance of objects, persons, or events (Bates, 1976). These intents are ini-tially expressed with simple gestures: reaching toward, to indicate a request, or pushing away, to indicate rejection. Next come more complex gestures, such as pointing a finger to request, or shaking the head to mean "no." The gestures are gradually accompanied by—and, in some cases, replaced by—vocalization and speech.

Another achievement that normally begins toward the end of the first year is the child's understanding of words. At first, children as-sociate words with games such as "pat-a-cake" or "so big" or with repetitive naming rituals ("Who is this?" [Daddy]). Children gradually become more active responders to these rou-tines (Bruner, 1975). By the time a child is 12 months old, merely hearing the words "Let's play pat-a-cake!" or "Show me your nose," without any gestural cue, will often elicit a spontaneous action such as clapping the hands or touching the nose.

First Words

Conventional use of language begins around age 12 months (see Table 9.1), which is when children usually say their first recognizable words and, by responding appropriately to spe-cific words outside the context of routine games, give the first clear evidence that they comprehend single words (Huttenlocher, 1974; Tomasello & Krueger, 1992). As shown in Table 9.1, 12- to 18-month-old children exhibit a rapid increase in both receptive and expres-sive vocabulary. Many of the words children learn during this period are names of objects and people with which or whom the child fre-quently interacts (Daddy, Mommy, cookie, ball) or descriptions of relationships among objects (all gone, more) (Fenson et al., 1994). Children also learn social words to be used in greetings and other rituals. Much like their early gestures, their first words often express ideas about appearance ("Uh-oh"), disappear-ance ("All gone"), and recurrence ("More") that are related to the child's developing

TABLE 9.1 A Summary of Milestones in Typical Language Development

	12 to 15 months	18 months	24 to 36 months	3 to 4 years	4 to 7 years
Semantics	Average expressive vocabulary size at 15 months: 10 words Average receptive vocabulary size at 15 months: 50 words Comprehension strategies include attending to objects named, and doing what is usually done	Average expressive vocabulary size at 18 months: 100 words (±105) Average receptive vocabulary size at 18 months: 300 words Comprehension strategies include acting on objects in the way mentioned, interpreting sentences as requests for child action	Average expressive vocabulary size at 24 months: 300 words (±75) Average receptive vocabulary size at 24 months: 900 words Comprehension strategies include interpreting sentences according to knowledge of probable events	Average expressive vocabulary size at 3 years: 900 words Comprehension strategies include supplying most probable missing information in answer to difficult questions	Average expressive vocabulary size at 6 years: 2,500 words Average receptive vocabulary size at 6 years: 8,000 words Comprehension strategies include overreliance on word order to process sentences that use unusual word order, such as passives
Syntax	First productions are single-word *holophrases*; one word carries the force of a whole sentence	Average age of first word combinations: 18 months (normal range: 14 to 24 months) First word combinations express basic semantic relations with consistent word order	Average MLU at 24 months: 1.92 (±0.5) Average MLU at 30 months: 2.54 (±0.6) Average MLU at 36 months: 3.16 (±0.7)	Average MLU at 4 years: 4.4 (±0.9) Grammatical morphemes become more consistent Mature forms of negatives and questions develop	Average MLU at 5 years: 5.6 (±1.2) Use of complex sentences increases from less than 10% to more than 20% of all utterances
Phonology	Most productions have CV or CVCV (consonant vowel/consonant vowel or consonant vowel vowel combinations, e.g., "ba" or "mama") form Front stops and nasals are most frequent consonants	Back stops, fricatives, and glides are added to the consonant inventory CVC syllable shapes begin to be used 50% of consonants are produced correctly	9 to 10 different consonants are used in initial position; 5 to 6 in final; stops at all places of articulation are used; liquids appear Two-syllable words and initial consonant clusters are used by a majority of children 70% of consonants are correct; speech is 50% intelligible	Most sounds are produced correctly Consonant blends are used Some phonological simplification processes may persist Speech is nearly 100% intelligible	Almost all sounds are produced correctly Phonological processes are no longer used; a few distortions on difficult sounds (/s/, /l/, /r/) may persist Phonological analysis skills are learned for reading and spelling

Pragmatics	Average rate of communications: 1 per minute Requests and comments are accomplished by combining gestures with speechlike vocalizations	Average rate of communications: 2 per minute Requests and comments are used; words predominate; gestural/vocal communication decreases	Average rate of communications: 5 per minute Requests and comments are used; children begin to ask questions and convey new information; word combinations predominate	Talk about past and future events increases More options for politeness are acquired New communicative functions (projecting, narrating, imagining, etc.) are expressed	Language is used to predict, reason, negotiate
Play	Conventional, functional play	Symbolic play using self as actor	Pretend play involving others and using multiple schemes	Sequences of events are played out (preparing food, setting table, eating) Child engages in dialogues, talking for all characters	Fantasy themes are played out Child or doll can take multiple roles Elaboration of planning and narrative story lines included in play

MLU = mean length of utterance
CV = consonant vowel
CVCV = consonant vowel consonant vowel

notions of object permanence (Bloom & Lahey, 1978).

As children advance toward 18 months, their average expressive vocabulary expands to include about 50 words (Fenson et al., 1994). A word explosion occurs when children begin to understand that some words describe characteristics of an object and can be used to communicate with others about that object (Nelson, 1973). Children begin to ask for names of things, verbally or by pointing. This behavior marks an important turning point: words are being used to get new information about the world (Halliday, 1975). By 16 to 19 months, children employ nonverbal cues, such as an adult's line of vision, to make quite fine distinctions between an object that an adult is naming and another object that happens to be present (Baldwin, 1991). Similar methods for learning words that describe actions have been reported for 2-year-olds (Tomasello & Kruger, 1992).

Even before they are 2 years old, most children begin forming two-word telegraphic sentences (Brown, 1973). A recent monograph, reporting on parents' observations of their children's early language development, using the MacArthur Communicative Development Inventory (Fenson et al., 1994), stated that 80% of the children observed were using two-word combinations ("sometimes" or "often") by 21 months. These sentences encode a limited range of meanings, such as possession ("Daddy shoe") and location ("Sit chair"). They are elaborations of the earlier gestures and single words that expressed existence, nonexistence, disappearance, and recurrence (Bloom, 1970). Thus, early language development, from gestures to single words to beginning sentences, is in many ways a remarkably organized process that reflects both how young children think about the world (e.g., how they recognize the coming and going of food and persons) and what is important to them (e.g., the things they can act on, or interesting events such as going outside or wiping up a spill). Individual differences exist among typically developing children, but language acquisition is not a random process. There are generally clear links between forms (i.e., gesture, words, syntax) and functions (e.g., why the child is trying to communicate) over time.

Toddlers often appear to understand everything they hear, but studies of early language comprehension in highly structured settings suggest that young children do not understand many more words than they are able to say (Bloom, 1974). However, when parents are asked to report the kinds of words and instructions their young children are able to understand, their estimates are typically much higher than the actual observations during formal testing. In response to a standard questionnaire (Fenson et al., 1994), parents estimated that their children, by 8 months, understood an average of 6 phrases and about 20 words, and, by 16 months, understood an average of 23 phrases and 169 words. There is no way to determine how much true comprehension was present, in the sense of discriminating minimal contrasts out of context (Tomasello & Mervis, 1994). Comprehension, in ordinary situations, may be achieved through a variety of nonlinguistic strategies. Children's responses to what their parents have said may, in fact, be responses to what their parents have done or what they know about the way things are usually accomplished (Chapman, 1978). Among the strategies children use are: looking at whatever the parent is looking at ("See the balloon!"), doing whatever is usually done in a particular situation ("Brush your teeth"), and interpreting sentences as a request ("Uh-oh, the door is open!" Better go shut it!). Few parents truly test their children's language comprehension by asking them to do things completely out of context (e.g., asking a child to get Mommy's keys from the bedroom during a family meal). Parents provide numerous redundant clues, such as shifts in gaze, intonation, gestures, and use of objects, when they communicate with infants and toddlers. All of these factors aid their children's comprehension.

The period from 18 months to 24 months also brings important changes in conversational ability. Children begin to understand the conversational obligation to answer speech with speech (Chapman, 1981). They reliably ask *and* answer routine questions ("Where's the doggy?" "What's this?" "What's the cow say?") and can begin to take their own part in a back-and-forth linguistic exchange.

The Acquisition of Linguistic Structures

In the preschool period (from 2 to 5 years), children's language evolves from primitive telegraphic utterances to fully grammatical forms. Their vocabulary expands rapidly, and they approximate more and more closely the syntax of the language spoken in the home. In their use of overgeneralized forms, such as "goed," "comed," and "mouses" (Cazden, 1968), they are not making these mistakes by imitating. They are creating novel, albeit wrong, forms by applying generative rules to words that happen to be exceptions to the usual rules for tenses and plurals.

As children's grammar becomes more complex, their sentence length increases (Loban, 1976; Miller & Chapman, 1981). Their simple sentences begin to approach the adult model of complex sentences that use embedded clauses ("Whoever wins can go first") and conjoined clauses ("Then it broke and we didn't have it any more") (Miller, 1981). As they learn to encode ideas syntactically ("Daddy's shoe" versus "Daddy shoe") and to connect thoughts within one utterance ("I'll go get it if you give me a bite of your candy"), children's language is freed from its earlier dependence on nonlinguistic contexts for interpretation. Before, an adult had to use knowledge of the child and the situation to interpret "Daddy shoe" (the shoe that's Daddy's? Daddy put on the shoe?); now, the syntactically marked "Daddy's shoe" is unambiguous and can be interpreted by anyone.

In addition to syntactic form, children between 3 and 5 years of age elaborate the ideas they express in their sentences. Their earlier sentences generally described actions and objects that were immediately present. During later preschool years, their sentence content expands to encompass remembered or imagined events that are remote in time and space. Using their language in more diverse ways (Dore, 1978), they begin to include imaginative, interpretive, and logical functions.

A variety of conversational skills emerge and become refined as children move toward age 5. Children increase their ability to maintain and add new information to a topic to clarify and request clarification of misunderstood utterances; to make their requests politely and indirectly; and to choose an appropriate speech style on the basis of the speaker's role and the listener's status (Bates, 1976). Their increasing comprehension skill is reflected in the expanding number of elements they can process in a simple sentence (Chapman, 1978). Also, their strategies for comprehending sentences change from relying on knowledge of the way things usually happen (they would give a correct interpretation to "The dog is patted by the child") to incorporating that knowledge into reliance on syntactic rules, such as word order (they misunderstand the passive "The dog is patted by the mother" because they treat it as the simple active sentence, "The dog pats the child") (Strohner & Nelson, 1974).

The Elaboration of Language

Children have acquired most of the sentence structure of their language by age 5, but their syntactic development continues into the school years as they learn how to elaborate on their simple statements and how to condense more information into each sentence by using dependent clauses (Loban, 1976). Children also gradually learn to use and to comprehend more complex, optional sentence types such as passives (Lempert, 1978). They learn to use syntactic cues not only to decode semantic relations within sentences but also to identify the connections between the elements in a particular sentence and the statements made previously in the discourse (Miller, 1981). These semantic and conversational abilities continue to develop throughout the school years (Loban, 1976). Vocabulary increases through education, exposure to communication media, reading, and conversation. School-age children gradually acquire the ability to communicate with precision and to take the listener's viewpoint into account when creating sentences (Asher, 1978).

Issues from the Study of Language Development in Typical Children

Several issues arise in determining how to fit the patterns of language development seen in children with autism (described below) into models of normal language acquisition. One source of confusion to parents and professionals is the question of consistency. Many autistic children occasionally show the behaviors observed in normally developing children. For example, new words may be used by toddlers once or twice, then never or very rarely be heard again. Are these real words? Does the child have them stored somewhere in the brain? Can they be recalled if the child is sufficiently motivated? Generally, words or sentences used very inconsistently do not lead to the development of useful communication. On the other hand, anyone who has ever tried to get a typical 15-month-old child to recite for Grandma all the new words learned that week can verify that normally developing toddlers and preschool children are not consistently able or willing to perform on demand.

Two questions arise:

1. How do we set standards for a reasonable level of consistency?
2. How broad do the contexts in which we can reliably expect a behavior have to be?

We might expect a 10-month-old child to understand "bubbles" only in the bathtub; but, by 18 months, the child should be able to say and understand the same word in a variety of different situations.

Development of these sorts of standards may be particularly helpful for parents and primary care professionals who are trying to evaluate the seriousness of a possible communication delay in a very young child.

Another source of confusion is that if one does not have a reasonable level of knowledge about the breadth and depth of typical language development, it is easy to fail to notice its absence. A child who occasionally (i.e., not every day) says five words, and does so without clear communicative intent, is very different from another child who can only say five different words but uses them to express a range of meanings (as described above) and links them to gestures, simple syntax, and intonation throughout each day. Variability is found within the normal range, primarily in the development of expressive language (Rutter & Lord, 1987). Minor differences have historically been associated with children's gender or birth order; however, individual differences are typically much greater than any group variability (Whitehurst & Fischel, 1994). Usually, on close inspection, individual differences within the normal range do not resemble the patterns of communication delay seen in autism. Among typical children, comprehension and the spontaneous expression of the range of ideas discussed above are much less variable than early production of words (Fenson et al., 1994)—however, normal individual differences do exist. Recognition of these differences should not lead to an underestimation of the communication delays usually seen in autism.

COMMUNICATION AND DEVELOPMENT IN AUTISM

Course and Developmental Change

Most individuals with autism begin to speak late and develop speech at a significantly slower rate than nonautistic persons (Le Couteur et al., 1989). Because autistic children are not usually diagnosed until age 3 or 4 years, relatively little information is available about very young children with autism. Various retrospective studies using parents' report and videotapes collected during infancy and toddler years suggest that the communication of most autistic children is different from that of other children by the second year of life (Dahlgren & Gillberg, 1989). Several studies have found that very young autistic children, when compared to other children as early as 1 year of age, are less responsive to their names or to hearing someone speak to them (Lord, 1995; Osterling & Dawson, 1994). In one study (Lord, Pickles, DiLavore, & Shulman, 1996), 2-year-old children judged very likely to have autism had mean expressive and receptive language ages of less than 9 months, in contrast to the age levels of other skills, which were between 16 and 21 months. Not only was their language severely delayed at the age of 2 years, but the young autistic children's expressive skills continued to develop at a slower rate through age 5, compared to nonautistic developmentally delayed children with similar nonverbal levels at age 2.

About 25% of children with autism are described by their parents as having some words at 12 or 18 months, and then losing them (Kurita, 1985). Generally, the regression is a gradual process in which the children do not learn new words and fail to engage in communicative routines in which they may have participated earlier. Some children gradually stop talking completely; others retain some old words. In a detailed study of this phenomenon, Kurita reports that for most autistic children, this disappearance of speech occurred when they had learned 10 or fewer words and had been using them for only a few months. This phenomenon is quite different from the regression associated with Childhood Disintegrative Disorder (CDD), in which the child moves from full communicative use of sentences, occurring in a variety of circumstances, to no speech at all (see Chapter 3). In CDD, other systems (such as motor behaviors or coordination) are affected as well. Although children with autism may have had only minimal speech skills before the regression, parents are often confused and heartbroken when the children lose any small component of communicative skill, fleeting though it may have been. To date, no attempts to relate this phenomenon to etiology or prognosis have been successful.

Much has been written in response to the finding that autistic children without speech by age 5 have a poor prognosis in terms of eventual independence. This conclusion continues to be supported across several different definitions of "speech before 5" and "outcome." In one follow-up study, the presence of fluent speech (defined as at least three-word utterances produced spontaneously, regularly, and communicatively) by the age of 5 predicted adaptive skills and academic achievement in adolescence equally as well as did early IQ or language tests (Venter, Lord, & Schopler, 1992). However, no study has systematically tested whether speech at age 4 or 3 or 7 or 10 years might be an even better predictor.

Other definitions of "useful speech" might be more appropriate. In one longitudinal study that followed autistic and nonautistic communication-handicapped children from preschool into elementary school years, the best predictor of receptive language at ages 7 to 12 was receptive vocabulary at ages 3 to 5. At the first assessment, when only preschool children who had no measurable vocabulary were the subjects of the analyses, the best predictor of developing a minimal (2-year-old) receptive vocabulary by ages 7 to 12 was the Vineland Social Maturity Scale (Lord & Schopler, 1989). This earlier version of the Vineland was a summary measure of adaptive and intellectual skills (Doll, 1965). Nonverbal joint attention and play skills within the preschool period also predict language acquisition for autistic children (Mundy, Sigman, & Kasari, 1990). Once children reach school age, many measures of language skill—standard verbal intelligence tests, specific measures of receptive vocabulary (e.g., the Peabody Picture Vocabulary Test; Dunn & Dunn, 1981), formal measures of language skill (such as the Reynell Scales; Reynell, 1978), or other broadly based language tests—can be used to predict adaptive outcome and achievement (Lord & Schopler, 1989).

Paul, Cohen, and Caparulo (1983), in a longitudinal study of children with aphasic and autistic disorders, showed that comprehension ability at early ages was related to degree of improvement in social relations in late adolescence and early adulthood. Paul and Cohen (1984a) suggested that both comprehension and expressive abilities continue to improve in these populations through adolescence and adulthood, but expressive abilities show greater rates of improvement. This pattern may occur because speech is more accessible than comprehension and is more often a direct target of remedial efforts. Another series of follow-up studies reported on a high-functioning group of autistic boys and a nonautistic but similarly language-handicapped group in the United Kingdom. Almost all the students showed substantial improvement in formal aspects of language into adulthood (Cantwell & Baker, 1989). However, the autistic group, as a whole, remained more severely language-delayed and had more severe behavioral limitations (Rutter, Mawhood, & Howlin, 1992). The language-handicapped group had a much broader range of outcome—from total independence and good language skill to severe psychiatric disorder and continued expressive language problems.

A well-circulated statistic predicts that about 50% of autistic individuals will eventually have useful speech. To some extent, the prediction is supported by epidemiological data (Bryson, Clark, & Smith, 1988), but its validity is clearly affected by variation among the subjects studied. What age(s) are the autistic participants? Are they recruited from special education services or clinics, or from broader populations? What measurable effects can be expected from education and treatment? How is *useful speech* defined? Do single words qualify? Simple sentences? How spontaneous do the utterances have to be? How often do they have to occur? How intelligible must they be?

Information about all these factors is needed before a statement about the proportion of autistic individuals with or without speech can be interpreted accurately. In a 3-hour school observation of categorical special education classes for 4- to 13-year-old children with autism, Stone and Caro-Martinez (1990) found that 21% of children with nonverbal IQs less than 50 and 53% of children with nonverbal IQs of 50 or greater spoke spontaneously. Other, more verbal children may have been placed in other classrooms, and some of the children may have been able to speak but did not do so during the visitors' observation. What seems clear is that a substantial minority of individuals with autism are not fluent speakers, as adolescents or adults. Spoken language is not their primary means of expressing themselves. Thus, a general focus on communication must encompass all available modes and forms of human expression. Nevertheless, anyone working with families that have young children tends to hope that the children's language will become sufficiently fluent and automatic for their participation in our heavily language-based society (see Chapters 23 to 25).

Another developmental change that takes place in the autistic population concerns the relationship between verbal IQ and other scores on formal intelligence tests. DeMyer and colleagues (DeMyer et al., 1973) found that performance scores were higher than verbal IQ scores in 135 autistic children whose mean age was 5.32 years. This result is not unexpected, given the preponderance of language deficits in this age group. Studies of older autistic individuals (Rumsey & Denckla, 1987; Rutter et al., 1992) suggest that some children and adults with autism, particularly those who are higher-

Relationship between Verbal IQ and Full-Scale IQ Scores

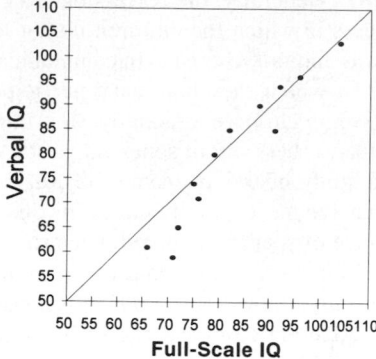

Figure 9.2 As IQ approaches 100 discrepancies between verbal and performance skills become less common.

functioning, improve in verbal IQ scores and may even have better verbal scores than performance scores. As shown in Figure 9.2, as IQ approaches 100, the discrepancy between verbal and performance skills lessens, and, in some samples, a discrepancy is more the exception than the rule (Siegel, Minshew, & Goldstein, 1996). Even so, individuals with autism still did poorly in Wechsler comprehension subtests and other tests that require social judgment or integration of information rather than verbal memory alone. An improved performance on verbal IQ measures does not imply that these individuals' use of language for communicative purposes is intact. On the contrary, poor social use of language continues to be one of the hallmarks of autism in adulthood.

Some children with autism develop far less language than would be expected, given their nonverbal skills (Lord & Schopler, 1989). Because of the small samples available and the tendency of researchers to group autistic children across a range of nonverbal abilities and chronological ages, information about these children is limited. Current research about specific language impairment in other populations may be useful for a better understanding of them.

Articulation

Among autistic children who speak, articulation may be normal or even precocious (Pierce & Bartolucci, 1977), although Bartak, Rutter, and Cox (1975) found articulation development to be somewhat slower than normal. Articulation abnormalities were more transient in a group of high-functioning autistic boys than in language-level-matched nonautistic boys with severe receptive-expressive delays in middle childhood (Rutter et al., 1992). Bartolucci, Pierce, Streiner and Tolkin-Eppel (1976) showed that the distributions of phoneme frequency and of phonological error types in 10 autistic children were similar to distributions in mentally handicapped and typical children matched for nonverbal mental age. The less frequently the phoneme occurred in the language, the greater was the number of errors. Phonological perception among the groups also was similar.

Two caveats should be noted. First, difficulties in articulation are relatively common in nonautistic, mentally handicapped children. Thus, the lack of statistically significant differences in articulation on comparisons of autistic and IQ-matched mentally handicapped children does not mean that autistic children have no articulation difficulties. Even if they are not specifically related to the autism, articulation difficulties can have very serious ramifications for the autistic child's ability to communicate effectively. For children with poor imitation skills and limited attention, improving articulation can be a particularly difficult task.

Second, a relatively small number of autistic children are identified as high-functioning on the basis of nonverbal tests during preschool but have extraordinary difficulty producing intelligible speech. These children are not likely to be included in many studies of language development because they are too rare to be treated as a separate group. Yet, by the time autistic children are 10 to 12 years old, fluent language is often an implicit criterion for the category of "high-functioning." These once-high-functioning children may account for the small number of autistic children whose IQ drops significantly after preschool because they cannot develop fluent speech (Lord & Schopler, 1989). Little is known about either the existence or the phenomenology of this pattern of development. When all information is considered together, phonological development in autism does not appear to differ from that seen in normal or mentally handicapped children except for the individual exceptions suggested above which require further documentation.

Word Use

Word use in autism can be observed by asking two rather different questions:

1. In their use and understanding of words, do autistic children assign words to the same categories that other people do?
2. Is there anything unusual about the way autistic individuals use words?

The answer to both questions is yes. Studies have shown that high-functioning autistic children use semantic groupings (e.g., such as bird, boat, food) in ways that are very similar to those used by nonautistic children to categorize and to retrieve words (Boucher, 1988; Minshew & Goldstein, 1993; Tager-Flusberg, 1985b). High-functioning autistic children and adolescents can score quite well on the Peabody Picture Vocabulary Test (Dunn & Dunn, 1981), for example (Fein & Waterhouse, 1979), although often not as well as they do on tests requiring less complex discriminations (Venter et al., 1992). Tager-Flusberg (1991) suggests that autistic children are able to represent word meanings in memory but fail to use meaning in a normal way in retrieval or organizational tasks.

Abnormal use of words and phrases has been described as a symptom of autism for many years (Rutter, 1970). In samples of high-functioning adolescents and adults, a significant minority has been shown to use words with special meanings (Rumsey, Rapoport, & Sceery, 1985; Volden & Lord, 1991). Most of these words or phrases were modifications of ordinary word roots or phrases that produced slightly odd-sounding but still comprehensible terms such as *commendment* for praise or *cuts and bluesers* for cuts and bruises. These terms were not radically different from those used occasionally by mentally handicapped or younger, nonhandicapped children of similar expressive language level, but they were more frequent in the autistic population. Only autistic subjects produced neologisms or odd phrases for which the root was not fairly obvious (e.g., calling a hair dryer a "poomba"), but these instances were relatively rare (Volden & Lord, 1991). One interesting finding was that increased language ability was associated with increased peculiarities and perseveration (proportions as well as absolute numbers) in autistic individuals. In a nonautistic mentally handicapped group, oddities decreased steadily as expressive language ability improved (Volden & Lord, 1991). Pedantic speech and excessive, rather concrete precision are descriptors frequently applied to individuals with high-functioning autism or Asperger's Syndrome (Ghaziuddin, Tsai, & Ghaziuddin, 1992). Though these qualities can be very difficult to quantify, listeners generally agree when they hear them; Mayes, Volkmar, Hooks, and Cicchetti (1993) found that peculiar language patterns was one of the best discriminators between Pervasive Developmental Disorder and language disability.

Several studies have measured autistic individuals' understanding of particular types of words. Hobson and Lee (1989) and Eskes, Bryson, and McCormick (1990) suggested that people with autism have specific difficulties in understanding social-emotional but not social-nonemotional terms, as measured on receptive vocabulary tests that require selection of an appropriate picture from among four choices. On one of the same tests, Van Lancker, Cornelius, and Needleman (1991) found that mental age accounted for differences between younger, school-age autistic children and nonautistic, mentally handicapped children in their comprehension of emotional terms. However, these authors also found that when parents were asked to identify the definitions of emotional terms provided by autistic youngsters (versus those given by nonautistic children), the parents performed as well as autism experts and slightly better than speech and language therapists.

Syntax and Morphology

Syntax in autism has been examined primarily by replicating earlier studies that investigated the occurrence, in continuous speech, of 14 grammatical morphemes. These were originally studied in typical children—longitudinally by Brown (1973) and cross-sectionally by de Villiers and de Villiers (1973). Several investigators, using small samples with relatively high rates of accuracy even on the most difficult morphemes (Fein & Waterhouse, 1979; Howlin, 1984), found no differences between groups of autistic children and matched controls (normal, schizophrenic) on these morphemes. A recent longitudinal study (Tager-Flusberg et al., 1990) compared six 3- to 6-year-old high-functioning autistic children and 6 children with Down syndrome, who were followed for about 2 years; these researchers stressed the similarities between the patterns of syntactic development in the autistic children and the children with Down syndrome, and those reported for typical children in the literature. Another paper reported that mean length of utterance (MLU) using morpheme counts overestimated grammatical complexity (per the Index of Productive Syntax) in autistic and mentally handicapped children, especially when MLU exceeded 3.0 (Scarborough, Rescorla, Tager-Flusberg, Fowler, & Sudhalter, 1991). This finding suggests that something is different in how developmentally delayed children use at least some grammatical markers, although the pattern may not be specific to autism.

In contrast to the other studies of the 14 morphemes, Bartolucci, Pierce, and Streiner (1980) found that, as a group, autistic children produced the 14 target morphemes in their obligatory contexts proportionately less often than did the matched mentally handicapped children. The morphemes that were most difficult for the autistic groups were those involving verb tense and articles. These are not typically the most difficult grammatical morphemes for children who do not have autism. The researchers suggest that the difficulty with such forms may be their deictic function—that is, their change of referent depending on the point of view of the speaker. Thus, this apparent morphological difference may, in fact, be semantically based.

Although they appear quite straightforward, these studies are in fact difficult to interpret. They are based on the assumption that all children create and fill, in the same way, obligatory contexts for the use of certain words and syntactic forms. Researchers must make many methodological decisions when they are counting frequencies of morphemes, particularly when numbers of occurrences or contexts are small and when the general context is not well controlled (e.g., a child may not mention possession or past occurrence because he or she does not understand the concept or has little interest in it). The assumptions about intentions and abilities, although appropriate for the typically developing children whose language formed the original database, may not be applicable to autistic children or to other children with delays.

One of the most important points emerging from this literature has been that difficulties with grammatical form do not alone cause difficulties with function. It is not true that if autistic children have knowledge about formal aspects of speech then all other communication difficulties disappear for them. In autism, the acquisition of grammar, in general, is quite dissociated from the development of functional aspects of language (Tager-Flusberg, 1994). However, differences in function may affect differences in form (see the later section on use of deictic terms). In the long run, results from research are dependent on how form is measured. Different results will be obtained if the frequencies measured are taken from spontaneous use, use in structured contexts, or use in obligatory contexts. Unusual use of form may possibly affect function in more general ways; that is, although more frequent grammatical errors (for example, using incorrect verb forms) may not affect a listener's understanding of a particular statement, these errors may affect the listener's perception of the competence or typicality of the speaker (Volden & Lord, 1991).

After making detailed investigations of verb tense in other populations of children with language difficulties, some researchers have proposed that omission of verb tense be considered a clinical marker for specific language impairment in English-speaking children (Rice, Wexler, & Cleave, 1995). Articles are of interest from a similar perspective but have not yet been analyzed in detail.

Studies of other sentence forms in spontaneous language have generally indicated that autistic children are similar to mental-age-matched normal, retarded, and aphasic young-sters in their acquisition of rule-governed syntactic systems (Bartak et al., 1975; Pierce & Bartolucci, 1977). Both mentally handicapped and autistic children lag in language development relative to their nonverbal mental age. Syntactic development in autistic children is very likely more similar than dissimilar to normal development. It proceeds at a slower pace and is related to developmental level more than to chronological age (although it may not keep pace with other areas of development) (Tager-Flusberg, 1981a). Studies of autistic adults (Paul & Cohen, 1984a) suggest that this development eventually reaches a plateau in at least some individuals. Adults with autism score significantly lower on measures of syntactic production in free speech than do mentally handicapped adults matched for nonverbal IQ.

The lags shown by autistic children and adolescents are often more severe than those of other children with comparable delays earlier in childhood. In research, these delays are often less obvious because autistic children who are not delayed on nonverbal tests are generally grouped with autistic children who are more severely delayed. The entire autism group is then compared to a more homogeneous control group of nonautistic children, all of whom are mentally handicapped (Lord & Pickles, 1996) and are matched to the autistic children on language measures. Within a group of ambulatory, not sensorily impaired, mentally handicapped children, the children who have the least language are almost always autistic (Lord et al., 1993; Wing & Gould, 1979).

Echolalia

One of the most salient aspects of deviant speech in autism is the occurrence of echolalia—the repetition, with similar intonation, of words or phrases that someone else has said. It can be immediate; for example, an autistic child may repeat her teacher's greeting to her, "Hi, Susie," exactly as it was said to her. Or, it can be delayed, as in the case of a child who, when he wants to be tickled, approaches his father and says, "I'm going to tickle you," repeating a phrase he has heard his parents say in the past. Echolalia was once viewed as an undesirable, nonfunctional behavior (Lovaas,

1977), and some instances of echolalia, such as repeating jingles from television commercials or parts of children's videos do not appear to serve any clear communicative function (Prizant & Duchan, 1981).

More recent approaches, however, beginning with Fay (1969) and elaborated by Prizant and colleagues (see Chapter 25), emphasize that echolalia, immediate or delayed, often accomplishes a purpose. These authors attempted to elucidate the functions that echolalia might serve. Prizant and Duchan (1981) presented six communicative functions they found to be served by immediate echolalia in autistic individuals: (a) turn-taking, (b) assertions, (c) affirmative answers, (d) requests, (e) rehearsal to aid processing, and (f) self-regulation. Delayed echoes can be used communicatively to request recreations of the scenes with which the remarks were originally associated, as when a child says, "You're okay" in a sympathetic tone of voice, after just falling down. They can serve other functions as well. Baltaxe and Simmons (1977) showed that the bedtime soliloquies of an 8-year-old autistic child contained frequent examples of delayed echolalia, much like those found in similar descriptions of bedtime soliloquies in a normally developing 2-year-old (Weir, 1962). The authors suggested that the child used these stored utterances as a base for analyzing linguistic forms that she was in the process of acquiring.

Although echolalia is one of the most classic symptoms of autism, not all autistic children echo, nor is echoing seen only in autism. Echoing, particularly immediate repetition, occurs in blind children, in children with other language impairments, in older persons with dementia, and, perhaps most important, in some normally developing children (Yule & Rutter, 1987). McEvoy, Loveland, and Landry (1988) found that immediate echolalia was most frequent in autistic children who have minimal expressive language and was not associated with chronological or nonverbal mental age. Shapiro (1977) and Carr, Schreibman, and Lovaas (1975) found that autistic children were most likely to echo immediately any questions or commands that they did not understand or for which they did not know the appropriate response. When the children these researchers studied were taught responses, they no longer echoed the questions. Bloom (see Bloom & Lahey, 1978) showed that some, but not most, normally developing young children will, in the early stages of language development, echo statements made by the current speaker. These echoes, however, are selective; primarily utterances containing forms that are slightly more advanced than those used in their spontaneous speech are repeated. Individual differences occur even among typical children in the extent to which they repeat phrases they hear.

A substantial minority of verbal autistic adolescents and adults are described by their parents as having engaged in delayed echolalia at some point in their development (Le Couteur et al., 1989). Immediate and delayed echoing are likely part of somewhat different developmental processes. Longitudinal observations would be helpful in explaining how these behaviors fit into language and other areas of development across time. Echolalia has been offered as evidence of gestalt processing in autism (Frith, 1989). Repeating long sections of frequently watched videotapes, with no social direction and no apparent meaning, would be an example of extreme reliance on gestalt processing (see Chapter 24). Researchers who study echolalia speculate that this reliance may arise partly from differences in cognitive capacity— that is, from a more restricted pattern of gestalt processing associated with autism as opposed to more analytic modes of processing.

Autistic children treat language segments as small gestalts or unanalyzed chunks—an approach that may be related to the failure of these children to engage in joint attentional activity. If autistic children do not attempt to direct another person's attention nor generally respond to another's attempts to direct their attention, they miss an important component of early social interaction. Consequently, they might receive fewer of the usual modifications made in speech directed to language-learning children. Adults (and even children) speaking to young children segment the speech stream deliberately—for example, "Oh, I see what you're pointing at. It's a bear! A teddy bear! Oh, a teddy bear just like the one you have at home! Does it look like your bear? Nice teddy bear!" This segmenting provides scaffolding from simple, early utterances to adult forms. When autistic children do not easily share attention with adults and do not attempt to direct adults' attention to objects in which they are interested, they miss the language-learning opportunities provided in this kind of interaction.

Some autistic children gain an ability to use the original memorized, unsegmented whole of a phrase to analyze the components of semantic and grammatical forms. Others may not ever become aware of the underlying symbolic nature of their echoed statements (Prizant, 1983). Children who mitigate or adjust their echoes to reflect their own perspectives (e.g., they echo "Do you want a drink of water?" as "Do I want a drink of water?") are likely to develop flexible spoken language sooner than children whose repetitions do not exhibit such adaptation (Bebko, 1990).

In summary, although immediate echolalia and delayed echolalia are salient features of autistic speech, they are neither synonymous with nor unique to this syndrome. Some echolalia in autism may appear to be nonfunctional or self-stimulatory, but both immediate and delayed echolalia can serve communicative purposes for the speaker. In addition, both forms of echolalia may function within a language acquisition strategy not entirely dissimilar from a style used by some typically developing children, although autistic children may use it to a greater degree and at different points in development.

Use of Deictic Terms

One of the most frequently mentioned language behaviors associated with autism is confusion and interchanging of personal pronouns, as when a child asks for a drink by saying, "Do you want a drink of water?" Like other aspects of deviant language, pronoun reversal sometimes occurs in children with language disorders other than autism and may be present briefly in the language of some normally developing children. It does not occur in all children with autism, but it is more common in this group than in persons with no or other disorders (Le Couteur et al., 1989; Lee, Hobson, & Chiat, 1994).

Kanner originally attributed pronoun reversals to echolalia. Some examples seem to reflect this relationship, as when a child says "Carry you!" Other accounts have attributed the confusion to the linguistic and/or information-processing demands of having to shift and mark reference (Lee, Hobson, & Chiat, 1994). However, difficulty using pronouns has been considered recently as part of a more general difficulty with deixis—the aspect of language that codes shifting reference between the speaker and the listener—and, sometimes, a third party. For example, in labeling an object or a person by name (e.g., "James"), the label remains the same without regard to who is speaking; for pronouns, however, James is referred to as "I" or "you," depending on whether he is the speaker of or the listener to a particular utterance.

Deixis is marked in different ways in other languages. In English, these ways include various articles (for example, whether a speaker uses "this" or "that," depending on previous reference or location of an object), selection of verbs (such as "come" and "go"), and verb tense. There is some evidence, discussed earlier, that deictic forms, such as articles or past-tense markings, may be particularly difficult for many individuals with autism, at least during specific periods of language development. Recent theoretical accounts have linked the use of deixis (and the acquisition of pronouns, in particular) with deficits in joint attention and understanding of others' perspectives (Hemphill, Picardi, & Tager-Flusberg, 1991; Loveland, 1984; Loveland & Landry, 1986), and with difficulty in conceptualizing the notion of self and other (Hobson, 1993; Lee et al., 1994).

Suprasegmental Aspects of Language

Paralinguistic features such as vocal quality, intonation, and stress patterns are other frequently noted speech characteristics of autistic individuals (Rutter et al., 1992). Clinically, odd intonation patterns associated with autism seem to be among the most immediately recognizable aspects of the disorder (for example, high-functioning adults with autism may be identifiable on the telephone because of the pitch and stress patterns of their speech).

However, defining what constitutes autism-related paralinguistic abnormalities so that clinicians can make reliable judgments about them has been quite difficult (Le Couteur et al., 1989; Volkmar et al., 1994). In part, this may be because language can sound unusual in a number of different ways. As an example of how researchers must carefully discriminate among different aspects of prosody, Thurber and Tager-Flusberg (1993) found that autistic children produced fewer nongrammatical pauses than did typical and mentally handicapped children matched on verbal mental age, when telling a story from a wordless picture book. There was no difference among the groups of children in their use of grammatical pauses (i.e., pauses between phrases). The authors interpreted the findings as demonstrating specific social cognitive deficits in autism that persist even when language level is controlled.

Intonational peculiarities frequently have been associated with autistic syndromes. The most frequently cited is monotony (see Fay & Schuler, 1980). Monotonous patterns were formerly attributed to emotional states believed to be present (or absent) in autistic individuals, and were originally thought to reflect flat affect, failure to express personality, and repressed anger (see Lord & Rutter, 1994). However, as Fay and Schuler (1980) pointed out, intonational phenomena serve a variety of functions beside the purely affective. They help to determine stress assignment within sentences, which in turn is used to mark topic or comment relations that aid listeners in processing discourse elements. They can indicate that sentences syntactically marked as assertions are in fact questions (e.g., "You're ready to go?"). They help to segment longer strings of discourse into processable units. Failure to use and appreciate intonational cues will likely not only affect the emotional tone of a verbal exchange but also hamper its comprehensibility.

There are variations in the deviant intonational patterns seen in autistic individuals. Fay and Schuler (1980) described a subset of autistic individuals who used a sing-song rather than a flat pattern. Goldfarb, Braunstein, and Lorge (1956) and Pronovost, Wakstein, and Wakstein (1966) found unusually high fundamental frequency levels in autistic speakers. Other voice disorders, such as hoarseness,

harshness, and hypernasality, have also been identified (Pronovost et al., 1966). Poor control of volume, with unexplained fluctuations, has also been reported (Pronovost et al., 1966). Fay (1969) found frequent whispering among autistic individuals who echoed.

The reasons behind these deficits in suprasegmental features remain obscure. Frith (1969) showed that autistic children, like normally developing children, recalled stressed words better than unstressed ones, especially when the stress was placed on content words. On the other hand, autistic children seemed less able than typical children to take advantage of stress cues for meaning. Baltaxe (1984), observing normal, autistic, and aphasic groups, found comparable use of stressed and nonstressed words in response to a yes/no question. Both disordered groups, however, did less well than the normal group. The autistic subjects performed most poorly and were more likely to produce more than one stress within a sentence. Paccia and Curcio (1982) used computer-assisted acoustic analyses to study prosodic features of echolalia responses in five autistic children. Their study revealed that four of the five subjects modified their intonation in echoing sentences.

Altogether, these formal studies do not completely account for the perceptions, by normal listeners, of marked deviance in autistic speech. The diversity of unusual characteristics is confusing. There is a relative lack of clinical sophistication in identifying the aspects of paralinguistic functioning that differentiate autism from other disorders, such as schizophrenia or mental handicap, and this lack may cause researchers within the field of autism to overestimate the specificity to autism of this type of problem. Deviance in intonation seems unlikely to result solely from simple perceptual or motor deficits. More fundamental aspects of the autistic syndrome may be reflected in higher-level language and communicative behaviors, such as understanding others and being able to plan and execute a complex action. These basic elements may also contribute to the ways autistic children learn to use intonation and other paralinguistic features.

On the other hand, there is definitely something different about the way people with autism produce the stream of sounds associated with speech. Ricks and Wing (1976), in one of the first studies in this area, examined parents' identification of the meaning of the prelinguistic vocalizations of autistic children. They discovered that parents of autistic children were unable to understand the preverbal vocalizations of other autistic children, even though they could understand their own child's messages. In contrast, parents of normally developing children could understand vocalizations of typical children who were not their own, as well as those of their own child.

Historically, autistic children have been described as babbling less frequently than other children during early childhood. In a recent study, Lord et al. (1996) found no difference in the frequency with which preverbal, developmentally delayed 2-year-olds, preverbal, normally developing 10- to 12-month-olds, and 2-year-olds with autism produced vocalizations during a standard diagnostic observation schedule (DiLavore, Lord, & Rutter, 1995). However, for each particular social situation, a smaller proportion of autistic children vocalized, compared with nonautistic children. The vocalizations that autistic children did produce were less likely to be paired with nonvocal communication, such as shifts in gaze or gesture, or changes in facial expression, than were the vocalizations by other children (Hellreigel, Tao, DiLavore, & Lord, 1995).

Lord et al. (1996) replicated a study by Ricks and Wing in which mothers of normally developing infants and toddlers listened to audio recordings of vocalizations made by children who were unfamiliar to them. The study showed that parents could identify, with much greater accuracy, the emotional context (e.g., delight, frustration, request) in which nonword vocalizations were made by typical and developmentally delayed children, as compared to those of preverbal children with autism. Vocalizations interpreted as indicating frustration were the most easily identified for children from all diagnostic groups; vocalizations associated with requests were the most difficult. The mothers were able to identify relatively easily the vocalizations made during solitary play by children with all three diagnoses; there were no differences in the mothers' accuracy in identifying vocalizations that were accompanied by other indications of social interest versus those that did

not seem to be socially directed (Arnold et al., 1993). Taken together, these findings suggest that the source of the differences between the vocalizations of the young children with autism and those of other young, nonverbal children was not just in social intent, but also in a more basic aspect of the form of the vocalization beginning very early in the child's development.

Language Comprehension in Autism

Most discussion of the language of autistic individuals centers on their productive capacities. Little attention has been focused on their understanding of speech. This omission is unfortunate because early response to language, a likely precursor to comprehension, is one of the strongest indicators of autism in very young children (Dahlgren & Gillberg, 1989; Lord, 1995). The continuation of significant delays in comprehension is also one of the strongest differentiators between high-functioning autism and specific language disorders (Rutter et al., 1992). Bartak and colleagues (Bartak et al., 1975) and Paul and Cohen (1984a) showed that autistic individuals performed more poorly on standardized measures of language comprehension than aphasic or mentally handicapped individuals at similar nonverbal mental age levels. In fact, delays in receptive as well as expressive language are often associated with social difficulties linked to the autism spectrum and pervasive developmental disorders, if not to a narrow diagnosis of autism (Cantwell et al., 1980; Wing & Gould, 1979).

Tager-Flusberg (1981b) conducted one of the few experimental studies of language comprehension in autistic children. Here, overall sentence comprehension was lower in the autistic group than in a normally developing comparison group matched for nonverbal mental age. Typical and autistic children were similar in their use of a word-order strategy for processing sentences (interpreting noun–verb–noun sequences as agent–action–object). However, autistic children were less likely than normally developing children to use a semantically based probable-event strategy, interpreting sentences based on the likelihood of occurrences in the real world (e.g., knowing that a mother is likely to pick up a baby but a baby will not pick up a mother). Tager-Flusberg (1981b) concluded that autistic children have difficulty applying their knowledge about the probability of real-world occurrences to the task of understanding sentences.

In a partial replication of this study, Gaddes (1984) showed that autistic children were much less consistent in identifying probable events that involved relationships between people (e.g., the mother feeds the baby) than were very young normally developing children with lower or equivalent expressive abilities. This inconsistency occurred when the relationships were acted out with dolls, even when no comprehension of language was required. Thus, the difficulties may lie in comprehending the situation (and what is probable in it) as well as the word order that depicts the situation. Paul, Fischer, and Cohen (1988) found that autistic and other children used similar strategies in sentence comprehension, but the autistic children always performed less competently. Together, these findings suggest that autistic children may have not only a limited ability to integrate linguistic input with real-world knowledge, but also, in some cases, a deficiency in knowledge about social events, which normally developing children use to enhance their emerging language skills and to acquire increasingly advanced linguistic structures (Lord, 1985a).

Sigman and Ungerer (1981) investigated language comprehension and sensorimotor performance in autistic children with mental ages of about 2 years. They found quite sophisticated performance on object permanence tasks (e.g., looking for a hidden object) and poor performance on receptive language measures such as naming pictures of objects. They suggested that sensorimotor skills play a small role in the acquisition of language. Play skills, on the other hand, were highly related to receptive language level, particularly those forms of play that were directed outward toward dolls. Thus, the more social aspects of cognition—those involving the creation of an imaginative scene with dolls, to represent interactions between people—appear to be more related to the understanding of language than are those involving knowledge about objects, which can be learned with very little social interaction. Other researchers have provided explanations of autism in terms of lack of a theory of mind (Baron-Cohen, Leslie, &

Frith, 1986; Tager-Flusberg & Sullivan, 1994) and have emphasized autism-specific deficits in social understanding to explain the symptoms.

Another perspective originates from interest in intermodal correspondence—the degree to which a child must integrate sources of information from different sensory systems to understand verbal input (e.g., noticing the smile on another's face; observing the way one person touches another; assessing the tone of a person's voice as well as the words spoken, to determine whether the person is being affectionate, is teasing, or is being aggressive). Deficits in putting these pieces of information together may affect a person's comprehension (Loveland, 1991; Ozonoff, Pennington, & Rogers, 1990; St. James & Tager-Flusberg, 1994).

Paul and Cohen (1985) researched the ability of autistic subjects and nonautistic, IQ-matched, mentally handicapped subjects to understand indirect requests for action ("Can you color this circle blue?") that had varying syntactic complexity. The two groups, with IQs in the mildly-to-moderately retarded range, performed similarly when the request intent of the utterance was made explicit ("I'm going to tell you to do some things. Can you . . . ?"). The autistic subjects did significantly worse when the same requests were presented in an unstructured context with no prefacing cue as to the intention of the utterance. Paul and Cohen concluded that, without explicit cues, the autistic subjects were deficient in their ability to determine the speaker's intention, over and above any syntactic comprehension deficit that might be present. This pattern may be an example of why, in their follow-up of high-functioning autistic individuals, Rutter et al. (1992) found a strong relationship between language comprehension and social functioning in adulthood, but no similar finding for adults identified as having specific receptive and expressive language impairment as children.

Recent longitudinal studies have examined very young children with autism (identified at 2 years of age and followed up at 3, 4, and 5 years). These children, when compared with other language-delayed children, have shown steady but slower increases in receptive language as measured by both parent report and direct testing (Lord et al., 1996). The trajectory of increases in comprehension was similar for autistic and nonautistic language-delayed children of equivalent chronological age, although the autistic children were always considerably lower in receptive skill than the other groups. Trajectories for the development of expressive language were more variable among the groups because a substantial minority of the children with autism did not gain much useful speech by age 5 years. Virtually no research has been done on the relationship between language comprehension and production in autistic children. There may be quite different courses of development for receptive and expressive language—and perhaps between areas of development (e.g., vocabulary, pragmatics)—within individuals with autism, and across individuals. Particularly for the nonverbal members of the autistic population, studies of language comprehension would be very useful in explaining the nature of communicative deficits more fully.

Language Use

Language use in autism has been studied from a variety of perspectives. Some of these topics are discussed elsewhere in this chapter; they include specific, unusual aspects of language use, such as delayed echolalia and neologisms, as well as language used to describe particular phenomena such as mental states or emotions. This section focuses on research on speech acts, referential communication, discourse, and narration.

One of the most interesting characteristics of language use in autism is that some aspects are constant across development and other aspects change. As with the development of social behavior (Lord, 1995), some of the changes occur because children improve in their communicative abilities; other changes occur because situational demands for communication are different for children of different ages and for adults, and they vary according to the contexts in which the individuals communicate. Thus, in considering deficits in language use, all factors—what individuals are expected to do, what they are given the opportunity to do, and what they usually do—must be considered.

Stone and Caro-Martinez (1990), in an observational study of the spontaneous communication of autistic children of varying abilities who were placed in special classrooms, found differences in the functions about which the children communicated. These differences were related to chronological age, nonverbal IQ, and whether the children's primary mode of communication was through speech or motor acts. Children who did not talk engaged in more social routines than did verbal children. Children with speech were more likely to use language to offer new information. They communicated to a greater number of different people (not just to the teacher) and were more likely to address their communications to peers as well as to adults than were the children without speech. Younger children made more requests than older children. McHale, Simeonsson, Marcus, and Olley (1980) observed that autistic students communicated more in the presence of their teachers than in their absence, and, in their study, directed their communication only to adults, not to peers.

Autistic children across different language levels also have important similarities. Despite deficits in spontaneous speech, most autistic children do attempt to use their language to communicate. Bernard-Opitz (1982) showed that the communicative performance of one autistic child varied with different interlocutors and different settings, indicating some social awareness in the child's use of language. However, the rate of initiation of spontaneous communications in autism is often described as very low. In the study by Stone and Caro-Martinez (1990), the modal frequency in school was two to three spontaneous communicative acts per child, per hour. In multiple observations, only half the children were ever seen to direct a communication to a peer. Several other investigators have shown that autistic children have less frequent and less varied speech acts than nonautistic children in free play or more open-ended situations, even when their responses to highly structured situations are similar to those of control groups (Landry & Loveland, 1989; Mermelstein, 1983). Children with autism, regardless of their level of verbal skill or modality, use a high proportion of their spontaneous communications in school to get attention and to comment on ongoing events (Stone & Caro-Martinez, 1990).

Similarities are also found in abnormalities in language use among verbal individuals with autism who show a range of expressive language abilities. Many children and adults with

autism have difficulties listening and following rules of politeness; they frequently make
irrelevant remarks or talk to themselves (Baltaxe, 1977; Rumsey, Rapoport, & Sceery,
1985). Shapiro and his colleagues were among
the first investigators to describe the contextual inappropriateness of the speech of young
autistic children (Shapiro, Chiarandini, &
Fish, 1974; Shapiro, Fish, & Ginsberg, 1972).
Autistic children and adults make few references to mental states (Storoschuk, Lord, &
Jaedicke, 1995; Tager-Flusberg, 1992; Tager-
Flusberg & Sullivan, 1994), and they use language less often to direct attention explicitly
to themselves in conversations at home. It is
interesting to note that this was not the case in
the one study carried out at school. More complex analyses of discourse might describe the
relationship between immediate context and
language in autism that may be problematic
and may contribute to this variability (Bishop
& Adams, 1989).

Autistic children and adolescents typically
perform less well on tasks of referential communication than do nonautistic individuals
(Loveland, McEvoy, Tunali, & Kelley, 1990),
although many can identify another person's
visual perspective (Baron-Cohen, 1989; Hobson, 1984). More social and/or more complex
aspects of referential communication, such as
those that affect narration and discourse, are
particularly affected (Hemphill et al., 1991).
Autistic children often have difficulty dealing
with new information (Tager-Flusberg & Anderson, 1991). They produce more noncontingent utterances. Their speech patterns are
similar to those of language-impaired children
but they have proportionately more errors
(Baltaxe & D'Angiola, 1992). Hurtig, Ensrud,
and Tomblin (1980) reported that persistent
and perseverative questioning generally did
not serve the purpose of requesting information in autistic children, but was communicative, often functioning as a means of initiating
interaction or getting attention.

Tager-Flusberg and Anderson (1991), in a
study of eight autistic children functioning in
the early stages of expressive language development, examined the children's communicative
competence in terms of discourse cohesion in
free conversation. Compared to normally developing 30-month-olds matched for expressive

language levels (MLU), the autistic children
were less likely to provide a relevant response
to an adult comment, to produce an expansion,
or to add new information; they were more
likely to imitate or not to respond at all. On the
other hand, there were no differences in the
overall amount of responding between the two
groups, and the autistic children were no more
likely than normal children to give noncontingent responses. The authors concluded that,
although the autistic children understood the
discourse requirements and were able to respond appropriately when adults provided a
structure in the form of simple questions, they
had relatively little to say, even though some
sophisticated syntactic forms were available to
them. Their rather primitive strategies for
maintaining the conversation were often like
those used by normal children at much lower
levels of syntactic development. Bishop and her
colleagues (Bishop, Hartley, & Weir, 1994)
studied a group of children with Semantic-
Pragmatic Disorder who had some social and
communicative behaviors that overlap with
autism and Pervasive Developmental Disorder.
They found, in these more verbally fluent children, a higher proportion of utterances that
were initiations rather than responses. This
finding seemed to account for how language-
impaired children, including some with autism,
could be considered talkative, even though the
total amount of language they produce is no
higher than that of other children.

Paul and Cohen (1984b) studied responses
to requests for clarification in eight autistic
adults and eight mentally handicapped adults
matched for nonverbal IQ. They found that, although the autistic subjects were just as likely
to respond to requests for clarification, their
answers were less specific than those of the retarded subjects. They were also less likely to
supply additional information that might be of
help to the listener. The autistic subjects, then,
attempted to respond to the listener's need for
clarification but had difficulty prejudging
what piece of information was relevant.

Paul and Feldman (1984) report that highly
verbal autistic adults, like the children studied
by Tager-Flusberg and Anderson (1991), show
difficulties identifying the topic initiated by
the autistic person's conversational partner
and providing a relevant comment. In response

to this difficulty, the autistic subjects developed a number of compensatory strategies. One strategy involved responding with some superordinate-level discourse marker ("I'll give you brief information about our group home"). It was as if, unsure that the choice of topic for their utterance was appropriate, they were attempting to orient the listener to what their comment would be about.

Additionally, these high-functioning autistic subjects had great difficulty complying with Grice's (1975) maxim of quantity. They were unable to judge—on the basis of (a) cues in the conversation and (b) general knowledge about what listeners could reasonably be expected to have in their knowledge store—how much information was the right amount to include in an utterance (Lord et al., 1989). For example, when asked the question, "Did you and your sister do anything besides rake leaves over the weekend?" an autistic adolescent responded, "Yes." This answer, although correct in a strictly syntactic sense, failed to appreciate the listener's real purpose in asking the question or to provide the socially appropriate amount of information in response. In contrast, another adolescent with autism, when asked how his day had gone, began the account with a description of the exact time when he awakened, the bathroom where he washed his face, and the color of his toothbrush.

Studies of the ability of individuals with autism to tell stories have also provided information about the ways people with autism organize their thoughts and convey them to others. In general, researchers have found that, commensurate with their language ability, children and adults with autism are able to narrate stories and follow simple scripts for common social events, such as a birthday party. However, participants in one study had particular difficulty in making causal statements (Tager-Flusberg, 1995), and, in two others, less frequent relevant remarks (Loveland & Tunali, 1991) and more frequent irrelevant remarks (Loveland et al., 1990) were made by children and adults with autism than by persons with other disorders.

Taken together, these studies of pragmatic skills in verbal autistic individuals echo the suggestions from studies of nonverbal communication in young autistic children. Although the basic intention to communicate often exists, the autistic person has *impaired* skill in participating in communicative activities that involve joint reference or shared topics. This deficit is particularly apparent when the autistic individual is supplying new information relevant to a listener's purposes. The strategies used by the person with autism to maintain conversation, as well as his or her ability to infer the interlocutor's implicit intentions, are less advanced than an apparent syntactic ability would predict.

One difference between individuals with autism and other populations with language impairments is that, in most groups with language impairment, the more a child talks, the less likely that his or her language usage will have unusual characteristics. In contrast, two studies with autistic children and adolescents showed that the subjects' unusual aspects of language and lack of cohesiveness increased with the amount of speech (Caplan, Guthrie, Shields, & Yudovin, 1994; Volden & Lord, 1991). In autism, difficulties in explaining and predicting behavior seem to be related both to general language deficits and to deficits in specific cognitive functions, such as metarepresentation and using the information at hand (Tager-Flusberg & Sullivan, 1994). Because most, but not all, individuals with autism have significant delays as well as deviance in language, they are doubly handicapped in communication.

Reading

Reading is an area of interest in autism because many young children with autism have an interest in letters, and some independently learn to read. Research has shown that decoding—that is, pronouncing written words (without any requirement for meaning)—and spelling are areas of relative strength for many individuals with autism. These strengths are especially remarkable when the autistic individuals are compared to other persons with similar histories of language delay. Several studies have shown high-functioning autistic children and adolescents to function at or near grade level in decoding and/or spelling (Minshew, Goldstein, Taylor, & Siegel, 1994; Rutter et al., 1992; Venter et al., 1992).

In contrast, reading comprehension is more problematic for the autistic population. Generally, even high-functioning autistic person's comprehension of written narratives is not at grade level, although these individuals often have somewhat more skill in understanding simple passages (Rutter et al., 1992; Venter et al., 1992). Unlike speech, written material has the advantage of remaining constant over time and making no immediate requirements for social attention. Thus, written material is a resource for intervention (see Chapter 19), but it is not a simple answer for the difficulties autistic individuals encounter in comprehending social communication or in following directions. Hyperlexia, the ability to read at a higher level than would normally be expected, is sometimes associated with autism (Fay & Schuler, 1980). The translation of print into speech in this condition, however, is usually accompanied by little comprehension of meaning. Tendencies toward hyperlexia in autism may explain why facilitated communication was thought to succeed in children with autism. However, almost all controlled studies showed that the children were actually engaged in little independent communication using this method (Vazquez, 1994). In any use of written text, the long-term functional use of the strategy must be considered. Thus, scripts for practicing social skills may be helpful initially but would be expected to have limited daily usefulness. On the other hand, making lists or outlines, or following recipes or complex written instructions, may be of practical value for adaptive or vocational situations.

Theories of Origin

Recently, increasingly sophisticated neuroimaging and neurophysiological measures have offered promise of eventual documentation of anatomical and functional differences in the brain in individuals with autism. This promise has not yet been fulfilled. A replicable, consistent, meaningful neuroanatomic and neurophysiological basis for autism has not yet been identified (Bailey, Phillips, & Rutter, 1996). However, when coupled with advances in molecular genetics, neurobiological techniques are likely to contribute directly to the understanding and treatment of autism in the next few years.

The new technological developments have affected, in several ways, the theories underlying autism and communication impairment. Ten or 20 years ago, theoretical explanations of autism were often based on neuropsychological explanations that used cognitive or behavioral patterns to infer neurobiological dysfunction. For example, theories of cerebral localization or temporal lobe dysfunction attempted to identify, by analogy, certain links between the effect of specific brain injury on language development and the communication abnormalities in autism (Fein et al., 1984). Currently, the focus in autism has been more on cognitive and developmental theories that will eventually be linked to neuroanatomy or physiology. Some of the theories associated with specific neurobiological findings also offer explanations of behavior patterns at an entirely different level. These theories may be useful in describing the nature of autism and the associated patterns in development, and in generating behavioral and educational treatments, regardless of whether their links with brain structure and function are verified as expected.

Any robust theoretical model for communication abnormalities in autism must have several characteristics. It needs to describe a course that goes awry very early in development and has a range of consequences—from severe language disability involving no representational-communication system to much milder abnormalities primarily affecting the pragmatics of connected discourse. It also needs to be related to other social and cognitive functions without being completely accounted for by other factors. There are children and adults without apparent syntactic and semantic difficulties who share the social difficulties seen in autism (as in Asperger's Syndrome). There are non-autistic children and adults with a severe-to-profound mental handicap, or with specific language disorders, who make substantial improvements in social areas and/or nonverbal cognitive functioning but who remain significantly impaired in spoken language. Thus, although the outcome and the severity of social and cognitive deficits in autism are apparently related to language level, these factors are also independent to some degree.

Two groups of theoretical orientations toward autism have provided accounts of the effects of particular cognitive deficits on social and communicative development in autistic persons (see Chapters 40, 41, and 42). One group emphasizes categorical differences in the ways individuals with autism think, compared with other persons (Hobson, 1991). Of particular interest are the ways in which these qualitative differences affect communication. This group would include researchers who characterize autism as an impairment principally defined by lack of theory of mind, metarepresentation, or ability to understand persons (Baron-Cohen, 1993; Hobson, 1991; Leslie & Happe, 1989). Each approach is somewhat different from the others, but all describe modular deficits that would limit a developing autistic child's understanding and use of language because of limitations in the knowledge of other persons' perspectives. The effects of such a deficit can most easily be seen in reduced use or understanding of the language employed to describe mental states (Happe, 1994; Tager-Flusberg, 1992) or to explain or predict behavior (Tager-Flusberg & Sullivan, 1994); they are also manifested in difficulties in discourse, such as narratives (Loveland & Tunali, 1991). Frith's theory of a lack of central coherence expands these perspectives into broader domains. The theory also has implications for further development in the ability to integrate segmented information into a whole (Frith, 1989; Shapiro & Hertzig, 1991).

Another group of theories about the cognitive dysfunction underlying autism and communication impairment arises from a neuropsychological approach to information processing. Building on a long history of cognitive research in autism (see Chapter 11), recent work on executive functioning (Ozonoff, 1995; Rumsey, 1992) and higher-order cognitive processes (Minshew & Goldstein, 1993) has offered explanations for how cognitive deficits could affect children's acquisition of meaningful words, and how deficits in flexibility could be manifested in difficulties in discourse (Ozonoff, Strayer, McMahon, & Filoux, in press). Because verbal tasks are used much more frequently than nonverbal tasks in studying complex cognitive activity, questions about the specificity of certain difficulties to verbal, auditory, or multimodal input are, for the most part, unresolved (Ameli, Courchesne, Lincoln, Kaufman, & Grillon, et al., 1988; Ozonoff et al., 1990).

CONCLUSION

The defining feature of the autistic syndrome is deviant social interaction (Cohen, Paul, & Volkmar, 1987). The primary function of language is to mediate social interaction. Language is the primary vehicle by which social interaction takes place among humans. The primacy of linguistic deficits in the autistic syndrome has often been questioned. Although, at one point, language deficits were thought to be the cause of the social withdrawal seen in autism, other evidence, such as the observation that young normal children communicate effectively nonverbally before they acquire language, has led away from this position. The evidence argues that, independent of cognitive functioning, at least some of the language and communicative deficits in autism arise from more fundamental disorders of human relating. If autistic children are unable to develop joint attentional routines, the limited functions about which they communicate (Curcio, 1978; Wetherby & Prutting, 1984) could be seen as a manifestation of a more basic disorder located at the intersection between cognition and social interaction. If autistic children have either little desire or limited means of achieving shared understanding with others, they have less need to learn language. Thus, the universal delays in language acquisition and/or use that are seen even in higher functioning autistic children may be affected by their difficulties in understanding the need to learn a system for establishing and elaborating joint reference.

The limited flexibility in play and imagination seen in autistic children (Wing, 1981) may also relate to autistic language deficits. Both play and language require the ability to create a cognitive space—play creates an internal world derived from experiences in the social world; language enters into a cooperative cognitive frame (Minsky, 1975) constructed around a shared topic. The forms of symbolic functioning at which some autistic children excel, such as drawing, do not require this creation of a shared cognitive space; rather, they involve representations that can be extracted from memory and reproduced, as Prizant (1983) suggests, holistically and without analysis. In children classified as having autism and other pervasive developmental disorders, this basic inability to enter into shared cognitive space may result in a persistent inability to enter the language system. Language input to the autistic child also may be less than optimal because of his or her failure to provide a parent with opportunities for using a style appropriately modified for a language-learning child. The difficulty in getting nonverbal autistic children to use signing or other alternative communication systems for purposes beyond requesting may be related to this basic failure to develop cognitive sharing abilities. Even the autistic child who eventually masters the verbal system can, to some extent, be seen as developing syntactic and phonological systems that do not quite link up with their semantic/pragmatic counterparts.

Curtis (1981) argues from data on mentally retarded and environmentally deprived children that semantic abilities appear to derive from capacities related to general conceptual development. However, syntax and morphological development appear dependent on language-specific acquisition mechanisms. Curtis finds that each mechanism—the general or conceptual and the language-specific—can operate independently in aberrant language development, although the two are highly integrated in the normal process. If syntax in verbal autistic individuals did arise from relatively specific language-learning strategies, it would be possible for sophisticated grammatical performance to be present, in the absence of semantic and pragmatic knowledge that accompanies it in normal development. The reality for most individuals with autism, however, is that both mechanisms are impaired.

Many questions remain to be answered about communication in autism. How is odd intonation related to deficits in communication and social cognition? How do linguistic comprehension deficits relate to the various aspects of deviant language seen in the syndrome? What triggers the initial failure of social cognition and joint attention that seems to be associated with such pervasive communicative difficulties? Like so many other questions about autism, the answers to these are likely to be neither simple nor universally true. A range of communicative behaviors is seen in the syndrome. Whatever the biological explanation, communication disorders in autism are most likely affected by deficits in the person's ability to process information about social situations and about how people behave when interacting with each other at every point in development. This deficit must be addressed in any attempt to remediate autistic communicative disorders. In addition, although they are integrally tied to broader cognitive and social deficits, delays in the ability to understand and produce words and sentences may have an even greater effect on the lives of individuals with autism than they do on persons with other handicaps. Because of the double handicap of delay and deviance in autism, it cannot be assumed that individuals with autism, or those who provide their linguistic environments, can naturally compensate for these deficits without carefully considered intervention. This intervention must include an understanding of how these deficits are manifested in particular children or adults and the communicative contexts in which each individual needs to function.

Cross-References

Aspects of classification and diagnosis are discussed in Chapters 1 to 7. Developmental changes in autism are described in Chapters 12 to 14, and language intervention is a key topic in Chapters 23 to 25.

REFERENCES

Ameli, R., Courchesne, E., Lincoln, A., Kaufman, A.S., & Grillon, C. (1988). Visual memory processes in high-functioning individuals with autism. *Journal of Autism and Developmental Disorders, 18,* 601–616.

Arnold, S.B., Elliott, M.J., Storoschuk, S.F., Pickles, A., Hellreigel, C., & Lord, C. (1993, November). *Social directedness and prelinguistic vocalization in autism.* Poster presentation at the annual meeting of the American Academy of Child and Adolescent Psychiatry, Santa Fe, NM.

Asher, S.R. (1978). Referential communication. In G.J. Whitehurst & B.J. Simmerman (Eds.), *The functions of language and cognition.* New York: Academic Press.

Bailey, A., Phillips, W., & Rutter, M. (1996). Autism: Towards an integration of clinical, genetic, neuropsychological, and neurobiological perspectives. *Journal of Child Psychology & Psychiatry & Allied Disciplines, 37,* 89–126.

Baldwin, D.A. (1991). Infants' contribution to the achievement of joint reference. *Child Development, 62,* 875–890.

Baltaxe, C. (1977). Pragmatic deficits in the language of autistic adolescents. *Journal of Pediatric Psychology, 2,* 176–180.

Baltaxe, C. (1984). Use of contrastive stress in normal, aphasic and autistic children. *Journal of Speech and Hearing Research, 24,* 97–105.

Baltaxe, C., & D'Angiola, N. (1992). Cohesion in the discourse interaction of autistic, specific language-impaired, and normal children. *Journal of Autism and Developmental Disorders, 22,* 1–22.

Baltaxe, C.A.M., & Simmons, J.Q. (1977). Bedtime soliloquies and linguistic competence in autism. *Journal of Speech and Hearing Disorders, 42,* 376–393.

Baron-Cohen, S. (1989). Perceptual role-taking and protodeclarative pointing in autism. *British Journal of Developmental Psychology, 7,* 113–127.

Baron-Cohen, S. (1993). From attention-goal psychology to belief-desire psychology: The development of a theory of mind, and its dysfunction. In S. Baron-Cohen, H. Tager-Flusberg, & D. Cohen (Eds.), *Understanding other minds: Perspectives from autism* (pp. 59–82). Oxford, England: Oxford University Press.

Baron-Cohen, S., Leslie, A.M., & Frith, U. (1986). Mechanical, behavioural and intentional understanding of picture stories in autistic children. *British Journal of Developmental Psychology, 4,* 113–125.

Bartak, L., Rutter, M., & Cox, A. (1975). A comparative study of infantile autism and specific developmental receptive language disorder: I. The children. *British Journal of Psychiatry, 126,* 127–145.

Bartolucci, G., Pierce, S.J., & Streiner, D. (1980). Cross-sectional studies of grammatical morphemes in autistic and mentally retarded children. *Journal of Autism and Developmental Disorders, 10,* 39–50.

Bartolucci, G., Pierce, S., Streiner, D., & Tolkin-Eppel, P. (1976). Phonological investigation of verbal autistic and mentally retarded subjects. *Journal of Autism and Childhood Schizophrenia, 6,* 303–315.

Bates, G. (1976). *Language in context.* New York: Academic Press.

Bebko, J.M. (1990). Echolalia, mitigation and autism: Indicators from child characteristics for the use of sign language and other augmentative language systems. *Sign Language Studies, 66,* 61–78.

Beitchman, J.H., & Inglis, A. (1991). The continuum of linguistic dysfunction from pervasive developmental disorders to dyslexia. *Psychiatric Clinics of North America, 14,* 95–111.

Bernard-Opitz, V. (1982). Pragmatic analysis of the communicative behavior of an autistic child. *Journal of Speech and Hearing Disorders, 47,* 99–109.

Bishop, D.V., & Adams, C. (1989). Conversational characteristics of children with Semantic-Pragmatic Disorder: 2. What features lead to a judgment of inappropriacy? *British Journal of Disorders of Communication, 24*(3), 241–263.

Bishop, D., Hartley, J., & Weir, F. (1994). Why and when do some language-impaired children seem talkative? A study of initiation in conversations of children with Semantic-Pragmatic Disorder. *Journal of Autism and Developmental Disorders, 24*(2), 177–197.

Bloom, L. (1970). *Language development: Form and function of emerging grammars.* Cambridge, MA: MIT Press.

Bloom, L. (1974). Talking, understanding and thinking. In R.C. Scheifelbusch & L.L. Lloyd (Eds.), *Language perspectives: Acquisition, retardation and intervention* (pp. 285–311). Baltimore: University Park Press.

Bloom, L., & Lahey, M. (1978). *Language development and language disorders.* New York: John Wiley & Sons.

Bolton, P., McDonald, H., Pickles, A., Rios, P., Goode, S., Crowson, M., Bailey, A., & Rutter, M. (1994). A case-control family history study of autism. *Journal of Child Psychology and Psychiatry, 35,* 877–900.

Boucher, J. (1988). Word fluency in high-functioning autistic children. *Journal of Autism and Developmental Disorders, 18,* 637–645.

Brown, R. (1973). *A first language.* Cambridge, MA: Harvard University Press.

Bruner, J.S. (1975). From communication to language—A psychological perspective. *Cognition, 3,* 255–289.

Bryson, S.E., Clark, B.S., & Smith, T.M. (1988). First report of a Canadian epidemiological study of autistic syndromes. *Journal of Child Psychology and Psychiatry, 29,* 433–445.

Cantwell, D.P., & Baker, L. (1989). Infantile autism and developmental receptive dysphasia: A comparative follow-up into middle childhood. *Journal of Autism and Developmental Disorders, 19,* 19–30.

Cantwell, D.P., Baker, L., & Mattison, R.E. (1980). Psychiatric disorders in children with speech and language retardation. *Archives of General Psychiatry, 37,* 423–426.

Caplan, R., Guthrie, D., Shields, W.D., & Yudovin, S. (1994). Communication deficits in pediatric complex partial seizure disorders and schizophrenia. *Development and Psychopathology, 6,* 499–517.

Carr, E., Shriebman, L., & Lovaas, O.L. (1975). Control of echolalic speech in psychotic children. *Journal of Abnormal Child Psychology, 3,* 331–351.

Cazden, C. (1968). The acquisition of noun and verb inflections. *Child Development, 39,* 443–448.

Chapman, R.S. (1978). Comprehension strategies in children. In J.F. Kavanagh & W. Strange (Eds.), *Speech and language in the laboratory, school and clinic* (pp. 308–327). Cambridge, MA: MIT Press.

Chapman, R. (1981). Exploring children's communicative intents. In J. Miller (Ed.), *Assessing language production in children: Experimental procedures.* Baltimore: University Park Press.

Cohen, D.J., Paul, R., & Volkmar, F.R. (1987). Issues in the classification of pervasive developmental disorders and associated conditions. In D.J. Cohen & A.M. Donnellan (Eds.), *Handbook of autism and pervasive developmental disorders* (pp. 20–40). New York: John Wiley & Sons.

Cohen, I.L., Sudhalter, V., Landon-Jimenez, D., & Keogh, M. (1993). A neural network approach to the classification of autism. *Journal of Autism and Developmental Disorders, 23,* 443–466.

Curcio, F. (1978). Sensorimotor functioning and communication in mute autistic children. *Journal of Autism and Childhood Schizophrenia, 8,* 281–292.

Curtis, S. (1981). Dissociations between language and cognition: Cases and implications. *Journal of Autism and Childhood Schizophrenia, 11,* 15–31.

Dahlgren, S.O., & Gillberg, C. (1989). Symptoms in the first two years of life: A preliminary population study of infantile autism. *European Archives of Psychiatric and Neurological Science, 283,* 169–174.

DeMyer, M.K., Barton, S., DeMyer, W.E., Norton, J.A., Allen, J., & Steel, R. (1973). Prognosis in autism: A follow-up study. *Journal of Autism and Childhood Schizophrenia, 3,* 199–245.

de Villiers, J.G., & de Villiers, P.A. (1973). A cross-sectional study of the acquisition of grammatical morphemes. *Journal of Psycholinguistic Research, 2,* 267–278.

DiLavore, P., Lord, C., & Opsahl, A. (1994, October). *The early diagnosis of autism: Year one.* Paper presented at the annual meeting of the American Academy of Child and Adolescent Psychiatry, New York.

DiLavore, P., Lord, C., & Rutter, M. (1995). Pre-Linguistic Autism Diagnostic Observation Schedule (PLADOS). *Journal of Autism and Developmental Disorders, 25,* 355–379.

Doll, E.A. (1965). *Vineland Social Maturity Scale.* Circle Pines, MN: American Guidance Service.

Dore, J. (1978). Requestive systems in nursery school conversations: Analysis of talk in its social context. In R. Campbell & P. Smith (Eds.), *Recent advances in the psychology of language* (pp. 139–164). New York: Plenum Press.

Dunn, L.M., & Dunn, L.M. (1981). *Peabody Picture Vocabulary Test—Revised: Manual for forms L and M.* Circle Pines, MN: American Guidance Service.

Eskes, G.A., Bryson, S.E., & McCormick, T.A. (1990). Comprehension of concrete and abstract words in autistic children. *Journal of Autism and Developmental Disorders, 20,* 61–73.

Fay, W. (1969). On the basis of autistic echolalia. *Journal of Communication Disorders, 2,* 38–47.

Fay, W., & Schuler, A.L. (1980). *Emerging language in autistic children.* Baltimore: University Park Press.

Fein, D., Humes, H., Kaplan, E., Lucci, D., & Waterhouse, L. (1984). The question of left hemisphere dysfunction in infantile autism. *Psychological Bulletin, 95,* 258–281.

Fein, D., & Waterhouse, L. (1979, October). *Autism is not a disorder of language.* Paper presented at the meeting of the New England Child Language Association, Boston.

Fenson, L., Dale, P., Reznick, J., Bates, E., Thal, D., & Pethick, S. (1994). Variability in early communicative development. *Monographs of the Society for Research in Child Development, 59* (5, Serial No. 242).

Frith, U. (1969). Emphasis and meaning in recall in normal and autistic children. *Language and Speech, 2,* 29–38.

Frith, U. (1989). *Autism: Explaining the enigma.* New York: Blackwell.

Gaddes, J. (1984). *Probable events and sentence comprehension in autistic children.* Unpublished senior honors thesis, University of Alberta, Edmonton, Alberta, Canada.

Ghaziuddin, M., Tsai, L., & Ghaziuddin, N. (1992). Brief report: A comparison of the diagnostic criteria for Asperger's Syndrome. *Journal of Autism and Developmental Disorders, 22,* 643–649.

Goldfarb, W., Braunstein, P., & Lorge, I. (1956). A study of speech patterns in a group of schizophrenic children. *American Journal of Orthopsychiatry, 26,* 544–555.

Grice, P. (1975). Logic and conversation. In J. Cole & P. Morgan (Eds.), *Syntax and semantics: Speech acts* (pp. 41–59). New York: Academic Press.

Halliday, M.A.K. (1975). *Learning how to mean: Exploration in the development of language.* London: Edward Arnold.

Happe, F.G.E. (1994). Wechsler IQ profile and theory of mind in autism: A research note. *Journal of Child Psychology and Psychiatry, 35,* 1461–1472.

Hellreigel, C., Tao, L., DiLavore, P., & Lord, C. (1995). *The effect of context on nonverbal social behaviors of very young autistic children.* Paper presented at the biannual meetings of the Society for Research in Child Development, Indianapolis, IN.

Hemphill, L., Picardi, N., & Tager-Flusberg, H. (1991). Narrative as an index of communicative competence in mildly mentally retarded children. *Applied Psycholinguistics, 12,* 263–279.

Hobson, R.P. (1984). Early childhood autism and the question of egocentrism. *Journal of Autism and Developmental Disorders, 14,* 85–104.

Hobson, R.P. (1991). Against the theory of "theory of mind." *British Journal of Developmental Psychology, 9,* 33–51.

Hobson, R.P. (1993). Understanding persons: The role of affect. In S. Baron-Cohen, H. Tager-Flusberg, & D. Cohen (Eds.), *Understanding other minds: Perspectives from autism* (pp. 204–227). Oxford, England: Oxford University Press.

Hobson, R.P., & Lee, A. (1989). Emotion-related and abstract concepts in autistic people: Evidence from the British Picture Vocabulary Scale. *Journal of Autism and Developmental Disorders, 19,* 601–623.

Howlin, P. (1984). The acquisition of grammatical morphemes in autistic children: A critique and replication of the findings of Bartolucci, Pierce, and Streiner, 1980. *Journal of Autism and Developmental Disorders, 14,* 127–136.

Hurtig, R., Ensrud, S., & Tomblin, J.B. (1980). The communicative function of question production in autistic children. *Journal of Autism and Developmental Disorders, 12,* 57–69.

Huttenlocher, J. (1974). The origins of language comprehension. In R.L. Solso (Ed.), *Theories in cognitive psychology* (pp. 331–368). Hillsdale, NJ: Erlbaum.

Kanner, L. (1943). Autistic disturbances of affective contact. *Nervous Child, 2,* 217–250.

Konstantareas, M., Zajdemann, H., Homatidis, S., & McCabe, A. (1988). Maternal speech to

verbal and higher-functioning versus nonverbal and lower-functioning autistic children. *Journal of Autism and Developmental Disorders, 18,* 647–656.

Kurita, H. (1985). Infantile autism with speech loss before the age of 30 months. *Journal of the American Academy of Child Psychiatry, 24,* 191–196.

Landa, R., Piven, J., Wzorek, M., Gayle, J.O., Chase, G.A., & Folstein, S.E. (1992). Social language use in parents of autistic individuals. *Psychological Medicine, 22,* 245–254.

Landry, S.H., & Loveland, K.A. (1989). The effect of social context on the functional communication skills of autistic children. *Journal of Autism and Developmental Disorders, 19*(2), 283–299.

Le Couteur, A., Rutter, M., Lord, C., Rios, P., Robertson, S., Holdgrafer, M., & McLennan, J.D. (1989). Autism Diagnostic Interview: A semi-structured interview for parents and caregivers of autistic persons. *Journal of Autism and Developmental Disorders, 19,* 363–387.

Lee, A., Hobson, R.P., & Chiat, S. (1994). I, you, me and autism: An experimental study. *Journal of Autism and Developmental Disorders, 24,* 155–176.

Lempert, H. (1978). Extrasyntactic factors affecting passive sentence comprehension in young children. *Child Development, 49,* 694–699.

Leslie, A.M., & Happé, F. (1989). Autism and ostensive communication: The relevance of metarepresentation. *Development and Psychopathology, 1,* 205–212.

Loban, W. (1976). *Language development: Kindergarten through grade 12.* Urbana, IL: National Council of Teachers of English.

Lord, C. (1985a). Autism and the comprehension of language. In E. Schopler & G. Mesibov (Eds.), *Communication problems in autism* (pp. 257–281). New York: Plenum Press.

Lord, C. (1985b). Contribution of behavioural approaches to the language and communication of persons with autism. In E. Schopler & G. Mesibov (Eds.), *Communication needs of persons with autism* (pp. 59–68). New York: Plenum Press.

Lord, C. (1995). Follow-up of two-year-olds referred for possible autism. *Journal of Child Psychology and Psychiatry, 36,* 1365–1382.

Lord, C., Elliott, M.J., Pickles, A., Arnold, S., Stulberg, D., Hellreigel, C., & Spencer, A. (1996). *Prelinguistic vocalizations in autistic children.* Manuscript submitted for publication.

Lord, C., Merrin, D.J., Vest, L., & Kelly, K.M. (1983). Communicative behavior of adults with an autistic four-year-old boy and his nonhandicapped twin brother. *Journal of Autism and Developmental Disorders, 13,* 1–17.

Lord, C., & Pickles, A. (1996). Language level and nonverbal social-communicative behaviors in autistic and language-delayed children. *Journal of the American Academy of Child and Adolescent Psychiatry, 35,* 1542–1550.

Lord, C., Pickles, A., DiLavore, P.C., & Shulman, C. (1996, August). *Longitudinal studies of young children referred for possible autism.* Paper presented at the biannual meetings of the International Society for Research in Child and Adolescent Psychopathology, Los Angeles, California.

Lord, C., & Rutter, M. (1994). Autism and pervasive developmental disorders. In M. Rutter, L. Hersov, & E. Taylor (Eds.), *Child and adolescent psychiatry: Modern approaches* (3rd ed.; pp. 569–593). Oxford, England: Blackwell.

Lord, C., Rutter, M., Goode, S., Heemsbergen, J., Jordan, H., Mawhood, L., & Schopler, E. (1989). Autism Diagnostic Observation Schedule: A standardized observation of communicative and social behavior. *Journal of Autism and Developmental Disorders, 19,* 185–212.

Lord, C., & Schopler, E. (1989). The role of age at assessment, developmental level, and test in the stability of intelligence scores in young autistic children from preschool years through early school age. *Journal of Autism and Developmental Disorders, 18,* 302–314.

Lord, C., Storoschuk, S., Rutter, M., & Pickles, A. (1993). Using the ADI-R to diagnose autism in preschool children. *Infant Mental Health Journal, 14,* 234–252.

Lord, C., & Venter, A. (1992). Outcome and follow-up studies of high-functioning autistic individuals. In E. Schopler & G. Mesibov (Eds.), *High-functioning individuals with autism* (pp. 187–199). New York: Plenum Press.

Lovaas, O.I. (1977). *The autistic child.* New York: Irvington.

Loveland, K. (1984). Learning about points of view: Spatial perspective and the acquisition of "I/you." *Journal of Child Language, 11,* 535–556.

Loveland, K.A. (1991). Social affordances and interaction: 2. Autism and the affordances of the human environment. *Ecological Psychology, 3,* 99–119.

Loveland, K., & Landry, S. (1986). Joint attention and language in autism and developmental language delay. *Journal of Autism and Developmental Disorders, 16,* 335–349.

Loveland, K.A., McEvoy, R.E., Tunali, B., & Kelley, M.L. (1990). Narrative storytelling in autism and Down syndrome. *British Journal of Developmental Psychology, 8,* 9–23.

Loveland, K.A., & Tunali, B. (1991). Social scripts for conversational interactions in autism and Down syndrome. *Journal of Autism and Developmental Disorders, 21,* 177–186.

Mayes, L., Volkmar, F., Hooks, M., & Cicchetti, D. (1993). Differentiating Pervasive Developmental Disorder Not Otherwise Specified from autism and language disorders. *Journal of Autism and Developmental Disorders, 23,* 79–90.

McEvoy, R.E., Loveland, K.A., & Landry, S.H. (1988). The functions of immediate echolalia in autistic children: A developmental perspective. *Journal of Autism and Developmental Disorders, 18,* 657–668.

McHale, S., Simeonsson, R.J., Marcus, L.M., & Olley, J.G. (1980). The social and symbolic quality of autistic children's communication. *Journal of Autism and Developmental Disorders, 10,* 299–310.

Mermelstein, R. (1983). *The relationship between syntactic and pragmatic development in autistic, retarded, and normal children.* Paper presented to the Eighth Annual Boston University Conference on Language Development, Boston.

Miller, J. (1981). *Assessing language production in children: Experimental procedures.* Boston: Allyn & Bacon.

Miller, J., & Chapman, R.S. (1981). The relation between age and mean length of utterance in morphemes. *Journal of Speech and Hearing Research, 24,* 154–162.

Minshew, N.J., & Goldstein, G. (1993). Is autism an amnesic disorder? Evidence from the California Verbal Learning Test. *Neuropsychology, 7,* 209–216.

Minshew, N.J., Goldstein, G., Taylor, H.G., & Siegel, D.J. (1994). Academic achievement in high-functioning autistic individuals. *Journal of Clinical Experimental Neuropsychology, 16,* 261–270.

Minsky, M. (1975). A framework for representing knowledge. In D. Winston (Ed.), *The psychology of computer vision* (pp. 144–175). New York: McGraw-Hill.

Mundy, P., Sigman, M., & Kasari, C. (1990). A longitudinal study of joint attention and language development in autistic children. *Journal of Autism and Developmental Disorders, 20,* 115–128.

Mundy, P., Sigman, M., & Kasari, C. (1994). Joint attention, developmental level, and symptom presentation in autism. *Development and Psychopathology, 6,* 389–401.

Nelson, K. (1973). Structure and strategy in learning to talk. *Monographs of the Society for Research in Child Development, 136*(1–2, Serial No. 149).

Osterling, J., & Dawson, G. (1994). Early recognition of children with autism: A study of first birthday home videotapes. *Journal of Autism and Developmental Disorders, 24,* 247–258.

Ozonoff, S. (1995). Executive functions in autism. In E. Schopler & G.B. Mesibov (Eds.), *Learning and cognition in autism* (pp. 199–219). New York: Plenum Press.

Ozonoff, S., Pennington, B.F., & Rogers, S.J. (1990). Are there emotion perception deficits in young autistic children? *Journal of Child Psychology and Psychiatry, 31,* 343–362.

Ozonoff, S., Strayer, D.L., McMahon, W.M., & Filoux, F. (in press). Executive function abilities in autism and Tourette Syndrome: An information processing approach. *Journal of Child Psychology and Psychiatry.*

Paccia, J., & Curcio, F. (1982). Language processing and forms of immediate echolalia in autistic children. *Journal of Speech and Hearing Research, 25,* 42–47.

Paul, R. (1987). Natural history. In D.J. Cohen & A. Donnellan (Eds.), *Handbook of autism and pervasive developmental disorders* (pp. 121–132). New York: John Wiley & Sons.

Paul, R., & Cohen, D.J. (1984a). Outcomes of severe disorders of language acquisition. *Journal of Autism and Developmental Disorders, 14,* 405–422.

Paul, R., & Cohen, D.J. (1984b). Responses to contingent queries in adults with mental retardation and pervasive developmental disorders. *Applied Psycholinguistics, 24,* 349–357.

Paul, R., & Cohen, D.J. (1985). Comprehension of indirect requests in adults with mental retardation and pervasive developmental disorders. *Journal of Speech and Hearing Research, 28,* 475–479.

Paul, R., Cohen, D.J., & Caparulo, B.K. (1983). A longitudinal study of patients with severe developmental disorders of language learning. *Journal of the American Academy of Child Psychiatry, 22,* 525–534.

Paul, R., & Feldman, C. (1984, March). *Communication deficits in autism.* Paper presented at the Institute for Communication Deficits in Autistic Youth. Columbia University, New York.

Paul, R., Fischer, M.L., & Cohen, D. (1988). Sentence comprehension strategies in children with autism and specific language disorders. *Journal of Autism and Developmental Disorders, 18,* 669–680.

Pierce, S., & Bartolucci, G. (1977). A syntactic investigation of verbal autistic, mentally retarded, and normal children. *Journal of Autism and Childhood Schizophrenia, 7,* 121–134.

Prizant, B.M. (1983). Echolalia in autism: Assessment and intervention. *Seminars in Speech and Language, 4,* 63–77.

Prizant, B., & Duchan, J. (1981). The functions of immediate echolalia in autistic children. *Journal of Speech and Hearing Disorders, 46,* 241–249.

Pronovost, W., Wakstein, M., & Wakstein, D. (1966). A longitudinal study of speech behavior and language comprehension in fourteen children diagnosed as atypical or autistic. *Exceptional Children, 33,* 19–26.

Reynell, J. (1978). *Reynell Developmental Language Scales—Revised.* Windsor, UK: National Foundation for Educational Research.

Rice, M.L., Wexler, K., & Cleave, P.L. (1995). Specific language impairment as a period of extended optional infinitive. *Journal of Speech and Hearing Research, 38,* 850–863.

Ricks, D.M., & Wing, L. (1976). Language, communication and use of symbols. In L. Wing (Ed.), *Early childhood autism* (pp. 93–134). Oxford, England: Pergamon Press.

Rumsey, J.M. (1992). Neuropsychological studies of high level autism. In E. Schopler & G.B. Mesibov (Eds.), *High-functioning individuals with autism* (pp. 41–64). New York: Plenum Press.

Rumsey, J., & Denckla, M. (1987). Neurobiological research priorities in autism. In E. Schopler & G.B. Mesibov (Eds.), *Neurobiological issues in autism.* New York: Plenum Press.

Rumsey, J., Duara, R., Grady, C., Rapoport, J., Margolin, R., Rapoport, S., & Cutler, N. (1985). Brain metabolism in autism. Testing cerebral glucose utilization rates as measured with positron emission tomography. *Archives of General Psychiatry, 42,* 448–455.

Rumsey, J.M., Rapoport, M.D., & Sceery, W.R. (1985). Autistic children as adults: Psychiatric, social, and behavioral outcomes. *Journal of the American Academy of Child Psychiatry, 24,* 465–473.

Rutter, M. (1970). Autistic children: Infancy to adulthood. *Seminars in Psychiatry, 2,* 435–450.

Rutter, M., & Lord, C. (1987). Language impairment associated with psychiatric disorder. In W. Yule, M. Rutter, & M. Bax (Eds.), *Language development and disorders. Clinic in Developmental Medicine, 101/102* (pp. 206–233). London: SIMP/Blackwell Scientific and Lippincott.

Rutter, M., Mawhood, L., & Howlin, P. (1992). Language delay and social development. In P. Fletcher & D. Hall (Eds.), *Specific speech and language disorders in children: Correlates, characteristics and outcomes* (pp. 63–78). London: Whurr.

St. James, P.J., & Tager-Flusberg, H. (1994). An observational study of humor in autism and Down syndrome, *Journal of Autism and Developmental Disorders, 24,* 603–617.

Scarborough, H.S., Rescorla, L., Tager-Flusberg, H., Fowler, A.E., & Sudhalter, V. (1991). The relation of utterance length to grammatical complexity in normal and language-disordered groups. *Applied Psycholinguistics, 12,* 23–45.

Shapiro, T. (1977). The quest for a linguistic model to study the speech of autistic children: Studies of echoing. *Journal of the American Academy of Child Psychiatry, 16,* 608–619.

Shapiro, T., Chiarandini, I., & Fish, B. (1974). Thirty severely disturbed children. *Archives of General Psychiatry, 30,* 819–825.

Shapiro, T., Fish, B., & Ginsberg, G.L. (1972). The speech of a schizophrenic child from two to six. *American Journal of Psychiatry, 128,* 92–98.

Shapiro, T., & Hertzig, M.E. (1991). Social deviance in autism: A central integrative failure as a model for social nonengagement. *Psychiatric Clinics of North America, 14,* 1, 19–32.

Short, C.B., & Schopler, E. (1988). Factors relating to age of onset in autism. *Journal of Autism and Developmental Disorders, 18,* 207–216.

Siegel, D.J., Minshew, N.J., & Goldstein, G. (1996). Wechsler IQ profiles in diagnosis of high-functioning autism. *Journal of Autism and Developmental Disorders, 26,* 389–406.

Siegel, B., Vukicevic, J., Elliott, G., & Kraemer, H. (1989). The use of signal detection theory to assess *DSM-III-R* criteria for autistic disorder. *Journal of the American Academy of Child and Adolescent Psychiatry, 28,* 542–548.

Sigman, M., & Ungerer, J. (1981). Sensorimotor skills and language comprehension in autistic children. *Journal of Abnormal Child Psychology, 9,* 149–166.

Stone, W.L., & Caro-Martinez, L.M. (1990). Naturalistic observations of spontaneous communication in autistic children. *Journal of Autism and Developmental Disorders, 20,* 437–453.

Storoschuk, S., Lord, C., & Jaedicke, S. (1995, March). *Autism and the use of mental verbs.* Paper presented at the Society for Research in Child Development, Indianapolis, IN.

Strohner, H., & Nelson, K. (1974). The young child's development of sentence comprehension: Influence of event probability, nonverbal context, syntactic form, and strategies. *Child Development, 45,* 567–576.

Tager-Flusberg, H. (1981a). On the nature of linguistic functioning in early infantile autism. *Journal of Autism and Developmental Disorders, 11,* 45–56.

Tager-Flusberg, H. (1981b). Sentence comprehension in autistic children. *Applied Psycholinguistics, 2,* 5–24.

Tager-Flusberg, H. (1985a). Psycholinguistic approaches to language and communication in autism. In E. Schopler & G. Mesibov (Eds.), *Communication problems in autism* (pp. 69–87). New York: Plenum Press.

Tager-Flusberg, H. (1985b). The conceptual basis for referential word meaning in children with autism. *Child Development, 56,* 1167–1178.

Tager-Flusberg, H. (1991). Semantic processing in the free recall of autistic children: Further evidence for a cognitive deficit. *British Journal of Developmental Psychology, 9,* 417–430.

Tager-Flusberg, H. (1992). Autistic children's talk about psychological states: Deficits in the early acquisition of a theory of mind. *Child Development, 63,* 161–172.

Tager-Flusberg, H. (1994). Mindreading from the perspective of cognitive neuroscience. *Cahiers de Psychologie, 13*(5), 718–723.

Tager-Flusberg, H. (1995). Dissociations in form and function in the acquisition of language by autistic children. In H. Tager-Flusberg (Ed.), *Constraints on language acquisition: Studies of atypical children* (pp. 175–194). Hillsdale, NJ: Erlbaum.

Tager-Flusberg, H., & Anderson, M. (1991). The development of contingent discourse ability in autistic children. *Journal of Child Psychology and Psychiatry, 32,* 1123–1134.

Tager-Flusberg, H., Calkins, S., Noin, I., Baumberger, T., Anderson, M., & Chadwick-Denis, A. (1990). A longitudinal study of language acquisition in autistic and Down syndrome children. *Journal of Autism and Developmental Disorders, 20,* 1–22.

Tager-Flusberg, H., & Sullivan, K. (1994). A second look at second-order belief attribution in autism. *Journal of Autism and Developmental Disorders, 24,* 577–586.

Thurber, C., & Tager-Flusberg, H. (1993). Pauses in the narratives produced by autistic, mentally retarded, and normal children as an index of cognitive demand, *Journal of Autism and Developmental Disorders, 23,* 309–322.

Tomasello, M., & Kruger, A.C. (1992). Joint attention on actions: Acquiring verbs in ostensive and non-ostensive contexts. *Journal of Child Language, 19,* 311–333.

Tomasello, M., & Mervis, C. (1994). The instrument is great, but measuring comprehension is still a problem. Variability in early communicative development [Commentary]. *Monographs of the Society of Research in Child Development, 59,* 174–179.

Van Lancker, D., Cornelius, C., & Needleman, R. (1991). Comprehension of verbal terms for emotions in normal, autistic, and schizophrenic children. *Developmental Neuropsychology, 7,* 1–18.

Vazquez, C.A. (1994). A multitask controlled evaluation of facilitated communication. *Journal of Autism and Developmental Disorders, 24,* 369–379.

Venter, A., Lord, C., & Schopler, E. (1992). A follow-up study of high-functioning autistic children. *Journal of Child Psychology and Psychiatry, 33,* 489–507.

Volden, J., & Lord, C. (1991). Neologisms and idiosyncratic language in autistic speakers. *Journal of Autism and Developmental Disorders, 21,* 109–130.

Volkmar, F.R., Klin, A., Siegal, B., Szatmari, P., Lord, C., Campbell, M., Freeman, B.J., Cicchetti, D.V., Rutter, M., Kline, W., Buitelaar, J., Hattab, Y., Fombonne, E., Fuentes, J.,

Werry, J., Stone, W., Kerbeshian, J., Hoshino, Y., Bregman, J., Loveland, K., Szymanski, L., & Towbin, K. (1994). Field trial for autistic disorder in *DSM-IV. American Journal of Psychiatry, 151,* 1361–1367.

Weir, R. (1962). *Language in the crib.* The Hague, The Netherlands: Mouton.

Wetherby, A.M., & Prutting, C.A. (1984). Profiles of communicative and cognitive-social abilities in autistic children. *Journal of Speech and Hearing Research, 27,* 364–377.

Whitehurst, G.J., & Fischel, J.E. (1994). Early developmental language delay: What, if anything, should the clinician do about it? *Journal of Child Psychology and Psychiatry, 35,* 613–648.

Wing, L. (1981). Language, social and cognitive impairments in autism and severe mental retardation. *Journal of Autism and Developmental Disorders, 11,* 31–44.

Wing, L., & Gould, J. (1979). Severe impairments of social interaction and associated abnormalities in children: Epidemiology and classification. *Journal of Autism and Developmental Disorders, 9,* 11–29.

Yule, W., & Rutter, M. (1987). *Language development and disorders.* London: MacKeith.

CHAPTER 10

Attention and Autism: Behavioral and Electrophysiological Evidence

JACOB A. BURACK, JAMES T. ENNS, JOHANNES E.A. STAUDER,
LAURENT MOTTRON, AND BETH RANDOLPH

Attentional processes are central to all aspects of information processing and, therefore, to virtually all domains of human function. A multiplicity of mechanisms and processes are attributed to *attention* which is considered essential to both typical and atypical development. Attention is studied with behavioral and electrophysiological paradigms and measures. Behavioral research on attention follows the information-processing tradition of rigorous control over stimuli and task performance. This research benefits from fine-grained analyses of cognitive components involved in a behavioral task, but suffers from the absence of clear links to everyday behavior. Electrophysiological research entails task analyses provided by information processing and by neurological underpinnings of cognitive tasks, but is limited by current knowledge of the neurological bases of attention.

WHAT IS ATTENTION?

Behavioral researchers of every discipline use the concept of attention. Ecological and ethological researchers utilize it to account for an organism's selection, from among several actions or options, of a choice that furthers survival within an environmental niche (Gibson,

1966). Cognitive and neuroscience researchers use it to explain how the limited sensory and information-processing systems of the brain cope with the barrage of information with which they are confronted (Broadbent, 1958; Treisman, 1988). Computational scientists require it because the execution of even the simplest tasks demands schedules and priorities (Marr, 1982; Ullman, 1984). Stimulus–response behaviorists are unable to escape attention in trying to explain why the same sensory stimulus does not always elicit the same action (Von Holst & Mittelstaedt, 1950). A comprehensive and fully acceptable definition of attention is elusive, but there appears to be consensus that attention is integrally related to processing selectivity.

Dimensions of Selectivity

A partitioning of processing selectivity into dimensions of modality, distribution, and function is shown in Figure 10.1 (for similar frameworks, see Coren, Ward, & Enns, 1994; Plude, Enns, & Brodeur, 1994). A fundamental dimension of this model is the modality or source of the processed information: visual, auditory, somatosensory, or memorial. In the everyday world, objects are often denoted

Jake Burack's work on this project was supported by a grant from the Social Sciences and Humanities Research Council of Canada and by a research grant from the Hebrew University of Jerusalem. The work was also supported in part by a Natural Sciences and Engineering Research Council of Canada operating grant to J.T. Enns. We thank Grace Iarocci, for her comments during various stages of the writing; Michelle O'Riordan and Kate Plaisted, for informing us of their unpublished data; and Julie Brennan, for coordinating the work among the contributors and for preparing the manuscript.

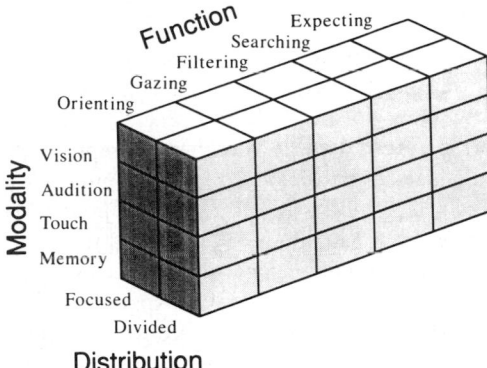

Figure 10.1 Multidimensional partitioning of processing selectivity into modality, distribution, and function.

simultaneously by information in more than one modality. For example, visual and auditory gestures associated with language are often present simultaneously, as are both the sounds and sights of an approaching object.

A second dimension is the distribution of attention over space and time. Processing may be focused on a specific object or visual-field location, or it may be divided among a number of objects and locations. Attention may be switched from one task or object to another, or it may be focused exclusively on a single target. In the model depicted in Figure 10.1, this dimension appears to be dichotomous but it is better represented as a continuum, ranging from exclusive focusing to complete distribution or division.

The third dimension is the various behavioral functions (often called tasks) that require specialized selection mechanisms. Included as examples on this dimension are orienting (adapting to particular visual field locations), gazing (focusing attention to a spatial area), filtering (selecting objects based on specific attributes), searching (for targets), and expecting information (of a certain kind or in a predesignated location). This list does not exhaust the potential tasks, but it illustrates the kinds that are most often studied.

The Attentional Components

The first two components of the model in Figure 10.1 are the most general since they apply

to all those that follow. The remaining components, the various tasks listed, are thought to be representative of attentional functions.

Arousal

A complex of behaviors is associated with the general level of an organism's arousal, which, in turn, has a direct effect on the nature and efficiency of selective information processing. At one extreme is the state of sleep. This state does not reflect the absence of arousal; even during sleep, predictable behaviors occur in response to the sudden onset of sensory stimulation. However, sleep represents the lowest possible form of arousal for a person who is not otherwise neurologically compromised. At the other extreme are the behaviors that occur in response to sudden and intense stimulation in an individual who is awake. These include changes in skin conductance, heart rate, blood flow, and breathing patterns (Donchin, 1981; Rohrbaugh, 1984). In addition to these stimulus-nonspecific behaviors, there are stimulus-orienting behaviors, such as body-, head-, and eye-turns toward (and sometimes away from) the environmental location of the sudden stimulus. Thus, arousal can be defined as a baseline that determines the levels of stimulus intensity needed to elicit attentional processes. With high arousal, even low stimulus intensity levels elicit attention; with low arousal, the intensity threshold is considerably higher.

Sustained Attention

This component concerns the focused/divided distribution dimension in Figure 10.1. When attention is sustained, sensory and cognitive resources are allocated, as exclusively as possible, to a particular task (and its associated stimuli) for an extended period of time. Although of considerable interest to researchers of atypical populations, this aspect of attention is historically not central to mainstream attention research and, accordingly, there is not yet a well developed theoretical framework for its study.

Orienting

One of the most primitive forms of visual selection involves aligning sensory receptors with certain locations in space. Reflexive visual and auditory orienting of this kind occurs whenever an event has an abrupt onset. A cat will prick up its ears, a newborn infant will slowly turn its head, and adults will involuntarily move their eyes and head toward the location of a flash of light or a sudden sound. Overt orienting behaviors can also be seen very early in human life, as when an infant responds to some symbolic cues, such as the gaze direction of another's eyes, or directed pointing. The key difference in this latter form of orienting lies in the cue that initiates the behavior. Reflexive orienting occurs in response to stimuli of abrupt onset; the signal value of the orienting cue is concrete in that it signals a location in space directly. Controlled orienting occurs in response to the signal value of a symbolic cue; the cue must first be "read" (interpreted). Only then is action taken, based on the acquired meaning of the cue. Other terms that are used to distinguish these two forms of orienting are exogenous, stimulus-driven, involuntary, or peripheral (referring to the visual-field location of the cue) for the reflexive kind, and endogenous, information-based, voluntary, or central (again referring to the visual-field location) for the controlled kind.

Overt forms of orienting (i.e., body, head, and eye movements) must also be distinguished from covert orienting, which involves an alignment of the mind's eye or ear in the absence of a physical alignment of the sensory receptor surfaces (Posner, 1980). This distinction can be combined orthogonally with that of the cue type, so that any orienting may in principle be classified as exogenous or endogenous (or their respective synonyms) or as overt or covert.

Gazing

This term is used in place of a variety of others (e.g., zoom lens, spotlight, mind's eye) because they all involve the metaphor of attention behaving in a way that is analogous to the eye. For example, visual acuity in an attentional gaze is highest at the center, with a decreasing gradient in the surround; to move from any point A to any point B, the attentional gaze must move through intermediate positions; and the attentional gaze cannot be centered on more than one location at a time (Coren et al., 1994).

Filtering

Many perceptual tasks require reporting or acting on the basis of certain object or scene attributes, to the exclusion of others. This is often referred to as filtering, to capture the implication that only certain perceptual attributes are permitted through a processing "gate." Although both orienting and the attentional gaze components involve filtering in this sense, albeit restricted to the spatial domain, filtering tasks deserve separate status because of the psychophysical (Bundesen, 1990; Nissen, 1985; Tsal, 1983) and neurological evidence (Mishkin, Ungerleider, & Macko, 1983; Ungerleider & Mishkin, 1982) pointing to the unique status of an object's attributes (e.g., size, color, pitch, and volume) from its location in the world or visual field.

Searching

In visual search tasks (e.g., Treisman, 1986; Treisman & Gormican, 1988), subjects are asked to look for a target item that is present on a random sampling (usually half) of the trials, and to respond with a simple "Present" or "Absent" response. The primary independent variable is the number of total items in the display. The rate at which performance declines (usually measured in terms of response time [RT] or response accuracy) as a function of the number of display items is taken to be indicative of search efficiency.

Expecting

Having some information about where, when, and which event will occur has a beneficial effect on perception. But this advantage applies only to perception when the expectation is fulfilled. When unexpected objects and events are involved, expectations hinder processing. Presumably, under these conditions, search images must be reformed, the attentional gaze must be reset, and search strategy must be reorganized. Thus, to examine this attention function systematically, the effects of different expectations are assessed.

EVENT-RELATED POTENTIALS AND ATTENTION

The prevailing view on the neural basis of attention is that processing selectivity is governed by a widely distributed network of interconnected subsystems (Gazzaniga, 1995; Posner & Raichle, 1994; Zeki, 1995). That is, attention is not considered the domain of a specific localized region of the brain; instead, it is seen as the outcome of communication among several such regions. For example, widely distributed regions of the brain must communicate in order to combine the appropriate attributes of shape, color, motion, and spatial location for a given object positioned in front of the viewer. The shape of the object is probably registered among neurons in the inferotemporal (IT) cortex; its color, in area V4; its motion, in area V5; and its location, in the parietal cortex. Thus, attending to the object because it is relevant to some action about to be performed appears to have the neural consequence of creating a confluence of activity in these widely distributed regions (Gilbert, 1995; Singer, 1995).

Event-Related Potential (ERP) Recordings

Event-related potential (ERP) recordings are only part of the spectacular developments that have occurred in brain-imaging techniques during the past three decades. Their principal advantage as a research tool is that they permit both noninvasive recording of brain activity in relation to a specific stimulus event, and fine-grained temporal analyses of activity that is time-locked to the stimulus. Their primary limitation is their relatively poor spatial resolution; beyond the most rudimentary brain area, localization becomes a difficult task. The spatial resolution of ERP recordings can be greatly improved with the use of multiple recording sites spread evenly across the scalp (Ciesielski, Knight, Prince, Harris, & Handmaker, 1995; Kemner, Verbaten, Cuperus, Camfferman, & van Engeland, 1994; Stauder, Molenaar, & van der Molen, 1989; Verbaten, Roelofs, van Engeland, Kenemans, & Slangen, 1991). However, even the best anatomical modeling of the underlying activity generators for the ERP wave involve centimeters of brain tissue, rather than millimeters.

The electrical brain activity recorded at the scalp originates principally from massive and synchronous postsynaptic activity that propagates toward the scalp via volume conduction.

Delays in the time resolution with which the electromagnetic neural activity can be recorded are due solely to limitations of the instrumentation (e.g., sampling, storage capacity) and not to physical constraints of the phenomena. This speed is essential for the direct study of information processing because a normal adult can detect, process, and react to a simple stimulus within one-third of a second. In addition, ERPs provide information about (a) the success of task performance independent of a behavioral response, and (b) the level of involvement and loci of the cerebral processes that occur before, between, and after stimulus presentation and response. ERPs are obtained by averaging multiple electroencephalogram (EEG) traces that are time-locked to specific events and recorded at a given location in the scalp. An ERP constitutes a series of amplitude peaks and dips in time that are denoted by their polarity (P = positive, N = negative) and their order of occurrence or timing (in milliseconds [ms]) after stimulus onset. For example, P1, also called P100, is the first major positive deflection, occurring around 100 ms after onset.

Most ERP waves appear to be modulated by attention. (For reviews of the multiple ERP approaches to attention, see Jennings & Coles, 1991; Meyer & Kornblum, 1993; Parasuraman & Davies, 1984.) The attention-related portions of the signal are independent of signals associated with other systems, such as those of sensory and motor activity. Thus, in a typical ERP study, stimulus and response parameters are held constant, and attention is modulated by task instructions.

The components of the ERP wave that can be seen in the first 50 to 100 ms (approximately) following the onset of a stimulus are mainly sensitive to the physical characteristics of the stimulus (e.g., its loudness, intensity, size, and so on). This portion of the signal is often referred to as the early, or exogenous (involuntary) portion. Thus, the P1 and N1 components are linked to visuospatial attention (Gunter, Wijers, Jackson, & Mulder, 1994; Harter & Aine, 1984), selective gating, and the control of gain in the visual pathways (Hillyard & Mangun, 1986). The portion of the signal beyond 100 ms is readily modulated by task manipulations and instructions and is referred to as the late, or endogenous (voluntary) portion. For example, N2 is typically evoked in auditory paradigms and is linked to the mismatch between a stimulus and an internal expectation based on a preceding presentation (Naatanen & Gaillard, 1974). The oft-studied P3 is considered to be proportional to the strength or amount of memory operations necessitated by a task (Curry & Polich, 1992), and its latency is used as a measure of stimulus evaluation time. (For a review, see van der Molen, Bashore, Halliday, & Callaway, 1991.) P3 is typically followed by a *slow wave* (SW), a large negative wave that increases in amplitude according to perceptual difficulty and the level of expectation associated with subsequent stimuli (Rosler & Heil, 1991). Although the ERP technique provides unique insights about the time-course of neural activity in attentional tasks, interpretations and comparisons across studies are complicated by differences in tasks and designs, discrepancies in number of electrodes, and the sensitivity of ERPs to a multitude of information-processing mechanisms and mental states.

METHODOLOGICAL ISSUES IN STUDYING ATTENTION IN PERSONS WITH AUTISM

As in the study of other areas of functioning among persons with autism, certain conceptual, methodological, and developmental issues need to be considered in evaluating the significance of empirical findings. Issues of ecological validity are particularly pertinent to the study of attention because of (a) its many different, often vaguely defined components, and (b) the discordance between performance on experimental tasks and attention in real-life settings (Swanson et al., 1990). The experimental study of attention entails the use of tasks that are typically designed to provide "pure" measures of specific aspect(s) or component(s) of attention, independent of other related and potentially confounding areas of functioning. These "stripped down" tasks, however, are limited with regard to ecological validity (e.g., Tipper & McLaren, 1990), and efficiency in attentional functioning in everyday life may not be reflected in performance on experimental tasks. Thus, attentional problems observed in

daily living may not be evidenced in performance on experimental tasks; conversely, deficiencies observed on experimental tasks may not be manifested as relevant impairments in the lives of the persons tested.

These issues of ecological validity are especially relevant when designing tasks for persons with pervasive developmental disorders, such as autism. They differ from other persons in their familiarity with and their ability to process perceptual, cognitive, and/or social information in the environment. Thus, researchers are faced with a methodological dilemma. Tests are designed with simple stimuli and instructions to minimize the a priori differences between persons with and without autism. However, these efforts typically result in simplistic paradigms that are not ecologically compelling because they do not reflect the intricacies inherent in the type of attending required for day-to-day living. Furthermore, because these constraints typically preclude the design of tasks that maximally tax attentional functioning, they limit the precision in understanding group differences and developmental change.

Although they are pertinent to all aspects of functioning among persons with autism, issues of development are particularly relevant to attentional functioning because efficiency of attention changes considerably with age (Brodeur, Trick, & Enns, in press; Enns, 1993; Plude, Enns, & Brodeur, 1994). Accordingly, consideration of the developmental levels of the persons included in each study is essential. Common or different levels of functioning among groups at one developmental level might not be evident at an earlier or later time. Precise matching by developmental level is essential to evaluating studies of attention in this group (Burack, 1994). The consequences of failing to do so were evident in the literature on the intuitively appealing and still widely held notion of a deficit in overselectivity among persons with autism (e.g., Lovaas, Koegel, & Schreibman, 1979). With matching for level of development, other researchers found that overselectivity was related to mental age (MA), but not to autism (e.g., Litrownik, McInnis, Wetzel-Pritchard, & Filipelli, 1978; Schover & Newsom, 1976).

RESEARCH ON ATTENTION
AND AUTISM

Origins of Research

The impetus for the study of attention in persons with autism comes from several origins that overlap to some degree. A primary origin is the underlying premise that efficiency of processing selectivity is essential to all aspects of human behavior and its development. Attention is then viewed as a potential candidate in the search for a core deficit associated with autism. In particular, the notion that attention is integral to the identification and selection of relevant information from the deluge of stimuli in the environment (Broadbent, 1971; Enns, 1990; James, 1890; Kahneman, 1973) appears relevant to the common observations that persons with autism typically act inappropriately within the environments in which they live, and that they are unable to benefit from those environments in the same way as other persons do (e.g., Gold & Gold, 1975).

Beginning with the initial definition of autism (Kanner, 1943), clinicians, educators, and relatives reported anecdotes that appeared to reflect specific attentional dysfunctions (e.g., Dawson & Lewy, 1989a, 1989b; Gold & Gold, 1975; National Society for Autistic Children [NSAC], 1978; van Engeland, 1984). These included fixating on apparently irrelevant stimuli, to the exclusion of other information in the environment (Bryson, Wainwright-Sharp, & Smith, 1990; Rosenblum et al., 1980); perseverating on self-initiated tasks and foci of interest (Casey, Gordon, Mannheim, & Rumsey, 1993); and difficulties in focusing on educational tasks (Hayes, 1987). These types of behaviors are often associated with criteria for diagnosis. Furthermore, recent interest in theory of mind deficits led to the notion that persons with autism may manifest basic deficiencies in the social or joint aspects of attention as early as infancy (e.g., Sigman, 1996).

A second origin stems from the observation that physiological and neurological components and mechanisms associated with attentional functioning often appear impaired among persons with autism. For example, the

operation of the reticular activating system (Hutt & Hutt, 1965; Ornitz, 1988; Ornitz & Ritvo, 1968) and electrodermal responses to the presentation of stimuli (Stevens & Gruzelier, 1984; van Engeland,1984) were studied both as indexes of impairment in specific aspects of attentional functioning among persons with autism and as reflecting primary deficits of the disorder. In more recent work, there is indirect evidence of links between attentional functioning and the "softer" neurological signs of executive functions that are increasingly cited as sources of impairments among persons with autism (e.g., Bryson, Landry, & Wainwright, in press; Ozonoff, Strayer, McMahon, & Filloux, 1995).

Although there have been attempts to provide unitary and comprehensive theories of attentional dysfunction in autism, the current knowledge of attentional functioning among persons with autism is, in our view, too limited to allow speculation about primary deficiencies or systemic differences. Instead, we present the available evidence as an initial step in examining and integrating the disparate types of research about the various aspects of attending.

Behavioral Research

Arousal

Initial interest in attention among persons with autism was largely focused on the relationship between symptoms of autism and atypical states and modulation of arousal. For example, Ornitz (1969) argued that sensorial information was inconsistently, inefficiently, or not at all filtered, thereby leading to high levels of arousal. Although this hypothesis was not supported in subsequent research (for a review, see Minshew, 1992), it was consistent with the prevailing notion of hyperarousal in persons with autism (e.g., Gold & Gold, 1975; Hutt, Hutt, Lee, & Ounsted, 1964), which was discussed with regard to hyperresponsiveness and slower habituation (Barry & James, 1988; James & Barry, 1980). Persons with autism were seen as turning attention inward and rejecting sensory stimulation to protect themselves from the overload of information that they faced (Cohen & Johnson, 1977; Kootz &

Cohen, 1981; van Engeland, 1984). Conversely, notions of underarousal (Rimland, 1964) and of faulty modulation of arousal (Kinsbourne, 1987; Ornitz & Ritvo, 1968) were also forwarded as integral to the manifestation of many of the symptoms of autism. In general, however, the study of arousal was abandoned during the past decade as researchers of autism focused on more specific attentional and/or physiological components.

Sustained Attention

Sustained attention is considered relevant to autism for at least two reasons, each of which would lead to a different hypothesis. The first reason involves the common observation of perseverative behaviors. These behaviors alone might suggest that persons with autism might be particularly capable of sustaining focus. However, it is unclear whether the level of concentration that is maintained is possible only for self-generated tasks or may also be applied to tasks imposed by others. The second, and opposing, reason concerns the suspected deficiencies in general arousal levels, which are seen as compromising the ability to maintain concentration over extended periods of time. Sustained attention is typically measured with continuous performance tasks (CPTs; see Nuechterlein, Parasuraman, & Jiang, 1983) characterized by repeated and rapid presentations of stimuli that include target stimuli (or sequences of stimuli) that have a relatively low probability of appearance.

Buchsbaum et al. (1992) assessed the CPT performance of 7 high-functioning persons with histories of diagnoses of autism, but with no histories of seizure disorders, neuroleptic use, or mental retardation, and compared the results to those of 13 adults with no history of autism, who were matched for socioeconomic status (SES) with the persons with autism. Although the IQs of the persons with autism were considerably lower than those of the comparison subjects, there were no significant group differences on task performance.

Casey et al. (1993) found only minor differences in sustained attention between a group of 10 relatively high-functioning male adult savants with autism, who had special calendar-calculating skills, and typical subjects matched for gender and age but not IQ. The persons with

autism performed well on a CPT and, compared to the age- and gender-matched subjects, displayed a minimally lower rate of hits and a similar number of false alarms, indicating relatively intact visual sustained attention. However, potential group differences were likely minimized by the attainment of ceiling levels of performance by all the persons in the typical group. Conversely, the group differences may be an artifact of the significantly lower IQs among the persons with autism who still performed close to the ceiling. More apparent differences in hits and false alarms were evident in auditory sustained attention. This is congruent with the notion that attentional deficits among persons with autism may be particularly pronounced on auditory tasks (Hermelin & O'Connor, 1970; Rutter, 1983), although this finding must be viewed as preliminary until replicated in studies with more representative groups of persons with autism and more precise matching with comparison groups.

Intact visual sustained attention was also found among lower-functioning persons with autism. Garretson, Fein, and Waterhouse (1990) examined performance on a CPT with various conditions of presentation speed and reward contingencies (social versus tangible) among 23 children and adolescents with autism and 23 typical children matched to the former group on gender and on the Draw-A-Design Test (DAD) of the McCarthy Scales of Children's Abilities (mean MAs of approximately 6 years; McCarthy, 1972). Level of performance was generally related to MA rather than to diagnosis. The performance of the children with autism, as a group, in relation to that of the comparison subjects, was neither deficient on most aspects of the CPT nor more variable within group or individuals. All children displayed the expected deterioration in performance over time and with a faster presentation of stimuli. The only group differences were evident in a later session, when the efficacy of social reinforcement declined at a steeper rate than that of tangible reinforcement.

Based on these few studies, all involving variants of the CPT, the efficiency of sustained visual attention appears to be largely related to level of cognitive development rather than to diagnosis among children functioning between the ages of 3 and 10 years. It also appears to be intact among high-functioning adults. There is preliminary evidence that abilities in auditory sustained attention may be deficient (Casey et al., 1993), but further evidence is required. In addition to developmental considerations, issues of motivation appear to be relevant to understanding performance on tasks of sustained attention among persons with autism, at least in childhood. This view is consistent with findings that motivational and personality characteristics are often implicated in deleterious task performance among children with developmental disabilities (e.g., Zigler & Hodapp, 1986). Thus, the efficiency of sustained attention among persons with autism appears largely contingent on several factors, including developmental level, motivational considerations, and modality.

Orienting

Reflexive visual orienting of both the physical eye (overt) and the mind's eye (covert) is of interest because of common reports that persons with autism perseverate in looking at and acting on idiosyncratic stimuli, are immune from distraction when so engaged, and appear to have problems in voluntarily shifting attention from one stimulus to another. These observations all point to a possible origin in the low-level mechanisms used to control eye movements and the locus of the attentional gaze. Of course, it is possible that the mechanisms used in reflexive orienting are intact, but are not controlled voluntarily in the same way by persons with and without autism.

Casey et al. (1993) examined reflexive shifting in both overt and covert orienting among the previously described savant persons with autism, and typical persons matched for chronological age but not IQ. The presentation of the target to the right or left of fixation was preceded by a valid, invalid, or neutral cue. The valid cue was a highlighted square presented on the same side as the target; the invalid cue was a highlighted square presented on the side opposite from the target; and the neutral cue entailed highlighted squares on both sides or on neither side of fixation. Two-thirds of the cues were valid, and the others were split evenly between invalid and neutral. The Stimulus Onset Asynchronies (SOAs)

between the presentation of the cue and the target were either 100 ms, permitting covert orienting to be tested before any overt eye movement could be made, or 800 ms, where an eye movement could accompany the movement of the attentional gaze. Across the two SOAs, the persons with autism displayed generally longer RTs and greater increases in RTs with the invalid cues (specifically, at the 100-ms SOA when the target was presented in the left visual field). These findings are consistent with a deficit in reflexively disengaging and shifting attention to visual targets in the periphery; however, the findings should be viewed as preliminary because of the a priori group differences in general level of functioning.

Contrary to Casey et al.'s (1993) findings, Burack and Iarocci (1995) found no deficits in reflexively disengaging and/or shifting covert attention to peripheral cues among 12 generally low-functioning persons with autism (with an approximate mean MA of 7 years) as compared to MA-matched groups of persons with developmental disabilities but without autism, and typical children. An exogenous nontarget symbol cue appeared for 50 ms to the left or right of, or at the fixation point, and was followed by the appearance of the target to the left or right of fixation at a 200-ms SOA, a time frame appropriate for the measurement of covert orienting. The nonneutral cues appeared on the same side as the target (left–left or right–right, as opposed to left–right or right–left) 50% of the time, thereby providing no information about the location of the subsequent target. Similarly, the neutral cue provided no information about target location because it appeared at the fixation point, where the target was never presented. Yet, all groups of persons displayed fastest RTs when the cue appeared in the same location as the target. The persons with autism showed patterns of responding similar to those in the other groups, indicating no specific deficit in reflexive disengaging and/or shifting of attention. A filtering component was also included in the task, but there were no interactions between this component and orienting attention.

Wainwright and Bryson (1996) identified differences between relatively high-functioning persons with autism (n = 9) or Asperger syndrome (n = 2) and chronological age (mean CA = 23.6 years) and mental age (MA; mean CA = 11.9 years) matched typical persons on a target-identification task with targets presented at the central fixation point, or to the right or left of fixation. The persons in the comparison groups responded with about equal rapidity to central and peripheral targets, whereas the persons with autism or Asperger syndrome responded more slowly to the peripheral targets. Evidently, the persons with autism shifted their attention more slowly to the peripheral target from the central location at the pre-display fixation point. However, even higher functioning persons with autism (n = 7), or Asperger syndrome (n = 4), as compared to an MA-matched (mean CA = 14.3 years) group of typical persons, did not show any deficits on a less demanding detection version of the task. This result suggests that deficiencies may be evident only in settings where processing capabilities are most taxed (Wainwright & Bryson, 1996). Alternatively, the failure to find differences in the latter task may be due to the higher level of functioning (as measured by Peabody Picture Vocabulary Test [PPVT] scores) among the persons with autism, indicating that differences in shifting attention evidenced at lower developmental levels are eventually overcome.

With regard to voluntary visual orienting, Wainwright-Sharp and Bryson (1993) report evidence of deficiencies in processing the symbolic information that is essential to performing such a task, among a group of relatively high-functioning adolescent/young adult males with autism (N = 8) or Asperger's Syndrome (N = 3), as compared to a group of typical males (N = 11) matched for chronological age and handedness, but not IQ (which was covaried). In 80% of the trials, a single endogenous cue (an arrow) was presented at fixation point in the middle of the screen and was used to provide correct (valid) or incorrect (invalid) information about the location of a subsequent target that could appear on either side of fixation. The ratio of valid:invalid cues was 4:1. In the other trials, a horizontal line appeared instead of an arrow and, because it provided no information about the position of the subsequent target, it was considered neutral. The

SOAs were either 100 ms for estimation of covert orienting or 800 ms for estimation of overt orienting. The RTs of the typical subjects were faster with valid as compared to invalid cues in both SOA conditions. However, this validity effect was only evident among the persons with autism or Asperger's Syndrome in the 800-ms SOA condition. Apparently, the persons with autism were unable to use the symbolic cues to orient covertly to the target location within the 100-ms window. Wainwright-Sharp and Bryson (1993) suggest that this result is consistent with the notion of a deficiency of some sort (e.g., speed, accuracy) in the use of controlled attentional processes (e.g., Hermelin & O'Connor, 1970), although an equally valid interpretation is that it reflects a more basic deficiency in the "reading" of briefly presented symbolic information.

In the 800-ms SOA condition, the validity effect was larger for the persons with autism. This finding was largely a function of longer RTs on invalid cue trials, because their RTs were typical in conditions with validly cued trials. Evidently, the simple engaging of attention necessary for revealing a processing benefit on valid trials is intact among persons with autism. However, something about the sequential operations of engage, shift, and disengage may be impaired. These findings are consistent with the notion of a deficiency in orienting attention to locations in space. Taken together with the findings of intact reflexive orienting, in which persons with autism differ little from MA-matched comparison subjects, these data (Wainwright-Sharp & Bryson, 1993) are at least suggestive of a spatial orienting deficit that may primarily be manifest when some aspect of voluntary control is needed for efficient task performance.

Gazing

The study of attentional gaze provides insight about the enduring notions of attentional overselectivity and narrowed vision among persons with autism. Rincover and Ducharme (1987) examined the sensitivity of visual conditioning (a form of automatic learning) to stimulus attributes (form or color) that were spatially separated or overlapping. Their subjects were low-functioning children and adolescents with autism and an MA-matched (mean = 3.5 years) group of children without autism. When the form and the color of the stimuli were separated in space, the persons with autism but not those without responded primarily to the form rather than the color. Rincover and Ducharme argued that the focus on one modality is indicative of overselectivity, and that its manifestation only when the two modalities are spatially separated is indicative of "tunnel vision," an excessive narrowing of attentional gaze. They noted that this notion of a small-diameter attentional gaze is consistent with the common observation that persons with autism can focus on a stimulus and seemingly ignore other, often more salient information in the environment. However, these phenomena may also be the consequents of a deficiency in voluntarily disengaging and reengaging attention on multiple items, and, therefore, may not be uniquely attributable to the question of breadth of attentional gaze.

In a more direct examination of attentional breadth, Burack (1994) examined target discrimination RT in several conditions that varied with regard to the presence of a spatial window cue and the number and location of nontarget distractors. Low-functioning persons with autism were compared to three MA-matched groups (approximate mean = 8 years): persons with organic retardation, persons with familial retardation, and persons of average intelligence. Based on the tunnel-vision hypothesis, persons with autism should be both less influenced by distractors and less able to benefit from the spatial cue that could be used to facilitate focus on the target. Relative to the performance of the persons in the other groups, the performance of the persons with autism improved the most with the presence of the spatial cue when no distractors were present. However, this effect was negated when distractors were present; in fact, the persons with autism showed greater distractor effects than the persons with familial retardation and the typical children, on all distractor conditions with the spatial cue. As is typically found in studies of attention, performance in all groups was impaired with close distractors (2 to 3 degrees of visual angle). In contrast, the performance of the persons with autism was impaired even with far distractors (6 to 9

degrees from target), although they did not affect the performance of the other groups of persons. Burack (1994) noted that some of the deficiencies might be related to organicity rather than to autism per se. The persons with organic retardation showed some increased distractibility on some conditions in the presence of distractors, as compared to persons with familial retardation or average intelligence, but not to the extent evidenced among the persons with autism.

The convergent data of the enhanced efficiency with the spatial window cue with no distractors present, and the impaired efficiency on conditions with (cue and) distractors, even those far from the target stimulus, are consistent with the notion of a deficit in appropriately sizing the attentional gaze (Burack, 1994). This impairment is not as simple as the unidimensional concept of tunnel vision, or the concept of failing to narrow the attentional gaze. It is also inconsistent with the idea that attentional deficits arise from encounters with complex, unpredictable, and novel stimuli, because the stimuli in this task were simple, redundant, and not novel. Rather, the impairment is consistent with a lack of voluntary control over the size of the attentional gaze that is appropriate for a given task (Enns & Girgus, 1985).

Filtering

Burack's (1994) findings were interpreted in the previous section as pointing to an impairment in appropriate sizing of the attentional gaze. However, the greater distractor effects among the persons with autism also could indicate a more general deficiency in filtering nontarget visual stimuli. Contrary to Burack's (1994) findings, however, filtering deficits were not evidenced among high-functioning adolescents with autism as compared to a CA- and IQ-matched group of typical adolescents on a similar task (Burack et al., 1996). Apparently, deficits in filtering (Burack, 1994) may be evident only at lower developmental levels (Bryson, Landry, & Wainwright, in press). Because filtering efficiency among typical persons improves during the childhood years and seems to function optimally by the time adolescence is reached (Enns & Akhtar, 1989; Pasto & Burack, 1995), it is likely that persons with autism eventually attain an efficient level of filtering, although later than other persons.

Filtering deficiencies were also not evident in a study of filtering and reflexive covert orienting in which distractors were presented at approximately 1.15 degrees from the target stimulus (Burack & Iarocci, 1995). Low functioning persons with autism, MA-matched (approximately 7 years) persons with developmental disabilities, and MA-matched typical children all displayed slower RTs in the presence of these distractors, which were located within a distance from the target that would cause distraction effects to be expected. Apparently, in situations where distractor effects are evident in all groups, no unique filtering deficit is evident among persons with autism. This result is consistent with the notion that when distractor effects are uniquely or primarily observed among persons with autism (Burack, 1994), they may likely be related to issues of breadth of attention rather than solely to those of filtering efficiency.

Filtering between Modalities

Ciesielski, Courchesne, and Elmasian (1990) initially trained 10 high-functioning adult males with autism and a group of typical males matched approximately for age (but not IQ) on a divided-attention task in which they identified the less frequently presented of two targets in each of the visual and auditory modalities. Subsequently, they administered a filtering task that necessitated attending to only one modality while ignoring the modality in which the target had been presented in the previous task. The adults with autism displayed slower RTs in both modalities, fewer correct detections in the selective auditory task, and significantly higher false-alarm rates in both modalities. The latter finding was largely due to false-positive responses to stimuli in the nontarget modality, indicating that the persons with autism were less able to filter the competing stimuli. In this case, the inability to filter stimuli from the distracting modality may largely be a function of the perseverative behaviors of the persons with autism, who continued to respond to the modality that was the target in the previous task, despite clear articulation of the need to

filter stimuli from that modality (Ciesielski et al., 1990). However, the implications of these findings are mitigated by those from a subsequent report in which there is no behavioral evidence of a deficit in filtering between modalities among 8 high-functioning adolescents and adults with autism, as compared to 11 typical adults with considerably higher IQs (Ciesielski et al., 1995).

Searching

In an initial study of visual search abilities among persons with autism, Plaisted, O'Riordan, and Baron-Cohen (1997b) tested the theory that persons with autism are good at processing unique features of a stimulus and relatively poor at processing features in common between two stimuli (Plaisted, O'Riordan, & Baron-Cohen, 1997a). They examined performance of 8 high-functioning children with autism (mean CA = 106 months), and a group of 8 typically developing children (mean CA = 81 months) in searching for a target presented among distractors in disjunctive and conjunctive conditions. The groups were matched on verbal MA (as measured by the British Picture Vocabulary Test); however, the children with autism were older and scored higher on a measure of spatial ability (the block design test of the Wechsler Intelligence Scale for Children—Revised [WISC-R]). In the disjunctive condition in which the target differed from all the distractors in terms of shape (a red S target with green X and red T distractors), the children with and without autism displayed search times independent of array size. The RTs of the persons with autism were marginally faster, although the difference was not statistically significant. Error rates in both groups were minimal and unrelated to RT. In the conjunctive task, the target was uniquely defined by the integration of its features (e.g., search for a red X target among red T and green X distractors). The children without autism displayed the typical pattern of linear increases in RTs with number of distractors; the RTs of the children with autism were not affected by the size of the array. One explanation for this difference is that the children without autism searched the display in serial, whereas those with autism were able to do so in parallel. (For these distinctions, see Treisman, 1982; Treisman & Gelade, 1980.) Alternatively, the groups may have both searched in parallel, but the children with autism were less affected by the increased difficulty inherent in this condition (see Duncan & Humphries, 1989). In either case, these findings apparently support Plaisted, O'Riordan, and Baron-Cohen's (1997a) notion that persons with autism are relatively more proficient at processing unique features. However, the effect on task performance of the initial group differences in spatial ability needs to be assessed.

Expecting

The role of expectation regarding target detection is examined in several importantly different ways among persons with autism. In one class of studies, targets are simply presented in two different modalities (e.g., vision and audition) and target-detection performance is examined for overall accuracy and for any modality-specific biases. The role of expectation is thus inferred indirectly from the observer's pattern of target accuracy: if one modality is favored, it suggests that the observer is deficient in switching attention from one modality (the expected one) to another (the unexpected one).

Two such studies are provided by Casey et al. (1993), who, as noted earlier, tested 10 male savants with autism and 10 typical adults matched on chronological age but not on IQ or MA. Persons with autism detected fewer targets, in both the visual and auditory modalities, in a divided-attention task. They apparently focused on one modality to the extent that it impaired detection of targets in the other. In a second task with the same subjects (Casey et al., 1993), discrimination accuracy and RT were recorded for one of two stimulus attributes (shape and closure). No group differences were found in either the accuracy of responding or the percentage of RT change between a shift in response set and a shift in target location alone. However, in both types of presentations, the persons with autism displayed slower overall RTs. With this combination of findings, the generally slower RTs were interpreted as reflecting a deficit in the

shifting of attention in visual space (Bryson et al., in press; Casey et al., 1993), although this explanation is only one of potentially many related to differences in general functioning between the groups.

In another type of study, targets are also presented in two modalities but expectations are manipulated more directly. For example, Courchesne, Townsend, Akshoomoff, Saitoh, et al. (1994) administered to persons with autism, and a comparison group of typical persons matched for CA and MA, a task in which rare and frequent items were presented in both the visual and the auditory modalities. The formal task was to detect only the rare targets, and the occurrence of a rare target served as a signal that the next target would appear in the opposite modality. To perform this task efficiently, observers had to (a) be vigilant for unusual items, (b) use the presence of a target as a symbolic cue to change their expectations about the modality of the next target, and (c) be successful in inhibiting expectations formed from previous target detections. When target accuracy was examined as a function of the time elapsed since the last correct detection, persons with autism displayed a relatively reduced hit rate within the first 2.5 seconds following the cue to shift attention to the other modality. At longer intervals, they performed like the persons in the comparison group, suggesting that they needed more time to change their expectations. A second finding was that observers with autism had an elevated false-alarm rate for the rare targets in the same modality that had been detected on previous trials. This result suggests that they were less able than comparison observers to inhibit the expectations formed on previous target occurrences.

In a related task in the same report, subjects were asked to detect targets in one modality (i.e., either vision or audition) during a 1-minute interval, and then detect targets in the other modality during the next minute. In each case, items that had been targets in the previous minute had to be ignored. Unlike results in the previous task, false-alarm rates did not differ between groups in either the visual or auditory modality. Courchesne, Townsend, Akshoomoff, Saitah, et al. (1994) suggest that the deficit evident among persons with autism is one of rapidly changing expectations from moment to moment.

The role of expectations has also been examined using a voluntary spatial orienting task. As summarized in an earlier section, Wainwright-Sharp and Bryson (1993) reported that relatively high-functioning persons with autism did not show orienting effects when a central arrow cue was presented 100 ms before the target, although they did when 800 ms elapsed between the arrow cue and the target. This finding is consistent with the view that persons with autism require more time to form the expectations that are at the heart of endogenous covert orienting. However, it is not clear why it takes them longer to do so. Perhaps they are limited by a deficiency in rapidly interpreting briefly presented information, or their limitation is in the ability to form the appropriate expectation. In this case, the expectation concerns the likely location of a target; in the Courchesne, Townsend, Akshoomoff, Saitah, et al. (1994) study, it involves an expectation about the likely modality of a target.

Event-Related Potential Recording Studies

The Exogenous Components

N1 is one of the earliest manifestations of selective gating in visual and auditory pathways at the cortical level, and its amplitude increases with the level of involvement of these selection processes. The study of N1 activity among persons with autism is characterized by inconsistencies between and even within research groups. Novick, Vaughan, Kurtzberg, and Simpson (1980) found no differences, between 5 less impaired adolescent males with autism and 5 age-matched typical males, for N1 amplitude to auditory stimulation. Two other groups of researchers reported mixed evidence of no differences and smaller N1 amplitudes between children (Bruneau, Garreau, Roux, & Lelord, 1987) or adolescents and young adults (13 to 25 years; Courchesne, Kilman, Galambos, & Lincoln, 1984; Courchesne, Lincoln, Kilman, & Galambos, 1985) with autism and typical subjects, on auditory tasks. In contrast, larger N1 amplitudes were found

among 7 relatively high-functioning children with autism (mean CA = 11 years, IQ = 90) as compared to age-matched children on an auditory oddball-type task (Oades, Walker, Geffin, & Stern, 1988). Increased N1 amplitudes were also evident with increased flash intensity among 5 children with autism (average CA = 6 to 14 years, IQ = 30 to 88), but not among gender- and age-matched comparison children (Pritchard, Raz, & August, 1987). Conversely, 17 children and adolescents with autism (CA = 8 to 18 years), as compared to typical children matched for age and gender, showed inverted N1 amplitudes (dominant at the right hemisphere) but no reduced patterns of hemispheric asymmetry (Dawson, Finley, Phillips, & Galpert, 1986).

Like N1 amplitude, P1 amplitude is also positively correlated with the efficiency of selective gating at the cortical level. Atypicalities in P1 amplitude were not reported with either the presentation of tone clicks to 5 adolescent males with autism and age-matched typical persons (Novick et al., 1980), or the administration of a visual habituation paradigm to 20 nonretarded children (CA = 5 to 15 years) with autism and 2 comparison groups of typical children categorized as externalizers or internalizers (Verbaten et al., 1991). However, larger-than-normal P1 enhancement of amplitudes at the attended location in a spatial-attention-choice RT task was evident among 5 persons with both autism and parietal abnormalities (Townsend & Courchesne, 1994). Similarly, increased P1 at the occipital area was evident with a visual oddball paradigm with differential manual responses to either of the stimulus conditions, among 16 high-functioning children and adults (8 to 36 years) with autism as compared to reference subjects matched for gender, age, and IQ (Stauder & Mottron, 1996). In addition, significant differences in P1 latency at the occipital area, between the rare and frequent stimulus conditions were found only among the persons with autism. The persons without autism displayed the typical pattern of similar P1 latencies in the two conditions. The P1 differences in amplitude and sensitivity to differences in stimulus conditions for latency are interpreted as reflecting qualitative differenc... in information processing specific to perceptual and early attentional mechanisms between the groups.

Although there is considerable inconsistency among the studies of the exogenous components among persons with autism, there is at least preliminary evidence of atypicalities. Persons with autism do not appear to show less efficient selective early-attention processes. However, the mechanisms seem to operate in qualitatively different ways, as indicated by the findings of hemispheric inversion, the specific enhancement at the attended location, and the significant oddball condition effect found only among persons with autism. These atypicalties in the exogenous components in autism were identified primarily in studies with more complex tasks, indicating that a certain level of task load needs to be attained to reveal group differences.

The Endogenous Components

In studies of the later endogenous components, there is relatively consistent evidence of atypicalities among persons with autism. With auditory oddball tasks, the P3 amplitudes are typically diminished among generally higher-functioning children, (Dawson, Finley, Phillips, Galpert, & Lewy, 1988; Lelord, Laffont, Jusseaume, & Stephant, 1973; Lincoln, Courchesne, Harms, & Allen, 1993; Martineau, Laffont, Bruneau, Roux, & Lelord, 1980; Novick, Kurtzberg, & Vaughan, 1979; Novick et al., 1980; Oades et al., 1988) adolescents and young adults with autism (Courchesne et al., 1984; Courchesne et al., 1985; Courchesne, Lincoln, Yeung-Courchesne, Elmasian, & Grillon, 1989). However, claims that these auditory phenomena are unique to persons with autism are attenuated by the generally common finding of reduced amplitudes to auditory stimulation among clinical groups (Holcomb, Ackerman, & Dykman, 1985). Nevertheless, Kemner, Verbaten, Cuperus, Camfferman, and van Engeland (1995) suggest that type (novel stimuli) and location (occipital) of the auditory P3 amplitude reductions may be unique to children with autism as compared to those with dyslexia or Attention Deficit Disorder with Hyperactivity (ADHD).

The manifestation of atypical endogenous ERPs specific to persons with autism is more apparent with visual oddball paradigms. In the initial visual oddball ERP study with persons with autism, three children with autism, compared to nonautistic subjects, displayed smaller P3 amplitudes at central parietal sites to omitted stimuli in a regular series of simple flashes (Novick et al., 1979). Conversely, in a visual ERP study in which the oddball was dissimilar from the standards but not missing, diminished visual P3 amplitudes were not evident among 5 children and adolescents with autism (Pritchard et al., 1987). On a task with both auditory and visual stimuli, Courchesne et al. (1985) found that 10 nonretarded adolescents and young adults with autism, as compared to comparison subjects, displayed diminished target visual P3 amplitudes at the central parietal electrode, although the reduction was less evidenced in the visual domain. Based on this preliminary evidence, they concluded that nonretarded persons with autism may have a limited capacity to process novel information and that the classification of simple visual information may be less impaired than in the auditory modality (Courchesne et al., 1985).

In subsequent studies with generally larger and more carefully matched subject groups and data from greater numbers of recording electrodes, there is consistent evidence of atypical ERPs to visual stimuli. Ciesielski, Courchesne, and Elmasian (1990) found significantly smaller P3 differences between attended and unattended rare stimuli in both the visual and auditory modality among 10 nonretarded males with autism as compared to 13 typical adults. Verbaten et al. (1991) found that 20 nonretarded children and adolescents (5 to 15 years of age, mean CA = 9.7 years) with autism, as compared to CA-matched groups of 20 children/adolescents with emotional problems (internalizers and externalizers) and 20 typical children/adolescents, showed smaller visual occipital P3 waves to standard stimuli on a non-task-relevant condition. They also displayed P3 waves to target stimuli that were diminished as compared to those of the typical comparison group but not different from those of the other two groups. The implications of these findings are questionable because the diminished P3 amplitude to target stimuli was not unique to the persons with autism and was evident only among a subgroup of persons with autism who were relatively poor performers. The other persons with autism showed typical P3 effects (Verbaten et al., 1991).

The use of multiple recording electrodes (up to 12) is instrumental in providing evidence of atypicalities specific to persons with autism, as compared to groups of typical and atypical persons. Kemner et al. (1994) reported that 20 children with autism—but not those in comparison groups of children with Attention Deficit Disorder, children with dyslexia, and typically developing children—showed both an oddball task effect on the visual P2N2 and larger P3s to novel (as compared to target) stimuli for both visual and somatosensory stimuli. Despite these differences, the behavioral performance of the children with autism was not impaired, indicating that they invoked processes not used by the other groups to attain the same level of speed and performance. However, the implications of these findings are limited by the generally lower levels of functioning among the children with autism as compared to the others.

The finding of smaller occipital P3 amplitudes to standard stimuli among persons with autism (Verbaten et al., 1991) was replicated with the standard stimuli in a visual oddball task by Stauder and Mottron (1996), who recorded ERPs from 30 recording electrodes across the scalps of 11 high-functioning persons with autism (CA = 10 to 20 years) and a group of typical persons matched for CA and IQ. The groups displayed similar RTs, number of errors, and ERP (P3 + SW) peak latencies. However, the persons with autism displayed a strongly reduced P3 condition effect at the right hemisphere. In contrast, their SW amplitudes were normal at the right hemisphere and more negative at the left hemisphere. In addition to the smaller P3 amplitudes at the occipital sites, the persons with autism displayed strongly reduced N2 amplitudes. A single-trial estimation technique revealed that most group differences in oddball-event differentiation occurred at the beginning of the task, and the P3 condition effect normalized toward the end of the task for the persons with autism. The increased P1 and reduced N2 amplitudes among the persons with autism remained significant across all task segments, suggesting more stable abnormalities for these components. Thus, persons with autism display atypicalities in early selective attention and orienting mechanisms that yield stable and significant group differences in ERP amplitudes, but do not seem to interfere with performance in simple-choice RT tasks.

Similarly, evidence is inconsistent among electrophysiological and behavioral findings regarding performance on a focused visual and auditory attention task and a visual and auditory divided-attention task, among 8 high-functioning persons with autism and a group of typical persons, matched for gender and age but not for IQ (Ciesielski et al., 1995). Although both groups performed well on the focused-attention tasks, the persons with autism displayed specific difficulties detecting targets (longer RTs, lower percentage of correct detections) in the cross-modal divided-attention conditions, as compared to those with one modality. A slow negative wave (SW) was the only negative component that reflected focused-versus-divided task effect among the comparison subjects; it was largest with stimuli in single channel-focused attention, intermediate when attention was divided, and smallest with unattended stimuli. The failure of persons with autism to modulate this slow negative wave in response to focused, divided, and ignored conditions; the presence of relatively normal morphology, despite the reduced amplitude of the P3b and other positive components; and the high level of correct target detections were interpreted as indicative of a selective inhibition deficit. Ciesielski et al. (1995) suggested that the selective attention system of persons with autism may rely on a more rudimentary kind of automatic processing, with less effective selective inhibition of irrelevant stimuli.

ERP studies can also be used to assess hypotheses regarding specific neurological deficits. For example, in order to examine the role of parietal abnormalities in the attentional functioning of persons with autism, Townsend and Courchesne (1994) administered a spatial-attention task to persons with autism with and without parietal abnormalities, and to a typical comparison group. Using 13 active electrodes, they identified earlier P3s to target stimuli and a larger-than-normal P1 effect among the persons with autism and parietal abnormalities. However, this evidence needs to be viewed as preliminary because there were only 5 persons with autism and parietal abnormalities and 3 without the parietal abnormalities, and the verbal and performance IQs among the persons with parietal damage were 20 points lower than those of the other groups.

In general, the ERP findings indicate evidence of atypicalities in early selective attention (N1 and P1 component), orienting response (N2), and late attention mechanisms (P3) in persons with autism, although the simultaneously recorded measures of behavioral performance seem generally unaffected. This reflects the unique contribution of ERP data to attention research.

SUMMARY AND
FUTURE DIRECTIONS

Despite a history of interest in attentional functioning among persons with autism that dates back as far as Kanner's (1943) landmark paper, the experimental study of this topic is still in the very early stages. The application of behavioral and electrophysiological paradigms, borrowed from the traditional experimental literature, marks only the beginning of the potentially informative study of the various phenomena associated with attention. In future work, researchers need to follow up on the initiated research, to more clearly delineate developmental and methodological implications, to broaden the work by integrating ideas from other areas of research, and to examine markers of attentional deficit that might be indicative of a more basic underlying deficit.

The evidence from the behavioral research is informative with regard to potential areas of attentional deficiencies that might help explain a wide range of the impairments and behaviors associated with autism. In particular, deficits and differences with regard to filtering and gazing behaviors, voluntary shifts of attention, and interpretation of symbolic information for predicting the whereabouts of relevant information can all be potentially implicated in the apparent problems involved in appropriately choosing, attending to, and

processing the most essential information from the stimulus-rich environments in which we live. In contrast, there is preliminary evidence that children with autism may be particularly adept at searching among a group of stimuli for one with unique features. These findings are preliminary, but there is relatively strong evidence from the ERP research of atypicalities in selective gating, the orienting response, and some later attentional mechanisms. The link between the behavioral and ERP research needs to be explored with more difficult tasks that would increase the likelihood of eliciting behavioral group differences and maximizing ERP differences. In particular, this strategy should be applied to selective attention and orienting tasks in which there is initial evidence of group differences.

The significance of future empirical work in this area will be largely dependent on researchers' success in addressing basic conceptual and methodological issues. There is a need for concordance with other tasks that tap into each of the cited components because these preliminary conclusions are based on a minimal number of studies or tasks. In addition, researchers must present a clearer developmental picture of attention among persons with autism, in which functioning and dysfunction are depicted at various developmental levels (MA) among subgroups differentiated by level of functioning (IQ) or other criteria, and in which there is careful delineation of both the target and comparison groups and precise matching by developmental level (Enns & Burack, in press). The value and utility of all these efforts are ultimately dependent on their ecological relevance to the daily lives of persons with autism.

Another direction for future research in attention among persons with autism is to examine this aspect of functioning in tandem with other related areas. The connection with joint attention is particularly obvious because this aspect of functioning, which is consistently inefficient among persons with autism (Sigman, 1996), is dependent on all the basic components of attending. The related notion of executive functioning is increasingly being studied in connection with attentional functioning (see Bryson et al., in press; Hughes & Russell, 1993; Ozonoff & Strayer, in press) because behaviors considered within that domain of functioning, including perseveration, planning, and inhibition are relevant to all aspects of attention. Similarly, there is considerable overlap between issues of attention and perception, such as hierarchic processing, and the relationships between the two are beginning to be explored (e.g., Burack et al., 1996; Mottron, Burack, Stauder, & Robaey, 1997). Indeed, the various findings involving particularities of filtering and visual search in autism may also be considered within the context of atypicalities in the construction of the perceptual representation of complex visual stimuli (Mottron & Belleville, 1993). Relevant to the issue of ecological validity, attention needs also to be examined with regard to the social nature of the stimuli. Persons with autism may be particularly deficient in attending to socially relevant information that is central to adaptive functioning (Dawson, Meltzoff, & Osterling, 1995). The consideration of attention in relation to these and other aspects of empirical work can only serve to broaden the understanding of functioning among persons with autism.

A third aspect of future research is the use of attentional and neurophysiological paradigms to isolate neurological or other physiological deficits that might be implicated as primary sources of the various deficiencies and behaviors associated with autism. For example, Courchesne and colleagues used attention tasks to isolate aspects of functioning that are specifically deficient among persons with autism and cerebellar (e.g., Courchesne, Townsend, Akshommoff, Yeung-Courchesne, et al., 1994) or parietal (Townsend & Courchesne, 1994) lesions. Although provocative, these findings are preliminary; they are based on small numbers of subjects, so there is a need for replication studies with greater numbers of subjects, more careful matching with comparison groups, and convergent evidence with other paradigms. However, the significance of identifying concordance between physiological anomalies of any type and specific areas of functioning are essential to understanding any type of disorder.

In sum, research on attention in persons with autism is still in its earliest stages. However, the initial evidence of difficulties in attending to information in our typically stimulus-rich environment suggests potential value for understanding a wide range of cognitive, social, and behavioral impairments associated with persons with autism. Although there is no consistent empirical evidence that persons with autism perform worse than those without autism on most experimental tasks used to date, this does not mean that they necessarily process information in a usual manner. The ERP data seem to support qualitative differences in several specific aspects of attentional functioning among persons with autism. Future research should be focused on developing more complex and sophisticated tasks that can elicit these potential qualitative atypicalities at the behavioral level.

Cross-References

Neurobiological aspects of syndrome expression in autism are discussed in Chapters 16, 39, and 40. Developmental changes in syndrome expression in autism are detailed in Chapters 12 through 14.

REFERENCES

American Psychiatric Association. (1994). *Diagnostic and statistical manual of mental disorders* (4th ed.). Washington, DC: Author.

Barry, R.J., & James, A.L. (1988). Coding of stimulus parameters in autistic, retarded, and normal children: Evidence for a two-factor theory of autism. *International Journal of Psychophysiology, 6,* 139–149.

Broadbent, D.E. (1958). *Perception and communication.* London: Pergamon Press.

Broadbent, D.E. (1971). *Decision and stress.* San Diego, CA: Academic Press.

Brodeur, D.A., Trick, L.M., & Enns, J.T. (in press). Selective attention over the lifespan. In J.A. Burack & J.T. Enns (Eds.), *Attention, development, and psychopathology.* New York: Guilford Press.

Bruneau, N., Garreau, B., Roux, S., & Lelord, G. (1987). Modulation of auditory evoked potentials with increasing stimulus intensity in autistic children. *Electroencephalography and Clinical Neuropsychology, 40,*(Suppl.) 584–589.

Bryson, S.E., Landry, R., & Wainwright, J.A. (in press). In J.A. Burack & J.T. Enns (Eds.), *Attention, development, and psychopathology.* New York: Guilford Press.

Bryson, S.E., Wainwright-Sharp, J.A., & Smith, I.M. (1990). Autism: A developmental spatial neglect syndrome? In J.T. Enns (Ed.), *The development of attention: Research and theory* (pp. 405–427). Amsterdam The Netherlands: Elsevier North Holland.

Buchsbaum, M.S., Siegel, B.V., Wu, J.C., Jr., Hazlett, E., Sicotte, N., & Haier, R. (1992). Brief report: Attention performance in autism and regional brain metabolic rate assessed by positron emission tomography. *Journal of Autism and Developmental Disorders, 22,* 115–125.

Bundesen, C. (1990). A theory of visual attention. *Psychological Review, 97,* 523–547.

Burack, J.A. (1994). Selective attention deficits in persons with autism: Preliminary evidence of an inefficient attentional lens. *Journal of Abnormal Psychology, 103,* 535–543.

Burack, J.A., & Enns, J.T. (Eds.). (in press). *Attention, development, and psychopathology.* New York: Guilford Press.

Burack, J.A., & Iarocci, G. (1995, March). *Visual filtering and covert orienting in autism.* Paper presented at the meeting of the Society for Research in Child Development, Indianapolis, IN.

Burack, J.A., Iarocci, G., Mottron, L., Stauder, J., Robaey, P., & Brennan, J.M. (1996, August). *Visual filtering in persons with autism: A developmental perspective.* Paper presented at the 26th International Congress of Psychology, Montreal, Canada.

Casey, B.J., Gordon, C.T., Mannheim, G.B., & Rumsey, J.M. (1993). Dysfunctional attention in autistic savants. *Journal of Clinical and Experimental Neuropsychology, 15,* 933–946.

Ciesielski, K.T., Courchesne, E., & Elmasian, R. (1990). Effects of focused selective attention tasks on event-related potentials in autistic and normal individuals. *Electroencephalography and Clinical Neurophysiology, 75,* 207–220.

Ciesielski, K.T., Knight, J.E., Prince, R.J., Harris, R.J., & Handmaker, S.D. (1995). Event-related potentials in cross-modal divided attention in autism. *Neuropsychologia, 33,* 225–246.

Cohen, D.J., & Johnson, W.T. (1977). Cardiovascular correlates of attention in normal and psychiatrically disturbed children. *Archives of General Psychiatry, 34,* 561–567.

Coren, S., Ward, L.M., & Enns, J.T. (1994). *Sensation and perception* (4th ed.). New York: Harcourt Brace.

Courchesne, E., Kilman, B.A., Galambos, R., & Lincoln, A.J. (1984). Autism: Processing of novel auditory information assessed by event-related brain potentials. *Electroencephalography and Clinical Neurophysiology: Evoked Potentials, 59,* 238–248.

Courchesne, E., Lincoln, A., Kilman, B.A., & Galambos, R. (1985). Event-related brain potential correlates of the processing of novel visual and auditory information in autism. *Journal of Autism and Developmental Disorders, 15,* 55–76.

Courchesne, E., Lincoln, A., Yeung-Courchesne, R., Elmasian, R., & Grillon, C. (1989). Pathophysiologic findings in non-retarded autism and receptive developmental language disorder. *Journal of Autism and Developmental Disorders, 19,* 1–17.

Courchesne, E., Townsend, J.P., Akshoomoff, N.A., Saitoh, O., Yeung-Courchesne, R., Lincoln, A.J., James, H.E., Haas, R.H., Schreibman, L., & Lau, L. (1994). Impairment in shifting attention in autistic and cerebellar patients. *Behavioral Neuroscience, 108,* 848–865.

Courchesne, E., Townsend, J.P., Akshoomoff, N.A., Yeung-Courchesne, R., Press, G.A., Murakami, J.W., Lincoln, A.J., James, H.E., Saitoh, O., Egaas, B., Haas, R.H., & Schreibman, L. (1994). A new finding: Impairment in shifting attention in autistic and cerebellar patients. In S.H. Broman & J. Grafman (Eds.), *Atypical cognitive deficits in developmental disorders: Implications for brain function* (pp. 101–137). Hillsdale, NJ: Erlbaum.

Curry. J.G., & Polich, J. (1992). P-300, Global probability and stimulus sequence effects in children. *Developmental Neuropsychology, 8,* 185–202.

Dawson, G., Finley, C., Phillips, S., & Galpert, L. (1986). Hemispheric specialization and the language abilities in autistic children. *Child Development, 57,* 1440–1453.

Dawson, G., Finley, C., Phillips, S., Galpert, L., & Lewy, A. (1988). Reduced P3 amplitude of the event-related brain potential: Its relationship to language ability in autism. *Journal of Autism and Developmental Disorders, 18,* 493–504.

Dawson, G., & Lewy, A. (1989a). Arousal, attention, and the socioemotional impairments of individuals with autism. In G. Dawson (Ed.), *Autism: Nature, diagnosis, and treatment* (pp. 49–74). New York: Guilford Press.

Dawson, G., & Lewy, A. (1989b). Reciprocal subcortical-cortical influences in autism. In G. Dawson (Ed.), *Autism: Nature, diagnosis, and treatment* (pp. 144–173). New York: Guilford Press.

Dawson, G., Meltzoff, A., & Osterling, J. (1995, April). *Children with autism fail to orient to naturally occurring social stimuli.* Paper presented at the meeting of the Society for Research in Child Development, Indianapolis, IN.

Donchin, E. (1981). Surprise! . . . Surprise? *Psychophysiology, 18*(5), 493–513.

Duncan, J., & Humphries, G. (1989). Visual search and stimulus similarity. *Psychological Review, 96,* 433–458.

Enns, J.T. (1990). Relations between components of attention. In J.T. Enns (Ed.), *The development of attention: Research and theory* (pp. 139–158). Amsterdam: The Netherlands: Elsevier North Holland.

Enns, J.T. (1993). What can be learned about attention from studying its development? *Canadian Psychology, 34,* 271–281.

Enns, J.T., & Akhtar, N. (1989). A developmental study of filtering in visual attention. *Child Development, 60,* 1188–1199.

Enns, J.T., & Burack, J.A. (in press). Attention, development, and psychopathology: Bridging disciplines. In J.A. Burack & J.T. Enns (Eds.), *Attention, development, and psychopathology.* New York: Guilford Press.

Enns, J.T., & Girgus, J.S. (1985). Developmental changes in selective and integrative visual attention. *Journal of Experimental Child Psychology, 40,* 319–337.

Garretson, H.B., Fein, D., & Waterhouse, L. (1990). Sustained attention in children with autism. *Journal of Autism and Developmental Disorders, 20,* 101–104.

Gazzaniga, M.S. (Ed.). (1995). *The cognitive neurosciences.* Cambridge, MA: MIT Press.

Gibson, J.J. (1966). *The senses considered as perceptual systems.* Boston: Houghton Mifflin.

Gilbert, C.D. (1995). Dynamic properties of adult visual cortex. In M.S. Gazzaniga (Ed.), *The cognitive neurosciences* (pp. 73–90). Cambridge, MA: MIT Press.

Gold, M.S., & Gold, J.R. (1975). Autism and attention: Theoretical considerations and a pilot study using set reaction time. *Child Psychiatry and Human Development, 6,* 68–80.

Gunter, T.C., Wijers, A.A., Jackson, J.L., & Mulder, G. (1994). Visual spatial attention to stimuli presented on the vertical and horizontal meridien: An ERP study. *Psychophysiology, 31,* 140–153.

Harter, M.R., & Aine, C.J. (1984). Brain mechanisms of visual selective attention. In R. Parasuraman & D.R. Davies (Eds.), *Varieties of attention* (pp. 293–321). Orlando, FL: Academic Press.

Hayes, R. (1987). Training for work. In D.J. Cohen and A.M. Donnellan (Eds.), *Handbook of autism and pervasive developmental disorders* (pp. 360–370). New York: John Wiley & Sons.

Hermelin, B., & O'Connor, N. (1970). *Psychological experiments with autistic children.* Oxford, England: Pergamon Press.

Hillyard, S.A., & Mangun, G.R. (1986). The neural basis of visual selective attention: A comment on Harter and Aine. *Biological Psychology, 23,* 265–279.

Holcomb, P.J., Ackerman, P.T., & Dykman, R.A. (1985). Cognitive event-related brain potentials in children with attention and reading deficits. *Psychophysiology, 22,* 656–667.

Hughes, C., & Russell, J. (1993). Autistic children's difficulty with mental disengagement from an object: Its implications for theories of autism. *Developmental Psychology, 29,* 498–510.

Hutt, C., & Hutt, S.J. (1965). Effects of environmental complexity on stereotyped behaviours in children. *Animal Behaviour, 13,* 1–4.

Hutt, C., Hutt, S.J., Lee, D., & Ounsted, C. (1964). Arousal and childhood autism. *Nature, 204,* 908–909.

James, A.L., & Barry, R.L. (1980). A review of psychophysiology in early onset psychosis. *Schizophrenia Bulletin, 6,* 506–525.

James, W. (1890). *Principles of psychology.* New York: Henry Holt.

Jennings, J.R., & Coles, M.G.H. (Eds.). (1991). *Handbook of cognitive psychophysiology: Central and autonomic nervous system approach.* Chichester, England: John Wiley & Sons.

Kahneman, D. (1973). *Attention and effort.* Englewood Cliffs, NJ: Prentice-Hall.

Kanner, L. (1943). Autistic disturbances of affective contact. *Nervous Child, 2,* 217–250.

Kemner, C., Verbaten, M.N., Cuperus, J.M., Camfferman, G., & van Engeland, H. (1994). Visual and somatosensory event-related brain potentials in autistic children and three different control groups. *Electroencephalography and Clinical Neurophysiology, 92,* 225–237.

Kemner, C., Verbaten, M.N., Cuperus, J.M., Camfferman, G., & van Engeland, H. (1995). Auditory event-related brain potentials in autistic children and three different control groups. *Biological Psychiatry, 38,* 150–165.

Kinsbourne, M. (1987). Cerebral-brainstem relations in infantile autism. In E. Schopler & G. Mesibov (Eds.), *Neurobiological issues in autism* (pp. 107–125). New York: Plenum Press.

Kootz, J.P., & Cohen, D.J. (1981). Modulation of sensory intake in autistic children: Cardiovascular and behavioral indices. *Journal of the American Academy of Child Psychiatry, 20,* 692–701.

Lelord, G., Laffont, F., Jusseaume, P., & Stephant, J.L. (1973). Comparative study of conditioning of averages evoked responses by coupling sound and light in normal and autistic children. *Psychophysiology, 10,* 415–425.

Lincoln, A.J., Courchesne, E., Harms, L., & Allen, M. (1993). Contextual probability evaluation in autistic, receptive language disorder, and control children: Event-related brain potential evidence. *Journal of Autism and Developmental Disorders, 23,* 37–58.

Litrownik, A.J., McInnis, E.T., Wetzel-Pritchard, A.M., & Filipelli, D.L. (1978). Restricted stimulus control and inferred attentional deficits in autistic and retarded children. *Journal of Abnormal Psychology, 87,* 554–562.

Lovaas, O.I., Koegel, R., & Schreibman, L. (1979). Stimulus overselectivity in autism: A review of research. *Psychological Bulletin, 86,* 1236–1254.

Marr, D. (1982). *Vision.* San Francisco: Freeman.

Martineau, J., Laffont, F., Bruneau, N., Roux, S., & Lelord, G. (1980). Event-related potentials evoked by sensory stimulation in normal, mentally retarded and autistic children. *Electroencephalography and Clinical Neurophysiology, 48,* 140–153.

McCarthy, P. (1972). Visual serial search performance for number and letter targets. *Journal of Experimental Psychology, 95,* 233–234.

Meyer, D.E., & Kornblum, S. (Eds.). (1993). *Attention and performance 14: Synergies in experimental psychology, artificial intelligence, and cognitive neuroscience.* Cambridge, MA: MIT Press.

Minshew, N.J. (1992). Neurological localization in autism. In E. Schopler & G.B. Mesibov (Eds.), *High-functioning individuals with autism* (pp. 65–89). New York: Plenum Press.

Mishkin, M., Ungerleider, L.G., & Macko, K.A. (1983). Object vision and spatial vision: Two cortical pathways. *Trends in Neurosciences, 6,* 414–417.

Mottron, L., & Belleville, S. (1993). A study of perceptual analysis in a high level autistic subject with exceptional graphic abilities. *Brain and Cognition, 23,* 279–309.

Mottron, L., Burack, J.A., Stauder, J.E., & Robaey, P. (1997). Perceptual processing among high functioning persons with autism. Manuscript submitted for publication.

Naatanen, R., & Gaillard, A.W. (1974). The relationship between the contingent negative variation and the reaction time under prolonged experimental conditions. *Biological Psychology, 1,* 277–291.

National Society for Autistic Children. (1978). National Society for Autistic Children definition of the syndrome of autism. *Journal of Autism and Developmental Disorders, 8,* 162–167.

Nissen, M.J. (1985). Assessing features and objects: Is location special? In M.J. Posner & O.S.M. Marin (Eds.), *Attention and performance* (pp. 205–219). Hillsdale, NJ: Erlbaum.

Novick, B., Kurtzberg, A., & Vaughan, H.G., Jr. (1979). An electrophysiologic indication of defective information storage in childhood autism. *Psychiatry Research, 1,* 101–108.

Novick, B., Vaughan, H.G., Kurtzberg, D., & Simpson, R. (1980). An electrophysiologic indication of auditory processing defects in autism. *Psychiatry Research, 3,* 107–114.

Nuechterlein, K.H., Parasuraman, R., & Jiang, Q. (1983). Visual sustained attention: Image degradation produces rapid sensitivity decrement over time. *Science, 220,* 344–358.

Oades, R.D., Walker, M.K., Geffin, L.B., & Stern, L.M. (1988). Event-related potentials in autistic and healthy children on an auditory choice reaction time task. *International Journal of Psychophysiology, 6,* 25–37.

Ornitz, E.M. (1969). Disorders of perception common to early infantile autism and schizophrenia. *Comprehensive Psychiatry, 10,* 259–274.

Ornitz, E.M. (1988) Autism: A disorder of directed attention. *Brain Dysfunction, 5–6,* 309–322.

Ornitz, E.M., & Ritvo, E.R. (1968). Perceptual inconstancy in early infantile autism. *Archives of General Psychiatry, 18,* 76–98.

Ozonoff, S., & Strayer, D.L. (in press). Inhibitory function in nonretarded children with autism. *Journal of Autism and Developmental Disorders.*

Ozonoff, S., Strayer, D.L., McMahon, W.M., & Filloux, F. (1995). Executive function abilities in autism and Tourette Syndrome: An information processing approach. *Journal of Child Psychology and Psychiatry, 35,* 1015–1037.

Parasuraman, R., & Davies, D.R. (Eds.). (1984). *Varieties of attention.* Orlando, FL: Academic Press.

Pasto, L., & Burack, J.A. (1995, June). *A developmental study of visual filtering: Can windows facilitate filtering efficiency?* Poster presented at the meeting of the Canadian Psychological Association, Charlottetown, Canada.

Plaisted, K.C., O'Riordan, M.A., & Baron-Cohen, S. (1997a). *Enhanced discrimination and reduced prototype effect in high functioning autistic individuals.* Manuscript submitted for publication.

Plaisted, K.C., O'Riordan, M.A., & Baron-Cohen, S. (1997b). *Looking for trees in the woods: Enhanced target detection in autistic individuals.* Manuscript submitted for publication.

Plude, D.J., Enns, J.T., & Brodeur, D. (1994). The development of selective attention: A life-span overview. *Acta Psychologica, 86,* 227–272.

Posner, M.I. (1980). Orienting of attention. *Quarterly Journal of Experimental Psychology, 32,* 3–25.

Posner, M.I., & Raichle, M.E. (1994). *Images of mind.* New York: Freeman.

Pritchard, W.S., Raz, N., & August, G.J. (1987). Visual augmenting/reducing and P300 in autistic children. *Journal of Autism and Developmental Disorders, 17,* 231–242.

Rimland, B. (1964). *Infantile autism.* New York: Appleton-Century-Crofts.

Rincover, A., & Ducharme, J.M. (1987). Variables influencing stimulus over-selectivity and "tunnel-vision" in developmentally delayed children. *American Journal of Mental Deficiency, 91,* 422–430.

Rohrbaugh, J.W. (1984). The orienting reflex: Performance and central nervous system manifestations. In R. Parasuraman & D.R. Davies (Eds.), *Varieties of attention* (pp. 323–373). Orlando, FL: Academic.

Rosenblum, S.M., Arick, J.R., Krug, D.A., Stubbs, E.G., Young, N.B., & Pelson, R.O. (1980). Auditory brainstem evoked responses in autistic children. *Journal of Autism and Developmental Disorders, 10,* 215–225.

Rosler, F., & Heil, M. (1991). Toward a functional categorization of slow waves: Taking into account past and future events. *Psychophysiology, 28,* 344–358.

Rutter, M. (1983). Cognitive deficits in the pathogenesis of autism. *Journal of Child Psychology and Psychiatry, 24*(4), 513–531.

Schover, L.R., & Newsom, C.D. (1976). Overselectivity, developmental level, and overtraining in autistic and normal children. *Journal of Abnormal Child Psychology, 4,* 289–298.

Sigman, M. (1996). Behavioral research in childhood autism. In M.F. Lenzenweger & J.J. Haugaard (Eds.), *Frontiers of developmental psychopathology* (pp. 190–208). New York: Oxford University Press.

Singer, W. (1995). Time as coding space in neocortical processing: A hypothesis. In M.S. Gazzaniga (Ed.), *The cognitive neurosciences* (pp. 91–104). Cambridge, MA: MIT Press.

Stauder, J.E., Molenaar, P.C., & van der Molen, W. (1989). Equivalent dipole modelling of topographic ERP-components: A developmental case study. *Journal of Psychophysiology, 3,* 361–368.

Stauder, J.E., & Mottron, L. (1996). *Event-related potentials to a visual oddball task in high functioning persons with autism.* Manuscript submitted for publication.

Stevens, S., & Gruzelier, J. (1984). Electrodermal activity to auditory stimuli in autistic, retarded, and normal children. *Journal of Autism and Developmental Disorders, 14,* 245–260.

Swanson, J.M., Shea, C., McBurnett, K., Potkin, S.G., Fiore, C., & Crinella, F. (1990). Attention and hyperactivity. In J.T. Enns (Ed.), *The development of attention: Research and theory* (pp. 383–403). Amsterdam, The Netherlands: Elsevier North Holland.

Tipper, S.P., & McLaren, J. (1990). Evidence for efficient visual selectivity in children. In J. T. Enns (Ed.), *The development of attention: Research and theory* (pp. 197–210). Amsterdam, The Netherlands: Elsevier North Holland.

Townsend, J., & Courchesne, E. (1994). Parietal damage and narrow "spotlight" spatial attention. *Journal of Cognitive Neuroscience, 6,* 220–232.

Treisman, A. (1982). Perceptual grouping and attention in visual search for features and for objects. *Journal of Experimental Psychology: Human Perception and Performance, 8,* 194–214.

Treisman, A. (1986). Features and objects in visual processing. *Scientific American, 255,* 114B–125.

Treisman, A. (1988). Features and objects: The fourteenth Bartlett memorial lecture. *Quarterly Journal of Experimental Psychology, 40A,* 201–237.

Treisman, A., & Gelade, G. (1980). A feature integration theory of attention. *Cognitive Psychology, 12,* 97–136.

Treisman, A., & Gormican, S. (1988). Feature analysis in early vision: Evidence from search asymmetries. *Psychological Review, 95,* 15–48.

Tsal, Y. (1983). Movements of attention across the visual field. *Journal of Experimental Psychology: Human Perception and Performance, 9,* 523–530.

Ullman, S. (1984). Visual routines. *Cognition, 18,* 97–159.

Ungerleider, L.G., & Mishkin, M. (1982). Two cortical visual systems. In D.J. Ingle, M.A. Goodale, & R.J.W. Mansfield (Eds.), *Analysis of visual behavior* (pp. 549–586). Cambridge, MA: MIT Press.

van der Molen, M.N., Bashore, T.R., Halliday, R., & Callaway, E. (1991). Chronopsychophysiology: Mental chronometry augmented by psychophysiological time markers. In R. Jennings & M.G.H. Coles (Eds.), *Handbook of cognitive psychophysiology: Central and autonomic nervous system approaches* (pp. 9–178). Chichester, England: John Wiley & Sons.

van Engeland, H. (1984). The electrodermal orienting response to auditive stimuli in autistic children, normal children, mentally retarded children, and child psychiatric patients. *Jour-*

nal of Autism and Developmental Disorders, 14, 261–279.

Verbaten, M.N., Roelofs, J.W., van Engeland, H., Kenemans, J.K., & Slangen, J.L. (1991). Abnormal visual event-related potentials of autistic children. Journal of Autism and Developmental Disorders, 21, 449–470.

Von Holst, E., & Mittelstaedt, H. (1950). Das reafferenz-princip. Die Naturwissenschaften, 20, 464–476.

Wainwright-Sharp, J.A., & Bryson, S.E. (1993). Visual orienting deficits in high-functioning people with autism. Journal of Autism and Developmental Disorders, 23, 1–13.

Wainwright-Sharp, J.A., & Bryson, S.E. (1996). Visual-spatial orienting in autism. Journal of Autism and Developmental Disorders, 26(4), 423–438.

Zeki, S. (1995). A vision of the brain. Boston: Blackwell.

Zigler, E., & Hodapp, R. (1986). Understanding mental retardation. New York: Cambridge University Press.

CHAPTER 11

Cognition and Emotion in Children and Adolescents with Autism

MARIAN SIGMAN, CHERYL DISSANAYAKE, SHOSHANA ARBELLE, AND ELLEN RUSKIN

The role of cognition in the syndrome of autism did not receive much attention until the 1970s. The earliest formulation of the syndrome, emphasizing the social and emotional aspects of the disorder (Bettelheim, 1967; Kanner, 1943), was succeeded by two major conceptualizations. One group of investigators viewed the autistic person's deviation in perceptual processing as the primary disorder (Ornitz & Ritvo, 1976); other theorists focused on the individual's problems in language development and usage (Churchill, 1972; Rutter, Bartak, & Newman, 1971). The significance of cognitive dysfunctions in autism became clear from research studies of perceptual and language deficits (Rutter, 1983). These studies showed that profound and syndrome-specific impairments were found only in higher-level perceptual processing. Furthermore, language disorders were shown to be restricted to those domains of language most closely tied to representational thought and communication (Baltaxe & Simmons, 1975; Prior, 1979; Tager-Flusberg, 1981). Thus, careful investigations of language and perception (Hermelin & O'Connor, 1970; Ornitz, Guthrie, & Farley, 1977) laid the foundation for studies of cognition in autistic populations.

This chapter begins with a review of research on cognition in autistic children. Studies of normal cognition have followed two lines of emphasis: (a) processes of knowledge acquisition or (b) products of cognitive processing. The first line of emphasis, exemplified in theories of learning and information processing, focuses on the ways in which individuals encode and maintain information; the second, conceptualized by Piagetian theories and theories of symbol formation, focuses on what the individual knows. The latter includes both knowledge about the world (concepts) and knowledge of how to act in the world (skills). Research on cognition in autistic individuals began with studies of processes of perception, learning, and memory, and these have been well surveyed by a number of authors (DeMyer, Hingtgen, & Jackson, 1981; Fein, Humes, Kaplan, Lucci, & Waterhouse, 1984; Prior, 1979, 1984). Research into the concepts and skills of autistic children is more recent; for this reason, it is the major area covered here. Research on the cognitive processes of autistic children is treated briefly, before discussion of the conceptualizations that autistic children hold about the inanimate environment, other people, and the self.

METHODOLOGICAL CONSIDERATIONS

The two major aims for studies of autistic individuals are: (a) to describe the clinical

Support for some of the research reported in this chapter was provided by Grants NS25243 from the National Institute of Neurological Disorders and Stroke and HD17662 from the National Institute of Child Health and Human Development.

syndrome as it is manifested in the majority of individuals affected, and (b) to describe the characteristics that are specific to the syndrome of autism. This distinction in aims is particularly crucial for investigations of autism because of the covariance of autism and mental retardation. The vast majority of autistic individuals are mentally retarded (Freeman & Ritvo, 1976; Rutter et al., 1971; Schreibman, Koegel, Charlop, & Egal, 1982). On standardized tests, about 70% to 80% achieve IQ scores in the mentally retarded range, with the major proportion scoring in the moderate to severe ranges of mental retardation (DeMyer et al., 1974; Wing & Gould, 1979).

If the aim of a study is to describe the clinical syndrome, researchers can observe autistic individuals without a comparison group. If the aim is to define the characteristics specific to autism, however, the performance of autistic subjects must be compared with that of control groups matched on mental age (MA) and chronological age (CA). The choice of control groups is difficult because certain matched groups may have deficits or idiosyncratic characteristics of their own; as a result, several control groups may be necessary. Furthermore, the selection of matching variables depends on the nature of the research question. Particular care must be taken to choose matching variables that differ from the dependent variables. Because the aim of this chapter is to discuss cognitive dysfunctions specific to autism, only studies that include appropriate control groups are reviewed.

The covariance of autism and mental retardation in many (but not all) individuals with autism complicates the interpretation of findings because individuals with autism vary as a function of their chronological age, degree of retardation, and severity of symptoms. Normal individuals show change with age and consequent mental development so that cognitive and emotional processes will vary, depending on the age and correlated level of development of the individual. However, there are retarded and nonretarded individuals with autism at all ages, so age and developmental level are only roughly correlated in groups of autistic individuals. If a cognitive or emotional process is disturbed in autism, it should

be disturbed regardless of the person's level of development. For this reason, evidence is needed to show that specific deficits are found in individuals with autism at all levels of retardation and at all ages. However, processes change with mental development so that, for example, symbolic functioning may be manifested in play at one age and in language use at another age. Therefore, we cannot expect to find identical group differences between individuals with autism and control subjects at all ages and levels of intelligence. In addition, some processes, such as symbolic functioning, do not emerge until a particular age or stage of development is reached, and, therefore, cannot be tested in particular groups. Certain deficits may not appear in older or more skillful individuals with autism because they use other abilities to overcome their deficiencies. Alternatively, deficits may be found in older individuals that are not primary but are secondary to the social and intellectual deprivation that often accompanies the disorder. This chapter considers these complications whenever there is enough evidence to do so.

COGNITIVE PROCESSING IN AUTISTIC INDIVIDUALS

Discrimination Learning and Short-Term Memory

Research suggests that autism is not associated with pervasive deficits in the capacity to discriminate stimuli. Autistic individuals easily learn simple discriminations of line position, length of line, and dimensionality (Hermelin & O'Connor, 1970; Maltz, 1981; Prior, 1979). In fact, in one study that employed three-dimensional stimuli, tangible rewards, and no verbal cues, performance of the autistic sample was superior to that of normal and retarded MA-matched controls (Prior & Chen, 1975). With three-dimensional stimuli, the autistic children were able to solve a conditional matching learning-set problem (Prior & McGillivray, 1980). Deficiencies in discrimination learning occur only when the stimuli to be differentiated are symbolic (Hermelin & O'Connor, 1970; Minshew, Goldstein, Muenz, & Payton, 1992; Prior, 1977), and these difficulties can be surmounted when the material is made concrete (Fein, Tinder, & Waterhouse, 1979). Thus, the limitation appears to be in the use of symbolic material rather than in the person's capacity to learn discriminations among stimuli. Autistic children are also able to learn both reversal and nonreversal shifts and do so at the appropriate ages (Charlop & Carlson, 1983).

The research literature also indicates that individuals with autism do not suffer from gross memory deficits. Memory for simple stimuli, particularly auditory stimuli (Hermelin & O'Connor, 1970; Prior, 1977), appears to be adequate. Repetitive rote memory for digits or simple phrases varies with the person's developmental level (Fyffe & Prior, 1978). When acquisition level is controlled, visual and auditory memory of autistic children is not different from that of MA-, CA-, and IQ-matched retarded controls. In addition, autistic children, especially those who are higher functioning, seem to be able to use semantic (Bryson, 1983) and syntactic cues to facilitate recall (Fyffe & Prior, 1978).

Sequencing of Information and Cross-Modal Transfer

Some studies have described limitations in autistic individuals' abilities to sequence information in both auditory and visual modalities (Frith, 1970, 1971, 1972). At times, autistic individuals appear to impose their own rules. Greater difficulties are demonstrated in temporal sequencing than in spatial sequencing. Deficits in cross-modal learning have been reported in some studies but not in others (Hermelin & O'Connor, 1970). In one study, participants had no problems in cross-modal transfer in visual or haptic modalities, and deficits in auditory-visual and auditory-haptic cross-modal learning could be attributed to poor original learning in the auditory modality (Herbert, cited in Prior, 1979).

Imitation

Imitation, or modeling, is one of the most frequent and ubiquitous routes for learning in normal children. The capacity to imitate allows the child to reproduce an action of another person and to internalize a representation of this action. Some argue that this ability is essential to the child's development of awareness of self and others (Barresi & Moore, 1996; Meltzoff & Gopnik, 1993). Autistic children rarely imitate spontaneously; however, observers are unsure whether they are unable or reluctant to do so. The experimental studies to date provide equivocal evidence for an imitation deficit. Many studies have shown that autistic children are much less likely to imitate body movements and actions on objects than are MA-matched controls (Bartak, Rutter, & Cox, 1975; Dawson & Adams, 1984; DeMyer et al., 1972; Hertzig, Snow, & Sherman, 1989; Jones & Prior, 1985; Ohta, 1987; Prior & Gajzago, 1974; Sigman & Ungerer, 1984b; Stone, Lemanck, Fishel, Fernandez, & Altemeier, 1990; Tubbs, 1966; Wing, 1978). However, some evidence suggests that autistic individuals have at least some basic imitation skills (Heimann, Ulstadius, Dahlgren, & Gillberg, 1992), especially when familiar actions are used (Dawson & Adams, 1984; Rogers & McEvoy, 1993). In a recent study, Charman and Baron-Cohen (1994) have demonstrated that autistic children are able to imitate both gestures and unfamiliar actions on objects, and Loveland et al. (1994) have shown good imitation of facial gestures in older autistic individuals. Dawson and Adams (1984) have also shown that certain intervention strategies enhance imitation. Thus, to date, it is unclear whether the development of imitation abilities is simply delayed or is deviant in autism. Moreover, research has not clarified whether the problem with imitation in this group is attributable to difficulty in attending to, perceiving, remembering, comprehending, or executing the modeled action. (See Smith & Bryson, 1994, for a review of this literature.)

STUDIES OF PERFORMANCE ON STANDARDIZED INTELLIGENCE TESTS

Standardized measures of intelligence provide information both about cognitive processes and about stored knowledge. Cognitive processes—fluid intelligence—have been measured by the Similarities and Block Design subtests of the Wechsler Intelligence Scales for Children—Revised (WISC-R), whereas stored knowledge—crystallized intelligence—

is manifested in the Vocabulary and Information subtests.

In addition, the subtests are designed to assess abilities in the verbal and performance domains. Research shows that autistic children have deficits both in cognitive processes and in stored knowledge, with the major impairments occurring in the verbal domain. To specify the nature of the cognitive disorder, researchers have compared the performance of nonretarded autistic children on standardized intelligence tests with that of nonpsychotic children matched for age, IQ, and sex (Gillies, 1965; Lockyer & Rutter, 1970; McDonald, Mundy, Kasari, & Sigman, 1989; Tymchuk, Simmons, & Neafsey, 1977; Wolf, Wenar, & Ruttenberg, 1972). In most studies, the autistic children had higher scores on performance scales than on verbal scales, whereas the nonpsychotic children's scores were roughly the same on both the verbal and the performance scales. On the verbal scales, autistic children scored best on the Digit Span, which assesses attention and short-term memory, and worst on the Comprehension scale, which assesses social knowledge. The nonpsychotic children scored highest on the Comprehension scale. On the WISC-R performance scale, autistic children were characterized by relatively high scores on Object Assembly and Block Design scales, which measure perceptual organization; the control group had relatively poor scores on Block Design.

Similar results were found with comparisons of nonretarded autistic children and children with developmental receptive language disorders (Bartak et al., 1975). Dysphasic children were studied to determine which aspects of the autistic child's deviant functioning were unique to autism and could not be accounted for solely by impaired language skills. Even with their language disorder, the dysphasic children performed better than the autistic group on all three verbal scales: Comprehension, Similarities, and Vocabulary. On the performance subscales, both groups performed more similarly. For the autistic children only, scores on the Block Design scale were significantly better than on all other performance scales. Rutter (1983) has interpreted the pattern of scores shown by autistic children on standardized intelligence tests and in other testing situations (Hermelin & O'Connor, 1970) as indicating special difficulties in sequencing and abstraction. Autistic children show few specific deficits in spatial performance, perceptual organization, and attentional short-term memory skills.

Object Knowledge

Knowledge of Object Permanence and Object Use

Piaget's theories concerning the development of perception and cognition during the sensorimotor, preoperational, and concrete operational periods have generated interest in the child's understanding of the world of objects. Piaget (1952) postulated that during the sensorimotor period, which occurs typically in the first two years of life, infants must develop the knowledge that objects exist outside their experience with them and that objects have an identity and permanence of their own. Infants also begin to differentiate between the means to a goal and the goal state. During the last stage, Stage 6, infants become able to form mental representations of objects and events, and consequently are capable of solving problems by mental activity rather than by trial and error with actual objects.

Researchers disagree about the actual age at which children achieve this understanding and about the nature of the changes in the infant's understanding (Baillargeon, 1994; Moore & Meltzoff, 1978); however, empirical studies have substantiated Piaget's behavioral observations regarding the child's search for hidden objects and the use of objects. The longitudinal progression noted by Piaget with his own children has been supported in controlled studies with larger samples (Decarie, 1967; Escalona & Corman, 1969; Uzgiris & Hunt, 1975). We have reported previously that a definite order is observable in children's sensorimotor attainments, but individual infants do backslide occasionally in test situations (Kopp, Sigman, & Parmelee, 1973, 1974).

Several studies have examined the sensorimotor knowledge of autistic children, and most report few differences in the abilities of mental-age-matched autistic, mentally retarded, and normal children (Dawson & Adams, 1984; Lancy & Goldstein, 1982;

Sigman & Ungerer, 1981, 1984b). Moreover, the results from one of our studies indicated that autistic children with mean MAs at 25 to 26 months had skills described by Piaget as representative of the sixth stage of sensorimotor development, as they passed the majority of the subtests at the Stage 6 level. Particularly noteworthy is that every child showed Stage 6 level skills on the subtest measuring object permanence. Thus, they showed no specific deficiency in sensorimotor knowledge, indicating that autistic children are capable of certain forms of representational thought.

Knowledge of Objects as Demonstrated in Play

Although sensorimotor skills do seem intact in children with autism, more advanced concepts, manifested in pretend play during the preoperational period, are impaired. The play of young children provides useful information for understanding the development of representational thought (Piaget, 1962). Research on play with objects in normal children 7 to 31 months of age indicates that qualitative, age-related changes occur in this period, providing a foundation for the emergence of symbolic play at approximately 20 months of age. Prior to 9 months of age, a child's play is characterized by close visual and tactile inspection of single objects, along with mouthing, waving, banging, and hand-to-hand manipulation. At 8 to 9 months of age, play advances to the relational use of objects in combination. At 12 to 13 months, infants begin to play with objects in a functionally appropriate or conventional manner, and, between 13 and 22 months of age, they develop play that is clearly symbolic (Inhelder, Lezine, Sinclair, & Stambak, 1972; Nicolich, 1977; Piaget, 1962; Sinclair, 1970; Ungerer, Zelazo, Kearsley, & O'Leary, 1981).

Most current studies of play use observations of four mutually exclusive categories, defined as follows:

1. Stereotypic play—mouthing, waving, banging, or fingering an object.
2. Relational play—the simultaneous association of two or more objects in a nonfunctional manner.
3. Functional play—use of a realistic toy in a functional or conventional manner (e.g.,
using a spoon to feed a doll; dialing the telephone and bringing the receiver to one's ear).
4. Symbolic play, including three different types of acts—use of one object to represent another, different object; acts implying that a doll is an agent of action; and acts implying the existence of imaginary objects.

The play of autistic children is markedly different from the play of children with similar developmental abilities (Riquet, Taylor, Benroya, & Klein, 1981; Wing, Gould, Yeates, & Brierly, 1977). First, children with autism show less exploration of objects in situations that are unstructured (Hermelin & O'Connor, 1970; Kasari, Sigman, & Yirmiya, 1993). When parents, experimenters, or teachers actively encourage object exploration by limiting the space in which the child can move and by handing objects to the child, object exploration increases and becomes equivalent to that shown by normal and mentally retarded children of the same developmental level. The exception to this is doll play, where even adult participation fails to engage autistic children to the same degree as it does control children (Sigman, Mundy, Sherman, & Ungerer, 1986).

Autistic children are capable of demonstrating a wide range of different play behaviors in both unstructured, free-play situations and in structured, one-to-one observation with an adult (Ungerer & Sigman, 1981). In addition to simple manipulation and relational use, these children also demonstrate a range of different functional acts and some symbolic play. However, autistic children distribute their play time differently from the control children, spending equal amounts of time in simple manipulation of objects, relational play, and functional play. In contrast, for MA-matched mentally retarded and normal children, more sophisticated forms of play, like functional and symbolic play, tend to dominate or to replace less sophisticated play behaviors like simple manipulation or relational play.

Young children with autism show evidence of a deficit in functional play. In one study, a group of 16 autistic children demonstrated less functional play in both unstructured and structured situations than a group of 16 mentally retarded children matched on mental and chronological age and a group of 16 normal children matched on mental age (Sigman & Ungerer, 1984b). In the unstructured situation, the autistic children engaged in less functional play and fewer sequences of three or more related functional acts than did the children in the other groups. The autistic children directed their functional play acts to another person or a doll fewer times than did the children in the other groups. They also performed less diverse play, demonstrating a smaller number of different functional acts. In the structured situation, objects in a toy set were presented to the child one at a time or in small groups of related items. The autistic children produced fewer different doll-directed functional acts as well as fewer different functional acts in general.

Studies of older, more developmentally advanced groups have had mixed results. Baron-Cohen (1987) did not find differences in functional play in an unstructured situation when autistic children were compared to a control group matched on verbal mental age. With an even more developmentally advanced sample, Lewis and Boucher (1988) observed play in both structured and unstructured situations. The autistic children had language abilities in the 4- to 5-year-old age range, and the control groups were matched on these language abilities. In the unstructured situation, the autistic children engaged in functional play less than the other two groups, although all but two of the autistic children engaged in at least some functional play.

Almost all studies have shown fewer symbolic play acts by autistic children than by control children. In our first study (Sigman & Ungerer, 1984b), autistic children showed fewer diverse symbolic play acts than did the controls in both unstructured and structured situations, although symbolic play increased in the structured situation. The number of symbolic acts performed in the structured situation was also lower for the autistic children in a second study in which the children were matched on both mental and verbal abilities (Mundy, Sigman, Ungerer, & Sherman, 1987). Baron-Cohen (1987) found that, compared to the normal and retarded control groups, significantly fewer autistic children produced any spontaneous symbolic play. Only two autistic

children demonstrated any pretend play, and only two children with Down syndrome and one normal child showed a complete lack of spontaneous symbolic play acts. In contrast, Lewis and Boucher (1988) reported fewer group differences in their study of older and more advanced subjects. In their unstructured situation, very few of the children in any group performed spontaneous symbolic play, a finding that suggests the toys or the situation were inappropriate for this age group. In the structured situation, no group differences were seen, and all the autistic children produced some symbolic play acts by making one object stand for another or imagining absent objects to be present. This study demonstrates that autistic children who achieve language abilities comparable to those of 5-year-olds are capable of using symbols in play, even though they may not often demonstrate this ability unless required by the task to do so.

Knowledge of Object Categories

Besides learning about object permanence and ways to use objects, infants must also learn to conceptualize and generalize about object properties in order to formulate categories. Children need to be able to note similarities among objects, in spite of perceived differences among them, to form categories or groupings that help them structure their thinking about the environment (Rosch, 1973). Ricciuti (1965) introduced a nonverbal technique for providing evidence that 12- to 24-month-old infants categorize objects when he observed toddlers applying sequential and spatial sorting to objects varying in size, form, and color.

To investigate children's knowledge of object categories, researchers have presented autistic, mentally retarded, and normal children with geometric forms and miniatures of common objects (Ungerer & Sigman, 1987). These were selected to represent four different colors, three different forms, and four different representational categories: animals, food, vehicles, and furniture. All children were tested individually while seated at a table next to the experimenter. A sorting trial consisted of giving the child four exemplars from each of two categories to sort (e.g., four red circles and four red squares for a form-sorting task, and four vehicles and four foods for a representational sorting task). No verbal instructions were given. A child's object manipulations on each trial were scored on both spatial and temporal groupings.

Children in all three groups showed numerous instances of sorting. Autistic children tended to sort shape and representational categories about equally and color categories somewhat less. In a series of comparisons of the sorting behaviors of the autistic, normal, and mentally retarded children, no significant differences appeared in how the groups sorted shape, color, or representational categories. Thus, the evidence from this paradigm and two other studies (Lancy & Goldstein, 1982; Slotnick, 1983) suggests that autistic children possess the perceptual and cognitive skills requisite for categorization.

Autistic adolescents and adults were also able to sort objects by geometric shape in a study carried out in Israel (Shulman, Yirmiya, & Greenbaum, 1995). The majority of this group's responses (74%) on a task of sorting representational objects (trees, beds, human figures, animals, tools, and vehicles) were correct, but they were less accurate than matched mentally retarded and normal subjects whose sorting of representational objects was nearly perfect (92% correct). In addition, individuals with autism had more difficulty with class inclusion problems than did mentally retarded and normal groups. Thus, although young children with autism are able to demonstrate functional knowledge of objects when the requirements are fairly minimal, some of this group may have difficulty when more sophisticated representational knowledge is required.

Conservation and Seriation

In a series of studies, Yirmiya and her colleagues (Shulman et al., 1995; Yirmiya & Shulman, 1996; Yirmiya, Sigman, Kasari, & Mundy, 1992; Yirmiya, Sigman, & Zacks, 1994) investigated object knowledge that is acquired during the period of concrete operations—from age 6 to 12 years in typically developing children. The results of these studies suggest that deficits in conservation and seriation are not specific to autism. Nonretarded autistic children and adolescents were as able as control subjects to do seriation tasks requiring them to place blocks in order by height, weight, and shade of color. Retarded autistic adolescents and adults were less accurate at seriation than the normal controls, but they were more skillful than the nonautistic mentally retarded subjects on seriation using multiple cues. Nonretarded autistic children and adults had severe problems with conservation tasks, demonstrating their limited knowledge about how object qualities such as number and weight are retained despite transformation in the appearance of the object. Only half the children with autism had mastered conservation of two-dimensional space, number, quantity, substance, and weight, despite having average intelligence. However, mentally retarded, nonautistic adolescents and adults were as seriously impaired on conservation tasks as were mentally retarded autistic subjects. Thus, both autism and mental retardation limit a person's understanding of conservation.

In summary, individuals with autism appear to be specifically deficient in certain object concepts and skills and not in others. The areas of cognitive development in which specific deficits are observed all involve representational knowledge. These deficits are particularly striking in forms of pretend play that usually develop early in childhood. This pattern of results raises several questions about the nature of symbolic play. The first question concerns the requirements that must be met for the child to use objects in pretend play. The second question concerns how these requirements differ from those necessary for understanding sensorimotor use of objects, object permanence, and object categories. Two major differences between symbolic play and other forms of object use can be considered. First, the ability to engage in pretend play may require the child to have some metarepresentational capacity. Leslie (1985) argues that a representational theory of play requires some way for the system to register that it is in the pretend mode. If this is true, then functional and symbolic play may differ from other forms of object use in terms of cognitive loading. Although autistic children may be able to perceive similarities and thus be able to categorize objects, and even to internalize action schemes, they may not have the cognitive capacity required for symbolic play.

A second difference between sensorimotor and category knowledge and the symbolic representation of objects in play may be the extent to which these different forms of object knowledge depend on social involvement. A child may be able to develop sensorimotor skills from observing and using objects, with little social input. Similarly, he or she may figure out many simple categories (e.g., food vs. nonfood) without much social involvement. On the other hand, symbolic play appears to develop in a social context. The demonstration of even simple object-directed functional play suggests that the child has observed the conventional use of objects by others in some detail. The direction of play outward to a doll or another person clearly requires social interaction. Thus, the social component may be more critical for development of symbolic play than for attainment of sensorimotor or category knowledge. Concepts and skills based on social involvement may be particularly impaired in autistic children.

KNOWLEDGE OF OTHER PEOPLE

For the normally developing infant, other people are particularly powerful stimuli. According to Bowlby's theories, an infant is born with an innate proclivity to respond to other human beings (Bowlby, 1969). Research evidence suggests that the young infant can differentiate between social and nonsocial objects (Wolff, 1969) as well as between sensations associated with familiar and unfamiliar people (McFarlane, 1977). The capacity to differentiate among facial expressions is usually considered to emerge at 5 to 6 months (La Barbara, Izard, Vietze, & Parisi, 1976; Young-Browne, Rosenfeld, & Horowitz, 1977), although one study reports that the ability is observed in neonates (Field, 1982). By the end of the first year of life, infants use their mother's emotional expressions to guide their behavior (Klinnert, Campos, Sorce, Emde, & Svejda, 1982). At this time, the infant appears to be capable of sharing perspective with other people by following another's line of regard or pointing finger (Scaife & Bruner, 1975). Infants also begin to point out objects

to others and to use a variety of looking behaviors and vocalizations to regulate the actions of other people (Bates, Benigni, Bretherton, Camaioni, & Volterra, 1979).

Social Communication Skills

An infant's knowledge of other people can be assessed by observing his or her prelinguistic social communication behaviors. Various categories of prelinguistic communication acts have been described and are reflected in the Early Social Communication Scales (ESCS; Seibert & Hogan, 1982), an instrument designed to evaluate skills that usually develop between 8 and 24 months of age. During the assessment, an experimenter presents the child with a series of structured situations designed to assess how well the child uses gestures and eye contact to achieve the following: (a) initiate joint attention—direct the adult's attention to objects or events; (b) initiate behavior regulation—request objects that are out of reach or ask for aid in activating mechanical toys; (c) initiate social interaction—initiate a social game involving physical contact such as a tickle game or one involving object exchange. The adult also presents situations designed to assess how well the child (d) responds to joint attention—responds to the adult's attempts to direct the child's visual attention; (e) responds to behavior regulation—complies with adult verbal and gestural requests or commands; and (f) responds to social interaction—requests repetition of an adult-initiated social game. Each administration of the ESCS lasts approximately 20 minutes and is videotaped for later scoring.

Deficits in joint attention skills were evident among two different groups of preschool children with autism (Mundy, Sigman, & Kasari, 1994; Mundy, Sigman, Ungerer, & Sherman, 1986). In the 1986 study, discriminant analyses comparing an autistic sample and MA-matched normal and mentally retarded samples indicated that joint attention behaviors, of all the types of nonverbal communication behaviors assessed, best discriminated the autistic children from the control groups. The autistic children displayed significant deficits on all the joint attention behaviors. Similar deficits were also shown in interactions with their caregivers (Sigman, Mundy, Sherman, & Ungerer, 1986).

Evidence of specific deficits in joint attention skills among autistic children has also been obtained in other studies (Van Engeland, Bodnar, & Bolhuis, 1985). Curcio (1978, p. 288) observed, in a sample of mute autistic children, a "striking absence" of protodeclaratives (i.e., pointing to indicate or show objects), but the use of protoimperatives (i.e., gestural requests for objects) was observed in all subjects. Wetherby and Prutting (1984) reported that 55% of the communicative acts observed in a small group of young autistic children were requests for objects or adult aid. However, no communicative acts to indicate were observed. Similar findings with somewhat older children and a matched control group of language-delayed children have been reported by Loveland and Landry (1986).

Thus, the evidence to date suggests that, in the preverbal phase of the development of joint attention skills, autistic children manifest specific deficits. In our research, young autistic children seemed quite capable of understanding object-related requests (such as "Give it to me") from an adult. However, when reference to objects or events was not goal-directed—the objective of the referential act was simply to share a focus of visual attention with another person—the autistic children were markedly impaired compared to mentally retarded children. The young autistic children seemed fairly able to understand other people as agents of action (someone to tickle me, someone to help me), but the children did not seem to understand other people as agents of contemplation; that is, they did not seem to realize that the other person had a perspective that could be shared.

With sufficient cognitive development, children with autism improve somewhat in terms of joint attention skills (Mundy et al., 1994), but whether older autistic children are able to intuit the spatial perspectives of others is unclear. Hobson (1984) reported that 7 autistic children, ranging in mental age from 6 to 9 years, were as able to determine a doll's visual perspective as were MA-matched subjects with Down syndrome. However, nonretarded 9- to 14-year-old children with autism had more difficulty reproducing the experimenter's image of a set of objects placed on a rotating circular table than did a matched control group (Yirmiya et al., 1994). Older children with autism clearly have limited awareness of the knowledge and intentions of others (see discussion in Chapter 42). Furthermore, even though older autistic children observed in a natural setting did show some use of pointing or indicating gestures, their total use of gesture was much less than that shown by normal or MA-matched controls with Down syndrome (Attwood, Frith, & Hermelin, 1988). Interestingly, the last two groups used gestures to express emotions. The autistic children never shared an emotional experience through gestural communication. This observation raises the question of whether autistic children distinguish among manifestations of emotion as shown in facial expressions and gestures.

Ability to Differentiate Facial Expressions

To assess the ability of nonverbal autistic children to differentiate facial expressions, the authors have used the familiarization-novelty test procedure developed for research with infants (Fantz, 1956), and have modified it to assess category-level knowledge. The autistic children were familiarized with a series of different faces, each showing the same expression. A slide series of photographed achromatic faces developed by Ekman and Friesen (1978) was used, and the two expressions tested were *happy* and *sad*. During the novelty preference trials, a new happy or sad face was paired with a new face with a neutral expression. If the child recognized the repeated facial expression and differentiated it from the novel expression, he or she was expected to look longer at faces with a neutral expression. Normal children, who were MA-matched with an autistic group, did show significant preferences for the face with a new expression. Autistic children did not show a significant preference for either the novel or the familiar facial expression, thereby giving no evidence that they differentiated between the facial expressions.

Young children with autism do not respond very much to individuals showing distress, fear, or discomfort. In a study of 90 children, normal and mentally retarded children were very attentive to adults posing these affects, but the children with autism attended much less and appeared much less concerned (Sigman, Kasari, Kwon, & Yirmiya, 1992). Similarly, children with autism responded differently from control children when they were praised after successfully completing a puzzle; the autistic children smiled less and turned less to their caregivers than did the control group. Even so, the autistic children had shown the same amount of pleasure as the control group after completing the task—before they were praised (Kasari, Sigman, Baumgartner, & Stipek, 1993). In fact, a few of the children with autism turned away or withdrew when they were praised, a behavior never shown by the control group. Thus, strong positive affect does not appear to attract the attention of many young autistic children any more than strong negative affect does.

Children with autism show individual differences in emotional responsiveness, and these differences are stable over time. Autistic children who seemed more concerned than other autistic children about the experimenter's distress during the first testing session were rated as more empathic to the experimenter's distress and anger 5 years later (Dissanayake, Sigman, & Kasari, 1996). This continuity existed independently of the children's level of intelligence. At the older age, the children with autism differentiated between the experimenter's pretense to be engaged in two telephone calls, one in which she acted angry and the other in which she was simply conversational. The children looked more at the angry experimenter and were rated as more empathic than when the experimenter remained neutral.

Older children with autism are also somewhat less skillful than control subjects at identifying affects correctly from photographs, drawings, and videotapes, although differences between groups are small when the groups have equivalent language abilities (Braverman, Fein, Lucci, & Waterhouse, 1989; Hobson, 1986a, 1986b; Ozonoff, Pennington, & Rogers, 1989; Prior, Dahlstrom, & Squires, 1990). Hobson (1986a, 1986b, 1993) has provided the strongest evidence that children with autism are less able to match particular components of particular feeling (facial expression, vocalization, gesture, and context). In line with this evidence, even autistic children of normal intelligence have more difficulty than controls

in identifying affects accurately, particularly when these are presented within a social situation (MacDonald et al., 1989; Ozonoff, Pennington, & Rogers, 1991). Nonretarded children with autism performed less well than controls on labeling the emotion shown by a child in a televised vignette, assuming the role of the televised child, and responding with empathy to this child (Yirmiya et al., 1992). Moreover, these children had difficulty talking about their own experiences of pride and embarrassment. They required more time and more prompts, their responses were more tentative and "scripted," and they displayed limited understanding of the salience of others in embarrassing situations (Capps, Yirmiya, & Sigman, 1992).

Social Interactions, Expressions of Emotions, and Attachment

On the basis of the foregoing results and in line with the popular conceptions about autism, one could hypothesize that autistic children are deviant whenever situations involve other people. Examination of social interactions in a variety of settings suggests, however, that there are ways in which autistic children behave more normally. First, children with autism are more responsive to direct bids for social engagement than is often appreciated. In situations in which parents or other adults initiate social interaction or maintain proximity, children with autism are as socially involved as mentally retarded and normal children of the same mental age. However, children with autism initiate social interactions much less than nonautistic children do, so that the groups differ when situations are unstructured (Kasari, Sigman, & Yirmiya, 1993).

Second, the facial expressions of children with autism do not seem to differ from those of other children in many situations. During the administration of the Early Social Communication Scale (described above), the children with autism showed mostly positive emotions, as did the other children tested (Yirmiya, Kasari, Sigman, & Mundy, 1989). They differed only in displaying somewhat more neutral facial expressions and some ambiguous emotions never shown by the other children. The most marked difference, also reported by other investigators (Dawson, Hill, Spencer, Galpert, & Watson, 1990; Snow, Hertzig, & Shapiro, 1987), was in the integration of affect and attention. Unlike the mentally retarded and control children who smiled when engaging in joint attention, the children with autism were less likely to show positive emotions during their infrequent engagements in joint attention (Kasari, Sigman, Mundy, & Yirmiya, 1990). Parents report that their children with autism show somewhat more negative and less positive emotion than control children (Capps, Kasari, Yirmiya, & Sigman, 1993), but there is little evidence that autism involves the "absence of emotional reactions" described in *DSM-III-R* (American Psychiatric Association, 1987, p. 35).

Third, children with autism are similar to other children in their attachment responses. Much of the clinical literature suggests that children with autism are unable to form attachments to others; numerous empirical studies, however, have shown that the reactions of children with autism to separation from and reunion with their caregivers are very similar to those shown by children of the same mental and chronological age (Dissanayake & Crossley, 1996a, 1996b; Rogers, Ozonoff, & Maslin-Cole, 1991, 1993; Shapiro, Sherman, Calamari, & Koch, 1987; Sigman & Mundy, 1989; Sigman & Ungerer, 1984a). Autistic children react to their caregiver's departure and direct more social behavior to the caregiver than to a stranger, and a majority increase their proximity-seeking behavior after separation from the caregiver. Many children with autism also appear to have secure attachments to their caregivers (Capps, Sigman, & Mundy, 1994; Rogers et al., 1991; Shapiro et al., 1987). The attachment classification was verified in one study where, in contrast to insecurely attached children, securely attached children initiated more social interactions with their mothers, who were more sensitive to their cues in a play session conducted independently of the attachment paradigm (Capps et al., 1994).

Knowledge of the Self

In the previous sections, we have discussed autistic children's knowledge of objects and of other people. Normal children also acquire some awareness of themselves as they develop cognitively and socially. Capacity for self-recognition, ability to differentiate the self from others, and awareness of the viewpoint of others may be precursors for the development of self-knowledge (Baldwin, 1897; Cohen, 1980; Rutter, 1983). Young autistic children are capable of self-recognition, as measured by their differential behaviors toward their mirror images when rouge was placed on their noses and created a contrast to their untransformed images (Neuman & Hill, 1978; Spiker & Ricks, 1984). They also seem able to distinguish themselves from others. However, their limited knowledge of others is a bar to understanding themselves. As Cohen has stated, "The lack of comprehension of the feelings and people in his life is the mirror image of the child's inability to form a stable, internal representation of the connectedness between his own inner states or a sense of himself as the locus of the organization of initiative, feelings, and thoughts" (1980, p. 390).

Nonretarded adolescents with autism are capable of more social understanding and are also able to compare themselves to others. Capps, Sigman, and Yirmiya (1995) found that autistic adolescents with normal intelligence considered themselves to be less competent socially and physically and to have lower overall self-worth than was true for control subjects. Only in the cognitive domain did they view themselves as being equally competent as the normal group, an accurate judgment because the two groups were matched on intelligence. More striking, the more able the adolescents were in terms of their intelligence, reported social adjustment, and ability to understand others, the more negatively they viewed themselves. Thus, a consequence of the strengths that accompany high intelligence in this group is that the adolescents are able to recognize some of their own shortcomings.

INTERPRETATION OF RESEARCH RESULTS

This review of research has attempted to specify the deficits of autistic children, particularly in regard to the concepts and skills that normally develop in the early years of life. As in the areas of perception and language, the cognitive deficits of autistic children are not evident across the entire gamut of cognitive functions. In terms of processing abilities, the autistic child does not have difficulty in learning discriminations or remembering material. The critical dysfunction in cognitive processing appears to be in deriving the abstract information necessary for sequencing material and in transforming this information into symbolic representations. Similarly, in terms of cognitive concepts, the autistic child appears to be able to learn about the functions of objects. Only when the child has to represent these functions in symbols does the cognitive deficiency appear.

On the basis of current research findings, the authors conclude that the kinds of intelligence affected in the autistic child are those most closely tied to social influences and those that require symbolic representation. Autistic children seem tremendously impaired in their ability to learn *from* other people and *about* other people. The deficits in symbol development may be related to this failure to learn from the social environment, in that symbol use may develop primarily as a function of social interactions (Werner & Kaplan, 1963). Thus, the limitation in abstract thought among autistic children may attest to the importance of social interchange for the development of symbolic concepts in all children. Alternatively, both social and symbolic knowledge may depend on a metarepresentational ability to perceive one's own views of actions from a different perspective.

In terms of social interchanges, individuals with autism are most profoundly impaired in those interactions that require knowledge of other people. If very simple social interchange is observed, autistic children are not so deficient. Social interchange requires social knowledge very early in a child's life. Furthermore, the kind of social knowledge that seems impaired is the most critical of all—the child's recognition that other people have thoughts and feelings of their own. In early infancy, this awareness requires only that a child recognize another individual's viewpoint, in the literal sense. Later in life, the impairment appears to be manifested in an inability to take into account the information that another person might have access to in particular situations. For the normal child, gestures and facial expressions may be meaningful because the child understands that these are manifestations of another person's feelings or state of mind. If the autistic child is unable to attribute intentions or emotional experiences to others, then gestures and facial expressions have little significance.

The origin of this deficit in social cognitive awareness remains an issue. One view is that the abnormalities stem from a cognitive dysfunction (Rutter, 1983). Most social and symbolic awareness requires a child to integrate two kinds of information simultaneously. For example, in pointing to an object, the child is able to see the object but has to keep in mind the other person with whom he or she is sharing this sight. Learning about other people is also difficult because the contingencies that must be learned are often initiated by others. The autistic child may associate an incorrect causal direction of effect or may have no idea which percepts to link. The cognitive requirements of social and symbolic learning may overload the information-processing capacities of the autistic child.

Another possible basis for the deficit in knowledge of others is a disorder in the affective system (Fein et al., 1984; Hermelin & O'-Connor, 1985; Hobson, 1989). Kanner's first description of autistic children was that they "have come into the world with innate inability to form the usual, biologically provided affective contact with people" (Kanner, 1943, p. 250). Hobson (1993) has suggested that only through empathic responsiveness do children come to be involved in personal relationships and, thereby, arrive at concepts of other people and of themselves. In this context, one could hypothesize that the autistic child does not experience the sort of empathic emotional responses that enable the normal child to know about other people.

Distinctions among etiological factors such as these are difficult to draw. Deficiencies in autistic children are evident in the kinds of knowledge about the world and other people that normal infants acquire by the age of 8 to 18 months. We do not know whether this knowledge derives from cognitive capacities or from emotional awareness in the normal infant. In fact, these forms of feelings and knowing may be inseparable. For this reason, a more useful approach may be to view the dysfunction in autism as a deficit in both the cognitive and affective domains. In our opinion, the investigation of the autistic child must continue to describe developing abilities and disabilities as specifically as possible, across a variety of settings and tasks, and in contrast to those of other children of similar developmental levels. Only in this way will we be able to understand the viewpoint of autistic children so that we can help them understand the viewpoint of others.

Cross-References

Acquisition of other developmental skills is addressed in Chapters 8 through 10. Psychological assessment is described in Chapter 19. Chapter 40 is on neuropsychology, and Chapter 41 discusses theory of mind in autism.

REFERENCES

American Psychiatric Association. (1987). *Diagnostic and statistical manual for mental disorders* (3rd ed., rev.). Washington, DC: Author.

Attwood, A., Frith, U., & Hermelin, B. (1988). The understanding of interpersonal gestures by autistic and Down syndrome children. *Journal of Autism and Developmental Disorders, 18,* 241–257.

Baillargeon, R. (1994). How do infants learn about the physical world? *Current Directions in Psychological Science, 3,* 133–140.

Baldwin, J.M. (1897). *Social and ethical interpretations in mental development.* New York: Macmillan.

Baltaxe, C.A., & Simmons, J.Q. (1975). Language in childhood psychosis: A review. *Journal of Speech and Hearing Disorders, 40,* 439–458.

Baron-Cohen, S. (1987). Autism and symbolic play. *British Journal of Developmental Psychology, 5,* 139–148.

Barresi, T., & Moore, C. (1996). Intentional relations and social understanding. *Behavioral and Brain Sciences, 19,* 107–154.

Bartak, L., Rutter, M., & Cox, A. (1975). Comparative study of infantile autism and specific developmental receptive language disorder: I. The children. *British Journal of Psychiatry, 126,* 127–145.

Bates, E., Benign, L., Bretherton, I., Camaioni, L., & Volterra, V. (1979). Cognition and communication from nine to thirteen months: Corre-lational findings. In E. Bates (Ed.), *The emergence of symbols: Cognition and communication in infancy* (pp. 69–140). New York: Academic Press.

Bettelheim, B. (1967). *The empty fortress: Infantile autism and the birth of the self.* New York: Free Press.

Bowlby, J. (1969). *Attachment and loss: Vol. 1. Attachment.* Harmondsworth, Middlesex, England: Penguin.

Braverman, M., Fein, D., Lucci, D., & Waterhouse, L. (1989). Affect comprehension in children with pervasive developmental disorders. *Journal of Autism and Developmental Disorders, 19,* 301–315.

Bryson, S.E. (1983). Interference effects in autistic children: Evidence for the comprehension of single stimuli. *Journal of Abnormal Psychology, 2,* 250–254.

Capps, L., Kasari, C., Yirmiya, N., & Sigman, M. (1993). Parental perception of emotional expressiveness in children with autism. *Journal of Consulting and Clinical Psychology, 61,* 475–484.

Capps, L., Sigman, M., & Mundy, P. (1994). Attachment security in children with autism. *Development and Psychopathology, 6,* 249–261.

Capps, L., Sigman, M., & Yirmiya, N. (1995). Self-competence and emotional understanding in high-functioning children with autism. *Development and Psychopathology, 7,* 137–149.

Capps, L., Yirmiya, N., & Sigman, M. (1992). Understanding of simple and complex emotions in non-retarded children with autism. *Journal of Child Psychology and Psychiatry, 33,* 1169–1182.

Charlop, M.H., & Carlson, J. (1983). Reversal and nonreversal shifts in autistic children. *Journal of Experimental Child Psychology, 36,* 56–57.

Charman, T., & Baron-Cohen, S. (1994). Another look at imitation in autism. *Development and Psychopathology, 6,* 403–413.

Churchill, D.W. (1972). The relation of infantile autism and early childhood schizophrenia to developmental language disorders of childhood. *Journal of Autism and Childhood Schizophrenia, 2,* 182–197.

Cohen, D.J. (1980). The pathology of the self in primary childhood autism and Gilles de la Tourette Syndrome. *Psychiatric Clinics of North America, 3,* 383–402.

Curcio, F. (1978). Sensorimotor functioning and communication in mute autistic children. *Journal of Autism and Childhood Schizophrenia, 8,* 282–292.

Dawson, G., & Adams, A. (1984). Imitation and social responsiveness in autistic children.

Journal of Abnormal Child Psychology, 12, 209–225.

Dawson, G., Hill, D., Spencer, A., Galpert, L., & Watson, L. (1990). Affective exchanges between young autistic children and their mothers. *Journal of Abnormal Child Psychology, 18,* 335–345.

Decarie, T.G. (1967). *Intelligence and affectivity in early childhood.* New York: International Universities Press.

DeMyer, M.K., Alpern, G.D., Barton, S., DeMyer, W.E., Churchill, D.W., Hingtgen, J.N., Bryson, C.Q., Pointius, W., & Kimberlin, C. (1972). Imitation in autistic, early schizophrenia, and non-psychotic subnormal children. *Journal of Autism and Childhood Schizophrenia, 2,* 264–287.

DeMyer, M.K., Barton, S., Alpern, G., Kimberlin, C., Allen, J., Yang, E., & Steele, R. (1974). The measured intelligence of autistic children. *Journal of Autism and Childhood Schizophrenia, 4,* 42–60.

DeMyer, M.K., Hingtgen, J.N., & Jackson, R.K. (1981). Infantile autism reviewed: A decade of research. *Schizophrenia Bulletin, 7,* 701–708.

Dissanayake, C., & Crossley, S.A. (1996a). Proximity and sociable behaviors in autism: Evidence for attachment. *Journal of Child Psychology and Psychiatry and Allied Disciplines, 37,* 149–156.

Dissanayake, C., & Crossley, S.A. (1996b). *Autistic children's responses to separation and reunion with their mothers.* Manuscript submitted for publication.

Dissanayake, C., Sigman, M.D., & Kasari, C. (1996). Long-term stability of individual differences in the emotional responsiveness of children with autism. *Journal of Child Psychology and Psychiatry and Allied Disciplines, 77,* 461–467.

Ekman, P., & Friesen, W.V. (1978). *Slides of facial expression.* Palo Alto, CA: Consulting Psychologists Press.

Escalona, S., & Corman, H. (1969). *Albert Einstein scales of sensorimotor development.* Unpublished manuscript.

Fantz, R.A. (1956). A method for studying early visual development. *Perceptual and Motor Skills, 6,* 13–15.

Fein, D., Humes, M., Kaplan, I., Lucci, D., & Waterhouse, L. (1984). The question of left hemisphere dysfunction in infantile autism. *Psychological Bulletin, 95,* 258–281.

Fein, D., Tinder, P., & Waterhouse, L. (1979). Stimulus generalization in autistic and normal children. *Journal of Child Psychology and Psychiatry, 20,* 325–355.

Field, T. (1982). Individual differences in the expressivity of neonates and young infants. In R.S. Feldman (Ed.), *Development of nonverbal behavior in children* (pp. 279–298). New York: Springer.

Freeman, B.J., & Ritvo, E.R. (1976). Cognitive assessment. In E.R. Ritvo, B.J. Freeman, E.M. Ornitz, & P.E. Tanguay (Eds.), *Autism: Diagnosis, current research and management* (pp. 27–33). New York: Spectrum.

Frith, U. (1970). Studies in pattern detection in normal and autistic children: 1. Immediate recall of auditory sequences. *Journal of Abnormal Psychology, 76,* 413–420.

Frith, U. (1971). Spontaneous patterns produced by autistic, normal, and subnormal children. In M. Rutter (Ed.), *Infantile autism: Concepts, characteristics, and treatment* (pp. 113–131). London: Churchill-Livingstone.

Frith, U. (1972). Cognitive mechanisms in autism: Experiments with color and tone sequence production. *Journal of Autism and Childhood Schizophrenia, 2,* 160–173.

Fyffe, C., & Prior, M.R. (1978). Evidence for language recoding in autistic, mentally retarded, and normal children: A re-examination. *British Journal of Psychology, 69,* 393–402.

Gillies, S. (1965). Some abilities of psychotic children and subnormal children. *Journal of Mental Deficiency Research, 9,* 89–101.

Heimann, M., Ulstadius, E., Dahlgren, S.O., & Gillberg, C. (1992). Imitation in autism: A preliminary research note. *Behavioral Neurology, 5,* 219–227.

Hermelin, B., & O'Connor, N. (1970). *Psychological experiments with autistic children.* New York: Pergamon Press.

Hermelin, B., & O'Connor, N. (1985). The logico-affective disorder in autism. In E. Schopler & G.B. Mesibov (Eds.), *Communication problems in autism* (pp. 283–310). New York: Plenum Press.

Hertzig, M.E., Snow, M.E., & Sherman, M. (1989). Affect and cognition in autism. *Journal of the American Academy of Child and Adolescent Psychiatry, 28,* 195–199.

Hobson, R.P. (1984). Early childhood autism and the question of egocentrism. *Journal of Autism and Developmental Disorders, 14,* 85–104.

Hobson, R.P. (1986a). The autistic child's appraisal of expressions of emotion. *Journal of Child Psychology and Psychiatry, 27,* 321–342.

Hobson, R.P. (1986b). The autistic child's appraisal of expression of emotion: A further study. *Journal of Child Psychology and Psychiatry, 27,* 671–680.

Hobson, R.P. (1989). Beyond cognition: A theory of autism. In G. Dawson (Ed.), *Nature, diagnosis and treatment* (pp. 22–48). New York: Guilford Press.

Hobson, R.P. (1993). *Autism and the development of mind.* Hillsdale, NJ: Erlbaum.

Inhelder, B., Lezine, I., Sinclair, H., & Stambak, M. (1972). Les debuts de la fonction symbolique. *Archives de Psychologie, 41,* 187–243.

Jones, V., & Prior, M.P. (1985). Motor imitation abilities and neurological signs in autistic children. *Journal of Autism and Developmental Disorders, 15,* 37–46.

Kanner, L. (1943). Autistic disturbances of affective contact. *Nervous Child, 2,* 217–250.

Kanner, L. (1949). Problems of nosology and psychodynamics of early infantile autism. *American Journal of Orthopsychiatry, 19,* 416–426.

Kasari, C., Sigman, M.D., Baumgartner, P., & Stipek, D.J. (1993a). Pride and mastery in children with autism. *Journal of Child Psychology and Psychiatry, 34,* 353–362.

Kasari, C., Sigman, M., Mundy, P., & Yirmiya, N. (1990). Affective sharing in the context of joint attention interactions of normal, autistic, and mentally retarded children. *Journal of Autism and Developmental Disorders, 20,* 87–100.

Kasari, C., Sigman, M., & Yirmiya, N. (1993). Focused and social attention of autistic children in interactions with familiar and unfamiliar adults: A comparison of autistic, mentally retarded, and normal children. *Development and Psychopathology, 5,* 403–414.

Klinnert, M.P., Campos, J.J., Sorce, J.F., Emde, R.N., & Svejda, M. (1982). Emotions as behavior regulators: Social referencing in infancy. In R. Plutchik & H. Kellerman (Eds.), *The emotions* (Vol. 2). New York: Academic Press.

Kopp, C.B., Sigman, M., & Parmelee, A.H. (1973). Ordinality and sensorimotor series. *Child Development, 44,* 821.

Kopp, C.B., Sigman, M., & Parmelee, A.H. (1974). Longitudinal study of sensorimotor development. *Developmental Psychology, 10,* 687–695.

La Barbara, J.D., Izard, C.E., Vietze, P., & Parisi, S.A. (1976). Four- and six-month-old infants' visual responses to joy, anger, and neutral expressions. *Child Development, 47,* 535–538.

Lancy, D.F., & Goldstein, G.I. (1982). The use of nonverbal Piagetian tasks to assess the cognitive development of autistic children. *Child Development, 53,* 1233–1241.

Leslie, A.M. (1985). Pretense and representation: The origins of "theory of mind." *Psychological Review, 94,* 412–426.

Lewis, V., & Boucher, J. (1988). Spontaneous, instructed, and elicited play in relatively able autistic children. *British Journal of Developmental Psychology, 6,* 325–339.

Lockyer, L., & Rutter, M. (1970). A five- to fifteen-year follow-up study of infantile psychosis: 4. Patterns of cognitive ability. *British Journal of Social and Clinical Psychology, 9,* 152–163.

Loveland, K., & Landry, S. (1986). Joint attention and language in autism and developmental language delay. *Journal of Autism and Developmental Disorders, 16,* 335–349.

Loveland, K., Tunali-Kotoski, B., Pearson, D.A., Brelsford, K.A., Ortegon, J., & Chen, R. (1994). Imitations and expression of facial affect in autism. *Development and Psychopathology, 6,* 433–444.

MacDonald, H., Rutter, M., Howlin, P., Rios, P., LeConteur, A., Evered, C., & Folstein, S. (1989). Recognition and expression of emotional cues by autistic and normal adults. *Journal of Child Psychology and Psychiatry, 30,* 865–877.

Maltz, A. (1981). Comparison of cognitive deficits among autistic and retarded children on the Arthur Adaptation of the Leiter International Performance Scales. *Journal of Autism and Developmental Disorders, 11,* 413–426.

McDonald, M.A., Mundy, P., Kasari, C., & Sigman, M. (1989). Psychometric scatter in retarded, autistic preschoolers as measured by the Cattell. *Journal of Child Psychology and Psychiatry, 4,* 599–684.

McFarlane, A. (1977). *The psychology of childbirth.* Cambridge, MA: Harvard University Press.

Meltzoff, A.N., & Gopnik, A. (1993). The role of imitation in understanding persons and developing a theory of mind. In S. Baron-Cohen, H. Tager-Flusberg, & D.J. Cohen (Eds.), *Understanding other minds* (pp. 335–366). New York: Oxford University Press.

Minshew, N.J., Goldstein, G., Muenz, L.R., & Payton, J.B. (1992). Neuropsychological functioning in nonmentally retarded autistic individuals. *Journal of Clinical and Experimental Neuropsychology, 14,* 749–761.

Moore, M., & Meltzoff, A.N. (1978). Object permanence, imitation, and language development: Toward a neo-Piagetian perspective of cognitive and communicative development. In F.D. Minifie & L.L. Lloyd (Eds.), *Communicative and cognitive abilities: Early behavioral assessment.* Baltimore: University Park Press.

Mundy, P., Sigman, M., & Kasari, C. (1994). Joint attention, developmental level, and symptom presentation in autism. *Development and Psychopathology, 6,* 389–401.

Mundy, P., Sigman, M., Ungerer, J.A., & Sherman, T. (1986). Defining the deficits of autism: The contribution of nonverbal communication measures. *Journal of Child Psychology and Psychiatry, 27,* 657–669.

Mundy, P., Sigman, M., Ungerer, J.A., & Sherman, T. (1987). Nonverbal communication and play correlates of language development in autistic children. *Journal of Autism and Developmental Disorders, 17,* 349–364.

Neuman, C.J., & Hill, S.D. (1978). Self-recognition and stimulus preference in autistic children. *Developmental Psychology, 11,* 571–578.

Nicolich, L. (1977). Beyond sensorimotor intelligence. *Merrill-Palmer Quarterly, 23,* 89–99.

Ohta, M. (1987). Cognitive disorders of infantile autism: A study of employing the WISC, spatial relationship conceptualization and gesture imitations. *Journal of Autism and Developmental Disorders, 17,* 45–62.

Ornitz, E.M., Guthrie, D., & Farley, A.H. (1977). Early development of autistic children. *Journal of Autism and Childhood Schizophrenia, 7,* 207–229.

Ornitz, E.M., & Ritvo, E. (1976). The syndrome of autism: A critical review. *American Journal of Psychiatry, 133,* 609–621.

Ozonoff, S., Pennington, B.F., & Rogers, S.J. (1989). Are there emotion perception deficits in young autistic children? *Journal of Child Psychology and Psychiatry, 51,* 343–361.

Ozonoff, S., Pennington, B.F., & Rogers, S.J. (1991). Executive function deficits in high-functioning autistic individuals: Relationship to theory of mind. *Journal of Child Psychology and Psychiatry, 32,* 1081–1105.

Piaget, J. (1952). *The origins of intelligence in children.* New York: Norton.

Piaget, J. (1962). *Play, dreams, and imitation in children.* New York: Norton.

Prior, M. (1977). Conditional matching learning set in autistic children. *Journal of Child Psychology and Psychiatry, 18,* 183–189.

Prior, M. (1979). Cognitive abilities and disabilities in infantile autism: A review. *Journal of Abnormal Child Psychology, 7,* 357–380.

Prior, M. (1984). Developing concepts of childhood autism: The influence of experimental cognitive research. *Journal of Consulting and Clinical Psychology, 52,* 4–17.

Prior, M., & Chen, C.S. (1975). Learning set acquisition in autistic children. *Journal of Abnormal Psychology, 84,* 701–708.

Prior, M., Dahlstrom, D., & Squires, T. (1990). Autistic children's knowledge of thinking and feeling states in other people. *Journal of Child Psychology and Psychiatry, 31,* 587–601.

Prior, M., & Gajzago, C. (1974). Recognition of autism. *Medical Journal of Australia, 8,* 183.

Prior, M., & McGillivray, J. (1980). The performance of autistic children on three learning set tasks. *Journal of Child Psychology and Psychiatry, 21,* 313–324.

Ricciuti, H.N. (1965). Object grouping and selective ordering behavior in infants 12 to 24 months old. *Merrill-Palmer Quarterly, 11,* 129–148.

Riquet, C.B., Taylor, N.D., Benroya, S., & Klein, L.S. (1981). Symbolic play in autistic, Down's, and normal children of equivalent mental age. *Journal of Autism and Developmental Disorders, 11,* 439–448.

Rogers, S.J., & McEvoy, R.E. (1993, March 15). *Praxis in high-functioning persons with autism.* Paper presented at the biennial meeting of the Society for Research in Child Development, New Orleans, LA.

Rogers, S.J., Ozonoff, S., & Maslin-Cole, C. (1991). A comparative study of attachment behavior in young children with autism or other psychiatric disorders. *Journal of the American Academy of Child and Adolescent Psychiatry, 30,* 483–488.

Rogers, S.J., Ozonoff, S., & Maslin-Cole, C. (1993). Developmental aspects of attachment behavior in young children with pervasive developmental disorders. *Journal of the American Academy of Child and Adolescent Psychiatry, 32,* 1274–1282.

Rosch, E. (1973). On the internal structure of perceptual and semantic categories. In T. Moore (Ed.), *Cognitive development and the acquisition of language* (pp. 111–144). New York: Academic Press.

Rutter, M. (1983). Cognitive deficits in the pathogenesis of autism. *Journal of Child Psychology and Psychiatry, 24,* 513–531.

Rutter, M., Bartak, L., & Newman, S. (1971). Autism: A central disorder of cognition and language? In M. Rutter (Ed.), *Infantile autism: Concepts, characteristics, and treatment* (pp. 148–171). London: Churchill-Livingstone.

Scaife, M., & Bruner, J.S. (1975). The capacity for joint visual attention in the infant. *Nature, 253,* 259–266.

Schreibman, L., Koegel, R.L., Charlop, M.H., & Egal, A.L. (1982). Autism. In A.S. Bellak, M. Hersan, & A.G. Kazdin (Eds.), *International handbook of behavior modification and therapy* (pp. 891–915). New York: Plenum Press.

Seibert, J.M., & Hogan, A.E. (1982). *Procedures manual for the Early Social-Communication*

Scales. Unpublished manuscript, University of Miami, Mailman Center for Child Development.

Shapiro, T., Sherman, M., Calamari, G., & Koch, D. (1987). Attachment in autism and other developmental disorders. *Journal of the American Academy of Child and Adolescent Psychiatry, 226,* 485–590.

Shulman, C., Yirmiya, N., & Greenbaum, C.W. (1995). From categorization to classification: A comparison among individuals with autism, mental retardation and normal development. *Journal of Abnormal Psychology, 104,* 601–609.

Sigman, M., Kasari, C., Kwon, J.H., & Yirmiya, N. (1992). Responses to the negative emotions of others by autistic, mentally retarded, and normal children. *Child Development, 63,* 796–807.

Sigman, M., & Mundy, P. (1989). Social attachments in autistic children. *Journal of the American Academy of Child and Adolescent Psychiatry, 28,* 74–81.

Sigman, M., Mundy, P., Sherman, T., & Ungerer, J.A. (1986). Social interactions of autistic mentally retarded, and normal children and their caregivers. *Journal of Child Psychology and Psychiatry, 27,* 647–656.

Sigman, M., & Ungerer, J. (1981). Sensorimotor skills and language comprehension in autistic children. *Journal of Abnormal Child Psychology, 9,* 149–165.

Sigman, M., & Ungerer, J.A. (1984a). Attachment behaviors in autistic children. *Journal of Autism and Developmental Disorders, 14,* 231–244.

Sigman, M., & Ungerer, J.A. (1984b). Cognitive and language skills in autistic, mentally retarded, and normal children. *Developmental Psychology, 20,* 293–302.

Sinclair, H. (1970). The transition from sensorimotor behavior to symbolic activity. *Interchange, 1,* 119–125.

Slotnick, L. (1983, April). *Spontaneous and provoked sorting behavior among autistic and normal children.* Paper presented at the biennial meeting of the Society for Research in Child Development, Detroit, Michigan.

Smith, I.M., & Bryson, S.E. (1994). Imitation and action in autism: A critical review. *Psychological Bulletin, 116,* 259–273.

Snow, M.E., Hertzig, M.E., & Shapiro, T. (1987). Expression of emotion in young autistic, mentally retarded and normal children and their caregivers. *Journal of the American Academy of Child and Adolescent Psychiatry, 26,* 836–838.

Spiker, D., & Ricks, M. (1984). Visual self-recognition in autistic children: Developmen-

tal relationships. *Child Development, 55,* 214–225.

Stone, W.L., Lemanck, K.L., Fishel, P.T., Fernandez, M.C., & Altemeier, W.A. (1990). Play and imitation skills in the diagnosis of autism in young children. *Pediatrics, 86,* 267–272.

Tager-Flusberg, H. (1981). On the nature of linguistic functioning in early infantile autism. *Journal of Autism and Developmental Disorders, 11,* 45–56.

Tubbs, V.K. (1966). Types of linguistic disability in psychotic children. *Journal of Mental Deficiency Research, 10,* 230–240.

Tymchuk, A., Simmons, J., & Neafsey, S. (1977). Intellectual characteristics of adolescent childhood psychotics with high verbal ability. *Journal of Mental Deficiency Research, 21,* 133–138.

Ungerer, J.A., & Sigman, M. (1981). Symbolic play and language comprehension in autistic children. *Journal of the American Academy of Child Psychiatry, 20,* 318–338.

Ungerer, J.A., & Sigman, M. (1987). Categorization skills and language development in autistic children. *Journal of Autism and Developmental Disorders, 17,* 3–16.

Ungerer, J.A., Zelazo, P.R., Kearsley, R.B., & O'Leary, K. (1981). Developmental changes in the representation of objects in symbolic play from 18 to 34 months of age. *Child Development, 52,* 186–195.

Uzgiris, I.C., & Hunt, J. McV. (1975). *Assessment in infancy.* Urbana: University of Illinois Press.

van Engeland, H., Bodnar, F.A., & Bolhuis, G. (1985). Some qualitative aspects of the social behavior of autistic children: An ethological approach. *Journal of Child Psychology and Psychiatry, 26,* 879–893.

Werner, H., & Kaplan, S. (1963). *Symbol formation.* New York: John Wiley & Sons.

Wetherby, A.M., & Prutting, C.A. (1984). Profiles of communicative and cognitive-social abilities in autistic children. *Journal of Speech and Hearing Research, 27,* 367–377.

Wing, L. (1978). Social, behavioral, and cognitive characteristics: An epidemiological approach. In M. Rutter & E. Schopler (Eds.), *Autism: A reappraisal of concepts and treatments* (pp. 27–45). New York: Plenum Press.

Wing, L., & Gould, J. (1979). Severe impairments of social interaction and associated abnormalities in children: Epidemiology and classification. *Journal of Autism and Developmental Disorders, 9,* 11–29.

Wing, L., Gould, J., Yeates, S.R., & Brierly, L.M. (1977). Symbolic play in severely mentally retarded and autistic children. *Journal of Child Psychology and Psychiatry, 18,* 167–178.

Wolf, E., Wenar, C., & Ruttenberg, B. (1972). A comparison of personality variables in autistic and mentally retarded children. *Journal of Autism and Childhood Schizophrenia, 2,* 92–108.

Wolff, P.H. (1969). The natural history of crying and other vocalizations in early infancy. In B.M. Foss (Ed.), *Determinants of infant behavior* (Vol. 4). London: Methuen.

Yirmiya, N., Kasari, C., Sigman, M., & Mundy, P. (1989). Facial expressions of affect in autistic, mentally retarded and normal children. *Journal of Child Psychology and Psychiatry, 30,* 725–735.

Yirmiya, N., & Shulman, C. (1996). Conservaton, seriation, and theory of mind abilities in individuals with autism, mental retardation, and normally developing children. *Child Development, 67,* 2045–2059.

Yirmiya, N., Sigman, M.D., Kasari, C., & Mundy, P. (1992). Empathy and cognition in high-functioning children with autism. *Child Development, 63,* 150–160.

Yirmiya, N., Sigman, M., & Zacks, D. (1994). Perceptual perspective-taking and seriation abilities in high-functioning children with autism. *Development and Psychopathology, 6,* 263–272.

Young-Browne, G., Rosenfeld, H.M., & Horowitz, F.D. (1977). Infant discrimination of facial expressions. *Child Development, 48,* 555–562.

CHAPTER 12

Autism in Infancy and Early Childhood

WENDY L. STONE

The notion that autism has its origins early in life is not new. In the first clinical description of autism, Leo Kanner (1943) proposed that, from early infancy, children with autism have an innate inability to form social relationships. Many parents of children with autism report an early onset of symptoms. Several studies based on parental report have identified the average age of symptom onset as between 16 and 20 months (Short & Schopler, 1988; Spitzer & Siegel, 1990; Volkmar, Cohen, Hoshino, Rende, & Paul, 1988). Moreover, onset in the children studied was reported to occur within the first year of life for 31% to 55% and within the first 2 years of life for 75% to 88% (DeMyer, 1979; Short & Schopler, 1988; Volkmar, Stier, & Cohen, 1985).

Despite autism's early onset, there have been relatively few empirical studies of the early features of autism. Research in this area has the potential to increase the conceptual and theoretical understanding of autism and to guide the development of early intervention services. In recent years, interest in identifying the manifestations of autism at young ages has increased, perhaps reflecting several political and scientific trends:

1. The availability of federal funding for early intervention programs has given children under 3 years old with disabilities increased access to services.
2. The success of specialized early intervention programs serving young children with autism (e.g., Lovaas, 1987; Rogers & Lewis, 1989; Strain, Hoyson, & Jamieson, 1985) has ignited interest in early identification and diagnosis.
3. The growth of the field of developmental psychopathology has led to increased recognition that the clinical expression of a disorder can change with age and maturation (Lewis & Miller, 1990; Sroufe & Rutter, 1984).

This chapter reviews the literature on the behavioral characteristics of autism in infancy and in early childhood. For the purpose of discussion, the period of infancy will be considered to extend from birth through 2 years, and early childhood will include the years from age 3 to approximately age 6.

INFANCY

One reason for the paucity of information about young children with autism is that children often do not receive a definitive diagnosis of autism until the age of 4 to 4½ years (Siegel, Pliner, Eschler, & Elliott, 1988; Stone & Rosenbaum, 1988). Formal diagnosis before the age of 2 years is difficult because diagnostic criteria require a certain level of cognitive and language development before particular deficiencies (e.g., peer relationship problems, language abnormalities) become apparent. However, a pattern of distinct social and communicative impairments may be observable within the first 2 years of life, even if formal diagnostic requirements are not met.

The preparation of this chapter was supported in part by NIMH Grant R29 MH50620.

Several different approaches have been used in attempts to circumvent the problem of studying children who are not yet diagnosed. The most common strategy has been to obtain retrospective reports from parents, through the use of questionnaires or interviews. Although this strategy affords a window into early infant behaviors, it is also associated with known liabilities related to distortions and inaccuracies of recall (Hart, Bax, & Jenkins, 1978; Mednick & Shaffer, 1963; Robbins, 1963). The study of home movies and videotapes taken of the child during infancy has received increasing attention in recent years. This methodology facilitates relatively objective behavioral ratings, but it is limited by the variability in content and quality from one home to another. Massie (1975, 1978) was the first to describe the systematic study of home movies of children later diagnosed as autistic or psychotic. Although Massie's case descriptions provide rich examples of disturbed interactions, in most cases the parents' behavior toward the infant was described as inappropriate from the child's first weeks of life. As a consequence, it is impossible to determine the extent to which the infants' behaviors reflected disturbed patterns of parenting or innate constitutional differences. Other studies have employed videotapes obtained serendiptiously through participation in unrelated research projects.

A more optimal approach toward studying the manifestation of autism in infancy is to design prospective studies that enable the collection of contemporaneous information over time and offer the opportunity to track the development of symptomatology. However, because of the low incidence of autism, this approach is feasible only for infants who are at high risk for developing autism, such as those with autistic siblings or those demonstrating some early features of the disorder.

In view of the scant empirical literature on infants with autism, case reports as well as controlled studies will be reviewed here. Clinical descriptions, which include case studies and other descriptive research in which comparison groups are not employed, are presented first, followed by studies that have included control groups. The number of studies employing developmentally comparable controls is quite low.

Clinical Descriptions

Case Studies

Kanner (1943) provided the first case descriptions of autism. Two specific patterns of behavior in infancy characterized the 11 children he studied: (a) failure to assume an anticipatory posture prior to being picked up by their parents, and (b) failure to adjust their body to conform to the contour or posture of their parents. On the basis of case history data, Clancy and McBride (1969) reported a lack of cuddling in the first year of life, along with lazy sucking, an absence of smiling, and a lack of responsiveness to human voices.

Kubicek (1980) studied mother–infant interactions in a pair of fraternal twins participating in a twin study, one of whom was later diagnosed with autism. Analysis of films made at the age of 4 months revealed several behavioral differences between the boys. The twin with autism evidenced a lack of eye contact with the mother, a neutral facial expression, and rigid posture. The give-and-take, mutual attending, and positive affect that characterized the mother's interaction with the nonautistic infant were not observed in her interaction with the autistic infant.

Sparling (1991) presented a case study of an infant who was assessed periodically from birth through age 3 years as part of a study on obstetric risk, and who later received a diagnosis of autism. Neonatal assessment using the Brazelton Scale revealed excessive tremulousness and startle behavior. A videotaped parent–child interaction at the age of 3 months revealed slight delays in expressive and receptive communication, and frustration tolerance. Further analysis of the videotape revealed limited eye contact on the part of the child and a high level of maternal energy required to sustain the interaction.

Not all children who demonstrate social disturbances in infancy receive a later diagnosis of autism. Zeanah, Davis, and Silverman (1988) presented a case study of Anna, a younger sibling of an autistic child. Early parental concerns included her infrequent smiling, unusual quietness, and failure to anticipate being picked up. At 8 months of age, Anna received a clinical evaluation that included developmental testing with the Bayley Scales and videotaped observations of mother–infant feedings. Clinic observations confirmed a lack of affective responsivity, as evidenced in limited eye contact, infrequent smiling, extreme wariness, muted affect, and quietness. Also observed were postural rigidity, lack of cuddling, and failure to assume an anticipatory posture when being picked up. However, Anna's clinical picture was quite different when she reached 12 to 15 months. By that time, she was initiating social games such as pat-a-cake, engaging in pretend play sequences and including others in her play, and pointing to objects for the purpose of requesting them or having them labeled for her. The only remaining social differences found at 18-month and 30-month follow-ups were limited smiling and initial reticence in interacting with unfamiliar adults.

Eriksson and de Chateau (1992) reported an opposite pattern: symptoms of autism became apparent in a young girl after a period of normal development. Parental report and analysis of home videotapes revealed that, by the age of 12 months, this infant was waving good-bye, playing peek-a-boo, babbling, and playing with toys appropriately. However, at 13 months, without apparent medical cause, she was described by her parents as losing interest in her surroundings. She was observed on the videotapes as being quiet, withdrawn, and less active in her play, and engaging in repetitive play activities. She received a formal diagnosis of autism during a clinic visit at the age of 2 years, 7 months.

Other Descriptive Reports

Adrien and colleagues (Adrien et al., 1991) examined home movies, made prior to the age of 2 years, of 12 children with pervasive developmental disorders. The coding system employed 5 categories of behavior that were rated on a 4-point scale of severity. The 9 children with autism all demonstrated disturbances in social interactions, expression and understanding of emotions, and visual or auditory behaviors prior to the age of 2 years. In addition, 8 of the 9 children were found to exhibit disordered motor behaviors and other atypical behaviors.

Gillberg and colleagues (Gillberg et al., 1990) conducted a prospective study in which 12 mothers of autistic children under 3 years old completed a 130-item questionnaire. Twenty-two items were endorsed by at least 10 of the 12 mothers, and were considered to be "high-load" items. These items included social behaviors (e.g., difficulty imitating movements, isolation from surroundings, limited eye contact, empty gaze, lack of smiling, indifference to the presence of others), communicative behaviors (e.g., late speech development, failure to attract attention to self-performed activities, failure to point to objects, inability to indicate wishes, failure to understand what people say), play behaviors (e.g., unusual play, play with only hard objects, interest limited to parts of objects, excessive interest in things that move), and sensory behaviors (e.g., overexcitement when tickled, evidence of possible deafness, failure to listen when spoken to). Several mothers reported that their children had exhibited symptomatology prior to 1 year of age; 5 of the 12 mothers reported abnormal eye contact, and 2 of the 12 mothers reported unusual reactions to sounds in early infancy.

Summary

These clinical descriptions of autism suggest different patterns of onset of symptomatology. In some children, symptoms became apparent within the first year; other children seemed to experience a period of normal development prior to the onset of symptoms. The presence of social or communicative symptomatology within the first year does not necessarily indicate autism, as demonstrated by Zeanah et al. (1988). The different developmental patterns illustrated in these case descriptions are consistent with those described by DeMyer (1979). In her sample, 35% of parents reported that their children had always seemed different, 45% described a specific turning point or setback, and 20% reported seemingly normal development for the first year of life, followed by a failure to keep up with normal developmental milestones.

An obvious limitation of the descriptive approach is that it provides little information about the *specificity* of the findings. Without comparison groups, it is unclear whether the behavioral abnormalities observed in autistic infants are unique to autism or also occur in normally developing infants or in those with other disabilities. For example, bland facial expressions may not be specific to infants with autism; preschizophrenic infants have also been found to exhibit reduced positive affect (Walker, Grimes, Davis, & Smith, 1993). Similarly, deficits in language development prior to 30 months have been found in the early histories of individuals with childhood onset schizophrenia (Watkins, Asarnow, & Tanguay, 1988). The following section reviews studies that have employed comparison groups.

Group Comparisons

Comparisons with Typically Developing Infants

Ornitz, Guthrie, and Farley (1977, 1978) used a written questionnaire to obtain retrospective information from parents of 74 children with autism (mean age = 45 months) and 38 typically developing children (mean age = 46 months). The questionnaire, which focused on behaviors observed within a child's first 30 months of life, was completed by parents before they had knowledge of their child's diagnosis. Numerous group differences were found in the areas of social relating, language, use of objects, sensory behaviors, and motoric behaviors. Except where indicated, this summary will focus on behaviors that differentiated the groups *and* that occurred in at least half of the autistic group.

Impaired social behaviors reported for the children with autism were: being hard to reach, ignoring or "looking through" people, avoiding eye contact, ignoring affection, and seeming unaware of the mother's absence (Ornitz et al., 1978). Although the autistic sample was less likely to respond to affection by smiling or cuddling, these appropriate social behaviors were reported for over half of the children with autism. No group differences were observed for gesturing to be picked up or for engaging in simple social games such as peek-a-boo. Communication disturbances included echolalia and the use of others' hands to acquire objects. Ignoring toys and engaging in repetitive activities with objects were

among the responses reported commonly for the autistic group. Sensory abnormalities included failing to respond to sounds, watching the motions of their own hands or fingers, staring into space, watching spinning objects, showing interest in minor details, scratching surfaces, and showing interest in the way things feel. Motor disturbances included hand-flapping, whirling around, and head or body rocking.

Significant delays in language and communication milestones were found for young children with autism (Ornitz et al., 1977). Emergence of first words occurred by the age of 16 months for 79% of the control children but for only 16% of the autistic children. Use of words to indicate desires occurred by 18 months for 69% of the control children but for only 3% of the autistic children. The use of pointing to indicate desires occurred in 69% of the control children by 16 months of age, but in only 10% of the autistic children. Understanding of simple commands was reported to occur by 13 months for all of the typically developing children but for only 53% of the autistic group.

DeMeyer (1979), using semistructured interviews, obtained retrospective reports of infant behaviors from 33 parents of children with autism and 33 parents of typically developing children. The mean age of the children at the time of the interviews was 4 years, 3 months. The groups were matched on several variables, including age, gender, race, number of siblings, ordinal position within the family, and socioeconomic level. Although no statistical analyses were performed, different patterns of early social behavior and speech development appeared to characterize the two groups. Infants with autism were more often described as socially underrespnosive (36% vs. 12%) or withdrawn (30% vs. 0%) relative to the control infants. In addition, fewer infants with autism were described as either extremely responsive or demanding of attention (18% vs. 39%), or as socially responsive but also content to play alone (15% vs. 48%). Social withdrawal reportedly began in the first year of life for 30% of the infants with autism and in the second year for an additional 54%. Temperamental differences within the autistic group were also described: 33% were reported to be overly passive or "too good," and 15% were described as overly irritable babies. Babbling and speech appeared to develop differently in the autistic group (DeMyer, 1979). The majority of the typically developing infants (79%) exhibited babbling that was similar to that of their siblings, compared with 30% of the autistic group. For about half of the autistic group (52%), babbling occurred less often or was qualitatively different from sibling babbling (compared with 9% of the control group). First words had emerged at 12 months or earlier for 82% of the control group, but for only 48% of the autistic group. About half of the autistic group did not use their first words meaningfully; this was not true for any of the control infants. By the age of 24 months, the majority of the children with autism (89%) used only 15 or fewer words.

Hoshino and colleagues (Hoshino et al., 1982) examined the development of pointing and imitation through retrospective parental interviews. All of the 150 typically developing children in their sample had acquired both behaviors by the age of 18 months. However, only 30% of the higher-functioning autistic children (i.e., children with a Developmental Quotient (DQ) of 70 or higher; $n = 27$) and 9% of the lower functioning autistic children (i.e., children with a DQ of 50 or lower; $n = 34$) were pointing by this age. Only 30% of the higher-functioning autistic children and 15% of the lower-functioning autistic children were imitating others by the age of 18 months.

Osterling and Dawson (1994) examined home videotapes of 11 children with autism and 11 typically developing children. Each videotape was made during a party celebrating the child's first birthday. Group differences in social behavior, joint attention behavior, and autistic symptomatology were found. Specifically, the children with autism were less likely to look at the face of another person, to show an object to another person, or to point to objects, and more likely to fail to orient to their name being called. These behaviors correctly classified 91% of the sample.

Adrien and colleagues (Adrien et al., 1993) used the Infant Behavior Summarized Evaluation (IBSE) scale to rate home movies of 12 children with autism and 12 typically developing children during the first 2 years of

life. Within the first year, significant group differences were found for: (a) poor social interactions, (b) no social smile, (c) lack of appropriate facial expressions, (d) hypotonia, and (e) unstable attention/distractibility. These same behaviors continued to differentiate the groups between the ages of 1 and 2 years. Other behaviors occurred more commonly in the autistic sample between years 1 and 2 of life: (a) ignores people, (b) prefers aloneness, (c) makes no eye contact, (d) lacks appropriate gestures or expressive postures, (e) is too calm, (f) exhibits unusual postures, (g) is hypoactive, and (h) shows no expression of emotion. The authors noted an increase in the frequency of most of the symptomatic behaviors during the second year, though the changes were not statistically significant.

Losche (1990) used home movies to compare the early development of motor action schemes and sensorimotor skills in 8 children with autism and 8 typically developing children. The home movies represented the age span from 4 months to 42 months. Differences between the groups became more apparent after the first year of life; the autistic group persisted in earlier behaviors that were outgrown by the control group. Children with autism demonstrated less sophisticated sensorimotor behaviors; they tended to repeat familiar means–end sequences rather than developing new means to achieve new outcomes. The autistic group also engaged in more actions that yielded continuous physical effects and initiated fewer goal-directed activities.

Baron-Cohen, Allen, and Gillberg (1992), in a prospective study, employed an instrument for screening for autism in 18-month-old children. The Checklist for Autism in Toddlers (CHAT) contains 9 items and assesses 5 behaviors that are deficient in autism: (a) social interest, (b) social play, (c) pretend play, (d) joint attention, and (e) protodeclarative pointing (i.e., pointing to indicate interest). The CHAT was administered to two groups of children: a high-risk group of 41 younger siblings of children with autism (mean age = 19 months), and 50 randomly selected normally developing children who had been brought for their 18-month medical checkups (mean age = 18 months). No group differences were found for any of the items. However, 4 children in the high-risk group missed 2 or more of the 5 diagnostically relevant items; no child in the control group missed more than one of these items. Follow-up at the age of 30 months revealed that these same 4 children had subsequently received an independent diagnosis of autism. The authors concluded that screening for autism can be performed effectively at 18 months of age.

Comparison with Clinical Samples

Prior, Boulton, Gajzago, and Perry (1975) used Rimland's Checklist to obtain information about past and present behaviors of 162 children with autism or other childhood psychiatric disorders. Two characteristics in infancy discriminated the children with autism from those with childhood psychoses: (a) abnormal responses to sensory stimuli and (b) failure to assume an anticipatory posture prior to being picked up. Other early behaviors associated with autism were: resistance to being held, a failure to imitate, and behaving as if deaf.

Johnson, Siddons, Frith, and Morton (1992) obtained information from routine infant vision and hearing screenings, in an attempt to predict the later diagnosis of autism. Early screening information was compiled for 13 children with autism, 19 children with developmental delays who were attending a program specializing in learning disorders, and 19 randomly selected children who were presumed to be developing normally. Current level of impairment, based on the British Picture Vocabulary Scales, was most severe in the group with autism. Information was available for 4 categories of development: (a) motor, (b) vision, (c) hearing and language, and (d) social. At the 6-month screening, no group differences in reported problems were found for any category. At the 12-month screening, problems in all categories were more common for the group with learning disorders. At the 18-month screening, the autistic group had a disproportionate number of problems reported in the social behavior category. These results suggest a possibility of early detection through simple routine screening.

Hoshino and colleagues (1982) conducted retrospective parental interviews to compare the development of 85 children with autism

with that of 64 children with mental retardation (MR) and 150 typically developing children. Questions focused on behaviors seen prior to the age of 2 years. The authors found 27 characteristics that differentiated the autistic sample from both comparison groups. Social behaviors more characteristic of the autistic sample included: not looking at others, not imitating others, fondness for being alone, no interest in playing peek-a-boo, and not liking to be held. Affective behaviors differentiating the autistic group from the others included: not smiling at others, an expressionless face, and an empty smile. Sensory behaviors reported more commonly for the children with autism included: no reaction to name being called, behaving as if deaf, insensitivity to pain, and hypersensitivity to the taste of foods. Behaviors characteristic of a "setback course" were reported more commonly for the autistic group: losing acquired words, losing the ability to point, and losing the ability to imitate.

Hoshino et al. (1982) also identified early behaviors that occurred more commonly in both the autistic and MR samples relative to the control group. These included communicative behaviors (e.g., little babbling, not pointing, and limited vocabulary), affective behaviors (e.g., not crying, unstable emotions, going into rages for no reason), and sensory behaviors (e.g., licking objects, covering ears to block out sounds, and insensitivity to cold or heat). These behaviors, therefore, may be more characteristic of general developmental delay than of autism.

Ohta, Nagai, Hara, and Sasaki (1987) used a questionnaire to obtain retrospective reports of early symptomotology of autism from 141 parents of children with autism. Their responses were compared with those obtained from 33 parents of children with MR. The most common early symptoms of the autistic sample were: delayed speech and other speech problems (84%), poor response to others (55%), restlessness and hyperactivity (45%), ignoring verbal comments as if deaf (32%), and difficulty forming personal relationships (26%). All of these behaviors were significantly more common in the autistic group than in the MR group. The most common early symptom reported for the MR sample was delayed speech and other speech problems (61%). Other early symptoms—delayed walking (42%) and delayed overall motor development (37%)—were significantly more common in the MR sample than in the autistic sample.

Dahlgren and Gillberg (1989) used a 130-item questionnaire to obtain retrospective information from parents about their children's development prior to the age of 2 years. Responses were obtained from parents of 26 autistic children, 17 developmentally matched children with MR, and 22 population-matched, typically developing children. Eighteen items discriminated the children with autism from the other two groups. These items included social behaviors (e.g., appearing isolated from surroundings, not smiling when expected, empty gaze, difficulty imitating movements, content if left alone, failure to attract attention to own activities), sensory behaviors (e.g., acting as if deaf, strange reactions to sounds, overexcited when tickled, little reaction to cold, unusual visual interest in objects, patterns, and movements), play behaviors (e.g., not playing like other children, showing attachments to unusual objects, playing only with hard objects), and sleep problems.

Adrien et al. (1992) rated videotapes of 39 children with autism, 33 children with MR, and 17 typically developing children using the IBSE. The ages of the children in the tapes ranged from 6 months to 48 months. The mean ages were: 2 years, 6 months for the autistic group; 1 year, 11 months for the MR group; and 1 year, 7 months for the control group. Global developmental quotients, obtained from a French adaptation of the Gesell Scales, were comparable for the autistic and MR groups (means = 48 and 50, respectively). The authors found that 19 items differentiated the autistic sample from the other groups. These items comprised social behaviors (e.g., imitates poorly, ignores people, prefers aloneness, and abnormal eye contact); affective behaviors (e.g., no social smile, lack of appropriate facial expressions, and no expression of emotions); communicative behaviors (e.g., lack of vocal communication and of appropriate gestures); motoric behaviors (e.g., stereotyped behavior, unusual postures, and inappropriate use of objects); sensory behaviors (e.g., no reaction or bizarre responses to auditory stimuli), and attentional behaviors (e.g., unstable attention/easily distracted). This set of behaviors correctly classified 83% of the sample as autistic vs. MR, and 95% of the sample as autistic vs. typically developing.

Summary

Most of the available research employing control groups has compared the behaviors of autism to those of typically developing infants. Although this type of comparison can control for behavioral differences associated with chronological age, children with autism also exhibit cognitive and language delays relative to normally developing children. Thus, any group differences that are found may be attributable to developmental delays in the autistic group, rather than to the autism itself.

More meaningful findings can be culled from studies employing developmentally comparable controls. A summary of these findings is presented in Table 12.1. It is evident from this research that autistic children under 3 years old can be differentiated from those with developmental delays or MR on the basis

TABLE 12.1   Behaviors Differentiating Autism from Developmental Delay in Children under 36 Months

Social Interactions and Reciprocity
Poor imitation
Abnormal eye contact
Poor relating or interactions
Underresponsive/Ignores others
Little interest in social games
Preference for being alone
Little interest in being held
Little smiling/Bland facial expression

Communication
Speech delays
Little use of gestures
Failure to attract attention to own activities

Restricted and Repetitive Interests and Behaviors
Motor stereotypies/Unusual postures
Inappropriate use of objects/Unusual play
Attachment to unusual objects
Unusual visual interests
Inconsistent response to sounds/Seems deaf
Insensitive to pain, cold, or heat
Hypersensitive to taste

of many behavioral and diagnostic features. Conspicuously absent from the table are behaviors indicative of disordered peer relationships, abnormal language features, and a need for sameness and routines. These behaviors are likely not yet apparent in children at such young ages (Lord, 1991; Stone & Hogan, 1993).

Despite the fact that very young children may not exhibit all of the diagnostic features of autism, there is evidence that the diagnosis of autism can be made reliably before the age of 3 years. Gillberg et al. (1990), in a study of 21 children who received a diagnosis of autism before their third birthdays, found that 20 children received the same diagnosis at follow-up 6 months to 13 years later. Lord (1991) found that 12 of 14 children who received a clinical diagnosis of possible or probable autism before the age of 3 years were diagnosed as autistic by a different clinician 12 to 18 months later. Adrien et al. (1992) reported that 11 children who received a diagnosis of autism at the age of 2 years received the same diagnosis after the age of 3 years. These results provide an impetus for continued investigation of the salient features of autism at young ages.

EARLY CHILDHOOD

This section reviews the behavioral characteristics of autistic children in the preschool years, the time when they are most likely to receive a definitive diagnosis. Although preschool-age children must meet the same general set of diagnostic criteria as older children with autism, it is widely recognized that the specific expression of characteristics may change as a function of age and developmental level (e.g., Siegel, 1991; Volkmar & Cohen, 1988; Wing, 1988). This section first describes research that has examined behavioral or diagnostic patterns in preschool-age children. Most of these studies have used broad-based parental interviews or questionnaires to obtain information across a wide range of behavioral domains. The second part of the section presents research focusing on specific behavioral features of young children with autism. This research consists primarily of observational studies of single behaviors or small clusters of behaviors.

Diagnostic Patterns

Several studies have used broad-based instruments as a means of gathering diagnostically relevant information about young children with autism. Most of the earlier studies relied on retrospective parental reports. More recent research has employed parental interviews to obtain contemporaneous information about the child's behavior.

Retrospective Parental Reports

Wing (1969) compared the behaviors of 2- to 5-year-old autistic children to those of typically developing children as well as children with MR, receptive or expressive aphasia, or dual sensory impairments (i.e., partially blind and deaf). Autistic children exhibited more impaired social relationships and more attachments to objects and routines, relative to all comparison groups. Autistic children also differed from all groups except the blind and deaf children in their emotional responses, understanding and use of communicative gestures, sensory responses, play, and motor behaviors.

From 50 parents of children with autism, Volkmar, Cohen, and Paul (1986) obtained information about behaviors exhibited by the children prior to the age of 6. Although no comparison groups were employed, support for the triad of diagnostic features was obtained. In the social realm, behaviors endorsed for over 75% of the children were: ignoring people, being emotionally distant, avoiding eye contact, looking through people, and failing to show affection or interest when held. Of the children who had acquired language, the majority evidenced unusual features such as poor speech tone or rhythm, pronoun confusion, and echolalia. With regard to restricted and repetitive activities, over 75% of the sample were reported as ignoring toys, demonstrating a preoccupation with spinning objects, and failing to respond to sounds.

Contemporaneous Parental Reports

Ohta et al. (1987) used a questionnaire to elicit information about the behaviors exhibited by 48 children with autism between the ages of 4 and 6 years. The most commonly reported deficits (94%) for this group of children were in the area of delayed speech or other speech problems. Social difficulties were common but by no means universal: 60% of the children were described as having poor interpersonal relationships, 46% were described as showing poor social responsiveness, and 40% were reported to have poor peer relationships. Unusual habits and patterns were reported for only 35% of the sample. A comparison of responses obtained from parents of 2- to 3-year-old children suggested that social deficits and unusual habits increased in frequency in the preschool years.

Lord, Rutter, and Le Couteur (1994) used the Autism Diagnostic Interview-Revised (ADI-R) to obtain contemporaneous reports of autistic symptomatology for 25 children with autism and 25 children with MR or language impairments (mean ages = 47 months and 45 months, respectively). The ADI-R is an investigator-based interview that was developed to correspond to *ICD-10* and *DSM-IV* diagnostic criteria. Behaviors representing the three primary features of autism differentiated the two groups. Within the *social* category, group differences were found for using nonverbal behaviors (e.g., eye gaze, smiling) to regulate social interactions, forming peer relationships, sharing one's own enjoyment with others (e.g., by directing attention), and demonstrating social-emotional reciprocity and modulation of behavior to the social context. *Communicative* behaviors differentiating the groups were: using gestures such as pointing and nodding one's head, interacting through social chat, and engaging in spontaneous make-believe play or social imitative play. In contrast, the groups did *not* differ in the stereotyped and repetitive use of language or in the ability to engage in reciprocal conversation (possibly because of the limited number of children with adequate language in the sample). Within the category of *restricted activities and interests,* the presence of verbal rituals, unusual sensory behaviors, hand and finger mannerisms, and whole-body mannerisms differentiated the groups. However, repetitive use of objects, presence of compulsions and rituals, and unusual preoccupations were *not* more common for the children with autism.

Stone and Hogan (1993) used the Parent Interview for Autism (PIA) to compare contemporaneous reports from 58 parents of children with autism and 36 parents of children with MR (mean ages = 39 months and 42 months, respectively). Group differences were found for the behavioral categories of social relating, imitation, peer interactions, nonverbal communication, language understanding, and imaginative play. Consistent with Lord et al. (1994), a need for sameness and routines did not differentiate the groups of young children. In contrast to the results obtained by Lord et al., unusual sensory responses and repetitive motor patterns were not found to differentiate the groups in this study.

Summary

Results obtained from both retrospective reports and contemporaneous reports provide support for the general pattern of autistic symptomatology in preschool-age children. All studies have reported significant deficits in the areas of social relating and communication, and most have also obtained evidence for the presence of some form of repetitive or restricted activities. However, there is little consistency from one study to another in terms of the specific *type* of restricted activity evidenced in the autistic samples. Certain behavioral manifestations appear to be less prominent in this age group than in older or mixed-age samples. In particular, the limited speech of many preschool-age children with autism precludes the observation of unusual language features. In addition, the presence of behavioral rituals or routines does not appear to differentiate preschool-age children with autism from those with other disabilities.

Despite the presence of the triad of diagnostic characteristics of autism, accurate diagnosis in the preschool years can be hampered by clinical features that overlap with those seen in children with other disabilities. Lord, Storoschuk, Rutter, and Pickles (1993) illustrated this point well by examining children who were misdiagnosed using the ADI-R. These authors reported the most difficulty in differentiating autism from developmental delay or language impairment in children who were nonverbal and who had mental ages below 18 months. The latter group of control children evidenced many "symptomatic" behaviors in all three diagnostic areas. To minimize the likelihood of misdiagnosis, these authors recommended the integration of direct behavioral observations and formal developmental assessment with parental report information, when conducting comprehensive diagnostic evaluations.

Specific Behavioral Features

The content of this section, which surveys the research focusing on specific behavioral characteristics of preschool-age children with autism, was determined by the availability of empirical literature. Behaviors within the social realm have received the most research attention; studies of joint attention, affective expression, and attachment have proliferated within the past 5 to 10 years. In contrast, very little research has focused on behaviors indicative of restricted activities and interests, with the exception of play skills.

Eye-to-Eye Gaze

One of the most salient aspects of social relating is the manner in which children use eye-to-eye gaze. Abnormal eye gaze is reported commonly by parents of young autistic children (Volkmar et al., 1986) and has been the subject of considerable research. Recent studies of young children have suggested that the use of eye gaze in children with autism is related to situational as well as developmental factors. For example, in structured situations with high adult involvement, the amount of eye contact directed toward adults is often similar for children with autism and for their controls (Dawson, Hill, Spencer, Galpert, & Watson, 1990; Sigman, Mundy, Sherman, & Ungerer, 1986). Moreover, autistic children have been found to demonstrate *more* eye contact than controls in certain situations (i.e., toward quiet, inactive adults, and toward adults following a tickle game; Mundy, Sigman, Ungerer, & Sherman, 1986). In contrast, deficits in eye-to-eye gaze in children with autism have been found during unstructured free-play situations (Kasari, Sigman, & Yirmiya, 1993).

There is also evidence that manipulation of the social context can affect the use of eye contact in young children with autism. In particular, child-centered interactions that involve imitation of the autistic child's actions appear to be facilitative of eye-to-eye gaze. Dawson and Adams (1984) found that autistic children who were poor imitators showed increased eye contact toward an experimenter during an interaction that involved simultaneous imitation

of their actions. A later study involving parents revealed that young children with autism looked at their mothers' faces for longer periods during imitative play compared with free play (Dawson & Galpert, 1990). In addition, increased eye contact was maintained following a 2-week intervention in which mothers engaged in imitative play at home for 20 minutes each day.

Developmental factors appear to influence the use of eye-to-eye gaze in children with autism. Increased frequency of eye contact in children with autism is associated with higher mental ages (Kasari et al., 1993; Mundy, Sigman, & Kasari, 1994), higher developmental quotients (Dawson & Galpert, 1990), and higher language levels (Dawson et al., 1990; Kasari et al., 1993). Mundy et al. (1994) found deficits in the use of eye contact only for autistic children with mental ages below 20 months.

Although absolute levels of eye contact do not consistently differentiate children with autism from their matched counterparts, deficits in the use of eye contact *for social or communicative purposes* have been found consistently in young autistic samples. For example, Phillips and colleagues found that autistic children used eye gaze less frequently than controls in ambiguous situations (i.e., when an experimenter blocked their actions by covering their hands or teased them by offering and then withdrawing toys) (Phillips, Baron-Cohen, & Rutter, 1992). The authors interpret these results as indicating a deficit in the use of eye contact to understand the purpose or goal underlying another person's behavior. Autistic children also have shown less frequent use of eye contact for the purpose of initiating joint attention with adults (i.e., to share attention while holding a toy or while watching an active mechanical toy; Mundy et al., 1986). Joint attention behavior is discussed in the following section.

Joint Attention

A significant feature of young autistic children is a deficiency in their ability to coordinate their attention when it is divided between another person and an object or event of interest. Coordinated attention, or joint attention, behavior serves the social function of indicating and sharing interest with another person; it is distinguished from behavior that serves the instrumental function of obtaining desired objects or actions (i.e., requesting). Young children with autism have been shown consistently to exhibit deficits in joint attention behaviors, such as showing objects, pointing to objects within reach, or alternating eye gaze between a person and an object of interest; moreover, these deficits appear to be specific to autism (Lewy & Dawson, 1992; McEvoy, Rogers, & Pennington, 1993; Mundy et al., 1986; Sigman et al., 1986; Wetherby, Yonclas, & Bryan, 1989). The *quality* of joint attention, when it occurs, is also different in children with autism. Autistic children are less likely to show positive affect during joint attention, suggesting that a disturbance in affective sharing may contribute to this deficit (Kasari, Sigman, Mundy, & Yirmiya, 1990).

The ability to engage in joint attention appears to be associated with developmental factors. Joint attention in young autistic children has been associated with mental age; more pervasive deficits have been found in children with mental ages below 20 months (Mundy et al., 1994). Joint attention skills in young autistic children have also been associated with concurrent language skills (Mundy, Sigman, Ungerer, & Sherman, 1987) and with the prediction of language development over a one-year period (Mundy, Sigman, & Kasari, 1990). In a recent study, McEvoy and colleagues (1993) revealed an association between joint attention and executive function skills and proposed that frontal lobe-mediated executive function skills may underlie the ability to engage in joint attention.

The importance of the social context in the expression of joint attention was highlighted by Lewy and Dawson (1992). These authors found that joint attention increased during child-centered play (i.e., imitating the child's actions) relative to adult-centered play, suggesting that this behavior may be responsive to environmental manipulation.

Understanding and Expression of Affect

A variety of deficits in the recognition and use of affect have been reported for young children with autism. With respect to the facial expression of emotion, children with autism have been found to display less positive affect (Snow, Hertzig, & Shapiro, 1987), more neutral affect (Yirmiya, Kasari, Sigman, & Mundy, 1989), and more incongruent combinations of affect (Yirmiya et al., 1989) relative to controls. Idiosyncratic affective vocalizations also have been reported for young children with autism (Ricks & Wing, 1975). Overall levels of positive affect do not always differentiate young children with autism from their controls, but differences are often found in the *social* aspects of positive affect. For example, Dawson et al. (1990) found no differences between children with autism and language-matched controls in the overall frequency or duration of smiling during interactions with their mothers; however, the children with autism were less likely to smile while looking at their mothers. Snow et al. (1987) found that young children with autism, relative to mental-age-matched controls, expressed positive affect less often during social interactions with adults, and more often during independent, self-absorbed activities.

The understanding of affect has been more difficult to assess directly in young children with autism because of their delays in cognitive and language development. Most of the work in this area has focused on the behavioral responses of children to positive or negative affective displays by adults. With regard to positive affect, children with autism were found to be less likely than controls to smile in response to their mothers' smiles (Dawson et al., 1990) and praise from adults (Kasari, Sigman, Baumgartner, & Stipek, 1993). In fact, children with autism were more likely than controls to look away or turn away from the adult providing the praise (Kasari et al., 1993). Children with autism also have been found to demonstrate qualitatively different responses to adults simulating negative affect. They were less likely than controls to look toward an adult feigning fear, distress, or discomfort (Sigman, Kasari, Kwon, & Yirmiya, 1992). Moreover, in the distress situation, which consisted of an adult pretending to hit herself with a toy hammer, children with autism showed less concern for the adult. They were more likely to play with the toy following the "accident."

Attachment

Research on attachment behavior has revealed that young children with autism are similar to other groups in attachment security (Rogers, Ozonoff, & Maslin-Cole, 1991, 1993; Shapiro,

Sherman, Calamari, & Koch, 1987; Sigman & Mundy, 1989; Sigman & Ungerer, 1984a). For example, they demonstrate increased proximity-seeking behavior upon reunion with their mothers, and they direct more proximity-seeking toward their mothers than toward strangers (Sigman & Mundy, 1989; Sigman & Ungerer, 1984a). However, their behavioral expression of attachment may take a form different from that seen in other children; for instance, they may demonstrate affective changes without seeking proximity or physical contact (Rogers et al., 1993). Attachment behavior in young children with autism has been associated with developmental level (Rogers et al., 1991, 1993), symbolic functioning (Sigman & Ungerer, 1984a), and language and communication skills (Capps, Sigman, & Mundy, 1994; Rogers et al., 1991). Information from parental reports suggests that the *perception* of attachment is not always present; the majority of parents report that their autistic children seem not to need their mothers (68%) and are unaware of their mothers' absence (58%; Volkmar et al., 1986).

Motor Imitation

Imitation has been referred to as a fundamental cognitive deficit that is specific to autism (Prior, 1979). Although many studies have documented motor imitation deficits in autism (see Smith & Bryson, 1994, for an excellent review), few have focused specifically on preschool-age children. A resurgence of interest in motor imitation has followed from recent recognition that imitation ability may be a precursor to the development of theory of mind (Meltzoff & Gopnik, 1993; Rogers & Pennington, 1991).

Studies of motor imitation in young children with autism have employed tasks involving the imitation of body movements as well as the imitation of actions with objects. Children with autism have been found to perform more poorly on both types of tasks relative to: control children with MR (DeMyer et al., 1972; Sigman & Ungerer, 1984b; Stone, Lemanek, Fishel, Fernandez, & Altemeier, 1990), mental-age-matched typically developing children (Sigman & Ungerer, 1984b), and developmentally delayed children matched on expressive language, chronological age, and

mental age (Stone, Ousley, & Littleford, 1995). In one study, imitation was found to be the best discriminator (among social and play measures) between children with autism and children with MR (Stone et al., 1990).

Imitation skills in children with autism appear to be related to other social and communicative behaviors. Among children with autism, better imitators tend to be more socially related and more communicative (Dawson & Adams, 1984) and to have better receptive language skills (Sigman & Ungerer, 1984b). However, there is little correspondence between imitation skills and other sensorimotor skills in young children with autism. For example, Dawson and Adams found weaker performance on motor imitation tasks than on other sensorimotor tasks (e.g., object permanence).

Only two studies have compared the performance of young children with autism on different types of motor imitation tasks. Autistic children have been found to perform more poorly on body imitation tasks compared to tasks involving actions with objects (DeMyer et al., 1972; Stone et al., 1995), and more poorly on nonmeaningful tasks relative to those involving meaningful actions (Stone et al., 1995). However, this pattern does not appear to be unique to autism. The same pattern was observed in developmentally delayed children matched on mental age, chronological age, and expressive language (Stone et al., 1995).

Although deficiencies in imitation skills seem to characterize young children with autism, there is evidence that these skills improve with age (Garfin, McCallon, & Cox, 1988). Consequently, deficient imitation may be more evident in infancy or early childhood than during later stages of development.

Functional and Symbolic Play

Young children with autism have been found to demonstrate less appropriate, less diverse, and more repetitive play than children with MR or typically developing children (Sherman, Shapiro, & Glassman, 1983; Stone et al., 1990; Tilton & Ottinger, 1964). In addition, autistic children are observed to engage in more oral manipulation and less combinational use of toys (Tilton & Ottinger, 1964). Studies investigating developmental levels of play have revealed that children with autism are less likely to engage in functional play relative to children with MR or typically developing children (Mundy et al., 1986; Sigman & Ungerer, 1984b; Stone et al., 1990). Deficits in functional play have been found to occur in unstructured (Sigman & Ungerer, 1984b; Stone et al., 1990) as well as structured (Mundy et al., 1986; Sigman & Ungerer, 1984b) settings. In addition, functional play skills have been associated with language skills in young autistic children (Sigman & Ungerer, 1984b).

Deficits in symbolic play also have been observed in children with autism (Mundy et al., 1986; Sherman et al., 1983; Sigman & Ungerer, 1984b), though the results have been less consistent. Symbolic play deficits are more likely to be apparent in structured settings than in unstructured play situations (Mundy et al., 1986; Sigman & Ungerer, 1984b; Stone et al., 1990). However, young children with autism—as well as the control groups—generally have been found to exhibit low levels of symbolic play in experimental situations (Mundy et al., 1986; Stone et al., 1990). Accordingly, the absence of functional play may be more meaningful than the absence of symbolic play in the evaluation or diagnosis of preschool-age children with autism.

Parents' reports of their young children's play skills generally are consistent with the results of observational studies. Children with autism have been reported to demonstrate less appropriate play, less variety in their play, and more perseverative, nonconstructive play (e.g., spinning or mouthing objects) than typically developing children (DeMyer, Mann, Tilton, & Loew, 1967). Fewer parents of autistic children (35%) report that their children engage in make-believe activities, compared with parents of children with MR (86%) (Stone & Lemanek, 1990). Dramatic play with dolls and role-play activities are reported substantially less frequently for autistic children than for typically developing children (3% vs. 67%, and 30% vs. 90%, respectively) (DeMyer et al., 1967).

SUMMARY

The study of preschool-age children with autism offers a unique opportunity for understanding the early features of the disorder. In fact, the preschool years may be the optimal time to observe certain important characteristics of autism—such as joint attention and imitation deficits—that tend to improve with advancing cognitive skills and chronological age.

Studies of preschool-age children have highlighted the subtle nature of the social and communicative deficits of autism. Many of the social and communicative impairments seen in young children with autism involve the *absence* of normative behaviors (e.g., failure to use nonverbal behaviors, failure to imitate), rather than the *presence* of noticeably unusual behaviors (e.g., peculiarities in the use of language). In addition, the extent to which deficits are apparent depends in large part on the context in which the behaviors are observed. For instance, deficits in eye contact and joint attention may not be evident during structured parent-child interactions or child-centered activities (Dawson & Galpert, 1990; Sigman et al., 1986). Moreover, the frequency with which certain social behaviors are observed appears to be less important than the way in which the behaviors are used. For example, whereas absolute levels of eye contact and positive affect may not differentiate young autistic children from other groups, the use of these behaviors for social purposes appears to be reduced.

Children within this age range generally show the triad of diagnostic features. However, social and communication impairments continue to be more prominent than restricted activities and interests. In particular, a need for sameness or routines is often *not* evident in preschool-age children with autism. Overall, the cluster of behaviors representative of restricted or repetitive activities has received very little research attention. A number of questions remain regarding the existence of developmental trends and continuity over time for these behaviors. For example, are certain forms of repetitive activities more likely to be manifested at particular ages or cognitive levels? Is the presence of a certain form of repetitive behavior in young children predictive of a different form in school-age children? Is the presence of repetitive activities in young children associated with other behavioral features of autism? Continued research employing a developmental framework and focusing on discrete age ranges can help answer these and many other questions about the early features of children with autism. The study of young children offers the potential benefits of contributing to earlier recognition of autism and facilitating a conceptual and theoretical understanding of the disorder.

Cross-References

Autism in school-age children and in adolescents and adults is discussed in Chapters 13 and 14. Developmental aspects of service needs are discussed in Chapter 45. Working with families and aspects of communication assessment and intervention are addressed in Chapters 9, 23 through 25, and 27.

REFERENCES

Adrien, J.L., Barthelemy, C., Perrot, A., Roux, S., Lenoir, P., Hameury, L., & Sauvage, D. (1992). Validity and reliability of the Infant Behavioral Summarized Evaluation (IBSE): A rating scale for the assessment of young children with autism and developmental disorders. *Journal of Autism and Developmental Disorders, 22,* 375–394.

Adrien, J.L., Fauré, M., Perrot, A., Hameury, L., Garreau, B., Barthelemy, C., & Sauvage, D. (1991). Autism and family home movies: Preliminary findings. *Journal of Autism and Developmental Disorders, 21,* 43–49.

Adrien, J.L., Lenoir, P., Martineau, J., Perrot, A., Hameury, L., Larmande, C., & Sauvage, D. (1993). Blind ratings of early symptoms of autism based upon family home movies. *Journal of the American Academy of Child and Adolescent Psychiatry, 33,* 617–626.

Baron-Cohen, S., Allen, J., & Gillberg, C. (1992). Can autism be detected at 18 months? The needle, the haystack, and the CHAT. *British Journal of Psychiatry, 161,* 839–843.

Capps, L., Sigman, M., & Mundy, P. (1994). Attachment security in children with autism. *Development and Psychopathology, 6,* 249–261.

Clancy, H., & McBride, G. (1969). The autistic process and its treatment. *Journal of Child Psychology and Psychiatry, 10,* 233–244.

Dahlgren, S.O., & Gillberg, C. (1989). Symptoms in the first two years of life. *European Archives of Psychiatry and Neurological Science, 238,* 169–174.

Dawson, G., & Adams, A. (1984). Imitation and social responsiveness in autistic children. *Journal of Abnormal Child Psychology, 12,* 209–226.

Dawson, G., & Galpert, L. (1990). Mothers' use of imitative play for facilitating social responsiveness and toy play in young autistic children. *Development and Psychopathology, 2,* 151–162.

Dawson, G., Hill, D., Spencer, A., Galpert, L., & Watson, L. (1990). Affective exchanges between young autistic children and their mothers. *Journal of Abnormal Child Psychology, 18,* 335–345.

DeMyer, M.K. (1979). *Parents and children in autism.* Washington, DC: Winston.

DeMyer, M.K., Alpern, G.D., Barton, S., DeMyer, W.E., Churchill, D.W., Hingtgen, J.N., Bryson, C.Q., Pontius, W., & Kimberlin, C. (1972). Imitation in autistic, early schizophrenic, and nonpsychotic subnormal children. *Journal of Autism and Childhood Schizophrenia, 2,* 264–287.

DeMyer, M.K., Mann, N.A., Tilton, J.R., & Loew, L.H. (1967). Toy-play behavior and use of body by autistic and normal children as reported by mothers. *Psychological Reports, 21,* 973–981.

Eriksson, A-S., & de Chateau, P. (1992). Brief report: A girl aged two years and seven months with autistic disorder videotaped from birth. *Journal of Autism and Developmental Disorders, 22,* 127–129.

Garfin, D.G., McCallon, D., & Cox, R. (1988). Validity and reliability of the Childhood Autism Rating Scale with autistic adolescents. *Journal of Autism and Developmental Disorders, 18,* 367–378.

Gillberg, C., Ehlers, S., Schaumann, H., Jakobsson, G., Dahlgren, S.O., Lindbolm, R., Bagenholm, A., Tjuus, T., & Blidner, E. (1990). Autism under age 3 years: A clinical study of 28 cases referred for autistic symptoms in infancy. *Journal of Child Psychology and Psychiatry, 31,* 921–934.

Hart, H., Bax, M., & Jenkins, S. (1978). The value of a developmental history. *Developmental Medicine and Child Neurology, 20,* 442–452.

Hoshino, Y., Kumashiro, H., Yashima, Y., Tachibana, R., Watanabe, M., & Furukawa, H. (1982). Early symptoms of autistic children and its diagnostic significance. *Folia Psychiatrica et Neurologica, 36,* 367–374.

Johnson, M.H., Siddons, F., Frith, U., & Morton, J. (1992). Can autism be predicted on the basis of infant screening tests? *Developmental Medicine and Child Neurology, 34,* 316–320.

Kanner, L. (1943). Autistic disturbances of affective contact. *Nervous Child, 2,* 217–250.

Kasari, C., Sigman, M.D., Baumgartner, P., & Stipek, D.J. (1993). Pride and mastery in children with autism. *Journal of Child Psychology and Psychiatry, 34,* 353–362.

Kasari, C., Sigman, M., Mundy, P., & Yirmiya, N. (1990). Affective sharing in the context of joint attention interactions of normal, autistic, and mentally retarded children. *Journal of Autism and Developmental Disorders, 20,* 87–100.

Kasari, C., Sigman, M., & Yirmiya, N. (1993). Focused and social attention of autistic children in interactions with familiar and unfamiliar adults: A comparison of autistic, mentally retarded, and normal children. *Development and Psychopathology, 5,* 401–412.

Kubicek, L.F. (1980). Organization in two mother–infant interactions involving a normal infant and his fraternal twin brother who was later diagnosed as autistic. In T. Field (Ed.), *High-risk infants and children* (pp. 99–110). New York: Academic Press.

Lewis, M., & Miller, S.M. (Eds.). (1990). Preface. *Handbook of developmental psychopathology* (pp. xiii–xvi). New York: Plenum Press.

Lewy, A.L., & Dawson, G. (1992). Social stimulation and joint attention in young autistic children. *Journal of Abnormal Child Psychology, 20,* 555–566.

Lord, C. (1991, April). *Follow-ups of two-year-olds referred for possible autism.* Paper presented at the meeting of the Society for Research in Child Development, Seattle, WA.

Lord, C., Rutter, M., & Le Couteur, A. (1994). Autism Diagnostic Interview-Revised: A revised version of a diagnostic interview for caregivers of individuals with possible pervasive developmental disorders. *Journal of Autism and Developmental Disorders, 24,* 659–685.

Lord, C., Storoschuk, S., Rutter, M., & Pickles, A. (1993). Using the ADI-R to diagnose autism in preschool children. *Infant Mental Health Journal, 14,* 234–252.

Losche, G. (1990). Sensorimotor and action development in autistic children from infancy to early childhood. *Journal of Child Psychology and Psychiatry, 31,* 749–761.

Lovaas, O.I. (1987). Behavioral treatment and normal educational and intellectual functioning in young autistic children. *Journal of Consulting and Clinical Psychology, 55,* 3–9.

Massie, H.N. (1975). The early natural history of childhood psychosis. *Journal of the American Academy of Child Psychiatry, 14,* 683–707.

Massie, H.N. (1978). Blind ratings of mother–infant interaction in home movies of pre-psychotic and normal infants. *American Journal of Psychiatry, 135,* 1371–1374.

McEvoy, R.E., Rogers, S.J., & Pennington, B.F. (1993). Executive function and social communication deficits in young autistic children. *Journal of Child Psychology and Psychiatry, 34,* 563–578.

Mednick, S.A., & Shaffer, J.B. (1963). Mothers' retrospective reports in child-rearing research. *American Journal of Orthopsychiatry, 33,* 457–461.

Meltzoff, A., & Gopnik, A. (1993). The role of imitation in understanding persons and developing a theory of mind. In S. Baron-Cohen, H. Tager-Flusberg, & D.J. Cohen (Eds.), *Understanding other minds: Perspectives from autism* (pp. 335–366). Oxford England: Oxford University Press.

Mundy, P., Sigman, M., & Kasari, C. (1990). A longitudinal study of joint attention and language development in autistic children. *Journal of Autism and Developmental Disorders, 20,* 115–128.

Mundy, P., Sigman, M., & Kasari, C. (1994). Joint attention, developmental level, and symptom presentation in autism. *Development and Psychopathology, 6,* 389–401.

Mundy, P., Sigman, M., Ungerer, J., & Sherman, T. (1986). Defining the social deficits of autism: The contribution of non-verbal communication measures. *Journal of Child Psychology and Psychiatry, 27,* 657–669.

Mundy, P., Sigman, M., Ungerer, J., & Sherman, T. (1987). Nonverbal communication and play correlates of language development in autistic children. *Journal of Autism and Developmental Disorders, 17,* 349–364.

Ohta, M., Nagai, Y., Hara, H., & Sasaki, M. (1987). Parental perception of behavioral symptoms in Japanese autistic children. *Journal of Autism and Developmental Disorders, 17,* 549–563.

Ornitz, E.M., Guthrie, D., & Farley, A.H. (1977). The early development of autistic children. *Journal of Autism and Childhood Schizophrenia, 7,* 207–229.

Ornitz, E.M., Guthrie, D., & Farley, A.J. (1978). The early symptoms of childhood autism. In G. Serban (Ed.), *Cognitive defects in the development of mental illness* (pp. 24–42). New York: Brunner/Mazel.

Osterling, J., & Dawson, G. (1994). Early recognition of children with autism: A study of first-birthday home videotapes. *Journal of Autism and Developmental Disorders, 24,* 247–257.

Phillips, W., Baron-Cohen, S., & Rutter, M. (1992). The role of eye contact in goal detection: Evidence from normal infants and children with autism or mental handicap. *Development and Psychopathology, 4,* 375–383.

Prior, M.R. (1979). Cognitive abilities and disabilities in infantile autism: A review. *Journal of Abnormal Child Psychology, 7,* 357–380.

Prior, M., Boulton, D., Gajzago, C., & Perry, D. (1975). The classification of childhood psychoses by numerical taxonomy. *Journal of Child Psychology and Psychiatry, 16,* 321–330.

Ricks, D.M., & Wing, L. (1975). Language, communication, and the use of symbols in normal and autistic children. *Journal of Autism and Childhood Schizophrenia, 5,* 191–221.

Robbins, L.C. (1963). The accuracy of parental recall of aspects of child development and of child-rearing practices. *Journal of Abnormal and Social Psychology, 66,* 261–270.

Rogers, S.J., & Lewis, H. (1989). An effective day treatment model for young children with pervasive developmental disorders. *Journal of the American Academy of Child and Adolescent Psychiatry, 28,* 207–214.

Rogers, S.J., Ozonoff, S., & Maslin-Cole, C. (1991). A comparative study of attachment behavior in young children with autism or other psychiatric disorders. *Journal of the American Academy of Child and Adolescent Psychiatry, 30,* 483–488.

Rogers, S.J., Ozonoff, S., & Maslin-Cole, C. (1993). Developmental aspects of attachment behavior in young children with pervasive developmental disorders. *Journal of the American Academy of Child and Adolescent Psychiatry, 32,* 1274–1282.

Rogers, S.J., & Pennington, B.F. (1991). A theoretical approach to the deficits in infantile autism. *Development and Psychopathology, 3,* 137–162.

Shapiro, T., Sherman, M., Calamari, G., & Koch, D. (1987). Attachment in autism and other developmental disorders. *Journal of the American Academy of Child and Adolescent Psychiatry, 26,* 480–484.

Sherman, M., Shapiro, T., & Glassman, M. (1983). Play and language in developmentally disordered preschoolers: A new approach to classification. *Journal of the American Academy of Child Psychiatry, 22,* 511–524.

Short, A.B., & Schopler, E. (1988). Factors relating to age of onset in autism. *Journal of Autism and Developmental Disabilities, 18,* 207–216.

Siegel, B. (1991). Toward *DSM-IV:* A developmental approach to autistic disorder. *Psychiatric Clinics of North America, 14,* 53–68.

Siegel, B., Pliner, C., Eschler, J., & Elliott, G.R. (1988). How children with autism are diagnosed: Difficulties in identification of children with multiple developmental delays. *Developmental and Behavioral Pediatrics, 9,* 199–204.

Sigman, M.D., Kasari, C., Kwon, J-H., & Yirmiya, N. (1992). Responses to the negative emotions of others by autistic, mentally retarded, and normal children. *Child Development, 63,* 796–807.

Sigman, M., & Mundy, P. (1989). Social attachments in autistic children. *Journal of the American Academy of Child and Adolescent Psychiatry, 28,* 74–81.

Sigman, M., Mundy, P., Sherman, T., & Ungerer, J. (1986). Social interactions of autistic, mentally retarded, and normal children and their caregivers. *Journal of Child Psychology and Psychiatry, 27,* 647–656.

Sigman, M., & Ungerer, J. (1984a). Attachment behaviors in autistic children. *Journal of Autism and Developmental Disorders, 14,* 231–244.

Sigman, M., & Ungerer, J.A. (1984b). Cognitive and language skills in autistic, mentally retarded, and normal children. *Developmental Psychology, 20,* 293–302.

Smith, I.M., & Bryson, S.E. (1994). Imitation and action in autism: A critical review. *Psychological Bulletin, 116,* 259–273.

Snow, M.E., Hertzig, M.E., & Shapiro, T. (1987). Expression of emotion in young autistic children. *Journal of the American Academy of Child and Adolescent Psychiatry, 26,* 836–838.

Sparling, J.W. (1991). Brief report: A prospective case report of infantile autism from pregnancy to four years. *Journal of Autism and Developmental Disorders, 21,* 229–236.

Spitzer, R.L., & Siegel, B. (1990). The *DSM-III-R* field trial of pervasive developmental disorders. *Journal of the American Academy of Child and Adolescent Psychiatry, 29,* 855–862.

Sroufe, L.A., & Rutter, M. (1984). The domain of developmental psychopathology. *Child Development, 55,* 17–29.

Stone, W.L., & Hogan, K.L. (1993). A structured parent interview for identifying young children with autism. *Journal of Autism and Developmental Disorders, 23,* 639–652.

Stone, W.L., & Lemanek, K.L. (1990). Parental report of social behaviors in autistic preschoolers. *Journal of Autism and Developmental Disorders, 20,* 513–522.

Stone, W.L., Lemanek, K.L., Fishel, P.T., Fernandez, M.C., & Altemeier, W.A. (1990). Play and imitation skills in the diagnosis of autism in young children. *Pediatrics, 86,* 267–272.

Stone, W.L., Ousley, O.Y., & Littleford, C. (1995, March). *A comparison of elicited imitation in young children with autism and developmental delay.* Poster session presented at the annual Gatlinburg Conference on Research and Theory in Mental Retardation and Developmental Disabilities, Gatlinburg, TN.

Stone, W.L., & Rosenbaum, J.L. (1988). A comparison of teacher and parent views of autism. *Journal of Autism and Developmental Disorders, 18,* 403–414.

Strain, P.S., Hoyson, M., & Jamieson, B. (1985, Spring). Normally developing preschoolers as intervention agents for autistic-like children: Effects on class deportment and social interaction. *Journal of the Division for Early Childhood,* 105–115.

Tilton, J.R., & Ottinger, D.R. (1964). Comparison of the toy play behavior of autistic, retarded, and normal children. *Psychological Reports, 15,* 967–975.

Volkmar, F.R., & Cohen, D.J. (1988). Classification and diagnosis of childhood autism. In E. Schopler & G.B. Mesibov (Eds.), *Diagnosis and assessment in autism* (pp. 71–89). New York: Plenum Press.

Volkmar, F.R., Cohen, D.J., Hoshino, Y., Rende, R.D., & Paul, R. (1988). Phenomenology and classification of the childhood psychoses. *Psychological Medicine, 18,* 191–201.

Volkmar, F.R., Cohen, D.J., & Paul, R. (1986). An evaluation of *DSM-III* criteria for infantile autism. *Journal of the American Academy of Child Psychiatry, 25,* 190–197.

Volkmar, F.R., Stier, D.M., & Cohen, D.J. (1985). Age of recognition of Pervasive Developmental Disorder. *American Journal of Psychiatry, 142,* 1450–1452.

Walker, E.F., Grimes, K.E., Davis, D.M., & Smith, A.J. (1993). Childhood precursors of schizophrenia: Facial expressions of emotion. *American Journal of Psychiatry, 150,* 1654–1660.

Watkins, J.M., Asarnow, R.F., & Tanguay, P.E. (1988). Symptom development in childhood-onset schizophrenia. *Journal of Child Psychology and Psychiatry, 29,* 865–878.

Wetherby, A.M., Yonclas, D.G., & Bryan, A.A. (1989). Communicative profiles of preschool children with handicaps: Implications for early identification. *Journal of Speech and Hearing Disorders, 54,* 148–158.

Wing, L. (1969). The handicaps of autistic children—A comparative study. *Journal of Child Psychology and Psychiatry, 10,* 1–40.

Wing, L. (1988). The continuum of autistic characteristics. In E. Schopler & G.B. Mesibov (Eds.), *Diagnosis and assessment in autism* (pp. 91–110). New York: Plenum Press.

Yirmiya, N., Kasari, C., Sigman, M., & Mundy, P. (1989). Facial expressions of affect in autistic, mentally retarded, and normal children. *Journal of Child Psychology and Psychiatry, 30,* 725–735.

Zeanah, C.H., Davis, S., & Silverman, M. (1988). The question of autism in an atypical infant. *American Journal of Psychotherapy, 42,* 135–150.

CHAPTER 13

The School-Age Child with Autism

KATHERINE A. LOVELAND AND BELGIN TUNALI-KOTOSKI

For the child with autism, the elementary school years bring challenges associated with the changing expectations that accompany increasing physical and behavioral maturity. From age 6 to age 12, the child with autism faces transitions to new learning environments, contact with new peers and adults, and departures from familiar places and routines. These changes affect many domains of functioning; the child is required to adapt to more complex and demanding social environments, to learn more sophisticated skills, to communicate at a higher level, and to process more information. Such experiences, which are common to children of school age, are particularly challenging for those with autism, who not only must contend with developmental delays in multiple domains but also have difficulty adjusting to changes in their environments.

Most children with autism make progress during the school years, acquiring new skills and learning to cope with new people, places, and events. The developmental path followed by an individual child during this period is difficult to predict; it is the complex product of a dynamic process linking neural maturation with environmental influences and the child's own self-regulatory activity (Cicchetti & Tucker, 1994). However, some trends in development can be projected.

By the age of 6, children with autism have begun to diverge from one another according to characteristics such as degree of language delay and intellectual deficit. These divergent developmental paths have much to do with later outcome; perhaps the best-known example of this divergence is the better outcome observed for those children who have acquired some oral language by age 5 (Rutter, Greenfield, & Lockyer, 1967). Thus, children with autism but without mental retardation (high-functioning autism) may be expected to respond to the challenges of the school years differently from those with both autism and mental retardation (lower-functioning autism).

The behavior of a child with autism in the school years is likely to be more obviously discrepant from that of nondisabled age-mates than it was earlier in life; that is, domains of development such as social and communicative functioning may become more, rather than less, divergent from their expected trajectories, particularly in the more severely autistic child. A lack of normal peer relationships, an absence or paucity of pretend play, the presence of repetitive behaviors or focused interests, and a marked impairment of social relatedness become clearly delineated in contrast to normative expectations for children in this age group. This increasing discrepancy is due in large part to changes in expectations for the child's behavior—that is, the inability to follow directions, to initiate interactions, or to inhibit motor stereotypies is much more obvious in an 8-year-old than in a 3-year-old.

Although such broad trends as those discussed above can be identified, tracing the so-called typical development of the school-age child with autism is complicated by the fact that classification of children on the autistic spectrum of disorders remains controversial (Tsai, 1992). Even though the syndrome of autism was identified more than 50 years ago (Kanner, 1943), there is surprisingly little agreement today about the nature of the syndrome or its relationship to other diagnostic categories, including mental retardation. This lack of agreement reflects in part a tension between categorical and dimensional approaches to classification. Research tends to support a picture of autism as multidimensional and multiply determined, but clinical and educational practice is based on assignment of children to discrete diagnostic categories. Despite the persistence of the diagnostic category of autism in clinical practice, there is evidence of considerable heterogeneity among persons diagnosed with autism (Gillberg & Coleman, 1992). The "spectrum of autistic disorder" (Wing & Gould, 1979) may include subtypes differing in etiology, clinical presentation, or developmental course as well as in the level of cognitive, social, or language disability (Volkmar et al., 1994). (These issues are explored in greater depth in other chapters of this Section.) For example, although both *DSM-IV* and *ICD-10* distinguish between Autistic Disorder (AD) and Asperger's Syndrome (AS), in practice, distinguishing these categories reliably and without overlap is difficult. In addition, some individuals, although manifesting symptoms of autism, do not qualify clearly for the diagnosis of AD or AS. At present, because of inconsistent methods of categorization across studies and insufficient information about the taxonomic validity of various categories, it is difficult to interpret the research literature with regard to the development of children in these possible subtypes. This state of affairs contributes to difficulty in identifying developmental expectations for children with autism in the school years.

This chapter reviews development in both lower- and higher-functioning school-age children with AD. The authors recognize, however, that the relevant literature will include studies of children diagnosed with atypical autism, Pervasive Developmental Disorder Not Otherwise Specified (PDD-NOS), Asperger's Syndrome, or other pervasive developmental disorders. As children develop during this period, the organization and trajectory of development in any number of domains may be expected to differ among higher- and lower-functioning children with autism. At the same time, however, continuities as well as discontinuities may become apparent between development in the school years, and earlier and later development. Although a wide-ranging literature provides information about the behavioral development of children with autism, the focus in this chapter is on several areas of particular interest in the development of these children from age 6 to age 12.

DEVELOPMENTAL ISSUES FOR THE SCHOOL-AGE CHILD WITH AUTISM

Social and Adaptive Skills

Deficits in social behavior and social understanding are particularly characteristic of persons with autism (see Chapter 8). Since autism was first described by Kanner (1943), these deficits have been recognized as an essential component of the syndrome. They first become obvious in the preschool years, when a failure to establish peer relationships, a lack of normal relatedness with familiar people, a preference for aloneness, poor eye contact and gesture, tactile defensiveness, and lack of initiative in communication become evident in most children with autism (Rutter, 1978; Wing & Gould, 1979). Social deficits may gradually decrease in severity during the school years, as the child begins to benefit from intervention and from learning to cope in familiar situations and with familiar people (Gillberg, 1984; Gillberg & Coleman, 1992). However, in general, the social deficits seen in the preschool child with autism tend to persist through the school years and beyond, even though the form in which they are manifested may change and the effects of the maturation and development of the individual may become evident (Rutter & Garmezy, 1983).

Although considerable heterogeneity occurs among children with autism in the presentation of their social behavior, some generalizations can be made. For example, Wing and colleagues have described three subtypes of autistic social behavior that capture many of the manifestations of autism seen in the school-age child (Wing & Attwood, 1987; Wing & Gould, 1979): (a) the aloof group, (b) the passive group, and (c) the active-but-odd group.

The *aloof* group are those most likely to be described as classically autistic. They do not seek, and may actively avoid, contact with others, and they may become very distressed if it is thrust on them. They do not initiate communication (even though some can speak), and much of their time may be occupied with stereotypies or other repetitive interests. These children with autism are noted for their unresponsiveness and their failure to initiate interactions with both peers and adults (Freitag, 1970; Loveland & Landry, 1986; Trad, Bernstein, Shapiro, & Hertzig, 1993). They often do not play with other children or demonstrate interest in friendships (Rutter, 1974). Deficits in their ability to use gaze and gesture appropriately in social situations lead to frequent failures to communicate (Buitelaar, van Engeland, de Kogel, de Vries, & van Hooff, 1991). Aloof children with autism may be so unresponsive that directing and maintaining their attention is very difficult; thus, it may be easier to get their attention using proximal rather than distal stimulation (e.g., touching a child's hand rather than pointing to something). These children may seem at times to be deaf, even though they are not. Lacking a complete participation in the usual set of social signals and routines that govern human interactions, aloof children with autism are distinctly handicapped in social situations. Although they may exhibit emotions, their emotions are not necessarily tied to contexts easily interpreted by others and can be puzzling and frustrating to caregivers. Tantrums are common, particularly when these children are frustrated by disruption of a routine or by other circumstances they cannot control. Individuals with these characteristics are most often seen in the preschool age group, but some continue in this manner into later childhood, adolescence, and adulthood; they are most likely to be persons with significant mental retardation. Quite often, they have a difficult and lengthy adjustment to a new school placement, and social problems are likely to arise in the new classroom.

In the *passive* group are children who do not actively avoid social contact with others, but who lack the spontaneous and intuitive grasp of social interaction that is shared by normally developing children. They will accept the social approaches of others but often do not have the skills to respond appropriately. Their communication and play behaviors are rigid and sometimes stereotyped. With more language

and fewer motor stereotypies, they tend to function at a somewhat higher developmental level than those in the aloof group, and they are, in general, easier to manage. Even so, passive children with autism require considerable help to relate to peers in the classroom or in other situations. Some children who start out displaying the aloof pattern of behavior later have a better fit with the passive group. Thus, presentation as aloof versus passive may depend to some extent on the child's developmental level or IQ, and a transition from one category to the other may reflect maturation as well as accumulation of social experiences.

The *active-but-odd* group are those who would usually be described as having high-functioning autism or, in some cases, Asperger's Syndrome. They actively seek out contact with others, but the form and quality of their social approaches are unusual and often inappropriate. These higher-functioning children with autism experience difficulty in relating socially to peers and others, even though they may have considerable language skills and may be interested in communicating with others. Characteristic of this group are such behaviors as repetitive questioning, inappropriate touching, conversation focused exclusively on their own narrow interests, and odd postures, gestures, and facial expressions. Their social behavior and communication seem to reflect a view of social interactions that is literal, concrete, and lacking in awareness of the feelings, thought, and motives of others. Because they are frequently intellectually able, their autistic characteristics are sometimes identified later than those of other children with autism. In contrast to lower-functioning children, active-but-odd children may be aware to some extent that they are different and not always accepted by others, and this knowledge can be a source of distress. They tend to prefer rigid and predictable routines; unexpected events, new people, and unfamiliar surroundings are very stressful to them. When they are highly stressed, they may regress to behaviors displayed at earlier ages (e.g., tantrums, self-stimulatory behaviors) or may even exhibit signs of psychosis (Wing & Attwood, 1987). Because they are relatively able, they are often placed in classes or other situations in which they are expected to exercise age-appropriate social judgment and social behavior. These situations can lead to difficulties for the school-age child who cannot meet the social expectations of peers.

Along with their many social deficits, children with autism have strengths in a number of areas and can make progress during the school years. For example, these children usually display signs of attachment to their parents and other caregivers, including distress upon separation (Volkmar, Cohen, & Paul, 1986). Studies have suggested that the attachment behavior of autistic children is not different in kind from that of other developmentally delayed children or of younger nondisabled children (Shapiro, Sherman, Calamari, & Koch, 1987; Sigman & Mundy, 1989; Sigman & Ungerer, 1984). Most autistic children do form such attachments. Moreover, autistic children respond differently to different persons and in different situations (Landry & Loveland, 1988; Sigman & Ungerer, 1984). They are not indifferent to other persons, but they are aware to some extent that different persons hold different significance for them. In addition, in the preschool and school years, they demonstrate mirror self-recognition, provided they have reached a mental age comparable to that at which nondisabled children achieve self-recognition (Dawson & McKissick, 1984; Ferrari & Matthews, 1983). Whatever the basis of their social deficits, they seem able to distinguish self from other(s). Thus, at least some of the foundations for normal social behavior appear to be present in children with autism.

Despite considerable clinical and research evidence that children with autism are deficient in social behavior, documentation of these deficits by use of standardized test instruments is needed (Volkmar & Klin, 1993) to reveal patterns of development across age groups and with reference to normative data. Research using adaptive behavior scales to study social behavior in autism has clearly shown that social and interpersonal skills of autistic persons are poorer than would be expected, based on their IQ and overall developmental level, and that people with autism are weaker in these areas than are comparable persons with other developmental disabilities (Ando & Yoshimura, 1979; Ando, Yoshimura, & Wakabayashi, 1980; Klin, Volkmar, & Sparrow, 1992; Loveland &

Kelley, 1988, 1991; Rodrigue, Morgan, & Geffken, 1991; Rumsey, Rapoport, & Sceery, 1985; Sparrow & Cicchetti, 1987; Volkmar et al., 1987). Moreover, evidence suggests that the socialization deficits of autism are not explainable as a result of overall developmental delay (Rodrigue et al., 1991) but appear to be a robust pattern that is associated with the syndrome of autism and persists over development in high- and low-functioning persons of both genders (Freeman et al., 1991; McLennan, Lord, & Schopler, 1993). Social delays seem to be more severe, relative to other domains of functioning, for those children with autism who also have mental retardation (Burack & Volkmar, 1992). In addition to this uneven pattern of development across domains, individuals with both autism and mental retardation may also exhibit more developmental regressions than do high-functioning individuals with autism.

In general, the social/adaptive skills of children with autism do not necessarily continue to improve with advancing age, as would ordinarily be expected. Some studies have shown little or no relationship between level of social-adaptive skills and chronological age in children or adolescents with autism (Jacobson & Ackerman, 1990; Loveland & Kelley, 1988, 1991). This pattern may reflect a tendency of these individuals to regress or to reach plateaus in development, or it may reflect the wide variability in performance often seen among children with autism. However, other studies have found that certain adaptive skills, such as communication and self-care, have a more predictable relationship with age—that is, older children have more skills than younger ones (Ando et al., 1980; Ando & Yoshimura, 1979; Loveland & Kelley, 1991). The literature clearly shows that the development of social skills is delayed in persons with autism; less clear, however, is what one should expect for the development of these skills in individual children.

Conclusions: Social and Adaptive Skills

Although deficits in social skills relative to other areas of functioning are characteristic of children with autism, their manifestations vary widely in the school-age child. These manifestations are linked to the severity of autism and each child's level of cognitive functioning. Some children with autism, particularly those with mental retardation, may exhibit regressions or plateaus in social development, with little progress being made over a period of time. In general, children with autism can be expected to make progress in social skills during the school years, but they will do so at a slower pace than their nondisabled age-mates.

Language and Communication

Deficits in language and communication are also characteristic of the school-age child with autism. Many children with autism have little language by age 5 or 6 years, and, in those children, deficits in nonverbal communication are usually also evident (Loveland & Landry, 1986). For example, lower-functioning and younger school-age children with autism may have continued difficulty in joint attention interactions, in which gestures such as pointing, showing, and gaze following are used to direct attention and establish a shared focus of interest (Landry & Loveland, 1988; Loveland & Landry, 1986; Mundy, Sigman, Ungerer, & Sherman, 1986). These children may fail to use or to respond to such gestural behaviors or may do so inconsistently, leading to marked difficulty in their maintaining social communicative interactions. These deficits in social communication are a significant barrier to learning because much effort must be expended just to direct and maintain the child's attention. Some children without oral language do successfully acquire a vocabulary of sign, or learn to use communicative aids such as pictures representing common requests (e.g., picture of a toilet to represent a request to go to the bathroom).

The presence of speech before age 5 is an indicator for a better prognosis in children with autism (Rutter, 1983) and is characteristic of those who become higher functioning. In school-age children with autism who do develop language, speech is likely to be pragmatically inappropriate as well as developmentally delayed. Among the characteristic features of language in children with autism are immediate and delayed echolalia; pronoun reversals; unusual intonation; bizarre, idiosyncratic, or metaphorical speech including neologisms; and stereotyped speech. High-functioning children who develop considerable language skills may primarily exhibit more subtle manifestations of language disorder, such as oddities of conversational interaction. The latter children, despite their pragmatic difficulties, may exhibit unusual strengths in some aspects of language development, such as word decoding skills that lead to unusually early reading or *hyperlexia* (Frith & Snowling, 1986; O'Connor & Hermelin, 1994). Some of the characteristics of language in children with autism are discussed in more detail below.

Echolalia

Although echolalic speech is considered characteristic of children with autism (Rutter, 1968), it is by no means present in all of them, nor is it independent of developmental level (Fay & Butler, 1968; Howlin, 1982; McEvoy, Loveland, & Landry, 1988). A number of studies have suggested that echolalia serves a purpose in the development of language in autistic children, possibly by allowing the child to take a conversational turn and thereby remain involved in a social communicative exchange (Fay, 1973; Prizant & Duchan, 1981). Prizant and Duchan (1981) and McEvoy et al., (1988) found that both immediate and delayed echolalia can serve a variety of functions in conversational exchanges: turn-taking, declarative statements, rehearsal, self-regulatory utterances, yes answers, and requests. One should be cautious in assigning specific meanings to the echolalic utterances of children with autism; such meanings depend to a large extent on contextual cues and the responses of the listener, and thus they can be open to a variety of interpretations (Loveland, Landry, Hughes, Hall, & McEvoy, 1988; McEvoy et al., 1988; Rydell & Mirenda, 1994). Echolalia may be best viewed as a communicative strategy used by children with autism who cannot consistently produce spontaneous speech. Another possibility is that echolalia itself aids the process of language acquisition, perhaps by sustaining the social-interactional context in which conversation (and learning) takes place (Rydell & Mirenda, 1994). However, a study by Tager-Flusberg and Calkins (1990), in which the utterances of children with autism were transcribed over the period of a year, found that the children's imitative utterances are not necessarily of greater length or complexity than their spontaneous speech. Thus, although echolalia may facilitate conversational skills, it does not necessarily facilitate grammatical development. Nevertheless, echolalic speech may be related in predictable ways to the development of language in children with autism. McEvoy et al., (1988) found that the proportion of echolalic language by children with autism was greatest at lower language levels, suggesting that as children acquire more language, less and less of it is echolalic. We should expect to see echolalic communication gradually replaced with spontaneous speech over time, in school-age children with autism who are continuing to acquire language.

Pronoun Errors

Errors in use of personal pronouns (i.e., I/you pronoun reversals) have long been described as characteristic of verbal persons with autism (Bartak & Rutter, 1974; Fay, 1979). Pronoun reversals occur in the course of normal development at around age 2, but, in most cases, not frequently and only for a limited time (Charney, 1980; Chiat, 1982; Loveland, 1984). Similarly, most persons with autism do not make pronoun reversals consistently or frequently (Lee, Hobson, & Chiat, 1994; Loveland & Landry, 1986; Tager-Flusberg, 1989). These errors are particularly striking when they occur in school-age children with autism because they usually seem to be out-of-keeping with the children's overall level of language development. Although autistic pronoun errors were interpreted in the past as indicating a confusion between the concepts of *I* and *you* (i.e., self and other; Bettelheim, 1967), more recently they have been interpreted to show a confusion of social roles, cognitive perspectives, or linguistic means of representing them (Charney, 1981; Fay, 1979; Loveland & Landry, 1986). Loveland and Landry showed that appropriate use of *I* and *you* by preschool and school-age autistic children was positively related to their ability to initiate joint attention interactions by means of gesture, suggesting that use of these terms is closely tied to the achievement of a basic social reciprocity. More recently, Lee et al., (1994) found that although autistic school-age children and adolescents

made few pronoun reversal errors in tests of pronoun use, they were reported to make them sporadically in their everyday life. This finding suggested that they know how to use the pronouns, but they may have difficulty identifying their own or others' social roles in some situations.

Conversational Skills

Many children with autism do not reach a level of development at which true conversational exchanges are possible. However, some forms of echolalic or stereotyped speech can function communicatively, and autistic children with little spontaneous language may use these forms of speech to engage in reciprocal communicative interactions (Hurtig, Ensrud, & Tomblin, 1982; Prizant & Duchan, 1981). This skill is highly important for school-age children with autism because with this skill, they acquire one of the keys for accessing the social world. Thus, it is important that lower-functioning, less verbal children with autism be encouraged to engage in whatever level of conversational interaction is possible for them and to use echolalia, stereotyped questions, delayed echoes, and other kinds of speech to scaffold their entry into this essential social experience.

In high-functioning persons with autism, a delay in social skills related to language use (language pragmatics) may be combined with relatively preserved grammar, a large vocabulary, and a high degree of fluency (Tager-Flusberg et al., 1990). Recent evidence suggests that this pattern of development in high-functioning persons with autism may reflect an adequate development of basic language skills such as knowledge of phonetics, but a specific impairment of more complex and interpretive language skills, including comprehension (Minshew, Goldstein, & Siegel, 1995). As a result, the high-functioning school-age child with autism is commonly described as "very verbal" but at the same time "a poor communicator."

Conversational speech of children with autism is usually described as deficient in a variety of ways. For example, the child's conversation may focus on limited topics of interest to no one but the child (e.g., reading maps); speech may be pedantic and formal in situations where this style is out of place; socially inappropriate statements or questions may be produced (e.g., "You've sure gotten fat!"); references may be hard to follow because of a failure to consider the speaker's point of view; intonation and prosody may be odd or uninformative (Fine, Bartolucci, Ginsberg, & Szatmari, 1991); and neologisms or other idiosyncratic speech may be used (Baltaxe, 1977; Fine et al., 1991; Loveland, Tunali, Kelley, & McEvoy, 1989). In addition, children with autism may be somewhat unresponsive to the speech of conversational partners, or they may respond in unexpected ways that suggest they have difficulty identifying and maintaining a topic of discourse. Even when children with autism are gaining structural language skills during their development, research suggests that they are not gaining discourse skills at a comparable rate (Tager-Flusberg & Anderson, 1991).

The conversational deficiencies of children with autism have been explained in various ways. A study by Fine, Bartolucci, Szatmari, and Ginsberg (1994) on cohesive links in the conversational discourse of children and adolescents with high-functioning autism or Asperger's Syndrome found that the high-functioning autism group did not tend to link their utterances to earlier statements in the conversation, suggesting that they may not be as attuned to the conversational context as a nonautistic speaker would be. The Asperger's group, by contrast, made errors such as referring to things for which there was no prior referent. These individuals seemed to have little awareness of the listener's need for information. Similar findings have resulted from studies of referential communication in verbal persons with autism. Loveland et al., (1989) asked children and adolescents with autism or Down syndrome (DS) to learn a game and teach it (verbally) to another person, with the learner giving three levels of increasingly specific prompts as needed. Even though autistic subjects had learned the game as well as DS subjects, they required much more specific prompting to convey the necessary target information to another person. Autistic subjects appeared to have difficulty selecting and organizing information to convey to a listener, even when

they knew the information. Their performance improved markedly, however, when they were given specific prompting that structured their responses. The Loveland et al. study also suggested that verbal persons with autism are less aware than nonautistic speakers of the listener's need for information. A study on the ability to make conversational responses within an accepted social framework (social scripts) found that children and adolescents with autism were less likely to give helpful or empathic responses to a conversational partner's distress than were comparison subjects with DS. Some of the autistic group did make empathic responses, however, after seeing such responses modeled (Loveland & Tunali, 1991). This study suggested that at least some persons with autism may be aware of the need to take into account a listener's point of view, but they may not know how to do so.

These studies all indicate that school-age children with autism are likely to have difficulty making the social judgments that ordinarily guide conversation. The specific reasons for this difficulty are not certain; however, there is consensus that it has something to do with a failure to understand other persons: their knowledge and beliefs, feelings, and other attributes that are not concretely observable. Research also suggests that conversational difficulties may arise from the children's confusion about how to act on what they know about others; when autistic children are given added structure or prompts, they can frequently speak more informatively. It is thus somewhat encouraging to conclude that, in many cases, children with autism actually know more than they say, and, with appropriate external structuring, they can communicate more effectively.

Narratives

A small but growing literature documents the ability of verbal children with autism to tell stories of various kinds. Story narratives are of special interest for the study of autism because they are an example of discourse for which fairly well-defined cultural expectations exist (for example, stories are expected to have a distinct beginning, middle, and end) and because they presuppose considerable interpersonal awareness between speakers, if the story is to be understood. Children with autism might be expected to have an imperfect grasp of cultural expectations as well as impaired interpersonal awareness. Thus, differences between the story narratives of children with and without autism should be expected.

Several studies have focused on storytelling. Tager-Flusberg and Quill (1987) and Bruner and Feldman (1993) found that persons with autism told stories that were less complex, were shorter, and contained more grammatical errors than those of nondisabled persons of a similar developmental level. Other researchers who examined the content of stories concluded that children with autism are likely to talk less about characters' mental states (Baron-Cohen, Leslie, & Frith, 1986); their narratives are pragmatically deficient and include neologisms and idiosyncratic expressions not usually found in the narratives of other children (Loveland, McEvoy, et al., 1990). Some verbal children and adolescents with autism, particularly those of lower IQ, apparently do not have any grasp of the conventional, culturally determined story schema. Loveland, McEvoy, et al., (1990) reported that some of their subjects with autism, when asked to tell the story of a puppet show, responded by describing the shape, color, or movements of the puppets ("Puppets. They are red and green. They go up and down . . .") but without conveying any kind of story. This response may indicate that these individuals lack a grasp of what a story *is,* perhaps reflecting a failure of acculturation (Bruner & Feldman, 1993; Loveland & Tunali, 1993). The study of story narratives in children with autism, though now only beginning, may eventually provide a window into the child's growing social and cultural awareness.

Conclusions: Language and Communication

Like their social skills, the communication skills of school-age children with autism vary widely according to degree of autistic impairment and level of development. Although many children with autism make considerable progress in communication during the school years, impairments of social aspects of communication remain a significant problem. Recent research suggests that verbal children with autism are capable of more sophisticated use of language (e.g., storytelling) than was previously thought, that they may communicate more effectively when given prompting or modeling of appropriate conversational language, and that even echolalic speech may contribute to the development of conversational skills.

Emotional Behavior

Emotional behavior, an essential part of a child's social development, provides a basis for communication and for an understanding of self and others. Children without autism engage in affective interactions from early in infancy (e.g., Stern, 1985). Before they reach preschool, they can not only produce readily recognizable facial expressions but also identify simple emotions in others. During the school years, these skills increase and may reach a ceiling in later childhood when emotional behaviors become similar to those of adults.

In individuals with autism, however, emotional development may be quite different. Because it has been hypothesized that children with autism are centrally deficient in relating emotionally to others (Hobson, 1993), much of the research on emotion in people with autism has been devoted to determining whether they do or do not have a special deficit in understanding or expressing emotion. This point remains controversial. Nevertheless, a clear finding is that children with autism display emotional responses that seem unusual, inappropriate, excessive, or inadequate compared with the responses of other children in similar situations. Also, they often behave in ways that suggest they are not aware of or concerned with the feelings of others, or that they do not understand the consequences of feelings in other people. Researchers have found that persons with autism have difficulty in recognizing the affective expressions of others and in sharing affect in communicative situations (Hobson, Ouston, & Lee, 1988; Loveland et al., 1995; Snow, Hertzig, & Shapiro, 1987; Weeks & Hobson, 1987). These individuals have also been found to have differences in their production of spontaneous and elicited affective expressions, with fewer positive expressions and more unusual or anomalous expressions than comparison subjects (Loveland et al.,

1994; Yirmiya, Kasari, Sigman, & Mundy, 1989). Although some studies have suggested that there may be an underlying deficit in perception of affect in children with autism (e.g., Loveland et al., 1995), other studies have not always reported such specific affective deficits, or have found no differences between persons with autism and comparison subjects matched for verbal mental age (MA) (Ozonoff, Pennington, & Rogers, 1990; Prior, Dahlstrom, & Squires, 1990). Also, persons with developmental disabilities other than autism (e.g., Down syndrome, learning disabilities) have also been found, in some studies, to have affective deficiencies (Hobson, Ouston, & Lee, 1989; Loveland, Fletcher, & Bailey, 1990). Thus, the affective deficiencies of children and adults with autism may partly reflect a developmental delay, and their affective development may be closely related to their level of language development.

Conclusions: Emotional Behavior

There is abundant clinical evidence that the affective development of children with autism differs from that of other children, but laboratory research studies on this topic have not consistently found evidence of affective deficiencies. In school-age children with autism, affective deficiencies could contribute to their difficulties in forming peer relationships. For example, children who fail to realize they have offended others will have difficulty making friends. More research is needed to explore the affective behavior and perceptions of children with autism in natural settings, so as to identify the consequences of affective deficiencies for the child's social development.

Academic Achievement

During the school years, children with autism experience significant changes in their cognitive, emotional, social, and adaptive development; consequently, their educational programs should be adapted to their changing needs over time. Because children with autism have unusual intellectual and academic skill profiles, their individual educational needs vary considerably. Most low-functioning children with autism require structure and individualized assistance in many, if not all, academic areas.

These children, as well as those with moderate levels of disability, may exhibit distinctly uneven profiles of ability; language-related skills especially are much more difficult for them than nonlanguage skills. Unfortunately, much classroom activity requires reading, listening, and speaking, and even arithmetic involves reading numerals. As a result, children whose nonverbal skills are much better developed than their verbal skills (particularly oral language) may be viewed as lower functioning than they really are, and they may be placed in classes that do not challenge them sufficiently in their areas of strength. Great care is needed in evaluating profiles of ability for children with autism. Their individual educational needs may not fit readily with the prepared programs of their school districts.

Many high-functioning school-age autistic children do not have significant delays in basic reading, spelling, and arithmetic skills. Instead, for such children, these skills are often intact or even precocious (Rumsey, 1992). For instance, a number of investigators have studied hyperlexia, in which the child displays exceptionally well-developed reading skills relative to IQ or mental age (Goldberg, 1987; O'Connor & Hermelin, 1994; Whitehouse & Harris, 1984). Hyperlexia is commonly found in a subgroup of high-functioning autistic children. O'Connor and Hermelin (1994) studied two children, ages 5 and 8, with high-functioning autism and hyperlexia. The children were paired for comparison with two normally developing children of average reading level. They were all tested at 6-month intervals over 2 years, and at ages 9 and 12. The reading ability of the children with autism, especially their phonological decoding skills, was very advanced for their chronological and mental ages. Their comprehension was also good, but at a level more commensurate with their mental age. Their reading was much faster than the comparison subjects' reading, especially with difficult material. These findings suggest some degree of dissociation between phonological decoding skills and semantic comprehension in these children. Additional research is needed to clarify the role of hyperlexia in the cognitive and language development of high-functioning children with autism and its implications for education.

Researchers have also studied dyslexia, in hopes of gaining a better understanding of the specific academic differences seen in school-age children with autism. In their comparative study of children with autism and children with dyslexia (matched for reading age), Frith and Snowling (1983) found that the dyslexic subjects had superior skills in comprehension and use of semantic context but had difficulties with phonological processing. The subjects with autism had problems in comprehension and the use of semantic context. This result is consistent with the findings from Rumsey and Hamburger's (1990) study, which found that high-functioning men with autism had better phonological and rote auditory memory skills than comparison subjects with severe dyslexia. These findings, taken together, suggest that verbal children with autism may have an advantage in some aspects of reading (i.e., phonological decoding) and a disadvantage in others (e.g., comprehension), relative to children without autism but of comparable mental age.

In general, children with autism do not necessarily share a characteristic set of academic difficulties; instead, they exhibit deficits that appear related to their individual patterns of strengths and weaknesses. Recently, a line of research has emerged that focuses on specific academic needs of and service delivery to individuals with autism and their families. As research has improved understanding of autism and the special needs of these children and their families, educational approaches to this group have changed significantly; however, educational systems did not begin to respond to their specific needs until the mid-1970s. Before this period, many public school programs were not accessible to children with autism (Schreibman, 1988). Families had to create their own resources through private organizations and were often left without guidance and support. Given this history, experiencing difficulties in dealing with school systems, finding appropriate programs, and gaining access to available services have historically been sources of frustration and stress for parents of school-age children with autism (Tunali & Power, 1993; Unger & Powell, 1980).

During the past several years, however, research on educating children with autism has provided a number of new and important educational directions (Schreibman, 1988). Among the major developments in education are emphases on comprehensive and functional curricula, teacher training and education (Dunlap, Koegel, & Egel, 1979; Halle, 1982), focus on the optimal educational environment and classroom instructions (e.g., inclusion, mainstreaming, emphasis on learning in the natural setting; Kamps, Walker, Maher, & Rotholtz, 1992), transition of the child and the services to less restrictive and more productive community-based settings (Schopler & Mesibov, 1983), and more comprehensive treatment combined with intervention that is longitudinal and age-appropriate (Schreibman, 1988). Despite these exciting changes, appropriate programs, much needed services, and the research to improve knowledge in teaching the school-age child with autism remain limited.

Conclusions: Academic Achievement

Because the individual educational needs of children with autism vary widely, meeting their needs in the classroom is often difficult. Both low-functioning and high-functioning children with autism are difficult to serve because they do not necessarily learn or develop in the same ways as other children (e.g., children with hyperlexia). More research is needed, on both the neurodevelopmental basis of learning in children with autism and on techniques to facilitate their learning of academic skills.

PSYCHIATRIC AND BEHAVIORAL PROBLEMS

Individuals with autism often exhibit social, emotional, and behavioral characteristics that overlap with those of other psychiatric disorders. Given their complexity and varying degrees of impairment, it can be a challenge to identify symptoms of autism and separate them from those of a potentially coexisting psychiatric disorder. In the developing child with autism, this task is particularly difficult, because of the changing manifestations of the disorder over time as well as the child's limited ability to give self-report. However, as the issue of comorbidity in autism begins to receive more interest and attention, studies have begun to focus on the relationship between autism and disorders such as schizophrenia, anxiety and mood disorders, and Obsessive-Compulsive Disorder. For instance, the risk of psychosis has been reported to be higher than expected in individuals with Asperger's Syndrome (approximately 3.5% of the reported cases; Clarke, Littlejohns, Corbett, & Joseph, 1989; Gillberg, 1985). Whereas mania occurs in 9% of individuals with high-functioning autism, the single most common psychiatric disorder is depression, which afflicts 15% (Frith, 1991). Anxiety disorders, mostly associated with depression, are also common in this population (7%; Frith, 1991). These and other findings emphasize that school-age children with autism are at risk for psychiatric disorders, and that it is important to identify and treat these disorders whenever possible.

Schizophrenia

Although autism and schizophrenia have been regarded as distinct and unrelated disorders (Rutter, 1972; Volkmar & Cohen, 1991), there is now controversy about the relationship between the two (Petty, Ornitz, Michelman, & Zimmerman, 1984). Over the years, autism has at various times been considered the earliest manifestation of childhood schizophrenia, or a syndrome having no relationship to schizophrenia (Petty et al., 1984; Rumsey et al., 1985; Rutter, 1972; Volkmar & Cohen, 1991). This relationship appears particularly ambiguous in regard to clinical and behavioral manifestations of autistic individuals who are described as high functioning. In addition to impairment in social relatedness and functioning, the presence of odd, idiosyncratic behaviors and preoccupations similar to those of people with schizophrenia makes this autistic group a diagnostic challenge, even in the absence of schizophrenic delusions and hallucinations. These observations have raised the possibility that autism is closely related to schizophrenia, or that persons with autism are at special risk for schizophrenia.

Despite some conflicting evidence, autism and schizophrenia have been considered clearly separate for a number of reasons: (a) autism has an earlier age of onset than childhood schizophrenia (Rutter, 1972); (b) mental retardation is common in autism but is not a usual feature of schizophrenia; similarly, schizophrenic patients often do not exhibit low adaptive skills in early childhood, with the exception of varying degrees of impairment in social relatedness and functioning; and (c) for individuals with autism, a family history of schizophrenia is rare (Kolvin, 1971). However, the recent neurodevelopmental approach to schizophrenia raises some interesting and challenging questions. Proponents of this approach speculate that, in schizophrenia, the impairment is present in the brain at a very young age, perhaps even before birth, but the clinical manifestations of the impairment change over time as the brain develops anatomically, physiologically, and functionally (Breslin & Weinberger, 1990). Such an approach holds promise for explaining why schizophrenia is usually manifested first in adolescence or later, whereas autism is present from infancy. Although as yet no agreement exists about the nature of the brain impairment present in schizophrenia or autism, this speculation has stimulated interest in both normal and abnormal development of the brain (Breslin & Weinberger, 1990).

In addition to unanswered questions on etiology, significant problems are currently encountered in defining schizophrenia. Because the nature and the degree of symptoms vary considerably among schizophrenic individuals, researchers disagree on who is and is not truly schizophrenic (Frith & Frith, 1992). Additional complications are introduced by findings from studies using different diagnostic criteria, further confusing the relationship of autism to schizophrenia. Certain studies that followed autistic children into adulthood found that some of them developed schizophrenia (Dahl, 1976; Rutter, 1970). However, in most of these studies, the diagnostic criteria for both disorders were not clearly defined (Petty et al., 1984). Thus, we cannot predict how many children with autism will later develop symptoms of schizophrenia.

In a limited number of longitudinal studies, the outcome of autism and autistic-like conditions was examined. Many of these studies are consistent in indicating that only a few individuals with autism eventually receive a formal diagnosis of schizophrenia (Asperger, 1944; Wing, 1981; Wolff & Chick, 1980). However, other studies have reported cases describing the coexistence of autistic disorder and schizophrenia-like psychosis (Clarke et al., 1989; Comings & Comings, 1991; Petty et al., 1984; Volkmar, Cohen, Hoshino, Rende, & Paul, 1988). Similarly, in a brief report, Sverd, Montero, and Gurevich (1993) described two children who were diagnosed as having co-occurring autistic disorder, schizophrenia-like psychosis, and Tourette's Syndrome. After reviewing the cases and recent literature on the topic, the researchers concluded that there appears to be a subgroup of autistic children who are at risk for developing schizophrenia-like symptoms and that Tourette's Syndrome may underlie the coexistence of the disorders in some patients. Other investigators have reported that high-functioning children and adults with autism are particularly at risk for episodic undifferentiated psychotic episodes under stressful circumstances. However, the individual usually returns to normal levels of functioning when the stressor is removed (Wing, 1981; Wolff & Chick, 1980).

Conclusions: Schizophrenia

Taken together, these studies indicate that the relationship of autism to schizophrenia is still not clear. Research suggests that at least some high-functioning individuals with autism may be at increased risk for schizophrenia or psychotic episodes. Less is known about the risks for lower-functioning individuals. New research focusing on neurodevelopmental aspects of schizophrenia offers the potential to trace neurobiological and developmental similarities and differences between persons with autism and those with adult-onset schizophrenia. Such research may help to illuminate the origins of both disorders.

The observation that stress can lead to schizophrenia-like symptoms serves to emphasize the importance of coping skills and social support for school-age children with autism. Situations that are not highly stressful for children without autism may be stressful for those with autism. For example, when social demands are high, or frequent changes in routine occur, children with autism experience a great deal of stress. Consideration of these factors is important in conceptualizing and treating psychotic episodes in children with autism.

Affective Disorders

Depression is one of the most common psychiatric disorders in persons with autism, particularly those who are high functioning. Despite their average/above-average levels of functioning in intellectual, language, adaptive, and academic areas, high-functioning individuals with autism experience chronic difficulties in social interactions and relatedness and are often painfully aware of their impairment. In the school years, when peer relationships and social skills become a crucial developmental task, developmental delays in this area generate a great deal of frustration, anxiety, and distress, which in turn increase the likelihood of psychiatric difficulties. However, when symptoms that are suggestive of an affective disorder develop, it is often difficult to make a formal diagnosis because of the autistic individual's difficulty in communicating his or her feelings (Lainhart & Folstein, 1994).

Comorbidity of affective disorders with Asperger's Syndrome has been reported (De-Long & Dwyer, 1988; Gillberg, 1985); in another case, an individual with autism had depression and trichotillomania (Hamden-Allen, 1991). Kurita and Nakayasu (1994) reported a rare case of a 20-year old autistic male presenting with seasonal affective disorder and trichotillomania. Lainhart and Folstein (1994) reviewed previously published cases of individuals with autism who had an additional diagnosis of affective disorder. Half these individuals were female, and almost all had some degree of mental retardation. The onset of affective disorder occurred during childhood for 35% of the subjects, and 50% had a family history of affective disorder or suicide. After their review, the investigators noted that the three critical features of an affective disorder—(a) a change in mood, (b) a change in the individual's view of self and the world, and (c) the appearance of vegetative symptoms—were rarely reported by the individuals themselves, which made the diagnostic assessment particularly challenging. These rare but important cases help emphasize that both high- and low-functioning individuals with autism are vulnerable to affective disorders.

Conclusions: Affective Disorders

Though apparently common in persons with autism, affective disorders are not easy to diagnose, particularly in children. There is a great need for research on methods of diagnosis and treatment of affective disorders in both high- and low-functioning individuals with autism.

Obsessive-Compulsive Disorder

Stereotyped, ritualistic behaviors similar to those found in Obsessive-Compulsive Disorder (OCD) are common in autism (Rutter, 1985; Wing & Gould, 1979). Both *DSM-III-R* (APA, 1987) and *DSM-IV* (APA, 1994) have included the presence of such behaviors as one of the major diagnostic criteria for pervasive developmental disorders. Bartak and Rutter (1976), in their study of 19 autistic children of average intelligence, stated that almost half of them had stereotypical movements and resisted changes in the environment. Unusually intense interest in subjects such as weather systems, maps, and geography, as well as unusual and repetitive play activity (e.g., reading the telephone book or train and bus schedules for fun, playing with the same toy repetitively), were all quite common. Mesibov and Shea (1980) reported that ritualistic and repetitive behaviors are more common and more intense during middle childhood and tend to diminish during adolescence and adulthood. However, other investigators report that these symptoms are often retained during adulthood. For instance, Rumsey, Rapoport, and Sceery (1985) found that many adult autistic men, regardless of their level of intellectual functioning, exhibited a number of ritualistic behaviors and compulsions, such as putting objects in certain places, hand-washing, and stereotyped touching. These behaviors can closely resemble those of persons with OCD, raising the question of a possible relationship between autism

and OCD, as well as the issue of differential diagnosis and treatment.

Some researchers claim that the stereotypies seen in autism, although superficially resembling the stereotypies of OCD, are less organized and less complex (Swedo & Rapoport, 1989). Whereas OCD behaviors are usually described as ego dystonic (i.e., recognized by the individual as undesirable), similar behaviors present in individuals with autism are thought to be ego syntonic (i.e., recognized by the individual as acceptable and desirable; Baron-Cohen, 1989; Swedo & Rapoport, 1989). However, recent research has produced findings that challenge this view of OCD in patients without autism. For instance, some researchers have observed that children with OCD do not always present with anxiety (Berg, Zahn, & Behar, 1986), and many patients with OCD have ego-syntonic obsessions and compulsions and may lack insight into the senselessness of their behaviors (Insel & Akiskal, 1986). Moreover, because of their social and communicative difficulties, even high-functioning individuals with autism may not appear to be resisting their compulsions or to be affected by associated emotional distress, making identification of a coexisting OCD difficult (Tsai, 1992). Some investigators have suggested conducting controlled studies of the efficacy of fluvoxamine and clomipramine (Gordon, Rapoport, Hamburger, State, & Mannheim, 1992) in persons with autism and OCD-like behaviors, to explore not only possible treatments but also neurochemical links between OCD and autism.

Conclusions: Obsessive-Compulsive Disorder

Ritualistic behaviors—a common characteristic of autism, especially in higher-functioning individuals—tend to become more intense during middle childhood, although they are present at other stages of development. The resemblance of these behaviors to those of persons with OCD, coupled with findings from recent limited but important studies, suggests possible similarities in underlying pathophysiology between the two disorders that require further investigation. Research is needed to investigate whether developmental continuities exist between the stereotyped movements commonly seen in younger and lower-functioning individuals with autism, and the ritualistic, OCD-like behaviors observed in more developed individuals with autism. In addition, more information is needed about the functions of these ritualistic behaviors in the daily lives of children with autism, so that appropriate decisions about treatment can be reached (whether, for example, the behaviors increase when the child is stressed or anxious, and whether the behaviors themselves serve to reduce anxiety).

Attention Deficit Hyperactivity Disorder

School-age children with autism frequently display characteristics that are associated with attention deficit hyperactivity disorder (ADHD). Symptoms such as inattention, hyperactivity, or impulsivity, as well as some associated features (e.g., low frustration tolerance, temper outbursts, mood lability, poor concentration, excessive insistence that requests be met), are observed in many settings, including school. These behaviors are among those most frequently reported by parents of children with autism, and they negatively affect the child's emotional well-being as well as his or her social and academic performance. They can be observed early in life and tend to continue through the school years, adolescence, and adulthood.

As in children without autism, attention deficits and hyperactivity in children with autism may present differently at different ages or levels of development. Whereas preschoolers may display a great deal of motor activity, older children are likely to become gradually less active, but to remain inattentive or distractible. Symptoms of attention deficit and hyperactivity often result in the placement of children with autism in self-contained or other highly structured classroom settings where distractions are minimized and tasks are presented in small steps.

The existing literature contains little discussion of the comorbidity of autism and ADHD, despite these clinical observations. One of the obvious reasons for this paucity is the way the *DSM* system defines these disorders. Like *DSM-III-R, DSM-IV* specifies that if the symptoms of inattention and hyperactivity occur during the course of a pervasive developmental disorder, an additional diagnosis

of ADHD is not given. This discourages the clinician from thinking of the child with autism as having an attention deficit, even when symptoms are severe.

Despite the difficulties inherent in diagnosing autism and ADHD comorbidly, there is now some evidence that impairments of attention and arousal may be involved in the underlying neurodevelopmental mechanisms of autism (Dawson & Lewy, 1989; Hutt, Hutt, Lee, & Ounsted, 1964; Rimland, 1964; Wainwright-Sharp & Bryson, 1993). Some investigators have studied the autonomic correlates of attention and arousal; others have investigated attention at the behavioral level in children with autism. Although it is not yet clear whether abnormalities in arousal play a role in autism (James & Barry, 1980), research suggests that persons with autism are impaired in basic information-processing and attentional operations (Wainwright-Sharp & Bryson, 1993), such that the response to sensory stimuli may be delayed or attenuated (Courchesne, 1987; Zahn, Rumsey, & Van Kannen, 1987). Given similar findings (i.e., attentuated responses) on tasks requiring selective attention (Ciesielski, Courchesne, & Elmasian, 1990), some researchers have suggested that although these individuals may not have difficulty registering information, they may have difficulties in processing it (Courchesne, Lincoln, Yeung-Courchesne, Elmasian, & Grillon, 1989; Wainwright-Sharp & Bryson, 1993). Another reported difficulty among this population is overselectivity and therefore limited usage of incoming information (Lovass, Schriebman, Koegal, & Rehm, 1971; Rincover & Ducharme, 1987). These studies emphasize that problems with attention may be present in all persons with autism to some degree, and that they are likely to affect numerous areas of functioning.

Conclusions: Attention Deficit Hyperactivity Disorder

Attention deficits and hyperactivity are among the most frequently reported and pervasive problems for children with autism. In the school years, hyperactivity usually diminishes, but problems in attention are likely to remain. Although current diagnostic practice discourages dual diagnosis of autism and

ADHD, recent research on the brain and attention in autism suggests that impairment of attention may play an important role in the development of the syndrome. The relationship of autism to attention deficits on a clinical level should receive further investigation.

EXAMPLES OF DEVELOPMENT IN THE SCHOOL-AGE CHILD WITH AUTISM

The trends in development of the child with autism during the school years are best observed through longitudinal follow-up. In the following cases, each child was seen from preschool through adolescence. These reports illustrate some of the issues that arise in the development of lower-functioning and higher-functioning children with autism, respectively. (Names of these individuals have been changed to protect confidentiality.)

A Girl with Autism and Moderate Mental Retardation

Joan was first seen at a medical center psychiatric clinic at the age of 4 years, 8 months. At the time of her first assessment, Joan lived with her mother and stepfather. Her parents had been divorced the year before. As an infant, Joan was reported to have had recurrent ear infections and delayed motor milestones. Between the ages of 12 and 18 months, she was reported to have displayed a sudden change in behavior, with loss of previously acquired language and onset of screaming episodes, running, twirling, spinning, and social withdrawal. At age 3 years, 6 months, Joan was enrolled in an early childhood intervention program, on the basis of her documented language delay. She was initially referred to the clinic for developmental evaluation and diagnosis, and she continued to receive follow-up evaluations at intervals over the succeeding 12 years. The records of these assessments depict the trends in her cognitive, social, and language development.

When first examined, Joan was restless, hyperactive, and uncooperative, with little eye contact and few signs of social relatedness. She explored her environment in an aimless manner, touching objects and spinning them. It was easier to get her attention using proximal rather than distal stimulation (e.g., touching her hand rather than pointing). She did not initiate social or communicative interaction by speech or gesture, but sometimes responded to initiations by others. Developmental testing required frequent breaks and the presentation of items in small units. She frequently did not attend and had to be reminded to look at what her hands were doing. She often perseverated, and her self-stimulatory and challenging behaviors tended to interfere with her testing. Joan often responded impulsively, but did not like to be asked to redo her work. However, with considerable structuring, her score fell above the 30-month level on the nonverbal items of the Bayley Scales of Infant Development, Mental Scale; she demonstrated receptive and expressive language at approximately a 24- to 30-month level, including both spontaneous language and echolalic speech. Her assessment led to a recommendation that she receive speech/language intervention and continue in a structured early childhood intervention program.

Joan was next seen at age 7 years, 1 month, after having been enrolled in school-based intervention for several years. She was then in a self-contained special education first-grade classroom for children with severe disabilities, where she was reported to display hyperactivity, short attention span, and behavior problems. Motor, cognitive, and social delays prevented her participation in age-appropriate physical play, such as riding bicycles and taking part in team sports. Joan also was not yet independent in toileting, dressing, or eating. On assessment, her expressive language was characterized primarily by echolalia, but she was sometimes able to respond to direct questions or commands and could point to named colors and parts of the body. Responses to gestures such as pointing were inconsistent, and she displayed little expressive gesture. Her language was found to be at a 30-month (expressive) to 36-month (receptive) level, although her nonverbal intelligence was at a mental age of 4 years, 9 months. At this point, Joan's behavior was characterized by repetitive behaviors such as spinning objects, by hyperactivity and distractibility, by some inappropriate affect, and by poor social relatedness.

At Joan's next evaluation at the clinic, she was 10 years, 7 months old. In the interval, she continued to be served in self-contained special education classrooms and to receive speech/language intervention. She was reported to have no friendships with peers at school at this time, although her behavior problems there had decreased. Her cooperativeness had distinctly improved since the previous evaluation, and she required much less external structuring to complete the assessment. She required more structure on tasks that were harder for her (verbal tasks) and less on those that were easier (nonverbal tasks). She exhibited little affect, but seemed to know when she was performing well; she said, "Good!" to herself whenever she responded correctly to an item. Despite continued problems in attention, Joan was able to attain a nonverbal mental age of 5 years, 9 months on the Leiter International Performance Scale (nonverbal IQ [NV IQ] = 55), demonstrating skills in matching by color, shape, and number, and in reproducing simple block designs. However, more abstract items, such as matching by use, were too difficult for her. Her language skills had improved to a 3- to 4-year-old level, with greater vocabulary, increased ability to respond to more complex questions and requests, skilled repetition of word- and number-strings, and decreased echolalia. More of Joan's language was now spontaneous, in 2- and 3-word utterances, although delayed echoes also appeared. Joan still rarely initiated communication, but her responsiveness to others had increased. Her receptive language was still better developed than her expressive language. Assessment of her adaptive behavior (Vineland Adaptive Behavior Scales) indicated that Joan had few skills for self-care (although she was now toilet-trained), and that her social skills were at a 2½-year level.

Joan was seen again a year later, at age 11 years, 6 months. Her cooperation at this evaluation was excellent, and her distractibility and hyperactivity were considerably reduced. Social relatedness with examiners was also improved, as shown by Joan's responsiveness to attempts to redirect her attention. Socially inappropriate behaviors were fewer, but still present (e.g., pulling her dress up over her head).

Nonverbal (NV) intelligence showed developmental progress (NV MA = 6 years, 3 months; NV IQ = 59), but language remained at a 3- to 4-year-old level, with echolalia and perseveration present in much of her speech. At the same time, Joan began to show signs of growing insight into her own behavior. For example, when frustrated by being unable to answer a question, she once said, "Joan is sad." Joan's adaptive skills also showed progress; she improved in self-care and social skills, and had notable strength in written communication skills, relative to oral skills.

At age 15 years, 2 months, Joan was seen again. At this time, she was enrolled in a self-contained life-skills class at her local high school, receiving individual speech therapy, occupational therapy, and adaptive physical education. She was mainstreamed for lunch, music, drama, and typing. During the school day, an educational aide accompanied Joan and assisted her individually in most of her activities. Joan was reported to have made significant advances in social behavior. For example, although she still rarely initiated conversation, she interacted with other students if placed in a group situation. Joan also seemed more interested in pleasing the examiners during her assessment, and she responded well to praise. Although she had greatly improved in her ability to attend and to remain on task, she still required structuring to complete more difficult tasks, both at school and during her assessment. In contrast to her earlier assessments, Joan's problems with attention and persistence now tended to take the form of distractibility and impulsive responding rather than hyperactivity. Her behavior also was improved, although some inappropriate affect and speech were still present. Joan's assessment revealed continued progress in nonverbal skills (NV MA = 7 years, 5 months; NV IQ = 57) but little progress in oral language skills, although her vocabulary had increased to about a 6-year level. Immediate and delayed echolalia were still present. Her academic achievement was found to be in the range of kindergarten to second grade, with strengths in spelling, word attack, and letter-word identification. Joan's adaptive skills had increased to a 4- to 7-year-old level, with particular weakness in interpersonal relationships.

Joan's most recent evaluation was at age 16 years, 4 months. She has made some progress in all areas, but her expressive language and social adaptive skills are still in the 4-year-old range. Joan continues to have significant difficulty with attention and concentration, expressive and receptive language, social skills, and adaptive behavior. Her overall IQ is in the moderate range of mental retardation. She is involved in extracurricular activities at her church and in Special Olympics, and she has begun to have friends in her class at school.

Interpretation

The case of Joan illustrates progression from a classically autistic presentation in the preschool years to a significantly improved, yet still autistic, presentation in adolescence. Joan exhibits many features typical of a child with autism who is moderately to severely impaired. She has a history of repetitive motor activities such as spinning objects; her language and communication are significantly more impaired than her nonverbal skills; it is difficult to direct and maintain her attention; she has been hyperactive and her behavior has been difficult to control; she has had few social relationships with peers; her play and exploration are very immature; she has inappropriate affect and poor social judgment. However, her development from the preschool years through the school years and into adolescence reveals developmental trends in a number of areas. Joan has gained nonverbal cognitive skills at a fairly constant rate throughout the period of study; her nonverbal IQ has remained stable between 55 and 60. Thus, she has continued to gain skill in nonverbal reasoning, and in visual-motor and constructional skills from preschool through adolescence. Her language has apparently reached a plateau at about a 4-year-old developmental level (attained by about age 12). She has greater weakness in expressive than in receptive language. As a result, on reaching adolescence, Joan is further behind her age-mates in academic progress than might be expected based on her nonverbal IQ. In addition, her significant language delay and autistic social deficits have combined to make her seem somewhat less intellectually able

than she may actually be; this appearance has meant that, over the years, she has received fewer opportunities to mix socially with nondisabled age-mates and has had somewhat lower expectations set for her in school than would be desirable. During the years from ages 6 to 12, the primary priorities of Joan's educational program were to develop her language and control her behavior.

Joan's adaptive skills have also increased over the years she has been assessed, but, like her language skills, they have progressed more slowly than her nonverbal skills and have reached an apparent plateau in adolescence. By age 12, she had mastered most basic self-care skills and had increased her social and communication skills; however, her recent slow progress in adaptive behavior may indicate that she is having difficulty making a transition to the greater independence, social judgment, and peer-oriented activities expected of adolescents.

Dramatic changes have taken place in Joan's attention and behavior. Starting from a state of hyperactivity, uncooperativeness, and frequent motor self-stimulation behaviors as a preschooler, she became in the school years significantly better controlled, better able to focus her attention and persist on tasks, and less disruptive in class. By adolescence, she was no longer hyperactive, although she still needed external structuring to persist on difficult tasks. Thus, over time, Joan developed improved *self*-control in a variety of situations, partly as a result of structured intervention and partly as a result of maturation.

Less dramatic but still significant changes have taken place in Joan's social behavior from preschool to adolescence. As a preschooler, Joan resembled the passive type of individual described by Wing: she rarely initiated but did respond to others. She has continued to be a relatively passive communicator, although her interest in others and her communication skills have both increased. Her assessments document steady increases in responsiveness, cooperativeness, social awareness, and relatedness as well as the beginnings of social insight and peer friendships. Some of these changes may have been facilitated by Joan's gradual increase in attentional and behavioral self-control, changes that may have helped her to benefit from both instruction and social experience.

A Boy with Pervasive Developmental Disorder and Above-Average Intelligence

James, the only child of his parents, was first brought to a medical center psychiatric outpatient clinic for an evaluation at the age of 5 years. His presenting problems were severe and frequent temper tantrums, extreme inattention and hyperactivity, restlessness, sleep difficulties, sensory abnormalities (e.g., he did not like to be touched, was overly sensitive to loud noises), extreme discomfort in response to changes in routines, and some self-stimulatory behaviors. Up to the age of 1 year, James reportedly had recurrent ear infections and was diagnosed with asthma at the age of 13 months. However, he reportedly never had a severe attack and did not have any asthma symptoms after age 2 years. Developmental milestones were met within the expected time frames, with some delays in socialization and toilet training. His parents reported that James was not very interested in interacting with his peers. They also reported that James taught himself how to read and write, could tell the day of the week that various dates fell on, and had an outstanding memory, recalling past events with every minor detail. At the age of 5, his level of nonverbal intelligence was measured by the Leiter International Performance Scale at an IQ of 145. Although the exact scores were not available, both his receptive and expressive language scores had been previously assessed to be "above age level." His preacademic skills assessed by the Wide Range Achievement Test (WRAT) were also significantly above average. During this time, James was described as a "somewhat anxious" child who was concerned about nuclear war and had some other fears (e.g., fear of heights). These anxieties were not severe enough to cause his parents concern. James was given a formal diagnosis of Pervasive Developmental Disorder Not Otherwise Specified (PDD-NOS) at the end of this evaluation.

At age 9, when he came for a follow-up evaluation, James had a set of more specific concerns. His parents reported that James had started to exhibit many unusual behaviors and

did not respond to medication (i.e., Ritalin) that was prescribed for his attentional difficulties and hyperactivity. He was often extremely anxious; he would suddenly dwell on a given thought, become restless, and (through a chain of associations) would reach a catastrophic conclusion that would create a state described as panicky. For example, while he was at school, he would look out the window on a sunny day and think of possible rain later. For James, rain meant destructive weather, which made him think of tornados. Consequently, he would become so anxious that he would not be able to remain in the classroom. James also displayed a significant amount of oppositional behavior and severe temper tantrums that lasted for hours. During the time since his previous evaluation, James had also developed a number of ritualistic and "obsessive-compulsive" behaviors that kept him preoccupied for long periods of time (e.g., touching the trash can a certain number of times before leaving the house, watching the weather channel for hours to avoid unexpected tornados).

During this time, James also became more interested in his age-mates and developed an intense but unrequited attachment to a female classmate, triggering the development of paranoid beliefs and experiences. These difficulties, which interfered significantly with his own and his family's daily lives, necessitated pharmacological and psychotherapeutic interventions. His second assessment at this time yielded a much more uneven profile, with intellectual skills in the high average range of the Wechsler Intelligence Scale for Children—Revised (WISC-R, full scale IQ = 111), but with social skills and social comprehension in the impaired range. His self-help and coping skills were also assessed to be much lower than expected levels. His academic scores, however, were significantly above average in all major areas. James was in regular classes (honors classes in some subjects) with no remedial academic assistance.

James was evaluated again at age 12. Significant improvement had occurred in many difficult behaviors (e.g., tantrums), but he had become more and more socially isolated, spending hours every day involved in his fantasy world of imaginary cities and countries.

He began to draw complicated maps of these places, discussing in great detail their populations, climates, imports, exports, and other characteristics. Although he showed an obvious desire to be with his peers, he simply did not know how to approach them. During this time, James also started to display appetite and sleep disturbances, decreased energy, and difficulty concentrating; he was prescribed antidepressant medication to which he responded well. His assessment scores continued to indicate above-average intellectual and language skills, and extremely well-developed academic skills. James was in honors classes in almost every subject. However, his adaptive behavior scores were in the impaired range in socialization and self-help skills. As a teenager, he worked closely with one of the chapter coauthors, receiving supportive therapy, medications, and social skills training. Socialization continues to be his major area of difficulty.

Interpretation

James's case highlights the many puzzling but fascinating developmental and diagnostic challenges of pervasive developmental disorders. At the age of 5, James presented as an extremely bright youngster who did not display many obvious developmental delays. Moreover, some skills, such as visuospatial memory and academic skills, were even precocious. However, he exhibited a number of unusual behaviors consistent with an autistic spectrum disorder that were relatively easy to identify. Although there was a gap between James and his peers in social skills, this deficit was not the major concern when compared with his other difficulties—such as lack of control in behavior (e.g., severe temper tantrums, no delay of gratification, inattention, and hyperactivity).

Over the years between preschool and adolescence, James continued to acquire skills in the cognitive and academic domains that kept him at or above the level of his nondisabled age-mates. Like Joan, he learned to control his behavior better in a variety of contexts. However, although his nondisabled age-mates made progress in the cognitive domain and overtook some of his early achievements, James' initial mild difficulties in the adaptive domain, especially socialization, became major handicaps over the years, making the gap between him and his norm group significantly wider.

Perhaps the most interesting aspect of James's case is the different presentation of autistic-like behaviors or characteristics in the course of his development. As James faced challenging developmental tasks (e.g., peer interaction and socialization experience), his well-developed intellectual capacity made him painfully aware of his deficiencies. This knowledge, in turn, made him more vulnerable to additional emotional discomfort, and he experienced feelings of isolation, withdrawal, sadness, and overall emotional distress. After his third evaluation, James met the diagnostic criteria for major depression in addition to his PDD diagnosis. Similarly, the intensity and the complexity of his obsessive rituals raised the question of comorbidity of Obsessive-Compulsive Disorder and PDD. Taken altogether, James's case requires examination of the relationships among different manifestations of his impaired functioning across the stages of development. Although some of the changes can be explained in terms of James's developmental maturation, many puzzling questions remain about the development of his autism and the eventual outcome for this intelligent young man.

CONCLUSIONS

Autism, like other developmental disorders, is not a static condition that, once visited upon the child, remains the same with increasing age. Instead, autism is manifested differently as the child develops, reflecting the maturation of neural and behavioral systems, the effects of learning and experience, the activity of the individual, and the reciprocal interactions of all these elements. This review of developmental issues for school-age children with autism suggests important directions for future research.

At present, much remains to be learned about the links between early behaviors and outcome in children with autism. For example, clinicians and others need to know more about precursors to later social skills that involve making inferences about what others know, feel, or believe. These skills, often described in relation to having a theory of mind, are known to be particularly difficult for children with autism to acquire. The main source of information on possible precursors to a theory of mind is the literature on joint attention (Baron-Cohen, 1991). Studies have repeatedly shown that young children with autism have deficits in such joint attention skills as pointing, showing, and gaze following (Landry & Loveland, 1988; Loveland & Landry, 1986; Mundy et al., 1986; Phillips, Baron-Cohen, & Rutter, 1992). The ability to engage in early interactive behaviors that establish joint awareness between parent and child may very possibly lead to a later, more explicit awareness of what others do and do not know. However, researchers have not yet determined the extent to which a person's early joint attention deficits are associated with deficits in theory of mind in the school years and later. Consequently, it is not clear whether joint attention should be regarded as having developmental continuity with theory of mind, based on empirical evidence. If issues such as this one are to be clarified, researchers must conduct longitudinal studies of early skills and behaviors hypothesized to be related to later skills and behaviors in children with autism.

Another research need is to link the longitudinal study of behavioral development in children with autism to the study of brain development, with respect to specific, known changes in the manifestations of autism over time. Although studies of the brain and of behavior have become increasingly more sophisticated over the years, these approaches have not been successfully integrated to form a more comprehensive neurodevelopmental model of autism. Such a model could help to explain, for example, what is centrally *autistic* about the various disorders on the autistic spectrum, and how the central deficit, if any, is related to developmental level; for example, differences in the characteristics of children with autism with and without mental retardation might reflect, in part, differences in the location and extent of brain impairment. In the construction of such a model, another important consideration is to examine not only the changing and reciprocal nature of the relationship between brain and behavior over development, but also the self-organizing activities of the developing child (Cicchetti & Tucker, 1994).

An additional need is to explore more thoroughly the interaction of mental retardation and autism over a person's development, so that the consequences of both having autism and being developmentally young can be better understood. For example, too little is known about the early development of very high-functioning children with autism and how it differs from that of lower-functioning children. This information would help to determine whether certain manifestations of autistic behavior, such as motor stereotypies, are linked to developmental level or to IQ in children with autism.

Despite the recent research emphasis on lack of social understanding in persons with autism, we still do not know enough about how children with autism actually view their world—how they interpret situations, make social judgments, understand what is said to them, and interpret the impact of their behaviors on others. Little is known about the person with autism as a member of a society or culture. The complexities and subtleties involved in social interactions may not be adequately captured in the laboratory with simple, easily controlled tasks. Moreover, the infrequent occurrence of certain behaviors (e.g., neologisms in speech, pronoun errors) may be highly important, even though these behaviors are not readily observed in the laboratory. Studies that are based on more natural situations, although still informed by current theoretical issues, could provide richer data, allowing a more realistic understanding of social functioning in autism. Such studies might make it possible to gain a better understanding of the more subtle social and communicative deficits observed in high-functioning persons with autism—deficits that are often difficult to document in the laboratory.

Research studies aimed at development of effective programs and services are critically needed. The school-age child with autism faces many and multidimensional challenges. To help this child deal successfully with school, peers, physical maturation, changing family relationships, and other challenges of the school years, programs must reflect an awareness not only of the deficits characteristic of autism, but also of the growing capabilities of the developing child.

Cross-References

Autism in infancy, adolescence, and adulthood is discussed in Chapters 12 and 14. Medical care of autistic children is reviewed in Chapter 33. Life-span issues are addressed in Chapter 45.

REFERENCES

American Psychiatric Association. (1987). *DSM-III-R: Diagnostic and statistical manual of mental disorders* (3rd ed., rev.). Washington, DC: Author.

American Psychiatric Association. (1994). *DSM-IV: Diagnostic and statistical manual of mental disorders* (4th ed.). Washington, DC: Author.

Ando, H., & Yoshimura, I. (1979). Effects of age on communication skill levels and prevalence of maladaptive behaviors in autistic and mentally retarded children. *Journal of Autism and Developmental Disorders, 9,* 83–93.

Ando, H., Yoshimura, I., & Wakabayashi, S. (1980). Effects of age on adaptive behavior levels and academic skill levels in autistic and mentally retarded children. *Journal of Autism and Developmental Disorders, 10,* 173–184.

Asperger, H. (1944). Die "autistischen Psychopathen" im Kindesalter. *Archiv für Psychiatrie und Nervenkrakheiten, 117,* 76–136.

Baltaxe, C. (1977). Pragmatic deficits in the language of autistic adolescents. *Journal of Pediatric Psychology, 2,* 176–180.

Baron-Cohen, S. (1989). Do autistic children have obsessions and compulsions? *British Journal of Child Psychology, 28,* 193–200.

Baron-Cohen, S. (1991). Precursors to a theory of mind: Understanding attention in others. In A. Whiten (Ed.), *Natural theories of mind* (pp. 233–252). Oxford, England: Basil Blackwell.

Baron-Cohen, S., Leslie, A., & Frith, U. (1986). Mechanical, behavioral, and intentional understanding of picture stories in autistic children. *British Journal of Developmental Psychology, 4,* 113–125.

Bartak, L., & Rutter, M. (1974). The use of personal pronouns by autistic children. *Journal of Autism and Childhood Schizophrenia, 4,* 217–222.

Bartak, L., & Rutter, M. (1976). Differences between mentally retarded and normally intelligent autistic children. *Journal of Autism and Childhood Schizophrenia, 6,* 109–120.

Berg, C.J., Zahn, T.P., & Behar, D. (1986). Childhood obsessive-compulsive disorder: An anxiety disorder? In R. Gittelman (Ed.), *Anxiety disorders of childhood* (pp. 126–135). New York: Guilford Press.

Bettelheim, B. (1967). *The empty fortress.* New York: Free Press.

Breslin, N.A., & Weinberger, D.R. (1990). Schizophrenia and the normal functional development of the prefrontal cortex. *Development and Psychopathology, 2,* 409–424.

Bruner, J., & Feldman, C. (1993). Theories of mind and the problem of autism. In S. Baron-Cohen, H. Tager-Flusberg, & D. Cohen (Eds.), *Understanding other minds: Perspectives from autism* (pp. 267–291). Oxford, England: Oxford University Press.

Buitelaar, J.K., van Engeland, H., de Kogel, K., de Vries, H., & Van Hooff (1991). Differences in the structure of social behaviour of autistic children and non-autistic retarded controls. *Journal of Child Psychology & Psychiatry & Allied Disciplines, 32,* 995–1015.

Burack, J., & Volkmar, F. (1992). Development of low- and high-functioning autistic children. *Journal of Child Psychology & Psychiatry & Allied Disciplines, 33,* 607–616.

Charney, R. (1980). Speech roles and the development of personal pronouns. *Journal of Child Language, 7,* 509–528.

Charney, R. (1981). Pronoun errors in autistic children: Support for a social explanation. *British Journal of Disorders of Communication, 15,* 39–43.

Chiat, S. (1982). If I were you and you were me: The analysis of pronouns in a pronoun-reversing child. *Journal of Child Language, 9,* 359–379.

Cicchetti, D., & Tucker, D. (1994). Development and self-regulatory structures of the mind. *Development and Psychopathology, 6,* 533–549.

Ciesielski, K.T., Courchesne, E., & Elmasian, R. (1990). Effects of focused selective attention tasks on event-related potentials in autistic and normal individuals. *Electroencephalography and Clinical Neurophysiology, 75,* 207–220.

Clarke, D.J., Littlejohns, C.S., Corbett, J.A., & Joseph, S. (1989). Pervasive developmental disorders and psychoses in adult life. *British Journal of Psychiatry, 155,* 692–699.

Comings, D.E., & Comings, B.G. (1991). Clinical and genetic relationships between autism-Pervasive Developmental Disorder and Tourette Syndrome: A study of 19 cases. *American Journal of Medical Genetics, 39,* 180–191.

Courchesne, E. (1987). A neurophysiological view of autism. In E. Schopler & G.B. Mesibov (Eds.), *Neurobiological issues in autism* (pp. 285–324). New York: Plenum Press.

Courchesne, E., Lincoln, A.J., Yeung-Courchesne, R., Elmasian, R., & Grillon, C. (1989). Pathophysiologic findings in nonretarded autism and receptive developmental language disorder. *Journal of Autism and Developmental Disorders, 19*, 1–17.

Dahl, V. (1976). A follow-up study of a child psychiatric clientele with special regard to the diagnosis of psychosis. *Acta Psychiatrica Scandinavica, 54*, 106–112.

Dawson, G., & Lewy (1989). Arousal, attention, and the socio-emotional impairments of individuals with autism. In G. Dawson (Ed.), *Autism: Nature, diagnosis and treatment* (pp. 49–79). New York: Guilford Press.

Dawson, G., & McKissick, F.C. (1984). Self-recognition in autistic children. *Journal of Autism and Developmental Disabilities, 14*, 383–395.

DeLong, G.R., & Dwyer, J.J. (1988). Correlation of family history with specific autistic subgroups: Asperger's Syndrome and bipolar affective disease. *Journal of Autism and Developmental Disabilities, 18*, 593–600.

Dunlap, G., Koegel, R.L., & Egel, A.L. (1979). Autistic children in school. *Exceptional Children, 45*, 552–558.

Fay, W. (1973). On the echolalia of the blind and of the autistic child. *Journal of Speech and Hearing Disorders, 38*, 478–489.

Fay, W. (1979). Personal pronouns and the autistic child. *Journal of Autism and Developmental Disorders, 9*, 247–260.

Fay, W., & Butler, B. (1968). Echolalia, IQ, and the developmental dichotomy of speech and language systems. *Journal of Speech and Hearing Research, 11*, 365–371.

Ferrari, M., & Matthews, W.S. (1983). Self-recognition deficits in autism: Syndrome specific or general developmental delay. *Journal of Autism and Developmental Disabilities, 13*, 317–324.

Fine, J., Bartolucci, G., Ginsberg, G., & Szatmari, P. (1991). The use of intonation to communicate in pervasive developmental disorders. *Journal of Child Psychology and Psychiatry, 32*, 771–782.

Fine, J., Bartolucci, G., Szatmari, P., & Ginsberg, G. (1994). Cohesive discourse in pervasive developmental disorders. *Journal of Autism and Developmental Disorders, 24*, 315–329.

Freeman, B.J., Rahbar, B., Ritvo, E.R., Bice, T.L., Yokota, A., & Ritvo, R. (1991). The stability of cognitive and behavioral parameters in autism: A twelve-year prospective study. *Journal of the American Academy of Child and Adolescent Psychiatry, 30*, 479–482.

Freitag, G. (1970). An experimental study of the social responsiveness of children with autistic behaviors. *Journal of Experimental Child Psychology, 9*, 436–453.

Frith, C., & Frith, U. (1992). Elective affinities in schizophrenia and childhood autism. In P.E. Bebbington (Ed.), *Social psychiatry: Theory, methodology and practice* (pp. 65–86). New Brunswick, NJ: Transaction.

Frith, U. (1991). *Autism and Asperger Syndrome.* London: Cambridge University Press.

Frith, U., & Snowling, M. (1983). Reading for meaning and reading for sound in autistic and dyslexic children. *British Journal of Developmental Psychology, 1*, 329–342.

Frith, U., & Snowling, M. (1986). Comprehension in hyperlexic readers. *Journal of Experimental Child Psychology, 42*, 392–415.

Gillberg, C. (1984). Autistic children growing up: Problems during puberty and adolescence. *Developmental Medicine and Child Neurology, 26*, 122–129.

Gillberg, C. (1985). Asperger's Syndrome and recurrent psychosis—A neuropsychiatric case study. *Journal of Autism and Developmental Disorders, 15*, 389–397.

Gillberg, C., & Coleman, M. (1992). *The biology of the autistic syndromes* (2nd ed.). New York: Cambridge University Press.

Goldberg, T.E. (1987). On hermetic reading abilities. *Journal of Autism and Developmental Disorders, 17*, 29–44.

Gordon, O.T., Rapoport, J.T., Hamburger, J.D., State, R.C., & Mannheim, G.B. (1992). Differential response of seven subjects with Autistic Disorder to clomipramine and desipramine. *American Journal of Psychiatry, 149*, 363–366.

Halle, J.W. (1982). Teaching functional language to the handicapped: An integrative model of the natural environment teaching techniques. *Journal of the Association for the Severely Handicapped, 7*, 29–36.

Hamden-Allen, G. (1991). Brief report: Trichotillomania in an autistic male. *Journal of Autism and Developmental Disorders, 21*, 79–82.

Hobson, R.P. (1993). *Autism and the development of mind.* Hove, England: Erlbaum.

Hobson, R.P., Ouston, J., & Lee, A. (1988). Emotion recognition in autism: Coordinating faces and voices. *Psychological Medicine, 18*, 911–923.

Hobson, R.P., Ouston, J., & Lee, A. (1989). Recognition of emotion by mentally retarded adolescents and young adults. *American Journal on Mental Retardation, 93*, 434–443.

Howlin, P. (1982). Echolalic and spontaneous phrase speech in autistic children. *Journal of Child Psychology and Psychiatry, 23*, 281–293.

Hurtig, R., Ensrud, S., & Tomblin, J.B. (1982). The communicative function of question production in autistic children. *Journal of Autism and Developmental Disorders, 12,* 57–69.

Hutt, C., Hutt, S.J., Lee, D., & Ounsted, C. (1964). Arousal and childhood autism. *Nature, 204,* 908–909.

Insel, T.R., & Akiskal, H.S. (1986). Obsessive-Compulsive Disorder with psychotic features: A phenomenologic analysis. *American Journal of Psychiatry, 143,* 1527–1533.

Jacobson, J., & Ackerman, L. (1990). Differences in adaptive functioning among people with autism or mental retardation. *Journal of Autism and Developmental Disorders, 20,* 205–219.

James, A.L., & Barry, R.J. (1980). A review of psychopathology in early onset psychosis. *Schizophrenia Bulletin, 6,* 506–525.

Kamps, D., Walker, D., Maher, J., & Rotholtz, D. (1992). Academic and environmental effects of small group arrangements in classrooms for students with autism and other developmental disabilities. *Journal of Autism and Developmental Disorders, 22,* 277–293.

Kanner, L. (1943). Autistic disturbances of affective contact. *Nervous Child, 2,* 217–250.

Klin, A., Volkmar, F.R., & Sparrow, S.S. (1992). Autistic social dysfunction: Some limitations of the theory of mind hypothesis. *Journal of Child Psychology and Psychiatry, 33,* 861–876.

Kolvin, I. (1971). Studies in the childhood psychoses: 1. Diagnostic criteria and classification. *British Journal of Psychiatry, 118,* 381–384.

Kurita, H., & Nakayasu, N. (1994). Brief report: An autistic male presenting Seasonal Affective Disorder (SAD) and trichotillomania. *Journal of Autism and Developmental Disorders, 24,* 687–692.

Lainhart, J.E., & Folstein, S.E. (1994). Affective disorders in people with autism: A review of published cases. *Journal of Autism and Developmental Disabilities, 24,* 587–601.

Landry, S., & Loveland, K. (1988). Communication behaviors in autism and developmental language delay. *Journal of Child Psychology & Psychiatry & Allied Disciplines, 29,* 621–634.

Lee, A., Hobson, R.P., & Chiat, S. (1994). I, you, me, and autism: An experimental study. *Journal of Autism and Developmental Disorders, 24,* 155–176.

Lovaas, O.I., Schreibman, L., Koegel, R., & Rehm, R. (1971). Selective responding by autistic children to multiple sensory input. *Journal of Abnormal Psychology, 77,* 211–222.

Loveland, K. (1984). Learning about points of view: Spatial perspective and the acquisition of "I/you." *Journal of Child Language, 2,* 535–556.

Loveland, K., Fletcher, J., & Bailey, V. (1990). Verbal and nonverbal communication of events in learning-disability subtypes. *Journal of Clinical and Experimental Neuropsychology, 12,* 433–447.

Loveland, K., & Kelley, M. (1988). Development of adaptive behavior in adolescents and young adults with autism and Down syndrome. *American Journal on Mental Retardation, 93,* 84–92.

Loveland, K., & Kelley, M. (1991). Development of adaptive behavior in preschoolers with autism and Down syndrome. *American Journal on Mental Retardation, 96,* 13–20.

Loveland, K., & Landry, S., (1986). Joint attention and communication in autism and language delay. *Journal of Autism and Developmental Disorders, 16,* 335–349.

Loveland, K., Landry, S., Hughes, S., Hall, S., & McEvoy, R. (1988). Speech acts and the pragmatic deficits of autism. *Journal of Speech & Hearing Research, 31,* 593–604.

Loveland, K., McEvoy, R., Tunali, B., & Kelley, M. (1990). Narrative story-telling in autism and Down syndrome. *British Journal of Developmental Psychology, 8,* 9–23.

Loveland, K., & Tunali, B. (1991). Social scripts for conversational interactions in autism and Down syndrome. *Journal of Autism and Developmental Disorders, 21,* 177–186.

Loveland, K., & Tunali, B. (1993). Narrative language in autism and the theory of mind hypothesis: A wider perspective. In S. Baron-Cohen, H. Tager-Flusberg, & D. Cohen (Eds.), *Understanding other minds: Perspectives from autism* (pp. 247–266). Oxford, England: Oxford University Press.

Loveland, K., Tunali, B., Kelley, M., & McEvoy, R. (1989). Referential communication and response adequacy in autism and Down syndrome. *Applied Psycholinguistics, 10,* 401–413.

Loveland, K., Tunali-Kotoski, B., Chen, R., Brelsford, K., Ortegon, J., & Pearson, D. (1995). Intermodal perception of affect in persons with autism or Down syndrome. *Development and Psychopathology, 7,* 409–418.

Loveland, K., Tunali-Kotoski, B., Pearson, D., Brelsford, K., Ortegon, J., & Chen, R. (1994). Imitation and expression of facial affect in autism. *Development and Psychopathology, 6,* 433–444.

McEvoy, R., Loveland, K., & Landry, S. (1988). Functions of immediate echolalia in autistic children. *Journal of Autism and Developmental Disorders, 18,* 657–688.

McLennan, J.D., Lord, C., & Schopler, E. (1993). Sex differences in higher-functioning people with autism. *Journal of Autism and Developmental Disorders, 23,* 217–227.

Mesibov, G.B., & Shea, V. (1980, March). *Social and interpersonal problems of autistic adolescents and adults.* Paper presented at the meeting of the Southeastern Psychological Association, Washington, DC.

Minshew, N., Goldstein, G., & Siegel, D. (1995). Speech and language in high-functioning autistic individuals. *Neuropsychology, 9,* 255–261.

Mundy, P., Sigman, M., Ungerer, J., & Sherman, T. (1986). Defining the social deficits of autism. *Journal of Child Psychology and Psychiatry, 27,* 657–669.

O'Connor, N., & Hermelin, B. (1994). Two autistic savant readers. *Journal of Autism and Developmental Disorders, 24,* 501–515.

Ozonoff, S., Pennington, B., & Rogers, S. (1990). Are there specific emotion perception deficits in young autistic children? *Journal of Child Psychology and Psychiatry, 31,* 343–361.

Petty, L.K., Ornitz, E.M., Michelman, J.D., & Zimmerman, E.G. (1984). Autistic children who become schizophrenic. *Archives of General Psychiatry, 41,* 129–135.

Phillips, W., Baron-Cohen, S., & Rutter, M. (1992). The role of eye-contact in goal detection: Evidence from normal infants and children with autism or mental handicap. *Development and Psychopathology, 4,* 375–383.

Prior, M., Dahlstrom, B., & Squires, T. (1990). Autistic children's knowledge of thinking and feeling states in other people. *Journal of Child Psychology & Psychiatry & Allied Disciplines, 31,* 587–601.

Prizant, B.M., & Duchan, J.F. (1981). The functions of immediate echolalia in autistic children. *Journal of Speech and Hearing Disorders, 46,* 241–249.

Rimland, B. (1964). *Infantile autism.* New York: Appleton-Century-Crofts.

Rincover, A., & Ducharme, J.M. (1987). Variables influencing stimulus overselectivity and "tunnel vision" in developmentally delayed children. *American Journal of Mental Deficiency, 91,* 422–430.

Rodrigue, J.R., Morgan, S.B., & Geffken, G.R. (1991). A comparative evaluation of adaptive behavior in children and adolescents with autism, Down syndrome, and normal development. *Journal of Autism and Developmental Disabilities, 21,* 187–196.

Rumsey, J.M. (1992). Neuropsychological studies of high-level autism. In E. Schopler & G. Mesibov (Eds.), *High-functioning individuals with autism* (pp. 41–64). New York: Plenum Press.

Rumsey, J.M., & Hamburger, S.D. (1990). Neuropsychological divergence of high-level autism and severe dyslexia. *Journal of Autism and Developmental Disorders, 20,* 155–168.

Rumsey, J.M., Rapoport, J.L., & Sceery, W.R. (1985). Autistic children as adults: Psychiatric, social, and behavioral outcomes. *Journal of the American Academy of Child Psychiatry, 24,* 465–473.

Rutter, M. (1968). Concepts of autism: A review of research. *Journal of Child Psychology and Psychiatry, 9,* 1–25.

Rutter, M. (1970). Autistic children: Infancy to adulthood. *Seminars in Psychiatry, 2,* 435–450.

Rutter, M. (1972). Childhood schizophrenia reconsidered. *Journal of Autism and Childhood Schizophrenia, 2,* 315–337.

Rutter, M. (1974). The development of infantile autism. *Psychological Medicine, 4,* 147–163.

Rutter, M. (1978). Diagnosis and definition. In M. Rutter & E. Schopler (Eds.), *Autism: A reappraisal of concepts and treatment* (pp. 1–25). New York: Plenum Press.

Rutter, M. (1983). Cognitive deficits in the pathogenesis of autism. *Journal of Child Psychology and Psychiatry, 24,* 513–531.

Rutter, M. (1985). Infantile autism and other pervasive developmental disorders. In M. Rutter & L. Hersov (Eds.), *Child and adolescent psychiatry: Modern approaches* (pp. 545–566). Oxford, England: Blackwell Scientific.

Rutter, M., & Garmezy, N. (1983). Developmental psychopathology. In E.M. Hetherington (Ed.), *Handbook of child psychology* (Vol. 4, pp. 775–911). New York: John Wiley & Sons.

Rutter, M., Greenfield, D., & Lockyer, L. (1967). A five- to fifteen-year follow-up study of infantile psychosis: II. Social and behavioral outcome. *British Journal of Psychiatry, 113,* 1187–1199.

Rydell, P.J., & Mirenda, P. (1994). Effects of high and low constraint utterances on the production of immediate and delayed echolalia in young children with autism. *Journal of Autism and Developmental Disorders, 24,* 719–735.

Schopler, E., & Mesibov, G.B. (1983). *Autism in adolescents and adults.* New York: Plenum Press.

Schreibman, L. (1988). *Autism.* Newbury Park, CA: Sage.

Shapiro, T., Sherman, M., Calamari, G., & Koch, D. (1987). Attachment in autism and other developmental disorders. *Journal of the American Academy of Child Psychiatry, 26,* 480–484.

Sigman, M., & Mundy, P. (1989). Social attachments in autistic children. *Journal of the*

American Academy of Child and Adolescent Psychiatry, 28, 74–81.

Sigman, M., & Ungerer, J.A. (1984). Attachment behaviors in autistic children. *Journal of Autism and Developmental Disorders, 14,* 231–244.

Snow, M.E., Hertzig, M.E., & Shapiro, T. (1987). Expression of emotion in young autistic children. *Journal of the American Academy of Child and Adolescent Psychiatry, 26,* 836–838.

Sparrow, S.S., & Cicchetti, D.V. (1987). Adaptive behavior and the psychologically disturbed child. *Journal of Special Education, 21,* 89–100.

Stern, D. (1985). *The interpersonal world of the infant.* New York: Basic Books.

Sverd, J., Montero, G., & Gurevich, N. (1993). Brief report: Cases for an association between Tourette Syndrome, Autistic Disorder, and Schizophrenia-Like Disorder. *Journal of Autism and Developmental Disabilities, 23,* 407–413.

Swedo, S.E., & Rapoport, J.L. (1989). Phenomenology and differential diagnosis of Obsessive-Compulsive Disorder in children and adolescents. In J.L. Rapoport (Ed.), *Obsessive-Compulsive Disorder in children and adolescents.* Washington, DC: American Psychiatric Press.

Tager-Flusberg, H. (1989, April). *An analysis of discourse ability and internal state lexicons in a longitudinal study of autistic children.* Paper presented to the Society for Research in Child Development, Kansas City, MO.

Tager-Flusberg, H., & Anderson, M. (1991). The development of contingent discourse ability in autistic children. *Journal of Child Psychology and Psychiatry, 32,* 1123–1134.

Tager-Flusberg, H., & Calkins, S. (1990). Does imitation facilitate the acquisition of grammar? Evidence from a study of autistic, Down's syndrome, and normal children. *Journal of Child Language, 17,* 591–606.

Tager-Flusberg, H., Calkins, S., Nolin, T., Baumberger, T., Anderson, M., & Chadwick-Dias, A. (1990). A longitudinal study of language acquisition in autistic and Down's syndrome children. *Journal of Autism and Developmental Disorders, 20,* 1–21.

Tager-Flusberg, H., & Quill, K. (1987, April). *Story-telling and narrative skills in verbal autistic children.* Paper presented to the Society for Research in Child Development, Baltimore, MD.

Trad, P.V., Bernstein, D., Shapiro, T., & Hertzig, M. (1993). Assessing the relationship between affective responsivity and social interaction in children with Pervasive Developmental Disorder. *Journal of Autism and Developmental Disorders, 23,* 361–377.

Tsai, L.Y. (1992). Diagnostic issues in high-functioning autism. In E. Schopler & G. Mesibov (Eds.), *High-functioning individuals with autism* (pp. 11–40). New York: Plenum Press.

Tunali, B., & Power, T. (1993). Creating satisfaction: A psychological perspective on stress and coping in families of handicapped children. *Journal of Child Psychology and Psychiatry, 34,* 945–957.

Unger, D.G., & Powell, D.R. (1980). Supporting families under stress: The role of social networks. *Family Relations, 29,* 566–574.

Volkmar, F.R., & Cohen, D.J. (1991). Debate and argument: The utility of the term Pervasive Developmental Disorder. *Journal of Child Psychology and Psychiatry, 32,* 1171–1172.

Volkmar, F.R., Cohen, D.J., Hoshino, Y., Rende, R., & Paul, R. (1988). Phenomenology and classification of the childhood psychoses. *Psychological Medicine, 18,* 191–201.

Volkmar, F.R., Cohen, D.J., & Paul, R. (1986). An evaluation of *DSM-III* criteria for infantile autism. *Journal of the American Academy of Child Psychiatry, 25,* 190–197.

Volkmar, F.R., & Klin, A. (1993). Social development in autism: Historical and clinical perspectives. In S. Baron-Cohen, H. Tager-Flusberg, & D. Cohen (Eds.), *Understanding other minds: Perspectives from autism* (pp. 40–55). Oxford, England: Oxford University Press.

Volkmar, F.R., Klin, A., Siegel, B., Szatmari, P., Lord, C., Campbell, M., Freeman, B.J., Cicchetti, D.V., Rutter, M., Kline, W., Buitelaar, J., Hattab, Y., Fombonne, E., Fuenter, J., Werry, J., Stone, W., Kerbeshian, J., Hoshino, Y., Bregman, J., Loveland, K., Szymanski, L., & Towbin, K. (1994). Field trial for Autistic Disorder in *DSM-IV. American Journal of Psychiatry, 151,* 1361–1367.

Volkmar, F.R., Sparrow, S.S., Goudreau, D., Cicchetti, D.V., Paul, R., & Cohen, D.J. (1987). Social deficits in autism: An operational approach using the Vineland Adaptive Behavior Scales. *Journal of the American Academy of Child and Adolescent Psychiatry, 26,* 156–161.

Wainwright-Sharp, J.A., & Bryson, S.E. (1993). Visual orienting deficits in high-functioning people with autism. *Journal of Autism and Developmental Disorders, 23,* 1–13.

Weeks, S., & Hobson, R.P. (1987). The salience of facial expression for autistic children. *Journal of Child Psychology & Psychiatry & Allied Disciplines, 28,* 137–151.

Whitehouse, D., & Harris, J.C. (1984). Hyperlexia in infantile autism. *Journal of Autism and Developmental Disabilities, 14,* 281–289.

Wing, L. (1981). Asperger's Syndrome: A clinical account. *Psychological Medicine, 11,* 115–130.

Wing, L., & Attwood, A. (1987). Syndromes of autism and atypical development. In D. Cohen, A. Donellan, & R. Paul (Eds.), *Handbook of autism and pervasive developmental disorders* (pp. 3–19). New York: John Wiley & Sons.

Wing, L., & Gould, J. (1979). Severe impairments of social interaction and associated abnormalities in children: Epidemiology and classification. *Journal of Autism and Developmental Disorders, 9,* 11–29.

Wolff, S., & Chick, J. (1980). Schizoid personality in childhood: A controlled follow-up study. *Psychological Medicine, 10,* 85–100.

Yirmiya, N., Kasari, C., Sigman, M., & Mundy, P. (1989). Facial expressions of affect in autistic, mentally retarded, and normal children. *Journal of Child Psychology and Psychiatry, 30,* 725–736.

Zahn, T.P., Rumsey, J.M., & Van Kannen, D.P. (1987). Autonomic nervous system activity in autistic, schizophrenic, and normal men: Effects of stimulus significance. *Journal of Abnormal Psychology, 96,* 135–144.

CHAPTER 14

Adolescents and Adults with Autism

GARY B. MESIBOV AND SARA HANDLAN

Only recently have adolescents and adults with autism been viewed as legitimate and appropriate subjects of inquiry. Research and clinical practice in autism originally focused on young children. The identification of autism has been easier with youngsters, and most professionals in the field have been trained to work with younger children. As an indication of the strong emphasis on children, until publication of *DSM-III-R* (American Psychiatric Association [APA], 1987), the term *Infantile Autism* was used exclusively to describe the disorder.

The current interest in adolescents and adults with autism has evolved for several reasons. The younger children first identified as being autistic in the 1970s and early 1980s have matured into adolescence and adulthood. They are receiving more attention now because there are many more of them than in earlier years. The need to provide services for today's increased population in this age group has instilled a growing awareness of and concern for their necessities of life. An earlier ignorance toward autistic adolescents and adults was not purposeful or intentional; it simply reflected a lack of information on and awareness of what was then a less populated age group. Efforts were concentrated on learning about and caring for the autistic individuals who were children at that time, perhaps with the hope that improvement in their condition would be accomplished by the time they were in the older age group.

As knowledge and information about adolescents and adults with autism increase, so does understanding of these critical periods and of how they fit into the overall developmental cycle for autism. This chapter focuses on diagnosis and assessment issues, critical research, and the effectiveness of various programs in dealing with the major issues in the field, as they apply to adolescents and adults with autism.

DIAGNOSIS AND ASSESSMENT

The terms *diagnosis* and *assessment* are used interchangeably by many people, although they represent different aspects of the evaluation process. Diagnosis is the part of an evaluation that is designed to determine appropriate grouping. Autism is a diagnosis. During the evaluation process, one tries to determine whether a client has a sufficient number of the agreed-on characteristics and whether they are present to an extent that allows classification in this group. Diagnosis examines the characteristics that people with autism share, and determines whether a particular individual fits appropriately into this category.

As part of an appropriate diagnosis and evaluation, most professionals want assessment information. Assessment is the process of understanding a client's unique characteristics in order to help establish an appropriate individualized intervention plan. Assessment investigates a client's unique learning characteristics, specific strengths, obvious deficits, work preferences, and other attributes that may contribute to the design of appropriate intervention. The diagnostic process determines appropriate groupings for individual clients; assessment identifies learning styles, strategies, and needs, independent of grouping.

Diagnosis

Diagnosing adolescent or adult clients with autism when they first come to a clinic is challenging. Young children with autism tend to have common characteristics. By the time autistic persons reach adulthood, their diversity and variations make systematic grouping difficult. The easiest persons to diagnose are those who have had careful workups as children or have knowledgeable parents or guardians who are reliable informants. Early history is still the most useful information. For those clients who did not have good workups as children, a comprehensive workup should be considered in adulthood. Among the many materials and methods available, the Childhood Autism Rating Scale (CARS; Schopler, Reichler, & Renner, 1988) is a behavior rating scale that is easy to administer and can be interpreted with a minimum of training. The CARS evaluates subjects on 15 scales:

1. Relating to People.
2. Imitation.
3. Emotional Response.
4. Body Use.
5. Object Use.
6. Adaptation to Change.
7. Visual Response.
8. Listening Response.
9. Taste, Smell, and Touch Response and Use.
10. Fear or Nervousness.
11. Verbal Communication.
12. Nonverbal Communication.
13. Activity Level.
14. Consistency of Intellectual Response.
15. General Impressions.

Each of these items is rated from 1 to 4, yielding a total score from 15 to 60. Cutoff scores on the CARS are: less than 30, nonautistic; 30 to 36.5, mildly to moderately autistic; 37 or greater, severely autistic.

Several studies have investigated the use of the CARS with adolescents and adults with autism. The TEACCH (Treatment and Education of Autistic and Related Communication Handicapped Children) program identified 89 subjects with CARS scores available before age 10 and again after age 13 (Mesibov, Schopler, Schaffer, & Michal, 1989). Most subjects showed a decrease in their CARS scores over time, suggesting that the characteristics of autism are less pronounced in older clients, at least if they have available the intensive structured training that characterizes North Carolina's TEACCH regimen. The average CARS rating decreased by 2.2 points over time, and a significant decrease was observed in 9 of the 15 CARS categories. Adjusting the CARS cutoff for autism (from 30 to 27), based on the average decrease, resulted in 92% of the adolescents or adults being diagnosed appropriately.

Garfin, McCallon, and Cox (1988) compared the scores of 22 autistic children (ages 6 to 10 years) and 22 adolescents (ages 13 to 22 years) matched on nonverbal IQ, sex, and ethnicity. CARS scores of 20 nonautistic handicapped youngsters were also computed. The CARS clearly discriminated between the two adolescent groups, suggesting that it is a useful diagnostic screening instrument. Of the 15 CARS items, only Consistency of Intellectual Response did not correlate well with the overall rating for these adolescent clients.

Two other instruments—the Autistic Diagnostic Interview—Revised (ADI-R; Lord, Rutter, & Le Couteur, 1994) and the Autism Diagnostic Observation Schedule (ADOS; Lord et al., 1989)—show promise, but no specific data have been presented for adolescents or adults with autism. The ADI-R is a semistructured interview directed at parents or caretakers of people for whom autism is a possible diagnosis. The ADOS is a standardized protocol for observation of social and communicative behaviors associated with autism.

Assessment

The goal of assessment is an individualized educational and behavioral program. Diagnosis examines common characteristics in people with autism; assessment looks at what makes each client unique. Historically, assessment of autistic people has been difficult because of their high activity levels, distractibility, and lack of interest in those aspects of the testing situation that typically motivate nonhandicapped people. Although great progress has been made in the assessment of young children (Schopler & Mesibov, 1988), assessment of adolescents and adults still presents many challenges and difficulties.

The AAPEP (Adolescent and Adult Psycho-educational Profile; Mesibov, Schopler, Schaffer, & Landrus, 1988), an assessment tool for adolescents and adults with autism, was developed by the TEACCH program. Designed along lines similar to those of the PEP-R for younger children (Schopler, Reichler, Bashford, Lansing, & Marcus, 1990), the AAPEP deemphasizes language, speed, and other areas of functioning that are consistently weak among clients with autism. Instead, the AAPEP emphasizes the visual and categorical skills that are traditionally stronger in these clients. Like the PEP-R, the AAPEP utilizes a "pass-emerge-fail" scoring system. The emerge rating is assigned when an individual has some knowledge of what is required to successfully complete a task, but lacks the skill necessary for complete mastery and understanding. Emerging skills, considered most likely to improve through instruction, become a major focus of intervention programs.

Administration of the AAPEP allows the examiner flexibility in adjusting the presentation of the materials as necessary while still remaining within the standardization guidelines. This flexibility allows autistic adolescents and adults, despite their deficits in communication and comprehension, to understand the test's expectations and perform at a level commensurate with their ability. In addition to the Direct Scale that is administered to the adolescent or adult with autism, the AAPEP has a Home Scale (administered to parents) and a School Scale (administered to teachers). People with autism are assessed in six functional areas: (a) Vocational Skills, (b) Independent Functioning, (c) Leisure Skills, (d) Vocational Behavior, (e) Functional Communication, and (f) Interpersonal Behavior.

The reliability and validity of the AAPEP were determined by testing 60 adolescents and adults with autism who were functioning in the moderate-to-severe range of mental retardation. Of this group, 30 were diagnosed as having autism, and 30 were diagnosed as mentally retarded without autism. Interrater reliability exceeded generally accepted requirements. To test for validity, professionals in the field were asked to examine recommendations based on the AAPEP and compare them to recommendations generated by school officials who had no access to the assessment information. Raters were blind to the condition. Results revealed a strong effect favoring recommendations generated from the AAPEP. This effect was stronger for the clients with autism than for the other group, but was significant for both.

In a longitudinal study, Martos-Perez and del-Sol-Fortea-Sevilla (1993) compared scores on the AAPEP with those achieved on the PEP when it was administered 5 years earlier. The eye–hand coordination scale of the PEP significantly predicted AAPEP scores on Vocational Skills, Independent Functioning, and Vocational Behavior. Imitation predicted Interpersonal Behavior; Fine Motor predicted Leisure Skills; and Cognitive Performance predicted Functional Communication. The study has important implications for adolescent and adult functioning.

CRITICAL RESEARCH—A REVIEW

Much research on adolescents and adults with autism has addressed their current status, skills, and general behaviors. Discussed here are studies that have focused on cognitive skills, behavior, medical status, language and communication, social and interpersonal skills, and, to a lesser extent, outcomes and follow-ups.

Cognitive Skills

For people with autism, IQ and academic changes during adolescence are similar to those typically seen in adolescents without autism. General performance during this period is consistent with middle childhood and remains relatively stable. Significant changes do occur in some students, but these are no greater than the fluctuations seen in the nonhandicapped population (DeMyer et al., 1972). Bartak and Rutter (1973) observed greater academic progress in higher-functioning adolescents with autism (IQs greater than 70) than in those functioning at lower cognitive levels. The higher-functioning group reported modest gains in reading accuracy and comprehension and in arithmetic (gains in arithmetic exceeded those in reading). Ando, Yoshimura, and Wakabayashi (1980), who also found greater improvement in arithmetic skills, specified that the improvement was in abilities with number concepts rather than in computational skills.

Wainwright-Sharp and Bryson (1993) examined attentional dysfunctions that might underlie learning difficulties in adolescents with autism. Studying 11 male high-functioning adolescents with autism and comparing them with matched controls, these investigators concluded that autistic adolescents and adults have difficulty in processing briefly presented information and in disengaging and shifting their attention. These findings could explain autistic persons' problems with sustaining attention in classroom settings and coping with environmental changes.

Several investigators have described substantial cognitive deterioration during adolescence in a subset of children with autism (Brown, 1969; Gillberg & Schaumann, 1981; Rutter, 1970). Estimates from these studies suggest that as many as 30% of the autistic population might experience cognitive deterioration during adolescence. Later reports seem to indicate that most people with autism who experience this decline regain their skills after a relatively brief period (Gillberg, 1984). Risk factors for cognitive deterioration are: high maternal age, female gender, and family history of affective disorders (Gillberg & Schaumann, 1981; Gillberg & Steffenberg, 1987).

Behavior

The behavior of people with autism is of concern because they sometimes threaten others and cause people with autism to be set apart from their communities (Schopler & Mesibov, 1994). These difficulties are especially problematic in adolescents and adults with autism whose large size and disruptive behaviors may be perceived as dangerous. A critical need in programs for adolescents and adults with autism is proper management of difficult behaviors.

Aggressive and Self-Injurious Behaviors

Of greatest concern among the behaviors of people with autism are aggressive and self-injurious behaviors, which are seen frequently in 10% to 20% of autistic people identified as showing deterioration during adolescence (Gillberg & Coleman, 1992). According to Gillberg and Coleman, increases in self-destructiveness and aggression also occur in many autistic adolescents and adults who do not show marked deterioration of other skills. Gillberg (1984) estimates that aggression and self-destruction increase during adolescence in about half of the students with autism. Although 10% to 20% of that group show continued deterioration, the rest begin to improve after a year or so of difficulties. Gillberg argues that periods of aggressiveness followed by calm are most frequently observed in clients with family histories of affective disorders.

Sexuality

Sexual maturation brings certain behavioral problems in autism, but they are not as severe as many parents anticipate. Although the onset of menstruation requires adjustments in females, Wing (1983) reports that these changes are usually accepted easily after proper hygienic instruction. The increase in sexual drive in males sometimes produces embarrassing moments if they expose themselves, masturbate in public, or touch other people's genital regions (Gillberg, 1984), but these behaviors are typically infrequent, and consistent behavioral teaching techniques, based on the recognition that people with autism typically lack appropriate social skills and understanding, can minimize their occurrence. Strategies that allow sexual needs to be met in socially acceptable ways, like seeking privacy before masturbating, can minimize inappropriate behavior in public.

Some research has focused on sexuality in adults with autism. Ousley and Mesibov (1991) interviewed 21 high-functioning adults with autism and 20 mildly to moderately mentally retarded adults without autism about dating, sexuality, and intimate interpersonal relationships. Both groups had equivalent knowledge about sexuality and interest in pursuing intimate relationships. Group differences were found in experience; more sexual experiences were reported among the mentally retarded adults without autism. In both groups, IQ was positively correlated with knowledge scores, and, compared to females, males had significantly greater interest in sexuality.

Haracopos (1989) has described the involvement of adults with autism in unsolicited homosexual contacts as resulting from their lack of suspiciousness, which makes them vulnerable to being taken advantage of sexually. A greater interest in same-sex peers or a biological orientation is not evident.

Activity Level

Changes in activity level frequently occur during adolescence. In general, activity level decreases during adolescence, especially in youngsters who were very active as young children (Ando & Yoshimura, 1979; Rutter, 1970). This change is sometimes quite dramatic, to the point of total inactivity or inertia. There sometimes can be an extreme degree of psychomotor retardation and a total lack of initiative (Gillberg & Coleman, 1992).

Medical Status

Seizures

Many people with autism, although seizure-free during childhood, develop seizures during adolescence or early adulthood. Estimates indicate that 25% to 40% of people with autism develop epilepsy before the age of 30 (Deykin & MacMahon, 1980; Gillberg & Steffenberg, 1987; Mesibov, 1983). People with autism and mental retardation are at higher risk for epilepsy than those functioning intellectually within the borderline-to-normal range, but seizures are also seen in persons of normal or even above-normal intelligence (Gillberg & Coleman, 1992). At present, there is no way of predicting which children with autism will develop seizures as adolescents or young adults, but there is a slight indication that the risk is higher for girls than for boys (Gillberg & Steffenberg, 1987).

Depression

The periods of marked underactivity sometimes seen in autistic adolescents have already been described (Rutter, 1970). For some professionals, these periods represent depression in nonverbal clients. Feelings of unhappiness, reported by verbal youngsters during adolescence (Wing, 1983), are most frequently seen in capable people with autism when they become aware of their differences from nonautistic adolescents. This depression is generally interpreted as a reaction to their unfulfilled need for friendships and peer relationships. Some people with autism go through major depressions during adolescence and young adulthood. This condition is most common in those with family histories of affective disorders and might represent a primary depressive disorder (Gillberg & Coleman, 1992).

Language and Communication

Problems with language and communication were among the most conspicuous symptoms that led to Kanner's (1943) identification of autism as a disorder distinct from Childhood Schizophrenia. Kanner was fascinated by these peculiarities of language and described them frequently in his writing. The earliest outcome studies highlighted the importance of language and communication skills for positive adult outcomes (Eisenberg & Kanner, 1956; Kanner, 1973). Follow-up studies of autistic children in adolescence and adulthood reveal continued communication difficulties such as echolalia, substitutions, literalness, repetitions, and problems with prosody (Eisenberg & Kanner, 1956; Kanner, 1973). In spite of continued difficulties, some adolescents and adults with autism develop relatively good language.

Fascination with language anomalies, the importance of speech to families, and outcome data have generated considerable research on language and communication in adolescents and adults with autism. Attwood, Frith, and Hermelin (1988) compared gestures of adolescents and young adults with autism to those of normal and Down syndrome controls. Almost all gestures were understood by normal children at age 5 years (and slightly later by the handicapped groups). The ability to initiate such gestures upon verbal request, however, was especially problematic for the adolescents with autism. The study by Attwood et al., which included observations in natural classroom settings where the autistic subjects almost never used expressive gestures, suggests that problems in communication are more pervasive in autistic students and persist through adolescence and young adulthood.

Semantic deficits have also been examined. The concreteness and literalness of autistic people were highlighted by Lord (1988), who also described autistic persons' dependence on immediate context and how this prevents generalization. Prosody problems have been described by Baltaxe and Guthrie (1987). Rumsey, Andreasen, and Rapoport (1986) also confirmed that poverty of speech and speech content were characteristics of adolescents with autism, along with excessive concreteness, reporting of details, and perseveration.

Other noteworthy features of communication, even for people with autism who have good language, are irregularities of delivery, usage, and understanding (Rutter & Schopler, 1978). Delivery problems include monotonic speech with little emotional expression, staccato speech, and lack of proper cadence or inflection. Language tends to be formal, stiff, pedantic, and unnatural. Obsessive questions are frequent, and abstract concepts are difficult to express or understand (Cox & Mesibov, 1995; Ricks & Wing, 1975; Shea & Mesibov, 1985).

Rutter (1970) feels that the most pervasive and basic deficiencies of communication in autism are those involving ordinary social communication. Autistic adolescents and adults are impaired in understanding rules, conducting dialogue, and distinguishing speaker-hearer roles in conversations. Beisler and Tsai (1983) identify the fundamental deficits as (a) not knowing how to take turns as part of social exchanges and (b) not understanding how communication can regulate the environment. Lack of understanding of relationships between rules and communication makes social dialogue extremely difficult.

There have been many attempts to mediate communication deficits in both verbal and nonverbal autistic clients. A variety of alternative communication systems have been used successfully with nonverbal adolescents and adults with autism: sign language, picture cards, and word cards, among others. Sign language, one of the earliest alternative communication approaches, has been effective because it adds visual and motor aspects to communication (Bonvillian & Nelson, 1976). Lancioni (1983) has trained severely impaired adolescents and adults with autism to associate picture cards with objects and then to point to the cards to indicate their choices of objects or activities. La Vigna (1977) has used word cards in a similar way. The TEACCH language curriculum (see below) incorporates several alternative communicative systems, based on individual clients' strengths and interests. Under this system, a student whose strength or peak skill is words would use a word system, another might use objects, and a third might use pictures. The TEACCH curriculum emphasizes training in natural settings so that communication becomes as meaningful as possible for the students with autism. The TEACCH curriculum particularly advocates the use of these alternative communication systems during highly motivating community-based outings.

Several approaches to communication training for verbal adolescents and adults with autism have focused on their ability to use language communicatively, rather than on improving their vocabulary or teaching them to speak in grammatically correct sentences. One area of emphasis is training in natural environments: teaching autistic people to communicate in the context of their everyday activities (Beisler & Tsai, 1983). This method makes words more meaningful and teaches autistic people the rules of social interaction. Intrinsically interesting materials and topics are emphasized so that autistic people are motivated and engaged. Once a paradigm is established, turn-taking activities are built into the training programs (Beisler & Tsai, 1983). Although difficult for people with autism to understand, reciprocal turn-taking is essential for effective communication.

Lord (1988) has developed communication training programs for adolescents (mid- to late teens) with autism. Lord's groups emphasize participation in social activities and the identification of appropriate conversation topics. The relationship among language, personal interests, and leisure activities is crucial. Increasing leisure interests and encouraging people with autism to discuss what they enjoy and think about are important motivational aspects of these training programs. Mesibov's (1984, 1986) social groups are based on similar concepts.

Krantz, Ramsland, and McClannahan (1989) evaluated the effectiveness of an adolescent peer prompter with autism in increasing conversational language skills of three other male verbal autistic adolescents. Participants who had paper-and-pencil mastery of the subject matter (sports) learned to include this information in their social interaction repertoires. Conversational skills also generalized to other groups, classrooms, and dyads. This study demonstrates that handicapped peers can be helpful in developing conversational skills, and that nonhandicapped peers are not always essential for the promotion of communication or social development.

Discovered in Australia and brought to the United States by Doug Biklen, Facilitated Communication (FC) has recently impacted the field of autism by promising latent communication skills previously unrevealed in severely handicapped people with autism. FC involves gently guiding the hand of a person with autism over a computer, a similar keyboard, or even a sheet of paper. This gentle guiding supposedly initiates communication and allows the client to express thoughts and ideas that no one believed possible. Most professionals working with FC clients did not previously think that the clients could even read or write. The problem with FC is in determining whether the message is coming from the client or is being influenced and determined by the facilitator. A recent study by Smith and Belcher (1993) is typical of the literature. They explored the use of FC with 8 adults with autism who had minimal verbal skills. FC training sessions occurred 1 to 3 times a week for a total of 7 to 12 weeks. In all cases, the typed communication was at or below the clients' levels of verbal communication. These results suggest that FC might not be effective in enhancing the communication of adults with autism. Other studies have obtained similar results (Mesibov, 1995; Shane, 1994) and

strongly suggest that most messages generated through FC are facilitator-, rather than client-initiated.

Social and Interpersonal Skills

Social and interpersonal deficits in autism have always been intriguing. They led Kanner (1943) to adopt the term *autism* to describe the youngsters in his program who exhibited these puzzling difficulties. Along with communication deficits, these are highlighted and enumerated in each definition and reinterpretation of the autism syndrome (APA, 1980, 1987, 1994; Creak, 1963; Ritvo & Freeman, 1978; Rutter, 1978; Schopler & Mesibov, 1988).

One of the most exciting findings from research focusing on adolescents and adults with autism is the observation that, during this period, social interests greatly expand and social skills continue to develop (Ando & Yoshimura, 1979; Mesibov, 1983; Mesibov & Schaffer, 1986; Schopler & Mesibov, 1983, 1986). Rutter (1970), describing data from his Maudsley sample, noted improvement in 50% of the cases. Park (1983) describes her daughter, Jessy, during adolescence: "If autism retains its root meaning of 'immured within the self,' Jessy is not autistic any more." Even when they have generally improved, adolescents and adults with autism continue to have difficulty in establishing and maintaining interpersonal relationships.

Rutter (1970) correlated observations of increased interest in social relationships during adolescence with a corresponding increase in skills:

Among those who had made the most progress, about half showed an interest, friendliness and involvement with other people; but they lack the skills in interpersonal relationships needed to proceed from acquaintanceship to friendship.

More recently, Rutter (1983) highlighted three social abnormalities most characteristic of adolescents and young adults with autism: (a) lack of reciprocity in social exchanges, (b) failure to seek physical contact, and (c) an inability to understand what others are thinking or feeling.

Other investigators have noted an important social deficit involving the inability of adolescents and adults with autism to extract meaningful rules from social situations (Hermelin & O'Connor, 1985; Lord & Allen, 1979). This is a crucial deficit because subtle and implicit rules govern so much of social behaviors. Individuals who have difficulty identifying and understanding these rules are highly disadvantaged in social situations.

Considering the importance of social relationships and the substantial deficits observed in people with autism, it is surprising that more intervention programs have not been designed to remediate these deficits. Duran (1986) established an all-day adolescent and adult program to help remediate social deficits. Her approach has a strong leisure activity component.

Mesibov (1984, 1992) has reported on a long-standing social and leisure skills training program for adolescents and adults with autism in Chapel Hill, North Carolina. This program focuses on practicing conversational skills, participating in social activities, understanding nuances of social behavior, and discussing social relationships. Humor is encouraged and discussed in the group, much to the enjoyment of the group members (Van Bourgondien & Mesibov, 1989). Perceptions of popularity among group members were assessed by sociograms in which perceived attractiveness and humor correlated positively with popularity. Subjects' assessments of these attributes, however, differed from those of the nonhandicapped group leaders.

McGee, Krantz, and McClannahan (1984) used simple game situations to teach positive and negative assertions. Their main training techniques included modeling and behavioral rehearsal. The leaders found that these techniques positively affected social interactions.

Outcomes and Follow-Ups

Only a limited number of outcome or follow-up studies have shown what happens to people with autism later in life. Venter, Lord, and Schopler (1992) evaluated the role of cognitive and behavioral factors in predicting later social-adaptive and academic achievement in higher-functioning adolescents and adults with autism. Early verbal skills were the best predictor of both academic functioning and adaptive behavior later in life. Nonverbal IQ was also positively related with outcome, but the effect was not as strong as for verbal skills. The academic performance of the children in the study was considerably stronger than in earlier outcome studies, suggesting positive effects of improved special education programs in the past decade.

Gillberg and Steffenberg (1987) reported relatively poor outcomes in social adjustment for 60% to 75% of the cases they followed into early adulthood. Of these, approximately 40% to 55% were institutionalized. Although the institutionalization figure for the 1990s is probably smaller, the number of adults with autism who are placed in institutions is still distressingly high.

Gillberg (1991) reports that mortality in the age range from 2 to 30 years has increased for people with autism, compared to the general population. This could be accounted for, at least in part, by severe medical conditions such as tuberous sclerosis. Studies by Rumsey and Hamburger (1988) and by Szatmari, Bartolucci, Brenner, Bond, and Rich (1989) suggest a slightly better outcome for people with autism, especially for a 25% subgroup of these authors' high-functioning sample.

SPECIAL PROGRAMS

Community-Based Programs

Division TEACCH, the Jay Nolen Center, and Community Services for Autistic Citizens (CSAC) are three widely known community-based models for serving adolescents and adults with autism. Division TEACCH, in North Carolina, is the largest and most comprehensive publicly supported statewide program that serves people with autism from cradle to grave in community settings. Established by state law in 1972, following a remarkably successful federal grant, the TEACCH program extended its mandate to adolescents and adults in 1982.

The Jay Nolen Center, in Los Angeles, California, is a privately funded, community-based organization with a full range of residential and vocational programs. CSAC also provides residential and vocational programming but is best known for its innovative vocational options.

Based in Rockville, Maryland, CSAC serves a limited number of adolescents and adults with autism in an intensive community-based model.

Division TEACCH

Division TEACCH includes a network of seven regional centers, a full continuum of educational programs, and a developing array of residential and vocational programs for adolescents and adults with autism. The TEACCH program emphasizes understanding autism and developing appropriate services to meet the full range of needs that these clients present. Individualization is essential because the goal of an effective intervention is to match the services to the specific strengths and unique needs of each client. For this reason, Division TEACCH has adapted its widely used assessment instrument, the PEP-R (Schopler et al., 1990), to meet the needs of adolescents and young adults (Mesibov et al., 1988). Division TEACCH has also adapted its diagnostic instrument, the CARS (Schopler et al., 1988), to more effectively identify adolescents and young adults with autism (Mesibov et al., 1989).

Division TEACCH offers a full continuum of vocational and residential options. The vocational programs are among the newest and most innovative in the field.

Jay Nolen Center

Established in Los Angeles, California, the privately funded Jay Nolen Center provides a full continuum of residential, vocational, recreational, and educational services for people with autism. The program is a collaborative effort shared by a local board and many community agencies. The Jay Nolen Center manages a wide range of group homes, apartments, occupational training programs, recreational programs, intensive intervention programs, and respite care.

Several important philosophical principles have guided this program: normalization, developmental programming, parent advocacy, and a problem-solving approach. Wolfensberger's (1972) normalization principle is a key foundation of the program. This principle supports community-based activities involving nonhandicapped peers in settings that are as age-appropriate as possible. Adherence to this principle requires that group homes are dispersed throughout the community with no home having more than six clients. The homes have no outward indication that they are different from the other homes in the community. So that clients also outwardly resemble other citizens in the community, care is taken to ensure that clients are dressed like other people of their age.

Developmental programming is organized toward a long-range goal of independent living and productive functioning in the community. Each client's skills are regularly evaluated, and programming is designed to help clients achieve the next step in the process toward independent living.

Parents established the Jay Nolen Center, and their advocacy remains a cornerstone of its success and effectiveness. The program grew out of an initiative by the local Los Angeles Parents' Group and has been controlled and expanded by parents since the outset. The majority of the Board are parents of autistic children, and their input is the major force guiding the organizational structure and program development.

Another feature of the program is careful analysis of current functioning through extensive data collection. Comprehensive data are collected and used in all aspects of the program. Administrators of the Jay Nolen Center believe that careful data analysis builds responsibility and accountability into their programming efforts.

Community Services for Autistic Citizens (CSAC)

CSAC was established in Rockville, Maryland, with the goal of providing a range of community-based services for adolescents and adults with autism. The main priority of the program is to facilitate the deinstitutionalization of people with autism by establishing a full continuum of residential and day programs. The innovative vocational model developed by CSAC has become nationally known because it has demonstrated that, with adequate supervision, people with autism can work in competitive employment.

Critical to the success of the CSAC model are the fully trained, nonhandicapped job counselors who work with clients in job settings to provide ongoing training, assistance, and support. Counselors are always available during the workday, and each counselor never has more than two clients to supervise. In addition to their supervisory responsibilities, job counselors assist workers in using public transportation, learning how to adjust to changes in routines, and developing relationships with coworkers. The wide range of vocational options available to clients in this program includes printing, library work, assembly work, and bookbinding.

Classroom and residential programs round out the CSAC options. CSAC is a powerful demonstration of what people with autism can achieve when appropriate community-based supports are available to them.

Self-Contained Residential Programs

Community-based models for adolescents and adults with autism also include several programs that are more self-contained. Although these programs are located within regular communities and the clients frequently interact with their nonhandicapped neighbors, they are described separately because the vocational and residential components share a single site. Benhaven, Bittersweet Farms, and the Carolina Living and Learning Center (CLLC) have expanded our understanding of the possibilities for people with autism by demonstrating that comprehensive programs do not always have to be dispersed throughout a community. These models extend the horizon for people with autism and their families.

Benhaven

Founded in 1967, in New Haven, Connecticut, Benhaven is primarily an educational and behavioral program offering a range of school, work, and agricultural environments. Individualized instruction in life skills is the cornerstone of the curriculum. As with many other comprehensive programs designed for adolescents and adults with autism, a major goal of Benhaven is to avoid institutionalization in large and impersonal state facilities. Benhaven accomplishes this goal through maximizing competence and independence in vocational, recreational, and residential skills in a day, residential, and school community.

Precision teaching is the main educational and behavioral intervention. Curriculum areas include academics, sex education, and vocational training. Total communication has been taught at Benhaven since 1971. Socialization and recreation are also important aspects of the program; all students at Benhaven are encouraged to enjoy and productively use their leisure time.

Bittersweet Farms

Established by a group of parents and professionals near Toledo, Ohio in 1975, Bittersweet Farms is an innovative model providing a comprehensive, holistic living environment for adolescents and adults with autism. Bittersweet Farms is modeled after Somerset Court, a program established by Sybil Elgar in Somerset, England. The general model is of a farm community where residents and staff together contribute to all aspects of the community, including meal preparation, farm maintenance, gardening, small animal care, leisure, and special tasks such as weaving and printing. One day, it is anticipated, the residents will operate shops where they can sell their goods.

Several aspects of the Bittersweet Farms model are especially appealing. Bittersweet Farms is a productive and exciting place where people with autism can live without major stress. (This climate would be difficult to achieve with autistic youngsters, who are easily disoriented and agitated.) All parts of the community are connected, to give residents the consistency that is so important to them. Because the activities of a farm community emphasize visual, fine motor, and gross motor skills, which are usually the strongest skills among adolescents and adults with autism, this community maximizes their possibilities for success. Although the farm is more removed from the mainstream than some people would like, it does not preclude extensive contact with neighbors and local towns. Residents of Bittersweet Farms have many opportunities to interact with townspeople when they shop, eat at restaurants, or participate in holiday and festival celebrations.

Carolina Living and Learning Center (CLLC)

The CLLC is an integrated and coordinated vocational and residential program designed specifically for adults with autism. It provides direct training to the clients, opportunities for professional development for community-based professionals, and an active research program. The CLLC is similar to Bittersweet Farms in that the basic program revolves around the outdoor activities that characterize rural agrarian communities in North Carolina.

Currently, the CLLC is funded to serve 15 adults with autism at all intellectual and adaptive functioning levels. A future plan is for 25 to 30 clients to be housed on this 88-acre property. Residential options include homelike environments with individual rooms for each client. The vocational program includes three primary areas of specialization: agriculture and horticulture, baking, and grounds and lawn maintenance.

The CLLC employs the highly successful TEACCH cotherapy model as its primary focus (Schopler & Reichler, 1971). The model emphasizes collaboration, which at the CLLC involves the relationships between staff and residents. Staff members work as cotherapists with their clients in an apprenticeship model. By working collaboratively with the residents, the staff have unique opportunities to teach new skills through the practice and active involvement approach that works best for these clients.

The agricultural community at the CLLC allows for vocational training in a variety of meaningful areas. Clients have a unique opportunity to sow the seeds, watch their plantings grow, and then harvest, prepare, and consume their produce. After-meals cleanup is part of their daily routine. For people with autism, who otherwise would have trouble figuring out and understanding how different aspects of their lives fit together, the CLLC is an opportunity for an integrated life.

The power of the CLLC model is in its integration of vocational and residential programs around activities that are reasonable and make sense to clients with autism. The large physical space is helpful; many clients prefer it to the crowds and noise of city life. This agriculture-based community is an exciting new approach to the treatment and education of adolescents and adults with autism.

SUMMARY

Although still in an early stage of evolution, research on adolescents and adults with autism is ongoing and expanding. This chapter has reviewed the status of current research on diagnosis and assessment, cognitive and social skills, behavior, related medical conditions, outcomes, and model programs. Current possibilities for adolescents and adults with autism are expanding, and their ability to benefit from services is increasing. Earlier and more effective intervention programs are having an impact, and the next decade should bring exciting new possibilities.

Cross-References

Developmental aspects of autism are addressed in Chapters 12 and 13. Vocational issues are reviewed in Chapter 28, and program administration and residential issues are discussed in Chapters 30 and 31. Life-span issues are treated in Chapter 45.

REFERENCES

American Psychiatric Association. (1980). *Diagnostic and statistical manual of mental disorders* (3rd ed.). Washington, DC: Author.

American Psychiatric Association. (1987). *Diagnostic and statistical manual of mental disorders* (3rd ed., rev.). Washington, DC: Author.

American Psychiatric Association. (1994). *Diagnostic and statistical manual of mental disorders* (4th ed.). Washington, DC: Author.

Ando, H., & Yoshimura, I. (1979). Effects of age on communication skill levels and prevalence of maladaptive behaviors in autistic and mentally retarded children. *Journal of Autism and Developmental Disorders, 9,* 83–93.

Ando, H., Yoshimura, I., & Wakabayashi, S. (1980). Effects of age on adaptive behavior levels and academic skill levels in autistic and mentally retarded children. *Journal of Autism and Developmental Disorders, 10,* 173–184.

Attwood, A., Frith, U., & Hermelin, B. (1988). The understanding and use of interpersonal gestures by autistic and Down's syndrome children. *Journal of Autism and Developmental Disorders, 18,* 241–257.

Baltaxe, C.A., & Guthrie, D. (1987). The use of primary sentence stress by normal, aphasic, and autistic children. *Journal of Autism and Developmental Disorders, 17,* 255–271.

Bartak, L., & Rutter, M. (1973). Special educational treatment of autistic children: A comparative study: 1. Design of study and characteristics of units. *Journal of Child Psychology and Psychiatry, 14,* 161–179.

Beisler, J.M., & Tsai, L.Y. (1983). A pragmatic approach to increase expressive language skills in young autistic children. *Journal of Autism and Developmental Disorders, 13,* 287–303.

Bonvillian, J.D., & Nelson, K.E. (1976). Sign language acquisition in a mute autistic boy. *Journal of Speech and Hearing Disorders, 41,* 339–347.

Brown, J.L. (1969). Adolescent development of children with infantile psychosis. *Seminars in Psychiatry, 1,* 79–89.

Cox, R.D., & Mesibov, G.B. (1995). Relationship between autism and learning disabilities. In E. Schopler & G.B. Mesibov (Eds.), *Learning and cognition in autism* (pp. 57–70). New York: Plenum Press.

Creak, E.M. (1963). Childhood psychosis: A review of 100 cases. *British Journal of Psychiatry, 109,* 84–89.

Cromer, R.F. (1981). Developmental language disorders: Cognitive processes, semantics, pragmatics, phonology, and syntax. *Journal of Autism and Developmental Disorders, 11,* 57–74.

DeMyer, M.K., Pontius, W., Norton, J.A., Barton, S., Allen, J., & Steele, R. (1972). Parental practices and innate activity in normal, autistic, and brain-damaged infants. *Journal of Autism and Childhood Schizophrenia, 2,* 49–66.

Deykin, E., & MacMahon, G. (1980). Pregnancy, delivery and neonatal complications among autistic children. *American Journal of Diseases of Children, 134,* 860–864.

Duran, E. (1986). Developing social skills in autistic adolescents with severe handicaps and limited English competencies. *Education, 107,* 203–207.

Eisenberg, L., & Kanner, L. (1956). Early infantile autism 1943–1955. *American Journal of Orthopsychiatry, 26,* 556–566.

Garfin, D.G., McCallon, D., & Cox, R. (1988). Validity and reliability of the Childhood Autism Rating Scale with autistic adolescents. *Journal of Autism and Developmental Disorders, 18,* 367–378.

Gillberg, C. (1984). Autistic children growing up: Problems during puberty and adolescence. *Developmental Medicine and Child Neurology, 26,* 122–129.

Gillberg, C. (1991). Outcome in autism and autistic-like conditions. *Journal of the American Academy of Child and Adolescent Psychiatry, 30,* 375–382.

Gillberg, C., & Coleman, M. (1992). *The biology of the autistic syndromes* (2nd ed.). London: MacKeith Press.

Gillberg, C., & Schaumann, H. (1981). Infantile autism and puberty. *Journal of Autism and Developmental Disorders, 11,* 365–371.

Gillberg, C., & Steffenberg, S. (1987). Outcome and prognostic factors in infantile autism and similar conditions: A population-based study of 46 cases followed through puberty. *Journal of Autism and Developmental Disorders, 17,* 273–287.

Haracopos, D. (1989). Comprehensive treatment program for autistic children and adults in Denmark. In C. Gillberg (Ed.), *Diagnosis and treatment of autism* (pp. 251–261). New York: Plenum Press.

Hermelin, B., & O'Connor, H.J. (1985). Inner language and nonverbal communication in autism. In E. Schopler & G.B. Mesibov (Eds.), *Communication problems in autism* (pp. 283–310). New York: Plenum Press.

Kanner, L. (1943). Autistic disturbances of affective contact. *Nervous Child, 2,* 217–250.

Kanner, L. (1973). *Childhood psychosis: Initial studies and new insights.* Washington, DC: Winston.

Krantz, P.J., Ramsland, S.E., & McClannahan, L.E. (1989). Conversational skills for autistic adolescents: An autistic peer as prompter. *Behavioral Residential Treatment, 4,* 171–189.

Lancioni, G.E. (1983). Using pictorial representation as communication means with low-functioning children. *Journal of Autism and Developmental Disorders, 13,* 87–105.

LaVigna, G.W. (1977). Communication training in mute autistic adolescents using the written word. *Journal of Autism and Childhood Schizophrenia, 7,* 135–150.

Lord, C. (1988). Enhancing communication in adolescents with autism. *Topics in Language Disorders, 9,* 72–81.

Lord, C., & Allen, J.A. (1979, March). *Comprehension of simple sentences in autistic children.* Paper presented at the meeting of the Midwestern Psychological Association, Chicago.

Lord, C., Rutter, M., Goode, S., Heemsbergen, J., Jordan, H., Mawhood, L., & Schopler, E. (1989). Autism Diagnostic Observation Scale:

A standardized observation of communicative and social behavior. *Journal of Autism and Developmental Disorders, 19,* 185–212.

Lord, C., Rutter, M., & Le Couteur, A. (1994). Autism diagnostic interview—revised: A revised version of a diagnostic interview for caregivers of individuals with possible pervasive developmental disorders. *Journal of Autism and Developmental Disorders, 24,* 659–685.

Martos-Perez, J., & del-Sol-Fortea-Sevilla, M. (1993). Psychological assessment of adolescents and adults with autism. *Journal of Autism and Developmental Disorders, 23,* 653–664.

McGee, G.G., Krantz, P.J., & McClannahan, L.E. (1984). Conversational skills for autistic adolescents: Teaching assertiveness in naturalistic game settings. *Journal of Autism and Developmental Disorders, 14,* 319–330.

Mesibov, G.B. (1983). Current perspectives and issues in autism and adolescence. In E. Schopler & G.B. Mesibov (Eds.), *Autism in adolescents and adults* (pp. 37–53). New York: Plenum Press.

Mesibov, G.B. (1984). Social skills training with verbal autistic adolescents and adults: A program model. *Journal of Autism and Developmental Disorders, 14,* 395–404.

Mesibov, G.B. (1986). A cognitive program for teaching social behaviors to verbal autistic adolescents and adults. In E. Schopler & G.B. Mesibov (Eds.), *Social behavior in autism* (pp. 265–303). New York: Plenum Press.

Mesibov, G.B. (1992). Treatment issues with high-functioning adolescents and adults with autism. In E. Schopler & G.B. Mesibov (Eds.), *High-functioning individuals with autism* (pp. 143–155). New York: Plenum Press.

Mesibov, G.B. (1995). Commentary: Facilitated communication: A warning for pediatric psychologists. *Journal of Pediatric Psychology, 20,* 127–130.

Mesibov, G.B., & Schaffer, B. (1986). Autism in adolescents and adults. In M.L. Wolraich & D.K. Routh (Eds.), *Advances in developmental and behavioral pediatrics* (Vol. 7, pp. 1–11). New York: Plenum Press.

Mesibov, G.B., Schopler, E., Schaffer, B., & Landrus, R. (1988). *Individualized assessment and treatment for autistic and developmentally disabled children: Vol. 4. Adolescent and Adult Psychoeducational Profile (AAPEP).* Austin, TX: Pro-Ed.

Mesibov, G.B., Schopler, E., Schaffer, B., & Michal, N. (1989). Use of the Childhood Autism Rating Scale (CARS) with autistic adolescents and adults. *Journal of the American Academy of Child and Adolescent Psychiatry, 28,* 538–541.

Ousley, O.Y., & Mesibov, G.B. (1991). Sexual attitudes and knowledge of high-functioning adolescents and adults with autism. *Journal of Autism and Developmental Disorders, 21,* 471–481.

Park, C.C. (1983). Growing out of autism. In E. Schopler & G.B. Mesibov (Eds.), *Autism in adolescents and adults* (pp. 279–295). New York: Plenum Press.

Ricks, D.M., & Wing, L. (1975). Language, communication, and the use of symbols in normal and autistic children. *Journal of Autism and Childhood Schizophrenia, 5,* 191–221.

Ritvo, E.R., & Freeman, B.J. (1978). National Society for Autistic Children definition of autism. *Journal of Autism and Developmental Disorders, 8,* 162–167.

Rumsey, J.M., Andreasen, N.C., & Rapoport, J.L. (1986). Thought, language, communication, and affective flattening in autistic adults. *Archives of General Psychiatry, 43,* 771–777.

Rumsey, J.M., & Hamburger, S.D. (1988). Neuropsychological findings in high-functioning men with infantile autism, residual state. *Journal of Clinical and Experimental Neuropsychology, 10,* 201–221.

Rutter, M. (1970). Autistic children: Infancy to adulthood. *Seminars in Psychiatry, 2,* 435–450.

Rutter, M. (1978). On confusion in the diagnosis of autism. *Journal of Autism and Childhood Schizophrenia, 8,* 137–161.

Rutter, M. (1983). Cognitive deficits in the pathogenesis of autism. *Journal of Child Psychology and Psychiatry, 24,* 513–531.

Rutter, M., & Schopler, E. (Eds.). (1978). *Autism: A reappraisal of concepts and treatment.* New York: Plenum Press.

Schopler, E., & Mesibov, G.B. (Eds.). (1983). *Autism in adolescents and adults.* New York: Plenum Press.

Schopler, E., & Mesibov, G.B. (Eds.). (1986). *Social behavior in autism.* New York: Plenum Press.

Schopler, E., & Mesibov, G.B. (Eds.). (1988). *Diagnosis and assessment in autism.* New York: Plenum Press.

Schopler, E., & Mesibov, G.B. (Eds.). (1992). *High-functioning individuals with autism.* New York: Plenum Press.

Schopler, E., & Mesibov, G.B. (Eds.). (1994). *Behavioral issues in autism.* New York: Plenum Press.

Schopler, E., & Reichler, R.J. (1971). Parents as co-therapists in the treatment of psychotic children. *Journal of Autism and Childhood Schizophrenia, 1,* 87–102.

Schopler, E., Reichler, R., Bashford, A., Lansing, M., & Marcus, L. (1990). *Individualized assessment and treatment for autistic and developmentally disabled children: Vol. 1. Psychoeducational Profile—Revised (PEP-R).* Austin, TX: Pro-Ed.

Schopler, E., Reichler, R.J., & Renner, B.R. (1988). *The Childhood Autism Rating Scale (CARS).* Los Angeles: Western Psychological Services.

Shane, H.C. (1994). *Facilitated communication: The clinical and social phenomenon.* San Diego: Singular.

Shea, V., & Mesibov, G.B. (1985). The relationship of learning disabilities and higher-level autism. *Journal of Autism and Developmental Disorders, 15,* 425–435.

Smith, M.D., & Belcher, R.G. (1993). Brief report: Facilitated communication with adults with autism. *Community Services for Autistic Adults & Children, 23,* 175–183.

Szatmari, P., Bartolucci, G., Brenner, R., Bond, S., & Rich, S. (1989). A follow-up study of high-functioning autistic children. *Journal of Autism and Developmental Disorders, 19,* 213–225.

Van Bourgondien, M.E., & Mesibov, G.B. (1989). Diagnosis and treatment of adolescents and adults with autism. In G. Dawson (Ed.), *Autism: New perspectives on diagnosis, nature, and treatment* (pp. 367–385). New York: Guilford Press.

Venter, A., Lord, C., & Schopler, E. (1992). A follow-up study of high-functioning autistic children. *Journal of Child Psychology and Psychiatry, 33,* 489–507.

Wainwright-Sharp, J.A., & Bryson, S.E. (1993). Visual orienting deficits in high-functioning people with autism. *Journal of Autism and Developmental Disorders, 23,* 1–13.

Wing, L. (1983). Social and interpersonal needs. In E. Schopler & G.B. Mesibov (Eds.), *Autism in adolescents and adults* (pp. 337–354). New York: Plenum Press.

Wolfensberger, W. (1972). *The principle of normalization in human services.* Toronto, Ontario, Canada: National Institute on Mental Retardation.

SECTION THREE

Neurobiology

Autism and other pervasive developmental disorders are brought to clinical attention and are diagnosed on the basis of distinctive disturbances in behavior and development. There is broad consensus among clinicians and researchers, however, that autism and associated syndromes represent the "surface" or "phenotypic" manifestations of underlying neurobiological diatheses or biological "genotypes." For this reason, these conditions are sometimes described as neurobehavioral or neuropsychiatric disorders, to emphasize the neurobiological underpinnings. As more is learned, we will be able to trace the expression of the underlying neurobiological dysfunctions in autism and these other conditions through each level of brain and behavioral organization—from the level of the gene(s) involved in brain formation and functioning, through the emergence and functioning of specific brain systems, to the appearance of symptoms and signs of the disorders during early childhood, and, finally, to the full picture of the clinical conditions.

Advances in molecular and behavioral genetics, neurochemistry, neuroimaging, and other related fields in the neurosciences are providing a deeper understanding of the normal development of the central nervous system (CNS) and the integrated functioning of the CNS during complex tasks (such as thinking, imagining, reading, listening, and inhibiting or planning behavior). There are fascinating leads about what particular brain systems are involved in normal processes and may be implicated in neurological, psychiatric, and developmental disorders. We are only at the first stages of understanding how regulatory genes guide the formation of brain structures, the

mechanisms underlying the laying down and pruning of pathways, the sensitive timing of brain connections and the formation of synapses, the ways in which the templates for higher cognitive processes are programmed, and the many interactions among parallel systems that relate to behavioral regulation (such as the cortico-striatal-thalamo-cortical pathways). The biology of uniquely human functioning—abstract thinking, mature social relations—is at the cutting edge of research. Newer methods of studying the functioning brain are already illuminating how the brain processes visual and auditory stimuli and the steps between physical sensation and conscious awareness, and how the parts of the brain are activated during different mental tasks. The availability of postmortem brains and the use of methods such as functional magnetic resonance imaging (MRI) will give new access to the study of brain structure and function and the integration of the findings with the functioning of the brain during life. We can look forward to being able to integrate these various neurobiological approaches with careful studies of behavior and development.

Far less is known, however, about the functioning of the brain during the first years of life and during the course of early development. The understanding of normal development and of the ways in which dysfunctions may arise during embryogenesis and postnatal life will provide a framework for understanding developmental disorders such as autism. Already, more than 1,000 forms of mental retardation are known and, for many of these forms, specific genetic and biological findings have helped to clarify their etiology. The hope is that similar, rigorous studies will help clarify the causal pathways that lead to the clinical syndrome of autism and the other pervasive developmental disorders. We are still a long way from reaching this goal, but the advances in the neurosciences have been explosive; we can anticipate that these findings will have direct relevance to subgroups of individuals with pervasive disorders.

The chapters in this section highlight major domains of neuroscience research—genetics, neurology, neurochemistry—relating to autism and pervasive disorders. One chapter also describes the medical conditions that are sometimes associated with autism and similar disorders. Only through basic neurobiological research will it be possible to provide firmly based genetic counseling, to diagnose pervasive disorders in utero, and to offer highly ameliorative and, hopefully, curative therapies that will fundamentally alter the natural history of these conditions.

CHAPTER 15

Neurochemical Studies of Autism

GEORGE M. ANDERSON AND YOSHIHIKO HOSHINO

The behavioral, emotional, and cognitive symptoms presented by autistic individuals clearly indicate that their central nervous system (CNS) functioning is altered. The early onset, pervasive nature, and chronicity of autism also point directly to brain abnormality. Furthermore, twin and family studies strongly suggest that autism has a genetic basis (Folstein & Piven, 1991; Rutter & Schopler, 1987; Young, Newcorn, & Leven, 1989; see also Chapter 17 of this volume).

Neurochemical studies of autistic individuals have been undertaken to examine the processes related to neural transmission in the CNS and peripheral nervous systems. The search for neurochemical alterations and causes in autism is given impetus by the rapid advance of basic neuroscience and the success of neuropharmacology in the relatively specific treatment of parkinsonism, schizophrenia, depression, and anxiety. The observation of neurochemical and neuroendocrine alterations has encouraged further research and prompted theories regarding neurochemical causes of these neuropsychiatric disorders.

In autism, an apparently less specific and less effective drug response has somewhat hindered the formulation of theories regarding possible neurochemical etiologies. However, a wide range of neurotransmitter and neuroendocrine systems has been examined. This examination, which we will review in detail, has made the elucidation of etiology its main goal, but it has also been carried on in the hope that particular measures might have diagnostic and prognostic utility in the future.

This chapter deals primarily with neurochemical studies measuring levels of neurotransmitters, their metabolites, and associated enzymes in blood, urine, or cerebrospinal fluid (CSF). Separate sections on neurochemistry cover, in order, each of the three major central monoamine neurotransmitters: serotonin, dopamine, and norepinephrine. Later sections concern research on the hypothalamic-pituitary axis, the peptides, amino acid metabolism, and the purines and related compounds.

Our review of these neurochemical and related neuroendocrine studies concentrates on recent findings and attempts to point out the promising areas for research. A number of prior reviews have covered the biochemical research of autism either exclusively (Anderson, 1992; Anderson, Horne, Chatterjee, & Cohen, 1990; Cook, 1990; McBride, Anderson, & Mann, 1990; Ritvo, 1977; Ritvo, Rabin, Yuwiler, Freeman, & Geller, 1978; Young, Kavanaugh, Anderson, Shaywitz, & Cohen, 1982; Yuwiler, Geller, & Ritvo, 1985) or as part of more general reviews (Cohen, Riddle, Laor, Young, & Shaywitz, 1983; Cohen & Young, 1977; DeMyer, Hingtgen, & Jackson, 1981; Guthrie & Wyatt, 1975; Piggott, 1979).

SEROTONIN

Serotonin (5-hydroxytryptamine; 5-HT) is an important neurotransmitter in the CNS, where it is involved in controlling a number of important functions and behaviors, including sleep, mood, body temperature, appetite, and hormone release (Iverson & Iverson, 1981). Cell bodies of most central neurons utilizing 5-HT as a neurotransmitter are located in the midbrain; however, the neurons make connections throughout the brain and spinal cord. Serotonin is synthesized from its amino acid precursor, tryptophan (TRP), by hydroxylation and decarboxylation. It is predominantly metabolized to 5-hydroxyindoleacetic acid (5-HIAA) by the enzyme monoamine oxidase (MAO).

Serotonin is the neurotransmitter that has stimulated the most neurochemical research in autism. Initial interest in the possible role of 5-HT in autism arose from consideration of its role in perception. The powerful effects of serotonergic hallucinogens, such as lysergic acid diethylamide (LSD), stimulated speculation around 5-HT and led to early studies of platelet 5-HT in autism (Schain & Freedman, 1961). Although much of the work has focused on the platelet hyperserotonemia of autism, a number of other observations have contributed to the increasing interest in 5-HT. Reports of a critical role for 5-HT during embryogenesis (Buznikov, 1984) and in the development of the CNS (Lauder, 1993; Whitaker-Azmitia, Lauder, Shemer, & Azmitia, 1987; Whitaker-Azmitia, Murphy, & Azmitia, 1992; Zhou, Auerbach, & Azmitia, 1987) have made 5-HT of special interest in developmental disorders such as autism.

Early studies of serotonergic drugs as possible therapeutic agents were not particularly promising. The 5-HT-releasing agent fenfluramine, despite initial enthusiasm, also has not been found to be of much use in treating autistic symptoms (Campbell, Anderson, & Small, 1990). However, in the past several years, a number of small treatment studies of 5-HT selective reuptake inhibitors—including clomipramine, fluvoxamine, and fluoxetine— have suggested that manipulation of the serotonergic system may be of some benefit (Cook, Rowlett, Jaselskis, & Leventhal, 1992; Gordon, Rapoport, Hamburger, State, & Mannheim, 1992; Markowitz, 1992; McDougle, Price, & Goodman, 1990; McDougle et al., 1992; Todd, 1991).

To assess brain 5-HT function in autism, researchers have measured CSF and urine levels of the major metabolite of 5-HT, 5-HIAA, and blood and urine levels of 5-HT itself. These studies, along with those examining the metabolism as well as the behavioral and neuroendocrine effects of the 5-HT precursors, TRP and 5-hydroxytryptophan (5-HTP), are reviewed below.

Blood 5-HT

The greatest number of 5-HT studies in autism concern the measurement of blood levels of 5-HT. A general consensus has been reached, dating from Schain and Freedman's original observation in 1961, that blood levels of 5-HT are increased in autism. Most of the subsequent research has been directed toward further characterizing the elevation and attempting to elucidate the causes.

Serotonin in blood derives from that synthesized in the wall of the gut; it is stored in platelets while circulating and is catabolizing to 5-HIAA by monoamine oxidase (MAO) after uptake into lung, liver, and capillary endothelium. These aspects of blood 5-HT, and the factor(s) that might cause the increase in autism, have been discussed in detail (Anderson, 1992; Anderson, Stevenson, & Cohen, 1987; Hanley, Stahl, & Freedman, 1977).

Research on the platelet storage of 5-HT has been extensive. At first, it appeared that there might be differences between normal and autistic subjects in terms of the number of platelets (Ritvo et al., 1970) and the platelet efflux of 5-HT (Boullin et al., 1971). However, at present, it appears that these platelet indexes, as well as the number of platelet 5-HT uptake sites, are normal in autism (Anderson, Minderaa, van Bentem, Volkmar, & Cohen, 1984; Boullin et al., 1982; Yuwiler et al., 1975). A more recent study of hyperserotonemic relatives of children with autism found some suggestive differences in platelet 5-HT uptake and the numbers of platelet 5-HT receptors in subgroups of the relatives (Cook et al., 1993).

No differences in platelet levels of the catabolic enzyme MAO have been found in autism (Giller et al., 1980; Young et al., 1982). Unfortunately, because 5-HT is principally metabolized by MAO-A rather than the form found in platelets, MAO-B, these studies of MAO are not definitive. Studies of 5-HT synthesis include those examining urine levels of 5-HIAA and 5-HT, and those in which TRP was administered.

Urine 5-HIAA and 5-HT

Because most 5-HT produced in the body is eventually metabolized to and excreted as

5-HIAA (Udenfriend, Titus, Weissbach, & Peterson, 1959), urine levels of 5-HIAA are a good indicator of the rate of 5-HT synthesis, at least as long as routes of metabolism and elimination are not altered significantly. There have been relatively few studies of urine 5-HIAA excretion in autistic subjects. One major study reported elevated levels (6.08 vs. 3.23 mg/day) of 5-HIAA in autistic subjects compared to mentally retarded individuals (Hanley et al., 1977). In addition, a greater increase in 5-HIAA was seen for the autistic subjects after a TRP load (12.95 vs. 6.52 mg/day). Two previous studies (Partington, Tu, & Wong, 1973; Schain & Freedman, 1961) had not detected differences in urine 5-HIAA excretion between autistic and normal individuals, although in one of the studies hyperserotonemic autistic subjects did have elevated urine 5-HIAA levels.

More recently, urinary excretion of 5-HIAA in a group of individuals with autism who were not receiving medication was observed to be very similar to that seen in an age-matched control group (Minderaa, Anderson, Volkmar, Akkerhuis, & Cohen, 1987). Furthermore, no correlation between urine 5-HIAA and whole blood 5-HT levels was observed in autistic or normal subjects, and hyperserotonemic autistic individuals did not have higher urine levels of 5-HIAA compared to other autistic subjects or to normals. These data regarding 5-HIAA suggest that normal amounts of 5-HT are produced in autistic individuals. In a subsequent study, no differences in urinary excretion of 5-HT itself were seen between autistic and control subjects (Anderson, Minderaa, Cho, Volkmar, & Cohen, 1989), and, in other related studies, no group differences were seen for free plasma levels of 5-HT (Cook, Leventhal, & Freedman, 1988). Taken together, these observations indicate that the platelet of autistic individuals is exposed to normal levels of 5-HT. This in turn suggests that there is an alteration in the platelet's handling of 5-HT, at least in some autistic patients.

Tryptophan Metabolism

Tryptophan, an essential amino acid, is the dietary precursor of 5-HT and of the vitamin nicotinic acid. It has been shown that the level of TRP in the brain is determined to some extent by plasma levels of free (non-protein-bound) TRP. Hoshino, Yamamoto, et al. (1984) determined plasma-free and total TRP levels and blood serotonin levels simultaneously, and reported that both plasma-free TRP and blood 5-HT levels were significantly higher in autistic children than in normal control subjects. In addition, there tended to be a significant correlation between the plasma-free TRP level and several clinical rating scales in autistic children, although there was no correlation between blood 5-HT and free TRP levels in these children. In contrast, Anderson, Volkmar, et al. (1987) reported that whole-blood TRP concentrations tended to be slightly (but not significantly) lower in unmedicated autistics compared to normal controls, although Takatsu, Onizawa, and Nakahato (1975) had previously reported that total-plasma TRP was reduced in autism. Sylvester, Jorgensen, Mellerup, and Rafaelsen (1970) have reported that psychotic children excreted significantly lower amounts of urinary TRP than controls. These results may not be inconsistent, given quite possible differences between free and total pools of plasma TRP.

Several investigators have attempted to demonstrate metabolic alterations in the serotonin metabolism of autistic children by administering large oral doses of L-tryptophan (L-TRP). Sutton, Read, and Arbor (1958) reported that an 18-month-old autistic girl excreted less urinary indoleacetic acid and 5-HIAA, compared with 4 nonpsychotic controls, after administration of a TRP load (0.25 g/kg). They suggested that the ability to metabolize TRP to 5-HIAA and indoleacetic acid might be disturbed in autistic children. However, Shaw, Lucas, and Rabinovitch (1959) examined the urine excretion of 5-HIAA in schizophrenic (autistic) and nonschizophrenic children after the administration of 3 g of oral TRP and found no significant difference between the groups with respect either to absolute amount excreted or to the extent of increase following TRP loading. Schain and Freedman (1961) also performed TRP (1 g) loading tests in autistic and mildly retarded children, but found no differences in blood 5-HT and urinary 5-HIAA concentration between the two groups. On the other hand, Hanley et al. (1977) reported that TRP (1 g) loading raised urinary 5-HT levels in hyperserotonemic autistic children but lowered urinary 5-HT levels in mildly retarded children who had normal levels of blood serotonin. In both groups, the TRP load caused a slight decrease of blood 5-HT and a marked increase of urinary 5-HIAA excretion. In a more recent study (Cook, Anderson, et al., 1992), an oral TRP load was not observed to increase blood 5-HT levels in relatives of autistic individuals. However, depletion of plasma TRP by the use of an amino acid drink has been reported to exacerbate symptoms in an autistic individual (McDougle et al., 1993).

The immediate precursor of 5-HT, 5-HTP, can pass from blood to brain. Once in the brain, 5-HTP can be decarboxylated to 5-HT, thereby increasing central serotonergic function. In an experiment with two autistic boys, Zarcone et al. (1973) administered oral D,L-5-HTP in a dosage of 3.0 mg/kg/day for 8 days. They reported that, during the treatment, increases in REM sleep were observed with no change in the clinical features. Sverd, Kupretz, Winsberg, Hurwic, and Becker (1978) examined the behavioral effects of L-5-HTP given with carbidopa in 3 autistic children, using direct behavioral observation and parental ratings. During the 20-week study, 2 of the children showed behavioral changes that appeared to be unrelated to drug treatment because there were no significant behavioral differences between L-5-HTP/carbidopa treatment and nonactive placebo.

Neuroendocrine Studies of Serotonergic Functioning

Hoshino and colleagues (Hoshino et al., 1983; Hoshino, Tachibana, et al., 1984) have examined the effect of L-5-HTP on serotonin metabolism and hypothalamo-pituitary function in autistic children. They administered L-5-HTP to autistic children and normal controls, and measured chronological changes of blood serotonin, plasma human growth hormone (HGH), and prolactin (PRL). After loading, blood serotonin showed a smaller increase compared with normal controls, although the baseline levels of blood serotonin were significantly higher in autistic children. The levels of plasma HGH observed after 5-HTP-stimulated release were similar in the groups studied, as were baseline HGH concentrations. However,

lower baseline levels of prolactin and a blunted prolactin response to 5-HTP were present in the autistic group (Hoshino et al., 1983; Hoshino, Tachibana, et al., 1984). These results might be explained on the basis of diminished central serotonergic functioning or enhanced activity of tuberoinfundibular dopamine neurons known to exert a powerful inhibitory control on prolactin release. In contrast, other researchers have found normal baseline levels of plasma prolactin and have observed an apparently normal increase in prolactin after chronic treatment with dopamine blockers (Minderaa et al., 1989). In a detailed study of the neuroendocrine response to the serotonergic agent fenfluramine, McBride and colleagues (1989) found that autistic subjects had a blunted prolactin response (with normal baseline prolactin levels). This was interpreted to suggest that central 5-HT type 2 receptor functioning might be reduced in autism. Simultaneous studies of the responsivity of the platelet 5-HT2 receptor also showed a blunted response in the autistic subjects.

CSF 5-HIAA

Levels of 5-HIAA and other monoamine metabolites have been widely measured in CSF in order to estimate brain turnover of the parent neurotransmitters (Garelis, Young, Lal, & Sourkes, 1974). Nearly all 5-HT is metabolized to 5-HIAA before elimination from the brain, and a substantial route for egress of brain 5-HIAA is through the CSF (Aizenstein & Korf, 1979; Meek & Neff, 1973). Certain drugs and treatments known to affect brain 5-HT turnover have corresponding effects on levels of CSF 5-HIAA (Young, Anderson, & Purdy, 1980), and it has been shown that CSF 5-HIAA is not contaminated with 5-HT or 5-HIAA arising elsewhere in the body. The close approach to the brain afforded by CSF measurements is attractive; however, the invasiveness of the required lumbar puncture has limited the number of studies carried out in autistic individuals.

Three studies have used probenecid to block the transport of 5-HIAA and other acidic compounds out of the CSF. In two of the studies, levels of 5-HIAA were observed to be similar (Cohen, Shaywitz, Johnson, & Bowers,

1974) or slightly lower (Cohen, Caparulo, Shaywitz, & Bowers, 1977) in autistic subjects, compared to nonautistic psychotic children. In the third probenecid study, no control groups were used; however, a few of the autistic subjects did not show the expected increase in 5-HIAA after probenecid administration (Winsberg, Sverd, Castells, Hurwic, & Perel, 1980). Although measurements made after probenecid administration are given more weight by some researchers, their interpretation is complicated by the varying levels of CSF probenecid observed in different subjects. In studies of baseline levels of CSF 5-HIAA, no significant differences have been observed between autistic and control subjects (Gillberg & Svennerholm, 1987; Gillberg, Svennerholm, & Hamilton-Hellberg, 1983; Narayan, Srinath, Anderson, & Meundi, 1993). In summary, the CSF studies suggest that if central 5-HT metabolism is altered in autism, it does not involve a widespread or marked change in 5-HT turnover.

DOPAMINE

Most dopamine (DA)-containing neurons lie in the midbrain. They appear to be especially important in the control of motor function, in cognition, and in the regulation of hormone release (Moore & Bloom, 1978). Dopamine is synthesized from dietary amino acids (phenylalanine or tyrosine) by hydroxylation and decarboxylation. Dopamine can be subsequently converted to norepinephrine and epinephrine by the action of the enzymes dopamine-B-hydroxylase and phenyl-ethanolamine-N-methyltransferase. Once released from the neuron, DA is enzymatically degraded by MAO and catechol-O-methyltransferase (COMT) to homovanillic acid (HVA) and 3,4-dihydroxy-phenylacetic acid (DOPAC).

The DA blockers (neuroleptics or major tranquilizers) have been observed to be effective in treating some aspects of autism. This result, and the fact that certain symptoms of autism—stereotypies and hyperactivity, for example—can be induced in animals by increasing DA function, has suggested that central DA neurons may be overactive in autism. Central dopamine function has been assessed in humans by several methods, including postmortem measurements of DA, its metabolites,

and receptors in brain tissue; positron emission tomography (PET scanning); CSF measurements of HVA and DOPAC; and blood or urine measures of DA, HVA, and DOPAC.

CSF HVA

Studies in humans and in animals have indicated that changes in central dopamine turnover are reflected to some extent in CSF levels of the principal dopamine metabolite, HVA (Garelis et al., 1974). In previously discussed studies of CSF 5-HIAA in autistic individuals, measurements of HVA also were made. In two of the three studies using probenecid to block transport of the acid metabolites out of CSF (Cohen et al., 1974; Cohen et al., 1977), no significant differences were observed between autistic children and various comparison groups. Comparison groups included nonautistic psychotic (atypical), aphasic, motor disordered, and neurologically disordered (contrast) children. In both studies, CSF HVA did tend to be lower in autistic children compared to nonautistic psychotic children, and in one of the studies (Cohen et al., 1974), HVA values were reported to be lower in the more disturbed autistic individuals. A third study employing the probenecid technique did not include measurements made in comparison groups; however, the increases in CSF HVA seen after probenecid administration appeared normal (Winsberg et al., 1980).

In more recent CSF studies, probenecid has not been administered. In a study carried out in Sweden, the baseline unperturbed concentrations of CSF HVA were observed to be elevated approximately 50% in the autistic group, compared to an age- and sex-matched control group of neurologically disordered children (Gillberg et al., 1983; Gillberg & Svennerholm, 1987). However, in two other studies of baseline CSF HVA in autism, significant elevations in autistic individuals compared to controls (Narayan, Srinath, et al., 1993; Ross, Klykylo, & Anderson, 1985) were not observed. This question of whether CSF levels are increased in autism is the subject of ongoing debate (Gillberg, 1993; Narayan, Anderson, & Srinath, 1993). Taken together, the CSF studies do not provide strong support for the idea that central DA turnover is increased in autism. However, the discrepancies among the studies suggest that further research in this area is warranted.

Plasma and Urine Measures of Dopamine Function

Unfortunately, the relationship of peripheral measures of DA, HVA, and DOPAC to central DA function is unclear. Although at least some of the HVA found in blood and urine arises from the brain, the exact proportion has not been well established. It has been estimated that approximately 25% of blood or urine HVA is of central origin (Elchisak, Polinsky, Ebert, Powers, & Kopin, 1978; Maas, Hattox, Greene, & Landis, 1980). On the other hand, peripheral DA itself is known to arise almost completely from the adrenal and the sympathetic nervous systems, rather than from the brain.

In the one study of plasma HVA levels in autism, no differences were observed between unmedicated autistic subjects and normal controls (Minderaa et al., 1989). Slight, nonsignificant increases in plasma HVA were seen in autistics medicated with neuroleptics. In two of three studies examining baseline plasma levels of prolactin, a hormone under powerful tonic inhibitory control by dopaminergic tuberinfidibular neurons, no group differences have been seen (McBride et al., 1989; Minderaa et al., 1989).

Although several groups have reported that the urinary excretion of HVA is increased in autism, a large study of urinary DA and HVA did not observe any differences between autistic and control groups in the rate of urinary excretion of these compounds (Minderaa et al., 1989). Studies of the catabolic enzyme COMT, which, along with MAO, converts DA to HVA, have found similar activities in red blood cells of autistic and control subjects (Giller et al., 1980; O'Brien, Semenuk, & Spector, 1976). A recent study of CSF levels of one form of tetrahydrobiopterin, a cofactor in the synthesis of DA, has found lower levels in autistic subjects (Tani, Fernell, Watanabe, Kanai, & Langstrom, 1994).

It is apparent that blood and urine measures of DA metabolites would give a better picture of central dopamine function if peripheral production of DA or its metabolites were lessened. Several groups have suggested that a reduction in the peripheral contribution might be brought about through the administration of debrisoquin (Riddle et al., 1986; Sternberg, Heninger, & Roth, 1983). As it stands, blood and urine levels of DA and HVA appear to be unchanged or only slightly altered in autism.

Neuroendocrine Studies of Dopamine Functioning

Ritvo et al. (1971) designed a study to assess neurochemical, behavioral, and neuroendocrine effects of L-Dopa administration. Following a 17-day placebo period, 4 hospitalized autistic boys received the DA precursor, L-Dopa, for 6 months. Results indicated a significant decrease in blood 5-HT concentrations and a significant increase in platelet counts. Urinary excretion of 5-HIAA decreased significantly in one patient, and a similar trend was noted in others. However, no changes were observed in the clinical course of the disorder, the amount of motility disturbances (stereotypic behavior), percentages of REM sleep time, or measures of endocrine function (plasma LH and FSH levels). In a study of the effects of L-Dopa on the secretion of growth hormone (HGH), Realmuto, Jensen, Reeve, and Garfinkel, (1990) found that, although autistic subjects had normal peak responses in plasma HGH, they had a delayed response compared to controls.

NOREPINEPHRINE

Norepinephrine (NE) is an important neurotransmitter in both the CNS and the peripheral sympathetic nervous system. Central and peripheral NE is produced from DA through the action of the enzyme dopamine-B-hydroxylase. Upon release, most central NE is metabolized by MAO and COMT to 3-methoxy-4-hydroxyphenylglycol (MHPG), whereas peripheral NE is predominantly converted to vanillylmandelic acid (VMA).

Most central NE-containing neurons have their cell bodies localized in one section of the hindbrain, the locus coeruleus. These neurons project in a diffuse manner to many areas of the brain and spinal cord and are crucial in processes related to arousal, anxiety, stress responses, and memory (Amaral & Sinnamon, 1977; Moore & Bloom, 1979). Drugs that lessen central NE function, such as clonidine, have been used to treat withdrawal symptoms (Redmond & Huang, 1979). Other agents that activate central NE neurons, such as yohimbine and desipramine, increase arousal or serve as antidepressants. Norepinephrine also serves as the major neurotransmitter in postganglionic sympathetic nervous neurons. These neurons serve to control autonomic functions and are balanced against cholinergic neurons that enervate the same organs. When sympathetic system activity predominates, the characteristic flight-or-fight response is elicited.

Activity of central NE neurons has been assessed by determining CSF levels of NE and MHPG. The CSF measures probably reflect NE activity in the spinal cord as well as in the brain, and some small contribution of blood MHPG to CSF MHPG has been demonstrated (Kopin, Gordon, Jimerson, & Polinsky, 1983). Blood and urine levels of MHPG also have been measured in order to gauge central NE function; however, the proportion of MHPG in these fluids that originates in the CNS relative to that arising from NE released by sympathetic neurons is not clear. Estimates of the central contribution have varied from 10% to 60% (Blomberry, Kopin, Gordon, Mackey, & Ebert, 1980; Maas et al., 1980; Maas & Leckman, 1983). Other NE metabolites—VMA and normetanephrine (NMN), along with MHPG—have been widely measured in urine to assess activity of the sympathetic nervous system.

The two studies of CSF MHPG in autism reported little or no difference between mean levels observed in autistic and control subjects. In a preliminary study, a mean MHPG concentration of 9.0 ng/ml, which is similar to group means observed in normal subjects, was reported for autistic subjects (Young, Cohen, Kavanaugh, et al., 1981). In a larger study using age- and sex-matched controls, quite similar group means were observed in autistic subjects and controls (Gillberg et al., 1983; Gillberg & Svennerholm, 1987). The two studies seem to indicate that central NE turnover is not grossly altered in autism. As mentioned,

CSF levels of MHPG might best reflect spinal cord NE. Dysfunction of brain NE, particularly dysfunction limited to small areas, cannot be ruled out on the basis of these results.

Studies of blood measures of noradrenaline and its metabolites are limited in number. Lake, Ziegler, and Murphy (1977), after examining blood levels of norepinephrine (NE) and dopamine-Ḃ-hydroxylase (DBH) in autistic and normal subjects, reported that significantly higher levels of blood NE were present in autistics when compared to normals. This suggested an overactive sympathetic nervous system; however, paradoxically, lower levels of DBH were observed in the autistic subjects. These findings were puzzling because both NE and DBH are thought to reflect sympathetic activity. The conflict might be resolved if one accepts the view that NE reflects acute sympathetic response, whereas DBH, with its longer plasma half-life, is indicative of long-term activity.

Two studies of plasma MHPG levels in autism reported seeing no significant differences between autistic and normal subjects. In the first study (Young, Cohen, Hattox, et al., 1981), group means of 3.7 ng/ml and 3.2 ng/ml were observed in the autistic and normal groups, respectively. This similarity of autistic and normal subjects was confirmed in a subsequent study (Minderaa, Anderson, Volkmar, Akkerhuis, & Cohen, 1994), which reported group mean plasma MHPG levels in unmedicated autistic (3.1 ± 0.6 ng/ml; N = 17), medicated autistic (3.3 ± 1.0 ng/ml; N = 23), and normal control groups (3.2 ± 1.2 ng/ml; N = 20). As with DBH, plasma MHPG levels tend to be less responsive to acute stress than NE, so time-related factors may have contributed to the apparent discrepancy between plasma MHPG and NE measures.

In a recent study (Minderaa et al., 1994) that examined MHPG, NE, and ephinephrine (EPI) levels in evening and overnight urines, only slightly lower excretion of NE and MHPG was seen in autistic subjects. Excretion rates in the medicated autistic group were similar to those in the unmedicated groups: neither autistic group had an excretion rate significantly lower than that of the normal group. The diurnal variation observed in normal children (11 P.M. to 7 A.M.) was also seen in autistic subjects. In all groups, overnight (11 P.M. to 7 A.M.) per-hour excretion was significantly lower (reduced from 40% to 70%) than in the evening (5 P.M. to 11 P.M.). Earlier studies (Young, Cohen, Brown, & Caparulo, 1978) had suggested that 24-hour catecholamine excretion was substantially reduced in autistic patients.

Overall, the CSF, plasma, and urine findings indicate that baseline noradrenergic function is probably not greatly altered in autism; however, there is some indication that, in a subgroup of autistic individuals, the sympathetic nervous system may be hyperresponsive to stress. This notion is consistent with reports that clonidine may be of some benefit in treating patients with autism (Frankhauser, Karumanchi, German, Yales, & Karumanchi, 1992).

STUDIES OF THE HYPOTHALAMIC-PITUITARY AXIS

Research examining hypothalamic-pituitary (HP) function in autism can be divided into two main categories: (a) studies that assess the stress response, and (b) studies directed toward determining the functioning of the neurochemical systems that are involved in the regulation of neuroendocrine secretion. The hypothalamic-pituitary-adrenal axis plays a critical role in the stress response and is closely interrelated with the sympathetic nervous system.

Cortisol Secretion

The glucocorticoid cortisol is released from the adrenal cortex in response to stress; increased amounts also are normally released in the early morning. The secretion is under the control of the adrenocorticotropin hormone (ACTH) released from the pituitary, and ACTH release, in turn, is under the control of corticotropin-releasing factor (CRF) produced in the hypothalamus. Levels of cortisol or its metabolites in plasma and urine, and plasma levels of ACTH, have been measured in order to assess hypothalamic-pituitary-adrenal (HPA) function. Normally, cortisol inhibits its own release by suppressing CRF and ACTH release. The status of this feedback system has been studied extensively in depression, using the dexamethasone suppression test (DST;

Gwirtsman, Gerner, & Sternbach, 1982). Studies in autism have examined basal levels of cortisol, diurnal variations, and the response to dexamethasone (a synthetic glucocorticoid) and other provocative agents.

A small study of three autistic-like (early-onset psychosis) children found normal plasma levels of ACTH but greatly reduced levels of urinary 17-hydroxy- and 17-ketocorticosteroids in all three subjects (Brambilla, Viani, & Rossotti, 1969). Hyposecretion was also observed after stimulation of ACTH with metyrapone. Similarly, Hill, Wagner, Shedlorski, and Sears (1977) found decreased levels of plasma cortisol in autistic subjects. However, the balance of the studies of autistic subjects report either normal or elevated baseline secretion of cortisol, and a failure to suppress cortisol release after dexamethasone. Maher, Harper, Macleay, and King (1975) reported an increased release of cortisol in response to insulin in autistic children, compared to retarded control subjects; Yamazaki, Saito, Okada, Fujiede, and Yamashita (1975) found a normal increase in 11-hydroxycorticosteroids (11-OHCS) after pyrogen stress in autistic subjects. The latter investigators also reported abnormal diurnal variations in 11-OHCS levels in the autistic individuals.

Several groups have performed the dexamethasone suppression test (DST) in autistic subjects. Hoshino, Ohno, et al. (1984) reported that, after DST, the low-functioning (IQ < 60) autistic individuals examined were nonsuppressors, whereas high-functioning autistic subjects had nearly normal suppression of cortisol secretion. Similarly, in a group of 12 low-functioning autistic individuals (IQ < 30), Jensen, Realmuto, and Garfinkel (1985) found 10 were nonsuppressors. In both studies, baseline cortisol levels observed in the autistic group were similar to those seen in the control groups (Hoshino, Ohno, et al., 1984; Jensen et al., 1985). Hoshino and colleagues (1989) reported similar abnormalities with the DST when measuring cortisol levels in saliva. In more recent studies, normal levels of plasma cortisol (Sandman, 1991) or slightly elevated levels of urinary cortisol (Richdale & Pryor, 1992) were found in the autistic group.

On the whole, it would appear that baseline secretions of cortisol and ACTH are not greatly altered in autism. However, questions regarding possible abnormalities in the diurnal rhythm remain to be addressed. It does seem clear that lower-IQ autistic subjects do not suppress cortisol secretion after dexamethasone to the same extent as normal or control subjects. Possible treatment effects of an ACTH analogue (Buitelaar, van Engeland, van Ree, de Wied, 1990) have added to the interest in this area.

Thyroid Hormone and TRH Test

Aspects of thyroid function in infantile autism and the efficacy of triiodothyronine (T3) treatment of autistic children have been studied by several investigators (Campbell, Small, et al., 1978; Sherwin, Flach, & Stokes, 1958). Kahn (1970) reported diminished values of T3 uptake in 45 of 62 autistic children. On the other hand, Abbassi, Linscheid, and Coleman (1978) and Cohen, Young, Lowe, and Harcherik (1980) investigated T3, T4, and TSH (thyroid stimulating hormone, thyrotropin) concentrations in 13 autistic children and found no clinical evidence for hypothyroidism; all subjects had levels within the normal range. Campbell, Small, et al. (1978) conducted a placebo-controlled crossover study of behavioral effects of T3 in 30 young, clinically euthyroid autistic children and reported that T3 did not differ from placebo, although, as a group, the lower-IQ autistic children responded to T3.

Campbell, Hollander, Ferris, and Greene (1978) performed the thyrotropin-releasing hormone (TRH) test in psychotic children. After administering synthetic TRH intravenously to 10 young psychotic children, plasma T3, TSH, and prolactin (PRL) were measured over time. In general, there were an elevated response to TSH and a delayed or blunted response of T3 in psychotic children. Suwa et al. (1984) examined hypothalamo-pituitary function by means of the TRH test in four children with autism. Hyperresponse of PRL to TRH was observed in one of the children with autism. Moreover, three of the four autistic children showed a hyperresponse of TSH to TRH. Similarly, Hoshino et al. (1983) reported that six autistic children showed an elevated response of TSH to TRH. Unlike Suwa et al. (1984), they found a blunted response of PRL to TRH. As Campbell, Hollander, et al.

(1978) and Hoshino et al. (1983) have postulated, these findings suggest that there may be some dysfunction or vulnerability of hypothalamo-pituitary function in autistic children.

Congenital hypothyroidism has been described in a number of patients with autism (Ritvo et al., 1990; Gillberg, Gillberg, & Koop, 1992; Gillberg & Coleman, 1992). If the finding is not coincidental, it may indicate that hypothyroidism increases the risk for autism in vulnerable individuals.

Sex Hormones

So far, there have been no reports on the therapeutic effect in autism of sex-related hormones such as luteinizing hormone (LH) and follicle-stimulating hormone (FSH). However, Hoshino et al. (1983) performed a LH-RH test in six autistic boys. They administered synthetic LH-RH intravenously and measured plasma release of LH and FSH; both LH and FSH exhibited a blunted response to LH-RH stimulation. In a recent study of plasma levels of the gonadal and the adrenal androgens, testosterone and dehydroepiandrosterone sulfate (DHEAS), Tordjman and colleagues (1995) found no differences between the autistic and control groups. The group similarities in the androgens were seen in both the pre- and postpubertal subjects.

NEUROPEPTIDE RESEARCH

The important role of peptides in central neurotransmission and neuromodulation is well established (Emson, 1979; Snyder & Childers, 1979). Neuropeptides have been shown to be crucial to processes related to emotion, appetite, pain perception, and sexual behavior. Measurement of CSF, plasma, and urine levels of specific or uncharacterized peptides in schizophrenia and depression has not clearly indicated whether peptides have etiological significance in these disorders. In autism, the work can be divided into studies of specific opioid peptides and more general studies of peptide excretion patterns.

Opioid peptides, such as the enkephalins and the endorphins, appear to be endogenous ligands for receptors activated by morphine and related compounds. Several investigators have theorized that the opioid peptides are involved in producing at least some of the symptoms of autism (Colette, 1978; Panksepp, 1979; Sandman, 1991, 1992). In particular, similarities between behaviors seen in opiate-injected animals and those displayed in autistic subjects (decreased pain perception, behavioral persistence, self-injurious behavior, poor social relations) have suggested that the opioid peptides are hyperfunctional in autism. The hypothesis has been tested by measuring levels of opioids in plasma and CSF, and by administering the opiate antagonist, naloxone, to self-injurious and autistic subjects.

Previous research on the plasma opioids yielded somewhat inconsistent results. Some investigators found elevations in autism, and others found little difference between groups (Barrett, Feinstein, & Hole, 1989; Bernstein, Hughes, Mitchell, & Thompson, 1987; Coid, Allolio, & Rees, 1983; LeBoyer, Bouvard, & Dupes, 1988; Sandman, Barron, Chicz-Demet, & Demet, 1990; Weizman et al., 1984). A study examining β-endorphin fragments in plasma has reported an extreme elevation in C-terminal fragments in autistic individuals (LeBoyer et al., 1994); further work on this aspect is warranted. Studies of CSF opioids have reported increased levels of met-enkephalin (Gillberg, Terenius, & Lonnerholm, 1985; Ross, Klykylo, & Hitzeman, 1987) and increased or unaltered (Nagamitsu, 1993) β-endorphin in autistic subjects. Although CSF opioids are presumably derived from central sources, plasma β-endorphin has a peripheral origin. In fact, β-endorphin appears to be released along with ACTH and probably should be considered a human stress hormone.

Initial tests of the effect of naloxone on self-injurious behavior in mentally retarded individuals were promising (Sandman et al., 1983). This result supported the idea of a hyperfunctional opioid system, at least with respect to this dimension of behavior. However, further studies of naloxone's effects have not tended to demonstrate clear clinical effects of the opioid antagonists in treating autism (Campbell, Anderson, Small, Locascio, et al., 1990; Herman, 1991; LeBoyer et al., 1992).

The urinary excretion of unidentified peptides and peptide complexes in autism has been described in a qualitative manner in several reports (Gillberg, Trygstad, & Foss, 1982; Isarangkun, Newman, Patel, Duruibe, & Abou-Issa, 1986; Reichelt et al., 1981; Reichelt, Saelid, Lindback, & Boler, 1986). Distinctive patterns of urinary peptides have been reported to occur in several childhood neuropsychiatric illnesses, including autism. Although there have been a number of reports of differences between autistic and control subjects in terms of their patterns of peptide excretion, the studies are far from definitive. The relatively nonspecific nature of the analytical separations and detection processes employed, and the nonquantitative aspect of the studies hinder interpretation. In a more recent collaborative study (LeCouteur, Trygstad, Evered, Gillberg, & Rutter, 1988), researchers did not find reproducible differences between autistic and control subjects' excretion of peptides. Any further research should be directed toward establishing which specific peptide species are increased or decreased in autistic subjects. Subsequent identification of the specific peptides that might be abnormal in autism would be desirable, in order to determine the etiological significance of the possible abnormalities.

AMINO ACID METABOLISM

A number of inborn errors of amino acid metabolism have been identified, and several of these disorders, such as phenylketonuria (PKU), histidinemia, and homocystinuria, affect the central nervous system and have severe behavioral consequences (Scriver & Rosenberg, 1973).

Sylvester et al. (1970) surveyed amino acid excretion in 178 children suffering from different psychiatric disorders, including psychosis, neurosis, character disorder, mental deficiency, and other functional disturbances. In no case was a specific hyperaminoaciduria found. Johnson, Wiersma, and Kraft (1974) analyzed amino acid composition of hair protein and found no significant differences between autistic and control children. In 1978, Perry, Hansen, and Christie measured amino compounds and organic acids in CSF, plasma, and urine of autistic and control children. Similar levels of most compounds were observed in the two groups; however, the mean concentration of ethanolamine in CSF was significantly higher in autistic children, compared to control subjects. Based on this finding, they suggested that a subgroup of autistic children may have a brain disorder involving ethanolamine metabolism.

Kotsopoulos and Kutty (1979) and Rutter and Bartak (1971) have reported cases showing features of infantile autism and also exhibiting histidinemia, with histidine blood levels several times higher than normal. It is not clear whether coexistence of autism and histidinemia is coincidental. If not merely coincidental, the histidinemia may have constituted a necessary but not sufficient factor leading to the clinical condition of autism.

An association between PKU and autism has been noted (Friedman, 1969). A subsequent survey of 65 children with pervasive developmental disturbance (Lowe, Tanaka, Seashore, Young, & Cohen, 1980) used standard urinary amino acid screening methods and found three children exhibiting PKU. The children were treated with low phenylalaine diets and showed improvement in functioning and developmental level after treatment. The study underlined the relevance of urinary amino acid screening for children being evaluated for serious developmental disturbances of childhood. Other work on aromatic amino acid precursors of the catecholamines (phenylalanine) and the indoleamines (TRP) found that autistic subjects had reduced intestinal absorption of the compounds (Naruse, Hayashi, Takesada, Nakane, & Yamazaki, 1989). Although an attempt was made to relate these peripheral findings to some central alteration in monoamine metabolism, such a relationship is not at all clear.

PURINES AND
RELATED COMPOUNDS

A good deal of attention has been paid to the role of cyclic AMP (adenosine-3′, 5′-cyclic monophosphate) as a second messenger in the mechanism of neural transmission. The enzymes involved in brain synthesis (adenylate cyclase) and decomposition (phosphodiesterase) of cyclic AMP are more active in the brain than in other body organs. Norepinephrine, among other neurotransmitters, elevates intracellular cyclic AMP after interacting with membrane receptors; the elevation of cyclic AMP appears

crucial to the subsequent neuronal firing. Cyclic GMP (guanosine-3′, 5′-cyclic monophosphate) is a nucleotide related to cyclic AMP and also has second-messenger properties.

In the psychiatric field to date, abnormal levels of cyclic AMP in the urine and CSF have been reported in patients with manic-depressive psychosis, epilepsy, and schizophrenia. Recently, the effect of psychotropic agents on the metabolism of cyclic AMP has also been investigated.

Winsberg et al. (1980) measured cyclic AMP in the CSF of autistic children and reported that levels were increased in all subjects by probenecid administration; however, no comparison to control groups was made. Hoshino, Kumashiro, and Kaneko (1979) determined plasma cyclic AMP levels in psychiatric diseases of children, such as early infantile autism, hyperkinetic mental retardation, Attention Deficit Disorder, and Down syndrome. The plasma cyclic AMP levels were higher in autistic and hyperkinetic mentally retarded children, compared to normal children, and were positively correlated with the hyperactivity score. In children with Attention Deficit Disorder, the plasma cyclic AMP level was significantly lower than in normal children and was not correlated with the hyperactivity score.

Goldberg, Hattab, Meir, Ebstein, and Belmaker (1984) reported that an examination of plasma cyclic AMP and cyclic GMP in 18 patients with childhood autism, 7 patients with Pervasive Developmental Disorder, and 12 age- and sex-matched healthy controls revealed that plasma cyclic AMP was significantly elevated (over 100%) in both groups of patients with childhood-onset psychoses, compared with controls, although plasma cyclic GMP was not elevated. They did not examine the correlation among plasma cyclic AMP, GMP, and clinical symptoms, including hyperkinesis. The origin of plasma cyclic AMP remains unclear; the compound has been assumed to be derived from peripheral organs, such as the liver, kidneys, lungs, and adrenals, as well as the brain.

Sankar (1971) determined red blood cell (erythrocyte) ATPase activity before and after lysing of the cells and reported that the level of ATPase in lyzate was significantly higher in autistic-like schizophrenic children, compared to normal controls. The addition of magnesium ions to the lyzate further increased the ATPase activity, especially among schizophrenic children. Based on this result, Sankar suggested that red cell membranes of schizophrenic children display decreased permeability either to ATP or to some other factor(s) necessary for ATPase activity in the cell.

Uric acid is the end product of all purine pathways, and hyperuricosuria (increased urinary excretion of uric acid) has been reported in about one-quarter of the autistic children studied in the United States and France (Rosenberger-Diesse & Coleman, 1986). Nyhan et al. (1969) described a 3-year-old boy with unusual autistic behavior, who was shown to have an excessive rate of uric acid synthesis due to an increase in the purine enzyme phosphoribosylpyrophosphate synthetase in his fibroblasts (Becker, Raivio, Bakay, Adams, & Nyhan, 1980). Other children with this enzyme abnormality have now been reported (Christen, Hanfeld, Duley, & Simmonds, 1992; Simmonds, Webster, Lingham, & Wilson, 1985).

Jaeken and Van den Berghe (1984) reported that succinyladenosine and succinylaminoimidazole carboxamide riboside were found in body fluids (CSF, plasma, and urine) in three children with severe infantile autism. Their presence indicates a deficiency of the enzyme adenylosuccinase, which is involved in both de novo synthesis of purines and the formation of adenosine monophosphate from inosine monophosphate. Moreover, according to their report, assays in one patient revealed markedly decreased adenylosuccinase activity in the liver, and absence of activity in the kidney. They suggested that the accumulation of both succinylpurines in the CSF implies a deficiency of this enzyme in the brain, and this may be the basic defect in a subgroup of children with autism. This work was followed up with a study of autistic siblings who had a markedly lowered Vmax of adenylosuccinase (Barshop, Alberts, & Gruber, 1989). Recently, the molecular basis of the three cases of severe retardation with autistic features has been identified: the affected children are homozygous for a point mutation, and their family members are heterozygous (Stone et al., 1992). The point mutation in the purine nucleotide biosynthetic enzyme, adenylosuccinate lyase, thus, segregates with the disorder.

SUMMARY

A survey of the field of neurochemical research in autism indicates how few replicated differences have been found between autistic and normal subjects. The studies reporting similarities between autistic and normal subjects should not be considered "negative studies"; they have served to narrow the field of investigation. The relatively few differences that have been reported tend to stand out. Most robust and well replicated is the increase in whole-blood 5-HT seen in autism. However, abnormalities also have been reported in peptide excretion and in neuroendocrine and HPA functioning, and some evidence suggests that central DA turnover might be increased.

An elucidation of the factor(s) causing the elevation of blood 5-HT would be of interest. The possibility of increased central dopamine function, which is supported by pharmacological and behavioral observations, also deserves further careful study. Additional studies of peptide excretion and hormone release seem warranted, given the abnormalities reported, their possible relevance to central neurotransmitter function, and the hormones' and peptides' physiological importance. Finally, the diurnal rhythms of, and the effects of stress on, NE, epinephrine (adrenaline), and cortisol appear to be potentially fruitful areas of research.

The direction of future research on the biochemical basis of autism no doubt will be influenced by advances in the basic neurosciences and by parallel studies in the biological psychiatry of other mental disorders. In the future, a greater consensus should be reached as to the exact aspects of neurochemical functioning that are abnormal in autism. The application of new techniques of neurochemical assessment also should allow a more complete picture to be drawn.

Cross-References

Neurologic and genetic aspects of autism are discussed in Chapters 16 and 17; medical conditions and autism is the topic of Chapter 18;

and psychopharmacology is covered in Chapter 32.

REFERENCES

Abbassi, V., Linscheid, T., & Coleman, M. (1978). Triiodothyronine (T3) concentration and therapy in autistic children. *Journal of Autism and Childhood Schizophrenia, 8,* 383–387.

Aizenstein, M.L. & Korf, J. (1979). On the elimination of centrally formed 5-hydroxyindoleacetic acid by cerebrospinal fluid and urine. *Journal of Neurochemistry, 32,* 1227–1233.

Amaral, D.G., & Sinnamon, H.M. (1977). The locus coeruleus: Neurobiology of a central noradrenergic nucleus. *Progress in Neurobiology, 9,* 147–196.

Anderson, G.M. (1992). Serotonin in autism: Research strategies. In H. Naruse & E.M. Ornitz (Eds.), *Neurobiology of infantile autism* (pp. 969–986). Tokyo: Excerpta Medica.

Anderson, G.M., Horne, W.C., Chatterjee, D., & Cohen, D.J. (1990). The hyperserotonemia of autism. *Annals of the New York Academy of Sciences, 600,* 333.

Anderson, G.M, Minderaa, R.B., Cho, S.C., Volkmar, F.R., & Cohen, D.J. (1989). The issue of hyperserotonemia and platelet serotonin exposure: A preliminary study. *Journal of Autism and Developmental Disorders, 19,* 349–351.

Anderson, G.M., Minderaa, R.B., van Bentem, P.-P.G., Volkmar, F.R., & Cohen, D.J. (1984). Platelet imipramine binding in autistic subjects. *Psychiatry Research, 11,* 133–141.

Anderson, G.M., Stevenson, J.M., & Cohen, D.J. (1987). Steady-state model for plasma-free and platelet serotonin in man. *Life Sciences, 41,* 1777–1785.

Anderson, G.M., Volkmar, F.R., Hoder, E.L., McPhedran, P., Minderaa, R.B., Young, J.G., Hansen, C.R., & Cohen, D.J. (1987). Whole blood serotonin in autistic and normal subjects. *Journal of Child Psychiatry and Psychology, 28,* 885–900.

Barrett, P.R., Feinstein, C., & Hole, W.T. (1989). Effects of naloxone and naltrexone on self-injury: A double-blind placebo-controlled analysis. *American Journal of Mental Retardation, 93,* 644–651.

Barshop, B.A., Alberts, A.S., & Gruber, H.E. (1989). Kinetic studies of mutant human adenylosuccinase. *Biochemica et Biophysica Acta, 999,* 19–23.

Becker, M.A., Raivio, K.O., Bakay, B., Adams, W.B., & Nyhan, W.L. (1980). Variant human phosphoribosylpyrophosphate synthetase altered in regulatory and catalytic functions. *Journal of Clinical Investigations, 65,* 109–120.

Bernstein, G.A., Hughes, J.R., Mitchell, J.E., & Thompson, T. (1987). Effects of narcotic antagonist on self-injurious behavior: A single case study. *Journal of the American Academy of Child and Adolescent Psychiatry, 26,* 886–889.

Blomberry, P.A., Kopin, I.J., Gordon, E.K., Mackey, S.P., & Ebert, M.E. (1980). Conversion of MHPG to vanillylmandelic acid: Implication for the importance of urinary MHPG. *Archives of General Psychiatry, 37,* 195–198.

Boullin, D.J., Coleman, M., O'Brien, R.A., & Rimland, B. (1971). Laboratory predictions of infantile autism based on 5-hydroxytryptamine efflux from blood platelets and their correlation with the Rimland E-2 score. *Journal of Autism and Childhood Schizophrenia, 1,* 63–71.

Boullin, D.J., Freeman, B.J., Geller, E., Ritvo, E., Rutter, M. & Yuwiler, A. (1982). Toward the resolution of conflicting findings. *Journal of Autism and Developmental Disorders, 12,* 97–98.

Brambilla, F., Viani, F., & Rossotti, V. (1969). Endocrine aspects of child psychoses. *Diseases of the Nervous System, 30,* 627–632.

Buitelaar, J.K., van Engeland, H., van Ree, J.M., & de Weid, D. (1990). Behavioral effects of Org 2766, a synthetic analog of the adrenocorticotrophic hormone (4–9), in 14 outpatient autistic children. *Journal of Autism and Developmental Disorders, 20,* 467–478.

Buznikov, G.A. (1984). The action of neurotransmitters and related substances on early embryogenesis. *Pharmacology and Therapeutics, 25,* 23–59.

Campbell, M., Anderson, L.T., & Small, A.M. (1990). Pharmacotherapy in autism. *Brain Dysfunction, 3,* 299–307.

Campbell, M., Anderson, L.T., Small, A.M., Locascio, J.J., Lynch, N.S., & Choroco, M.C. (1990). Naltrexone in autistic children: A double-blind and placebo-controlled study. *Psychopharmacology Bulletin, 26,* 130–135.

Campbell, M., Hollander, C.S., Ferris, S., & Greene, L.W. (1978). Response to thyrotropin-releasing hormone stimulation in young psychotic children: A pilot study. *Psychoneuroendocrinology, 3,* 195–201.

Campbell, M., Small, A.M., Hollander, C.S., Korein, J., Cohen, I.L., Kalmijn, M., & Ferris, S. (1978). A controlled crossover study of triiodothyronine in autistic children. *Journal of Autism and Childhood Schizophrenia, 8,* 371–381.

Christen, H.J., Hanfeld, F., Duley, J.A., & Simmonds, H.A. (1992). Distinct neurological syndrome in two brothers with hyperuricaemia. *Lancet, 340,* 1167–1168.

Cohen, D.J., Caparulo, B.K., Shaywitz, B.A., & Bowers, M.B., Jr. (1977). Dopamine and serotonin metabolism in neuropsychiatrically disturbed children: CSF homovanillic acid and 5-hydroxyindoleacetic acid. *Archives of General Psychiatry, 34,* 545–550.

Cohen, D.J., Riddle, M.A., Laor, N., Young, J.G., & Shaywitz, B.A. (1983). Neurobiological perspectives on neuropsychiatric disorders of childhood. In H. Hoppius & G. Winokur (Eds.), *Psychopharmacology: Vol. 1, Part 2. Clinical Psychopharmacology* (pp. 53–73). Amsterdam: Excerpta Medica.

Cohen, D.J., Shaywitz, B.A., Johnson, W.T., & Bowers, M.B., Jr. (1974). Biogenic amines in autistic and atypical children: Cerebrospinal fluid measures of homovanillic acid and 5-hydroxyindoleacetic acid. *Archives of General Psychiatry, 31,* 845–853.

Cohen, D.J., & Young, J.G. (1977). Neurochemistry and child psychiatry. *Journal of the American Academy of Child Psychiatry, 16,* 353–411.

Cohen, D.J., Young, J.G., Lowe, T.L., & Harcherik, D. (1980). Thyroid hormone in autistic children. *Journal of Autism and Developmental Disorders, 10,* 445–450.

Coid, J., Allolio, B., & Rees, L.H. (1983). Raised plasma met-enkephalin in patients who habitually mutilate themselves. *Lancet, 2,* 545.

Colette, J.W., (1978). Speculation on similarities between autism and opiate addiction. *Journal of Autism and Childhood Schizophrenia, 8,* 477–479.

Cook, E.H. (1990). Autism: Review of neurochemical investigation [Review]. *Synapse, 6,* 292–308.

Cook, E.H., Anderson, G.M., Heninger, G.R., Fletcher, K.E., Freedman, D.X., & Leventhal, B.L. (1992). Tryptophan loading in hyperserotonemic and normoserotonemic adults. *Biological Psychiatry, 31,* 525–528.

Cook, E.H., Arora, R.C., Anderson, G.M., Berry-Kravis, E.M., Yan, S., Yeoh, H.C., Sklena, J.P., Charak, D.A., & Leventhal, B.L. (1993). Platelet serotonin in hyperserotonemic relatives of children with autistic disorder. *Life Sciences, 52,* 2005–2015.

Cook, E.H., Leventhal, B.L., & Freedman, D.X. (1988). Free serotonin in plasma: Autistic children and their first-degree relatives. *Biological Psychiatry, 24,* 488–491.

Cook, E.H., Rowlett, R., Jaselskis, C., & Leventhal, B.L. (1992). Fluoxetine treatment of children and adults with autistic disorder and mental retardation. *Journal of the American Academy of Child and Adolescent Psychiatry, 31,* 739–745.

DeMyer, M.K., Hingtgen, J.N., & Jackson, R.K. (1981). Infantile autism reviewed: A decade of research. *Schizophrenia Bulletin, 7,* 388–451.

Elchisak, M.A., Polinsky, R.J., Ebert, M.H., Powers, J., & Kopin, I.J. (1978). Contribution of plasma homovanillic acid (HVA) to urine and CSF HVA in the monkey and its pharmacokinetic disposition. *Life Sciences, 23,* 2339–2348.

Emson, P. (1979). Peptides as neurotransmitter candidates in the mammalian CNS. *Progress in Neurobiology, 13,* 61–116.

Folstein, S.E., & Piven, J (1991). Etiology of autism: Genetic influences. *Pediatrics, 87, (Suppl.),* 767–773.

Frankhauser, M.P., Karumanchi, V.C., German, M.L., Yales, A., & Karumanchi, S.D. (1992). A double-blind, placebo-controlled study of the efficacy of transdermal clonidine in autism. *Journal of Clinical Psychiatry, 53,* 77–82.

Friedman, E. (1969). The "autistic syndrome" and phenylketonuria. *Schizophrenia, 1,* 249–261.

Garelis, E., Young, S.N., Lal, S., & Sourkes, T.L. (1974). Monoamine metabolites in lumbar CSF: The question of their origin in relation to clinical studies. *Brain Research, 79,* 1–8.

Gillberg, C. (1993). Comment on CSF HVA. *Biological Psychiatry, 34,* 746.

Gillberg, C., & Coleman, M. (1992). *The biology of the autistic syndromes* (2nd ed., p. 131). London: Mac Keith Press.

Gillberg, C., & Svennerholm, L. (1987). CSF monoamines in autistic syndromes and other pervasive developmental disorders of early childhood. *British Journal of Psychiatry, 151,* 89–94.

Gillberg, C., Svennerholm, L., & Hamilton-Hellberg, C. (1983). Childhood psychosis and monoamine metabolites in spinal fluid. *Journal of Autism and Developmental Disorders, 13,* 38–96.

Gillberg, C., Terenius, L., & Lonnerholm, G. (1985). Endorphin activity in childhood psychosis. *Archives of General Psychiatry, 42,* 780–783.

Gillberg, C., Trygstad, O., & Foss, J. (1982). Childhood psychosis and urinary excretion of peptides and protein-associated peptide complexes. *Journal of Autism and Developmental Disorders, 12,* 229–241.

Gillberg, I.C., Gillberg, C. & Koop, S. (1992). Hypothyroidism and autism spectrum disorders.

Journal of Child Psychology & Psychiatry & Allied Disciplines, 33, 531–542.

Giller, E.L., Young, J.G., Breakefield, X.O., Carbonari, C., Braverman, M., & Cohen, D.J. (1980). Monoamine oxidase and catechol-O-methyltransferase activities in cultured fibroblasts and blood cells from children with autism and the Gilles de la Tourette syndrome. *Psychiatry Research, 2,* 187–197.

Goldberg, M., Hattab, J., Meir, D., Ebstein, R.P., & Belmaker, R.H. (1984). Plasma cyclic AMP and cyclic GMP in childhood-onset psychoses. *Journal of Autism and Developmental Disorders, 14,* 159–164.

Gordon, C.T., Rapoport, J.L., Hamburger, S.D., State, R.C., & Mannheim, G.B. (1992). Differential response of seven subjects with Autistic Disorder to clomipramine and desipramine. *American Journal of Psychiatry, 149,* 363–366.

Guthrie, R.D., & Wyatt, R.J. (1975). Biochemistry and schizophrenia: III. A review of childhood psychosis. *Schizophrenia Bulletin, 12,* 18–32.

Gwirtsman, H., Gerner, R.H., & Sternbach, H. (1982). The overnight dexamethasone suppression test: Clinical and theoretical review. *Journal of Clinical Psychiatry, 48,* 321–327.

Hanley, H.G., Stahl, S.M., & Freedman, D.X. (1977). Hyperserotonemia and amine metabolites in autistic and retarded children. *Archives of General Psychiatry, 34,* 521–531.

Heeley, A.F., & Roberts, G.E. (1966). A study of tryptophan metabolism in psychotic children. *Developmental Medicine and Child Neurology, 8,* 708–718.

Herman, B.H. (1991). Effects of opioid receptor antagonists on the treatment of autism and self-injurious behavior. In J.J. Ratey (Ed.), *Mental retardation: Developing pharmacotherapies, progress in psychiatry* (Vol. 32, pp. 107–137). Washington, DC: American Psychiatric Press.

Hill, S.D., Wagner, E.A., Shedlorski, J.G., & Sears, S.P. (1977). Diurnal cortisol and temperature variation of normal and autistic children. *Developmental Psychobiology, 10,* 579–583.

Hoshino, Y., Kumashiro, H., & Kaneko, M. (1979). Serum serotonin, free tryptophan plasma cyclic AMP levels in autistic children. *Fukushima Journal of Medical Science, 26,* 79–91.

Hoshino, Y., Kumashiro, H., Yashima, Y., Kaneko, M., Numato, Y., Oshima, N., & Watanabe, A. (1980). Plasma cyclic AMP level in psychiatric diseases of childhood. *Folia Psychiatrica et Neurologica Japonica, 34,* 9–16.

Hoshino, Y., Ohno, Y., Yamamoto, T., Tachibana, R., Murata, S., Yokoyama, F., Kaneko, M., & Kumashiro, H. (1984). Dexamethasone suppression test in autistic children. *Japanese Journal of Clinical Psychiatry, 26,* 100–102.

Hoshino, Y., Tachibana, R., Watanabe, M., Murata, S., Yokoyama, F., Kaneko, M., Yashima, Y., & Kumashiro, H. (1984). Serotonin metabolism and hypothalamic-pituitary function in children with infantile autism and minimal brain dysfunction. *Japanese Journal of Psychiatry, 26,* 937–945.

Hoshino, Y., Watanabe, M., Tachibana, R., Murata, S., Kaneko, M., Yashima, Y., & Kumashiro, H. (1983). A study of the hypothalamus-pituitary function in autistic children by the loading test of 5HTP, TRH and LH-RH. *Japanese Journal of Brain Research, 9,* 94–95.

Hoshino, Y., Yamamoto, T., Kaneko, M., Tachibana, R., Watanabe, M., Ono, Y., & Kumashiro, H. (1984). Blood serotonin and free tryptophan concentration in autistic children. *Neuropsychobiology, 11,* 22–27.

Isarangkun, P.P., Newman, H.A., Patel, S.T., Duruibe, V.A., & Abou-Issa, H. (1986). Potential biochemical markers for infantile autism. *Neurochemical Pathology, 5,* 51–70.

Iverson, S.D., & Iverson, L.L. (1981). *Behavioral pharmacology* (2nd ed.). New York: Oxford University Press.

Jaeken, J., & Van den Berghe, G. (1984). An infantile autistic syndrome characterized by the presence of succinylpurines in body fluids. *Lancet, 2,* 1058–1061.

Jensen, J.B., Realmuto, G.M., & Garfinkel, B.D. (1985). The dexamethasone suppression test in infantile autism. *Journal of the American Academy of Child Psychiatry, 24,* 263–265.

Johnson, R.J., Wiersma, V., & Kraft, I.A. (1974). Hair amino acids in childhood autism. *Journal of Autism and Childhood Schizophrenia, 4,* 187–188.

Kahn, A.A. (1970). Thyroid dysfunction. *British Medical Journal, 4,* 495.

Kopin, I.J., Gordon, E.K., Jimerson, D.C., & Polinsky, R.J. (1983). Relationship between plasma and cerebrospinal fluid levels of 3-methoxy-4-hydroxyphenylglycol. *Science, 219,* 73–75.

Kotsopoulos, S., & Kutty, K.M. (1979). Histidinemia and infantile autism. *Journal of Autism and Developmental Disorders, 9,* 55–60.

Lake, R., Ziegler, M.G., & Murphy, D.L. (1977). Increased norepinephrine levels and decreased DBH activity in primary autism. *Archives of General Psychiatry, 35,* 553–556.

Lauder, J.M., (1993). Neurotransmitters as growth regulatory signals: Role of receptors and second messengers. *Trends in Neuroscience, 15,* 233–240.

LeBoyer, M., Bouvard, M.P., & Dupes, M. (1988). Effects of naltrexone on infantile autism. *Lancet, 1,* 715.

LeBoyer, M., Bouvard, M.P., Launay, J.M., Tabuteau, F., Waller, D., Dugas, M., Kerdelhue, B., Lensing, P., & Panksepp, J. (1992). Brief report: A double-blind study of naltrexone on infantile autism. *Journal of Autism and Developmental Disorders, 22,* 309–319.

LeBoyer, M., Bouvard, M.P., Recasens, C., Philippe, A., Guilloud-Bataille, M., Bondoux, D., Tabuteau, F., Dugas, M., Panksepp, J., & Launay, J.M. (1994). Differences between plasma N- and C-terminally directed beta-endorphin immunoreactivity in infantile autism. *American Journal of Psychiatry, 151,* 1797–1801.

LeCouteur, A., Trygstad, O., Evered, C., Gillberg, C., & Rutter, M. (1988). Infantile autism and urinary excretion of peptides and protein-associated peptide complexes. *Journal of Autism and Developmental Disorders, 18,* 181–190.

Lowe, T.L., Tanaka, K., Seashore, M.R., Young, J.G., & Cohen, D.J. (1980). Detection of phenylketonuria in autistic and psychotic children. *Journal of the American Medical Association, 243,* 126–128.

Maas, J.W., Hattox, S.E, Greene, N.M., & Landis, B.H. (1980). Estimates of dopamine and serotonin synthesis by the awake human brain. *Journal of Neurochemistry, 34,* 1547–1549.

Maas, J.W., & Leckman, J.F. (1983). Relationships between CNS noradrenergic function and plasma and urine MHPG and other norepinephrine metabolites. In J.W. Maas (Ed.), *MHPG: Basal mechanisms and psychopathology* (pp. 33–43). New York: Academic Press.

Maher, K.R., Harper, J.F., Macleay, A., & King, M.G. (1975). Peculiarities in the endocrine response to insulin stress in early infantile autism. *Journal of Nervous and Mental Disease, 161,* 180–184.

Markowitz, P. I. (1992). Effect of fluoxetine on self-injurious behavior in the developmentally disabled: A preliminary study. *Journal of Clinical Psychopharmacology, 12,* 27–31.

McBride, A.P., Anderson, G.M., Hertzig, M.E., Sweeney, J.A., Kream, J., Cohen, D.J., & Mann, J.J. (1989). Serotonergic responsivity in male young adults with autistic disorder. *Archives of General Psychiatry, 46,* 213–221.

McBride, A.P., Anderson, G.M., & Mann, J.J. (1990). Serotonin in autism. In E. F. Coccaro & D.L. Murphy (Eds.), *Serotonin in major psychiatric disorders* (pp. 49–68). Washington, DC: American Psychiatric Press.

McDougle, C.J, Naylor, S.T., Goodman, W.K., Volkmar, F.R., Cohen, D.J., & Price, L.H. (1993). Acute tryptophan depletion in autistic disorder: A controlled case study. *Biological Psychiatry, 33,* 547–550.

McDougle, C.J, Price, L.H., & Goodman, W.K. (1990). Fluvoxamine treatment of coincident autistic disorder and obsessive-compulsive disorder: A case report, *Journal of Autism and Developmental Disorders, 20,* 537–543.

McDougle, C.J., Price, L.H., Volkmar, F.R, Goodman, W.K., Ward-O'Brien, D., Nielson, J.R., Bergman, J.D., & Cohen, D.J. (1992). Clomipramine in autism: Preliminary evidence of efficiency. *Journal of Child and Adolescent Psychiatry, 31,* 746–750.

Meek, J.L. & Neff, N.H. (1973). Is cerebrospinal fluid the major avenue for the removal of S-hydroxyindoleacetic acid from the brain? *Neuropharmacology, 12,* 497–499.

Minderaa, R.B., Anderson, G.M., Volkmar, F.R., Akkerhuis, G.W., & Cohen, D.J. (1987). Urinary 5-HIAA and whole-blood 5-HT and tryptophan in autism and normal subjects. *Biological Psychiatry, 22,* 933–940.

Minderaa, R.B., Anderson, G.M., Volkmar, F.R., Akkerhuis, G.W., & Cohen D.J. (1994). Noradrenergic and adrenergic functioning in autism. *Biological Psychiatry, 36,* 237–241.

Minderaa, R.B., Anderson, G.M., Volkmar, F.R., Harcherik, D., Akkerhuis, C.W., & Cohen, D.J. (1989). Neurochemical study of dopamine functioning in autistic and normal subjects. *Journal of the American Academy of Child and Adolescent Psychiatry, 28,* 200–206.

Moore, R.Y., & Bloom, F.E. (1978). Central catecholamine neuron systems: Anatomy and physiology of the dopamine systems. *Annual Review of Neuroscience, 1,* 129–169.

Moore, R.Y., & Bloom, F.E. (1979). Central catecholamine neuron systems: Anatomy and physiology of the norepinephrine and epinephrine systems. *Annual Review of Neuroscience, 2,* 113–168.

Nagamitsu, S. (1993). CSF beta-endorphin levels in pediatric neurologic disorders. *Kurume Medical Journal, 40,* 223–241.

Narayan, M., Anderson, G.M., & Srinath, S. (1993). CSF HVA in autism (in reply). *Biological Psychiatry, 34,* 746–747.

Narayan, M., Srinath, S., Anderson, G.M., & Meundi, D.B. (1993). Cerebrospinal fluid levels of homovanillic acid and 5-hydroxyindoleacetic acid in autism. *Biological Psychiatry, 33,* 630–635.

Naruse, H., Hayashi, T., Takesada, M., Nakane, A., & Yamazaki, K. (1989). Metabolic changes in aromatic amino acids and monoamines in infantile autism and development of new treatment related to the finding. *No to Hattatsu [Brain and Development], 21,* 181–189.

Nyhan, W.L., Jones, J.A., Teberg, A.J., Sweetman, L., & Nelson, L.G. (1969). A new disorder of purine metabolism with behavioral manifestations. *Journal of Pediatrics, 74,* 20–27.

O'Brien, R.A., Semenuk, G., & Spector, S. (1976). Catechol-0-methyltransferase activity in erythrocytes of children with autism. In E. Coleman (Ed.), *The autistic syndromes* (pp. 43–49). Amsterdam, The Netherlands: North-Holland.

Panksepp, J. (1979). A neurochemical theory of autism. *Trends in Neuroscience, 2,* 174–177.

Partington, M.W., Tu, J.B., & Wong, C.Y. (1973). Blood serotonin levels in severe mental retardation. *Developmental Medicine and Child Neurology, 15,* 616–627.

Perry, T.L., Hansen, S., & Christie, R.G. (1978). Amino compounds and organic acids in CSF, plasma, and urine of autistic children. *Biological Psychiatry, 13,* 575–586.

Piggott, L.R. (1979). Overview of selected basic research in autism. *Journal of Autism and Developmental Disorders, 9,* 199–218.

Realmuto, G.M., Jensen, J.B., Reeve, E., & Garfinkel, B.D. (1990). Growth hormone response to L-dopa and clonidine in autistic children. *Journal of Autism and Developmental Disorders, 20,* 455–465.

Redmond, D.E., Jr., & Huang, Y.W. (1979). New evidence for a locus coeruleus-norepinephrine connection with anxiety. *Life Sciences, 25,* 2149–2162.

Reichelt, K.L., Hole, K., Hamberger, A., Saelid, G., Edminson, P.D., Braestrup, C.B., Linsjaerde, O., Ledaal, P., & Orbeck, H. (1981). Biologically active peptide-containing fractions in schizophrenia and childhood autism. *Advances in Biochemistry and Psychopharmacology, 28,* 627–643.

Reichelt, K.L., Saelid, G., Lindback, T., & Boler, J.B. (1986). Childhood autism: A complex disorder. *Biological Psychiatry, 21,* 1279–1290.

Richdale, A.L., & Prior, M.R. (1992). Urinary cortisol circadian rhythm in a group of high-functioning children with autism. *Journal of Autism and Developmental Disorders, 22,* 433–446.

Riddle, M.A., Leckman, J.F., Anderson, G.M., Shaywitz, B.A., Caruso, K.A., Ort, S., & Cohen, D.J. (1986). Debrisoquin loading to assess central dopaminergic function in Tourette's Syndrome. *Life Sciences, 38,* 1041–1048.

Ritvo, E.R. (1977). Biochemical studies of children with the syndromes of autism, childhood schizophrenia and related developmental disabilities: A review. *Journal of Child Psychology and Psychiatry 13,* 373–379.

Ritvo, E.R., Mason-Brothers, A., Freeman, B.J., Pingree, C., Jenson, W.R., McMahon, W.M., Peterson, P.B., Jorde, L.B., Mo, A., & Ritvo, A. (1990). The UCLA-University of Utah epidemiologic survey of autism: The etiologic role of rare diseases. *American Journal of Psychiatry, 147,* 1614–1621.

Ritvo, E.R., Rabin, K., Yuwiler, A., Freeman, B.J., & Geller, E. (1978). Biochemical and hematological studies: A critical review. In M. Rutter & E. Schopler (Eds.), *Autism: A reappraisal of concepts and treatment* (pp. 163–183). New York: Plenum Press.

Ritvo, E.R., Yuwiler, A, Geller, E., Kales, A., Rashkis, S., Schicor, A., Plotkin, S., Axlerod, R., & Howard, C. (1971). Effects of L-Dopa in autism. *Journal of Autism and Childhood Schizophrenia, 1,* 190–205.

Ritvo, E.R., Yuwiler, A., Geller, E., Ornitz, E.M., Saeger, K., & Plotkin, S. (1970). Increased blood serotonin and platelets in early infantile autism. *Archives of General Psychiatry, 23,* 566–572.

Rosenberger-Diesse, J., & Coleman, M. (1986). Brief report: Preliminary evidence for multiple etiologies in autism. *Journal of Autism and Developmental Disorders, 16,* 385–392.

Ross, D.L., Klykylo, W.M., & Anderson, G.M. (1985). Cerebrospinal fluid indoleamine and monoamine effects in fenfluramine treatment of autism. *Annals of Neurology, 18,* 394.

Ross, D.L., Klykylo, W.M., & Hitzeman, R. (1987). Reduction of elevated CSF beta-endorphin by fenfluramine in infantile autism. *Pediatric Neurology, 3,* 83–86.

Rutter, M., & Bartak, L. (1971). Causes of infantile autism: Some considerations from recent research. *Journal of Autism and Childhood Schizophrenia, 1,* 20–32.

Rutter, M., & Schopler, E. (1987). Autism and pervasive developmental disorders: Concepts and diagnostic issues. *Journal of Autism and Developmental Disorders, 17,* 159–186.

Sandman, C.A. (1991). The opiate hypothesis in autism and self-injury. *Journal of Child and Adolescent Psychopharmacology, 1,* 237–248.

Sandman, C.A. (1992). Various endogenous opioids and autistic behavior: A response to Gillberg. *Journal of Autism and Developmental Disorders, 22,* 132–133.

Sandman, C.A., Barron, J.L., Chicz-Demet, A., & Demet, E.M. (1990). Plasma β-endorphin levels in patients with self-injurious behavior and sterotypy. *American Journal on Mental Retardation, 95,* 84–92.

Sandman, C.A., Patta, P.C., Banon, J., Hoehler, F.K., Williams, C., & Swanson, J.M. (1983). Naloxone attenuates self-abusive behavior in developmentally disabled clients. *Applied Research in Mental Retardation, 4,* 5–11.

Sankar, D.V.S. (1971). Studies on blood platelets, blood enzymes, and leukocyte chromosome breakage in childhood schizophrenia. *Behavioral Neuropsychiatry, 2,* 2–10.

Schain, R.J., & Freedman, D.X. (1961). Studies on 5-hydroxyindole metabolism in autistic and other mentally retarded children. *Journal of Pediatrics, 58,* 315–320.

Scriver, C.R., & Rosenberg, L.E. (1973). *Amino acid metabolism and its disorders.* Philadelphia: Saunders.

Seifert, W.E., Foxx, J.L., & Butler, I.J. (1980). Age effect on dopamine and serotonin metabolite levels in cerebrospinal fluid. *Annals of Neurology, 8,* 38–42.

Shaw, C.R., Lucas, J., & Rabinovitch, R.D. (1959). Metabolic studies in childhood schizophrenia. *Archives of General Psychiatry, 1,* 366–371.

Sherwin, A.C., Flach, F.F., & Stokes, P.E. (1958). Treatment of psychoses in early childhood with triiodothyronine. *American Journal of Psychiatry, 115,* 166–167.

Simmonds, H.A., Webster, D.R., Lingham, S., & Wilson, J. (1985). An inborn error of purine metabolism, deafness and neurodevelopmental abnormality. *Neuropediatrics, 16,* 106–108.

Snyder, S.H., & Childers, S. (1979). Opiate receptors and endorphins. *Annual Review of Neuroscience, 2,* 35–64.

Sternberg, D.E., Heninger, G.H., & Roth, R.H. (1983). Plasma homovanillic acid as an index of brain dopamine metabolism: Enhancement with debrisoquin. *Life Sciences, 32,* 2447–2452.

Stone, R.L., Aimi, J., Barshop, B.A., Jaeken, J., Van den Berghe, G., Zalkin, H., & Dixon, J.E. (1992). A mutation in adenylosuccinate lyase associated with mental retardation and autistic features. *Nature Genetics, 1,* 59–63.

Sutton, H.E., Read, J.H., & Arbor, A. (1958). Abnormal amino acid metabolism in a case suggesting autism. *American Journal of Diseases of Children, 96,* 23–28.

Suwa, S., Naruse, H., Ohura, T., Tsuruhara, T., Takesoda, M., Yamazake, K., & Mikuni, M. (1984). Influence of pimozide on hypothalamo-pituitary function in children with behavioral disorders. *Psychoneuroendocrinology, 9,* 37–44.

Sverd, J., Kupretz, S.S., Winsberg, B.G., Hurwic, M.J., & Becker, L. (1978). Effect of L-5-hydroxytryptophan in autistic children. *Journal of Autism and Childhood Schizophrenia, 8,* 171–180.

Sylvester, O., Jorgensen, E., Mellerup, T., & Rafaelsen, O.J. (1970). Amino acid excretion in urine of children with various psychiatric diseases. *Danish Medical Bulletin, 17,* 166–170.

Takatsu, T., Onizawa, J., & Nakahato, M. (1975). Tryptophan metabolism disorder and therapeutic diet in children with infantile autism. *Amino Acids, 5,* 13–14.

Tani, Y., Fernell, E., Watanabe, Y., Kanai, T., & Langstrom, B. (1994). Decrease in 6R-5, 6, 7, 8-tetrahydrobiopterin content in cerebrospinal fluid of autistic patients. *Neuroscience Letters, 181,* 169–172.

Todd, R.D. (1991). Fluoxetine in autism. *American Journal of Psychiatry, 148,* 8.

Tordjman, S., Anderson, G.M., McBride, A.P., Hall, L.M., Ferrari, P., & Cohen, D.J. (1995). Plasma androgens in autism. *Journal of Autism and Developmental Disorders, 25,* 295–304.

Udenfriend, S., Titus, E., Weissbach, H., & Peterson, R.E. (1959). Biogenesis and metabolism of 5-hydroxyindole compounds. *Journal of Biological Chemistry, 219,* 335–344.

Weizman, R., Weizman, A., Tyrano, S., Szekely, B., Weissman, B.A., & Sarne, Y. (1984). Humoral-endorphin blood levels in autistic, schizophrenic and healthy subjects. *Psychopharmacology (Berlin), 82,* 368–370.

Whitaker-Azmitia, P.M., Lauder, J.M., Shemer, A., & Azmitia, E.C. (1987). Postnatal changes in serotonin, receptors following prenatal alterations in serotonin levels: Further evidence for functional fetal serotonin, receptors. *Developmental Brain Research, 33,* 285–289.

Whitaker-Azmitia, P.M., Murphy, R., & Azmitia, E.C. (1992). Stimulation of astroglial 5-HT$_{1A}$ receptors releases in the serotonergic growth factor, protein S-100, and alters astroglial morphology. *Brain Research, 528,* 155–158.

Winsberg, B.G., Sverd, J., Castells, S., Hurwic, M., & Perel, J.M. (1980). Estimation of monoamine and cyclic-AMP turnover and amino acid concentrations of spinal fluid in autistic children. *Neuropediatrics, 11,* 250–255.

Yamazake, K., Saito, Y., Okada, F., Fujiede, T., & Yamashita, T. (1975). An application of neuroendocrinological studies in autistic children and Heller's Syndrome. *Journal of Autism and Childhood Schizophrenia, 5,* 323–332.

Young, J.G., Cohen, D.J., Brown, S.L., & Caparulo, B.K. (1978). Decreased urinary free catecholamines in childhood autism. *Journal of the American Academy of Child Psychiatry, 17,* 671–678.

Young, J.G., Cohen, D.J., Hattox, S.E., Kavanaugh, M.E., Anderson, G.M., Shaywitz, B.A., & Maas, J.W. (1981). Plasma free MHPG and neuroendocrine responses to challenge doses of clonidine in Tourette's Syndrome: Preliminary report. *Life Sciences, 29,* 1467–1475.

Young, J.G., Cohen, D.J., Kavanaugh, M.E., Landis, H.D., Shaywitz, B.A., & Maas, J.W. (1981). Cerebrospinal fluid, plasma, and urinary MHPG in children. *Life Sciences, 28,* 2837–2845.

Young, J.G., Kavanaugh, M.E., Anderson, G.M., Shaywitz, B.A., & Cohen, D.J. (1982). Clinical neurochemistry of autism and associated disorders. *Journal of Autism and Developmental Disorders, 12,* 147–165.

Young, J.G., Newcorn, J.H., & Leven, L. (1989). Pervasive developmental disorders. In H.I. Kaplan & B.J. Saddock (Eds.), *Comprehensive textbook of psychiatry* (pp. 1772–1787). Baltimore: Williams & Wilkins.

Young, S.N., Anderson, G.M., & Purdy, W.C. (1980). Indoleamine metabolism in rat brain studied through measurements of tryptophan, 5-hydroxynidoleactic acid and indoleactetic acid in cerebrospinal fluid. *Journal of Neurochemistry, 34,* 309–315.

Yuwiler, A., Geller, E., & Ritvo, E. (1985). Biochemical studies of autism. In E. Lajtha (Ed.), *Handbook of neurochemistry* (pp. 671–691). New York: Plenum Press.

Yuwiler, A., Ritvo, E.R., Geller, E., Glousman, R., Schneidermann, G., & Matsuno, D. (1975). Uptake and efflux of serotonin from platelets of autistic and nonautistic children. *Journal of Autism and Childhood Schizophrenia, 5,* 83–98.

Yuwiler, A., Shih, J.C., Chen, C., Ritvo, E.R., Hanna, G., Ellison, G.W., & King, B.H. (1992). Hyperserotonemia and antiserotonin antibodies in autism and other disorders. *Journal of Autism and Developmental Disorders, 22,* 33–45.

Zarcone, V., Kales, A., Scharf, M., Tan, T.L., Simmons, J.O., & Dement, W.C. (1973). Repeated oral ingestion of 5-hydroxytryptophan. *Archives of General Psychiatry, 28,* 843–846.

Zhou, E.C., Auerbach, S., & Azmitia, E.C. (1987). Denervation of serotonergic fibers in the hippocampus induced a trophic factor which enhance the maturation of transplanted serotonergic neurons but not norepinephrine neurons. *Journal of Neuroscience Research, 17,* 235–246.

CHAPTER 16

Neurological Aspects of Autism

NANCY J. MINSHEW, JOHN A. SWEENEY, AND MARGARET L. BAUMAN

Autism is now generally accepted to be a disorder of brain development, and hence of neurologic origin. Neuropathologic abnormalities have been described, providing definitive evidence of a brain basis for this disorder and categorizing it as a disorder of neuronal organization. Several aspects of neuronal organization have been implicated by the neuropathologic and neuroimaging abnormalities in autism, in particular the elaboration of dendritic and axonal ramifications, the establishment of synaptic connections, and the selective elimination of neuronal processes. The developmental pathophysiology of these structural abnormalities remains to be defined.

Autism is, furthermore, a sporadic disorder faithfully reproduced both neuropathologically and clinically from case to case, suggesting a common pathophysiology that originates at the level of DNA or its transcription for brain development. Several associated findings are likely related to autism at this biologic level, in particular, the prominent incidence of mood disorder in first degree relatives, the expression of pieces of the clinical syndrome in first degree relatives, and the frequent occurrence of autistic symptomatology in tuberous sclerosis, a disorder also characterized by overgrowth of cerebral white matter. Identification of the gene sequence involved in tuberous sclerosis or affective disorder may identify regions of DNA of increased likelihood for containing the genetic sequences related to the neuronal organization error in autism and the impairments exhibited by less affected relatives.

Substantial progress has been made toward defining the pathophysiology of the clinical manifestations of autism. Over the past 15 years, the neurologic characterization of autism has changed substantially, reflecting advances in research diagnostic methods and criteria used to define autistic subjects and the evolution in technology for the *in vivo* study of central nervous system function and structure. Studies in the past 15 years using functional methodologies have uniformly implicated disturbances in late information processing, neocortical circuitry, and higher order cognitive abilities in the pathophysiology of autism. Structural studies have provided evidence of increased supratentorial brain volume, increased cerebral cortical grey and white matter volumes, increased brain weight, and above average head circumference, on the one hand, and, on the other, truncation of the dendritic tree development of neurons in limbic structures and decreased neuronal number in the cerebellum. This constellation of functional and structural findings has defined two "paradoxes," the first being the dissociation between the CNS localizations of functional and structural findings, and the second the contrast between "too much brain" in some regions and "too little brain" in other regions. These paradoxes are in defiance of conventions established on the basis of studies of acquired brain damage, but are likely to be

The careful and dedicated technical assistance of Evelyn Herbert is acknowledged and appreciated. The support of the National Institute of Neurologic Disorders and Stroke grant #NS33355 to Nancy Minshew is also gratefully acknowledged.

typical of disturbances in the developmental dynamics of neuronal organization. The identification of such paradoxes attests to the considerable progress achieved in recent years in defining the developmental neuropathology of autism, and to the insights that are likely to result from the study of autism with respect to the development of the brain organization subserving higher-order cognitive abilities.

Neurologic conceptualizations or models for the clinical pathophysiology of autism have evolved in response to the changing structural and functional characterization of autism. Current neurobiologic theories postulate single or multiple primary deficits in complex or higher-order cognitive abilities, dysfunction at the neural systems level of brain organization, and a central role for cerebral cortex in the final common pathophysiology of the clinical manifestations. Such theories represent a closer approximation of the pathophysiology of autism, but certainly not the final step. A particular challenge at present is the provision of data that define the link between laboratory deficits and behavioral abnormalities in autism. Ultimately, research can be expected to define the pathophysiology of the clinical syndrome, the developmental pathophysiology of the structural and functional brain abnormalities underlying the clinical syndrome, and the genetic mechanisms and related etiologies that trigger the disruption in brain development leading to these abnormalities. This knowledge will result in substantial improvements in diagnosis and in all phases of intervention, and will pave the way for the development of definitive neurobiologic interventions designed to ameliorate the brain abnormalities underlying autism.

CENTRAL NERVOUS SYSTEM FUNCTION IN AUTISM

The neurophysiologic integrity of neural pathways in the brain can be investigated with several methods, most commonly with evoked potentials and oculomotor paradigms. These methods provide information about neural pathways at multiple levels of the neuraxis and about the function of the sensory and motor systems and cognitive functions. Both of these methods were originally applied to autism

shortly after they were introduced to medical science. The first era of this research in autism, ending in the early to mid-1980s, largely documented the results of clinical studies with problematic experimental design, since the majority of abnormalities were ultimately attributed to these methodologic limitations. Research studies since 1980 using contemporary methodology have defined a neurophysiologic profile in autism that is characterized by bilaterally symmetrical abnormalities in cognitive potentials and neocortical circuitry, and deficits in complex cognitive abilities, with intact early information processing potentials, posterior fossa circuitry, and simple cognitive abilities.

Neuropsychologic studies investigate brain function at a level beyond the more basic unit of function assessed with neurophysiologic methods, and thus provide an intermediate step between neurophysiologic deficits and the clinical syndrome. Studies of the profile of neuropsychologic functioning in autism are a relatively recent contribution that has provided evidence of generalized difficulty with complex cognitive abilities with preservation of simpler abilities in the same functional domains, intact information acquisition abilities, and sparing of the visual-spatial domain.

All of these methods of study have been dependent on the capabilities and cooperation of high-functioning autistic individuals. These individuals provide the opportunity for maximally defining the qualitative features of the deficits and intact abilities that are specifically related to autism, and not to the presence of mental retardation or to an infectious, metabolic, or genetic disorder sometimes associated with autism. Because high-functioning autistic individuals have the same neuropathology, imaging, and family history characteristics as lower ability autistic individuals, findings in high functioning autistic individuals have major implications for the neurobiology of autism as a whole.

Evoked Potentials: Sensory System and Cognitive Processing

Evoked potentials are recordings from an array of scalp electrodes of the neural response to a sensory stimulus or cognitive challenge task.

These electrical potentials are time-locked to stimuli and thus can be averaged to distinguish them from the background electroencephographic activity. Sensory stimuli trigger electrical activity with a typical time-course at many locations in the brain. Many of the potentials overlap in time and spatial distribution, and thus reflect the activity and contributions of many different neural systems rather than of a single system that is sequentially activated as information is conducted to the cortex. Each potential has a characteristic latency range and spatial distribution. Amplitude varies with the characteristics of the stimulus or cognitive task, and, in the case of the cognitive potentials, with various subject characteristics. Some potentials also have a developmental trajectory, which adds yet another dimension to experimental design and data interpretation.

Evoked potentials are typically classified as either exogenous or endogenous. Exogenous potentials occur within the first 200 msec of the stimulus and are typically an obligatory response of brain neurons to a sensory stimulus. Their amplitude and latency are influenced by the physical properties of the stimulus, specifically its intensity, duration, and frequency. These potentials are affected by the auditory or visual acuity of the subject but are minimally affected by attention, motivation, and level of consciousness. Endogenous potentials are elicited by stimulus paradigms that require the subject to perform a perceptual analysis of stimuli, such as distinguishing one stimulus from a group of others. These potentials occur between 30 msec and 1 sec following the stimulus, and depend primarily on the setting in which the stimulus occurs. They are relatively independent of the physical properties of the stimulus and are influenced by subject attention, comprehension of the task, past experience with the task, importance of task performance to the subject, and the subject's ability level and knowledge. Thus, all the various sources of influence on human perception may have an influence on the endogenous potentials.

With few exceptions, evoked potential research in autism to date has been confined to the study of auditory brainstem potentials, auditory endogenous potentials primarily to tasks involving attentional control and modulation, and, to a very limited extent, the visual endogenous potentials. Notable for their relative absence from the neurophysiologic literature in autism are studies of the social, language, and reasoning deficits inherent to the definition of this disorder. A major limitation of evoked potentials as a methodology has been the unknown localization of the generators of these potentials, which precludes conclusions about the origin of evoked potential abnormalities. Significant limitations in the design of event related potential (ERP) studies in autism to date have been the use of only a few recording sites, the reliance on small sample sizes, and inconsistency of the methods across studies.

Auditory Brainstem Evoked Potentials

These potentials are generated within the first 10 msec following a click stimulus and reflect early neural activity in the auditory pathway. Waves I and II represent activity in the eighth nerve and thus are commonly used to assess hearing in infants and noncooperative children. Wave III is thought to result from activity in the lower pons and in the area of the superior olive, and wave V from activity in the upper pons and area of the inferior colliculus. Waves I, III, and V are the most reliable wave forms. At lower stimulus intensities or higher stimulation rates, only wave V remains clinically reliable (Courchesne, Lincoln, Kilman, & Galambos, 1985; Galambos & Hecox, 1978; Starr, Sohmer, & Celesia, 1978; Stockard, Stockard, & Sharbrough, 1978). Waves II and IV are often not measured because of lack of established clinical utility (Chiappa & Gladstone, 1978; Rumsey, Grimes, Pikus, Duara, & Ismond, 1984). The most reliable measurements are the latencies of the waves, particularly wave V, and the interpeak intervals between waves I, III, and V, which are used to assess the integrity of the brainstem auditory pathway. In healthy individuals, the latencies of waves I and V achieve adult values by 2 years of age. The maturation of the I-V interpeak latency exhibits two phases, one completed by 1 year of age and the second by 3 years, which may reflect different aspects of brainstem maturation (Aminoff, 1992; Zimmerman, Morgan, & Dubno, 1987). Gender also impacts on the norms for these potentials, with females generally having shorter latencies with higher amplitudes and shorter I-V and III-V intervals compared to males. Middle ear, cochlear, eighth nerve, and brainstem pathology involving or immediately adjacent to the auditory pathways may cause abnormalities in these potentials.

The first studies of auditory brainstem evoked potentials in autism reported normal results (Ornitz, Mo, & Olson, 1980; Ornitz & Walter, 1975), but were followed by many studies emphasizing abnormalities (Gillberg, Rosenthal, & Johansson, 1983; Rosenblum et al., 1980; Skoff, Mirsky, & Turner, 1980; Student & Sohmer, 1978, 1979; Tanguay & Edwards, 1982; Tanguay, Edwards, Buchwald, Schwafel, & Allen, 1982; Taylor, Rosenblatt, & Linschoten, 1982; Thivierge, Bedard, Cote, & Maziade, 1990; Wong & Wong, 1991). The latter studies reported abnormalities in 20% to 60% of the autistic subjects, consisting of moderate to severe abnormalities or absence of wave I (sensorineural deafness) and delays in brainstem transmission time. Over time, the abnormalities described in these studies were traced to various methodologic limitations. The abnormalities reported by Student and Sohmer (1978) were found to be secondary to equipment error and were retracted (Student & Sohmer, 1979). The abnormal findings of the other studies were traced to limitations in subject selection or ERP methodology; subject selection procedures often failed to exclude autistic subjects with causes of brain damage other than autism, assess audiologic function, exclude individuals with hearing loss, and match autistic and control subjects on age and gender. As was typical of the subject samples in these studies, 5 of the 15 autistic subjects in Student and Sohmer's study (1978) had an absence of wave I, and the remaining 10 had significant prolongation. The high incidence in these early studies of sensorineural deafness reflected the prevalence of fetal rubella and complicated postnatal bacterial meningitis among individuals diagnosed with autism during that era, and possibly also the increased incidence of recurrent otitis media in mentally retarded individuals and its less aggressive diagnosis and treatment at the time. Technical limitations of these early studies included: the failure to consider the impact of age and gender on measurements; the failure to differentiate between brainstem transmission times that were too short and too long when determining the incidence of abnormalities; the failure to assess measurement reliability; and the use of unreliable or idiosyncratic evoked potential measurements or procedures. The largest and well controlled of the early studies (Tanguay & Edwards, 1982; Tanguay, Edwards, et al., 1982) emphasized abnormalities in their interpretation but actually found very few abnormal brainstem transmission values except at the lowest stimulus intensity, and these abnormal values were in both directions. When the autistic and control groups in this study were matched on both age and gender, no statistically significant abnormalities were present.

These various design and methodologic issues were rigorously addressed in the studies of Rumsey et al. (1984) and Courchesne et al. (1985). In a study of 25 children and adults with a wide range of autism severity, Rumsey et al. found prolonged brainstem transmission times (>3 S.D. of laboratory norms) in one autistic subject and one normal control. Three autistic subjects were found to have shortened brainstem transmission times, and these data accounted for the few group differences observed. Based on the review of prior work and the results of their study, Rumsey et al. concluded that "reports of prolonged transmission times in a substantial percentage of autistic children may be attributable to concomitant identifiable neurological disease and peripheral hearing impairments, inadequately matched control groups, high artifact levels, and poor reliability of measurements" (p. 1416). In 1985, Courchesne et al. evaluated the auditory brainstem evoked responses of 14 high functioning (Performance IQ > 70) and 14 normal control adolescents and young adults at slow, medium, and fast rates of stimulation; soft, medium, and loud stimulus intensities; right and left ear stimulation; and rarefaction and compression clicks. The authors also controlled for body temperature. This study found no group differences in the auditory brainstem evoked potentials between the autistic subjects, the normal controls, and clinical norms under any of the stimulus conditions. Examination of the individual cases further revealed that every autistic subject in the study had normal auditory evoked potentials. Courchesne et al. (1985) concluded that there was unlikely to be an abnormality in autism in the auditory brainstem pathways that generate these ERPs, and that abnormalities in brainstem auditory ERPs were neither necessary nor sufficient to produce autism. These authors also noted that previously demonstrated abnormalities in long latency sensory and cognitive ERPs in these same autistic subjects were not, therefore, the downstream consequence of abnormalities in brainstem auditory pathways but were instead the result of an abnormality in higher auditory processing pathways (Courchesne, Kilman, Galambos, & Lincoln, 1984). In a follow-up study, Courchesne and colleagues emphasized the limitations of using small numbers of normal subjects to represent population norms in earlier ERP studies in autism (Grillon, Courchesne, & Akshoomoff, 1989).

Reports of abnormal brainstem auditory evoked potentials have re-emerged recently (McClelland, Eyre, Watson, Calvert, & Sherrard, 1992; Thivierge et al., 1990; Wong & Wong, 1991). Again, it is difficult to interpret the significance of these findings for autism because of the inclusion of individuals with tuberous sclerosis, fetal cytomegalovirus, Rett's Disorder, and Fragile X Syndrome (Wong & Wong, 1991), and the use of idiosyncratic methodology with unclear physiologic significance (Thivierge et al., 1990). McClelland et al. (1992) reported normal brainstem auditory evoked potentials in all autistic subjects under age 14 years and in all high functioning autistic subjects, but emphasized the failure of brainstem ERP latencies in the autistic group to decrease after 14 years of age as occurred in the normal control group of 54 children. However, age effects on these potentials are largely confined to the first 3 years of life, suggesting that the differences noted between autistic and control subjects after 14 years of age may be a function of subject factors, such as the representativeness of the control group for normative values. The investigators interpreted these data as evidence of a delay in brainstem myelination. However, myelination of the brainstem is a very early developmental event that is complete within the first years of life. In addition, the absence

of evidence of abnormal maturation prior to age 14 also would seem inconsistent with delayed myelination as an explanation. Alternatively, this pattern of findings, if demonstrated to be valid, might correspond to the histoanatomic observations of Bauman and Kemper (1994) of the persistence of a fetal pattern in inferior olivary circuits that might be vulnerable to deterioration during the teen years.

In conclusion, the research evidence for the presence and pathophysiologic significance of abnormalities in brainstem ERPs in autism is essentially negative at this point.

Auditory Middle Latency Potentials

The middle latency auditory potentials occur 10 to 50 msec following a click stimulus and consist of several positive and negative waves of which Na (10-25 msec), Pa (25-40 msec), Nb (40-50 msec) and P1 (50-65 msec) are the major components. These potentials are thought to represent activity in the thalamus, thalamocortical radiations, and primary auditory cortex, respectively.

Only two studies have investigated middle latency potentials in autism, and only in small numbers of subjects (Buchwald et al., 1992; Grillon et al., 1989). Grillon et al. found no abnormalities in Na, Pa, and Nb latencies or in wave Na-Pa and Pa-Nb amplitudes in their study of 8 autistic young adults. Buchwald et al. studied Pa and P1 in 11 high functioning autistic subjects and reported normal Pa amplitude and latency; P1 was reported to be smaller in amplitude in the autistic subjects and did not habituate with increasing stimulus rate. The failure to demonstrate habituation was interpreted as evidence of a disturbance in the input of the brainstem ascending reticular activating system cholinergic neurons to thalamus. However, the data in this study are equally consistent with diminished thalamic and auditory cortical feedback inhibition on P1 generators, additional data are necessary to differentiate between these two possibilities.

Long Latency Auditory Potentials

The long latency potentials to a frequent stimulus occur after 50 msec and consist of a large negative (N1)-positive (P2) complex that is maximal in amplitude at the vertex (Goodin,

1992). The generators of these potentials are unknown, but at least part of this activity is from neural areas that can be activated by more than one sensory modality. Like the early and middle latency ERPs, this complex is a stimulus-related response. Thus, the amplitude and latency of these potentials are related to stimulus intensity and frequency and are relatively independent of subject attention. The long latency potentials to the frequent stimulus reach adult levels by 5 to 6 years, if not before (Courchesne, 1978; Finley, Faux, Hutcheson, & Amstutz, 1985; Goodin, Squires, & Starr, 1978; Kurtzberg et al., 1984; Polich & Starr, 1984). In the midteens to early twenties, the P2 latency begins to increase linearly with age. Gender also has a significant impact on these potentials (Stockard et al., 1978).

The auditory N1 and P2 potentials to frequent tones have been examined in autism in only a few studies. Courchesne et al. (1984, 1985, 1989) did not find any differences in N1 or P2 amplitude or latency between autistic subjects and normal controls to a listening task and a two-tone task.

Auditory Cognitive Potentials

The long latency response to the rare auditory stimulus is considerably different from the response to the frequent stimulus, consisting of a negative (N1)-positive (apparent P2)-negative (N2)-positive (P3) complex (Goodin, 1992). The apparent P2 is so named because it represents the sum of the stimulus-related P2 and the event-related P165. The P3 component has a latency of 300 to 400 msec after a rare or "oddball" stimulus, and its amplitude is maximal in the midline over the central and parietal scalp regions. The P3 peak can be further resolved into two components, P3a and P3b. The P3a subcomponent appears to be constant regardless of subject attention, whereas the P3b component appears to be sensitive to task requirements (Squires, Squires, & Hillyard, 1975). These long latency ERPs can be recorded to stimuli in any of the sensory modalities. They also can be recorded without the stimulus-related long latency potentials in response to the unexpected omission of an anticipated stimulus. These potentials are relatively insensitive to stimulus intensity, but are very sensitive to change in the ease with which targets can be distinguished from non-targets, by alterations in the ratio of target to non-target stimuli, or by fluctuations in subject attention to the stimulus. The N2 and P3 components are markedly prolonged in young children, and decrease in latency with increasing age until reaching adult values in the teens and early twenties. Thereafter, there is a linear increase in latency with increasing age. Gender does not impact on latency, but P3 amplitude tends to be larger in females.

A fifth potential Nc has been the subject of more recent investigation in autism (Courchesne, Elmasian, & Yeung-Courchesne, 1987; Courchesne et al., 1989). Nc is the earliest endogenous component to appear developmentally and can be elicited in infants. It occurs in response to surprising, interesting, or important pictures or sounds. Nc has an onset at around 100 to 200 msec, a peak amplitude at about 350 to 450 msec, and is maximal in amplitude over frontal scalp regions.

Abnormalities in cognitive potentials have been a consistent neurophysiologic finding in autism for the past 15 years. Abnormal auditory P300 potentials to rare tones and missing stimuli in autism were first reported by Novick, Kurtzberg, and Vaughan (1979) and Novick, Vaughan, Kurtzberg, and Simson (1980), and confirmed by Courchesne et al. (1984, 1985). In a subsequent study, Lincoln, Courchesne, Harms, and Allen (1993) reported decreased amplitudes of P3b responses to auditory stimuli in young non-retarded autistic children, suggesting difficulty in modifying expectancies to contextually relevant sequences of auditory information, and perhaps a more general disturbance in habituation processes that interfere with the discrimination of novel information. The reaction times of responses to odd-ball stimuli by the autistic children in this study were normal, indicating intact sensory processing and task compliance. Similar findings have been reported by other investigators (Ciesielski, Courchesne, & Elmasian, 1990; Courchesne et al., 1989; Dawson, Finley, Phillips, Galpert, & Lewy, 1988).

Nc abnormalities also appear to be a prominent cognitive ERP finding in autism. Courchesne et al. (1987, 1989) have reported Nc to be small and often absent to auditory and visual stimuli, and to the omission of auditory and visual stimuli. P3b was also documented to be small in these same subjects, thus demonstrating the coexistence of abnormalities in these two cognitive potentials in autism.

Only two studies have examined neurophysiologic functioning in response to language stimuli. One study using simple affective and nonaffective prosodic language discriminations in adult autistic individuals of normal intelligence reported normal P3 responses (Erwin et al., 1991). However, the language tasks used in this study presented were of low difficulty and well within the abilities of these non-mentally retarded adult autistic individuals, whose deficits typically involve higher-order linguistic and prosodic discriminations. Interestingly, one study (Strandburg et al., 1993) reported *increased* P3 responses to oddball stimuli in a visual continuous performance task (CPT) and a visually presented idiom recognition task. In contrast to the simple prosodic discriminations of the previous study, idiomatic language is a well documented feature of the language deficits in high functioning autistic individuals; the increase in P3 amplitude under these circumstances could reflect the surprise element that may result from a literal interpretation of idiomatic language. Alternatively, the increase in P3 with these tasks could indicate a modality effect with different P3 effects to visual stimuli than to auditory stimuli, or an indication that there may be some situations where autistics may have a greater allocation of attention to some tasks to compensate for dysfunction in cognitive processes that interfere with task performance.

Visual and Somatosensory Cognitive Potentials

Few ERP studies have been conducted with visual stimuli. Some data have suggested that visual ERPs (P3b) to novel stimuli are abnormal (Novick et al., 1979; Verbaten, Roelofs, van Engeland, Kenemans, & Slangen, 1991), but less impaired than the auditory P3b (Courchesne, Lincoln, Kilman, & Galambos, 1985; Courchesne et al., 1989). However, it is not clear whether task difficulty for the auditory and visual ERP studies was equivalent (Dunn, 1994). Studies of somatosensory ERPs in

autism have been rare but one recent study reported abnormal somatosensory P3 responses (Kemner, Verbaten, Cuperus, Camfferman, & van Engeland, 1994).

Evoked Potential Profile

Evoked potential studies in autism have largely been confined to the auditory system, although similar findings have been reported for the visual and somatosensory systems. The neurophysiologic profile defined for autism is characterized by bilaterally symmetrical abnormalities in cognitive potentials and intact early and middle latency potentials. These findings have provided evidence of abnormalities in higher auditory, visual, and somatosensory processing and neural pathways and integrity of brainstem processing and pathways.

Oculomotor and Postural Physiology: Motor and Cognitive Systems

Eye movement studies can be performed to assess the functional integrity of the vestibular system by monitoring eye movement responses to caloric challenge or to rotation of the head or body. The duration and amplitude of the procedure-induced nystagmus and the velocity of the slow phase component are then measured. Eye movement paradigms also are used to provide important information about nonreflexive eye movements and the status of the well established cortical and subcortical origins of these parameters.

For quantitative eye movement studies, patients are typically taken to a dark room, their heads are comfortably restrained so that head and eye movements are not confounded, and various eye movement tasks are performed. Eye movements can be recorded by electrooculography (EOG) procedures (similar to those used in EEG studies to identify eye movement "artifacts"), camera-based recording systems, or direct monitoring of the reflection of an infra-red light source from the corneal-scleral margin. Responses to lights moving abruptly from one point to another can be measured (latency, accuracy, peak velocity) to assess the integrity of saccadic eye movements, and the tracking of slowly but steadily moving targets can be evaluated to assess smooth pursuit eye movements (Leigh & Zee, 1991). These procedures approximate those used in neurological examinations, but are conducted under controlled conditions and in ways that are amenable to quantitative analysis. Examining semi-reflexive saccadic responses to unpredictable lights can be informative about the integrity of subcortical regions involved in basic oculomotor control. By varying saccadic eye movement tasks in different ways, such as by instructing subjects to look away from lights, requiring delayed responses to locations that need to be remembered for brief periods of time, and cueing locations where targets will be presented, various neocortical systems related to complex visual attentional processes or working memory can be evaluated.

Eye Movement Studies

As with evoked potential research in autism, eye movement studies during the 1960s and 1970s frequently reported abnormalities in post-rotatory nystagmus and nystagmus during REM sleep (Ornitz, Brown, Mason, & Putnam, 1974; Ornitz, Forsythe, & de la Pena, 1973; Ornitz & Ritvo, 1968a, 1968b; Ornitz, Ritvo, Brown, et al., 1969; Ornitz, Ritvo, Panman, et al., 1968; Ritvo, Ornitz, Eviatar, et al., 1969). Subsequently, these investigators concluded that these abnormal findings were the result of idiosyncratic methods. A repetition of these studies using accepted methodology revealed only one statistically significant result (Ornitz, Atwell, Kaplan, & Westlake, 1985).

Recent studies have included analysis of the oculomotor effects of vestibular challenge that bear on the functional integrity of the cerebellum (Minshew, Furman, Goldstein, & Payton, 1990; Ornitz et al., 1985), a small number of studies of saccadic and pursuit responses to visual stimuli that assess the functional integrity of the brainstem and basal ganglia (Minshew et al., 1990; Rosenhall, Johansson, & Gillberg, 1988), and a preliminary study of volitional saccadic eye movement subserved by frontal and parietal cortex (Minshew, Sweeney, & Furman, 1995; Sweeney et al., 1995).

Ornitz et al. (1985) tested 22 autistic patients and reported slightly prolonged post-rotatory nystagmus, though there was no disturbance in gain of the slow component. In addition, the statistically significant difference was confined to one parameter, the vestibulo-ocular reflex time constant, and appeared to be the result of two outliers in the data rather than a trend for the group as a whole.

Rosenhall et al. (1988) reported normal pursuit eye movements but hypometric horizontal visually guided saccades to unpredictable targets in 6 of 11 mentally retarded autistic children. However, some patients were taking CNS-active medications that affect eye movements, cooperation was frequently a problem, and the control subjects had normal IQs in comparison to the high rates of mental retardation in the autistic subjects.

In two independent studies of 85 and 15 autistic subjects from separate laboratories, Minshew et al. (1990) and Minshew et al. (1995) found no abnormalities of vestibulo-ocular reflexes, or in pursuit or visually-guided saccadic eye movements. However, a study of voluntary saccadic eye movements known to be subserved by discrete regions in frontal and parietal cortex (Goldman-Rakic, 1987; Sweeney et al., 1995) revealed significant abnormalities in cortically controlled eye movements in 15 autistic subjects compared to age- and gender-matched controls. The autistic subjects demonstrated significant impairments in the ability both to willfully suppress saccades to unpredictable targets (executive function) and to shift gaze to remembered target locations (working memory). These findings, together with the demonstrated integrity of visually guided saccades in these same autistic subjects, provide evidence for a significant disturbance in the cortical connectivity of neocortical systems and the integrity of subcortical systems.

Startle Modulation

One study has reported results of startle modulation (Ornitz, Lane, Sugiyama, & de Traversay, 1993). This study was designed to investigate the brainstem and cerebellar physiology. The findings of this study were normal, with the exception of only two values that were outside the normal range. Based on the findings, the study concluded that there was no evidence of dysfunction in the primary startle pathway in the brainstem. The two significant differences in this study, involving prolongation of unmodulated startle onset latency and a slower rate of short-term habituation of startle onset latency in some of the experiments, provided only equivocal evidence of brainstem dysfunction. There was no evidence from this study to support cerebellar dysfunction. In particular, the investigators noted the absence of differences in long-term habituation of startle as evidence of the absence of dysfunction related to the cerebellar vermis. They also noted that atrophic cerebellar lesions are associated with short time constants of nystagmus, whereas Ornitz et al. (1985) had documented prolonged time constants. Thus, the findings of this study using a third method for investigating the function of brainstem-cerebellar circuits have provided negative results that are consistent with evoked potential and reflex eye movement data in autism.

Postural Physiology

Studies of postural functions are another method for providing direct and specific evidence of the physiologic integrity of the vestibular system, including the cerebellum. Although posterior fossa circuitry contributes significantly to postural function, contributions from more widespread regions are also important. Kohen-Raz, Volkmar, and Cohen (1992) conducted a study of 91 autistic children and adolescents using a computerized posturographic procedure that evaluated the effects of various stresses to this system. Computerized recording of postural sway (recorded as changes in weight distribution) performed as subjects stood on 4 plates, one for the heel and toe of each foot. Results of this study indicated poorer postural stability with greater variability in overall posture. Oddly, autistic subjects demonstrated the paradoxical effect of improved rather than impaired function when they were stressed by procedures such as standing on elastic pads with occluded vision. This is the opposite of the effect observed in normal individuals and in patients with known vestibular disease, so the etiology of variable posture when standing on a firm surface demonstrated by the autistic patients remains unclear. There were several methodologic limitations to this study that

may have contributed to this finding. Roughly one-third of the sample was taking neuroleptic medications, the majority appeared to have been mentally retarded, and compliance/cooperation with procedures was questionable in some cases.

Oculomotor Profile

As with evoked potentials, studies of oculomotor physiology in autism have defined bilaterally symmetric abnormalities in functions dependent on neocortical circuitry, with subtle or no abnormalities in parameters dependent on widely distributed pathways between posterior fossa and cortex, and intact oculovestibular reflexes and posterior fossa circuitry. This profile demonstrates a similar pattern of findings involving motor pathways as were demonstrated for sensory pathways with evoked potentials.

Profile of Neuropsychologic Functioning in Autism

Comprehensive studies of neuropsychologic functioning in autism are relatively recent and few, having awaited a consensus on the diagnostic criteria and research methods for defining autism in verbal individuals with average IQ scores. The first such study of 10 autistic men with Full Scale and Verbal IQ scores of 103 reported a pattern of neuropsychologic functioning characterized by the predominance of deficits in abstraction and conceptual reasoning, relative sparing of memory and language, and intact visuospatial, sensoriperceptual and motor abilities (Rumsey & Hamburger 1988, 1990). This general profile of relative deficits and abilities was confirmed by several other laboratories (Minshew, Goldstein, Muenz, & Payton, 1992; Ozonoff, Pennington, & Rogers, 1991; Prior & Hoffman, 1990).

In a more detailed examination of each neuropsychologic domain and of both the auditory and visual modalities, Minshew, Goldstein, and Siegel (1995) reported evidence in 33 autistic individuals of deficits in complex tasks across domains involving both the visual and auditory modalities and preserved function on tests of simpler abilities in these same domains and in the visual-spatial domain. Thus, deficits were documented in concept formation and cognitive flexibility, complex or higher order language abilities, working memory and memory for complex information, and complex motor abilities or praxis. Simpler abilities in these same domains were intact, as were information acquisition and visual spatial abilities. This pattern of generalized deficits in complex abilities was not that of a general deficit syndrome or mental retardation, since autistic subjects did as well or better than age- and IQ-matched controls in preserved areas and performance in deficit areas was substantially below expectations based on age and IQ. This profile of deficits and intact abilities also is not compatible with a deficit in a single cognitive or sensory domain. This profile is most consistent with multiple primary deficits in complex abilities across multiple domains and with a disorder of complex information processing. This neuropsychologic profile is analogous to the pattern of ERP abnormalities in late, endogenous evoked potentials and intact early and mid-latency potentials, which suggests that autism is furthermore a disorder of late information processing.

Many other studies over the past two decades have examined neuropsychologic functioning in individual cognitive domains, and have provided evidence of the above documented deficits in different subject samples. The above study examining neuropsychologic function across domains within the same subjects has provided evidence of the co-occurrence of these deficits. Some studies have provided evidence of deficits in the simpler cognitive abilities demonstrated to be intact in the above study. However, examination of these studies generally reveals that the subjects were of lower ability, supporting the need for documenting deficits in relation to the subjects' general level of function and function in other cognitive domains, rather than in isolation.

CENTRAL NERVOUS SYSTEM STRUCTURE IN AUTISM

Neuropathology

For many years, autism was believed to be related to parenting and environmental factors. However, over the past 25 years, there has been an increasing recognition of the neurological basis for this disorder. Based on clinical features and evidence from neurophysiologic studies, a number of regions of the brain were hypothesized as possible sites of abnormality in the 1960s and 1970s. Proposed localizations included the basal ganglia (Vilensky, Damasio, & Maurer, 1981), the vestibular system (Ornitz & Ritvo, 1968a, 1968b), and medial temporal lobe (Boucher & Warrington, 1976; Damasio & Maurer, 1978; Delong, 1978; Maurer & Damasio, 1982). The few autopsy studies reported in the mid-1970s showed sparse and inconsistent findings; microscopic analysis of tissue obtained from a frontal lobe biopsy showed slight thickening of the arterioles, some increase of connective tissue in the leptomeninges, and some increased cellularity (Aarkrog, 1968). Subsequently, Darby (1976) reviewed 33 cases of childhood psychosis and suggested that there might be a relationship between limbic system lesions and the affective component of autism, but no specific pathologic abnormalities were described. In 1980, Williams, Hauser, Purpura, Delong, and Swisher examined autopsy material from 4 individuals with autistic features, looking primarily for gliosis. No consistent abnormalities were observed.

More recently, quantitative analysis of glial and neuronal cell number was performed in multiple areas of the cerebral cortex in a single autistic patient and compared with similar observations in two age- and sex-matched controls (Coleman, Romano, Lapham, & Simon, 1985). No differences were observed, and the authors concluded that abnormalities in the early stages of central nervous system development and in neuronal migration were not features of the developmental pathophysiology of autism. They hypothesized that the probable pathogenetic process responsible for this disorder was more likely to occur later in development, during the elaboration of neuronal processes and synapses.

In a study of the microscopic anatomy of the cerebellum, Ritvo et al. (1986) noted decreased numbers of Purkinje cells in 4 autistic subjects when compared with neurologically healthy controls. These investigators speculated on the relationship of these cerebellar abnormalities to the clinical syndrome of autism.

In 1984, the results of a systematic analysis of the brain of a 29-year-old man with well-documented autism, studied in comparison with an identically processed age- and sex-matched control, was reported (Bauman & Kemper, 1984). A more detailed description of this study was published in 1985 (Bauman & Kemper, 1985). Since that initial report, eight additional cases have been similarly studied (Bauman & Kemper, 1994). Abnormalities have been consistently observed in the limbic system and in the cerebellum and related inferior olive. When compared with controls, the autistic subjects showed reduced neuronal size and increased cell packing density in the hippocampus, amygdala, mammillary body, anterior cingulate cortex, and septum; all of these areas are known to be related to each other by interconnecting circuits and make up a major portion of the limbic system of the brain.

Studies of the CA1 and CA4 pyramidal neurons of the hippocampus, using the rapid Golgi technique, have demonstrated reduced complexity and extent of dendritic arbors in these cells (Bauman & Kemper, 1994). Although small cell size and increased cell packing density were found in the medial septal nucleus (MSN) in the autistic persons' brains, a different pattern of abnormality was observed in the nucleus of the diagonal band of Broca (NDB). Enlarged but otherwise normal appearing neurons were found in the NBD of all autistic subjects under the age of 12 years; in contrast, these same neurons were noted to be small in size and markedly reduced in number in all of the autistic subjects over the age of 22 years (Bauman & Kemper, 1994).

Outside of the forebrain, the only additional abnormalities have been confined to the cerebellum and related inferior olive. A significant reduction in the number of Purkinje cells has been demonstrated throughout the cerebellar hemispheres, most prominently in the posteriolateral neocerebellar cortex and adjacent archiocerebellar cortex (Arin, Bauman, & Kemper, 1991). In contrast to the findings in the hemispheres, detailed quantitative analysis of Purkinje cell numbers in the vermis has demonstrated no statistically significant differences in comparison with age- and sex-matched controls (Bauman & Kemper, 1996). In addition to these observations, abnormalities have

been found in the fastigial, globose, and emboliform nuclei in the roof of the cerebellum, which, like the findings in the NDB of the septum, appear to differ with the age of the patient. As in the NDB, small pale neurons that are reduced in number, have been observed in all young adult subjects. In all of the younger subjects, however, these neurons, as well as those of the dentate nucleus, are enlarged in size and present in adequate numbers (Bauman & Kemper, 1994).

No evidence of retrograde cell loss or atrophy has been found in the principal olivary nucleus of the brainstem in any of the autistic brains, areas which are known to be related to the abnormal regions of the cerebellar cortex (Holmes & Stewart, 1988). In human pathology, neuronal cell loss and atrophy of the inferior olive has been invariably observed following perinatal and postnatal Purkinje cell loss (Greenfield, 1954; Norman, 1940). This cell loss is presumably due to the close relationship of the olivary climbing fiber axons to the Purkinje cell dendrites (Eccles, Iro, & Szentagothai, 1967). The olivary neurons in the young adult autistic brains were small but present in adequate numbers, while those in the younger persons' brains were significantly enlarged but otherwise normal in appearance and number.

To date, postmortem studies of the brain in autism have failed to show any abnormalities of gross brain structure. Myelination has been found to be comparable to controls in all cases (Bauman & Kemper, 1994). However, in 1993, Bailey, Luthert, Bolton, Le Couteur, and Rutter reported that three out of four autopsied brains from autistic subjects were heavier than expected for age and sex. Although the authors suggested that their observations could be coincidental, they noted that their findings were supported by clinical studies in which large head circumference was recorded in autistic children under the age of 16 years (Bailey et al., 1993, 1995; Bolton et al., 1994). More recently, in a review of 19 autopsy cases, brains from autistic subjects less than 12 years of age were found to be heavier than expected for age and this difference was statistically significant (Bauman & Kemper, 1995). In contrast, however, brains of adult autistic subjects were lighter in weight by approximately 100 to 200 grams than expected for age. Thus, brain weight may be reflective of the age of the patient and may be associated with as yet undetermined pathogenetic mechanisms in autism.

Theories of Pathogenesis

What theories can be derived from the available neuroanatomic observations to date? First, the pattern of abnormality seen in the limbic system suggests a curtailment of development in this circuitry. Studies in animals, humans, and non-human primates support a role for medial temporal lobe structures, particularly the hippocampus and the amygdala, in cognition, behavior, emotion, and learning in autism. Second, based on what is known about the relationship of the Purkinje cells and the olivary neurons, the observation of reduced numbers of cerebellar Purkinje cells in the face of preserved olivary neurons strongly suggests that the process that resulted in the brain abnormalities in autism had its onset before birth. Third, there is growing evidence that the cerebellum may play a role in the mediation and modulation of some aspects of learning and affective behavior. Although the effects of prenatal abnormalities of the limbic system and cerebellum on development are unknown, early dysfunction in these circuits could have a significant impact on the acquisition and processing of information during life and could account for many of the clinical features of autism.

Questions for the Future

While substantial progress has been made in autism research, particularly within the past 10 years, many significant questions remain to be answered before we can truly understand the underlying neural mechanisms that result in the clinical features of autism. Given the substantially limited quantity of autopsy material, research would be significantly aided by the availability of an animal model for anatomic, neurochemical, and neurophysiological study. Neurochemical analyses of blood, urine, and spinal fluid has shown inconsistent abnormalities in a variety of neurochemical substances, and related neuropharmacological research has been discouraging in most instances. To date, neurochemical analysis of brain tissue from autistic patients has yet to be performed. However, given improved technology and known structural location of anatomic abnormalities in the autistic brain, such studies should be possible in the future.

Future neuroanatomic research in autism should continue to systematically correlate the location and degree of histologic abnormality with the clinical characteristics of the patient, thereby increasing our understanding of the relationships between site-specific brain dysfunction and behavior. Autopsy material obtained from subjects of varying ages and degrees of clinical severity will need to be carefully analyzed in order to better understand the timing and significance of brain changes that appear to be age-related. Whether more profoundly affected patients show significantly different abnormalities than those who are high functioning, and how phenotypic differences may be expressed within the brain, should be major areas of interest. Finally, with increased knowledge of the pathogenesis of this disorder, it is likely that a better understanding of the maturational mechanisms inherent to the normal and abnormal nervous system will be achieved.

Research Imaging

As with evoked potential and eye movement research in autism, the first era of imaging research from the 1960s through the early 1980s largely demonstrated the relationship of gross anatomic abnormalities to causes of brain damage other than autism (see Minshew & Dombrowski, 1994, for a detailed review). Radiologic abnormalities of the brain in autism were first documented with pneumoencephalography (PEG) beginning in the 1950s and continuing through the mid-1970s. One such study reported pneumoencephalographic abnormalities in 54% of 46 children with infantile psychosis (Aarkrog, 1968). Studies such as this played an important role in supporting the shift in conceptualization toward autism as a disorder of neurologic origin. The overly broad diagnostic criteria for autism at that time and the high frequency of a wide variety of neurologic, infectious, and genetic disorders among the autistic subjects, otherwise limited the biologic implications of such studies. The last of the PEG studies (Hauser, DeLong, & Rosman, 1975) reported left lateral ventricular enlargement in 13 of 18 developmentally disabled children with autistic symptoms, thus beginning the brief phase in imaging research investigating brain asymmetries as a neurologic basis of autism. Frontal and parieto-occipital brain asymmetries were a focus of early CT imaging research in autism (Damasio, Maurer, Damasio, & Chui, 1980; Hier, LeMay, & Rosenberger, 1979; Rumsey et al., 1988; Tsai, Jacoby, & Stewart, 1983). Ultimately, these studies failed to provide evidence of brain asymmetries as a basis for autism, an outcome that was consistent with emerging neuropathologic (Bauman & Kemper, 1985) and neurophysiologic (Courchesne et al., 1984) evidence of bilaterally symmetrical brain abnormalities. A second theme emanating from early CT studies in autism was the frequent presence of assorted gross brain abnormalities in subjects diagnosed with autism at that time (Damasio et al., 1980; Gillberg & Svendsen, 1983), echoing the observations of the initial PEG studies. During the early 1980s, a series of studies documented the relationship of such abnormalities to the inclusion of autistic subjects with readily identifiable neurologic, infectious, and genetic causes of brain abnormalities (Campbell et al., 1982; Creasey et al., 1986; Damasio, 1984; Damasio et al., 1980; Gaffney & Tsai, 1987; Harcherik et al., 1985; Prior, Tress, Hoffman, & Boldt, 1984). The study by Damasio et al. (1980) was ultimately pivotal in demonstrating that the presence of gross brain abnormalities on CT scan in autism were related to the inclusion of autistic individuals with other causes of brain damage. The screening of research subjects for infectious, metabolic, genetic, and neurologic disorders other than autism was a general policy in imaging research by 1982, and the incidence of gross structural abnormalities in reports dropped dramatically thereafter.

The first imaging studies to employ rigorous screening procedures were those of Campbell et al. (1982) and Rosenbloom, Campbell, and George (1984). With the exception of a low incidence of ventricular enlargement, the CT scans of the 58 autistic children in these two studies were normal.

Mild to moderate ventricular enlargement was present in 25% of the 45 subjects in the Campbell et al. study and 15% of the 13 autistic subjects in the Rosenbloom et al. study. In both studies, ventricular size was unrelated to all clinical indices examined, and thus its implications for the pathophysiology of autism are unknown. These two studies were followed by the negative report of Prior et al. (1984) on 9 carefully screened, high functioning autistic boys, designed to exclude the potential confounding influence of mental retardation on imaging findings. This study was complemented by those of Harcherik et al. (1985) and Creasey et al. (1986) of respectively 14 and 12 carefully screened autistic individuals who spanned the IQ spectrum. These studies concluded that autistic individuals without other neurologic conditions were "very unlikely to have detectable CT abnormalities" (Harcherik et al., 1985) and that the "cerebral defect in autism was likely to be microscopic without major gross anatomic correlate" (Creasey et al., 1986). These conclusions were consistent with neuropathologic findings of Bauman and Kemper (1985) of abnormalities at the microscopic level but no gross structural abnormalities other than a 100 to 200 gm increase in brain weight.

The current era of imaging research began with the introduction of magnetic resonance imaging (MRI) technology and morphometric methodology for deriving volumetric measurements of brain structures. These methodologies remain in evolution, with the goals of developing an imaging sequence that generates a true or near-true volumetric data set with isotropic voxels and morphometric measurement methods that have demonstrated reliability and validity. Another methodologic need is for the development of a representative normative database of brain measurements that documents all relevant influences on brain structure size, specifically age, gender, IQ, height, and possibly socioeconomic status. During the transition period of technology development, imaging research in autism must move with caution and maintain a clear awareness of existing limitations.

MRI research in autism, using quantitative rather than qualitative measurement procedures and up-to-date methods for screening and diagnosis of autistic subjects, has been quite limited. Thus far, no studies are available that provide a comprehensive analysis of the whole brain and its component structures. Such an overview is essential for interpreting the significance of findings related to isolated brain structures, particularly in a developmental disorder such as autism, which, from all other evidence, involves multiple levels of the neuraxis and brain organization and function at the neural systems level. A few MRI studies, reporting quantitative measurements of isolated brain structures and total brain size, comprise the research findings in autism to date.

Total Brain Area and Volume

In 1992, Piven and colleagues reported an increase in the midsagittal, supratentorial brain area in 15 high functioning autistic men compared to well matched control groups (Piven et al., 1992). More recently, Piven and colleagues have reported an increase in the total brain volume above the lower boundary of the brainstem in 22 autistic male adolescents and young adults (Piven et al., 1995); this increase reflected an increase in tissue volume and in increase in lateral ventricular volume. In a follow-up to this study, Piven et al. (in press) reported that the enlargement of the cerebral hemispheres was regional and involved occipital, parietal and temporal regions but not the frontal lobe. These findings are consistent with the preliminary report of increased supratentorial brain volume and increased cortical grey and white matter volumes by Filipek et al. (1992), the 100 to 200 gm increase reported in autopsy brain weight (Bailey et al., 1993; Bauman & Kemper, 1985, unpublished data), and reports of above average head circumference in autism (Bailey et al., 1993, 1995).

Cerebellar Vermis

In a series of studies since 1988, Courchesne and colleagues have reported a selective decrease in the midsagittal area of vermal lobules vi and vii (Ciesielski, Allen, et al., 1990; Courchesne, Yeung-Courchesne, Press, Hesselink, & Jernigan, 1988; Murakami, Courchesne, Press, Yeung-Courchesne, & Hesselink, 1989; Saitoh, Courchesne, Egaas, Lincoln, & Schreibman, 1995) in the absence of an alteration in the midsagittal area of the pons (Hsu, Yeung-Courchesne, Courchesne, & Press, 1991), and have proposed an intrinsic

abnormality of neocerebellar vermis as important in the pathophysiology of autism. Subsequently, Courchesne and colleagues reported two types of abnormalities of the neocerebellar vermis, a selective hypoplasia in most cases and a selective hyperplasia in a minority of cases (Courchesne et al., 1994). However, these findings have not been independently replicated; in fact, four studies collectively examining vermal size in a wide age and IQ range of autistic subjects failed to replicate these results, when autistic and control subjects were well matched on age, gender, and IQ (Garber & Ritvo, 1992; Garber et al., 1989; Holttum, Minshew, Sanders, & Phillips, 1992; Kleiman, Neff, & Rosman, 1992; Piven et al., 1992). A reanalysis (Courchesne et al., 1994) of the data from two of these negative studies (Kleiman et al., 1992; Piven et al., 1992) by Courchesne and colleagues reported positive results, but failed to include the IQ matched control groups from the original studies in the reanalysis. Thus, the different results obtained in the reanalysis of these data reflected the failure to control for age and IQ, and not the failure of the original studies to identify abnormalities present in their samples.

A recent imaging study (Hashimoto et al., 1995) reported a decrease in the size of the brainstem in toto; of the midbrain, pons, and medulla individually; of the cerebellar vermis in toto; and of lobules I–V, VI–VII, and VIII–X individually in mentally retarded individuals with autism when compared to normally developing children of average intellectual ability. Although cited as supportive of the findings of Courchesne and colleagues, the generalized reduction in the brainstem and cerebellum size reported in by Hashimoto et al. is not consistent with the findings of Courchesne et al. of selective alterations in the size of the neocerebellar vermis, which furthermore emphasized the absence of alterations in the size of the pons as evidence of the intrinsic origin of the neocerebellar vermis abnormalities (Hsu et al., 1991). The study of Hashimoto et al. (1995) suffered from major design limitations, which could explain differences between autistic subjects and controls: the comparison of mentally retarded autistic patients with normal IQ children; the unequal gender composition of subject and control groups; and the failure to compare brainstem and cerebellar measurements to overall brain size. A generalized reduction in brainstem and cerebellar size in mentally retarded individuals would have few implications, if any, for autism if it represented a generalized reduction in brain size.

When reports of imaging abnormalities of the cerebellum first appeared, it was initially assumed that the imaging findings were a reflection of the histologic findings previously reported in the cerebellum (Bauman & Kemper, 1985; Ritvo et al., 1986). However, it subsequently became clear that the imaging findings were not equivalent in location (cerebellar hemispheres versus vermis) or in nature (cell number versus tissue area) to the abnormalities reported by postmortem studies. Whereas imaging studies reported selective reduction in the area of neocerebellar vermis, the neuropathologic studies have documented no reduction in cell numbers in any of the three vermal segments but a significant decrease in neuronal number in the cerebellar hemispheres (Bauman & Kemper, 1996).

A recent imaging study of the cerebellum in a number of neurogenetic syndromes has reported cerebellar hypoplasia in a number of disorders, suggesting that such abnormalities may be common in developmental cognitive disorders. Ciesielski and Knight (1994) have also observed cerebellar abnormalities following treatment of brain malignancies in early childhood and have suggested that such abnormalities may also be a nonspecific effect of early brain damage.

In summary, the disparity in findings across imaging studies with respect to posterior fossa structures appears therefore to be primarily related to the selection of controls, specifically to their comparability or lack of comparability to the autistic subjects on IQ, age, and possibly also gender, and to the absence of a representative normative data base for imaging measurements establishing the normal biologic variability in the size of these structures.

Brainstem

The brainstem has been measured in a few studies, with some finding a decrease in area (Gaffney, Kuperman, Tsai, & Minchin, 1988; Hashimoto et al., 1995) but most finding no differences (Garber & Ritvo, 1992; Garber et al., 1989; Hsu et al., 1991; Piven et al., 1992).

Corpus Callosum

Three studies have provided data on the corpus callosum in autism. Gaffney, Kuperman, Tsai, Minchin, and Hassanein (1987) reported no difference in the midsagittal area of the corpus callosum. Saitoh et al. (1995) found no differences in the total midsagittal area of the corpus callosum or in anterior and middle subregions (Clarke, Kraftsik, Van der Loos, & Innocenti 1989), but reported a decrease in the area of the most posterior region. In the third study, Piven, Bailey, Ranson, and Arndt (in press) reported decreased areas of the middle and posterior regions of the corpus callosum when measurements were adjusted for total brain volume. These subjects were the same subjects demonstrated in a previous study to have an increase in the volumes of the parietal, temporal, and occipital lobes but not the frontal lobes (Piven et al., in press). The dissociation between the sizes of the cerebral cortex and corpus callosum was interpreted as evidence of abnormal development of neural connectivity between the hemispheres.

Hippocampus

Only two MRI studies have reported imaging data for the hippocampus, and only one of these involved volume measurements. The first study found no differences in the cross sectional area of the hippocampal formation measured in a single slice in 33 autistic subjects compared to normal controls (Saitoh et al., 1995). The second study (Piven, Bailey, Ranson, & Arndt, submitted) measured the volume of the hippocampus in 35 autistic and 36 control subjects and found no inter-group differences between the volume of the hippocampus with or without correction for total brain volume.

Summary

Research imaging studies have entered an exciting new era in autism with the emergence of volume based measurements and of reports of regional increases in the volumes of the parietal, temporal, and occipital lobes of the cortex but not of frontal lobes, corpus callosum, or hippocampus. The increase in cerebral cortical volume is independently supported by reports of increased brain weight and head circumference from multiple centers and is an intriguing contrast with neuropathologic evidence of truncation in dendritic tree development in the limbic system and decrease in neuronal cell number in neocerebellar hemispheres. Collectively, the current neurobiologic characterization of autism provides repeated evidence of the disruption of the normal dynamics of neuronal organization events underlying the development of brain organization at the neural systems level. In the upcoming years, imaging studies can be expected to define the profile of structure size across brain regions, so that the volumes of the various CNS structures can be considered in relation to each other within a neural systems framework. To achieve this goal in the least amount of time, it is essential that imaging studies use volumetric measurements, rigorously control for the effects of age, IQ, and gender on measurements, and initially provide measurements of individual structures within the broader context of total brain volume. Ultimately, it is hoped that such studies will achieve a profile of measurements of all key brain structures within their respective subject populations so that the pattern of relationships between structures can emerge. Simultaneously, carefully designed MRI studies can be used to explore the integrity of neural systems from a functional perspective and ^{31}P and ^{1}H magnetic resonance spectroscopy can be used to investigate the metabolic dynamics of brain membrane production and turnover and neuronal number in these same brain regions.

CLINICAL NEUROLOGY

The Neurologic Examination

The neurologic examination in autism is remarkable for the absence of findings, other than the manifestations of autism, and for above average head circumference in many but not all individuals with autism (Bailey et al., 1993, 1995; Davidovitch et al., in press; Lainhart et al., in press; Woodhouse et al., 1996). The mean head circumference in a sample of 91 autistic individuals between 3 and 38 years of age was 67% with 14.3% having head circumferences above 97% (Lainhart et al., in press). The age at which head growth accelerates to produce an above average head circumference in autism is not clear, as this finding does not appear to be present at birth or shortly after birth (Mason-Brothers et al., 1987, 1990), suggesting that the abnormality in brain growth is associated with later events in brain development.

Microcephaly is not, however, part of this syndrome, and its presence should suggest the existence of another cause for this finding, such as fetal infection with rubella or cytomegalovirus, or Rett's Disorder. Muscle tone is generally but subtly decreased in autism. Deep tendon reflexes are either generally increased (3+), or absent in the upper extremities and at the knees but brisk at the ankles. Babinski signs are absent.

Clinical Imaging

In the absence of an associated disorder such as tuberous sclerosis or fetal rubella, the most common neuroradiologic finding in autism is of normal neuroanatomy. As mentioned in the section on research imaging, a minority of autistic individuals will have ventricular enlargement, but because it is not related to increased intracranial pressure and is nonspecific to autism, it has no diagnostic or treatment implications. Very rarely, other findings such as an arachnoid cyst may be present, but, without clinical manifestations referrable to this focal abnormality, management and treatment are unchanged. Such focal abnormalities are not etiologic of autism, which, from all available data, is the result of a bilaterally symmetrical neurobiologic abnormality involving multiple levels of the neuraxis. Thus, in the absence of an unusual clinical course such as the late appearance of symptoms or a progressive or fluctuating course (Volkmar, 1992, 1994), or evidence on history or examination of an associated disorder such as tuberous sclerosis or postnatal meningitis, clinical imaging is unlikely to be useful and should not be a routine part of the neurologic evaluation of autistic children (Rapin, 1991).

Electroencephalography

The electroencephalogram (EEG) was one of the first methods used to investigate the status of the brain in autism. The documentation of a high incidence of EEG abnormalities and of seizure disorders in autism was among the earliest evidence in support of a biologic basis for this syndrome. The first such study, in 1964 (White, DeMeyer, & DeMeyer, 1964), reported EEG abnormalities in 58% and epilepsy in 19% of the 58 young autistic children in this series. In the ensuing decade, the incidence of EEG abnormalities in various studies ranged from 10% to 83%, depending on the method of subject selection and criteria for interpretation of the EEGs, and the incidence of epilepsy ranged from 19% to 25% (Creak & Pampiglione, 1969; Fish & Shapiro, 1965; Gubbay, Lobascher, & Kingerlee, 1970; Hutt, Hutt, Lee, & Ounsted, 1965; Ritvo, Ornitz, Walter, & Hanley, 1970; Small, 1968; Stevens & Milstein, 1970). In 1975, Small reported paroxysmal EEG abnormalities in 65% of 147 autistic children who had two or more EEGs. Two factors were found to have a bearing on the documentation of EEG abnormalities in these cases: (a) the number of recordings and (b) sampling from all three states of alertness (awake, drowsy, and sleep). Specifically, EEG abnormalities were present in 40% of the autistic sample if a single recording was used, 60% for two recordings, and 80% for three or more recordings of good quality. Small (1975) also documented a relationship between EEG status and IQ, in that 75% of autistic subjects with abnormal EEGs were mentally retarded, whereas only 58% of the subjects with normal EEGs were mentally retarded. Hence, the incidence of abnormal EEGs was significantly higher in mentally retarded autistic individuals but was by no means inconsequential in non-mentally retarded autistic individuals. The relationship between EEG status and autism severity was examined in a number of other studies (Brown, 1963; DeMeyer, 1975; Lotter, 1974; Small, 1975; Tsai & Stewart, 1982). The most probable interpretation of these data is that the more severely impaired autistic children have more extensive evidence of brain abnormalities on most indices of function.

The most recent EEG studies (Olsson, Steffenburg, & Gillberg, 1988; Tsai & Stewart, 1982; Tsai, Tsai, & August, 1985; Waldo et al., 1978), based primarily on single recordings, have reported abnormalities in 32% to 45% of autistic children, a range comparable to the earlier findings of Small (1975) for single recordings. The largest and most recent of these studies found EEG abnormalities in 43 of 100 autistic children (Tsai et al., 1985). Abnormalities included diffuse or focal spikes or slow waves and a paroxysmal spike wave activity; a mixed discharge was the most common pattern. The abnormalities tended to be bilateral; when unilateral, they did not show a consistent predilection for any particular brain region. Although data based on subjects selected according to current diagnostic practices in autism research are not available, the existing data indicate a significant incidence of EEG abnormalities far exceeding the known incidence of seizures in autistic individuals. The early EEG and seizure literature emphasizing the prevalence of hypsarrhythmia and infantile spasms in autism likely reflected the inclusion of individuals with tuberous sclerosis, and thus such findings are not likely to have implications for autism outside of the context of tuberous sclerosis. The tendency of these early studies to include cases of autism with a wide range of causes of brain damage and abnormality other than autism make it difficult to determine what EEG patterns and seizure types are related to autism. A study of EEG patterns and seizure types, using current diagnostic criteria for autism and separately considered cases identified as having causes of brain damage other than autism, would be helpful in updating the understanding of these issues and their implications for current assessment and treatment of the majority of autism cases, in which such disorders are not present.

Neurologic Complications: Epilepsy

The development of epilepsy in autism has been well documented and is estimated to have a cumulative prevalence by young adulthood of 20% to 35% of the autism population, based on the occurrence of readily identifiable major motor seizures. Two longitudinal studies that followed autistic individuals from early childhood into early adulthood have provided evidence of seizure onset at all ages and a cumulative incidence of 25% (Lockyer & Rutter, 1970) and 33% (Gillberg & Steffenburg, 1987). As with EEG abnormalities, the occurrence of epilepsy was more common in the more severely impaired individuals. Early childhood (Volkmar & Nelson, 1990) and adolescence (Deykin & MacMahon, 1979) have been reported to be peak periods of seizure onset (Gillberg & Steffenburg, 1987; Rutter, 1970), but seizures can begin at any age in autism, as demonstrated by the longitudinal studies.

The Lockyer and Rutter (1970) longitudinal study also reported the occurrence of neurologic regression during adolescence in 12% of the subjects, usually in association with the onset of seizures: "The deterioration usually began with a loss of language skills associated with inertia and intellectual decline. In half of these cases, the deterioration was accompanied by the development of fits." Little else appears in the literature concerning the prevalence of such cases or the etiology of the deterioration.

Recent papers on seizures in autism have emphasized the occurrence of partial complex seizures. The first such report resulted from the serendipitous observation of electrographic seizures in two autistic children hospitalized for behavior problems (Gillberg & Schaumann, 1983). With the guidance of telemetry, clinical seizures corresponding to the epileptiform discharges were identified. Control of the seizures with anticonvulsant medication resulted in major improvement in the level of function and severity of the autistic symptoms in these two cases. Gillberg and Schaumann (1983) emphasized the difficulty in recognizing this type of seizure in the autistic population, because the behavioral manifestations of these seizures were likely to be attributed to autism.

In a population-based study of children with autism and autistic-like conditions that included cases due to tuberous sclerosis and other causes of brain abnormality, Olsson et al. (1988) found psychomotor seizures in 20% of cases. Psychomotor seizures commonly accompanied other types of seizures, and thus a mixed seizure pattern was the most common pattern in their population. Consistent with the clinical observation of partial complex seizure activity, the EEG abnormalities in this population had a predilection for the temporal lobe and phylogenetically older regions of the brain. In addition to the previously recognized prevalence of partial complex seizures, this study emphasized that the association between epilepsy and autism was with the autism, and not with the concomitant mental retardation.

The clinical recognition of complex partial seizures in the autistic population is complicated by the lack of sufficient clinical familiarity with autism on the part of most neurologists consulted to evaluate seizures; the lack of familiarity of psychiatrists and psychologists with complex partial seizures; the tendency by all professionals to automatically attribute abnormal behavior to autism; and the lack of 1:1 correspondence between clinical seizures and EEG abnormalities, with disparities in both directions, i.e., abnormal EEGs without epilepsy and epilepsy without electrographic correlate using routine recording techniques. Staring (with or without conjugate deviation of the eyes) and arrest of activity, or episodes of irritability evolving to aggression are typical clinical manifestations of such seizures in autistic individuals.

The association of one particular seizure type, infantile spasms, with autism was common in the early epilepsy and EEG literature in autism. Such cases were most likely related to the inclusion of individuals with tuberous sclerosis, who frequently exhibit autistic symptomatology. The presence of infantile spasms or jacknife seizures, in which the infant or young child suddenly bends forward at the waist, should therefore suggest the possibility of tuberous sclerosis. A Wood's lamp examination of the skin for signs of tuberous sclerosis should be a routine part of the pediatrician's assessment of autistic and autistic-like children.

Recently, a few articles have appeared suggesting that some cases of autism, Pervasive Developmental Disorder, and Childhood Disintegrative Disorder presenting with language regression are cases of Landau-Kleffner syndrome, or epileptic aphasia, and that such cases may be amenable to corticosteroid treatment. The first issue raised is whether a diagnostic error has been made. The pervasive developmental disorders are clinically defined disorders, and it is well established that a small proportion of individuals with this clinical syndrome have one of a wide range of identifiable etiologies. However, the presence of such an etiology does not preclude the individual from also having the clinical syndrome of Pervasive Developmental Disorder. The issue therefore is not one of errors in clinical diagnosis, where cases of Landau-Kleffner syndrome are mistaken for Autism Disorder or Pervasive Developmental Disorder Not Otherwise Specified.

The second issue raised is whether seizures cause the regression that occurs in approximately one-third of individuals presenting with autism and Pervasive Developmental Disorder. Even within the population of individuals with Landau-Kleffner syndrome, seizures appear only in some cases to be etiologic of the aphasia, as evidenced by onset of seizures followed by a fluctuating aphasia which resolves with anticonvulsant control of the seizures. In other cases, however, either there are no seizures or EEG abnormalities, or the seizures appear to be a consequence of the same process that has caused the aphasia. Seizures and epileptiform EEG abnormalities thus do not appear to be the etiologic agent causing language regression in many cases of Landau-Kleffner syndrome. The presence and causal relationship of EEG abnormalities and seizures to the language regression has also been observed to be highly variable in the pervasive developmental disorders (Tuchman, 1995).

Rather than diagnostic accuracy or seizures, the major scientific and clinical issue in need of consideration at present is whether children presenting with language regression might have a pathophysiologic mechanism that can be treated with the administration of steroids. The normal or near normal development of these children prior to the regression suggests that they have the genetic capacity and mechanisms to produce normal brain structure, but that something happens to destabilize and disrupt the synaptic connections. It is theoretically feasible, therefore, that corticosteroids could interrupt this destabilization and deterioration process, since corticosteroids are known to stabilize neuronal connections and are protective against the neurologic deterioration of Alzheimer's disease. However, this is a hypothesis and little to no data exist in autism to provide an answer. However, the morbidity and mortality associated with the use of high dose steroids have been well documented in the treatment of infantile spasms, and are not to be taken lightly. The exploration of this possible experimental treatment should proceed with caution within the context of carefully controlled trials in which subjects are clinically well characterized at presentation and at each follow-up by experts in the clinical diagnosis of autism, who are independent of the treating physicians. In addition, it is important that a comparable control group be followed to define outcome in the absence of such treatment.

Cases presenting with regression past 3 years of age should be carefully evaluated for degenerative neurologic diseases of childhood, some of which have specific treatments. Cases of language regression clearly related to epileptiform EEGs and clinical seizures should be treated first with traditional anticonvulsants before more risky treatment is considered.

CONTEMPORARY NEUROBIOLOGIC MODELS FOR AUTISM

Early theories of the clinical pathophysiology of autism generally postulated a single primary deficit in basic cognitive abilities associated with information acquisition, with the responsible neuropathology in a localized region of the brain. Current neurobiologic theories postulate single or multiple primary clinical deficits in higher-order cognitive processing abilities, abnormalities at the neural systems level or in multiple structures at several levels of the neuraxis, and the involvement of cerebral cortex in the final common pathway for the clinical symptomatology. These theories are hypotheses based on recently generated data, but key aspects of each of these theories are speculation and are not supported by empirical data. A particular gap is in the lack of objective data documenting a relationship between laboratory test abnormalities and "real life" behavioral abnormalities. Cognitive psychology research has provided some examples of how this gap can be bridged. For example, research on referential looking, the analysis of executive dysfunction using an information processing approach, and theory of mind deficits have contributed significantly to the understanding of the basis of abnormal behavior in autism.

At present, four theories are conceptualized in neurologic terms: (a) the executive function-frontal systems theory proposed by Ozonoff, Pennington, and Rogers; (b) the control mechanisms of attention-frontal cortex, parietal cortex-neocerebellum theory proposed by Courchesne and colleagues; (c) the representational memory-limbic system theory proposed by Bauman and Kemper, DeLong, and Bachivalier; and (d) the complex information processing-neocortical systems theory proposed by Minshew, Goldstein, and Siegel.

Fundamentally, the first two theories, the executive function and control of attention theories, hypothesize a basic deficit in a subunit of cognitive processing as underlying all the clinical deficits in autism, thus unifying the social, language, cognitive, and behavioral abnormalities at a clinical level. Although introduced as two entirely separate deficits and theories, the cognitive flexibility and shifting attention deficits described by these theories seem to be different terms for the same cognitive phenomenon. The term *shifting attention* suggests that the deficit is in a simple shift of attentional focus at the perceptual level, but the task paradigm used to support this model actually involves a complex set of contingencies with significant working memory and executive function demands. Regardless of the identity (or lack of identity) of these deficits, the tasks used to demonstrate the executive function and the complex attentional deficits are both widely considered to assess frontal lobe function.

The third model proposes a central role for the limbic system in the association of meaning to information. However, the neuropsychologic deficits attributed to a representational memory deficit in this theory involve tests that are classified as higher-order language and conceptual reasoning tests according to neuropsychologic convention. Thus, this model lacks construct validity at the clinical level. In addition, there is no data to document that the limbic system functions in the manner proposed.

The last theory proposes multiple primary deficits in higher order cognitive abilities as a result of a generalized deficit in the processing of complex information, and thus proposes that the syndrome will be unified at the biologic level by a common dependence on a specialized type of dendritic architecture rather than at the clinical level by a single primary deficit in one cognitive function.

These several theories reflect many new findings but also large residual gaps in the data, which allow multiple potentially feasible interpretations. Nonetheless, there have been major strides in the clinical and neurologic understanding of autism over the past 15 years. Future research will likely clarify existing ambiguities, witness the exploration of the developmental pathophysiology of autism, and examine the pathophysiology at the genetic level along with the various mechanisms that can trigger the pathophysiology of autism. These future research developments hold the key to the development of new clinical and neurobiologic interventions that can substantially affect the quality of life of these individuals and, ultimately, the fundamental course of this disorder.

Cross-References

Other aspects of the neurobiology of autism are discussed in Chapters 15, 17, and 18. Pharmacological treatment and routine health care are addressed in Chapters 32 and 33, respectively. Issues related to the spectrum of Pervasive Developmental Disorders and neuropsychology can be found in Chapters 39 and 40.

REFERENCES

Aarkrog, T. (1968). Organic factors in infantile psychoses and borderline psychoses. *Danish Medical Bulletin, 15,* 283–288.

Aminoff, M.J. (1992). *Electrodiagnosis in clinical neurology.* New York: Churchill Livingston.

Arin, D.M., Bauman, M.L., & Kemper, T.L. (1991). The distribution of Purkinje cell loss in the cerebellum in autism. *Neurology, 41,* 307 (Abstract No. 676P).

Bailey, A., Le Couteur, A., Gottesman, I., Bolton, P., Simonoff, E., Yuzda, E., & Rutter, M. (1995). Autism as a strongly genetic disorder: Evidence from a British twin study. *Psychological Medicine, 25,* 63–78.

Bailey, A., Luthert, P., Bolton, P., Le Couteur, A., Rutter, M. (1993). Autism and megalencephaly. *Lancet, 341,* 1225–1226.

Bauman, M.L., & Kemper, T.L. (1984). The brain in infantile autism: A histoanatomic report. *Neurology, 34,* 275 (Abstract No. 10).

Bauman, M.L., & Kemper, T.L. (1985). Histoanatomic observations of the brain in early infantile autism. *Neurology, 35,* 866–874.

Bauman, M.L., & Kemper, T.L. (Eds.). (1994). Neuroanatomic observations of the brain in autism. *The neurobiology of autism* (pp. 119–145). Baltimore: Johns Hopkins University Press.

Bauman, M.L., & Kemper, T.L. (1995). Brain weight appears to abnormally alter with age in autism. Personal communication.

Bauman, M.L., & Kemper, T.L. (1996). Observations on the Purkinje cells in the cerebellar vermis in autism. *Journal of Neuropathology and Experimental Neurology, 55,* 613 (Abstract No. 34).

Bolton, P., MacDonald, H., Pickles, A., Rios, P., Hoode, S., Crowson, M., Bailey, A., & Rutter, M. (1994). A case-control family history study of autism. *Journal of Child Psychology and Psychiatry, 35,* 877–900.

Boucher, J., & Warrington, E.K. (1976). Memory deficits in early infantile autism: Some similarities to the amnestic syndrome. *British Journal of Psychology, 67,* 73–87.

Brown, J.L. (1963). Follow-up of children with atypical development (infantile psychosis). *American Journal of Orthopsychiatry, 33,* 855.

Buchwald, J.S., Erwin, R., Van Lancker, D., Guthrie, D., Schwafel, J., & Tanguay, P. (1992). Midlatency auditory evoked responses: P1 abnormalities in adult autistic subjects. *Electroencephalography and Clinical Neurophysiology, 84,* 164–171.

Campbell, M.S., Rosenbloom, S., Perry, R., George, A.E., Kricheff, I.I., Anderson, L., Small, A.M., & Jennings, S.J. (1982). Computerized axial tomography in young autistic children. *American Journal of Psychiatry, 139,* 510–512.

Chiappa, K., & Gladstone, K. (1978). The limits of normal variations in waves I through VII of the human brain stem auditory response. *Neurology, 28,* 402.

Ciesielski, K.T., Allen, P.S., Sinclair, B.D., Pabst, H.F., Yanossky, R., & Ludwig, R. (1990). Hypoplasia of cerebellar vermis in autism and childhood leukemia. In *Proceedings of the 5th International Child Neurology Congress,* Tokyo, Japan, (Abstract No. 650).

Ciesielski, K.T., Courchesne, E., & Elmasian, R. (1990). Effects of focused selective attention tasks on event-related potentials in autistic and normal individuals. *Electroencephalography and Clinical Neurophysiology, 75,* 207–220.

Ciesielski, K.T., & Knight, J.E. (1994). Cerebellar abnormality in autism: A nonspecific effect of early brain damage. *Acta Neurobiologiae Experimentalis (Warszawa), 54,* 151–154.

Clarke, S., Kraftsik, R., Van der Loos, H., & Innocenti, G.M. (1989). Forms and measures of adult and developing human corpus callosum: Is there sexual dimorphism? *Journal of Comparative Neurology, 280,* 213–230.

Coleman, M. (1979). Studies of the autistic syndromes. In R. Katzman (Ed.), *Congenital and acquired cognitive disorders* (pp. 265–303). New York: Raven Press.

Coleman, P.D., Romano, J., Lapham, L., & Simon, W. (1985). Cell counts in cerebral cortex in an autistic patient. *Journal of Autism and Developmental Disorders, 15,* 245–255.

Courchesne, E. (1978). Neurophysiological correlates of cognitive development: Changes in long-latency event-related potentials from childhood to adulthood. *Electroencephalography and Clinical Neurophysiology, 45,* 468–482.

Courchesne, E., Courchesne, R.Y., Hicks, G., & Lincoln, A.J. (1985). Functioning of the brainstem auditory pathway in non-retarded autistic individuals. *Electroencephalography and Clinical Neurophysiology, 61,* 491–501.

Courchesne, E., Elmasian, R., & Yeung-Courchesne, R. (1987). Electrophysiological correlates of cognitive processing: P3b and Nc, basic, clinical, and developmental research. In A.M. Halliday, S.R. Butler, & R. Paul (Eds.), *A textbook of clinical neurophysiology* (pp. 645–676). New York: John Wiley & Sons.

Courchesne, E., Kilman, B.A., Galambos, R., & Lincoln, A.J. (1984). Autism: Processing of novel auditory information assessed by event-related brain potentials. *Electroencephalography and Clinical Neurophysiology, 59,* 238–248.

Courchesne, E., Lincoln, A.J., Kilman, B.A., & Galambos, R. (1985). Event-related brain potential correlates of the processing of novel visual and auditory information in autism. *Journal of Autism and Developmental Disorders, 15,* 55–76.

Courchesne, E., Lincoln, A.J., Yeung-Courchesne, R., Elmasian, R., & Grillon, C. (1989). Pathophysiologic findings in non-retarded autism and receptive developmental language disorders. *Journal of Autism and Developmental Disorders, 19,* 1–17.

Courchesne, E., Saitoh, O., Yeung-Courchesne, R., Press, G.A., Lincoln, A.J., Haas, R.H., & Schreibman, L. (1994). Abnormality of cerebellar vermian lobules VI and VII in patients with infantile autism: Identification of hypoplastic and hyperplastic subgroups with MR

Imaging. *American Journal of Roentgenology, 162,* 123–130.

Courchesne, E., Yeung-Courchesne, R., Press, G.A., Hesselink, J.R., & Jernigan, T.L. (1988). Hypoplasia of cerebellar vermal lobules VI and VII in autism. *New England Journal of Medicine, 318,* 1349–1354.

Creak, M., & Pampiglione, G. (1969). Clinical and EEG studies on a group of 35 psychotic children. *Developmental Medicine and Child Neurology, 11,* 218–227.

Creasey, J., Rumsey, J.M., Schwartz, M., Duara, R., Rapoport, J.L., & Rapoport, S.I. (1986). Brain morphometry in autistic men as measured by volumetric computed tomography. *Archives of Neurology, 32,* 669–672.

Damasio, A.R. (1984). Autism [Editorial]. *Archives of Neurology, 41,* 481.

Damasio, A.R., & Maurer, R.G. (1978). A neurological model for childhood autism. *Archives of Neurology, 35,* 777–786.

Damasio, H., Maurer, R.G., Damasio, A.R., & Chui, H.C. (1980). Computerized tomographic scan findings in patients with autistic behavior. *Archives of Neurology, 37,* 504–510.

Darby, J.H. (1976). Neuropathological aspects of psychosis in childhood. *Journal of Autism and Childhood Schizophrenia, 6,* 339–352.

Davidovitch, M., Patterson, B., & Gartside, P. (in press). Head circumference measurements in children with autism. *Journal of Child Neurology.*

Dawson, G., Finley, C., Phillips, S., Galpert, L., & Lewy, A. (1988). Reduced P3 amplitude of the event-related brain potential: Its relationship to language ability in autism. *Journal of Autism and Developmental Disorders, 18,* 493–504.

Delong, G.R. (1978). A neuropsychological interpretation of infantile autism. In M. Rutter & E. Schopler (Eds.), *Autism* (pp. 207–218). New York: Plenum Press.

DeMyer, M.K. (1975). Research in infantile autism: A strategy and its results. *Biological Psychiatry, 10,* 433–452.

Deykin, E.Y., & MacMahon, G. (1979). The incidence of seizure, among children with autistic symptoms. *American Journal of Psychiatry, 136,* 1310–1312.

Dunn, M. (1994). Neurophysiologic observations in autism and implications for neurologic dysfunction. In M.L. Bauman & T.L. Kemper (Eds.), *The neurobiology of autism* (pp. 45–65). Baltimore: Johns Hopkins University Press.

Eccles, J.C., Iro, M., & Szentagothai, J. (1967). *The cerebellum as a neuronal machine.* New York: Springer.

Erwin, R., Van Lancker, D., Guthrie, D., Schwafel, J., Tanguay, P., & Buchwald, J.S. (1991). P3 responses to prosodic stimuli in adult autistic subjects. *Electroencephalography and Clinical Neurophysiology, 80,* 561–571.

Filipek, P.A., Richelme, C., Kennedy, D.N., Rademacher, J., Pitcher, D.A., Zidel, S., & Caviness, V.S. (1992). Morphometric analysis of the brain in developmental language disorders and autism. *Annals of Neurology, 32,* 475 (Abstract No. 166).

Finley, W.W., Faux, S.F., Hutcheson, J., & Amstutz, L. (1985). Long-latency event-related potentials in the evaluation of cognitive function in children. *Neurology, 35,* 323.

Fish, B., & Shapiro, T. (1965). A typology of children's psychiatric disorders. *Journal of the American Academy of Child Psychiatry, 4,* 32–52.

Gaffney, G.R., Kuperman, S., Tsai, L.Y., & Minchin, S. (1988). Morphological evidence for brainstem involvement in infantile autism. *Biological Psychiatry, 24,* 578–586.

Gaffney, G.R., Kuperman, S., Tsai, L.Y., Minchin, S., & Hassanein, K.M. (1987). Midsagittal magnetic resonance imaging of autism. *British Journal of Psychiatry, 151,* 831–833.

Gaffney, G.R., & Tsai, L.Y. (1987). Brief report: Magnetic resonance imaging of high-level autism. *Journal of Autism and Developmental Disorders, 17,* 433–438.

Galambos, R., & Hecox, K.E. (1978). Clinical applications of the auditory brain stem response. *Otolaryngological Clinics of North America, 11,* 709–722.

Garber, H.J., & Ritvo, E.R. (1992). Magnetic resonance imaging of the posterior fossa in autistic adults. *American Journal of Psychiatry, 149,* 245–247.

Garber, H.J., Ritvo, E.R., Chui, L.C., Griswold, V.J., Kashanian, A., & Oldendorf, W.H. (1989). A magnetic resonance imaging study of autism: Normal fourth ventricle size and absence of pathology. *American Journal of Psychiatry, 146,* 532–535.

Gillberg, C., Rosenthal, U., & Johansson, E. (1983). Auditory brainstem responses in childhood psychosis. *Journal of Autism and Developmental Disorders, 13,* 181–195.

Gillberg, C., & Schaumann, H. (1983). Epilepsy presenting as infantile autism? Two case studies. *Neuropaediatrics, 14,* 206–212.

Gillberg, C., & Steffenburg, S. (1987). Outcome and prognostic factors in infantile autism and similar conditions: A population-based study of 46 cases followed through puberty. *Journal of Autism and Developmental Disorders, 17,* 273–287.

Gillberg, C., & Svendsen, P. (1983). Childhood psychosis and computed tomographic brain scan findings. *Journal of Autism and Developmental Disorders, 13,* 19–33.

Goldman-Rakic, P.S. (1987). Circuitry of primate prefrontal cortex and regulation of behavior by representational memory. In V.B. Mountcastle, F. Plum, & S.R. Geiger (Eds.), *Handbook of physiology: Section 1. The nervous system: Vol. 5. Higher functions of the brain, Part 1* (pp. 373–417). Bethesda, MD: American Physiology Society.

Goodin, D.S. (1992). Event-related (endogenous) potentials. In M.J. Aminoff (Ed.), *Electrodiagnosis in clinical neurology* (pp. 627–648). New York: Churchill Livingstone.

Goodin, D.S., Squires, K., & Starr, A. (1978). Long latency event-related components of the auditory evoked potential in dementia. *Brain, 101,* 635–648.

Greenfield, J.G. (1954). *The spino-cerebellar degenerations.* Springfield, IL: Charles Thomas.

Grillon, C., Courchesne, E., & Akshoomoff, N. (1989). Brainstem and middle latency auditory evoked potentials in autism and developmental language disorder. *Journal of Autism and Developmental Disorders, 19,* 255–269.

Gubbay, S.S., Lobascher, M., & Kingerlee, P. (1970). A neurological appraisal of autistic children: Results of a western Australian survey. *Developmental Medicine and Child Neurology, 12,* 422–429.

Harcherik, D.F., Cohen, D.J., Ort, S., Paul, R., Shaywitz, B.A., Volkmar, F.R., Rothman, S.L.G., & Leckman, J.F. (1985). Computed tomographic brain scanning in four neuropsychiatric disorders of childhood. *American Journal of Psychiatry, 142,* 731–734.

Hashimoto, T., Tayama, M., Murakawa, K., Yoshimoto, T., Miyazaki, M., Harada, M., & Kuroda, Y. (1995). Development of the brainstem and cerebellum in autistic patients. *Journal of Autism and Developmental Disorders, 25,* 1–18.

Hauser, S.L., DeLong, G.R., & Rosman, N.P. (1975). Pneumographic findings in the infantile autism syndrome: A correlation with temporal lobe disease. *Brain, 98,* 677–688.

Hier, D.B., LeMay, M., & Rosenberger, P.B. (1979). Autism and unfavorable left-right asymmetries of the brain. *Journal of Autism and Developmental Disorders, 9,* 153–159.

Holmes, G., & Stewart, T.G. (1988). On the connection of the inferior olives to the cerebellum in man. *Brain, 31,* 125–137.

Holttum, J.R., Minshew, N.J., Sanders, R.S., & Phillips, N.E. (1992). Magnetic resonance imaging of the posterior fossa in autism. *Biological Psychiatry, 32,* 1091–1101.

Hsu, M., Yeung-Courchesne, R., Courchesne, E., & Press, G.A. (1991). Absence of pontine abnormality in infantile autism. *Archives of Neurology, 48,* 1160–1163.

Hutt, S.J., Hutt, C., Lee, D., & Ounsted, C. (1965). A behavioral and electroencephalographic study of autistic children. *Journal of Psychiatric Research, 3,* 181–197.

Kemner, C., Verbaten, M.N., Cuperus, J.M., Camfferman, G., & van Engeland, H. (1994). Visual and somatosensory event-related brain potentials in autistic children and three different control groups. *Electroencephalography and Clinical Neurophysiology, 92,* 225–237.

Kleiman, M.D., Neff, S., & Rosman, N.P. (1992). The brain in infantile autism: Is the cerebellum really abnormal? *Neurology, 2,* 753–760.

Kohen-Raz, R., Volkmar, F.R., & Cohen, D.J. (1992). Postural control in children with autism. *Journal of Autism and Developmental Disorders, 22,* 419–432.

Kurtzberg, D., Vaughan, H.G., Jr., Courchesne, E., Friedman, D., Harter, M.R., & Putnam, L.E. (1984). Normal and aberrant development: Developmental aspects of event-related potentials. *Annals of the New York Academy of Science, 425,* 300–318.

Lainhart, J.E., Piven, J., Wzorek, M., Landa, R., Santangelo, S.L., Coon, H., & Folstein, S.E. (in press). Macrocephaly in children and adults with autism. *Journal of Child and Adolescent Psychiatry.*

Leigh, R.J., & Zee, D.S. (1991). *The neurology of eye movements* (2nd ed.). Philadelphia: Davis.

Lincoln, A.J., Courchesne, E., Harms, L., & Allen, M. (1993). Contextual probability evaluation in autistic, receptive developmental language disorder, and control children: Event-related brain potential evidence. *Journal of Autism and Developmental Disorders, 23,* 37–58.

Lockyer, L., & Rutter, M. (1970). A five to fifteen-year follow-up study of infantile psychosis: Patterns of cognitive ability. *British Journal of Social and Clinical Psychology, 9,* 152–163.

Lotter, V. (1974). Factors related to outcome in autistic children. *Journal of Autism and Child Schizophrenia, 4,* 263–277.

Mason-Brothers, A., Ritvo, E.R., Guze, B., Mo, A., Freeman, B.J., Funderburk, S.J., & Schroth, P.C. (1987). Pre-, peri-, and postnatal factors in 184 autistic patients from single and multiple incidence families. *Journal of*

American Academy of Child and Adolescent Psychiatry, 26, 39–42.

Mason-Brothers, A., Ritvo, E.R., Pingree, C., Petersen, P.B., Jenson, W.R., McMahon, W.M., Freeman, B.J., Jorde, L.B., Spencer, M.J., Mo, A., & Ritvo, A. (1990). The UCLA-University of Utah epidemiologic survey of autism: prenatal, pernatal, and postnatal factors. *Pediatrics, 86,* 514–519.

Maurer, R.G., & Demasio, A.R. (1982). Childhood autism from the point of view of behavioral neurology. *Journal of Autism and Developmental Disorders, 12,* 195–205.

McClelland, R.J., Eyre, D.G., Watson, D., Calvert, G.J., & Sherrard, F. (1992). Central conduction time in childhood autism. *British Journal of Psychiatry, 160,* 659–663.

Minshew, N.J., & Dombrowski, S.M. (1994). In vivo neuroanatomy of autism: Imaging studies. In M. Bauman & T.L. Kemper (Eds.), *The neurobiology of autism* (pp. 66–85). Baltimore: Johns Hopkins University Press.

Minshew, N.J., Furman, J.M., Goldstein, G., & Payton, J.B. (1990). The cerebellum in autism: A central role or an epiphenomenon? *Neurology, 40,* 173, (Abstract No. 204S).

Minshew, N.J., Goldstein, G., Muenz, L.R., & Payton, J.B. (1992). Neuropsychological functioning in non-mentally-retarded autistic individuals. *Journal of Clinical and Experimental Neuropsychology, 14,* 749–761.

Minshew, N.J., Goldstein, G., & Siegel, D.J. (1995). Neuropsychological functioning in autism: Evidence for a generalized deficit in complex information processing. *Society for Research and Child Development, 147.*

Minshew, N.J., Sweeney, J.A., & Furman, J.M. (in press). Evidence for a primary neocortical system abnormality in autism. *Society for Neuroscience Abstracts, 21,* 735 (Abstract No. 293.13).

Murakami, J.W., Courchesne, E., Press, G.A., Yeung-Courchesne, R., & Hesselink, J.R. (1989). Reduced cerebellar hemisphere size and its relationship to vermal hypoplasia in autism. *Archives of Neurology, 46,* 689–694.

Norman, R.M. (1940). Cerebellar atrophy associated with *état marbre* of the basal ganglia. *Journal of Neurological Psychiatry, 3,* 311–318.

Novick, B., Kurtzberg, A., & Vaughan, H.G., Jr. (1979). An electrophysiologic indication of defective information storage in childhood autism. *Psychiatry Research, 1,* 101–108.

Novick, B., Vaughan, H.G., Jr., Kurtzberg, D., & Simson, R. (1980). An electrophysiologic

indication of auditory processing defects in autism. *Psychiatry Research, 3,* 107–114.

Olsson, I., Steffenburg, S., & Gillberg, C. (1988). Epilepsy in autism and autistic-like conditions. *Archives of Neurology, 45,* 666–668.

Ornitz, E.M., Atwell, C.W., Kaplan, A.R., & Westlake, J.R. (1985). Brain-stem dysfunction in autism. *Archives of General Psychiatry, 42,* 1018–1025.

Ornitz, E.M., Brown, M.B., Mason, A., & Putnam, N.H. (1974). Effect of visual input on vestibular nystagmus in autistic children. *Archives of General Psychiatry, 31,* 369–375.

Ornitz, E.M., Forsythe, A.B., & de la Pena, A. (1973). The effect of vestibular and auditory stimulation on the rapid eye movements of REM sleep in normal children. *Electroencephalography and Clinical Neurophysiology, 34,* 379–390.

Ornitz, E.M., Lane, S.J., Sugiyama, T., & de Traversay, J. (1993). Startle modulation studies in autism. *Journal of Autism and Developmental Disorders, 23,* 619–637.

Ornitz, E.M., Mo, A., & Olson, S.T. (1980). Influence of click sound pressure direction on brainstem responses in children. *Audiology, 19,* 245–254.

Ornitz, E.M., & Ritvo, E.R. (1968a). Neurophysiologic mechanisms underlying perceptual inconstancy in autistic and schizophrenic children. *Archives of General Psychiatry, 19,* 22–27.

Ornitz, E.M., & Ritvo, E.R. (1968b). Perceptual inconstancy in early infantile autism. *Archives of General Psychiatry, 18,* 76–98.

Ornitz, E.M., Ritvo, E., Brown, M., La Franchi, S., Parmelee, T., & Walter, R. (1969). The EEG and rapid eye movements during REM sleep in autistic and normal children. *Electroencephalography and Clinical Neurophysiology, 26,* 167–175.

Ornitz, E.M., Ritvo, E.R., Panman, L.E., Lee, Y.H., Carr, E.M., & Walker, R.D. (1968). The auditory evoked response in normal and autistic children during sleep. *Electroencephalography and Clinical Neurophysiology, 25,* 221–230.

Ornitz, E.M., & Walter, D.O. (1975). The effect of sound pressure waveform on human brainstem auditory evoked responses. *Brain Research, 92,* 490–498.

Ozonoff, S., Pennington, B.F., & Rogers, S.J. (1991). Executive function deficits in high-functioning autistic individuals: Relationship to theory of mind. *Journal of Child Psychology and Psychiatry, 32,* 1081–1105.

Piven, J., Arndt, S., Bailey, J., Havercamp, S., Andreasen, N.C., & Palmer, P. (1995). An MRI study of brain size in autism. *American Journal of Psychiatry, 152,* 1145–1149.

Piven, J., Bailey, J., Ranson, B.J., & Arndt, S. (in press). An MRI Study of the Corpus Callosum in Autism. *Journal of Autism and Developmental Disorders.*

Piven, J., Bailey, J., Ranson, B.J., & Arndt, S. (submitted). No difference in hippocampus volume detected on MRI in autistic individuals.

Piven, J., Nehme, E., Simon, J., Barta, P., Pearlson, G., & Folstein, S.E. (1992). Magnetic resonance imaging in autism: Measurement of the cerebellum, pons, and fourth ventricle. *Biological Psychiatry, 31,* 491–504.

Polich, J., & Starr, A. (1984). Evoked potentials in aging. In M.L. Albert (Ed.), *Clinical Neurology of Aging* (p. 149). New York: Oxford University Press.

Prior, M., & Hoffmann, W. (1990). Brief report: Neuropsychological testing of autistic children through an exploration with frontal lobe tests. *Journal of Autism and Developmental Disorders, 4,* 581–590.

Prior, M.R., Tress, B., Hoffman, W.L., & Boldt, D. (1984). Computed tomographic study of children with classic autism. *Archives of Neurology, 41,* 482–484.

Rapin, I. (1991). Autistic children: Diagnostic and clinical features. *Pediatrics, 87*(Suppl), 751–760.

Raymond, G., Bauman, M.L., & Kemper, T.L. (1989). The hippocampus in autism: Golgi analysis. *Annals of Neurology, 26,* 483–484.

Ritvo, E., Freeman, B.J., Scheibel, A., Duong, T., Robinson, H., Guthrie, D., & Ritvo, A. (1986). Lower Purkinje cell counts in the cerebella of four autistic subjects: Initial finding of the UCLA-NSAC autopsy research report. *American Journal of Psychiatry, 143,* 862–866.

Ritvo, E.R., Ornitz, E.M., Eviatar, A., Markham, C.H., Brown, M.B., & Mason, A. (1969). Decreased postrotatory nystagmus in early infantile autism. *Neurology, 19,* 653–658.

Ritvo, E.R., Ornitz, E.M., Walter, R.D., & Hanley, J. (1970). Correlation of psychiatric diagnoses and EEG findings: A double-blind study of 184 hospitalized children. *American Journal of Psychiatry, 126,* 112–120.

Rosenbloom, S., Campbell, M., & George, A.E. (1984). High resolution CT scanning in infantile autism: A quantitative approach. *Journal of the American Academy of Child Psychiatry, 23,* 72–77.

Rosenblum, S.M., Arick, J.R., Krug, D.A., Stubbs, E.G., Young, N.B., & Pelson, R.O. (1980). Auditory brainstem evoked responses in autistic children. *Journal of Autism and Developmental Disorders, 10,* 215–225.

Rosenhall, U., Johansson, E., & Gillberg, C. (1988). Oculomotor findings in autistic children. *Journal of Laryngology and Otology, 102,* 435–439.

Rumsey, J.M., Creasey, H., Stepanek, J.S., Dorwart, R., Patronas, N., Hamburger, S.D., & Duara, R. (1988). Hemispheric asymmetries, fourth ventricular size, and cerebellar morphology in autism. *Journal of Autism and Developmental Disorders, 18,* 127–137.

Rumsey, J.M., Grimes, A.M., Pikus, A.M., Duara, R., & Ismond, D.R. (1984). Auditory brainstem responses in pervasive developmental disorders. *Biological Psychiatry, 19,* 1403–1418.

Rumsey, J.M., & Hamburger, S.D. (1988). Neuropsychological findings in high-functioning men with infantile autism, residual state. *Journal of Clinical and Experimental Neuropsychology, 10,* 201–221.

Rumsey, J.M., & Hamburger, S.D. (1990). Neuropsychological divergence of high-level autism and severe dyslexia. *Journal of Autism and Developmental Disorders, 20,* 155–168.

Rutter, M. (1970). Autistic children. Infancy to adulthood. *Seminars in Psychiatry, 2,* 435–450.

Saitoh, O., Courchesne, E., Egaas, B., Lincoln, A.J., & Schreibman, L. (1995). Cross-sectional area of the posterior hippocampus in autistic patients with cerebellar and corpus callosum abnormalities. *Neurology, 45,* 317–324.

Schaeffer, G.B., Thompson, J.N., Bodensteiner, J.B., McConnell, J.M., Kimberling, W.J., Gay, C.T., Dutton, W.D., Hutchings, D.C., & Gray, S.B. (1996). Hypoplasia of the cerebellar vermis in neurogenetic syndromes. *Annals of Neurology, 39,* 382–385.

Skoff, B.F., Mirsky, A.F., & Turner, D. (1980). Prolonged brainstem transmission time in autism. *Psychiatric Research, 2,* 157–166.

Small, J.G. (1968). Epileptiform electroencephalographic abnormalities in mentally ill children. *Journal of Nervous and Mental Disorders, 147,* 341–348.

Small, J.G. (1975). EEG and neurophysiological studies of early infantile autism. *Biological Psychiatry, 10,* 355–397.

Squires, N., Squires, K., & Hillyard, S.A. (1975). Two varieties of long-latency positive waves evoked by unpredictable auditory stimuli in man. *Electroencephalography and Clinical Neurophysiology, 38,* 387–401.

Starr, A., Sohmer, H., & Celesia, G.G. (1978). Some applications of evoked potentials to patients with neurological and sensory impairment. In E. Callaway, P. Tueting, & S.H. Koslow (Eds.), *Event-related brain* potentials in man (pp. 155–196). San Francisco: Academic Press.

Stevens, J.R., & Milstein, V. (1970). Severe psychiatric disorders of childhood. *American Journal of Diseases of Children, 120,* 182.

Stockard, J.J., Stockard, J.E., & Sharbrough, F.W. (1978). Nonpathologic factors influencing brainstem auditory evoked potentials. *American Journal of EEG Technology, 18,* 177–209.

Strandburg, R.J., Marsh, J.T., Brown, W.S., Asarnow, R.F., Guthrie, D., & Higa, J. (1993). Event-related potentials in high-functioning adult autistics: Linguistic and nonlinguistic visual information processing tasks. *Neuropsychologia, 31,* 413–434.

Student, M., & Sohmer, H. (1978). Evidence from auditory nerve and brainstem evoked responses for an organic brain lesion in children with autistic traits. *Journal of Autism and Childhood Schizophrenia, 8,* 13–20.

Student, M., & Sohmer, H. (1979). Erratum. *Journal of Autism and Developmental Disorders, 9,* 309.

Sweeney, J.A., Mintun, M.A., Kwee, S., Wiseman, M.B., Brown, D.L., Rosenberg, D.R., & Carl, J.R. (1995). A positron emission tomography study of voluntary saccadic eye movements and spatial working memory. *Journal of Neurophysiology, 75,* 454–468.

Tanguay, P.E., & Edwards, R. (1982). Electrophysiological studies of autism: The whisper of the bang. *Journal of Autism and Developmental Disorders, 12,* 177–184.

Tanguay, P.E., Edwards, R.M., Buchwald, J., Schwafel, J., & Allen, V. (1982). Auditory brainstem responses in autistic children. *Archives of General Psychiatry, 39,* 174–180.

Taylor, M.J., Rosenblatt, B., & Linschoten, L. (1982). Electrophysiological study of the auditory system in autistic children. In A. Rothenberger (Ed.), *Event-related potentials in children.* Amsterdam, The Netherlands: Elsevier.

Thivierge, J., Bedard, C., Cote, R., & Maziade, M. (1990). Brainstem auditory evoked response and subcortical abnormalities in autism. *American Journal of Psychiatry, 12,* 1609–1613.

Tsai, L.Y., Jacoby, O.G., & Stewart, M.A. (1983). Morphological cerebral asymmetries in autistic children. *Biological Psychiatry, 18,* 317–327.

Tsai, L.Y., & Stewart, M.A. (1982). Handedness and EEG correlation in autistic children. *Biological Psychiatry, 17,* 595–598.

Tsai, L.Y., Tsai, M.C., & August, G.J. (1985). Brief report: Implications of EEG diagnoses in the subclassification of infantile autism. *Journal of Autism and Developmental Disorders, 15,* 339–344.

Tuchman, R.F. (1995). Regression in pervasive developmental disorders: Is there a relationship with Landau-Kleffner syndrome? *Annals of Neurology, 38,* 526 (Abstract No. 95).

Verbaten, M.N., Roelofs, J.W., van Engeland, H., Kenemans, J.K., & Slangen, J.L. (1991). Abnormal visual event-related potentials of autistic children. *Journal of Autism and Developmental Disorders, 21,* 449–470.

Vilensky, J.A., Damasio, A.R., & Maurer, R.G. (1981). Gait disturbances in patients with autistic behavior. *Archives of Neurology, 38,* 646–649.

Volkmar, F.R. (1992). Childhood Disintegrative Disorder: Issues for *DSM-IV. Journal of Autism and Developmental Disorders, 22,* 625–642.

Volkmar, F.R. (1994). Childhood Disintegrative Disorder. *Child and Adolescent Psychiatric Clinics of North America, 3,* 119–129.

Volkmar, F.R., & Nelson, D.S. (1990). Seizure disorders in autism. *Journal of the American Academy of Child and Adolescent Psychiatry, 1,* 127–129.

Waldo, M.C., Cohen, D.J., Caparulo, B.K., Young, G., Prichard, J.W., & Shaywitz, B.A. (1978). EEG profiles of neuropsychiatrically disturbed children. *American Academy of Child Psychiatry, 17,* 656–670.

White, P.T., DeMeyer, W., & DeMeyer, M. (1964). EEG abnormalities in early childhood schizophrenia. *American Journal of Psychiatry, 120,* 950–958.

Williams, R.S., Hauser, S.L., Purpura, D.P., Delong, G.R., & Swisher, C.N. (1980). Autism and mental retardation. *Archives of Neurology, 37,* 749–753.

Wong, V., & Wong, S.N. (1991). Brainstem auditory evoked potential study in children with autistic disorder. *Journal of Autism and Developmental Disorders, 21,* 329–340.

Woodhouse, W., Bailey, A., Rutter, M., Bolton, P., Baird, G., & Le Couteur, A. (1996). Head circumference in autism and other pervasive developmental disorders. *The Journal of Child Psychology and Psychiatry, 37,* 665–671.

Zimmerman, M.C., Morgan, D.E., & Dubno, J.R. (1987). Auditory brainstem evoked response characteristics in developing infants. *Annals of Otology Rhinology and Laryngology, 96,* 291.

CHAPTER 17

Genetic Influences and Autism

MICHAEL RUTTER, ANTHONY BAILEY, EMILY SIMONOFF, AND ANDREW PICKLES

In the first report that described autism, Kanner (1943) postulated that it was an inborn disorder. Yet, for many years, little attention was paid to possible genetic factors because occurrences of two autistic children in the same family were so infrequent (some 2% of cases in the literature reviewed by Smalley, Asarnow, & Spence, 1988). Early chromosome studies also failed to reveal any abnormalities.

Three developments changed the situation radically. First, aware that even a 2% rate of autism in siblings meant a huge increase in relative risk compared to the general population, Folstein and Rutter (1977a, 1977b) conducted the first systematic, general-population-based twin study and provided evidence of a strong genetic component. Second, discovery of the Fragile X anomaly led to the finding that a substantial minority of autistic individuals had this anomaly (Blomquist et al., 1985). From the early (albeit mistaken) belief that a stronger association existed between autism and the Fragile X than between mental retardation and the Fragile X, there evolved a major research interest in the associations as well as a renewal of interest in other chromosome anomalies that might be associated with autism (Gillberg & Wahlström, 1985). Third, clinical investigations encouraged a growing awareness that some cases of autism were associated with single-gene medical disorders that showed a Mendelian pattern (see Folstein & Piven, 1991; Folstein & Rutter, 1988).

Some of the claims made in these three areas of research were short-lived (see below). It is universally accepted now that genetic factors play a major role in autism even when no associated genetic disease such as Fragile X or tuberous sclerosis is evident. Indeed, autism is the most strongly genetic of all multifactorial psychiatric disorders (Rutter, Bailey, Bolton, & Le Couteur, 1993). Attention has turned, accordingly, to a more detailed consideration of specific issues relating to the role of genetic factors.

ASSOCIATIONS WITH SPECIFIC GENETIC DISORDERS

Two conditions make the strongest case for an association with autism: (a) the Fragile X anomaly (see Simonoff, Bolton, & Rutter, 1996, for an account of the several genetic abnormalities involved) and (b) tuberous sclerosis. For each condition, a detailed consideration of the evidence is informative for understanding the broad implications as well as the specific findings.

Fragile X Anomaly

The Fragile X anomaly occurs with about the same frequency as autism, is associated with mental retardation (both mild and severe), and receives its name from the appearance of a fragile site on the long arm of the X chromosome

A major portion of this chapter is based on "Autism: Towards an Integration of Clinical, Genetic, Neuropsychological and Neurobiological Perspectives," by A.J. Bailey, W. Phillips, and M. Rutter, 1996, *Journal of Child Psychology and Psychiatry.* Reproduced with permission.

when cultured in low-folate media (Warren & Nelson, 1994). The first reports of a link between the Fragile X anomaly and autism suggested that the anomaly occurred in at least 16% of autistic persons (Gillberg & Wahlström, 1985). When a larger number of subjects were pooled a few years later, the estimate dropped to 7% (Bolton & Rutter, 1990; Brown et al., 1986). Current estimates, based on new data, put the true rate at about 2.5%, and almost certainly below 5% (Bailey et al., 1993; Piven et al., 1991). The first point to consider, therefore, is why the estimate has fallen so dramatically.

Rutter, Bailey, Bolton, and Le Couteur (1994) suggested four reasons:

1. A publishing bias exists; positive associations tend to be published and negative ones are not.
2. With a small sample size, typical of these early studies, the proportion of false positives in the findings is higher than that with large samples (see Pocock, 1983).
3. Early reports were based on inclusion of very low (1% to 3%) rates of Fragile X expression, which do not have the same significance as rates of 4% and above. This was first evident from statistical analyses using latent class methods (Bolton et al., 1992), but it is no longer necessary to rely on demonstration of a Fragile X site using low-folate media. The Fragile X anomaly originates from a trinucleotide repeat sequence in the region containing the FMR-1 gene (Davies, 1991), which means that DNA methods can be used. These methods have shown that individuals with low rates of Fragile X expression do not have this abnormality (Gurling et al., 1997, submitted).
4. The initial reports of autism in individuals who were so identified because they had the Fragile X anomaly were mainly based on clinical impression rather than systematic standardized assessment. It is now apparent that, although Fragile X individuals can show typical autism, their pattern of social and communicative abnormalities more often takes a different form (Hagerman, 1990). Marked social anxiety, gaze avoidance, and an ambivalent social approach combined with a turning away of the face seem to be particularly characteristic (Cohen, Vietze, Sudhalter, Jenkins, & Brown, 1989; Sudhalter, Cohen, Silverman, & Wolfschein, 1990; Wolff, Gardner, Paccia, & Lappen, 1989). The cognitive features associated with the social deficits that accompany the Fragile X anomaly may also be different from those found in autism (Mazzocco, Pennington, & Hagerman, 1994).

Given this evidence of a lower rate of the Fragile X anomaly in individuals with autism, it is necessary to reconsider whether there is any specific association between the two. Einfeld, Malony, and Hall (1989) compared Fragile X males with controls matched for age and IQ. When no differences in autistic symptomatology were found between the two groups, these authors argued for a lack of a meaningful causal association. On the other hand, a 2.5% rate of Fragile X in autistic persons is well above the general population figures. The alternative is that the association arises only because both autism and the Fragile X are associated with mental retardation. In other words, the suggestion is that the basic association is between mental retardation and Fragile X, and the association between autism and Fragile X is secondary. In support of that possibility is the finding that the great majority of autistic individuals with the Fragile X are mentally retarded. On the other hand, there is no direct relationship between IQ and autism. For example, trisomy 21, the most common cause of mental retardation, is only infrequently associated with autism. It seems fair to conclude that: (a) there may be some specific association between Fragile X and autism, but (b) the association does not point strongly to any genetic mechanisms that may be involved in autism. A molecular genetic study of multiplex families by Hallmayer et al. (1994) appeared to exclude linkage to the FMR-1 gene (the gene associated with Fragile X) in the sample investigated.

For many years, there have been clinical reports of autistic features in individuals with tuberous sclerosis. This single-gene, autosomal-dominant, neurocutaneous disorder occurs in about 1 per 7,000 individuals (Osborne, Fryer, & Webb, 1991). It is characterized by a combination of skin lesions and neurological features, but protean abnormalities in other organs of the body also occur. Depigmented maculas that show up best in ultraviolet light are usually the earliest and most common skin lesion (but they occur occasionally in the general population). Facial angiofibromatosis, typically in a butterfly distribution, is often striking but may not appear until adolescence or adult life. Fibrous plaques on the forehead, shagreen patches (thickened skin) on the lower back, and fibromas of the nails also occur. Retinal hamartomas (phakomas), usually near the optic disk, may be revealed in an ophthalmoscopic examination. Glial nodules along the lateral walls of the lateral ventricles are present in some four-fifths of cases. They usually calcify and are identifiable on a cranial CT scan. About two-thirds of patients develop epileptic seizures, and a general learning disability is present in about two-fifths. About three-fourths of cases derive from new mutations (i.e., there is no family history). The physical manifestations of tuberous sclerosis vary greatly from individual to individual, even within the same family. A very mild condition may be manifest only in hypomelanotic maculas (Smalley, Burger, & Smith, 1994). Gene loci have been discovered on chromosome 9 (Fryer et al., 1987) and chromosome 16 (European Chromosome 16 TS Consortium, 1993). Each accounts for about half the cases.

Hunt and Dennis (1987), who used a checklist approach, reported that 50% of children with tuberous sclerosis showed autistic behavior. A later more systematic study (Hunt & Shepherd, 1993) showed that 24% of children with tuberous sclerosis met *DSM-III-R* criteria for autism, and an additional 19% showed autistic traits. The findings of Smalley and colleagues (Smalley, Smith, & Tanguay, 1991; Smalley, Tanguay, Smith, & Gutierrez, 1992) are broadly similar and Gillberg, Gillberg, and Ahlsén (1994) reported that 61% showed autism. There are fewer data on the proportion of autistic individuals with tuberous sclerosis and it has been necessary to make various extrapolations. These have produced figures ranging from 3% (Smalley et al., 1992) to 9% (Gillberg et al., 1994). Currently available data do not provide a precise figure, although it is probably nearer the bottom than the top of the range mentioned. A low percentage would

still establish a more specific association than has been found to date with any other genetically determined medical condition.

Again, the question must be raised: What does the association mean? It is likely to be causal in some way (because of its relative strength) but it is noteworthy that the main association occurs when tuberous sclerosis is accompanied by both mental retardation and epilepsy. It has been reported in the absence of mental retardation (Gillberg, Steffenburg, & Jakobsson, 1987); nevertheless, autism seems much less common when tuberous sclerosis is associated with normal intelligence, especially if epilepsy is not found. The latter observation suggests that the risk for autism arises through the brain disorder accompanying tuberous sclerosis and not because a gene for autism is closely associated with the locus of one of the two genes known to be linked with tuberous sclerosis.

Other Genetic Conditions and Chromosome Abnormalities

The literature includes reports of autistic features in individuals with untreated phenylketonuria (see Folstein & Rutter, 1988), but because none of the reports was based on standardized assessments of autism, the strength of the association, and perhaps even its reality, must be in some doubt. Untreated phenylketonuria is now a rare occurrence; hence, it must be an even rarer cause of autism. Gillberg and Forsell (1984) published case reports of two children with autism and a third with an autistic-like condition who showed neurofibromatosis. A few similar cases have been reported, but there are no systematic studies that would allow any estimate of the validity, or strength, of the association. Possibly, the association is real, even if it does not account for many cases; as with tuberous sclerosis, a combination of skin lesions and neural tumors is involved, which may be relevant. A diverse range of other genetically determined medical conditions have been reported from time to time to be associated with autism (see the systematic review by Gillberg & Coleman, 1992) but in no case is there good evidence of a strong association.

It is quite likely that autism is associated with some increase in the rate of chromosome anomalies. Probably the rate is something of the order of 5%, in addition to the Fragile X (Gillberg & Coleman, 1992). That figure is high enough to warrant routine examination of the chromosomes in the clinical assessment of autistic individuals, but the meaning of the association remains in considerable doubt. Many of the abnormalities reported are of quite uncertain clinical significance. Thus, some are balanced translocations (i.e., they involve exchange, but not loss, of chromosomal material) and these and other anomalies are known to arise in individuals without handicap. It might have been hoped that the particular chromosome abnormalities associated with autism would provide clues to the possible locus of the gene or genes that underlie autism. Unfortunately, they do not; autism has been associated with anomalies involving almost all chromosomes. Perhaps the only chromosome in which there is any suggestion of a stronger specific association is chromosome 15. There are reports that autism is sometimes associated with an extra marker chromosome deriving from chromosome 15 (Baker, Piven, Schwartz, & Patil, 1994; Gillberg et al., 1991; Hotopf & Bolton, 1995).

QUANTIFICATION OF GENETIC RISK IN IDIOPATHIC CASES

Evidence on the strength of the genetic component in cases of autism that are unassociated with a known medical condition derives from both family and twin studies. Clinical reports initially put the rate of autism in siblings at about 2% (Smalley et al., 1988). However, this figure was not based on systematic assessment of all siblings. Bolton et al. (1994) studied the 153 siblings of 99 autistic subjects, of whom 2.9% showed autism, and a further 2.9% showed atypical autism, with a 0% rate of both in the 65 siblings in the Down syndrome comparison group. Piven et al. (1990) found a 3% rate of autism in siblings and a 4% rate of severe social impairment. Szatmari et al. (1993) found a rate of 5.3% pervasive developmental disorder (PDD) in siblings compared with 0% in controls. Jorde et al. (1991), reporting data from a large-scale Utah family study, reported a recurrence risk of 3.7% if the first autistic child was male and 7.0% if female. It may be concluded that the rate in siblings is probably in the region of 3% to 7%, which represents a

50-fold to 100-fold increase in risk. Although it does not seem likely that this could be environmentally mediated, family studies cannot separate genetic and nongenetic influences, and it is necessary to turn to twin data.

There have been three general-population-based twin studies of idiopathic autism. Folstein and Rutter (1977a, 1977b), in a British study, found a 36% pairwise concordance rate in monozygotic (MZ) twins and a 0% rate in same-sex dizygotic (DZ) twins. Steffenburg et al. (1989), in a Nordic study, reported a 91% pairwise concordance rate for autism in MZ twins and a 0% concordance rate in same sex DZ twins. In a more recent British study, Bailey et al. (1995) found an MZ pairwise concordance rate of 69%, and, again, 0% in DZ pairs. Pooling the two British studies, and using the rate of autism among the siblings of autistic singletons as the basis for the DZ rate, Bailey et al. (1995) calculated a heritability of 91% to 93% for an underlying liability to autism (the variation in estimate stemmed from different assumptions about the base rate of autism). Clearly, this represents a very strong genetic component. Several issues should be tackled before concluding that the genetic effect is as strong as these calculations seem to indicate. To begin with, the possibility that the findings could stem, at least in part, from obstetric complications needs to be considered. This possibility particularly arises because both the original Folstein and Rutter (1977a, 1977b) study, and the study by Steffenburg et al. (1989), showed that obstetric complications differentiated twins with autism from their cotwins without autism. In both studies, this was interpreted as indicating the possible role of environmentally induced brain damage. This possibility now seems unlikely for the following reasons:

1. Most of the obstetric complications were quite minor, the association with obstetric complications in singletons is weak, and it mainly applies to minor complications (Nelson, 1991; Tsai, 1987).
2. The association in singletons may be a function of maternal parity (Piven et al., 1993), although this seemed not to be so in the study by Bolton et al. (in press).
3. Within the Bailey et al. (1995) twin sample, obstetric complications were associated

with congenital anomalies, most of which were likely to derive from aberrations in early pregnancy.

4. In the Bolton et al. (1994, in press) family study, the familial loading was greater in the case of autistic subjects with obstetric complications.

Other evidence has shown that genetically abnormal fetuses (e.g., with Down syndrome) may give rise to an increased rate of obstetric and perinatal complications (Bolton & Holland, 1994). The totality of the evidence strongly suggests that the minor obstetric complications derive from a genetically abnormal fetus rather than from an environmental risk process (Bolton et al., in press). Isolated cases of autism may stem from neonatal brain damage that is associated with serious perinatal complications or very low-birth-weight, but such cases seem to be uncommon.

A further approach to the possible role of physical environmental factors is provided by a study of various specific infectious risks. Probably the best documented is a report by Chess, Korn, and Fernandez (1971) that autism is quite common in children with congenital rubella. However, the significance of this finding was modified by follow-up data (Chess, 1977) indicating that, as they grew older, many of the children with congenital rubella ceased to exhibit autism (a rare occurrence among autistic persons). In its course and, to some extent, in the details of its clinical features, the autism associated with rubella is atypical. Because congenital rubella is uncommon these days, it could constitute only a rare cause of autism. Deykin and MacMahon (1979) undertook a systematic study of possible associations with maternal infections during pregnancy, but the results were essentially negative. Several studies have reported seasonal variations in the births of children with autism and this has been taken to suggest an environmental pathogen may be operative during pregnancy (e.g., Gillberg & Coleman, 1992). Bolton et al. (1992) examined the postulated association in detail and concluded that it was far less definite than had been claimed and that it does not provide strong evidence for an environmental cause. A possible association between autism and the cytomegalovirus has been suggested, but this is, at best, a quite infrequent cause of autism (Gillberg & Coleman, 1992). Cases of autism associated with postnatal encephalitis have also been reported, but they, too, appear quite rare.

Psychosocial environmental risk factors are only rarely influential (see reviews by Cantwell, Rutter, & Baker, 1978; Koegel, Schreibman, O'Neill, & Burke, 1983). Early suggestions that autism might be an effect of parental neglect, rejection, or indifference have long since been abandoned. Numerous studies have failed to show any association between autism and qualities of upbringing or frequency of stress experiences. Accordingly, it seems most unlikely that environmentally mediated psychological experiences play any significant role in autism. An apparent exception to that widely accepted generalization is provided by a report (Rutter and the ERA team, 1997, submitted) that some children adopted from Romanian orphanages into UK families exhibited an autistic-like syndrome. Although this was very much a minority pattern, the rate was clearly raised in relation to the general population. Nevertheless, its relevance in relation to the broad run of autism is very doubtful because the clinical pattern was usually atypical in certain important features and, more especially, because the autistic features often faded as the children grew older. The children had suffered quite exceptional physical and psychological privation and it is not clear which aspect of their early experiences led to their being at risk for this atypical pattern. Grossly depriving experiences are not ordinarily found among autistic individuals. In general, psychosocial stressors and adversities play no significant role in the etiology of autism.

Another approach is provided by examination of the concordance rate in MZ pairs. The 91% pairwise concordance rate for autism in MZ twins, found by Steffenburg et al. (1989), would seem to leave little room for nongenetic influences, whereas the 69% pairwise concordance rate found by Bailey et al. (1995) allows more scope. However, as discussed below, the great majority of the non-autistic twins in discordant MZ pairs showed cognitive and social deficits of autistic quality, albeit of lesser degree. It may be concluded that, in the great majority of cases of autism, genetic influences predominate in the etiology of autism.

What Is the Phenotype?

The findings discussed so far all apply to autism as traditionally diagnosed. Folstein and Rutter (1977a, 1977b) noted, however, that most of the MZ pairs that were not concordant for autism were concordant for some type of cognitive deficit, usually involving language delay. By contrast, this applied to only 1 in 10 of the discordant DZ pairs. The implication was that it might not be autism as such that was inherited, but rather some broader type of cognitive abnormality including, but not restricted to, autism. The more recent British twin study undertaken by Bailey et al. (1995) found the same but also demonstrated that the cognitive deficits were usually associated with a persistent social impairment that continued into adult life (Le Couteur et al., 1996). Of the MZ pairs, 76% were concordant for a *combined* social and cognitive disorder, compared with 0% of the DZ pairs. Conversely, in only 8% of MZ pairs was the cotwin *without* either a social or a cognitive disorder, compared with 90% of the DZ pairs.

The family studies have also strongly suggested that the genetic liability applies to a range of social and cognitive abnormalities in individuals of normal intelligence. These abnormalities are very similar in quality to those found in autism, but they are very different in degree of handicap (for reviews, see Bolton et al., 1994; Folstein & Piven, 1991; Rutter et al., 1993). A parallel may be drawn with the association between schizophrenia and schizotypal personality disorder (Kendler, Gruenberg, & Kinney, 1994). Bolton et al. (1994) found that between 12% and 20% of the siblings of autistic probands (compared with 2% to 3% of the Down syndrome siblings) exhibited this lesser variant of autism. The exact figures were dependent on the stringency of definition. Other family studies vary in the extent to which the disorders in relatives have involved social, language, and/or cognitive deficits.

There has been some variability in whether these are mainly evident in parents or in siblings, but nearly all have shown a much increased rate of abnormalities (Landa, Piven, Wzorek, Gayle, Chase, & Folstein, 1992; Landa, Wzorek, Piven, Folstein, & Isaacs, 1991; Murphy, Bolton, Pickles, & Rutter, 1997, submitted; Narayan, Moyes, & Wolff, 1990; Piven et al., 1994; Silliman, Campbell, & Mitchell, 1989; Wolff, Narayan, & Moyes, 1988). Thus, the social characteristics have included a lack of empathy, rapport, and emotional responsiveness; hypersensitivity; and single-minded pursuit of special interests. Communication difficulties have primarily involved pragmatic deficiencies, overcommunicativeness and undercommunicativeness, excessive guardedness and disinhibition. Language-related cognitive deficits have also been present but, strikingly, neither mental retardation nor general cognitive impairment has been evident (Fombonne, Bolton, Prior, Jordan, & Rutter, in press; Freeman et al., 1989; Szatmari, Jones, Tuff, Bartolucci, Fisman, & Mahoney, 1993). Perhaps surprisingly, the pattern of verbal and visuospatial skills is not helpful in the diagnosis of the broader phenotype of autism and, possibly, the relatives of autistic individuals may tend to have slightly superior verbal skills, rather than the verbal deficits that are characteristic of autism itself (Fombonne et al., in press).

Only two studies have yielded essentially negative findings. Gillberg, Gillberg, and Steffenburg (1992) found few differences in a rather small-scale study, but over one-third of their sample had a known medical syndrome and half were severely retarded. Szatmari et al. (1993) compared the unaffected siblings and parents of 52 probands with PDD and 33 Down's syndrome and low-birth-weight controls. No significant differences were found between the groups. It is not clear why the findings are so different from most of the other studies, but it is notable that the probands were clinically more heterogeneous, and the findings on siblings were not internally coherent. For example, speech delay was nearly three times as common in the siblings of PDD subjects (16.3% versus 6.8%), but reading problems were far less frequent (3.8% versus 20.5%). Rates of special education were also very high in both groups (10.0% in the PDD subjects and 18.2% in the controls). In addition, Spiker et al. (1994), in their study of multiplex families, argued that autism was either present or absent, and there was no need to involve the concept of a broader phenotype. However, their own data showed a substantial number of individuals who were clearly not autistic (at least as usually diagnosed) but were equally far from normal (see Le Couteur et al., 1996).

Although there are some inconsistencies, the twin and family studies, taken together, strongly suggest that the autism phenotype extends well beyond the traditional diagnosis. The extension involves characteristics that are closely similar to autism in quality but markedly different in degree, and which are found in individuals of normal intelligence. The clinical picture chiefly differs from autism (as traditionally diagnosed) in the following ways: lack of abnormal nonpragmatic language features (such as pronominal reversal and delayed echolalia); less striking stereotyped repetitive behavioral patterns; subtler social deficits; and lack of an association with epilepsy. Nevertheless, there are three main reasons for confidence in the assumption that this clinical picture is indeed part of autism: (a) the social abnormalities have been found to persist into adult life; (b) the concordance in MZ pairs for the broader phenotype, even after exclusion of autism and PDD, is much higher than in DZ pairs (Le Couteur et al., 1996); and (c) family data show a much increased loading for the broader phenotype compared with Down syndrome families (see, e.g., Bolton et al., 1994).

The boundaries of the broader phenotype remain to be determined. Questions remain on whether it may be evident in language abnormalities, social deficits, or circumscribed interest patterns in isolation, or whether its manifestation requires two or more of these. In each of this trio of abnormalities, what specific qualities are pathognomonic of autism? Even more basic, are such features categorically present or absent, or are they more appropriately considered in terms of a dimension? There is a need to differentiate the broader phenotype (or lesser variant) of autism from other forms of social abnormality and especially from schizotypal personality disorder, a quite different disorder that is

associated with schizophrenia rather than with autism. (The broader phenotype of autism appears clinically different, as follows: it is first manifest in early childhood; it is associated with circumscribed interests rather than ideas of reference, magical thinking, and unusual perceptual experiences; and deficits in social reciprocity and pragmatic aspects of communication are prominent. However, systematic comparisons have yet to be undertaken.) Some means of validation of the broader phenotype of autism would be helpful. Potentially, this validation might be provided by patterns of psychological abnormality (with respect, for example, to "theory of mind," executive planning, central coherence, or pragmatic aspects of language; see Bailey, Phillips, & Rutter, 1996), but that research remains a task for the future.

More surprisingly, several studies (Bolton, Pickles, Murphy, & Rutter, 1997, submitted; DeLong, 1994; DeLong & Nohria, 1994; Murphy et al., 1997, submitted; Piven et al., 1990; Smalley, McCracken, & Tanguay, 1995) have reported an apparently increased familial loading for affective disorders and for social phobia/anxiety traits and disorders, but it is not yet clear whether this is genetically mediated. Smalley et al. (1995) compared 36 families with an autistic child with 21 families with a nonautistic child who showed either tuberous sclerosis or epilepsy. Major affective disorder was three times as common in the first-degree relatives of the autistic individuals. In nearly two-thirds of the parents with affective disorder, the onset preceded the birth of an autistic child. Social phobia was also much increased in the autism families when the autism was unaccompanied by mental retardation. Bolton et al. (1997, submitted), using both standardized interview (Schedule for Affective Disorders and Schizophrenia Lifetime Version (SADS-L) and pedigree methods, showed that the raised rate of major affective disorders in the first- and second-degree relatives of autistic individuals, compared with the relatives of individuals with Down syndrome, was not a function of the broader phenotype as defined in terms of cognitive and social abnormalities. Moreover, unlike the broader phenotype, affective disorder was more frequent in females and had a different pattern of correlates.

At first sight, it would seem unlikely that autism and affective disorders could constitute different manifestations of the same underlying genotype. Rather, the increased familial loading for depressive disorders might reflect the strains and stresses associated with rearing an autistic child and there is some evidence that, possibly, this may constitute part of the explanation (Bolton et al., 1997, submitted). Nevertheless, despite the apparent implausibility of the association, four findings suggest that it may be real: (a) the increase in affective disorders applies to second-degree, as well as first-degree, relatives; (b) the increase applies to bipolar and severe unipolar disorders as much as to milder depressive disorders; (c) the increase applies to affective disorders with an onset before the birth of the autistic individual as well as those arising afterwards; and (d) the increase has been noted in studies using quite different samples. Accordingly, although few of the investigations included adequate controls, the apparent association between autism and affective disorders clearly requires further study. One crucial test would be provided by examining the association from a different perspective. If autism and major depression are truly genetically associated, there should be an increased loading for autism in the families of individuals with major depressive disorders (although the low base rate of autism would make this difficult to detect). There are no reports that that is the case but systematic studies have yet to be undertaken. If the association between autism and affective disorders is confirmed, it will be important to examine competing hypotheses on the underlying mechanisms. Bolton et al. (1997, submitted) showed that the raised rate of affective disorders was probably not just a function of the broader phenotype as defined in terms of cognitive and social abnormalities. Nevertheless, there are many possibilities of artifact in the findings, and further research is needed both to test the reality of the association and to investigate its meaning if confirmed.

In addition, there have been suggestions that the phenotype should be extended to include Tourette's syndrome (Comings & Comings, 1991) and anorexia nervosa (Gillberg, 1992) but in neither case is the evidence particularly convincing.

Given the likelihood that the phenotype does extend beyond autism, questions must be raised about the connections between autism as traditionally diagnosed and the so-called lesser variant. The latter shares a number of features with autism proper; for example, it, too, is much more common in males than in females (although this is less true of the milder degrees of the phenotype), and the features are usually evident from early childhood onward. On the other hand, there are at least two marked differences; (a) the relatives who showed this broader phenotype in the various studies have been of normal intelligence, and (b) no association with epilepsy has been found. This could represent simply a lower "dose" of the genetic predisposition, but the possibility of some kind of "two-hit" mechanism must also be considered; that is, one set of causal factors may predispose to the broader phenotype, and a separate set of causal factors may be involved in the transition to the handicapping condition of autism proper. At one time, it was thought that this second step might involve perinatal complications (Folstein & Rutter, 1977a, 1977b; Steffenburg et al., 1989), but, for the reasons given above, that possibility now seems unlikely. The issue is unresolved, but there is an apparent paradox in the fact that most cases of autism occur in individuals who are also mentally retarded and who have a much increased rate of epilepsy, but the familial loading mainly involves qualitatively similar abnormalities in individuals without epilepsy and of normal intelligence.

GENETIC HETEROGENEITY

The history of medical genetics strongly suggests that genetic heterogeneity is to be expected in autism. There are numerous examples of different genetic abnormalities all leading to what appears to be the same clinical picture. Thus, as already noted, some cases of tuberous sclerosis are associated with a gene locus on chromosome 9, and others are associated with a locus on chromosome 16. Other neurological conditions show even greater genetic heterogeneity (see Simonoff et al., 1996). Some genetic heterogeneity has already been demonstrated insofar as autism is associated with the Fragile X anomaly, tuberous sclerosis, and various other genetic conditions. Claims have been made that more than one-third of cases of autism are associated with such known medical conditions (Gillberg, 1992) but review of the evidence suggests that the true rate of known medical conditions in autism is probably about 10% (Rutter et al., 1994). On the other hand, the rate may be higher in atypical cases of autism and in autism associated with profound mental retardation. The question then is whether there are currently any clinical indicators of heterogeneity in the remaining 90% of cases of idiopathic autism. One way to tackle this issue is to examine the variabilities in clinical expression within MZ pairs, a strategy followed by Le Couteur and colleagues (1996). In brief, they compared the variability within MZ pairs with the variability between MZ pairs. If the clinical variations index genetic heterogeneity, it would be expected that the between-pair variation should be much greater than the within-pair variation. That is because MZ cotwins will necessarily share all their genes whereas that will not be the case across pairs. The findings showed that, with respect to both autistic symptoms and verbal IQ, there was almost as much variation within pairs as there was between pairs. Differences in verbal and nonverbal IQ within concordant MZ pairs ranged up to more than 50 points. These findings strongly pointed to a wide range of phenotypic expression and provided few clinical pointers on possible clinical indicators of genetic heterogeneity. One possible exception was provided by epilepsy where there was a greater tendency for concordance within pairs. On the other hand, the presence of epilepsy was not associated with any other indications of meaningful differences, and the Bolton et al. (1994) family study showed no variation in familial loading by epilepsy. Spiker et al. (1994) used a somewhat similar strategy with respect to differences between affected family members in families that were multiplex for autism. Again, substantial variation within

pairs of affected relatives was found for both clinical features and IQ. It may be concluded that the *same* genes involved in liability to autism can give rise to a surprisingly wide range of clinical manifestations. The same evidence makes it unlikely that the several different genes involved in autism (see below) give rise to different facets of the clinical syndrome.

There is some slight suggestion that autism associated either with profound mental retardation or with a lack of useful spoken language may be different. Thus, Bolton et al. (1994) found that, although the familial loading was strongly associated with the symptom score in verbal probands, this was not so in those without useful language. August and his colleagues (August, Stewart, & Tsai, 1981; Baird & August, 1985) found a raised rate of severe mental retardation in the siblings of autistic probands who were also severely retarded, something that has not been evident in any of the studies of less retarded subjects. Their findings were based on a very small number of cases and cannot be taken as anything more than a possibility worth examining further. About one-third of autistic individuals have hyperserotoninaemia, and there is some evidence that this may be a familial trait to some extent (Cook, 1990). Although untested, this might prove to be a marker of genetic heterogeneity; but again, this is no more than a suggestion worth following up. Genetic heterogeneity is likely to be proven eventually but, so far, there are no strong leads on how this might be indexed in terms of phenotypic characteristics, and variable expression will make its identification a hard task.

ARE THE GENETIC INFLUENCES AUTISM-SPECIFIC?

A somewhat related question is whether the genetic influences are autism-specific. Clearly they are not to the extent that autism is secondary to conditions such as tuberous sclerosis or the Fragile X anomaly, but these account for only 1 in 10 cases. It has been suggested that autism is no more than a final common pathway for a heterogeneous range of etiological processes and that there is no point in searching for autism-specific causal factors (Coleman,

1990; Gillberg, 1992). The available evidence, however, suggests that this conclusion is not valid. Four key sets of data are relevant:

1. Neither brain pathology nor mental retardation carries a consistent risk for autism. Some conditions (such as cerebral palsy or Down syndrome) carry only a small additional risk (but see Howlin, Wing, & Gould, 1995); for others (such as tuberous sclerosis), the risk is much higher.
2. The twin and family studies show strong associations with a relatively specific pattern of social and cognitive deficits, but not with mental retardation or brain disease more generally.
3. The concordance for the broader phenotype of autism in MZ pairs is very high (over 90%).
4. Although there is considerable variability of phenotypic expression within MZ pairs (and within multiplex families), the variability is within the range of autistic features and does not extend to other psychiatric manifestations of brain pathology. Also, both twin and family studies have failed to find any association between autism and cognitive impairment when the latter is not accompanied by autism.

In the great majority of cases, the genetic influences are likely to prove to be autism-specific, even though it is probable that they will be multiple.

Mode of Genetic Transmission

The last issue with respect to genetics concerns the mode of genetic transmission. A segregation analysis undertaken by Ritvo et al. (1985), using families that had two or more affected siblings, suggested autosomal recessive inheritance and apparently ruled out a multifactorial model. However, the biased nature of the sample, together with a nonexclusion of cases due to known medical conditions and uncertainties about diagnosis (including a failure to take into account the possibility of a broader phenotype), calls for caution in accepting the conclusions. Also, a further study by the same research group (Jorde et al., 1990) produced a different set of conclusions. An additional

complication may be the tendency of families to stop having children after an autistic child is borne (Jones & Szatmari, 1988), although this was not found by Bolton et al. (1994) in a study with limited statistical power to detect the effect. Altogether, the evidence suggests that multiple interacting genes are a much more likely cause than a single gene operating in Mendelian fashion. Two main findings point to that conclusion. First, there is a marked decline in rate, going from MZ cotwins to DZ cotwins or siblings (Bailey et al., 1995; Folstein & Rutter, 1977a, 1977b; Steffenburg et al., 1989), and a further decline occurs going from first-degree to second-degree relatives (Jorde et al., 1990; Pickles et al., 1995; Pickles, Bolton, Macdonald, Rios, Storoschuk, & Rutter, 1997, submitted). Using a development of the Risch (1990) approach based on a decline in rates, Pickles et al. (1995) estimated that a three-gene model was most likely, although the range could be anywhere between two and ten genes. The rationale for this inference is that, whereas MZ twins share all their genes and therefore all combinations of genes, DZ twins (or singleton siblings), on average share only half their genes. This necessarily means that they will share only one-quarter of any specified two-gene combinations and only one-eighth of any specified three-gene combinations. Hence, the marked decline suggests the likelihood that particular combinations of genes underlie autism, and not just one major gene. However, the estimate of approximately three genes provides only a rough guide to the likely number because the calculations are necessarily affected by the strength of effect of each gene and by the degree of genetic heterogeneity.

Second, Bolton et al. (1994) found that the familial loading increased with the severity of the autism as measured in terms of the number of autism-diagnostic interview algorithm symptoms. This, too, suggests that the severity indexes the number of genes. However, this finding does not tally well with the hypothesis that *specific combinations* of genes are required for autism to occur. The one finding that does not seem consistent with that model is that the familial loading seems only slightly greater in the families of female autistic subjects (the sex difference is nonsignificant in most studies). This is apparently inconsistent because a multifactorial threshold model leads to the expectation that the loading should be higher in the less often affected sex—namely females. On the other hand, the statistical power to detect a sex difference was low in all studies, and the matter remains unresolved (see Rutter et al., 1993).

SCREENING FOR GENETIC ABNORMALITIES

A key clinical issue that derives from the genetic findings is what assessments, or investigations, should be undertaken as part of the initial diagnostic assessment. The first requirement is to combine a careful, systematic, searching of clinical history with a thorough medical examination. Particular attention needs to be paid to the possibility of tuberous sclerosis, and this requires careful examination of dermatological features. Use of Wood's light when looking for depigmented leaf-shaped maculas is essential, because differential diagnosis is often quite difficult on the basis of inspection alone. If epileptic seizures have occurred, a skull X ray or CT scan (to look for calcified lesions), as well as an EEG, may be informative, although a negative picture does not rule out tuberous sclerosis. Chromosomal examination, together with DNA study for the Fragile X anomaly, should be undertaken routinely. Although only some 5% of cases of autism are associated with Fragile X, the implications are sufficiently important to rule it out (or identify it) in all cases. As noted, some 1 in 20 other cases of autism may have associated chromosome anomalies, and this is a sufficient ratio to justify screening for them. However, in most cases, their clinical meaning is quite uncertain, and a major etiological role should not necessarily be assumed.

It has been traditional in many medical centers to screen all individuals presenting with either autism or mental retardation for metabolic abnormalities (using a range of urinary and blood tests). Clearly, screening *is* indicated if the clinical history or examination suggests the possibility of a medical condition that would be detected by these means. On the other hand, because the detection rate in the absence of clinical indications is so low as to cast doubt on the value of routine

screening (Scott, 1994), the use of such screening now needs to be re-evaluated (Bailey, 1994).

Some commentators (e.g., Gillberg, 1990) have even recommended the routine use of cerebrospinal fluid (CSF) examinations and brain scans. Although it is important not to miss etiologically relevant medical conditions, there is a lack of evidence that these more invasive or stressful investigations detect diseases that would otherwise be missed. We recommend that they should be undertaken only if there are clinical indications.

The personal history should include a detailed account of the pregnancy and neonatal period, always supplemented by the medical records made at the time. The crucial issue is not so much whether obstetric or perinatal complications occurred, as whether they were associated at the time with either brain-imaging evidence of brain damage (usually through ultrasound studies) or clinical evidence of the same (neonatal convulsions, neurological abnormalities, and so on).

GENETIC COUNSELING

Families should be given information on the role of genetic factors in autism, and genetic counseling should be made available to those who request it. Such counseling needs to start with a careful diagnostic assessment, because some individuals thought to have autism turn out to have some other disorder when a systematic evaluation is undertaken. If the autism is causally associated with some genetically determined medical condition (such as the Fragile X or tuberous sclerosis), the genetic risks should be discussed in terms of that condition. Also, when it is possible to test relatives directly (as is the case, for example, with the Fragile X anomaly), this possibility should be offered. Knowledge of patterns of Mendelian inheritance allows quantitative advice on risks when the mode of inheritance is known (see Simonoff, McGuffin, & Gottesman, 1994). However, the possibility of new mutations (common with tuberous sclerosis) and the effects of intergenerational change (as with the Fragile X, in which the risk of having an affected child seems to be related to the number of maternal trinucleatide repeats;

Warren & Nelson, 1994) should be carefully taken into account.

In the great majority of cases, however, autism is not associated with any known medical condition. In these circumstances, counseling is less straightforward. The first task is usually to explain that although the *relative* risk of autism in other family members is very greatly raised in relation to the general population, the *absolute* risk is rather low. Thus, if the issue is risk of recurrence with respect to future children born to the same biological parents, this can be stated as an approximate increase of 50 to 100 times overall, but still only a 1-in-20 chance. Because, at first hearing, that fact is hard to grasp, it is usually helpful to go on to explain, in simple terms, how this arises with conditions in which combinations of several genes are required. Although it is not known for certain that that is so with autism, it appears very likely, and this should be explained.

Several other issues need to be considered. Families will want to know whether the risks in their particular family are greater or less than the overall average. That question rarely has an easy answer. It seems reasonable to suppose that the risks may be lower if the autism is associated with some definite nongenetic cause, but that inference is not straightforward. In the unusual circumstance that such a definite cause can be identified (as with congenital rubella or early encephalitis), a lower risk can reasonably be assumed. More commonly, however, the story is one of obstetric complications, or an onset following immunization or some unknown fever. In this situation, the inferred causal role is usually in doubt. Unless there is contemporaneous clinical or imaging evidence of organic brain pathology, it would be unwise to assume a nongenetic etiology (Bailey, 1994). In particular, mild obstetric complications may derive from a genetically abnormal fetus (see above) and not reflect any environmental risk mechanism. Again, great caution should be exercised in making any causal inference. There is no convincing evidence that autism can be caused by any ordinarily stressful life circumstances (such as hospital admission, family discord, or loss of an attachment figure). In rare instances, an autism-like syndrome can develop

as a result of unusually severe and prolonged physical and psychological privation, but, even here, the clinical picture is usually somewhat atypical. Nevertheless, in this very rare circumstance, a lower risk may be inferred.

Equally important is the need to consider whether the absence of any case of autism, including its broader phenotype, in the extended family lowers the risk, or, conversely, whether the occurrence of several such cases increases the risk. Two problems immediately arise. First, there is bound to be huge individual variation across families in the number of affected members. Accordingly, an unusually high or low familial loading does not necessarily mean anything and little weight can be attached to it. That is especially the case with respect to a lack of other affected members in the family because this will often be so simply because autism has a low base rate.

Second, given the considerable uncertainties regarding the boundaries of the broader phenotype it may be quite difficult to decide which family members are affected. Thus, there will necessarily be doubt about whether to include isolated instances of severe language delay or social oddity in the absence of a clear indication that these are autistic in type. The main situation in which the possibility of an increased risk needs to be considered is when there are definite cases of autism on both sides of the family or when one or both parents are themselves affected. Even here, empirical evidence is lacking that the risk is actually increased, although it would seem prudent to assume that it may be. The absence of a family loading, however, should not be taken to imply a reduced risk.

A further consideration is whether the risk needs to be adjusted up or down on the grounds that the autism is atypical in some respect, or that it is unusually severe or unusually mild. Bolton et al. (1994) found that, other things being equal, the risks tended to be greater if the autism was severe, although possibly not so much greater if the affected individual was nonverbal. There is also some slight suggestion (see above) that at least some cases of autism associated with profound mental retardation may be genetically different (although that does not necessarily mean that the *level* of risk is different). The point is an important one, but, in the present state of knowledge, there are no solid grounds for concluding that the risk is any different (although it may be so) when the clinical picture is atypical in some way or is unusually mild.

Queries often arise regarding four particular points. First, families want to know whether any investigations can be undertaken to measure or identify genetic risk. At the present time, regrettably, no such test is possible in idiopathic cases, although identification of the gene should make that possible, and, with the advances in molecular genetics, that is likely to happen during the next decade. Second, a frequent concern centers on possible risks to the offspring of nonaffected siblings (i.e., nephews or nieces or second-degree relatives). The few available data on second-degree relatives (Jorde et al., 1991; Pickles et al., 1997, submitted) indicate a rate of probably less than 1 in 500. However, the figure is necessarily a most uncertain one, and it is unclear how much the risk is influenced by the fact that parents are likely to have been selected on the basis of not being affected (or being less affected) themselves (see Pickles et al., 1997, submitted). The limited available evidence suggests that siblings who exhibit all but the mildest phenotypic expression are less likely than unaffected siblings to marry (or cohabit) and have children.

A third query concerns the risks in other family members for milder problems that are part of the autistic spectrum but not autism as traditionally diagnosed. The family and twin data (Bailey et al., 1995; Bolton et al., 1994) indicate that the risks are substantially greater than for autism itself, but, given the uncertainties over how far the broader phenotype extends, no precise figure is possible. Probably, however, the risk in siblings for the lesser manifestations of autism may be in the 10% to 20% range. It should be emphasized to families that most such affected individuals are *not* seriously handicapped, and the great majority go on to live fulfilling lives as independent and self-sufficient adults.

The fourth query concerns whether some *specific* family member (usually a sibling) who has been delayed in speaking, or is socially unusual, or has idiosyncratic circumscribed interests, does or does not suffer from some variant of autism. Often, that question constitutes a quite difficult clinical decision. The only guideline is that the closer the specific social or communicative qualities of the deficit or abnormality are to those found in autism, and the greater the extent to which the abnormalities extend across all three domains of reciprocal social relationships, communication, and repetitive or stereotyped interest patterns, the greater the likelihood that the picture does represent autism. Because autism is so strongly associated with specific cognitive patterns (see Bailey et al., 1996), there is the possibility that the diagnosis of the broader phenotype could be validated through cognitive testing (see above). That is quite likely to become possible in the future, but it will require adaptation of the cognitive tests to make them suitable for nonhandicapped individuals of normal intelligence.

Three other points need to be made about genetic counseling:

1. If is often helpful to put the risks into perspective by expressing them in positive terms (i.e., a 19-out-of-20 chance that a future child will *not* be autistic).
2. It is not the job of the counselor to make decisions for the family. Rather, his/her responsibility is to provide the family with (a) the factual information that will allow them to come to their own decisions, and (b) the clinical context in which there can be a sensitive discussion of the dilemmas involved and the individual family members' own feelings about them.
3. There must be ethical concern over the inappropriateness of counseling one family member on behalf of some other member who has not asked for such information (including those who are still too young to ask for genetic counseling).

CLINICAL VALUE OF GENETIC KNOWLEDGE

At present, genetic influences are known to be strong in autism, the precise genetic mechanisms involved have yet to be determined. That situation is likely to change during the next decade as a result of advances in molecular genetics (see Bailey et al., 1996; Rutter,

1994). Accordingly, it is necessary to consider the usefulness of identifying the gene (or, more likely, several genes) involved in a liability to autism. Merely knowing where such genes are to be found (i.e., their loci on particular chromosomes) will not in itself be clinically very useful. The point, however, is that this constitutes a necessary first step in order to identify the gene itself, and the identification, in turn, constitutes a key step in the search for how the gene leads to autism. In other words, it will then be possible to determine the gene product and find out *how* that leads to autism; whether specific environmental features interact with genetic susceptibility, and why the cognitive impairment associated with autism varies from severe and general to mild and specific. An understanding of that process is likely to carry very important implications for prevention and treatment. Therein lies the enormous potential value of molecular genetics.

CONCLUSION

Our understanding of the role of genetic factors in the liability to autism has increased greatly over the last decade, although basic questions have yet to be answered. It is now clear that genetic factors play a very important role in the causation of autism; indeed, autism is probably the most strongly genetic of all non-Mendelian psychiatric disorders. Evidence has also shown that the phenotype extends beyond (perhaps quite a long way beyond) autism as traditionally diagnosed, and that several (but probably a small number of) interacting genes are responsible. In a minority of cases, however, autism arises on the basis of some single-gene medical condition. These findings already have important implications for the diagnosis of autism and for genetic counseling, and they need to be appreciated by practitioners as well as researchers. Identification of the precise genetic mechanisms will have an even greater impact on clinical practice.

Cross-References

Neurological aspects of autism and medical conditions frequently associated with autism are discussed in Chapters 16 and 18.

REFERENCES

August, G.J., Stewart, M.A., & Tsai, L. (1981). The incidence of cognitive disabilities in the siblings of autistic children. *British Journal of Psychiatry, 138,* 416–422.

Bailey, A.J. (1994). Physical examination and medical investigations. In M. Rutter, E. Taylor, & L. Hersov (Eds.), *Child and adolescent psychiatry: Modern approaches* (3rd ed., pp. 79–93). Oxford: Blackwell Scientific.

Bailey, A.J., Bolton, P., Butler, L., Le Couteur, A., Murphy, M., Scott, S., Webb, T., & Rutter, M. (1993). Prevalence of the Fragile X anomaly amongst autistic twins and singletons. *Journal of Child Psychology and Psychiatry, 34,* 673–688.

Bailey, A., Le Couteur, A., Gottesman, I., Bolton, P., Simonoff, E., Yuzda, E., & Rutter, M. (1995). Autism as a strongly genetic disorder: Evidence from a British twin study. *Psychological Medicine, 25,* 63–78.

Bailey, A., Phillips, W., & Rutter, M. (1996). Autism: Towards an integration of clinical, genetic, neuropsychological and neurobiological perspectives. *Journal of Child Psychology and Psychiatry Annual Research Review, 37,* 89–126.

Baird, T.D., & August, G.J. (1985). Familial heterogeneity in infantile autism. *Journal of Autism and Developmental Disorders, 15,* 315–321.

Baker, P., Piven, J., Schwartz, S., & Patil, S. (1994). Duplication of chromosome 15q11-13 in two individuals with autistic disorder. *Journal of Autism and Developmental Disorders, 24,* 529–535.

Blomquist, H.K., Bohman, M., Edvinsson, S.O., Gillberg, C., Gustavson, K.H., Holmgren, G., & Wahlström, J. (1985). Frequency of the Fragile X syndrome in infantile autism: A Swedish multicenter study. *Clinical Genetics, 27,* 113–117.

Bolton, P., & Holland, A. (1994). Chromosomal abnormalities. In M. Rutter, E. Taylor, & L. Hersov (Eds.), *Child and adolescent psychiatry: Modern approaches* (3rd ed., pp. 152–171). Oxford: Blackwell Scientific.

Bolton, P., MacDonald, H., Pickles, A., Rios, P., Goode, S., Crowson, M., Bailey, A., & Rutter, M. (1994). A case-control family history study of autism. *Journal of Child Psychology and Psychiatry, 35,* 877–900.

Bolton, P., Murphy, M., MacDonald, H., Whitlock, B., Pickles, A., & Rutter, M. (in press). Obstetric complications in autism: Consequences or causes of the condition. *Journal of the American Academy of Child and Adolescent Psychiatry.*

Bolton, P., Pickles, A., Murphy, M., & Rutter, M. (1997, submitted). *Autism, affective and other psychiatric disorders: Patterns of familial aggregation.*

Bolton, P., Pickles, A., Rutter, M., Butler, L., Summers, S., Lord, C., & Webb, T. (1992). Fragile X in families multiplex for autism and autism-related phenotypes: Prevalence and criteria for cytogenetic diagnosis. *Psychiatric Genetics, 2,* 277–300.

Bolton, P., & Rutter, M. (1990). Genetic influences in autism. *International Review of Psychiatry, 2,* 65–78.

Brown, W.T., Jenkins, E.C., Cohen, I.L., Fisch, G.S., Wolf-Schein, E.G., Gross, A., Waterhouse, L., Fein, D., Mason-Brothers, A., Ritvo, E. et al. (1986). Fragile X and autism: A multicenter survey. *American Journal of Medical Genetics, 23,* 341–352.

Cantwell, D., Rutter, M., & Baker, L. (1978). Family factors. In M. Rutter & E. Schopler (Eds.), *Autism: A reappraisal of concepts and treatment* (pp. 269–296). New York: Plenum.

Chess, S. (1977). Follow-up report on autism in congenital rubella. *Journal of Autism and Childhood Schizophrenia, 7,* 68–81.

Chess, S., Korn, S.J., & Fernandez, P.B. (1971). *Psychiatric disorders of children with congenital rubella.* New York: Brunner/Mazel.

Cohen, I.L., Vietze, P.M., Sudhalter, V., Jenkins, E.C., & Brown, W.T. (1989). Parent-child dyadic gaze patterns in Fragile X males and in non-Fragile X males with autistic disorder. *Journal of Child Psychology and Psychiatry, 30,* 845–856.

Coleman, M. (1990). Is classical Rett Syndrome ever present in males? *Brain and Development, 12,* 31–32.

Comings, D.E., & Comings, B.G. (1991). Clinical and genetic relationships between autism-pervasive developmental disorder and Tourette Syndrome: A study of 19 cases. *American Journal of Medical Genetics, 39,* 180–191.

Cook, E.H. (1990). Autism: Review of neurochemical investigations. *Synapse, 6,* 292–308.

Davies, K. (1991). Breaking the Fragile-X. *Nature, 351,* 439–440.

DeLong, R. (1994). Children with autistic spectrum disorder and a family history of affective disorder. *Developmental Medicine & Child Neurology, 36,* 674–687.

DeLong, R., & Nohria, C. (1994). Psychiatric family history and neurological disease in autistic spectrum disorders. *Developmental Medicine & Child Neurology, 36,* 441–448.

Deykin, E.Y., & MacMahon, B. (1979). The incidence of seizures among children with autistic symptoms. *American Journal of Psychiatry, 136,* 1310–1312.

Einfeld, S., Malony, H., & Hall, W. (1989). Autism is not associated with the Fragile X syndrome. *American Journal of Medical Genetics, 34,* 187–193.

European Chromosome 16 TS Consortium. (1993). Identification and characterization of the tuberous sclerosis gene on chromosome 16. *Cell, 75,* 1305–1315.

Folstein, S., & Piven, J. (1991). Etiology of autism: Genetic influences. *Pediatrics, 87*(Suppl.5), 767–773.

Folstein, S., & Rutter, M. (1977a). Infantile autism: A genetic study of 21 twin pairs. *Journal of Child Psychology and Psychiatry, 18,* 297–321.

Folstein, S., & Rutter, M. (1977b). Genetic influences and infantile autism. *Nature, 265,* 726–728.

Folstein, S., & Rutter, M. (1988). Autism: Familial aggregation and genetic implications. *Journal of Autism and Developmental Disorders, 18,* 3–30.

Fombonne, E., Bolton, P., Prior, J., Jordan, H., & Rutter, M. (in press). Family study of autism: Cognitive patterns and levels in parents and siblings. *Journal of Child Psychology and Psychiatry.*

Freeman, B.J., Ritvo, E.R., Mason-Brothers, A., Pingree, C., Yokota, A., Jenson, W.R., McMahon, W.M., Petersen, P.B., Mo, A., & Schroth, P. (1989). Psychometric assessment of first-degree relatives of 62 autistic probands in Utah. *American Journal of Psychiatry, 146,* 361–364.

Fryer, A.E., Chalmers, A., Connor, J.M., Fraser, I., Povey, S., Yates, A.D., Yates, J.R., & Osborne, J.P. (1987). Evidence that the gene for tuberous sclerosis is on chromosome 9. *Lancet, 21,* 659–661.

Gillberg, C. (1990). Medical work-up in children with autism and Asperger Syndrome. *Brain Dysfunction, 3,* 249–260.

Gillberg, C. (1992). Autism and autism-like conditions: Sub-classes among disorders of empathy. *Journal of Child Psychology and Psychiatry, 33,* 813–842.

Gillberg, C., & Coleman, M. (1992). *The biology of autistic syndromes* (2nd ed.). London: MacKeith Press.

Gillberg, C., & Forsell, C. (1984). Childhood psychosis and neurofibromatosis—more than a coincidence? *Journal of Autism and Developmental Disorders, 14,* 1–8.

Gillberg, C., Gillberg, I.C., & Steffenburg, S. (1992). Siblings and parents of children with autism: A controlled population-based study. *Developmental Medicine and Child Neurology, 34,* 389–398.

Gillberg, C., Steffenburg, S., & Jakobsson, G. (1987). Neurobiological findings in 20 relatively gifted children with Kanner-type autism or Asperger Syndrome. *Developmental Medicine and Child Neurology, 29,* 641–649.

Gillberg, C., Steffenburg, S., Wahlström, J., Sjöstedt, A., Gillberg, I.C., Martinsson, T., Liedgren, S., & Eeg-Olofsson, O. (1991). Autism associated with marker chromosome. *Journal of the American Academy of Child and Adolescent Psychiatry, 30,* 489–494.

Gillberg, C., & Wahlström, J. (1985). Chromosome abnormalities in infantile autism and other childhood psychoses: A population study of 66 cases. *Developmental Medicine and Child Neurology, 27,* 293–304.

Gillberg, I.C., Gillberg, C., & Ahlsén, G. (1994). Autistic behaviour and attention deficits in tuberous sclerosis: A population-based study. *Developmental Medicine and Child Neurology, 36,* 50–56.

Gurling, H.M.G., Bolton, P.F., Vincent, J., Melmer, G., & Rutter, M. (1997, submitted). *Molecular and cytogenic investigations of the fragile X region in families multiplex for autism and related phenotypes.*

Hagerman, R.J. (1990). The association between autism and Fragile X syndrome. *Brain Dysfunction, 3,* 219–227.

Hallmayer, J., Pintado, E., Lotspeich, L., Spiker, D., McMahon, W., Petersen, P.B., Nicholas, P., Pingree, C., Kraemer, H.C., Wong, D.L., Ritvo, E., Lin, A., Hebert, J., Cavalli-Sforza, L.L., & Ciaranello, R.D. (1994). Molecular analysis and test of linkage between the FMR-1 gene and infantile autism in multiplex families. *American Journal of Human Genetics, 55,* 951–959.

Hotopf, M., & Bolton, P. (1995). A case of autism associated with partial tetrasomy 15. *Journal of Autism and Developmental Disorders, 25,* 41–49.

Howlin, P., Wing, L., & Gould, J. (1995). The recognition of autism in children with Down syndrome—implications for intervention and some speculations about pathology. *Developmental Medicine and Child Neurology, 37,* 406–414.

Hunt, A., & Dennis, J. (1987). Psychiatric disorder among children with tuberous sclerosis. *Developmental Medicine and Child Neurology, 29,* 190–198.

Hunt, A., & Shepherd, C. (1993). A prevalence study of autism in tuberous sclerosis. *Journal of Autism and Developmental Disorders, 23,* 329–339.

Jones, M.B., & Szatmari, P. (1988). Stoppage rules and genetic studies of autism. *Journal of Autism and Developmental Disorders, 18,* 31–40.

Jorde, L.B., Hasstedt, S.J., Ritvo, E.R., Mason-Brothers, A., Freeman, B.J., Pingree, C., McMahon, W.M., Peterson, B., Jenson, W.R., & Moll, A. (1991). Complex segregation analysis of autism. *American Journal of Human Genetics, 49,* 932–938.

Jorde, L.B., Mason-Brothers, A., Waldman, R., Ritvo, E.R., Freeman, B.J., Pingree, C., McMahon, M.W., Petersen, P.B., Jenson, W.R., & Mo, A. (1990). The UCLA–University of Utah epidemiologic survey of autism: Genealogical analysis of familial aggregation. *American Journal of Medical Genetics, 36,* 85–88.

Kanner, L. (1943). Autistic disturbances of affective contact. *Nervous Child, 2,* 217–250.

Kendler, K.S., Gruenberg, A.M., & Kinney, D.K. (1994). Independent diagnosis of adoptees and relatives as defined by *DSM-III* in the provincial and national samples of the Danish adoption study of schizophrenia. *Archives of General Psychiatry, 51,* 456–468.

Koegel, R., Schreibman, L., O'Neill, R.E., & Burke, J.C. (1983). The personality and family-interaction characteristics of parents of autistic children. *Journal of Consulting and Clinical Psychology, 51,* 683–692.

Landa, R., Piven, J., Wzorek, M., Gayle, J.O., Chase, G.A., & Folstein, S.E. (1992). Social language use in parents of autistic individuals. *Psychological Medicine, 22,* 245–254.

Landa, R., Wzorek, M., Piven, J., Folstein, S., & Isaacs, C. (1991). Spontaneous narrative discourse characteristics of parents of autistic individuals. *Journal of Speech and Hearing Research, 34,* 1339–1345.

Le Couteur, A., Bailey, A., Goode, S., Pickles, A., Robertson, S., Gottesman, I., & Rutter, M. (1996). A broader phenotype of autism: The clinical spectrum in twins. *Journal of Child Psychology and Psychiatry, 37,* 785–801.

Mazzocco, M.M.M., Pennington, B.F., & Hagerman, R.J. (1994). Social cognition skills among females with Fragile X. *Journal of Autism and Developmental Disorders, 24,* 473–485.

Murphy, M., Bolton, P., Pickles, A., & Rutter, M. (1997, submitted). *Personality traits of relatives of autistic probands.*

Narayan, S., Moyes, B., & Wolff, S. (1990). Family characteristics of autistic children: A further report. *Journal of Autism and Developmental Disorders, 20,* 523–536.

Nelson, K. (1991). Prenatal and perinatal factors in the etiology of autism. *Pediatrics, 87,* 761–766.

Osborne, J.P., Fryer, A.E., & Webb, D. (1991). Epidemiology of tuberous sclerosis. *Annals of the New York Academy of Sciences, 615,* 125–127.

Pickles, A., Bolton, P., MacDonald, H., Bailey, A., Le Couteur, A., Sim, C-H., & Rutter, M. (1995). Latent class analysis of recurrence risks for complex phenotypes with selection and measurement error: A twin and family history study of autism. *American Journal of Human Genetics, 57,* 717–726.

Pickles, A., Bolton, P., MacDonald, H., Rios, P., Storoschuk, S., & Rutter, M. (1997, submitted). *A case control family history study of autism: Further findings from extended pedigrees.*

Piven, J., Chase, G.A., Landa, R., Wzorek, M., Gayle, J., Cloud, D., & Folstein, S. (1991). Psychiatric disorders in the parents of autistic individuals. *Journal of the American Academy of Child and Adolescent Psychiatry, 30,* 471–478.

Piven, J., Gayle, J., Chase, J., Fink, B., Landa, R., Wzorek, M., & Folstein, S. (1990). A family history study of neuropsychiatric disorders in the adult siblings of autistic individuals. *Journal of the American Academy of Child and Adolescent Psychiatry, 29,* 177–183.

Piven, J., Simon, J., Chase, G.A., Wzorek, M., Landa, R., Gayle, J., & Folstein, S. (1993). The etiology of autism: Pre-, peri- and neonatal factors. *Journal of the American Academy of Child and Adolescent Psychiatry, 32,* 1256–1263.

Piven, J., Wzorek, M., Landa, R., Lainhart, J., Bolton, P., Chase, G.A., & Folstein, S. (1994). Personality characteristics of the parents of autistic individuals [Preliminary communication]. *Psychological Medicine, 24,* 783–795.

Pocock, S.J. (1983). *Clinical trials: A practical approach.* Chichester: John Wiley & Sons.

Risch, N. (1990). Linkage strategies for genetically complex traits. *American Journal of Human Genetics, 46,* 222–253.

Ritvo, E.R., Spence, M.A., Freeman, B.J., Mason-Brothers, A., Mo, A., & Marazita, M.L. (1985). Evidence for autosomal recessive inheritance in 46 families with multiple incidences of autism. *American Journal of Psychiatry, 142,* 187–192.

Rutter, M. (1994). Psychiatric genetics: Research challenges and pathways forward. *American Journal of Medical Genetics (Neuropsychiatric Genetics), 54,* 185–198.

Rutter, M., & the English and Romanian Adoptees (E.R.A.) Study Team. (1997, submitted). *Quasi-autistic patterns following severe privation.*

Rutter, M., Bailey, A., Bolton, P., & Le Couteur, A. (1993). Autism: Syndrome definition and possible genetic mechanisms. In R. Plomin & G.E. McClearn (Eds.), *Nature, nurture, and psychology* (pp. 269–284). Washington, DC: APA Books.

Rutter, M., Bailey, A., Bolton, P., & Le Couteur, A. (1994). Autism and known medical conditions: Myth and substance. *Journal of Child Psychology and Psychiatry, 35,* 311–322.

Scott, S. (1994). Mental retardation. In M. Rutter, E. Taylor & L. Hersov (Eds.), *Child and adolescent psychiatry: Modern approaches* (3rd ed., pp. 616–646). Oxford: Blackwell Scientific.

Silliman, E.R., Campbell, M., & Mitchell, R.S. (1989). Genetic influences in autism and assessment of metalinguistic performance in siblings of autistic children. In G. Dawson (Ed.), *Autism: Nature, diagnosis & treatment* (pp. 225–259). New York: Guilford Press.

Simonoff, E., Bolton, P., & Rutter, M. (1996). Mental retardation: Genetic findings, clinical implications, and research agenda. *Journal of Child Psychology and Psychiatry, 37,* 259–280.

Simonoff, E., McGuffin, P., & Gottesman, I.I. (1994). Genetic influences on normal and abnormal development. In M. Rutter, E. Taylor & L. Hersov (Eds.), *Child and adolescent psychiatry: Modern approaches* (3rd ed., pp. 129–151). Oxford: Blackwell Scientific.

Smalley, S., Asarnow, R., & Spence, M. (1988). Autism and genetics: A decade of research. *Archives of General Psychiatry, 45,* 953–961.

Smalley, S., McCracken, J., & Tanguay, P. (1995). Autism, affective disorders, and social phobia. *American Journal of Medical Genetics (Neuropsychiatric Genetics), 60,* 19–26.

Smalley, S., Smith, M., & Tanguay, P. (1991). Autism and psychiatric disorders in tuberous sclerosis. *Annals of New York Academy of Science, 615,* 382–383.

Smalley, S. L., Burger, F., & Smith, M. (1994). Phenotypic variation of tuberous sclerosis in a single extended kindred. *Journal of Medical Genetics, 31,* 761–765.

Smalley, S.L., Tanguay, P.E., Smith, M., & Gutierrez, G. (1992). Autism and tuberous sclerosis. *Journal of Autism and Developmental Disorders, 22,* 339–355.

Spiker, D., Lotspeich, L., Kraemer, H.C., Hallmayer, J., McMahon, W., Petersen, P.B., Nicholas, P.,

Pingree, C., Wiese-Slater, S., Chiotti, C., Wong, D.L., Dimicelli, S., Ritvo, E., Cavalli-Sforza, L.L., & Ciaranello, R.D. (1994). Genetics of autism: Characteristics of affected and unaffected children from 37 multiplex families. *American Journal of Medical Genetics, 54,* 27–35.

Steffenburg, S., Gillberg, C., Helgren, L., Anderson, L., Gillberg, L., Jakobsson, G., & Bohman, M. (1989). A twin study of autism in Denmark, Finland, Iceland, Norway, and Sweden. *Journal of Child Psychology and Psychiatry, 30,* 405–416.

Sudhalter, V., Cohen, I.L., Silverman, W., & Wolfschein, E.G. (1990). Conversational analyses of males with Fragile X, Down syndrome, and autism: Comparison of the emergence of deviant language. *American Journal on Mental Retardation, 94,* 431–441.

Szatmari, P., Jones, M.B., Tuff, L., Bartolucci, G., Fisman, S., & Mahoney, W. (1993). Lack of cognitive impairment in first-degree relatives of children with pervasive developmental disorders. *Journal of the American Academy of Child and Adolescent Psychiatry, 32,* 1264–1273.

Tsai, L. (1987). Pre-, peri-, and neonatal factors in autism. In E. Schopler & G.B. Mesibov (Eds.), *Neurobiological issues in autism* (pp. 180–189). New York: Plenum Press.

Warren, S.T., & Nelson, D.L. (1994). Advances in molecular analysis of Fragile X syndrome. *The Journal of the American Medical Association, 271,* 536–542.

Wolff, P.H., Gardner, J., Paccia, J., & Lappen, J. (1989). The greeting behavior of Fragile X males. *American Journal of Mental Retardation, 93,* 406–411.

Wolff, S., Narayan, S., & Moyes, B. (1988). Personality characteristics of parents of autistic children. *Journal of Child Psychology and Psychiatry, 29,* 143–154.

CHAPTER 18

Medical Conditions Associated with Autism

ELISABETH M. DYKENS AND FRED R. VOLKMAR

For nearly three decades, it has been clear that autism is often associated with neurobiological correlates and central nervous system dysfunctions. These include high rates of seizures in individuals with autism as well as other, less specific symptoms and signs, such as persistent primitive reflexes, delayed development of hand dominance, and other neurological soft signs (see Chapter 16). Of particular importance is the observation that as many as 25% of persons with autism develop seizures during adolescence (Deykin & MacMahon, 1979; Rutter, 1970; Volkmar & Nelson, 1990). The unusual pattern of onset and the frequency of seizures in persons with autism are strong indications of a neuropathological process.

Over the past two decades, autism has been associated with a number of medical conditions, and genetic factors have also been implicated in the pathogenesis of this disorder (Bailey, 1993; Dawson, 1990; Gillberg & Coleman, 1992; Rutter, Bailey, Bolton, & Le Couteur, 1994; see also Chapter 17). Researchers are in general agreement on the neurobiological basis of autism, but they often disagree on the extent and nature of medical and neurobiological features associated with autism (see Rutter, 1996).

This chapter provides a selective review of these issues. Studies that screen autistic subjects for various medical conditions are reviewed, and methodologic problems in interpreting these studies are discussed. The relationship of autism to four different conditions is addressed in some detail. These syndromes are chosen either because of the apparent frequency with which they are associated with autism (fragile X syndrome, tuberous sclerosis) or because of the apparent *infrequency* of such associations (Down syndrome, Williams syndrome). Following the syndrome review, implications for future research are discussed. Neurological conditions associated with autism and neurochemical aspects of autism (discussed in Chapters 16 and 15, respectively) are not extensively reviewed here, nor are conditions such as plumbism, which seem more likely to be results of autism rather than causes (Accardo, Whitman, Caul, & Rolfe, 1988).

ASSOCIATIONS OF AUTISM AND VARIOUS MEDICAL CONDITIONS

Researchers generally agree that autism is the result of some neurobiological factor or factors. Individuals with autism are clearly at increased risk for seizures, but considerable controversy surrounds the frequency and significance of other conditions associated with autism. Gillberg (1990a, 1990b, 1992b), for example, argues that more than one-third of cases of autism are due to some identifiable medical condition and further suggests that it may be possible to develop a subtyping system for autism, based on such conditions (Gillberg, 1992a, 1992b). In contrast, Rutter and colleagues (1994) find that only about 10% of autism cases are associated with known medical causes.

The authors thank Robert M. Hodapp, Ph.D., for his helpful comments on an earlier draft of this manuscript.

Examining these discrepancies in more detail, several studies have compared the frequency of medical conditions in autistic subjects to samples exhibiting other developmental disorders. Wing and Gould (1979) found a much lower rate of known medical problems in their autistic sample relative to nonautistic subjects (17% versus 71%, respectively). Disorders such as phenylketonuria and tuberous sclerosis were found only in the nonautistic group. In contrast, Tuchman, Rapin, and Shinnar (1991) compared groups of children with autism to those with developmental language disorder and found similar rates of medical conditions, about 5%, across groups. Similarly, in a study comparing autistic children to students with special educational needs, Fombonne and Mazaurbrun (1992) noted that these groups did not differ in the frequency of most medical conditions, including congenital rubella or chromosomal abnormalities. The autistic group, however, was significantly less likely to have Down syndrome or cerebral palsy, and all cases of neurofibromatosis and phenylketonuria (PKU) were found in the nonautistic group.

In a series of studies, Bolton et al. (1991) and Rutter, Bailey, Bolton, and Le Couteur (1993) conducted extensive evaluations on 151 individuals with autism. They found that 8.1% showed medical conditions that were likely to be causal factors of autism, including fragile X syndrome, bilateral deafness, cerebral palsy, multiple congenital abnormalities, and chromosomal anomalies. About 3.8% had other medical concerns that were less likely to be etiologic factors. The overall rate of medical conditions, 11.9%, is similar to the rate found in a study of medical conditions in twins with autism (12.9%) (Bailey et al., 1991).

Rates of medical conditions associated with autism seem associated with IQ level. Although some find that IQ is not related to medical risk (e.g., Steffenburg, 1991), others find more medical conditions among autistic persons at lower IQ levels. In an epidemiologic study of autism, Ritvo et al. (1990) demonstrated that medical conditions were more frequent in persons with severe mental retardation. These findings are consistent with those of other researchers (Rutter et al., 1994; Wing & Gould, 1979), yet two warnings are in

order. First, it is more difficult to diagnose autism in persons with severe levels of mental retardation. Second, the possibility of finding any associated medical condition rises with increasing degrees of mental retardation and approaches 50% among persons at the severe and profound levels (Scott, 1994). In brief, studies have found that the rates of medical conditions in autism range from 5% to 33%. IQ level may be one complicating factor, but variability in rates is also likely to be associated with other methodologic problems.

METHODOLOGIC PROBLEMS

Several methodologic factors may account for discrepancies in rates of associated medical conditions in autism. Studies using small sample sizes may have limited generalizability, and larger studies may fall prey to ascertainment bias, such as when only clinic samples are used. Many studies, including epidemiologic surveys, often rely on previous assessments of autism, and these a priori diagnoses are typically based on different diagnostic criteria. Not only do criteria differ across studies, but some diagnostic criteria are more systematic and rigorous than others.

DSM-III-R criteria are clearly less stringent than *DSM-III, ICD-10,* or *DSM-IV* criteria. In particular, *DSM-III-R* criteria overdiagnose autism in individuals with severe and profound mental retardation. Indeed, in the *DSM-IV* field trial, the *DSM-III-R* criteria had close to a 60% false-positive rate in persons with profound mental retardation. Given the rather broad diagnostic net cast by *DSM-III-R* (American Psychiatric Association [APA], 1987), it would seem likely that high rates of associated medical conditions might be a function of the diagnostic criteria used. This hypothesis has been supported in one study comparing *DSM-III, III-R,* and *ICD-10* criteria, i.e., *DSM-III-R* criteria were more likely to "overdiagnose" autism among more severely mentally handicapped persons and this group was, in turn, more likely to exhibit associated medical conditions (Barton & Volkmar, 1996). Thus it appears that a large part of the discrepancy arises in the group of cases with "atypical autism," particularly when associated with severe mental handicap (see Rutter, 1996 for a discussion).

Gillberg and Coleman (1996) have more recently suggested that the rate of associated medical condition in autism averaged over a number of studied is approximately 25% with higher rates observed in subjects with more severe retardation; however, they did not unequivocally observer higher rates in atypical autism.

In addition, it is not always clear whether medical conditions are causal in nature. Seizures, for example, are often cited in studies as being causal, yet seizure disorders in autism usually start many years after autism is diagnosed.

Finally, because of their relative scarcity, medical problems in autism are often initially reported as case studies. As Rutter et al. (1994) note, however, multiple reporting of single cases sometimes conveys an impression of stronger associations than are actually observed. Single-case reports linking autism to other medical conditions are often readily published, but their significance may be rather limited since data on risk in the larger population of persons with autism is not addressed.

Given these problems, initial positive reports linking autism to other conditions have often been reevaluated, with different results. This reappraisal is seen rather dramatically in fragile X syndrome (see below). In other syndromes, early reports suggested that autism was more common than expected in children with congenital rubella (Chess, Korn, & Fernandez, 1971). On follow-up, however, autistic features were less prominent (Chess, 1977), raising some doubt about the initial diagnoses. Witt-Engerström and Gillberg (1987) initially suggested that over three-fourths of girls with Rett's Syndrome had autism or autistic features, but this view has not been supported subsequently (Olsson & Rett, 1985).

Several methodologic problems are thus prominent in studies of medical conditions in autism. These problems include small sample sizes, ascertainment bias, complexities in making autism diagnoses, ambiguities regarding causal medical conditions, and multiple reporting of single cases. As demonstrated in the next section, however, the primary issue is not whether autism is ever associated with a particular condition such as fragile X syndrome, congenital rubella, or Down syndrome. Rather, the critical issue is whether these associations

are significantly more frequent (or, possibly, less frequent) than would be expected on the basis of chance alone.

SYNDROME REVIEW

This section reviews relations between autism and fragile X syndrome, Williams syndrome, Down syndrome, and tuberous sclerosis. Even though these syndromes show remarkably diverse behavioral features (Dykens, 1995), each is connected to autism in work that ranges from case reports to large-scale epidemiologic studies.

Fragile X syndrome has received more than a decade of intense autism research. Yet the fragile X–autism controversy is only now being settled, in part because of new work examining a broader range of behavior in this syndrome. Williams syndrome and Down syndrome show the importance of following up initial autism case reports with systematic research. These syndromes also have behavioral phenotypes that argue against an increased risk of autism, above and beyond the risk associated with mental retardation. In contrast to these disorders, research to date in tuberous sclerosis finds rather promising ties to autism. This section first reviews the autism controversy in fragile X syndrome; this syndrome, more than any other, highlights the methodologic problems described above.

Fragile X Syndrome

As the most common inherited cause of mental retardation, fragile X syndrome is second only to Down syndrome in terms of a known chromosomal cause of mental retardation (Sherman, 1992). With the discovery of the fragile X gene, it is now known that most cases of this syndrome are caused by an amplification or excessive repetition of two nucleotides that make up DNA: cytosine (C) and guanine (G). Above a certain threshold of these triplet CGG repeats, people have "premutations" and may be affected or unaffected carriers of the syndrome, depending on the mode of inheritance and other genetic factors (see Caskey, Pizzuti, Fu, Fenwich, & Nelson, 1992, for a review).

Early descriptions of fragile X syndrome focused on fully affected males and their many autistic-like features. These included poor eye contact; language delay, perseveration, and echolalia; self-abuse (e.g., hand and arm biting); stereotypies (e.g., hand flapping and body rocking); hypersensitivity to auditory stimuli or environmental change; tactile defensiveness; preoccupations with a narrow range of stimuli; and poor social relating (Borghgraef, Fryns, Dielkens, Pych, & Van den Berghe, 1987; Fryns, Jacobs, Klecklowska, & Van den Berghe, 1984; Gillberg, Persson, & Wahlstrom, 1986; Hagerman, Jackson, Levitas, Rimland, & Braden, 1986). Indeed, early case studies described several fragile X boys who met *DSM-III* criteria for autism (e.g., August & Lockhart, 1984; Meryash, Szymanski, & Gerald, 1982).

These early reports and case studies generated much excitement among researchers who hypothesized that fragile X syndrome might be a common genetic cause of autism. This hypothesis was tested in more than a decade of research, and findings sparked much debate about the overlap between these two disorders. The relevant studies examined either the prevalence of fragile X syndrome in autistic samples, or the prevalence of autism in fragile X samples.

Table 18.1 summarizes studies that screened autistic males for fragile X syndrome. As shown in the table, prevalence rates for fragile X syndrome among these autistic samples ranged from 0% to 16%, with a median of about 4%.

Studies using the opposite approach—diagnosing autism in fragile X syndrome—are summarized in Table 18.2. To an even greater extent than in the first approach, the prevalence rates of autism among fragile X males varied considerably from one study to another, ranging from 5% to 60%.

Variability in prevalence rates in both tables is associated with several methodologic problems. Of some concern are differences in sample sizes, particularly among studies in Table 18.1 that screened autistic samples for the fragile X marker (Fisch, Cohen, Jenkins, & Brown, 1988). Most of these studies were conducted prior to more accurate molecular testing for fragile X syndrome, when cytogenetic laboratories often used different criteria for making fragile X diagnoses (Frisch et al., 1988). Also, because many studies in Table 18.2 used fragile X males presenting

TABLE 18.1 Studies of Fragile X Syndrome in Autism

Study	Number of Autistic Subjects	Percentage with Fragile X Syndrome
Jorgensen et al., 1984	23	4.0%
Venter et al., 1984	40	0
Watson et al., 1984	76	5.3
Blomquist et al., 1985	102	16.0
Goldfine et al., 1985	37	0
Pueschel et al., 1985	18	0
Brown et al., 1986	183	13.1
Fisch et al., 1986	144	12.5
McGillivary et al., 1986	33	9.0
Wahlstrom et al., 1986	143	13.0
Wright et al., 1986	40	2.5
Ho & Kalousek, 1989	45	2.0
Payton et al., 1989	85	2.4
Wahlstrom et al., 1989	52	9.0
Cantu et al., 1990	67	1.0
Tranebjaerg & Kure, 1991	32	6.0
Bailey et al., 1993	123	1.6

*All references cited in Tables 18.1–18.5 appear in their entirety in the References section at the end of the chapter.

for clinical services, ascertainment biases may have inflated the estimates of autism.

Of primary concern, however, is these studies' use of inconsistent or unclear diagnostic criteria for autism. Studies in Table 18.1 typically did not report how a priori diagnoses of autism were made. For studies assessing autism in fragile X samples (Table 18.2), diagnostic criteria ranged from systematic approaches (e.g., *DSM-III*) to informal methods (e.g., presence of two behaviors). Informal methods are particularly susceptible to bias because of researchers' different opinions regarding the primary deficit in autism. Only two studies addressed interrater reliability in making autism diagnoses.

Despite these many methodologic problems, researchers used these prevalence studies to determine whether fragile X syndrome was a common cause of autism. In particular, workers compared differential prevalence rates of fragile X syndrome in autism versus rates in mental retardation in general. Blomquist et al. (1985) and Gillberg and Wahlstrom

TABLE 18.2   Studies of Autism in Fragile X Syndrome

Study	Number of Fragile X Subjects	Percentages of Subjects with Autism	Autism Diagnosis Criteria
Brown et al., 1982	22	23%	Rutter
Fryns & Van den Berghe, 1983	30	16	Not stated
Jacobs et al., 1983	9	22	Not stated
Levitas et al., 1983	10	60	*DSM-III*
Nielsen, 1983	27	33	Four behaviors
Fryns et al., 1984	21	14	Two behaviors
Partington, 1984	61	5	Three behaviors
Rhoads, 1984	17	18	Not stated
Benezech & Noel, 1985	28	53	*DSM-III*
Brown et al., 1986	150	17	*DSM-III*
Hagerman et al., 1986	50	46	*DSM-III*
Borghgraef et al., 1987	23	39	Autiscale
Bregman et al., 1988	14	7	*DSM-III*
Reiss & Freund, 1990	17	18%	*DSM-III-R*

(1985) asserted that their prevalence rates of fragile X and autism—16% to 20%—far exceeded the 4.5% to 7.0% of severely and mildly retarded males with fragile X syndrome. These and other researchers (e.g., Fisch et al., 1988) concluded that fragile X syndrome was more strongly associated with autism than with mental retardation.

In contrast to these researchers, Watson et al. (1984) and Payton, Steele, Wenger, and Minshew (1989) claimed that their prevalence rates of autism and fragile X (3.0% and 5.3%, respectively) were no higher than the rate of fragile X syndrome among mentally retarded males. This group argued, then, that fragile X syndrome should not increase the risk of autism above and beyond the risk associated with mental retardation.

Recent work supports this latter position. Examining 123 autistic subjects, Bailey et al. (1993) found that 1.6% had fragile X syndrome; and that fragile X was not found in more than 2.5% of any of the subsamples that comprised their subject population. These rates are lower than the rates of fragile X syndrome in the population of persons with mental retardation. Einfeld, Malony, and Hall (1989) found comparable rates of autism in appropriately matched groups of fragile X and non-fragile X males. Summarizing data across 40 studies, Fisch (1992) found virtually identical pooled proportions of fragile X syndrome in autistic males and in mentally retarded males in general.

These studies suggest that autism and fragile X syndrome indeed co-occur but the prevalence of these cases is much lower than originally thought. In contrast to early hypotheses, it is unlikely that fragile X syndrome is a major etiologic factor in autism. Of note, however, is that fragile X syndrome may account for more females in the autistic population than has previously been appreciated (Bailey et al., 1993; Cohen, Brown, et al., 1989).

Instead of full-blown autism per se, individuals with fragile X syndrome show a wide range of learning and behavioral problems. For example, attention deficits and hyperactivity are often seen, especially in males (Bregman, Leckman, & Ort, 1988; Dorn, Mazzocco, & Hagerman, 1994), and some females show vulnerabilities to depression (Reiss, Hagerman, Vinogradov, Abrams, & King, 1988). More pertinent to the autism debate, however, is that affected individuals often show varying degrees of social dysfunction, primarily shyness, social and performance anxiety, withdrawal, social avoidance, and gaze aversion.

Among males, Cohen and his colleagues (Cohen, Vietze, Sudhalter, Jenkins, & Brown, 1989, 1991) found that gaze aversion persisted throughout development and was seen in males with high and low levels of communicative abilities (Cohen et al., 1991). Unlike a comparison group of autistic subjects, fragile X males were more attuned and responsive to parental gaze and social cues. Fragile X males also showed a level of wariness toward strangers that was not exhibited by their less discriminating autistic counterparts (Cohen et al., 1991).

Other researchers have identified excessive shyness and socially related anxieties in their fragile X samples (e.g., Bregman, Leckman, & Ort, 1988; Einfeld, 1988; Nielsen, 1983); some males met criteria for avoidant, overanxious, and generalized anxiety disorders. Many males, however, become less shy and more sociable as their familiarity with others increases (Einfeld et al., 1989; Jacobs, Mayer, Matsuura, Rhoads, & Yee, 1983; Rhoads, 1984). This slow-to-warm stance contrasts with the persistent aloofness and social indifference more typically found in autism.

Many girls and women with fragile X syndrome are also shy, withdrawn, and socially anxious, and they show poor or fleeting eye contact (Borghgraef, Fryns, & Van den Berghe, 1990; Hagerman et al., 1992; Lachiewicz, 1992). Relative to controls, fragile X women appear to have poorer social and interpersonal skills, more lability and withdrawal, and increased risks of schizotypal personality disorder (Freund, Reiss, Hagerman, & Vinogradov, 1992; Reiss et al., 1988). Withdrawal, anxiety, and gaze avoidance may be more apparent among fully affected women relative to women with premutations (Freund, Reiss, & Abrams, 1993; Sobesky, Pennington, Porter, Hull, & Hagerman, 1994).

Growing evidence thus indicates that shyness, social avoidance, gaze aversion, and withdrawal characterize many males and females with fragile X syndrome. Symptoms are milder and more variably expressed among persons with premutations. After more than a decade of debate, it now appears that fragile X syndrome involves a spectrum of socially avoidant behavior that ranges in severity from autism at one extreme to shyness at the other. These features suggest a distinctive fragile X behavioral phenotype that is only rarely associated with full-blown autism per se.

Williams Syndrome

Williams syndrome affects about 1 in 20,000 people and is caused in most cases by a deletion on one of the chromosome 7s that includes the gene for elastin (Ewart et al., 1993). Persons with Williams syndrome often show a distinctive cognitive profile, hyperacusis, cardiovascular disease, hypercalcemia, and characteristic facial features described as "elfin-like" and appealing (Pober & Dykens, 1996).

Relations between Williams syndrome and autism have not yet been widely studied. To date, six cases have been reported in which patients with Williams syndrome met *DSM-III* criteria for autistic disorder (Gillberg & Rasmussen, 1994; Reiss, Feinstein, Rosenbaum, Borengasser-Caruso, & Goldsmith, 1985). Yet, as previously noted, multiple reporting of single cases may create an impression of a stronger overlap between disorders than is actually the case. Indeed, many of Williams syndrome's phenotypic features argue against a heightened risk of autism.

In particular, Williams syndrome and autism show opposite patterns of cognitive strength and weakness, as well as dissimilar maladaptive behaviors. Persons with autism often have relatively poor verbal skills (e.g., Lerea, 1987). In contrast, many individuals with Williams syndrome show remarkable strengths in expressive language and linguistic functioning. These strengths include high-level syntax and semantics (e.g., Bellugi, Marks, Bihrle, & Sabo, 1988); storytelling and narrative enrichment strategies involving affective prosody and a sense of drama (Reilly, Klima, & Bellugi, 1990); and reliance on stereotypic, adult phrases (Udwin & Yule, 1990).

Further, certain nonverbal perceptual skills are often relative strengths in autism (e.g., Frith & Baron-Cohen, 1987); however, these same skills are typically weak in Williams syndrome. Many persons with Williams syndrome have marked difficulties in visual-spatial processing, especially integrating details into a whole (e.g., Bihrle, Bellugi, Delis, & Marks, 1989). Yet some visual-spatial skills seem well-preserved, even within this area of deficit.

In particular, persons with Williams syndrome generally excel on facial perception and recognition tasks (Bellugi, Wang, & Jernigan, 1994; Udwin & Yule, 1991), and they often look intently at the faces of both strangers and familiar people (Bellugi, Bihrle, Neville, Jernigan, & Doherty, 1992; Bertrand, Mervis, Rice, & Adamson, 1993). Marked interest in human faces likely facilitates the ability of many persons with Williams syndrome to be "acutely attentive to the emotional states of others" (Bellugi et al., 1994, p. 35) and "responsive to any and all facial cues" (p. 46). In contrast, profound difficulty with facial and affective recognition (e.g., Sigman, Ungerer, Mundy, & Sherman, 1987) is among the social deficits that are hallmarks of autistic disorder.

Finally, the personality and maladaptive features seen in Williams syndrome are not particularly characteristic of autism. Consistent with their verbal and facial recognition strengths, individuals with Williams syndrome are often described as pleasant, friendly, affectionate, engaging, and charming (e.g., Dilts, Morris, & Leonard, 1990; Udwin, Yule, & Martin, 1987). Although they are sociable, many persons with Williams syndrome have difficulties in sustaining friendships, and they also show impulsivity, distractibility, and anxiety. Anxiety symptoms include excessive worrying and preoccupations about future events or unfamiliar situations, as well as excessive crying, fearfulness, and somatic complaints (e.g., Brewer, Levine, & Pober, 1994; Einfeld, Tonge, & Florio, 1992; Plissart, Borghgraef, Volke, Van den Berghe, & Fryns, 1994; Preuss, 1984; Tomc, Williamson, & Pauli, 1990; Udwin, 1990; Udwin et al., 1987).

Although not strikingly autistic, some of these maladaptive features may be described as autistic-like. The latter include obsessive worrying, perseveration, difficulties relating to peers, and body-rocking and other repetitive behaviors seen in highly anxious persons (Pober & Dykens, 1996). These behaviors in Williams syndrome need further study, including how they might relate to high-functioning or atypical autism.

For the most part, however, Williams syndrome and autistic disorder have many features that set them apart from one another. The disorders show opposite patterns of strength and weakness in both verbal and nonverbal functioning, especially in facial and affective recognition. Different personality and maladaptive features are also seen. Although further research is needed, it seems unlikely that the six cases noted above represent an increased risk of autism above and beyond the overlap associated with mental retardation.

Down Syndrome

Unlike Williams syndrome and other recently delineated syndromes, Down syndrome has a 130-year history of research. In addition to this rich history, work on Down syndrome is facilitated by the high prevalence of this disorder, its frequent detection at birth, and the relative genetic homogeneity of trisomy 21 cases. Indeed, of the behavioral research articles on specific syndromes published between 1985 and 1990, 47% were devoted to Down syndrome (Hodapp & Dykens, 1994).

In all this research, however, autism is rarely noted. Over the years, only a handful of histories have been reported on children or adults with Down syndrome and autism. From the late 1970s to the present, 10 cases of co-occurring autism and Down syndrome have been published by five different research groups (Bregman & Volkmar, 1988; Ghaziuddin, Tsai, & Ghaziuddin, 1992; Howlin, Wing, & Gould, 1995; Wakabayashi, 1979; Wing & Gould, 1979).

Large-scale prevalence studies have also screened samples with Down syndrome and, as summarized in Table 18.3, have found relatively low rates of autism. In studies screening large numbers of Down syndrome using *DSM-* or *ICD*-based diagnostic criteria, autism rates have ranged from 1.0% to 2.2%. Using another approach, Fombonne and Mazaubrun (1992) screened 152 subjects with autism, and found just 2 subjects with Down syndrome (1.3%).

Altogether, these published case reports and epidemiologic studies found 33 subjects with Down syndrome and autism. This number is remarkably low, given that Down syndrome, which occurs in approximately 1 in 800 births (Hook, 1982), is the most common chromosomal cause of mental retardation.

Rates of other psychiatric disorders are similarly low among persons with Down syndrome,

TABLE 18.3 Autism and Down Syndrome

Studies of Autism in Down Syndrome			
Study	Number of Down Syndrome Subjects	Percentage of Subjects with Autism	Autism Diagnostic Criteria
Gath & Gumley, 1986	193	1.0%	*ICD-9* and *DSM-III*
Gillberg, Grufman, & Themner, 1986	20	5.0	*DSM-III*
Lund, 1988	44	11.4	MRC Schedule[a]
Meyers & Pueschel, 1991	497	1.0	*DSM-III-R*
Collacott et al., 1992	371	2.2	*ICD-9*

Study of Down Syndrome in Autism		
Study	Number of Autistic Subjects	Percentage with Down Syndrome
Fombonne & Mazaubrun, 1992	152	1.3%

[a] MRC Handicaps, Behavior, and Skills Schedule (Wing, 1980).

even as compared to groups with other types of developmental delay (Collacott, Cooper, & McGrother, 1992; Grizenko, Cvejic, Vida, & Sayegh, 1991; Meyers & Pueschel, 1991). Some children, however, may be prone to attentional difficulties, overactivity, oppositionality, and anxiety (Gath & Gumley, 1986; Meyers & Pueschel, 1991; Pueschel, Bernier, & Pezzullo, 1991), and adults with Down syndrome may be particularly vulnerable to depression and Alzheimer-type dementia (Warren, Holroyd, & Folstein, 1989; Zigman, Schupf, Zigman, & Silverman, 1993).

Although the reasons for low rates of autism and other psychiatric disorders are unclear, they may be related to a commonly held clinical opinion about the nature of Down syndrome; that is, many persons with this condition are perceived as outgoing, affectionate, easygoing, placid, and cheerful—like "Prince Charming" (Gibbs & Thorpe, 1983; Menolascino, 1965). Recent research, however, calls this stereotype into question. Mothers, for example, describe their children with Down syndrome as having a wide range of personality features (Rogers, 1987; Wishart & Johnston, 1990). Some children are easygoing, but others are more active and distractible and have difficult temperaments (see Ganiban, Wagner, & Cicchetti, 1990, for a review). A variety of personality and temperament profiles have emerged, and no single description is adequate for all persons with the syndrome.

Yet the stereotype persists and may actually contribute to professionals' overlooking certain psychiatric disorders like autism in persons with Down syndrome. Indeed, although autism diagnoses are typically made in the preschool years, Howlin et al. (1995) note later ages at which autism was diagnosed in their four Down syndrome cases, as well as in all cases reported in the literature (age range from 7 years to adulthood). This "diagnostic overshadowing" creates unnecessary stress for families, and prevents them from using supports and interventions available to families with an autistic child. Even though autism is rare in persons with Down syndrome, it should be considered in the range of diagnostic possibilities for persons with this syndrome. Somewhat paradoxically, this condition may, ultimately, prove of greater interest to research in autism because of the relative lack of association.

Tuberous Sclerosis

Tuberous sclerosis affects as many as 1 in 10,000 people and is characterized by abnormal tissue growth, or benign tumors (hamartomas), in the brain and in many other organs such as the skin, kidneys, eyes, heart, and lung (Hunt, 1990). These tumors are variably expressed; they can result in a changeable phenotype that ranges from mild skin problems or seizures to severe mental retardation and intractable seizures (Short, Richardson, Haines, & Kwiatowski, 1995). Between 50% and 60% of affected individuals show mental retardation, and 80% have seizures; those with mental retardation invariably have seizures (Gomez, 1988). Tuberous sclerosis is an autosomal dominant disorder, and recent molecular genetic breakthroughs have identified two tuberous sclerosis genes: one on chromosome 9 (9q34), and another on chromosome 16 (16p13.3) (see Short et al., 1995, for a review).

Autistic-like symptoms were first described in patients with tuberous sclerosis a decade before Kanner's classic delineation of infantile autism (Critchley & Earl, 1932). These early-noted symptoms included stereotypies, absent or abnormal speech, withdrawal, and impaired social interactions. In subsequent years, over 50 case reports of co-occurring autism and tuberous sclerosis were published, and surveys were conducted of autistic-like and other maladaptive behaviors (e.g., Hunt, 1983). Reviewing this early work, Smalley, Tanguay, Smith, and Gutierrez (1992) found three predominant types of behavioral dysfunction in tuberous sclerosis: (a) autism or autistic-like behaviors; (b) hyperactivity and impulsivity; and (c) aggression and uncooperative behavior.

Building on these early observations, current work includes population-based prevalence studies of tuberous sclerosis in autism, as well as systematic assessments of autism in tuberous sclerosis. Almost all of these studies focus on tuberous sclerosis subjects with co-occurring mental retardation and seizures. As summarized in Table 18.4, epidemiologic studies of autistic subjects find between 0.4% to 2.8% who are diagnosed with tuberous sclerosis. Rates are higher (from 8% to 14%) in studies that include only autistic subjects with seizure disorders. Frequencies of tuberous sclerosis found in autistic samples are higher than the frequencies found in the general population (Smalley et al., 1992), suggesting a possible association between these two disorders.

Further ties between the two disorders are shown in several studies that examined autism in subjects with tuberous sclerosis. As summarized in Table 18.5, rates of autism in tuberous sclerosis samples range from 17% to 61%. All

TABLE 18.4   Studies of Tuberous Sclerosis in Autism

Studies	Number of Autistic Subjects	Percentage with Tuberous Sclerosis
Epidemiologic studies		
Lotter, 1967	32	3.0%
Ollson, Steffenburg, & Gillberg, 1988	35	2.8
Ritvo et al., 1990	233	0.4
Gillberg, Steffenburg, & Schaumann, 1991	55	1.9
Studies of autistic subjects with seizures		
Riikonen & Amnell, 1981	24	8.0
Gillberg, 1991	66	14.0

of these studies used well-established diagnostic criteria for autism, and some were quite rigorous in their use of multiple diagnostic criteria for autism (e.g., Gillberg, Gillberg, & Ahlsen, 1994; Smalley et al., 1992).

Autism in tuberous sclerosis seems to affect males and females about equally (Gillberg et al., 1994; Hunt and Shephard, 1993); similarly, tuberous sclerosis is equally distributed between the sexes in the general population. Some studies, however, find more males than females with co-occurring tuberous sclerosis and autism (Smalley et al., 1992). Further work is needed to show the extent to which this disorder afflicts both males and females in the autistic population.

In contrast to studies of persons with tuberous sclerosis and mental retardation, data are limited on autism in tuberous sclerosis subjects without mental retardation. Of the 6 tuberous sclerosis subjects with average IQs studied by Gillberg et al. (1994), 3 had nonsignificant psychiatric evaluations, 1 met criteria for Asperger's Syndrome, 1 had a history of elective mutism, and 1 was autistic-like. Atypical autism was also recently described in a case report of a girl with tuberous sclerosis and average intelligence (Williamson & Bolton, 1995). Although autistic-spectrum

TABLE 18.5   Studies of Autism in Tuberous Sclerosis

Study	Number of Tuberous Sclerosis Subjects	Percentage of Subjects with Autism	Autism Diagnostic Criteria
Hunt & Dennis, 1987	69	58%	Rutter
Riikonen & Simell, 1990	24	17	Rutter
Curatolo et al., 1991	23	26	Rutter
Smalley et al., 1991	24	21	ABC[a]
Smalley et al., 1992	18	39	ADI[b], *ICD-10*
Hunt & Shepard, 1993	21[c]	24	*DSM-III-R*
Gillberg et al., 1994	28[d]	61	*DSM-III-R,* ABC[a], CARS[e]

[a] Autism Behavior Checklist.
[b] Autism Diagnostic Inventory.
[c] Includes 9 nonretarded subjects, none showed autism.
[d] Includes 6 nonretarded subjects, none showed autism.
[e] Childhood Autism Rating Scale.

problems are suggested in persons with tuberous sclerosis and average IQs, Hunt and Shepherd (1993) found no such vulnerabilities in 9 average-IQ tuberous sclerosis subjects. Instead, 5 of these subjects were described as overactive by their parents.

Smalley, Burger, and Smith (1994) recently did an in-depth study of the range of phenotypic expression in nonretarded individuals with tuberous sclerosis. Examining a large extended family showing tuberous sclerosis markers on chromosome 16, they compared psychiatric symptoms between affected and unaffected family members. Among the members with tuberous sclerosis, physical symptoms were mild and were generally limited to skin problems. Yet, relative to unaffected family members, the tuberous sclerosis subjects showed significantly higher rates of psychiatric disorder, primarily anxiety disorders, and to a lesser extent, mood disorders. Among nonretarded tuberous sclerosis persons with markers on chromosome 16, then, a phenotype of mild physical symptoms and increased risk of anxiety disorders is suggested.

Although further work is needed, research to date finds promising ties between tuberous sclerosis and autism, primarily in persons with tuberous sclerosis and mental retardation. Preliminary new data and case reports also suggest increased risks of autistic-like symptoms and anxiety disorders among nonretarded persons with tuberous sclerosis.

AUTISM AND OTHER MEDICAL RISK

Obstetrical Factors

Several studies have suggested that children with autism come from pregnancies that are at increased risk (Nelson, 1991; Tsai, 1987). Obstetrical risk factors that have been reported to be significantly increased in autism include older maternal age, pre- or post-maturity, bleeding during the pregnancy, meconium staining during delivery, and so forth (Tsai, 1987). Interestingly, autism has not apparently been particularly associated with perinatal factors (other than those entailed in prematurity; Goodman, 1990; Nelson, 1991). On balance, the data suggest that problems noted at birth are more strongly related to problems in the fetus rather than to labor and delivery (e.g., Bailey, Le Couteur, Gottesman & Bolton, 1995; Goodman, 1990; Rutter, et al., 1993).

Disorders of Metabolism

Various inborn errors of metabolism have been associated either with autism or with autistic features. Several problems complicate the interpretation of available data. As noted by Gillberg and Coleman (1992), various factors may result in a somewhat later presentation of developmental or behavioral disturbance than is typical in "classical" autism; for example, the metabolic abnormality may not be of sufficient severity to result in clinical symptoms for some months after the child's birth. A second complication is that the degree of associated cognitive delay is often very severe in such conditions, and the diagnosis of autism (not just the rather nonspecific presence of "autistic-features") may be difficult to establish.

Disorders that have been associated with autism or autistic-features include PKU (Lowe, Tanaka, Seashore, Young, & Cohen, 1980; Pueschel, Herman, & Groden, 1985), histidinemia (Kotsopoulous & Kutty, 1979), Lesch-Nyhan syndrome (Nyhan, James, Teberg, Sweetman, & Nelson, 1969), and others (see Gillberg & Coleman, 1992; Visconti, Piazzi, Posar, & Santi, 1994). It appears to be appropriate to consider screening for inborn errors of metabolism in all children with severe developmental delay, but the specific relationship of such conditions to autism remains to be clearly established.

Infections

The claim has been made that a small but significant proportion of children develop autism as a result of pre- or post-natal infections—for example, with rubella, cytomegalovirus, herpes simplex, HIV, and so on (see Gillberg & Coleman, 1992, for a review of claims). The limited available evidence regarding seasonality of birth of autistic children (e.g., Gillberg, 1990a; Konstantareas, Hauser, Lennox, & Homatidis, 1986) has similarly been taken to suggest a potential contribution of maternal viral infection (see Gillberg & Coleman, 1992). However, more recent studies, e.g., Bolton, Pickles, Harrington, McDonald, and Rutter (1992) have not shown consistent patterns. Reported associations with congenital infections such as rubella (Chess, 1971) or other agents (Stubbs, 1978) must be interpreted with some caution, for several reasons. Cases initially identified appear to have more frequently exhibited the nonspecific autistic-features clinical picture (Deykin & MacMahon, 1979); importantly, such cases may be less likely to exhibit such features at follow-up (e.g., Chess, 1977).

Immunological Association

Interest in the immune system and autism arises from the various case reports in which infections (and possibly altered immune response) are associated with the development of autism or autistic features (Marchetti, Scifo, Batticane, & Scapagnini, 1990; Menage et al., 1992; Singh, Warren, Odell, Warren, & Cole, 1993). However, the few studies conducted have yielded inconsistent or contradictory findings.

IMPLICATIONS FOR FUTURE RESEARCH AND CLINICAL PRACTICE

This review of the association of autism with various medical conditions suggests many areas that need to be addressed in future research. First, standard diagnostic criteria for autism need to be used in studies devoted to specific conditions; this need was seen most dramatically in fragile X syndrome, where diagnostic imprecision contributed to an impression of a much stronger association than actually appears to exist. Consistent use of standard diagnostic criteria would also facilitate comparisons of autism rates across different disorders.

Second, research needs to reflect a greater appreciation for diagnostic complexities at either end of the IQ spectrum. Autism is particularly difficult to assess in persons with severe and profound mental retardation; these same individuals show increased risks of medical complications. Yet studies are also needed that examine a wide range of social and communicative dysfunctions in high-functioning persons with autism and related disorders. This need was seen in nonretarded persons with tuberous sclerosis and fragile X syndrome, where suggestions of atypical autism, Asperger's syndrome, and social anxieties were found.

Although case reports are clinically relevant, they should be interpreted with considerable caution. Case studies tying autism to a specific medical condition do not prove an increased vulnerability to autism in others with this medical condition. Instead, case reports may provide a first step toward more systematic research. In Williams syndrome, for example, the case reports suggest some overlap with autism. Yet, to determine whether this overlap is higher than expected due to chance alone, studies are needed that examine large, representative samples of Williams syndrome subjects for autism, and that screen autistic samples for deletions in the Williams-syndrome critical region on chromosome 7.

Finally, the behavioral phenotypes associated with specific disorders often complicate autism research. In particular, phenotypes may predispose researchers to either overdiagnose or underdiagnose autism. On the one hand, there may be a premature rush to diagnose autism in disorders that show many autistic-like traits, such as fragile X syndrome or tuberous sclerosis. Despite early claims of high rates of autism in fragile X syndrome, we now know that autism is rare relative to more common phenotypic features of social anxiety, shyness, and gaze aversion. Similarly, tuberous sclerosis has long been characterized by phenotypic variability, and it is not yet clear how autism relates to the wide range of expression of this disorder. Although current official diagnostic systems and categories are clearly applicable to severely handicapped persons, it also is clear that the psychiatric and behavioral difficulties of many of these persons are not always adequately reflected in current diagnostic systems (Volkmar & Schwab-Stone, 1996).

On the other hand, the phenotypes of some disorders are not at all suggestive of autism, and in these syndromes autism may be underdiagnosed. Williams syndrome and Down syndrome have features that set them apart from autism. These differences may preclude many researchers from even considering an autism diagnosis in persons with these syndromes, reflecting a type of diagnostic overshadowing. Even though autism may be rare in Down syndrome or Williams syndrome, overlooking an autism diagnosis poses particular hardships for patients and their families. Phenotypes can lead to missing an autism diagnosis, or to inflated autism estimates, and future work

needs to take phenotypic predispositions into account.

Studies linking autism to various medical conditions have important implications for clinical practice, especially for evaluating persons with autism and related disorders. Unfortunately, results to date are rather contradictory, and some (e.g., Gillberg, 1992a, 1992b) argue for very extensive clinical evaluations on a routine basis. Such assessments, which might include collection of cerebrospinal fluid or other more intrusive procedures, put the individual at some risk. They also pose a financial burden for families and for the healthcare system, and it could reasonably be contended that funds for vast numbers of unnecessary medical or laboratory tests might better be spent in supporting programs for screening and early intervention. In some instances, findings of such associations may have important implications for the individual (e.g., in treating PKU) or, more commonly, for the family (e.g., in terms of recurrence risk for fragile X).

Given the currently markedly divergent findings on the association of autism with medical conditions, what is reasonable clinical practice? Informed clinical practice should reflect a knowledge of reported associations as guided by history and examination of the individual. Unfortunately, the extent of diagnostic medical investigation in children with *any* form of developmental difficulty is controversial. Most studies have suggested that there is a greater likelihood of positive findings in individuals with more severe mental retardation (Levy, 1996). Given the potential importance of the identification of such problems to affected children and their families, the initial assessment of individuals with autism, particularly young children, should be particularly thorough. This assessment shares many of the features relevant to the pediatric assessment of developmental delay (see Levy, 1996).

Information gathering should include family history as well as the developmental and medical history of the individual. Developmental assessment and physical examination may suggest specific laboratory studies. The physical examination should be conducted with careful attention to symptoms and signs of specific conditions, such as staring spells suggestive of epilepsy, or dysmorphic features suggestive of fragile X or other genetic syndromes. For example, a family history of developmental delay, particularly if associated with characteristic features in the individual, may suggest the need for fragile X screening or chromosomal analysis. A history of staring spells may suggest the need for an EEG examination. Other investigations, conducted routinely, should be modified as appropriate for the patients' history and examination. These investigations include screening for hearing and visual impairment and for fragile X syndrome and other chromosomal anomalies. Electroencephalographic (EEG) studies are clearly indicated in the presence of potential seizures, or if there is a question of language loss and marked developmental regression. Otherwise, the specific yield of EEGs is rather low. Findings on physical examination that may guide the assessment include skin abnormalities, unusual head size, focal or lateralizing findings on neurological examination, and so forth.

In certain circumstances, medical evaluations should err on the side of being very extensive. This is true if the disorder has an unusual or atypical presentation, if the course is a deteriorating one, or if a prolonged period of normal development precedes the onset of the disorder. The likelihood of finding associated medical conditions appears to increase if the degree of associated handicap is more severe, if a deteriorating course is observed, or if specific signs and symptoms suggestive of such conditions are present on examination. Unless clinically indicated, more extensive or invasive procedures such as brain scan or magnetic resonance imaging (MRI) should probably not be done in the absence of clinical indications.

Many careful studies have already included screening autistic samples for medical concerns, and diagnosing autism in specific disorders such as fragile X syndrome, tuberous sclerosis, and Down syndrome. Yet more work is needed in these and other syndromes, especially work that takes diagnostic difficulties into account in both very low- and high-functioning persons. There is a clear need for risk-versus-benefit analyses of the results of various screening and assessment procedures done in the context of carefully controlled studies. This future work has important implications for theories regarding the etiology of autism, and for practical considerations in clinical practice.

Cross-References

Neurochemical, neurological, and genetic aspects of autism and related conditions are discussed in Chapters 15, 16, and 17, respectively. Associations of autism and other conditions with psychiatric and medical conditions are also discussed in Chapters 1 through 7.

REFERENCES

Accardo, P., Whitman, B., Caul, J., & Rolfe, U. (1988). Autism and plumbism: A possible association. *Clinical Pediatrics, 27*(1), 41–44.

American Psychiatric Association. (1987). *Diagnostic and statistical manual of mental disorders* (3rd ed., rev.). Washington, DC: Author.

August, G.L., & Lockhart, L.H. (1984). Familial autism and the fragile X chromosome. *Journal of Autism and Developmental Disorders, 14,* 197–204.

Bailey, A. (1993). The biology of autism. *Psychological Medicine, 23,* 7–11.

Bailey, A., Bolton, P., Butler, L., Le Couteur, A., Murphy, M., Scott, S., Webb, T., & Rutter, M. (1993). Prevalence of the fragile X anomaly amongst autistic twins and singletons. *Journal of Child Psychology and Psychiatry, 34,* 673–688.

Bailey, A., Le Couteur, A., Gottesman, I., & Bolton, P. (1995). Autism as a strongly genetic disorder: Evidence from a British twin study. *Psychological Medicine, 25*(1), 63–77.

Bailey, A., Le Couteur, A., Rutter, M., Pickles, A., Uuzda, E., Schmidt, D., & Gottesman, I. (1991). Obstetric and neurodevelopmental data from the British Twin Study of Autism. *Psychiatric Genetics, 2,* S7A/1.

Barton, M., & Volkmar, F.R. (1996, October). *Autism and associated medical conditions.* Paper presented at the Annual Meeting of the American Academy of Child and Adolescent Psychiatry, Philadelphia, PA.

Bellugi, U., Bihrle, A.M., Neville, H., Jernigan, T., & Doherty, S. (1992). Language, cognition and brain organization in a neurodevelopmental disorder. In M. Gumnnar & C. Nelson (Eds.), *Developmental brain neuroscience* (pp. 201–232). Hillsdale, NJ: Erlbaum.

Bellugi, U., Marks, S., Bihrle, A.M., & Sabo, H. (1988). Dissociation between language and cognitive functions in Williams syndrome. In D. Bishop & K. Mogfont (Eds.), *Language development in exceptional circumstances* (pp. 177–189). London: Churchill Livingstone.

Bellugi, U., Wang, P., & Jernigan, T.L. (1994). Williams syndrome: An unusual neuropsychological profile. In S.H. Browman & J. Grafram (Eds.), *Atypical cognitive deficits in developmental disorders* (pp. 23–56). Hillsdale, NJ: Erlbaum.

Benezech, M., & Noel, B. (1985). Fra(X) syndrome and autism. *Clinical Genetics, 28,* 93.

Bertrand, J., Mervis, C., Rice, C., & Adamson, L. (1993, March). *Development of joint attention by a toddler with Williams syndrome.* Paper presented to the Gatlinburg Conferences on Research and Theory in Mental Retardation and Developmental Disabilities, Gatlinburg, TN.

Bihrle, A.M., Bellugi, U., Delis, D., & Marks, S. (1989). Seeing either the forest or the trees: Dissociation in visuospatial processing. *Brain Cognition, 11,* 37–49.

Blomquist, H.K., Bohman, M., Edvinsson, S.O., Gillberg, C., Gustavson, K.H., Holgren, G., & Wahlstrom, J. (1985). Frequency of the fragile X syndrome in infantile autism: A Swedish multicenter study. *Clinical Genetics, 27,* 113–117.

Bolton, P., MacDonald, H., Murphy, M., Scott, S., Yuzda, E., Whitlock, B., Pickles, A., & Rutter, M. (1991). Genetic findings and heterogeneity in autism. *Psychiatric Genetics, 2,* S7A/2.

Bolton, P., Pickles, A., Harrington, R., MacDonald, H., & Rutter, M. (1992). Season of birth: Issues, approaches and findings for autism. *Journal of Child Psychology and Psychiatry, 33*(3), 509-530.

Borghgraef, M., Fryns, J.P., Dielkens, A., Pych, K., & Van den Berghe, H. (1987). Fragile X syndrome: A study of the psychological profile in 23 prepubertal patients. *Clinical Genetics, 32,* 179–186.

Borghgraef, M., Fryns, J.P., & Van den Berghe, H. (1990). The female and the fragile X syndrome: Data on clinical and psychological findings in 7 fragile X carriers. *Clinical Genetics, 37,* 341–346.

Bregman, J.D., Leckman, J.F., & Ort, S.I. (1988). Fragile X syndrome: Genetic predisposition to psychopathology. *Journal of Autism and Developmental Disorders, 18,* 343–354.

Bregman, J.D., & Volkmar, F.R. (1988). Autistic social dysfunction and Down syndrome. *Journal of the American Academy of Child and Adolescent Psychiatry, 27,* 440–441.

Brewer, J.L., Levine, K., & Pober, B. (1994, July). *Parental survey of psychiatric problems in the adult with Williams syndrome.* Paper presented to the Sixth International Conference of the Williams Syndrome Association, San Diego, CA.

Brown, W.T., Greer, M.K., Aylward, E.H., Fisch, G.S., Wolf-Schein, E.G., Gross, A., Waterhouse, L., Fein, D., Mason-Brothers, A., Ritvo, E., Ruttenberg, B.A., Bentley, W., & Castells, S. (1986). Fragile X syndrome and autism: A multicenter study. *American Journal of Medical Genetics, 23,* 341–352.

Brown, W.T., Jenkins, E.C., Friedman, E., Brooks, J., Wisniewski, K., Raguthu, S., & French, J. (1982). Autism is associated with the fragile X syndrome. *Journal of Autism and Developmental Disorders, 12,* 303–307.

Cantu, E.S., Stone, J.W., Wing, A.A., Langee, H.R., & Williams, C.A. (1990). Cytogenetic survey for autistic fragile X carriers in a mental retardation center. *American Journal on Mental Retardation, 94,* 442–447.

Caskey, C.T., Pizzuti, A., Fu, Y.H., Fenwich, R.G., & Nelson, D.L. (1992). Triplet repeat mutations in human disease. *Science, 256,* 784–789.

Chess, S. (1971, January). Autism in children with congenital rubella. *Journal of Autism and Childhood Schizophrenia, 1*(1), 33–47.

Chess, S. (1977). Follow-up report on autism in congenital rubella. *Journal of Autism and Childhood Schizophrenia, 7,* 69–81.

Chess, S., Korn, S.J., & Fernandez, P.B. (1971). *Psychiatric disorders of children with congenital rubella.* New York: Brunner/Mazel.

Cohen, I.L., Brown, W.T., Jenkins, E.C., Krawczun, M.S., French, J.H., Raguthu, S., Wolf-Schein, E.G., Sudhalter, V., Fisch, G., & Wisniewski, K. (1989). Fragile X syndrome in autistic females. *American Journal of Medical Genetics, 34,* 302–303.

Cohen, I.L., Vietze, P.M., Sudhalter, V., Jenkins, E.C., & Brown, W.T. (1989). Parent–child dyadic gaze patterns in fragile X males and in non-fragile X males with autistic disorder. *Journal of Child Psychology and Psychiatry, 30,* 845–856.

Cohen, I.L., Vietze, P.M., Sudhalter, V., Jenkins, E.C., & Brown, W.T. (1991). Effects of age and communication level on eye contact in fragile X males and non-fragile X autistic males. *American Journal of Medical Genetics, 38,* 498–502.

Coleman, M. (1990). Delineation of the subgroups of the autistic syndrome. *Brain Dysfunction, 3,* 208–217.

Collacott, R.A., Cooper, S.A., & McGrother, C. (1992). Differential rates of psychiatric disorders in adults with Down's syndrome compared with other mentally handicapped adults. *British Journal of Psychiatry, 161,* 671–674.

Critchley, M., & Earl, C.J. (1932). Tuberous sclerosis and allied conditions. *Brain, 55,* 311–346.

Curatolo, P., Cusmai, R., Cortesi, F., Chiron, C., Jambeque, I., & Dulac, O. (1991). Neuropsychiatric aspects of tuberous sclerosis. In W.G. Johnson & M.R. Gomez (Eds.), *Tuberous scelerosis and allied disorders* (pp. 8–16). New York: New York Academy of Sciences.

Dawson, G. (Ed.). (1990). *Autism: Nature, diagnosis and treatment.* New York: Guilford Press.

Deykin, E., & MacMahon, B. (1979). The incidence of seizures among children with autistic symptoms. *American Journal of Psychiatry, 136,* 1310–1312.

Dilts, C.V., Morris, C.A., & Leonard, C.O. (1990). Hypothesis for development of a behavioral phenotype in Williams syndrome. *American Journal of Medical Genetics, 6,* 126–131.

Doherty, S., & Bellugi, U. (1992). Trajectories of early language development in Williams and Down syndromes. *Journal of Clinical and Experimental Neuropsychology, 14,* 103.

Dorn, M.B., Mazzocco, M.M., & Hagerman, R.J. (1994). Behavioral and psychiatric disorders in adult male carriers of fragile X. *Journal of the American Academy of Child and Adolescent Psychiatry, 33,* 256–264.

Dykens, E.M. (1995). Measuring behavioral phenotypes: Provocations from the "new genetics." *American Journal on Mental Retardation, 99,* 522–532.

Dykens, E.M. (1996). DNA meets *DSM:* The growing importance of genetic syndromes in dual diagnosis. *Mental Retardation, 34,* 125–127.

Dykens, E.M., Hodapp, R.M., & Leckman, J.F. (1994). *Behavior and development in fragile X syndrome.* Thousand Oaks, CA: Sage.

Dykens, E.M., Leckman, J.F., & Cassidy, S.B. (1996). Obsessions and compulsions in Prader-Willi syndrome. *Journal of Child Psychology and Psychiatry, 37,* 995–1002.

Einfeld, S.L. (1988). Autism and the fragile X syndrome [letter to the editor]. *American Journal of Medical Genetics, 30,* 237–238.

Einfeld, S.L., Molony, H., & Hall, W. (1989). Autism is not associated with the fragile X syndrome. *American Journal of Medical Genetics, 19*(34), 187–193.

Einfeld, S.L., Tonge, B.J., & Florio, T. (1992, November). *Behavioural and emotional problems in Williams syndrome.* Paper presented to the Society for the Study of Behavioural Phenotypes Second International Symposium, Welshpool, United Kingdom.

Ewart, A.K., Morris, C.A., Atkinson, D., Jin, W., Sternes, K., Spallone, P., Stock, A., Leppart, M., & Keating, M. (1993). Hemizygosity at the elastin gene locus in a developmental disorder, Williams syndrome. *Nature Genetics, 5,* 11–16.

Fisch, G.S. (1992). Is autism associated with the fragile X syndrome? *American Journal of Medical Genetics, 43,* 47–55.

Fisch, G.S., Cohen, I.L., Jenkins, E.C., & Brown, W.T. (1988). Screening developmentally disabled male populations for the fragile X syndrome: The effect of sample size. *American Journal of Medical Genetics, 30,* 655–633.

Fisch, G.S., Cohen, I.L., Wolf, E.G., Brown, W.T., Jenkins, E.C., & Gross, A. (1986). Autism and the fragile X syndrome. *American Journal of Psychiatry, 143,* 71–73.

Fombonne, E., & Mazaubrun, C. (1992). Prevalence of infantile autism in four French regions. *Social Psychiatry and Psychiatric Epidemiology, 27,* 203–210.

Freund, L.S., Reiss, A.L., & Abrams, M.T. (1993). Psychiatric disorders associated with fragile X in the young female. *Pediatrics, 91,* 321–329.

Freund, L., Reiss, A.L., Hagerman, R.J., & Vinogradov, S. (1992). Chromosome fragility and psychopathology in obligate female carriers of the fragile X chromosome. *Archives of General Psychiatry, 49,* 54–60.

Frith, U., & Baron-Cohen, S. (1987). Perception in autistic children. In D.J. Cohen, A.M. Donnellan, & R. Paul (Eds.), *Handbook of autism and pervasive developmental disorders* (pp. 85–102). New York: John Wiley & Sons.

Fryns, J.P., Jacobs, J., Klecklowska, A., & Van den Berghe, H. (1984). The psychological profile of the fragile X syndrome. *Clinical Genetics, 25,* 131–134.

Fryns, J.P., & Van den Berghe, H. (1983). X-linked mental retardation and fragile Xq27 site. *Clinical Genetics, 23,* 203–206.

Ganiban, J., Wagner, S., & Cicchetti, D. (1990). Temperament and Down syndrome. In D. Cicchetti & M. Beeghly (Eds.), *Children with Down syndrome: A developmental perspective* (pp. 63–100). New York: Cambridge University Press.

Gath, A., & Gumley, D. (1986). Behaviour problems in retarded children with special reference to Down's syndrome. *British Journal of Psychiatry, 149,* 151–156.

Ghaziuddin, M., Tsai, L., & Ghaziuddin, N. (1992). Autism in Down's syndrome: Presentation and diagnosis. *Journal of Intellectual Disability Research, 36,* 449–456.

Gibbs, M.V., & Thorpe, J.G. (1983). Personality stereotype of noninstitutionalized Down syndrome children. *American Journal of Mental Deficiency, 87,* 601–605.

Gillberg, C. (1990). Do children with autism have March birthdays? *Acta Psychiatrica Scandinavica, 82*(2), 152–156.

Gillberg, C. (1990a). Autism and pervasive developmental disorders. *Journal of Child Psychology and Psychiatry, 33,* 813–842.

Gillberg, C. (1990b). Medical work-up in children with autism and Asperger Syndrome. *Brain Dysfunction, 3,* 249–260.

Gillberg, C. (1991). The treatment of epilepsy in autism. *Journal of Autism and Developmental Disorders, 21,* 61–77.

Gillberg, C. (1992a). Subgroups in autism: are there behavioural phenotypes typical of underlying medical conditions? *Journal of Intellectual Disability Research, 36*(pt 3), 201–214.

Gillberg, C. (1992b). The Emanuel Miller Memorial Lecture 1991: Autism and autistic-like conditions: Subclasses among disorders of empathy. *Journal of Child Psychology and Psychiatry and Allied Disciplines, 33*(5), 813–842.

Gillberg, C., & Coleman, M. (1992). *The biology of the autistic syndromes.* London: MacKeith Press.

Gillberg, C., & Coleman, M. (1996). Autism and medical disorders: A review of the literature. *Developmental Medicine and Child Neurologyn, 38,* 181–202.

Gillberg, C., & Gillberg, I.C. (1991, June). Note on the relationship between population-based and clinical studies: The question of reduced optimality in autism. *Journal of Autism and Developmental Disorders, 21*(2), 251–253.

Gillberg, C., Gillberg, I.C., & Ahlsen, G. (1994). Autistic behavior and attention deficits in tuberous scelerosis: A population-based study. *Developmental Medicine and Child Neurology, 36,* 50–56.

Gillberg, C., Grufman, M., & Themner, U. (1986). Psychiatric disorders in mildly and severely mentally retarded urban children and adolescents: Epidemiological aspects. *British Journal of Psychiatry, 149,* 68–74.

Gillberg, C., Persson, E., & Wahlstrom, J. (1986). The autism fragile X syndrome: A population-based study of 10 boys. *Journal of Mental Deficiency Research, 30,* 27–39.

Gillberg, C., & Rasmussen, P. (1994). Brief report: Four case histories and a literature review of Williams syndrome and autistic behavior.

Journal of Autism and Developmental Disorders, 24, 381–393.

Gillberg, C., Steffenburg, S., & Schaumann, H. (1991). Is autism more common now than ten years ago? *British Journal of Psychiatry, 158,* 403–409.

Gillberg, C., & Wahlstrom, J. (1985). Chromosome abnormalities in infantile autism and other childhood psychoses: A population study of 66 cases. *Developmental Medicine and Child Neurology, 27,* 293–304.

Goldfine, P.E., McPherson, P.M., Heath, G.A., Hardesty, V.A., Beauregard, L.J., & Gordon, B. (1985). Association of the fragile X syndrome with autism. *American Journal of Psychiatry, 142,* 108–110.

Gomez, M.R. (1988). Neurologic and psychiatric features in tuberous sclerosis. In M.R. Gomez (Ed.), *Tuberous sclerosis* (2nd ed., pp. 21–36). New York: Raven Press.

Gosch, A., & Pankau, R. (1994). Social-emotional and behavioral adjustment in children with Williams-Beuren syndrome. *American Journal of Medical Genetics, 53,* 335–339.

Gosch, A., Stading, G., & Pankau, R. (1994). Linguistic abilities in children with Williams-Beuren syndrome. *American Journal of Medical Genetics, 52,* 291–296.

Grizenko, N., Cvejic, H., Vida, S., & Sayegh, L. (1991). Behavior problems in the mentally retarded. *Canadian Journal of Psychiatry, 36,* 712–717.

Hagerman, R.J., Jackson, A.W., Amiri, K., Silverman, A.C., O'Connor, R., & Sobesky, W. (1992). Girls with fragile X syndrome: Physical and neurocognitive status and outcome. *Pediatrics, 89,* 395–400.

Hagerman, R.J., Jackson, A.W., Levitas, A., Rimland, B., & Braden, M. (1986). An analysis of autism in 50 males with the fragile X syndrome. *American Journal of Medical Genetics, 23,* 359–374.

Ho, H.H., & Kalousek, D.K. (1989). Fragile X syndrome in autistic boys. *Journal of Autism and Developmental Disorders, 19,* 343–347.

Hodapp, R.M., & Dykens, E.M. (1994). Mental retardation's two cultures of behavioral research. *American Journal of Mental Retardation, 98,* 675–687.

Hook, E. (1982). The epidemiology of Down syndrome. In S. Pueschel & J. Rynders (Eds.), *Down syndrome: Advances in biomedicine and the behavioral sciences* (pp. 11–88). Cambridge, MA: Ware Press.

Howlin, P., Wing, L., & Gould, J. (1995). The recognition of autism in children with Down syndrome: Implications for intervention and some speculations about pathology. *Developmental Medicine and Child Neurology, 37,* 398–414.

Hunt, A. (1983). Tuberous sclerosis: A survey of 97 cases: I: Seizures, pertussis immunization and handicap. *Developmental Medicine and Child Neurology, 25,* 346–349.

Hunt, A. (1990). Tuberous scelerosis. In J. Hogg, J. Sebba, & L. Lambe (Eds.), *Profound retardation and multiple impairment* (Vol. 3, pp. 69–81). London: Chapman and Hall.

Hunt, A., & Dennis, J. (1987). Psychiatric disorder among children with tuberous sclerosis. *Developmental Medicine and Child Neurology, 29,* 190–198.

Hunt, A., & Shepherd, C. (1993). A prevalence study of autism in tuberous sclerosis. *Journal of Autism and Developmental Disorders, 23,* 323–339.

Jacobs, P.A., Mayer, M., Matsuura, J., Rhoads, F., & Yee, S.C. (1983). A cytogenetic study of a population of mentally retarded males with special reference to the marker (X) chromosome. *Human Genetics, 63,* 139–148.

Jorgensen, J.W., Nielsen, K.B., Isager, T., & Mouridsen, S.E. (1984). Fragile X chromosome among child patients with disturbance of language and social relationships. *Acta Psychiatrica Scandinavica, 70,* 510–514.

Karmiloff-Smith, A., Grant, J., Berthoud, I., Bouthers, B., & Stevens, T. (1994, July). *The complex picture of the linguistic profile of individuals with Williams syndrome.* Paper presented to the Sixth International Professional Meeting of the Williams Syndrome Association, San Diego, CA.

Konstantareas, M.M., Hauser, P., Lennox, C., & Homatidis, S. (1986, Fall). Season of birth in infantile autism. *Child Psychiatry and Human Development, 17*(1), 53–65.

Kotsopoulos, S., & Kutty, K.M. (1979, March). Histidinemia and infantile autism. *Journal of Autism and Developmental Disorders, 9*(1), 55–60.

Lachiewicz, A.M. (1992). Abnormal behavior of young girls with fragile X syndrome. *American Journal of Medical Genetics, 43,* 72–77.

Lerea, L.E. (1987). The behavioral assessment of autistic children. In D.J. Cohen, A.M. Donnellan, & R. Paul (Eds.), *Handbook of autism and pervasive developmental disorders* (pp. 273–288). New York: John Wiley & Sons.

Levine, K. (1994). *Williams syndrome: Information for teachers.* Clawson, MI: Williams Syndrome Association.

Levine, K., & Castro, R. (1994, July). *Towards a social skills profile of school age children with Williams syndrome.* Paper presented to the Sixth International Conference of the Williams Syndrome Association, San Diego, CA.

Levitas, A., Hagerman, R.J., Braden, M., Rimland, B., McBogg, P., & Matus, I. (1983). Autism and the fragile X syndrome. *Developmental and Behavioral Pediatrics, 4,* 151–158.

Levy, S. (1991). Note on obstetrical records and autism: A response to Gillberg and Gillberg, *Journal of Autism and Developmental Disorders, 21*(2), 253.

Levy, S. (1996). Pediatric assessment of the child with developmental delay. *Child and Adolescent Psychiatry Clinics of North America, 5*(4), 809–826.

Levy, S., Zoltak, B., & Saelens, T. (1988, December). A comparison of obstetrical records of autistic and nonautistic. *Journal of Autism and Developmental Disorders, 18*(4), 573–581.

Lotter, V. (1967). Epidemiology of autistic conditions in young children: Some characteristics of the children and their parents. *Social Psychiatry, 1,* 163–173.

Lowe, T.L., Tanaka, K., Seashore, R., Young, J.G., & Cohen, D.J. (1980). Detection on phenylketonuria in autistic and psychotic children. *Journal of the American Medical Association, 243,* 126–128.

Lund, J. (1985). The prevalence of psychiatric morbidity in mentally retarded adults. *Acta Psychiatria Scandanavia, 72,* 563–570.

Lund, J. (1988). Psychiatric aspects of Down syndrome. *Acta Psychiatrica Scandinavica, 78,* 369–374.

Marchetti, B., Scifo, R., Batticane, N., & Scapagnini, U. (1990). Immunological significance of opioid peptide dysfunction in infantile autism. *Brain Dysfunction, 3*(5-6), 346–354.

Mazzocco, M.M., Hagerman, R.J., Cronister-Silverman, A., & Pennington, B.F. (1992). Specific frontal lobe deficits among women with the fragile X gene. *Journal of the American Academy of Child and Adolescent Psychiatry, 31,* 1141–1148.

McGillivary, B.C., Herbst, D.S., Dill, F.J., Sandercock, H.J., & Tischler, B. (1986). Infantile autism: An occasional manifestation of fragile X mental retardation. *American Journal of Medical Genetics, 23,* 353–358.

Menage, P., Thibault, G., Martineau, J., Herault, J., Muh, J.P., Barthelemy, C., LeLond, G., & Bardos, P. (1992). An IgE mechanism in autistic hypersensitivity? *Biological Psychiatry, 31*(2), 210–212.

Menolascino, F.J. (1965). Psychiatric aspects of mongolism. *American Journal of Mental Deficiency, 69,* 653–660.

Mervis, C., & Bertrand, J. (in press). Relations between cognition and language: A developmental perspective. In L.B. Adamson & M.A. Romski (Eds.), *Research on communication and language disorders: Contributions to theories of language development.* New York: Brookes.

Meryash, D.L., Szymanski, L.S., & Gerald, P. (1982). Infantile autism associated with the fragile X syndrome. *Journal of Autism and Developmental Disorders, 12,* 349–355.

Meyers, B.A., & Pueschel, S.M. (1991). Psychiatric disorders in persons with Down syndrome. *The Journal of Nervous and Mental Disease, 179,* 609–613.

Morris, C.A., Demsey, S.A., Leonard, C.O., Dilts, C., & Blackburn, B.L. (1988). Natural history of Williams syndrome: Physical characteristics. *Journal of Pediatrics, 113,* 318–326.

Morris, C.A., Leonard, C.O., Dilts, C., & Demsey, S.A. (1990). Adults with Williams syndrome. *American Journal of Medical Genetics, 6,* 102–107.

Nielsen, K.B. (1983). Diagnosis of the fragile X syndrome (Martin Bell syndrome): Clinical findings in 27 males with the fragile site at Xq28. *Journal of Mental Deficiency Research, 27,* 211–226.

Nyhan, W.L., James, J.A., Teberg, A.J., Sweetman, L., & Nelson, L.G., (1969). A new disorder of purine metabolism with behavioral manifestations. *Journal of Pediatrics, 74,* 20–27.

Olsson, B., & Rett, A. (1985). Behavioral observations concerning differential diagnosis between the Rett's Syndrome and autism. *Brain and Development, 7,* 281–289.

Olsson, I., Steffenburg, S., & Gillberg, C. (1988). Epilepsy in autism and autistic-like condition: A population-based study. *Archives of Neurology, 45,* 666–668.

Pagon, R.A., Bennett, F.C., LaVeck, B., Stewart, K.B., & Johnson, J. (1987). Williams syndrome: Features in late childhood and early adolescence. *Pediatrics, 80,* 85–91.

Partington, M.W. (1984). The fragile X syndrome: II. Preliminary data on growth and development in males. *American Journal of Medical Genetics, 17,* 175–194.

Pary, R. (1992). Differential diagnosis of functional decline in Down syndrome. *The Habilitative Mental Healthcare Newsletter, 11,* 37–41.

Payton, J.B., Steele, M.W., Wenger, S.L., & Minshew, N.J. (1989). The fragile X marker and autism in perspective. *Journal of the American Academy of Child and Adolsecent Psychiatry, 28,* 417–468.

Plissart, L., Borghgraef, M., Volcke, P., Van den Berghe, H., & Fryns, J.P. (1994). Adults with Williams-Beuren syndrome: Evaluation of the medical, psychological and behavioral aspects. *Clinical Genetics, 46,* 161–167.

Pober, B.R., & Dykens, E.M. (1996). Williams syndrome. *Child and Adolescent Psychiatry Clinics of North America, 5,* 929–944.

Preus, M. (1984). The Williams syndrome: Objective definition and diagnosis. *Clinical Genetics, 25,* 422–428.

Pueschel, S.M., Bernier, J.C., & Pezzullo, J.C. (1991). Behavioral observations in children with Down's syndrome. *Journal of Mental Deficiency Research, 35,* 502–511.

Pueschel, S.M., Herman, R., & Groden, G. (1985). Screening children with autism for fragile X syndrome and phenylketonuria. *Journal of Autism and Developmental Disorders, 15,* 335–338.

Reilly, J., Klima, E.S., & Bellugi, U. (1990). Once more with feeling: Affect and language in atypical populations. *Development and Psychopathology, 2,* 367–391.

Reiss, A.L., Feinstein, C., Rosenbaum, K.N., Borengasser-Caruso, M.A., & Goldsmith, B.M. (1985). Autism associated with Williams syndrome. *The Journal of Pediatrics, 106,* 247–249.

Reiss, A.L., & Freund, L. (1990). Fragile X syndrome, *DSM-III-R* and autism. *Journal of the American Academy of Child and Adolescent Psychiatry, 29,* 885–891.

Reiss, A.L., Hagerman, R.J., Vinogradov, S., Abrams, M., & King, R.J. (1988). Psychiatric disability in female carriers of the fragile X chromosome. *Archives of General Psychiatry, 45,* 697–705.

Rhoads, F.A. (1984). Fragile X syndrome in Hawaii: A summary of clinical experience. *American Journal of Medical Genetics, 17,* 209–214.

Riikonen, R., & Amnell, G. (1981). Psychiatric disorders in children with earlier infantile spasms. *Developmental Medicine and Child Neurology, 23,* 747–760.

Riikonen, R., & Simell, O. (1990). Tuberous scelerosis and infantile spasms. *Developmental Medicine and Child Neurology, 32,* 203–209.

Ritvo, E.R., Mason-Brothers, A., Freeman, B.J., Pingree, C., Jenson, W.R., McMahon, W., Peterson, P.B., Jorder, L.B., Mo, A., & Ritvo, A. (1990). UCLA–University of Utah Epidemiologic Survey of Autism: Etiologic role of rare diseases. *American Journal of Psychiatry, 147,* 1614–1621.

Rogers, C. (1987). Maternal support for the Down's syndrome stereotype: The effect of direct experience on the condition. *Journal of Mental Deficiency Research, 31,* 271–278.

Rutter, M. (1970). Autistic children: Infancy to adulthood. *Seminars in Psychiatry, 2,* 435–450.

Rutter, M. (1991). Autism: Pathways from syndrome definition to pathogenesis. *Comprehensive Mental Health Care, 1*(1), 5–26.

Rutter, M. (1996). Autism research: prospects and priorities. *Journal of Autism and Developmental Disorders, 26*(2), 257–275.

Rutter, M., Bailey, A., Bolton, P., & Le Couteur, A. (1993). Autism: Syndrome of definition and possible genetic mechanisms. In R. Plomin & G.E. McLearn (Eds.), *Nature, nurture and psychology.* Washington, DC: American Psychological Association Press.

Rutter, M., Bailey, A., Bolton, P., & Le Couteur, A. (1994). Autism and known medical conditions: Myth and substance. *Journal of Child Psychology and Psychiatry, 35,* 311–322.

Scott, S. (1994). Mental retardation. In M. Rutter, E. Taylor, & L. Hersov (Eds.), *Child and Adolescent Psychiatry: Modern Approaches* (3rd ed., pp. 616–646). Oxford: Blackwell Scientific Publications.

Sherman, S.L. (1992, June). *Epidemiology and screening.* Paper presented to the Third International Fragile X Conference, Snowmass Resort, CO.

Short, M.P., Richardson, E.P., Haines, J.L., & Kwiatowski, D.J. (1995). Clinical, neuropathological and genetic aspects of the tuberous scelerosis complex. *Brain Pathology, 5,* 173–179.

Sigman, M., Ungerer, J.A., Mundy, P., & Sherman, Y. (1987). Cognition in autistic children. In D.J. Cohen, A.M. Donnellan, & R. Paul (Eds.), *Handbook of autism and pervasive developmental disorders* (pp. 103–120). New York: John Wiley & Sons.

Singh, V.K., Warren, R.P., Odell, J.D., Warren, W.L., & Cole, D. (1993). Antibodies to myelin basic protein in children with autistic behavior. *Brain, Behavior and Immunity, 7*(1), 97–103.

Smalley, S.L., Burger, F., & Smith, M. (1994). Phenotypic variation of tuberous sclerosis in a single extended kindred. *Journal of Medical Genetics, 31,* 761–765.

Smalley, S.L., Smith, M., & Tanguay, P.E. (1991). Autism and psychiatric disorders in tuberous sclerosis. *Annals of New York Academy of Science, 615,* 382–383.

Smalley, S.L., Tanguay, P.E., Smith, M., & Gutierrez, G. (1992). Autism and tuberous sclerosis. *Journal of Autism and Developmental Disorders, 22,* 339–355.

Sobesky, W.E., Hull, C.E., & Hagerman, R.J. (1994). Symptoms of schizotypal personality disorder in fragile X women. *Journal of the American Academy of Child and Adolescent Psychiatry, 33,* 247–255.

Sobesky, W.E., Pennington, B.F., Porter, D., Hull, C.E., & Hagerman, R.J. (1994). Emotional and neurosensitive deficits in fragile X. *American Journal of Medical Genetics, 51,* 378–385.

Steffenburg, S. (1991). Neuropsychiatric assessments of children with autism: A population-based study. *Developmental Medicine and Child Neurology, 33,* 495–511.

Stubbs, E.G. (1978). Autistic symptoms in a child with congenital cytomegalovirus infection. *Journal of Autism and Developmental Disorders, 8*(1), 37–43.

Tager-Flusberg, H. (in press). Early language development in children with mental retardation. In J.A. Burack, R.M. Hodapp, & E. Zigler (Eds.), *Handbook of development and mental retardation.* New York: Cambridge University Press.

Tomc, S.A., Williamson, N.K., & Pauli, R.M. (1990). Temperament in Williams syndrome. *American Journal of Medical Genetics, 36,* 345–352.

Tranebjaerg, L., & Kure, P. (1991). Prevalence of fra(X) and other specific diagnoses in autistic individuals in a Danish county. *American Journal of Medical Genetics, 38,* 212–214.

Tuchman, R., Rapin, I., & Shinnar, S. (1991). Autistic and dysphasic children: II. Epilepsy. *Pediatrics, 88,* 1219–1225.

Udwin, O. (1990). A survey of adults with Williams syndrome and idiopathic infantile hypercalcaemia. *Developmental Medicine and Child Neurology, 32,* 129–141.

Udwin, O., & Yule, W. (1990). Expressive language of children with Williams syndrome. *American Journal of Medical Genetics, 6,* 108–114.

Udwin, O., & Yule, W. (1991). A cognitive and behavioral phenotype on Williams syndrome. *Journal of Clinical and Experimental Neuropsychology, 13,* 232–244.

Udwin, O., Yule, W., & Martin, N. (1987). Cognitive abilities and behavioral characteristics of children with idiopathic infantile hypercalcaemia. *Journal of Child Psychology and Psychiatry, 28,* 297–309.

Venter, P.A., Op'lHof, J., Coezee, D.S., Van de Wa, H.C., & Retie, F. (1984). No marker X chromosome in autistic children. *Human Genetics, 67,* 107.

Visconti, P., Piazzi, S., Posar, A., & Santi, A. (1994). Amino acids and infantile autism. *Developmental Brain Dysfunction, 7,* 86–92.

Volkmar, F.R., & Nelson, D.S. (1990). Seizure disorders in autism. *Journal of the American Academy of Child and Adolescent Psychiatry, 29,* 127–129.

Volkmar, F.R., Schwab-Stone, M. (1996). Annotation: Childhood disorders in *DSM-IV. Journal of Child Psychology and Psychiatry, 37*(7), 779–784.

Wahlstrom, J., Gillberg, C., Gustavson, K.H., & Holgren, G. (1986). Infantile autism and the fragile X: A Swedish multicenter study. *American Journal of Medical Genetics, 23,* 403–408.

Wahlstrom, J., Steffenburg, S., Helgren, L., & Gillberg, C. (1989). Chromosome findings in twins with early-onset autistic disorder. *American Journal of Medical Genetics, 32,* 19–21.

Wakabayashi, S. (1979). A case of infantile autism associated with Down's syndrome. *Journal of Autism and Developmental Disorders, 9,* 31–36.

Warren, A.C., Holroyd, S., & Folstein, M.F. (1989). Major depression in Down's syndrome. *British Journal of Psychiatry, 155,* 202–205.

Watson, M.S., Leckman, J.F., Annex, B., Breg, R.W., Boles, D., Volkmar, R.R., Cohen, D.J., & Carter, C. (1984). Fragile X syndrome in a survey of 75 autistic males. *New England Journal of Medicine, 301,* 1462.

Williamson, D.A., & Bolton, P. (1995). Brief report: Atypical autism and tuberous sclerosis in a sibling pair. *Journal of Autism and Developmental Disorders, 25,* 435–441.

Wing, L. (1980). The MRC handicaps, behavior, and skills (BSH) schedule. In E. Strömgren, A. Dupont, & Nielson, J.A. (Eds.), Epidemidosical research as basis for the organization of extramural psychiatry. *Acta Psychiatrica Scandinavica* (Suppl. *285,* 241–247).

Wing, L., & Gould, J. (1979). Severe impairment of social interaction and associated abnormalities in children: Epidemiology and classification. *Journal of Autism and Developmental Disorders, 9,* 11–29.

Wishart, J.G., & Johnston, F.H. (1990). The effects of experience on attribution of a stereotyped personality to children with Down's syndrome. *Journal of Mental Deficiency Research, 34,* 409–420.

Witt-Engerström, I., & Gillberg, C. (1987). Letter: Rett Syndrome in Sweden. *Journal of Autism and Developmental Disorders, 17,* 149–150.

Wright, H.H., Young, S.R., Edwards, J.G., Abramson, R.K., & Duncan, J. (1986). Fragile X syndrome in a population of autistic children. *Journal of the American Academy of Child and Adolescent Psychiatry, 25,* 641–644.

Zigman, W.B., Schupf, N., Zigman, A., & Silverman, W. (1993). Aging and Alzheimer disease in people with mental retardation. *International Review of Research in Mental Retardation, 19,* 41–70.

SECTION FOUR

Assessment

The assessment of individuals with autism and other pervasive developmental disorders calls on the expertise of various disciplines, including child and adolescent psychiatry, psychology, speech and language, education, pediatrics, neurology, physical rehabilitation, and others. The specific forms of assessment implemented in some of these fields are also described in other sections of this volume, for example, the close relations between communication evaluation and interventions are covered in Section Six. The following section focuses on the rigorous assessment of psychological functioning, communication, and behavior—the core symptom areas of impairment in individuals with autism and associated conditions.

Categorical diagnosis (as described in Section One of this volume) provides useful information that places an individual in a class. The classification decision has important implications for intervention, prognosis, and other areas, including legal rights; classification also may be critical for various approaches to etiological and other research. However, classification, by its nature, reduces individuality in order to achieve generality.

An important goal of assessment is to move beyond global descriptions to more refined, precise documentation of an individual's functioning in various domains (e.g., from global intellectual level to specific verbal and performance abilities; social competence; receptive and expressive language skills and social use of language; self-care and other abilities of daily living; and so on). Assessment techniques provide valuable information that is descriptive—and often prescriptive—for a particular individual.

Assessment is also informative when it allows the information about a particular individual to be placed within a broader developmental or normative framework. In this approach, the child's functioning (and not only the impairments) is placed in context. The child's "scores" and behavior are compared with those that might be expected from normal children of the same age or at the same level of mental development. This developmental approach to assessment augments the usual pathographic description of problems, symptoms, difficulties, or deficiencies that marks the person off from the normal population.

When rigorous assessments are done with many children from the same diagnostic group, it is possible to integrate findings into a valid multidimensional description of the class. This process enriches categorical diagnoses; empirical findings from such assessment research are not simply restatements of the diagnostic criteria but expand the knowledge about the disorder. For example, studies on the neuropsychological functioning of individuals who are classified as Asperger's Syndrome reveal patterns of psychological functioning that may underlie the clinical phenomenology and that are not simply predictable by the diagnostic criteria (Chapter 6). Eventually, these findings may be useful in defining the class, along with (or instead of) the current diagnostic criteria.

Studies of large numbers of children from the same diagnostic group also allow for comparisons of specific dimensions (e.g., receptive language abilities) across groups, thereby indicating whether drawing a specific diagnostic boundary between closely related diagnostic groups (e.g., between Asperger's Syndrome and high-functioning autism) is valid.

To perform a formal behavioral or psychological assessment, the diagnostician must have expertise in the use of specific methods for acquiring the psychological and behavioral data, knowledge of the range of disorders, and clinical skills in forming relationships with individuals with disabilities. It is important to observe their approach to tasks, their styles of performance, and what they can achieve, and to understand the meaning of findings that derive from the testing and observing. For the assessor to then use the data to create a formulation based on assessments, she or he must have an understanding of development and developmental psychopathology and of the ways in which various domains or processes (language, cognition, social judgment, etc.) may relate to each other over the course of an individual's life and as revealed in current testing.

The results of assessments must be placed in the context of the opportunities that the individual with autism and associated disorders has had to develop, including the individual's opportunities for social relations, learning, recreation, and formal and informal learning about the world. We can anticipate that children who have had the advantage of enriched programs, aimed at facilitating their competence, will appear quite different on assessments than those who have had less optimal or even restricted resources. Findings on assessment are a complex function of the individual's constitutional and neurobiological endowment, maturation, and personal history and experiences at home, in school, and in the community. Used appropriately, objective and rigorous assessment methodology can help guide and monitor effective intervention.

CHAPTER 19

Developmentally Based Assessments

Children with autism and other pervasive developmental disorders present unique issues for assessment. Unusual developmental profiles are common in this population, and behavior problems can present major challenges for examiners. However, developmentally based assessments of cognitive, social, and communicative skills provide information that is important for diagnosis and for program planning. Observations of the child's unique strengths and weaknesses can have a major impact on the design of effective intervention programs. The closely related sections presented here summarize the overall approaches to assessment as well as the methods of psychological and communicative assessment.

By grouping these sections together with a common bibliography, we emphasize the importance of an integrated, interdisciplinary approach to assessment in autism. In our experience, the clinical assessment of children with such disorders is most effectively conducted by an experienced interdisciplinary team (Klin & Shepard, 1994) that adopts a developmental and comprehensive approach (Sparrow, Carter, Racusin, & Morris, 1995). The efforts of professionals from various other disciplines—neurology, pediatrics, audiology, physical and occupational therapy—are often needed, and the issue of coverage here is, to some extent, arbitrary. Psychological and communicative assessments are, however, those that are most frequently obtained, and, in conjunction with behavioral and other assessments (see Chapter 20), they provide the basis for intervention programs (Volkmar, Klin, Marans, & Cohen, 1996). Other chapters in this volume address issues of psychiatric diagnosis, neurological

problems, and the efforts of specific disciplines with regard to certain conditions, and touch on aspects of cognitive, communicative, and behavioral development and assessment. The focus here is on the *general approach* to assessment of individuals with autism and the uses of standardized, norm-referenced instruments.

FRED VOLKMAR
DONALD COHEN

19.1 ASSESSMENT ISSUES IN CHILDREN WITH AUTISM

*Ami Klin, Alice Carter, Fred R. Volkmar,
Donald J. Cohen, Wendy D. Marans,
and Sara S. Sparrow*

Children with autism and related conditions typically exhibit problems in multiple ares of development. This section outlines the principles of a comprehensive assessment approach and the aspects of autism that are mostly commonly encountered by a clinical evaluator. We concentrate primarily on the practical clinical issues that are involved in developmentally based evaluations of children with autism. However, we believe that these clinical issues are best addressed within the context of the research literature related to the clinical phenomena of autism, which are described in greater depth throughout this volume. Our emphasis on practical clinical issues was adopted in response to the currently limited resources available to clinicians who are seeking specific information about how to conduct an effective evaluation and manage the complexities and challenges that an evaluation of a child with autism may present. The paucity of information on practical aspects of assessment contrasts markedly with the voluminous literature on phenomenological descriptions and research-based discussions related to the diagnosis and clinical assessment of children with autism (e.g., Schopler & Mesibov, 1988).

THE COMPREHENSIVE DEVELOPMENTAL APPROACH

Employing a comprehensive developmental approach to assessment involves evaluating multiple areas of functioning that are relevant to the child's adaptation, taking the developmental aspects of each of these areas into consideration, and analyzing interrelationships between domains. The comprehensive developmental approach also emphasizes the need to delineate the available resources and the implications of the child's deficits and needs for his or her real-life adaptation (Sparrow et al., 1995). This approach is particularly well suited to the assessment of children with autism because their psychological profile is often very variable within and across domains, and is inconsistent across settings. The following principles define this approach in the context of autistic children's assessment:

- *Assessment of multiple areas of functioning.* The pervasive nature of the disability affecting children with autism implies a need to assess multiple areas of functioning, including current abilities (e.g., intellectual and communicative skills), behavioral presentation (e.g., compliance, distractibility, disruptive behaviors), and functional adjustment (e.g., adaptive skills as demonstrated in day-to-day life).
- *Adoption of a developmental perspective.* Given the presence of mental retardation in the majority of individuals with autism, (Volkmar, 1996) it is important to interpret their functioning, in the various domains assessed, in terms of normative expectations for performance at these children's developmental level (Cicchetti, 1984). Hence, the overall developmental or intellectual level establishes the frame within

which one may interpret more meaningfully the performance obtained and the behaviors observed during the assessment.
- *Variability of skills.* The profiles of children with autism often involve skills that are greatly scattered across different domains (e.g., relative strengths on sensorimotor tasks contrasting with significant weaknesses in conceptual or language tasks). It is important, therefore, to delineate a profile of assets and deficits rather than simply presenting an overall (often misleading) summary score or measure, because such global scores may represent the average of highly discrepant skills. Similarly, it is important not to generalize from an isolated performance (e.g., a "splinter" skill) to an overall impression of the level of functioning. This, too, may be a gross misrepresentation of the child's capacities for learning and adaptation.
- *Variability across settings.* The nature, demands, and configuration of the settings in which the child is observed vary in terms of familiarity, degree of structure imposed, number of adults present, and complexity of the environment, and the child's behavior and performance are likely to vary as well. Hence, the assessment should not only report levels of demonstrated performance but also address the issue of optimal environments that are likely to maximize learning and/or diminish disruptive behaviors. Equally important, detrimental environments should be discussed as a reference point when appraising the pros and cons of the particular programs or services offered to a child.
- *Functional adjustment.* An understanding of findings related to specific skills measured in the assessment must evolve in the context of the child's adjustment to everyday situations and real-life demands. This entails at least three factors: (a) a thorough assessment of the child's adaptive behaviors—his or her ability to translate capacities into consistent, habitual behaviors fostering self-sufficiency in naturalistic settings; (b) a view of assessment findings in the context of their impact on the child's ongoing adaptation, learning, and behavioral adjustment; the interrelatedness of

assessment and intervention should be emphasized, with the goal of translating findings into directives for treatment or remedial approaches; (c) because the central, defining symptom of autism is a pervasive impairment of socialization (Chapter 8), it is important to explore the interrelationship between social emotional functioning and the other areas assessed, so as to identify any contributors to social deficits and deviance and, conversely, to consider the impact of the social disability on the child's behavior and performance in the various procedures that compromise the assessment. Adequate consideration of these issues strengthens the interpretation of the assessment findings. In many cases, this approach informs intervention and the communication of the intervention rationale, transforming the evaluation from a potentially anxiety-provoking experience into a supportive, constructive, and focused process.

- *Delays and deviance.* Even though this distinction is implied in the developmental principles outlined above, it is important to explicitly frame the assessment in terms of both the normative course of development and deviant patterns of development and behavior (Klin & Volkmar, 1993; Volkmar, Carter, Sparrow, & Cicchetti, 1993). The normative approach places the child's resources in the context of abilities and skills that emerge systematically (e.g., walking at around 11 to 13 months, 2-word combinations at around 18 to 24 months, pretend play at around 3 to 4 years) and describes advances or delays in the acquisition of normative behaviors. In contrast, the deviance approach refers to departures from normal expectations—behaviors that are not typically observed in normally developing children of any age. These deviant behaviors are most often described in terms of the specific symptomatological pattern of the disorder that is exhibited by the child. Normative behaviors are usually measured in a standardized fashion. In contrast, the deviant behaviors observed in autism can rarely be measured with a standardized instrument because abnormal behaviors have very low base rates and do not follow systematic patterns across settings

and developmental levels. Normative capacities such as intellectual functioning or adaptive behavior can be measured using normed instruments, but information concerning deviant behaviors must be obtained through diagnostic instruments (ADI-R; Lord et al., 1994) or behavioral rating checklists (ABC; Krug, Arick, & Almond, 1980). These instruments are not normed, but they can (and should) be administered in a standardized fashion.

GENERAL GUIDELINES FOR THE ASSESSMENT OF CHILDREN WITH AUTISM

The phenotypic expression of autism and related conditions covers a range of developmental abilities that spans the entire IQ spectrum as well as varying degrees of symptom severity, communicative skills, and self-sufficiency (Volkmar, 1996). This variability of presentation and the nature of the symptoms defining autism pose a considerable challenge for assessment methods and for the evaluating clinicians (Cohen, Paul, & Volkmar, 1987). To address these challenges meaningfully, principles regarding the quality of the measures obtained, parental involvement, interdisciplinary collaboration and cohesion, and continuous contact should be adopted in the evaluation of these children.

Quality of Measures Obtained

Decisions as to how to obtain the most reliable and valid measure of a child's functioning must be based on experienced clinical judgment relative to the individual child. Because attentional and behavioral difficulties are often a significant obstacle to evaluation, the specific techniques employed must ensure the child's interest and investment in the tasks that are administered. The use of effective reinforcers as rewards for attention and compliance (e.g., social praise, food reinforcers, or careful utilization of the child's stereotypic use of a favorite toy) may be advisable. Pacing of task presentation should follow the child's own rhythm while still making optimal use of prime testing time by efficiently administering evaluative tasks, shifting between task stimuli, sustaining interest, and progressing continuously through seamless transitions. For most children, structure (e.g., creation of a standard routine, adoption of a reward system, and firm redirection) facilitates improved performance.

The level and intensity of the social demands imposed in the testing procedures (e.g., attending to instructions, learning from demonstration, or imitating) need to be considered. For children with autism, an examination of patterns of performance relative to the social demands of particular tasks can be quite illuminating. Depending on the social demands involved, a child may demonstrate highly variable performance across two tasks that are designed to assess a similar underlying ability. In almost all cases of autism, increased social demands are associated with a decrement in performance. Hence, it is essential to include at least some procedures that minimize direct social contact by shifting the focus of the interaction to the materials employed. The examiner's tone of voice and volume of speech are additional variables. They should be attuned to the child's individual style, with a goal of facilitating further engagement and comfort. In the same vein, transitions between tests or subtests must be managed skillfully, given autistic children's typical difficulty in shifting from task to task.

Simplification of the testing environment is an additional consideration. A stimulus-rich room may be very distracting to the child, especially over the course of the several assessment sessions that may be required. Children with autism typically exhibit variability and it may be critical to see a child on more than one occasion in order to adequately describe his or her range of functioning.

Parental Involvement

When there is a possibility of a diagnosis of autism, parents should be encouraged, to the extent possible, to observe the evaluation of their child (Morgan, 1988). Participation of parents helps to demystify assessment procedures and provides a common set of observations for subsequent discussion. The rationale for specific tests and procedures and the meaning of specific observations can then be reviewed with the parents in a more efficient and engaging fashion. Additionally, the parents' usual focus on problematic behaviors and their implications for the educational and home environments forces the clinicians to think carefully and continuously about the interrelatedness between assessment and intervention.

An important phase of the assessment concerns the presentation and interpretation of test results to parents (Shea, 1993). It is very important to schedule a parent conference that allows enough time for a thorough discussion of: the results, and the parents' concerns; specific problem-solving and counseling regarding the individual situation of the child and the family; and the prospective intervention program(s) available. If possible, only the adults should be present at this conference. Parents should be reassured that the information on their child will be transmitted in the form of an accessible written report, and that the professionals will be available for further discussion and consultation at a later date. Professional consultation must be especially available after the parents have had an opportunity to reflect on the verbal feedback, review the written report, discuss various concerns among themselves and with other adults who know the child well (e.g., teachers, relatives, child care providers), and initiate contacts with intervention programs. A sense of continuity of care should be conveyed, to allay the parents' anxieties and to establish a reassuring partnership of care that involves all those concerned, including the clinicians. Ideally, the evaluator (or a member of the evaluation team) will have the opportunity to discuss the results and recommendations with one of the individuals involved in implementing the recommended intervention.

Interdisciplinary Collaboration and Cohesion

The findings of the interdisciplinary evaluation should be translated into a single coherent view of the child. Reports should be easily understood, detailed, and concrete, and recommendations should be realistic. Depending on the nature of the child's individual needs, the services of various professionals may be needed. In optimal conditions, when a multidisciplinary team is conducting the evaluation, team members must maintain close communication with each other and avoid fragmentation or duplication of efforts. More importantly, the findings obtained by the different evaluators (e.g., cognitive profile, communicative functioning, and clinical presentation) should be integrated and discussed in terms of the shared implications of findings within each discipline, and with emphasis on the interrelationship of all abilities and disabilities assessed. The evaluation should be sufficiently integrated so that parents receive a single coherent picture of the child's strengths and difficulties. A plethora of individual reports is less helpful than a longer report that integrates input from all members of the evaluation team. The latter format also facilitates discussion among team members, who must be able to reconcile, or understand, apparent discrepancies in their results. When writing their reports, professionals should strive to relate the implications of their findings to the child's day-to-day adaptation and learning. Although quantitative findings across instruments must be presented so that future evaluators can trace the child's development, technical language should be avoided to the extent possible. A brief narrative summary, presenting succinctly the child's competencies and problems across domains, should be included in all psychological reports.

Continuous Contact

The typical complexity of the child's clinical presentation may necessitate direct and continuous contact, from assessment to intervention, with the various professionals who implement the recommended intervention (e.g., teachers, speech pathologists, and occupational therapists). This type of team approach not only maximizes the efficacy of the interventions adopted, but also establishes a partnership among all those involved in clarifying objectives, aiding in specific problem-solving, and monitoring the child's progress. The team approach also reassures parents, who have the complex task of processing a great amount of poignant and often technical information and acquainting themselves with the various health and educational systems whose services are required for their child.

CLINICAL ASSESSMENT OF CHILDREN WITH AUTISM: AN OVERVIEW

Several general areas must be covered within a comprehensive evaluation of an autistic child: a thorough developmental and health history, a psychological assessment, a diagnostic examination, a psychiatric evaluation, and, in some cases, additional consultation regarding motor or neuropsychological functioning. This section addresses these areas in some detail.

History

A careful developmental and health history should include, at a minimum, information related to the pregnancy and neonatal period, the quality and characteristics of attainment of typical developmental milestones (e.g., walking, talking, feeding, toileting), and a detailed medical and family health history. For example: Was the baby very "easy" and content to be left alone? Was it hard to get a response from the child? Did the child smile responsively? Was it hard to feed the baby? Information on the nature and timing of the apparent onset of the condition can provide important data relevant to differential diagnosis. For example: Did the child exhibit a prolonged period of normal development prior to the onset of the condition? (This pattern occurs in Child Disintegrative Disorder; see Chapter 3.) The history should also inquire about normally expected skills (e.g., early social interest, babbling and early prelinguistic communicative behaviors, motor development) as well as deviant behaviors (e.g., excessive echoing, motor mannerisms, peculiar interests, repetitive patterns of behavior).

Questions about development can sometimes be framed for parents around a specific time or well-remembered event, such as the child's first birthday. The most useful questions are those that address specific everyday situations that parents can describe in detail. This type of response allows the clinician to make a judgment about the quality of the child's behavior (Le Couteur et al., 1989) and has the advantage of not requiring the parents to make general statements regarding the normalcy or abnormality of the child's behavior.

Instead, the focus is on real examples of behavior, about which parents have been shown to often provide very accurate descriptions (Schopler & Reichler, 1972). The process of taking the history should convey to parents a sense that the information they provide is both helpful and welcome; the history taking can help the clinician establish a collaborative relationship with parents.

To make maximal use of time, developmental and behavioral inventories may be forwarded to the parents prior to their first visit. They may help to plan the assessment and to elicit and frame observations that can then be further elaborated with the help of the examiner. When parents are willing to share videotapes of representative situations at home or at school, the videotapes can provide essential historical and behavioral information for the purpose of differential diagnosis. Optimally, parents are included in the evaluation process in two complementary ways: (a) as informants, e.g., for semistructured interviews such as the Autism Diagnostic Interview—Revised (ADI-R; Lord et al., 1994) or the Vineland (Sparrow et al., 1984), and (b) as observers who can contextualize the behaviors exhibited by the child during the evaluation.

Psychological Assessment

The psychological assessment focuses on establishing the overall level of intellectual and adaptive functioning as well as describing the child's strengths and weaknesses. The psychological assessment should describe patterns of both verbal and nonverbal functioning across the following domains: (a) problem solving (Can the child generate strategies and integrate information?); (b) concept formation (Can the child group objects by class, color, and so on, or generalize knowledge from one context to another?); (c) style of learning (Can the child learn from modeling or imitation?); and (d) memory skills (How many items of information can the child retain, and is there a difference in the child's ability to recognize inanimate geometric forms versus human faces and related stimuli?) Other areas of interest include adaptive functioning, motor and visual-motor skills, play, and social cognition. A description of results should include not only quantified information but also a judgment of how representative of the child's functioning the measure appears to be, and a description of the conditions that are likely to foster optimal and diminished performance on the part of the child. (The various procedures and some of the available instruments that are suitable for the psychological assessment of children are presented in more detail below.)

Diagnostic Examination

The diagnostic examination should include observations of the child during more and less structured periods (e.g., while interacting with parents, and while engaged in assessments with other members of the evaluating team). Social deficits and deviances typically are most apparent during unstructured times and when observations are focused on the child's *own* overtures and approaches. Thus, the child must have an opportunity to be left to his or her own devices for a period of time (e.g., to handle toy materials). Whether the child becomes absorbed in isolated play or attempts to involve the adults, the nature of the isolated activities (e.g., repetitive, stereotypic play) and of the self-initiated contacts with others (e.g., physical proximity versus shared attention and engagement) constitutes an important diagnostic observation. The professionals should be aware that social problems may not be immediately recognizable because of the structure and initiative taken by sensitive parents and other adults who develop compensatory strategies when interacting with very young children who respond positively to structure (Kasari, Sigman, Mundy, & Yirmiya, 1988).

Areas for observation and inquiry with parents include: (a) social development (e.g., interest in social interaction, patterns of gaze, differential attachments, style of social interaction); (b) communication (e.g., receptive and expressive language, nonverbal and pragmatic communication, communicative intents, echolalia); (c) responses to the environment (e.g., idiosyncratic responses, resistance to change); (d) play skills (e.g., nonfunctional or idiosyncratic uses of play materials); (e) the child's capacities for self-awareness (e.g., interest in mirror image, awareness of his or her own body); (f) motor behaviors (e.g., stereotypic movements such as hand flapping, finger flicking, body twirling, body awareness); and (g) problem behaviors that are likely to interfere with remedial programming (e.g., marked aggression or problems in attention and activity level).

To structure and quantify their observations, clinicians may utilize one of the several diagnostic instruments that have been developed with reference to autism (see Parks, 1983, and Chapter 21). Most diagnostic instruments are designed with parents as informants or rely on direct observations of the child. The Autism Diagnostic Interview—Revised (ADI-R; Lord et al., 1994) is a semistructured interview that focuses on parents' descriptions of children's behavior in social as well as other areas. Although it is designed for the purpose of making a diagnosis, it also provides relevant information regarding the child's developmental and behavioral history; current difficulties in social, communicative, and behavioral areas; and the parents' perceptions of the child's behaviors and difficulties. It has excellent validity and reliability and is currently the instrument of choice in both clinical and research settings (Lord et al., 1994). For the Autism Diagnostic Observation Schedule (ADOS; Lord et al., 1989)—a standardized schedule for the observation of communicative and social behaviors of autistic children—the examiner follows a semistructured protocol involving verbal exchange and play sequences. This instrument was developed for children with verbal mental ages of at least 3 years. A downward extension of the ADOS is currently being evaluated, the Prelinguistic Autism Diagnostic Observation Schedule (PL-ADOS; DiLavore, Lord, & Rutter, 1995). The PL-ADOS was developed for the assessment of children whose language functioning is at the preverbal level. Its diagnostic value and psychometric properties are not yet known. (These instruments are reviewed extensively in Chapter 21.)

Further Consultation

For younger children, consultations with other medical professionals, such as pediatric neurologists or geneticists, may be indicated. History or examination may suggest the need for consultation to obtain specific laboratory studies or medical procedures. For example, the presence of severe mental retardation or dysmorphic features in the child, or a family history of mental retardation, indicates a need for genetic screening and chromosome analysis (including screening for Fragile X). Symptoms suggestive of seizures (e.g., apparent periodic unresponsiveness) suggest the need for an EEG and possible neurological consultation. Neuroimaging, via a CT scan or MRI, may be indicated, and sometimes, though not often, these procedures may reveal disorders such as tuberous sclerosis or degenerative CNS disease. A careful history of the pregnancy and neonatal period should be obtained, to ascertain possible pre- or postnatal infections such as congenital rubella. Usually, the child's hearing is tested prior to the comprehensive evaluation. If this has not been done, or if it was not possible to elicit the child's cooperation, alternative audiometric procedures independent of the child's cooperation should be adopted. In such instances, auditory Brainstem Evoked Responses (BSERs) should be obtained, to rule out sensory loss (Klin, 1993).

Although autism is associated with a number of other medical conditions (Coleman, 1987), in most instances even extensive medical evaluations fail to reveal an underlying organic etiologic factor (see Chapter 18). On the other hand, certain features may suggest the importance of extensive medical investigations (e.g., the abrupt behavioral and developmental deterioration of a child who was previously developing normally; Volkmar, 1996). Given the invasive nature of some of these procedures and the typical heightened reactivity displayed by children with autism, as well as the low probability of positive findings, the clinician should exercise reasonable judgment in seeking additional medical assessments, which should be considered in terms of their cost:benefit value (see Chapter 18).

Differential Diagnosis

The differential diagnosis of autism and other pervasive developmental disorders includes language and other specific developmental disorders, mental retardation, sensory impairments (particularly deafness), and reactive attachment disorder. Usually, children with language disorders do not exhibit the pattern of serious social deviance and deficits found in autism; indeed, nonverbal communicative abilities are often an area of relative strength. In mental retardation, social and communicative skills are usually on a par with cognitive skills. Deaf children may exhibit some difficulties in social interaction and some repetitive activities; however, they are usually interested in social interaction and may use gestures for communicative purposes. Children with reactive attachment disorders have, by definition, experienced marked psychosocial deprivation, which results in deficits in social interaction, most notably in attachment (expressed as either withdrawal or indiscriminate friendliness). However, the quality of the social deficit is different than in autism, and the disturbance tends to remit or diminish significantly after an appropriately responsive and nurturing psychosocial environment is provided.

In young children, the task of differential diagnosis is complicated by the typical rapid change and rate of development, the frequency of autistic-like behaviors in other psychiatric conditions, and the fact that autism can be associated with deafness and, particularly, mental retardation. In many instances, the issue of diagnosis is clarified with certainty only over time and after a period of intervention. It is appropriate to share with parents a sense of the clinician's degree of confidence in the diagnosis. It is also important to realize that the diagnosis may have important, if not necessarily intended, implications for a host of other purposes: educational placement and programming, eligibility for special services in the community, and so forth. It is critical that the importance of educational and other interventions be emphasized, regardless of how "classically" autistic, or low-functioning, the child appears to be. (Chapters 1 through 7 provide a detailed review of aspects of differential diagnosis of autism and other pervasive developmental disorders.)

Summary of Clinical Assessment

The multifaceted nature of the clinical assessment of autistic children underscores the need for integration of the often voluminous information produced by the various clinicians. To prevent fragmentation, the contribution of each professional should not be confined to his or her own area of specialty (e.g., test scores); rather, the team should strive to pool clinical observations, despite the redundancy incurred, in order to obtain a more valid clinical picture in terms of the child's presentation across different settings and persons, and over time.

19.2 PSYCHOLOGICAL ASSESSMENT

Ami Klin, Alice Carter, and Sara S. Sparrow

THE ROLE OF PSYCHOLOGICAL ASSESSMENT

The assessment of intellectual functioning, developmental level, adaptive behavior, and other areas comprising the psychological assessment play an important role in the clinical evaluation of an autistic child. The primary goal of the psychological assessment is to provide a frame for the clinical observations by describing the child's overall level of cognitive functioning. This description is particularly important for a child with autism. For example, intellectual skills are associated with pattern of skill acquisition (Rutter, 1985), severity of symptomatology (Volkmar & Cohen, 1988), level of self-sufficiency (Volkmar, Sparrow, Goudreau, Cicchetti, Paul, & Cohen, 1987), and outcome in autistic persons (Lotter, 1978). In addition to being a central explanatory element of phenotypic expression, intellectual level is an integrated component of diagnosis because the diagnostic category of autism should be applied only to a child whose social disability exceeds what might be expected from someone with his or her level of cognitive functioning (Rutter, 1978).

A careful assessment of overall cognitive functioning is, however, merely the first step in the interpretation of intelligence tests. Variability and consistencies across the various areas of intellectual functioning contribute importantly to the planning and implementation of educational and other interventions. The purpose is to create an individualized profile of strengths and weaknesses, which can be used to maximize the child's learning potential and to optimize the learning environment. The creation of an optimal environment for learning makes it possible for the child to achieve a sense of mastery and self-control, regardless of his or her level of disability. Another area of importance in the psychological assessment concern documenting eligibility for services. In most jurisdictions, legislation mandating services for handicapped children requires a careful assessment of cognitive skills and level of self-sufficiency. With respect to research, appropriate control for intellectual level is an essential component of virtually all investigations, including neurobiological, experimental, and intervention studies.

HISTORICAL PERSPECTIVES

In his original description of autistic children, Kanner (1943) was careful to place his clinical observations within a developmental context. By contrasting the limited social skills of his first autistic patients with the normative skills emerging very early in normally developing children, he was able to characterize autism in terms of both social deviance and developmental deficits. Despite his careful observations, however, certain aspects of his report suggested false leads for research. Central among these was his belief that autism was not accompanied by mental retardation. Interestingly, despite an overwhelming body of literature documenting the intellectual deficits of the majority of autistic children (Lockyer & Rutter, 1969), this belief has persisted in some clinical quarters and resurfaces periodically following the upsurge of innovative, though often unsubstantiated, therapeutic techniques (Cohen, Volkmar, Anderson, & Klin, 1993).

Several factors have contributed to the enduring assumption that most children with autism are not retarded. A frequently voiced belief is that children with autism are "untestable" because of their inherent "negativism" or "noncompliance" (see Volkmar, 1987, for a discussion). However, research studies (e.g., Volkmar, Hoder, & Cohen, 1985) question this view and point to intellectual limitations, rather than volitional noncompliance, as the source of autistic children's difficulties on various cognitive tasks. In fact, when compared to developmentally matched nonautistic peers, these children appear to be more, not less, compliant, and more focused and competent in situations characterized by a high degree of structure and interpersonal involvement (Clark & Rutter, 1981). With respect to testing, it has become clear that intellectual level in autistic children can be assessed, provided that adequate instruments are utilized and the clinician is willing to explore lower-level developmental skills using techniques adapted to children with developmental disabilities.

A second factor that has contributed to a general overevaluation of autistic children's intellectual abilities resulted from observations made originally by Kanner (1943) and Scheerer, Rothman, and Goldstein (1945), regarding some areas of special ability, or "splinter skills," exhibited by many autistic children. For most autistic children, such isolated talents are not of a "savant" nature (Treffert, 1988), but they stand in stark contrast to their skills in other areas of functioning. The range of such skills tends to be quite narrow and usually involves memory for concrete events or trivial information (e.g., numbers, calendars), visual-spatial or manipulative skills (e.g., jigsaw puzzles), or a precocious interest in letters and numbers. Faced with the expressions of these isolated areas of skills, parents and professionals alike are tempted to believe they are evidence against a diagnosis of mental retardation. However impressive the splinter skills are, they are often dissociated from the child's other cognitive skills, and they typically contribute very little to the child's overall real-life adaptation. The psychological evaluator must document such areas of strength but must also contextualize them in terms of broader skill areas that are often significantly deficient. For example, a precocious ability to recognize letters and numbers (i.e., reading decoding) might be unaccompanied by the ability to combine letters into words and sentences, understand what is correctly read (i.e., reading comprehension), and use the words and sentences for the purpose of communication. Similarly, an unusual facility with numerical computation may not transfer to the application of numerical skills to day-to-day tasks such as managing money. Educationally, there is a need to emphasize that a narrow encouragement of these skills must not replace broader intervention efforts aimed at preparing the child to function independently.

The importance of obtaining a comprehensive sample of the child's abilities and disabilities cannot be overemphasized. Only in this context can the targets of intervention that foster social, emotional, and cognitive adaptation be selected and intensively facilitated. Through a developmental understanding of multiple areas of functioning, and an appreciation of the interrelationship among these areas and their direct implications for adaptation, a balanced appraisal of the various factors affecting the child's life can be constructively understood, and any undue importance ascribed to isolated findings can be prevented.

ISSUES IN PSYCHOLOGICAL ASSESSMENT OF AUTISTIC CHILDREN

Psychological assessments are analogous to single-subject experimental designs in which conditions are kept constant, allowing the child's abilities to provide the only source of variance. The advantages of utilizing standardized procedures lie in the fact that the evaluator, utilizing normative tables, can then compare the child's performance to the performance of other children of the same age. Adherence to standardized procedures is of paramount importance for the valid and justified use of normative information. Although deviations from standard procedures should be avoided, it is sometimes necessary, however, to make minor clinical modifications. Such adaptions should only be considered in situations when other supports that maintain standard administration (e.g., breaks, distraction free setting) are not sufficient to obtain an adequate assessment. However, the examiner should be aware that, as a consequence of a break with standardized administration, the results obtained should be viewed with some caution, and the accompanying interpretation should make any deviations from standard administration explicit to the reader.

In testing sessions, it is always critical to consider the child's level of interest and engagement. When working with children with autism, the usual verbal instructions and social reinforcements might not be effective in eliciting optimal cooperation and effort. To successfully conduct the evaluation, it is often necessary to empirically establish potential reinforcers for a particular child. For example, visual-spatial or "hands-on" tasks might have to be interspersed with verbally mediated measures to maintain an acceptable level of effort and engagement. Operant techniques may be particularly useful if an effective reinforcement can be defined, and, though not a primary choice, food reinforcers or even stereotypic interests and activities (e.g., winding up a music box, manipulating a spin top) may be used to motivate the child.

A thorough knowledge of available psychological instruments not typically employed with the normative population may be crucial in conducting the evaluation of a child with autism. Several factors should be considered when choosing a test: (a) the level of language skills required; (b) the complexity of the instructions and the tasks; (c) the level of social demands; (d) the utilization of timed tasks; and (e) the number of shifts from one subtest or format to another. As an informal rule, instruments that require less language mediation and imitative skills (i.e., modeling), are more concrete and straightforward, depend more on visual than on auditory skills, and require fewer attentional and cognitive shifts tend to be more appropriate for the majority of children with autism. Because of the different level of social demands included in the administration of each of the tests, one may obtain different results on tests that tap the same psychological construct. For example, the Hand Movements subtest of the Kaufman—Assessment Battery for Children (K-ABC) and the Bead Memory subtest for the Stanford-Binet share the focus on short-term memory for sequential visual stimuli. However, in the former, the child is required to reproduce a sequence of movements demonstrated by the examiner; in the latter, the child reproduces a sequence from a photograph or plastic model. This single difference in social demands would likely result in higher performance on the Bead Memory test.

Within each testing session, a large amount of extremely important qualitative information is gathered. Nearly every aspect of the events taking place can be viewed as empirically derived information that may prove useful for the purpose of intervention. For example, the child's responses to the amount of structure imposed by the adult, the optimal pace for presentation of tasks, successful strategies to facilitate learning from modeling and demonstrations, effective ways of containing off-task and maladaptive behaviors, are all important observations that can be extremely useful for designing an appropriate intervention program.

AREAS OF ASSESSMENT

Traditional psychological evaluations comprise measures in the areas of intelligence (intellectual profile), adaptive behavior (level of self-sufficiency in real-life situations), achievement (proficiency in academic areas taught at school), additional neuropsychological functioning (abilities of specific higher cognitive or psychomotor processes), and personality (intrapersonal conflicts, emotional presentation, and style of social adaptation). With the exception of intelligence and adaptive behavior, which are essential components of any psychological evaluation, the other areas may or may not be included in the evaluation of an autistic child, depending on clinical and other practical considerations. Depending on the individual's age and level of functioning, other areas of assessment may be important. Among the most prominent are vocational evaluations for programming (Hayes, 1987), behavioral assessment of problematic behaviors (Powers, 1988), and family assessment (Harris, 1988). Although these areas of evaluation are often extremely important in developing program intervention for the autistic individual, they are not typically part of psychological batteries and, therefore, are not discussed here. Achievement testing is also excluded, given that when these measures are appropriate in the case of an autistic child, the instruments adopted and the procedures followed do not differ in a significant way from those employed with the normative population.

The following discussion of the use of various measures in assessing the central domains of psychological functioning is not intended to be comprehensive; rather, it highlights those instruments and procedures that have been proven to be of particular utility in the assessment of children with autism.

Intelligence

Definitions of intelligence are almost as numerous as the theorists who strive to define the concept (Sattler, 1988), but there is a high degree of consensus among psychologists as to the specific, operationalized capacities that should be measured in order to obtain a useful indicator of a child's intellectual level (Snyderman & Rothman, 1987). These include: verbal and nonverbal reasoning or abstract/conceptual thinking; problem-solving; the capacity to acquire knowledge; linguistic competence; mathematical competence; memory; mental speed; and perceptual discrimination. Most intelligence batteries currently in use include these areas in varying degrees. The various instruments differ, however, in terms of emphasis placed on linguistic skills, speed of performance (i.e., timed tasks), reliance on visual or auditory presentation, and number of constructs tested.

As noted previously, autistic individuals as a group cover the entire spectrum of intellectual functioning and formal language capacities. Nevertheless, the great majority of children presenting for evaluation typically exhibit very significant language delays, difficulties in social interaction, poor imitation skills, high levels of distractibility and off-task behaviors, and low tolerance for prolonged periods of testing. Accordingly, testing procedures and instruments should be chosen in order to circumvent such difficulties while safeguarding validity and maximizing the sampling of skills.

Among the various intelligence batteries currently in use, the age-proven Wechsler scales—Wechsler Preschool and Primary Scale of Intelligence (WPPSI-R, 1989), and Wechsler Intelligence Scale for Children—III (WISC-III, 1991)—and the fourth edition of the Stanford-Binet (Thorndike, Hagen, & Sattler, 1986) provide the standards for the testing of intelligence in terms of psychometric properties, standardization procedures, and extent of research. Whenever possible, these batteries should be utilized. They provide valid measures across a large number of relevant constructs, and they yield profiles of functioning that can be readily translated into intervention objectives. The Wechsler scales' division of the various tasks into verbal and performance (visual-perceptual) scales offers a useful conceptualization of autistic children's strengths and weaknesses. The verbal scale usually corresponds to a much lower level of performance, compared to the performance scale (Prior, 1979). Because of the preponderance of scatter (i.e., marked variability in subtest scores) in the Wechsler scales of intelligence (McDonald, Mundy, Kasari, & Sigman, 1989), global indexes of verbal and performance functioning may misrepresent these children's cognitive abilities. Depending on the degree and nature of the scatter, factor scores (as discussed by Kaufman, 1994) may provide a more accurate description of the child's functioning. However, even factor scores may be biased by the presence of isolated strengths or weaknesses. The inclusion of a verbal task examining the child's understanding of social conventions (Comprehension) and a nonverbal task exploring the child's ability to sequence social situations (Picture Arrangement) helps determine the level of discrepancy between the child's comprehension of social versus nonsocial situations (Dean, 1977). The Stanford-Binet has the added advantage of containing scales that extend to the 2-year level (in comparison to the 4-year level in the WPPSI-R); hence, enough simple items are provided, and they can be very useful when there is a need to document reliably a very low level of functioning. Despite these advantages, the emphasis on verbal instructions and linguistic capacities usually diminishes the usefulness of this battery in the assessment of children with autism.

The Wechsler scales and the Stanford-Binet are often not viable for this population, not only because of language requirements but also because they rely on timed tasks, knowledge of specific content, and a number of tests that are exclusively auditory in nature (and, thus, more susceptible to the disruptive effects of distractibility and poor rapport). Hence the importance of alternative batteries that can provide measures of intellectual level with varying degrees of comprehensiveness. The Kaufman-Assessment Battery for Children (K-ABC; Kaufman & Kaufman, 1983) is particularly useful because of its wide age range (2½ to 12 years), reduced emphasis on verbal abilities and acquired knowledge, attractive and straightforward stimuli, and close association with neuropsychological processes. In addition, a provision in the standardization procedure makes it possible for the examiner to teach and demonstrate initial items to the child. The K-ABC also offers a profile of learning style in terms of sequential and simultaneous processing of information that can be very useful in devising optimal teaching techniques. Although the K-ABC does not include a measure of understanding of social situations per se, it does contain a test of face recognition that appears to be very sensitive to the diagnosis of autism, irrespective of developmental level (Klin, Volkmar, Sparrow, de Bild, & Cicchetti, 1996). For the cooperative autistic child who has sufficient verbal skills, the Comprehension and Picture Arrangement subtests of the Wechsler scales may be a valuable addition to the K-ABC profile.

For children with very low levels of linguistic skills, the Leiter International Performance Scale (Leiter, 1980) offers an acceptable measure of nonverbal intelligence. The Leiter scale is based on a visual matching procedure that remains the same for the entire age range of the test (year 2 to year 18). Items range from pairings of colors, shapes, and figures at early levels to items involving analogies and concepts at later levels. Apart from its ability to attract and maintain the attention of more uncooperative autistic children, the Leiter scale has many advantages among this population (Shah & Holmes, 1985): (a) no speech is required from the examiner or the child (i.e., instructions are given in pantomime, if needed at all); (b) the tasks are self-explanatory and, for the initial items, unlimited demonstration is permitted; (c) with the exception of four items at higher levels, there are no timed tasks or time limits (a very useful attribute for children who do not understand the need for speed or have fleeting attention, or whose stereotypies interfere with their performance); (d) only minimal record keeping is required, and the tasks can be introduced casually and in a playlike manner. These are useful attributes when testing children with attentional and behavioral problems as well as high levels of activity.

Unfortunately, these advantages arc counterbalanced by several limitations, including the following: (a) the scale measures primarily nonverbal skills and should not be seen as a measure of general intellectual ability; (b) there are too few items at each age level, which may lead to an inaccurate estimate of mental age; (c) the items' difficulty level is not constant; (d) many of the pictures used are outdated; and (e) unlike other psychological batteries, a ratio IQ is used rather than standard scores. Despite these shortcomings, the Leiter scale is often the only viable alternative at a clinician's disposal, and its forthcoming revision is expected to rectify some of the limitations while safeguarding the proven advantages. Profiles obtained with the Leiter scale may be of diagnostic value for children with autism (Maltz, 1981). When other batteries prove impractical, the combination of the Leiter scale with measures of listening vocabulary, such as the Peabody Picture Vocabulary Test—Revised (PPVT-R; Dunn & Dunn, 1981), may provide an estimate of the child's overall intellectual level. It should be noted, however, that both the Leiter scale and the PPVT-R tend to inflate the scores of autistic children (see Shah & Holmes, 1985, and Klin, Volkmar, Marans, & South, 1996). Although the norms of the Leiter scale are outdated, a revised version, including new norms and some innovations in the testing materials, will be available in 1997.

For very low-functioning individuals, other tests may provide useful information about cognitive functioning. These include: (a) the Extended Merrill-Palmer Scale (Ball, Merrifield, & Stott, 1978), which is primarily a performance test involving puzzles and pegboards; (b) developmental tests such as the Bayley Scales of Infant Development, 2nd Edition (Bayley, 1993), a test designed primarily for children with mental ages under $3\frac{1}{2}$ years, and the Uzgiris-Hunt Ordinal Scale of Infant Development (Uzgiris & Hunt, 1975), which is based on Piagetian concepts. Although such tests provide acceptable measures of current developmental level, they often have poor predictive value and stability over time. More importantly, the use of developmental tests

with severely retarded adolescents and adults is particularly problematic because the profiles obtained carry little relevance to the day-to-day real life of these individuals. Unfortunately, a more relevant test of intellectual functioning is not yet available for employment with this group of very low-functioning individuals.

Despite the difficulties inherent in the intellectual testing of autistic children, several studies have substantiated the validity and predictive usefulness of intelligence scores (Lord & Schopler, 1988). Clinicians should be aware that the larger the sampling of cognitive skills (i.e., comprehensiveness of the test or combination of tasks), the higher the validity and accuracy of the estimate of intellectual functioning.

Several measurement peculiarities may be encountered in the assessment of autistic children. First, it should not be assumed that the correlations between different batteries, as reported in the test manuals, are directly applicable to this group of children. The patterns of strengths and weaknesses typically observed among children with autism do not allow that application. For example, the PPVT-R in typical populations is very highly correlated with overall measures of both intelligence and language comprehension (Sattler, 1988). In the case of autistic children, however, correlations are much lower. Indeed, the PPVT-R often provides an inflated measure of cognitive and linguistic ability because it does not require a verbal response nor sentence or syntax comprehension (Klin, Volkmar, Marans, et al., 1996).

Second, it is not unusual to observe a drop in standard scores over time. This phenomenon usually does not indicate a loss of acquired skills; rather, it suggests that the child's intellectual gains are not commensurate (i.e., they are at a slower rate) with gains in chronological age.

Third, given autistic children's usual strengths in visual perceptual tasks and weaknesses in conceptual and reasoning tasks, it is not uncommon to observe a drop in standard scores at around school-entry level. This follows the typical developmental organization of test batteries that reduce the number of items dependent on perceptual discrimination and increase the number of items requiring transformation of verbal information at this point in the developmental course. This observation underscores the importance of emphasizing reasoning, conceptualization, and generalization in programming for autistic children.

Adaptive Behavior

Adaptive functioning refers to capacities for personal and social self-sufficiency in real-life situations. The importance of this component of the clinical assessment cannot be overemphasized. Its aim is to obtain a measure of the child's typical patterns of functioning in familiar and representative environments, such as the home and the school, which may contrast markedly with the demonstrated level of performance and presentation in the clinic. It provides the clinician with an essential indicator of the extent to which the child is able to utilize his or her potential, as measured in the assessment, in the process of adaptation to environmental demands. A large discrepancy between intellectual level and adaptive level signifies that priority should be given to instruction within the context of naturally occurring situations, in order to foster and facilitate the use of skills to enhance quality of life. In most circumstances, a measure of adaptive level is required in order to establish a child's entitlement to services.

The most widely employed instrument to assess adaptive behavior is the Vineland Adaptive Behavior Scales (Sparrow, Balla, & Cicchetti, 1984a). "The Vineland" assesses capacities for self-sufficiency in various domains of functioning, including Communication (receptive, expressive, and written language), Daily Living Skills (personal, domestic, and community skills), Socialization (interpersonal relationships, play and leisure time, and coping skills), and Motor Skills (gross and fine). These capacities are assessed on the basis of the individual's current daily functioning, using a semistructured interview administered to a parent or other primary caregiver. The Vineland is available in three editions: (a) a survey form to be used primarily as a diagnostic and classification tool for normal to low-functioning children or adults (Sparrow et al., 1984a); (b) an expanded form for use in the development of individual education or rehabilitative planning (Sparrow et al., 1984b); and (c) a classroom edition to be used by teachers (Sparrow et al., 1985). Among the various editions, the expanded form is the most useful for autistic children, whose level of adaptive functioning is usually much lower than their demonstrated intellectual level (Volkmar et al., 1993). Using a child's developmental level as a point of reference, this form makes it possible for the clinician to plan intervention on the basis of skills that the child should have acquired, given his or her intellectual level. Because the items of the Vineland were selected on the basis of their immediate relevance to real-life adaptation, the skills described therein can be readily incorporated into the child's intervention plan.

Several research studies (e.g., Volkmar et al., 1987) have helped delineate the usual profile obtained for autistic children. This profile typically consists of relative strengths in the areas of Daily Living and Motor skills, and significant deficits in the areas of Socialization and, to a lesser extent, Communication. Recent studies (Klin, Volkmar, & Sparrow, 1992; Volkmar et al., 1993) have also demonstrated the utility of the Vineland for diagnostic purposes. Vineland supplementary norms for autistic individuals are now available (Carter, Volkmar, Sparrow, & Cicchetti, 1996).

Neuropsychological Assessment

Along with intelligence batteries, neuropsychological assessments may be used to complement a psychological assessment when there are concerns about specific patterns of behavioral deficits, or when there are indications of possible and identifiable neurological involvement affecting specific brain systems. These measures may include sensory-perceptual functions (tactile, visual, and auditory modalities); laterality and psychomotor functions related to speed and visual-motor integration; motor functioning relating to speed, strength, and coordination of movement; attention in the various sensory modalities; specific language and memory skills; concept formation and planning, or executive functions such as forward planning, categorization, strategy generation, and mental shifting. Such measures may also be indicated to explore the nature of a child's learning disability in detail. Several comprehensive batteries are available, but because they were developed initially for use with adults, their use with children is limited (Pennington, 1991).

For the majority of autistic children presenting for evaluation at a clinic, these batteries do not offer a contribution that is significant enough to justify the cost, in time and effort, for their use. Nevertheless, the employment of single tasks from these batteries, or the use of brief tests to explore the child's visual-motor skills or motor functioning can be of great value for some children whose learning and adaptation appear to be hindered by deficits in these skills. For example, the Beery-Buktenica Developmental Test of Visual-Motor Integration (VMI; Beery & Buktenica, 1989) and the Bender Visual Motor Gestalt Test (Bender, 1938) provide a quick assessment of the child's graphic and motor skills, perceptual accuracy, and hand–eye coordination. Perseverative behaviors, laterality problems, and distortions that may indicate neurological involvement may also be revealed (Stellern, Vasa, & Little, 1976). The Bruininks-Oseretsky Test of Motor Proficiency (Bruininks, 1978) provides useful measures of gross and fine motor skills and is indicated whenever a child appears to present with deficits in coordination (e.g., is often "clumsy" or tends to "bump into other children") and in other motor skills.

For the "classically autistic" child, motor functioning is often a strength relative to other areas of functioning; however, the clinician may see children whose motor skills lag behind the development of other skills and who often have a higher IQ and less severe social dysfunction. For these children, the provision of physical and occupational therapy (PT and OT) may be a beneficial element of their educational program, given the important role played by motor and coordination skills in learning processes, particularly for the young child. In this context, there is a need to integrate the various components of the educational program, with a view toward maximizing learning opportunities and encouraging skills in areas that are typically weak among children with autism. For example, occupational therapy may include activities focused on the teaching of conceptual terms (e.g., quantity, position, size), problem solving, and awareness of self and others (e.g., body awareness, motor planning). This learning may be achieved with the use of large three-dimensional objects or structures that can be moved, positioned, and played with. The intent is to teach a concept via multiple sensory modalities in a "hands-on" and exaggerated fashion.

In the past few years, a great deal of attention has been given to a subgroup of the autistic population: individuals with IQs within, or close to, the normal range (Schopler & Mesibov, 1992). These individuals appear to fall within two distinct diagnostic categories, based on their phenomenological presentation, namely, high functioning autism and Asperger's Syndrome (Klin, 1994). Recent research has suggested that the phenomenological distinctions may be accounted for by the different patterns of neuropsychological skills and disabilities obtained for these two groups (Klin, Volkmar, Sparrow, Cicchetti, & Rourke, 1995). If corroborated by additional studies, neuropsychological assessments might prove to be of greater clinical value than was previously discerned for this small group of individuals. This outcome would bring the clinical and research fields closer together, because the investigation of neuropsychological functioning in normal-IQ individuals with autism has witnessed a great upsurge of research studies in the past several years (Rumsey, 1992).

Social Emotional Functioning

Traditional methods of personality assessment are generally not very useful in the evaluation of autistic children because of these children's typically limited linguistic skills and concreteness. Nevertheless, at least a few studies (e.g., Dykens, Volkmar, & Glick, 1991) have suggested the usefulness of projective instruments such as the Rorschach Inkblot Test (Exner, 1990) in the diagnosis of disorganized thinking for a small group of higher-functioning autistic individuals. More commonly, though, the use of simpler projective techniques, such as drawings and play sessions, may be more revealing with regard to social-cognitive skills, emotional presentation, and intrapsychic preoccupations that are typically not explored during other sections of the evaluation. These data can only be appropriately interpreted, however, within the context of the child's developmental level and psychomotor skills.

Drawings may provide some information about cognitive level, interests, understanding of social life, and primary attachments—and even some diagnostic information. Several specific guidelines should be kept in mind when requesting the autistic child to draw and when interpreting the work produced. The child should have an opportunity to draw spontaneously before a specific request is made. The resultant work may be a perseverative interest ranging from, for example, an oval stroke, drawn repeatedly, to meaningful figures representing inanimate objects such as clocks or machinery. This work should be analyzed in terms of its perseveration quality, salience of social versus inanimate elements, visual-perceptual coherence, and presence of unusual qualities, given the child's age and developmental level. Unusual features may include a precocious sense of perspective and "realistic" representations such as visual occlusion (e.g., an object is partially superimposed on another with no overlapping lines; they appear as they might be perceived if one were actually looking at them). Such features are important because normally developing children's drawings often reflect their symbolic or cognitive understanding of an object (e.g., a person's body parts are drawn first and then clothed, resulting in overlapping strokes). In contrast, visual occlusion is thought to reflect the predominance of perceptual, rather than cognitive, determinants in visual representation (Selfe, 1978), and is thought to be typical of at least some autistic children.

The child should then be requested to draw a person, then self, and then his or her family. This work can be analyzed in terms of traditional cognitive scoring systems (Harris, 1963), but also, and more importantly, in terms of the difference in quality between the inanimate and the social drawings. Particular attention should be paid to the sense of coherence of the human body, the sophistication of the work, and any emotional quality that is represented in the drawing. It is also important to question a verbal child, to the extent that

this is possible, about the drawing. Often, indistinguishable strokes may actually represent the child's effort to comply with the request to draw a person.

Play activities offer innumerable opportunities to explore aspects of the child's development and behavior, especially cognitive quality (e.g., functional/manipulative versus representative and imaginative) and the presence of role-play (Fein, 1981), which may characterize the child's ability to take the perspective of others. This social-cognitive skill is essential for adequate interaction with others and for development of self-understanding (Klin, 1989; Selman, Lavin, & Brion-Meisels, 1982). If opportunities to observe these phenomena are not available in the child's spontaneous play, the examiner may initiate play situations in order to directly explore the child's understanding of social-emotional phenomena. For example, a puppet setting can be used to elicit the child's responses to situations of joy and distress, as well as to explore the child's ability to impute mental states (e.g., beliefs, intentions) to others and predict their behavior accordingly (Baron-Cohen, 1989).

Unstructured play is also an essential aspect of the diagnostic assessment. The clinician should be primarily interested in the child's behavior patterns in unstructured situations that contrast with the structured testing procedure. Relevant issues are the capacity for self-control and self-monitoring, habitual patterns of behavior observed when the child is left to his or her own devices, as well as the need (or absence thereof) to include the examiner in play activities. In contrast to other children, whose performance in a testing situation may be less than optimal because of the anxiety caused by the unfamiliar setting, autistic children may, in fact, perform at optimal levels because of the rigid, one-to-one, socially structured situation. Such a setting is rarely duplicated in a naturalistic environment such as school, where the presence of other children and less adult control place increased demands on the child's capacities for self-regulation. The use of less structured projective and play techniques often provides a richer view of the child's overall functioning and behavioral presentation.

SUMMARY

This chapter unit presents an overview of the psychological assessment within the broader context of assessment in autism. We advocate a comprehensive developmental approach that applies the following core principles:

1. The adaptive and maladaptive functioning of individuals with autism must be interpreted in terms of the interrelationship between normative developmental expectations and the delays and typical deviant patterns of behavior associated with this condition.
2. To fully capture an individual's psychological functioning, it is critical to assess, in an integrated fashion, multiple domains of functioning. The selection of relevant domains of functioning should be based on state-of-the-art knowledge of typical psychological profiles observed in individuals with autism as well as the presenting problems of the specific individual. The tests chosen should be developmentally appropriate and should maximize the sampling of a wide range of skills.
3. In light of the variability in performance across time and settings that is typically observed in individuals with autism, it is essential to gather information from multiple sources, particularly those related to the individual's familiar settings (e.g., school and home).
4. In the administration and interpretation of specific tasks, conditions that optimize or diminish performance (e.g., level of structure, social demands, and task shifts) should be given particular attention.

19.3 COMMUNICATION ASSESSMENT

Wendy Dalton Marans

Impaired communicative competence is a central feature of autism. Noted by Kanner in his original (1943) report, unusual communicative characteristics continue to be one of the essential features of the condition (American Psychiatric Association [APA], 1994; World Health Organization [WHO], 1990). Communicative deficits do not operate in isolation. They interact in complex ways with the disordered social development and restricted patterns of behavior and interest in an autistic individual, and they impact on his or her adaptive and behavioral functioning and educational achievement. An accurate assessment and understanding of particular strengths and needs in a challenging task for parents, evaluators, and teachers, but meaningful information about the autistic person's communicative functioning is critical for effective program planning and intervention. The individual's competencies and needs must be considered in the context of a whole person who is a member of the family and community. This broad view of assessment is important because patterns of development are uneven and developmental inconsistencies are common in individuals with autism. If viewed in isolation, splinter skills or isolated strengths may be misinterpreted and may lead to inappropriate expectations (see Chapter 24 for a discussion). Broader approaches to assessment have been advanced by the development of transactional, functional, and ecological models (Crais & Roberts, 1991; Prizant & Rydell, 1993) that do not isolate communicative behaviors from the contexts in which they occur or from the people to whom they are directed.

This chapter unit addresses the challenges inherent in the process of assessing communication in individuals with autism and Pervasive Developmental Disorder (PDD), describes some of the standardized, criterion-referenced, and observational assessment measures and methods available, and serves as an introduction to this complex topic. Additional information on particular assessment approaches and instruments is provided in Chapters 18, 20, 21, and 23–25.

Standardized tests constitute only one part of a comprehensive assessment of persons with autism. These instruments may not always capture the whole spectrum of the pragmatic and functional deficits entailed in social interaction. In addition, to be successful, the administration of these tests may require some modifications to the standard presentation. However, the selection of appropriate tests, combined with a comprehensive understanding of autism and of developmental processes, can yield information that is helpful for both diagnostic assessment and educational or vocational planning.

ISSUES IN ASSESSMENT

Communicative Impairments

Idiosyncratic but disorder-specific communicative behaviors are common in children and adults with autism. Approximately 50% of affected individuals do not speak (Paul, 1987). The presence of speech by age 6 years is a positive prognostic factor. For children who are mute, an accurate assessment of comprehension is especially important. Where an appropriate alternative or augmentative communicative system is needed, the skills that are required to support such a system—level of symbolic understanding, imitation, eye–hand coordination, reading skills, ability to use computers, and so on—must be evaluated. In addition, the presence of motor-speech difficulties above and beyond the child's social and communicative needs will influence decisions regarding focus of therapy and primary mode of communication.

From the earliest stages of development, prosodic and paralinguistic features are notably atypical in this population (Tager-Flusberg, 1989), although Szatmari and colleagues (Fein, Bartolucci, Ginsberg, & Szatmari, 1991) found that, under controlled conditions, individuals with autism were able to recognize meanings conveyed through prosody. Even babble and cry behaviors have been shown to be idiosyncratic and unusual in autistic children, when compared with mentally retarded and normally developing controls (Ricks, 1975). In communication, prosody and paralinguistic devices are central in (a) marking new versus old information; (b) dividing utterances into meaningful units, which makes it easier to process the incoming auditory signal; and (c) conveying affective and emotional expression. Even in autistic individuals who develop higher-level language skills, prosodic differences may remain intractable. Standardized measures are not widely available, but these aspects of language and communication are important to observe and characterize so that, in higher-functioning individuals, they can be addressed explicitly. For example, learning when and where to reduce volume; developing an awareness of which word is stressed in the sentence and what that means; appreciating the use of pausing as a signal that the next speaker can take a turn, etc.

Well before verbal language is achieved, children show an intent to communicate. In children who are autistic, development of intentionality may be delayed, and the range of intents conveyed may be restricted in terms of their function, frequency of occurrence, and means used (Wetherby & Prizant, 1990; Wetherby, Yonclas, & Bryan, 1989). Reaching and, later, more specific pointing are means of conveying needs and wants, or of drawing someone's attention to some aspect of the environment. Studies have investigated understanding and use of protoimperative versus protodeclarative pointing behaviors (*give me* as opposed to *show me; get me* as opposed to *look at that;* see Chapter 41). Young children with autism understood and used protoimperative pointing as did their nonautistic counterparts but, unlike them, the autistic children did not appreciate or use the more social, protodeclarative pointing, presumably because of a lack of interest in joint attention. In an attempt to elicit and sample communicative intents, many recently developed assessment instruments have established "communicative temptations" or "presses" (Lord et al., 1989; Wetherby & Prizant, 1990). The information obtained by using these techniques can help in developing treatment goals, and it serves as a baseline against which to measure progress. For example, the number of intentional acts per 10-minute period, or spontaneous versus elicited means used for each act, can be systematically addressed as a focus of intervention.

Echolalia is considered a hallmark of early expressive language in many children with autism. An early study estimated that 75% of autistic individuals may be echolalic, and this phenomenon has now been extensively studied (e.g., Prizant & Duchan, 1981; Prizant & Rydell, 1993; Schuler & Prizant, 1985). Echolalia is not limited to autistic children. It occurs early in normal language development, but decreases in frequency as the spontaneous output of the typically developing child increases. In children with autism, echolalia tends to be more pronounced and sustained. Examiners must remain aware of the various functions echolalia can serve; their own demands on a child may contribute to the behavior. Violette and Swisher (1992) found that immediate echolalia in autism increased when examiners were more directive and the vocabulary used was less familiar. Rydell and Mirenda (1994) reported that a directive and constraining linguistic style on the part of the adult increased students' use of unconventional verbal behavior. Conversely, favorable effects can occur when adult intervention is more child-focused. Dawson and Galpert (1990) reported increased imitation by the children, and greater eye contact and gaze shifts directed toward the adults when adults imitated young autistic children's behaviors during spontaneous play with objects. During communication assessments, any variables that may influence the children's or the adults' performance must be considered. Variables may include task demands, language levels, setting, interpersonal demands, and methods of analyzing data.

Observations of communicative and language behaviors within the broader contexts in which they occur have led to greater appreciation of what students with autism understand and convey. For example, higher-functioning children and adults with autism do produce many of the relational meanings and grammatical forms (Tager-Flusberg, 1989) used by mental-age-matched peers, even when prosody and sociocommunicative behaviors continue to pose difficulties. At higher language levels, the control of variables continues to make a difference. In controlled conditions with explicit instructions, students with autism have been able to demonstrate abilities that may not always be possible for them in spontaneously occurring situations. Paul and Cohen (1985) assessed comprehension of indirect requests and contingent queries and found that, if preparation for the task was provided, the subjects recognized and responded appropriately to the requests. The inability to respond spontaneously when incoming stimuli (linguistic, social, and contextual) require rapid on-line integration leads to breakdowns in communication. Pragmatic communication deficits also tend to be more pervasive. They include (a) the use of unconventional means to communicate a limited range of functions, (b) a limited ability to sustain discourse, and (c) problems in interpretation of nonliteral language forms (humor, idiomatic language, inferencing, sarcasm, and so on). Comprehension in children and adults can range from significant delays in understanding verbal input to stronger, age-appropriate abilities, if conventional, contextual cues are optimal. Even in the latter instance, there is a tendency toward being concrete and overliteral, and difficulties may be noted in understanding of deictic terms which have shifting reference, for example, pronouns, relative and spatial, and temporal concepts (Menyuk & Quill, 1985). Assumptions regarding comprehension of certain concepts and statements, therefore, should not be made without adequate sampling across different linguistic/social contexts. Discrepancies in performance at home, at school, and at the testing site may result from (a) level of comfort, (b) familiarity (with the examiner or the setting), or (c) the support of context or routine. Understanding the source, when variability in performance is present, is the first step in determining how to develop context-independent comprehension and encourage generalization of skills to more consistent and advanced levels across settings.

When considering the communicative aspects of the assessment, it is important for the examiner to use a range of means for the evaluation, drawing on parental and staff reports as well as direct testing and observation. Standardized, developmental, criterion-based, and observational data should be integrated with information about cognitive status and other factors that may have an impact on potential.

Social Impairment

Assessment of anyone with autism must include information about sociocommunicative and socioaffective behaviors that are part of the person's repertoire, and consideration of social components and their impact on the responses to testing. The inherent drive toward sociability, seen in most infants, is typically lacking in children with autism. However, not all children are actively avoidant (Wing & Gould, 1979). Children whose styles are more passive may be easier to assess because they can tolerate the tester's participation. A child who finds such involvement intrusive and upsetting may respond in less adaptive ways to the testing situation. A passive student may demand less attention in a classroom setting, compared to an active, behaviorally challenging student who immediately commands involvement on the part of the staff, albeit sometimes in maladaptive ways. Some recent studies have pinpointed the sociocommunicative behaviors that may distinguish autistic and nonautistic youngsters. Videotapes from home or school settings are useful additions to the assessment process, particularly when direct observation in these settings is not possible. Retrospective review of videotaped first-birthday parties of children subsequently diagnosed with autism (Osterling & Dawson, 1994) revealed that certain prosocial behaviors occurred less frequently in these children; there was reduced eye contact, decreased pointing for the purpose of showing (joint attention), and failure to orient to their names. Lord (1995), looking at the accuracy of different methods of diagnosis (clinical versus interview) for children 2 and 3 years of age, found sociocommunicative abnormalities to be the best discriminators between nonautistic and autistic subjects. Directing attention, attention to voice, and pointing behaviors were most sensitive, and stereotypies were less discriminative. Studies of facial expression in children with autism suggest that a narrower range of expressions occurs and reactions are frequently confused or merged, making it difficult for the partner in an interaction to "read" the cues correctly (Kasari, Yirmiya, Mundy, & Sigman, 1986).

Assessment of nonverbal communication must therefore include observation of sociocommunicative and socioaffective behaviors. In light of the interactive nature of testing, assessors may need to adapt their own behaviors, or the approaches they use when testing, to maximize the likelihood that the testee will be able to respond. Adaptations may include having a parent in the room, allowing time during which interpersonal demands on the child are minimal, avoiding direct eye contact until the child is comfortable, using appealing toy materials as intermediaries or as channels for some reciprocal involvement, setting up communicative temptations (Wetherby, Cain, Yonclas, & Walker, 1988; Wetherby & Prizant, 1990),

imitating the child's spontaneous behaviors, and moving gradually to more formal assessment activities (if appropriate). During the assessment, it is often helpful to observe the child and parents together, without a nonfamilial adult present. To form impressions and complete the process, more than one session is often needed. With higher-functioning students with autism, formal testing (which should include assessment of nonliteral and higher-level language skills, where deficits are more likely to be apparent) may be less stressful than spontaneous language sampling. Structured activities are not as open-ended, are more predictable, and require less participation at a social level than spontaneous conversation sampling, which should be reserved for later in the session, when the student is presumably more comfortable. Flexibility on the part of the tester, and sensitivity to the child's style and reactions, can allow for ongoing adaptation in order to maximize the useful information obtained.

Restricted Patterns of Behavior, Interest, and Activities

Assessment outside of the individual's home, school, or work setting constitutes a novel environment that is unfamiliar, unpredictable, and likely to generate anxiety. The anxiety is exacerbated when unfamiliar individuals assign cognitive, social, and linguistic tasks during the assessment. Their demands may have a negative impact on the student's attention, processing, sociability, ability, and/or willingness to engage. Other factors pose significant challenges to obtaining optimal and representative samples of behavior. They include:

1. Difficulties with state regulation because of heightened sensitivities and responses to various sensory stimulation.
2. Poor frustration tolerance.
3. Limited capacity for modulation of mood and affect.

Individuals' responses to stress will vary; they must be recognized and understood when possible. For example, stereotypic behaviors may increase as a means of self-soothing or withdrawal from social contact—or, they may signal excessive task difficulty (Dawson & Lewy,

1989). Under these circumstances, gauging the representativeness of the results and knowing whether performance is an indicator of potential or an artifact of anxiety can be difficult. Prior knowledge, gained from parents or through video review, of the activities, methods, and management techniques that are most effective in calming and stabilizing the child can allow the evaluator(s) to try to replicate, as much as possible, optimal conditions within the unfamiliar environment. The level to which change disrupts a given individual becomes, in and of itself, a part of the assessment data and a target for intervention.

Play

Research has revealed parallels in the development of language and symbolic play, especially during the first 2 years of life (Bates, 1979). These parallels are apparent in children with and without a range of disabilities such as mental retardation, Down syndrome, and hearing impairment. Synchronies are found between the timing of first words and the appearance of play gestures and between syntactic complexity and play schemes or sequences, and the capacity to have an object represent something other than itself. Toddlers with specific expressive language impairment (but with age-appropriate comprehension) exhibited less frequent play directed toward a doll or other toy (decentered play), a reduced number of play sequences, and fewer symbolic play transformations (Rescorla & Goossens, 1992); that is, there was more manipulative exploration and less representational or social play among the children with expressive language delays. Evaluation of play behaviors in children with autism is important because the behaviors pertain to their level of symbolic awareness (choice of medium for communication), have implications for language readiness, and reveal ramifications in terms of social awareness. Uneven patterns of play behaviors—for example, advanced manipulation or mechanical skills in the absence of any pretending—are often observed. They can be used in planning effective reinforcement and teaching strategies, and in determining the materials and methods that are most likely to be effective. The child's flexibility within play, especially his or her willingness to take on other roles, to appreciate another person's point of view, and to suspend disbelief, should also be observed. These capacities have been discussed within the context of theory of mind, which proposes a potential underlying deficit in autism: the inability to appreciate others' states of mind (see Chapter 41).

Behavioral Issues

Adaptive and maladaptive behaviors must be understood within the context of individuals' abilities, needs, and responses to stress, and the demands of the situation. Despite the frequent reports of high levels of noncompliance in children with autism, such behaviors, when viewed in a broader context, are relatively uncommon. Misattribution of noncompliance may take place when unconventional, and often unrecognized, attempts to comply occur (Volkmar, Hoder, & Cohen, 1985). Various factors can contribute to unconventional verbal or other behaviors. These may include failure to comprehend, demands that are too great or overwhelming, or an inability to communicate more adaptively and conventionally. Keeping developmental expectations in mind, and using appropriate behavioral methods to provide structure and support, can help to reduce stress, to increase the individual's sense of order, and to promote optimal performance. Similarly, it is important to be sure that requested skills do not exceed the individual's capacity, particularly during the early phase of assessment. Repeated experience of failure can lead to frustration, exacerbation of maladaptive behavioral patterns, and underestimates of more typical abilities. It is important to emphasize that a behavioral analysis, in and of itself, may constitute part of the evaluation. All behaviors during the course of the assessment process can be informative: how tasks are approached; when the individual evidences shifts in attention, mood, or behavior; what behavioral strategies prove helpful. These behaviors become part of the planning process for bridging assessment and programming.

ASSESSMENT

The communication assessment should be one component of a transdisciplinary or multidisciplinary evaluation. At a minimum, this evaluation should include psychological and psychiatric components and should involve the parents as collaborators in the process (see Chapter 19.1). Investigations for the presence of any potentially comorbid or contributory conditions should include audiological testing (pure tone, tympanometry, and BSER if necessary) to determine any hearing impairment, neurological consultation, and physical and occupational therapy evaluations as appropriate.

If possible, an oral motor assessment for apraxia should be conducted within the context of the communication evaluation, particularly if the child is verbal but is having clear difficulties in formulating sounds and words. Obtaining imitation of oral motor movements may be problematic and may be limited initially to observational data. Information about oral motor control, however, has direct implications in determining whether additional augmentative systems are required for communication. If this is the case, then, before deciding on the systems of choice, an assessment of fine motor skills, intentionality and imitation, and preference for stimulus or system type (e.g., sign versus picture/photo) will need to be done.

The use of standardized testing continues to be important in establishing a need for services (Public Law 94-457). The complications in assessing younger children (birth to 3 years of age) and children with autism or pervasive development disorders have, however, been recognized. State guidelines generally allow for qualitative information (criterion-referenced assessment, clinical observation) to be used in lieu of quantitative data in such cases. The impetus to develop more reliable tools for the birth-to-3-years population has led to a proliferation of developmental assessment and criterion-referenced checklists that are to be used as alternatives or additions to standardized testing. Some of the more useful instruments for children with autism are based on collection of information on sociocommunicative and socioaffective functioning. Observation of unstructured or semistructured play for signs of communicative intent (Coggins & Carpenter, 1981; Wetherby & Prizant, 1990) and developmental play levels (McCune-Nicholich, & Carroll, 1981; Westby, 1988) can provide valuable data.

Specific instruments developed for assessment of students with autism have been based on operationalized play (Lord et al., 1989), ecological assessment, and functional communication profiles (Prizant & Rydell, 1984).

When selecting materials to be used for testing, developmental functioning must be considered. One advantage of working as part of a multidisciplinary team is that such information may already have been collected and can inform assessments of communicative functioning. Although 75% of children with autism also exhibit overall cognitive delay, the unevenness in any individual's profile is key. Given the current resources and an understanding of how autism can manifest, no child should be considered "untestable." Instead, the tester needs to adapt and use any and all available methods to develop a profile of the given child and his or her needs. Higher-functioning autistic individuals may have age-appropriate skills on many tests of formal language properties—articulation, fluency, grammatical form, vocabulary knowledge, reading decoding (Minshew, Goldstein, & Siegel, 1995). If only structural aspects of language are tested, findings are likely to be inconclusive at best and misleading at worst. It is essential to select instruments that tap higher-level language abilities such as nonliteral skills—inferencing, understanding ambiguity and metaphor, interpreting texts (reading between the lines), and providing explanations that are appropriate and comprehensive and take the listener's perspective into account, i.e., through discourse analysis (Paul, 1995). Observational data regarding interactions with family, peers, or staff provide input as to how such students are able to use their language for the purposes of socializing, learning, and coping. The consistency of performance across settings can be tapped via reporting instruments such as the Vineland Adaptive Behavior Scales (Sparrow et al., 1984), which can be completed by caretakers and teachers. Discrepancies in levels of functioning in one setting or another should lead to an objective of generalizing optimal skill levels across settings.

Parent Interviews and Checklists

Interviews vary in terms of whether they use open-ended questions or require only Yes/No answers, and they may or may not be standardized. Open-ended interviews tend to be more time-consuming and more informative, particularly where specific examples of behaviors are required in order to score any given item (e.g., Lord et al., 1989; Sparrow et al., 1984). Open-ended interviews require more operationalizing and training of administrators to ensure reliability.

Questionnaires requiring only categorical Yes/No responses are often easier and quicker to administer and score, but they do not usually yield equally rich information. In some cases, they can be completed independently by the parent or caretaker, but it is essential to determine that the respondent can read and fully understand the questions. The examiner should make sure that all items are completed and should provide an opportunity for the respondent to ask questions about any items that may have been unclear. The utility of the instrument will depend on the comprehensiveness, sensitivity, and specificity of the items, their relevance to the population under investigation, and the accuracy of the respondent.

When selecting any instrument requiring parental report, users should be aware that information regarding current skills is more reliable than retrospective reporting, and recognition is more reliable than recall (e.g., "Does your child do X or Y?" as opposed to "What does your child do under X circumstances?"). Table 19.1 lists some parental reports and interviews. (Additional information regarding autism-related instruments appears in Chapter 21.)

Assessment of Prelinguistic/ Preverbal Children

This group includes children who are mute and children who are not yet using words but may be vocalizing and will use language at some later date. Social, communicative, and play behaviors become the focus of the assessment (Bruner, 1981; Wetherby et al., 1988). The goal is to set up a situation and elicit behaviors, or to observe a spontaneous situation that allows assessing the following characteristics:

1. Level of comprehension or awareness of sociocommunicative bids from others (gestures, words and sentences, affective expression).
2. Intentionality—whether the child has a sense of his or her own ability—through regulating others' behaviors, social routines, and establishment of joint attention (Bruner, 1981)—to have an impact on people in their environment.
3. Means used to convey intentional communicative bids—behavioral, vocal, gestural, signed, verbal, or some combination.
4. Quality of communicative bids—conventionality, adaptability, persistence, and effectiveness.
5. Functions served by communicative bids—regulating others' social routines, establishing joint attention.
6. Sociability—Does the child appreciate or use eye contact, gaze shifts, and other nonverbal communicative behaviors to reference others? Are reciprocal games enjoyed, initiated, and responded to? If so, is the response different, depending on the nature of the game (physical versus more social) or the child's familiarity with the other player?
7. Sensorimotor skills—means and ends, object permanence, spatial awareness, and imitative abilities. Are they different when they involve objects rather than people (e.g., the child manages to turn and push buttons in imitation of the adult, but will not imitate body movements, gestures, vocal or verbal behaviors)?
8. Play behaviors and preferences—Is there evidence of symbolic behavior that might pave the way for using symbols for communicative purposes?

Several instruments designed to be used specifically with younger children, or this particular population, are summarized in Table 19.2.

Assessment of Verbal Children

Social and play behaviors continue to be important areas of observation, but more standardized instruments become options for children who are using multiword utterances. Information can be obtained regarding comprehension and expressive language, vocabulary and semantic relations, syntax and

TABLE 19.1   Parent Interviews/Inventories

Name/Author	Age Range	Area Assessed	Comments
Receptive Expressive Emergent Language Scales—2 (Bzoch & League, 1971)	0 to 36 months	Parent interview: Yes/No questions divided into receptive and expressive language scales.	Does not tap pragmatics comprehensively and may therefore overestimate levels. No examples of behavior are elicited. Weak psychometrics.
MacArthur Communicative Development Inventories (Fenson et al., 1993)	8 to 16 months	Checklist for Comprehension of Lengthy Lists, Vocabulary, Vocabulary Production, and Gestural Communication.	Scoring by hand or machine yields percentiles. *Authors caution re* application of norms to children from low education/socioeconomic households.
	16 to 30 months	Checklist for Expressive Vocabulary, Sentence Complexity, and MLU.	
Language Development Survey (Rescorla, 1989)	24 months	Expressive Vocabulary Checklist designed to screen for distinction between "late bloomers" at 24 months and "at risk" for language delay (< 50 words/2-word utterance criteria).	Reliability and validity data established across socioeconomic groups. Single-page survey is manageable, and words are divided into categories. Serves as useful baseline.
Autism Diagnostic Interview (Le Couteur et al., 1989)	5 years to early adulthood	Assesses range of behaviors relevant to the differential diagnosis of PDD. Three primary areas are: (a) reciprocal social interaction, (b) communication and language, (c) repetitive, restricted, and stereotyped behaviors.	Standardized investigator-based interview. Operationalized coding based on descriptions of actual behaviors from caretakers. Requires training to maintain reliability. May be used in conjunction with ADOS/ PLAY-DOS.
Vineland Adaptive Behavior Scales (Sparrow et al., 1984)	Birth to adulthood	Structured Interview to assess Adaptive, Communication, Socialization, Daily Living, and Motor skills (< 5 years)—typical, as opposed to optimal, behaviors.	Well-standardized, open-ended interview that yields standard scores, percentiles, and age equivalents. Can provide useful information for goals in program planning. Three versions (Survey, Expanded, and Teacher) allow for comparison across home and school settings.

MLU = Mean Length of Utterance

morphology, pragmatics, articulation, and prosody. Choice of instrument will depend on the developmental stage and chronological age of the student being assessed. (See Tables 19.3 and 19.4.) Discrepancies between developmental levels and chronological age lead to instances where a test is developmentally appropriate although standardized for a younger population. Decisions then have to be made regarding whether the information to be gained from the instrument is sufficiently useful to warrant administration even though standard scores will not apply. If a decision is made to use the instrument, the rational and necessary caution regarding interpretation of findings must be documented in the report. In the same vein, any changes to the standardized administration procedures must be reported, and the resulting caution in interpreting standardized scores must be mentioned. Every attempt should be made to follow the standardized presentation as strictly as possible, but

TABLE 19.2   Measures of Sensorimotor Skills, Play, and Communicative Intent

Name/Author	Age Range	Area Assessed	Comments
Uzgiris-Hunt Scales of Infant Development (Dunst, 1980)	0 to 24 months	Object permanence, means–ends, spatial awareness, imitation.	Informal measure of cognitive skills related to early language development and intentionality.
Symbolic Play Test (Lowe & Costello, 1976)	12 to 36 months	Level of symbolic awareness and sequences of pretend play.	Informal measure of level of symbolic awareness and capacity to use pretend.
Symbolic Play Scale (Westby, 1988)	17 months to 5 years	From spontaneous play sample. Assesses decontextualization, thematic content, organization, self–other relations, and language forms and meanings.	Informal but operationalized play assessment usefully integrates information in these areas, focusing on the child's level of social knowledge and his or her capacity to integrate incoming information.
Play Scale (Carpenter, 1987)		Symbolic behavior in nonverbal children through play observation.	Informal but semistructured parent–child play sample with specific props. Ages at which a given percentage of children demonstrate certain play behaviors can be used.
Communicative Intention Inventory (Coggins & Carpenter, 1981)		Communicative intent, function, means, frequency.	Operationalizes observation of play/social interaction (as regards communicative intent) and provides frequency counts.
The Rossetti Infant Toddler Language Scale (Rossetti, 1990)	0 to 36 months	Measures communication and interaction, receptive and expressive language, infant–caretaker interaction, play behavior, pragmatics, gesture, comprehension, language expression.	Not standardized, but well-operationalized assessment tool that uses elicited, spontaneously occurring, and reported information.
Communication and Symbolic Behavior Scales (Wetherby & Prizant, 1993)	8 to 24 months	Determines children "at risk" for developing communication impairment and gives a profile of the following communicative functions: gestural communicative means, vocal communicative means, verbal communicative means, reciprocity, social affective signaling, symbolic behavior.	Standardized—yields raw scores, scaled and normed scores, profile of strengths/needs, 5-point rating scales. Caregiver Questionnaire scales include setting up communicative temptations, book sharing, symbolic play, language comprehension. Probes constructive/combinatorial play. Appealing materials, well-organized process. Time consuming rating from videotape—60–90 minutes. Reliability and validity reported.
Autism Diagnostic Observation Schedule (Lord et al., 1989)	30 months to adult	Includes greetings, elicited communicative/social behavior, pretend, social demonstration, conversation, appreciation of humor and nonliteral language.	Used in conjunction with ADI. Structured and semistructured "presses" for interaction are coded—use of algorithm yields differential diagnostic information.
Prelinguistic Autism Diagnostic Schedule (DiLavore, Lord, & Rutter, 1995)		Standardized protocol for observation of social and communicative behavior associated with autism.	Downward extension of ADOS for younger students.

TABLE 19.3   Tests of Vocabulary and Verbal Concepts

Name/Author	Age Range (Years–Months)	Area Assessed	Comments
Language Development Survey (Rescorla, 1989)	2 years	Expressive Vocabulary Checklist designed to screen for distinction between "late bloomers" at 24 months and "at risk" for language delay (< 50 words/2-word utterance criteria).	Reliability and validity data established across socioeconomic groups. Single-page survey is manageable, and words are divided into categories. Serves as useful baseline.
Peabody Picture Vocabulary Test—Revised (PPVT-R) (Dunn & Dunn, 1981)	2–6 to Adult	Receptive vocabulary through picture identification (one of four pictures).	Yields standard score, or percentile rank, and age equivalent. Large standardization sample. Should not be used as measure of language. Vocabulary recognition may be a strength and may suggest higher skills than in other areas. Spanish version—selected items translated from original.
Receptive One-Word Picture Vocabulary Test (Gardner, 1985)	2–11 to 12	Receptive vocabulary through picture identification.	Yields standard score, percentile, language age. Smaller standardization sample than PPVT-R. Spanish version available.
Receptive One-Word Picture Vocabulary Test—Upper Extension (Gardner, & Brownell, 1987)	12 to 15–11	Receptive vocabulary through picture identification.	Yields standard score, percentile, language age. Smaller standardization sample than PPVT-R. Spanish version available.
Expressive One-Word Picture Vocabulary Test—Revised (EOW-PVT-R) (Gardner, 1990)	2 to 12	Expressive vocabulary through naming of line drawings presented one to a page.	Yields standard score, percentile, age equivalent. Analysis of error types (informal) can yield useful information.
Expressive One-Word Picture Vocabulary Test—Upper Extension (Gardner & Brownell, 1983)	12 to 15–11	See EOWPVT-R.	See EOWPVT-R.
The Word Test-R Elementary (Jorgensen, Barrett, Huising, & Zachman, 1981)	7 to 11	Expressive vocabulary and semantics—associations, synonyms, antonyms, semantic absurdities, definitions, and multiple definitions.	Yields standard score, percentile rank, and age equivalent. Limited standardization sample.
The Word Test—Adolescent (Zachman et al., 1989)	12 to 17	Expressive vocabulary and semantics—brand names, synonyms, signs of times, definitions.	Yields standard score, percentile, age equivalent. May provide some useful information re functional ? for older subjects.
Test of Word Finding (German, 1991)	6 to 12	Diagnoses word-finding difficulties—picture naming—nouns and verbs, sentence completion, naming, description and category naming.	Yields standard score and percentile rank for age and grade. First subtest yields information re accuracy and speed of retrieval. Standardization sample > 1,000.

TABLE 19.3   *(Continued)*

Name/Author	Age Range (Years–Months)	Area Assessed	Comments
Test of Adolescent/Adult Word Finding (German, 1990)	12 to 80	Diagnosis of word-finding disorders; subtests—as above.	As above—smaller standardization sample.
Vocabulary Comprehension Scale (Bangs, 1975)	2 to 6	Receptive vocabulary—conceptual terms relating to position, size, quantity, quality (heavy, etc.), and pronouns.	Appealing 3-D materials. Child acts on objects in response to directions. No standard scores. Limited sampling of each concept.
Boehm Test of Basic Concepts—Preschool and Revised Versions, (Boehm, 1986)	3 to 5 K–Grade 12	Receptive vocabulary—concepts; spatial, temporal, and quantitative terms.	Yields T-score, percentile, and age equivalent. Preschool by age. Revised by grade. Normative sample = 433 students. Picture identification task.
Assessing Semantic Skills Through Everyday Themes (Barrett, Zachman, & Huisingh, 1988)	3 to 9	Receptive and expressive vocabulary and semantics. Labels, categories, attributes, functions, and definitions.	Yields standard score, percentile, and age equivalent. Normative sample = 2,500 students. Thematic pictures used to assess concepts.

TABLE 19.4   **Receptive and Expressive Language Tests**

Name/Author	Age Range (Years—Months)	Area Assessed	Comments
Preschool Language Scale—3 (Zimmerman, Steiner, & Pond, 1992)	0–6	Receptive and Expressive Language. Articulation Screen, Language Sample Checklist, Parent Questionnaire. Tasks arranged in developmental sequence.	Yields standard score, percentile rank, and age equivalent. Normed on 1,200+ children. Toy and picture materials at earliest levels. Story retelling task useful. Spanish version available. Commonly used in schools.
Sequenced Inventory of Communicative Development—Revised (Hedrick, Prather, & Tobin, 1975)	4 to 48 mo.	Receptive—sound and speech discrimination, awareness, and understanding. Expressive—imitating, imitating and responding: MLU, syntax, and articulation.	Yields age norms for both scales. Small standardization sample (n = 252). Uses pictures and 3-D materials, plus information from parental report. Spanish version available.
Reynell Developmental Language Scales—U.S. Edition (Reynell & Gruber, 1990)	12 mo. to 6	Receptive and Expressive Scales. Expressive is divided into Structure, Vocabulary, and Content.	Yields standard score, percentile rank, and developmental age score. Normed on 600 children. Materials are highly motivating. Comprehension is measured by action on objects, rather than recognition of pictures. Some gender stereotyping. Not culturally sensitive.

Continued

TABLE 19.4 *(Continued)*

Name/Author	Age Range (Years–Months)	Area Assessed	Comments
Clinical Evaluation of Language Fundamentals—Preschool (Wiig, Secord, & Semel, 1989)	3 to 6	Six subtests tap Receptive and Expressive Language—Semantics, Syntax, Memory; Basic Concepts, Sentence Structure, Word Structure, Formulating Labels, Recalling Sentences in Context, Linguistic Concepts.	Yields standard score, percentile rank and age equivalent. Normed on >1,500 children. Uses 2-D materials in full color.
Test of Auditory Comprehension of Language—Revised (Carrow-Woolfolk, 1985)	3 to 9	Receptive Language—Word Meanings and Relations, Grammatical Morphemes, Elaborated Sentences.	Yields standard score, percentile rank for age/grade, and age equivalent. Picture recognition/identification task (1 of 3 choices).
Utah Test of Language Development—3 (Mecham, 1989)	3 to 9–11	Receptive and Expressive Language.	Yields standard score and percentile rank.
Token Test for Children (DiSimoni, 1978)	3 to 12	Receptive Language Concepts—Spatial and Temporal.	Age and grade equivalent score. Normative sample = 1,300+ subjects. Uses 3-D, color.
Test of Language Development—2 Primary (Newcomer & Hammill, 1991)	4 to 8	Receptive and Expressive Language—Semantics and Syntax: Picture Vocabulary, Oral Vocabulary, Grammatic Understanding, Sentence Imitation, Grammatic Completion, Word Discrimination, Word Articulation.	Yields standard score, percentile. Normative group >2,000 children.
Test of Language Development—2 Intermediate (Newcomer & Hammill, 1991)	8–6 to 12–11	Receptive and Expressive—Semantics and Syntax: Sentence Combining, Vocabulary, Word Ordering, Grammatic Completion, Malapropisms.	Yields standard score, percentile rank. Standardized on >1,000 children.
Clinical Evaluation of Language Fundamentals—3 (Semel, Wiig, & Secord, 1995)	6 to 21	Receptive and Expressive Language—Semantics and Syntax: Additional Rapid Automatic Naming Task optional.	Yields standard score and percentile rank for total. Receptive and Expressive Language subtests have their own standard score. Normative sample = 2,400 students. Formulated Sentences provides opportunity to observe perspective. Listening to Paragraphs provides some information re inferencing and predicting.

there may be times when modifications are necessary in order to obtain information. Changes might include:

1. Repetition of the verbal stimulus more often than allowed in standardized administration given.

2. Altering the order of presentation (in a test that is not developmental)—for example, starting with a comprehension scale and shifting between this and an expressive scale, to match the child's response pattern.
3. Adding a gestural cue when making requests for objects (if the goal is comprehension of

object labels as opposed to recognizing a request).

4. Rephrasing a question.
5. Providing additional demonstration items in order to establish the response set needed.
6. Using behavioral reinforcers.

Areas to be assessed will include:

1. Vocabulary and semantics.
2. Receptive language—syntax and morphology.
3. Expressive language—syntax and morphology.
4. Pragmatics.
5. Spontaneous language sampling.
6. Articulation and Prosody.

Assessment of Fluent, Higher-Functioning Individuals

An individual who is functioning at higher levels may show fewer difficulties with the formal properties of language—vocabulary and syntax. As a result, tests of vocabulary and syntax alone may overestimate his or her language skills because these tests tap strengths in memory for objects and events. The very unfortunate effect may be that the test results would mislead the persons who design the intervention program. Even areas of residual weakness, such as nonliteral language skills and pragmatic functions, for which there are some assessment tools, may be measured best during real-life events and interactions. The structure inherent in testing provides optimal conditions for some subjects, and the testing makes explicit the aspects under investigation, preparing the individual in advance. The testing situation therefore cannot mirror the requirements of online information processing in spontaneous social situations and must be supplemented by additional observations and sampling methods.

In selecting measures, it is important to consider whether the task requires recognition of potential answers/solutions or demands a more self-generated problem-solving strategy (e.g., picture identification versus acting on objects in response to directions, or identifying which of four given solutions explains a given situation versus offering a spontaneous

explanation). Using tests that have a range of tasks (to sample comprehension and expressive output) will provide more information about what conditions or demands allow for the best performance. This decision will have implications in planning teaching methods and in developing ways to promote generalization of strengths. Some of the formal instruments available are listed in Table 19.5.

Sampling of narratives—verbal and written, with and without specific constraints regarding content—may highlight subtle deficits in cases where formal language measures are insufficiently sensitive. Deficits might include difficulties with cohesion (e.g., failing to use pronominal reference clearly; Loveland, McEvoy, Kelley, & Tunali, 1990) and presuppositional errors because the individual has failed to take into account the conversational partner's or reader's perspective and expectable prior knowledge or experience (Landa, Mastin, Minshew, & Goldstein, 1995). Methods for analyzing narratives have been well documented since Stein and Glenn's early work in 1979. Particular attention should be paid to the individual's ability to produce a logical, sequentially organized and coherent account with predictions, solutions, and any appreciation of cause and effect and motivations. The information obtained can then be applied to real-life events and pragmatic skill development.

When arranging to observe within school or work settings, consideration should be given to:

1. The ability to manage conversational interchanges—topic management, initiation:response ratios, shifting, maintenance, and extension.
2. The ability to recognize and respond to clarification requests, or to request clarification.
3. The ability to demonstrate appropriate interactions that illustrate Grice's maxims of relevance (contingency): quantity, quality, and manner.
4. The ability to interpret nonliteral language accurately—humor, sarcasm, irony, indirect requests, polite forms, ambiguity, inferencing, and implicature.
5. The ability to recognize indirect and polite forms.
6. The awareness of a need for shifts in register that are person- and context-dependent in their style and manner (teacher/boss

TABLE 19.5   Tests of Higher-Level, Nonliteral Language Skills and Pragmatic Skills

Name/Author	Age Range (Years—Months)	Area Assessed	Comments
Test of Language Competence Expanded Edition Level 1 Level 2 (Wiig & Secord, 1989)	5 to 9–11 9 to 18–11	Metalinguistic—higher-level language skills—interpreting and recognizing ambiguity, inferencing, conversational sentence production, interpreting figurative expressions.	Yields standard score, percentile rank, and overall age equivalent. Total and subtest norms. Screening—use of 2 subtests. Use of both interpretation and recognition responses to same stimulus can provide useful information. Inferencing involves recognition of 2 of 4 choices, rather than self-generated ideas.
Preschool Language Assessment Instrument (Blank, Rose, & Berlin, 1978)	3 to 6	Identification of language needs that interfere with classroom performance: integration of semantics and syntax, comprehension of directions, reflecting on given information and problem solving.	Yields percentile rank. Spanish version available.
Test of Pragmatic Language (Phelps-Terasaki & Phelps-Gunn, 1992)	5 to 13–11	Pragmatics—core components—physical setting, audience, topic, purpose (speech acts), visual gestural cues, abstraction.	Yields standard score, percentile rank. Normative sample = 1,016 subjects. Can also be used as criterion reference instrument for older clients. Picture display and verbal prompt as stimuli to the presented dilemma.
Test of Problem Solving—Elementary (Zachman et al., 1986)	6 to 11	Assesses use of language for problem solving: predicting outcomes, determining solutions, using content cues, making inferences, understanding-why questions, empathizing.	Yields standard score for total test, percentile rank, age equivalent. Normative sample = 2,400 children. Students respond to questions about 14 familiar situations depicted in black and white photos. Useful tool for planning goals.
Adolescent Test of Problem Solving (Zachman, Barrett, Huisingh, Orman, & Blagden, 1991)	12 to 17	Language for reasoning: clarifying, evaluating, fair-mindedness, analyzing, thinking independently, affect.	Yields standard score (for total test), percentile rank, age equivalent. Normative sample = 1,700 subjects. Students have to answer open-ended questions about passages.

versus peers, individual versus group, familiar versus unfamiliar partner; home versus school or work; formal versus informal).

7. The capacity to modulate tone and volume and other prosodic features according to context, topic, or emotional valence.

8. The flexibility of the individual in dealing with a range of different situations, and his or her capacity to use language to modulate the responses given.

9. The individual's ability to use language for purposes of learning or managing work routines, problem solving, predicting, reframing, and similar tasks.

Rating instruments are currently under development to provide a more operationalized and reliable assessment of pragmatics (e.g., the Pragmatic Rating Scale; Landa, 1996). The information obtained, when combined with other data from standardized testing, will provide a basis from which to build sociocommunicative goals that can enhance real-life skills and levels of functioning.

SUMMARY

A comprehensive communication evaluation, as part of a multidisciplinary assessment for individuals with autism, should (a) provide a reliable baseline of strengths and weaknesses; (b) identify appropriate goals and objectives to be addressed across settings; and (c) inform service providers and parents how best to achieve these goals in a continuous and consistent manner. The continuing support and availability of the assessment team as the proposed program plans are implemented should be considered essential to ensuring their utility and effectiveness.

Cross-References

Communication in autism is discussed in Chapter 9. Aspects of assessment and intervention are reviewed in Chapters 23 through 25.

REFERENCES

American Psychiatric Association. (1994). *Diagnostic and statistical manual of mental disorders* (4th Ed.). Washington, DC: Author.

Arthur, G. (1949). The Arthur adaptation of the Leiter International Performance Scale. *Journal of Clinical Psychology, 5,* 345–349.

Baker, A.F. (1983). Psychological assessment of autistic children. *Clinical Psychology Review, 3,* 41–59.

Ball, R.S., Merrifield, P., & Stott, L.H. (1978). *Extended Merrill-Palmner Scale.* Chicago: Stoelting.

Baltaxe, C., & Simmons, J. (1985). Prosodic development in normal and autistic children. In E. Schopler & G. Mesibov (Eds.), *Communication problems in autism* (pp. 95–125). New York: Plenum Press.

Bangs, T. (1975). *Vocabulary Comprehension Scale.* Chicago: Riverside.

Baron-Cohen, S. (1989). The autistic child's theory of mind: A case of specific developmental delay. *Journal of Child Psychology and Psychiatry, 30,* 285–297.

Barrett, M., Zachman, L., & Huisingh, R. (1988). *Assessing semantic skills through everyday themes.* East Moline, IL: Linguisystems.

Bates, E. (1976). *Language in context: Studies in the acquisition of pragmatics.* New York: Academic Press.

Bates, E. (1979). *The emergence of symbols: Cognition and communication in infancy.* New York: Academic Press.

Bayley, N. (1993). *Bayley Scales of Infant Development* (2nd ed.). San Antonio, TX: Psychological Corporation.

Bender, L. (1938). *A Visual Motor Gestalt Test and its clinical use.* American Orthopsychiatric Association Research Monograph, No. 3.

Berry, K.E. (1982). *Revised administration, scoring, and teaching manual for the Developmental Test of Motor Integration.* Cleveland, OH: Modern Curriculum Press.

Blank, S., Rose, M., & Berlin, L. (1978). *Preschool Language Assessment Instrument.* San Antonio, TX: Psychological Corporation, Harcourt Brace.

Boehm, A. (1986). *Boehm Test of Basic Concepts: Preschool.* San Antonio, TX: Psychological Corporation, Harcourt Brace.

Brownell, C.A. (1986). Convergent developments: Cognitive–developmental correlates of growth in infant/toddler peer skills. *Child Development, 57,* 275–286.

Bruininks, R.H. (1978). *Bruininks-Oseretsky Test of Motor Profesiciency.* Circle Pines, MN: American Guidance Service.

Bruner, J. (1981). Intention in the structure of action and interaction. *Advances in Infancy Research, 1,* 41–56.

Bzoch, K., & League, R. (1971). *The Receptive-Expressive Emergent Language Scale.* Gainesville, FL: Computer Management Corporation, Language Education Division.

Carpenter, T. (1987). Play Scale. In L. Olswang, C. Stoel-Gammon, T. Coggins, & R. Carpenter (Eds.), *Assessing prelinguistic and early behaviors in developmentally young children* (pp. 44–77). Seattle: University of Washington Press.

Carrow, E. (1973). *Test for Auditory Comprehension of Language* (5th ed.). Austin, TX: Learning Concepts.

Carrow-Woolfolk, E. (1985). *Test of Auditory Comprehension of Language* (Rev.). Austin, TX: Pro-Ed.

Carter, A.S., Gillham, J.E., Sparrow, S.S., & Volkmar, F.R. (1996). Adaptive behavior in autism. *Child and Adolescent Psychiatry Clinics of North America, 5*(4), 945–962.

Carter, A.S., Volkmar, F.R., Sparrow, S.S., Cicchetti, D.V. (1996). *Vineland Adaptive Behavior Scores: Supplementary norms for individuals with autism.* Manuscript in preparation.

Cicchetti, D. (1984). The emergence of developmental psychopathology. *Child Development, 55,* 1–7.

Cicchetti, D., & Serafica, F.C. (1981). Interplay among behavioral systems: Illustrations from the study of attachment, affiliation, and wariness in young children with Down's syndrome. *Developmental Psychology, 17,* 36–49.

Clark, P., & Rutter, M. (1981). Autistic children's responses to structure and to interpersonal demands. *Journal of Autism and Developmental Disorders, 11,* 201–217.

Coggins, T., & Carpenter, R. (1981). The Communicative Intention Inventory: A system for observing and coding children's early intentional communication. *Applied Psycholinguistics, 2,* 235–251.

Cohen, D.J., Paul, R., & Volkmar, F.R. (1987). Issues in the classification of pervasive developmental disorders and associated conditions. In D.J. Cohen & A.M. Donnellan (Eds.), *Handbook of autism and pervasive developmental disorders* (pp. 20–40). New York: John Wiley & Sons.

Cohen, D.J., Volkmar, F., Anderson, G.M., & Klin, A. (1993). Integrating biological and behavioral perspectives in the study and care of autistic individuals: The future. *Israel Journal of Psychiatry and Related Sciences, 30*(1), 15–32.

Crais, E., & Roberts, J. (1991). Decision making in assessment and early intervention planning. *Language, Speech and Hearing Services in Schools, 22,* 19–30.

Dawson, G., & Galpert, L. (1990). Mother's use of imitative play for facilitating social responsiveness and toy play in young autistic children. *Development and Psychopathology, 2,* 151–162.

Dawson, G., & Lewy, A. (1989). Arousal, attention and socioemotional impairments of individuals with autism. In G. Dawson (Ed.), *Autism—nature, diagnoses and treatment* (pp. 49–74). New York: Guilford Press.

Dean, R.S. (1977). Patterns of emotional disturbance on the WISC-R. *Journal of Clinical Psychology, 33,* 486–490.

DeMyer, M.K., Barton, S., Alpern, G.D., Kimberlin, C., Allen, J., Yang, E., & Steele, R. (1974). The measured intelligence of autistic children. *Journal of Autism and Childhood Schizophrenia, 4,* 42–60.

DiLavore, P., Lord, C., & Rutter, M. (1995). Pre-Linguistic Autism Diagnostic Observation Schedule (PL-ADOS). *Journal of Autism and Developmental Disorders, 25,* 355–379.

DiSimoni, F. (1978). *Token Test for Children.* Austin, TX: Pro-Ed.

Dunn, L. (1965). *Peabody Picture Vocabulary Test.* Circle Pines, MN: American Guidance Service.

Dunn, L., & Dunn, L. (1981). *Peabody Picture Vocabulary Test—Revised.* Circle Pines, MN: American Guidance Service.

Dunst, C. (1980). *A clinical and educational manual for use with the Uzgiris and Hunt Scales of Infant Psychological Development.* Austin, TX: Pro-Ed.

Dykens, E., Volkmar, F.R., & Glick, M. (1991). Thought disorder in high-functioning autistic adults. *Journal of Autism and Developmental Disorders, 21,* 291–302.

Exner, J.E. (1990). *A Rorsachach workbook for the comprehensive system* (3rd ed.). Asheville, NC: Author.

Fein, G.G. (1981). Pretend play in childhood: An integrative review. *Child Development, 52,* 1095–1102.

Fein, J., Bartolucci, G., Ginsberg, G., & Szatmari, P. (1991). The use of intonation to communicate in pervasive developmental disorders. *Journal of Child Psychology and Psychiatry & Allied Disciplines, 32*(5), 771–782.

Fenson, L., Dale, P., Reznick, S., Thal, D., Bates, E., Hartung, S., Pethick, S., & Reilly, J. (1993). *MacArthur Communicative Development Inventories.* San Diego, CA: Singular Publishing Group.

Fey, M. (1992). Infantile autism. In D. Bishop & K. Mogford (Eds.), *Language development in exceptional circumstances* (pp. 190–202). Hillsdale, NJ: Erlbaum.

Gardner, M. (1985). *Receptive One-Word Picture Vocabulary Test.* Los Angeles, CA: Western Psychological Services.

Gardner, M. (1990). *Expressive One-Word Picture Vocabulary Test.* Los Angeles, CA: Western Psychological Services.

Gardner, M., & Brownell, R. (1987). *Expressive One-Word Picture Vocabulary Test—Upper Extension.* Los Angeles, CA: Western Psychological Service.

Gardner, M., & Brownell, R. (1989). *Receptive One-Word Picture Vocabulary Test—Upper Extension.* Los Angeles, CA: Western Psychological Services.

German, D. (1990). *Test of Adolescent/Adult Word Finding.* San Antonio, TX: Psychological Corporation, Harcourt Brace.

German, D. (1991). *Test of Word Finding.* San Antonio, TX: Psychological Corporation, Harcourt Brace.

Happe, F.G. (1995). The role of age and verbal ability in the theory of mind task performance of subjects with autism. *Child Development, 66,* 843–855.

Harris, D.B. (1963). *Children's drawings as a measure of intelletual maturity: A revision and extension of the Goodenough Draw-a-Man Test.* New York: Harcourt, Brace, & World.

Hayes, R. (1987). Training for work. In D. Cohen & A.M. Donnellan (Eds.), *Handbook of autism and pervasive developmental disorders* (1st ed., pp. 360–370). New York: John Wiley & Sons.

Hedrick, D., Prather, E., & Tobin, A. (1975). *Sequenced Inventory of Communication Development.* New York: Slosson Ed. Publishers.

Hobson, R.P. (1986). The autistic child's appraisal of expressions of emotion. *Journal of Child Psychology and Psychiatry, 27,* 321–342.

Jorgensen, C., Barrett, M., Huising, R., & Zachman, L. (1981). *The Word Test.* Moline, IL: Linguisystems.

Kanner, L. (1943). Autistic disturbances of affective contact. *Nervous Child, 2,* 217–250.

Kasari, C., Sigman, M., Mundy, P., & Yirmiya, N. (1988). Caregiver interactions with autistic children. *Journal of Abnormal Child Psychology, 16,* 45–56.

Kasari, C., Yirmiya, N., Mundy, P., & Sigman, M. (1986). *Affect expressions: A comparison of autistic, MR and normal children.* Paper presented at the annual meeting of the American Psychological Association, Washington, DC.

Kaufman, A.S. (1994). *Intelligent testing with the WISC-III.* New York: John Wiley & Sons.

Kaufman, A.S., & Kaufman, N.L. (1983). *K-ABC: Kaufman—Assessment Battery for Children.* Circle Pines, MN: American Guidance Service.

Klin, A. (1993). Auditory brain stem responses in autism: Brain stem dysfunction or peripheral hearing loss? *Journal of Autism and Developmental Disorders, 23*(1), 15–35.

Klin, A. (1994). Asperger syndrome. *Child and Adolescent Psychiatry Clinics of North America, 3*(1), 131–148.

Klin, A., & Shepard, B.A. (1994). Psychological assessment of autistic children. *Child and Adolescent Psychiatric Clinics of North America, 3*(1), 53–70.

Klin, A., Volkmar, F.R., Marans, W.D., & South, M. (1996). *Research Note: Using the PPVT-R or BPVT-R to match children with autism with children with other disorders on verbally mediated experimental tasks.* Manuscript in preparation.

Klin, A., Volkmar, F.R., & Sparrow, S.S. (1992). Autistic social dysfunction: Some limitations of the Theory of Mind Hypothesis. *Journal of Child Psychology & Psychiatry, 33*(5), 861–876.

Klin, A., Volkmar, F.R., Sparrow, S.S., Cicchetti, D.V., & Rourke, B.P. (1995). Validity and neuropsychological characterization of Asperger syndrome. *Journal of Child Psychology and Psychiatry, 36*(7), 1127–1140.

Klin, A., Volkmar, F.R., Sparrow, S.S., de Bild, A., & Cicchetti, D.V. (1996). *A normed assessment of facial recognition in children with autism using the K-ABC.* Manuscript in preparation.

Krug, D.A., Arick, J.R., & Almond, P.J. (1980). Behavior checklist for identifying severely handicapped individuals with high levels of autistic behavior. *Journal of Child Psychology and Psychiatry, 21,* 221–229.

Landa, R. (1996). *The Pragmatic Rating Scale.* Author.

Landa, R., Mastin, M., Minshew, N., & Goldstein, G. (1995, March). *Discourse and abstract language ability in nonretarded individuals with autism.* Paper presented at the meeting of Society for Research in Child Development, Indianapolis, IN.

Le Couteur, A., Rutter, M., Lord, C., Rios, P., Robertson, S., Holdgrafer, M., & McLennan, J.D. (1989). Autism Diagnostic Interview: A standardized investigator-based instrument. *Journal of Autism and Developmental Disorders, 19,* 363–387.

Leiter, R.G. (1980). *Leiter International Performance Scale, instruction manual.* Chicago: Stoelting.

Leslie, A. (1988). Some implication of pretense for mechanisms underlying the child's theory of mind. In J.W. Astington, P.L. Harris, & D.R. Olsen (Eds.), *Developing theories of mind* (pp. 19–46). New York: Cambridge University Press.

Lockyer, L., & Rutter, M. (1969). A five- to fifteen-year follow-up study of infantile psychosis: III. Psychological aspects. *British Journal of Psychiatry, 115,* 865–882.

Lockyer, L., & Rutter, M. (1970). A five- to fifteen-year follow-up study of infantile psychosis: IV. Patterns of cognitive ability. *British Journal of Social and Clinical Psychology, 9,* 152–163.

Lord, C. (1995). Follow-up of two-year-olds referred for possible autism. *Journal of Child Psychology and Psychiatry, 36,* 1365–1382.

Lord, C., Pickles, A., McLennan, J., Rutter, M., Bregman, J., Folstein, S., Fombonne, E., Leboyer, M., & Minshew, N. (1994). Diagnosis of autism: Analyses of data from the

Autism Diagnostic Interviews. In American Psychiatric Association (Eds.), *DSM-IV source book*. Washington, DC: American Psychiatric Association.

Lord, C., Rutter, M., Goode, S., Heemsbergen, J., Jordan, H., & Mawhood, L. (1989). Autism Diagnostic Observation Schedule: A standardized observation of communicative and social behavior. *Journal of Autism and Developmental Disorders, 19,* 185–212.

Lord, C., & Schopler, E. (1988). Intellectual and developmental assessment of children from preschool to schoolage: Clinical implications of two follow-up studies. In E. Schopler & G.B. Mesibov (Eds.), *Diagnosis and assessment in autism* (pp. 167–182). New York: Plenum Press.

Lotter, V. (1978). Follow-up studies. In M. Rutter & E. Schopler (Eds.), *Autism: A reappraisal of concepts and treatment* (pp. 475–495). New York: Plenum Press.

Loveland, K.A., McEvoy, R.E., Kelley, M.K., & Tunali, B. (1990). Narrative storytelling in autism and Down syndrome. *British Journal of Psychiatry, 8,* 9–23.

Lowe, M., & Costello, A. (1976). *Manual for the Symbolic Play Test* (Experimental ed.). London: NFER Nelson.

Maltz, A. (1981). Comparison of cognitive deficits among autistic and retarded children in the Arthur adaptation of the Leiter International Performance Scales. *Journal of Autism and Developmental Disorders, 11,* 413–426.

McCune-Nicholich, L., & Carroll, S. (1981). Development of symbolic play: Implications for the language specialist. *Topics in Language Disorders, 2,* 1–15.

McDonald, M.A., Mundy, P., Kasari, C., & Sigman, M. (1989). Psychometric scatter in retarded, autistic preschoolers as measured by the Catell. *Journal of Child Psychology and Psychiatry, 30*(4), 599–604.

Mecham, M. (1989). *Utah Test of Language Development—3*. Austin, TX: Pro-Ed.

Menyuk, P., & Quill, K. (1985). Semantic problems in autistic children. In E. Schopler & G. Mesibov (Eds.), *Communication problems in autism* (pp. 127–145). New York: Plenum Press.

Minshew, N.J., Goldstein, G., & Siegel, D.J. (1995). Speech and language in high-functioning autistic individuals. *Neuropsychology, 9*(2), 255–261.

Morgan, S. (1988). Diagnostic assessment of autism: A review of objective scales. *Journal of Psychoeducational Assessment, 6*(2), 139–151.

Morgan, S.B. (1984). Helping parents understand the diagnosis of autism. *Journal of Developmental and Behavioral Pediatrics, 5*(2), 78–85.

Mundy, P., & Sigman, M. (1989). Specifying the nature of the social impairment in autism. In G. Dawson (Ed.), *Autism: Nature, diagnosis and treatment*. New York: Guilford Press.

Newcomer, P., & Hammill, D. (1991). *Test of Language Development—2: Primary and Intermediate*. Austin, TX: Pro-Ed.

Osterling, J., & Dawson, G. (1994). Early recognition of children with autism: A study of first birthday home videotapes. *Journal of Autism and Developmental Disorders, 24,* 247–257.

Parks, S.L. (1983). The assessment of autistic children: A selective review of available instruments. *Journal of Autism and Developmental Disorders, 13,* 255–267.

Paul, R. (1987). Communication. In D.J. Cohen & A.M. Donnellan (Eds.), *Handbook of autism and pervasive developmental disorders* (pp. 61–84). New York: John Wiley & Sons.

Paul, R. (1995). *Language disorders: From infancy through adolescence*. St. Louis: Mosby.

Paul, R., & Cohen, D. (1984). Outcomes of severe disorders of language acquisition. *Journal of Autism and Developmental Disorders, 14,* 405–421.

Paul, R., & Cohen, D. (1985). Comprehension of indirect requests in adults with mental retardation and pervasive developmental disorders. *Journal of Speech and Hearing Research, 28,* 475–479.

Paul, R., Cohen, D., & Caparulo, B. (1983). A longitudinal study of patients with severe disorders of language learning. *Journal of American Academy of Child Psychiatry, 22,* 525–534.

Pennington, B.F. (1991). *Diagnosis of learning disorders: A neuropsychological framework*. New York: Guilford.

Phelps-Terasaki, L., & Phelps-Gunn, T. (1992). *Test of Pragmatic Language*. Austin, TX: Pro-Ed.

Powers, M.D. (1988). Behavioral assessment of autism. In E. Schopler & G.B. Mesibov (Eds.), *Diagnosis and assessment in autism* (pp. 139–165). New York: Plenum Press.

Prior, M. (1979). Cognitive abilities and disabilities in infantile autism: A review. *Journal of Abnormal Child Psychology, 7,* 357–380.

Prior, M., & Ozonoff, S. (in press). Cognitive development. In F. Volkmar (Ed.), *Autism and Pervasive Developmental Disorders*. Cambridge, England: Cambridge University Press.

Prizant, B. (1983). Language acquisition and communicative behavior in autism: Toward an understanding of the "whole" of it. *Journal of Speech and Hearing Disorders, 48,* 296–307.

Prizant, B. (1988). Communication in the autistic client. In N. Lass, L. McReynolds, J. Northern, & D. Yoder (Eds.), *Handbook of speech–language pathology and audiology* (pp. 114–139). Philadelphia: Decker.

Prizant, B., & Duchan, J. (1981). The functions of immediate echolalia in autistic children. *Journal of Speech and Hearing Disorders, 46,* 241–249.

Prizant, B., & Rydell, P. (1984). An analysis of the functions of delayed echolalia in autistic children. *Journal of Speech and Hearing Research, 27,* 183–192.

Prizant, B., & Rydell, P. (1993). Assessment and intervention: Considerations for unconventional verbal behavior. In J. Reichle & D. Wacker (Eds.), *Communicative alternatives to challenging behavior: Integrating functional assessment and intervention strategies* (pp. 263–298). Baltimore: Paul H. Brookes.

Prizant, B.M., & Schuler, A. (1987). Facilitating communication: Theoretical foundations. In D. Cohen & A. Donnellan (Eds.), *Handbook of autism and pervasive developmental disorders* (pp. 289–300). New York: John Wiley & Sons.

Prizant, B.M., & Wetherby, A.M. (1989). Enhancing language and communication in autism: From theory to practice. In G. Dawson (Ed.), *Autism: New perspectives on diagnosis, nature, and treatment* (pp. 282–309). New York: Guilford Press.

Prizant, B.M., & Wetherby, A.M. (1993). Communication assessment for young children. *Infants and Young Children, 5,* 20–34.

Rescorla, L. (1989). The Language Development Survey: A screening tool for delayed language development in toddlers. *Journal of Speech and Hearing Disorders, 54,* 587–599.

Rescorla, L., & Goossens, M. (1992). Symbolic play development in toddlers with expressive specific language impairment. *Journal of Speech and Hearing Research, 35,* 1290–1302.

Reynell, J., & Gruber, C. (1990). *Reynell Developmental Language Scales* (U.S. ed.). Los Angeles, CA: Western Psychological Services.

Ricks, D. (1975). Vocal communication in preverbal normal and autistic children. In N. O'Connor (Ed.), *Language, cognitive deficits and retardation* (pp. 75–80). London: Butterworths.

Rossetti, L. (1990). *The Rossetti Infant-Toddler Language Scale: A measure of communication and interaction.* East Moline, IL: Linguisystems.

Rumsey, J.M. (1992). Neuropsychological studies of high-level autism. In E. Schopler & G.B. Mesibov (Eds.), *High-functioning individuals with autism* (pp. 41–64). New York: Plenum.

Rutter, M. (1978). Diagnosis and definition of childhood autism. *Journal of Autism and Childhood Schizophrenia, 8,* 139–161.

Rutter, M. (1985). Infantile autism and other pervasive developmental disorders. In M. Rutter & L. Hersov (Eds.), *Child and adolescent psychiatry: Modern approaches* (2nd ed., pp. 367–379). Oxford, England: Blackwell.

Rydell, P., & Mirenda, P. (1994). Effects of high and low constraint utterances on the production of *immediate* and delayed echolalia in young children with autism. *Journal of Autism and Developmental Disorders, 24,* 719–735.

Sattler, J.M. (1988). *Assessment of children* (3rd ed.). San Diego: Author.

Scheerer, M., Rothman, E., & Goldstein, J. (1945). A case of 'idiot savant': An experimental study of personality organization. *Psychological Monographs, 58*(4), 1–63.

Schopler, E., & Mesibov, G.B. (Eds.). (1988). *Diagnosis and assessment in autism.* New York: Plenum Press.

Schopler, E., & Mesibov, G.B. (Eds.). (1992). *High-functioning individuals with autism.* New York: Plenum.

Schopler, E., & Reichler, R.J. (1972). How well do parents understand their own psychotic child? *Journal of Autism and Childhood Schizophrenia, 2,* 387–400.

Schuler, A., & Prizant, B. (1985). Echolalia. In E. Schopler & G. Mesibov (Eds.), *Communication problems in autism* (pp. 163–186). New York: Plenum Press.

Schuler, A., Prizant, B., & Wetherby, A. (1997, this volume).

Selfe, L. (1978). *Nadia: A case of extraordinary drawing ability in an autistic child.* New York: Academic Press.

Selman, R.L., Lavin, D.R., & Brion-Meisels, S. (1982). Troubled children's use of self reflection. In F.C. Serafica (Ed.), *Social-cognitive development in context* (pp. 62–99). New York: Guilford Press.

Semel, E., Wiig, E., & Secord, W. (1995). *Clinical Evaluation of Language Fundamentals—3.* San Antonio, TX: Psychological Corporation, Harcourt Brace.

Shah, A., & Holmes, N. (1985). Brief report: The use of the Leiter International Performance Scale with children. *Journal of Autism and Developmental Disorders, 15,* 195–203.

Shea, V. (1993). Interpreting results to parents of preschool children. In E. Schopler, M.E. Van Bourgondien, & M. Bristol (Eds.), *Preschool issues in autism* (pp. 195–203). New York: Plenum Press.

Snyderman, M., & Rothman, S. (1987). Survey of expert opinion on intelligence and aptitude testing. *American Psychologist, 42,* 137–144.

Sparrow, S., Balla, D., & Cicchetti, D. (1984a). *Vineland Adaptive Behavior Scales* (Survey ed.). Circle Pines, MN: American Guidance Service.

Sparrow, S., Balla, D., & Cicchetti, D. (1984b). *Vineland Adaptive Behavior Scales* (Expanded ed.). Circle Pines, MN: American Guidance Service.

Sparrow, S., Balla, D., & Cicchetti, D. (1985). *Vineland Adaptive Behavior Scales* (Classroom ed.). Circle Pines, MN: American Guidance Service.

Sparrow, S., Carter, A.S., Racusin, G., & Morris, R. (1995). Comprehensive psychological assessment through the life span: A developmental approach. In D. Cicchetti & D.J. Cohen (Eds.), *Developmental psychopathology* (Vol. 1, pp. 81–108). New York: John Wiley & Sons.

Stellern, J., Vasa, S.F., & Little, J. (1976). *Introduction to diagnostic-prescriptive teaching and programming.* Glen Ridge, NJ: Exceptional Press.

Tager-Flusberg, H. (1989). A psycholinguistic perspective on language development in the autistic child. In G. Dawson (Ed.), *Autism: Nature, diagnosis and treatment,* 92–118. New York: Guilford Press.

Thorndike, R.L., Hagen, E.P., & Sattler, J.M. (1986). *Guide for administering and scoring the Stanford-Binet Intelligence Scale* (4th ed.). Chicago: Riverside.

Thorum, A. (1986). *Fullerton Language Test for Adolescents.* Chicago: Riverside.

Treffert, D.A. (1988). The idiot savant: A review of the syndrome. *American Journal of Psychiatry, 145,* 563–572.

Tsai, L., & Beisler, J.M. (1984). Research in infantile autism: A methodological problem in using language comprehension as the basis for selecting matched controls. *Journal of the American Academy of Child Psychiatry, 23,* 700–703.

Uzgiris, I.C., & Hunt, J. McV. (1975). *Assessment in infancy: Ordinal scales of psychological development.* Urbana: University of Illinois Press.

Violette, J., & Swisher, L. (1992). Echolalic responses by a child with autism to four experimental conditions of sociolinguistic input. *Journal of Speech and Hearing Research, 35,* 139–147.

Volkmar, F.R. (1987). Social development. In D.J. Cohen & A.M. Donnellan (Eds.), *Hand-book of autism and pervasive developmental disorders* (pp. 41–60). New York: John Wiley & Sons.

Volkmar, F.R. (1996). Autism and the pervasive developmental disorders. In M. Lewis (Ed.), *Child and adolescent psychiatry: A comprehensive textbook* (2nd ed., pp. 489–497). Baltimore: Williams & Wilkins.

Volkmar, F.R., Carter, A., Sparrow, S.S., & Cicchetti, D.V. (1993). Quantifying social development in autism. *Journal of the American Academy of Child and Adolescent Psychiatry, 32,* 627–632.

Volkmar, F.R., & Cohen, D.J. (1988). Diagnosis of pervasive developmental disorders. In B. Lahey & A. Kazdin (Eds.), *Advances in clinical child psychology* (pp. 249–284). New York: Plenum Press.

Volkmar, F., & Cohen, D. (1994). Autism: Current concepts. In F. Volkmar (Ed.), *Child and Adolescent Psychiatric Clinics of North America: Psychoses and Developmental Disorders, 3,* 43–52.

Volkmar, F., Hoder, L., & Cohen, D. (1985). Compliance, "negativism" and the effects of treatment and structure in autism: A naturalistic behavior study. *Journal of Child Psychology and Psychiatry, 26,* 865–877.

Volkmar, F.R., Klin, A., Marans, W., & Cohen, D.J. (1996). The pervasive developmental disorders: Diagnosis and assessment. *Child and Adolescent Psychiatry Clinics of North America, 5*(4), 963–978.

Volkmar, F.R., Sparrow, S.A., Goudreau, D., Cicchetti, D.V., Paul, R., & Cohen, D.J. (1987). Social deficits in autism: An operational approach using the Vineland Adaptive Behavior Scales. *Journal of the American Academy of Child and Adolescent Psychiatry, 26,* 156–161.

Waterhouse, L., & Fein, D. (1984). Developmental trends in cognitive skills for children diagnosed as autistic and schizophrenic. *Child Development, 55,* 236–248.

Wechsler, D. (1989). *Weschler Preschool and Primary Scale of Intelligence.* San Antonio, TX: Psychological Corporation.

Wechsler, D. (1991). *Weschler Intelligence Scale for Children* (3rd ed.). San Antonio, TX: Psychological Corporation.

Wenar, C., Ruttenberg, R. A., Kalish-Weiss, B., & Wolf, E.G. (1986). The development of normal and autistic children: A comparative study. *Journal of Autism and Developmental Disorders, 16,* 317–334.

Westby, C. (1988). Children's play: Reflections of social competence. In *Seminars in speech and language* (pp. 1–13). New York: Thieme Medical Publishers.

Wetherby, A., Cain, D., Yonclas, D., & Walker, V. (1988). Analysis of intentional communication of normal children from the prelinguistic to the multiword stage. *Journal of Speech and Hearing Research, 31,* 240–252.

Wetherby, A., Koegel, R.L., & Mendel, M. (1981). Central auditory nervous system dysfunction in echolalic autistic individuals. *Journal of Speech and Hearing Research, 24,* 420–429.

Wetherby, A., & Prizant, B.M. (1989). The expression of communicative intent: Assessment guidelines. *Seminars in Speech and Language, 10,* 77–91.

Wetherby, A., & Prizant, B.M. (1990). *Communication and Symbolic Behavior Scales.* Chicago: Riverside.

Wetherby, A., & Prizant, B.M. (1992). Profiling young children's communicative competence. In S. Warren & J. Riechle (Eds.), *Causes and effects in communication and language intervention* (pp. 217–253). Baltimore: Paul Brookes.

Wetherby, A., & Prizant, B.M. (1993). *Communication and Symbolic Behavior Scales* (Normed ed.). Chicago: Riverside.

Wetherby, A., Yonclas, D., & Bryan, A. (1989). Communication profiles of preschool children with handicaps: Implication for early identification. *Journal of Speech and Hearing Disorders, 54,* 148–158.

Wiig, E., & Secord, W. (1989). *Test of Language Competence* (Expanded ed.). San Antonio, TX: Psychological Corporation, Harcourt Brace.

Wiig, E., Secord, W., & Semel, E. (1989). *Clinical Evaluation of Language Fundamentals—Preschool.* San Antonio, TX: Psychological Corporation, Harcourt Brace.

Wing, L., & Gould, J. (1979). Severe impairments of social interaction and associated abnormalities in children: Epidemiology and classification. *Journal of Autism and Developmental Disorders, 9,* 11–29.

World Health Organization. (1990). *International classification of diseases. Mental and behavioural disorders. Diagnostic criteria for research* [Draft] (10th ed., Vol. 5). Geneva: Author.

Yule, W. (1978). Research methodology: What are the "correct controls"? In M. Rutter & E. Schopler (Eds.), *Autism: A reappraisal of concepts and treatment* (pp. 155–162). New York: Plenum Press.

Zachman, L., Barrett, M., & Huisingh, R. (1984). *Test of Problem Solving—Elementary.* East Moline, IL: Linguisystems.

Zachman, L., Barrett, M., Huisingh, R., Orman, J., & Blagden, C. (1991). *Test of Problem Solving—Adolescent.* San Antonio, TX: Psychological Corporation, Harcourt Brace.

Zachman, L., Huisingh, R., Barrett, M., Orman, J., & Blagden, C. (1981). *The Word Test—Adolescent.* East Moline, IL: Linguisystems.

Zimmerman, J., Steiner, V., & Pond, R. (1992). *Preschool Language Scale—3.* San Antonio. TX: Psychological Corporation, Harcourt Brace.

CHAPTER 20

Behavioral Assessment of Individuals with Autism

MICHAEL D. POWERS

Behavioral assessment is an ongoing process designed to guide treatment planning by providing predictive, formative, and summative information about the behavior of an individual with autism. It is predictive in that data gathered prior to intervention are used to guide the development of individualized treatment plans. Over the course of treatment, ongoing progress is used in a formative manner to guide refinements and alterations to the treatment protocol. Behavioral assessment also provides a method for the formal summation of treatment effects by emphasizing the comparison of pre- and posttreatment performance or behavior rates. By emphasizing a multimethod approach for gathering information, behavioral assessment data can be comprehensive in scope. A reliance on objective and empirically valid methods of evaluation and analysis ensures both internal and external validity of assessment findings. The inclusion of developmental considerations in the assessment process ensures that factors such as age expectations, developmental discontinuity, and the plasticity of behavior at various ages will be considered in the treatment planning process.

In contrast to more traditional methods of assessment, behavioral assessment emphasizes description of stimulus (or antecedent) and consequent control over behavior. Thus, factors such as physical space configurations, heat and light, sensory acuity, fatigue and hunger, and the communicative intent of the behavior itself are all understood to affect behavior rates, as are reinforcers and punishers. By emphasizing a hypothesis-testing process in which decision making is grounded in objective and verifiable data, the role of inference is minimized. By

appreciating both the temporal and the contextual bases of behavior, this approach permits more careful consideration of events that may either inhibit or facilitate generalization and maintenance of behavior.

This chapter describes the characteristics of contemporary behavioral assessment for individuals with autism from a functional ecological perspective. A broadband framework for assessment is provided, and then domains of assessment are described. Lastly, the relationship between assessment data and intervention planning is reviewed.

CHARACTERISTICS OF BEHAVIORAL ASSESSMENT: A FUNCTIONAL ECOLOGICAL APPROACH

Assessment of the behavior of an individual with autism involves four steps: (a) identification and description of the target behavior(s); (b) determination of setting events, and antecedent and consequent stimuli controlling the target behavior; (c) development and implementation of an intervention plan; and (d) evaluation of intervention effects (Powers & Handleman, 1984).

Earlier conceptualizations of behavioral assessment have emphasized descriptions of behavior and consequences, with less attention to antecedent environmental, organismic, and interactional variables. Unfortunately, these conceptualizations often led to narrow treatment strategies, more limited generalization of effects, and less-than-optimal maintenance of treatment outcomes.

A functional ecological approach to assessment increases the likelihood that assessment methods (and the resultant data), intervention strategies, and outcomes are useful across the various environments that the individual with autism encounters.

To integrate the four steps within a functional ecological context, the assessment process should address several critical dimensions. These are described below.

Developmental Sensitivity

Autism is characterized by developmental discontinuity. Although behavioral assessment methods have traditionally been criticized for underemphasizing developmental factors in autism (Harris & Ferrari, 1983), more recent efforts at nomothetic assessment (e.g., Childhood Autism Rating Scale, Schopler, Reichler, & Renner, 1986; Behavioral Development Questionnaire, Castelloe & Dawson, 1993) and idiographic assessment (e.g., Powers, 1988) have stressed the need to evaluate the child's behavior within a broader developmental context. Typical and atypical developmental sequelae within cognitive, social, communicative, adaptive, and perceptual domains all must be considered in order to best describe the behavior of a *particular* individual within *specific* situations.

Emphasis on the Criterion of Ultimate Functioning

The criterion of ultimate functioning (Brown, Nietupski, & Hamre-Nietupski, 1976) emphasizes that assessment efforts and intervention objectives should specifically target behavior that will be functional in real environments for the individual with a disability. In particular, the target behaviors identified to be increased should be those that will have longitudinal value, will replace problematic behavior with more adaptive response alternatives, and will facilitate integration into community settings with maximum independence.

Attention to Molar and Molecular Levels of Analysis

Behavioral assessment must integrate the specifics of a target behavior into the environments within which the behavior occurs. At the molecular level, the clinician considers the behavior and its controlling variables by describing the behavior along six dimensions: (a) behavioral unity, (b) duration, (c) interresponse time, (d) latency, (e) intensity, and (f) topography. Behavioral unity describes the predictability of sequential target behavior onsets and offsets. Duration refers to the period of time covered by a response, and interresponse time refers to the amount of time separating one target behavior from another. Latency refers to the interval of time that elapses between the stimulus that occasions (or "triggers") a behavior and the occurrence of that behavior. Intensity refers to the magnitude of behavior. Assessment of intensity can be a rather subjective enterprise because of differences in perception and/or tolerance by observers. To objectify this situation, it is advisable to use permanent products or other verifiable indexes whenever possible (e.g., the number of tissue breaks caused by self-injury; the distance covered by the hand before striking an object or another person, and so on). A description of the topography of a behavior highlights the physical actions undertaken when emitting that behavior. Often, this dimension entails a description of exactly what the individual does when performing the behavior. For example, in describing the topography of aggression, one might note that the individual with autism picked up an object not intended for throwing, and threw it at another person, covering a distance greater than 12 inches. This approach may appear to be reductionistic, but it should be recalled that, for behavioral assessment to better predict treatment outcomes, precision in the description of the behavior to be consequated must be emphasized.

Molar assessment evaluates the pervasiveness of a specific target behavior by understanding it within broader ecological contexts. These can include different environments (home, school, or community) as well as a view of the behavior within a normative developmental context in those environments. For example, the target behavior of hand flapping may occur across multiple environments but is observed to be more frequent in different situations in each of those environments. At home, it may occur most frequently when the child's favorite television program is on. At school, it may occur during periods of heightened stress or unpredictability. The behavior may look exactly alike in both situations, but the cause of the behavior may be vastly different. Treatment options for the same behavior may be different in these two situations because treatment must follow behavioral function, not behavioral form.

Setting events are conditions that occasion behavior but do not themselves exert control over it (Halle & Spradlin, 1993). For example, physical conditions such as hunger, fatigue, and sensory acuity are organismic setting events. Time of day, particular classrooms or staff configurations, and so on, are environmental setting events. These conditions may not exert contingent control over the target behavior, but they set the stage for the behavior to occur. For example, face slapping may be most likely to occur between 11:30 A.M. and 12:30 P.M., Monday through Friday. Functional analysis of this behavior (described in a later section of this chapter) identifies access to social attention as the maintaining variable. However, the high-probability setting (school, between 11:30 A.M. and 12:30 P.M.) sets the stage for this behavior because the student:teacher ratio in the classroom decreases significantly (staff take their lunch breaks during this hour). With fewer staff present, less attention is available for any particular student, increasing the probability that a student will use face slapping to access the social attention he or she desires.

Emphasis on Multidimensional Assessment

A functional ecological assessment is multidimensional by design. In addition to conducting molecular and molar analyses of behavior, various contextual factors must be considered in order to address the functional analytic issues in assessment. These include an assessment of the high- and low-probability times for the behavior's occurrence (Repp & Karsh, 1990); whether the behavior is part of a regular or predictable chain (Charlop & Trasowech, 1991); the learning history for the target behavior (Powers & Handleman, 1984); the functional consequence of the behavior for the client and for others (Iwata, Pace, Kalsher,

Cowdery, & Cataldo, 1990); the communicative intent of the behavior (Durand & Carr, 1991); and any sensory or perceptual factors that may inhibit or occasion the behavior (Favell, McGimsey, & Schell, 1982). Response covariation among (a) motor, (b) physiological, and (c) verbal-cognitive processes cannot be assumed. Comprehensive behavioral assessment includes measures of each of these three domains, within the context of multimethod assessment. Evans (1986) provides a thoughtful discussion of this issue and its limitations. Attention to these factors allows the clinician to address maintaining variables more efficiently and comprehensively, in order to promote generalization and maintenance.

Assessment across Multiple Systems of Interaction

Many variables contribute to the highly individualized behavioral, cognitive, and adaptive profile presented by an individual with autism. In recent years, increasing attention has been given to expanding the behavioral assessment and treatment process to include various systems of interaction *beyond* the level of the individual client with a particular target behavior (Powers, 1988). These include assessment of: the family system (Harris, 1988, 1994); the family's readiness for change (Powers & Handleman, 1984); the classroom curriculum (Dunlap, Kern-Dunlap, Clarke, & Robbins, 1991); the needs of siblings (Harris, 1994); peer reactions (McHale & Simeonsson, 1980); and the child's position within the family life cycle (Harris & Powers, 1984). Explicit consideration of child, family, environmental, and interactional variables facilitates an understanding of the reciprocal, bidirectional nature of behavior. Treatment planning that accounts for this reciprocity can thereby be directed toward *both* the individual with autism and those persons or events in his or her environment that impact the behavior.

Emphasis on Strengths and Needs

Behavioral treatment that simply reduces or eliminates a problem behavior is inadequate to meet the life needs of the individual with autism. To facilitate long-term maintenance and generalization, the intervention must *also* teach new skills that are functionally equivalent response alternatives—skills that address and satisfy the motivators of the problem behavior (Dunlap, 1993). To accomplish this substitution, the behavioral assessment process must identify functional strengths, skills, and preferences to be incorporated into the treatment plan. This approach will increase the likelihood that prosocial behavior is taught *explicitly* as a replacement for the problem behavior that is targeted to be reduced. Where the targeted behavior is a skill deficit not currently in the child's repertoire, attention to functional strengths and individual preferences provides information that can be used: to select new behaviors that can be taught; to create optimal teaching environments; to choose reinforcers; and generally to effect a better "fit" between the skill to be taught and the learner's environment.

Use of Multiple Sources of Data

If individualized behavioral intervention protocols are the objectives of assessment, then the behavioral assessment process must generate as descriptive a data resource as possible. Molar and molecular analysis of behavior will generate a broadband understanding of the target behavior within its environment(s). However, other data sources may be considered as well, including information from psychological evaluations (Powers, 1988), family assessments (Harris, 1988), and diagnostic material (Volkmar & Cohen, 1988). Individual profiles of information processing/cognitive strengths and weaknesses, derived from standardized psychological evaluations, provide useful information about learning issues. Data from family assessments can offer information on family coping style, use of resources, and family adaptability and cohesion (Powers & Egel, 1989). Diagnostic information can also be of value. Powers (1984) has described the advantages of incorporating syndromal diagnosis into the behavioral assessment process. The specificity and developmental sensitivity of the *DSM-IV* criteria for autism and related pervasive developmental disorders provide a framework for understanding the breadth of symptoms presented by a child that co-occur

(and thus may be related functionally) with the target behavior. Other nomothetic measures, such as the Childhood Autism Rating Scale (CARS; Schopler, Reichler, & Renner, 1986) and the Behavioral Development Questionnaire (Castelloe & Dawson, 1993), also provide information useful to the treatment planning process.

Interdisciplinary Collaboration: An Essential Factor

Behavioral assessment serves treatment planning. As noted earlier in this chapter, broad-based intervention increases the likelihood that the results of treatment will generalize and maintain. Recent advances in the understanding of (a) the biological correlates of behavior and psychopharmacologic treatment (McDougle, Price, & Volkmar, 1994), (b) the complex relationship between severe behavior problems and communicative intent (Carr et al., 1994), (c) the relationship between sensory preferences and learning rate (Dyer, 1987), and (d) the continuing development of effective instructional strategies (Snell, 1992) all highlight the need for integrating information from various disciplines in order to develop a more comprehensive treatment plan.

DOMAINS OF BEHAVIORAL ASSESSMENT

As noted in the introduction to the dimensions of the assessment process, completion of a comprehensive behavioral assessment involves four steps: (a) identification of the target behavior, (b) determination of variables controlling the target behavior, (c) development of a treatment plan, and (d) evaluation of the effectiveness of the treatment plan. Each step is discussed below.

Identification of the Target Behavior

The precision implicit in behavioral treatment requires a clear, objective, verifiable, and operationalized definition of the target behavior. The behavior must be described with sufficient detail that two independent observers would agree that the behavior had just been (or had not been) emitted by the client.

Where two or more behaviors are identified as targets, they must be evaluated to determine whether they serve the same behavioral function. For example, the construct "aggressive and destructive behavior" may include aggression toward others as well as self-injurious behavior. Both of these behaviors may function to gain escape (or avoidance) of demand situations. In contrast, to the individual with autism, aggression may function to gain escape while self-injury functions to provide sensory feedback. In this latter case, these two behaviors may be part of two different response classes and will require two different assessment and intervention protocols. By identifying the *form* the behavior takes (its topography, intensity, duration, and frequency), the clinician sets the stage for assessment of behavioral *function* in the next step.

The process of prioritizing target behavior includes description of several factors, including risk to the client and others, the resources available and necessary, and the social validity of the target behavior. Wolf (1978) has proposed three broad areas for consideration when assessing social validity: (a) acceptability of treatment goals for target behavior selection, (b) acceptability of treatment procedures, (c) acceptability of treatment outcomes. Assessment of the acceptability of goals, target behaviors, and procedures *prior* to implementation should increase the likelihood that consumers and families will support treatment efforts. Assessment of the social acceptability of intervention outcomes during and following treatment is more related to maintenance and generalization of those effects. Runco and Schreibman (1983, 1987) and Schriebman, Koegel, Mills, and Burke (1981) provide excellent examples of social validation with individuals with autism.

Although social validity can be evaluated anecdotally and less formally, several methods for more systematic assessment have been proposed. Norm-based comparisons involve identification of competent models and determination of criterion levels of performance on target behaviors that are of importance to the child with autism (Van Houten, 1979). Subjective evaluation (Kazdin, 1977) provides a global judgment as to whether observed behavior changes are seen as important to those

individuals with whom the person with autism interacts.

Social validation is an important adjunct to the behavioral assessment process. Evaluation of social validity prior to beginning treatment provides a check-and-balance unit, increasing the likelihood that successful treatment will be both empirically and clinically meaningful to the person with autism and to the significant others in his or her life. When used with appropriate limitations (Kazdin, 1977; Wolf, 1978), social validation provides synthetic validity (Anastasi, 1976) for objectively derived data, enhancing the value and generality of results obtained.

Determination of Variables Controlling the Target Behavior

This step involves an ecological assessment (investigating the physical environment, antecedent and consequent stimulus events, organismic events, contingencies of reinforcement, the learning environment and learning history, and temporal analysis); indirect analysis using behavioral interviewing about the target behavior, with specific reference to its communicative value; reinforcer assessment, with a special emphasis on sensory preferences; and functional analysis of the behavior, where the hypotheses generated with existing assessment data are tested empirically *prior to* proceeding with implementation of the treatment plan. Using indirect methods, descriptive analysis, and functional analysis (Halle & Spradlin, 1993; Iwata, Vollmer, & Zarcone, 1990; Mace, Lalli, Pinter-Lalli, & Shea, 1993; O'Neill, Horner, Albin, Storey, & Sprague, 1990), this step provides a comprehensive basis for gathering information for treatment planning.

The physical, structural environment should be assessed to determine whether conditions such as noise, crowding, open (vs. small and confined) workspaces, and so on, are related to the occurrence of the target behavior. For example, physical spaces that produce echoes (locker rooms, gyms, stairwells) may increase the probability of behavior such as covering one's ears, running away, motor stereotypies, and so on. To the extent that this hypothesis can be demonstrated functionally, a potential intervention might include altering the physical environment by using other space, or by masking or attenuating the (presumably aversive) auditory stimulus with headphones.

Conditions that immediately precede the occurrence of the target behavior (antecedent stimuli) and conditions that occur immediately following the target behavior (consequent stimuli) are considered. Antecedent stimuli can be classified as discriminative stimuli or as elicitors. Discriminative stimuli predict the expectation of a particular response for a person, because that person has learned that the stimulus provokes a response on his or her part that leads to a certain consequence originating from someone else. Elicitors, in contrast, evoke automatic emotional or physiological responses (e.g., tachycardia, sweating, and dilation of the pupils). These types of responses are important in the assessment of the individual with autism because target behavior maintained by sensory or "automatic" reinforcement (arousal reduction or induction) can be among the most difficult to treat. Identification of the automatic "triggers" that are elicited by environmental events may allow the clinician to intervene by removing the "trigger" or by teaching the client to exert control over his or her own more purposeful (and less automatic) responses.

Consequent stimulus events are those imposed on the individual with autism after the target behavior has been emitted. These stimuli can be environmental or organismic. For example, the social attention, gentle touch, and soothing talk provided a person immediately after a self-injurious episode may serve as reinforcing consequences of a more external nature, and may maintain the self-injury at unacceptable levels. In contrast, the self-injury may be reinforced by the sensory consequence it provides, quite independent from any external environmental event.

Organismic variables have been underrepresented in the behavioral assessment of autism (Powers & Handleman, 1984). Conditions that have a specific effect on the form and function of behavior (e.g., Tourette's Disorder, seizures, sensory impairments, gastroesophageal reflux, Fragile X syndrome) must be accounted for in the assessment process so that treatment planning can reflect the relationship between environmental factors and genetic, neurological, or biological factors that might exert control over the target behavior.

When assessing antecedent and consequent stimuli, it is important to identify any behavior chains within which the target behavior may be embedded (Charlop & Trasowech, 1991). For antecedent stimuli, this is done by determining whether there is a pattern of predictable behavior immediately preceding the target behavior. Thus, aggression that reliably occurs after the client has been frustrated in an attempt to obtain something—followed, in turn, by shouting, then menacing physical gestures, then physical aggression—offers the clinician the option of intervening earlier in the chain (i.e., before the aggression occurs), in an attempt to preempt the response. When assessing for consequent stimulus behavior chains, it is useful to consider not only which consequence followed the target behavior, but also the *client's response* to that consequence. This allows assessment of ongoing clinician behavior that unwittingly may be reinforcing or punishing the behavior.

Contingencies of reinforcement refer to the particular conditions of reinforcement that influence the probability that a correct behavior or response will occur. Included here are schedules of reinforcement (Koegel, Schreibman, Britten, & Laitenen, 1979), reinforcer variation (Egel, 1981), task variation (Winterling, Dunlap, & O'Neill, 1987), and the use of sensory reinforcers (Durand & Carr, 1985; Dyer, 1987). By understanding the role and importance of reinforcement in learning the target behavior, the clinician may be able to intervene by altering reinforcement contingencies *prior to* the occurrence of the behavior.

Comprehensive assessment considers the teaching and learning environments the person with autism may participate in, because these situations may exert control over the target behavior (Horner, Sprague, & Flannery, 1993). Task ease or difficulty, boredom and fatigue, fast or slow pacing of presentation of instructional material, novelty of material, excessive auditory processing (vs. visual processing) demands, a reliance on simultaneous processing (vs. sequential processing), curriculum that is poorly matched to learner ability, and so forth, may increase the likelihood that the targeted behavior will occur. To the extent that one or more of these dimensions is implicated, intervention can be tailored to this issue, again preempting the function of the target behavior by replacing it with a more appropriate response alternative.

Temporal analysis investigates the target behavior across time and within specific time periods. For example, the frequency of a behavior can be entered on a data sheet that divides the entire day into 30-minute intervals. Over the course of one or two weeks, patterns may be evident signaling high- and low-probability times for a target behavior's occurrence. These intervals can be keyed to specific events throughout the day or week, permitting additional assessment into those situations. Touchette, MacDonald, and Langer (1985) developed the scatterplot to organize temporal data. The scatterplot is a grid with time intervals on the ordinate that monitors individuals for rate or frequency of target behaviors throughout their day. These frequencies are then keyed to activities and activity changes. The visual display that results provides information on high- and low-frequency behavior times as these relate to environmental variables.

Indirect methods, such as behavioral interviewing about the target behavior, provide information on the social and interpersonal factors that maintain or motivate behavioral performance and nonperformance across different situations. Information gathered in the behavioral assessment thus far has contributed to this understanding by providing convergent information on maintaining variables. More formal assessment of these variables can provide even more information, however. The Motivation Assessment Scale (MAS; Durand & Crimmins, 1988) is a 16-item questionnaire that provides information about these specific behavioral functions: (a) positive reinforcement by social attention or by access to material reinforcers; (b) escape from demands, and (c) sensory consequences. Responses by caregivers are made on a Likert scale, and the relative impact of each of these functions is determined. As an adjunct to direct observation of the target behavior, the MAS provides useful information for treatment selection, particularly if used to understand communicative function.

That is, treatment planning can address the communicative intent of the target behavior and be designed to teach alternative and more adaptive behavior, thus serving a communicative function identical to that of the problem behavior (Carr & Durand, 1985). O'Neill et al. (1990) have developed the Function Analysis Interview to provide a structured format for assessing antecedent and consequent events. Both of these methods share common advantages. They are structured and relatively straightforward to administer, and they provide broadband information pertinent to treatment planning. Their common disadvantage is their reliance on interview or reporting data (instead of direct observations).

Because behavioral assessment is intended ultimately to facilitate treatment planning, an assessment of reinforcer preferences must be an integral part of the process. Earlier, more simplistic reinforcer surveys identified materials and activities by form or type. For example, one might determine that a client preferred access to a particular toy, food, or television program. Dyer (1987) has broadened this process and has proposed that reinforcers be assessed by their stimulus preferences, including a wide range of *sensory conditions* for consideration. The wisdom of this is evident if one recalls that autism is a disorder characterized by atypical responses to the sensory environment. Indeed, deviant responses to auditory, tactile, deep-pressure proprioceptive, vestibular, olfactory, and gustatory sensory events are not uncommon in the behavioral profiles of individuals within the autism spectrum. By conducting a functional assessment of stimulus (sensory) preferences, clinicians have access to a more specifically tailored set of material and sensory reinforcers, and these reinforcers have demonstrated value for the particular individual.

The final step in determining controlling variables involves conducting a functional analysis. Functional analysis is the systematic, objective, empirical manipulation of variables presumed to exert influence over the target behavior in controlled settings. These variables are generated by the indirect and descriptive analysis methods described above, and they permit the clinician to extend the assessment process *beyond* a description of factors *correlated* with the target behavior, to factors exerting functional *control* over the target behavior. Functional analysis involves creating controlled analog conditions designed to "test" functions presumed to control behavior. For example, Iwata, Dorsey, Slifer, Bauman, and Richman (1982) evaluated four conditions presumed related to self-injurious behavior: (a) social disapproval, (b) task demand, (c) unstructured play with materials, and (d) sensory consequences. Each 15-minute condition was presented twice per day. Frequencies of self-injury were then calculated across the four conditions, and determinations were made as to which condition exerted more stimulus control over the behavior. Advantages of controlled analog analysis are related to the precision and specificity obtained. Some have argued that this step is always necessary (Iwata, Vollmer, & Zarcone, 1990); others have noted that analog analysis may require more of a commitment of human and financial resources than is necessary (or available), and that concise and appropriate behavioral interventions can sometimes be inferred from observation and indirect methods (O'Neill et al., 1990).

Development of a Treatment Plan

Behavioral assessment data provide the basis for intervention planning and evaluation. Thus, not only does assessment serve the predictive function noted at the beginning of this chapter, but it also provides the basis for ongoing (formative) and summative evaluation of intervention effectiveness. A functional ecological approach generates a wealth of information to be incorporated into the treatment plan. Interventions must address the controlling variables identified and the contextual information related to behavior performance and nonperformance. Strategies to teach functional alternative communicative responses must be incorporated. The use of differential reinforcement procedures to strengthen behaviors that are functionally, physically, and topographically incompatible is essential. Altering stimulus (antecedent) conditions formally addresses the ecological variables identified. Finally, the incorporation of consequent procedures that are func-

tionally compatible with desired outcomes is necessary.

Evaluation of the Effectiveness of the Treatment Plan

Behavioral assessment begins with the identification of dependent measures that are objective, valid, and reliable. Once the target behavior is identified, defined operationally, and observed in a baseline or pretreatment setting, this baseline becomes the yardstick against which efficacy is measured. Behavioral assessment methods include anecdotal recording, direct observation of the target behavior in natural or analog settings, and analysis of permanent products (e.g., incident reports, nursing notes, number of skin breaks caused by biting).

The use of direct observation procedures is considered a hallmark in behavioral assessment and treatment, but certain issues must be considered. Reactivity to direct observation methods can influence both client (subject) and observer behavior. Client awareness of the observer or of changes in the environment occasioned by the observer (e.g., the presence of a video camera with a red light that blinks while recording) can impact client behavior in ways atypical to the natural (unobserved) environment. Reactivity can also influence the observer and impact the reliability of data obtained.

Even when direct observation methods are used, the data obtained may not be accurate. Central to this issue is the concept of reliability, which describes the internal consistency of behavior observations or the interobserver agreement that the target behavior did in fact occur. Reliability of data is a core concept in behavioral assessment, because these data are used to predict and evaluate the efficacy of treatment. High rates of interobserver agreement are indicative of higher-quality observational data. Foster and Cone (1986) describe several factors that may influence reliability of observations. These include: observers' expectations that *their* performance will be evaluated; awareness of the identity of the rater; unsupervised collection of data; observer fatigue; setting variables in the observation environment; observer expectations;

interactions among the observers, experimenters, and subjects of the observation; and demand characteristics of the experimental situation.

Various methods are used to calculate reliability for categorical data (i.e., data that are recorded as observed, or not observed during established intervals). These include overall percentage agreement, percentage occurrence agreement, Kappa (K), and Phi (Φ). For data that are aggregated over an entire session, however, product–moment correlations (r) or generalizability analyses are often used (Foster & Cone, 1986).

Despite well-defined target behaviors and careful training of observers, the accuracy of observations and the inclusion or exclusion of ambiguous or borderline responses may shift subtly over time. Observer "drift" increases the systematic (and accidental) error of measured responses and represents a threat to the quality of obtained data. A comprehensive review of factors affecting interobserver reliability and of methods for assessment of observer drift and reactivity is beyond the scope of this chapter. Foster and Cone (1986) provide a detailed review and analysis of these issues. Finally, evaluation should occur in the context of an experimental or quasi-experimental design appropriate to the dependent measure (see Barlow & Hersen, 1984). Choice of method is determined by the resources available, the risk associated with using a less precise method, and the degree of experimental control necessary to make valid outcome statements.

RELATED ISSUES FOR COMPREHENSIVE ASSESSMENT

In addition to determining the effect on the target behavior, a functional ecological approach suggests evaluation of procedural reliability, ecological validity, and generalization and maintenance. Procedural reliability represents the degree to which the intervention plan was carried out correctly by all intervenors (Billingsly, White, & Munson, 1980). The assessment of procedural reliability should be conducted while treatment is in progress, in order to better inform ongoing decision making and interpretation of treatment effect.

Ecological validity refers to the extent to which the targets and settings addressed are functional in the individuals' everyday environment. The concept of ecobehavioral analysis (Rogers-Warren, 1984) provides strategies to increase the ecological validity of interventions. Specifically, behavioral assessment is conducted in the context of natural environments and situations the individuals currently (or will in the near future) participate in. After first conducting an inventory of relevant environments (e.g., school) and subenvironments (e.g., small group instruction), the clinician proceeds to describe the activities performed in those subenvironments (e.g., completing an assessment independently and correctly) and the skills that will be necessary (e.g., read the material, ask for assistance when needed). The clients' *current* skill repertoire is then evaluated against these criteria, and treatment is provided to develop the skills that are missing.

For target behavior to be functional in nontreatment settings, it must generalize and maintain over time. Unfortunately, attention to these important concepts is often given less emphasis by clinicians than the demonstration of initial changes in targeted behavior. Because problems with generalization are endemic to individuals with autism, greater emphasis is warranted.

Generalization and maintenance go hand-in-hand. Simply put, skills taught that do not become broadly useful, in nontraining environments, or those that do not last over time, are of limited value. Behavioral assessment of generalization and maintenance is not merely summative; that is, it is insufficient to become concerned about whether a skill transferred and maintained only *after* it was acquired. Stokes and Baer (1977) note that the "train and hope" strategy can be supplanted by a technology of generalization designed to facilitate orderly transfer of skills. A more proactive (and predictive) strategy involves assessing three broad areas described by Stokes and Osnes (1988): (a) an assessment of natural functional contingencies or reinforcement; (b) an assessment of diverse training opportunities; and (c) an assessment of common stimuli that may serve as functional mediators of newly learned behavior.

An assessment of natural communities of reinforcement provides information on the type, frequency, and variety of reinforcers that are already available in the clients' environment. For example, if high rates of social approval are available (and low rates of material or food reinforcers are not widely used), the clinician may wish to exploit social approval as a reinforcer if it is functional to the client. Subsequent training would then provide social approval for the target behavior in both training and nontraining environments. Stokes and Osnes (1988) note that generalization is facilitated by training with sufficient exemplars. This implies programming explicitly with a diverse range of people, environments, settings, and materials. Prior identification of those training opportunities allows the clinician to vary systematically those stimulus dimensions that may otherwise control responding, so that rigid and artificial conditions of treatment are avoided.

Identifying stimuli that can serve as potential functional mediators to untrained settings is the third area described by Stokes and Osnes (1988). Functional mediators are stimuli that facilitate generalization, most likely because they serve as discriminative stimuli for targeted behavior. These can include objects or people in the physical environment, present in both trained and untrained settings, that help the client determine the behavior that is expected (e.g., picture prompts, peer tutors). Once these objects or people are identified in the assessment, they can be incorporated into training protocols to promote generalization.

Expanding the scope of behavioral assessment to include procedural reliability, ecological validity, and generalization and maintenance moves the assessment process beyond the molecular analysis of the target behavior and places it within the social context wherein the client operates. This in turn facilitates a more comprehensive understanding of treatment effectiveness and treatment failures.

Comprehensive, lasting change in the lives of individuals with autism should be the goal of intervention efforts. A functional ecological approach to behavioral assessment provides a framework for understanding be-

havioral excesses, deficits, and strengths from a broader systemic perspective, creating an educative base for intervention efforts. As interventions for behavioral challenges more precisely target and teach adaptive and functional response alternatives, the distinctions between behavioral treatment and effective education will fade.

Cross-Reference

Behavioral intervention planning and evaluation are discussed in Chapter 26.

REFERENCES

Anastasi, A. (1976). *Psychological testing* (4th ed.). New York: Macmillan.

Barlow, D., & Hersen, M. (1984). *Single-case experimental designs: Strategies for studying behavior change.* New York: Pergamon.

Billingsly, F., White, O.R., & Munson, R. (1980). Procedural reliability: A rationale and an example. *Behavioral Assessment, 2,* 229–241.

Brown, L., Nietupski, J., & Hamre-Nietupski, S. (1976). Criterion of ultimate functioning and public school services for severely handicapped students. In M.A. Thomas (Ed.), *Hey, don't forget about me* (pp. 2–15). Reston, VA: Council for Exceptional Children.

Carr, E.G., & Durand, V.M. (1985). Reducing behavior problems through functional communication training. *Journal of Applied Behavior Analysis, 18,* 111–126.

Carr, E.G., Levin, L., McConnachie, G., Carlson, J.I., Kemp, D.C., & Smith, C.E. (1994). *Communication-based intervention for problem behavior.* Baltimore: Brookes.

Castelloe, P., & Dawson, G. (1993). Subclassification of children with autism and Pervasive Developmental Disorder: A questionnaire based on Wing's subgrouping scheme. *Journal of Autism and Developmental Disorders, 23,* 229–241.

Charlop, M.H., & Trasowech, J.E. (1991). Increasing autistic children's daily spontaneous speech. *Journal of Applied Behavior Analysis, 24,* 747–761.

Dunlap, G. (1993). Promoting generalization. In R. Van Houten & S. Axelrod (Eds.), *Behavior analysis and treatment* (pp. 269–296). New York: Plenum Press.

Dunlap, G., Kern-Dunlap, L., Clarke, S., & Robbins, F.R. (1991). Functional assessment, curricular revision, and severe behavior problems.

Journal of Applied Behavior Analysis, 24, 387–397.

Durand, V.M., & Carr, E.G. (1985). Self-injurious behavior: Motivating conditions and guidelines for treatment. *School Psychology Review, 14,* 171–176.

Durand, V.M., & Carr, E.G. (1991). Functional communication training to reduce challenging behavior: Maintenance and application in new settings. *Journal of Applied Behavior Analysis, 24,* 251–264.

Durand, V.M., & Crimmins, D.B. (1988). Identifying the variables maintaining self-injurious behavior. *Journal of Autism and Developmental Disorders, 18,* 99–117.

Dyer, K. (1987). The competition of autistic stereotyped behavior with usual and specially assessed reinforcers. *Research in Developmental Disabilities, 8,* 607–626.

Egel, A.L. (1981). Reinforcer variation: Implications for motivating developmentally disabled children. *Journal of Applied Behavior Analysis, 14,* 345–350.

Epstein, R. (1985). The positive side effects of reinforcement: A commentary on Balsam and Bondy. *Journal of Applied Behavior Analysis, 18,* 71–78.

Evans, I.M. (1986). Response structure and the triple-response-mode concept. In R.D. Nelson & Steven C. Hayes (Eds.), *Conceptual foundations of behavioral assessment* (pp. 131–155). New York: Guilford Press.

Favell, J.E., McGimsey, J., & Schell, R. (1982). Treatment of self-injury by providing alternative sensory activities. *Analysis and Intervention in Developmental Disabilities, 2,* 83–104.

Foster, S.L., & Cone, J.D. (1986). Design and use of direct observation procedures. In A.R. Ciminero, K.S. Calhoun, & H.E. Adams (Eds.), *Handbook of behavioral assessment* (2nd ed., pp. 253–324). New York: John Wiley & Sons.

Halle, J.W., & Spradlin, J.E. (1993). Identifying stimulus control of challenging behavior. In J. Reichle & D.P. Wacker (Eds.), *Communicative approaches to challenging behavior* (pp. 83–109). Baltimore: Brookes.

Harris, S.L. (1988). Family assessment in autism. In E. Schopler & G.B. Mesibov (Eds.), *Diagnosis and assessment in autism* (pp. 199–210). New York: Plenum Press.

Harris, S.L. (1994). *Siblings of children with autism.* Bethesda, MD: Woodbine.

Harris, S.L., & Ferrari, M. (1983). Developmental factors in child behavior therapy. *Behavior Therapy, 14,* 54–72.

Harris, S.L., & Powers, M.D. (1984). Behavior therapists look at the impact of the autistic child on the family system. In E. Schopler & G.B. Mesibov (Eds.), *The effects of autism on the family* (pp. 207–220). New York: Plenum Press.

Horner, R.H., Sprague, J.R., & Flannery, K.B. (1993). Building functional curricula for students with severe intellectual disabilities and severe problem behaviors. In R. Van Houten & S. Axelrod (Eds.), *Behavior analysis and treatment* (pp. 47–71). New York: Plenum Press.

Iwata, B.A., Dorsey, M.F., Slifer, K.J., Bauman, K.E., & Richman, G.S. (1982). Toward a functional analysis of self-injury. *Analysis and Intervention in Developmental Disabilities, 2,* 3–20.

Iwata, B.A., Pace, G.M., Kalsher, M.J., Cowdery, G.E., & Cataldo, M.F. (1990). Experimental analysis and extinction of self-injurious escape behavior. *Journal of Applied Behavior Analysis, 23,* 11–27.

Iwata, B.A., Vollmer, T.R., & Zarcone, J.R. (1990). The experimental (functional) analysis of behavior disorders: Methodology, applications, and limitations. In A.C. Repp & N.N. Singh (Eds.), *Perspectives on the use of nonaversive and aversive interventions for persons with developmental disabilities* (pp. 301–330). Sycamore, IL: Sycamore.

Kazdin, A.E. (1977). Assessing the clinical or applied importance of behavior change through social validation. *Behavior Modification, 1,* 427–451.

Koegel, R.L., Schreibman, L., Britten, K., & Laitenen, R. (1979). The effect of schedule of reinforcement on stimulus over selectivity in autistic children. *Journal of Autism and Developmental Disorders, 9,* 383–397.

Mace, F.C., Lalli, J.S., Pinter-Lalli, E., & Shea, M.C. (1993). Functional analysis and treatment of aberrant behavior. In R. Van Houten & S. Axelrod (Eds.), *Behavior analysis and treatment* (pp. 75–99). New York: Plenum Press.

McDougle, C., Price, L.H., & Volkmar, F.R. (1994). Recent advances in the pharmacotherapy of autism and related disorders. *Child and Adolescent Psychiatric Clinics of North America, 3,* 71–89.

McHale, S.M., & Simeonsson, R.J. (1980). Effects of interaction on nonhandicapped children's attitudes toward autistic children. *American Journal of Mental Deficiency, 85,* 18–24.

O'Neill, R.E., Horner, R.H., Albin, R.W., Storey, K., & Sprague, J.R. (1990). *Functional analysis of problem behavior: A practical assessment guide.* Sycamore, IL: Sycamore.

Powers, M.D. (1984). Syndromal diagnosis and the behavioral assessment of childhood disorders. *Child and Family Behavior Therapy, 6,* 1–15.

Powers, M.D. (1988). Behavioral assessment of autism. In E. Schopler & G.B. Mesibov (Eds.), *Diagnosis and assessment of autism* (pp. 139–165). New York: Plenum Press.

Powers, M.D., & Egel, A.L. (1989, May). *Stress, coping and conflict in families of young autistic children.* Paper presented at the annual conference of the Association for Behavior Analysis, Philadelphia.

Powers, M.D., & Handleman, J.S. (1984). *Behavioral assessment of severe developmental disabilities.* Rockville, MD: Aspen.

Repp, A.C., & Karsh, K.G. (1990). A taxonomic approach to the nonaversive treatment of maladaptive behavior of persons with developmental disabilities. In A.C. Repp & N.N. Singh (Eds.), *Perspectives on the use of nonaversive and aversive interventions for persons with developmental disabilities* (pp. 381–402). Sycamore, IL: Sycamore.

Rogers-Warren, A.K. (1984). Ecobehavioral analysis. *Education and Treatment of Children, 7,* 283–303.

Runco, M.A., & Schreibman, L. (1983). Parental judgments of behavior therapy efficacy with autistic children: A social validation. *Journal of Autism and Developmental Disorders, 13,* 237–248.

Runco, M.A., & Schreibman, L. (1987). Socially validating behavioral objectives in the treatment of autistic children. *Journal of Autism and Developmental Disorders, 17,* 141–147.

Schopler, E., Reichler, R.J., & Renner, B.R. (1986). *The Childhood Autism Rating Scale (CARS) for diagnostic screening and classification of autism.* New York: Irvington.

Schreibman, L., Koegel, R.L., Mills, J., & Burke, J.C. (1981). Social validation of behavior therapy with autistic children. *Behavior Therapy, 12,* 610–624.

Snell, M. (Ed.). (1992). *Instruction of students with severe disabilities* (4th ed.). New York: Macmillan.

Stokes, T.F., & Baer, D.M. (1977). An implicit technology of generalization. *Journal of Applied Behavior Anlaysis, 10,* 349–367.

Stokes, T.F., & Osnes, P.G. (1988). The developing applied technology of generalization and maintenance. In R.H. Horner, G. Dunlap, & R.L. Koegel (Eds.), *Generalization and maintenance* (pp. 5–19). Baltimore: Brookes.

Touchette, P.E., MacDonald, R.F., & Langer, S.N. (1985). A scatterplot for identifying stimulus control of problem behavior. *Journal of Applied Behavior Analysis, 18,* 343–351.

Van Houten, R. (1979). Social validation: The evolution of standards of competency for target behaviors. *Journal of Applied Behavior Analysis, 12,* 581–591.

Volkmar, F.R., & Cohen, D.J. (1988). Classification and diagnosis of childhood autism. In E. Schopler & G.B. Mesibov (Eds.), *Diagnosis and assessment in autism* (pp. 71–89). New York: Plenum Press.

Winterling, V., Dunlap, G., & O'Neill, R.E. (1987). The influence of task variation on the aberrant behavior of autistic students. *Education and Treatment of Children, 10,* 105–119.

Wolf, M.M. (1978). Social validity: The case for subjective judgment or how applied behavior analysis is finding its heart. *Journal of Applied Behavior Analysis, 11,* 203–214.

CHAPTER 21

Diagnostic Instruments in Autism Spectrum Disorders

CATHERINE LORD

The development of diagnostic instruments in the past 30 years is an example of the interplay between clinical and research needs in the field of autism. When judged from case reports, autism is one of the most reliably diagnosed disorders in child psychiatry (Mattison, Cantwell, Russell, & Will, 1979). However, many diagnostic aspects of the disorder provide unique challenges, as well as presenting issues shared with other childhood-onset disorders. This chapter considers general and specific issues in designing and selecting a diagnostic instrument for autism spectrum disorders. A brief historical review of some of the first standardized instruments used for diagnosis of autism is included, along with short descriptions of some of the most commonly used diagnostic instruments. The chapter concludes with information about instruments employed for specific purposes (i.e., measuring change; general screening) and a discussion of current implementation. Because the emphasis of the chapter is on issues in the design and selection of diagnostic measures, discussion of individual instruments is not intended to be comprehensive. Readers are referred to review articles by Parks (1988) and Teal and Wiebe (1986), as well as original works cited in the text, for further information on specific instruments.

GENERAL ISSUES IN DIAGNOSIS OF AUTISM SPECTRUM DISORDERS

Implications of Autism/PDD as Disorders of Development

Autism and other pervasive developmental disorders (PDD) are associated with a broad range of intellectual and language skills, particularly across time. This range affects the ways in which the disorders' defining symptoms are manifested. Because autism spectrum disorders typically begin when children are infants or toddlers, and continue into adulthood, it has been difficult to identify precisely defined behaviors that are necessary and sufficient to diagnoses across developmental levels (Lord et al., in press; Volkmar et al., 1994). For example, although deficits in simple pretense (e.g., having a tea party) and elicited imitation are typical of most autistic children at certain points in development, these impairments do not necessarily discriminate autism from other disorders at either very simple levels of development (i.e., age equivalents of under 12 months) or at much more sophisticated levels of development (i.e., very high-functioning verbal adults) (Boucher, in press; Smith & Bryson, 1994).

Changes in development in autism present issues similar to those that affect the measurement of general intellectual development in all children. Years of investigation, access to large populations, and a focus on normative data have allowed the development of instruments such as the Wechsler tests (Wechsler, 1981, 1991), which contain different tasks for different children at different levels. Standard scores are computed according to small gradations of age. In autism spectrum disorders, with the exception of the revised Autism Diagnostic Observation Schedule (ADOS-G; Lord, Rutter, & DiLavore, 1996), such grading has not yet been attempted—and may not be feasible, given the incidence of the disorders.

As discussed in detail below, issues arise about how best to define any comparison group in order to generate norms appropriate to autism. Providing normative data based on chronological age, as is done for most well-known general intellectual assessments, is clearly not sufficient, because autism spectrum disorders are often associated with mental handicap. Thus, differences between autistic, mentally handicapped children and chronological-age-matched nonautistic children who are not mentally handicapped may be attributed to autism, mental handicap, or both. Yet the generation of norms based on all combinations of chronological age and level of mental handicap is not feasible.

A further factor is language delay. Even when level of mental handicap is addressed through a research design, children with autism-related disorders almost always (with a few notable exceptions) show more severe language delays than other children of equivalent nonverbal level. Any diagnostic instrument that relies heavily on behaviors associated with receptive or expressive language competence must take this into account. However, exactly how to do so becomes a complex decision (Happé, 1995; Hobson, 1991). Trying to control for language delay may also "control for" autism itself or result in comparisons that are invalid for other reasons (e.g., comparing 2-year-olds with autism to nonhandicapped 8-month-olds of equivalent receptive language skill).

In general, classification systems and diagnostic instruments for pervasive developmental disorders have been most accurate in addressing autism in somewhat verbal, mildly to moderately mentally handicapped school-age children. Classification systems and diagnostic instruments decrease in interpretability according to how far one moves away from this group (Lord & Rutter, 1994). Unfortunately, well-standardized diagnostic instruments are most needed for children and adults who are not included in this group. As discussed below, consumers who use diagnostic instruments must take into account the biases that an instrument shows for populations outside of this group of children with autism—for example, children with nonautism pervasive developmental disorders, such as Asperger's Syndrome

and PDD-NOS. Although they are less relevant for Rett's Syndrome and Fragile X, which have biological markers, the difficulties still hold true for questions of when and how children with these disorders have autism.

Issues in Selecting the Appropriate Focus and Level of Analysis

An alternative to building diagnostic instruments around very specific behaviors is to use broadly defined deficits, such as impairments in social reciprocity or circumscribed interests, that are relevant to the behaviors of individuals across a range of chronological ages and developmental levels. However, interpreting such broad terms may be difficult for naïve observers, particularly nonexpert clinicians (Volkmar et al., 1994) and parents (Schopler & Reichler, 1972). In diagnoses of young children (see DiLavore, Lord, & Rutter, 1995; Lord, Storoschuk, Rutter, & Pickles, 1993), it may be especially difficult to disentangle well-coordinated social behaviors produced as part of familiar physical routines, from spontaneous and socially motivated interactions. For example, in a study comparing parent report in a structured interview to direct observations, good agreement across the two methods for the occurrence of abnormalities emerged for only 3 of 16 items taken from *DSM-III-R*: (a) abnormal social play, (b) stereotyped body movements, and (c) restricted range of interests (Stone & Lemanek, 1990). For adults, differentiation between deficits specific to autism and those associated with any severe chronic psychiatric disorder that drastically limits social contact and everyday opportunities, also becomes more difficult (Rutter, Mawhood, & Howlin, 1992; Volkmar et al., 1994).

Parent and child reports are not interchangeable. This issue is most relevant to high-functioning older children, adolescents, and adults with autism and pervasive developmental disorders who can be asked to describe their own symptoms and concerns. For certain behaviors, parent report may be more valid and reliable over time (e.g., reports of friendships, development of play; Lord et al., 1989); for other behaviors, either direct observation (such as of very young children with autism; DiLavore, Lord, & Opsahl, 1994) or individual reports (such as for mood and interest in the opposite sex; Mawhood, 1994) may be more accurate indicators. In other areas of developmental psychopathology, with a few notable exceptions (e.g., self-reports of depressive feelings), informant accounts have often been better discriminators than alternative methods (Bird, Gould, & Staghezza, 1992).

Use of multiple sources may address some of these issues by helping to place diagnostic information in developmental and social contexts. For example, if a child appears fascinated by pencils during an observation, a parent's account of the child's fascination with sticklike materials at home would be important in evaluating whether a consistent focus or a brief interest had been observed. Information about very limited social interaction beginning in early childhood will help place reports of social isolation into context for an adult patient. From the reverse perspective, observation of a child's response when a parent is asked to call the child's name may be a helpful complement to the parent's description of how the child responds when family members attempt to get his or her attention at home. Ideally, diagnostic instruments would maximize use of direct observations and parents' and teachers' descriptions, while not requiring informants to draw inferences that they do not have the knowledge (e.g., about the nature of autism and the applicability of that term to a particular child). However, how best to combine information from multiple sources is not obvious (Kraemer, 1992).

Instruments may differ in the degree to which they emphasize the presence of observable abnormalities or the absence of normally developing features. This distinction may be arbitrary, as in descriptions of the use of gaze by children with autism, for example, "unusual eye contact" or "failure to use gaze to regulate social interaction in subtle ways." The former describes the presence of an abnormality; the latter describes the absence of a prosocial behavior. For other diagnostic features, the presence of clear abnormalities and the absence of normal development may be strongly related, but the two factors may not necessarily be the same and may occur independently. For example, developmental and behavioral intervention studies would suggest that the presence of unusual preoccupations and restricted interests

is associated with the absence of early social play. A child who is taught developmentally appropriate play skills will show fewer stereotyped behaviors (Schopler, 1976). To our knowledge, this assumption has not been directly tested outside of evaluations of specific interventions.

Even though the two approaches (computing the presence of abnormalities versus computing the absence of prosocial features) are clearly related, they have somewhat different implications for diagnostic instruments. Social-communicative features of autism tend to be described in terms of absences, and oddities in interest and behavior, as well as a few specific characteristics of language (e.g., stereotypic speech), tend to be described in terms of the presence of abnormalities. When odd behaviors occur, such as hand and finger mannerisms or repeated smelling of objects, they may be more striking and more obviously abnormal than the lack of typical development in a particular area. However, such obviously abnormal behaviors, even if a child or adult engages in them frequently at home or in school, may not always occur during a relatively brief observation. For example, in one study, only 60% of verbal, mildly mentally handicapped adolescents with autism and 35% of very high-functioning, verbal adolescents with autism exhibited clearly observable repetitive behaviors during a half-hour structured observation (Lord et al., 1989), although all of these individuals were described by their parents as engaging in such behaviors on a regular basis at home. None of the language and chronological-age-matched mentally handicapped and normally developing adolescents exhibited these behaviors during the observation. The *presence* of these behaviors was important diagnostically, but the *absence* during one observation was not interpretable.

In addition, at lease in autism, there is reason to believe that such abnormalities are less directly related to clinical outcome than are social impairments and more broadly based aspects of communication (Venter, Lord, & Schopler, 1992). Brief descriptions of clearly abnormal behaviors, particularly sensory reactions to environmental stimuli, are more amenable to checklists and screening measures (Rimland, 1971) than are longer-winded descriptions of subtle differences in nonverbal social behaviors, but, compared to other measures, they may be less indicative of outcome and of diagnoses made by experienced clinicians.

It is important to remember that, in a diagnosis, a clinician gets what is looked for or asked about. The content and the nature of the behaviors that are observed (or described) and of the ways in which they are reduced or "coded" affect the end product of diagnosis. Scales that employ linear approaches to scores (e.g., using a single total with a single cut-off) more easily measure severity of dysfunction, but are more likely affected by factors outside autism (most notably, co-occurring mental retardation) than are instruments that require thresholds in different areas. On the other hand, scales that require coordination of multiple thresholds are more tied to specific diagnostic theory (i.e., as stated in *DSM-IV* and *ICD-10*) and may underestimate cases because of the requirements for the distribution of scores.

For example, a recent study showed that both the Childhood Autism Rating Scale (CARS; Schopler, Reichler, & Renner, 1988) and the Autism Diagnostic Interview—Revised (ADI-R; Lord, Rutter, & Le Couteur, 1994) were concordant with clinician's judgments in diagnosing autism in children at age 3 years (Lord, 1995). Both were less accurate for children 2 years younger, but for somewhat different reasons. The CARS consistently overdiagnosed nonautistic mentally handicapped children as having autism at age 2; CARS diagnoses of these children became more accurate by age 3 years, but were still less specific than has been reported for older children. The ADI-R was more accurate than the CARS with nonautistic children at age 2 years, but was also overinclusive for mentally handicapped and/or language-delayed children. The ADI-R also failed to diagnose autism in about 10% of 2-year-olds who later met formal diagnostic criteria for the disorder. Agreement between the ADI-R and CARS was in fact quite high; the difference was whether a simple total or thresholds across several areas (i.e., social reciprocity, communication, restricted and repetitive behaviors) were required for a diagnosis. As will be discussed later in the chapter, decisions on which approach is most appropriate may differ, depending on the needs of the clinician or researcher

and the developmental level of the child or adult being assessed.

Implications of Information from Other Areas of Research for Diagnostic Instruments

Without a well-established biological marker, decisions about classification of autism and pervasive developmental disorders have often been based on the need to identify appropriate populations for services and research, rather than on empirical bases (American Psychiatric Association, 1994; Volkmar et al., 1994; Wing & Gould, 1979). Eventually, neurobiological factors may result in changes in diagnoses in autism and PDD, but biological heterogeneity is expected within and among the spectrum disorders. Thus, clinicians will be dependent on descriptions of social and other behaviors for the near future.

The behavioral boundaries between autism and other disorders in the spectrum, such as Pervasive Developmental Disorder Not Otherwise Specified (PDD-NOS) and Asperger's Syndrome, are not clearly defined, particularly when developmental changes are taken into account (see Ghaziuddin, Tsai, & Ghaziuddin, 1992; Volkmar, Chapter 1, this volume). Information, such as developmental trajectories and clustering of symptoms, that arises out of studies conducted with diagnostic instruments may influence classification systems in the near future (Lord et al., in press; Szatmari, Archer, Fishman, Streiner, & Wilson, 1995; Mahoney et al., in press). The instruments themselves can be expected to change as more information is acquired.

Furthermore, priorities for the results of diagnoses may be different for clinical and research purposes. A clinical diagnosis offers families access to general information about their children and is the entry point to services. A priority for families and diagnosticians is to ensure that children or adults are not being excluded from appropriate services because of a particular label or classification (Wing & Attwood, 1987). From the perspective of service providers, a diagnosis is a basis for allocating limited resources.

Researchers often prefer narrow diagnoses because they provide better cross-site reliability, eliminate outliers, and reduce overlap with control groups. On the other hand, researchers seek populations of particular sizes and are interested in maximizing the number of participants who meet their criteria. All of these forces affect the goals addressed by diagnostic instruments and the ways in which they are used.

There is an urgent need for instruments to address diagnoses beyond autism, particularly PDD-NOS and Asperger's Syndrome. In part, the absence of replicable, reliable, and valid instruments in this area is related to the absence of clear diagnostic criteria for these disorders (Szatmari, 1995). A lack of empirical data affects the ability to discriminate these disorders from autism and from disorders outside the autism spectrum (e.g., severe attention deficit; severe communication impairment). In turn, the development of criteria and the operationalization of these criteria are affected adversely.

Numerous diagnostic proposals for PDDs, especially for Asperger's Syndrome, suggest conceptualizations but do not directly address the overlap with autism. In contrast, *DSM-IV* and *ICD-10* criteria define Asperger's Syndrome purely in terms of its relationship with autism, but provide little conceptualization. Conceptualizations of schizoid disorder and atypical development are given, but without clear indications of the relationship with autism. The *DSM-IV* criteria for PDD-NOS and the *ICD-10* criteria for Atypical Autism are based solely on just missing the autism criteria.

Instruments tend to follow the same pattern, which proves to be truly a vicious cycle. Without reliable diagnostic criteria and measures, empirical findings are very difficult to interpret; yet, without empirical data about the course and characteristics of nonautism PDDs, attempts to draw clear boundaries for autism will not be effective. Data from genetic and family studies, as well as other neurobiological approaches, may make this task easier but are also affected by instrumentation. Thus, researchers must arrive at working agreements that allow them to proceed forward in a reliable fashion.

In the face of these difficulties, autism as a field has the strength of its intense research history and the benefit of investigation of similar questions by different research teams from around the world. Descriptive and experimental research has offered solutions to some of these difficulties, for example, by identifying developmentally meaningful behaviors that discriminate autism from other disorders at various points in development. There is promise of other knowledge, from new statistical techniques to neuroimaging to DNA typing. As perspectives on autism have shifted to reflect new theories and empirical findings, strategies and content of instruments used for diagnosis of autism have been adapted in numerous ways. However, in the newer instruments, roots can almost always be traced to strategies begun in earlier work. Science offers clinicians the opportunity to learn from investigators and the opportunity to test findings as they emerge.

PSYCHOMETRIC ISSUES

The American Psychological Association has issued guidelines for the development of psychometric instruments in the United States. Selected standards of reliability and validity, from these guidelines, are presented in Tables 21.1 and 21.2, respectively. Many diagnostic instruments used for autism/PDD have addressed some of these issues, but few (or none) have addressed all of them. In part, this lack of information is understandable because of difficulties in achieving sufficiently large, well-documented samples; but, in part, it reflects the short history of instrument development in autism.

A number of factors affect the psychometric appropriateness of an instrument. Issues of reliability and validity are raised here, as they apply to diagnostic instruments for the autism spectrum in general. More specific discussions of selected instruments appear in the next section.

Reliability

Reliability, or the degree to which a score or decision is free from errors of measurement, requires assessment in a number of forms, including across raters, across time, and within an instrument. Often, the term *reliability* is used to describe all these separate aspects of the stability of the results of an instrument, as if they were interchangeable. They are not. For example, the degree to which different raters concur

TABLE 21.1   Reliability and Errors of Measurement: Issues Related to Diagnosis of Autism Spectrum Disorders[a]

1. For each total score, subscore, or combination of scores that is reported, estimates of relevant reliabilities and standard errors of measurement should be provided in adequate detail to enable the test user to judge whether scores are sufficiently accurate for the intended use of the test.

2. The procedures that are used to obtain samples of individuals, groups, or observations for the purpose of estimating reliabilities and standard errors of measurement, as well as the nature of the populations involved, should be described.

3. The conditions under which the reliability estimate was obtained, and the situations to which it may be applicable, should be explained clearly.

4. Coefficients based on internal analysis should not be interpreted as substitutes for alternate-form reliability or estimates of stability over time, unless other evidence supports that interpretation in a particular context.

5. Where judgmental processes enter into the scoring of a test, evidence on the degree of agreement between independent scorings should be provided.

6. Where cut scores are specified for selection or classification, the standard errors of measurement should be reported for score levels at or near the cut score. For dichotomous decisions, estimates should be provided to indicate the percentage of test takers who are classified in the same way on two occasions or on alternate forms of the test.

[a] Selected and adapted from American Educational Research Association (AERA), American Psychological Association (APA), & NCME. (1985). *Standards for educational and psychological testing*. Washington, DC: American Psychological Association.

TABLE 21.2   Validity: Issues Related to Diagnosis of Autism Spectrum Disorders[a]

1. Evidence of validity should be presented for the major types of inferences for which the use of a test is recommended.

2. If validity for some common interpretation has not been investigated, that fact should be made clear, and potential users should be cautioned about making such interpretations.

3. The composition of the validation sample should be described, in as much detail as is practicable.

4. When criteria are composed of rater judgments, the relevant training, experience, and qualifications of the raters should be described.

5. When a test is proposed as a measure of a construct, that construct should be distinguished from other constructs. Evidence should be presented to show that a test does not depend heavily on extraneous constructs. If evidence indicates that a criterion measure is affected to a substantial degree by irrelevant factors, this evidence should be reported.

6. When criteria are composed of rater judgments, the degree of knowledge that raters have concerning rate performance should be reported.

7. If specific cut scores are recommended for decision making (for example, in differential diagnosis), the instructions should caution that the rates of misclassification will vary depending on the percentage of individuals tested who actually belong in each category.

[a] Selected and adapted from American Educational Research Association (AERA), American Psychological Association (APA), & NCME. (1985). *Standards for educational and psychological testing*. Washington, DC: American Psychological Association.

when using the same instrument cannot be determined by looking at the internal characteristics of a test. The internal consistency of an instrument (i.e., the degree to which different items on a scale measure the same concept) can be quite high, even though the interrater reliability is low. In a disorder such as autism, which is defined by a pattern of difficulties across several areas (i.e., communication, social interaction, behavior), internal consistency in a scale is a worthwhile endeavor, but it does not have the same meaning as in a scale that is not designed to describe a pattern of deficits.

In the past, reliability estimates were often reported as correlations (i.e., as a measure of whether the rankings of different individuals

are similar across different raters). The difficulty with correlations is that the absolute scores of raters can be quite different (resulting in different diagnoses) even though they are highly correlated. For example, if one rater rates all participants relatively high and another rates them all relatively low, and they follow the same rankings among participants, the correlation of the two raters' scores will be high. If diagnosis is based on exceeding a certain threshold, the fact that the raters agreed in the rankings would not prevent the scores from resulting in different diagnoses for the same individual. Thus, although correlations provide an important index of the relationship among scores, it is not sufficient to show agreement when scores are used to make categorical judgments about diagnoses.

In place of correlations, many investigators now employ a percent-of-agreement measure between pairs or among larger groupings of raters. Agreement is defined at a level commensurate with the aims of the instrument. It may be exact agreement or agreement within a certain number of points, depending on how scores are to be used. Clinicians and researchers then evaluate the frequency with which their coding agrees with that of another person for a given individual. There are no set standards for levels of agreement, but generally, in self-report and interview studies, researchers have been able to achieve 90% or greater agreement on individual categorical measures and at least 80% on individual observational codes, with greater agreement attained for pooled or summary scores.

The difficulty with using percent-of-agreement as a metric is the role of chance. If there is a high frequency of extreme scores without much variation within different populations (e.g., almost all zeros for nonautism or all high scores for autism), correlation and percent-of-agreement among raters can be quite high because of the good chance of agreement based on using an extreme score, without attention to individual differences. That is, having seen a child's performance on the first item of the test, a rater might predict that, because the child looked quite autistic on the first item, he or she will receive high scores on all further measures of abnormality. Having seen a typically developing child's behavior on the same first item, a rater might predict, based on the child's "normal" reaction to the first task, that he or she will receive normal scores on the same measures. If there is little variation across tasks and little overlap across populations, two raters might get better agreement using this strategy than by actually observing and coding the children. Specific statistics, called kappas (Cicchetti & Sparrow, 1981), allow some control of this phenomenon.

There is no simple answer to address these problems. Although kappas control for chance, they are sensitive to distributions and so, as with any statistic, must be interpreted in light of other information. Another strategy using reliability coefficients does not address the intersection between individual participants and individual raters, but allows quantification of the effects of each separately (Mundy, Sigman, Ungerer, & Sherman, 1986).

These issues illustrate the importance of the nature of the samples on which psychometric analyses are conducted. Autism across the life span affects individuals who have a range of language and cognitive skills. If samples are not well-matched and not relevant to the clinical or research contexts in which the instrument will be used, there will generally be little overlap in scores. If instruments are developed using only very easily discriminable populations, documentation of reliable ratings will be difficult to achieve when statistics that take distributions into account are employed, although they may look good in terms of absolute agreement.

For many scales, reliability estimates are presented only for totals, even when subscales are described. For clinicians or researchers who want to base interpretations on specific items or subscales, data about reliability for particular items must be available. If they are not available, then it is important for the test user to interpret his or her results within the context of what is available.

Sometimes, the reverse result occurs. Researchers present detailed psychometric data for items, but do not present reliability for the diagnostic categorization for which the scale is intended. This is particularly problematic for autism and PDDs. It is not difficult to find an instrument that identifies autism spectrum behaviors as abnormal in some way; however, that is not the goal. To be useful diagnostically, instruments must discriminate children with autism or PDD from nonautistic, severely mentally handicapped, language-impaired children. Because it is often difficult to set a threshold that keeps mildly autistic children identified as such and excludes nonautistic, severely mentally handicapped children, the consistency across raters and across time with which an individual falls in or out of the category of autism or PDD must be measured directly.

The issue of test–retest reliability in autism is complex. Changes in behavior due to development would be expected, if administrations of a test are separated by substantial amounts of time. Some learning may occur within the testing situation; a child asked to carry out the same actions again may not behave the same way. This is different from an error in measurement, but still must be taken into account. In some cases, the fact that the instrument has been administered already may change the nature of the interaction when it is used a second time. For example, in the Autism Diagnostic Observation Schedule for nonverbal children (ADOS-G, module 1; Lord et al., 1996), children are taught a routine of bringing a balloon to the examiner if they do not do so spontaneously. If they are presented with the same task several weeks later, they may respond differently because of learning, not because of error in measurement. However, the examiner still needs to adjust his or her expectations accordingly. Ideally, information about stability and expected changes across multiple administrations should be available for all instruments.

For diagnostic instruments, this information must be presented at the level of each individual's score and resulting diagnosis. Just because a task or instrument has been used in many studies, it cannot be assumed that it is reliable on an individual level or achieves a standard that is appropriate for diagnostic work. Many experimental studies in psychology and psychiatry are primarily concerned with identifying group differences. If they address issues at an individual level at all, the amount of detail they give is minimal. For example, two papers recently reported substantial intraindividual variability, across tasks and time, in standard tasks used to assess theory of mind (see Chapter 41 for discussion of this concept) in autism (Holroyd & Baron-Cohen, 1993; Mayes & Zigler, 1992). Group effects on false-belief tasks have been replicated across studies internationally and have had a major impact on the conceptualization of social-cognitive deficits in autism. Yet, in neither of these recent studies were these effects sufficiently replicable within individuals to meet reasonable clinical standards for classification.

An important aspect of reliability is specification of exactly how and under what circumstances diagnostic instruments are to be used and how they are to be scored. Procedures reported in journal articles are often described so briefly that it is difficult to determine what exactly was done and who did it. Differences in

procedures—such as whether coding is carried out live or from videotape, or how experienced in autism the raters are—can make marked differences in scoring (Sanchez et al., 1995; Volkmar et al., 1994). Users of instruments may benefit from knowing how they might be expected to develop and judge their own reliability with an instrument.

In studies of reliability and validity, raters should be unaware of children's diagnostic categories or their scores on other diagnostic instruments, unless this information would typically be available prior to use of the instrument. If other information is assumed to be critical for proper use of the instrument, this needs to be stated clearly in the procedural instructions. For example, for the ADOS-G, general information about a participant's likely level of expressive language is crucial in selecting the appropriate module and so is considered part of the assessment. How this information is used is specified in the manual. In addition, descriptions of the training required for a rater and the circumstances of the training and the administration are critical aspects of reliability.

Another factor to be considered in autism and PDDs is parents' awareness of their child's diagnosis. In many research samples, parents of previously diagnosed autistic children are well-versed in the characteristics of autism and how their children fit into the diagnostic schema. If a parent-report instrument is intended to be used in initial diagnosis, it is appropriate that it has been shown to be reliable and valid with caregivers who have not yet received a formal diagnosis.

Validity

Validity, or the degree to which evidence supports inferences drawn from the scores, is the most important aspect of a diagnostic instrument. How validity is best measured is inherently related to the uses for which the instrument is intended. Validity is often grouped into categories of content, construct, and criterion-related evidence. For the diagnosis of autism and PDDs, questions of construct validity are related to the concepts that underlie the diagnostic framework on which the instrument is based. For example, the ADI-R uses the concept of social reciprocity, as derived from theories of autism (see Lord & Rutter, 1994) and as operationalized in terms of specific questions to parents and caregivers about behaviors such as joint attention, shared enjoyment, comforting, and friendship. Data from studies of the ADI (Lord et al., in press) contributed to the understanding of this construct during preparation of *DSM-IV* and *ICD-10* criteria. Along with the results of observational studies and field trials, these data showed that traditional measures of attachment were not strongly related to other measures of social reciprocity (Lord et al., 1993; Sigman & Ungerer, 1984; Volkmar et al., 1994). A further study suggested that parental reports on the ADI, detailing autistic children's responses to separation and reunion (which were intended to be linked theoretically to conceptualizations of attachment), were more highly correlated with their children's communicative competence than the same children's observed responses to separation and reunion in a standardized setting (e.g., during administration of the Pre-Linguistic Autism Observation Schedule; PL-ADOS; DiLavore et al., 1995; Spencer, 1993).

Internal consistency for items within a diagnostic instrument can be used to support an assertion that a test measures a single construct. In autism, this has meant support for differentiation of the autism spectrum from other developmental disorders, or support for the three domains (social reciprocity, communication, and restricted, repetitive behaviors) that define the syndrome. Measures of internal consistency for the instruments most commonly used in the diagnosis of autism—the ADI-R, the Autism Behavior Checklist (ABC), and the Childhood Autism Rating Scale (CARS)—have been consistently high.

Content validity has to do with the degree to which a sample of items, tasks, or questions in an instrument is representative of a defined domain. In most cases, this domain is autism, either narrowly or broadly defined (i.e., autism spectrum disorder or pervasive developmental disorder). For the purposes of this review, content validity is most clearly related to the degree to which different instruments represent diagnostic criteria for autism spectrum disorders. Most of the instruments reviewed here predated the release of *DSM-IV*

and *ICD-10* criteria for autism and so do not correspond to the three-domain approach specified in these diagnostic systems. The exceptions are the ADI-R and ADOS-G. These are special cases because interpretation of results from the original versions of these instruments (the ADI and ADOS/PL-ADOS) influenced strategies tested in the *DSM-IV* field trials and the *ICD-10* revisions.

Concurrent aspects of the criterion-related validity of instruments have been most commonly addressed in the broad area of autism by looking at the convergence of diagnostic categorizations yielded by another diagnostic instrument or with clinical judgment. As shown in Table 21.3, convergent validity for three of the most common diagnostic instruments (ADI-R, ADOS, and CARS) available in English has been quite good. Convergence between the CARS and several other instruments (e.g., the Autism Behavior Checklist; Krug, Arick, & Almond, 1980; the Real-Life Rating Scale or RLRS; Freeman, Ritvo, Yokota, & Ritvo, 1986) has also been good. Also, as depicted in Table 21.3, all of the diagnostic instruments have been shown to be adequate in identifying clinically diagnosed children with autism, and have yielded relatively rare false negatives within a "prototypical" group of mildly to moderately mentally handicapped school-age children with autism.

There is more variability as instruments are used with younger (Lord, 1995; Lord et al., 1993) and older (CARS; Garfin, McCallon, & Cox, 1988; Piven, Harper, Palmer, & Arndt, 1996) populations, and with higher-functioning (Lord et al., in press; Yirmiya, Sigman, & Freeman, 1994) and lower-functioning groups (Fombonne, 1992; Lord et al., 1993). This pattern is not unique to the instruments; it reflects general difficulty in the application of standard diagnostic criteria to various developmental levels. More detailed information about this issue is included in the descriptions of particular instruments. Sometimes, this information may have been available, but the way in which data were reported, or the very small sample sizes when subsets of subjects were addressed, precluded interpretation.

An even more serious, though less widespread, issue is that of false positives. Instruments differ considerably in the number of

TABLE 21.3 Diagnostic Instruments in Autism

Instrument	Reliability			Validity			General Information			
	Interrater	Test–Retest	Internal Consistency	Construct/Content	Convergent	Discriminant Matched Sample	Published Guidelines for Diagnostic Decision	Subscales	Most Appropriate For	Level of Expertise
ABC Autism Behavior Checklist	T: variable	~	T: good S: poor	~	~		Yes	2/5	Measuring maladaptive behavior	Minimal
ADI-R Autism Diagnostic Interview—Revised	T: high I: high	High High	T: unpublished S: high	DSM-IV ICD-10	CARS	AUT/MR	Yes	3	Diagnostic clinics/research across developmental level	Requires training
ADOS-G Autism Diagnostic Observation Schedule—Generic	~	~	Unpublished	DSM-IV ICD-10	~		In progress	Not available	Specialists in any setting	Requires training
ADOS Autism Diagnostic Observation Schedule	T: good I: good	T: good I: good	Unpublished	DSM-IV ICD-10	ADI	AUT/MR HFA/LANG DEL	Yes	2	Specialists in any setting	Requires training
PL-ADOS Pre-Linguistic Autism Diagnostic Observation Schedule	T: high I: good	Unpublished	Unpublished	DSM-IV ICD-10	ADI CARS	AUT/MR/LD	Yes	2	Symptoms for research	Requires training
BSE Behavioral Summarized Evaluation	T: high I: good	~	T: factor analysis	~	~	AUT/MR/MP	~		Symptoms for research	Requires training
IRSE Infant Behavior Summarized Evaluation									Symptoms for research	
BOS Behavior Observation Scale	I: good	~		ASA	~	Limited	~	4	Screening/ nonspecialists	
BEIAAC Behavior Rating Instrument for Autistic and Atypical Children	S: good		S: variable	~	~	Limited	Yes	8	Current observation	Requires training
CARS Childhood Autism Rating Scale	T: high		T: high	DSM-III-R	ABC ADI	AUT/MR	Yes	4	Screening	Minimal/ video available
HBS Handicaps, Behavior & Skills Schedule	S: good	~	~	General	VABS	~	~	42	Services-oriented clinic	Requires training
E-2 Rimland's E-2 form	Unpublished	Unpublished	Unpublished	Kanner	~	Poor	~	~	Screening	Parent checklist
RLRS Real-Life Rating Scale	T: moderate I: marginal		T: good S: poor	ASA	CARS	AUT/MR/TYP	~	3/5	Screening	Minimal

Note: All instruments are discussed in detail in text; T = total; I = item; S = subscale; AUT = autistic; MR = mentally retarded; LANG DEL = language delayed; MP = multiple handicap; TYP = typical.

studies that include comparison groups. They also differ in the degree to which the comparison groups represent typical populations for whom a diagnosis of autism or PDD might be considered and rejected. Often, studies included a comparison group of nonautistic mentally handicapped or language-impaired subjects, without sufficient information to determine the degree to which these subjects were comparable to the autistic individuals in ways other than the characteristics of autism. Autism is associated with particularly severe communication difficulties, and it is well-established that the triad of deficits that define autism increases in frequency as the level of mental retardation increases (in individuals without cerebral palsy or genetic/chromosomal syndromes; Wing & Gould, 1979). Consequently, there is reason to be concerned that, without deliberate stratification, most comparison groups of nonautistic individuals will have markedly higher communication skills, adaptive abilities, and perhaps even general intellectual skills, than autistic participants. Thus, comparisons of such samples, even though they may be representative of the population at hand, could yield differences interpreted as specific to autism that may be more accurately linked to severity of mental handicap or communication impairment (Lord et al., 1993). This is another reason why data concerning the size, characteristics, and ascertainment of samples are especially important in evaluating instruments for the diagnosis of autism spectrum disorders. In addition, more sophisticated statistical techniques, such as latent class analyses and logistic regression, may allow researchers to take into account both the positive and the negative predictive values within a single metric (while continuing to be dependent on adequate samples on which to make comparisons).

Except for a few studies using the ADI, little information concerning the predictive validity of diagnostic instruments in autism exists. Our own follow-up study of 2-year-olds who were referred to a pediatric clinic for an evaluation of possible autism showed that both the ADI and the CARS tended to overdiagnose autism in mentally handicapped children at age 2 years (Lord, 1995). This was much less the case by age 3 years, and was less true for

the ADI (in part, because of the requirement for a "triad" of deficits) than for the CARS. On the other hand, Baron-Cohen found ADI diagnoses to be quite stable from 18 months to 3 years, for a select, possibly higher-functioning group of children identified as having autism via a screening instrument called the CHAT (Checklist for Autism in Toddlers; Baron-Cohen et al., 1996).

A follow-up study from early school age showed that retrospective ADI scores describing behavior at 4 to 5 years of age significantly predicted academic achievement and adaptive scores in adolescence and young adulthood in a group of mildly mentally handicapped to high-functioning autistic individuals (Venter et al., 1992). It was interesting that social and communication deviance at age 5 made independent contributions (in addition to various measures of expressive and receptive language and nonverbal IQ) to adaptive skill, whereas the severity of restricted and repetitive behaviors added to the predictive value of verbal and nonverbal predictors of academic achievement.

In the next section, instruments used in the diagnosis of autism and autism spectrum disorders are discussed briefly, in the approximate chronology of their introduction to the public and according to general categories of method. Descriptions are not meant to be comprehensive; some instruments are described primarily as examples of kinds of measures or novel approaches. (For more detailed information, the reader is referred to specific publications about each instrument or to a chapter by Parks, 1988, which describes many of the older instruments). Following the descriptions of some of the most frequently used instruments within general categories is a discussion of goals, and issues in the future, for the development of diagnostic instruments in autism and PDDs. When several versions of the same or a similar scale have been disseminated, the focus is on the most recent version.

DIAGNOSTIC INSTRUMENTS FOR AUTISM

Early Rating Scales and Questionnaires

The Rimland Diagnostic Form for Behavior-Disturbed Children (Form E-1) was the first widely used scale for the identification of autism (Rimland, 1968). It made an important contribution as the first systematic diagnostic assessment that focused on a carefully selected range of symptoms rather than on more abstract and inconsistently defined concepts, especially of emotional withdrawal. A revised form, Form E-2, is now available and is scored for parents, without charge, by the Autism Research Institute, in San Diego, California. The form consists of 80 multiple-choice questions about social interaction, speech patterns, and symptom development. Each item receives a plus or a minus, depending on whether it is associated with the presence or absence of autism. The total score is additive across all questions; scores ranging from −42 to +45 have been reported (Rimland, 1971). A cutoff of +20 has been set as an indication of autism. The scale is based on the core symptoms defined by Kanner in 1943 and his belief (Kanner, 1962, as cited in Rimland, 1971), that only a relatively small percentage of children labeled as autistic have "pure" autism.

Many parents have found information from the Autism Research Institute to be helpful. Comparisons with other scales suggest that the diagnosis yielded by the E-2 form is different from those offered by most other instruments. In the original validation study of the Childhood Autism Rating Scale (CARS; Schopler, Reichler, DeVellis, & Daly, 1980; also see below), over 200 children who met autism criteria and another 200 children who did not meet the criteria, received classifications on the E-2 form. Only 8 children were considered autistic by Rimland, using the E-2 form. Of those 8 children, 3 were considered nonautistic on the CARS. In another study, diagnostic overlap with the Behavior Rating Instrument for Autistic and Atypical Children (BRIAAC; Ruttenberg, Dratman, Frakner, & Wenar, 1966) was low (Cohen et al., 1978).

Basic psychometric data and scoring information for the E-2 form have not been published in scientific journals (Masters & Miller, 1970). Several studies suggested differences between reports of parents and staff using the scale (Davids, 1975; Prior & Bence, 1975), and limited differentiation between children with autism and children with other disorders. Although current diagnostic

frameworks such as *DSM-IV* and *ICD-10* continue to build on Kanner's original descriptions of autism (Kanner, 1943), the ways in which symptoms are operationalized and weighted have changed substantially. Thus, the E-2 form may be most useful to parents who are beginning to familiarize themselves with behaviors associated with autism, rather than as a measure of standard diagnoses of autism or related disorders.

Another scale that was created about the same time as Rimland's first diagnostic checklist is the Behavior Rating Instrument for Autistic and Atypical Children (BRIAAC; Ruttenberg et al., 1966; Ruttenberg, Kalish, Wenar, & Wolf, 1977). It consists of eight subscales that measure behavior in different areas, yielding a diagnosis of autism. A trained rater completes the scale after substantial observations.

The BRIAAC was important historically because it used direct observations of behaviors, defined on the basis of descriptions in case notes (Parks, 1988). Psychometrics were computed on various samples; at least one study compared autistic, mentally handicapped, and normally developing children. Reliability estimates in the form of correlations have consistently been high, although the scoring criteria are complex. More sophisticated estimates of interrater or test–retest reliability are not yet published. Results from validity studies have not indicated that diagnostic classifications based on the BRIAAC correspond to those yielded by other instruments or by clinical judgment (Cohen et al., 1978). Because it is based only on current observations, the BRIAAC has the potential to be used as a measure of therapeutic effectiveness (Wenar, Ruttenberg, Dratman, & Wolf, 1976), if it can meet more up-to-date, rigorous standards for reliability.

Another scale that has been extremely influential in the field of autism spectrum disorders is the Handicaps, Behavior, and Skills (HBS) schedule (Wing & Gould, 1978), the first widely distributed semistructured interview for parents and caregivers of children who were mentally retarded or autistic (referred to as "psychotic" at the time). It was used in the Camberwell epidemiological study and, as the source of data for that study, has had a significant effect on our understanding of the "triad of impairments" seen in autism and related disorders (Wing & Gould, 1979). A revised version is currently being completed.

The HBS is not a diagnostic instrument; it is a "framework for eliciting, systematically, clinical information to be used in conjunction with appropriate psychological tests for assessment and diagnosis" (Wing & Gould, 1978, p. 81). It provides standard questions and topics so that an interviewer can elicit from a parent or caregiver sufficient information to make an appropriate rating for each item. Formal scoring is mapped onto the Vineland Social Maturity Scale (Doll, 1965). The schedule does not yield a formal diagnosis; it results in a pattern of developmental skills and behavioral abnormalities that can be compared to typical profiles of individuals with autism-related disorders.

The HBS takes several hours to administer. Its 31 sections include questions about both diagnostic and developmental issues. Psychometrics are based on 171 children between 2 and 15 years of age who comprised an epidemiological sample of children with IQs below 50 and/or who were receiving special services in the London borough of Camberwell. Many of the children were mentally handicapped but did not have autism; a relatively small number had autism but were not mentally handicapped.

Reliability, judged on the basis of comparisons between pairs of ratings by parents, professional workers, and the authors of the HBS, averaged from 77% to 81%. Summary ratings across informants, and observations in the form of 3-point scales for each section, showed near-perfect agreement. Indexes of association were stronger for the absence of skills than for their presence, except for social development. Developmental variables were generally more reliable than ratings of behavioral abnormalities.

An unusual aspect of the reported research was the comparisons among professionals' reports, parents' reports, and the authors' direct observation of relevant behaviors. Parents tended to describe their children as more socially and emotionally responsive than did the professionals, but the parents reported more stereotyped movements and abnormal responses to sensory stimuli. The more severe the child's impairment, the better was the agreement among the reports. The mechanism for combining scores from different environments is unique and may contribute to the scale's usefulness in documenting changes in behavior.

A final scale that was important in the first group of diagnostic instruments that emerged in the 1970s was the Behavior Observation Scale (BOS; Freeman, Ritvo, Guthrie, Schroth, & Ball, 1978). An early version that consisted of a checklist of 67 behaviors was modified to create a 24-item rating of behaviors, carried out at 10-second intervals of a videotaped free play session. The BOS made a significant contribution in acknowledging the importance of controlling the environment in which a child was observed, as well as standardizing what was observed. It was an attempt to introduce quantitative techniques by using frequencies to differentiate among diagnostic groups. However, the authors noted that this approach was not completely successful, for several reasons. Frequencies of many behaviors were associated with developmental level as much as with diagnosis. In some cases, behaviors that occurred only rarely were very important, suggesting that frequency was a less critical variable than the quality of behavior.

The same authors developed another scale, the Ritvo-Freeman Real-Life Rating Scale (Freeman et al., 1986), for the purpose of assessing more accurately the behaviors that characterize autism. Emphasis is on unusual sensory behaviors. This scale can be used after observation of a 30-minute free play period. Marginal-to-adequate reliability was found for individual items; adequate subscale and total interrater reliability resulted from using kappas (Freeman et al., 1986; Sevin, Matson, Coe, Fee, & Sevin, 1991) for relatively brief samples of behavior carried out by raters with minimal training. In a sample of 24 children and adolescents with autism, 7 of 38 items did not occur at all, and 4 others were very rare. Interrater reliability for another 9 items was not significant (Seven et al., 1991). On the other hand, the correlation with the CARS total score was .77 for an autistic sample. Three (of 5) subscales—social relationships, sensory, and language—and the total had adequate-to-high internal consistency (Sturmey,

Matson, & Sevin, 1992). No specific cutoffs for diagnosis are provided. Thus, the instrument is primarily useful as a general index of diagnostic features rather than as an independent method of classification.

Childhood Autism Rating Scale

The Childhood Autism Rating Scale (CARS; Schopler, Reichler, & Renner, 1988) is the strongest, best documented, and most widely used rating scale for behaviors associated with autism. It consists of 15 items on which children and adults are rated, generally after observation, on a 4-point scale. The scale requires minimal training, which is available on videotape or in brief workshops. Points are added, and a standard cutoff of 30 points has been suggested and validated with various samples (Garfin et al., 1988; Schopler et al., 1980). Minor modifications have been suggested in which cutoffs are moved up (a few points) for very young children (Lord, 1995) and down for high-functioning adolescents and adults (Mesibov, Schopler, Schaffer, & Michal, 1989).

Most of the information about the CARS is from studies of autistic children who function in the mild-to-moderate range of mental handicap. Studies of discriminant validity from carefully matched comparison groups are not yet available, but the CARS has been shown to discriminate autistic children from children without autism who have some mental handicap (Schopler et al., 1988; Teal & Wiebe, 1986). Convergence between the CARS and the Autism Diagnostic Interview (ADI; Le Couteur et al., 1989; Lord, 1995; Sevin et al., 1991; Venter et al., 1992) and correlation between CARS total scores and RLRS total scores (Sevin et al., 1991) were good for autistic children, but less good for young, nonautistic, mentally handicapped children (Lord, 1995). Thus, the evidence that the CARS accurately identifies children with autism is stronger than the evidence that it discriminates between children with autism and mental-age-matched children with other disorders.

The CARS was created before the introduction of the DSM-IV and ICD-10 diagnostic frameworks. It shows good agreement with clinicians' judgments using DSM-III-R, though it

is somewhat overinclusive compared to strict application of the criteria (Van Bourgondien, Marcus, & Schopler, 1992). With the exception of the Van Bourgondien et al. paper, DSM-III-R has been found to be more inclusive than clinicians' judgments of autism (Herztig, Snow, New, & Shapiro, 1990; Volkmar, Cicchetti, Bregman, & Cohen, 1992). This finding suggests that, compared to the currently accepted three-domain diagnostic framework (e.g., using separate scores for social reciprocity, communicative deviance, and restricted, repetitive behaviors), the CARS probably identifies more children as having autism. Children with minimal verbal skills and/or moderate-to-severe mental handicap may be more likely to fall into the range of autism, in part because items on the CARS that rate language skill and mental handicap comprise part of the total score. For the purposes of screening or determining services, this is the direction in which error should be made (Wing & Gould, 1979). Implications may be different for research. The CARS cannot be used alone to make discriminations for complex diagnostic cases in which DSM-IV or ICD-10 criteria are the standard; however, as discussed earlier, multiple sources are important in any diagnostic decision making.

Over the years, despite repeated, careful examination by numerous investigators, the CARS total score has held up as internally consistent (Kurita, Kita, & Miyake, 1992; Sturmey et al., 1992) and reliable across raters (Kurita et al., 1992; Garfin et al., 1988; Sevin et al., 1991). Interrater reliability for individual items has been found to be more variable. Some of the scales (e.g., Relating to People, Imitation) have consistently shown high correlations among different raters' scores. Statistics such as kappas, which control for base rates, have not yet been employed (Garfin et al., 1988; Sevin et al., 1991). One of the important contributions of the CARS was the provision of specific anchor points for each item in a way that allows the rater to take into account developmental level. The difficulty with this strategy is that the definition of anchor points differs across items. Interpretation of scores on individual items, particularly given the inconsistent evidence of reliability at this level, must be carried out with care.

Besides direct observation by a clinician, for which it was designed, the CARS has been used in chart review, scored by parents and teachers, and used as part of a parent interview (Schopler et al., 1988). On the whole, classifications and correlations between raters for total scores have been relatively high across different procedures. Several studies have suggested that, compared to fathers and mothers, clinicians tend to rate behaviors as more severe (Bebko, Konstantareas, & Springer, 1987; Konstantareas & Homatidis, 1989). Other studies have found few differences (Freeman, Perry, & Factor, 1991; Schopler et al., 1988).

Overall, the CARS is probably the most widely employed rating of autism in the United States. Versions are also available in numerous languages. It has been repeatedly documented as a reliable screening instrument that can be used with minimal training across a range of situations. Its scores do not correspond to current formal diagnostic frameworks for autism, such as *DSM-IV* and *ICD-10*. For research purposes, it may identify a somewhat different population than is suggested by those systems.

Autism Behavior Checklist

The Autism Behavior Checklist (ABC) is one component of the Autism Screening Instrument for Educational Planning (ASIEP; Krug et al., 1980)—and the only one that has been evaluated psychometrically. It builds on Rimland's Form E-2, the original Kanner (1943) criteria, the Behavior Observation Schedule (Freeman et al., 1978), the BRIAAC (Ruttenberg et al., 1977), and several other sources. It contains 57 items in 5 areas: (a) sensory, (b) relating, (c) body and object use, (d) language, and (e) social interaction and self-help. No special training is required. It was intended to be completed by teachers as an initial step in educational planning. It has also been used with parents on a current basis (scores are somewhat higher than with teachers; Volkmar et al., 1988) and, retrospectively, with high-functioning children (Yirmiya et al., 1994). The rater completes dichotomous ratings that are weighted differentially according to the authors' data, and a total score is calculated. Ranges, on the basis of a very

large but unspecified sample, are provided for a high probability of autism (scores of 67 or greater), a low probability of autism (under 53) and a mixed probability. Norms and standard profiles are provided for samples of autistic, typical, deaf, and blind students.

Initial estimates for interrater reliability were high, but they were based on small samples and did not control for chance (Krug et al., 1980). Later estimates were less high (Volkmar et al., 1988). Discriminant validity has been variable, in part, depending on whether investigators generated discriminant functions from data within a group, or used the cutoffs suggested by the authors. In the latter case, there was considerable overlap between autistic and mentally handicapped populations (Volkmar et al., 1988). In the former case, diagnostic differentiation was, not surprisingly, better (Wadden, Bryson, & Rodgers, 1991). Current scores on the ABC did not meet the criteria for most of a group of high-functioning autistic adolescents, but retrospective accounts did (Yirmiya et al., 1994). Differences in studies may also be related to (a) the use of a somewhat broader definition of autism, in which case the ABC becomes more accurate in diagnosing autism, and (b) inclusion of subjects with Down syndrome, which may decrease the false positive rate (Wadden et al., 1991).

Internal consistency for the total scale is good. Various investigations have yielded different results in internal consistency and intercorrelations of the five areas; both chronological and mental age may account for much of the variance. Subscales of relating and object/body use were the strongest in one study (Sturmey et al., 1992) in terms of interitem correlations and lack of rogue items. Several investigators have suggested that discriminant validity may be equally good using even fewer items (Volkmar et al., 1994; Wadden et al., 1991).

Convergent validity between the ABC and other instruments has been measured for the CARS and the RLRS and found to be poor, suggesting that the ABC's usefulness as an independent diagnostic instrument may be limited, particularly because it was constructed before current theoretical frameworks for autism were proposed. For high-functioning autistic adolescents, retrospective parent ratings on the ABC related to whether children were considered to have "residual" autism, but diagnosis did not correspond to the cutoffs suggested by the authors of the scale (Yirmiya et al., 1994).

In emphasizing autistic symptomatology rather than prosocial behaviors, the ABC is quite different from several of the other instruments—for example, the ADI and the Vineland Adaptive Behavior Scales. Because of its emphasis on observable features associated with but not limited to autism, the ABC may be helpful in documenting changes, particularly changes in the presence of abnormal behaviors. Unlike several other autism scales that showed more consistent convergent validity with each other, the ABC is correlated with the American Association for Mental Deficiency (AAMD) Adaptive Behavior Scale—School Version (Sevin et al., 1991). In part, because of its lack of strength as a diagnostic instrument, the ABC may be useful in documenting response to treatment and educational programming.

BEHAVIORAL SUMMARIZED EVALUATION (BSE)/INFANT BEHAVIORAL SUMMARIZED EVALUATION (IBSE)

These overlapping rating scales are primarily designed to document behavioral symptoms associated with autism as they relate to neurophysiological measures. The scales are only available in French and have been used in many basic research investigations of children with autism in France. There are 20 items in the BSE, the form for older children and adults (Barthelemy et al., 1990), and 19 items within the autism factor (33 total) in the IBSE, the form for children under four years of age (Adrien et al., 1992). Items are scored on a 5-point scale. They are administered by trained raters who have experience with autistic persons; they employ direct (for the BSE) or videotaped (for the IBSE) observation, discussion of history, and access to information from multiple sources. With trained raters, most individual items have shown very good interreliability. Interrater reliability for total scores has been excellent, although ratings were not typically based on independently acquired information.

Factor analyses have shown loadings within a single autism factor, which would suggest that internal consistency has been adequate (Barthelemy et al., 1990; Adrien et al., 1992). Discriminant function analyses accurately grouped 80% to 85% of autistic and mentally handicapped children using the IBSE (Adrien et al., 1992). BSE scores were correlated with expert ratings of severity of autism (Barthelemy et al., 1990); however, specific cutoff scores for autism are not yet available. Convergent validity with other measures is not yet published. There is some suggestion that the BSE may be particularly helpful in measuring response to treatment (Boiron, Barthelemy, Adrien, Martineau, & Lelord, 1992).

Autism Diagnostic Interview—Revised (ADI-R)

The ADI-R is a semistructured, investigator-based interview for caregivers of children and adults for whom autism or PDD is a possible diagnosis. Originally developed as a research diagnostic instrument (the ADI; Le Couteur et al., 1989), the ADI-R has been modified to be appropriate for a broader age range of children. It is linked specifically to *ICD-10* and *DSM-IV* criteria (Lord, Rutter, & Le Couteur, 1994). A shortened version, consisting of about 40 items, is now available; however, even this version takes an experienced interviewer about 90 minutes to administer, which limits its usefulness for screening. Researchers are required to participate in training workshops and to establish reliability with investigators from other centers; however, clinicians may use the instrument without intensive training. Effective administration of the ADI-R requires general experience in both interviewing and working with autistic individuals.

Psychometric data for the ADI and ADI-R have been carefully acquired with attention to matching across samples and maintaining as much rater "blindness" as possible, but the data are based on very small samples. This limitation is compensated for slightly by similar psychometric findings in other major research centers that have used the ADI or

ADI-R as diagnostic instruments (Minshew & Goldstein, 1993; Piven et al., 1992; Smalley, Tanguay, Smith, & Gutierrez, 1992; Spiker et al., 1994). Interrater reliability has been good to excellent for individual items and excellent for overall scores, including those for each of the three subscales: (a) social reciprocity, (b) communication, and (c) restricted, repetitive behaviors that correspond to the *DSM-IV* and *ICD-10* domains. Test–retest reliability, on a very small sample, was also good. Change over time is reflected in items that ask whether a behavior "ever" occurred, and items that focus on "current" manifestation. On the whole, however, the ADI-R is not intended to measure change. There has been a deliberate attempt to include items that will reflect autism of varying levels of severity and at varying points in development.

Internal consistency is excellent within the three domains. Differentiation between autistic and mentally handicapped children and adults is excellent; the only restriction is that the instrument tends to be overinclusive for individuals with mental ages of less than 18 months (Lord et al., 1993). One study found that the ADI was slightly underinclusive with very high-functioning children with autism or PDDs (Yirmiya et al., 1994); another study reported that it was overinclusive (Mahoney et al., in press). Convergent validity with the CARS was excellent after age 3 years (Lord, 1995); convergent validity with the Autism Diagnostic Observation Schedule (see below) has also been good (Lord et al., 1989). ADI scores were also related to ABC scores, given by history, for a group of high-functioning children (Yirmiya et al., 1994). Because of its clear links to *DSM-IV* and *ICD-10* and its multidimensional approach, the ADI-R has the potential to provide empirical information and diagnostic guidance about other PDDs besides autism. However, cutoffs for nonautism PDDs are not yet established.

Autism Diagnostic Observation Schedule (ADOS; ADOS-G)/Pre-Linguistic Autism Diagnosis Observation Schedule (PL-ADOS)

The ADOS and PL-ADOS are standardized protocols for the observation of social and communicative behavior of children for whom a diagnosis of autism or PDDs is in question (Lord et al., 1989; DiLavore et al., 1995). The ADOS was originally developed for use with children who had fluent phrase speech; the PL-ADOS was intended for preschool children who had little or no expressive language. Recently, the two schedules have been combined and extended within a single instrument, the Autism Diagnostic Observation Schedule—Generic (ADOS-G; Lord et al., 1996). The PL-ADOS comprises most of Module 1; the ADOS comprises most of Module 3; and new modules have been added for children with some language but not fluent spontaneous speech (Module 2) and for high-functioning adolescents and adults (Module 4). The ADOS-G provides the same information as the ADOS and PL-ADOS for individuals ranging in age and development from nonverbal toddlers to verbally fluent adults of normal intelligence. Because psychometric information is not yet available for the ADOS-G, the focus of this section will be on the earlier instruments.

The ADOS and PL-ADOS were developed as companion instruments for the ADI/ADI-R. Their purpose is to provide a series of structured and semistructured "presses" for social interaction, communication, and play that can be coded online (although, often videotapes are made as well). They are scored in the context of a diagnostic algorithm for autism. The rationale is that context can have very significant effects on social-communicative behaviors. Consequently, it is important to standardize contexts as well as judgments in any diagnostic observation of these behaviors. Both instruments can be administered by a trained examiner in about 30 to 45 minutes. Training and establishment of reliability with another center are required for research, but not for clinical use. A substantial amount of experience and skill in working with individuals with autism or PDD is necessary to use either instrument effectively.

For both instruments, interrater reliability has been good for individual items and excellent for totals. Internal consistency for both instruments, within domains of social-communicative and restricted-repetitive behaviors, has also been good. Test–retest reliability has been adequate for the ADOS but has not yet been tested for the PL-ADOS. Discriminant validity has been good for diagnostic algorithms using social-communicative scores only for the ADOS, and using both social-communicative and restricted-repetitive behaviors for the PL-ADOS. There are developmental differences in the appropriateness of various cutoffs. This was one reason for the expansion of the instruments into the four modules that comprise the ADOS-G. Diagnostic algorithms for the PL-ADOS were underinclusive for children with phrase speech; about 80% accuracy was realized for autistic and/or nonautistic mentally handicapped 3–4-year-olds. For the ADOS, the diagnostic algorithm was overinclusive for children with mental handicap and difficult behaviors, and underinclusive for very high-functioning adolescents; accuracy in comparing autistic to mentally handicapped and behavior-disordered, language-impaired children was about 87%. Like the ADI/ADI-R, the ADOS and PL-ADOS are not intended to measure change or response to treatment. Also like the ADI, it is hoped that multidimensional scoring may allow quantification of nonautism PDDs, most notably PDD-NOS and Asperger's Syndrome. The ADOS and PL-ADOS may be helpful in providing to parents, therapists, and teachers useful information concerning social and communicative functioning, collected in a positive but standard context.

OTHER ISSUES

Two other issues related to measurement in autism spectrum disorders involve measuring change and providing initial screening with very young children. Often, investigators have attempted to use diagnostic instruments to measure change in response to treatment. On the whole, this approach has not been very successful. In part, success has been lacking because most diagnostic instruments were designed to include a wide range of deficits associated with autism and are not sufficiently sensitive to changes within an individual. In addition, expectations and contexts for behavior, especially among young children, frequently change with time. A child may be showing substantial improvement and acquisition of specific behaviors, but this improvement may not be measurable if the basis of comparison is the quality of interaction seen in typical children.

A number of well-known instruments measure behaviors that are not specific to autism but are frequently found in association with it. These instruments have often been used in medication research. The most prominent one is the Aberrant Behavior Checklist (ABC; Aman, 1994; Aman & Singh, 1986). The Autism Behavior Checklist (also known as the ABC; Krug et al., 1980), although found to be less appropriate as a diagnostic instrument, has been helpful in indicating the degree of overtly abnormal or impairing behaviors produced by autistic youngsters, particularly those who are both autistic and mentally handicapped. The Children's Global Assessment Scale (Shaffer et al., 1983) gives a general measure of impairment that may be helpful for some investigators. The Maladaptive Behavior Scale, from the Vineland Adaptive Behavior Scale (Perry & Factor, 1989), provides counts of particular adaptive behaviors. The author's own research has revealed more quantifiable changes if identical items are readministered over extended time periods (several years) on the direct observation schedules (e.g., ADOS) than are found in parents' reports of the ADI, because of the ADI's very broad focus. The Real-Life Rating Scale (Freeman et al., 1986) has also been used toward this goal. Most of these scales were not designed for this purpose and do not have psychometric data to support this use. The exception is the Aberrant Behavior Checklist.

Another very complex issue is the question of screening. Several authors have attempted to identify those few items on various scales that best indicate autism. This effort has been more of an intellectual enterprise than a question of direct screening, but it has suggested that one can obtain a relatively good initial identification of possibly autistic "populations" by asking general questions about social reciprocity, about looking through and being aware of people, and about a particular combination of sensory deficits (Oswald & Volkmar, 1991; Siegel, Vukicevic, Elliot, & Kramer, 1989). In all of these instances, "screening" was done by trained coders reading records written by experienced clinicians.

Their activity was "screening" only in the sense that they scored a few items; they were not nonexperts assessing large numbers of children.

Recently, the CHAT (Checklist for Autism in Toddlers; Baron-Cohen, Allen, & Gillberg, 1992; Baron-Cohen et al., 1996), a measure intended as a screening instrument for 18-month-olds, has been introduced. These investigators have carried out a large-scale epidemiological study in the United Kingdom. Their screening procedures have been very successful in correctly identifying relatively high-functioning "autistic" children. These authors emphasize the initiation of joint attention through pointing, as well as the absence of pretend play. The results have been influential in bringing early childhood researchers' attention to the possibility and need of assessing, in a quite specific way, some aspects of social behavior in very young children. However, there are several concerns. First, across the two papers that described use of the CHAT, three different ways of calculating who might and might not have autism are suggested. However, why and how use of these methods changed has not been discussed explicitly.

Second, the sequential steps that the investigators employed in order to reach the final number of "autistic" children are not clearly described. In the latest study (Baron-Cohen et al., 1996), children were identified through administration of the CHAT by nurses, but additional screening to eliminate inappropriate cases was carried out on the telephone by an experienced clinical psychologist. It may be that, in any screening for autism, it will be necessary to have a standard measure and then a follow-up, perhaps on the telephone, by an experienced clinician, in order to decide who receives further evaluation. Until this procedure is as clearly described as any other part of the research, it is not possible to judge the accuracy of the instrument.

Third, the population was not representative of children with autism or autism spectrum disorders. In the epidemiological study (Baron-Cohen et al., 1996), most mentally handicapped children were not included in the sample. There was a significantly higher proportion of children who were autistic but not mentally handicapped than one would expect in a typical population of autistic persons. Because many autistic children who are mentally handicapped are not known to be so until they are diagnosed with autism, it is not quite clear how these children were excluded or why these investigators had such an unusual distribution. The major differentiation needed is not in identifying autistic persons from normal persons, but rather, identifying them from persons with delays. The current approach may therefore be of limited practical usefulness, until it is applied to more relevant populations.

Attention to specific social variables, as in the CHAT, can clearly be very useful in helping nonexpert professionals notice possible autism and begin to identify, very early on, who may benefit from services. It will be important for investigators and clinicians interested in the method to get more detailed information about what was actually done, and with whom, in order to make informed decisions about the usefulness of the procedure.

CONCLUSIONS

Overall, there is a wealth of information and options for the diagnosis of autism, but much remains to be done to make the present techniques stronger and broader in scope. There will always be trade-offs between getting the maximum amount of meaningful information and the highest validity versus being able to replicably record and make repeatable decisions about information. Users of diagnostic instruments must be aware of the needs of their particular situation and population in order to make the most informed choice of instruments. In general, as instruments are evaluated, keeping examiners "blind" to diagnosis, attempting to use instruments with parents who have not yet received a diagnosis, and expecting measurements of test–retest reliability and appropriate analysis of reliability statistics, will aid in the interpretability of the instruments. Clear descriptions of exactly how instruments have been used and are intended to be used, including cutoffs if categorical discriminations are implied, are also critical.

It seems particularly important to recognize that a variety of needs having to do with formal diagnoses may not be met by a single instrument. Screening of large populations for possible autism is most likely to occur with very young children. It must be coordinated with developmental screening because delays in language are inherently entwined with the recognition of autism in many children. Procedures for early diagnosis, after a child has been identified as possibly having an autism spectrum disorder, may be quite different from screening methods. Diagnostic procedures involve far fewer children and need to have closer links to individual education and treatment plans, as well as to possible multiaxial diagnoses.

For research purposes, there is a need for lifetime diagnoses and standard procedures that presumably yield the same final interpretation (though not necessarily the same raw data) for the same individual at multiple points in his or her life. In contrast, there is also a need for measurements of change. It seems very unlikely that any one instrument will accomplish all these purposes. However, for each of these needs, there are promising candidates. Ensuring that the relationship between various instruments and goals is well understood will also increase the usefulness of the endeavor. Recognizing that other factors, particularly the level of development and language skill, have marked effects on most measurements in autism and PDDs is an important step in considering the meaning of any clinical or research result.

Finally, there is a great need for extension of the current instruments to diagnosis of disorders other than autism that are within the autism spectrum. Part of the difficulty, as discussed in later chapters, is that the definitions of these disorders, and their discrimination from autism, are not as clear as we would like. However, reliable ways of formally substantiating diagnoses such as PDD-NOS, Asperger's Syndrome, and Atypical Autism are needed so that researchers and clinicians can make informed decisions about the usefulness of these concepts. Various instruments have been proposed to study these disorders, but, at this point, they have little relationship to each other, have not been found to be reliable, and offer only limited scientific usefulness. Priority should be given to researchers' working together to derive operationalized definitions and specific proposals for how their approaches add

to or fit in with those of others. In the meantime, clinicians need to keep informed about the kind of information a particular instrument provides and to consider whether that information is appropriate for their immediate clinical needs.

Cross-References

Categorical diagnostic systems are discussed in Chapters 1–7; other aspects of assessments are addressed in Chapters 19 and 20.

REFERENCES

Adrien, J.L., Barthelemy, C., Perrot, A., Roux, S., Lenoir, P., Hameury, L., & Sauvage, D. (1992). Validity and reliability of the Infant Behavioral Summarized Evaluation (IBSE): A rating scale for the assessment of young children with autism and development disorders. *Journal of Autism and Developmental Disorders, 22*, 375–394.

Aman, M.G. (1994). Instruments for assessing treatment effects in developmentally disabled populations. *Assessment in Rehabilitation and Exceptionality, 1*, 1–20.

Aman, M.G., & Singh, N.N. (1986). *Manual for the Aberrant Behavior Checklist.* East Aurora, NY: Slosson Educational Publications.

American Psychiatric Association. (1994). *Diagnostic and statistical manual of mental disorders* (4th ed.). Washington, DC: Author.

Baron-Cohen, S., Allen, J., & Gillberg, C. (1992). Can autism be detected at 18 months? The needle, the haystack, and the CHAT. *British Journal of Psychiatry, 161*, 839–843.

Baron-Cohen, S., Cox, A., Baird, G., Swettenham, J., Nightingale, N., Morgan, K., Auriol, D., & Charman, T. (1996). Psychological markers in the detection of autism in infancy in a large population. *British Journal of Psychiatry, 168*, 158–163.

Barthelemy, C., Adrien, J.L., Tanguay, P., Garreau, B., Fermanian, J., Roux, S., Sauvage, D., & Lelord, G. (1990). The Behavioral Summarized Evaluation: Validity and reliability of a scale for the assessment of autistic behaviors. *Journal of Autism and Developmental Disorders, 20*, 189–204.

Bebko, J.M., Konstantareas, M.M., & Springer, J. (1987). Parent and professional evaluations of family stress associated with characteristics of autism. *Journal of Autism and Developmental Disorders, 17*, 565–576.

Bird, H.R., Gould, M.S., & Staghezza, B. (1992). Aggregating data from multiple informants in child psychiatry epidemiological research. *Journal of the American Academy of Child and Adolescent Psychiatry, 31,* 78–85.

Borion, M., Barthelemy, C., Adrien, J.L., Martineau, J., & Lelord, G. (1992). The assessment of psychophysiological dysfunction in children using the BSE scale before and during therapy. *Acta Paedopsychiatrica, 55,* 203–206.

Boucher, J. (in press). Language profiles in autistic and mentally retarded children: Implications for research methodology. *Journal of Autism and Developmental Disabilities.*

Cicchetti, D.V., & Sparrow, S.A. (1981). Developing criteria for establishing interrater reliability of specific items: Applications to assessment of adaptive behavior. *American Journal of Mental Deficiency, 86,* 127–137.

Cohen, D.J., Caparulo, B.K., Gold, J.R., Waldo, M.C., Shaywitz, B., Ruttenberg, B.A., & Rimland, B. (1978). Agreement in diagnosis: Clinical assessment and behavior rating scales for pervasively disturbed children. *Journal of the American Academy of Child Psychiatry, 17,* 589–603.

Davids, A. (1975). Childhood psychosis: The problem of differential diagnosis. *Journal of Autism and Childhood Schizophrenia, 5,* 129–138.

DiLavore, P., Lord, C., & Opsahl, A. (1994). *The early diagnosis of autism: Year one.* Paper presented at the annual meeting of the American Academy of Child and Adolescent Psychiatry, New York.

DiLavore, P., Lord, C., & Rutter, M. (1995). Pre-Linguistic Autism Diagnostic Observation Schedule (PL/ADOS). *Journal of Autism and Developmental Disorders, 25,* 355–379.

Doll, E.A. (1965). *Vineland Social Maturity Scale.* Circle Pines, MN: American Guidance Service.

Fombonne, E. (1992). Diagnostic assessment in a sample of autistic and developmentally impaired adolescents. *Journal of Autism and Developmental Disorders, 22,* 563–582.

Freeman, B.J., Ritvo, E.R., Guthrie, D., Schroth, P., & Ball, J. (1978). The Behavior Observation Scale for autism: Initial methodology, data analysis, and preliminary findings on 89 children. *Journal of the American Academy of Child Psychiatry, 17,* 576–588.

Freeman, B.J., Ritvo, E.R., Yokota, A., & Ritvo, A. (1986). A scale for rating symptoms of patients with the syndrome of autism in real-life settings. *Journal of the American Academy of Child Psychiatry, 25,* 130–136.

Freeman, N.L., Perry, A., & Factor, D.C. (1991). Child behavior as stressors: Replicating and extending the use of the CARS as a measure of stress: A research note. *Journal of Child Psychology & Psychiatry & Allied Disciplines, 32,* 1025–1030.

Garfin, D.G., McCallon, D., & Cox, R. (1988). Validity and reliability of the Childhood Autism Rating Scale with autistic adolescents. *Journal of Autism and Developmental Disorders, 18,* 367–378.

Ghaziuddin, M., Tsai, L., & Ghaziuddin, N. (1992). Brief report: A comparison of the diagnostic criteria for Asperger's Syndrome. *Journal of Autism and Developmental Disorders, 22*(4), 643–649.

Happé, F.G.E. (1995). The role of age and mental ability in the theory of mind task performance of subjects with autism. *Child Development, 66,* 843–855.

Hertzig, M.E., Snow, M.E., New, E., & Shapiro, T. (1990). *DSM-III* and *DSM-III-R* diagnosis of autism and Pervasive Developmental Disorder in nursery school children. *Journal of the American Academy of Child Psychiatry, 29,* 123–126.

Hobson, R.P. (1991). Methodological issues for experiments on autistic individuals' perception and understanding of emotion. *Journal of the American Academy of Child and Adolescent Psychiatry, 32,* 1135–1158.

Holroyd, S., & Baron-Cohen, S. (1993). Brief report: How far can people with autism go in developing a theory of mind? *Journal of Autism and Developmental Disorders, 23,* 379–385.

Kanner, L. (1943). Autistic disturbances of affective contact. *Nervous Child, 2,* 217–250.

Konstantareas, M.M., & Homatidis, S. (1989). Assessing child symptom severity and its stress in parents of autistic children. *Journal of Child Psychology and Psychiatry, 30,* 459–470.

Kraemer, H.C. (1992). Measurement of reliability for categorical data in medical research. *Statistical Methods in Medical Research, 1,* 183–199.

Krug, D.A., Arick, J., & Almond, P. (1980). Behavior checklist for identifying severely handicapped individuals with high levels of autistic behavior. *Journal of Child Psychology and Psychiatry, 21,* 221–229.

Kurita, H., Kita, M., & Miyake, Y. (1992). A comparative study of development and symptoms among disintegrative psychosis, and infantile autism with and without speech loss. *Journal of Autism and Developmental Disorders, 22,* 175–188.

Le Couteur, A., Rutter, M., Lord, C., Rios, P., Robertson, S., Holdgrafer, M., & McLennan,

J.D. (1989). Autism Diagnostic Interview: A semistructured interview for parents and caregivers of autistic persons. *Journal of Autism and Developmental Disorders, 19,* 363–387.

Lord, C. (1995). Follow-up of two-year-olds referred for possible autism. *Journal of Child Psychology and Psychiatry, 36,* 1365–1382.

Lord, C., Pickles, A., McLennan, J., Rutter, M., Bregman, J., Folstein, S., Fombonne, E., Leboyer, M., & Minshew, N. (in press). Diagnosing autism: Analysis of data from the Autism Diagnostic Interview. *Journal of Autism and Developmental Disorders.*

Lord, C., & Rutter, M. (1994). Autism and pervasive developmental disorders. In M. Rutter, L. Hersov, & E. Taylor (Eds.), *Child and adolescent psychiatry: Modern approaches* (3rd ed., pp. 569–593). Oxford, England: Blackwell.

Lord, C., Rutter, M., & DiLavore, P. (1996). *Autism Diagnostic Observation Schedule—Generic (ADOS-G).* Unpublished manuscript, University of Chicago.

Lord, C., Rutter, M., Goode, S., Heemsbergen, J., Jordan, H., Mawhood, L., & Schopler, E. (1989). Autism Diagnostic Observation Schedule: A standardized observation of communicative and social behavior. *Journal of Autism and Developmental Disorders, 19,* 185–212.

Lord, C., Rutter, M., & Le Couteur, A. (1994). Autism Diagnostic Interview—Revised: A revised version of a diagnostic interview for caregivers of individuals with possible pervasive developmental disorders. *Journal of Autism and Developmental Disorders, 24,* 659–685.

Lord, C., Storoschuk, S., Rutter, M., & Pickles, A. (1993). Using the ADI-R to diagnose autism in preschool children. *Infant Mental Health Journal, 14,* 234–252.

Mahoney, W., Szatmari, P., Maclean, J., Bryson, S., Bartolucci, G., Walter, S., Hoult, L., & Jones, M. (in press). *Reliability and accuracy of differentiating pervasive developmental disorder subtypes.* Unpublished manuscript, McMaster University.

Masters, J.C., & Miller, D.E. (1970). Early infantile autism: A methodological critique. *Journal of Abnormal Psychology, 75,* 342–343.

Mattison, R., Cantwell, D.P., Russell, A.T., & Will, L. (1979). A comparison of *DSM-II* and *DSM-III* in the diagnosis of childhood psychiatric disorders: 2. Interrater agreement. *Archives of General Psychiatry, 36,* 1217–1222.

Mawhood, L. (1994). *Follow-up of high-functioning autistic children and children with severe language impairment into adulthood.* Unpublished doctoral dissertation, University of London.

Mayes, L.C., & Zigler, E. (1992). An observational study of the affective concomitants of mastery in infants. *Journal of Child Psychology & Psychiatry & Allied Disciplines, 33,* 659–667.

Mesibov, G., Schopler, E., Schaffer, B., & Michal, N. (1989). Use of the Childhood Autism Rating Scale with autistic adolescents and adults. *Journal of the American Academy of Child and Adolescent Psychiatry, 28,* 538–541.

Minshew, N.J., & Goldstein, G. (1993). Is autism an amnesic disorder? Evidence from the California Verbal Learning Test. *Neuropsychology, 7,* 209–216.

Mundy, P., Sigman, M.D., Ungerer, J., & Sherman, T. (1986). Defining the social deficits of autism: The contribution of non-verbal communication measures. *Journal of Child Psychology & Psychiatry & Allied Disciplines, 27,* 657–669.

Oswald, D., & Volkmar, F. (1991). Brief report: Signal detection analysis of items from the Autism Behavior Checklist. *Journal of Autism and Developmental Disorders, 21,* 543–549.

Parks, S.L. (1988). Psychometric instruments available for the assessment of autistic children. In E. Schopler & G. Mesibov (Eds.), *Diagnosis and assessment in autism* (pp. 123–136). New York: Plenum Press.

Perry, A., & Factor, D.C. (1989). Psychometric validity and clinical usefulness of the Vineland Adaptive Behavior Scale and the AAMD Adaptive Behavior Scale for an autistic sample. *Journal of Autism and Developmental Disorders 19,* 41–55.

Piven, J., Harper, J., Palmer, P., & Arndt, S. (1996). Course of behavioral change in autism: A retrospective study of high-IQ adolescents and adults. *Journal of the American Academy of Child and Adolescent Psychiatry, 35,* 523–529.

Piven, J., Nehme, E., Simon, J., Barta, P., Pearlson, G., & Folstein, S.E. (1992). Magnetic resonance imaging in autism: Measurement of the cerebellum, pons and fourth ventricle. *Biological Psychiatry, 31,* 491–504.

Prior, M., & Bence, R. (1975). A note on the validity of the Rimland Diagnostic Checklist. *Journal of Clinical Psychology, 31,* 510–513.

Rimland, B. (1968). On the objective diagnosis of infantile autism. *Acta Paedopsychiatrica, 35,* 146–161.

Rimland, B. (1971). The differentiation of childhood psychoses: An analysis of checklists for

2,218 psychotic children. *Journal of Autism and Childhood Schizophrenia, 1,* 161–174.

Ruttenberg, B.A., Dratman, R., Frakner, T.A., & Wenar, C. (1966). An instrument for evaluating autistic children. *Journal of the American Academy of Child Psychiatry, 5,* 453–478.

Ruttenberg, B.A., Kalish, B.I., Wenar, C., & Wolf, E.G. (1977). *Behavior rating instrument for autistic and other atypical children* (rev. ed.). Philadelphia: Developmental Center for Autistic Children.

Rutter, M., Mawhood, L., & Howlin, P. (1992). Language delay and social development. In P. Fletcher & D. Hall (Eds.), *Specific speech and language disorders in children: Correlates, characteristics and outcomes* (pp. 63–78). London: Whurr.

Sanchez, L.E., Adams, P.B., Uysal, S., Hallin, A., Campbell, M., & Small, A.M. (1995). A comparison of live and videotape ratings: Comipramine and halperidol in autism. *Psychopharmacology Bulletin, 31,* 371–378.

Schopler, E. (1976). Towards reducing behavior problems in autistic children. In L. Wing (Ed.), *Early childhood autism* (pp. 221–246). London: Pergamon Press.

Schopler, E., & Reichler, R.J. (1972). How well do parents understand their own psychotic child? *Journal of Autism and Childhood Schizophrenia, 2,* 387–400.

Schopler, E., Reichler, R., DeVellis, R., & Daly, K. (1980). Toward objective classification of childhood autism: Childhood Autism Rating Scale (CARS). *Journal of Autism and Developmental Disorders, 10,* 91–103.

Schopler, E., Reichler, R.J., & Renner, B.R. (1988). *The Childhood Autism Rating Scale (CARS).* Los Angeles: Western Psychological Services.

Sevin, J.A., Matson, J.L., Coe, D.A., Fee, V.E., & Sevin, B.M. (1991). A comparison and evaluation of three commonly used autism scales. *Journal of Autism and Developmental Disorders, 21,* 417–432.

Shaffer, D., Gould, M., Brasic, J., Ambrosini, P., Fisher, P., Bird, H., & Aluwahlia, S. (1983). A Children's Global Assessment Scale (CGAS). *Archives of General Psychiatry, 40,* 1228–1231.

Siegel, B., Vukicevic, J., Elliot, G., & Kramer, H. (1989). The use of signal detection theory to assess DSM-III-R criteria for autistic disorder. *American Academy of Child and Adolescent Psychiatry, 28,* 542–548.

Sigman, M., & Ungerer, J. (1984). Attachment behaviors in autistic children. *Journal of Autism and Developmental Disorders, 14,* 231–244.

Smalley, S.L., Tanguay, P.E., Smith, M., & Gutierrez, G. (1992). Autism and tuberous sclerosis. *Journal of Autism and Developmental Disorders, 22,* 339–355.

Smith, I.M., & Bryson, S.E. (1994). Imitation and action in autism: A critical review. *Psychological Bulletin, 116,* 259–273.

Spencer, A. (1993). *Separation and reunion in autistic two-year-olds.* Unpublished doctoral dissertation, University of North Carolina, Chapel Hill.

Spiker, D., Lotspeich, L., Kraemer, H.C., Hallmayer, J., McMahon, W., Peterson, B., Nicholas, P., Pingree, C., Wiese-Slater, S., Chiotti, C., Lee Wong, D., Dimicelli, S., Ritvo, E., Cavalli-Sforza, L.L., & Ciaranello, R. (1994). Genetics of autism: Characteristics of affected and unaffected children from 37 multiplex families. *American Journal of Medical Genetics, 54,* 27–35.

Stone, W.L., & Lemanek, K.L. (1990). Parental report of social behaviors in autistic preschoolers. *Journal of Autism and Developmental Disorders, 20,* 513–522.

Sturmey, P., Matson, J.L., & Sevin, J.A. (1992). Brief report: Analysis of the internal consistency of three autism scales. *Journal of Autism and Developmental Disorders, 22,* 321–328.

Szatmari, P., Archer, L., Fishman, S., Streiner, D.L., & Wilson, F. (1995). Asperger's Syndrome and autism: Differences in behavior, cognition, and adaptive functioning. *Journal of the American Academy of Child and Adolescent Psychiatry, 34,* 1662–1671.

Teal, M.B., & Wiebe, M.J. (1986). A validity analysis of selected instruments used to assess autism. *Journal of Autism and Developmental Disorders, 16,* 485–494.

Van Bourgondien, M.E., Marcus, L., & Schopler, E. (1992). Comparison of *DSM-III-R* and Childhood Autism Rating Scale diagnoses of autism. *Journal of Autism and Developmental Disorders, 22,* 493–506.

Venter, A., Lord, C., & Schopler, E. (1992). A follow-up study of high-functioning autistic children. *Journal of Child Psychology and Psychiatry, 33,* 489–507.

Volkmar, F. (1997). In F. Volkmar & D. Cohen (Eds.), *The handbook of autism and pervasive developmental disorders.* New York: John Wiley & Sons.

Volkmar, F.R., Cicchetti, D.V., Bregman, J., & Cohen, D.J. (1992). Three diagnostic systems for autism: *DSM-III, DSM-III-R, and ICD-10. Journal of Autism and Developmental Disorders, 22,* 483–492.

Volkmar, F.R., Cicchetti, D.V., Dykens, E., Sparrow, S., Leckman, J.F., & Cohen, D.F. (1988). An evaluation of the Autism Behavior Checklist. *Journal of Autism and Developmental Disorders, 18,* 81–97.

Volkmar, F.R., Klin, A., Siegal, B., Szatmari, P., Lord, C., Campbell, M., Freeman, B.J., Cicchetti, D.V., Rutter, M., Kline, W., Buitelaar, J., Hattab, Y., Fombonne, E., Fuentes, J., Werry, J., Stone, W., Kerbeshian, J., Hoshino, Y., Bregman, J., Loveland, K., Szymanski, L., & Towbin, K. (1994). Field trial for autistic disorder in *DSM-IV. American Journal of Psychiatry, 151*(9), 1361–1367.

Wadden, N., Bryson, S., & Rodgers, R. (1991). A closer look at the Autism Behavior Checklist: Discriminant validity and factor structure. *Journal of Autism and Developmental Disorders, 21,* 529–542.

Wechsler, D. (1981). *Manual for the Wechsler Intelligence Scale-Revised.* San Antonio, TX: Psychological Corporation.

Wechsler, D. (1991). *Manual for the Wechsler Intelligence Scale for Children* (3rd ed.). San Antonio, TX: Psychological Corporation.

Wenar, C., Ruttenberg, B., Dratman, M., & Wolf, E.G. (1967). Changing autistic behavior: The effectiveness of three milieus. *Archives of General Psychiatry, 17,* 26–34.

Wing, L., & Attwood, A. (1987). Syndromes of autism and atypical development. In D.J. Cohen & A.M. Donnellan (Eds.), *Handbook of autism and pervasive developmental disorders.* New York: Wiley.

Wing, L., & Gould, J. (1978). Systematic recording of behaviors and skills of retarded and psychotic children. *Journal of Autism and Childhood Schizophrenia, 8,* 79–97.

Wing, L., & Gould, J. (1979). Severe impairments of social interaction and associated abnormalities in children: Epidemiology and classification. *Journal of Autism and Developmental Disorders, 9,* 11–29.

Yirmiya, N., Sigman, M., & Freeman, B.J. (1994). Comparison between diagnostic instruments for identifying high-functioning children with autism. *Journal of Autism and Developmental Disorders, 24,* 281–291.

CHAPTER 22

Issues of Curriculum and Classroom Structure

J. GREGORY OLLEY AND CHRISTINE E. REEVE

For over 50 years, research on autism and the education of children with autism has emphasized *methods* of instruction more than *content* of instruction. Curriculum has taken a back seat to methods of treatment. Competing approaches to instruction have vied for acceptance, sometimes on the basis of strong research, more often not. Schopler (1994) identified 28 approaches to treatment of individuals with autism. Although most of these 28 have enjoyed a brief time in the headlines of newspapers and have been featured on television programs, few offer any objective evidence for their effectiveness. Furthermore, surprisingly few approaches have specified exactly what it is that they expect to improve. In other words, they do not have an explicit curriculum.

In fairness, it should be emphasized that research on the effectiveness of education or any other treatment approach for autism is very difficult and lengthy. Most well-designed research has been carried out in an effort to teach a small number of skills to a small number of children. Few comprehensive curricula for students with autism have been evaluated objectively. Yet curriculum is an essential component of any effective education or treatment plan.

This chapter reviews the major published approaches to curriculum and classroom structure for children and youth with autism. The emphasis is on approaches that have been thoroughly researched, but because there are many gaps in the research literature, the chapter also notes widely accepted practices that lack thorough evaluation. Finally, the chapter reviews individual studies that have demonstrated how to teach important skills to children with autism, although such skills may not have been integrated into a formal curriculum.

CURRICULUM, METHODS, AND THEIR APPLICATIONS

In addition to the focus on methods, or how to teach children with autism, educational approaches must also have explicit or implicit content. The content and the sequence of instruction are the elements of curriculum.

Research in recent years has identified effective curricula and methods, and the professional community has come to demand evidence of effectiveness. The Association for Behavior Analysis Position Statement on Clients' Rights to Effective Behavioral Treatment emphasizes "an obligation to use only those procedures demonstrated by research to be effective" (Van Houten et al., 1988). Despite this strong professional stand, a scientific research base is not a requirement for popularity of treatment approaches. In fact, proponents of some approaches to the treatment of autism, such as gentle teaching (McGee, Menolascino, Hobbs, & Menousek, 1987), facilitated communication (Biklen, 1991), and the option method (Kaufman, 1976), have been unsupportive or have actively discouraged research, arguing that it is not in the best interests of consumers. In such a climate of opinion, it is essential to identify those approaches that have proven effectiveness and to make knowledge about such programs available to parents and policy makers.

APPROACHES TO CURRICULUM

As education for students with autism has become more available in the past three decades, curricula have changed. Viewpoints on curriculum have been diverse, but most do have some common features. Curricula are usually tied closely to the remediation of the learning deficits that are central to autism. They primarily address either language or social skill deficits, or both. Earlier curricula put a more explicit emphasis on the elimination of problem or interfering behavior as a prerequisite to learning adaptive skills (Lovaas, 1981). More recent curricula, as we shall see, have incorporated the management of difficult behavior into their ongoing instruction. Further, most published research on curriculum has been oriented toward young children, but innovative approaches exist for all ages.

The curricular emphasis for students with autism has been, alternately, on the normal developmental sequence and on the unusual learning problems of autism. Other recent approaches, borrowing from curricula for students with severe mental retardation, have emphasized individual design based on functional skills that will be needed throughout life. As in all research on autism treatment, issues of curriculum, teaching methods, and assessment become intertwined. In some respects, this conceptual overlap has been beneficial because it has led to integrated rather than competing approaches.

The Developmental Approach

Most educators, particularly those working with young children, are highly aware of the typical pattern and sequence of learning. Because assessment instruments are usually based on developmental milestones, curricula have often reflected the typical sequence of development. This approach is intuitively appealing because it allows curriculum to be individualized. If a child is shown to be developing more slowly than peers in certain areas, the developmental curriculum can address those areas of deficit. Several writers have noted the advantages and limitations of the developmental approach (Dyer & Peck, 1987; Mirenda & Donnellan, 1987; Peck et al., 1986). This approach is based on the assumption that certain developmental skills are prerequisites to learning the next step, but this assumption is not always valid. Steps or sequences seen in the typical child may or may not apply to children with autism. Deficits identified by developmental tests may or may not be important areas for development or for school learning. Despite their intuitive appeal, curricula based on developmental sequences are not universally effective.

Curricula Designed for the Special Characteristics of Autism

Because the learning and development of children with autism are in many ways different from those of the typical child, some curricula have been designed to address these unusual characteristics.

TEACCH

The most widely disseminated approach of this type is that of Eric Schopler and his colleagues at Division TEACCH (Treatment and Education of Autistic and related Communication handicapped CHildren) of the University of North Carolina at Chapel Hill. In this model, each child receives an individualized assessment designed for the special learning characteristics of autism (Schopler, Reichler, Bashford, Lansing, & Marcus, 1990). Using this assessment and ongoing classroom observation, a curriculum is designed for each child, based on areas of deficit and learning style (Schopler, Reichler, & Lansing, 1980). The curriculum is further influenced by parents' knowledge of their own child and ranking of their child's needs (Schopler, Mesibov, Shigley, & Bashford, 1984). Although Schopler and his colleagues (Schopler, Lansing, & Waters, 1983) have published examples of teaching activities, the TEACCH curriculum is quite individualized. The teaching is directed to each child's strengths, which are often in the motor and visual areas, and to "emerging" skills in which the student is likely to experience success. Thus, TEACCH combines some elements of the developmental model with approaches that address the special learning problems of children with autism.

Schopler and his colleagues have not conducted research using control groups to evaluate the overall effectiveness of the TEACCH classroom approach, but most of the elements of the TEACCH approach to curriculum are well supported in the research literature. Lord and Schopler (1994) cited developmental gains in follow-up of students in TEACCH preschool services. These studies (and the evaluation data of other autism programs) were not designed to examine the effects of curriculum.

Cognitive Curricula

Whereas the TEACCH approach addresses many aspects of autism, two recent approaches have focused on remediation of the "cognitive" deficits in autism. Powell and Jordan (1992) described their application of a problem-solving approach to curriculum. Rather than focusing on the development of skills, these writers emphasized teaching flexible thinking and the use of strategies in an effort to develop more independent learners. They cited no research evidence for their approach, which is based on the theory of mind research of Baron-Cohen (1988).

Butera and Haywood (1992, 1995) have also offered a cognitive approach through the application of aspects of their Bright Start curriculum to students with autism. The authors cited research on the effectiveness of Bright Start for preschool-age children from environments that put them at risk for developmental and learning problems. They have begun to apply aspects of the curriculum to children with autism, although no outcome studies are yet available. This curriculum addresses several learning areas that commonly present problems in autism: deficits in attention/arousal, social interaction, communication, and motivation. Unlike curricula based on specific developmental skill deficits, cognitive curricula aim to develop thinking skills or cognitive processes that are typically very weak in children with autism. Although research data are not yet available, the goals of this approach are quite ambitious. In their efforts to teach children with autism to think and solve problems like typical children, these researchers are attempting to remediate some of the central characteristics of autism.

Daily Life Therapy

Daily Life Therapy was originated in Japan, in 1964, by the late Kiyo Kitahara. In 1987, this approach began to be replicated (in most respects) when the Boston Higashi School opened, in Lexington, Massachusetts. Whereas the Japanese application of this approach integrates autistic students with typically developing students, the Massachusetts school serves only students with autism. Quill, Gurry, and Larkin (1989) gave a detailed description of the Massachusetts program in response to many American parents' difficulties in understanding Kitahara's writings. Quill and her colleagues did not attempt to evaluate the program's effectiveness and noted that "It appears to be as much a philosophy of education as a curriculum for children with autism." In fact, it is less a curriculum designed for the special characteristics of autism and more an expression of Japanese culture. The Daily Life Therapy curriculum emphasizes physical training and art forms in a group format. The music instruction is in choral singing. The diverse physical activities are intended to decrease self-stimulation, self-injury, and hyperactivity. The academic curriculum in the elementary and secondary grades includes social studies, mathematics, and language. The Japanese emphasis on moral development is expressed in goals such as harmony and opening the hearts of the children.

Unlike the American emphasis on individualized curriculum and intensive teaching for each child, Daily Life Therapy emphasizes group participation and consistency of curriculum. The frequently repeated patterns of group activities are intended to lead to uniformity of behavior. Teaching is done in highly structured group routines, usually involving motor exercises. There are few materials, and emphasis is more on worksheets than on manipulation of materials.

Quill et al. (1989) noted other ways in which Daily Life Therapy differs from most Western approaches to autism. The lack of emphasis on language skills, developmental sequences, and functional skills was noteworthy. To date, no objective evaluation of the effectiveness of Daily Life Therapy has been reported.

Ecological Approaches

Curriculum for students with severe disabilities (including autism) has been greatly influenced by the work of Lou Brown and his colleagues at the University of Wisconsin (e.g., Brown, Branston, Baumgart, et al., 1979; Brown, Branston, Hamre-Nietupski, et al., 1979). Although the ecological approach does not address the specific learning characteristics of students with autism, it has been widely adopted for this population.

An ecological approach emphasizes teaching functional skills—those for which the student will have a need throughout life. Like the TEACCH approach, the ecological approach is based on assessment of skill deficits, but the assessment emphasizes the student's ability to use functional skills in natural environments. The assessment (or "ecological inventory") takes place in the community or home, rather than in the classroom or clinic, and it is criterion-referenced; that is, the important outcome is how well the student can perform functional skills in community, recreation/leisure, domestic, and vocational settings. The resulting individualized curriculum emphasizes useful skills. In using this approach, the teacher of students with autism will have to make some important adaptions to be sure that the individual steps being taught and the methods of instruction are appropriate. Whereas the developmental curriculum approach has been mostly applied to young children, the ecological approach has been emphasized more in adolescence, when the shift to work skills and independent living becomes critical (Dalrymple, 1989; Porco, 1989).

Integration of Approaches

Each of the approaches to curriculum noted above has advantages for children with autism, and, collectively, the approaches share some features in common. Thus, there may be no "pure" examples of any of these models. Most curricula have combined various approaches and have done so with some success. Dyer and Peck (1987) suggested an "integrative view" of curriculum for social and language skills. Regarding language curricula, they cited experimental and quasi-experimental data showing that some developmentally determined objectives were achieved more readily than were "nondevelopmentally determined" objectives. Their examples were phonetic sounds and syntactic structures. They concluded that

some developmental language sequences and cognitive skills (e.g., object permanence and limitation) must be taken into consideration when designing curriculum.

Dyer and Peck (1987) also took the emphasis in curriculum away from teaching *forms* of behavior (individual skills) and put it on the *functions* of behavior. This emphasis has been strong in recent curricula on language and autism (e.g., Watson, Lord, Schaffer, & Schopler, 1989) as well as in the behavioral literature. The form of behavior is defined by its topography; the function of behavior is defined by the effect that it has on the environment. Examples of language functions may include requesting, protesting, and commenting. Self-help functions may include obtaining nourishment and getting dressed. Nearly all functions can be achieved in more than one way; for example, requesting may take the form of speaking, gesturing, writing, or pulling at another's hand. Thus, most curriculum in recent years has emphasized more flexible approaches to achieving functions, rather than rigidly taught task analyses of skills.

Dyer and Peck (1987) made the important point that a curriculum based on teaching functions can be empirically evaluated. Successful learning of a function can be measured by its impact on the world. Whether curricula are determined by developmental theory, remediation of cognitive deficits, or instruction in the least restrictive setting, their outcome is judged by the extent to which children learn to "function" outside the classroom. Horner, Sprague, and Flannery (1993) pointed out that there is extensive agreement on the expected outcomes of various curricula. A successful outcome is more than the acquisition of discrete skills or the reduction of problem behavior; it is a meaningful change in *lifestyle*. Horner and his colleagues emphasized that curriculum should be planned to affect "how the individual will work, play, learn, make friends, and be part of his or her ongoing community life" (p. 53).

IMPACT

A good example of a curriculum that integrates several approaches is Neel and Billingsley's (1989) IMPACT curriculum. This program is designed for students with moderate and severe disabilities, including autism. It emphasizes social and language skills but does not offer a curriculum in the form of developmentally sequenced skills. Rather, it is a guide to assessment of each child and to the development of individualized teaching goals that are functional in each student's environment. The program's use of assessment and instruction in natural settings clearly shows the influence of the ecological approach advocated by Brown and his colleagues, described earlier. It also integrates contemporary research on autism, although it does not offer follow-up data to show its effectiveness over time.

COMMON ISSUES IN CURRICULUM

Most of the detailed descriptions of curriculum have been published by individual programs and have not been widely disseminated. These publications have offered useful descriptions of individual programs but little evaluative data. In contrast, the well-researched aspects of curriculum have usually addressed very specific topics and their effects on a small number of children. Thus, the field is made up of a mix of conventional wisdom, careful research, and controversial issues.

Conventional Wisdom

The conventional wisdom is drawn from published program descriptions (e.g., Harris & Handleman, 1994; Schopler et al., 1980) and from a variety of informal publications and presentations.

Structure

Although most programs for students with autism emphasize structure, the term is not uniformly defined. In a structured program, the curriculum (activities and schedule) is very clear to the students and the teachers. A very rough measure of the adequacy of classroom structure can be obtained by observing a class for about 10 minutes. After this time, if the observer is not sure what each student is supposed to be doing, it is likely that the students are not sure either. Such a classroom has inadequate structure.

The clarity that is typically associated with structure helps the student with autism to gain a sense of order and predictability. Students can perform best when they understand where things belong, what will happen and in what sequence, how long activities will last, how familiar or how difficult the activities will be, who will be in the room or nearby, what is expected of them, and what the consequences are for appropriate or inappropriate behavior. Structure requires planning and organization, but it should not be confused with an authoritarian approach. A structured program can include variety, choice-making, instruction in natural settings, functional activities, and many other components that make instruction individualized and effective.

Physical Space

Most programs that serve children with autism (whether in an integrated or a separate format) give very careful attention to the use and arrangement of space. Activities are commonly arranged around "centers" that are clearly designated by distinctive colors, room dividers, signs, pictures, or other identifying markers. Centers for preschoolers may designate separate work areas and play areas. For adolescents, the centers may identify different types of vocational tasks. Each center indicates a place where certain activities and materials are located. Careful use of space can limit distractions.

Most students find it important to have a place to put private belongings and special tools, and a clearly marked area to go to at the start of the schoolday. For the teacher, it is important to have any gathering spaces arranged to allow a clear view of each student and each exit. Some very creatively designed classroom spaces have proved to be confusing and even unsafe for students with autism.

Materials

The needs of the individual child should dictate the curriculum, and the curriculum should dictate the materials. This statement may seem obvious, but in some programs, the preference for certain materials has dictated the curriculum. For example, students with autism often seem to understand and more easily complete visual-motor tasks rather than tasks requiring language or the application of abstract principles. As a result, activities requiring hand manipulation may predominate in the curriculum. These activities and their accompanying materials have practical advantages. They are likely to have a clear beginning and end. They may lend themselves to the repeated practice necessary for mastery. They may facilitate general goals, such as learning to work from left to right, or matching, or learning to count. Students may work with such materials with less direct teacher supervision.

Despite these advantages, use of the materials should not be an end in itself. The materials should be used to help students learn essential skills. For example, students with autism may not spontaneously enjoy tasks requiring language and social interaction, but these are essential parts of curricula, beginning at the earliest ages. When manipulative materials and visual cues are included in activities to teach language and social skills, particularly for very young children, the tasks become a bit more comfortable for students with autism.

Another generally accepted aspect of material selection is their age-appropriateness. As students get older, it is important—for their learning and for the way they are viewed by others—to avoid child-oriented materials. Because it is hard to find commercially distributed materials that are age-appropriate for older students with disabilities, teachers often make materials and rely on the natural materials required for functional tasks (e.g., pans for cooking).

Scheduling

An education program, whether in a classroom, community setting, or work site, can be a confusing experience without the predictability of a schedule. Students with autism typically catch on to the routine of the schoolday and begin to experience more success and fewer signs of distress when the schedule is consistent. Even nonspeaking students show anticipation of what activity comes next.

Students who work well on scheduled activities may show distress when they are required to make a transition from one activity to the next. Further experience with the schedule can help this problem somewhat, but the teacher may have to plan carefully for transitions. Alternating preferred activities with those that are more demanding, and keeping the demanding activities short, may help students learn to tolerate difficult work in anticipation of the activity to follow. Schedules typically mix work time with lunch or snack, toilet use, nap, and playtime for younger students. A schedule that uses words, pictures, or objects can remind students of transition times, and teachers may find it helpful to give warnings or "foreshadowing" of upcoming changes (e.g., "Three minutes until clean-up time."). Some students also benefit from holding a "transition object" that they can carry to the next activity (e.g., a spoon to bring to the cafeteria).

Comparing various age groups, the schedule is typically more rigid for young children. As students learn to follow the prescribed routine, the schedule becomes more flexible, to teach them to tolerate change and make choices. The predictability of a schedule can be combined with exposure to new experiences and choices from a range of opportunities.

Finally, a schedule ensures that there will be adequate instructional time and that the time will be reasonably distributed among several priorities—social learning, independent work, new skills vs. review, vocational objectives, self-help, generalization, and so on. Fredericks, Anderson, and Baldwin (1979), in a study of students with severe disabilities, showed that the factor most related to achievement of instructional objectives was the amount of instructional time in the day. Without a schedule, the caretaking demands of the day can take away from planned teaching. Adherence to a schedule ensures that teacher time is well distributed among students and that sufficient time is allotted for recording data on students' progress. For further reading on this topic, Van Bourgondien (1993) has provided a thorough, practical description of the use of schedules for young students with autism.

Students with autism may not easily understand the meaning of a schedule, but MacDuff, Krantz, and McClannahan (1993) demonstrated that, using graduated guidance, a picture schedule could be taught to four boys with autism. The boys learned to associate the pictures with scheduled activities, sustain engagement in tasks, and generalize their knowledge to a new sequence of the pictures and to new pictures. Krantz, MacDuff, and McClannahan

(1993) taught parents to use photo activity schedules with their children at home. This approach resulted in more engagement and social initiation and less disruptive behavior over a 10-month follow-up.

Instructional Content

In addition to teaching language and social skills, which are particular concerns for students with autism, most autism programs have taught the same skills that other youngsters with severe learning problems require. These include self-help, recreation and leisure, functional academic skills, activities of daily living (e.g., meal preparation, hygiene, cleaning, safety), vocational skills, community functioning (e.g., transportation, money use and management), and sexuality.

Empirical Research

Beyond the guidelines of conventional wisdom, curriculum has been developed through well-controlled studies. Slowly, these research findings are becoming common features of curriculum in public schools. Much of the current research looks at new ways to structure the environment for teaching the skills that conventional wisdom has emphasized for years. The familiar emphasis on language and social skills can be found in nearly every study.

Prerequisites for Success

Are there certain skills that are essential for later success? Schreibman (1988) pointed to the importance of being able to learn in a group and being able to work without constant teacher supervision. Teachers often find it difficult to teach the planned curriculum because their students do not follow oral instructions and engage in behavior that interferes with learning. For this reason, much of the early research on autism emphasized compliance to instructions and the elimination of interfering behavior (e.g., self-stimulation, being out of an assigned seat, and so on). In Ivar Lovaas's (1993) description of his research project on autism at UCLA (ongoing for more than 30 years now), he emphasized the importance of some prerequisites for later learning: eliminating interfering behavior, and teaching children to comply to simple instructions and to remain in their seats. In his early work, Lovaas used punishment (mild slaps to the bottom and, in rare cases, electric shock). As such approaches became more controversial and the effects of punishment were found to be short-lived, Lovaas and others in the field shifted their approach. In recent years, teaching new skills through positive reinforcement and curricular change has become the preferred approach to reducing behavior problems. This change in emphasis has had a profound impact. Current approaches still recognize that certain problem behaviors interfere with learning, but the elimination of such behavior is now done by building up adaptive skills (Carr, Robinson, Taylor, & Carlson, 1990). This change has given a new importance to curriculum. No longer merely a collection of skills needed for later living curriculum is often the key to managing problem behavior that would otherwise interfere with many aspects of development.

Although there appears to be agreement that certain problem behaviors are incompatible with learning, the issue of critical skills or prerequisites for success is not entirely clear. Lovaas (1993) noted that the students who showed greatest progress in his program were those who acquired the skill of verbal imitation within the first 3 months of his intensive treatment program. Children who entered his program with echolalia already demonstrated verbal imitation, and they tended to show better progress than the nonverbal children. Because all of the children in his program were taught verbal imitation, Lovaas (1993, 1994) found this to be a learning trait on which children naturally differed, not a curriculum issue. He distinguished between "auditory learners," who showed good progress in his program, and "visual learners," who did not. He suggested that a more visually oriented curriculum might work better for the visual learners.

Curriculum Based on Assessment

Design of curriculum is commonly based on an assessment of the student; for example, the TEACCH approach assesses the individual child's developmental skills as well as the characteristics associated with autism (Schopler et al., 1980). Behavioral assessment has typically included measures of skills and problem behavior, as well as assessment of reinforcing and punishing consequences (Wisocki, 1988). The ecological inventory approach to assessment was evaluated earlier.

Curriculum Based on a Functional Analysis of Behavior

Functional analysis of behavior is a complement to behavioral assessment. This highly individualized approach takes into account many aspects of curriculum. A functional analysis involves: (a) a clear definition of the behavior to be changed, (b) assessment of the antecedent factors that affect the targeted behavior, and (c) measures of the consequences (reinforcers) that motivate the student to engage in this or any other behavior (Pyles & Bailey, 1990). This approach is based on an understanding of the *function* (or purpose) of the problem behavior. The earliest behavioral treatment programs were based on the assumption that problem behavior could be eliminated and adaptive behavior could be taught, given the right schedule and application of punishment and reinforcement. More recent research has shown that effective treatment requires assessment of the function of problem behavior (Pyles & Bailey, 1990). Common functions include acquiring attention or sensory consequences or access to objects or activities (positive reinforcement) and escape from tasks (negative reinforcement).

As an aside, it may be helpful to acknowledge some confusion in the use of the term *functional.* The autism literature refers to *functional curriculum* (curriculum that is practical and useful), to teaching forms and *functions* (classes of behavior that have the same effect on the environment), and to assessment of the *function* of behavior (its purpose or consequence). Although these uses of the term are similar, their slightly different meanings can be a source of confusion.

Functional analysis can be used to determine curricular changes that will reduce interfering behavior. An example may be found in a study by Lalli, Casey, Goh, and Merlino (1994). These researchers worked with two 18-year-old men who had mild mental retardation and severe aberrant behavior (physical aggression, disruption, property destruction). Their functional analysis revealed that, for both men, aberrant behavior served the function of escape from demands. The researchers used two procedures: (a) escape extinction (i.e., the aberrant behavior no longer led to escape from the task) and (b) an activity schedule (a curricular change). The schedule served to make the tasks and their duration clearer to the students. The results of these combined procedures were: a significant reduction in problem behavior, and an increase in compliance to scheduled activities. In other words, a functional analysis has been the basis for an individualized approach that teaches skills and reduces problem behavior without a need for punishment.

In the functional analytic approach, the curriculum is seen as one of the major factors influencing student performance. Researchers have carried out functional analyses by systematically changing the curriculum (activities), the antecedents to the target behavior, and the consequences that follow the behavior. Such careful changes in the natural environment reveal the factors that affect learning for an individual student. Dunlap, Kern-Dunlap, Clarke, and Robbins (1991) demonstrated this approach with Jill, a 12-year-old girl with mental retardation and severe behavior problems. In their functional analysis, they sought to determine the relationship between the curriculum and four classes of student behavior: (a) disruption, (b) on/off task, (c) social interactions, and (d) inappropriate vocalizations. The researchers developed and confirmed four hypotheses about the relationship between the curriculum and the student's behavior: "(a) Jill is better behaved when she is engaged in large motor as opposed to fine motor activities, (b) Jill is better behaved when her fine motor and academic requirements are brief as opposed to lengthy, (c) Jill is better behaved when she is engaged in functional activities resulting in concrete and preferred outcomes, and (d) Jill is better behaved when she has some choice regarding her activities" (p. 389). The study confirmed each of these hypotheses and demonstrated the practical importance of a functional analysis in determining curriculum and improving performance of students with disabilities and problem behavior.

A functional analysis that is carried out in such detail is not practical for most teachers. However, very useful information about the factors affecting learning can be obtained by informal observation, questionnaires, and interviews of parents and of teachers who know the student well (O'Neill, Horner, Albin, Storey, & Sprague, 1990). Such informal functional analyses provide tentative findings that can be explored further in the classroom. The study by Dunlap et al. (1991) illustrated the importance of several aspects of curriculum for one student, and further research has confirmed and extended these findings.

Sequencing Activities

Experience with the conventional wisdom on topics such as schedules has led to research on some specific aspects of curriculum. For example, teachers for many years have used the Premack Principle (Sulzer-Azaroff & Mayer, 1991) to sequence activities. This principle indicates that high-probability activities (e.g., playing with Legos™) may serve as a reinforcer for low-probability responses (e.g., cleaning up). The result has been a sequence in which "fun" activities are alternated with "work," and student performance improves.

Recent research has applied variations of this principle in creative ways. Dunlap (1984) demonstrated that interspersing maintenance tasks (those already mastered) with acquisition tasks improved motivation and learning. Charlop, Kurtz, and Milstein (1992) further demonstrated that learning and management of problem behavior were effective when the interspersed new (acquisition) tasks were reinforced, and reinforcement was greatly reduced for the maintenance tasks. These approaches to improving performance and minimizing external reinforcers are valuable steps toward teaching skills for independent work. They are also very practical for teachers to implement. Teachers have typically welcomed curricular suggestions that allow them to avoid an exclusively 1:1 teaching format. The strategy of interspersing familiar tasks with new ones and reinforcing primarily the new tasks is helpful to both students and teachers.

Sequencing Requests

Sequencing requests is another variation on sequencing tasks. Davis, Brady, Williams, and Hamilton (1992) identified requests that were likely to be followed and others that were not, and took advantage of a phenomenon known as "behavioral momentum." They sequenced their requests so that a series of 3 to 5 high-probability requests was followed by a low-probability request. The result was a rapid increase in compliance to requests across multiple trainers. In a follow-up study, Davis, Brady, Hamilton, McEvoy, and Williams (1994) used a similar procedure to increase the rate of social initiations to peers in 3 boys with autism. The change generalized to peers who had not been involved in the training and to new situations. This is another line of research that has very practical implications for teaching. In addition to the content, the curricular sequence can have an important impact on learning.

Task Size

Sweeney and LeBlanc (1995) have recently provided evidence for the conventional wisdom that children with autism respond better to tasks of reasonable size. This is such a commonsense notion that it is likely to apply to virtually all learners. When the task appears to be overwhelmingly large, the student is likely to be less motivated and more inclined to engage in disruptive behavior. Sweeney and LeBlanc (1995) offered 5 children with autism (ages 7 and 8) a bead-stringing task of either 36 beads or 250 beads, with no tangible reinforcement for their work. The smaller task resulted in more on-task behavior and better work rate. The larger task resulted in more inappropriate use of materials and some other disruptive behavior, although there were notable differences among students. This finding is congruent with the conventional wisdom on curriculum, which suggests that students be given tasks of an appropriate length and level of difficulty.

Student Preference and Choice

A common assumption is that the teacher chooses the curriculum and it is the student's responsibility to comply with the teacher's instructions. Recent research has shown that, for many students with autism and other severe disabilities, performance is better on preferred activities and on activities that the student chooses. Teachers have noticed for years that children with autism find idiosyncratic consequences, preferred activities, and being in control of an activity to be reinforcing.

Conventional wisdom dictates that children with disabilities (and probably everyone else) are more motivated, productive, attentive, and free of disruptive behavior when engaged in preferred activities. (This is also an implication of the Premack Principle mentioned earlier.) Activities are identified as preferred based on (a) the amount of time the student spends on them when given a choice, (b) initiations toward the materials, and (c) opposition when the activity is taken away (Dyer, 1987). A study by Foster-Johnson, Ferro, and Dunlap (1994) is a good example of the effect of preferred activities. The three students in this study (aged 9, 14, and 15 years) showed more desirable behavior (e.g., appropriate use of materials, vocalizations, direction following) and less problem behavior (e.g., off task, disruption) when preferred activities were available. Because preferred activities appear to result in better student performance, a next logical step is to offer students choices.

Dyer, Dunlap, and Winterling (1990) found that offering choices of activities and reinforcers reduced the severe problem behaviors (aggression, self-injury, tantrums) of three school-age children with autism. Choice did not affect the rate of correct responding. It should be noted that, in this study, the children knew how to make a choice; but some students do not. Teaching children the skill of making a choice (pointing or selecting in some way) must include experiencing the consequences of that choice. Once the skill and the concept of choice are established, choice making can become an important part of the curriculum and an activity that will be used throughout life.

Self-Management

Most curricula for students with autism, particularly those derived from a behavioral approach, have been composed of many skills that are broken down into small, sequenced steps (task-analyzed) and taught individually. Teachers and parents have sometimes found this approach frustrating; the skills are learned slowly, and by the time most students leave school, they have not been prepared adequately for adult living. Researchers have sought strategies that would allow students with autism to learn a small number of key skills that will readily generalize to new skills

(response generalization) and to new people, materials, and settings (stimulus generalization). In describing his early work in teaching children with autism, Lovaas (1994) noted that he taught speech in the hope that the children would then use it spontaneously and make significant breakthroughs in other areas. These breakthroughs did not occur.

Recent research has shown self-management to be a promising solution to this problem. Students who can manage their own behavior learn in ways similar to those of nondisabled students. They take initiative, and they require little supervision from teachers. Research in autism has used the same approaches to self-management that have been thoroughly studied in other populations: relaxation, self-recording, and self-reinforcement.

Baron, Groden, and Cautela (1988) described the program that is operative at the Groden Center, in Providence, Rhode Island. Large numbers of children, adolescents, and adults have been taught systematic relaxation as an alternative to impulsive or disruptive behavior. Once they have learned to cue themselves to relax in the presence of stimuli that used to lead to anger, aggression, or other disruptive behavior, the students are taught adaptive coping strategies. The result has been greater opportunities for independent functioning.

Several researchers have demonstrated the effectiveness of a self-management package made up of differential reinforcement, self-recording, and self-reinforcement. In this approach, the students are taught a behavior (usually a social communication skill) and prompted to record when they have done it correctly. When they have made enough correct self-recordings, they may choose a reinforcer.

R.L. Koegel and Koegel (1990) applied self-management to the reduction of stereotypy. Stahmer and Schreibman (1992) used the self-management package with differential reinforcement and prompts to teach toy play to three children ages 7 to 13. The children not only learned to play appropriately with toys, but they generalized these changes across settings and toys, and maintained the skills to unsupervised posttreatment sessions.

L.K. Koegel, Koegel, Hurley, and Frea (1992) used a similar self-management package to teach children to respond appropriately to questions from typically developing peers. Although the training and reinforcement took place in the clinic, the social behavior and the self-management took place in community, home, and clinic. In addition to these significant changes in social behavior, the authors noted dramatic reduction in disruptive behavior. Many people who have experience in teaching children with autism may find these results hard to believe. Children with autism do not appear to have the "insight" required to monitor their own behavior accurately. Yet this body of research reminds us that such skills do not depend on insight. In some respects, their rigid dependence on routine and their interest in counting things may help children with autism to become accurate recorders of their own behavior. The earliest report of such a self-management program may have been by a parent. Park (1974) reported that his daughter, Jessy, was very accurate in her use of a self-counting program. Koegel et al. (1992) also found that their students could very accurately record their correct responses (72% to 89% accurate) and the nonoccurrences of the target behavior (69% to 95%).

As a final example, R.L. Koegel and Frea (1993) used the self-management package to teach two high-functioning teenage boys to improve the "social communicative" behaviors that their parents thought were significant concerns (e.g., nonverbal mannerisms, perseveration of topic, intensity of voice volume, and so on). The boys learned to keep a written record of their social behavior targets in community settings and earned quarters to play video games when their performance was good. The appropriate target behavior increased to nearly 100% of intervals during training, and nontargeted social communicative behavior also increased markedly.

The success of these researchers in teaching self-management of social behavior as a "pivotal skill" deserves some emphasis. In many ways, it achieves Lovaas's (1994) desire for a skill that will generalize enough to lead to breakthroughs in other skill areas. R.L. Koegel and Frea (1993) offered two possible explanations for their findings. First, from a behavioral perspective, social communication encompasses a large class of behaviors that serve a function. When one behavior in this class is reinforced, other behaviors in the same functional class may be strengthened. As a result, the student will begin to demonstrate new (generalized) skills. Second, Koegel and Frea (1993) pointed out that teaching pivotal social skills gives students with autism an opportunity to be successful in social situations that they had previously found to be very aversive and, thus, had avoided. Their new social skills "simplify conversational exchanges," make social situations less aversive, and make it less likely that the student will attempt to escape from them. These findings also fit well with the research of Carr and his colleagues (Carr et al., 1994), who indicated that problem behavior that serves the function of communication will diminish when other, more efficient functional communication skills are learned.

LANGUAGE CURRICULA

Contemporary research on language curricula is the product of current views of language development in autism, described in Chapters 23, 24, and 25 of this volume. This section describes the few available comprehensive language curricula for students with autism, as well as examples of recent research on teaching specific communication skills.

Recent Research Issues Related to Language Curriculum

Many issues in language curriculum are the same as those discussed in regard to social skills, vocational skills, community living skills, and so on. The emphasis is on acquiring functional communication that can be used in a variety of settings and that will lead to as much independent functioning as possible. Among the current language curriculum issues is the teaching of "efficient" communication skills and of communication that will be maintained (reinforced) in the student's natural environment.

Efficiency of Communication Response

Previous discussions in this chapter have noted the growing emphasis on functional skills and teaching routines—on activities or functions rather than discrete skills (Horner et al.,

1993). One important consideration in choosing activities for language instruction is the efficiency of the language responses being taught. The efficiency of a response is measured by how quickly and consistently it gains reinforcement and the physical effort required to exhibit the response. Several studies have pointed to the importance of efficiency in teaching communication.

Horner, Sprague, O'Brien, and Heathfield (1990) taught an adolescent boy to request help for tasks from which he had previously tried to escape. The boy was taught two methods of requesting help: (a) to type out the words on a keyboard, which was very difficult and time-consuming (due in part to mild cerebral palsy) or (b) to press, on the same keyboard, a button that emitted the same statement. Systematic manipulations showed that the student exhibited fewer behavior problems when he used the more efficient strategy of pressing a single button. When required to type the whole statement, he usually engaged in the aggression that had, in the past, allowed him to escape from the task immediately. In addition, Carr, Reeve, and Palumbo (in Carr, Reeve, & Magito-McLaughlin, 1996) showed that the efficiency of a communication response was a key factor in determining whether the response would increase while problem behavior decreased. They worked with three young children who had developmental delays in addition to idiosyncratic types of gestural communication (i.e., they used a sign to request an item but did not execute the sign correctly). When unfamiliar adults were informed of the meaning of each child's gesture, the gesture led to reinforcement quickly, with little effort, and consistently across these adults (i.e., efficiently). When the adults were not informed of the meaning of each child's communication, the signs led to longer delays, the adults offered wrong items, and the children showed more behavior problems. A side observation of this study was that some children who were screened for the study often "shut down" when their communication was not readily understood; that is, they refused to repeat their gesture or to use other methods to communicate their intent. It seems reasonable to assume that an inefficient communication response will not be reinforced and, therefore, will not maintain

or generalize well to other settings. This issue is important for individuals with autism who have difficulty engaging in spontaneous communication at the start. To encourage communication, the communicative form should be as efficient as possible.

Several variables contribute to the efficiency of a communicative response. As in the example above, one such variable is the interpretability of the child's response. Efficiency is also affected by the context in which the communication occurs. For example, pointing is efficient when there is an open shelf but not when there are closed cabinets with which the child is unfamiliar. Also, taking an adult by the hand and pushing the hand in the direction of a desired object is efficient when there is one item on an open shelf but not when there are several (Palumbo, Reeve, & Carr, 1991). Similarly, it may be more efficient to allow an individual who has speech, but has serious articulation difficulties, to use an electronic augmentative communication device (e.g., Touch Talker™) to communicate frequent requests, instead of demanding that he or she use speech.

Opportunities for Natural Reinforcement

Another factor to consider when deciding the content of communication curriculum is the opportunity for the response to be reinforced in the natural environment. That is, students with autism should be taught communication responses that evoke reinforcement from the environment naturally, such as requesting a favorite toy. Instruction can also involve structuring the environment so that the child's communication is reinforced (e.g., ensuring that an adult is available to attend to a child who is learning to communicate requests for attention). In addition, the curriculum should be structured to elicit increasingly sophisticated forms of communication. For example, a child's taking an adult's hand and pushing it in the direction of a cookie jar should be viewed as communication, and the child should be prompted and encouraged to point toward the cookie jar and then receive a cookie (Carr, 1985). Similarly, if the child is learning to point, desired items can be placed just out of reach. This structure encourages the child to engage an adult for help, thereby making it more likely that the child will point, or allowing the adult to prompt pointing.

Increasing Opportunities

Children with autism are likely to require repeated trials or opportunities to learn. Therefore, it is beneficial to structure the classroom or community to make available many and varied situations that encourage communication and that lead to natural consequences for communication. This approach, called *multiple exemplar training* in behavioral terms, has been consistently shown to increase generalization of skills for people with autism who have difficulty using new skills in new situations (Carr, 1985; Stokes & Baer, 1977).

Formal Curricula

Communication is a part of nearly all instruction for students with autism, but few comprehensive curricula on language have been published. The following three curricula represent somewhat different approaches.

TEACCH Language Curriculum

The TEACCH curriculum (Watson et al., 1989) is like the rest of the TEACCH program in that it begins with assessment and it emphasizes teaching to children's strengths in order to enhance their weaknesses. The curriculum was designed for children with communication skills that range from nonverbal to simple sentence use, and it contains steps based on developmental theory. The curriculum also has some very practical appeal; it was designed to be carried out by special education teachers in collaboration with language specialists. Parents are considered an integral part of the assessment and goal planning process, and they receive training in how to work on the objectives with the student at home. Each child has an individual program of objectives based on his or her existing skills and long-term goals.

The curriculum is multidimensional and focuses on (a) the purpose of communication, (b) the context in which communication occurs, (c) categories of meaning, (d) words, gestures, or signs the child uses to communicate, and (e) the form of communication (e.g., pictures, gestures, words). Principles for setting objectives

for training include choosing logical steps toward reaching individual goals, and building on the student's existing spontaneous communication skills. The curriculum is designed to teach the child only one new skill in one dimension while using preexisting skills in other dimensions. TEACCH focuses on a "real-world" view to teaching communication so that children will communicate better in naturally occurring situations. Watson and her colleagues described ways to "engineer" the environment so that the students encounter frequent natural opportunities to use their language skills. Hence, the curriculum reflects an interactive view of language development.

The TEACCH Language Curriculum, based on current research in language and autism, was developed through extensive pilot work in TEACCH classrooms. Research on its long-term effectiveness has not yet been published.

Behavioral Language Curricula

In contrast to the TEACCH curriculum, behavioral approaches to language are generally not based on a developmental model. Instead, they are based on the view that autism is a learning disorder and that the student has already failed to learn language in the natural setting. Hence, behavioral models focus on teaching language in simplified instructional situations to promote success. Behaviorists use reinforcement in discrete trials, prompting, fading, shaping, and chaining to teach specific, and measurable, skills (Lovaas, 1977, 1981; T. Smith, 1993).

Lovaas's (1977, 1981, 1987) approach is not a classroom-based curriculum; it is an intensive behavioral program that begins with one-to-one instruction of children under 40 months old, and prepares them for school entry. Although language is a central element of the curriculum, many other skills are emphasized. The program begins by teaching basic or prerequisite skills, such as imitation and attention. The students are then taught to imitate words, use words for labeling, and combine words in simple sentences. When students master these skills, the teachers move on to instruction of abstract language use—plurals, adjectives, prepositions, and pronouns.

Later steps include asking questions and engaging in simple conversations (Smith, 1993).

Lovaas's program applies behavioral techniques to the teaching of language and social skills as well as to the reduction of inappropriate behavior, such as echolalia and aggression. Lovaas and Smith (1989) estimated that therapists teach about 500 different skills in the course of treatment.

Lovaas has not published a recent description of his curriculum, and, like other researchers, he has not evaluated the effects of the curriculum separately from the other components of the treatment package. His evaluation of the overall program has followed children at age 7 (Lovaas, 1987) and age 13 (McEachin, Smith, & Lovaas, 1993). At both ages, children in his intensive treatment group were superior to controls on several measures, including success in regular education programs, IQ, and adaptive behavior (including adaptive communication). Although Lovaas's experimental design has been stronger than that of other program evaluations in autism, he has been criticized, primarily, for failure to assign children randomly to treatment conditions (Schopler, Short, & Mesibov, 1989).

Functional Communication Training

Behavioral approaches to language teaching have been criticized for viewing the child as a passive learner. Functional communication training (FCT; Carr et al., 1994) represents an effort to combine the more "interactive" approaches to language remediation with behavioral methods. To date, the research on FCT has been focused on the reduction of severe behavior problems. A full language curriculum has not been offered. However, a discussion of the fundamental principles underlying functional communication training may be helpful in illuminating the path the field appears to be taking. Like other recent approaches to teaching language and social skills to children with autism, FCT has emphasized the function of the skills being taught, rather than the form of the behavior. This trend can also be seen in the teaching of sign language (Carr, 1979) and other forms of augmentative communication (Beukelman & Mirenda, 1992; Reichle, York,

& Sigafoos, 1991) to help individuals with autism communicate effectively.

As noted earlier, functional analysis of behavior has been an effective approach to revealing the function or purpose of behavior in autism. Some behaviors seen in autism, such as aggression and self-injury, had previously been viewed as bizarre and aberrant, but recent research has shown that many, if not most, of these behaviors serve a communicative function. Hence, when the individual learns to use communicative responses that are more appropriate, that serve the same function as the behavior problem, and that lead to reinforcement more efficiently than the problem behavior, the frequency of communication responses has been found to increase while the frequency of problem behavior decreases (Carr & Durand, 1985). Although FCT has been used primarily to develop curriculum for professionals and paraprofessionals to use in treating severe behavior problems, it also serves the purpose of increasing students' communication (Carr et al., 1994).

The approach begins with a functional analysis assessment, to determine the function of the behavior problem. The assumption behind the model is that the function for communication already exists, but the form used to obtain the function is inappropriate. Hence, the teaching is designed to develop a more appropriate form to serve the same function. After the function is identified, an appropriate communication strategy must be identified that will be readily interpretable by others and will efficiently gain the function of the response in as many settings as possible (Carr et al., 1996). The form is then taught in a manner similar to incidental teaching methods in behavioral models (Hart & Risley, 1975; McGee, Daly, & Jacobs, 1994).

Functional communication training is similar to the TEACCH Language Curriculum (Watson et al., 1989) in that it provides the student with many opportunities when he or she is likely to communicate. Specific teaching sessions are set up to elicit the function of the desired communication response. For example, if the child's behavior problems serve the function of gaining attention from an adult, and the adult wishes to teach the child to tap his shoulder instead, the adult would design a situation in which the child usually seeks attention. The adult would then prompt the child to tap his shoulder and would reinforce the shoulder-tapping response with attention. On the other hand, attention would be withheld for tantrums (the identified behavior problem), making them a less immediate and less efficient way to communicate. At best, tantrums would only gain attention after a lengthy delay and frequent repetition. Extension of these steps would be easy to accomplish for other functional skills. Indeed, teaching of functional communication skills has been suggested as a crucial element in early intervention programs as a method to develop curriculum and prevent severe behavior problems (Dunlap, Johnson, & Robbins, 1990).

Little research has been conducted on the effectiveness of FCT as a method for teaching language, but numerous studies have shown it to be an effective method for increasing communication responses and decreasing behavior problems (reviewed by Carr et al., 1994; Carr, McConnachie, Levin, & Kemp, 1993). As an approach to curriculum development, Carr and his colleagues (1994) have field-tested FCT at two residential settings for individuals with autism.

Despite promising signs of its effectiveness, several issues must be addressed before FCT can be placed in the same category as other whole-language curricula. For example, FCT generally acts on functions that are already exhibited by the individual. What if the student with autism does not currently exhibit the function that one wishes to teach? Can a function be created? This question will be important when FCT is used to teach language (e.g., pronouns) that is not directly related to the common functions addressed in the literature (e.g., escape, attention, tangibles).

In summary, these approaches to curriculum all have unique characteristics. the TEACCH curriculum uses an interactive style with a developmental model to teach to the child's strengths. Lovaas's behavioral approach has more data on its effectiveness than are available on the other approaches. It does not apply an interactional model, and the details of its current curriculum have not yet been published. FCT, although not completely

developed as a curriculum, combines an interactive approach with an emphasis on functions of communication rather than form.

SOCIAL SKILLS CURRICULA

Difficulty in interaction with others is so central to autism that it is reflected in most classroom activities and in a large portion of the research in autism. Social interaction deficits are also intertwined with the language problems and narrowness of interests that make up most current definitions of autism. The following review of this large topic focuses first on some recent research on specific social skills and then identifies more comprehensive approaches that have used curriculum to improve social functioning.

Many of the recent advances in teaching social skills to children and adults with autism are natural extensions of the empirical work described earlier. Examples have been given of the work of Davis and her colleagues, using behavioral momentum, and of Koegel and his colleagues, using self-management to teach social skills.

Play and Social Initiation

Parents, teachers, and researchers have often pointed out both the slowness in the development of play skills and the oddness of the social interaction that characterize autism (Jarrold, Boucher, & Smith, 1993; Stone, Lemanek, Fishel, Fernandez, & Altemeier, 1990). Curricula that increase social behavior, social responsiveness, and sensitivity to social cues offer promise for significant and practical changes in everyday functioning for students with autism.

Self-Monitoring of Play

Strain, Kohler, Storey, and Danko (1994) extended the use of self-management to preschool-age children. They taught three children with autism (ages 3, 4, and 5 years) a social skills package at school and at home. Children learned to make (a) "play organizer suggestions" (suggesting an activity or a place to play), (b) "share offers and requests" (offering or requesting an object from another child), and (c) "assistance offers and requests."

Children were taught to place a disk with their picture on it in a container each time they engaged in one of the targeted social behaviors. Each disk in the container could be exchanged for a small edible reward. The reinforcement schedule was slowly faded so that children had to engage in more extended social contact before receiving the reinforcer. The self-monitoring strategy resulted in increased social behavior toward peers in the classroom and toward siblings at home.

Scripts to Teach Play Initiation

The research on social skills illustrates some innovative methods of teaching and an emphasis on social skills that are naturally observed in children and are useful in natural settings. For example, Krantz and McClannahan (1993) taught four boys with autism (ages 9 to 12 years) to make initiations to peers. Their method was to offer detailed scripts and, initially, to prompt each student to follow the script. The method also had an element of self-monitoring; the students checked off each element of the script as they completed it. The use of scripts increased social initiations, and, as scripts were faded, initiations generalized to new students and new settings. The initiations also generalized beyond the scripted comments to more "original" social comments, including teasing.

Symbolic Play

Another aspect of play in autism that distinguishes it from that of typical children is a failure to engage in complex actions or to use materials in a "pretend" manner to symbolize other materials (e.g., making "mud pies"). A more advanced form of play is sociodramatic play, in which groups of children use symbolic play to act out themes and play roles. Goldstein and Cisar (1992) used scripts to increase sociodramatic play in preschool children with autism. The children learned the scripted social behavior and also showed some elaborations on the theme and on their roles.

Pivotal response training (R.L. Koegel, O'Dell, & Koegel, 1987) has been applied in two recent studies to increase these higher levels of play. Stahmer (1995) applied this teaching package to increase symbolic play in 7 boys, ages 4 to 7 years. The package combines many elements discussed earlier in this chapter (e.g., reinforcing, varying tasks, offering choices, and interspersing new tasks with maintenance tasks). The design of the study allowed for a comparison of pivotal response training for language and for symbolic play. The results indicated that language training had no effect on symbolic play, but when the pivotal response training package was directed to symbolic play, all 7 children showed increases in symbolic play and in complexity of play.

In a closely related study, Thorp, Stahmer, and Schreibman (1995) used pivotal response training to teach sociodramatic play to 3 boys, ages 3, 8, and 9 years. These authors used several measures to demonstrate increases in sociodramatic play, spontaneous speech, and social behavior. Further, these sophisticated play and social skills generalized to a new setting, new adults, and new toys.

These two studies are significant in several respects. Although Stahmer (1995) and Thorp et al. (1995) used reinforcement procedures, the behaviors targeted for change (symbolic play and sociodramatic play) were those more typically addressed by researchers with a cognitive perspective. In addition, these authors noted the importance of developmental prerequisites, such as language skills, for success in this program. Such research reflects the increasing integration of approaches to curriculum that is resulting in significant educational and social progress for children with autism. Thorp et al.'s (1995) instructional package required only 16 hours of individual instruction for each student. This relatively small investment of time resulted in significant gains that generalized in meaningful ways.

Offering Assistance

The research on cognitive aspects of autism has emphasized the difficulty that children and adults with autism have in recognizing and responding to social cues in others (e.g., Baron-Cohen, 1988). Harris, Handleman, and Alessandri 1990) taught 3 boys (ages 13 and 14 years) to discriminate situations in which others needed assistance, and then to offer assistance. The youths generalized this social behavior to new people and new settings, including offers to assist their mothers at home. This study highlights another operational similarity among various approaches to autism. Harris and her colleagues used behavioral procedures to teach a "cognitive" skill—recognizing and acting on another's point of view.

Self-Evaluation for Peers

Self-evaluation is a variation on the self-management approach used by Koegel and his colleagues (e.g., R.L. Koegel & Koegel, 1990), which was reviewed earlier. Sainato, Goldstein, and Strain (1992) used self-evaluation to assist typically developing peers in teaching social behavior to preschoolers with autism. They taught the peers strategies, such as how to get the attention of the children with autism, organize play, share, and respond to playmates. The peers self-evaluated by indicating whether they had been successful in using these strategies. The peers received stickers for accurate reporting, which they later traded for prizes. The use of self-evaluation enabled typical preschoolers to learn a rather sophisticated set of social skills, use them in interaction with 3- and 4-year-old children with autism, and improve the social behavior of the autistic children. The improvement was primarily in social responsiveness rather than in social initiation. Self-evaluation also seemed to help the peers to use social strategies with other children, without teacher assistance. As in other research with self-monitoring, these young children generalized their behavior in ways that are encouraging for teachers.

The use of self-monitoring for children with autism (R.L. Koegel & Frea, 1993), self-evaluation for peers (Sainato et al., 1992), and teaching in routines or activities in natural contexts—all these have led to impressive gains in independent behavior and generalization of social skills.

Teaching a Theory of Mind

Ozonoff and Miller (1995) described a social skills group for a small number of adolescents with autism and average (above 70) IQ. Their 14-session program taught conversational skills (e.g., speaking in turn, listening, giving compliments) but also gave instruction intended to overcome problems in theory of mind and perspective taking that have been identified by other researchers (e.g., Baron-Cohen, 1988). The group instruction used explanation of principles, modeling, role playing, and videotaped feedback to teach the adolescents that others have a perspective that is different from their own. The instruction made these abstract principles concrete with examples and exercises, to illustrate that "what one sees or hears determines what one knows" (p. 422).

The authors concluded, with caution, that the 5 adolescents had improved (compared to 4 control subjects) on 4 theory of mind measures, but had not generalized their gains to a more broadly improved social competence. Despite these limited findings, Ozonoff and Miller have added a useful component to social skills instruction, and future research will, no doubt, extend their approach.

Examples of Social Skills Curricula

As noted earlier, curricula for language and social skills overlap greatly. Lovaas's (1987, 1993) work, which was reviewed in the section on language curricula, also contains many elements of social skills. Carr's (Carr et al., 1994; Carr et al., 1993) use of functional communication training, which was also described earlier as a language curriculum, is in many ways an approach to increase appropriate social behavior. The following two examples address social skills but also have been applied to other aspects of autism.

Pivotal Response Training

Several examples of the application of pivotal response training to language and social skills have been noted earlier in this chapter. R.L. Koegel and Koegel (1995) have recently published an extensive summary of their work, which combines many of the effective elements of curriculum that have been described in individual studies. Koegel and Koegel have taken into consideration the choice of tasks and materials, scheduling of activities, sequencing of requests, student preferences and choices, and self-management, and their curriculum has targeted critical language and social skills. As a result, they have not only increased these skills, they have shown generalization, flexibility, and a spontaneity of responding that is remarkable for students with autism.

Koegel and Koegel and their colleagues have integrated several approaches to curriculum. The important issues of developmental prerequisites, cognitive skills, and teaching functional skills in natural settings are all reflected in their work. The effectiveness of their approach is shown in many individual, well-controlled research studies. Although their reports have included follow-up several months later, they have not applied their approach to a group of students and followed them, with a control group, over an extensive time. Nevertheless, their work must be recognized for its strong research base and its integration of approaches to curriculum.

LEAP Preschool

Learning Experiences: An Alternative Program for Preschoolers and Parents (LEAP) was developed by Phillip Strain and colleagues in Pittsburgh (Hoyson, Jamieson, & Strain, 1984), in 1982. Since that time, it has served over 48 preschool children with autism or pervasive developmental disorders (Strain & Cordisco, 1994). Although much of LEAP's emphasis has been on social skill development, its comprehensive curriculum consists of functional skills (e.g., transition from one activity to another, selection of play activities), independent play and work skills, social interaction, language skills, adaptive behavior, and prevention of behavior problems (Strain & Cordisco, 1994).

Kohler and Strain (1993) described the specific aspects of their social skills curriculum in the Early Childhood Social Skills Program. This program contains a clear sequence of instruction for specific social skills, in addition to methods of instruction that rely on interactions between typical preschoolers and peers with autism or other significant social interaction problems.

In the approaches to language instruction, reviewed earlier, the form of communication was deemphasized; any form that accomplished a useful communication function was encouraged. In contrast, Strain's curriculum

has a very clear content and sequence, and it is taught using prescribed activities and methods. The Early Childhood Social Skills Program contains curricular elements that Strain and his colleagues have investigated for over 20 years. The social skills "include (a) making offers and requests to share; (b) offering play suggestions; (c) making offers and requests to give assistance; (d) showing affection; and (e) giving compliments" (Kohler & Strain, 1993, p. 41). Although other researchers have demonstrated the effectiveness of some of these individual skills, Strain has examined them as a curriculum; that is, all the children are taught each skill in the above sequence. This work is another example of the integration of curricular approaches. The targeted social skills, their sequence, and the overall goals of the program have been influenced by developmental researchers such as Hartup (1983). The targeted skills are those that are typically lacking in young children with autism. The structured nature of the instruction and the methods of instruction are distinctly behavioral.

Strain's research on LEAP and the Early Childhood Social Skills Program is different, in several respects, from much that has been written about curriculum. First, the curriculum is taught in an integrated setting. Classrooms consist of children with disabilities and typical children. Second, Strain's research has been a mix of individual studies regarding instruction of small numbers of children and follow-up of experimental and control students for many years. Strain (Strain & Cordisco, 1994) and Lovaas (McEachin et al., 1993) have been the only researchers to follow their preschool students well into the school years. Third, the LEAP preschool model has been widely replicated in several states.

Although the LEAP curriculum has been well specified, follow-up research cannot determine the effects of curriculum, because (as in other programs) the curriculum effects are confounded with other components of the program. Nevertheless, the long-term effects of LEAP have been impressive. After 2 years in the preschool, most children no longer meet the diagnostic criteria for autism. Graduates of the preschool have made better progress on measures of intellectual, language, and social skills than control children. These gains have been maintained during long-term follow-up with the students (up to fifth grade; Strain & Cordisco, 1994).

CURRICULUM FOR EARLY EDUCATION

The programs for children with autism that have the most clearly defined curriculum, the most empirical basis for treatment, and the most extensive follow-up of students have been early education programs. The programs of Strain, Lovaas, and Koegel have been described earlier. Many other preschool programs exist throughout the United States and Canada (Harris & Handleman, 1994; Olley, Robbins, & Morelli-Robbins, 1993), and although their findings have not been as extensively disseminated as those of Strain, Lovaas, and Koegel, they are serving an important role in demonstrating curriculum and other aspects of services for young children. The consensus from well-controlled studies and informal demonstrations is that early intervention and appropriate curriculum are essential to realizing significant gains for students with autism.

The preschool programs described by Harris and Handleman (1994) and Olley et al. (1993) are notably different from other programs in that their curriculum content and sequence tend to be more uniformly prescribed than in programs for older children. That is, they specify the things that the children are supposed to learn, and there is less variation in the individual child's curriculum than is found in programs for older children.

PREPARATION FOR ADULTHOOD

The characteristics of autism are present throughout life for nearly all affected individuals, although the manifestations of the disorder vary at different stages of development (Paul, 1987). Thus, curriculum for adolescents and adults should receive careful attention. Unlike the extensive descriptions of curriculum in the preschool and school years, however, the process of transition to adulthood has been less fully described and lacking in controlled research. Most of the published information on curriculum appears to be influenced by the ecological approach of Brown and his

colleagues. For example, Berkell (1992) described the following curricular domains: (a) life skills for integrated community living, (b) vocational preparation, (c) functional academics, and (d) community-based instruction to aid generalization.

The work of Berkell (1987) and M.D. Smith (1992; M.D. Smith, Belcher, & Juhrs, 1995) illustrates the use of curriculum based on an ecological approach with adaptations for the learning and social characteristics of autism. Berkell described the READDY curriculum, which contains job skills, interpersonal social skills, and job-related activities of daily living. Berkell and Smith have both emphasized the preparation of students with autism for supported employment and the importance of community living skills, including recreation.

In contrast to the preschool curricula that specify skills expected of every student, curricula for adolescents and adults with autism are much more individualized. Berkell (1987) and M.D. Smith (1992; M.D. Smith et al., 1995) emphasized the importance of individualized assessment and matching of individuals to jobs. Social skills and independent work skills are of obvious importance in adulthood, but continuity in curriculum planning must be emphasized. The social skills, language skills, and skills for working in a group that are emphasized in early education are important foundations for later learning and for successful community living and employment. Early education and adult education look very different but share many essential themes.

With regard to the outcome research on curriculum for adolescents and adults, the literature consists of descriptions of programs, such as M.D. Smith et al.'s (1995) Community Services for Autistic Adults and Children, in Maryland. The descriptions are helpful in replicating adult services, and they illustrate individual cases of successful employment and adult living. Although these programs can point to more anecdotal success for their participants than is realized by employees of sheltered workshops or other models, well-controlled comparisons have not been carried out.

CONCLUSION

In the past decade, several important changes have occurred that have made curriculum and classroom structure more effective aspects of education for students with autism. First, and most striking, is the integration of several approaches to curricula. Although writers continue to refer to developmental or cognitive or behavioral, or other approaches, contemporary curricula have borrowed heavily from each other. The result has been combined and integrated approaches that have produced impressive effects on the learning of children and adults. Virtually all curricula that have been the subject of empirical research (a) have been influenced by developmental sequences, (b) address the unusual learning characteristics of autism, (c) use a structured approach, (d) include social and communication skills, and (e) emphasize skills that will generalize and be useful throughout the student's life.

Second, results of well-controlled research on curriculum and structure are being more widely applied in demonstration programs as well as in public schools. This change is very timely because of public and professional concern about the use of punishment in the classroom. Classroom structure and an individualized curriculum have several clear benefits. They are positive approaches that encourage adaptive skills, rather than punishing maladaptive behavior. They are practical for use by teachers who do not typically have extensive resources. They have been shown to have more lasting benefits than other approaches.

Third, recent curricula have moved from teaching many individual developmental skills to teaching the critical skills that are related to autism. Researchers from cognitive, developmental, and behavioral orientations have taught children to be more flexible, to solve novel problems, to initiate social interaction and respond to social cues, and to act spontaneously.

Fourth, the criteria for evaluation of education programs have shifted in recent years from the reduction of problem behavior and skill development in isolation to meaningful changes in quality of life (Horner et al., 1993). An emphasis on curriculum ensures that the outcome of education will be useful in adulthood and throughout life. Recent research has shown that children with autism can learn social, language, and independent work skills that generalize across settings and people. These new approaches open up, for the first

time, the possibility that some children with autism will make friends, achieve in school, and live satisfying adult lives without special services and without the label of autism

Fifth, in evaluating curriculum, one must consider how efficient or practical the curriculum is for the average teacher who wishes to implement it. Many of the curricula that have shown effectiveness have required many hours of individual instruction, or access to resources that are not usually available in schools. In contrast, some approaches, such as pivotal response training, have shown impressive changes in social and language skills that generalize to new people and settings. These changes have followed relatively short periods of instruction. Recent research has shown the benefit of early education, instruction in critical social and language skills, self-management, naturally available reinforcers, and instruction in natural settings. These aspects of curriculum are efficient in the long run because of their impact on the individual's ability to function with greater independence throughout life.

Many more questions remain unanswered about the best curricular approaches in autism. The most thorough and best controlled research has been on children receiving early education services. Programs such as those of Strain (Strain & Cordisco, 1994) and Lovaas (McEachin et al., 1993), and others described by Harris and Handleman (1994), have shared many important elements with other parallel efforts, but they have stood apart in the uniformity of their curriculum. These programs combine a clear structure and curriculum with an expectation that children will acquire certain skills before going on to the next level of learning. Does this outcome mean that there are prerequisite skills for later learning? Or, is there an early "critical period" for learning? The research to date does not answer these questions, but it does open important pathways for the next decade of research and practice.

Cross-References

Aspects of social development are discussed in Chapters 8, 39, and 43. Assessment issues are explored in Chapters 19 through 21. Communication and behavioral intervention are the topics of Chapters 23 through 26, and Chapter 44.

REFERENCES

Baron, M.G., Groden, J., & Cautela, J.R. (1988). Behavioral programming: Expanding our clinical repertoire. In G. Groden & M.G. Baron (Eds.), *Autism: Strategies for change* (pp. 49–73). New York: Gardner.

Baron-Cohen, S. (1988). Social and pragmatic deficits in autism: Cognitive or affective? *Journal of Autism and Developmental Disorders, 18,* 379–402.

Berkell, D.E. (1987). Career development for youth with autism. *Journal of Career Development, 13*(4), 14–20.

Berkell, D.E. (1992). Instructional planning: Goals and practice. In D.E. Berkell (Ed.), *Autism: Identification, education, and treatment* (pp. 89–105). Hillsdale, NJ: Erlbaum.

Beukelman, D.R., & Mirenda, P. (1992). *Augmentative and alternative communication: Management of severe communication disorders in children and adults.* Baltimore: Brookes.

Biklen, D. (1991). Communication unbound: Autism and praxis. *Harvard Educational Review, 60,* 291–314.

Brown, L., Branston, M.B., Baumgart, D., Vincent, L., Falvey, M., & Schroeder, J. (1979). Utilizing the characteristics of a variety of current and subsequent least restrictive environments as factors in the development of curricular content for severely handicapped students. *Association for the Education of the Severely and Profoundly Handicapped Review, 4,* 55–62.

Brown, L., Branston, M.B., Hamre-Nietupski, S., Pumpian, I., Certo, N., & Gruenewald, L. (1979). A strategy for developing chronological age-appropriate functional curricular content for severely handicapped adolescents and young adults. *Journal of Special Education, 13,* 81–90.

Butera, G., & Haywood, H.C. (1992). A cognitive approach to the education of young children with autism. *Focus on Autistic Behavior, 6*(6), 1–14.

Butera, G., & Haywood, H.C. (1995). Cognitive education of young children with autism: An application of Bright Start. In E. Schopler & G.B. Mesibov (Eds.), *Learning and cognition in autism* (pp. 269–292). New York: Plenum Press.

Carr, E.G. (1979). Teaching autistic children to use sign language: Some research issues. *Journal of Autism and Developmental Disorders, 9,* 345–359.

Carr, E.G. (1985). Behavioral approaches to language and communication. In E. Schopler & G.B. Mesibov (Eds.), *Communication problems in autism* (pp. 37–57). New York: Plenum Press.

Carr, E.G., & Durand, V.M. (1985). Reducing behavior problems through functional communication training. *Journal of Applied Behavior Analysis, 18,* 111–126.

Carr, E.G., Levin, L., McConnachie, G., Carlson, J.I., Kemp, D.C., & Smith, C.E. (1994). *Communication-based intervention for problem behavior: A user's guide for producing positive change.* Baltimore: Brookes.

Carr, E.G., McConnachie, G., Levin, L., & Kemp, D.C. (1993). Communication-based treatment of severe behavior problems. In R. Van Houten & S. Axelrod (Eds.), *Behavior analysis and treatment* (pp. 231–267). New York: Plenum Press.

Carr, E.G., Reeve, C.E., & Magito-McLaughlin, D. (1996). Contextual influences on problem behavior in people with developmental disabilities. In L.K. Koegel, R.L. Koegel, & G. Dunlap (Eds.), *Positive behavioral support: Including people with difficult behavior in the community* (pp. 402–423). Baltimore: Brookes.

Carr, E.G., Robinson, S., Taylor, J.C., & Carlson, J.I. (1990). Positive approaches to the treatment of severe behavior problems in persons with developmental disabilities: A review and analysis of reinforcement and stimulus-based procedures. *Monographs of the Association for Persons with Severe Handicaps,* (Monograph No. 4).

Charlop, M.H., Kurtz, P.F., & Milstein, J.P. (1992). Too much reinforcement, too little behavior: Assessing task interspersal procedures in conjunction with different reinforcement schedules with autistic children. *Journal of Applied Behavior Analysis, 25,* 795–808.

Dalrymple, N. (1989). *Developing a functional and longitudinal individual plan. Functional programming for people with autism: A series.* Bloomington: Indiana Resource Center for Autism.

Davis, C.A., Brady, M.P., Hamilton, R., McEvoy, M.A., & Williams, R.E. (1994). Effects of high-probability requests on the social interactions of young children with severe disabilities. *Journal of Applied Behavior Analysis, 27,* 619–637.

Davis, C.A., Brady, M.P., Williams, R.E., & Hamilton, R. (1992). Effects of high-probability requests on the acquisition and generalization of responses to requests in young children with behavior disorders. *Journal of Applied Behavior Analysis, 25,* 905–916.

Dunlap, G. (1984). The influence of task variation and maintenance tasks on the learning and affect of autistic children. *Journal of Experimental Child Psychology, 37,* 41–64.

Dunlap, G., Johnson, L.F., & Robbins, F.R. (1990). Preventing serious behavior problems through skill development and early interventions. In A.C. Repp & N.N. Singh (Eds.), *Perspectives on the use of nonaversive and aversive interventions for persons with developmental disabilities* (pp. 273–286). Sycamore, IL: Sycamore.

Dunlap, G., Kern-Dunlap, L., Clarke, S., & Robbins, F.R. (1991). Functional assessment, curricular revisions, and severe behavior problems. *Journal of Applied Behavior Analysis, 24,* 387–397.

Dyer, K. (1987). The competition of autistic stereotyped behavior with usual and specially assessed reinforcers. *Research in Developmental Disabilities, 8,* 607–626.

Dyer, K., Dunlap, G., & Winterling, V. (1990). Effects of choice making on the serious problem behaviors of students with severe handicaps. *Journal of Applied Behavior Analysis, 23,* 515–524.

Dyer, K., & Peck, C.A. (1987). Current perspectives on social/communication curricula for students with autism and severe handicaps. *Education and Treatment of Children, 10,* 338–351.

Foster-Johnson, L., Ferro, J., & Dunlap, G. (1994). Preferred curricular activities and reduced problem behaviors in students with intellectual disabilities. *Journal of Applied Behavior Analysis, 27,* 493–504.

Fredericks, H.D.B., Anderson, R., & Baldwin, V. (1979). Identifying competency indicators of teachers of the severely handicapped. *Association for the Education for the Severely and Profoundly Handicapped Review, 4,* 81–95.

Goldstein, H., & Cisar, C.L. (1992). Promoting interaction during sociodramatic play: Teaching scripts to typical preschoolers and classmates with disabilities. *Journal of Applied Behavior Analysis, 25,* 265–280.

Harris, S.L., & Handleman, J.S. (1994). *Preschool education programs for children with autism.* Austin, TX: Pro-Ed.

Harris, S.L., Handleman, J.S., & Alessandri, M. (1990). Teaching youths with autism to offer assistance. *Journal of Applied Behavior Analysis, 23,* 297–305.

Hart, B.M., & Risley, T.R. (1975). Incidental teaching of language in the preschool. *Journal of Applied Behavior Analysis, 8,* 411–420.

Hartup, W.W. (1983). Peer relations. In P.H. Mussen (Ed.), *Handbook of child psychology* (Vol. 4, pp. 103–196). New York: John Wiley & Sons.

Horner, R.H., Sprague, J.R., & Flannery, K.B. (1993). Building functional curriculum for students with severe intellectual disabilities and severe problem behaviors. In R. Van Houten & S. Axelrod (Eds.), *Behavior analysis and treatment* (pp. 47–71). New York: Plenum Press.

Horner, R.H., Sprague, J.R., O'Brien, M., & Heathfield, L.T. (1990). The role of response efficiency in the reduction of problem behaviors through functional equivalence training: A case study. *Journal of the Association for Persons with Severe Handicaps, 15,* 91–97.

Hoyson, M., Jamieson, B., & Strain, P.S. (1984). Individualized group instruction of normally developing and autistic-like children: The LEAP curriculum model. *Journal of the Division of Early Childhood, 8,* 157–172.

Jarrold, C., Boucher, J., & Smith, P. (1993). Symbolic play in autism: A review. *Journal of Autism and Developmental Disorders, 23,* 281–307.

Kaufman, B. (1976). *Son-rise.* New York: Harper & Row.

Koegel, L.K., Koegel, R.L., Hurley, C., & Frea, W.D. (1992). Improving social skills and disruptive behavior in children with autism through self-management. *Journal of Applied Behavior Analysis, 25,* 341–353.

Koegel, R.L., & Frea, W.D. (1993). Treatment of social behavior in autism through the modification of pivotal social skills. *Journal of Applied Behavior Analysis, 26,* 369–377.

Koegel, R.L., & Koegel, L.K. (1990). Extended reductions in stereotyped behavior of students with autism through a self-management package. *Journal of Applied Behavior Analysis, 23,* 119–127.

Koegel, R.L., & Koegel, L.K. (Eds.). (1995). *Teaching children with autism: Strategies for initiating positive interactions and improving learning opportunities.* Baltimore: Brookes.

Koegel, R.L., O'Dell, M.C., & Koegel, L.K. (1987). A natural language teaching paradigm for nonverbal autistic children. *Journal of Autism and Developmental Disorders, 17,* 187–200.

Kohler, F.W., & Strain, P.S. (1993). The Early Childhood Social Skills Program: Making friends during the early childhood years. *Teaching Exceptional Children, 25,* 41–42.

Krantz, P.J., MacDuff, M.T., & McClannahan, L.E. (1993). Programming participation in family activities for children with autism: Parents' use of photographic activity schedules. *Journal of Applied Behavior Analysis, 26,* 137–138.

Krantz, P.J., & McClannahan, L.E. (1993). Teaching children with autism to initiate to peers: Effects of a script-fading procedure. *Journal of Applied Behavior Analysis, 26,* 121–132.

Lalli, J.S., Casey, S., Goh, H., & Merlino, J. (1994). Treatment of escape-maintained aberrant behavior with escape extinction and predictable routines. *Journal of Applied Behavior Analysis, 27,* 705–714.

Lord, C., & Schopler, E. (1994). TEACCH services for preschool children. In S.L. Harris & J.S. Handleman (Eds.), *Preschool education for children with autism* (pp. 87–106). Austin, TX: Pro-Ed.

Lovaas, O.I. (1977). *The autistic child: Language development through behavior modification.* New York: Irvington.

Lovaas, O.I. (with Ackerman, A., Alexander, D., Firestone, P., Perkins, M., Young, D.B., Carr, E.G., & Newsom, C.). (1981). *Teaching developmentally disabled children: The ME book.* Baltimore: University Park Press.

Lovaas, O.I. (1987). Behavioral treatment and normal educational and intellectual functioning in young autistic children. *Journal of Consulting and Clinical Psychology, 55,* 3–9.

Lovaas, O.I. (1993). The development of a treatment-research project for developmentally disabled and autistic children. *Journal of Applied Behavior Analysis, 26,* 617–630.

Lovaas, O.I. (1994). Interview with Ivar Lovaas continued. *The Advocate: Newsletter of the Autism Society of America, Inc., 26*(6), 19–23.

Lovaas, O.I., & Smith, T. (1989). A comprehensive behavioral theory of autistic children: Paradigm for research and treatment. *Journal of Behavior Therapy and Experimental Psychiatry, 20,* 17–29.

MacDuff, G.S., Krantz, P.J., & McClannahan, L.E. (1993). Teaching children with autism to use photographic activity schedules: Maintenance and generalization of complex response chains. *Journal of Applied Behavior Analysis, 26,* 89–97.

McEachin, J.J., Smith, T., & Lovaas, O.I. (1993). Long-term outcome for children with autism who received early intensive behavioral treatment. *American Journal on Mental Retardation, 97,* 359–372.

McGee, G.G., Daly, T., & Jacobs, H.A. (1994). The Walden Preschool. In S.L. Harris & J.S. Handleman (Eds.), *Preschool education programs for children with autism* (pp. 127–162). Austin, TX: Pro-Ed.

McGee, J.J., Menolascino, F.J., Hobbs, D.C., & Menousek, P.E. (1987). *Gentle teaching: A nonaversive approach to helping people with mental retardation.* New York: Human Sciences Press.

Mirenda, P.L., & Donnellan, A.M. (1987). Issues in curriculum development. In D.J. Cohen & A.M. Donnellan (Eds.), *Handbook of autism and pervasive developmental disorders* (pp. 211–226). New York: John Wiley & Sons.

Neel, R.S., & Billingsley, F.F. (1989). *IMPACT: A functional curriculum handbook for students with moderate to severe disabilities.* Baltimore: Brookes.

Olley, J.G., Robbins, F.R., & Morelli-Robbins, M. (1993). Current practices in early intervention for children with autism. In E. Schopler, M.E. Van Bourgondien, & M.M. Bristol (Eds.), *Preschool issues in autism* (pp. 223–245). New York: Plenum Press.

O'Neill, R.E., Horner, R.H., Albin, R.W., Storey, K., & Sprague, J.R. (1990). *Functional analysis: A practical assessment guide.* Sycamore, IL: Sycamore.

Ozonoff, S., & Miller, J.N. (1995). Teaching theory of mind: A new approach to social skills training for individuals with autism. *Journal of Autism and Developmental Disorders, 25,* 415–433.

Palumbo, L.W., Reeve, C.E., & Carr, E.G. (1991, April). *Effects of context on communicative efficiency and behavior problems.* Poster presented at City University of New York (Queens), New York.

Park, D. (1974). Operant conditioning of a speaking autistic child. *Journal of Autism and Childhood Schizophrenia, 4,* 189–191.

Paul, R. (1987). Natural history. In D.J. Cohen & A.M. Donnellan (Eds.), *Handbook of autism and pervasive developmental disorders* (pp. 121–130). New York: John Wiley & Sons.

Peck, C.A., Schuler, A.L., Haring, T.G., Willard, C., Theimer, R.K., & Semmel, M.I. (1986). Teaching social/communicative skills to children with autism and severe handicaps: Issues in assessment and curriculum selection. *Child Study Journal, 16,* 297–313.

Porco, B. (1989). *Growing towards independence by learning functional skills and behaviors. Functional programming for people with autism. Revised: A series.* Bloomington: Indiana Resource Center for Autism.

Powell, S.D., & Jordan, R.R. (1992). Remediating the thinking of pupils with autism: Principles into practice. *Journal of Autism and Developmental Disorders, 22,* 413–418.

Pyles, D.A.M., & Bailey, J.S. (1990). Diagnosing severe behavior problems. In A.C. Repp & N.N. Singh (Eds.), *Perspectives on the use of nonaversive and aversive interventions for persons with developmental disabilities* (pp. 381–401). Sycamore, IL: Sycamore.

Quill, K., Gurry, S., & Larkin, A. (1989). Daily Life Therapy: A Japanese model for educating children with autism. *Journal of Autism and Developmental Disorders, 19,* 625–635.

Reichle, J., York, J., & Sigafoos, J. (1991). *Implementing augmentative and alternative communication: Strategies for learners with severe disabilities.* Baltimore: Brookes.

Sainato, D.M., Goldstein, H., & Strain, P.S. (1992). Effects of self-evaluation on preschool children's use of social interaction strategies with their classmates with autism. *Journal of Applied Behavior Analysis, 25,* 127–141.

Schopler, E. (1994). Behavioral priorities for autism and related developmental disorders. In E. Schopler & G.B. Mesibov (Eds.), *Behavioral issues in autism* (pp. 55–77). New York: Plenum Press.

Schopler, E., Lansing, M., & Waters, L. (1983). *Individualized assessment and treatment for autistic and developmentally disabled children: Vol. 3. Teaching activities for autistic children.* Austin, TX: Pro-Ed.

Schopler, E., Mesibov, G.B., Shigley, H., & Bashford, A. (1984). Helping autistic children through their parents: The TEACCH model. In E. Schopler & G.B. Mesibov (Eds.), *The effects of autism on the family* (pp. 65–81). New York: Plenum Press.

Schopler, E., Reichler, R.J., Bashford, A., Lansing, M., & Marcus, L.M. (1990). *Individualized assessment and treatment for autistic and developmentally disabled children: Vol. 1. Psychoeducational Profile Revised.* Austin, TX: Pro-Ed.

Schopler, E., Reichler, R.J., & Lansing, M. (1980). *Individualized assessment and treatment for autistic and developmentally disabled children: Vol. 2. Teaching strategies for parents and professionals.* Baltimore: University Park Press.

Schopler, E., Short, A., & Mesibov, G.B. (1989). Relation of behavioral treatment to "normal functioning": Comment on Lovaas. *Journal of Consulting and Clinical Psychology, 57,* 162–164.

Schreibman, L. (1988). *Autism.* Newbury Park, CA: Sage.

Smith, M.D. (1992). Community integration and supported employment. In D.E. Berkell (Ed.),

Autism: Identification, education, and treatment (pp. 253–271). Hillsdale, NJ: Erlbaum.

Smith, M.D., Belcher, R.G., & Juhrs, P.D. (1995). *A guide to successful employment for individuals with autism.* Baltimore: Brookes.

Smith, T. (1993). Autism. In T.R. Giles (Ed.), *Effective psychotherapies* (pp. 107–133). New York: Plenum Press.

Stahmer, A.C. (1995). Teaching symbolic play skills to children with autism using pivotal response training. *Journal of Autism and Developmental Disorders, 25,* 123–141.

Stahmer, A.C., & Schreibman, L. (1992). Teaching children with autism appropriate play in unsupervised environments using a self-management treatment package. *Journal of Applied Behavior Analysis, 25,* 447–459.

Stokes, T.F., & Baer, D.M. (1977). An implicit technology of generalization. *Journal of Applied Behavior Analysis, 10,* 349–367.

Stone, W.L., Lemanek, K.L., Fishel, P.T., Fernandez, M.C., & Altemeier, W.A. (1990). Play and imitation skills in the diagnosis of autism in young children. *Pediatrics, 86,* 267–272.

Strain, P.S., & Cordisco, L.K. (1994). LEAP preschool. In S.L. Harris & J.S. Handleman (Eds.), *Preschool education programs for children with autism* (pp. 225–244). Austin, TX: Pro-Ed.

Strain, P.S., Kohler, F.W., Storey, K., & Danko, C.D. (1994). Teaching preschoolers with autism to self-monitor their social interactions: An analysis of results in home and school settings. *Journal of Emotional and Behavioral Disorders, 2,* 78–88.

Sulzer-Azaroff, B., & Mayer, G.R. (1991). *Behavior analysis for lasting change.* Fort Worth, TX: Holt, Rinehart and Winston.

Sweeney, H.M., & LeBlanc, J.M. (1995). Effects of task size on work-related and aberrant behaviors of youths with autism and mental retardation. *Research in Developmental Disabilities, 16,* 97–115.

Thorp, D.M., Stahmer, A.C., & Schreibman, L. (1995). Effects of sociodramatic play training on children with autism. *Journal of Autism and Developmental Disorders, 25,* 265–282.

Van Bourgondien, M.E. (1993). Behavior management in the preschool years. In E. Schopler & M.E. Van Bourgondien (Eds.), *Preschool issues in autism* (pp. 129–145). New York: Plenum Press.

Van Houten, R., Axelrod, S., Bailey, J.S., Favell, J.E., Foxx, R.M., Iwata, B.A., & Lovaas, O.I. (1988). Association for Behavior Analysis position statement on clients' rights to effective behavioral treatment. *Journal of Applied Behavior Analysis, 21,* 381–384.

Watson, L.R., Lord, C., Schaffer, B., & Schopler, E. (1989). *Teaching spontaneous communication to autistic and developmentally handicapped children.* New York: Irvington.

Wisocki, P. (1988). Behavioral assessment procedures for the evaluation of children with autism. In G. Groden & M.G. Baron (Eds.), *Autism: Strategies for change* (pp. 21–48). New York: Gardner.

SECTION FIVE

Interventions

The driving force for research on autism and pervasive developmental disorders is the provision of increasingly effective treatment and interventions. This goal is extremely challenging. The impairments of individuals with autism start at the dawn of development, in the first year or two of life. They are severe and broad-based interferences in the unfolding of basic competencies in socialization and communication, and are compounded by intellectual disability. They are of unknown origin and life-long duration.

The planning of an intervention strategy must be carefully related to the assessment of a child's or adult's current level of functioning; an understanding of the individual's strengths and difficulties; a theoretical and pragmatic model for planning and delivering long-term, stage-by-stage programming; and a vision of the individual's potential future. To be effective, an intervention strategy must be broad-gauged and related to the full range of an individual's impairments. The interventions must recognize individual domains of difficulties (e.g., speech and language, or motor skills) as well as the interaction among domains (e.g., the ways in which social and language development proceed). Because autism starts early and persists, the interventions must be thoughtfully adapted to the individual's chronological age and developmental phase. A program of education and socialization that is suitable for a 5-year-old child would be incongruous with a young adult.

The types and strategies for intervention are guided primarily by a pragmatic concern for what is useful in promoting development and adaptation. The primary locus for intervention is almost always educational, and the central professionals involved in intervention are educators. Through the application of scientific knowledge about learning and development, special educators aim at helping individuals with autism and other pervasive disorders to use their areas of competence, to expand their skills and capacities, and to develop approaches to circumventing areas of difficulty in order to move ahead in their personal and social adaptation. In this endeavor, special educators are equipped with theories about social, language, and other types of learning, as well as models for teaching (curricula).

Approaches to intervention are guided by theories of developmental psychopathology that focus attention on particular domains. Thus, there is a general emphasis on the importance of social cognition, on learning communicative and social skills, and on enhancing motivation to achieve a reduction of interfering and maladaptive behaviors. Intervention is also shaped by ideological considerations that relate to the importance of preparing individuals to remain as fully participative in their communities as possible; to be able to take an active role in their families and in a broader social world; and to develop the skills necessary for independence and productivity in their adult life, to the degree that is possible.

Throughout the life of an individual with autism, parents remain vital to the person's welfare and development. A well-functioning strategy for intervention represents a collaboration between family and professionals, and it reflects the values, style, and goals of the family. Only through such partnership can there be suitable and sensitive resolution of issues relating to: the methods that might be used to deal with specific maladaptive behaviors, the potential for an individual to live within the family, the expression of sexual and other intimate behaviors, the types of work and the exposures to risks that are acceptable, the role for medication, and similar concerns.

Having an autistic child or sibling places unique and sometimes quite difficult burdens on families. When families are full partners in a program for intervention, their own special needs are also recognized and they are provided with suitable support and guidance. There is a delicate balance—varying among different families and according to the various stages of an individual's and a family's life—between, on one hand, the model that emphasizes collaboration between professionals and families, and, on the other hand, the model that recognizes and meets the needs of parents and siblings and sees them as requiring and deserving care in their own right. Encouraging parents to clearly define their views and wishes is an important step in resolving the tensions that can arise between the "collaborative" and "clinical" paradigms. The provision of fully informed consent is ethically central to all clinical and professional intervention with individuals with autism and their families.

In the United States, and in most other nations in the world today, autistic children and others with severe developmental problems live at home and participate in family life. Generally, they attend neighborhood schools and programs, sometimes spending all or part of their days with normal children who are close to them in age. In some nations, and for some children in the United States, programming takes place in specialized day settings—for younger children, in therapeutic nurseries and day programs; for older children, in special classes or specialized schools for individuals with developmental disabilities. It is unusual in the United States, and in most other nations, for children with autism and similar disorders to require extended (or even *any*) out-of-home placement, or to enter residential programs (such as hospitals, therapeutic treatment centers, or longer-term facilities). However, occasional respite care and camps are useful for the family and for the autistic individual. Some autistic persons have such extremely severe behavioral difficulties that residential or hospital treatment is required. Also, although home residence may seem optimal, exceptions need to be respected. There are children without families, children whose families are unable to provide a suitable setting for them, children who themselves do better outside of the family, and children for whom foster care or other settings, including residential treatment, are clearly indicated. As individuals with autism mature and reach adulthood, and as their parents mature and reach old age, it is natural for them to have a transition from family life to another setting, such as a group home, a supported apartment, or a residential program.

Wherever a child or adult lives and is cared for, intervention strategies and the atmosphere of the program must respect the individual's humanity and personal value; programs must appreciate and enhance the individual's personal autonomy and individuality. Toward individuals with severe behavioral problems and intellectual disabilities, maintaining this attitude of concern, empathy, and respect is not a simple matter in any setting, whether a school, a hospital, or a residential program. Constant attention, consciousness raising, monitoring, and excellent administration are required. Without such vigilance, it is easy for humane standards to slip, as has occurred all too often not only in large institutions but also in nursing homes, special schools, group homes, independent living settings, and residential programs, as well as, tragically, in the context of a stressed family.

Care for the whole person with a developmental disability requires special consideration of his or her physical and general health needs. Individuals with autism, mental retardation, and other disabilities deserve high-quality, comprehensive health care, including routine preventive health measures (such as immunizations and dental care) and special health evaluation and treatment (vision, hearing, nutrition, and orthopedic examinations). Family practitioners may provide "routine" evaluation, monitoring, and treatment, but individuals with developmental disabilities often require the episodic or continuing special expertise of physicians with training and professional interest in autism and developmental disabilities. This level of care is particularly important when there are complicated comorbid conditions—such as a seizure or a metabolic disorder—or behavioral and psychiatric problems that require psychopharmacological treatment in combination with other behavioral approaches. It is important for medical management to be closely integrated with other strategies for intervention, and for prescribing physicians to work as members of the treatment team. Medication should be prescribed only in the context of an individual's full profile—his or her experiences at home and in school, plus other ongoing and planned interventions that may be aimed at the same targets, for example, reduction of stereotypic, compulsive, or self-injurious behavior. An advocate (a nurse, educator, physician, social worker, or other professional) working closely with parents can help coordinate the range of interventions and ensure communication and collaboration among professionals and settings of care.

There is no cure for autism. Thus, clinicians must strive to ameliorate difficulties and help the individual with autism cope to the highest degree possible. Families and professionals need to be realistic about what can be achieved using current knowledge and methods; yet they should maintain reasonable hope for future advances.

Where there is no cure, however, there are often countless treatments, especially when the clinical problems are urgent, as with autism. Autism can be a heartbreaking disorder. Professionals and others wish to be helpful, and, in this field, as with other types of incurable medical disorders, hoping and wishing can breed belief in the benefits of an unproven therapy or a "miracle cure." Routinely, parents and professionals will hear about "breakthroughs" and "alternatives" that promise striking success but for which no rigorous studies or data are available.

Many treatments start on the basis of chance observation, and anecdotal reports may contain important truths. In the usual course of science, these hunches and observations become hypotheses that are rigorously tested for their efficacy and safety. Only when the objective data about benefits and dangers are available should a potential treatment be undertaken outside of a careful research setting.

One aspect of showing respect for individuals with autism and other disorders is to ensure that interventions withstand the tests of rigorous investigation, publication of findings for peer review, and replication. The gradual improvement of interventions for individuals with autism and associated disorders, as described in this section, is testimony to the value of this scientific approach.

CHAPTER 23

Enhancing Language and Communication Development: Theoretical Foundations

AMY M. WETHERBY, ADRIANA L. SCHULER, AND BARRY M. PRIZANT

Communicative competence may be the primary factor determining the extent to which individuals with autism and Pervasive Developmental Disorder (PDD) can develop relationships with others and can participate in daily activities and routines at school, at home, and in the community. The level of communicative competence achieved by persons with autism and PDD is closely related to the development of social behavior (Garfin & Lord, 1986) and measures of outcome (Lotter, 1978; McEachin, Smith, & Lovaas, 1993). Moreover, gains in communication skills seem to be directly related to the reduction of challenging behavior (Carr & Durand, 1986; Smith, 1985).

Providing effective programming for communication enhancement for individuals with autism and related disorders is an extremely challenging endeavor. Although there is a clear consensus on the importance of enhancing communication abilities for persons with autism and PDD, intervention approaches vary greatly and may even appear diametrically opposed to the specific goals and procedures that are advocated. Past efforts at speech and language intervention have focused primarily on the form or structural dimensions of speech and language; that is, on building labeling vocabulary, phrases, and clauses through repetition and rote training. However, individuals with autism and PDD are most challenged by their limited understanding of the conventions of communication, including its communicative and cognitive functions. In addition to limitations in the development of conventional gestures and words, difficulties in the social use of nonverbal and verbal behavior have a major impact on communicative effectiveness (Prizant & Wetherby, 1987). Because of these dual challenges, the focus of communication enhancement efforts must be the development of functional communication abilities, rather than just the development of communicative means or behaviors.

The developmental and social-cognitive differences associated with autism and PDD must also be taken into account. The social-cognitive style demonstrated by many individuals with autism and PDD has a profound effect on the acquisition of symbols and communication systems, and possibly an even greater effect on the ability to use language effectively in social interactions. Caregivers and practitioners—and, indeed, persons with autism and PDD—are challenged by a complex interaction of communicative and language limitations, behavior problems, and an uneven profile of learning strengths and weaknesses. Such cognitive discrepancies—as reflected by the ability of many persons to reproduce, by rote, memorized speech in specific contexts—may mask the true communicative limitations and may result in challenging behavior that arises when expectations about a person's ability to communicate are unrealistic. This chapter examines communicative and social-cognitive differences from a communication enhancement perspective. The intent here is to establish the conceptual and philosophical basis for the next two chapters, in which more specific guidelines for assessment and communication enhancement are provided.

SOCIAL COMMUNICATION FRAMEWORK: A TRANSACTIONAL PERSPECTIVE

Approaches to communication enhancement must be rooted in sound theory or philosophy (Prizant & Wetherby, 1989); otherwise, clinical efforts will be unsystematic, ineffective, or inefficient, and may be frustrating to all involved. The philosophy should emphasize and focus on the social-affective basis of verbal and nonverbal communication in real-life contexts, rather than merely on the structural dimensions of speech and language training received in artificial and contrived settings (e.g., training of speech repetition). Professionals who wish to work effectively with individuals with autism and PDD must understand how and why these individuals communicate. Enhancing communication is not merely a matter of expanding a repertoire of words and sentences. Such skills are mostly superfluous if an individual has limited understanding of how to use them in a communicative interaction. This section addresses the importance of understanding the learning style and characteristics of individuals with autism and PDD in order to make an effective communication enhancement effort. Later sections review pertinent issues underlying the advocated intervention philosophy and approaches, which will be discussed in detail in Chapter 24 (on nonspeaking individuals) and Chapter 25 (on persons at language levels).

Understanding Communication in Autism and PDD

Earlier publications have suggested that the constructs of *intentionality* and *conventionality* contribute significantly to understanding communicative behavior of persons with autism (Prizant & Wetherby, 1987; Schuler & Prizant, 1985). Bates (1979) defined communicative intent as "signaling behavior in which the sender is aware a priori of the effect that a signal will have on his listener, and he persists in that behavior until the effect is obtained or failure is clearly indicated" (p. 36). However, not all communicative behaviors are intentional. Any behavior can serve a communicative function, regardless of whether the effect was intended (Dunst, Lowe, & Bartholomew, 1990). Alterna-

tively, communicative behavior may fail to accomplish the purpose or function originally intended. Communicative competence is greatly determined by the ability to evaluate and monitor one's own communicative effectiveness, and, when necessary, to fix or "repair" failed communicative attempts. The more effective the communicator, the more likely communicative behaviors will serve intended purposes.

Many individuals with autism and PDD show limited expression of communicative intentions that involve social goals, such as sharing experiences. This is especially true for young children and for persons with autism who have great limitations in communicative ability. Additionally, there may be particular difficulty in following and using common indicating strategies (e.g., pointing) to establish a joint focus of attention with communicative partners. Communicative acts, especially in early stages of communication and language development, are heavily skewed toward behavior regulation functions or need-based functions, such as requesting an object or protesting an event, as opposed to functions that are more social in nature, such as commenting, describing, or sharing emotions (Curcio, 1978; Mundy, Sigman, & Kasari, 1990; Wetherby & Prutting, 1984). This communicative pattern appears to be closely tied to social-cognitive differences; that is, motivations to communicate are focused on immediate needs and properties of the physical world rather than on social interactions and socioemotional concerns. This focus is analogous with Kanner's (1943) early claims of dissociations between person and object intelligence in autism.

Conventionality in communicative signaling refers to the degree to which the meaning of signals is shared or understood by a social community. At its most basic level, communicative behavior may be conceptualized along two dimensions: (a) as communicative means, or the behaviors used to communicate (e.g., gestures, words); and (b) as communicative function, or the goals that are actually accomplished through those means (e.g., requesting objects or actions, providing information). Typically developing children acquire communicative intentions on the basis of observed function—that is, children learn to communicate through the predictable reactions of others, first in response to their preintentional signals produced without specific purposes in mind, and eventually in response to intentional and purposeful prelinguistic and linguistic signals. Early in development, caregivers assign meaning to a range of vocal as well as nonvocal behaviors, and communicative means become increasingly conventionalized through reciprocal social exchanges (Ainsworth & Bell, 1974; Bates, 1979; Bruner, 1975; McLean, 1990).

It is now widely accepted that individuals with autism and PDD acquire unconventional behaviors to express communicative intentions in the absence of more conventional means (Prizant & Wetherby, 1987). Even speech production (e.g., delayed echolalia) may be unconventional in both form and function (Prizant & Rydell, 1993). In addition, nonverbal and paralinguistic behavior, including gesture, facial expression, intonation, and body orientation, typically is limited in augmenting communicative effectiveness (Fay & Schuler, 1980; Prizant, 1988; Ricks & Wing, 1975). The development of idiosyncratic communication patterns, which commonly incorporate unconventional and often undesirable communicative means, is frequently observed. These patterns may possibly emerge from the limited ability in imitating others and in social learning. Certain behaviors, previously dismissed as aberrant and nonfunctional, have been found through functional assessment to serve a variety of communicative purposes (Donnellan, Mirenda, Mesaros, & Fassbender, 1984). The use of unconventional and idiosyncratic communicative means places a greater burden on the communicative partner to be sensitive to body language and other subtle, difficult-to-read signals.

Contributions of a Developmental Framework

The burgeoning literature in social, communicative, and cognitive development provides a theoretical foundation both for understanding communication problems and for implementing effective and developmentally appropriate interventions. Three significant principles, drawn from the literature on communication development, are seen as crucial to understanding and enhancing the communication abilities of persons with autism (Prizant & Wetherby, 1989). First, communication development involves continuity from preverbal to verbal communication; that is, the development of preverbal communication is a necessary precursor to the development of the intentional use of language to communicate. Words should be mapped onto preverbal communication skills. For individuals with autism who do not speak, emphasis should be placed on developing preverbal social and communication skills. Second, a competent communicator is the product of a developmental interaction of cognitive, social-affective, and linguistic capacities. An individual's developmental profile across these domains should provide the basis for decision making for communication enhancement. Third, in a developmental framework, all behavior should be viewed in reference to the individual's relative level of functioning across developmental domains. Many of the challenging behaviors developed by individuals with autism and PDD can be understood as attempts to communicate if such behaviors are interpreted relative to developmental discrepancies and as coping strategies in the face of significant communicative limitations.

In attempting to understand the limitations in communicative intentions displayed by individuals with autism, it is helpful to consider the predictable sequences through which typically developing children acquire various communication skills (see Bates, O'Connell, & Shore, 1987; Lahey, 1988; and McLean, 1990, for reviews). As noted, research has documented that the development of preverbal communication is a necessary precursor to the development of the intentional use of language to communicate (Bates, 1979; Harding & Golinkoff, 1979). Children who are developing normally use prelinguistic gestures and vocalizations to communicate intentionally for a variety of purposes. Bruner (1981) suggested that three "innate communicative intentions" emerge during the first year of life:

1. Behavior regulation—communication used to regulate another's behavior for purposes of obtaining or restricting environmental goals.
2. Social interaction—communication used to direct another's attention to oneself for affiliative purposes.

3. Joint attention—communication used to direct another's attention for purposes of sharing the focus on an entity or event.

Prior to the emergence of words, normally developing children use intentional communicative signals for these three major functions (Wetherby, Cain, Yonclas, & Walker, 1988). Over the second year of life, these communicative intentions are expressed with more sophisticated and conventional signals, paving the way for the acquisition of symbolic communication.

Wetherby (1986) suggested that the easiest and first emerging communicative intention for persons with autism is behavior regulation, and the most difficult is joint attention, presumably because of the differing social underpinnings of these respective abilities. A lack of joint attention skills has become a hallmark of autism, as accumulated studies have documented this deficit in children with autism and PDD (Loveland & Landry, 1986; Mundy et al., 1990; Wetherby & Prutting, 1984). Because of the early emergence of joint attention in normal development, this limitation has important implications for early identification of autism and PDD (Baron-Cohen, Allen, & Gillberg, 1992; DiLavore, Lord, & Rutter, 1995; Mundy, Kasari, & Sigman, 1992; Prizant & Wetherby, 1987; Wetherby & Prizant, 1993). Furthermore, an individual's range of communicative intentions should be considered in deciding how to enhance communication development. Rather than setting goals based on form alone (e.g., gestures, words), enhancement should begin with an emphasis on function and form, such as use of gestures for behavior regulation, which is an easier-to-master and more specific functional goal for persons with autism and PDD. Once gains are made in behavior regulation, greater emphasis should be placed on communicating for more social purposes of social interaction and joint attention.

Pragmatic-social interactive theories since the late 1970s have focused on the role of social interaction in language development and have emphasized that successful communication involves reciprocity and mutual negotiation (Lahey, 1988; McLean, 1990). Joint action between the child and caregiver forms the social context in which children learn to talk (Bruner, 1978). From early in life, infants make deliberate attempts to share experiences with caregivers by sharing attention and affective states (Stern, 1985). Early displays of affect and directed eye gaze serve as signals to regulate interaction and help the caregiver read the infant's emotional state (Tronick, 1989). Children are viewed as active participants who learn to affect the behavior and ideas of others through active signaling, and who gradually acquire more sophisticated and conventional means to communicate, given the caregivers' contingent social responsiveness (Dunst et al., 1990). Thus, the combination of the readability of the child's signals and the caregiver's contingent social responsiveness influences the successful acquisition of communication and language.

Communication development reflects the mutual interaction of the child and significant others. The transactional model of development proposed by Sameroff (Sameroff, 1987; Sameroff & Chandler, 1975) underscores the developmental interplay between a child and his or her social environment. This model emphasizes child effects, implying that a child's behavior influences the caregiver's responsiveness, which, in turn, significantly influences the child's development. A compromised biology of early socialization will thus serve to transform the caregiving environment in a transactional fashion. The caregivers' ability to counteract these transactional effects and, ultimately, to foster successful communication will depend on the formal and informal supports available to them (Dunst et al., 1990).

The recent focus on encouraging individuals with autism to initiate more and to take a more active role in communicating should lead to the acquisition of greater knowledge of the reciprocal nature of communicative interactions, and, ultimately, conversation (Dawson & Galpert, 1986; Mirenda & Donnellan, 1986). Numerous intervention studies have demonstrated that providing opportunities to initiate communication and then responding contingently can result in meaningful gains in eye gaze and communicative behavior (Dawson & Adams, 1984; Klinger & Dawson, 1992; Mirenda & Donnellan, 1986; Peck, 1985). If responses to a child's communicative efforts are clear, consistent, and contingent on the meaning and intention expressed, the child is more likely to learn about the most effective way to express intentions successfully (Prizant & Wetherby, 1989).

The process of language acquisition may also be viewed from a broader cultural perspective. One of the unique qualities of humans is their ability to transmit and acquire knowledge from others, and to consider the perspective of others (Bruner, 1975; Vygotsky, 1934/1962). This capacity has been referred to as cultural learning. Tomasello, Kruger, and Ratner (1993) have recently described the ontogeny of cultural learning as progressing through three stages:

1. Imitative learning, in which learners imitate models provided.
2. Instructed learning, in which learners internalize the rules of the instructor and regulate their own attentional and learning strategies.
3. Collaborative learning, in which learners construct new meanings or ideas with other learners.

A child's emerging communicative competence reflects the child's developing capacity for cultural learning. Communication and language development in autism and PDD must be approached within a broad social-cognitive context that affords opportunities for cultural learning.

Understanding Challenging Behavior from a Communicative Perspective

Despite the fact that as many as 50% of individuals with autism display some functional speech and language skills (Prizant, 1988), problem behaviors such as aggression and self-injury may be used to procure attention, to escape from a task or situation, to protest against changes of schedule and routine, or to regulate social interactions in a predictable manner. For example, Carr and Durand (1985) reported that aggression, tantrums, and self-injury were more likely to occur in situations with a high level of task difficulty and a low level of adult attention. These challenging behaviors may range on a continuum, from automatic and nondeliberate to preintentional expression of internal states (such as frustration, boredom, or anxiety), and to intentional communication (e.g., protesting) used to deliberately affect others' behaviors (Prizant & Wetherby, 1987; Wetherby, 1986).

Given that unconventional forms of behavior often serve communicative purposes, efforts to manage behavior problems should acknowledge the functions that the problematic behavior might serve. Long-term solutions to many behavior problems ultimately involve the development of communicative skills, both to replace challenging behaviors used to communicate intent, and to prevent the further development of behavior problems. Positive, nonaversive, and respectful approaches to the management of challenging behaviors are becoming widely accepted as *best practices* for individuals with severe disabilities (see Carr et al., 1994; Horner et al., 1990; Reichle & Wacker, 1993). The expanded use and improved technology of functional assessment of challenging behavior have led to a variety of alternatives to using punishment as a way of precluding or managing difficult behavior (see Carr et al., 1994; Horner et al., 1990; Meyer & Evans, 1986; Reichle & Wacker, 1993). One effective intervention derived from a functional assessment has been to teach functional equivalents of, or replacements for, the challenging behaviors (Carr & Durand, 1986; Horner et al., 1990; Prizant & Rydell, 1993). For example, some challenging behaviors are determined through a functional assessment to serve a communicative function (i.e., either to request an object or attention, or to "escape" from a boring or frustrating activity). Functional communication training entails teaching the individual an alternative, appropriate communicative means to express the function(s) served by the challenging behaviors (Carr & Durand, 1985; Durand, 1990). A significant body of literature has demonstrated how functional communication training can lead to (a) a reduction in problem behavior, (b) generalization across people and social contexts, and (c) maintenance of acquired skills over time (see Durand, Berotti, & Weiner, 1993, for a review). It has been demonstrated that the challenging behavior will be reduced only if the alternative communicative means serves the same function as the challenging behavior (Carr & Durand, 1985).

Challenging behaviors do not always serve communicative ends; they may reflect internal states or environmental variables rather than the expression of communicative intentions. However, the boundary between intentional and preintentional behavior is not precise. Preintentional behavior may eventually be used intentionally when the effects or outcome of these behaviors become anticipated as a result of previous experience with others' reactions. Intentionality is thus a matter of degree rather than an all-or-nothing phenomenon (Prizant & Wetherby, 1985; Wetherby & Prizant, 1989). For instance, rather elaborate speech may reflect only limited communicative intent, such as when the same phrase is literally repeated over and over without any adjustment to allow for greater communicative efficacy. Typically, the greater the intent, the greater the persistence, repair, and diversification of the behavior if initial attempts are unsuccessful or if anticipated outcomes are violated (Wetherby & Prizant, 1989).

The nature and extent of the challenging behaviors of individuals with autism and PDD are certainly primary determinants of the extent of independence that can be achieved in domestic, educational, and, eventually, vocational settings. Assessment and communication enhancement efforts should thus examine an individual's communicative system as a whole, including apparently unconventional and/or challenging behaviors, which may serve communicative and/or cognitive functions. Because these matters are most critical for individuals with severe communicative and cognitive disabilities, they are discussed in considerable detail in Chapter 24 (on prelanguage approaches). Nevertheless, for verbal as well as nonverbal individuals, the basic tenet accepted is that behavior problems should always be examined in the context of an individual's repertoire of communicative means and functions, and how these are used in a natural context. To acquire a more fully integrated picture of communicative abilities, cognitive differences also must be considered.

DEVELOPMENTAL DISCONTINUITY AND COGNITIVE STYLE

A broad understanding of communication from a functional perspective needs to be combined with knowledge of the developmental discrepancies and discontinuities associated with autism and PDD. Behavioral and communicative differences can only be understood in reference to social-cognitive differences, because of their common roots. Evidence for cognitive differences has been gathered from a number of sources, including (a) intelligence testing (see DeMyer, 1975; Prior, 1979) and claims of generalized cognitive deficits (Rimland, 1964; Rutter, 1968, 1983); (b) applied learning research on persistent generalization problems (for a discussion, see Koegel, Rincover, & Egel, 1982) and so-called stimulus-overselectivity (for a review, see Lovaas, Koegel, & Schreibman, 1979); (c) research on information processing and theory of mind (Baron-Cohen, Leslie, & Frith, 1985); and (d) developmental discontinuity, as evidenced by specific patterns of abilities and disabilities (see Schuler, 1995, for a review).

Developmental discontinuity has intrigued caregivers as well as professionals ever since the publication of Kanner's first case studies (1943), in which he referred to his subjects as cognitively "well endowed," based on observations of isolated specific ability. Approximately two-thirds of all individuals with autism have subsequently been described as intellectually impaired, based on their performance on standard IQ tests (DeMyer, 1975). Although some of the commonly observed areas of relative ability have been discarded as "splinter skills," the true nature of the cognitive differences and cognitive impairments continues to challenge researchers and practitioners. The often striking contradictions between apparent intellectual promise (based on observation of specific skills) and significant limitations in communicative and adaptive skills are a source of great interest and promise—and frustration—for those closely involved with people with autism and PDD.

The patterns of relative strengths and weaknesses identified in the literature provide some insight into this matter. Commonly cited abilities of autistic persons include an excellent rote memory for both visual and auditory information, and proficiency in tasks demanding visual-spatial judgment and pattern recognition (Grandin, 1995; Prior, 1979; Prizant, 1983b). Specific skills related to these abilities include both recognition and reproduction of melodic patterns; construction of visual-spatial arrays from samples (e.g., elaborate arrangements of blocks); and solution of jigsaw puzzles, form boards, block design tasks, and so forth.

Information processing research, capitalizing on a now classic series of experiments conducted by Hermelin and O'Connor (1970) and Frith (1971), has further clarified the cognitive traits of individuals with autism and PDD. These individuals perform well on tasks that rely on spatial location and simultaneous information processing, but they have difficulty with the coding and categorization of sequential information. Furthermore, autistic children performed equally well when recalling nonsense as opposed to meaningful series of information, regardless of whether visual or auditory stimulus input was presented (Hermelin, 1976). Control groups did better in the recall of meaningful series. In other words, the autistic children employed a rote memorization strategy that was not aided by meaningful stimuli. This outcome has been interpreted by Hermelin as reflecting an impairment with the coding and categorization of information.

Based on extensive nonverbal investigations of the conceptual and representational abilities of a mute adolescent with autism, and on larger-scale follow-up studies, Schuler (Schuler, 1979, 1995; Schuler & Bormann, 1983) has suggested that individuals with autism seem to perform considerably better with nontransient rather than transient stimulus input, and when only judgment of object and material properties and spatial orientation is required, rather than judgment about the impact of one's own and others' action. An understanding of social causality requires processing of temporally organized, sequential cues. An understanding of object properties and spatial relations is acquired more readily by individuals with autism because of the nontransient nature of the discriminations involved. Reports of this pattern of ability and disability are commensurate with the discrepancies reported by Kanner (1943). That is, strengths tend to revolve around object manipulation and object knowledge, whereas apparent weaknesses are related to the development of social cognitive constructs (for a discussion of the differences between thinking about people and thinking about objects, see Hoffman, 1981). It may be speculated that, at least in part, specific weaknesses are noted in social communicative domains because signals that regulate social interactions are largely transient, as are the interactions themselves.

Metarepresentation as an Explanatory Theory

Frith (1989) interprets the extremely literal ways in which people with autism process information as indicative of a reduced awareness of their own thoughts in relation to the thoughts of others. In experiments designed to measure the construct of *theory of mind,* children with autism have been found to have difficulty understanding the beliefs and desires of others (Baron-Cohen et al., 1985; Baron-Cohen, Leslie, & Firth, 1986). In an experiment utilizing various dolls and props, Wimmer and Perner (1983) presented the following scenario to typically developing 3- and 4-year-olds:

A girl named Sally enters the stage. She leaves after putting a marble into her basket. Next a different girl named Anne appears, who takes the marble out of Sally's basket to hide it in her own box.

Subsequently, the 3- and 4-year-olds were asked the following questions: "Where is the marble really?" and "Where was the marble in the beginning?" Although these questions did not present any trouble to either age group, the subsequent question proved to be hard for the 3-year-olds to answer: "Where will Sally look for her marble?" The younger children found it difficult to apprehend that Sally's picture of the world doesn't match reality. A better understanding of Sally's beliefs and intentions was shown by 4- and 5-year-olds.

When this same scenario was presented to a group of children with autism, who were compared to developmentally matched normal children and to children with Down syndrome, 80% of the children with autism predicated that Sally would look for the marble in its actual location rather than where she would be expected to look (Baron-Cohen et al., 1985). Similarly, when asked to sequence pictures that dealt with people as opposed to objects, children with autism did poorly when it was necessary to comprehend the beliefs of others

(Baron-Cohen et al., 1986). These selected impairments in understanding the beliefs of others have been reported by other researchers and have been extended to include the desires of others (e.g., Harris, 1993).

Confirming the validity of Kanner's theory on the early differentiation between objects and people, Hobson (1990) has suggested that the impaired social and communicative abilities in autism may result from a deficit in *affective* relations with others, compared to a relative strength in relations with the physical world. Based on the theory of mind research findings, Baron-Cohen (1988) has proposed that the primary deficit in autism is cognitive and that it involves a selective impairment in the capacity for *metarepresentation* or beliefs about other people's mental states. Baron-Cohen attributed the deficits in joint attention and other pragmatic skills, as well as the deficits in symbolic play and theory of mind, to an impaired metarepresentational capacity, and urged an integration of the cognitive and affective theories. In consideration of the relatively early emergence of joint attention, it is plausible that the impairment in joint attention in early development underlies the impairment in theory of mind in later development. Sigman and Kasari (1995) suggest that the joint attention deficit in autism reflects the demands of integrating attention and cognition with affect.

Differences in Style of Cognitive Processing

Frequently cited characteristics of language and communicative behavior in autism can be understood in reference to analogous differences in the cognitive and language acquisition styles of normally developing children. A differentiation between gestalt versus analytic forms has been made in reference to differences in styles of language acquisition (i.e., gestalt vs. analytic styles; Peters, 1983). Gestalt language forms are multiword utterances that are memorized and produced as single units or chunks, with little analysis of their internal linguistic structure and with little or no comprehension of the utterances themselves. Analytic forms, on the other hand, are generated on the basis of the appli-

cation of (a) linguistic rules that presume greater comprehension of constituent structure, and (b) the specific meanings encoded by those utterances and their component parts. These two different forms of language, gestalt and analytic, have been noted to be used by typically developing children, and appear highly relevant to the understanding of language acquisition strategies in populations with various disabilities (Prizant, 1983b; Schuler & Prizant, 1985; Wills, 1979).

Prizant (1983b) proposed that children with autism use a gestalt strategy in early language learning by imitating unanalyzed chunks or multiword units of speech and subsequently breaking down these units into meaningful segments. Most verbal individuals with autism seem to demonstrate a gestalt style of language acquisition in that their early utterances are typically rigidly echolalic (Ricks & Wing, 1975), and their early communicative functions tend to be expressed through immediate and delayed echolalia (Prizant, 1987; Schuler & Prizant, 1985). This cognitive style is a relatively inflexible mode of information processing that results in the memorization of unanalyzed chunks of information, including speech stimulus as well as visual stimulus input. In contrast, a more analytic style allows for decoding the specific meanings of the component parts of a sequence in relation to each other. This process is based on extraction of the meaning or "gist" of experiences by interrelating the relevant pieces of information and references to previous experiences, and not by simply storing information to be reproduced later in an identical fashion (Fay & Schuler, 1980; Prizant, 1983a). Prizant (1983b) suggested that, for many verbal children with autism, language acquisition progresses from (a) the predominant use of echolalia, with little evidence of comprehension or communicative intent, to (b) the use of echolalia for a variety of communicative functions, and later to (c) a decrease in echolalia co-occurring with an increase in creative, spontaneously generated utterances. Pronoun reversals, stereotypic utterances, and insistence on certain verbal routines—all common characteristics of language use of verbal individuals—may also reflect a gestalt strategy in acquisition and use. The prevalence of gestalt forms can thus be conceptualized as variation at the extreme end of the normal continuum, which apparently corresponds with differences in cognitive style.

Weaknesses in processing transient signals may also contribute to gestalt patterns. Processing of transient signals is critical to comprehension of the constituent structure of utterances and to construction of a generative grammatical system. Construction of a linguistic rule system requires rapid processing of both auditory and visual transient information (speech as well as nonverbal cues) and presumes an ability to focus on consistencies and variations within speech and nonverbal behavior as they occur relative to objects and social or nonsocial environmental events. A gestalt mode of processing is ill-suited to the apprehension of transient signals and is clearly counterproductive when it comes to unraveling the temporally coded segmental structure of spoken language as well as the temporal structure of social interaction. Common reports on precocious written-word skills, or even on so-called hyperlexia (Aram & Healy, 1988), are of relevance in this context. A major difference between written and spoken language lies within the coding mechanisms involved— that is, in the utilization of nontransient versus transient signals. Because the processing of written language is not as dependent on sequential analyses, superior written-word skills in individuals with autism are readily explained.

The preference for nontransient signals and the associated information processing style may impede the acquisition of rule-governed systems of linguistic and social knowledge. On the other hand, it could be argued that the prevalent cognitive style in autism results from impaired social interaction, if early social experience is viewed as a primary determinant of more flexible social and linguistic rule systems and the modes of processing associated therewith. In other words, social interaction limitations can partially be explained on the basis of cognitive style differences, or cognitive style differences can be explained on the basis of early and pervasive limitations in joint attention and social interaction. Whatever the case, approaches to communication enhancement that address the cognitive discrepancies (taking into account both strengths and weaknesses) and the gestalt style of language acquisition and use would seem to be "best-fit" interventions, considering the distinctly different learning style of persons with autism and PDD (Grandin, 1995; Prizant & Wetherby, 1989; Schuler, 1995). Commonly cited challenges— lack of flexibility in communication and language; development of unconventional verbal behavior, including echolalia; insistence on preservation of sameness; and overreliance on social routines and rituals—need to be approached and understood as resulting from these cognitive differences.

IMPLICATIONS FOR COMMUNICATION ASSESSMENT AND ENHANCEMENT

Advances in the conceptualization of autism and PDD as developmental disabilities involving impairments of social interaction, communication, and symbolic abilities have had a great influence on approaches to language intervention (Prizant & Wetherby, 1988). Contemporary language intervention approaches differ dramatically from the traditional operant behavioral approaches to language and communication "training" that dominated the 1970s and early 1980s. One of the most critical differences is the emphasis on successful communicative interactions in natural contexts, which affects all aspects of programming, from targeting goals to designing the contexts of intervention. The developmental idiosyncrasies associated with autism tend to complicate intervention efforts; the communicative and social limitations are often masked by much higher skills, leading to frustration and unrealistic expectations. Consequently, individuals with autism have often been considered noncompliant, which has led to a focus on compliance training. As a result, much potential ability may be used in a maladaptive way—for example, in learning to escape from extremely didactic and demanding teaching sessions that are experienced as aversive (because they may not make sense to the individual involved and do not lead to an increased sense of control).

The cognitive and communicative discrepancies discussed above raise a host of other issues. Communication problems experienced by people with autism and PDD are not simply a matter of isolated deficits; they reflect underlying social-cognitive limitations that impact on social interaction and communication. Therefore, a deficiency remediation model does not suffice. Rather, communication assessment and enhancement practices should be guided by efforts to understand, modify, and expand current social/communicative, linguistic, and cognitive systems, acknowledging the functions served by an individual's current behavioral repertoire and coping strategies. The advocated approach is *transactional* in nature: it addresses the individual with autism or PDD, the social environment, and the interaction between the individual and the environment. A transactional approach is a *constructivist model* that addresses *interactive* and *functional* dimensions of communication.

The term *constructivist* is used because learning is viewed as an active process by which individuals "construct" or build knowledge and meanings based on interactions with people and experiences in their environment (Brown, Bransford, Ferrara, & Campione, 1983; De Ruiter & Wansart, 1983; Piaget, 1971; Rogoff, 1990; Wertsch, 1985). If newly acquired skills are to be integrated within one's current behavioral repertoire and cognitive understanding, teaching should extend current knowledge and incorporate self-generated behaviors. Because communication is rooted within such cognitive understanding, the primary focus is on helping individuals communicate about things they know or emotions they feel. Similarly, language should be taught as a tool to help organize experiences and to plan and regulate behavior, allowing for the integration of experiences across different environments and times of occurrence. Language experience is thus used to mediate thinking and problem solving (Brown et al., 1983; Rogoff, 1990; Vygotsky, 1934/1962) and, ultimately, to increase the capacity for cultural learning, moving the individual from imitative and instructed to more collaborative forms of learning that allow for the broadest developmental impact (Tomasello et al., 1993).

The advocated intervention approach is *interactive* because social interaction is viewed as the medium of language learning; the reactions of others refine and reinforce communicative behaviors in terms of function and structure. Through social interaction, individuals experience and come to understand the impact of their communicative attempts on their environment. (For a more detailed discussion of interactive approaches to language learning, see Snow, Midkiff-Borunda, Small, & Proctor, 1984.) This interactive dimension underscores the need for consistent and clear responses to the communicative endeavors of individuals with autism and PDD, allowing them to form hypotheses about the behaviors and intentions of others, to perceive the structure of social interaction, and to participate in interactive "scripts" (Nelson, 1981). The predictability inherent in structured intervention sessions may help provide the roots of communication as the individuals involved learn to anticipate the behavior of others and to observe the outcome of their own communicative bids. Further expansion and refinement of scripts are acquired in peer play.

Because of the transactional nature of communication, communication enhancement should focus not only on the behavior of the individual with autism, but also on the communicative partner. Knowledge of language structure is facilitated through semantic contingency between the initiations of the autistic individuals involved and the responses of others. Communicative partners must be responsive to the intentions as well as to the semantic content of an autistic individual's utterances. Contingent responses of others not only serve to acknowledge initiations but also may help to restructure inflexible and stereotyped utterances. Goals for communicative partners should include learning to: create opportunities for communication, wait for the initiation of communication, read the communicative attempts of the individual with autism or PDD, and then respond in a supportive manner. Significant others need to understand an individual's language abilities across contexts, in order to adjust their own language and to foster language and communication goals that are developmentally appropriate.

The advocated approach is *functional* because intervention should be built around actual communicative needs that pertain to everyday living routines and environments.

There is then a clear and natural incentive to communicate. Stated differently, the perspective of the learner should be adopted. Instruction should be learner-centered more than "teacher"-imposed (and thus unrelated to daily communicative needs and motivations to communicate). Given that many individuals are limited in their grasp of communication as a purposeful and collaborative social transaction, a primary focus needs to be placed on the establishment of an interest in communication based on experiencing socially and emotionally satisfying interactions. That is, communicative exchanges must make sense in events that make sense, and the exchanges must foster the development of secure and trusting relationships before too much emphasis is placed on producing the correct word or sentence, or articulating clearly, or other requirements.

Assessment Principles

To provide for the type of communication enhancement approach advocated here, (a) assessment should focus on communicative needs in a variety of natural environments and (b) current communication strategies should be examined. The primary function of assessment is to provide information that can be directly translated into goals for communication enhancement and that can be used in the evaluation of intervention efforts. In fact, assessment and intervention are dynamically interwoven: assessment guides intervention, and intervention continues to refine and expand assessment questions. Assessment is thus an ongoing process rather than a brief, episodic exercise. Therefore, assessment should not focus on tasks that may be completely unrelated to actual communicative behavior, or on molecular fragments of behavior that have lost their meaning and function because they are devoid of relevant context. Assessment that attempts to diagnose only deficiency will likely not contribute to the enhancement of communication abilities.

Caution should be applied in using more traditional norm-referenced and/or standardized assessment tools, which are often based on assumptions that do not hold true for individuals with autism or PDD. For normally developing children, advances in one domain of development are typically paralleled by similar gains in related areas. This synchrony is often absent in persons with autism or PDD. Normal or near-normal development in areas such as motor development and speech production may occur alongside profound delays in the development of relatively simple social/communicative skills such as imitation, joint attention, communicative gesturing, and turn-taking. In fact, relatively advanced skills in one area may pose serious problems for assessment, because less apparent deficiencies are then easily overlooked. Given these discontinuities, assumptions about synchronous development across domains may be violated.

A second problem lies in the behavioral challenges that may seriously interfere with the completion of any assessment in a standardized manner. The disruption of familiar routines, which is inherent to testing situations, and the novel demands posed may cause confusion and distress, leading to so-called noncompliant behavior. A third problem lies in the lack of comprehension of not only verbal, but also nonverbal communication, including pointing and other gesturing. Very few formal tests are truly nonverbal; they often presume social imitative abilities that may be limited in some individuals with autism. A fourth related problem has to do with limited comprehension of social conventions. Whereas normally developing children may perform to please the examiner, even if the testing situation does not make any sense from a child's perspective, individuals with autism and PDD may not do so (for a discussion, see Donaldson, 1978). Generalization problems are another obstacle; although certain skills may be observed in more natural contexts, they may not be observed during formal assessments. Nevertheless, for purposes other than intervention planning (diagnostic or predictive purposes, for example), standardized tests may be of some value. For those purposes, tests should be carefully selected and adapted as needed.

The assessment process, in this view, is guided by some central core questions that are continuously redefined on the basis of overall developmental level, environmental needs, and preliminary assessment outcome. These core assessment questions pertain to the communicative/social, cognitive, and linguistic domains and the interrelations among those domains, so that areas of greatest needs and greatest strengths are identified. Table 23.1 summarizes these basic domains in their most general form and provides a framework for assessment concerns. (Chapters 24 and 25 demonstrate how these domains become more detailed regarding overall functioning levels, preliminary assessment outcome, and individual differences.) Because assessment is viewed as a tool rather than as an end in itself, many different assessment approaches may be used: observational or experimental, formal or informal, structured or less structured. A useful initial method for gathering information about an individual's communication and language abilities is to interview significant others who are familiar with the subtle

nuances of communicative behaviors. The natural variation in behavior across contexts and interactants necessitates the use of multiple assessment tools and strategies in different contexts. (For a further discussion of these issues, see Lund & Duchan, 1993.) Furthermore, performance variables related to context and interactional style deserve to be investigated, because communication is a dyadic phenomenon closely tied to, and determined by, social context. Assessment, therefore, should not be limited to the evaluation of student variables; it should be extended to contextual and interactional variables.

Developmental and Functional Considerations for Communication Enhancement

In recent years, clinicians and educators have debated the question of how goals and objectives for persons with autism and related disabilities should be derived. At one extreme are those who focus primarily on the functional needs of a person relative to his or her chronological age (Brown et al., 1979), placing minimal emphasis on potential contributions from literature on normal language and communication development. At the other extreme are developmentally oriented clinicians, especially those with expertise in language and communication development, who have tended to focus on approaches that attempt to move children along a developmental track based on research on language and communication development (Lahey, 1988).

Information on language and communication development offers an organizational framework for assessment and intervention. Too rigid an interpretation of a developmental model has resulted in "readiness models," which require a student to reach a certain level of ability before working on a subsequent skill. A distinction must be made between working within a developmental model, which is the advocated approach, and teaching according to a developmental checklist. Rather than merely offering a guideline for sequencing communication goals, developmental information can provide a frame of reference for understanding an individual's behavioral competencies and for setting appropriate goals.

TABLE 23.1   Core Assessment Domains

Language and Communication Domains

Expressive language and communication:

    use of idiosyncratic/conventional gestures

    quality of vocal means

    complexity of verbal means (words, sentences, conversation)

    modality strengths and preferences (verbal, gestural, graphic)

Receptive language and communication:

    use of nonlinguistic response strategies

    understanding of conventional meanings

    engagement in discourse

Sociocommunicative and Socioemotional Domains

Range of communicative functions expressed

Reciprocity of interaction evident in rate of communicating and use of repair strategies

Use of social-affective signals for social referencing and for regulating interaction

Comprehension of and expression of emotion in language and play

Use of self- and mutual-regulatory strategies to modulate arousal and emotional state

Language-Related Cognitive Domain

Evidence of symbolic representation in symbolic or constructive play

Imitation strategies

Anticipation of routines/ event knowledge

Attention in social and nonsocial contexts

Prizant and Wetherby (1989) have argued that so-called functional approaches (which tend to be behaviorally oriented) and developmental approaches need not be viewed as mutually exclusive. However, many educators and clinicians tend to lean heavily toward either developmental approaches or functional/behavioral approaches, to the virtual exclusion of integrating the best practices from both approaches. Nevertheless, the two perspectives can be integrated. Intervention goals and contexts for communication enhancement can and should be selected on the basis of functional as well as developmental criteria. Developmental considerations should contribute to, but not mandate, the selection of goals, and they should serve to guide the choice of task adaptation and the selection of appropriate contextual supports (e.g., visual aids such as picture schedules, choice boards, and so on). Goals should be selected on the basis of functional considerations, particularly when dealing with teenagers and adults.

For communication enhancement activities to be most relevant for children with autism and their families, approaches must be directed toward increasing functional skills to enhance independence, and reducing stress on the family by providing appropriate tangible and psychosocial supports. Functional criteria should be based on the assessment information obtained from caregivers' and professionals' knowledge of an individual's communicative needs. On the other hand, developmental considerations will have great bearing on the specific communicative means targeted. Without careful attention to developmental issues, communication enhancement efforts can target competencies that are considerably above or below an individual's capabilities. However, the uneven profile of abilities and disabilities in cognitive and communicative functioning, which, in part, is definitive of autism and PDD, should caution against the adoption of too narrow a developmental focus. The validity of intervention goals will be questioned if they fail to account for functional as well as developmental issues.

Contemporary approaches to treatment are guided by a growing appreciation of both social and linguistic aspects of communicative competence. As noted, the communicative characteristics and related social-cognitive style of individuals with autism and PDD suggest that the function and meaning underlying communicative acts should always supersede their form, when considering the nature of "true" communicative growth. A rigid preoccupation with speech development and correct language structure or form is counterproductive if individuals are striving to experience the power of communication in controlling their living environments and developing meaningful relationships with others. Therefore, communication enhancement efforts, emerging from behavioral (Charlop & Haymes, 1994; Koegel & Johnson, 1989; Koegel, O'Dell, & Koegel, 1987) as well as developmental traditions (Klinger & Dawson, 1992; Prizant, 1988; Wetherby & Prizant, 1992), have increasingly emphasized and incorporated more pragmatic dimensions of communication, including social reciprocity, and a greater variety of communicative functions and social contexts. This functional-pragmatic orientation was highly influential in moving communication enhancement efforts to consider the communicative meaning of challenging behavior, which has become a joint focus for combining interventions that address both behavioral issues and communicative growth (Prizant & Wetherby, 1987). To enhance effective communication, alternative (nonspeech) means of communication may need to be explored, such as gestures, signs, and pictorial or written modes of exchange. In addition, even the subtlest and often unconventional or idiosyncratic modes of communication need to be recognized, for they may provide the foundation for communication enhancement based on understanding and respecting a person's efforts to communicate. By providing consistent responses to communicative initiations and replacing undesirable means of communication with more conventional or socially acceptable ones, communicative success is more likely to occur.

Communicative Events and Functions

Because individuals with autism and PDD, at all ability levels, are so challenged in their understanding of communicative events in social context, communication enhancement efforts must be concerned with all dimensions of communication—that is, with enhancing communicative means and providing a better understanding of the function of communicative behavior and of the dyadic structure of communicative events. Communicative events occur when two or more participants engage in social interactions cooperatively, to accomplish particular goals (e.g., sharing information, solving a problem, playing a game, and so on). The structure of such events involves reciprocal exchanges. Each participant must have some understanding that he or she has a role and a responsibility to fulfill in the exchange toward a shared goal. Approaches such as task analysis, which breaks down teaching procedures and responses into minute steps, may be counterproductive when applied to communication development, because they do not help children to make sense out of communicative transactions (Donaldson, 1978; Duchan, 1986).

Because individuals with autism evidence cognitive discontinuities and a limited grasp of communicative events, functionality of communication should always be the primary consideration. (For a more detailed discussion of functionality issues, see Goetz, Schuler, & Sailor, 1979; Prizant & Wetherby, 1989.) Verbal and nonverbal communicative behavior should always be surrounded by a natural incentive that serves to highlight the communicative function served, be it a request, a directive, a protest, or another communicative function. Providing language intervention is thus not so much a matter of specifying desirable response topographies as of providing motivating contexts, including opportunities and needs to communicate (McLean & Snyder-McLean, 1978). This implies that language intervention should largely take place in the natural environment, capitalizing on the notion of incidental teaching and joint activity routines (see Cavallaro, 1983; Hart, 1985; Koegel, O'Dell, & Koegel, 1987; Snyder-McLean, McLean, Etter-Schroeder, & Rogers, 1984).

Cued Response Training versus Communication Enhancement

Traditional behavioral treatment programs that predominated in the 1970s and 1980s utilized imitation, prompting, and reinforcement techniques within a discrete-trial teaching format that targeted speech or language as an operant behavior (Charlop & Haymes, 1994). It is important to distinguish between (a) the learning of cue-dependent response topographies, as is characteristic of traditional behavioral programs (e.g., Lovaas, 1981), and (b) the acquisition of true communicative, linguistic, and social knowledge. Because many autistic individuals do quite well with the situation-specific recall of unanalyzed memorized phrases, they may easily learn specific responses to visual or auditory cues that may be mistaken for truly communicative behaviors. Unfortunately, many traditional language-training programs view such responses as indicative of linguistic or communicative progress, applying success criteria that fail to reflect spontaneous and communicative use of creative forms. Subsequent to situation-specific training, which results in the reproduction of specified response topographies, "generalization" training is often identified as the final step of the program. Our position is that truly functional communicative and linguistic behavior *is defined* by flexibility in use and generalization across contexts. Consequently, communicative advances cannot be claimed solely on the basis of situation-specific responses. Furthermore, we believe that elaborate training of situation-specific responses can be misleading both to parents and to professionals who may not understand the limited impact that such response training may have on the life of a person with autism or PDD. For persons unfamiliar with autism and the associated discrepancies in learning and development, exposure to an elaborate verbal repertoire may lead to attempts at interaction that are far too complex to understand. The results will be frustration and interactional breakdown for the parties involved.

The major dimensions that distinguish a developmental/social-pragmatic approach (from which we draw heavily) from a traditional operant behavioral approach, are delineated in Table 23.2. More contemporary behavioral approaches, in contrast, have moved away from the discrete-trial format which focuses on compliance training and readiness skills, and toward a more naturalistic approach to language and communication enhancement—an

TABLE 23.2   Dimensions to Consider in Planning and Implementing Communication and Language Programs for Individuals with Autism

Dimension	Developmental/Social-Pragmatic Approach	Traditional Behavioral Approach
Theoretical underpinnings	Developmental and social-pragmatic theory; transactional teaching model	Learning theory: applied behavioral analysis; unidirectional teaching model
Degree of prescription vs. flexibility in teaching	Strategies applied systematically but flexibly; capitalize on natural or simulated opportunities	Highly prescribed—content and procedures determined on an a priori basis as part of program with minimal variation
Adult- vs. child-centered	Content influenced by child's level of development; when possible, follow child's lead	Adult initiates "topic," determines focus of attention; adult control reduced in time
Child role—initiate vs. respond	Priority placed on child initiation, in appropriate balance to responding	Initially, train responding; later, train "spontaneity"
Response to child's behavior	Consequences depend on child's communicative intent	Consequences depend on predetermined procedures
Naturalness of context	Learning contexts reflect natural interactions and events to the extent possible	Initially contrived, discrete trial training; eventual movement to more natural situations
Relevance of information on child development	Developmental information and individual child's learning strategies used to select goals and teaching procedures	Not of primary relevance; goals and procedures based on predetermined program or child's perceived needs
Social context of intervention	Groups of different social complexity—one-to-one, small group, large group—depending on child's ability	Primarily one-to-one, especially in early stages; movement to more complex social groupings
Carryover and generalization to other environments	Skills taught across environments and persons, from early in program	Generalization programmed for after child reaches criterion in initial training context
Intensity—extent and frequency of direct teaching	Varies greatly according to child: staff ratio and skill of staff in programming learning opportunities in natural environments	Intensity is determined by nature of specific program; focus on one-to-one direct teaching
Utilization of child's strengths	Activities based on child's preferences and strengths; follow child's interests	Reinforcers selected on basis of child's preferences; activities may not be
Type of reinforcement	Focus on natural reinforcers, including responding to child's intent; social reinforcement	Initial use of artificial reinforcers, then artificial and pairing of social, and, finally, movement to social
Treatment of challenging behavior	Understand behavior from developmental perspective and child's communicative intent; if intent can be determined, modify environment/task and/or replace with socially acceptable form	Understand behavior by identifying maintaining variables; ignore (extinguish) or punish challenging behavior. If functional analysis is performed, replace with socially acceptable form

Continued

TABLE 23.2   (*Continued*)

Dimension	Developmental/Social-Pragmatic Approach	Traditional Behavioral Approach
Type and intensity of data collection—documentation of progress	Varies from informal impressions to on-line time sampling. May use language–communication sampling and analysis to determine changes in level of functioning or in developmental patterns	Typically, intensive, ongoing, online data collection, or time sampling; focus is on frequency counts of discrete behaviors; Looking for increases or decreases in target behaviors
Consideration of individual differences in learning	Attempts made to determine differences in learning style, with program modifications made according to differences	Individual preferences used in selecting reinforcers; however, program and child needs determine program content and procedures
Role of typical or developmentally advanced peers	Peers seen as positive developmental influence; more focus on natural or semistructured play interactions	Initially, peers play minimal (if any) role; eventually, peers may be trained to play role in structured teaching
Parent involvement	Parents taught to understand child's developmental patterns and to use natural routines and developmental strategies	Parents taught principles of behavior modification and encouraged to carry out prescribed teaching program

From "Dimensions to Consider in Planning and Implementing Communication and Language Programs for Individuals with Autism and PDD," by B.M. Prizant, October 1994, Seminar presented for State of Connecticut Special Education Directors, Fairfield, CT.

approach that draws from, and is closely aligned with, the description of a developmental social-pragmatic approach (for example, see Koegel, Camarata, & Koegel, 1994; Koegel & Johnson, 1989).

Nonspeech Communication Modes (Augmentative and Alternative Communication)

Traditional behavioral interventions have focused on increasing speech output (see Charlop & Haymes, 1994; Schuler, Gonsier-Gerdin, & Wolfberg, 1990, for reviews). Researchers are increasingly recognizing, however, that training speech production does not necessarily enhance communicative competence, and that communication development can be fostered by, and proceed through, nonspeech means. The increased use of communication augmentation speaks to this realization, acknowledging the value of nonspeech means of communication. After all, meaningful language and communication growth (i.e., initiated and spontaneous use of language for a

variety of communicative purposes) cannot be determined on the basis of pre- and posttreatment comparison data collected in contrived and controlled training sessions. Too narrow a focus on training discrete instances of observable behavior may lead one to the misleading assumption that discrimination training or compliance training is equal to language learning and communication development. In such an approach, responses may be void of communicative intent, social motivation, and understanding.

Selection of a communication and/or language system should be based on an individual's social, communicative, cognitive, and motoric abilities. Because considerations of function tend to override structural concerns, special attention should be given to the use of nonspeech communication systems. Lack of communicative understanding is reflected in limitations of verbal as well as nonverbal behavior. Therefore, introduction of augmentative or alternative communication systems is by no means a panacea. Progress may be slow, especially for individuals with more severe social-cognitive limitations. Nevertheless, for most nonspeaking persons, a nonspeech means to communicate may be a tremendous asset: it can demonstrate the power of communication without requiring neuromuscular coordination and motor planning, which are involved in speech production. Although nonspeech communication systems may be extremely helpful in teaching communication—and have actually been documented to do so (Kiernan, 1983; Layton, 1987; Reichle, York, & Sigafoos, 1991)—no specific recommendations can be made regarding implementing specific systems for persons with autism or PDD, as a group. Matches between individuals and systems need to be made carefully, and selected systems may need to be continuously adapted to the needs of individuals.

Nevertheless, some general principles apply when selecting suitable systems for individuals with autism and PDD. Given the fact that so many individuals with autism are limited in their use of gestures, facial expression, body orientation, and other nonverbal means of communication, enhancing the use of nonverbal communicative means as an augmentative system, prior to or along with introduction of an alternative formal nonspeech communication system, may be appropriate. Furthermore, given that many individuals seem better able to process visuospatially coded information, written words, pictorial systems, communication boards, and other systems that incorporate nontransient signals (e.g., visual displays) may be preferable (Prizant & Wetherby, 1989; Quill, 1995).

Recently, the issue of facilitated communication (FC) has been at the center of much attention and heated debate. We recommend that the notion of communicative intent be considered in understanding and interpreting communicative behavior of individuals with autism, whether the communication entails natural gestures or other nonverbal behavior, speech, written or typed communication, or some other augmentative communication system (Prizant, Wetherby, & Rydell, 1994). An individual's communicative competence should be documented multidimensionally, reflecting the range of intentions expressed, the conventionality of means used to express intent, and the degree of intentionality evidenced. With

evidence of independent success, an individual's use of FC should then be considered in relation to the individual's full repertoire of communicative behavior. Although some reported cases of success with FC indicate unexpected literacy skills, many are within the realm of what would be expected, given a person's symbolic level with other means of communicating. Significant discrepancies between level of communication expressed with FC and with other means of communication need to be examined carefully. The issue of facilitator influence warrants serious scrutiny, and, of course, is at the heart of claims that FC is a fraudulent educational practice. A recent report provides a comprehensive consideration of research and practice in FC (Calculator, Fabry, Glennon, Prizant, & Schubert, 1995).

Competence Model

When communication enhancement is approached in a more interactive, supportive, and competency-oriented manner, interventionists are more likely to respond and assign meaning to communicative initiations from others. The advocated approach starts with the competencies of the individual, identifies current learning strengths and communicative strategies, and builds on the strategies that may be effective in serving important communicative functions. Additionally, motivating learning contexts must be identified and expanded to encourage independence by providing opportunities for communication, and by gradually eliminating supports provided to increase communicative effectiveness. Recent research findings suggest that, for children, naturalistic play contexts that facilitate social and communicative success may be a more effective means of enhancing communication and language development than direct instruction in designated language forms (Wolfberg & Schuler, 1993). Whether language gains can indeed be promoted by gains in social interaction and symbolic play across a wide range of individuals deserves to be a primary focus of future treatment research.

The support and assumed competence of the communication partner are very important contributors to the enhancement of communicative competence. Success in communicative encounters is critical in developing communicative competence, and treatment efforts should set the stage for this success. Some controversial treatment approaches, such as facilitated communication, are more consistent with human intuitions about communication as a joint enterprise than with prevailing teaching practices, which favor independent task mastery without contextual support. This factor may account for some of the recent popularity of facilitated communication, even though reports have identified the unwitting influence of some facilitators on communicative output (Calculator et al., 1995). One positive lesson learned from the experience of facilitated communication is that, rather than putting the burden of communication on the less capable participant in the exchange, the more capable one may have to work harder, providing the amount of compensation necessary to make both communication partners successful (Duchan, 1993). Nevertheless, even as more relevant communicative functions and contexts are increasingly incorporated into intervention programs, the burden of communicative change generally remains on the less competent communicative partner.

This lack of accommodation indicates the insidious power of prevailing linear notions of instruction that favor step-by-step progression contingent on completion of prior program stages and independent task mastery. Such notions of direct instruction may be useful in teaching practical skills that can be effectively task-analyzed, but they may be ill-suited to the teaching of communication and social interaction skills that are more hierarchical and reciprocal in nature. The acquisition of symbolic modes of interaction cannot be divorced from the cultural contexts in which those modes of representation have evolved. As pointed out by Tomasello and colleagues (1993), cultural learning embodies more than earlier conceptualization of social learning, where the child's attention is drawn to specific objects and/or locations in the environment, which otherwise might have gone unnoticed. Although social interactions are critical for this type of learning, the mechanisms involved remain essentially solitary because the specific strategies or methods followed, and the reflection involved, are not shared. According to Tomasello

et al., cultural learning involves the adoption of the other's perspective so that one learns through and with another rather than merely from another. The shared perspective allows for the reciprocity inherent in joint attention and turn-taking, and implies the simulation of the other's mental states and eventually the emergence of a theory of mind (Baron-Cohen et al., 1985; Wimmer & Perner, 1983). We argue for the adoption of more reciprocal and collaborative modes of learning to be eventually superimposed on more solitary and object-based modes of learning, which seem more readily established and still predominate in many treatment approaches.

To eventually arrive at more cultural modes of learning, instruction should be built around the interests and initiatives of the individuals involved, even when most or all of such initiatives take unconventional forms. Because the individual with autism or PDD may initially be incapable of establishing a joint focus of attention, reciprocity will fail to be established without such accommodations; communication will remain a one-way enterprise. Close observation and ongoing evaluations of current levels of understanding and competence are, therefore, critical. Such observation should be designed to determine the highest level of competence, given the optimal amount of social assistance and allowing for scaffolded performance within the zone of proximal development, as defined by Vygotsky (1934/1962).

To accomplish these goals, clinicians, educators, and caregivers need to examine their own level of discomfort when common behavior expectations and norms are violated. Are our efforts to impose structure a reflection of our own anxiety and uneasiness, motivating us to reestablish control on our own terms? A directive and controlling stance might make us feel more at ease, but typically leads to power struggles. To provide individuals with autism or PDD with a sense of control and a structure that serves *their* needs, rather than the needs of more competent partners, motivating tasks and activity contexts that support a sense of competence can be selected. Additionally, communicative partners must be willing to scrutinize their own motivations, language use, and communicative style, and then make the necessary adaptations to foster success. Consequently, communicative growth is pursued as a collaborative endeavor based on conscious reflection that respects the humanity of persons with autism and PDD.

Family-Centered Principles

Communication enhancement is one dimension of a comprehensive intervention plan for an individual with autism or PDD, and his or her family. The degree of successful communication and interaction between a child and his or her caregivers, peers, and siblings has a significant impact on the parents' sense of competence, the well-being of the family, and the social and emotional well-being of the child (Theadore, Maher, & Prizant, 1990). Thus, the family should be at the center of intervention efforts. Public Law 99-457 (Noonan & McCormick, 1993) and its mandate for interdisciplinary cooperation within a family-centered framework in preschool and early intervention services holds great promise for making the fragmentation of services a thing of the past (Bailey, 1991; Crais, 1991; Kaufmann & McGonigel, 1991). Family centered practice entails the following major principles: (a) to provide services and supports to the family, as well as the affected child; (b) to foster the family's sense of competence and independence; (c) to respect the parents' right and responsibility to decide what is best for their child; (d) to help mobilize resources for coordinated, normalized service delivery; and (e) to develop a collaborative relationship with the family (Crais, 1991; Dunst, Trivette, & Deal, 1988).

Successful approaches to communication enhancement are achieved through caregiver–professional partnerships. Caregivers should be viewed as primary intervention agents. Whether services are provided in a home- or center-based program, caregivers possess the greatest potential for actuating positive change in the child's communicative abilities (Dunst et al., 1990). Caregivers' ability to enhance communication will be influenced by the formal and informal supports available to them (Bristol & Schopler, 1983; Dunst et al., 1990). Stresses on the family change with the child's age; thus, issues regarding family

support are related to specific needs at different points in the life of the family. Families with younger children may just be beginning to experience a grieving process, and may be undergoing dramatic shifts in emotional well-being (Moses, 1981; Prizant & Tiegerman, 1984). Development of communication is critical for younger children; it relates to day-to-day stresses of the family and to long-term prognosis. Stresses on the families of older children and adolescents have been found to be even greater, because of the need to plan for future care and the great demands on a family that is caring for a youth with autism or PDD (Bristol & Schopler, 1983).

Because of the severity of the disabilities that may be associated with autism, it is critical for communication enhancement efforts to address skills that will enhance the individual's ability to be a more effective communicator. Coordination is needed in (a) the use of an interactive style that is most conducive to a child's active participation and communicative growth; (b) the development of strategies for arranging learning environments; and (c) the use of specific approaches to help a child develop more sophisticated means of communication. Some caregivers' perceptions of children's communicative abilities may be skewed toward attributing less or greater competence than is observed by a clinician. In these situations, an important goal is to help caregivers in developing more accurate perceptions or in redefining their perceptions of the children's abilities in a supportive and collaborative problem-solving climate (Theadore et al., 1990).

Providing Services in Inclusive Settings

Over the past decade, there has been a general movement toward providing services for individuals with severe disabilities, including autism and PDD, in inclusive educational and work settings. Inclusive education is mandated by the Individuals with Disabilities Education Act (IDEA) and is considered best practice because it reflects principles of normalization. Inclusive education allows students with disabilities to attend the school that their siblings attend, and to become members of a regular class while receiving individualized adaptations and support (Ford & Davern, 1989). For a child with autism or PDD, this environment offers actual opportunities to interact with typical peers who can provide appropriate models and be responsive partners when support is needed (Goldstein & Kaczmarek, 1992; Udvari-Solner, 1994; Wolfberg & Schuler, 1993). Research has demonstrated that physical integration, which places students with disabilities among typical nondisabled students, does not ensure social integration, particularly for children with moderate to severe disabilities (Gaylord-Ross, 1989; Odom & McEvoy, 1988; Stainback, Stainback, & Forest, 1989).

The movement toward inclusive education parallels the movement toward positive/nonaversive behavior management. Approaches to discipline must be considered from the perspective of what is acceptable to the community, so that practices can be administered in inclusive settings without infantilizing or stigmatizing an individual. Community-referenced behavioral support should lead to changes that impact on the individual's access to community settings, opportunities for social interaction, and choices of activities to participate in (Horner et al., 1990; Wehman & Kregel, 1985). Ideally, communication intervention should enhance communication so that greater access is provided to a variety of people, places, and events, thereby enhancing the quality of life of individuals with disabilities.

FINAL CONSIDERATIONS

An understanding of the limitations surrounding communication, as well as of the cognitive and developmental idiosyncrasies and the associated behavior problems, is critical in work with persons with autism and PDD, particularly when the focus is on speech and language. For those living or working with persons with autism and PDD, the difficulties discussed herein present a dilemma: much of what it is hoped persons with autism will learn about language and communication, such as greater flexibility in language production and language use, and the ability to adjust communicative behavior to situational contexts, may be particularly difficult because of the social cognitive requirements involved. Stated another way, the flexibility and mutual negotiation that characterize communication in daily interactions may exceed the learning and coping strategies of many persons with autism and PDD, because of the nature of their disability.

Progress in communication and language development must be conceptualized in reference to how far an individual has come in the acquisition of flexible, conventional communicative abilities, rather than by gauging progress on cued production of speech or expectations based primarily on normal developmental milestones. For instance, it is difficult to estimate the extent to which some individuals will be able to engage in uses of language for primarily social ends. Literature on language of more able individuals indicates that language appearing to be social in nature is very often used to carry out predictable routines; the motivation is in the execution of routines rather than in the true social "togetherness" that communication affords. Furthermore, it is not known to what extent a history of frustration and stress experienced in social interactions may inhibit interest and participation in further interaction.

In determining the success of any intervention, it is essential to consider whether the intervention has resulted in meaningful outcomes, not just demonstrable changes. Meyer and Evans (1993) describe a meaningful outcome as a significant change in the individual's lifestyle and human condition. Communication programming should impact on the individual's lifestyle by enhancing meaningful progress in communication abilities that increases access to a variety of people, places, and events. Evans and Meyer (1990) warn that "lifestyle enhancement, such as teaching communication within responsive environments, not 'functional communication training' in isolation, is the fundamental intervention" (p. 135). Ultimately, the individual's competence in social interaction, and his or her capacity to cope with stress by using flexible communicative strategies, will determine the level of independence that can be achieved in adulthood. Chapters 24 and 25 discuss, in greater detail, content areas and specific approaches to the assessment and development of the communication ability of individuals with autism and PDD. Readers are urged to consider the next two chapters in relation to the theoretical perspectives and treatment philosophy presented here.

Cross-References

General aspects of communicative development are discussed in Chapter 9. Issues in assessment are delineated in Chapters 19 through 21, and curriculum development is treated in Chapter 22. Other aspects of communication interventions are developed further in Chapters 24 and 25.

REFERENCES

Ainsworth, M.D.S., & Bell, S.M. (1974). Mother–infant interaction and the development of competence. In J.J. Connelly & J. Bruner (Eds.), *The growth of competence* (pp. 97–118). New York: Academic Press.

Aram, D.M., & Healy, J.F. (1988). Hyperlexia: A review of extraordinary word recognition. In L.K. Obler & D. Fein (Eds.), *The exceptional brain: Neuropsychology of talent and special abilities* (pp. 70–102). New York: Guilford Press.

Bailey, D. (1991). Building positive relationships between professionals and families. In M. McGonigel, R. Kaufmann, & B. Johnson (Eds.), *Guidelines and recommended practices for the individualized family service plan* (2nd ed., pp. 29–38). Bethesda, MD: Association for the Care of Children's Health.

Baron-Cohen, S. (1988). Social and pragmatic deficits in autism: Cognitive or affective? *Journal of Autism and Developmental Disorders, 18,* 379–402.

Baron-Cohen, S., Allen, J., & Gillberg, C. (1992). Can autism be detected at 18 months?: The needle, the haystack, and the CHAT. *British Journal of Psychiatry, 161,* 839–843.

Baron-Cohen, S., Leslie, A.M., & Frith, U. (1985). Does the autistic child have a theory of mind? *Cognition, 21,* 37–46.

Baron-Cohen, S., Leslie, A.M., & Frith, U. (1986). Mechanical, behavioral and intentional understanding of picture stories in autistic children. *British Journal of Developmental Psychology, 4,* 113–115.

Bates, E. (1979). *The emergence of symbols: Cognition and communication in infancy.* New York: Academic Press.

Bates, E., O'Connell, B., & Shore, C. (1987). Language and communication in infancy. In J. Osofsky (Ed.), *Handbook of infant development* (pp. 149–203). New York: John Wiley & Sons.

Bristol, M.M., & Schopler, E. (1983). Stress and coping in families of autistic adolescents. In E. Schopler & G.B. Mesibov (Eds.), *Autism in adolescents and adults* (pp. 251–278). New York: Plenum Press.

Brown, A.L., Bransford, J.D., Ferrara, R.A., & Campione, J.C. (1983). Learning, remembering, and understanding. In P.H. Mussen (Ed.), *Carmichael's manual of child psychology: Vol. 3. Cognitive development* (pp. 77–166). New York: John Wiley & Sons.

Brown, L., Branston, M.B., Hamre-Nietupski, S., Pumpian, L., Certo, N., & Gruenewald, L. (1979). A strategy for developing chronological age-appropriate and functional curricular content for severely handicapped adolescents and young adults. *Journal of Special Education, 13,* 81–90.

Bruner, J. (1975). From communication to language: A psychological perspective. *Cognition, 3,* 255–289.

Bruner, J. (1978). From communication to language: A psychological perspective. In I. Markova (Ed.), *The social context of language.* Chichester, England: John Wiley & Sons.

Bruner, J. (1981). The social context of language acquisition. *Language and Communication, 1,* 155–178.

Calculator, S., Fabry, D., Glennon, S., Prizant, B.M., & Schubert, A. (1995). *Technical report on standards of practice for facilitated communication.* Rockville, MD: American Speech-Language-Hearing Association.

Carr, E.G., & Durand, V.M. (1985). Reducing behavior problems through functional communication training. *Journal of Applied Behavior Analysis, 18,* 111–126.

Carr, E.G., & Durand, V.M. (1986). The social-communicative basis of severe behavior problems in children. In S. Reiss & R. Bootzin (Eds.), *Theoretical issues in behavior therapy* (pp. 219–254). New York: Academic Press.

Carr, E.G., Levin, L., McConnachie, G., Carlson, J., Kemp, D., & Smith, C. (1994). *Communication-based intervention for problem behavior: A user's guide for producing positive change.* Baltimore, MD: Brookes.

Cavallaro, C. (1983). Language intervention in natural settings. *Teaching Exceptional Children, 49,* 65–70.

Charlop, M.H., & Haymes, L.K. (1994). Speech and language acquisition and intervention:

Behavioral approaches. In J. Matson (Ed.), *Autism in children and adults: Etiology, assessment, and intervention* (pp. 213–240). Pacific Grove, CA: Brooks/Cole.

Crais, E. (1991, September). Moving from "parent involvement" to family-centered services. *American Journal of Speech-Language Pathology, 1,* 5–7.

Curcio, A. (1978). A study of sensorimotor functioning and communication in mute autistic children. *Journal of Autism and Childhood Schizophrenia, 8,* 281–292.

Dawson, G., & Adams, A. (1984). Imitation and social responsiveness in autistic children. *Journal of Abnormal Child Psychology, 12,* 209–226.

Dawson, G., & Galpert, L. (1986). A developmental model for facilitating the social behavior of autistic children. In E. Schopler & G.B. Mesibov (Eds.), *Social behavior in autism* (pp. 237–261). New York: Plenum Press.

De Ruiter, J., & Wansart, H. (1983). *The psychology of learning disabilities.* Rockville, MD: Aspen Press.

DeMyer, M.K. (1975). The nature of neuropsychological disability in autistic children. *Journal of Autism and Childhood Schizophrenia, 8,* 109–128.

DiLavore, P.C., Lord, C., & Rutter, M. (1995). The Pre-Linguistic Autism Diagnostic Observation Schedule. *Journal of Autism and Developmental Disabilities, 25,* 355–379.

Donaldson, M. (1978). *Children's minds.* New York: Norton.

Donnellan, A., Mirenda, P., Mesaros, R., & Fassbender, L. (1984). Analyzing the communicative functions of aberrant behavior. *Journal of the Association for Persons with Severe Handicaps, 9,* 201–212.

Duchan, J.F. (1986). Language intervention through sensemaking and finetuning. In R. Schiefelbusch (Ed.), *Communicative competence: Assessment and language intervention.* Baltimore: University Park Press.

Duchan, J.F. (1993). Issues raised by facilitated communication for theorizing and research on autism. *Journal of Speech and Hearing Research, 36,* 1108–1119.

Dunlap, G., & Kern, L. (1993). Assessment and intervention for children within the instructional curriculum. In J. Reichle & D.P. Wacker (Eds.), *Communicative alternative to challenging behavior—Integrating functional assessment and intervention strategies* (pp. 177–203). Baltimore: Brookes.

Dunst, C., Lowe, E., & Bartholomew, P. (1990). Contingent social responsiveness, family ecology, and infant communicative competence. *National Student Speech Language Hearing Association, 17,* 39–49.

Dunst, C., Trivette, C., & Deal, A. (1988). *Enabling and empowering families: Principles and guidelines for practice.* Cambridge, MA: Brookline Books.

Durand, V.M. (1990). *Severe behavior problems: A functional communication training approach.* New York: Guilford Press.

Durand, V.M., Berotti, D., & Weiner, J. (1993). Functional communication training: Factors affecting effectiveness, generalization and maintenance. In J. Reichle & D.P. Wacker (Eds.), *Communicative alternative to challenging behavior—Integrating functional assessment and intervention strategies* (pp. 317–340). Baltimore: Brookes.

Evans, I.M., & Meyer, L.H. (1985). *An educative approach to behavior problems: A practical decision model for intervention with severely handicapped learners.* Baltimore: Brookes.

Evans, I.M., & Meyer, L.H. (1990). Toward a science in support of meaningful outcomes: A response to Horner et al. *Journal of the Association for Persons with Severe Handicaps, 15,* 133–135.

Fay, W.H., & Schuler, A.L. (1980). *Emerging language in autistic children.* Baltimore: University Park Press.

Ford, A., & Davern, L. (1989). Moving forward with school integration: Strategies for involving students with severe handicaps in the life of the school. In R.G. Ross (Ed.), *Integration strategies for students with handicaps* (pp. 11–31). Baltimore: Brookes.

Frith, U. (1971). Spontaneous patterns produced by autistic, normal, and subnormal children. In M. Rutter (Ed.), *Infantile autism: Concepts, characteristics, and treatment* (pp. 113–133). London: Churchill Livingstone.

Frith, U. (1989). *Autism: Explaining the enigma.* Oxford, England: Blackwell.

Garfin, D., & Lord, C. (1986). Communication as a social problem in autism. In E. Schopler & G. Mesibov (Eds.), *Social behavior in autism* (pp. 237–261). New York: Plenum Press.

Gaylord-Ross, R. (Ed.). (1989). *Integration strategies for students with handicaps.* Baltimore: Brookes.

Goetz, L., Schuler, A.L., & Sailor, W. (1979). Teaching functional speech to the severely handicapped: Current issues. *Journal of Autism and Developmental Disorders, 9,* 325–343.

Goldstein, H., & Kaczmarek, L. (1992). Promoting communicative interaction among children in integrated intervention settings. In S. Warren

& J. Reichle (Eds.), *Causes and effects in communication and language intervention* (pp. 81–111). Baltimore: Brookes.

Grandin, T. (1995). The learning style of people with autism: An autobiography. In K. Quill (Ed.), *Teaching children with autism: Methods to enhance communication and socialization.* Albany, NY: Delmar.

Harding, C., & Golinkoff, R. (1979). The origins of intentional vocalizations in prelinguistic infants. *Child Development, 50,* 33–40.

Harris, P. (1993). Pretending and planning. In S. Baron-Cohen, H. Tager-Flusberg, & D. Cohen (Eds.), *Understanding other minds: Perspectives from autism* (pp. 228–247). New York: Oxford Press.

Hart, B. (1985). Naturalistic language training techniques. In S. Warren & A.K. Rogers-Warren (Eds.), *Teaching functional language: Generalization and maintenance of language skills* (pp. 63–88). Baltimore: University Park Press.

Hart, B., & Risley, T. (1975). Incidental teaching of language in the preschool. *Journal of Applied Behavioral Analysis, 8,* 411–420.

Hermelin, B., & O'Connor, N. (1970). *Psychological experiments with autistic children.* Oxford, England: Pergamon Press.

Hobson, R.P. (1990). On the origins of self and the case of autism. *Development and Psychopathology, 2,* 163–182.

Hoffman, M.L. (1981). Perspectives on the difference between understanding people and understanding things: The role of affect. In J.H. Flavell & L. Ross (Eds.), *Social cognitive development* (pp. 67–82). Cambridge, England: Cambridge University Press.

Horner, R., Dunlap, G., Koegel, R., Carr, E., Sailor, W., Anderson, J., Albin, R., & O'Neill, R. (1990). Toward a technology of "nonaversive" behavioral support. *Journal of the Association for Persons with Severe Handicaps, 15,* 125–147.

Hubbell, R. (1981). *Children's language disorders: An integrated approach.* Engelwood Cliffs, NJ: Prentice-Hall.

Kanner, L. (1943). Autistic disturbances of affective contact. *Nervous Child, 2,* 217–250.

Kaufmann, R., & McGonigel, M. (1991). Identifying family concerns, priorities, and resources. In M. McGonigel, R. Kaufmann, & B. Johnson (Eds.), *Guidelines and recommended practices for the individualized family service plan* (2nd ed., pp. 47–55). Bethesda, MD: Association for the Care of Children's Health.

Kiernan, C. (1983). The use of nonvocal communication techniques with autistic individuals.

Journal of Child Psychology and Child Psychiatry, 24, 339–373.

Klinger, L., & Dawson, G. (1992). Facilitating early social and communicative development in children with autism. In S. Warren & J. Reichle (Ed.), *Causes and effects in communication and language intervention* (pp. 157–186). Baltimore: Brookes.

Koegel, R.L., Camarata, S.M., & Koegel, L.K. (1994). Aggression and noncompliance: Behavior modification through naturalistic language remediation. In J. Matson (Ed.), *Autism in children and adults: Etiology, assessment, and intervention* (pp. 165–180). Pacific Grove, CA: Brooks/Cole.

Koegel, R.L., & Johnson, J. (1989). Motivating language use in autistic children. In G. Dawson (Ed.), *Autism: New perspectives on diagnosis, nature and treatment* (pp. 310–325). New York: Guilford Press.

Koegel, R.L., O'Dell, M.C., & Koegel, L.K. (1987). A natural language paradigm for teaching nonverbal autistic children. *Journal of Autism and Developmental Disorders, 17,* 187–199.

Koegel, R.L., Rincover, A., & Egel, A.L. (1982). *Educating and understanding autistic children.* San Diego, CA: College Hill.

Lahey, M. (1988). Language disorders and language development. New York: Macmillan.

Layton, T.L. (1987). Manual communication. In T. Layton (Ed.), *Language and treatment of autistic and developmentally disordered children* (pp. 189–213). Springfield, IL: Thomas.

Lotter, V. (1978). Follow-up studies. In M. Rutter & E. Schopler (Eds.), *Autism: A reappraisal of concepts and treatment* (pp. 475–495). New York: Plenum Press.

Lovaas, O.I. (1977). *The autistic child: Language development through behavior modification.* New York: Irvington Press.

Lovaas, O.I. (1981). *Teaching developmentally disabled children. The "Me" Book.* Baltimore: University Park Press.

Lovaas, O.I., Koegel, R., & Schreibman, L. (1979). Stimulus overselectivity in autism: A review of research. *Psychological Bulletin, 86,* 1236–1254.

Loveland, K., & Landry, S. (1986). Joint attention and language in autism and developmental language delay. *Journal of Autism and Developmental Disorders, 16,* 335–349.

Lund, N., & Duchan, J. (1993). *Assessing children's language in naturalistic contexts* (3rd ed.). Englewood Cliffs, NJ: Prentice-Hall.

McEachin, J.J., Smith, T., & Lovaas, O.I. (1993). Long-term outcome for children with autism who received early intensive behavioral treatment. *American Journal on Mental Retardation, 97,* 359–372.

McLean, J., & Snyder-McLean, L. (1978). *A transactional approach to early language training: Derivation of a model system.* Columbus, OH: Charles Merrill.

McLean, L.K.S. (1990). Communication development in the first two years of life: A transactional process. *Zero to Three, 11*(1), 13–19.

Meyer, L., & Evans, I. (1986). Modification of excess behavior: An adaptive and functional approach for educational and community contexts. In R. Horner, L. Meyer, & H. Fredericks (Eds.), *Education of learners with severe handicaps: Exemplary service strategies* (pp. 315–350). Baltimore: Brookes.

Meyer, L., & Evans, I. (1993). Meaningful outcomes in behavioral intervention: Evaluating positive approaches to the remediation of challenging behaviors. In J. Reichle & D.P. Wacker (Eds.), *Communicative alternative to challenging behavior—Integrating functional assessment and intervention strategies* (pp. 407–428). Baltimore: Brookes.

Mirenda, P., & Donnellan, A. (1986). Effects of adult interaction style on conversational behavior in students with severe communication problems. *Language, Speech, and Hearing Services in Schools, 17,* 126–141.

Moses, K. (1981, April). *Mourning theory as related to parents of autistic children.* Paper presented at the National Society for Autistic Children Midwest Regional Conference, Chicago, IL.

Mundy, P., Kasari, C., & Sigman, M. (1992). Joint attention, affective sharing, and intersubjectivity. *Infant Behavior and Development, 15,* 377–381.

Mundy, P., Sigman, M., & Kasari, C. (1990). A longitudinal study of joint attention and language development in autistic children. *Journal of Autism and Developmental Disorders, 20,* 115–128.

Nelson, K. (1981). Social cognition in a script framework. In J.H. Flavell & L. Ross (Eds.), *Social cognitive development* (pp. 97–119). Cambridge, England: Cambridge University Press.

Noonan, M.J., & McCormick, L. (1993). *Early intervention in natural environments.* Pacific Grove, CA: Brooks/Cole.

Odom, S., & McEvoy, M. (1988). Integration of young children with handicaps and normally developing children. In S. Odom & M. Karnes (Eds.), *Early intervention for infants and children with handicaps* (pp. 241–267). Baltimore: Brookes.

Peck, C. (1985). Increasing opportunities for social control by children with autism and severe handicaps: Effects on student behavior and perceived classroom climate. *Journal of the Association for Persons with Severe Handicaps, 4,* 183–193.

Peters, A. (1983). *The units of language acquisition.* London: Cambridge University Press.

Piaget, J. (1971). *The language and thought of the child.* New York: World.

Prior, M. (1979). Cognitive abilities and disabilities in autism: A review. *Journal of Abnormal Child Psychology, 2,* 357–380.

Prizant, B. (1982). Speech-language pathologists and autistic children: What is our role? Part 1. *American Speech-Language-Hearing Association, 24,* 463–468.

Prizant, B. (1983a). Echolalia in autism: Assessment and intervention. *Seminars in Speech and Language, 4,* 63–77.

Prizant, B. (1983b). Language acquisition and communicative behavior in autism: Toward an understanding of the "whole" of it. *Journal of Speech and Hearing Disorders, 48,* 296–307.

Prizant, B. (1987). Theoretical and clinical implications of echolalic behavior in autism. In T. Layton (Ed.), *Language and treatment of autistic and developmentally disordered children* (pp. 65–88). Springfield, IL: Thomas.

Prizant, B. (1988). Communication in autistic clients. In N. Lass, L. McReynolds, J. Northern, & D. Yoder (Eds.), *The handbook of speech-language pathology* (pp. 1014–1039). Toronto, Ontario, Canada: BC Decker.

Prizant, B. (1994, October). *Dimensions to consider in planning and implementing communication and language programs for individuals with autism and PDD.* Seminar presented for State of Connecticut Special Education Directors, Fairfield, CT.

Prizant, B., & Rydell, P. (1984). Analysis of the functions of delayed echolalia in autistic children. *Journal of Speech and Hearing Research, 27,* 183–192.

Prizant, B.M., & Rydell, P.J. (1993). Assessment and intervention considerations for unconventional verbal behavior. In J. Reichle & D. Wacker (Eds.), *Communicative alternatives to challenging behavior: Integrating functional assessment and intervention strategies* (pp. 263–297). Baltimore: Brookes.

Prizant, B., & Tiegerman, E. (1984). Working with language-impaired children: Problems/issues often encountered but (too) rarely discussed.

Journal of the National Student Speech Language Hearing Association, 11, 18–32.

Prizant, B., & Wetherby, A. (1985). Intentional communicative behavior of children with autism: Theoretical and practical issues. *Australian Journal of Human Communication Disorders, 13,* 21–59.

Prizant, B.M., & Wetherby, A. (1987). Communicative intent: A framework for understanding social-communicative behavior in autism. *Journal of the American Academy of Child Psychiatry, 26,* 472–479.

Prizant, B., & Wetherby, A. (1988). Providing services to children with autism (0 to 2 years) and their families. *Topics in Language Disorders, 9,* 1–23.

Prizant, B., & Wetherby, A. (1989). Enhancing language and communication in autism: From theory to practice. In G. Dawson (Ed.), *Autism: Nature, diagnosis, and treatment* (pp. 282–309). New York: Guilford Press.

Prizant, B., Wetherby, A., & Rydell, P.J. (1994). Implications of facilitated communication for education and communication enhancement practices for persons with autism. In H. Shane (Ed.), *Facilitated communication: The clinical and social phenomenon* (pp. 123–155). San Diego, CA: Singular Publishing Group.

Quill, K. (Ed.). (1995). *Teaching children with autism: Methods to enhance communication and socialization.* Albany, NY: Delmar.

Reichle, J., & Wacker, D.P. (Eds.). (1993). *Communicative alternative to challenging behavior— Integrating functional assessment and intervention strategies.* Baltimore: Brookes.

Reichle, J., York, J., & Sigafoos, J. (1991). *Implementing augmentative and alternative communication: Strategies for learners with severe disabilities.* Baltimore: Brookes.

Ricks, D., & Wing, L. (1975). Language, communication and the use of symbols in normal autistic children. *Journal of Autism and Childhood Schizophrenia, 5,* 191–221.

Rimland, B. (1964). *Early infantile autism.* Englewood Cliffs, NJ: Prentice-Hall.

Rogoff, B. (1990). *Apprenticeship in thinking: Cognitive development in a social context.* New York: Oxford University Press.

Rutter, M. (1968). Concepts of autism: A review of research. *Child Psychiatry, 9,* 1–25.

Rutter, M. (1983). Cognitive deficits in the pathogenesis of autism. *Journal of Child Psychology & Psychiatry & Allied Disciplines, 4,* 513–531.

Sameroff, A. (1987). The social context of development. In N. Eisenburg (Ed.), *Contemporary topics in development* (pp. 273–291). New York: John Wiley & Sons.

Sameroff, A., & Chandler, M.J. (1975). Reproductive risk and the continuum of care taking causality. In F. Horowicz, M. Hetherington, F. Scarr-Salapatek, & G. Siegel (Eds.), *Review of child development research* (Vol. 4, 187–244). Chicago: University of Chicago Press.

Schuler, A.L. (1979). *An experimental analysis of conceptual and representational abilities in a mute autistic adolescent: A serial vs. a simultaneous mode of processing.* Unpublished doctoral dissertation, University of California, Santa Barbara.

Schuler, A.L. (1981, November). *The relations between disruptive behavior and communicative deficiencies.* Paper presented at the annual convention of the American Speech-Language-Hearing Association, Los Angeles.

Schuler, A.L. (1995). Thinking in autism: Differences in learning and development. In K. Quill (Ed.) *Teaching children with autism: Methods to enhance communication and socialization* (pp. 11–32). Albany, NY: Delmar.

Schuler, A.L., & Bormann, C. (1983). The interrelations between cognitive and communicative development; Some implications of the study of a mute autistic adolescent. In C.L. Thew & C.E. Johnson (Eds.), *Proceedings of the Second International Congress on the Study of Child Language* (Vol. 2, pp. 269–282). Washington, DC: University Press of America.

Schuler, A.L., & Goetz, L. (1981). The assessment of severe language disabilities: Communicative and cognitive considerations. *Analysis and Intervention in Developmental Disabilities, 1,* 333–346.

Schuler, A., Gonsier-Gerdin, & Wolfberg, P. (1990). Efficacy of speech and language intervention: Autism. *Seminars in Speech and Language, 11,* 242–251.

Schuler, A.L., & Prizant, B. (1985). Echolalia. In E. Schopler & G. Mesibov (Eds.), *Communication problems in autism* (pp. 163–184). New York: Plenum Press.

Sigman, M., & Kasari, C. (1995). Joint attention across contexts in normal and autistic children. In C. Moore & P. Dunham (Eds.), *Joint attention: Its origins and role in development* (pp. 189–203). Hillsdale, NJ: Erlbaum.

Smith, M. (1985). Managing the aggressive and self-injurious behavior of adults disabled by autism. *Journal of the Association for Persons with Severe Handicaps, 4,* 228–232.

Snow, C., Midkiff-Borunda, S., Small, A., & Proctor, A. (1984). Therapy as social interaction:

Analyzing the context for language remediation. *Topics in Language Disorders, 3,* 72–85.

Snyder-McLean, L., McLean, J., Etter-Schroeder, R., & Rogers, N. (1984). Structuring joint action routines: A strategy for facilitating communication in the classroom. *Seminars in Speech and Language, 5,* 213–228.

Stainback, S., & Stainback, W. (1985). *Integration of students with severe handicaps into regular schools.* Reston, VA: Council for Exceptional Children.

Stainback, S., Stainback, W., & Forest, M. (Eds.). (1989). *Educating all students in the mainstream of regular education.* Baltimore: Brookes.

Stern, D. (1985). *The interpersonal world of the infant.* New York: Basic Books.

Tanguay, P. (1984). Toward a new classification of serious psychopathology in children. *Journal of the American Academy of Child Psychiatry, 23,* 373–384.

Theadore, G., Maher, S., & Prizant, B. (1990). Early assessment and intervention with emotional and behavioral disorders and communication disorders. *Topics in Language Disorders, 10,* 42–56.

Tomasello, M., Kruger, A.C., & Ratner, H.H. (1993). Cultural learning. *Behavioral and Brain Sciences, 16,* 495–552.

Tronick, E. (1989). Emotions and emotional communication in infancy. *American Psychologist, 44,* 112–119.

Turnbull, A. (1991). Identifying children's strengths and needs. In M. McGonigel, R. Kaufmann, & B. Johnson (Eds.), *Guidelines and recommended practices for the individualized family service plan* (2nd ed., pp. 39–46). Bethesda, MD: Association for the Care of Children's Health.

Udvari-Solner, A. (1994). A decision-making model for curricular adaptations in cooperative groups. In J. Thousand, R. Villa, & A. Nevin (Eds.), *Creativity and collaboration: A practical guide to empowering students and teachers* (pp. 59–77). Baltimore: Brookes.

Vygotsky, L.S. (1962). *Thought and language.* Cambridge, MA: MIT Press. (Original work published 1934)

Wehman, P., & Kregel, J. (1985). A supported work approach to competitive employment of individuals with moderate and severe handicaps. *Journal of the Association for Persons with Severe Handicaps, 10*(1), 3–11.

Wertsch, J.V. (Ed.). (1985). *Culture, communication, and cognition: Vygotskian perspectives.* Cambridge, England: Cambridge University Press.

Wetherby, A. (1986). The ontogeny of communicative functions in autism. *Journal of Autism and Developmental Disorders, 16,* 295–316.

Wetherby, A., Cain, D., Yonclas, D., & Walker, V. (1988). Analysis of intentional communication of normal children from the prelinguistic to the multi-word stage. *Journal of Speech and Hearing Research, 31,* 240–252.

Wetherby, A., & Prizant, B. (1989). The expression of communicative intent: Assessment guidelines. *Seminars in Speech and Language, 10,* 77–91.

Wetherby, A., & Prizant, B. (1992). Facilitating language and communication development in autism: Assessment and intervention guidelines. In D. Berkell (Ed.), *Autism: Identification, education, and treatment.* Hillsdale, NJ: Erlbaum.

Wetherby, A., & Prizant, B. (1993). Profiling communication and symbolic abilities in young children. *Journal of Childhood Communication Disorders, 15,* 23–32.

Wetherby, A., & Prutting, C. (1984). Profiles of communicative and cognitive-social abilities in autistic children. *Journal of Speech and Hearing Research, 27,* 364–377.

Wills, D.M. (1979). Early speech development in blind children. *Psychoanalytic Studies of the Child, 34,* 85–117.

Wimmer, H., & Perner, J. (1983). Beliefs about beliefs: Representation and constraining function of wrong beliefs in young children's understanding of deception. *Cognition, 13,* 103–128.

Wing, L., & Gould, J. (1979). Severe impairments of social interaction and associated abnormalities in children: Epidemiology and classification. *Journal of Autism and Developmental Disorders, 9,* 11–29.

Wolfberg, P.J., & Schuler, A.L. (1993). Integrated play groups: A model for promoting the social and cognitive dimensions of play in children with autism. *Journal of Autism and Developmental Disorders, 23,* 467–489.

CHAPTER 24

Enhancing Language and Communication Development: Prelinguistic Approaches

ADRIANA L. SCHULER, BARRY M. PRIZANT, AND AMY M. WETHERBY

This chapter focuses on individuals with autism and Pervasive Developmental Disorder (PDD) who exhibit the greatest limitations in communication. They are described as prelinguistic or, in the most extreme cases, preintentional (those who do not yet communicate with clear purposes or intentions). Enhancing the communication abilities of these persons is indeed a challenge; thus far, intervention efforts have met with only limited success. In the past, many prelinguistic individuals were excluded from language intervention services because of the severity of their attentional and behavioral challenges. Contemporary approaches have integrated communication and behavioral goals, replacing fragmented remedial efforts with more comprehensive and holistic approaches to communication enhancement. Highly structured data-based interventions with a behavioral orientation have typically included the most severely communication-impaired persons with autism and PDD, but these efforts have only been partially successful, at least as far as can be ascertained from the data reported (Goetz, Schuler, & Sailor, 1979; Schuler, Gonsier-Gerdin, & Wolfberg, 1990).

The effectiveness of traditional behavioral approaches in systematic skill building and behavioral control for individuals with severe disabilities has been amply documented; however, fewer advances have been made when similar techniques have been applied to the domains of communication and language. Treatment outcome has typically been disappointing when criteria of spontaneous use and generalization have been applied (Howlin, 1981;

Schuler et al., 1990). As discussed in Chapter 23, a disproportionate emphasis on training of externally cued response topographies in contrived rather than natural social contexts may be at fault. This type of approach, although useful for specific instruction in discrete skills, runs counter to the dynamic and interactive nature of communicative transactions.

Shifting philosophies and treatment perspectives are reflected in more current efforts. Primarily, a greater appreciation of the functions of communication is apparent both among developmental treatment approaches, as evidenced by an increased focus on the pragmatics of communication, and within contemporary behavioral circles (Reichle & Wacker, 1993). Innovations in the use of behavioral treatment practices, drawing largely from the pragmatics of communication literature, acknowledge the various functions of communicative acts in more natural environments and the primacy of self-initiated and reciprocal communication as opposed to compliance training. These innovations have served to mitigate and even preclude some of the commonly encountered behavior problems that may be observed in autism and PDD. (For a more detailed discussion, see Carr, 1985; Carr & Carlson, 1993; Charlop & Haymes, 1994; Hart, 1981; Koegel, Camarata, & Koegel, 1994.) As discussed in Chapter 23, these recent trends are incorporated into the treatment philosophy and guidelines presented in this chapter. The approaches espoused in this chapter are also augmented by these other sources: (a) a pragmatic view of communicative competence, referring to the use of multiple communicative means serving multiple communicative functions or purposes; (b) insights into early communicative development, with emphasis on the importance of supportive scaffolded interactions with relevant others (Bruner, 1975; Dunst, Lowe, & Bartholomew, 1990; Snow, Midkiff-Borunda, Small, & Proctor, 1984); (c) the explosion of technology supporting communication enhancement practices that recognize that nonverbal modes of communication must be utilized when prognosis for the development of functional speech is limited (Beukelman & Mirenda, 1992; Reichle, Sigafoos, & York, 1991); (d) an emerging understanding of the learning mechanisms involved in the acquisition of cultural as opposed to more object-referenced knowledge (Tomasello, Kruger, & Ratner, 1993); and (e) insights that have been acquired from recent research dealing with the "culture of play" and play-based interventions for children (Wolfberg, 1995; Wolfberg & Schuler, 1993).

This chapter first discusses the interrelationships between the severe communication disability associated with preverbal levels of representation and the related behavioral difficulties. This is followed by a discussion of the particular challenges presented by individuals who may be not only prelinguistic but also preintentional. The key themes of these discussions pertain to: limitations in the expression of communicative intent, the unevenness of developmental profiles, the associated behavior excesses frequently observed, and the challenges these issues present for both assessment and intervention efforts. Next, assessment principles and practices, and related intervention approaches, are discussed. Specific examples will be given of how communication goals are selected that are commensurate with the assessed levels of communication skills. While close interrelationships exist between communication assessment and intervention, these issues are, however, discussed separately for the sake of organizational clarity.

The term *communication,* denoting a range of purposeful behavior, is used with varying degrees of intentionality within the structure of social exchange to transmit information, observations, or internal states, or to bring about changes in the immediate physical environment. Verbal as well as nonverbal behaviors are

included, as long as some intent, evidenced by anticipation of outcome, can be inferred. This usage implies that not all vocalizations (or even all speech) qualify as intentional communicative behavior. Not all vocalizations are used for communicative purposes; they may be produced in the context of other "self-stimulatory" or self-directed behavior for no apparent purpose other than the provision of sensory feedback.

The term *prelanguage* is used to denote communicative behavior that lacks formal grammatical organization and symbolic reference. For instance, an individual might effectively use certain memorized echolalic or "gestalt" phrases for communicative purposes, but is unable to segment them into the individual words that constitute their internal makeup. Chapter 25 addresses the communicative behaviors of more able individuals—those who are capable of intentional linguistic communication, and who are functioning at the one-word or short-phrase level, or beyond, thus demonstrating at least the roots of symbolic thinking.

CHALLENGES AND ISSUES AT PRELINGUISTIC LEVELS

Establishing Intentionality

A prime challenge in working with nonspeaking individuals with autism and PDD is that many are preintentional as well as prelinguistic. This may well be the ultimate communication disorder; not only do more effective means of communication need to be learned, but, most importantly, the basic notion of communication has not yet been acknowledged. Because communication hinges on the anticipation of outcomes of one's own and of others' behavior, progress can be inferred when the autistic individual starts to anticipate particular memorized outcomes in association with his or her own behavior (e.g., hand and body movements, vocalizations). When the individual is starting to look for the effect of his or her actions, significant progress is being made toward intentional communication. Further progress is indicated when he or she realizes that the anticipated outcomes are mediated by the actions of communication partners. For instance, anticipation is evident when approaching a snack an individual starts to touch a communication picture symbol in anticipation and/or manually approximates the sign "eat." The most critical progress is made when that same individual is starting to shift his or her gaze between the snack and an adult who is close by, particularly when that gaze is accompanied by a reaching motion and/or a change in body orientation.

To promote true communicative progress, communicative function should supersede form or structure. Too often, individuals are drilled on the correct production of particular speech sounds, words, signs, or even a "whole sentence" without any grasp of intentional communication. As impressive as the speech produced may sound, this kind of drill is counterproductive because it is likely to generate situation-specific behavior that fails to generalize or to be used spontaneously (Fay & Schuler, 1980; Greenspan, 1992; Prizant, 1982). Moreover, the prompted behaviors may be produced out of context—for example, when a particular level of distress or agitation is being associated with one well-memorized phrase, such as "May I go potty, please," that is being uttered as a preintentional protest against the unpredictability of a change in routine. Thus, apparent gains in speech may mask minimal communicative competence, foster negative attention, and due to unrealistic expectations, invite behavior problems.

Uneven Developmental Profiles (Developmental Discontinuities)

Communicative limitations are often not recognized because so many individuals with autism and PDD have proficiencies in other areas, and these proficiencies may mask their lack of understanding of the world of person-related cause and effect and intentionality. This masking occurs especially when the individual involved is occasionally observed to repeat the speech of others, but not for communicative purposes. For instance, an individual may say "Don't hit," when close to another individual who is being hit, but without paying any attention to the unfolding scene. As explained by Prizant and Rydell (1984, 1995), such a delayed echolalic act of

speech production may function merely as a "situation association" echo—a situation-specific memorization of a particular phrase, which may further be associated with certain states of arousal or agitation.

When the delayed echolalic nature of the utterance is not understood by others, there may be considerable confusion about the level of communicative competence to be inferred. Typically, an individual may be accused of "negativism," of "withholding," or of simply not doing his or her best when failing to use language. Such attributions are readily made when excellent situational recall skills allow for the production of contextually appropriate utterances. These may, nevertheless, be created without specific communicative intentions. Unfortunately, this type of echolalia may lead parents, clinicians, and teachers to believe that these individuals would be able to talk creatively if they were sufficiently pressured. Such false assumptions can easily lead to unproductive power struggles. This type of scenario may serve to underscore the importance of a comprehensive assessment designed to provide a true picture of communication skills and related levels of development across contexts.

The magnitude of the developmental discontinuities encountered in autism and PDD makes the gathering of pertinent and valid assessment data most challenging. In making comparisons across areas of assessment, differentiations need to be made between domains of knowledge that are dependent on social knowledge as opposed to knowledge of objects and spatial relations. The authors have found many discrepancies along those dimensions. Consistent with Kanner's (1943) seminal writings, object knowledge almost always exceeds person knowledge. The most extreme discrepancy we ever encountered pertained to a preintentional level of communicative and social knowledge (roughly estimated at a 6 months age level) in the presence of astounding knowledge of objects and spatial relations (roughly estimated at beyond 9 years of age). (For an in-depth discussion, the reader is referred to Fay & Schuler, 1980; Papy, Papy, & Schuler, 1995; Schuler, 1995; or Schuler & Watanabe, 1995.) A pervasive lack of communicative understanding and of the related skill discrepancies sets the stage for the severe behavioral challenges that are so commonly encountered, especially in preverbal individuals.

Behavior Ramifications

As pointed out in Chapter 23, the close interrelationships between communicative deficiency and challenging behavior often have been overlooked. What should be taken into account is that much "aberrant" behavior may serve communicative functions in a preintentional or semi-intentional way. For instance, self-injury, tantrums, stereotyped echolalic routines, and so on, may be the only available means by which an individual with autism or PDD can create an impact on the environment, or at least make predictions about it and test his or her hypotheses. Such behaviors may serve to terminate an unpleasant situation, to secure physical contact and/or attention, to initiate or regulate a social interaction, and so on. (For a more detailed discussion of these issues, see Carr, 1977; Carr et al., 1994; Schuler & Goetz, 1981; Schuler & Prizant, 1985; Weeks & Gaylord-Ross, 1981.)

The prevalence of undesirable communicative means suggests that communicative competence would be enhanced if such inappropriate means could be replaced by more socially acceptable, conventional, and mutually satisfactory forms of communication. This suggestion implies that behavior management and communication skill-building efforts are interdependent and closely integrated. In other words, the functional analysis of challenging behavior should guide communication programming (Durand, 1990). For instance, if an individual's temper tantrums and self-injurious behaviors typically occur when daily schedules are violated, or when activities are imposed that seem to be disliked, these behaviors are likely to serve a protest function. Functional analysis of the pattern of behaviors and situational context involved should be completed, including antecedents as well as consequences. (For detailed guidelines, see Carr et al., 1994; Durand, 1990.) If the behaviors involved indeed serve a protest function, more appropriate means to express protest functions need to be taught. For instance, a pictorial or written-word symbol, or a formalized hand or other body movement may be introduced.

The most effective behavior management approach is one that incorporates an analysis of the communicative functions of the behaviors of concern into a comprehensive program that involves teaching more mutually satisfying and more adaptive alternatives. The selection of teaching activities that are functional, meaningful, and motivating, as well as manageable, will serve to prevent many behavior problems.

Alternatives to Speech Communication

In many cases, speech may not be the most viable mode of communication and may not constitute a reasonable short-term objective. It is generally assumed that about half of all persons with autism and PDD never develop functional speech (Fay & Schuler, 1980; Prizant, 1988). Not only do we often observe a lack of expressive speech, but the comprehension of others' speech tends also to be limited despite some situational understanding. Language is often only understood in highly familiar contexts, and, most likely, the individual is not responding to the speech but to the routine within its situational context, or to other cues such as gestures and location in space. Our own clinical experience has convinced us that, for prelinguistic individuals, it is desirable to reduce and/or simplify speech input and to supplement it with visual information, manual demonstration, and contextual support. Another accommodation to the limited comprehension of speech lies in the use of a highly structured—and therefore predictable—environment that incorporates routine interactions, predictable time schedules, and clear spatial layouts of living and learning spaces, schedules, and so on.

When speech does not seem feasible as a primary mode of communication, alternative or augmentative modes of expression need to be introduced along with the expansion of natural gestures. Research and clinical reports have documented the effective use of nonspeech means to augment communication and develop literacy skills in sign language, communication boards, picture books, and computers for persons with autism, PDD, and other disabilities. (For reviews, see Bedrosian, 1996; Beukelman & Mirenda, 1992; Bishop,

Rankin, & Mirenda, 1994; Koppenhaver & Yoder, 1992; McNaughton & Lindsay, 1995; Mirenda & Schuler, 1988; Reichle et al., 1991; Schuler & Baldwin, 1981; Schuler, Gonsier-Gerdin, & Wolfberg, 1990.) Despite encouraging findings, many people continue to fear that the introduction of a nonspeech mode of communication will inhibit speech development. Fortunately, this fear is not supported by the available research or by our own clinical experience. Spontaneous increases in speech or vocal output are typically observed in about one-third to one-half of those nonspeaking individuals who learn to express themselves through other modes.

Decisions about specific modes and systems of communication should be made on an individual basis (Beukelman & Mirenda, 1992; Reichle et al., 1991; Schuler, 1985; Schuler, Peck, Willard, & Theimer, 1989). As will be discussed in more detail, those decisions should be based on a careful examination of current communicative repertoires and of the demands of current and subsequent living and learning environments. Nevertheless, many individuals with autism and PDD have been found to benefit most from those forms of augmentation that code information in a visual-spatial manner. This term is used in reference to visual stimuli that remain present over time, allowing for repeated visual examination. This feature distinguishes picture boards, written words, or related symbol systems from sign language, which also incorporates transient or fleeting visual information. (For a more detailed discussion, see Mirenda & Schuler, 1988.) The recent interest in facilitated communication (FC) is at least partially explained by the fact that it incorporates written words, graphic symbols, and/or keyboards, all of which are presented in a visual-spatial mode.

Joint Attention and Action

The biggest challenge in enhancing communicative competence probably lies in the need to expand the repertoire of communicative functions to include more social purposes, allowing for greater reciprocity and mutual enjoyment of communication (Wetherby & Prizant, 1993b). Typically, the greatest success is in teaching

more socially acceptable ways to request objects or actions, as well as ways to protest against changes in environment, interruptions of routines, increased demands, and so on. In other words, communication alternatives are most easily acquired as long as the communication centers around objects and the maintenance of order in the physical environment. However, more socially referenced forms of communication are often lacking in the communicative repertoire and present much greater challenges. When more advanced communicative behaviors appear, the range of communicative functions displayed typically remains restricted to immediate needs and environmental ends (i.e., communicating to regulate others' behavior; Fay & Schuler, 1980; Wetherby, 1986). To allow for the conventionalization of behavior and affect, it is critical that communication is established to share experiences (i.e., to establish joint attention) and to increase reciprocity between an autistic individual and a caregiver. It is important for the individual to learn to take turns and to participate in shared activities and, ultimately, shared affect. Our own research suggests that supported play with more competent peers (Wolfberg & Schuler, 1993) may be not only the most effective but also a most enjoyable vehicle for teaching more socially referenced communication and for normalizing affect.

ASSESSMENT AND INTERVENTION DOMAINS AND APPROACHES AT PRELINGUISTIC LEVELS

Before embarking on a more detailed discussion of assessment and intervention strategies, our guiding philosophy should be stated clearly. We believe that, first and foremost, the competencies and needs of the individuals involved should be considered. Second, environments that invite and are responsive to social and communicative interactions should be created, to help foster communicative competence.

Promoting Competence

When dealing with individuals with severe communicative limitations, the experience of communicative success is of paramount importance. As discussed in Chapter 23, to accomplish this goal, we advocate moving away from orientations that focus too narrowly on deficiencies, despite the obvious severity of the disabilities involved. A person's learning strengths, motivations, and preferred activities and relationships should be acknowledged. It is equally important to reexamine communication as a transactional phenomenon that involves at least two or more individuals and serves a range of different social and cognitive functions. Although the burden of changing behavior has traditionally been placed on the most disabled communication partner, important accommodations for communicative success can be made by pertinent others. Both the context and the interactional style of the communication partners need to be targeted in intervention efforts. (For a discussion of these matters, see Duchan, 1989; Kaiser & Goetz, 1993; Peck, 1986.) After all, communication is a transaction between two or more individuals in a given social context (Prizant & Wetherby, 1989) that allows the more competent partners to compensate for the disabled partner's communicative limitations. In doing so a scaffold is provided for the development of new skills.

Concerning interaction style variables, nurturant response styles that acknowledge even the most minimal initiations are most likely to enhance communicative skills than are less responsive and more controlling response styles, especially for persons with very limited communication ability (Duchan, 1983; Dunst et al., 1990; Peck, 1989). Similarly, play interventions that incorporate adult-mediated peer responses to even the slightest approximations of appropriate play interactions were found to be highly effective in promoting play behaviors (Wolfberg & Schuler, 1993). The design of interventions to promote play and social interactions thus becomes a matter not only of specifying desirable changes in child behavior, but also of specifying desired changes in adult interaction style.

Concerning context variables, we need to determine which contexts and learning situations invite the most competent communicative initiations (Koegel & Johnson, 1989; Peck, 1989; Rowland & Schweigert, 1993). In doing

so, a combination of motivational and cognitive issues should be considered. For instance, an individual with limitations in means–end behavior may exhibit communicative behavior only in a structured routine context and not in a more generative, spontaneous manner, because his or her understanding of communication as a process to achieve specific goals is limited. Similarly, an individual without object permanence will lack the motivation to request objects and/or activities that are remote and abstract. The task of the communicative partner (i.e., the caregiver, clinician, teacher) is to stage contexts that invite success and, ultimately, the experience of communicative efficacy. Developmental information is thus sought in an effort to select a proper level of task adaptation rather than as a goal by itself. The social and cognitive approach we advocate in Chapter 23 demands that current knowledge and cognitions are taken into account so that successful learning can be planned in a context that makes sense to the individual involved.

To provide the type of intervention approach that is advocated, alternatives to standardized and other traditional forms of assessment tools must be used. (For a further discussion of these issues, see Halle, 1993; Prizant & Wetherby, 1985, 1993a; Schuler & Perez, 1991.) For instance, the value of traditional behavior checklists, which reduce assessment to measuring the frequency of desirable and/or undesirable behaviors, and which tend to be context-free, is questionable for our purposes. Rather than identify and/or measure deficiencies, assessment should pinpoint enabling factors. The tools selected should allow for the evaluation of communicative behavior in natural contexts that demand close involvement of teachers, parents, siblings, peers, and pertinent others who may have important observations to share. Similarly, it is imperative that interventions are not limited to one specific setting, so that the individual involved is able to experience communicative success throughout the day. Use of a number of different settings and interactants creates an environment that is conducive as well as responsive to communicative and social initiations. Again, these concerns demand close collaboration with parents and family members or other pertinent caregivers. For such collaboration to take place, it is critical that parents or pertinent others have an active voice in the assessment process as well as in the design of the overall intervention program.

Because people with autism and PDD are more limited in their ability to acquire skills that are normally "assimilated" from interactions with others, the primary goal of an intervention program is to break down modes of noninteraction or minimal interaction and to provide for more social modes of communication. When these modes are not accessed, the lack of socially constructed knowledge becomes only more profound over time. Intensive interventions that support social learning—for example, incidental teaching (for a discussion, see Halle, 1993), use of joint action routines, and other socially based strategies—are thus of critical importance, particularly when services are provided to very young children and their families (Harris & Handleman, 1994). Fortunately, increasing numbers of children and their families are being identified and served at a much earlier age. Encouraging results from intense early intervention efforts have been documented in the literature (see Birnbrauer & Leach, 1993; Greenspan, 1992; Kalmanson & Pekarsky, 1987; Lovaas, 1987; McEachin, Smith, & Lovaas, 1993; Rogers, 1995; Scheinkoph & Siegel, in press; Siegel, 1996) and have been observed in our clinical practice. The earlier parents are supported in establishing more reciprocal modes of interaction and more conventionalized patterns of actions and attention, the greater the chances of self-regulation and communicative efficacy (Dunst et al., 1990; Greenspan, 1992; Prizant & Meyer, 1993).

Assessment Principles

Traditional formal communication assessment approaches focus primarily on the structure or form of language and rely on elicited responses. Because communication impairments associated with autism and PDD are most apparent in the area of social use of communicative acts, most formal communication assessment instruments have limited utility other than for establishing developmental levels, particularly for preverbal individuals. Wetherby and Prizant (1993a) identified

several major limitations of the most frequently used formal communication assessment instruments for individuals with limited language abilities. First, most instruments are not family-centered. They do not allow for the family to collaborate in decisions about the assessment process, nor to participate to the extent desired by the family members. Second, most instruments involving direct assessment are primarily clinician-directed. The individual being evaluated is placed in a respondent role, which limits observations of spontaneously initiated communication. Third, most formal instruments emphasize language milestones and forms of communication (e.g., number of different gestures, sounds, words, word combinations), rather than use of communicative acts in everyday interactions, and the social-communicative and symbolic foundations of language and communicative competence.

Current theories on how children acquire language (Bates, 1979; Lahey, 1988) suggest that the following features are critical to the assessment of language and communication in individuals with significant social-communicative problems:

1. Communication and language should be assessed within an interactive, meaningful context in which each person is encouraged to initiate communication.
2. If possible, the caregiver should be integrally involved in the assessment as an active participant, as an informant about the individual's competence and performance, and as a collaborator in decision making;
3. Assessment should not only identify relative developmental weaknesses, but should also provide information about relative strengths in communication and related areas of development.
4. Assessment should be viewed as a dynamic process in which an individual's capacity for developing communicative competence is understood over time.

Thus, there is a critical need (a) to move toward more authentic assessment of persons with autism and PDD by ensuring the ecological validity of assessment practices (Damico, Secord, & Wiig, 1992), and (b) to utilize dynamic assessment to explore aspects of contexts that support or impede an individual's acquisition of communicative competence (Olswang, Bain, & Johnson, 1992; Schuler, 1989).

Assessment of social communication and related abilities is most relevant when it pinpoints specific treatment goals and teaching strategies—that is, when it provides specific directions for intervention. The limitations in intentional communication and language comprehension, and the associated developmental discontinuities and behavior problems make it very difficult to use standardized instruments. A variety of assessment techniques may be used, as long as they are indicative of current ability levels and provide direction for how communication abilities may be expanded.

The framework presented in the previous chapter (see Table 23.1) can be used as a guide for determining domains that need to be assessed. (More specific assessment questions that need to be addressed at this level are summarized in Table 24.1.) Following is an overview of important considerations for assessment of prelinguistic individuals with autism and PDD, using a social communication assessment framework.

Assessment Domains

Expressive Communicative Means

Preverbal individuals, by definition, show limited ability to express themselves through oral

TABLE 24.1   Examples of Core Prelanguage Assessment Questions

Does the student exhibit intentional communicative behavior?

Through which means does the student communicate?

Which communicative functions may be inferred from behavioral observations?

Does the student utilize multiple means to achieve communicative functions? If so, for which functions?

Does the student exhibit repair strategies when communicative ends fail to be met? If so, which ones?

Is the student able to initiate, respond, and/or maintain a communicative exchange?

Which contexts are most facilitative of communicative behavior?

language. Therefore, communication assessment should identify the range of communicative means or behaviors used to express intentions (see Table 24.2). Persons with autism and PDD often use unconventional, idiosyncratic, or challenging behavior to communicate for various functions (Carr & Durand, 1985; Donnellan, Mirenda, Mesaros, & Fassbender, 1984; Schuler & Goetz, 1981; Wetherby & Prutting, 1984). Therefore, a lack of conventionality or social acceptability should not preclude the possibility that a behavior is being used purposefully to communicate. The degree of conventionality and social acceptability of the individual's entire repertoire of communicative behaviors should be considered. Additionally, the sophistication of preverbal communication should be considered. Gestures may range from primitive contact gestures, such as physical manipulation of another person's hand, to distal gestures in which there is no physical contact, such as pointing or depictive gestures (i.e., pantomime gestures). Vocal communication may range from vowels that are differentiated on the basis of affective state (e.g., excitement versus distress) to mono- or multisyllabic vocalizations of consonants and/or vowels, some of which may approximate speechlike forms.

As far as speech output is concerned, pertinent questions revolve around the ability to repeat or approximate speech, and, perhaps more importantly, to use vocalizations for intentional purposes. It should be determined whether vocalizations and/or some form of echoing may be used intentionally for communicative purposes. (See Chapter 25 for further discussion of echolalia and other forms of unconventional verbal behavior.) For instance, can some form of speech imitation be prompted? Is there any evidence of apraxic involvement that affects the motor-planning capacities of the oral musculature, as well as bodily movement and coordination?

Receptive Language and Communication

It is also important to assess the level of language comprehension so that service providers and family members can use this information to adjust their language level to promote successful interactions. It should first be determined whether the individual's language

TABLE 24.2   Summary of Communicative Means, with Some Examples and Definitions

Communicative Means	Description
Crying, tantrums/Self-injury, proximity	Physical closeness to others and/or objects.
Passive gaze	Eye contact without attempts to direct the other's gaze or focus of attention.
Active gaze	Eye contact with attempts to direct the gaze of others.
Grabs/Reaches	May be responded to by others as being a request for an object, particularly when combined with gaze and/or vocalization.
Vocalization	A wide range of vocal acts and/or "noises."
Self-removal	Running away or disappearance may be used as a form of protest.
Reenactment (rituals)	Reenactment of partial or entire behavior sequences associated with a desired outcome (e.g., requesting to go out shopping by collecting jacket, car keys, etc.).
Physical manipulation	Physically moving other person to have him or her perform a desired action. May also be a reenactment (e.g., requesting to be tickled by placing someone else's hand on the desired location).
Giving/Showing objects	Handing a toy to someone in an effort to establish joint attention and reference.
Pointing (contact or distal)	Indicative hand gesture denoting attention toward or request for object or action. Distinct from reaching and actual physical contact.
Gesturing	Natural gestures such as pushing away, making a palm-up request, giving; distinct from signing and stereotyped body manipulations.
Intonation	Variations in vocal pitch, volume, or duration.
Aggression	Pushing, kicking, biting, pinching directed toward another individual.
Echolalia	Delayed or immediate repetition of the speech of others; may vary in situational appropriateness and degree of intent.
Single-word speech	
Single-word signs	
AAC system use (e.g., pictures)	

Note: The behaviors listed, particularly those that are least conventional and symbolic, may vary in intentionality.

comprehension is at a prelinguistic or linguistic level (Lord, 1985). Assessment of receptive communication should include an individual's ability to receive and respond to others' communicative signals. A full audiological assessment relevant to an individual's developmental level may need to be conducted to assess hearing status. An individual's ability to respond to communicative signals in natural environments—for example, communicative gestures, vocalizations, words, and multiword utterances—should also be documented. A primary determination is whether speech signals convey any information to the autistic individual. Although this seems a rather straightforward matter, such determinations are not always easily made. Because many individuals have good recall of sequences of events and may

learn to respond to an overall contextual "gestalt," they may respond appropriately to everyday instructions given in a predictable context. The linguistic comprehension skills of individuals can be easily overestimated because of their use of situational cues and their memorization of daily routines. A correlate of gestalt processing may be inferred when individuals show a contextual comprehension of an utterance as a whole but are unable to respond correctly when a few words are altered, intonation is changed, or other minor revisions occur. An in-depth assessment of comprehension skills should thus examine what happens when standard instructions are altered in a variety of daily contexts. (For a more detailed discussion of assessment strategies, see Peck & Schuler, 1987; Peck, Schuler, Tomlinson,

Theimer, & Haring, 1983; Wetherby & Prizant, 1992a; for a more detailed discussion of nonlinguistic comprehension strategies, see Chapter 25.)

When an individual can comprehend linguistic aspects of a message, it is important to determine whether he or she is able to comprehend single words within the message, multiword combinations guided by semantic relations (i.e., understanding based on knowledge about word classes and relations), grammatical constructions (i.e., syntactic and morphological rules), or connected discourse. The individual's language comprehension level should contribute to the selection of suitable augmentative communication systems; that is, individuals with greater comprehension skills show more readiness for a symbolic communication system.

Social-Communicative and Socioemotional Abilities

Assessment of communication should determine the communicative functions expressed by an individual as well as the repertoire of behaviors used for communicating. If an individual is at a preintentional level (i.e., does not demonstrate any deliberate, goal-directed communication), assessment should identify behaviors that serve a communicative function based on others' interpretation of these behaviors. The triad of functions defined by Bruner (1981)—behavior regulation, social interaction, and joint attention—is particularly useful in assessing individuals with autism and PDD. Wetherby (1986) has suggested that, for individuals with autism and PDD, the easiest and first emerging communicative function is behavior regulation, and the most difficult function is referencing joint attention, presumably because of the differing social underpinnings of these abilities.

Persons with autism and PDD also evidence difficulty with the reciprocity of communication. Assessment should consider the individual's ability to synchronize and regulate turn-taking interactions (Dawson & Galpert, 1986). Additionally, it is important to assess the individual's ability to repair communication breakdowns; that is, when an individual's attempt to communicate is unsuccessful, what strategies are used to repair? Does the individual at least repeat the communicative signal

to persist in communicating, or is the individual able to modify the signal to clarify the communicative intention? Because individuals with autism may be faced frequently with communication breakdowns, repair strategies are critical for successful communicative interactions.

Use of social-affective signals, including facial expression and displays of affect, gaze behavior, vocalizations, and other behavior reflecting emotional and physiological states, should be assessed. Individuals with autism often demonstrate limited use of gaze shifts to regulate interactions, and their emotional states may be difficult to read because of a limited range of affect expression (Prizant & Wetherby, 1990).

Assessment of social relatedness is an important component of a thorough communication assessment because communicative competence will depend, to a great extent, on an individual's social knowledge and social relationships. Social relatedness may be defined as an individual's motivation to be with, to be like, to share feelings with, and to learn from others (Prizant, 1986; Prizant & Meyer, 1993). This entails knowledge of social conventions of behavior and an understanding of others' motivations and intentions. Dimensions of social relatedness that may be assessed include social orientation (interest in being with or observing others), attachment (selective orientation toward an individual who may serve as a base of security), joint reference (the ability to establish and maintain shared attention with others), imitation (the ability to repeat actions or speech of others for social ends, or to learn from others), emotional expression (the ability to express emotional states in a readable manner), empathy (the ability to understand the emotional perspective of others), and knowledge of social rules and conventions (understanding rules of social behavior in different contexts and modifying behavior accordingly) (see Chapter 25 for further discussion). The appropriateness of nonverbal behavior in communicative interactions may also be assessed as to its role in supporting or inhibiting social exchange and communication interactions (Wetherby & Prizant, 1990).

In assessing social interaction, the present authors have mostly relied on direct observation in unstructured and semistructured contexts. The Social Interaction Observation Guide (see also Peck & Schuler, 1987) or, more formally, the Communication and Symbolic Behavior Scales for younger children (Wetherby & Prizant, 1993a, 1993b) have been helpful for organizing our observations. We look for the behaviors that are used to initiate, respond to, maintain, or terminate social interactions, as well as the use of gaze and the expression of affect in social interactions.

The observational framework shown in Table 24.3 was not designed to quantify the behaviors involved. Instead, it provides detailed descriptions of response topographies and related contextual variables, which will help to pinpoint productive intervention contexts.

Language-Related Cognitive Abilities/Symbolic Representation

Assessment of cognitive strengths and weaknesses is of extreme relevance, particularly for individuals at preverbal levels. It is important to determine an individual's understanding of characteristics and categorizations of objects, events, and persons, and how such understanding is brought into his or her social interactions. Therefore, communication abilities should be considered in the context of cognitive abilities, including attentional capacities, symbolic play and object use, and understanding of cause–effect relations (Bates, 1979). Both cognitive and social skills are pertinent to the emergence of symbolic play, and distinct correspondences have been observed in the appearances of increasingly sophisticated forms of language and play (McCune, 1995; McCune-Nicolich, 1981).

Persons with autism and PDD have been found to have relative weaknesses in symbolic play (make-believe play in which one object is used to stand for and represent an absent object), presumably because of the greater social demands of symbolic play (Dawson & Adams, 1984; Sigman & Ungerer, 1984; Wetherby & Prutting, 1984; Wing & Gould, 1979), and in symbolic representational capacities (Frith, 1989). Relative strengths are observed in constructive play (combining objects to create a product such as a drawing, a block construction, or a puzzle assembly; Schuler, 1995). For children with autism and PDD, it is important to assess play skills at preschool and early

school age, and to compare their cognitive level of symbolic play separate from their constructive play. Because participation in symbolic play diminishes during late childhood, it is not appropriate to evaluate symbolic play in adolescents and adults with autism and PDD, even if they have cognitive limitations. It is possible to assess knowledge of object use and level of sequential organization in daily living skills (e.g., setting the table and doing laundry) and in recreation and leisure skills, to provide information about nonverbal mental representation. Extreme insistence on identical routines is generally suggestive of limited symbolization, and spontaneous manipulations of "novel" objects may provide another index of levels of representation.

It is our position that the cognitive status of individuals should never dictate teaching content, and that cognitive objectives that are removed from a context of functional communicative exchanges are undesirable. On the other hand, neglect of cognitive abilities and styles may backfire, because only situation-specific communicative behaviors may be learned when content is developmentally inappropriate. Such communicative acts are not likely to generalize or be used spontaneously in interactive contexts. Therefore, we believe that assessment of cognitive levels is of critical importance in planning intervention when assessing persons at prelanguage levels (see Table 24.4; also see Chapter 19).

Assessment Practices and Strategies

For persons at preverbal levels, assessments that depend solely on verbal instructions or verbal output are not suitable. In addition, the characteristics of preverbal individuals make assessments that depend on modeling or imitation questionable. Familiarity with typical profiles of persons with autism and PDD often allows slight modification of the tasks and protocols, to obtain the information sought. It should be kept in mind, however, that such adaptations make the findings more difficult to interpret. Congruent with the cognitive profile and the associated learning style, as discussed earlier, we find that tasks that are visual and that involve a spatial layout of the information presented are most manageable.

TABLE 24.3   Social Interaction Observation Guide

Name: _____

Observer: _____

Length of Observation: _____

Context: _____ Date: _____

INITIATION SKILLS (e.g., Approaches, Touches, Offers Object, Gestures, Vocalizes, Signs/Speaks, Other)

Description/Context:

RESPONDING SKILLS (e.g., Reorients Toward, Imitates, Complies with Directives, Gestures, Vocalizes, Signs/Speaks, Other)

Description/Context:

MAINTENANCE SKILLS (e.g., Maintains Proximity, Follows, Imitates, Alternates or Reciprocates Action, Takes Turns, Offers Objects, Vocalizes, Signs/Speaks, Other)

Description/Context:

TERMINATION SKILLS (e.g., Moves Away, Gestures, Signs/Speaks, Other)

Description/Context:

LEVEL OF PLAY (e.g., Unoccupied, Isolate, Onlooker, Parallel, Associative, Cooperative)

Description/Context:

TABLE 24.4   Major Questions for an Interview to Assess Cognitive Status

1. Does the individual realize that objects and/or people continue to exist even when out of sight? (Objective and people permanence)
2. Does the individual realize and anticipate the impact of his or her own and other people's actions?
3. Does the individual understand that different looking objects can belong in the same conceptual category/class because of shared features?
4. Does the individual remember and utilize concrete spatial information (e.g., location, shape, etc.)? Does the individual remember and utilize less tangible, fleeting information (e.g., facial expressions and gestures)?
5. Does the individual insist on the strict maintenance of routines/rituals, or can creative rearrangements of events be tolerated?
6. Does the individual demonstrate object manipulations that are largely stereotyped and/or exploratory, or, instead, functional and pretend forms of object manipulations?
7. Does the individual imitate novel actions vs. actions already observed within his or her behavioral repertoire?

Assessment of activities that require relatively simple motor responses is important because our own clinical experience is consistent with literature claiming the existence of additional motor planning problems (e.g., Biklen, 1990; Grandin, 1995b), including oral and limb apraxias that negatively impact on motor planning, coordination, and execution.

The difficulties inherent in assessment mandate validating assessment findings through other sources. The use of multiple types of assessments carried out in multiple contexts serves to reduce the chances of situational artifacts and measurement error. Such variation in assessment formats and contexts has additional value in a dynamic sense: it may serve to identify optimal learning contexts and supports. It is also important to look at the effects of externally imposed structure. Assessment formats that are highly externally structured may present a very different clinical picture than more loosely structured formats, which require individuals to impose their own structure, that is, to regulate and organize their own behavior. (For an in-depth discussion of this issue, see Schuler & Perez, 1991.)

Because of the difficulty in assessing language, communicative, social, and related symbolic abilities of individuals with autism, we recommend use of a combination of assessment strategies (Peck & Schuler, 1987; Wetherby & Prizant, 1992b), varying from direct observations of naturally occurring behavior samples throughout the day to ratings of behaviors observed in semistructured or staged communicative contexts. If possible, such situations should be videotaped for later analysis. Assessment of these abilities should occur in the home, the classroom, and the community, and should involve significant others in order to determine what abilities an individual can and will need to use in his or her natural environments.

Interviews

An initial method for gathering information about an individual's communicative and symbolic behavior is to interview significant others. Because of their extensive experience under a range of circumstances, the input of family members and teachers is critical in providing a highly representative picture of an individual's communicative repertoire and profile. For these reasons, we have made extensive use of structured interview formats to assess communicative competence (Schuler, 1981, 1985; Schuler et al., 1989; Wetherby & Prizant, 1993b). The completion of an interview sets the stage for close collaboration among parents, other caretakers, and pertinent professionals. Because the knowledge of many valued informants tends to be intuitive and not formalized, we have found it helpful to operationalize the questions and avoid any queries that are too open-ended. Table 24.5 displays the questions used; together with the means presented in Table 24.2, they constitute the core of our interview format.

The process of completing an interview has, in our experience, been most valuable because informants become typically more cognizant of their interaction and communication patterns when they respond to the questions posed. This type of awareness is most critical to effective incidental teaching in naturalistic contexts.

Naturalistic Observation

A second assessment strategy is observation during performance of routine activities, using a checklist or inventory of possible

TABLE 24.5   Overview of Probed Communicative Functions and Corresponding Situational Contexts

Requests for Affection and Interaction	Requests for Adult Action
What if S. wants:	*What if S. wants:*
An adult to sit close?	Help with dressing?
A peer to sit near adult to pay attention?	To have a book ready?
A cuddle or hug?	An adult to perform a favorite action/activity?
To sit on an adult's lap?	An adult to look in a certain direction?
To be closer to peers?	An adult to move or remove himself or herself?
To interact with peers?	An adult to play a record or sing a song?
To play ball or another game with an adult or peer?	Other?
Other?	

Requests for Food, Toys, or Other Items	Protests (Reversed Requests)
What if S. wants:	*What if:*
An object (toy) out of reach?	A common routine is dropped or changed?
A door/container opened to get something?	A favorite food is removed?
A favorite food or drink?	A favorite toy is removed?
Keys, books, or other toys that are out of sight?	S. is taken out for a ride when he/she doesn't want to go?
Other?	Other?

Declaratives/Comments
What if S. wants:
To show an adult a favorite toy?
To look at what he or she is doing?
To direct an adult's attention to something that is happening or has happened?
Other?

Note: These questions are asked in conjunction with the summary of communicative means.

communicative and symbolic behaviors. Observation during regularly scheduled activities provides information about an individual's communicative, social, and symbolic behavior, as well as the adequacy of the natural environment to provide opportunities that foster spontaneous communication. For children, peer play contexts provide ideal opportunities to obtain measures of communication, social interaction, and object use. Table 24.6 provides an example of the framework we have used in our own research and demonstration activities (Wolfberg & Schuler, 1993).

Observations in natural contexts provide meaningful information about an individual's spontaneous communicative behavior; however, collecting this information may be very time-consuming. Furthermore, because an individual may not display particular behaviors during even an extended observation period, semistructured assessments of communicative behavior, which we refer to as *communication behavior sampling,* are an important adjunct to interviewing and naturalistic observation.

Communication Behavior Sampling

Measures of communicative behavior in staged communicative situations or during "communicative temptations" are obtained by creating situations that necessitate some communicative response, such as putting desired objects out of reach, or placing a favorite toy or piece of candy in a "see-through" container that is tightly closed. These procedures are similar to those described by Curcio (1978), Peck and Schuler (1987), Sugarman (1984), and Wetherby and Prizant (1993b). The purpose is to create a situation that is highly enticing to an individual, while requiring some active signaling directed toward the partner. Once the individual anticipates that the communicative partner may act in a predictable way (e.g., by opening the container, by rolling back a ball, or by blowing more bubbles), the situation be-

TABLE 24.6   Definitions of Dimensions of Cognitive and Social Play

Cognitive Play with Objects	Social Play with Peers
No Interaction	*Isolation*
The child does not touch or play with toys. The child engages in self-stimulatory behavior that does not involve toys (e.g., the child stares at hands; rocks body; waves or flaps arms or hands; stares at toys).	Child appears to be oblivious or unaware of others. May occupy self by watching anything of momentary interest, playing with own body, or playing alone (e.g., child wanders, gets on and off chair, sits quietly, plays with back to peers).
Manipulation	*Orientation*
Exploratory play with toys ranges from simple to quite complex interactions. There is an apparent motivation to control the physical world. Child shows an interest in toys, but does not use them in conventional ways (e.g., holds and gazes at toys; mouths, waves, shakes, or bangs toys; stacks blocks or bangs them together; lines up objects).	Child has an awareness of the other children, as evidenced by looking at them or at their play materials or activities. The child does not enter into play (e.g., child quietly watches other children, child turns whole body facing children).
Functional	*Parallel Location/Proximity*
Complex and conventional use of toys in which one response is definitely dependent on another. There is a quality of delayed imitation while actions are performed that include simple pretense (e.g., puts teacup to mouth; puts brush to hair; connects train sections and pushes train; arranges pieces of furniture in dollhouse; constructs a building with blocks).	Child plays independently, beside rather than with the other children. There is simultaneous use of the same play space or materials as peers. There may be occasional imitation, showing of objects, or alternation of actions with peers (e.g., one child plays with a ball while sitting close to another child who plays with a train; one child brushes a doll's hair while another pushes a doll in a carriage).
Symbolic/Pretend	*Common Focus*
The child pretends to do something or to be someone or something else, with an intent that is representational. Mature pretense involves role playing and includes movements, vocalizations, or verbalizations that are substituted for real objects (e.g., child makes hand move to mouth, signifying drinking from teacup; makes a puppet talk; uses a toy person or doll to represent self; uses block as a car accompanied by engine sounds).	Child engages in activities directly involving one or more peers, including: informal turn-taking, giving and receiving assistance and directives, and active sharing of materials. There is a common focus or attention on the play (e.g., each child plays with blocks and shares blocks, each plays with dolls and touches others' dolls; they take turns playing beanbag toss).

gins to make sense (Donaldson, 1978; Duchan, 1986). The partner then violates the interactional "contract," probing to determine what the individual will do to fix or repair the interaction. For instance, the individual may reach over and move the partner's hand toward the container. This would be recorded as a "reenactment" strategy or a physical manipulation. Alternatively, the individual might point to the jar, sign "eat," vocalize, passively gaze at the adult, actively gaze back and forth between the jar and the adult, or engage in context-appropriate or marginally related stereotyped and/or echolalic speech. On the other hand, minimal active signaling may be observed. The individual may keep trying to open the container, shake it, or mouth it; he or she may even seem to forget about the contents. In addition, agitation or some form of challenging behavior, such as self-injury, tantrums, or aggression, may be observed. Table 24.6 summarizes actual behaviors that have been observed in such contexts. It may be helpful to use a standard protocol that specifies the behaviors observed across repeated trials, allowing examination of behavior gains over time. (For a more detailed description of this assessment approach, see Peck et al., 1983; Sugarman, 1984; Wetherby & Prizant, 1993b.)

Assessment should be considered an exploratory process and should be ongoing, particularly when assessing unconventional and primitive communicative behaviors. Assessment using a combination of interviewing, observing, and sampling provides information about an individual's profile of strengths and weaknesses in language, communication, social relatedness, and symbolic capacity, as well as information about the interaction style of significant others and the adequacy of natural environments to provide opportunities for communicating. Such assessment information provides the basis for decisions about intervention goals and strategies.

Communication and Symbolic Behavior Scales

To accomplish the assessment goals discussed above, and to provide an alternative to currently available formal assessment tools for developmentally young children, we developed the Communication and Symbolic Behavior Scales (CSBS) (Wetherby & Prizant, 1993a) to formalize a more authentic, yet efficient approach to assessment. The CSBS is designed to examine communicative, social/affective, and symbolic abilities of individuals whose functional communication abilities range from emerging prelinguistic intentional communication to early stages of language acquisition. This assessment instrument is designed to meet the goals of the diagnostic assesment as well as assessment for purposes of intervention planning. A developmental screening version of the CSBS is forthcoming.

The CSBS utilizes a standard but flexible format for gathering data, using a combination of a caregiver questionnaire and behavior sampling procedures. Through the use of a questionnaire that can be given to the family ahead of time or on the same day as the direct assessment, information is gathered from the caregiver about the individual's communicative and symbolic competence, using descriptive questions that solicit examples of typical behaviors. The direct assessment involves varying degrees of relatively structured and unstructured sampling procedures that resemble natural interactions and provide opportunities for documenting an individual's use of a variety of communicative and symbolic behaviors. The CSBS sampling procedures allow for dynamic assessment of the

effects of contextual factors on an individual's communicative abilities. Examples of how dynamic assessment is integrated within the CSBS sampling procedures include: (a) comparisons of the individual's communication during structured communicative opportunities as opposed to unstructured play contexts within the sample; (b) when the individual's communicative attempts are not responded to as intended, opportunities to examine the individual's ability to persist and repair are created; and (c) if the individual does not initiate communication during structured opportunities, a hierarchy of verbal and gestural cues is offered, and the individual's response to these cues can be examined.

The caregiver is present during the entire sampling and is encouraged to respond naturally to the individual's bids for interaction. After the sample is collected, the caregiver rates how typical the individual's behavior was during the sample, along seven dimensions: (a) alertness, (b) emotional reaction, (c) level of interest and attention, (d) comfort level, (e) level of activity, (f) overall level of communication, and (g) play behavior. The caregiver's perception rating allows the caregiver to validate the representativeness of the individual's behavior during direct assessment. Thus, the assessment procedures enable the clinician to engage the parent as an interactant during the direct assessment with the individual and as an informant by using the caregiver questionnaire and the caregiver perception rating. Having the caregiver present as a participant during the sampling provides an opportunity for the clinician and caregiver to build consensus on perceptions of the individual's communicative strengths and weaknesses, as displayed during the sample, and to compare these patterns with information provided on the caregiver questionnaire.

Behaviors collected in the sample are rated along a number of parameters and are converted to scores on 22 5-point rating scales of communication and symbolic behaviors. Seven cluster scores are derived from the 22 scales; the first six contribute to the individual's profile of communication and the last one relates to the individual's profile of symbolic behaviors. The clusters are: Communicative Functions, Communicative Means—Gestural,

Communicative Means—Vocal, Communicative Means—Verbal, Reciprocity, Social-Affective Signaling, and Symbolic Behavior. Table 24.7 lists the scale clusters and individual scales used on the CSBS.

Normative data on a sample of almost 300 normally developing American English-speaking children from 8 to 24 months of age and 30 children with developmental disabilities from 18 to 30 months of age have been published (Wetherby & Prizant, 1993a). In addition to norms referenced to chronological age, the CSBS presents norms based on the following language stages: prelinguistic, early one-word, late one-word, and multiword.

Summarizing Assessment Data

By summarizing the assessment information gathered across the various domains, the interrelations between domains and the meaning of the emerging profiles will become clearer. Two similar, yet different, case illustrations may serve to clarify these points.

Mark is a 3-year-old who has not yet grasped the idea of intentional communication. His communicative signals include proximity and passive gaze, combined with posturing and stereotypic motor behaviors—highly rhythmic finger-tapping as well as occasional hand-biting when apparently frustrated and upset. So far, Mark doesn't seem able to regulate his own emotions. He depends on the structure provided by others to prevent and manage behavior escalations. No social initiation of any type is noted, but there is some responsiveness to initiations of others in routine contexts, such as a "peekaboo" routine initiated by his little sister. In those instances, Mark has been observed to smile and cover his sister's face with her hands in an apparent attempt to continue the routine. This is the only context in which notable positive social affect has been observed.

Regarding imitation, Mark will mimick the hand motions of others when they are imitating him. In more technical terms, Mark demonstrates emerging imitation skills within the constraints of his own repertoire of behaviors. Although the behaviors demonstrated are indicative of severe delays, his performance with objects in nonsocial domains is more advanced. As is common in autism, Mark is fascinated with objects and explores them actively. He has a pretty good notion of object permanence, as evidenced by his ability to remember the exact location of his favorite toys and preferred reinforcers at his school program. This object knowledge may not be readily apparent in a more formalized assessment context, because of his limited understanding of the physical impact of his own actions or the actions of others. For instance, he would not be able to retrieve a hidden object, as is often required in a more formal assessment context, because he would not understand that his own actions could serve to retrieve the item. Instead, he is more likely to demonstrate his knowledge of object location by hovering around a storage cabinet, climbing on it, or even unlocking it. Nevertheless, not knowing how to do so, he would never actively seek out the assistance of others to help him access his treasures.

Mark is able to match identical objects and has performed a variety of tasks that require visuospatial skill, as long as the tasks were presented nonverbally and laid out spatially. Although Mark demonstrates only functional and conventional object use in the context of routines (e.g., when making brownies with his mother at home), motorically sophisticated and unconventional, if not creative, forms of object use were observed in free play. However, when approached by peers, Mark generally tries to "escape"; the proximity of peers seems hard to tolerate. The greatest proximity to peers has been observed in the sandbox, one of Mark's favorite spots. In this location, he has occasionally demonstrated some parallel play, when a preschool peer was imitating his sand-sifting routine. In that context, Mark has been noted to cast an occasional glance at the other child.

In the speech domain, Mark has produced a few context-specific but only marginally intelligible vocalizations, which might have functioned like delayed echolalia. When his vocalizations are imitated, in an attempt to establish vocal turn-taking, he seems intrigued but, so far, has not reciprocated these "echoes." His speech comprehension appears extremely limited. Yet, because of his uncanny ability to recall routinized actions in response

TABLE 24.7   Assessment Clusters and Scales in the Communication and Symbolic Behavior Scales (Wetherby & Prizant, 1993)

I.   Communicative Functions

1. *Behavioral Regulation.* Communicative acts used to regulate behavior of another person to obtain or restrict an environmental goal.
2. *Joint Attention.* Communicative acts used to direct another's attention to an object, an event, or a topic of a communicative act.
3. *Sociability of Functions.* Proportion of communicative acts used for social interaction plus joint attention.

II.   Communicative Means—Gestural

4. *Conventional Gestures.* Gestural communicative acts whose meaning is shared by a general community, including giving, showing, pushing away, open-hand reaching, pointing, waving, nodding head, and shaking head.
5. *Distal Gestures.* Gestural communicative acts in which the child's hand does not touch a person or object (e.g., open-hand reaching, pointing at a distance, waving).
6. *Coordination of Gesture and Vocal Acts.* Communicative acts that are composed of a gesture and a vocalization produced simultaneously or overlapping in time.

III.   Communicative Means—Vocal

7. *Vocal Acts without Gestures.* Transcribable vowels or vowel-plus-consonant combinations that are used as a communicative act and are not accompanied by a gesture.
8. *Inventory of Different Consonants.* The total number of different consonants produced as part of communicative acts.
9. *Syllables with Consonants.* Vocal communicative acts that are transcribable vowel-plus-consonant combinations.
10. *Multisyllables.* Vocal communicative acts that contain two or more syllables that may be vowels only, or a vowel plus a consonant.

IV.   Communicative Means—Verbal

11. *Inventory of Different Words.* The total number of different words used (i.e., spoken or signed) in communicative acts; a word or word approximation must be used to refer to a specific object, action, or attribute and only to that word class.
12. *Inventory of Different Word Combinations.* The total number of different multiword combinations produced in communicative acts.

V.   Reciprocity

13. *Respondent Acts.* Communicative acts that are in response to the adult's conventional gestures or speech.
14. *Rate.* The frequency of communicative acts displayed per minute.
15. *Repair Strategies.* A measure of the child's ability to repeat and/or modify a previous communicative act when a goal is not achieved.

VI.   Social-Affective Signaling

16. *Gaze Shifts.* Alternating eye gaze between a person and an object (i.e., either person-object-person or object-person-object).
17. *Shared Positive Affect.* Clear facial expressions of pleasure or excitement, accompanied or unaccompanied by a vocalization, that are directed toward the adult with eye gaze.
18. *Episodes of Negative Affect.* Clear vocal expressions of distress or frustration that commence when the vocalization begins and continue until the child has recovered and has displayed a neutral or positive affect.

VII.   Symbolic Behavior

19. *Language Comprehension.* A measure of comprehension of contextual cues, single words, and multiword utterances.
20. *Inventory of Different Action Schemes.* The total number of different action schemes used with objects in symbolic play.
21. *Complexity of Action Schemes.* A measure of the child's use of action schemes with objects, toward self or other agents, and the child's ability to sequence different action schemes in pretend play.
22. *Constructive Play.* A measure of the child's ability to use objects in combination to construct a product (e.g., a tower).

to specific situational cues, his abilities in this domain are often overestimated by others.

David, a 10-year-old, demonstrates a similar profile but functions overall at a somewhat higher level. David exhibits more intentional forms of communication, indicating an emerging understanding of means–end and causality relationships, but almost no understanding of social agency. His reenactment strategies are used deliberately in anticipation of a desired outcome, but he does not realize how the actions of others contribute to the outcome. For instance, David communicates his desire to be taken out to the shopping center by physically pulling his dad toward the door, and by piling up his father's car keys and coat in the entrance hall. David is highly attached to routines and becomes quite agitated when his routines are disrupted. His receptive skills are a bit higher than Mark's, but, again, they tend to be overestimated because of David's ability to pick up on extraneous cues.

As for David's speech and language skills, he produces some stereotyped speech (delayed echolalia) and signs within the context of predictable routines, and more intentional forms of communication in concrete contexts related to objects and physical events (e.g., to request food). In other contexts, more primitive signaling occurs. David initiates social interaction by seating himself next to a favorite person and then climbing on the person's lap and physically moving his or her face in his direction.

Within the cognitive domain, David is able to perform rather sophisticated categorization and matching tasks, as long as only judgment with regard to physical properties (not the functional use of the object) is concerned. For instance, although able to match broken and whole objects as well as objects that complement each other, such as the bottom and the top of a jar, he is unable to match a crayon and a pen on the basis of their shared writing functions. He demonstrates a number of functional object manipulations, such as "driving" toy cars and making airplanes fly. He will also make a brushing motion when presented with a hairbrush and a sucking motion when presented with a baby bottle (he has a baby sister at home). However, he does not demonstrate any pretend actions. Regarding the

social dimensions of his play, he tolerates the close proximity of other children in the play area and has demonstrated some parallel play, as well as turn-taking, when toy cars are involved. In that same context, he has been observed to share a common focus (a toy parking garage) with a neighborhood "friend" who frequently visits his house. He and his friend take turns moving cars down the ramp. In these contexts, David smiles and appears content. Negative affect is demonstrated when confronted with violations of routine, or when other children interfere with his rather rigid play routines. He has not yet learned to regulate his emotional state but has been noted to engage in delayed echolalic vocalizations such as "Be OK, be OK," indicative of potential emotional regulation through self-talk.

From Assessment to Intervention

Once a profile of an individual's strengths and weaknesses in communication and related areas is determined, goals and strategies for communication enhancement may be considered. As discussed in Chapter 23, developmental and functional considerations need to be integrated, and professionals and caregivers should collaborate in this process. Assessment serves to determine initial goals and strategies that can be modified and refined over time, based on the success of communication enhancement efforts and the specific changes in an individual's communication profile. The profile serves to select and fine-tune instructional goals and objectives. For instance, the overall communication objectives for Mark and David will be rather similar, but individual adaptations will have to be made with regard to the level and type of task presentation, the degrees to which contexts need to be staged and/or routinized, and the interaction styles to be adopted.

COMMUNICATION ENHANCEMENT AT PRELINGUISTIC LEVELS

In Chapter 23, we reviewed our basic philosophy of intervention for individuals at both prelinguistic and language levels. This chapter focuses more specifically on goals and communication enhancement strategies at prelinguistic levels, with concentration on communicative means and functions. Goals for other communication-related domains are suggested in a more cursory form. No strict sequence of goals is implied; some may be approached simultaneously. However, the goals in this section are organized, in general, from less to more sophisticated dimensions of communication and social reciprocity.

Establish Anticipatory and Early Intentional Behaviors

In working with individuals who communicate at a preintentional level, it is essential that communication enhancement efforts take place in contexts of predictable routines—everyday living routines, as well as contrived activities engineered to support the development of communication skills. The focus of initial intervention should be the establishment of (a) anticipatory behaviors, indicating that the individuals involved are starting to make predictions about sequences of activities and events, and (b) communicative behaviors, which are necessary to reach desired goals during such events. The persons learning to communicate must become cognizant of the effects of their own as well as other people's actions. Typically developing infants learn to do so in the context of highly repetitive interactive routines, such as those commonly encountered in feeding and bathing (Bruner, 1981). The anticipation of highly predictable behavior sequences sets the stage for intentional communication. When the routines involved are slowed down or otherwise violated, an individual may be prompted to continue the routine by vocalizing, or by body movements, which are responded to as if they are intentional signals, serving to restore the anticipated sequence of behavior.

For individuals with the most severe communicative limitations, as described above in the case of Mark, anticipation of communicative outcomes should be established in a highly routinized format. The initial goal is not to request independently (e.g., a piece of food), but rather to attend closely to the concomitant interaction sequences, which eventually lead to the desired outcome or reinforcing event. For instance, a banana is sliced up in a tantalizing

way in front of a child like Mark, who is fond of bananas. These slices are offered one at a time, in a highly ritualized and dramatic way, to ensure that Mark's attention is indeed captured. Initially, the banana is offered with no strings attached; the only goal is for Mark to start anticipating the routinized transactions—by leaning forward, extending the palm of his hand, making eye contact, and so on. When some anticipation of the interactive routine is evidenced, Mark will be required to respond more actively. Increasing time delays will be introduced before the next slice of banana is offered. These delays give an opportunity to watch for any initiations and/or agitation from Mark. To restate this more formally, the violation of the established routine now becomes a context for incidental assessment as well as incidental teaching. Based on what is observed in the staged assessment context, a more active response is now required: a pointing motion in the direction of, or a mere touch of, the banana; an extended hand; an active gaze shift from the banana to, or in the direction of, the adult's face; and/or a vocalization or head movement. Simple communicative gestures that are readily initiated and can easily be used across contexts, such as reaching motions or physical manipulations, are more suitable for establishing early intentional communicative acts than more formalized communication systems, such as communication boards and booklets, which are not always immediately accessible.

An alternative to the establishment of routines for the sake of communication enhancement is the use of already existing instructional routines. When the anticipated routine sequence of events is interrupted, the motivation to complete the established routines may mobilize communicative initiative (Halle, 1984; Prizant, 1982). Motivating contexts may readily be identified through collaboration of caregivers, teachers, speech and language specialists, and others involved with the individual. What is being stressed in dealing with minimally communicative individuals is the need to communicate more actively through *any* means (preferably, more conventional and socially appropriate means), and to establish increasingly intentional forms of communication.

Replace Idiosyncratic Communicative Means

Reenactments and other idiosyncratic means of communicating need to be replaced by more conventional and intentional gestures, such as an extended hand or a pointing gesture. Replacement of idiosyncratic patterns of communication by more appropriate means warrants some closer discussion. For instance, if challenging or otherwise socially unacceptable behavior serves to secure attention or to protest, the individual may be taught, for instance, how to secure physical contact by asking or signing for a hug, or may learn to communicate "no" or "stop" when an undesirable item is being presented (e.g., a push-away gesture). Although short-term behavioral interventions may need to zero in on the elimination of a possibly harm-inflicting behavior, longer-term teaching efforts should be tailored toward the establishment of more appropriate communicative alternatives. (For detailed discussions and examples, see Carr et al., 1994; Durand, 1990; Reichle & Wacker, 1993.)

Depending on the intensity of the behavior, the state of arousal associated with it, and the availability of clearly observable antecedent cues, behavior reduction efforts may be directly combined with communication skill-building efforts. For instance, jumping and flapping may be replaced by pointing and looking in the direction of the desired item, when a favorite toy or food is being requested. If the behavior is relatively harmless, behavior replacement strategies are readily used in incidental contexts. Carr et al. (1994) and Durand (1990) have provided numerous examples of such behavior intervention strategies, referring to them as "differential reinforcement of communicative behavior." If the behavior of concern is more severe and/or dangerous, replacement strategies may only work when antecedents can be detected in time to divert the undesirable behavior by helping an individual to communicate more appropriately, or to calm down. If this is not the case, more conventional behavior management strategies may be combined with the teaching of relevant communicative behaviors in more manageable contexts.

When assessment results indicate, as in the case of David, a reliance on reenactment behaviors, use of conventional gestures may be targeted. This route can be pursued by frequent modeling of, for example, pointing and showing gestures, and the accompanying gaze and body orientation in suitable activities. Physical prompts and ritual violations (as described above) may be used when modeling does not suffice. Yet, it is important that the individuals involved start to observe others' use of gestures and to experience the immediate success of their own use of communicative gestures. Activities and strategies that may help to foster use of conventional gestures have been described by Willard and Schuler (1987). Examples include: (a) give-and-take exchanges; (b) commenting on and pointing at pictures and objects; (c) offering desirable and undesirable foods or toys to elicit gestural or vocal requests, or push-away gestures, head shakes, or head nods; and (d) modeling and prompting a hand wave for greeting when a person enters a room, or for farewell when a person leaves or favorite activity objects are put away.

The use of natural gestures, such as body orientation, pointing, and gaze to direct the behavior of others, should be emphasized for David. His reliance on reenactment strategies is indicative of his limitations in understanding social agency. Pointing and gaze can be added through incidental teaching in suitable contexts, but the introduction of a spatially organized communication board or booklet, or a simple set of pictures (see later discussion), may provide an extra incentive. Such salient referents can promote highly concrete pointing and gaze behaviors.

Establish Multiple Means of Communication

The development of conventional vocalizations—the addition of vocalizations to nonvocal means—requires clear, if not, emphatic, modeling of both words and intonation patterns during communicative exchanges. Although it is not expected that all individuals will clearly imitate and acquire a wide variety of conventional forms of words at this stage, imitation of sounds and approximations of words in highly repetitive routines can be encouraged. As with gestures, partners need to provide clearly visible models by being at an individual's physical level, encouraging (not coercing) face-to-face gaze, and producing words slowly, clearly, and repetitively in communicative exchanges. In doing so, specific speech imitation training may be useful. A number of different strategies may be used; selection should be based on an individual's chronological age and learning style. Strategies that may heighten an individual's attention to speech and foster vocal imitation and approximation include:

1. Imitating an individual's vocalizations and gradually modifying them in a playful turn-taking context.
2. Using short, relevant phrases and introducing interesting and simple intonation patterns.
3. Using stereotypic or ritualized utterances in routines (e.g., saying "What's *that?*" with exaggerated intonation while looking at pictures in a book, "Uh-oh" when something falls down, "All finished" when completing an activity).
4. Modeling short utterances, in synchrony with body movement, during gross motor and physical games, or sensory integration activities.
5. Singing songs and/or reciting rhymes that have predictable slots for words or sounds to be filled in.

With appropriate modeling and opportunities to vocalize and imitate, most individuals at this level, if they have the requisite oral-motor skills, should begin to produce varied and frequent vocalizations, with increased imitation and/or approximation of adult models within highly routinized contexts. Highly limited or restricted vocal production, in the presence of clear intentional gestural communication, may be indicative of motor speech problems. An in-depth consideration of oral-motor function, and immediate consideration of a more formal augmentative communication system (discussed in a later section), would then be required.

Expand the Range of Communicative Functions

As noted earlier, one important aspect of communicative competence is the range of purposes or functions for which an individual communicates (Prizant & Wetherby, 1990). Individuals with autism and PDD have been found to communicate for a relatively narrow range of functions or purposes (i.e., primarily for behavioral regulation). When individuals communicate for fewer purposes and these purposes serve relatively nonsocial functions, fewer opportunities to engage others in social interaction are created, resulting in fewer opportunities to learn about the reciprocal nature of communication. For example, an individual may communicate primarily to request or protest to satisfy immediate physical needs. Typically, this individual will have difficulty bringing attention to self to request social games or comfort from others, or to bring attention to events for the purpose of sharing those experiences with others. The transactional impact of such a limited range of functions is that communicative partners have few opportunities to model a broader range of communicative behaviors and/or expand on communicative initiations exhibited. Therefore, an important goal for individuals at a prelinguistic intentional communicative level is expansion of the range of functions.

Communication for a wider variety of purposes provides a special challenge to communicative partners, who must create needs and opportunities, provide intensive modeling, and, if necessary, prompt conventional prelinguistic gestures and salient language models. The functional breakdown of communicative acts for (a) behavioral regulation, (b) social interaction, and (c) joint attention (Bruner, 1981; Wetherby & Prizant, 1993b) is useful in setting specific goals because it helps to delineate the least social (behavioral regulation) from the most social forms of communication (joint attention). Some types of activities provide opportunities to elicit and model communicative acts across all categories. Final activity selections must be made according to their chronological and developmental appropriateness for individuals at prelinguistic and at early language levels. Based on an individual's motivations, needs, and learning strengths (see Table 24.8), additional activities may be included.

The desire to establish an interest in joint attention and action underscores the need to include families, siblings, and peers, and it calls particular attention to the importance of play. Play is the ultimate context for joint as well as reciprocal action, as best demonstrated by common play scenarios. For instance, two children may be gazing at a block tower that they are constructing together. By taking turns in stacking blocks, they jointly create suspense as they watch the tower getting so tall that it might

TABLE 24.8   Activities to Expand Communicative Functions

Characteristics of Activities for Behavioral Regulation

1. Opportunities to request food or objects.
2. Opportunities to make choices among alternatives.
3. Opportunities to protest actions or to reject objects or food.
4. Opportunities to request cessation of an activity.
5. Opportunities or needs to request assistance.

Characteristics of Activities for Social Interaction

1. Opportunities to request social games or routines, or continuation of games or routines.
2. Opportunities to practice greeting behaviors verbally or nonverbally.
3. Opportunities or needs to bring attention to self through calling others or requesting comfort verbally or nonverbally.
4. Opportunities to "show off" during games (e.g., hide-and-seek, peekaboo, dressing up, face painting, show and tell).

Characteristics of Activities for Joint Attention

1. Opportunities or needs to give or transfer objects, or to follow another person's focus of attention.
2. Opportunities or needs to use gestures or vocalizations to bring attention to objects or events (e.g., looking at books, going to the zoo, looking out a window onto a busy street).
3. Opportunities to comment on events introducing novelty and change (e.g., taking new toys out of a cloth bag, performing interesting actions on objects).
4. Opportunities or needs to request information or clarification (for children with higher-level abilities).

collapse. The joint attention culminates when the tower does indeed collapse. The children share their excitement by looking at each other and at the collapsed tower. Common play scenarios of tea parties and grocery shopping are hard to imagine without joint attention and action.

Our experiences with play have been very encouraging; besides advances in play, we have observed the most positive changes in communicative behaviors that were not specifically being targeted for intervention. Initially, we were quite skeptical about our chances to enhance play in school-age children who lacked both the social and cognitive dimensions of play. We were most encouraged by the gains in play behavior that we were able to document (Wolfberg & Schuler, 1993), and we believe that these gains were accompanied by gains in the social dimensions of communication because play offers a natural context for joint attention and joint action.

The subjects of our case illustrations, Mark and David, need to learn to play. The approaches prescribed will be very similar; we do not advocate a strictly developmental approach. We believe that children should be immersed in play through the peer and contextual support provided. Nevertheless, individual adaptations are based on our overall observations and on the assessment findings. In the case of David, we are faced with a relatively rich play repertoire, including functional rather than self-stimulatory object manipulations, and an emerging play scenario involving toy cars and a garage as well as toy airplanes. These play routines are still rather repetitive, but David's tolerance of peers allows him to acquire a more diverse repertoire, including emerging pretense and related story schemes. To promote that kind of narrative understanding and emerging "theory of mind" (Frith, 1989), support needs to be provided through peer coaching, modeling, and the selection of suitable play props and settings.

Mark's relative lack of play provides more challenges, although they are offset a bit by his age. We have found interactions with younger peers often helpful, since so many of the younger kids are prone to the type of physical rather than verbal play and/or highly rulebound play that we typically find in older children. Nevertheless, even play with younger peers still needs to be supported—for example, by selecting an optimal physical space and suitable toys and activities, and by carefully choosing (and limiting) the number of peers involved. Based on the assessment findings, we might suggest a sandbox setting for Mark and provide him with a variety of containers and a modeling of sand play scenarios to the peer(s) selected. Parallel play and turntaking would be targeted here, but attempts would be made to frame Mark's still stereotypic actions into a larger peer play scenario. (For further suggestions, see Wolfberg, 1995, and also Sheridan, Foley, & Radlinsky, 1995.)

Develop Strategies to Persist in Communication and to Repair Breakdowns

Many factors may interfere with an individual's ability to communicate intentions successfully; for example, environmental distractions, inability to secure a partner's attention, or production of unclear or unconventional communicative signals (e.g., unintelligible speech, idiosyncratic gestures) may undermine communicative effectiveness. Therefore, a goal for prelinguistic individuals is the development of repair strategies, or an ability to persist, through repeating or modifying communicative signals, when initial communication is unsuccessful. An individual who demonstrates limited repair strategies may not realize his or her communicative potential even though the basic requisite communicative skills are present. Often, such individuals may appear passive, lethargic, or easily distracted. Once again, intervention strategies to develop the motivation to persist, and to repair communicative breakdowns, are predicated on frequent opportunities to do so in the presence of sufficient contextual, instructional, and interactive support, which puts more demands on the communication partner. These opportunities may occur naturally, but an extra effort should be made by partners who, by pretending not to understand, create opportunities for supported repair efforts.

It is important for individuals to clearly demonstrate intentional goal-directed communication before working on repair strategies.

The underlying assumption is that intentional communication is already established, and persistence in communicating is the next major challenge. Individuals at emerging intentional levels should be responded to immediately, even if intent is assigned or imputed. Suggestions for developing repair strategies for both prelinguistic individuals and individuals in early language stages include:

1. Utilize preferred and highly motivating activities that are likely to keep an individual interested and focused.
2. Begin to require an increase in clear and conventional signals before responding to or imputing intent to unclear or subtle signals. However, acknowledge verbally or nonverbally that the individual has made an attempt to communicate. Respond with "What?" or "I don't understand," along with a questioning look, shrugged shoulders, and so on.
3. If the attempts to elicit a repair do not work, say "Show me" (and extend a hand) or "Say it again," whichever is appropriate to an individual's communicative level. If the unsuccessful communicative act involves requesting an object, the object may be presented again, and a simple reach may be followed by modeling or prompting an appropriate communicative act.
4. Partners' requests for repair should never be demanding, withholding, or negatively cast through disapproving facial expression or tone of voice, because some individuals will withdraw under such conditions. Any initial attempt at persistence should be supported by subsequent physical prompting of more appropriate gestures or clear modeling of speech at or slightly above an individual's expressive level.
5. Opportunities for repair may be set up by:
   a. Delaying responses to initial unclear communicative attempts.
   b. Intentionally responding incorrectly in a playful manner (e.g., heading toward the bathroom when an individual signals a wish for a drink at the water fountain).
   c. Offering undesired foods or items when an individual points or reaches in the direction of many items that are out of reach on a table or shelf.

At higher levels of repair, an individual may be required to first get attention (e.g., by tapping an arm or calling a name) prior to receiving a response.

Use Aided, Augmentative, and/or Alternative Communication (AAC)

It is beyond the scope of this chapter to provide a comprehensive discussion of the variety of augmentative or alternative communication (AAC) systems and instructional strategies available for persons with autism and PDD. AAC technology has proliferated over the past decade, especially for persons with more severe disabilities and communicative limitations (see Beukelman & Mirenda, 1992; Reichle et al., 1991; and Watson, Lord, Schaeffer, & Schopler, 1989; for more specific information). While opinions and practices do diverge, it is becoming increasingly clear that the selection of a suitable formal communication system is most critical when an individual: (a) is clearly communicating intentionally, possibly using multiple prelinguistic unconventional communicative means to express different functions; (b) uses communicative repair, pursing communicative alternatives when goals are not met; and (c) demonstrates the ability to understand some degree of representation (e.g., photographs or picture symbols), either through trial teaching or less formal exposure in daily routines. We are not implying that individuals must meet these requirements before an AAC system can be introduced; rather, persons demonstrating these abilities are likely to benefit greatly from the introduction of some type of system. For individuals with more significant limitations (e.g., no recognition of representations such as photographs), a system or mode must be chosen carefully after trial periods of modeling and ongoing diagnostic teaching. The system selected must suit the individual's communicative profile in terms of conceptual as well as motor and perceptual considerations (Schuler, 1985), and must be accessible to all pertinent communication partners, allowing for high rates of communicative initiations and responses. (For a more detailed discussion of these issues as they pertain to autism, see Bedrosian, 1996; Beukelman & Mirenda, 1992;

TABLE 24.9   AAC Options for Nonspeaking Individuals

1. Objects for exchange or indication—a cup for a drink, cookies in a plastic bag (point or touch), and so on.
2. Pictures/Picture symbols for exchange or indicative gesture.
3. Signs.
4. Printed words.
5. Computers or other electronic aids; using overlays of pictures/words (with the option of vocal output).
6. Letter boards or electronic keyboards.

Mirenda & Schuler, 1988; Schuler, 1985; Schuler & Baldwin, 1981.) Table 24.9 lists the commonly used AAC options for persons with autism and PDD.

The selection of one particular system does not necessarily exclude the introduction of an additional system. We have been successful in using concrete visuospatial systems that incorporate drawings, written words, magazine pictures, and photographs. These are most helpful in relaying concrete information—requests for objects, comments on observations, and so on. When other less tangible communicative functions are involved, such as emotional expression, these means may not allow for sufficient immediate expressive powers. We have used signs and sign adaptations in reference to emotional states such as anger, frustration, happiness, and so on. When a sign is designed to express an initial message, the message may be followed up by more specific messages through combinations of pictures, written words, and other systems. Rapid advances in technology allow increasing use of computer-assisted systems and/or some type of voice output, which can be most empowering.

Implement AAC Options

Frequent problems that limit an individual's full potential use of augmentative devices include: (a) a fragmented approach to designing systems for individuals rather than considering daily activities and routines in the context of day care or classroom settings, and (b) the partner's limited modeling of interactive use of symbols (Goossens, 1990). The following guidelines for arranging or "engineering" environments to support interactive augmentative communication are based on the work of Goossens' (1990). She has provided numerous suggestions for ensuring that preschool individuals' augmentative communication needs are fulfilled, and she promotes the use of "aided language stimulation" on an ongoing basis. Her approach refers to the interactive modeling of augmentative systems, highlighting pictures or picture symbols on an individual's communication display while providing appropriate oral language input. General guidelines for using this approach include: (a) using simple utterances about ongoing activities; (b) speaking slowly; (c) commenting about activities rather than using primarily questions or directives; (d) pausing frequently to allow the individual to take turns; and (e) expanding on the individual's utterances. Initially, the vocabulary used should be relevant to the activity and should reflect early semantic functions and relations. For highly distractible individuals, Goossens recommends using handheld lights or noise-makers to bring an individual's attention to a target picture.

Additional suggestions made by Goossens are:

1. Requesting should be a first expressive goal and frequent opportunities for choice-making should be provided. Requesting is highly motivating and allows individuals to experience the power of communication. Within these contexts, opportunities to reject should also be provided.
2. In addition to the specific devices selected for individuals, a variety of representations should be made available in reference to common objects and activities. For developmentally younger individuals, real objects may be the most effective means; photographs or line drawings (e.g., picture communication symbols) may be used for persons capable of responding to more abstract representations. Similarly, when individuals receive services in a center-based or classroom setting, the full range of representations should be made available to accommodate all individuals with special needs.
3. Lower- and higher-level representations should be paired, to enable individuals to move to higher-level representations. For

example, real objects may be paired with photographs on a display in which individuals make choices through manual pointing. An ultimate goal (in addition to speech acquisition) is movement to more abstract line drawings, or to the written word.
4. Predictable play routines or caregiving routines should be the primary contexts for facilitating acquisition of augmentative system use, and techniques of cuing, prompting, and fading of cues and prompts should be used systematically within the routines.
5. Larger arrays of vocabulary items should be made available to more capable individuals when they are engaged in activities that involve more complex joint activity routines (e.g., food preparation) and symbolic play. In addition, increased opportunities for repairing communication breakdowns, and for using multiword utterances and more complex language functions (e.g., requesting information), should be modeled and reinforced.

Selecting and Using Communication Aids

Teaching an individual to use a communication board or a similar communication aid follows the basic pattern of any good instructional program that uses direct and naturalistic teaching approaches. The specific communicative behaviors to be used by an individual should be clearly defined. For example, the specific symbols, pictures, or other referents to be used need to be carefully specified, as do the specific behaviors to be demonstrated by the individual in selecting and manipulating those symbols. The communicative function of an individual's behavior should be demonstrated contingent on the occurrence of the prompted and/or modeled communicative behaviors. For example, an individual could be encouraged, through modeling and prompting, to point to a picture of food or juice and immediately be presented with the desired items. Likewise, the individual should be taught to point to a picture of a favorite toy and immediately be allowed to play with that toy. The experience of functional consequences is critical to subsequent spontaneous use. In addition, as noted above in the discussion on aided language stimulation, an adult's use of the communication aid along with an appropriate level of speech input should be modeled throughout the day in relevant contexts.

In designing and teaching the use of communication aids, the following points should be remembered:

1. The individual must have ready access to a device if it is to become a meaningful communication tool. For example, if a communication board is used only in limited activities, the probability of generalization becomes very small. If the board itself is not readily available, the individual should always have a means to request the board, through gestures, vocalization or verbalization, or other signals (e.g., a light or buzzer).
2. The symbol system used on the board should be accessible and appropriate to the individual's level of cognitive development and learning style.
3. The symbols on the board should represent ideas or wishes the individual frequently needs to express.
4. The family and other significant persons in the individual's environment should be involved in the selection of an appropriate communication aid or system.
5. Decisions about the modes and systems of communication used should always be guided by the results of trial teaching sessions and the input and feedback of all involved parties.

OTHER GOALS FOR COMMUNICATION-RELATED DOMAINS

The expansion of communicative means and functions is of prime importance, but other communicative and communication-related objectives also warrant consideration. A detailed discussion of a greater variety of goals related to communication extends beyond the scope of this chapter; nevertheless, examples are included, organized according to the domains in the Social Communication Assessment-Intervention Framework presented in Chapter 25. Table 24.10 provides examples of different objectives, across those domains, that are relevant to individuals at prelinguistic lev-

els. For further discussion of goals and strategies for persons at prelinguistic levels, see Watson et al. (1989), Quill (1995), and Prizant and Wetherby (1988, 1993a, 1993b).

SUMMARY AND CONCLUSIONS

This chapter has focused on assessment and intervention issues specific to the social, communicative, and cognitive characteristics of individuals with autism and PDD who are at prelinguistic levels. But communication goals should never be defined only in terms of these intrinsic considerations. We advocate a more ecological orientation. Intervention efforts should try to identify which contexts and which styles of interaction and language use most facilitate communicative exchanges. One goal is important: that the individuals involved learn to be more active participants in the social interactions taking place around them. The combined force of responsive communication partners and the motivating social contexts makes the enhancement of communication a collaborative rather than a solitary effort, and therefore a truly interactive process.

Efforts to enhance communication should be based directly on an individual's current behavioral and communicative repertoire, and on future needs. More specific decisions regarding content and context of intervention efforts should be fine-tuned, based on the assessment of related cognitive and socioemotional abilities and ongoing diagnostic teaching. Another intervention consideration in selecting content lies in the individual's perspective of the world. Too often, utterances and exchanges targeted for intervention are based solely on a predetermined program that may be peripheral to an individual's daily experiences and interests. The most logical content for communicative behavior lies in communicating about events that make sense, and with people who matter to an individual.

Cross-References

General aspects of communicative development are discussed in Chapter 9. Issues in assessment are dealt with in Chapters 19 through 21. Curriculum development is detailed in Chapter 22. Other aspects of communication

TABLE 24.10   Goals for Communication and Related Domains for Persons at Prelinguistic Levels

Language and Communication	
Expressive	Receptive
Establishes anticipatory and early intentional behaviors. Replaces idiosyncratic communicative means (such as reenactments) with more conventional and intentional gestures, such as an extended hand or a pointing gesture. Establishes multiple means of communication by adding vocalizations to nonvocal means. Expands the range of functions or purposes for communication. Develops strategies to persist in communication and to repair breakdowns. Develops use of aided or more formal AAC systems to communicate intentions.	Responds to gestures and/or gaze of others. Responds to picture/written-word symbols of other augmentative means presented by others. Responds to own name when called by others. Associates single words, or short phrases, with their referents when used in context. Recognizes basic written-word labels, including own name, names of family members, and basic objects in daily environment.

Cognitive Abilities/Symbolic Representation			
Symbolic Play	Combinatorial/ Constructive Play	Imitation	Anticipation of Routines/ Event Knowledge
Uses objects in non-stereotypic functional ways. Plays in proximity to adult or peers. Shares toy or other focus of joint attention. Displays pretend behaviors with toys or common objects.	Plays with blocks or other construction toys for longer periods of time. Plays with blocks or other construction toys in closer proximity to peers. Creates more elaborate constructions.	Imitates when own behavior is imitated by adults or peers. Imitates when prompted. Imitates spontaneously. Imitates for purposes of problem solving. Imitates for social purposes.	Shows anticipation of routine completion. Initiates corrective action when routine is violated. Demonstrates anticipation of simple peekaboo, tickle, or hand-slap ("high-five") routine. Demonstrates recognition of simple story plot and/or video sequence (either oral or visual).

Social-Communicative and Socioemotional				
Communicative Functions— Behavior Regulation	Communicative Functions— Joint Attention	Reciprocity	Social-Affective Signaling	Emotional Expression/ Regulation
Expresses basic request for favorite item in sight. Expresses basic request for favorite item just removed from sight. Expresses basic request for desired adult action. Expresses basic request for adult/peer/sibling to sit near/be close. Behavioral regulation.	Looks at same toy that parent or peer is looking at (and touches or explores that toy together?). Draws adult or peer attention to focus of current attention (e.g., point or vocalize to toy, display).	Increases number of intentional communicative acts. Restores an interrupted routine. Repeats acts, utilizing an additional communicative means when communicative initiation is not responded to. Responds to communicative initiations of others when approached verbally and/or nonverbally at a specified level.	Adds gaze (active or passive) to turn-taking interaction. Increases display of positive affect in playlike situations. Decreases display of unregulated negative affect.	Responds appropriately to display of marked affect by parents, peers, or other caregivers. Attunes to affect of interactant in playlike interaction. Responds to others' efforts to calm when emotionally aroused. Develops self-regulatory strategies to calm when aroused.

interventions are the subject of Chapters 23 and 25.

REFERENCES

Bates, E. (1976). *Language and context: The acquisition of pragmatics.* New York: Academic Press.

Bates, E. (1979). *The emergence of symbols: Cognition and communication in infancy.* New York: Academic Press.

Bedrosian, J. (1996). Efficacy of emergent literacy intervention with young AAC system users. *Proceedings from 7th Biennial Conference of the International Society for Augmentative and Alternative Communication,* Vancouver, August 7–10, 207–208.

Beukelman, D., & Mirenda, P. (1992). *Augmentative and alternative communication: Management of severe communication disorders in children and adults.* Baltimore: Brookes.

Biklen, D. (1990). Communication unbound: Autism and praxis. *Harvard Educational Review, 60,* 291–314.

Birnbrauer, J. S., & Leach, D. J. (1993). The Murdoch early intervention program after 2 years. *Behaviour Change, 10*(2), 63–74.

Bishop, K., Rankin, J., & Mirenda, P. (1994). Impact of graphic symbol use on reading acquisition. *Augmentative and Alternative Communication (AAC), 10*(2), 113–125.

Bricker, W.A., Macke, P.R., & Levin, J.A. (1981). The modifiability of intelligent behavior. *Journal of Special Education, 10,* 145–162.

Bruner, J. (1975). From communication to language: A psychological perspective. *Cognition, 3,* 255–289.

Bruner, J. (1981). The social context of language acquisition. *Language and Communication, 1,* 155–178.

Carr, E.G. (1977). The motivation of self-injurious behavior: A review of some hypotheses. *Psychological Bulletin, 84,* 800–816.

Carr, E.G. (1985). Behavioral approaches to language and communication. In E. Schopler & G. Mesibov (Eds.), *Communication problems in autism* (pp. 37–59). New York: Plenum Press.

Carr, E.G., & Carlson, J.I. (1993). Reduction of severe behavior problems in the community using a multicomponent treatment approach. *Journal of Applied Behavior Analysis, 26,* 157–172.

Carr, E.G., & Durand, V.M. (1985). Reducing behavior problems through functional communication training. *Journal of Applied Behavior Analysis, 18,* 111–126.

Carr, E.G., Levin, L., McConnachie, G., Carlson, J.I., Kemp, D.C., & Smith, C.A. (1994). *Communication-based intervention for problem behavior: A user's guide for producing positive change.* Baltimore: Brookes.

Charlop, M.H., & Haymes, L.K. (1994). Speech and language acquisition and intervention. Behavioral approaches. In J. Matson (Ed.), *Autism in children and adults: Etiology, assessment and intervention.* Pacific Grove, CA: Brooks/Cole.

Curcio, A. (1978). A study of sensorimotor functioning and communication in mute autistic children. *Journal of Autism and Childhood Schizophrenia, 8,* 281–292.

Damico, J., Secord, W., & Wiig, E. (1992). Descriptive language assessment at school: Characteristics and design. In W. Secord (Ed.), *Best practices in school speech-language pathology* (pp. 1–8). San Antonio, TX: Psychological Corp.

Dawson, G., & Adams, A. (1984). Imitation and social responsiveness in autistic children. *Journal of Abnormal Child Psychology, 12,* 209–226.

Dawson, G., & Galpert, L. (1986). A developmental model for facilitating the social behavior of autistic children. In E. Schopler & G.B. Mesibov (Eds.), *Social behavior in autism* (pp. 237–261). New York: Plenum Press.

Donaldson, M. (1978). *Children's minds.* Glasgow, Scotland: Fontana.

Donnellan, A., Mirenda, P., Mesaros, R., & Fassbender, L. (1984). Analyzing the communicative functions of aberrant behavior. *Journal of the Association for Persons with Severe Handicaps, 9,* 201–212.

Duchan, J.F. (1983). Autistic children are noninteractive: Or so we say. *Seminars in Speech and Language, 4,* 63–78.

Duchan, J.F. (1986). Language intervention through sensemaking and finetuning. In R. Schiefelbusch (Ed.), *Assessment and language intervention* (pp. 187–213). Baltimore: University Park Press.

Duchan, J.F. (1989). Evaluating adults' talk to children: Assessing adult attunement. *Seminars in Speech and Language, 10,* 17–27.

Dunst, C.J., Lowe, L.W., & Bartholomew, P.C. (1990). Contingent social responsiveness, family ecology, and infant communicative competence. *National Student Speech Language Hearing Association Journal, 17,* 39–49.

Durand, V.M. (1990). *Severe behavior problems: A functional communication training approach.* New York: Guilford Press.

Durand, V.M., & Carr, E.G. (1992). An analysis of maintenance following functional communication training. *Journal of Applied Behavior Analysis, 25,* 777–794.

Fay, W.H., & Schuler, A.L. (1980). *Emerging language in autistic children.* Baltimore: University Park Press.

Frith, U. (1989). *Autism: Explaining the enigma.* Oxford, England: Blackwell.

Goetz, L., Schuler, A.L., & Sailor, W. (1979). Teaching functional speech to the severely handicapped: Current issues. *Journal of Autism and Developmental Disorders, 9,* 325–343.

Goossens, C. (1990, March). *Engineering the preschool classroom environment for interactive symbolic communication.* Workshop presented at Bradley Hospital, East Providence, RI.

Grandin, T. (1995a). The learning style of persons with autism: An autobiography. In K. Quill (Ed.)., *Teaching children with autism: Strategies to enhance communication and social behavior.* Albany, NY: Delmar.

Grandin, T. (1995b). *Thinking in pictures and other reports of my life with autism.* New York: Doubleday.

Greenspan, S.I. (1992). Reconsidering the diagnosis and treatment of very young children with autism spectrum or Pervasive Developmental Disorder. *Zero to Three, 13,* 1–9.

Halle, J.W. (1984). Arranging the natural environment to occasion language. Giving severely language delayed children reasons to communicate. *Seminars in Speech and Language, 5,* 185–197.

Halle, J.W. (1993). Innovative assessment measures and practices designed with the goal of achieving functional communication and integration. In L. Kupper (Ed.), *The National Symposium on Effective Communication for Children and Youth with Severe Disabilities.* Washington, DC: U.S. Department of Education, Office of Special Education & Rehabilitative Services (OSERS).

Harris, S.L., & Handelman, J.S. (1994). *Preschool education programs for children with autism.* Austin, TX: Pro-Ed.

Hart, B. (1981). Pragmatics and language development: How language is used. *Analysis and Intervention in Developmental Disabilities, 1,* 299–313.

Howlin, P. (1981). The effectiveness of parent language training with autistic children. *Journal of Autism and Developmental Disorders, 11,* 54–69.

Kahn, J.V. (1975). Relationship of Piaget's sensorimotor period to language acquisition of profoundly retarded children. *American Journal of Mental Deficiency, 79,* 640–643.

Kaiser, A.P., & Goetz, L. (1993). Enhancing communication with persons labeled severely disabled. *Journal of the Association for Persons with Severe Handicaps, 18,* 137–142.

Kalmanson, B., & Pekarsky, J.H. (1987, Winter). Infant parent psychotherapy with an autistic toddler. *Infant Mental Health Journal, 8*(4), 18–27.

Kanner, L. (1943). Autistic disturbances of affective contact. *Nervous Child, 2,* 217–250.

Koegel, R.L., Camarata, S.M., & Koegel, L.K. (1994). Aggression and noncompliance: Behavior modification through naturalistic language remediation. In J. Matson (Ed.), *Autism in children and adults: Etiology, assessment and intervention* (pp. 165–180). Pacific Grove, CA: Brooks/Cole.

Koegel, R.L., & Johnson, J. (1989). Motivating language use in autistic children. In G. Dawson (Ed.), *Autism: New perspectives on diagnosis, nature and treatment.* New York: Guilford Press.

Koppenhaver, D., & Yoder, D. (1992). Literacy learning. *Seminars in Speech and Langauge, 13*(2), 143–164.

Lahey, M. (1988). *Language disorders and language development.* New York: Macmillan.

Lord, C. (1985). Autism and the comprehension of language. In E. Schopler & G.B. Mesibov (Eds.), *Communication problems in autism* (pp. 257–281). New York: Plenum Press.

Lovaas, O.I. (1987). Behavioral treatment and normal educational and intellectual functioning in young autistic children. *Journal of Consulting and Clinical Psychology, 55,* 3–9.

McCune, L. (1995). A normative study of representational play at the transition to language. *Developmental Psychology, 31,* 198–206.

McCune-Nicolich, L. (1981). Toward symbolic functioning: Structure of early pretend games and potential parallels with language. *Child Development, 52,* 785–797.

McEachin, J.J., Smith, T., & Lovaas, O.J. (1993). Long-term outcome for children who received early intensive behavioral treatment. *American Journal on Mental Retardation, 97,* 359–372.

McNaughton, S., & Lindsay, P. (1995). Approaching literacy with AAC graphics. *Augmentative and Alternative Communication (AAC), 11*(4), 212–228.

Mirenda, P., & Donnellan, A. (1986). Effects of adult interactional style on conversational behavior in students with severe communication problems. *Language, Speech and Hearing Services in Schools, 17,* 126–141.

Mirenda, P., & Schuler, A.L. (1988). Augmenting communication for persons with autism: Issues and strategies. *Topics in Language Disorders, 9,* 24–43.

Olswang, L., Bain, B., & Johnson, G. (1992). Using dynamic assessment with children with language disorders. In S. Warren & J. Reichle (Eds.), *Causes and effects in communication and language intervention* (pp. 187–215). Baltimore: Brookes.

Papy, F., Papy, G., & Schuler, A.L. (1995). *La pensee hors language de l'enfant autiste.* Paris: Bayard Press.

Papy, F., Schuler, A., & Papy, G. (1994). *Pensiero autistico senza linguaggio: Incontri con spiriti non fertilizzati dalla necessita di stabilire relazioni sociali.* Bologna, Italy: Pitagora Editrice Bologna.

Peck, C.A. (1986). *Student control in classrooms for children with severe handicaps: Effects on student behavior and perceived social climate.* Unpublished doctoral dissertation, University of California, Santa Barbara.

Peck, C.A. (1989). Assessment of social communicative competence: Evaluating environments. *Seminars in Speech and Language, 10,* 1–15.

Peck, C.A., & Schuler, A.L. (1987). Assessment of social/communicative behavior for students with autism and severe handicaps: The importance of asking the right question. In T. Layton (Ed.), *Language and treatment of autistic and developmentally disordered children* (pp. 35–58). Springfield, IL: Thomas.

Peck, C.A., Schuler, A.L., Tomlinson, C., Theimer, K., & Haring, T. (1983). *Social competence curriculum project: Assessment handbook.* Santa Barbara: University of California, Special Education Research Institute.

Prizant, B.M. (1982). Speech-language pathologists and autistic children: What is our role? Part 1. *American Speech & Hearing Association, 24,* 463–468.

Prizant, B.M. (1986). *Social relatedness and communicatively impaired children.* Paper presented at the Third Sino-American Symposium on Speech Pathology and Communication Disorders, Taipei, Taiwan.

Prizant, B.M. (1988). Communication in autistic clients. In N. Lass, L. McReynolds, J. Northern, & D. Yoder (Eds.), *The handbook of speech-language pathology.* Toronto, Ontario, Canada: BC Decker.

Prizant, B.M., & Meyer, E. (1993). Socioemotional aspects of communication disorders in young children. *American Journal of Speech-Language Pathology, 2,* 56–71.

Prizant, B.M., & Wetherby, A.M. (1985). Intentional communicative behavior of children with autism: Theoretical and applied issues. *Australian Journal of Human Communication Disorders, 13,* 21–58.

Prizant, B.M., & Wetherby, A.M. (1988). Providing services to children with autism (ages 0 to 2 years) and their families. *Topics in Language Disorders, 9,* 1–23.

Prizant, B.M., & Wetherby, A.M. (1989). Enhancing language and communication in autism: From theory to practice. In G. Dawson (Ed.), *Autism: Nature, diagnosis, and treatment* (pp. 282–309). New York: Guilford Press.

Prizant, B.M., & Wetherby, A.M. (1990). Toward an integrated view of early language, communication and socioemotional development. *Topics in Language Disorders, 10,* 1–16.

Prizant, B.M., & Wetherby, A.M. (1993a). Communication and language assessment for young children. *Infants and Young Children, 5,* 20–34.

Prizant, B.M., & Wetherby, A.M. (1993b). Communication in preschool autistic children. In E. Schopler, M. van Bourgandien, & M. Bristol (Eds.), *Preschool issues in autism* (pp. 95–128). New York: Plenum Press.

Quill, K. (1995). Enhancing children's social-communicative interactions. In K. Quill (Ed.), *Teaching children with autism: Methods to enhance communication and socialization.* Albany, NY: Delmar.

Reichle, J., Sigafoos, J., & York, J. (1991). *Implementing augmentative and alternative communication: Strategies for learners with severe disabilities.* Baltimore: Brookes.

Reichle, J., & Wacker, D.P. (Eds.). (1993). *Communicative alternatives to challenging behavior—Integrating functional assessment and intervention strategies.* Baltimore: Brookes.

Rice, M.L., & Kemper, S. (1984). *Child language and cognition.* Baltimore: University Park Press.

Rogers, S.J. (1996). Brief report: Early intervention in autism. *Journal of Autism and Developmental Disorders, 26*(2), 243–246.

Rowland, C., & Schweigert, P. (1993). Analyzing the communication environment to increase functional communication. *Journal of the Association for Persons with Severe Handicaps, 18,* 161–176.

Rydell, P., & Prizant, B. (1995). Assessment and intervention strategies for children who use echolalia. In K.A. Quill (Ed.), *Teaching children with autism: Strategies to enhance communication and socialization.* Albany, NY: Delmar.

Sameroff, S.A., & Chandler, M.J. (1975). Reproductive risks and the continuum of caretaking casualty. In Horowitz (Ed.), *Review of child development research* (pp. 187–244). Chicago: University Press.

Scheinkoph, S., & Siegel, B. (in press). Home based behavioral treatment of children with autism. *Journal of Autism and Developmental Disorders.*

Schiefelbusch, R., & Hollis, J. (1979). *Language from ape to man.* Baltimore: University Park Press.

Schuler, A.L. (1979). *An experimental analysis of conceptual and representational abilities in a mute autistic adolescent: A serial versus a simultaneous mode of processing.* Unpublished doctoral dissertation, University of California, Santa Barbara.

Schuler, A.L. (1980). Teaching functional speech. In B. Wilcox & A. Thompson (Eds.), *Critical issues in teaching autistic children and youth.* Washington, DC: U.S. Department of Education.

Schuler, A.L. (1981, November). *The relations between disruptive behavior and communicative deficiencies.* Paper presented at the National Convention of the American Speech and Hearing Association, Los Angeles, CA.

Schuler, A.L. (1985, December). Selecting alternative communication systems on the basis of current communicative means and functions. *Australian Journal of Human Communication Disorders.*

Schuler, A.L. (1989). Assessment considerations. *Seminars in Speech and Language, 10,* 1–4.

Schuler, A.L. (1995). Thinking in autism: Differences in learning and development. In K. Quill (Ed.), *Teaching children with autism: Strategies to enhance communication and socialization.* Albany, NY: Delmar.

Schuler, A.L., & Baldwin, M. (1981). Non-speech communication and childhood autism. *Language, Speech and Hearing Services in the Schools, 12,* 246–257.

Schuler, A.L., & Bormann, C. (1983). The interrelations between cognitive and communicative development: Some implications of the study of a mute autistic adolescent. In C.L. Thew & C.E. Johnson (Eds.), *Proceedings of the Second International Congress on the Study of Child Language* (pp. 269–282). Washington, DC: University Press of America.

Schuler, A.L., & Goetz, L. (1981). The assessment of several language disabilities: Communicative and cognitive considerations. *Analysis and Intervention in Developmental Disabilities, 1,* 333–346.

Schuler, A.L., Gonsier-Gerdin, J., & Wolfberg, P. (1990). The efficacy of speech and language intervention: Autism. *Seminars in Speech and Language, 11,* 242–251.

Schuler, A.L., Peck, C.A., Willard, C.T., & Theimer, K. (1989). Assessment of communicative means and functions through interview: Assessing the communicative capabilities of individuals with limited language. *Seminars in Speech and Language, 10,* 51–63.

Schuler, A.L., & Perez, L. (1991). Assessment: Current concerns and future directions. In L.H. Meyer, C.A. Peck, & L. Brown (Eds.), *Critical issues in the lives of people with severe disabilities* (pp. 101–106). Baltimore: Brookes.

Schuler, A.L., & Prizant, B.M. (1985). Echolalia. In E. Schopler & G. Mesibov (Eds.), *Communication problems in autism* (pp. 163–182). New York: Plenum Press.

Schuler, A.L., & Watanabe, A. (1995). Beyond Rainman: Thinking about people versus thinking about objects. *College of Education Review, 2,* 90–100.

Sheridan, M.J., Foley, G.M., & Radlinsky, S.A. (1995). *Using the supportive play model: Individual intervention and early childhood practice.* Teachers College Press, New York: Columbia University.

Siegel, B. (1996). *The world of the autistic child.* New York: Oxford Press.

Sigman, M., & Ungerer, J. (1984). Cognitive and language skills in autistic, mentally retarded and normal children. *Developmental Psychology, 20,* 293–302.

Snow, C., Midkiff-Borunda, S., Small, A., & Proctor, A. (1984). Therapy as social interaction: Analyzing the contexts for language remediation. *Topics in Language Disorders, 2,* 45–56.

Sugarman, S. (1984). The development of preverbal communication. In R. Schiefelbusch & J. Pickar (Eds.), *The acquisition of communicative competence* (pp. 23–67). Baltimore: University Park Press.

Tomasello, M., Kruger, A.C., & Ratner, H.H. (1993). Imitative learning of action as objects by children, chimpanzees, and enculturated chimpanzees. *Child Development, 64,* 1688–1705.

Warren, S.F., & Kaiser, A.P. (1986). Incidental language teaching: A critical review. *Journal of Speech and Hearing Disorders, 51,* 291–299.

Watson, L., Lord, C., Schaeffer, B., & Schopler, E. (1989). *Teaching spontaneous communication to autistic and developmentally handicapped children.* New York: Irvington.

Weeks, M., & Gaylord-Ross, R. (1981). Task difficulty and aberrant behavior in severely handicapped students. *Journal of Applied Behavior Analysis, 14,* 449–463.

Wetherby, A.M. (1983). *Cognitive and communicative/social development in autistic children.* Unpublished doctoral dissertation, University of California, San Francisco.

Wetherby, A.M. (1986). Ontogeny of communicative functions in autism. *Journal of Autism and Developmental Disorders, 16,* 295–316.

Wetherby, A.M., & Prizant, B.M. (1989). The expression of communicative intent: Assessment guidelines. *Seminars in Speech and Language, 10,* 77–91.

Wetherby, A.M., & Prizant, B. (1992a). Profiling young children's communicative competence. In S. Warren & J. Reichle (Eds.), *Perspective on communication and language intervention: Development, assessment, and intervention* (pp. 217–251). Baltimore: Brookes.

Wetherby, A.M., & Prizant, B. (1992b). Facilitating language and communication development in autism: Assessment and intervention guidelines. In D.E. Berkell (Ed.), *Autism: Identification, education, and treatment* (pp. 107–134). Hillsdale, NJ: Erlbaum.

Wetherby, A.M., & Prizant, B. (1993a). *Communication and Symbolic Behavior Scales* (Normed ed.). Chicago: Riverside.

Wetherby, A.M., & Prizant, B. (1993b). Profiling communication and symbolic abilities in young children. *Journal of Childhood Communication Disorders, 15,* 23–32.

Wetherby, A.M., & Prutting, C. (1984). Profiles of communicative and cognitive-social abilities in autistic children. *Journal of Speech and Hearing Research, 27,* 364–377.

Willard, C., & Schuler, A.L. (1987). Social transactions: A vehicle for intervention. In T. Layton (Ed.), *Language and treatment of autistic and developmentally disordered children* (pp. 265–287). Springfield, IL: Thomas.

Wing, L., & Gould, J. (1979). Severe impairments of social interaction and associated abnormalities in children: Epidemiology and classification. *Journal of Autism and Developmental Disorders, 9,* 11–29.

Wolfberg, P. (1995). Enhancing children's play. In K.A. Quill (Ed.), *Teaching children with autism: Strategies to enhance communication and socialization* (pp. 193–218). Albany, NY: Delmar.

Wolfberg, P.J., & Schuler, A.L. (1993). Integrated play groups: A model for promoting the social and cognitive dimensions of play in children with autism. *Journal of Autism and Developmental Disorders, 23,* 467–489.

CHAPTER 25

Enhancing Language and Communication Development: Language Approaches

BARRY M. PRIZANT, ADRIANA L. SCHULER, AMY M. WETHERBY,
AND PATRICK RYDELL

This chapter considers individuals with autism and Pervasive Developmental Disorder (PDD) who are relatively more advanced in communicative and language-related cognitive abilities; that is, they can communicate through language. Included in this group are persons at emerging language levels who show evidence of the acquisition of a conventional symbolic system for communication, and persons who are beyond emerging and early stages of language acquisition and are able to use language (both expressively and receptively) as a primary mode of acquiring and conveying information, and of expressing needs and desires to others. We will consider individuals who have achieved at least a single-word utterance stage in expressive linguistic ability, as well as those who are able to use language in conversations.

Many persons within this group's range of ability also produce echolalia and other forms of unconventional verbal behavior (UVB; Prizant & Rydell, 1993), or have progressed through periods of echolalia in language development (Baltaxe & Simmons, 1981; Prizant, 1983b). These individuals may be literate or may have the potential to develop literacy skills. Initially, emerging literacy abilities may take the form of hyperlexia (defined as a precocious and self-taught ability to decode written language with limited comprehension) co-occurring with a significant language disability (Aram & Healy, 1988). The chronological ages of persons within this ability range may vary from preschool children to adolescents and adults. This variety of age groups

greatly influences assessment and communication enhancement decisions because chronological age is a major factor in determining functional communicative needs (Prizant & Wetherby, 1993).

Persons with autism who are at language levels pose a different set of challenges in assessment and intervention than persons who are primarily preverbal and nonspeaking. As noted in Chapter 24, acquisition of the concept of communicative intentionality is a major concern when autistic persons are at preverbal levels. In contrast, individuals using language demonstrate knowledge of the "power" of communication in their intentional use of linguistic means to communicate (i.e., to affect others with specific goals in mind; Bates, 1979). However, the range of purposes for which they communicate may be restricted (Wetherby, 1986; Wetherby & Prutting, 1984). For persons with linguistic ability, the acquisition of conventional and socially acceptable symbolic means to communicate intent, and the appropriate social use of language in different contexts, are major concerns.

Two general levels of expressive language ability are of interest here. At the first level, which we will refer to as the *emerging and early language level*, are individuals with expressive abilities ranging from the emergence of a stable, core vocabulary of single words used with comprehension and intent, to the production of early multiword utterances or sign–symbol combinations that demonstrate the acquisition of early semantic–syntactic knowledge. At this first level, echolalia and other forms of UVB may comprise a significant portion of expressive utterances, and may be used, along with single and multiword utterances, to serve different communicative functions or purposes. The second level, which we will refer to as *more advanced language levels,* ranges from the production of more grammatically complete simple utterances and different sentence types, to the use of language as part of conversational and narrative discourse. Language production at more advanced language levels may reflect relatively sophisticated knowledge of linguistic structure (e.g., production and comprehension of different sentence types, including declaratives, questions, negatives, and even complex sentence forms), although significant difficulties in pragmatics or social use of language may remain (Chapter 9; Prizant, 1988; Tager-Flusberg, 1987; Watson, 1987).

The purpose of this two-level breakdown is to highlight different assessment and intervention challenges: first, for persons at emerging language levels who may be communicating primarily through early language forms and echolalia; and second, for persons at more advanced linguistic levels who have acquired the ability to communicate more consistently through generative and creative linguistic means. It is important to recognize, however, that there is a continuum of communicative ability in persons with autism and PDD at language stages, rather than a clear dichotomy. Furthermore, great variation and individual differences in social communicative and language profiles must be taken into account in assessment and communication enhancement practices.

Challenges and Issues at Emerging Language Levels

The major challenges for assessment and communication enhancement at emerging language levels are presented here, so that they are understood at the outset.

1. The shift from preverbal communication to language may be slow. It represents a shift from sensorimotor communication to symbolic communication, and persons with

autism show evidence of specific symbolic deficits affecting language acquisition and use (Frith, 1989; Schuler, 1995). Thus, as described in Chapter 24, presymbolic sensorimotor communication (e.g., gestures, physical manipulation) may remain an important strategy for communication, even after language is acquired. An important goal of communication enhancement is the development of linguistically based conventional communication that will eventually replace sensorimotor communication, which tends to be idiosyncratic, less readable, and more context-bound than linguistic communication.

2. At the emerging language level, and even at more advanced language levels, unconventional verbal behavior (UVB), including immediate and delayed echolalic utterances, perseverative speech, idiosyncratic language (Volden & Lord, 1991), and so-called metaphorical language or language with "private meanings" (Kanner, 1946), may be produced for communicative as well as noncommunicative purposes (Prizant & Rydell, 1993). Within the category of UVB, there is a continuum of behavior ranging from (a) highly unconventional and noninteractive speech patterns, which may appear to be noncommunicative or irrelevant to listeners, to (b) speech characterized by varying degrees of conventionality, which is produced with communicative intent but violates some conventions of language meaning and use, and thus may be functional only with frequent communicative partners (i.e., those who are familiar with the idiosyncrasies of an individual's communicative system), and then to (c) speech patterns that are produced with clear intent and are close enough to conventional forms that most listeners (frequent or new) understand the speaker's purpose and meaning. Thus, the communicative success of individuals at emerging language levels will vary greatly, depending on the presence of UVB and the degree of conventionality and intentionality achieved. When the language produced has only limited relevance to the context in which it is used, communicative success is more limited. Table 25.1 defines and gives examples of unconventional verbal behavior.

3. Early creative language and gestalt forms (i.e., memorized and repeated language

TABLE 25.1   Forms and Definitions of Unconventional Verbal Behavior (UVB)

Form of UVB	Definition
Immediate Echolalia	Repetition of speech that: a. is produced either following immediately, or within two turns of original production; b. involves exact repetition (pure echolalia), or minimal structural change (mitigated immediate echolalia); and c. may serve a variety of communicative and cognitive functions.

Example: Child repeats, "Want some juice?" immediately following adult's question. The child's nonverbal behavior (i.e., reaching toward juice bottle) indicates child was repeating the utterance in order to acquire juice, thus serving the function of affirmation (Kanner, 1943) or "yes-answer" (Prizant & Duchan, 1981).

Delayed Echolalia	Repetition of speech that: a. is repeated at a significantly later time (i.e., at least three turns following original utterance, but more typically hours, days, or even weeks later); b. involves exact repetition (pure echolalia), or minimal structural change (mitigated delayed echolalia); and c. may serve a variety of communicative and cognitive functions.

Example: Child pulls teacher to the classroom door and states, "Time to go for a walk," as a request to get a drink of water. The utterance is a repetition of what his teacher said to him two weeks earlier, prior to leaving the room for a drink. This utterance is used to serve a request function (Prizant & Rydell, 1984).

Perseverative Speech	Persistent repetition of a speech pattern that: a. consists of a word, phrase, or combination of utterances that is imitated (echolalia) or self-generated; b. is produced in a cyclical, recurring manner; and c. is produced with no evidence of communicative intent or expectation of a response from the partner.

Example: Child states repeatedly, "We must clean up the mess," while pacing in a corner of the classroom, away from the other students and the teacher. The teacher had said this to him a month before, in the same location, after he spilled some juice. In this example, the perseverative utterance is also a delayed echo based on a "situation association" (Prizant & Rydell, 1984).

Incessant (Repetitive) Questioning	Repeated verbal inquiries that: a. are directed toward the communicative partner; b. are produced with communicative intent, with an expectation of a response; and c. persist either immediately following a response or after a short respite, even though a response was provided.

Example: Over a two-hour period, a child asks his mother repeatedly, "Going swimming after lunch?" after his mother indicated they would go to the beach that afternoon. The questioning continues despite affirmative responses from his mother.

units, including echolalia) are first acquired within frequently experienced routines and contexts, and generalization of these forms to new situations and communicative partners may be slow. Furthermore, early word forms may be acquired and then "lost," prior to the development of the ability to communicate consistently through linguistic means. For reasons that remain unclear, some children who lose language never regain oral language abilities (Kurita, 1985).

4. Early language forms are typically used for a limited range of communicative functions or purposes. Linguistic communication initially serves the function of regulating others' behavior for tangible ends and immediate needs (e.g., requesting objects and actions, protesting). Communication for such instrumental purposes typically is acquired earlier than communication for more social purposes such as sharing feelings, requesting permission, or sharing observations and experiences (Wetherby, 1986).

5. Although language may be used in a symbolic or quasi-symbolic manner, use of language forms rarely approaches the flexibility of language that is necessary to be consistently effective in communicative exchanges across settings and persons. The social-cognitive learning style associated with autism and PDD limits, to varying degrees, symbolic thinking and decontextualized learning. As a result, the language forms and usage that are acquired are often concrete, cue-dependent, and context-bound (Prizant, 1983b; Schuler, 1995). It is not uncommon for caregivers to report language abilities observed in the home context that are discrepant from communicative abilities observed in educational or clinical settings.

6. Early language use may be influenced greatly by socioemotional and situational variables (e.g., level of emotional arousal, familiarity of partner, and so on). Great variability in communicative competence is to be expected relative to these factors (Prizant & Meyer, 1993).

7. In addition to challenges in expressive communication, difficulties in comprehending communicative partners' language and nonverbal signals may limit the reciprocity and ultimate success of interpersonal communication and social and emotional relatedness.

Given these challenges, the primary purpose of communication and language assessment for persons at emerging and more advanced language levels is to construct a profile of communication and language-related abilities, and to determine the extent to which the challenges noted above are operative. With knowledge of an individual's relative strengths and needs, caregivers and professionals may then collaborate to determine intervention goals, interactive styles, and strategies for communication enhancement.

ASSESSMENT DOMAINS AND APPROACHES AT EMERGING AND EARLY LANGUAGE LEVELS

The generic framework for assessment (see Table 25.2) identifies major domains for documenting strengths and weaknesses, and for determining communication and language goals at emerging language levels. It is beyond the scope of this chapter to address assessment procedures and domains in depth. (See Prizant & Meyer, 1993; Prizant & Rydell, 1993; Prizant & Wetherby, 1993; Twachtman, 1995; and Wetherby & Prizant, 1992, for details on communication assessment domains and strategies.) Important domains specific to this level are addressed. They include: expressive language and communication, receptive language and communication, social-communicative and socioemotional abilities, and language-related cognitive abilities/symbolic representation.

Expressive Language and Communication

Unconventional Verbal Behavior (UVB) and Gestalt Language Use

Echolalia, which is the most common form of UVB, is the most frequently discussed characteristic of children with autism and PDD who acquire speech (Prizant, 1983a). Based on Peters's (1983) work on normal language acquisition, we have referred to echolalia as "gestalt language forms" (Prizant, 1983b) because echolalic speech is mostly comprised of unanalyzed units of speech that may be repeated immediately (i.e., immediate echolalia) or at some time after an utterance was heard (i.e., delayed echolalia). A wide range of abilities is evident in persons who produce echolalia. Some individuals demonstrate very primitive and noncommunicative echolalic behavior and are not truly functioning at a linguistic level in communication (Schuler & Prizant, 1985). However, many persons demonstrate evidence of progressive change in their echolalic utterances, leading to the emergence of some degree of more creative, rule-governed linguistic behavior. For the latter group, the major considerations are, first, how echolalia may function in communicative interactions, and, second, what role echolalia may play in language acquisition.

An analysis of echolalic behavior can provide two types of information about an individual's communicative abilities. The first type of information pertains to an individual's knowledge of language and communicative function. That is, functional analyses of echolalic behavior observed in different contexts can provide information about the range of

TABLE 25.2   Social Communication Assessment—Intervention Framework for Early Language Levels

I. Language and Communication
   A. Expressive Language and Communication
      1. Gestural means—idiosyncratic/conventional gestures; contact/distal gestures
      2. Vocal means
         a. inventory of consonants
         b. syllabic structure and complexity
         c. coordination of gestural and vocal acts
      3. Verbal means—lexicon, linguistic complexity, unconventional verbal behavior (UVB)
      4. Graphic means
         a. picture/picture symbol systems
         b. written language—manual/typed
   B. Receptive Language and Communication
      1. Nonlinguistic response strategies
      2. Lexicon
      3. Semantic relations
      4. Discourse

II. Social-Communicative and Socioemotional Abilities
   A. Communicative Functions
      1. Range of functions—behavioral regulation, social interaction, joint attention
      2. Sociability of communicative acts (acts for joint attention + social interaction/all acts)
   B. Reciprocity
      1. Rate of communicative acts
      2. Persistence and repair strategies
      3. Respondent acts
   C. Social-Affective Signaling
      1. Use of gaze and gaze shifts for social referencing and to regulate interaction
      2. Display of affect—sociability of positive affect
      3. Display of affect—episodes of negative affect
   D. Emotional Expression
      1. Comprehension of and response to others' emotional expressions
      2. Expression of emotion in language use and play
   E. Emotion Regulation and Communicative Competence
      1. Communicative competence as a function of situational or relationship context
      2. Communicative competence as a function of degree of emotional arousal (positive or negative)
      3. Use of self-regulatory strategies to modulate arousal
      4. Use of mutual regulatory strategies to modulate arousal

III. Language-Related Cognitive Abilities/Symbolic Representation
   A. Symbolic Play
   B. Combinatorial/Constructive Play
   C. Imitation
   D. Anticipation of Routines/ Event Knowledge
   E. Attention in Social and Nonsocial Contexts

functions an individual is learning to express, even if the means of expression is through immediate and delayed echolalia. The second type of information provided by an analysis of echolalic behavior pertains to an individual's knowledge of language structure, and evolving linguistic competence. That is, analyses of language samples over time can help to document movement from primarily echolalic behavior to the emergence of more creative and generative language forms. The greater the creativity and generativity demonstrated in linguistic production, the greater the evidence that a person is progressively acquiring a rule-based linguistic system. Procedures for functional and structural analyses of echolalia are summarized by Prizant and Rydell (1993), and Rydell and Prizant (1995) based on analyses performed by Prizant and Duchan (1981), Prizant and Rydell (1984), and Rydell and Mirenda (1991).

To reflect the multiple factors that underlie the occurrence of echolalia and other forms of UVB, assessment must address: (a) situational determinants and antecedent conditions associated with UVB; (b) the range of intentionality and of communicative functions served by UVB; (c) how UVB "fits" into an individual's communicative profile; and (d) the developmental relationship between UVB and other communicative behavior over time (i.e., is UVB a transitional phenomenon reflecting an individual's growing communicative competence?).

1. *Situational determinants and antecedent conditions associated with UVB.* Research has indicated that UVB is more likely to occur in some situational and communicative contexts than in others (Charlop, 1983; Rydell & Mirenda, 1991). Specific contextual features that correspond to the production of UVB should be documented. An individual may be more likely to produce UVB when faced with unfamiliar situations, challenging tasks, relatively unstructured time, transitions, or unmotivating or boring activities. Specific interpersonal interactive styles or social and linguistic demands also are factors associated with UVB. These include a partner's use of complex language (Roberts, 1989), utterances of high constraint (Rydell & Mirenda, 1991), or excessive task demands (Durand & Crimmins, 1987).

2. *The range of intentionality and of communicative functions served by UVB.* Differing degrees of intent may underlie the production of UVB, depending on an individual's awareness of a specific goal and the effectiveness of a communicative act in achieving that goal. Therefore, it is not uncommon for some forms of UVB to be produced initially with limited intent and used later with increased intentionality. Increased intentional usage may result when an individual experiences and learns the consistent effect of the UVB on the behavior of others. For example, an individual may repeat an utterance (e.g., "Do you want a drink?") immediately following an adult query (immediate echolalia), with little evidence of comprehension or intent. If the repetition is followed by obtaining a drink, the same utterance may be used in future situations as a request for a drink. UVB may also be produced noninteractively, serving intrapersonal functions such as anxiety reduction (i.e., emotional regulation) or rehearsal (Donnellan, Mirenda, Mesaros, & Fassbender, 1984; Prizant, 1987).

3. *How unconventional verbal behavior "fits" into an individual's communicative profile.* UVB must be considered as one aspect of a person's communicative system, which most often includes conventional as well as unconventional means of communicating intentions (Donnellan et al., 1984; Prizant & Rydell, 1993). Therefore, UVB should be considered in relation to both nonlinguistic and linguistic means of expressing intentions.

5. *The developmental relationship between UVB and other communicative behavior over time.* Some patterns of UVB, especially when observed in young children, may represent a transitional phenomenon (Prizant, 1983b) and a positive prognostic indicator for further communicative growth and change (Howlin, 1981; McEachin, Smith, & Lovaas, 1993; Prizant, 1983b). Prizant (1983b) described the transition of echolalic speech as following a predictable progression. Early speech typically is predominantly echolalic and serves limited communicative functions. As cognitive and linguistic growth occurs, echolalic speech is enlisted for a greater variety of communicative functions, and more creative patterns begin to emerge. With the development of a more rule-governed and generative linguistic

system, spontaneous language gradually increases, echolalic speech decreases, and speech repetition becomes more flexible and less rigidly produced (i.e., echolalia is mitigated: as echolalia reflecting change and modification increases, exact reproductions decrease). For persons who are able to move on to primarily creative and spontaneous language, echolalia may not fully disappear, but may be observed primarily during states of confusion and fatigue, when it serves the function of conversational turn-taking. However, for some persons, patterns of echolalia and other forms of UVB may remain static, with minimal progressive change. These forms may be considered to be interfering or challenging by many communicative partners. Intervention strategies therefore must be based on systematic analyses of echolalia and other forms of UVB, taking individual differences and situational factors into account.

Additional assessment dimensions and strategies relevant to UVB have been discussed in literature on analysis of the communicative functions of challenging behavior (Carr et al., 1994; Donnellan et al., 1984; Prizant & Rydell, 1993; Prizant & Wetherby, 1987; Reichle & Wacker, 1993). Assessment practice must account for co-occurrence of and dynamic interaction among the factors associated with the production of UVB. Clear agreement must be reached about the definition of the behavior being evaluated for both assessment and intervention. Reference to general categories such as echolalia or perseverative speech may not address situational determinants and individual differences in usage of utterances that fall under general headings. The strategy of obtaining language samples (including the more conventional forms of emerging language) in the different settings in which UVB occurs most frequently is important for acquiring a picture of expressive language abilities, including UVB.

Analysis of Conventional Language Forms

In addition to UVB, language samples of the more conventional language forms used should be collected and analyzed. Detailed procedures for analyzing the phonological, semantic, syntactic, morphological, and pragmatic dimensions of early conventional language forms are available, and will not be reviewed here (Lund & Duchan, 1993; Owens, 1995; Retherford, 1993). Nonverbal means of communication should be documented as well; they comprise a significant proportion of communicative strategies at this level (see Chapter 24). It is essential that samples be collected in different contexts and during a variety of familiar life events and routines. Expert informants, including caregivers and other professionals, must be involved in constructing a profile of expressive language and communication abilities that results in a representative picture of an individual's expressive communication system.

Receptive Language and Communication

Assessment of receptive language and communication involves determining a person's level of language comprehension and documenting the strategies the individual uses in responding to language. This information provides direction for parents, teachers, and professionals to target appropriate goals and to make adjustments in their language and communicative behavior that will enhance the individual's comprehension and participation in communicative exchange.

Assessment of receptive language is important for a number of reasons. First, language complexity may be contributing to nonresponsiveness to speech (Klin, 1991). Unfortunately, nonresponsiveness to speech and to complex language often results in a person's being labeled as "noncompliant." Second, if an individual is aware that demands are being made through language, but cannot understand the language, confusion, anxiety, and behavioral problems may result. Third, as indicated, one cannot learn language and learn *from* language that is too complex. Fourth, if they have an estimate of an individual's comprehension abilities, communicative partners can adjust their own language accordingly and can add nonlinguistic cues as needed to aid in comprehension.

Some individuals with autism and PDD are able to respond appropriately to language by referring to other cues available in the environment (Prizant & Schuler, 1987). For example, when appropriate responses seem to be based on comprehension of linguistic forms, the individual may be responding to a familiar routine, to gestural cues used by others, to particular words in an utterance that is supported by environmental cues, or to intonational cues, such as rising inflections when questions are asked (Chapman, 1981). For this level, the major concerns to be addressed in assessment include the range of vocabulary understood, the level of comprehension of various semantic–syntactic structures (e.g., question forms, negatives), and the comprehension of language pertaining to events in the immediate environment versus past and future events.

The most relevant information about an individual's comprehension of language and other supportive cues should be gathered from informal assessments in motivating and naturalistic interactions, as well as more formal assessments of language comprehension appropriate to the estimated level of an individual's linguistic comprehension. More controlled systematic assessment of language comprehension, involving systematic manipulation of situational and gestural cues, can provide information about the cues an individual relies on or refers to when responding to language. Miller and Paul (1995) provide a detailed consideration of and specific strategies for assessing receptive language and communication.

Social-Communicative and Socioemotional Abilities

Assessment of abilities in this domain involves determining an individual's expression of communicative functions, reciprocity, social-affective signaling, emotional expression, and emotional regulation. It is important to document the functions or purposes of an individual's communicative acts, whether verbal or preverbal. Analysis of functions of UVB was discussed earlier. Functions of challenging behavior and preverbal behavior, as discussed in Chapter 24, remain relevant at this level, because persons at emerging language levels will continue to use unconventional and preverbal communicative means to a great extent. An individual's abilities in communicative reciprocity—including persistence and repair when communication breaks down, and the types of strategies used to repeat or modify commu-

nicative acts—should be documented. Frequency or rate of communicative acts also provides important information relevant to reciprocity.

Additional dimensions of socioemotional abilities related to communicative competence include social relatedness, emotional expression and relatedness, sociability of communicative functions, emotional regulation and communicative competence, and expression of emotion in language and play (Prizant & Meyer, 1993). Table 25.3 identifies some key dimensions of socioemotional functioning, related to communication, that may be addressed in assessment.

Language-Related Cognitive Abilities/Symbolic Representation

The final domain of assessment relevant to this level provides information about an individual's ability to represent experiences through symbolic or imaginative play (Westby, 1988) and to use visuospatial and configurational abilities in problem solving and in daily activities. The profile of abilities for most persons with autism and PDD typically indicates weaknesses in their symbolic and abstract representational ability, especially when language is used as a mode of representation and when information involves knowledge of persons and social situations rather than knowledge about objects and the nonsocial world (Schuler, 1995). Relative strengths are often observed in visuospatial problem solving and in tasks that can be accomplished through visual representation and imagery (Grandin, 1995). The extent to which this pattern holds for an individual is important for planning intervention activities and for determining the relationship of language and communicative abilities to nonverbal cognitive functions. Additional abilities that should be assessed for their relevance in planning intervention include: the use of imitation as a strategy for learning; anticipation of routines and event knowledge; and attention in activities in both social and nonsocial contexts. Documentation of abilities and needs in these cognitive domains, across contexts, provides important information relevant to intervention planning.

TABLE 25.3   Socioemotional Dimensions in Communication Assessment

I. Social Relatedness
  A. Social and Communicative Motivation
    1. Does the individual typically prefer to be in proximity of others, or alone?
    2. Does the individual bring attention to self for social engagement?
    3. Does the individual respond to and initiate social games and social routines?
    4. Does the individual visually orient to others (face-to-face gaze)?
    5. Does the individual regularly use gaze shifts to reference the attention of others?
    6. Is the frequency of communicative acts directed to adults and other persons?
  B. Joint Attention
    1. Does the individual follow adults' visual line of regard or observe adults' or other persons' activities?
    2. Does the individual communicate to establish joint attention, verbally or preverbally, by commenting, requesting information, or providing information?
    3. Is the individual able to respond to the preverbal or verbal signals of others, to establish shared attention?
    4. Is the individual able to maintain and follow up topics introduced by others?
  C. Social Imitation
    1. Does the individual imitate actions, vocalizations, and/or verbalizations with some evidence of social orientation (e.g., gaze checks, sharing of affect, verbal communication)?

II. Emotional Expression and Relatedness
  A. Attachment
    1. Does the individual seek out caregivers or others for comfort and emotional "refueling"?
    2. After a reasonable period of time, does the individual learn to see new acquaintances as a base of security?
  B. Emotional Expression
    1. Does the individual express different emotions through facial expression, vocalization, and/or verbalization, and are these expressions appropriate to the situational and interpersonal context?
    2. Does the individual share emotional states by directing displays of affect to others?
    3. Does the individual understand and respond appropriately to the emotional expressions of others?
  C. Empathy
    1. Does the individual demonstrate concern for, or actively attempt to soothe, another individual who has been hurt or is otherwise in distress?

III. Sociability of Communicative Functions
  A. Does the individual communicate for the functions of:
    1. Behavioral regulation (i.e., requesting objects/actions, protesting)?
    2. Social interaction (i.e., greeting, calling, requesting social routine, requesting comfort)?
    3. Joint attention (i.e., commenting, requesting, providing information)?
  B. Does the individual communicate for all three general functions or primarily for behavioral regulation, which may be indicative of a limited sociability in communication?

IV. Emotion Regulation and Communicative Competence
  A. Does communicative competence vary significantly with different communicative partners?
  B. Does communicative competence vary significantly in comfortable/familiar contexts as opposed to unfamiliar/emotionally arousing contexts?
  C. How does degree of emotional arousal (positive or negative) influence communicative competence (e.g., the individual withdraws, speech becomes disorganized, the individual uses developmentally less sophisticated means, and so on)?
  D. Does the individual demonstrate self-regulatory strategies to modulate arousal?
  E. Does the individual demonstrate mutual regulatory strategies?
  F. What are the most effective means others can use to help the individual to modulate extreme states of arousal?

V. Expression of Emotion in Language and Play
  A. Does the individual use vocabulary to talk about emotional states (self or other)?
  B. Do emotional themes emerge consistently in play, and are they an attempt to understand stressful life events?

Adapted from Prizant and Meyer (1993) and Wetherby and Prizant (1992).

COMMUNICATION ENHANCEMENT AT EMERGING AND EARLY LANGUAGE LEVELS

The overriding goal for persons at emerging and early language levels is acquisition and effective use of a language-based system of communication. Within most communities, spoken and written language are the most conventional forms of communication. Therefore, competence with oral and/or written language modes will allow for participation in communicative interactions with family members, peers, and other community members who share knowledge of the same language system. Beyond the general goal of acquiring a language-based system for communication, this chapter discusses generic goals and appropriate strategies for achieving them. By generic goals, we mean abilities that address typical needs and challenges faced by most persons with autism and PDD in language-based social interaction. We have identified these needs and challenges based on our clinical experience and on the extant literature on communication and language abilities of persons with autism and PDD. Specific goals for any individual can be determined only after a careful assessment of that person's current profile of abilities and functional communicative needs. Information for that profile must be gathered from family members, educators, clinicians, caregivers, and, whenever possible, the person with autism or PDD.

Although the assessment framework presented earlier addresses domains in addition to language and communication (i.e., socioemotional and related cognitive abilities), expressive and receptive language and communication abilities are the specific focus of this discussion of generic goals. Socioemotional and cognitive concerns will be integrated in the discussion where appropriate.

Expansion of Vocabulary

The expansion of personal vocabulary is based on meanings and intentions expressed through preverbal means of communication and through functional needs. Persons at emerging language levels need to acquire a core vocabulary that they can use effectively in everyday interactions. Selection of vocabulary should be based on a variety of criteria, including meanings that are currently expressed through nonverbal means and can be practiced often (e.g., names of familiar objects and persons; functional actions; words for social control—"stop," "help," "more"—and emotion words—"happy," "sad," "mad"). Establishing the words for social control (i.e., to protest or reject) and for expression of emotion is particularly critical in autism and PDD. Because of the risk that disruptive and challenging behavior may develop, acquisition of vocabulary that could preclude or replace behavior that serves a protest or escape function is a high priority. Additional criteria for vocabulary selection are listed in Table 25.4.

TABLE 25.4   Criteria for Vocabulary Selection

1. Words that express early semantic functions such as nonexistence or disappearance (e.g., "all gone," "no"), recurrence (e.g., "more," "again"), existence (e.g., object labels, "there"), rejection (e.g., "no"), possession (e.g., "mine"), action (e.g.,"open"), and locative action (e.g., "up," "out").
2. Words to request motivating foods, objects, or activities.
3. Words for routine independent living activities (e.g., "eat," "drink," "sleep/tired," "bathroom/potty").
4. Words that can express functions currently expressed through socially unacceptable means (e.g., "no" for rejection/protest, "all done" or "stop" for cessation).
5. Words for expressing agreement or affirmation (e.g., "yes," "OK").
6. Names of significant others.
7. Words to request assistance (e.g., "help"), affection or comfort (e.g., "hug," "kiss"), or interaction (e.g., "play").
8. Words for common environments (e.g., "home," "school," "pool").
9. Action words of general application (e.g., "close," "go," "give").
10. Words of attribution (e.g., "hot," "dirty").
11. Words to express feelings or internal states (e.g., "want," "mad," "happy," "scared").

Adapted from "Facilitating the Acquisition and Use of Communication Skills," by B.M. Prizant and D. Bailey, 1992, in D. Bailey and M. Wolery (Eds.), *Teaching Infants and Toddlers with Handicaps*. New York: Merrill.

Production of Communicative Acts

The ability to produce intelligible or unambiguous communicative acts may be exhibited in spoken words, signing, or pointing to a board or a desired object. The acquisition of expressive vocabulary is of little use unless the act of communicating (through speech or via nonspeech alternative means) is intelligible to listeners. Refining intelligibility is an ongoing process that requires careful use of modeling and of prompting more intelligible forms. However, caution is advised when requiring responses that are too refined, especially in early stages of language acquisition. Koegel, O'Dell, and Dunlap (1988) found that, compared to reinforcement based on *correctness of form,* reinforcement of *efforts to use speech* resulted in increased attempts to produce speech. This finding is consistent with the social-communicative philosophy underlying these chapters, and illustrates the need to build a sense of the power of communication and an emphasis on function more than form.

Expansion of Communicative Functions

A characteristic of the communicative patterns of persons with autism and PDD is their limited range of purposes for communicating. Most typically, communication for self-needs and environmental ends (i.e., for purposes of behavioral regulation) comprises the great majority of communicative acts. Communication to bring attention to self for affiliative purposes (i.e., social interaction) or to share an event or experience (i.e., joint attention) is more limited or is absent. For example, communication that serves to request objects or actions, or to protest (i.e., behavioral regulation), is more likely to be observed than communication to request comfort or greeting (i.e., social interaction), or communication to comment or to provide information (i.e., joint attention). One measure of communicative effectiveness and social relatedness is the variety of purposes for which one communicates, including both social and relatively nonsocial purposes. Therefore, increasing the range of purposes, which typically involves expansion from behavioral regulation to social interaction and joint attention, becomes an important goal. Specific functional goals involving

expansion of communicative functions are determined based on an individual's needs and life activities.

Direction of Attention

The ability to direct attention to self, or to secure others' attention prior to communicating, is referred to as the calling function. This ability, a fundamental requirement of effective communication, falls under the quasi-social intentional category of social interaction. Calling may be accomplished through verbal means (e.g., calling someone's name) or nonverbal means (e.g., a tap on the shoulder). Unfortunately, one of the pragmatic difficulties experienced by persons with autism—and one that has a detrimental impact on communication effectiveness—is their limited ability to bring attention to self, or their use of unconventional or socially inappropriate strategies to do so (Hurtig, Ensrud, & Tomblin, 1982). This goal may be approached through modeling and prompting by adult partners and peers, and by offering frequent practice opportunities in both contrived and more natural situations.

Combination of Communication Elements

The ability to combine words, signs, and pictures creatively enhances the expression of relational concepts. In early stages, a major achievement in language development is movement from single-unit communication (i.e., single words, gestalt or memorized forms) to a combination of units, reflecting knowledge of early semantic–syntactic relationships. The ability to produce multiword utterances, especially when they emerge from agent–action and action–object relationships, is the foundation for realizing the creative potential of language as a hierarchical, rather than a linear system (Lahey, 1988). Thus, movement from single-unit communication to multiword communication is an important goal for individuals who have established a solid single-word/unit vocabulary used communicatively. Once again, this goal may be approached through clear modeling of multiword utterances—in natural as well as contrived contexts, and based on both developmental and functional needs—and through expansion of single-unit language in contrived and naturalistic learning opportunities. In particular, a natural need to use multiword utterances, in order to achieve more explicit communication, creates a natural motivation to expand expressive language use. For example, opportunities for requesting objects or actions may require that more specific information be provided to designate desired objects or actions among a number of alternatives (e.g., a drink of orange juice in a cup, rather than a drink of milk in a glass; bouncing a ball versus rolling a ball). (See Lahey, 1988, for more specific suggestions in addressing this goal.)

Production of Sentence Types

The ability to produce different sentence types serves different communicative functions. Movement beyond single-word stages to multi-word utterances is also characterized by the acquisition of different sentence types: declaratives, negatives, wh-questions, yes–no questions, and imperatives (commands). From a communicative perspective, syntactic marking of different sentence types is essential in communicating clearly and explicitly to serve different communicative functions. For example, rejection and protest (serving the function of behavioral regulation) may require clear marking of negation; requesting comfort or permission (serving the function of social interaction) and requesting information (serving the function of joint attention) may require production of wh- and yes–no questions; and commenting (joint attention) is achieved through declarative sentence production. More specific goals and procedures are discussed by Lahey (1988), Nelson (1993), Owens (1995), and Watson, Lord, Schaeffer, and Schopler (1989).

Development of Emergent Literacy Skills

An area of language competence frequently neglected in intervention with persons with disabilities is the development of language skills in the visual modality (Koppenhaver, Coleman, Kalmin, & Yoder, 1991). Many persons with disabilities remain illiterate even when they may have the requisite linguistic knowledge to develop literacy skills. Literacy skills provide an important means of acquiring and transmitting information, and they are essential for

school and vocational success in our culture. The intensive interest and motivation of many persons with autism and PDD to manipulate and learn written symbols and text are well documented (Aram & Healy, 1988; Tirosh & Canby, 1993). Unfortunately, such interest and ability, although closely related to the learning strengths of persons with autism, is often devalued as a "splinter skill," and the potential for exploiting such skills for functional communicative purposes has only recently been addressed (Berger, 1994). We agree with Koppenhaver et al. (1991) that strategies for language and communication enhancement must address literacy development, and such development involves direct teaching as well as creating literacy-rich environments that encourage incidental learning. We will return to this issue in our later discussion of intervention at more advanced language levels.

More Conventional Use of Repetition to Express Intentions

Because of the cognitive style and language-learning style observed in autism and PDD, it is highly likely that persons at language stages will rely on echolalia (i.e., repetition of speech) in interacting with others. As noted earlier, some forms of echolalia will be highly unconventional, and therefore may be barriers to effective communication. However, other forms are clearly produced with intent and will be more readable because of their greater conventionality and relevance to the communicative context. Therefore, a major goal is to help persons use repetition more conventionally to achieve communicative goals. Our approach is to respect the learning style so characteristic in language use, and exploit tendencies to repeat speech by helping persons to learn forms that can be used as tools in communication. Charlop (1983) and Scherer and Olswang (1989) have used gestalt forms to teach both receptive labeling and expressive language forms.

Gestalt Forms

Eventual segmentation of gestalt forms with rule induction allows for greater creativity and generativity in language production. A language system that is limited to primarily gestalt forms, in contrast to more creative and spontaneously generated forms, will restrict communicative effectiveness over time. Therefore, it is imperative that gestalt language users be supported in moving to the acquisition of rule-governed, creative language use. Expansion and reduction of gestalt forms have been shown to be effective strategies in helping children with autism or PDD to produce more creative, rule-governed utterances (Scherer & Olswang, 1989).

STRATEGIES FOR ACHIEVING GOALS AT EMERGING AND EARLY LANGUAGE LEVELS

We believe that functional language use and active participation in communicative exchange are learned most effectively within activities and routines that are encountered regularly or can be scheduled to occur as part of a person's daily experiences (Duchan, 1991; Prizant, 1982). These include activities of high motivation and interest, as well as activities that must be engaged in because they meet a person's life needs for learning, independence, safety, security, and nutrition. When it is not possible to utilize naturally occurring events in a person's daily schedule, the next best solution is to replicate routines and activities in somewhat contrived situations to foster carryover to similar natural contexts. Current "best practices" involve utilizing natural learning contexts and events as a first priority, and using engineered or staged events whenever necessary (Charlop & Haymes, 1994; Duchan, 1986; Elliott, Hall & Soper, 1991; Koegel & Johnson, 1989; Prizant & Wetherby, 1989; Twachtman, 1995; Wolfberg & Schuler, 1993). This approach is in sharp contrast to the traditional behavioral model of discrete trial training, which reduces language teaching to isolated, respondent behaviors under the control of instructor preferences and instructor-selected contingent reinforcement (Lovaas, 1977). We have long believed that measurement of true communicative success is more a matter of communicative initiation and reciprocity than of use of correct grammatical forms or response to predetermined training protocols (Fay & Schuler, 1980; Prizant, 1982; Prizant & Wetherby, 1985). Thus, communicative success across events or activity routines gains precedence over judgments of behavioral correctness in discrete trials. In other words, the whole is greater than the sum of the parts when considering acquisition of communicative competence, because successful communication and social interaction occur over multiple turns in communicative exchange, rather than single isolated trials.

In pragmatic event-based communication enhancement efforts, the role of the communicative partner (e.g., parent, clinician, or teacher) is to "engineer" situations and routines that create the motivation, as well as opportunities and needs for communication (McDonald, 1989; Snyder-McLean, McLean, Etter-Schroeder, & Rogers, 1984; Twachtman, 1995). In such contexts, communicative partners (e.g., adults, peers) model the appropriate use of communicative forms (e.g., words, multiword utterances, graphic symbols, and other visually depicted concepts) with subsequent prompting to enable the emerging-language individual to experience some degree of communicative success and, when necessary, to repair communicative breakdowns. For persons at this level, learning situations may involve predictable goal-directed activities. Although the ultimate goal is to enhance language-based communication, active participation and learning within the context of events and routines provide the structure and motivation. This issue will be addressed in greater depth in the discussion of persons at more advanced language levels.

Addressing Unconventional Verbal Behavior in Communication Enhancement

Approaches addressing UVB should always be viewed as only one dimension of a coordinated approach to communication enhancement (Prizant & Rydell, 1993; Rydell & Prizant, 1985); this is a basic tenet that often has not been followed in more fragmented approaches to unconventional communicative behavior (Burke, 1990). Interventionists must consider the interrelationships among social-cognitive, socioemotional, and linguistic factors and their cumulative effect on the communicative competence of individuals with UVB. Thus, when considered as part of a more comprehensive approach to enhancement of social-communicative competence, strategies for addressing UVB may not involve only direct interventions, but should be viewed on a continuum from indirect to direct strategies. Some strategies may be utilized prior to the production of UVB (i.e., antecedent strategies), and others, in response to the production of UVB (e.g., consequential strategies).

Antecedent Strategies

Antecedent strategies do not necessarily involve direct intervention. These strategies are analogous to what have been referred to as antecedent manipulations (Horner et al., 1990). They address interactive and situational determinants of UVB (antecedent conditions), and, if necessary, alter those conditions to promote the use of more conventional forms of communication (Prizant & Wetherby, 1988). Determinants of UVB for an individual must be derived from assessment, and ongoing monitoring of changes in UVB should follow the implementation of strategies. The following are examples of antecedent strategies.

1. *Modify a situation if it is known to result in challenging UVB.* When challenging UVB is associated with an emotionally arousing (i.e., confusing or disorganizing) situation, modification of the situation may be an effective first-line strategy to reduce its occurrence. For example, reducing or dampening aversive sensory stimulation (e.g., loud noises), heightening structure and routine in unstructured activities, or simplifying new and difficult tasks or routines may serve to reduce UVB if it is found to be precipitated by anxiety associated with these types of circumstances.

2. *Prepare the individual for potential emotionally arousing situations.* When patterns of UVB are found to be correlated with specific situational determinants or events that cannot be changed, such as unplanned violation of regular routines, or other "must do" events that may be negatively emotionally arousing, an individual can be prepared to anticipate such events. Strategies to achieve this end may include the use of picture or written-word schedules with some discussion about the event(s), or the use of relaxation procedures (Cautela & Groden, 1981). The primary goal

is to help an individual remain calm or self-regulate emotionally. Achieving emotional self-regulation is supported by the predictability of events and by a learner's ability to anticipate and plan cognitively for their occurrence (Prizant & Wetherby, 1990). Anticipation and planning may be fostered by using supports such as calendars and daily schedules and should result in fewer negatively arousing incidents precipitated by unpredictability of, or change in, scheduled activities or events (Prizant & Schuler, 1987).

3. *Simplify language input and vary adult interaction style. Simplify language input* is a cardinal rule when interacting with individuals who have communication impairments. However, an individual's comprehension and production abilities may be overestimated because of the apparent (but not real) complexity of some forms of UVB, especially echolalia. Overestimation of linguistic competence may result in the partner's use of language that is too complex for the individual to comprehend. For example, an individual who uses delayed echoic utterances of up to eight words in length may actually be at a one- to three-word utterance level of generative language (Prizant & Rydell, 1984), yet the production of these longer utterances may lead others to overestimate his or her language comprehension and production abilities. As mentioned earlier, a factor found to result in greater occurrence of UVB is comprehension difficulty. Thus, reducing complexity of language input is a major intervention consideration. Furthermore, when UVB is indicative of limited comprehension and results from interpersonal communicative demands, appropriate modifications in communicative partners' interactive style are warranted. For instance, facilitative styles of verbal interaction have been found to promote increased occurrences of communicative initiations, topic initiations, and unprompted requesting and providing of information. Conventional verbal behavior occurs with greater frequency within less demanding, adult-facilitative interaction contexts (Rydell, 1989; Rydell & Mirenda, 1991).

With individuals who are extremely passive and show little or no evidence of social-communicative initiation, a more directive adult style may be warranted. A higher level of adult social-communicative control and structure may be needed to elicit verbal interaction for these individuals. In such situations, UVB may serve a useful purpose in reducing the information-processing load associated with high-demand interaction contexts while allowing a passive individual to experience some degree of reciprocity in social exchange. Furthermore, UVB may eventually serve a variety of cognitive and social-communicative functions and may become the vehicle by which an individual acquires more conventional forms.

4. *Provide relevant language during activities that allow for decision making and choice making.* A major challenge faced by persons with UVB is the acquisition of language forms that relate to objects and events in appropriate contexts. Given that UVB often is "borrowed" language, based on the repetition of others' speech, it is essential that the language environment includes models that are relevant and meaningful in context. Decision making and choice making in daily activities provide a motivating context for individuals to learn to use conventional forms of verbal behavior with clear consequences. Because of the tendency of persons with UVB to repeat utterances when highly motivated, developmentally appropriate language models, provided in contexts of requesting or rejecting items, form an intervention strategy that can promote a conventional verbal repertoire. Choices of foods for lunch, leisure activities, and so on, can be offered throughout the day. Relevant and clear language should be modeled, along with visual supports (e.g., pictures) if necessary, when presenting possible choices to an individual.

Consequential Strategies

Consequential strategies are more direct and are implemented by communicative partners as specific responses to the production of UVB in naturalistic contexts. They may also include the following teaching activities, which attempt to replace UVB with more conventional and appropriate communicative forms.

1. *Replace challenging UVB with more conventional means to communicate.* As noted in Chapter 23, a basic theme underlying approaches to challenging behavior is the need to help an individual to acquire more conventional

forms that serve the same communicative function (Burke, 1990; Donnellan et al., 1984; Durand & Crimmins, 1987; Evans & Meyer, 1985; Prizant & Wetherby, 1985). Available approaches to challenging and unconventional behavior that help individuals acquire more conventional communicative forms are clearly relevant to UVB (see Carr et al., 1994; Reichle & Wacker, 1993, for detailed information on communicative alternatives to challenging behavior). For example, situations may be set up to teach an individual to state "Work all finished," rather than protesting through unconventional UVB and/or nonverbal means.

2. *Respond to communicative intent and relate UVB to objects and events in the environment.* If UVB is produced with apparent communicative intent, we recommend that communicative partners respond with contingent simplification of utterances approximating an individual's true language level and processing capacity. If possible, communicative partners should attempt to emphasize the relationships between UVB and environmental referents (objects, actions, people). While providing a simplified model or recast model of UVB, demonstrative gestures (e.g., pointing, touching) and action demonstration can be used to relate utterances to the immediate context. Modeling language in a context of active involvement and in synchrony with relevant action patterns is a powerful teaching strategy for children who produce UVB (Fay & Schuler, 1980). If UVB is noninteractive and not relevant to the situational context, and if its production interferes with a person's ability to participate in educational and social activities, it may be necessary to redirect the individual's attention and provide language models that are more relevant to ongoing activities.

3. *Augment verbal communicative behavior with conventional nonspeech communicative means.* When a systemic view is taken regarding UVB, introduction of nonspeech augmentative communicative means may be an important strategy for helping individuals with UVB to communicate in more conventional ways. Unfortunately, because an individual may be producing some recognizable speech, interventions sometimes focus too narrowly on oral language development. We are not aware of any published research that directly addresses

the effect of augmentative system use on UVB. However, in our experience, two general benefits are apparent. First, individuals with highly unconventional and challenging UVB are able to communicate intentions more efficiently and conventionally through augmentative means, with a concomitant reduction in challenging UVB. Second, for individuals whose UVB is clearly functional and transitional, and co-occurs with functional language, augmentative means may provide a backup or "safety-net" function in difficult or stressful circumstances, and may also help an individual to participate more actively in communicative exchange while transitioning to primarily oral language means over time. This latter pattern appears more typical for younger individuals. (For a comprehensive consideration of these and other issues in augmentative communication, see Beukelman & Mirenda, 1992, and Reichle, Sigafoos, & York, 1991.)

4. *Make interventions for UVB positive and supportive.* Research has demonstrated that UVB often is socially motivated and functional, and, in some cases, may represent a transitional phase to more conventional communication. Therefore, an individual should never be punished for producing UVB. Whether it is intentional and interactive, or is a primary strategy for communication, the use of punishment amounts to admonishing a person for his or her limitations in acquiring conventional means to communicate. Direct intervention and physical redirection may be necessary to counteract production of highly stereotypic repetitive UVB; however, this type of UVB usually comprises a small portion of an individual's verbal production and most typically occurs during unstructured or transitional periods, or periods of high arousal. Use of positive interventions, including the strategies discussed above, should be sufficient to address even the most challenging forms of UVB.

In summary, communicative intervention strategies and goals addressing UVB should include methods that involve the modification of environmental and situational determinants of UVB, including partners' interactive style, to help preclude the production of UVB when it is a function of limited comprehension, or when it becomes challenging. Additional strategies include helping an individual acquire more conventional language forms, and, when appropriate, augmentative communication options. Concurrently, interventions must take into account that many forms of UVB (e.g., echolalia) may be important compensatory strategies that are part of an individual's natural transition to more conventional communication.

Addressing Comprehension Problems

Specific activities can be planned to improve comprehension of lexical and semantic–syntactic forms. Modifications in daily routines and activities may serve to enhance comprehension of functional vocabulary and relational meaning in multiword utterances, at a level appropriate to an individual's needs. For many individuals at emerging language levels, the use of visual supports to facilitate language comprehension and language use can be helpful (Hodgdon, 1995). Comprehension of language will be most greatly affected by the type of language input a person is exposed to, and the strategies used by communicative partners to optimize attention. Additionally, cues accompanying verbal messages enhance comprehension. Therefore, language adjustments and gestural and situational cues used by communicative partners will have a great influence on comprehension. Table 25.5 provides some guidelines for how communicative partners may adjust language to support comprehension for individuals at this level.

Summary of Assessment and Intervention for Emerging and Early Language Levels

The significant assessment concerns at this level include developing a profile of communication abilities and weaknesses that addresses expressive and receptive language, social-communicative behavior and socioemotional issues, and language-related cognitive skills. Intervention concerns for persons at emerging and early language levels include development and expansion of verbal communicative means and functions, strategies to deal with unconventional verbal behavior, and ways to enhance comprehension. We believe strongly that the interrelationships between communicative and socioemotional competence must be scrutinized for each individual,

TABLE 25.5   Guidelines for Simplifying Language Input for Emerging Language Levels

1. Adjust the complexity of language to the level of the individual:
   a. through language structure (how you talk)
   b. through language content (what you talk about).
2. Avoid excessive talking; speak in clearly articulated utterances.
3. Attempt to get an individual's attention before beginning to speak:
   a. call his or her name
   b. use physical direction if necessary.
4. Talk about relevant topics—what he or she:
   a. is doing or attending to
   b. is about to do
   c. has just done
   d. is familiar with.
5. Use repetition, redundancy, and paraphrasing.
6. Use "buildups" and "breakdowns" to help an individual learn about language structure:
   a. buildup: "Put on. Shoe on. Put shoe on."
   b. breakdown: "Take your spoon and eat the cereal. Take spoon, spoon [with point], take cereal, eat cereal."
7. If possible, relate utterances to objects, actions, and events in the environment through gestures, touching, and action demonstration.
8. If possible, relate echolalia to aspects of the environment, through simplification of such utterances, and action demonstration.
9. Segment utterances clearly by using stress, intonation, and pause.
10. If an individual does something negative, "bite your lip." Indicate displeasure through a lower, serious voice, and facial expression. Do not create a display of exaggerated volume and pitch, and exaggerated anger.
11. If necessary, use gestures to supplement speech.
12. Let an individual know that you are a willing listener by attending to his or her communicative attempts.
13. If an individual cannot communicate through speech or signs, encourage him or her to "show" you, and provide the words.
14. If requests or demands cannot be fulfilled, respond simply and consistently (e.g., "No juice now").
15. Use language to help an individual anticipate future events, especially unexpected changes in routine.
16. Use language to review completed events, by discussing, for example, a trip you have taken, people you have visited, and so on.

Note: These guidelines pertain to speech, to sign language, and/or to total communication.

for progress in communication has been shown to preclude behavioral difficulties, and to contribute to emotional regulation. For further information regarding the selection of specific programmatic content and strategies for persons at emerging and early language levels, see Charlop and Haymes (1994), Koegel and Johnson (1989), Prizant (1988), Twachtman (1995), Watson et al., (1989), and Wetherby and Prizant (1992).

ASSESSMENT AND INTERVENTION ISSUES FOR PERSONS AT MORE ADVANCED LANGUAGE LEVELS

Challenges and Issues at More Advanced Language Levels

For individuals beyond emerging and early language stages, more sophisticated linguistic ability may not necessarily ensure consistently effective and successful communicative interactions. The social use of language in natural interactions remains a significant challenge. Social-communicative difficulties are believed to be closely tied to the social-cognitive limitations inherent to autism and PDD (Frith, 1989). Difficulties that remain in important areas of social-communicative interactions may preclude communicative success, and typically are exacerbated when communicative interactions occur in unfamiliar settings, with unfamiliar listeners, and in stressful or anxiety-arousing circumstances. Such difficulties include: (a) understanding the communicative needs of listeners (e.g., how much information to provide, adjustments relative to familiar vs. unfamiliar listeners, recognizing and repairing breakdowns); (b) understanding the communicative requirements of different social situations (e.g., politeness vs. directness in language use); and (c) understanding and adhering to conventions of conversational interactions (e.g., initiating, maintaining, and terminating conversations; topic maintenance skills). Problems may also remain in the use of language forms that are idiosyncratic (i.e., unconventional forms) and therefore meaningful only to listeners familiar with an individual's communicative patterns. The following are more specific challenges and issues that should be addressed in assessment and intervention for individuals who are beyond emerging language stages.

1. Language comprehension and social-cognitive limitations experienced by persons with autism and PDD adversely affect conversational ability. The difficulties in comprehension and use of verbal and nonverbal behavior (Tantam, Holmes, & Cordess, 1993), and the limited understanding of socially embedded events and routines (Loveland & Tunali, 1991) make participation in conversational interactions challenging. Typically, both the content and the structure of conversational exchange are supported by reading a partner's nonverbal behavior to determine when adjustments and repairs are necessary. Furthermore, understanding of social contexts and events supports conversations. Difficulties in both these areas are confounding factors in considering conversational competence.

2. Verbal and nonverbal conventions of discourse may be violated by persons with autism and PDD, thereby affecting the success of communicative exchanges. Limited knowledge and inflexible use of conversational openings and closings may affect the social acceptability of communicative exchange (Hurtig et al., 1982). Conversation may be limited to specific topics of interest, and communicative partners' efforts to shift attention to new topics, or to topics of limited interest to an individual, may not succeed (Prizant, 1988).

3. For some individuals, learned verbal "scripts" may be applied too rigidly, with few, if any, adjustments for different communicative or situational contexts. For example, question asking may be repetitive or incessant, or there may be expectations regarding specific answers previously provided by others.

4. Ability to recognize and repair communication breakdowns may be limited. When one is not able to take the communicative perspective of others, recognition of unsuccessful communicative attempts may occur only infrequently. Even when breakdowns are recognized, strategies to repair those breakdowns may be few, and may be applied inappropriately.

5. Unconventional verbal forms used with clear intent may be difficult to "read," especially for unfamiliar partners. Many forms may be idiosyncratic or "metaphorical," with little apparent relevance to the context. These challenges, which we discussed earlier and which first appear with movement to linguistically based communication, may continue, even as language abilities increase (Kanner, 1946; Prizant & Rydell, 1993; Volden & Lord, 1991).

6. Language use in more complex and less familiar social situations may be especially challenging. The requirements of communicative exchange involving multiple partners across different social situations compound difficulties. Engaging appropriately in different discourse genres (e.g., storytelling, open-ended conversations, describing personally experienced events) may pose further difficulties because of the advanced social-cognitive and linguistic knowledge necessary to participate successfully in different types of discourse (Lund & Duchan, 1993).

Thus, because of the myriad of challenges faced by more able persons with autism or PDD, clinicians, educators, and caregivers must be clear in selecting, for communication enhancement, goals that will have the greatest positive impact on an individual's communicative competence. Goals will therefore vary relative to an individual's developmental profile of strengths and needs, and functional needs in situations and contexts experienced most frequently. Assessment must be directed toward determining the most crucial goals.

Assessment Domains

For persons who have acquired sufficient linguistic knowledge to be able to generate novel utterances consistently, and who, therefore, use echolalia and other forms of UVB only under limited circumstances (e.g., during states of confusion or fatigue, or as a turn-filling strategy), the focus in assessment and intervention efforts shifts to the following concerns: (a) the appropriate use of language and nonverbal communicative behaviors in a wide range of conversational contexts, (b) the acquisition of the ability to make metacommunicative judgments about communicative effectiveness and appropriate behavior to support conversational interactions, and to develop strategies to repair breakdowns; and

(c) the use of both spoken and written language as tools for learning, planning, and anticipating events, and for emotional regulation.

To some degree, these concerns also are relevant for those at emerging language levels; however, the distinction is a matter of emphasis and expectation of progress in planning for intervention. In general, for more able individuals, one would expect increased ability to engage in longer cohesive sequences of linguistic exchange and social interaction, and to take greater responsibility in fulfilling a role as an interactional partner. Furthermore, because persons of greater ability are expected to engage in a broader range of interactive experiences with greater independence, there is an increased need to be able to judge the communicative demands of different situations as well as to reflect on the success of communicative exchanges. Along with relevant assessment domains discussed earlier under emerging language issues, assessment should address language and communicative abilities in the areas discussed in the following sections.

Communication about Past and Future Events

The social, cognitive, and linguistic requirements of communicating about past or future events far exceed the requirements of communicating about events in the immediate environment. Therefore, significant discrepancies between communication abilities are to be expected, depending on whether discourse is supported by events in the immediate environment. These abilities must be addressed in constructing the picture of an individual's communication system.

Conversational Abilities Necessary for Successful Communication in More Complex Interactions

The literature on conversational abilities and on analysis of nonverbal behavior in human communication has proliferated over the past decade (Gallagher & Prutting, 1983; Lund & Duchan, 1993). This literature has helped to provide greater insight into the difficulties that individuals with autism and PDD experience with both verbal and nonverbal aspects of communication. It may be unreasonable to expect individuals who are so challenged in understanding and processing subtle social cues and social events to be able to learn and understand the requirements of conversational interactions across social contexts. However, from this recent literature, which offers a clearer understanding of what constitutes effective dyadic and larger group interactions, frameworks are provided for assessing abilities and for planning facilitative contexts for the acquisition of knowledge of verbal and nonverbal dimensions of conversational interactions.

Abilities required for successful conversational exchange include aspects of both verbal and nonverbal behavior. Specific abilities examined in assessment depend on an individual's level of communicative competence, as well as communicative needs and requirements in typical interactions. Lapidus (1985) and Brinton and Fujiki (1989) provided frameworks for analyzing conversational skills. Both frameworks were developed for analysis of conversational behavior of persons with developmental disabilities, including autism and PDD, and are based on literature in pragmatics. A primary purpose of this type of analysis is to identify major sources of breakdowns within, or barriers to, conversational and social interactions. Specific barriers that are most relevant to autism and PDD are listed in Table 25.6. These barriers involve behavior of both communicative partners, for, as noted in Chapter 23, we believe that each partner plays a major role in contributing to and supporting successful communicative transactions.

For analyzing discourse strategies, Lapidus (1985) provided a detailed framework that is divided into verbal and nonverbal domains (see Table 25.7). The verbal domain includes such general areas as attending, turn-taking, initiating conversation, maintaining conversation, recognizing breakdowns, developing strategies to repair conversational breakdowns, acquiring metalinguistic knowledge, acquiring sociolinguistic sensitivity while allowing for style adjustments, and using politeness and knowledge of conventions for terminating conversations. Domains of nonverbal behavior in this framework include use of gestures, eye gaze, facial expression, head

TABLE 25.6 Major Sources of Conversational and Interactional Breakdowns

1. Inflexibility of routines (verbal or nonverbal).
2. Competing motor stereotypies, postural and movement violations.
3. Gaze aversion.
4. Inability or unwillingness to shift focus of attention (agenda differences resulting in lack of joint reference).
5. Inability to shift topic or focus of discussion to partner's topic.
6. Inability to maintain topic of interaction once established.
7. Use of unconventional verbal behavior.
8. Insufficient provision of background information.
9. Partner's inability to adjust language level at semantic–syntactic levels.
10. Partner's inability to allow sufficient time for processing of language.
11. Deficient or minimal use of repair strategies.

nods, posture, proximity, bodily contact, head and body orientation, and paralanguage.

Topic Management Skills

A basic requirement of successful discourse is the ability to clearly introduce topics, follow up and maintain topics introduced by others, add new and relevant information appropriate to the topic of focus, and mark topic shifts as necessary. The ability to manage a topic in communicative exchange is a more generic skill that cuts across different types or genres of conversational and narrative discourse. Unfortunately, topic management difficulties often result in communication breakdowns, and assessment of such skills is necessary for intervention planning.

Knowledge of Situational and Communicative "Scripts"

In language-based communication enhancement, there is an increasing focus on knowledge of communicative events and on the discourse requirements of events, rather than on teaching language skills in isolated "context-stripped" situations (Duchan, 1991; Sonnenmeier, 1994). This literature is supported by a number of basic premises. First, real-life situations typically are organized into cohesive events; therefore, there is potential for greater carryover and generalization to everyday experiences when intervention is focused on events. Second, it makes sense to emphasize the meaning and functionality of events, rather than isolated behaviors. It is well accepted that persons with autism and PDD have particular difficulties in deriving meaning from, and understanding relationships within and among, social events. Finally, some important events that are a part of daily experiences are characterized by relatively fixed communicative exchanges, both in turn structure and in the content of language used. Examples include using a telephone, ordering food in a restaurant, engaging in the discourse of classroom instruction and response, and so on. Specific conventions of discourse, including verbal and nonverbal behavior, vary according to different social contexts. The types of events that a person engages in, and successes and breakdowns in these real-life contexts, should be documented to prioritize intervention goals.

Use of Language to Plan, Problem Solve, and Organize Life Schedules and Routines

For more able and older persons, there are greater expectations for problem solving, planning and achieving goals, and participating in daily routines independently. The most common language-based tools used for planning and in self-organization are written language and internalized or "inner language," by which one can represent, through symbolic means, "lists" of activities and events to be performed, goals to be accomplished, obligations to be met, and the like. More able individuals with autism and PDD may not spontaneously develop strategies for dealing with life schedules and routines. On the other hand, many persons with autism and PDD become so obsessed with life routines and schedules that the primary goal often appears to be to stay rigidly on schedule rather than to enjoy activities. We have found that some individuals who do not develop strategies to externalize schedules (e.g., keep a written list of activities) often become so preoccupied with thinking

TABLE 25.7   Assessment and Intervention Domains for Verbal and Nonverbal Discourse Skills

Verbal Discourse Skills

1. Attending
   Attends to partner.
   Secures other's attention.
   Modifies signals based on cues of attention.

2. Turn-taking
   Initiates greetings.
   Responds to greetings.
   Follows partner's turn with appropriate utterance.
   Yields turn when appropriate.
   Allows partner to complete turn without
      interrupting.
   Can participate in discourse over multiple turns.

3. Initiating conversation
   Introduces/establishes conversation or topic:
      a. Uses attention getters.
      b. Uses comments.
      c. Requests information.
      d. Uses variety of strategies.
   Selects appropriate topic.
   Takes listener's perspective by focusing on new
      information.
   Can discuss a variety of topics.

4. Maintaining conversation
   Acknowledges others' comments.
   Questions appropriately.
   Uses contingent responses/comments.
   Presents appropriate amounts of information.
   Presents valid and relevant information.
   Signals topic shift.
   Uses repetition (echolalia) to maintain
      conversation.
   Requests clarification.
   Responds to clarification requests.

5. Breakdown and repair
   Recognizes breakdown.
   Requests clarification.
   Responds to request for clarification.

6. Metalinguistic knowledge
   Uses/understands metaphors or idioms.
   Tells/Understands jokes.
   Understands teasing.
   Gives/Understands warnings.
   Gives/Understands hints.

7. Sociolinguistic sensitivity
   Adjusts speaking style according to listener's
      age, status, sex, and familiarity.
   Uses politeness markers and forms.
   Uses appropriate vocal volume and intonation.
   Avoids socially inappropriate topics.

8. Terminates conversations appropriately

Nonverbal Discourse Skills

1. Use of gestures
   Points to support language use.
   Gestures for size and distance.
   Does not use extraneous movements that interfere
      with communication.

2. Eye gaze
   Establishes eye contact prior to initiating
      communication.
   Looks at speaker when listening.
   Uses gaze checks to signal attention to speaker.
   Uses gaze appropriately (duration and timing).

3. Facial expression
   Display of affect is appropriate to situation.
   Does not display extraneous facial movements.

4. Use of head nods and head shakes
   To signal affirmation.
   To signal denial/refusal.
   To signal attention to speaker and comprehension
      of message.

5. Posture
   Is conducive to face-to-face interaction.
   Stands or sits appropriately in situation.

6. Proximity
   Moves closer to initiate interaction.
   Uses appropriate distance.
   Moves away to terminate interaction.

7. Bodily contact
   Shakes hands appropriately.
   Uses touch to secure attention.
   Does not exhibit inappropriate touching during
      interaction.

8. Orientation
   Uses appropriate head and body orientation when
      seated or standing.

9. Paralanguage
   Uses appropriate features for:
      a. Volume.
      b. Intonation.
      c. Pitch.
      d. Vocal quality.
      e. Stress.
      f. Rate.
   Speaks fluently.
   Does not produce extraneous sounds or jargon.

Note: Adapted from "Developing Communication and Language Skills in Autism," by D. Lapidus, 1985, unpublished manuscript, Nassau Center for Developmental Disabilities. New York, NY.

about routine that it may become difficult for them to shift attention to the needs of the moment. Such abilities must be addressed in assessment, especially because of their significance in living independently and taking greater responsibility in making decisions.

Use of Language for Emotional Expression and Emotional Regulation across Socioemotional Contexts

Prizant and Meyer (1993) discussed a number of assessment questions that address the relationships among language and communicative competence, emotional expression, and emotional regulation (see Table 25.3). Issues that are particularly relevant at more advanced language levels include:

1. Does communicative competence vary significantly with different communicative partners? The nature of relationships with others may have a great influence on communicative motivation and ability.
2. Does communicative competence vary significantly in comfortable or familiar contexts as opposed to unfamiliar emotionally arousing contexts? Emotional arousal relative to different situations will likely affect communication ability.
3. How does degree of emotional arousal (positive or negative) influence communicative competence (e.g., the person withdraws, speech becomes disorganized, the person uses developmentally less sophisticated means to express intentions, and so on)?
4. Does a person demonstrate use of self-regulatory strategies to modulate arousal? Self-regulatory strategies may include reference to a personal calendar or organizer when temporally disorganized, or use of self-calming or self-soothing strategies such as rehearsing potentially difficult circumstances.
5. Does a person demonstrate mutual regulatory strategies to modulate arousal? Mutual regulatory strategies may include requesting assistance from others to reduce anxiety, or communicating one's emotional state (using language to express fear, anger, excitement, and so on, rather than acting

out or withdrawing) so that communicative partners may respond in a supportive manner.
6. What are the most effective strategies communicative partners can use to help an individual regulate extreme states of arousal? Is language an effective tool to help a person stay calm and relaxed when aroused (e.g., through reassuring, reasoning), or are other strategies necessary (e.g., distraction, such as listening to music; leaving a situation, etc.)?

It is essential to address socioemotional issues in documenting communicative competence for persons who are at more advanced language levels. Regardless of a person's abilities in familiar and routine situations, emotionally dysregulating circumstances may have a major impact on language comprehension and use. In the most extreme circumstances, we have observed persons who are quite verbal when calm and relaxed become selectively mute when confused or upset. Intervention strategies can help persons stay calm or be prepared for such situations.

In summary, for persons beyond emerging language stages, assessment focuses on the ability to communicate about past and future events, to follow social conventions of verbal and nonverbal behavior that contribute to appropriate and effective communication in everyday conversational exchange, to use language as a tool for problem solving and planning, and to regulate emotional arousal through language and communication.

COMMUNICATION ENHANCEMENT AT MORE ADVANCED LANGUAGE LEVELS

For persons at emerging and early language levels, a primary goal is the acquisition of linguistic means to communicate and the effective use of those skills in interactions with others. At more advanced language levels, the focus of communication enhancement shifts to effective use of language and nonverbal communicative skills in conversational interactions involving more complex and decontextualized topics. Effective language use is determined by the appropriateness of language and communicative behavior relative to the social demands and conventions of social contexts; therefore, intervention must also address understanding of social situations (Duchan, 1986; Gray, 1995). Language for learning (i.e., to acquire information through oral and written modalities and to problem solve; Westby, 1991) and for emotional regulation (Prizant & Meyer, 1993) also are major foci of intervention efforts. Continued development of new vocabulary and more advanced linguistic knowledge in expressive and receptive modalities is also relevant; however, such learning should be embedded in the social use of language across interpersonal and situational contexts (Brinton & Fujiki, 1994). The choice of specific goals must be informed by a number of factors related to an individual, including: (a) chronological age; (b) communicative needs based on typical communicative challenges faced in daily interactions, and (c) developmental abilities, to ensure that new communicative skills are within the "zone of proximal development" (Vygotsky, 1933/ 1978, 1986) and not too far below or too far beyond a person's capabilities. The generic goals described in the following subsections are relevant and should be considered for most persons within this range of abilities.

Ability to Convey Information about Past and Future Events

A hallmark of more advanced communication is language use referring to past and future events. As the transition is made between early language levels and more advanced language use, individuals will begin to refer to just-completed events and anticipated events. Language use referring to past and future events typically first occurs within the context of familiar and frequently recurring routines, and indicates a person's ability to internally represent and recall events—initially, with the support of the immediate context, and eventually, without available contextual cues. Because of the symbolic and representational requirements of past and future language use, movement beyond contextually supported language use is a difficult hurdle for many persons with autism and PDD. Interestingly, many persons

are quite able to replicate past utterances or events in a rote and unanalyzed manner, even though the ability to reflect on and discuss events from a metarepresentational perspective may be limited.

This ability may be approached through frequent practice in reviewing and discussing, first, recently completed events or routine events that are about to occur, and, eventually, events more removed in time and space. The use of visual and organizational supports such as calendars, picture schedules, photographs, and journals is typically quite effective, especially when caregivers and communicative partners systematically model language to discuss past and future events. As an aid to language acquisition and language use, visual representation of events may provide the necessary support to enable an individual to discuss past and future events when the cognitive demands for recall, prediction, or expression about such events may be too difficult in an oral language mode. Coordination between different living environments, such as school and home, further enhances opportunities to develop skills in this area. Table 25.8 offers additional guidelines for encouraging communication about past and future events.

Acquisition of Conversational Skills and Strategies

Conversations involve coordinated, multifaceted, and interwoven aspects of verbal and nonverbal behavior reflecting a person's knowledge of requirements of social situations as well as social conventions of behavior. Ongoing adjustments in conversational exchange are necessary to respond to partners' changing contributions to the exchange; they are not unlike the adjustments necessary to exchange volleys in various sports (Lund & Duchan, 1993). In intervention, at least three areas might be addressed for persons at more advanced language levels:

1. Verbal conventions for initiating interactions, exchanging turns during interactions, and terminating interactions.
2. Use of nonverbal and paralinguistic behavior to support social interactions.

TABLE 25.8   Strategies to Encourage Communication about Past and Future Events

1. Review a sequence of activities or steps within an activity prior to, and following completion of, the activity. Start with a number of sequences within a person's processing capacity.

2. Use external supports such as activity boards or picture schedules, and refer to these for persons who have not yet internally represented this information.

3. For special events or activities, develop books with photographs to review these events and to plan for future similar events.

4. Mark special events, holidays, and activities, and discuss how much time will pass before they occur. Always use visual displays (e.g., calendars) to support this discussion.

5. Exchange information between home and school, to encourage discussion about events that occur in other environments. Depending on a person's language abilities, strategies might include:
    a. Using a communication book, or "fill-in" worksheets, so that parents can share with school staff relevant information about events at home, and vice versa.
    b. Sending photographs from home to school, and vice versa.
    c. Setting up conversation or "show and tell" times for persons to share information about activities at home or special family activities. The supports noted above can be used in demonstrations.

6. Provide practice activities to convey information to other staff or other persons. For example, a student may be asked to go to another classroom to deliver a message.

7. Introduce ongoing projects that may take days or even weeks to complete. Prior to each return to the project, review what has been done and what needs to be done.

8. Leave open slots in a person's schedule so that he or she may have the opportunity to select a future activity.

9. Initially, use concrete words to specify future time (e.g., after lunch, or at two o'clock, rather than "later"). Time words with shifting reference (e.g., yesterday, today, tomorrow, earlier, later) may initially be difficult for some persons to understand.

10. Introduce concepts of conditional and causal links between events, when discussing past and future events (e.g.,"If it rains, we will not go swimming. We'll go to the gym." "We went for ice cream because you stayed with the class at the park.").

11. Provide opportunities to plan trips or special events, and increase requirements for children's participation, depending on their abilities (e.g., planning to buy Christmas gifts for family members).

3. Strategies for repairing communication breakdowns.

Verbal Conventions for Initiating Interactions, Exchanging Turns during Interactions, and Terminating Interactions

Conversations are governed by a variety of rules pertaining to these structural dimensions (Brinton & Fujiki, 1989). Because of the sociolinguistic sensitivity and adjustments required for appropriate participation, persons with autism and PDD often violate conversational conventions. Their violations may involve inappropriate use or absence of organizational devices such as conversational openers (e.g., "Hi! Good to see you.") or closings (e.g., "I have to get going now. It was good to see you."). Violations also may occur at the content level, for example, when a person talks repeatedly on the same topic, fails to follow up on the topic introduced by the partner, or suddenly shifts the topic without using a conversational device (e.g., "Oh, by the way," or "Did I mention that I saw Mary?") to mark the topic shift. Unfortunately, given the social-cognitive disabilities definitive of autism and PDD, such challenges are difficult to remediate because the individual must monitor and process multiple levels of social information. These may include subtle nonverbal cues communicating the partner's degree of interest or lack of interest, the topical flow of the exchange, and the degree to which both partners are following and understanding the exchange. However, by focusing on the major challenges and barriers to successful conversational exchange, teaching new skills, and heightening the individual's awareness of appropriate conversational behavior, much progress can be made. These goals may be approached through specially designed activities as well as by providing feedback during naturally occurring conversational exchange. The next generic goal is also an important aspect of conversational interaction.

Use of Nonverbal and Paralinguistic Behavior to Support Social Interactions

Problems in nonverbal and paralinguistic aspects of communicative behavior (e.g., body posture and orientation, eye contact, vocal volume) are frequently cited barriers to successful communication for persons with autism and PDD. The degree to which such challenges are present varies greatly from one individual to another. Assessment that documents the presence, absence, and appropriateness of these skills for an individual will help determine whether specific aspects of nonverbal and paralinguistic behavior need to be flagged as intervention goals (Lapidus, 1985; see Table 25.7). Intervention must address whether a behavior that is not occurring needs to occur (e.g., a person shows no visual regard to the partner), whether modifications and adjustments need to be made (e.g., a speaker stands at an inappropriate distance from the partner), or whether an interfering pattern of behavior needs to be controlled (e.g., a person moves incessantly while speaking, and distracts the listener). Intervention must then address whether an individual is aware of an interfering behavior, can be made aware of the behavior, and is able to learn rules that should be followed to enhance communicative effectiveness. Whether a pattern of behavior is interfering or inappropriate depends on factors such as the specific situation (e.g., it is inappropriate to speak loudly in a library but not in a gym) and the relationship status of the communicative partner (e.g., standing close to and touching a person may be acceptable behavior toward a friend but not toward a stranger).

If it is determined that particular patterns of behavior should be addressed in communication enhancement, a variety of strategies may be used. Many persons with autism and PDD may not engage spontaneously and frequently in interactions with others, especially unfamiliar persons. Therefore, we assume the need to structure somewhat contrived interactive situations periodically, so that more frequent opportunities are available for acquiring and applying social knowledge relative to conversational activities. Conversational activities can be derived from an individual's daily routines as well as from social experiences that have not yet occurred but are likely to be encountered, such as a job interview. Furthermore, activities must be viewed in terms of their cognitive demands and their levels of conversational complexity. For example, conversational language that is goal-directed, in which two or more individuals are working physically on a project together, may be more inherently motivating and less complex (due to contextual support) than language that is purely social with little or no relevance to the immediate context or instrumental goals (e.g., discussing past and future events, favorite activities, and so on). Opportunities for many types of conversational activities should be made available; however, the differing demands of each situation should be kept in mind. Table 25.9 provides a variety of dimensions to be considered in conversational activities. Berlin, Blank, and Rose (1980) also provide guidelines for analyzing the complexity of conversational dialogue.

It is often helpful to provide opportunities for individuals to be able to observe themselves or others, and make determinations about appropriate behavior. Charlop and Milstein (1989) used video modeling to help children with autism acquire conversational skills. Lapidus (1985) used videotape review (during interaction of small social groups) and role-playing activities to provide somewhat structured but rich interactive contexts for adolescents and adults with autism. Lapidus focused on helping individuals to acquire knowledge about appropriate behavior during conversational interactions, and to make metacommunicative judgments about their own and others' behavior in social interaction. General conversational conventions—use of eye contact, topic maintenance, and appropriate gestures—as well as behavior more specific to the style of individuals are discussed and practiced in social groups. This approach addresses the requisite abilities for appropriate interactions, as well as the significant problems of individual group members.

Perhaps because of the cognitive style in autism and PDD, there is a potential danger in teaching conversational behaviors in isolation:

TABLE 25.9   Some Dimensions of Complexity of Conversational Interactions

Less Complex	More Complex
Discussing observable events, aspects of the environment.	Discussing events outside of the immediate environment (temporally and spatially distant).
Discussing activities of considerable interest.	Discussing activities of little interest.
Discussing frequently recurring events.	Discussing hypothetical events or events that rarely occur.
Stating own preferences or attitudes.	Inferring other's preferences or attitudes.
Commenting on observable attributes or events.	Making judgments regarding logical relationships between events (e.g., causality, conditionality).
Dyadic interaction or small group interaction.	Larger group interaction.

the behaviors may be learned and then used either in inappropriate situations or to too extreme a degree (e.g., greeting every person encountered, maintaining eye contact for too long). Such problems are more likely to occur when isolated behaviors are trained out of context and in lieu of focusing on the purpose of the behaviors in relation to communicative events. Duchan (1986) discussed the concept of "sensemaking," which refers to what participants in an interaction think is going on in the interaction, and what ideas structure that thinking. Conversational breakdowns are more likely to occur when participants' sense of the event differs. On the other hand, if the larger purpose or the goal of a conversational interaction is understood, an individual will more likely be able to, or be motivated to recognize and repair conversation breakdowns. Thus, facilitation of conversational abilities and interactive strategies should occur in the context of communicative events in which the purpose or goal of the interaction is emphasized. In that way, conversational activities become a means of meeting particular goals. This transition can occur in regularly scheduled activities (e.g., cooking, crafts) or through role playing around typical activities (e.g., eating at a restaurant, purchasing items at a store), with subsequent carryover to more natural environments.

Strategies for Repairing Communication Breakdowns

Some of the most important—and most difficult to acquire—abilities relative to con-

versational behavior are those involving self-monitoring and self-evaluation, leading to the recognition and repair of breakdowns. Persons without significant linguistic disabilities may be poor communicators simply because of their inability to reflect on their own communicative behavior and utilize cues from others to modify their communicative behavior. The extent to which self-evaluation of communicative effectiveness is possible with persons with autism or PDD varies with the individual and the behavior in question. For example, it may be easier to self-monitor and adjust gaze behavior, and to understand its importance, than to provide feedback and signals of interest to the listener through head nods and other back-channel responses (e.g., "Yeah," "Uh-huh," and so on). Again, intervention priorities must be set based on careful assessment of factors that contribute to breakdowns in communication, and on an individual's current level of understanding of what constitutes effective communicative interactions.

The ability to recognize breakdowns in communication and utilize appropriate repair strategies is an essential part of conversational competence (Brinton & Fujiki, 1989). Typically, both partners must utilize strategies in order to ensure that successful exchange will continue; however, one must initially have the ability to recognize that a breakdown has occurred, in order to then attempt repair. Breakdowns may occur for a variety of reasons, and intervention efforts must address specific patterns determined to be operative for a person, based on assessment findings. As with other aspects of conversational behavior, increasing awareness of conversational breakdowns and teaching of repair strategies may occur within the context of contrived as well as naturalistic routines and activities, and may be incorporated in role playing and social skills groups.

Knowledge of Communicative Events, and Use of "Scripts" Specific to Particular Events

Recent approaches to intervention have moved toward utilizing typical and frequently occurring life events as the context and support for communication enhancement efforts (Duchan, 1991). Communication enhancement approaches utilizing this theme for persons with autism, PDD, and other developmental disabilities include "Joint Activity Routines" (Snyder-McLean et al., 1984), "Integrated Play Groups" (Wolfberg & Schuler, 1993), "Script-based Language Intervention" (Sonnenmeier, 1994), and "Sociodramatic Play" (Culatta, 1994; Goldstein & Strain, 1988). Although such strategies are useful for persons at prelinguistic and early language levels, they are particularly relevant for persons at more advanced language levels.

Common events that are experienced, or that may be planned, include typically occurring experiences such as domestic family routines (e.g., meals, self-care activities); activities associated with restaurants, stores, or visits to healthcare professionals such as doctors or dentists; and traveling or leisure activities with friends or family (Sonnenmeier, 1994). Interactions with persons without disabilities are often an important part of these efforts because of the movement toward providing educational services in inclusive settings, and the benefits of the linguistic and social models provided by persons who do not have communication disabilities. Within such routines, specific vocabulary, language structures serving relevant communicative functions, and specific discourse events may be modeled and practiced. When events are characterized by relatively fixed verbal exchanges and routines, such as ordering food at a restaurant, using the telephone, purchasing a bus ticket, and so on, the specific language requirements of each event first need to be determined, and can then be modeled and taught through role playing, with carryover to real-life contexts.

The approaches noted above use different teaching strategies with varying degrees of facilitator support (e.g., physical, gestural, verbal, graphic, or written prompts) and varying degrees of structure and prescription (e.g., loosely structured play to specifically scripted interactions). Although the topic has not been explored empirically, the relative efficacy of the different approaches is likely to vary according to factors such as the level of communicative and social ability of the participants, and the social complexity of the events. The major commonality is that each approach has as its goal the development of functional and spontaneous conversational skills and of the social knowledge necessary to participate actively and independently in the daily routines of living. At the same time, efforts are made to emphasize the goal of participation and the internal coherence of each event by not focusing too narrowly on discrete behaviors in lieu of the sense and purpose of the event.

Use of Reading and Writing Skills for Intrapersonal and Interpersonal Communicative Functions

We have emphasized that the cognitive style of persons with autism and PDD seems better suited to the processing of information in visuospatial formats because such information is less transient and less abstract than auditory information, and may take advantage of the superior visual processing skills of many individuals (Schuler, 1995). Resources are now available that specifically address these skills for enhancing communication (Hodgdon, 1995). As discussed earlier, many more able persons with autism have been reported to use or to understand written language prior to the use and comprehension of oral language. Some persons who acquire this ability without direct instruction at young ages evidence symptoms of hyperlexia; they may develop an ability to decode written language prior to understanding the linguistic forms that they are reading (Aram & Healy, 1988). Other individuals may not develop this ability spontaneously, but many more able persons demonstrate little difficulty in learning to read and to recognize graphic symbols, although comprehension may be somewhat limited. It is not uncommon for many persons to be highly motivated to engage in activities involving written words and symbols, probably because of their relative strengths in visuospatial processing and configurational processing, and the nontransient and fixed nature of such stimuli.

Some success with the use of graphic symbols with individuals with limited communicative abilities has been reported (LaVigna, 1977), yet there are few reports of the potential variety of uses of written language for more able persons with autism. Reports of particular approaches for persons with autism and PDD are beginning to appear (Berger, 1994), some of which utilize technology such as computers as learning tools. For individuals at prelinguistic and early language levels, pictures or written words can be used to generate daily or weekly schedules, to note changes that are occurring in regular routines, and even as a primary mode of communication for speakers who experience great difficulty in face-to-face interaction (see Chapter 24). For more able individuals, the use of written language—either as a cognitive or organizational tool, or as a communication tool—should always be considered as a possibility if it aids an individual in communicating more effectively and with greater efficiency. Although our clinical experience clearly indicates that much greater attention is being paid to the development of literacy skills for acquiring information, self-organization, and planning, it is our opinion that the potential of written language systems and literacy training for noncommunicative functions has not yet been fully realized for persons with autism and other developmental disabilities (Koppenhaver et al., 1991). Specific to more able individuals, use of computers in employment or everyday life activities may provide a modality that is readily accessible because the requirements of such activities are closely related to the relative learning strengths of persons with autism and PDD. However, in implementing programs directed toward the development of literacy skills, direct instruction is not enough. Persons must be immersed in literacy-rich environments so that learning can occur incidentally as well as

through direct instruction (Koppenhaver et al., 1991).

LANGUAGE AS A TOOL FOR EMOTIONAL REGULATION

Efforts to enhance language abilities among persons with language disabilities have traditionally emphasized functions of communication to express needs and share information. Little attention has been given to the potential function of language for emotional regulation. Prizant and Meyer (1993) defined emotional regulatory capacities as individuals' ability to develop and use various means to control or modulate their level of emotional arousal. Such capacities allow an individual to stay calm and focused, to problem-solve, to communicate, to maintain social engagement, and to be more "available" for learning.

Researchers have identified two types of emotional regulatory capacities that are believed to be essential for maintaining emotional regulation, especially during confusing or stressful circumstances (Garber & Dodge, 1991; Tronick, 1989) . Self-regulatory capacities involve the use of language to cope with potentially upsetting or dysregulating events by planning for such events. Mutual regulatory capacities involve the ability to solicit and secure the assistance of others in regulating emotional arousal. Self and mutual regulatory capacities can be mediated by the use of language (Garber & Dodge, 1991). Intervention strategies have begun to address emotional regulation through the use of pictures and imagery (Groden & LeVasseur, 1995) and relaxation procedures (Cautela & Groden, 1981). For more able individuals, the following language-based strategies may be helpful for both mutual and self-regulation.

1. *Development of vocabulary to share emotional states and experiences with others.* The acquisition of emotion words enables persons to objectify emotions, which may be an important step toward being able to develop some mastery over emotional arousal, rather than being at its mercy (Stern, 1985). Bretherton, Fritz, Zahn-Wexler, and Ridgeway (1986) noted that children whose parents used emotion words in relevant contexts acquired and

used emotion words earlier. Because of the potential relevance of emotional language to a person's socioemotional development, the development of the ability to express emotional states and categorize emotional experiences should be incorporated in intervention efforts. This may be accomplished by appropriate modeling of emotion words relative to a person's experiences, or by discussing and reviewing emotionally arousing circumstances while teaching alternative strategies to cope with such conditions.

2. *Preparing individuals for changes in routine.* Common problems involving emotional dysregulation include violations of schedule or routine, and confusion caused by the social requirements and rules of different situations. One of the great difficulties that many individuals experience is understanding changes in time schedules—either systematic changes, such as holidays or weekends, or, even worse, unpredictable changes such as cancellation of activities, teacher absences, or breaks in schedule. A cardinal rule regarding unexpected change or violations of routine is: Use language and visual aids to help individuals prepare for changes. Use of visual supports may help to concretize abstract concepts such as the time schedule or temporal structure of one's life routine. By seeing a depiction of time on a visuospatial dimension (e.g., denoting a daily schedule by a sequence of pictures or words relevant to particular events during the day), an individual may be able to feel more cognitively "comfortable" by being cognizant of and prepared for events. In addition, such displays may give individuals the power to rearrange schedules or routines according to their preference. Offering clear alternatives involving activities of interest often is helpful in dealing with these potentially emotionally arousing circumstances.

3. *Providing opportunities to review, understand, and discuss potentially problematic situations.* In addition to dealing with unpredictable change, communication enhancement efforts must encompass efforts to help individuals understand and cope with confusing or problematic social situations. Gray (1995) developed a multicomponent intervention approach, which she calls "Social Reading," to

deal with problem situations for persons with autism and PDD. The "Social Reading" approach involves the use of visually presented materials to improve social skills in problem situations. Three areas of instructional activities are utilized in this format: (a) "Social Stories," involving the development of personalized stories, written by professionals or caregivers, regarding difficult and confusing situations for persons with autism and PDD, and strategies and alternative responses for coping in such circumstances; (b) "Social Review," involving videotape recordings of problem situations, with subsequent review of tape segments to identify problem behavior and support the development of new social skills; and (c) "Social Assistance Activities," providing modifications and supports that utilize visual aids and computer work to both preclude the potential for confusion and problem behavior, and target circumstances that have proven to be problematic. In all cases, efforts are made to understand the perspective of the person with autism or PDD, while identifying and supporting the development of needed skills. Such activities focus on the development of both mutual and self-regulatory abilities through the identification and review of problem situations, and the development of appropriate language skills to manage in such circumstances.

4. *Use of language to request assistance and comfort.* An additional emotional regulatory strategy that helps to preclude or mitigate negative emotion is language use to request assistance and to request comfort. Unfortunately, more able persons with autism and PDD do not spontaneously develop these abilities, although their language may appear to be sufficiently developed to serve these functions. In both contrived and naturalistic learning contexts, strategies may be modeled and taught appropriate to a person's language abilities. Simply being able to ask for help—to indicate that "I don't understand," or "I need a break"—may preclude problematic reactions. When appropriate to a person's age, asking for a hug or for feedback on performance ("Am I doing OK?") may support emotional regulation. The ultimate goal is to enable a person to develop the means to maintain emotional

homeostasis under stressful situations, and language can play a major role toward achieving that goal.

In summary, for persons at more advanced language stages, major issues in language and communication assessment and intervention include: (a) communicating about past and future events; (b) identifying major sources of breakdown in conversational interactions in both verbal and nonverbal domains; (c) acquisition of appropriate conversational skills, including use of appropriate nonverbal and paralinguistic behavior in conversational interactions; (d) acquisition of some ability to make judgments about one's own communicative effectiveness, along with strategies to repair communication breakdowns; (e) developing an understanding of communicative events relative to typical conversational interactions that occur in such events; (f) use of written language as a tool for acquiring information and planning sequences of events; and (g) use of language for emotional regulation.

SUMMARY AND CONCLUSIONS

For most people, the acquisition of a flexible language system and an effective communicative style is of little concern. Our world is built largely on effective communication through spoken language and other symbol systems. It is somewhat of a paradox that for more able individuals with autism and PDD who have acquired language, the communicative disability may seem particularly pronounced because they have accomplished what appears to be a most difficult task—acquisition of the "tools" for communicating. However, knowledge of a linguistic system does not guarantee that an individual will be able to apply this knowledge effectively in everyday communicative interactions.

For the range of ability discussed in this chapter, initial concerns included acquisition of the requisite abilities (i.e., knowledge to formulate utterances and to comprehend others' utterances) and application of these abilities across a variety of contexts and interactive partners. For individuals with greater potential and ability, the focus shifts to larger units

of interaction in which individuals must take greater responsibility as interactive partners in adhering to social conventions in communication as well as in adjusting communicative style appropriately according to the needs of a situation. Only through recurring interactive experiences will persons with autism have a chance to acquire these abilities, and only to the extent that they experience some success in social endeavors will they be willing and motivated to communicate with others.

For professionals, the difficulty is finding the balance between understanding and respecting the manner by which a person with autism or PDD copes with the challenge of language acquisition and interpersonal communication, and the need to make prescriptive judgments about the abilities needed to function as independently as possible. Only professionals who have such understanding and respect have a right to support caregivers and persons with autism or PDD in the often frustrating processes of language acquisition and social communication.

Cross-References

General aspects of communicative development are discussed in Chapter 9. For issues in assessment, see Chapters 19 through 21. Curriculum development is the topic of Chapter 22. Other aspects of communication interventions are covered in Chapters 23 and 24.

REFERENCES

Aram, D.M., & Healy, J.F. (1988). Hyperlexia: A review of extraordinary word recognition. In L.K. Obler & D. Fein (Eds.), *The exceptional brain: Neuropsychology of talent and special abilities* (pp. 70–102). New York: Guilford Press.

Baltaxe, C.A.M., & Simmons, J.G. (1981). Disorders of language and childhood psychosis: Current concepts and approaches. In J. Darby (Ed.), *Speech evaluation in psychiatry* (pp. 285–328). New York: Grune & Stratton.

Bates, E. (1979). *The emergence of symbols: Cognition and communication in infancy.* New York: Academic Press.

Berger, C. (1994, July). *Teaching reading and writing skills to students with autism.* Paper presented at the Annual Convention of the Autism Society of America, Las Vegas, NV.

Berlin, L., Blank, M., & Rose, S. (1980). The language of instruction: The hidden complexity. *Topics in Language Disorders and Language Disabilities, 1,* 47–58.

Beukelman, D., & Mirenda, P. (1992). *Augmentative and alternative communication: Management of severe communication disorders in children and adults.* Baltimore: Brookes.

Bretherton, I., Fritz, J., Zahn-Wexler, C., & Ridgeway, D. (1986). Learning to talk about emotions: A functionalist perspective. *Child Development, 57,* 529–548.

Brinton, B., & Fujiki, M. (1989). Conversational management with language-impaired children: Pragmatic assessment and intervention. Rockville, MD: Aspen.

Brinton, B., & Fujiki, M. (1994). Ways to teach conversation. In J. Duchan, L. Hewitt, & R. Sonnenmeier (Eds.), *Pragmatics: From theory to practice* (pp. 59–71). Englewood Cliffs, NJ: Prentice-Hall.

Burke, G. (1990). Unconventional behavior: A communicative interpretation in individuals with severe disabilities. *Topics in Language Disorders, 10,* 75–86.

Carr, E., Levin, L., McConachaie, G., Carlson, J., Kemp, D., & Smith, C. (1994). *Communication-based intervention for problem behavior: A user's guide for producing positive change.* Baltimore: Brookes.

Cautela, J., & Groden, J. (1981). *Relaxation procedures for persons with developmental disabilities.* Champaign, IL: Research Press.

Chapman, R. (1981). Exploring children's communicative intent. In J. Miller (Ed.), *Assessing language production in children* (pp. 111–136). Baltimore: University Park Press.

Charlop, M. (1983). The effect of echolalia on acquisition and generalization of receptive labeling in autistic children. *Journal of Applied Behavior Analysis, 16,* 111–126.

Charlop, M., & Haymes, L.K. (1994). Speech and language acquisition and intervention: Behavioral approaches. In J. Matson (Ed.), *Autism in children and adults: Etiology, assessment, and intervention* (pp. 213–240). Pacific Grove, CA: Brooks/Cole.

Charlop, M., & Milstein, J. (1989). Teaching autistic children conversational speech using video modeling. *Journal of Applied Behavior Analysis, 22,* 275–285.

Culatta, B. (1994). Representational play and story enactments: Formats for language intervention. In J. Duchan, L. Hewitt, & R. Sonnen-

meier (Eds.), *Pragmatics: From theory to practice* (pp. 105–119). Englewood Cliffs, NJ: Prentice-Hall.

Donnellan, A., Mirenda, P., Mesaros, R., & Fassbender, L. (1984). Analyzing the communicative functions of aberrant behavior. *Journal of the Association for Persons with Severe Handicaps, 9,* 201–220.

Duchan, J.F. (1986). Language intervention through sensemaking and finetuning. In R. Schiefelbusch (Ed.), *Communicative competence: Assessment and language intervention* (pp. 182–212). Baltimore: University Park Press.

Duchan, J.F. (1991). Everyday events: Their role in language assessment and intervention. In T.M. Gallagher (Ed.), *Pragmatics of language: Clinical practice issues* (pp. 43–98). San Diego, CA: Singular Publishing Group.

Durand, V.M., & Crimmins, D. (1987). Assessment and treatment of psychotic speech in an autistic child. *Journal of Autism and Developmental Disorders, 17,* 17–28.

Elliott, R., Hall, K., & Soper, H. (1991). Analog language teaching vs. natural language teaching: Generalization and retention of language learning for adults with autism and mental retardation. *Journal of Autism and Developmental Disorders, 21,* 433–447.

Evans, I., & Meyer, L. (1985). *An educative approach to behavior problems: A practical decision model for interventions with severely handicapped learners.* Baltimore: Brookes.

Fay, W., & Schuler, A.L. (1980). *Emerging language in autistic children.* Baltimore: University Park Press.

Frith, U. (1989). *Autism: Explaining the enigma.* Oxford, England: Blackwell.

Gallagher, T., & Prutting, C. (Eds.). (1983). *Pragmatic assessment and intervention issues in language.* San Diego, CA: College Hill Press.

Garber, J., & Dodge, K. (1991). *The development of emotion regulation and dysregulation.* Cambridge, England: Cambridge University Press.

Goldstein, H., & Strain, P. (1988). Peers as communication intervention agents: Some new strategies and research findings. *Topics in Language Disorders, 9,* 44–57.

Grandin, T. (1995). The learning style of students with autism. In K. Quill (Ed.), *Teaching children with autism: Strategies to enhance communication and socialization.* Albany, NY: Delmar.

Gray, C. (1995). Teaching children with autism to "read" social situations. In K. Quill (Ed.), *Teaching children with autism: Strategies to enhance communication and socialization.* Albany, NY: Delmar.

Groden, J., & LeVasseur, P. (1995). Cognitive picture rehearsal: A system to teach self-control. In K. Quill (Ed.), *Teaching children with autism: Strategies to enhance communication and socialization.* Albany, NY: Delmar.

Hodgdon, L. (1995). *Visual strategies for improving communication—Volume 1.* Troy, MI: Quirk Roberts Publishing.

Horner, R.H., Dunlap, G., Koegel, R.L., Carr, E.G., Sailor, W., Anderson, J., Albin, R.W., & O'Neill, R.E. (1990). Toward a technology of "nonaversive" behavioral support. *Journal of the Association for Persons with Severe Handicaps, 15,* 125–132.

Howlin, P. (1981). The effectiveness of operant language training with autistic children. *Journal of Autism and Developmental Disorders, 11,* 89–106.

Hurtig, R., Ensrud, S., & Tomblin, B. (1982). The communicative function of question production in autistic children. *Journal of Autism and Developmental Disorders, 12,* 57–69.

Kanner, L. (1943). Autistic disturbances of affective contact. *Nervous Child, 2,* 217–250.

Kanner, L. (1946). Relevant and metaphorical language in early infantile autism. *American Journal of Psychiatry, 103,* 242–246.

Klin, A. (1991). Young autistic children's listening preferences in regard to speech: A possible characterization of the symptom of social withdrawal. *Journal of Autism and Developmental Disorders, 21,* 29–42.

Koegel, R., & Johnson, J. (1989). Motivating language use in autistic children. In G. Dawson (Ed.), *Autism: New perspectives on diagnosis, nature and treatment* (pp. 310–325). New York: Guilford Press.

Koegel, R., O'Dell, N., & Dunlap, G. (1988). Producing speech use in nonverbal autistic children by reinforcing attempts. *Journal of Autism and Developmental Disorders, 18,* 525–538.

Koppenhaver, D., Coleman, P., Kalmin, S., & Yoder, T. (1991) The implications of emergent literacy research with developmental disabilities. *American Journal of Speech-Language Pathology, 1,* 38–44.

Kurita, H. (1985). Infantile autism with speech loss after 30 months. *Journal of the American Academy of Child Psychiatry, 24,* 191–196.

Lahey, M. (1988). *Language disorders and language development.* New York: Macmillan.

Lapidus, D. (1985). *Developing communication and language skills in autism.* Unpublished manuscript. Nassau Center for Developmental Disabilities, Long Island, NY.

LaVigna, G.,(1977). Communication training in mute autistic adolescents using the written word. *Journal of Autism and Childhood Schizophrenia, 7,* 135–149.

Lord, C., & O'Neill, P. (1983). Language and communication needs of adolescents with autism. In E. Schopler & G. Mesibov (Eds.), *Autism in adolescents and adults* (pp. 57–77). New York: Plenum Press.

Lovaas, O.I. (1977). *The autistic child: Language development through behavior modification.* New York: Irvington.

Loveland, K., & Tunali, B. (1991). Social scripts for conversational interactions for autism and Down syndrome. *Journal of Autism and Developmental Disorders, 21,* 177–186.

Lund, N., & Duchan, J. (1993). *Assessing children's language in naturalistic contexts* (3rd ed.). Englewood Cliffs, NJ: Prentice-Hall.

McDonald, J. (1989). *Becoming conversational partners with children.* Chicago: Riverside.

McEachin, J.J., Smith, T., & Lovaas, O.I. (1993). Long-term outcome for children with autism who received early intensive behavioral treatment. *American Journal on Mental Retardation, 97,* 359–372.

Miller, J., & Paul, R. (1995). *The clinical assessment of language comprehension.* Baltimore: Brookes.

Nelson, N. (1993). *Childhood language disorders in context.* Columbus, OH: Merrill.

Owens, R. (1995). *Language disorders: A functional approach to assessment and intervention* (2nd ed.). Boston: Allyn & Bacon.

Peters, A. (1983). *The units of language acquisition:* Cambridge, England: Cambridge University Press.

Prizant, B.M. (1982). Speech-language pathologists and autistic children: What is our role? Part 1. *American Speech-Language Hearing Association Journal, 24,* 463–468.

Prizant, B.M. (1983a). Echolalia in autism: Assessment and intervention. *Seminars in Speech and Language, 4,* 63–77.

Prizant, B.M. (1983b). Language acquisition and communicative behavior in autism: Toward an understanding of the "whole" of it. *Journal of Speech and Hearing Disorders, 48,* 296–307.

Prizant, B.M. (1987). Clinical implications of echolalic behavior in autism. In T. Layton (Ed.), *Language and treatment of autistic and developmentally disordered children* (pp. 65–88). Springfield, IL: Thomas.

Prizant, B.M. (1988). Communication in autistic clients. In N. Lass, L. McReynolds, J. Northern, & D. Yoder (Eds.), *The handbook of speech-language pathology* (pp. 1014–1039). Toronto, Ontario, Canada: BC Decker.

Prizant, B.M., & Bailey, D. (1992). Facilitating the acquisition and use of communication skills. In D. Bailey & M. Wolery (Eds.), *Teaching infants and toddlers with handicaps* (pp. 299–361). New York: Merrill.

Prizant, B.M., & Duchan, J. (1981). The functions of immediate echolalia in autistic children. *Journal of Speech and Hearing Disorders, 46,* 241–249.

Prizant, B.M., & Meyer, E. (1993). Socioemotional aspects of communication disorders in young children. *American Journal of Speech-Language Pathology, 2,* 56–71.

Prizant, B.M., & Rydell, P.J. (1984). An analysis of the functions of delayed echolalia in autistic children. *Journal of Speech and Hearing Research, 27,* 183–192.

Prizant, B.M., & Rydell, P. (1993). Assessment and intervention strategies for unconventional verbal behavior. In S. Warren & J. Reichle (Eds.), *Communicative alternatives to challenging behavior* (pp. 263–298). Baltimore: Brookes.

Prizant, B.M., & Schuler, A.L. (1987). Facilitating communication: Language approaches. In D. Cohen & A. Donnellan (Eds.), *Handbook of autism and pervasive developmental disorders* (pp. 316–332). New York: John Wiley & Sons.

Prizant, B.M., & Wetherby, A.M. (1985). Intentional communicative behavior of children with autism: Theoretical and applied issues. *Australian Journal of Human Communication Disorders, 13,* 21–58.

Prizant, B.M., & Wetherby, A.M. (1987). Communicative intent: A framework for understanding social-communicative behavior in autism. *Journal of the American Academy of Child Psychiatry, 26,* 472–479.

Prizant, B.M., & Wetherby, A.M. (1988). Providing services to children with autism (0–2 years) and their families. *Topics in Language Disorders, 9,* 1–23.

Prizant, B.M., & Wetherby, A.M. (1989). Enhancing communication: From theory to practice. In G. Dawson (Ed.), *Autism: New perspectives on diagnosis, nature and treatment* (pp. 282–309). New York: Guilford Press.

Prizant, B.M., & Wetherby, A.M. (1990). Toward an integrated view of early communication, language and socioemotional development. *Topics in Language Disorders, 10,* 1–16.

Prizant, B.M., & Wetherby, A.M. (1993). Communication in preschool autistic children. In E. Schopler, M. van Bourgandien, & M. Bristol (Eds.), *Preschool issues in autism* (pp. 95–128). New York: Plenum Press.

Reichle, J., Sigafoos, J., & York, J. (1991). *Implementing augmentative and alternative communication: Strategies for learners with severe disabilities.* Baltimore: Brookes.

Reichle, J., & Wacker, D.P. (Eds.). (1993). *Communicative alternatives to challenging behavior—Integrating functional assessment and intervention strategies.* Baltimore: Brookes.

Retherford, K. (1993). *A guide to analysis of language transcripts* (2nd ed.). Eau Claire, WI: Thinking Publications.

Roberts, J. (1989). Echolalia and comprehension in autistic children. *Journal of Autism and Developmental Disorders, 19,* 271–281.

Rydell, P.J. (1989). *Social-communicative control and its effect on echolalia in children with autism.* Unpublished doctoral dissertation, University of Nebraska—Lincoln.

Rydell, P.J., & Mirenda, P. (1991). The effects of two levels of linguistic constraint on echolalia and generative language production in children with autism. *Journal of Autism and Developmental Disorders, 21,* 131–158.

Rydell, P., & Prizant, B.M. (1995). Assessment and intervention strategies for children who use echolalia. In K. Quill (Ed.) *Teaching children with autism: Methods to enhance communication and socialization.* Albany, NY: Delmar.

Scherer, N., & Olswang, L. (1989). Using structured discourse as a language intervention technique with autistic children. *Journal of Speech and Hearing Disorders, 54,* 383–394.

Schuler, A.L. (1995). Thinking in autism: Differences in learning and development. In K. Quill (Ed.), *Teaching children with autism: Methods to enhance communication and socialization* (pp. 11–32). Albany, NY: Delmar.

Schuler, A.L., Gonsier-Gerdin, J., & Wolfberg, P. (1990). The efficacy of speech and language intervention: Autism. *Seminars in Speech and Language, 11,* 242–251.

Schuler, A.L., & Prizant, B.M. (1985). Echolalia. In E. Schopler & G. Mesibov (Eds.), *Communication problems in autism* (pp. 163–185). New York: Plenum Press.

Snyder-McLean, L., McLean, J., Etter-Schroeder, R., & Rogers, N. (1984). Structuring joint action routines: A strategy for facilitating communication in the classroom. *Seminars in Speech and Language, 5,* 213–228.

Sonnenmeier, R. (1994). Script-based language intervention: Learning to participate in life events. In J. Duchan, L. Hewitt, & R. Sonnenmeier (Eds.), *Pragmatics: From theory to practice* (pp. 134–148). Englewood Cliffs, NJ: Prentice-Hall.

Stern, D. (1985). *The interpersonal world of the infant.* New York: Basic Books.

Tager-Flusberg, H. (1987). On the nature of a language acquisition disorder: The example of autism. In F. Kessel (Ed.), *The development of language and language researchers* (pp. 249–267). Hillsdale, NJ: Erlbaum.

Tantam, D., Holmes, D., & Cordess, C. (1993). Nonverbal expression in autism of Asperger type. *Journal of Autism and Developmental Disorders, 23,* 111–133.

Tirosh, E., & Canby, J. (1993). Autism with hyperlexia: A distinct syndrome? *American Journal on Mental Retardation, 98,* 84–92.

Tronick, E. (1989). Emotion and emotional communication in infants. *American Psychologist, 44,* 112–119.

Twachtman, D. (1995). Methods to enhance communication in verbal children. In K. Quill (Ed.), *Teaching children with autism: Methods to enhance communication and socialization* (pp. 133–162). Albany, NY: Delmar.

Volden, J., & Lord, C. (1991). Neologisms and idiosyncratic language in autistic speakers. *Journal of Autism and Developmental Disorders, 21,* 109–130.

Vygotsky, L. (1978). *Mind in society: The development of higher psychological processes.* Cambridge, MA: Harvard University Press. (Original work published in Russian in 1933)

Vygotsky, L. (1986). *Thought and language* (A. Kozulin, Ed. and Trans.). Cambridge, MA: Harvard University Press.

Watson, L.R. (1987). Pragmatic abilities and disabilities of autistic children. In T. Layton (Ed.), *Language and treatment of autistic and developmentally disordered children* (pp. 89–127). Springfield, IL: Thomas.

Watson, L., Lord, C., Schaeffer, B., & Schopler, E. (1989). *Teaching spontaneous communication to autistic and developmentally handicapped children.* New York: Irvington.

Westby, C. (1988). Children's play: Reflections of social competence. *Seminars in Speech and Language, 9,* 1–13.

Westby, C. (1991). Learning to talk—talking to learn. Oral-literate language differences. In C. Simon (Ed.), *Communication skills and classroom success* (pp. 334–357). Eau Claire, WI: Thinkings Publications.

Wetherby, A.M. (1986). The ontogeny of communicative functions in autism. *Journal of Autism and Developmental Disorders, 16,* 295–316.

Wetherby, A.M., & Prizant, B. (1992). Facilitating language and communication development in autism: Assessment and intervention guidelines. In D. Berkell (Ed.), *Autism: Identification, education, and treatment* (pp. 107–134). Hillsdale, NJ: Erlbaum.

Wetherby, A.M., & Prutting, C. (1984). Profiles of communicative and cognitive-social abilities in autistic children. *Journal of Speech and Hearing Research, 27,* 364–377.

Wolfberg, P.J., & Schuler, A.L. (1993). Integrated play groups: A model for promoting the social and cognitive dimensions of play in children with autism. *Journal of Autism and Developmental Disorders, 23,* 467–489.

CHAPTER 26

Behavioral Interventions

JOEL D. BREGMAN AND JOHN GERDTZ

During the past 10 years, behavioral interventions have become the predominant treatment approach for promoting the social, adaptive, and behavioral functioning of children and adults with autism. The sophistication of these strategies has increased substantially, reflecting advancements in technique and refinements in behavioral assessment. Of particular importance has been the development of improved methods of identifying environmental factors and events that precipitate and maintain maladaptive patterns of behavior.

Behavioral approaches have been adopted increasingly for enhancing personal independence and responsible choice through skill development and habilitative training, increasing repertoires of prosocial behavior and leisure activities, and teaching methods of self-control and relaxation. In addition, behavioral interventions have been employed for reinforcing adaptive responses and suppressing maladaptive ones. The targets of treatment have included social, communicative, and behavioral responses.

This chapter reviews the recent literature regarding specific behavioral interventions developed to ameliorate the core features of autism and reduce the behavioral symptoms frequently associated with the syndrome (e.g., aggression, self-injury, destructive behavior, noncompliance, agitation, stereotypy, and so on). Discussions of learning theory, behavioral assessment, and educational interventions, found in other chapters of this volume, should be referred to for the theoretical principles that underlie behavioral treatment, educational approaches for teaching adaptive skills,

and methods of analyzing the functions of behavior in individual cases. It should be stressed that the success of a well-designed behavioral intervention program rests on the completion of a thorough functional analysis of behavior. The functional analysis serves as the blueprint for identifying the behavioral interventions that are most likely to influence the antecedent and consequent factors responsible for maintaining maladaptive patterns of behavior.

A few words should be said about the methodology of the published behavioral studies. Most of the studies involve either single-case designs or reports of very small sample size. Treatment failures are rarely published, and few studies attempt to uncover demographic or clinical variables that are predictive of a favorable response. Therefore, although conclusions can be drawn regarding the efficacy of specific procedures in the individual cases presented, generalization to the broader population of persons with autism is difficult. Nonetheless, as different research groups report successes for similar behavioral interventions, support for efficacy to the broader population with autism accrues.

Articles were ascertained by a comprehensive computer search of several databases and a manual search of the relevant professional journals published between 1984 and 1995. The following criteria were used to select studies for this review: (a) inclusion of subjects with a diagnosis of either autism or a related pervasive developmental disorder, or the presence of "autistic-like behavior"; (b) the use of at least one intervention type generally accepted as a valid behavioral procedure by professionals in the field of behavior modification or applied behavior analysis (studies employing several interventions needed to include at least one accepted procedure); (c) publication in a refereed professional journal or as a contributed chapter in a professionally reviewed book, or a paper presented at a conference, following professional review; and (d) a publication date from 1984 through early 1995. Although studies with methodological flaws (e.g., inadequate documentation of generalization and maintenance) were not excluded, these factors are critiqued in the chapter.

The various behavioral strategies reviewed in this chapter are divided into the following general categories: antecedent interventions (those that are implemented before a target behavior is likely to occur, in an effort to avert problems), consequence interventions (those that are implemented following the occurrence of a target behavior), and skill development interventions (behavioral programs designed to teach alternative, adaptive behaviors, thereby reducing the frequency and severity of maladaptive responses). Most of the recently published studies report on the efficacy of behavioral programs that include elements of all three major intervention types (antecedent, consequence, and skill development procedures). However, for purposes of this discussion, the interventions will be classified according to the primary focus of the treatment package.

ANTECEDENT INTERVENTIONS

Antecedent interventions, as the name implies, involve procedures that are implemented before a target behavior occurs. The antecedent interventions can be further subdivided into those that are implemented relatively distant in time from the target behaviors and those that are implemented immediately before the target behaviors are expected to occur. The former procedures are sometimes known as ecological or setting event interventions, whereas the latter are often termed immediate antecedents.

A number of setting event, or remote antecedent interventions may be helpful in reducing problem behaviors exhibited by children and adults with autism. For example, Duker and Rasing (1989) reported that environmental changes designed to reduce visual distractions led to a decrease in self-stimulatory behavior and an increase in on-task behavior among three adolescents and adults with autism. In a review of studies on environmental modifications in the classroom, Olley (1987) concluded that educational progress and adaptive behavior are enhanced by an identification and modification of environmental factors that precipitate and maintain problem behaviors (see Gerhardt & Holmes, 1994, for an example of a comprehensive behavioral evaluation program that includes an assessment of environmental factors).

Early intervention services are antecedent interventions that are becoming increasingly important because of their potential for reducing the likelihood that problem behaviors will arise later in life. There is now some evidence that young children with autism who receive early intervention and educational services that focus on the development of functional communication, social skills, and personal independence may exhibit fewer behavioral problems as they grow older (Dunlap, Johnson, & Robbins, 1990; McGee, Daly, & Jacobs, 1994). These preliminary reports are encouraging. However, much more research in this area is necessary in order to confirm the long-term preventive effects of early intervention and to determine which specific interventions of the treatment packages are responsible for a more favorable outcome. In this regard, one potentially valuable remote antecedent intervention involves exposure to children who can serve as adaptive role models. For example, it has been reported that young children with autism who are in close proximity to typically (i.e., normally) developing peers display significantly lower rates of aberrant behavior, such as stereotypy (Lanquetot, 1989; McGee, Paradis, & Feldman, 1993). Exposure to typical peers was definitely beneficial, but was not sufficient to maintain clinically significant behavioral change without the addition of intensive behavioral treatment. Therefore, exposure to normal social role models may represent a useful antecedent procedure that enhances the success of an intensive and well-designed early intervention program. It should be noted that this research is still very preliminary and more studies in this area are needed.

In an effort to identify successful antecedent interventions, Touchette, MacDonald, and Langer (1985) developed a simple "scatter plot" data collection system to help identify possible situations and events in a daily schedule that may precipitate problem behaviors. The scatter plot data collection system can be used in a variety of clinical settings with relatively minor modifications. The authors provided case examples for using the scatter plot technique of data collection to identify antecedents for self-injurious and aggressive behaviors of three adolescents and adults with autism. Based on the information derived from the scatter plot, the authors modified several environmental factors, including staffing patterns and task assignments, resulting in a significant reduction in subjects' self-injury and aggression. Brown (1991) described another type of data collection method for identifying antecedents of problem behaviors exhibited by adults with developmental disabilities, including autism. The findings prompted modifications in the daily schedules of the subjects, which enhanced the success of a behavioral program in significantly decreasing problem behaviors. Based on a review of clinical research, Flannery and Horner (1994) concluded that adherence to a predictable daily schedule of events and activities can result in a reduction of disruptive behavior among persons with severe developmental disabilities.

There has been considerable interest in the role of antecedent exercise for improving the physical health and reducing the frequency and severity of behavioral problems of persons with autism and other developmental disabilities. There is evidence that antecedent exercise can reduce self-stimulatory behavior among children with autism (R.L. Koegel & Koegel, 1989) and aggressive behavior and stereotypy among adults with autism and mental retardation (Allison, Basile, & MacDonald, 1991; Elliott, Dobbin, Rose, & Soper, 1994). In the Allison et al. study, exercise was superior to the antianxiety medication lorazepam in reducing the frequency and severity of aggression manifested by an adult with autism and mental retardation. Unfortunately, because of staffing problems, the exercise program had to be abandoned, and the aggressive behaviors

returned to previous levels (Hittner, 1994, pp. 125–126). There are indications that the exercise regime must be vigorous to be effective (Elliott et al., 1994). In a literature review of this topic, Gabler-Halle, Halle, and Chung (1993) found evidence to support the efficacy of antecedent exercise in reducing problem behaviors; however, the beneficial effects appear to be relatively short-term. In addition, many of the reported studies suffer from methodological design problems, which limit the generalization of findings. Nonetheless, antecedent aerobic exercise has potential as a relatively nonintrusive antecedent intervention for problem behavior, with the additional benefit of enhancing physical health and conditioning. Further research on this topic clearly is warranted.

Immediate antecedent events and situations also have been identified in the literature as influencing the frequency and severity of behavioral problems. In a comprehensive review, Munk and Repp (1994) uncovered several factors in a teaching situation that influence the prevalence of behavioral difficulties. A number of these factors, including student choice of activities, variation in teaching lessons, task difficulty, and the interspersal of mastered tasks with novel tasks, fall into the immediate antecedent category. Munk and Repp also outlined a useful framework for conducting functional analyses of problem behaviors in teaching environments and designing behavioral interventions to address these problems. (See Chapter 20 for a thorough discussion of functional analysis.)

Studies involving children with autism have confirmed the influence of immediate antecedents in teaching situations. Robbins and Dunlap (1992) found that parents were able to teach young children with autism new tasks at home with appropriate professional support; however, problem behaviors increased significantly during the teaching process. These behaviors could be partially averted through the implementation of antecedent interventions, including the use of errorless learning techniques and the interspersal of mastered tasks with the new tasks being taught. Robbins and Dunlap have argued that, in some cases, it may be preferable for parents to practice mastered skills that have already been taught to the children by professionals. Other investigators also have re-ported that systematic variation in the presen-tation of new tasks and mastered skills promotes learning and reduces behavioral problems among children and adults with autism (Dunlap, 1984; Weber & Thorpe, 1992; Winterling, Dunlap, & O'Neill, 1987). Other immediate antecedent interventions, such as the opportunity to express personal choice, ap-pear to be effective in reducing the likelihood of disruptive behavior. For example, Dyer, Dunlap, and Winterling (1990) found that when students with autism and mental retarda-tion were given the opportunity to choose the particular task to be taught, as well as the rein-forcer to be earned for success, the frequency of problem behaviors decreased significantly.

The importance of conducting a proper functional analysis of antecedent variables and problem behaviors was highlighted by Taylor, Ekdahl, Romanczyk, and Miller (1994). In a study of four students with autism, the authors found that escape from the demands of teach-ing sessions was a common motivating factor for a variety of problem behaviors, including noncompliance, aggression, and the destruc-tion of teaching materials. The object of the escape behavior was different among the stu-dents, however. Two of the students were moti-vated by escape from the task demands themselves, whereas the two other students were motivated by escape from social inter-action with the teacher. These latter two stu-dents would perform the tasks if they were able to avoid social contact. Taylor et al. dis-cussed possible antecedent interventions to ad-dress each type of escape behavior.

There are circumstances under which a specific setting event will precipitate behav-ioral problems for persons with autism. Kennedy and Itkonnen (1993) conducted func-tional analyses for two young adults with de-velopmental disabilities (one with autism) in order to identify possible antecedent motiva-tors of aggression and self-injury. For the sub-ject with autism, the authors found that oversleeping in the morning set up a negative chain of events that often resulted in behav-ioral problems at school. With the implementa-tion of a positive reinforcement program to reward the young adult for getting up at the correct time, the frequency and severity of

problem behaviors later in the day decreased considerably. In a related study, Kennedy (1994) found that demands from staff to begin work or other tasks often resulted in problem behaviors (e.g., aggression, self-injury, non-compliance) for three subjects with mental re-tardation (two of whom also had autism). Social comments from staff generally did not elicit problem behaviors. Kennedy reduced the number of task demands and increased the number of social comments directed toward the subjects. Problem behaviors decreased sig-nificantly and remained at relatively low lev-els, despite the gradual reintroduction of task demands.

Behavioral momentum, or high-probability (high-p) requests, constitute another potentially powerful class of antecedent interventions, es-pecially for the treatment of noncompliance. This type of procedure, which is relatively straightforward to implement, involves request-ing the performance of a series of simple tasks ("Say hi," "Give me five," and so on) in a fairly rapid sequence. A low-probability (low-p) task (i.e., a task that has been previously resisted) is then introduced into the sequence of requests. In many instances, the previously noncompliant individual will proceed to complete the low-p task that has been embedded in the series of high-p tasks. In a review of research on the use of behavioral momentum procedures to treat noncompliant behavior among adults with men-tal retardation, Mace et al. (1988) found con-vincing support for the success of high-p requests as antecedent interventions. Studies also document the success of behavioral mo-mentum procedures among persons with autism. Davis, Brady, Williams, and Hamilton (1992) used high-p requests with two preschool chil-dren with autism to promote appropriate re-sponses to adult requests. The high-p requests were effective and, in fact, generalized outside of the treatment setting. Houlihan, Jacobson, and Brandon (1994) also reported the success-ful use of high-p requests with preschool chil-dren with autism. The authors noted that a short interprompt interval (5 seconds) was more ef-fective than a longer interval (20 seconds) in es-tablishing the effectiveness of high-p requests. However, there are situations in which high-p requests may not be effective. For example, in their treatment program for noncompliance and self-injurious behavior motivated by escape, Zarcone, Iwata, Mazaleski, and Smith (1994) found that high-p requests were not effective until an extinction component was added (i.e., prevention of physical escape from demands).

Appropriate antecedent interventions are particularly important in the behavioral treatment of rumination (the voluntary regurgitation, rechewing, and reswallowing of partially digested food). Rumination is relatively rare, but can lead to serious health complications if left untreated (see Rast, 1992, for review). Effective behavioral treatment of rumination begins with a functional analysis. Based on the specific findings, antecedent interventions can be developed to target the identified factors, which typically include the amount of food consumed at mealtimes, the presence of distractions, the types of foods and liquids consumed, and the pace at which foods are presented (Luiselli, Medeiros, Jasinowski, Smith, & Cameron, 1994; McKeegan, Estill, & Campbell, 1987). In the treatment of rumination, antecedent interventions usually need to be supplemented by reinforcement programs delivered either alone (McKeegan et al.) or in combination with extinction of escape through emesis (Luiselli et al.). The combined treatment intervention was found to be effective in reducing high-frequency rumination to a zero level at four to six months' follow-up (Luiselli et al.).

The usefulness of other antecedent interventions has been documented in the behavioral literature. For the treatment of rectal digging and sniffing exhibited by a woman with autism, Smith (1986) reported the efficacy of providing a variety of desirable odors (perfumes and soaps) on a fixed schedule while ignoring behavioral episodes. The target behaviors were maintained at near zero levels through 14 months of follow-up.

The manner in which skills are taught can serve as a powerful antecedent for children and adults with autism. For example, Chen and Bernard-Opitz (1993) found that four elementary school children with autism exhibited significantly fewer behavioral problems (especially noncompliance) when task instructions were presented by a computer instead of by a teacher.

Stimulus Change Procedures

Stimulus change procedures usually involve the presentation of a novel or unfamiliar stimulus that is not directly antecedent or consequent to the specific problem behavior. (For theoretical discussions of stimulus change procedures, see Carr, Robinson, & Polumbo, 1990; LaVigna & Donnellan, 1986.) Relatively straightforward stimulus change procedures offer the behavioral clinician strategies that have the potential for rapidly reducing the frequency and/or severity of problem behaviors. Carr et al. and LaVigna and Donnellan noted that stimulus change procedures may be particularly effective as crisis intervention techniques. Stimulus change techniques do not by themselves permanently alter behavior; however, they do offer a "window of opportunity" for the implementation of other interventions. For example, stimulus change can be used to interrupt a pattern of high-frequency problem behavior, thereby providing an opportunity to teach alternative skills or to reward alternative positive behaviors. Stimulus change techniques offer the potential for rapidly altering behavior and can be implemented in a variety of clinical settings with relative ease. Further research on this technique is, therefore, warranted. A variation of the stimulus change procedure was used by Van Houten (1993) in the treatment of severe self-injury (face slapping) exhibited by a child with autism. A functional analysis indicated that the high-frequency face slapping was motivated by the sensory reinforcement provided by the behavior. Van Houten placed small padded weights (1.5 pounds) on the child's wrists. This change in stimulus was sufficient to reduce face slaps to near-zero levels for five months of follow-up.

CONSEQUENCE-BASED INTERVENTIONS

Consequence-based interventions are behavioral procedures that are implemented following the initiation or completion of a problem behavior. The most effective behavioral intervention package is likely to include a combination of antecedent and consequence-based interventions. The articles reviewed in this section highlight consequence-based interventions as the primary treatment procedures.

Interruption and Redirection

Interventions involving interruption and redirection usually include physical prevention of the targeted behavior and redirection to another activity. Sensory extinction is one type of interruption that involves elimination of the sensory feedback obtained from certain repetitive aberrant behaviors. For example, if a person is reinforced by the vibrations and sounds of repetitively knocking on a table, it may be possible to reduce or eliminate the problem behavior by simply padding the table to eliminate the sensory feedback. The benefits and potential limitations of interruption and redirection were illustrated in the research of Maag, Wolchik, Rutherford, and Parks (1986). These authors studied the effects of a sensory extinction procedure on the self-stimulatory behavior of two boys with autism. Highly variable results were reported: some self-stimulatory behaviors decreased, whereas others actually increased slightly.

Interruption procedures can be as direct as simply blocking the problem behavior. Mulick and Meinhold (1994) conducted a functional analysis of chronic hand-mouthing manifested by a woman with autism and profound mental retardation. The behavior had resulted in serious medical problems. The functional analysis suggested that this behavior was primarily motivated by automatic, sensory reinforcement. The authors implemented a simple program to physically block attempts at hand-mouthing. This procedure resulted in a significant decrease in hand-mouthing, as well as an increase in academic engagement.

An interruption program was used by Bebko and Lennox (1988) to treat chronic bruxism (tooth grinding) in two young children with autism. The intervention consisted of a physical cue (i.e., a light touch of the chin) to prompt the children to open the mouth (a behavioral response that competes with bruxism). This intervention did not generalize until the cue was used in all environmental settings. As a result of this intervention, bruxism was reduced considerably, and a two-year

follow-up indicated that bruxism remained at low levels.

Reinforcement-Based Interventions

A reinforcer can be defined as "a consequent stimulus that increases or maintains the future rate and/or probability of occurrence of a behavior" (Alberto & Troutman, 1990, p. 454). In general terms, a reinforcer is a situation or event that follows a particular behavior, resulting in an increased likelihood that the behavior will recur in the future. The goal of most behavioral interventions is to systematically reinforce desirable behaviors, and reduce or eliminate reinforcers associated with undesirable behaviors.

A reinforcer-based intervention will only be successful if the reinforcer(s) used is powerful enough to significantly motivate the individual to perform certain behaviors. Comprehensive guides to behavioral assessment that include interview and observational techniques for identifying potential reinforcers are available (Mason, McGee, Farmer-Dougan, & Risley, 1989; O'Neill, Horner, Albin, Storey, & Sprague, 1990; Willis, LaVigna, & Donnellan, 1989). Mason et al. developed a rapid and effective observational method for identifying reinforcers for young children with autism. The authors then taught the children a number of specific tasks and used the reinforcers identified during the observations as rewards for task completion. The reinforcement program resulted in a significant increase in skill development and a corresponding decrease in behavioral problems exhibited during teaching sessions. Because the problem behaviors were not specifically targeted for intervention, the implementation of structured teaching procedures and the use of reinforcers may serve to suppress problem behaviors during teaching sessions.

Durand, Crimmins, Caulfield, and Taylor (1989) suggested that the nature of problem behaviors themselves (e.g., self-stimulation, stereotypy) may provide important information for identifying potential reinforcers. This approach was followed by Charlop, Kurtz, and Casey (1990), who provided children with autism brief periods of time during which they could engage in stereotypy, echolalia, and perseveration as reinforcement for appropriate behavior at other times of the day. This brief access (five seconds) served as a powerful reinforcer and resulted in a significant increase in appropriate behavior for all students. Behavioral problems did not increase and there were no difficulties terminating access to the preferred behaviors at the end of five seconds. As Charlop et al. (1990) and Durand et al. (1989) have noted, serious behavior problems, such as aggression and self-injury, cannot be used as reinforcers. In such cases, appropriate reinforcers would need to be identified by a functional analysis.

A variety of reinforcement-based interventions are known as Differential Reinforcement procedures. As the name implies, these procedures are designed to provide reinforcement in some situations but not in others. The main categories of Differential Reinforcement procedures currently utilized are: Differential Reinforcement of Other Behavior (DRO), Differential Reinforcement of Incompatible Behavior (DRI), Differential Reinforcement of Alternative Behavior (DRAlt or DRA), and Differential Reinforcement of Low Rates of Responding (DRL). Some behavioral intervention programs employ one type of Differential Reinforcement procedure; others employ several, at times in conjunction with antecedent interventions, skill development procedures, and/or punishment. For the purposes of this discussion, the interventions will be reviewed according to general type. Interventions with multiple elements will be classified according to the main element of the behavioral program.

Differential Reinforcement of Other Behavior (DRO) is defined as "reinforcement for engaging in any response other than the target behavior for a set period of time" (LaVigna & Donnellan, 1986, p. 58). Of all the Differential Reinforcement interventions, DRO has received the most research attention and has been demonstrated to be effective for a variety of behavioral problems manifested by a diverse group of subject populations (LaVigna & Donnellan). Critical factors in the success of a DRO program include selection of appropriate reinforcers and use of proper reinforcement intervals, to ensure motivation and avoid satiation. LaVigna and Donnellan, and Repp,

Felce, and Barton (1991), provide useful guidelines for the design of DRO programs, including methods for determining optimal reinforcer intervals. A number of studies utilizing DRO procedures have been reported for the treatment of children and adults with autism. Haring, Breen, Pitts-Conway, and Gaylord-Ross (1986) found that DRO procedures implemented during teaching situations significantly reduced the frequency and severity of stereotypy exhibited by students with autism. Wong, Floyd, Innocent, and Woolsey (1992) reported that a treatment program that combined DRO with compliance training (i.e., systematic reinforcement for following directions) was effective in reducing the severe aggression, self-injury, and property damage of a hospitalized adult with autism. The benefits of this program were maintained at a one-year follow-up. Kennedy and Haring (1993) conducted functional analyses on three high school students with autism who exhibited behavioral problems at school, including aggression, disruptive vocalizations, and stereotypy. The analyses indicated that reinforcers for these behaviors included access to certain rewards, as well as escape from demands. The authors implemented a DRO program with a token economy, which enabled the students to earn tokens for refraining from disruptive behavior. The tokens could be exchanged for access to desired objects or for limited periods of escape from classroom demands. The DRO schedule was most effective when students had access to both types of reinforcement. The importance of a functional analysis (including assessment of environmental contexts) was supported by a study conducted by Haring and Kennedy (1990). Two students with severe disabilities (including autism) were studied in a classroom situation and in an after-school leisure program. In the classroom setting, DRO was effective in reducing disruptive behavior, whereas time-out was ineffective. However, in the after-school program, the reverse was true. Smith (1985) reported on the efficacy of a DRO program implemented in conjunction with a variety of antecedent interventions in the treatment of aggression and self-injury manifested by two group-home residents with autism and mental retardation. The DRO program involved the delivery of reinforcers contingent on the absence of aggression and self-injury. The antecedent interventions included the scheduling of activities with the aid of pictures, food satiation, and the interspersal of preferred with unpreferred tasks. The treatment program succeeded in significantly reducing the frequency and severity of aggression and self-injury.

Although DRO is rather easy to understand on a conceptual level, it can be difficult to implement in some clinical settings. Paisey, Fox, Curran, Hooper, and Whitney (1991) used a DRO program, antecedent interventions (e.g., posted good-behavior rules, relaxation procedures), and physical intervention techniques to treat the severe aggression of an 11-year-old boy with autism. The interventions were designed to be implemented at home by the parents. Although the interventions were conducted faithfully, they were not successful. An alternative program, which combined compliance training with extinction of escape from demands, was implemented by professional staff in the family home and proved to be successful. In view of these results, Paisey et al. advised caution in recommending that parents implement DRO programs for target behaviors such as severe aggression.

DRO programs can rapidly reduce the frequency and severity of problem behaviors in a variety of clinical settings. However, there are two major disadvantages in using DRO schedules of reinforcement. First, although DRO interventions focus on the problem or target behaviors, they do not teach alternative, adaptive behavioral responses. Second, DRO procedures result in the reinforcement of all behaviors (other than the target behaviors) that occur during reinforcement intervals. Problem behaviors that have not been directly targeted for intervention, may, therefore, be inadvertently reinforced.

Other Differential Reinforcement techniques have been developed to address the major problems related to the use of DRO. Differential Reinforcement of Incompatible Behavior (DRI) interventions provide reinforcement for the *occurrence* of a behavior that is physically incompatible with the target behavior. The theoretical assumption underlying DRI is that an individual cannot simultaneously engage in the target behavior and the incompatible behavior.

Although conceptually straightforward, DRI procedures can be difficult to implement. Determination of the proper reinforcement interval can be critical to the success of the intervention. Furthermore, it may be extremely difficult to identify a behavior that is entirely incompatible with the target behavior. Finally, research support for the effectiveness of DRI is much less convincing than the support for DRO (LaVigna & Donnellan, 1986).

During the past 10 years, a number of studies involving the use of DRI with children and adults with autism have been published. Azrin, Besalel, Janner, and Caputo (1988) studied a group of nine adolescents and adults with a variety of severe disabilities (including autism), who exhibited severe self-injurious behavior (SIB). The authors found that a behavioral intervention that combined response interruption (i.e., physical blocking of the SIB) with reinforcement of incompatible behaviors (DRI) was the most effective behavioral intervention for the treatment of the self-injury. Underwood, Figueroa, Thyer, and Nzeocha (1989) used the response interruption–DRI program described by Azrin et al. to treat SIB manifested by two adolescents diagnosed with autism and mental retardation. This intervention was effective for one subject but not for the other. The nonresponder engaged in self-restraint behavior, and Underwood et al. hypothesized that self-injury accompanied by such self-restraint may represent a subtype of SIB that is relatively resistant to this intervention strategy.

McNally, Calamari, Hansen, and Keliher (1988) used a DRI schedule of reinforcement to treat polydipsia (excessive water consumption) in a woman with autism and mental retardation. The polydipsia was so severe that the woman was in danger of potentially fatal water intoxication. The authors provided edible reinforcers and a reduction in activity demands as rewards for the incompatible behavior of refusing offers of water. The woman's water consumption returned to normal levels. Smith (1987) successfully used a combined intervention of DRI plus Differential Reinforcement of Alternative Behavior (DRA) to treat the pica (consumption of nonfood items) of a man with autism and mental retardation. Reinforcers for this study included edibles, access to desired activities, and praise from staff. The subject received reinforcement for a "clean mouth" (DRI), plus reinforcers for remaining in his assigned workstation, keeping his hands on his work, and working quickly (DRA). Pica decreased and work productivity increased when the DRI/DRA programs were in effect. Pica increased when the reinforcement schedule was withdrawn, and again diminished when the program was reinstated.

DRA is a version of DRI in which the alternative (rewarded) behavior is not completely incompatible with the target (problem) behavior. DRA can be used to reward a variety of positive alternative behaviors. Choosing an appropriate reinforcement interval is as important for DRA as it is for DRO and DRI. The obvious benefit of a DRA schedule is that the program can be used to teach the individual a variety of adaptive responses. However, DRA shares with DRI several drawbacks in comparison with DRO, including a slower rate of response and less empirical support. Dunlap, Koegel, Johnson, and O'Neill (1987) used a DRA program in combination with verbal reprimand to increase the on-task behavior of adults with autism who were participating in a vocational program. With the motivation provided by the DRA schedule (and reprimands delivered at home), the subjects remained on-task for up to eight hours, allowing staff members to gradually fade their supervision. Hittner (1994) used a combination of DRA, DRO, and medication (imipramine) to treat the severe aggression and self-injury of a man diagnosed with autism and mental retardation. The DRA schedule involved rewarding the subject every 30 minutes for remaining on-task and following his schedule, and the DRO program provided reinforcers for the absence of aggression and self-injury during the same period. Both target behaviors decreased significantly and remained suppressed at a five-month follow-up. It is difficult to separate the effect of the medication from the effects of the behavioral interventions in this study. However, significant suppression of problem behaviors did not begin until the DRA and DRO programs were added to the treatment plan.

The complexities of designing and combining behavioral treatment interventions were illustrated in the work of Vollmer, Marcus, and LeBlanc (1994). These authors conducted a functional analysis of the self-injurious behavior of three preschool children (one with "autistic-like" behaviors). The functional analyses were inconclusive as to the possible functions of the problem behaviors. Vollmer et al. then used reinforcer assessments to identify preferred items for each child. Self-injury decreased when the children were given access to the preferred items. In order for clinically significant reductions in the problem behaviors to occur, one child required a DRA schedule to reinforce appropriate toy play, and another required time-out as a consequence for his self-injurious behavior.

Differential Reinforcement of Low Rates of Responding (DRL) is another Differential Reinforcement technique that rewards low rates of a target behavior. This intervention is appropriate only for behaviors that are essentially acceptable but can be disruptive if they occur frequently or at high levels of intensity (e.g., asking frequent questions in class). When used appropriately, DRL is a potentially powerful technique that can result in a relatively rapid reduction in the rate of behavioral problems. Choosing the appropriate reinforcement interval is important, as it is for all the Differential Reinforcement techniques. Among the problems associated with the use of DRL is a limited foundation of research documenting efficacy, as compared with DRO (LaVigna & Donnellan, 1986). Another problem with DRL is that this intervention does not, by itself, teach alternative positive behaviors. The published research on the DRL treatment of behavioral disturbances associated with autism is limited in comparison with the research published for other Differential Reinforcement techniques. Rotholz and Luce (1983) used tokens successfully to reward reductions in the self-stimulatory behavior of two boys with autism and mental retardation. Handen, Apolito, and Seltzer (1984) used a token program and DRL to systematically reduce the repetitive speech of an adolescent with autism. When the DRL program was withdrawn, the repetitive speech returned to baseline levels. When the program was reinstated, the repetitive speech again decreased significantly and remained at low levels at a 14-month follow-up.

Differential Reinforcement programs represent potentially powerful interventions that can often be implemented across clinical settings. Donnellan, LaVigna, Zambito, and Thvedt (1985) described an intensive behavioral intervention program designed to serve children and adults with different diagnoses (including autism) who exhibited a variety of serious problem behaviors. Behavioral interventions were administered in home and community settings. The program was generally effective in reducing or eliminating problem behaviors. A two-year follow-up indicated that most of the clinical gains had been maintained. The programs included several different behavioral strategies, including DRO, DRI, DRA, stimulus change, and relaxation procedures.

Extinction Procedures

Extinction as a behavioral procedure can be defined as "withholding reinforcement for a previously reinforced behavior to reduce the occurrence of that behavior" (Alberto & Troutman, 1990, p. 452). Extinction procedures can be time-consuming and difficult to implement in clinical settings, and they may actually result in a transient increase in behavioral problems before the problems are finally extinguished. Extinction does not teach alternative adaptive behaviors, unless it is used in combination with other interventions. However, these problems can be addressed through the graduated introduction of extinction procedures and the addition of Differential Reinforcement programs (Ducharme & Van Houten, 1994).

Several studies have reported benefits related to the use of extinction. Iwata, Pace, Cowdery, and Miltenberger (1994) discussed the use of extinction for the treatment of severe self-injury. A functional analysis often indicates that extinction of attention, extinction of escape from demands, or extinction of sensory reinforcement may be necessary for the effective treatment of many forms of severe self-injury. As previously discussed, this use of the extinction procedure was illustrated by Zarcone et al. (1994), who found that behavioral momentum was not an effective treatment for escape-motivated self-injury until

extinction from escape was added to the treatment program. The escape extinction involved physically preventing the subject from escaping task demands through self-injury. Lalli, Casey, Goh, and Merlino (1994) found that antecedent activity schedules were not effective in controlling the aggression and property destruction of adolescents with mild mental retardation until escape-motivated behaviors were extinguished. Given the findings reported above, additional research regarding extinction procedures in clinical and community settings is warranted.

Noncontingent Reinforcement

Noncontingent reinforcement is rarely used, and few studies of this type of reinforcement have been conducted in the area of autism and other disabilities. Noncontingent reinforcement involves the provision of reinforcement on a fixed schedule or routine, despite the presence of problem behaviors. There are a number of obvious difficulties with this intervention. First, it may be difficult to motivate parents or clinical staff to provide ongoing reinforcement even when problem behaviors are occurring. The natural temptation is to stop the reinforcement and implement other interventions (usually punishment). Second, the intervention may accidentally reinforce untargeted problem behaviors that may require additional interventions at a later time. Third, this intervention does not, by itself, teach alternative positive behaviors. Although there is little published research on noncontingent reinforcement, there are reasons to believe that this intervention may be useful in some circumstances. Noncontingent reinforcement is relatively easy to implement on a consistent basis and, when effective, results in rapid behavioral change. These factors improve the likelihood that parents and staff members will implement the program faithfully. Hagopian, Fisher, and Legacy (1994) described an interesting intervention using noncontingent reinforcement with 5-year-old quadruplets diagnosed with mental retardation and Pervasive Developmental Disorder (PDD). The target behaviors were aggression and self-injury. A functional analysis indicated that these behaviors were primarily motivated by access to attention from adults. The investigators designed a program to provide the children with attention on a dense schedule of reinforcement (every 10 seconds). This schedule was gradually faded to noncontingent attention every 5 minutes. The program was implemented in the family home, and problem behaviors decreased significantly. The parents also found that the program was relatively easy to implement. Behavioral improvement was maintained at one and two months' follow-up. Hagopian et al. recommended that if noncontingent reinforcement is used in a clinical setting, it should begin with a very dense schedule of reinforcement and gradually be faded to a leaner schedule as problem behaviors decrease.

Punishment Procedures

The use of punishment is one of the most controversial issues in the behavioral literature. Clinicians and ethicists have seriously questioned the use of these procedures. Some state that punishment should never be used; others suggest that punishment may be indicated in the short-term treatment of serious behavioral disturbances, when used in conjunction with appropriate education, training, and reinforcement procedures. (A more complete discussion of this issue appears at the end of this chapter.)

Punishment is defined in behavioral terms as "a consequent stimulus that decreases the future rate and/or probability of a behavior" (Alberto & Troutman, 1990, p. 454). As is the case for other behavioral interventions, punishment is rarely implemented alone. Rather, it is typically used together with reinforcement-based interventions, antecedent procedures, and skill development programs.

Similar to reinforcement, punishment (and what is experienced as punishing) can vary greatly from individual to individual. In an effort to identify punishers for the treatment of pica manifested by three young developmentally disabled children (two with pervasive developmental disorders), Fisher et al., (1994) conducted a systematic evaluation to identify both reinforcers and mild punishers for each child. A DRI schedule was implemented in order to provide reinforcement to the children for appropriate eating. Opportunities for pica were presented in a "baited environment," and children who engaged in pica received a

punisher. Pica decreased rapidly with generalization of the benefits into the children's homes. Even though the program was successful, pica was not entirely eliminated, and safety precautions to prevent ingestion of inedible objects continued to be necessary at home and school.

Punishers seem to be more effective if they are systematically varied over time. Charlop, Burgio, Iwata, and Ivancic (1988) designed a program to reduce aggression and object throwing exhibited by three children with developmental disabilities (two of whom had autism). The authors identified a number of mild potential punishers (verbal reprimand, overcorrection, time-out) and compared the effects of using one punisher consistently with those of varying punishers over time. The use of varied punishers appeared to be more effective than the use of one type of punisher. The schedule used to deliver the punisher may also influence efficacy. Cipani, Brendlinger, McDowell, and Usher (1991) compared the effects of continuous and intermittent schedules of punishment on the self-injury of a 6-year-old with autism. Lemon juice squirted in the mouth, contingent on self-injury, immediately suppressed the behavior on both a continuous and an intermittent schedule. Manual guidance overcorrection as a punisher for self-injury was immediately effective if implemented continuously, but took longer to become effective if implemented intermittently.

Punishment procedures can be effective even if implemented some time after the problem behavior has occurred. Van Houten and Rolider (1988) treated three preschool children for biting and stomping on the feet of other children in the class. The punisher was movement suppression time-out in which the child had to face the wall for a specific period of time and not move or make a noise during that time. The child also received a verbal reprimand. If the aggressive behavior occurred at another time, the authors attempted to "recreate the scene" of the problem behavior as much as possible, and then implement the time-out procedure. The frequency of the aggression was reduced to zero, and this was maintained at one and four months' follow-up. A previous study by Rolider and Van Houten (1985) found that movement suppression time-out was more effective than simple corner time-out in reducing the aggressive behavior of three children with severe disabilities. In addition to movement suppression time-out, the authors used a DRO schedule to reinforce the absence of aggressive behavior. Movement suppression time-out has also been used in treatment programs for adults. Matson and Keyes (1988) used this intervention in conjunction with highly structured activities, DRO, and choice making in a daily schedule to treat the severe aggression, self-injury, and property destruction of a man with autism and mental retardation. DRO and antecedent interventions were not effective in reducing the problem behavior. When a movement suppression time-out component involving contingent mechanical restraint was added, the behavioral problems decreased rapidly. The use of time-out was faded, and the positive benefits were maintained at a 10-month follow-up. Simple time-out may also be effective in treating some problem behaviors. For example, Mulick and Meinhold (1994) found that simple time-out eliminated the attention-motivated screaming and self-injury of a 30-month-old child diagnosed with pervasive developmental disorder.

Chapman, Fisher, Piazza, and Kurtz (1993) used a combination of punishment and reinforcement-based interventions to treat the potentially life-threatening ingestion of drugs by an adolescent with mental retardation and autism. A functional analysis indicated that escape from task demands (especially work-related demands) was one of the primary motivators of this behavior. The subject was placed on a DRA schedule of reinforcement for completing work assignments, a DRI schedule for turning in any medication he found, and a punisher (performing his least favorite work activity) if he ingested medication. This intervention was effective in eliminating the ingestion of medication.

The efficacy of other punishment procedures has been studied. Rojahn, McGonigle, Curcio, and Dixon (1987) found that contingent water mist was more effective than aromatic ammonia in suppressing the pica of an adolescent with autism and severe mental retardation. There was no increase in other problem behaviors with the use of water mist, and the problem behaviors remained suppressed at a three-month follow-up. Jenson, Rovner, Cameron, Petersen, and Keskr (1985) found

that contingent fine water mist, verbal reprimand, and praise for appropriate behavior, delivered on a DRO schedule, were effective in eliminating severe self-injury (biting) manifested by a young girl with autism. The reduction in self-injury generalized across staff members and settings, and was maintained at a six-month follow-up.

Punishers are sometimes used in combination with medication to reduce behavioral problems. Holttum, Lubetsky, and Eastman (1994) successfully used medication (clomipramine) plus contingent exercise to treat the severe trichotillomania (hair pulling) of a preschool girl with autism. When used alone, neither the medication nor the behavioral intervention was successful in reducing trichotillomania to acceptable levels. However, when used in combination, the interventions were effective in decreasing the behavior substantially.

The use of contingent electric shock as a punisher is occasionally reported in the behavioral literature. Williams, Kirkpatrick-Sanchez, and Crocker (1994) reported a treatment program for the severe self-injury of a young woman with autism and mental retardation. The program involved contingent electric shock, verbal reprimand, and contingent restraint for self-injurious behaviors. The procedure resulted in a significant reduction in self-injury, allowing discontinuation of the contingent shock following 30 months of treatment. Self-injury remained suppressed at follow-up six years later. However, another treatment program for severe self-injury, using contingent electric shock, compliance training, DRO, and extinction of escape, was not as successful (Williams, Kirkpatrick-Sanchez, & Iwata, 1993). The authors reported that, after a period of initial success, the self-injurious behavior increased again at six months, despite the implementation of contingent shock. Although the self-injury did not return to baseline levels, the use of contingent shock did not result in a clinically significant reduction in the target behaviors.

SKILL ACQUISITION

This type of intervention emphasizes the development of alternative positive behavioral skills to compete with, and ideally replace, problem behaviors. Skill acquisition is often used in conjunction with antecedent and consequence interventions, but, at times, the acquisition of new skills alone can reduce the frequency and severity of problem behaviors. An example of a skill acquisition program can be found in the work of Santarcangelo, Dyer, and Luce (1987). The investigators taught a group of young children with autism to play appropriately with toys. The teaching prompts were faded and the children continued to be able to play in unsupervised settings. A reduction in disruptive behaviors also occurred, although these behaviors were not specifically targeted for intervention.

The skill acquisition programs reviewed in this chapter have been specifically designed to address various problem behaviors. General educational programs to teach new skills to persons with autism are reviewed in other chapters in this volume.

Skill acquisition programs generally fall into the following main categories: language and communication skills, self-management skills, and social skills. A comprehensive behavior management program may include interventions from all three categories. Once again, studies will be reviewed according to the major focus of the intervention package.

Language and Communication Skills

The development of functional language and communication skills to reduce the frequency and severity of problem behavior is one of the fastest growing areas in the field of behavioral intervention. The benefits of this type of intervention were illustrated in the report of McMorrow and Foxx (1986) on the treatment of echolalia exhibited by adults with autism. Using a systematic program of shaping, reinforcement, and extinction, the authors were able to significantly decrease echolalia and increase functional language (which generalized outside of the immediate treatment setting).

Functional Communication Training (FCT) involves teaching a communicative response as an alternative to maladaptive behavior. Many problem behaviors, such as self-injury and aggression, serve a communicative function by expressing desires (e.g., for objects, activities, attention), representing a form of protest, or serving as a means of escaping task demands.

FCT is not simply the replacement of a problem behavior; it is also an effective means of gaining access to reinforcers (Carr, 1988). Because many persons with autism and other severe disabilities do not have effective communication skills, an effective behavioral intervention will often require instruction in functional communication, as well as methods to deal with the problem behaviors (Doss & Reichle, 1989).

Carr and Durand (1985) conducted some of the early work in FCT. In one study, a functional analysis indicated that the disruptive behavior exhibited by four children with disabilities (one with autism) was motivated by escape from task demands, and, in one case, a desire for attention from adults. The students were taught short phrases to request breaks from activities and attention, and the disruptive behavior declined. Carr and Durand emphasized the importance of conducting a functional analysis and teaching functionally equivalent communicative behavior (communication that is effective and efficient).

Durand and Crimmins (1987) taught a boy with autism and escape-motivated behaviors the phrase "Help me." Use of this phrase resulted in being excused from task demands. As the child gained adaptive control in this manner, the frequency of the escape behaviors declined. Under some circumstances, stereotyped behaviors, such as body rocking and hand flapping, may respond to FCT. Durand and Carr (1987) found that the stereotyped behavior of children with autism increased during task demands and difficult requests, and declined during easier tasks. A communication training program to enable the children to request assistance with difficult tasks resulted in a decline in the frequency of stereotypy.

Functional Communication Training has been adapted for teaching nonverbal communication, to supplement instruction in speech. For example, Carr and Kemp (1989) taught four preschool children with autism to point to a desired toy rather than engage in "autistic leading." Once a pointing response was established, the autistic leading of all four children declined significantly. Horner and Budd (1985) taught simple manual signs to an 11-year-old boy with autism, who engaged in grabbing and yelling in school when he wanted particular items. Manual sign communication was taught most effectively in the actual school setting in which the signs were to be used. The authors found that once the student had mastered several simple signs, the frequency and severity of grabbing and yelling declined substantially.

FCT can be combined with a variety of antecedent, consequence, and other skill acquisition programs in the development of a comprehensive and effective behavioral intervention. Jayne, Schloss, Alper, and Menscher (1994) developed a comprehensive treatment program for elementary school students (several with autism or pervasive developmental disorders) who engaged in a variety of disruptive behaviors, such as screaming, hitting, and throwing objects. The program included systematic teaching procedures (system of least prompts), communication training to request help, and DRA reinforcement to reward appropriate communication. This program was successful in reducing the problem behaviors in the classroom. L.K. Koegel, Koegel, Hurley, and Frea (1992) used a combination of FCT, social skills training, self-management training, and differential reinforcement to improve the social skills of children with autism in community settings. As the children's communication and social skills improved, disruptive behaviors declined, even though these behaviors were not directly targeted for intervention. Carr and Carlson (1993) described an intensive behavioral treatment program for three adolescents with autism who exhibited aggression, property destruction, disruptive screaming, and elopement behavior. The program, which was implemented in a community setting, involved a number of antecedent, consequence, and skill acquisition components, including FCT, procedures for improving frustration tolerance, behavioral momentum, and other related interventions. Although this was a sophisticated behavioral program, the intervention was implemented by general group-home staff in a community setting. The program resulted in an almost total elimination of problem behaviors, and a corresponding increase in on-task performance and other adaptive behaviors.

The complexity of behavior problems that can result from communication deficits was illustrated in a report by Day, Horner, and O'Neill (1994), who conducted a functional analysis of self-injury and aggression manifested by three persons with mental retardation (one of whom also had autism). The functional analysis indicated that the behaviors were motivated by access to food or objects in one setting, and escape from demands in other settings. FCT was not effective until the subjects were taught communication skills sufficient to make requests for desired items and breaks from required tasks. This study, and the others discussed previously, emphasize the importance of a functional analysis in designing effective behavioral interventions.

Sprague and Horner (1992) found that FCT was effective in reducing a number of problem behaviors (e.g., hitting self and others, screaming) exhibited by a child with autism. The authors of this study also found that attempts to eliminate one problem behavior resulted in an increase in other maladaptive behaviors of the same response class (i.e., behaviors that had similar effects in gaining reinforcement). Only FCT was effective in the overall suppression of the problem behaviors. Campbell and Lutzker (1993) found that FCT in combination with activities planning was effective in reducing the tantrums and property destruction of an 8-year-old boy with autism. This program was successfully implemented by a parent in the family home.

Durand and Carr (1991) demonstrated the potential long-term effectiveness of FCT in their study of three children with disabilities who engaged in disruptive behavior motivated by escape from demands and a desire for attention. The progress achieved in adaptive behavior and functional communication was maintained across settings at 18 and 24 months' follow-up.

Although FCT is quite beneficial in expanding the communicative repertoires of persons with disabilities, and secondarily, in reducing a variety of behavioral problems, there are limitations to its effectiveness. Vollmer (1994) has suggested that FCT alone is not an appropriate treatment for maladaptive behaviors that are motivated by automatic or sensory reinforcement. In this regard, Wacker et al. (1990) and Fisher et al. (1993) found that FCT was not effective without a punishment component for their subjects. However, when combined with other behavioral approaches, FCT and related interventions are effective in expanding communication skills and reducing maladaptive behavior across a variety of home and community settings.

Social Skills Training

A major impact in the behavioral functioning of children and adults with autism can be achieved by expanding their range of adaptive social skills. This seems quite logical, given the fact that deficient social reciprocity represents one of the core features of the syndrome. In a recent review of social skills training in children with autism, Matson and Swiezy (1994) found that, although the field is in its infancy, the available research findings are quite promising. As investigators reach consensus regarding the definition and assessment of social skills, significant progress should be made. Presently, much of the current research on social skills in autism is focused on the preschool population. Several intriguing methods of training social skills among preschool children have been reported. Lefebre and Strain (1989) found that typically developing preschool children could be taught to initiate social interactions with their peers with autism. The general improvement in social behavior demonstrated by the children with autism was maintained by group contingencies and teacher prompts. Oke and Schreibman (1990) reported that the disruptive behavior of a young boy with autism decreased after he was taught adaptive methods of initiating social contact with his peers.

Some social skills programs have been developed for adolescents and adults with autism. Agran, Salzberg, and Stowitschek (1987) used a combination of social skills training and self-management procedures to teach a group of adults with disabilities (one with autism) appropriate social behaviors on a work site. The behavioral gains were maintained at three to four months' follow-up. Dunlap et al., (1987) taught adolescents and adults with autism to respond appropriately to the social initiatives and task requests of untrained staff in community settings. The positive social behaviors were maintained in community settings by using infrequent and delayed contingency reinforcement programs.

One method of social skills training, pivotal response training (PRT), emphasizes responsiveness to multiple cues and improved motivation. PRT represents a potentially powerful approach to teaching social skills to persons with autism (R.L. Koegel et al., 1989).

R.L. Koegel and Frea (1993) used PRT to teach basic social skills to two adolescents with autism. The training resulted in a significant improvement in social behavior and communication (e.g., reductions in verbal perseveration, inappropriate facial expressions, and so on), which generalized beyond the immediate treatment setting. Schreibman, Kaneko, and Koegel (1991) found that parents appeared happier and more relaxed when they used PRT methods with their children than when they used more structured teaching techniques.

There is some research evidence indicating long-term effectiveness of social skills training strategies. For example, Foxx and Faw (1992) reported that improvements in social skills were maintained for eight years, following the completion of a social skills training program for adults with mental retardation.

Self-Management Procedures

Self-management procedures are behavioral strategies in which individuals take responsibility for monitoring their own behavior and administering contingent rewards and consequences. The major benefits of this type of intervention include increased independence, better generalization of treatment progress outside of the immediate treatment setting, and greater success in addressing several problem behaviors simultaneously (L.K. Koegel, Koegel, & Parks, 1992; R.L. Koegel, Frea, & Surratt, 1994). These strategies are potentially beneficial for children and adults with autism. Self-management programs developed for persons with autism often make use of aids to assist in the self-monitoring process, such as pictorial or written schedules, task analyses, wrist-mounted counting devices, and so on. For example, MacDuff, Krantz, and McClannahan (1993) introduced photographic activity schedules to four boys with autism. With the aid of these schedules, the students learned to perform complex tasks, mastered a number of new behaviors, and experienced a decrease in disruptive behavior. In a follow-up study, Krantz, MacDuff, and McClannahan (1993) trained the parents of three boys with autism to implement picture activity schedules within the home. The parents successfully taught their children to follow the schedules and, as a result, reported an increase in social engagement and a decrease in disruptive behavior (tantrums, aggression, property destruction). Stahmer and Schreibman (1992) used self-management procedures to teach children with autism appropriate, independent toy play. The children learned to play appropriately in unsupervised settings, and continued to do so at a one-month follow-up. Pierce and Schreibman (1994) used picture schedules and other self-management procedures to teach daily living skills to children with autism. The children began using the newly learned skills in a variety of unsupervised settings, and their stereotypic behavior decreased.

RESPONDENT CONDITIONING PROCEDURES

Most of the behavioral interventions described in this chapter are based on the principles of operant conditioning; however, several behavioral strategies used in clinical practice follow classical or respondent conditioning theory. (See Alberto & Troutman, 1990, pp. 30–35, for a discussion.)

Clinical behavioral interventions based on respondent conditioning tend to involve covert imagery or relaxation procedures. Although respondent conditioning procedures have been applied infrequently to persons with autism, several have proven to be useful. In some studies, behavioral programs incorporate interventions that reflect both respondent and operant principles.

Groden and Cautela (1988) used a covert conditioning program that involved imagining positive consequences for appropriate social behaviors in order to increase the verbal interactions of a group of three adolescents with autism. The program was successful in increasing appropriate social interactions with peers. In a recent case series, Groden, Cautela, Prince, and Berryman (1994) reported that social skills training and relaxation procedures decreased the disruptive behavior of subjects with autism and related handicaps. Lindsay, Fee, Michie, and Heap (1994) found that adults

with severe mental retardation could learn simple relaxation techniques and apply them so as to reduce their level of disruptive behavior. Love, Matson, and West (1990) used a combination of operant strategies (modeling, reinforcement) and respondent conditioning (in vivo desensitization) to treat the phobias of two children with autism. The mothers of the children were taught to implement the procedures at home. The significant reduction in phobic anxiety that resulted was maintained at a one-year follow-up.

Procedures based on respondent conditioning offer a number of advantages over other behavioral interventions. First, because these procedures can be used in a variety of clinical settings, they result in improved maintenance and generalization of adaptive behavioral responses. Second, the personal independence of many people with autism can be enhanced by successful self-monitoring and the implementation of relaxation and covert conditioning responses. However, considerably more research is needed to identify the demographic and clinical factors that are predictive of a beneficial outcome to respondent procedures (Miranda, 1986).

DIFFERENTIAL EFFICACY OF BEHAVIORAL STRATEGIES

It is of particular importance for the treating clinician to have access to data outlining a hierarchy of behavioral strategies that are successful for treating specific behavioral problems. Unfortunately, there has been little research in this area. The literature is dominated by single-case designs and small case series that rarely include comparisons of different behavioral interventions or evaluations of the influence of specific demographic and clinical variables on treatment outcome. However, several meta-analyses have been published that offer preliminary insight regarding these important issues among persons with developmental disorders (Gorman-Smith & Matson, 1985; Lennox, Miltenberger, Spengler, & Erfanian, 1988; Matson & Gorman-Smith, 1986). These studies suggest that the most responsive target behaviors include hyperactivity, stereotypy, and toileting problems, whereas the least responsive include self-injury and aggression (Lennox et al.; Matson & Gorman-Smith). Specific intervention types may be most effective for particular problems. For example, differential reinforcement procedures, physical prompting, redirection, and skill training may be most efficacious for the treatment of anxiety, dysphoria, and inappropriate social behavior; extinction, social disapproval, and overcorrection for physiological problems (for example, enuresis and encopresis); and more intensive punishment procedures (such as time-out and restraint) for destructive behavior (including self-injury and aggression; Lennox et al.). There is a definite need for more studies to clarify the relationship between the types of behavior interventions and clinical variables (specific problem behaviors, demographics, and so on).

CURRENT AND FUTURE ISSUES IN BEHAVIORAL INTERVENTION

The research studies reviewed in this chapter demonstrate the utility and effectiveness of behavioral interventions in enhancing the adaptive behavior, productivity, and independence of children and adults with autism. The remainder of this chapter will focus on issues that are central to the field of behavioral intervention.

Maintenance and Generalization of Behavioral Interventions

Functional analysis assessment procedures are generally accepted as the basis for effective behavioral interventions. Despite its importance, functional analysis has received little attention in the research literature. During recent years, however, the number of systematic studies has been increasing (Hile & Desrochers, 1993; Peterson & Martens, 1995).

Maintenance refers to the length of time, following the end of initial treatment, during which clinical benefits continue. Generalization refers to the degree to which positive behavioral change extends beyond the immediate treatment setting. Although it is theoretically and clinically possible for long-term maintenance to occur without generalization, and for generalization to occur without long-term maintenance, the optimal outcome is for both to follow the initial treatment phase.

Reviews of behavioral research in the field of developmental disabilities have indicated that the published research in this area does not clearly document the generalization and maintenance of positive behavior change (Scotti, Evans, Meyer, & Walker, 1991; Werry & Wollersheim, 1989). Scotti et al. reported that fewer than half of the published studies in their comprehensive review of behavioral interventions included documentation of maintenance and generalization of treatment effects. Furthermore, those studies that did include follow-up rarely reported data for more than six months. Scotti et al. recommended that future studies include more information about the subjects, a formal functional analysis, and objective measures of follow-up extended to a minimum of six months to a year after initial treatment.

There is some support for the long-term effectiveness of behavioral interventions. For example, McEachin, Smith, and Lovaas (1993) published a six-year follow-up of young children with autism who received intensive early behavioral treatment. A comparison group consisted of children who received less intensive intervention. The outcomes clearly favored the intensive treatment group, even after six years. However, controversy surrounds various aspects of the research design of the study. (For commentary, see Baer, 1993; Foxx, 1993; Kazdin, 1993; Mesibov, 1993; Mundy, 1993.)

Future behavioral research should focus on documenting the long-term maintenance and generalization of positive behavioral change. For the present, there is ample preliminary evidence indicating that behavioral procedures are the most effective treatment interventions for a variety of behavioral symptoms associated with autism.

Aversive and Nonaversive Interventions

During the past 10 years, a great deal of time and energy has been devoted to discussions and debate regarding the appropriateness of punishment procedures as behavioral treatment strategies (see Repp & Singh, 1990, for an overview). The major issues underlying this controversy will be presented; however, a thorough review is beyond the scope of this chapter. (For a more complete review, see Matson and Taras, 1989.) Some professional organizations have advocated that punishment procedures never be used, and many states have adopted regulations that either ban or restrict their implementation. Currently, there is little justification for using aversive procedures as the sole treatment intervention; they do not teach problem-solving strategies, communication skills, or adaptive ways of dealing with frustrations and stress. Even those who support a role for aversive interventions strongly support the development of effective nonaversive treatment approaches (e.g., Smith, T., 1990). Most would agree that, when used, aversive procedures should be reserved for serious behavioral problems (e.g., severe aggression, self-injury) and be part of a comprehensive program of alternative skill development and positive reinforcement. In addition, they should be implemented appropriately and reviewed regularly to ensure continuing efficacy and need. The controversy over punishment procedures has, in itself, stimulated some changes in the field. For example, it has encouraged the development of sophisticated, multi-element, behavioral interventions for severe problem behaviors that can be implemented in community settings.

Guidelines for the use of behavior reduction procedures (including punishment) were presented by a panel of experts in the field of developmental disabilities who participated in a Consensus Development Conference on the Treatment of Destructive Behaviors in Persons with Developmental Disabilities, sponsored by the National Institutes of Health in 1989 (National Institutes of Health, 1991). Among their recommendations were the following:

1. Most successful approaches to treatment are likely to involve multiple elements of therapy (behavioral and psychopharmacological), environmental change, and education.
2. Treatment methods may require techniques for enhancing desired behaviors; for producing changes in social, physical, and educational environments; and for reducing or eliminating destructive behaviors.
3. Treatments should be based on an analysis of medical and psychiatric conditions, environmental situations, consequences, and skill deficits. In the application of any of these treatments, an essential step involves a functional analysis of existing behavioral patterns.
4. Behavior-reduction procedures should be selected for their rapid effectiveness *only*

if the exigencies of the clinical situation require such restrictive interventions and *only* after appropriate review. These interventions should *only* be used in the context of a comprehensive treatment package.

The controversy over aversive interventions is likely to continue.

Social Validity

There is an increasing awareness that behavioral interventions should not only reduce the frequency and severity of problem behaviors, but also be valued by those who receive the services, their families, and the larger community. Therefore, the outcome of behavioral interventions should document change in specific behaviors and, whenever possible, improve the support and options available to a child or adult with autism. As part of a comprehensive behavioral treatment program, these options should include, throughout the day, opportunities for a child or adult to make choices, learn new skills, and gain access to appropriate reinforcement. Meyer and Evans (1989) presented a useful discussion of methods for assessing, documenting, and implementing positive changes in a person's lifestyle. Schreibman (1994) also discussed several helpful methods for assessing the social validity of behavioral interventions and their outcomes.

Behavioral Interventions in the Community

A survey of families of children and adults with autism, conducted by Dunlap, Robbins, and Darrow (1994), found that families frequently deal with problem behaviors. However, most of the families reported that they had little or no access to regular behavioral consultation. This is unfortunate because research indicates that behavioral consultation in community settings is effective for the treatment of many behavioral problems, and can be delivered in an efficient manner (Derby et al., 1992; Harchik, Sherman, Sheldon, & Strouse, 1992; Northup et al., 1994).

In the absence of direct behavioral consultation, families rely most heavily on teachers, other family members, and published materials for behavioral information. As one of these resources, behavioral treatment manuals constitute an important source of information for families and behavioral clinicians (e.g., Carr et al., 1994; Dalrymple, 1991; Foxx, 1982a, 1982b; M.D. Smith, 1990). However, it has become increasingly important that behavioral analysts not only promote the development of "user-friendly" treatment manuals, but also assist in the development of programs that make behavioral support more readily available to families and professionals in the community.

Computer Applications

Computers can be used to enhance the usefulness and efficiency of behavioral intervention programs. For example, computer programs can assist with data collection, the documentation of interventions, staff scheduling, and a variety of administrative tasks in programs for persons with developmental disabilities (Romanczyk, 1984). Some computer programs simplify the collection of direct observational data and provide an efficient method of data analysis (Repp & Karsh, 1990). In addition, sophisticated computer software systems have been developed to assist behavioral clinicians in locating and evaluating treatment programs (Hofmeister et al., 1994). In the future, advanced software programs will play an increasingly important role in the development of behavioral interventions.

During recent years, behavioral treatment approaches for persons with autism have become more effective and more complex. Advances in behavioral treatment are likely to continue into the future. However, the most important measure of success of such approaches will be the documented improvement they bring to the lives of children and adults with autism.

Cross-References

Issues in psychological and behavioral assessment are discussed in Chapters 19 and 20. Aspects of curriculum and communication interventions are addressed in Chapters 22 through 25. Program administration is discussed in Chapter 30. Theoretical perspectives on behavioral interventions are addressed in Chapters 44 and 45.

REFERENCES

Agran, M., Salzberg, C.L., & Stowitschek, J.J. (1987). An analysis of the effects of a social skills training program using self-instructions on the acquisition and generalization of two social behaviors in a work setting. *Journal of the Association for Persons with Severe Handicaps, 12,* 131–139.

Alberto, P.A., & Troutman, A.C. (1990). *Applied behavior analysis for teachers.* New York: Macmillan.

Allison, D.B., Basile, V.C., & MacDonald, R.B. (1991). Brief report: Comparative effects of antecedent exercise and lorazepam on the aggressive behavior of an autistic man. *Journal of Autism and Developmental Disorders, 21,* 89–94.

Azrin, N.H., Besalel, V.A., Janner, J.P., & Caputo, J.N. (1988). Comparative study of behavioral methods of treating severe self-injury. *Behavioral Residential Treatment, 3,* 119–152.

Baer, D.M. (1993). Quasi-random assignment can be as convincing as random assignment. *American Journal on Mental Retardation, 97,* 373–375.

Bebko, J.M., & Lennox, C. (1988). Teaching the control of diurnal bruxism to two children with autism using a simple cueing procedure. *Behavior Therapy, 19,* 249–255.

Brown, F. (1991). Creative daily scheduling: A nonintrusive approach to challenging behaviors in community residences. *Journal of the Association for Persons with Severe Handicaps, 16,* 75–84.

Campbell, R.V., & Lutzker, J.R. (1993). Using functional equivalence training to reduce severe challenging behavior: A case study. *Journal of Developmental and Physical Disabilities, 5,* 208–216.

Carr, E.G. (1988). Functional equivalence as a mechanism of response generalization. In R.H. Horner, G. Dunlap, & R.L. Koegel (Eds.), *Generalization and maintenance: Life-style changes in applied settings* (pp. 221–241). Baltimore: Brookes.

Carr, E.G., & Carlson, J.I. (1993). Reduction of severe behavior problems in the community using a multicomponent treatment approach. *Journal of Applied Behavior Analysis, 26,* 157–172.

Carr, E.G., & Durand, V.M. (1985). Reducing behavior problems through functional communication training. *Journal of Applied Behavior Analysis, 18,* 111–126.

Carr, E.G., & Kemp, D.C. (1989). Functional equivalence of autistic leading and communicative pointing: Analysis and treatment. *Journal of Autism and Developmental Disorders, 19,* 561–578.

Carr, E.G., Levin, L., McConnachie, G., Carlson, J.I., Kemp, D.C., & Smith, C.E. (1994). *Communication-based interventions for problem behavior. A user's guide for producing positive change.* Baltimore: Brookes.

Carr, E.G., Robinson, S., & Palumbo, L.W. (1990). The wrong issue: Aversive versus nonaversive treatment. The right issue: Functional versus nonfunctional treatment. In A.C. Repp & N.N. Singh (Eds.), *Perspectives on the use of nonaversive and aversive interventions for persons with developmental disabilities* (pp. 361–379). Sycamore, IL: Sycamore.

Chapman, S., Fisher, W., Piazza, C.C., & Kurtz, P.F. (1993). Functional assessment and treatment of life-threatening drug ingestion in a dually diagnosed youth. *Journal of Applied Behavior Analysis, 26,* 255–256.

Charlop, M.H., Burgio, L.D., Iwata, B.A., & Ivancic, M.T. (1988). Stimulus variation as a means of enhancing punishment effects. *Journal of Applied Behavior Analysis, 21,* 89–95.

Charlop, M.H., Kurtz, P.F., & Casey, F.G. (1990). Using aberrant behaviors as reinforcers for autistic children. *Journal of Applied Behavior Analysis, 23,* 163–181.

Chen, S.H.A., & Bernard-Opitz, V. (1993). Comparison of personal and computer-assisted instruction for children with autism. *Mental Retardation, 31,* 368–376.

Cipani, E., Brendlinger, J., McDowell, L., & Usher, S. (1991). Continuous versus intermittent punishment: A case study. *Journal of Developmental and Physical Disabilities, 3,* 147–156.

Dalrymple, N.J. (1991). *Helping people with autism manage their behavior* (3rd ed.). Bloomington: Indiana Resource Center for Autism.

Davis, C.A., Brady, M.P., Williams, R.E., & Hamilton, R. (1992). Effects of high-probability requests on the acquisition and generalization of responses to requests in young children with behavior disorders. *Journal of Applied Behavior Analysis, 25,* 905–916.

Day, H.M., Horner, R.H., & O'Neill, R.E. (1994). Multiple functions of problem behaviors: Assessment and intervention. *Journal of Applied Behavior Analysis, 27,* 279–289.

Derby, K.M., Wacker, D.P., Sasso, G., Steege, M., Northup, J., Gigrand, K., & Asmus, J. (1992).

Brief functional assessment techniques to evaluate aberrant behavior in an outpatient setting: A summary of 79 cases. *Journal of Applied Behavior Analysis, 25,* 713–721.

Donnellan, A.M., LaVigna, G.W., Zambito, J., & Thvedt, J. (1985). A time-limited intensive intervention program model to support community placement for persons with severe behavior problems. *Journal of the Association for Persons with Severe Handicaps, 10,* 123–131.

Doss, S., & Reichle, J. (1989). Establishing communicative alternatives to the emission of socially motivated excess behavior: A review. *Journal of the Association for Persons with Severe Handicaps, 14*(2), 101–112.

Ducharme, J.M., & Van Houten, R. (1994). Operant extinction in the treatment of severe maladaptive behavior. *Behavior Modification, 18,* 139–170.

Duker, P.C., & Rasing, E. (1989). Effects of redesigning the physical environment on self-stimulation and on-task behavior in three autistic-type developmentally disabled individuals. *Journal of Autism and Developmental Disorders, 19,* 449–460.

Dunlap, G. (1984). The influence of task variation and maintenance tasks on the learning and affect of autistic children. *Journal of Experimental Child Psychology, 37,* 41–64.

Dunlap, G., Johnson, L.F., & Robbins, F.R. (1990). Preventing serious behavior problems through skill development and early intervention. In A.C. Repp & N.N. Singh (Eds.), *Perspectives on the use of nonaversive and aversive interventions for persons with developmental disabilities* (pp. 273–286). Sycamore, IL: Sycamore.

Dunlap, G., Koegel, R.L., Johnson, J., & O'Neill, R.E. (1987). Maintaining performance of autistic clients in community settings with delayed contingencies. *Journal of Applied Behavior Analysis, 20,* 185–191.

Dunlap, G., Robbins, F.R., & Darrow, M.A. (1994). Parents' reports of their children's challenging behaviors: Results of a statewide survey. *Mental Retardation, 32,* 206–212.

Durand, V.M., & Carr, E.G. (1987). Social influences on "self-stimulatory" behavior: Analysis and treatment application. *Journal of Applied Behavior Analysis, 20,* 119–132.

Durand, V.M., & Carr, E.G. (1991). Functional communication training to reduce challenging behavior: Maintenance and application in new settings. *Journal of Applied Behavior Analysis, 24,* 251–264.

Durand, V.M., & Crimmins, D.B. (1987). Assessment and treatment of psychotic speech in an autistic child. *Journal of Autism and Developmental Disorders, 17,* 17–28.

Durand, V.M., Crimmins, D.B., Caulfield, M., & Taylor, J. (1989). Reinforcer assessment 1: Using problem behavior to select reinforcers. *Journal of the Association for Persons with Severe Handicaps, 14,* 113–126.

Dyer, K., Dunlap, G., & Winterling, V. (1990). Effects of choice making on the serious problem behaviors of students with severe handicaps. *Journal of Applied Behavior Analysis, 23,* 515–524.

Elliott, R.O., Jr., Dobbin, A.R., Rose, G.D., & Soper, H.V. (1994). Vigorous, aerobic exercise versus general motor training activities: Effects on maladaptive and stereotypic behaviors of adults with both autism and mental retardation. *Journal of Autism and Developmental Disorders, 24,* 565–574.

Fisher, W.W., Piazza, C.C., Bowman, L.G., Kurtz, P.F., Sherer, M.R., & Lachman, S.R. (1994). A preliminary evaluation of empirically derived consequences for the treatment of pica. *Journal of Applied Behavior Analysis, 27,* 447–457.

Fisher, W.W., Piazza, C.C., Cataldo, M., Harrell, R., Jefferson, G., & Conner, R. (1993). Functional communication training with and without extinction and punishment. *Journal of Applied Behavior Analysis, 26,* 23–36.

Flannery, K.B., & Horner, R.H. (1994). The relationship between predictability and problem behavior for students with severe disabilities. *Journal of Behavioral Education, 4,* 157–176.

Foxx, R.M. (1982a). *Increasing behaviors of persons with severe mental retardation and autism.* Champaign, IL: Research Press.

Foxx, R.M. (1982b). *Decreasing behaviors of persons with severe mental retardation and autism.* Champaign, IL: Research Press.

Foxx, R.M. (1993). Sapid effects awaiting independent replication. *American Journal on Mental Retardation, 97,* 375–376.

Foxx, R.M., & Faw, G.D. (1992). An eight-year follow-up of three social skills training studies. *Mental Retardation, 30*(2), 63–66.

Gabler-Halle, D., Halle, J., & Chung, Y.B. (1993). The effects of aerobic exercise on psychological and behavioral variables of individuals with developmental disabilities: A critical review. *Research in Developmental Disabilities, 14,* 359–386.

Gerhardt, P., & Holmes, D.L. (1994). The Eden Decision Model. A decision model with practical applications for the development of behavior decelerative strategies. In E. Schopler & G.B. Mesibov (Eds.), *Behavioral issues in autism* (pp. 247–276). New York: Plenum Press.

Gorman-Smith, D., & Matson, J.L. (1985). A review of treatment research for self-injurious and stereotyped responding. *Journal of Mental Deficiency Research, 29,* 295–308.

Groden, J., & Cautela, J. (1988). Procedures to increase social interaction among adolescents with autism: A multiple baseline analysis. *Journal of Behavior Therapy and Experimental Psychiatry, 19,* 87–93.

Groden, J., Cautela, J., Prince, S., & Berryman, J. (1994). The impact of stress and anxiety on individuals with autism and developmental disabilities. In E. Schopler & G.B. Mesibov (Eds.), *Behavioral issues in autism* (pp. 177–194). New York: Plenum Press.

Hagopian, L.P., Fisher, W.W., & Legacy, S.M. (1994). Schedule effects of noncontingent reinforcement on attention-maintained destructive behavior in identical quadruplets. *Journal of Applied Behavior Analysis, 27,* 317–325.

Handen, B.L., Apolito, P.M., & Seltzer, G.B. (1984). Use of differential reinforcement of low rates of behavior to decrease repetitive speech in an autistic adolescent. *Journal of Behavior Therapy and Experimental Psychiatry, 15,* 359–364.

Harchik, A.E., Sherman, J.A., Sheldon, J.B., & Strouse, M.C. (1992). Ongoing consultation as a method of improving performance of staff members in a group home. *Journal of Applied Behavior Analysis, 25,* 599–610.

Haring, T.G., Breen, C.G., Pitts-Conway, V., & Gaylord-Ross, R. (1986). Use of differential reinforcement of other behavior during dyadic instruction to reduce stereotyped behavior of autistic students. *American Journal of Mental Deficiency, 90,* 694–702.

Haring, T.G., & Kennedy, C.H. (1990). Contextual control of problem behavior in students with severe disabilities. *Journal of Applied Behavior Analysis, 23,* 235–243.

Hile, M.G., & Desrochers, M.N. (1993). The relationship between functional assessment and treatment selection for aggressive behaviors. *Research in Developmental Disabilities, 14,* 265–274.

Hittner, J.B. (1994). Case study: The combined use of imipramine and behavior modification to reduce aggression in an adult male diagnosed as having Autistic Disorder. *Behavioral Interventions, 9,* 123–139.

Hofmeister, A.M., Althouse, R.B., Likins, M., Morgan, D.B., Ferrara, J.M., Jenson, W.R., & Rollins, E. (1994). SMH.PAL: An expert system for identifying treatment procedures for students with severe disabilities. *Exceptional Children, 61,* 174–181.

Holttum, J.R., Lubetsky, M.J., & Eastman, L.E. (1994). Comprehensive management of tricho-tillomania in a young autistic girl. *Journal of the American Academy of Child and Adolescent Psychiatry, 33,* 577–581.

Horner, R.H., & Budd, C.M. (1985). Acquisition of manual sign use: Collateral reduction of maladaptive behavior, and factors limiting generalization. *Education and Training of the Mentally Retarded, 20,* 39–47.

Houlihan, D., Jacobson, L., & Brandon, P.K. (1994). Replication of a high-probability request sequence with varied interprompt times in a preschool setting. *Journal of Applied Behavior Analysis, 27,* 737–738.

Iwata, B.A., Pace, G.M., Cowdery, G.E., & Miltenberger, R.G. (1994). What makes extinction work: An analysis of procedural form and function. *Journal of Applied Behavior Analysis, 27,* 131–144.

Jayne, D., Schloss, P.J., Alper, S., & Menscher, S. (1994). Reducing disruptive behaviors by training students to request assistance. *Behavior Modification, 18,* 320–338.

Jenson, W.R., Rovner, L., Cameron, S., Petersen, B.P., & Keskr, J. (1985). Reduction of self-injurious behavior in an autistic girl using a multifaceted treatment program. *Journal of Behavior Therapy and Experimental Psychiatry, 16,* 77–80.

Kazdin, A.E. (1993). Replication and extension of behavioral treatment of autistic disorder. *American Journal on Mental Retardation, 97,* 377–379.

Kennedy, C.H. (1994). Manipulating antecedent conditions to alter the stimulus control of problem behavior. *Journal of Applied Behavior Analysis, 27,* 161–170.

Kennedy, C.H., & Haring, T.G. (1993). Combining reward and escape DRO to reduce the problem behavior of students with severe disabilities. *Journal of the Association for Persons with Severe Handicaps, 18,* 85–92.

Kennedy, C.H., & Itkonnen, T. (1993). Effects of setting events on the problem behavior of students with severe disabilities. *Journal of Applied Behavior Analysis, 26,* 321–327.

Koegel, L.K., Koegel, R.L., Hurley, C., & Frea, W.D. (1992). Improving social skills and disruptive behavior in children with autism through self-management. *Journal of Applied Behavior Analysis, 25,* 341–353.

Koegel, L.K., Koegel, R.L., & Parks, D.R. (1992). *How to teach self-management to people with severe disabilities: A training manual.* Santa Barbara: University of California, Graduate School of Education, Counseling/Clinical/School Psychology Program.

Koegel, R.L., & Frea, W.D. (1993). Treatment of social behavior in autism through modification of pivotal social skills. *Journal of Applied Behavior Analysis, 26,* 369–377.

Koegel, R.L., Frea, W.D., & Surratt, A.V. (1994). Self-management of problematic social behavior. In E. Schopler & G.B. Mesibov (Eds.), *Behavioral issues in autism* (pp. 81–97). New York: Plenum Press.

Koegel, R.L., & Koegel, L.K. (1989). Community-referenced research on self-stimulation. In E. Cipani (Ed.), *The treatment of severe behavior disorders. Behavior analysis approaches* (pp. 129–150). Washington, DC: American Association on Mental Retardation (Monograph No. 12).

Koegel, R.L., Schreibman, L., Good, A., Cerniglia, L., Murphy, C., & Koegel, L.K. (1989). *How to teach pivotal behaviors to children with autism: A training manual.* Santa Barbara: University of California, Graduate School of Education, Counseling/Clinical/School Psychology Program.

Krantz, P.J., MacDuff, M.T., & McClannahan, L.E. (1993). Programming participation in family activities for children with autism: Parents' use of photographic activity schedules. *Journal of Applied Behavior Analysis, 26,* 137–138.

Lalli, J.S., Casey, S., Goh, H., & Merlino, J. (1994). Treatment of escape-maintained aberrant behavior with escape extinction and predictable routines. *Journal of Applied Behavior Analysis, 27,* 705–714.

Lanquetot, R. (1989). The effectiveness of peer modeling with autistic children. *Journal of the Multihandicapped Person, 2*(1), 25–34.

LaVigna, G.W., & Donnellan, A.M. (1986). *Alternatives to punishment: Solving behavior problems with non-aversive strategies.* New York: Irvington.

Lefebre, D., & Strain, P. (1989). Effects of a group contingency on the frequency of social interactions among autistic and nonhandicapped preschool children: Making LRE efficacious. *Journal of Early Intervention, 13,* 329–341.

Lennox, D.B., Miltenberger, R.G., Spengler, P., & Erfanian, N. (1988). Decelerative treatment practices with persons who have mental retardation: A review of five years of the literature. *American Journal on Mental Retardation, 92,* 492–501.

Lindsay, W.R., Fee, M., Michie, A., & Heap, I. (1994). The effects of cue control relaxation on adults with severe mental retardation.

Research in Developmental Disabilities, 15, 425–437.

Lovaas, O.I. (1981). *Teaching developmentally disabled children. The ME book.* Austin, TX: Pro-Ed.

Love, S.R., Matson, J.L., & West, D. (1990). Mothers as effective therapists for autistic children's phobias. *Journal of Applied Behavior Analysis, 23,* 379–385.

Luiselli, J.K., Medeiros, J., Jasinowski, C., Smith, A., & Cameron, M.J. (1994). Behavioral medicine treatment of ruminative vomiting and associated weight loss in an adolescent with autism. *Journal of Autism and Developmental Disorders, 24,* 619–629.

Maag, J.W., Wolchik, S.A., Rutherford, J.B., Jr., & Parks, B.T. (1986). Response covariation on self-stimulatory behaviors during sensory extinction procedures. *Journal of Autism and Developmental Disorders, 16,* 145–154.

MacDuff, G.S., Krantz, P.J., & McClannahan, L.E. (1993). Teaching children with autism to use photographic activity schedules: Maintenance and generalization of complex response chains. *Journal of Applied Behavior Analysis, 26,* 89–97.

Mace, F.C., Hock, M.L., Lalli, J.S., West, B.J., Belfiore, P., Pinter, E., & Brown, D.K. (1988). Behavioral momentum in the treatment of noncompliance. *Journal of Applied Behavior Analysis, 21,* 123–141.

Mason, S.S., McGee, G.G., Farmer-Dougan, V., & Risley, T.R. (1989). A practical strategy for ongoing reinforcer assessment. *Journal of Applied Behavior Analysis, 22,* 171–179.

Matson, J.L., & Gorman-Smith, D. (1986). A review of treatment research for aggressive and disruptive behavior in the mentally retarded. *Applied Research in Mental Retardation, 7,* 95–103.

Matson, J.L., & Keyes, J. (1988). Contingent reinforcement and contingent restraint to treat severe aggression and self-injury in mentally retarded and autistic adults. *Journal of the Multihandicapped Person, 1,* 141–153.

Matson, J.L., & Swiezy, N. (1994). Social skills training with autistic children. In J.L. Matson (Ed.), *Autism in adults and children. Etiology, assessment and intervention* (pp. 241–260). Pacific Grove, CA: Brooks/Cole.

Matson, J.L., & Taras, M.E. (1989). A 20-year review of punishment and alternative methods to treat problem behaviors in developmentally delayed persons. *Research in Developmental Disabilities, 10,* 85–104.

McEachin, J.J., Smith, T., & Lovaas, O.I. (1993). Long-term outcome for children with autism who received early intensive behavioral treatment. *American Journal on Mental Retardation, 97,* 359–372.

McGee, G.G., Daly, T., & Jacobs, H.A. (1994). The Walden Preschool. In S.L. Harris & J.S. Handleman (Eds.), *Preschool education programs for children with autism* (pp. 127–162). Austin, TX: Pro-Ed.

McGee, G.G., Paradis, T., & Feldman, R.S. (1993). Free effects of integration on levels of autistic behavior. *Topics in Early Childhood Special Education, 13*(1), 57–67.

McKeegan, G.F., Estill, K., & Campbell, B. (1987). Elimination of rumination by controlled eating and differential reinforcement. *Journal of Behavior Therapy and Experimental Psychiatry, 18,* 143–148.

McMorrow, M.J., & Foxx, R.M. (1986). Some direct and generalized effects of replacing an autistic man's echolalia with correct responses to questions. *Journal of Applied Behavior Analysis, 19,* 289–297.

McNally, R.J., Calamari, J.E., Hansen, P.M., & Keliher, C. (1988). Behavioral treatment of psychogenic polydipsia. *Journal of Behavior Therapy and Experimental Psychiatry, 19,* 57–61.

Mesibov, G.B. (1993). Treatment outcome is encouraging. *American Journal on Mental Retardation, 97,* 379–380.

Meyer, L.H., & Evans, I.M. (1989). *Nonaversive interventions for behavior problems. A manual for home and community.* Baltimore: Brookes.

Mirenda, P. (1986). Covert conditioning. In G.W. LaVigna & A.M. Donnellan (Eds.), *Alternatives to punishment: Solving behavior problems with nonaversive strategies* (pp. 157–167). New York: Irvington.

Mulick, J.A., & Meinhold, P.M. (1994). Developmental disorders and broad effects of the environment on learning and treatment effectiveness. In E. Schopler & G.B. Mesibov (Eds.), *Behavioral issues in autism* (pp. 99–128). New York: Plenum Press.

Mundy, P. (1993). Normal versus high-functioning status in children with autism. *American Journal on Mental Retardation, 97,* 381–384.

Munk, D.D., & Repp, A.C. (1994). The relationship between instructional variables and problem behavior: A review. *Exceptional Children, 60,* 390–401.

National Institutes of Health. (1991). *Treatment of destructive behaviors in persons with developmental disabilities. NIH Consensus Development Conference.* Washington, DC: U.S. Department of Health and Human Services.

Northup, J., Wacker, D.P., Berg, W.K., Kelly, L., Sasso, G., & DeRaad, A. (1994). The treatment of severe behavior problems in school settings using a technical assistance model. *Journal of Applied Behavior Analysis, 27,* 33–47.

Oke, N.J., & Schreibman, L. (1990). Training social initiations to a high-functioning autistic child: Assessment of collateral behavior change and generalization in a case study. *Journal of Autism and Developmental Disorders, 20,* 479–497.

Olley, J.G. (1987). Classroom structure and autism. In D.J. Cohen & A.M. Donnellan (Eds.), *Handbook of autism and pervasive developmental disorders* (pp. 411–417). New York: John Wiley & Sons.

O'Neill, R.E., Horner, R.H., Albin, R.W., Storey, K., & Sprague, J.R. (1990). *Functional analysis of problem behavior. A practical assessment guide.* Sycamore, IL: Sycamore.

Paisey, T.J., Fox, S., Curran, C., Hooper, K., & Whitney, R. (1991). Reinforcement control of severe aggression exhibited by a child with autism in a family home. *Behavioral Residential Treatment, 6,* 289–302.

Peterson, F.M., & Martens, B.K. (1995). A comparison of behavioral interventions in treatment studies for adults with developmental disabilities. *Research in Developmental Disabilities, 16,* 27–41.

Pierce, K.L., & Schreibman, L. (1994). Teaching daily living skills to children with autism in unsupervised settings through pictorial self-management. *Journal of Applied Behavior Analysis, 27,* 471–481.

Rast, J. (1992). Rumination. In E.A. Konarski, J.E. Favell, & J.E. Favell (Eds.), *Manual for the assessment and treatment of the behavior disorders of people with mental retardation* (pp. 1–9). Morganton, NC: Western Carolina Center Foundation.

Repp, A.C., Felce, D., & Barton, L.E. (1991). The effect of initial interval size on the efficacy of DRO schedules of reinforcement. *Exceptional Children, 57,* 417–425.

Repp, A.C., & Karsh, K.G. (1990). A taxonomic approach to the nonaversive treatment of maladaptive behavior of persons with developmental disabilities. In A.C. Repp & N.N. Singh (Eds.), *Perspectives on the use of nonaversive and aversive interventions for persons with developmental disabilities* (pp. 331–347). Sycamore, IL: Sycamore.

Repp, A.C., & Singh, N.N. (1990). *Perspectives on the use of nonaversive and aversive interventions for persons with developmental disabilities.* Sycamore, IL: Sycamore.

Rincover, A., & Newsom, C.D. (1985). The relative motivational properties of sensory and edible reinforcers in teaching autistic children. *Journal of Applied Behavior Analysis, 18,* 237–248.

Robbins, F.R., & Dunlap, G. (1992). Effects of task difficulty on parent teaching skills and child behavior problems in young children with autism. *American Journal on Mental Retardation, 96,* 631–643.

Rojahn, J., McGonigle, J.J., Curcio, C., & Dixon, J.M. (1987). Suppression of pica by water mist and aromatic ammonia: A comparative analysis. *Behavior Modification, 11,* 65–74.

Rolider, A., & Van Houten, R. (1985). Movement suppression time-out for undesirable behavior in psychotic and severely developmentally delayed children. *Journal of Applied Behavior Analysis, 18,* 275–288.

Romanczyk, R.G. (1984). Micro-computers and behavior therapy: A powerful alliance. *Behavior Therapist, 7*(4), 59–64.

Rotholz, D.A., & Luce, S.C. (1983). Alternative reinforcement strategies for reduction of self-stimulatory behavior in an autistic youth. *Education and Treatment of Children, 6,* 363–377.

Santarcangelo, S., Dyer, K., & Luce, S.C. (1987). Generalized reduction of disruptive behavior in unsupervised settings through specific toy training. *Journal of the Association for Persons with Severe Handicaps, 12,* 38–44.

Schreibman, L. (1994). General principles of behavior management. In E. Schopler & G.B. Mesibov (Eds.), *Behavioral issues in autism* (pp. 11–38). New York: Plenum Press.

Schreibman, L., Kaneko, W.M., & Koegel, R.L. (1991). Positive affect of parents of autistic children: Comparison across two teaching techniques. *Behavior Therapy, 22,* 479–490.

Scotti, J.R., Evans, I.M., Meyer, L.H., & Walker, P. (1991). A meta-analysis of intervention research with problem behavior: Treatment validity and standards of practice. *American Journal on Mental Retardation, 96,* 233–256.

Smith, M.D. (1985). Managing the aggressive and self-injurious behavior of adults disabled by autism. *Journal of the Association for Persons with Severe Handicaps, 10,* 228–232.

Smith, M.D. (1986). Use of similar sensory stimuli in the community-based treatment of self-stimulatory behavior in an adult disabled by autism. *Journal of Behavior Therapy and Experimental Psychiatry, 17,* 121–125.

Smith, M.D. (1987). Treatment of pica in an adult disabled by autism by differential reinforcement of incompatible behavior. *Journal of Behavior Therapy and Experimental Psychiatry, 18,* 285–288.

Smith, M.D. (1990). *Autism and life in the community*. Baltimore: Brookes.

Smith, T. (1990). When and when not to consider the use of aversive interventions in the behavioral treatment of autistic children. In A.C. Repp & N.N. Singh (Eds.), *Perspectives on the use of nonaversive and aversive interventions with persons with developmental disabilities* (pp. 287–297). Sycamore, IL: Sycamore.

Sprague, J.R., & Horner, R.H. (1992). Covariation within functional response classes: Implications for treatment of severe problem behavior. *Journal of Applied Behavior Analysis, 25,* 735–745.

Stahmer, A.C., & Schreibman, L. (1992). Teaching children with autism appropriate play in unsupervised environments using a self-management treatment package. *Journal of Applied Behavior Analysis, 25,* 447–459.

Taylor, J.C., Ekdahl, M.M., Romanczyk, R., & Miller, M.L. (1994). Escape behavior in task situations: Task versus social antecedents. *Journal of Autism and Developmental Disorders, 24,* 331–344.

Touchette, P.E., MacDonald, R.F., & Langer, S.N. (1985). A scatter plot for identifying stimulus control of problem behavior. *Journal of Applied Behavior Analysis, 18,* 343–351.

Underwood, L.A., Figueroa, R.G., Thyer, B.A., & Nzeocha, A. (1989). Interruption and DRI in the treatment of self-injurious behavior among mentally retarded and autistic self-restrainers. *Behavior Modification, 13,* 471–481.

Van Houten, R. (1993). The use of wrist weights to reduce self-injury maintained by sensory reinforcement. *Journal of Applied Behavior Analysis, 26,* 197–203.

Van Houten, R., & Rolider, A. (1988). Recreating the scene: An effective way to provide delayed punishment for inappropriate motor behavior. *Journal of Applied Behavior Analysis, 21,* 187–192.

Vollmer, T.R. (1994). The concept of automatic reinforcement: Implications for research in developmental disabilities. *Research in Developmental Disabilities, 15,* 187–207.

Vollmer, T.R., Marcus, B.A., & LeBlanc, L. (1994). Treatment of self-injury and hand mouthing following inconclusive functional analyses. *Journal of Applied Behavioral Analysis, 27,* 331–344.

Wacker, D.P., Steege, M.W., Northrup, J., Sasso, G., Berg, W., Reimers, T., Cooper, L., Gigrand, K., & Doun, L. (1990). A component analysis of functional communication training across three typographies of severe behavior problems. *Journal of Applied Behavior Analysis, 23,* 417–429.

Weber, R.C., & Thorpe, J. (1992). Teaching children with autism through task variation in physical education. *Exceptional Children, 59,* 77–86.

Werry, J.S., & Wollersheim, J.P. (1989). Behavior therapy with children and adolescents: A twenty-year overview. *Journal of the American Academy of Child and Adolescent Psychiatry, 28*(1), 1–18.

Williams, D.E., Kirkpatrick-Sanchez, S., & Crocker, W.T. (1994). A long-term follow-up of treatment for severe self-injury. *Research in Developmental Disabilities, 15,* 487–501.

Williams, D.E., Kirkpatrick-Sanchez, S., & Iwata, B.A. (1993). A comparison of shock intensity in the treatment of longstanding and severe self-injurious behavior. *Research in Developmental Disabilities, 14,* 207–209.

Willis, T.J., LaVigna, G.W., & Donnellan, A.M. (1989). *Behavior assessment guide*. Los Angeles, CA: Institute for Applied Behavior Analysis.

Winterling, V., Dunlap, G., & O'Neill, R.E. (1987). The influence of task variation on the aberrant behaviors of autistic students. *Education and Treatment of Children, 10,* 105–119.

Wong, S.E., Floyd, J., Innocent, A.J., & Woolsey, J.E. (1992). Applying a DRO schedule and compliance training to reduce aggressive and self-injurious behavior in an autistic man: A case report. *Journal of Behavior Therapy and Experimental Psychiatry, 22,* 299–304.

Zarcone, J.R., Iwata, B.A., Mazaleski, J.L., & Smith, R.G. (1994). Momentum and extinction effects on self-injurious escape behavior and noncompliance. *Journal of Applied Behavior Analysis, 27,* 649–658.

CHAPTER 27

Working with Families

LEE M. MARCUS, LINDA J. KUNCE, AND ERIC SCHOPLER

Approaches to working with parents of autistic individuals have undergone significant changes over the past two decades. Paralleling the recognition of autism as a developmental disorder with diverse etiologies (Coleman & Gillberg, 1985; Schopler & Mesibov, 1987; Taft, 1993), rather than as an emotional disturbance, has been the involvement of parents directly in the treatment process of their child (Harris, 1994; Howlin, 1989; Kozloff, 1984; Lovaas, 1987; Marcus & Schopler, 1989; Schopler, Mesibov, Shigley, & Bashford, 1984; Schopler & Reichler, 1971; Schreibman, Koegel, Mills, & Burke, 1984). Parents, no longer viewed as the cause of their child's biologically based problems, now are recognized as being able to play a key role in the effective treatment of their child with autism. This chapter draws from the 30-year experience of Division TEACCH (*T*reatment and *Edu*cation of *A*utistic and Related *C*ommunication-handicapped *CH*ildren) in the Department of Psychiatry at the University of North Carolina School of Medicine, and its predecessor, the Child Research Project (Reichler & Schopler, 1976; Schopler, 1987), as well as from the research and clinical literature.

In this chapter, we first review the literature on work with families whose children exhibit a wide variety of conditions. We then discuss the unique stressors that face families with an autistic child, to provide a framework for understanding the specialized principles and approaches needed to help these families. Using the three decades of experience of the TEACCH program, we continue by covering basic concepts and strategies of support. We

conclude by providing a developmental perspective, from early childhood through adulthood, to highlight crucial intervention issues over the life span of the child and the family.

AN OVERVIEW OF PARENT TRAINING

Over the past three decades, training parents to become cotherapists has become a viable option for treating children with conditions as diverse as enuresis (Azrin, Sneed, & Foxx, 1974), oppositional defiant disorder (Barkley, 1987), motor tics (Levine & Ramirez, 1989), childhood depression (e.g., Cunningham, 1989), and autism (Short, 1984). Indeed, reviews of the clinical and research literature on parent training almost lead to the impression that there are few childhood disorders to which parent training has *not* been applied (see, e.g., Graziano & Diament, 1992; Schaefer & Briesmeister, 1989; Webster-Stratton & Herbert, 1993).

Shared Characteristics of Parent Training Programs

Despite the broad spectrum of targeted behavior problems, a number of assumptions and procedures are shared by a majority of parent training programs. First, the collaborative nature of the relationship between parents and professionals is emphasized. Schaefer and Briesmeister (1989) liken this relationship to a consumer model of service delivery, stating that professionals must listen closely to parents' views, present multiple treatment options to parents, and help parents identify solutions that are in line with family goals and priorities. Placing similar stress on the importance of collaboration, Webster-Stratton and Herbert (1993) suggest that the functions of the professional in parent training are more akin to those of a coach—teaching, empowering, and supporting—than to those of an expert who advises parents on how to best manage their children.

Second, parent training programs tend to share a common perspective on parent–child relationships: they are understood in terms of interactional (e.g., Anastopoulos & Barkley, 1989; Bell & Harper, 1977) or transactional models. For example, children with externalizing disorders exhibit above-average levels of oppositional behaviors, and research evidence suggests that their parents are more likely to experience marital problems and to be more critical, and are less likely to reinforce their child's appropriate behavior (e.g., Griest, Forehand, Wells, & McMahon, 1980; Patterson, 1982). From an interactional or transactional perspective, these patterns of parent and child behavior are viewed as becoming established and maintained over time, through a cycle of mutual influences. It would be naïve to assume that the relative impact of parent-versus-child behaviors on interactional patterns stays constant across disorders, individuals, or time. Nevertheless, use of this type of model helps parents and professionals to collaborate, to lay aside issues of "blame" regarding the cause of the child's problems, and to focus attention on ways in which the parents can develop more effective and satisfying patterns of interaction with their child.

A third characteristic that tends to be similar across parent training programs is the sequence of events that precedes parent training itself; that is, most programs emphasize the importance of a thorough assessment followed by a collaborative decision regarding participation in treatment (e.g., Cunningham, 1989). In line with the close association between parent training and the behavioral tradition in psychology, assessment generally includes not only a traditional diagnostic workup but also close attention to situational factors surrounding child behavior (e.g., Barkley, 1987; Eyberg & Boggs, 1989). In addition, because parent training requires a high degree of commitment from the parents, the assessment process typically involves gathering information about parental concerns, beliefs, and problem-solving skills, as well as factors that may affect the parents' ability to take on a therapist role, such as the need to care for other children in the family, employment responsibilities and travel requirements, lack of extended family support, and so forth (e.g., Eyberg & Boggs, 1989; Webster-Stratton & Herbert, 1993).

Following the assessment, the parent and professional typically enter into a collaborative decision-making process wherein the professional provides a detailed explanation of the available parent training program (e.g., Cunningham, 1989). Whether the decision is to begin, delay, or defer parent training, the professional ensures that parents who are ready to work on other issues, such as marital discord, drug abuse, or accessing general social services, are referred to appropriate persons or agencies (e.g., Azar, 1989).

Parent Training Approaches and Techniques

Not surprisingly, it is the actual *content* of parent training programs that varies most across programs, especially when different disorders or interactional problems are targeted. Schaefer and Briesmeister (1989) divided parent training programs into two major categories: behavior modification approach and relationship enhancement approach. Table 27.1—which adds two additional categories, educational approach and cognitive approach—provides a sampling of the skills taught to parents under each of the four approaches. In reviewing Table 27.1, readers should keep in mind that the four-category division is somewhat artificial because many parent training programs include elements from more than one approach. Further, a single technique may sometimes be used in service of more than one approach (e.g., differential social attention is a behavior modification technique, but it is frequently used to achieve the goal of enhancing the parent–child relationship). Finally, the list in Table 27.1 is meant to be illustrative and representative rather than exhaustive.

An *educational* approach, whether standing alone or used as part of a more comprehensive parent training program, provides parents with

TABLE 27.1   General Approaches to Parent Training and the Accompanying Skills Learned by Parents

Educational Approach. Topics include:

Nature of child's disorder/problems.

General child development.

Child development in respect to the disorder.

General learning principles.

Transactional model of parent–child relationships.

Behavior Modification Approach. Skills include:

Shaping techniques.

Extinction/Ignoring.

Positive reinforcement (social, tangible, token systems).

Differential reinforcement.

Time-out from positive reinforcement.

Contingent negative practice (repetition of undesired behavior).

Positive practice (repetition of desired behavior).

Overlearning.

Relaxation procedures.

Relationship Enhancement Approach. Skills include:

Attending skills ("play therapist" skills such as use of nondirective, descriptive, reflective comments).

Use of a child-directed play time.

Delivery of effective commands.

Establishing clear expectations (e.g., house rules).

Use of therapeutic games/books (parent with child).

Cognitive Approach. Skills include:

Problem-solving skills.

Cognitive restructuring.

Self-monitoring.

Setting realistic expectations.

Topics or skills listed under each approach are meant to be illustrative and representative, rather than exhaustive.

basic information drawn from the clinical research literature and presented in an accessible format. (See Schroeder & Gordon, 1991, for an extensive bibliography of books written for parents and addressing a wide range of issues.) A *behavior modification* approach helps parents to apply principles of learning to day-to-day child rearing as well as to specific problem behaviors. For example, a parent might coach the child in relaxation procedures (Cautela & Groden, 1978), use a time-out from

positive reinforcement to increase child compliance (e.g., Barkley, 1987), or implement a contingent negative practice program to help the child reduce motor tics (e.g., Levine & Ramirez, 1989). Parent training programs that include an emphasis on *relationship enhancement* seek to increase the positive valence and decrease the negative aspects of the parent–child relationship, through teaching the parent such techniques as "attending" or "play therapist" skills (Barkley, 1987; Eyberg & Boggs, 1989). More recently, research has begun to suggest that training parents in a number of *cognitive* and cognitive-behavioral techniques can increase their motivation and persistence in using techniques taught during parent training (e.g., Anastopoulos & Barkley, 1989; Azar, 1989; Williams, Williams, & McLaughlin, 1991). For example, parents may be taught self-monitoring and problem-solving strategies so that they can manage future problems more effectively and independently (Schopler, 1995).

There are both commonalities and differences among parent training programs in how professionals help parents learn and master the skills that they will use in helping their child change. Reading materials, videos, and discussions are frequently used in educating parents about child development and disorders. In presenting new skills, professionals may utilize modeling (live or videotaped), role playing, and discussion. Parents are helped to master skills through the use of role playing, in-session practice with their child, coaching, feedback, and homework assignments (stressing in vivo practice of skills at home and in other settings). Finally, to assess change and encourage use of skills, parents are often encouraged to gather data on their child's behavior, their own behaviors, and the child's responses to intervention attempts. (The reader is referred to Schaefer and Briesmeister's (1989) parent training handbook, and Graziano and Diament's (1992) review, for a sampling of the numerous studies that have used these techniques.)

Advantages of Parent Training

Research and clinical practice indicate that teaching parents to serve as active change agents in their child's treatment can have positive effects beyond improvement in the child's condition. For example, the parents develop feelings of competence and self-efficacy; there is potential for treatment gains to be maintained and generalized as parents apply the recommended techniques over time; and the treatment may favorably influence other behaviors or other children in the family (e.g., Dadds, Sanders, & James, 1987; Humphreys, Forehand, McMahon, & Roberts, 1978). Finally, in a time of limited resources for intervention, parent training can be a relatively cost-effective treatment approach.

Summary and Relevance for Parents of Children with Autism

The standard parent training goals—decreasing inappropriate child behavior, improving the quality of parent–child relationships, and enlisting parents in the change process—are clearly applicable to working with parents of children with autism. Many, if not most, of the teaching techniques used in other parent training programs—such as modeling, coaching, and bibliotherapy—apply to families with a child who has autism. On the other hand, parent training is apt to be ineffective, and perhaps even harmful, if a parent is trained in behavior modification and relationship enhancement approaches without simultaneous education regarding the unique characteristics associated with autism.

For example, if a parent of an autistic child attempts to use time-out procedures to punish self-stimulatory behavior, or relies on social praise to encourage child communication, the parent is apt to become increasingly frustrated when these methods fail to yield the desired results (or even result in a worsening of the child's symptoms). Parents of autistic children face a number of special stressors, not the least of which is the failure of some of the most "tried and true" parenting techniques to work for their child.

In reviewing the effectiveness of parent training for parents of children with mental retardation, Graziano and Diament (1992) argue that the parents do not benefit from "general behavioral training" but they *do* profit from practically oriented training that is specific to their unique situation. Similarly, for parents of children with autism, we believe that effective parent training will take place in a context of understanding regarding (a) the unique characteristics of autism and (b) the unique stressors and challenges faced by the parents of autistic children. These unique stressors are highlighted in the following section.

STRESSORS UNIQUE TO FAMILIES WITH AN AUTISTIC CHILD

Although all parents who have children with behavioral or health-related problems share some common concerns, the parents of an autistic child struggle with many concerns that are unique to their situation. Some of the more stressful factors are described below.

Diagnostic Confusion

Despite current widespread publicity and media attention to the problem of autism, parents, all too often, are not given an accurate, clear, and informative description and definition of their child's problems. Parents usually suspect early on that their child has a significant developmental problem, but they often find their observations unsupported by pediatricians or other health professionals. Later, when the problems begin to escalate and referrals are made to other professionals, the diagnosis of autism may be buried in terms such as the more generic Pervasive Developmental Disorder, or "developmental delays in social and language areas," or other equally unhelpful labels. The failure to establish or communicate the diagnosis of autism adds to the stress of coping with the difficult behaviors and learning problems of their child.

Uneven and Unusual Course of Development

Autism is a disorder marked by delays and deviancies in development that cut across a variety of areas of functioning. The course of development can vary from apparently early normal development followed by plateauing or regression, to generally slow development with the gradual unfolding of the autism character-istics (DeMyer, 1979). These atypical patterns are accompanied by unevenness across skill areas, such as relatively intact visual, spatial, and motor skills alongside deficient language, social, and problem-solving abilities (Wing, 1989). Such variability across skills and time is confusing to parents, whose natural inclina-tion is to expect normal development and deny significant problems. When their child's devel-opment seems to be slowing, parents usually will consider such a process to be temporary. When they see their child solve a complex puz-zle or remember a route to a fast-food restau-rant, they understandably will overlook the receptive language delays or weak imitation skills. The child's uneven profile can prove frustrating to the parents, who may feel that their child will soon catch up. Gauging appro-priate expectations is difficult; for example, although the child may have adequate motor skills for being toilet trained, he or she may not be ready if an understanding of cause and effect is limited. In communicating with their child, parents usually use spoken language, along with emotional expression; however, their autistic child is not likely to respond ade-quately to either form of communication, thereby heightening the parents' anxiety and confusion.

The "Can't vs. Won't" Dilemma

Related to the confusion generated by the child's uneven developmental pattern is the question of whether the child is unable to do something (e.g., respond to a request) or is simply refusing. Typically, a parent reacts to a child's failure to follow through by assuming that the child is unmotivated or is being stub-born. This interpretation is compounded by the child's inconsistent responses and occasional impression of understanding what is being asked. The child may also pick up on contex-tual cues (e.g., "Time to eat" is said as food is placed on the table) and may seem to have a greater understanding of language than is the case. When parents assume that their child is being willful and obstinate, their discipline techniques are often confrontational and tend to result in negatively charged situations.

Appropriate intervention can help parents rec-ognize which behaviors are the result of lack of understanding or ability, and which are oppositional. In the absence of such profes-sional guidance, parents experience consider-able stress.

Attractive Appearance

Because most autistic children appear normal, are attractive, and, from the strictly physical standpoint, do not stand out from their peers, parents experience additional frustration and stress when their child acts unusual or seems to mimic a much younger child. Unlike obvious impairments such as blindness or cerebral palsy, autism is almost invisible; it creates expectations of average social and communi-cative behavior that are rarely met. The dis-crepancy between these expectations and the reality of the disability increases the burden on the family as they seek to understand the child's condition and learn how to deal with it.

Behavior in Public

A constant source of stress for parents is the potentially embarrassing behavior of their autistic child in public places. Anxiety can be highest in parents whose child has not been di-agnosed or who have not yet developed the "thick skin" necessary to cope with the myriad of predictable and unpredictable situations that develop in clear view of the community. When the child has a major tantrum, disrupts a church service, approaches strangers indis-criminately, or is loud or intrusive, the day-to-day stress on families intensifies. Parents understandably worry that they are being judged by others as not being able to control what appears, physically, to be a normal child. In addition, completing daily chores, such as shopping, can be a monumental task, so family life is further disrupted.

Professional Turfism

Obtaining an accurate diagnosis can be diffi-cult, as noted above. Adding to this stressful experience may be disagreements among pro-fessionals, even after the proper diagnosis is made. Given the complexity of the disorder and its effect on multiple aspects of development, it is not surprising that professionals from various disciplines will urge use of treatment techniques and goals that reflect their particular perspective. Unfortunately, varying perspectives can conflict, leaving parents struggling for clarification and support. For example, a pediatric neurologist might view a seizure disorder in an autistic child as primary, treatable, and contraindicating the diagnosis of autism, even though autism and seizures often co-occur. Parents naturally will latch onto a more hopeful prognosis and develop doubts about the professionals who made the autism diagnosis. Another example might be a recommended treatment of sensory integration therapy, with the goal of effecting global change in all areas of the child's functioning (not simply to help with a specific behavior, such as increasing the child's ability to tolerate a certain texture), a choice that seems incompatible with empirically validated educational techniques. Again, parents may be forced to choose, largely because instead of working collaboratively, professionals are committed to their methods and "turf." In these situations, the family and the autistic child ultimately suffer.

Fads and Unproven Therapies

Like other chronic or incurable disorders, autism has been the target for quick-fix practitioners whose techniques end up victimizing families who are desperate for easy answers to difficult questions. The past decade seems to have spawned an extraordinary number of promised cures or solutions, far more than the previous decades. Popular coverage of autism by the news media and the recent proliferation of electronic communication have added to the speed with which information, both accurate and distorted, is obtained. Children are being identified and diagnosed much earlier (Marcus & Stone, 1993), and, in seeking out as much information as possible, parents become susceptible to the promotions of specific therapies that usually have little to offer other than hope.

Schopler (1995) has discussed several factors that these therapies have in common:

1. The technique used appears to be a good idea at first impression, or it may have been helpful in its application to a certain condition and is now assumed to be generalizable to autistic individuals.

2. Reports of effectiveness are invariably anecdotal and not based on careful empirical research. One or two cases of a "cure" are sufficient to capture the attention of vulnerable families. But without systematic investigation, it cannot be clarified what (if any) factors specific to the treatment worked, or what would happen over time with multiple cases. Printed periodicals and television "magazines" are not interested in a new technique that has failed. As Schopler (1995) has noted, "replications are often based on unlikely hypotheses, without adequate theoretical bases, but promoted mainly by hype and hope. Regardless of how the techniques are repeated, not a single treatment technique has been effective with all or even most autistic children" (p. 14).

3. The techniques invariably have negative and costly side effects. For example, the inevitable outcome of the indiscriminate use of facilitated communication (FC) has been unwarranted and unfounded accusations of sexual abuse against families whose lives have been all but destroyed. The excitement over inclusion as the single option for educating all autistic students has resulted in a failure to provide many students with meaningful, individualized instruction (Mesibov & Shea, 1996).

Their efforts to sort through the claims of the various widely touted therapies add to parents' stress. They are diverted from dealing with the fundamental needs of their child and focusing their energies in useful teaching and behavioral approaches.

BASIC CONCEPTS AND PRINCIPLES OF THE TEACCH PROGRAM

To help parents handle these special stressors and to support them in their efforts to effectively deal with their child's problems, the TEACCH program has evolved a number of principles and concepts that guide our treatment efforts and philosophy (Marcus & Schopler, 1989).

Understanding Autism as a Developmental Disability

Perhaps the single most important concept for parents and other professionals to grasp is that autism is a disorder of development and not a psychiatric disturbance. The nature of the disorder is such that the cognitive, communicative, and social learning processes are impaired at least to a mild degree and often more seriously. A primary implication of these deficits is that the deviant behaviors manifested by autistic individuals are the result of inadequate coping and maladaptive response patterns. Behavior problems, often the main identifying or presenting characteristic, are best viewed as the children's inability to effectively deal with their environments because of failure to adequately understand and communicate with others.

A second implication of the concept of a developmental disability is that autism is a chronic disorder that can be adapted to without being totally removed. Therefore, parents need to expect to have to deal with their child's developmental problems to some extent over the child's lifetime. In collaboration with parents, professionals need to be sensitive to the long-term nature of the condition and to the realities that the parents will face over an indefinite period of years.

A third implication is that autism is pervasive; that is, it occurs across all settings and needs to be treated accordingly. A total program requires implementation in various community settings as well as in the home.

INDIVIDUALIZATION AND FLEXIBILITY

Autism may be the most heterogeneous of the developmental disabilities (Wing, 1976). Although it is defined by a core set of characteristics, the wide range of manifestations of each of the major features, within and across individuals, reduces the likelihood that any two autistic individuals will be very similar. In addition, the intelligence levels vary widely, from the profound range of mental retardation to above-average abilities. Associated medical conditions, such as seizure disorders, or sensory impairments, such as blindness, can occur with autism. Autistic individuals can be hyperactive or hypoactive or may fluctuate between the two. Autistic persons come from the entire socioeconomic spectrum, and family resources vary. Therefore, in helping families, it is necessary to recognize their individual differences. A highly individualized and flexible approach requires an in-depth understanding of the child and his or her family as a point of departure during the assessment process. This type of approach implies that ideological positions and packaged training methods may interfere with the helping process by de-emphasizing the uniqueness of each situation. It also assumes that a trial-and-error approach based on an open and collaborative relationship between parent and professional is most appropriate.

Importance of Structure

A central teaching concept in the TEACCH program involves the use of structure (Mesibov, Schopler, & Hearsey, 1994; Schopler, Brehm, Kinsbourne, & Reichler, 1971; Schopler, Mesibov, & Hearsey, 1995). Structured teaching includes the consistent use of a predictable work routine; physical placement and arrangement of materials, and demonstration of the action requested; and/or physically helping the child through the activity. Structure is used to compensate for an autistic child's difficulties in organizing and understanding his or her world. Autistic individuals tend to get fixed into routines, probably as a means of establishing predictability for themselves. The maladaptive form of that tendency is an obsessive preoccupation with maintaining sameness or a strong reaction to change. By establishing positive routines through structured teaching, parents can capitalize on this need in their child and help develop competencies and improved learning patterns. The implication of this concept for parent training is that a clinician working with parents should use methods that effectively demonstrate the structured teaching process.

The Developmental Continuum

Not only is it important for the professional to understand autism from a developmental perspective, it is also helpful to consider developmental stages in the life cycle of a family with an autistic child, and the role the professional can play at different points. During early childhood, primacy is placed on early diagnosis, emotional support during the grief process, and parent training and counseling. The elementary or middle school years emphasize understanding and dealing with behavior and learning problems and home–teacher relationships. The adolescent and adult periods are a time for focusing on maximizing independence and obtaining relevant residential and work opportunities. This perspective will be elaborated on later in the chapter.

Parent–Professional Collaboration

The overriding principle of the TEACCH approach to family work involves adherence to the goal of building a collaborative relationship between parents and professionals (Marcus & Schopler, 1989; Schopler, 1995; Schopler et al., 1984). The belief in a partnership based on mutual respect and trust is paramount.

Over the years, four types of relationships have been identified. First, parents relate to professionals as trainees, with an emphasis on home teaching programs, behavior management, and related activities. Second, parents serve as trainers of professionals with emphasis on sharing information with staff and broadening the professionals' understanding of autism and of how families cope. Third, parents and professionals provide mutual emotional support, utilizing techniques of ongoing discussions, parent counseling, and support groups. Fourth, parents develop advocacy skills as a means of promoting improved services and other social action issues. No set formula can be applied to every case, but TEACCH staff therapists and parents usually shift among these different roles in attempting to facilitate the strengthening of the parent–child relationship and to help families cope effectively with this chronic disorder.

Competencies and Coping

The focus of intervention should be on the development and building of potential survival skills and competencies in the child and the family. The emphasis should be on pragmatic, problem-solving approaches, which necessitate action-oriented approaches rather than strictly verbal interactions.

Professional as Guide, Not Expert

There is a need to respect the parental perspective and priorities and to seek out and consider parental opinion and interpretation of behavior or proposed method. The professional has experience with a wide range of handicapped individuals, and a breadth of knowledge of what has been effective or ineffective. The parents have a deep and unique perspective on their own child's development, idiosyncrasies, likes, and dislikes. The sensitive merging of these two sources of information strengthens the parent–professional relationship toward improving the child's adaptation.

Consideration of Total Family Needs

There is a need for awareness of other pressures and demands on the family that are unrelated to the autistic child. It is easy to neglect other facets of a parent's identity and life circumstances, such as economic, social, and emotional pressures. There is also a need to understand the child and family beyond the clinic or classroom; that is, the clinician should be alert to and concerned about the impact of the child on normal siblings (Mates, 1990; McHale, Sloan, & Simeonsson, 1984; Rodrigue, Geffken, & Morgan, 1993) or others in the home, and the effects of the child on the parents' marital, social, and work situations. In addition, the personal or psychological implications of coping with an autistic child on a daily basis (Bristol, 1984) should be considered.

In summary, the techniques and methods developed in the 30-year experience of the TEACCH program share many features with other parent training programs described above: (a) parents and professionals seek to form a collaborative relationship; (b) parents and children are understood as mutually influencing one another (a bidirectional model), and (c) a complete initial assessment is an essential part of the treatment process. It is important to apply these principles and approaches to families of autistic individuals across stages of development. The problems faced by families, and the possible solutions or strategies across time, form the basis of the remainder of the chapter.

EARLY CHILDHOOD

Diagnosis

Increased understanding, by professionals, of autism and its manifestations in the early years (ages 2 to 4) has been beneficial to families (Marcus & Stone, 1993). Although clinicians might not be certain whether the problems should be called autism or another pervasive developmental disorder variant, they are able to convey to parents the need for appropriate intervention and enable them to begin the process of obtaining services and gathering further information. During this period, parents often are dealing with a number of stressful circumstances: the ambiguity of the handicap, fatigue caused by the child's irregular sleep patterns and high activity level, lack of an effective communication system, lack of fear in the child, which places the child at risk (e.g., for the danger of running into the street), peculiar food habits, and lack of adequate (and willing) babysitters or respite care (Bristol & Schopler, 1984).

Early diagnosis and assessment is the crucial first step in helping parents develop awareness of what they face as parents of an autistic child. The manner in which they receive this information is, of course, important, although it is likely that the weight of the news of having a chronically handicapped child cannot be mitigated fully by any particular approach. Still, the initial conference should be structured in a way that presents the data clearly, descriptively, and sensitively, without underplaying the seriousness of the situation (Morgan, 1984; Shea, 1993). The age of the child, the severity of the degree of autism, and the level of intellectual and adaptive impairment control prognostic implications to some extent, but the essential nature of the condition needs to be explained.

During this session, parents should be told that even though a precise cause may not be known, their child's disorder did not result from improper parenting or related environmental circumstances. Even if parents do not express a prior sense of guilt, there are likely to be many recriminations that they attribute to themselves or live with daily. They may feel that they have not provided sufficient stimulation or should have identified the problem sooner or sought out help more aggressively. Extended family may be adding to parents' self-imposed pressure by suggesting that they are "spoiling" the child by giving in to the child's demands. The clinician who is interpreting diagnostic findings to the parents needs to be sensitive to these background factors.

Along with the long-range implications of autism, parents must understand the unique learning patterns of their autistic child. Most likely, they have been confused by the atypical pattern of higher skills in motor development and visual memory, and deficits in language and abstract problem solving (DeMyer, 1979; Wing, 1989). Like professionals, parents assume that the relative proficiencies suggest normal intelligence and that the child's failure to perform well in the other areas is caused by a temporary phenomenon, a lack of motivation, or an emotional disturbance. Parents must understand the implications of the uneven developmental profile; in particular, they must know that adequate gross motor skills should not be interpreted as potential for normal cognitive and communicative development. One of the first steps in helping parents deal effectively with their child is to establish appropriate expectations. By simplifying language demands and individualizing their teaching approach based on a realistic appraisal of developmental functioning, parents can initiate a process that will facilitate improved behavior as well as basic competencies (Schopler et al., 1984).

Although many questions are often raised at an interpretive conference, and detailed explanations should be provided, parents vary in their understanding of, and receptivity to, the facts and opinions presented. The emotional impact of discovering that their child has a chronic disorder that may involve mental retardation as well as autism should not be underestimated (Akerley, 1975). Although some families can respond with remarkable calm, it is natural to react with worry, anger, or a form of denial. In the clinic, such feelings may not be manifested, but they are likely to emerge over time. Thus, the clinician must be available for follow-up, to continue to discuss the findings and the family response, and to plan an intervention program.

The clinician should be careful not to destroy the hope and optimism parents need to work with their handicapped child. There is a thin line between making a "realistic prognosis" and undermining hope, and the clinician should be guided by a simple principle: Do not disturb parental expectations except when they interfere with appropriate current management.

Treatment

Along with a complete and sensitive explanation of the child's condition, the clinician, with the active collaboration of the family, should develop a systematic plan of action (Marcus & Schopler, 1989). Although they may feel overwhelmed and helpless at the point of diagnosis, parents require involvement in decision making and in intervention strategies. At the outset, the momentum is provided by the professional, but parents should be given as much responsibility as they can realistically be expected to handle at this stage.

Minimally, they should be informed about, and their feelings and opinions solicited about, any treatment or additional diagnostic procedures. For example, a series of medical procedures might be recommended, including an inpatient hospital stay; but if the family is apprehensive, this plan should be postponed unless considered essential. If a preschool classroom is being considered, the parents should be encouraged to visit, ask questions of the director, and freely discuss concerns and hopes with the clinician. If a parent training, education, or counseling program is recommended, the family's schedule, other demands

and priorities that affect their time, and willingness to participate should be reviewed.

During this first stage, most families are eager for maximum participation, unless other circumstances greatly prohibit their presence. Parents of young autistic children are themselves usually young, have more energy, and are more hopeful than parents of older autistic children. It is typical of parents to be actively involved in teaching their preschool child and in carefully scrutinizing available support services. When parents have just received a diagnosis, it is important to capitalize on their normal reaction—a wish to possibly reverse the course of the disorder and to gain control over the situation—before the reality of the long-term implications of the condition is established. Although not every family is capable of learning specialized teaching and management skills or of becoming articulate advocates, parents of younger autistic children tend to be well suited to carry out such tasks.

Direct parent involvement in the treatment of autistic children has become accepted as a sound and often necessary component of a total intervention program (Kozloff, 1984; Lovaas, 1987; Marcus & Schopler, 1989; Schopler et al., 1984). Although the models may vary in terms of methodology and content, there is no longer any dispute that the earlier psychodynamically oriented approaches (e.g., DesLauriers & Carlson, 1969) have been superseded by strategies that give parents control over the teaching and therapy of their child.

There are essentially two approaches in working with parents as therapists: (a) clinic-based (e.g., Schopler et al., 1984) and (b) home-based (e.g., Howlin, 1989). The clinic-based method involves the use of a training center, where techniques can be demonstrated and parents can be coached to develop effective ways of teaching and managing their child. Parents are then expected to carry out these methods at home. Home visits by clinic staff supplement the center teaching, but the evaluation of effectiveness derives primarily from parental report of progress at home and observation of change in teaching/management skills in the clinic setting. The main advantages of this approach are that it makes full use of the clinic resources, and it provides an atmosphere free of distractions and cues that can interfere with training in a home setting.

The home-based approach brings trainers into the natural daily environment, where demonstration and instruction take place. The obvious advantage is that generalization of training occurs immediately, and staff can recognize and adapt their methods to the setting under observation. Whereas the limitation of the clinic-based model is the artificiality of the clinic playroom, the drawbacks of the home-based approach include the potential distractions of the natural setting and the child's fixed patterns of behavior, which may interfere with new learning. The clinic-based approach is more efficient from a service delivery standpoint; however, it also requires a greater commitment of time from the family, who may be discouraged from participation. In the absence of conclusive evidence of the superiority of one model over the other, a logical intermediate strategy would include elements of both and would permit flexibility of approach, depending on family needs and circumstances.

An alternate approach involves working with parents in groups (e.g., Kozloff, 1984). In this approach, a combination of lectures and discussions with homework assignments provides the material a family can utilize in dealing with their autistic child. The advantages of such an approach include its economy and efficiency and the use of the group for emotional and logistical support. Its disadvantages include the loss of individualization and the high cost to families who miss sessions. A group approach can, of course, be integrated with the individualized methods described above. Most families need opportunities to share experiences and feelings with other families in a comparable situation. Often, ingenious solutions to problems can be suggested by other parents (Schopler, 1995). In other circumstances, simply realizing that a family is not alone can be a source of relief. This need for group support, although covering the age spectrum, is extremely important in the early years, as the family slowly comes to grips with the impact of having an autistic child.

The TEACCH program has been involved in a support group for mothers of autistic children for 10 years (Marcus, Wertheimer, Clement, & Kuhr, 1995). This group has evolved from a small group of 8 to 10 mothers into a large network of parents who have ongoing contact with one another, take retreat-type trips together, and have produced a useful resource guide for parents of newly diagnosed children. The regular meeting times of the group provide a structured format for discussion and emotional support, but the informal contacts and networking outside the group setting are equally important.

As noted earlier, during these first years, parents seem particularly vulnerable to quick solutions or promises of miracle cures. Some may seem far-fetched or magical; others appear grounded in preliminary empirical (e.g., Geller, Ritvo, Freeman, & Yuwiler, 1982) or clinical (e.g., Kaufman, 1976) evidence. The reality is that autism is too variable and complex a condition for any one treatment to possibly address all cases. However, from the parental perspective, the popular literature or news media fail to critically evaluate claims for treatment success, and parents appropriately seek out advice from professionals as they pursue the best available services for their child. Professionals have a responsibility to keep abreast of such developments and, while keeping a critical if open mind, to be ready to handle parental questions in a frank but not overly judgmental way. Above all, the parents' wish to find an answer or partial solution needs to be acknowledged, without encouraging them to actively pursue every lead or unsubstantiated promise of a cure.

Community Services

The need for a wide range of community-based services is somewhat less during the early years than during adolescence and adulthood. Nevertheless, parents need support in beginning to deal with day care programs, early childhood public school programs, and dental and specialized medical services. It is not uncommon, for example, for an autistic child not to have had a complete medical examination because of the child's lack of cooperation. Ongoing pediatric or dental care requires, for many autistic children, sensitive health professionals who are willing to listen to parents and to become familiar with autism. The professional working with the parents should be available both to provide names of physicians and dentists experienced with the handicapped and to discuss with these professionals relevant aspects of the child's condition.

Similarly, parents usually require support in searching for and placing the child in an appropriate preschool setting (Lord, Bristol, & Schopler, 1993). The decision to try a typical preschool program versus a specialized one is complicated, and the pros and cons of each alternative need discussion. For many parents, entrusting the child's early education to an "outside" agency can arouse anxiety, and the emotional support of the professional can facilitate this process. As with health providers, the clinician should work with the preschool program, not just to consult around issues concerning the child but to ensure that the parental views and concerns are being considered. Parents of autistic children will have many years of coordinating their efforts with the educational establishment; the initial school experience can set the tone for developing sound practices in the teacher–parent dialogue.

The early years for families are thus characterized by the emotional stress of discovering that they have a seriously handicapped child, working through the initial period of grief while assuming the challenge of helping the child at home, finding community services, and anticipating what the future might bring. The helping clinician needs to be a part of this process, guiding and supporting the family through this difficult stage.

THE ELEMENTARY SCHOOL YEARS

For many families, the elementary school years are relatively less stressful than the preschool years, particularly if an adequate school program is available (DeMyer, 1979). As the child develops cognitively and socially, behavioral difficulties often diminish in intensity and frequency. If parents have had early identification and support, they have learned basic management and coping skills, and the child is prepared for adjusting to the public school environment. If early services have not at all been provided, then families continue in

a state of limbo, and pressures mount. Fortunately, in the past decade, improved early diagnosis and intervention services have reduced the likelihood of complete absence of services for most families with an autistic child.

The transition to the public school system is not necessarily a uniformly positive experience. Although parents are satisfied that their child is a part of a community system, they are again reminded of the chronicity and severity of their child's handicap, since, for many autistic children, education means placement in a special class or a special school. In addition to the normal anxieties parents face when their child goes to school for the first time, parents of the autistic child have to deal with the recognition that theirs is an atypical child who is not truly integrated in the mainstream. Parents whose children are fully included in a typical classroom setting also have a number of experiences that emphasize their child's atypical development. For many parents, these events reawaken the anguish associated with the first awareness of having a handicapped child and provide further evidence that the future course of development will not be normal.

The public school system is more impersonal than the typical preschool environment, and parents are far less likely to have the built-in support network they have previously experienced. Many parents who have had their child served in a developmental day care program or public school preschool program with additional family support services have appreciated the informal, caring atmosphere of a small program, often staffed with a social worker or parent coordinator. Because the main business of public schools is education, ancillary personnel are in shorter supply and are spread thinly across large numbers of children, whether normal or handicapped.

Parents need to be prepared for this change, and the helping clinician again should be available for advice and guidance. As in the selection of a preschool program, the clinician should be knowledgeable about the variety of early elementary programs that are appropriate and should explore these possibilities with the parents, school system personnel, and preschool teacher or other representatives. Again, parents should be central to the decision-making process, although reality usually results in relatively few options, many of which may be unacceptable or at least far from ideal. The active intervention of the clinician at this stage in transition can ease the concerns of parents who are justifiably worried about their child's adaptation to public school, establish a foundation for a satisfactory relationship between home and school, and indicate to the school system that the family and child have an outside advocate whose support they can draw on when school begins.

If such groundwork is successfully laid, the clinician can facilitate the development of a smooth relationship between the family and teacher. Sometimes the autistic child's elementary school classroom does not change, and if a teacher remains with a program, the child may have the same teacher for as many as 5 to 7 years. This arrangement may have advantages of continuity and consistency, but, from the standpoint of parent–teacher relationships, there will be a natural tendency for conflicts to occur and possible competitive feelings to arise. The clinician should be alert to such tensions and be ready, at times, to serve as a mediator or troubleshooter, to make certain that the teacher and the family understand the other's perspective. If the child and family are no longer seen regularly by the clinician, it may be useful to conduct an annual evaluation involving the teacher, to provide an objective forum for reviewing everyone's concerns. For the teacher, questions concerning medications or possible development of seizures may arise, and the clinician should help explore these questions in conjunction with the parents.

Many school systems advocate full inclusion (Kauffman & Hallahan, 1995; Mesibov & Shea, 1996) of all special education students, including those with autism. Although inclusion seems to be defined in various ways, its strict interpretation is full-time placement in regular education with whatever supports are necessary. Parents whose children are fully included may have mixed feelings about this arrangement: on the one hand, they are excited and hopeful about the opportunity for their child to be educated alongside typically developing peers; on the other hand, they are worried about whether their child will get the individualized attention he or she needs and

about how successful the integrated experience will be. The professional engaged with the family whose child is included needs to be alert to the parental emotions about the situation as well as available to help the school program handle the variety of problems that will inevitably occur.

In addition to promoting a strong home–school relationship, the clinician should be available to continue to help the family with the child's at-home functioning. As the responsibility for education shifts from home to school, the focus of intervention correspondingly shifts from home teaching of the child to activities and methods that facilitate the child's continued survival and growth in the family system. Some parents may wish to remain active in basic skills training, in order to supplement the school program or as a means for feeling they are an integral part of the child's development. Parents have recognized that structured teaching and home routines enhance their personal interactions with their children, who typically do not respond to normal conversation interchanges or family leisure events (Davis & Marcus, 1980).

For most families, this stage is an auspicious time to build daily living and functional communication skills because they have come to realize the importance of these areas for their child's future adaptation. Many parents, after being frustrated in their efforts to teach complex cognitive skills, are gratified at the relative ease with which their autistic child learns household routines and tasks. The autistic individual's predilection toward orderliness can be recognized by the family as a pleasant quality that fits in with everyday chores. The clinician can help by encouraging parents to work on these skills and by suggesting task analysis and other teaching techniques.

Although not confined to the elementary school years, issues involving siblings often take on increased significance during the autistic child's elementary school years. As the autistic child grows older, the developmental delays and deviancies become more obvious, especially in social relationships. Depending on their age, siblings may become increasingly sensitive to having a brother or sister who behaves oddly, demands considerable time from their parents, and is not a normal playmate.

Siblings, like their parents, have common worries and concerns that professionals need to be aware of and, when indicated, to deal with (Powell & Ogle, 1985). These include the reason(s) for their handicapped sibling's problems; whether they might also have similar problems; what the future holds regarding a long-term responsibility for care; and how they should behave toward their autistic sibling. Normal sibling interactional patterns can be distorted or altered because of the presence of the cognitive, play, and social disabilities of the autistic child. Parents, who are struggling with their own reactions and stress, have the additional burden of making sure their nonaffected children are having their personal and developmental needs met. The professional can and should be helping by advising parents on how to communicate with their normal children and by providing individualized counseling or a support group for the siblings. Bristol and Schopler (1989) note that, based on the research literature (e.g., Mates, 1990; McHale et al., 1984), it may not be necessary in many, if not most cases, to provide for specialized services for siblings, but that it is appropriate for counseling or training to be an optional part of a comprehensive program for autistic children.

ADOLESCENCE

Over the past decade, there has been a dramatic increase in the awareness of autism in adolescence and a proliferation of writing on this topic (e.g., Schopler & Mesibov, 1983). This surge of interest has been stimulated, in large part, by the openly expressed needs of parents whose younger autistic children were now growing older and continuing to show the major problems of autism. Basically, this same group of parents previously helped build public awareness and program support for younger autistic children. Now, faced with issues of managing and dealing with their adolescent and adult autistic children, these parents approach the professional community for methods and services to help with the next stages in their child's development (Mesibov, Schopler, & Sloan, 1983).

The problems and concerns raised by families during the adolescent period reflect the continuation of earlier issues such as the chronicity of the basic deficits, the need for specialized services, dealing with the community, and the realization that the disorder is lifelong. Added to these are newer factors brought by the physical changes in adolescence: increasing sexuality and inappropriate ways of expressing it, the stress of many years of raising an autistic child, the emerging sense of independence in someone who lacks many of the prerequisites for self-direction, onset of seizures (for some adolescents), and an increased awareness of the parents' own mortality. Research has indicated that this period produces additional stress for families of autistic individuals (Bristol & Schopler, 1983; DeMyer & Goldberg, 1983). The need for ongoing parental support is perhaps even greater as the parents' energy level decreases and their potential for burnout increases (Marcus, 1984).

Behavioral matters that are likely to emerge include increased sexual awareness, aggressiveness and openly expressed defiance, and striving for independence despite limitations imposed by the handicap (Mesibov, 1983). These issues, of course, are common to normal adolescence, but the individual hampered by dysfunctions in communication, social understanding, and cognitive facility cannot cope as readily with the profound biological changes this stage brings.

The direct help that can be provided by the clinician at this point includes discussion (with parents) of the implications of adolescence for an autistic person; suggestions on behavior management geared to the practical realities of the home situation; sex management and counseling; relaxation and/or cognitive behavioral therapy; consideration of medication, which often becomes more necessary during this period; information regarding respite care, including after-school, weekend, and summer programs; and work toward obtaining a future residential placement. The latter consideration often comes as a jolt to families who, during the preadolescent years, rarely thought that their child could not remain at home indefinitely. The combination of their own decreasing control of the situation, other family needs and priorities, and the visible daily reminder that their child is becoming a young adult has an unexpected impact that few families have anticipated.

For many families, there is a need to develop a plan of action regarding residential placement that takes into account both logistical and emotional considerations. From the practical standpoint, appropriate group homes or other residential options may not be available, and parents need to work with community agencies to develop such a program (LaVigna, 1983; Mesibov et al., 1983; Wall, 1990). The clinician has to collaborate with the parent in this effort. Emotionally, parents need to know that placement outside the home is a natural and logical next step in the move toward independence of the child, and is not the result of the family's failure to provide a good home. Unfortunately, emergencies often allow little opportunity for adequate preparation, and placement occurs in a somewhat traumatic manner. The clinician needs to be sensitive to the emotional pain experienced by parents in these circumstances, and should thoughtfully counsel them through the crisis. As with parents of younger children, support groups for the parents of adolescents remain crucial because they continue to seek solutions to daily problems and quality services (Marcus et al., 1995).

The other area for parental support involves the changing educational needs of the autistic adolescent. Parents who have worked tirelessly to obtain adequate early school programs often have to follow the same route to continue their child's education into secondary schools. If the school system has not planned ahead, the autistic adolescent may be left adrift or kept in the elementary school setting despite the chronological age discrepancy. In addition, with increased age, the type of curriculum must shift—in most cases, away from academic and toward prevocational and vocational (Fredericks, Buckley, Baldwin, Moore, & Stremel-Campbell, 1983). Parents should be prepared for this as early as possible and should be supported by the clinician, outside the educational system, in their efforts to obtain the suitable educational setting and curriculum.

Finally, in the absence of full-time residential care, the professional should help locate adequate respite and emergency relief services, after-school and recreational programs, and summer programs. These services are required to some extent at all stages of development, but they become particularly critical as the child grows older.

From the standpoint of the role of the professional over time, although the need to remain engaged in a partnership remains constant, the scope of activities broadens. There is less emphasis on direct treatment of the child and greater initiative in interacting with the community and maintaining alertness to crisis situations.

ADULTHOOD

Compared to early childhood, relatively little has been written about autism in adulthood, beyond outcome studies (Lotter, 1978), parental narratives (e.g., Park, 1982), and aspects of treatment and care (Holmes & Carr, 1991; Schopler & Mesibov, 1983). More recently, autobiographies of high-functioning persons with autism have become popular and have highlighted coping and adjustment problems in this subgroup (e.g., Grandin & Scariano, 1986). What is known is that the problems of autism continue to some extent, that mental retardation in cognitive and social adaptation persists, and that the needs for long-range sheltered care and supervised employment pertain to the majority. The assistance that families require is consistent with the help required during the adolescent period, but the ability of most families to continue to take the initiative in procuring services is considerably compromised by their declining strength.

Historically, by adulthood, most autistic individuals have been institutionalized (DeMyer & Goldberg, 1983); however, the current trend toward deinstitutionalization is likely to all but eliminate that option, and the responsibility of the home and community to arrange for residential care and vocational opportunities will become more prevalent. Thus, there is a greater urgency for the professional to explore these options with families and, more so than ever before, to take a leadership role in creating opportunities and advocating in the community. By their early adulthood years, autistic persons should have the opportunity to live independently, whether in a group home, an apartment complex with supervision, or a comparable facility. Parents of autistic adults should be able to have the same expectation as parents of normal individuals: to see their adult offspring live his or her life away from home.

With school services no longer available, job training and placement become a top priority, and although some families have options available, in most situations the autistic adult will be at home, increasing the burden on the parents. The professional must anticipate this situation before the conclusion of the school years and work toward an appropriate day program, and, it is hoped, meaningful employment.

Parents also must become involved in estate planning, guardianship, and related matters that affect the future of their autistic adult child (Frolile, 1983; Turnbull, Turnbull, Bronicki, Summers, & Roeder-Gordon, 1989). Again, the professional can be available to remind the parents of this need, and should be able to make a referral to legal counsel experienced in this area.

Direct services that can be helpful include individual counseling with higher-functioning adults (Mesibov, 1992), social skills training and related social activities experiences (Mesibov, 1984), and parent support groups (Harris, 1994). If the autistic adult has received adequate educational services and parents have been actively involved in their child's programs and have received good support for themselves, then the shift into adulthood can be smooth and rewarding. The parent–professional partnership can continue to be productive.

CONCLUSIONS

This chapter has reviewed the sources of stress, the needs of families across the developmental spectrum, and the roles and strategies that can be adopted by the helping professional. The importance of working as partners with the parents cannot be emphasized enough, nor can the necessity of maintaining a flexible attitude and a willingness to avoid building barriers. Professionals should be knowledgeable about the range and variety of parent training, counseling, and treatment approaches described earlier in this chapter. Professionals also need

to be prepared to deal with families whose problems extend beyond the stresses of having an autistic child, such as marital discord, maladaptive perceptions (e.g., belief that the family has no control over the events in their life), or dysfunctional balance (Harris, 1994). As families in the 1990s contend with reckless promoters of faddish therapies and the pressure to find a cure, both of which reinforce the natural tendency to doubt or deny the chronicity of the disorder, professionals must remain sensitive to the vulnerable situation parents are placed in and their need for support and for sound, empirically based interventions.

The developmental perspective presented in this chapter is a useful framework: in early childhood, the emphasis is on early diagnosis, emotional support during the grief process, and parent training, counseling, and networking; the elementary and middle school years emphasize understanding and dealing with behavior and learning problems, home–teacher relationships, and awareness of sibling issues; and the adolescent and adult period is a time for focusing on maximizing independence and obtaining relevant vocational opportunities. As our knowledge of the condition of autism continues to grow, and effective interventions for those affected by it are documented and replicated, professionals will always need to be available for families throughout the life span of the person with autism. Professionals knowledgeable about and sensitive to the needs of these families will be major contributors to successful outcomes.

Cross-References

Developmental aspects of syndrome expression are discussed in Chapters 12 through 14; issues in development of curriculum, behavioral, and vocational interventions appear in Chapters 22, 26, and 28; interventions focused on communication skills are described in Chapters 23 through 25. Residential treatment is detailed in Chapter 31; pharmacological and routine medical care are dealt with in Chapters 32 and 33, respectively. Issues for parents are addressed in Chapter 34, and the Division TEACCH program is summarized in Chapter 35. Rights to service are discussed in Chapter 37.

REFERENCES

Akerley, M. (1975). The invulnerable parent. *Journal of Autism and Childhood Schizophrenia, 5,* 275–281.

Anastopoulos, A.D., & Barkley, R.A. (1989). A training program for parents of children with attention deficit hyperactivity disorder. In C.E. Schaefer & J.M. Briesmeister (Eds.), *Handbook of parent training: Parents as cotherapists for children's behavior problems* (pp. 83–104). New York: John Wiley & Sons.

Azar, S.T. (1989). Training parents of abused children. In C.E. Schaefer & J.M. Briesmeister (Eds.), *Handbook of parent training: Parents as co-therapists for children's behavior problems* (pp. 414–441). New York: John Wiley & Sons.

Azrin, N.H., Sneed, T.J., & Foxx, R.M. (1974). Dry-bed training: A rapid method of eliminating bedwetting (enuresis) of the retarded. *Behaviour Research and Therapy, 11,* 427–434.

Barkley, R.A. (1987). *Defiant children: A clinician's manual for parent training.* New York: Guilford Press.

Bell, R.Q., & Harper, L.V. (1977). *Child effects on adults.* Hillsdale, NJ: Erlbaum.

Bristol, M.M. (1984). Family resources and successful adaptation to autistic children. In E. Schopler & G.B. Mesibov (Eds.), *The effects of autism on the family* (pp. 289–310). New York: Plenum Press.

Bristol, M.M., & Schopler, E. (1983). Family resources and successful adaptation in autistic children. In E. Schopler & G.B. Mesibov (Eds.), *Autism in adolescents and adults* (pp. 251–279). New York: Plenum Press.

Bristol, M.M., & Schopler, E. (1984). Developmental perspective on stress and coping in families of autistic children. In J. Blacher (Ed.), *Families of severely handicapped children: Review of research* (pp. 91–134). New York: Academic Press.

Bristol, M.M., & Schopler, E. (1989). The family in the treatment of autism. In American Psychiatric Association, *Treatment of psychiatric disorders: A task force report of the American Psychiatric Association* (pp. 249–266). Washington, DC: American Psychiatric Association.

Cautela, J.R., & Groden, J. (1978). *Relaxation: A comprehensive manual for adults, children, and children with special needs.* Champaign, IL: Research Press.

Coleman, M., & Gillberg, C. (1985). *The biology of the autistic syndromes.* New York: Praeger.

Cunningham, C.E. (1989). A family-systems-oriented training program for parents of language-delayed children with behavior problems. In C.E. Schaefer & J.M. Briesmeister (Eds.), *Handbook of parent training: Parents as co-therapists for children's behavior problems* (pp. 133–176). New York: John Wiley & Sons.

Dadds, M.R., Sanders, M.R., & James, J.E. (1987). The generalization of treatment effects in parent training with multidistressed parents. *Behavioural Psychotherapy, 15,* 289–313.

Davis, S., & Marcus, L.M. (1980). Involving parents in the treatment of severely communication-disordered children. *Journal of Pediatric Psychology, 5,* 189–197.

DeMyer, M.K. (1979). *Parents and children in autism.* New York: John Wiley & Sons.

DeMyer, M.K., & Goldberg, P. (1983). Family needs of the autistic adolescent. In E. Schopler & G.B. Mesibov (Eds.), *Autism in adolescents and adults* (pp. 225–250). New York: Plenum Press.

DesLauriers, A.M., & Carlson, C.F. (1969). *Your child is asleep: Early infantile autism.* Homewood, IL: Dorsey.

Eyberg, S.M., & Boggs, S.R. (1989). Parent training for oppositional-defiant preschoolers. In C.E. Schaefer & J.M. Briesmeister (Eds.), *Handbook of parent training: Parents as co-therapists for children's behavior problems* (pp. 105–132). New York: John Wiley & Sons.

Forehand, R., & McMahon, R.J. (1981). *Helping the noncompliant child: A clinician's guide to parent training.* New York: Guilford Press.

Fredericks, H.D., Buckley, J., Baldwin, V.L., Moore, W., & Stremel-Campbell, K. (1983). In E. Schopler & G.B. Mesibov (Eds.), *Autism in adolescents and adults* (pp. 79–109). New York: Plenum Press.

Frolile, L.A. (1983). Legal needs. In E. Schopler & G.B. Mesibov (Eds.), *Autism in adolescents and adults* (pp. 319–334). New York: Plenum Press.

Geller, E., Ritvo, E.R., Freeman, B.J., & Yuwiler, A. (1982). Preliminary observations on the effect of fenfluramine on blood serotonin and symptoms in three autistic boys. *New England Journal of Medicine, 307,* 165–169.

Grandin, T., & Scariano, M. (1986). *Emergence: Labelled autistic.* Novato, CA: Arena.

Graziano, A.M., & Diament, D.M. (1992). Parent behavioral training: An examination of the paradigm. *Behavior Modification, 16,* 3–38.

Griest, D.L., Forehand, R., Wells, K.C., & McMahon, R.J. (1980). An examination of differences between nonclinic and behavior-problem clinic-referred children and their mothers. *Journal of Abnormal Psychology, 89,* 497–500.

Harris, S.L. (1994). Treatment of family problems in autism. In E. Schopler & G.B. Mesibov (Eds.), *Behavioral issues in autism* (pp. 161–175). New York: Plenum Press.

Holmes, N., & Carr, J. (1991). The pattern of care in families of adults with a mental handicap: A comparison between families of autistic adults and Down syndrome adults. *Journal of Autism and Developmental Disorders, 21,* 187–196.

Howlin, P. (1989). Help for the family. In C. Gillberg (Ed.), *Diagnosis and treatment of autism* (pp. 185–202). New York: Plenum Press.

Humphreys, L., Forehand, R., McMahon, R., & Roberts, M. (1978). Parent behavioral training to modify child noncompliance: Effects on untreated siblings. *Journal of Behavior Therapy and Experimental Psychiatry, 9,* 235–238.

Kaufman, B.N. (1976). *Son-rise.* New York: Warner.

Kauffman, J.M., & Hallahan, D.P. (1995). *The illusion of full inclusion.* Austin, TX: Pro-Ed.

Kozloff, M.A. (1984). A training program for families of children with autism: Responding to family needs. In E. Schopler & G.B. Mesibov (Eds.), *The effects of autism on the family* (pp. 163–186). New York: Plenum Press.

LaVigna, G.W. (1983). The Jay Nolan Center: A community-based program. In E. Schopler & G.B. Mesibov (Eds.), *Autism in adolescents and adults* (pp. 381–410). New York: Plenum Press.

Levine, F.M., & Ramirez, R. (1989). Contingent negative practice as a home-based treatment of tics and stuttering. In C.E. Schaefer & J.M. Briesmeister (Eds.), *Handbook of parent training: Parents as co-therapists for children's behavior problems* (pp. 38–59). New York: John Wiley & Sons.

Lord, C., Bristol, M.M., & Schopler, E. (1993). Early intervention for children with autism and related developmental disorders. In E. Schopler, M.E. Van Bourgondien, & M.M. Bristol (Eds.), *Preschool issues in autism* (pp. 199–221). New York: Plenum Press.

Lotter, V. (1978). Follow-up studies. In M. Rutter & E. Schopler (Eds.), *Autism: A reappraisal of concepts and treatment* (pp. 475–495). New York: Plenum Press.

Lovaas, O.I. (1987). Behavioral treatment and normal education and intellectual functioning in young autistic children. *Journal of Consulting and Clinical Psychology, 55,* 3–9.

Marcus, L.M. (1984). Coping with burnout. In E. Schopler & G.B. Mesibov (Eds.), *The effects of autism on the family* (pp. 311–326). New York: Plenum Press.

Marcus, L.M., & Schopler, E. (1989). Parents as co-therapists with autistic children. In C.E. Schaefer & J.M. Briesmeister (Eds.), *Handbook of parent training: Parents as co-therapists for children's behavior problems* (pp. 337–360). New York: John Wiley & Sons.

Marcus, L.M., & Stone, W.L. (1993). Assessment of the young autistic child. In E. Schopler, M.E. Van Bourgondien, & M.M. Bristol (Eds.), *Preschool issues in autism* (pp. 149–173). New York: Plenum Press.

Marcus, L.M., Wertheimer, A., Clement, S., & Kuhr, R. (1995, July). *Support groups for parents of autistic children from preschool to adulthood.* Presented at the annual meeting of the Autism Society of America, Greensboro, NC.

Mates, T.E. (1990). Siblings of autistic children: Their adjustment and performance at home and in school. *Journal of Autism and Developmental Disorders, 20,* 545–553.

McHale, S.M., Sloan, J., & Simeonsson, R.J. (1984). Sibling relationships of children with autistic, mentally retarded, and nonhandicapped brothers and sisters. *Journal of Autism and Developmental Disorders, 16,* 399–413.

Mesibov, G.B. (1983). Current perspectives and issues in autism and adolescence. In E. Schopler & G.B. Mesibov (Eds.), *Autism in adolescents and adults* (pp. 37–53). New York: Plenum Press.

Mesibov, G.B. (1984). Social skills training with verbal autistic adolescents and adults: A program model. *Journal of Autism and Developmental Disorders, 14,* 395–404.

Mesibov, G.B. (1992). Treatment issues with high-functioning adolescents and adults with autism. In E. Schopler & G.B. Mesibov (Eds.), *High-functioning individuals with autism* (pp. 143–155). New York: Plenum Press.

Mesibov, G.B., Schopler, E., & Hearsey, K. (1994). Structured teaching. In E. Schopler & G.B. Mesibov (Eds.), *Behavioral issues in autism* (pp. 195–207). New York: Plenum Press.

Mesibov, G.B., Schopler, E., & Sloan, J.L. (1983). Service development for adolescents and adults in North Carolina's TEACCH Program. In E. Schopler & G.B. Mesibov (Eds.), *Autism in adolescents and adults* (pp. 411–432). New York: Plenum Press.

Mesibov, G.B., & Shea, V. (1996). Full inclusion and students with autism. *Journal of Autism and Developmental Disorders, 26,* 337–346.

Morgan, S.B. (1984). Helping parents understand the diagnosis of autism. *Developmental and Behavioral Pediatrics, 5,* 78–85.

Park, C.C. (1982). *The siege*. Boston: Little, Brown.

Patterson, G. (1982). *Coercive family process*. Eugene, OR: Castalia.

Powell, T.H., & Ogle, P.A. (1985). *Brothers and sisters—A special part of exceptional families*. Baltimore: Brookes.

Reichler, R.J., & Schopler, E. (1976). Developmental therapy: A program model for providing individual services in the community. In E. Schopler & R.J. Reichler (Eds.), *Psychopathology and child development: Research and treatment* (pp. 347–372). New York: Plenum Press.

Rodrigue, J.R., Geffken, G.R., & Morgan, S.B. (1993). Perceived competence and behavioral adjustment of siblings of children with autism. *Journal of Autism and Developmental Disorders, 23*, 665–674.

Schaefer, C.E., & Briesmeister, J.M. (Eds.). (1989). *Handbook of parent training: Parents as co-therapists for children's behavior problems*. New York: John Wiley & Sons.

Schopler, E. (1987). Specific and nonspecific factors in the effectiveness of a treatment system. *American Psychologist, 42*, 376–383.

Schopler, E. (1995). *Parent survival manual: A guide to crisis resolution in autism and related developmental disorders*. New York: Plenum Press.

Schopler, E., Brehm, S., Kinsbourne, M., & Reichler, R.J. (1971). Effect of treatment structure on development in autistic children. *Archives of General Psychiatry, 24*, 415–421.

Schopler, E., & Mesibov, G.B. (1983). *Autism in adolescents and adults*. New York: Plenum Press.

Schopler, E., & Mesibov, G.B. (Eds.). (1987). *Neurobiological issues in autism*. New York: Plenum Press.

Schopler, E., Mesibov, G.B., & Hearsey, K. (1995). Structured teaching in the TEACCH system. In E. Schopler & G.B. Mesibov (Eds.), *Learning and cognition in autism* (pp. 243–268). New York: Plenum Press.

Schopler, E., Mesibov, G.B., Shigley, R.H., & Bashford, A. (1984). Helping autistic children through their parents: The TEACCH model. In E. Schopler & G.B. Mesibov (Eds.), *The effects of autism on the family* (pp. 65–81). New York: Plenum Press.

Schopler, E., & Reichler, R.J. (1971). Parents-as-cotherapists in the treatment of autistic children. In S. Chess & A. Thomas (Eds.), *Annual progress in child psychiatry and child development* (pp. 679–697). New York: Brunner/Mazel.

Schreibman, L., Koegel, R.L., Mills, D.L., & Burke, J.C. (1984). Training parent-child interactions. In E. Schopler & G.B. Mesibov (Eds.), *The effects of autism on the family* (pp. 187–205). New York: Plenum Press.

Schroeder, C.D., & Gordon, B.N. (1991). *Assessment and treatment of childhood problems*. New York: Guilford Press.

Shea, V. (1993). Interpreting results to parents of preschoolers. In E. Schopler, M.E. Van Bourgondien, & M.M. Bristol (Eds.), *Preschool issues in autism* (pp. 185–198). New York: Plenum Press.

Short, A.B. (1984). Short-term treatment outcome using parents as co-therapists for their own autistic children. *Journal of Child Psychology and Psychiatry, 25*, 443–458.

Taft, L.T. (1993). Medical syndromes in young autistic children. In E. Schopler, M.E. Van Bourgondien, & M.M. Bristol (Eds.), *Preschool issues in autism* (pp. 175–183). New York: Plenum Press.

Turnbull, H.R., Turnbull, A.P., Bronicki, G.J., Summers, J.A., & Roeder-Gordon, C. (1989). *Disability and the family: A guide to decisions for adulthood*. Baltimore: Brookes.

Wall, A.J. (1990). Group homes in North Carolina for children and adults with autism. *Journal of Autism and Developmental Disorders, 20*, 353–366.

Webster-Stratton, C., & Herbert, M. (1993). What really happens in parent training? *Behavior Modification, 17*, 407–456.

Williams, B.F., Williams, R.L., & McLaughlin, T.F. (1991). *Journal of Developmental and Physical Disabilities, 3*, 385–407.

Wing, L. (1976). Diagnosis, clinical description, and prognosis. In L. Wing (Ed.), *Early child autism* (2nd ed., pp. 15–64). New York: Pergamon.

Wing, L. (1989). The continuum of autistic characteristics. In E. Schopler & G. B. Mesibov (Eds.), *Diagnosis and assessment in autism* (pp. 91–110). New York: Plenum Press.

CHAPTER 28

Employment: Options and Issues for Adolescents and Adults with Autism

PETER F. GERHARDT AND DAVID L. HOLMES

Children with autism grow up and, subsequently, develop needs beyond the reaches of the educational system. Unfortunately, for many persons with autism, this transition from school to the adult world is often a confusing maze of misinformation, limited opportunities, insufficient resources, and inappropriate or time-limited services. Despite these barriers, one fact remains unalterable: throughout their adult lives persons with autism can and do continue to grow and develop as individuals, and when provided with both the opportunity and the necessary supports, they have an increasing repertoire of new skills and abilities (Holmes, 1989).

In the United States, participation in employment and the resulting job-related social status and increased financial independence are generally seen as integral components of an individual's postschool life (Inge, Banks, Wehman, Hill, & Shafer, 1988; Kiernan & Stark, 1986a; Levy, 1983). For many individuals with autism, however, employment and employment-related services remain elusive (Wolf & Goldberg, 1986). Peraino (1992), in reviewing postschool outcome studies of persons with autism, noted that the majority of reported cases had "poor outcomes, including . . . poor occupational achievement." Surprisingly, the majority of those for whom these assessments were conducted would generally be acknowledged as being "high-functioning" (i.e., IQ > 70) individuals and, consequently, would be assumed to have a greater potential for more positive employment outcomes. Occupational outcomes for individuals with autism who may present more serious cognitive or behavior challenges could, therefore, be assumed to be even less favorable.

This failure to obtain greater occupational status should not be viewed in terms of the limitations of persons with autism but, instead, in terms of the limitations of the system that has been charged with providing the necessary educational and vocational training and supports so that persons with autism can achieve increasingly more valued and complex employment outcomes. This chapter reviews the issues that most directly impact the provision of more proactive vocational services, which can result in greater employment outcomes for persons with autism, and the obstacles to their implementation. Following a brief historical review of adult services, relevant legislation and the components of a functional school-to-work transition project are discussed. Lastly, the current state of adult services and of employment support for persons with autism is reviewed, and some recommendations for the future are presented.

We would like to express our sincere appreciation to the individuals with autism who are provided employment support through the Eden W.E.R.C.s Employment Service, their families, and the faculty of Eden W.E.R.C.s, for all their help and inspiration in the preparation of this chapter. In addition, we would like to express our sincere appreciation to our wives, Caroline and Karen, whose patience and understanding make much of what we do seem easy.

HISTORICAL OVERVIEW

Despite the recognition of autism as a distinct diagnostic entity over 50 years ago (Kanner, 1943), only in the past decade or so has there been general recognition of the fact that children with autism grow into adults with autism (Hayes, 1987) and require specialized services similar to those provided to children with autism (e.g., Schopler & Mesibov 1983). As to why this apparent "denial of adulthood," has occurred, Holmes (1989) contends that, in the past, adults with autism were often misdiagnosed and labeled as mentally retarded, schizophrenic, or otherwise "disturbed," and were institutionalized, thereby concealing their presence. It has, in fact, been estimated that as recently as two decades ago, up to 98% of all adults with autism were institutionalized (National Society for Autistic Children, 1977). As a result, the early history of services for adults with autism must be viewed as mirroring the history of individuals with mental retardation in the later decades of this century.

During the late 19th century and early 20th century, the public perception of individuals with disabilities as generally nonproductive and best suited for custodial care resulted in the growth of institutions as the primary service system for persons with mental retardation and other disabilities (Janicki, Castellani & Norris, 1983; Schopler, & Hennick, 1990). Individuals with autism, with their myriad behavior, learning, and social idiosyncrasies, were among the many persons who were routinely placed in such custodial settings (Holmes, 1990; Sullivan, 1981) with little or no voice in the decision and almost no opportunity for proactive programming once placed.

By the late 1960s, the deinstitutionalization movement was gaining professional and popular acceptance, and a transition from the institution to the community had begun (Mesibov, 1990). However, although an understanding of the needs of individuals with mental retardation may have entered a new era, the needs of persons with autism remained unaddressed (Schopler & Hennick, 1990). The bulk of literature available at that time focused primarily on theoretical perspectives of etiology and classification of autism (Celiberti, Alessandri, Fong, & Gill, 1993). With the critical exception of the debate regarding psychodynamic models of intervention (Rimland, 1964) and the noteworthy early investigations into the efficacy of behavioral systems of learning (e.g., Ferster & DeMyer, 1962; Lovaas & Simmons, 1969), treatment literature at that time was hard to come by, and, in the case of psychodynamic interventions (Bettelheim, 1967), was misdirected and ultimately harmful.

Celiberti, Alessandri, Fong, and Gill (1993), in their review of the behavioral treatment literature, note that not until the mid- to late 1970s was a more comprehensive body of literature specifically devoted to addressing the educational and behavioral needs of children with autism. From these early investigations (e.g., Carr, Binkoff, Kologinsky, & Eddy, 1978; Solnick, Rincover, & Peterson, 1977) came the basis for our understanding of many of the systems of education, training, and support currently in use today (e.g., the use of applied behavior analysis in the classroom).

As the cohort of children referenced in these early studies aged beyond the capacities of the available educational services, the attention of their families, interested professionals, and, most importantly, the individuals themselves turned to issues relevant to adulthood. Despite a tendency to view these "new adults" with autism as larger versions of the children with whom there may have been a degree of comfort and familiarity, that view, quite obviously, was inadequate (Markowitz, Gerhardt, Christopher, Christopher, & McKean, 1994). Subsequently, service delivery entered a new phase; the differing needs of individuals with autism across the life span began to be recognized (Holmes, 1989).

As part of this new attention to life-span issues, the 1980s brought a national emphasis on the school-to-work transition process for all special needs learners (e.g., Lagomarcino & Rusch, 1987; Will, 1984). Recognition of the appropriateness and subsequent benefits of employment for many individuals with disabilities prompted the development, nationwide, of a variety of supported employment initiatives intended to provide individuals with severe disabilities access to the world of work. This process continues today.

Unfortunately, despite the growing recognition of the employment-related needs and abilities of adolescents and adults with autism, the development of employment-related services for persons with autism in the 1990s has continued to lag far behind the opportunities currently available for persons with less severe disabilities (Kregel & Wehman, 1989; Mank, 1994; Wehman & Kregel, 1988). This disparity between what can be done and what is being done, in terms of services for adults with autism, represents the critical challenge to the field as the 21st century approaches.

LEGISLATION

Lamentably, there are no federal laws or regulations designed to specifically address the needs and rights of adolescents and adults with autism in the vocational and employment arena. These specific concerns are generally subsumed under the laws that provide personal and systemic protection for individuals with disabilities in general (Kaplan & Moore, 1989). Included in this cadre of relevant disability legislation are: (a) The Education of All Handicapped Children Act (PL 94-142), now the Individuals with Disabilities Education Act (PL 101-476); (b) The Vocational Rehabilitation Act of 1973 (PL 93-112) and its subsequent Amendments (1986, 1992); and (c) The Americans with Disabilities Act (PL 101-336). Other legislative initiatives exist (e.g., Perkins Vocational Education Act, and Job Training Partnership Act), but their impact on services for individuals with autism has proven to be somewhat less extensive than that of the three leading legislative initiatives.

The Individuals with Disabilities Education Act (IDEA)

Congress, in 1975, passed the Education of all Handicapped Children Act (PL 94-142), which mandated that all children with disabilities, through their 21st birthday, are to be provided with free appropriate public education in the least restrictive environment available. In 1990, PL 94-142 was reauthorized as PL 101-476 and renamed the Individuals with Disabilities Education Act (IDEA). In addition to including children with autism as being eligible for special education services (a significant event in and of itself), IDEA introduced wording requiring the provision of transition planning as part of a student's Individualized Education Program (IEP), with the planning to begin no later than the student's 16th birthday.

Transition services, according to the law, are defined as:

a coordinated set of activities for the student, designed within an outcome-oriented process, which promotes movement from school to post-school activities, including post-secondary education, education, vocational training, integrated employment including supported employment, continuing adult education, adult services, independent living or community participation. The coordinated set of activities shall be based on the individual student's needs, taking into account the student's preferences and interests. . . . (PL 101-476, 20 U.S.C. 1401 [a][19])

DeStefano and Wermuth (1992) contend that IDEA's definition of transition services is important on a number of counts. Of primary importance, these authors state, is the legislative acknowledgment of the need for a "coordinated set of activities" to address inherent complexities in providing functional transition planning. Comprehensive planning, parental involvement, and interagency coordination all comprise components of this coordinated set of activities. As discussed later in the chapter, given the diverse and sometimes enigmatic challenges presented by students with autism, the importance of effective interagency coordination, coupled with comprehensive planning and parent input in transition programming, cannot be overstated.

Second, IDEA requires transition planning to be an "outcome-oriented process," based on the anticipated demands of the postschool environment. Previously, secondary special education tended to rely more on the continued provision of skill training in activities that may have been of more use in the classroom than in the adult life (e.g., Brown, Nietupski, & Hamre-Nietupski, 1976). Potentially successful students were produced, but successful graduates often failed to materialize. Outcome-oriented transition planning incorporates the needs of the learner and the demands of the next environment so that more effective transition planning may be undertaken.

Lastly, DeStefano and Wermuth (1992) note that transition planning, as defined, is a process that is to be based on individual needs, preferences, and interests. For each individual learner with autism, this definition requires, to the extent possible, active participation in the transition process through such activities as job sampling, family input, comprehensive vocational assessments, and the provision of structured community experience.

IDEA is the legislative architect of school-based responsibility for the provision of transition planning. In addition, IDEA has served to highlight the need for transition services to be developed and provided in a comprehensive, thoughtful, and consumer-based manner, and has stimulated greater public and professional awareness of the issues surrounding transition planning. The practical impact of functional transition planning as mandated by IDEA will only be seen in the coming years, as greater numbers of learners with autism graduate from a system mandated by law to more effectively meet their postschool needs.

The Vocational Rehabilitation Act of 1973 (PL 93-112)

The Vocational Rehabilitation Act of 1973 (PL 93-112) provided access for individuals with disabilities to any program, service, or activity receiving federal funds. One component in particular (Section 504) is known as the "Bill of Rights" for individuals with disabilities because of its strong, antidiscrimination language. In 1986, Congress authorized a set of Amendments (PL 99-506) to the Rehabilitation Act which, by including language on the importance of transition and transition services, "offered a major avenue of transition opportunity for young adults" (Wehman, 1992, p. 10). In particular, Title I of PL 99-506 specifically allowed states to fund supported employment services from the basic state grant program.

Most recently, the Rehabilitation Act Amendments of 1992 (PL 102-569) can be expected to have an even greater impact on the provision of functional transition and postschool services to individuals with autism (Smith, Belcher, & Juhrs, 1995). Of particular importance are: the assumption of employability, regardless of the severity of the disability, and the removal of time limits on supports provided under the legislation's state grant program.

The Americans with Disabilities Act (PL 101-336)

The Americans with Disabilities Act (ADA; PL 101-336) has been called the "capstone" to a public policy promoting access and participation by people with disabilities within their community (Ward, 1992). Under the ADA, individuals with disabilities cannot be discriminated against in the areas of employment, transportation, public accommodations, public services, and telecommunications. According to the employment provisions, employers are unable to discriminate, on the basis of a disability, against potentially qualified employees. In addition, employers are required by law to provide "reasonable accommodations" to workers who are able, with such accommodations, to perform the essential functions of a job.

The impact of ADA on the employment of individuals with autism remains to be seen. Compared to more cognitive or behavioral disabilities such as autism, far greater public attention has been paid to issues associated with the access and accommodation of persons with physical disabilities. Physical accessibility standards exist and are enforced, but questions as to what may constitute a reasonable accommodation for a person with autism (e.g., flex time, more/less frequent breaks, modified production standards) remain unanswered (and can, in actuality, only be answered on a case-by-case basis). Although ADA represents great promise, the promise is yet to be filled for many individuals with autism.

Summary

Federal legislation, in the form of IDEA, mandates the provision of school-to-work transition services for all individuals with autism, beginning no later than age 16. Beyond that, however, both the Vocational Rehabilitation Act and ADA mandate only equal access, and not the provision of necessary services and supports once access is obtained. Equal access then should be viewed as only half the battle. What would appear to be essential is some form of employment services legislation, whereby funding is made available so that individuals with autism and other disabilities may take full advantage of the access granted them, as citizens, by the ADA and the Vocational Rehabilitation Act.

THE SCHOOL-TO-WORK TRANSITION

As provided for by IDEA, the process by which a student with autism is to make the transition from the classroom to the post-21 world of work must begin no later than age 16. A key issue then is: What constitutes functional transition planning for individuals with autism? Berkell (1992) cites several potential challenges as being relevant to the provision of transition services to individuals with autism. Among these are high anticipated costs due to anticipated lower teacher:student ratios; societal misperceptions regarding the nature and needs of individuals with autism; the need for, in many cases, intensive social/communication skills and behavior management training; and concerns regarding personnel preparation.

In terms of shared needs, several authors (e.g., Rusch, DeStefano, Chadsey-Rusch, Phelps, & Szymanski, 1992; Steere, Wood, Pancsofar, & Rucker, 1993; Wehman, Kregel, & Barcus, 1985) have written on the overall importance of the transition process in obtaining desired postsecondary outcomes. Wehman, Kregel, and Barcus (1985), in discussing the essential components of a functional transition, emphasize the importance of developing a formal, comprehensive transition plan that incorporates input from both the individual and the family, and delineates the steps necessary for effective interagency cooperation. Comprehensive planning, these authors contend, is so important that failure to develop a comprehensive plan functionally negates the potential significance of all other aspects of transition services.

Stowitschek (1992), in his review of the literature on transition planning, presents a consensus list of best practices in transition planning. Items contained in this list can generally be grouped together in relation to (a) transition planning; (b) transition implementation, or (c) transition evaluation. Included in transition planning are: the development of appropriate long-term goals and short-term objectives, the development of a plan to ensure eligibility for posttransition services, the provision of case management services, and the development of a timeline for transition activities. Implementation items cited by Stowitschek include the provision of appropriate vocational, leisure, and residential options; transportation training; money management training; and vocationally relevant social skills training. Long-term support and follow-up of the transition process and specific outcome evaluations (as appropriate to each transition program) comprise the evaluatory component of the transition process.

Planning and Coordination

Returning to the issue of comprehensive planning and interagency coordination (e.g., DeStefano & Wermuth, 1992; Snauwaert, 1992; Wehman, Kregel, & Barcus, 1985), a practical dilemma presents itself: To what is the learner with autism transitioning? As noted by Lagomarcino and Rusch (1987), even the best school-based employment development programs will not benefit students if they do not coordinate their activities beyond the school years. Although some states have recognized the importance of the adult services component of transition planning (Wehman, 1991), issues relating to the availability of post-21 (i.e., post-IDEA) funds, the length of service(s) available, and the degree of individualization and appropriateness of available services remain unresolved. In many states, waiting lists for postgraduation services act as barriers to the continuation of transition programming to its desired employment outcome (Moore, 1994; Thomas & Halloran, 1987). The best planning cannot overcome the prospect of nothing on the other side of transition.

Recognizing the concerns generated by the lack of a post-21 mandate for services, Bates, Bronkema, Ames, and Hess (1992) state that the "focus [of transition] must be on assisting agencies to work more efficiently in coordination with one another" (p. 128). These authors note that, as a general rule, state agencies tend to act as isolated entities and not as cooperative units. As a result, the complexities of transition, especially for those with more complex needs, are not fully addressed, and strategies that are developed may be destined for failure.

Bates et al. (1992) note several steps that they consider integral to the resolution of this challenge. The development of a state interagency transition committee, comprised of representatives from all concerned agencies, with the mission of identifying and resolving areas of concern and/or competition among agencies, is discussed as a first but important step. As a product of this committee, formal written agreements regarding interagency responsibilities in the transition process need to be developed and enforced by member agencies. Lastly, these authors contend that comprehensive statewide assessments of transition needs and resources must be completed, with special attention to the degree to which individual needs may or may not be met by existing specialized and generic services. In this way, generally scarce resources may be directed to those areas of most critical need, and the duplication of existing services is avoided. By enacting such steps, the question—To what are learners with autism transitioning?—may be more readily answered.

The Role of the Family

Several authors have written about the important role of the family in the transition-to-work process (Brotherson et al., 1988; Hosack & Malkmus, 1992; Irvin, Thorin, & Singer, 1993; Turnbull & Turnbull, 1988). Wehman (1991), however, while fully acknowledging the importance of parental involvement, asserts that although parents, in general, are not excluded, neither have they come "fully on board" (p. 7) with the transition process. This lack of active involvement, whether by choice or by limited access, can result in significant familial concerns regarding such issues as safety and security on the job site and loss of entitlement benefits. These concerns, if identified, may be effectively addressed in a manner that encourages parents' continued participation in, and support of, the transition-to-work process for their son or daughter (Sowers & Powers, 1991).

Perhaps the most important contribution that parents (and family members) can make in the transition-to-work process is in their continuing role as advocates for their child (Friedlander, 1989). It can be argued that, in the advocacy process, the voice of one insistent parent is louder and often more effective than that of 10 professionals. Despite a multitude of new stressors that may appear as their child enters the transition years (e.g., an unfamiliarity with the adult system of services and supports, the potential inability of this system to meet the needs of a nearly-adult-age child, and the stress associated with life-cycle transitions in general [Brotherson et al., 1988] and with the uncertainty of the future [Fong, Wilgosh, & Sobsey, 1993]), parents' role as forceful advocates on behalf of their son or daughter does not, in most instances, diminish with age. In point of fact, given the systemic challenges that they and their child with autism will face in the transition process, the need for parental advocacy may be even more critical than it had previously been. From ensuring the provision of job sampling services to the development, to the extent possible, of interagency cooperative planning, parents' support, input, and advocacy are critical.

Summary

Although a good degree of attention has been given to the transition needs and process of and for special needs learners in general (Snauwaert, 1992), much still needs to be done. Comprehensive planning must include the learners with autism, their parents and teachers, and representatives from all concerned agencies. Given the often complex and long-term needs of many individuals with autism, of particular importance are the development and maintenance of systems of interagency cooperation that will best provide for a continuity of services on the other side of transition. Practical considerations for the transitioning learner with autism include the provision of structured community experience, community-referenced behavior management and social skills training (Berkell, 1992), and the incorporation of individual choice in the job development process (Winking, O'Reilly, & Moon, 1993).

Unfortunately, despite the best efforts and intentions of many schools to provide transition programming, the process, in many cases, remains incomplete and employment remains a clearly defined but functionally unobtainable goal. If the transition planning requirement of IDEA is to be consistently and effectively implemented, the discrepancy between legislative intent and systemic practice needs to be fully resolved so that the necessary resources and services are more readily available on the terminal side of transition.

ADULT SERVICES AND EMPLOYMENT

Although individuals with autism, as a group, share a recognizable set of behavioral characteristics (American Psychiatric Association, 1994), the diversity within this group is great. In fact, individuals with autism are as different from one another as members of any group with shared interests or characteristics. Individuals with autism, first and foremost, are individuals; they have divergent strengths, limitations, likes and dislikes (Gerhardt & Holmes, 1995). Therefore, although employment should be considered the goal of adult services, it is arguable that no single system of adult employment-related service would be sufficient to meet the needs of all adults with autism. Beyond institution-based services, the current employment-related service options usually provided to adults with autism are: the sheltered workshop, secure employment training (Holmes, 1989), and supported models of employment.

Sheltered Workshops

Levy (1983), in discussing the appropriateness of a sheltered workshop or activity-center-based program for individuals with autism, argues that ongoing concerns—the lack of functional work tasks and employment training, the scant attention to training beyond the skills for minimal production, and the insufficient levels of staff training and expertise—may indicate that the sheltered workshop is a less than desirable option for many individuals with autism. Others (Bellamy, Rhodes, Bourbeau, & Mank, 1986; Gold, 1975) claim

that, in addition, sheltered workshops tend to function more as final placements for individuals with disabilities rather than as the transitional service (to a less restrictive employment placement) they were meant to be. Perhaps more importantly, critics such as Moore (1994) and Gerhardt and Markowitz (1993) argue that the sheltered workshop system appears to be a system geared toward fostering dependence within a tightly supervised and nontherapuetic environment rather than encouraging independence in the less supervised community at large.

Although still quite common, the sheltered workshop as an appropriate workplace for many people with autism is being questioned. Concerns with sheltered workshops are apparently twofold: (a) an apparent lack of training and supports that would allow sheltered employees to move beyond the physical and social confines of the workshop, and (b) the basic design, wherein large numbers of persons with disabilities, isolated from more nomalized daily events and interactions, work on repetitive tasks with limited reinforcement or supervision. The sheltered workshop simply does not appear to offer an optimal program model for individuals with autism if continued personal growth and the development of real employment opportunities are the accepted goals of adult services for persons with autism (Gerhardt & Markowitz, 1993).

Secure Employment

As an alternative to the sheltered workshop, Holmes (1989) proposes an approach to employment-related services that he refers to as "secure employment" (p. 263). Tenets of this system include a commitment to: (a) individualized assessments, planning, and services; (b) increasingly less restrictive environments and increasingly more normalized life experiences; (c) the provision of a personally compatible physical environment; (d) the provision of remedial programming to the extent necessary; (e) supportive appropriate behavior across environments; and (f) a lifetime of continually evolving services designed to meet changing needs.

Holmes (in press) describes the hallmark of secure employment as being its ecobehavioral approach to employment-related services for individuals with autism. These individuals are able to participate in a variety of employment (subcontracted, supported, and competitive) and/or employment development and training activities (e.g., from personal hygiene training to the development of appropriate interviewing skills [Holmes et al., 1994]) within a system designed to meet their particular needs at their particular point in life. Holmes also argues for a commitment to life-span services and a continuum of services in order to provide a "safety net" (1989, p. 261) so that job loss or the challenges associated with aggressive behavior would not result in a loss of services.

The secure employment paradigm, with its multiple options (including supported and competitive employment) and individualized approach to employment development and support, appears to be a significant and viable option for those individuals with autism (and their families) who value the employment security and life-span commitment that this model offers.

Supported Employment

Supported employment (SE) can generally be defined as "an employment option that recognizes the capacity of the adult with developmental disabilities while acknowledging his or her need for ongoing support" (Kiernan & Stark, 1986b, p. 109). Over the past decade, increasing numbers of individuals with developmental disabilities, including autism (e.g., Burt, Fuller, & Lewis, 1991; Smith, Belcher, & Juhrs, 1995; Wehman & Kregel, 1988), have obtained employment within the general workforce through SE initiatives (Revell, Wehman, Kregel, West, & Rayfield, 1994). Among the reasons most often cited for this increase are: changing societal perceptions of the employability of individuals with disabilities (Hopkins, 1992), improved employment assessment processes (Menchetti & Flynn, 1990), the noted emphasis on school-to-work transitions (Lagomarcino & Rusch, 1987), the development of increasingly sophisticated employment strategies (Buckley, Mank, & Sandow, 1990), a heightened awareness of the role of social competence in the maintenance of employment (Herbert & Ishikawa, 1991), and the reported

cost efficiency of supported employment as a service option (Tines, Rusch, McCaughrin, & Conley, 1990).

Models of Supported Employment

Rusch and Hughes (1990) describe four models of supported employment placement that are applicable to individuals with autism: (a) an individual placement model, (b) a clustered placement or enclave model, (c) a mobile crew; and (d) an entrepreneurial model. In the individual placement model, a job coach works to develop a job for an individual with a disability within a private-sector enterprise. Intensive on-site training and support provided by the job coach in a one:one setting are subsequently faded as job competencies increase, freeing up the job coach to "job-develop" for another individual. In general, social integration is high in the individual placement model, as is the degree of individuality. Troublesome, however, is the desire to fade support over a relatively brief period of time. This would, in effect, eliminate all but the most able individuals from participation in the individualized placement model. A modification of the model to provide the long-term individualized supports often required by persons with autism would present a much more functional application.

In the clustered or enclave model, instead of working with one individual, the job coach works to support a small group of individuals (usually two to six persons) with disabilities at a private-sector location. Job coach support is generally provided for the length of employment, although more intensive supervision may be faded over time. Social integration may be high, but limitations associated with the physical setup of a clustered placement may restrict more normalized interactions. For this reason, the clustered model has been criticized as being a "private-sector sheltered workshop" and perhaps less ideal than the individual placement model for some individuals.

Similar to clustered placements, mobile crews generally consist of a small number of individuals who provide an agreed-on level of contracted services (e.g., office cleaning) throughout a specific geographic area. Because of the nature of many of the services offered by mobile crews, and the fact that many of these jobs are generally accomplished during times when few people may be working, the level of social integration tends to be somewhat limited under this model.

The entrepreneurial model involves the development of a small, often specialized, business for the purposes of (a) meeting a specific business need, and (b) providing paid employment to persons with disabilities. Of all models, the entrepreneurial model provides the lowest level of social integration because it requires, in effect, a "reverse integration" (D.L. Holmes, personal communication) of the community into the entrepreneurial business. The entrepreneurial model is often seen as an option for those individuals with "the most severe disabilities who require intensive, continuous supervision" (Rusch, 1990, p. 10); however, this description may be dependent on the nature and needs of the developed business.

Research on Supported Employment for Persons with Autism.

Individuals with autism may present significant challenges to the development and maintenance of employment—supported or not. Communication and social deficits, inappropriate behaviors, poor attentional skills, and issues related to the generalization and maintenance of learned skills may impact the perceived employability of an adult with autism (Smith, Belcher, & Juhrs, 1994). Although limited, the research on employment does support the argument that many persons with autism can, indeed, be gainfully employed when provided the necessary training and supports.

Wehman and Kregel (1988) documented the process by which an individual with autism and limited verbal skills, who functioned in the range of moderate mental retardation, was able to access employment with a local bank. Beginning in his last year of school, and using an individualized, long-term model of employment training and support, these authors documented this individual's ability to maintain employment (average of 30 hours/week) over the course of 21 months. Wehman and Kregel report that, following the

720 hours of job-related intervention provided, the supported employee was "performing the job at 95% accuracy and his production rate was approaching the standards of the employer" (p. 6).

Burt, Fuller, and Lewis (1991) reported on the employment of four individuals with autism who displayed "low to moderate levels of autistic behavior" (p. 237) and were reported as being at or above borderline levels of intellectual functioning. Following an intensive training program, all four individuals had been able to maintain competitive employment for periods ranging from 6 to 30 months. Factors noted as having positively impacted the efficacy of the employment training included family and workplace support, good interpersonal and communication skills, and an ability to control undesirable behaviors. Factors noted as negatively impacting employment included a lack of motivation, a lack of task flexibility, and specific behavior challenges (in this case, encopresis).

Of particular interest in both investigations are the high levels of training and support that were required for employment, despite the fact that all five individuals functioned at or above the moderate range of mental retardation. This would support the contention that, independent of levels of cognitive functioning, autism, in and of itself, constitutes a severe disability that presents a significant challenge within the context of community employment. The question left unanswered then is: What levels and types of supports are necessary for individuals with autism who display more significant cognitive, behavioral, and social challenges than those currently reported in the literature? Although the simple, yet accurate, answer would be *a lifetime of supports* (Holmes, 1989), there exists a critical need for further research to address this question, if those adults with autism who may present such challenges are to be provided the most effective systems of employment programming.

Current Issues in Supported Employment for Persons with Autism

Some literature endorses the active involvement of persons with autism in supported employment, but much of the endorsement comes from a programmatic belief that employment, in general, is a normalized, desirable, valued, and obtainable event. If that premise is accepted, what issues, specific to individuals with autism, may impact their participation in supported community-based employment?

Employment-Readiness

Gerhardt and Markowitz (1993), in reviewing the issues relevant to the provision of effective supported employment services to persons with autism who present more significant cognitive and behavioral challenges, propose that a reexamination of the concept of "employment-readiness" may be necessary if increasing numbers of individuals with autism are to access employment. Historically, employment-readiness was used to identify that cohort of skills deemed necessary for community employment (e.g., production skills). Gerhardt and Markowitz contend that, in a very pragmatic sense, many of the skills necessary to obtain and maintain employment can only be identified, let alone taught, in the community, usually at potential job sites. Earlier interpretations of employment-readiness, unfortunately, resulted in a situation where, because certain skills had not yet been acquired, community access and participation were not realized, and, subsequently, new and perhaps more beneficial skills could not be taught and an individual's actual potential for employment was reduced. These authors question the appropriateness of maintaining a concept of employment-readiness that may effectively function as a barrier to employment for many individuals with autism. In its place, they recommend that the practice of ongoing job development for all individuals, whereby attempts are made to integrate job and employer demands with current individual skills and abilities, become the standard of practice for the field.

Job-Match

Throughout the supported employment literature, a number of authors (see, e.g., Rusch, 1990) note the importance of the job-match in supporting employment opportunities for individuals with autism and other disabilities. Job-match generally refers to the development of

employment opportunities that meet the preferences of the potential supported employee. Among the many considerations in developing an appropriate job-match are hours of employment (Is the individual not a morning person?), the level of coworker involvement (With whom and to what extent will cooperative action be required?), level of physical involvement (Is lifting required?), social environment (With whom and to what extent will the individual be required to socially interact?), noise or activity levels (Is the job too loud or too quiet?), production demands (What is the level of quality control required?), and work schedules (How many hours per week are required?). Especially for a more behaviorally challenged individual with autism, the development of an appropriate job-match, and the resulting intrinsic reinforcement that may then be associated with the job, would appear crucial to successful employment.

The importance of establishing an appropriate job-match should not be given short shrift. Although economic variables (i.e., pay) do play a role in maintaining long-term employment motivation, the importance of the paycheck for many employees with disabilities is, at best, idiosyncratic (Ford, Dineen, & Hall, 1984). For employees with autism, factors such as supportive surroundings, a comfortable work space, clearly defined job expectations, interesting and challenging work, and improved coworker and societal perceptions may offer far greater employment motivation than can be associated with a biweekly paycheck. In developing employment opportunities for individuals with autism, it is critical to identify as many potential individual employment preferences as possible. The greater the percentage of individual employment preferences a particular job potentially meets (i.e., the better the job-match), the greater the potential for long-term job success and, subsequently, the greater the possibility that the employment will result in positive changes in an individual's perception of his or her own quality of life (Shalock & Jensen, 1986).

Social Competence

Social competence appears to play a critical role in employment maintenance, according to the literature on job loss in supported employment (Hill, Wehman, Hill, & Goodall, 1986; Salzberg, Llikins, McConaughy, & Lignugaris-Kraft, 1986). In fact, social competence has been seen as so integral to job success that, according to McConaughy, Stowitschek, Salzberg, and Peatross (1989), "social employment skills simply cannot be separated from the performance of job tasks" (p. 13). Given that persons with autism, as a group, present significant social deficits, the role that social competence plays in their employment may appear particularly daunting.

Holmes (1988) proposes that, in order to address this issue, job coaches need to also assume the role of "social coaches." Social coaching, as described by Holmes (1989), requires the identification of problematic social situations, the development of situation-specific strategies, coaching to promote reinforcement, errorless navigation of the situation, and the gradual fading of coaching as specific social competencies and strategies are acquired. Smith, Belcher, and Juhrs (1995), in addition to stressing the importance of skill development, note that employer and coworker training in the nature of autism may help reduce employer concerns related to employees' social deficits.

Behavior Management

The aggression, self-injury, and other inappropriate behavior that may be displayed by adults with autism may, in the majority of instances, be incompatible with the needs of a community employer (Smith & Coleman, 1986). The reduction of these problematic behaviors in a manner that is acceptable to the community at large is another crucial issue (Horner, Sprague, & Flannery, 1993) in employment. Significant advances in the understanding and applied use of functional analysis technology (e.g., Mace, Lalli, Lalli, & Shea, 1993) has allowed more effective identification and development of behavioral strategies that may be more functional and appropriate in the workplace than other, potentially more intrusive strategies. Absent a comprehensive review of the surrounding issues (which may be found elsewhere in this volume), suffice it to say that the issue of behavior management for persons with autism who display potentially dangerous

behaviors within a community-referenced context remains an area in need of further, well designed investigations.

Summary

The services currently available for adults with autism range from the traditional sheltered workshop or activity-center program to the various models of community-based, paid, supported employment. Holmes (1989), in his discussion of secure employment, presents a compendium of employment-related services designed to meet individual needs across the life span.

Although a large body of research on the employment of individuals with autism is lacking (as opposed to that for individuals with mental retardation), the field as a whole is moving toward supported employment as being the service of choice for the majority of adults with autism. Programmatic issues that may impact the ability of the adult with autism to access and maintain employment include: restrictive definitions of employment-readiness, the complexities involved in developing an appropriate job-match, issues related to social competence, and behavior management concerns. Additional research, amplifying published anecdotal reports and informing on the best practices for providing employment programming to individuals with autism, particularly those who pose significant intellectual or behavioral challenges, is of critical importance at this time.

DISCUSSION

Children with autism become adults with autism, and, as adults, they have differing needs, one of which is the ability to access some form of employment opportunity. Although IDEA requires the provision of transition-to-work services for all individuals with autism, there are continuing issues regarding the efficacy of many transition plans, due, in large part, to difficulties associated with the interagency coordination of transition services and the availability of appropriate services on the terminal side of transition. Adult employment services legislation appears to be necessary (perhaps the *I*ndividuals with *D*isabilities

Employment Act or IDEA II), if the flow of learners with autism transitioning to inappropriate services or to no services at all is to be stopped and more appropriate employment-related services are to be consistently available. Not only would such legislation be philosophically appropriate in terms of normalization and community integration, but the fiscal advantages to supporting individuals with autism to move beyond being "consumers" of services and become wage-earning "producers" of services (and, ultimately, taxpayers) would appear difficult to dispute.

Although much has been written regarding supported employment for persons with mental retardation, a significant body of research on the employment needs of individuals with autism, particularly those with more severe cognitive and behavioral challenges, is lacking. Consequently, there is a critical need for published, well-designed reports and investigations regarding such issues as the duration and types of supports necessary to attain employment, the provision of social skills and behavior management training in the workplace, issues in the development of a functional job-match, and issues related to personnel preparation and other administrative concerns.

In practice, although published reports indicate that participation in supported employment initiatives has increased in the past decade, the majority of individuals with autism continue to be excluded from accessing these potentially appropriate services. That is not to say, however, that more specialized employment services are not being provided to some individuals at locations across the country. For example, Eden W.E.R.C.s, an employment service for adults with autism in New Jersey (based on the secure employment model of service delivery), offers community-supported employment services to over 35 adults with autism, the majority of whom function within the severe range of mental retardation and present various degrees of behavioral challenges, including aggression and self-injury. It is now incumbent on such providers to "get the message out" (e.g., Ball, Gerhardt, Holmes, & Alessandri, 1994; Smith, Belcher, & Juhrs, 1995) as to how best to accomplish this daunting, yet attainable and very necessary task.

The field has changed dramatically in 25 years. A system once rooted in institution-based services has moved to one focused on a system of community-integrated services and supports. There is no "silver bullet" when it comes to adult service options, and it would certainly appear that the diversity that is autism supports the need for programmatic diversity in employment opportunities. The challenge now is to provide a mechanism by which increasing numbers of adolescents and adults with autism may best assess the option that meets their needs, so that increasingly more promising postgraduation employment outcomes are realized.

Cross-References

Autism in adolescents and adults is discussed in Chapter 14. Issues in behavioral and pharmacological intervention are explored in Chapters 26 and 32. Behavioral assessment is the topic of Chapter 20, and issues in program administration are further discussed in Chapter 30.

REFERENCES

American Psychiatric Association. (1994). *Diagnostic and statistical manual of mental disorders* (4th ed.). Washington, DC: Author.

Ball, J., Gerhardt, P.F., Holmes, D.L., & Alessandri, M. (1994). *A parent's guide to the Social Security Administration and Social Security Work Incentive Programs.* Princeton, NJ: Eden Press.

Bates, P.E., Bronkema, J., Ames, T., & Hess, C. (1992). State-level interagency planning models. In F.R. Rusch, L. DeStefano, J. Chadsey-Rusch, L.A. Phelps, & E. Szymanski (Eds.), *Transition from school to adult life: Models, linkages, and policy* (pp. 115–129). Sycamore, IL: Sycamore.

Bellamy, G.T., Rhodes, L.E., Bourbeau, P.E., & Mank, D.M. (1986). Mental retardation services in sheltered and day activity programs: Consumer benefits and policy alternatives. In F.R. Rusch (Ed.), *Competitive employment issues and strategies.* Baltimore: Brookes.

Berkell, D.E. (1992). Transition issues for secondary school students with autism and developmental disabilities. In F.R. Rusch, L. DeStefano, J. Chadsey-Rusch, L.A. Phelps, & E. Szymanski (Eds.), *Transition from* school to adult life: Models, linkages, and policy* (pp. 460–472). Sycamore, IL: Sycamore.

Bettelheim, B. (1967). *The empty fortress.* New York: Free Press.

Brotherson, M.J., Turnbull, A.P., Bronicki, G.J., Houghton, J., Roeder-Gordon, C., Summers, S.A., & Turnbull, H.R. (1988). Transition into adulthood: Parental planning for sons and daughters with disabilities. *Education and Training in Mental Retardation, 23,* 165–174.

Brown, L., Nietupski, J., & Hamre-Nietupski. (1976). The criterion of ultimate functioning. In M.A. Thomas (Ed.), *Hey, don't forget about me!* (pp. 2–15). Reston, VA: Council for Exceptional Children.

Buckley, J., Mank, D., & Sandow, D. (1990). Developing and implementing support strategies. In F.R. Rusch (Ed.), *Supported employment: Methods, models and issues* (pp. 131–144). Sycamore IL: Sycamore.

Burt, D.B., Fuller, P., & Lewis, K.R. (1991). Brief report: Competitive employment of adults with autism. *Journal of Autism and Developmental Disorders, 21,* 237–242.

Carr, E.G., Binkoff, J.A., Kologinsky, E., & Eddy, M. (1978). Acquisition of sign language by autistic children: 1. Expressive labeling. *Journal of Applied Behavior Analysis, 11,* 489–501.

Celiberti, D.A., Alessandri, M.O., Fong, P.L., & Gill, M.J. (1993). Past, current, and future trends in the behavioral treatment of autism. *The Behavior Therapist, 16,* 127–132.

DeStefano, L., & Wermuth, T.R. (1992). IDEA (PL 101-476): Defining a second generation of transition services. In F.R. Rusch, L. DeStefano, J. Chadsey-Rusch, L.A. Phelps, & E. Szymanski (Eds.), *Transition from school to adult life: Models, linkages, and policy* (pp. 537–549). Sycamore IL: Sycamore.

Ferster, C.B., & DeMyer, M.K. (1962). A method for the experimental analysis of the behavior of autistic children. *American Journal of Orthopsychiatry, 32,* 89–98.

Fong, L., Wilgosh, L., & Sobsey, D. (1993). The experience of parenting an adolescent with autism. *International Journal of Disability, Development and Education, 40,* 105–113.

Ford, L., Dineen, J., & Hall, J. (1984). Is there life after placement? *Education and Training in Mental Retardation, 19,* 291–296.

Friedlander, B. (1989). Becoming an advocate. In M. Powers (Ed.), *Children with autism: A parent's guide* (pp. 231–252). Rockville, MD: Woodbine House.

Gerhardt, P.F., & Holmes, A.S. Through the lifespan: Managing communication and social issues in autism. *ADVANCE for Speech-Language Pathologists & Audiologists, 5,* 13, 17.

Gerhardt, P.F., & Markowitz, J. (1993). Employment programming and the adult with autism: Options, issues and challenges. In *1993 International Conference Proceedings: Autism—A World of Options* (pp. 93–97). Arlington, TX: Future Education.

Gold, M.W. (1975). Vocational training. In J. Wortis (Ed.), *Mental retardation and developmental disabilities: An annual review* (pp. 254–264). New York: Brunner/Mazel.

Hayes, R.P. (1987). Training for work. In D.J. Cohen & A.M. Donnellan (Eds.), *Handbook of autism and pervasive developmental disorders* (pp. 360–370). New York: John Wiley & Sons.

Herbert, J.T., & Ishikawa, T. (1991). Employment-related interpersonal competence among workers with mental retardation. *Vocational Evaluation and Work Adjustment Bulletin, 24,* 87–94.

Hill, J.W., Wehman, P., Hill, M., & Goodall, P. (1986). Differential reasons for job separation of previously employed persons with mental retardation. *Mental Retardation, 24,* 347–351.

Holmes, D.L. (1988). Social coaching as a method of promoting community involvement in persons with autism. Princeton, NJ: Eden Press.

Holmes, D.L. (1989). The years ahead: Adults with autism. In M.D. Powers (Ed.), *Children with autism: A parents' guide* (pp. 253–273). Rockville, MD: Woodbine House.

Holmes, D.L. (1990). Community-based services for children and adults with autism: The Eden family of programs. *Journal of Autism and Developmental Disorders, 20,* 339–351.

Holmes, D.L. (in press). *Life-span services for children and adults with autism: The Eden Services model.* Rockville, MD: Woodbine House.

Holmes, D.L., Storm, K., Milton, R., Gerhardt, P., Holmes, A.S., Cohen, M., & Bomba, C. (1994). *The Eden Services Employment Curriculum.* Princeton, NJ: Eden Press.

Hopkins, K.R. (1992). *Willing to act: A summary of the 1991 Harris Survey on public attitudes towards people with disabilities.* (Available from the National Organization on Disability, 910 Sixteenth St. NW, Washington, DC, 20006)

Horner, R.H., Sprague, J.R., & Flannery, K.B. (1993). Building functional curricula for students with severe intellectual disabilities and severe behavior problems. In R. VanHouten & S. Axelrod (Eds.), *Behavior analysis and treatment* (pp. 47–71). New York: Plenum Press.

Hosack, K., & Malkmus, D. (1992). Vocational rehabilitation of persons with disabilities:

Family inclusion. *Journal of Vocational Rehabilitation, 2,* 11–17.

Inge, K.J., Banks, P.D., Wehman, P., Hill, J.W., & Shafer, M.S. (1988). Quality of life for individuals who are labeled mentally retarded: Evaluating competitive employment versus sheltered employment. *Education and Training in Mental Retardation, 23,* 97–104.

Irvin, L.K., Thorin, E., & Singer, G.H.S. (1993). Family-related roles and considerations: Transition to adulthood by youth with developmental disabilities. *Journal of Vocational Rehabilitation, 3,* 38–46.

Janicki, M.P., Castellani, P.J., & Norris, R.G. (1983). Organization and administration of service delivery systems. In J. Matson & J. Mulick (Eds.), *Handbook of mental retardation* (1st ed., pp. 3–23). New York: Pergamon.

Kanner, L. (1943). Autistic disturbances of affective contact. *Nervous Child, 2,* 217–250.

Kaplan, J.E., & Moore, R.J. (1989). Legal rights and hurdles. In M.D. Powers (Ed.), *Children with autism: A parents' guide* (pp. 203–228). Rockville, MD: Woodbine House.

Kiernan, W.E., & Stark, J.A. (1986a). Comprehensive design for the future. In W. Kiernan & J. Stark (Eds.), *Pathways to employment for adults with developmental disabilities* (pp. 103–111). Baltimore: Brookes.

Kiernan, W.E., & Stark, J.A. (1986b). Demographic characteristics. In W. Kiernan & J. Stark (Eds.), *Pathways to employment for adults with developmental disabilities* (pp. 21–50). Baltimore: Brookes.

Kregel, J., & Wehman, P. (1989). Supported employment: Promises deferred for persons with severe disabilities. *Journal of the Association of Persons with Severe Handicaps, 14,* 293–303.

Lagomarcino, T., & Rusch, F.R. (1987). Supported employment: Transition from school to work. *American Rehabilitation, 13,* 4–5, 26–27.

Levy, S.M. (1983). School doesn't last forever: Then what? Some vocational alternatives. In I.E. Schopler & G.B. Mesibov (Eds.), *Autism in adolescents and adults* (pp. 133–148). New York: Plenum Press.

Lovaas, O.I., & Simmons, J.Q. (1969). Manipulation of self-destruction in three retarded children. *Journal of Applied Behavior Analysis, 2,* 143–157.

Mace, F.C., Lalli, J.S., Lalli, E.P., & Shea, M.C. (1993). Functional analysis and treatment of aberrant behavior. In R. Van Houten & S. Axelrod (Eds.), *Behavior analysis and treatment* (pp. 75–99). New York: Plenum Press.

Mank, D. (1994). The underachievement of supported employment: A call for reinvestment. *Journal of Disability Policy Studies, 5,* 1–24.

Markowitz, J., Gerhardt, P.F., Christopher, W., Christopher, B., & McKean, T. (1994). Quality of life issues for adults with autism. *1994 Autism Society of America Conference Proceedings: A new dawn of awakening* (pp. 89–90). Arlington, TX: Future Education.

McConaughy, E.K., Stowitschek, J.J., Salzberg, C.L., & Peatross, D.K. (1989). Work supervisor's ratings of social behaviors related to employment success. *Rehabilitation Psychology, 34,* 3–15.

Menchetti, B.M., & Flynn, B.M. (1990). Vocational evaluation. In F.R. Rusch (Ed.), *Supported employment. Methods, models and issues* (pp. 111–130). Sycamore IL: Sycamore.

Mesibov, G.B. (1990). Normalization and its relevance today. *Journal of Autism and Developmental Disorders, 20,* 379–390.

Moore, S.C. (1994). Adult services: Opportunities to demonstrate competence. In L.J. Hayes, G.J. Hayes, S.C. Moore, & P.M. Ghezzi (Eds.), *Ethical issues in developmental disabilities* (pp. 135–134). Reno, NV: Context Press.

National Society for Autistic Children. (1977). *A short definition of autism.* Bethesda MD: Author.

Peraino, J.M. (1992). Post-21 follow-up studies: How do special education graduates fare? In P. Wehman (Ed.), *Life beyond the classroom: Transition strategies for young people with disabilities* (pp. 21–70). Baltimore: Brookes.

Pollack, R. (1997). *The creation of Dr. B: A biography of Bruno Bettelheim.* New York: Simon & Schuster.

Revell, W.G., Wehman, P., Kregel, J., West, M., & Rayfield, R. (1994). Supported employment for persons with severe disabilities: Positive trends in wages, models and funding. *Education and Training in Mental Retardation and Developmental Disabilities, 29,* 256–264.

Rimland, B. (1964). *Infantile autism: The syndrome and its implications for a neural theory of behavior.* New York: Appleton-Century-Crofts.

Rusch, F.R. (Ed.). (1990). *Supported employment: Methods, models and issues.* Sycamore IL: Sycamore.

Rusch, F.R., DeStefano, L., Chadsey-Rusch, J., Phelps, L.A., & Szymanski, E. (1992). *Transition from school to adult life: Models, linkages, and policy.* Sycamore, IL: Sycamore.

Rusch, F.R., & Hughes, C. (1990). Historical overview of supported employment. In F.R. Rusch (Ed.), *Supported employment: Methods, models and issues* (pp. 5–14). Sycamore IL: Sycamore.

Salzberg, C.L., Llikins, M., McConaughy, E.K., & Lignugaris-Kraft, B. (1986). Social competence and employment of retarded persons. *International Review of Research in Mental Retardation. 7,* 32–41.

Schopler, E., & Hennick, J.M. (1990). Past and present trends in residential treatment. *Journal of Autism and Developmental Disorders, 20,* 291–298.

Schopler, E., & Mesibov, G.B. (1983). *Autism in adolescents and adult.* New York: Plenum Press.

Shalock, R.L., & Jensen, C.M. (1986). Assessing the goodness-of-fit between persons and their environment. *Journal of the Association for Persons with Severe Handicaps, 11,* 103–109.

Smith, M.D., Belcher, R.G., & Juhrs, P.D. (1995). *A guide to successful employment for individuals with autism.* Baltimore: Brookes.

Smith, M.D., & Coleman, D. (1986). Managing the behavior of adults with autism. *Journal of Autism and Developmental Disorders, 16,* 145–154.

Snauwaert, D.T. (1992). Transition policy. In F.R. Rusch, L. DeStefano, J. Chadsey-Rusch, L.A. Phelps, & E. Szymanski (Eds.), *Transition from school to adult life: Models, linkages, and policy* (pp. 509–517). Sycamore, IL: Sycamore.

Solnick, J.V., Rincover, A., & Peterson, C.R. (1977). Some determinants of the reinforcing and punishing effects of timeout. *Journal of Applied Behavior Analysis, 10,* 415–424.

Sowers, J., & Powers, L. (1992). *Vocational preparation and employment of students with physical and multiple disabilities.* Baltimore: Brookes.

Steere, D.E., Wood, R., Pancsofar, E.L., & Rucker, R.E. (1993). Vocational training for secondary-level students with severe disabilities. *Teaching Exceptional Children, 25,* 7–11.

Stowitschek, J.J. (1992). Policy and planning in transition programs at the state agency level. In F.R. Rusch, L. DeStefano, J. Chadsey-Rusch, L.A. Phelps, & E. Szymanski (Eds.), *Transition from school to adult life: Models, linkages, and policy* (pp. 519–536). Sycamore, IL: Sycamore.

Sullivan, R.C. (1981). What does institutionalization mean for our children? *Journal of Autism and Developmental Disabilities, 11,* 347–356.

Thomas, M.A., & Halloran, W. (1987). Facts and attitudes about adult services for people with severe disabilities. *American Rehabilitation, 13,* 20–25.

Tines, J., Rusch, F.R., McCaughrin, W., & Conley, R.W. (1990). Benefit-cost analysis of supported employment in Illinois: A statewide evaluation. *American Journal on Mental Retardation, 95,* 44–54.

Turnbull, A.P., & Turnbull, H.R. (1988). Toward great expectations for vocational opportunities: Family professional partnerships. *Mental Retardation, 26,* 337–342.

Ward, M.J. (1992). Introduction to secondary special education and transition issues. In F.R. Rusch, L. DeStefano, J. Chadsey-Rusch, L.A. Phelps, & E. Szymanski (Eds.), *Transition from school to adult life: Models, linkages, and policy* (pp. 387–389). Sycamore IL: Sycamore.

Wehman, P. (1991). Transition: What lies ahead in the 1990's. *Journal of Vocational Rehabilitation, 1,* 7–8.

Wehman, P. (1992). *Life beyond the classroom: Transition strategies for young people with disabilities.* Baltimore: Brookes.

Wehman, P., & Kregel, J. (1988). Supported competitive employment for individuals with autism and sever retardation: Two case studies. *Focus on Autistic Behavior, 3,* 1–11.

Wehman, P., Kregel, J., & Barcus, M.J. (1985). From school to work: A vocational transition model for handicapped students. *Exceptional Children, 52,* 25–37.

Will, M. (1984). *OSERS programming for the transition of youth with disabilities: Bridges from school to working life.* Washington, DC: U.S. Department of Education.

Winking, D.L., O'Reilly, B., & Moon, M.S. (1993). Preference: The missing link in the job match process for individuals without functional communication skills. *Journal of Vocational Rehabilitation, 3,* 27–42.

Wolf, L., & Goldberg, B. (1986). Autistic children grow up: An 8- to 24-year follow-up study. *Canadian Journal of Psychiatry, 31,* 550–556.

CHAPTER 29

Helping Children with Autism Enter the Mainstream

SANDRA L. HARRIS AND JAN S. HANDLEMAN

Educators and psychologists are increasingly adept at preparing children with autism to enter mainstream educational settings. Developments in applied behavior analysis enable some very young children to be fully included with their normally developing peers when they reach kindergarten or first grade (e.g., Fenske, Zalenski, Krantz, & McClannahan, 1985; Harris & Handleman, 1994; Lovaas, 1987). Other children, although not making such dramatic changes, can nonetheless function, at least in part, within the same classes as their peers. This chapter reviews current empirically based technology for including children with autism in the mainstream, and describes several models for this process.

Definitions

There is variation in how the terms *mainstream, inclusion,* and *integration* are used in the educational literature. No single set of terminology has yet emerged. In an early article, Odom and Speltz (1983) recommended that a class be called an *integrated special education class* when children with a disability predominate but there are some normally developing peers. A class in the regular education system that has one or more children with special needs is called a *mainstreamed special education class.* Mainstreamed classes are built around the regular education model; integrated classes are developed within an individualized special education model. We use that vocabulary in the present chapter. We also use the term *inclusion* to refer to any situation that brings children with autism together with their peers for specific educational purposes. We

will review the literature on the development of social skills in children with autism, suggestions for social inclusion, and models of inclusion. These issues are at the heart of effectively involving children with autism in regular educational settings.

SOCIAL SKILLS

Competent social skills are essential for effective inclusion of children with autism in mainstreamed classes. Even children with Autistic Disorder or Asperger's Disorder who are of normal intellectual ability have grave problems understanding the social transactions of childhood. These limitations make them stand out among their peers and can lead to rejection by other children.

Mastering social skills appears daunting. Not only must the child learn a full range of skills that should be generalized to a bewildering variety of settings and people, but these skills should also extend beyond the memorizing of rote responses, to spontaneous behavior in novel contexts. Among the social skills documented to be useful for children with autism are: playing games (Coe, Matson, Fee, Manikam, & Linarello, 1990), being affectionate (McEvoy et al., 1988), responding to greetings (Nientimp & Cole, 1992), being assertive in conversation and play (McGee, Krantz, & McClannahan, 1984), and recognizing other people's needs (Harris, Handleman, & Alessandri, 1990).

An important decision in teaching social skills is the extent to which the teacher, peer, or child with autism is the primary locus of instruction. For example, early strategies for teaching social behaviors to children who were deficient in these skills relied heavily on adult mediation to reinforce appropriate behavior (e.g., Strain, Shores, & Kerr, 1976; Strain & Timm, 1974). This strategy had limited durability because the interactions were dependent on adult reinforcement, and when that was withdrawn, the social behavior of the child with autism declined (e.g., Odom, Hoyson, Jamieson, & Strain, 1985).

Another approach to teaching social skills focuses on teaching normally developing peers to initiate interactions with children with autism (e.g., Odom & Strain, 1986; Strain, 1983; Strain, Kerr, & Ragland, 1979). Early studies of these interventions were often limited by the unwillingness of a peer to initiate, and did not result in increased initiations by the child with autism. From these early studies, it became clear that it was important for the child with autism to become an initiator of interactions, rather than remaining a passive respondent.

Educationally, there is no good reason to separate the domains of teacher-, peer-, or child-focused intervention. Although we review each area of research separately, in an optimal setting one would combine adult mediation, responsive peers, and a well-prepared child with autism. In our experience, the well-prepared child with autism has an interest in other children, can learn in a small group, and does not engage in a great many intrusive or disruptive behaviors that might frighten peer children.

Peers Initiation

Normally developing peers are valuable for modeling social skills and language for children with autism. Much of this research has been done with preschool-age children (e.g., Odom et al., 1985; Odom & Strain, 1986). Some studies have observed older, elementary school-age children (e.g., Blew, Schwartz, & Luce, 1985; Lord & Hopkins, 1986; Sasso & Rude, 1987); in other studies, children who have mild disabilities have served as models for more impaired youngsters (e.g., Shafer, Egel, & Neef, 1984).

Physical proximity alone is not sufficient to allow children with autism to benefit from the modeling of their peers; special training helps peers be effective models. For example, Carr

and Darcy (1990) used peer modeling and prompting to teach children with autism to play "Follow the Leader." Having the peer ask the child with autism to watch him or her was not sufficient to teach the new skill; the peer had to model and physically prompt the child with autism. McGee, Almeida, Sulzer-Azaroff, and Feldman (1992) taught normally developing preschoolers to use incidental teaching strategies when interacting with classmates who had autism. The peers learned to request responses and praise the child with autism for appropriate behaviors during free play. Adult supervision helped establish the skills, but was then faded. Although they were effective in the play setting, the peers did not show spontaneous generalization of initiations when the lunch table was the setting. McGee and her colleagues (1992) found that being a peer tutor did not have a negative effect on a child's popularity with other classmates.

In a study by Goldstein, Kaczmarek, Pennington, and Shafer (1992), peers learned to make comments that did not demand a response from the child with autism to the extent that a question or request might. Increases in non-demanding social initiations by the peers led to a substantial increase in the social behaviors of the children with autism. This study broadened the potential repertoire of helpful peer behaviors to include comments and acknowledgments along with the initiations of play and other requests used in previous studies.

Interventions used with older children, to teach them more advanced social skills, require different methods than those used to teach preschoolers how to play. Haring and Breen (1992) recruited normally developing junior high school students to create a school-based social network for youngsters with autism. These adolescents discussed with an adult facilitator strategies for promoting greater social interaction, and then self-monitored their activities with their classmates who had disabilities. The study found an increase in the frequency and appropriateness of interactions in natural settings when the social network was used. When the project was completed, many peers described their classmate with a disability as a friend, and were likely to initiate interactions that were not assigned by the adult facilitator.

Self-monitoring of social initiations can be effective for preschoolers as well as older peers. Sainato, Goldstein, and Strain (1992) taught young peers how to get the attention of a child with autism, initiate a play activity with the child, and respond to the child. After the peers mastered these skills, they learned to evaluate their own performance. These self-evaluation strategies improved the peers' use of social interaction skills. Although teacher prompts are important for helping preschool peers initiate a social skills intervention, after the children have started to interact effectively, the prompts should be faded systematically (Odom, Chandler, Ostrosky, McConnell, & Reaney, 1992; Odom & Watts, 1991). McGee and her colleagues (1992) found that adult prompts risk being intrusive if continued after the peers have mastered the requisite skills. Adult attention may adversely influence the richness of the child-to-child exchange (Kliewer, 1995).

Younger peers need more adult support than older ones (Odom & Watts, 1991). Lord and Hopkins (1986) reported that children ages 10 to 12 years were more effective than children 5 to 6 years of age in adapting their behavior to the needs of a developmentally disabled partner. Meyer and her colleagues (1987) similarly found that adult supervision was not essential for elementary school-age children. With older children, it may be important to use high-social-status peers as models. Sasso and Rude (1987) reported that higher-status peers based on classmate nomination made more initiations toward the children with autism than did lower-status peers in an elementary school.

Classwide Intervention

Interventions designed to help children with autism may also be beneficial to their normally developing peers. In the academic realm, Harris, Handleman, Gordon, Kristoff, and Fuentes (1991) reported that peers, as well as children with autism, showed significant developmental gains in language after being together in an integrated class. The children with autism, but not the peers, also showed an increase in IQ after one school year.

Working with school-age children, Kamps, Barbetta, Leonard, and Delquadri (1994) designed a peer tutoring program in which tutor–learner pairs worked together on reading skills. This was a classwide intervention that included three high-functioning children with autism. The intervention, valued by students and teacher alike, improved reading fluency for both children with autism and typical peers. Similarly, in a study of fourth-grade cooperative learning groups, both children with autism and their peers showed increased mastery of information and increased frequency of interaction in a small-group context (Dugan et al., 1995). These studies are creative demonstrations of the possibility of enhancing overall classroom functioning while mainstreaming children with autism among their peers.

In another study, Kamps and her colleagues (1992) used social skills groups to teach first-grade children with autism, and their peers, to increase their interactions. All of the children learned to initiate, respond, and sustain interactions. They also learned to greet others and discuss a variety of subjects. Giving and receiving compliments, turn taking, offering and requesting assistance were included. As a result of training, the children with autism increased their social initiations and responses to their peers, and the peers in turn increased their responsiveness to the children with autism.

Another tool for increasing independent, generalized social interactions among children with autism and normally developing preschool peers is social scripts. Goldstein and Cisar (1992) taught children with autism, and their peers, verbal and nonverbal scripts for pretend play. After the children mastered the scripts, they showed improved social interaction and communication. The use of scripts may be valuable for teaching fantasy play, a skill that is especially challenging for many children with autism.

Initiations by the Child with Autism

Because trained peers are not always available in the real world, it is helpful when children with autism can initiate interactions, in addition to responding to the initiations of others. The role of self-initiation was shown by Oke and Schreibman (1990), who first taught non-handicapped peers to initiate interactions with a child with autism. Although there was an initial increase in level of social interaction by both the peers and the child with autism, there was a subsequent decline in responding by the child with autism when the peers, who were no longer reinforced for initiating interactions, decreased their initiations. In the next phase of the study, when the child with autism learned to make initiations, his level of responding rose again, and this time was accompanied by a decline in his disruptive behavior. An interesting aspect of this research was the use of videotaped feedback to help the child with autism learn appropriate play skills. Similar benefits from videotaped feedback were found by Kern-Dunlap et al. (1992) with children having severe emotional and behavioral problems.

Belchic and Harris (1994) taught children with autism to initiate and sustain an interaction with a normally developing peer in an integrated preschool by first teaching the children to initiate play with the adult trainer, and then transferring this skill to other children. The children with autism generalized social initiations from the classroom to the playground, to an untrained child with autism, and to their brother or sister at home.

Teaching self-management of social skills can be effective for older children as well as preschoolers. Koegel, Koegel, Hurley, and Frea (1992) taught school-age children with autism who had severe social deficits how to increase appropriate social behavior in the community. The children learned to monitor their own social responses and showed a collateral decrease in inappropriate behavior. Like the work of Belchic and Harris (1994) with preschool children, this technique put the locus of control for social initiation in the hands of the child with autism, not the peers. It therefore has the potential to be valuable in settings where naïve peers do not initiate contact.

Suggestions for Social Inclusion

Based on her clinical experience, Lord (1995) makes a series of suggestions for social inclusion of children with autism. These guidelines concern the context, the role of the peers, the role of the adult, and the needs of the child with autism. In terms of the context, one recommendation is to ensure that the activities are interesting and attractive (Carr & Darcy, 1990). These should be things that all of the children might enjoy, and should not demand responses too complex for the children with autism. Carr and Darcy (1990) point to the importance of using multiple training objects to attract the attention of the peers. Lord (1995) reports that having a theme for the group activity (e.g., holidays, community helpers) can provide an organizing format for the session. The physical environment should be arranged to increase proximity among the children, and the activities should be ones that require cooperation or interaction (Demchak & Drinkwater, 1992). Group activities should be relatively brief, with very young children having 5- or 10-minute sessions, and older children going as long as a half-hour. Lord (1995) suggests that, in her experience, frequent meetings increase a sense of group identity as does having group rituals that are part of every meeting.

In effective inclusion, peers are given general instructions such as persisting in their effort to engage the child with autism, joining in the autistic child's activities, using simple language, praising efforts to interact, and calling an adult if there are problems. Lord (1995) suggests that children with autism comprise less than half the group.

Among the essentials for effective inclusion is preparation of the classroom teacher (Hundert & Hopkins, 1992). Demchak and Drinkwater (1992) urge that teachers learn inclusion techniques and behavior management skills before children with disabilities are brought into the regular classroom. Lord (1995) describes the adult's role as one of a mediator rather than an active participant in the interaction. She suggests that the adult respond to the child with autism primarily through the peers or through the arrangement of the environment rather than by direct intervention.

TEACHERS' AND PARENTS' PERSPECTIVES

The attitudes of special education and regular education teachers can stall or facilitate inclusion (Odom & McEvoy, 1990), and these two groups of educators may differ on the criteria for this goal. For example, the competencies for entering a mainstreamed class are viewed differently by regular and special education teachers, and vary by the child's age. In setting criteria for inclusion in second- or third-grade classes, regular education teachers give higher priority to the ability to read and write, and to the absence of behavior problems, than do special education teachers (Hanrahan, Goodman, & Rapagna, 1990). In contrast, when asked about the criteria for mainstreaming the kindergarten child, regular education teachers rate academic preparation as less important than do the special education teachers (Hanrahan, Goodman, & Rapagna, 1985). Kindergarten teachers may be more concerned about the social adjustment of their students; second- and third-grade teachers recognize that academic competence is important to a child's effective classroom functioning (Hanrahan et al., 1990).

Parents may be ambivalent about where their child belongs on the spectrum of inclusion. That perspective is an important consideration in the placement process. Guralnick, Connor, and Hammond (1995) interviewed parents of preschool-age children with disabilities. They found that mothers of children in inclusive programs and of those in specialized programs viewed their child's educational setting as valuable in helping the child establish peer relationships and friendships. Mothers of children in the inclusive settings reported that their child played better and was more social because of the peer children. However, both groups of mothers were concerned about their child's social rejection. Guralnick et al. (1995) point out that although parents want their children exposed to the real world, they fear their youngsters will suffer painful rejection in that setting. These fears are not without foundation. For example, Guralnick and Groom (1987) found that children with mild disabilities are less accepted and more rejected than their peers in a play group. Rejection and social isolation may occur in any setting. It is therefore critical that administrators and staff be sensitive to the needs of every person who is part of a social setting. For many families, the primary concern may not be the location of services, but the excellence of services regardless of setting.

OUTCOMES OF INCLUSION

Data on the benefits of inclusion for language development, general development, and social development of children with disabilities are limited, and only a few of these studies involve children with autism. Durbach and Pence (1991) found that young children with various disabilities used more language in a segregated setting than in an inclusive one; they also noted that an adult mediator was important in supporting language in either setting. Harris, Handleman, Kristoff, Bass, and Gordon (1990) reported that children with autism made equivalent language gains over one school year, regardless of whether they were in an integrated or segregated setting. Changes in general developmental level in children with a variety of disabilities show a similar pattern, with no clear benefits for inclusive settings (Buysse & Bailey, 1993).

Social behavior appears to be the domain with the greatest potential to benefit from inclusion in the preschool years. Buysse and Bailey (1993) report that, for preschool children with a variety of disabilities, growth in social behavior and play skills is greater in inclusive than in segregated settings. These authors caution that research has not shown the extent to which increased social exchanges enable children to establish true friendships and enduring social inclusion. This is of special concern for children with autism.

MODELS OF INCLUSION

The striking benefits from early and intensive intervention have led to a number of programs for including these youngsters with typically developing peers (Lovaas, 1987; Strain, 1983). Many of these programs are contributing to our understanding of key variables for success in inclusion. For example, most discussions of methods of inclusion typically recognize a continuum of options ranging from part-time community experiences to full inclusion in regular classes (Harris & Handleman, 1994). This sensitivity to the highly individual nature of the inclusion process promotes the careful planning and monitoring that are central to the education of students with autism (Handleman & Harris, 1986).

The educational programs discussed in the present section emphasize different features and strategies. They are located in a variety of settings, including public schools, private special education facilities, and universities, but each program maintains a strong commitment to supportive inclusive programming, and they all have a proven track record of effectiveness. Although we have highlighted special features of each program for didactic purposes, there is considerable overlap in methods from one program to the next, and components linked with one program are likely to be found in others as well.

Individualized Comprehensive Programming

Two decades of research and clinical experience have confirmed the value of comprehensive behavioral programming for children with autism (Harris & Handleman, 1994). This value is illustrated in programs operated by the Princeton Child Development Institute (McClannahan & Krantz, 1994) and the Children's Unit for Treatment and Evaluation (Romanczyk, Matey, & Lockshin, 1994), which emphasize individualized planning for effective community education. Inclusive education is viewed by these programs as a function of a child's needs and should be solely assessed and provided on an individual basis.

The programs at the Princeton Child Development Institute and the Children's Unit emphasize the building of skills that can promote participation in community life. For example, being able to follow instructions, to generalize concepts, and to delay reinforcement are viewed as important prerequisites to responding to the multitude of experiences in a typical school or social setting. Both preschool programs follow a detailed curriculum designed to promote systematic developmental and behavioral progress.

Transition activities by the Princeton Child Development Institute and the Children's Unit reflect a continuum of options and typically include initial involvement in local day camps, religious schools, or other neighborhood activities. Like many of the other preschool models, decisions about inclusive education are based on systematic assessment, planning, and implementation. Movement to alternate programs

is guided by a carefully monitored transition plan.

Early Inclusion

Classes operated by the Walden Preschool (McGee, Daly, & Jacobs, 1994) and the LEAP Preschool (Strain & Cordisco, 1994) support the commitment to inclusive education by enrolling students with a range of developmental needs in the same class from the very start. The approach of these programs reflects the philosophy that typical children are very good intervention agents for children with autism, and that inclusive settings offer these students the benefits of enriched experiences.

Both the Walden and LEAP programs have a curriculum that includes careful planning and scheduling of activities to promote social inclusion. Emphasizing, for example, the importance of developmentally appropriate goals and strategies, experiences at the LEAP preschool include early childhood activities and behavioral programming. Intervention at Walden involves the systematic use of incidental teaching procedures (McGee, Krantz, & McClannahan, 1986). Both programs promote the continuum of inclusive opportunities by developing and implementing systematic transitional plans to community placements.

A hallmark of the Walden and LEAP programs, as well as most other exemplary programs, is their commitment to staff training. Careful planning and preparation of educational experiences are viewed as critical variables for program effectiveness. For example, maintaining enthusiasm, making complex teaching judgments, and accurately tracking student progress are some of the very important teacher competencies that are encouraged by these programs.

Steps to Inclusion

The May Center for Early Childhood Education (Anderson, Campbell, & O'Malley Cannon, 1994) and the Douglass Developmental Disabilities Center (Handleman & Harris, 1994) are examples of programs that provide a progression of experiences for preschoolers, from segregated to inclusive programming. These programs' approach to inclusion reflects the philosophy that, for some children, initial segregated intervention may increase their ability to benefit from subsequent inclusive opportunities. Instruction is initially designed to include fundamental skills that will eventually enhance responsiveness to community-based applications. Placement along a continuum of classroom settings is then based on a child's readiness for a curriculum that includes systematically guided inclusion experiences.

Both programs provide sequential movement from individual to small-group and then to inclusive programming. For example, classes at the Douglass Developmental Disabilities Center include a prep class that offers exclusive one-to-one teaching, a small-group preschool that provides instruction in groups of increasing size, and the Small Wonders program, where students with autism attend school with typically developing peers. The May Center operates very similar classes. In both programs, as children move along the continuum, the complexity of the curriculum systematically increases, toward the goal of approximating community-based experiences.

Transition to mainstream settings is carefully orchestrated by both the May and Douglass programs. A highly systematic process includes initial assessment visits by the teacher to public and private settings, and then the development of a comprehensive transition plan. There are many variables to consider, such as staff/student ratio, classroom structure, and school-life activities. After a complete assessment of the skills needed in the identified setting, the child's requisite skills are evaluated, and the curriculum is modified accordingly. The transition process is further enhanced by having the student attend the new school for increasing periods of time prior to enrollment. Formal follow-up support services are provided by both programs. The success of this inclusion effort, however, often relies on advocacy efforts and educational support services, as well as the preparation of the child.

Statewide Services

The Delaware Autistic Program (Bondy & Frost, 1994) and TEACCH in North Carolina (Lord & Schopler, 1994) are models of statewide service delivery for students with autism. Both programs, which are responsible for providing educational services for students throughout their respective states, share the common philosophy that a continuum of services from complete inclusion to highly specialized programming should be available. This full range of resources is believed to enable both states to meet the federal mandate for a free and appropriate education within the least restrictive environment on an individual basis.

Providing statewide programs presents the challenges of matching the needs of students with the resources of the local community. Consideration for variables such as population, distance, and services for typical children increases the complexity of these statewide systems. For example, one town may share the same elementary school; another may provide resources on a regional basis. Developing a statewide continuum of program options often reflects these and other demographic and logistical concerns.

Both the Delaware and North Carolina models support the commitment to providing inclusive options for students with autism through a continuum of services and placements. Specialized categorical programs are supplemented with local mainstreaming experiences in day care centers or preschools, and some communities provide full inclusive experiences. In addition, some students may receive home intervention services on either an exclusive or part-time basis.

Planning Inclusion Activities

As reflected by the variety of models, meeting the challenges of inclusive education is dependent on many issues that determine the ultimate complexion of the preschool program. For example, one feature that is highlighted by the Montgomery County Public School System Preschool for Children with Autism (Egel, 1994) is the comprehensive system of inclusive activities. Classroom events in this preschool program are conducted in the context of naturally occurring situations such as free play, lunch, storytime, and recess.

When designing educational experiences for the children, the staff of the Montgomery program considers variables such as the student:teacher ratio, the rate of attention, and the type of materials used in the integrated setting. This information is then assessed in order to modify the child's program activities and approximate those conducted in the community Headstart class. Children then attend Headstart as early as possible, according to an integration plan that specifies time, activities, and staffing.

The Role of Peers

All of the programs presented in this chapter value the importance of the typical peer as a model. This issue is particularly exemplified by the Berkshire Hills Learning Center (Powers, 1994). Program development efforts for this inclusive preschool class consider peer-specific variables such as age, developmental level, social comfort, and effective modeling skills. Peer-training activities are then matched to educational need and targeted for instruction. The curriculum that emerges provides rich educational experiences both for the children with autism and the peers.

Follow-up services are also a critical feature of inclusive programming in the Berkshire Hills program. For example, in-class supports and consultation services are among the resources that are available to families and agencies after graduation. The ultimate success of the transition process is viewed as being dependent on the ongoing review and monitoring of student progress.

The various programs presented here produce a wide range of student outcomes. Many schools report, each year, a number of students who are able to be fully included with varying levels of support. Also, part-time mainstreaming experiences are described by most agencies. Each of the programs also identifies children who continue to require specialized programming beyond the preschool years. All of these findings support the view that successful inclusive education for the young child with autism is a function of individual need and response to intervention.

The range of program options offered by the distinguished service providers we have described reflect current thinking regarding integrated education for the preschooler with autism. Whether provided on a local or statewide basis, or in the private school or university, variables such as segregated programming, peer modeling, and the exclusivity of the included experience become common concerns of this intricate issue. The continued evolution of the continuum of program options should provide the clarification that is needed to answer the many questions regarding integrated education.

SUMMARY

Including children with autism in classes with their normally developing peers has been found helpful in improving the social skills of these children. A significant body of research exists to guide the educator in facilitating social interactions among children with disabilities and their classmates. Benefits in the domains of language and general development are not as well documented. An important focus of social skills training appears to be teaching the child with autism to initiate interactions and to respond to the efforts of his or her peers. Adult support for both the peers and the children with autism, especially in the early stages of learning, is important. It is also important to have receptive peers who will be patient with the awkward initial efforts of the child with autism. Although shown to be effective for some children, especially those who are very young, the benefits of inclusion are not yet fully explored. For example, we do not know the optimal blend or sequencing of special and regular educational experience for the child with autism. A variety of models have been developed, with little comparative data among them. Thus, much of the research to evaluate inclusion remains to be done (Buysse & Bailey, 1993).

In the absence of definitive data, we believe the extent of inclusion is best adjusted to fit each child and may vary at different points in the child's education. Very young children with autism require an initial intensity of instruction that may best be done one-to-one (e.g. Harris & Handleman, 1994; Lovaas, 1987). After that, the best setting will be dictated by the child's skills and the best available resources. Higher-functioning children with autism who have good cognitive abilities, few disruptive behaviors, and some awareness of other people, might profitably spend the full school day with their peers in a regular class. These children will need some special support in the classroom, especially for their social development, but can often benefit from the full academic curriculum. Other children with autism might share some classes with normally developing peers, and return to a specialized setting for other experiences. The most impaired children might share cafeteria and recreational services with their peers, but do other work in a segregated class. A child's age, cognitive abilities, behavior problems, and social awareness should all be considered in making these plans.

Cross-References

Assessment issues are discussed in Chapters 19 through 21. Curriculum development is covered in Chapter 22, behavioral issues in Chapter 26, and working with families in Chapter 27. Theoretical issues relative to inclusion are addressed in Chapter 36.

REFERENCES

Anderson, S.R., Campbell, S., & O'Malley Cannon, B. (1994). The May Center for Early Childhood Education. In S.L. Harris & J.S. Handleman (Eds.), *Preschool education programs for children with autism* (pp. 15–36). Austin, TX: Pro-Ed.

Belchic, J.K., & Harris, S.L. (1994). The use of multiple peer exemplars to enhance the generalization of play skills to the siblings of children with autism. *Child and Family Behavior Therapy, 16,* 1–25.

Blew, P., Schwartz, I.S., & Luce, S. (1985). Teaching functional community skills to autistic children using nonhandicapped peer tutors. *Journal of Applied Behavior Analysis, 18,* 337–342.

Bondy, A.S., & Frost, L.A. (1994). The Delaware autistic program. In S.L. Harris & J.S. Handleman (Eds.), *Preschool education programs for children with autism* (pp. 37–54) Austin, TX: Pro-Ed.

Buysse, V., & Bailey, D.B. (1993). Behavioral and developmental outcomes in young children with disabilities in integrated and segregated settings: A review of comparative studies. *Journal of Special Education, 26,* 434–461.

Carr, E.G., & Darcy, M. (1990). Setting generality of peer modeling in children with autism. *Journal of Autism and Developmental Disorders, 20,* 45–59.

Coe, D., Matson, J., Fee, V., Manikam, R., & Linarello, C. (1990). Training nonverbal and verbal play skills to mentally retarded and autistic children. *Journal of Autism and Developmental Disorders, 20,* 177–187.

Demchak, M., & Drinkwater, S. (1992). Preschoolers with severe disabilities: The case against segregation. *Topics in Early Childhood Education, 11*(4), 70–83.

Dugan, E., Kamps, D., Leonard, B., Watkins, N., Rheinberger, A., & Stackhaus, J. (1995). Effects of cooperative learning groups during social studies for students with autism and their fourth-grade peers. *Journal of Applied Behavior Analysis, 28,* 175–188.

Durbach, M., & Pence, A.R. (1991). A comparison of language production skills of preschoolers with special needs in segregated and integrated settings. *Early Child Development and Care, 68,* 49–69.

Egel, A.L. (1994). The Montgomery County Public School System Preschool for Children with Autism. In S.L. Harris & J.S. Handleman (Eds), *Preschool education programs for children with autism* (pp. 55–70). Austin, TX: Pro-Ed.

Fenske, E.C., Zalenski, S., Krantz, P.J., & McClannahan, L.E. (1985). Age at intervention and treatment outcome for autistic children in a comprehensive intervention program. *Analysis and Intervention in Developmental Disabilities, 5,* 49–58.

Goldstein, H., & Cisar, C.L. (1992). Promoting interaction during sociodramatic play: Teaching scripts to typical preschoolers and classmates with disabilities. *Journal of Applied Behavior Analysis, 25,* 265–280.

Goldstein, H., Kaczmarek, L., Pennington, R., & Shafer, K. (1992). Peer-mediated intervention: Attending to, commenting on, and acknowledging the behavior of preschoolers with autism. *Journal of Applied Behavior Analysis, 25,* 289–305.

Guralnick, M.J., Connor, R.T., & Hammond, M. (1995). Parent perspectives of peer relationships and friendships in integrated and specialized programs. *American Journal on Mental Retardation, 99,* 457–476.

Guralnick, M.J., & Groom, J.M. (1987). The peer relations of mildly delayed and nonhandicapped children in mainstreamed play groups. *Child Development, 58,* 1556–1575.

Handleman, J.S., & Harris, S.L. (1986). *Educating the developmentally disabled: Meeting the needs of children and families.* San Diego, CA: College Hill.

Handleman, J.S., & Harris, S.L. (1994). The Douglass Developmental Disabilities Center. In S.L. Harris & J.S. Handleman (Eds.), *Preschool education programs for children with autism* (pp. 71–86). Austin, TX: Pro-Ed.

Hanrahan, J., Goodman, W., & Rapagna, S. (1985). Instructional priorities for the integration of mentally handicapped children as judged by special class teachers and regular class teachers. *Canadian Journal of Special Education, 1,* 101–108.

Hanrahan, J., Goodman, W., & Rapagna, S. (1990). Preparing mentally retarded students for mainstreaming: Priorities of regular and special school teachers. *American Association on Mental Retardation, 94,* 470–474.

Haring, T.G., & Breen, C.G. (1992). A peer-mediated social network intervention to enhance the social integration of persons with moderate and severe disabilities. *Journal of Applied Behavior Analysis, 25,* 319–333.

Harris, S.L., & Handleman, J.S. (Eds.). (1994). *Preschool education programs for children with autism.* Austin, TX: Pro-Ed.

Harris, S.L., Handleman, J.S., & Alessandri, M. (1990). Teaching youths with autism to offer assistance. *Journal of Applied Behavior Analysis, 23,* 297–305.

Harris, S.L., Handleman, J.S., Gordon, R., Kristoff, B., & Fuentes, F. (1991). Changes in cognitive and language functioning of preschool children with autism. *Journal of Autism and Developmental Disorders, 21,* 281–290.

Harris, S.L., Handleman, J.S., Kristoff, B., Bass, L., & Gordon, R. (1990). Changes in language development among autistic and peer children in segregated and integrated preschool settings. *Journal of Autism and Developmental Disorders, 20,* 23–31.

Hundert, J., & Hopkins, B. (1992). Training supervisors in a collaborative team approach to promote peer interactions of children with disabilities in integrated preschools. *Journal of Applied Behavior Analysis, 25,* 385–400.

Kamps, D.M., Barbetta, P.M., Leonard, B.R., & Delquadri, J. (1994). Classwide peer tutoring: An integration strategy to improve reading skills and promote peer interactions among students with autism and general education peers. *Journal of Applied Behavior Analysis, 27,* 49–61.

Kamps, D.M., Leonard, B.R., Vernon, S., Dugan, E.P., Delquadri, J.C., Gershon, B., Wade, L., & Folk, L. (1992). Teaching social skills to students with autism to increase peer interactions in an integrated first-grade classroom. *Journal of Applied Behavior Analysis, 25,* 281–288.

Kern-Dunlap, L., Dunlap, G., Clarke, S., Childs, K.E., White, R.L., & Stewart, M.P. (1992). Effects of a videotape feedback package on the peer interactions of children with serious behavioral and emotional challenges. *Journal of Applied Behavior Analysis, 25,* 355–364.

Kliewer, C. (1995). Young children's communication and literacy: A qualitative study of language in the inclusive preschool. *Mental Retardation, 33,* 143–152.

Koegel, L.K., Koegel, R.L., Hurley, C., & Frea, W.D. (1992). Improving social skills and disruptive behavior in children with autism through self-management. *Journal of Applied Behavior Analysis, 25,* 341–353.

Lord, C. (1995). Facilitating social inclusion. In E. Schopler & G.B. Mesibov (Eds.), *Learning and cognition in autism* (pp. 221–240). New York: Plenum Press.

Lord, C., & Hopkins, J.M. (1986). The social behavior of autistic children with younger and same-age nonhandicapped peers. *Journal of Autism and Developmental Disorders, 16,* 249–262.

Lord, C., & Schopler, E. (1994). TEACCH Services for Preschool Children. In S.L. Harris & J.S. Handleman (Eds.), *Preschool education programs for children with autism* (pp. 87–106). Austin, TX: Pro-Ed.

Lovaas, O.I. (1987). Behavioral treatment and normal educational and intellectual functioning in young autistic children. *Journal of Consulting and Clinical Psychology, 55,* 3–9.

McClannahan, L.E., & Krantz, P.J. (1994). The Princeton Child Development Institute. In S.L. Harris & J.S. Handleman (Eds.), *Preschool education programs for children with autism* (pp. 107–126). Austin, TX: Pro-Ed.

McEvoy, M.A., Nordquist, V.M., Twardosz, S., Heckaman, K.A., Wehby, J.H., & Denny, R.K. (1988). Promoting autistic children's peer interactions in an integrated early childhood setting using affection activities. *Journal of Applied Behavior Analysis, 21,* 193–200.

McGee, G.C., Almeida, M.C., Sulzer-Azaroff, B., & Feldman, R.S. (1992). Prompting reciprocal interactions via peer incidental teaching. *Journal of Applied Behavior Analysis, 25,* 117–126.

McGee, G.G., Daly, T., & Jacobs, H.A. (1994). The Walden Preschool. In S.L. Harris & J.S. Handleman (Eds.), *Preschool education programs for children with autism* (pp. 127–162). Austin, TX: Pro-Ed.

McGee, G.G., Krantz, P.J., & McClannahan, L.E. (1984). Conversational skills for autistic adolescents: Teaching assertiveness in naturalistic game settings. *Journal of Autism and Developmental Disorders, 14,* 319–330.

McGee, G.G., Krantz, P.J., & McClannahan, L.E. (1986). An extension of incidental teaching procedures to reading instruction for autistic children. *Journal of Applied Behavior Analysis, 19,* 147–157.

Meyer, L.H., Fox, A., Schermer, A., Ketelsen, D., Montan, N., Maley, K., & Cole, D. (1987). The effects of teacher intrusion on social play interactions between children with autism and their nonhandicapped peers. *Journal of Autism and Developmental Disorders, 17,* 315–332.

Nientimp, E.G., & Cole, C.L. (1992). Teaching socially valid social interaction responses to students with severe disabilities in an integrated school setting. *Journal of School Psychology, 30,* 343–354.

Odom, S.L., Chandler, L.K., Ostrosky, M., McConnell, S.R., & Reaney, S. (1992). Fading teacher prompts from peer-initiation interactions for children with disabilities. *Journal of Applied Behavior Analysis, 25,* 307–317.

Odom, S.L., Hoyson, M., Jamieson, B., & Strain, P.S. (1985). Increasing handicapped preschoolers' peer social interactions: Cross-setting and component analysis. *Journal of Applied Behavior Analysis, 18,* 3–16.

Odom, S.L., & McEvoy, M.A. (1990). Mainstreaming at the preschool level: Potential barriers and tasks for the field. *Topics in Early Childhood Special Education, 10*(2), 48–61.

Odom, S.L., & Speltz, M.L. (1983). Program variations in preschools for handicapped and nonhandicapped children: Mainstreamed vs. integrated special education. *Analysis and Intervention in Developmental Disabilities, 3,* 89–103.

Odom, S.L., & Strain, P.S. (1986). A comparison of peer-initiation and teacher-antecedent intervention for promoting reciprocal social interactions of autistic preschoolers. *Journal of Applied Behavior Analysis, 19,* 59–71.

Odom, S.L., & Watts, E. (1991). Reducing teacher prompts in peer-mediated interventions for young children with autism. *Journal of Special Education, 25,* 26–43.

Oke, N.J., & Schreibman, L. (1990). Training social initiations to a high-functioning autistic child: Assessment of collateral behavior change and generalization in a case study.

Journal of Autism and Developmental Disorders, 20, 479–497.

Powers, M.D. (1994). The Berkshire Hills Learning Center. In S.L. Harris & J.S. Handleman (Eds.), *Preschool education programs for children with autism* (pp. 163–180). Austin, TX: Pro-Ed.

Romanczyk, R.G., Matey, L., & Lockshin, S.B. (1994). The Children's Unit for Treatment and Evaluation. In S.L. Harris & J.S. Handleman (Eds.), *Preschool education programs for children with autism* (pp. 181–224). Austin, TX: Pro-Ed.

Sainato, D.M., Goldstein, H., & Strain, P.S. (1992). Effects of self-evaluation on preschool children's use of social interaction strategies with their classmates with autism. *Journal of Applied Behavior Analysis, 25,* 127–141.

Sasso, G.M., & Rude, H.A. (1987). Unprogrammed effects of training high-status peers to interact with severely handicapped children. *Journal of Applied Behavior Analysis, 20,* 35–44.

Shafer, M.S., Egel, A.L., & Neef, N.A. (1984). Training mildly handicapped peers to facilitate changes in the social interaction skills of autistic children. *Journal of Applied Behavior Analysis, 17,* 461–476.

Strain, P.S. (1983). Generalization of autistic children's social behavior change: Effects of developmentally integrated and segregated settings. *Analysis and Intervention in Developmental Disabilities, 3,* 23–34.

Strain, P.S., & Cordisco, L.K. (1994). LEAP Preschool. In S.L. Harris & J.S. Handleman (Eds.), *Preschool education programs for children with autism* (pp. 225–244). Austin, TX: Pro-Ed.

Strain, P.S., Kerr, M.M., & Ragland, E.U. (1979). Effects of peer-mediated social initiations and prompting/reinforcement procedures on the social behavior of autistic children. *Journal of Autism and Developmental Disorders, 9,* 41–54.

Strain, P.S., Shores, R.E., & Kerr, M.M. (1976). An experimental analysis of "spill over" effects on the social interaction of behaviorally handicapped preschool children. *Journal of Applied Behavior Analysis, 9,* 31–40.

Strain, P.S., & Timm, M.A. (1974). An experimental analysis of social interaction between a behaviorally disordered preschool child and her classroom peers. *Journal of Applied Behavior Analysis, 7,* 583–590.

CHAPTER 30

Initiating and Administering Programs: Alternative Settings

JUNE GRODEN AND GERALD GRODEN

Private programs for children with autism and related disorders were usually identified with schools and treatment centers that were located in isolated settings, apart from families and community life. Such programs did not prepare these individuals for social and economic life in normalized community settings and weakened the bonds between the children and their families.

An alternative model for the private school and treatment center is presented in this chapter. The Groden Center, in Providence, Rhode Island, is described here as a model program. We believe that this presentation illustrates an ecologically sound, clinically appropriate, and dynamic model for private service agencies for children and adults with autism. In this chapter, we suggest that when a community encourages the development of such private specialized services, it maximizes what it can provide. In addition, with the current philosophy of inclusion of all children into public education, the private program must supplement, complement, and collaborate with the public school system's home community (Billingsley, 1993; Rankin et al., 1994).

THE GRODEN CENTER AS A MODEL FOR PRIVATE PROGRAMS: A COMMUNITY-BASED APPROACH

The Groden Center was created in 1976, when professionals and other advocates within Rhode Island recognized the need for a community-based day educational and treatment program for children with autism and related disorders.

The creation of a private service facility such as the Groden Center represented a shift from the isolated institutional model to a community-based model. Furthermore, the founders of the Groden Center required that its education and treatment programs incorporate new proven procedures and research monitoring capabilities. Although many models emerged in the 1960s and 1970s that had considered accountability, to a great extent there still existed a void in programs that effectively utilized systems analysis and systems theory. The Groden Center feedback loop model (J. Groden, Baron, Pentecost, & Stevenson, 1988) is an organized structure of administration. The activities of (a) assessment, (b) plan development, (c) program implementation, and (d) ongoing data analysis are defined and integrated. Each activity in the system "feeds back" information, which is then used in the next phase. The process does not end with the fourth phase (ongoing data analysis) but returns to the first assessment phase and repeats each activity. This creates a data-based flexible system that incorporates checkpoints at each phase to ensure the quality of treatment.

The Groden Center program was shaped by bringing together professionals who had previous experience in a range of human services, training, and research settings. Key philosophic and pragmatic principles (J. Groden, Groden, Baron, & Stevenson, 1984) were as follows:

1. The most well-developed, reliable, and effective modes of intervention were those behavioral procedures developed under the rubrics of *behavior therapy* and *applied behavior analysis.*
2. There has been a growing awareness that *human ecology* (Rogers-Warren & Warren, 1977) could merge productively with a behavioral technology.
3. The program would be designed in accordance with current knowledge of developmental principles, emphasizing that growth is organized and evolves through a series of systematic stages.
4. Treatment programs are built on a *biobehavioral* model that provides a data-based setting for the application of the most current research and technology in neurological functioning and psychopharmacology.
5. A wide range and continuum of services would be *flexible in schedule or setting* as necessary and appropriate to meet the unique and changing needs of the child and family.

These principles serve as the basis of the Groden Center's philosophy. They lay the groundwork for the spectrum of services provided. The primary goal of the Groden Center is to maximize each individual's chances of inclusive and effective functioning in a relevant social network. The primary service must effectively come to grips with the pragmatic day-to-day needs and problems of children and adults with autism and other developmental disabilities, and their families. The settings in which services are provided, in addition to center-based programs, are each child's functioning life environment, including home, school, or job-training site, and the local community. The change agents who provide treatment include not only the trained therapists and teachers but also the children's parents and siblings, and, as much as possible, the children and adults themselves.

The Private Program's Spectrum of Services to Meet Unique Needs

Children and adults with autism evidence unique and severe problems. Programs serving them must provide a wide range of intensive and coordinated services to meet these needs.

Clinical services should be tailored to the needs of each individual and carefully integrated with other aspects of his or her program.

Research indicates that families play a vital role in the positive development of children with autism, and that family participation in education and treatment efforts is essential to the overall effectiveness of a day treatment program (Harris, 1994; Lovaas, Koegel, Simmons, & Long, 1973). Even with parent education, however, families often find it impossible to maintain their child at home without additional support. Programs such as the Groden Center respond to this need by providing a broad spectrum of services not usually delivered by public education. The provision of these comprehensive services often makes it possible for children with autism to remain with their families in natural environments.

The Groden Center's Support Services

Transdisciplinary Assessment

Standardized and criterion-referenced assessments are conducted by a transdisciplinary team at the time a child enters the program, and are carried out for a six-week period in the home, at the Groden Center, and in community-based environments.

Extended Day and Saturday Program

Families who have children with autism and other challenging behaviors often need services besides the regular schoolday program to enable them to keep their children at home. The usual schoolday ends at 2:00 or 2:30 P.M., which means that these children need to be cared for until bedtime—a sizable amount of time. To assist these families, the Groden Center offers recreational, arts and crafts, and leisure skill programs in the afternoon. A Saturday program is also offered so that families can spend time with their other children or attend to home matters. Saturday programs are devoted to therapeutic recreation and focus on the learning of appropriate skills in community settings.

Respite Services

Numerous types of respite are possible, ranging from a few hours to a few weeks in the child's home or a provider's home. All providers are trained in specialized techniques of behavioral management.

Data-Based Systems

All curriculum and behavioral areas incorporate data-based systems for recording progress, thus providing the basis to define objectives and track changes (J. Groden, Groden et al., 1984).

Family Therapy

Individual or family sessions are based on the needs of the family and include family dynamics, coping mechanisms, and sibling and parent interaction.

Family Education and Support Groups

Parents and other family members, as appropriate, are taught behavioral and educational skills to use in home and community settings. In addition to support groups, parents attend the Groden Center's programs and participate in community activities such as restaurant trips and recreational activities. Or, teachers/therapists may provide training in the student's home. A number of variables are taken into consideration in planning programs: amount of involvement desired by the family, work schedules, number of siblings, number of parents, extended family resources, and so on. Informal parent groups are formed to provide support and to share ideas, solutions, and similar experiences.

Vocational Services

The purpose of the vocational program at the Groden Center is to maximize an individual's employability. This goal is accomplished through comprehensive assessment and training, in both school and community settings, for each individual beginning at 14 years of age. Vocational planning is done in accordance with and is integrated into academic, social, and behavioral instruction. The philosophy of the vocational program is that learning will be most effective if it occurs in the natural setting. For that reason, vocational training activities occur primarily in actual work settings in the community.

Initial community-based vocational activities include assessment and training at nonpaid work sites—hospitals, public parks and greenhouses, and the community food bank. Activities at these sites focus on assessing a student's abilities and interest, as well as his or her ability to identify and manage work-related stressors. Program staff supervise students at each of these sites and help to facilitate social interactions between students and employers. Upon determination of a student's interest, program goals for skill acquisition, production, and independence are developed and implemented. Program goals related to social interaction, communication, and stress management are also developed for each student on an individual basis.

Most students in the program participate in supported employment upon completion of their assessment and training. The level of support provided is determined by the needs of the individual, but it is generally more intensive at the beginning of the job and less intensive as the student becomes more integrated and more independent. In addition to providing direct instruction and support to a student at a job site, job coaches may facilitate the development of "natural supports," a process in which a supervisor or coworker already at the job site provides much of the instruction and support that an individual needs to maintain a job. As a natural support relationship develops, the job coach decreases the time spent at the site and alters his or her role to that of coordinator of natural support services between the student and the employer.

Among the jobs obtained by students in the program are the following: data entry processor, office worker, grocery packer, delivery person, retail store clothing assembler, dishwasher, park maintenance worker, and indoor and outdoor maintenance person. In addition, several individuals have begun to organize their own window washing business.

Community-Based Residential Alternatives

Although the main thrust of the Groden Center's program is to maintain individuals in their own homes, it is often necessary to provide residential services. These services are needed because of many factors, such as changing home environments (as a result of divorce, death of a parent, illness, and so on), severity of a behavioral problem with which the family is no longer able to cope (this may happen with an adolescent), or appearance of new behavioral problems that necessitate short-term intensive therapy. Residential placement is often needed when a child lacks the social supports of an organized and functional family or caregiver system.

The Groden Center provides a continuum of residential services, depending on the needs of the individual. Small group residences located in the community serve four or six persons in a homelike setting. Residence staff provide structured and intensive training to prepare these persons for less restrictive settings. Programs in living skills, social interaction, communication, recreation, and leisure are incorporated into the lifestyle planning process (Malette et al., 1992; O'Brien & Lyle, 1987). A second residential option is the Professional Family Living Arrangement program (PFLA; Stevenson & Ruby, 1994), which provides short- to long-term placement for children outside of their own homes, with other families. The children's own families participate in the therapeutic process along with the professional family team. PFLA providers act as therapeutic foster parents and are recruited, monitored, and trained by the Groden Center. PFLA families receive support from the Center in the form of case managers to coordinate services, program development, weekly respite, and ongoing in-home training. Staffed apartments are another residential option. They are suited to persons who are more independent and want to live in an area where they have access to stores, transportation, and other community services.

Community Consultation Services (CCS)

A wide range of consultative services supports the Center's overall goal to promote inclusion and community-based treatment and educational services. Referrals for these services are made by schools, agencies, health professionals, families, and individuals. Often, the clinical expertise provided by the CCS program prevents an individual's being placed outside of the local school district, service area, or family home, and gains admission into a more integrated setting. Teams of Groden Center psychologists and clinical and educational specialists provide on-site expertise in

behavioral management, special education, vocational and transitional services, self-control and stress management, and strategic inclusion planning. Services include comprehensive behavioral evaluation and program design, multidisciplinary assessments, on-site staff training, and grant-preparation support. Workshops are also provided on behavioral analysis, ecological assessment, curriculum development, self-control procedures (including relaxation training and imagery-based techniques), systematic program development, and vocational program design and implementation. Funding for these services typically comes from public school departments, state agencies, private health plans, federal and state grants, and private individuals.

Public schools, in adopting the concept of wraparound, have also begun to recognize the services needed to keep children with autism and other disabilities in their home communities. Wraparound refers to the provision of a seamless array of services for youth and family in their natural home, school, and community environments. "Parent-driven individualized service plans, creative use of resources and natural environments are the common attributes which characterize nationally recognized service systems based on wraparound" (Eber, 1994). Private agencies can work with school systems to consult or contract parts of these wraparound services. The Groden Center has developed the skill and technology to implement, and consult to schools to provide, programs such as in-school respite, family advocacy, and behavioral interventions to support the development of desired behaviors. An important consultative service provided by the Groden Center (and essential to the success of wraparound services) is case coordination. Often, the role of the Groden Center clinical administrator is to identify and bring together a variety of agencies to participate in a particular case. The ongoing management of services provided by multiple agencies ensures that programs and services are cohesive and coordinated.

Early Intervention

Research has shown that the early years (birth to 3 years) are crucial for developing language and social behaviors for children with autism

(G. Groden, Dominigue, Chesnick, Groden, & Baron, 1983; McEachin, Smith, & Lovaas, 1993). The early intervention programs provide needed services for the young child. The Groden Center Early Intervention staff work with parents and siblings in their own homes and also offer center-based group and individual training. The first child enrolled in this program, who began at age 2 with serious behavioral difficulties and intellectual limitations, is now integrated into a general education program.

Physical Education and Recreational Services

The Groden Center's physical education (PE) programs focus on physical fitness and competitive and noncompetitive sports. Two adaptive physical education teachers are employed full-time in the PE department. Physical fitness programs are designed for each person, with input from the physical therapist, and then an individual educational plan is written for each person. Sports activities include swim programs, bowling, ice and floor hockey, and roller skating. There are also competitive teams for baseball, basketball, floor hockey, skiing, and speed skating. At first, it was difficult to form teams and organize cooperative sports. However, over the years, these have become favorite activities, and being on a basketball, baseball, or hockey team is something many of the students enjoy. These teams play in Special Olympics and intramural competitions. Some of the students also play on unified teams, which combine typical children and those with developmental disabilities. Among the many advantages to participation in PE programs are: improved muscle tone and strength, reduced stress, aid in coordination, and instruction in spatial relationships. Team sports also assist in teaching cooperation and fostering peer relationships. Participation necessitates being aware of other people, concentrating on what they are doing and how they are moving, and working cooperatively with them. Persons with autism have deficits in these areas and receive much benefit from these programs.

Recreational programs are included in the daily schedule and offer the students opportunities to participate in the many field trips that are available. These trips are to museums, movies, special events such as ice shows, or other recreational and social activities. During the summer months, there is a heavy concentration on recreational activities, with frequent trips to parks and beaches. Recreation time is an opportunity to practice social skills, communication, and other interaction skills in the natural community. It also offers a natural change of pace from the typical school year.

In conclusion, support services are comprehensive and are geared to the personalized needs of the individuals with autism and their families. The Groden Center's programs are unique in their accent on curricula geared to functional needs taught in natural settings; their use of natural reinforcers; their focus on field-based research in contrast to laboratory research; and their focus on flexible instructional arrangements and support services. The result is that children have been brought back from out-of-state programs, and many other children are able to remain in their own homes and communities.

ADVANTAGES OF HAVING PRIVATE AGENCIES AS PART OF THE SERVICE SYSTEM

Source for Leadership, Innovation, Research, and Training

Excellence and innovation in autism, as in other fields, often emerge or are systematically fostered in nonmainstream settings. In fact, program development facilities such as research laboratories, think tanks, training and proving grounds, and intensive and experimental service sites are routinely assumed and accepted (and often heavily funded) in other areas of science, medicine, industry, and education. In autism, centers of higher learning, with their emphases on systematic, closely evaluated, state-of-the-art programming and personnel preparation, contribute disproportionately to the available literature on models for programs and services. Similarly, many advances in the field, especially program-related advances, have come from the private sector. Persons involved in developing and operating private programs are frequently highly motivated individuals who are intent on making a difference. Indeed, a review of the list of con-tributors to the *Handbook of Autism and Per-vasive Developmental Disorders* (Cohen & Donnellan, 1987), judged to be one of the ten most important books in the field (Pfieffer & Nelson, 1992), shows that 19 of the 76 con-tributors represent private programs. The re-mainder of the contributors represent mainly universities. A review of the presenters at the Autism Society of America's 1996 annual meeting revealed that more presenters repre-sented private agencies than any other affilia-tion, except universities, which had only a slightly higher number of presentations.

The Groden Center, as an example, has pio-neered treatment and research in the develop-ment of self-control procedures (described in another section). Contributions have also been made in the area of behavioral assessment. Noting the critical importance of assessment for effective behavioral programming, and the relative neglect of adequate assessment in the literature and in practice, procedures were developed by Center personnel to encourage and improve comprehensive behavioral assess-ment procedures (G. Groden, 1989; G. Gro-den, Stevenson, & Groden, 1996) and were then disseminated to sites throughout the country.

Being associated with universities and with personnel representing many disciplines also facilitates applied research efforts that are po-tentially advantageous to the field. As an ex-ample, among other research activities, the Center participated in a multisite investigation into the efficacy of fenfluramine on autism (G. Groden et al., 1987).

Undoubtedly, the setting described is an ideal site for training personnel. The Groden Center, as well as similar private centers throughout the country, is continuously in-volved in the preparation of treatment staff (Stevenson, Groden, & Groden, 1992) who will, in their turn, contribute to the field.

High Degree of Responsivity to Needs

Private agencies typically have been created as timely responses to known service gaps. The driving forces behind these programs were concerned people (frequently parents and/or professionals) who were impatient with the extent to which service needs were being addressed in their communities. Private agen-cies are generally relatively small and not part of a governmental bureaucracy. Once in opera-tion, they have the flexibility to continue to re-spond more rapidly to existing and emerging needs than do most public school systems. Pri-vate agency staffing and service patterns, for example, can be readily altered should they not appear practical for a given situation or popu-lation. Similarly, such agencies can rapidly expand services or programs as needs become evident. Several of the programs that the Groden Center has added, such as respite and early intervention, are examples. By identify-ing consumer needs and rapidly providing quality services to meet them, private agencies play an entrepreneurial role in the marketplace of services to the developmentally disabled.

The commitment of private agencies to per-sons with autism and other developmental dis-abilities has resulted in their attempts to serve the multiple needs of these individuals seam-lessly, as opposed to the provision of more limited services, such as education, therapy, or social services by different agencies in sepa-rate settings. This approach, reflected in the array of Groden Center services described above, might not be maintained, were private services to suddenly disappear. Zigler (1978) had similar reservations when he argued stren-uously against a move to place Head Start within the Department of Education. More specifically, in testimony before the United States Senate Committee on Governmental Af-fairs, he stated that "Head Start's inclusion in a Department of Education would jeopardize the program's unique status as a national labo-ratory for all children's services." In light of the above, consumers are well advised to insist that, for the present, private agencies should continue to be encouraged to provide services and to aspire to be models of innovation and excellence.

Their size and flexibility are not the only reasons private agencies can respond quickly and effectively to service needs. Because they are not a part of any government agency, pri-vate programs can creatively seek and com-bine funds from different governmental and private sources to develop the components of a comprehensive continuum of services. At the Groden Center, for example, funding for respite, day treatment, and residential services are provided by three different agencies, one for each respective service.

Provision of Options to Consumers and Employees

The presence of private agencies is also advantageous in that they increase consumer options. For instance, there might be only one placement for a particular child, depending on his or her needs, within a particular school system. If parents or other advocates feel that the placement is not satisfactory, no other options may exist. Private agencies increase consumer choice by providing options; they also provide a standard for consumer comparison. Even if private placement is not the goal, consumers can compare programs and request that their children be provided with commensurate services.

In addition, private agencies provide alternative employment and training sites for teachers. Private agencies afford teachers an opportunity to make temporary or permanent changes in their employment setting. Because these settings are frequently quite different with respect to administrative and service delivery supports, such changes allow personnel to vary and broaden their experience. Such transitions also frequently benefit public school systems, because teachers from private agencies can bring into public systems an extensive range of skills, some of which are not widely available in the school systems they enter.

PROBLEMS IN THE PROVISION OF COMMUNITY-BASED PRIVATE SERVICES

Difficulties are, of course, encountered in providing private services such as those just outlined. Some of these difficulties are presented below.

Personnel

Private agencies are not usually funded at levels that are appropriate for provision of the kinds of services that are considered necessary. If a high quality of care is to be maintained, a high staff-to-child ratio is needed. This ratio often results in low pay and few benefits. To recruit and maintain staff, private agencies must provide motivation and make the experience rewarding. Because of the specialized tasks assigned to staff members, and the consultants available to them, staff can experience the satisfaction of seeing behavior change in the individuals they treat and of working with knowledgeable colleagues. This experience often compensates for the long hours and low pay. It is also important to provide staff reinforcement in the form of recognition for achievements, benefits such as conference fee and tuition reimbursements, and recreational and social activities. Tuition and conference fee reimbursements help to attract staff who are interested in advancing in the field through graduate training. In addition, staff members' satisfaction is increased when they are involved in developing child and agency goals. The fulfillment of these goals helps the staff to realize their own personal and professional objectives (Broskowski, 1984). The creative, efficient use of limited funds to solve perennial personnel issues presents an ongoing challenge to private programs.

Community Acceptance

The ecological approach sees children and adults in relation to their environment. Focusing attention on the problems that persons with developmental disabilities have in dealing with the community is a crucial component of a program. But how the community feels about and interacts with persons with developmental disabilities is equally important. It is essential for persons with developmental disabilities to learn to feel comfortable and to act appropriately in the community, and for the people in the community to learn to accept these individuals and some of their behaviors, even though they deviate from the norm. Many community-based programs, especially residential programs, have failed because of lack of acceptance by the community (Graziano, 1974). To combat these problems, it is important to make sure that staffing is adequate and that children are optimally prepared for particular community activities. In addition, the community needs to be made aware of the field of autism and helped to feel ownership in the progress of the individuals. Community members should be encouraged to visit and observe programs. A community outreach worker employed by the Groden Center speaks at Rotary Clubs, Kiwanis Clubs, church guilds, and other community social settings, and makes appearances at schools, on TV, and on radio to acquaint people with the aims and goals of the program. Once educated, the people in the community can be called on to support the Groden Center and are encouraged to participate in its social and recreational programs.

The problem of community acceptance is shared by public and private programs. Private programs can take advantage of their flexibility in staffing arrangements and scheduling to introduce persons with autism and other developmental disabilities into community settings, and they can thereby prevent possible negative reactions to the students.

Family Participation

Families play a major role in effectively maintaining individuals in community settings. They should be encouraged to participate in the treatment and educational programs. The families of children and adolescents enrolled in private residential programs should also be expected to have their children with them for holidays and vacations, and for one weekend a month, if possible. This encourages the maintenance of strong family ties and the continuity of the family unit. Unfortunately, all families are not always willing or able to fulfill this expectation. A center may not want to exclude a child because of the limited participation of his or her family, but the center should recognize, in turn, that the success of the program will be limited by the family's nonparticipation, and plans should include the development of more effective methods to increase family involvement. A center may provide additional in-home services or consider the use of arrangements such as short-term foster parents, when appropriate.

Funding Agency Relationship

A number of problems are encountered in the provision of innovative services that are dependent on funding from local, state, or federal governmental agencies. Four of these problems are discussed here.

1. Private agencies often find that bureaucratic personnel in a position to grant funds are not receptive to new programming approaches and narrowly interpret the funding regulations. For example, dollars available for residential services often can only be utilized for funding out-of-home residential programs and cannot be applied to in-home support services that might enable children to remain in their natural home environment. Fortunately, the need for flexible service provision is increasingly being recognized, and more creative solutions to this problem are beginning to emerge.

2. Active resistance is sometimes encountered from established professionals who have been a part of traditional service systems and who feel threatened by change.

3. Administrative changes in major funding agencies are frequent. Changes can occur when funding responsibility for the private agency is shifted to another existing or newly created agency or when agency leadership changes. The shift in funding responsibility, of course, is more traumatic because no (or few) persons in the new agency may be familiar with, or sympathetic to, the private agency's philosophy and operation. In either case, an important item in the private agency's agenda becomes orientation of the staff and leadership of the new funding agency. Timely and effective orientation is essential. Otherwise, decisions might be made that would threaten the private agency's effectiveness or even its existence. These transitions can occur with such frequency that it is wise for private agencies to anticipate them and to have orientation strategies and materials available in advance. It is essential for private agencies to develop a constituency of parent groups and community friends who form a support network that can help in these efforts.

4. Some spokespersons have argued that *only* public school services for children with developmental disabilities should be supported by public funds. We feel that this is a drastic move, and, no matter how well-intentioned, would be detrimental to persons needing services. To limit funding in this way would, in effect, create a public monopoly and, further,

would create conditions or laws that would inhibit entrepreneurship and innovations. In the business world, it has been determined that such a situation is detrimental to consumers, and laws have been devised to discourage it. Similarly, educational monopolies would be detrimental to consumers of educational services and would deprive them of the advantages of a dual public/private nonprofit system. It is interesting that, quite recently, private alternatives in the field of public education are currently being proposed as a result of perceived problems in both the quality and cost of general education services. There is no reason why persons with special needs should not have access to these same alternatives.

RELATIONSHIPS BETWEEN PUBLIC EDUCATIONAL AND PRIVATE SERVICE AGENCIES

Prerequisites and Potential Obstacles

The expertise and technology available from private agencies such as the Groden Center offer the possibility of multiple productive relationships with local and state educational agencies. For these relationships to be useful, they must be positive and collaborative in nature. There are potential obstacles for the realization of these ideals, however. State educational agencies are responsible for licensing and may impose seemingly impeding requirements on private agencies. Local public school personnel may be pressured by parents or legal advocates demanding private agency involvement or placement that the public personnel may feel is unnecessary or difficult to arrange. Private agency staff occasionally are called on to provide testimony unsupportive of public school positions in court proceedings, which may arouse ill feelings. Such threats to positive collaboration need not impede collaboration, however, if lines of communication remain open and there is an atmosphere of trust among the involved parties.

Collaboration of the Public and Private Sectors

Private agencies depend on local and state educational agencies for financing and referrals, and the local educational specialized agencies depend on private agencies as an additional resource in providing advanced methodology, adequate comprehensive services, and the technology their students need. Without collaboration, each could not serve the other's needs and, ultimately, the children's needs. Collaboration is also required for such activities as mutual decision making in selecting students to refer to private agencies, as well as in determining which children are ready to return to public schools. Collaborative efforts additionally are required when each system functions in the other's setting to effect smooth transitions of children between settings.

There are many other benefits of collaboration for both public educational and private agencies. The following examples are drawn from the Groden Center's cooperative efforts with public school systems.

Consultation and Training

Private agencies develop expertise in a particular field, such as autism, and can provide consultation and training to school personnel. This ranges from assistance regarding a problem with a particular student to training staff in the use of general procedures, such as self-control techniques.

Establishing Ethical Codes and Systems to Guarantee the Protection of Human Rights

Ensuring the rights of the person with autism is of mutual concern to the public and private sector. Establishment of ethical systems should be an area of collaboration. The Groden Center has developed human rights policies that have been shared with local and state educational personnel to help create systems for statewide use (Baron & Stevenson, 1983).

Collaboration on Grants and the Development of Innovative Programs

Private and public agencies can and do collaborate in expanding funding bases to improve services. Following are some examples of areas in which the Groden Center and local educational administrations (LEAs) have been funded for grants that are mutually beneficial.

At the present time, the Groden Center has located several classes at a local regular education school and preschool site staffed by Groden Center personnel. Although these are segregated classrooms, the children are integrated during recreation, lunch, projects (such as peer tutoring), special events, and appropriate educational activities. The long-term goal is to "transition" these children into public schools, with the Groden Center serving in a consulting capacity.

Two local school systems and the Groden Center have received a grant in which Groden Center students receive work adjustment training in the local high school, along with special students from the high school. All of the students are then placed in various jobs at community vocational training sites, where they work alongside staff. The Groden Center provides the on-site technology and supervision for all the students (J. Groden, Snow, Pentecost, & Smith, 1984).

When a joint decision has been made for Groden Center students to reenter the public school system, a transition program is designed. A year before the student is transitioned, the new setting is analyzed to determine the necessary skills in that environment. The child is then instructed in these skills and curriculum areas. During the year, the Groden Center staff and the child make visits to the new program, gradually increasing the public school's responsibility. The following year, when the child is transitioned fully, the Groden Center is available for consultation.

FUTURE TRENDS FOR PRIVATE SERVICES

The adequacy of a human service program model should not be judged only by the range or quality of services it currently provides. Its heuristic value as a base for generating future services should also be considered. Armed with the overriding advantage of flexibility, a community-based private program can contribute to future developments in areas such as the following.

Collaboration with Other Agencies

Private agencies will join with school systems, universities, mental health centers, hospitals, and so on, to promote a full range of services. Collaboration will offer the possibilities of joint funding and the pooling of expertise.

Increased Collaboration between Behaviorally and Biologically Oriented Specialists

As both fields become increasingly sophisticated, greater communication and coordination between them will be necessary for maximizing effective service delivery. In the biological sphere, for example, psychopharmacology and imaging techniques are stretching frontiers. The power of behavioral strategies to produce important and sometimes dramatic changes is still being demonstrated.

Technologically Advanced Training Programs

Computer networking systems, interactive television, and other innovations in technology provide opportunities for the private agency to disseminate information in many different ways. During in-service sessions and seminars, participants can be anywhere in the country and still take advantage of training courses and materials. In this way, private providers can share their technology and information with learners who would not normally have access to these resources. Clinicians can use videotapes of persons in their own facility or at a location anywhere in the world. These videos can be used for assessment purposes (e.g., observing persons with disruptive behaviors in their natural environment), training (e.g., observing people engaged in therapy and critiquing procedures), and illustration and prescription of treatment procedures.

Options and Choices

Consumers will have the advantage of participating in making decisions on flexible services and where the services will take place. In Rhode Island, the CHOICES (Citizens, Health, Opportunities, Interdependence, Choices, Environments, Support) program will spur the transition of the current service delivery system from one that is provider-driven to one that is more consumer-driven. This change will increase opportunities for consumers to build on natural supports and to take more control over their lives by making their own decisions, to the extent possible, about the services they want (Carson, 1994). Consumers will be allocated a specific amount of money (or a voucher), and they will select the services that are affordable within the range of available funds. In this way, voucher systems will empower parents and persons with autism to select the types of services they feel are relevant. These services may combine public school and private services, such as having academics in the public school, and participating in a vocational program at a private agency. These same choices will be available in residential programming and in recreational and leisure activities. As innovators of a range of service options designed to maximize the potential of persons with autism, the private agencies will have an important role in the provision of these services.

Individuals with autism will increasingly have more choices in determining their own curriculum, job placements, and living arrangements. Programs to teach decision making will be important, to enable these individuals to make beneficial choices. Abilities for gathering information and for sampling available options are necessary when persons must make informed decisions.

Necessary Supports to Achieve Inclusion

The philosophy of inclusion is defined as the education of all students in neighborhood classrooms and schools (Stainback & Stainback, 1990). It emphasizes inclusion educationally, physically, and socially, regardless of abilities or level of functioning. There is debate presently on whether full inclusion is appropriate for all students with autism. Some educators advocate inclusion under all circumstances; others feel that it is important to have options and alternatives and to select the proper placement based on individual needs (Martin, 1994; Rimland, 1994; Shanker, 1994). Shanker, president of the American Federation of Teachers, states, "The movement in American education that is taking hold the fastest and is likely to have the profoundest—and most destructive—effect is not what you might think. It's the rush towards full inclusion of disabled children in regular classrooms." For full inclusion to be effective, adaptations and supports, both educational and physical, should be provided (i.e., one-to-

one teacher aides, visual supports, adapted curriculum, and so on). In practice, these supports are sometimes not provided. Dr. Tom Hehir of the Office for Special Education Programs (OSEP) in Washington, DC, states, "I support the idea of options, I also support inclusion. . . . Parents do have a problem though in getting a good inclusive program" (as cited in Kownacki, 1995). Advocates see inclusion as providing each student with the opportunity to learn to live and work with his or her peers in natural, integrated, educational community settings. Vandercook, Fleetham, Sinclair, and Tetlie's study (as cited in Stainback & Stainback, 1990) noted: "In included classrooms all children are enriched by having the opportunity to learn from one another, grow to care for one another, and gain the attitudes, skills, and values necessary for our communities to support the inclusion of all citizens."

At the Groden Center, our approach has been to evaluate each person on an individual basis, to review the real options that are available (evaluate the classroom conditions, and the teacher, and the adaptations that could be made), and to suggest the most appropriate setting. Through our years of experience, we have found that persons with autism need flexible services. They may do very well in an included setting for a number of years, and may then need additional support or short-term intensive service. Once a student is in a regular education classroom, the Center provides an array of support based on the needs of the classroom and the individual. The following case study is an example.

Case Study

James was first evaluated while he was in a preschool. At that time, he showed the classic characteristics of autism. He did not interact with his peers, had stereotypic behavior, little language, and frequent tantrums. Weekly consultation by the Center, following a careful behavioral assessment, took the form of providing assistance in behavioral management, stress reduction, (the use of relaxation and imagery programs), and training in social interactions. As James moved into regular first grade, he was assigned a one-to-one teaching assistant who was trained by the Groden Center. Each year, a representative from the Center addressed the entire school personnel. Teachers, cafeteria aides, bus aides, resource personnel, and so on, came to the meeting, which provided them with information on autism and suggestions for coping strategies when James appeared to be distressed. James's teacher's aide reported, "All of the teachers, including the principal at the school, know James and are willing to take an extra minute or two when needed to explain something to him. There have been several times [when] Mr. Kling, the principal, has taken the time to calm James down before sending him home on the bus. One time James was upset because one of his friends did not wait for him. Mr. Kling pointed out to him that the friend did not say he would wait. It took James a few seconds to think about it and then he calmed down" (S. Bougery, personal communication, 1987). James's parents were included in the school training and received specific instruction in the use of relaxation and imagery-based techniques (Cautela & Groden, 1978; J. Groden, Cautela, LeVasseur, Groden, & Bausman, 1991). James did very well academically and was able to keep up with his peers. He also learned to write his own imagery scenes (Quill, 1995). The support of the consultant and the one-to-one teaching assistant were gradually faded. When James reached fifth grade, he no longer needed special education services and has continued to high school in all included classrooms.

In summary, the consultant on this case performed the following four functions:

1. Education in the area of autism to the family and school personnel (teachers, administrators, resource personnel, and auxiliary staff).
2. Family support and training.
3. "Translator" to the staff so that many of the behaviors that had been labeled as disruptive were explained in terms of communication deficits, stress and anxiety, or sensory problems related to autism. Given this understanding, staff made new attributions, and new approaches to problems were put into place.
4. Prescription of interventions and programs that focused on academic, communication, behavioral, and social needs.

This is one example of the flexible supports for inclusion that are already in place at the Groden Center. A wide array of options is provided to school systems and programs. Resource personnel such as speech and language clinicians, because of their knowledge of autism, often consult. At times, a Groden Center staff member works in the classroom at the public school. Vocational programs foster cooperation between the regular classroom and the vocational program, so that the student might attend the Groden Center's on-site vocational program for part of a week and then spend another part in his or her own homeroom.

An additional option is the inclusion of nondisabled students into the private agency. Presently, few if any schools for nondisabled students have experience with autism. However, private programs that have this expertise in autism can also serve nondisabled children. If private programs become fully integrated, services to all children can benefit from programs that are individualized, ecologically sound, and responsive to changing developmental and situational needs.

Multidisciplinary Field-Based Training

Both Donnellan (1980) and Olley (1980) cited inadequacies of then-current professional preparation programs. University programs concentrating in preparing teachers to work with the severely handicapped child have still not targeted those specialized needs of the child with autism. Without a theme or "gestalt," these programs consist of disjointed, functionally irrelevant "behavioral targets" (Donnellan, 1980). Many teachers certified in special education must then receive specialized training in autism. The private program, with its staff of specialists in autism, provides the resources to fill this training gap. The Groden Center model provides a pool of professionals to augment special education pretraining programs at local colleges and universities, as well as in-service programs at local school departments. It also offers opportunities for hands-on training at the Groden Center in the form of practica and internships.

An innovative model for specialized training in autism would entail academic and on-the-job training that would be offered at the private facility. This type of model has been gaining favor in the business community, in companies such as American Telephone and Telegraph (AT&T) and McDonald's (the "McDonald College").

An Ecological Approach to Flexible Support Systems

To provide personalized services that can meet the wide range of cognitive and behavioral problems present in individuals with autism, there needs to be a similarly wide range of services available. Some of these have been described above, among the community-based residential alternatives. There is, however, a concurrent need for alternative therapeutic and academic programs.

Therapy can be available for as little as an hour a week or in intensive, full-time programs. Socialization programs may be needed for those who can live independently but do not have the social or leisure skills to occupy their free time. In all cases, therapeutic interventions with an underlying ecological philosophy should be available to permit changes from intensive therapy to less intensive therapy and perhaps back again. To provide personalized services that meet the wide range of cognitive and behavioral problems present in individuals with autism, an equally wide range of services must be available. As one works in the field of autism, it becomes apparent that differing needs appear during the life cycle of an individual with autism. The agencies providing services must recognize these changing needs and have flexible services already in place.

Within a few years, during the life of a person with developmental disabilities, the best service to meet his or her full-life needs may vary from intensive 24-hour interventions to transition programs, to short-term foster placement with intense individual therapy and vocational instruction, to residential placement with social support and training sessions. Smooth and effective transitions from intensive to less intensive services, and sometimes back again, would certainly maximize the quality of services provided and would also diminish detrimental "downtime" while service decisions and placements are being made.

A community-based private service agency can more easily focus its energies on adapting its services to meet the ever-changing service needs of the person with autism. Private programs may be particularly effective in developing the following services: (a) in-home supports and parent training; (b) therapeutic foster care; (c) small, community-based residential alternatives, including apartment living; (d) expansion of service options before and after legally mandated services are provided (these options would increase services at both ends of the age spectrum—early intervention and over 21); and (e) individualized vocational placement.

In conclusion, private agencies have contributed significantly to services for children with autism and their families and will undoubtedly continue these contributions, as well as expand on them, in the future. Benefits to this population will be increased to the degree that public and private systems can work collaboratively in the development and implementation of services.

Cross-References

Issues in curriculum development, behavioral and vocational intervention, and residential programming are discussed in Chapters 22, 28, and 31, respectively.

REFERENCES

Baron, G., & Stevenson, S. (1983, May). *A human rights model with clinical and administrative process analysis.* Paper presented to the annual conference of the Association for Behavior Analysis, Milwaukee, WI.

Billingsley, F. (1993). Reader response in my dreams: A response to some current trends in education. *Journal of the Association for Persons with Severe Handicaps, 18,* 61–63.

Broskowski, A. (1984). Organizational controls and leadership. *Professional Psychology: Research and Practice, 15,* 645–663.

Carson, S.A. (1994, December). Rhode Island's CHOICES proposal awaits final approval. *New Directions, 27,* 1–3.

Cautela, J., & Groden, G. (1978). *Relaxation: A comprehensive manual for adults, children, and children with special needs.* Champaign, IL: Research Press.

Cohen, D.J., & Donnellan, A.M. (Eds.). (1987). *Handbook of autism and pervasive developmental disorders.* New York: John Wiley & Sons.

Donnellan, A. (1980). An educational perspective of autism: Implications for curriculum development and personnel development. In B. Wilcox & A. Thompson (Eds.), *Critical issues in educating autistic children and youth* (pp. 53–88). Washington, DC: National Society for Autistic Children

Eber, L. (1994, Fall). The wraparound approach toward effective school inclusion. *Claiming Children:The Nation's Mental Health Advocate for Children and Families, 1,* 4–9.

Graziano, A. (1974). *Child without tomorrow.* New York: Pergamon.

Groden, G. (1989). A guide for conducting a comprehensive behavioral analysis of a target behavior. *Journal of Behavior Therapy and Experimental Psychiatry, 20*(2), 163–169.

Groden, G., Dominigue, D., Chesnick, M., Groden, J., & Baron, M.G. (1983). Early intervention with autistic children: A case presentation with pre-program, program, and follow-up data. *Psychological Reports, 53,* 715–722.

Groden, G., Pueschel, S., Groden, J., Dondey, M., Zane, T., & Velicer, W. (1987). Effects of fenfluramine on the behavior of autistic individuals. *Research in Developmental Disabilities, 8,* 203–211.

Groden, G., Stevenson, S., & Groden, J. (1996). *Understanding challenging behavior: A step-by-step analysis guide.* Worthington, OH: IDS Publishing Company.

Groden, J., Baron, G., Pentecost, A., & Stevenson, S. (1988). A systems approach for educators and clinicians working with persons with autism: Putting it all together. In G. Groden & G. Baron (Eds.), *Autism strategies for change* (pp. 203–236). New York: Gardner Press.

Groden, J., Cautela, J.R., LeVasseur, P., Groden, G., & Bausman, M. (1991). *Video guide to Breaking the Barriers II.* Champaign, IL: Research Press.

Groden, J., Groden, G., Baron, M.G., & Stevenson, S. (1984). Day treatment services for children with severe behavior disorders. In W.T. Christian, G.T. Hannah, & T.J. Glahn (Eds.), *Programming effective human services* (pp. 337–355). New York: Plenum Press.

Groden, J., Snow, W., Pentecost, A., & Smith, M. (1984). *Project COVE: Cooperative on-site vocational education.* Providence, RI: BDC Press.

Harris, S.L. (1994). Treatment of family problems in autism. In E. Schopler & G.B. Mesibov (Eds.), *Behavioral issues in autism* (pp. 161–175). New York: Plenum Press.

Kownacki, S. (1995, January/February). An interview with Dr. Tom Hehir, director of the Office of Special Education Programs (OSEP) in Washington, DC. *Advocate, Newsletter of the Autism Society of America, Inc., 27,* 1, 3.

Lovaas, O.I., Koegel, R.L., Simmons, J.Q., & Long, J.S. (1973). Some generalizations and follow-up measures on autistic children in behavior therapy. *Journal of Applied Behavior Analysis, 6,* 1–36.

Malette, P., Mirenda, P., Kandborg, T., Jones, P., Bunz, T., & Rogow, S. (1992). Application of a lifestyle development process for persons with severe intellectual disabilities: A case study report. *Journal of the Association for Persons with Severe Handicaps, 17,* 179–191.

Martin, E. (1994, April). Inclusion: Rhetoric and reality. *Exceptional Parent, 24*(4), 39–42.

McEachin, J.J., Smith, T., & Lovaas, O.I. (1993). Long-term outcome for children with autism who received early intensive behavioral treatment. *American Journal on Mental Retardation, 97,* 359–372.

O'Brien, J., & Lyle, C. (1987). *Framework for accomplishment.* Decatur, GA: Responsive Systems Associates.

Olley, J.G. (1980). Organization of educational services for autistic children and youth. In B. Wilcox & A. Thompson (Eds.), *Critical issues in educating autistic children and youth* (pp. 53–88). Washington, DC: National Society for Autistic Children.

Pfieffer, S.I., & Nelson, D.D. (1992). The cutting edge in services for people with autism. *Journal of Autism and Developmental Disorders, 22,* 95–105.

Quill, K. (1995). Teaching children with autism: Methods to enhance learning, communication and socialization. Albany, NY: Delmar.

Rankin, D., Hallick, A., Ban, S., Hartley, P., Bost, C., & Uggla, N. (1994). Who's dreaming? A general education perspective on inclusion. *Journal of the Association for Persons with Severe Handicaps, 19,* 235–237.

Rimland, B. (1994). Inclusive education: Right for some. *Autism Research Review International, 7,* 3.

Rogers-Warren, A., & Warren, S. (1977). The developing ecobehavioral psychology. In A. Rogers-Warren & S. Warren (Eds.), *Eco logical perspectives in behavioral analysis* (pp. 3–9). Baltimore: University Park Press.

Shanker, A. (1994, February 6). Where we stand. *The New York Times,* p. 14.

Stainback, S., & Stainback, W. (1990). Inclusive schooling. In W. Stainback & S. Stainback

(Eds.), *Support networks for inclusive schooling* (pp. 3–23). New York: Brooks.

Stevenson, S., Groden, G., & Groden, J. (1992). Staff training: Meeting the needs of personnel, clients and service providers. *Association for Advancement of Behavior Therapy's Autism Special Interest Group Newsletter, 7*(2), 1–8.

Stevenson, S., & Ruby, B. (1994, July). *Specialized home care: A natural alternative to residential placement.* Paper presented at the national conference of the Autism Society of America, Las Vegas, NV.

Zigler, E. (1978, April 27). Statement of Dr. Edward Zigler, Yale University, before the Senate Committee on Governmental Affairs. *Hearings before the Committee on Governmental Affairs United States Senate,* 95th Congress, Second Session on S. 991, S. 225, S. 300, S. 894, and S. 1685.

CHAPTER 31

Residential Treatment for Individuals with Autism

MARY E. VAN BOURGONDIEN AND NANCY C. REICHLE

As children with autism grow up to be adults with autism, families are faced with the complex issue of how to best meet their offspring's need for an appropriate living environment.

This chapter describes the history and unique needs of individuals with autism in residential care. An overview of autism-specific treatment options is then provided, to highlight the variety of clinical issues and empirical findings that must be considered in residential treatment.

HISTORY OF RESIDENTIAL TREATMENT OF INDIVIDUALS WITH AUTISM

Residential care of individuals with developmental disabilities can be traced back to the early 1800s (Hilton, 1987). However, only in the past 30 to 40 years have distinctions been made between the diagnosis and treatment of autism versus other developmental disabilities (Schopler & Hennike, 1990). The treatment of children with autism started with Kanner's (1943) description of the unique features of this group of individuals. Unfortunately, at that time, autism was viewed as an emotional disorder caused by cold and unresponsive parenting. As a result, early treatment approaches emphasized removing these children from their parents, considered the source of the problem, and placing them permanently in residential treatment (Bettelheim, 1967).

Rimland (1964) and Schopler (1971) were among the first to recognize that the psychoanalytic approach to working with individuals with autism was not effective and was based on a misunderstanding of the nature of autism.

Autism was redefined as a biologically based disorder, and parents were not only *not* the cause of the disorder, but were instrumental in the treatment of these children (Schopler & Reichler, 1971).

With the demonstration that structured teaching was an effective approach to education of autistic children (Schopler, Brehm, Kinsbourne, & Reichler, 1971) came the first public school education for this population in North Carolina in 1971 (Reichler & Schopler, 1976). Several years later, the passage of Public Law 94-142 gave children with handicaps across the United States the right to an appropriate public school education. The recognition that families were an important part of the treatment process, along with access to the public schools, meant that more children were beginning to be served in the community. For young children, this meant living at home with their families and attending public schools. These events coincided with the popularization of the mainstreaming and deinstitutionalization movements (Wolfensberger, 1972).

Although the rate of institutionalization decreased with the availability of public school options and supports for families, appropriate community-based residential options for adults with autism have been slow to develop. Lotter (1978), in a review of outcome studies of people with autism, indicated that 50% to 75% were placed in large institutions and very few were receiving appropriate residential and vocational services. A survey done at the request of the North Carolina Mental Health Study Commission, in the early 1980s, estimated that there were over 4,000 adults with autism in the state. Of the 393 persons located, less than 15% were in group homes, and, at best, between 30% and 50% were in day treatment programs. Although less than 10% were in institutions and most were at home with their families, the concern of the Mental Health Study Commission centered around the lack of appropriate community-based alternatives.

UNIQUE DIFFICULTIES OF ADULTS WITH AUTISM IN RESIDENTIAL CARE

One of the factors that has impeded the adaptation of adults with autism into community settings is that most available residential and vocational training programs have been designed to serve clients with mental retardation without autism. As a result, these programs have typically either not accepted residents with autism or accepted them but had difficulty maintaining them in a program not specifically designed for their needs. In many instances, the adults with autism who have been placed and appropriately served in programs for adults with mental retardation have been individuals who have relatively high intelligence and few behavior problems (Van Bourgondien & Elgar, 1990). Teachers and house managers who have successfully worked with clients with autism in community-based programs report that even individuals with relatively more developed skills require significantly more time and effort than individuals with mental retardation without autism (Mesibov & Shea, 1980).

To date, a limited amount of research has systematically examined the factors that contribute to the person with autism's difficulty in adapting to community-based services. The literature that does exist is primarily based on case studies or clinical observations (Everard, 1976; Kanner, Rodriquez, & Ashenden, 1972; Mesibov & Shea, 1980; Van Bourgondien & Elgar, 1990). The literature suggests that, in settings that are not specifically designed for this population, the caregivers have a difficult time managing the resident's tendency to talk too much and to exhibit ritualistic behaviors, anxiety, and agitation. These behaviors were reported to create major problems in the group-home settings (Mesibov & Shea).

Additional problems noted for the residents with autism involved their difficulties in processing the language of others, often leading to their moving at a slower pace than those around them. Their overattention to details, inappropriate social behaviors, poor money management, and self-stimulating behaviors have also contributed to their adjustment problems (Everard, 1976; Kanner, Rodriquez, & Ashenden, 1972; Mesibov & Shea, 1980). These results were based on clinical impressions rather than a direct comparative study of the clients with autism versus those without autism in the same homes.

Van Bourgondien, Mesibov, and Castelloe (1989) conducted a study to determine the types of behavior problems individuals with autism exhibit in group homes, compared to residents with mental retardation without autism. The behavior problems of residents with autism, described as either typical or challenging by their caregivers, were compared to typical or challenging behaviors of residents with mental retardation without autism. A second objective of the study was to determine the manner and degree to which group-home environments differed, depending on the clients they served. Group homes that served exclusively clients with autism were compared to programs that served exclusively clients with mental retardation without autism and to programs that served both residents with autism and residents with mental retardation without autism.

The results demonstrated that, in residential settings, individuals with autism exhibited problem behaviors that were significantly different from those of individuals with mental retardation without autism. The most frequent and most problematic behaviors exhibited by individuals with autism were rituals and other behaviors emphasizing sameness, and a tendency to get easily upset and agitated. These behaviors were significantly more frequent in individuals with autism versus individuals with mental retardation without autism. In addition, isolating behavior was found to be significantly more problematic for subjects with autism compared to those without autism.

It is interesting to note that there were no differences, based on diagnosis, on items well known to affect adaptation, such as aggression, inappropriate sexual behaviors, and uncooperative behaviors. There were significant interactions for these behaviors. Typical individuals with mental retardation exhibited significantly fewer behavior problems than challenging individuals with mental retardation and typical or challenging individuals with autism.

The comparison among the treatment programs (autism, mental retardation, mixed homes) also showed important differences. Programs designed for individuals with autism had a tendency to use more augmentative communications systems (e.g., pictures), adapt their language, and use more gestures than did programs that were designed for persons with mental retardation, even if they served some clients with autism. Compared to programs for either of the other two groups, those designed for individuals with autism used significantly more visual structure in the form of individualized client schedules and visual directions.

Behavior management approaches also varied according to the type of home. Compared to programs that served only clients with mental retardation, autism-specific programs used significantly more preventive approaches to controlling behaviors; for example, the behavior programs utilized proactive, nonintrusive techniques that emphasized providing structure for the individual *before* a behavior problem occurred. The behavior programs in the homes for persons with mental retardation were more reactive than preventive, with emphasis on the use of consequences.

In summary, Van Bourgondien et al. (1989) found that, in residential settings, individuals with autism exhibited problem behaviors that were significantly different from those of individuals with mental retardation without autism. The finding of a greater difference between typical and challenging individuals with mental retardation than between typical and challenging individuals with autism fits with the perceptions of direct care workers who find that even the most typical individuals with autism present challenges for their caregivers. The fact that programs designed for individuals with other types of developmental disabilities utilized different behavioral and instructional strategies helps to explain why individuals with autism have had difficulty in these settings.

AUTISM-SPECIFIC RESIDENTIAL TREATMENT PROGRAMS

In recognition of the different needs of individuals with autism, residential programs specifically designed for individuals with autism have been developed throughout the world. The initiative for most of these programs came from parents and teachers who were concerned about the future of their children and students as they prepared to leave school.

Benhaven was one of the earliest residential programs specifically designed for individuals with autism (Lettick, 1983; Rumanoff-Simonson, Simonson, & Volkmar, 1990). Amy Lettick, a teacher and the mother of a son with autism, started Benhaven as a school in 1967 in Connecticut. A residential component was added in 1972. As of 1990, the residential program had expanded to include 36 residents living in 6 different group homes located in both rural and urban settings (Rumanoff-Simonson et al.). Gradually, during the late 1970s and 1980s, a number of other autism-specific community-based residential programs were developed across the United States—the Jay Nolen Center, California (LaVigna, 1983), the Eden Family of Programs, New Jersey (Holmes, 1990), and, in Maryland, the Community Services for Autistic Adults and Children (CSAAC, 1995; Juhrs, 1988), to name a few. In an effort to promote maximum integration into the community, most of these programs have group homes located in urban or suburban settings with no more than 6 clients in each home (LaVigna, 1983; Wall, 1990). Some prefer smaller groupings of either 4 residents per home, or garden apartments and town homes with 2 or 3 residents in each unit (CSAAC, 1995).

These community-based programs usually share common goals, including creating a homelike atmosphere (Sloan & Schopler, 1977), optimizing development in each individual through maximizing independence and competence in a variety of areas (Lettick, 1983), and facilitating the process of becoming an independent, productive, and valued member of the community (LaVigna, 1983). In many instances, the residents are seen as active "participants" in the program (Holmes, 1990), sharing in all the activities necessary to maintain a home (Wall, 1990). The treatment programs emphasize the use of special education, developmental, and behavioral techniques, including careful assessment and positive behavioral techniques (Holmes, 1990; LaVigna, 1983; Lettick, 1983).

In recognition of the fact that individuals with autism are a very diverse group with a variety of needs, other types of community-based residential programs have been developed. In contrast to the previously mentioned group homes and apartment programs, which are located primarily in urban settings, a number of programs designed specifically for individuals with autism have chosen more rural farmstead models. Bittersweet Farms in Ohio (Kay, 1990), the Carolina Living and Learning Center in North Carolina (Van Bourgondien & Reichle, 1996), and Ny Allergard in Denmark (Giddan & Giddan, 1993) are examples of the farmstead approach to autism.

Bittersweet Farms opened in 1982 and was based on the model of Somerset Court in England and the classroom experience of Bettye Ruth Kay, the founder (Kay, 1990). The goal of Bittersweet Farms is to meet the needs of adults with autism for growth in every area of life by using the rural, extended-family community as the model. The daily farming activities on this 80-acre farm are seen as an integral part of the overall program of care and training and not as a vocational program that can be described separately.

The Carolina Living and Learning Center (CLLC; Van Bourgondien & Reichle, 1996; Van Bourgondien & Woods, 1992) is an integrated residential and vocational training program for adults with autism. As part of Division TEACCH (Treatment and Education of Autistic and Related Communications Handicapped CHildren) of the University of North Carolina at Chapel Hill, the CLLC is also actively involved in professional training and research.

In Europe, a variety of the residential programs designed to serve individuals with autism emphasize farming as a major component (Giddan & Giddan, 1993). Ny Allergard in Denmark is an example of one of these programs. Founded in 1983 by Mogens Anderson and a group of parents, Ny Allergard emphasizes the importance of setting realistic and humane expectations for development and of having effective communication and collaboration between staff members and parents. The program was built in the belief that respect for personal needs, values, and goals is essential (Giddan & Giddan).

All of the farm communities are located in settings where farming is one of the predominant activities of nonhandicapped individuals. The programs emphasize the same goals as the more urban settings—maximizing the quality of life, improving the skills and independent functioning of the residents, and helping them to be integrated members of their local communities (Kay, 1990; Van Bourgondien & Reichle, 1996). These rural programs tend to be slightly larger in size than the typical group-home settings. Bittersweet Farms currently serves 15 individuals with moderate to low abilities in a main house, and 5 relatively more able individuals in a cooperative home (Kay). The CLLC serves 5 individuals in one home and is currently building a second home for 10 individuals. Ny Allergard serves 15 residents, divided into groups of 5, in 3 separate living areas.

The larger groups are seen as beneficial because they provide increased opportunities for social contacts among individuals who have a tendency to isolate themselves socially. Also, the groups are large enough to allow for natural subgroups of 2 to 4 people for social and work participation around common interests and skills. The greater number of residents also allows for a larger number of staff members who can provide the program with a variety of background skills. In addition, the larger nucleus makes it possible to provide more flexible supervision (Kay, 1990).

Despite their rural location, the farm programs compare favorably to group homes in their emphasis on integrating their residents into the larger community through their work, recreational, and household activities. Mobile landscaping crews and small business ventures (e.g., an engine repair business, or farm stands at local markets) bring the residents into frequent contact with the community. The residents in these farm programs also utilize the same community resources—stores, churches, parks, and recreational activities—as their nonhandicapped neighbors.

OPTIONS FOR INDIVIDUALS WITH SEVERE BEHAVIOR PROBLEMS

Limited research or literature is available describing treatment options for individuals with autism with the most severe behavior problems. Many of these individuals eventually are served in institutional settings, typically institutions designed for individuals with mental retardation. There continues to be a need for settings that have a physical structure that cannot be easily destroyed by the breaking, throwing, slamming, biting, kicking, and other persistent destructive behaviors of some individuals with autism. Schopler and Hennike (1990) point out the need for institutional settings as a resource for consultation to the community setting in times of crisis, and, at times, as a respite service while the community-based program reassesses and restructures its approach.

Based on clinical experience, some of the most severe behavior problems may be exhibited by adults with autism who do not have mental retardation. Until the definition of developmental disabilities was expanded to include autism in the Developmental Disability Act of 1977, these individuals often were denied access to services for individuals with mental retardation, and were inappropriately placed in services for individuals with mental illness—or denied services entirely.

Programs have been developed that serve these very challenging individuals with autism together with individuals who have other developmental disabilities with extreme behavior disorders. An example of a private model is the Au Clair Palms program (Au Clair, 1994), which is part of a network of private facilities along Florida's east coast. Individuals with extreme behavior disorders are placed in the program on a contract basis, often with the local community or state agency.

In North Carolina, a new residential program for individuals with severe behavior problems, including persons with autism, is being developed by the Department of Human Resources Mental Retardation/Developmental Disabilities (MR/DD) Division, on the grounds of one of the state institutions for individuals with developmental disabilities. This Behaviorally Advanced Residential Treatment (BART) program will serve a number of average-intelligence individuals with autism who exhibit extreme behavior difficulties. In both the Au Clair and BART programs, the treatment facility has been specially designed and built to serve this highly destructive population. The staffing patterns and availability of specialized consultants are much higher than in typical community settings.

ISSUES IN RESIDENTIAL TREATMENT

The programs mentioned thus far represent a sampling of the autism-specific residential options that have been developed over the past 20 years. In reviewing these programs, a number of areas of similarity as well as a number of areas of variability warrant closer attention.

Client Selection

In selecting clients for community-based residential facilities for persons with autism, most programs recommend seeking a balance of skill levels in the home (LaVigna, 1983; Van Bourgondien & Schopler, 1990; Wall, 1990). According to Wall, the effectiveness of instructional and management efforts is maximized when the client group is composed of persons with varying degrees of supervisory and instructional needs. Important areas to consider in achieving a balance are the prospective residents' skills in the areas of self-help and communication, and the level of behavioral difficulties (LaVigna).

Selecting a balanced group of residents for a home helps ensure that each resident will be able to experience the individualized programming that is essential for persons with autism (Van Bourgondien & Schopler, 1990). In addition, the staff members of group homes, who often work for long periods without breaks, may be less likely to experience burnout when the group of residents is varied in skill level and behavioral needs (Wall, 1990).

Determinants of Out-of-Home Placement

In recent years, the proponents of normalization have advocated maintaining individuals with developmental disabilities in the least restrictive environment (Sherman, 1988). Therefore, even through adulthood, more families are continuing to care for their members with developmental disabilities at home. For some families of adults with autism, however, the selection of a residential placement outside of the home is perceived as a natural developmental progression. Others seek out-of-home placement for children or adults as the result of many factors, including child/adult characteristics, family characteristics, and support resources (Bromley & Blacher, 1991).

In comparing families who had placed their adult child in residential programs with those who had not, Sherman (1988) reported that the more severely disabled, the more behaviorally disruptive, and the older adult children were significantly more likely to be placed outside of the home. An examination of specific disorders revealed that autism was three times more prevalent in the out-of-home group than in those living at home. Families whose adult offspring continue to live at home reported having significantly more informal sources of assistance with caregiving, and receiving more formal client services as well (Sherman).

Heller and Factor (1993) determined that support resources play a significant role in reducing the perceived caregiving burden of older parents of an adult child with mental retardation living at home and therefore contribute to the out-of-home placement preferences. Specifically, a higher number of unmet needs was associated with higher burden and greater preference for out-of-home placement. Maladaptive behaviors were also a strong determinant of increased caregiving burden over time.

Investigating the urgency of out-of-home placement needs for families with children and adults with developmental disabilities, Kobe, Rojahn, and Schroeder (1991) documented caregiver stress as the main predictor. Other significant correlates with urgency of placement need were child behavior problems and lack of support services. Bromley and Blacher (1991) found similar results with a sample of children with severe handicaps who were recently placed outside of the home. Parental interviews revealed that parents' daily stress, the children's low level of functioning, and the children's behavior problems were the strongest influences on the placement decision.

The results of these studies suggest that, consistent with Sherman's finding (1988), persons with autism may be more likely to be placed in residential settings than other persons with disabilities. Persons with autism are more likely to exhibit maladaptive behaviors, possibly creating an excessive caretaker burden for parents and other family members. In addition, appropriate support services for persons with autism are often lacking in the community. The combination of problem behaviors and unmet service needs is likely to result in more frequent placement of persons with autism outside of the family home.

Transitions

Moving from one residential program to another, or from the family home to a residential program, may cause high stress and disruption for the resident and for his or her family. For persons with developmental disabilities, the most common reactions may be in the emotional and behavioral areas and may typically last for several months (Heller, 1988).

For persons with autism, however, a residential program transition may be even more difficult. Their communication deficits may make it hard for them to understand the move and the reasons for moving. In addition, the characteristics of autism—being bound to routines and resistant to change—may contribute to the disruption of a move to a new program. The nature and duration of the transition reaction, therefore, may be different for persons with autism.

Some persons with autism have been described as having an initial "honeymoon" period immediately following the move, a time when they show initial positive adaptation (Van Bourgondien & Reichle, 1993). However, once the new resident begins to have expectations in the new setting, behavioral issues may occur. As much as is possible, appropriate programming expectations for the residents should be in place from the time of admission so that residents do not have to go through more than one period of adaptation.

Other persons with autism may have an immediate negative reaction to a move, which may last for a significant length of time. Anecdotal reports from caregivers suggest that it may take up to 18 months for residents to begin to show positive developments in the new setting (Van Bourgondien & Reichle, 1993). Programs may need additional staffing during periods of transition to help ensure success in the new setting.

Heller (1988) suggests some ways to help facilitate the residential transition for persons with developmental disabilities. Preparatory strategies that may be useful include counseling, site visits, and staff visits prior to the move. Such strategies, however, require that a move be anticipated in advance. For persons with autism who are living at home with their families, it may be advisable to explore residential options prior to a family crisis that may necessitate immediate placement.

Other suggestions for helping with transitions for persons with developmental disabilities (Heller, 1988) include maintaining continuity in vocational or day programs when possible, and giving the residents choices when available, for example, regarding attributes of their bedroom and participation in social activities. These suggestions may be beneficial as well for persons with autism. Using calendars and other visual cues to communicate when home visits and other family contact will occur may also reduce the anxiety of the person with autism and facilitate the transition. In addition, making any necessary environmental adaptations as soon as possible may help ease adjustment to the new setting.

Another important consideration in residential transitions is the difficulties persons with autism may have in generalizing previously learned skills to a new environment (LaVigna, 1983; Van Bourgondien & Reichle, 1993). In addition to knowing the skills and abilities of the incoming residents, staff members at the new setting will need to know how the resident learned the skills, and the prompts and reinforcements that maintain the skills, so they can promote the generalization of the skills to the new setting.

Curriculum

Programs designed specifically for individuals with autism emphasize the importance of understanding autism and of providing an individualized program based on a careful assessment of the adults' skills, needs, and interests (Holmes, 1990; LaVigna, 1983; Lettick, 1983; Wall, 1990). The curriculum areas addressed in different autism-specific programs have extensive overlap with most programs providing training in self-care and domestic skills, communication skills, leisure, recreation, and social skills. Although labeled differently, most autism-specific residential facilities promote the development of skills and behaviors that will enhance the individual's involvement and acceptance in the larger community.

Variations in curriculum are often difficult to perceive from written descriptions in the literature and may be better understood as a difference in emphasis at any given moment in time. For example, sex education appears to have more emphasis in some programs (Lettick, 1983), but this may merely be a reflection of differential needs of the residents served at a particular point in time. Development of expressive communication skills seems to be a focus in established programs with residents who are well known to the staff. Receptive communication, helping the clients understand the staff members, is typically emphasized early in most settings. Some areas of curriculum emphasis, however, do differ by program. The farm programs, such as Bittersweet Farms (Kay, 1990) and the Carolina Living and Learning Center (Van Bourgondien & Reichle, 1996), emphasize the importance of physical exercise. Strenuous physical activities play a major role in not only their vocational curricula, but also in their recreational activities, which include weekly hikes, swimming, and other sports (Kay, 1990; Van Bourgondien & Reichle, 1996). There is evidence to suggest that the residents are not only healthier, but have fewer behavior problems and fewer rituals when they engage in physical exercise (Kay, 1990; McGimsey & Favell, 1988).

Independence training is an area of the curriculum that requires greater clarification. Most programs have independence as a stated goal (Holmes, 1990; LaVigna, 1983; Lettick, 1983; Van Bourgondien & Reichle, 1996), but there is little information on how independence is developed. For some programs, independence may be defined as the acquisition of specific skills that allow the individual to care for his or her own needs, such as dressing, toileting, or feeding oneself. Many individuals with autism may learn these specific self-care, domestic, or communication skills, but because of their difficulties with initiation, sequencing, and organization, they do not utilize their skills independently. Often, these residents become dependent on their caregivers to prompt them to begin activities, to move to the next step, or to stop an activity. An individual is not truly independent if someone else needs to be present to say when to start, what to do next, and when to finish an activity.

The Structured Teaching techniques developed by Division TEACCH (Mesibov, Schopler, & Hearsey, 1994) were specifically designed to help the individual with autism learn to use his or her skills independently. Instead of relying on another person, the individual is taught to use individualized visual cues in order to know where to go, what to do and in what sequence, when activities are finished, and how to complete each activity. The visual schedules, visual lists, and visual instructions are seen as prosthetic devices, much like glasses, that help the person with autism "see" and understand the world independently. Both the CLLC (Van Bourgondien & Reichle, 1996) and Ny Allergard (Giddan & Giddan, 1993) have adapted these structured teaching techniques to increase the independence and to meet the needs of the adults in their residential and vocational settings.

Another area requiring greater clarification relates to teaching strategies utilized to help residents learn to handle changes. Routines have been shown to help some individuals with autism learn specific skills (e.g., toothbrushing, showering), but they may often be misused as a way of helping the individual have appropriate expectations for the day's events. Residential programs that rely on routines as the primary way an individual knows what will happen on a given night (e.g., Tuesday is swimming night) inevitably run into problems when the routine needs to be changed (e.g., the pool is closed, a staff member is ill), or when an individual has memory skills that are inconsistent. A more helpful approach is to make the world more predictable through the use of visual schedules (featuring written messages, pictures, or objects; Mesibov et al, 1994; Van Bourgondien & Reichle, 1996). Through the use of visual systems, the daily activities can and should change from day to day. The resident learns to anticipate and predict the activities through the visual cues rather than relying on their memory. By emphasizing predictability over routines, the individual can become more flexible and is often better able to handle changes.

Vocational Programs

Perhaps the greatest variability in residential care is in the approach and curricula of the vocational programs. Many autism-specific programs also administer their own day programs (Holmes, 1990; Kay, 1990). This overlap in administration between residential and vocational programs is not necessarily typical of most community-based programs, many of which are administered, located, and staffed by totally different agencies. The advantage of having the same administration for both the residential and vocational programs is the greater likelihood of consistency throughout the day (Van Bourgondien & Schopler, 1990). A 24-hour consistency is likely to be an asset for individuals with autism, who have difficulty generalizing skills across settings and people. The hope is that a single administrative unit allows for a coherent philosophy and treatment program across settings.

Despite this similarity in administrative structure, there is an increasing variability in the vocational treatment options available to adults with autism. Some of these options involve individual, paired, or small-group employment in community settings (Juhrs, 1988); others emphasize a more supervised setting. The farm programs such as Ny Allergard, Bittersweet Farms, and the CLLC have been created as additional options on the continuum of services. These programs emphasize a vocational curriculum—farming and landscaping—that is consistent with the typical occupations of nonhandicapped individuals in their respective communities. Also, by including mobile landscaping crews, the CLLC and Bittersweet Farms demonstrate that a farm model can be consistent with a supported employment approach.

Just as a continuum of residential options is needed to meet the needs of a heterogeneous group of individuals with autism, a similar continuum of vocational alternatives is essential as well. (For a more detailed look at vocational issues, see Chapter 28.)

In exploring residential and vocational options for adults with autism, the problems with generalizing skills across settings and the importance of contextual cues in learning indicate that there may not be a direct relationship between an individual's residential and vocational needs (Van Bourgondien & Schopler, 1990). The degree and type of supervision or support needed in one environment cannot necessarily be predicted from performance in the other setting. Someone who needs close supervision in a residential setting may do very well in supported employment if an appropriate job is found. Conversely, someone who requires minimal supervision in the home may require more support and supervision in a job site. It is important to assess the individual's vocational needs independently of his or her residential needs.

Family Involvement

Family involvement in residential settings has been a neglected topic of study where persons with developmental disabilities are concerned. Baker and Blacher (1988) suggest that residential placement should not mean a severing of family ties; they recommend additional research on family roles throughout the life cycle.

The involvement of families in residential programs may vary, depending on the age of the child or adult. In studying family involvement with children in residential settings, Baker and Blacher (1993) reported increased involvement over earlier studies. They hypothesized that families who are accustomed to involvement in their child's school setting may

also be more involved when their child is placed in a residential setting.

Several studies of families of adults, however, have documented that many adults with developmental disabilities who are living in community settings have limited contact with their families (Hill, Rotegard, & Bruininks, 1984; Stoneman & Crapps, 1990). In their study of adults with developmental disabilities living in family care homes, Stoneman and Crapps discovered that nearly half of the residents were never visited by family members and did not go home to visit relatives. In addition, residents who did have contact with their families experienced a decrease in the contact across the life span.

The involvement of family members with persons with autism in residential settings, however, may be affected by their role in the development of residential services for their children. Many group homes and residential programs designed specifically for persons with autism have been started with parental initiatives and have created parental advisory boards to operate many of the nonprofit programs (Kay, 1990; Rumanoff-Simonson et al., 1990; Wall, 1990). Negotiating the roles of families who have been involved in the creation and administration of the program and are working together with staff members requires open communication and an understanding of the perspectives of both groups.

Some authors have suggested that increasing family involvement should be a priority for residential programs (Hill et al., 1984). Recommendations for increasing family involvement include providing reasons and opportunities for family visits, using family visits to promote positive staff–family interactions, and involving families in decision making whenever possible (Hill et al. 1984). Considering the involvement of siblings and other family members is important as well. Stoneman and Crapps (1990) found that involvement was higher when families participated in the placement process and when providers actively encouraged family involvement.

However, the individualization of family involvement merits consideration as well (Hill et al., 1984). Family involvement should be individualized according to the placement setting, the needs of the resident, and the needs of the other family members. Varying levels of family involvement should be accepted without staff members making families feel guilty (Hill et al.). Parents of adult children without disabilities often have little involvement with their adult children. Parents of adult children with disabilities should have a similar right to less involvement (Van Bourgondien & Schopler, 1990).

Van Bourgondien and Schopler (1990) promote the individualization of family involvement in residential settings designed specifically for persons with autism. Some families may feel guilty about placing their son or daughter in a residential setting and may be either very involved or more detached as a result of their feelings. Continuing family involvement may take different forms; the family may be a social outlet for their offspring rather than a continuing caretaker, or the family may be actively involved in the treatment program through frequent contact or through yearly attendance at the goal-planning meetings.

Assessing preferences regarding the type and amount of family involvement desired is critical in working with families in residential settings. In addition, continuing to reassess families' involvement is valuable because families' ability and desire for involvement may change over time (Reichle & Campbell, 1993).

Location and Size

The deinstitutionalization movement provided an opportunity for researchers to prospectively study the effects of smaller, community-based residential services for persons with developmental disabilities (Landesman, 1988). In addition, many cross-sectional studies comparing outcomes for residents living in large, congregate facilities (typically, 90 or more residents) versus smaller, community-based facilities (typically, 15 or fewer residents) have been conducted (e.g., Barber & Hupp, 1993; Lakin, Hill, & Bruininks, 1986).

Results of these comparison studies have generally favored the smaller settings, which have been associated with improvements in adaptive skills, especially in the areas of self-care, social behavior, and communication (Lakin et al., 1986); increases in the number of close friends of the residents (Barber & Hupp, 1993); and enhancements of individual

dignity and increased community involvement of the residents (Bowd, 1989).

Within the community-based programs designed for adults with autism, there is diversity in the number of residents in each home and in the location of the homes. The numbers range from apartments with 1 to 3 residents (CSAAC, 1995) to group homes with 4 to 6 residents in one home (Holmes, 1990; LaVigna, 1983). Some of the rural settings have 10 to 15 residents (Kay, 1990; Van Bourgondien & Reichle, 1996). Some homes are in urban or suburban settings; others, reflecting the trend in their states, have a rural location.

Limited research is available regarding the effects of size at this level, for individuals with autism. Within the developmental disability literature, a review by Landesman-Dwyer, Sackett, and Kleinman (1980) reported that among programs with fewer than 20 clients, the relatively bigger programs had some advantages. Residents in the larger homes demonstrated more appropriate social interactions with others than did the clients in the smaller programs. In addition, larger staff-to-client ratios (that is, more staff members available to fewer residents) did not lead to more staff contact with the residents.

Comparisons between the treatment effectiveness of urban and rural settings for persons with autism have not been conducted to date. For the general population of individuals with developmental disabilities, there is no evidence that rural settings are more segregated or limit the opportunities for community involvement (Landesman-Dwyer, Stein & Sackett, 1978). In fact, parents of residents of the rural Carolina Living and Learning Center were significantly more satisfied with their children's community involvement than were parents of individuals living in institutions or group homes that were in more residential areas (Van Bourgondien, Reichle, Schopler, & Mesibov, 1996). Based on the descriptions of the programs mentioned previously, it appears that both types of settings emphasize similar skill development and provide equivalent opportunities to interact with neighbors and other members of the local communities. Rather than deciding whether one option is better for everyone with autism, a more effective strategy would be to continue to develop an array of options and match the individual to the setting, based on the individual's and his or her family's needs and preferences.

In approaching residential services for persons with autism, the conclusion of Landesman and Butterfield (1987) seems appropriate:

The size and location of a residence are not what matter most; what does matter is the actual care and treatment an individual receives. Rather then prematurely narrowing our treatment approaches, we should encourage the development of diverse and innovative residential programs. (p. 815)

Staff Recruitment and Training

Recruiting, selecting, training, managing, and retaining direct care staff members have been described as frequent problems of residential programs for persons with developmental disabilities (Lakin, 1988). The importance of addressing this problem is emphasized by the heavy influence of the direct care staff performance on the quality of living and habilitation of the residents (Arco & Birnbrauer, 1990).

Recruiting staff members for direct care positions in residential settings for persons with developmental disabilities can be a difficult task for program administrators (Wall, 1990). The typical low salaries and limited benefits and the atypical work hours (often early mornings, evenings, and weekends) may limit the pool of quality applicants. According to Wall, direct care staff working in group homes for persons with autism should have the following characteristics: a positive attitude, commitment and dependability, high levels of energy, flexibility, an ability to take initiative and function independently as well as an ability to recognize when help is needed, a strong sense of ethics and compassion, and good organizational skills.

High turnover of direct care staff is a significant problem in residential programs serving persons with developmental disabilities (e.g., Larson & Lakin, 1992; Mitchell & Braddock, 1992, 1993, 1994; Razza, 1993). Among the many negative effects that may occur as a result of high staff turnover are: discontinuity in treatment and care, staff shortages, administrative intensity in personnel replacement, and the financial burden of staff replacement (Lakin, 1988). Turnover of direct care staff may be even more problematic for persons with autism, for whom coping with change is

often very challenging. Skills that residents with autism have mastered may not readily generalize to new staff members. The communication limitations of persons with autism may make forming relationships with staff more challenging and time-consuming. When staff members leave the program, this challenging and time-consuming process must begin again.

These serious consequences have motivated investigators to study the potential causes of high staff turnover, in the hope of beginning to solve the problem (e.g., Hatton & Emerson, 1993; Jacobson & Ackerman, 1992; Razza, 1993). One potential cause of high staff turnover is staff burnout, described by Maslach (1982) as a syndrome of emotional exhaustion that can occur when a person works extensively with distressed individuals. In a survey of staff in community residential facilities, Edwards and Miltenberger (1991) found a moderate degree of burnout among direct care providers. These authors documented the need for effective programs to prevent or combat burnout on the job. Proactive programs for preventing burnout may be especially important for staff members working in programs designed specifically for persons with autism because of the potential frequency and intensity of behavioral outbursts in the population.

Many residential programs designed specifically for persons with autism have developed strategies for maintaining staff and preventing burnout. Bittersweet Farms (Kay, 1990) and Benhaven (Rumanoff-Simonson et al., 1990) have large, diverse staff groups, an approach that provides opportunities for advancement within the program and allows staff members to work with a variety of clients, reducing the potential for staff burnout. Maintaining staff continuity is facilitated at the CLLC (Van Bourgondien & Reichle, 1996) by beginning with student volunteers and part-time staff members who often are promoted into full-time permanent staff positions when they graduate. Holmes (1990) found that live-in staff members appear more committed to the program and give the neighbors a greater sense of security and comfort than do rotating shifts.

The provision of both pre- and in-service staff training programs is crucial for staff working in residential programs. According to

Levy, Levy, Freeman, Feiman, and Samowitz (1988), preservice training programs should include the agency's philosophy, principles, and rules. For staff members working in programs for persons with autism, it is important to provide preservice and ongoing training about the characteristics of autism and the treatment strategies that relate to those characteristics (Van Bourgondien & Schopler, 1990). Van Bourgondien et al. (1989) found that staff members' knowledge about autism as a developmental disorder was related to greater use of developmental assessment and planning, more preventive than reactive management techniques, and greater family involvement in treatment.

According to Wall (1990), training should include the characteristics and etiology of autism and its remediation, with an emphasis on social and communication deficits; instructional and behavioral techniques centered on the use of visual structure; preparation for the potential slow rate of behavioral and skill changes; and techniques for staff communication and collaboration. Adequate training is crucial in maintaining the longevity of competent staff.

In addition to an adequate training program, administrative support of direct care staff members is important throughout the tenure of the program (Holmes, 1990; Wall, 1990). Group-home administrators should provide feedback to staff members on a regular basis, indicating areas of good performance and making suggestions for improving areas of difficulty. Programs that promote staff morale, such as employee award programs, also may be useful (Hatton & Emerson, 1993). Involving direct care staff in decision making is another effective method for improving staff morale and program success. Wall stated that the most successful group homes are those whose management staff make an effort to involve direct care staff in decision making and information exchange.

Financing

Funding for most community-based residential programs generally comes from a combination of state and federal sources (Wall, 1990). Medicaid has been a source of funding for a variety of programs (Yohalem, 1987). In some states, Medicaid funds have been available on a program level through the Intermediate Care Facilities for the Mentally Retarded and Developmentally Disabled (ICF/MR, ICF/DD) program (Grants to the States for Medical Assistance Programs, 42 U.S.C. § 1396d [d]). Each state has approached the development of ICF-MR group homes differently, so this is not an option in all states (Yohalem, 1987).

Another source of Medicaid funding that is increasing is the Medicaid Community Services Waiver. Known by different names in different states, the waiver money can be used to provide services to an individual in order to avoid institutional care (Yohalem, 1987). The waiver money can be used to provide a variety of supports and services but cannot be used to pay for room and board.

State monies are often used to support group homes that serve individuals with less severe disabilities, who need less intensive treatment (Wall, 1990). Often, state mental health dollars are combined with Supplemental Security Income (SSI), a federal resource, to cover the cost of apartments or group homes with more limited numbers of staff members than ICF-MR staffing patterns (Social Security Act, 1974). SSI is often used to fund room and board costs for individuals whose treatment services are covered by the waiver program.

Most group homes rely on state and federal money for the bulk of their operational funding. Many programs also engage in some type of fund-raising activities to supplement these services.

PROGRAM EVALUATION RESEARCH

There is a limited research base that documents the effectiveness of residential treatment models for individuals with autism. The relative effectiveness of residential versus home-based and outpatient treatment conditions was explored for young children with autism (Sherman, Barker, Lorimer, Swinson, & Factor, 1988). Behavioral observation and psychological assessment indicated that all three types of treatment were nearly equally effective, and that both nonresidential groups achieved slightly better results. The authors recommended outpatient treatment as the treatment of choice for both clinical and economical reasons (Sherman et al., 1988).

For adults with autism, a study is in progress comparing the effectiveness of the Carolina Living and Learning Center (CLLC)—the model residential and vocational program developed and operated by Division TEACCH (*T*reatment and *E*ducation of *A*utistic and Related *C*ommunication Handicapped *CH*ildren) at the University of North Carolina at Chapel Hill—to the effectiveness of other residential settings, including family homes, group homes, and institutions (Van Bourgondien, Reichle, Schopler, & Mesibov, 1996). Results indicated that the CLLC treatment environment provided significantly more individualized communication programming, visual structure, socialization training, and preventative behavior intervention strategies than the control settings. For all study participants, the increased use of these autism-specific teaching strategies was significantly related to a decrease in negative behaviors.

Another indication of program effectiveness is the degree of family satisfaction. In the CLLC comparison study (Van Bourgondien et al., 1996), families of CLLC residents were significantly more satisfied with the care their sons received than were families whose sons or daughters lived in the control settings. Further data analyses of the CLLC effectiveness are in progress.

Brown (1991) utilized case studies to demonstrate the importance of considering, when designing daily activities and routines, the lifestyle preferences of individuals with disabilities who are living in residential programs. Many of the case examples described individuals with autism and demonstrated that manipulation of their daily routine, utilizing the concepts of communication, choice, and refusal, can provide an effective strategy for reducing challenging behaviors. Brown indicated that further research in the area is needed.

Several studies have investigated the skill acquisition of adults with autism within specific residential programs (LaVigna, 1983; Smith & Belcher, 1985). Smith and Belcher studied the implementation of a training program for teaching life skills to 5 adults with

autism in community group-home settings in the CSAAC program in Maryland. House counselors served as trainers after receiving instruction on the teaching methods, which included task analysis of domestic and self-care skills and a systematic prompting procedure. The data collection procedures involved recording the type of prompting required per step of the tasks. Over time, all subjects in the study (2 males, 3 females) showed a gradual increase in the number of steps performed with no assistance, prompting the authors to conclude that the training model is a viable method for teaching independent living skills to adults with autism.

LaVigna (1983) also reported successful skill acquisition in his study of the first 6 adult residents of the Jay Nolen Center residential program in California. The training program was based on Mark Gold's task-analysis procedures (Gold, 1976), in which tasks are reduced to sequential steps and trainers provide the minimal assistance required for the resident to complete each step successfully. Before providing assistance, staff members encourage the residents to "try another way." The degree of assistance required for each step of the task is recorded by staff members.

The results indicated that the skill development of the residents in the areas of self-help, home care, and cooking showed continuous developmental growth at intervals of 6 months, 1 year, and 2 years. The 6 residents began with a total of fewer than 15 skills mastered, and they progressed to nearly 100 skills mastered overall. In fact, 2 of the 6 residents were ready to move into homes that have less staff supervision. LaVigna (1983) concluded that the results provide encouraging evidence that adults with autism can continue to develop.

SUMMARY AND CONCLUSIONS

During the past 20 years, great strides have been made in recognizing the unique needs of adults with autism, and a variety of treatment options have been developed to address these needs. Given the heterogeneity of the individuals with autism, no single residential treatment approach will be appropriate for everyone with autism. Each person needs assessment and planning based on his or her individual strengths, needs, and interests. Continued efforts to expand the continuum of options are essential.

Within residential programs, future challenges include maximizing the growth and quality of life of those residents with the most severe cognitive and/or behavioral difficulties. To ensure the long-term success and stability of these approaches to residential care, ways to improve the quality and stability of direct care staff members need to be developed and empirically validated.

Cross-References

Chapters 12 through 15 provide a summary of developmental changes in syndrome expression. Behavioral interventions are summarized in Chapter 26, working with families is discussed in Chapter 27, and vocational intervention issues are explored in Chapter 28.

REFERENCES

Arco, L., & Birnbrauer, J.S. (1990). Performance feedback and maintenance of staff behavior in residential settings. *Behavioral and Residential Treatment, 5,* 207–217.

Au Clair. (1994). *Au Clair Programs* [Brochure]. Mount Dora, FL: Author.

Baker, B.L., & Blacher, J. (1988). Family involvement with community residential programs. In M.P. Janicki, M.W. Krauss, & M.M. Seltzer (Eds.), *Community residences for persons with developmental disabilities: Here to stay* (pp. 173–188). Baltimore: Brookes.

Baker, B.L., & Blacher, J.B. (1993). Out-of-home placement for children with mental retardation: Dimensions of family involvement. *American Journal on Mental Retardation, 98,* 368–377.

Barber, D., & Hupp, S.C. (1993). A comparison of friendship patterns of individuals with developmental disabilities. *Education and Training in Mental Retardation, 28,* 13–22.

Bettleheim, B. (1967). *The empty fortress—Infantile autism and the birth of self.* New York: Free Press.

Bowd, A.D. (1989). Client satisfaction and normalization of residential services for persons with developmental handicaps. *Canadian Journal of Community Mental Health, 8,* 63–73.

Bromley, B.E., & Blacher, J. (1991). Parental reasons for out-of-home placement of children with severe handicaps. *Mental Retardation, 29,* 275–280.

Brown, F. (1991). Creative daily scheduling: A nonintrusive approach to challenging behaviors in community residences. *Journal of the Association for Persons with Severe Handicaps, 16,* 75–84.

Community Services for Autistic Adults and Children (CSAAC). (1995). *Adult residential program, Adult vocational program* [Brochure]. Rockville, MD: Author.

Edwards, P., & Miltenberger, R. (1991). Burnout among staff members at community residential facilities for persons with mental retardation. *Mental Retardation, 29,* 125–128.

Everard, M.P. (1976, July). *Mildly autistic young people and their problems.* Paper presented at the International Symposium on Autism, St. Gallen, Switzerland.

Giddan, J.J., & Giddan, N.S. (1993). *European farm communities for autism.* Toledo: Medical College of Ohio Press.

Gold, M.W. (1976). Task analysis of a complex assembly task by the retarded blind. *Exceptional Children, 43,* 78–84.

Hatton, C., & Emerson, E. (1993). Organizational predictors of staff stress, satisfaction, and intended turnover in a service for people with multiple disabilities. *Mental Retardation, 31,* 388–395.

Heller, T. (1988). Transitions: Coming in and going out of community residences. In M.P. Janicki, M.W. Krauss, & M.M. Seltzer (Eds.), *Community residences for persons with developmental disabilities: Here to stay* (pp. 149–158). Baltimore: Brookes.

Heller, T., & Factor, A. (1993). Aging family caregivers: Support resources and changes in burden and placement desire. *American Journal on Mental Retardation, 98,* 417–426.

Hill, B.K., Rotegard, L.L., & Bruininks, R.H. (1984). The quality of life of mentally retarded people in residential care. *Social Work, 29,* 275–280.

Hilton, A. (1987). Residential facilities. In C.R. Reynolds & C. Mann (Eds.), *Encyclopedia of special education* (pp. 1350–1351). New York: John Wiley & Sons.

Holmes, D.L. (1990). Community-based services for children and adults with autism: The Eden family of programs. *Journal of Autism and Developmental Disorders, 20,* 339–351.

Jacobson, J.W., & Ackerman, L.J. (1992). Factors associated with staff tenure in group homes serving people with developmental disabilities. *Adult Residential Care Journal, 6,* 45–60.

Juhrs, P.D. (1988). *Community Services for Autistic Adults and Children Vocational Program Overview.* Unpublished manuscript.

Kanner, L. (1943). Autistic disturbances of affective contact. *Nervous Child, 2,* 217–250.

Kanner, L., Rodriquez, A., & Ashenden, B. (1972). How far can autistic children go in matters of social adaptation? *Journal of Autism and Childhood Schizophrenia, 2,* 9–33.

Kay, B.R. (1990). Bittersweet Farms. *Journal of Autism and Developmental Disorders, 20,* 309–322.

Kobe, F.H., Rojahn, J., & Schroeder, S.R. (1991). Predictors of urgency of out-of-home placement needs. *Mental Retardation, 6,* 323–328.

Lakin, K.C. (1988). Strategies for promoting the stability of direct care staff. In M.P. Janicki, M.W. Krauss, & M.M. Seltzer (Eds.), *Community residences for persons with developmental disabilities: Here to stay* (pp. 231–238). Baltimore: Brookes.

Lakin, K.C., Hill, B.K., & Bruininks, R.H. (1986). Habilitative functions and effects of residential services. *Remedial and Special Education, 7,* 54–62.

Landesman, S. (1988). Preventing "institutionalization" in the community. In M.P. Janicki, M.W. Krauss, & M.M. Seltzer (Eds.), *Community residences for persons with developmental disabilities: Here to stay* (pp. 105–116). Baltimore: Brookes.

Landesman, S., & Butterfield, E.C. (1987). Normalization and deinstitutionalization of mentally retarded individuals. *American Psychologist, 42,* 809–816.

Landesman-Dwyer, S., Sackett, C.P., & Kleinman, J.S. (1980). Relationship of size to resident and staff behavior in small community residences. *American Journal of Mental Deficiency, 85,* 6–17.

Landesman-Dwyer, S., Stein, J., & Sackett, C.P. (1978). A behavioral and ecological study of group homes. In G.P. Sackett (Ed.), *Observing behavior: Vol. 1. Theory and applications in mental retardation* (pp. 349–377). Baltimore: University Park Press.

Larson, S., & Lakin, K. (1992). Direct-care staff in a national sample of small group homes. *Mental Retardation, 30,* 13–22.

LaVigna, G.W. (1983). The Jay Nolen Center: A community-based program. In E. Schopler & G.B. Mesibov (Eds.), *Autism in adolescents and adults* (pp. 381–410). New York: Plenum Press.

Lettick, A.L. (1983). Benhaven. In E. Schopler & G.B. Mesibov (Eds.), *Autism in adolescents and adults* (pp. 355–379). New York: Plenum Press.

Levy, P.H., Levy, J.M., Freeman, S., Feiman, J., & Samowitz, P. (1988). Training and managing community residence staff. In M.P. Janicki, M.W. Krauss, & M.M. Seltzer (Eds.), *Community residences for persons with developmental disabilities: Here to stay* (pp. 239–250). Baltimore: Brookes.

Lotter, V. (1978). Follow-up studies. In M. Rutter & E. Schopler (Eds.), *Autism: A reappraisal of concepts and treatment* (pp. 475–495). New York: Plenum Press.

Maslach, C. (1982). Understanding burnout: Definitional issues in analyzing a complex phenomenon. In W.S. Paine (Ed.), *Job stress and burnout: Research, theory, and intervention perspectives* (pp. 29–40). Beverly Hills, CA: Sage.

McGimsey, J.F., & Favell, J.E. (1988). The effects of increased physical exercise on disruptive behavior in retarded persons. *Journal of Autism and Developmental Disorders, 18,* 167–180.

Mesibov, G.B., Schopler, E., & Hearsey, K.A. (1994). Structured teaching. In E. Schopler & G.B. Mesibov (Eds.), *Behavioral issues in autism* (pp. 195–207). New York: Plenum Press.

Mesibov, G.B., & Shea, V. (1980, March). *Social and interpersonal problems of autistic adolescents.* Paper presented at the meeting of the Southeastern Psychological Association, Washington, DC.

Mitchell, D., & Braddock, D. (1992). Review of research on compensation and turnover. In M.J. Begab (Ed.), *Residential services and developmental disabilities in the United States* (pp. 1–43). Washington, DC: American Association on Mental Retardation.

Mitchell, D., & Braddock, D. (1993). Compensation and turnover of direct-care staff in developmental disabilities residential facilities: I. Wages and benefits. *Mental Retardation, 31,* 429–437.

Mitchell, D., & Braddock, D. (1994). Compensation and turnover of direct-care staff in developmental disabilities residential facilities in the United States: II. Turnover. *Mental Retardation, 32,* 34–42.

Razza, N.J. (1993). Determinants of direct-care staff turnover in group homes for individuals with mental retardation. *Mental Retardation, 31,* 284–291.

Reichle, N.C., & Campbell, D.G. (1993, February). *Working with families in residential settings.* A paper presentation at the TEACCH Winter inservice meeting, Brown Summit, NC.

Reichler, R.J., & Schopler, E. (1976). Developmental therapy: A program model for providing individual services in the community. In E. Schopler & R.J. Reichler (Eds.), *Psychopathology and child development: Research and treatment* (pp. 347–372). New York: Plenum Press.

Rimland, B. (1964). *Infantile autism.* New York: Appleton-Century-Crofts.

Rumanoff-Simonson, L., Simonson, S.M., & Volkmar, F.R. (1990). Benhaven's residential program. *Journal of Autism and Developmental Disorders, 20,* 323–338.

Schopler, E. (1971). Parents of psychotic children as scapegoats. *Journal of Contemporary Psychotherapy, 4,* 17–22.

Schopler, E., Brehm, S.S., Kinsbourne, M., & Reichler, R.J. (1971). Effect of treatment structure on development in autistic children. *Archives of General Psychiatry, 24,* 415–421.

Schopler, E., & Hennike, J.M. (1990). Past and present trends in residential treatment. *Journal of Autism and Developmental Disorders, 20,* 291–298.

Schopler, E., & Reichler, R.J. (1971). Parents as cotherapists in the treatment of psychotic children. *Journal of Autism and Childhood Schizophrenia, 1,* 87–102.

Sherman, B.R. (1988). Predictors of the decision to place developmentally disabled family members in residential care. *American Journal on Mental Retardation, 92,* 344–351.

Sherman, J., Barker, P., Lorimer, P., Swinson, R., & Factor, D.C. (1988). Treatment of autistic children: Relative effectiveness of residential, out-patient, and home-based interventions. *Child Psychiatry and Human Development, 19,* 109–125.

Sloan, J.L., & Schopler, E. (1977). Some thoughts about developing programs for autistic adolescents. *Journal of Pediatric Psychology, 2,* 187–190.

Smith, M.D., & Belcher, R. (1985). Teaching life skills to adults disabled by autism. *Journal of Autism and Developmental Disorders, 15,* 163–175.

Social Security Act, 42 U.S.C. §§ 1381–1383 (1974).

Stoneman, Z., & Crapps, J.M. (1990). Mentally retarded individuals in family care homes: Relationships with the family-of-origin. *American Journal on Mental Retardation, 94,* 420–430.

Van Bourgondien, M.E., & Elgar, S. (1990). The relationship between existing residential services and the needs of autistic adults. *Journal of Autism and Developmental Disorders, 20,* 299–308.

Van Bourgondien, M.E., Mesibov, G.B., & Castelloe, P. (1989, July). *Adaptation of clients with autism to group home settings.* Paper presented at the national conference of the Autism Society of America, Seattle, WA.

Van Bourgondien, M.E., & Reichle, N.C. (1993, June). *Making changes: Adolescents and adults with autism in transition.* A presentation at the annual conference of the American Association on Mental Retardation (AAMR), Washington, DC.

Van Bourgondien, M.E., & Reichle, N.C. (1996). The Carolina Living and Learning Center: An example of the TEACCH approach to residential and vocational training for adults with autism. In G. Kristoffersen & E. Kristoffersen, (Eds.), *Status Pa Garden* (pp. 155–169). Copenhagen: Parentes.

Van Bourgondien, M.E., Reichle, N.C., Schopler, E., & Mesibov, G.B. (1996). The effectiveness of a model treatment program on adults with autism. Manuscript in preparation, University of North Carolina at Chapel Hill.

Van Bourgondien, M.E., & Schopler, E. (1990). Critical issues in the residential care of people with autism. *Journal of Autism and Developmental Disorders, 20,* 391–400.

Van Bourgondien, M.E., & Woods, A.V. (1992). Vocational possibilities for high-functioning adults with autism. In E. Schopler & G.B. Mesibov (Eds.), *High-functioning individuals with autism* (pp. 227–239). New York: Plenum Press.

Wall, A.J. (1990). Group homes in North Carolina for children and adults with autism. *Journal of Autism and Developmental Disorders, 20,* 353–366.

Wolfensberger, W. (1972). *The principle of normalization in human services.* Toronto, Ontario, Canada: National Institute on Mental Retardation.

Yohalem, J.B. (1987). Federal funding for community-based residential services. In D.J. Cohen & A.M. Donnellan (Eds.), *Handbook of autism and pervasive developmental disorders* (pp. 625–631). New York: John Wiley & Sons.

CHAPTER 32

Psychopharmacology

CHRISTOPHER J. McDOUGLE

Effective pharmacotherapy of neuropsychiatric disorders involves the use of drugs to stabilize those dysregulated neuronal systems believed to underlie the abnormal behavior. Although research over the past 35 years has shown the etiology of autism to be multifactorial (Rubenstein, Lotspeich, & Ciaranello, 1990), direct and indirect lines of evidence suggest that certain neurochemical systems are of particular relevance to the pathophysiology of autism (Cook, 1990). Although there is currently no cure for autism, the appropriate use of medication, in the context of a comprehensive individualized treatment program, can enhance the autistic person's ability to benefit from educational and behavior modification interventions. The combination of appropriate pharmacotherapy and an individualized psychosocial treatment plan can reduce many of the behavioral disturbances of the syndrome, resulting in an improved quality of life for the person and his or her family members (McDougle, Price, & Volkmar, 1994). This chapter reviews psychopharmacology research in Autistic Disorder from the perspective of specific neurochemical systems.

DRUGS AFFECTING SEROTONIN FUNCTION

Little is definitively known regarding the pathophysiology of the syndrome of autism,

but abnormalities in the serotonin (5-hydroxytryptamine [5-HT]) neurotransmitter system have been identified in a subset of patients. Schain and Freedman (1961) first reported elevated levels of whole blood 5-HT (WBS) in the peripheral vascular system of autistic children. Others have replicated this finding in studies that compared groups of autistic children with normal controls (Anderson et al., 1987). Antibodies against human brain 5-HT receptors were identified in the blood and cerebrospinal fluid (CSF) of a child with autism (Todd & Ciaranello, 1985), although subsequent studies found no difference in the degree of immunoglobulin inhibition of binding of the 5-HT1A agonist [^{3}H]-8-hydroxy-N,N-dipropyl-2-aminotetralin (DPAT) to 5-HT1A receptors between autistic patients and controls (Cook, Perry, Dawson, Wainwright, & Leventhal, 1993; Yuwiler et al., 1992). Blunted neuroendocrine responses to pharmacological probes of the 5-HT system have been observed in autistic children (Hoshino et al., 1984) and adults (McBride et al., 1989) compared with normal subjects. Finally, acute dietary depletion of the 5-HT precursor tryptophan has been associated with an exacerbation of behavioral symptoms in drug-free autistic adults (McDougle, Naylor, Cohen, Aghajanian, et al. 1996). Based on evidence implicating a dysregulation in 5-HT function in some patients

The author wishes to thank Elizabeth Kyle for preparing the manuscript, and Elizabeth Ruff and Sally Vegso for the graphics work. This work was supported by a National Alliance for Research on Schizophrenia and Depression Young Investigator Award (Dr. McDougle), the State of Connecticut Department of Mental Health and Addiction Services, the Korczak Foundation for Autism and Related Disorders, and National Institutes of Health grants M01 RR06022-33, P50 MH30929-18, HD 03008-27, and P01 MH25642.

with autism, drugs that affect this system have been studied.

Fenfluramine

Fenfluramine is an indirect 5-HT receptor agonist that releases 5-HT presynaptically and blocks its reuptake from 5-HT neurons. Although fenfluramine increases 5-HT neurotransmission acutely, ongoing administration results in a reduction in brain 5-HT.

Enthusiasm for the drug as a potential treatment for autism was generated in 1982, following a published description of its effects in three hyperserotonemic autistic boys (Geller, Ritvo, Freeman, & Yuwiler, 1982). The first child showed an increase in social responsivity during treatment with fenfluramine (up to 40 mg/day for 2 weeks), with a return to baseline levels of maladaptive symptoms upon drug discontinuation. Following a 2-week placebo period and 3 weeks of dosage adjustment, the two other boys received a fixed dose of fenfluramine for 8 additional weeks, followed by 6 weeks of placebo. Both boys showed improvement on IQ testing and in disturbances of motor, social, affective, speech, language, communication, object-relations, and sensory modulation function. Assessment at 3 months posttreatment found that a significant return of symptoms had occurred.

To follow up these preliminary findings, a large, multicenter, single-blind, A-B-A design study of fenfluramine was conducted at 18 sites. Following a 2-week open placebo baseline period, patients received 4 additional weeks of placebo, 16 weeks of fenfluramine (1.5 mg/kg in 2 divided doses), and 8 weeks of placebo. Ritvo and colleagues published a report describing their center's experience with 14 autistic patients in this study (Ritvo, Freeman, Geller, & Yuwiler, 1983). A significant decrease in abnormal motor movements was found, and improvement was seen on scales measuring social and sensory function. WBS concentrations decreased an average of 51% after 1 month of fenfluramine and returned to baseline values within 4 weeks after return to placebo. Patients with both normal and elevated baseline WBS levels showed clinical improvement. No adverse reactions or clinically significant side effects were reported.

In a subsequent report, results from 9 of the participating centers were described (Ritvo et al., 1986). Data from 64 boys and 17 girls with autism, ranging in age from 33 months to 24 years (mean, 8.8 years), were presented. The mean values of the overall, motor, social, and sensory scales of the Ritvo-Freeman Real-Life Rating Scale (Freeman, Ritvo, Yokota, & Ritvo, 1986) showed significant improvement with fenfluramine. Mean changes on the affect and language scales did not reach significance. IQ testing showed slight but statistically significant increases during drug treatment. On categorical measures of patient response, 27 (33%) were "strong responders," 42 (52%) were "moderate responders," and 12 (15%) were "nonresponders." Lethargy and irritability were the most frequently reported side effects. Mean WBS concentrations fell 46% from baseline after 2 months, and 57% after 4 months, of fenfluramine administration. Baseline WBS concentrations showed a significant inverse correlation with clinical response categories (lowest in the "strong responders," intermediate in the "moderate responders," and highest in the "nonresponders").

More recent controlled studies of fenfluramine in autism have not been as encouraging. Employing a double-blind, placebo-controlled, parallel-groups design, Campbell and colleagues studied the effects of fenfluramine on the core symptoms of autism and discrimination learning (Campbell, Adams, Small, et al., 1988). The sample included 28 hospitalized children (22 boys, 6 girls) with autism, aged 2.6 to 6.7 years (mean, 4.6 years), whose intelligence ranged from severely mentally retarded to dull normal. Following a 2-week placebo baseline period, patients were randomly assigned to fenfluramine or placebo for 8 weeks. This was followed by a 2-week posttreatment placebo period. Fourteen children were randomized to fenfluramine (mean dose, 1.7 mg/kg/day; maximum dose, 50 mg/day), and 14 to placebo. The most common side effects were weight loss, excessive sedation, loose stools, and irritability. Fenfluramine was associated with a significant decrease in fidgetiness and withdrawal, although no difference between fenfluramine and placebo was found for ratings of stereotypy or the core symptoms of autism. Furthermore, fenfluramine had a retarding effect on discrimination learning.

Ekman, Miranda-Linné, Gillberg, Garle, and Wetterberg (1989) also reported results suggesting that fenfluramine is not an effective treatment for most patients with Autistic Disorder. Eighteen boys and 2 girls with autism, aged 1.5 to 10.5 years (mean, 6.3 years), participated in this outpatient study. The mean IQ of the 20 children at baseline was 40 (range, 9 to 94). A double-blind, placebo-controlled, crossover A-B-A design was used, with each treatment segment lasting 16 weeks. Fenfluramine (1.5 mg/kg) was given in 2 daily divided doses. Three of the patients dropped out of the study due to oversedation, increased aberrant behavior, and stomach pains and elimination problems, respectively. Although no major adverse reactions occurred, 14 of the 20 patients experienced some side effects, primarily sedation and decreased appetite. WBS levels decreased by 53% during fenfluramine administration. A significant decrease in abnormal motor movements occurred, but no significant improvement in social relatedness, affectual response, sensory response, language, or IQ was found. Additional double blind, placebo-controlled, crossover studies of fenfluramine for 4 weeks (15 autistic children; Sherman, Factor, Swinson, & Darjes, 1989) and 5 to 12 weeks (11 children with autism; Duker, Welles, Seys, Rensen, & Vis, 1991) failed to show significant drug–placebo differences despite significant decreases in WBS levels.

Fenfluramine has been shown to lead to significant reductions in brain 5-HT content and to produce potentially irreversible changes in 5-HT neurons in certain regions of the brain in rats, guinea pigs, and rhesus monkeys (Schuster, Lewis, & Seiden, 1986). In humans, Chase and Shoulson (1975) demonstrated that CSF levels of 5-hydroxyindoleacetic acid (5-HIAA), the principal metabolite of 5-HT in the brain, were significantly reduced after 7 days of treatment with fenfluramine. In addition, Leventhal et al. (1993) found that plasma norepinephrine (NE) levels were decreased as long as 8 weeks after fenfluramine treatment in autistic children. Based on the potential risk of long-term, possibly irreversible changes in 5-HT and, possibly, catecholaminergic neurons, together with controlled studies demonstrating that fenfluramine is no better than placebo in reducing the core symptoms of autism, this drug cannot be recommended as a routine treatment for most patients with autistic disorder (Campbell, 1988).

Methysergide

Methysergide, a 5-HT receptor antagonist, is currently used in the treatment of migraine headaches. In 1969, Fish, Campbell, Shapiro, and Floyd described the effects of methysergide in 11 hospitalized autistic children aged 2 to 5 years. A daily dosage of 2 to 4 mg was administered for an average of 6 weeks. Of the 11 children, the 2 most retarded, mute, "psychotic" children were considered to be improved. Three children, however, showed no change, and 6 were worse. The 2 improved patients showed increased alertness, affective responsiveness, and goal-directed activity. Of the patients who did not improve, many were more talkative and active, although the content of the speech was more "bizarre," and the activity was disorganized and not goal-directed.

Imipramine

Imipramine is a nonselective tricyclic that blocks presynaptic neuronal uptake of both NE and 5-HT. Campbell, Fish, Shaprio, and Floyd (1971) gave imipramine (mean maximum tolerated dose = 34.5 mg/day) to 10 autistic children (8 boys, 2 girls), aged 2 to 6 years (mean, 3.5 years), for an average of 10.5 weeks. Two of the children were rated as markedly improved; the others were rated as unchanged or worse. The authors concluded that imipramine is not a useful drug for most patients with autism. In some of the children, imipramine decreased affective blunting, anergy, and withdrawal, and stimulated speech production; in others, it increased "psychotic speech," behavioral disorganization, and excitation. Any therapeutic effect was usually outweighed by toxic effects, including grand mal seizures in one case.

Buspirone

Buspirone, a 5-HT1A receptor partial agonist, has been shown in preclinical studies to increase 5-HT function (Blier, de Montigny, & Chaput, 1990). It is marketed in the United States for the treatment of generalized anxiety disorder. A 4-week open-label study of bus-pirone was conducted in 4 autistic children (3 boys, 1 girl), aged 9 to 10 years, in doses of 15 mg/day (Realmuto, August, & Garfinkel, 1989). Two children showed a reduction in hy-peractivity, one showed a reduction in stereo-typic behavior, and the fourth showed no significant change. No adverse effects were observed.

In an open-label study of buspirone in 14 de-velopmentally disabled, self-injurious adults (age range, 23 to 63 years; 3 adults with autism) 9 persons showed some improvement with the drug (Ratey, Sovner, Mikkelsen, & Chmielin-ski, 1989). The dose of buspirone ranged from 15 to 45 mg/day; of the 9 responders, 7 were on concomitant psychoactive medication. The au-thors stated that the effect of buspirone allowed for the reduction or discontinuation of neu-roleptic and facilitated a more adaptive exis-tence for many of the patients.

Clomipramine

Clomipramine is a nonselective tricyclic agent that has been shown in double-blind, placebo-controlled trials to be efficacious in the treat-ment of depression and Obsessive-Compulsive Disorder (OCD; DeVeaugh-Geiss et al., 1991). In addition, clomipramine has been reported to be effective in reducing some forms of self-injurious behavior (Lipinski, 1991). Although clomipramine affects NE and dopamine (DA) neuronal uptake, its most potent action is to inhibit 5-HT uptake.

Reports have described the potential use-fulness of clomipramine in the treatment of children and adults with Autistic Disorder. In the first published controlled study of clomipramine in autism, Gordon, State, Nel-son, Hamburger, and Rapoport (1993) found clomipramine (152 ± 56 mg/day) superior to the relatively selective NE-uptake-inhibitor desipramine (127 ± 52 mg/day) and placebo in a 10-week (5 weeks on each drug or placebo), randomized, crossover study in children with autism (mean age, 9.6 years). In the comparison of clomipramine with placebo, significant improvement was found in the core symptoms of autism, anger/unco-operativeness, hyperactivity, and obsessive-compulsive symptoms. When clomipramine

was compared with desipramine, significant changes in the core symptoms of autism, anger/uncooperativeness, and obsessive-com-pulsive symptoms were also observed. There was no significant difference between the two drugs in the treatment of hyperactivity. Ad-verse effects from clomipramine included prolongation of the corrected QT interval, tachycardia, and a grand mal seizure; with de-sipramine, irritability, temper outbursts, and uncharacteristic aggression were seen.

A Yale University research group (McDougle et al., 1992) found that 4 of 5 young adults with a *Diagnostic and Statistical Manual of Mental Disorders* (*DSM-III-R;* American Psychiatric Association [APA], 1987) diagnosis of autism, presenting with disturbances in social related-ness, repetitive thoughts and behavior, and/or impulsive aggression, had a significant im-provement in symptomatology with open-label clomipramine treatment. The fifth patient re-mained unchanged. Up to 12 weeks of treatment with clomipramine was necessary in some cases before appreciable change occurred. The dose of clomipramine in the 4 responders ranged from 75 to 250 mg/day, with a mean dose of 185 mg/day. Other than dry mouth in two cases, the patients tolerated the drug well and had no adverse effects. Four patients showed a sig-nificant improvement in social interaction, 3 demonstrated a clinically meaningful decrease in aggression, and 4 had a significant reduc-tion in repetitive behavior with clomipramine treatment.

We recently completed the first systematic study of clomipramine in adults with perva-sive developmental disorders, including autism (Brodkin, McDougle, Naylor, Cohen, & Price, 1995). Thirty-five subjects, 24 men and 11 women, who met *Diagnostic and Statistical Manual of Mental Disorders* (*DSM-IV;* APA, 1994) criteria for Pervasive Developmental Disorder entered a 12-week open-label trial of clomipramine. The mean age of the group was 30.2 years, with a range of 18 to 44 years. Clomipramine was begun at 50 mg/day and dosage was increased by 50 mg/week to a max-imum dose of 250 mg/day, based on clinical response and side effects. Behavioral mea-sures of global improvement, repetitive thoughts and behavior, aggression, and social relatedness were obtained at baseline and then every 4 weeks throughout the trial. Of the 33 patients who completed the 12-week trial, 18 (55%) were responders based on Clinical Global Impression (CGI) Scale (Guy, 1976) scores of "much" or "very much improved." Improvement was seen in repetitive thoughts and behavior, aggression, and social relatedness. The mean dose of clomipramine for the group was 139.4 ± 50.4 mg/day. Two patients had grand mal seizures and one had an exacerbation of absence seizures. No adverse cardiac events occurred. These preliminary data suggest that clomipramine may be effective in reducing interfering behaviors in many adults with pervasive developmental disorders, but careful monitoring for the induction or exacerbation of seizures is necessary.

Fluvoxamine

Fluvoxamine is a potent and selective 5-HT uptake inhibitor that has little or no affinity for 5-HT, DA, adrenergic, histaminic, or muscarinic receptors, and no known clinically active metabolites (Benfield & Ward, 1986). Its in vitro potency for blocking 5-HT uptake is equivalent to that of clomipramine, and it causes minimal inhibition of DA or NE uptake. Fluvoxamine has been shown to be effective in the treatment of refractory depression (Delgado, Price, Charney, & Heninger, 1988), and more efficacious than placebo (Goodman, Price, Rasmussen, Delgado, et al., 1989) and desipramine (Goodman, Price, et al., 1990) in the treatment of OCD. Importantly, a recent controlled study found fluvoxamine more effective than placebo in the treatment of social phobia (van Vliet, den Boer, & Westenberg, 1994), a disorder that may occur more frequently in first-degree relatives of autistic probands than in relatives of control probands (Smalley, McCracken, & Tanguay, 1995).

In the first report to describe the use of a 5-HT uptake inhibitor in Autistic Disorder, our group found fluvoxamine effective in the treatment of a 30-year-old man with autism and comorbid OCD (McDougle, Price, & Goodman, 1990). The patient had become obsessed with having the fingernails on each hand trimmed and manicured exactly the same as the corresponding nail on the opposite hand. He would typically spend up to 12 to 15 hours a day attending to his nails. If a hangnail or scab developed, the patient would gouge the opposite hand, to the point of bleeding, in order to "even it up." He realized that this behavior was excessive and irrational, but felt he had to perform the rituals in order to avoid the emergence of extreme anxiety. In addition, the patient had frequent aggressive outbursts, often resulting in physical injury to family members. He was extremely withdrawn socially and had no friends. After treatment with fluvoxamine (up to 150 mg/day), the patient showed a significant reduction in obsessive-compulsive symptoms and aggressivity. His parents reported the emergence of a desire to pursue social relationships, improved interpersonal interaction, and less withdrawal from human contact.

We recently completed the first double-blind, placebo-controlled investigation of fluvoxamine in patients with Autistic Disorder (McDougle, Naylor, Cohen, Volkmar, et al., 1996). The sample consisted of 27 men and 3 women, aged 18 to 53 years (mean, 30.1 years), with a diagnosis of Autistic Disorder based on *DSM-III-R,* Autism Diagnostic Interview (ADI; Le Couteur et al., 1989), and Autism Diagnostic Observation Schedule (ADOS; Lord et al., 1989) criteria. Each patient's symptoms were at least "moderate" in severity, as defined by global severity of illness rating on the CGI scale. The Autism Behavior Checklist (ABC; Krug, Arick, & Almond, 1980) was completed with the parent or legal guardian of each patient to determine the patient's level of autistic behavior. Full-scale IQ was measured with the Wechsler Adult Intelligence Scale—Revised (WAIS-R; Wechsler, 1981) in the 26 verbal patients. The Leiter International Performance Scale (Leiter, 1948) was used to assess IQ in the 4 nonverbal patients. Patients were psychotropic drug-free for at least 4 weeks prior to the start of the trial. One male patient had Fragile X syndrome; none of the other patients had a diagnosed genetic, metabolic, or neurological etiology for their syndrome.

After baseline behavioral ratings were obtained, patients were randomized to 12 weeks of double-blind treatment with fluvoxamine or placebo. The drug was started at 50 mg every night, and the dosage was then increased by 50 mg daily every 3 or 4 days, to a maximum dosage of 300 mg/day. Thus, the maximum dosage of fluvoxamine was attained within 3 weeks and patients received this dose for a minimum of 9 weeks.

Behavioral ratings were obtained every 4 weeks throughout the 12-week study. Repetitive thoughts and behavior were rated with a modified version of the Yale–Brown Obsessive Compulsive Scale (Y-BOCS; Goodman, Price, Rasmussen, Mazure, Delgado, et al., 1989; Goodman, Price, Rasmussen, Mazure, Fleischmann, et al., 1989), a 10-item, semistructured, clinician-rated questionnaire that is valid and reliable for assessing the severity of obsessive-compulsive symptoms in patients with OCD. Based on previous findings (McDougle, Kresch, et al., 1995), the ego-dystonicity diagnostic criterion for OCD was eliminated in rating the repetitive thoughts and behavior of the autistic patients. Aggression was rated with a modified version of the Brown Aggression Scale, a 9-category instrument that assesses different aspects of aggressive behavior (Brown, Goodwin, Ballenger, Goyer, & Major, 1979). The Ritvo-Freeman Real-Life Rating Scale served as an in vivo observational measure of a variety of symptoms of autism, including sensory motor behaviors, social relationship to people, affectual reactions, sensory responses, and language. The Vineland Adaptive Behavior Scale (Sparrow, Balla, & Cicchetti, 1984) Maladaptive Behavior Subscales (Part 1 and Part 2) were also administered at each assessment time-point. Finally, the CGI global improvement item (7 = "very much worse" to 1 = "very much improved") was recorded at each rating session following the baseline period. Treatment response was determined by scores obtained at the end of the last week of the study on the CGI. Patients with CGI scores of "much improved" or "very much improved" were categorized as responders.

All 30 patients completed the 12-week study and were thus included in the efficacy analysis. Fifteen patients were randomized to fluvoxamine and 15 received placebo. There was no significant difference in dosage between patients randomized to fluvoxamine (276.7 ± 41.7 mg/day) versus placebo (283.3 ± 36.2 mg/day). The fluvoxamine group (age, 30.1 ± 7.1 years) contained 2 women and 13

men, and the placebo group (age, 30.1 ± 8.4 years) consisted of 1 woman and 14 men. There were no significant differences in age, gender distribution, ABC scores, or full-scale IQ scores between the two groups.

Ratings on the CGI showed fluvoxamine superior to placebo beginning at week 4 and continuing at weeks 8 and 12 (Figure 32.1). Eight out of 15 (53%) of the fluvoxamine patients were categorized as responders compared with 0 out of 15 in the placebo group. Treatment response was not correlated with age, level of autistic behavior, or full-scale IQ.

As measured by reduction in total Y-BOCS scores, fluvoxamine was superior to placebo in the treatment of repetitive thoughts and behavior beginning at week 8 and continuing at week 12 of treatment (Figure 32.2). Fluvoxamine was more effective than placebo in reducing Y-BOCS subscale scores for both repetitive thoughts and repetitive behavior.

On the Vineland Maladaptive Behavior Subscales (Part 1 and Part 2), fluvoxamine was more effective than placebo beginning at week 4 and continuing through weeks 8 and 12. As measured by total score on the Brown Aggression Scale, fluvoxamine was also superior to placebo in reducing aggression beginning at week 4 and continuing through weeks 8 and 12.

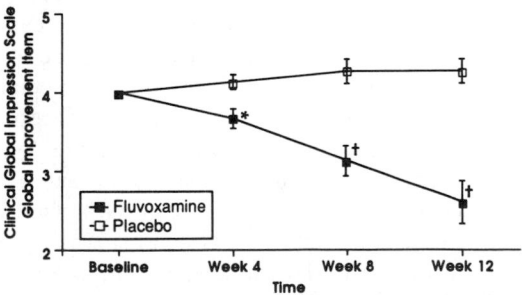

Figure 32.1 Global improvement in autistic patients given fluvoxamine (closed squares) or placebo (open squares) for 12 weeks, as measured on the Clinical Global Impression Scale global improvement item. * = p < .006, change from baseline, fluvoxamine vs. placebo, Student's t test; † = p < .0001, change from baseline, fluvoxamine vs. placebo, Student's t test. All tests are two-tailed.

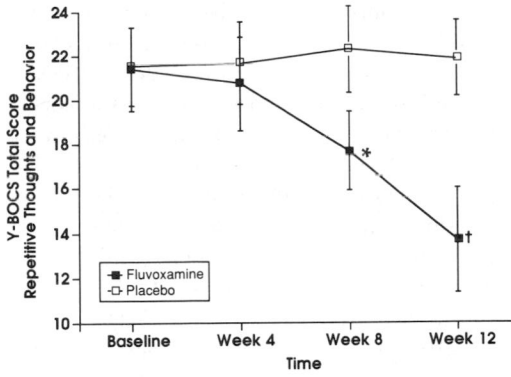

Figure 32.2 Change in severity of repetitive thoughts and behavior in autistic patients given fluvoxamine (closed squares) or placebo (open squares) for 12 weeks, as measured on the Yale–Brown Obsessive Compulsive Scale (Y-BOCS; range: 0 = no symptoms, 40 = most severe). * = p < .01, change from baseline, fluvoxamine vs. placebo, analysis of covariance; † = p < .001, change from baseline, fluvoxamine vs. placebo, analysis of covariance.

Fluvoxamine was superior to placebo in improving the behavioral symptoms of Autistic Disorder as measured by the Ritvo-Freeman Scale overall score. There was a trend for fluvoxamine to be superior to placebo beginning after 8 weeks, and, following 12 weeks, fluvoxamine was significantly better than placebo. In particular, fluvoxamine was superior to placebo in improving language usage (Subscale V) beginning at week 4 and continuing at weeks 8 and 12.

Fluvoxamine was well tolerated, with no medically significant adverse events. Four patients reported nausea (3 on active drug, 1 on placebo) during the first 2 weeks, but they developed tolerance and were able to continue. Three different patients developed moderate sedation (2 on active drug, 1 on placebo), which also was resolved. No anticholinergic side effects developed, and no significant changes in pulse or sitting and standing blood pressure occurred. No laboratory or electrocardiographic changes could be attributed to fluvoxamine. No dyskinesias, adverse cardiovascular events, or seizures occurred. The lack of seizures with fluvoxamine is noteworthy because nearly one-third of autistic patients develop seizures at some point in their lifetime (Volkmar & Nelson, 1990).

Fluoxetine

Fluoxetine is a potent and selective 5-HT uptake inhibitor that has been shown in double-blind, placebo-controlled investigations to be effective in the treatment of depression and OCD (Tollefson et al., 1994). Preliminary open-label studies and case reports suggest that fluoxetine may be useful in the treatment of some patients with Autistic Disorder (Cook, Rowlett, Jaselskis, & Leventhal, 1992; Ghaziuddin, Tsai, & Ghaziuddin, 1991; Hamdan-Allen, 1991; Mehlinger, Scheftner, & Poznanski, 1990; Todd, 1991).

Mehlinger et al. (1990) reported that fluoxetine (20 mg every other day) was useful in reducing ritualistic behavior and in improving mood in a 26-year-old autistic woman. Hamdan-Allen (1991) described marked improvement in trichotillomania in an 18-year-old man with autism who had been resistant to a 6-month trial of imipramine at therapeutic blood levels. Todd (1991) reported that 3 out of 4 patients with autism showed a significant reduction in ritualistic behavior or increased tolerance of changes in routine with fluoxetine treatment. Ghaziuddin et al. (1991) found fluoxetine (20 to 40 mg/day) effective in reducing depressive symptoms in adolescents with Autistic Disorder, although many of the core features of autism remained unchanged.

In a larger open-label case series, Cook et al. (1992) found that fluoxetine, in doses ranging from 20 mg every other day to 80 mg/day, led to significant improvement in subjects with Autistic Disorder and in subjects with mental retardation without autism. The autistic subjects ranged in age from 7 to 28 years (mean, 15.9 years) and those with mental retardation ranged in age from 4.8 to 52 years (mean, 21 years). Subjects with autism and those with mental retardation alone had been treated with fluoxetine for approximately 6 months at the time of rating. In subjects with Autistic Disorder, fluoxetine led to an improvement in CGI severity scale scores in 15 out of 23 subjects. Ten of 16 mentally retarded subjects had an improvement of 1 point or more on CGI overall severity ratings, including improvement in impulse control, attention span, and ability to tolerate frustration. Six of 23 subjects with autism and 3 of 16 subjects with mental retardation had side effects, consisting primarily of restlessness, hyperactivity, agitation, decreased appetite, and insomnia.

Sertraline

Sertraline is a potent and selective 5-HT uptake inhibitor that has been shown in double-blind, placebo-controlled studies to be effective in the treatment of depression and OCD (Greist et al., 1995). Preliminary results from our group suggest that sertraline may be useful for improving the symptoms of impaired reciprocal social interaction, aggression, and repetitive behavior in some adults with pervasive developmental disorders, including autism (McDougle et al., 1997). In an open-label study, 24 of 42 adults (57%) were rated as "much" or "very much improved" on the global improvement item of the CGI following 12 weeks of treatment with sertraline (50 to 200 mg/day). Five patients ended the trial prematurely because of the emergence of interfering anxiety (N = 3), syncope (N = 1), and noncompliance (N = 1), respectively. No other significant side effects or adverse reactions occurred.

Lithium

Although lithium's actions on neurotransmitter systems are diverse and the biologic basis for its clinical efficacy is unknown, lithium's antidepressant properties are mediated in part by an enhancement of 5-HT function (Price & Heninger, 1994). We recently described a 27-year-old man with autism who was treated with fluvoxamine (200 mg/day for 12 weeks) with minimal clinical response. When lithium (900 mg/day) was added to the fluvoxamine, a substantial clinical improvement in social relatedness and a marked reduction in aggressive and impulsive behavior were observed after 2 weeks. At the end of 4 weeks of treatment with fluvoxamine and lithium, the patient was rated as much improved on several rating scales. He maintained this clinically meaningful improvement at a 12-month follow-up, with no significant adverse effects (Epperson et al., 1994).

The combination of the facilitatory effect of lithium on presynaptic 5-HT neurons (Blier & de Montigny, 1985) with the desensitization of inhibitory presynaptic 5-HT autoreceptors by fluvoxamine (Chaput, de Montigny, & Blier, 1986) has been hypothesized to be a mechanism by which brain 5-HT neurotransmission might be enhanced during lithium augmentation of 5-HT uptake inhibitors (de Montigny, Cournoyer, Morissette, Langlois, & Caille, 1983).

Although this patient's response to lithium augmentation of fluvoxamine appeared to be clinically impressive, a number of potentially limiting factors need to be considered in interpreting this finding. It is possible that his improvement in social relatedness and reduction in aggressivity simply represent an "antidepressant" response to lithium augmentation. Prior to the initiation of treatment, however, he did not meet criteria for major depression, either clinically or based on structured ratings. Similarly, the patient had no consistent history of symptoms that would be indicative of bipolar disorder. It is also possible that lithium treatment alone led to the reduction in symptoms. However, the majority of reports of lithium monotherapy in Autistic Disorder have not been encouraging (Campbell et al., 1972), unless there was a personal or family history of bipolar illness (Kerbeshian, Burd, & Fisher, 1987; Steingard & Biederman, 1987).

In summary, although much further controlled research is necessary to determine whether potent 5-HT uptake inhibitors and other drugs affecting 5-HT function have efficacy for improving any of the interfering behavioral symptoms of autism, the data reviewed above suggest that this line of approach warrants further investigation. In support of this suggestion, indirect evidence from related areas of preclinical and clinical research supports a role for central 5-HT in the neuromodulation of many of the clinical characteristics of autism, including aggression, social dysfunction, and repetitive thoughts and behavior. For example, CSF levels of 5-HIAA are reduced in children with conduct and other aggressive behavioral disorders (Kruesi et al., 1990; Kruesi et al., 1992), in humans who demonstrate impulsive vs. nonimpulsive violent behavior (Linnoila et al., 1983), and in aggressive and impulsive free-ranging male rhesus monkeys (Mehlman et al., 1994). The selective 5-HT uptake inhibitors—fluvoxamine (McDougle, Naylor, Cohen, Volkmar, et al., 1996), fluoxetine (Markowitz, 1992), sertraline (Kelley, Hellings, Gabrielli, & Kilgore, 1993), and paroxetine (Snead, Boon, & Presberg, 1994)—as well as the nonselective 5-HT uptake inhibitor clomipramine (Garber, McGonigle, Slomka, & Monteverde, 1992), all of which increase synaptic 5-HT in the brain, have been reported to reduce aggression and self-injurious behavior in patients with autism and other developmental disabilities.

Many consider the core disturbance in Autistic Disorder to be impaired reciprocal verbal and nonverbal social interaction (Volkmar, 1987). Central 5-HT has been found to contribute to the regulation of social behavior and social hierarchies in animals. For example, the tryptophan hydroxylase enzyme inhibitor, p-chlorophenylalanine (PCPA), resulted in decreased grooming, approaching, resting, and eating behavior, and increased locomotion, solitariness, vigilance, and avoiding, when administered to vervet monkeys. Fluoxetine, tryptophan, and the 5-HT receptor agonist quipazine had the opposite effect (Raleigh et al., 1980). The autistic patients' improvement with 5-HT uptake inhibitors suggests that enhancement of central 5-HT function may be important for facilitating certain aspects of social interaction in some patients.

Brain 5-HT has also been hypothesized to be involved in modulating repetitive thoughts and behavior. Although the types, frequency, and quality of repetitive thoughts and behavior of age- and sex-matched adults with OCD and Autistic Disorder have been shown to be different (McDougle, Kresch, et al., 1995), these interfering symptoms often improve with 5-HT uptake inhibitor treatment in both diagnostic groups (Goodman, Price, Rasmussen, Delgado, et al., 1989; McDougle, Naylor, Cohen, Volkmar, et al., 1996). Given the adaptive changes in receptor function that occur during chronic administration of 5-HT uptake inhibitors, coupled with the delayed onset of improvement in repetitive thoughts and behavior in OCD (Goodman, Price, Rasmussen, Delgado, et al., 1989) and autistic patients (McDougle, Naylor, Cohen, Volkmar, et al.,

1996), it is unclear what changes in 5-HT function are ultimately associated with improvement in these symptoms. It may be that variation in the time course of 5-HT receptor adaptation in neuroanatomical regions hypothesized to subserve repetitive thoughts and behavior contributes to this delayed response to 5-HT uptake inhibitors. For example, El Mansari, Bouchard, and Blier (1994) recently showed that 8 (but not 3) weeks of treatment with the 5-HT uptake inhibitor paroxetine enhanced 5-HT release, secondary to desensitization of the 5-HT autoreceptor, in the orbitofrontal cortex of guinea pigs. Alternatively, the 5-HT uptake inhibitors may act indirectly on another system more closely tied to the pathophysiology of the disorders (e.g., DA), or they may compensate for dysfunction in one system by enhancing function of a different intact system (Goodman, McDougle, et al., 1990). In any case, central 5-HT appears to be significantly involved in the treatment, if not the pathophysiology, of repetitive thoughts and behavior.

DRUGS AFFECTING DOPAMINE FUNCTION

Evidence from clinical neurobiological studies and drug treatment response data suggest that DA function may be increased in some patients with Autistic Disorder. Gillberg, Svennerholm, and Hamilton-Hellberg (1983) found that mean basal CSF concentrations of homovanillic acid (HVA), the primary metabolite of brain DA, were elevated in 13 medication-free autistic children in comparison to matched controls. In addition, the indirect DA receptor agonist amphetamine has been shown to exacerbate stereotypic motor symptoms and hyperactivity in some autistic children, whereas controlled studies of DA receptor antagonists have found these drugs effective in improving some of the behavioral symptoms associated with Autistic Disorder.

Haloperidol

The DA receptor antagonist haloperidol has been extensively studied in controlled clinical trials in children with Autistic Disorder. Campbell et al. (1978) completed a 12-week, double-blind, placebo-controlled study of haloperidol in 40 hospitalized autistic children (32 boys and 8 girls) aged 2.6 to 7.2 years (mean, 4.5 years). Patients were randomly assigned to 1 of 4 treatment groups, based on drug (haloperidol vs. placebo) and level of concomitant language training (response-contingent reinforcement vs. response-independent [placebo] reinforcement). Following a 2-week drug-free period, haloperidol (0.5 mg) or placebo was given in identical-appearing tablets. Dosage was increased twice weekly during the first 3 weeks to a maximum of 4 mg/day (mean optimal dose = 1.65 mg/day), depending on therapeutic response or the development of untoward side effects. Haloperidol was found to be superior to placebo in reducing stereotypies and withdrawal, particularly for children above 4.5 years of age. In addition, the combination of haloperidol and behavioral language training was more effective than haloperidol or behavioral therapy alone in facilitating the imitation of new words in training sessions. Twelve children experienced dose-dependent sedation, and 2 had acute dystonic reactions.

In an attempt to replicate the findings of the first study, Cohen et al. (1980) conducted a double-blind, placebo-controlled, within-subjects reversal (A-B-A-B) design study of haloperidol. Ten hospitalized autistic children (6 girls and 4 boys), aged 2.1 to 7.0 years (mean, 4.7 years), who were mildly to profoundly retarded, completed the study. Following a 2-week placebo period, patients were randomly assigned to alternating treatment periods of haloperidol or placebo at 2-week intervals. Haloperidol was begun at 0.5 mg/day and increased to a maximum of 4.0 mg/day within the first week of treatment. The mean optimal dose of haloperidol was 1.65 mg/day during the initial administration period and 1.90 mg/day upon repeat administration. Eight of 10 children experienced excessive sedation during haloperidol treatment, and 1 had two episodes of acute dystonia relieved by diphenhydramine (25 mg I.M.). Haloperidol was effective in reducing stereotypies and in helping the children to orient attention to a rater's requests. As in the initial study, the older children responded better to haloperidol than the younger patients.

Anderson et al. (1984) conducted a 12-week follow-up study to determine whether learning was facilitated because haloperidol reduced stereotypies and withdrawal, or because of a direct effect on attentional mechanisms. Following a 2-week placebo period, 40 autistic children (29 boys, 11 girls), aged 2.3 to 6.9 years (mean, 4.6 years), entered a double-blind, crossover study of haloperidol versus placebo. Patients were started on haloperidol (0.5 mg/day) or placebo, and dosage was adjusted until clinical improvement or untoward side effects were observed. The maximum dose of haloperidol was 4.0 mg/day, and the optimal dose was 1.1 mg/day. The most frequent side effects were excessive sedation and increased irritability, although these were reported to occur only during dosage adjustment or above-optimal doses. Acute dystonic reactions occurred in 11 children. Haloperidol led to a significant decrease in symptoms of withdrawal, stereotypies, hyperactivity, abnormal object relationships, fidgetiness, negativism, angry affect, and lability of mood. Furthermore, haloperidol produced greater facilitation and retention of discrimination learning in a structured laboratory setting. These findings led the authors to suggest that the effect of haloperidol on learning was not a function of its decreasing maladaptive behaviors but rather a direct effect on attentional mechanisms.

A subsequent double-blind, placebo-controlled investigation of haloperidol was conducted by Anderson and Campbell (1989). The sample consisted of 45 autistic children (35 boys, 10 girls), aged 2.0 to 7.6 years (mean, 4.5 years), of whom 42 were at least mildly mentally retarded. The starting dose of haloperidol was 0.5 mg/day, and dosage was increased to a maximum of 4.0 mg/day or until therapeutic or untoward effects were observed. The mean optimal dose of haloperidol was 0.8 mg/day. No adverse side effects were observed at these doses. Haloperidol was associated with decreases in hyperactivity, temper tantrums, withdrawal, and stereotypies, and an increase in social relatedness. Although haloperidol did not have an adverse effect on learning in this study, it also did not have generalized facilitating effects on discrimination learning.

Because longer-term administration of medication is often needed in moderately to severely affected autistic children, Perry and colleagues (1989) studied the effects when haloperidol was given for 6 months to a large group of children with autism. Sixty children with autistic disorder (48 boys, 12 girls), aged 2.3 to 7.9 years (mean, 5.1 years), who had previously shown clinically significant improvement on haloperidol, completed the study as outpatients. Intellectual functioning ranged from severe mental retardation to dull normal, as measured on the Gesell Developmental Schedules. The children were randomly assigned to two groups: Group I received haloperidol on a continuous basis, and Group II was on a discontinuous schedule consisting of 5 days of haloperidol alternating with 2 days of placebo. Following the 6-month treatment period, both groups were placed on placebo for 4 weeks. Haloperidol doses ranged from 0.5 to 4.0 mg/day (mean optimal dose = 1.23 mg/day). At these doses, sedation and parkinsonian side effects were not observed. Twelve children developed haloperidol-related dyskinesias, 3 during haloperidol administration and 9 upon discontinuation. Long-term haloperidol administration was found to be effective in reducing maladaptive symptoms in these autistic children. Improvement was seen in 71.5% of children, 20% showed no improvement, and 8.5% were rated as worse. The discontinuous drug administration did not reduce the efficacy of haloperidol, and there was no difference in side effects between children who received continuous versus discontinuous treatment. Fifty-nine percent of the children had a significant return of symptoms during the 4-week placebo period. In particular, those children who had demonstrated angry affect, lability of affect, loud voice, and negative and uncooperative symptoms showed more marked behavioral deterioration during haloperidol withdrawal. The authors concluded that, because of the emergence of drug-related dyskinesias, safer and more effective drugs need to be developed for autistic children who require medication as an adjunct to special education and behavior modification.

In an attempt to more carefully define the occurrence of drug-related dyskinesias in this patient group, Campbell, Adams, Perry, Spencer, and Overall, (1988) conducted a prospective study of 82 autistic children whose ages ranged from 2.3 to 8.2 years at the time of entry into the study. Patients received haloperidol (0.25 to 10.5 mg/day; mean, 0.054 mg/kg/day) for 0.8 to 78.5 months (mean, 18.1 months). Twenty-four of the 82 children developed dyskinesias, 21% during haloperidol administration and 79% during drug withdrawal. The dyskinesias tended to occur in the orofacial muscles, the tongue, and the upper extremities, and females showed a trend toward greater risk. All of the dyskinesias were reversible, but the time course for this to occur varied from 7 days to 7.5 months.

Pimozide

Like haloperidol, pimozide is a DA receptor antagonist that is currently receiving attention as a potential treatment for Autistic Disorder. In a multicenter investigation, Naruse et al. (1982) conducted a double-blind, crossover study of pimozide, haloperidol, and placebo in children with behavior disorders. The patients ranged in age from 3 to 16 years and included 34 autistic children. The doses of pimozide ranged from 1 to 9 mg/day. A significant reduction occurred in some types of aggression, including "injury and violence to others" and "breaking furniture," although self-mutilation was not significantly improved.

In an open-label pilot study, Ernst and colleagues (1992) found pimozide in doses of 3 to 6 mg/day (mean, 4.9 mg/day) to be helpful for hospitalized autistic children. Eight moderately to profoundly retarded boys, aged 4.2 to 8.3 years (mean, 5.7 years), completed the 3-week study. Untoward side effects were minimal and transient, and clinical improvement was found on global measures of behavioral change.

L-Dopa

Ritvo and colleagues (1971) administered L-dopa, a precursor to DA, to 4 hospitalized autistic boys, aged 3, 4, 9, and 13 years. Following 16 days of placebo, patients were begun on L-dopa (300 to 500 mg/day). Doses were then increased to maximum tolerable daily levels of 2.0 grams, 3.25 grams, 4.0 grams, and 3.25 grams, respectively, administered for 6 months. The dose-limiting factor was the onset of emesis, which began approximately 1 hour after drug administration. Although WBS levels decreased in 3 out of the 4 patients, no changes in behavior were observed.

Campbell and colleagues (1976) also studied the effects of L-dopa in children with autism. Twelve autistic children (10 boys, 2 girls), aged 3 to 6 years (mean, 5.4 years), received L-dopa (mean, 1.49 grams/day) and levoamphetamine (mean, 13.4 mg/day) in a double-blind, crossover design. Each drug was given for an average of 7.5 weeks, and active drug administration was separated by a 4-week placebo washout period. Based on global ratings, 5 children showed improvement, 5 were unchanged, and 2 were worse with L-dopa treatment. The particular therapeutic effects of L-dopa were those involving stimulation of play, energy, and motor initiation in hypoactive children, as well as an increase in language production, vocabulary, and affective responsiveness. Of the 11 children who received levoamphetamine, only 2 showed improvement on the CGI. Clinically significant changes on optimal dosages were minor, if they occurred at all, and were usually outweighed by a worsening of preexisting symptoms.

Amisulpride versus Bromocriptine

Dollfus and Petit (1992) published a study comparing the effects of the DA receptor antagonist amisulpride with those of bromocriptine, a DA receptor agonist, in 9 children with autism (4 girls, 5 boys; age range, 4 to 13 years; mean age, 6.9 years). Following a 1-week single-blind placebo period, patients were randomly assigned to 4 weeks of amisulpride (1.5 mg/kg/day) or bromocriptine (0.15 to 0.20 mg/kg/day). After a 6-week double-blind, placebo-washout period, patients received 4 weeks of the alternate drug. Both treatments were generally well tolerated. Amisulpride was associated with an improvement on the specific autistic scale of the Behavioral Summarized Evaluation (behavioral inhibition and withdrawal symptomatology), and bromocriptine treatment was associated with improvement in symptoms of hyperactivity and inattention on the Connors Parent–Teacher Questionnaire.

Stimulants

Stimulant medications, such as dextroamphetamine and methylphenidate, affect a number of neurotransmitter systems, although their most potent effect is to enhance DA neurotransmission. Reports describing the efficacy of stimulants for treating symptoms of hyperactivity in autistic children are equivocal. As described above, Campbell et al. (1976) found that levoamphetamine worsened negativism in 8 of 11 autistic children, although 5 of 7 subjects who had hyperactivity showed a reduction of that symptom. Strayhorn, Rapp, Donina, and Strain (1988) described a 6-year-old autistic boy who showed improvement in attention and motor hyperactivity, and a reduction in destructive behavior and stereotyped movements on methylphenidate (10 mg twice a day). In addition to these positive effects, however, the child became more depressed and had an increase in temper tantrums. Controlled studies of stimulants in larger numbers of autistic children are needed to determine whether a reduction in inattentiveness and hyperactivity can be consistently attained, and whether these effects outweigh potential increases in negativism and dysphoria.

Risperidone

Risperidone, an atypical neuroleptic agent, is a highly potent DA D2/5-HT2 receptor antagonist (Leysen et al., 1988) that has been shown in controlled clinical trials to have efficacy in improving both the positive and negative symptoms of schizophrenia (Chouinard et al., 1993). In addition, its side effect profile appears superior to those of typical neuroleptics (Moller, Pelzer, Kissling, Riehl, & Wernicke, 1991). A recent controlled study found risperidone significantly better than placebo in reducing persistent behavioral disturbances, when added to existing medication in patients with severe to profound mental retardation (Vanden Borre et al., 1993). We have observed a robust and sustained clinical improvement in several adults with autism-spectrum disorders treated with open-label risperidone (McDougle, Brodkin, et al., 1995). In addition, Purdon, Lit, Labelle, and Jones (1994) described the favorable clinical response to risperidone in two adult males with pervasive developmental disorder and mental retardation. A 30-year-old man showed a marked decrease in ritualistic behaviors, facial grimacing, verbal perseveration, and obsessive preoccupation on a combination of risperidone (8 mg/day), methotrimeprazine (37.5 mg/day), and clonazepam (1 mg/day). The other patient, a 29-year-old man, exhibited a marked decline in psychomotor agitation, self-directed speech, rocking, and facial stereotypies on a combination of risperidone (6 mg/day) and clomipramine (50 mg/day). Results from a recent prospective, open-label study suggest that low-dose risperidone (mean, 1.8 mg/day) may also be helpful to children and adolescents with autism-spectrum disorders (McDougle, Holmes, et al., in press).

Risperidone has been shown to improve the negative symptoms of schizophrenia, including blunted affect, emotional withdrawal, poor rapport, passive/apathetic social withdrawal, difficulty in abstract thinking, lack of spontaneity and flow of conversation, and stereotyped thinking (Chouinard et al., 1993), which is of interest with regard to the impairment in reciprocal social interaction that characterizes autism. It has been hypothesized that the unique ratio of 5-HT2 to DA D2 receptor antagonism, which characterizes risperidone, may account for its efficacy in improving the negative symptoms of schizophrenia and its lack of prominent acute (dystonia, akathisia) and chronic (tardive dyskinesia) extrapyramidal side effects (Moller et al., 1991).

Risperidone has been shown to enhance social interaction behavior in preclinical studies, as well as in clinical populations. In rodents, for example, risperidone significantly increased social interaction behavior between pairs of unfamiliar, but not familiar, rats (Corbett et al., 1993). In contrast, the typical antipsychotic agents haloperidol and chlorpromazine and the selective DA D1 and D2 receptor antagonists, SCH23390 and raclopride, respectively, decreased social behavior in unfamiliar rats. Interestingly, the 5-HT2 receptor antagonist ritanserin had no effect on social behavior in this paradigm. Thus, perhaps a critical ratio of central DA/5-HT neurochemical function is necessary for optimal enhancement of some forms of social interaction behavior.

In addition to impaired social relatedness, it is not uncommon for autistic patients to have interfering repetitive thoughts and behavior. Risperidone has recently been reported to improve repetitive thoughts and behavior in

OCD patients who are unresponsive to the 5-HT uptake inhibitor fluvoxamine (McDougle, Fleischmann, et al., 1995). Importantly, risperidone may be effective in reducing these symptoms in adults with pervasive developmental disorders.

Impulsive aggression is often a presenting complaint for many patients with developmental disabilities. A double-blind, placebo-controlled, crossover study of risperidone addition to the ongoing medication regimen (butyrophenones, phenothiazines, and benzodiazepines) of 37 severely to profoundly mentally retarded patients found the drug significantly more effective than placebo (Vanden Borre et al., 1993). Specifically, improvement was seen in hostility, aggressivity, irritability, agitation, hyperactivity, automutilation, and "autism." The mean dose of risperidone in the study was 8.3 mg/day, and there was no significant difference in extrapyramidal symptoms between risperidone and placebo.

The single-dose pharmacokinetics and safety of risperidone have been previously established in autistic children (Casaer, Walleghem, Vandenbussche, Huang, & De Smedt, 1994). Six children, aged 3 to 7 years, received single oral doses of risperidone (0.015 mg/kg, 3 subjects; 0.030 mg/kg, 3 subjects). No clinically important changes were observed in any of the investigated laboratory and cardiovascular safety parameters, except for a transient increase in heart rate in 2 patients 1 to 2 hours after drug intake. Somnolence was the adverse event that was most frequently reported (5 subjects).

Prospective double-blind, placebo-controlled trials of risperidone are necessary to determine its efficacy in the treatment of patients with autism and other pervasive developmental disorders. These preliminary results suggest, however, that continued investigation into the role of DA and 5-HT in the pathophysiology and treatment of autism are warranted.

Drugs Affecting Norepinephrine Function

Studies investigating norepinephrine (NE) function and the response to drugs that affect this system suggest that NE may not be significantly involved in the pathophysiology and treatment of autistic disorder (Minderaa, Anderson, Volkmar, Akkerhuis, & Cohen, 1994). Although Lake, Ziegler, and Murphy (1977) found elevated levels of plasma NE in autistic patients compared with age-matched controls, not all of these patients were drug-free at the time of the study. Young et al. (1981) showed that levels of plasma-free 3-methoxy-4-hydroxyphenethylene glycol (MHPG), the principal metabolite of brain NE, were no different between autistic patients and normal controls. Gillberg et al. (1983) found no difference in CSF MHPG levels in autistic children compared with control subjects. As mentioned previously, Gordon and colleagues (1993) found the 5-HT uptake inhibitor clomipramine superior to the NE uptake inhibitor desipramine in the treatment of autistic children. Additional studies of drugs that affect NE function are reviewed below.

Beta-Blockers

Beta-blockers are drugs that block NE receptors and reduce overall NE neurotransmission. Ratey and colleagues (Ratey, Bemporad, et al. 1987; Ratey, Mikkelsen, et al., 1987) described a reduction in aggressive, impulsive, and self-injurious behavior, and an improvement in speech and socialization in 8 hospitalized adults with autism who were treated with open-label propranolol or nadolol. Seven of the 8 patients were receiving concomitant neuroleptic or mood-stabilizing drugs during the trial. Patients were started on propranolol or nadolol (40 mg/day) and the dose was increased weekly or biweekly in 40-mg increments until clinical effect or hypotension occurred. Final doses of propranolol ranged from 100 to 420 mg/day (mean, 225 mg/day). The mean duration of treatment at the time of assessment was 14.2 months. All 8 patients showed a moderate to marked reduction in aggressivity, 6 of the 8 improved their social skills and sought more human contact, and 4 of the 8 improved their speech. Five patients were able to have their dose of neuroleptic reduced, and 1 patient was able to discontinue neuroleptic. The authors speculated that the observed clinical improvement was a result of a decrease in chronic hyperarousal.

Clonidine

Clonidine is an alpha-2 noradrenergic receptor agonist that has been shown to decrease NE neurotransmission. In a double-blind, placebo-controlled, crossover study, clonidine was given to 8 autistic boys (age range, 5.0 to 13.4 years; mean, 8.1 years) who demonstrated symptoms of inattention, impulsivity, and hyperactivity, which limited the effectiveness of educational and behavioral interventions (Jaselskis, Cook, Fletcher, & Leventhal, 1992). All of the children had been previously treated with methylphenidate, neuroleptic, or desipramine without effect. Clonidine (0.15 to 0.20 mg/day) or placebo was given 3 times a day for 6 weeks, and, following a 1-week washout, the alternate treatment was given for 6 weeks. Teacher and parent ratings showed modest improvement of hyperactivity and irritability during clonidine treatment. Clinician ratings of behavior during videotaped sessions, however, were not significantly different between clonidine and placebo. Sedation and decreased blood pressure were the most frequent side effects. In addition, many of the patients eventually developed tolerance to the therapeutic effects of clonidine, as well as an associated increase in irritability. The authors concluded that, because of these factors, the use of clonidine to treat symptoms of hyperactivity in autistic children may be limited. Guanfacine is another alpha-2 noradrenergic receptor agonist that has recently been reported to improve comorbid symptoms of Attention Deficit Hyperactivity Disorder in patients with Tourette's Disorder (Chappell et al., 1995). Compared with clonidine, guanfacine may have less sedating and hypotensive effects (Arnstein, Cai, & Goldman-Rakic, 1988).

Drugs Affecting Neuropeptide Function

To date, the opioid system has been the most extensively studied peptidergic system with respect to Autistic Disorder. Weizman et al. (1984) found significantly decreased blood levels of endorphin H in autistic and schizophrenic patients, compared with controls. Gillberg, Terenius, and Lonnerholm (1985) identified elevated CSF endorphin fraction II levels in autistic children in comparison with controls. The 55% of patients with autism who had CSF endorphin levels above the highest control value also demonstrated decreased pain sensitivity. Ross, Klykylo, and Hitzeman (1987), after finding elevated CSF beta-endorphin levels in autistic children compared with controls, hypothesized that a defect in the maturation of brain endorphin systems may underlie some of the symptoms of autism. Adrenocorticotrophic hormone (ACTH) analogs have also received attention as potential treatments for some symptoms of autism.

Naltrexone

In an open-label study, Campbell et al. (1989) evaluated the safety and efficacy of the opiate receptor antagonist naltrexone in 10 hospitalized autistic boys aged 3.4 to 6.5 years (mean, 5.0 years). Following a 2-week baseline period during which behavioral ratings were obtained, patients received single oral doses of naltrexone (0.5 mg/kg/day, 1.0 mg/kg/day, and 2.0 mg/kg/day, in ascending order) once a week. Seven children showed mild sedation and 1 became hypoactive. No changes in liver function tests, electrocardiograms, or vital signs occurred. Naltrexone resulted in a reduction in withdrawal across all three doses, increased verbal production at the 0.5 mg/kg/day dose, and reduced stereotypies at the 2.0 mg/kg/day dose. The authors stated that these changes were independent of the slight and transient sedation that occurred with naltrexone. At baseline, 8 of the 10 children displayed mild to severe aggression, and 5 of the 10 evidenced self-injurious behavior. The authors' clinical impression was that there was only a slight reduction in these behaviors with naltrexone. Overall, 8 of the 10 children were judged to show a positive response to naltrexone.

Borghese and colleagues (1991) studied the acute effects of naltrexone (0.5, 1.0, 1.5, and 2.0 mg/kg) in 13 autistic children. Scores on the Childhood Autism Rating Scale (CARS) were significantly lower in response to the 1.0, 1.5, and 2.0 mg/kg doses of naltrexone, compared with placebo. However, a detailed assessment of eye contact and social avoidance showed no difference between naltrexone and placebo. The authors concluded that these data failed to confirm the hypothesis of opioid involvement in the social dysfunction characteristic of autism. In a study of similar design, this same research group demonstrated that naltrexone was more effective than placebo in reducing the locomotor hyperactivity characteristic of many autistic children (Asleson, Herman, Borghese, Allen, & Arthur-Smith, 1991).

In a double-blind, randomized study, Leboyer et al. (1992) administered naltrexone (0.5 mg/kg/day, 1.0 mg/kg/day, and 2.0 mg/kg/day) and placebo, for 1 week each, to 4 autistic children (3 boys, 1 girl), aged 4, 12, 12, and 19 years. All 4 children had self-injurious behavior. Three patients had elevated levels of blood beta-endorphin at baseline, and each of these children demonstrated a significant improvement in symptoms at the lowest and highest doses of naltrexone. The one patient who had a normal blood level of beta-endorphin showed no clinical improvement. There was no change in behavior during placebo for any of the children, and there were no adverse effects during naltrexone administration. The 3 responders showed increased socialization, improved eye contact, increased verbalization, increased attentiveness, and decreased restlessness and self-injurious behavior.

In a double-blind, placebo-controlled study in 41 autistic children, Campbell et al. (1993) found naltrexone useful only for symptoms of hyperactivity; it had no effect on discrimination learning. The authors reported that there was a suggestion that naltrexone had a beneficial effect on self-injurious behavior, but further study would be necessary. Untoward effects of naltrexone were mild and transient.

Willemsen-Swinkels, Buitclaar, Nijhof, and van Engeland (1995) described a 4-week, double-blind, placebo-controlled trial of naltrexone (50 mg/day or 150 mg/day) in 32 adult subjects (7 with autism, 16 with autism and self-injurious behavior, and 9 with self-injurious behavior alone). Naltrexone had no therapeutic effects on autistic symptoms or self-injurious behavior, and it increased the incidence of stereotypic behavior (Willemsen-Swinkels et al., 1995). In summary, most controlled studies suggest that the core symptoms of autism and self-injurious behavior are not significantly affected by naltrexone. A reduction of motor hyperactivity may occur in some autistic children who receive the drug.

ACTH Analog (Org 2766)

In a double-blind, placebo-controlled, crossover study, Buitelaar, van Engeland, van Ree, and de Wied (1990) studied Org 2766, a synthetic analog of ACTH 4-9, in 14 children with autism. The subchronic administration of ACTH 4-9 had been previously shown to improve mood and to increase gregariousness, sociability, feelings of competence, and cooperation in mentally retarded adults (Sandman, Walker, & Lawton, 1980), although no anxiolytic effects were found in patients with social phobia (den Boer, Westenberg, & De Vries, 1992). Following a 2-week, single-blind, placebo period, Org 2766 (20 mg/day) or placebo was given for 4 weeks in a randomized manner. Patients were then crossed over to the alternate treatment. Org 2766 seemed to have an activating and stimulating effect on behavior, as evidenced by increases in locomotion, changing toys, and talkativeness. A decrease in stereotypic behavior was also observed. Parents rated 11 of the 14 patients as improved, and investigators rated 8 of the 14 patients as showing improvement with Org 2766. No adverse events or side effects were observed. In a subsequent report, Buitelaar et al. (1992) documented an improvement in the coordination of gaze behaviors, resulting in increased eye contact, an increase in mutual smiling, and a decrease in the interactional role of stereotyped behaviors with Org 2766 administration.

SUMMARY

Preliminary evidence suggests that drugs that increase 5-HT neurotransmission, such as the 5-HT uptake inhibitors clomipramine, fluvoxamine, fluoxetine, and sertraline, as well as 5-HT receptor agonists such as buspirone, may be useful in reducing interfering repetitive behavior and aggression and in improving social relatedness in some children and adults with Autistic Disorder. To date, only two controlled studies have been conducted with these drugs.

Clomipramine was found to be more effective than desipramine, a relatively selective NE uptake inhibitor, and placebo for improving the core symptoms of autism, anger, and obsessive-compulsive symptoms in children with autism. Fluvoxamine was superior to placebo for reducing aggressive impulsivity and interfering repetitive thoughts and behavior, and for enhancing social relatedness, particularly language usage, in adults with autism. Clomipramine can lower the seizure threshold and affect cardiac conduction, making it imperative to utilize close monitoring for these adverse effects. Otherwise, these medications are generally well tolerated and are not associated with significant short- or long-term side effects. Double-blind, placebo-controlled trials of clomipramine in autistic adults, and of fluvoxamine in autistic children and adolescents, are necessary to evaluate the impact of brain developmental changes on response to these drugs. Controlled studies of fluoxetine, sertraline, paroxetine, and buspirone in children, adolescents, or adults with autism have yet to be published.

Well-designed controlled studies have demonstrated that DA receptor antagonists such as haloperidol are effective in reducing many of the maladaptive behaviors of autistic children. Because of the relatively high percentage of drug-induced and withdrawal-related dyskinesias associated with this class of drugs, however, safer agents are needed. The recent development of alternative drugs that modulate DA transmission and have significantly lower risks of extrapyramidal side effects and tardive dyskinesia (e.g., risperidone) may prove useful in some patients with Autistic Disorder. Controlled studies of risperidone in children and adults with autism are currently under way. The role of stimulants, such as dextroamphetamine and methylphenidate, for treating symptoms of hyperactivity in autistic children needs to be clarified. Clinical lore has suggested that these agents typically exacerbate restlessness and impulsivity, but recent reports describe more favorable results. Because distractibility and hyperactivity are often prominent interfering symptoms in autistic children, controlled studies of stimulants in larger numbers of patients appear warranted.

Investigations of drugs that affect NE function have not suggested a primary role for these agents in treating the core symptoms of autism. Controlled studies of beta-blockers have not been conducted to determine whether these drugs are useful for reducing aggression and self-injury in patients with Autistic Disorder. Because of the potential for adverse cardiac effects and the availability of safer agents, beta-blockers currently have a limited role in the pharmacotherapy of autism. Studies of the alpha-2 receptor agonist clonidine have suggested that symptoms of hyperactivity might show initial improvement, but tolerance and irritability often develop with ongoing treatment. Controlled studies of guanfacine, which may have less sedating and hypotensive effects than clonidine, are needed to determine its efficacy for improving symptoms of hyperactivity and inattentiveness in autistic children.

The opiate receptor antagonist naltrexone has been shown to be useful in reducing hyperactivity in some children with autism, although recent evidence indicates that its prosocial effects and ability to improve self-injurious and aggressive behavior may be minimal. Preliminary findings suggest that ACTH analogs may play some role in the treatment of impaired social relatedness. Speculation about the prosocial effects of the nonapeptide oxytocin (Insel, 1992) may warrant further thought with respect to autism (Panksepp, 1993).

Cross-Reference

Neurochemical studies of autism are described in Chapter 15.

REFERENCES

American Psychiatric Association. (1987). *Diagnostic and statistical manual of mental disorders* (3rd ed., rev.). Washington, DC: Author.

American Psychiatric Association. (1994). *Diagnostic and statistical manual of mental disorders* (4th ed.). Washington, DC: Author.

Anderson, G.M., Freedman, D.X., Cohen, D.J., Volkmar, F.R., Hoder, E.L., McPhedran, P., Minderaa, R.B., Hansen, C.R., & Young, J.G. (1987). Whole blood serotonin in autistic and normal subjects. *Journal of Child Psychology and Psychiatry, 28,* 885–900.

Anderson, L., & Campbell, M. (1989). The effects of haloperidol on discrimination learning and behavioral symptoms in autistic children. *Journal of Autism and Developmental Disorders, 19,* 227–239.

Anderson, L., Campbell, M., Grega, D., Perry, R., Small, A., & Green, W. (1984). Haloperidol in the treatment of infantile autism: Effects on learning and behavioral symptoms. *American Journal of Psychiatry, 141,* 1195–1202.

Arnstein, A.F.T., Cai, J.X., & Goldman-Rakic, P.S. (1988). The alpha-2 adrenergic agonist, guanfacine improves memory in aged monkeys without sedative or hypotensive side effects: Evidence for alpha-2 receptor subtypes. *Journal of Neuroscience, 8,* 4287–4298.

Asleson, G.S., Herman, B.H., Borghese, I.F., Allen, R.P., & Arthur-Smith, A. (1991). Effects of acute naltrexone on locomotor activity in autistic children. *Society for Neuroscience Abstracts, 17*(2), 1346.

Benfield, P., & Ward, A. (1986). Fluvoxamine: A review of its pharmacodynamic and pharmacokinetic properties, and therapeutic efficacy in depressive illness. *Drugs, 32,* 313–334.

Blier, P., & de Montigny, C. (1985). Short-term lithium administration enhances serotonergic neurotransmission: Electrophysiological evidence in the rat CNS. *European Journal of Pharmacology, 113,* 69–77.

Blier, P., de Montigny, C., & Chaput, Y. (1990). A role for the serotonin system in the mechanism of action of antidepressant treatments: Preclinical evidence. *Journal of Clinical Psychiatry, 51,* 14–20.

Borghese, I.F., Herman, B.H., Asleson, G.S., Chatoor, I., Benoit, M.B., Papero, P., & McNulty, G. (1991). Effects of acutely administered naltrexone on social behavior of autistic children. *Society for Neuroscience Abstracts, 17*(2), 1252.

Brodkin, E.S., McDougle, C.J., Naylor, S.T., Cohen, D.J., & Price, L.H. (1995). Clomipramine in adults with Pervasive Developmental Disorder. *American Psychiatric Association New Research Abstracts, NR76,* 74.

Brown, G.L., Goodwin, F.K., Ballenger, J.C., Goyer, P.F., & Major, L.F. (1979). Aggression in humans correlates with cerebrospinal fluid amine metabolites. *Psychiatry Research, 1,* 131–139.

Buitelaar, J.K., van Engeland, H., de Kogel, K.H., de Vries, H., van Hooff, J.A.R.A.M., & van Ree, J.M. (1992). The use of adrenocorticotrophic hormone (4-9) Analog ORG 2766 in autistic children: Effects on the organization of behavior. *Biological Psychiatry, 31,* 1119–1129.

Buitelaar, J.K., van Engeland, H., van Ree, J.M., & de Wied, D. (1990). Behavioral effects of Org 2766, a synthetic analog of the adrenocorticotrophic hormone (4-9), in 14 outpatient autistic children. *Journal of Autism and Developmental Disorders, 20,* 467–478.

Campbell, M. (1988). Fenfluramine treatment of autism. *Journal of Child Psychology and Psychiatry, 29,* 1–10.

Campbell, M., Adams, P., Perry, R., Spencer, E.K., & Overall, J.E. (1988). Tardive and withdrawal dyskinesia in autistic children: A prospective study. *Psychopharmacology Bulletin, 24,* 251–255.

Campbell, M., Adams, P., Small, A.M., Curren, E.L., Overall, J., Anderson, L.T., Lynch, N., & Perry, R. (1988). Efficacy and safety of fenfluramine in autistic children. *Journal of the American Academy of Child and Adolescent Psychiatry, 27,* 434–439.

Campbell, M., Anderson, L., Meier, M., Cohen, I., Small, A., Samit, C., & Sachar, E. (1978). A comparison of haloperidol and behavior therapy and their interaction in autistic children. *Journal of the American Academy of Child and Adolescent Psychiatry, 17,* 640–655.

Campbell, M., Anderson, L., Small, A.M., Adams, P., Gonzalez, N.M., & Ernst, M. (1993). Naltrexone in autistic children: Behavioral symptoms and attentional learning. *Journal of the American Academy of Child and Adolescent Psychiatry, 32,* 1283–1291.

Campbell, M., Fish, B., Korein, J., Shapiro, T., Collins, P., & Kob, C. (1972). Lithium and chlorpromazine: A controlled crossover study of hyperactive severely disturbed young children. *Journal of Autism and Childhood Schizophrenia, 2,* 234–263.

Campbell, M., Fish, B., Shapiro, T., & Floyd, A.J. (1971). Imipramine in preschool autistic and schizophrenic children. *Journal of Autism and Childhood Schizophrenia, 1,* 267–282.

Campbell, M., Overall, J.E., Small, A.M., Sokol, M.S., Spencer, E.K., Adams, P., Foltz, R.L., Monti, K.M., Perry, R., Nobler, M., & Roberts, E. (1989). Naltrexone in autistic children: An acute open dose range tolerance trial. *Journal of the American Academy of Child and Adolescent Psychiatry, 28,* 200–206.

Campbell, M., Small, A.M., Collins, P.J., Friedman, E., David, R., & Genieser, N. (1976). Levodopa and levoamphetamine: A crossover study in young schizophrenic children. *Current Therapeutic Research, 19,* 70–83.

Casaer, P., Walleghem, D., Vandenbussche, I., Huang, M.-L., & De Smedt, G. (1994). Pharmacokinetics and safety of risperidone in autistic children. *Pediatric Neurology, 11*(2), 89.

Chappell, P.B., Riddle, M.A., Scahill, L., Lynch, K.A., Schultz, R., Arnsten, A., Leckman, J.F., & Cohen, D.J. (1995). Guanfacine treatment of comorbid Attention Deficit Hyperactivity Disorder and Tourette's Syndrome: Preliminary clinical experience. *Journal of the American Academy of Child and Adolescent Psychiatry, 34,* 1140–1146.

Chaput, Y., de Montigny, C., & Blier, P. (1986). Effects of a selective 5-HT uptake blocker, citalopram, on the sensitivity of 5-HT autoreceptors: Electrophysiological studies in the rat. *Naunyn Schmiedebergs Archives of Pharmacology, 333,* 342–345.

Chase, T.M., & Shoulson, I. (1975). Behavioral and biochemical effects of fenfluramine in patients with neurologic disease. *Postgraduate Medical Journal, 51,* 105–109.

Chouinard, G., Jones, B., Remington, G., Bloom, D., Addington, D., MacEwan, G.W., Labelle, A., Beauclair, L., & Arnott, W. (1993). A Canadian multicenter placebo-controlled study of fixed doses of risperidone and haloperidol in the treatment of chronic schizophrenic patients. *Journal of Clinical Psychopharmacology, 13,* 25–40.

Cohen, I.L., Campbell, M., Posner, D., Small, A.M., Triebel, D., & Anderson, L.T. (1980). Behavioral effects of haloperidol in young autistic children. *Journal of the American Academy of Child and Adolescent Psychiatry, 19,* 665–677.

Cook, E.H. (1990). Autism: Review of neurochemical investigation. *Synapse, 6,* 292–308.

Cook, E.H., Perry, B.D., Dawson, G., Wainwright, M.S., & Leventhal, B.L. (1993). Receptor inhibition by immunoglobulins: Specific inhibition by autistic children, their relatives, and control subjects. *Journal of Autism and Developmental Disabilities, 23,* 67–78.

Cook, E.H., Rowlett, R., Jaselskis, C., & Leventhal, B.L. (1992). Fluoxetine treatment of children and adults with Autistic Disorder and mental retardation. *Journal of the American Academy of Child and Adolescent Psychiatry, 31,* 739–745.

Corbett, R., Hartman, H., Kerman, L.L., Woods, A.T., Strupczewski, J.T., Helsley, G.C., Conway, P.C., & Dunn, R.W. (1993). Effects of atypical antipsychotic agents on social behavior in rodents. *Pharmacology, Biochemistry and Behavior, 45,* 9–17.

Delgado, P.L., Price, L.H., Charney, D.S., & Heninger, G.R. (1988). Efficacy of fluvoxamine in treatment of refractory depression. *Journal of Affective Disorders, 15,* 55–60.

de Montigny, C., Cournoyer, G., Morissette, R., Langlois, R., & Caille, G. (1983). Lithium carbonate addition in tricyclic antidepressant-resistant unipolar depression. *Archives of General Psychiatry, 40,* 1327–1334.

den Boer, J.A., Westenberg, H.G.M., & De Vries, H. (1992). The MSH/ACTH analog ORG 2766 in anxiety disorders. *Peptides, 13,* 109–112.

DeVeaugh-Geiss, J., Katz, R., Landau, P., Akiskal, H., Ananth, J., Ballenger, J., Betts, W.C., Diamond, B., Feiger, A., Foa, E., Fogelson, D., Goodman, W., Greist, J., Himmelhoch, J., Hoehn-Saric, R., Jenike, M., Kim, S.W., Liebowitz, M., Mavissakalian, M., Noyes, R., Rasmussen, S., Ringold, A., Shear, K., & The Clomipramine Collaborative Study Group. (1991). Clomipramine in the treatment of patients with Obsessive-Compulsive Disorder. *Archives of General Psychiatry, 48,* 730–738.

Dollfus, S., & Petit, M. (1992). Amisulpride versus bromocriptine in infantile autism: A controlled crossover comparative study of two drugs with opposite effects on dopaminergic function. *Journal of Autism and Developmental Disorders, 22,* 47–60.

Duker, P., Welles, K., Seys, D., Rensen, H., & Vis, A. (1991) Brief report: Effects of fenfluramine on communicative, stereotypic, and inappropriate behaviors of autistic-type mentally handicapped individuals. *Journal of Autism and Developmental Disorders, 21,* 355–363.

Ekman, G., Miranda-Linné, F., Gillberg, C., Garle, M., & Wetterberg, L. (1989). Fenfluramine treatment of twenty children with autism. *Journal of Autism and Developmental Disorders, 19,* 511–532.

El Mansari, M., Bouchard, C., & Blier, P. (1994). Alteration of serotonin release in the orbitofrontal cortex by paroxetine: Relevance to Obsessive-Compulsive Disorder. *Society for Neuroscience Abstracts, 20*(1), 226.

Epperson, C.N., McDougle, C.J., Anand, A., Marek, G.J., Naylor, S.T., Volkmar, F.R., Cohen, D.J., & Price, L.H. (1994). Lithium augmentation of fluvoxamine in Autistic Disorder: A case report. *Journal of Child and Adolescent Psychopharmacology, 4,* 201–207.

Ernst, M., Magee, H.J., Gonzalez, N.M., Locascio, J.J., Rosenberg, C.R., & Campbell, M. (1992). Pimozide in autistic children. *Psychopharmacology Bulletin, 28,* 187–191.

Fish, B., Campbell, M., Shapiro, T., & Floyd, A.J. (1969, August). Schizophrenic children treated with methysergide (Sansert). *Diseases of the Nervous System, 30,* 534–540.

Freeman, B.J., Ritvo, E.R., Yokota, A., & Ritvo, A. (1986). A scale for rating symptoms of patients with the syndrome of autism in real life settings. *Journal of the American Academy of Child and Adolescent Psychiatry, 25,* 130–136.

Garber, H.J., McGonigle, J.J., Slomka, G.T., & Monteverde, E. (1992). Clomipramine treatment of stereotypic behaviors and self-injury in patients with developmental disabilities. *Journal of the American Academy of Child and Adolescent Psychiatry, 31*(6), 1157–1160.

Geller, E., Ritvo, E., Freeman, B., & Yuwiler, A. (1982). Preliminary observations on the effect of fenfluramine on blood serotonin and symptoms in three autistic boys. *New England Journal of Medicine, 307,* 165–169.

Ghaziuddin, M., Tsai, L., & Ghaziuddin, N. (1991). Fluoxetine in autism with depression [letter]. *Journal of the American Academy of Child and Adolescent Psychiatry, 30,* 3.

Gillberg, C., Svennerholm, L., & Hamilton-Hellberg, C. (1983). Childhood psychosis and monoamine metabolites in spinal fluid. *Journal of Autism and Developmental Disorders, 13,* 383–396.

Gillberg, C., Terenius, L., & Lonnerholm, G. (1985). Endorphin activity in childhood psychosis. *Archives of General Psychiatry, 42,* 780–783.

Goodman, W.K., McDougle, C.J., Price, L.H., Riddle, M.A., Pauls, D.L., & Leckman, J.F. (1990). Beyond the serotonin hypothesis: A role for dopamine in some forms of Obsessive Compulsive Disorder? *Journal of Clinical Psychiatry, 51,* 36–43.

Goodman, W.K., Price, L.H., Delgado, P.L., Palumbo, J., Krystal, J.H., Nagy, L.M., Rasmussen, S.A., Heninger, G.R., & Charney, D.S. (1990). Specificity of serotonin reuptake inhibitors in the treatment of Obsessive Compulsive Disorder: Comparison of fluvoxamine and desipramine. *Archives of General Psychiatry, 47,* 577–585.

Goodman, W.K., Price, L.H., Rasmussen, S.A., Delgado, P.L., Heninger, G.R., & Charney, D.S. (1989). Efficacy of fluvoxamine in Obsessive-Compulsive Disorder: A double-blind comparison with placebo. *Archives of General Psychiatry, 46,* 36–43.

Goodman, W.K., Price, L.H., Rasmussen, S.A., Mazure, C., Delgado, P., Heninger, G.R., & Charney, D.S. (1989). The Yale-Brown Obsessive Compulsive Scale (Y-BOCS): Part 2. Validity. *Archives of General Psychiatry, 46,* 1012–1016.

Goodman, W.K., Price, L.H., Rasmussen, S.A., Mazure, C., Fleischmann, R., Hill, C., Heninger, G.R., & Charney, D.S. (1989). The Yale-Brown Obsessive Compulsive Scale (Y-BOCS): Part 1. Development, use, and reliability. *Archives of General Psychiatry, 46,* 1006–1011.

Gordon, C.T., State, R.C., Nelson, J.E., Hamburger, S.D., & Rapoport, J.L. (1993). A double-blind comparison of clomipramine, desipramine, and placebo in the treatment of Autistic Disorder. *Archives of General Psychiatry, 50,* 441–447.

Greist, J., Chouinard, G., DuBoff, E., Halaris, A., Kim, S.W., Koran, L., Liebowitz, M., Lydiard, R.B., Rasmussen, S., White, K., & Sikes, C. (1995). Double-blind parallel comparison of three dosages of sertraline and placebo in outpatients with Obsessive-Compulsive Disorder. *Archives of General Psychiatry, 52,* 289–295.

Guy, W. (1976). *ECDEU assessment manual for psychopharmacology* (NIMH Publication No. 76-338). Washington, DC: U.S. Department of Health, Education and Welfare, National Institute of Mental Health.

Hamdan-Allen, G. (1991). Brief report: Trichotillomania in an autistic male. *Journal of Autism and Developmental Disorders, 21,* 79–82.

Hoshino, Y., Tachibana, J.R., Watanabe, M., Murata, S., Yokoyama, F., Kaneko, M., Yashima, Y., & Kumoshiro, H. (1984). Serotonin metabolism and hypothalamic-pituitary function in children with infantile autism and minimal brain dysfunction. *Japanese Journal of Psychiatry and Neurology, 26,* 937–945.

Insel, T.R. (1992). Oxytocin—A neuropeptide for affiliation: Evidence from behavioral, receptor autoradiographic, and comparative studies. *Psychoneuroendocrinology, 17,* 3–35.

Jaselskis, C.A., Cook, E.H., Jr., Fletcher, K.E., & Leventhal, B.L. (1992). Clonidine treatment of hyperactive and impulsive children with Autistic Disorder. *Journal of Clinical Psychopharmacology, 12,* 322–327.

Kelley, L.A., Hellings, J.A., Gabrielli, W.F., & Kilgore, E. (1993). Sertraline response in mentally retarded adults. *American Psychiatric Association New Research Abstracts, NR173,* 103.

Kerbeshian, J., Burd, L., & Fisher, W. (1987). Lithium carbonate in the treatment of two patients with infantile autism and atypical bipolar symptomatology. *Journal of Clinical Psychopharmacology,* 401–405.

Kruesi, M.J., Hibbs, E.D., Zahn, T.P., Keysor, C.S., Hamburger, S.D., Bartko, J.J., & Rapoport, J.L. (1992). A 2-year prospective follow-up study of children and adolescents with disruptive behavior disorders: Prediction by cerebrospinal fluid 5-hydroxyindoleacetic acid, homovanillic acid, and autonomic measures? *Archives of General Psychiatry, 49,* 429–435.

Kruesi, M.J., Rapoport, J.L., Hamburger, S., Hibbs, E., Potter, W.Z., Lenane, M., & Brown, G.L. (1990). Cerebrospinal fluid monoamine metabolites, aggression, and impulsivity in disruptive behavior disorders of children and adolescents. *Archives of General Psychiatry, 47,* 419–426.

Krug, D.A., Arick, J.R., & Almond, P.J. (1980). *Autism screening instrument for education planning.* Portland, OR: ASIEP Educational.

Lake, C.R., Ziegler, M.G., & Murphy, D.L. (1977). Increased norepinephrine levels and decreased dopamine-β-hydroxylase activity in primary autism. *Archives of General Psychiatry, 34,* 553–556.

Leboyer, M., Bouvard, M.P., Launay, J.-M., Tabuteau, F., Waller, D., Dugas, M., Kerdelhue, B., Lensing, P., & Panksepp, J. (1992). Brief report: A double-blind study of naltrexone in infantile autism. *Journal of Autism and Developmental Disorders, 22,* 309–319.

Le Couteur, A., Rutter, M., Lord, C., Rios, P., Robertson, S., Holdgrafer, M., & McLennan, J. (1989). Autism Diagnostic Interview: A standardized investigator-based instrument. *Journal of Autism and Developmental Disorders, 19,* 363–387.

Leiter, R.G. (1948). *Leiter International Performance Scale.* Chicago, IL: Stoelting.

Leventhal, B.L., Cook, E.H., Morford, M., Ravitz, A.J., Heller, W., & Freedman, D.X. (1993). *Journal of Neuropsychiatry and Clinical Neurosciences, 5,* 307–315.

Leysen, J.E., Gommeren, W., Eens, A., De Chaffoy De Courcelles, D., Stoof, J.C., & Janssen, P.A.J. (1988). Biochemical profile of risperidone, a new antipsychotic. *Journal of Pharmacology and Experimental Therapeutics, 247,* 661–670.

Linnoila, M., Virkkunen, M., Scheinin, M., Nuutila, A., Rimon, R., & Goodwin, F.K. (1983). Low cerebrospinal fluid 5-hydroxyindoleacetic acid concentration differentiates impulsive from nonimpulsive violent behavior. *Life Sciences, 33,* 2609–2614.

Lipinski, J.F., Jr. (1991). Clomipramine in the treatment of self-mutilating behaviors [letter]. *New England Journal of Medicine, 324,* 1441.

Lord, C., Rutter, M., Goode, S., Heemsbergen, J., Jordan, H., Mawhood, L., & Schopler, E. (1989). Autism Diagnostic Observation Schedule: A standardized observation of communicative and social behavior. *Journal of Autism and Developmental Disorders, 19,* 185–212.

Markowitz, P.I. (1992). Effect of fluoxetine on self-injurious behavior in the developmentally disabled: A preliminary study. *Journal of Clinical Psychopharmacology, 12,* 27–31.

McBride, P.A., Anderson, G.M., Hertzig, M.E., Sweeney, J.A., Kream, J., Cohen, D.J., & Mann, J.J. (1989). Serotonergic responsivity in male young adults with Autistic Disorder: Results of a pilot study. *Archives of General Psychiatry, 46,* 213–221.

McDougle, C.J., Brodkin, E.S., Naylor, S.T., Carlson, D.C., Cohen, D.J., & Price, L.H. (1997). *Sertraline in adults with pervasive developmental disorders.* Unpublished data.

McDougle, C.J., Brodkin, E.S., Yeung, P.P., Naylor, S.T., Cohen, D.J., & Price, L.H. (1995). Risperidone in adults with autism or pervasive developmental disorder. *Journal of Child and Adolescent Psychopharmacology, 5*(4), 273–282.

McDougle, C.J., Fleischmann, R.L., Epperson, C.N., Wasylink, S., Leckman, J.F., & Price, L.H. (1995). Risperidone addition in fluvoxamine-refractory Obsessive Compulsive Disorder: Three cases. *Journal of Clinical Psychiatry, 56,* 526–528.

McDougle, C.J., Holmes, J.P., Bronson, M.R., Anderson, G.M., Volkmar, F.R., Price, L.H., & Cohen, D.J. (in press). Risperidone treatment of children and adolescents with pervasive developmental disorders: A prospective open-label study. *Journal of the American Academy of Child and Adolescent Psychiatry.*

McDougle, C.J., Kresch, L.E., Goodman, W.K., Naylor, S.T., Volkmar, F.R., Cohen, D.J., & Price, L.H. (1995). A case-controlled study of repetitive thoughts and behavior in adults with Autistic Disorder and Obsessive-Compulsive Disorder. *American Journal of Psychiatry, 152,* 772–777.

McDougle, C.J., Naylor, S.T., Cohen, D.J., Aghajanian, G.K., Heninger, G.R., & Price, L.H. (1996). Effects of tryptophan depletion in drug-free adults with autistic disorder. *Archives of General Psychiatry, 53,* 993–1000.

McDougle, C.J., Naylor, S.T., Cohen, D.J., Volkmar, F.R., Heninger, G.R., & Price, L.H. (1996). A double-blind, placebo-controlled study of fluvoxamine in adults with autistic disorder. *Archives of General Psychiatry, 53,* 1001–1008.

McDougle, C.J., Price, L.H., & Goodman, W.K. (1990). Fluvoxamine treatment of coincident Autistic Disorder and Obsessive Compulsive Disorder: A case report. *Journal of Autism and Developmental Disorders, 20,* 537–543.

McDougle, C.J., Price, L.H., & Volkmar, F.R. (1994). Recent advances in the pharmacotherapy of autism and related conditions. In

F.R. Volkmar (Ed.), *Child and Adolescent Psychiatric Clinics of North America, 3*(1), Psychoses and pervasive developmental disorders, (pp. 71–89). Philadelphia: Saunders.

McDougle, C.J., Price, L.H., Volkmar, F.R., Goodman, W.K., Ward-O'Brien, D., Nielsen, J., Bregman, J., & Cohen, D.J. (1992). Clomipramine in autism: Preliminary evidence of efficacy. *Journal of the American Academy of Child and Adolescent Psychiatry, 31,* 746–750.

Mehlinger, R., Scheftner, W.A., & Poznanski, E. (1990). Fluoxetine and autism [letter]. *Journal of the American Academy of Child and Adolescent Psychiatry, 29,* 985.

Mehlman, P.T., Higley, J.D., Faucher, I., Lilly, A.A., Taub, D.M., Vickers, J., Suomi, S.J., & Linnoila, M. (1994). Low CSF 5-HIAA concentrations and severe aggression and impaired impulse control in nonhuman primates. *American Journal of Psychiatry, 151,* 1485–1491.

Minderaa, R.B., Anderson, G.M., Volkmar, F.R., Akkerhuis, G.W., & Cohen, D.J. (1994). Noradrenergic and adrenergic functioning in autism. *Biological Psychiatry, 36,* 237–241.

Moller, H.J., Pelzer, E., Kissling, W., Riehl, T., & Wernicke, T. (1991). Efficacy and tolerability of a new antipsychotic compound (risperidone): Results of a pilot study. *Pharmacopsychiatry, 24,* 185–189.

Naruse, H., Nagahata, M., Nakane, Y., Shirahashi, K., Takesada, M., & Yamazaki, K. (1982). A multi-center double-blind trial of pimozide (Orap), haloperidol and placebo in children with behavior disorders, using crossover design. *Acta Paedopsychiatrica, 48,* 173–184.

Panksepp, J. (1993). Commentary on the possible role of oxytocin in autism [letter]. *Journal of Autism and Developmental Disorders, 23,* 567–569.

Perry, R., Campbell, M., Adams, P., Lynch, N., Spencer, E.K., Curren, E.L., & Overall, J.E. (1989). Long-term efficacy of haloperidol in autistic children: Continuous versus discontinuous drug administration. *Journal of the American Academy of Child and Adolescent Psychiatry, 28,* 87–92.

Price, L.H., & Heninger, G.R. (1994). Lithium in the treatment of mood disorders. *New England Journal of Medicine, 331,* 591–598.

Purdon, S.E., Lit, W., Labelle, A., & Jones, D.W. (1994). Risperidone in the treatment of Pervasive Developmental Disorder. *Canadian Journal of Psychiatry, 39,* 400–405.

Raleigh, M.J., Brammer, G.L., Yuwiler, A., Flannery, J.W., McGuire, M.T., & Geller, E. (1980). Serotonergic influences on the social behavior of vervet monkeys (Cercopithecus aethiops sabaeus). *Experimental Neurology, 68,* 322–324.

Ratey, J.J., Bemporad, J., Sorgi, P., Bick, P., Polakoff, S., O'Driscoll, G., & Mikkelsen, E. (1987). Brief report: Open trial effects of beta-blockers on speech and social behaviors in 8 autistic adults. *Journal of Autism and Developmental Disorders, 17,* 439–446.

Ratey, J.J., Mikkelsen, E., Sorgi, P., Zuckerman, H.S., Polakoff, S., Bemporad, J., Bick, P., & Kadish, W. (1987). Autism: The treatment of aggressive behaviors. *Journal of Clinical Psychopharmacology, 7*(1), 35–41.

Ratey, J.J., Sovner, R., Mikkelsen, E., & Chmielinski, H.E. (1989). Buspirone therapy for maladaptive behavior and anxiety in developmentally disabled persons. *Journal of Clinical Psychiatry, 50,* 382–384.

Realmuto, G.M., August, G.J., & Garfinkel, B.D. (1989). Clinical effect of buspirone in autistic children. *Journal of Clinical Psychopharmacology, 9,* 122–125.

Ritvo, E.R., Freeman, B.J., Geller, E., & Yuwiler, A. (1983). Effects of fenfluramine on 14 outpatients with the syndrome of autism. *Journal of the American Academy of Child and Adolescent Psychiatry, 22,* 549–558.

Ritvo, E.R., Freeman, B.J., Yuwiler, A., Geller, E., Schroth, P., Yokota, A., Mason-Brothers, A., August, G.J., Klykylo, W., Leventhal, B., Lewis, K., Piggott, L., Realmuto, G., Stubbs, E.G., & Umansky, R. (1986). Fenfluramine treatment of autism: UCLA collaborative study of 81 patients at nine medical centers. *Psychopharmacology Bulletin, 22,* 133–140.

Ritvo, E.R., Yuwiler, A., Geller, E., Kales, A., Rashkis, S., Schicor, A., Plotkin, S., Axelrod, R., & Howard, C. (1971). Effects of L-dopa in autism. *Journal of Autism and Childhood Schizophrenia, 1*(2), 190–205.

Ross, D.L., Klykylo, W.M., & Hitzemann, R. (1987). Reduction of elevated CSF beta-endorphin by fenfluramine in infantile autism. *Pediatric Neurology, 3,* 83–86.

Rubenstein, J.L.R., Lotspeich, L., & Ciaranello, R.D. (1990). The neurobiology of developmental disorders. In B.B. Lahey & A.E. Kazdin (Ed.), *Advances in clinical child psychology* (Vol. 13, pp. 1–52), New York: Plenum Press.

Sandman, C.A., Walker, B.B., & Lawton, C.A. (1980). An analog of MSH/ACTH 4-9 enhances interpersonal and environmental awareness in mentally retarded adults. *Peptides, 1,* 109–114.

Schain, R.J., & Freedman, D.X. (1961). Studies on 5-hydroxyindole metabolism in autistic and other mentally retarded children. *Journal of Pediatrics, 58,* 315–320.

Schuster, C., Lewis, M., & Seiden, L. (1986). Fenfluramine: Neurotoxicity. *Psychopharmacology Bulletin, 22,* 148–151.

Sherman, J., Factor, D., Swinson, R., & Darjes, R. (1989). The effects of fenfluramine (hydrochloride) on the behaviors of fifteen autistic children. *Journal of Autism and Developmental Disorders, 19,* 533–543.

Smalley, S.L., McCracken, J., & Tanguay, P. (1995). Autism, affective disorders, and social phobia. *American Journal of Medical Genetics (Neuropsychiatric Genetics), 60,* 19–26.

Snead, R.W., Boon, F., & Presberg, J. (1994). Paroxetine for self-injurious behavior [letter]. *Journal of the American Academy of Child and Adolescent Psychiatry, 33*(6), 909–910.

Sparrow, S.S., Balla, D.A., & Cicchetti, D.V. (1984). *Vineland Adaptive Behavior Scales* (A revision of the Vineland Social Maturity Scale by Edgar A. Doll). Circle Pines, MN: American Guidance Service.

Steingard, R., & Biederman, J. (1987). Lithium responsive manic-like symptoms in two individuals with autism and mental retardation: Case report. *Journal of the American Academy of Child and Adolescent Psychiatry, 26,* 932–935.

Strayhorn, J.M., Rapp, N., Donina, W., & Strain, P.S. (1988). Randomized trial of methylphenidate for an autistic child. *Journal of the American Academy of Child and Adolescent Psychiatry, 27,* 244–247.

Todd, R.D. (1991). Fluoxetine in autism [letter]. *American Journal of Psychiatry, 148,* 1089.

Todd, R.D., & Ciaranello, R.D. (1985). Demonstration of inter- and intraspecies differences in serotonin binding sites by antibodies from an autistic child. *Proceedings of the National Academy of Sciences USA, 82,* 612–616.

Tollefson, G.D., Rampey, A.H., Jr., Potvin, J.H., Jenike, M.A., Rush, A.J., Dominguez, R.A., Koran, L.M., Shear, M.K., Goodman, W., & Genduso, L.A. (1994). A multicenter investigation of fixed-dose fluoxetine in the treatment of Obsessive-Compulsive Disorder. *Archives of General Psychiatry, 51,* 559–567.

Vanden Borre, R., Vermote, R., Buttiëns, M., Thiry, P., Dierick, G., Geutjens, J., Sieben, G., & Heylen, S. (1993). Risperidone as add-on therapy in behavioural disturbances in mental retardation: A double-blind placebo-controlled cross-over study. *Acta Psychiatrica Scandinavia, 87,* 167–171.

van Vliet, I.M., den Boer, J.A., & Westenberg, H.G.M. (1994). Psychopharmacological treatment of social phobia: A double-blind placebo-controlled study with fluvoxamine. *Psychopharmacology, 115,* 128–134.

Volkmar, F.R. (1987). Social development. In D. Cohen & A. Donnellan (Eds.), *Handbook of autism and pervasive developmental disorders* (pp. 41–60). New York: John Wiley & Sons.

Volkmar, F.R., & Nelson, D.S. (1990). Seizure disorders in autism. *Journal of the American Academy of Child and Adolescent Psychiatry, 1,* 127–129.

Wechsler, D. (1981). *Manual for the Wechsler Adult Intelligence Scale-Revised.* San Antonio, TX: Psychological Corp.

Weizman, R., Weizman, A., Thano, S., Szekely, G., Weissman, B.A., & Sarne, Y. (1984). Humoral-endorphin blood levels in autistic, schizophrenic and healthy subjects. *Psychopharmacology, 82,* 368–370.

Willemsen-Swinkels, S.H.N., Buitelaar, J.K., Nijhof, G.J., & van Engeland, H. (1995). Failure of naltrexone hydrochloride to reduce self-injurious and autistic behavior in mentally retarded adults: Double-blind placebo-controlled studies. *Archives of General Psychiatry, 52,* 766–773.

Young, J.G., Cohen, D.J., Kavanagh, M.E., Landis, H.D., Shaywitz, B.A., & Maas, J.W. (1981). Cerebrospinal fluid, plasma, and urinary MHPG in children. *Life Sciences, 28,* 2837–2845.

Yuwiler, A., Shih, J.C., Chen, C.-H., Ritvo, E.R., Hanna, G., Ellison, G.W., & King, B.H. (1992). Hyperserotoninemia and antiserotonin antibodies in autism and other disorders. *Journal of Autism and Developmental Disorders, 22,* 33–45.

CHAPTER 33

Routine Health Care

ROBERT G. LA CAMERA AND ANN COBB LA CAMERA

The patient with autism or other pervasive developmental disorders differs little from other patients in his or her need for good and comprehensive health care. In many ways, evaluation and care are no more difficult than for children with no autistic tendencies. However, the history, approach to the patient, physical evaluation, and type of treatment must be considered in the broad context of autism, to enable provision of appropriate and effective medical care.

The examiner or primary caregiver always must be aware of the autistic patient's similarities—in physical structure, developmental advances and plateaus, and even many behavioral patterns—to children without developmental disorders, but also must be alert to the uniqueness of the autistic patient and the very broad dimensions of variation within the diagnosis of pervasive developmental disorders.

Wing (1972) has indicated that variations in behavior and development occur similarly in the normal and in the autistic child. The normal child eventually discards the abnormal variations, however, whereas the autistic child may retain them for many years. An understanding of this observation will provide guidance to families and other appropriate persons during diagnosis and supervision of health care.

MEDICAL HISTORY

Medical personnel must listen to the "family" of the patient when assessing the health of a child or adult. The family may be the blood or adoptive relatives, the current caregivers in a residential or day school program, or others who have tangential but important relationships to the patient. All may provide valuable information about the patient's daily and episodic health. For the primary caregiver, usually a person who has been supervising health care since the child was young, much of the past and continuing history already will be known; however, the family needs to provide an accurate and thorough updating on occasion.

The history rarely can be provided by the patient, regardless of age or ability to communicate. A careful review of past and family history can be more revealing than the physical examination (Dalldorf, 1993), both in the early years when the diagnosis is being determined and in later years when general health issues are being delineated.

Should the autistic child be admitted to a school or a residential community, the past history becomes an imperative part of admission. It should be available to the school in advance and certainly no later than on the day the child arrives. The child's usual pattern of response to infection, allergies, food idiosyncrasies, neurological history with emphasis on seizures (even if none has occurred in recent years), current medications of any type, history of surgery or injury even if well healed, and complete immunization record should be available along with psychological and developmental reports. This information may need revision when events (e.g., unusual illness, reactions to medication, stresses in the life of the patient such as severe illness or death in the family, change in caregiver status) occur that may affect the physical and emotional well-being of the patient.

PHYSICAL ASSESSMENT

The following description of physical assessment is presented in the order of a routine examination of an autistic child or adult. Patients with autism vary in severity of impairment. The examiner must be flexible and adjust the order of examination to the individual patient's reactions and behavior on the day of assessment.

The examination begins as the patient enters the medical office. The patient's mode of entering the waiting room should be observed closely, including fine and gross motor movements; how the patient relates to and communicates with the accompanying caregiver; what he or she is doing while waiting (picking up a toy or magazine, playing with it appropriately or inappropriately, relating or not relating to others in the room), and how the patient responds to the office staff.

Observations about the patient's entry into the examination room provide information. How does he or she respond to the examiner? Is the patient willing to be weighed and measured? How does he or she climb onto the scale, onto the examination table?

The physician's approach is important. A brusque entrance into the room can alarm the patient, especially if the examiner is unfamiliar. Quick movements during the examination frequently are upsetting to children without developmental disorders and are more so to an autistic child or adult. Many autistic patients are tactilely defensive, and an attempt to place hands on the patient is more successful if the approach is cautious, yet confident. An easy reaching out to the patient, with open hands, unencumbered by examining instruments and accompanied by easy conversation with the patient and caregiver, often predisposes the patient to see the physician as a friend rather than as an adversary.

Despite a careful approach, the examiner may be confronted by an intimidating patient. Awkward patients may suddenly grab those within reach. It is crucial that the examiner, except in dire emergencies, have present an assistant who knows the patient. This calms the patient and enables the examiner to proceed with more concentration on the patient. The caregiver can distract the patient when

necessary, try various kinds of communication, and, together with the examiner, demonstrate to the patient the kinds of movements that are essential to the examination. If the patient is not compliant with a request to sit on a chair or an examining table, the examiner may need to go to the patient, that is, examine the patient wherever he or she is located in the room. When an evaluation must be made while a patient is medicated, a repeat or continuation of the examination may need to be arranged at a future date.

It is advantageous for the patient to undress himself or herself in the presence of the examiner, to allow observation of motor skills, effect of physical movement on respiration, and general affect while following (or disregarding) instructions.

Brief explanations of what is occurring during the various phases of the examination often are helpful in eliciting the cooperation of the patient. If information about size is less important than a cardiac assessment in an unwilling patient, skip the height and weight until another opportunity is present. It is best to examine areas that require "invasion" (e.g., ears and mouth) at the end of the examination, just as one would for an anxious toddler.

REVIEW OF SYSTEMS

Skin and Dermatologic Problems

The skin is a vulnerable area of self-abuse. The hands and lower arms often are the sites of callus formation or open lesions caused by biting. Infection of the lesions is common. The areas and lymph nodes proximal to the lesion must be observed frequently for signs of inflammation, because the warning symptom of pain may not be communicated by the autistic patient.

Insect bites, contact inflammations such as poison ivy, and burns need to be looked for on a regular basis to ensure adequate treatment. Topical treatment and dressings may not be feasible: ointments frequently are licked off, and dressings may be pulled off and even swallowed. Dressings and lesions attract attention, often resulting in the patient's picking at the skin, delaying healing. Warm-water play often is the only way an autistic patient will permit moist heat application to a lesion. Elbow restraints can be effective but should be used only when they do not interfere with a training or behavior modification program.

Less vigorous treatment with close observation over a longer period of time may be preferable to intensive treatment over a short time span but resulting in poor patient acceptance or modification of program.

Mild acne requires no special treatment. Moderate to severe acne deserves help. Good skin cleansing without irritation plus careful use of topical medications, such as benzoyl peroxide and retinoic acid A, or oral medications, such as tetracycline and isotretinoin (Tunnessen, 1984), can be effective. Increased sun exposure requires close monitoring of these medications because they induce heightened susceptibility to the harmful effects of direct sunlight. Careful evaluation of the appropriate therapeutic approach should be discussed with the caregiver, dermatologist, and primary medical personnel before a program is begun.

Chest and Heart

The chest and heart examination can be very simple or may require ingenuity. If the patient becomes willing to have a stethoscope placed on his or her chest, he or she may still be unwilling or unable to cooperate in producing deep respirations. Extraneous noises produced at will by the patient interfere with auscultation, and great perseverance is required to obtain even fleeting moments of clear observation. A patient may permit random contact with an instrument but refuse human contact to evaluate radial pulses.

Blood pressure is difficult to determine when agitation results from unfamiliarity with the examiner or equipment. The best tactic is an easy, slow approach when applying the cuff; repeated attempts at inflation, which provide familiarity with the procedure; and arranging for the presence of a familiar caregiver to assist in communicating with and calming the patient. The actual reading may be impossible using the threatening stethoscope, and visual reading of the gauge may be a necessary compromise.

Gastrointestinal Examination

Because most of the abdominal examination is by palpation or percussion after simple observation and auscultation, history is crucial if the tactilely defensive posture of the patient prevents even percussion. Abdominal ultrasound studies should be reserved for the more serious concerns.

Bowel movements should be examined at least grossly on occasion. Blood from fissures or higher lesions usually is ignored by the patient. Diarrhea, because of frequency, odor, and occasional accident, is more likely to be discovered. Persistence of postprandial pain might indicate *Giardia lamblia* infestation, and bowel movement examination for parasites of all types is indicated if unexplained behavioral changes occur.

Examination of the anal area should be part of a routine assessment. Fissures, external hemorrhoids, venereal warts, and other surface lesions do not require the "invasive" examining finger for diagnosis. The warts may be the only clue that sexual contact is occurring. Too often, the assumption is made that the rather sequestered lifestyle of an autistic person precludes sexual involvement, either heterosexual or homosexual. Family members and trusted caregivers should not be excluded from an expected involvement; they have more contact with and often receive more trust from the patient than casual visitors can earn.

Genitalia

Genitalia need evaluation on a regular basis. Patients should be checked for hernias, specific or nonspecific discharge, and irritation or scratches, which can be masturbatory or caused by another's contact.

The testicles and penis should have regular evaluation. Because the autistic young man usually is unaware of lumps and masses, a caregiver should be taught to observe and examine the genitalia fairly frequently (for abnormalities such as scrotal masses, changes in testicular size, and true genital tenderness) and not rely on the annual physical assessment. The observation can be done casually during dressing, changing into bathing suits, and so on. It need not be an attention-drawing project. When hernias or hydrocele are present, should they be repaired? The potential for strangulation of a hernia is greater with autistic men and women, because they may not recognize or communicate their discomfort. Emergencies like strangulation require treatment with as considerate care as possible, usually with a familiar caregiver around for communication and comforting presence.

The gynecologic assessment for young adolescents need not include a complete gynecologic examination or Papanicolaou smear if the patient is not sexually active (Goldfarb, 1983). At the assessment of older adolescents and young women for vaginal discharge or other gynecologic variations, a more complete examination of the pelvis or other invasive procedure (with occasional demonstration, if warranted) is desirable and may be necessary for an accurate exam (Dahlquist, Gil, Kalfus, Blount, & Boyd, 1984).

The preteen can have almost cyclic abdominal pain, usually in the right ovarian area, long before the onset of menarche but rarely requiring therapy. Painful menstruation can be minimized by analgesic medication taken at the *beginning* of discomfort. Menstrual irregularities with accompanying mood changes and anemia can be as upsetting to autistic young women and caregivers as to nonautistic women (Blackwell, 1979).

The approach of menarche is anticipated with dread by many parents. Will periods be "normal" in length or flow? Will there be distress that cannot be communicated well by the developing young woman? Even with instruction, will she be able to care for herself? Will her caregivers at school or at an institution keep her clean? Will she be abused and even sexually molested? Can she or will she become pregnant? Should she be prevented from conceiving? If so, by what method? Can she or should she be sterilized? What are the moral or legal implications?

The elective surgical or other medical procedure demands careful consideration. The difficulty of explaining and coping with hospitalization, discomfort, probability of restraints, and IV tubing all contribute to critical questions: Is this procedure really necessary? Can it be accomplished with relative ease or at least with careful planning? Will the end result be worthwhile?

The trend toward outpatient surgery should benefit an already defensive and communication-poor autistic surgical patient. Decreasing the hours away from the familiar home or facility and the number of "strange" hospital contacts is possible with carefully planned and controlled one-day surgery.

Orthopedic Examination

Orthopedic assessment evaluates bone and joint structure, musculature, and postural variations that may be behavioral or true physical abnormalities. Fractures and other injuries do occur even among the rather sedentary autistic population. As more programs for autistic children and adults develop, injuries will increase. At such well-supervised activities as the commendable Special Olympics, injuries are more likely to be noticed quickly. The child or adult who frequently is independent of a supervised group may be injured while essentially alone and unnoticed by the responsible adult. It is not uncommon for a fracture to remain undetected until callus formation is present. Therefore, routine observation of body structure and movement by the patient's family, school, or workshop advocate is recommended.

Most injuries should be handled as one would handle those of any patient, including casting when indicated. If the patient is tempted to remove supports and bandages, casting may be necessary to maintain position, even though it ordinarily would not be used in such circumstances.

Simple pes planus and/or pronation require no correction if asymptomatic. Some gait abnormalities are the result of poor motor skills or behavioral patterns, and usually do not require or benefit from shoe correction. Correction of shoes or addition of orthotics should be considered to assist a structurally abnormal extremity, especially if symptomatic.

Scoliosis presents a dilemma. Mild structural scoliosis usually will require no treatment. Scoliosis due to leg length inequality may require only a simple shoe lift. Moderate to severe scoliosis that might require exercises, bracing, or surgery presents a difficult choice. Many autistic children will not be able to perform the necessary exercises with consistency. If bracing is required, compliance in wearing the brace is a necessity. The reasoning for wearing a brace is difficult to convey to many autistic children; for some, such a device might be considered a "shackle" or at least a punishment.

Should the autistic child be subject to major scoliosis surgery and prolonged convalescence? If not corrected, the deformity often increases to the point of impingement on pulmonary function and back pain. Yet, surgery usually does not correct the curvature completely, and subsequent surgery, with associated increased risk and difficulty, may be necessary. Each scoliotic patient must be evaluated individually, with assessment at intervals no longer than 6 months during the teenage growing years and more frequently in rapidly changing children.

Postural scoliosis is more apparent than real. Close observation will reveal the changing patterns in muscle position on a behavioral rather than a structural basis. It is the examiner's responsibility to rule out organic causes, including muscle pain and spasm, when changes occur.

Neurologic Examination

The diagnosis of autism does not preclude the presence of associated neurologic disorders. The classic neurologic examination should be part of any routine physical assessment. Even though it may not provide information clarifying a diagnosis or assisting in treatment plans, it does provide a baseline for evaluating changes. The autistic child's occasional lack of response to pain and other tactile sensations requires the examiner to be very patient, observant, and even ingenious.

Behavioral changes always should suggest the possibility of a variation in neurologic status. Even if no definite seizures are observed, these and other pathologies, such as neoplasm, abscesses, vascular anomaly, and so on, should be ruled out by careful history and laboratory studies.

Medication and treatment to control neurologic disease must be chosen to suit the total needs and program of the patient. It may be necessary *not* to treat nonthreatening neurological disease, to avoid detrimental effects of treatment.

Eyes

The eyes pose special problems for the medical team. Accurate assessment of vision can be very important in planning programs, especially fine-motor-skill activity. Testing visual acuity by the usual methods, however, can be very trying and even impossible. Techniques (e.g., STYCAR) used in assessing vision in young, nonverbal children can help (Accardo & Capute, 1979).

A very simple aid to the assessment of visual acuity is the Benhaven Eye Chart (see Figure 33.1), which is similar to the standard chart but differs in utilizing uncomplicated figures (such as an ice cream cone or a ball)

Notice: This 8-inch × 13-inch chart should be viewed at 15 feet.

Figure 33.1   The Benhaven eye chart.

often found in daily life and identified readily by many autistic persons. The person being examined stands 15 feet from the eye chart and covers one eye at a time with a wooden cooking spoon. When the examiner points first to a large figure and then to other figures of diminishing size the examinee attempts to identify the figures verbally or by sign language.

Obvious injury or infection on the surface of the eye can be identified readily, although many autistic patients will not permit close inspection, let alone the use of an ophthalmoscope or even a magnifying glass. Instillation of drops, ointment application, or even bathing the eye can be as difficult as maintaining a dressing on the eye, unless restraints are used.

Close observation to determine the presence of injury to the interior of the eye is of great importance. Self-abusive behavior may result in hitting of the eye with the hand or fist, and an interior hemorrhage can occur without evidence externally. The autistic patient may not indicate that vision is distorted or pain is present, Even if hemorrhage is suspected, ophthalmoscopic examination of the interior of the eye may be impossible without sedation or even anesthesia.

External examination to determine internal hemorrhage can be assisted by the use of the ophthalmoscope set at 0 or +1 and held about 3 feet from the eye. A normal red reflex on the unaffected eye contrasts with a dark reflex on the suspect eye.

The afferent or Marcus-Gunn pupil defect is present essentially when there is an ailment such as major retinal disease or injury, whose ultimate effect is on the optic nerve. A light directed to the pupil of the suspected diseased eye results in both pupils being larger. A light directed to the suspected normal eye causes both pupils to be smaller.

Ears

The ears are one of the last areas evaluated, because, for greatest accuracy, the auditory canal usually must be "invaded" by an ear speculum. Very rarely can a satisfactory exam be made using an ordinary flashlight, though if the canal is large and rather straight, a magnifying lens held close to the pinna will suffice. If the ear speculum is rejected by the patient, a more complete examination may

have to be attempted at another time. If there is a question of serious or acute involvement of the ear of a strong, muscular young adult, anesthesia may be necessary.

Many programs for autistic persons include swimming and water activities, which can increase the incidence of external ear infections, especially in geographic areas where the climate is damp and the ears do not dry readily. Pain on palpation of the pinna should suggest the possibility of external otitis, which usually is treated adequately by external ear drops or occasional oral medication. Swimming may need to be continued while the patient is under treatment, if the appropriate behavioral program requires continuity. Otitis media usually is revealed through pain, but even if not readily apparent, it may be indicated by change in posture or balance or by evidence of hearing loss. A change in hearing patterns always suggests the possibility of fluid and/or infection behind the drum or in the eustachian tube.

Because autistic children frequently do not show a response to sound in the usual manner, hearing loss can be overlooked on the assumption that lack of response is part of the autism. Traditional office evaluation of the spoken voice, with close observation for response to a variety of sounds in the room or outside the building, will give a rough determination of hearing. More specific etiologic testing may need to be repeated a number of times for accurate determination. If results still are uncertain, testing for brain stem evoked response (BSER) or auditory evoked potential (EP; Batshaw & Perret, 1981) can be attempted, but sedation may be required.

The use of hand signing should not be overlooked as an aid in more accurate hearing testing in the primary care office. Most medical personnel do not sign, but the significant parent, teacher, or caregiver accompanying the patient to the office can assist in interpreting the patient's response.

Nose

The nose receives injuries because it is always exposed and it is easily accessible for self-abuse. Diagnosis of obvious injuries requires little contact with the defensive patient. Nasal fractures must be considered even if the nasal structure is not distorted, especially if breathing is compromised. Most fractures do not require immediate treatment; several days are available for explanation and preparation of the patient for necessary studies and treatment.

A foreign body in the nostril should be suspected if a discharge or foul odor is persistent. Epistaxis control can be enhanced by the use of oral decongestants for a few days after the acute episode. Cauterization may be necessary because the autistic patient may not respond to instructions to avoid repeating the trauma or picking the nose.

Sinusitis, both acute and chronic, allergic or infectious, should be considered if the patient gives evidence of headache, persisting discharge without obvious source, or unexplained fever. Sinus X rays and/or cultures may be advantageous in early diagnosis, but they will not be obtained easily. Treatment need not depend on such tests to begin. Warm showers, or application of warm wet washcloths or compresses to the sinus area provide comfort and encourage drainage, as do decongestants. Antibiotics may need to be tried without benefit of culture if other treatment fails or is not tolerated. Allergic sinusitis may respond to pure antihistamines, but these medications should not be used unless the patient's total program is considered, because patients may become either agitated or drowsy.

Throat

Most oral cavity diseases have the virtue of being visible, though only fleeting glimpses of the interior may be possible. Ideally, cultures should precede treatment of infection, but good judgment without cultures may often be necessary unless restraining by force is employed. For example, laryngitis usually is viral rather than bacterial but also may be caused by a foreign body. Acute epiglottitis, characterized by inability to swallow or control saliva, absence of hoarseness, rapidly progressive respiratory obstruction, and a cherry-red epiglottis, is a medical emergency usually not recognized by the patient and often not by medical personnel. Both of these diagnoses can be made without lab studies, though X ray can aid in specificity.

Repeated tonsillitis and/or streptococcal infections pose a dilemma. Is it better to treat repeated infections with appropriate antibiotics, even if difficult to accomplish, or to consider tonsillectomy with the difficulties of surgery, particularly for an autistic patient?

DENTAL CARE

Good dental care is difficult to maintain unless the autistic patient is cooperative. Some, but not all, patients do carry out good hygienic techniques. Hygiene is particularly important if the patient is receiving diphenylhydantoin for seizure control or is involved in a behavior modification program with excessive reliance on sweets for reward. With the introduction of fluoridated drinking water, fluoride oral preparations for home use, and fluoridated toothpaste, the incidence of tooth decay has been decreased. For autistic children and adults, this is important in minimizing corrective procedures, which are psychologically threatening to some patients. Even simple procedures like tooth cleaning and gum treatments by a competent dental hygienist can be difficult.

Overlooking or avoiding dental care because of the difficulty in examination or treatment can lead to major dental problems, such as abscesses and other infections, marked malocclusion, painful jaw movement, and gum disease, with resultant loss of teeth and of ability to chew food.

Careful dental staff preparation, through the use of techniques such as the dental team concept, patient management strategies, and practice with simulated patient situations (Lange, Entwistle, & Lipson, 1983), will assist the team in working with the patient. To help the patient adapt to the dental team, the dental treatment room, and the equipment, simulation of the dental procedures, by family or other caregivers, may need to be repeated a number of times before the patient is ready to attempt the actual procedures.

Routine examination and/or treatment may not be able to be accomplished in the dental office. If more than simple dental care needs to be performed, anesthesia often is necessary. General anesthesia should not be performed in the dentist's office unless adequate emergency help is present on the scene. Dental procedures requiring general anesthesia are best performed in hospitals or short-stay outpatient facilities where assistance is available immediately should a complication arise.

Orthodontia is not just the rearrangement of teeth to improve appearance even if commendable. Severe malocclusion, potential for infection, speech impediments, and so on, all are important for the autistic patient. Kostoro (1977) clearly indicates the interrelationship of the patient's multidisciplinary team with successful orthodontic management of the handicapped patient. The benefits and disadvantages need to be explored carefully before an orthodontic program is begun.

ALLERGY

When allergy is present, the decision for or against treatment should be considered carefully. Mild allergy, resulting in occasional rhinorrhea, coughing, itching, and so on, should require no treatment unless the patient is unusually sensitive. Changes in pattern and severity should be monitored. Moderate allergy, resulting in definite distress that either is of short duration or is relieved by treatment, usually requires only medication. However, antihistamines may cause drowsiness or, conversely, occasional stimulation, and they may interfere with other medication or with a training program. Severe allergy, for which effective medication causes too many undesirable side effects or for which standard treatment is ineffective, may require a vigorous plan of control. If, after careful consideration, a program of desensitization is indicated, the decision on mode of administration (injections or, very rarely, oral or sublingual) must be made on clinical judgment plus probability of successful outcome. It is important that all injections be given by the same person if at all possible.

Allergy not only causes discomfort but also may interfere with the patient's ability to participate in educational, vocational, or training programs. Careful history—and, especially, a visit by the medical care provider, to the home, residential home, or school and/or workshop—can be very effective in identifying actual or possible allergens. If environmental adjustments can be made judiciously, they should be made only after consideration of the patient's total program. For example, removal of a pet

animal may assist in reduction of allergic signs or symptoms but may be destructive in the patient's psychologic or training programs.

NUTRITION AND WEIGHT-RELATED ISSUES

Nutrition and the control of weight pose special problems. Fortunately, a wide variety of foods is available, and nutritional supplements are relatively easy to administer. Food requirements vary at different ages. A caregiver has the problem of providing appropriate caloric intake for a steadily growing, but overweight, younger child and much larger iron, protein, and caloric intake for a rapidly growing adolescent who is often eating at the same table. The younger child may feel punished by even limited food restriction when the older tablemate is encouraged to eat more.

Overeating is sometimes a problem with autistic persons. Many autistic children and adults do not participate spontaneously in physical activity. Because mealtime and the intake of food often are part of the total program of an autistic person, any variation in meal planning must be coordinated between those responsible for nutrition and health and those responsible for the program. Weight control is advisable, but food restriction should not be instituted just to eliminate a few pounds of extra weight if the restriction interferes with the overall behavioral program of the patient.

During school and workshop hours, when activities are programmed tightly or in closely monitored residential programs, unrestricted food intake can be controlled if staff has a good understanding of nutrition and needs. Less control is likely in private homes, where family members are trying to live their own lives. Weight control then depends on the skill of family members to monitor the activity of the autistic member without unduly restricting activity of the rest of the family. There is the occasional husky young adult who becomes aggressive if food and snacks are denied. The sheer size and determination of some young adults is intimidating, so programming must be established specifically to address the prohibition.

The possibility of metabolic variation as a source of overweight or underweight must not be overlooked in the concentration on behavior and education. A thyroid screen can be reassuring if negative, and important if abnormal. Attention to basic groups of foods, supplemented with vitamins, usually provides the nutrients necessary for growth and health.

PUBLIC HEALTH

The simple act of hand washing must not be forgotten as an aid in decreasing the incidence of infection. Respiratory infections do spread through hand contact as well as droplet spray, and poor toileting hygiene may result in gastrointestinal disease. Exposure to numbers of people with infections, at school or workshop, is balanced by the fact that autistic groups usually are fairly circumscribed; they are monitored closely, and infectious diseases are more likely to be discovered than in the random population, permitting early isolation of the infected member. However, because obtaining a willing and competent "sitter" while parents work can be very difficult when the autistic member is ill, some parents may ignore the illness that should be isolated at home and send the ill member off to school or workshop.

Pinworm and other parasitic infestations can contribute to behavioral changes among the affected students and their caregivers, sometimes involving an entire unit of a school. Parasitic infestation can be undetected unless the organism is seen or a relatively easy-to-obtain stool specimen is examined for ova and parasites. Caregivers need to watch for external signs, such as organisms in the feces or perineal itching, and be aware that postmeal abdominal pain warrants examination of the stool for *Giardia lamblia*.

Preventive immunizations should be kept current rather than relying on providing the immunization only when an incident or epidemic occurs. Tuberculosis screening, especially in residential settings, remains a viable procedure. Because residents of institutions have been found to be at high risk for hepatitis B, all who enter a program should be screened on entrance for hepatitis antigens and antibodies, unless they have been evaluated very recently or never have been in contact with other institutionalized patients or their classmates.

Blood count and urinalysis screening need not be obtained yearly if the care providers are alert to subtle changes in behavior or health of the patient. Blood counts and differentials, drug levels, and liver function studies are important for patients on drugs for control of seizures or behavior.

Cohen, Paul, Anderson, and Harcherick (1982) have reminded us that patients with pervasive developmental disorders have been found to have blood lead levels significantly higher than those of their normal siblings. A blood lead level should be part of the initial blood workup and should be followed by periodic screening, especially of those patients exhibiting pica.

HOSPITALIZATION

An admission to the hospital must be planned carefully beforehand. Consistency of approach for the autistic patient is important (Cohen, 1973), Repetition of activities, conversations, and events can be comforting and, for some, almost essential.

Preparation of the hospital staff to cope with the patient—and of the parents or caregiver(s) to cope with the hospital—is crucial to creating an optimal experience (Gabriel & Gluck, 1973). If all concerned with the care of the patient share an understanding of each other's roles—the positive possibilities as well as the problems that each faces—the hospitalization can be accomplished much more smoothly. The patient can be informed about the impending hospital trip in a calm manner, not necessarily in detail, but providing at the least some idea of what to expect. The timing and extent of patient explanations will depend on knowledge of how to ease the agitation and fearfulness of the patient.

The autistic patient must be accompanied by a person with whom he or she is familiar and through whom some type of communication with the patient can take place. The person may be a family member, teacher, school advocate, or friend. The presence of such a person not only will give the patient a much easier transition into the hospital but also can ensure a more accurate history of the patient's behavior patterns, thus facilitating enabling hospital care. Depending on the patient's needs, the "care person" may room with the patient during the hospital stay, to provide continuity of a familiar presence, easier communication with a nonverbal patient, and ready history, should nonfamiliar staff require it for unexpected needs. Many hospitals provide "sitters" to assist family members. The sitter for autistic patients should be qualified, that is, have some familiarity with autistic patients even if unable to communicate easily with them by voice or by hand signing.

Even minimal words and sounds can have meaning and can be interpreted by sensitive staff. Warning signs such as humming or hissing can indicate fright or, more ominously, anger about to erupt into quick and sometimes violent action. Staff and patient may use art or music, as well as gestures, sign language, and verbal communication to express themselves.

Admission to the hospital does not preclude continuation of prior patterns of behavior by the patient or treatment by the caregivers. Awareness of many aspects of the patient's life may be vital to a successful hospitalization. The hospital staff should want to know the patient's routines and time schedules; activities of daily living and the assistance required to carry them out; toileting patterns, including frequency and character of urination or bowel movements and type of gestures or noises that indicate the time or need for toileting; sleep patterns, including the need for light or music or favorite blanket for comforting; type of amusement or objects of play that are desirable; and so on.

The hospital staff should have information about current medication and the easiest way to administer it, and a history of effects of or reactions to previous medications, including sedation if the patient will undergo procedures requiring cooperation.

Special Safety Considerations for Hospitalization

What will be required for safety? Does the patient need restraints full- or part-time? Are sitters required in addition to regular nursing staff? Does the patient need protected windows, padded side rails or crib rails on the bed,

or removal of some room furniture? Are helmets or hand mitts necessary? Is the patient likely to harm himself or herself, or caregivers, or strangers in the hospital? Does the patient respond to behavior modification techniques for reward or to avoid harmful activity? Which ones have been effective or ineffective?

Blood drawing usually requires assistance from a familiar caregiver, aided, if necessary, by strong assistants. Before beginning, determine whether the patient will be most cooperative if the procedure is explained carefully or whether an attempt with minimal delay is better. The patient should be informed of what is occurring. Diversional activity can help, and the patient may need constant positive reinforcement during and after the procedure.

Uncomfortable procedures such as lumbar punctures and throat cultures ideally should not be done in the patient's room. A treatment room, with a favorite toy or familiar objects visible, is preferable. Everything should be ready before the patient enters the room, though the patient may need time to become familiar with the room and staff before the procedure begins.

Because studies such as electroencephalograms, computer tomography (CT) scans, and magnetic resonance imaging (MRI) require an extended period of time, sedation may be necessary. The patient usually responds better if a familiar caregiver accompanies him or her to the lab. If there are several opportunities to visit the lab room prior to the procedure, patient distress and agitation may be minimized. Similar visits to the operating suite and recovery room and introduction to their staffs are recommended.

Even though an autistic patient may not or cannot communicate with conversation and does not seem to be absorbing the conversations around him or her, much if not all of a conversation is being received by the patient. Therefore, it is crucial not to converse openly about medical plans, especially potentially intrusive or painful ones, in front of the patient unless it is time to notify him or her of the rapidly approaching procedures. Similarly, conversation about the status of the patient—intellect, emotional status, concerns about medical status, especially if it is serious—

should not be discussed in front of even the most apparently unresponsive patient unless the conversation is meant to be overheard by the patient.

A decision for surgery must be made on the basis of the best interest of the patient. Surgery never should be denied because the patient is autistic, It might be denied if after careful evaluation of all options the medical team, family, and caregivers decide the procedure, hospitalization, postoperative care, and potential end results do not warrant the disruption of the patient's program and emotional status, the inevitable discomfort, and the potential for infection and complication.

Cross-References

Developmental aspects of the expression of autism are discussed in Chapters 12 through 14. Issues relative to specific syndromes, medical and neurological conditions, and genetic factors are reviewed in Chapters 1 though 7 and 16 through 18. Pharmacological interventions are reviewed in Chapter 33.

REFERENCES

Accardo, P.J., & Capute, A.J. (1979). *The pediatrician and the developmentally delayed child.* Baltimore: University Park Press.

Batshaw, M.L., & Perret, Y.M. (1981). *Children with handicaps. A medical primer.* Baltimore: Brookes.

Blackwell, M.W. (1979). *Care of the mentally retarded.* Boston: Little, Brown.

Cohen, D.J. (1973). The medical care of autistic children. A commentary on Gabriel & Gluck, "Management of an autistic child undergoing open heart surgery." *Pediatrics, 31,* 278–280.

Cohen, D.J., Paul, R., Anderson, G.M., & Harcherik, D.F. (1982). Blood lead in autistic children. *Lancet, 8289,* 94–95.

Dahlquist, L.M., Gil, K.M., Kalfus, O.R., Blount, M.A., & Boyd, M.S. (1984). Enhancing an autistic girl's cooperation with gynecological examinations: A clinical note. *Clinical Pediatrics, 23,* 203.

Dalldorf, J.S. (1983). Medical needs of the autistic adolescent. In E. Schopler & G.B. Mesibov (Eds.), *Autism in adolescents and adults.* New York: Plenum Press.

Gabriel, H.P., & Gluck, R. (1973). Management of an autistic child undergoing open heart surgery. *Pediatrics, 51,* 251–253.

Goldfarb, A.F. (1983). The initial encounter. In A.M. Bongiovanni (Ed.), *Adolescent gynecology: A guide for clinicians.* New York: Plenum Press.

Kostoro, S. (1977). Orthodontia treatment of handicapped persons. In S.H.Y. Wei & J. Casko (Eds.), *Orthodontic care for handicapped persons: Proceedings of a workshop held at the University of Iowa.* Iowa City: University of Iowa.

Lange, B.M., Entwistle, B.M., & Lipson, L.F. (1983). *Dental management of the handicapped. Approaches for dental auxiliaries.* Philadelphia: Lea & Febinger.

Tunnessen, W.W., Jr. (1984). Help your acne patients help themselves. *Contemporary Pediatrics, 1,* 10–25.

Wing, L. (1972). *Autistic children: A guide for parents.* New York: Brunner/Mazel.

Public Policy Perspectives

Public policy defines a society's beliefs, values, and practices. In relation to individuals with developmental disabilities, such as autism and pervasive developmental disorders, public policy also reflects emerging knowledge about causes, course, and outcome. Policy is shaped by various forces—a society's ethical commitments, its legal and judicial traditions, competition and balancing among groups for setting priorities and allocating resources, and the processes of political action. Policy reflects the success of advocates—parents, professionals, and organizations—in having their own views become established in law, practice, and budget.

A major force in shaping public policy has been the recognition that particular types of interventions are able to facilitate the development of individuals with autism, mental retardation, and other developmental disorders. These interventions emphasize the potential of individuals with disabilities to learn, to have pleasures and successes in the mainstream of society, to cope with challenges and failures, to achieve vocational skills, and to be able to work toward and take pride in personal independence.

There are, among individuals with autism and pervasive disorders, differences in the degree to which these potentials are actualized. For the most severely retarded and behavior-disordered individuals, life remains terribly compromised and often recurrently painful. For individuals at the other end of the autistic spectrum—such as those with Asperger's Syndrome, the milder variants of Pervasive Developmental Disorder, or higher functioning autism—life in the mainstream of society,

including holding a job and competing with normal individuals, is more often achieved.

As recently as 20 or 30 years ago, public policy that foresaw only very protected, limited lives in public institutions for individuals with retardation led to public and family actions that almost assured lower levels of adaptation. Placed in large institutions, individuals with retardation tended to lose personal motivation and to comply with routines; they were not expected to assert themselves as individuals; and they often did not achieve the level of personal adaptation that they might otherwise have been capable of.

Public policy recognized the dangers of low expectations of individuals with disabilities and of their isolation. This recognition has shaped policy, and the concept of self-fulfilling expectations has altered the course of disability law.

Living at home or in their own apartments, individuals with autism and retardation are more likely to be able to function in the broader communal context, to act like others and respond to the natural contingencies of life—to be able to shop, ride public transportation, try new things, decide when and what to eat, deal with disappointments and hurt feelings, and use their successes as well as their errors and mistakes to help alter their behavior.

There has been virtually universal acceptance of the goal of inclusion or mainstreaming as the target for public policy in relation to individuals with disabilities. Such a model, of course, makes important demands on services, organizations, and professionals, as well as parents. Between an ideology and a successful system are many intervening steps, often

741

costly in time, energy, and money. Simply placing children in a classroom with normal children, or adults in a single-room-occupancy hotel, will not ensure inclusion or promote competence. Rather, supports are needed to develop prosthetic environments that will help lead to success; without ramps for physically handicapped children and aids for those with severe behavioral problems, inclusion is not possible. Similarly, education and interventions with "normal" peers are needed to help them include the individual with disabilities and accept special provisions that may be needed in the classroom.

Inclusion is embodied in law and regulations, but there are situations in which specialized programs and services are preferable or needed. Just as when children have distinctive medical needs, treatment in more restrictive environments occasionally may be required for individuals with developmental disabilities. When the "standard model" is for inclusion, as it is today, the use of a more restrictive environment needs to be justified and accepted by everyone involved, including the families and the individuals themselves.

In a society that has dealt adequately with the needs of individuals with disabilities, there should be a spectrum of services from least to more restrictive, from fully inclusive to more specialized. A long-standing debate has tended to pit advocates of two poles—full inclusion versus segregated services—against each other. Today, the inclusion viewpoint is the paradigm. Families, professionals, and advocates generally recognize the value of an available spectrum of educational, living, and rehabilitation services to meet individual needs to the degree possible, especially when the goal of these services is ultimate integration.

Research in relation to the development of individuals with mental retardation showed the value of thinking about retarded individuals as whole people (Zigler & Hodapp, 1986). This ideology captured an important set of empirical findings about the role of motivation and personality in shaping behavior of individuals with retardation. It was found that an individual's intelligence is only one factor in determining adaptation and ultimate level of functioning. In addition, motivational factors and phenomena such as self-direction,

effectance, esteem, modeling normal behavior, and history of success made enormous differences in functioning. Indeed, within a broad range of IQ scores, the level of adaptive functioning has less to do with intelligence than with these psychological characteristics and the presence of maladaptive behavior. The developmental approach to understanding individuals with intellectual disabilities also emphasizes the importance of enhancing the experiences and the environments of individuals with disabilities. An extension of the research and policy concerning individuals with intellectual disabilities has been seeing the "autistic child as a whole person." This now is a cornerstone of public policy and underlies the most innovative programs, as described in this Section.

Ethical considerations have profound effects on personal, social, and professional activities. Usually, ethics are implicit in daily life and in most social relations. However, in the study, care, and treatment of individuals with disabilities, ethics need to be made explicit. Through the discussion of ethical issues, professionals and families are able to articulate their personal values and define a shared perspective. This is particularly relevant to complex issues where there are more shades of gray than clearly right-versus-wrong answers—for example, in the use of new and unproven therapies and in decisions about participation of persons with intellectual and behavioral disabilities in research.

Ethical discussion highlights issues and possibilities, but cannot be expected to provide an authoritative conclusion. Rather, ethical discourse is an important process of societal and personal self-reflection. In relation to autism and other severe developmental disorders, ethical discussions emphasize the importance of appreciating the humanity of those who are most different from the normal while working to try to improve their future.

Contemporary legal understanding of the rights of individuals with disabilities, including those with autism and pervasive developmental disorders, is the result of a process of politics, advocacy, and scientific and educational advancements. Current law reflects many convergent forces, including the legal analysis of the dangers of previous special educational and institutional practices, the extension of civil rights to the disabled, and the success of advocates and, increasingly, self-advocates, in shaping legislation. The available legislative mandates and legal remedies are powerful forces for influencing the services and programs delivered to individuals with disabilities and their rights for inclusion and participation. However, there are enormous gaps between rights and practice, between what might be hoped for and what actually exists. Even in the most affluent and programmatically advanced nations, educational and therapeutic services for children and adolescents with disabilities are often limited and are far from what the law may mandate. Almost everywhere, the special educational, vocational, social, therapeutic, and living opportunities for adults are far more limited than for children and adolescents.

Public policy is expressed in laws, regulations, budgets, and programs; it also defines shared public goals and aspirations. Public policy has changed over the past years and will continue to reflect new knowledge and changing values and priorities. The study of the history of public policy and differences in policies among communities and nations can help shape the future directions of public attitudes and guide informed public policy.

REFERENCES

Zigler, E., & Hodapp, R. (1986). *Understanding mental retardation.* Cambridge, England: Cambridge University Press.

CHAPTER 34

Coping with the Diagnosis of Autism

BRYNA SIEGEL

It is ironic how our changing understanding of the causes of autism may have influenced how parents come to cope with having a child with autism. Three decades ago, the disorder was blamed on cold, rejecting, "refrigerator parents" who supposedly caused their children to withdraw into their own autistic worlds (cf., Bettelheim, 1967, 1974; Szurek, Berlin, & Boatman, 1971). Today, a more psychodynamically enlightened, neurobiological model for the causes of autism has replaced the outmoded experiential model of the etiology of autism. Indeed, research has shown that autistic children engender reactive depressions and other signs of stress response in their mothers—rather than the influence being the other way around (Bristol, Gallagher, & Holt, 1993; DeMeyer, 1979; Holroyd & McArthur, 1976). In response to the early model, in which parents were blamed, there has been an opposite reaction—almost no attention to parental psychodynamics in response to the diagnosis of their child's autism, instead of a complete focus upon it. Parents of autistic children today have parenting experiences similar to those of 30 years ago. Fortunately, today, we may recast these basic emotional responses to the autistic child as resulting from the sense of loss that is experienced when a parent learns that his or her child is not expected to develop typically, and is likely to have lifelong and severe impairments in adaptive functioning.

The presence of an autistic child may have a profound influence on the functioning of his or her family. Distress about the child's difficulties first arises during the period of time in which the symptoms of autism are first being recognized. Often, they seem to crescendo at the time of diagnosis. Thereafter, the imprint of the child's diagnosis may mark family functioning in various ways and may present special challenges not only in raising the child, but also in the maintenance of equilibrium in the parent's marriage, and the quality of life for the siblings. Having and raising an autistic child precipitates some reorganization of each parent's intrapsychic functioning as they adapt to their autistic child's special needs. We will examine the period of time in which the diagnosis of autism is first received, and parental responses to the diagnosis, with the goal of identifying how coping with such an unexpected and stressful life event may best be achieved. The information in this chapter is designed to guide clinicians who are helping families of children with autism work through their grief process and also to directly help parents understand the progress of their own changing emotional responses to their child's disability.

There is virtually no empirical research on how parents come to cope successfully with receiving a diagnosis of autism, though, clinically, having a child diagnosed with a serious developmental disability is universally seen as highly stressful. To develop a model for successful coping with the diagnosis of autism, research and theory from several related areas have been brought together. There is some research on family coping with developmental disability, and with autism, but it has centered more on long-term adjustment than on the period of initial response to the diagnosis. There is research on bereavement responses to the diagnosis of a severe chronic physical illness in a child, or to the death of a child. The adult bereavement literature, which mostly focuses on the death of spouses and adults' parents, can also be tapped for a theoretical perspective that allows receiving the diagnosis of autism to be viewed, initially, as a kind of bereavement. From these existing bodies of research, as well as from existing theory and clinical work, it is possible to put together a picture of what likely happens when a parent receives a diagnosis of autism, how that diagnosis subsequently may resonate over the life span of the family, and how families may resolve initial intense feelings of grief and learn to cope well with autism as a stressor life event. Treatment implications for understanding the period around the diagnosis of autism are discussed, as are types of future research that may provide empirical validation of models of coping with the diagnosis of a developmental disorder.

In coping with the diagnosis of autism, parents deal with accepting a deeply felt loss, much in the same way that parents do when a child dies. However, with autism, parents experience the loss of their "idealized" or "hoped-for" child. Psychological adaptation to autism is a process of accepting that the "hoped-for" child does not exist, and that a substantially different child exists instead. In some respects, the "refrigerator mother" theory of 30 years ago held out more hope for a resolution of parental distress at the child's difficulties: A "talking" cure would supposedly restore the child to normalcy—an easier path to follow than acceptance of a permanent loss of the "hoped-for" child due to a biological defect. Although the contemporary neurobiological explanation of autism definitively removes parental blame based on inadequate parenting, it also deprives parents of the feeling that they can heal the harm they have "caused" by improving their parenting, or by obtaining intensive psychotherapy for the child or themselves.

This chapter discusses parental coping with the initial diagnosis of autism. The coping includes several stages:

1. The process of bringing into consciousness the realization that a disability may exist, and the psychological correlates of the process of being able to consciously formulate concerns.

2. The process of actively seeking help for the child.
3. Outcry responses or other psychological reactions to initially getting a diagnosis.
4. The initiation of positive coping in the form of functional adaptations to the child's needs, such as accepting special education, or making changes in family planning.
5. Over time, recognition and acceptance of how fully the child with autism will ultimately develop.

RESEARCH RELEVANT TO UNDERSTANDING PARENTAL GRIEVING FOR AN AUTISTIC CHILD

Five bodies of research bear on development of an understanding of parental coping in response to the birth of an autistic child. No direct research, however, has been carried out on the specific grief and subsequent coping responses of parents with autistic children, and on how the initial responses of parents of autistic children may be different from the reactions of parents with other types of developmentally disabled children, although clinical descriptions of this difference have been provided (Siegel, 1996; Siegel & Silverstein, 1994). The five areas of research that will be reviewed here are:

1. Studies of families' coping with developmental disabilities (e.g., Crnic, Friedrich, & Greenberg, 1983; Donovan, 1988; Gallagher, Beckman-Bell, & Cross, 1983; Kazak, 1987; Longo & Bond, 1984; Mink, Nihira, & Meyer, 1983; Wikler, 1981).
2. Studies of families' coping with autism (e.g., Bristol, 1984; Donovan, 1988; Fisman & Wolf, 1991; Holroyd & McArthur, 1976; Konstantareas & Homatidis, 1991; Konstantareas, Homatidis, & Plowright, 1992).
3. Studies of bereavement reactions to the diagnosis of a developmental disorder (e.g., Bruce, Schultz, Smyrnios, & Schultz, 1994; Emde & Brown, 1978; Fortier & Wanlass, 1984; Wikler, 1981).
4. Studies of bereavement reactions to the diagnosis of a chronic physical disorder (Clubb, 1991; Delight & Goodall, 1990; Drotar, Baskiewitz, Irvin, Kennell, & Klaus, 1975; Parks, 1977; Young, 1987) or death of

a child (e.g., Downey, Silver, & Wortman, 1990; Fish, 1986; Hazzard, Weston, & Gutterres, 1992; Kachoyeanos & Selden, 1993; Lchman, Wortman, & Williams, 1987; Littlefield & Rushton, 1986; Rando, 1983; Schiff, 1977).

5. Research on coping in caregivers of mentally disabled adult family members, such as the demented elderly (Grafstrom, Norberg, & Hagberg, 1993; Haley & Pardo, 1989; Pruchno & Potashnik, 1989; Semple, 1992), or a child who becomes schizophrenic (Atkinson, 1994).

Each of these areas of research contributes to a partial understanding of the experience of parents when their child is diagnosed with autism. For each of these areas of research, an overview will be given, and specific studies that contribute to an understanding of stages of parental coping with an autistic child will be examined. We extrapolate from the existing literature in order to speculate how potential risk or protective factors—such as parental personality traits, previous sensitizing life events, marital satisfaction, prediagnosis family structure, extrafamilial social supports, or cultural factors—may be expected to predict the course of initial grief and longer-term coping.

Families' Coping with Developmental Disabilities

The research on family coping with developmental disabilities has generally demonstrated that developmental disabilities often present a more difficult challenge than caring for a child with a chronic physical condition (cf., Murphy, 1982). A child with a physical disability may require extra physical care, but lack of intellectual handicap often ameliorates the perceived burden to parents, or perhaps—compared to autism—the more normal course of social maturation helps. The lack or delay of milestones in the life of a developmentally disabled child may present to parents more concerns about the child's ultimate adjustment than are experienced by parents of children with chronic physical conditions, for whom a physical prognosis may be more definable. Stress, therefore, seems to derive from uncertainty about what to do presently

for the developmentally disabled child and what the future will be like.

Research on coping with developmental disabilities also has emphasized the importance of the family's social ecology (Bronfenbrenner, 1979), defined in this case as (a) the microsystem of the family itself; (b) the mesosystem of teachers, caseworkers, therapists, and support group members; (c) the exosystem of schools, healthcare, and developmental disabilities service agencies; and (d) the macrosystem consisting of cultural, socioeconomic, and religious influences on attitudes toward developmental disability (Konstantareas & Homatidis, 1991).

Families' Coping with Autism

As already indicated, a smaller amount of research has examined the specific psychosocial stressors faced by parents of autistic children. This research consistently suggests that, compared to other developmental or learning disorders, autism is a more difficult disorder for parents to face (e.g., Donovan, 1988; Holroyd & McArthur, 1976). Parents of children with autism, as discussed in detail later, face many challenges in child rearing that are not faced by parents of children with other developmental disorders. These differences stem largely from the fact that autism is a disorder of social relatedness, and parent–child communication and attachment are disequilibrated more than in other mental retardation or learning disabilities syndromes.

Bereavement Reactions to the Diagnosis of a Developmental Disorder

Compared to longer-term family coping with developmental disabilities, relatively less research has focused on the inception of the coping process—the period in which the parent learns of the child's disability and begins an initial process of grieving. Study of grief responses, as will be described below, is an important part of understanding the larger picture of successful coping with a diagnosis of autism. It will be argued that recognition of the response to the diagnosis as a grief process allows parental energy to begin to be reinvested into proactive coping, that is, treatment for the child's autism.

A few studies have examined initial grief responses and have suggested that the time of initial diagnosis is a period of family crisis and tends to be subject to the types of responses the family is predisposed to make to other major life stressors, given the family ecology (e.g., Konstantareas & Homatidis, 1991). Some research regards the initial grief response to the diagnosis of a developmental disability as the starting point for an infinite course of grief that will wax and wane at various times in the child's and parents' lives (e.g., Olshansky, 1962; Wikler, 1981; Wikler, Wasow, & Hatfield, 1981). These researchers argue that, because a developmental disability does not end and is not final in the way that death is, the onset of grief may be more like a bereavement reaction due to a death, but, over time, may have less of a chance of a more complete resolution.

Whether grief is seen as diminishing in intensity over time, or as an ebbing and flowing phenomenon, it is important to consider the qualities of the initial grieving process as potentially predictive of later family adaptation or risk. A better understanding of the prognostic value of initial grief response to a diagnosis of autism or other developmental disability may also help clinicians differentiate typical and atypical patterns of grief response, and make effective interventions when an atypical pattern of grief response begins to emerge.

Bereavement Reactions to the Diagnosis of a Chronic Physical Disorder or Death of a Child

The specific stages of the grieving process itself have been studied somewhat more in parents who have had a child die of illness or injury, or whose child was stillborn (e.g., Layne, 1990), or born prematurely (e.g., Fraley, 1990), or with a stigmatizing birth defect such as spina bifida (e.g., Delight & Goodall, 1990) or cleft palate (e.g., Riski, 1991; Young, 1987). These studies suggest discrete stages of outcry, denial, and working through, derived from the larger literature on adult bereavement responses when a spouse or other loved one is lost (e.g., Zisook & Shuchter, 1991a, 1991b). These studies suggest that there is a discrete nature to the initial stages of coping with loss. These studies may be only partly relevant to understanding parental responses to the diagnosis of autism because the recognition of autism is not itself a discrete event. First, the recognition of autism, unlike the death of a child, or the birth of a child with a clearly visible defect, is not a unitary event, but a growing series of fears and concerns culminating at the moment the dreaded diagnosis is first given. Second, unlike a death or even a physical defect for which a series of corrective surgeries may exist, the outcome of a diagnosis of autism is much more open-ended. Third, the autistic child remains, in some ways, "normal" (i.e., in physical appearance), throwing constant doubt on exactly what it is that has been lost. The literature on the death of a child often emphasizes a working-through phase—when parents come to terms with the fullness of their sense of loss and then eventually begin to experience decreasing intensity of grief symptoms as the permanence of the loss is assimilated. While this may not occur in the same way when the child still lives—albeit in a handicapped condition, a working through, and with it, the initiation of proactive coping, is likely to begin as it becomes clear that the child's condition is not temporary. Although there will be some working through or assimilation of the reality of the situation, the loss, in the case of a developmentally disabled child, is by its nature incomplete because the child is, in some ways, *not* "lost." The incompleteness of the loss itself may, in some instances, inhibit a full working through. The child with autism may appear "normal" more moments of the day than he may appear to be disabled. As the child watches TV, eats, sleeps, sits in a car seat, he may seem like other children. Only in those moments when the child may fail to speak or understand, display stereotyped motor movements, play oddly with toys, or ignore peers, and so on, are the clear stigmata of autism unavoidably forced into parental awareness.

When a child dies, the parent has the actual memory of a whole child who once existed. Although the whole is lost, it really once existed—and recollection of the "whole" child is often cited as a great source of comfort to parents whose children die (Schiff, 1977). By contrast, the parent of the autistic child also "loses" a "whole" child, but, in the case of autism, the "whole" child has only existed as an idealized, hoped-for, fantazied child. This idealization may be a factor in cases where the working through or acceptance of the new reality that includes the child's disability is only partly achieved.

Coping in Caregivers of Mentally Disabled Adult Family Members

Germane similarities are faced by parents of autistic children and by adult children who are caregivers of their demented parents. Both are caregivers for difficult family members who show little or no acknowledgment of, or reciprocity for, the care and love directed toward them. Both situations require providing care to someone who is loved but is not the person he or she once was—or, in the case of autism, was once believed to have been. The coping process shares some key dynamics in both these situations. In both, grief resolution is inhibited from completion by the continued presence of the person being cared for. The demented patient was clearly once normal. The autistic patient was either considered normal until the onset of concern about symptoms or may in fact have been normal prior to onset of symptoms of a childhood-onset disintegrative disorder (Volkmar, 1992) or a period of developmental setback (Kurita, Kita, & Miyake, 1992). In both cases, caregivers have to cope with the presence of the person requiring significant care, who constantly serves as a negatively cathected metaphor for the loved and lost ideal. Caregivers of demented parents can ameliorate their sense of loss by looking back to a time when their loved one was normal, that is, when the idealized love object existed as such. Parents of autistic children face additional challenges to effective grief resolution and coping because they have no period to look back on, no time when the idealized object was unquestionably real, or gave love to them and benefited from their loving care.

Graftstrom and colleagues (1993) studied the coping process in family members caring for an elderly demented parent or spouse. Their findings suggested that the ability to engage in a one-way, nurturant sort of "mothering" care,

and to acknowledge the ongoing nature of the grieving process was a psychologically protective response to the challenge of a generally nonresponsive and sometimes combative family member with Alzheimer's disease. Caregivers who did not engage in mothering care expressed less grief and less guilt about problems in care, were more likely to distance themselves from and objectify their ill parent or spouse, and were considered at greater risk to abuse their charges. These patterns may apply to children with autism as well. An ability to deliver unconditional mothering, such as is associated with the care of an infant, may be a positive means for coping with the autistic child. Therefore, responding to the autistic child more in terms of his or her social age (rather than chronological age) may benefit the parent faced with caring for a relatively unresponsive child with autism. Conversely, it may be particularly important to consider the relationship between blocked grief turned to anger and the potential for child abuse that may be flagged through parenting characterized by objectifying and distancing from the autistic child.

A SPECTRUM OF PARENTAL COPING WITH AUTISM

The existing empirical research that has been cited can be woven together to give some insight into how parents cope with altered expectations in a child, how autism in particular is a difficult disorder for parents to adjust to, and how studies of family stress and coping, and of bereavement, can help explain how parents develop means to cope positively and proactively with their child's autism. In addition to empirical studies, some theoretical work has provided a basis for interpreting empirical research results in the context of a specific understanding of the coping process as it relates to the diagnosis of autism. Three kinds of theories may be applied to studying the intrapsychic processes of parents of children with autism. These theories involve (a) the psychoanalytic perspective of seeing the child's disability as a narcissistic injury to the parent, which must be resolved; (b) the chronic sorrow model wherein long-term positive coping is interwoven with recurrent reawakenings to the child's limitations; and (c) the complicated coping or pathological grief model in which mastery of initially strong symptoms of avoidance, intrusive thoughts, and a failure to face realities must be resolved before positive coping can occur. Each of these theories is discussed in turn in the following subsections.

Psychoanalytic Perspective

The first theory is psychoanalytically derived and was first presented by Solnit and Stark (1961). Their psychoanalytic perspective has had an enduring impact on research on coping with loss. The birth of the defective child is seen as a crisis to which the parent eventually accommodates, through the deployment of intrapsychic mechanisms of defense. Emotionally healthy individuals would be predicted to use adaptive defenses resulting in the most positive coping. Those with more disorganized ego defenses to begin with would be seen as most at risk to defend poorly against this new stressor. Solnit and Stark's perspective on coping with the birth of a disabled child is based on the concept of narcissistic involvement, particularly by the mother, in her expected baby. Pregnancy, according to the psychoanalytic model, is a time of psychological rearrangements for the expectant mother, involving development of a specific notion of who the infant will be relative to her own sense of self. The mother forms an image of her awaited child which is comprised of representations of the self and the mother's own love objects (mother, husband, father, and siblings). When the awaited child is "defective," not only is there the loss of the baby that was expected, and the sudden presence of an unknown and feared infant, but the mother's own preparation for her new role as a parent is revealed as insufficient for the actual event. Solnit and Stark saw this as a process where the newly established (prospective) libidinal pathways and attachments were precipitously terminated, and where, at the same time, the mother faced demands for a new kind of libidinal cathexes. They argued that the demand for investing in the "new" (disabled) child as a love object was thus likely to be overwhelming. Further, the demands of

caring for a disabled child who was more difficult than a normal child constrained resources for the process of grieving for the narcissistically invested and prepared-for infant. Thus, the more difficult the disabled infant turned out to be, the longer it might take for the parents to accept the reality that their hoped-for infant was never to materialize.

From this perspective, the birth of the autistic child, whose early infancy may be perceived as normal, does not involve immediate narcissistic injury or reschematization of expectations for the parent, because the child is initially viewed as the expected child. In fact, compared to the birth of an infant who is diagnosed as disabled at birth, the parents of the autistic infant have an extended period in which to consolidate the representation of the narcissistically invested child that began to form prenatally. The blow to the parents' sense of self and the potential disturbance to the attachment to the child come after a period of growing discontinuity between expectation and realization, and may therefore be even more difficult to accept because there has been a longer period in which to consolidate fantasy and expectation-based beliefs about who the child is (or should be). This may be especially true when some of the child's initial traits of autism, such as lining things up, are seen as early signs of unusually high intelligence; or when other traits of autism, such as a fascination with pushing buttons on a computer are seen as a precursor of aptitudes one of the parents may possess.

Solnit and Stark (1961) described acceptance of the reality of the existing child along with the intrapsychic loss of the desired child as a slow process of mental work, involving repeated review of memories and discharge of intense feelings. In addition to the initial loss of the prepared-for child, Solnit and Stark believed that there was an ongoing narcissistic injury to the mother from the difficulties involved in caring for the (not-prepared-for) child, which could further identify her to herself as a defective or inadequate mother. They suggested that the role of professionals was to lessen this sense of "defectiveness" through providing as much information about the child's disorder as possible. By increasing parental competence in the special care of the disabled child, the parent may experience healing of the narcissistic injury around being an incompetent parent. Thus, early implementation of parent training programs may be expected to facilitate parental coping as well as achieving the more overt goal of remediating aspects of the child's disability. Later, as the sense of narcissistic injury decreases, increased acceptance of the "actual" child clears the way for increasing acceptance of the child for who he or she really is, as evidenced by parents who take pleasure in special (albeit odd) competencies and interests of their autistic child, such as memorizing pages of the *Encyclopedia Britannica,* or drawing nothing but highly accurate sketches of backhoes for months on end.

The Chronic Sorrow Model

The second theoretical perspective for understanding parental reactions to the birth of a disabled child originates in a short paper by Olshansky (1962), who introduced the construct of "chronic sorrow," proposing that parents can never fully resolve the grief initiated by the birth of a disabled child; instead, grief waxes and wanes in response to various changes in the child, other family stressors, and life events. In contrast to Solnit and Stark's (1961) clearly intra-psychic formulation of parental grieving as an injury to the self, Olshansky focused more on how grief varied with extra-psychic events in the social ecology of the family. He and others delineated this response as a more time-bound phenomenon, and placed major emphasis instead on the effects of sorrow as an ongoing emotional state. Olshansky argued that the everyday reality of caring for a disabled child caused most parents to suffer from chronic sorrow. In writing about parents of mentally retarded children, Olshansky characterized "chronic sorrow" as a normal, lifelong psychological reaction to a tragic occurrence, varying in severity based on social and personality factors within families. Olshansky noted that chronic sorrow did not prevent parents from taking satisfaction and pride in the disabled child's development, but that realistic concern over the child's future led to concomitant lasting feelings of sorrow. The chronic sorrow model does not preclude stages

of working through and acceptance, but it sees chronic sorrow as an overlay that is interwoven with more positive aspects of adaptation and coping.

The chronic sorrow model gained momentum in the 1960s, when there were relatively fewer special education services, and when parents of autistic and other mentally retarded children did indeed face a lifetime in which they could expect relatively little improvement in their child's adaptive functioning. The chronic sorrow model implied a very protracted period of adjustment to the diagnosis of a developmental disorder, as well as a fairly static state of continuing grief that corresponded to the fairly static state of the child's disability. The chronic sorrow model emphasized that parents had a lifetime in which to learn to deal with the needs and problems of a mentally disabled child; therefore, giving parents several years to go through an initial grief process was felt to have little downside risk. Olshansky's (1962) recommendation for how to treat parental response to the diagnosis of a disability was pragmatic for a time when little treatment and virtually no early intervention programs were available. Perhaps because of the lack of treatments, Olshansky apparently did not consider the benefits of working through initial grief by refocusing parental cathexis in the child's disability to cathexis in the child's improvements—however small. A key difficulty with early chronic sorrow theory, from a clinical-treatment point of view, is its "cup half-empty" perspective, which perpetuates a focus on what is not there.

More recent developments in theory about chronic sorrow suggest that coping is akin to a ride on a roller coaster: the impact of the diagnosis of the disorder is followed by denial, and then by grief—which again makes real the impact of the diagnosis (Copley & Bodensteiner, 1987). Over time, this cycling is described as moving toward an outward focus (in the case of the autistic child, readiness to engage in treatment). In doing so, the whole grief resolution process is seen as growing closer to closure and to more positive coping.

Some empirical proof for the concept of chronic sorrow has been established, and the idea has also gained clinical acceptance in nursing and in social work practice with parents of children with chronic physical disabilities (Clubb, 1991; Fraley, 1990) or developmental disorders (Copley & Bodensteiner, 1987; Wikler, 1981). In a study of parental responses to developmental disabilities, Wikler, Wasow, and Hatfield (1981) conducted a questionnaire survey of parents of cognitively delayed children. Their findings support the idea that chronic sorrow persists, although it is interwoven with signs of positive coping that vary in intensity, based on life events, changes in the family situation, and, specifically, developmental events in the life of the mentally retarded child. These authors identified stressor events that triggered periodic renewed grieving in the families they studied. Not surprisingly, the stressor events were those that reawakened memories of the idealized child, such as the child's failing to meet developmental milestones of walking, talking, or starting school; and, at later ages, discussions of residential placement, and the twenty-first birthday. Wikler et al. also proposed that there were intensifications of chronic sorrow at a time of crisis (such as when the formal diagnosis was made) and when special interventions were needed (the first psychoactive medications, or behavioral intervention for help with out-of-control behaviors). Routine life events were also believed to trigger intensifications of chronic sorrow, such as when younger siblings developmentally surpassed the handicapped child, or when the handicapped child was viewed by others at family events and compared to familial agemates, or even when a mother of a developmentally disabled child heard other mothers of same-age children talking about everyday things that her child could not yet do.

These findings on episodic reactivity to the autistic child's condition can sensitize clinicians working with parents to times when a parent of an autistic child may be more likely to perceive the child's future more darkly, or minimize progress, or seemingly withdraw from the child. Parents may even, at these times, unconsciously transfer their reawakened sense of distress into active anger toward those who may be seen irrationally, as "preventing" the autistic child's milestones. This group may include teachers, who may be seen as thwarting mainstreaming; caseworkers, who suggest residential placement; or siblings, who, by being "normal" may highlight the autistic child's deficiencies.

Wikler et al. (1981) also surveyed social workers' perceptions of the family coping process and found that although social workers identified time of diagnosis as the time when parents would experience the greatest coping difficulties, families self-reported experiencing the most difficulty coping later in the child's life—at one of the later transitional periods mentioned above. These findings also may reflect the protracted nature of the coping process, in which feelings of denial protect families from overwhelming grief at the time of diagnosis. It also seems possible that Wikler et al.'s results may be influenced by the fact that recently recalled events may still be more intensely felt than distant events (which may be partly repressed). More current events are then invested with emotions from both the past and the present. Thus, what is called chronic sorrow may in fact be a transfer of old feelings onto certain critical triggering current events.

The Complicated Coping Model

The third theory of coping with an autistic child's diagnosis is based on the notion of pathological grief or what is referred to here as complicated grief. The concept of pathological grief derives from a theory of personal and interpersonal schemas that represent dynamic and static aspects of views of self and others (Horowitz, Bonnano, & Holen, 1993). Prolongations or complications of unresolved grief and subsequent inadequate coping can be described as "pathological grief." In cases of such complicated grief, schemas may be blocked from modification so that, when a loved one dies, the schemas used for understanding that person in relation to the self may remain in place, rather than changing with the objective knowledge that the love object no longer exists. Complicated coping therefore can be associated with persistent difficulties in adaptive functioning that arise in response to the loss, which, in this case, would be the specific "loss" of the idealized or hoped-for child to the diagnosis of autism. Signs of complicated grief (or pathological grief) have been shown to take three general forms: (a) avoidances, (b) intrusive thoughts, and (c) failures to adapt (Horowitz, Siegel, Holen, & Bonnano, 1997).

Complications or intensifications of avoidance responses may take the form of denial of the diagnosis or avoidance of people, places, or situations where the child's diagnosis will be evident. Examples might include avoiding the company of relatives or friends who might ask after the child's development; taking the child out of a regular school where he or she has been identified as different; avoiding playgrounds, restaurants, malls, or movies where the child's behavior might be seen as unacceptable for his or her age; or simply emotionally walling off information that professionals have provided about the nature of the child's disability by dismissing professional opinions as wrong, incomplete, or based on inadequate data.

Intrusive thoughts are another complication or intensification of coping responses. Around the time of diagnoses, intrusive phenomena may include flashbacks to events surrounding the pregnancy or delivery that the parent feels may be etiological—and perhaps, in the parent's mind, were preventable. Parents of autistic and other developmentally delayed children may experience intrusive unwanted and unpleasant thoughts ranging from a desire to be somewhere away from the child to uncontrollable fantasies in which they hurt or even kill the child. As suggested by the chronic sorrow model, parents may be especially prone to intrusive phenomena when a particularly landmark event occurs in the life of a sibling or other child, triggering unintended rumination on the autistic child's failure to (ever) reach that same goal.

Coping may also be complicated by failure to adapt to the realities presented by the autistic child. This failure could take the form of not implementing behavioral controls that the parent has been taught, resulting in uncontrollable tantrums, aggression, or self-injury by the child. Failure to adapt may also be represented by the pursuit of "miracle cures" for autism that have no scientific support, with energy directed away from the known treatments for autism that are "just" palliative, and focused instead on "cures" that have no solid foundation in well-accepted science or logic.

When coping with grief proceeds beyond the possible complications described, a re-schematization of the lost loved one results (Horowitz, Bonnano, & Holen, 1993). In successful grief resolution, the schema or attributes of the hoped-for child would therefore change, or re-schematize, to reflect who the child "is" now.

Time-Bound, Completed Grief

Where coping is not complicated by a prolonged period of avoidant, intrusive, or other maladaptive responses, the grieving process is more time-bound. Fortier and Wanlass (1984) describe stages of time-bound grief in response to the diagnosis of a handicap in a child: the impact of the diagnosis, denial, grief, focusing outward (the parents begin to seek information and help for the child), and closure (the parents accept the new status quo). Eventually, a parent who has the social support and intrapsychic resources to undertake a healthy coping process will form a new schema comprised of the attributes of the autistic child, to replace the schema for the hoped-for child. The new schema of the child as autistic incorporate traits of the autism as an integral part of the child's identity. Once a new, revised schema is in place, a phenomenon such as chronic sorrow is not likely to be operative because the old schema of the child is virtually "dead" and is not part of the dynamic cognitive process that has formed and will maintain the current schema of the now "real" autistic child. Chronic sorrow can best be explained in the context of complicated grief by the idea that subordinate schema are maintained and become activated only by certain critical events that serve as triggers.

SPECIAL FEATURES OF GRIEF AROUND THE DIAGNOSIS OF AUTISM

Specific diagnostic features of autism present parents with special difficulties in accepting their child's disability. Many traits of autism exacerbate the most challenging aspects of parenting any child. These traits may engender feelings of latent or overt hostility toward the child, or, at the very least, parental confusion and uncertainty about whether negative feelings about the child are the result of what the child is doing as part of the disability, or what the parent is failing to do to make the child behave to the best of his or her ability. Several of the diagnostic traits of autism prevent parents from experiencing the child as if the child is the idealized or hoped-for child because the child behaves so differently. Over time, the autistic traits erode the schema for the hoped-for child, actively driving the grief process toward a point where a new schema for the child must be adopted, or where staunch pathological degrees of denial, walling-off, or compartmentalization must be adopted to avoid recognition of the child as he or she really is.

Physical Appearance

Compared to children with other developmental disabilities, the autistic child physically appears normal and lacks the dysmorphisms that mark other well-described mental retardation syndromes. This allows the child to appear normal when behavioral symptoms are not actively manifest. Thus, the autistic child's physical appearance constantly challenges the parent's knowledge that something is physically wrong with the child.

Social Responsiveness

Autistic children lack the typical social responsiveness to parents that is so critical in motivating high-quality aspects of parenting behavior. Besides failing to seek parental attention normally, autistic children can actively reject social overtures by the parent that typically developing children readily accept. Parents are sometimes struck with the autistic child's lack of empathy or guilt, and with what instead seems like very self-centered, self-serving behavior. Parents can be unnerved by the child's apparent lack of caring for others (e.g., biting an infant sibling because he is crying). Parents can also feel helpless when the usual social appeals to be a "good boy" or a "big girl" seem to fall on deaf ears because the autistic child lacks social reference. Parents of autistic children rate their children as less adaptable and acceptable, and more demanding, compared to parents' ratings of their children with Down syndrome (Noh, Dumas,

Wolf, & Fisman, 1989). Conversely, parents are often confused by the autistic child's instrumental seeking of affection—seeking hugs and kisses when he or she initiates them, but, more often than not, rejecting such interaction when it's the parent's idea. Such behavior may complicate coping because of an uncertainty about what the child really is or is not capable of doing.

Excessive Independence

Young autistic children often lack a sense of danger, and when coupled with a lack of need for parental proximity and a lack of ability to read parental non-verbal cues of warning, they may tend to run off in unfamiliar and sometimes dangerous places. The assurance of their physical safety is then a nerve-wracking and physically exhausting task for their parents. Public interactions with the child may be experienced by the parents as socially stigmatizing because others may not readily comprehend that the child's "misbehavior" is due to autism or some other unseen problem and may view the parents as overly restrictive or punitive or conversely, as overly-permissive or unattentive. Some parents, especially parents of earlier-born children, may view excessive independence as a lack of attachment, which may be taken as a personal rejection, or which may produce a sense of guilt that the parent has not cared for the child sufficiently.

Parenting Milestones

Parents of autistic children lack parenting milestones—the experiences that parents look forward to sharing with their child as their child develops, such as discussing firefighters, or acting out favorite fairy tales. Parenting style may also be modified: Rather than adopting the permissive, laissez-faire, or authoritative parenting style that may have been used with older siblings, parents of a newly diagnosed autistic child find they must adopt teaching and behavior management techniques that may be relatively more authoritarian and run against their grain as parents. Parents of autistic children miss out on comparing their parenting experiences to those of friends and relatives. (One of the benefits of joining a parent support group, such as an Autism Society of America chapter, is the amelioration of this difficulty through identification of one's parenting experiences with other parents in the same situation.) Parents of autistic children are also less able to rely on their own experiences of being parented, when they were children, to know whether what they are doing with their autistic child is "right."

Because autistic children vary so much in symptom expression, not all parents of autistic children will be exposed to the same challenges. The actual symptoms of a particular child's autism are just one set of factors that may affect how that child's parents adjust to autism. Other factors related to the social ecology of the family, as well as personality variables (cf., Alarcon, 1987), may also predict response to the diagnosis, and these will now be examined.

RISK AND PROTECTIVE FACTORS IN SUCCESSFUL COPING WITH AUTISM

A number of studies of families with physically disabled or other developmentally disabled children point to demographic and other sociological factors that may promote successful coping or ameliorate parents' stress responses to the diagnosis of autism (e.g., Bristol, 1984; Crnic et al., 1983; Donovan, 1988; Fisman & Wolf, 1991; Gallagher et al., 1983; Kazak, 1987; Konstantareas et al., 1992; Mink et al., 1983; Noh et al., 1989). These studies generally have not specifically examined coping, grief, or outcry responses at the time of diagnosis, nor focused exclusively on autistic children; nonetheless, they contribute to developing a broader picture of factors that exacerbate or ameliorate stress associated with rearing a handicapped child. Parental personality or habitual styles of defensive functioning prior to the birth of the autistic child may predict qualities of coping and adaptation to the handicapped child, because research on other types of emotional loss (e.g., marital loss) suggests that preloss personality is a major variable in subsequent adjusting (cf., Alarcon, 1987).

Social Support

The degree of social support experienced by the family prior to the child's diagnosis (family and community contacts) and after the diagnosis (specialized support groups) seems to be a key set of variables because families risk isolation from traditional forms of social support as they take on the role of parents and siblings of a handicapped child (Kazak, 1987; see also Chapter 48). Several specific parent and family variables that will now be discussed seem to influence perceived social support in general, and risk for poor coping with the diagnosis of autism in particular.

Parent and Child Gender Differences

Mothers tend to experience more distress in parenting a child with disabilities than fathers. Most research attributes this to the typically greater amount of time the mother spends with a child, as well as the greater burden of prolonged care (Konstantareas & Homatidis, 1988; Levy-Schiff, 1986; Price-Bonham & Addison, 1978). Murphy (1982) showed that the increased stress response in mothers versus fathers was exacerbated in families where the child had a cognitive disability, compared to families with children with chronic physical illness.

One study suggested that mothers more clearly show a coping response more congruent with chronic sorrow, while fathers more often show more time-bound grief resolution (Fraley, 1990). In our clinical experience, at the time of diagnosis, fathers more often ask about what the child's future as an adult will be like, and mothers more often focus on their fear of not being able to improve the currently most maladaptive symptoms (e.g., prolonged tantrums) and self-endangering behaviors (e.g., carelessly running away). This may be support for Fraley's conclusion that fathers are actively producing a time-bound "map" of the child's life course, to which they must accommodate. Mothers focus more on the successes or failures of the current moment, which would be more congruent with the concept of chronic sorrow and exacerbations that may occur when developmental milestones are missed. Each milestone the child achieves or fails to achieve then marks a new reality to which the parents must accommodate.

The gender of the handicapped child (Fish, 1986) or the child who dies (Littlefield & Rushton, 1986) is also a factor in parental coping responses. These studies have suggested that, especially for fathers, grief responses are more marked when a boy, rather than a girl, is affected. Clinical experience with families with autistic children is skewed by the fact that the vast majority are boys. It also may be clinically significant to an evaluation of the parents' coping responses to consider the relative value of males and females in a particular family's cultural or ethnic group, and whether the child, particularly a male, is the firstborn, or the father's namesake.

Marital Satisfaction and Support

Some research has examined the role of marital satisfaction and the quality of marital support that the mother and father are likely to find in one another as additional stress is placed on their marriage by the extra care and burdens associated with their child's handicap. Longo and Bond (1984) reviewed research and suggested that marital support was mediated by maternal stress, with more distressed mothers being less able to give and get marital support. Mothers with lower levels of marital support reported decreased feelings of intimacy in their marriages, as well as lower self-esteem—factors that seem also to point to poorer adjustment to their child's diagnosis (Fisman, Wolf, & Noh, 1989). Interestingly, Longo and Bond's review refutes a notion that is often held clinically: Parents of handicapped children do not seem to divorce more frequently than the general population, despite higher stress levels. Whether it is that lower divorce rates in these high-stress marriages may be related to the prominent role that the desire for successful coping with the autistic child may play in family life or guilt over abandoning a spouse in such a difficult situation, has not been directly studied, but, clinically, seems quite possible.

Social Class

Social class differences in adjustment to the diagnosis of a developmental disorder have been noted: Parents of higher socioeconomic status (SES) have been described as more action-oriented in response to a diagnosis of a child's disability, and parents of lower SES can be characterized as more acceptance-oriented (Parkes, 1975; Steele, 1983). Action-oriented families cope with the diagnosis by more immediately seeking services, and they invest hope that the child's condition may be improved markedly if the right treatments are undertaken. Acceptance-oriented families deal with the child as he or she is, and they expect less improvement in behavior. Each of these approaches may have relative benefits and drawbacks. Action-oriented higher-SES families may experience greater disappointment if they seek all sorts of "miracle cures" that ultimately do not work. On the other hand, they may more readily organize the emotional resources necessary to devote themselves to the more intensive treatment programs that may differentially benefit a subset of children with autism. Acceptance-oriented lower-SES families may more readily see the disabled child as relatively less disabled in comparison to higher-SES families. If a father is a janitor, the prospect of a son who may be a janitorial assistant someday is less narcissistically injuring than for a father who is an attorney. On the downside, too-ready acceptance of the child's disability may be associated with a sense of helplessness and a subsequent failure to follow through on simple recommendations made by teachers and behaviorists, because the child's condition is viewed as static. This may result in more problematic behavior on the part of the autistic child, and, subsequently, more difficulties to cope with in rearing the child. Such lower-SES families have been described as disadvantaged, with low morale (Mink et al., 1983).

Religious Faith

Another factor in acceptance of the diagnosis of a child's disability is the family's degree of religious faith (Bristol, 1984). When families subscribe to or practice an organized religion, those who identify themselves as more invested in belief in a higher organization or purpose have been reported to cope better with a diagnosis of a disability in their child. This makes sense phenomenologically in the context of Western religions. However, clinically, we have seen many Asian families who are influenced by the Buddhist tradition, which suggests that ancestral wrongdoings may later be punished in the form of a handicapped child, and, therefore, having a handicapped child is shameful. There appears to be no cross-cultural research on the meaning of a handicapped child that might support this clinical observation. In Western culture, however, religiously observant families may benefit not only from the philosophical advantage of seeing meaning in the handicapped child's condition as a test of altruism of self-sacrifice, but also from having additional material and social support from members of their church or synagogue.

Locus of Control

The variability in adjustment to a child's diagnosis that is explained by a parent's degree of religious faith may be a specific case of a more general phenomenon in adjustment to the diagnosis of autism, and may be related to internal versus external locus of control (Rotter, 1966). Parents with more internal locus of control have been described as engaging in more self-blame for their child's condition; parents with more external locus of control engage in more fate-blame (Konstantareas & Homatidis, 1991). The parent who feels personally responsible for his or her child's disability must painfully revise a self-schema to reflect being more defective than previously believed, in addition to forming and accepting a schema of the child as defective. As a case in point, parents with an already-diagnosed child with autism or another developmental disability may feel particularly self-blaming when a second child is diagnosed with the same or possibly related disability.

COPING WITH THE DIAGNOSIS— EFFECTS ON INTRA- AND INTERPERSONAL FUNCTIONING

All parents can be expected to experience outcry and a sense of loss at the news that their child is autistic. Therefore, professionals are faced with negotiating the Scylla and Charybdis of parental need for time and emotional resources to process their feelings versus the need to face the child's disability fully enough so that appropriate and early intervention can be initiated. An important task of the clinician

involved with parents at the time of their child's diagnosis of autism is to delineate the supportive or risk factors that may predict each family's ability to garner their resources to help their child. This has become relatively more important as advances in early treatment (for autism in particular, and for infant stimulation programs in general) have become increasingly available and effective (e.g., Lovaas, 1993; McEachin, Smith, & Lovaas, 1993; Vietze & Vaughn, 1988).

Empirical research clearly supports implementation of early interventions. However, some early interventions come to be viewed by parents as strategies for "recovering" the child from his state of disability. There may be particular risks to progress of the grief resolution and reschematiziation process for parents with strong beliefs in their autistic child's full recovery. Belief in recovery likely puts the grief process on hold. It remains unclear what the psychological effects may be of diverting intra-psychic energies in this fashion, especially as hope of "recovery" may prove false.

In the absence of specific empirical data, clinical experience plus existing research in the areas that have been reviewed here can be used to generate hypotheses about how coping responses to the diagnosis of autism might influence the view of the self, changes in the quality of the marital relationship, quality of care provided to siblings, functioning outside the home, and, most obviously, the ability to provide care for the autistic child. Each of these domains of functioning will be examined to enumerate ways in which, clinically, we have observed sequelae of a possibly complicated coping response to the diagnosis of autism. These observations are intended as guidelines for further clinical observations, and as potential, testable research hypotheses.

View of the Self

In response to the diagnosis of autism, many parents immediately search for a reason. In doing so, blame is sometimes put on the other parent for less-than-perfect prenatal care, for delivery complications, or for some aspect of family history that might suggest whose "side" the autism comes from. Some parents, especially mothers, come to focus on a fact that makes them allegedly responsible for their child's autism (e.g., drinking before the pregnancy was diagnosed). Internalization of this belief may result in a lowering of their appraisal of self-worth, or a sense of helplessness and depression about the present circumstances. This response may be intensified for the parent who wanted the pregnancy, if the other parent did not as actively wish it.

The Marital Relationship

Guilt about the child's autism, or a lack of acceptance, or blame placed by one parent on the other may initiate a marital rift. Conversely, one parent may feel so guilty about the child's condition that he or she martyrs self and/or the marital relationship, as if punishing the marriage that created the child will make amends. This may be manifest in families where the autistic child sleeps with the parents, or where one parent sleeps with the child, or where only one parent is in charge of coordinating all the special services the autistic child needs, while the other parent focuses on the other siblings. Marital tension may be particularly likely when one parent engages in prolonged grieving, either by failing to relinquish the schema of the idealized child, or otherwise denying that there is a severe developmental problem, while the other parent views the child more realistically. Thus, one parent may persist in talking about how the autism is a passing problem of slowness, or is something he or she expects will be resolved by the time the child is kindergarten age, while the other parent wants to invest energy in treatment.

Care of Siblings

In families where inadequate coping with the reality of an autistic child's condition continues, the rearing of siblings may be marginalized (Siegel & Silverstein, 1994). Siblings may adapt by becoming parentified (i.e., coopted into being a caregiver, helper, or teacher)—the only effective way they can earn positive parental regard. Other siblings may be pressed into overachievement, to gain parental attention as well as to compensate for the narcissistic insult of having a child who is disabled.

Some siblings—especially those younger, who have not experienced a period of care that has not been overshadowed by the needs of the autistic child—may become depressed or withdrawn. They may be helpless to get parental attention, or to control their own space, if their autistic sibling is active and unaware of personal boundaries (as many are). Other siblings may act out and rebel. Older siblings may prematurely separate from their families. Some younger siblings may actively provoke their autistic sibling because, for them, getting negative parental attention is better than getting no attention at all.

Functioning Outside the Home

In response to the care demands of an autistic child, some parents may quit their jobs to have more time to work with the autistic child, especially when the child is very young. However, some parents come to feel marginalized from society and do not return to work or finish their education. Other families radically change their family's social network, possibly because it is too painful to spend time with friends who have normally developing children of the same age, or because they perceive others as unaccepting or hypercritical of their care of their autistic child.

Care of the Autistic Child

Clinically, the domain of functioning that is perhaps most affected by a complicated coping response is the care of the autistic child. Parents who are unable to accept their child's autism seem to maintain a homonculus theory of autism, maintaining a belief that a fully-cognizant individual resides inside the exterior child who produces the problematic behavior. Such parents hold onto (and perhaps elaborate) their schema of their idealized child, and look constantly for a tool to tear down the facade of false schema representing who the child only appears to be. Such parents are susceptible to quick fixes for autism, such as the recent facilitated communication (F/C) fad, or other treatments not supported by empirical data, such as auditory training and various diets or dietary supplements. Parents with this type of blocked adaptive response may be more likely to try quick fixes than proven (though only palliative) treatments. In extreme cases, parents may forgo treatments that may help at least somewhat (e.g., refusing oral speech therapy for a nonverbal child who is seen as already "communicating" with facilitated communication).

A THEORETICAL MODEL FOR STAGES OF HEALTHY VERSUS COMPLICATED COPING WITH THE DIAGNOSIS OF AUTISM

Table 34.1 presents a stage-oriented model for normal and complicated coping responses to the diagnosis of autism, as a way of summarizing the stages of response and adaptation experienced as parents adjust to their child's autism.

Stages of Adaptation

The initial *outcry* period is characterized by intense feelings of loss, which echo the helplessness and despair inherent in facing a lifelong stressor. Outcry is normal, but persisting outcry or outcry turned into anger toward self or others is less likely to be adaptive.

Initially, *denial* may be a healthy mechanism in coping, because it provides a means of self-titration of painful news. When maladaptive intensifications of denial occur, the diagnosis and its treatments are marginalized or rendered invalid. Waves of denial first may begin moments after the diagnosis, sometimes persisting until events that take place months or years later make the realization of the diagnosis inevitable. Denial is the inverse of acceptance. Vacillating cycles of denial are bolstered by moments of the child's normal or near-normal behavior. These alternate with moments of increasing insight and resignation to or acceptance of the child's autism. Although denial serves to titrate painful information, the press of this information will lead to "break-throughs" when the parent will be flooded with fears and uncontrollable thoughts about the child. Denial may become interspersed with *intrusive thoughts* about the feared diagnosis and its meaning. When intrusive thinking takes over, feelings of shame, guilt, and anger may guide behavior, making

rational reaction to the child less probable. Child abuse then becomes a real possibility for some parents who may try to externalize these unwanted and painful feelings.

Over time, most parents *work through* intense feelings. Denial consumes less psychic effort. Intrusions become less frequent and less painful, and they occur at more predictable times (such as visits to family members who will be taking a "fresh" look at the child). At this stage, the intrusive episodes of unwanted thoughts that are experienced resemble the recurrent grief that has been described as chronic sorrow. This type of response probably is not as intensely painful as intrusive thoughts that occurred closer to the time of diagnosis, but are still inescapable and inevitable. Formalized ways of controlling unwanted cognitions are likely to develop as the phase of working through begins, and eventually can be consciously employed. Parents who are not able to meaningfully work through their reactions to the diagnosis become trapped in a conundrum of "miracle cures" or other false hopes and expectations, and may experience a sense of alienation from social supports that otherwise would allow the parent to create functional defenses against painful feelings.

Attainment of a Stasis

Coping is substantially achieved when the cascade of responses just described reaches a relatively static state. Sadness may not be completely resolved, as suggested by the chronic sorrow model, but acceptance of the child characterizes everyday functioning. In the best cases, the child's autism and personality may be seen as a unified whole; that is, both are seen as "real" parts of the whole child. In cases where coping remains complicated, and where completion of coping stages has not occurred, the parents' lives may revolve around the child in a way that reflects an unrealistic view of who the child is.

Implications for Clinical Work

The research reviewed here, as well as our clinical understanding of parents' responses to the diagnosis of autism, point to several recommendations that the clinician can

TABLE 34.1   Normal and Complicated, Intensified Responses to the Diagnosis of Autism

Stage	Normal Responses	Complicated, Intensified Responses
Outcry	Crying; intense feelings of loss.	Numbing/shutdown in response to news.
	Protective action toward child in response to diagnostic "threat."	"Kill the messenger"; invalidate credibility of diagnostician.
	"Why me?"; questioning of etiology and bad odds.	Clinical distancing from child.
		Abandon spouse and child.
Denial	Continue to seek further diagnostic opinions.	Avoid contact with helping professionals.
	Avoid situations where child may look "different."	Resist recommended special education.
	Try not to think about the child's future.	Persist in belief that child will outgrow autism.
	Don't talk about it to siblings unless they ask.	Resist/refuse a "label," even if dealing with professionals.
Intrusion	Fear that the child will develop self-injurious symptoms.	Recurring and intense shame and guilt at negative thoughts about the child.
	Fear for the child's future after parents die.	Real fear of harming child and/or self (uncontrollable rage).
	Vividly imagined reenactment of possible "causal" events.	Uncontrollable and unfounded diffuse anxiety about the child.
	Wishing child were dead.	Anger/irritation, not pride in success of siblings or relatives' children.
	Reexperiencing the moment when it was realized the child was autistic.	Recurrent nightmares about fate of child.
	Bad dreams about child.	
Working Through	Realization that child can change but that hard work is needed.	Continued hope for a "cure"; pursuit of illogical, long-shot "miracle" cures.
	Realization that intrusive fears can be handled and learned from.	Child becomes "feral" from lack of intervention, confirming worst fears.
	Recognition of situations that may trigger renewed sadness about child.	Feeling that no one is helping; system is out to thwart parents.
	Ability to seek and accept support from family, friends, and system.	
Stasis vs. Chronic Sorrow	Acceptance of autism as part of child's "personality."	Inability to feel that child is doing as well as can be expected.
	Enjoyment of "quirks."	Unable to utilize social support when offered.
	Realistic expectations for child's future.	"Martyr"; devotes self entirely to autistic child.
	Rational balance between child and other aspects of life (e.g., having a new baby).	Can accept other family members only insofar as they are also devoted to autistic child.
	Sadness but acceptance of how child's future will differ from others.	Numbness in response to accomplishments of other children.

implement when first explaining the diagnosis of autism to parents. Clinicians must recognize that the diagnosis of autism provokes the acute responses that have been the focus here, as well as being a long-term stressor life event.

Understanding the Nature of Autism

Parents must be helped to understand what autism is and, to the best of our current understanding, what may have caused it in their particular child. The first step in this process is to convey a realization that autism is a physical problem that can't be undone, and that the parents did not consciously or unconsciously choose to cause it. The symptoms of autism need to be explained so that the parents can clearly delineate between the child's inability to respond socially, or inability to respond because of a communication deficit, and a willful intention not to respond. This understanding is important in priming the parents for revision of their schemas of the child so they can begin to realistically appraise and accept what the autistic child's strengths and weakness are.

Therefore, before giving a diagnosis of autism, the clinician should establish what (if any) diagnoses have been given in the past, whether autism has ever been ruled out, and what diagnoses the parents already believe the child may have, in order to establish what types of schema the parents currently may have for assimilating their observations about their child's atypical behavior. Prior to discussion of the diagnosis of autism, finding out what the parent knows (or believes) autism is will help build an accurate account of what the parent subsequently may attribute to the child's disability, personality, or response to the environment.

Autism and Mental Retardation

Another important factor at the point of giving parents a diagnosis of autism is whether the parents will also be learning that their child has some degree of mental retardation in addition to autism. Parents may suspect autism, and may have already evidenced a partial acceptance of the term *autism* or *autistic-like* prior to receiving a formal diagnosis, but this may be partly serving to ward off the possibility of a diagnosis of mental retardation which may be seen as a separate, not necessarily concomitant disorder. Autism may be more of a "black box" or may have some mystique to parents who know relatively little about it. A diagnosis of mental retardation is likely to be more uniformly feared. The clinician should be sensitive to the fact that parental preparedness for the diagnosis of autism does not necessarily mean the parents are equally prepared for a diagnosis of some degree of mental retardation.

Further, many early intervention specialists prefer the term *developmental delay* over mental retardation. Parents who accept that their child is developmentally delayed may not realize that the term is often used as a euphemism for mental retardation and will be hit hard if the clinician begins to use the noneuphemistic term in a matter-of-fact manner.

Brush Strokes of a Long-Term View

Parents can benefit from contact with a clinician who has extensive experience with autistic children and can give the parents a realistic picture of what may be expected, based on his or her own experience with a cross-section of autistic children and knowledge of the research literature. The brush strokes of such an initial portrait of the child's future may be very broad if a child is just 3 years old, but there should be a framing of reality based on the child's apparent level of mental retardation, the presence of any concomitant conditions, the degree to which language has spontaneously developed, and the child's level of curiosity about the world. Many, if not most, parents ask the "crystal ball" question, indicating that they seek this information to develop a new schema of their child's future. Giving parents realistic parameters allows them to appreciate the progress the child does make, even if it is measured in centimeters rather than inches.

Titration of Diagnostic and Treatment Information

At the time of diagnosis, parents are likely to be flooded with emotion and may reach a threshold beyond which no further information can be assimilated. Giving the parents time to cry and recover, sit quietly, or hold their child after they have heard the diagnosis can help to contain some of the immediate feelings of being flooded, and subsequent information (that might bear on treatment recommendations, for example) may be better assimilated.

For some parents, concrete aids, such as using a tape recorder to tape the diagnostic debriefing, or receiving summary notes of what has been said on the day of the diagnostic assessment, may facilitate titrated assimilation of information that may initially and unconsciously have been defensively blocked to protect against further feelings of devastation.

Recognition of the Coping Process as Normal

Parents may need to be assisted in recognizing that the emotional outcry they are experiencing is part of an expected coping process that will take time. For some, the acknowledgment that they must engage in working through what is a very personal loss is itself sometimes too painful to face. Such parents may lash out at the system and identify their intense feelings as being angry at earlier doctors who gave wrong or incomplete diagnoses; or, they may experience their intense feelings as self-blame for not having recognized the problem earlier and sought help sooner.

To resolve their grief, parents need to understand that a sense of loss is central to what they are experiencing emotionally, that outcry is normal, and that what has been lost is their idealized or hoped-for child. Although the idealized child may be lost, parents may be helped by being encouraged to recognize behaviors, parts of behaviors, or contexts where the child resembles the ideal by looking or acting normally (e.g., a teenage autistic girl who spends hours looking at herself in the mirror, a 5-year-old autistic boy who collects every Matchbox™ car there is, or an autistic toddler who giggles hilariously when tickled). As working through of grief proceeds, parents may at first develop dual schemas for the child—one set encompassing the more normal behaviors, and one set encompassing the more atypical behaviors. It may take a long time for parents to realize that these schemas may also be integrated into a noncontradictory view of the child as a "whole" child. Contact with other parents of autistic children, especially parents of somewhat older autistic children, may be able to provide parents of newly diagnosed autistic children with needed assurance that the emotional changes experienced during the stages of the coping process are normal and importantly, that the intense emotions of grief will decline in intensity over time.

Initiation of Treatment to Promote Working Through

Parents should be encouraged to pursue treatment for their child as soon as possible. In the initial outcry in response to the diagnosis, parents are likely to feel overwhelmed and helpless. Giving the parents a concrete strategy to pursue—such as tips on behavior modification techniques, or steps to establishing an individualized educational program (IEP) with the child's school district, can ameliorate the feeling that "nothing can be done" or that there is a dumbfounding finality or terminality to having been given the diagnosis of autism. The sooner treatment is undertaken, the sooner there likely will be some improvement in the child, illustrating to the parents that their mental representation of the child should indeed be dynamic and developmental, as it is for all children, and not some sort of dead-end reality. Seeing the child make some improvement is a tangible indicator that the parents themselves must, in some way, be successfully coping.

Recurrent Intensifications of Grief Responses

A central implication of the chronic sorrow model suggests that parents will episodically need help beyond the time of initial diagnosis. At these later times, parents may need to further alter their expectations as their schemas for their child shift and they realize the child may not fulfill roles they once hoped possible.

Times of major life events that are specific to autism do indeed seem to be when parents experience renewed sadness about their child's autism—for example, when parents may realize that special education rather than inclusion is more effective, or must decide on the first use of a psychoactive medication, or are faced with planning for the 22-year-old who is no longer eligible for special education.

Research has emphasized how life events may trigger recurrent periods of sadness, but life events may also periodically provide boosts toward positive adaptations and successful coping. Parents of autistic children may be particularly proud when they see their child has actually met his or her IEP goals, or when they watch an old home video and realize that certain maladaptive behaviors that used to greatly interfere with family functioning have resolved. Helping other families with more newly diagnosed children "learn the ropes" of the developmental disabilities system can promote positive coping through altruistic activity. Parents may also cope by developing a related positive cathexis in the autistic child's siblings' accomplishments, feeling relieved and pleased each time a sibling reaches a milestone never achieved by the autistic child. In families with older children, a sibling who becomes a social worker or an attorney may give parents assurance that there will be a caring family member who can handle the developmental disabilities service system on the autistic brother's or sister's behalf after the parents become too old or die.

FUTURE RESEARCH

To date, research studies on autism (or on other developmental disabilities) have not examined how typical or complicated coping responses (as measured by inventories of grief symptoms or stress response syndromes) may predict subsequent functioning. Based on clinical experience, it would seem worthwhile to generate hypotheses for research on how a complicated coping process may manifest itself in domains of everyday functioning with respect to the child's special care needs in particular, and family functioning in general. For example, it would be quite informative to compare parents of autistic children, who have a range of responses to the diagnosis of autism, on domain-specific measures such as the Grief Experiences Inventory (GEI; Sanders, Mauger, & Strong, 1979) or the Parental Experience Assessment Form (PEAF; Rando, 1983), which have been used in earlier coping research on families of handicapped children; or modified versions of other grief-specific measures like the Texas Revised Inventory of Grief (TRIG; Faschingbauer, 1981), the Reaction to Loss Inventory (RLI; Horowitz, Field, & Fridhandler, 1991), or the Pathological Grief Module for the Structured Clinical Interview for Diagnoses (PG-SCID; Holen & Bonnano, 1993). Such data could be used to study complications of coping over time and to predict families most at risk for severe dysfunction as a result of the distress associated with the autistic child's disability.

Receiving the diagnosis of autism is clearly a major stressor life event. In certain ways, the diagnosis is made even more painful and difficult to accept by the open-endedness and uncertainty that are raised by the variety of outcomes inherent among autistic children. The lifetime of care that parents can expect to provide for the child, as well as the arrangements they will need to make to provide for the child after they themselves die, is an overwhelming prospect that likely cannot be fully appreciated by anyone not faced with it. The reality of the child's limited life, the loss of expectations for the child the parents had hoped to have, and the burden of care for the autistic child are all imprinted on the parent at the time of diagnosis. Understanding this difficult phase in the life cycle of families dealing with autism is an important component in being able to promote a good quality of life for families with an autistic child.

Cross-References

Developmental aspects of autism are discussed in Chapters 12 to 14, and issues in working with families are addressed in Chapter 27.

REFERENCES

Alarcon, R.D. (1987). Personality disorder as a pathogenic factor in bereavement. *Journal of Nervous and Mental Disease, 172,* 45–47.

Atkinson, S.D. (1994). Grieving and loss in parents with a schizophrenic child. *American Journal of Psychiatry, 151*(8), 1137–1139.

Bettelheim, B. (1967). *The empty fortress.* New York: Free Press.

Bettelheim, B. (1974). *Home for the heart.* New York: Knopf.

Bristol, M.M. (1984). Family resources and successful adaptation to autistic children. In E. Schopler & G. Mesibov (Eds.), *The effects of autism on the family* (pp. 289–310). New York: Plenum Press.

Bristol, M.M., Gallagher, J.J., & Holt, S. (1993). Maternal depressive symptoms in autism: Response to psychotherapy. *Journal of Rehabilitative Psychology, 38,* 3–10.

Bronfenbrenner, U. (1979). *The ecology of human development.* Cambridge, MA: Harvard University Press.

Bruce, E.J., Schultz, C.L., Smyrnios, K.X., & Schultz, N.C. (1994). Grieving related to development: A preliminary comparison of three age cohorts of parents of children with intellectual disability. *British Journal of Medical Psychology, 67*(1), 37–52.

Clubb, R.L. (1991). Chronic sorrow: Adaptation patterns of parents with chronically ill children. *Pediatric Nursing, 17*(5), 461–466.

Copley, M.F., & Bodensteiner, J.B. (1987). Chronic sorrow in families of disabled children. *Journal of Child Neurology, 2,* 67–70.

Crnic, R.A., Friedrich, W.N., & Greenberg, M.T. (1983). Adaptation of families with mentally retarded children: A model of stress coping and family ecology. *American Journal of Mental Deficiency, 88,* 125–138.

Delight, E., & Goodall, J. (1990). Love and loss: Conversations with parents of babies with spina bifida managed without surgery: 1971–1981. *Developmental Medicine and Child Neurology, 61,* 1–58.

DeMeyer, M. (1979). *Parents and children in autism.* Washington, DC: Winston.

Donovan, A.M. (1988). Family stress and ways of coping with adolescents who have handicaps: Maternal perceptions. *American Journal of Mental Retardation, 92,* 502–509.

Downey, G., Silver, R.C., & Wortman, C.B. (1990). Reconsidering the attribution-adjustment relation following a major negative event: Coping with the loss of a child. *Journal of Personality and Social Psychology, 59,* 925–940.

Drotar, D., Baskiewitz, A., Irvin, N., Kennell, J., & Klaus, M. (1975). The adaptation of parents to the birth of a child with a congenital malformation: A hypothetical model. *Pediatrics, 56,* 710–717.

Emde, R., & Brown, C. (1978). Adaptation to the birth of a Downs syndrome infant: Grieving and maternal attachment. *Journal of the Academy of Child and Adolescent Psychiatry, 17,* 299–323.

Faschingbauer, T.R. (1981). *Texas Revised Inventory of Grief manual.* Houston, TX: Honeycomb.

Fish, W. (1986). Differences in grief intensity in bereaved parents. In T. Rando (Ed.), *Parental loss of a child* (pp. 323–371). Champaign, IL: Research Press.

Fisman, S., & Wolf, L. (1991). The handicapped child: Psychological effects of parental, marital, and sibling relationships. In M.M. Konstantareas & J.H. Beitchman (Eds.), *The Psychiatric Clinics of North America: Pervasive Developmental Disorders, 14*(1), 199–217.

Fisman, S., Wolf, L., & Noh, S. (1989). Marital intimacy in parents of exceptional children. *Canadian Journal of Psychiatry, 34*(6), 519–525.

Fortier, L.M., & Wanlass, R.L. (1984). Family crisis following the diagnosis of a handicapped child. *Family Relations, 33,* 13–24.

Fraley, A.M. (1990). Chronic sorrow: Parental response. *Journal of Pediatric Nursing, 5*(4), 268–273.

Gallagher, J.J., Beckman-Bell, P., & Cross, A. (1983). Families of handicapped children: Sources of stress and its amelioration. *Exceptional Children, 50,* 10–19.

Graftstrom, M., Norberg, A., & Hagberg, B. (1993). Relationships between demented elderly people and their families: A follow-up study of caregivers who had previously reported abuse when caring for their spouses and parents. *Journal of Advanced Nursing, 18*(11), 1747–1757.

Haley, W.E., & Pardo, K.M. (1989). The relationship of severity of dementia to caregiving stressors. *Psychology and Aging, 4*(4), 389–392.

Hazzard, A., Weston, J., & Gutterres, C. (1992). After a child's death: Factors related to parental bereavement. *Journal of Developmental and Behavioral Pediatrics, 13*(1), 24–30.

Holen, A., & Bonnano, G. (1993). *The Pathological Grief module for the Structured Clinical Interview for Diagnoses* (PG-SCID). San Francisco: University of California, Center for the Study of Neuroses.

Holroyd, J. (1974). The questionnaire on resources and stress: An instrument to measure family response to a handicapped member. *American Journal of Community Pscyhology, 2,* 92–94.

Holroyd, J., & McArthur, D. (1976). Mental retardation and stress on parents: A contrast between Downs syndrome and childhood autism. *American Journal of Mental Deficiency, 80,* 431–436.

Horowitz, M.J., Bonnano, G.A., & Holen, A. (1993). Pathological grief: Diagnosis and explanation. *Psychosomatic Medicine, 55,* 260–273.

Horowitz, M.J., Field, N., & Fridhandler, S. (1991). *The reaction to loss inventory.* San Francisco: University of California, Center for the Study of Neuroses.

Horowitz, M.J., Siegel, B., Holen, A., & Bonnano, G. (1997). *Complicated grief: A proposal of diagnostic criteria.* Manuscript submitted for publication.

Kachoyeanos, M.K., & Selden, F.E. (1993). Life transitions of parents at the unexpected death of a school-aged or older child. *Journal of Pediatric Nursing, 8*(1), 41–49.

Kazak, A.E. (1987). Families with disabled children: Stress and social networks in three samples. *Journal of Abnormal Child Psychology, 15,* 137–146.

Konstantareas, M.M., & Homatidis, S. (1988). Stress and differential parent involvement in families of autistic and learning disabled children. In E.D. Hibbs (Ed.), *Children and families: Studies in prevention and intervention* (pp. 321–336). Madison, WI: International Universities Press.

Konstantareas, M.M., & Homatidis, S. (1991). Effects of developmental disorder on parents: Theoretical and applied considerations. In M.M. Konstantareas & J.H. Beitchman (Eds.), *The Psychiatric Clinics of North America: Pervasive Developmental Disorders, 14*(1), 183–198.

Konstantareas, M.M., Homatidis, S., & Plowright, C.M.S. (1992). Assessing resources and stress in parents of severely dysfunctional children through the Clarke modification of Holroyd's Questionnaire on Resources and Stress. *Journal of Autism and Developmental Disorders, 22*(2), 217–234.

Kurita, H., Kita, M., & Miyake, Y. (1992). A comparative study of the development and symptoms among disintegrative psychosis and infantile autism with and without speech loss. *Journal of Autism and Developmental Disorders, 22*(2), 175–188.

Layne, L.L. (1990). Motherhood lost: Cultural dimensions of miscarriage and stillbirth in America. *Women and Health, 16*(3/4), 69–98.

Lehman, D.R., Wortman, C.B., & Williams, A.F. (1987). Long-term effects of losing a spouse or child in a motor vehicle crash. *Journal of Personality and Social Psychology, 52*, 218–231.

Levy-Schiff, R. (1986). Mother–father–child interactions in families with a mentally retarded young child. *American Journal of Mental Deficiency, 91*, 141–149.

Littlefield, C., & Rushton, J.P. (1986) When a child dies: The sociobiology of bereavement. *Journal of Personality and Social Psychology, 4*, 797–802.

Longo, D.C., & Bond, L. (1984). Families of the handicapped child: Research and practice. *Family Relations, 33*, 57–65.

Lovaas, O.I. (1993). The development of a treatment-research project for developmentally disabled and autistic children, *Journal of Applied Behavioral Analysis, 26*(4), 617–630.

McEachin, J.J., Smith, T., & Lovaas, O.I. (1993). Long-term outcome for children with autism who received early intensive behavioral treatment. *American Journal of Mental Retardation, 97*(4), 359–372.

Minde, K.K., Hackett, J.D., Killou, D., & Silver, S. (1972). How they grow up: 41 physically handicapped children and their families. *American Journal of Psychiatry, 128*, 1554–1560.

Mink, I.T., Nihira, K., & Meyer, C.E. (1983). Taxonomy of family life style: 1. Homes with TMR children. *American Journal of Mental Deficiency, 87*, 484–497.

Murphy, M. (1982). The family with a handicapped child: A review of the literature. *Journal of Developmental and Behavioral Pediatrics, 3*, 73–81.

Noh, S., Dumas, J.E., Wolf, L., & Fisman, S. (1989). Delineating sources of stress in parents of exceptional children. *Family Relations, 38*, 456–461.

Olshansky, S. (1962). Chronic sorrow: A response to having a mentally defective child. *Social Casework, 43*, 190–193.

Parkes, C.M. (1975). Determinants of outcome following bereavement. *Omega, 6*, 303–323.

Parks, R. (1977). Parental reactions to the birth of a handicapped child. *Health & Social Work, 2*, 52–66.

Price-Bonham, S., & Addison, S. (1978). Families and mentally retarded children: Emphasis on the father. *The Family Coordinator, 27*, 221–230.

Pruchno, R.A., & Potashnik, S.L. (1989). Caregiving spouses: Physical and mental health in perspective. *Journal of the American Geriatric Society, 37*(8), 697–705.

Rando, T. (1983). An investigation of grief and adaptation in parents whose children have died of cancer. *Journal of Pediatric Psychology, 8*(3), 3–20.

Riski, J.E. (1991). Parents of children with cleft lip and palate. *Clinics in Communication Disorders, 1*(3), 42–47.

Rotter, J.B. (1966). Generalized expectancies for external versus internal control of reinforcement. *Psychological Monographs, 86*, 609.

Sanders, C., Mauger, P., & Strong, P. (1979). A manual for the Grief Experience Inventory. (Available from C. Saunders, 1021 S. Kings Dr., Doctors Bldg., Ste. 801, Charlotte, NC 28283).

Schiff, H.S. (1977). *The bereaved parent.* New York: Crown.

Semple, S.J. (1992). Conflict in Alzheimer's caregiving families: Its dimensions and consequences. *The Gerontologist, 32*(5), 648–655.

Siegel, B. (1996). *The world of the autistic child: Understanding and treating autistic spectrum disorders.* New York: Oxford University Press.

Siegel, B., & Silverstein, S. (1994). *What about me? Siblings of developmentally disabled children.* New York: Insight Books/Plenum Press.

Solnit, A., & Stark, M. (1961). Mourning and the birth of the defective child. *The Psychoanalytical Study of the Child, 16*, 523–537.

Spanier, G.B. (1976). Measuring dyadic adjustment: New scales for assessing the quality of marriage and similar dyads. *Journal of Marriage and the Family, 38*(1), 15–28.

Steele, S. (1983). *Health promotion of the child with a long-term illness.* Norwalk, CT: Appleton-Century-Crofts.

Szurek, S.A., Berlin, I.N., & Boatman, M.J. (1971). Inpatient care for the psychotic child. *The Langley Porter Child Psychiatry Series,* Vol. 5. Palo Alto: Science and Behavior Books.

Vietze, P.M., & Vaughn, H.G. (1988). *Early identification of infants with developmental disabilities.* Philadelphia: Grune & Stratton.

Volkmar, F. (1992). Childhood Disintegrative Disorder. Issues for *DSM-IV. Journal of Autism and Developmental Disorders, 22*(4), 625–642.

Wikler, L. (1981). Chronic stress of families of mentally retarded children. *Family Relations, 30,* 281–288.

Wikler, L., Wasow, M., & Hatfield, E. (1981). Chronic sorrow revisited: Attitudes of parents and professionals about adjustment to mental retardation. *American Journal of Orthopsychiatry, 51,* 63–70.

Young, R.K. (1987). Intervening with families of infants with cleft lip and palate. In L.M. Wright & M. Leahey (Eds.), *Families and chronic illness.* Bethlehem, PA: Springhouse.

Zisook, S., & Shuchter, S. (1991a). Depression through the first year after the death of a spouse. *American Journal of Psychiatry, 148,* 1346–1352.

Zisook, S., & Shuchter, S. (1991b). Early psychological reaction to the stress of widowhood. *Psychiatry, 54,* 320–333.

CHAPTER 35

Implementation of TEACCH Philosophy

ERIC SCHOPLER

North Carolina's statewide program for the Treatment and Education of Autistic and Related Communication Handicapped CHildren (Division TEACCH) is the only university-based statewide program mandated by law to provide services, research, and multidisciplinary training on behalf of autism and related developmental disorders. TEACCH was developed in response to the needs of individuals and families struggling with the stresses, confusion, and frustration generated by this most severe of the developmental disabilities (Rutter & Schopler, 1978, 1992). The effects of this struggle impinge not only on the individuals and families involved, but also on the community in which they live. When these special needs are ignored or misunderstood, the costs for all concerned increase and multiply.

Division TEACCH was evolved over 30 years ago in response to a misunderstanding widely accepted throughout the mental health establishment. According to erroneous psychoanalytic assumptions, parents were believed to induce autistic symptoms in their children through pathologic unconscious impulses and rejection. Children were thought to require separation from their parents by residential placement (Bettelheim, 1967). These erroneous Freudian assumptions lacked empirical support. They assigned psychogenic bases for what was soon demonstrated to be a developmental disorder, one determined by multiple biologic processes rather than being of emotional origins. In addition, autism was confused with childhood schizophrenia or psychosis. This monumental confusion and misunderstanding increased both the stress and the cost of the disorder for all concerned, until the accumulation of research evidence was sufficient to change the title of the *Journal of Autism and Childhood Schizophrenia* to the *Journal of Autism and Developmental Disorders* (Schopler, Rutter, & Chess, 1979).

This chapter is a survey of the TEACCH program, starting with its early history and origins, and tracing how it evolved to meet current needs. The various facets of the program's philosophy are described. A major source of the program's success and long-term viability has been the implementation of the TEACCH philosophy into program structure, clinical research, and empirical research. These elements are described in some detail because they both reinforce and teach the program's philosophy without ideological preaching and administrative coercion. The resulting service functions, research, and training activities are summarized, and TEACCH program evaluation and outcome data are reviewed.

BACKGROUND

Division TEACCH formed its tap root in Eric Schopler's graduate education, where he found Bettelheim an eloquent though negative role model (1993). The confusion of autism and childhood schizophrenia inspired Schopler (1965, 1966) to conduct one of the first studies to focus on the perceptual rather than the emotional source of the autism syndrome. Impairments in perceptual processes correlated significantly with impaired human relatedness (Reichler & Schopler, 1971).

Eric Schopler, founder of Division TEACCH, joined the faculty of the Psychiatry Department of the University of North Carolina in 1964. At that time, children with autism, and their parents, were seen in group therapy (Speers & Lansing, 1965). Autism was still viewed as a form of social withdrawal from dysfunctional parents. Children were seen in a group where free expression of feelings was permitted, with the expectation that the resulting regression would have therapeutic effects. Unfortunately, the ensuing chaos frequently only increased anxiety levels in both staff and children. Parents drove great distances twice a week to participate in this process with their children. The most noticeable results from this procedure was that a group of parents committed to helping their children became more demoralized, and a significant number of mothers were being hospitalized for a period of psychiatric inpatient care.

It became apparent that such psychodynamic interventions and their underlying theoretical orientations were fundamentally flawed and ineffective. When parents expressed themselves in confused language about their children, they were considered to be suffering from disordered thinking, which in turn caused disordered language in their children (Goldfarb, 1958). Schopler and Loftin (1969) demonstrated empirically that parents of autistic children had no more indications of thought disorders than did parents of retarded children, and that higher scores on disordered thinking were attributable to a "test anxiety" response associated with Freudian assumptions of parental blame and resulting scapegoating (Schopler, 1971).

I teamed up with a young child psychiatry fellow, Robert Reichler, who had had his critical faculties nurtured by attending the University of Chicago, and who was willing to undertake the inevitable career risks of noting that the Freudian emperor was nude of substance. Based on our experience and observations, we adopted the radical proposition that autism was not caused by parental pathology, but rather by some form of brain abnormality (Schopler & Reichler, 1971c). Parents were not the agents of the disorder, deserving to be treated as patients; they were instead the agents of recovery and were to be treated as collaborators. Rather than being subjected to unstructured psychotherapy, children needed educational structure (Schopler,

Brehm, Kinsbourne, & Reichler, 1971). We demonstrated that parents understood their children better than did most professionals, by comparing parental estimates of their child's level of development with formal psychological testing (Schopler & Reichler, 1972). Schopler was able to obtain the support of the National Institute of Mental Health for what was then considered a radical and innovative approach: these children could achieve optimum development when their parents were trained as cotherapists (Schopler & Reichler, 1971b). This proposal led to establishment of the Child Research Project, advocating parent-professional collaboration designed to pool information and resources in order to develop and implement individualized treatment programs for each child, with parental input and collaboration. Parents were trained in special educational procedures and advised on how to manage troublesome behavior problems like temper tantrums and toileting difficulties.

At the completion of the federal grant, word of this exciting new experiment spread around North Carolina, and parents became active in transforming the project's educational group sessions into a social action group whose purpose was to continue the program with the North Carolina legislature's support. One of the parents' most innovative ideas was to organize a Sunday breakfast, attended by parents, children, and program staff, to which members of the legislature would be invited. The resulting legislation was a tribute to the energy, persistence, and commitment of the parents' group and their professional collaborators. In 1972, Division TEACCH received its legislative mandate from the North Carolina legislature as the country's first statewide program for diagnosis, treatment, training, and education of autistic children and their families. When a formal NIMH review of Division TEACCH was published, it emphasized the importance of a federally funded treatment program being continued by the state, and the need to expand the program gradually without loss of individualization. This unusual relationship between university research and state policy, as reviewed by Schopler (1986), developed along the following organizational priorities.

ORGANIZATIONAL STRUCTURES

TEACCH program priorities included establishing comprehensive services for autistic children via parent involvement from preschool to adulthood, conducting related research, and offering multidisciplinary training. Successive development priorities arose from the parents' perspective in the three main areas of each client's life: (a) home adjustment, (b) education, and (c) community adaptation. This goal was pursued via relevant organizational structures (Reichler & Schopler, 1976).

Home Adjustment

Helping families cope with the special needs presented by their child was the first order of concern raised by the parents. This assistance was realized through the establishment of seven regional TEACCH centers geographically distributed around the state. Each center is housed near three important collaborating resources: (a) a branch of the University of North Carolina system—a source of research collaboration, training, and staff development; (b) a Developmental Evaluation Clinic (DEC), mandated to evaluate young handicapped children; and (c) an Area Health Education Center (AHEC), designed to provide up-to-date healthcare to all areas of the state.

Each TEACCH center provides diagnostic assessment, parent training and support, consultation, and professional training. At each center, the direct services of social skills training, vocational training, case management, and support groups for parents and siblings are available. The centers also collaborate with other agencies involved in the provision of services for people with developmental disabilities, such as the Department of Public Instructions, the Division of Developmental Disabilities, and the Division of Vocational Rehabilitation Services.

The regional TEACCH centers are coordinated by an Administrative and Research Unit, directed by Gary Mesibov and Eric Schopler, both professors of psychology at the University of North Carolina at Chapel Hill. This unit is responsible for the overall administration, direction, and coordination of the program, including national and international consultation, and it is the main liaison with the North Carolina State Legislature and the Autism Society of North Carolina.

Each regional center is directed by a doctoral-level psychologist who supervises a staff of five to seven therapists with backgrounds in serving handicapped people and those with autism. Staff members come from various disciplines, including special education, social work, speech and hearing, psychology, occupational therapy, child development, vocational therapy, and rehabilitation counseling. Although most TEACCH therapists have specialized professional training, they are taught to function as generalists and are expected to deal with the entire range of problems created by autism in a manner that reflects the social expectations of the parent role.

Education

The second area of concern for TEACCH is the child's education. When the program began, autistic children were considered to be in the province of mental health rather than public school education. The children were usually managed through psychiatric facilities and excluded from public schools, and their special educational needs were not recognized. When the legislative mandate created TEACCH in 1972, eleven public school classrooms were also funded. These funds provided for a teacher and assistant teacher for four to six children. Although these classes were located in the public schools, they were affiliated with TEACCH according to contracts made with each school.

The contracts may vary by location, but usually have these provisions: (a) TEACCH and the school are to be involved in hiring the teacher; (b) each teacher is to complete the intensive five-day training on the needs and teaching techniques for the problems of autism; (c) the children are to be placed in the classroom after the center has completed the diagnostic assessment and the center staff has participated in the formulation of each Individualized Educational Plan (IEP); (d) consultation is to be provided from each center to the classrooms in its region. Because of the consistent effectiveness of these classrooms in providing community-integrated education, there are now more than 265 TEACCH affiliated classrooms in North Carolina. The centers also provide assistance, support, and training to the many children being educated in non-TEACCH affiliated classrooms.

Community Adaptation

The third area for which parents requested professional help was the relationship between the community and their autistic child. The main purpose of this priority was a twofold advocacy: first, to help the community recognize and understand the special needs of this population, and, second, to develop cost-effective services where none was available. During the past 25 years, this initiative has involved classrooms in the public school, summer recreation facilities (including camp and recreational groups), services for adolescents, supported employment for adults, job coaches, group homes, and the residential-vocational options in the Carolina Living and Learning Center. More recently, preschool services received new initiatives from federal legislation, reflected also at the local level (Schopler, Van Bourgondien, & Bristol, 1993).

Organizationally, this effort is facilitated by the relationship between TEACCH staff and parent groups. Each center and each classroom has a parents' group, which also belongs to the Autism Society of North Carolina, a chapter of the national Autism Society of America (ASA). The organizational structures described in this section emphasize parent-professional collaboration and the bond created by sharing the generalist orientation. Pyramidal hierarchy is minimized so as to maximize staff responsibility with each child and family at the local level and with community integration. By being located in the university system, the program also contributes to research and new knowledge. New treatment interventions are evaluated, both from direct experience and published research. Those that appear sound and have a reasonable cost:benefit ratio can be introduced into the program without beureaucratic delay.

Being based at the University of North Carolina and having its leaders on the faculty, the program is involved in all of the traditional university functions, including research,

teaching, and clinical work. This unique university–service model is a powerful combination. It exemplifies in many ways how university resources can directly impact citizens throughout a state.

The combined university and community-based service program also offers important advantages in continuity for both staff and consumers. Because future professionals are trained to understand the same theoretical principles and practice the same techniques used by practitioners in the field, their experiences and university training are relevant for later professional work. TEACCH liaison with other agencies involved with autistic and similar people provides for a common approach. Therefore, children with autism can move from preschool to public school to adult vocational and residential programs with a common focus and orientation. The sustained long-term consistency provided by Division TEACCH is unusual in the human services and vital for maximal client development.

POPULATION SERVED

Division TEACCH serves people of all ages and levels of functioning who have received the diagnosis of autism or related communication handicaps. Since Division TEACCH was established, over 3,500 people with these diagnoses have received direct and indirect services. However, before we describe this population, it is worth noting that during the 30-year period covered in this chapter, diagnostic labels have stayed on the move. In the background section, we referred to Schopler's early work (1965, 1966) on perceptual processes and receptor preference. During that period, autism was considered the earliest form of childhood schizophrenia, and no formal distinction was made between the two. Some children in that ambiguous group were also labeled as psychotic. Neither the first *Diagnostic and Statistical Manual of Mental Disorders (DSM)*, published in 1952, nor *DSM-II*, in 1968, identified autism as a separate diagnostic category, thus adding to the diagnostic overlap. There is little doubt that children diagnosed as schizophrenic or psychotic during that period would be primarily identified within the autism or pervasive developmental disability classification today.

With the publication of *DSM-III* (American Psychiatric Association [APA], 1980), autism was recognized as a separate diagnostic category, defined by four criteria: (a) lack of relatedness, (b) communication handicaps, (c) perseverative behavior, and (d) age of onset under 30 months. These four criteria, sometimes referred to as the Rutter criteria, were confined to the young age group. Dissatisfaction with *DSM-III* became the basis of further revisions in *DSM-III-R* (APA, 1987) and *DSM-IV* (APA, 1994). However, by 1980, the APA had made a service commitment to base any future changes on research data and empirical evidence. A significant accumulation of research evidence, described below, has resulted in broadening the autism definition.

DEMOGRAPHIC CHARACTERISTICS

The characteristics of the TEACCH population described below come from the data published in our annual report (TEACCH, 1990), updated to the present.

Age

TEACCH clients range in age from 16 months to 60 years. Numbers in both the adult and preschool age groups have grown during the past decade.

IQ

From 3,083 consecutive referrals, the IQ distribution was about 39% with IQ of 70 or higher, in the near-normal range; 41.7% with IQ of 40 to 69, in the moderate range of retardation; and 18.6% less than 40, in the severe range of retardation. During the post-World War II period, autism and mental retardation were considered to be dichotomous diagnoses. However, in subsequent years, most centers saw larger numbers of autistic children and reported that autism and mental retardation could and did coexist. This finding had the effect of including in the autism diagnosis children who had previously been excluded, thus broadening the diagnostic base.

Socioeconomic Status

In Kanner's (1943) paper, where he first reported a series of children with the autism features, he also noted that all the children came from highly educated and economically advantaged families, with certain religious preference. In our sample, however, only 18% came from families in the advantaged class, 56% were from the middle class, and 26% were from the lower-income group. Our racial distribution was 63.8% White, 31.6% Black, and 4.6% others. We found possible selection factors that could skew for the selective distribution described by Kanner. Moreover, the distribution of our sample was similar to that of the overall population of North Carolina (Schopler, Andrews, & Strupp, 1979).

Age of Onset

DSM-III (1980) listed age of onset under 30 months as a defining feature of autism. However, in our sample, 15% had age of onset after 30 months (Short & Schopler, 1988), comparable to findings by Volkmar, Stier, and Cohen (1985). Age of onset was dropped as a defining feature of autism in *DSM-III-R*, thus removing another restricting characteristic in the definition of autism.

Gender

In our sample, 76% were boys and only 24% were girls. This is similar to the male:female ratio reported from virtually all samples with larger numbers of autistic individuals.

Diagnosis at Referral

In a sample of consecutive referrals from 15 years ago, 56% were diagnosed with autism, and 44% were in the related communications handicapped category. This latter group would now be described primarily as PDD-NOS (Van Bourgondien, Marcus, & Schopler, 1992). However, from a more recent sample, the percentage of referrals diagnosed autistic has been increasing to more than 76%. The changes in the definition of autism, based on empirical research reviewed above, have had the effect of broadening the definition. It is perhaps not surprising that the Autism Society of America used a prevalence rate of 4 in 10,000 persons for autism 20 years ago. Today, the rate used is 15 to 20 per 10,000 persons.

PHILOSOPHY

Probably the clearest discussion of the TEACCH philosophy emerges from reviewing the shared values and attitudes we teach, model, and search for when we hire and train staff and faculty. Moreover, one of the leading factors in the unusual effectiveness of the TEACCH Program has been our consistent effort to develop both organizational and clinical structures that will support and reinforce these values. They include:

1. Understanding characteristics of autism from observations of the child rather than from professional theories.
2. Parent-professional collaboration.
3. Improving the child's adaptation both through teaching new skills and through environmental accommodation to deficits.
4. Assessment for individualized treatment.
5. Use of structured teaching.
6. Priority for cognitive and behavior theory.
7. Skill enhancement and acceptance of deficits.
8. Holistic orientation.
9. Lifelong community-based service.

This section reviews these shared values. Their structural implementation is described in the next section.

Characteristics of Autism

We share an awareness that the historical misunderstanding of autism, when it was explained in terms of Freudian theories of parental rejection and unconscious parental wishes, was destructive. When Kanner (1943) first introduced autism into the professional literature, his most important contribution was probably that he described the children as having clear and lucid behavioral characteristics, which enabled clinicians in other countries to identify similar children with good

consistency. These clinical descriptions provided the basis for a growing accumulation of empirical evidence showing that autism was based in various neurobiological processes. We shared a belief in the importance of empirical evidence. When new treatment based on ideological social policy is proposed, we expect supporting research evidence. Examples of the destructive effects when a specific treatment technique is extended past supporting evidence can be seen in psychoanalytic therapy, facilitated communication, total inclusion, intensive behavior therapy, and others discussed elsewhere (Schopler, 1994).

Parent-Professional Collaboration

When parents' relationship to their children's autism was misinterpreted by the mental health establishment in the period from 1940 to the 1960s, parents often had the experience of being scapegoated by professionals (Schopler, 1971). If we were going to challenge and change these fixed assumptions, it was clear that parent-professional collaboration was both desirable and necessary. This collaborative effort has continued for the past two decades and is responsible for many advances in services for people with autism in North Carolina (Schopler, Mesibov, Shigley, & Bashford, 1984) and other regions. During the beginning stages of the TEACCH program, when we teamed up with parents against professional misunderstanding, our collaboration was spontaneous and required little articulation (Schopler & Reichler, 1971b). Unfortunately, today, parent-professional relationships have become more acrimonious and litigious, and collaboration is more difficult to achieve. It requires the ability to see the other group's point of view and to modify each group's perspectives for the welfare of the larger whole. Currently, when differences are so often resolved by litigation using an adversarial procedure, productive parent-professional collaboration is harder to come by. However, we have found that by keeping this relationship central in our philosophy, other program ramifications have been possible, with long-term benefits for all concerned. The shared value of the importance of parent-professional collaboration goes back to the very beginning of this program and hence overlaps with more aspects of TEACCH philosophy than any other component.

Goal of Improved Adaptation

As the biologic bases of autism became more widely established, it became evident that a meaningful treatment program would need to be long-term and no priority could be given to finding a quick fix. Possible cures should, of course, be researched, but they should not be used as the primary rationale for research funding, as was the case with many federal grants in the past. Equally important, the biologic basis of autism produced certain problems of learning and cognitive styles that were highly resistant to change. It was important that professionals first learn about these cognitive characteristics before becoming active in changing them. By stressing adaptation, we emphasize that improved adaptation has two elements. One is achieved by teaching new interests and skills. But when an autism deficit blocks the learning of a new skill, the second approach is to accommodate the environment to that deficit. Both of these approaches form essential components of improved adaptation, and must be recognized from the outset if they are to be realized in a treatment program.

Assessment for Individualization

Central to the effort of improving adaptation is the knowledge of what skill to teach, or what deficit should receive environmental accommodation. People do not want to wear glasses if their vision is satisfactory. The decision of when to overcome a learning problem by teaching a better skill and when to overcome it by environmental accommodation can best be reached with the use of the most appropriate diagnostic assessment. This assessment can be done through formal instruments that have been field-tested or standardized. It can also be done by informal means, making careful observation of the child in various situations. From parents' and teachers' thoughtful and accurate observations, we get the most useful information. From a parent, usually we obtain the most consistent longitudinal observations

of a child, and when we know the individual's unique history, we can formulate the most appropriate individualized treatment program.

Structured Teaching

From formal and informal assessment, we can identify priorities for teaching the individual new skills for communication, social interaction, and daily living. We can find some of the autism-related deficits, including difficulties with organization, auditory processing, attention, and memory. These are minimized by using the frequently found learning strengths in visual processing, rote memory, and special interests (Grandin, 1995; Schopler, Mesibov, & Hearsey, 1995). Visual structures for organizing physical space, schedules, work-learning systems, and task organization have been most useful for their application across the life span and their potential for individualization. They can be modified or faded out as needed for an individual.

Priority for Cognitive and Behavior Theory

The importance of both cognitive and behavior theory is that they are useful for guiding both intervention and empirical research. Both are accountable to the rules of evidence. In recent years, behavioral and cognitive research have become more integrated. This integration was eloquently reviewed by Gardner (1985) and can be seen increasingly in the inventive work of traditional behaviorists, for example, in studying self-management (Koegel, Frea, & Surratt, 1994) and teaching natural language (Koegel, O'Dell, & Koegel, 1987).

Skill Enhancement and Acceptance of Deficit

The most effective treatment approach is to give priority to recognition and enhancement of children's skills and to recognize and accept their deficits and shortcomings. For several reasons, this is an important and enduring value for TEACCH staff.

First, it is parallel to one of the important findings of behavioral treatment: the treatment is said to be most effective when positive reinforcements or rewards are used far more frequently than any other response. We have learned that the restricted interests found in most autistic individuals often lead to special skills that may be used as a bridge to teaching other skills. Skill enhancement broadens the use of frequent positive reinforcement, with the reminder that competence provides its own reinforcement and motivation (White, 1959).

From our clinical work, we know that the emphasis on competence helps to enhance child-rearing efforts. We learned early that parents would show signs of "thought disorder" when tested in the context of psychoanalytic therapy, which sought to bring them insight into their dysfunctional child-rearing efforts. On the other hand, when these parents were first interviewed about the secrets of their success in also raising nonautistic siblings, before they were tested for thought disorder, their thought impairment scores washed out (Schopler & Loftin, 1969). Both formal research and informal clinical observation showed that parents responded productively and constructively with their children when their effective child-rearing efforts were identified, supported, and praised. Under these circumstances, most parents were also willing to modify their child-rearing behavior when useful changes were suggested by their parent-consultant.

The philosophy of emphasizing skills while accepting or minimizing deficits has generated constructive responses in both children and their parents. However, it has turned out to be equally important to our TEACCH staff. All of us have talents that we would prefer to use in our work, rather than display the weaknesses we have not yet conquered, which can be accepted in the meantime.

Holistic Orientation

The TEACCH program was begun in reaction to professional misunderstanding of autism. Parents' unconscious wishes and attitudes, as extensions of psychoanalytic theory, were seen as the primary causal agent for the autism symptoms. However, parental complaints were not confined to Freudian sources of misunderstanding. In their search for help, the parents

had seen other professionals from a variety of disciplines who viewed their children narrowly through the focus of their specific discipline. Rather than seeing a whole child, many professionals, overreacting to their specialized training, saw a behavior problem, a speech deficit, a perceptual motor impairment, or a new medical syndrome. Few took the extra trouble to see the whole child in the context of a unique family.

By sharing a holistic approach, the TEACCH staff considers the children's aggregate skills, learning problems, deficits or weaknesses, and personality attributes—all interacting with a family. The holistic approach is taught and demonstrated with the generalist model—the expectation that every trainee, regardless of professional discipline, will become familiar with the whole range of problems occurring with autistic children, and with all the specific treatment techniques currently being experimented with or used.

This important value initially met considerable opposition, especially from representatives of special disciplines. However, insofar as they could recall their own experience with the parent role, they could remember that parents are expected to function as generalists. For example, they must decide about the relative need of orthodontics for their child, without first going to dental school. The generalist model requires professionals to see children more as their parents do, to learn better how to use specialists as consultants. The model binds parental and professional perspectives closer together.

Lifelong Community-Based Service

Autism, as of this time, is still a lifelong disability for which no cure has yet been found. In TEACCH's early years, both parents and staff soon recognized that most autistic individuals and their families will require some special help from cradle to grave (Mesibov, 1983). Such services are most cost-effective when coordinated with consistency in teaching strategies and support systems throughout each child's life. Autism involves special problems not only in social relations and communications, but also in the areas of cognition, learning, sensory processing, behavior, organization, and planning. When demands and expectations involve understanding of these problems and uniform remediation and support, later teaching can build on what has already been learned, thus optimizing the individual's possibilities and learning potential. The shared staff value of providing life-span support and services is a natural corollary to a constructive parents' perspective and to the holistic philosophy that animates the TEACCH program.

IMPLEMENTATION OF PHILOSOPHY

The nine-faceted philosophy described in the previous section is taught to new staff through training, reading, and observation. We have been fortunate in that the fascinating complexities of autism continue to draw the interest of an unusually talented cadre of professionals and students. However, the remarkable success of the TEACCH program would not have been possible if program organization and service delivery procedures had not continued to reinforce and facilitate the implementation of the program's philosophy. Philosophical guidelines were formulated to give direction both to empirical research and to accountable service delivery. In this section, we describe the administrative structures, service procedures, and empirical research that maintained and facilitated the nine facets of the program philosophy reviewed above.

Characteristics of Autism

When new applicants for a therapist or consultant position are being screened, we are searching for persons with special interest in this population, along with relevant experience and education. At the beginning of the program, not many applicants familiar with autism were available. We developed a hiring procedure that was eventually accepted by the university personnel department. After screening for interest, relevant experience, and training, the two or three finalists were asked to meet with one of our children and his or her parents. After observing the child through a one-way window, the applicant was asked to interact with the child for 15 minutes for the purpose of forming some initial impression of both the child's learning problems and what

kind of educational approach might be helpful. Upon completing the session, the applicant was asked to write up briefly the interaction, the learning problems observed and the teaching strategies that might be considered. The applicant was to provide supporting evidence only from the child's behavior observed during the 15-minute period. Members of the recruiting committee and the child's parents observed through the one-way window.

Next, the applicant was asked to conduct a 30-minute interview with the child's parents, for the purpose of forming an initial impression of what sorts of problems the parents were struggling with and how to begin helping them. A written report parallel to the one after the child's interview was required, with evidence for recommendations based only on direct interview observations. After the interview, parents were asked for input on the applicant's suitability for the position, and parents' recommendations were given equal weight with those of members of the recruiting committee. Observation (through the one-way window) of this miniature job sample usually resulted in high agreement between staff and parents regarding the best applicant. Although more applicants with relevant experience and education are now available, the staff still use this selection procedure and have extended it to the hiring of new clinical directors, a faculty position. This aspect of our hiring process helps in the selection of applicants who can make inferences from observed behavior.

The recognition of autism characteristics is also structured into our formal diagnostic process. In the past, the diagnosis of autism was primarily made by psychiatrists of the psychoanalytic persuasion—and usually on the basis of subjective Freudian assumptions. To make the diagnosis more public and more consistent with Kanner's behavioral description, we developed the Childhood Autism Rating Scale (CARS; Schopler, Reichler, DeVellis, & Daly, 1980). The reliability and validity of this 15-scale rating system has been replicated and confirmed (Morgan, 1988; Parks, 1988). Because the CARS is based on direct observation, valid ratings can be made under alternate conditions, including a one-hour observation during a diagnostic session or in the child's classroom; or from parent interviews or case history charts; or by applying various disciplines (Schopler, Reichler, & Renner, 1988).

From using the CARS, a new TEACCH staff member will learn diagnostic procedures based on direct observations. CARS is taught via workshops, supervised usage, and two training tapes—one demonstrating the scale (Schopler, 1981a) and the other offering practice for scoring (Schopler, 1981b). Our personnel selection procedures and our programwide, uniform use of and training with the CARS constitute structural implementations of the philosophy of understanding characteristics of autism on the basis of direct behavioral observation.

Parent-Professional Collaboration

This element has been the cornerstone of the TEACCH system from the very beginning and therefore has more structural implementations than other facets of the program philosophy.

1. The one-way observation method is used in every TEACCH center. Parents observe the diagnostic interview and participate in the process. Therapists do not ask parents to use educational techniques they themselves cannot first demonstrate with the child while the parents observe. Subsequently, parents may find effective teaching activities that neither therapists nor the child's teachers have considered. The parent then demonstrates these activities while the professionals observe through the one-way window. This creates a kind of dialogue between the therapist and the parent as the child's actual learning response is used to find the optimum teaching strategy for each child. This one-way observational procedure fosters equal discussion between staff and parents. It also presents a serious obstacle to the excesses of traditional consultation, which took place in the privacy of a therapist's office, where it was only too easy to offer advice from a position of authority. If the advice was ineffective, blame was placed on the parents' misapplication or misunderstanding. This sequence is most unlikely when teaching or behavioral interventions are demonstrated and written out.

2. A second powerful structural support to parent-professional collaboration is the therapist's job description. It includes four types of

interactions with parents (described in more detail in Schopler et al., 1984). These are: (a) the traditional interactions in which the parent is the new trainee and the therapist is the expert trainer. These interactions occur in situations in which the therapist is required to use his or her education, knowledge of the field, and experience with many more similar children than are available to parents, and also when the therapist has general information on the understanding and treatment of autism. (b) Parent as trainer and therapist as trainee is a reversal of the previous form and is less familiar. It is based on the recognition that parents, in most cases, are the foremost experts on their own child's behavior, and have the highest motivation for living in some degree of harmony with their child. This form of interaction is used when parents provide assessment information to staff, demonstrate to the staff effective behavior interventions they have observed or used (as part of their assistance in training new staff members), or talk to legislators. (c) Reciprocal emotional support between professionals and parents is based on the recognition that the children's slow and uneven learning, sometimes slow progress, and resulting frustrations can be a threat or challenge to both parental and professional roles. Once they both understand this, their mutual support for each other is usually spontaneous and survives technical differences over treatment and management. (d) Community advocacy is a parent-professional collaboration role that is written into the therapist's job description. Here, the objective is to develop community understanding and acceptance of the child's special problems and, concurrently, the needed cost-effective services. A common front emerges from the previous three aspects of the relationship, and social-role differences are at a minimum here. Parents' contributions are as versatile as their careers, be they writers, lawyers, or politicians (Surratt, 1984). Parents, more than professionals, are considered to represent a political constituency; professionals are often thought of as meeting the constituents' needs.

3. In addition to functioning as cotherapists (Schopler & Reichler, 1971a), parents collaborate with the classroom teacher according to individual need. Collaboration has ranged from parents' functioning as assistant

teachers twice a week, or participating in special events or community trips, to regular conferences at least once a month, or to daily diaries carried over from school to home (Schopler et al., 1984; Schopler & Olley, 1982).

4. Another structural support for parent-professional collaboration has been maintenance of open records or medical charts. No longer does any staff person make a chart entry that might not be reviewed by the parents of the child. This has helped to curb the tendency to make unsubstantiated interpretations, so common in psychodynamic clinic records.

5. Parents' diagnostic observations are incorporated in TEACCH evaluation reports. In the beginning of the TEACCH program, Schopler and Reichler (1972) studied parents' ability to evaluate their own child's level of functioning. During the first diagnostic interview, mothers and fathers were asked to estimate, independently of each other, the age level at which their child was functioning in daily living skills, social interaction, communication, and motor abilities. Parents' developmental estimates were then compared with formal testing done subsequently. Parents' estimates correlated significantly with test-based estimates, were found clinically most useful, and are still used in all TEACCH centers to this day, over 20 years after the completion of the research project for which they were developed.

6. Parents' perspective has also been represented through chapters written by articulate parents in the 11 volumes of our Plenum Press Autism Series (see Table 35.3, later in this chapter), thus advancing what we felt was a demonstrated essential principle of our program.

These are some of the more prominent program structures and procedures for informing new staff on the importance of parent-professional collaboration as a philosophic principle.

Striving for Optimum Adaptation

This value refers to the TEACCH staff's commitment to two related efforts: (a) to improve each individual's acquisition of skills and (b) to develop and evaluate all new therapies and teaching techniques promoted for achieving this aim. Insofar as any autism-related deficit is blocking such skill development, the environment can be modified to accommodate that deficit. Both of these efforts are essential to achieve optimum adaptation. Program structural supports were evolved for both components of this guiding value.

Skill Enhancement and Acceptance of Deficit

During the past few decades, more than two dozen therapies for autism have been developed and identified (Schopler, 1994). Especially when first introduced, these techniques have often been heralded with great excitement, either by parents convinced they were witnessing a miraculous improvement or by professionals hoping they were on the way to finding a cure. Such events are often attended by excessive media hype and extension beyond all outcome data, which leads to unnecessary costs, unexpected parental disappointment, and misdirected social policy. TEACCH staff are involved with the collection of outcome data and experience, and its dissemination to any inquiring parent or colleague. For example, the limits, negative side effects, and overzealous marketing of techniques such as psychodynamic therapy, facilitated communication (FC), total inclusion, and intensive behavior therapy were discussed in Schopler (1994). This knowledge enables both parents and staff to make the most informed choice for optimum individualized treatment, designed for optimum skill development of each child.

Ways to distinguish between potential for skill development and deficits that need to be neutralized through environmental change are structured into TEACCH assessment procedures (Mesibov, Schopler, Schaffer, & Michal, 1989; Schopler, Reichler, Bashford, Lansing, & Marcus, 1990). For these instruments, the scoring is adapted to the needed distinction by using a three-way scoring method. On each test item, the individual is scored *pass* or *fail,* as is typical of most standard tests. However, a third score is applied when the individual's completion of the item is only partially correct or merely shows some inkling of what the task is about. Such a response is scored as *emerging,* and the emerging profile becomes the basis for the individualized educational program. The passed or established skills are designed to interact with and improve the emerging skills, and the failed items indicate areas that require environmental accommodations. This scoring is also taught in several training tapes and directs attention toward budding skills (Schopler, 1981c, 1981d). The scoring of an emerging response represents an environmental accommodation. The most consistent environmental adjustment used in the TEACCH system is discussed below.

The use of skill recognition and deficit acceptance has had far-reaching implications beyond teaching autistic children. Parents have reported many incidents in which they handled difficult behavior problems successfully by using environmental accommodations (Schopler, 1995). In addition, parents were energized and more productive when their positive qualities were recognized and used (Schopler & Loftin, 1969). It soon became self-evident that this response was also occurring among TEACCH staff. In fact, all of us perform better when tasks involve our skills and interests, especially when our weaknesses can be recognized and accepted. With a broad and comprehensive program like TEACCH, job descriptions can be more easily adapted to an individual's stronger skills than with a program that has a more restricted mandate.

Assessment

The TEACCH approach, based on thoughtful observation and understanding of clients, has a number of structural program supports. In their first training session, staff are taught both formal and informal evaluation. Formal or standardized testing is separated into two types. One is *diagnosis*—identifying those features the children share with each other, for the purpose of diagnostic grouping. Because this is insufficient information for an individualized treatment plan, each child is also evaluated for all other characteristics of learning and cognition. This is referred to as *the assessment process.* The Childhood Autism Rating Scale (CARS; Schopler et al., 1988), discussed earlier, is employed because of its strong psychometric properties. CARS is central to the diagnostic process as it distinguishes autism from other disorders of childhood. Formal

assessment of other learning characteristics is conducted by using the Psychoeducational Profile—Revised (PEP-R; Schopler et al., 1990). It produces a learning profile of seven different functions in which emerging skills are distinguished from those that have been accomplished and those that are not yet available. Both of these instruments are also taught on training tapes (Schopler, 1981a, 1981b, 1981c). The PEP-R was extended to the adolescent and adult population through use of the Adolescent and Adult Psychoeducational Profile (AAPEP), by Mesibov, Schopler, Schaffer, and Landrus (1988), for the purpose of evaluating each individual for placement in the best vocational and living arrangements. Diagnostic data are obtained from three different sources: (a) direct test observation, (b) the home, and (c) the training–work situation. Staff from three different locations evaluate each client on the same function areas (vocational skills, independent functioning, leisure skills, vocational behaviors, functional communication, and interpersonal behavior). Emerging skills requiring further training are distinguished from accomplished skills and from deficits, as they are on the PEP-R.

These three formal assessment instruments-CARS, PEP-R, and AAPEP—reinforce the philosophic priority of emphasizing observable characteristics of autism. Throughout the life span, the scoring on the assessment instruments maintains staff attention on the use of the *emerging* rating as an alternative to the traditional *pass/fail* scoring dichotomy.

The transition between formal and informal assessment is used in our teaching of communication skills (Watson, Lord, Schaffer, & Schopler, 1989). Here we use a communication sample, usually a 2-hour observation period or the time needed for 50 spontaneous communications by the student to be evaluated. This is combined with a parent assessment—eliciting parents' observation and communication priorities for their child. Informal assessments by parents have already been referred to. They include parents' assessment of their child's level of functioning (Schopler & Reichler, 1972), and parents' direct participation in the diagnostic process. In the TEACCH training, discussed below formal evaluation is taught in didactic sessions, while informal assessment is taught during hands-on experience with the children. These formal and informal observation structures support the program philosophy of understanding the child from observation rather than from theory, and of making a meaningful distinction between teaching emphasis and environmental accommodation to deficits.

Structured Teaching

Prior to the formation of TEACCH in 1972, autistic children were frequently placed in unstructured "therapeutic" settings, with the expectation that their emotional barriers would be resolved and a nonhandicapped child would emerge. Because this result was achieved only rarely, we studied the effects of structure and found that autistic individuals learned better in structured than in unstructured settings (Schopler et al., 1971), a finding soon replicated by others (Bartak, 1978; Bartak & Rutter, 1973). Moreover, an accumulation of learning profiles and individualized teaching programs (Schopler, Lansing, & Waters, 1983) showed that a large number of autistic children had similar profiles on several characteristics. They showed weaknesses in organization and in memory of things unrelated to their special interest, and they had difficulty with auditory processing. On the other hand, they had strengths in visual processing, special interests, and related memory skills that could be structured to neutralize their difficulties. Of special benefit has been the use of visual structures, involving the physical layout of space, schedules for when activities occur, visual learning systems, and visual organization of materials. These are incorporated in all TEACCH training and have been spelled out by Mesibov, Schopler, and Hearsey (1994) and Schopler et al. (1995), and is shown operating in schools and homes in documentaries made by Asahi Shimbun Welfare Foundation (Schopler & Sasaki, 1990a, 1990b).

The principle of structured teaching has special program importance, as it integrates, teaches, and reinforces a number of other principles central to the TEACCH system. Visual structures provide environmental accommodations to the autism deficits discussed above. These structures foster independence,

especially from nagging, negative interactions with supervising adults. The student is freed to enhance skills, special interests, and social interactions. Structures can be individualized from assessment information and they offer an important bridge for generalizing between home, school, and work placement. While structured teaching is important, it is sometimes mistaken as the essential meaning of TEACCH. It is perhaps the easiest of the nine principles to demonstrate, visualize, and implement. Although it is a central treatment technique, it cannot produce long-term program viability that comes from implementing our other principles as well. All nine are needed to achieve long-term program stability, while at the same time incorporating new knowledge and effective new treatment techniques that will be developed in the future.

Priority for Cognitive and Behavior Theory

The integrated use of behavior and cognitive theory is reinforced in the program's application of behavior management and communication training. For reducing behavior problems, we emphasize prevention by understanding each individual child and structuring his or her educational experience accordingly (Schopler et al., 1995). Behavior problems that occur in spite of structured teaching are reduced according to the procedures shown by the iceberg metaphor in Figure 35.1.

Above the waterline are specific behaviors that can appear in the tantrums problem area: screams without apparent cause, is self-injurious, destroys toys, and so on. Below the waterline are explanatory inferences or autism-related deficits that may account for the behavior: inability to communicate needs, emotional inconsistency, poor understanding, strong need for sameness, low frustration levels, and so on. Careful observation by professionals or parents will enable them to make accurate inferences about the causal trigger mechanisms of the behaviors. For example, if a child destroys one of his Power Ranger™ toys, careful observation may show that a favorite blue one had disappeared and was inadvertently replaced by a red one. If the caretaker can find the blue one, the

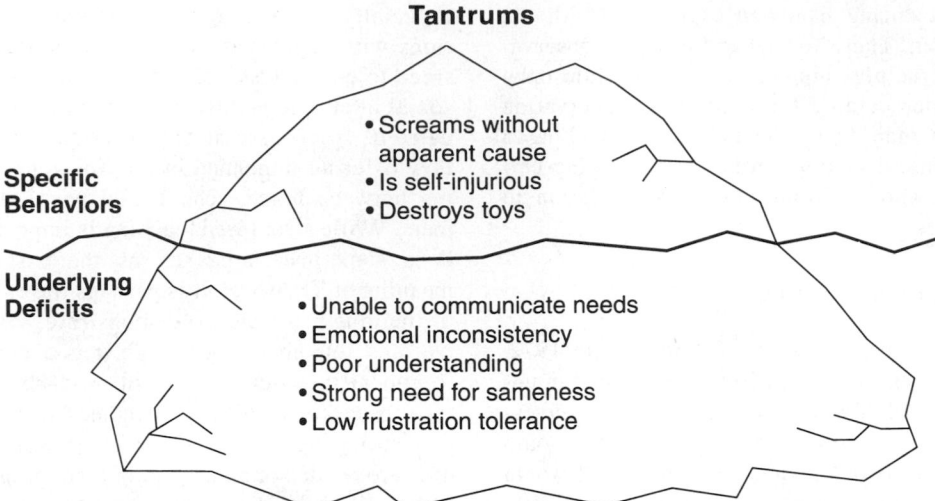

Figure 35.1 The "iceberg" of specific behaviors and underlying deficits. *Source:* Copyright © 1987, Division TEACCH.

child's stress from having his restricted interests disrupted will be alleviated. If this intervention does not reduce or stop the tantrums, additional observation or history information should provide an alternate explanatory hypothesis, one that permits a different intervention. This process is used by both professionals and parents (Schopler, 1995).

Cognitive theory in the form of psycholinguistics directs our language training. That communication is not only taught by conditioning verbal behavior is shown in our curriculum for increasing spontaneous communication (Watson et al., 1989). Each child's communication level is carefully observed and recorded, whether he or she relies on body posture, gesture, signs, pictures, or words. The communicative intent is recorded along with the semantic category used and the context in which the communication took place. Figure 35.2 shows a sample of an assessment form. This information is implemented for teaching a new communication unit in a context to which the child is accustomed. Only after it is established is that unit taught in a new context; until then, new communications are taught in the old context, be it school or grandmother's house. Both examples of teaching and implementing behavior intervention and communication training require priority for behavior and cognitive theory.

Holistic Orientation

Somewhat different program structures are used for implementing a holistic orientation for staff and trainees. The TEACCH staff therapist job description was first rewritten to integrate the traditional child psychiatric clinic division of labor. Under this traditional practice, psychiatrists conducted therapy with the child, social workers saw families, and psychologists did diagnostic evaluations. Before 1970, TEACCH therapists were trained to work with children and parents, and to conduct the assessment procedures described above, regardless of the professional discipline in which they had obtained their primary training. This therapist job description has proven to be viable and is still in use.

Another example of implementing the generalist principle is the opening interaction in a diagnostic evaluation initiated by a parent. The clinical director, who conducts the diagnostic session, asks the parents at the beginning of the session what questions they hope to have answered from the evaluation. These questions are written down and kept in mind throughout the several phases of the evaluation. They are addressed in the interpretive conference along with issues identified by the staff as potentially helpful. This practice requires the

Student: _____	Functions							Semantic Categories				
Observer: _____ Date: _____ Time began: _____ Time ended: _____	Request	Getting Attention	Reject	Comment	Give Information	Seek Information	Other					
Context | What Student Said or Did								Object	Action	Person	Location	Other

Figure 35.2 Communication Assessment Sample.

diagnostic team to consider the whole range of problems raised by autism as a parent would, rather than as representatives of a special discipline.

TEACCH training, discussed more fully below, has been thoroughly structured to teach the generalist model. Regardless of their primary discipline, all trainees rotate through four professional roles in an intensive training experience that combines didactic sessions on eight generalist related topics with direct hands-on experience. This training program has been made into a documentary film by Asahi Shimbun (1990). Its use in Japan and other countries has contributed to successful implementation across cultural and language barriers. The training is adapted to preschool, school-age, and adult-age groups and is a vital connection for integrating lifelong community-based service across our service programs.

Lifelong Community Service

Although autism characteristics can be modified, no cure has been validated. Accordingly, the parents' perspective on this chronic condition soon requires long-range plans and services. Moreover, we have found that structured teaching can bridge the gap between school attendance and living/working arrangements for adults. A holistic orientation minimizes the need for dividing child and adult services. The emphasis on skill development can best be implemented when staff can transfer to different service functions in a life-span community service without leaving the job.

This section has identified some of the program structures and procedures that reinforce and support various facets of the TEACCH philosophy. The next section summarizes TEACCH services and interagency collaboration.

TEACCH SERVICES

Because the TEACCH program evolved from parent-professional collaboration, it was soon required to provide North Carolina families with services from cradle to grave. As a result, TEACCH staff members were increasingly called on to collaborate with other state agencies. This assumed a special value for our families because children's needs for specific agencies change as they grow. TEACCH staff, on the other hand, maintain a collaborative relationship with each family through their child's lifetime, and provide the services summarized in the following subsections.

Diagnostic Clinic

All TEACCH service programs had their beginning in working to resolve the special family stresses arising from autism and from professional misunderstanding of the disorder. For families who had just observed signs of developmental problems in the newest member of the family, the question of what was wrong and how it could be corrected was foremost.

This resulted in the diagnostic parent-professional collaboration procedures used in all seven regional TEACCH centers (Marcus, Lansing, & Schopler, 1993). Following a referral from a physician, a family, a school program, or an evaluation clinic, the child comes, with both parents, for a full-day evaluation, after first submitting a history form, descriptions of special problems and special strengths shown by the child in a typical day, and previous evaluations of any kind.

The diagnostic day involves several steps. First, the family starts the visit with a brief introductory session with the clinic team, which consists of the clinical director, a child therapist, and a parent consultant. They all hear the specific questions the parents hope to have answered from the evaluation. The child therapist takes the child to the one-way observation room, where the diagnostic testing takes place, usually without parents present. (A parent is included in the rare case that the child has trouble separating.) The diagnostic evaluation and screening is done with the Childhood Autism Rating Scale (CARS; Schopler et al., 1988), with scoring adjusted as necessary for adults and adolescents (Mesibov et al., 1989). The CARS is used to determine whether the referred child fits the accepted criteria for autism. Each child's unique characteristics are assessed with the Psychoeducational Profile–Revised (PEP-R; Schopler et al., 1990) for the young child, and with the Adolescent and Adult Psychoeducational Profile (AAPEP; Mesibov et al., 1988) for adolescents and adults. Other assessment procedures are used as needed. The primary purpose of the assessment process for the young child is to identify individual learning problems and to design a starting individualized educational program.

While the child or adolescent is being tested, parents complete a history of developmental functions based on the Vineland Social Maturity Scale (Sparrow, Balla, & Cicchetti, 1984) and focused specifically around functions the child has accomplished and others that are presenting difficulties or behavior problems.

Next, each parent is asked to interact with the child behind the one-way observation window for 15 minutes, and on a signal, to ask the child to stop and help put away materials. This session provides a comparison between the child's reaction to a familiar person versus a stranger, and information on how the parents interact with their child. After this session, the clinic team meets to discuss preliminary observations and test results. Next, the team meets with the family for an interpretive conference conducted by the clinical director. Recommendations for educational procedures, school collaboration, and living or working arrangements are discussed, in light of the questions raised by parents at the outset.

Extended Diagnostic

After the interpretive session, the family is offered an intensive, extended diagnostic session to increase understanding and teaching skills with their child. Parents practice their implementation of a home teaching program, as written out by the staff after the diagnostic session. They then demonstrate their use of the teaching program while staff observe through a one-way window. Parents are also encouraged to demonstrate revisions or additions to the home teaching program that they found useful during their sessions at home. Through this interaction, both staff and parents achieve the best possible understanding of the child and the available teaching skills. When the child is already enrolled in school, the teacher is included in the extended diagnostic whenever possible, and the teaching program is adapted for classroom use (Schopler & Olley, 1980).

During the diagnostic period, other parental concerns and special treatment techniques of interest to the parents are discussed, and experience and research publications are pooled to help families separate fads from feasible interventions (Schopler, 1989, 1994). The parent consultant helps the family to cope with the range of problems presented by the child's autism and to organize their priorities and intervention goals so as to be most beneficial for their child and the family.

Classroom Program

When the child enters school, collaboration shifts to include the parent-teacher relationship. Although several models of school programs are available, the most popular one was developed through annual contracts between TEACCH and the local school (Schopler & Olley, 1982). These contracts usually provide for joint hiring of teachers (and provision of a week of intensive training, as described below), diagnostic evaluations done between regional TEACCH centers and the school system, and consultation from TEACCH centers to the classroom. These classrooms, located in the public school, usually accommodate 5 to 7 children with a teacher and assistant teacher. There are currently about 265 such TEACCH-affiliated classrooms in 65 school systems.

Other classroom models are available, depending on the region. Some children with autism (generally, the higher-functioning group) are included in regular classrooms. Of those mainstreamed, some receive no extra assistance, some have one-to-one assistance throughout the schoolday, and others are mainstreamed without assistance but spend extensive time in resource rooms. Some children are in learning disability programs for moderately mentally retarded students. The number and type of classrooms available in any one location depend on the tax base of that region and the activity level of particular parent groups. The TEACCH goal in school placement is to find the combination of programs that best fits the needs of each individual child.

Residential Programs

TEACCH collaborates with the North Carolina Department of Human Resources to provide a range of residential options. The Department of Human Resources administers many of these programs, and TEACCH staff provide consultation in program development, implementation, and in-service staff training.

The most common type of residential facility in North Carolina is the small community-based group home for adults, serving 5 to 6 residents. The residence is viewed as a permanent home and is staffed according to clients' needs and skills. When capable of living in less restrictive settings, the clients may move to sheltered apartments, occupied by 2 or 3 adults together. A responsible staff person lives nearby but not in the same apartment. These clients work in the community, shop, cook, and generally function independently with a minimum of supervision or assistance. As individuals mature through the TEACCH system, a growing number are becoming qualified for this lifestyle.

A new and exciting residential option developed and administered by TEACCH is the Carolina Living and Learning Center (Van Bourgondien & Reichle, 1996; Van Bourgondien & Woods, 1992). Located on 70 acres and part of the University-TEACCH system, the Center offers the opportunity for 30 residents to live on a farm and to obtain training in work that involves different levels of functioning. Using a vocational apprenticeship interaction, at the simplest level are gardening and other farm activities. However, training will soon be available in a bakery, in use of office equipment, and in the activities of cleaning crews. This residential program was, in part, inspired by Somerset Court in England (Van Bourgondien & Elgar, 1990) and Bittersweet Farm in Ohio (Kay, 1990). TEACCH's Carolina Living and Learning Center has some distinct advantages over the group home option, in that it offers a greater concentration of professional resources, allowing for program variety and continuity in the absence of individual staff.

Because residential programs are costly, the number of available residential units is limited and unable to meet the compelling demand. Need for residential care can be decreased through support, training, and respite care, but these are often insufficient when the parents of the autistic adults are older and are tired of the struggles that are increased during a lifetime of raising a child with special needs.

Respite Care

This service is designed to enable parents to take a vacation or a similar break from the special demands of autism. A parent may either leave the child with another family for a weekend or longer, or the respite care worker may come to the home while the parents go somewhere else. Sometimes, a bed is reserved for respite care in a group home, but this has the disadvantage of the renewed adjustment required for the respite care client and the group home residents.

VOCATIONAL PLACEMENT

One of the productive consequences of having a program committed to individuals over the life span is the ability to develop relatively smooth transitions from school to work placement. Through hard experience, we learned that an optimum individualized educational plan needs to have an approximation of vocational goals long before the client reaches age 18. The use of structured teaching, with emphasis on visual structures as discussed before, offers a practical and useful transition from school to work. Visual structures can be adapted to the individual and to age requirements. They can easily be discontinued when not useful.

Division TEACCH has developed a range of models to meet the needs of autistic adults in North Carolina (Mesibov, 1996). The adults represent a continuum, from those requiring minimal supervision to those needing intensive support. Supported employment models include job coaches, enclaves, small businesses, mobile crews, and structured or sheltered workshops.

Job Coaches

A job coach assists a client in identifying appropriate jobs, completing application processes, and rehearsing phone calls and job interviews. Once the client is hired, the job coach visits the work setting daily to help the client learn the job responsibilities and adjust to the setting. The job coach also helps nonhandicapped employees and management to understand the autistic worker.

The job coach model is generally used with higher-functioning individuals because it requires their becoming independent after a relatively brief training period. Over 100 individuals have been placed into jobs with this job coach model; this total is increased by approximately 15 persons per year. Job coaches need approximately 150 hours, on average, to train a worker, depending on his or her needs. This model is funded by the Division of Vocational Rehabilitation in collaboration with TEACCH. It is cost-effective, especially in the TEACCH system, which, through structured teaching, starts early to work with clients toward independent functioning throughout the program.

Enclaves

Although most clients coming through the job coach program have successfully maintained their placements, a few have had enough problems to prevent continued employment. The enclave model evolved from experience with clients who were not yet ready for competitive employment. (These clients currently work in two large food service operations, at a university and at a nursing home.) In each of the settings, 5 to 8 clients have been brought together with a full-time TEACCH job coach, who prevents or manages any disruptions.

The enclave programs have been highly successful. Management has become increasingly supportive, and competitive employment is made possible for individuals not yet able to function on a job without continuous support. Clients work in many different aspects of food service: busing tables, washing dishes, serving food, taking inventory, and operating equipment. Given the diversity of the work, clients have a chance to interact with nonhandicapped employees, with customers, and with each other. As employees of large corporations, clients earn more than the minimum wage and have the same benefits as anyone working for the same company at their level.

Small Businesses

This structure is similar to the enclave, except that the business organization is established to employ handicapped workers. Rather than hiring handicapped workers to supplement the nonhandicapped staff, in such a small business, the nonhandicapped are hired to supplement the efforts of the handicapped clients. As owners, advocates for the clients have more control over factors that might help (or hinder) the clients' adaptation. They also have more influence with nonhandicapped workers and require them to provide more support and supervision than are possible in enclaves. Bakeries that follow this model are already in operation, and one is planned for the Carolina Living and Learning Center, discussed above.

Mobile Crews

This model provides more support than either enclaves or small businesses. A mobile crew is a group of supervised clients who provide a service in different settings. Chapel Hill is both a university town and a retirement community. The TEACCH mobile crew—1 to 3 handicapped individuals under the supervision of a coach—cleans houses. There is less noise and distraction than in less sheltered work,

and the clients' special work interests, such as preferring to do windows or bathroom floors, can be satisfied. The presence of a job coach ensures additional structure, assistance, and training. Mobile crews have also been effective doing yard work, janitorial work, laundry, and animal care. The work fills a community need, and the TEACCH clients are paid at least minimum wage.

Sheltered Workshops

Sheltered workshops are too often harshly criticized as segregated, stagnant, and demeaning, based on political ideology. Although there are obvious limitations to sheltered workshops for many handicapped people, these are still an option on the continuum of services, and they can meet important needs for some individuals. In our experience, sheltered workshops, organized as an extension of a structured teaching approach (Mesibov et al., 1994; Schopler et al., 1995), can be made into an effective and productive vocational setting. One of these workshops produces the rather complex test material for the PEP and AAPEP, discussed earlier. These materials are produced at a high level of quality, bringing both financial and job satisfaction to the clients involved.

TEACCH PROGRAM EVALUATION

Evaluating the outcome and effectiveness of a large and complex program like TEACCH is difficult. No single component can represent the outcome for all our clients. Instead, multiple outcome criteria offer the most reasonable approach to program evaluation. Accordingly, we have used the following outcome measures: formal empirical studies of specific program components, outcome data as reported in parents' evaluations, peer review indicators, and informal anecdotal and statistical information about the impact of Division TEACCH.

Formal Research

Starting with his doctoral dissertation, Schopler (1965, 1966; Reichler & Schopler, 1971) demonstrated the importance of understanding sensory processes for overcoming autism-related handicaps, rather than the misrepresentations of the accepted Freudian theories. In a subsequent study, Schopler and colleagues (1971) alternated structured and nonstructured teaching programs with autistic children. They found improved attending, relatedness, affect, and general behavior when comparing the effects of the structured with the unstructured learning situation. This finding was confirmed by Bartak and Rutter (1973) and Rutter and Bartak (1973) when they compared three classrooms with varying degrees of structure (Bartak, 1978). This knowledge was integrated into the very first TEACCH classrooms, and refined into the sophisticated emphasis on visual structures in use today (Mesibov et al., 1994; Schopler et al., 1995).

After the effectiveness of structured teaching for autism-related learning problems was established in the early years of the TEACCH program, the next important question was whether the children's parents could be taught to develop skills for teaching their own child. Marcus, Lansing, Andrews, and Schopler (1978) used pre- and posttest videotapes of parent-child interactions to assess the impact of 6 to 8 hours of parent training. The results of that study showed clearly improved effectiveness in the parents' use of structured teaching techniques following training. In addition to the parent-child interactions becoming more positive and enjoyable, there was an increase in the child's cooperation and compliance.

The parent training sessions and the Marcus et al. (1978) research were conducted in the clinic. The question then arose: Would the training effects carry over into the home? Short (1984) examined the carryover of parent training in structured teaching to the home. Through a systematic analysis of videotapes made in the home, Short compared child behaviors in the time interval before the first diagnostic evaluation and after the parent training sessions. The comparison showed that the children's increase in appropriate, cooperative behavior was similar to the improvement documented after training sessions in the clinic. A dramatic example of carryover from clinic to home was documented in a film made by Asahi Shimbun (1990). A child's father not only carried over visual structures carefully into his home teaching, but also used the process to overcome his son's toilet-training problems, both at home and at school.

Parents' Evaluation

Parents' evaluations of the effectiveness of structured teaching and the TEACCH intervention program were examined in several outcome studies. Schopler, Mesibov, DeVellis, and Short (1981) analyzed questionnaires from 348 families who had participated in the TEACCH program. With consistent enthusiasm, parents reported that interventions with TEACCH were positive, productive, and extremely helpful. Most impressive was the high percentage of adolescents and adults who were still functioning in community-based programs. Of the families with older children, 93% reported that their children were still living in their local communities; 7% required a more restrictive residential placement. This outcome was compared with five published follow-up studies in which between 39% and 78% of the autistic populations had to be institutionalized after they became adults (DeMyer et al., 1973; Lotter, 1974; Rutter, 1970; Rutter, Greenfield, & Lockyer, 1967). This comparison showed that a community-based program like TEACCH can avoid the more costly and restrictive placement used in the regions in which these follow-up studies were conducted.

The relationship between family stress and availability of support networks was studied in consecutive referrals to the TEACCH program (Bristol & Schopler, 1983). Parents reported that, among the formal and informal support systems, TEACCH was the most helpful in reducing their stress. In a later study, Bristol, Gallagher, and Holt (1993) found a decrease in depressive symptoms, over time, for parents participating in the TEACCH program. In contrast, mothers without this intervention showed no change in depressive symptoms over time.

Peer Review

Supplementing these rigorous and systematic outcome studies are the more informal but equally demanding evaluations of effectiveness for special recognition of excellence, offered by peer review.

The program was first recognized with awards for excellence, nationally and internationally, in 1972, when the Gold Achievement Award was given to TEACCH by the American Psychiatric Association for "the establishment of productive research on developmental disorders of children and the implementation of an effective clinical application."

In 1985, the founder and then director of TEACCH, Eric Schopler, received the Gardner Award, the only statewide honor given to a faculty member by the Board of Governors of the Consolidated State University system for "the greatest contribution to human welfare." In the same year, he also received the Distinguished Professional Contribution to Public Service Award from the American Psychological Association. The award is conferred on individual members "whose distinguished contributions have served to advance psychology as a profession in the areas of knowledge, public service, and professional practice." Similar recognition as a model program was recently given by the APA Section on Clinical Child Psychology. In 1988, Schopler received the Hargrave Mental Health Research Award, and, in 1989, the J.M. Foundation's National Award for Outstanding Community-Based Work Services. In 1993, he received North Carolina's "highest honor the state can bestow," the Governor's Award, for his exemplary work of public service in establishing TEACCH. The program's current director, Gary Mesibov, was recently recognized with the highest achievement award of the North Carolina Psychological Association and the Opleidungscentrum in Belgium.

Another measure for evaluating effectiveness is the number and value of federal grants awarded for research and training. TEACCH's federal grants, amounting to approximately $4.2 million, have paid for the study of: parents as cotherapists, classroom structure, early identification, the extension of the TEACCH model to residential care, and multidisciplinary training. TEACCH receives state support for seven regional centers, a coordinating unit in Chapel Hill, and a residential living and learning center. For each dollar the state provides for Division TEACCH, the program raises an additional dollar from state and federal contracts and grants, training activities,

private foundations, and individual donations. Division TEACCH's international recognition as a model for research, training, and service delivery provides yet another source of revenue and peer review evaluation, in the form of visitors from other states and other countries. In 1996 alone, 1,214 visitors came from all over the world to observe the program. They came from 32 states and 24 foreign countries, including every continent and major region of the world. An additional 727 parents and professionals attended the annual TEACCH conference or summer training sessions. International film producers from Japan and Belgium have made a total of eight documentary films about the program, for international dissemination.

Another indication of peer endorsement can be seen when an intervention process once considered marginal and alien is accepted by the mental health establishment. The American Psychiatric Association has been publishing a compendium of psychiatric treatments and a companion volume to the *Diagnostic and Statistical Manual of Mental Disorders*. Essential components of the TEACCH approach were detailed in Campbell and Schopler (1989) and for the companion volume to *DSM-IV* (Campbell, Schopler, Mesibov, & Sanchez, 1995).

Informal Indicators of Program Effectiveness

Supplementing empirical outcome studies and peer-reviewed financial support are more informal measures of the effectiveness of the TEACCH program. In a 1971 letter supporting the legislation creating Division TEACCH, Dr. Leo Kanner wrote, ". . . their educational approach, including parents, offers the best treatment available for these children to date."

Presenting TEACCH to the 1980 White House Conference on the Family, in a National Institute of Mental Health publication, Runck (1979) wrote:

Division TEACCH . . . is one of the rare cases where a successful, federally funded, experimental treatment program was expanded and continued as an ongoing part of state and local services. . . . The importance of this achievement should be emphasized. The transition was orderly, the expansion was gradual, and there were few breaks in service to the children in the experimental program. Even more remarkable, the TEACCH program has been extended to serve most of the state without sacrificing its ability to treat one child at a time according to his or her needs. Because it offers services democratically and has resisted the pressure toward becoming bureaucratic and uniform, Division TEACCH may be the most effective statewide program available to autistic children in this country.

Professionals from abroad have been enthusiastic about the impact of Division TEACCH in their countries. A child psychiatrist from Tokyo wrote: "If we consider that the TEACCH program had its start in Japan with the visit of a Japanese team 10 years ago (1984), we can consider that a revolution has occurred in the teaching of autistic children in Japan over the past 10 years." A professional in Belgium has summarized the perceptions in the international community: "TEACCH has become a synonym for quality and many TEACCH-inspired services now stand as models for many European countries including France, Denmark, Switzerland, Sweden, and Norway."

Testimonials to TEACCH's effectiveness have also come from within the University of North Carolina. After joining TEACCH's social club (founded for social skills training of adolescents and adults with autism) for a barbecue (to which some foreign visitors were also invited), the Chairman of Psychiatry wrote, in November 1992:

Not only was it totally enjoyable, but completely exemplified TEACCH's rare combination of love and respect for its patients/clients, its international reputation as a world leader in the field of autism, and its devotion to training and teaching. I doubt there is a treatment institution in the world which would have such a rare combination of people come together to have a great time.

The Chancellor of the University of North Carolina at Chapel Hill recently wrote, "Your insights gained locally, through individual children and their teachers, have meaning for others everywhere. Does that not epitomize what collaboration, at its best, does for the whole human race?"

Parents have participated generously in all aspects of research relating to the program. They have also offered numerous spontaneous expressions of appreciation, especially for the positive TEACCH approach, the staff's dedication, and the comprehensiveness of the program. Just a few examples are cited below. One mother wrote about her son to their therapist:

A's illness was such a frightening thing, the early years so heartbreaking. Even with all A has gone through plus the effect on the family, I can truly say today that it has given us something in our lives that we would never have had otherwise. He has especially brought much into my life, given me new insight, strength, and compassion. And all through this you were leading us along this road of challenge to a goal that even I was afraid to hope for. You have given us the greatest gift anyone could ever give us—you have given us our A. I only hope that in the future I can be of some help to you in helping others like A. These children are very dear to my heart as I know they are to yours. Your concept of wholly integrating the parents in the treatment of the children is so necessary and precious to the parents. It gives them purpose and effectiveness in helping and living with their children.

Other typical letters from parents had these excerpts:

Nowhere have we found another program which matches TEACCH's emphasis on the strengths and the abilities—not the weakness—of disabled persons. Nowhere else have we seen an agency match the success TEACCH has in helping handicap [sic] persons develop their potential.

The lives of many people we know who have disabilities, and their families, have been enriched substantially by TEACCH services. TEACCH greatly expands its influence, and contributes to other missions of the University, by integrating service activities with teaching and research.

In the 20 years of living in and out of different places I have had numerous agencies, organizations, doctors, social groups, advocates, and schools make promises to call me or follow through on something they had committed to. Almost all of them never even bothered to pick up a phone and call me to let me know what was happening. Now that I am in North Carolina I have slowly begun to trust people. I sincerely want to thank all concerned with TEACCH for caring, thoughtfulness, and professionalism in dealing with people with autism and their families. TEACCH has reinstated my faith in humankind and I now feel that there is hope for the future.

RESEARCH

Four sources of autism evaluated evidence have been reviewed for the improvement of life quality and adaptation, with the TEACCH system, for individuals with autism and related problems. No one of these indications represents conclusive evidence, but cumulatively they show this to be a most effective program for clients, their families, and communities.

Although it is generally regarded as undesirable, conflict between research and practice is all too common. It follows from the different requirements imposed by the two enterprises. Clinical practice involves coping with different needs, which vary among individuals in an uncontrolled environment; research usually involves finding different subjects' common responses to controlled conditions. This means that staffing, time allocation, and procedures are frequently quite different for the two activities.

In the TEACCH program, from the outset, research was considered an important and necessary component of services, in part because we recognized that we were initiating a new direction in the treatment of autism and new research questions would arise from the process. Nevertheless, on those occasions when service and research aims appeared incompatible, we tended to stay with the service priority, even though this may have resulted in fewer publications than if we had embraced the "basic" research priority. Although theoretical and experimental studies were conducted and published, the majority of TEACCH faculty publications were designed for service applications.

During the first 25 years of the TEACCH program, or until 1990, TEACCH faculty had published abut 281 books and articles. These are summarized in the TEACCH Research Report (1996), on the topics identified in Table 35.1.

These publications were intended not only as contributions to the understanding and

treatment of autism but also as reflections of the priorities of the TEACCH philosophy. For example, 55 publications (20%) were on family factors and parent involvement; 41 (15%) were on autism characteristics; 35 (12%) were on assessment; and 56 (20%) were on treatment issues.

Our research mandate was conceptualized broadly. Therapists, parent consultants, teachers, and vocational and residential staff were considered important contributors to our research effort. There were two components to this broad involvement: (a) the formulation of new ideas or problems and (b) field testing of new instruments.

New Ideas

The staff working on the front lines, in schools and in the community, have been encouraged to keep track of any new procedure or special problem they have experienced and feel may be of use to other TEACCH staff. They are invited to present such an issue at our winter in-service, held annually for TEACCH and affiliated staff. These 3-day in-service sessions are held in February and have been in place for over 25 years. A major speaker is usually invited and is requested to present his or her special interest, for possible application in our TEACCH system. One year, for example, the outside speaker was a music therapist specializing in autism, who was asked for a presentation to enhance TEACCH's use of music and rhythm in public school classrooms. The other presentations come from TEACCH staff, who share their insights on procedures they have tried during the year, which they believe will be of possible use or interest to others. Those experienced as useful may be converted into formal research in the Administration and Research section of the program. These winter in-service presentations are often at a higher and more interesting level than presentations at professional conferences. Attendance has gradually increased from 60 in 1972 to 490 in 1995.

Field Testing

Besides the definition of research being broadened to include formal presentations of new ideas that are potentially useful to other staff

TABLE 35.1   TEACCH Publications 1966–1996

Adolescence and Adulthood	18	Family Factors	36
Autism Theory	26	General Studies	33
Autistic Characteristics	15	Language	21
Behavior Management	16	Parent Involvement	19
Biomedical Factors	10	Teaching Factors	12
Diagnostic Assessment	35	Treatment of Autism	6
		Treatment Model	34

and workers in the trenches, expansion has included front-line staff in reviewing formal research designed and produced in the TEACCH Administration and Research section. The most recent example, the Psychoeducational Profile (PEP), will illustrate the process.

At the winter in-service of 1989, a presentation of the PEP (Schopler & Reichler, 1979) criticized this test for its limited use with a preschool population. With a growing interest in preschool, reflected also in federal initiatives, staff complained that there were insufficient test items below the $2\frac{1}{2}$-year age level. The low number of items in that age range could penalize preschoolers, lowering their scores if they missed only a few items. The PEP had been found most useful, and was translated into more than a half-dozen languages during 20 years of use. PEP authors were not especially interested in what seemed belated criticism. However, when this complaint was verified by other Center staff, revisions and additions of test items were undertaken. These were developed and field-tested at TEACCH Administration and Research and then tried and critiqued by regional center staff. All new items were modified according to users' criticisms and the new version was sent out for another field trial. Although this process slowed down the publication of the revised PEP (Schopler et al., 1990), the resulting product was more useful and consumer-friendly.

We had used total staff involvement from the outset, and other TEACCH instruments developed by this process included the CARS (Schopler et al., 1988), the PEP (Schopler & Reichler, 1979), the AAPEP (Mesibov et al., 1988), the index of teaching activities (Schopler et al., 1983), and the communication curriculum (Watson et al., 1989). The communication curriculum was field-tested in several classrooms, revised, and redistributed throughout the TEACCH classroom system for an additional year of field trial before the final published version was produced.

This apparently unwieldy research process has repeatedly raised a question from visitors and observers: Is it reasonable to expect teachers, group home workers, and others already feeling overworked to take on the added research requests? Some do refuse participation. But the majority, including the "most overworked," participate with surprising enthusiasm. It gives their work a broader perspective and enables them to relate more easily to visitors and colleagues from other countries. More important, there is always the unharnessed desire to show that those working in the protected halls of the ivory towers know less about what is going on than do the less academically prepared who are working in the trenches. They seem genuinely to enjoy criticizing our research.

TRAINING

The importance of disseminating corrective information for the misunderstanding of autism, propagated by the Freudian ideology, was obvious from the beginning. Psychodynamic misinterpretations frequently demoralized and confused parents, increased behavior problems, and glossed over the intriguing differences among autistic children. Moreover, the misunderstandings of autism were reflected in a number of professional disciplines and the university preparation offered for particular careers. Autism training for multidisciplinary purposes was developed for both preservice and in-service functions.

Preservice

This training involves interested undergraduates and students in professional programs, including education, social work, psychiatry, pediatrics, speech pathology, occupational therapy, and others. It includes lectures and introductory courses for undergraduates and for professional schools. From the outset, one of the most valuable educational experiences is to offer undergraduates opportunities to babysit at parent meetings and, more recently, in recreational social groups and as peer models for socially appropriate behavior (Mesibov, 1995).

TEACCH faculty provide advanced training as practicum or internship experiences for interested graduate students from various disciplines. Available opportunities range from brief part-time placements to full-time, year-long placement in one of the eight regional units. Foreign students from Australia, Belgium, Brazil, China, France, Korea, Japan, and Israel have availed themselves of these opportunities, often with special TEACCH training stipends provided by their governments.

The most condensed and effective training component is the intensive one-week program first organized for preparing North Carolina leaders and group home staff for their new responsibilities involving autism. This training most reflects the TEACCH philosophy for understanding and teaching autistic individuals. Under the outstanding leadership of Gary Mesibov, didactic lectures covering the topics needed for the generalist orientation are thoughtfully integrated with hands-on experience with preschool, elementary school, or adolescent children. The week includes the eight didactic sessions basic to the generalist orientation (see Table 35.2).

The topics are presented in part of each day, and their application is demonstrated in hands-on experience with a group of 5 children. Each training week typically includes 20 trainees. Four trainees in different roles are assigned to a child. One trainee only has hands-on work with the child, the second one does informal assessment of the interaction, the third trainee represents the parents' perspective, and the fourth takes notes on all observations. All the trainees rotate through the four roles during the week. During the last day, each team organizes a party for the children; party games are individualized for the participation of each child. Discussions under the supervision of the most experienced staff follow each of these training sessions.

Originally designed for training new North Carolina teachers and group home staff, the one-week training is now attended also by psychologists, physicians, speech therapists, administrators, and others interested in implementing the TEACCH system in their region. It has been used in many other countries

and readily transcends barriers of language and cultural differences.

In-Service Training

In-service training is important and necessary, not only because most professionals begin working with this population without adequate preparation, but also because of the need to stay up-to-date in the ever-changing area of specific treatment techniques and new research information. In addition, the ever-present risk of waning enthusiasm, because of the intensity and demands of the work, is lessened. The in-service program not only provides new information, but also energizes staff from their interaction with presenters and with each other, as they participate in research.

TEACCH sponsors two major statewide in-service training activities each year. They now include not only participants from North Carolina, but also professionals from TEACCH-affiliated programs in different countries around the world. The first is the winter in-service, comprising $2\frac{1}{2}$ days of seminars, lectures, and discussions. As discussed earlier, an outside speaker is generally invited to provide a new perspective. However, most of the program consists of presentations by TEACCH staff, whose innovative solutions to difficulties experienced during the year are offered for use by other colleagues.

The other major in-service activity is the annual TEACCH May Conference, which is organized around one topic that is of major interest to autism. Knowledgeable speakers are invited from other states or countries to present relevant topics during the two-day Conference. Each May Conference topic is converted into a volume in our Autism Series, which includes chapters contributed by other experts not attending the conference. The result is a 11-volume series edited by Eric Schopler and Gary Mesibov and published by Plenum Press. The titles of the volumes published to date are listed on Table 35.3.

SUMMARY AND CONCLUSIONS

This chapter has reviewed the only comprehensive, statewide program for individuals and families struggling with the special problems of

TABLE 35.2   Topics for Generalist Training in Autism

1. Characteristics of autism	6. Independence and vocational training
2. Family work	7. Social and leisure training
3. Structured teaching	
4. Assessment	8. Behavior management
5. Communication	

TABLE 35.3   Plenum Press: Current Issues in Autism Series, Titles to Date

Autism in Adolescents	High-Functioning Individuals with Autism
The Effect of Autism on the Family	
Communication Problems in Autism	Preschool Issues in Autism
Social Behavior in Autism	Behavioral Issues in Autism
Neurobiological Issues in Autism	Learning and Cognition in Autism
Diagnosis and Assessment in Autism	Asperger Disorder and High Functioning Autism

autism and related communication handicaps. It has described the background that inspired the development of this program's organizational structure, and the population served. However, because the program has survived a rocky political road, maintaining its base in both the university and the community for a longer period than any comparable program, the chapter has focused on the nine-faceted philosophy that guides program service, research, and training. The values involved are: (a) characteristics of autism from observation rather than theory; (b) parent-professional collaboration; (c) goal of improved adaptation; (d) assessment for individualized treatment; (e) use of structured teaching; (f) priority for cognitive and behavior theory; (g) emphasis on skill enhancement; (h) holistic orientation; and (i) lifelong community service.

TEACCH's long-term viability and continued effectiveness are due to the high quality of the staff and the traditional strong collaboration between the University of North Carolina and the state legislature. However, in large measure, the program's effectiveness is also due to the extent to which the guiding philosophy has been implemented through organizational structures, intervention procedures, and empirical research. The structural implementation of the guiding philosophic principles provides both direction and shaping of staff and avoids a coercive ideology enforced by administrative authority. The latter is all too common, especially in programs without the mediating influence of scholarship and research provided by university mandate and connection. The chapter's focus on

implementing program philosophy was spelled out in some detail in the hope that it may provide heuristic guidance to others struggling with similar problems.

Cross-References

Issues in assessment are discussed in Chapters 19 through 21. Curriculum development is treated in Chapter 22, and communication is detailed in Chapters 23 through 25. Behavioral intervention is addressed in Chapter 26, and working with families, in Chapter 27.

REFERENCES

American Psychiatric Association. (1980). *Diagnostic and statistical manual of mental disorders* (3rd ed.). Washington, DC: Author.

American Psychiatric Association. (1987). *Diagnostic and statistical manual of mental disorders* (3rd ed., rev). Washington, DC: Author.

American Psychiatric Association. (1994). *Diagnostic and statistical manual of mental disorders* (4th ed.). Washington, DC: Author.

Bartak, L. (1978). Educational approaches. In M. Rutter & E. Schopler (Eds.), *Autism: A reappraisal of concept and treatment* (pp. 423–438). New York: Plenum Press.

Bartak, L., & Rutter, M. (1973). Special educational treatment of autistic children: A comparative study. *Journal of Child Psychology & Psychiatry, 14,* 162–179.

Bettelheim, B. (1967). *The empty fortress: Infantile autism and the birth of self.* New York: Free Press.

Bristol, M.M., Gallagher, J.J., & Holt, K.D. (1993). Maternal depressive symptoms in autism: Response to psychoeducational intervention. *Rehabilitation Psychology, 38,* 8–10.

Bristol, M.M., & Schopler, E. (1983). Stress and coping in families of autistic adolescents. In E. Schopler & G.B. Mesibov (Eds.), *Autism in adolescents and adults* (pp. 251–278). New York: Plenum Press.

Campbell, M., & Schopler, E. (Eds.). (1989). Section 2: Pervasive developmental disorders. In American Psychiatric Association, *Treatments of psychiatric disorders: A taskforce report of the American Psychiatric Association* (pp. 179–294). Washington, DC: American Psychiatric Association.

Campbell, M., Schopler, E., Mesibov, G.B., & Sanchez, L.E. (1995). Pervasive developmental disorders. In G.O. Gabbard (Ed.), *Treatment of psychiatric disorders: The DSM-IV*

Edition (pp. 151–178). Washington, DC: American Psychiatric Press.

DeMyer, M.K., Barton, S., DeMyer, W.E., Norton, S.A., Allen, J., & Steele, R. (1973). Prognosis in autism: A follow-up study. *Journal of Autism & Childhood Schizophrenia, 3,* 199–246.

Gardner, H. (1985). *The mind's new science: A history of the cognitive revolution.* New York: Basic Books.

Goldfarb, W. (1958). Parental perplexity and childhood confusion. In A.H. Esmond (Ed.), *New frontiers in child guidance* (pp. 316–331). New York: International University Press.

Grandin, T. (1995). *Thinking in pictures.* New York: Doubleday Dell.

Kanner, L. (1943). Autistic disturbances of affective contact. *Nervous Child, 2,* 217–250.

Kay, B.R. (1990). Bittersweet Farms. *Journal of Autism and Developmental Disorders, 20*(3), 309–321.

Koegel, R.L., Frea, W.D., & Surratt, A.V. (1994). Self management of problematic social behavior. In E. Schopler & G.B. Mesibov (Eds.), *Behavioral issues in autism* (pp. 81–95). New York: Plenum Press.

Koegel, R.L., O'Dell, M.C., & Koegel, L.N. (1987). A natural language teaching paradigm for nonverbal autistic children. *Journal of Autism and Developmental Disorders, 17,* 187–200.

Lotter, V. (1974). Factors related to outcome in autistic children. *Journal of Autism and Childhood Schizophrenia,* Vol. 4, pp. 263–277.

Marcus, L., Lansing, M., Andrews, C., & Schopler, E. (1978). Improvement of teaching effectiveness in parents of autistic children. *Journal of the American Academy of Child Psychiatry, 17,* 625–639.

Marcus, L., Lansing, M., & Schopler, E. (1993). Assessment of the autistic and pervasive developmental disordered child. In J. Culbertson & D. Willis (Eds.), *Testing young children* (pp. 319–344). Austin, TX: Pro-Ed.

Mesibov, G.B. (1983). Current perspectives and issues in autism and adolescence. In E. Schopler & G.B. Mesibov (Eds.), *Autism in adolescents and adults* (pp. 37–53). New York: Plenum Press.

Mesibov, G.B. (1995). A comprehensive program for serving people with autism and their families: The TEACCH model. In J.L. Matson (Ed.), *Autism in children and adults: Etiology, assessment, and intervention* (pp. 85–97). Belmont, CA: Brooks/Cole.

Mesibov, G.B. (1996). Division TEACCH: A collaborative model program for service delivery, training, and research for people with autism

and related communication handicaps. In M.C. Roberts (Ed.), *Model programs in child and family mental health* (pp. 215–230). Mahawah, NJ: Erlbaum.

Mesibov, G.B., Schopler, E., & Hearsey, K.A. (1994). Structured teaching. In E. Schopler & G.B. Mesibov (Eds.), *Behavioral issues in autism.* New York: Plenum Press.

Mesibov, G.B., Schopler, E., Schaffer, B., & Landrus, R. (1988). *Adolescent and Adult Psychoeducational Profile (AAPEP).* Austin, TX: Pro-Ed.

Mesibov, G.B., Schopler, E., Schaffer, B., & Michal, N. (1989). Use of Childhood Autism Rating Scale with autistic adolescents and adults. *Journal of the American Academy of Child and Adolescent Psychiatry, 28,* 538–541.

Morgan, S. (1988). Diagnostic assessment in autism: A review of objective scales. *Journal of Psychoeducational Assessment, 6,* 139–151.

Parks, S.L. (1988). Psychometric instruments available for the diagnosis and assessment of autistic children. In E. Schopler & G.B. Mesibov (Eds.), *Diagnosis and assessment in autism* (pp. 123–135). New York: Plenum Press.

Reichler, R.J., & Schopler, E. (1971). Observations on the nature of human relatedness. *Journal of Autism and Childhood Schizophrenia, 1,* 283–296.

Reichler, R.J., & Schopler, E. (1976). Developmental therapy: A program model for providing individual services in the community. In E. Schopler & R.J. Reichler (Eds.), *Psychopathology and child development: Research and treatment* (pp. 347–372). New York: Plenum Press.

Runck, B. (1979). Basic training for parents of psychotic children. In K. Caufman (Ed.), *Families today: A research sampler on families and children* (DHEW Publication No. ADM 79-815, pp. 767–809). Washington, DC: U.S. Government Printing Office.

Rutter, M. (1970). Autistic children: Infancy to adulthood. *Seminars in Psychiatry, 2,* 435–450.

Rutter, M., & Bartak, L. (1973). Special educational treatment of autistic children: A comparative study: 2. Follow-up findings and implications for services. *Journal of Child Psychology and Psychiatry, 14,* 246–270.

Rutter, M., Greenfield, D., & Lockyer, L. (1967). A five to 15-year follow-up study of infantile autism. *British Journal of Psychiatry, 113,* 1183–1199.

Rutter, M., & Schopler, E. (Eds.). (1978). *Autism: Reappraisal of concept and treatment.* New York: Plenum Press.

Rutter, M., & Schopler, E. (1992). Some concepts and practical considerations of pervasive developmental disorders. *Journal of Autism and Developmental Disorders, 22,* 459–482.

Schopler, E. (1965). Early infantile autism and receptor processes. *Archives of General Psychiatry, 13,* 327–335.

Schopler, E. (1966). Visual versus tactile receptor preference in normal and schizophrenic children. *Journal of Abnormal Psychology, 71,* 108–114.

Schopler, E. (1971). Parents of psychotic children as scapegoats. *Journal of Contemporary Psychotherapy, 4,* 17–22.

Schopler, E. (1981a). *Childhood Autism Rating Scale (CARS): A demonstration tape* [28 min.]. Chapel Hill, NC: Health Science Consortium.

Schopler, E. (1981b). *Childhood Autism Rating Scale (CARS): Practice tape* [37 min.]. Chapel Hill, NC: Health Science Consortium.

Schopler, E. (1981c). *The Psychoeducational Profile. Scoring the PEP: Test tape* [55 min.]. Chapel Hill, NC: Health Science Consortium.

Schopler, E. (1981d). *The Psychoeducational Profile. Scoring the PEP: Training tape* [35 min.]. Chapel Hill, NC: Health Science Consortium.

Schopler, E. (1986). Relationship between university research and social policy: Division TEACCH (*T*reatment and *E*ducation of *A*utistic and related *C*ommunication handicapped *CH*ildren). *Popular Government, 51*(4), 23–32.

Schopler, E. (1989). Principles for directing both educational treatment and research. In C. Gillberg (Ed.), *Diagnosis and Treatment of Autism* (pp. 167–183). New York: Plenum Press.

Schopler, E. (1993). The anatomy of a negative role model. In G. Brannigan & M. Merrens (Eds.), *The undaunted psychologist* (pp. 173–186). New York: McGraw-Hill.

Schopler, E. (1994). Behavioral priorities for autism and related developmental disorders. In E. Schopler & G.B. Mesibov (Eds.), *Behavioral issues in autism* (pp. 55–77). New York: Plenum Press.

Schopler, E. (1995). *Parents' survival manual: A guide to crisis resolution in autism and related developmental disorders.* New York: Plenum Press.

Schopler, E., Andrews, C., & Strupp, K. (1979). Do autistic children come from upper middle class parents? *Journal of Autism and Developmental Disorders, 9,* 139–152.

Schopler, E., Brehm, S.S., Kinsbourne, M., & Reichler, R.S. (1971). Effects of treatment structure on development in autistic children. *Archives of General Psychiatry, 24,* 415–421.

Schopler, E., Lansing, M., & Waters, L. (1983). *Individualized assessment and treatment for autistic and developmentally disabled children: Vol. 3. Teaching activities for autistic children.* Austin, TX: Pro-Ed.

Schopler, E., & Loftin, J. (1969). Thought disorders in parents of psychotic children: A function of test anxiety. *Archives of General Psychiatry, 20,* 174–181.

Schopler, E., Mesibov, G.B., De Vellis, R., & Short, A. (1981). Treatment outcome for autistic children and their families. In P. Mittler (Ed.), *Frontiers of knowledge in mental retardation: Vol. 1. Social, educational, and behavioral aspects* (pp. 293–301). Baltimore: University Park Press.

Schopler, E., Mesibov, G.B., & Hearsey, K.A. (1995). Structured teaching in the TEACCH system. In E. Schopler & G.B. Mesibov (Eds.), *Learning and cognition in Autism* (pp. 243–1268). New York: Plenum Press.

Schopler, E., Mesibov, G.B., Shigley, H., & Bashford, A. (1984). Helping autistic children through their parents: The TEACCH model. In E. Schopler & G.B. Mesibov (Eds.), *The effects of autism on the family* (pp. 65–81). New York: Plenum Press.

Schopler, E., & Olley, J.G. (1980). Public school programming for autistic children. *Exceptional Children, 46,* 461–463.

Schopler, E., & Olley, J.G. (1982). Comprehensive educational services for autistic children: The TEACCH model. In C.R. Reynolds & T.R. Gutkin (Eds.), *The handbook of school psychology* (pp. 629–643). New York: John Wiley & Sons.

Schopler, E., & Reichler, R.J. (1971a). Developmental therapy by parents with their own autistic child. In M. Rutter (Ed.), *Infantile autism: Concepts, characteristics, and treatment* (pp. 206–227). London: Churchill-Livingston.

Schopler, E., & Reichler, R.J. (1971b). Parents as cotherapists in the treatment of psychotic children. *Journal of Autism and Childhood Schizophrenia, 2,* 387–400.

Schopler, E., & Reichler, R.J. (1971c). Psychological referents for the treatment of autism. In D.W. Churchill, G.D. Alpern, & M.K. Demyer (Eds.), *Infantile autism* (pp. 243–264). Springfield, IL: Thomas.

Schopler, E., & Reichler, R.J. (1972). How well do parents understand their own psychotic child? *Journal of Autism and Childhood Schizophrenia, 2,* 387–400.

Schopler, E., & Reichler, R.J. (1979). *Individualized assessment and treatment for autistic and* developmentally disabled children: Vol. 1. Psychoeducational profile. Austin, TX: Pro-Ed.

Schopler, E., Reichler, R.J., Bashford, A., Lansing, M.D., & Marcus, L.M. (1990). Psychoeducational Profile Revised (PEP-R). Austin, TX: Pro-Ed.

Schopler, E., Reichler, R.J., DeVellis, R., & Daly, K. (1980). Toward objective classification of childhood autism: Childhood Autism Rating Scale (CARS). Journal of Autism and Developmental Disorders, 10, 91–103.

Schopler, E., Reichler, R.J., & Renner, B.R. (1988). The Childhood Autism Rating Scale (CARS). Los Angeles: Western Psychological Services.

Schopler, E., Rutter, M., & Chess, S. (1979). Editorial: Change of journal scope and title. Journal of Autism and Developmental Disorders, 9, 1–10.

Schopler, E., & Sasaki, M. (1990a). TEACCH Program for Teachers. Asahi Shimbun Production [45 min. video]. Chapel Hill, NC: Health Science Consortium.

Schopler, E., & Sasaki, M. (1990b). TEACCH Program for Parents. Asahi Shimbun Production [45 min. video]. Chapel Hill, NC: Health Science Consortium.

Schopler, E., Van Bourgondien, M.E., & Bristol, M.M. (Eds.). (1993). Preschool issues in autism. New York: Plenum Press.

Shimbun, A. (Producer), Schopler, E., & Sasaki, M. (Eds.). (1990). TEACCH for parents [Film].

Short, A. (1984). Short-term treatment outcome using parents as cotherapists for their own autistic children. Journal of Child Psychology & Psychiatry & Allied Disciplines, 25, 443–458.

Short, A., & Schopler, E. (1988). Factors relating to age of onset in autism. Journal of Autism and Developmental Disorders, 18(2), 207–216.

Sparrow, S.S., Balla, D.A., & Cicchetti, D.V. (1984). A revision of the Vineland Social Maturity Scale by Edgar A. Dall. Circle Pines, MN: American Guidance Services.

Speers, R.W., & Lansing, C. (1965). Group therapy in childhood psychosis. Chapel Hill: University of North Carolina Press.

Surratt, J.E. (1984). Advocacy: Effectively changing the system. In E. Schopler & G.B. Mesibov (Eds.), The effects of autism on the family (pp. 129–141). New York: Plenum Press.

TEACCH. (1990). Annual report of Division TEACCH: Treatment and Education of Autistic and related Communication handicapped CHildren. Chapel Hill: University of North Carolina, Department of Psychiatry.

TEACCH. (1996). Research report of Division TEACCH: Treatment and Education of Autistic and related Communication handicapped CHildren. Chapel Hill: University of North Carolina, Department of Psychiatry.

Van Bourgondien, M.E., & Elgar, S. (1990). The relationship between existing residential services and the needs of autistic adults. Journal of Autism and Developmental Disorders, 20(3), 299–308.

Van Bourgondien, M.E., Marcus, L.M., & Schopler, E. (1992). Comparison of DSM-III-R and Childhood Autism Rating Scale diagnoses of autism. Journal of Autism and Developmental Disorders, 22(4), 493–506.

Van Bourgondien, M.E., & Reichle, N.C. (1996). The Carolina Living and Learning Center: An example of the TEACCH approach to residential and vocational training for adults with autism. In G. Kristofferson & E. Kristofferson (Eds.), Status På Gården (pp. 155–169). Copenhagen: Parentes.

Van Bourgondien, M.E., & Woods, A. (1992). Vocational possibilities for high-functioning adults with autism. In E. Schopler & G.B. Mesibov (Eds.), High-functioning individuals with autism (pp. 227–239). New York: Plenum Press.

Volkmar, F.R., Stier, D.M., & Cohen, D.J. (1985). Age of recognition of Pervasive Developmental Disorder. American Journal of Psychiatry, 142, 1450–1452.

Watson, L., Lord, C., Schaffer, B., & Schopler, E. (1989). Teaching spontaneous communication to autistic and developmentally handicapped children. Austin, TX: Pro-Ed.

White, R.W. (1959). Motivation reconsidered: The concept of competence. Psychology Review, 66, 297–335.

CHAPTER 36

Inclusive Education for Students with Autism: Reviewing Ideological, Empirical, and Community Considerations

JACOB A. BURACK, RHODA ROOT, AND EDWARD ZIGLER

The nature of optimal educational practices for children and adolescents with special needs, including those with autism, is an active area of investigation and discussion among educators, advocates, researchers, and parents (see Chapter 22, and others in this volume; for further reviews, see Burack & Derevensky, 1992; Stainback & Stainback, 1992a). There is broad-based agreement about general features of education for individuals with autism and similar disorders. These include the importance of individualized curricula, concern about many domains of functioning (social, cognitive, communicative, prevocational, adaptive, and so on), and thoughtful planning to ensure that programs are well implemented and monitored. Also, there is a consensus that educational initiatives should facilitate the child and adolescent's overall development and aim at allowing the individual to function within as normal an environment as possible. This particular emphasis on inclusion has become an internationally shared objective for all individuals with disabilities—including physical and intellectual disabilities—and has been extended, most recently, to individuals with

autism and pervasive developmental disorders. The concepts of inclusion, mainstreaming, and least restrictive environment have not only been supported by educators and families throughout the world; these social policies have become embedded in the language of legislation.

In spite of these agreements, there are differences of view about the specific ways in which the goals of facilitating development and promoting inclusion should be achieved. At times, these differences have taken the tone of a debate about one specific question: To what extent should children with special needs be included in regular classrooms? Most advocates today argue that full inclusion of these children in mainstream classrooms should be the standard approach; based on research and experience, others (admittedly, now probably a minority) feel that inclusion is only one factor among many that need to be considered in school placement, and that longer-term goals may be more readily achieved when the child is provided with more specialized, albeit segregated, programs. The contrasting viewpoints on this issue reflect differences in ideology,

Jake Burack's work was supported by a grant from the Social Sciences and Humanities Research Council of Canada. The authors thank Perry Leslie for his thoughtful and informative critiques of earlier drafts, and also thank Julie Brennan and Jessica Steinberg for editing the manuscript. Jake Burack thanks the EPSE 513 class (Fall 1994) at the University of British Columbia for their insightful discussions on this topic.

beliefs, traditions, and worldviews (Burack, Kurtz, & Derevensky, 1992; Hodapp & Zigler, 1992). Empirical studies are relevant to resolving the differences, but they cannot fully resolve the controversy because criteria for assessing the alternatives are often diverse and do not provide common ground for evaluating programs.

The practice of inclusion is based on the philosophy that all children have the right to learn and to belong in the mainstream of school and community life (see Stainback & Stainback, 1992b). Inclusive school programs are based on a sense of a community to which everyone belongs and in which diversity is valued. Students are viewed and treated as individuals with unique needs, interests, and capabilities that, optimally, are appreciated within natural, normal settings. These schools are aimed at fostering interdependence, natural support networks, collaboration, and cooperation among all students and staff. The courts, state legislatures, and the U.S. Congress have impacted greatly on the development of the current educational policies of inclusion for all students with special needs. The Civil Rights of Institutionalized Persons Act, The Individuals with Disabilities Education Act, and The Americans with Disabilities Act all affirm the nation's commitment that each and every person should have the opportunity to participate in the mainstream of life (see Chapter 37). This approach is widely advocated for all types of children with special needs, including those with autism.

Conversely, the full-inclusion model has been criticized as an overarching political and philosophical ideal. Critics of this model feel that, although it is sensible in theory, it may not, in practice, ensure the most optimal approach to the education of all children with special needs. These critics highlight the diversity and major differences in levels of functioning and types of handicaps presented by children with autism and other disabilities, and their need and right to special treatment. For these scholars and educators, empirical research should guide the acceptance or modification of the full-inclusion model as the sole philosophy of choice for the education of children with special needs.

ARGUMENTS FOR INCLUSION

The advocates of inclusion argue that it is the inherent human right of all children to be educated in a setting with their peers (e.g., Lusthaus, Gazith, & Lusthaus, 1992). To them, "it is the fair, ethical, and equitable thing to do . . . when one single individual, who has not broken any laws, is excluded from the mainstream of school and community life, we all become vulnerable" (Stainback & Stainback, 1992b, p. 32). In North America, these proponents may be characterized as being within the traditions established by the civil rights movement of the 1950s, 1960s, and 1970s, in which the fundamental rights of individuals were asserted in many areas. During this period, there were significant, albeit insufficient, gains in ensuring the rights of and reducing prejudices toward individuals on the basis of ethnicity, race, religion, or gender. Legislative activity and legal findings helped to ensure that individuals were not discriminated against on these bases and that efforts were made to integrate these groups of persons into all aspects of mainstream American society, including educational settings, where the specific educational goals were to ensure that all children had the same access to all public education programs and that all schools were open to all children. Although the goals of this effort have not been completely realized, the philosophy and achievements are noteworthy; this era marked an exciting and progressive moment in the beginnings of equal educational opportunities and, subsequently, "more equal" employment opportunities.

The movement toward integration of children with disabilities such as autism and related special needs became prominent in the 1970s with the passage of PL 94-142. This landmark legislation, which formally introduced the notion of a least restrictive environment, reflected and enhanced the growing influence of the normalization principle: everyone should be allowed to lead a life that is as typical as possible (Blatt, 1987; Nirje, 1969; Simpson & Sasso, 1992; Wolfensberger, 1972). This legislative thrust, and the judicial and regulatory actions related to it, marked the formal beginning of the systematic quest for desegregated forms of education for students with special needs (Wolfensberger, 1972). The implementation of PL 94-142 led to an expansion of services for many different types of students with special needs. For example, educational services for children with autism and/or other severely handicapped students were expanded to include integrated classrooms at the preschool level, special classrooms for older students in regular schools, and integrated programs outside the classroom (Egel & Gradel, 1988). The increased success in independent functioning, skill generalization, and maintenance in natural, integrated settings provided a challenge to the common use of segregated settings for students with disabilities (Brown, Nietupski, & Hamre-Nietupski, 1976).

In the 1980s, projects that were focused on the enhancement of social skills training, interaction opportunities, and nondisabled students' attitudes in integrated settings received considerable funding (Stainback, Stainback, & Bunch, 1989). By the end of the decade, the trend toward full inclusion of all students into the mainstream of regular education had gained considerable momentum. The proponents of this movement emphasized the need for increasing the capabilities of the regular education mainstream to meet the unique needs of all students. They argued that full inclusion benefits both the educational and the social development of students with special needs, and it increases the social awareness of nonhandicapped students who are exposed to students with special needs (Egel & Gradel, 1988; Sailor, 1991).

With appropriate educational experiences and support, students with special needs in integrated (as compared to segregated) programs are better able to learn, accept individual differences, interact, communicate, and develop friendships. Concordantly, they are less likely to experience the adverse effects on self-perceptions that are thought to be associated with placement in segregated settings—lack of self-confidence, of motivation, and of expectations for achievement (Stainback & Stainback, 1992b). Many of these contentions have been highlighted by self-advocates who frequently speak out against the inherent degradation that is often associated with segregated settings (e.g., Lusthaus, Gazith, & Lusthaus, 1992; Wizner & Lucht, 1992).

CRITICISMS OF FULL INCLUSION

Despite claims of the ethical necessity for full inclusion (Stainback & Stainback, 1992a) and of conclusive empirical support (Egel & Gradel, 1988; Lusthaus, Gazith, & Lusthaus, 1992; Sailor, 1991), criticisms of inclusive education persist. In particular, critics argue that the model places too much emphasis on values and has not been based sufficiently on scientific validation (Hodapp & Zigler, 1992; Mesibov, 1990; Simpson & Sasso, 1992). Also, critics warn there is an overemphasis on ethical and moral imperatives and a relative lack of concern for meeting individualized needs. There are parents and professionals who have felt that, for some children, full-inclusion programs in general education classes cannot meet special and divergent needs (see Fuchs & Fuchs, 1994; Leiberman, 1992; Simpson & Myles, 1990; Vergason & Anderegg, 1992). Instead of a universal, inclusive approach, these critics argue for a continuum of services and service options for students with a wide range of needs (e.g., Leiberman, 1992; Mesibov, 1976). Regular classrooms, they say, cannot accommodate all children with special needs because some students require highly specialized skills that are best taught by specially trained teachers, others might never respond to the demands of an academic curriculum, others might require an inordinate amount of time and attention from a regular class teacher, and others might respond best to a peer group that is more like themselves. Many of these concerns are most apparent for children with the most severe behavioral difficulties, who are likely to display maladaptive and disruptive behavior, as is common among persons with autism.

Although some empirical studies document benefits of inclusion, other studies are equivocal in support of inclusion of students with special needs into regular education programs (Meyers, MacMillan, & Yoshida, 1980; Porter, Ramsey, Tremblay, Iaccobo, & Crawley, 1978; Zigler & Hodapp, 1986). Inclusion has been championed as integral to improving the social and academic development of students with and without special needs (e.g., Egel & Gradel, 1988; Sailor, 1991); however, Gottlieb (1990) concludes, from a review of empirical studies, that "the data are clear that in the absence of specialized interventions merely placing an educable mentally retarded child in a regular education classroom does not improve academic performance . . . the mere placement into a classroom of nonhandicapped children does not improve social acceptance by classmates."

The limitations of some inclusion programs to promote socialization has been documented in both academic and popular publications. For example, in one empirical study, Sainato, Goldstein, and Strain (1992) indicated that nonhandicapped peers tend to play with one another during free-play periods and often ignore or reject classmates with handicaps. Similarly, in a review of the literature on educational mainstreaming, Zigler and Hodapp (1987) concluded that the nonhandicapped children in mainstreamed classrooms do not interact even with high-functioning children with mental retardation, do not choose them as friends, and identify them as least liked (see also Iano, Ayers, Heller, McGetigan, & Walker, 1974). They argued that children who are not as high functioning are even less likely to be included in the recreational activities of their nonhandicapped peers. Simply placing children with mental retardation and children of average intelligence together in the same environment does not guarantee cross-group peer imitation and interaction (Snyder, Apolloni, & Cooke, 1977). This is even more relevant to children with autism, who often require specialized training programs in order to develop social skills.

Currently, regular education settings are not sufficiently structured nor equipped to meet the unique needs of all students successfully. Perhaps this is particularly true in urban settings where budgets are limited and teachers are already stressed. For any classroom and school, the successful inclusion of a child with a disability often requires extensive adaptation, including teacher training, preparation of classmates, and suitable alterations in the physical setting, depending on the nature of the disability. Similarly, the teaching staff may need to be augmented by a specially trained educator or an aide with access to consultation (Stainback & Stainback, 1989).

THE ROLE OF TEACHERS IN THE MAINSTREAMING PROCESS

In addition to the acceptance by and participation of other children, the success of inclusive school settings is largely contingent on the positive attitude and cooperation of teachers in the integration process. For example, classroom teachers need to consider themselves active participants in the development of the educational programming, otherwise they perceive the integration process as another mandate that requires more work without extra time or resources (Miller, 1990). In the case of students with autism, teachers need to be introduced to the general characteristics of the disorder—specific academic and behavioral strengths and weaknesses; anticipated behaviors that might be evident in the classroom, cafeteria, bathrooms, or halls; and ways to explain these atypical behaviors to the other students.

It is an optimistic sign that 86% of the general educators surveyed were willing to accept a student with a disability in their classrooms on a full-time basis if appropriate support and training were provided (Myles & Simpson, 1989). However, without the support and training, less than 33% of the teachers were willing to accept the same students. This is consistent with the lower level of acceptance of integrated classrooms among general educators (as compared to special educators), who perceive themselves as less competent than the support staff to teach children with handicaps (Whinnery, Fuchs, & Fuchs, 1991). This lack of confidence among regular schoolteachers is evidenced by the fact that they are less likely to make specific modifications in their instruction, use of materials, or environment (Schumm & Vaughn, 1991), even though they are generally willing to accept mildly and moderately handicapped mainstreamed students within whole-class activities and to provide encouragement and support for their academic success.

In carefully controlled studies of social interaction between students with special needs and their peers, teachers were required to provide prompts several times a minute (for a brief review, see Sainato et al., 1992). Thus, it is evident that successful implementation of the integration process is contingent on the effective education and training of the regular schoolteachers and their willingness and motivation to participate in this endeavor.

INCLUSIVE EDUCATION FOR STUDENTS WITH AUTISM

The wide range of positions regarding inclusion in general is represented among educators and parents of students with autism. As is the case with other students with special needs, there are many advocates of full inclusion for students with autism. In addition, most other educators agree that many children with autism can and should be integrated into appropriate regular class settings when possible. However, there is recognition that inclusion, despite its inherent advantages, is not appropriate for all students with autism (Simpson & Myles, 1993; Zigler & Hodapp, 1987). Critics of mandatory full inclusion contend that inclusive education, or any single approach to education, is unlikely to be the most effective treatment for all students with autism, who vary greatly with regard to general level of functioning and specific strengths and weaknesses (Mesibov, 1976, 1990).

Persons with autism have IQs that range from severe mental retardation to superior intellectual functioning; they display considerable unevenness in development across domains of behavioral, social, and cognitive functioning (Burack & Volkmar, 1992); and they often manifest a wide range of severe behavior problems (Klin, Volkmar, & Sparrow, 1992). Within this diverse context, the insistence for inclusion for all persons with autism is considered by some to be too simplistic an approach for a uniquely complex and varied disorder (Mesibov, 1990). Rather, there needs to be an increased emphasis on individualized programs that foster development in all domains of functioning (Zigler & Hodapp, 1987). With this approach, continual assessments of

the educational and behavioral changes are essential to the validation of integrated, or any other type of, educational setting.

Evaluation of inclusive programs for children with autism is difficult, for both conceptual and practical reasons. As with other groups of students with special needs, there is a lack of consensus regarding prioritizing the assessment criteria. For the advocates of inclusion, the common experiences provided in the integrated settings between the students with and without autism are in themselves indexes of success. Evidence of academic and behavioral benefits is important (e.g., Egel & Gradel, 1988), but may be of secondary value in the decisions to implement integrated classrooms. Conversely, developmentalists and other educators emphasize that documented improvements in academic, behavioral, and social functioning should be the primary criteria of success and that there is insufficient evidence to justify large-scale programs of inclusion.

The goal of providing empirical evidence to assess the "real-world" effectiveness of inclusive schools is limited by a variety of real-world considerations. Most obvious, the relatively low incidence of children with autism precludes extensive research programs for evaluating large-scale implementation of inclusive classrooms. Accordingly, many of the studies are limited to small experimental programs that involve only a few children and rarely include control subjects. Similarly, the experimental settings are often situations of reverse mainstreaming because the nonautistic peers are brought to the special education classrooms or other isolated environments, which are antithetical to the inclusive education ideals. And, in studies in which children with and without autism are integrated, the setting is typically preschools, day cares, or recess/free play in primary schools, rather than regular classrooms. In many of the studies, only high-functioning students with autism—or sometimes only with autistic-like behaviors—are included, providing little basis for generalization to the whole population of children with autism. These considerations highlight difficulties in both implementing and studying large-scale educational programming for students with autism, and they reflect the need for caution in assessing the relevant empirical evidence.

Effects of Interacting with Nonhandicapped Age-Mates: The Study of Social Inclusion

A primary objective in integrated programs for children with autism, as with students who have other types of special needs, is the increased frequency of the social interactions of these children with their nonhandicapped peers (Odom & Watts, 1991). Through this peer contact, children with autism may observe more appropriate models for social behavior, have access to responsive social partners, and engage in more normalized social experiences than would occur with autistic peers alone. Accordingly, evaluations of integration efforts with students with autism are typically focused on changes in social skills and reciprocal social interaction among the children with autism and/or their nonhandicapped age-mates in small group formats.

In an attempt to promote appropriate valid social interactions with nonhandicapped peers, Nientimp and Cole (1992) taught 3 young adolescents with autism, autistic-like behaviors, or Pervasive Developmental Disorder, appropriate social responses in self-contained classrooms. All of these students showed an increase in independent appropriate social interaction responses and a decrease in echolalic responding.

Other researchers have focused their intervention on the nonhandicapped peers as well as on the students with autism. Brady, Shores, McEvoy, Ellis, and Fox (1987) prepared nonhandicapped children in sixth grade to interact with two severely handicapped students with autism, aged 8 and 10 years, in a playroom outside the regular classroom. The children were taught to recognize and respond to initiations and were provided with additional instruction in social initiation strategies. This intervention resulted in increases in spontaneous interactions, initiation rates, and the percentage of time spent in extended interactions. Similarly, a program for teaching typical peers social strategies (mutual attention, commenting and acknowledging skills) to direct to the children with autism was effective in promoting improved and more frequent social interactions and enhanced interaction on the part of the preschoolers with autism (Goldstein, Kaczmarek, Pennington, & Schafer, 1992). In this program, 5 triads of 2 nonhandicapped peers and 1 target student with autism or autistic-like behaviors were established in 2 integrated preschool classrooms. Improved rates of social interaction during play, for 4 of the 5 students with autism, were associated with this peer intervention.

Kamps, Leonard, Vernon, Dugan, and Delquadri (1992) developed social skills groups to promote increased social interactions for 3 high-functioning students with autism and their 11 nonhandicapped peers in an integrated classroom that also included 2 children with physical disabilities. All students were trained in (a) initiating, responding, and keeping interactions going; (b) greetings, conversations, and topics; (c) giving and accepting compliments; (d) taking turns and sharing; (e) helping others and asking for help; and (f) including others in activities. Both groups of students displayed improved social performance with increases in the frequency and duration of social interactions. In addition, the children with autism displayed increases in levels of initiations and responses, and the peers showed increases in their responsivity to the children with autism.

In a study of larger-scale integration, Strain (1983) alternately placed students with autism into integrated or segregated free play/recess situations. The classmates in the integrated setting included 24 nonhandicapped children who had received peer initiation training. The students with autism were more responsive to initiations in this setting as compared to the segregated one. Furthermore, the nonhandicapped classmates were more likely than the classmates in the segregated setting to both initiate interactions with and respond to initiations from the students with autism.

The studies of development of social skills of children with autism and their nonhandicapped peers are evidence for the many potential benefits of programs that integrate children with and without autism. However, the implications are limited because many of these studies were not conducted in actual classrooms, in which effective skills training and prompting would be more difficult. Empirical data from classrooms across a variety of communities are still necessary in order to establish the utility and benefits of inclusive education.

Teachers' and Peers' Roles in Successful Social Integration

The studies of social skills training are evidence of the potential for increased positive social interactions between students with autism and their classmates with highly systematic approaches and well-planned interventions. However, it is also apparent that the maintenance of these improvements is often contingent on teacher's prompting of peers to direct social initiations to the children with special needs (Odom & Watts, 1991). For example, Odom and colleagues (Odom, Hoyson, Jamieson, & Strain, 1985; Odom & Watts, 1991) found increases in peer initiations and social interactions between the peers and children with autism when teachers verbally prompted the initiations in the intervention setting, but no increases when these verbal prompts were not provided.

Sainato and colleagues (1992) contend that attempts to promote and generalize social interactions are hindered by a technology that has inadvertently produced prompt-dependent behavior. They investigated the effects of a self-evaluation procedure on preschool children's use of social interaction strategies with their classmates with autism. Peers were taught strategies such as getting their friend's attention, getting their friend to play, sharing with their friend, and talking to their friend. After the strategies were taught, each child practiced using the strategy with the experimenter until the child was able to demonstrate successful use of the strategies on three consecutive opportunities without teacher prompting. Self-evaluation training was provided after the children practiced the newly acquired strategies with a target child. In the self-evaluation, each child had to evaluate whether he or she was successful at implementing the strategy, by marking yes (happy face) or no (sad face) in a self-evaluation book. Teaching peer confederates strategies

alone was not sufficient to facilitate their use of the strategies with their handicapped classmates. Increases in the use of the strategies occurred only after the self-evaluation intervention was introduced. Untrained peers demonstrated little change in their social behavior, indicating a need to train all peers grouped with target children. The results also indicated a lower rate of teacher prompting of peer confederates throughout the study. Changes in the social behavior of the children with autism occurred primarily in their responsiveness; however, no clear improvements were demonstrated in their initiations to peers. There were difficulties with the analysis of generalization across playtimes and children, due to the fact that children left the program at the end of the school year.

Other researchers have also found that the nonhandicapped classmates do not show across-peer generalized interactions (Brady et al., 1987) or generalized correct responses from teacher-initiated greetings to greetings from nonhandicapped peers (Nientimp & Cole, 1992). Kamps, Walker, Maher, and Rotholz (1992) indicated that positive interactions between students with and students without autism were maintained only when the peers were monitored and given feedback on social performance.

Academic Benefits

Although the empirical focus has been predominantly on social benefits, researchers are increasingly aware of the need to demonstrate the academic benefits of full inclusion. Accordingly, recent studies focus on various academic benefits of integrated education for children with autism.

Harris, Handleman, Kristoff, Bass, and Gordon (1990) compared developmental changes in language ability of high-functioning preschool children with autism after the implementation of an intensive language curriculum in segregated and integrated classes. The assignment of the children with autism to the two groups was based on the manifestations of behavior problems. The children who posed substantial management problems that required individual attention and were considered to be potentially disruptive to class functioning in a less intensively staffed setting were placed in the segregated classroom. All of the children in both classes were exposed to formal, structured group language instruction in the classroom, including a weekly group led by the speech and language specialist. The children with autism from the two classroom settings displayed similarly substantial changes in language abilities. Harris et al. argue that these findings reflect the value of matching the appropriate educational setting to the individual child. The integrated setting was beneficial, and therefore the one of choice, for the children with less severe behavior problems. However, they argue that the children with more severe problem behaviors were only able to learn as much as the other children because of the opportunities afforded in a segregated classroom.

In a study of the effects of classwide peer tutoring on reading skills of high-functioning students with autism and their general education classroom peers, Kamps, Barbetta, Leonard, and Delquadri (1994) measured the effects of the classwide peer tutoring on the frequency and duration of social interactions that occurred during unstructured free time following classwide peer tutoring. They found that classwide peer tutoring increased reading fluency and correct responses to reading comprehension questions for all students. In addition, increases in the total duration of free-time social interactions for all children were noted. Although classwide peer tutoring was associated with significant improvements, Kamps et al. question whether lower-functioning students with autism would exhibit similar improvements with this type of program.

Dugan and colleagues (1995) examined the effects of using cooperative learning groups as an instructional format for students with autism, fully included in a fourth-grade social studies general education classroom. Comparing cooperative learning groups versus teacher–student discussion and traditional lecture formats, Dugan et al. found that increased learning occurred for two students with autism, and their peers, in the cooperative learning groups. Students scored two to four times more correct items on weekly quizzes during the intervention. The highest gains

occurred during the final condition. Improvements made by students with autism were noted in the area of social studies vocabulary recognition, but comprehension of the word through sentence formulation remained difficult. Additionally, higher levels of active engagement and social interaction among the group members were promoted in the cooperative learning groups.

These findings support earlier reports, and common sense, that successfully integrating students with autism requires teachers' adaptation of instruction and curricula for students and social skills training, as well as systematic guidance and encouragement of interactions among students with and without autism.

Attempts at Developing Integrated Programs

There is considerable evidence and consensus that, given the "right conditions," many children and adolescents with autism may be successfully assigned to general educational settings (Simpson & Myles, 1993) This has led educators to suggest possible models of successful inclusion programs, and several factors are common to various integrated programs.

Quill (1990) described an integration model for children with autism that was implemented in a Massachusetts school district. The program has six primary components:

1. Parents are actively involved in the development and implementation of the program. Among other duties, the parents are responsible for presenting the new program and the children with autism to the school's faculty and students, prioritizing educational goals, and serving as coteachers.
2. Consultative services and technical support are available for all school faculty and family members. The support includes a special educator who acts as a parent liaison educator, two specialized educators working as program consultants, and a team consisting of a physical therapist, an occupational therapist, and a speech and language pathologist, who work in cooperation with the program consultants.
3. An individually designed integration plan is used to match children's learning styles

and interests to their curriculum of daily activities with typical peers.

4. A peer buddy program is instituted in an effort to improve social acceptance among peers with and without handicaps.

5. An ecological approach is used for curriculum development.

6. Challenging behaviors are creatively managed by a new program.

Simpson and Myles (1993) formed the Autism Mainstreaming Collaboration Model, an example of a program that can be designed to support general educators in their work with students with autism. The model's major components include mainstreaming modifications and general education classroom support, attitudinal and social support, and coordinated team commitment. Support for general education teachers should include availability of appropriately trained support personnel, reduced class size, access to collaborative problem-solving relationships, adequate teacher planning time, paraprofessional availability, and in-service training.

The models presented by Quill (1990) and Simpson and Myles (1993) are comprehensive, and, given the appropriate funding and training circumstances, they could allow for the successful inclusion of many students with autism. However, both proposals highlight the extensive resources that are essential to the development of effective inclusion programs and the need to expand the evaluations of the benefits of these programs to include their appropriateness for the teachers, schools, parents, and community.

SUMMARY AND DIRECTIONS FOR FUTURE RESEARCH

Integration, normalization, and inclusion have been central to the improved and more normalized conditions and educational programs for children with autism and other special needs (Mesibov, 1990). Within this orientation, persons from all aspects of society, including educators, legislators, and parents, have become more sensitized to the need to provide children with special needs the opportunities for a more typical lifestyle. Increasingly, these children are no longer as marginalized in society,

nor are they educated only in secluded settings, separated from other children and from most of society. Rather, with increased interaction with nonhandicapped peers and adults, and with additional exposure to more typical environments, students with special needs often show better self-concepts and are able to function, at least to some extent, in typical situations.

The recognition of the value, and the legal requirement, to normalize the lives of persons with special needs to the maximum extent possible is particularly significant in light of the poor conditions and degraded existence that were common for persons with special needs throughout the 1900s and into the 1950s and 1960s. Many persons with special needs were confined to segregated residences, often distant from other communities, regardless of their ability to function independently or semi-independently. Similarly, children with special needs were educated in separate schools or in segregated classrooms sequestered far from other classes in a regular school. Despite the efforts of the administrators, clinicians, and educators in these settings, these programs were typically doomed to mediocrity or even to failure. There was usually little support from educational administrators and virtually no interaction between special and regular educators. The message that the education, self-images, and rights of students with special needs were not societal priorities was clearly evident to the students as well as to their parents and teachers. The advocates of normalization, integration, and inclusion have been instrumental in initiating attempts to correct this situation by increasing awareness of the rights of persons with special needs, sensitivity to their desires, and acceptance of them within the general communities.

These changes in societal attitudes have been reflected in educational programming that is increasingly oriented to meeting the specific needs of the individual students. In many cases, this programming entails inclusive education (Quill, 1990; Simpson & Myles, 1993) or less extensive integration in which students with autism attend the same school as their nonhandicapped peers, but spend only a part of the schoolday with these children and the rest in separate classes or resource rooms.

There are also segregated schools exclusively for children with autism and other related types of special needs. In most of these schools, the goal is to provide the students with sufficient educational and social backgrounds to allow them to be successfully included in regular school settings. In all cases, greater attention is being paid to respecting the rights of the students with special needs and to providing them an opportunity for a normalized life.

This continuum of educational programs appears to be consistent with both the PL 94-192 notion of least restrictive environment and Nirje's (1969) notion of a lifestyle that is normal to the extent possible, and would seem to be appropriate for the education of a group as diverse in level of functioning and strengths and weaknesses as are children with autism. However, the partially integrated and, even more so, the segregated educational programs, continue to be attacked by the supporters of inclusion. To these educators and advocates, any separation, isolation, or differentiation of children with autism from their peers is unacceptable.

The lack of full agreement about the efficacy of various levels of integrated/segregated classrooms suggests the need for further studies of educational strategies for students with autism. In the absence of strong evidence of potential harm or other special reasons, the inclusive approach to education is considered by many to be the educational program of choice. However, can one approach be optimal for all children with autism, and suitable for all classes, schools, or communities?

Special education schools are costly to operate at a high degree of quality. There are those who argue that integration will be seen as a money-saving, rather than a developmentally optimal, method. "As in mainstreaming we fear that least restrictive may translate into least costly when it comes to providing services for autistic children" (Zigler & Hodapp, 1987, p. 673).

At times, advocates of inclusion minimize the complexity of implementing inclusive programs within a community. The decentralization of special education programs results in the diffusion of expertise throughout the larger school system and the need to involve much greater numbers of participants. Although an exemplary goal, the effective integration of students with autism into regular classrooms requires substantial commitment that extends beyond the already extensive demands on general educators. Additional demands for resources are particularly taxing at present because of current economic difficulties. Many communities have been forced to cut education budgets, although the cost of teacher salaries continues to rise. The consequents of these predicaments are already evidenced in school systems where teachers are faced with increased numbers of students in regular classrooms, but are provided with fewer resources. With these types of constraints, inclusive education is unlikely to be embraced enthusiastically enough for it to be universally successful. Accordingly, responsible advocacy is needed to ascertain which situations are likely to be appropriate for effective inclusive education and which need to be targeted for modification and adaptation to be able to meet diverse student needs and include all children. Although inclusive education is certainly a goal to strive for, it is necessary for educators to consider student capabilities, empirical findings, teacher attitudes, parental wishes, community resources, societal values, and a host of other factors before inclusive education can be accepted as the sole educational setting for children with autism and related disorders.

Cross-References

Issues of integration of children with autism are discussed in Chapter 29, and curriculum development and behavioral intervention issues are topics in Chapters 22 and 26, respectively. Working with families is addressed in Chapter 27.

REFERENCES

Blatt, B (1987) *The conquest of mental retardation.* Austin, TX: Pro-Ed.

Brady, M.P., Shores, R.E., McEvoy, M.A., Ellis, D., & Fox, J.J. (1987). Increasing social interactions of severely handicapped autistic children. *Journal of Autism and Developmental Disorders, 17,* 375–390.

Brown, L., Nietupski, J., & Hamre-Nietupski, S. (1976). The criterion of ultimate functioning and public school services for severely handicapped students. In L. Brown, N. Certo, K. Belmore, & T. Crowner (Eds.), *Madison alternative for zero exclusion: Papers and programs related to public school services for secondary age severely handicapped students*. Madison, WI: Madison Public Schools.

Burack, J.A., & Derevensky, J.L. (Eds.). (1992). Providing services for persons with mental retardation: Looking to the 21st century [Special issue]. *McGill Journal of Education, 27*.

Burack, J.A., Kurtz, L., & Derevensky, J.L. (1992). Services for persons with mental retardation: A debate for all seasons. *McGill Journal of Education, 27*, 275–278.

Burack, J.A., & Volkmar, F.R. (1992). Development of low- and high-functioning autistic children. *Journal of Child Psychology and Psychiatry, 33*, 607–616.

Cook, T.P., Apolloni, T., & Cooke, S.A. (1987). Normal preschool children as behavioral models for retarded peers. *Exceptional Children, 43*, 531–532.

Dugan, E., Kamps, D., Leonard, B., Watkins, N., Rheinberger, A., & Stackhaus, J. (1995). Effects of cooperative learning groups during social studies for students with autism and fourth grade peers. *Journal of Applied Behavior Analysis, 28*, 175–188.

Egel, A.L., & Gradel, K. (1988). Social integration of autistic children: Evaluation and recommendations. *The Behavior Therapist, 11*, 7–11.

Fuchs, D., & Fuchs, L.S. (1994). Inclusive schools movement and the radicalization of special education reform. *Exceptional Children, 60*, 294–309.

Goldstein, H., Kaczmarek, L., Pennington, R., & Schafer, K. (1992). Peer-mediated intervention: Attending to, commenting on and acknowledging the behavior of preschoolers with autism. *Journal of Applied Behavior Analysis, 25*, 289–305.

Gottlieb, J. (1990). Mainstreaming and quality education. *American Journal on Mental Retardation, 95*, 16–17.

Harris, S.L., Handleman, J.S., Kristoff, B., Bass, L., & Gordon, R. (1990). Changes in language development among autistic and peer children in segregated and integrated preschool settings. *Journal of Autism and Developmental Disorders, 20*, 23–31.

Hodapp, R.M., & Zigler, E. (1992). Integration and development: Reconciling two conflicting perspectives. *McGill Journal of Education, 27*, 279–291.

Iano, R., Ayers, D., Heller, J., McGetigan, J., & Walker, V. (1974). Sociometric status of retarded children in an integrative program. *Exceptional Children, 40*, 267–271.

Kamps, D.M., Barbetta, P.M., Leonard, B.R., & Delquadri, J. (1994). Classwide peer tutoring: An integration strategy to improve reading skills and promote peer interactions among students with autism and general education peers. *Journal of Applied Behavior Analysis, 27*, 49–61.

Kamps, D.M., Leonard, B.R., Vernon, S., Dugan, E.P., & Delquadri, J.C. (1992). Teaching social skills to students with autism to increase peer interactions in an integrated first-grade classroom. *Journal of Applied Behavior Analysis, 25*, 281–288.

Kamps, D., Walker, D., Maher, J., & Rotholz, D.A. (1992). Academic and environmental effects of small group arrangements in classrooms for students with autism and other developmental disabilities. *Journal of Autism and Developmental Disorders, 22*, 277–293.

Klin, A., Volkmar, F.R., & Sparrow, S. (1992). Autistic social dysfunction: Some limitations of the theory of mind hypothesis. *Journal of Child Psychology and Psychiatry, 33*, 861–876.

Leiberman, L.M. (1992). Preserving special education . . . For those who need it. In S. Stainback & W. Stainback (Eds.), *Controversial issues confronting special education*. Boston: Allyn & Bacon.

Lusthaus, E., Gazith, K., & Lusthaus, C. (1992). Each belongs: A rationale for full inclusion. *McGill Journal of Education, 27*, 293–309.

Mesibov, G.B. (1976). Implications of the normalization principle for psychotic children. *Journal of Autism and Childhood Schizophrenia, 6*, 360–365.

Mesibov, G.B. (1990). Normalization and its relevance today. *Journal of Autism and Developmental Disorders, 20*, 379–390

Meyers, C., MacMillan, D., & Yoshida, R. (1980). Regular class placement of E.M.R. students, from efficacy to mainstreaming: A review of issues and research. In J. Gottlieb (Ed.), *Educating mentally retarded persons in the mainstream*. Baltimore: University Park Press.

Miller, L. (1990). The regular education initiative and school reform: Lessons from the mainstream. *Remedial and Special Education, 11*, 17–22.

Myles, B.S., & Simpson, R.L. (1989). Regular educators' modification preferences for mainstreaming mildly handicapped children. *The Journal of Special Education, 22*, 479–492.

Nientimp, E.G., & Cole, C.L. (1992). Teaching socially valid social interaction responses to students with severe disabilities in an integrated school setting. *Journal of School Psychology, 30*, 343–354.

Nirje, B. (1969). The normalization principle and its human management implications. In R. Kugel & W. Wolfensberger (Eds.), *Changing patterns in residential services for the mentally retarded*. Washington, DC: U.S. Government Printing Office.

Odom, S.L., Hoyson, M., Jamieson, B., & Strain, P.S. (1985). Promoting the social interaction of handicapped preschool children: Cross-setting and component analysis. *Journal of Applied Behavior Analysis, 18*, 3–16.

Odom, S.L., & Watts, E. (1991). Reducing teacher prompts in peer-mediated interventions for young children with autism. *The Journal of Special Education, 25*, 26–43.

Porter, R.H., Ramsey, B., Tremblay, A., Iaccobo, M., & Crawley, S. (1978). Social interactions in heterogeneous groups of retarded and normally developing children: An observational study. In G.P. Sackett (Ed.), *Observing behavior: Theory and applications in mental retardation*. Baltimore: University Park Press.

Quill, K.A. (1990). A model for integrating children with autism. *Focus on Autistic Behavior, 5*, 1–19.

Sailor, W. (1991). Special education in the restructured school. *Remedial and Special Education, 12*, 8–22.

Sainato, D.M., Goldstein, H., & Strain, P.S. (1992). Effects of self-evaluation on preschool children's use of social interaction strategies with their classmates with autism. *Journal of Applied Behavior Analysis, 25*, 127–141.

Schumm, J.S., & Vaughn, S. (1991). Making adaptations for mainstreamed students: General classroom teachers' perspectives. *Remedial and Special Education, 12*, 18–25.

Simpson, R.L., & Myles, B.S. (1990). The General Education Collaboration Model: A model for successful mainstreaming. *Focus on Exceptional Children, 23*, 1–10.

Simpson, R.L., & Myles, B.S. (1993). Successful integration of children and youth with autism in mainstreamed settings. *Focus on Autistic Behavior, 7*, 1–13.

Simpson, R.L., & Sasso, G.M. (1992). Full inclusion of students with autism in general education settings: Values versus science. *Focus on Autistic Behavior, 7*, 1–13.

Snyder, L., Apolloni, T., & Cooke, T.P. (1977). Integrated settings at the early childhood level:

The role of nonretarded peers. *Exceptional Children, 43*, 262–266.

Stainback, S., & Stainback, W. (1989). Integration of students with mild and moderate handicaps. In D.K. Pipsky & A. Gartner (Eds.), *Beyond separate education: Quality education for all* (pp. 41–52). Baltimore: Brookes.

Stainback, S., & Stainback, W. (1992a). *Controversial issues confronting special education*. Boston: Allyn & Bacon.

Stainback, S., & Stainback, W. (1992b). Schools as inclusive communities. In S. Stainback & W. Stainback (Eds.), *Controversial issues confronting special education* (pp. 29–43). Boston: Allyn & Bacon.

Stainback, S., Stainback, W., & Bunch, G. (1989). Introduction and historical background. In S. Stainback, W. Stainback, & M. Forest (Eds.), *Educating all students in the mainstream of regular education*. Baltimore: Brookes.

Strain, P. (1983). Generalization of autistic children's social behavior change: Effects of developmentally integrated and segregated settings. *Analysis and Intervention in Developmental Disabilities, 3*, 23–24.

Vergason, G.A., & Anderegg, M.L. (1992). Preserving the least restrictive environment. In S. Stainback & W. Stainback (Eds.), *Controversial issues confronting special education* (pp. 45–54). Boston: Allyn & Bacon.

Whinnery, K.W., Fuchs, L.S., & Fuchs, D. (1991). General, special and remedial teachers' acceptance of behavioral and instructional strategies for mainstreaming students with mild handicaps. *Remedial and Special Education, 12*, 6–13.

Wizner, S., & Lucht, C.L. (1992). Of scarce resources and gilded cages: A case study. *McGill Journal of Education, 27*, 377–388.

Wolfensberger, W. (1972). *The principle of normalization in human services*. Toronto, Ontario, Canada: National Institute on Mental Retardation.

Zigler, E., & Hodapp, R.M. (1986). *Understanding mental retardation*. New York: Cambridge University Press.

Zigler, E., & Hodapp, R.M. (1987). The developmental implications of integrating autistic children within the public schools. In D.J. Cohen & A.M. Donnellan (Eds.), *Handbook of autism and pervasive developmental disorders* (pp. 668–674). New York: John Wiley & Sons.

CHAPTER 37

The Legal Rights of Children with Disabilities
to Education and Developmental Services

MIRIAM BERKMAN

The Individuals with Disabilities Education Act (IDEA) provides a federal legal right to special education and related services for school-age children with disabilities. The related Infants and Toddlers with Disabilities Act provides a similar, though somewhat more limited, right to early intervention services for children from birth to 3 years old whose development is significantly delayed. Taken together, these federal statutes create a powerful legal mechanism for obtaining necessary and timely services to promote the development of children with autism and other developmental disabilities. Other federal laws that more generally prohibit discrimination against individuals with disabilities (i.e., Section 504 of the Rehabilitation Act, and the Americans with Disabilities Act [ADA]) provide additional protection for some children. Because early diagnosis and engagement in developmentally appropriate services is so central to long-term developmental progress, it is important for both the parents of children with pervasive developmental disorders and the many professionals of different disciplines who come in contact with these children to have basic familiarity and access to information about the laws related to special education. This chapter describes the law's basic provisions and discusses some of the issues that commonly arise for parents, advocates, and clinicians in trying to secure the rights of individual children.

SPECIAL EDUCATION FOR SCHOOL-AGE CHILDREN

In 1975, Congress enacted the Education for All Handicapped Children Act (EAHCA) (the IDEA's precursor) to remedy years of gross neglect of the educational needs of children with disabilities, including the outright exclusion of many children from public education. At that time, Congress found that:

- More than half of the 8 million children with disabilities in the United States do not receive appropriate educational services.
- One million of these children are excluded entirely from the public school system.
- Many children in regular school programs have undetected disabilities that prevent them from having success in school.
- Because of the lack of adequate services within the public school system, families are often forced to find services outside the system, often at great distance from their residence and at their own expense.
- State and local educational agencies have a responsibility to provide education for all children with disabilities but lack the financial resources to do so. (20 U.S.C. Sec. 1400(b))

Federal law now provides a system of grants-in-aid to the states, to be used for special education services for children with disabilities.

Federal funding is coupled with a legal right to special education for these children, as well as a variety of procedural protections to ensure that children with disabilities receive services appropriate to their individual needs, and that parents are included in the educational planning process. The statute is remarkable in that it articulates an individualized right to a "free appropriate public education" for all children who require special education or related services as a result of their disabilities, regardless of the severity of disability, and notwithstanding the extraordinary cost that may be entailed in meeting some students' educational needs. The statute is also remarkable in its provision of an individualized right to administrative appeal and, ultimately, to litigate in court the content of the plan to meet each student's unique needs. The legal power of the IDEA to make complex and comprehensive services available to children with autism and other disabilities contrasts with the much more limited legal rights and remedies available to adults with similar disabilities. The legal mandates of the IDEA do not, however, automatically result in good education for children with disabilities. Disparities in communities' resources, as well as in families' knowledge; access to expert consultation and legal representation; and capacity to advocate on behalf of the children often lead to limitations and disparities in the quality of special education provided.

THE RIGHT TO A FREE APPROPRIATE PUBLIC EDUCATION

Eligibility

To receive federal assistance, the IDEA requires states to guarantee special education at public expense to all children between the ages of 3 and 21 years who require special education or related services as a result of their disabilities. Services are not mandatory for children under 5 or over 18 years, however, to the extent that such a requirement would be inconsistent with state law [20 U.S.C. Sec. 1412(2)(B)]. (For example, if state law does not authorize use of state funds to provide any services for nondisabled children between 3 and 5 years, it would not be required to make

special education services available for this age group.)

Under the statute, eligible "children with disabilities" are defined as those who fall within one of a large number of disability categories and, as a result of their impairments, are in need of special education and related services. Autism is explicitly listed among the disabilities that may qualify a child for special services [20 U.S.C. Sec. 1401(a)(1)(A)]. In addition, the states may, at their discretion, expand the eligibility criteria to include children between 3 and 5 years who experience more generalized delays in their physical, cognitive, communicative, social or emotional, and/or adaptive development (e.g., children who may not meet formal criteria for autism or other pervasive developmental disorders, but who are experiencing significant difficulties and would benefit from early access to developmental interventions) [20 U.S.C. Sec. 1401(a)(1)(B)]. For purposes of a child's educational rights, autism is defined, by federal regulation, not with reference to professional clinical criteria, but as "a developmental disability significantly affecting verbal and non-verbal communication and social interaction, generally evident before age 3, that adversely affects a child's educational performance. Other characteristics often associated with autism are engagement in repetitive activities and stereotyped movements, resistance to environmental change or change in daily routines, and unusual responses to sensory experiences . . ." [34 C.F.R. Sec. 300.7(b)(1)].

Most children with pervasive developmental disorders will either meet this definition, or will be eligible for services under the IDEA on the basis of mental retardation, speech and language impairment, learning disability, or serious emotional disturbance, all of which are also covered by the defining statute and regulations [20 U.S.C. Sec. 1401 (a)(1)(A); 34 C.F.R. Secs. 300.7(b)(5); 300.7(b)(9); 300.7(b)(10); 300.7(b)(11)]. There are, however, some high-functioning children with pervasive developmental disorders who do not meet the IDEA's eligibility criteria because they are able to make significant educational progress without special education and therefore do not "need special education and related services." Although these children are not protected by the very specific provisions of the IDEA, they are protected from discrimination by Section 504 of the Rehabilitation Act and by the ADA. (See discussion below.)

Defining the Right to a Free Appropriate Public Education

The federally mandated services for children with disabilities include "special education," defined as "specially designed instruction . . . to meet the unique needs of a child with a disability" [20 U.S.C. Sec. 1401(a)(16)], and "related services," defined broadly to include "such developmental, corrective, and other supportive services . . . as may be required to assist a child with a disability to benefit from special education" [20 U.S.C. Sec. 1401(a)(17)]. Related services specifically include transportation to and from school, physical and occupational therapy, speech pathology, social work, assistive technology, psychology and counseling services for children, early identification and assessment of disabling conditions in children, as well as counseling and training for parents [20 U.S.C. Sec. 1401(a)(17); 34 C.F.R. Sec. 300.16]. Other services not expressly listed in the regulations may also qualify if they are necessary to enable a child to benefit from special education. Depending on a child's particular needs, special education may include not only academic instruction, but also a wide range of additional activities, including (but not limited to) services aimed at facilitating social and emotional development, daily living skills, and basic behavioral controls. Instruction may take place at school, at home, in summer camps, in residential institutions, or in hospitals; some children may require the school day to extend beyond traditional school hours, for the school year to extend into traditional vacation periods, for school programs to be coordinated explicitly with parents' management of a child at home, or, in extreme situations, for the child's education to extend to 24 hours a day, 365 days a year.

Mandated services include transition services (beginning no later than age 16, and earlier if appropriate), which consist of coordinated activities designed to anticipate, prepare for, and facilitate the student's movement from school to postschool activities, such as employment, independent living, continuing education, and community activities [20 U.S.C. Sec. 1401(a)(19); 34 C.F.R. Sec. 300.18]. Transition services include such activities as vocational assessments and training; community-based experiences, such as supported employment; services to prepare for and make the transition to independent living, or to identify and prepare for supported group living; and liaison between school programs and public or private agencies that provide services to adults with disabilities.

Federal law describes a broad range of services that may be required, but it says little to prescribe what must be provided in individual cases. Decisions are individualized and fact-specific. What is legally prescribed is not educational content but a process of multidisciplinary collaboration, including a child's parents, school personnel, and experts, to determine what education is appropriate for each particular child. This approach leaves room for different educational philosophies to be applied in different communities, and it provides opportunities for discussion, disagreement, and negotiation among educators, parents, and clinicians regarding a child's difficulties and the appropriateness of various educational approaches. Federal regulations specifically caution that the IDEA provides a right to educational opportunity, not a guarantee of a successful outcome (34 C.F.R. Sec. 300.350).

The Rowley *Standard*

Though limited, there are a few basic legal principles that define the scope of federally mandated services. First, the Supreme Court has held that appropriate services are those that are designed to provide children with disabilities with a "basic floor of opportunity" to achieve educational progress through a program "individually designed to provide educational benefit to the handicapped child" (*Board of Education of Hendrick Hudson Central School District v. Rowley*, 1982, p. 200). As interpreted by the Court, the statute does not create a right to optimal services or to maximization of a child's educational potential, but rather a right to obtain some demonstrable educational benefit. Specifically, the Court in *Rowley* held that a very bright hearing-impaired child was not entitled to a sign-language interpreter in order to facilitate her best possible academic performance, where she was doing better-than-average schoolwork in a regular class without the interpreter. Although some of the Supreme Court's language in the *Rowley* opinion could be taken to require only formal access to some education or minimal educational benefit, courts and administrative hearing officers since the *Rowley* decision have further defined the entitlement to educational benefit so as to make it a meaningful right to education (*Abrahamson v. Hirshman,* 1983; *Oberti v. Board of Education of Borough of Clementon School District,* 1993; *Town of Burlington v. Department of Education,* 1984).

Some states have interpreted their own laws regarding special education to impose a higher standard than the federal minimum. Michigan, for example, requires its schools to provide special education designed to enable the student to develop to his or her "maximum potential" (*Barwacz v. Michigan Department of Education,* 1988). Massachusetts, New Jersey, and North Carolina apply similar standards (*Geis v. Board of Education of Parsippany–Troy Hills, Morris County,* 1985; *Harrell v. Wilson County School,* 1982; *Town of Burlington v. Department of Education,* 1984). Courts in other states (e.g., Tennessee) have, however, interpreted state laws that appear to set a "maximizing" standard as imposing a requirement identical with federal law (*Doe v. Board of Education of Tullahoma City Schools,* 1993).

Least Restrictive Environments

The IDEA also adopts as federal policy a principle of integrating children with disabilities into the mainstream of public education to the "maximum extent appropriate." Children with disabilities are to be placed in special classes or separate schools, or otherwise removed from the regular school environment "only when the nature or the severity of the disability is such that education in regular classes with the use of supplementary aids and services cannot be achieved satisfactorily" [20 U.S.C. Sec. 1412(5)(B); 34 C.F.R. Sec. 300.550]. Nonacademic activities, such as recess, meals, and physical education are likewise required to be integrated to the maximum extent possible (34 C.F.R. Sec. 300.553). To give effect to the principle of educating children with disabilities in the least restrictive environment, local school systems must make available a continuum of educational placements, including instruction in regular classes, special classes, special schools, and institutions, and must provide for supplementary services, such as resource rooms, classroom aides, modified curricula, and assistive technology, to augment regular classroom placements (34 C.F.R. Sec. 300.551).

In choosing the appropriate (and least restrictive) educational placement for a child with a disability, federal regulations direct the public schools (a) to base the decision on the child's individual needs, as defined by the child's individualized educational program (IEP); (b) to place the child as close as possible to home; (c) to place the child in the school the child would have attended if not disabled, unless the child requires some other arrangement; and (d) to consider any potential harmful effect of the placement on the child or on the quality of services that he or she needs (34 C.F.R. Sec. 300.552). Imbedded in the law is a continuing tension between the principles of maximum integration and individualization. Taken as a whole, however, these provisions create a rebuttable presumption in favor of maximum integration, which can be overridden if experience demonstrates that the child's individual educational needs demand a different course of action.

As with the more general requirements of free appropriate public education, the least restrictive environment regulations offer innumerable opportunities for disagreement, negotiation, and individual, fact-specific decision making. Because educators, parents, clinicians, and advocates differ in the relative value that they assign to a child's exposure to and participation in an integrated setting, as opposed to the value they assign to the individualized services that may be more easily provided in a separate setting, they will necessarily disagree about when it is appropriate or necessary to remove a child from the regular class for all or part of the child's education. Some parents seek greater inclusion for their severely impaired children in order to provide opportunities for socialization and modeling of nondisabled behavior, and to facilitate greater understanding among nondisabled children and lessen the stigma of disability. These parents argue for extensive modifications of regular classes to accommodate children with disabilities, for example, individual aides, assistive technology, modified curricula, provision of individual therapies such as speech and language within the regular classroom rather than removing the child, and so on (Detroit, Michigan Public Schools, 1993; *Mavis v. Sobol,* 1994; *Oberti v. Board of Education of Borough of Clementon School District,* 1993; *Sacramento City School District v. Rachel H.,* 1994; Sudbury, Massachusetts Public Schools, 1993). Other parents, believing it unlikely that the intensive needs of seriously disabled children can be met adequately in the regular classroom, seek segregated placements in order to obtain greater individual attention, greater specialization of educational program, and potentially greater expertise of educational staff (*Learning Disabilities Association of Maryland v. Board of Education of Baltimore County,* 1993; *Roland M. v. Concord School Committee,* 1990). A wide range of intermediate plans may also be arranged, in which a child with a disability spends part of the day in an integrated setting and the remainder in separate special education activities. Courts approach disputes regarding the least restrictive environment with multiple-factor balancing tests that weigh the costs and benefits of integrated education against the costs and benefits of separate education, taking into account the nonacademic benefits, to both disabled and nondisabled children, of integrated education; the extent to which the school system has attempted to meet the child's needs in the regular classroom through supplemental aids and services; and the disruption a child with a disability may cause to nondisabled students (*Daniel R.R. v. El Paso Independent School District,* 1989; *Greer v. Rome City School District,* 1991; *Oberti v. Board of Education of Borough of Clementon School District,* 1993; *Roncker v. Walter,* 1983; *Sacramento City School District v. Rachel H.,* 1994).

Because of the very high value that federal law places on integration, a school may not remove a child from the regular classroom against a parent's wishes simply because he or she would make greater *academic* progress in a segregated setting (*Oberti v. Board of Education of Borough of Clementon School District,* 1993; *Roland M. v. Concord School Committee,* 1990). However, because of the relative frequency with which children with autism and other pervasive developmental disorders do require very structured settings, protection from overstimulation, education relating to basic activities of daily living and basic communication, and intensive behavior management, it is more likely that segregated or partially segregated placements will be found appropriate for children with this group of disorders than for many others. Parents and educators may also agree to segregated placements that would not have been compelled over the objection of one party or the other. (Other chapters in this volume discuss the issue of integration in detail.)

Special Issues Related to Special Education for Children with Autism

As discussed above, decisions regarding the appropriate program for an individual child revolve around determinations of the child's specific strengths and weaknesses, setting realistic goals for the child's education, and designing the education and related services that will permit the child an opportunity to achieve his or her goals. A few of the specific issues that may arise in making educational plans for children with autism are discussed below.

Choice of Educational Methods

Educators, clinicians, and parents often disagree about which of several competing educational methods will best serve the needs of a child with a disability. This issue has arisen frequently in disputes over various methods of language instruction for hearing-impaired students and also in several recent cases regarding parents' requests for Lovaas training (an individualized behavioral intervention program for young children, which ordinarily involves intensive training for both the child and his or her parents in school and home settings) for young children with pervasive developmental disorders (Calavaras Unified School District, 1993; *Delaware County Intermediate Unit #25 v. Martin and Melinda K.,* 1993). In general, although the views of the child's parents are important and must be considered by the school, parents cannot compel a school system to implement the educational approach of their choice as long as the approach chosen by the school is "appropriate" to the child's needs (*Board of Education of Hendrick Hudson Central School District v. Rowley,* 1982; *Delaware County Intermediate Unit #25 v. Martin and Melinda K.,* 1993; *Lachman v. Illinois Board of Education,* 1988; *Petersen v. Hastings Public Schools,* 1994). Ultimately, under the IDEA, questions of appropriateness are determined in administrative or judicial appeals based on expert testimony and on evidence regarding whether the services offered by the school were "reasonably calculated to provide educational benefit" (*Board of Education of Hendrick Hudson Central School District,* 1982). Parents may succeed in enforcing their choice of educational method if they can convince a hearing officer or court that the method chosen by the school is not supported by competent professional evidence or is not being implemented according to accepted professional norms (*Delaware County Intermediate Unit #25 v. Martin and Melinda K.,* 1993).

Extended School Year

Many children with disabilities, including autism, require a continuation of their schooling beyond the traditional school year, in order to maintain their educational progress and avoid the regression in their skills that would take place if their education were to be interrupted for lengthy vacation periods. Factors that may be considered include the nature of the child's disability, the child's rate of educational progress and need for consistent structure, any history of regression during breaks in schooling, critical periods in the child's education (e.g., acquisition of language, transition from school to adult living, and so on) (*Alamo Heights Independent School District v. State Board of Education,* 1986; *Battle v. Pennsylvania,* 1980; *Georgia Association of Retarded Citizens v. McDaniel,* 1983; *Houston Independent

School District,* 1994; *Johnson v. Independent School District,* 1990). Similar considerations also apply to requests for extended week and extended day programming (Houston Independent School District, 1994).

Private Placement

Private school programs may be required if the public school system cannot provide an appropriate educational program for a child with a disability. Under the least restrictive environment regulations, a school system may not remove a child from a public school against the parents' wishes without first attempting to devise a system of aids and services that will enable the child to function in the most integrated setting (see above). Similarly, a parent may not obtain a private placement at public expense without showing that the public school program will not enable the child to benefit from his or her education (34 C.F.R. Sec. 300.403; *Town of Burlington v. Department of Education,* 1984). Where, however, the public school system fails to offer any program or offers an inappropriate program, or where the child's parents and the school system can agree that a private program is the best alternative, private school placements and associated transportation costs must be funded by the school system (*Town of Burlington v. Department of Education,* 1984; *Union School District v. Smith,* 1994). Similar standards have been applied in the cases noted above, in which parents have requested intensive, home-based Lovaas training for their children. Lovaas has been found an appropriate instructional approach and has been ordered where the alternative proposed by the school system was inadequate (*Delaware County Intermediate Unit #25 v. Martin and Melinda K.,* 1993).

Parent Counseling and Training

Many children with pervasive developmental disorders require education relating to activities of daily living, have difficulty generalizing from one environment to another, and learn best when skills learned at school are consistently reinforced at home. These children's education will be facilitated by services, such as counseling and training, that assist their parents in developing and maintaining a consistent environment at home and in applying the same behavioral management techniques that school staff have found useful (Houston Independent School District, 1994). Parent counseling or training will be ordered as a related service for those children who require such coordination between school and home in order to benefit from their education. Explicit and structured coordination of children's school programs with their management and support at home may also either avoid a need for residential placement or assist in determining that no less restrictive alternative is capable of providing educational benefit.

Residential Placement

The most intensive and costly special education placements possible are in 24-hour residential settings. Although such intensive and restrictive placements are required for only a small number of the most severely disabled children, they are often the focus of disagreement because of their cost. Federal regulations specifically provide that "if placement in a public or private residential program is necessary to provide special education and related services to a child with a disability, the program, including non-medical care and room and board, must be at no cost to the parents of the child" (34 C.F.R. Sec. 300.302). Residential programs are "necessary" under the *Rowley* standard and the least restrictive environment regulations, when the child cannot otherwise benefit from special education (*Abrahamson v. Hirshman*, 1983; *Angevine v. Jenkins*, 1990; *Ash v. Lake Oswego School District*, 1992; *B.G. by F.G. v. Cranford Board of Education*, 1988; *Cremeans v. Fairland Local School Board*, 1993; *Kruelle v. New Castle County School District*, 1981). Generally, residential placements will not be ordered, either at the parent's behest or the school's, without evidence that less intensive and restrictive alternatives have been tried and that they do not permit the child to make sufficient educational progress. When less restrictive options have been tried and have failed, such factors as difficulty generalizing from one context to another, persistent dangerous behaviors, need for instruction in basic life skills such as eating and toileting, and behavioral deterioration in response to such small environmental changes as

necessarily take place when a child travels back and forth from home to school argue in support of the need for residential placement. Residential placements may also be required when no appropriate program is available for a child within daily commuting distance of the child's home (*Ojai Unified School District v. Johnson*, 1993; *Union School District v. Smith*, 1994).

Psychotherapy as a Related Service

Some children with pervasive developmental disorders require ongoing psychotherapy in order to be able to maintain their functioning in school. It is often difficult if not impossible, however, to differentiate mental health services that are necessary to support school progress from more generalized mental health treatments, which may also be necessary to support the child's development and family relationships but are not the financial responsibility of the local school system. Where a child suffers from serious psychological symptoms that directly impede school functioning and social and emotional goals have been recognized as part of the child's program, psychotherapy may be required as a related service at no charge to the parent (*Doe v. Anrig*, 1987; *Papacoda v. State of Connecticut*, 1981; *T.G. v. Board of Education of Piscataway, New Jersey*, 1983; Richardson, Texas Independent School District, 1994). Intensive treatments that are primarily for psychiatric rather than educational reasons (e.g., acute hospitalizations) are not within the ambit of related services, although treatment does enable the child to proceed with his or her education (*Field v. Haddonfield Board of Education*, 1991; *Tice v. Botetourt County School Board*, 1990).

PARENTS' RIGHTS WITHIN THE EDUCATIONAL PLANNING PROCESS

In large part, the IDEA applies a procedural approach to ensuring the appropriate education of children with disabilities, relying on (a) the inclusion of individuals with varying experience and perspectives on the child's needs to develop a full understanding of the child and (b) the interest of parents to safeguard their children's rights. The statute sets out a detailed process through which educators, parents, and other experts, if necessary, come together to make decisions concerning the nature of the child's needs and the appropriate methods of addressing those needs and evaluating the child's progress. The statute also prescribes detailed procedures for resolving disputes between parents and school systems.

Notice to Parents

Whenever a school system either proposes to change or refuses to change a child's identification, evaluation, or placement, or the nature of a child's individualized program, the school must provide the child's parent(s) with written notice, in their native language, describing the school's decision and the reasons for that decision. Notices must also inform parents of their rights to participate in meetings concerning the child, to object to decisions made by the school, and to invoke the procedural safeguards associated with the appeal process (described below) (34 C.F.R. Secs. 300.504; 300.505).

Identification and Evaluation of Children with Disabilities

Either the school system or a child's parent(s) may first identify a child as potentially in need of special education and related services. Once a child has been identified, a meeting must be convened with the child's parent(s) to determine the content of the evaluation to be conducted and the personnel who will conduct it. The school system must then conduct, at no cost to the parents, an evaluation that addresses the areas of concern regarding the child. No evaluation may be conducted without the parent's informed written consent (34 C.F.R. Sec. 300.504). In the case of children suspected of having pervasive developmental disorders, evaluations should broadly address all developmental domains of cognitive, communicative, social/emotional, and adaptive functioning, and should include psychiatric, psychological, and speech and language assessments. Neurological examinations may also be required. Comprehensive evaluations should include standardized testing, behavioral observations, and parent interviews (for a complete developmental history).

Parents who bring the potential disability of their child to the attention of the school may have already obtained comprehensive evaluations and recommendations from pediatricians and other clinicians. These may be accepted by the school system, and they must be considered in making any decisions concerning the child (34 C.F.R. Sec. 300.503). When parents disagree with the results of the school's evaluation of their child, they have a right to obtain independent evaluations at the school system's expense, to be conducted by personnel not employed by the school system, and they must be provided with information about relevant local experts who may conduct independent evaluations. If the school system objects to the independent evaluation, it may initiate a hearing, and if a hearing officer agrees that the school system's evaluation was appropriate, the parent may be required to assume the cost of the additional evaluation (34 C.F.R. Sec. 300.503). Children receiving special education must also be reevaluated at least once every 3 years in order to assess changes in the nature and degree of their disabilities and associated changes in their educational needs (34 C.F.R. Sec. 300.534).

Individualized Educational Programs

The central provision of the IDEA is the requirement that each child with a disability is to have a written individualized educational program (IEP) that has been developed at a multidisciplinary meeting which the child's parent(s) are requested to attend.

Content of the IEP

An IEP is a written document that includes (a) a statement of the child's current levels of performance; (b) a statement of annual educational goals and measurable short-term instructional objectives; (c) a statement of the specific kind and amount of educational services to be provided to the child (including related services) and the extent to which the child will participate in regular educational programs (including any modifications that will be made in the regular program to accommodate the child); (d) a statement of the needed transitional services for students, beginning no later than age 16; (e) the projected date for beginning services, and their expected duration; and (f) objective criteria and evaluation procedures and schedules for determining whether instructional objectives are being met (20 U.S.C. Sec. 1401(a)(20); 34 C.F.R. Sec. 300.346; 34 C.F.R. Part 300, Appendix C, Sec. 300.346). Where a child's IEP addresses transition planning, it must include goals and objectives regarding (a) instruction; (b) community experiences; (c) employment and other postschool living objectives; and (d) if appropriate, acquisition of daily living skills (34 C.F.R. Secs. 300.18; 300.346).

The IEP is the blueprint for the child's education. It allows parents to know what to expect the school to provide and with what aim. It sets standards for both parents and teachers to assess when the child's program is working and when it is not. It also provides a record of the school's efforts on behalf of the child, which may be the subject of administrative or judicial review.

IEP Meetings

IEP meetings are the forum for discussions aimed toward developing an IEP for each student. Ideally, they provide structured opportunities for parents, teachers, administrators, and evaluators to discuss the child's needs and progress and to resolve differences between schools and parents regarding the appropriate educational program for the child. Less optimally, the meetings provide a record of the parties' differences and attempts to reach an agreement, and offer a basis for appeals through administrative and/or judicial channels. IEP meetings must take place (a) within 30 days of the initial determination that a child is in need of special education; (b) at least once each year after the child's first determination of eligibility; and (c) at other times, at the request of the parent or the school, when revisions of the child's program may be necessary, for example, changes in school placement, additions or modifications of educational services, revisions of educational goals, or decisions to conduct additional evaluations (34 C.F.R. Sec. 300.343 and Appendix C, Sec. 300.343).

Participants in IEP meetings are intended to include those who are necessary to a meaningful discussion of the issues that are to be considered (i.e., the nature of the child's disability and its effects on the child's learning; the child's goals for the next year and the modes of assisting the child to reach those goals). At a regular annual IEP meeting, participants must include (a) a representative of the school system, other than the child's teacher; (b) the child's teacher; (c) the child's parent(s); and (d) the child, if appropriate [34 C.F.R. Sec. 300.344(a)]. At the discretion of the school or the parent(s), other individuals may be included: additional teachers of the child or providers of related services, independent evaluators, private therapists, representatives of out-of-district programs that are being considered for the child, and lawyers or lay advocates. In addition, the IEP meeting following a child's first evaluation must include a member of the team that evaluated the child or a school staff person familiar with the evaluation [34 C.F.R. Sec. 300.344(b)]. Any independent evaluators should also be invited at that time (or their reports should be submitted). Similarly, when the purpose of the meeting is to consider transition services for an older child, the school must invite the student and a representative of any other agency that is likely to be responsible for providing or paying for transition services [34 C.F.R. Sec. 300.344(c)]. Such additional participants may include representatives of the relevant state or local child welfare agency; governmental agencies responsible for services to adults with mental retardation or mental illness, vocational rehabilitation, and/or adult education; as well as private providers of supported employment, supported housing, day programs for adults with disabilities, and similar facilities.

In keeping with the emphasis of the IDEA on the centrality of parents to safeguarding the rights of children with disabilities, schools are required to make substantial efforts to include parents in IEP meetings. These include timely notification of parents of the date, time, and purpose of the meeting; meeting times that are reasonably convenient for the parent; provision of alternate means of participation for parents who cannot attend (e.g., conference telephone calls); and provision of foreign-language or sign-language interpreters for parents who do not speak English or are hearing-impaired or mute (34 C.F.R. Sec. 300.345). If a meeting is conducted without either of the child's parents present, the school must document its efforts to persuade the parent(s) to come, supplying records of telephone calls, correspondence, and home visits [34 C.F.R. Sec. 300.345(d)]. When a child does not have a parent who can possibly participate in the IEP process—because no parent has been identified, the parents' whereabouts are unknown, or the child is a ward of the state—the state is required to provide a mechanism for assigning the child a "surrogate parent," someone who is independent of both the school system and any child care agency that is responsible for the child, and who will act in place of the parent in advocating for the child's educational needs [20 U.S.C. Sec. 1415(b)(1)(B); 34 C.F.R. Sec. 300.514].

At the IEP meeting, the child's parent(s) and representatives of the parent(s), such as independent evaluators or attorneys, may participate in the discussion and present any disagreements with the school's approach to educating the child. If the parties do not reach an agreement regarding the child's IEP, either the parent(s) or the school system may appeal, as described below.

Due Process

Whenever a child's parent(s) and the responsible local school system cannot agree regarding the identification, evaluation, placement, or appropriate services to be provided for a child with a disability, either the parent(s) or the school system may initiate an appeal. An administrative hearing will then be conducted by an impartial hearing officer. Prior to the hearing, the parent(s) must be provided with written notice of the school system's decision regarding their child's education, including the reasons for that decision; must have an opportunity to examine all records relevant to the child's evaluation, placement, and educational program; must be notified of their procedural rights at the hearing; and must be provided with information regarding the availability of free or low-cost legal representation to assist them [20 U.S.C. Sec. 1415(b); 34 C.F.R. Secs. 300.505; 300.506]. At the hearing, both the parent(s) and the school system are entitled:

- To be accompanied by counsel and by experts who have special knowledge concerning children with disabilities.
- To present documentary evidence, to confront and cross-examine, and to compel the attendance of witnesses.
- To obtain a written or electronic verbatim record of the hearing.
- To obtain written findings of fact and decisions within 45 days of the request for a hearing. (20 U.S.C. Sec. 1415(d); 34 C.F.R. Sec. 300.508, 300.512)

A parent or school system that is not satisfied with the decision of the hearing officer may request an administrative review of the decision by the state educational agency (unless it was the state that conducted the hearing) [20 U.S.C. Sec. 1415(c)], and may then appeal either in a state court or in federal court [20 U.S.C. Sec. 1415(e)(2); 34 C.F.R. Sec. 300.512]. The court must consider the record of the administrative proceedings and may, at the request of the parties, hear additional evidence.

In some states, there are procedures in place to attempt to resolve disputes concerning a child's educational program through informal mediation rather than through adversarial hearings. Generally, participation in mediation is voluntary. In situations in which school personnel and parents have become personally invested and hardened in their opposition to each other, mediation often offers an opportunity to resolve impasses through the engagement of an impartial facilitator. It may also provide an opportunity for the parties to assess the relative strength of the evidence that will be presented in the hearing if the mediation is unsuccessful, and to negotiate a solution at less cost than a contested hearing would incur.

Child's Placement during the Appeal Period—The "Stay Put" Rule

There may be a lengthy period between the initial disagreement between parent and school system regarding a child's placement, and the final resolution of the dispute by a court. The

IDEA provides that, during this period, unless the school system and the parents agree on a different placement, the child is to remain in his or her then-current educational placement. If the child is applying for initial admission to public school and therefore has no current placement, the child must, with the parents' consent, be placed in the public school program pending completion of due process procedures [20 U.S.C. Sec. 1415(e)(3); 34 C.F.R. Sec. 300.513]. The purpose of the "stay put" rule is to protect the continuity of the child's education and to avoid repeated temporary changes in a child's educational placement, which might otherwise result from the litigation process (e.g., if a parent prevails in an administrative hearing, the school system prevails in a trial court, and the parent prevails again in the appeals court). The rule may operate in favor of either the school or the parent, depending on whether the disputed decision is the school system's proposal to change the child's placement or a refusal to grant a parent's request for a changed placement.

The Gun-Free Schools Act of 1994 [20 U.S.C. Sec. 1415(e)(3)(B)] provides an exception to the stay put rule for children who are determined to have brought a gun to school. In such cases, the child may be removed from his or her current placement and placed in an alternative educational setting for up to 45 days. If the child's parent(s) then request a due process hearing, the child must stay put in the alternative placement pending the hearing, unless the school and parent(s) agree otherwise.

Remedies for Violation of the Right to Free Appropriate Public Education

Attorneys' Fees

When a parent disputes a school system's decision regarding the appropriate education for a child with a disability and the parent prevails, whether in an administrative hearing, a mediation, or a court case, the parent may be awarded reasonable attorneys' fees to compensate the parent for the costs of litigation [20 U.S.C. Sec. 1415(e)(4)]. The requirement that schools reimburse parents for their attorneys' fees makes it possible for parents who are not eligible for free legal services and who would not otherwise be able to afford legal representation to pursue their children's rights under the IDEA.

Reimbursement for Unilateral Placement

If a local school system makes a free appropriate public education available to a child with a disability, and the child's parents choose not to enroll the child in the public school but to place their child unilaterally in a different program, the parents are not entitled to reimbursement from the school system for the costs incurred in the private program (34 C.F.R. Sec. 300.403). If, however, the school system offers a program that is found through due process to be inappropriate to the child's needs, the school may be required to reimburse the parents for the costs of a unilateral private placement, as long as the program chosen by the parent was an appropriate one (*School Committee of the Town of Burlington v. Massachusetts Department of Education*, 1985). As the Supreme Court has explained, reimbursement may be required in order to give effect to the law's guarantee of a free appropriate public education, and to remove parents from the dilemma of either leaving their child in a program they believe to be inappropriate or forgoing their entitlement to public education. A parental decision to place a child unilaterally in a private program always carries with it the risk that the cost will not be reimbursed.

Compensatory Education

When a child with a disability has been denied an education—through the provision of no program, a substantially inappropriate program, or gross procedural violations amounting to no education—a court may, as an additional remedy, order the school system to provide compensatory education in the form of extra assistance, such as summer school or tutoring (*Hall v. Detroit Public Schools*, 1993; *Johnson v. Bismarck Public School District*, 1991), or to continue the child's special education and related services beyond the date when he or she would otherwise no longer be eligible (i.e., beyond age 21; *Hall v. Knott County Board of Education*, 1991; *Jefferson County Board of Education v. Breen*, 1988; *Lester H. v. Gilhool*, 1990; *Miener v. State of Missouri*, 1986; *Pihl v. Massachusetts Department of Education*,

1993). The provision of compensatory education is another way of implementing the IDEA's general mandate to provide special education to children with disabilities at public expense, and offers the only means of redress for children from families who cannot afford to pay for unilateral placements in the hope of eventual reimbursement.

LEGAL PROHIBITIONS AGAINST DISCRIMINATION ON THE BASIS OF DISABILITY

As noted above, most but not all children with pervasive developmental disorders will qualify for special education services under the IDEA. For those children who do not meet the IDEA's eligibility criteria, two additional federal statutes provide protection against discrimination on the basis of disability: (a) Section 504 of the Rehabilitation Act (29 U.S.C. Sec. 794) prohibits discrimination on the basis of disability in any program receiving federal funds; and (b) the Americans with Disabilities Act (ADA; 42 U.S.C. Sec. 12101, et seq.) extends the prohibitions of Section 504 to all state and local government entities regardless of their receipt of federal funds. Both statutes define persons with disabilities more broadly than the IDEA; they include "any person who has a physical or mental impairment which substantially limits one or more major life activities; has a record of such impairment; or is regarded as having such impairment" [29 U.S.C. Sec. 706(8)(B); 42 U.S.C. Sec. 12102(2)]. Children with disabilities who do not "need special education and related services" or who do not fall within one of the disability categories listed in the IDEA are therefore covered by these antidiscrimination laws.

Regulations implementing Section 504 of the Rehabilitation Act (hereafter, "Section 504") specifically require the provision of free appropriate public education to children with disabilities and define an appropriate education to include "regular or special education and related aids and services that . . . are designed to meet individual educational needs of handicapped persons as adequately as the needs of nonhandicapped persons are met" [34 C.F.R. Sec. 104.33(1)]. Like the IDEA, Section 504 requires that public education be provided in the most integrated setting appropriate to the disabled child's needs, that supplemental aids and services be used to facilitate integration, and that nonacademic and extracurricular activities be integrated as well as classroom activities (34 C.F.R. Sec. 104.34). Section 504 also provides procedural safeguards for parents of children with disabilities, including the rights to notice, to inspect records, and to impartial hearings with opportunities to participate and to be represented by counsel (34 C.F.R. Sec. 104.36). Adherence to the procedural requirements of the IDEA is one method of compliance with Section 504 [34 C.F.R. Sec. 104.33(2)]. However, Section 504 does not require written IEPs and does not include a stay put rule.

In practice, Section 504 provides a source of rights for children who do not otherwise qualify under the IDEA, and it provides a forum for addressing such school-related issues as a child's need for resource room help, supplemental instructions for assignments, modified testing procedures, modified class schedules, or other accommodations and supportive services that will allow a child with a disability to make educational progress.

"BIRTH-TO-THREE" SERVICES FOR CHILDREN

Amendments to the IDEA, passed in 1986 [20 U.S.C. Secs. 1471 et seq.], provide additional federal funds to the states for the purposes of increasing the availability of developmental services for very young children; developing a statewide system to coordinate referrals, evaluations and services for infants and toddlers with disabilities; identifying children under 3 years of age who are experiencing developmental delays; and coordinating the provision of early intervention services to these children and their families. The statute is founded on these premises: that early identification and provision of services will lead to increased ability of families to provide appropriate care for young children with disabilities; that early intervention will lead to decreased need for special education and related services when these children reach school age; and that early intervention will lead to increased long-term independence for individuals with disabilities and decreased need for institutional care [20 U.S.C. Sec. 1471(a)]. For children with autism and other pervasive developmental disorders, as well as many other children with disabilities, these assumptions are substantially in keeping with clinical experience. The wider availability of services for very young children with disabilities is likely to result in earlier identification of many autistic children and the provision of more appropriate services as soon as these children are identified.

Although the law providing for services for children under 3 years of age is in many respects modeled on the public education sections of the IDEA, there are important differences. First, because very young children are necessarily more dependent on their families and because their development is intimately involved with their family relationships, appropriate services for infants and toddlers necessarily involve parents to a greater degree than public school programs do. This difference is reflected in an explicit family focus during assessments of a child's needs and in substantially increased use of home-based modes of intervention. Second, unlike schooling for older children, which is compulsory under state law, early intervention services are entirely voluntary on the part of a child's parents; parents may therefore accept or decline any or all of the services offered by the relevant agency, with no right of appeal for the service agency. Third, because there is neither a tradition nor an established institutional structure to provide publicly funded services to children under 3 years who are not disabled, and therefore there is no claim to early intervention services as a remedy for discrimination, services for infants and toddlers need not be made available completely free of charge to a child's parents. Rather, the law prescribes a system of coordinating financial resources from many sources, including the child's family.

Eligibility

Early intervention services are available to children under 3 years who are experiencing delays in their cognitive, physical, communicative, social or emotional, or adaptive development, and to children under 3 years who "have

a diagnosed physical or mental condition which has a high probability of resulting in developmental delay" [20 U.S.C. Sec. 1472(1)(A)]. At the state's discretion, eligibility may be expanded to include infants and toddlers who are "at risk" of having substantial developmental delays if services are not provided [20 U.S.C. Sec. 1472(1)(B)]. Developmental delays in the various domains are to be defined by the state along with procedures for assessment. There is little question that young children who are suspected to have pervasive developmental disorders will be covered by these definitions.

Scope of Services

Early intervention services are defined broadly to include a wide variety of services in a range of disciplines that share the goal of promoting or facilitating young children's cognitive, physical, communicative, social/emotional, or adaptive development [20 U.S.C. Sec. 1472(2)(C)]. Covered services include special instruction, speech pathology and audiology, occupational and physical therapy, parent training and counseling, psychological services, medical services for diagnostic purposes, nursing services, case management services, early identification and screening, social work services, vision services, assistive technology devices, and transportation and related costs [20 U.S.C. Sec. 1472(2)(E),(F)]. As modeled on the least restrictive environment principle of special education, the statute requires that early intervention services "to the maximum extent appropriate, are provided in natural environments, including the home, and community settings in which children without disabilities participate" [20 U.S.C. Sec. 1472(2)(G)]. Like the IEP of special education, early intervention services are to be provided according to an individualized family service plan (IFSP) [20 U.S.C. Sec. 1472(2)(H)].

In addition to establishing procedures for evaluating and planning for individual infants and toddlers with disabilities, states are required, as a condition of federal funding, to undertake such systemic reforms as the development of a comprehensive "child find" system, a public awareness program focusing on early identification of young children with disabilities, a central directory of service resources, a comprehensive system of personnel development to increase local capacity to identify and serve infants and toddlers with disabilities, and the coordination of multiple public and private service providers under the leadership of a single lead agency (20 U.S.C. Sec. 1476). Such systemic developments are necessary because most states have no established system of early intervention services that is analogous to the public school system.

Financial Responsibility for Services

Individual states must establish policies regarding payment for early intervention services. Federal regulations mandate that the following services are provided free of charge: (a) child find; (b) evaluation and assessment; (c) service coordination; (d) administrative activities related to the development of IFSPs and implementation of procedural safeguards for parents; and (e) direct developmental services for children and families *if* state law requires the provision of free appropriate public education to children with disabilities from birth. Other services (i.e., direct intervention or therapeutic services in most states) may be subject to sliding fee scales (34 C.F.R. Sec. 303.521). The lead agency in every state is charged with the responsibility of identifying and coordinating all available resources to provide early intervention services. These may include federal funds provided under the early intervention program, Maternal and Child Health funds, Medicaid funds, Head Start resources, special education resources, and other education resources (34 C.F.R. Sec. 303.522). Although families may be asked to pay for some services, the inability of a child's family to pay may not result in the denial of necessary services to the child [34 C.F.R. Sec. 303.520(b)(3)(ii)].

Individualized Family Service Plan (IFSP)

Like the IEP, the IFSP is a written document that is developed, according to a prescribed process, by a multidisciplinary team that includes the child's parents.

Content of the IFSP

The IFSP must contain: (a) a statement of the infant's or toddler's current levels of cognitive, physical, communicative, social or emotional, and adaptive development, based on objective criteria; (b) a statement of the family's resources, priorities, and concerns for enhancing the child's development; (c) a statement of the major outcomes expected to be achieved for the child and family, and the criteria and procedures for measuring progress; (d) a statement of the specific early intervention services that are necessary to meet the unique needs of the infant or toddler and the family, including the location, frequency, and intensity of services, and the payment arrangements (if any); (e) a statement of the natural environment in which services will be provided, such as the home or a preschool; (f) projected dates for beginning services, and their expected duration; (g) the name of the service coordinator who will be responsible for implementing and coordinating the plan; and (h) the steps to be taken to support the transition of the child to special education, if appropriate, including preparing the child for changes in his or her environment and providing information to the local public school system, with parental consent (34 C.F.R. Sec. 303.344). In addition to the services that are identified as necessary in the IFSP, the IFSP should also document other services (e.g., medical services) that the child needs, which are not required under the early intervention program, and the funding sources that will be used to obtain those services or the steps that will be taken to obtain funding for those services [34 C.F.R. Sec. 303.344(e)]. Like the IEP for special education, the IFSP provides a blueprint—for the family, the service coordinator, and the multiple service providers who may be involved—of the overall plan for assisting the child. In the case of disagreements, the IFSP provides a record on which to base an appeal.

Process of Developing the IFSP

Each state must develop a coordinated system of early intervention services, including a child find system—the procedures for how parents and primary referral sources, such as hospitals and pediatricians, are to make referrals of infants and toddlers with disabilities to the appropriate agency for evaluation. Once a referral is received, a service coordinator must be assigned, and the child must receive a multidisciplinary evaluation of his or her strengths and needs in all developmental domains within 45 days. No evaluation may be conducted without the consent of the child's parents. With parental consent, an assessment of family resources, priorities, and concerns is also conducted, to determine what services are needed to assist the family to understand and meet the developmental needs of their disabled infant or toddler (34 C.F.R. Secs. 303.321; 303.322). If a child needs early intervention services immediately, those services may begin prior to completing the child's evaluation, provided that the child's parent(s) consent, an interim IFSP is written, a service coordinator is identified, and completion of the evaluation is not delayed (34 C.F.R. Sec. 303.345).

Following completion of the evaluation, an IFSP meeting must be held to consider the results of the evaluation and to design an early intervention program for the child. The child's family must be invited to the meeting by written notice in their native language, and the meeting should be held at a time and place that are convenient for them (34 C.F.R. Sec. 303.342). Participants in the meeting must include (a) the child's parent(s); (b) other family members, as requested by the parent; (c) an advocate for the parent, if requested; (d) the service coordinator who has been working with the child and family; (e) persons directly involved in conducting the evaluation; and (f) persons who will be providing services to the child and family, if appropriate (34 C.F.R. Sec. 303.343). At the meeting, the child's needs are discussed with the aim of arriving at a service plan. Like IEP meetings, IFSP meetings ideally offer an opportunity for family members and professionals to discuss the child's development from their varied perspectives in order to obtain the fullest understanding of the child's needs and to develop a plan that will address the identified areas of need. The child's parents may consent to or decline the services offered, and no service may be provided without parental consent. If a child's parents consent to some but not all

services that have been recommended, those services to which the parents consent must be provided [34 C.F.R. Sec. 303.342(e)]. Parents must also be provided with an opportunity to examine any records regarding their child's evaluation or eligibility determination, and the development or implementation of a service plan (34 C.F.R. Sec. 303.402).

Due Process

If a parent is not satisfied with the child's evaluation or with the services identified as necessary by the multidisciplinary team, and the parent seeks additional or different services for the child, the parent may request an administrative hearing to be conducted by an impartial hearing officer. At the hearing, the parent has the same rights as at a special education hearing:

- To be accompanied by counsel and by persons who have special knowledge of early intervention services.
- To present documentary evidence, to confront and cross-examine, and to compel the attendance of witnesses.
- To obtain a written or electronic verbatim record of the hearing.
- To obtain written findings of fact and decisions within 30 days of the filing of the request for the hearing. (34 C.F.R. Secs. 303.422; 303.423)

Any party who disagrees with the decision of the hearing officer in an administrative appeal may file an action in state or federal court. As in the case of special education for school-age children, an infant or toddler whose program is in dispute will remain in his or her current program during the period of administrative or judicial appeals, unless the service agency and the parent agree to a different interim program. If the dispute concerns an initial application for services, the child must receive those services that are not in dispute (34 C.F.R. Sec. 303.425). For a variety of reasons, including the relative novelty of the "birth-to-three" program, the voluntary nature of the services provided, the more limited availability of services for very young children in many communities, the short period in which a child is eligible for birth-to-three services, and the hope of parents and professionals that beginning any services will facilitate developmental gains, there is far less litigation concerning the birth-to-three program than concerning special education for older children.

ADVOCACY ISSUES

As described above, federal law creates a right to individualized special education services for children with disabilities and a set of complex procedures to enable parents to enforce that right. In practice, it is often not easy to obtain quality special education for children with disabilities, particularly severe disabilities, especially if the children's families are poor, uneducated, and unfamiliar with developmental and educational issues. The potential impediments to service for children make it essential that all of the professionals involved with a child, as well as the child's parents, collaborate actively in advocating for the child. Some of the potential difficulties and inequalities in the distribution of resources are discussed below.

Costs of Free Appropriate
Public Education

Although federal funding contributes to the costs of special education, substantial state and local funds are also required to meet the federal mandate. The IDEA mandates that each child with a disability is to receive the services appropriate to his or her individual needs, without balancing one child's needs against another's; however, this requirement creates a dilemma for educators, who, with a finite budget, must provide education to all children within their jurisdiction. Especially when very intensive services are needed, such as one-on-one aides or specialized private or residential programs, the needs of one seriously disabled child may threaten to overwhelm the school's special education budget, and the educational needs of a single child may therefore conflict with the needs (and rights) of many other children in and out of special education. In these circumstances, it is not unusual or surprising for school systems to resist

paying for the very intensive and costly programs that some children need.

Some may argue that the current law results in an inefficient allocation of educational resources, to the detriment of many children, but it does provide a mechanism for obtaining comprehensive services in individual cases. Under current law, children with very serious disabilities are most likely to receive the most intensive services when they have educated parents who are aware of their procedural rights and when parents are both assisted by advocates and supported by knowledgeable clinical experts independent of the school system. Such comprehensive adult support is, of course, not always available to the children who need it most.

Parents' Difficulties in Assuming
the Role of Advocate

The IDEA is based on a participatory model, which assigns parents a central role in educational planning for their children. It implicitly adopts the presumptions that parents know as much about their children's strengths and weaknesses as professionals do; that parents will freely join discussions regarding such issues as evaluation, intervention, and assessment of progress; and that parents' motivation to obtain the best for their children makes them the best advocates for their children's rights. These presumptions are generally sensible, but many parents have difficulty advocating effectively for their children—not only because of practical barriers, such as lack of transportation, need for child care for preschool siblings, and language difficulties, but also because they lack knowledge about their children's rights and may face psychological barriers as well.

Effective advocacy for a child with a serious disability requires a realistic, objective assessment of the child's strengths and needs, coupled with a willingness to express and argue for one's understanding of the child, both of which can be extremely difficult for parents. For example, some parents' hopes and wishes for their child's healthy development may lead them to minimize the child's difficulties and reject appropriately intensive services, or, conversely, to make unrealistic demands on the school system to produce an extraordinary program. Other parents' hopelessness, depression, or ambivalence about the child may lead to disengagement or passivity at just the time when a vocal advocate might make a difference. Many parents do not feel themselves to be knowledgeable enough about their children's educational needs to disagree with school-based experts, even when they are not satisfied with their child's educational program. They experience school personnel as intimidating authority figures, rather than as partners in working with their child; consequently, they have difficulty making use of the formal opportunities for parent input that are mandated by the IDEA. In addition, parents may worry that active advocacy on behalf of their child, which may include disagreement with school officials or even litigation, will result in an atmosphere of animosity between the school and family that will detract from the child's education in the long run. These parents may forgo opportunities to voice concerns or disagreements that might lead to improvements in their child's program. For all of these reasons, many parents find the IEP process much easier to bear, as well as more productive, if they are accompanied by advocates and/or by professionals who know their child and can assume some of the burden of thinking objectively and speaking up.

Access to Legal Representation and Expert Assistance

As noted previously, legal representation and expert assistance are not always accessible to the families of children with disabilities. For families who cannot afford to pay for professional services, advocates may be available from several sources. Some free legal assistance programs represent children and families in special education disputes. Information regarding free and low-cost legal services must be provided to parents who challenge their child's IEP. Information about legal resources is usually also available from the relevant state department of education, the state agency for protection and advocacy, or disability rights organizations and local support groups for parents of children with disabili-

ties. Eligibility for free legal services is usually determined by the family's income, and is often limited to indigent families.

Some private attorneys will also agree to represent families in these cases on a contingency fee basis, taking no fees in advance and relying on the possibility of obtaining payment from the school system if they are successful in an appeal. It may be difficult for parents to find these attorneys, however, particularly those who have knowledge and experience regarding the substantive and procedural issues involved in special education. Also, because attorneys' fees are potentially available from the school system only for legal costs incurred in pursuing an appeal (i.e., after the IEP meeting at which the dispute becomes defined), many private attorneys will be unwilling to spend uncompensated time advising and accompanying parents to IEP meetings. In some communities, lay advocates, some of whom are extremely knowledgeable, can be found through state protection and advocacy groups, nonprofit disability rights organizations, or social service agencies.

Qualified experts are also difficult to engage if families cannot afford to pay. Although parents who disagree with the school system's evaluation of their child have a right to obtain an independent evaluation, this will rarely result in the involvement of a clinical professional who consults extensively with the parent(s), attends and participates in IEP meetings, and/or observes the child in school. Moreover, the family's statutory right to an independent evaluation of their *child* does not encompass a right to an independent expert's assessment of the quality of the *program* being offered by the school. The unavailability of free expert consultation is therefore likely to compound the difficulty some parents experience in advocating effectively for their children. Medical insurance, including public assistance, may cover some limited professional fees, including some consultations with parents. The costs of expert witnesses' preparation and testimony are also recoverable, along with attorneys' fees, if the case is appealed and the parents prevail; however, this will not result in reimbursement for the expert's initial consultations with the parents or his or her attendance at IEP meetings.

Some professionals who are familiar with and invested in a child will be willing to consult with the child's parents and with the school without compensation, especially if the child is particularly at risk. Unfortunately, many of the parents who most need the extensive support of knowledgeable professionals in order to participate meaningfully in the IEP process have least access to their services.

Early Identification of Children with Disabilities

The IDEA imposes a specific obligation on the states and local school systems to take steps to identify, locate, and evaluate all children with disabilities in order that they will be provided with services that will facilitate their development and education [20 U.S.C. Sec. 1414(a)(1); 34 C.F.R. Sec. 300.220]. Child-find procedures may include surveys or education of pediatricians and other health care providers in order that early referrals will be made. Health care, day care, and early childhood education professionals are likely to be in the best position to make the earliest identifications and referrals of children with serious developmental disabilities. It is important for these professionals to have knowledge about the availability of special services for children and to discuss with the parents their concerns about a child's developmental difficulties in a way that supports the parents to seek help for the child rather than to take offense at the suggestion that something is wrong. For families who have least access to health care and other early childhood services, or least capacity, because of poverty, language, racial or ethnic barriers, geographic isolation, or the parent's own disability, to form trusting relationships with the various professionals in contact with their children, early identification of children with disabilities is likely to be most problematic. Unfortunately, these are the same families who are least likely to have independent understanding of their children's need for special educational services, and most likely to send their children to impoverished school systems, where the burden of identifying and serving children with disabilities is particularly acute.

Access to a Range of Good Programs Close to Home

Communities differ widely in the availability of good special education programs within the public school system or in an area that requires minimal travel. Despite the federal mandate to make available a continuum of educational placements, it is particularly difficult for small, rural, or very poor school systems to offer programs appropriate to children with a full range of disabilities, including the most severe. Where established programs do not exist, educators must either invest substantial resources in developing and implementing new programs or pay costly out-of-district tuition, with associated transportation costs. Knowledgeable experts can be particularly helpful, both to school systems and to individual families, in addressing these dilemmas. Broader group advocacy efforts are necessary to improve the range and quality of services available in many communities.

CONCLUSION

Federal law articulates a remarkable right to comprehensive, individualized, publicly funded special education for children with disabilities. The law's statements of principles may not always match up with the experience of individual families, however, particularly in an era of shrinking budgets for social services and increasing inequalities in the distribution of essential resources. Under these circumstances, children with serious disabilities will have the best chance of obtaining the educational services they need to maximize their developmental potential when all the adults involved in their care work collaboratively to define and meet the child's needs, and when forceful advocacy is available to enforce the rights guaranteed by law if discussion and collaboration fail.

Cross-References

Development during the school years is discussed in Chapter 13; autism in adolescents and adults, in Chapter 14; and family issues in autism, in Chapter 34.

REFERENCES

Abrahamson v. Hirshman, 701 F.2d 223 (1st Cir. 1983).

Alamo Heights Independent School District v. State Board of Education, 790 F.2d 1153 (5th Cir. 1986).

Americans with Disabilities Act, 42 U.S.C. Sec. 12101, et seq. (1994).

Angevine v. Jenkins, 752 F. Supp. 24 (D.D.C. 1990).

Ash v. Lake Oswego School District, 980 F.2d 585 (9th Cir. 1992).

B.G. by F.G. v. Cranford Board of Education, 702 F. Supp. 1140 (D.N.J. 1988).

Barwacz v. Michigan Department of Education, 681 F. Supp. 427 (W.D. Mich. 1988).

Battle v. Pennsylvania, 629 F.2d 269 (3d Cir.), *on remand,* 513 F. Supp. 425 (E.D.Pa. 1980), *cert. den. sub nom Scanlon v. Battle,* 452 U.S. 968 (1981).

Board of Education of Hendrick Hudson Central School District v. Rowley, 458 U.S. 176 (1982).

Calavaras Unified School District, 21 IDELR 211 (1993).

Code of Federal Regulations, 28 C.F.R. Secs. 35.101 et seq. (1994).

Code of Federal Regulations, 34 C.F.R. Secs. 104.1 et seq. (1994).

Code of Federal Regulations, 34 C.F.R. Secs. 300.1 et seq. (1994).

Code of Federal Regulations, 34 C.F.R. Secs. 303.1 et seq. (1994).

Cremeans v. Fairland Local School Board, 91 Ohio App. 3d 668 (1993).

Daniel R.R. v. El Paso Independent School District, 874 F.2d 1036 (5th Cir 1989).

Delaware County Intermediate Unit #25 v. Martin and Melinda K., 20 IDELR 363 (E.D. Pa. 1993).

Detroit, Michigan Public Schools, 20 IDELR 406 (1993).

Doe v. Anrig, 651 F. Supp. 424 (D. Mass. 1987).

Doe v. Board of Education of Tullahoma City Schools, 9 F.3d 455 (6th Cir. 1993).

Education for All Handicapped Children Act (EAHCA), 20 U.S.C. Secs. 1400 et seq.

Field v. Haddonfield Board of Education, 769 F. Supp. 1313 (D.N.J. 1991).

Geis v. Board of Education of Parsippany–Troy Hills, Morris County, 774 F.2d 575 (1985).

Georgia Association of Retarded Citizens v. McDaniel, 716 F.2d 1565 (11th Cir. 1983), *modified on other grounds,* 740 F.2d 902 (1984).

Greer v. Rome City School District, 950 F.2d 688, *withdrawn,* 956 F.2d 1025 (11th Cir. 1991), *reinstated,* 967 F.2d 470 (1992).

Gun-Free Schools Act of 1994, 20 U.S.C. Sec. 1415(e)(3)(B).

Hall v. Detroit Public Schools, 823 F. Supp. 1377 (E.D. Mich. 1993).

Hall v. Knott County Board of Education, 941 F.2d 402 (6th Cir. 1991), *cert. den.,* 112 S.Ct. 982.

Harrell v . Wilson County Schools, 293 S.E.2d 687 (N.C. 1982).

Houston Independent School District, 21 IDELR 208 (1994).

Individuals with Disabilities Education Act (IDEA), 20 U.S.C. Secs. 1400 et seq.

Infants and Toddlers with Disabilities Act, 20 U.S.C. Secs. 1471 et seq.

Jefferson County Board of Education v. Breen, 853 F.2d 853 (11th Cir. 1988).

Johnson v. Bismarck Public School District, 949 F.2d 1000 (8th Cir. 1991).

Johnson v. Independent School District, 921 F.2d 1022 (10th Cir. 1990).

Kruelle v. New Castle County School District, 642 F.2d 687 (3d Cir. 1981).

Lachman v. Illinois Board of Education, 852 F.2d 290 (7th Cir. 1988).

Learning Disabilities Association of Maryland v. Board of Education of Baltimore County, 837 F. Supp. 717. (D.Md. 1993).

Lester H. v. Gilhool, 916 F.2d 865 (3d Cir. 1990), *cert. den. sub nom Chester Upland School District v. Lester H.,* 111 S.Ct. 1317.

Mavis v. Sobol, 839 F. Supp. 968 (N.D.N.Y. 1994).

Miener v. State of Missouri, 800 F.2d 749 (8th Cir. 1986).

Oberti v. Board of Education of Borough of Clementon School District, 995 F.2d 1204 (3d Cir. 1993).

Ojai Unified School District v. Johnson, 4 F.3d 1467 (9th Cir. 1993).

Papacoda v. State of Connecticut, 528 F. Supp. 68 (D. Conn. 1981).

Petersen v. Hastings Public Schools, 21 IDELR 377 (8th Cir. 1994).

Pihl v. Massachusetts Department of Education, 9 F.3d 184 (1st Cir. 1993).

Rehabilitation Act of 1973, 29 U.S.C. Secs. 706(8); 794 (1994).

Richardson, Texas Independent School District, 21 IDELR 333 (1994).

Roland M. v. Concord School Commission, 910 F.2d 983 (1st Cir. 1990).

Roncker v. Walter, 700 F.2d 1058 (6th Cir.), *cert. den.,* 464 U.S. 864 (1983).

Sacramento City School District v. Rachel H., 14 F.3d 1398 (9th Cir. 1994), *cert. den.*, 114 S.Ct. 2679 (1994).

School Committee of the Town of Burlington v. Massachusetts Department of Education, 471 U.S. 359 (1985).

Sudbury, Massachusetts Public Schools, 20 IDELR 948 (1993).

T.G. v. Board of Education of Piscataway, N.J., 576 F. Supp. 420 (D.N.J. 1983), *aff'd.*, 738 F.2d 420, *cert. den.*, 469 U.S. 1086.

Tice v. Botetourt County School Board, 908 F.2d 1200 (4th Cir. 1990).

Town of Burlington v. Department of Education, 736 F.2d 773 (1st Cir. 1984), *aff'd.* 471 U.S. 359 (1985).

Union School District v. Smith, 15 F.3d 1519 (9th Cir. 1994).

United States Code, 20 U.S.C. Secs. 1400 et seq. (1994).

United States Code, 20 U.S.C. Secs. 1471 et seq. (1994).

United States Code, 29 U.S.C. Sec. 794 (1994).

United States Code, 42 U.S.C. Secs. 12101 et seq. (1994).

CHAPTER 38

Ethical Issues in Research and Treatment

AMI KLIN AND DONALD J. COHEN

Individuals with autism, and their families, are in a particularly vulnerable position as eager consumers of clinical services. Forms of treatment in use with individuals with autism have ranged from the well researched and documented to the unresearched and charismatic and even to the bizarre. There is a need for ethical and quality control standards, particularly because so many forms of treatment fall in the gray area of the well-meaning but unproven. The availability and wide use of unproven treatments are evidence of a failure, within the mental health and scientific community and by government, to study and regulate clinical services before they are made widely available.

The use of treatment techniques that have not been systematically investigated places individuals with autism at risk. Research on the causes and treatment of autism also presents risk. Finally, doing nothing places individuals at the greatest risk of continuing or progressive disability. Investigators, families, clinicians, advocates, and the patients/clients themselves must consider and balance all these factors—the dangers of research, of unproven treatments, and of inaction—in deciding on a course of action.

This chapter discusses some ethical considerations involved in research and treatment of autism. It covers the need to investigate and regulate the forms of treatment available in autism as well as the need to promote research on the condition, utilizing the latest developments of neurobiological technology. As a devastating medical condition, autism deserves the same type of rigorous, systematic research that has led to major improvements in the care of children with other biological disorders.

ETHICAL ISSUES IN RESEARCH WITH CHILDREN

In the past 15 years, there has been an increasing awareness of the value of safeguards and regulations protecting participants of studies in the behavioral and medical sciences. Classic behavioral studies conducted in the 1960s and 1970s, such as Milgram's (1974) research on obedience to authority, Zimbardo's research on role play (Zimbardo, Ebbesen, & Maslach, 1977), or even Harlow's (1971) and Gallup's studies involving nonhuman primates (Gallup & McClure, 1971), would probably raise concerns and might not be approved by most Institutional Review Boards (IRBs) today. This trend toward "higher standards" for approval of research was given regulatory status by the National Commission for the Protection of Human Subjects of Biomedical and Behavioral Research (National Commission, 1977), which defined the basic ethical principles that should guide research involving human subjects. "Respect for persons" and the inalienable rights of subjects to privacy, confidentiality, and informed consent were established as the necessary requirements protecting individuals from being "used merely as means" to the researcher's goals. In practice, investigators today are required, both ethically and legally, to ensure that research subjects provide informed consent, which signifies the participant's volitional embrace of the investigator's scientific goals. Procedures judged as entailing risk of any form, or deception; samples that are not demographically representative of the distribution of gender or ethnicity among the general population; and the involvement of particularly vulnerable populations who are not able to fulfill the requirement of "informed consent" (such as children and the mentally impaired), are all particularly scrutinized to prevent injustices affronting societal consensus on appropriate norms of scientific conduct.

These moral values are valuable counterweights against thoughtless and potentially dangerous pursuit of studies that may harm individuals or distort the scientific search for truth. There is good reason for concern about unregulated research. The Nazi experiments stand out as the most painful examples of immoral research. But before the era of ethical scrutiny of research, and in isolated instances since then, individual rights have been ignored by some investigators in the course of pursuing studies. Studies have been done with individuals with mental retardation or serious medical illnesses, and other vulnerable populations, as well as with individuals who did not know that they were being exposed to potentially dangerous research, as in the military, without suitable consent and oversight. Some studies may have been important and might have been accomplished with suitable scientific and ethical safeguards. Other studies have been done that could not be scientifically or ethically justified, as with the exposure of children and adults to various types of radiation or the deprivation of appropriate medication to individuals with curable diseases (Advisory Committee on Human Radiation Experiments, 1995).

We believe that research involving individuals with autism and similar disorders must pass the highest standards of ethical review. No unproven or nonstandard behavioral or biological treatments should be used, and no systematic research should be undertaken without formal review and approval by an Institutional Review Board (IRB, sometimes called a Human Investigation Committee [HIC] or, in Europe and elsewhere, a Helsinki Committee). Indeed, it would be reasonable to consider whether IRB review might be appropriate in relation to some currently used treatments that may not be considered "investigatory" but perhaps should be.

As important as the process of informed consent and review of research is, the implementation of procedures of regulation has had some inadvertent deleterious impact on the field of human research. Also, by framing the questions primarily in terms of the protection of individuals exposed to research, the scientific investigators who are the protagonists of scientific research may be cast, as a group, as being more dangerous than beneficent. Yet, the goal of ethical regulations is not the needless burdening of scientific progress or the elimination of research. Rather, it is the pursuit of an acceptable balance between trying to ensure that humans are not endangered or their autonomy reduced, on the one hand, and the quest for understanding the unknown and the benefits that may accrue from knowledge based on empirical, systematic, and creative research, on the other hand. Research is not supposed to be judged as unduly intrusive, nor are investigators to be perceived as in need of scrutiny to prevent them from unethical pursuit of dehumanized science. Nevertheless, the cultural pendulum may at times have swung too far from the central societal commitment to the fundamental value of the scientific enterprise: to probe the unknown—responsibly and respectfully, but also unrelentingly—in order to make knowledge the property of not only a given culture, but, and particularly, of those members of the society who are most in need of its benefits.

In a field as young and uncharted as developmental psychopathology and the clinical fields of child and adolescent psychiatry, and pediatric neurology and psychology, the balance between the known and the unknown still tilts heavily toward the latter. The population that is of concern to these professions is probably the one most in need of protection. Yet, a cultural aversion directed at research with children may leave whole areas of behavior, pathology, and potential treatments barred to systematic examination. We believe that, along with rigorous review of proposed research, an acknowledgment of the extent of the unknown carries with it a responsibility, a moral mandate, to conduct research.

The dilemma defined by the equally valid ethical principles of the protection of subjects and the need for knowledge is nowhere more acute than when subjects of research are children. Here, uncertainty about the propriety of clinical investigation has led to some ethically untenable results. One extreme example of overconformance to safety considerations is provided by what Shirkey (1968) called the "therapeutic orphans of our expanding pharmacopoeia" (p. 119), a situation created by investigators' great reluctance to conduct studies to determine the safety and efficacy of drugs in children. Mirkin (1975) reported that more than 80% of drugs prescribed for children had a clause such as "not to be used in children" in their prescribing information. Such a "orphaning clause" would appear to imply that childhood is an anomalous and rare state of being and that the diseases of childhood are of secondary importance. As Levine (1986, pp. 239–241) points out, if we consider the availability of drugs proved safe and effective through the devices of modern clinical pharmacology and clinical trials a benefit, then it is unjust to deprive classes of persons—e.g., children—of this benefit. The practical implication of this void in knowledge is that practitioners often ignore labels that warn of the unknown effects of drugs on children. By so doing, a tendency is created to expose children to unknown risks of drugs. This possibly maximizes the frequency of unsuspected side effects in children and minimizes the probability of their early and systematic detection. Most drugs proved safe and effective in adults do not produce unexpected adverse reactions in children (Levine, 1978); yet, when they do, the numbers of harmed children may be higher than would be the case had the drugs been researched systematically and their therapeutic dosage and side-effect profiles determined, before their introduction into clinical practice (Cohen, 1977). At times, the use of a medication for an orphan indication may lead to quite surprising side effects that would not have been risked if the full implications were known beforehand, as was the case when desipramine was associated with sudden death among hyperactive children (Riddle, Geller, & Ryan, 1993). Also, only through the study of children can the long-term effects on maturation and development be defined (such as ultimate height, eventual appearance of disturbances

in blood pressure, alterations in the timing of puberty, or subtle effects on central nervous system [CNS] development). When drugs are tested only with adults, the impact on maturation is completely ignored. Finally, the increasing use of more than one drug at a time—so-called "poly-pharmacy"—raises questions about drug interactions in developing individuals that may not be apparent in adults. On the other side, there may be drugs that are useful early in the course of an illness (as with autistic children during the first years of life) but may not be recognized as efficacious when tested with adults. Thus, children may be deprived of benefits, or exposed to unknown side effects, if drugs are studied only with adults.

Clinical practice and research with children should obviously strive to exemplify a high level of ethical concern. But there is a danger that such principles might serve as self-justification for inaction, reinforced by an often unflattering portrayal of researchers and fear of malpractice litigation. Our ethical sensitivities, however, should be as much aroused by the persistence of acknowledged ignorance as by the wish to avoid unethical research. The ethical pride we might take in avoiding human investigation with children will bring no solace to children afflicted by developmental or psychiatric disorders or to their families.

The view that research and human welfare are at odds contradicts the premises of research in child and adolescent psychiatry. Both rigorous research and clinical care are aimed at reducing human suffering. Responsible clinical concern for patients' welfare may be said to impose an ethical imperative to conduct, or at least support, research, at the same time that it imposes an obligation for the research to be conducted in an ethical manner. This issue has been discussed by a work group convened at the National Institute of Mental Health (Arnold et al., 1995), which adopted a position of "advocacy for children's right to research access while recognizing that this advocacy must be tempered by thoughtful protection for children and adolescent subjects" (p. 929). The American Academy of Pediatrics (1995) adopted similar guidelines for drug research in pediatric populations. While acknowledging the need for strict protection of child subjects, the Academy guidelines also specify that these responsibilities "should not be reasons for the pharmaceutical company, IRB, or the investigator to exclude children from drug research and its potential benefits" (p. 294). The guidelines also express a hope for an increase in the number of drug investigations in children, and endorse the view that it is unethical to deny children appropriate access to existing and new therapeutic agents.

Although drug therapies and other medical procedures are often strictly regulated and controlled, a wide range of therapeutic modalities that can be broadly referred to as behavior treatments are much less regulated and are implemented under much less scrutiny. We use the term *behavior treatment* to denote a host of nonpharmacological forms of treatment, and not merely the group of therapies commonly known as behavioral therapies (e.g., operant and classical conditioning). A marked proliferation of alternative forms of treatment for all sorts of disorders and ailments has occurred, and it mirrors the cultural trends of the society and follows its waves of fashion and popular paradigm shifts. This situation, of course, prevails in all societies and cultures. However, as such alternative forms of treatment become more influential and begin to assume a pseudomedical and pseudoscientific appeal to consumers, while remaining unchallenged by the rules and regulations of the medical profession, there is the attending danger that mental health patients and their families might fall prey to unscrupulous or well-meaning zealot practitioners of such unscrutinized treatments. Although the medical profession often quickly dismisses any responsibility for these fringes of clinical practice, the question remains whether the consumers should be left to struggle alone with the myriad alternative paths of treatment that are often costly in human and financial terms and that fill the void left by the unavailability of cures for chronic ailments and developmental disorders.

Of all the sources for behavior treatments, possibly the only practitioners' group that is relatively self-regulated is the one engaged in the cluster of operant conditioning methods (those that involve a number of behavior modification strategies; Mash, 1989) and classical conditioning techniques (such as are used in anxiety reduction, aversive techniques, and biofeedback). In an effort to regulate the practice of behavioral therapy and provide some guidelines for ethical implementation, the Association for Advancement of Behavior Therapy (AABT) provided a set questions for the practitioner to ponder while preparing to engage in clinical service delivery (AABT, 1977). Given their roots in the psychological laboratories conducting quantified research of behavior, these therapies are empirical in nature, and a great deal of attention is given to explicit definition of goals and careful measuring of results. Finally, there is great concern about the training of professionals as behavioral therapists or consultants not only in behavioral techniques but also in child development and the disorders addressed, as well as in supervision and monitoring of the implementation of programs (Konarski, Favell, & Favell, 1992). Despite these guidelines, however, there are a number of shortcomings in the practice of these forms of treatment, including substandard implementation of programs, reductionism that sometimes ignores some aspects of human learning and development (such as functional aspects of behavior, generalization, and social adjustment), reduced clinical judgment, and lack of training and supervision (Marcus & Schopler, 1994).

These pitfalls notwithstanding, the empirical, explicit, and well-documented nature of behavioral therapies lends them to regulation and evaluative research. This is not the case for other forms of behavior treatments, whose practitioners sometimes not only fail to evaluate their procedures, but also, on occasion, decry the attempts of others to assess the efficacy of their methods, sometimes resorting to issues of faith and belief. When families are encouraged to accept a treatment on the basis of faith, the stage is set for unprotected clinical practice that may result in sincere but spurious effects, at best, or deceitful charlatanism, at worst. The lack of regulation, documentation, and empirical evaluation of such nonpharmacological forms of treatment leaves consumers of clinical service at the mercy of the practitioners. How can the freedoms of an open society be reconciled with the need to regulate clinical practice that may ultimately victimize the sufferers of chronic disorders for which the medical establishment has no answer?

ETHICAL ISSUES IN RESEARCH AND TREATMENT OF AUTISM

Autism is characterized by typical patterns of delay and deviance affecting social, affective, communicative, and, in most cases, intellectual development. It is both the most severe and most researched psychiatric disorder of early onset, serving as the paradigmatic condition against which a broader group of disorders characterized by social disabilities—the pervasive developmental disorders—are defined. In the 50 years since Kanner's original description of the syndrome (1943), the research literature on autism has grown to voluminous size. The trends in autism research have more often reflected cultural shifts occurring within the behavioral sciences—from psychoanalytic concepts to the more recent computational metaphors of the cognitive sciences—than paradigmatic shifts resulting from validated scientific discoveries. As a result, even though we may now assert that a great deal more is known about autism than during the 1940s, our understanding of the etiology, pathogenesis, and treatment of autism remains limited.

To fundamentally improve the quality of care and treatment and the prognosis for individuals with autism, it is important to encourage the advancement of knowledge through systematic research. Advances in the clinical neurosciences have provided and will continue to provide new approaches to studying brain development and functioning, including techniques such as neuroimaging, neurochemical assessment of CNS functioning, and molecular biological approaches to studying genetic factors involved in brain formation and activity. Some of these methodologies may carry a price of discomfort for the patients and their families. Invasive procedures, from blood drawing to interviews of the extended family, may pose psychological and varying degrees of biological risk, and thus should raise concerns among families, advocates, child psychiatrists, and others involved with children's care. After all, such medical procedures are usually deemed justified only for specific therapeutic indications—for example, the diagnosis of suspected brain lesions or treatable diseases.

And yet, autism is a serious and quality-of-life threatening condition with a presumably neurobiological etiology. Few if any disorders of childhood are more devastating to a child's development and a family's life. Yet, the investment of the scientific community in research has been less intense than for other equally or more infrequent conditions, such as childhood cancers. Had a biological marker been found for the disorder, as in the case of metabolic (e.g., PKU) or infectious (e.g., HIV) diseases, the commitment to new approaches, and the willingness to make use of the most recent methodologies available, would probably be of a different order of magnitude.

From an ethical standpoint, acknowledgment of the devastating impact of autism and of its medical nature is essential to understanding the calculus of risk and benefit in relation to research. Seeing autism as a chronic life-disruptive disorder of unknown origin places it in the context of disorders such as cystic fibrosis and muscular dystrophy, which are the objects of large, sustained (and increasingly illuminating) research commitments in major medical centers.

With disorders as severe and mysterious as autism, clinicians and investigators have found a sense of self-justification and comfort through the pursuit of new knowledge. But how far are we willing to go, how strong is the ethical mandate justifying research of autism, and what safeguards are necessary to protect this vulnerable population?

Interestingly, systematic research has done much to dispel one of the most harmful misconceptions of the origins of autism. Based on the prevalent notions of child development at the time, several authors (e.g., Bettelheim, 1967) suggested a potential role of parental psychopathology in the pathogenesis of the disorder. Specifically, the social withdrawal typical of autistic children was hypothesized to be the result of emotionally unresponsive and inadequate parenting. Already burdened by their children's disabilities, caregivers were also faced with the accusation that they had actually contributed to, if not caused, the disorder afflicting their child. Terms such as "refrigerator parents" were used in clinical discussion. Only with the advent of epidemiological studies showing that the disorder did not discriminate in terms of social class or culture; further studies showing no evidence of increased parental psychopathology; of psychological research demonstrating that the ubiquitous mental retardation was a reality not attributable to "negativism" or noncompliance; and medical research documenting the association of the disorder with a host of medical conditions such as congenital rubella and Fragile X syndrome, as well as with a higher risk for seizure disorders and other neurological abnormalities, was this misconception rectified. Autism was redefined as a condition of "organic," neurobiological etiology.

Most recently, issues about the familial contributions to autism have arisen in relation to the field of human genetics of complex disorders. The early impression that autism had no genetic aspects is now increasingly questioned by research (e.g., Bailey et al., 1995) showing that siblings are at a significantly greater risk for also exhibiting autism and other developmental difficulties (Chapter 17, this volume). Familial links in milder forms of autism, such as Asperger's Syndrome (Chapter 5, this volume) appear even more pronounced. These findings require a rethinking of the ways in which the vulnerability to autism may be transmitted within families and the range of expression of the disorder. Thus, the early observations of higher aggregation of individuals with unusual social relations within families of autistic individuals may have been valid. If these findings are sustained, parents will have to face a new era of dealing with their contributions to the onset and nature of the disorder. Advances in this area may have profound implications for genetic counseling as well as for suggesting newer approaches to remediation once the specific gene(s) are identified.

Research on autism is complicated by the very early onset of symptoms and by pervasive impact on the emergence of most developmental processes. A typical time lag before diagnosis may range from several months to years. Autistic children come to the attention of the specialist only after an average of 3 to 4 years from the onset or recognition of the disorder

(Siegel, Pliner, Eschler, & Elliot, 1988); the crucially important early aspects of the syndrome are outside the realm of direct investigation in these children. Although they are helpful, parental reports and nontraditional sources of information such as home videos made by parents prior to diagnosis are associated with methodological difficulties (Chapter 12, this volume). Given the low prevalence of the disorder, prospective studies are economically prohibitive except if carried out with a high-risk population—in this case, with the younger siblings of autistic individuals. Such forms of research require a degree of intrusion and intervention that raises ethical considerations, and will inevitably arouse parental concerns (which can, nevertheless, be appropriately addressed with sensitive genetic counseling). In other fields of medicine, genetic counseling and monitoring are seen as obligations of the health professional. A prevailing assumption that the intrusion accompanying research in autism is resented by potential participants has so far gone unexamined systematically; in our experience, research is generally welcomed by families who are eager to increase knowledge and pleased to be able to actively do something that may aid their child or others.

Neurobiological research on autism, with its inevitably invasive methodologies, provides only a fragmentary collection of findings and no specific site for the etiology of the disorder. A range of neuroanatomical findings and hypotheses is available, as is a range of suggestive neurochemical findings (Chapters 15 and 39, this volume). Advancements in technology and methodology, and refinement in descriptive phenomenology and classification, increase the potential value of carefully designed studies of sufficiently large numbers of patients. Because autism occurs in early childhood and both the brain and the child's behavior change during the course of the first years, it is ethically indicated to include children as subjects in neurobiological research. Methods of ethical review and of building a consensus about the severity of the condition and the need for research are required, to ensure that children are not excluded from being studied and that their rights are protected during the course of research.

The need to make such an assertion would probably not arise in relation to obviously medical conditions, such as childhood malignancies and congenital heart disease. For these conditions, rigorous and invasive research has proven its value. In the 1960s, when leukemia was an almost certainly fatal illness, leukemic children underwent highly experimental treatment trials that promised little benefit and were often associated with a great deal of suffering, discomfort, and perhaps even earlier death from drug side effects. Those concerned with children's right to die in peace resisted their participation in studies. Yet, as a result of this effort and the sacrifice of families and children who participated in research on antimetabolite and other drugs, the child oncologist today is able to (happily) inform parents that certain forms of leukemia affecting the large majority of afflicted children are potentially curable. Had overzealous research regulations curbed investigations, would the prognosis for this disorder have been so dramatically altered? In other words, if an uncompromising view of unconditional subject protection had been adopted by clinical researchers and the advocates for children, leukemic children would have won the battle against human experimentation and lost their war. The life-threatening nature of cancer muted ethical objections.

The commitment of medical researchers and funding agencies to leukemia contrasts with their attitude toward autism and other serious neuropsychiatric disorders. In some crucial manner, throughout the world and in the United States, autism is viewed by government and others (including insurers) as a less medical and less debilitating condition than childhood cancer. But autism gives rise to terrible suffering for the afflicted individual and his or her family—suffering that persists over years and decades, and costs a fortune in direct services, family burdens, and pain and suffering.

Research on the etiology and pathogenesis of autism should be scrutinized in terms of its potential contributory value to the understanding of the disorder. Similarly, studies of intervention and treatment should be monitored so that gains can be assessed independently of theoretical biases or cultural ideologies, with only the individual client's progress in mind. Such systematic follow-up protects the child from unexamined assumptions based on changeable educational currents.

In the area of intervention, research protects the subject. All forms of treatment, pharmacological as well as behavioral, should be properly scrutinized by human investigation committees, and their proponents should be called on to justify their actions in terms of empirical information. Let us consider a few illustrations that substantiate this ethical stance.

The 1975 (U.S.) Public Law 94-142 (1977) regulations, mandating least restrictive placements for individuals with disabilities, have often been interpreted as a mandate to provide mainstreaming for all autistic children (see Chapters 36 and 37). The premises underlying this notion are commendable and have made a major impact on the lives of individuals with developmental and intellectual disabilities. Yet, the implementation of this approach has often not received the careful scrutiny that a therapeutic intervention requires, possibly because the general value has been judged to be too important or too apparent to require systematic research. Do we know when, for whom, and in what type of settings mainstreaming is optimal, or what supports are needed in practice to make mainstreaming work? (See Chapter 36.) Autism has a wide range of phenotypic expression, in terms of both intellectual level and range of symptom severity. For many and perhaps the majority of autistic children, the decision about a suitable placement is a complex process; the value of specialized settings and the potential benefits of degrees of mainstreaming require careful consideration. Yet, the data may be quite limited, and ideology may prevail over obvious limitations. Where research does exist, it may run against ideology for some children. For example, research on educational strategies indicates unequivocally that intensive individual and behavioral approaches provide the conditions for a far more beneficial intervention than could be possible in a regular classroom (Rogers, 1996). When issues such as this are at stake, research is necessary both to document the impact of the intervention technique and to protect the individual child from falling victim to ideologic determinations distant from the child's condition and educational needs.

Considerable dangers are posed to the individual child and family in the area of treatment, particularly by unconventional forms of treatment. Despite strong claims, by partisans of particular treatment approaches, that much dedicated effort has gone into their implementation, no treatment has been demonstrated to produce major alterations in the natural course of autism (DeMyer, Hingtgen, & Jackson, 1981; Rutter, 1985). In the absence of a definitive cure, there are a thousand treatments. With the exception of a few approaches (notably, behavior modification and pharmacological intervention, and, to a lesser degree, educational guidelines), proposed interventions have not been rigorously studied. Most worrisome are treatments that disrupt educational routines, are costly, make unwarranted claims of success, and discard systematic research as an unsuitable form of evaluation.

In a 100-mile radius of our own clinical center, over a dozen major unconventional treatment interventions are available for children with autism and their families. These include megavitamin and other nutritional supplementation therapies, hugging therapy, auditory training, visual training, facilitated communication (FC), physical exertion, discipline and group regimentation, patterning of psychomotor skills, 'round-the-clock stimulation within a confined space, dolphin therapy, allergic desensitization, environmental decontamination therapies, antimonilia therapy, harsh use of aversives, and a host of medication and drug combination therapies. The propounders of these approaches tend to be hostile to systematic evaluations conducted by independent researchers; they aggressively market their approach with little if any rigorous, peer-reviewed, replicable evidence substantiating their claims of success. Such claims fall on the very vulnerable ears of parents and educators whose hopes and dedication may lead them to embrace the approach, along with its cost in both material and human terms. Many among the sponsors of these approaches discard researchers' protests, arguing that systematic studies are inherently flawed to measure gains and progress because they imply a disbelief in the approach, interfere with the treatment

process, or underestimate the child's potential to the point of compromising the whole enterprise. Desperately in search of a spark of hope, many parents adopt these arguments. They invest their time, feelings, and commitment, and often large sums of money, to "give it a try." After all, what caring parent would leave a stone unturned in the hope of finding a cure for his or her child's devastating ailment?

These circumstances can and have caused a great deal of suffering. In the unconventional therapy called facilitated communication (FC; Biklen, 1990), a child's hand is placed on a letter board or typewriter keyboard and guided by the hand of an educator or "facilitator." Words and sentences are spelled out by the child's hand while the child may be looking away into space and engaged in stereotypic behavior. The level of complexity of the messages is far beyond what the child shows that he or she is capable of in other ways. For example, autistic children who are mute, self-injurious, and not toilet-trained may, through FC produce complex sentences about abstract concepts, describe their feelings, and even ask for specific pharmacological treatments. Their behavior may demonstrate IQs in the 30s, but their language, through the keyboard, may put the child's IQ into the 130s. How is this remarkable disparity possible?

Many studies (e.g., Crews et al., 1995; Regal, Rooney, & Wandas, 1994; Smith, Haas, & Belcher, 1994; Wheeler, Jacobson, Paglieri, & Schwartz, 1993) have shown that the communication from the typewriter or special keyboard originates from the individual who guides the child's hand and fingers rather than from the retarded, autistic child (see also Cummins & Prior, 1992). Sometimes, the messages that are spelled out with this Ouija-board method are critical of parents or other caregivers, and cause them emotional pain. In a large number of cases, the facilitators who have guided the child's hands have spelled out accusations of sexual abuse that have led to court action against parents and other teachers (e.g., Siegel, 1995). An atmosphere similar to that of a witch trial can be created by an accusation of abuse, and the person led to the stake is quite often a parent or teacher most committed to the care of the child. Colleagues critical of the FC approach and doubtful of its validity have often been pressured into conformity or otherwise faced ostracism by those who are true believers in the method; skeptics may be judged incompetent, when their only fault is to feel that their professional responsibility entails validating the adopted treatment approach and not acting by blind belief. Parents who have already mourned because of their child's illness and accepted the implications of the disability have been led to believe that their previous acceptance of the diagnosis was the result of a mental health professional's misleading them. Through the "miracle" of FC, parents have been given a false sense that their child is really not retarded, but has a bright, even brilliant, mind captured in an autistic body. The individuals who do the "facilitation"—usually well-meaning teachers, but sometimes parents or others—seem genuinely to believe that the message comes from the child, rather than from themselves. As in mass hysteria, their hands guide the fingers of the autistic individual into writing out messages that originate in their own unconscious and fantasies. Some "facilitators" may have doubts about the process, but others are convinced that the message, in some way, is the result of the child's mentation, not their own. Legal loopholes and the pressure for a cure have often disarmed investigators concerned with testing the significance of the messages produced through FC. Just as with other nontraditional therapies, however, rigorous research was often blocked by a call to belief. In the past 2 years or so, some highly publicized cases of injustices committed against loving caregivers, and the increasing pressure that parents and educators, reacting to media coverage, exercised on clinicians with a view to obtaining referrals, justifying educational spending, and so forth, finally led to the trickle of studies that completely debunked the premises of FC. It remains to be seen how parents and educational agencies and professionals will react to this development. Quite likely, many will become disillusioned with the prospect of any progress in the field, and might find it difficult to return to the well-proven but slow and hard progress associated with more traditional educational interventions. Had FC been evaluated early on, its widespread use, and now, the widespread disil-

lusionment and suffering, might have been prevented.

Facilitated Communication is similar to many other so-called treatments and magical "cures" that have emerged over the decades; most, although not all, sooner or later fade away. Their victims are the children and their parents. Precious money is wasted, parents are exhausted, hopes are raised and dashed, and, at the end, parents feel shattered and betrayed. Those who now have been led to believe, through FC, that their retarded autistic child is brilliant will feel the pain of losing their child to autism again; they will suffer as they accept the fact, just as they did when the diagnosis was first made. The need for systematic study is not only an ethical imperative but a necessary step to protect a vulnerable population of children and parents. And those investigators who defy the pressure to give in, even if by so doing they arouse the ire of hostile (though dedicated) treaters, are making a strong moral statement and putting their skills to their best use, namely, protecting the well-being of disabled children and their families.

One widespread practice that needs urgent scrutiny stems from the view that behavior treatments, as long as they are nonpharmacological or nonmedical forms of treatment, need not be closely examined because there is no risk of chemical, radioactive, or other harmful side effects. Doctors' experiences with thalidomide in the 1950s ushered in an era of cautionary and regulatory safeguards in pharmacology. No equivalent landmark can be found in the realm of unconventional, behavioral, dietary, or similar treatments. Anatomic anomalies are easily photographed and a medical mistake can be laid bare in its visual cruelty. Unfortunately, we cannot take photographs of parents' anguish when they face accusations of mistreatment of their loved ones, or of the crushing of their high, spuriously encouraged hopes for a cure, or of the stagnation or regression of children's development because conventional forms of treatment have been abandoned for the sake of miracle cures. Thalidomide-like equivalent landmarks in the realm of unconventional treatments often go undocumented and unexposed, remaining the private misery of parents and powerless clinicians who are called on to counsel the parents when things go awry.

SOME ETHICAL CONSIDERATIONS CONFRONTING THE CLINICIAN

Although most responsible clinicians adopt a conservative approach regarding forms of treatment for autism, it is important to acknowledge that a cursory dismissal of unconventional treatment procedures may not suffice to protect parents and service providers from the enticement of attractive but unwarranted claims of magical cures or astounding overnight progress. A number of principles delineating the best available forms of intervention in autism are now available (see Chapters 22 through 26), and the new follow-up studies of these interventions have revealed quite positive results (Rogers, 1996), though still involving slow and incremental progress, and certainly no cures. It is important to emphasize to caregivers that these interventions should be made available to the child, and that any form of additional or alternative treatment should not come at the expense of this core program. Treatment strategies that have very little data to support their efficacy (e.g., megavitamin therapy; Rimland, 1988) but are generally innocuous may be discussed with parents, with a view to acquainting them with the limitations of the approach and the limited amount of information available on its efficacy. The clinician should not withhold his or her reservations about the approach, but should stress that, insofar as the treatment does not cause harm to the child or the family (in terms of material and emotional costs) and does not take away any of the components of the core intervention program, it should be the family's decision to invest in it or not. This principle can be called the "necessary intervention provision." Forms of treatment for which there are no efficacy data—if they do not detract from the above principle, and if they contain aspects that could be pleasurable to the child or could enhance his or her quality of life (e.g., "hippotherapy," swimming)—may be presented as attractive additions to the child's routine and program, but care should be taken in explaining to parents that such strategies are not addressing the disorder per se; rather, they create pleasurable experiences, which in themselves have a very positive value for the child.

In contrast, if the treatment approach encroaches on the "necessary intervention provision" principle, or is associated with unrealistic and irresponsible claims, or is too costly in human or material terms, it is the responsibility of the clinician to avail himself or herself of empirical knowledge and clinical judgment. This may lead the clinician to warn the family or, when necessary, to condemn the approach, in a sensitive and supportive fashion, but unequivocally and decisively. This may be easier when truly bizarre treatment approaches are brought up for discussion. For example, we have had to discuss, with a few clients originating from Central America, an approach based on the transplantation of sheep cerebellar cells into the brains of children with autism. Thankfully, the procedure did not involve neurosurgery, only the intramuscular injection of a suspicious solution. However, families traveled to a central European country, had to pay exorbitant sums for each injection, and, of course, had to rely solely on placebo effects. Less bizarre but equally unsubstantiated approaches, combining threads of scientific ideas with unwarranted conclusions and sensationalist but empty results, are available in the market. The clinician should be as unambiguously critical of such approaches as of the more fantastic ones. We do not think that it is in the patient's or family's best interests for knowledge to be withheld in the spirit of being "open-minded" or supportive of the family.

Such guidelines may be viewed by some as narrow-minded and inflexible, or even arrogant. Why should clinicians and scientists be the purveyors of truth? This view might be justified were it not for the unfortunate history of fads that come and go in the field of autism, and leave behind a trail of failed expectations. For example, the promulgation of psychoanalytic residential treatment for individuals with autism by Bettelheim (1967) was based on flawed research and, we believe, perhaps intentionally inaccurate reporting of benefits. These studies were uncontrolled, nonreplicable, hidden from peer review, without objective measures, and the like; they were conducted by "therapists" who did not have the benefit of scientific consultation and suitable methods. Bettelheim's concepts of the pathogenic role of parents and the need to remove children from their families for their therapy caused his own clients, and other families, great distress; the continued citation of his evocatively written material in other nations perpetuates the harm. Bettelheim's work is now discredited, but the field as a whole has not internalized the most important lesson: rigorous research on treatments, however intuitively good they may seem, protects children and eventually benefits them.

The promoter of an innovative treatment technique bears the major responsibility for systematically researching the approach and showing its efficacy in empirical or otherwise clinically sound ways that will stand the scrutiny of peer review. The investigator must make the principles and details of the procedure explicit so that others may replicate the studies in order to corroborate (or not) the claims commending the treatment procedure. There may be shortcomings to this process, including slowness of progress and of institution of new treatment regimes; however, such an effect may in fact benefit the field of autism, which has seen more than its share of spurious findings and irresponsible claims.

ENSURING ETHICAL PRACTICES IN RESEARCH

There is a well-described canon of practice in the ethical review of medical research with children and other vulnerable populations. This process guides the conduct of IRBs, in medical centers, universities, and research institutions. Research on autism carries with it no major differences in principle from research on other medical conditions, but it may be useful to cite several considerations that may arise.

Much of the therapeutic and behavioral research done with autistic children and adolescents is done in schools and other educational settings. Often, an improvisation of a behavioral treatment or an application of a behavioral or educational method may not seem "experimental" and in need of systematic research. Such an innovation may not be "research" and may not need systematic review. However, sometimes the pursuit of new techniques would be best served by review. When educators, therapists, and others engage in a major innovation, the question of IRB scrutiny

should come to mind. This is especially an issue when the innovation is used with a scientific or investigatory goal, in addition to any particular therapeutic goal; when the findings are generalized to other clients; or when the results are announced at a meeting or are published.

Schools and other treatment settings, including outpatient clinical settings, may not be formally affiliated with an institution that has an active IRB. How, then, can a suitable review of their studies proceed? An ad hoc approach to review may not be acceptable, and individuals are not able to be their own reviewers, however competent and concerned they may be. We believe that such settings should work in collaboration with medical schools, hospitals, research institutions, or similar programs that have well-organized, effective methods for research review and a suitably composed IRB that meets federal agency standards. A well-organized, serious IRB is not only a safeguard for the clients; it also provides assurance for investigators that their work is both scientifically and ethically defensible and meets community standards for ethical human investigation. Such an assurance is useful when and if criticisms are later raised, or at the time of publication, when IRB review is required.

Systematic research review requires specific documentation of the background, scientific justification, and methodology for the research, including potential dangers and potential benefits for the individuals who are participating and for relevant others. This research protocol includes specification of the subjects (clients, patients) to be included, those who may be excluded for medical or other reasons, and monitoring procedures for side effects. A critical component of the review materials and process is documentation of informed consent. For individuals who have intellectual disabilities and for children, the question of informed consent and assent must take into consideration the competencies of the individual and the involvement of others who may provide consent for them. We believe that it is useful to try to ensure that all individuals involved in research are brought into the decision making as much as possible. For children, research can be explained and their assent obtained to the degree possible. At times, this may be impossible—for example, for very young children and those with serious disabilities, and for many autistic individuals. However, for some autistic individuals, especially those with higher functioning, a research project can be explained in detail and full consent can be obtained. The investigator should operate under the presumption that the research subject should be involved and consenting; when not possible, this should be documented. It is critically important for a competent adult to provide fully informed consent for all research. This involves the opportunity for the research to be presented in detail, for all questions to be answered, and for the protocol to be provided for study and clarification. Written consent should not be considered a mere formality; instead, it is the culmination of a process of discussion and trust-building.

At times, there may be no one who feels able to provide consent for an individual with autism. This situation may arise for individuals who are living in government programs, or whose parents are dead or unavailable and whose guardianship is held by someone who is not the parent and who feels unable to provide, or is prevented from providing, consent for any type of research. In these and other situations, the possibility of engaging an individual with autism in research is limited. When this occurs, the individual may be deprived of the benefits of new treatments and increased attention that may accompany research participation. The most difficult situation occurs when a class of individuals is deprived of the opportunity of being involved in research because of bureaucratic procedures that make it virtually impossible for consent to be provided—for example, individuals who are living in some state programs. These limitations, in the name of protection, are the result of well-meaning procedures, and must be respected.

The procedures of human investigation represent the voice of the community, as embodied in law, regulations, and practice. The open, public pursuit of research—including discussion of planned research among colleagues, formally written protocols, IRB review, and monitoring—has a high moral value. The publication of findings—negative as well as positive results—in peer-reviewed journals is an important step in this process; experience becomes scientific knowledge only when it stands the test of a challenge that leads to either refutation or replication.

CONCLUSION

Clinicians, parents, advocates, and clients/patients are eager for new treatments to be developed and quickly applied. They often feel that there is little time for the niceties of rigorous, long-term, skeptical, hypothesis-testing research, let alone the difficulties of control groups and double-blind methods. Given the suffering imposed by autism, how could one withhold a potentially useful treatment until it is demonstrated? Or enroll an individual with autism in a double-blind study?

Similarly, the burdens of scientific research may sometimes seem to compound the suffering of individuals with a disorder. It is a great burden on a family to enroll a child in a double-blind study of anticancer agents, when what they want is the assurance that their child will receive the best available care.

Yet, in relation to medical illness, we recognize that systematic research has been the major protection against children's being exposed unduly to dangerous side effects, and that new and more effective treatments can be based on advancing knowledge. Basic research has led to vaccines; providing state-of-the-art care would have confined generations of children to iron lungs. Over the next few years, gene therapy will bring new challenges and dangers, but also new hope for other disorders.

The history of autism has been plagued by too many treatments, too-quick introduction of unproven therapies, and too few rigorous studies on causes, course, and treatment. For us, research is the best guarantee of continuously expanding knowledge and improving therapies.

There is sometimes an implicit assumption that protection of subjects and of the research enterprise represents confrontative values. Proponents of unproven therapies argue that research inaction in clinical practice is not an ethically neutral stance; the lack of serious research may, and often does, signify a willingness of society to consign children to chronic suffering. Unexamined hypotheses about etiology and treatment, even if they represent the "state of the art" and the "standard of care," represent a willingness by clinicians and society to live with ignorance. The pursuit of rigorous scientific study is fully compatible with a high standard of ethical and humane concern; indeed, we believe it may exemplify the highest degree of such concern and care.

Cross-References

Current research issues and theories are reviewed in Chapters 39–45.

REFERENCES

Advisory Committee on Human Radiation Experiments. (1995, October). Final report. Washington, DC: U.S. Government Printing Office.

American Academy of Pediatrics. (1995). Guidelines for the ethical conduct of studies to evaluate drugs in pediatric populations: Committee on drugs. *Pediatrics, 95*(2), 286–294.

Arnold, L.E., Stoff, D.M., Cook, E., Jr., Cohen, D.J., Kruesi, M., Wright, C., Hattab, J., Graham, P., Zametkin, A., Castellanos, X., McMahon, W., & Leckman, J.F. (1995). Ethical issues in biological psychiatric research with children and adolescents. *Journal of the American Academy of Child and Adolescent Psychiatry, 34*(7), 929–939.

Association for the Advancement of Behavior Therapy. (1977). Ethical issues for human services. *Behavior Therapy, 8,* 763–764.

Bailey, A., Le Couteur, A., Gottesman, I., Bolton, P., Simonoff, E., Yuzda, E., & Rutter, M. (1995). Autism as a strongly genetic disorder: Evidence from a British twin study. *Psychological Medicine, 25*(1), 63–77.

Bettelheim, B. (1967). *The empty fortress.* New York: Free Press.

Biklen, D. (1990). Communication unbound: Autism and praxis. *Harvard Educational Review, 60,* 291–314.

Cohen, S.N. (1977). Development of drug therapy for children. *Federation Proceedings, 36,* 2356–2358.

Crews, W.D., Jr., Sanders, E., Hensley, L.G., Johnson, Y.M., Bonaventura, S., Rhodes, R.D., & Garren, M.P. (1995). An evaluation of facilitated communication in a group of nonverbal individuals with mental retardation. *Journal of Autism and Developmental Disorders, 25*(2), 205–213.

Cummins, R., & Prior, M. (1992). Autism and assisted communication: A reply to Biklen. *Harvard Educational Review, 62,* 228–241.

DeMyer, M.K., Hingtgen, J.N., & Jackson, R.K. (1981). Infantile autism reviewed: A decade of research. *Schizophrenia Bulletin, 7,* 388–451.

Gallup, G.G., Jr., & McClure, M.K. (1971). Preference for mirror-image stimulation in differentially reared Rhesus monkeys. *Journal of Comparative and Physiological Psychology, 75,* 403–407.

Harlow, H.F. (1971). *Learning to love.* San Francisco: Albion.

Kanner, L. (1943). Autistic disturbances of affective contact. *Nervous Child, 2,* 217–250.

Konarski, E.A., Jr., Favell, J.E., & Favell, J.E. (1992). *Manual for the assessment and treatment of the behavior disorders of people with mental retardation.* Morganton, NC: Western Carolina Center Foundation.

Levine, R.J. (1978). Appropriate guidelines for the selection of human subjects for participation in biomedical and behavioral research. In The National Commission for the Protection of Human Subjects of Biomedical and Behavioral Research, *The Belmont report: Ethical principles and guidelines for the protection of human subjects of research* (DHEW Publication No. OS 78-0013, Appendix I, pp. 4.1–4.103). Washington, DC: U.S. Department of Health, Education, and Welfare.

Levine, R.J. (1986). *Ethics and regulation of clinical research* (2nd ed.). Baltimore: Urban & Schwarzenberg.

Marcus, L.M., & Schopler, E. (1994). Ethics and behavior therapy with children. In J.Y. Hattab (Ed.), *Ethics and child mental health* (pp. 166–176). Jerusalem: Gefen.

Mash, E.J. (1989). Treatment of child and family disturbance: A behavioral-systems perspective. In E.J. Mash & R.A. Barkley (Eds.), *Treatment of childhood disorders* (pp. 3–36). New York: Guilford Press.

Milgram, S. (1974). *Obedience to authority: An experimental view.* New York: Harper & Row.

Mirkin, B.L. (1975). Drug therapy and the developing human: Who cares? *Clinical Research, 23,* 106–113.

National Commission for the Protection of Human Subjects of Biomedical and Behavioral Research. (1977). *Research involving children: Report and recommendations* (DHEW Publication No. OS 77-0004). Washington, DC: U.S. Department of Health, Education, and Welfare.

Prior, M., & Cummins, R. (1992). Questions about facilitated communication and autism. *Journal of Autism and Developmental Disorders, 22,* 331–336.

Public Law 94-142: The Education for All Handicapped Children Act of 1975 (1977, August 23). *Federal Register, 42*(163).

Regal, R.A., Rooney, J.R., & Wandas, T. (1994). Facilitated communication: An experimental evaluation. *Journal of Autism and Developmental Disorders, 24*(3), 345–355.

Riddle, M.A., Geller, B., & Ryan, N. (1993). Another sudden death in a child treated with desipramine. *Journal of the American Academy of Child and Adolescent Psychiatry, 32,* 792–797.

Rimland, B. (1988). Controversies in the treatment of autistic children: Vitamin and drug therapy. *Journal of Child Neurology, 3,* S68–S72.

Rogers, S. (1996). Follow-up studies in autism. *Journal of Autism and Developmental Disorders, 26*(2), 243–246.

Rutter, M. (1985). The treatment of autistic children. *Journal of Child Psychology and Psychiatry, 26,* 193–214.

Shirkey, H.C. (1968). Therapeutic orphans. *Journal of Pediatrics, 72,* 119–120.

Siegel, B. (1995). Brief report: Assessing allegations of sexual molestation made through facilitated communication. *Journal of Autism and Developmental Disorders, 25*(3), 319–326.

Siegel, B., Pliner, C., Eschler, J., & Elliot, G.R. (1988). How autistic children are diagnosed: Difficulties in identification of children with multiple developmental delays. *Journal of Developmental and Behavioral Pediatrics, 9,* 199–204.

Smith, M.D., Haas, P.J., & Belcher, R.G. (1994). Facilitated communication: The effects of facilitator knowledge and level of assistance on output. *Journal of Autism and Developmental Disorders, 24*(3), 357–367.

Wheeler, D.L., Jacobson, J.W., Paglieri, R.A., & Schwartz, A.A. (1993). An experimental assessment of facilitated communication. *Mental Retardation, 31,* 49–60.

Zimbardo, P.G., Ebbesen, E.B., & Maslach, C. (1977). *Influencing attitudes and changing behavior* (2nd ed.). Reading, MA: Addison-Wesley.

Theoretical Perspectives

Theory is an attempt to understand and integrate observable phenomena. In turn, theories focus the attention of researchers and clinicians on particular types of data. New methodologies generate new data, and challenge theories; in turn, intellectual curiosity and theoretical questions lead investigators to perform new studies and create new methods. Autism has been a testing ground for every theory of social and affective development; in turn, studies of autism have led to new theoretical issues in relation to the preconditions and course of normal development.

The major domains of behavioral and psychological difficulties of individuals with autism and similar conditions have been recognized throughout the world since the time of Kanner's original descriptions. These include a particular profile of cognitive functioning with relative sparing of some areas that call on perceptual abilities (exemplified by the block design tests of the WISC intelligence tests) and profound difficulties with activities that require social judgment (as shown in difficulties in understanding the plot line of picture arrangement tasks, as in the WISC). The presence of specific neuropsychological profiles has motivated a major stream of research and provides a rich source of theoretical speculation about the underlying basis of autism.

In general, the difficulties of individuals with autism are most apparent when they are called on to understand the implicit intention in a social situation, to use abstract reasoning and apply concepts to novel situations, to analytically describe an experience or observation, or to intuitively understand what another person knows, wants, and expects from a query

or the like. However bright an individual with autism may be, there are difficulties in spontaneous, nonprogrammed, social interactions. Such individuals may be stymied by subtle humor, by when and how to repair the common breakdowns and missed communications of ordinary discourse, and by the subplots of ambivalent relationships. Gifted as they may be in work with computers and math, for autistic individuals the intuitive algebra of belief, knowledge, desire, and intent may remain wholly or partly elusive. They have trouble in understanding how their own minds and the minds of others work.

Early in the life of an autistic child, the parents become aware, sometimes gradually and then with a sense of horror, that something is going wrong at the heart of social relations. They initially may think their child is deaf or worry over his or her language; they then sense and can describe that the child is not socially present the way other children are. Children's social abilities and interests are represented in the most subtle and moving ways: calming down in the parents' arms; anticipating and enjoying the approach, touch, and hug of someone offering affection; paying attention to what interests another and hoping to focus the other's attention on something wished for or specially attractive; playing and working alongside a peer; expressing dislike, annoyance, and anger in ways that make the point without destroying self or other; coping with depression and anxiety, often with the help of others; falling in love with parents and then with others, and, as happens, falling out of love, mourning a loss and making new friendships. The developmental line from first relations to mature relations is the personal novel written by each individual, with fewer or more subplots. For individuals with autism, it is markedly more limited, predictable, and often tragic, a frequent replay of early-appearing failures and inadequacies. The task of theory is to understand at what point, and for what reasons, the developmental pathway from being cared for to becoming capable of passionate love is disrupted.

Other behavioral processes that are dysfunctional in autism include the capacity to engage in imaginative and creative play, to find pleasure in diverse activities, to be able to move from one topic (interest, activity, hobby) to another, over time and in different situations, to be able to appreciate that others may not share one's passionate interest or preoccupation. Thus, individuals with autism tend to be narrow in their interests and focus and to be obsessively preoccupied by details of their own hobby (train schedules, sports statistics, historical events). Their perceptual abilities, perseverance in the face of obstacles, and single-mindedness may lead to personal achievements (such as remarkable mastery of a body of knowledge) and vocational advancement (in fields that call for hard work, care, honesty, memory, detail, and so on, and are suited to the individual's intellectual level).

There are broad variations and blurred areas between "normal" and "atypical." Traits such as obsessiveness and preoccupation with one's favorite sports team or historical epoch are not restricted to individuals with autism; on the other hand, there are autistic individuals with genuine talents (finding artistic talents) that reveal imagination and creativity, a special way of seeing the world and conveying it to others. From a theoretical perspective, what etiological relations exist between difficulties in imagination and restriction of interest and other areas of difficulty, including the modulation of affects and the forming of flexible relations?

All these psychological functions are closely tied in with basic intellectual competence in complex manners. A developmental approach to understanding the more sophisticated mental difficulties shown by autistic individuals must start with consideration of IQ, mental age, or underlying cognitive capacity.

These intellectual abilities may be conceptualized as a single, basic, general level of intelligence (as in classical formulations of a "G factor" in intelligence) or as multiple, only partially correlated types of intelligences. From whatever theoretical perspective, it is important to recognize that some aspects of the psychological problems of autistic individuals are shared with other individuals who also have cognitive and adaptive problems (those with mental retardation), while others seem distinctive. Thus, patterns or subtypes of behavioral functioning, as explicated by Wing, may, in large part, be related to general intellectual level. However, IQ alone does not predict the full range of impairments nor the specific pattern of impairment or competence.

The most distinctively human competence is the ability to use language—to ask for things, to plan, to fantasize, to engage in abstract thinking; to share thoughts and feelings in speech; to read, write, and translate; to argue, compromise, deceive, seduce, and insult; to record our histories in our mind and on paper. Babies in utero hear their mothers' voices and respond to sounds. And from the very first months of life, children engage in communication in which language becomes quickly implicated. They understand words and phrases and soon have a small vocabulary; around 18 months or so, they begin to sprout words like weeds and become active language users. From then on, language and communication through speech affects every domain of mental and behavioral life.

Standing back from all that is known about autism, surely the most salient fact would be that up to 40% of autistic individuals are mute. Those who do speak exhibit a range of communication and language difficulties—in prosody, narrative, and the social use of language. Some of the language and communicative difficulties were already apparent to Kanner; others have been clearly defined over the past decades. Because communication is so deeply encoded biologically and so relevant to all social functioning, it is natural to place heavy emphasis on communication in the pathogenesis of autism. Are these difficulties at the core? Do they reflect some deeper or more proximal disturbance in socialization?

In the history of theories in the field of autism, there has been a tendency to highlight one domain at the expense of others. In science, theories are generally meant to explain only a circumscribed set of data, and one should not ask too much of a good theory. In the field of autism, the breadth of data is enormous. There are many domains of functioning that are impaired, and there are areas that are relatively spared; behavior and psychological functioning change over the course of development; there is enormous heterogeneity in clinical severity, intelligence, adaptive functioning, and, presumably, etiology. One should not expect any single theory to do justice to all of these domains. A useful theory, such as one that relates aspects of autistic social dysfunction to impairments in acquiring a theory of how another's mind operates, can be pushed beyond its limits if asked to explain why the majority of individuals with autism suffer from intellectual disability. A theory aimed at problems in communication may or may not have any relevance to understanding stereotypies, motor clumsiness, or other executive skills. Eventually, there will be further clarification of the neurobiological templates underlying the domains of behavior and the interconnections among systems that lead to emerging social, intellectual, and communicative competencies. The rapid technological and theoretical advances of many biomedical and behavioral fields—developmental neuroscience, neuroimaging of the functioning brain, cognitive sciences, to name a few—will surely lead to new data concerning normal development and impairments in autism and associated disorders. These data will generate new theories and, hopefully, increasingly comprehensive and useful understanding of autistic children's development, the connections across domains, and sensitive points for therapeutic intervention.

CHAPTER 39

Classification and Causal Issues in Autism

ISABELLE RAPIN

Autism is now viewed as but one of the behaviorally defined developmental disorders of early childhood. As is true of other developmental disorders—dysphasia, dyslexia, attention deficit disorder, mental deficiency, and many others—autistic symptomatology expresses the atypical function of an affected individual's brain; in turn, this atypical organization and function of the brain reflect the interaction of the genetic programs and environmental events that shaped its maturation.

Autism was erroneously thought to be very rare until epidemiologic studies carried out during the past decade indicated that its prevalence may be as high as 1 to 2 per 1,000 children, if less severely affected children are included (Gillberg, 1993; Gillberg & Coleman, 1992; Sugiyama & Abe, 1989; Sugiyama, Takei, & Abe, 1992). The current estimate is considerably higher than the widely quoted figure of 2 to 5 per 10,000 children. Progress toward defining the limits of the autistic spectrum[1] (Wing, 1988, 1993) and understanding its neurologic basis remains modest, despite recent multidisciplinary studies of its behavioral symptomatology, pathophysiology, anatomic basis, and etiologies. At this juncture, theories about the basis of autism have far outstripped fact, a feature of the field of which the public at large is generally unaware and which results in many misconceptions.

This chapter addresses some controversial issues about autism: diagnosis and classification, and the many overlapping and competing theories about autism's causation. Classification issues arise from the fact that autism is defined behaviorally on the basis of dimensional criteria. There is no single biologic marker or "gold standard" that would provide dichotomous diagnostic criteria to distinguish autism and its subtypes from other developmental disorders of early childhood. Yet, despite a wide range of severity, behaviorally defined autism (a) has a commonality of symptomatology that crosses all ages and makes it unmistakable to clinicians who know it well, and (b) hints at a unique underlying neurobiology. Some of the reasons for the difficulty in developing objective and widely accepted diagnostic criteria for autism and its subtypes will be discussed.

The chapter also focuses on some of the many current and past theories about the fundamental cause of autism, and points out that the term *cause* is used with somewhat different meanings in different fields. Some of these many theories are complementary rather than

Editor's note: As indicated in Chapter 1, *ICD-10* and *DSM-IV* terms are used interchangeably in this work. Rett's Syndrome and Asperger's Syndrome, used in *ICD-10,* appear as Rett's Disorder and Asperger's Disorder in *DSM-IV.*

Preparation of this chapter was supported in part by NIH Program Project NS 20489 from the National Institute of Neurologic Disorders and Stroke and by a grant from the Jack and Mimi Leviton Amsterdam Foundation.

[1] The term *autistic spectrum* refers in this chapter to a range of disorders that share similar behavioral symptomatology. It roughly corresponds to the term Pervasive Developmental Disorder in *DSM-IV.* The terms *autism* and *autistic* refer to the autistic spectrum. Unless specified, they are not used in the more restricted sense of Autistic Disorder *(DSM-IV)* or Childhood Autism *(ICD-10).*

competing, provided one takes into account the level of causation at which one is operating. There are indeed several levels of causation that are at least partially independent: (a) the behavioral/neuropsychologic level, (b) the neural/pathophysiologic level, and (c) the etiologic level. Professionals from different disciplines, constrained by the optics of their field of expertise, tend to consider one or another of these levels in their theorizing, unaware that elucidating causation at one level will not necessarily shed light on causation at another level. This compartmental approach has contributed some unnecessary confusion to the field. A full understanding of autism requires that all levels be studied, each in its own right, because each is required for an integrated understanding of autism.

AUTISM VERSUS NONAUTISM: BEHAVIORAL CLASSIFICATION ISSUES

As just stated, experienced clinicians and investigators can spot (i.e., diagnose) a prototypically autistic person rapidly and reliably because both severely and mildly affected persons share a common nucleus of salient behavioral characteristics that makes them stand out among other developmentally handicapped children. But, as is true for all psychopathologic disorders, there is no "acid test"—no pathognomonic chemical test or brain image—to validate this behaviorally based diagnosis. To further communication and reliability among investigators and clinicians, and to ensure consistency in the use of diagnostic labels for psychopathologic disorders, investigators and clinicians created the successive versions of the *Developmental and Statistical Manual of Mental Disorders (DSM)*, published by the American Psychiatric Association (APA; most recent edition, *DSM-IV*, 1994), and of the *International Classification of Diseases (ICD)*, published by the World Health Organization (WHO; most recent edition, *ICD-10*, 1993). Both sources have gone through several editions to weed out ambiguities and inconsistencies brought out in field trials and in practical application. Diagnosis, according to both *DSM* and *ICD* criteria, requires a minimum number of symptoms taken from a list of possible characteristics encompassing several realms of behavior. In the case of the autistic spectrum disorders (Pervasive Developmental Disorder, or PDD, in *DSM-IV*; APA, 1994), a diagnosis of "nuclear autism" (Autistic Disorder, or AD, in *DSM-IV*; Childhood Autism in *ICD-10*; WHO, 1993) requires severe qualitative deficits in three core areas that specify the condition:

1. Reciprocal social interaction.
2. Communication and symbolic or social imitative play.
3. Stereotyped behaviors, range of interests, and activities.

The high degree of interrelation of these three areas of deficit suggests that they may share a common underlying neurologic basis.

DSM-IV and *ICD-10* are parsimonious; they list only a dozen highly discriminating characteristics on which to base the diagnosis of Autistic Disorder. None of these alone suffices for the diagnosis of autism; the presence of a defined number of deficits in all three categories is required. Besides deficiencies in these core areas, autistic persons regularly exhibit a variety of additional characteristics that amplify the description of the individual, and are helpful in making a diagnosis, and defining subtypes within the autistic spectrum. These inconstant yet characteristic traits are not pathognomonic of autism and often occur in other conditions. Some of the individual traits, such as echolalia and hand flapping, are normal in infants and toddlers and may even be seen, occasionally and in isolation, in otherwise normal older children. These additional characteristics belong to two main categories: (a) those related to (or secondary manifestations of) core symptoms, and (b) concomitant consequences of an unselective dysfunction affecting brain circuits other than those responsible for the autistic symptomatology. For example, motor clumsiness and mental deficiency belong to the second type inasmuch as they are co-occurrent (comorbid) symptoms in an autistic individual with rather diffuse brain malfunction. On the other hand, the typical echolalia with pronominal reversal evidenced in many verbal autistic children is an example of a related or secondary feature;

it may serve as a compensatory strategy exploiting an excellent rote memory to mitigate inadequate comprehension and in-depth processing of language (Prizant & Duchan, 1981).

A number of well-standardized autism questionnaires and observational checklists (e.g., Childhood Autism Rating Scale [CARS; Schopler, Reichler, & Renner, 1986]; Autistic Diagnostic Observation Schedule [ADOS; Lord et al., 1989]; Autism Diagnostic Interview—Revised [ADI-R; Lord, Rutter, & Le Couteur, 1994]), have been designed to be filled out by parents, caretakers, educators, or professionals from many disciplines. These instruments (a) provide longer, more detailed lists of traits and aberrant behaviors than either *DSM-IV* or *ICD-10*, (b) specify the number of checkmarks required for a diagnosis of autism, and (c) yield a measure of severity. The diagnosis of autism based on any of these "objective" instruments is thus scalar or dimensional along a continuum of severity. This guarantees that there will be a gray area on either side of the scale's arbitrary cut-point, even though the point was chosen on the basis of standardization tests to minimize the number of false-positive (Type I error) and false-negative (Type II error) diagnoses. Any nondichotomous (dimensional) diagnosis implies a spectrum around prototypical cases and a margin of disagreement in case ascertainment.

Diagnostic agreement is excellent for typical cases, using any one of these structured instruments, but their coverage varies. For example, *DSM-III* (APA, 1980) used more stringent criteria than did *DSM-III-R* (APA, 1987) for the diagnosis of Autistic Disorder and therefore captured a smaller sample of individuals on the autistic spectrum when both sets of criteria were applied to the same sample of children (Waterhouse et al., 1996). How stringently one chooses to diagnose autism depends on one's goal. If the goal is research on the neurologic or biochemical basis of autism, one will accept only prototypic cases so as to minimize variance as much as possible. If the goal is to provide services to all affected children, one will use less stringent criteria, yet worry about flooding resources with mildly affected children who might get by without expensive services. Finally, if the goal is epidemiology or classification, one will cast the net as broadly as possible so as not to prejudice the findings.

Classification difficulty arises at the "edges" of the syndrome, where the symptomatology of autism overlaps not only with normalcy but also with other behaviorally defined syndromes such as severe mental deficiency, receptive-expressive and semantic-pragmatic language disorders (Bartak, Rutter, & Cox, 1977; Bishop & Adams, 1989; Rapin & Allen, 1983; Tanguay, 1990), Tourette's Syndrome and Obsessive-Compulsive Syndrome (Baron-Cohen, 1989; Comings & Comings, 1991; Singer, 1994; Sverd, 1991), the syndrome of nonverbal learning disability (Rourke, 1989; Semrud-Klikeman & Hynd, 1990), childhood manic-depressive syndrome (DeLong, 1994; Kennard, Emslie, & Weinberg, 1992), early-onset schizophrenia (Asarnow, 1992; Volkmar, Cohen, Hoshino, Rende, & Paul, 1988), and overfocused or socially gauche individuals (Kinsbourne, 1991) whose peculiarities are too restricted to earn them a psychopathologic label in the *DSM* system. Some individuals fulfill criteria for more than a single syndrome—an example of comorbidity—which brings up the reality of common etiologies producing different phenotypes and, conversely, different etiologies producing common phenotypes. For example, DeLong (1994) suggests that, in some cases, Asperger's Syndrome may be an early manifestation of manic-depressive syndrome, and Sverd (1991) and Comings and Comings (1991) speculate that some cases of autism may be the phenotypic expression of homozygosity of the gene for Tourette's Syndrome.

DSM-IV, like its predecessors, *DSM-III* and *DSM-III-R,* specifies no exclusionary criterion for a diagnosis of Pervasive Developmental Disorder (PDD), the umbrella category that encompasses autism (Autistic Disorder, or AD) and other disorders on the autistic spectrum. This means that behaviorally defined autism can exist in persons with blindness, deafness, structural brain lesions, genetic diseases like PKU and tuberous sclerosis, motor handicaps, and other conditions with overt evidence of an insult to the immature brain (coded in *DSM-IV* on Axis III). In particular, there is no cognitive exclusionary criterion (Mental Retardation is to be coded on Axis II, separately from autism, which is coded on Axis I together with other developmental disorders). This implies that autism can exist in severely mentally deficient persons as well as in those of superior intelligence. Yet *DSM* specifies that PDD is to be diagnosed only if symptoms are out of proportion to the person's cognitive level (mental age). Under Mental Retardation, *DSM* lists behaviors such as stereotypies and inadequate socialization and communication, which are core features of autism. When visiting a center for the severely to profoundly mentally deficient, one will see that many of the residents exhibit these autistic behaviors, yet they are not to be diagnosed as such according to the *DSM* system because these behaviors are not out of proportion to the severe mental deficiency. It is the case that, on purely statistical grounds, the more diffuse the damage to the brain, the more likely it will also affect the network(s) responsible for the appearance of autistic symptomatology. *DSM* provides for comorbidity of Mental Retardation and Autistic Disorder on separate axes but implies that autism is not the primary diagnosis in these profoundly brain-damaged individuals. Yet, inasmuch as the definition of autism is strictly behavioral, autistic behaviors in the profoundly mentally deficient population should be acknowledged as such. This issue is related to the contentious issue of primary versus secondary autism, which is discussed later.

BEHAVIORALLY DEFINED *DSM-IV* AUTISM SUBTYPES: CLASSIFICATION ISSUES

DSM-IV and *ICD-10* classify persons on the autistic (PDD) spectrum into several subtypes. Autistic Disorder in *DSM-IV* requires 6 or more checks among 12 listed symptoms, including at least 2 in sociability and 1 each in the communication and restricted-pattern-of-activities domains; it also specifies that delay or qualitative deficit in social interaction, communicative language, or symbolic or imaginative play must have appeared before the age of 3 years.

Entirely normal development, including language, up to or beyond age 2 years, followed by the loss of language and the appearance of autistic behaviors prior to age 10 years, is referred to as Childhood Disintegrative Disorder (CDD) in *DSM-IV* and *ICD-10*. But is CDD truly distinct from Autistic Disorder? The age-cut at 2 years is arbitrary, and it overlaps with the age at which regression is reported by at least one-third of parents of autistic children (Burack & Volkmar, 1992; Kurita, 1985, 1988; Kurita, Kita, & Miyake, 1992; Tuchman & Rapin, in press; Tuchman, Rapin, & Shinnar, 1991a, 1991b; Volkmar & Cohen, 1989). Parents of these classically autistic children relate that regression (or, in some cases, a prolonged stagnation) affected language, sociability, and play—but not motor skills—usually between ages 1 and 3 years. In some children, regression took place against a background of preexisting, less severe, and usually overlooked autistic symptoms; in other children, there was no premonitory sign of autism. In a few children, regression occurred suddenly, after a presumably traumatic event such as a hospitalization or the temporary absence of a parent; more often, it was insidious and had no recognized triggering illness of other deleterious antecedent. Development resumed after months or even years, but full recovery was never achieved and autistic characteristics of greater or lesser severity were permanent. Thus, the distinction between autistic and disintegrative disorders is at least partly age-related in *DSM-IV* and *ICD-10*—a unique and rather controversial discriminating factor for conditions with a biologic basis. This distinction is presumably temporary, pending the discovery of a biologic marker to define the specificity (or lack thereof) of the two conditions.

The cause of autistic regression, whether before or after age 3 years, is rarely known. In a minority of cases, regression may be associated with clinical seizures or with subclinical epilepsy manifested by paroxysmal discharges in the EEG. The EEG abnormality may be of the type seen in children with acquired epileptic aphasia (Landau & Kleffner, 1957) and may be characterized by unilateral or bilateral independent or synchronous spikes, spike/waves, or sharp waves in the Rolandic areas (e.g., Deonna, 1991; Dugas, Gerard, Franc, & Sagar, 1991; Rapin, Mattis, Rowan, & Golden, 1977; van Dongen, De Wijngaert, &

Wennekes, 1991). Sleep characteristically activates the electrical paraoxysmal activity, and. occasionally, this activity may take on the features of electrical status epilepticus in slow-wave sleep (ESES; Beaumanoir, Bureau, Deonna, Mira, & Tassinari, 1995; Jayakar & Seshia, 1991; Roulet Perez, Davidoff, Despland, & Deonna, 1993). Besides the overlap in timing between the onset of autistic regression and of disintegrative disorder, there is an overlap of autistic regression with classic acquired epileptic aphasia (Landau-Kleffner Syndrome). Classic acquired epileptic aphasia itself may or may not be associated with a behavioral disorder or even with autistic symptomatology (if it is associated with autistic symptomatology, it fulfills the criteria for disintegrative disorder; Aicardi, 1994; Roulet Perez et al., 1993). It is tempting to speculate that the extent of clinical disability (language alone or language + behavior and cognition) depends on the extent of the underlying brain dysfunction (or of the epileptic activity per se? [Deonna, 1993]): Does it involve limbic structures such as the amygdala and mesial frontal cortex (Paquier, van Dongen, & Loonen, 1992; Roulet Perez et al., 1993) as well as the lateral temporal cortex? Perhaps functional studies like SPECT (cerebral single photon emission tomography; Lou, 1992) and PET (positron emission tomography; Maquet et al., 1990) will shed light on the mechanism of this distressing condition.

Children who have fewer than 6 checkmarks on the *DSM-IV* list, or who do not have them in all 3 categories, are to be classified as Pervasive Developmental Disorder Not Otherwise Specified (PDD-NOS). This less severely, less typically autistic group is likely to be verbal and to have a higher IQ and better prognosis than the children with AD. *DSM-IV* specifies that older individuals who used to fulfill criteria for a developmental disorder (which includes Autistic Disorder) should continue to carry this diagnosis even though they may have improved enough to no longer fulfill criteria for the full diagnosis (DeMyer et al., 1973; Gonzalez, Alpert, Shay, Campbell, & Small, 1993). Parents of these improved children would most certainly protest that this practice would stigmatize their children; yet, some intelligent mildly autistic persons have welcomed an explanation for persistent social

difficulties that remained inexplicable to them until their difficulty acquired a name. *DSM-III* dealt with this issue by having Residual State categories, which were dropped in subsequent editions; *DSM-IV* suggests adding a specifier, "In Partial Remission," to the diagnosis of a developmental disorder when it is present in attenuated or residual form.

There are practical reasons, such as the provision of adequate educational services and the communication of prognostic information to parents, for separating severely autistic individuals from those more mildly affected, but whether PDD-NOS is fundamentally different from AD or, instead, represents the upper part of an autistic spectrum, is debatable (Wing 1988, 1991). In a multidisciplinary study of 176 preschool autistic children selected to meet *DSM-III-R* criteria for AD and 18 similarly studied children who fulfilled PDD-NOS criteria, there were high- and low-functioning children in both the AD and PDD-NOS groups, and a lack of a fundamental difference between the groups was noted (Allen, Rapin, & Steinberg, 1997). How much these two diagnostic categories will differ in outcome remains to be determined.

Although *DSM-IV* and *ICD-10* do not subclassify autistic individuals on the basis of their cognitive ability, many investigators propose that a severely affected ("low-functioning") group of individuals with AD whose full-scale IQ is below 70 (or even below 50; Burack & Volkmar, 1992) should be separated from a less severely affected ("high-functioning") group with an IQ above 70 (Cohen, Paul, & Volkmar, 1987; Rutter, 1979; Rutter & Garmezy, 1983; Tsai, 1992). There is evidence that severity of autistic symptoms and intelligence level are partially correlated, but, as just pointed out, PDD-NOS and "high-functioning" do not overlap exactly; intelligence and sociability are partially independent. The IQ cut at 70 is arbitrary, yet studies comparing low- and high-functioning children indicate that the two groups differ in a number of respects, including prognosis (DeMyer et al., 1972; Lockyer & Rutter, 1970; Lord & Venter, 1992; Lotter, 1978). In a multidisciplinary study of the 194 children on the autistic spectrum just mentioned (Rapin, 1996), multivariate regression-mixture analysis suggest that the most discriminating IQ cut between a less severely affected (AutA) group and a more severely affected (AutB) group at preschool is a nonverbal IQ of 65.

Asperger's Syndrome is listed separately in both *DSM-IV* and *ICD-10,* although *DSM-IV* views it as a subtype of PDD-NOS. This label applies to children with severe social impairment who do not have a history of delayed language acquisition (but generally still have higher-order processing and pragmatic disorders) and who have a particularly narrow range of interests (Frith, 1991). In contrast to the majority of children with AD who are mentally deficient, those with Asperger's Syndrome have average, close to average, or even superior cognitive skills, self-help skills, and interest in the environment. Some of these children may be clumsy and some have had delayed motor milestones. It has not been shown definitely that children with Asperger's Syndrome are nosologically distinct from relatively intelligent children with AD or PDD-NOS whose language development was quite delayed but who then progressed rapidly to fluent speech without notable phonologic or syntactic errors (Tager-Flusberg, 1994). Therefore, the term is often used loosely in the clinic and is applied to all relatively high-functioning children, inasmuch as it is viewed as a less stigmatizing diagnosis than autism.

In more mildly affected children, diagnostic overlaps with disorders outside the autistic spectrum are particularly problematic. Some children with Asperger's Syndrome or PDD-NOS who have reasonable social skills may overlap with those diagnosed with Obsessive-Compulsive Disorder because of their rigidity, perfectionism, and narrowly focused interests. DeLong (1994) proposes that at least some of these children suffer from early-onset genetic manic-depressive psychosis. Whether Asperger's Syndrome will turn out to be the upper tail of the autistic spectrum distribution or a genetically or neurologically valid subgroup(s) of autism remains unresolved.

DSM-IV and *ICD-10* identify Rett's Syndrome (RS) as a separate PDD syndrome. Unlike other disorders on the autistic spectrum, where the predominance of boys is of the order of 4:1, RS affects girls, by present consensus, exclusively. A regression in sociability and hand use almost always takes place before age 1 year (Hagberg, 1993; Hagberg, Aicardi, Dias, & Ramos, 1983). Mental deficiency is severe to profound, language is rudimentary or absent, and seizures are frequent. Other characteristic features include postnatal deceleration of head (and brain) growth; marked hypotonia and scoliosis; small, cold, cyanosed feet; and episodic hyperventilation. It is said that sociability improves as the girls become older (Witt Engerström, 1993), but this is also true of typical autism (e.g., DeMyer et al., 1973). RS does not appear to be a classic degenerative disease of the brain inasmuch as adult, even middle-aged women with the condition are being identified in increasing numbers, although unexpected and unexplained early death is frequent. Of all the autistic spectrum disorders listed in *DSM-IV* and *ICD-10,* RS is the only one for which the defining criteria are not strictly behavioral. Because there is at least suggestive evidence that RS may be traceable to a specific genetic defect, it would seem logical to list it on Axis III, among the many etiologies of autism, rather than as a subvariant of the behaviorally defined autistic spectrum. A differential diagnosis between severe autism with regression in a girl and RS may be difficult early in life (Burd, Fisher, & Kerbeshian, 1989; Hagberg & Gillberg, 1993). The regression in RS occurs earlier and is more severe than in autism, and it is associated with the biologic marker of impaired brain growth that is absent in garden-variety autism, where measurements of head circumference (Bailey, Luthert, Bolton, Le Couteur, & Rutter, 1993; Rapin, 1996) and MRI hemispheric volume (Filipek et al., 1992) are usually normal or even larger than normal. Thus, regression in RS seems to differ fundamentally from regression in Autistic Disorder and in Childhood Disintegrative Disorder, but the neurologic basis of the regression is unknown in all three disorders.

LEVELS OF CAUSATION

Perhaps one of the reasons for what are often interpreted as many disparate or even conflicting theories about the cause of autism is that different fields use the term *causation* in somewhat different ways and are concerned with different levels of causation. In medicine, cause means etiology, or causation of disease by a specific agent—for example, a particular infectious agent like the measles virus, a defined form of cancer, vitamin C deficiency (which causes scorbut), or, in the case of Huntington disease, the mutation of a single gene. Etiologies fall into only three basic categories: (a) genetic, (b) environmentally determined (e.g., trauma, infection, intoxication) or (c) more often, a combination of (a) and (b) (e.g., a given bacterium can cause disease of vastly different severity, depending on the immune makeup of the host). Most likely, RS is a particular genetic (?) etiology of autism, whereas congenital rubella represents a specific environmental cause.

Even in the case of highly specific etiologies, there is a loose connection between etiology and symptomatology. A reason for this, besides variable susceptibility of the host, is that clinical symptoms depend on what parts of the anatomy are affected. Clinically, strep throat has nothing in common with streptococcal infection of the uterus, whereas one needs a bacteriologic test to differentiate streptococcal from viral pharyngitis, two distinct etiologies for a sore throat. Therefore, it comes as no surprise that autism, which, like pharyngitis, is defined by its symptoms, has many etiologies, and that defining the etiology of autism in a particular individual provides little information about that autistic person's behavioral symptoms.

There is increasing evidence for genetics playing a major etiologic role in autism (e.g., Bailey et al., 1995; Lotspeich & Cianarello, 1993). It was thought until recently that a genetically defined disease had a unique etiology: one gene, one protein or enzyme, one disease. Progress in molecular biology is uncovering increasing inadequacies of this dogma. For example, allelic mutations and deletions in the dystrophin gene responsible for X-linked muscular dystrophy are responsible for two distinct phenotypes ("diseases"), and symptoms and severity vary within each. In addition to classic lethal Duchenne muscular dystrophy of young boys—which tends to be associated with specific neuropsychologic deficits (Mehler & Dunn, 1995) and, in a minority of cases, with subnormal intelligence (Karagan, 1979) or,

rarely, classic autism (Komoto, Usui, Otsuki, & Terao, 1984, and personal observations)—other mutations and deletions of the same gene cause Becker muscular dystrophy, which is much more slowly progressive (Nicholson et al., 1993) and is unassociated with cognitive deficits. The gene alterations affect the synthesis of dystrophin, a structural cellular protein normally found in muscle and in the brain, notably in cerebellar Purkinje cells and in pyramidal cells of the hippocampus and frontal lobe. In stark contrast with the divergent phenotypes arising from alterations in the one dystrophin gene, different genetic illnesses can produce the same phenotype. For example, what was thought of as a single disorder, Sanfilippo disease, which is a genetic dementing neuronal storage disease of childhood and adolescence, turns out to be genetically heterogeneous inasmuch as it has four genetically and enzymatically distinct etiologies. Thus, not only can one have a single illness with several genetic etiologies, but the mutation of a single gene can result in several phenotypes (diseases).

In the case of the brain, the behavioral manifestations of diseases depend not on etiology but on what parts or systems of the brain are affected, because they determine behavioral symptomatology. This is the level of pathophysiologic causation. Parkinsonism, which is a behaviorally defined syndrome, may be caused by any one of several genetic disorders, by a previous viral encephalitis, by neural dropout associated with aging, by overmedication with dopamine-receptor blocking drugs like haloperidol and chlorpromazine, by intoxication with the heroin adulterant MPTP, or even by a tumor. All these etiologic agents, whether they are genetic, biochemical, or structural, share common symptoms because they all impair function of the dopaminergic nigro-striatal pathway or its targets.

CAUSATION IN AUTISM: CONFLICTING OR COMPLEMENTARY THEORIES?

Many theories have been proposed to explain the disorders of the autistic spectrum. Behavioral theories attempt to explain autistic symptoms on the basis of underlying psychologic/cognitive mechanisms. Neurologic/

pathophysiologic theories draw on information regarding the neural basis of particular skills and behaviors, and enlist neuroimaging, neurophysiology, neuropathology, and neurochemistry to identify the responsible dysfunctional circuit(s). The *behavioral level* is thus closely related to and correlated with the *neurologic/pathophysiologic level,* and progress at the neural/pathophysiologic level will illuminate the neural basis of the developmental disorders, including autism, and provide a basis for rational pharmacologic intervention. Contributions at the *etiologic level* have an impact on prevention, genetic counseling, and epidemiology, but they do not explain behavior. Far from being competitive or mutually exclusive, theories at these three levels are complementary. Problems arise when any one theory is touted as *the* cause of autism, or when hybrid theories that unwittingly span causal levels are propounded.

Explanatory Theories at the Behavioral/Neuropsychologic Level

Autism research at the behavioral/neuropsychologic level has led to the largest number of theories about *the* fundamental deficit in autism. A great deal of effort has been and is being devoted at the behavioral level to attempts to determine which of the many symptoms of autism are manifestations (i.e., consequences) of a common underlying neuropsychologic deficit, and which may be primary (i.e., causal). Repeated attempts have been made to elevate individual behavioral symptoms to the position of a basic mechanism. The search for that basic mechanism is by no means over (see Rumsey, 1992, for a recent review of neuropsychologic theories of autism).

The earliest causal theories were strictly behavioral and blamed early affective deprivation on inadequate parenting in infancy or early childhood (e.g., Bettelheim, 1967). These theories were subsequently refuted by empirical research on the parenting skills of autistic children's parents (Cantwell, Baker, & Rutter, 1979; DeMyer et al., 1972). Then came perceptual theories that invoked aberrant vestibular, visual, auditory, and somatosensory processing (reviewed in Ornitz, 1989; see also Grandin & Scariano, 1986, for a firsthand account). Perceptual causal theories still have their proponents today; witness the vast sums of money being spent on auditory desensitization (Auditory Integration Training; Stehli, 1991), special eyeglasses, vestibular stimulation, and brushing of the skin to decrease tactile defensiveness (Ayres & Tickle, 1980; Slavik, Kitsuwa-Lowe, Danner, Green, & Ayres, 1984). Despite the reality of aberrant responses (both too little and too much) of autistic children to a variety of sensory inputs, and despite their prominence in the public's eye and in the schools, there is little to suggest that perceptual aberrations are primary causes of autistic symptomatology.

Deficits of attention and arousal may contribute to the unevenness of autistic persons' responses to sensory inputs and to their disordered circadian sleep patterns (Segawa, Katoh, Katoh, & Nomura, 1992). Overfocused attention on and obliviousness of the environment (Kinsbourne, 1991), failure of joint attention (Mundy & Sigman, 1989; Mundy, Sigman, & Kasari, 1993), and slowness or difficulty in shifting attentional set (Akshoomoff & Courchesne, 1992) are often prominent. That this deficit in intermodality attentional shifting is fundamental to autism and can explain all of its many symptoms adequately requires more evidence.

Lack of social drive, impaired perception or interpretation of facial expression and tone of voice (Hobson, Ouston, & Lee, 1988, 1989), and blunting of the experience of pleasure and pain (Hobson, 1993) have all been considered important or even fundamental deficits in autism. These social and affective deficits may contribute to autistic children's inadequate learning of language and deficient responsiveness to social cues, inasmuch as learning depends to such a large extent on the pleasurable awareness of mastery and on the experience of social and tangible rewards. The reported success of educational approaches based on classic conditioning paradigms (Lovaas, 1981, 1987) casts some doubt on the adequacy of this explanation, but does not invalidate the prominence of affective deficits, especially affective lability, in autism. The previously mentioned theory of DeLong (1994), concerning genetic linkage between manic-depressive disorder and high-functioning autism, is potentially relevant in this context.

Learning theories of autism (e.g., DeLong, 1992) have been bolstered by Bauman and Kemper's (1985, 1994) finding of hippocampal and diencephalic pathology in autistic brains. Subtle deficits in the organization of semantic memory (Dunn, Gomes, & Sebastian, in press), together with impaired affective modulation, may contribute to the deficient verbal skills of many autistic children. Declarative/representational memory depends on lateral prefrontal/hippocampal circuits (Goldman-Rakic, Funahashi, & Bruce, 1990), which seem to be affected in autism. Even within declarative memory, there are significant dissociations in autism; verbal memory is generally more deficient than visual-spatial memory (Killiany & Moss, 1994). Some autistic individuals have remarkable rote verbal, musical, and visual-spatial memories and, as a result, may be hyperlexic and read with little comprehension (Aram & Healy, 1988); become mnemonists (Treffert, 1989); play music after a single hearing, without a score and without knowing musical notation (Miller, 1989); or call on a superior ideitic memory to draw a scene with extraordinary precision after only a brief exposure (Obler & Fein, 1988; O'Connor & Hermelin, 1987). This dissociation between representational/declarative and procedural/rote memory in autism reflects the well-known survival of procedural (habit/rote) memory functions following bilateral hippocampectomy (Milner, 1965), which, at least for automatized motor tasks, may involve the neostriatum, neocerebellum, and parietal cortex (Sanes, Dimitrov, & Hallett, 1990). The fact that declarative memory matures later and more gradually than procedural memory, which is demonstrable soon after birth (Killiany & Moss, 1994), may be relevant to autistic regression, which always affects language but does not affect motor skills and is most likely to occur in toddlers.

Language disorders are prominent features of autism in virtually every preschooler. The children's ubiquitous lack of sociability and drive to communicate no doubt contributes to their inadequate pragmatic skills (communicative intent) but provides an insufficient explanation for the variety of their language deficits (Allen & Rapin, 1992). Some children are essentially word-deaf and therefore nonverbal. Others with less profoundly impaired comprehension have severely deficient phonologic and syntactic skills and, consequently, limited fluency and vocabulary. Children with either of these language deficits are very different from those with adequate phonology and syntax, whose deficits involve higher-order language processing, such as organization of the lexicon (repository of word meanings in long-term memory) (Dunn, Gomes, & Sebastian, 1996), comprehension at the level of the sentence rather than at the word or phrase level, and ability to formulate coherent discourse (Tager-Flusberg, 1994). These higher-level language deficits occur at the intersection of cognitive, social, and language competence (Rumsey, Andreason, & Rapoport, 1986). Inadequate language comprehension is often blamed for the behavioral deficits of autistic children, but autism cannot be ascribed to this factor alone. Congenital deafness and progressive hearing loss, as well as many cases of acquired epileptic aphasia with verbal auditory agnosia (all of which preclude or severely jeopardize language comprehension), do not cause autism.

Cognitive deficits are salient in autism, and, as discussed earlier, the more severe the mental deficiency, the more likely it is associated with frankly autistic behaviors. Yet, the majority of mildly to moderately mentally deficient persons have no autistic features, so overall cognitive incompetence does not provide a satisfactory explanation for autism. Neuropsychologic studies indicate that a consistent feature of autism is an uneven profile of skills, with generally better nonverbal than verbal skills, especially among lower-functioning persons (Rumsey, 1992). The pattern of test scores emphasizes adequate rote memory and visual-spatial skills but highlights deficient abstract comprehension, problem solving, and cognitive flexibility, resulting in faulty abstract reasoning and difficulty in making contextual inferences from partial data (Minshew, Goldstein, Muenz, & Payton, 1992). The pattern of neuropsychologic deficits in autism has suggested that autism may be caused by a fundamental deficit in complex information processing (Minshew, 1992).

One of the features of deficient abstract cognition is impaired executive function (Ozonoff & McEvoy, 1994; Ozonoff, Pennington, & Rogers, 1991). Executive function, the ability to consider alternatives in planning, calls for keeping a number of items in working memory, allocating attention to competing stimuli, balancing priorities, weighing the consequences of alternative courses of action, considering available resources realistically, and thinking of possible options before taking action. In contrast to rote memory, where items are stored more or less unselectively, selective storage for efficient retrieval requires preanalysis in working memory so as to link new items to old for assignment to appropriate networks. Deficient executive function is salient in autism, and accounts for some but not all of its features.

Baron-Cohen, Leslie, and Frith (1985); Leslie and Frith (1988); Frith (1993); and others (see Baron-Cohen, Tager-Flusberg, & Cohen, 1993) propose that a prominently defective feature of abstract cognition, which they call "theory of mind," represents *the* fundamental deficit in autism. Theory of mind refers to the ability to imagine what another person may be thinking and how one's behavior may impact on that person. Indeed, very young autistic children typically have no idea that they have means at their disposal, other than screaming, to influence what another person will do for them—for example, fulfill a want or need. Impaired theory of mind provides a credible explanation for a number of autistic features, such as deficient social pragmatics, failure to read facial expression and tone of voice, inadequate socialization and social learning, and failure of joint attention; but the claim that theory of mind can explain all of the complexities of autism is less convincing (Klin, Volkmar, & Sparrow, 1992).

This brief survey indicates that, despite many claims to the contrary, overwhelming evidence supporting any one of the sensory, attentional, social/affective, language, learning, or cognitive theories as *the* fundamental deficit in autism is lacking. Each of these theories provides a plausible explanation for a number of the symptoms of autism, but none seems fully adequate to account for all of them. Each represents a facet of what is behaviorally wrong in autism, but more work will be required to determine which, if any, of the proposed underlying behavioral/neuropsychologic deficits is primary.

Causal Theories at the Neural/Pathophysiologic Level

Contributions to an understanding of the neurologic basis of autism, recently reviewed in Bauman and Kemper (1994), come from a variety of sources: neuroimaging (CT, MRI, PET, SPECT), neurophysiology (EEG, ERP, MEG), neuropathology, and neurochemistry. Early theories focused on the temporal lobes because of the prominence of receptive language disorders, presumed to involve auditory association and posterior language areas, and because of the proximity of the temporal lobes to the hippocampus, amygdala, and diencephalon, viewed as likely sources for the affective, social, and learning deficits and the frequent epilepsy of autistic persons. Hauser, DeLong, and Rosman (1975) described atrophy of the left temporal lobe on pneumoencephalographic (air) studies, a finding not corroborated in most later imaging studies (e.g., Courchesne, 1991; Filipek et al., 1992). Recently, the animal model created by Bachevalier and Merjanian (1994), who performed bilateral temporal ablations in neonatal monkeys, as well as the rare human infant or adult surviving inadequately treated herpes encephalitis with bilateral temporal damage (personal observation; DeLong, Bean, & Brown, 1981; Gillberg, 1991) and presenting with behavioral features typical of severe autism, have revived interest in the relevance of medial temporal lobe structures to autism. These studies and the observations of Bauman and Kemper (1985, 1994) of cellular pathology in the hippocampus and amygdala appear to lend support to a learning/memory/affective theory of autism (DeLong, 1992; Deonna, Ziegler, Moura-Serra, & Innocenti, 1993; Waterhouse, Fein, & Modahl, 1996). Electrophysiologic studies of patients with verbal auditory agnosia (word deafness) with and without autistic behaviors showed unilateral (not necessarily left) or bilateral paroxysmal EEG discharges in the temporal-parietal regions (Klein, Tuchman, & Rapin, 1989), abnormality of early (Klein, et al., 1995) and late (Novick, Kurtzberg, & Vaughan, 1979) components of the auditory-evoked potentials, and decreased cerebral blood flow on SPECT imaging (Lou, 1992). An inadequately explored but approachable issue, with therapeutic implications at the pathophysiologic level, is the potential role of epilepsy in autistic subtypes associated with regression.

Attentional and sleep deficits in autism (Segawa et al., 1992) have put the spotlight on brain stem arousal systems and also on right frontal and anterior cingulate regions (Mesulam, 1990). PET studies in young adults with autism (Rumsey et al., 1985) suggested less cortical hemispheric asymmetry for glucose metabolism than expected, because of the lack of an expected higher metabolic rate on the right, notably in the right basal ganglia and right frontal cortex, an asymmetry characteristic of normal subjects during the performance of a visual vigilance task. High-functioning autistic subjects, even though they performed this task almost as well as controls, did not show this asymmetry (Siegel et al., 1992). Furthermore, these subjects also had decreased metabolism in the right gyrus rectus, a part of the frontal ventro/medial region heavily interconnected with the limbic system, where damage impairs reasoning/decision making and emotion/feeling (Damasio, 1994; Damasio & Maurer, 1978). The striking feature of all these metabolic imaging studies was intersubject inconsistencies, suggesting heterogeneous pathophysiologies and the need for further studies in rigidly selected subjects performing highly specific cognitive tasks that dissect out particular behavioral demands if one is to evaluate the generality of findings (see Raichle, 1994).

The MRI study of Courchesne, Yeung-Courchesne, Press, Hesselink, and Jernigan (1988) drew attention to a potential role of the cerebellum in autism. These investigators reported that the mean *areas* of lobules VI and VII of the cerebellar vermis on midline sagittal MRI images were smaller in 14 of 18 autistic men than in normal controls. In a later study, Courchesne, Townsend, and Saitoh (1994) found that the distribution of mean areas was smaller in the majority of autistic persons (85%), and that a minority (12%) showed larger areas than controls. In a preliminary morphometric study in which *DSM-III-R* Autistic Disorder school-age children were compared to language-impaired and normal controls, Filipek et al. (1992; Filipek, 1995 and personal communication) found no difference in *mean volumes* of areas VI and VII, nor in the volumes of any other cerebellar region. Other studies of brain stem and cerebellar structures have yielded inconsistent results (e.g., Filipek, 1995; Hashimoto et al., 1993; Holtum, Minshew, Sanders, & Phillips, 1992; Hsu, Yeung-Courchesne, Courchesne, & Press, 1991; Piven et al., 1992).

There is evidence for cellular pathology of the cerebellum in autism. Early case studies by Williams, Hauser, Purpura, DeLong, and Swisher (1980); Ritvo et al. (1986); and Bauman and Kemper (1985) revealed a paucity of Purkinje and granular cells in the cerebellar hemispheres. The most up-to-date pathologic study (of 6 brains; Bauman & Kemper, 1994) stresses some differences in the findings in children under 12 years and in adults above 22 years (no brains at intermediate ages have become available to date). In the children, neurons of the inferior olivary nucleus (a major cerebellar afferent) and in the cerebellar roof nuclei (cerebellar outflow) were larger than in controls; in the adult brains, these neurons were smaller, paler, and reduced in number. Paucity of Purkinje cells and some decrease of granular neurons in the cerebellar hemispheres, especially in the posterior inferior neocerebellar cortex and archicerebellum, were seen in both adults and children. There was no evidence for an expected gliosis or for transneuronal retrograde degeneration in the inferior olive, which Bauman and Kemper interpreted as evidence for the persistence of an immature fetal olivo-cerebellar circuit involving the deep cerebellar nuclei and for timing of the abnormality before 30 weeks of gestation.

These MRI and pathologic studies have drawn attention to an unsuspected role of the cerebellum in autism and in higher cerebral functions in general. For example, recent PET studies of cerebral blood flow, using ^{15}O water in normal adults, illustrate the participation of the cerebellum for language—not just speech—in that there was right cerebellar hemispheric activation during the generation of verbs (Raichle, 1994). The cerebellum is now known to play a role in conditioned learning, word generation, and a variety of cognitive tasks (Kim, Ugurbil, & Strick, 1994; Schmahmann, 1994), and to be connected not only with midbrain and thalamic nuclei but with the hippocampus and neocortex as well. It is fair to say, however, that the behavioral correlates of cerebellar pathology in autism are still largely speculative.

In the limbic system, Bauman and Kemper (1994) found a pattern of cellular abnormalities that provides support for the learning and affective theories of autism. Cells in the hippocampus, parts of the amygdala, the subiculum, entorhinal cortex, mammillary bodies, septum, and anterior cingulate cortex were smaller and more closely packed, with stunted arbors in some pyramidal cells of the hippocampus. These findings were interpreted as evidence of curtailed development. Age differences were limited to the diagonal band of Broca in the septum, with large cells in the brains of young subjects and small, sparser cells in the brains of older subjects. Bauman and Kemper did not find any cellular changes in the neocortex, but they point out that there are extensive connections between limbic and neocortical association areas whose function may be disrupted without anatomic counterpart. In contrast, MRI imaging (Courchesne, Press, & Yeung-Courchesne, 1994; Piven et al., 1990), electrophysiologic experiments (reviewed in Dunn, 1994), imaging of cerebral blood flow (Mountz, Tolbert, Lill, Katholi, & Liu, 1995) and MRI spectroscopy studies of high-energy phosphate metabolism (Minshew, 1994) provide some evidence for abnormalities of the association neocortex in autism. It would be difficult to explain the cognitive deficits and the existence of true language disorders in autism—not just a deficient drive to communicate—in the absence of any cortical dysfunction, although subcortical contributions to developmental language disorders similar to those in some of the acquired language disorders

of adults with subcortical lesions (Crosson, 1985) have yet to attract much attention.

Because most autistic children do not have obvious focal or diffuse abnormalities on imaging or EEG studies, and because complex behaviors such as those deficient in autism engage so many brain systems, the possibility of biochemical aberrations of a neurotransmitter or neuromodulator affecting a particular distributed neural network(s) has gained favor. Biochemical and anatomic theories are complementary, not mutually exclusive, because neurotransmitters and neuromodulators are expressed selectively in some circuits and not others. As a result, anatomic and chemical lesions in a given network are likely to have similar behavioral consequences. A putative biochemical theory of autism will still require determining the identity of the affected neural network. Abnormalities of serotonin, catecholamines, acetylcholine, enkephalins, oxytocin, and growth factors have all been invoked as potential explanations for autism (see Anderson, 1994, and Waterhouse, Fein, & Modahl, 1996, for reviews), but, again, evidence for any one of these as *the* fundamental deficit in autism is lacking. Identification of biochemical factors in autism is, of course, critical for the development of rational approaches to pharmacotherapy and perhaps, ultimately, chemical remediation.

Minshew (1992) has speculated, on the basis of a review of neuroanatomic, neurophysiologic, neuroimaging, and neuropsychologic evidence, that one should seek the fundamental neurologic dysfunction in autism in a distributed network responsible for the processing of complex information of all types. Although speculative, this view would have the virtue of encompassing rival pathophysiologic theories about the cause of autism. Identifying such a network will not be easy, given the dearth of pathologic material, cost of functional neuroimaging studies, practical difficulty finding suitable subjects for behavioral and imaging tests, and laboriousness of electrophysiologic studies. New approaches such as magnetoencephalography (Gordon, Rennie, & Collins, 1990), brain electric source analysis (BESA; Scherg & Picton, 1991), and functional MRI (Turner, 1994), which integrate imaging and electrophysiologic technologies, open exciting new windows on brain function in autism for the future.

As was true of attempts to define the fundamental cause of autism at the behavioral level, studies aimed at uncovering its neural basis have not yet succeeded. At the neural level, there is evidence to support a number of the behavioral hypotheses, and findings have suggested new behavioral theories, but an overarching theory remains elusive.

Issues at the Etiologic Level

Autism has many known etiologies (for reviews, see Gillberg, 1992; Gillberg & Coleman, 1992), yet etiology is unknown in most affected persons. Structural brain lesions, such as hydrocephalus (Fernell, Gillberg, & von Wendt, 1991), and other conditions producing diffuse or multifocal damage to the immature brain; biochemical lesions like PKU, adenylsuccinase deficiency, histidinemia, and others; the sequelae of infections including congenital rubella (Chess, Korn, & Fernandez, 1971); some disorders of neuronal migration, such as lissencephaly, tuberous sclerosis, hypomelanosis of Ito, and incontinentia pigmenti; a host of genetic syndromes, such as Williams Syndrome, Norrie Syndrome, and Rett's Syndrome; chromosome anomalies like Fragile X, Angelman Syndrome, and, occasionally, Down syndrome, account for a small minority of children with autistic symptomatology (Rutter, Bailey, Bolton, & Le Couteur, 1994). The role of epilepsy as a cause for autism is well accepted for infantile spasms (Taft & Cohen, 1971), although epilepsy seems to account for a minority of the children who undergo autistic regression or Childhood Disintegrative Disorder (personal observation; Rapin, 1995; Tuchman & Rapin, in press). It is critical to keep in mind that by no means are all children with these etiologic conditions autistic. Again, one is forced to conclude that the identity of the affected brain circuitry, and not what rendered it dysfunctional, determines whether the condition is associated with autistic symptomatology.

Epidemiologic studies and studies in monozygotic and same-sex dizygotic twins (Bailey et al., 1995; Folstein & Piven, 1991; Folstein & Rutter, 1977) indicate that genetics plays an important part in the etiology of so-called "primary" autism. The fact that monozygotic twins are not universally concordant or, if concordant, may be affected to quite a different degree, indicates that simple Mendelian inheritance does not provide a full explanation (nor does it in schizophrenia; Gottesman, 1991). Pedigrees show that Mendelian genetics do not account for the majority of families, although there are occasional families with patterns compatible with classic dominant or recessive inheritance (Ritvo, Brothers, & Pingree, 1988; Ritvo et al., 1985; Spiker et al., 1994). The strong predominance of autism in boys, which is more likely to have a genetic rather than an environmental basis, remains unexplained to date. Because environmental triggers appear to account for at least some cases of autistic regression, it would seem reasonable to invoke epigenetic environmental stressors affecting a genetically vulnerable child as a unifying etiologic theory for at least some cases of autistic regression and, perhaps, for autism in general.

What is clear is that etiology does not determine the behavioral autistic phenotype. Yet, some investigators would like to sort children into "primary" (etiology unknown, genetic?) and "secondary" autism (known specific etiology or nature of the underlying brain pathology). As more and more etiologies of autism are defined, "primary" autism will shrink to a residue as "secondary" autism grows; or, the designation of "primary" autism may be reserved for the almost-certainly-multiple genetic etiologies responsible for autism without overt evidence of structural brain malformation or damage. This brings us back to the behavioral definition of autism and to reiterating that etiologic and pathophysiologic considerations need to be kept separate from those at the behavioral level.

In short, studies at the etiologic level have shown that there is no unifying etiology for autism. A multiplicity of acquired and genetic insults can be associated with the behavioral phenotype. It may be that specific behaviorally defined *DSM-IV* subtypes such as Asperger's Syndrome and Rett's Syndrome (the latter more likely a biologic cause rather than a legitimate subtype) may be associated with particular genetic traits. However, until it has been determined at the behavioral level that subtypes of the autistic spectrum are more than arbitrarily defined clusters, their fuzziness will make phenotype–genotype correlations difficult.

CONCLUSIONS

Classification is a necessary first step toward the identification of an organism, phenomenon, or disorder to be studied. This review has brought out some of the problems inherent in the classification and subclassification of the disorders on the autism spectrum because of their fuzzy borders and their overlap with other disorders with which they share some symptomatology. Some of the problems of behavioral classification that depend on arbitrary cutoffs along dimensional continua have been emphasized; in general, categorical diagnostic criteria are nonexistent in behavioral classifications. Many of the disparate theories about *the* cause of autism are complementary rather than contradictory because they are concerned with distinct, entirely separate levels of causality. Etiology does not map onto behavior. There may never be *one* chemical, genetic, electrophysiologic, or neuroimaging test for autism; tests of this type may specify the etiology or neural basis of autism in a particular individual or group of individuals, but not its diagnosis, because the diagnosis of autism rests on behavioral criteria. There is clearly a much closer relation between neural pathophysiology and behavior, which inform one another, than between etiology and either behavior or pathophysiology. Etiology is critical for genetic counseling and, one hopes, ultimately, for prevention. Rational neuropharmacologic intervention depends on identification of the network(s) whose malfunction underlies autism and its neurotransmitter(s) or neuromodulator(s). Habilitation tailored to the individual requires neuropsychologic analysis of language and cognitive deficits and the devising of more effective ways to influence behavior. Research addressing all of the many facets of autism needs to be pursued at multiple levels and integrated, with a clear understanding of the complementarity and indispensability but separateness of the biologic and behavioral levels of investigation.

Cross-References

Issues of diagnosis and classification are discussed in Chapters 1 through 7. Neurobiological aspects of autism are discussed in Chapters 15 through 18.

REFERENCES

Aicardi, J. (1994). Syndrome of acquired aphasia with seizure disorder (epileptic aphasia, Landau-Kleffner Syndrome, verbal auditory agnosia with convulsive disorder), and continuous spike-waves during slow sleep ("electrical status epilepticus of slow sleep"). In J. Aicardi, *Epilepsy in children* (2nd ed., pp. 207–216). New York: Raven Press.

Akshoomoff, N.A., & Courchesne, E. (1992). A new role of the cerebellum in cognitive operations. *Behavioral Neuroscience, 106,* 157–168.

Allen, D.A., & Rapin, I. (1992). Autistic children are also dysphasic. In H. Naruse & E. Ornitz (Eds.), *Neurobiology of infantile autism* (pp. 157–168). Amsterdam, The Netherlands: Excerpta Medica.

Allen, D.A., Rapin, I., & Steinberg, M. (1997). *Autistic disorder versus PDD-NOS in preschool children: Same or different?*

American Psychiatric Association. (1980). *Diagnostic and statistical manual of mental disorders* (3rd ed.). Washington, DC: Author.

American Psychiatric Association. (1987). *Diagnostic and statistical manual of mental disorders* (3rd ed. rev.). Washington, DC: Author.

American Psychiatric Association. (1994). *Diagnostic and statistical manual of mental disorders* (4th ed.). Washington, DC: Author.

Anderson, G.M. (1994). Studies on the neurochemistry of autism. In M.L. Bauman & T.L. Kemper (Eds.), *The neurobiology of autism* (pp. 227–242). Baltimore: Johns Hopkins University Press.

Aram, D.M., & Healy, J.M. (1988). Hyperlexia: A review of extraordinary word recognition. In L.K. Obler & D. Fein (Eds.), *The exceptional brain: Neuropsychology of talent and special abilities* (pp. 70–102). New York: Guilford Press.

Asarnow, R. (1992). Childhood-onset schizophrenia. In S.J. Segalowitz & I. Rapin (Eds.), *Handbook of neuropsychology: Vol. 7. Child neuropsychology* (pp. 443–456). Amsterdam, The Netherlands: Elsevier Science.

Ayres, J.A., & Tickle, L.S. (1980). Hyper-responsivity to touch and vestibular stimuli as a predictor of positive response to sensory integration procedures by autistic children. *American Journal of Occupational Therapy, 34,* 375–386.

Bachevalier, J., & Merjanian, P.M. (1994). The contribution of medial temporal lobe structures in infantile autism: A neurobehavioral study in primates. In M.L. Bauman & T.L. Kemper (Eds.), *The neurobiology of autism* (pp. 146–169). Baltimore: Johns Hopkins University Press.

Bailey, A., Le Couteur, A., Gottesman, I., Bolton, P., Simonoff, E., Yuzda, E., & Rutter, M. (1995). Autism as a strongly genetic disorder: Evidence from a British twin study. *Psychological Medicine, 25,* 63–77.

Bailey, A., Luthert, P., Bolton, P., Le Couteur, A., & Rutter, M. (1993). Autism and megalencephaly. *Lancet, 341,* 1225–1226.

Baron-Cohen, S. (1989). Do autistic children have obsessions and compulsions? *British Journal of Clinical Psychology, 28,* 193–200.

Baron-Cohen, S., Leslie, A.M., & Frith, U. (1985). Does the autistic child have a "theory of mind"? *Cognition, 21,* 37–46.

Baron-Cohen, S., Tager-Flusberg, H., & Cohen, D.J. (Eds.). (1993). *Understanding other minds: Perspectives from autism.* Oxford, England: Oxford University Press.

Bartak, L., Rutter, M., & Cox, A. (1977). A comparative study of infantile autism and specific developmental receptive language disorders: 3. Discriminant function analysis. *Journal of Autism and Childhood Schizophrenia, 7,* 383–396.

Bauman, M.L., & Kemper, T.L. (1985). Histoanatomic observations of the brain in early infantile autism. *Neurology, 35,* 866–874.

Bauman, M.L., & Kemper, T.L. (1994). Neuroanatomic observations of the brain in autism. In M.L. Bauman & T.L. Kemper (Eds.), *The neurobiology of autism* (pp. 119–145). Baltimore: Johns Hopkins University Press.

Beaumanoir, A., Bureau, H., Deonna, T., Mira, L., & Tassinari, C.A. (Eds.). (1995). *Continuous spikes and waves during slow sleep: Acquired epileptic aphasia and related conditions.* London: John Libbey.

Bettelheim, B. (1967). *The empty fortress.* New York: Free Press.

Bishop, D.V.M., & Adams, C. (1989). Conversational characteristics of children with Semantic-Pragmatic Disorder: 2. What factors lead to a judgement of inappropriacy? *British Journal of Disorders of Communication, 24,* 241–263.

Burack, J.A., & Volkmar, F.R. (1992). Development of low- and high-functioning autistic children. *Journal of Child Psychology & Psychiatry & Allied Disciplines, 33,* 607–616.

Burd, L., Fisher, W., & Kerbeshian, J. (1989). Pervasive Disintegrative Disorder: Are Rett Syndrome and Heller dementia infantilis subtypes? *Developmental Medicine and Child Neurology, 31,* 609–616.

Cantwell, D.P., Baker, L., & Rutter, M. (1979). Families of autistic and dysphasic children: 1. Family life and interaction patterns. *Archives of General Psychiatry, 36,* 682–687.

Chess, S., Korn, S.J., & Fernandez, P.B. (1971). *Psychiatric disorders of children with congenital rubella.* New York: Brunner/Mazel.

Cohen, D.J., Paul, R., & Volkmar, F.R. (1987). Issues in the classification of pervasive developmental disorders and associated conditions. In D.J. Cohen, A.M. Donnellan, & R. Paul (Eds.), *Handbook of autism and pervasive developmental disorders* (pp. 20–40). New York: John Wiley & Sons.

Cohen, D.J., Volkmar, F., Anderson, G., & Klin, A. (1993). Integrating biological and behavioral perspectives in the study and care of autistic individuals: The future. *Israel Journal of Psychiatry and Related Sciences, 30,* 15–32.

Comings, D.E., & Comings, B.C. (1991). Clinical and genetic relationships between Autism-Pervasive Developmental Disorder and Tourette Syndrome: A study of 19 cases. *American Journal of Medical Genetics, 39,* 180–191.

Courchesne, E. (1991). Neuroanatomic imaging in autism. *Pediatrics, 87,* 781–790.

Courchesne, E., Press, G.A., & Yeung-Courchesne, R. (1994). Parietal lobe abnormalities detected with MR in patients with infantile autism. *American Journal of Roentgenology, 162,* 236–237.

Courchesne, E., Townsend, J., & Saitoh, O. (1994). The brain in infantile autism: Posterior fossa structures are abnormal. *Neurology, 44,* 214–223.

Courchesne, E., Yeung-Courchesne, R., Press, G.A., Hesselink, M.D., & Jernigan, T.L. (1988). Hypoplasia of cerebellar vermal lobules VI and VII in autism. *New England Journal of Medicine, 318,* 1349–1354.

Crosson, B. (1985). Subcortical functions in language: A working model. *Brain & Language, 25,* 257–292.

Damasio, A.R. (1994). *Descartes' error: Emotion, reason, and the human brain.* New York: Putnam.

Damasio, A.R., & Maurer, R.G. (1978). A neurological model for childhood autism. *Archives of Neurology, 35,* 777–786.

DeLong, G.R. (1992). Autism, amnesia, hippocampus, and learning. *Neuroscience Biobehavioral Review, 16,* 63–70.

DeLong, G.R. (1994). Children with autistic spectrum disorder and a family history of affective disorder. *Developmental Medicine and Child Neurology, 36,* 674–688.

DeLong, G.R., Bean, S.C., & Brown, F.R.I. (1981). Acquired reversible autistic syndrome in acute encephalopathic illness in children. *Archives of Neurology, 38,* 191–194.

DeMyer, M.K., Barton, S., DeMyer, W.E., Norton, J.A., Allen, J., & Steele, R. (1973). Prognosis in autism: A followup study. *Journal of Autism and Childhood Schizophrenia, 3,* 199–246.

DeMyer, M.K., Pontius, W., Norton, J.A., Barton, S., Allen, J., & Steele, R. (1972). Parental practices and innate activity in normal, autistic, and brain-damaged infants. *Journal of Autism and Childhood Schizophrenia, 2,* 49–66.

Deonna, T. (1991). Acquired epileptic aphasia in children (Landau-Kleffner Syndrome). *Journal of Clinical Neurophysiology, 8,* 288–298.

Deonna, T. (1993). Annotation: Cognitive and behavioural correlates of epileptic activity in children. *Journal of Clinical Neurophysiology, 34,* 611–620.

Deonna, T., Ziegler, A.L., Moura-Serra, J., & Innocenti, G. (1993). Autistic regression in relation to limbic pathology and epilepsy: Report of two cases. *Developmental Medicine and Child Neurology, 35,* 166–176.

Dugas, M., Gerard, C.L., Franc, S., & Sagar, D. (1991). Natural history, course and prognosis of the Landau and Kleffner Syndrome. In I. Pavao Martins, A. Castro-Caldas, H.R. van Dongen, & A. van Hout (Eds.), *Acquired aphasia in children: Acquisition and breakdown of language in the developing brain* (pp. 263–277). Dordrecht, The Netherlands: Kluwer Academic Publishers.

Dunn, M. (1994). Neurophysiologic observations in autism and implications for neurologic dysfunction. In M.L. Bauman & T.L. Kemper (Eds.), *The neurobiology of autism* (pp. 45–65). Baltimore: Johns Hopkins University Press.

Dunn, M., Gomes, H., & Sebastian, M. (1996). Prototypicality of responses in autistic language-disordered and normal children in a verbal fluency task. *Child Neuropsychology, 2,* 99–108.

Fernell, E., Gillberg, C., & von Wendt, L. (1991). Autistic symptoms in children with infantile hydrocephalus. *Acta Paediatrica Scandinavica, 80,* 451–457.

Filipek, P.A. (1995). Quantitative MRI in autism: The cerebellar vermis. *Current Opinion in Neurology, 2,* 134–138.

Filipek, P.A., Richelme, C., Kennedy, D.N., Rademacher, L., Pitcher, D.A., Zidel, S.Y., & Caviness, V.S.J. (1992). Morphometric analysis of the brain in developmental language disorders and autism [Abstract]. *Annals of Neurology, 32,* 475.

Folstein, S.E., & Piven, J. (1991). Etiology of autism: Genetic influences. *Pediatrics, 87,* 767–773.

Folstein, S.E., & Rutter, M. (1977). Infantile autism: A genetic study of 21 twin pairs. *Journal of Child Psychology and Psychiatry, 18,* 297–321.

Frith, U. (Ed.). (1991). *Autism and Asperger Syndrome.* Cambridge, England: Cambridge University Press.

Frith, U. (1993, June). Autism: Autistic individuals suffer from a biological defect. Although they cannot be cured, much can be done to make life more hospitable for them. *Scientific American, 6,* 108–114.

Gillberg, C. (1991). Autistic syndrome with onset at age 31 years: Herpes encephalitis as a possible model for childhood autism. *Developmental Medicine and Child Neurology, 33,* 920–924.

Gillberg, C. (1992). Subgroups of autism: Are there behavioral phenotypes typical of underlying medical conditions? *Journal of Intellectual Disability Research, 36,* 201–214.

Gillberg, C. (1993). Autism and related behaviours. *Journal of Intellectual Disability Research, 37,* 343–372.

Gillberg, C., & Coleman, M. (1992). *The biology of the autistic syndromes* (2nd ed., Clinics in Developmental Medicine No. 126). London: Mac Keith Press.

Goldman-Rakic, P.S., Funahashi, S., & Bruce, C.J. (1990). Neocortical memory circuits. *Cold Spring Harbor Symposium on Quantitative Biology, 55,* 1025–1038.

Gonzalez, N.M., Alpert, M., Shay, J., Campbell, M., & Small, A.M. (1993). Autistic children on follow-up: Change in diagnosis. *Psychopharmacology Bulletin, 29,* 353–358.

Gordon, E., Rennie, C., & Collins, L. (1990). Magnetoencephalography and late component

ERPs. *Clinical and Experimental Neurology, 27,* 113–120.

Gottesman, I.I. (1991). *Schizophrenia genesis: The origins of madness.* New York: W.H. Freeman.

Grandin, T., & Scariano, M.M. (1986). *Emergence: Labeled autistic.* Arena, CA: Arena Press.

Hagberg, B. (Ed.). (1993). *Rett Syndrome—Clinical and biological aspects* (Clinics in Developmental Medicine No. 127). London: Mac Keith Press.

Hagberg, B., Aicardi, J., Dias, K., & Ramos, O. (1983). A progressive syndrome of autism, dementia, ataxia, and loss of purposeful hand use in girls: Rett's Syndrome: Report of 35 cases. *Annals of Neurology, 14,* 471–479.

Hagberg, B., & Gillberg, C. (1993). Rett variants—Rettoid phenotypes. In B. Hagberg (Ed.), *Rett Syndrome—Clinical and biological aspects* (pp. 40–60). London: Mac Keith Press.

Hashimoto, T., Tayama, M., Miyazaki, M., Murakawa, K., Shimakawa, S., Yoneda, Y., & Kuroda, Y. (1993). Brain stem involvement in high-functioning autistic children. *Acta Neurologica Scandinavica, 88,* 123–128.

Hauser, S.L., DeLong, G.R., & Rosman, N.P. (1975). Pneumographic finding in the infantile autism syndrome: A correlation with temporal lobe disease. *Brain, 98,* 667–688.

Hobson, P. (1993). Understanding persons: The role of affect. In S. Baron-Cohen, H. Tager-Flusberg, & D.J. Cohen (Eds.), *Understanding other minds: Perspectives from autism* (pp. 204–227). Oxford, England: Oxford University Press.

Hobson, R.P., Ouston, J., & Lee, A. (1988). Emotion recognition in autism: Coordinating faces and voices. *Psychological Medicine, 18,* 911–923.

Hobson, R.P., Ouston, J., & Lee, A. (1989). Naming emotion in faces with voices: Abilities and disabilities in autism and mental retardation. *British Journal of Developmental Psychology, 7,* 237–250.

Holtum, J.R., Minshew, N.J., Sanders, R.S., & Phillips, N.E. (1992). Magnetic resonance imaging of the posterior fossa in autism. *Biological Psychiatry, 32,* 1091–1101.

Hsu, M., Yeung-Courchesne, R., Courchesne, E., & Press, G.A. (1991). Absence of magnetic resonance evidence of pontine abnormality in infantile autism. *Archives of Neurology, 48,* 1160–1163.

Jayakar, P., & Seshia, S.S. (1991). Electrical status epilepticus during slow-wave sleep: A review. *Journal of Clinical Neurophysiology, 8,* 299–311.

Karagan, N.J. (1979). Intellectual functioning in Duchenne muscular dystrophy. *Psychological Bulletin, 86,* 250–259.

Kennard, B.D., Emslie, G.J., & Weinberg, W.A. (1992). Mood, affect, and their disorders in children and adolescents. In S.J. Segalowitz & I. Rapin (Eds.), *Handbook of Neuropsychology: Vol. 7. Child neuropsychology* (pp. 331–355). Amsterdam, The Netherlands: Elsevier Science.

Killiany, R.J., & Moss, M.B. (1994). Memory functions and autism. In M.L. Bauman & T.L. Kemper (Eds.), *The neurobiology of autism* (pp. 170–194). Baltimore: Johns Hopkins University Press.

Kim, S., Ugurbil, K., & Strick, P.L. (1994). Activation of cerebellar output nucleus during cognitive processing. *Science, 265,* 949–951.

Kinsbourne, M. (1991). Overfocusing: An apparent subtype of Attention Deficit-Hyperactivity Disorder. In N. Amir, I. Rapin, & D. Branski (Eds.), *Pediatric neurology: Behavior and cognition of the child with brain dysfunction* (pp. 18–35). Basel, Switzerland: Karger.

Klein, S.K., Kurtzberg, D., Brattson, A., Kreuzer, J.A., Stapells, D.R., Dunn, M.A., Rapin, I., & Vaughan, H.G.J. (1995). Electrophysiologic manifestations of impaired temporal lobe auditory processing in verbal auditory agnosia. *Brain & Language, 51,* 383–405.

Klein, S.K., Tuchman, R.F., & Rapin, I. (1989). *The influence of premorbid language skills and behavior on language recovery in children with verbal auditory agnosia.*

Klin, A., Volkmar, F.R., & Sparrow, S.S. (1992). Autistic social dysfunction: Some limitations of the theory of mind hypothesis. *Journal of Child Psychology & Psychiatry & Allied Disciplines, 33,* 861–876.

Komoto, J., Usui, S., Otsuki, S., & Terao, A. (1984). Infantile autism and Duchenne muscular dystrophy. *Journal of Autism and Developmental Disorders, 14,* 191–195.

Kurita, H. (1985). Infantile autism with speech loss before the age of thirty months. *Journal of the American Academy of Child Psychiatry, 24,* 191–196.

Kurita, H. (1988). The concept and nosology of Heller's Syndrome: Review of articles and report of two cases. *Japanese Journal of Psychiatry and Neurology, 42,* 785–793.

Kurita, H., Kita, M., & Miyake, Y. (1992). A comparative study of development and symptoms among disintegrative psychosis and infantile autism with and without speech loss. *Journal of Autism and Developmental Disorders, 22,* 175–188.

Landau, W.M., & Kleffner, F.R. (1957). Syndrome of acquired aphasia with convulsive disorder in children. *Neurology, 7,* 523–530.

Leslie, A.M., & Frith, U. (1988). Autistic children's understanding of seeing, knowing and believing. *British Journal of Clinical Psychology, 6,* 315–324.

Lockyer, L., & Rutter, M. (1970). A five- to fifteen-year follow-up study of infantile psychosis: IV. Patterns of cognitive ability. *British Journal of Social and Clinical Psychology, 9,* 152–163.

Lord, C., Rutter, M., Goode, S., Heemsbergen, J., Jordan, H., Mawhood, L., & Schopler, E. (1989). Autistic Diagnostic Observation Schedule: A standardized observation of communicative and social behavior. *Journal of Autism and Developmental Disorders, 19,* 185–212.

Lord, C., Rutter, M., & Le Couteur, A. (1994). Autism Diagnostic Interview—Revised: A revised version of a diagnostic interview for caregivers of individuals with possible pervasive developmental disorders. *Journal of Autism and Developmental Disorders, 24,* 659–685.

Lord, C., & Venter, A. (1992). Outcome and follow-up studies of high-functioning autistic individuals. In E. Schopler & G.B. Mesibov (Eds.), *High-functioning individuals with autism* (pp. 187–199). New York: Plenum Press.

Lotspeich, L.J., & Cianarello, R.D. (1993). The neurobiology and genetics of infantile autism. *International Review of Neurobiology, 35,* 87–129.

Lotter, V. (1978). Follow-up studies. In M. Rutter & E. Schopler (Eds.), *Autism: A reappraisal of concepts and treatment* (pp. 475–495). New York: Plenum Press.

Lou, H. (1992). Cerebral single photon emission tomography (SPECT) and positron emission tomography (PET) during development and in learning disorders. In I. Rapin & S.J. Segalowitz (Eds.), *Handbook of neuropsychology: Vol. 6. Child neuropsychology* (pp. 331–338). Amsterdam, The Netherlands: Elsevier Science.

Lovaas, O.I. (1981). *Teaching developmentally disabled children: The me book.* Austin, TX: Pro-Ed.

Lovaas, O.I. (1987). Behavioral treatment and normal educational and intellectual functioning in young autistic children. *Journal of Consulting and Clinical Psychology, 55,* 3–9.

Maquet, P., Hirsch, E., Dive, D., Salmon, E., Marescaux, C., & Frank, G. (1990). Cerebral glucose utilization during sleep in Landau-Kleffner Syndrome. *Epilepsia, 31,* 778–783.

Mehler, M., & Dunn, M. (1995). *Cognitive and linguistic profiles of boys with Duchenne dystrophy.*

Mesulam, M.M. (1990). Large-scale neurocognitive networks and distributed processing for attention, language, and memory. *Annals of Neurology, 28,* 597–613.

Miller, L.K. (1989). *Musical savants: Exceptional skill in the mentally retarded.* Hillsdale, NJ: Erlbaum.

Milner, B. (1965). Visually-guided maze learning in man: Effects of bilateral hippocampal, bilateral frontal and unilateral cerebral lesions. *Neuropsychologia, 3,* 317–338.

Minshew, N.J. (1992). Neurological localization in autism. In E. Schopler & G.B. Mesibov (Eds.), *High-functioning individuals with autism* (pp. 65–89). New York: Plenum Press.

Minshew, N.J. (1994). In vivo brain chemistry of autism: ^{31}P magnetic resonance spectroscopy studies. In M.L. Bauman & T.L. Kemper (Eds.), *The neurobiology of autism* (pp. 86–101). Baltimore: Johns Hopkins University Press.

Minshew, N.J., Goldstein, G., Muenz, L.R., & Payton, J.B. (1992). Neuropsychological functioning in nonmentally retarded autistic individuals. *Journal of Clinical and Experimental Neuropsychology, 14,* 749–761.

Mountz, J.M., Tolbert, L.C., Lill, D.W., Katholi, C.R., & Liu, H.G. (1995). Functional deficits in autistic disorder: Characterization by technetium—99m—HMPAO and SPECT. *Journal of Nuclear Medicine, 36,* 1156–1162.

Mundy, P., & Sigman, M. (1989). The theoretical implications of joint-attention deficits in autism. *Development and Psychopathology, 1,* 173–183.

Mundy, P., Sigman, M., & Kasari, C. (1993). The theory of mind and joint-attention deficits in autism. In S. Baron-Cohen, H. Tager-Flusberg, & D.J. Cohen (Eds.), *Understanding other minds: Perspectives from autism* (pp. 181–203). Oxford, England: Oxford University Press.

Nicholson, L.V., Johnson, M.A., Bishby, K.M., Gardner-Medwin, D., Curtis, A., Ginjaar, I.B., den Dunnen, J.T., Welch, J.L., Butler, T.J., Bakker, E., van Ommen, G.-J.B., & Harris, J.B. (1993). Integrated study of 100 patients with Xp21 linked muscular dystrophy using clinical, genetic, immunochemical, and histopathological data: Part 1. Trends across the clinical groups. *Journal of Medical Genetics, 30,* 728–736.

Novick, B., Kurtzberg, D., & Vaughan, H.G. Jr. (1979). An electrophysiologic indication of auditory processing defects in autism. *Psychiatric Research, 1,* 101–108.

Obler, L.K., & Fein, D. (1988). *The exceptional brain: Neuropsychology of talent and special abilities.* New York: Guilford Press.

O'Connor, N., & Hermelin, B. (1987). Visual and graphic abilities of the idiot savant artist. *Psychological Medicine, 17,* 79–90.

Ornitz, E.M. (1989). Autism as the interface between sensory and information processing. In G. Dawson (Ed.), *Autism: Nature, diagnosis, and treatment* (pp. 174–207). New York: Guilford Press.

Ozonoff, S., & McEvoy, R.E. (1994). A longitudinal study of executive function and theory of mind development in autism. *Development and Psychopathology, 6,* 415–431.

Ozonoff, S., Pennington, B.F., & Rogers, S.J. (1991). Executive function deficits in high-functioning autistic individuals: Relationship to theory of mind. *Journal of Child Psychology and Psychiatry, 32,* 1081–1105.

Paquier, P.F., van Dongen, H.R., & Loonen, C.B. (1992). The Landau-Kleffner Syndrome or acquired aphasia with convulsive disorder. *Archives of Neurology, 49,* 354–359.

Piven, J., Berthier, M.L., Starkstein, S.E., Nehme, E., Pearlson, G., & Folstein, S. (1990). Magnetic resonance imaging evidence for a defect of cerebral cortical development in autism. *American Journal of Psychiatry, 147,* 734–739.

Piven, J., Nehme, E., Simon, J., Barta, P., Pearlson, G., & Folstein, S.E. (1992). Magnetic resonance imaging in autism: Measurement of the cerebellum, pons, and fourth ventricle. *Biological Psychiatry, 31,* 491–504.

Prizant, B., & Duchan, J.F. (1981). The functions of immediate echolalia in autistic children. *Journal of Speech and Hearing Research, 46,* 241–249.

Raichle, M.E. (1994). Positron emission tomographic studies of verbal response selection. In D.C. Gajdusek, G.M. McKhann, & L.C. Bolis (Eds.), *Evolution and neurology of language* (Discussions in Neuroscience, Vol. 10, pp. 130–136). Amsterdam, The Netherlands: Elsevier.

Rapin, I. (1995). Autistic regression and Disintegrative Disorder: How important the role of epilepsy? *Seminars in Pediatric Neurology, 2,* 278–285.

Rapin, I. (Ed.). (1996). *Preschool children with inadequate communication: Developmental language disorder, autism, mental deficiency*

(Clinics in Developmental Medicine No. 139). London: Mac Keith Press.

Rapin, I., & Allen, D.A. (1983). Developmental language disorders: Nosologic considerations. In U. Kirk (Ed.), *Neuropsychology of language, reading, and spelling* (pp. 155–184). New York: Academic Press.

Rapin, I., Mattis, S., Rowan, A.J., & Golden, G.S. (1977). Verbal auditory agnosia in children. *Developmental Medicine and Child Neurology, 19,* 192–207.

Ritvo, E.R., Brothers, A.M., & Pingree, C. (1988). Eleven possibly autistic parents. *Journal of Autism and Developmental Disorders, 18,* 139–141.

Ritvo, E.R., Freeman, B.J., Scheibel, A.B., Duong, T., Robinson, H., Guthrie, D., & Ritvo, A. (1986). Lower Purkinje cell counts in the cerebella of four autistic subjects: Initial findings of the UCLA–NSAC autopsy research report. *American Journal of Psychiatry, 143,* 862–866.

Ritvo, E.R., Spence, M.A., Freeman, B.J., Mason-Brothers, A.M., Mo, A., & Marazita, M.L. (1985). Evidence for autosomal recessive inheritance in 46 families with multiple incidences of autism. *American Journal of Psychiatry, 142,* 187–192.

Roulet Perez, E., Davidoff, V., Despland, P., & Deonna, T. (1993). Mental and behavioural deterioration in children with epilepsy and CSWS: Acquired epileptic frontal syndrome. *Developmental Medicine and Child Neurology, 35,* 661–674.

Rourke, B.P. (1989). *Nonverbal learning disabilities: The syndrome and the model.* New York: Guilford Press.

Rumsey, J.M. (1992). Neuropsychological studies in high-level autism. In E. Schopler & G.B. Mesibov (Eds.), *High-functioning individuals with autism* (pp. 41–64). New York: Plenum Press.

Rumsey, J.M., Andreason, N., & Rapoport, J. (1986). Thought, language, communication, and affective flattening in autistic adults. *Archives of General Psychiatry, 43,* 771–777.

Rumsey, J.M., Duara, R., Grady, C., Rapoport, J.L., Margolin, R.A., Rapoport, S.I., & Cutler, N.R. (1985). Brain metabolism in autism. *Archives of General Psychiatry, 42,* 448–455.

Rutter, M. (1979). Language, cognition, and autism. In R. Katzman (Ed.), *Congenital and acquired cognitive disorders* (pp. 247–264). New York: Raven Press.

Rutter, M., Bailey, A., Bolton, P., & Le Couteur, A. (1994). Autism and known medical conditions:

Myth and substance. *Journal of Child Psychology & Psychiatry & Allied Disciplines, 35,* 311–322.

Rutter, M., & Garmezy, N. (1983). Developmental psychopathology. In E.M. Hetherington (Ed.), *Socialization, personality, and social development. Mussen's handbook of child psychology* (4th ed., Vol. 4, pp. 775–911). New York: John Wiley & Sons.

Sanes, J.N., Dimitrov, B., & Hallett, M. (1990). Motor learning in patients with cerebellar dysfunction. *Brain, 113,* 103–120.

Scherg, M., & Picton, T.W. (1991). Separation and identification of event-related potential components by brain electric source analysis. In C.H.M. Brunia, G. Mulder, & M.N. Verbaten (Eds.), *Event-related potentials in the brain* (pp. 24–37). Amsterdam, The Netherlands: Elsevier.

Schmahmann, J. (1994). The cerebellum in autism: Clinical and anatomic perspectives. In M.L. Bauman & T.L. Kemper (Eds.), *The neurobiology of autism* (pp. 195–226). Baltimore: Johns Hopkins University Press.

Schopler, E., Reichler, R.J., & Renner, B.R. (1986). *The Childhood Autism Rating Scale (CARS) for diagnostic screening and classification in autism.* New York: Irvington.

Segawa, M., Katoh, M., Katoh, J., & Nomura, Y. (1992). Early modulation of sleep parameters and its importance in later behavior. *Brain Dysfunction, 5,* 211–223.

Semrud-Klikeman, M., & Hynd, G.W. (1990). Right hemisphere dysfunction in nonverbal learning disabilities: Social, academic and adaptive functioning in adults and children. *Psychological Bulletin, 107,* 196–209.

Siegel, B.V. Jr., Asarnow, R., Tanguay, P., Call, J.D., Abel, L., Ho, A., Lott, I., & Buchsbaum, M.S. (1992). Regional cerebral glucose metabolism and attention in adults with a history of childhood autism. *Journal of Neuropsychiatry and Clinical Neuroscience, 4,* 406–414.

Singer, H.S. (1994). Neurobiological issues in Tourette Syndrome. *Brain & Development, 16,* 353–364.

Slavik, B.A., Kitsuwa-Lowe, J., Danner, P.T., Green, J., & Ayres, A.J. (1984). Vestibular stimulation and eye contact in autistic children. *Neuropediatrics, 15,* 33–36.

Spiker, D., Lotspeich, L., Kraemer, H.C., Hallmayer, J., McMahon, W., Petersen, P.B., Nicholas, P., Pingree, C., Wiese-Slater, S., Chiotti, C., Wong, D.L., Dimiceli, S., Ritvo, E.R., Cavalli-Sforza, L.L., & Ciaranello, R.D. (1994). Genetics of autism: Characteristics of affected and unaffected children from 37 multiplex families. *American Journal of Medical Genetics, 54,* 27–35.

Stehli, A. (1991). *The sound of a miracle.* New York: Doubleday.

Sugiyama, T., & Abe, A. (1989). The prevalence of autism in Nagoya, Japan: A total population study. *Journal of Autism and Developmental Disorders, 19,* 87–96.

Sugiyama, T., Takei, Y., & Abe, T. (1992). The prevalence of autism in Nagoya, Japan: 2. A total population study for 10 years. In H. Naruse & E.M. Ornitz (Eds.), *Neurobiology of infantile autism* (pp. 181–184). Amsterdam, The Netherlands: Excerpta Medica.

Sverd, J. (1991). Tourette Syndrome and Autistic Disorder: A significant relationship. *American Journal of Medical Genetics, 39,* 173–179.

Taft, L.T., & Cohen, H.J. (1971). Hypsarrhythmia and childhood autism: A clinical report. *Journal of Autism and Childhood Schizophrenia, 1,* 327–336.

Tager-Flusberg, H. (1994). Dissociation in form and function in the acquisition of language by autistic children. In H. Tager-Flusberg (Ed.), *Constraints on language acquisition: Studies of atypical children* (pp. 175–194). Hillsdale, NJ: Erlbaum.

Tanguay, P. (1990). Infantile autism and social communication spectrum disorder. *Journal of the American Academy of Child and Adolescent Psychiatry, 29,* 854.

Treffert, D.A. (1989). *Extraordinary people: Understanding "idiots savants."* New York: Harper & Row.

Tsai, L. (1992). Diagnostic issues in high-functioning autism. In E. Schopler & G. Mesibov (Eds.), *High-functioning individuals with autism* (pp. 11–40). New York: Plenum Press.

Tuchman, R.F., & Rapin, I. (in press). Regression in Pervasive Developmental Disorders: Seizures and epileptiform EEG correlates. *Pediatrics.*

Tuchman, R.F., Rapin, I., & Shinnar, S. (1991a). Autistic and dysphasic children: I. Clinical characteristics. *Pediatrics, 88,* 1211–1218.

Tuchman, R.F., Rapin, I., & Shinnar, S. (1991b). Autistic and dysphasic children: II. Epilepsy. *Pediatrics, 88,* 1219–1225.

Turner, R. (1994). Magnetic resonance imaging of brain function. *Annals of Neurology, 35,* 637–638.

van Dongen, H.R., De Wijngaert, E., & Wennekes, M.J. (1991). Landau and Kleffner Syndrome: Diagnostic considerations. In I. Pavao Martins, A. Castro-Caldas, H.R. van Dongen, & A. van Hout (Eds.), *Acquired aphasia in children: Acquisition and breakdown of language in the developing brain* (pp. 253–261). Dordrecht, The Netherlands: Kluwer Academic Publishers.

Volkmar, F.R., Carter, A., Sparrow, S.S., & Cichetti, D.V. (1993). Quantifying social development in autism. *Journal of the American Academy of Child and Adolescent Psychiatry, 32,* 627–632.

Volkmar, F.R., & Cohen, D.J. (1989). Disintegrative disorder or "late onset" autism. *Journal of Child Psychology and Psychiatry, 30,* 717–724.

Volkmar, F.R., Cohen, D.J., Hoshino, Y., Rende, R.D., & Paul, R. (1988). Phenomenology and classification of the childhood psychoses. *Psychological Medicine, 18,* 191–201.

Waterhouse, L., Fein, D., & Modahl, C. (1996). Neurofunctional mechanisms in autism. *Psychological Reviews, 103,* 457–489.

Waterhouse, L., Morris, R., Allen, D.A., Fein, D., Dunn, M., Feinstein, C., Rapin, I., & Wing, L. (1996). Diagnosis and classification of autism. *Journal of Autism and Developmental Disorders, 26,* 59–86.

Williams, R.S., Hauser, S.L., Purpura, D.P., DeLong, G.R., & Swisher, C.W. (1980). Autism and mental retardation: Neuropathologic studies performed in four retarded persons with autistic behavior. *Archives of Neurology, 37,* 749–753.

Wing, L. (1988). The continuum of autistic characteristics. In E. Schopler & G. Mesibov (Eds.), *Diagnosis and assessment in autism* (pp. 91–110). New York: Plenum Press.

Wing, L. (1991). The relationship between Asperger's Syndrome and Kanner's autism. In U. Frith (Ed.), *Autism and Asperger Syndrome* (pp. 93–121). Cambridge, England: Cambridge University Press.

Wing, L. (1993). The definition and prevalence of autism: A review. *European Child and Adolescent Psychiatry, 2,* 61–74.

Witt Engerström, I. (1993). Evolution of clinical signs. In B. Hagberg (Ed.), *Rett Syndrome— Clinical and biological aspects* (Clinics in Developmental Medicine No. 127, pp. 26–39). London: Mac Keith Press.

World Health Organization. (1993). *Mental disorders: Glossary and guide to their classification in accordance with the tenth revision of the international classification of diseases.* Geneva, Switzerland: Author.

CHAPTER 40

Causal Mechanisms of Autism: Unifying Perspectives from an Information-Processing Framework

SALLY OZONOFF

Information processing paradigms have been used to identify the cognitive underpinnings of psychopathological conditions, such as schizophrenia (Goldberg, Gold, & Braff, 1991), depression (Ingram & Reed, 1986), and Attention Deficit Hyperactivity Disorder (ADHD; Schachar & Logan, 1990; Swanson et al., 1991), and to study autism as well (Burack, 1994; Courchesne, Akshoomoff, & Ciesielski, 1990; Hermelin & O'Connor, 1970; Ozonoff, Strayer, McMahon, & Filloux, 1994; Wainwright-Sharp, & Bryson, 1993). This chapter examines the utility of an information processing perspective for exploring the cognitive deficits of autism. First, the information processing framework is described. This is followed by an overview of previous research on causal mechanisms of autism. Issues that remain unresolved or require further clarification are highlighted. Recent work that has adopted an information processing framework to understand autism is then reviewed. Finally, how this perspective may be helpful in unifying previous empirical results and elucidating common underlying mechanisms is explored.

THE INFORMATION PROCESSING APPROACH

The information processing approach focuses on an understanding of the sequence of mental operations involved in the performance of a particular cognitive task (e.g., information input, encoding, transformation, selection, retrieval, and output). The information processing perspective is not a specific model or theory; rather, it is a broad framework for understanding cognition. It provides relatively theory-independent methods and specific experimental paradigms for understanding complex behavior (Anderson & Bower, 1973; Ingram, 1989). Thus, a variety of different cognitive models and constructs can be articulated and tested from within this framework.

One central methodologic strategy of the information processing approach is *component process analysis* (Farah, 1984; Friedrich & Rader, 1996). The goal of component process analysis is decomposition of complex cognitive functions into the elementary operations that appear to underlie them, the time course and relationship of these component processes to each other, and the internal representations, schemas, or codes they act upon (Friedrich & Rader, 1996). The component process approach has been used for many years in the fields of experimental psychology and cognitive neuropsychology. As explored below, this perspective has relevance for elucidating causal mechanisms of autism as well.

Preparation of this manuscript and the work described in it were supported by an NIMH FIRST Award (5R29MH52229-02). The author gratefully acknowledges the assistance of Fran Friedrich, who read and commented on an earlier draft of this chapter.

THE STUDY OF CAUSAL MECHANISMS IN AUTISM

In investigating the causal bases of any form of psychopathology, an interdependent set of analytic levels must be considered. Causal mechanisms operate at multiple levels, including genetic, neurological, cognitive, and behavioral levels (Pennington & Ozonoff, 1991). Reciprocal relationships exist among these different levels, such that anomalies at one level affect other levels. So, for example, genetic abnormalities may be expressed as neurological, cognitive, and/or behavioral abnormalities; likewise, cognitive dysfunction may have its roots in neurological or genetic dysfunction, and so on.

Research at the behavioral level, also known as phenotype analysis, is critical to investigations at all other levels (Rutter & Bailey, 1993). Before it is possible to isolate genetic or neurological mechanisms, the core or primary deficits of a disorder must be clearly differentiated from less central characteristics (Pennington & Ozonoff, 1991; Rapin, 1987; Sigman, 1994). So-called "primary symptoms" of a disorder are those that are: universally found among affected individuals, relatively specific to the disorder, present from an early age, and persistent throughout development. Associated secondary and correlated symptoms, on the other hand, are found in only a subset of affected individuals, may be present in other conditions, may markedly improve with age, and are not essential for diagnosis. In recent years, much progress has been made toward a taxonomy of autistic symptoms; there is general consensus that primary features include abnormalities in social reciprocity, pragmatic communication, and range of interests and behaviors (American Psychiatric Association, 1994; Rutter & Bailey, 1993; Rutter & Schopler, 1992). It should be noted, however, that relatively great behavioral heterogeneity exists within the autistic population. To the extent that phenotypic heterogeneity is a reflection of etiologic heterogeneity, the search for a universal and specific substrate of autism may be, at best, complicated, and, at worst, doomed to failure.

Research on autism conducted at the genetic level of analysis suggests that genetic factors play some role in development of the disorder (see Chapter 17). Progress has also been made at the neurological level of investigation (see Chapters 16 and 39). It has been assumed that the cause of autism would emerge from biological research, as this appeared to be the most direct, least inferential path of investigation. Given the size and complexity of the human genome and central nervous system, however, it is perhaps not surprising that this research has been so difficult. What is needed is some way to **focus** the search for biological substrates of the disorder. Frith (1989) has suggested that a better understanding of the cognitive bases of autism may inform biological studies. Cognitive and neuropsychological research has been used to inform, guide, and stimulate neurobiological and genetic investigations. Cognitive deficits are not thought to *cause* autism but may drive a cascade of developmental sequelae that result in particular symptoms of the disorder.

Many theories have been put forth regarding the nature of the cognitive dysfunction underlying autism (see Chapters 6 through 11). Candidates have included impairments in sensory modulation (Ornitz, 1985), arousal and attention (Dawson & Lewy, 1989), affective and interpersonal relatedness (Hobson, 1989), and language (Rutter, 1978). Recently, a candidate for a primary cognitive deficit was identified in the domain of mental state processing or "theory of mind." Early studies demonstrated that autistic children were unable to correctly predict the beliefs of others, while controls of lower mental age had little difficulty doing so (Baron-Cohen, Leslie, & Frith, 1985, 1986). This finding has since been replicated with several additional false-belief paradigms (Baron-Cohen, 1989; Harris & Muncer, 1988; Leekam & Perner, 1991; Leslie & Frith, 1989; Perner, Frith, Leslie, & Leekam, 1989).

Another candidate for a central cognitive deficit of autism is executive function impairment (Hughes, Russell, & Robbins, 1994; Ozonoff, 1995). Executive function is the cognitive construct used to describe goal-directed, future-oriented behaviors thought to be mediated by the frontal lobes (Duncan, 1986), including planning, inhibition of prepotent responses, flexibility, organized search, and use of working memory (Baddeley, 1986; Goldman-Rakic, 1987; Pennington, 1994). The striking similarity between the behavior of autistic individuals and that of patients with prefrontal damage has led to the suggestion that executive function impairment may be central to autism (Damasio & Maurer, 1978; Ozonoff, 1995). Like individuals with prefrontal lobe disorder, autistic individuals often appear rigid and inflexible, perseverative, narrowly focused on details, impulsive, and deficient in the ability to inhibit familiar or overlearned responses.

Supporting this behavioral analogy are several empirical reports of deficits in executive function in autistic people. Ozonoff, Pennington, and Rogers (1991) found that intellectually normal children with autism were highly deficient relative to controls on two executive function tasks, the Wisconsin Card Sorting Test and the Tower of Hanoi. Similar impairment has been found in preschoolers (McEvoy, Rogers, & Pennington, 1993), children and adolescents (Hughes et al., 1994; Hughes & Russell, 1993; Prior & Hoffman 1990), and adults (Rumsey, 1985; Rumsey & Hamburger, 1988) with autism on a variety of additional measures presumed to tap executive function. Ozonoff, Rogers, Farnham, and Pennington (1993) also found that executive function variables were best able to discriminate siblings of autistic subjects from siblings of learning disabled control subjects, indicating a possible subclinical marker of autism in the executive function domain. This growing body of research has led several investigators to hypothesize that executive function impairment, possibly mediated by prefrontal cortical dysfunction, underlies many symptoms of autism (Damasio & Maurer, 1978; Harris, 1993; Ozonoff, 1995; Pennington, 1994).

REMAINING ISSUES TO BE RESOLVED

A number of issues are yet to be resolved. First, the relationship between theory of mind and executive function impairment has not been clearly determined. The deficits may be independent modular cognitive operations that are parallel central impairments of autism, or one deficit may be generated by the other, or both may be driven by a third shared impairment (Ozonoff, 1995; Rutter & Bailey, 1993).

Second, the cognitive tasks typically employed suffer from great measurement imprecision. Most tap more than one cognitive operation, usually without specific scoring systems that permit individual variance to be parceled out and examined independently; an example is the Wisconsin Card Sorting Test (WCST), the most widely used measure of executive function in autism. Although the WCST is generally considered a test of cognitive flexibility, other operations appear to be required for successful performance, including attribute identification, categorization, working memory, inhibition, selective attention, and encoding of verbal feedback (Bond & Buchtel, 1984; Dehaene & Changeux, 1991; Ozonoff, 1995; Perrine, 1993; van der Does & van den Bosch, 1992).

Third, for a causal mechanism to have explanatory power, it should be relatively specific to the disorder it is intended to explain (Pennington & Ozonoff, 1991). Yet, difficulties in executive function are seen in a wide variety of disorders (Pennington, Bennetto, McAleer, & Roberts, 1996), including ADHD (Chelune, Ferguson, Koon, & Dickey, 1986), conduct disorders (Lueger & Gill, 1990), early-treated phenylketonuria (Welsh, Pennington, Ozonoff, Rouse, & McCabe, 1990), Obsessive-Compulsive Disorder (Head, Bolton, & Hymas, 1989), Tourette Syndrome (Bornstein, 1990; Gladstone et al., 1993), and schizophrenia (Axelrod, Goldman, Tompkins, & Jiron, 1994; Beatty, Jocic, Monson, & Katzung, 1994). If deficits in executive function generally distinguish "normal" from "abnormal," but are not specific indicators that distinguish one syndrome from another, their explanatory power is diminished.

Finally, identification of cognitive impairments should help predict and explain causal mechanisms at other analytic levels. One of the goals of cognitive analysis is to shed light on potential biological substrates of autism. Bailey (1993) has emphasized that neurobiological findings must help explain cognitive deficits, but the converse also applies: cognitive evidence should help elucidate affected neural structures, functions, or circuits. So far, this goal has not been attained.

BENEFITS OF AN INFORMATION PROCESSING APPROACH

The information processing approach and the use of component process analyses may be helpful in addressing the problems just identified in studying the causal mechanisms of autism.

How Are Executive Function and Theory of Mind Impairment Related?

At a superficial level of analysis, executive function and theory of mind appear rather dissimilar. Focusing on the content of the domains may, however, obscure similarities that exist at a process level of analysis.

The Smarties task is a standard false-belief measure (Perner et al., 1989). Subjects are shown a box of Smarties (similar to the American candy, M&M's) and asked what it contains. After a response is given, the box is opened to reveal that it actually holds a pencil. Subjects are then asked to predict what the next subject, who has never seen the box, will think it contains. A pass is scored if the subject responds, "Candy."

An analysis of this task (following Frye, Zelazo, & Palfai, in press) suggests that successful performance requires consideration of two mental perspectives and two types of cognitive judgments. The subject must attend to two different perspectives about the contents of the box—his or her own perspective and that of the other person—and must also make two types of judgments—what is *thought to be* in the box and *what is really* in the box. As Frye et al. (in press) explain, subjects must employ two recursive if–then rules to solve the problem correctly. Using only one or the other rule will result in an incorrect answer. Successful performance requires that the rules be considered in an embedded and sequential manner, for example, "If the question is about me, and if it is asking what the contents really are, then the answer is a pencil" versus "If the question is about someone else, and if it is asking what the contents are thought to be, then the answer is candy." Thus, a critical skill to successful solution of this false-belief task is *embedded use of if–then rules* (Frye et al., in press).

The Tower of Hanoi is a standard executive function measure in which subjects must sequentially move disks among pegs to duplicate a goal state determined by the experimenter. To receive a high score on this task, subjects must predict intermediate disk configurations produced by different potential moves, consider their implications for future disk configurations, and evaluate their utility toward eventual attainment of the goal state (Harris, 1993). Embedded rules, applied recursively, must again be used, for example, "If I move the blue disk to peg 3, then it will leave peg 1 open for the yellow disk, thus freeing up the red disk" (etc.).

This component process analysis suggests that theory of mind and executive function tasks, which appear rather different at the content level, may be quite similar at the process level. Tasks in both domains appear to require recursive or sequential analysis of information and embedded rule use (Frye et al., in press; Hughes & Russell, 1993). The focus is not on *what type* of information is processed, but on *how* it is processed. Thus, an important distinction between content and process is introduced by the information processing approach. Other impairments of autism that appear different at the macroanalytic, surface, or content level may be related at the microanalytic or process level.

Imprecision of Measurement

Information processing paradigms and component process analyses may also be helpful in reducing the measurement variance associated with standard neuropsychological tasks typically used in studies of autism. At least two advantages of information processing tasks are apparent. First, the methods employed help to minimize error variance that can be introduced during data collection. Information processing tasks are typically presented by computer, and precise reaction time and accuracy data are recorded. Thus, there is less opportunity for the administration and scoring errors that can occur during traditional neuropsychological testing. Second, information processing tasks measure very specific processes, such as target detection or response inhibition, and thus reduce unintentional measurement of other cognitive operations. Researchers can use component process analyses to identify the underlying cognitive operations that appear requisite to performance of a complex test and develop new tasks that isolate and selectively measure these individual components (Friedrich & Rader, 1996).

Hermelin and O'Connor (1970) conducted a pioneering series of investigations that explored perceptual, sensory, linguistic, attentional, and memorial functions in children with autism. This research was conducted prior to the era of computerized tasks, but the methods were similar to more recent information processing studies in the precision with which experimental paradigms selectively measured different components of cognitive function. Interest in cognition in autism was stimulated by Hermelin and O'Connor, but few researchers after them employed equally sophisticated experimental paradigms that carefully analyzed and measured specific elements of cognition. Cognitive research in the 1980s, especially the research on executive functions, was dominated by the use of neuropsychological tests, which tend to be less precise in their measurement characteristics than information processing paradigms.

Recently, researchers studying executive functions have adopted an information processing approach to explore the determinants of poor performance on standard executive function tasks, such as the WCST. As discussed above, the WCST appears to measure more than cognitive flexibility. To perform well on this task, subjects must be able to classify stimuli according to the abstract principles of color, shape, and number, inhibit previously reinforced responses, selectively attend to appropriate dimensions of the stimulus materials, and use verbal feedback provided in the context of a social interaction. When an individual receives a poor score on the WCST, it is difficult to determine which cognitive operations were responsible. Several information processing studies explore this question through decomposition of the WCST into its more elementary operations.

Ozonoff et al. (1994) used a Go–NoGo information processing task to examine inhibition and flexibility, two executive function component skills that appear important to

WCST performance. The Go–NoGo task consisted of three test conditions with a hierarchy of processing demands: (a) a "neutral inhibition" condition required subjects to respond to a neutral stimulus while simultaneously inhibiting responses to another neutral stimulus (this condition required no shifting of cognitive set); (b) a "prepotent inhibition" condition required inhibition of a previously reinforced, well-learned response; and (c) a "flexibility" condition necessitated frequent shifting from one response pattern to another and placed higher demands on cognitive flexibility.

Ozonoff et al. (1994) found that individuals with autism performed as well as controls when inhibiting neutral responses, but were moderately impaired when inhibiting prepotent responses, and very deficient in shifting their response set. Interpretation of these results was complicated, however, by a confounding of the inhibition and flexibility conditions. Specifically, the prepotent inhibition condition also required flexibility (i.e., when shifting from the response pattern required in the neutral inhibition condition to the new response mode necessitated by the prepotent inhibition condition). Because the two constructs were not measured independently, it was difficult to determine which cognitive operation, inhibition or flexibility, contributed more to the poor performance of the prepotent inhibition condition.

Ozonoff and Strayer (in press) conducted a second study that isolated inhibition and flexibility operations more completely. Two inhibition tasks were administered to a group of nonretarded children with autism and a matched sample of normally developing children. In the Stop–Signal measure (Logan, 1994; Logan, Cowan, & Davis, 1984), subjects were engaged in a simple task in which they categorized words as names of animals or nonanimals by pressing keys on a two-choice response box. On a subset of trials, an auditory signal was presented to indicate that responses to the primary task should be inhibited on that trial. Thus, this task measured the ability to control a voluntary motor response and did not require any flexibility.

The Negative Priming task (Tipper, 1985) measured a central cognitive inhibitory mechanism (Neill, Lissner, & Beck, 1990). In this task, subjects saw a five-letter string (e.g., TVTVT) and were asked to judge whether the second and fourth letters were "the same" or "different." On some trials, the target stimuli (letters 2 and 4) were the same as the distractor stimuli (letters 1, 3, and 5) from the immediately preceding trial. It has been demonstrated that when distractors from previous trials become targets on subsequent trials, performance is slower and less accurate than if the stimuli had not been previously seen (Tipper, 1985). This disruption in performance, termed the *negative priming effect,* is thought to be due to the "costs" of actively inhibiting attention to the stimulus when it was a distractor in earlier trials. Thus, a weak negative priming effect indicates deficient *cognitive inhibition* (Neill et al., 1990).

Ozonoff and Strayer (in press) found that subjects with autism were unimpaired, relative to age- and IQ-matched normal controls, on both tests of inhibition. On the Stop–Signal task, no group differences were evident in the likelihood of responding on signal trials (i.e., when responses should have been withheld). On the Negative Priming task, both groups demonstrated an intact negative priming effect and there were no significant group differences in the magnitude of this effect. When distractors on one trial became targets on subsequent trials, the act of previously ignoring these stimuli slowed reaction time and increased error rate to a similar extent in both groups. Thus, across tasks measuring both motor and cognitive components of inhibition, the inhibitory capacity of the autistic group was similar to that of matched normal controls.

Consistent results have been found by two other research teams employing different information processing paradigms. Hughes et al. (1994) used a computerized set-shifting task that measured flexibility while controlling for other cognitive processes that might be important to task performance. They found their autistic sample to be highly perseverative, which they attributed to deficits in flexibility "rather than low level motoric inhibition" (p. 488). Burack and Iarocci (1995) found no differences between autistic and matched mentally retarded individuals in their ability to filter distractors during an attentional task. Taken together, these results suggest that

inhibition may be a spared component of executive function in autism, standing in contrast to the impairments in flexibility that have been found in other studies (Hughes et al., 1994; Ozonoff et al., 1994). This body of research begins to clarify the cognitive dysfunction underlying the poor WCST performance of autistic individuals (Ozonoff et al., 1991; Prior & Hoffmann, 1990; Rumsey, 1985; Rumsey & Hamburger, 1988), suggesting that inhibitory dysfunction is not instrumental in driving this impairment.

Lack of Specificity of Causal Mechanisms

Certain putative primary deficits, especially those in the executive function realm, do not appear specific to the disorder. The umbrella category of executive function is composed of a variety of loosely related cognitive functions, such as planning, inhibition, organization, flexibility, and working memory. If the large construct of executive function is parsed into more unitary and functionally independent cognitive operations, it is possible that different neurodevelopmental disorders will be associated with different profiles of strength and weakness in executive function.

For example, as discussed above, evidence suggests that inhibitory function may be intact in individuals with autism (Burack & Iarocci, 1995; Ozonoff & Strayer, in press). In contrast, performance on the Negative Priming and Stop–Signal paradigms is deficient in adults with schizophrenia and children with attention problems (Beech, Powell, McWilliam, & Claridge, 1989; Schachar & Logan, 1990). These studies provide preliminary evidence that component executive functions are not only dissociable, but also are selectively associated with different disorders.

Just as the broad domain of executive function impairment is not specific to autism, neither is impairment in attentional processes. Attention deficits are a cardinal feature, of course, of ADHD, and are also prominent in Tourette Syndrome (Comings & Comings, 1987), schizophrenia (Bellak, 1994; Cornblatt & Keilp, 1994), and other disorders. Fortunately, research on attention in autism that has employed information processing paradigms has isolated and measured dissociable components of attention. As detailed below, paradigms first developed by cognitive psychologists to examine different types of attention (e.g., visuospatial vs. semantic, location-based vs. object-based, divided vs. focused, and so on) are now being used with samples of children with autism and other disorders. This research suggests that, just as with executive function, there are some distinctive relationships between different disorders and specific components of attention.

Courchesne et al. (1990, 1994) were the first to employ information processing paradigms to study attention in autistic people. They were particularly interested in how individuals with autism shifted or moved attention. As suggested by Posner (1980), orientation of attention requires that it be disengaged from its current location, moved to the new location, and reengaged there. Courchesne et al. (1990, 1994) found that nonretarded autistic adults performed as well as normal controls on a focused attention task that required no shifting. Performance was over six standard deviations below that of controls, however, on a task that required rapid alternation of attention between auditory and visual channels. The task was designed so that the disengage, move, and reengage components of attention could be examined relatively independently. Specifically, subjects were told to monitor one modality (either auditory or visual) until an oddball target was detected, and then immediately shift their attention to the other modality. "False alarm" errors occurred when subjects failed to disengage attention from the first modality and inappropriately continued to respond to old targets, and "misses" occurred when subjects failed to quickly move or reengage attention in the new channel, resulting in failure to detect new targets. Results suggested that the deficit of the autistic group was specific to the disengage operation, as evidenced by a high false alarm rate but a normal miss rate.

Another paradigm that has been used to study attention shifting in individuals with autism is the visuospatial orienting task of Posner (1980). In this task, two boxes are positioned on either side of a central fixation cross on a computer screen. Targets appear in one of the two boxes and subjects are instructed to respond to them as quickly as possible. A visuospatial cue is presented just before the target appears, indicating where attention should be directed. On valid cue trials, one of the boxes is brightened, followed by presentation of the target in that box. On invalid cue trials, one of the boxes is brightened, followed by presentation of the target in the opposite box. On neutral trials, both boxes brighten, rendering the cue uninformative. Typically, a validity effect is obtained, in which targets are processed more quickly on valid than on neutral trials and more slowly on invalid than on neutral trials.

Using Posner's paradigm (1980), Wainwright-Sharp and Bryson (1993) found no validity effect for autistic subjects when the cue was presented very briefly (100 msec), but a robust validity effect when the cue was presented for longer duration (800 msec). This suggested that autistic subjects took longer than controls to disengage attention from the fixation cross and move it to the location indicated by the cue. Very similar results were obtained by others using the same paradigm (Casey, Gordon, Mannheim, & Rumsey, 1993), reinforcing the suggestion that the disengage/move component of attention is dysfunctional in autism.

How specific is this particular attentional deficit to autism? Interestingly, the disengage/move operation appears unimpaired in children with ADHD on Posner's paradigm (Swanson et al., 1991). In contrast, ADHD subjects have difficulty with sustained attention and impulse control (Douglas & Peters, 1979), which appear to be relatively spared functions in autism (Buchsbaum et al., 1992; Casey et al., 1993; Garretson, Fein, & Waterhouse, 1990). Thus, considering attention as a multidimensional rather than a unitary construct has helped obtain more precision in the nature of the attentional dysfunction associated with autism, and has provided a preliminary double-dissociation between the attentional strengths and weaknesses of autism and ADHD.

Establishing Links with Other Analytic Levels

Component process analyses may be useful in elucidating brain–behavior relationships

(Friedrich, 1990). Complex tasks require distributed and integrated neural function for successful performance. When complex tasks are broken down into basic operations, the relationship between component cognitive functions and neural systems may be clearer. Posner (1987, cited in Friedrich, 1990) has suggested that component process analyses permit a mapping of cognitive and brain functions. For example, if component operations have separate neural substrates, their neurological underpinnings may be masked if the subcomponents are not dissociated and examined separately. In fact, the research of Posner and colleagues (Posner, 1980; Posner, Walker, Friedrich, & Rafal, 1984, 1987) has demonstrated that the disengage, move, and reengage components of spatial attention are, to some degree, functionally independent and dissociable. Selective brain damage can impair one component while sparing the others (Posner, 1988; Posner, Petersen, Fox, & Raichle, 1988).

Similarly, Fuster (1989) hypothesized that dissociable components of executive function are associated with specific prefrontal circuits and topographic cortical representation. Although this hypothesis is speculative, it suggests why previous research has not been more successful in identifying a common neural substrate for executive function deficits. Inhibition impairments may reflect different neural circuitry than flexibility or working memory deficits, for example.

Information processing approaches may also be useful in functional neuroimaging studies. Because information processing tasks are typically administered by computer, can be performed independently, and involve only minimal motor response on the part of subjects, they may be compatible with the requirements of imaging technology.

Information processing paradigms appear sensitive to individual differences (Friedrich & Rader, 1996); as such, they may be useful in genetic studies. An active search for subclinical markers of autism that may be more proximal to the presumed genotype is ongoing (Smalley & Asarnow, 1990). If a component of executive dysfunction is identified that is universal and specific to autism, information processing paradigms measuring this ability could be administered to nonautistic family members.

CONCLUSION

One goal of the information processing perspective is to identify basic cognitive operations that are dysfunctional in autism. A further objective of this approach is to elucidate relationships among genetic, neurobiological, and behavioral deficits of autism, tying them together in a way not previously possible. The identification of one cognitive process or operation responsible for all manifestations of the syndrome of autism is unlikely and unrealistic. However, as both Frith (1989) and Bailey (1993) have written, identification of specific cognitive impairments associated with autism may be a critical first step in understanding what causes this puzzling disorder. While we are still far from a unifying account of autism, the information processing approach provides new paradigms and general frameworks that may permit continued progress toward that goal.

Cross-References

Cognitive development in autism is discussed in Chapter 8. Psychological assessment methods are described in Chapter 19. Theory of mind in autism, and cognitive models of social dysfunction, are addressed in Chapters 41 and 43, respectively.

REFERENCES

American Psychiatric Association. (1994). *Diagnostic and statistical manual of mental disorders* (4th ed.). Washington, DC: Author.

Anderson, J.R., & Bower, G.H. (1973). *Human associative memory.* Hillsdale, NJ: Erlbaum.

Axelrod, B.N., Goldman, R.S., Tompkins, L.M., & Jiron, C.C. (1994). Poor differential performance on the Wisconsin Card Sorting Test in schizophrenia, mood disorder, and traumatic brain injury. *Neuropsychiatry, Neuropsychology, and Behavioral Neurology, 7,* 20–24.

Baddeley, A.D. (1986). *Working memory.* Oxford, England: Clarendon Press.

Bailey, A.J. (1993). The biology of autism. *Psychological Medicine, 23,* 7–10.

Baron-Cohen, S. (1989). Are autistic children behaviorists? An examination of their mental-physical and appearance-reality distinctions. *Journal of Autism and Developmental Disorders, 19,* 579–600.

Baron-Cohen, S., Leslie, A.M., & Frith, U. (1985). Does the autistic child have a "theory of mind?" *Cognition, 21,* 37–46.

Baron-Cohen, S., Leslie, A.M., & Frith, U. (1986). Mechanical, behavioral and intentional understanding of picture stories in autistic children. *British Journal of Developmental Psychology, 4,* 113–125.

Beatty, W.W., Jocic, Z., Monson, N., & Katzung, V.M. (1994). Problem solving by schizophrenic and schizoaffective patients on the Wisconsin and California Card Sorting Tests. *Neuropsychology, 8,* 49–54.

Beech, A., Powell, T., McWilliam, J., & Claridge, G. (1989). Evidence of reduced cognitive inhibition in schizophrenia. *British Journal of Clinical Psychology, 28,* 109–116.

Bellak, L. (1994). The schizophrenic syndrome and Attention Deficit Disorder: Thesis, antithesis, and synthesis? *American Psychologist, 49,* 25–29.

Bond, J.A., & Buchtel, H.A. (1984). Comparison of the Wisconsin Card Sorting Test and the Halstead Category Test. *Journal of Clinical Psychology, 40,* 1251–1255.

Bornstein, R.A. (1990). Neuropsychological performance in children with Tourette Syndrome. *Psychiatry Research, 33,* 73–81.

Buchsbaum, M.S., Siegel, B.V., Wu, J.C., Hazlett, E., Sicotte, N., Haier, R., Tanguay, P., Asarnow, R., Cadorette, T., Donoghue, D., Lagunas-Solar, M., Lott, I., Paek, J., & Sabalesky, D. (1992). Attention performance in autism and regional brain metabolic rate assessed by positron emission tomography. *Journal of Autism and Developmental Disorders, 22,* 115–125.

Burack, J.A. (1994). Selective attention deficits in persons with autism: Preliminary evidence of an inefficient attentional lens. *Journal of Abnormal Psychology, 103,* 535–543.

Burack, J.A., & Iarocci, G. (1995, March). *Visual filtering and covert orienting in developmentally disordered persons with and without autism.* Paper presented at the meeting of the Society for Research in Child Development, Indianapolis, IN.

Casey, B.J., Gordon, C.T., Mannheim, G.B., & Rumsey, J.M. (1993). Dysfunctional attention in autistic savants. *Journal of Clinical and Experimental Neuropsychology, 15,* 933–946.

Chelune, G.J., Ferguson, W., Koon, R., & Dickey, T.O. (1986). Frontal lobe disinhibition in Attention Deficit Disorder. *Child Psychiatry and Human Development, 16,* 221–234.

Comings, D.E., & Comings, B.G. (1987). A controlled study of Tourette Syndrome: Attention Deficit Disorder, learning disorders, and school problems. *American Journal of Human Genetics, 41,* 701–741.

Cornblatt, B.A., & Keilp, J.G. (1994). Impaired attention, genetics and the pathophysiology of schizophrenia. *Schizophrenia Bulletin, 20,* 31–46.

Courchesne, E., Akshoomoff, N.A., & Ciesielski, K. (1990). Shifting attention abnormalities in autism: ERP and performance evidence. *Journal of Clinical and Experimental Neuropsychology, 12,* 77.

Courchesne, E., Townsend, J.P., Akshoomoff, N.A., Yeung-Courchesne, R., Press, G.A., Murakami, J.W., Lincoln, A.J., James, H.E., Saitoh, O., Haas, R.H., & Schreibman, L. (1994). A new finding in autism: Impairment in shifting attention. In S.H. Broman & J. Grafman (Eds.), *Atypical cognitive deficits in developmental disorders: Implications for brain function* (pp. 101–137). Hillsdale, NJ: Erlbaum.

Damasio, A.R., & Maurer, R.G. (1978). A neurological model for childhood autism. *Archives of Neurology, 35,* 777–786.

Dawson, G., & Lewy, A. (1989). Arousal, attention and the socioemotional impairments of individuals with autism. In G. Dawson (Ed.), *Autism: Nature, diagnosis and treatment* (pp. 49–74). New York: Guilford Press.

Dehaene, S., & Changeux, J.P. (1991). The Wisconsin Card Sorting Test: Theoretical analysis and modeling in a neuronal network. *Cerebral Cortex, 1,* 62–79.

Douglas, V.I., & Peters, K.G. (1979). Toward a clearer definition of the attentional deficit of hyperactive children. In G.A. Hale & M. Lewis (Eds.), *Attention and cognitive development* (pp. 173–247). New York: Plenum Press.

Duncan, J. (1986). Disorganization of behavior after frontal lobe damage. *Cognitive Neuropsychology, 3,* 271–290.

Farah, M.J. (1984). The neurological basis of mental imagery: A componential analysis. *Cognition, 18,* 245–272.

Friedrich, F.J. (1990). Frameworks for the study of human spatial impairments. In R.P. Kesner & D.S. Olton (Eds.), *Neurobiology of comparative cognition* (pp. 317–337). Hillsdale, NJ: Erlbaum.

Friedrich, F.J., & Rader, S. (1996). Component process analysis in experimental and clinical neuropsychology. In M. Maruish & J. Moses (Eds.), *Theoretical foundations of clinical neuropsychology for clinical practitioners* (pp. 59–79) Hillsdale, NJ: Erlbaum.

Frith, U. (1989). *Autism: Explaining the enigma.* Oxford, England: Basil-Blackwell.

Frye, D., Zelazo, P.D., & Palfai, T. (in press). Theory of mind and rule-based reasoning. *Cognitive Development.*

Fuster, J.M. (1989). *The prefrontal cortex: Anatomy, physiology, and neuropsychology of the frontal lobe* (2nd ed.). New York: Raven Press.

Garretson, H.B., Fein, D., & Waterhouse, L. (1990). Sustained attention in children with autism. *Journal of Autism and Developmental Disorders, 20,* 101–114.

Gladstone, M., Carter, A.S., Schultz, R.T., Riddle, M., Scahill, L., & Pauls, D.L. (1993, February). *Neuropsychological functioning of children affected with Tourette Syndrome and Obsessive Compulsive Disorder.* Paper presented at the meeting of the International Neuropsychological Society, Galveston, TX.

Goldberg, T.E., Gold, J.M., & Braff, D.L. (1991). Neuropsychological functioning and time-linked information processing in schizophrenia. *Review of Psychiatry, 10,* 60–78.

Goldman-Rakic, P.S. (1987). Circuitry of primate prefrontal cortex and regulation of behavior by representational memory. In V.B. Mountcastle, F. Plum, & S.R. Geiger (Eds.), *Handbook of physiology: The nervous system* (pp. 373–417). Bethesda, MD: American Physiological Society.

Harris, P. (1993). Pretending and planning. In S. Baron-Cohen, H. Tager-Flusberg, & D.J. Cohen (Eds.), *Understanding other minds: Perspectives from autism* (pp. 228–246). New York: Oxford University Press.

Harris, P., & Muncer, A. (1988). *Autistic children's understanding of beliefs and desires.* Paper presented at the meeting of the British Psychological Society, Coleg Harlech.

Head, D., Bolton, D., & Hymas, N. (1989). Deficit in cognitive shifting ability in patients with Obsessive-Compulsive Disorder. *Biological Psychiatry, 25,* 929–937.

Hermelin, B., & O'Connor, N. (1970). *Psychological experiments with autistic children.* New York: Pergamon.

Hobson, R.P. (1989). Beyond cognition: A theory of autism. In G. Dawson (Ed.), *Autism: Nature, diagnosis and treatment* (pp. 22–48). New York: Guilford Press.

Hughes, C., & Russell, J. (1993). Autistic children's difficulty with mental disengagement from an object: Its implications for theories of autism. *Developmental Psychology, 29,* 498–510.

Hughes, C., Russell, J., & Robbins, T.W. (1994). Evidence for executive dysfunction in autism. *Neuropsychologia, 32,* 477–492.

Ingram, R.E. (1989). Information processing as a theoretical framework for child and adolescent psychiatry. In M.H. Schmidt & H. Remschmidt (Eds.), *Needs and prospects of child and adolescent psychiatry* (pp. 25–36). Lewiston, NY: Hogrefe and Huber.

Ingram, R.E., & Reed, M. (1986). Information encoding and retrieval processes in depression: Findings, issues, and future directions. In R.E. Ingram (Ed.), *Information processing approaches to clinical psychology* (pp. 3–21). Orlando, FL: Academic Press.

Leekam, S., & Perner, J. (1991). Does the autistic child have a theory of representation? *Cognition, 40,* 203–218.

Leslie, A., & Frith, U. (1989). Autistic children's understanding of seeing, knowing, and believing. *British Journal of Developmental Psychology, 6,* 315–324.

Logan, G. (1994). On the ability to inhibit thought and action: A user's guide to the stop-signal paradigm. In D. Dagenbach & T.H. Carr (Eds.), *Inhibitory processes in attention, memory and language* (pp. 189–239). San Diego: Academic Press.

Logan, G., Cowan, W.B., & Davis, K.A. (1984). On the ability to inhibit simple and choice reaction time responses: A model and a method. *Journal of Experimental Psychology: Human Perception and Performance, 10,* 276–291.

Lueger, R.J., & Gill, K.J. (1990). Frontal lobe cognitive dysfunction in conduct disorder adolescents. *Journal of Clinical Psychology, 46,* 696–706.

McEvoy, R.E., Rogers, S.J., & Pennington, B.F. (1993). Executive function and social communication deficits in young autistic children. *Journal of Child Psychology and Psychiatry, 34,* 563–578.

Neill, W.T., Lissner, L.S., & Beck, J.L. (1990). Negative priming in same-different matching: Further evidence for a central locus of inhibition. *Perception and Psychophysics, 48,* 398–400.

Ornitz, E.M. (1985). Neurophysiology of infantile autism. *Journal of the American Academy of Child Psychiatry, 24,* 251–262.

Ozonoff, S. (1995). Executive functions in autism. In E. Schopler & G.B. Mesibov (Eds.), *Learn-*

ing and cognition in autism (pp. 199–219). New York: Plenum Press.

Ozonoff, S. (1995). Reliability and validity of the Wisconsin Card Sorting Test in studies of autism. *Neuropsychology, 9,* 491–500.

Ozonoff, S., Pennington, B.F., & Rogers, S.J. (1991). Executive function deficits in high-functioning autistic individuals: Relationship to theory of mind. *Journal of Child Psychology and Psychiatry, 32,* 1081–1105.

Ozonoff, S., Rogers, S.J., Farnham, J.M., & Pennington, B.F. (1993). Can standard measures identify subclinical markers of autism? *Journal of Autism and Developmental Disorders, 23,* 429–441.

Ozonoff, S., & Strayer, D.L. (in press). Inhibitory function in nonretarded children with autism. *Journal of Autism and Developmental Disorders.*

Ozonoff, S., Strayer, D.L., McMahon, W.M., & Filloux, F. (1994). Executive function abilities in autism: An information processing approach. *Journal of Child Psychology and Psychiatry, 35,* 1015–1031.

Pennington, B.F. (1994). The working memory function of the prefrontal cortices: Implications for developmental and individual differences in cognition. In M.M. Haith, J. Benson, R. Roberts, & B.F. Pennington (Eds.), *Future-oriented processes in development* (pp. 243–289). Chicago: University of Chicago Press.

Pennington, B.F., Bennetto, L., McAleer, O., & Roberts, R.J. (1996). Executive functions and working memory: Theoretical and measurement issues. In G.R. Lyon & N.A. Krasnegor (Eds.), *Attention, memory, and executive function* (pp. 327–348). Baltimore: Brookes.

Pennington, B.F., & Ozonoff, S. (1991). A neuroscientific perspective on continuity and discontinuity in developmental psychopathology. In D. Cicchetti & S.L. Toth (Eds.), *Rochester Symposium on Developmental Psychopathology: Vol. 3. Models and integrations* (pp. 117–159). Rochester, NY: University of Rochester Press.

Perner, J., Frith, U., Leslie, A.M., & Leekam, S.R. (1989). Exploration of the autistic child's theory of mind: Knowledge, belief and communication. *Child Development, 60,* 689–700.

Perrine, K. (1993). Differential aspects of conceptual processing in the Category Test and Wisconsin Card Sorting Test. *Journal of Clinical and Experimental Neuropsychology, 15,* 461–473.

Posner, M.I. (1980). Orienting of attention. *Quarterly Journal of Experimental Psychology, 32,* 3–25.

Posner, M.I. (1988). Structures and functions of selective attention. In T. Boll & D.K. Bryant (Eds.), *Clinical neuropsychology and brain function: Research, assessment and practice* (pp. 173–202). Washington DC: American Psychological Association.

Posner, M.I., Petersen, S.E., Fox, P.T., & Raichle, M.E. (1988). Localization of cognitive operations in the human brain. *Science, 240,* 1627–1631.

Posner, M.I., Walker, J.A., Friedrich, F.J., & Rafal, R.D. (1984). Effects of parietal injury on covert orienting of attention. *Journal of Neuroscience, 4,* 1863–1874.

Posner, M.I., Walker, J.A., Friedrich, F.J., & Rafal, R.D. (1987). How do the parietal lobes direct covert attention? *Neuropsychologia, 25,* 134–145.

Prior, M.R., & Hoffmann, W. (1990). Neuropsychological testing of autistic children through an exploration with frontal lobe tests. *Journal of Autism and Developmental Disorders, 20,* 581–590.

Rapin, I. (1987). Searching for the cause of autism: A neurologic perspective. In D.J. Cohen & A.M. Donnellan (Eds.), *Handbook of autism and pervasive developmental disorders* (pp. 710–717). New York: John Wiley & Sons.

Rumsey, J.M. (1985). Conceptual problem-solving in highly verbal, nonretarded autistic men. *Journal of Autism and Developmental Disorders, 15,* 23–36.

Rumsey, J.M., & Hamburger, S.D. (1988). Neuropsychological findings in high-functioning autistic men with infantile autism, residual state. *Journal of Clinical and Experimental Neuropsychology, 10,* 201–221.

Rutter, M. (1978). Language disorder and infantile autism. In M. Rutter & E. Schopler (Eds.), *Autism: A reappraisal of concepts and treatment* (pp. 85–104). New York: Plenum Press.

Rutter, M., & Bailey, A. (1993). Thinking and relationships: Mind and brain (some reflections on theory of mind and autism). In S. Baron-Cohen, H. Tager-Flusberg, & D.J. Cohen (Eds.), *Understanding other minds: Perspectives from autism* (pp. 481–504). New York: Oxford University Press.

Rutter, M., & Schopler, E. (1992). Classification of pervasive developmental disorders: Some concepts and practical considerations. *Journal of Autism and Developmental Disorders, 22,* 459–482.

Schachar, R., & Logan, G.D. (1990). Impulsivity and inhibitory control in normal development and childhood psychopathology. *Developmental Psychology, 26,* 710–720.

Sigman, M. (1994). What are the core deficits in autism? In S.H. Broman & J. Grafman (Eds.), *Atypical cognitive deficits in developmental disorders: Implications for brain function* (pp. 139–157). Hillsdale, NJ: Erlbaum.

Smalley, S.L., & Asarnow, R.F. (1990). Cognitive subclinical markers in autism. *Journal of Autism and Developmental Disorders, 20,* 271–278.

Swanson, J.M., Posner, M., Potkin, S., Bonforte, S., Youpa, D., Fiore, C., Cantwell, D., & Crinella, F. (1991). Activating tasks for the study of visual-spatial attention in ADHD children: A cognitive anatomic approach. *Journal of Child Neurology, 6(Suppl.),* S119–S127.

Tipper, S.P. (1985). The negative priming effect: Inhibitory priming by ignored objects. *Quar-*

terly Journal of Experimental Psychology, 37, 571–590.

van der Does, A.W., & van den Bosch, R.J. (1992). What determines Wisconsin Card Sorting Test performance in schizophrenia? *Clinical Psychology Review, 12,* 567–583.

Wainwright-Sharp, J.A., & Bryson, S.E. (1993). Visual orienting deficits in high-functioning people with autism. *Journal of Autism and Developmental Disorders, 23,* 1–13.

Welsh, M.C., Pennington, B.F., Ozonoff, S., Rouse, B., & McCabe, E.R.B. (1990). Neuropsychology of early-treated PKU: Specific executive function deficits. *Child Development, 61,* 1697–1713.

CHAPTER 41

Theory of Mind in Autism: Its Relationship to Executive Function and Central Coherence

SIMON BARON-COHEN AND JOHN SWETTENHAM

Over the past decade, an important area of research in the psychology of autism has emerged, generating a considerable amount of scientific attention. This concerns the ability of children with autism (a) to appreciate their own and other people's mental states—such as their beliefs, desires, intentions, knowledge, pretense, and perception; and (b) to understand the links between mental states and action. This area is, for shorthand reasons, referred to as "theory of mind." This phrase was coined by Premack and Woodruff (1978). They suggested that the ability to reflect on mental states was theory-like because mental states are *unobservable* entities which we infer to be underlying people's actions; and because reference to mental states allows us to *explain and predict* other people's behavior with remarkable power. This gives it at least some of the properties of a theory.

In 1987, with the first edition of this book, work in theory of mind and autism had already begun. It did not surface there because of the time lag familiar in academic publishing. Thus, in reviewing this area, we will cite work from the mid-1980s. We begin with the review, and we then consider the relationship of this aspect of cognition in autism to two other cognitive processes: "executive function," and "central coherence." Like theory of mind, both of these have also emerged as important domains over the past decade of psychological research in autism.

DOES THE AUTISTIC CHILD HAVE A THEORY OF MIND?

This was the question—and the title of the paper—that opened this area (Baron-Cohen, Leslie, & Frith, 1985). The question was asked because of the interest that was developing concerning the normal child's understanding of mental states. Indeed, two years before this was asked of children with autism, the related question had been asked of normal 4-year-olds. To make this issue tractable, Wimmer and Perner (1983) had devised an elegant paradigm in which the child was presented with a short story, with the simplest of plots. The story essentially involved one character who was not present when an object was moved, and therefore did not *know* that the object was in a new location. The subject being tested is asked where the character thinks the object is. Wimmer and Perner called this the False Belief test; the focus was on the subject's ability to infer a story character's mistaken belief about a situation. These authors found that normal 4-year-olds could correctly infer that the character would think the object was where the character had last left it, rather than where it actually was. This was impressive evidence for the normal child's ability to distinguish between his or her own knowledge (about reality) and someone else's false belief (about reality).

The screening studies reported herein were supported by three sequential project grants from the Medical Research Council (MRC) (1988–1996).

When this test was given to a sample of children with autism, with mild degrees of mental handicap, a large majority of them "failed" the test by indicating that the character would think the object was where it actually was (Baron-Cohen et al., 1985). That is, they appeared to disregard the important information that, by virtue of being *absent* during the critical moving, the character's mental state would be different from the child's own mental state. In contrast, a control group of children with Down syndrome, with moderate degrees of mental handicap, passed this test as easily as the normal children. The implication was that the ability to infer mental states may be an aspect of social intelligence that is relatively independent of general intelligence (Cosmides, 1989), and that children with autism might be specifically impaired in the theory-of-mind domain.

Simply failing one test would not necessarily mean that children with autism lacked a theory of mind. One swallow does not make a summer. There might be many reasons for failure on such a test. (Interestingly, control questions in the original procedure ruled out memory, or language difficulties, or inattention as possible causes of failure.) The conclusion that children with autism are indeed impaired in the development of a theory of mind only becomes possible because of the convergence of results from widely differing experimental paradigms. These are reviewed in detail in an edited volume (Baron-Cohen, Tager-Flusberg, & Cohen, 1993) and for that reason are only briefly summarized in the next section.

SUMMARY OF RESULTS ON AUTISM AND THEORY OF MIND[1]

The majority of children with autism have the following characteristics:

1. They are at chance on tests of the *mental–physical distinction* (Baron-Cohen, 1989a); that is, they do not show a clear understanding of how physical objects differ from *thoughts* about objects.

[1] In the following list of studies, all of the tests mentioned are at the level of a normal 4-year-old child.

2. They have an appropriate understanding of the functions of the brain, but have a poor understanding of the functions of the mind (Baron-Cohen, 1989a); that is, they recognize that the brain's physical function is to make a person move and do things, but they do not spontaneously mention *the mind's mental function* (in thinking, dreaming, wishing, deceiving, and so on).

3. They also fail to make the *appearance–reality distinction* (Baron-Cohen, 1989a), meaning that, in their description of misleading objects (like a red candle in the shape of an apple), they do not distinguish between what the object *looks* like, and what they *know* it really is.

4. They fail a range of *first-order false belief* tasks, of the kind described in the previous section (Baron-Cohen et al., 1985, 1986; Leekam & Perner, 1991; Perner, Frith, Leslie, & Leekam, 1989; Reed & Peterson, 1990; Swettenham, 1996).

5. They also fail tests that assess whether they understand the principle that "seeing leads to knowing" (Baron-Cohen & Goodhart, 1994; Leslie & Frith, 1988). For example, when presented with two dolls, one of whom touches a box, and the other of whom *looks inside* the box, and when asked, "Which one *knows* what's inside the box?" they are at chance in their response. In contrast, normal children, at 3 to 4 years of age, correctly judge that the doll who looked is the one who knows what's in the box. (See Figure 41.1).

6. They are at chance in *recognizing mental state words* (like "think," "know," and "imagine") in a word list (Baron-Cohen et al., 1994).

7. They do not *produce* the same range of mental state words in their spontaneous speech (Baron-Cohen et al., 1986; Tager-Flusberg, 1992).

8. They are impaired in the production of *spontaneous pretend play* (Baron-Cohen, 1987; Lewis & Boucher, 1988; Wing, Gould, Yeates, & Brierley, 1977). Pretend play is relevant here simply because it is thought to involve understanding the mental state of *pretending*.

9. Although they can understand simple causes of emotion (such as situations and

The question:
which one knows what is in the box?

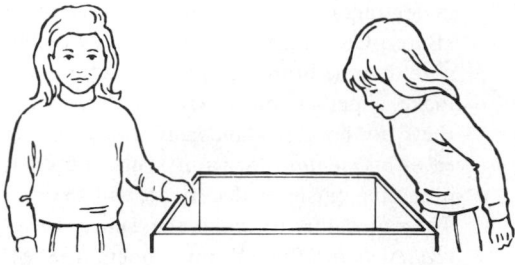

Sally touches   Anne looks
the box   inside the box

Figure 41.1 The "seeing-leads-to-knowing" test. After Baron-Cohen and Goodhart (1994). Adapted from Pratt and Bryant (1990).

desires), children with autism have difficulty understanding more *complex causes of emotion* (such as beliefs; Baron-Cohen, 1991a; Baron-Cohen, Spitz, & Cross, 1993). For example, they can understand that if Jane falls over and cuts her knee, she will feel sad, and that if John gets what he wants, he will feel happy. But they are poor at understanding that if John *thinks* he's getting what he wants (even if in reality he is not), he will feel happy.

10. They fail to recognize *the eye-region of the face* as indicating when a person is *thinking* and what a person might *want* (Baron-Cohen, Campbell, Karmiloff-Smith, Grant, & Walker, 1995; Baron-Cohen & Cross, 1992). For example, unlike normal 4-year-olds, they do not correctly judge which person is thinking in Figure 41.2, or which candy the cartoon character Charlie wants in Figure 41.3. Children and adults without autism use gaze to infer both of these mental states.

11. They fail to make the *accidental–intentional distinction* (Phillips, 1993); that is, they are poor at distinguishing whether someone "meant" to do something, or whether it simply happened accidentally.

12. They seem unable to *deceive* (Baron-Cohen, 1992; Sodian & Frith, 1992), a result that would be expected if they are unaware that people's beliefs can differ and therefore can be manipulated.

13. They fail tests of understanding metaphor, sarcasm, and irony, which are all *intentionally nonliteral statements* (Happé, 1994).

14. They fail to produce most aspects of *pragmatics* in their speech (reviewed in Baron-Cohen, 1988; see also Tager-Flusberg,

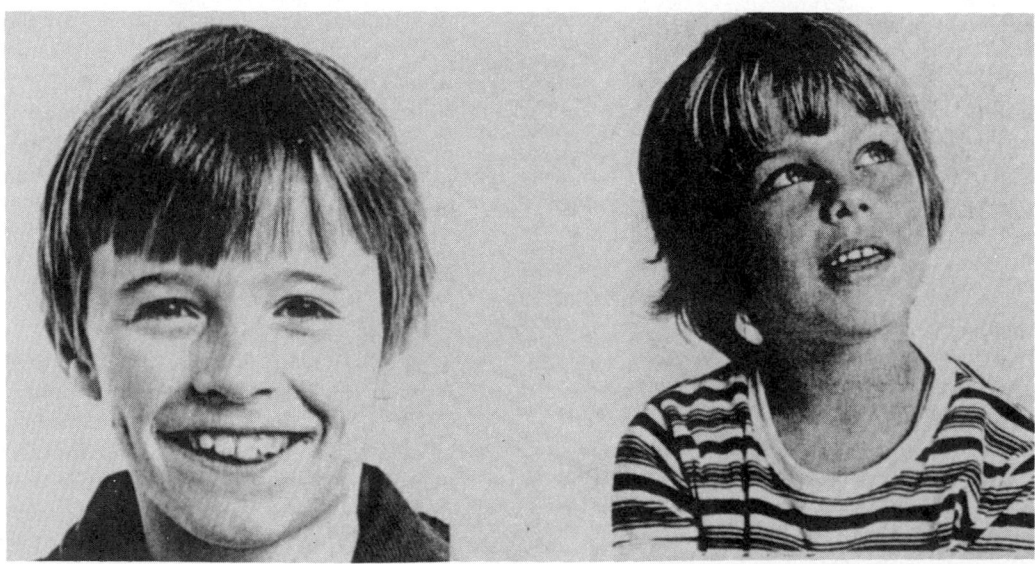

Figure 41.2 The "Which one is thinking?" test. From Baron-Cohen and Cross (1992).

Figure 41.3 The "Which candy does Charlie want?" test. From Baron-Cohen, Campbell, Karmiloff-Smith, Grant, and Walker (1995).

1993), and fail to recognize violations of pragmatic rules, such as the Gricean Maxims of conversational cooperation (Surian, Baron-Cohen, & Van der Lely, 1996). For example, if a character replies to a question with an irrelevant answer, normal young children are very sensitive to this pragmatic failure, but most children with autism are not. Because many pragmatic rules involve tailoring one's speech to what the listener needs to *know,* or might be *interested* in, this can be seen as intrinsically linked to a theory of mind.

This long list of experiments provides strong evidence for there being a theory of mind deficit in autism. For this reason, autism can be conceptualized as involving degrees of *mindblindness* (Baron-Cohen, 1990, 1995). One possibility arising from these studies is that there may be a particular part of the brain which, in the normal case, is responsible for understanding mental states, and which is specifically impaired in autism. If this view is correct, the assumption is that this may be for genetic reasons, because autism appears to be strongly heritable (see Chapter 17). The idea that the development of theory of mind is under genetic/biological control in the normal case is consistent with evidence from cross-cultural studies: Normally developing children from markedly different cultures seem to pass tests of theory of mind at roughly the same ages (Avis & Harris,

1991). The exact part of the brain that might be involved in this is not yet clear, although candidate regions include right orbitofrontal cortex, which is active when subjects are thinking about mental state terms during functional imaging using single photon emission tomography (SPECT; Baron-Cohen et al., 1994); and left medial frontal cortex, which is active when subjects are drawing inferences about thoughts while being PET- (positron emission tomography) scanned (Fletcher et al., 1995; Goel, Grafman, Sadato, & Hallett, 1995). Other candidate regions include the superior temporal sulcus and the amygdala (for reasons explained below). These regions may form parts of a neural *circuit* supporting theory-of-mind processing (Baron-Cohen & Ring, 1994). Finally, it is possible that the development of a theory of mind involves input from lower-level social perception systems, some of which may be impaired in autism (Baron-Cohen, 1994; Klin & Volkmar, 1993).

It is important to mention data that do not easily fit the strong form of the theory-of-mind hypothesis. First, a small minority of children or adults with autism pass first-order false-belief tests. (First-order tests involve inferring what one person thinks.) However, these individuals often fail second-order false-belief tests (Baron-Cohen, 1989b), that is, tests of understanding what one character thinks another character thinks. Such second-order reasoning is usually understood by normal children of 5 to 6 years of age, and yet these tests are failed by individuals with autism with a mental age above this level. We can therefore interpret these results in terms of there being a *specific developmental delay* in theory of mind at a number of different points.

Some individuals with autism who are very high-functioning (in terms of IQ and language level), and who are usually adults, may pass even second-order tests (Bowler, 1992; Happé, 1993; Ozonoff, Pennington, & Rogers, 1991). Those who can pass second-order tests correspondingly may have difficulties understanding figurative language (Happé, 1993), suggesting they do not have a normal theory of mind. Appropriate adult tests of theory of mind reveal these persisting deficits (Baron-

Cohen, Jolliffe, Mortimore, & Robertson, in press; Baron-Cohen & Hammer, in press).

In summary, the theory-of-mind deficit in the majority of cases with autism is very severe. It has the potential to explain the social, communicative, and imaginative abnormalities that are diagnostic of the condition, because being able to reflect on one's own mental states (and those of others) would appear to be essential in all of these domains. The theory-of-mind deficit has been found to correlate with real-life social skills, as measured by a modified version of the Vineland Adaptive Behavior Scales (Frith, Happé, & Siddons, 1994). In the next section, we consider the developmental origins of this cognitive deficit.

DEVELOPMENTAL ORIGINS OF THEORY OF MIND

In an influential article, Leslie (1987) proposed that, in the normal case, the developmental origins of theory of mind lay in the capacity for pretense, and that, in the case of children with autism, the developmental origins of the theory-of-mind deficit lay in their inability to pretend. In his model, pretense was the crucible for theory of mind because both involved the same computational complexity. Thus, to understand that someone else might *think* "This banana is real," or might *pretend* "This banana is real," the child (according to Leslie) would need to be able to represent the agent's *mental attitude* toward the proposition. One idea, then, is that theory of mind is first evident from about 18 to 24 months of age, in the normal toddler's emerging pretend play.

However, there is some evidence that theory of mind might have even earlier developmental origins. Soon after the first demonstrations of a theory-of-mind impairment in autism— and again, too late for inclusion into the first edition of this *Handbook*—Marian Sigman and her colleagues at UCLA reported severe deficits in *joint attention* skills in children with autism (Sigman, Mundy, Ungerer, & Sherman, 1986). Joint attention skills are behaviors, produced by the child, which involve monitoring or directing the target of attention of another person, so as to coordinate the

child's own attention with that of somebody else (Bruner, 1983). Such behaviors include the pointing gesture, gaze monitoring, and showing gestures, most of which are absent in most children with autism. This was an important discovery because joint attention behaviors are normally fully developed by about 14 months of age (Butterworth, 1991; Scaife & Bruner, 1975), so their absence in autism signifies a very early-occurring deficit. This was also important because the traditional theory-of-mind skills referred to above are mostly those one would expect to see in a 3- to 4-year-old normal child. Deficits in these areas cannot therefore be the developmentally earliest signs of autism, because we know that autism is present from at least the second year of life, if not earlier.

Implicit in the idea of joint attention deficits in autism was the notion that these might relate to a failure to appreciate other people's point of view (Sigman et al., 1986). Bretherton, McNew, and Beeghly-Smith (1981) had also suggested that joint attention should be understood as an implicit theory of mind. Baron-Cohen (1989c, 1989d, 1991b) explicitly argued that the joint attention and theory-of-mind deficits in autism were no coincidence, and proposed that joint attention was a *precursor* to the development of a theory of mind. In that study (Baron-Cohen, 1989c), young children (under 5 years old) with autism were shown to produce one form of the pointing gesture (imperative pointing, or pointing to request) while failing to produce another form of pointing (declarative pointing, or pointing to share interest). This dissociation was interpreted in terms of the declarative form of pointing being an indicator of the child's monitoring of another person's mental state—in this case, the mental state of "interest," or "attention." More recent laboratory studies have confirmed the lack of spontaneous gaze-monitoring (Leekam, Baron-Cohen, Brown, Perrett, & Milders, 1997; Phillips, Baron-Cohen, & Rutter, 1992). The demonstration of a joint attention deficit in autism and of the role that the superior temporal sulcus in the monkey brain plays in the monitoring of gaze direction (Perrett et al., 1985) has led to the idea that the superior temporal sulcus may be involved in the development of a theory of mind

(Baron-Cohen, 1994, 1995; Baron-Cohen & Ring, 1994).

AN APPLICATION TO THE EARLY DIAGNOSIS OF AUTISM

The work on the developmental origins of theory of mind is important not only for its theoretical interest (in terms of understanding normal development), but also for its value as a tool in lowering, into infancy, the age of diagnosis of autism. Thus, at 18 months of age, absence of joint attention, in combination with an absence of pretend play, is a very strong predictor of autism, both in a high-risk study of siblings who were undiagnosed (Baron-Cohen, Allen, & Gillberg, 1992), and in a random population study (Baron-Cohen, Cox, et al., 1996). In the latter study, 16,000 children were screened by their health visitors for these behaviors, using the Checklist for Autism in Toddlers (CHAT). Just 12 children out of the total population lacked joint attention and pretend play, of whom 10 were discovered to have clear autism. (The other two cases were not normal, but did not meet research criteria for autism.)

THEORY OF MIND, EXECUTIVE FUNCTION, AND CENTRAL COHERENCE

While there is now considerable evidence for the theory-of-mind deficit in autism, it is also clear that this is not the only cognitive deficit in autism. Two others have emerged as important in the past 5 years: (a) children with autism fail tests of "executive function," and (b) they also fail tests of "central coherence." Each of these is reviewed briefly below (see also Chapter 40). These additional deficits are important because although the theory-of-mind deficits may account for aspects of the social, communicative, and imaginative abnormalities, there are other symptoms (such as repetitive behavior, and unusual perception) that are not easily explained by the theory-of-mind deficits.

Executive Function and Autism

Executive function is the postulated mechanism that enables the normal person to shift attention flexibly, inhibit prepotent responses, generate goal-directed behavior, and solve problems in a planful, strategic way (see Baddeley, 1991; Shallice, 1988). The basic idea, developed by Norman and Shallice (1980), is that without a "central executive," or a "Supervisory Attentional System" (SAS) as it is also called, actions are controlled by the environment, and the organism simply responds to cues that elicit behavior. Without an SAS, action schemas or motor programs "contend" between themselves for execution. This takes place in a system known as the Contention Scheduling System (CSS). Shallice's notion is that the CSS is broadly a basal-ganglia function, and the SAS is basically a frontal lobe function. The SAS allows inhibition of routine (CSS) actions. The claim that the SAS is a frontal lobe function derives from the evidence that patients with frontal lobe damage fail tests of SAS (or executive) function.

Tests of executive function include the following:

1. The Wisconsin Card Sorting Test (Milner, 1964), in which the subject has to shift card-sorting strategies flexibly.
2. The Tower of Hanoi (and its modified version, the Tower of London; Shallice, 1982), in which the subject has to solve problems by planning before acting.
3. The Verbal Fluency Test (or F-A-S test; see Perret, 1974), in which the subject has to generate, in a fixed time period, novel examples of words beginning with a given letter.
4. The Detour Reaching Test (Diamond, 1991), in which the subject has to inhibit reaching straight for a visible goal, and must take a detour route to the goal instead.

Patients with frontal lobe damage fail on these tasks (reviewed in Shallice, 1988), and so do patients with autism (Hughes & Russell, 1993; Hughes, Russell, & Robbins, 1994; Ozonoff, Pennington, & Rogers, 1991; Prior & Hoffman, 1990; Rumsey & Hamburger, 1988). This observation has led to the conclusion that children with autism might have frontal lobe damage. Hughes and Russell (1993) have suggested that they might fail theory-of-mind tests listed earlier because they cannot "disengage from the salience of reality."

There seems little doubt that there is an executive dysfunction in autism, and that this is likely to be a sign of frontal pathology. However, it is important to note that executive dysfunction occurs in a large number of clinical disorders, and in this respect it is not specific to autism. Thus, the following eight patient groups all show impairments on different tests of executive function:

1. Schizophrenia (Elliot, McKenna, Robbins, & Sahakian, 1995; Frith, 1992; see Elliot & Sahakian, 1995, for a review).
2. Treated patients with PKU (Diamond, 1994; Pennington, van Doorninck, McCabe, & McCabe, 1985; Welsh, Pennington, Ozonoff, Rouse, & McCabe, 1990).
3. Obsessive-Compulsive Disorder (Christensen, Kim, Dysken, & Hoover, 1992; Head, Bolton, & Hymas, 1989; Zelinski, Taylor, & Juzwin, 1991).
4. Tourette's Syndrome (Baron-Cohen, Moriarty, Mortimore, & Robertson, 1995; Baron-Cohen & Robertson, 1995; Bornstein, 1990, 1991).
5. Attention Deficit with Hyperactivity Disorder (ADHD) (Chelune, Ferguson, Koon, & Dickey, 1986; Gorenstein, Mammato, & Sandy, 1989; Grodzinsky & Diamond, 1992; Loge, Staton, & Beatty, 1990).
6. Parkinson's disease (Downes et al., 1989).
7. Frontal lobe syndrome (Owen, Roberts, Polkey, Sahakian, & Robbins (1991).
8. Children and adults with mental handicap (Borys, Spitz, & Dorans, 1982).

This list implies that there is no specific mapping between psychiatric classification and the concept of what Baddeley and Wilson (1988) call a "dysexecutive syndrome" (Baron-Cohen & Moriarty, 1995). Because all of these conditions involve an executive impairment, and yet do not lead to autism, it follows that, by itself, an impairment in executive function cannot explain autism. In addition, because some studies now show a dissociation between executive function and theory of mind in some disorders (e.g., Tourette's Syndrome; Baron-Cohen, Moriarty,

et al., 1995), this means that they may be relatively independent processes.[2]

As presently construed, the concept of executive function may be too broad a level of analysis. The model suggests the presence of several component processes (generativity, attention shifting, disengaging, and so on), and perhaps specificity of deficit will be more apparent at this more fine-grained level of analysis. One example of a component process hypothesis is that, in autism, there is a deficit in "disengaging from the salience of reality." However, this cannot be correct in its strong form because, in a number of studies, subjects have to do just this, and yet children with autism *pass* these tests. The tests include:

1. Visual perspective taking (Baron-Cohen, 1989c, 1991c; Hobson, 1984; Tan & Harris, 1991). In these tasks, the child has to infer what someone else can see from his or her spatial position, even if this view is different from what the child currently sees.
2. False photograph tests (Leekam & Perner, 1991; Leslie & Thaiss, 1992; Swettenham, Baron-Cohen, Gomez, & Walsh, 1996). In these tasks, the child has to infer where something will be in an outdated photograph of reality, when the child knows that reality has been changed and the object is actually in a new position.
3. False map tests (Leekam & Perner, 1991; Leslie & Thaiss, 1992). This test uses a map instead of a photograph to measure the same ability as in the false photograph task.
4. False drawing tests (Charman & Baron-Cohen, 1992). These tasks test the same ability as the false photograph task, but a drawing is used instead of a photograph.
5. False model tests (Charman & Baron-Cohen, 1995). These tasks test the same ability as the false photograph task, but a model is used instead of a photograph.
6. Intellectual realism tests in drawing (Charman & Baron-Cohen, 1993). In these tasks,

---

[2] A further confound within the field of autism research is that many tests of theory of mind involve some attention shifting, and many tests of executive function involve taking into account one's own mental states, such as one's plans and thoughts.

the subject is asked to draw an object that is partially occluded—for example, a coffee mug whose handle is out of view. Children with autism show "intellectual realism" at the same mental age as do children without autism (i.e., below a mental age of about 6 years); they include the occluded part or object even though it is out of view. For example, they draw the handle of the coffee mug, even when it is not visible. (Not until after a mental age of about 6 years has been achieved will subjects (with or without autism) show "visual realism," drawing only what they see, not what they know about.) This task is relevant in that if children with autism were "prisoners" of reality, they would show precocious visual realism, which they do not.

For these reasons, it is likely that theory of mind is not reducible to executive function. Rather, executive function deficits in autism may cooccur with theory-of-mind deficits because of their shared frontal origin in the brain. Despite these provisos, the executive hypothesis of autism is important because of its potential to explain the perseverative, repetitive behaviors in this condition, which are not accounted for by the theory of mind hypothesis. Perseveration and repetitive behaviors are symptomatic of frontal lobe syndrome, in which executive dysfunction is also seen (Shallice, 1988). In this view, the two cognitive deficits may be separately responsible for different types of abnormal behavior.

Central Coherence and Autism

The third and last area of cognitive deficit in autism that is reviewed here is in what Frith (1989) calls "central coherence." This is a slippery notion to define; the essence of it is the normal drive to integrate information into context, gist, gestalt, and meaning. Frith argues that the autistic person's superior ability on the Embedded Figures Test (Shah & Frith, 1983; Jolliffe & Baron-Cohen, in press) and on an unsegmented version of the Block Design subtest in the Wechsler Intelligence Scale for Children (WISC) and Wechsler Adult Intelligence Scale (WAIS) (Shah &

Frith, 1993) arises because of a relative immunity to context effects in autism. Happé (in press) also reports a failure, by people with autism, to use context in reading, such that homophones are mispronounced (e.g., "There was a *tear* in her eye" might be misread so as to sound like "There was a *tear* in her dress"). A recent study has shown that children with autism are equally good at judging the identity of familiar faces in photographs, whether they are given the whole face or just part of the face. Nonautistic controls show a "global advantage" on such a test, performing significantly better when given the whole face, not just the parts of the face (Campbell, Baron-Cohen, & Walker, 1995). The central coherence account of autism is attractive in having the potential to explain the nonholistic, piecemeal, perceptual style characteristic of autism, and the unusual cognitive profile seen in this condition (including the islets of ability).

As with the other two theories, it appears that a strong version of the central coherence account cannot be correct because children with autism perform in line with their mental age on a range of tasks that would seem to involve integration across context. These include: (a) *transitive inference* tests (Scott & Baron-Cohen, 1996); (b) *analogical reasoning* tests (Scott & Baron-Cohen, 1996); and (c) *counterfactual syllogistic reasoning* tests (Scott, Baron-Cohen, & Leslie, 1995).

Happé (in press) reports that some high-functioning patients with autism who pass second-order theory-of-mind tasks nevertheless fail tasks of central coherence, such as the homophone task mentioned earlier. This dissociation implies that theory of mind and central coherence may also be relatively independent processes (Frith & Happé, 1994). In sum, a strong version of the central coherence theory would suggest that individuals with autism should be unable to recognize whole objects, and only perceive their parts, which we know does not occur. Instead, a weak form of central coherence theory seems likely to be correct, disabling individuals with autism from making full use of context. Whether this can account for islets of ability in autism (and even in Idiot Savant Syndrome) remains to be investigated in detail.

SUMMARY AND FUTURE DIRECTIONS

In this chapter, we have reviewed evidence for a theory-of-mind deficit in autism. We have also looked at two other cognitive deficits, in executive function and central coherence and have concluded that the theory of mind, executive function, and central coherence deficits are relatively independent of one another. Given this independence, one possibility is that there is a specific theory-of-mind mechanism (ToMM; Leslie, 1987, 1991; Leslie & Roth, 1993) and it is specifically damaged in autism. Leslie suggests that the function of such a mechanism is to represent information in a data structure, as shown in the following example:

Agent—Attitude—"Proposition"

Fred thinks "the safe is behind the Picasso."

Such a proposal is sufficient to allow representation of the full range of mental states in the Attitude slot. Explaining exactly how the brain is able to implement such a process will be important for future research, not only in relation to understanding the normal brain, but also in relation to autism. Circumventing theory-of-mind deficits through the use of carefully designed teaching methods will also be an important goal for applied research in this area. This research is already underway, with some promising results (Hadwin, Baron-Cohen, Howlin, & Hill, 1995; Swettenham, 1996; Swettenham et al., 1996). Ultimately, any biological theory of autism will have to account not only for specific genetic abnormalities, but also for how such abnormalities cause brain damage of the type that causes the specific cognitive deficits reviewed above.

We close with four questions for future research.

1. If, in autism, there are cognitive deficits in all three domains reviewed here (theory of mind, executive function, and central coherence), which of these are *necessary and sufficient* for the development (and diagnosis) of autism? We can clarify this question using the Venn diagram method in Figure 41.4. In which

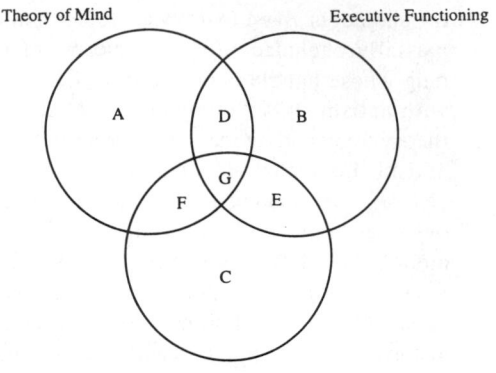

Figure 41.4   A Venn diagram of the possible relationship among deficits in theory of mind, executive function, and central coherence. Different diagnostic groups and subgroups may correspond to the different regions in the diagram. For example, autism may only occur in regions A, D, F and G, and these may reflect subtly different subgroups. See text for details.

regions of the diagram do individuals with autism fall? Only in regions A, D, F, and G? Are these different subtypes of autism?

2. Related to the first question, how do cognitive deficits in each of these three areas map on to areas of abnormal behavior? Do the three cognitive domains correlate with the three behavioral domains to which they have been theoretically tied? (To recap, the theory-of-mind deficit has been theoretically tied to the abnormal social, communicative, and imaginative development; the central coherence deficit has been theoretically tied to the abnormalities in perception and in processing contextual information; and the executive function deficit has been theoretically tied to the presence of repetitive behavior and cognitive inflexibility.) Do correlational studies bear out these mappings between cognition and behavior?

3. Which other psychiatric conditions might correspond to the "pure" or combined forms of executive function, central coherence, or theory-of-mind deficits? Can one derive any specificity between diagnosis and type of cognitive deficit, for each of the lettered regions in Figure 41.4?

4. Are these three domains of cognition really independent of each other, as the Venn

diagram implies? Double dissociations should be possible among all of these, if they are truly independent processes. If not, how might they relate to one another? We hope that such questions will be answerable in the next edition of the *Handbook*.

Cross-References

Aspects of social development in autism and a critique of theory of mind are provided in Chapters 8 and 43. Cognitive aspects of autism are discussed in Chapters 11 and 19. Executive function studies are reviewed in Chapter 40, and language aspects of theory of mind are discussed in Chapter 42.

REFERENCES

Avis, J., & Harris, P. (1991). Belief–desire reasoning among Baka children: Evidence for a universal conception of mind. *Child Development, 62,* 460–467.

Baddeley, A. (1991). *Human memory: Theory and practice.* Hillsdale, NJ: Erlbaum.

Baddeley, A., & Wilson, B. (1988). Frontal amnesia and the dysexecutive syndrome. *Brain and Cognition, 7,* 212–230.

Baron-Cohen, S. (1987). Autism and symbolic play. *British Journal of Developmental Psychology, 5,* 139–148.

Baron-Cohen, S. (1988). Social and pragmatic deficits in autism: Cognitive or affective? *Journal of Autism and Developmental Disorders, 18,* 379–402.

Baron-Cohen, S. (1989a). Are autistic children behaviorists? An examination of their mental-physical and appearance-reality distinctions. *Journal of Autism and Developmental Disorders, 19,* 579–600.

Baron-Cohen, S. (1989b). The autistic child's theory of mind: A case of specific developmental delay. *Journal of Child Psychology and Psychiatry, 30,* 285–298.

Baron-Cohen, S. (1989c). Perceptual role-taking and protodeclarative pointing in autism. *British Journal of Developmental Psychology, 7,* 113–127.

Baron-Cohen, S. (1989d). Joint attention deficits in autism: Towards a cognitive analysis. *Development and Psychopathology, 1,* 185–189.

Baron-Cohen, S. (1990). Autism: A specific cognitive disorder of "mindblindness." *International Review of Psychiatry, 2,* 79–88.

Baron-Cohen, S. (1991a). Do people with autism understand what causes emotion? *Child Development, 62,* 385–395.

Baron-Cohen, S. (1991b). Precursors to a theory of mind: Understanding attention in others. In A. Whiten (Ed.), *Natural theories of mind* (pp. 233–252). Oxford, England: Basil Blackwell.

Baron-Cohen, S. (1991c). The development of a theory of mind in autism: Deviance and delay? *Psychiatric Clinics of North America, 14,* 33–51.

Baron-Cohen, S. (1992). Out of sight or out of mind: Another look at deception in autism. *Journal of Child Psychology and Psychiatry, 33,* 1141–1155.

Baron-Cohen, S. (1994). How to build a baby that can read minds: Cognitive mechanisms in mindreading. *Cahiers de Psychologie Cognitive/Current Psychology of Cognition, 13*(5), 513–552.

Baron-Cohen, S. (1995). *Mindblindness: An essay on autism and theory of mind.* Cambridge, MA: MIT Press.

Baron-Cohen, S., Allen, J., & Gillberg, C. (1992). Can autism be detected at 18 months? The needle, the haystack, and the CHAT. *British Journal of Psychiatry, 161,* 839–843.

Baron-Cohen, S., Campbell, R., Karmiloff-Smith, A., Grant, J., & Walker, J. (1995). Are children with autism blind to the mentalistic significance of the eyes? *British Journal of Developmental Psychology, 13,* 379–398.

Baron-Cohen, S., Cox, A., Baird, G., Swettenham, J., Morgan, K., Drew, A., Charman, T., & Nightingale, N. (1996). Psychological markers of autism at 18 months of age in a large population. *British Journal of Psychiatry, 168,* 158–163.

Baron-Cohen, S., & Cross, P. (1992). Reading the eyes: Evidence for the role of perception in the development of a theory of mind. *Mind and Language, 6,* 173–186.

Baron-Cohen, S., & Goodhart, F. (1994). The "seeing leads to knowing" deficit in autism: The Pratt and Bryant probe. *British Journal of Developmental Psychology, 12,* 397–402.

Baron-Cohen, S., & Hammer, J. (in press). Parents of children with Asperger syndrome: What is the cognitive phenotype? *Journal of Cognitive Neuroscience.*

Baron-Cohen, S., Jolliffe, T., Mortimore, C., & Robertson, M. (in press). Another advanced test of theory of mind: Evidence from high functioning adults with autism or Asperger syndrome. *Journal of Child Psychology and Psychiatry.*

Baron-Cohen, S., Leslie, A.M., & Frith, U. (1985). Does the autistic child have a "theory of mind?" *Cognition, 21,* 37–46.

Baron-Cohen, S., Leslie, A.M., & Frith, U. (1986). Mechanical, behavioral and Intentional understanding of picture stories in autistic children. *British Journal of Developmental Psychology, 4,* 113–125.

Baron-Cohen, S., & Moriarty, J. (1995). Developmental dysexecutive syndrome: Does it exist? A neuropsychological perspective. In M. Robertson & V. Eapen (Eds.), *Movement and allied disorders in childhood.* Chichester, England: John Wiley & Sons.

Baron-Cohen, S., Moriarty, J., Mortimore, C., & Robertson, M. (1995). *An investigation of executive function in Gilles de la Tourette Syndrome.* Manuscript submitted for publication, University of Cambridge, Cambridge, England.

Baron-Cohen, S., & Ring, H. (1994). A model of the mindreading system: neuropsychological and neurobiological perspectives. In P. Mitchell & C. Lewis (Eds.), *Origins of an understanding of mind* (pp. 305–316). Hillsdale, NJ: Erlbaum.

Baron-Cohen, S., Ring, H., Moriarty, J., Shmitz, P., Costa, D., & Ell, P. (1994). Recognition of mental state terms: A clinical study of autism, and a functional neuroimaging study of normal adults. *British Journal of Psychiatry, 165,* 640–649.

Baron-Cohen, S., & Robertson, M. (1995). Children with either autism, Gilles de la Tourette Syndrome, or both: Mapping cognition to specific syndromes. *Neurocase, 1,* 101–104.

Baron-Cohen, S., Spitz, A., & Cross, P. (1993). Can children with autism recognize surprise? *Cognition and Emotion, 7,* 507–516.

Baron-Cohen, S., Tager-Flusberg, H., & Cohen, D.J. (Eds.). (1993). *Understanding other minds: Perspectives from autism.* Oxford: Oxford University Press.

Bornstein, R. (1990). Neuropsychological performance in children with Tourette Syndrome. *Psychiatry Research, 33,* 73–81.

Bornstein, R. (1991). Neuropsychological correlates of obsessive characteristics in Tourette Syndrome. *Journal of Neuropsychiatry and Clinical Neurosciences, 3,* 157–162.

Borys, S., Spitz, H., & Dorans, B. (1982). Tower of Hanoi performance of retarded young adults and nonretarded children as a function of solution length and goal state. *Journal of Experimental Psychology, 33,* 87–110.

Bowler, D.M. (1992). Theory of mind in Asperger Syndrome. *Journal of Child Psychology and Psychiatry, 33,* 877–893.

Bretherton, I., McNew, S., & Beeghly-Smith, M. (1981). Early person knowledge as expressed in gestural and verbal communication: When do infants acquire a "theory of mind?" In M. Lamb & L. Sharrod (Eds.), *Infant social cognition* (pp. 333–374). Hillsdale, NJ: Erlbaum.

Bruner, J. (1983). *Child's talk.* Oxford: Oxford University Press.

Butterworth, G. (1991). What minds have in common is space. *British Journal of Developmental Psychology, 9,* 55–72.

Campbell, R., Baron-Cohen, S., & Walker, J. (1995). *Do people with autism show a whole face advantage in recognition of familiar faces and their parts? A test of central coherence theory.* Unpublished manuscript, University of London, Goldsmiths College.

Charman, T., & Baron-Cohen, S. (1992). Understanding beliefs and drawings: A further test of the metarepresentation theory of autism. *Journal of Child Psychology and Psychiatry, 33,* 1105–1112.

Charman, T., & Baron-Cohen, S. (1993). Drawing development in autism: The intellectual to visual realism shift. *British Journal of Developmental Psychology, 11,* 171–185.

Charman, T., & Baron-Cohen, S. (1995). Understanding models, photos, and beliefs: A test of the modularity thesis of metarepresentation. *Cognitive Development, 10,* 287–298.

Chelune, G., Ferguson, W., Koon, R., & Dickey, T. (1986). Frontal lobe disinhibition in Attention Deficit Disorder. *Child Psychiatry and Human Development, 16,* 221–234.

Christensen, K., Kim, S., Dysken, M., & Hoover, K. (1992). Neuropsychological performance in Obsessive Compulsive Disorder. *Biological Psychiatry, 31,* 4–18.

Cosmides, L. (1989). The logic of social exchange: Has natural selection shaped how humans reason? Studies with the Wason Selection Task. *Cognition, 31,* 187–276.

Diamond, A., (1991). Neuropsychological insights into the meaning of object concept development. In S. Carey & R. Gelman (Eds.), *The epigenesis of mind: Essays on biology and knowledge* (pp. 67–110). Hillsdale, NJ: Erlbaum.

Diamond, A., (1994). Phenylaline levels of 6–10 mg/dl may not be as benign as once thought. *Acta Paediatrica, 83,* 89–91.

Downes, J., Roberts, A., Sahakian, B., Evenden, J., Morris, R., & Robbins, T. (1989). Impaired extra-dimensional shift performance in medicated and unmedicated Parkinson's disease: Evidence for a specific attentional dysfunction. *Neuropsychologia, 27,* 1329–1343.

Elliot, R., McKenna, P., Robbins, T., & Sahakian, B. (1995). Neuropsychological evidence for frontostriatal dysfunction in schizophrenia. *Psychological Medicine, 25.*

Elliot, R., & Sahakian, B. (1995). The neuropsychology of schizophrenia: Relations with clinical and neurobiological dimensions. *Psychological Medicine, 25.*

Fletcher, P., Happé, F., Frith, U., Baker, S., Dolan, R., Frackowiak, R., & Frith, C. (1995). Other minds in the brain: A functional imaging study of "theory of mind" in story comprehension. *Cognition, 57,* 109–128.

Frith, U. (1989). *Autism: Explaining the enigma.* Oxford, England: Basil Blackwell.

Frith, U., & Happé, F. (1994). Autism: Beyond "theory of mind." *Cognition, 50,* 115–132.

Frith, U., Happé, F., & Siddons, F. (1994). Autism and theory of mind in everyday life. *Social Development, 3,* 108–124.

Goel, V., Grafman, J., Sadato, N., & Hallett, M. (1995). Modeling other minds. *Neuroreport, 6,* 1741–1746.

Gorenstein, E., Mammato, C., & Sandy, J. (1989). Performance of inattentive-overactive children on selected measures of prefrontal type. *Journal of Clinical Psychology, 45,* 619–632.

Grodzinsky, G., & Diamond, A. (1992). Frontal lobe functioning in boys with Attention Deficit Hyperactivity Disorder. *Developmental Neuropsychology, 8,* 427–445.

Hadwin, J., Baron-Cohen, S., Howlin, P., & Hill, K. (1996). Can we teach children with autism to understand emotions, belief, or pretence? *Development and Psychopathology, 8,* 345–365.

Happé, F. (1993). Communicative competence and theory of mind in autism: A test of relevance theory. *Cognition, 48,* 101–119.

Happé, F. (1994). An advanced test of theory of mind: Understanding of story characters' thoughts and feelings by able autistic, mentally handicapped, and normal children and adults. *Journal of Autism and Developmental Disorders, 24,* 129–154.

Happé, F. (in press). Central coherence and theory of mind in autism. *British Journal of Developmental Psychology.*

Head, D., Bolton, D., & Hymas, N. (1989). Deficit in cognitive shifting ability in patients with Obsessive-Compulsive Disorder. *Biological Psychiatry, 25,* 929–937.

Hobson, R.P. (1984). Early childhood autism and the question of egocentrism. *Journal of Autism and Developmental Disorders, 14,* 85–104.

Hughes, C., & Russell, J. (1993). Autistic children's difficulty with mental disengagement from an object: Its implications for theories of autism. *Developmental Psychology, 29,* 498–510.

Hughes, C., Russell, J., & Robbins, T. (1994). Specific planning deficit in autism: Evidence of a central executive dysfunction. *Neuropsychologia, 3,* 477–492.

Jolliffe, T., & Baron-Cohen, S. (in press). Are high functioning adults with autism or Asperger syndrome faster than normal on the Embedded Figures Test? *Journal of Child Psychology and Psychiatry.*

Klin, A., & Volkmar, F. (1993). The development of individuals with autism: implications for the theory of mind hypothesis. In S. Baron-Cohen, H. Tager-Flusberg, & D. Cohen (Eds.), *Understanding other minds: Perspectives from autism* (pp. 317–332). Oxford: Oxford University Press.

Leekam, S., Baron-Cohen, S., Brown, S., Perrett, D., & Milders, M. (1997). Eye-direction detection: A dissociation between geometric and joint-attention skills in autism. *British Journal of Developmental Psychology.*

Leekam, S., & Perner, J. (1991). Does the autistic child have a metarepresentational deficit? *Cognition, 40,* 203–218.

Leslie, A.M. (1987). Pretence and representation: The origins of "theory of mind." *Psychological Review, 94,* 412–426.

Leslie, A.M. (1991). The theory of mind impairment in autism: Evidence for a modular mechanism of development? In A. Whiten (Ed.), *Natural theories of mind* (pp. 63–78). Oxford, England: Basil Blackwell.

Leslie, A.M., & Frith, U. (1988). Autistic children's understanding of seeing, knowing, and believing. *British Journal of Developmental Psychology, 6,* 315–324.

Leslie, A., & Roth, D. (1993). What can autism teach us about metarepresentation? In S. Baron-Cohen, H. Tager-Flusberg, & D. Cohen (Eds.), *Understanding other minds: Perspectives from autism* (pp. 83–111). Oxford, England: Oxford Medical Publications.

Leslie, A.M., & Thaiss, L. (1992). Domain specificity in conceptual development: Evidence from autism. *Cognition, 43,* 225–251.

Lewis, V., & Boucher, J. (1988). Spontaneous, instructed and elicited play in relatively able autistic children. *British Journal of Developmental Psychology, 6,* 325–339.

Loge, D., Staton, D., & Beatty, W. (1990). Performance of children with ADHD on tests sensitive to frontal lobe dysfunction. *Journal of the American Academy of Child and Adolescent Psychiatry, 29,* 540–545.

Milner, B. (1964). Some effects of frontal lobectomy in man. In J. Warren & K. Akert (Eds.), *The frontal granular cortex and behaviour.* New York: McGraw-Hill.

Norman, D., & Shallice, T. (1980). Attention to action: Willed and automatic control of behavior. In R. Davidson, G. Schwartz, & D. Shapiro (Eds.), *Consciousness and self-regulation* (Vol. 4). New York: Plenum Press.

Owen, A., Roberts, A., Polkey, C., Sahakian, B., & Robbins, T. (1991). Extradimensional versus intradimensional set shifting performance following frontal lobe excisions, temporal lobe excisions, or amygdalo-hippocampectomy in man. *Neuropsychologia, 10,* 99–1006.

Ozonoff, S. (1997, this volume).

Ozonoff, S., Pennington, B., & Rogers, S. (1991). Executive function deficits in high-functioning autistic children: Relationship to theory of mind. *Journal of Child Psychology and Psychiatry, 32,* 1081–1106.

Ozonoff, S., Strayer, L., McMahon, A., & Filloux, F. (1994). Executive function abilities in autism and Tourette Syndrome: An information processing approach. *Journal of Child Psychology and Psychiatry, 35,* 1015–1032.

Pennington, B., van Doorninck, W., McCabe, L., & McCabe, E. (1985). Neurological deficits in early treated phenylketonurics. *American Journal of Mental Deficiency, 89,* 467–474.

Perner, J., Frith, U., Leslie, A.M., & Leekam, S. (1989). Exploration of the autistic child's theory of mind: Knowledge, belief, and communication. *Child Development, 60,* 689–700.

Perret, E. (1974). The left frontal lobe of man and the suppression of habitual responses in verbal categorical behaviour. *Neuropsychologia, 16,* 527–537.

Perrett, D., Smith, P., Potter, D., Mistlin, A., Head, A., Milner, A., & Jeeves, M. (1985). Visual cells in the temporal cortex sensitive to face view and gaze direction. *Proceedings of the Royal Society of London, B223,* 293–317.

Phillips, W. (1993). *Understanding intention and desire by children with autism.* Unpublished doctoral dissertation, University of London, Institute of Psychiatry.

Phillips, W., Baron-Cohen, S., & Rutter, M. (1992). The role of eye-contact in the detection of goals: Evidence from normal toddlers, and children with autism or mental handicap. *Development and Psychopathology, 4,* 375–383.

Pratt, C., & Bryant, P. (1990). Young children understand that looking leads to knowing (so long as they are looking into a single barrel). *Child Development, 61,* 973–983.

Premack, D., & Woodruff, G. (1978). Does the chimpanzee have a "theory of mind?" *Behaviour and Brain Sciences, 4,* 515–526.

Prior, M., & Hoffman, W. (1990). Neuropsychological testing of autistic children through exploration with frontal lobe tests. *Journal of Autism and Developmental Disorders, 20,* 581–590.

Reed, T., & Peterson, C. (1990). A comparative study of autistic subjects' performance at two levels of visual and cognitive perspective taking. *Journal of Autism and Developmental Disorders, 20,* 555–568.

Rumsey, J., & Hamburger, S. (1988). Neuropsychological findings in high-functioning men with infantile autism, residual state. *Journal of Clinical and Experimental Nueuropsychology, 10,* 201–221.

Rumsey, J., & Hamburger, S. (1990). Neuropsychological divergence of high-level autism and severe dyslexia. *Journal of Autism and Developmental Disorders, 20,* 155–168.

Scaife, M., & Bruner, J. (1975). The capacity for joint visual attention in the infant. *Nature, 253,* 265–266.

Scott, F., & Baron-Cohen, S. (1996). Logical, analogical, and psychological reasoning in autism: A test of the Cosmides theory. *Development and Psychopathology, 8,* 235–246.

Scott, F., Baron-Cohen, S., & Leslie, A. (1995). *"If pigs could fly": An examination of imagination and counterfactual reasoning in autism.* Unpublished manuscript, University of London.

Shah, A., & Frith, U. (1983). An islet of ability in autism: A research note. *Journal of Child Psychology and Psychiatry, 24,* 613–620.

Shah, A., & Frith, U. (1993). Why do autistic individuals show superior performance on the block design test? *Journal of Child Psychology and Psychiatry, 34,* 1351–1364.

Shallice, T. (1982). Specific impairments of planning. *Philosophical Transactions of the Royal Society of London, B298,* 199–209.

Shallice, T. (1988). *From neuropsychology to mental structure.* Cambridge, England: Cambridge University Press.

Sigman, M., Mundy, P., Ungerer, J., & Sherman, T. (1986). Social interactions of autistic, mentally retarded, and normal children and their caregivers. *Journal of Child Psychology and Psychiatry, 27,* 647–656.

Sodian, B., & Frith, U. (1992). Deception and sabotage in autistic, retarded, and normal children. *Journal of Child Psychology and Psychiatry, 33,* 591–606.

Surian, L., Baron-Cohen, S., & Van der Lely, H. (1996). Are children with autism deaf to Gricean Maxims? *Cognitive Neuropsychiatry, 1,* 55–72.

Swettenham, J. (1996). Can children be taught to understand false belief using computers? *Journal of Child Psychology and Psychiatry.*

Swettenham, J., Baron-Cohen, S., Gomez, J.-C., & Walsh, S. (1996). What's inside a person's head? Conceiving of the mind as a camera helps children with autism develop an alternative theory of mind. *Cognitive Neuropsychiatry, 1,* 73–88.

Tager-Flusberg, H. (1989). A psycholinguistic perspective on language development in the autistic child. In G. Dawson (Ed.), *Autism: Nature, diagnosis, and treatment* (pp. 92–118). New York: Guilford Press.

Tager-Flusberg, H. (1992). Autistic children's talk about psychological states: Deficits in the early acquisition of a theory of mind. *Child Development, 63,* 161–172.

Tager-Flusberg, H. (1993). What language reveals about the understanding of minds in children with autism. In S. Baron-Cohen, H. Tager-Flusberg, & D.J. Cohen (Eds.), *Understanding other minds: Perspectives from autism* (pp. 138–157). Oxford: Oxford University Press.

Tan, J., & Harris, P. (1991). Autistic children understand seeing and wanting. *Development and Psychopathology, 3,* 163–174.

Welsh, M., Pennington, B., Ozonoff, S., Rouse, B., & McCabe, E. (1990). Neuropsychology of early-treated phenylketonuria: Specific executive function deficits. *Child Development, 61,* 1679–1713.

Wimmer, H., & Perner, J. (1983). Beliefs about beliefs: Representation and constraining function of wrong beliefs in young children's understanding of deception. *Cognition, 13,* 103–128.

Wing, L., Gould, J., Yeates, S.R., & Brierley, L.M. (1977). Symbolic play in severely mentally retarded and in autistic children. *Journal of Child Psychology and Psychiatry, 18,* 167–178.

Zelinski, C., Taylor, M., & Juzwin, K. (1991). Neuropsychological deficits in Obsessive-Compulsive Disorder. *Neuropsychiatry, Neuropsychology and Behavioural Neurology, 4,* 110–126.

CHAPTER 42

Perspectives on Language and Communication in Autism

HELEN TAGER-FLUSBERG

Over the past decade, studies on language acquisition and communicative functioning in autism have increased exponentially. De Villiers and de Villiers (1987), in their commentary on this topic, focused on two questions: (1) What can be learned about the process of normal language through the study of autistic language? and (2) What is the contribution of work in normal language acquisition to research and intervention with autistic children? (p. 697)

These questions are still timely, although the answers to them have changed considerably in the past decade, as shown in the core chapters in this volume that address basic research and interventions in the domain of language and communication (see Chapter 9 and Chapters 23 through 25). In this commentary, I consider these questions once again, as they have been illuminated by a decade of significant progress. Much has been learned both in the field of autism and in the field of language acquisition, but I end by considering the questions that remain for research to address in future years.

CONTRIBUTIONS FROM AUTISM TO NORMAL LANGUAGE ACQUISITION

Role of Theory of Mind in Language Acquisition

It has become increasingly clear that autism involves primary impairments in the development of a theory of mind (see Chapter 41), which have been used to explain the core social deficits that define the syndrome. One significant influence of the theory-of-mind hypothesis is its provision of a theoretical framework within which the language and communicative deficits in autism can also be explained (Happé, 1993, 1994; Tager-Flusberg, 1993). This framework provides a unifying way of interpreting both what is clearly impaired in the language of autistic individuals, and the larger pattern of what is spared (see Table 42.1). Studies conducted over the past few decades have shown that those autistic children who do develop some functional language have relatively little difficulty acquiring the formal, rule-governed components of language—namely, phonology and syntax. In contrast, as illustrated in the relevant chapters in this volume, certain pragmatic aspects of language—those that entail an understanding of others' minds—are specifically and uniquely impaired in autism.

Work on language deficits in autism has highlighted the role of a theory of mind in the acquisition of language, not only among autistic children but also among normally developing children. It has been accorded an important theoretical status because it is considered critical for providing the major motivation for learning language (Locke, 1993). By the end of infancy, normally developing infants understand that people are intentional, and that others may attend to the world and

Support for the preparation of this chapter was provided by a grant from the National Institute on Deafness and Other Communication Disorders (RO1 DC01234).

TABLE 42.1 Examples of Spared and Impaired Components of Language and Communication in Autism

Spared	Impaired
Speech sounds (phonology)	Intonation/Voice quality (prosody)
Linguistic form (syntax)	Linguistic function (pragmatics)
Questions for requests	Questions seeking information
Turn-taking abilities	Adding to conversational topic
Protoimperatives (requests, commands)	Protodeclaratives (comments, informing)
Instrumental gestures	Expressive gestures

experience it in different ways than they do. This incipient mentalistic view of people provides one key impetus to the infant to communicate with others, to learn about their view of the world as well as to share their own (Baldwin, 1993, 1995). Not all communication depends on this social understanding and so we see that even nonverbal autistic individuals can engage in some aspects of communication, particularly in expressing their own instrumental needs (see Chapter 25). Nevertheless, it seems clear that profound impairments in theory of mind leave many autistic children with an extremely limited capacity to communicate, even at the prelinguistic level.

There is still considerable debate about the underlying factors that are critical in acquiring a theory of mind. However, data from recent studies make it increasingly clear that the earliest and most enduring impairments that can be identified in autism involve a failure to orient toward social stimuli (Dawson, Meltzoff, & Osterling, 1995) and to integrate the expression of positive emotions in interactions with others (Dawson, Hill, Spencer, Galpert, & Watson, 1990; Kasari, Sigman, Mundy, & Yirmiya, 1990; Kasari, Sigman, & Yirmiya, 1993; Snow, Hertzig, & Shapiro, 1987). Such impairments suggest that, at its foundation, a theory of mind entails affective and cognitive components that are indivisible from one another, and that these components are the key to developing communicative aspects of language functioning.

Dissociations between the acquisition of linguistic form and function are characteristic even of high-functioning verbal autistic children (Tager-Flusberg, 1994). These kinds of dissociations underscore the view that language depends on complex interactions among a number of independent neurocognitive mechanisms. One is a computational system dedicated to processing hierarchical linguistic information, as in phonological and grammatical structures. The second mechanism is amodal, and it involves more general cognitive systems that are critical in building conceptual structures. These structures are the foundation for categorization and the lexical-semantic components of language (Jackendoff, 1983). Autism's deficits are primarily in the third mechanism, which is involved in understanding mental states. This third system processes both visual and vocal information about people and builds conceptual representations of social stimuli. It is also critical for effective communication (Locke, 1993). Thus, research on dissociations in the language of autistic individuals provides key evidence for a multicomponential view of language (Tager-Flusberg, 1997).

Constraints on Language Development

Early clinical descriptions of autistic language focused on its atypical characteristics—for example, echolalia, pronoun reversals, use of stereotyped language, and unusual meanings (Kanner, 1946; Pronovost, Wakstein, & Wakstein, 1966; Wolf & Chess, 1965). Some researchers went on to argue that even the *process* of development was different in autism; that is, children with autism who acquire language do not follow the same stages or developmental patterns as do other children (Menyuk & Quill, 1985; Simon, 1975).

Recent studies, however, have demonstrated that autistic children exhibit much greater similarity to other children, even normally developing children; they acquire more of the computational and semantic aspects of language than was previously thought. In our detailed longitudinal study of six autistic boys, we found that these children followed the same developmental path as the Down syndrome children who were being compared as part of the study, and normally developing children drawn from the extant literature (Tager-Flusberg et al., 1990). In looking at their grammatical development, we found that both the autistic and Down syndrome children showed similar growth curves in the length of their utterances, which is usually taken as a hallmark measure of grammatical development. Not surprisingly, however, for most of the children, the *rate* of growth was slower than in normally developing children. We also found that the autistic and Down syndrome children acquired grammatical structures in the same order as normally developing children: the order of acquisition of syntactic and morphological aspects of language is determined by linguistic complexity. More detailed analyses of the developmental patterns and a comparison of spontaneous and imitative (or echolalic) utterances suggested that even the processes involved in grammatical development in the autistic children were similar to those of normally developing children (Tager-Flusberg & Calkins, 1990). In this longitudinal study, and in earlier related work on semantic and conceptual development in autistic subjects, we found that their lexical growth and semantic representations also showed similar developmental patterns (Tager-Flusberg, 1985, 1986).

These findings underscore the powerful constraints that operate on syntactic and semantic development. It is interesting to note that studies of numerous other populations in recent years have also revealed these kinds of similarities in developmental patterns, particular in syntactic development (Tager-Flusberg, 1994). Taken together, studies on atypical children suggest that constraints in the linguistic system and the biological substrate for the computational and conceptual basis of language limit variations in possible patterns of development.

This view of language development has replaced older views about *deviance* in the acquisition of language in autism, with the idea that the language impairment may be more accurately conceptualized in terms of *asynchrony* or *dissociations* between the acquisition of form and function, or between computational and pragmatic aspects of language. In autism, one component of language, the pragmatic component, shows serious developmental delays or even arrested development, which then impacts other areas of language. The concept of deviance is no longer seen as useful either for describing and understanding the underlying problems in language development or for designing and implementing successful intervention programs.

CONTRIBUTIONS OF NORMAL LANGUAGE ACQUISITION TO AUTISM

Theories and Methods

About two decades ago, during the period when empirical studies of language in autism were just beginning, the field of language acquisition was dominated by cognitive-developmental and social-interactionist theories. According to these theories, language development could be accounted for in terms of either general cognitive developmental processes (e.g., Cromer, 1974; Sinclair-de-Zwart, 1969) or social interaction patterns between caregivers and their children (e.g., Bruner, 1975; Lock, 1980; Snow, 1979). The role of cognitive development (mental age) and the kind of language input provided by caregivers were regarded as quite central to explaining how children acquired this rich and complex system of communication in just a few short years.

Within a few years, studies began revealing serious limitations in both these theories (Cromer 1988; Shatz, 1982), which paved the way for the current, more complex view of language as involving a number of independent systems. The hypothesis that syntax represents a relatively autonomous component can be traced back to the earliest writings of Chomsky (1957, 1965), though his ideas have often been received with considerable skepticism among many child language researchers. More recently, Locke (1993) proposed the "dual specialization" hypothesis, a comprehensive account of how children come to acquire spoken language. Two critical mechanisms are outlined by Locke; one is a grammatical analysis module (based on a Chomskyian perspective), and the other is a social cognitive mechanism that is akin to a theory-of-mind system.

Theories of normal language acquisition, which propose that language is founded on more than one relatively autonomous mechanism, have opened the doors to our current view, that language deficits in autism involve specific impairments in the pragmatic system. Unlike the earlier social-interactionist models, however, these deficits are no longer seen as resulting from external factors—particularly, differences in the input language. Instead, theories such as Locke's highlight the role of theory of mind in language acquisition, in which the social and related language deficits are linked to mechanisms internal to the child.

Studies of language and communicative functioning in autism have benefited significantly from the methodological advances that have been made in the broader field of language acquisition. It is now standard to utilize a combination of experimental and naturalistic approaches (see Chapter 9), with each one contributing complementary information about how autistic children understand and produce language. The availability of specialized software programs (e.g., SALT, Miller & Chapman, 1985; CHAT/CLAN, MacWhinney, 1995) has greatly facilitated the acquisition and analysis of lengthy samples of speech, which have contributed important detailed information about language use in autism. Because of the existence of an international computerized database of language samples from large numbers of normally developing children and from populations of language-impaired children, we are now able to compare autistic children and other groups in ways that were previously not possible (MacWhinney, 1995). This has been particularly important, given the relative rarity of rich language samples from well-defined autistic children.

In the past decade, language acquisition researchers have turned their attention beyond naturalistic conversation to other forms of discourse. Studies of narrative discourse, such as storytelling and personal narratives, have expanded our views and have demonstrated that language acquisition extends well into the middle childhood years in normally developing children (e.g., Berman & Slobin, 1994). Narrative discourse entails the integration of linguistic, paralinguistic, conceptual, and social knowledge, and often reveals wide individual variation in both style and success. Because complex integration of multiple sources of information is required for producing a coherent narrative, it is not surprising that recent studies of stories told by autistic individuals reveal a wide array of problems (e.g., Bruner & Feldman, 1993; Loveland, McEvoy, Tunali, & Kelley, 1990; Tager-Flusberg, 1995; Tager-Flusberg & Sullivan, 1995). With these newer methodological approaches to the study of language, we have learned more about the kinds of communicative problems that even high-functioning autistic individuals experience in their everyday lives.

Understanding Impairments in Autism

Studies of normally developing children have afforded us highly detailed pictures of the stages and processes of language acquisition. The rich perspectives provided by these studies, particularly studies of the earliest periods of development, may be especially helpful in understanding why so many autistic children have difficulty developing beyond a limited repertoire of simple words or other symbols.

Research on early lexical development in normally developing children has highlighted two distinct phases. At the onset of spoken language, children acquire new lexical terms quite slowly. They learn labels for only the most significant objects, people, and events in their lives, and these are often not widely generalized nor used very systematically (Barrett, 1995; Nelson, 1973). These words, and sometimes whole phrases, are learned one at a time in an associative way, using general cognitive or learning abilities. By the time the lexicon has grown to between 50 and 100 words, a qualitative shift can be observed. At this point, children have reached what is referred to in the literature as the "vocabulary spurt," when the rate of lexical development begins increasing exponentially (Dromi, 1987; Fenson et al., 1994). After the onset of the vocabulary spurt, many new words are acquired daily with little effort. New words are often acquired after only a single exposure and are widely generalized to new exemplars (though not always with the same extensions as adults). Researchers argue that this new phase is facilitated by a set of principles that guides the child's lexical semantic development by constraining the hypotheses about how words map onto underlying meanings (e.g., Golinkoff, Mervis, & Hirsh-Pasek, 1994). Indeed, this *qualitative* change in how words are learned, now based on language-specific principles, is viewed as a central component of our species-specific ability to acquire language.

Within the field of autism, case histories sometimes document that a child followed a normal developmental pathway for the first year or 15 months of life, even to the stage of beginning to acquire language. In such cases, it seems as though development comes to a stop and the child appears to regress, losing whatever language had been acquired. It is interesting to note that, compared to the framework provided by studies of normal language acquisition, this sudden change typically occurs *prior to* the vocabulary spurt, when the autistic child knows only a few words. Thus, the loss of language at this early developmental stage suggests that the autistic child had not reached the point when acquisition is guided by domain-specific principles, but is still relying on associative learning mechanisms. Those autistic children who, even later in life, make relatively little progress in acquiring more than a small lexicon that is used in limited ways, are also still depending on associative learning, not language-specific mechanisms. It is as if these children have not yet gained insight into what human language is and how it functions. The challenge for intervention programs is to move these autistic children beyond this barrier.

Chapters 24 and 25, detailing the methods and approaches to language intervention with autistic children, demonstrate the remarkable progress that has been made in this area. Drawing from current literature on language development in normally developing children, researchers in this field have argued that the goal of therapy is to emphasize the central role of *context* in the development of communicative competence. The focus of language intervention is not limited to the use of language, but extends back to the development of prelinguistic communication as the core foundation on which language develops. Because these approaches are grounded in current theoretical and empirical work on normal language acquisition, they have led to far greater success than the earlier behaviorally based intervention programs.

FUTURE RESEARCH

Despite the progress made over the past decade, there is still much to be learned about the nature of the language impairments in autism. The close relationship between research on autism and research on language acquisition in normally developing children and other populations will undoubtedly continue over the next decade to foster further advances in this area.

One key issue remains relatively unstudied, yet quite central to an understanding of language impairment in autism: To what extent do autistic individuals have particular deficits in *comprehension?* Numerous experimental studies have found that autistic subjects have difficulties understanding spoken or written language (see Chapter 9), but the findings are not consistent across studies or on standardized measures of receptive language. We do not know whether the reported difficulties are linguistically based problems that are related to syntactic or semantic deficits. Alternatively, comprehension deficits in autism may be better understood in terms of difficulties integrating language with the social and environmental context. These different interpretations have profound implications for the kinds of interventions that should be designed to increase comprehension.

New studies that take advantage of new technologies need to be conducted in this area, so that our knowledge of comprehension matches the advances that have been made in interpreting expressive language deficits in autism. Within the field of language acquisition, important methodological advances have been made in the study of language comprehension. The use of techniques such as the preferential-looking paradigm have been successfully employed to test lexical and syntactic comprehension even in preverbal infants (Golinkoff, Hirsh-Pasek, Cauley, & Gordon, 1987). These newer methodologies should be explored as one way in which we might better assess language comprehension in autism, with the goal of understanding the underlying problems that autistic individuals may have in this area.

The greatest challenge that still remains is how to bring all of those autistic individuals across the barrier that so limits their ability to understand and express themselves through language. How do we teach them what language is for, the functions of communication, and the beauty and power of limitless expression? The impact of success in this area will not only be felt in the domain of language, but will also enhance the social competence and broaden the horizons of many individuals with autism.

Cross-References

Communication skills in autism are discussed in Chapter 9. Assessment and intervention issues are addressed in Chapters 19 and 23 through 25. Social development in autism is reviewed in Chapter 8 and theory of mind in autism is discussed in Chapter 41.

REFERENCES

Baldwin, D. (1993). Early referential understanding: Infants' ability to recognize referential acts for what they are. *Developmental Psychology, 29,* 832–843.

Baldwin, D. (1995). Understanding the link between joint attention and language. In C. Moore & P.J. Dunham (Eds.), *Joint attention: Its origins and role in development* (pp. 131–158). Hillsdale, NJ: Erlbaum.

Barrett, M. (1995). Early lexical development. In P. Fletcher & B. MacWhinney (Eds.), *The handbook of child language* (pp. 362–392). Oxford, England: Blackwell.

Berman, R., & Slobin, D.I. (1994). *Relating events in narrative: A cross-linguistic developmental study.* Hillsdale, NJ: Erlbaum.

Bruner, J. (1975). From communication to language: A psychological perspective. *Cognition, 3,* 255–287.

Bruner, J., & Feldman, C. (1993). Theories of mind and the problem of autism. In S. Baron-Cohen, H. Tager-Flusberg, & D.J. Cohen (Eds.), *Understanding other minds: Perspectives from autism* (pp. 267–291). Oxford, England: Oxford University Press.

Chomsky, N. (1957). *Syntactic structures.* The Hague: Mouton.

Chomsky, N. (1965). *Aspects of the theory of syntax.* Cambridge, MA: MIT Press.

Cromer, R. (1974). The development of language and cognition: The cognition hypothesis. In B. Foss (Ed.), *New perspectives in child development* (pp. 184–252). London: Penguin.

Cromer, R. (1988). The cognition hypothesis revisited. In F. Kessel (Ed.), *The development of language and language researchers: Essays in honor of Roger Brown* (pp. 223–248). Hillsdale, NJ: Erlbaum.

Dawson, G., Hill, D., Spencer, A., Galpert, L., & Watson, L. (1990). Affective exchanges between young autistic children and their mothers. *Journal of Abnormal Child Psychology, 18,* 335–345.

Dawson, G., Meltzoff, A., & Osterling, J. (1995, April). *Children with autism fail to orient to naturally-occurring social stimuli.* Paper presented at the biennial meeting of the Society for Research in Child Development, Indianapolis, IN.

de Villiers, P.A., & de Villiers, J.G. (1987). Commentary on language and autism. In D.J. Cohen & A.M. Donnellan (Eds.), *Handbook of autism and pervasive developmental disorders* (pp. 697–702). New York: John Wiley & Sons.

Dromi, E. (1987). *Early lexical development.* Cambridge, England: Cambridge University Press.

Fenson, L., Dale, P., Reznick, S., Bates, E., Thal, D., & Pethick, S.J. (1994). Variability in early communicative development. *Monographs of the Society for Research in Child Development, 59*(5, Serial No. 242).

Golinkoff, R., Hirsh-Pasek, K., Cauley, K.M., & Gordon, L. (1987). The eyes have it: Lexical and syntactic comprehension in a new paradigm. *Journal of Child Language, 14,* 23–45.

Golinkoff, R., Mervis, C.C., & Hirsh-Pasek, K. (1994). Early object labels: The case for a developmental lexical principles framework. *Journal of Child Language, 21,* 125–155.

Happé, F. (1993). Communicative competence and theory of mind in autism: A test of relevance theory. *Cognition, 48,* 101–119.

Happé, F. (1994). An advanced test of theory of mind: Understanding of story characters' thoughts and feelings by able autistic, mentally handicapped and normal children and adults. *Journal of Autism and Developmental Disorders, 24,* 129–154.

Jackendoff, R. (1983). *Semantics and cognition.* Cambridge, MA: MIT Press.

Kanner, L. (1946). Irrelevant and metaphorical language in early infantile autism. *American Journal of Psychiatry, 103,* 242–246.

Kasari, C., Sigman, M., Mundy, P., & Yirmiya, N. (1990). Affective sharing in the context of joint attention interactions of normal, autistic, and mentally retarded children. *Journal of Autism and Developmental Disorders, 20,* 87–100.

Kasari, C., Sigman, M., & Yirmiya, N. (1993). Focused and social attention of autistic children in interactions with familiar and unfamiliar adults: A comparison of autistic, mentally retarded, and normal children. *Development and Psychopathology, 5,* 403–414.

Lock, A. (1980). *The guided invention of language.* London: Academic Press.

Locke, J. (1993). *The child's path to spoken language.* Cambridge, MA: Harvard University Press.

Loveland, K.A., McEvoy, R.E., Tunali, B., & Kelley, M.L. (1990). Narrative story telling in autism and Down's syndrome. *British Journal of Developmental Psychology, 8,* 9–23.

MacWhinney, B. (1995). *The CHILDES project: Tools for analyzing talk* (2nd ed.). Hillsdale, NJ: Erlbaum.

Menyuk, P., & Quill, K. (1985). Semantic problems in autistic children. In E. Schopler & G. Mesibov (Eds.), *Communication problems in autism* (pp. 127–146). New York: Plenum Press.

Miller, J., & Chapman, R. (1985). *SALT: User's guide.* Madison, WI: University of Wisconsin Language Analysis Laboratory.

Nelson, K. (1973). Structure and strategy in learning to talk. *Monographs of the Society for Research in Child Development, 38*(1–2, Serial No. 149).

Pronovost, W., Wakstein, M.P., & Wakstein, D.J. (1966). A longitudinal study of speech behavior and language comprehension in fourteen children diagnosed atypical or autistic. *Exceptional Children, 33,* 19–26.

Shatz, M. (1982). On mechanisms of language acquisition: Can features of the communicative environment account for development? In E. Wanner & L. Gleitman (Eds.), *Language acquisition: The state of the art* (pp. 102–127). New York: Cambridge University Press.

Simon, N. (1975). Echolalic speech in childhood autism: Consideration of possible underlying loci of brain damage. *Archives of General Psychiatry, 32,* 1439–1446.

Sinclair-de-Zwart, H. (1969). Developmental psycholinguistics. In D. Elkind & J. Flavell (Eds.), *Studies in cognitive development* (pp. 315–336). New York: Holt, Rinehart & Winston.

Snow, C. (1979). The role of social interaction in language acquisition. In W.A. Collins (Ed.), *Children's language and communication* (pp. 157–182). Hillsdale, NJ: Erlbaum.

Snow, M., Hertzig, M., & Shapiro, T. (1987). Expression of emotion in young autistic children. *Journal of the Academy of Child and Adolescent Psychiatry, 26,* 836–838.

Tager-Flusberg, H. (1985). The conceptual basis for referential word meaning in children with autism. *Child Development, 56,* 1167–1178.

Tager-Flusberg, H. (1986). Constraints on the representation of word meaning: Evidence from autistic and mentally retarded children. In S.A. Kuczaj & M. Barrett (Eds.), *The development of word meaning* (pp. 139–166). New York: Springer-Verlag.

Tager-Flusberg, H. (1993). What language reveals about the understanding of mind in children with autism. In S. Baron-Cohen, H. Tager-Flusberg, & D.J. Cohen (Eds.), *Understanding other minds: Perspectives from autism* (pp. 138–157). Oxford, England: Oxford University Press.

Tager-Flusberg, H. (1994). Dissociations in form and function in the acquisition of language by autistic children. In H. Tager-Flusberg (Ed.), *Constraints on language acquisition: Studies of atypical children* (pp. 175–194). Hillsdale, NJ: Erlbaum.

Tager-Flusberg, H. (1995). "Once upon a ribbit": Stories narrated by autistic children. *British Journal of Developmental Psychology, 13,* 45–59.

Tager-Flusberg, H. (1997). The role of theory of mind in language acquisition: Contributions from the study of autism. In L. Adamson & M.A. Romski (Eds.), *Research on communication and language disorders: Contributions to theories of language development* (pp. 133–158). Baltimore: Brookes.

Tager-Flusberg, H., & Calkins, S. (1990). Does imitation facilitate the acquisition of grammar? Evidence from a study of autistic, Down syndrome and normal children. *Journal of Child Language, 17,* 591–606.

Tager-Flusberg, H., Calkins, S., Nolin, T., Baumberger, T., Anderson, M., & Chadwick-Dias, A. (1990). A longitudinal study of language acquisition in autistic and Downs syndrome children. *Journal of Autism and Developmental Disorders, 20,* 1–21.

Tager-Flusberg, H., & Sullivan, K. (1995). Attributing mental states to story characters: A comparison of narratives produced by autistic and mentally retarded individuals. *Applied Psycholinguistics, 16,* 241–256.

Wolf, S., & Chess, S. (1965). An analysis of the language of fourteen schizophrenic children. *Journal of Child Psychology and Psychiatry, 6,* 29–41.

CHAPTER 43

Perspectives on Social Impairment

LYNN WATERHOUSE AND DEBORAH FEIN

This chapter reviews current models of social impairment in autism and considers the implications of debates about human social behavior generated by new theoretical frameworks in evolutionary psychology and cognitive neurosciences. The two goals of the chapter are (a) to provide a critical evaluation of models of social impairment, and (b) to explore potential frameworks for more comprehensive models of social skills and social impairment.

CURRENT MODELS OF SOCIAL IMPAIRMENT IN AUTISM

It is generally agreed that social impairment in autism stems from abnormal brain function, but there are variant interpretations of social impairment. We have categorized current views in terms of their assumptions:

1. Social impairments are assumed to be a secondary effect of a primary deficit in attention, arousal, sensory function, pain system function, memory, executive function, or information processing (Courchesne et al., 1994; Dawson & Lewy, 1989; DeLong, 1992; Frith, 1989; Happé, 1994; Kinsbourne, 1987; Minshew, 1991; Ornitz, 1985, 1988; Ozonoff, 1995; Ozonoff, Pennington, & Rogers, 1991; Ozonoff, Strayer, McMahon, & Filloux, 1994; Panksepp & Sahley, 1987; Shah & Frith, 1993).
2. Impairment in social cognition is assumed to be the primary deficit (Baron-Cohen, 1995; Baron-Cohen, Leslie, & Frith, 1985; Happé, 1994, 1995; Happé & Frith, 1995; Leslie, 1993; Perner, 1993).

3. Impairment in affective sociability and impairment in social cognition together are assumed to be the primary deficit (Brothers, 1989, 1995; Brothers & Ring, 1992; Hobson, 1993; Sigman, Yirmiya, & Capps, 1995).
4. Social impairments are assumed to be the most salient of a set of deficits (Bachevalier & Merjanian, 1994; Fein, 1994; Fein, Pennington, & Waterhouse, 1987; Modahl, Fein, Waterhouse, & Newton, 1992; Waterhouse, 1994a, 1994b; Waterhouse, Fein, & Modahl, 1996).

Before the advent of these models, during the 20 years from Kanner's identification of autism in 1943 until Rimland's argument for an organic etiology of the syndrome in 1964, social impairment in autism was generally hypothesized to be the result of cold, hyperrational parents who provided "a mechanical type of attention to material needs only . . . mechanized service of the kind that is rendered by an overconscientious gasoline station attendant" (Kanner, 1949, pp. 424–425). Rimland argued that Kanner's psychogenic hypothesis did not account for the existence of warm and unintellectual parents of autistic children, for normal siblings of autistic children, for normal children of cold, hyper-rational parents, for autism in children with known brain damage, or for the consistent ratio of four autistic boys to one autistic girl (Rimland, 1964, pp. 51–52).

Rimland's (1964) argument for biological causation has been accepted, and impaired social behavior in autism is now assumed to arise from neurological impairment. However, as yet, there is no single, clear model of the developmental path that leads to autism. Key unresolved issues include (a) the relationship between heritabililty and heterogeneity, (b) the multiplicity of neural deficits identified, and (c) the effect of systemic developmental interactions. These unresolved issues limit current understanding of the sources of social impairment in autism.

Heritability and Heterogeneity

Recent studies have reported that approximately 6% of the siblings of autistic individuals are autistic or autistic-like (Bolton et al., 1994; Rapin, 1996), and twin studies in autism have reported significant concordance rates (Bailey et al., 1995). However, the specific genetic basis (or bases) for autism is not yet understood (Piven & Folstein, 1994). Moreover, because of the cognitive, social, motor, and associated symptom heterogeneity within autism, it has been difficult to determine what should count as a genetic minor variant of autism in the family members of autistic individuals. Plomin (1995b) outlined a way of thinking about complex disorders that could obviate the heritability/heterogeneity problem: quantitative trait loci (QTL). Quantitative trait loci models posit that behavioral syndromes such as autism are caused by multiple genes that have varying effect sizes, wherein no one gene is necessary or may be sufficient to cause the disorder. More importantly, QTL effects are "probabilistic propensities" (Plomin, 1995b, p. 116), and thus their impact is dimensional, not dichotomous. A QTL model of autism would view the heterogeneity of symptoms in autism and the heterogeneity of minor social, cognitive, and other deficits in family members as related dimensional expressions of the multigene system underlying the autistic syndrome.

Multiplicity of Neural Deficits Identified

Autism has been found in association with a wide variety of neural deficits (Piven et al., 1995; Reichler & Lee, 1987; Waterhouse, Fein, et al., 1996). Given a QTL model, as described above, all neural deficits identified could possibly contribute to the aberrant diagnostic behaviors of autism. Alternatively, subgroups of autistic individuals may have distinct causal neural deficits (Bolton et al., 1994; Waterhouse, Morris, et al., 1996). Most current models, however, have argued for a unitary neural source for autism (amygdala—Brothers, 1995; cerebellum—Courchesne, 1995; hippocampus—DeLong, 1992). Whether based in many, some, or one deficit, the neural dysfunction underpinning social impairment in autism remains, at present, a matter for speculation.

Systemic Developmental Interactions

Two types of interactions make neural function in developmental disorders difficult to model. First, brain mechanisms for the control of behavior are likely to be restructured continuously as the individual engages in the behavior (Kass, 1995). Thus, as an autistic individual expresses a deviant or delayed behavior, the disordered neural source for that behavior will actively reconfigure itself. Although such reconfiguration could be beneficent, it is more likely that feedback from impaired functioning will drive source mechanisms into further dysfunction. Second, neural behavior control mechanisms that are delayed or disordered may negatively affect correlative emergent developmental skills. For example, abnormal or delayed language development will negatively affect social and cognitive development.

Although the four current approaches considered in this chapter assume that neural deficit is the source of social impairment, none is designed to explain systemic neurobehavioral developmental interactions, and none proposes a model of possible genetic bases for social impairment. These models do offer distinct interpretations of social behavior, and variant constructions of brain–behavior relationships.

SOCIAL IMPAIRMENT AS THE SECONDARY EFFECT OF A PRIMARY DEFICIT

Social impairment may be the secondary effect of a primary deficit in attention, arousal, sensory function, pain system function, memory, executive function, or information processing. Secondary effect models of social impairment assume that human social behavior crucially depends on a more basic psychological function, such as memory or attention, or a basic unitary neural function, such as brainstem or beta endorphin, and proponents argue that social impairment is a by-product of deficit in the more basic function. Courchesne and colleagues (1994) proposed that impaired attention is the primary deficit. Dawson and Lewy (1989) suggested that arousal level and attentional processes are abnormal in autism. Ornitz (1985, 1988) posited brainstem sensory processing as the core dysfunction. Panksepp and Sahley (1987) argued that autism is caused by excessive amounts of striatal beta endorphin. DeLong (1992) claimed that memory management is the key deficit in autism. Ozonoff and colleagues (Ozonoff, 1995; Ozonoff et al., 1991; Ozonoff et al., 1994) claimed that the failure of executive function skills is the core of the syndrome and the basis for social impairment. Minshew (1991) argued that the syndrome is based on failed information processing. Frith (1989) hypothesized that autism rests on a failure of central coherence of information processing. Each of these models is discussed in the following subsections.

Primacy of Attention Deficit

Courchesne and colleagues (1994) hypothesized that the key deficit in autism is an inability to shift attention from one modality to another. Along with other researchers (see Courchesne, 1995, and Minshew & Dombrowski, 1994, for summaries), Courchesne et al. reported findings for abnormal development of neocerebellar structures in autism. On this basis, they proposed that the neocerebellum determines the voluntary shifting of attention which, in turn, determines the ability to engage in joint social attention. In their model, impaired social behavior arises from impaired attention shifting, which stems from aberrant over- or underdevelopment of neocerebellar tissue (Courchesne, 1995; Courchesne et al., 1994).

Courchesne and colleagues (1994) also reported parietal abnormality for a subgroup of autistic individuals, where parietal abnormality was correlated with indexes of impaired attention. Still other findings (Hashimoto et al., 1995) suggest an association between abnormal brainstem development and cerebellar hypoplasia in autism.

There is abundant evidence for cerebellar abnormality in autism, and the cerebellum has been implicated in conditioning, in motor skill acquisition, in the timing of behavior, in error detection (Fiez, Peterson, Cheney, & Raichle, 1992), and in the enhancement of mental functioning generally, as well as frontal lobe functioning specifically (Leiner & Leiner, 1993). However, in six studies of autistic subjects, no cerebellar abnormalities were found (Courchesne, 1995; Reiss, Lee, & Freund, 1994; and see review by Minshew & Dombrowski, 1994), and no connection with social skills has been reported for the cerebellum (Schmahman, 1994). The model posits that impaired joint attention is caused by attention-shifting difficulties—a logical hypothesis. Attention-shifting problems by themselves, however, do not yield severe social impairment. Down syndrome children experience abnormal difficulty in shifting attention from visual fixation (Klinger & Dawson, 1995) and yet are sociable. Children with frank Attention Deficit Disorder, who have severe difficulty with attention shifting, are usually normally sociable and like to play with friends even when joint attention cannot be consistently maintained (American Psychiatric Association, 1994; Barkley, 1990).

Primacy of Arousal Deficit

Dawson and Lewy (1989) and Kinsbourne (1987) proposed that the essential social behaviors are negatively affected by overarousal. In this view, the primary deficits of autism are overarousal and impaired attention. The model postulates that arousal from social interactions is too great for the impaired arousal system of autistic individuals; therefore, social interchanges become aversive and are avoided. Dawson and Lewy proposed that, although the autistic child's bond with mother is severely and permanently disrupted by this avoidance, nonetheless the autistic child may prefer interaction with mother over strangers because exposure to mother has made her effectively less arousing.

This is a reasonable and well-thought-out hypothesis. Attention and arousal problems are key nondiagnostic deficits found in autism. The Dawson–Lewy model (1989) provides an explanation for one segment of the range of social impairment in autism: the aloof and hyperaroused individual. Kinsbourne (1987) additionally accounts for the socially interested but intrusively awkward type of autistic child by arguing that such an individual is attentionally overfocused. However the passive, unaroused child who exhibits focal attention to objects and not people (Wing, 1988) remains to be accounted for in these models.

Primacy of Sensory Deficit

Ornitz (1985, 1988) reported a significant association between number of sensory processing deficits and number of social deficits, and proposed autism to be a continuum based on relative severity of impairment of sensory information processing.

Ornitz and Ritvo (1968) earlier argued that aberrant sensory modulation arising from impaired brain stem attentional mechanisms was the basis for autism. Ornitz (1988) outlined a modification of this model: autism originates in the failure of thalamic and reticular structures "to adequately modulate sensory input, transmit this dysmodulation to limbic structures mediating interest and motivation, and that together reticular and limbic (medial temporal lobe) structures transmit the dysmodulation of processing sensory input to cortical structures" (p. 311).

Failed sensory integration appears to be a major disability for many autistic individuals (Frankel, Simmons, Fichter, & Freeman, 1984; Lovaas, Koegel, & Schreibman, 1979; Ornitz, 1985, 1988). Ornitz developed a clear and interesting model that can account for this disability and for brainstem abnormalities. However, there are also findings for abnormalities in the cerebellum, the medial temporal lobe, and the association cortex in autism. Thus, it remains a question whether the medial temporal lobe and the association cortex, if abnormal, will function only as passive downstream recipients of sensory dysmodulation forwarded from the brainstem. It would also be helpful if the specific mechanisms whereby sensory dysmodulation generates impaired social function were to be outlined in this model.

Primacy of Pain/Reward System Abnormalities

Panksepp and Sahley (1987) argued that autism is caused by the prenatal or neonatal production of excessive amounts of striatal beta endorphin, a primary internal reinforcer. In this model, autistic individuals are socially impaired because their own excessive level of internal reinforcement (beta endorphin) is so high that it exceeds any reward value that could come from social interaction (Panksepp & Sahley, 1987; Sahley & Panksepp, 1987).

Panksepp and Sahley (1987) proposed that the social withdrawal caused by excess beta endorphin negates both affective sociability (the emotional drive to be with others) and social cognition, and also leads to self-injurious behavior. They outlined an evolutionary model in which the neurophysiological basis for pain mediation (beta endorphin) came to serve mammalian social attachment, and attachment processes served as a basis for the evolution of language skills in humans.

Sahley and Panksepp (1987) argued that, because attachment and language have evolved out of the opioid-based pain control system, damage to the opioid system in autism impairs both social attachment and language functions. This is a fascinating theoretical assumption, but it needs supporting data. The model must also either exclude some subgroups of autistic individuals or specify how the withdrawal caused by elevated beta endorphin could generate (a) autistic developmental regression, (b) socially eager but perseveratively odd autistic individuals, and (c) autistic individuals who have normal pain responses.

Primacy of Memory Management Deficit

DeLong (1992) defined memory management as the primary deficit of autism. He proposed that hippocampal damage in autistic individuals cuts off access to memories, and thus all autistic behavior is limited to stimulus–response habits. DeLong argued that because autistic individuals lack memories of their own prior generalized patterns of behavior, they can produce only inflexibly rote or repetitive behavioral sequences in language and social interaction.

DeLong's (1992) model provides an impressively persuasive account of the behavioral effects of medial temporal lobe abnormalities in autism. The model would be more powerful if it were extended to explain how (a) abnormalities in attachment and sociability might be generated by hippocampal damage, and how (b) many autistic individuals have better "rote" spatial memory than "rote" verbal memory, and up to 10% have savant "rote" memory. The model would also be more powerful if it included a consideration of possible effects of deficit in other brain areas, such as association cortex, or cerebellum, or other limbic structures demonstrated to be affected in autism. Finally, the model should exclude subgroups or explain how some autistic individuals do use language flexibly to express needs and peculiar interests, while others with good rote language skills often fail to learn even rote behavioral sequences associated with normal ritualized patterns of social interaction, such as "Hi, how are you?" "Fine, and you?"

Primacy of Executive Function Deficit

Ozonoff and colleagues (Ozonoff, 1995; Ozonoff, Pennington, & Rogers, 1991; Ozonoff et al., 1994) reported that nonretarded autistic individuals express a selective deficit in executive function. The frontal lobe is understood as the mediator of executive function; it guides behavior by selectively activating plans and schemas extant in working memory or long-term memory.

Ozonoff (1995) argued that because nonautistic children with frontal lobe damage are like autistic children in that they cannot understand the viewpoints of others and they do not express normal empathy (Grattan & Eslinger, 1992), therefore findings for impaired executive function that imply frontal damage in autism can account for the social impairments in autism. Ozonoff (1995) attributed autistic social skill impairments in the perception of emotion, imitation, pretend play, intersubjectivity, joint attention, and theory of mind to impaired executive function.

Ozonoff and colleagues (Ozonoff, 1995; Ozonoff et al., 1991; Ozonoff et al., 1994) have developed substantial evidence that supports executive function deficits in high-functioning autistic individuals. Although there are, at present, no neuroimaging or neuroanatomical findings that document discrete anatomic or physiologic abnormality in the frontal lobes of autistic individuals (Minshew & Dombrowski, 1994), a study of five preschool autistic children (Zilbovicious et al., 1995) reported evidence for transient hypoperfusion of frontal lobes, suggesting maturational delay in frontal cortex development. Furthermore, limbic system and temporal lobe processing deficits could add to frontal lobe dysfunction (Horowitz & Rumsey, 1994).

This model is both plausible and intriguing. It would be stronger if it offered an explanation for cerebellar deficit and medial temporal lobe deficit. Most importantly the model needs to be expanded to account for the autistic symptoms of the 70% to 75% of autistic individuals who are retarded. Executive function impairment would appear to be insufficient to explain severe autistic social withdrawal bound to severe cognitive dysfunction found in the majority of autistic individuals.

Primacy of Information Processing Deficit

Two models propose deficits in information processing as primary in autism: (a) Minshew's proposal (1991) that information processing per se is the core problem in autism, and (b) Frith's suggestion (1989) that lack of central coherence in information processing is the basis for the syndrome.

Minshew (1991) proposed that association cortex deficit is the basis of autism, and has claimed that "all of the clinical manifestations of autism can be accounted for by dysfunction of association cortex . . . and are not attributable to dysfunction at the hippocampal or subcortical levels" (p. 779). She further claimed that the cell development abnormalities and "decrease in neural connectivity observed in the hippocampus" only serve to reflect "deficits in the larger neural network of association cortex involved in complex information organization and processing" (p. 779).

Minshew (1991) reported that her model was based on research findings obtained in studies of high-functioning autistic individuals. In these studies, auditory, visual, and somatosensory evoked potentials showed normal conduction through subcortical pathways, with no evidence for abnormal transmission to the cerebral cortex (p. 778).

Minshew's model raises an important point that no theorist in the field should ignore. Given the evidence for aberrant comprehension across a variety of forms of content, autism, de facto, must be a disorder of information processing. A question that remains is the presence of extremely variant information processing skill across autistic individuals. For example, why do many autistic individuals process a complex visual design significantly better than a frowning human face, and why do some autistic individuals perform better than normal age-peers on block design measures (Shah & Frith, 1993)? Minshew's model needs to provide an explanation for such variation, as well as a mechanism whereby general information-processing impairment gives rise to the specific social impairments associated with autism.

Minshew's model is based on studies of high-functioning autistic individuals as representing "pure autism." As with Ozonoff and colleagues' executive function model, however, this leaves the information-processing deficits of low-functioning autistic individuals unexplained. At the neural level, the evidence for medial temporal lobe deficit (Bauman & Kemper, 1994; Reiss et al., 1994) and cerebellar deficit (Courchesne, 1995) is essentially rejected in this model.

Primacy of Failed Central Coherence Faculty

Frith (1989) proposed the existence of "a force (imagine a strong flowing river) which pulls together large amounts of information (many tributaries)" (p. 97). She argued that this cohesive force is abnormally weak in autism, and is impaired relative to local cohesive forces of perceptual information processing. Frith concluded that autism is a failure of central coherence.

Shah and Frith (1993) reported that high-functioning autistic individuals performed better than normal children and adults on the Block Design task of the Wechsler Intelligence

Scale for Children—Revised (WISC-R). They suggested that high-functioning autistic individuals constructed block designs bottom-up, with supernormal speed and accuracy, because they lack a central coherence faculty (which would effectively slow down piece-assembly construction by generating the mental image of the whole design).

Frith's model is appealing because it is consonant with global clinical and research perceptions of autistic individuals. The model makes no distinction between social and nonsocial information processing, but Frith argues that weak central coherence leads to failure to understand context which, in turn, impairs social interaction. The model is psychological, not neurobiological. However, if a psychological faculty of central coherence exists, it must have a neural basis. Identification of that neural locus is crucial both for understanding what central coherence may be, and for understanding its relationship to the full range of symptomatology in autism.

IMPAIRED SOCIAL COGNITION AS THE PRIMARY DEFICIT OF AUTISM

A subcomponent of social behavior is social cognition—understanding the meaningful communicative verbal and nonverbal behavior of other people. Three models have been constructed in which impaired social cognition is assumed to be the primary deficit of autism. Leslie (1993) proposed that autistic children lack a brain module that forms a theory of mind of other people. Perner (1993) suggested that autistic individuals lack understanding of abstract representation. Baron-Cohen (1995) proposed that autistic children are impaired in four evolved brain modules needed for normal social cognition: (a) an intention detector, (b) an eye direction detector, (c) a shared attention mechanism, and (d) a theory-of-mind mechanism.

Leslie's Theory-of-Mind Model

Leslie (1993) proposed a "Theory of Mind Mechanism" (ToMM) that infers the state of mind of other people by using two subsystems: (a) comprehension of the explicit behavior of others; and (b) an M-representational system by which the presumed mental states of another person, such as pretense or belief, are encoded as concepts. Leslie also proposed the existence of a selection processor (SP), which selects the memory appropriate for understanding a current situation. The SP then sends that memory either to the ToMM, when people's thoughts need to be understood on the basis of prior information, or to the CDRA—the "component that deals with representational (non-human, non-agent) artifacts" (p. 101)—when objects need to be understood. Leslie further hypothesized that executive functions form still another mental module (EF), which operates separately from the SP, ToMM, and CDRA.

Perner's Model of Impaired Metarepresentation Skill

Perner (1993) posited that very young normal children are situation theorists, and children over the age of 4 years develop the skill to be representation theorists (p. 128). Perner claimed that after age 4, throughout development and adulthood, we remain situation theorists who can move into a representational view when pushed. He proposed that autistic individuals remain forever limited to situation interpretation because they cannot represent that something is a representation. Thus, for Perner, the key deficit in autism is a general inability to operate symbolically (i.e., a metarepresentational deficit).

Baron-Cohen's Four-Module Mechanism for Social Cognition

Baron-Cohen (1995) outlined four innate brain function modules as requisite for the development of normal social cognition:

1. An Intentionality Detector (ID), which interprets perceived motion in terms of the primitive volitional mental states of goal and desire.
2. An Eye-Direction Detector (EDD), which (a) detects the presence of eye-like stimuli, (b) computes the directionality of the eye-like stimulus, and (c) infers that if another organism's eyes are directed at something, the other organism sees that same thing.
3. A Shared-Attention Mechanism (SAM), which builds triadic representations of self-plus-other-plus-object (or another).

4. A "Theory of Mind Mechanism" (ToMM) that integrates the products of ID, EDD, and SAM with representations of epistemic mental states (i.e., pretending, thinking, guessing).

Baron-Cohen (1995, p. 56) postulates a developmental sequence in which the infant has ID and EDD from birth to 9 months, adds SAM during the period from 9 to 18 months, and develops ToMM as triggered by SAM during the period from 18 to 48 months.

Three Theory-of-Mind Models

Because theory-of-mind models are backed by considerable findings (Charman & Baron-Cohen, 1995; Happé, 1994, 1995), and because they are consistent with current views of brain function modularity in evolutionary and cognitive psychology (Cosmides & Tooby, 1992), they compel attention. The hypothesis that a theory-of-mind deficit defines autism has motivated more than 40 published studies to date (Baron-Cohen et al., 1985) to 1995 (Peterson & Siegal, 1995; Sparrevohn & Howie, 1995; for reviews see Happé, 1994, 1995; Happé & Frith, 1995; and Klin & Volkmar, 1993). Happé and Frith (1995) concluded that the triad of impairments seen in autism (impaired sociability, communication, and imagination) is adequately explained by theory-of-mind models. They also proposed that, beyond the triad of impairments, "much of the autistic person's strange behavior can be better understood if we remember that he or she cannot mind-read the way most of us do" (p. 193).

Six types of data, however, challenge the theory-of-mind paradigm as a core deficit in autism:

1. Of autistic individuals tested, 15% to 60% pass theory-of-mind tests (Happé, 1995; Happé & Frith, 1995).
2. Peterson and Siegal (1995) have reported that deaf and autistic children have comparable rates of failure on theory-of-mind tests. Peterson and Siegal attribute the deaf children's failure to impoverished conversation—conversation that is limited to the concrete, visible, and tangible; they attribute autistic children's failure to the

absence of normal conversation. They have proposed that conversation teaches children how to report and label states of mind (p. 470).

3. Sparrevohn and Howie (1995) have reported (a) evidence that verbal ability is a significant correlate of theory-of-mind skill in autism, and that theory-of-mind skill acquisition follows a developmental sequence in autism; and (b) no correlation between social skills and theory-of-mind skills.

4. Hughes and Russell (1993) have claimed that autistic children fail on theory-of-mind tasks because they form an abnormal perceptual fixation on a task object in its actual location, and cannot therefore identify the empty location, which would be the correct task answer.

5. Klin, Volkmar, and Sparrow (1992) have reported that many autistic children do not show normal social skills in infancy and toddlerhood. This suggests that social impairment predates impaired theory of mind in autism.

6. Home video studies of very young children later diagnosed as autistic (Adrien et al., 1993; Osterling & Dawson, 1994) support Klin et al. (1992). The videos reveal that many autistic infants and toddlers: (a) express a wider range of abnormal symptomatology (including social withdrawal, motor stereotypy, lack of attachment) than can be accounted for by ToMM models—even by Baron-Cohen's ID, EDD, and SAM; and (b) express specific precursors to the development of theory of mind—for example, eye gaze, pointing, orienting, and means–end behavior (Frye, 1993)—but with less frequency than do normal children seen on home videos (Osterling & Dawson, 1994).

If social impairment appears much earlier in development than theory-of-mind skill (Adrien et al., 1993; Klin et al., 1992; Osterling & Dawson, 1994), and social skill is not correlated with theory-of-mind skill (Sparrevohn & Howie, 1995), theory of mind cannot account for social impairment. If theory-of-mind skill behavioral precursors appear (albeit with less frequency) in autistic toddlers (Osterling & Dawson, 1994), and ToMM is developmentally associated with verbal skill

(Happé, 1995; Sparrevohn & Howie, 1995) and with time spent in conversation (Peterson & Siegal, 1995), theory-of-mind skill may be, in large part, a function of social learning acquired through language use, for which many autistic children have inadequate but not absent development. If theory-of-mind task failure is, in part, a function of abnormal object fixity (as is posited by Hughes & Russell, 1993), the neural deficit must occur at an earlier point of information processing than the higher cognitive function machinery envisioned for a theory-of-mind brain module (Baron-Cohen, 1995; Happé, 1994; Happé & Frith, 1995; Leslie, 1993; Perner, 1993). Finally, if a significant, verbal subgroup of autistic individuals can pass theory-of-mind tests (Happé, 1995; Happé & Frith, 1995), then theory-of-mind failure cannot be argued to be the single pathognomonic defining feature of autism.

It has been claimed that autistic individuals master theory-of-mind tasks via nonnormal means (Happé, 1995). This hypothesis requires new tests. At present, this claim is tantamount to saying that theory-of-mind tests are not valid indicators of theory-of-mind skill, but only measure a behavior which makes it seem as if individuals have theory-of-mind skill.

Taken together, these data suggest that theory-of-mind skill depends on a number of subskills, which have not been defined as components of theory-of-mind mechanisms (Baron-Cohen, 1995): (a) the ability to inhibit a response to immediate stimuli in favor of an alternate working memory construct (Goldman-Rakic, 1995; Zelazo, Reznick, & Pinon, 1995); (b) the ability to learn and use a belief/desire vocabulary (Peterson & Siegal, 1995); (c) the ability to construct means–end relationships from the observed behavior of others (Frye, 1993); and (d) the language-based ability to infer the existence of intangibles (Clark, 1996).

IMPAIRED AFFECT AND SOCIAL COGNITION AS THE PRIMARY DEFICIT

Impaired sociability and social cognition together may be the primary diagnostic deficit of autism. Two models offer accounts of the relationship of affective sociability and social cognition: (a) Brothers and Ring's "hot" theory of mind (1992), and (b) Hobson's intersubjectivity model (1993). Each model frames the development of impaired social behavior in different ways.

Brothers and Ring's "Hot" Theory of Mind

Brothers (1989) posited the amygdala as the source of empathy and suggested that lack of empathic concern for others is a central feature of autism. Brothers and Ring (1992) and Brothers (1995) theorized that the lack of concern for others results from the lack of a "hot" theory of mind. In this model, humans read evaluative attitudes and intentions from the facial expressions and eye-gaze directions of others, and from this reading they form a social situation representation (SSR). This representation (a form of a theory of mind), in turn, is bound in memory—through the amygdala, anterior cingulate, and orbitofrontal cortex—to an associated emotional response (R) or hot reaction, which is triggered by the activation of the SSR. Brothers (1995) proposed that, although there can be innumerable SSR/R links in a normal individual's mind, autistic individuals cannot form SSR/Rs.

Sigman and colleagues (1995) argued that their findings for social knowledge in high-functioning autistic children support Brothers's hot theory of mind: "In our view, the only children who achieve metarepresentation and social comprehension without recourse to the nearly automatic emotional understanding that most normal people possess are autistic children" (p. 174).

The hot theory of mind offers an articulate model of a mechanism to explain the abnormal social reactivity of autistic individuals. Moreover, nearly all autistic individuals do lack empathy. However, empathy is unlikely to be a simple function; it is more likely to be a complex developmental acquisition based on many elements, including hypothalamic and neuroendocrine function, amygdala function and SSR/Rs, imaginative mental models construction, as well as complex social contextual (non-SSR/R) learning. The peculiarities of cognitive development found in many autistic individuals, such as superior skill in visual pattern recognition, are not accounted for in this model, and the most severely avoidant social withdrawal—found in many autistic individuals—cannot be adequately characterized as a failure of empathy, or even as a failure to establish SSR/Rs.

Hobson's I–Thou Intersubjectivity Model

Hobson (1993) postulated that the mind of a normal newborn contains two modes of information processing: (a) an I–Thou process for understanding people, and (b) an I–It process for understanding objects. Hobson asserted that the I–Thou and I–It processes normally fuse early in development, and their fusion is a necessary precondition to enable the child to construct a theory of the minds of others, and to manipulate symbols imaginatively in language use.

Hobson (1993) argued that the autistic infant experiences abnormal I–Thou information processing. Consequently, the autistic child cannot fuse I–Thou and I–It information-processing mechanisms, and thus (a) can never establish normal social intersubjectivity, (b) cannot form a theory of the minds of others, and (c) will not develop normal linguistic or social skills, or normal skill for symbolic cognition. Hobson theorizes that the neural base of I–thou processing could be either subcortical structures coordinating body and mind, or a set of subcortical and cortical structures that indirectly control intersubjective communication (p. 15).

This insightful and detailed model provides an account of how affective and social cognitive impairment may be linked in autism. However, the model excludes autistic children who express normal attachment to their mothers (Rogers, Ozonoff, & Maslin-Cole, 1993), because attachment would indicate normal I–Thou information processing. The model also excludes autistic individuals who have exhibited theory-of-mind skill (Baron-Cohen, 1995; Happé, 1995), because, according to Hobson's theoretical framework, I–Thou and I–It systems must have developed and fused in these autistic individuals. Lewis and Boucher (1988) reported that a significant subgroup of autistic children express symbolic play, a skill that—in Hobson's model—could only develop after normal I–Thou and I–It fusion.

SOCIAL IMPAIRMENT AS ONE OF SEVERAL PRIMARY DEFICITS

One important issue has involved determining the place of social impairment in the realm of autistic disabilities. Autism includes a wide variety of motor, vegetative, cognitive, and social impairments. The first group of models discussed in this chapter assumes that social impairment is an indirect by-product of another, more fundamental deficit in mental functioning. The second and third groups of models assume that social impairment is the direct and primary deficit of the syndrome. This last set of models assumes that the causal neurological source(s) of the syndrome generate a set of separate dysfunctions, of which social impairment is the most salient. Our research group (Fein, 1994; Modahl et al., 1992; Waterhouse, 1994a, 1994b) and Bachevalier and Merjanian (1994) have proposed models wherein social impairment is one of a set of impairments arising from specified neural deficits. These are examined next.

Waterhouse, Fein, and Modahl's Multiple Source Model

In our model, a subgroup of behavioral deficits in autism is theorized to result from four neurofunctional impairments: (a) canalesthesia, wherein abnormal hippocampal function "canalizes" sensory records, disrupting integration of information; (b) impaired assignment of the affective significance of stimuli, wherein abnormal amygdala function disrupts affect association; (c) asociality, wherein impaired oxytocin-vasopressin system function flattens social bonding and affiliativeness; and (d) extended selective attention, wherein abnormal cortical organization disrupts normal processing of representations and attention shifting. These four mechanisms are proposed to impair information processing, pair bonding, social imitation, and communication. The mechanisms are not proposed as mutually exclusive or exhaustive, and it is possible that behavioral or cognitive subtypes of autism result from different

relative contributions of these impairments (Waterhouse, Fein, et al., 1996).

In this model, abnormal neuronal organization in medial temporal lobe tissues and association cortex is hypothesized to generate autistic symptomatology, and cerebellar abnormalities are hypothesized to add to the severity of all information-processing deficits. We have noted, however, that "the potential for learning and memory in the absence of the cerebellum may seem so considerable that the cerebellum should be regarded as at best a minor member of the set of mechanisms that taken as a whole constitute intelligence" (Macphail, 1993, p. 186).

There are a number of problematic aspects of our model. (a) We have relegated cerebellar impairment to nonsyndromic status. If future studies find that cerebellar dysfunction does generate symptoms unique to autism, our model would not provide an adequate explanation. (b) We outlined four neural mechanisms and have proposed the existence of two neurobiologically distinct subtypes of autism (Waterhouse, 1994b; Waterhouse, Fein, et al., 1996). If future enhanced imaging and pathology studies were to determine that there was a single necessary or sufficient neural locus for all cases of autism, parts of our model would have to be dismantled. (c) We eschew discrete social behavior brain modules, and alternately have proposed that neuroanatomical and neurochemical systems affected in autism (medial temporal lobe structures, oxytocin system, association cortex) support both processing of "social" and "nonsocial" stimuli. If a discrete organic basis for a theory-of-mind module were to be discovered, it would argue against our model.

Bachevalier and Merjanian's Limbic System Model

Bachevalier and Merjanian (1994) concluded that the impaired behaviors of monkeys with bilateral removal of amygdala and hippocampus early in infancy, which include withdrawal from other monkeys, lack of eye contact, and motor stereotypies, are similar to the aberrant behaviors of autistic individuals. Bachevalier (1995) also suggested that autistic behavior parallels the Kluver-Bucy syndrome (resulting from bilateral removal of the temporal lobes) in symptoms of psychic blindness, severe changes in emotional behavior, oral exploration of objects, and dietary changes. In sum, this model presents hippocampus-plus-amygdala as determinants of (a) the medial temporal lobe (limbic) memory system, (b) development and governance of social behavior, and (c) emotions and emotional expression (Bachevalier, 1995; Bachevalier & Merjanian, 1994). These researchers proposed that, because all autistic persons share the same behavioral impairments, they, like the monkeys and like Kluver-Bucy syndrome cases, all suffer from limbic system deficit (Bachevalier, 1995; Bachevalier & Merjanian, 1994).

Autopsy studies (Bauman & Kemper, 1994) and imaging studies (Reiss, Lee, & Freund, 1994) have reported medial temporal lobe deficit in some autistic individuals, and many autistic individuals experience some of the symptoms profiled in the model (Rapin, 1991). Bachevalier and Merjanian's model makes good sense of medial temporal lobe deficit, but it would be stronger if it went beyond the animal model/adult pathology analogies to outline a functional mechanism whereby medial temporal lobe deficit engenders the specific social impairments found in autism.

COMPARISON OF THE FOUR APPROACHES

All models considered here generate research questions on social impairment in autism. The plurality of models in contention is valuable; it forces specificity of assumptions and clarification of what new data are needed. Nonetheless, it is clear from the preceding brief review that the majority of models of social impairment in autism have failed to incorporate (a) current knowledge of neural function, (b) the range of autistic symptoms, neural deficits, and associated etiologies, or (c) full-scale models of human social behavior in their theoretical frameworks.

Observing the Constraints of Neurobiology

Social impairments in autism are now assumed to originate in neural deficit, but despite advances in knowledge of brain function, the majority of models considered in this chapter have been formulated at the psychological level, without any regard for neurobiological constraints on psychological functions. Psychological models should limit speculation to what is neurofunctionally possible and plausible. If an eye-direction detector is proposed (as per Baron-Cohen's 1995 model), the proposal for that psychological module should depend on current findings from research on neural domains of the visual system, such as those reported as identifying object-centered spatial awareness in neuronal eye-fields (Olson & Gettner, 1995). If psychological models do not respect the constraints of neurobiology, they reprise the fallacy of Cartesian dualism.

Respecting the Full Complexity of the Syndrome

At present, most models of social impairment seek to explain autism as a unitary disorder with a unitary cause. The precedents for unitary models are negative. The complexity of the pattern of autistic symptomatology has not yielded to models of either a unitary psychological or a unitary neurological deficit. There is consistent evidence for patterns of behavioral variation within the syndrome (Green, Fein, Joy, & Waterhouse, 1995; Klin & Volkmar, 1993; Rapin, 1996; Waterhouse, 1994a; Wing, 1988), and evidence for many varied associated neurological deficits (Minshew & Dombrowski, 1994) and associated etiological agents (Gillberg, 1992). Even idiopathic autism is not homogeneous; it only identifies autism with unknown etiology. Future models of social impairment should expand their frameworks to include a wider understanding of the autistic spectrum behavioral phenomena.

Most importantly, the full range and relationship of "social" and "cognitive" symptoms have not yet been adequately accounted for in current models of social impairment in autism. Happé (1994) reviewed evidence for three groups of psychological models—executive function, central coherence, and theory of mind—and concluded that all three models may be needed to account for the impaired social cognition and impaired cognitive style found in autistic individuals. If all three models are needed, none has been sufficiently comprehensive to explain the phenomena of autistic symptoms.

Establishing a Comprehensive Model of Human Social Behavior

Models of social impairment in autism have taken a magpie approach to ideas about social behavior. They pick up attractive conceptualizations (attachment, hyperarousal, opioid reward, intersubjectivity, joint attention, empathy, theory of mind) and bring them in as a means of offering striking, unifying, and unitary evidence concerning autistic social development. Admittedly, there is no single "standard science" paradigm for understanding human social behavior. However, when discrete developmental aspects of the complexity that is human social behavior are isolated, the explanatory limitations of these conceptualized "bits" should be recognized. More importantly, efforts to model a comprehensive framework for human social behavior are needed.

NEW IDEAS ABOUT HUMAN SOCIAL BEHAVIOR

The second goal of this chapter is to outline potential frameworks for more comprehensive models of social skills and social impairment. To that end, we consider three current relevant questions concerning human social behavior:

1. Was the evolution of human cognition driven by selection for social skills?
2. Are there discrete brain systems for social behaviors?
3. Are normal individual differences in social behavior innate?

Was the Evolution of Human Cognition Driven by Selection for Social Skills?

Brain size "is a superb estimator of the total neural information processing capacity of the brain in mammals" (Jerison, 1995, p. 196), but it is not a good estimator of degree of social organization across all mammalian species. In humans and the great apes,

however, individual social skill does reflect information-processing skill in the form of strategic judgment: the ability to consider alternate possible lines of action, and, within every social interchange, to select the course of action most likely to yield the least effort and most reward in food, safety, mating, comfort, or social status (Quiatt & Reynolds, 1995, p. 7).

If social interchange requires strategic judgment, was the human increase in cognitive skill and brain size selected for by the pressures of both competitive and cooperative social interchange? At present, there are a variety of answers to this question. Wilkins and Wakefield (1995) have argued that the need to understand the world drove the development of an amodal association area in the brain, which produced cognitive structure, which permitted language, which, in turn, supported social interchange. Jerison (1995), however, has argued that a hominid environment "selected" language as an adaptive (social) trait in very early, small-brained australopithecines. Quiatt and Reynolds (1995) have posited that social life increased intelligence. Although increasingly complex social cooperation improved the survival rates of group members, it increased the individual's need for multiple rapid nonconscious calculations. Damasio (1994) has proposed that social cognition operates on emotionally marked information, limiting our access to behavioral sequences marked with negative affective associations, and LeDoux (1995) has suggested that the generation of internal affective states is a rapid means of information processing in both social and nonsocial contexts where rapid behavioral choice is important.

If every productive social interchange represents a self-versus-other or self-versus-group computation of relative advantage (e.g., What will I gain or lose here? What does the other want? What will be the outcome for my position in the social group?), even if prior aversively marked behavioral options are eliminated (Damasio, 1994; Tranel & Damasio, 1993) and our decisions are guided by rapidly formed affective states (LeDoux, 1995), the calculations needed in social interchange will be more numerous and more variable than those needed in nonsocial contexts.

This debate has two important implications for the study of social impairment in autism. The first is the hypothesis that the greatest information-processing load imposed on the primate or hominid is social interaction. In fact, nonautistic severely retarded individuals may be affectionate and affiliative, but they are not strategic interactants. Insel (1992) proposed that there is a neurochemical basis for mammalian social attachment and affiliativeness (the oxytocin-vasopressin system) and that it varies across mammalian species. Most autistic individuals are neither affiliative nor strategic. Models of social impairment need to consider the distinction between affiliativeness and strategic interaction, because affiliativeness can occur even in individuals with poor information-processing skills. Future models should also consider seriously the information-processing demands of strategic human social interaction. The associations between aspects of social impairment and measured intelligence in autism may be indexes of developmental status (Volkmar, Carter, Sparrow, & Cicchetti, 1993), but should also be explored as significant aspects of the syndrome (Klin & Volkmar, 1993; Minshew, 1991; Rapin, 1996).

The second important implication is that the need for rapid choices for behavior is likely to have shifted selection pressures away from built-in behavior control mechanisms and toward social learning mechanisms. Heyes (1994) has defined social learning as the acquisition of behavior patterns by observation of, or interaction with, a group member (p. 207). Heyes proposed that social learning uses the same central nervous system mechanisms as asocial learning, and falls into three categories: (a) stimulus enhancement—if B watches A eat Y, B will be more likely to eat Y; (b) observational Pavlovian conditioning—if B observes that A is fearful around lakes, B may be fearful around lakes; and (c) observational instrumental conditioning—if B observes A digging, B will imitate A in digging, and may or may not be rewarded by finding an edible root.

Comparative social learning studies have not been conducted in autism, but experimental work has revealed impaired or absent social imitation (see Smith & Bryson, 1994, for a review) and impaired or absent social attention to the behavior of others (Frith, 1989; Rapin, 1996; Wing, 1988). Social learning cannot take place without both social attention and social imitation. Although essential affiliativeness is unlikely to be a function of social learning, perhaps a significant portion of aberrant social behavior in autism represents the failure of social learning.

Are There Discrete Brain Systems for Social Behavior?

Cosmides and Tooby (1992) have argued for the existence of specific brain modules for social interchange, and Fiske (1992) and Haslam (1994) have claimed the existence of a limited set of strategic social exchange processes. Cosmides and Tooby (1992) have proposed that there are myriad discrete brain modules, including (but not limited to) modules engaged in: (a) computation of social permission and obligations; (b) computation of social threats and warnings; (c) computation of social event frequencies; (d) computation of social danger avoidance; (e) computation of the emotions of others; (f) computation of a theory of the minds of others; (g) recognition of the faces of others; (h) computation of the semantics of what others say; and (i) computation of the syntax of what others say.

Thus, for Cosmides and Tooby's model, if autistic individuals are impaired in the brain module that constructs a theory of the minds of others, they need not have any difficulty in language comprehension, face recognition, understanding threats and promises, or computing incipient social dangers. Theory-of-mind studies in autism, to date, however, have contrasted theory-of-mind skill with object recognition, object memory, and object inference, but have not contrasted theory-of-mind skill with any other of Cosmides and Tooby's proposed modular social skills.

Haslam (1994) and Fiske (1992) have proposed that there are four forms of social exchange: (a) communal sharing (one for all and all for one); (b) equality matching (50–50 turn taking); (c) authority ranking (one is the leader); and (d) market pricing (participation in a relationship when it is worthwhile to do so). They have not proposed that these are discrete brain modules, but Fiske has argued (1992) that these four schemas provide an information-processing framework through which to initiate social action, to make sense of the social actions of others, and to coordinate and evaluate social interchanges.

These four schemas can be seen as mechanisms by which individuals strategically balance self-needs with group needs. Fiske (1992) has argued that they unfold in order in a developmental sequence in childhood. Fiske's categories have not been studied in autism, but it is likely that few autistic individuals would be able to understand or enact even sharing or matching relationships without extensive programmatic instruction. Although there is evidence that some autistic individuals make functional use of other people to obtain needs (Frith, 1989), and some depend on their mothers, who may engage in strategic interactions on their behalf (Rogers et al., 1993), there is no evidence that autistic individuals employ cost–benefit analysis or engage in strategic interaction with others.

There is evidence for modularity in many aspects of brain function (Goldman-Rakic, 1995). The modules suggested by neurological research are tangible and identifiable (e.g., the amygdala), and their proposed mental functions are built from research findings. The modules proposed at the psychological level largely ignore organic constraints but provide more immediately satisfying explanatory models of behavior.

It would be neither creative nor adequately productive to limit theorizing to neurologically supported modules. The field should, however, design research to explore the links among: (a) social learning, asocial learning, and neural function; (b) measures of intelligence, measures of skill in social interchange, and neural function; and (c) affiliativeness, strategic skills in interaction, and neural function.

Are Normal Individual Differences in Social Behavior Innate?

Kagan (1994) has presented a cogent argument for the presence of dimensions of social reactivity as part of human temperament: "[I]nfants seem to inherit two independent qualities: ease of arousal, on the one hand, and valence of the (affective) state that follows arousal, on the

other" (p. 235). Kagan has claimed that inhibited children, who are normal but very shy in social interactions, have high sympathetic arousal and negative valence affect; uninhibited, gregarious children have low arousal and positive valence affect.

The presence of normal underlying individual variation in temperament is rarely considered in the assessment of the social impairments of autism. It is tacitly assumed that the neural deficits swamp individual variation, and this may not be the case. The same neuropathological process might result in different phenotypic presentations in children who would have been shy if not autistic, than in children who would have been gregarious and uninhibited if not autistic. A complicating factor, of course, is that a key neural basis for reactivity in normal temperament in Kagan's model is the amygdala, which is proposed as the source of abnormal social behavior in a variety of existing models (Bachevalier & Merjanian, 1994; Brothers & Ring, 1992; Fein, 1994; Waterhouse, Fein, et al., 1996).

An equally complex question involves the developmental interaction of children's genotype, neural organization, sociability, social learning, and elicited environmental effects. Scarr (1992) proposed that children's own genotypes may determine their environments: passively in infancy, evocatively in childhood, and selectively in adolescence. Autistic infants may or may not evoke dysfunctional environmental reactions. In childhood, however, when both synaptogenesis and synaptic pruning are at their peak (Blakeslee, 1995), and when the impaired language, cognition, sociability, and impaired social learning of autistic children must evoke a less spontaneous and less rich pattern of stimulation from those around them, the environmentally triggered synaptic reorganization that takes place is likely to be nonnormal. In adolescence, autistic individuals have far fewer chances to select environments for themselves than do normal young adults; thus, they are likely to remain in the position of evoking reactive behaviors of others in environments they did not choose.

Plomin's quantitative trait loci (QTL) model (1995b), which argues for a multigene basis for the dimensional expression of complex disorders such as autism, raises still another issue. It is possible that, in those cases where autism has a genetic basis, a parent or other family member of the autistic individual might experience some minor language, cognitive, or sociability difficulties (Bolton et al., 1994). Unlike Kanner's initial hypothesis that impaired parenting was the cause of autistic behavior (1949), (a) very few parents are likely to be affected (Bolton et al., 1994), and (b) where such minor cognitive, linguistic, or social deficits do occur in a parent, they are likely to add very little to the developmental variance of the autistic individual (Plomin, 1995a, 1995b). The child's genotype for impaired neural/behavioral functioning, and the evocative effects of the abnormal functioning of that genotype in all environments (i.e., all family members, school, and society) will be the chief determinants of the child's developmental trajectory of neural and behavior dysfunction (Plomin, 1995a). Furthermore, although the autistic individual will have diminished ability to evoke a unique environment under strictly regulated conditions such as behavioral modification programs, even such programs—in a larger sense—can be said to be evoked by the child's impairments.

In sum, the new ideas concerning human behavior considered here have suggested several possibilities for new lines of research. If the greatest information-processing load for human beings is social interaction, then hypotheses concerning information-processing loads, working memory, hippocampal function, and frontal lobe function should be investigated. If there are many discrete social modules in human brains, then research designs to compare types of social skills, and to explore neural functioning in relation to those presumptively discrete skills should be developed. Finally, if autistic children do further impair their already impaired neural development through the abnormally limited "evocativeness" of their abnormal social functioning, then family studies and school program studies should be conducted to attempt to develop the most beneficial programmatic environmental structures.

CONCLUSIONS

This chapter evaluated models designed to explain social impairment in autism. The models reviewed were based on four distinct assumptions: (a) that social impairments are a secondary effect of a primary deficit in attention, arousal, sensory function, pain system function, memory, executive function, or information processing; (b) that impairment in social cognition is the primary deficit; (c) that impairments in affective sociability and social cognition together are the primary deficits; and, (d) that social impairments are the most salient of a set of core deficits.

The critical review led to three conclusions about current models of social impairment. First, the majority of models have been constructed without adequate regard for current knowledge of neural function. At present, little is known about the neurobiological basis of human social behavior; nonetheless, what is known should be addressed in models of social impairment in autism. Second, the full extent and interrelationship of "social" and "cognitive" symptoms has not yet been adequately accounted for in current models of social impairment in autism. Here again, it must be noted that until we fully understand the source of social and cognitive behaviors, we will not be able to adequately distinguish related groups of expressed behaviors. Finally, a number of models of social impairment in autism have focused on one element of social behavior as the source of autistic impairment. Given the heterogeneity of social impairment in autism, this is unlikely to be the case. It remains the burden of researchers in the field to understand the full range of human social behaviors, and to model the ways in which social behaviors are aberrant, delayed, or absent in autism.

The chapter also reviewed a number of current models of human social behavior. We suggested that future research on social impairment in autism should consider the implications of these current conceptualizations: (a) the greatest information-processing load imposed on humans is social interaction (Quiatt & Reynolds, 1995); (b) affiliativeness is likely to be a discrete, innate system (Insel, 1992), that is distinct from strategic interaction skill; (c) social learning, which involves imitation and attention to others, is a key vehicle for acquisition of behavior (Heyes, 1994); (d) of the many brain modules theorized to control social behavior, theory of mind is the only one that has been tested in autism (Cosmides & Tooby, 1992); (e) components of individual temperament have not been explored in studies of social impairment in autism (Kagan, 1994); and (f) the functioning of children evokes the unique environments they develop within (Scarr, 1992), and these environments serve, in turn, to reconfigure the functional neural bases for their ongoing development.

Cross-References

Social development in autism is reviewed in Chapter 8, and cognitive development is the subject of Chapter 10. Executive function deficits and theory of mind are discussed in Chapters 40 through 42, and a personal perspective on autism is provided in Chapter 49.

REFERENCES

Adrien, J.L., Lenoir, P., Martineau, J., Perrot, A., Hameury, L., Larmande, C., & Sauvage, D. (1993). Blind ratings of early symptoms of autism based upon family home movies. *Journal of American Academy of Child Adolescent Psychiatry, 32,* 617–626.

American Psychiatric Association. (1994). *Diagnostic and statistical manual of mental disorders* (4th ed.). Washington, DC: Author.

Bachevalier, J. (1995, February 8). *Neuropsychological indices of medial temporal lobe functions.* Paper presented at the meeting of the International Neuropsychology Society Workshop, Seattle, WA.

Bachevalier, J., & Merjanian, P. (1994). The contribution of medial temporal lobe structures in infantile autism: A neurobehavioral study in primates. In M.L. Bauman & T.L. Kemper (Eds.), *The neurobiology of autism* (pp. 146–169). Baltimore: Johns Hopkins University Press.

Bailey, A., Le Couteur, A., Gottesman, I., Bolton, P., Simonoff, E., Yuzda, E., & Rutter, M. (1995). Autism as a strongly genetic disorder: Evidence from a British twin study. *Psychological Medicine, 25,* 63–77.

Barkley, R. (1990). *Attention Deficit Hyperactivity Disorder: A handbook for diagnosis and treatment.* New York: Guilford Press.

Baron-Cohen, S. (1995). *Mindblindness.* Cambridge, MA: MIT Press.

Baron-Cohen, S., Leslie, A.M., & Frith, U. (1985). Does the autistic child have a "theory of mind?" *Cognition, 21,* 37–46.

Bauman, M.L., & Kemper, T.L. (1994). Neuroanatomic observations of the brain in autism. In M.L. Bauman & T.L. Kemper (Eds.), *The neurobiology of autism* (pp. 119–145). Baltimore: Johns Hopkins University Press.

Blakeslee, S. (1995, August 29). In brain's early growth, timetable may be crucial. *New York Times Science Times,* pp. C1, C3.

Bolton, P., MacDonald, H., Pickles, A., Rios, P., Goode, S., Crowson, M., Bailey, A., & Rutter, M. (1994). A case-control family history study of autism. *Journal of Child Psychology and Psychiatry, 35,* 877–900.

Brothers, L. (1989). A biological perspective on empathy. *American Journal of Psychiatry, 146,* 10–19.

Brothers, L. (1995). Neurophysiology of the perceptions of intentions by primates. In M. Gazzaniga (Ed.), *The cognitive neurosciences* (pp. 1107–1115). Cambridge, MA: MIT Press.

Brothers, L., & Ring, B. (1992). A neuroethological framework for the representation of minds. *Journal of Cognitive Neuroscience, 4,* 107–118.

Charman, T., & Baron-Cohen, S. (1995). Understanding photos, models, and beliefs: A test of the modularity thesis of the theory of mind. *Cognitive Development, 10,* 287–298.

Clark, H.H. (1996). *Using language.* New York: Cambridge University Press.

Cosmides, L., & Tooby, J. (1992). Cognitive adaptations for social exchange. In J.H. Barkow, L. Cosmides, & J. Tooby (Eds.), *The adapted mind* (pp. 163–228). New York: Oxford University Press.

Courchesne, E. (1995). New evidence of cerebellar and brainstem hypoplasia in autistic infants, children, and adolescents: The MR imaging study by Hashimoto and colleagues. *Journal of Autism and Developmental Disorders, 25,* 19–22.

Courchesne, E., Townsend, J., Akshoomoff, N.A., Yeung-Courchesne, R., Murakami, G.A., Lincoln, A., James, H.E., Saitoh, O., Haas, R.H., Schreibman, L., & Lau, L. (1994). A new finding in autism: Impairment in shifting attention. In S.H. Broman & J. Grafman (Eds.), *Atypical cognitive deficits in developmental disorders: Implications for brain function* (pp. 101–138). Hillsdale, NJ: Erlbaum.

Damasio, A. (1994). *Descartes' error.* New York: Grosset/Putnam.

Dawson, G., & Lewy A. (1989). Arousal, attention, and socioemotional impairments of individuals with autism. In G. Dawson (Ed.), *Autism: Nature, diagnosis and treatment* (pp. 49–74). New York: Guilford Press.

DeLong, R.G. (1992). Autism, amnesia, hippocampus and learning. *Neuroscience and Biobehavioral Review, 16,* 63–70.

Fein, D. (1994, March 16). Evaluating the role of memory and attention in social competence. In L. Waterhouse (Organizer), *Social competence: A neurobehavioral perspective.* Symposium conducted at the meeting of the Learning Disabilities Association of American Research, Washington, DC.

Fein, D., Pennington, B., & Waterhouse, L. (1987). Implications of social deficits in autism for neurological dysfunction. In E. Schopler & G. Mesibov (Eds.), *Neurobiological issues in autism* (pp. 127–144). New York: Plenum Press.

Fiez, J.A., Peterson, S.E., Cheney, M.K., & Raichle, M.E. (1992). Impaired non-motor learning and impaired error detection associated with cerebellar damage. *Brain, 115,* 155–178.

Fiske, A. (1992). The four elementary forms of sociality: Framework for a unified theory of social relations. *Psychological Review, 99,* 689–723.

Frankel, F., Simmons, J.Q., Fichter, M., & Freeman, B.J. (1984). Stimulus overselectivity in autistic and mentally retarded children: A research note. *Journal of Child Psychology and Psychiatry, 25,* 147–155.

Frith, U. (1989). *Autism: Explaining the enigma.* London: Basil Blackwell.

Frye, D. (1993). Causes and precursors of children's theories of mind. In D.F. Hay & A. Angold (Eds.), *Precursors and causes in development and psychopathology* (pp. 145–168). New York: John Wiley & Sons.

Gillberg, C. (1992). Subgroups in autism: Are there behavioral phenotypes typical of underlying medical conditions? *Journal of Intellectual Disability Research, 36,* 201–214.

Goldman-Rakic, P. (1995). Neurobiology of representation. In H. Morowitz & J.L. Singer (Eds.), *The mind, the brain and complex adaptive systems* (pp. 51–62). Reading, MA: Addison-Wesley.

Grattan, L.M., & Eslinger, P.J. (1992). Long term psychosocial consequences of childhood frontal lobe lesion inpatient DT. *Brain and Cognition, 20,* 185–195.

Green, L., Fein, D., Joy, S., & Waterhouse, L. (1995). Cognitive functioning in autism: An overview. In E. Schopler & G. Mesibov (Eds.), *Learning and cognition in autism* (pp. 13–31). New York: Plenum Press.

Happé, F.G.E. (1994). Annotation: Current psychological theories of autism: The "theory of mind" account and rival theories. *Journal of Child Psychology and Psychiatry, 35,* 215–229.

Happé, F.G.E. (1995). The role of age and verbal ability in the theory of mind task performance of subjects with autism. *Child Development, 66,* 843–855.

Happé, F.G.E., & Frith, U. (1995). Theory of mind in autism. In E. Schopler & G.B. Mesibov (Eds.), *Learning and cognition in autism* (pp. 177–198). New York: Plenum Press.

Hashimoto, T., Tayama, M., Murakawa, K., Yoshimoto, T., Miyazaki, M., Harada, M., & Kuroda, Y. (1995). Development of the brainstem and cerebellum in autistic patients. *Journal of Autism and Developmental Disorders, 25,* 1–18.

Haslam, N. (1994). Categories of social relationship. *Cognition, 53,* 59–90.

Heyes, C.M. (1994). Social learning in animals: Categories and mechanisms. *Biological Reviews, 69,* 207–231.

Hobson, R.P. (1993). *Autism and the development of mind.* Hove, England: Erlbaum.

Horowitz, B., & Rumsey, J.M. (1994). Positron emission tomography: Implications for cerebral dysfunction in autism. In M.L. Bauman & T.L. Kemper (Eds.), *The neurobiology of autism* (pp. 102–118). Baltimore: Johns Hopkins University Press.

Hughes, C.H., & Russell, J. (1993). Autistic children's difficulty with mental disengagement from an object: Its implications for theories of autism. *Developmental Psychology, 29,* 498–510.

Insel, T.R. (1992). Oxytocin—A neuropeptide for affiliation: Evidence from behavioral, receptor autoradiographic, and comparative studies. *Psychoneuroendocrinology, 17,* 3–35.

Jerison, H.J. (1995). Issues in neo- and paleoneurology of language. Commentary on Wilkins, W.K., & Wakefield, J., Brain evolution and neurolinguistic preconditions. *Behavioral and Brain Sciences, 18,* 195–196.

Kagan, J. (1994). *Galen's prophecy.* New York: Basic Books.

Kanner, L. (1943). Autistic disturbances of affective contact. *Nervous Child, 2,* 217–250.

Kanner, L. (1949). Problems of nosology and psychodynamics of early infantile autism. *American Journal of Orthopsychiatry, 19,* 416–426.

Kass, J. (1995). The reorganization of sensory and motor maps in adult animals. In M. Gazzaniga (Ed.), *The cognitive neurosciences* (pp. 51–71). Cambridge, MA: MIT Press.

Kinsbourne, M. (1987). Cerebral-brainstem relations in infantile autism. In E. Schopler & G.B. Mesibov (Eds.), *Neurobiological issues in autism* (pp. 107–125). New York: Plenum Press.

Klin, A., & Volkmar, F. (1993). The development of individuals with autism: Implications for the theory of mind hypothesis. In S. Baron-Cohen, H. Tager-Flusberg, & D.J. Cohen (Eds.), *Understanding other minds* (pp. 317–331). New York: Oxford University Press.

Klin, A., Volkmar, F., & Sparrow, S.S. (1992). Autistic social dysfunction: Some limitations of the theory of mind hypothesis. *Journal of Child Psychology and Psychiatry, 33,* 861–876.

Klinger, L.G., & Dawson, G. (1995). A fresh look at categorization abilities in persons with autism. In E. Schopler & G.B. Mesibov (Eds.), *Learning and cognition in autism* (pp. 119–136). New York: Plenum Press.

LeDoux, J.E. (1995). In search of an emotional system in the brain: Leaping from fear to emotion to consciousness. In M. Gazzaniga (Ed.), *The cognitive neurosciences* (pp. 1049–1062). Cambridge, MA: MIT Press.

Leiner, H., & Leiner, A. (1993). Cognitive and language functions of the human cerebellum. *Trends in Neurosciences, 16,* 444–447.

Leslie, A. (1993). What autism teaches us about meta-representation. In S. Baron-Cohen, H. Tager-Flusberg, & D.J. Cohen (Eds.), *Understanding other minds* (pp. 83–111). New York: Oxford University Press.

Lewis, V., & Boucher, J. (1988). Spontaneous, instructed and elicited play in relatively able autistic children. *British Journal of Developmental Psychology, 6,* 325–339.

Lovaas, L., Koegel, R., & Schreibman, L. (1979). Stimulus overselectivity in autism: A review of research. *Psychological Bulletin, 86,* 1236–1254.

Macphail, E. (1993). *The neuroscience of animal intelligence.* New York: Columbia University Press.

Minshew, N.J. (1991). Indices of neural function in autism: Clinical and biological implications. *Pediatrics, 87*(Suppl.), 774–780.

Minshew, N.J., & Dombrowski, S.M. (1994). In vivo neuroanatomy of autism: Neuroimaging studies. In M.L. Bauman & T.L. Kemper (Eds.), *The neurobiology of autism* (pp. 66–85). Baltimore: Johns Hopkins University Press.

Modahl, C., Fein, D., Waterhouse, L., & Newton, N. (1992). Does oxytocin deficiency mediate social deficits in autism? *Journal of Autism and Developmental Disorders, 24,* 449–451.

Olson, C.R., & Gettner, S.N. (1995). Object-centered direction selectivity in the macaque supplementary eye field. *Science, 269,* 985–988.

Ornitz, E.M. (1985). Neurophysiology of infantile autism. *Journal of the American Academy of Child Psychiatry, 24,* 251–262.

Ornitz, E.M. (1988). Autism: A disorder of directed attention. *Brain Dysfunction, 1,* 309–322.

Ornitz, E.M., & Ritvo, E.R. (1968). Neurophysiologic mechanisms underlying perceptual inconsistency in autistic and schizophrenic children. *Archives of General Psychiatry, 19,* 22–27.

Osterling, J., & Dawson, G. (1994). Early recognition of children with autism: A study of first birthday home videotapes. *Journal of Autism and Developmental Disorders, 24,* 247–258.

Ozonoff, S. (1995). Executive functions in autism. In E. Schopler & G.B. Mesibov (Eds.), *Learning and cognition in autism* (pp. 199–219). New York: Plenum Press.

Ozonoff, S., Pennington, B., & Rogers, S. (1991). Executive function deficits in high-functioning autistic individuals: Relationship to theory of mind. *Journal of Child Psychology and Psychiatry, 32,* 1081–1105.

Ozonoff, S., Strayer, D.L., McMahon, W.M., & Filloux, F. (1994). Executive function abilities in autism and Tourette syndrome: An information processing approach. *Journal of Child Psychology and Psychiatry, 35,* 1015–1032.

Panksepp, J., & Sahley, T.L. (1987). Possible brain opioid involvement in disrupted social intent and language development of autism. In E. Schopler & G. Mesibov (Eds.), *Neurobiological issues in autism* (pp. 357–372). New York: Plenum Press.

Perner, J. (1993). The theory of mind deficit in autism: Rethinking the metarepresentation theory. In S. Baron-Cohen, H. Tager-Flusberg, & D.J. Cohen (Eds.), *Understanding other minds* (pp. 112–137). New York: Oxford University Press.

Peterson, C., & Siegal, M. (1995). Deafness, conversation and theory of mind. *Journal of Child Psychology and Psychiatry, 36,* 459–474.

Piven, J., Arndt, S., Bailey, J., Havercamp, S., Andreasen, N., & Palmer, P. (1995). An MRI study of brain size in autism. *American Journal of Psychiatry, 152,* 1145–1149.

Piven, J., & Folstein, S. (1994). The genetics of autism. In M.L. Bauman & T.L. Kemper (Eds.), *The neurobiology of autism* (pp. 18–44). Baltimore: Johns Hopkins University Press.

Plomin, R. (1995a). Genetics and children's experiences in the family. *Journal of Child Psychology and Psychiatry, 36,* 33–68.

Plomin, R. (1995b). Molecular genetics and psychology. *Current Directions in Psychological Science, 4,* 114–117.

Quiatt, D., & Reynolds, V. (1995). *Primate behaviour.* Cambridge, England: Cambridge University Press.

Rapin, I. (1991). Autistic children: Diagnosis and clinical features. *Pediatrics, 87*(Suppl.), 751–760.

Rapin, I. (Ed.). (1996). *Preschool children with inadequate communication.* London: Cambridge University Press.

Reichler, R.J., & Lee, M.C.L. (1987). Overview of biomedical issues in autism. In E. Schopler & G.B. Mesibov (Eds.), *Neurobiological issues in autism* (pp. 14–43). New York: Plenum Press.

Reiss, A.L., Lee, J., & Freund, L. (1994). Neuroanatomy of Fragile (X) syndrome: The temporal lobe. *Neurology, 44,* 1317–1324.

Rimland, B. (1964). *Infantile autism: The syndrome and its implications.* New York: Appleton-Century-Crofts.

Rogers, S.J., Ozonoff, S., & Maslin-Cole, C. (1993). Developmental aspects of attachment behavior in young children and pervasive developmental disorders. *Journal of the American Academy of Child and Adolescent Psychiatry, 32,* 1274–1282.

Sahley, T.L., & Panksepp, J. (1987). Brain opioids and autism: An updated analysis of possible linkages. *Journal of Autism and Developmental Disorders, 17,* 201–216.

Scarr, S. (1992). Developmental theories for the 1990s: Development and individual differences. *Child Development, 63,* 1–19.

Schmahman, J. (1994). The cerebellum in autism: Clinical and anatomic perspectives. In M.L. Bauman & T.L. Kemper (Eds.), *The neurobiology of autism* (pp. 195–226). Baltimore: Johns Hopkins University Press.

Shah, A., & Frith, U. (1993). Why do autistic children show a superior performance on the block design task? *Journal of Child Psychology and Psychiatry, 34,* 1351–1364.

Sigman, M., Yirmiya, N., & Capps, L. (1995). Social and cognitive understanding in high-functioning children with autism. In E. Schopler & G.B. Mesibov (Eds.), *Learning and cognition in autism* (pp. 159–176). New York: Plenum Press.

Smith, I.M., & Bryson, S.E. (1994). Imitation and action in autism: A critical review. *Psychological Bulletin, 116,* 259–273.

Sparrevohn, R., & Howie, P.H. (1995). Theory of mind in children with Autistic Disorder: Evidence of developmental progression and the role of verbal ability. *Journal of Child Psychology and Psychiatry, 36,* 249–263.

Tranel, D., & Damasio, A.R. (1993). The covert learning of affective valence does not require structures in hippocampal system or amygdala. *Journal of Cognitive Neuroscience, 5,* 79–88.

Volkmar, F.R., Carter, A., Sparrow, S.S., & Cicchetti, D. (1993). Quantifying social development in autism. *Journal of the American Academy of Child and Adolescent Psychiatry, 32,* 627–632.

Waterhouse, L. (1994a). Severity of impairment in autistic spectrum disorders. In S.H. Broman & J. Grafman (Eds.), *Atypical cognitive deficits in developmental disorders: Implications for brain function* (pp. 159–182). Hillsdale, NJ: Erlbaum.

Waterhouse, L. (1994b, March 16). Models of the biological basis of human social behavior. In L. Waterhouse (Organizer), *Social competence: A neurobehavioral perspective.* Symposium conducted at the meeting of the Learning Disabilities Association of American Research, Washington, DC.

Waterhouse, L., Fein, D., & Modahl, C. (1996). Neurofunctional mechanisms in autism. *Psychological Review, 103,* 457–489.

Waterhouse, L., Morris, R., Allen, D., Dunn, M., Fein, D., Feinstein, C., Rapin, I., & Wing, L. (1996). Diagnosis and classification in autism. *Journal of Autism and Developmental Disorders, 26,* 59–86.

Wilkins, W.K., & Wakefield, J. (1995). Brain evolution and neurolinguistic preconditions. *Behavioral and Brain Sciences, 18,* 161–226.

Wing, L. (1988). The continuum of autistic characteristics. In E. Schopler & G. Mesibov (Eds.), *Diagnosis and assessment in autism* (pp. 91–110). New York: Plenum Press.

Zelazo, P.D., Reznick, J.S., & Pinon, D.E. (1995). Response control and the execution of rules. *Developmental Psychology, 31,* 508–517.

Zilbovicious, M., Garreau, B., Samson, Y., Remy, P., Barthelmey, C., Syrota, A., & LeLord, G. (1995). Delayed maturation of the frontal cortex in childhood autism. *American Journal of Psychiatry, 152,* 258–252.

CHAPTER 44

Theoretical Perspectives on Behavioral Intervention for Individuals with Autism

LAURA SCHREIBMAN

Few people involved with the treatment of autism would deny that, at this time, the treatment of choice is based on a behavioral model, reflecting the fact that behavioral treatment has been empirically demonstrated to be effective with this population (Bristol et al., 1996; Schreibman, 1988). Behavioral procedures do not cure the disorder, but they have been shown to be extremely effective in substantially improving the lives of autistic people and the lives of those around them. The application of behavioral techniques to autism, like the diagnosis itself, has a relatively short history. However, the progress in the development and refinement of behavioral treatment has been swift and impressive. The objectives of this chapter are: to reflect on important recent contributions of the behavioral approach to the treatment of autism, and to identify challenges for the future of this intervention model.

Behavioral treatment is essentially the application of the psychological principles of learning to human behavior. Specifically, behavioral treatment (often called "behavior modification" or "behavior therapy") is derived from the experimental analysis of behavior, which is a science dedicated to understanding the laws by which behavior is determined by environmental events. Identification of these laws allows for the prediction and control of behavior, and thus, logically, for the systematic application of these laws to change behavior. The application of these laws to the improvement of socially important behaviors is referred to as *applied behavior analysis,* and the development of the behavioral treatment of autism is largely the result of this field of science (see Chapter 26).

The application of learning theory to autism resulted from several events. First, there was the failure of treatments based on the popular early concept that autism was of psychogenic origin (i.e., the "parent-causation" hypothesis); treatments based on this model (e.g., Bettelheim, 1967) were notoriously ineffective (see Schreibman, 1988). Second, the fact remained that, prior to behavioral intervention, no effective treatment existed for autistic children, some of whom exhibited profound behavioral deficits and seriously disruptive behaviors. The severity of these problems resulted in most of these individuals being placed in highly restrictive environments (e.g., institutions) because there were no effective clinical programs, the schools were not equipped to teach these children, and the parents simply could not keep the children in the home and eventually were forced to place them outside the home. Third, the pervasive nature of the disorder and the specific deficits in what are

Preparation of this chapter was facilitated by U.S.P.H.S. Research Grant MH43943 from the National Institute of Mental Health. The author is indebted to Drs. Aubyn Stahmer and Karen Pierce and to Laura Campbell and Michelle Sherer for helpful comments on an earlier version of this work.

typically deemed as the most basic of human behaviors (social attachment and communication) proved irresistible to behavioral scientists interested in studying how such elemental behaviors interact with the environment. This led to the popularity of autism with behavioral researchers.

Many strengths are associated with the behavioral approach to understanding and treating individuals with autism. Most basic is the fact that the approach is based on the experimental analysis of behavior and the specific procedures have been subjected to rigorous study and careful conclusions. Thus, there already exists a comprehensive foundation of research to support the characteristics of specific treatments and treatment outcomes.

Further, forward progress in treatment development is guaranteed because of the self-analytic and self-critical nature of research in this area. Because of the emphases on detailed operational definitions of behavior, specific description of treatment procedures, and careful objective assessment of treatment outcome, behavioral researchers and clinicians are in a position to look very closely and critically at treatment effects. This, in turn, allows for closer examination of the interrelationships that may exist among characteristics of target behavior, treatment procedures, and outcome. Based on these findings, the parameters of treatment effectiveness and limitations are determined. These limitations and qualifications regarding effectiveness are then used to inform future directions of study aimed at improving the efficacy and efficiency of treatment. Constant refinement and improvement enable the field to advance in a systematic forward direction.

In addition, because of the objectivity of measurement and the detailed description of treatment procedures, the behavioral researcher or clinician knows exactly what he or she did in treating any particular case and can replicate the treatment effects. Because of the specificity of description of population, target behavior(s), treatment procedures, and outcome, others in the field will be able to assess replicability to their cases. Such replicability is essential to the development of the field as a directional whole, as opposed to an array of disparate parts.

EARLY CONTRIBUTIONS

To fully appreciate how far the behavioral approach to the treatment of autism has come over a relatively short period of time, it is informative to take a brief look at early efforts in the area. The earliest efforts were considered very dramatic and highly speculative because they directly contradicted the earlier psychogenic approach to the development of the disorder and the earlier prescribed psychodynamic treatment. Early behavioral researchers viewed autism not as a disease entity caused by pathological parental behavior, but as a syndrome of specific behaviors that could be related to environmental determinants. With this perspective, it was possible to consider changing behaviors by manipulating environmental events. For example, Ferster and DeMyer (1961, 1962) were among the first to demonstrate that children with autism could learn if the systematic application of operant discrimination learning techniques were employed. They demonstrated that these children could learn new behaviors under conditions where correct responses to a discrimination task were followed by contingent applications of reinforcement. Later, other behavioral researchers demonstrated the utility of the systematic application of reinforcement, prompting, fading, chaining, and other behavioral procedures (see Schreibman, 1988, for a review). Lovaas and his colleagues (e.g., Lovaas, 1977; Lovaas, Berberich, Perloff, & Schaeffer, 1966; Lovaas, Freitag, Gold, & Kassorla, 1965; Lovaas, Koegel, Simmons, & Long, 1973) were the first to develop a comprehensive, systematic package of behavioral interventions that addressed a range of behaviors in children with autism. Such interventions were associated with substantial decreases in inappropriate behaviors such as self-injury, self-stimulation, aggression, and tantrums as well as substantial increases in language, social, play, and academic skills.

The results of much of this early work are widely known and cited. However, despite its proven effectiveness, some aspects of behavioral intervention have remained controversial (e.g., use of aversives) and have sometimes limited the acceptance of the approach. Fortunately, the very nature of the approach itself has led to some reduction of controversy and to a widening of acceptance. The self-evaluating, forward-directing nature of behavioral intervention has allowed for the development of a broadened, more effective, and more efficient treatment approach.

FROM SIMPLE DEMONSTRATIONS TO COMPREHENSIVE TREATMENT

Because of the preliminary and tentative nature of the first demonstrations of behavioral intervention with autism (in the 1960s), the procedures used were limited, as were the target behaviors to which the interventions were applied. Thus, a simple positive reinforcement procedure was implemented to teach a young boy with autism to wear glasses (Wolf, Risley, & Mees, 1964). The procedure was effective, but we do not know to what extent the behavior change was maintained over time; what other areas of the child's behaviors may have been affected; how difficult the treatment was to implement; or how change in this behavior affected the child's overall adaptation. The fact that the techniques utilized in these early treatments were based on relatively simple principles of learning applied to individual behaviors also contributed to the perception of behavioral intervention as the "simplistic" use of "reward and punishment." Although this early perception of behavioral intervention was somewhat unfair, it is in fact the case that, compared to behavioral intervention now, these early studies were indeed simplistic. Current behavioral treatment is infinitely more comprehensive and complex; it involves broad-based behavioral assessment, utilizes a variety of procedures (individually or in package form), addresses more comprehensive behavioral repertoires, and seeks more generalized treatment outcome. (Chapters 20 and 26 give the specifics of these advances.)

Increased Reliance on Functional Analysis

One of the most significant directions in relatively recent behavior analysis and treatment is the widespread use of functional analysis strategies (e.g., Carr, 1994). As noted in Chapters 20 and 26, functional analysis is a systematic determination of the function of a particular behavior in relation to the environment. Once the function(s) is(are) determined, the environment may be altered in a manner designed to alter the behavior. For example, Iwata, Dorsey, Slifer, Bauman, and Richman (1982) assessed the function of self-injury for several children with autism. These investigators found that self-injurious behavior (SIB) served different, and even multiple, functions for different children. To illustrate, one child engaged in SIB as a means to escape demands. Another child engaged in SIB as a means to obtain attention. Essentially, a topographically similar behavior (SIB) was maintained by different consequences, and we might expect that the behavior of different children might respond to a single manipulation in very different ways. Removing attention contingent on SIB would likely lead to an *increase* in SIB for the first child, and the same procedure might lead to a *decrease* in SIB for the second child. These results point to the importance of understanding the functional relationship between a behavior and the environment. The technology of functional analysis allows us to identify just these kinds of relationships. A functional analysis may prevent the unsuccessful treatment of the behavior and greatly increase the chances that an effective treatment is applied first.

The use of functional assessment has allowed for a more accurate treatment prescription as well as detailed prediction of treatment outcome, thus reducing the variability in effectiveness sometimes noted in early behavioral work. We will see in the following sections that functional analysis has largely affected almost all areas of behavioral intervention.

Decreased Reliance on Aversive Stimulation and Punishment

One of the most hotly debated aspects of behavioral intervention has been the use of aversive procedures. This controversy is not surprising, when the application of painful stimuli to children with disabilities is involved. The very early work in this area includes studies in which children with autism who displayed extremely serious, even life-threatening, behaviors were given painful consequences in order to obtain rapid control over the behavior. For example, in one of the most well-known studies, Lovaas and Simmons (1969) reported immediate reductions of dangerous SIB with the application of painful, but harmless, contingent localized electric shocks. In these early studies, understanding of other methods to control these behaviors was limited. Punishment is a procedure that, by definition, leads to a rapid reduction in behavior, and there was little doubt that immediate control of some of these highly dangerous behaviors was essential. Other forms of punishment involving aversive procedures (but not including the application of painful stimuli) were also developed and utilized. They included time out, overcorrection, and punishment by withdrawal (sometimes called response cost).

In behavioral technology, "punishment" is defined as a procedure in which an aversive stimulus is applied contingent on and directly following a behavior, for the purpose of effecting reduction in the probability of the behavior. Thus, it is procedurally defined. There is nothing inherent in the term *punishment* that denotes pain; the requirement for *aversive* is only that the recipient find it unpleasant. We all use punishment every day of our lives. If we tell a child "no" when she dashes into the street, we are administering punishment. Something as mild as a frown or a look of disappointment may be a very effective punisher. In most cases, critics who have faulted behavioral intervention for using punishment are really commenting on the use of aversive stimulation to effect behavior change. In the more recent behavioral literature, very few studies involve the use of painful aversives. In fact, far fewer studies involve the use of *any* form of punishment. The reasons for this reduction in the use of punishment and aversives are many.

As noted above, behavioral interventions now are much more likely to employ functional analyses to determine the function of a behavior, and to utilize positive procedures to effect behavior change. In the past, a behavior might have been viewed more in isolation (e.g., a child is hitting himself), and a procedure known to be reductive in effect (e.g., contingent application of a known aversive) was applied. Now, however, a functional analysis would yield information allowing for positive programming and would obviate the need for a punishment procedure. To illustrate, Durand and Carr (1991) studied three boys with mental retardation and Pervasive Developmental Disorder or autism, who engaged in severely challenging behaviors such as SIB and aggression. These investigators conducted a functional analysis and determined that the challenging behaviors of all the boys served the function of allowing escape from demands. In addition, for one boy, the behavior served to elicit attention. Using this information, the investigators systematically taught the boys to request assistance (i.e., saying, "Help me") in demand situations, or to seek attention in a more appropriate manner (i.e., "Am I doing good work?"). This training, referred to as "functional communication training," was effective in reducing the challenging behaviors. Importantly, the behaviors were reduced without the use of aversive procedures. The inappropriate behaviors were replaced by appropriate responses that served the same function, that is, they accomplished the same environmental effect as had the original challenging behaviors. (The reader is referred to Carr, 1988; Carr & Durand, 1985; and Carr et al., 1994, for discussions of functional communication training.) Functional analysis allowed for the use of more positive procedures where more aversive procedures may have previously been the main treatment chosen.

Another reason for the decrease in the use of punishment and aversives is the increasing emphasis given to antecedent stimulus control. From a behavioral perspective, the operant paradigm involves an antecedent stimulus, the behavior, and a consequent stimulus. Much of the earlier work in the area focused on manipulating environmental consequences (i.e., reinforcement, extinction, punishment). More recently, however, the field has turned to antecedent stimulus manipulation to alter behavior. This approach has several advantages: (a) it often obviates the need for employing an aversive consequence; (b) it can be used to change behaviors when a controlling consequence cannot be identified or several consequences may be involved; (c) it can be used to change behaviors when the maintaining consequence cannot be controlled by the treatment provider; and (d) it can lead to immediate change in behavior. Touchette, MacDonald, and Langer (1985) demonstrated the assessment of antecedent situations associated with zero-rate or low-rate levels of severe behavior problems in several children with developmental disabilities. By programming these same situations to replace antecedent situations assessed to be associated with high rates of disruptive behavior, these investigators were able to effect an immediate reduction in the behavior problems. Thus, rapid reductions in the problematic behaviors were achieved without punishment or other consequence manipulation. Carr, Newsom, and Binkoff (1980) found that therapist demands during teaching situations cued SIB in a young boy with autism and mental retardation. The investigators found that if they embedded the demands in enjoyable "conversation," the child responded to the demands and did not engage in SIB.

Related to this is the emphasis on understanding setting events that affect the occurrence of behaviors. A setting event is an environmental stimulus that affects the control of a specific antecedent in evoking a behavior. Thus, perhaps a child responds well to instructional demands in a teaching situation, unless he or she is not feeling well (a setting event to which we all can relate), at which times the child engages in tantrum behavior. The behavioral treatment provider might determine this relationship from a behavioral assessment (e.g., "scatterplot"; see Chapter 20) and find that resistance to instructions is associated with fever and other symptoms. In short, the treatment provider may decide against presenting instructions during times when the child is ill. This would obviate the necessity of providing consequences to decrease disruptive behavior. Or, conversely, a treatment provider may be able to increase the power of an antecedent stimulus by adding a setting event. For example, perhaps a child does better on school tasks if he or she is in a "good mood." Putting the child in such a mood (setting event) by engaging in play activity prior to school might improve school-task performance. Operations aimed at increasing motivation are another example of this systematic approach to increasing the effectiveness of interventions (Koegel, O'Dell, & Koegel, 1987). Behavioral researchers have been aware of the influence of setting events for quite some time, but the systematic assessment and use of setting events in treatment has seen a large increase in recent years.

In sum, recently, there has been increased utilization of functional analysis technology, adoption of functional communication training, increased utilization of stimulus control procedures, and incorporation of more effective and efficient procedures for increasing competing positive behaviors. All of these have allowed for reduction in the use of aversives in programs to reduce challenging behaviors.

Enhancing Generalization of Intervention Effects

One of the oft-noted limitations of many early behavioral interventions was the failure of newly established behaviors to demonstrate adequate generalization. Thus, newly taught behaviors might not generalize to different environments, people, or related behaviors, or over time. The behavioral community, utilizing the data that accompany such interventions, noted this limitation and addressed the problem by actively focusing research on the enhancement of generalized treatment effects. In 1977, Stokes and Baer specified a variety of behavioral procedures designed to increase generalization. Since publication of that seminal paper, the field has advanced even further.

One way in which behavior researchers and clinicians have recently addressed the problem of limited generalization is to focus on behavioral aggregates as opposed to single target behaviors. This emphasis represents a shift from treatment strategies that focus on teaching individual behaviors (either successively or concurrently) to treatment strategies that are more efficient in simultaneously effecting a range of behaviors. For example, Pivotal Response Training (Koegel, Koegel, & Schreibman, 1991; Koegel, Schreibman, et al., 1989; Schreibman & Koegel, 1996) is a multicomponent treatment package involving specific procedures designed to increase the "pivotal" behaviors of *motivation* and *responsivity to multiple cues*. These are considered pivotal behaviors in that increases in each are associated with improvements in a wide array of specific behaviors. An individual who is motivated is likely to engage in more learning attempts, be more successful in learning new behaviors, and generalize these behaviors widely (Schreibman & Koegel, 1996). Also, because many individuals with autism have difficulty responding to multiple stimulus input ("stimulus overselectivity"; see Lovaas, Koegel, & Schreibman, 1979; and Schreibman, 1988, for reviews), expanding their use of environmental cues will serve to "normalize" their attention and help them learn in a manner more similar to that of nonautistic people. To illustrate, it has been shown that training children with autism to broaden their attentional focus (i.e., responding to simultaneous multiple cues) leads to more normalized learning (e.g., Schreibman, Charlop, & Koegel, 1982) and to increased social responsiveness (Burke & Cerniglia, 1990). Thus, focusing treatment efforts on broader behavioral targets leads to more rapid and more generalized treatment effects.

Another relatively recent strategy to increase generalization is to move away from the more laboratory-based, discrete-trial style of training and toward more naturalistic strategies that allow the individual with autism to learn behaviors in their natural context under more natural conditions. The more traditional form of training involves a highly structured, repetitively-practiced paradigm (e.g., Lovaas, 1977). Although this approach has been shown to be highly effective in establishing specific behavioral repertoires, the reported lack of generalization may be directly related to the specificity that characterizes the approach. Because behaviors are taught in a very carefully designed and typically repetitive manner, the behaviors are unlikely to generalize to the natural environment, where more variability in terms of antecedent stimuli, behavioral requirements, and consequences is present. Naturalistic strategies incorporate a variety of antecedents, responses, and consequences during the actual training so that the individual is able to sample and learns a spectrum of these events. To illustrate, the concept of "red" may be effectively taught using a discrete trial approach that includes colored blocks, colored flashcards, and so on, and the generalized concept of "red" is learned via training with a variety of colored stimuli. However, the concept of "red" may also be taught in a more naturalistic format that mimicks the natural environments in which "red" is encountered. Thus, one may note that a toy car is red, a toothbrush is red, a leaf can be red, and so on. Because the red stimulus is observed in its naturally occurring circumstance, generalization of the concept is more likely to occur without specific training for generalization. Similarly, early (and to some extent, current) discrete-trial behavioral interventions utilize indirect reinforcers to strengthen behavior. An indirect reinforcer is one that may be a desired stimulus but is unrelated to the behavior being taught. Receiving a piece of candy for saying "car" is an example. More recently, behavioral researchers and clinicians have used direct reinforcement wherein the reinforcer is directly related to the behavior (Koegel & Williams, 1980). Receiving access to a toy car for saying "car" is an example. (Candy would be a direct reinforcer for saying "candy" or some other candy-related response.) When one considers that most of us acquire and use generalized language because of the direct effect on the environment, it seems reasonable that direct reinforcement would lead to enhanced generalization. When most of us say "Please give me the book," it is because we want the book, not someone saying "Good talking" and handing us an M&M. Further, in the naturalistic strategies, the child is allowed to sample more variability in the response itself. Several variations on the correct response may be acceptable and thus reinforced. This, in turn, enhances response generalization. These procedures allow for the contingencies in the natural environment to acquire control over behavior and greatly enhance generalization. Versions of this type of training have been developed in different laboratories across the country and have been referred to by a number of names, including "incidental teaching" (McGee, Krantz, & McClannahan, 1985), "milieu" training (Kaiser, Yoder, & Keetz, 1992), and "Pivotal Response Training" (Schreibman & Koegel, 1996). These procedures all have in common the training of behavioral repertoires in the environment where they would naturally occur and the use of the same principles of behavior as before, yet now using natural contingencies. Essentially, acquisition and generalization of new behaviors are trained simultaneously.

Because true generalization of treatment effects means the exhibition of newly acquired behaviors in a variety of settings and in the presence of a variety of people, it makes sense that behavioral interventions have involved expansion of the role of treatment provider to include parents, teachers, siblings, and peers. Behavioral methodology, with its basis in the relatively easy-to-train principles of learning, lends itself nicely to the incorporation of a diverse set of treatment providers. The behavioral literature is rich in accounts of successful training of, and successful implementation by, these individuals. A follow-up study of behavioral intervention for children with autism (Lovaas et al., 1973) demonstrated that treatment gains for children whose parents had not been involved in implementing treatment were subsequently lost. However, if parents were taught to provide treatment for their children, the treatment gains were maintained over time. This dramatically illustrated the fact that parent training made not only intuitive sense, in that parents could help their children, but it also was essential to the long-term maintenance and generalization of treatment gains. Since that original demonstration, there has been an expanded emphasis on parent training in programs for children with autism (e.g., Baker, 1989). Teachers represent another population that has been the focus of behavioral intervention training. This also makes intuitive sense, given that the role of the teacher is mainly to teach and the teacher is around the child for much of the day. Accordingly, behavioral procedures have been adapted for teacher use in classroom situations (e.g., Koegel & Rincover, 1974). Because children spend a good deal of time in the presence of siblings and peers, it certainly makes sense to recruit the siblings and peers as treatment agents. Behavioral techniques have been successfully taught to siblings (Oke, 1993; Schreibman, O'Neill, & Koegel, 1983), to expand general skills, and to peers, to increase social behaviors (Pierce & Schreibman, 1995; Strain, Kerr, & Ragland, 1979). In essence, if treatment is provided when the child is with the parents, at school, with siblings, and with peers, an almost total treatment environment is created and it is likely to promote successful generalization.

Another behavioral intervention aimed at enhancing the generalization of treatment effectiveness is the utilization of self-management procedures. With self-management, the autistic individual can literally take the treatment along into all settings and at any time. Essentially, this technique involves teaching the individual to discriminate the presence or absence of the target behavior, correctly monitor successful behavior change, record performance, and self-reinforce if appropriate (e.g., Koegel, Koegel, & Parks, 1989). Self-management has been widely used for many years, but only relatively recently have the procedures been applied with children and adults with autism (Koegel & Koegel, 1990; Stahmer & Schreibman, 1992). In fact, it has been demonstrated that the procedures can be adapted so that even children who are more severely affected with autism may benefit (Krantz, MacDuff, & McClannahan, 1993; Pierce & Schreibman, 1994). Another obvious advantage of self-management is that it allows the child to be independent, which not only enhances generalization because of the absence of a treatment provider, but also reduces the burden of parents and others who otherwise might have to supervise the child.

Advances in Assessment

As discussed in Chapter 20, behavioral assessment has expanded substantially over recent years. Early behavioral assessments consisted largely of relatively simple, but extremely careful, measurement of discrete behavioral and environmental events. These assessments allowed for precise determination of target behaviors, specificity in treatment implementation, and evaluation of intervention effects. More recent advances in assessment reflect not only the sophistication and complexity of the questions we ask, but also an increasing receptivity to the society within which we operate.

Probably the single most important addition to our assessment arsenal is functional assessment. As noted earlier, this form of careful assessment and the incorporation of functional analysis into treatment strategies have made it possible for the field of applied behavior analysis to progress in a variety of important ways. These include: (a) progress in increasing emphasis on positive behavioral programming (due to the greatly reduced reliance on aversive procedures); (b) an overall increase in treatment effectiveness due to greater specificity of controlling variables, including setting events, antecedent stimulus control, and maintaining contingencies; (c) identification of multiple and complex functional relations, and (d) illumination of relations that merit investigation. Just as important as the contribution of functional assessment in the design and implementation of effective treatments is the fact that the technology of conducting functional assessments can be taught to "front-line" personnel who are immediately responsible for treatment delivery. This includes parents, teachers, and others who do not have advanced training in behavior analysis.

Another extremely important addition to our assessment is social validation—the determination of the social acceptability of our treatment procedures and the social importance of our treatment targets and our treatment effects. When behavioral interventions were first implemented, the determination of treatment targets (populations and specific target behaviors), treatment procedures, and treatment effectiveness was made by the behavioral researcher or clinician applying the treatment. However, controversy over some specific procedures (i.e., aversives) made it clear that behaviorists were perhaps not being properly responsive to the social environment. In essence, what was needed was a set of assessment procedures that would allow for relevant consumer input regarding the focus, nature, and evaluation of our treatment (see Schwartz & Baer, 1991, and the *Journal of Applied Behavior Analysis* special edition on social validation [1991], Volume 24, Number 2, for excellent discussions of this work). Schreibman, Koegel, Mills, and Burke (1981) provided a social validation assessment of the effects of behavioral treatment with a group of children with autism. These investigators had accumulated the usual objective behavioral assessments of treatment effectiveness but wanted to determine whether the nature and amount of treatment gains made by the children were apparent to other members of the community who were not familiar with autism or with behavior therapy. Would the subjective judgments of members of the general public (in this case, college undergraduates) agree with the objective assessments of the investigators? The investigators showed the judges videotapes of children with autism before and after a period of behavior therapy. The judges rated the children on a Likert scale across a variety of specific behaviors (e.g., "To what extent does this child engage in repetitious behavior?") and on more global questions (e.g., "To what extent does this child appear to be abnormal?" and "I would be willing to babysit for this child."). The investigators found that the judges rated those children who showed substantial improvement, as determined by objective assessments, as greatly improved in specific behaviors, and they responded more favorably on the global questions. Similarly, they judged those children who showed minimal or no progress as not showing much improvement. Importantly, the judges rated changes in specific behaviors, such as language use, much the same as did the objective assessments, indicating that the behaviors assessed by the investigators were important in the judgment of the raters. One might argue whether college undergraduate students are "relevant consumers" of treatment of autism. This investigation was replicated with parents (Runco & Schreibman, 1983) and with teachers (Schreibman, Runco, Mills, & Koegel, 1982) with similar results. Social validation is important, but there may be some limits as to the extent behavioral researchers and clinicians should be guided by information supplied by consumers. To illustrate, Runco and Schreibman (1987) asked parents to judge which behaviors of children with autism were important to focus on for treatment. The parents viewed videotapes of children with autism (not their own) and were asked to rate the importance of several behaviors for intervention. Behavior therapists and special education teachers were asked to do likewise. The results indicated that the different groups of judges had different priorities for intervention. Parents did not rate the importance of verbal behaviors and self-stimulation as highly as they did noninteractive behaviors such as ignoring mother and noncompliance. However, we know that improvements in language are more closely tied with favorable prognosis than are improvements in compliance and cooperation.

Thus, this social validation assessment suggested the importance of educating this group of consumers regarding important treatment targets. The balancing of what consumers want, need, accept, and use is delicate indeed, and behavioral researchers must weigh these issues carefully. Issues in the area of social validation may be complex but we must attend to them if behavioral intervention is to remain in tune with the society within which it operates and within which individuals with autism live.

FUTURE DIRECTIONS AND CHALLENGES AHEAD

The past 10 to 15 years have brought a tremendous broadening and sophistication of behavioral technology as it is applied to people with autism. The earlier work in the area has laid the foundation for the current state-of-the-art and for what will follow. The fact that we now view some of our early efforts as relatively "simplistic" and are now much more effective and efficient in providing treatment should in no way be considered as criticisms of these earlier efforts. Quite the contrary. We are not moving *away* from our early efforts; rather, we are moving *beyond* them. Simply put, we would not be where we are now, if we had not been there first.

What can the field of autism treatment expect from future behavioral interventions? If one extrapolates from the present trends in treatment development, it is quite clear where we are going. The broadening of treatment focus and treatment packages, the increased efforts to specify important child variables and how they may relate to treatment procedures and outcome, the increased interest in understanding the role of expanded environmental variables (including family, culture, school), and the more detailed study of treatment variables—all point in the direction of a greater emphasis on the *individualization* of treatment.

Individualization of Treatment

The focus on subject variables is evident when one considers the increased emphasis on differentiating subpopulations within the broad autism spectrum disorders category (e.g., Bristol et al., 1996; Volkmar & Cohen, 1994). The heterogeneity of the population of autism and the variability of treatment effectiveness reported over the years speak to the fact that child characteristics interact with treatment effectiveness in ways we do not yet fully understand. As we learn more about how certain child characteristics interact with specific treatment procedures, we will be in a better position to enter this relationship into the treatment equation. To give some examples, we know that early identification and early intervention are important indicators of treatment benefits (Bristol et al., 1996). Perhaps some individuals with severe cognitive impairment will not benefit from self-management training (Schreibman & Koegel, 1996). Children who are overselective in their attention may be the ones to benefit most from training in responsivity to multiple cues (Schreibman, Charlop, & Koegel, 1982). Recent information about neuroanatomic abnormalities and attentional deficits (Courchesne et al., 1994; Townsend & Courchesne, 1994) have treatment implications suggesting that different instructional procedures may eventually be tailored to the child's neuroanatomic status. Certain communication deficits will be more or less responsive to certain treatment procedures (Kaiser et al., 1992).

Further, we have begun to focus more on how family variables interact with treatment effectiveness. The effects of ethnicity, culture, marital status, parental attitudes, parental age, level of education, socioeconomic status, and other factors all may affect how treatment is best delivered and the ultimate effectiveness of the treatment. To illustrate, training in self-management may be more successfully implemented by parents for whom child independence is important (Schreibman & Koegel, 1996). However, certain cultures may not place a strong emphasis on child independence; thus, the parents may not choose to use self-management with their child or may use it ineffectively. Another example is the effect of stress. It has been shown that parents of children with autism report being under stress (e.g., Koegel et al., 1992). Perhaps parents who are under a good deal of stress at a point in time would be poor candidates to implement training with their child; a clinician may then be the treatment provider of choice. At a later time, if the stress is reduced, these parents could perhaps very effectively implement treatment.

Treatment variables and how they interact with child and family characteristics are also crucial elements in the individualized treatment equation. Our ultimate goal is to be in a position to determine a priori which treatment procedures will be most effective and efficient with a particular child and a particular family situation.

One combination of treatment and child characteristics that has led to a good deal of attention in recent years is the combination of intensive discrete-trial behavioral intervention and early chronological age of the child. Lovaas (1987) reported that 47% of very young (under 46 months of age) children receiving intensive (40 hours per week) behavioral intervention achieved "normal" functioning, defined as an IQ in the normal range and successful performance in a regular first-grade classroom. These results are impressive, but the study remains controversial (e.g., Foxx, 1993; Kazdin, 1993; Schopler, Short, & Mesibov, 1989). Before our level of enthusiasm is determined, true independent replication of the reported treatment effects is required, along with a direct comparison of this type of training with other forms of behavioral treatment also delivered at this early age (Bristol et al., 1996). Another form of treatment may be as effective as, or perhaps even more effective than, the intensive discrete-trial treatment. Perhaps not. The fact that not all of the children benefited to the same extent suggests that important child variables remain to be accounted for. What are the characteristics of the children who do or do not show substantial improvement with this type of treatment? In short, more research relating treatment variables and child variables should help us untangle this situation. What about the influence of family variables for this treatment? What happens when families cannot afford this intensive treatment? What about children who are not diagnosed at an early age or for whom the parents were unable to obtain early intensive intervention? What options are available for them? All of these issues need careful consideration because they all hold important implications for the provision of effective treatment.

We have some way to go in our research. Ultimately, we would like to be able to tailor our treatments to the child and family in such a way that all relevant variables are entered into our equation. This would be ideal, and although the ideal is still far off, it is nonetheless coming closer all the time. Importantly, the field of applied behavior analysis is progressing in all of these areas. Continued research will be the key to developing individualized treatments for all children and adults with autism.

Increasing Adoption of Behavioral Intervention

One challenge for behavioral intervention that remains important is: How do we, as behavior analysts and interventionists, effect widespread adoption of our methodology? We possess a quite impressive arsenal of effective treatments, and we are continually improving them. Yet, it takes a great deal of time for the procedures we develop to be implemented with the population we seek to help. Some people seem to resist behavioral treatment because they see it as "mechanistic," or simplistic, or merely a bag of "tricks." There are several remedies we might consider, to counteract this perception and thus increase the acceptance of our treatments.

One improvement would be more careful consideration of the people applying our treatments. If we want people to adopt our procedures, we must consider how much effort they require, how intrusive they are in family situations, how pleasant or unpleasant the treatment provider finds the procedures, and so on. A treatment that is difficult to implement, intrusive or stigmatizing, and/or unpleasant to implement is a treatment unlikely to be used. Thus, we might develop truly outstanding treatments, but they will be ineffective if they are never put into practice.

Behavior analysts are aware of these problems and are working to ensure that the behavioral interventions we develop are acceptable to those implementing them. As an important step, some behavior analysts are attempting to make our terminology more "friendly" (while maintaining the technical precision required). There is no doubt that a treatment approach with terms such as *punishment, extinction, manipulation, control,* and *aversives* does not evoke the positive emotions that may be associated with other forms of treatment (Foxx, 1995). A behavior analyst is no less a humanist just because of the technical jargon associated with the approach.

We must assess how the treatments are viewed by the intended treatment provider. Social validation methodology is an excellent way to obtain such "consumer satisfaction" information (Schwartz & Baer, 1991). If people do not view the treatment as acceptable for some reason, we must address the problem by making the treatment more acceptable. Schreibman, Kaneko, and Koegel (1991) used social validation methodology to assess how parents responded during application of treatment. In this study, parents were videotaped while teaching their children. One of two forms of treatment was used: (a) repetitive practice discrete-trial training or (b) Pivotal Response Training. Judges (undergraduate students) viewed the videotapes and rated the parents on how enthusiastic, happy, and interested they appeared to be while working with their child. Parents implementing Pivotal Response Training were judged as showing significantly more positive affect than parents implementing discrete-trial training. This result might suggest that parents would be more likely to use Pivotal Response Training because they seem to enjoy implementing it.

Dissemination of Behavioral Intervention Technology

Another extremely important issue is: How can we rapidly disseminate our findings so that they are widely applied? Like most scientific disciplines, behavioral interventions are developed and reported in professional journals. However, parents, teachers, and other front-line treatment providers are unlikely to be among the audience of these journals. We need to specifically target outlets that reach these personnel. Thus, publication of our work in media outlets and the popular press might be quite effective in making our treatments

known. For example, the publication of a single book (Maurice, 1993) describing the personal history of the effects of early intensive discrete-trial training led to widespread attention to that intervention.

This dissemination issue is particularly vexing because one of the positive features of behavioral intervention is that the methodology is built on the relatively straightforward principles of learning. These principles are logical, the laws are for the most part very well understood, and the methodology has been readily taught to students, parents, teachers, and children. Given that our technology can be presented in such a manner, why do we seem to be having difficulty getting our message across? The market is filled with "how-to" books based on behavioral principles as applied to a wide variety of typical behaviors. Why do we not have this same widespread acceptance and ready adoption of behavioral technology for autism? What is needed is an increased emphasis on the clear and convincing presentation of our methodology to our direct consumers (parents, teachers, clinicians) and to the general public.

Development of Nonaversive Technology

A continuing challenge to behavior analysts is the development of a totally nonaversive treatment technology. We have made great strides in developing treatments that obviate or greatly reduce reliance on aversive procedures, but the fact remains that, as yet, we have not accomplished this goal (Horner et al., 1990). There are some serious behavioral challenges for which aversive procedures need to be implemented. As we increase our ability to develop comprehensive treatments that take into account the characteristics of the behavior, the client, the environment, and the treatment provider, we will ultimately be able to discontinue completely the use of aversives. Success in this endeavor will certainly serve to increase the adoption and acceptance of behavioral interventions.

The biggest challenge behavioral intervention faces is to be successful in these areas. We must continue to prove our effectiveness with sound science, develop procedures that are acceptable to practitioners (and society), and disseminate information about our techniques accurately, clearly, and widely. These strategies will not only promote the utilization of behavioral interventions but will likely reduce the possibility that bogus "treatments" such as Facilitated Communication (Jacobson, Mulick, & Schwartz, 1995) and other treatments *du jour* will be adopted for children with autism. The fact that parents embrace these false hopes is indicative of our continuing failure to meet these challenges.

Many challenges lie ahead, but confidence in the forward progress of behavior analyses can only suggest that these challenges will be met successfully. The next years promise to be exciting ones indeed.

Cross-References

Behavioral assessment is discussed in detail in Chapter 20, and behavioral interventions are reviewed in Chapter 26.

REFERENCES

Baker, B.L. (1989). *Parent training and developmental disabilities.* Washington, DC: American Association on Mental Retardation (AAMR) Monographs.

Bettelheim, B. (1967). *The empty fortress.* New York: Free Press.

Bristol, M.M., Cohen, D.J., Costello, E.J., Denckla, M., Eckberg, T.J., Kallen, R., Kraemer, H.C., Lord, C., Maurer, R., McIlvane, W.J., Minshew, N., Sigman, M., & Spence, M.A. (1996). State-of-the-science in autism: A report to the National Institutes of Health. *Journal of Autism and Developmental Disorders, 26,* 121–154.

Burke, J.C., & Cerniglia, L. (1990). Stimulus complexity and autistic children's responsivity: Assessing and training a pivotal behavior. *Journal of Autism and Developmental Disorders, 20,* 233–253.

Carr, E.G. (1988). Functional equivalence as a mechanism of response generalization. In R.H. Horner, G. Dunlap, & R.L. Koegel (Eds.), *Generalization and maintenance: Lifestyle changes in applied settings* (pp. 221–241). Baltimore: Brookes.

Carr, E.G. (1994). Emerging themes in the functional analysis of problem behavior. Special

issue: Functional analysis approaches to behavioral assessment and treatment. *Journal of Applied Behavior Analysis, 27,* 393–399.

Carr, E.G., & Durand, V.M. (1985). Reducing behavior problems through functional communication training. *Journal of Applied Behavior Analysis, 18,* 111–126.

Carr, E.G., Levin, L., McConnachie, G., Carlson, J.I., Kemp, D.C., & Smith, C.E. (1994). *Communication-based intervention for problem behavior: A user's guide for producing positive change.* Baltimore: Brookes.

Carr, E.G., Newsom, C.D., & Binkoff, J.A. (1980). Escape as a factor in the aggressive behavior of two retarded children. *Journal of Applied Behavior Analysis, 13,* 101–117.

Courchesne, E., Townsend, J., Akshoomoff, N.A., Saitoh, O., Yeung-Courchesne, R., Lincoln, A.J., James, H.E., Haas, R.H., Schreibman, L., & Lau, L. (1994). Impairment in shifting attention in autistic and cerebellar patients. *Behavioral Neuroscience, 108,* 848–865.

Durand, V.M., & Carr, E.G. (1991). Functional communication training to reduce challenging behavior: Maintenance and application in new settings. *Journal of Applied Behavior Analysis, 24,* 251–264.

Ferster, C.B., & DeMyer, M.K. (1961). The development of performance in autistic children in an automatically controlled environment. *Journal of Chronic Diseases, 13,* 312–345.

Ferster, C.B., & DeMyer, M.K. (1962). A method for the experimental analysis of the behavior of autistic children. *American Journal of Orthopsychiatry, 32,* 89–98.

Foxx, R.M. (1993). Sapid effects awaiting independent replication. *American Journal on Mental Retardation, 97,* 375–376.

Foxx, R.M. (1995, May). *Translating the covenant.* Presidential address delivered at the annual convention of the Association for Behavior Analysis, Washington, DC.

Horner, R.H., Dunlap, G., Koegel, R.L., Carr, E.G., Sailor, W., Anderson, J., Albin, R.W., & O'Neill, R.E. (1990). Toward a technology of "nonaversive" behavioral support. *Journal of the Association for Persons with Severe Handicaps, 15,* 125–132.

Iwata, B.A., Dorsey, M.F., Slifer, K.J., Bauman, K.E., & Richman, G.S. (1982). Toward a functional analysis of self-injury. *Analysis and Intervention in Developmental Disabilities, 2,* 3–20.

Jacobson, J.W., Mulick, J.A., & Schwartz, A.A. (1995). A history of facilitated communication:

Science, pseudoscience, and antiscience. *The American Psychologist, 50,* 750–765.

Kaiser, A.P., Yoder, P.J., & Keetz, A. (1992). Evaluating milieu training. In S.F. Warren & J. Reichle (Eds.), *Causes and effects in communication and language intervention.* Baltimore: Brookes.

Kazdin, A.E. (1993). Replication and extension of behavioral treatment of autistic disorder. *American Journal on Mental Retardation, 97,* 377–379.

Koegel, R.L., & Koegel, L.K. (1990). Extended reductions in stereotypic behaviors through self-management in multiple community settings. *Journal of Applied Behavior Analysis, 23,* 119–127.

Koegel, L.K., Koegel, R.L., & Parks, D.R. (1989). *How to teach self-management to people with severe disabilities: A training manual.* Santa Barbara: University of California.

Koegel, R.L., Koegel, L.K., & Schreibman, L. (1991). Assessing and training parents in teaching pivotal behaviors. In R.J. Prinz (Ed.), *Advances in behavioral assessment of children and families* (pp. 65–82). Greenwich, CT: JAI Press.

Koegel, R.L., O'Dell, M.C., & Koegel, L.K. (1987). A natural language paradigm for teaching nonverbal autistic children. *Journal of Autism and Developmental Disorders, 17,* 187–199.

Koegel, R.L., & Rincover, A. (1974). Treatment of psychotic children in a classroom environment: I. Learning in a large group. *Journal of Applied Behavior Analysis, 7,* 45–59.

Koegel, R.L., Schreibman, L., Loos, L.M., Dirlich-Wilhelm, H., Dunlap, G., Robbins, F.R., & Plienis, A.J. (1992). Consistent stress profiles in mothers of children with autism. *Journal of Autism and Developmental Disorders, 22,* 205–216.

Koegel, R.L., Schreibman, L., Good, A.B., Cerniglia, L., Murphy, C., & Koegel, L.K. (1989). *How to teach pivotal behaviors to autistic children: A training manual.* Santa Barbara: University of California.

Koegel, R.L., & Williams, J. (1980). Direct vs. indirect response-reinforcer relationships in teaching autistic children. *Journal of Abnormal Child Psychology, 4,* 536–547.

Krantz, P.J., MacDuff, G.S., & McClannahan, L.I. (1993). Programming participation in family activities for children with autism: Parents' use of photographic activity schedules. *Journal of Applied Behavior Analysis, 26,* 137–148.

Lovaas, O.I. (1977). *The autistic child.* New York: Irvington.

Lovaas, O.I. (1987). Behavioral treatment and normal educational and intellectual functioning in young autistic children. *Journal of Autism and Developmental Disorders, 9,* 315–323.

Lovaas, O.I., Berberich, J.P., Perloff, B.F., & Schaeffer, B. (1966). Acquisition of imitative speech in schizophrenic children. *Science, 151,* 705–707.

Lovaas, O.I., Freitag, G., Gold, V.J., & Kassorla, I.C. (1965). Experimental studies in childhood schizophrenia. I. Analysis of self-destructive behavior. *Journal of Experimental Child Psychology, 2,* 67–84.

Lovaas, O.I., Koegel, R.L., & Schreibman, L. (1979). Stimulus overselectivity in autism: A review of research. *Psychological Bulletin, 86,* 1236–1254.

Lovaas, O.I., Koegel, R.L., Simmons, J.Q., & Long, J.S. (1973). Some generalization and follow-up measures on autistic children in behavior therapy. *Journal of Applied Behavior Analysis, 6,* 131–166.

Lovaas, O.I., & Simmons, J.Q. (1969). Manipulation of self-destruction in three retarded children. *Journal of Applied Behavior Analysis, 2,* 143–157.

Maurice, C. (1993). *Let me hear your voice: A family's triumph over autism.* New York: Knopf.

McGee, G.G., Krantz, P.J., & McClannahan, L.E. (1985). The facilitative effects of incidental teaching on preposition use by autistic children. *Journal of Applied Behavior Analysis, 18,* 17–31.

Oke, N.J. (1993). *A group training program for siblings of children with autism: Acquisition of language training procedures and related behavior change.* Unpublished doctoral dissertation, University of California, San Diego.

Pierce, K., & Schreibman, L. (1994). Teaching children with autism daily living skills in unsupervised settings through pictorial self-management. *Journal of Applied Behavior Analysis, 27,* 471–481.

Pierce, K., & Schreibman, L. (1995). Increasing complex social behaviors in children with autism: Effects of peer-implemented Pivotal Response Training. *Journal of Applied Behavior Analysis, 28,* 285–295.

Runco, M.A., & Schreibman, L. (1983). Parental judgments of behavior therapy efficacy with autistic children: A social validation. *Journal of Autism and Developmental Disorders, 134,* 237–248.

Runco, M.A., & Schreibman, L. (1987). Brief report: Socially validating behavioral objectives in the treatment of autistic children. *Journal of Autism and Developmental Disorders, 17,* 141–147.

Schopler, E., Short, A., & Mesibov, G. (1989). Relation of behavioral treatment to "normal" functioning: Comment on Lovaas. *Journal of Consulting and Clinical Psychology, 57,* 162–164.

Schreibman, L. (1988). *Autism.* Newbury Park, CA: Sage.

Schreibman, L., Charlop, M.H., & Koegel, R.L. (1982). Teaching autistic children to use extra-stimulus prompts. *Journal of Experimental Child Psychology, 33,* 475–491.

Schreibman, L., Kaneko, W.M., & Koegel, R.L. (1991). Positive affect of parents of autistic children: A comparison across two teaching techniques. *Behavior Therapy, 22,* 479–490.

Schreibman, L., & Koegel, R.L. (1996). Fostering self-management: Parent-delivered Pivotal Response Training for children with autistic disorder. In E.D. Hibbs & P.S. Jensen (Eds.), *Psychosocial treatment for child and adolescent disorders: Empirically based approaches* (pp. 525–552). Washington, DC: American Psychological Association.

Schreibman, L., Koegel, R.L., Mills, J.I., & Burke, J. (1981). The social validation of behavior therapy with autistic children. *Behavior Therapy, 12,* 610–624.

Schreibman, L., O'Neill, R.E., & Koegel, R.L. (1983). Behavioral training for siblings of autistic children. *Journal of Applied Behavior Analysis, 16,* 129–138.

Schreibman, L., Runco, M.A., Mills, J.I., & Koegel, R.L. (1982). Teachers' judgments of improvements in autistic children in behavior therapy: A social validation. In R.L. Koegel, A. Rincover, & A.L. Egel (Eds.), *Educating and understanding autistic children* (pp. 78–87). San Diego, CA: College Hill Press.

Schwartz, I.S., & Baer, D.M. (1991). Social validity assessment: Is current practice state of the art? *Journal of Applied Behavior Analysis, 24,* 189–204.

Stahmer, A.C., & Schreibman, L. (1992). Teaching children with autism appropriate play in unsupervised environments using a self-management treatment package. *Journal of Applied Behavior Analysis, 25,* 447–459.

Stokes, T.F., & Baer, D.M. (1977). An implicit technology of generalization. *Journal of Applied Behavior Analysis, 10,* 349–368.

Strain, P.S., Kerr, M.M., & Ragland, E.U. (1979). Effects of peer-mediated social initiations and prompting/reinforcement procedures on the social behavior of autistic children. *Journal of Autism and Developmental Disorders, 9,* 41–54.

Touchette, P.E., MacDonald, R.F., & Langer, S.N. (1985). A scatter plot for identifying stimulus control of problem behavior. *Journal of Applied Behavior Analysis, 18,* 343–351.

Townsend, J., & Courchesne, E. (1994). Parietal damage and narrow "spotlight" of spatial attention. *Journal of Cognitive Neuroscience, 6,* 218–230.

Volkmar, F.R., & Cohen, D.J. (1994). Autism: Current concepts. *Psychoses and Pervasive Developmental Disorders, 3,* 43–51.

Wolf, M.M., Risley, T.R., & Mees, H. (1964). Applications of operant conditioning procedures to the behavior problems of an autistic child. *Behaviour Research and Therapy, 1,* 305–312.

CHAPTER 45

A Life-Span Approach in the Education and Treatment of Persons with Autism

JUDITH M. LEBLANC, STEPHEN R. SCHROEDER, AND LILIANA MAYO

When we think of typical development, we naturally organize the life span into stages of infancy, childhood, adolescence, adulthood, and aging. *Stage* refers to a circumscribed period of life in which important interactions among biological maturation, environmental opportunities, and behavior result in key advances in development, for example, birth, language, puberty, and so on (Schroeder, 1993). If a child does not pass these milestones within the expected age range, we say the child is at risk for developmental delay.

We frequently think of these maturational stages in conjunction with age-related education and service programs. We further compartmentalize them into stages related to childhood and stages related to adulthood (see Table 45.1). Programs related to childhood include child care or early intervention, leaving home or preschool, primary school, junior high, and high school. Settings related to adult life include vocational training, employment, and retirement. Education and services for persons with autism are thus divided into stage categories that, in turn, define professional training and roles (e.g., preschool, primary and secondary teachers, and vocational trainers). Programs and professionals tend to focus on only one particular stage of life. As a person developmentally ages, milestones are reached and it becomes necessary to move from the educational and service programs designed for one age group into those designed for another. These moves require persons with autism, and their families, to make transitions from one set of program variables to another.

The term *transition* comes from the study of problems people have in making changes and adjustments to different environments and expectations of society at different developmental stages. Recognizing the difficulty persons with autism, and their families, may have when moving from one to another age-related educational and service program, we have created research programs on special transition services to support them at these times.

For the person with autism, the study of transitions should perhaps involve more than moving from one age-related program to another. It should, for example, involve looking at the ecocultural niche of the child and the family, as well as the service settings as they change throughout development. Do professionals need to focus on the changes a person faces when moving from one program to another across the life span? Or should we be more concerned with the gradual transformation from one developmental stage to another, which includes smaller transitions from a set of interrelated environmental and interpersonal variables such as moves from one neighborhood to another, changes in the makeup of the family living within the home, illnesses that occur, or changes from one teacher or caseworker to another? Perhaps autistic individuals need continual "on-call" transitional services, available from birth through adulthood, dictated by individual and family needs rather than only by movement across delineated age-related programs. This requires changing emphasis from *program* to *life-span requirements* and focusing on the goal of

TABLE 45.1   Life Stages and Transitions in the United States

No Disability		Age	Disability	
Transitions	Stages		Stages	Transitions
Infancy and Childhood				
Child Care ←	*Normal Development*	0–2	*Early Intervention* →	*NICU Follow-up
Leaving Home ←	*Preschool*	3	*Preschool* →	Leaving Home
		4	*Head Start* →	School Classes
School Life ←	*Kindergarten*	5	*Kindergarten* →	School Life
	Elementary School 6 or 8 years	6		
School Choice ←			*Elementary and Secondary Special Education:* →	School Placement
	Junior High 3-Year / Junior High 2-Year	12		
		14	Regular Classes Separate Classes Separate Schools Other Placements	
	Voc. Tech. School (3-Year) / Regular 4-Year High School	15		
College or Job ←		18	*Employment* →	Work Evaluation
Adulthood				
School Choice ←	Voc.Tech Junior College / Regular 4-Year	18	Vocational Training →	Work Adjustment
	Undergraduate Study in College or University			
Advanced Study or Job ←		22	→	Adult Life
	Graduate or Postgraduate Study (1–6 years)			
Adult Life ←				
	Employment Independence Productivity Marriage Children Home Ownership		Employment? Independence? Productivity? Marriage? Children? Home Ownership?	
		65		
Adjustment ←	Retirement		Retirement →	Adjustment
	Self-Esteem Loss of Function Death of Loved One		Self-Esteem Loss of Function Death of Loved One	

*Neonatal Intensive Care Unit

quality of life as it is dictated by each person's needs.

Risley (1995) proposed that quality of life can be achieved when programs and services focus on life arrangements rather than on behavioral change—for example, the Oregon Neighborhood Living Project (Bellamy, Newton, LeBaron, & Horner, 1990), which is based on quality-of-life tracking measures. Life arrangement interventions, according to Risley, include "patterns of the persons' weekly and monthly life, and of their interactions with the people, places and things they prefer or despise, are the units of consideration. And the programming at this level is to arrange for a life reduced in stress, deprivation and fear; enriched in those things that attract and engage the person's interest and repertoire; and richly responsive to their activities." Such a life would provide varied and complex experiences in the person's reinforcers, repertoires, and fluency. Risley further indicated the need for a lifetime coach to assist in flexible, individually driven education and service programs, as well as flexible and cooperative funding sources. He further predicted that the small menu of prespecified, available services for persons with developmental disabilities is a temporary state of affairs as "successful examples and successful lawsuits build on each other to provide flexible funding for real individualized services" (Risley, 1995).

When applied to program planning and implementation, the *continual* transition view implies early identification of lifetime goals that guide the education and treatment services implemented at each age-related stage of life. It also suggests the necessity of predicting, at the early childhood stage, developmental problems that might occur along life's way. Necessary treatment and educational programs can then be implemented *before* family and/or individual problems expand to trap professionals with treatment goals focused on problem resolution rather than on positive development of individual abilities and family adaptation. This approach challenges us to provide *cooperative* lifetime programs. Risley (1995) notes that "helping a consumer design a life is not hard—getting everyone else to agree is."

To take this broader and longer planning view, we must continually ask: "Where are we going?" and "Are the treatment or educational goals we suggest functional in the life-span development of the person with whom we are working?"

Only *one* lifetime comprehensive ecobehavioral educational and treatment plan is necessary for implementation in each person's complex network of human relationships and environments. The plan should travel with persons with autism and their families across all of life's changes, a kind of map for ensuring that service providers are always aiming toward quality-of-life and life-span goals that are constantly defined and redefined by ever-changing individual abilities and choices, and family life styles.

Life-span plans dictate that all education and services follow a prespecified sequence of behavioral objectives established by and for the individuals and their families, with each service building on those previously achieved. This continuity then becomes the driving force in the process of development, replacing separate expectations drawn from circumscribed programs operating at each developmental stage. Basic goals for persons with autism, and their families, will generally remain the same along the developmental journey, with adjustments made for: (a) ecocultural dimensions of the person's daily life; and (b) gradual or abrupt daily life changes that can occur in ability levels, family situations, educational opportunities, and so on. Each of these adjustments would be based on past accomplishments but would remain focused on previously established general life-span goals. The "client" in this approach is thus not only the individual with autism, but also *that* individual within the context of the family, "and more often than not, the extended family, the neighbors, the school and the entire larger community" (Schroeder & Schroeder, 1990, p. 368).

The development of service or educational delivery models to meet the demands of a life-span individualized plan requires continuity that can best be served by one or more individuals whose job is to guarantee consistency of service and who can advocate for the individual and family when needed. This centralized system is similar to the brokerage system proposed by Schroeder and Schroeder (1990) when they created the Annie Sullivan Enterprises in North Carolina. Such systems are based on a resource networking concept described in the 1976 annual report of the President's Committee on Mental Retardation. The broker, or life arrangement coach as proposed by Risley (1995), is responsible for each person's life-span program. When individual or family situations require program changes or additions, this person must develop a set of alternatives from which the consumers (the persons with autism and their families) can choose. Ideally, the broker identifies these alternatives from currently available services in the geographical location of the persons being served. If local services do not match the needs of individuals and their families, the broker must either convince providers to adapt their programs to these needs or find other professionals willing to design more compatible services. If neither of these alternatives works, as a last resort the broker must find ways to design and implement new services to meet the needs. The broker thus guarantees that persons with autism, and their families, receive appropriate lifetime services.

ESTABLISHMENT OF LIFE-SPAN GOALS

Services provided for persons with autism throughout life should establish skill and concept objectives leading to real and realistic adult objectives. These should be generally the same for all, with adjustments made for individual differences in ability levels. To establish general life-span objectives, it is essential to identify the skills and concepts the individual needs to live effectively.

The goals for persons with autism, like all persons, must include the capacity for gainful employment when they leave school. They can build self-esteem through meaningful work, which, in turn, will promote independence and mobility. Relationships and a sensitivity to life-span changes in relationships are also important as people move from the school years into adulthood. Typically, young adults are expected to independently identify friends, socially network with people, and initiate social activities that require adaptive social skills. Similarly, the development of self-esteem and sexuality are important as individuals move into adulthood. Limitations in this area clearly can cause stress and anxiety for persons with autism.

PROFESSIONAL ORIENTATION TRENDS

Some trends in professional orientation have historically affected the education and treatment of persons with autism. Parents and advocates have succeeded in creating the possibility of life-span programs. Changes in values have guided treatment of people with disabilities over the past 100 years (Turnbull, 1991). These changes are summarized in Table 45.2.

Today, we believe that a person's disability must be accommodated by society so as to minimize its handicapping condition. Social policy has changed from a view of inherent disability, to rehabilitation and education, to social inclusion and participation. Persons with disabilities are now viewed *within* the context of the person, the family, and society

TABLE 45.2 Changing Perspectives on Disabilities in the United States

The Distant Past	The Recent Past	The Present
Inherently disabled	Able to learn and be productive	Able to contribute to society
Focus on the person	Focus on the person and the family	Focus on person, family, and community
Segregation	Integration	Inclusion
Removal from family	Adoption, foster care	Family preservation
Dependence	Independence	Interdependence
Medical model	Developmental model	Ecological model
Charity motive	Rights motive	Rights and compassion
Second-class citizen	More equality	Full citizenship
No autonomy	Partial autonomy	Protection and advocacy
No rights	Negative rights	Positive rights

as a whole, rather than as burdens requiring special institutions. They and their families have special needs and rights that can help adults with autism to be integrated within and included in the lives and activities of others. A major policy theme of the past decades has been the move from segregation to integration and to inclusion.

RESEARCH AND PROGRAMS INVOLVING TOTAL ENVIRONMENT ACROSS THE LIFE SPAN

Education and treatment needs change across the life span of families with members having autism. Families may need more special help during some periods. At the time of first diagnosis, family support is critical for maintaining positive but realistic parental expectations of the child. Parents should be helped to assume an active role in the education and treatment of the child, and should be presented with educational and treatment alternatives that can assist the child with autism to achieve his or her maximum potential.

As the child moves into the school years, parents are concerned with finding education programs that best fit the child's and the family's needs. They may have to face difficult choices between segregated programs, which provide no normal peer models but do provide intensive one-on-one and, perhaps more functional teaching, and integrated programs, which provide social models but perhaps less functional education. In many cases, parents discover that they assume a major role in educating the educators about the needs of their children. Professionals should help parents in this process.

As a child's abilities become more apparent and as a family's situation changes, it will sometimes be necessary to alter choices of education and treatment. Each time this occurs, the professional is ready to work with the individual and the family to make whatever adjustments are appropriate.

As noted by Risley (1995), the life-span family orientation should attempt to reduce stress. Regardless of how it is produced, the appearance of undue stress in the family is a "marker variable" (Baer, 1984), perhaps indicating the need for intervention. Caution in assessing this need is indicated, and intervention

may need to be focused on very specific areas such as dependency, management, cognitive impairment, limits on family free time, and life-span caregiving (Bristol, 1979; DeMyer, 1979; Koegel et al., 1992; Marcus, 1977; Robbins, Dunlap, & Plienis, 1991; Wolf & Goldberg, 1986; Wolf, Noh, Fisman, & Speechley, 1989). In this regard, it is important to note that families without a severely disabled child also experience stress (Koegel, Schreibman, O'Neill, & Burke, 1983).

CURRENT TRENDS IN LIFE-SPAN APPROACHES: WHAT'S BEING DONE AND WHAT NEEDS TO BE DONE

To implement individualized life-span development plans for all persons with autism, we must consider what has been and needs to be accomplished in the areas of assessment, individualized education, treatment and vocational programs, and family involvement.

Diagnosis and Assessment

The defining features of autism have been subject to debate (Sturmey & Sevin, 1994). The broader diagnostic concept employed in *DSM-III-R* may have significantly increased its estimated incidence (Schreibman & Charlop, 1987). Burd and Kerbeshian (1988) note the need for continued refinement of these diagnostic criteria. The *DSM-IV* criteria are a considerable refinement over *DSM-III-R* (see Chapter 1). The early identification of children at risk for autism (Osterling & Dawson, 1994) will permit the design of life-span programs starting at a much younger age. In about 50% of cases, parents of children with autism are concerned about their child before age 1 year (Ornitz, Guthrie, & Farley, 1977), and most parents have expressed concern to pediatricians by the time the child is 18 months old (Siegel, Pliner, Eschler, & Elliot, 1988). Pediatricians and early childhood educators should be educated about early identification because they are most likely to have early contact with children.

As persons with autism, and their families, enter into educational programs, assessments should identify *strengths* to be enhanced rather than only skill deficits, so programs can be designed to reach maximum potentials. The importance of individual behavioral assessments rather than only norm-referenced assessments of skill level was suggested as early as 1972 by Bijou. Most behavioral assessments, however, focus only on specific skills that are expected to occur at equally specific stages of development. Assessments should view the individual in the context of the total environment with its changes across the life span. Continuous behavioral assessment should take place before, during, and after the teaching of specific skills (Harris, Belchic, Blum, & Celiberti, 1994). Finally, we need a broader assessment of the abilities and progress of persons with autism as they develop (see Chapter 19). Information on individual interests and abilities can suggest objectives, to strengthen and enhance the opportunities for obtaining jobs as an adult. Finally, we need methods for assessing the social abilities of persons with autism that are based in reality.

Educational Programs

The research literature provides many procedures for teaching persons with autism new skills (Doyle, Wolery, Ault, & Gast, 1988), pivotal behaviors (Koegel et al., 1989), and behaviors that promote generalization and maintenance (Horner, Dunlap, & Koegel, 1988). For these procedures to be incorporated into educational services, professionals must be taught to use them effectively. Continual assessment of the use of skills in a variety of ecological settings can ensure: (a) that the skills are useful and are used in the student's daily environment, and (b) that the student is sufficiently motivated to use learned skills by engaging in interesting and enjoyable activities.

Behavioral skill fluency is an area of concern. Skills must be fluently executed to meet the ultimate competition that will be faced on jobs. Fluency, although based primarily on ability, is also highly influenced by motivation (i.e., whether the person is interested in doing the skill). Thus, it is important to look at a person's strengths and interests when determining lifetime objectives.

It is also important to teach skills in their natural sequence (Koegel, O'Dell, & Koegel,

1987; LeBlanc, 1990, 1991; Schreibman, 1988; Snell & Zirpoli, 1987), with natural consequences (Carr, 1980; Koegel, Camarata, & Koegel, 1994; LeBlanc, 1990, 1991; Litt & Schreibman, 1981), to ensure generalization of the skills to new environments. Teaching in community-and-work places is effective (Horner, McDonnell, & Bellamy, 1986) for functional skill development; when this is not practical or economically feasible, an emerging research literature shows that simulated environments can accomplish the same outcome (Domaracki & Lyon, 1992; Neef, Lensbower, Hockersmith, DePalma, & Gray, 1990). It has been suggested that a good comprehensive lifetime curriculum will result in good behavior (LeBlanc, 1990). What are needed are more empirical outcome data testing this hypothesis.

There currently is a debate regarding inclusion/integration versus segregation in the education of persons with autism (Sailor, Gee, & Karasoff, 1993). What program will best prepare persons with autism for future work and social adaptation? Programs of inclusion and integration have difficulty providing intensive skill training, and segregated programs offer few opportunities for normal social interaction. Perhaps the best solution is a mixture of these two approaches.

Vocational and Adult Living Programs

Capturing the abilities of individuals with autism in real workplaces results in changes of coworker attitudes regarding the social value of persons with autism (Wehman, 1992). The expectation that the individual should *and* does actually work like anyone else can effectively reduce even the most severe self-aggressive behaviors (Kane, personal communication, July, 1992). Advocates must work with businesspeople to do this economically and realistically (Lynch, October 1994).

Life consists of more than work. Researchers are now developing ways to increase the independence of and provide more choices for persons with autism by teaching them how to live in apartments, such as the Community Living Opportunities, Inc. (Harchik, Sherman, Sheldon, & Strouse, 1992; Sherman, Sheldon, & Strouse, 1988).

Although many of these vocational and daily-living programs are research-based and change with societal and professional changes in values and orientation, there is still a problem for persons with autism, and their families, in making transitions into vocational programs from educational programs that do not teach functional skills for work and daily living. More research is needed on the transitions from school life to adult, work-oriented life, as well as research that focuses on how school-based programs can best prepare persons with autism for adult life. A life-span perspective in education and treatment involves input and program planning from professionals working at all stages of development as the first step in this regard.

Family Involvement and Participation

The family is central for the development of individuals with autism in at least ten domains:

1. Family subsistence and financial base.
2. Access to public health and educational services.
3. Home and neighborhood safety.
4. Domestic tasks and chores.
5. The child's play groups.
6. Marital role relationships.
7. Support networks.
8. Sources of cultural influence.
9. Sources of information for parents.
10. Community participation and inclusion. (Schroeder, 1993)

Parents must make choices regarding the programs they feel will be best for their child. Professionals with a life-span perspective may have important input in this process. However, when professionals provide treatment suggestions to families, a delicate balance must be maintained between the professional's preferences and what the lifestyle and choices of the family dictate.

Families provide the best continuity for persons in daily living environments as well as across the life span. When parents have full-time jobs, when there is only one parent, or when there are many other children, there will be understandable limitations on the choice of a program and on parent and family participation

in the education and treatment of their child. These issues should be viewed as challenges for professionals to create ways for families to be involved despite limitations.

Children with autism are constantly learning. Whether families teach what they intend to teach depends on whether they know how to use successful teaching procedures. Active and successful family participation in the education of children with autism requires family educational programs (Schreibman, 1988). This need for parent education is addressed in the large literature on parent training techniques (Altman & Mira, 1983; Baker, 1984; Dangel & Polster, 1984; Gordon & Davidson, 1981; Graziano, 1977; Moreland, Schwebel, Beck, & Wells, 1982; O'Dell, 1985; Sanders & James, 1983). There is, however, limited research indicating whether parent and child behavioral changes obtained in training are maintained for long periods. Long-term follow-up data, like those presented by Mayo (1996), are required. Finding ways to provide continual family training and support throughout the life span is critical, because the needs of the individual and family change as the person with autism grows and develops.

Currently, we have many excellent examples of parent and family education, and they report major immediate success and, sometimes, short-term maintenance (Rickert et al., 1988; Schreibman, 1988). If we utilize the life-span orientation in parent and family education, however, we must be committed to continually refreshing and maintaining parent and family skills.

SOME PROGRAMS THAT FOCUS ON LIFE-SPAN DEVELOPMENT

The Ann Sullivan Center of Peru, trains parents and maintains active parent and family participation in the education of the child with autism. It provides a comprehensive and continual educational and service program for persons with autism and their families throughout the life span, thus requiring no transitions between programs. The Center requires family participation in the education of their member with autism and provides 90 hours of parent education annually to ensure that the teaching that occurs within the family unit is of high quality and mirrors the approach that is used during the students' 10 to 16 hours (weekly) of center-based education. The students spend more time in family and community activities than they do at the Center, thereby creating integration of their learning into their life. This Center provides all of the education and psychological treatment for students and their families. When students move to integrated school environments or into work placements in the community, the Center offers the necessary continual services. Commitment to continual support is needed to make a life-span program work.

Programs such as TEACCH, in North Carolina (Mesibov, 1994; see Chapter 35) the Delaware Program for Autism (Bondy & Frost, 1994) and the May Institute, Inc. of Massachusetts (Anderson, Campbell, & O'Malley-Cannon, 1994) provide new educational and rehabilitative programs for individuals with autism, and enhance their ability to participate more fully in normalized settings across the life span. The programs' commitment to research and procedural changes provides an excellent context for developing and implementing individualized life-span plans for education and treatment. The key elements that make these and similar programs appropriate for life-span programming are: (a) they directly provide the education and treatment programs or work with those who do; (b) the programs they provide span all developmental stages; (c) most of the professional staff members who work with the children with autism have been taught the same procedures and orientation; (d) they involve families at least in decision making, and they provide some parent education; and (e) they all are developing ways to reduce restrictions placed on persons with autism and to enhance their inclusion into school and community life.

The long-term treatment outcome achieved by Lovaas (1987) indicated very substantial improvement in nearly 50% of the intensively treated group who had received 40 hours of intensive treatment per week. Another outcome of this research was that the children whose parents were trained in behavior therapy techniques maintained their skills and advanced, but those who were institutionalized did not, thus providing a compelling reason for the inclusion of parents and families in the education and treatment of their children with autism. Although there has been some controversy over this research (Lovaas, Calouri, & Jada, 1989; McEachin, 1987; Schreibman, 1988) work of this kind sets a new standard for the field (Romanczyk, Ekdahl, & Lockshin, 1992).

THE FUTURE

Establishment of life-span goals and of programs to accomplish them must be coupled with intensive family education and support, to broaden the spectrum of comprehensive and continual education of persons with autism. Romanczyk and colleagues (1992) called for a focus, in the next decade, on "establishing the critical components of treatment strategies as they relate to outcome" (p. 45). They concede that recovery is not a realistic goal for the vast majority of persons with autism, but call for endorsement of the goal of functioning in typical environments without support services. As Risley (1995) indicated, the necessary tools to make life plans and provide life coaching are low-tech and require little training.

ASPECTS OF SOCIAL POLICY THAT FACILITATE OR IMPEDE RESEARCH IN AUTISM

The ability to create and develop life-span educational and service programs is constricted by traditional systems of service provision and funding. Flexibility is the key to creating new approaches. Funds are needed to motivate professionals and researchers to try new and innovative service approaches, to collect life-span data in order to determine what the outcomes really are, and to challenge researchers to find ways to make persons with autism more independent and productive and thus more normal in their interactions in family and community life. Such emphasis in funding would provide the motivation for persons to try entirely new program development and research, in an attempt to find what really results in success.

Cross-References

Developmental issues are discussed in Chapters 12 through 14. Assessment issues are enumerated in Chapters 19 through 21, and behavioral interventions, in Chapter 26. Vocational interventions, integration issues, program administration, and residential interventions are addressed in Chapters 28 through 31. A perspective on behavioral intervention is provided in Chapter 44.

REFERENCES

Altman, K., & Mira, M. (1983). Training parents of developmentally disabled children. In J.L. Matson & F. Andrasik (Eds.), *Treatment issues and innovations in mental retardation* (pp. 303–372). New York: Plenum Press.

Anderson, S.R., Campbell, S., & O'Malley-Cannon, B. (1994). The May Center for Early Childhood Education. In S. Harris & J.S. Handleman (Eds.), *Preschool education programs for children with autism* (pp. 15–36). Austin, TX: Pro-Ed.

Baer, D.M. (1984). Future directions?: Or, Is it useful to ask, "Where did we go wrong?" before we go? In R.F. Dangel & R.A. Polster (Eds.), *Parent training: Foundations of research and practice* (pp. 417–442). New York: Guilford Press.

Baker, B.L. (1984). Intervention with families with young, severely handicapped children. In J. Blacher (Ed.), *Severely handicapped young children and their families: Research in review* (pp. 317–375). Orlando, FL: Academic Press.

Bellamy, G.T., Newton, J.S., LeBaron, N., & Horner, R.H. (1990). Quality of life and lifestyle outcomes: A challenge for residential programs. In R. Schalock (Ed.), *Quality of life: Perspectives and issues* (pp. 421–443). Washington, DC: American Association on Mental Retardation.

Bijou, S.W. (1972). The technology of teaching young handicapped children. In S.W. Bijou & E. Ribes-Iñesta (Eds.), *Behavior modification: Issues and extensions* (pp. 27–42). New York: Academic Press.

Bondy, A., & Frost, L. (1994). The Delaware Autistic Program. In S. Harris & J.S. Handleman (Eds.), *Preschool education programs for children with autism* (pp. 37–54). Austin, TX: Pro-Ed.

Bristol, M.M. (1979). *Maternal coping with autistic children: The effect of child characteristics and interpersonal support.* Unpublished doctoral dissertation, University of North Carolina at Chapel Hill.

Burd, L., & Kerbeshian, J. (1988). Diagnosis of autism and other pervasive developmental disorders. *Neuroscience and Biobehavioral Reviews, 12,* 275–282.

Carr, E.G. (1980, November). Generalization of treatment effects following educational intervention with autistic children and youth. In B. Wilcox & A. Thompson (Eds.), *Critical issues in educating autistic children and youth* (pp. 118–134). Washington, DC: U.S. Department of Education, Office of Special Education.

Dangel, R.F., & Polster, R.A. (1984). *Parent training: Foundations of research and practice.* New York: Guilford Press.

DeMyer, M.K. (1979). *Parents and children in autism.* New York: John Wiley & Sons.

Domaracki, J.W., & Lyon, S. (1992). A comparative analysis of general case simulation instruction and naturalistic instruction. *Research in Developmental Disabilities, 13,* 363–379.

Doyle, P.M., Wolery, M., Ault, M.J., & Gast, D.L. (1988). System of least prompts: A literature review of procedural parameters. *Journal of the Association for Persons with Severe Handicaps, 13*(1), 28–40.

Gordon, S.B., & Davidson, N. (1981). Behavior parent training. In A.S. Gurman & D.P. Kniskern (Eds.), *Handbook of family therapy* (pp. 78–122). New York: Brunner/Mazel.

Graziano, A.M. (1977). Parents as behavior therapists. In M. Hersen, R.M. Eisler, & P.M. Miller (Eds.), *Progress in behavior modification* (pp. 251–298). New York: Academic Press.

Harchik, A.E., Sherman, J.A., Sheldon, J.B., & Strouse, M. (1992). Ongoing consultation as a method of improving performance of staff members in a group home. *Journal of Applied Behavior Analysis, 25,* 599–610.

Harris, S.L., Belchic, J., Blum, L., & Celiberti, D. (1994). Behavioral assessment of autistic disorder. In J.L. Matson (Ed.), *Autism in children and adults* (pp. 127–146). Pacific Grove, CA: Brooks/Cole.

Horner, R.H., Dunlap, G., & Koegel, R.L. (Eds.). (1988). *Generalization and maintenance.* Baltimore: Brookes.

Horner, R.H., McDonnell, J.J., & Bellamy, G.T. (1986). Teaching generalized skills: General case instruction in simulation and community settings. In R.H. Horner, L.H. Meyer, & H.D.B. Fredericks (Eds.), *Education of learners with severe handicaps: Exemplary service strategies* (pp. 289–314). Baltimore: Brookes.

Kanner, L. (1943). Autistic disturbances of affective contact. *Nervous Child, 2,* 217–250.

Koegel, R.L., Camarata, S.M., & Koegel, L.K. (1994). Aggression and noncompliance: Behavior modification through naturalistic language remediation. In J.L. Matson (Ed.),

Autism in children and adults (pp. 165–191). Pacific Grove, CA: Brooks/Cole.

Koegel, R.L., O'Dell, M.C., & Koegel, L.K. (1987). A natural language teaching paradigm for nonverbal autistic children. *Journal of Autism and Developmental Disorders, 17,* 187–200.

Koegel, R.L., Schreibman, L., Good, A.B., Cerniglia, L., Murphy, C., & Koegel, L.K. (1989). *How to teach pivotal behaviors to autistic children: A training manual.* University of California, Santa Barbara, Graduate School of Education.

Koegel, R.L., Schreibman, L., Loos, L.M., Dirlich-Wilhelm, H., Dunlap, G., Robbins, F.R., & Plienis, A.J. (1992). Consistent stress profiles in mothers of children with autism. *Journal of Autism and Developmental Disorders, 22*(2), 205–216.

Koegel, R.L., Schreibman, L., O'Neill, R.E., & Burke, J.C. (1983). The personality and family-interaction characteristics of parents of autistic children. *Journal of Consulting and Clinical Psychology, 51*(5), 683–692.

LeBlanc, J.M. (1986, October). *Teaching children who have difficulties learning.* Presented at the Seminario Internacional de Educación Especial y Dificultades el Aprendizaic, Universidad Nacional de San Agustin, Facultad de Ciencias en la Educación, (International Seminar of Special Education and Difficulties in Understanding, National University of Saint Augustine, Faculty of the Sciences in Education) Arequipa, Peru.

LeBlanc, J.M. (1990, September). *A good curriculum equals good behavior and maximum skill acquisition for children with retardation and autism.* Special arranged presentation for parents, teachers, and professionals in Kobe, Japan.

LeBlanc, J.M. (1991, November). *Functional curriculum in the education of persons with retardation.* Keynote address, Fourth Congress of Mental Deficiencies, COANIL, Foundation for Helping Children with Limitations, Santiago, Chile.

LeBlanc, J.M. (1992). *Goals for preparing persons for adult life integration.* Paper presented at the meeting of the Special Task Force for Integration, Peruvian Ministry of Education, Lima, Peru.

Litt, M.D., & Schreibman, L. (1981). Stimulus-specific reinforcement in the acquisition of receptive labels by autistic children. *Analysis and Intervention in Developmental Disabilities, 1,* 171–186.

Lovaas, O.I. (1987). Behavioral treatment and normal education and intellectual functioning in young autistic children. *Journal of Consulting and Clinical Psychology, 55,* 3–9.

Lovaas, O.I., Calouri, K., & Jada, J. (1989). The nature of behavioral treatment and research with young autistic persons. In C. Gillberg (Ed.), *Diagnosis and treatment of autism* (pp. 285–306). New York: Plenum Press.

Lynch, C. (1994, October). *Supported employment.* Workshop given at the Ann Sullivan Center, Lima, Peru.

Marcus, L. (1977). Patterns of coping in families of psychotic children. *American Journal of Orthopsychiatry, 47,* 383–399.

Mayo, L. (1996). *Long term follow-up in parent training: A low cost alternative for parents in developing countries.* Unpublished doctoral dissertation, University of Kansas, Lawrence.

McEachin, J.J. (1987). *Outcome of autistic children receiving intensive behavioral treatment: Residual deficits.* Unpublished doctoral dissertation, University of California, Los Angeles.

Mesibov, G.B. (1994). A comprehensive program for serving people with autism and their families: The TEACCH Model. In J.L. Matson (Ed.), *Autism in children and adults* (pp. 85 97). Pacific Grove, CA: Brooks/Cole.

Moreland, J.R., Schwebel, A.I., Beck, S., & Wells, R. (1982). Parents as therapists: A review of the behavior therapy parent training literature—1975 to 1981. *Behavior Modification, 6*(2), 250–276.

Neef, N.A., Lensbower, J., Hockersmith, I., De-Palma, V., & Gray, K. (1990). In vivo versus simulation training: An interactional analysis of range and type of training exemplars. *Journal of Applied Behavior Analysis, 23,* 447–458.

O'Dell, S.L. (1985). Progress in parent training. In M. Hersen, R.M. Eisler, & P.M. Miller (Eds.), *Progress in behavior modification* (pp. 57–108). New York: Academic Press.

Ornitz, E.M., Guthrie, D., & Farley, A.H. (1977). The early development of autistic children. *Journal of Autism and Childhood Schizophrenia, 7,* 207–229.

Osterling, J., & Dawson, G. (1994). Early recognition of children with autism: A study of first birthday home videotapes. *Journal of Autism and Developmental Disorders, 24*(3), 247–257.

Rickert, V.I., Stollano, D.C., Parrish, J.M., Riley, A.W., Hunt, F.M., & Pelco, L.E. (1988). Training parents to become better behavior managers: The need for a competency-based approach. *Behavior Modification, 12,* 475–496.

Risley, T. (1995). Get a life! Positive behavioral intervention for challenging behavior through life arrangement and life coaching. In L.K. Koegel, R.L. Koegel, & G. Dunlap (Eds.), *Community, school, family, and social inclusion through positive behavioral support* (pp. 425–438). Baltimore: Brookes.

Robbins, F.R., Dunlap, G., & Plienis, A.J. (1991). Family characteristics, family training, and the progress of young children with autism. *Journal of Early Intervention, 15*(2), 173–184.

Romanczyk, R.G., Ekdahl, M., & Lockshin, S.B. (1992). Perspectives on research in autism: Current trends and future directions. In D.E. Berkell (Ed.), *Autism: Identification, education and treatment* (pp. 21–51). Hillsdale, NJ: Erlbaum.

Sailor, W., Gee, K., & Karasoff, P. (1993). Full inclusion and school restructuring. In M. Snell (Ed.), *Instruction of students with severe disabilities* (pp. 1–30). New York: Macmillan.

Sanders, M.R., & James, J.E. (1983). The modification of parent behavior. A review of generalization and maintenance. *Behavior Modification, 7,* 3–27.

Schreibman, L. (1988). *Autism.* Newbury Park, CA: Sage.

Schreibman, L., & Charlop, M.H. (1987). Autism. In V.B.V. Hasselt & M. Hersen (Eds.), *Psychological evaluation of the developmentally and physically disabled* (pp. 236–260). New York: Plenum Press.

Schroeder, C.S., & Schroeder, S.R. (1990). The future of children is now. *Journal of Autism and Developmental Disorders, 20,* 367–378.

Schroeder, S.R. (1993). *Stages and transitions across the life span for persons with problems in development: U.S. and Latin American perspectives.* Paper presented at the Third International Symposium of the Ann Sullivan Center, Lima, Peru.

Sherman, J.A., Sheldon, J.B., & Strouse, M.C. (1988). *Implementing the teaching-family model for people with developmental disabilities.* Topeka: Kansas Planning Council on Developmental Disabilities Services.

Siegel, B., Pliner, C., Eschler, J., & Elliot, G.R. (1988). How children with autism are diagnosed: Difficulties in identification of children with multiple developmental delays. *Developmental and Behavioral Pediatrics, 9*(4), 199–204.

Snell, M.E., & Zirpoli, T.J. (1987). Intervention strategies. In M. Snell (Ed.), *Systematic instruction of persons with severe handicaps* (pp. 110–149). Columbus, OH: Merrill.

Sturmey, P., & Sevin, J.A. (1994). Defining and assessing autism. In J.L. Matson (Ed.), *Autism in children and adults* (pp. 13–36). Pacific Grove, CA: Brooks/Cole.

Turnbull, H.R. (1991). *The communitarian perspective: Thoughts on the future for people with developmental disabilities.* Invited address, North Carolina Developmental Disabilities Planning Council, Raleigh, NC.

Wehman, P. (1992). *Life beyond the classroom.* Baltimore: Brookes.

Wolf, L.C., & Goldberg, B.D. (1986). Autistic children grow up: An eight- to twenty-four-year follow-up study. *Canadian Journal of Psychiatry, 31,* 550–556.

Wolf, L.C., Noh, S., Fisman, S.N., & Speechley, M. (1989). Brief report: Psychological effects of parenting stress on parents of autistic children. *Journal of Autism and Developmental Disorders, 19*(1), 157–166.

International Perspectives

CHAPTER 46

Conceptualizations of Autism and Intervention Practices: International Perspectives

INTRODUCTION

Donald J. Cohen and Fred Volkmar

Individuals with autism have been recognized in every region of the world since the time of the first description of the syndrome 50 years ago. The essential features and natural history of autism have been consistent wherever they have been studied. Professional disciplines, as well as nations, have gone through similar processes of development as they have recognized and responded to the needs of autistic individuals and their families. With remarkable consistency worldwide, parents have organized themselves as the most effective advocates for their autistic children and have taken the lead in shaping national policies and creating programs dedicated to research, education, and understanding.

A comparative, cross-national analysis of the history and current status of knowledge, programs, and theories concerning autism reveals both broadly shared features and areas of individuality related to differing resources and theories, and to cultural and historical variances. The study of autism thus offers a unique perspective on the spread and sharing of knowledge about serious clinical problems while illustrating how ideas and practice are shaped by national traditions and cultural differences.

The comparative study of autism benefits immeasurably from publication of conceptions of diagnosis. Diagnostic schema developed during the past 15 years have enhanced communication and are unifying the world's literature. The introduction of the *Diagnostic and Statistical Manual of Mental Disorders* (DSM) of the American Psychiatric Association (APA) in 1980 and its revisions in *DSM-III-R* (APA, 1987) and, most recently, *DSM-IV* (APA, 1994) have led the way in the operational definition of autism and in the creation of the concept of Pervasive Developmental Disorder. The *International Classification of Diseases,* most recently revised as *ICD-10* (World Health Organization [WHO], 1992), has similarly provided an approach to diagnosis of autism within the broader medical nosology. Fortunately, in their most recent versions, the diagnoses of autism in these two dominant systems of nosology have converged. This is a major achievement of the international scientific community. The criteria are largely based on a unique, multinational field trial conducted for *DSM-IV.* The international collaboration demonstrated that clinicians everywhere are able to achieve good reliability in the diagnosis of autism. The *DSM* and *ICD* systems are supplemented by regional approaches (most particularly in France), which contribute their own emphases.

There is no other developmental or psychiatric disorder of children (or, perhaps, of persons of any age) for which such well-grounded and internationally accepted diagnostic criteria exist. The availability of these diagnostic standards allows important comparisons in epidemiology, natural history, treatment methods and systems, and research findings, and it facilitates international sharing of knowledge.

The contributed sections of this chapter provide a broad survey of the field of autism in more than 15 nations: Australia, Canada, China, France, Germany, Israel, Italy, Japan, Latin America, the Nordic Nations, Spain, and the United Kingdom. Prominent clinicians and leaders in the field of autism were invited to discuss a series of topics: the history of autism in their country or region; the current status of diagnosis and treatment services; research and theory; parents' organizations; and publications in the field. We encouraged the contributors to respond to the topic in a way that conveyed their own national situation.

In each case, their responses reflect their national orientations and their personal perspectives and interests. Similarities across nations are apparent in the nearly universal acceptance of the diagnostic conventions of *DSM* and *ICD* and the general approaches to diagnosis and treatment. The interesting differences in theoretical and treatment emphasis, however, make this first comparative study especially intriguing. For example, the contributions from France and from several nations in Latin America emphasize the contributions of psychoanalytic theory to understanding the inner experience of autistic individuals and psychological pathogenesis; the contributions from other nations are relatively silent on these matters, or they emphasize a pragmatic or more empirical approach. Other areas of national difference relate to emphases on education, treatment, and the role of parents. Major differences across nations concern the availability of resources and access to them, and the full inclusion of individuals with autism in a national medical and mental health system.

The national reports given here do not include accounts from the United States or Africa. The latter omission reflects the limited resources in most of Africa, and the paucity of professional contacts, which we hope in the future to remedy. In contrast, a history of autism in the United States deserves a scholarly study beyond the scope of a short chapter. An outline of this history and its effect on most of the world's continents emerges from all the chapters in this volume. We present here a very condensed, selective review, particularly for the benefit of those who have not lived this history directly.

AUTISM IN THE UNITED STATES

As in many other areas of clinical medicine, the brilliant observations of one pioneer mark the starting point. The history of autism began with Leo Kanner's (1943) intuitive application of the emerging field of developmental research, including the charting of social behavior by Arnold Gesell. In his first reports, Kanner was struck by a particular childhood pattern of social disabilities in forming relationships, accompanied by areas of unexpected competence (such as rote memory and duplication of patterns). He highlighted the inborn nature of the children's social disturbance and selected the term *autism,* from the field of schizophrenia, as the hallmark of the new syndrome. Recognizing the unusual nature of the concomitant family interactions, Kanner initially—and wrongly—attributed the disorder to environmental, particularly parental, influences. He later revised his opinion when he came to appreciate how the child's abnormality influenced the family environment, and parental behavior. More recent research, reviewed in this volume, has returned attention to the contributions of genetically transmitted vulnerabilities and to shared difficulties in emotional engagement within families, which are particularly evident in Asperger's Syndrome. Kanner also dealt with the complex relations between autism and mental retardation, initially distinguishing these conditions sharply and later acknowledging that most autistic individuals are, and remain, cognitively disabled and that intellectual level is a major determinant of later functioning.

Kanner's first papers attracted wide attention. Within a few years, many clinicians and clinical centers were replicating his observations. Throughout the 1950s, the major emphasis in the field was on working with very young and preschool children; the full lifetime course of the disorder was not yet apparent. The major theoretical approach was drawn from the broader field of child psychoanalytic theory, and clinicians and investigators attempted to understand pathogenesis and to provide intervention within a psychodynamic framework. At times, and in certain places, this approach was associated with a causal theory that led to attributing a child's disorder to particular, often subtle, patterns of parental interaction.

Decades later, this "blaming" of parents continues to be remembered and resurrected in the criticisms of some child mental health professionals and in various therapeutic approaches. A major force underlying the parental blaming was Bruno Bettelheim. His published papers and books about his work with autistic children (e.g., Bettelheim, 1967) achieved great international popularity because of their literary power and therapeutic claims. It is now recognized that his reports of therapeutic success with autistic children who were removed from what he considered pathogenic families are grossly inaccurate and perhaps intentionally deceptive. Yet, they remain cited outside the United States and are a source of continuing misunderstanding. Their fame is a black mark on the history of autism in the United States.

By the 1960s, limitations in available theories and treatments had become apparent. The landmark book on autism by Bernard Rimland (1964), a parent and an advocate, heralded a new era in research and treatment. Rimland argued for a biological base, postulated a specific pathogenesis, and advocated a more rational and empirical treatment approach. The new era was also facilitated by the observation, in 1961, by Daniel X. Freedman, a biological psychiatrist and pharmacologist, of elevated whole blood serotonin among autistic individuals (Schain & Freedman, 1961). This finding remains the single consistently replicated biological finding in international research.

Within a few years, the field of autism was enriched by a growing cadre of biologically and psychologically sophisticated researchers and clinicians. Research programs were increasingly broadened to include methods from associated fields of neurobiological and behavioral research, which focused on the range of developmental deviations among autistic children. New approaches to studying brain development (including assessment of neurotransmitters and metabolites), language, and other psychological processes were applied to individuals with autism.

Concurrently, during the 1960s, a national society was created by parents, with the support of professionals. The National Society for Autistic Children (NSAC), whose name and scope have changed over the years to reflect recognition of adults with autism, succeeded as a major voice for parent advocacy. Parents created new educational programs; influenced local, state, and national policy; challenged legislation and policies that excluded autistic individuals from services; and encouraged researchers.

During the 1970s, access to services dramatically increased. The nature of these services was influenced heavily by emerging theories and methods from operant conditioning and applied behavioral analysis. By the mid-1970s, research focusing on autism was in the mainstream of child psychiatric and special educational programs, and large numbers of psychologists, educators, and child and adolescent psychiatrists devoted their attention to research and intervention. The large number of publications concerning autism, always remarkable from the earliest years of the field, now found a special home in a journal devoted to this work and were welcome in other, general publications. Numerous books were devoted to research, clinical descriptions, and, increasingly, parental accounts.

Research on autism has continued to expand along with new knowledge about brain development, new techniques for studying neurobiology of brain functioning, theories of cognitive and social development, innovative methods for intervention that emphasize adaptive functioning and normalizing life experiences, genetic methods that can be applied to complex disorders, pharmacological approaches to symptom reduction, and other advances in the behavioral and medical world. Today, clinicians and educators take a lifetime perspective on autistic individuals and recognize the multiple influences on personal outcomes.

The range of services and programs for individuals with autism has expanded enormously over the past decade. Judicial and legislative mandates ensure, at least in theory, that all autistic individuals will have the right to education within the least restrictive environments. For many autistic individuals, these rights do in fact lead to optimally delivered services, and programs are available into adulthood. For too many others, these advantages are still quite limited. Throughout the United States are found exemplary educational programs and varied models of longer-term, supported living. Numerous autistic individuals are now able to function as productive members of society in fully mainstreamed life situations. But even as these achievements are noted, it must be recognized that large numbers of autistic adults are in inadequate situations and, for autistic children and adults with the most severe behavioral problems (such as self-abuse) and the lowest levels of functioning, opportunities and outlook remain bleak.

With advances have come various controversies. Virtually every theory of human development that has emerged during the past five decades has been applied to autism and has, at least for a while, attracted adherents. Numerous therapeutic enthusiasms have been consciously imported from other branches of medicine. Others, carried in the turbulent air over the field of autism, have taken root, often without firm empirical soil and nurtured only by a passionate commitment that had equal parts of distress and hope. Often, parents and their advocates have been caught in a maelstrom of different or opposite viewpoints: mainstreaming has competed with specialized services; parents hear reports of cures achieved in intensive, short-term programs, even as they educate themselves about the lifelong nature of their autistic child's problems; young parents face decisions about whether to pursue dietary treatments, allergic treatments, hugging and holding, use or nonuse of aversive methods, the dangers or benefits of medications, and a host of different other modalities, including (in a return to some of the extremes of the 1950s) claims that autistic individuals are really brilliant people who are held captive by their autism and who can, if given the right chance, express profound truths about their inner life.

As the new century approaches, the power of modern molecular biology and other scientific methods offers new opportunities to study the basis for developmental disorders such as autism. The entire field of the study of autism will no doubt benefit greatly from current scientific advances. At the same time, in the United States, heated controversies continue among well-intentioned advocates and professionals.

Why has autism had such a history, and what accounts for its current status?

In large part, the controversies reflect a simple fact: where there is no cure, there are a hundred treatments. In spite of major advances in understanding the history and psychological features of autism, effective behavioral and pharmacological remediation is limited, and there is no cure. Behavioral and other approaches provide amelioration and habilitation, but we do not know how to fundamentally alter natural history. The distress of parents, the psychological suffering of individuals with autism, and clinicians' and other professionals' wish to be helpful fuel the development of new ideas, new approaches, and, regrettably, unfounded and overenthusiastic claims. The only antidote, and the source of greatest hope has three parts: (a) empirical, rigorous, scientific investigation by well-trained multidisciplinary teams; (b) the translation of scientific knowledge into clinical intervention; and (c) a full, honest sharing of knowledge that will overcome ignorance about autism among professionals, parents, and advocates.

COMPARATIVE STUDIES OF AUTISM

In the following sections, leading clinicians and researchers from throughout the world reflect on specific domains of interest—epidemiology, diagnosis, treatment, and theory. Their appreciation of shared interests and knowledge, as well as their differences in emphasis and view, should encourage further international exchanges, as well as a tolerance for differences. International pooling of concepts and knowledge should accelerate the rate of change in the field of autism and should help to disseminate knowledge to clinicians, educators, and parents across national and language boundaries. For 50 years, autism has been a shared focus of attention for clinicians and researchers throughout the world. We hope that the enhanced communication on autism, across nations, will serve as a model of international collaboration in relation to other psychiatric problems and concerns.

REFERENCES

American Psychiatric Association. (1980). *Diagnostic and statistical manual of mental disorders* (3rd ed.). Washington, DC: Author.

American Psychiatric Association. (1987). *Diagnostic and statistical manual of mental disorders* (3rd ed., rev.). Washington, DC: Author.

American Psychiatric Association. (1994). *Diagnostic and statistical manual of mental disorders* (4th ed.). Washington, DC: Author.

Bettelheim, B. (1967). *The empty fortress.* New York: Free Press.

Kanner, L. (1943). Autistic disturbances of affective contact. *Nervous Child, 2,* 217–250.

Rimland, B. (1964). *Infantile autism.* New York: Appleton-Century-Crofts.

Schain, R., & Freedman, D.X. (1961). Studies on 5-hydroxyindole metabolism in autistic and other mentally retarded children. *Journal of Pediatrics, 58,* 315–320.

World Health Organization. (1992). *Manual of the international statistical classification of diseases and related health problems.* (10th ed., Vol. 1). Geneva, Switzerland: Author.

AUSTRALIA

Bruce J. Tonge and Avril V. Brereton

CONTEXT

Australia covers an area almost the size of the U.S. mainland. Much of the land on this island continent is semiarid and arid bush and grasslands, or desert. The population is around 17 million, of which the great majority live in the cities of Brisbane, Sydney, Melbourne, and Adelaide, on the eastern and southern seaboards, and in Perth, in the southwest. The society is multicultural as a result of progressive immigration from many parts of the world, including Great Britain, Ireland, Europe, the Middle East, Southeast Asia, the Indian subcontinent, and South America. There is also an indigenous population of Australian Aborigines.

The governing and administration of society is based on a federation of states (New South Wales, Queensland, South Australia, Tasmania, Victoria, and Western Australia, and the Australian Capital Territory). The country elects a national parliament and a parliament in each of the states and territories. Delivery of the predominantly free health, education, and welfare services is administered by each State Government, but the Commonwealth Government provides a range of social service benefits and pensions, as well as reimbursement (through an organization called Medicare) for part of the costs of private medical and pharmaceutical services. This system in general delivers a high standard of health, education, and welfare services throughout the nation, but variations in services provided—for example, to persons with autism and their families—do occur between states, because of different service delivery policies, and among urban, rural, and far outback areas, because of access to services.

PREVALENCE AND EPIDEMIOLOGY

There is some evidence that the prevalence of Pervasive Developmental Disorder (Autism) (PDD Autism) in Australia is somewhat higher than the 0.04% reported by Wing (1981) in Great Britain, but more consistent with the level of around 0.07% reported by Gillberg (1984) in Sweden. To determine the prevalence of autism in the Australian population, the authors used the Developmental Behaviour Checklist (DBC; Einfeld & Tonge, 1991, 1994, 1995), a reliable and valid 96-item checklist to be completed by parents or caregivers. The DBC is designed to assess a broad range of behavioral and emotional disturbances in children and adolescents with intellectual disabilities.

The capacity of the DBC to act as a screening instrument for autism has been investigated. The subjects comprised 97 children and adolescents who met the *DSM-III-R* (APA, 1987) criteria for PDD Autism, based on a combination of observation of the child, interview with the parents or caregivers, and information from others, such as teachers. This sample was matched for age, gender, and IQ range with nonautistic children who were part of an epidemiological representative sample of Australian children with intellectual disability. The mean age of the autistic and control subjects was 9.3 years; 81% were males. DBC items were included as predictor variables in a discriminant function analysis if there was a statistically significant univariate difference between the autistic and control subject scores on that item. This provided a list of canonical loadings for 48 items, sorted by magnitude of their discriminating power. The discriminant function was highly significant, and the analysis correctly classified 92% of the autistic and the control subjects—an indication that the DBC can be used to differentiate autistic children from intellectually disabled nonautistic children with a high degree of precision. In a companion study on the use of a neural network for making a diagnosis of autism in the same sample, an accurate classification of

95% was made (Florio, Tonge, Brereton, & Einfeld, in press).

DBC data were available from an epidemiological sample of 514 intellectually disabled children, ages 4 to 18 years (Einfeld & Tonge, 1994). The authors were confident about virtually complete ascertainment of children with moderate intellectual disability (IQ less than 52), but, as with any population survey of intellectually disabled children, the completeness of ascertainment of children with mild-borderline intellectual disability is less certain. These children lived in selected census areas in New South Wales which, when taken together, represented a cross-section of social class and urban and rural distribution that reflected the Australian community. The total population of children and adolescents was 172,914 persons, ages 4 to 18 years. Using the results from the linear discriminant function analysis, a total of 116 (23%) of the epidemiological sample of 514 children were identified as autistic on the basis of their DBC profile. This is equivalent to a prevalence for PDD Autism of 6.7 per 10,000 Australian children. This figure is likely to be an underestimate of the prevalence of autism in the Australian population because it was confined to a survey of intellectually disabled children. Estimates of the proportion of children with autism who have normal intellectual ability are 20% to 30% (DeMyer, Hington, & Jackson, 1981). Taking this into account, the prevalence of autism in Australian children, across the full spectrum of intellectual abilities, might be around 9.5 to 10 per 10,000 children.

ASSESSMENT AND DIAGNOSIS

Although each state and territory has its own approach to assessment, there is much in common in the philosophy and standards applied, and a general picture of the Australian approach to assessment can be described. A national umbrella organization of nongovernment autism associations has a unit in each state. These state associations bring together groups of parents and professionals who are actively involved in the assessment, management, and education of children, adolescents, and adults with autism. The associations either provide (on the basis of government grants) their own assessment services—often associated with early intervention, education, employment, and social skills programs—or are active participants in the government health, education, and welfare management advisory committees that run a range of publicly funded services for persons with disabilities, including autism. The aim is to provide, as early as possible, a comprehensive assessment of children suspected of having autism and to organize an early program of intervention and family support. Prior to assessment, most families have sought help from a range of early childhood community services. Referrals for assessment usually come from maternal and child health nurses, preschool teachers, speech therapists, general medical practitioners, and pediatricians.

Early detection depends on professionals who work in early childhood services and who have some knowledge of autism. The state associations actively provide various autism awareness programs. For example, the autism associations in Victoria and South Australia have produced quality videotapes and educational material for use in undergraduate and continuing professional education. Seminars on autism are in the curriculum of all Australian medical schools and professional training programs for pediatricians, psychiatrists, and clinical psychologists.

The majority of children with autism in Australia are now detected and assessed during the preschool years, before entry into primary school at age 5 or 6 years. Some children are still not diagnosed until later years of primary school or even until adolescence. This delay usually occurs when the child has a normal level of intellectual ability and above-average language development, or has Asperger's Syndrome, or lives in a relatively isolated rural setting, or is a member of a recently arrived immigrant or refugee family from a country that has more limited services for children.

In most cases, the assessment is multidisciplinary. Apart from a diagnosis, assessment of the child's language, social, and cognitive skills, as well as his or her health and medical status is necessary in order to plan the most effective and comprehensive management program. An assessment may be undertaken: (a) by a multidisciplinary team funded specifically for that purpose, (b) by a variety of professionals, in both public and private practice, whose assessments are brought together and coordinated by professionals working for the state autism association, or (c) by staff working for a state or regional child and adolescent mental health service. In general, an assessment has the following components (Tonge, Dissanayake, & Brereton, 1994):

1. Pediatric medical assessment. A full physical assessment, laboratory investigation, and chromosome analysis are done, including a search for Fragile X chromosome, in order to screen for known causes of intellectual disability. When indicated on clinical grounds, more complex investigations such as EEG and MRI scans are ordered. In most instances, an audiological assessment is also done.
2. Cognitive assessment. The cognitive ability and profile of the child are assessed by a psychologist or a special educator using psychological tests that are appropriate to the child's developmental level and behavior, such as the Psycho Educational Profile (Schopler) or the WISC-R (4th edition).
3. Communication assessment. An assessment of communication skills and language development is often undertaken by a speech pathologist.
4. Sensory integrative and motor assessment. Some centers have occupational therapists or physiotherapists available to undertake these assessments, which can be informative in the development of a comprehensive treatment program.
5. Diagnostic consultation. A child psychiatrist or a pediatrician or clinical psychologist with expertise in the assessment of children with autism is usually asked to consult. Information on direct behavioral observations of the child in the preschool and home setting is available, together with the results of the other assessments. The diagnostic consultation includes an interview with the parents or caregivers to obtain a developmental history and assess the psychosocial context as well as the direct behavioral and mental status examination of the child. Rating scales are also used to gain a comprehensive description of the child's

behavior. Among them are the Developmental Behavior Checklist (Einfeld & Tonge, 1994), completed by the parents or caregivers, and the Autistic Behavior Checklist (Krug, Arick, & Almond, 1980) and Childhood Autism Rating Scale (Schopler, Reichler, & Renner, 1988), completed by the clinician.

Following this assessment procedure, it is common for the clinician responsible for the diagnostic consultation, or the coordinator of the autism assessment clinic, to call together a multidisciplinary case conference in which the diagnosis is discussed, the management and therapy program is planned, and consultation with other agencies and support for the family are arranged. A clinician is identified to be responsible for providing the parents with feedback with the opportunity to discuss the diagnosis and management plan, and, often, to remain available to provide further advice and support for the parents if necessary. In the capital cities, such as Melbourne, specialized multidisciplinary teams provide this full and comprehensive assessment and diagnostic service. These teams usually undertake the assessment together, using a one-way observation screen so that all members of the team can observe the various components of the assessment. This method can also serve as a training exercise for students and professionals coming from less specialized settings. It is not always possible for a comprehensive assessment to be undertaken in more isolated rural areas. Children and their families in these locales must travel to a capital city, such as Sydney, for an assessment, or, alternatively, a specialist, such as a child psychiatrist, may travel to a country center on a regular basis to consult with local health, education, and welfare professionals and participate in the assessment of local children with developmental problems.

Although the professional backgrounds of the clinicians and their approach to information gathering may vary from team to team, in general, throughout Australia, the diagnosis of autism and allied disorders is based on *DSM-IV* criteria (APA, 1994) and on the *International Classification of Diseases,* 10th edition (WHO, 1992).

APPROACHES TO MANAGEMENT

Early intervention and the provision of appropriate education form the centerpiece of the management of children with autism in Australia. Early intervention usually is centered around part-time attendance at a preschool, where a teacher's aide provides one-to-one help and support for the child. In the capital cities and the larger country centers, some preschools provide special programs for young children with developmental disabilities. A range of ancillary therapy, such as speech therapy and motor skills programs, is provided when appropriate, to supplement the preschool program. Advice on behavioral management, and the provision of family support, home help, and respite care are further services available to families, to enable them to effectively care for their autistic child.

The delivery of school-based educational programs can vary from state to state, but essentially it is determined by the cognitive and communicative ability of the child. For children with moderate and greater levels of intellectual impairment, educational programs are available in a normal class setting with the one-to-one assistance of an integration teacher's aide, in a special small class within a normal school, or in a special school setting. In both Melbourne and Sydney, some special schools are dedicated exclusively to children with autism, but all have the aim of preparing the child for integration into a more normal setting as soon as possible. Educational and treatment programs, including several residential schools, have been available in Australia since the 1960s. This long experience of service delivery informs current practice and has facilitated the development of new services and research.

All schools are able to receive advice and consultation on educational programs and behavioral management from psychologists and special educators and, to some extent, from speech therapists. Services for the management of more severe behavioral problems and psychopathology are more patchy and less well distributed. Each of the capital cities has a well-developed network of child and adolescent psychiatric clinics, many of which provide secondary consultation services to country areas.

The government service for intellectually disabled persons in each state also employs psychologists and other professionals to provide advice on behavioral management. Child psychiatrists and pediatricians with an interest in behavioral pediatrics, supported by general medical practitioners, are available in the capital cities and major population centers to provide behavioral advice and pharmacotherapy. In most parts of rural Australia, medical services are predominantly provided by general medical practitioners, but telephone consultation with city-based specialists, who also provide secondary consultation visits to country areas, is available. Overall, in Australia, although more resources could be available, the great majority of children with autism, and their families, have access to a good range of essentially free education, welfare, and health services that are further supported by a vigorous system of private medical and psychology services.

An innovative and augmentative communication system was developed in Australia in 1982. Computerized picture graphs, in the form of stylized single-line drawings, were used to symbolically represent a range of concrete objects, emotions, actions, and social interchanges. This system, referred to as COMPIC, forms the basis of an effective alternative channel of communication for autistic children who have delayed and disordered language and communication skills (COMPIC, 1992).

In line with international experience, various unsubstantiated and expensive treatment fads are found in Australia, but they must buck an Australian tradition of wariness toward cure-alls and exaggerated claims for improvement. Currently, active research being conducted in Australia is investigating auditory training (Bettison, in press), facilitated communication (Hudson, 1994), and Vitamin B group therapy. The autism associations remain well informed of the international literature and provide summaries of articles to parents in periodic newsletters and seminars.

RESEARCH

Australian academics have made a contribution to the international literature on autism. Autism research in Australia is most diverse, covering a broad range of biopsychosocial fields and education. Although it would not be appropriate, in the confines of this chapter, to mention all those academics working in Australia who have published in the field, several leading researchers deserve mention. Bartak, who has an academic appointment at Monash University, undertook landmark studies in the education of children with autism and continues to foster a range of educational and psychological studies (Bartak & Rutter, 1973). Prior (1987; Prior & Tonge, 1990), first at Latrobe and now at the University of Melbourne, has led a number of important neurobiological and psychological research projects into autism and allied conditions.

CONCLUSIONS

The services provided to persons with autism in Australia are based on a comprehensive assessment, using internationally recognized criteria for diagnosis, and on an understanding that education and the acquisition of social skills and communication ability are central to management. Strong parent associations, together with professionals, are active in lobbying and in developing and coordinating a range of services, community and professional education, and family support. These programs are generally supported by research and academic programs based predominantly in the universities. The need for a wider range of services for adults is becoming apparent as the identified autistic population ages. As in a number of other countries, the refinement of diagnostic classification, such as the introduction of criteria for Asperger's Syndrome, and the recognition of comorbidity are raising new assessment and service delivery challenges.

Cross-References

International approaches to diagnosis are addressed in Chapters 1–7.

REFERENCES

American Psychiatric Association. (1987). *Diagnostic and statistical manual of mental disorders* (3rd ed., rev.). Washington, DC: Author.

American Psychiatric Association. (1994). *Diagnostic and statistical manual of mental disorders* (4th ed.). Washington, DC: Author.

Bartak, L., & Rutter, M. (1973). Special educational treatment of autistic children. *Journal of Child Psychology and Psychiatry, 14,* 161–179.

Bettison, S. (in press). The long-term effects of auditory training on children with autism. *Journal of Autism and Developmental Disorders.*

COMPIC. (1992). *Your guide to COMPIC.* Melbourne, Australia: Spastic Society of Victoria.

DeMyer, M.K., Hington, J.N., & Jackson, R.K. (1981). Infantile autism reviewed: A decade of research. *Schizophrenia Bulletin, 7,* 388–451.

Einfeld, S.L., & Tonge, B.J. (1991). Psychometric and clinical assessment of psychopathology in developmentally disabled children. *Australian and New Zealand Journal of Developmental Disability, 17*(2), 147–154.

Einfeld, S.L., & Tonge, B.J. (1994). *Manual for the Developmental Behavior Checklist.* University of New South Wales Department of Child and Adolescent Psychiatry, School of Psychiatry; and Monash University, Centre for Developmental Psychiatry.

Einfeld, S.L., & Tonge, B.J. (1995). The Developmental Behavior Checklist: The development and validation of an instrument to assess behavioral and emotional disturbance in children and adolescents with mental retardation. *Journal of Autism and Developmental Disabilities, 25*(2), 81–104.

Florio, T.M., Tonge, B.J., Brereton, A.V., & Einfeld, S.L. (in press). Neural network diagnosis of autism: A replication and extension. *Journal of Autism and Developmental Disorders.*

Gillberg, C. (1984). Infantile autism and other childhood psychoses in a Swedish urban region: Epidemiological aspects. *Journal of Child Psychology and Psychiatry, 25,* 35–43.

Hudson, A. (1994). Disability and facilitated communication: A critique. In T.H. Ollendick & R.J. Prinz (Eds.), *Advances in clinical child psychology* (Vol. 17, pp. 197–232). New York: Plenum Press.

Krug, D., Arick, J.R., & Almond, P.J. (1980). Behavior checklist for identifying severely handicapped individuals with high levels of autistic behavior. *Journal of Child Psychology and Psychiatry, 21,* 221–229.

Prior, M. (1987). Biological and neurophysiological approaches to childhood autism. *British Journal of Psychiatry, 150,* 8–17.

Prior, M., & Tonge, B.J. (1990). Pervasive developmental disorders. In B.J. Tonge, G.D. Burrows, & J. Werry (Eds.), *Handbook of studies in child psychiatry* (pp. 193–208). Amsterdam: Elsevier.

Schopler, E., Reichler, R.J., & Renner, B.R. (1988). *The Childhood Autism Rating Scale (CARS).* Los Angeles: Western Psychological Services.

Tonge, B.J., Dissanayake, C., & Brereton, A.V. (1994). Autism: Fifty years on from Kanner. *Journal of Pediatrics and Child Health, 30,* 102–107.

Wing, L. (1981). Sex ratios in early childhood autism and related conditions. *Psychiatry Research, 5,* 129–137.

World Health Organization. (1992). *The international classification of diseases: Classification of mental and behavioral disorders* (10th ed.). Geneva: Author.

CANADA

Peter Szatmari

The care of children with autism in Canada has been influenced by both the advance of scientific knowledge and government policy. The first clinic to take a special interest in the diagnosis and treatment of children with autism was established at the West End Creche in Toronto by Dr. Milada Havelkova, who emigrated to Canada from Czechoslovakia after World War II. She was given an appointment in the Department of Psychiatry at the University of Toronto and did her clinical work at the West End Creche (perhaps the oldest mental health center for preschool children in Canada). Havelkova developed a keen and abiding interest in children with developmental problems and worked at the Creche for over 30 years. She was the first child psychiatrist in Canada to initiate studies into the etiology and natural history of children with infantile autism, and these studies resulted in several important early publications.

The first major influence that profoundly transformed the care of children with autism was the introduction of universal healthcare to Canada during the 1950s. This single-tier system aimed to provide comprehensive, accessible, and universally available medical services to all citizens, regardless of income. Although private health insurance was still available, it became increasingly irrelevant. The impact of this financing arrangement was that every family with an autistic child could receive both diagnostic and treatment services.

The second major influence on the development of services for children with autism was that treatment programming generally developed in community mental health clinics rather than in general psychiatric hospitals. Diagnostic and assessment services were often carried out in a children's hospital, in a large metropolitan center, by pediatricians and child psychiatrists, whereas treatment programs often took place in community settings or schools. There were very few hospital-based treatment centers that provided either residential or day programming for children with autism and other forms of developmental disabilities. Instead, several large institutions that serviced developmentally disabled children and adults were established in rural settings. Many of the residents of these facilities qualified for a diagnosis of autism, although a review of records often revealed a diagnosis of mental retardation or mental handicap instead. However, with recent changes in funding and a move to "least restrictive environments," many of these large institutions have either closed or now care for a very much smaller number of severely disabled adults who cannot be cared for in community settings. Very few community resources are now available for adults with autism.

This separation between diagnostic and treatment services has had the unfortunate consequence of not promoting the training of physicians with expertise in developmental handicap in general, and autism in particular. Compared to the United Kingdom, for example, few pediatricians or child psychiatrists in Canada have specialized expertise in the diagnosis and assessment of children with autism. Very little instruction is provided in medical school, and subspecialty training programs in both psychiatry and pediatrics have tended to emphasize acute illnesses rather than chronic developmental disabilities.

The third major influence on the delivery of services for children with autism in Canada has been the emphasis on integration of disabled children within community settings. This emphasis has arisen from a number of sources, including advocacy movements for integration in the United States, the lack of hospital-based residential services, and the pioneering work on integration done by several school boards in Ontario. In most parts of Canada, schools are administered by two separate, publicly funded systems, generally divided along religious lines. Public school boards are open to children of all religious affiliations, but children in

Catholic families are usually served by Catholic school boards. Many of these boards have taken a forceful role in integrating children with developmental handicaps into the regular school system. For example, the Hamilton-Wentworth Roman Cathologic Separate School Board has been integrating children with severe mental and physical disabilities into community classrooms since the early 1970s. Specialized support services were available for these children, and the schools have learned to accommodate the children's special needs in a creative way. Although the move away from segregated classrooms for autistic children has been slow in several school regions, the integration of children with autism into regular classrooms has been accomplished now in many parts of Canada. Unfortunately, due to the nature of the disability, many children with autism continue to languish in segregated settings without the kind of treatment programming that is needed for these types of disabilities. In addition, resources available to support the integration of children with autism appear to be diminishing in some jurisdictions.

The fourth important influence on the delivery of services was the introduction of the *Diagnostic and Statistical Manual of Mental Disorders* (DSM; 3rd ed.) of the American Psychiatric Association (APA) in 1980. Prior to *DSM-III,* there was considerable confusion and lack of clarity in Canada and elsewhere about the diagnostic criteria for autism. Different diagnostic labels such as childhood psychosis, brain dysfunction, childhood schizophrenia, and infantile autism were used in a haphazard way. Moreover, the use of diagnostic categories often divided along professional lines. For example, pediatricians tended to use the term *infantile autism* infrequently but used instead labels such as *autistic tendencies* or *autistic features* to identify large numbers of developmentally handicapped children. Similarly, child psychiatrists preferred to use *childhood schizophrenia* or *childhood psychosis* rather than autism, and interpreted the disorder along psychodynamic lines. With *DSM-III,* however, specific diagnostic criteria for autism became available and could be relatively easily applied. In addition, the term Pervasive Developmental Disorder (PDD), introduced in *DSM-III* to identify a spectrum of conditions that shared features of the "autistic continuum," gained wide acceptance. As a result, the number of children given a diagnosis of autism increased, and there was further interest in the characterization of children with other forms of PDD. Indeed, in Canada, the term PDD has gained considerable popularity and no distinction is made between autism and PDD in terms of access to services or school programs. With the broadening of the criteria for autism in *DSM-III-R* (APA, 1987), the number of children who received a diagnosis of autism increased substantially, as did the number of children who received a diagnosis of Pervasive Developmental Disorder Not Otherwise Specified (PDD-NOS). However, these children were generally given a diagnosis of PDD instead, and autism and PDD were often seen as mutually exclusive terms by both the lay and professional communities. This confusion persists to this day, but may improve with the recent publication of *DSM-IV* (APA, 1994). The end result of these changes in classification is that the number of children with autism and other forms of PDD has grown substantially. There is now much greater recognition of the disorder among those who provide services for preschool children and considerable interest in creating programs for these children in community preschools and day care centers. The current demand for services for children with PDD has grown substantially, and the available treatment centers and services are finding it difficult to cope with this increasing demand.

Throughout these developments, an important role has been played by parent organizations. The Autism Society of Ontario was founded in 1973, and a national organization was started in 1976. Currently, there are autism parent societies in all ten provinces, and a national organization receives funding from both the private sector and the federal government. These organizations have provided an extremely important forum for education, a means of disseminating information, and parental support; on many occasions, they have also provided direct treatment such as summer camps and other recreational activities. As government funding for hospital-based and community-based services decreases, it is anticipated that these voluntary organizations will become even more important in the delivery of services to children with autism in the future.

REFERENCES

American Psychiatric Association. (1980). *Diagnostic and statistical manual of mental disorders* (3rd ed.). Washington, DC: Author.

American Psychiatric Association. (1987). *Diagnostic and statistical manual of mental disorders* (3rd ed., rev.). Washington, DC: Author.

American Psychiatric Association. (1994). *Diagnostic and statistical manual of mental disorders* (4th ed.). Washington, DC: Author.

Bryson, S.E., Clark, B.S., & Smith, I. (1988). First report of a Canadian epidemiological study of autistic syndromes. *Journal of Child Psychology and Psychiatry, 29,* 433–446.

Havelkova, M. (1968). Follow-up study of 71 children diagnosed as psychotic in preschool age. *American Journal of Orthopsychiatry, 38,* 846–857.

Szatmari, P., Archer, L., Fisman, S., Streiner, D.L., & Wilson, F. (1995). Asperger's Syndrome and autism: Differences in behavior, cognition, and adaptive functioning. *Journal of the American Academy of Child and Adolescent Psychiatry, 34,* 1662–1671.

CHINA

Kuo-Tai Tao and Xiao-Ling Yang

Infantile and early childhood autism as a pervasive developmental disorder were unknown to most people and even to medical professionals in China until the past decade. Programs of clinical studies, treatment, and rehabilitation training have now been started, but are just at an early developmental stage.

DIAGNOSTIC CONCEPT

Kanner (1943) described a group of 11 children with a previously unrecognized disorder, and he noted a number of characteristic features in these children to which he first gave the diagnosis of early infantile autism. This diagnostic concept was introduced into China as late as 1982 by one of the authors (Tao), in an article on "Issues of Diagnosis and Classification of Infantile Autism." The article, published in a Chinese journal, described 4 cases and emphasized the qualitative change in behaviors for the purpose of differentiation from other developmental and mental disorders in childhood. In a later article, Tao (1987) provided a brief report on 15 cases. It was news to the rest of the world that infantile autism definitely existed and was being diagnosed in mainland China. Following this report, Yang (1990) reported on an additional 30 cases of children with autism. From this time onward, other reports have appeared in journals for special education teachers, and articles about autism have been published in magazines and newspapers. Most people, except those who are illiterate, now have some idea of autism.

RARITY OF AUTISM IN CHINA

In China, most people cannot imagine that a disorder such as autism can occur in infancy and early childhood. This denial has also influenced the thinking of many pediatricians and psychiatrists. Because child psychiatry developed quite recently in China, most professionals working with children have no child psychiatry training. The few child psychiatrists working in China are located in large cities. Both of the present authors had the opportunity for training in the United States, and many autistic children are referred to us from different parts of China. These children have been diagnosed as having mental retardation, hyperactive syndrome, childhood schizophrenia, sporadic encephalitis, and other conditions.

In China, children usually are sent by their parents to a clinic, for evaluation and treatment: The first step of professional recognition of this disorder is largely dependent on whether the parents consider the behavior of their children somewhat abnormal and seek help from medical professionals. In fact, only a few of the parents in our series have shown this awareness. There are several reasons for this unfortunate history:

1. Most parents do not have scientific knowledge about the developmental milestones of the first 2 years of their children's lives, so they cannot recognize problems that might raise a suspicion of a disorder unless their children do not speak by the time they are 3

or 4 years of age. Usually, delayed speech leads to otolaryngological examination of hearing and, if this is found to be normal, to psychiatric help.

2. Knowing that there are different speeds of normal development of children, some parents think that their children's maturational lag will be made up in the future. So they wait.

3. Perhaps in line with the Chinese biological-medical model, parents pay more attention to physical symptoms of illness than to behavioral symptoms. Also, a stigma is still attached to mental disorder, especially in undeveloped areas. Young parents feel guilty or ashamed and try to hide their children's behavioral problems from the outside world.

These factors may influence the early recognition and diagnosis of autism. Both of us (working in Nanjing and Beijing, respectively) have found that autistic children come to the clinics an average of 3 years after parents have noticed abnormal behavior in their children.

The difficulties in early recognition and evaluation have given an impression that autism is very rare in China, but it does seem likely that autism is actually less common in China than elsewhere. Tao reported 15 cases, and only 2 came from Nanjing, a city with a population over 4 million; similarly, the population of Beijing was 11 million in 1990, and Yang reported 30 cases, with only 10 coming from Beijing. The rarity of autism in China needs to be studied in further detail.

CLASSIFICATION AND DIAGNOSTIC CRITERIA

The first draft of a Chinese classification of mental disorders was proposed in 1958. It classified mental disorders exclusively in relation to mental retardation. The first official classification, published in 1981 as CCMD-1 (Chinese Classification of Mental Disorders), included other childhood mental disorders besides mental retardation. In 1989, CCMD-2 was published and the diagnostic category of Childhood Autism (Pervasive Developmental Disorder) first appeared, with diagnostic

criteria essentially adopted from *ICD-9*. In 1994, CCMD-2-R was prepared. One of the most important features is its provision of more detailed diagnostic criteria than CCMD-2. To improve the reliability of diagnostic judgment, the clinician has two tasks: (a) to determine the presence or absence of specific clinical features, and (b) then to use the criteria provided as guidelines for making the diagnosis. The term Childhood Autism is adopted from *ICD-10,* the diagnostic criteria are close to *ICD-10,* and *DSM-III-R* is used as a major reference.

DIAGNOSTIC PROCEDURES

The diagnostic procedures of our clinics are essentially the same as those in the United States. The importance of histories of development, present illness, and psychiatric examination (unstructured and structured) is emphasized. The data gathered are usually supplemented by physical examination and laboratory tests. Formal psychological tests include the Denver Developmental Screening Tests (DDST), Bayley, Wechsler Preschool and Primary Scale of Intelligence (WPPSI), and the Japanese Social Adaptive Ability Test (Chinese Version). The autistic children we have examined belong mostly to lower or moderate functional levels and cannot cooperate with psychological testing. We also use rating scales and other methods, including the Autism Behavior Checklist (ABC), the Childhood Autism Rating Scale (CARS), and the Clancy Behavior Scale.

As indicated, we perform biological tests, including chromosome and Fragile X testing, EEG, CT, MRI, and other tests.

TREATMENT AND CARE SERVICES

China is a vast country with a population of 1.8 billion. Services are just beginning to be developed.

In Nanjing and Beijing, we have developed parent counseling services for parents who seek help. We send parents a questionnaire covering family history; parents' education level, economic status, and relationship with the child; developmental and present illness; and so on. If we believe the child is possibly autistic, we send a packet of available written material about autism and the care and training of autistic children, and we ask parents to seek help from local rehabilitation centers for handicapped children or similar facilities. If they come back to Nanjing or Beijing, our clinic has several kinds of services—an outpatient clinic, a day hospital, and an inpatient treatment service. These services are provided by a group that includes child psychiatrists, special teachers, and psychologists. The rehabilitation training program includes behavior modification; sometimes, psychotropic drugs are used to control overactivity and aggressive self-injurious and stereotyped behaviors.

At present, the medical treatment and care services are limited, but they include both inpatient and outpatient care. They consist of:

1. Medical treatment services. Several kinds of limited medical treatment services are offered to autistic children in a few of China's largest cities.
2. Hospitals and centers specializing in psychological analysis and health offer hospital treatments for short periods (about 2 months) for autistic children. The parents or foster parents of the autistic child must accompany the child. The purposes of the hospital treatment are:

   - Observation. During the period of hospitalization, psychologists and parents observe the autistic child. The psychologists help the parents to analyze the child's developmental level and behavioral characteristics, develop a detailed program for training, and show how to train the child at home.
   - Medical treatment. After detailed investigation of the child, the psychiatrists choose proper medicines and doses for children who have serious withdrawal, emotional instability, anxiety, and impulsiveness. The most widely used medicines are neuroleptics (e.g., haloperidol, sulpiride, thioridazine), which are found to have some beneficial influence.
   - Psychological adjustment of the parents. During the period of hospitalization, the psychiatrists and psychologists help the parents to improve their ability to give

more love, patience, time, and knowledge to their child.

3. Outpatient services. The range of outpatient care is again limited. It includes:

   - Clinic consultation. Normally, parents bring their children to clinics, but there are no assigned doctors and no fixed consultation times, so medical examinations are often not possible. Systematic help and instruction for autistic children is problematical, and the results are very difficult to evaluate. Unfortunately, most autistic children are treated in this way.
   - Daytime medical treatment and training. The medical treatments and training in the psychological hospitals and centers are like those in the special education schools. The children are offered a combination of medical treatments, perceptual exercises, and physical exercise. Most of these services are full-day; some are half-day.
   - Service in kindergarten and social centers. Some children who have difficulties are able to enter normal kindergartens or primary schools. The service offered could be a half-day (or shorter time) of observation and training.

EDUCATION AND EMPLOYMENT OF THE HANDICAPPED

The education law in China provides obligatory education for 9 years. In the past decade, special education has developed very rapidly in big cities. There are schools for blind, deaf, handicapped, and mentally retarded children. For diverse reasons, autistic children are not included in the national special education project. Since 1994, however, the Ministry of Education of China has begun a research program to investigate how to educate and train autistic children, in order to gain experience in this field, preparatory to proposing a national autistic education program. In Beijing, several schools and kindergartens accept autistic children. These children receive treatments and training in special programs, but the number of acceptances is limited. Some autistic children with more serious syndromes cannot enter schools and must be cared for by their families.

Employment is very difficult for autistic adolescents, even after they have received special education for several years. Their social protection is not yet established, and their families must take care of them.

PARENTS' ASSOCIATION

The preparation and foundation of a parents' association began in 1991. Dr. Yang Xiao-Ling of the Institute of Mental Health of Beijing Medical University has united a group of parents to form an association for autistic children. By organizing meetings, video shows, and discussions, the parents and medical specialists have improved understanding of autism and of what can be done for autistic children by exchange of information between parents and doctors. The parents receive not only knowledge, experience, and confidence about medical treatments, education, and training; they also become friends and are released from their feelings of helplessness, isolation, and depression. This support eases the parents' difficult situation and improves their psychological health.

Parents have recognized that, for their autistic children's healthcare, education, and other rights, they should unite and work together, and an official association is a necessity. In December 1993, the Beijing Rehabilitation Association for Autistic Children was officially inscribed and funded. Currently, the association has 120 members (about half are from other cities and provinces). The purposes of this association are to improve the material and social environments for autistic children, ensure their equality in social life, and create rehabilitation, education, and medical care conditions that will help them achieve their highest possible level of living.

The tasks of the association are: (a) to investigate the social situation of autistic children; (b) to present wishes and requests of autistic children to local and central governments; (c) to exchange information and to give consultative services of rehabilitation, education, and social care of autistic children; (d) to promote coordination among members and exert pressure for governmental projects concerning autistic children; (e) to promote international scientific exchange, and (f) to support research on autism.

LAW FOR PROTECTION OF DISABLED

The Chinese government has attached great importance to the welfare of the disabled. This policy has been implemented in various legislation, including the laws of 1991. A full plan developed between 1988 and 1992 includes national work programs for the disabled that offer rehabilitation and education as well as employment. Compulsory education will be ensured to most children and teenagers with various disabilities, including autistic disorder. The major problems have been the recognition of individuals with autism and the creation of sufficient services.

REFERENCES

Kanner, L. (1943). Autistic disturbances of affective contact. *Nervous Child, 2,* 217–250.

Tao, Kuo-Tai. (1987). Infantile autism in China. *Journal of Autism and Developmental Disorders, 2,* 289.

Yang, Xiao-Ling. (1990). Clinical analysis of 30 cases of childhood autism. *Chinese Journal of Mental Health, 6,* 250.

FRANCE

Pierre Ferrari

HISTORY AND CLASSIFICATION

Psychotic disorders of early childhood were long ignored in France as well as in the rest of the world. During the past century, intellectual deficiency was the banner under which all child mental pathology was grouped, and clinical studies were limited to the description of different forms of mental retardation. In 1888, the French alienist Moreau de Tours, in his famous treatise, "La Folie chez l'enfant" ("Madness in the Child"), deemed inconceivable that anyone could refer to the possible existence of psychosis in the child. In his view, psychotic manifestations could only be exceptionally observed, and only in children close to puberty.

During the first half of the 20th century, French clinicians recognized and described the existence of a schizophrenia in the child that was similar to the same condition in an adult but had a childhood onset. This led G. Heuyer to describe forms of schizophrenia beginning around the age of 10. During the 1950s and 1960s, when Kanner's research was ongoing in the United States, French child psychiatrists, who often had a psychoanalytic orientation, became interested in psychotic manifestations of very early childhood, and created a nosographic frame for early childhood psychoses (R. Diakine, S. Lebovici, J.L. Lang, & R. Mises). Their research has led to the recent construction of a French classification of child and adolescent mental disorders (R. Mises). This classification, comprising two axes (Axis I is devoted to basic clinical categories, and Axis II takes into account possibly etiological associated factors), regroups child psychoses and separates them into five categories:

1. Autism.
2. Atypical forms of autism.
3. Psychoses with mental deficiency.
4. Dysharmonic psychoses.
5. Child schizophrenia.

This classification differs somewhat from the classifications suggested by *DSM-III-R* and *ICD-10*.

The form of autism that was described by Leo Kanner maintains a central place in the French nosology. The criteria that have been retained for this diagnosis are: onset during the first year of life, with organization of a full picture before the age of 3; and presence of all the characteristic features, including major autistic withdrawal, immutability, stereotypies, absence of language (or specific language disorders), and cognitive development dysharmony.

In addition to autism, other forms of early psychoses and of dysharmonies have been characterized.

In the *early psychoses with mental deficiency,* aspects and mechanisms of psychoses are implicated, from the onset, with severe disorders in the organization of cognitive and instrumental functions. These forms are characterized by association with two patterns:

(a) a syndrome involving severe mental retardation (marked by intellectual deficiency and severe instrumental deficits), or (b) symptoms suggesting the presence of a psychotic nucleus.

Symptoms associated with a psychotic nucleus include withdrawal attitudes, denoting important communication difficulties; the presence of major anxieties that increase the withdrawal attitudes, the regressive behaviors, the impulsive behaviors, and, mainly, the self-aggressive behaviors; and the presence of certain language disorders evocative of a psychotic dimension of language (mutism, soliloquy, verbal stereotypies).

The characterization of the *psychotic dysharmonies* as forms of child psychosis (similar in some respects to Other Pervasive Developmental Disorders in *ICD-10*) is one of the original features of the French classification. French authors have considered that these forms differ from autism, as well as from other developmental disorders, because of the following characteristics:

1. Their later onset, around the age of 3 to 4 years, often after a seemingly normal period of early development.
2. Their frequency: twice to three times greater than that of autism.
3. The variety of symptomatic manifestations: major psychomotor instability or, conversely, important psychomotor inhibition; severe pseudoneurotic manifestations (with overwhelming phobia or severe obsessive symptoms, severe language disorders characteristic of psychotic language, intolerance to frustration accompanied by violent fits of anger, important mood changes, failure of the first attempts at schooling).
4. Behind this varying series of symptoms, a diagnosis based on a close psychopathological examination that makes it possible to reveal, beyond the symptoms, the presence of the following psychotic mechanisms:

   • Contact with reality and capacities of adaption to reality are always fragile; relatively maintained at certain moments, contact with reality is severely disorganized at other times by the invasion of psychotic processes.

- Relation with others, apparently possible at certain moments, seems at other moments completely disrupted. Generally speaking, relation with others, when it is possible, takes place in a poorly differentiated dual way.
- Anxieties are always important but they are of a variety of natures (annihilation anxiety, depressive anxieties of object loss, separation anxieties).
- Thought processes are invaded and overwhelmed by very crude and intense affects, fantasies, and representations (often marked by the importance of aggressive and destructive instincts).

The main feature of this French classification is that it maintains the term Early Psychosis rather than Pervasive Developmental Disorder, used in *DSM-III-R* and *DSM-IV*. The term *psychosis* was preferred (a) to better indicate that the specificity of the disorder is related to the presence of a psychotic process underlying the developmental disorders and delays, and (b) to emphasize the unity of the group of early psychoses, marked by the existence of a continuum and of forms of passage between autism and psychotic dysharmony. Therefore, the aim of the French classification is not to mark the boundaries of entities that strictly exclude each other and are stable over time, but rather to enable the identification of different psychopathological modes of organization that can essentially evolve and change into each other, under the effect of therapy.

RESEARCH

The investigations of French child psychiatrists have been oriented during recent decades in several directions: toward biology, clinical practice, and therapeutics. These investigations are based on a multifactorial conceptualization of the origin of child psychosis and emphasize the close interdependence of factors originating in the field of social relations as well as factors originating in the field of biology, during the first period of the infant's mental life. Inside the interactive melting pot where the beginning of the child's psyche becomes organized, two aspects become interactively engaged: (a) the newborn's competence

and possible failures, whether the latter are biological or of another nature, and (b) the components of the relational field, with their possible failures, wherever they originate.

In the field of biological research, several research teams are interested in the study of visual-auditory evoked potentials in the cortex and the cerebral stem (Lelord & Sauvage, 1990). Others have centered their research on the study of genetic factors involved in child psychosis (J. Mallet). Finally, other studies have focused on alterations in the systems of neurotransmitters (serotonin, epinephrine and norepinephrine, endorphins), and the correlations of these findings with clinical data (P. Ferrari & C. Bursztejn) as well as a possible dysfunction of the hypothalamic-pituitary-adrenal axis (Torgman et al., in press).

French clinicians have emphasized the necessity to carry out a very early diagnosis, during the first 2 years of the child's life. The precocity of the diagnosis allows for early therapeutic care, which will itself condition, at least in part, the quality of the natural history of the disorder. According to this point of view, different authors have applied themselves to specific, very early symptoms of autistic evolution, through a careful observation of child–parent interactions during the first 18 months of life. These symptoms are:

1. In the realm of psychomotricity, absence of anticipatory attitudes and of postural adaptation.
2. In the realm of perceptive communication, abnormalities concerning gaze and reactions to sounds and to the human voice.
3. Nonappearance of Spitz's organizers (such as separation distress).
4. Absence of interest in objects and the surrounding world.
5. Presence of massive and poorly organized phobias.
6. Lack of expression and of understanding of emotions.
7. Gesture stereotypies and visual and auditory self-stimulations.
8. Lack of development of transitional and play activities.

Despite the multiplicity of these symptoms, French researchers have stressed the difficulty in making a very early diagnosis, because symptoms vary, are inconspicuous, or sometimes lack specificity. Thus, investigators suggest that, rather than speaking of early signs of autism, it might be preferable to speak of "early interactive dysfunctions with a risk of autistic evolution." Autism would then appear less as an independent disease, strictly speaking, than as one pathological evolution, among others, of certain severe and early interactive disturbances.

In the realm of psychopathology, French clinical researchers have applied themselves to understand, with the help of psychoanalytic concepts, the psychopathological mechanisms of autistic and psychotic states. They emphasize the importance of this understanding for good treatment planning. This understanding notably calls on the concepts of the Kleinian and post-Kleinian theories of F. Tustin and D. Meltzer. This viewpoint has developed in France under the influence of the ideas of D. Anzieu, D. Houzel, and G. Haag (1984), among others.

This perspective on psychopathology has recognized the value of some concepts for the understanding of autistic states—for example, adhesive identification, self-sensoriality, the feeling of bodily discontinuity (black hole), a self with no envelope and no interior. Concerning psychotic dysharmonies, these authors have stressed the importance of mechanisms such as splitting, projective identification, the depressive position, and "instinctual disintrication."

DIAGNOSIS

The diagnosis of early psychosis in France is formulated by the child psychiatrist on the basis of a diagnostic process that involves the following steps:

1. An anamnestic inquiry, in order to specify the child's and the family's past record.
2. A search for early signs of autism previous to the consultation.
3. A psychiatric clinical examination, in search of clinical signs and relational modalities that could support the diagnosis. This clinical examination is completed by an assessment of the psychopathological mechanisms underlying the symptoms.

4. An organic clinical examination in search of an associated organic disease (encephalopathy, sensorial deficiencies, malformations, other biological abnormalities, and so on).
5. A psychological evaluation, with a range of important aims, including:

   - Projective tests for specifying the characteristics of the child's personality and the nature of the psychopathological mechanisms that are operating.
   - Cognitive assessment to evaluate the child's intellectual level and cognitive capacities, using standardized psychological tests such as the Brunet-Lezine, EDEI, WISC, WPPSI, or K-ABC.
   - Assessment of psychomotor behavior.
   - Language assessment (including the psycholinguistic assessment set of Chevry-Muller).
   - Other assessment methods, including rating scales for autistic symptoms Childhood Autism Rating Scale (CARS), structured interviewing and observational methods Autism Diagnostic Interview (ADI), and measures of adaptive functioning (Vineland scales).

6. Organic tests, as indicated by the clinical picture, including:

   - Search for genetic abnormalities.
   - Electroencephalogram (EEG), as well as studies of evoked potentials in the cortex and the brain stem.
   - Neuroimaging (CT scan or MRI).
   - Neurochemical studies (neurotransmitter metabolism).

TREATMENT

The goals of treatment are quite broad. They include the following:

1. Enabling the child to recognize self as a subject and to gain the means to reach a genuine communication with others. For this, the child must be recognized as a subject with a unique personal history who is endowed with a specific psychic life that organizes his or her relationship modalities with the environment. The psychoanalytic theory is an important tool for the understanding of this psychological functioning.

2. Offering the child the educative measures necessary to become autonomous.
3. Offering the child the pedagogic and academic measures necessary for eventual academic, professional, and social insertion.

Although the broader, therapeutic goal remains essential, the contribution of educative measures should not be neglected. These educative measures are part of an exchange that takes into account the nature of the child's relation with the environment, in order to enable the child to integrate these educative measures. The pedagogic and academic approaches are considered essential to help the child achieve autonomy and become integrated into society. They are offered to the child according to individual learning abilities.

The presence of a multidisciplinary mental health team is a guarantee that each child will be approached as a whole person. A heterogeneity of points of view within the same team, in which educators, nurses, teachers, psychiatrists, psychologists, and occupational therapists come into contact with each other, helps assure a nonrestrictive, more global vision of the child.

The varied *treatment settings* and methods of delivering care include:

1. The Day Hospital (*Hôpital de Jour*). This is the most flexible approach and offers the greatest chance of maintaining the child in the family. It is thus the most favored solution whenever possible.
2. The Therapeutic Living-In Facility (*Internat Therapeutique*). Separation of the child from the family environment and admission to a therapeutic, living-in facility is justified in some cases (e.g., extreme severity of the pathology, absent or deeply pathogenic family).
3. Part-Time Therapeutic "Welcoming" Centers (*Centres d'Accueil Therapeutique à Temps Partiel*). These less intensive facilities deliver part-time care and, at the same time, enable the continuation of the child's academic integration in a normal environment.
4. Therapeutic Family Placement ("Welcoming") (*Accueil Familial Therapeutique*). This setting may be indicated for the very young child when the family conditions make it impossible to maintain the child in a more natural environment, and when the child's very young age does not allow his or her admission to a living-in facility. The maternal workers (*assistantes maternelles*), paid by the hospital, receive supervision and support from the sector's psychiatric team. (Since 1972, public regional sectors of child psychiatry have covered the totality of France and form the pillar of child mental health.)
5. When early mother–baby interactive dysfunctions, with a "psychotic potential," have been discovered, early mother–baby therapy by specially trained psychotherapists may be implemented, possibly in the child's home.

The *specific aims of institutional treatment* for autistic individuals include:

1. The institution as a meeting space. The aim of the treatment is to put into place new modes of mental functioning that are correlative for the establishment of new exchange modalities with others.
2. The institution as a stimulus barrier. The institution is a protecting and protected frame that sets a sort of nondistorting but attenuating filter between the child and the outside world. It aims at protecting the child against the return of experiences the traumatic character of which could not be mastered by his or her psyche.
3. The institution as a containing function. This function implies on the part of the mental health workers a true capacity to welcome, contain, and live the nonorganized emotions and affects felt by the child, to verbalize them and give them meaning in order to return them to the child in a form that can be assimilated. This enables the child to build a personal psychic space and to organize his or her emotional life.
4. The institution as a mothering function. This function implies an exchange and communication, through bodily care, that enables the child to effect a libidinal cathexis and take possession of his or her own body.
5. The institution as a transitional space. The institution should enable the child to practice primary creativity while being

confronted with perception of the reality of objects in the world.

The performance and the stability of the health workers are basic conditions if the therapeutic processes in the institution are to succeed. The child should be able to recover, through everyday relations with the team members, stable reference figures that will instill a feeling of security.

The *schooling of psychotic child* may take place in two different settings:

1. Inside the day hospital or the therapeutic living-in facility. Pedagogic help is given by teachers who depend on the Ministry of National Education and who work in close collaboration with all the team members.
2. The integration of a psychotic child in a normal schooling system is sometimes accomplished. The success of such an integration depends, among other things, on the quality of the exchanges and the cooperation that have been established between the team members and the teachers who welcome the child.

Along with the care of the child, parents also require the following interventions:

1. Parental guidance measures that aim at supporting the parents in their educative task with their child are implemented.
2. Specific therapeutic measures are offered to the parents and aim at:

   - Enabling them to recover their capacity for anticipatory illusion toward their child, in order to perceive, understand, and accept the fluctuations in their child's evolution.
   - Restoring their self-esteem (narcissism), which has been deeply wounded by the arrival of a psychotic child.

It should be mentioned that the care offered to psychotic children in the different public mental health institutions is free; the expenditures are totally taken in charge by the social security agencies as long as necessary. Also, a special pension for education may be allocated, in certain conditions, to parents of psychotic children.

In France, medication is little used. It is administered only during limited periods, and only to lessen certain symptoms that are particularly bothersome. Medications include sedative neuroleptics, antianxiety remedies, and antidepressants.

EVOLUTION AND RESULTS

The evolution of psychotic dysharmonies is quite favorable. Almost half these children may, when leaving mental health institutions, integrate within a normal academic or professional environment. Other children are professionally integrated in a protected environment.

The evolution of autistic children and those with psychoses with mental retardation is more severe.

A small number of autistic children evolve little, if at all; when they do, it is toward a picture of retardation (50%). When they become adults, these patients are referred either to "life settings" (*lieux de vie*) or to psychiatric hospitals. The other half succeed in acquiring language, and their life becomes enriched with relations with others. When they are adults, these patients may become integrated in a protective environment.

PARENTS' ASSOCIATIONS

The first association for parents of psychotic children was created in 1963 under the name ASITP (*Association su Service des Enfants Inadaptes ayant des Troubles de la Personnalité*; Association at the Service of Maladjusted Children with Personality Disorders). The parents who founded ASITP wanted in this way to end their isolation and to promote institutions adapted to their children's specific problems. On these parents' initiative, one of the first day hospitals in Paris was established.

At the beginning of the 1980s, controversies pertaining to the importance that should be given to education in the treatment of psychotic children led to a schism inside ASITP and, eventually, to two parents' associations in France:

1. *Autisme-France* tends to promote the establishment of integrated school classes in which the main recommended educative approach, inspired by the Treatment and

Education of Autistic and Related Communications Handicapped CHildren (TEACCH) method, aims at giving the children an "educative prosthesis" in order to improve their socialization and understanding of the world;

2. *Sesame Autisme (Federation Française Autisme et Psychose Infantile)* comprises 24 regional associations. The federation publishes a quarterly journal, Sesame, with the collaboration of many child psychiatrists. Today, 1,200 families, regrouped in regional associations, belong to *Sesame Autisme*. In 1985, its national committee adopted the charter of a national movement on autism and child psychoses, with the following goals:

- To improve the well-being of persons handicapped because of autistic disorders and child psychoses, and help them reach the best accomplishments possible.
- To improve them socially as much as possible.
- To place at the children's and their families' disposal a large range of therapeutic means that may satisfy their needs while offering adequate guarantees.

Sesame Autisme encourages close cooperation between parents and professionals. Its approach respects children's educative needs and helps them to progress in the relational realm and in the domain of psychic functioning.

REFERENCES

Ferrari P. (1993). Psychoses infantiles. In P. Ferrari & C. Epelbaum (Eds.), *Psychiatrie de l'Enfant et de l'Adolescent.* Paris: Medicine-Science-Flammarion.

Geissmann, C., & Geissman, P. (1984). *L'enfant et sa psychose.* Paris: Dunod.

Haag, G. (1984). Autisme infantile precoce et phenomenes autistiques. Reflexions psychoanalytiques. *Psychiatrie Infantile, 27*(2), 293–354.

Hochmann, J. (1984). *Pour soigner l'enfant psychotique.* Toulouse: Privately published.

Lang, J.L. (1987). *Aux frontières de la psychose infantile.* Paris: University of France Press.

Launay, A.M., Ferrari, P., & Haimart, M. (1988). Serotonin metabolism and other biochemical parameters in infantile autism: A controlled study of 22 autistic children. *Biological Psychiatry, 20,* 1–11.

Lelord, G., & Sauvage, D. (1990). *L'autisme de l'enfant.* Paris: Masson.

Mises, R. (1993). Le cure en institution (2nd ed.). Paris: ESF.

Mises, R., & Quemada, N. (1993). Classification Française des Troubles Mentaux de l'Enfant et de l'Adolescent. Classification Internationale des Troubles Mentaux et du Comportement (ch. V de la CIM 10-O.M.S.). Paris: C.T.N.E.R.H.I.

Torgman, S., Anderson, G.M., McBride, P.A., Hertzig, M.E., Snow, M.E., Hall, L., Ferrari, P., & Cohen, D.J. (in press). Plasma β endorphin, adrenocorticotropin hormone, and cortisol in autism. *Biological Psychiatry.*

GERMANY AND AUSTRIA

Martin Schmidt

INTRODUCTION OF THE DIAGNOSTIC CONCEPT

Through the relations of the Marburg child and adolescent psychiatrist Hermann Stutte with the Dutch child and adolescent psychiatrist Van Krevelen, the diagnostic concept of autism was introduced in Germany very soon after World War II. From 1947 onward, Doris Weber from Marburg studied the diagnosis of "autistic" children; she delimited this classification from the traditional diagnosis of dementia infantilis of Heller (Childhood Disintegrative Disorder), which was frequently given to autistic children at that time. In the 1950s, Bosch, in Frankfurt, started to work on the differentiation of Kanner's autism and schizophrenia. In the 1960s, Nissen originally described the distinction between Kanner's infantile autism and Asperger's Syndrome, and between somatogenic and psychogenic autism. Until the mid-1980s, nosological considerations in Germany followed the concepts of the *International Classification of Diseases (ICD-9),* in which autism was seen as the earliest and most extensive form of infantile psychosis. Since the 1980s, Kanner's autism has increasingly been regarded as a developmental disorder. Recently, specialists have started to focus on other pervasive developmental disorders, but little research has yet been done.

The concept of Asperger's Syndrome was not used in Germany until the early 1960s. Autistic psychopathy, as described by Hans

Asperger in 1943, is amazingly similar to the present diagnostic criteria, although more attention has focused on the B-criteria listed in *DSM-IV* than on the A-criteria, which are more characteristic for the diagnosis in childhood. Until the introduction of *ICD-10,* this disorder was mostly treated as equivalent to an infantile form of schizoid personality disorder. In Germany today, Asperger's Syndrome in adults is generally regarded as a variant of schizoid personality disorder.

Within Germany, there is broad acceptance of the view that autism may reflect a common final pathway of various underlying disorders and dispositions (as suggested by Nissen and, more recently, by Gillberg).

HISTORY OF CARE OF INDIVIDUALS WITH AUTISM AND RELATED DISORDERS

Originally, autistic children were diagnosed and treated in university hospitals, but soon institutions for long-term residential care were established. These followed the example of the pioneering Swiss institution created by Lutz in the 1950s. Many autistic children were placed in institutions for the mentally retarded, but it became more acceptable for many parents to have a child diagnosed as autistic rather than as mentally retarded. In the 1960s, a parent association for mentally retarded children opened the Kerstin-Haus in Marburg, an institution caring for both mentally retarded and autistic children. There, Doris Weber carried out a great part of her follow-up studies on autistic children. For a long time, there was no apparent need for special preschool programs, because autism was not generally diagnosed until school age nor was it differentiated from mental retardation. In some regions, day care centers for autistic schoolchildren were set up to combine school and therapeutic interventions. Medical treatments were tried in some of these centers, with varying success. Starting in the late 1960s, the Max Planck Institute for Psychiatry was the first institution to utilize behavior therapy methods with autistic children, using American concepts of this approach. The first main focus of therapy was the reduction of stereotyped behavior and rituals; later, methods were aimed at improving the child's development and modeling behavioral patterns. This change in therapy paralleled the change in concept of the disorder from infantile psychosis to developmental disorder.

Unlike France, where children with Kanner's autism were treated by psychoanalysis, Germany had no special psychoanalytic institutions for the treatment of autism. Today, in Germany, the treatment of an autistic child only on the basis of psychoanalysis is, as a rule, attributed to misdiagnosis.

CURRENT STATUS OF TREATMENT SERVICES

In Germany, treatment services for autistic individuals can be separated into four types. (a) Most treatment services have been organized by the Parent Society of Autistic Children. At present, special outpatient clinics and mobile support services of the Parent Society are in charge of many autistic individuals of preschool age. Only a minority of these younger children are cared for by early health promotion services and social-pediatric centers. (b) Autistic individuals of school age occasionally are treated within child guidance clinics; more frequently, their care is within child psychiatric outpatient or inpatient clinics. (c) Special school classes provide day care. (d) Long-term residential care offers many programs for psychiatrically ill or behaviorally disordered children. These facilities have special units for autistic children—mainly high-functioning autistic children who do not fit into the local schools for mentally retarded or behaviorally disturbed children.

Appropriate care for high-functioning autistic children remains a great problem for treatment services. Extradomestic placement is required in most cases. Lately, attempts to integrate high-functioning autistic children into normal schools are on the increase, but most such attempts only work well when specially trained additional staff can be hired.

WHEN AND BY WHOM IS THE CONDITION DIAGNOSED?

Most cases of autism are diagnosed by child psychiatrists or clinical psychologists working in special outpatient clinics of the Parent Society of Autistic Children; only seldom is a diagnosis given by early health promotion services of social pedagogical centers or pediatric clinics. In spite of educational efforts, very early diagnosis of autism is quite unusual. Autism is diagnosed mostly at 5 or 6 years of age. In 3-year-olds, autism is hardly ever suspected; in 4-year-olds, it can be diagnosed if autistic behavior is accompanied by mental retardation. Asperger's Syndrome is diagnosed mostly at age 7 or 8 years, if special restricted interests are the predominating symptom and interfere with school to a great extent, and at ages 9 to 11 years or later, if the social deficits predominate.

SPECIFIC NATIONAL AND THEORETICAL ISSUES

Changes in therapeutic concepts for autism have mirrored changing trends and ideologies. Two examples are worth mentioning:

1. The integration of high-functioning autistic children has been pushed along as the ideology of integrating other handicapped children into normal schools has been implemented. This procedure requires additional staff and sometimes leads to the misinterpretation that all autistic children ought to be integrated into normal schools.
2. The policy of the parent organizations has been (correctly) to insist that autism is a multiple handicap and not only a mental handicap. The intended effect of this policy is to counteract the ideology of psychogenic causation (still proposed by educators, in contrast with psychologists and medical doctors). The parents' emphasis helps to guarantee a multilevel approach to care, and continued services after school age.

SERVICES OVER THE LIFE SPAN AND BARRIERS TO SERVICES

The transition from adolescence to adulthood is the highest barrier for treatment services of autistic individuals. They lack housing possibilities, especially in the absence of mental retardation, as well as sheltered workplaces. Therefore, most of them live in institutions

run by the Parent Society for Mentally Retarded People. Few autistic adults receive proper treatment, often limited to psychopharmacology. Different institutions for autistic adults without mental retardation have been established, chiefly by the Parent Society. Their aim is not therapy and "normalization" but provision of a suitable, lifelong residence for autistic adults. Currently, a bottleneck in the system of care has occurred where services are required for crisis intervention in case of autoaggressive or violent behavior. Many psychiatrists lack knowledge of autistic disorders; the situation is comparable to the difficulties surrounding treatment of adults with hyperkinetic disorder.

PARENTS' ASSOCIATION

In 1970, parents of autistic children founded the Parent Society for Mentally Retarded People. At present, the Society counts 3,200 members and 35 regional agencies spread all over Germany. Initially, the main task was to educate doctors, psychologists, and pedagogues about the importance of early diagnosis of autistic disorders. The second focus was promoting social integration and nonacademic opportunities. The Parent Society cooperated with health insurance and other state agencies bearing financial responsibility for handicapped people, but little has been achieved for full school integration. The third main task of the Parent Society was the establishment of regional outpatient clinics, and the fourth goal was setting up services for autistic adults. At present, the central concerns are the relationship of autistic individuals with their families, and their lifelong care.

The national Parent Society is in constant exchange with the European International Parent Society; its scientific committee processes specialist literature about autism and Asperger's Syndrome and passes on important information to concerned groups. Scientific investigations on autistic individuals—for example, studies on the genetics of autistic disorders—are also supported by the Parent Society. Another goal is to move legislation toward accepting autistic individuals as generally multiply handicapped people. The Parent Society does not include the concerns of children with Rett's Syndrome, for whom there is a separate parent organization, nor does it deal with other pervasive developmental disorders.

HISTORY AND STATUS OF TREATMENT SERVICES IN AUSTRIA

In Austria, a special concept of treatment services was established in 1975, the "Wiener Modell" (Vienna model), which uses the same standardized concept from early childhood to adulthood. Apart from client-centered therapeutic and family therapeutic approaches, the main elements of this concept are involvement therapy and learning by model. The Vienna Model can be divided into four phases. (a) In 1975, it started with an orthopedagogic, outpatient clinic that provided special consultation services for autistic preschool children. (b) As the children grew older, further services were required. Therefore, a day care center for autistic preschool and school-age children was opened in 1983. (c) A special school for autistic children was set up in 1986. At present, it has 7 classes, with 8 pupils and 2 teachers per class. (d) The latest section, established in 1993, is Rain Man's Home, an institution for vocational and social integration of autistic adolescents and adults, initiated by the parent society of the same name.

NATIONAL PARENT SOCIETY

In the early 1990s the parent society called Rain Man's Home was founded in Austria. The parents of autistic adolescents took this urgent step, motivated by the massive problems of autistic adolescents at the threshold of their work life. The main task of the parent society is to enable autistic adolescents and adults to live a positive and meaningful life.

REFERENCES

Bormann-Kischkel, C. (1990). *Erhennen autistische Kinder Personen und Emotionenen?* [Can autistic children recognize persons and emotions?]. Regensburg: Verlag S. Roderer.

DeMyer, M.K. (1986). *Familien mit autistischen Kindern* [Families with autistic children]. U. & H. Remschmidt, Trans. Stuttgard: Ferdinand Enke Verlag.

Hebborn-Brass, U. (1993). *Autistische Kinder in stationärer Langzeit-behandluneine empirishe Längsschnittuntersuchung und Erfahrungsberichte* [Long-term inpatient treatment of autistic children]. München: Quintessenz-Verlag.

Kehrer, H.E. (1989). *Autismus—Diagnostische, therapeutische und soziale aspekte* [Autism—Diagnostic, therapeutical and social aspects]. Heidelberg: Roland Asanger Verlag.

Weber, D. (1985). Autistische syndrome [Autistic syndromes]. In *Kinder und Jugendpsychiatrie in Klinik und Praxis*. Stuttgart: Georg Thieme Verlag.

ISRAEL

Tamar Moses and Samuel Tyano

BACKGROUND

Psychiatric wards for children were established in Israel in the mid-1950s. A legal ruling separated the administrative responsibility for the care of retarded children from responsibility for the care of psychotic children. The care of retarded children was placed in the hands of the Ministry of Welfare, and the care given to the "mentally ill" remained under the responsibility of the Ministry of Health. The distinction between the two groups of patients was based on a diagnosis of "mental illness" according to the "Bleulerian" approach, and a diagnosis of retardation by testing of cognitive function (Rahav, Cohen, & Porat, 1981).

In the early 1960s, autistic children began to be identified and diagnosed according to the description of Kanner. At that time, the number of diagnosed children was small, and they were treated primarily in combined psychiatric-educational settings. Later, the diagnostic approach broadened, and the term *autism* was used to refer to isolation from the environment in disproportion to the child's mental ability.

Three main groups of children were identified: (a) a "Kannerian" group; (b) aphasic children who exhibit a tendency to introversion and behave "autistically," but who still have some motivation to develop and "get out" of this syndrome; and (c) retarded children with some brain damage, where the socialization level is in disproportion to the level of retardation. The different treatment approaches developed in accordance with these categories included both the educational and the psychiatric aspects of care. The overall approach was not to separate the treatment of autistic children from that of children who suffer from other syndromes, but to give treatment in accordance with the functional level (Rahav et al., 1981).

In 1974, a National Organization for Autistic Children (ALUT) was established by parents and advocates. This organization opposed the conception that autism is part of a spectrum of mental illness. ALUT viewed autism as a developmental disorder, for which the recommended treatments are educational as well as rehabilitative. ALUT's main targets were: to establish educational and rehabilitation centers for autistic children, to prepare professionals to work in the field, and to provide help to the families.

In 1974, the first school for autistic children, Yachdav, was established with the help of the Ministry of Education and the Tel-Aviv Municipality. With time, more schools, special classes, and kindergartens were opened throughout the country. The basic approach of these programs has been educational and rehabilitative; an effort has been made to offer each child a program that meets his or her individual needs. As the students in the schools grew older, the system developed boarding houses, hostels, day care centers, and employment facilities for autistic adults.

In 1990, counseling centers for autism (MILA) were established by the Ministry of Education, in cooperation with the parents' organization, ALUT. MILA's goals are both professional and educational. The organization sponsors professional seminars, plans and develops databases, and formulates new concepts. It also distributes up-to-date information to professionals as well as to the lay communities. In cooperation with ALUT, MILA offers counseling and deals with issues related to the care of the different age groups of autistic individuals.

In 1991, another parents' organization, Foundation for Children at Risk, was established, with similar goals, especially the promotion and development of services for preschool children. In the beginning, treatment was limited to children suffering from the autistic syndrome as diagnosed by Kannerian criteria; in time, services were extended to individuals with the diagnosis of Pervasive Developmental Disorder (PDD).

Controversies concerning diagnosis and treatment continue among the medical psychiatric establishment, the educational system, and the parents' organizations.

ORGANIZATION OF SERVICES

Three government authorities share responsibility for the care of autistic children. In 1992, a joint committee was set up by the Director of the Ministry of Health. The committee includes representatives from the ministries of Education, Health, and Welfare. The main indications for the establishment of this committee were:

1. Traditionally, the care of autistic patients was the responsibility of the Ministry of Health's Mental Health Service. Although this service generally provided the psychiatric and other mental health needs of the patients, it did not cover important needs in the areas of welfare, education, and housing.
2. Various community services were missing, and no special resources were allocated for this population.
3. The spheres of responsibility of the various governmental ministries were unclear, especially in light of the complex demands imposed by the autistic syndrome.

The committee agreed that autism represents a clinical syndrome that has complex behavioral and dysfunctional manifestations. There was also agreement that optimal treatment of this multidimensional and complex disorder requires a coordinated and multidisciplinary team approach. The committee concluded that, in this approach, the autistic population should be divided according to age groups and developmental-functional levels. The assigned areas of responsibility are: the Ministry of Health is responsible for the developmental and mental health domain; the Ministry of Education, for educational needs; and the Ministry of Welfare, for rehabilitation.

PARENTS' ORGANIZATIONS

The parents' groups and the counseling service for the autistic population (MILA) work hand-in-hand with the government offices. They advocate the opening of new programs for different age groups, and they distribute information within the organization. They also support seminars for professionals from Israel and abroad, as well as the development of professional educational materials and their distribution.

Epidemiology

In 1993, a survey studied all the existing known programs for autism in Israel. The survey identified 378 individuals with the clinical diagnosis of autism (Cohen & Levinson, 1993). The age group distribution was as follows:

Ages in Years	Number of Cases
0 to 3	64
4 to 6	62
7 to 21	158
22–	94

This survey did not deal with the complexity in the definition of autism because the diagnosis was made in different programs. Currently, 10 to 12 autistic children are born every year in Israel (Cohen & Levinson, 1993).

FRAMEWORKS FOR TREATMENT OF AUTISM

Programs for treatment are based on a two-dimensional approach: age groups and clinical condition. There is a wide spectrum of programs. At one end are special kindergartens and psychiatric day care centers, which combine ambulatory therapy and participation in the activities of the local kindergarten. There are also classes in the regular schools, specially designed for autistic children, as well as day care and employment centers for the adolescents and adults. On the other end of the spectrum are programs with full hospitalization, day hospitalization, and a lifetime care center.

The framework for the adult autistic population is also varied; it includes:

1. Sheltered day workshops for those who are able to remain in the family home.
2. Hostels that provide a protected live-in community. Residents work in local sheltered workshops.
3. A village (Kfar Ofarim) for 75 young adults who require a more protected environment, but are capable of some self-care management and some occupational training.
4. A lifetime care center for autistic adults who require a total protected environment.

It may be possible to combine various programs, such as full hospitalization with attendance at special schools or rehabilitation centers. This would enable the system to tailor the treatment to individuals' needs. The survey data indicate that, prior to the development of ambulatory wards and special kindergartens, most autistic patients were institutionalized or hospitalized for life. Presently, the low number (10 children) of autistic children hospitalized in psychiatric wards gives testimony to the efficiency of community intervention and care, and reflects the community's preparedness to make an appropriate investment in the care and rehabilitation of this group of vulnerable individuals.

IDENTIFICATION

A network of well baby clinics provides medical and developmental follow-up for most of the pediatric population of Israel until age 3 years. When a developmental disorder is detected, the child is referred to one of the 25 existing, widely dispersed child development centers that offer neurologic and psychiatric evaluation and counseling. If the need arises, the child is referred to a local psychiatric clinic. If the disorder is in the autistic spectrum but no psychiatric treatment is needed, the child is referred to the appropriate educational institution.

DIAGNOSIS

The *ICD* system provides the official criteria for psychiatric disorders, as dictated by the Ministry of Health. In the light of other diagnostic criteria and the desire to reach a common language, the use of the concept of PDD was introduced as defined in *DSM-III-R* and, later, in *DSM-IV*. Social diagnoses are based on functional criteria, with emphasis on the nature of the illness as a social disturbance. In autism, the emphasis is on the developmental disturbance of socialization skills relative to those that are expected at a given mental age. Treatment and rehabilitation programs are linked with the diagnostic assessments.

TREATMENTS

A range of treatments is offered in Israel to autistic children. At the core of all methods, a basic educational and cognitive treatment that relies heavily on behavioral and developmental approaches is coupled with an openness to existing approaches worldwide. There is a willingness to consider less conventional approaches.

In psychiatric cases, pharmacological treatment is included in accordance with symptomatology. Each institution tends to offer a broad spectrum of therapeutic options to suit the individual patient's needs.

RESEARCH

Research plays an important role in enhancing the treatment of autism. Over the past several years, relevant studies concerning the biological and behavioral aspects of this disorder have been conducted in Israel.

A series of studies on the psychobiology of autism—specifically, the presence of autoantibodies to basic myelin protein—was demonstrated in some autistic patients (A. Weizman, Weizman, Szekely, et al., 1982), and reduced plasma levels of endogenous opioids were detected in autistic children, as compared to normal controls and nonautistic children (R. Weizman, Weizman, Tyano, et al., 1984; R. Weizman, Gil-Ad, Dick, et al., 1988). Despite the responsiveness of Obsessive-Compulsive Disorder (OCD) symptoms in autistic children to serotonin reuptake inhibitors, no alteration was found in the expression of the platelet serotonin transporter (A. Weizman, Gonen, Tyano, et al., 1987).

Studies on cyclical birth rate, in patients with autistic disorder born in Israel during the period of 1964 to 1986, demonstrated significant increase for autistic children born in March and August (Barak, Ring, Sulkes, & Gabbay, 1995). The studies found an annual periodicity of 17.6 years, 3.2 years, and 4.1 years.

Israel was a site for the international collaborative research project on the criteria for *DSM-IV*. Through this collaboration, investigators in Israel are able to utilize the current nosology with a high level of expertise (Volkmar, Klin, Siegel, et al., 1994).

REFERENCES

Barak, Y., Ring, A., Sulkes, J., & Gabbay, U. (1995). Season of birth and Autistic Disorder in the Middle East. *American Journal of Psychiatry, 152*(5), 798–800.

Cohen, Y., & Levinson, D. (1993). *Planning programs for autistic population for the year 2000.* Jerusalem: Israel Ministry of Health.

Rahav, M., Cohen, Y., & Porat, S. (1981). *Autism in Israel.* Jerusalem: Israel Ministry of Health.

Volkmar, F.R., Klin, A., Siegel, B., et al. (1994). Field trial for Autistic Disorder in *DSM-IV*. *American Journal of Psychiatry, 151*(9), 1361–1367.

Weizman, A., Gonen, N., Tyano, S., et al. (1987). Platelet (H3) imipramine binding in autistic and schizophrenic children. *Psychopharmacology, 91,* 101–103.

Weizman, A., Weizman, R., Szekely, G.A., et al. (1982). Abnormal immune response to brain tissue antigen in syndrome of autism. *American Journal of Psychiatry, 139,* 1462–1465.

Weizman, R., Gil-Ad, I., Dick, J., et al. (1988). Low plasma immunoreactive B-endorphin levels in autism. *Journal of the American Academy of Child & Adolescent Psychiatry, 27,* 430–433.

Weizman, R., Weizman, A., Tyano, S., et al. (1984). Humoral endorphin blood levels in autistic, schizophrenic and healthy subjects. *Psychopharmacology, 82,* 368–370.

ITALY

Gabriel Levi and Paola Bernabei

BACKGROUND AND HISTORY

Between 1905 and 1910, F. De Sanctis described 22 cases, aged 4 to 10 years, exhibiting features that were different from those exhibited by children with mental retardation. De Sanctis stressed that these children's behavioral disorders and emotional and cognitive problems were linked to an early psychotic disturbance.

One of De Sanctis's students, Maria Montessori, became interested (between 1899 and 1907) in the educational problems of mentally retarded children after graduating with a degree in medicine. She developed her theories and educational methods with the aim of promoting a great project of mental health for all children from 2 to 6 years of age. The diffusion of kindergartens in which her methods were applied made it easier to identify atypical children.

At the end of the 1940s and during the 1950s, an interesting debate on Kanner's and especially on Asperger's work took place among Italian clinicians. There was broad agreement on childhood psychosis as a nosographic entity that could be diagnosed before 4 years of age. Many clinicians thought that a psychotic breakdown (with autism, delusions, and hallucinations as cardinal signs) marked the beginning of autistic disorder; others maintained that the disorder depended on a psychotic development.

In 1967, Professor G. Bollea pointed out that, on the basis of a peculiar vulnerability occurring during the first year of life, some children could develop a cognitive disturbance and others a psychotic disturbance, depending on the type of perceptual integration and affective interactions they experienced.

In 1975, G. Levi's study of 30 autistic children, aged 3 to 7 at diagnosis, included a 4-year follow-up. He found that there are different degrees of severity in the autistic disorder and that autistic children develop cognitive and emotional skills according to a sequence of recognizable evolutionary phases. The degree of severity and the type of prognosis are correlated with the interval that separates the atypical phases, and each phase of the psychotic development is characterized by learning strategies and a sense of identity that are in some ways coherent.

In the 1980s, two viewpoints emerged in Italy. The majority of Italian neuropsychiatrists, following Tustin's and Meltzer's theories, considered that childhood psychoses were linked to an emotional catastrophe occurring during the first year of life, and that

the treatment of choice, even for low-functioning cases, was psychoanalytic psychotherapy (often for both mother and child). A minority position related the autistic disorder to an atypical development of communicative and symbolic skills and to a noninteractive development of verbal comprehension (Levi, Bernabei, Fabrizi, & Zollinger, 1984).

During the past few years, Italian researchers have been involved in the worldwide debates on *ICD* and *DSM* that have brought about interesting discussions on subtypes and on diagnostic criteria.

TREATMENT APPROACHES

Until 1977, autistic children attended special schools and special institutions, as did any other handicapped child in Italy. The main therapeutic models were based on special pedagogy (strongly affected by Montessori's methods) and on psychoanalytic psychotherapy.

Legislation introduced in 1977 required that all handicapped children attend normal schools and classes. Autistic children today are supposed to be in classrooms with no more than 15 children, instead of the standard 25. A remedial teacher is provided for at least 2 hours a day; this teacher tries to link the autistic child's work to other children's work, to improve learning and socialization potentialities. Concurrent with this integration, the idea spread that behavioral conditioning techniques may provide some therapeutic success, but it is now felt that they tend to implement imitative, echopraxic, and echolalic behavior and prevent identification processes.

In spite of much improvisation, and enthusiasm not always supported by practical technique, the wide diffusion of kindergartens and the integration of handicapped children have brought advantages. More than half of the autistic children are now recognized as atypical between 2.6 and 3 years of age, before they enter kindergarten, and nearly all autistic children start a treatment program between 5.6 and 6 years of age, before they enter elementary school. By that age, most high-functioning autistic children are known to schools and community centers. Autistic children start elementary school 1 or 2 years later than normal children, to allow a greater development of their communicative and symbolic skills.

Lively discussion continues regarding treatment strategies for low-functioning children and the tendency toward a drastic reduction of psychoanalytical psychotherapies. The following criteria prevail in choosing the type and time of intervention: (a) correlation among mental age, symbolic and communicative development, and chronological age; (b) development of verbal comprehension; and (c) cognitive skills and interaction and identification mechanisms in the peer group (Levi, 1993). Early treatment in small groups is gaining in acceptance, and great emphasis is put on the integration of nonverbal and verbal communication. The central roles of communication and symbolization dysfunctions in the autistic disorder give importance to interactions during play and in imitation and identification processes in small groups. Behaviorally based teaching methods (such as TEACCH) are quite frequently used, and are in many cases integrated with active pedagogical methodologies such as Montessori's; methods based on group work; and psychodynamic models that do not use verbal interpretation, but focus on the verbalization of affects and the awareness of the self.

DIAGNOSIS

Autism is diagnosed by child neuropsychiatrists who usually see the child and the parents; a clinical psychologist and a therapist who specializes in communication disorders also see the child. Most cases are referred by schools or pediatricians, but parents often come to the service on their own. Sometimes, usually in private practice, diagnoses are made by psychotherapists. In Italy, there are nearly 150 community centers and about 40 Child neuropsychiatry units in hospitals and universities. There are approximately 900 to 1,000 neuropsychiatrists in community centers (the ratio is between 1:5,000 and 1:12,000 children, depending on the area). More than 4,000 clinical psychologists and therapists work in teams with child neuropsychiatrists, and more than 50,000 remedial teachers are on staff in state schools.

Specialized centers for autistic children are available only at universities and about 20 community centers. In the other centers, great attention is given to the problem of autism.

The 1977 law requiring the integration of handicapped children has allowed earlier diagnosis and treatment for autistic children. Between 1975 and 1988, the prevalence of autism was, however, grossly overestimated; children with mental retardation and emotional disorders were frequently diagnosed as autistic, as were children with behavioral disorders and environmental isolation. Increased attention to standard diagnostic criteria (*ICD* and *DSM*) has contributed to progressive refinement of diagnostic assessment, and recent epidemiological research has shown that the prevalence of autism in Italy tallies with international data.

Communication disorders and specific language disorders tend to be referred quite early in Italy because of particular sensitivity in the general population. This attitude helps identify a group of children, in the age range from 18 to 30 months, who have features of language disorder, Pervasive Developmental Disorder, and mild or moderate mental retardation.

PARENTS' ASSOCIATION

A parents' association for autistic children was created in Italy as a reaction against the dominant psychoanalytical approach to autism. The association supports the parents of autistic children through a self-help strategy and educational plans based on short- and medium-term goals. Parent associations for different kinds of handicap also exist, and they are usually prepared to recognize and treat possible comorbidity with autism in their centers.

Laws that regulate the assistance provided to autistic children and adults are the same as for other kinds of handicaps. Individuals with autism may get a monthly allowance, and their integration in work settings is promoted by law. Legislation passed in 1992 formalized the relationship between schools and community centers, stressed the right to education for handicapped people, and defined the role of remedial teachers within this process. In addition, one parent is entitled to stay at home during the first 3 years of life of a handicapped child, without losing his or her job, and can have 3 paid days off a month after returning to work.

CONCLUSION

Regarding services, autistic children in Italy generally receive an early diagnosis and an early start on treatment. The policy of promoting integration of all handicapped children permits autistic children to have an intensive and prolonged educational treatment that is focused on social skills. This approach is yielding interesting results with low- and medium-functioning autistic children. During the past 10 years, there has been an excessive investment in individual psychotherapies. At the moment, group therapy, based on interactions with peers, intentional exchanges, and mutual identifications, is also available.

The use of *DSM* criteria in diagnosis is progressively gaining acceptance. There is a strong trend to add to a *DSM* diagnosis a cognitive and neuropsychological evaluation and an emotional assessment. Clinical groups that evaluate and treat very young children (between 8 and 20 months) tend to look for possible symbolization and communication disorder, from which an autistic or other disorder might develop.

Regarding research, recent debates have focused on three problems: (a) autism is a multiphase disorder, with developmental phases that may be reconstructed and may be anticipated; this model emphasizes the importance of understanding natural history; (b) autistic children with communication problems (preverbal, extraverbal, or an integration of nonverbal and verbal) and supposed left-hemisphere involvement should be distinguished from autistic children who exhibit early dyspractic problems and supposed right-hemisphere involvement (Bernabei, Levi, Mazzoncini, & Penge, 1994); treatment of the dyspractic core may lessen the severity of the autistic component; and (c) low- and high-functioning autistic children should be diagnostically separated. It is currently being debated whether, among low-functioning children, it is possible to distinguish children with an early cognitive impairment from children who, because of mental retardation, are more vulnerable to an autistic disorder.

REFERENCES

Bernabei, P., Levi, G., Mazzoncini, B., & Penge, R. (1994). Un nucleo disprattico nei disturbi generalizzati dello sviluppo [The core dyspractic disturbance in pervasive developmental disorders]. *Psichiatria dell'Infanzia e dell'Adolescenza, 61,* 337–346.

Levi, G. (1973). Sviluppo psicotico e sviluppo cognitivo [Psychotic development and cognitive development]. *Neuropsichiatria Infantile, 147,* 661–677.

Levi, G. (1993). Psicosi infantili precoci (Early childhood psychosis). In *Enciclopedia Medica Italiana, 4,* 6208–6220. Florence, Italy: USES, Edizioni Scientifiche Firenze.

Levi, G., Bernabei, P., Fabrizi, A., & Zollinger, B. (1984). Disturbi precoci di simbolizzazione: Un nucleo patogenetico comune per i disturbi di sviluppo e le disarmonie evolutive [Early symbolization disorders: A common pathogenetic core for developmental disorders]. *Psichiatria dell'Infanzia e dell'Adolescenza, 51,* 179–187.

JAPAN

Yoshihiko Hoshino and Shin-chi Niwa

Autism is one of the major research objectives in child psychiatry in Japan; in fact, it is no exaggeration to state that there is no child psychiatrist in Japan who is not interested in autism. Among the studies of this clinical entity, the subjects of particular concern include the early signs in infancy and early childhood, developmental regression, psychopathology, problems of social adaptation among youths, biological research, and investigation of pharmacological treatments.

EARLY SYMPTOMS

Studies of the early symptoms of autism are considered important for discovering children with this clinical entity and initiating appropriate therapy at an early stage. Yamazaki (1992), after conducting a retrospective study of the early symptoms of autism by analyzing home videos that had been recorded by family members, reported that, in contrast to normal children or those with other types of developmental disorders, autistic children more frequently exhibit early symptoms. These include: "a lack of response when called by their names," "absence of interest in a game of peek-a-boo," "uncooperative response when an adult approaches to pick [them] up," "a lack of eye-to-eye contact," "a loss of meaningful taste expressions that were acquired by the age of 1 to 2 years," and "sudden outbursts of laughter or crying without any obvious reasons." Shirataki, Taira, and Kashiwagi (1984) employed the strange situation procedure (SSP) that was designed by Ainsworth et al. (1978) and evaluated the mother–child bonding pattern involving children around the age of 2 years who were at high risk for infantile autism. In contrast to the control group, the children with a high risk for infantile autism lacked emotional expression at scenes of separation from their mothers or from strangers, and at subsequent encounter with them. Specifically, they stated that "they failed to smile when they meet their mothers after a brief separation," "they frequently approach strangers," and "they were indifferent to the presence of their mothers."

Hoshino et al. (1982) also investigated early symptoms of autistic children up to 2 years of age, and recognized that, unlike normal or mentally retarded children, they frequently exhibited behavior such as "refusal to make eye contact," "absence of pointing behavior," "a lack of body imitation behavior," "refusal to be held by . . . parents," "indifference to . . . parent's presence," "no fear of strangers," "short and irregular sleeping times," "insensitive to being left alone," "a limited smiling response," and "a loss of the spoken words that have already been acquired."

Studies on the early symptoms of autism are useful in the discovery and treatment of young autistic children as well as in delineating pathophysiology.

SETBACK COURSE AND DEVELOPMENTAL REGRESSION

Studies have been actively conducted in Japan on the setback course and developmental regression associated with autism from the 1970s to the present. The pioneering activities are represented by Ishii (1987), who reported that 25% to 30% of autistic children undergo a "setback course" by the age of 2 years: language that they have already acquired becomes extinct. These children, in comparison with other autistic infants, suffer from lower developmental or intelligence levels and their long-term prognosis is rather poor. Kobayashi (1993b) and Hoshino, Kaneko, Yashima, Kumashiro, Volkmar, and Cohen (1987) reported similar research results. Specifically, they recognized that autism with a setback course is frequently associated with the development of epilepsy as well as perinatal abnormalities, suggesting a strong possibility that an organic brain disorder is implicated. Kurita (1985), on the other hand, compared the percentage of development of setback courses among 164 autistic children, 114 children with other pervasive developmental disorders (OPDD), 16 children with disintegrative psychoses, and 62 children with mental retardation without association of PDD. The occurrence of a setback course was much higher in autism (24.4%) in comparison with mental retardation (1.6%); not significantly different from OPDD (21.7%); but significantly lower than in disintegrative psychoses (100%). In view of these results, Kurita concluded that the setback course is not specific to autism but is commonly recognized in disintegrative psychoses and other pervasive developmental disorders.

PSYCHOPATHOLOGY

It is difficult to conduct a detailed psychopathological study on autism with individuals who have a low language development level. Recently in Japan, however, several psychopathological studies were conducted on autistic children with high intellectual levels. To cite a few, Sugiyama (1994) pointed out that some autistic children or youths suddenly remember events that occurred in the past (sometimes several years ago) and consider them as if they had taken place only recently. Sugiyama has assigned the term, "time slip phenomenon" to this psychopathological event and believes that the phenomenon represents a disorder of the memory function associated with autism. The so-called delayed echolalia and sudden panic attack are also most likely caused by this phenomenon. Kobayashi (1993a) cited the "phenomenon of sensory distortion" for sensory abnormalities that are unique to autism. These abnormalities include a "distorted visual perception phenomenon" (the patient gazes at or examines an object from an oblique angle as if he or she had never seen it before); a "distorted auditory perception phenomenon" (the patient expresses extreme pain when exposed to a certain voice or sound, or exhibits sensitivity when he or she becomes the topic of conversation); and a "distorted situational phenomenon" (an exaggerated confusion at a situation that leads to a pathological state suggestive of a delusion of persecution). Kobayashi states that these perception-distorting phenomena suggest the mode of perception by autistic children. They perceive the environment differently from the way they had discerned it earlier.

Nagai (1983) and Hoshino, Komatsu, and Kumashiro (1992) investigated the psychopathology of autistic children by observing their patterns of food preference or abnormal eating behavior. In their surveys, the following abnormal behavior patterns were recognized: "persistence on certain food," "insistence on sniffing food before eating," "refusing drinks except for a selected few types of beverages," "disregarding the appearance of food (contrary to the expected behavior of normal children)," "liberal use of certain condiments," and "refusal to eat food unless it is flavored in a certain manner." These behavior patterns suggest an obsessive desire for the maintenance of sameness, as well as perceptual immaturity: the child relies more heavily on the proximal perceptions (such as gustatory and olfactory perceptions) than on distal perception (such as visual and auditory perceptions).

PROBLEMS OF SOCIAL ADAPTATION DURING EARLY ADULTHOOD

It has been noted recently in Japan that autistic individuals who have reached adolescence and early adulthood experience various psychiatric problems and exhibit social maladaptation. These problems occur more frequently among highly intelligent autistic individuals who attend regular elementary, middle, and high schools. They constitute a serious obstacle to their social adaptation.

Kamio et al. (1993) noted conditions such as obsessive-compulsive disorder, mood disorder, conversion disorder, Tourette's disorder, and schizophrenia-like reactions in autistic individuals who had reached early adulthood. Yokota et al. (1989) report that these individuals in adolescence or early adulthood exhibit exaggerated aggressive or self-mutilative behavior when their obsessive-compulsive acts are restrained. Kusunoki (1988) and Hoshino and Kumashiro (1989) also state that autistic individuals with high intellectual capacities are unable to adapt to the school environment or to interpersonal relations and often develop neurosis-like reactions during adolescence or in early adulthood.

Kobayashi, Oshima, and Kaneko (1992) describe a female autistic patient who developed anorexia nervosa at 23 years of age. In this patient they noted a negative emotion toward her mother, which suggested the presence of a personality disorder or delusional behavior. Yashima et al. (1991) also reported on an autistic child who became obsessed with the concept of death following the sudden demise of a family member, and subsequently suffered from a demented or panic state.

BIOLOGICAL STUDIES

Biological studies of autism are scarce in Japan, because of a high degree of consideration in relation to ethical problems. However, a few neuroendocrinological studies and those using magnetoencephalographic (MEG) technology have recently been published.

The early studies in this area are represented by Hoshino, Kaneko, Kumashiro, et al. (1987), who determined circadian rhythms in the salivary cortisol contents and the response to the dexamethasone suppression test in high- and low-functioning groups of autistic individuals, those with mental retardation, and normal controls, to investigate their hypothalamo-hypophyseal-adrenocortical function. Those in the low-functioning autistic group exhibited abnormal circadian rhythms in the salivary cortisol level and aberrations in the response to the dexamethasone suppression test. In contrast, the high-functioning autistic group and the group with mental retardation showed normal circadian rhythms in the salivary cortisol levels and reacted normally to the dexamethasone suppression test. These findings suggest the presence of abnormalities in the hypothalamo-hypophyseal-adrenocortical functions in the low-functioning autistic individuals.

Kawasaki et al. (1994) followed 158 autistic children up to the age of 15 years, and investigated their electroencephalographic abnormalities. "Paroxysm at F" (paroxysm at the frontal lobe) was found in 75 patients and coincided with the development of epileptic seizures. However, other patients exhibited the paroxysm at F without epileptic complications. Kawasaki et al. also conducted a MEG study on 4 autistic patients and found that, in all subjects, the focus of the paroxysm at F was either at the cingulate gyrus or at the superior frontal gyrus. According to these investigators, their findings indicate that autistic lesions are located in the frontal area, especially the fronto-limbic system.

PHARMACOLOGY

In Japan, as in the United States, major tranquilizers such as haloperidol and pimozide are used as the first choice in the treatment of autism. When complicated with epilepsy, diphenylhydantoin, carbamazepine, and sodium valproate are also employed.

Recently, the co-enzyme therapy of autism has been attempted and has produced a marked efficacy in certain cases in Japan. Naruse et al. (1989) first analyzed the in vivo metabolic turnover using an aromatic amine that had been labeled with a stable isotope (deuterium, ^{13}C). They recognized reductions in cerebral catecholamine and serotonin metabolism in some of the autistic children. Based on this finding, they administered R-tetrahydrodiopterin (a coenzyme for three dehydrogenases of phenylalanine, tyrosine, and tryptophan, and closely related to cerebral catecholamine and serotonin synthesis) and compared the result in a double-blind study using a placebo. They proved a significant efficacy for this agent in the treatment of autism, especially in those under the age of 5 years. In a subsequent follow-up employing a double-blind multicenter study, however, the result was not favorable. The reason for this therapeutic failure is unknown, but the inadequacy of the survey table for abnormal behavior of children, used to rate the symptoms (autistic symptoms, subtle changes in language functions, and variability in the diagnostic concept of autism were assessed in each facility, thus resulting in a lack of homogeneity in the patient group), may explain the discrepancy. Perhaps another double-blind test will be conducted in the future and will take these factors into consideration.

CONCLUSION

As described above, studies conducted on autism in Japan have approached it from various angles. Researchers are actively engaged in psychopathological and phenomenological studies, but biological research and investigations on the chemotherapy for the disease are still scarce. It is hoped that more energetic research activities will also be directed toward this end.

REFERENCES

Ainsworth, M.D.S., Blehar, M.C., Waters, E., et al. (1978). *Patterns of attachment: A psychological study of the stranger situation.* Hillsdale, NJ: Erlbaum.

Hoshino, Y., Kaneko, M., Kumashiro, H., et al. (1987). The diurnal variation and the response to dexamethasone suppression test of saliva cortisol level in autistic children. *Folia Psychiatrica Japonica, 41,* 227.

Hoshino, Y., Kaneko, M., Yashima, Y., Kumashiro, H., Volkmar, F.R., & Cohen, O.J., (1987). Clinical features of autistic children with setback course in their infancy. *Japanese Journal of Psychiatric Neurology, 41,* 237–246.

Hoshino, Y., Komatsu, F., & Kumashiro, H. (1992). The investigation on unbalanced diet and abnormal dietary behavior in autistic children. *Psychiatric Pediatric Neurology, Japan, (Neurologica Pediatrica Japonica), 32,* 59–67.

Hoshino, Y., & Kumashiro, H. (1989). *Clinic of infantile autism.* Tokyo: Shinko-Igaku-Shuppan Sha.

Hoshino, Y., Kumashiro, H., Yashima, Y., et al. (1982). The early symptoms of autistic children and their diagnostic significance. *Folia Psychiatrica Neurologica Japonica, 36,* 367–374.

Ishii, T. (1987). Long-term prognosis of infantile autism. *Japanese Journal Clinical Psychiatry, 7,* 907.

Kamio, Y., Ishizaka, Y., Koshimoto, T., et al. (1993). *The mental disorders of autistic children in their adolescence.* Proceedings of the 34th Association of Japanese Child and Adolescent Psychiatry, p. 72.

Kawasaki, Y., Shinomiya, M., Niwa, S., et al. (1994). *Regions of EEG paroxysms in autism—evidence for possible frontal lobe involvement in the pathogenesis of autism.* Proceedings of 13th International Association for Child & Adolescent Psychiatry & Allied Professions, p. 19.

Kobayashi, R. (1993a). Phenomenological study on the perception. Metamorphosis phenomena in autism. *Japanese Journal of Clinical Psychiatry, 35,* 804–811.

Kobayashi, R. (1993b). Setback phenomena in and the long-term prognoses for autistic children. *Japanese Journal of Child and Adolescent Psychiatry, 34,* 239–248.

Kobayashi, R. (1994). Physiognomic perception, delusional perception and affective communication in autism. *Japanese Journal of Clinical Psychiatry 36,* 829–836.

Kobayashi, R., Oshima, M., & Kaneko, S. (1992). Developmental psychopathology as related to the eating disorder of an autistic adult. *Japanese Journal of Child and Adolescent Psychiatry, 33,* 311–320.

Kurita, H. (1985). Infantile autism with speech loss before the age of 30 months. *Journal of American Academy of Child Psychiatry, 24,* 191–196.

Kusunoki, T. (1988). *Neurotic maladaptation state in a group setting of adolescent autism.* Proceedings of 29th Association of Japanese Child and Adolescent Psychiatry, p. 57.

Nagai, Y. (1983). The characteristics and mechanism of food preference in infantile autism. *Japanese Journal of Child and Adolescent Psychiatry, 24,* 260–278.

Naruse, H., Hayashi, T., Takesada, M., et al. (1989). Metabolic changes of aromatic amino acids and monoamines in infantile autism, and development of new treatment related to the finding. *Japanese Journal of Child Neurology, 21,* 181–189.

Shirataki, S., Taira, R., & Kashiwagi, H. (1984). *Abnormal attachment relationship as an early sign of autistic disorders.* Proceedings of 13th International Association for Child &

Adolescent Psychiatry & Allied Professions, p. 53.

Sugiyama, T. (1994). *A strange recollection phenomenon seen in autistic patients: The time slip phenomenon in autism.* Proceedings of 13th International Association for Child & Adolescent Psychiatry & Allied Professions, p. 21.

Yamazaki, K. (1992). Early signs of infantile autism. In H. Naruse & E.M. Ornitz (Eds.), *Neurobiology of infantile autism* (pp. 165–175). Amsterdam: Elsevier Science.

Yashima, Y., Hoshino, Y., Murata, S., et al. (1991). *The various problems of the death of autistic children.* Proceedings of the 32nd Association of Japanese Child and Adolescent Psychiatry, p. 16.

Yokota, K., Sakaguchi, M., Nagai, Y., et al. (1989). *The aggressive behavior of autistic adolescents.* Proceedings of the 30th Association of Japanese Child and Adolescent Psychiatry, p. 20.

KOREA

Soo Churl Cho

INTRODUCTION OF DIAGNOSTIC CONCEPT

The diagnostic concept for autism was introduced in 1979, when Dr. Michael Hong returned to Korea from the United States, where he completed his training and was on the faculty of a leading medical school. In Korea, he established an academic clinical and training program for children with psychiatric disorders. In 1981, the first care unit for individuals with autism was founded in Seoul National University Hospital. Previously, autistic children were diagnosed by social workers and teachers in special schools; many children were classified as "emotionally disturbed" or "mentally retarded."

HISTORY OF THE CARE OF INDIVIDUALS WITH AUTISM

In the 1970s, there were no special education programs for children with autism or other pervasive developmental disorders. Autism and related developmental disorders were often undiagnosed. Autistic children were typically admitted to a treatment center for mentally retarded children, and their condition was considered to be a variant of mental retardation. In the 1980s, five centers for autistic children were founded, and the number of treatment centers for autism started to increase later in that decade.

CURRENT STATUS OF TREATMENT SERVICES

Today, Korea has about 250 treatment programs for children with autism and other pervasive developmental disorders. Three universities have more intensive treatment and service programs for autism. Of about 240 private treatment centers, 60% to 70% are centered around Seoul City. The other centers arc located in rural areas. The number of autistic children who are cared for by these programs differs, but the average capacity is about 10 autistic children. Thus, nationwide, 2,500 autistic and similar children receive special treatment. One group home, founded by parents of autistic children, is located near Seoul City.

A TREATMENT PROGRAM: THE DAY CARE CENTER OF SEOUL NATIONAL UNIVERSITY HOSPITAL

The Seoul National University Hospital is Korea's leading academic center for child and adolescent psychiatry. In the autism program, there are two classes; each serves about 6 to 8 children with autism and a wide range of developmental disorders, including Rett's Disorder, Childhood Disintegrative Disorder, and Reactive Attachment Disorders. The children range in age from 24 to 72 months. The ratio of staff to patients remains at 1:2 to 1:3. The program provides 3 hours of service daily.

Administratively, the program is headed by a Medical Director from the faculty of the Division of Child Psychiatry, who has overall medical responsibility for all patients in the Day Care Center. The Director develops and administers the educational treatment program, teaching, and research, and is responsible for the daily functioning of the Center, as well as long-term planning and treatment. A

fellow in training in child psychiatry is the primary physician for up to 3 children and acts as the team leader for these patients. The fellow writes all orders for his or her patients, including admission and discharge orders. Special educators and nurses have received training in the management of autistic children and are directly involved in the treatment of the children and the education and guidance of parents. They meet weekly with the Medical Director or child psychiatry fellow for supervision.

Before being admitted to the Day Care Center, the children receive a thorough diagnostic assessment as prescribed by the child psychiatrists. The diagnostic system used is either *DSM-IV* or *ICD-10*. After admission, the special educator or the nurse specialist who is responsible for the child administers Krug's Autism Behavior Checklist (ABC), Schopler's Childhood Autism Rating Scale (CARS), or the Psychoeducational Profile (PEP), to further evaluate the child. Psychologists evaluate intelligence, using the Wechsler Intelligence Scale for Children—Revised (WISC-R), Wechsler Preschool and Primary Scale of Intelligence (WPPSI), and Peabody Picture Vocabulary Test (PPVT). The Social Maturation Scale (SMS) is administered to assess social functioning.

Many types of individualized educational programs are used; most are based on a developmental approach. The programs provide training in behavior control and in various skills, including communication, social, motor, and academic skills. Various nonaversive behavioral techniques are frequently used; positive or negative reinforcement, stimulus control, and shaping are most commonly applied. Sometimes, low doses of major tranquilizers (mainly, haloperidol) are prescribed when behavioral problems of the children are so severe that they cannot be controlled effectively with behavioral methods.

A Parent Education Program aims at instructing parents, both intellectually and behaviorally, and providing them with specific training for postdischarge management of their children. Child psychiatrists, individual therapists, social workers, and nurses are involved in this program, which provides education in normal development as well as language, social, motor, and self-care development. Parents are helped to understand the concepts of Autistic Disorder and related pervasive developmental disorders, the principles of behavior modification, and how to interact with a problem child.

WHEN AND BY WHOM IS AUTISM DIAGNOSED?

Usually, child psychiatrists are responsible for making the diagnosis of autism. Nine universities, all over the country, have child psychiatrists, and about 30 child psychiatrists are practicing in local clinics. When children suspected of having autism or other pervasive developmental disorders are brought to the treatment centers, they are referred to these child psychiatrists for a specific diagnosis.

NATIONAL OR THEORETICAL ISSUES

Korea has no specific national policy that relates to classification or services. There are recent plans to establish one national treatment center for autistic children at the Korean National Institute of Mental Health. About 40 to 50 autistic children would be treated at this center.

NATIONAL PARENTS' SOCIETY

In Korea, a National Parents' Society has about 600 families as members. The main purposes of this society are: (a) helping each other emotionally; (b) educating the parent-members; (c) exchanging information; (d) promoting early detection and treatment; and (e) raising research funds.

CENTRAL AMERICA AND SOUTH AMERICA

Miguel Cherro Aguerre and Natalia Trenchi

This section reviews the current situation concerning autism in Central America and South America. The discussion is based on information received from institutions in the region, from a computer search of the literature, and from personal experience in the field.

BACKGROUND AND HISTORY OF CONCEPT

Mills Costa (1989), from Brazil, offers a good synthesis about autism in Latin America. She explicates three important aspects of the history and current situation: (a) the decisive influence of the North American and European ideas on Latin American concepts about autism; (b) the relatively recent consideration of the entity in Latin America, together with a lack of institutional resources; and (c) the general lack of specific legislation that would permit fully adequate care of autistic individuals.

The diagnostic concept of autism was introduced to Uruguay by Professor Luis E. Prego Silva in 1951, when he returned from a psychiatric fellowship at the Harriet Lane Clinic of John Hopkins Medical School in Baltimore, Maryland. A multidisciplinary team was created in the Child Psychiatric Clinic of the Dr. Pedro Visca Hospital with the purpose of doing research and treating autistic children on an outpatient basis. Since then, other public and private groups have worked in the field. In 1989, a parents' association (AUPPAI) was created, and its members have worked hard and effectively for autistic individuals' welfare.

Uruguay has health systems with programs and projects launched by the Department of Public Health, as well as laws that protect the handicapped. However, the coverage from both sources is partial and insufficient, and a restructuring is needed to gain adequate care for the complex needs of autistic individuals. Similarly, the intentions for institutional resources are good, but the resources themselves are not really suitable. It is our impression that the situation in the rest of Latin America is not very different from that in Uruguay.

ASSESSMENT

An older tendency of talking about autism in a general fashion is now being abandoned. Instead, diagnosis within Latin America is mainly based on the *DSM* or *ICD* criteria. In their discussion of the *DSM* criteria for autism, Tallis and Soprano (1991) of Argentina wonder about the value of not including autism in the ambiguous field of psychoses, but placing it among the pervasive developmental disorders instead. Is the latter a less ambiguous field? In these authors' opinion, this approach implies that there is a deficit of cognitive competence in autism, and that autism is related to some kind of biological dysfunction. These ideas exclude the concept that autism can be found in a biologically intact organism.

We believe that pediatricians and teachers, and the multidisciplinary teams working in the mental health services, should be properly trained to recognize any feature suggesting autism at an early stage. A child psychiatrist should provide the formal diagnostic assessment.

ETIOLOGY AND PSYCHOPATHOLOGY

Prego Silva, influenced in his work by D.W. Winnicott, distinguishes between *psychosis* and *the psychotic*. He conceptualizes the psychotic as a way of reacting when looking for solutions and when faced with the consequences of very difficult environmental conditions. Mendilaharsu and de Mendilaharsu (1987), reflecting the ideas of W. Bion, hypothesize an "amalgamatic nucleus" that constitutes the destructive part of the personality. This nucleus, generally disorganizing and destructive, is related to the ego in various ways. The massive introjection of the amalgamatic nucleus stops the normal construction of the psychological system. As long as the malignant introjections remain "encapsulated," they permit the development of the mental apparatus, until the destructive element invades and disorganizes it.

In another psychoanalytic conception, Garbarino (1990) maintains that the psychological apparatus as conceived by S. Freud accounts for mental disorders in subjects who retain their psychological coherence as individuals; this model of the mind, he contends, is not always useful to understand some other types of patients. According to Freud, one is born with an id, and the ego appears after a "new psychological action" configurates it. Freud's id is delimited so that it can get into the psychological apparatus. For Garbarino, one is born with an unlimited id which is perceived by the newly born and favored by the narcissistic imbalance provoked by birth. He calls this original narcissism a *narcissism of the Being (Ser)*, which is not endowed with one's own image but with a sense of the universe in an unlimited centrifugal movement. That internal perception of the unlimited id originates in an instance called Being. The Being constitutes a presentiment of presence, for at birth there is not yet an ego capable of perceiving feelings. The inner perception of sensations of the id would originate in this dark presentiment of presence, before the psychological apparatus is formed. In autism, where the interaction of the mother–child dyad fails, the first interhuman identification cannot be made. The incipient psychological ego then relates more to the cosmic order than to the interhuman order.

In Argentina, Bleger (1972), in an article written shortly before his death, says that, in autism, there is a lack of discrimination between the outer and the inner worlds, between the ego and the objects. In the autistic individual, there is not a loss of the sense of reality, but a construction of his or her own sense of reality. As a whole, Bleger calls the phenomenon "syncretism": something might seem a confusion for the observer, but is not confusing to the patient. Bleger thinks that autism has a syncretic structure.

Dio Bleichmar (1987) recognizes that we have not arrived at the ultimate foundation—the genesis—of the dysfunction that leads to the psychotic process in childhood. However, she assigns prime relevance to the intersubjective failure in the distortion or absence of psychological representations of the child's own body, the mother's body as a separate being, and reality. The symbolic function that permits the location of oneself and the other is disturbed in such a way that the child seems submerged in a world of sensorial and physical stimuli without categorization.

Oelsner (1989), influenced by the concepts of D.W. Winnicott, W. Bion, and F. Tustin, states that the psychological birth implies the notion of separation. In the Winnicottian sense, in being "one" separated from "mother," the infant experiences the loss of the object that ensured the illusion of omnipotence, of being one who had everything. Normally, the mother's mind serves as a substitute uterine matrix and contains the baby, allowing the baby to maintain the idea of being one until it is mature enough to tolerate the separation and to then accept that they are two persons. If this uterine relationship is prematurely interrupted, by either inner or outer causes, the continuity of the Being is threatened; in response, the ego that is in the process of blossoming might capitulate and develop a protection against itself that becomes the autistic capsule. The essential problem is that the child then comes to separation at a stage that is still dominated by its self-generated sensuality. The premature and abrupt disillusionment hinders the development of transitional activities and the creation of transitional objects as the child's first nonego possessions. The hard reality, the hard nonego compared to the pleasant and soft sensuality, opens a gap in the primitive bodily ego and creates unthinkable anxieties. Extreme vulnerability forces the child to wrap itself into a hard nonego formed by a capsular cover, or a fusion, and interpenetration with soft objects. In both cases, the results are inaccessibility to the outside world, interruption of the psychological development, and alienation.

Jarast (1990), following the ideas of E. Bick and D. Anzieu, contrasts the ego-skin with the second muscular skin. Normally, the first skin, through the bond with the mother, has a constraining and cohesive function that allows the baby to acquire a notion of its inner self and to approach the separation of self and object, each contained in its own skin. However, if the constraining motherly functions are not properly accomplished, there is a permanent pathologic identification that creates a confusion of identity. States of nonintegration persist, with a consequent desperate search by the baby for an object (light, voice, smell) that maintains a unifying attention on the parts of his or her body. The inadequate performance of the first skin drives the baby to form a second, muscular skin that replaces the dependency on the constraining object with a pseudo-dependency.

Tallis and Soprano (1991) divide the etiologic theories of autism into major subtypes. They consider two different types of primary pathways into autism: (a) problems of the psychological surroundings of the child (genetic or environmental factors) and (b) organic problems specifically linked with genetic

problems. Another major pathway includes the group of psychological and psychophysiological dysfunctions that create cognitive deficits affecting both language and symbolic abilities. These cognitive dysfunctions result in a limited capacity to establish relations between new and previously experienced stimuli, and a weak capacity to establish relations between the basic mechanisms of communication and verbal language. The cognitive deficits are hypothesized to result from a biological dysfunction of the central nervous system, from a different organization of the brain, and/or from clear organic disorders related to different pathologies and heterogeneous groups of biological disorders. These biological factors are also influenced by psychosocial factors.

In Perú, Gomberoff, Noemi, and de Gomberoff (1991) make use of Tustin's conceptualizations of the autistic object. They differentiate the autistic object from other objects, such as the autosensorial, the transitional, and the fetishistic, and they use the concept of autistic object to explain resistances as well as transference and countertransference reactions that are found in some patients. In the autosensorial stage, a very early stage of normal human development, the baby perceives objects as sensation-objects. For example, the nipple-breast of the mother, like the pacifier, is an autosensorial object joined to the tongue-mouth of the baby. The origin of the autistic object is found in the substitution for the loss of a part of the feeding mother, which is felt as a loss of a part of the child's own body, and which produces in the child a sense of desolate anguish. The autistic object produces a massive mental restriction with lack of motivation and of basic confidence. Like a crust, the autistic object blocks the intolerable injury provoked by the physical separation from the mother, which is experienced as a violent tear. That same crust or scar obstructs the healing relationship between parent and child. The autistic object helps the child avoid the pain produced by the consciousness of the nonego, felt as a tear of the self; it is used as a permanent replacement instead of as a transitory substitute for the parental functions. The transitional object, on the other hand, is used to regulate and handle the tension produced by the awareness of normal separation. The fetishistic object, as pathological as the autistic one, is experienced by the child as an external object that is foreign to the self; it represents or substitutes for the absent mother or part of her. This type of object allows the child to satisfy sexual impulses that are prohibited with the real mother.

In Brazil, Pinto (1982) uses neuroscience and embryological research to revive Kanner's hypothesis about the high intellectual level of autistic parents. He thinks that the autistic syndrome may be present in children whose brain (a) is not only mature but also ready for socialization and (b) did not receive adequate stimulation during intrauterine life. In this hypothesis, the child develops behaviors similar to those of animals that do not establish imprinting during a critical period. Pinto, citing the work of K. Lorenz, suggests that the disorder arises from a situation as if the child developed imprinting on his or her own hands (mannerisms, rhythmic games, a search for sameness).

In Mexico, Marcin (1991) suggests that autism is a primary cognitive disorder that involves the perceptual processes and communication systems. He lists findings that originate in the neurosciences and points out that it is not possible to draw definite conclusions yet. The goal of assessment is to take into account the multiple therapeutic strategies required by each child, according to his or her own special rhythm and need for therapeutic timing. Also in Mexico, Guisa Cruz et al. (1991) studied a sample of 20 subjects defined as autistic according to the *DSM-III-R* criteria. They verified alterations in brain-evoked potentials and brain stem conduction. They also found EEG evidence for possible structural damage, as well as signs of epileptic activity.

In Colombia, Villareal and Gaviria (1987) have analyzed the characteristics of the learning process that accompany autistic children's idiosyncratic way of interacting with the environment. These authors describe the processes of stimulus control and motivation, paying special attention to the factors that should be taken into account to achieve efficiency in treatment strategies. Villareal and Gaviria consider learning as a process of stimulus control that can be affected by the following factors:

1. *Overselectivity of stimuli.* Autistic individuals respond to one feature or component of the stimulus array while ignoring the others. This leads to adaptive disadvantage because the majority of environmental stimuli have a complex configuration. Learning is interfered with because the autistic child does not respond functionally to the different signals or because his or her behavior remains under the control of irrelevant incidental stimuli.

2. *Perseveration of inaccurate response strategies.* The child repeatedly emits a response or responds repeatedly to a determined stimulus, independent of the reinforcement. Autistic children choose a determined response instead of exploring other possibilities. This leads to a limited behavioral repertoire and constitutes an important handicap for learning and socialization.

3. *Abnormalities of the motivation that is basic for learning.* The motivational structure of autistic individuals is characterized by an orientation to solely self-stimulating behavior, with a sequence that alternates between different types of behavior in the same behavioral line and periods of rest without any activity. The reinforcement of the self-stimulating behaviors reduces the power of diverse potential sources of reinforcement.

TREATMENT

In Latin America, there has been a gradual transition from uni- to multidisciplinary types of treatment. Together with the spread of multidisciplinary approaches and the organization of teams, a need for institutional frameworks at both the public and private levels has emerged.

The organization of teams has proved to be effective because it allows for sharing knowledge and coordinating efforts. However, the team approach has also brought difficulties, such as contradictions and confrontations among team members. These can be resolved as long as a true team spirit, with real respect for each of the disciplines and orientations, can be created.

Various publications exemplify different types of approaches: psychoanalytic, behavioral, cognitive-behavioral, linguistic, psychomotor, musical therapy, and so on. In Uruguay, the psychoanalytical approach has been the most widely accepted. A synthesis by C. Marcin (1991), from Mexico, is relevant. Marcin offers a view of psychotherapy and associated controversies. He affirms the importance of carefully evaluating the child's situation holistically; psychotherapy is most beneficial for patients who have a high level of functioning, and whose cognitive and verbal capacities are adequate for understanding and expressing thoughts and emotions. In psychotherapy, a very special bond is created and there is work that requires symbolic capacities—work with fantasy and with the past; in a sense, psychotherapy is a cryptic game that represents the bonds between the self and its objects. In the treatment of an autistic child, there are two stages. The first stage aims at establishing a significant relationship focused on the organization of the presence of an object that talks, listens, and helps differentiate the ego from the nonego. The therapist encloses and holds. The therapist's thoughts mediate between the child and the outside world, providing protection and techniques for experiencing security that the child can incorporate through routine. These techniques are support and withdrawal mechanisms that help the child deal with his or her impulses, and help set the child free from aberrant behaviors.

In the second stage, after the concrete and archaic modes of functioning have been established, the therapist works with the incipient identification processes, the omnipotent primitive mechanisms, the analysis of unusual stages in the formation of symbols, the fear of physical disintegration, unifying relationships, the progressive creation of the imaginary world, and the emergence of the self as a unique entity that is ideally integrated for the establishment of genuine relationships. In short, the later stages are an attempt to find the path that leads to the psychological development.

Marcin insists on the relevance of an accurate evaluation before initiating treatment. He also mentions that it is necessary to recognize other therapeutic options with autistic individuals. He describes the aims of the work carried out at the Mexican Clinic of Autism (CLIMA), and points out that the connotation that the acronym has in Spanish (it means *climate*) suggests an environmental purpose of the institution. The therapeutic models used at CLIMA are related to the severity of each case. They involve structured therapies, sensory integration, the "forced embrace" therapy and psychotherapy, individual and family. Marcin highlights that therapists must be open to all contributions that prove effective for the different levels and types of autism. The treatment is not chosen by theoretical favoritism, but by thoughtful analysis of the pathology of the child, the needs of the family, and a deep respect for individuality.

Also in Mexico, de Plá (1991) considers the autistic individual as a willing being; she argues for the role of the unconscious dimension. Nonetheless, she postulates a multidisciplinary approach and describes the general conditions under which the personalized teaching of an autistic child should be carried out. She also points out that the personalization of the bond, the openness to learning and to change, implies conflict and causes psychological pain that the child, his or her parents, and those who care for the child must be ready to assume.

In Argentina, Wernicke (1991) proposes a holistic therapeutic approach aimed at solving diverse psychopathologic conditions, including autism. It consists of a multimodal approach that includes neurologic and pharmacologic treatments, orientation to parents, rehabilitation, and the technique after which the approach has been named—the "forced" or "fastening embrace." This technique uses the embrace of the mother in a process that has several steps: confrontation, rejection, and reconciliation. Through this process, there is an intention to create a "flooding of security."

In Chile, Donovan and Olivari (1989) propose a treatment model in which professional procedures are minimized and the work is contextualized in the family and the immediate social world of the child. Parents and significant others are integrated in the therapy. The model encourages that the changes in the interaction introduced by the treatment should be kept in the family world through the "live" learning of the parents, using an unidirectional mirror. The therapy aims at helping the child establish meaning in acts and things. The parents are encouraged to discover abilities in the child, so they will not become hopeless from the very beginning. At the proper moment, a "labeling procedure" is started, so that the parents' expectations meet the real possibilities of the child.

In Ecuador, a Directory has been published (FEPAPDEM, 1992–1993) that contains a list of institutions that take care of mentally handicapped persons. The list mentions 78 institutions spread throughout the country; 5 include autism as a condition treated.

It is generally recognized in Latin America that the treatment should respond to both the child and his or her environment. Parents and teachers should be trained properly. In Panama, Audero (1980) proposes a workshop-seminar model to train personnel who will work with parents and teachers. The model is based on the behavioral conceptualization of autism, and mainly uses the operant conditioning paradigm.

In Colombia, Villareal and Gaviria (1987) propose an approach to treatment based on their analysis of the learning process of autistic children. From their concept of problems in stimulus control and overselectivity of stimuli, they advise a careful use of support procedures when guiding the responses during the first stages of the programs. They warn that the autistic child might respond to the supports instead of the specific stimuli of the task. They suggest inserting supports in the stimulus for the task, then fading them progressively in such a way that the response is finally controlled by the relevant characteristics of the stimulus. Likewise, they warn not to presuppose that a child has actually learned a behavior until it is known which stimuli control the behavior. The other feature that has therapeutic implications is the perseveration of responses. In this respect, they underline the need for structuring objectives in order to help the child learn key strategies of exploration and response. Another prime objective is the amplification of the motivational structure. Finally, to facilitate learning therapeutic activities, they advise the creation of a situation that limits potential competition—a clear separation between work and free activities, and strategies that maximize the reinforcement used by the therapist.

Our own therapeutic work (Cherro Aguerre, Trenchi, & Grobert, 1990) is influenced by the theory of attachment. Our therapeutic team includes child psychiatrists and psychologists with different theoretical orientations, psychoanalytic and cognitive-behavioral. We emphasize work with the child and parents through various techniques. For example, we videotape sequences of daily-life interactions between the child and parents (free play, bathing, feeding) and then view and discuss the film with parents. This allows parents to examine their own behavior and to think about their relationships with the child. The aim is to establish, as much as possible, a facilitating child–parent relationship.

CONCLUSIONS

The current status of research and clinical work in Latin America emphasizes the importance of consistency in classification to allow for accurate exchange of information. The availability of *DSM-IV* and *ICD-10* will assist in achieving this goal. Further epidemiological research is needed to guide the creation of national policies. Within therapeutic centers, there should be multidisciplinary teams created on the basis of a respect for the contributions of each discipline.

Finally, the active participation of parents and of resources within communities is an important element in efforts to implement optimal health policies. Undoubtedly, laws will have to be passed, and services transformed, so that they meet the real needs of the autistic child, his or her family, and the community.

REFERENCES

Audero, M.A. (1980). Seminario taller de tratamiento conductual a niños y adolescentes autistas. *Edes Revista Educación Especial, 2,* 131–164.

de Bagattini, M.C.M. (1990). *Clínica y Psicopatología del Autismo y la Psicosis Infantil.* Montevideo, Uruguay: Biblioteca de Psicoanálisis.

Bleger, J. (1972). Esquizofrenia, autismo y psicosis, enfoque psicoanalítico. *Acta Psiquiátrica Psicológica de América Latina, 18*(4), 227–231.

Cherro Aguerre, M., (1990). Therapeutic approach of an Autistic Syndrome. Paper presented to the 12th International Congress of the International Association of Child & Adolescent Psychiatry & Allied Professions, Kyoto, Japan.

Cherro Aguerre, M., Trenchi, N., & Grobert, M. (1990). Interactions parents-baby in an autism case. Paper presented to the 12th International Congress of the International Association of Child & Adolescent Psychiatry & Allied Professions, Kyoto, Japan.

de Plá, E.P. (1991). El niño psicótico y la escuela: Un enfoque psicoanalítico. *Psicosis y Retardo Mental, AMERPI, 3,* 1–47.

Dio Bleichmar, E. (1987). Psicosis y Autismo. In N. Fejerman & E. Fernandez Alvarez (Eds.), *Fronteras entre neuropediatría y psicología* (pp. 193–213). Buenos Aires, Argentina: Edic. Nueva Visión.

Donovan, L., & Olivari, C. (1989). Autismo Infantil. Un proceso co-terapéutico a dos voces. *Revista Terapia Psicológica, 8*(12), 44–49.

FEPAPDEM (Federacion Ecuatorian Pro Atencion a la Person con Deficiencia Mental). (1992–1993). *Directorio.* (p. 81). Quito, Ecuador.

Garbarino, H. (1990). *El Ser en Psicoanálisis.* Montevideo, Uruguay: EPPAL.

Gomberoff, M., Noemi, C., & de Gomberoff, L.P. (1991). "Detección del objeto autista en el análisis de una niña psicótica. *Transiciones, 2,* 36–52.

Guisa Cruz, V. M., et al. (1991). Potenciales evocados auditivos y electroencéfalograma en el niño autista. *AMERPI (Association Mexicana del Estudio del Retraso Mental y la Psicosis Infantil), 3,* 47–64.

Jarast, R. (1990). Yo-piel psicótico infantil. *Diarios Clínicos, Revista de Psicoanálisis con niños y adolescentes, 1,* 107–113.

Marcin, C. (1991). Modelos de intervención terapéutica en el autismo. *AMERPI, 3,* 65–85.

Mendilaharsu, C., & de Mendilaharsu, S.A. (1987). Reflexiones sobre el Psicoanálisis de la Psicosis. *Rev. Uruguaya de Psicoanálisis, 66,* 9–37.

Mills Costa, N. (1989). Educacao especial e tratamento da crianca autista. *Integracao, 2*(4), 7–8.

Oelsner, R.R. (1989). Vulnerabilidad y fenómenos autistas. *Psicoanalysis, 11*(1), 177–190.

Pinto Pereira, J.L. (1982). O autismo infantil. Análise de uma hipótese etiopatogenética. Consideracoes sobre a neurobiologia da senso-percepcao. *Journal Brasileiro de Psiquiatria, 31*(2), 79–85.

Prego Silva, L.E. (1980). ¿Qué es lo posicótico del punto de vista clínico?" *Rev. APPIA, 7*(1–2), 83–90.

Tallis, J., & Soprano, A.M. (1991). *Neuropediatría, Neuropsicología y aprendizaje.* Buenos Aires, Argentina: Edic. Nueva Visión.

Villarreal, L., & Gaviria, P. (1987). Características del aprendizaje en los niños autistas: Sus implicaciones para las estrategias de tratamiento. *Encuentro Nacional de Educación Especial,* Colombia, pp. 35–63.

Wernicke, C. (1991). El autismo y la terapia de contención. In G. Fernandez (Ed.), *Autismo,¿un síntoma?* (pp. 149–157). Buenos Aires, Argentina: Ed. Gabas.

THE NETHERLANDS

Herman van Engeland

Insofar as it can be established, the term *autism* was used in the pedagogical institute in Nijmegen, Holland, as early as 1937 to 1940, to indicate certain forms of child behavior. The term was applied to children who were excessively self-absorbed and who had markedly stereotyped behavior, excessive anxiety, impaired social interaction with their environment, and retarded development of communicative abilities, and whose form perception and form control were remarkably better developed than their other functions.

And yet, not until 1952 was the first case study published—Van Krevelen's case of a four-year old boy who fulfilled all the criteria of infantile autism as published by Kanner in 1943. Van Krevelen noted that, in his opinion, this was not an early case of schizophrenia because there were no signs of dementia and, in some areas, there was developmental progress.

In 1953, Kamp showed that some autistic children are not characterized by massive aloofness, but demonstrate "symbiotic empty clinging" in their contact with their primary caregiver. Kamp suggested the term *autistic continuum.* The continuum was supposed to have two extremes: on the one hand, the children as described by Kanner, and, on the other hand, Rank's atypical children and the symbiotic psychotic children as described by Margaret Mahler. He suggested that this continuum be indicated by the term *developmental psychosis,* and, with Van Krevelen, he was convinced that this was a developmental disorder, not dementia or regression of functions as in schizophrenia.

Since then, the autistic syndrome has been the subject of numerous studies; more than 10 doctoral dissertations have been published focusing on pedagogic, psychophysiological, neurochemical, pharmacological, psychometric, and cognitive psychological aspects. Autism can be regarded as the syndrome that has been examined most extensively in Dutch child and adolescent psychiatry.

The term *developmental psychosis* proposed by Kamp was used until the early 1980s; since then, the *DSM-III* (and, since 1994, the *DSM-IV*) terminology and diagnostic criteria have been used.

Not only have the diagnostic criteria changed over the years, the treatment of the autistic disorder has also altered. Until the early 1980s, psychotherapy (often on psychoanalytical lines) was used particularly for autistic children functioning at a higher level. Their parents received intensive parental guidance. The idea behind this approach was that the autistic disorder could be seen as a form of fixation or regression to what was considered to be an autistic stage of the child's development; that is, autism was conceptualized as a "developmental arrest" that could be treated by intensive psychotherapy. By the mid-1980s, this view had been relegated to obscurity. Currently, autism is regarded as a congenital developmental disorder in which behavior therapy and "home training," combined with specialized day care, are used to optimize the child's cognitive development, to improve his or her communicative skills, and to restrict bizarre, unmanageable, and unacceptable behavior. Tools used in this treatment approach are the TEACCH programs developed by Schopler, and pharmacotherapy as an adjunct, when necessary.

HISTORY OF CARE

In the early 1970s, the parents of autistic children founded support groups in various places in the Netherlands, usually supported by child psychiatrists and psychologists. These Foundations for Autism had a strong regional character. They were geared to increasing awareness of the autistic disorder and the possibilities for diagnosis and treatment, as well as to stimulating research.

In 1974, a Foundation, Hulp aan Autistische Kinderen en Adolescenten (Help for Autistic Children and Adolescents), was licensed to establish a psychiatric clinic for autistic adolescents: The Dr. Leo Kannerhuis, in Oosterbeek. In this clinic, adolescents from the age of 16, who have a performance intelligence within the normal range, can receive intensive treatment, in the hope that they ultimately will be able to live and work independently. Treatment mainly consists of remedial teaching and behavior therapy; emphasis is on rehabilitation, job training, and training in social skills. In the 1980s, a Work Home was created as a necessary extension of the treatment program. The treatment started with much enthusiasm and effort, but the Dr. Leo Kannerhuis unfortunately did not lead to completely independent and autonomous functioning for adult autistics. It was realized that adults with autism still required continuous support and protection, which is a goal of the Work Home. A number of autistic people now live in similar Work Homes under the guidance of group leaders. They work on the land (e.g., their own gardens), keep cattle, and do simple handicrafts. They try to sell the products. The Work Homes are subsidized by the government. At present, several Work Homes (usually affiliated with psychiatric hospitals) have been or are in the process of being established throughout the Netherlands.

In the early 1980s, the National Parents' Association for Autism (NVA) was established. The Association works in close cooperation with autism experts, and an estimated 80% of parents of autistic children are members. The Association organizes regional support groups in which parents are informed about the possibilities of home treatment options, weekend and holiday care, and new treatments.

Because of intensive contact with experts in the field of autism, the possibility of referrals for parents who are having problems with their child have improved considerably. The parents' association publishes a professional-looking magazine in which parents are kept up to date about the latest developments in diagnosis and treatment. Some parents write about their experiences, and autistic people sometimes contribute first-person accounts or publish their artistic products (drawings, paintings, and poems). The NVA has made a considerable contribution to improving the care given to autistic persons.

TREATMENT SERVICES

The NVA's political lobby influenced the Dutch government to publish an Autism Memorandum in 1984. This Memorandum regulates that each Regional Institution for Outpatient Mental Health Care (RIAGG) must make facilities available for diagnosis of and assistance for autistic people. The Netherlands has a population of 15 million and there are 60 RIAGGs throughout the country. In most cases, 3 or 4 RIAGG juvenile care teams have combined to form a Regional Autism Team. Each regional team consists of a child psychiatrist, a child psychologist, a remedial teacher, and a social worker. They usually work in close cooperation with university centers for child and adolescent psychiatry. The autism teams focus on diagnosis, treatment, and guidance of the autistic people and their parents. Diagnosis is usually made in a university center for child and adolescent psychiatry so that the medical aspects of the diagnosis are fully integrated. Treatment and guidance consist mainly of conducting home-training projects, organizing day care, placing the children in special educational centers, and assisting in organizing admission of poorly functioning autistic persons to mental institutions. By now, all of the Netherlands is covered by these regional autism teams. They are easily accessible to parents, and they provide assistance free of charge. (They receive funding through the AWBZ—the Exceptional Medical Expenses Act.) Unfortunately, the teams' capacity is rather restricted. Waiting lists indicate a delay of 2 to 6 months after application for assistance.

The Autism Memorandum also generated a special subsidy regulation for schools that have autistic children as pupils. Special "autism schools" have not been established in the Netherlands. However, the subsidy regulation has the effect of making some schools—mainly special education schools (schools for children with speech or language disorders and with learning and educational problems)—more or less specialized in dealing with autistic children. Some of these schools have even created special classes for autistic children. However, autism classes or autism groups are not limited to schools. Special autism groups have been created in some medical kindergarten day care centers, in day care centers for the mentally

handicapped, and in institutions for the mentally deficient.

Departments of child and adolescent psychiatry generally offer the possibility of extensive diagnosis and special treatment (pharmacotherapy) for children with complicated problems whose treatment requires a special approach. Usually, admission to child psychiatry centers is relatively brief, and treatment is then continued by the outpatient autism teams.

Help for the autistic child or adolescent is currently well organized in the Netherlands and is actively stimulated by the government. Nevertheless, a number of bottlenecks remain in the provision of assistance. In particular, help and backup systems for autistic adolescents and adults are much in need of improvement. Although the number of Work Homes is being increased, accessibility to sheltered workplaces and social workplaces could be improved.

Another problem is the care for children with disorders closely related to autism (Pervasive Developmental Disorders Not Otherwise Specified, or PDD-NOS). The subsidy regulations implemented by the Autism Memorandum apply only to children who have been diagnosed as autistic. Children with an autism-related disorder such as PDD-NOS fall outside the subsidy terms; their special education is not compensated, and a special teacher cannot be appointed. In these days of fiscal cutbacks, it does not seem likely that these bottlenecks in the service system will be resolved in the foreseeable future.

REFERENCES

Kamp, L.N.J. (1953). Les psychoses chex l'enfant. *Acta Neurologica et Psychiatrica, Belgium, 53,* 309–330.

van Engeland, H. (1981). *Over ontwikkelingspsychosen.* Acco: Leuven.

van Krevelen, D. (1952). Een geval van "Early Infantile Autism." *Nederlands Tijdschrift voor Geneeskunde, 96,* 202–206.

SPAIN

Joaquin Fuentes

BACKGROUND AND CONCEPT

Modern interest in autism as an identifiable disorder to be studied empirically originated in Spain soon after a national meeting held in Madrid in 1977. Prior to this date, sporadic papers were published in the Spanish psychiatric journals in 1955, 1965, and 1974, but the disorder was considered extremely rare and not deserving of a great deal of interest. In fact, it has been pointed out (Cobo, 1981) that, in Spain, interest in autism arose not from the field of psychiatry but from psychology.

Three elements that coincided in the Madrid Conference influenced the future unfolding of the situation in Spain:

1. Many international experts were present, mainly from the Anglo-Saxon scientific community, which led to the establishment of professional bonds.
2. The Conference served as the initial melting pot for many psychologists, teachers, and psychiatrists interested in autism, who later founded AETAPI, the Spanish National Society of Therapists of Autism and Childhood Psychosis.
3. The Conference gave birth to many parents' associations which have played a very significant role.

This triple configuration of new scientific data, interested professionals, and determined parents, needs to be considered within the framework of the historical events of that time. Spain, after many years of dictatorship, underwent a profound political change. Democracy led to decentralization of State services, and the nation was organized according to a quasi-federal model. The new political leaders, influenced by the fast growing economical bonanza and the spirit of renaissance, were sensitive to consumers' initiatives. The whole country was involved in a modernization effort, related to full participation in the European arena, and the changes that occurred in the education, health, and social programs were very relevant to the field of autism.

Decentralization, nevertheless, generated very diverse conditions, depending on the geographical area under consideration. Parents' and professionals' local initiatives had varying impacts and were met with different degrees of support by respective authorities. Because of this diversity, it is erroneous to speak of Spain as a homogeneous country. As in other countries, highly developed and qualified services, in some communities, coexist with severe deficiencies in others.

SERVICES

In contrast to neighboring countries, in Spain, it was readily accepted that autism is a pervasive developmental disorder closely linked to other handicaps such as mental retardation, and best managed within an educational framework. Very few families had to suffer the interpretative abuse of psychoanalysis; in general, the vast majority of them had to cope more with sheer ignorance on the part of professionals, rather than with a skewed and guilt-provoking view of the problem.

It is interesting to probe the reason behind this lack of rejection of the modern view of autism. Official psychiatry in the old regime could hardly be described as innovative. The predominant model was biologically oriented, and public psychiatric assistance was limited to institutionalization in state hospitals. Psychoanalysis, which had an incipient influence during the Spanish Republic, did not really develop later (in part, because many of its leading proponents had to flee the country during the Civil War). Only in some big cities, such as Barcelona and Madrid, did psychoanalysis have some influence; even there, it was restricted to private practice and had no real presence in the academic world. Psychiatric assistance was not really considered a health matter; it was linked to the regional departments of social welfare. The national health system of that time did not even consider psychiatry as a separate specialty. It was linked to neurology, in a medical specialty called neuropsychiatry. The neuropsychiatrists of the national health system's outpatient clinics had to deal with a vast number of patients and the only treatment basically available was psychopharmacology. Little time was available to individualize the needs of the patients.

The beginning of the 1980s coincided with the progressive acceptance of a community psychiatry model. Credit for this has to be given to different mental health professionals (many of them trained abroad), who initiated what was known as the "psychiatry reform." Originating in Galicia and Asturias, this effort contested the old predominant model, in much the same way that other European radical psychiatry alternatives were developing at the same time.

In a simplistic manner, it can be said that the community psychiatry movement proposed ideas such as decentralization of resources, coordination with other community services, deinstitutionalization, and so forth. In a parallel way, other means of intervention, besides psychopharmacology, were promoted. The steps taken have been slow, and, although many significant advances have been made, much remains to be achieved in the area of public psychiatry in Spain.

The lack of community psychiatry resources coincided with the limited educational services available for students with severe learning difficulties, such as those diagnosed with autism. The majority of these students were excluded from the first special schools that opened for children with mental retardation in the 1970s and were sent, if anywhere at all, to residential centers that were dependent on social services and were characterized by their almost nonexistent educational interest.

Given these antecedents, it can be more easily understood that, after the Madrid Conference, focus was centered on the development of the first schools for students with autism, which were established in major Spanish cities in the 1980s. The model frequently entailed the initial organization of a parents' association, which then hired professionals to manage services largely covered by public funds. This alternative has both advantages and risks, but it has proven to be an effective way to initiate programs in underserved areas.

The new national Law on Social Services, passed by the democratic Parliament, introduced many innovative concepts and led the way to an integrative approach to handicaps. Consumers were acknowledged for their role in innovation, and planning and funding responsibilities were assigned to local authorities.

The first years of the Centers for Persons with Autism in Spain were characterized by adherence to the predominant approach utilized in many Anglo-Saxon countries at that time. Thus, behavior modification techniques were used to teach self-help skills and language. A very small number of schools, mainly in the Catalonia area, followed a psychoanalytic orientation, but it is fair to say that, in general, the few programs that were created sustained a behavioral-linguistic approach.

The mid-1980s were associated with a strong movement in favor of school integration. The educational authorities accepted—little by little, and in agreement with the guidelines of the European Union—the principle of nonexclusion in catering to the needs of all students. A new language emerged that was educational rather than clinical, and many initiatives to provide schooling, hopefully in a minimally restrictive environment, were developed. Students with autism and other pervasive developmental disorders were recognized as deserving of a high teacher-to-student ratio, but were excluded from the integration effort by many local authorities, who felt that these students posed too many difficulties and would be better served in special schools.

A particular region of Spain, the Basque Country, did consider all students, including those with autism, in its integrative approach. For example, by the end of the 1980s, the small Basque province of Guipuzcoa had a network of special classes, run by the GAUTENA Autistic Society, located in ordinary schools, and availability for individual integration was available, with different degrees of support, in many schools. In conjunction with this network, inspired by the TEACCH program, families had access to other services such as home programs, respite care, adult services, group homes, and leisure opportunities.

In recent years, the British concept of "special educational needs" has had an enormous impact in Spain, both in special education at large and in the particular domain of autism. The initial move of the 1980s from a clinical perspective to a more socioeducational approach has become stabilized. For many (although not all) involved, this is a positive and irreversible achievement. Educational authorities have recognized autism and have opened sections on autism in their special education resources centers. Many people feel that, at this point, problems are related more to resource limitations and lack of well-trained staff with proper institutional support rather than to confusion about the model to follow.

In a parallel way, many changes have occurred in the conceptualization of autism. Initial emphasis on language and cognitive skills has been replaced by aspects such as socioemotional deficits, theory of mind, visually supported learning, alternative communication means, normal peer tutoring, adaptation to national curriculum, functionality, incidental teaching, and so on. Advances in the field find quick application in the majority of available programs, and the rigid behaviorism of 15 years ago has disappeared.

AETAPI, the Spanish National Society of Therapists of Autism and Childhood Psychosis, remains the key influential channel for the dissemination of innovative research and services models. The society has more than 100 members from all related professions and, in 1995, held its 8th Congress. Also, in 1994, a national federation of parents' associations, named AUTISM-SPAIN, was constituted to coordinate local efforts and influence national policy. This national society has now eleven regional societies as members, and hopes to incorporate all parents' initiatives.

SUMMARY

Autism in Spain enjoys the active participation of many involved parents and professionals. Despite the fact that underserved areas still remain in the country, there are elements that allow anticipation of a brighter future. Autism is recognized and diagnosed following internationally accepted criteria (*DSM-IV* and *ICD-10*), there are structured organizations for parents and professionals, and the general attitude of authorities and laypersons toward autism is a positive one. The challenge now is to extend throughout the country the model programs that are currently providing services in certain areas. In a time of economic uncertainty and social welfare restrictions, joint lobbying by parents and professionals, as well as fluent international communication, will still be needed, much to the same degree that they proved essential in the past.

REFERENCES

Cobo, C. (1981, September 21–27). Ser hoy niño autista en Espana. *Profesion Medica*, 27–30.

Fuentes, J. (1994). Portrait: GAUTENA, Association du Pays Basque en Espagne. *AUTISME-EUROPE, Link, 15*, 4–7.

SWEDEN AND OTHER NORDIC NATIONS

Per-Anders Rydelius

INTRODUCTION

The history of child and adolescent psychiatry and of the theories used to explain psychiatric disorders in the Nordic countries (Sweden, Finland, Norway, Denmark, and Iceland) provides an important context for understanding the treatment of autism and pervasive developmental disorders.

Although the Nordic countries have had much in common, including religious, ethnic, cultural, and social aspects and closely related languages (except Finnish), there are important differences. Child and adolescent psychiatry in the five countries has been an independent medical discipline since the beginning of the 1950s, but the situation in Finland and Sweden is different from that in Norway, Denmark, and Iceland (Hannesdóttir, 1993; Piha & Almqvist, 1994; Rydelius, 1993; Smedegaard, Hansen, & Isager, 1993; Vandvik & Spurkland, 1993).

In Norway, Denmark, and Iceland, as in Great Britain and the United States, child and adolescent psychiatry is closer to general psychiatry. In Sweden and Finland, for a long time, child and adolescent psychiatry has been far closer to pediatrics. It could be said that the main influence on Swedish and Finnish child and adolescent psychiatry originated from central Europe, a situation that is partly relevant also for Denmark, but the British and American influence has been stronger on the establishment of child and adolescent psychiatry in Norway and Iceland.

In Sweden, child and adolescent psychiatry was established as a medical discipline in 1951. The initiatives for the establishment of a "new" discipline originated from pediatrics, school mental health work, child social welfare, and general psychiatry—in that order, starting with Ellen Key's book (Key, 1909) introducing the 20th century as "The Century of the Child." As shown by the pamphlet *Broken Minds,* the strongest influence came from pediatrics and not from general psychiatry. In 1915, Jundell (chairman of the Department of Pediatrics at the Karolinska Institute) presented his arguments, based on a pediatric developmental perspective, for a new discipline dedicated to understanding childhood mental health problems. The history of child and adolescent psychiatry has been very much influenced by the corresponding histories of the discipline's development in Austria, France, Germany, and Switzerland.

FROM "HÄILPAEDAGOGIE" (CURATIVE EDUCATION) TO A PSYCHODYNAMIC APPROACH TO UNDERSTANDING AND TREATING CHILD PSYCHIATRIC DISORDERS

Over the past 100 years, several historical periods can be delineated in relation to the theories and ideas used in Central Europe, the Nordic countries, and Sweden to explain and treat child psychiatric disorders.

At the beginning of the 20th century, the ideas of *Häilpaedagogie,* or curative education, had a major influence on the development of child and adolescent psychiatry. In Sweden, the "phase of curative education," later influenced by the mental health movement originating in the United States, was succeeded in the 1930s by a "genetic phase" and theories based on genetic explanations for child psychiatric disorders. In turn, this period was followed by a "neuropsychiatric phase" in the 1940s and the 1950s.

A SHIFT IN THE USE OF THE SCIENTIFIC LANGUAGE IN THE NORDIC COUNTRIES AFTER WORLD WAR II

Until World War II, German was the main scientific language in all five Nordic countries. Thus, there are historical similarities between these nations and Central Europe. During the 1950s, new ideas were introduced for explaining child psychiatric problems. Clinicians began to use a psychoanalytically oriented frame of reference. There was also a shift of the main scientific language as British and

American scientific literature became most important. Swedish child psychiatrists were influenced by Kanner's *Textbook in Child Psychiatry,* 2nd edition (Kanner, 1948), which replaced the German textbooks, *Lehrbuch der Psychopathologie des Kindesalters* (Benjamin, Hanselmann, Isserlin, Lutz, & Ronald, 1938) and *Lehrbuch der allgemeinen Kinderpsychiatrie* (Tramer, 1942). The shift in the use of scientific language also meant that child psychiatrists, in their clinical work, became more dependent on the practice of child psychiatry in the United States and Great Britain, and the close connections to general psychiatry in those countries.

THE CONCEPT OF CHILDHOOD PSYCHOSIS

In the Nordic countries, until the introduction of infantile autism by Kanner in the United States, and Autistische Psychopathie by Asperger in Austria, psychotic disorders in childhood were mainly categorized as Dementia Infantilis (described by Heller in 1908), Dementia Praecox (suggested by Kraepelin), or Dementia Praecocissima (suggested by Sante De Sanctis). These disorders were distinguished clinically. In the psychosis of Heller, the child had normal development for the first 3 to 4 years of life and then deteriorated, lost speech, developed an autistic status, and successively showed "dementia." The disorder most often showed itself in children who had a degenerative brain disorder. Dementia Praecox and Dementia Praecocissima (although in some cases organic brain disorder was included) were descriptions of what later was called childhood schizophrenia.

Later, the Danish psychiatrist Strömgren suggested the following categorization of childhood psychotic disorders: psychosis of psychogenic origin; psychosis of physiogenic-"organic" origin (including Heller's disorder); psychosis of cryptogenic origin (including schizophrenia, manic-depressive disorders, and early infantile autism—the Kanner Syndrome). The diagnosis of a childhood psychosis required the appearance of symptoms before the age of 10 to 11 years (Annell, 1958).

Children with these psychotic disorders were looked on as mentally ill, not as mentally handicapped. This was still the case when two new Parliament Acts, passed in the 1960s, gave special services and support to the mentally retarded and transferred the responsibility for psychiatric hospitals and psychiatric care in Sweden from the government to the county councils. Also, according to *ICD-7* and *ICD-8,* children with childhood psychosis were still looked on as mentally ill. In 1986, a new law was passed to support the mentally retarded, and children with childhood psychosis were considered mentally handicapped.

The *ICD* system of classification has been used in all Nordic countries. However, beginning in 1980, the American *DSM-III/DSM-III-R* systems were increasingly taken into consideration in daily clinical work. The multiaxial system for child psychiatric diagnoses proposed by Rutter, Schaffer, and Sturge was also translated into Swedish and used simultaneously with *DSM.* In 1987, after a study of the *ICD* and *DSM* systems, the Swedish Association of Child and Adolescent Psychiatry adopted the *DSM* approach to diagnostic considerations. Thus, the concept of pervasive developmental disorders was introduced, followed by the change from Infantile Autism *(DSM-III)* to Autistic Disorders *(DSM-III-R).*

The most important treatment program for autistic children in Sweden since the 1930s has been curative education, Häilpaedagogie (in its anthroposophical form). This treatment approach continues to link Sweden with child psychiatry in Central Europe and with European concepts of nosology. In the second edition of the German textbook *Lehrbuch der speziellen Kinder- und Jugendpsychiatrie* (Harbauer, Lempp, Nissen, & Strunk, 1974), Nissen makes the following clinically helpful suggestions about differentiation of autistic disorders. Autistic factors can be manifested in a spectrum ranging from psychogenic autism (autistic reaction) at one pole, through Asperger's Syndrome, Kanner Syndrome, Somatic Autism, Infantile Autism, and Pseudo-Autism.

Nissen hypothesized that the autistic syndromes depend on an autistic hereditary factor that shows itself with different degrees of penetration. This factor results in an autistic psychogenic reaction (a) if psychosocial environmental factors are severe or (b) through

Asperger's Syndrome or Kanner's Syndrome. In children with brain disorders, the same autistic factor could give a somatic form of brain-organic autism. He uses the term *pseudo-autism* for an autistic state without the influence of a hereditary autistic factor, in which autism is found together with other severe handicaps such as mental retardation, deafness, or blindness.

TREATMENT OF CHILDHOOD PSYCHOSIS

During the first decades of this century, no specific treatment was given to children with childhood psychosis. Until the 1930s, these patients were mainly cared for in mental hospitals or in special homes for the mentally retarded. Curative education has been the major approach to children with childhood psychosis since the 1930s. Also, during the past 20 to 30 years, as a consequence of the orientation toward theories originating from psychoanalysis, psychodynamic approaches have had a major influence on the treatment of child psychiatric disorders, including the treatment of childhood psychosis and autistic disorders, in all Nordic countries.

HÄILPAEDAGOGIE (CURATIVE EDUCATION)

In Central Europe, curative education (Hanselmann, 1933) has been used for a long time to treat and take care of children with handicaps. Heller and Asperger, in Vienna (Harbauer et al., 1974; Remschmidt & Schmidt, 1988), suggested Häilpaedagogie to treat children with childhood psychosis. The concept of curative education was also used by Steiner (*Antroposofisk läkepedagogik och socialterapi i Norden,* 1991), who combined Häilpaedagogie with his anthroposophical philosophy. His variant of curative education remains the most important form of treatment of children with autistic disorders, especially in Sweden.

Beginning in 1935, treatment homes based on anthroposophical curative education were established in all the Nordic countries. Today, there are more than 50 such treatment homes. In Sweden, a "center" south of Stockholm has almost 20 independent treatment homes arranged in villages. For the first 15 years of their existence, the activities' main goal was to support mentally handicapped children and youth. Beginning in the 1950s, mentally handicapped adults were also included, because the children who came to these homes tended to stay for their lifetime. Since the 1980's, these anthroposophical "villages" in Järna have become national centers for the treatment of autistic children. Since 1967, the Stockholm County Council has had a special agreement with five of these treatment homes to offer treatment and care to autistic children from the Stockholm area.

In a research report in 1986 (Rydelius, 1986), the patients attending the programs in 4 of the treatment homes, and the treatment they were receiving, were described from a child psychiatric point of view. At that time, 136 children, youth, and adults stayed in these 4 homes. The population investigated consisted of 101 male and 35 female patients ranging from 4 to 62 years. Two-thirds were between 4 and 19 years. Among the youngest, up to the age of 16 years, 15 of 39 boys and 6 of 23 girls met the criteria for the *DSM-III* diagnosis of infantile autism. Two boys and 1 girl had infantile autism, residual state; another 4 boys and 1 girl fulfilled the criteria for childhood onset pervasive disorder. The remaining patients suffered from other disorders and handicaps.

The treatment program in these villages is based on an individual plan for each patient. The programs are evaluated regularly, and they follow the anthroposophical view that children develop in 3 periods of 7 years each, from birth to adulthood, and that different support is needed during each period. In the treatment, the staff must adjust to each patient according to the patient's own capacity. School, occupational therapy, *eurytmi* (a kind of training to support attention, concentration, and motoric control), and other group activities are added to the individual supportive program. With the daily care given on an individual basis, the children seem to function on a maximum personal level. The majority of the patients in the villages were admitted because of severe behavioral symptoms, such as hyperactive/restless/aggressive behavior, or sleeping and eating problems. Their symptoms diminished or disappeared soon after their arrival. If necessary, the patients were treated with anthroposophical pharmacology and/or "ordinary" drugs. Because the staff had very long experience with autistic children (some of them had lived and worked with autistic children for their entire work life), it was interesting to find out that they had learned to predict prognosis in a way that was comparable to the *DSM* system. They said that an early onset of language and a short period of an "autistic echo-speech" indicated a capacity for development.

The majority of the patients in these programs have had lifelong handicaps and are in need of a 24-hour supportive program. However, some have developed rather well and need only day care as adults. A very few can handle their life situation as adults, with only limited support.

The programs of these treatment homes resemble programs in different child psychiatric centers in Europe and in the United States, from psychiatric, psychological, pedagogical, and social points of view. The main differences are the Nordic emphases on anthroposophical treatment. In Sweden, there has been recent criticism concerning the fact that the children staying in these villages are segregated from and will not have influences from normal society. Another major concern is the absence of supportive programs for families.

TWO UNUSUAL AUTISTIC PATIENTS

Members of one village staff were responsible in the 1950s for the care of a 4-year-old girl with an autistic state. She had been carefully investigated by pediatricians and child psychiatrists at the Crown Princess Lovisas' Hospital in Stockholm (the university department for child and adolescent psychiatry at that time), and was given the diagnosis of early infantile autism (Kanner's Syndrome). Expressive aphasia also had been discussed as a possible differential diagnosis, but the clinical picture was better captured by Kanner's Syndrome. The girl started to speak at age 6 years. She successively improved and could attend normal school. In her teen years, she had individual psychotherapy. When the research report was done, she was married and working, but had no children. A retrospective review of her file (by myself, in 1984) revealed that the clinical picture in the 1950s fulfilled the *DSM-III* criteria for Infantile Autism. So far, no other child coming to these treatment homes has had such a good development.

Sweden's oldest known individual with an autistic disorder lives at one of the treatment homes. In the middle of the 1930s at the age of 12 years, he was admitted to the Mikaelgården, the oldest of the Swedish anthroposophical treatment homes. As he grew older, he became the first patient who needed a program for autistic adults, and he has stayed in this program for his whole life. He is still living there, but now is considered "retired." This individual was born in 1923 into a very wealthy and capable family. He had a late development of language, developed "echo-speech" when he was around 3 years of age, and could, at the age of 4 years, say words but could not communicate. As a preschooler (in Sweden until 7 years of age), he had temper outbursts and stereotyped behavior. He was impulsive and played monotonously and alone, even if other children were there. He was placed in a Montessori kindergarten, but had to be taken out of the group. Although he could not communicate through language, he learned poems by heart and could read before the age of 7 years. In 1929, at the age of 6 and after an examination at the pediatric university department in Stockholm, he was given the diagnosis of Dementia Praecox. He was admitted to a hospital for the mentally retarded, and then went to Beckomberga, a newly built mental hospital in Stockholm, for one year before he came to the treatment home. For his whole life, he has had stereotyped behavior, rituals, and severely disturbed language without communicative skills. As a child, he walked on tiptoe. During his 20s, he showed strong emotional affection for one staff member, but after some time he again lost interest in other persons. He has had a tendency toward anxiety paroxysms all his life, and is especially afraid of certain noises. Yet he has always been interested in music and, even as a child, he could listen in a very concentrated fashion and "be absorbed" by classical music. Over the years, he showed mood changes. Periods of very passive behavior were

interspersed with periods of aggressive outbursts with impulsive behavior and self-damaging incidents. As an adult, his behavior has raised suspicions of hallucinations, and he has been treated with phenothiazines and lithium. His neurological status is normal, without epileptic seizures, and his cognitive level in the 1970s was severe mental retardation.

From a clinical point of view, he fulfilled the criteria for Infantile Autism as a child and those for Childhood Onset Pervasive Developmental Disorder (according to *DSM-III*) later on. Today, he presents a "schizophrenic autistic" impression. His behavior has been slightly improved by medication. In retrospect, it is hard to say whether this has been the life history of a child with a severe form of an autistic disorder or whether this child had an early form of schizophrenia and the diagnosis of Dementia Praecox, in 1929, when he was 6 years old, was correct. The information given by the now deceased head of the treatment home where he has spent his life—someone who knew him from the 1930s—favors the diagnosis of Infantile Autism.

This patient still lives at the same treatment home where he was admitted in the early 1940s. When he became 67, the age of retirement in Sweden, he too became aware of his "new status" and adjusted himself and his habits to gentler activities.

TREATMENT PROGRAMS BASED ON A PSYCHODYNAMIC APPROACH

In the 1960s, when the shift toward a psychodynamic view on child psychiatric problems had been firmly established in clinical practice in the Nordic countries, the treatment of childhood psychosis was also influenced by these views. Although the emphasis was on habilitation and not on cure, strong influences came from Bettelheim's view on Infantile Autism and from Mahler's theory of separation-individuation (Bettelheim, 1967; Mahler, 1952, 1955). In Stockholm, a psychoanalytically based treatment program was offered at the Ericastiftelsen (a private foundation instituted in 1934 for Häilpaedagogie and child and adolescent psychiatric treatment; today, it is also a training-institute for psychotherapy) between 1976 and 1981. As part of this program, there was a scientifically based evaluation of Mahler's model of development, recently presented as a doctoral dissertation in psychology. A comparison of normal preschool children and children with severely disturbed development (including autistic disorders) could not confirm Mahler's model of development. However, Mahler's theory, used in a dimensional model, was found to be of interest when studying and assessing children's development during psychotherapy (Elwin, 1994).

CURRENT TREATMENT

Since the 1980s, alternatives to curative education and to the psychodynamic approaches have been successively developed. From studies in different parts of Sweden (Bohman, Bohman, & Sjöholm-Lif, 1988; Gillberg, 1994; Magnusson, Rydell, & Dahlin, 1975) and in the other Nordic countries (Sommerschild & Grøholt, 1989), habilitation programs have been based on early diagnosis, support for the families, pedagogically based day care programs for the children, and education in special classes. The treatment programs today are similar to those given in other countries, and are influenced by the current British and American views on autistic disorders. In a way, they are similar to the programs given at the anthroposophical curative education treatment homes, especially in their pedagogical aspects. The major differences are: (a) the children are more integrated in the normal society and (b) support to the parents and families is emphasized. National parent societies have been established in Sweden since 1973, and have been very important in the development of better services for autistic children and their parents.

REFERENCES

Annell, A.-L. (1958). *Elementär barnpsykiatri.* Stockholm: Norstedts.

Antroposofisk läkepedagogik och socialterapi i Norden. (1991). Södertälje: Telleby bokförlag.

Benjamin, E., Hanselmann, H., Isserlin, M., Lutz, J. & Ronald, A. (1938). *Lehrbuch der Psychopathologie des Kindesalters für Ärzte und Erzieher.* Erlenbach-Zürich und Leipzig: Rotapfel-Verlag.

Bettelheim, B. (1967). *The empty fortress—Infantile autism and the birth of the self.* New York: Free Press, Collier-Macmillan.

Bohman, M., Bohman, I.-L., & Sjöholm-Lif, E. (1988). *Barndomspsykos—Att känna igen, förstå och behandla.* Stockholm: Almqvist & Wiksell.

Elwin, B. (1994). *Separation-individuation according to Mahler. Empirical studies of normal and pathological development in early childhood.* Doctoral dissertation, Stockholm University, Dept. of Psychology. Akademitryck AB, Edsburk.

Gillberg, C. (1994). *Autism och autismliknande tillstånd hos barn, ungdomar och vuxna* (2nd ed.). Stockholm: Natur & Kultur.

Hannesdóttir, H. (1993). Child and adolescent psychiatry in Iceland—The state of the art, past, present, and future. *Nordic Journal of Psychiatry, 47*(1), 9–13. Oslo: Scandinavian University Press.

Hanselmann, H. (1933). *Einführung in die Heilpädagogik.* Erlenbach-Zürich und Leipzig: Rotapfel-Verlag.

Harbauer, H., Lempp, R., Nissen, G., & Strunk, P. (1974). *Lehrbuch der speciellen Kinder- und Jugendpsychiatrie.* Heidelberg: Springer-Verlag.

Jundell, I. (1915). *Broken minds.* Stockholm: Barnens Dagblad.

Kanner, L. (1948). *Child psychiatry.* Springfield, IL: Charles C Thomas.

Key, E. (1909). *The century of the child.* London: G.P. Putnam's Sons.

Magnusson, K., Rydell, A.-M., & Dahlin, G. (1975). *Autism hos barn. Teorier, vård och behandling.* Stockholm: Natur & Kultur.

Mahler, M. (1952). On child psychosis and schizophrenia: Autistic and symbiotic infantiel psychosis. *The Psychoanalytic Study of the Child, 7,* 286–305. New York: International Universities Press.

Mahler, M. (1955). On the symbiotic child psychosis: Genetic, dynamic and restitutive aspects. *Psychoanalytical Study of the Child, 10,* 195–211.

Piha, J., & Almqvist, F. (1994). Child psychiatry as an academic and clinical discipline in Finland. *Nordic Journal of Psychiatry, 48*(1), 3–8. Oslo: Scandinavian University Press.

Remschmidt, H., & Schmidt, M. (1988). *Kinder- und Jugendpsychiatrie in Klinik und Praxis. In drei Bänden.* Stuttgart: Georg Thieme Verlag.

Rydelius, P.-A. (1986). *Barn, ungdomar och vuxna vid fyra läkepedagogiska behandlingshem i Järna.* Stockholm: Karolinska Institutet, Institutionen för barn- och ungdomspsykiatri, Forskningsrapport Nr: 5, ISSN 1103–0887.

Rydelius, P.-A. (1993). Child and adolescent psychiatry in Sweden—from yesterday until today. *Nordic Journal of Psychiatry, 47*(6), 395–404. Oslo: Scandinavian University Press.

Smedegaard, N., Hansen, N., & Isager, T. (1993). Danish child psychiatry—Past, present, future. *Nordic Journal of Psychiatry, 47*(2), 75–79. Oslo: Scandinavian University Press.

Sommerschild, H., & Grøholt, B. (1989). *Laërebok i barnepsykiatri.* Tano.

Vandvik, I.H., & Spurkland, I. (1993). Child and adolescent psychiatry in Norway—Today and tomorrow. *Nordic Journal of Psychiatry, 47*(3), 155–160. Oslo: Scandinavian University Press.

Tramer, M. (1942). *Lehrbuch der allgemeinen Kinderpsychiatrie—einschliesslich der allgemeinen Psychiatrie der Pubertät und Adoleszenz.* Basel: Benno Schwabe & Co Verlag.

THE UNITED KINGDOM

Richard Mills and Lorna Wing

INTRODUCTION OF THE DIAGNOSTIC CONCEPT

In the 1940s and 1950s, interest in autism in the United Kingdom (UK) was limited. Autism was generally considered to be a manifestation of early-onset schizophrenia (Cameron, 1955). Changes in the diagnostic concept and acceleration in the growth of interest can be dated from the beginning of the 1960s, when two separate influential events occurred. First, Creak (1961, 1964) chaired a working party of professionals in the field of child psychiatry. The ostensible aim of the project was to clarify the use of the term *psychosis* in childhood. The members chose the term *schizophrenic syndrome of childhood.* The diagnostic criteria they produced, known as the Nine Points, listed the major features of what are now known as autistic spectrum conditions. Despite this confusion over terminology, the Nine Points represented the first attempt to introduce operational criteria for autistic disorders.

Second, a group of parents of children with autism decided, in 1962, to form an association. The group has evolved into the British National Autistic Society, has both parent and professional members, and is concerned with adults as well as children. The structure now comprises the National Society and a large number of local autistic societies, almost all of which are associated with the National Society.

In the 1960s, the events described above took place against a backdrop of the struggle between those professionals who accepted and those who rejected the diagnostic concept of autism. A common belief among professionals at that time was that autism was a middle-class euphemism for mental retardation. The newly formed Society had to battle against this prejudice.

The concept of autism began to acquire scientific respectability with the publication of well-designed research in the field. One of these studies in the UK was the epidemiological work of Lotter (1966, 1967), which identified children with typical autism. Wing and Gould (1979) carried out another epidemiological study and introduced the concept of a wider spectrum of autistic disorders, which have in common a triad of impairments of social interaction, communication, and imagination, and a repetitive pattern of activities. Twelve years later, Wing (1981) published an account of the syndrome originally described by and named after Asperger (1944; translated by Frith, 1991). This expanded even more the concept of an autistic spectrum. Ehlers and Gillberg (1993) carried out the first epidemiological study of this syndrome. Other aspects of research were the clarification of the clinical picture of typical childhood autism, and a follow-up into adolescence and early adult life (Rutter, 1968, 1970, 1978).

Despite the volume of publications in the field from the 1960s to the present, the level of awareness within the general professional community remains low. A recently published evaluation of community care services (Baldwin & Hattersley, 1991) contains no reference to autism.

CARE OF INDIVIDUALS WITH AUTISTIC DISORDERS

Before the 1960s, there were no services specifically for people with autism. Probably the single most commonly used residential placements were the long-stay institutions for the mentally retarded. The "treatments" varied from psychoanalysis to Electro-Convulsive Therapy (ECT), depending on the belief systems of the therapists involved. However, the only methods that have been subject to controlled investigation are: (a) structured education (Bartak & Rutter, 1971; Rutter & Bartak, 1973) and (b) behavior management based on behavioral techniques (Howlin & Rutter, 1987).

Well before the Bartak and Rutter studies of education, some teachers had found, through intuition and trial-and-error, methods that were helpful for children with autistic disorders. The members of the parents' association were more impressed by the results of education than by those of any other approaches. From the outset, they had decided to use all their resources for setting up specialized schools. In 1964, the National Autism Society started the first school for children with autistic disorders. One of the major problems in the early years was that children with severe learning disabilities or disruptive behavior could be excluded from education. Parents struggled to persuade the education authorities that their children should be funded to attend a special school. In 1970, in England and Wales, an Act of Parliament established the right of all children to education in schools. Scotland and Northern Ireland passed similar laws later. More schools (with day care and/or residential places) and some special classes were set up following the success of the first school. Most schools are run by the national or local autistic societies, but some are sponsored by other voluntary or private bodies or by local education authorities.

In the early 1970s, a team of workers at the Institute of Psychiatry began to develop a program in which parents were helped, through advice and guidance in their own homes, to improve their management strategies by using behavioral methods in a flexible way (Howlin et al., 1973). This started as a research project but is now carried on as a clinical service within the National Health Service (Howlin & Rutter, 1987). The service is much appreciated by parents but has been copied in very few other areas of the country.

After some years, it became apparent that many children with autistic disorders would never become independent, so efforts to develop services for adults were begun. The first adult residential community was started in 1974. Other specialized residential and day services have followed; almost all of them are set up and run by the national or local autistic societies.

CURRENT STATUS OF TREATMENT SERVICES

Currently in the UK, the only treatments dedicated to autistic disorders are: the specialized schools and adult centers; the home-based service described above; a very few therapeutic groups run for more able adolescents or adults; and a newly begun National Society scheme to organize supported employment for those able to benefit. There are no schemes for early intervention, apart from some preschool units for children with all kinds of language problems. The national and local autistic societies arrange parent support groups, meetings and weekend courses for parents and professional workers, and various other social or educational activities. Overall, despite the success of the specialized service, they provide for only a tiny proportion of children and adults with autistic disorders. Most are cared for within the generic education, health, or social services, although such places have a hard struggle to provide a suitable environment for those with autistic disorders, even if their special needs are recognized. The generic psychiatric services in hospitals or outpatient clinics provide most of the advice on behavior management and medication. Only a minority of the professionals involved have any knowledge of or interest in autistic disorders. There are no specialized services for the adolescents or adults who develop superimposed psychiatric illnesses that can occur in adolescence or adult life. The generic adult psychiatric hospitals and clinics have to be used and are often not equipped to cope.

The first residential centers for adults were for groups of 20 or more residents in large houses with large grounds. Currently, the national and local autistic societies are working in conjunction with housing associations to develop small group homes or individual apartments with staff supervision. These have proved beneficial for more able individuals with autistic disorders, including Asperger's Syndrome. However, the larger homes in their own grounds are still needed for many adults with more marked levels of disability and behavior disturbance. A range of community services catering to a spectrum of needs is still awaited (Landesman-Dwyer, 1981).

There are some advantages, for some people, from the emphasis on community-based approaches, but one unfortunate result has been that relatives are placed in the front line of care for individuals with highly complex needs, many of whom require intensive specialist resources that are rarely available. The development of community-based services for individuals with severe behavioral disorders has posed a particular challenge. Evaluation of some of these services, notably by the Special Development Team at the University of Kent, has demonstrated the high cost and scarcity of such provision (Emerson, McGill, & Mansell, 1994). There has been growing awareness of autistic disorders in the forensic field. Offenders with such conditions were specifically mentioned for the first time in a major policy review of services by Reed (1994). The National Autistic Society has recently collaborated with the Special Hospitals Authority (the government agency responsible for secure provision for mentally disordered offenders) in organizing a conference to raise awareness among the staff of the Special Hospitals. The National Society is soon to open a unit for adults with autistic disorders who need a secure placement, and is working closely with the authorities involved in this field.

As already mentioned, those who started the original parents' association were firm in their belief that structured education was the most important way of helping their children. In recent years, as it has become clear that autistic disorders have lifelong effects, a number of different approaches that have promised either cures or remarkable improvements have appealed to some parents who want to pursue any line that offers hope. These include holding therapy, facilitated communication, auditory integration training, the options method, and treatment with various medications. None of the claims made has been validated by properly controlled research. So far, the British,

with their typical caution, have tended to show less uncritical enthusiasm for these treatments than has been seen in some other countries.

Over the past 3 years, in addition to the long recognized emphasis on structure, consistency, reduction of disturbing stimuli, and a high degree of organization, the approach in the National Autistic Society schools and adult centers has concentrated on specific programs to overcome or reduce the effects of the impairments of imagination, communication, and social skills that underlie autistic behavior (Wing & Gould, 1979). This has proved helpful because it provides a clear framework for the staff working with children and adults.

PROBLEMS OF DIAGNOSIS

In 1962, when the parents' association was formed, few people had heard of autism. Now, as a result of the efforts of the national and local autistic societies and the popularity of the film *Rain Man,* almost everyone has. Despite this change, parents still often have major difficulties in obtaining a diagnosis, and many children and adults remain undiagnosed, especially those with Asperger's Syndrome or variants other than typical autism. Many different pathways are followed by children with autistic disorders, depending on the type and severity of their condition and the degree of their mental retardation. They may be referred at any age to pediatric, psychiatric, educational, or social service professionals. Recognition of the autistic disorder depends on the depth of interest, and experience in the field, of the professional concerned. Before they learned the truth, many parents have had years of struggle and distress in which they were made to feel that they had caused their child's behavior. There is some evidence of a positive reluctance in some quarters to recognize autism as a clinical condition requiring a specialized approach, possibly because of the financial implications of the services concerned.

In the early 1990s, in response to the parents' problems in obtaining diagnoses, the National Society set up the Center for Social and Communication Disorders in Bromley. Its function is to make detailed diagnostic assessments and give advice on service needs. Individuals of all ages are seen. Three other centers specializing in the diagnosis of autistic disorders are located in Radlett, Southampton, and Nottingham, respectively. They see children but not adults. A few child psychiatric clinics, such as that at the Maudsley Hospital, have a special interest in autism but see other childhood psychiatric conditions as well.

NATIONAL POLICIES

In recent years, changes in government policies on health, education, social welfare, and economics have had some positive but many negative effects on services for people with autistic disorders. The importance of early assessment and diagnosis and of education appropriate for the needs of children with disabilities has been emphasized in legislation, but cuts in local government funding have militated against the implementation of these ideals. This is especially true for children with autistic disorders who have expensive needs.

A further complication has been government support for integrating children with disabilities in mainstream schools. This works for some children with autistic disorders but has been detrimental for many more. One piece of evidence for this is the growing number of referrals to the special schools of children who have failed in mainstream, including more able children with Asperger's Syndrome, whose social difficulties set them apart from their peers.

Similar pressures have affected the services for adults. The normalization philosophy (Wolfensberger, 1972; Wolfensberger & Thomas, 1983), coupled with rising costs, resulted in government agendas to close institutions. Community-based services for more able individuals who were the first to be moved out of the institutions worked well and were economical in cost. However, this policy has resulted in major problems for people with autistic disorders and disturbed behavior. The change of environment and the lack of a structured routine were more than they could cope with (Wing, 1989). The eventual costs were much higher than anticipated.

On the positive side, the Department of Health has supported initiatives in the field of autistic disorders, including an evaluation of the effects of legislation on services for children and adults with these conditions. The Department has also helped finance the accreditation process piloted by the National Autistic Society to develop, demonstrate, and disseminate models of good practice within specialist and other services catering to individuals with autistic disorders.

SERVICES OVER THE LIFE SPAN

From this account, it can be seen that all types of services for individuals with autistic disorders, from diagnosis onward, are patchily distributed. They vary widely throughout the country, being excellent in a few places and virtually nonexistent elsewhere. Children with special needs have a statutory right to education from 5 to 19 years, but no legal right to preschool or adult services.

The crisis points for parents are, first, when their child approaches school age. They usually have to battle to obtain the type of education they believe is needed, and they may not succeed. Some parents have moved their household to an area where there is a special school. The second crisis is at the school-leaving age, when the battle for appropriate services, day or residential, begins all over again. Even for the most able group, there are many difficulties upon entering adult life. The National Autistic Society and its affiliated network of local autism societies continues to expand and develop specialist provision. Despite their efforts, the great majority of individuals are not given specialist help but are fitted into whatever services are available in their local area, have room, and are willing to keep them. People with autistic disorders are to be found in schools, hostels, hospitals, day centers, lodging houses for the homeless, and, unfortunately, living on the streets. The precise numbers in these different settings are unknown. Even so, children and adults with autistic disorders are more likely to find some kind of help in a country like the UK, which still preserves some aspect of the welfare state, than in countries with no similar provision. How the situation will evolve in the uncertain future is impossible to predict.

REFERENCES

Asperger, H. (1944). Die "autistischen psychopathen" im kindersalter. *Archives fur psychiatrie und Nervenkrankheiten, 117,* 76–136.

Baldwin, S., & Hattersley, J. (Eds.). (1991). *Mental handicap: Social science perspectives*. London: Tavistock/Routledge.

Bartak, L., & Rutter, M. (1971). Education treatment of autistic children. In M. Rutter (Ed.), *Infantile autism: Concepts, characteristics and treatment*. London: Churchill.

Cameron, K. (1955, September). Psychosis in infancy and early childhood. *The Medical Press,* 280–283.

Creak, E.M. (Chairman). (1961, April). Schizophrenic syndrome in childhood: Progress report of a working party. *Cerebral Palsy Bulletin, 3,* 501–504.

Creak, E.M. (1964, April). Schizophrenic syndrome in childhood: Further progress report of a working party. *Developmental Medicine and Child Neurology, 6,* 530–535.

Ehlers, S., & Gillberg, C. (1993). The epidemiology of Asperger Syndrome. A total population study. *Journal of Child Psychology and Psychiatry, 34,* 1327–1350.

Emerson, E., McGill, P., & Mansell, J. (Eds.). (1994). *Severe learning disabilities and challenging behaviours: Designing high quality services*. Chapman and Hall.

Frith, U. (1991). Asperger and his syndrome. In U. Frith (Ed.), *Autism and Asperger syndrome*. Cambridge, England: Cambridge University Press.

Howlin, P., Marchant, R., Rutter, M., Berger, M., Hersov, L., & Yule, W. (1973). A home-based approach to the treatment of autistic children. *Journal of Autism and Childhood Schizophrenia, 4,* 308–336.

Howlin, P., & Rutter, M. (1987). *Treatment of autistic children*. New York: John Wiley & Sons.

Kanner, L. (1943). Autistic disturbances of affective contact. *Nervous Child, 2,* 217–250.

Landesman-Dwyer, S. (1981). Living in the community. *American Journal of Mental Deficiency, 86*(3), 223–234.

Lotter, V. (1966). Epidemiology of autistic conditions in young children: 1. Prevalence. *Social Psychiatry, 1,* 124–137.

Lotter, V. (1967). Epidemiology of autistic conditions in young children: 2. Some characteristics of the parents and children. *Social Psychiatry, 1,* 163–173.

Reed, J. (Chairman). (1994). People with learning disabilities (mental handicap) or with autism. In *Review of health and social services for mentally disordered attendees and others requiring similar services* (Vol. 17). London: H.M.S.O.

Rutter, M. (1968). Concepts of autism: A review of research. *Journal of Psychology and Psychiatry, 9,* 1–25.

Rutter, M. (1970). Autistic children: Infancy to adulthood. *Seminars in Psychiatry, 2,* 435–450.

Rutter, M. (1978). Diagnosis and definition. In M. Rutter & E. Schopler (Eds.), *Autism: A reappraisal of concepts and treatment* (pp. 1–26). New York: Plenum Press.

Rutter, M., & Bartak, L. (1973). Special educational treatment of autistic children: A comparative study. 11. Follow-up findings and implications for services. *Journal of Child Psychology and Psychiatry, 14,* 241–270.

Wing, L. (1981). Asperger's Syndrome: A clinical account. *Psychological Medicine, 11,* 115–130.

Wing, L. (1989). *Hospital closure and the effects on the residents*. Aldershot: Avebury.

Wing, L., & Gould, J. (1979). Severe impairments of social interaction and associated abnormalities in children: Epidemiology and classification. *Journal of Autism and Childhood Schizophrenia, 9,* 11–29.

Wolfensberger, W. (1972). *The principle of normalization in human services*. Toronto, Ontario, Canada: NIMR.

Wolfensberger, W., & Thomas. (1983). *Programme analysis of service systems implementation of normalization goals*. Toronto, Ontario, Canada: NIMR.

Personal Perspectives

Clinicians and researchers have a great deal to contribute to the understanding and care of individuals with autism. Yet, the authentic voice of individuals who have lived with autism has an unmistakable authority. The descriptions provided by individuals with autism, and by their families and teachers, convey the full meaning of the disorder as a way of being in the world and the impact of the disorder on all who care about and live with an autistic person. These descriptions are also the source of rich understanding of how the various domains and dimensions of the disorder come together in a full person.

The autistic individual is cut off from others, even those who are closest, in a fundamental way. Fortunately, some autistic individuals have the capacity to express their sense of being different or "other," their unique modes of experiencing sounds and sights, how they navigate through the social world, and their attempts to communicate their thoughts and worries to others. From these descriptions, we can cautiously try to extrapolate to the dilemmas of those who are less able to communicate—the retarded and behaviorally disordered autistic individuals who remain far more detached from ordinary social intercourse.

Being the parent of an autistic child is almost always felt as a terrible, indeed crushing, burden. What can be more painful than recognizing that one's sweet infant will never fully reciprocate the love bestowed on him? That he will never fully experience the pleasures of life? That his life, and one's own, will forever be shaped by the crises and challenges of a handicapping condition? Advocates, today, rightly emphasize the strides that have been made in supporting parents during the crisis of diagnosis and those first years of uncertainty about prognosis. Yet, can anyone diminish the pain of young parents at the birth of a child with multiple defects, or erase from memory the grief that surrounds the results of tests that reveal a brain lesion, cancer, or abnormal chromosomes? The recognition that one's child has autism is deeply painful; it is the kind of pain that extended families and clinicians can only in part share.

During the 1960s, parents joined together with clinicians to form a national parents' advocacy organization in the United States. During the 1970s and 1980s, similar organizations were created in other countries. These parent advocacy organizations have had tremendous impact. Parents have organized, sponsored, and supported schools and other treatment programs; have challenged laws and helped to enact new legislation and regulations; and have encouraged and facilitated research. They have supported each other, disseminated knowledge, and helped to overcome the feeling of isolation that accompanies personal tragedy. By becoming active, they have also helped reduce their sense of being passive victims of forces completely beyond their control.

Having a sibling with autism is unfair. An autistic sibling becomes the focal point of family life and drains the parents' energies, finances, and time. It is often difficult to bring friends home, and parents may have little surplus energy for outings or activities with the normal child. A normal sibling, younger or older, is often recruited into being the parents' helper, at substantial personal expense. The childhood years, especially, may be prematurely terminated or truncated. It is especially difficult when an autistic sibling is self-injurious, aggressive, or destructive.

Remarkably, many siblings of autistic and similar children rise to the challenge and eventually take pride in their abilities to understand and help their brother or sister. Others remain angry and feel that they were cheated of their childhood. Perhaps most siblings are in between. They recognize that they have been deepened and made more sensitive by growing up with a handicapped sibling; they also are aware of how their family life and childhood was adversely affected. Having the testimonies of siblings is quite helpful in providing guidance to families about coping with an autistic child and appreciating the needs and individual differences among family members.

There are teachers who have devoted their entire professional lives to trying to bring out the capabilities of autistic individuals and to collaborating with and supporting parents. Some of these teachers have worked for decades with autistic individuals. They have experimented with theories and methods in devising their own approaches. The best, most devoted teachers can almost read the minds of their autistic students. They interpret small changes in behavior and expression; and they know how to maintain limits and provide structure while satisfying the child's needs for emotional contact and security. Those who have worked with autistic children in the classroom also have the most detailed knowledge of what they actually can do, including the surprising exceptions to the rule, those episodes that reveal another facet of the child. Older teachers also have the advantage of a longitudinal perspective: they know what children can achieve, they can take a balanced view of today's crisis, and they can convey the variations in natural history to others.

The following chapters capture the voices of those who have lived with autism—individuals with autism themselves, who are now speaking out; parents and siblings; and devoted teachers. Listen to them well.

CHAPTER 47

Diagnosis Autism: You Can Handle It!

RUTH CHRIST SULLIVAN

Unlike newborns and young babies with obvious handicaps, those with autism usually appear physically intact and indeed are often strikingly handsome children. As far as you or your doctor can tell, you have the normal, healthy baby you hoped and prayed for.

In looking back, after the diagnosis, you may remember that he[1] may have been slightly jaundiced, did not nurse well, and seemed to not want to be held, but nothing was significant enough to give you a clue about what was in store for you and your child.

In autism, the realization that your child is not developing right usually comes gradually. Unless you are well versed in the early signs of the syndrome (or were fortunate enough, in those early days, to meet a professional or someone who knew autism), the signs are easily overlooked. For instance, you may be concerned that your baby seems happiest when left alone, or does not reach out to be picked up, or stiffens when you hold him, or rocks very hard in his bed, or seems not to want to make eye contact, or bangs his head, or screams through the night for no known reason, or is eerily absorbed with visual stimuli such as a dust ball, or prefers objects to you. He seems to not hear, and you suspect deafness. All of these signs can be explained away. You tell yourself he's just a good baby, exploring his environment. But you begin to be uneasy about the accumulation of odd behaviors.

They are subtle and you may be unsure of your observations. Your family, your neighbors, or your doctor may dismiss your worries with, "He'll grow out of it; you're just an overanxious parent."

He is likely to reach his motor milestones right on schedule, or may even be precocious in his physical skills—such as sitting up or walking early—but as the months roll on, your uneasiness turns into real concern. Once you get professionals to listen and take you seriously, they are likely to suggest autism. Not all. There are still plenty who are not yet well enough informed to recognize the early manifestations of the syndrome. They may put you off, maybe even suggesting you're too "uptight" about your child.

Finally, the nagging suspicion that something is not right, combined with the reality of what you are seeing makes you take action to find out what's going on. Your child may have begun to talk—even talk unusually well—at one year, but stops at about 18 months. He won't cuddle and begins to disappear from the household. He doesn't seem to enjoy the company of others, preferring to be alone. He's probably hyperactive. His tantrum behavior increases. It's embarrassing to take him out because you have so little control of his behavior. He gets into things and is destructive. Your house is a wreck. As he approaches age 2 or 3 years, he might hurt babies or small animals. He seems out of control.

At this point, you are desperate for help.

Eventually, you get a name for what's wrong. If the professional doing the diagnosing knows a great deal about autism, the label will

---

[1] Because there is not a good pronoun for both "he" and "she," and because three out of four persons with autism are male, I use "he" to mean male or female.

probably be "autism." If the professional is not knowledgeable about the subject, the diagnosis will probably be "autistic-like" or "pervasive developmental disorder" (PDD). Whichever way you hear it, at least you'll have a label to work with and you'll know that what is wrong has a name. It's not just your imagination.

Many professionals are extremely reluctant to tell parents that their child is or may be autistic. They know autism is a severe disorder, still poorly understood, which brings with it a relatively poor prognosis—unless there is help. Only a few of the professionals know how to give significant help beyond a diagnosis.

But the label brings you to some help sooner. Most pediatricians, psychiatrists, psychologists, or speech and hearing professionals (those most likely to see your young child at this stage) now can refer you to parent groups, like the Autism Society of America (ASA) and its state and local chapters.[2]

The sooner you meet other parents, the better. It is comforting to know that others have been through what you're now experiencing and have survived. They will know your grief and frustrations. They will help you through the early tasks of finding understanding and knowledgeable service providers, such as pediatricians, barbers, and dentists. (The first time I brought my son in to have his teeth checked, the family dentist reacted as though I'd put a rattlesnake in his chair.) The veteran parents you meet will be able to talk with you about what worked for them, and what didn't. You'll probably be interested in speaking to those whose child is most like yours. A collection of these parents is almost always an excellent accumulation of practical wisdom. The storytelling alone is worth the effort spent getting to a meeting.

And the humor!

At an NSAC annual meeting in the early 1970s, I was standing on a street corner with a group of parents, waiting for a shuttle bus to take us across the university campus. We were exchanging funny stories about our autistic children and the laughter convulsed us all. A young man stood with us, a little aside, clearly

not feeling as though he "belonged." Soon he was listening to each story and joining in the merriment. Later, sitting on the bus beside me, he told me he was a psychologist. He confided that this was his first autism conference and he had only reluctantly decided to attend. He said he had assumed a gathering of parents of these children would be too gloomy for him to bear.

For several years, in the 1970s, I edited a monthly publication called *Gleanings,* in which I included a "Bittersweet" with each issue. Those were little stories written by parents who briefly chronicled some of their extraordinary, mostly very funny, experiences with their autistic child. The vignettes poured in and I was never at a loss for one for each issue. Here are two of my favorites.

This one came from Debra Price, at that time president, Concho Valley Chapter of NSAC, San Angelo, Texas. Her autistic son, Kit, was then 13.

Kit has always been a runner and a climber. One day when he was just under 18 months old, while we were living in an apartment building with a large backyard with no fence, I was hanging out clothes with Kit in his harness locked to the clothesline pole as usual. When I went back into the apartment for some more clothespins, Kit somehow wriggled out of his harness and I returned to find him running across the yard, heading for a very large tree in the opposite corner. I immediately ran after him, but by the time I reached the tree, Kit was climbing fast. In a few seconds he reached the top of the tree, where he proceeded to shed his diaper and shirt and drop them to the ground. Kit has always been, and in fact still is, a nudist at heart. I stood there for a few minutes, very pregnant with my second child, and unable to climb after Kit. There was no one home in the building at that time of day who could climb up and get him, so I called the fire department. They arrived a few minutes later, glanced at me on the ground, looked up at Kit in the top of the tree happily contemplating a leaf in his birthday suit, and one of them accusingly said to me, "Who put that baby in the tree?" Although I assured them that baby put himself in the tree, it was obvious that they found it hard to believe. I often wonder what they put in their report when they got back to the station house.

The following is my own story:

It was confirmation day at our parish chapel on the university campus. The church was full of proud relatives and happy new "soldiers of Christ." The visiting

[2] Until July 1987, ASA was known as NSAC, the National Society for Autistic Children.

white-haired bishop was elegant in his brilliant red episcopal robe. The congregation filed out slowly so each could shake the bishop's hand and exchange a pleasantry. We were among the last of the crowd and as our turn came nearer, I could see that our 16-year-old autistic son, Joseph, was excited. Finally, able to wait no longer, he stretched his arm past three persons, shook the bishop's hand, and said in his happy voice, "French toast!" What the startled prelate didn't know is that eating French toast is one of Joseph's greatest pleasures. He probably felt the "vibes" of the occasion and decided that to be an appropriate comment.

Two little volumes of such parent-written stories came out recently (Gilpin, 1993, 1994) and are fun to read.

Autism is no laughing matter, of course, but other parents can help you get some perspective on how you and your special child fit into the larger scheme of things. You will probably have your own collection of stories by the time you read this.

EMOTIONAL REACTIONS TO THE DIAGNOSIS OF AUTISM

If you know what autism is before you receive a diagnosis, you are likely to have thought of it long before you presented your child for a label. Quite possibly, you'll even be relieved that someone else has corroborated what you already suspected, even though it confirms your worst fears. Professionals are sometimes surprised at this relief, and may even mistake it in a parent as insensitivity—or refer to you as "aloof" in their notes.

If you hear the word "autism" for the first time at diagnosis, you may not have the slightest notion of the severity of the disorder. In my case, upon questioning the psychiatrist, he said only, "He'll be a little odd." Joseph was not yet 3 years old at the time, and I already knew he was "a little odd." I can live with "odd," I remember thinking at the time. Little did I know the meaning of the "odd" I was to later experience. This was 1963 and I was given no literature to read. (Truthfully, there was very little available at the time.) I was referred, however, to an article by "a Dr. Leo Kanner." And so my education began.

Today, you will most likely get literature in the diagnostician's office or a referral to some

information, or to a group or person. Your local library is likely to have *something*—probably outdated, but at least a starting point.

Autism Services Center, the agency I founded in 1979 and currently direct, often gets calls from parents who have just been told their child is autistic. We send pertinent information and try to link callers to parents in their locality. It is not unusual to get letters or calls later saying they spent hours on the phone (sometimes long-distance) talking to that first other parent.

Whichever way you learn it, once you understand the gravity of the diagnosis, you are likely to be stunned, shocked, and even unbelieving. You thought you were prepared to deal with whatever you were told. After all, you've been seeing this strange, even bizarre, behavior for months, maybe years, before you got a word for it. But, you'll think, disorders, handicaps, severe illnesses happen to other people's children, not mine.

You had probably not thought much about your baby's future, except that he would of course grow up to be a pride and joy to his parents. All of a sudden, those years ahead are dark, unknown, ominous, troublesome. Your parenthood is not going to be like everyone else's. Will you have the strength, the support of your spouse, your family?

If you are the mother (and if you are reading this, you probably are—mothers are more likely than fathers to read "how-to" books on parenting), you may wonder about returning to or pursuing the career you had planned "after the children are in school." You may think, "What about my and my husband's old age? Will we be caring for a severely handicapped adult all of our 'golden' years? Will we never be free of the care of our eternal child? Who will care for him after we're gone? What will my parents/brothers/sisters/aunts/uncles/friends/colleagues/neighbors think? Will my other children be embarrassed to bring friends home? How will they feel about having children of their own?"

You will probably feel grief for the child you lost—the one who would have graduated from Harvard and gone on to be a U.S. senator. All the hopes and dreams for a good life for your precious baby are now dashed. A cruel fate has moved in on his future.

You may feel resentment. If your child had died, or had a life-threatening illness, or was in a terrible accident, your grief would be shared lovingly by many. You would get cards of sympathy, special caring treatment, gifts of food, offers of help. But the news about your child's autism does not get announced in the local paper. There is no gathering of family and friends at which your pastor solemnly announces the diagnosis, or formally asks for prayers. The news sits heavy on your shoulders, and it's up to you to decide how and when, or even *if,* you announce it.

Some parents find themselves being resentful of parents of normal children who complain about their child's diaper rash or turned-in foot. "Get real," you want to say. "You don't know what a problem *is.*" You may resent these parents' seeming to be cavalier about their children, taking them so much for granted.

Some parents get angry at and blame God— "Why us?" or "How could You do this to us?"—and stop going to church.

The time of reckoning can strain marital relationships. The more nurturing partner may experience diminished or no support from the other partner. Anger or withdrawal, or both, might result in friction and distancing of the couple. The articulate one wants to talk. The quiet one wants to be alone. Some sulk. Some blame the partner. ("We never had anything like that in *my* family.") Or try to find a cause, like the mother's having continued to work during the pregnancy, or the father's drinking.

The parents and grandparents and other close kin may react clumsily or not at all, adding hurt to an already painful situation. They may not know what to say, so say nothing, hoping that somehow you'll understand their omission.

A family friend (I'll call him Tom) had an extremely disabled son who, at age 10, was no larger than an 18-month-old. We had heard about this son but because Tom lived several states away, we had never seen the child, nor had we any idea of the severity of his handicap.

One year, during the Christmas holidays, Tom rang our doorbell. My sister, alone in the house at the time, answered and saw him standing there with a small child in his arms. She invited him in and once in the light, realized the "baby" was his un-grown, severely

deformed son. She grasped, unsuccessfully, for the right words. Tom was quite drunk. My sister still tells the story of her complete inability to find an appropriate way to react to the small visitor. Instead, with great effort, she looked only at Tom and did not again drop her eyes to the child he was holding. Neither of them mentioned the helpless being. They exchanged a few pleasantries, swapped family news, wished each other "Merry Christmas," and without having even taken a seat during the brief encounter, Tom left as suddenly as he came.

I've often thought of that episode. Now, with several decades' experience behind me, I believe Tom wanted us, his old friends, to meet his son, but was afraid of our reaction, so came only when he had the courage given him by too much alcohol. I wonder, too, how I would have behaved then if I had opened that door—before I had any personal experience with people who have handicaps. I hope I would have been kind. My sister, college age at the time, did not mean to seem unfeeling. She had no preparation for the sudden scenario and in the panic of the moment could not think of the right lines.

Most people do not wish to hurt. If they stare, we must remember it is a natural human thing to do when your eyes light on a novel sight. If they don't say gracious words, it's probably more a lack of quick thinking than unkindness. If you try to put yourself in *their* place, it helps to understand they are not deliberately being thoughtless or mean.

For parents of autistic children, that lesson comes hard. One can't *see* autism, and its major manifestation—especially in children— is the behavior. The child looks normal, often handsome and quite graceful, and probably is extremely physically active. There are no visible clues, like a limp, a wheelchair, crutches, or hearing aids. There are no deformities to tip off an observer. The child seems to be just plain bratty. You are likely to get a look that says Lady-why-don't-you-smack-his-bottom, or If-he-were-mine-he'd-never-get-away-with-that-kind-of-behavior. Many parents of autistic children report that they were actually *told* such things. Some parents eventually stop taking their child out except for necessities.

After several such encounters while out in public with Joseph when he was a young child, I decided to carry in my purse copies of the NSAC brochure which briefly described autism. If someone was particularly unpleasant about his behavior, I handed the person a brochure and tried for a quick exit.

Once, when all my children were young, the one just younger than Joseph (then about 7 years old) suddenly needed an item of clothing for the next day. The only way to get it was to pick her up from school at noon, during her lunch hour, and with Joseph in tow (this was pre-Public Law 94-142, the federal mandatory education act, and he was home a lot), dash to a department store, choose a garment, and have her try it on. Joseph was into everything—underneath counters, upsetting displays, or running off when my back was turned. I couldn't chase Joseph and be in the dressing room too. Then suddenly my problem was solved. A ten-foot stepladder had been left in an aisle and my sure-footed, athletic, uncommonly agile Joseph climbed straight to the top. He never fell or hurt himself, so I knew he'd be safe as well as entertained sitting on his high seat for a few moments. I dashed into the dressing room, made a final decision with my daughter, and was ready to leave.

Joseph wasn't.

Sitting atop the tall structure was extremely exciting to him, and it took all the skill I could muster to talk him down. By this time, a small crowd had gathered and the store manager was himself directing traffic, all the while loudly chastising me for "letting" my young child be in such danger.

I handed the manager and a particularly hostile woman customer copies of the NSAC brochure. Shaking, and struggling for self-control, I walked quickly, with the two children, across the store to the cashier.

That experience, and many others, taught me to spend more time in planning outings with Joseph. It's hard enough to rush normal young children; it's next to impossible to rush those with autism. I could have planned several options but I didn't feel they were available at the time. For example, my husband or a sitter could have relieved me of Joseph's care for that hour, or I could have asked a friend to sit in the car with Joseph while I shopped.

I now suggest to mothers that they shop or go on outings with other mothers of autistic children. There is significantly less stress when there are two of you. The world is much easier to face if you're not alone. And, interestingly, the public perceives you differently. Your "enclave" is in control of the situation.

Fathers having public outings with their "acting-up" autistic child are more likely to receive sympathy. Mothers are more likely to receive blame.

Another piece of advice: A mother once told me that when she was out alone with her "acting-up" child, she pretended to be his aunt.[3] She found public reaction considerably kinder. After all, an "aunt" is doing society's work. By temporarily relieving a parent of the care of this hard-to-manage child, she is engaged in a noble act. Right? Right!

GETTING SERVICES

Most of the above discussion has been about the early years—realizing something's not right, having it confirmed and then labeled, and dealing with the changes in your old perception of how your life *was* going to be.

In my experience with families, most diagnoses now occur at about age 3 years. With more and better education and training of professionals, however, and as more widespread attention is given to the subject in the popular press, it is not uncommon these days to hear from parents of children age 2 years (and, occasionally, even younger) who already have a diagnosis.

By the time your child is 4 or 5 years old, you have begun to deal with the sharp-edged pain and the grief you previously thought unbearable. You have probably gathered enough information about autism to know more about it than most professionals. You have begun to ask questions and find resources. Now you've started the what-can-be-done phase. You may find there's nothing, or very little, or inappropriate assistance in your community, especially if you're not in a large city or near a university. You may be pleasantly surprised,

---

[3] I said this during one of my conference presentations and was later confronted by an upset mother who said she'd never do that because it might hurt her autistic child's feelings.

however, that some less populated areas have good programs. Almost always, it is because of the advocacy of parent groups.

In this phase, it is important that you learn as much about the disorder and its treatment as you can. Some parents go after self-education more vigorously than others, but it is critical that you are well informed. *You* will probably be the child's major advocate for the rest of your life.

Most articles and books written for parents of handicapped children talk about how to gain access to and choose the right community services. In autism, you often have little or nothing to choose from. I call this section "Getting Services," *not* "Finding Services." There are still very few communities where you can find appropriate services for children like yours. That's why you need to know how to be a systems changer. I've discussed that briefly above and will go into it more, shortly.

If you don't know what a state-of-the-art program is like, you might be happy to accept something inadequate, thinking what you have is all that you can expect.

If you don't know what progress children like yours make in model programs, how can you know what to expect of your child? Only a decade ago—and occasionally even now—parents were advised to "Put him away. Go home and have more children. Think of your other children, etc. Forget he was ever born." Some believed those "experts" who told them nothing more could be done. You need to know what to ask for, push for. If you don't know what children with autism are capable of, how can you persuade a teacher, for instance, that your child *can* learn to stop tantrumming, or banging his head, and *can* learn to attend to a task, like tying shoes, or dressing himself?

Once your child reaches school age, another "career" starts for you. These days, you don't have to persuade school officials that your child deserves their charity. A generation of parents before you (if your child was school age after 1975) have ensured your child's federally mandated *right* to an appropriate education, at public expense, in the least restrictive environment. That law is the Education for Handicapped Act (EHA), now called the Individuals with Disabilities Education Act (IDEA). It was *reluctantly* signed

by President Gerald Ford.[4] Get your own copies of both the federal law and your state's adaptation of it. Study them *well*.

The children of those parents, by the way, are now adults, aged-out of the education system their parents fought so hard for, with no place to go. If you help them, maybe by the time your child reaches that age they'll have solved the problem of severe lack of postschool services, again just in time for your child to benefit.

One full year before your child is school age, notify the director of special education that your child will be in the system within the year. Ask what is available for him. Check it out. Is the program he will be in isolated and segregated from nondisabled students? Is the teacher trained in autism? If not, does the school system plan to have a trained (in autism) teacher by the time your son arrives? What is the ratio of students to teacher? Does your state have a mandated ratio (e.g., no more than 4 pupils with 1 teacher and an aide)? Is this school district in compliance with state regulations? Try to meet the parents of the children in that classroom. Because of confidentiality, you will probably not be given those parents' names, but you could request that the teacher give *your* name to those parents so they can voluntarily contact you.

If you've joined a local group of parents of handicapped children (especially the local chapter of the Autism Society of America,[5] if there is one in your town), you will most likely have a head start on meeting parents. Though not all join parent groups, the active parents usually know who those parents are.

If you feel your son's education is in good hands for his beginning school year, start thinking about the next year, and the next. What is your school district and your state

---

[4] The former long-term Senator Jennings Randolph (WV) told me President Ford had a veto message ready to return to Congress with the unsigned bill, but after learning from Senator Randolph that the veto would be overwhelmingly overturned, the president signed it.

[5] If not in your town, join one closest to you, or become a member-at-large of the state or local organization of the Autism Society of America. The newsletters alone are worth the price of membership.

doing about recruiting and/or training teachers for pupils with autism at every level in the system? A few states have made impressive progress, again mostly because of parent pressure.

An active and well-run volunteer organization can move mountains. In my state (West Virginia), where we have a lot of mountains, our organization was responsible for the nation's first (1969) educational mandate to serve pupils with autism, even before the landmark federal legislation, Education for All Handicapped Act (Public Law 94-142) in 1975. We were instrumental in getting funds set aside to begin an autism-specific program in our state institutional system. We have requested and received from several state agencies, for more than 10 years, funds to sponsor annual statewide autism conferences. We have lobbied for and received funds to pay parents' expenses to travel to those conferences. We have had two state-funded state plans for autism—one for education, and one "comprehensive" for all other services (Sullivan & Mabee, 1982; Sullivan & Rowe, 1981). Almost all of the recommendations from those plans are now in place.

My agency, Autism Services Center (ASC), which I founded in 1979, opened the state's first autism group home in 1988. We now have seven more, in addition to other residential autism programs and other services. ASC is a community-integrated center, providing comprehensive developmental disabilities (DD) services to approximately 425 individuals, about 50 of whom have a diagnosis of autism or PDD. In addition to group homes (no more than 3 individuals to a house) we provide case management services, in-home training, respite, supported employment, personal care, family support, and a National Autism Hotline.

In 1983 (during West Virginia's worst economic recession since the Great Depression!), we organized an all-out lobbying effort to establish an Autism Training Center, located at Marshall University, in Huntington, where a team made up of parents/child/teacher or other professionals go, for up to three weeks, with campus accommodations, to be trained to work with that specific child. Follow-along services after the training are an important element of the program. Satellite offices are now located around the state.

The TEACCH project in North Carolina, begun in 1972, is a good example of what a parent/professional coalition can accomplish. That state probably has the most comprehensive statewide services now available for people with autism. Because of those services, the state of North Carolina probably has more autism per capita than any other state. I, for one, don't hesitate to recommend it[6] for parents who are wanting to relocate, so I stand "guilty" of helping to cause that state's swelling autism population. Today, I am also accused of causing a high autism population in Huntington, West Virginia. There is still a great deal to be done, of course, like establishing many more adult community services and supported employment, but the above description was to help demonstrate the strength in unity, the power of coalitions, and the worthiness and accomplishments of such organizational endeavors.

As a veteran of over three decades of such activity, I'm not naïve about the time, energy, and other resources needed for such work. What is the alternative? Sitting at home complaining about lack of services? If your child never really gets what he deserves, are you prepared to live with the knowledge that you never lifted a finger, or did very little, to help those parents and their professional allies struggling to make the system change to serve *all* citizens with autism, including your child?

Or are you going to go it alone? A few successes have come about that way (usually through litigation), but the parents I know who went *first* to the courts, spent *more* resources, especially financial, than those who were successful in getting services by working with a group.

It is not easy being a good advocate. It is costly in time and energy. It often is stressful. And because the work is almost always done as a volunteer, it can be financially draining. The volunteer must be available during regular business hours for telephone calls and for travel to meetings, appointments, and hearings. If the volunteer is employed, she or he must have a very flexible job, with lots of available

---

[6] I do this *after* I fail to convince them to stay and fight for services where they are. Some of them are military families returned from overseas assignments.

daytime hours. What it boils down to is that most long-term advocates are mothers who do not have full-time out-of-home employment. Besides being unemployed, they probably have child care expenses because most will have autistic children who are still living at home. Unless they are independently wealthy or married to a good provider, their advocacy puts them at economic risk should their husband's support get interrupted (through loss of a job, illness, divorce, or death). It is almost impossible for a single, working parent to spend much time on advocacy outside of ASA chapter activity. In these days when most families have two working parents, it means the family has chosen to live on one income. If and when the advocate-mother goes to a paying job, there is always the risk she will be penalized for having been out of the job market for a long period. It is easy to understand why there are so few long-term advocates in autism.

But lest you be left with the feeling that advocacy is all a long dirge, let me assure you that there are rich (though almost always nonmonetary) rewards. The first time you and your group are successful in getting a regulation changed (like getting autism as a separate category in your state's mandatory education law), or a new appropriation for a summer camp program, or a commitment to send teachers off (or bring a trainer in) for autism training, or an agreement to include autistic pupils at the school assembly, or funds from your legislature for a statewide needs assessment and state plan, or any of the myriad other things you can work on—you will be so well "paid" you will redouble your efforts and excitedly recruit more helpers. Your success will inspire others. And your crusade is in high gear.

There are personal rewards, too. You no longer feel trapped, or as vulnerable as before. You have learned to "work" the system for your child and others. If one strategy doesn't work, you have learned there are several others available. You are now knowledgeable and sure of your information. You are a parent-colleague. (It is when we feel cornered that we get scared, teary, angry, hostile, depressed.) You have multiplied your options. In helping your child, you have helped others. And your family. And yourself.

A fellow parent, Margaret Dewey, a gifted writer whose advocacy took the form of exquisite analytic papers on autism, once wrote me that one day, when her "career" in autism was getting established, the phone rang while the family was having dinner. She returned to the table to happily announce she'd just been invited to speak at a prestigious professional conference. The family was discussing the good news, when her high-functioning son, Jack, piped up and said, "I've done something nice for you, haven't I?"

And that's part of the reward—having your efforts pay off by receiving affirmation that your work interests and is valued by others, especially those who can make a difference in your child's life.

Systems don't change easily. And when they do make significant changes, like accepting handicapped children as equal school-citizens, it is almost always because of external pressure. Very few significant changes in the system come from within. Advocacy drives services. Advocacy drives services. Advocacy drives **services.**

UNTRADITIONAL, UNTAPPED, AVAILABLE COMMUNITY RESOURCES

When Joseph reached teen-age, I began to recruit high school or college students as companions for him. His siblings, themselves going through some crucial years, could not be expected to include him very much in their routine social activities, though he was warmly accepted by most of their friends when they visited our home. We live in a university town, which helped, but except for very rural areas, most communities will have a pool of young people from which to recruit. In addition to high schools, junior colleges, and institutions of higher education, there are organizations such as church groups, 4H clubs, social clubs, or Big Brothers/Big Sisters in most towns and cities.

You can always consider the children of your friends and neighbors, just as you did when you looked for sitters for your nondisabled children. I am continually amazed at the large percentage of young people who are the human services type. I have never had a serious problem finding them for Joseph and, subsequently, for the clients served by Autism Services Center. My town has a population of about 53,000. The local university enrollment is about 13,000. Your helpers are in your community, too, if you look for them.

Most of your recruits (and probably their instructors, if you're using students) will not know much about autism, so you need to do your homework. Gather material for handouts. Make their first visit to your home one of introduction. You might suggest they bring a little gift (which you either buy or reimburse), which you know will be particularly pleasing to your child. You can set up a brief activity (like spinning a top, or pushing your child on the backyard swing) that you know your child will enjoy. This is a trial visit, to see whether there is mutual compatibility. If not, try someone else.

If the companion is working for class credit, find out how you can help that student get a good grade. A satisfied student and instructor can help you with future recruitment. Some may need only a documented record of hours spent with your child. Others might be doing this project as a term paper. Help with the necessary reference material. Set up interviews with other parents and children with autism so that the student's experience can be broadened beyond a one-subject project. Joseph's student-companions' class reports and papers have informed many a fellow classmate, as well as instructors. They almost always got a good grade.

If you're lucky, you might have a student[7] for a whole semester. During such an assignment, Joseph learned how to use public transportation. We wrote out a detailed schedule based on what today would be called a functional analysis. There was always an incentive plan for him to get to town—buying an album, or a favorite edible, or going to a movie. The student taught him appropriate bus behavior as well as how to use proper coins, when to get off, how to choose the right bus, and so on.

After being satisfied that he had learned the rules, she allowed him to sit alone on the bus one day while she sat at the rear to observe. Later, he "soloed," with her following in the car. Even later, she followed without his knowing it. Finally, he checked out. It took several companions and almost two years.[8]

One student companion (a physical education major) taught Joseph how to swim and dive. A succession of others taught him the rules of the road for bicycle riding, which he has done alone since about age 14. The cycling has given him immense freedom. I am acutely aware of his vulnerability, but it is a risk worth taking. So far, there have been no major problems. In a larger city, he would have needed more training and probably more instruction about off-limits areas.

Some of his companions have voluntarily returned after their assignments in school to take Joseph out for a coke or a country drive. They have invited him to Sunday dinner at their apartments or their families' homes, to their weddings and baby showers, and to parties.

One student, a single mother with a 4-year-old son and a boyfriend, took Joseph on an overnight train excursion to a distant city. (We paid.) All of them had a wonderful time. She got college credit for her paper.

College recruits for the position of companion have come from the fields of speech and hearing, psychology, counseling, adaptive physical education (or regular physical education), music, art, nursing, religion and philosophy, criminal justice, business, accounting, home economics, and teacher education. We have recruited for part-time work (weekends, holidays) special education teachers who want to get autism experience. Our part-time "staff" has included two public school, Master's-level teachers—one in gifted education, one in special education. Both expressed an interest in eventually going into full-time teaching of people with autism.

An interesting and gratifying spin-off from this system of using college students for this

---

[7] If the student was female, I asked for two. One young woman out alone with a tall autistic teenage boy whom she doesn't know well can be frightening. Having two makes the job easier. I prefer a male/female team. It's "safer" all around.

[8] Joseph is high-functioning and is one of two autism models studied in depth by Dustin Hoffman when developing the character of Raymond in the film "Rain Man." More disabled individuals would probably not be able to go out into the community unattended.

work is that roughly 10% of the staff we hire (that is, those I have personally recruited for Joseph and those recruited through my agency, Autism Services Center) *change* their major to a field in human services. Some decide to go into the field of autism specifically. Their part-time work with us has helped some students to focus their career goals. One high school senior had no idea what she wanted to do in college. After four months with ASC (working with one of the most difficult clients I have ever encountered), she changed her major to special education.

One of the main reasons I have written so much about using students is to stress the fact that programs for our children do not have to have a roomful of experienced Ph.D.- or Master's-level professionals. You need *one* knowledgeable key person: to plan, train, design programs, supervise, and give good and intense staff support. That person could be you.

Selection and training of staff are critical. We look for people with a high energy level, physical stamina, maturity, generally good mental health, a high threshold for frustration, and a commitment to excellence. We want intelligent, curious people who are problem solvers and self-starters. We look for staff who are comfortable treating our clients with respect and dignity. We find them. So can you.

This idea of a companion led us, in 1981, to decide to try Joseph in a job at the library with a companion, a job he still holds today. We now call that position a job coach. Joseph had just graduated from high school (special education diploma) with no further services in sight, when I approached the Division of Rehabilitation Services (DRS) to ask for training. Because it was not likely he could work on his own after the relatively short-term training was finished, his application was stalled. I set up a meeting with the director and made the case for autism and Joseph. He doesn't need leg braces, I said, or an artificial limb, or a crutch, or a wheelchair, or grab bars in bathrooms. The "prosthesis" he needs in his job is a human being who can teach him to understand how to behave among fellow workers and how to do what his boss wants him to do. With extraordinary math and spatial skills, he

didn't need much instruction to learn the Dewey Decimal System or where books belong on the shelf. He needed someone to teach him such things as not to spend his 15-minute breaks in the restroom washing his hands, or perseverating, such as wiping book covers with a wet paper towel.

I finished by asking the director how much it cost his agency to send a blind man and his dog (I'd just heard of an actual case) off for several months' training at a center in another state. He left the room and, after a while, came back and said Joseph could be admitted to the program—the first rehabilitation client in our state's DRS agency with a diagnosis of autism. Years later, Joseph got a state award as their "Client of the Year."

These days, parents of children older than school age are struggling with the same issue. The federal Rehabilitation Services Agency still can give only time-limited training. Most adults with autism will need supported employment much longer than the state DRS agency is able to pay. Unfortunately, the federal Medicaid program will not pay for a job coach at all, unless a person has been in an institution. Families who kept their children at home are penalized, though some states contribute *state* dollars for job coaches and supported employment. States prefer, of course, to spend their funds where they are matched with federal funds.

The lack of funding for job coaches is one of the most pressing issues for adults with autism in this nation. Perhaps this problem will be solved by the time your young autistic child ages out of school.

Every spring, I get numerous requests for a list of summer camps for children with autism. There aren't many, and private-pay ones are extremely expensive. Publicly funded camps are usually limited to those who live within the geographic area of the funding source. I suggest to parents they use our model—sending kids to *regular* camps (e.g., 4H, Boy Scout, Girl Scout, church camps) with paid companions. Autism Services Center ran a summer camp program for seven years. We sent two counselors with each autistic child. That way, they can fit into almost any camp; you don't need one especially for autistic children. You will need to carefully recruit, train, and supervise the counselor-companions if they have no autism experience. But, quite possibly, you can recruit your child's classroom aide (she probably won't have a summer job), or even the teacher, or another special education teacher who wants the experience and could use the extra money. If these professionals are enrolled in university classes, they may even arrange to get credit for the experience, especially if the supervisor (you?) is someone who is experienced in autism and has a graduate degree.

Having your child in a nearby camp is much less stressful and less expensive than paying the costs of traveling two states (or more) away. If you're going to spend money[9] on camp anyway, one close to home gives you more opportunity to visit and to be more available in case of emergency, *and* it helps train local people to work with your child—and others.

Additionally, we were pleasantly surprised to learn that the camp directors, once they learned we would furnish our own staff for each child, were quite happy to have us. Many camps have their campers work on projects that earn badges. One of them is a badge for working with people who are handicapped. It is still a relatively new badge, apparently, and some of the camp directors were delighted to be able to offer it by having the regular campers do activities with our campers. We were invited back for each of our seven years.

One of our campers is mute, but a fluent finger speller. He taught every boy in his troop to finger spell his own name.

These unusual campers have been the subjects of local TV and newspaper stories, giving the camps some good publicity and giving autism some much needed public exposure. Over the years, our campers have "educated" several thousand nondisabled campers (and their staff), including, quite possibly, future legislators, judges, teachers, principals, businesspeople, neighbors, or even future parents or relatives of children with autism. Some of

those nondisabled campers no doubt "educated" their families and neighbors when they got back home.

WHAT'S AHEAD

In a 1984 study I conducted (Sullivan, 1984), I looked at outcomes for 30 adults with autism. It was the first such study in the 10 years since mandatory education. Before that time, there had been 25 follow-up studies—a surprising statistic, considering the low incidence of autism. I was astonished to find no study had been done since 1973.

Needless to say, those studies reported gloomy outcomes. I wanted to find out whether education made a difference. Were the outcomes for the first generation of autistic students after Public Law 94-142 still as unyielding and forbidding?

I am happy to report that this investigation indicated outcomes had gotten impressively better. I based my findings on levels of functioning. In the earlier studies, an average of 65% of the subjects had a "worst" outcome (continued institutionalization, severe lack of communication, few social or life skills). In my study, only 30% fell under "worst" outcome.

I fully expect that if a similar study were done today, the percentage will fall even further.

In the past few years, occasional reports in the autism literature have used the word "recovered," and even "cured." The latter is claimed by UCLA's Ivar Lovaas, whose work in the autism field has spanned 30-plus years. In an experiment with 19 autistic children under age 3½, he reported (Lovaas, 1987) that 9 (47%) had achieved "normal cognitive functioning"; by all standard measures of IQ and reasoning, they were normal. He had provided intensive behavior modification for these young children, as much as 40 hours a week, for 2 or more years. Long-term follow-up studies (McEachin, Smith, & Lovaas, 1993) done when these 9 were in their teens, show them to be indistinguishable from their normal peers, in their social skills as well as their academic skills.

In 1993, a New York City mother published her story (Maurice, 1993) about recovering

---

[9] These days, parents may be granted funds for camp from their state or local Family Support Programs. Ask for assistance from your regional or state office serving individuals with developmental disabilities.

her young daughter Anne-Marie from autism, and, subsequently, her next child, Michel, a son. Using the Lovaas method, she, too, uses the term "recovered" or "cured." The family later moved out of New York City to an undisclosed place so that when the children reached school age, no one would know their history of autism. Ms. Maurice reports they are in a normal school, doing well. Bernard Rimland (1993), who has visited the Maurice children, writes in the Foreword of Catherine Maurice's book:

I . . . have visited the Maurice home and seen the children, *delightful* children, on several occasions, and did not (thank heaven!) detect any . . . residual signs [of autism]. (p. xiv)

So dramatic is the new notion that recovery from autism *is* possible if treatment is started at a young age that the first reports were met with great skepticism, incredulity, and even hostility. Statements began to appear saying the children could not have been autistic in the first place. As a result, three of the professionals, some well-known names in autism, who first saw and diagnosed Anne-Marie and Michel, have written (Perry, Cohen, & DeCarlo, 1995) to confirm their original diagnoses, and to confirm the children's amazing progress. They, too, call it recovery.

Maybe we should not be so surprised. Annie Sullivan successfully used what would now be called intensive "behavior therapy" with her famous student, Helen Keller. Parents and professionals with long-term connections to autism can identify remarkable progress[10] made when there is significant, intensive, consistent, respectful, and persistent help—at any age. And though it is a leap to "cured," we will probably see more and more such reports, especially as children more routinely get a

---

[10] See "Out of the Darkness: The Jeff Matney Story," a video, produced in 1994 by Autism Services Center, about an extremely violent young man who, after four years in a small community group home with a structured program, has made significant progress. The 12-minute tape is available for purchase. In 1996 it won Honorable Mention at the Columbus International Film Festival and won one of the two media awards at the annual conference of the Association for the Severely Handicapped (TASH) in New Orleans.

diagnosis before age 3 years, and "treatment" starts early.

Already parents of young children are pushing school systems to use intensive and *early* interventions like the Lovaas method. Dr. Mary Jane Weiss, at Rutgers University, has developed a training program specifically to teach families, therapists, and teachers how to educate these very young students.

A significant court case was won, in September 1993, by a law professor-father of a preschool child with a diagnosis of PDD. The case, known as *Delaware County Intermediate Unit No. 25 v. Martin and Melinda K., individually and as Parents and Guardians of Paul K.*, was heard in the U.S. District Court, Eastern District of Pennsylvania. The parents of 5-year-old Paul K. wanted reimbursement from the Intermediate Unit (IU) for providing their son, at their own expense, education using the Lovaas method. The IU wanted to provide Paul K. with the TEACCH system, a statewide program in North Carolina, developed by Dr. Eric Schopler and his colleagues. A state review panel decision ordered the IU to provide the Lovaas method. The U.S. District Court agreed with the parents (*Individuals with Disabilities Education Law Report,* 1993):

. . . the Lovaas model was appropriate, and . . . the parents were entitled to reimbursement for the costs of providing the student with a Lovaas-based program. (p. 363)

Martin Kotler later wrote at length about the case, in the *Journal of Law Reform* (Kotler, 1994), using material from the autism literature and other pertinent case law in disability issues. His article basically reviews the Education for All Handicapped Act (EHA) of 1975 and proposes changes. In my opinion, it is an excellent resource for parents, professionals, or any serious student of educational rights for individuals with autism or other disabilities.

Another eastern seaboard school system recently settled out-of-court with another family. Several more cases involving very young children are now in due process or are seeking relief in the civil courts.

The future for all persons with handicaps, our children included, is probably brighter than it has ever been in human history. We have good laws, a good body of successful court cases, a growing interest by legislative bodies (driven by advocacy) to enhance the lives of citizens with disabilities, and a growing commitment by government agencies to offer adequate services—albeit sometimes driven by parents' court cases.

Most importantly, consumers and their families now have heightened awareness of their power and are increasingly setting higher expectations for what can be done for their children with autism.

For example, who would have thought, only a decade ago, that community integrated competitive employment (with the support of job coaches where necessary) would be a goal of advocacy organizations? As of 1987, it is also the goal of OSERS, the federal Office of Special Education and Rehabilitation Services. It helped, no doubt, that the chief officer of OSERS at that time was Madeleine Will, the parent of a child with a severe handicap.

Since 1988, no mention of increased public awareness of autism should fail to mention the Academy Award-winning film, *Rain Man.* It did more to tell the world about autism than all of us working in the field for 25 years had been able to accomplish. Dustin Hoffman's portrayal of Raymond, an autistic young man with savant skills, was accurate, moving, and beautifully effective. Three directors had given up trying to make sense of a commercial film, for public consumption, with a mostly nonspeaking main character. Barry Levinson earned an Oscar for his successful direction of *Rain Man.* My son Joseph, also a savant, was one of two main autistic models studied by Dustin Hoffman for his role as Raymond. *Rain Man* premiered in Huntington, West Virginia, as a benefit for the Autism Services Center. With the proceeds, ASC was able to make a down payment on a house which has become home for Joseph and two other young men with developmental disabilities.

CONCLUSION

Having a child with autism was not in your life plan, but here you are. How it goes for you and your child will depend on many things, quite a few of which are under your control. Getting control is what I hope this chapter has helped

you do. Each victory brings you closer to what your child needs. As the writer, Denise Levertov, says in one of her poems, "Every step [is] an arrival."

Cross-References

Interventions are discussed in Chapters 22 through 33. Division TEACCH is described in detail in Chapter 35. Advocacy and legal issues, and research and ethical issues in treatment are addressed in Chapters 37 and 38, respectively. Aspects of behavioral intervention are discussed in Chapter 44, and life-span developmental issues, in Chapter 45.

REFERENCES

Delaware County Intermediate Unit (I.U.) #25. v. Martin & Melinda K. Civ. A. No. 92-3866 U.S. Dist., E.D. PA, Sept. 15, 1993 (831 F. Supp., pp. 1206–1231).

Gilpin, W. (1993). *Laughing and loving with autism.* (Available from FutureEducation, Inc., Arlington, TX 76011)

Gilpin, W. (1994). *More laughing and loving with autism.* (Available from FutureEducation, Inc., Arlington, TX 76011)

Individuals with Disabilities Education Law Report. (1993, November 18). *20*(5), 363.

Kotler, M. (1994). The Individuals with Disabilities Act: A parent's perspective and proposal for change. *Journal of Law Reform, 27*(2), 331–397. Ann Arbor: University of Michigan Press.

Levertov, D. (1979). *Collected earlier poems* (p. 55). New York: New Directions.

Lovaas, I. (1981). *The me book.* Austin, TX: Pro-Ed.

Lovaas, I. (1987). Behavioral treatment and normal educational and intellectual functioning in young autistic children. *Journal of Consulting and Clinical Psychology, 55, 3 9.*

Maurice, C. (1993). *Let me hear your voice.* New York: Knopf.

McEachin, J., Smith, T., & Lovaas, O. (1993). Long-term outcome for children with autism who received early intensive behavioral treatment. *American Journal of Mental Retardation, 97,* 359–373.

Perry, R., Cohen, I., & DeCarlo, R. (1995). Case study: Deterioration, autism, and recovery in two siblings. *Journal of American Child and Adolescent Psychiatry, 34*(2), 232 237.

Rimland, B. (1993). Foreword. In C. Maurice, *Let me hear your voice* (p. xiv). New York: Knopf.

Sullivan, R. (1984). *Are there identifiable factors in autism which can predict outcomes and are they changing?* Unpublished doctoral dissertation, Ohio University, Athens.

Sullivan, R., & Mabee, B. (1982). *Opening doors for West Virginians with autism: A comprehen-* *sive plan.* Charleston: West Virginia Department of Health.

Sullivan, R., & Rowe, L. (1981). *Recommendations for the delivery of appropriate educational services for school-age West Virginians with autism: A state plan.* Charleston: West Virginia Department of Education.

CHAPTER 48

A Sibling's Perspective on Autism

JASON B. KONIDARIS

When I was 2 years old, I had bite marks on my back. We had no dog or other household pets at that time. My parents were alarmed and took me to the pediatrician. The pediatrician attributed the situation to severe sibling rivalry. My brother had been doing the biting.

My brother was diagnosed as autistic in 1974, at the Developmental Evaluation Clinic of the Aid for the Retarded, in Stamford, Connecticut. Sent by his pediatrician because of questionable hyperactivity and emotional overlay, he was first seen by a team consisting of a neurologist, a speech pathologist, a psychologist, a social worker, and a family relations counselor. He was reevaluated by Dr. Donald Cohen's team at the Yale University Child Study Center and was diagnosed as a "classic case" of childhood autism. He was 3½ years old; I was a year younger.

RESPONSIBILITY

"Who left the front door open? How long was it open? Where is he? He's gone! Jason, did you leave the front door open? He's lost now!" The hysteria that ensued remains a vivid memory. I had left the front door unlocked on a rainy afternoon, and my brother had run away. Not yet 4 years old, I had called out to the 5-year-old runaway from our front porch. He was volatile, nonverbal, barefoot, and gone. Slowly, a sickening feeling washed over me. My brother was lost forever and it was my fault. It was the first and only time I resented my parents and their handling of the relationship between their two children. I was clearly blamed for my brother's disappearance. I learned later that, in this kind of sibling rela-

tionship, the "normal" child commonly bears the burden of the autistic child's actions.

A far-off neighbor brought my brother back to us after we had spent hours searching for him. The isolated incident sent my life in an entirely new direction. From that early age, I was consumed by a self-imposed sense of responsibility for my brother's safety and well-being. No demand was placed on me by my parents; my attitude, as a younger sibling, to care for an older one was not common, but it became a focus and priority—a given—within my life.

I began trying to figure my brother out. What does he want? What does he feel? Why does he not seem to love me? My brother's complete inability to understand social conventions was matched by my inability to understand him. Day by day, I kept a mental journal of my brother's peculiar habits—those we now identify as typical characteristics of autism. I was 5 years old, he was 6. He refused to make eye contact with me—or anyone else. I learned not to be offended by it. He was echolalic and would repeat, for hours on end, the TV commercials he had heard. I learned to appreciate his precision and even laughed at his antics at times. He broke anything and everything he could get his hands on. I learned to put my things out of his reach. He had pica and ate Play-Doh, among other things. I learned to work with clay. He ate staples. I learned to berate him without guilt because I drew the line at his health and well-being. By the age of 8, he still refused to use the toilet. I learned to clean up after him. He feared strange surroundings. I learned to comfort him and talked him through new experiences. I learned to challenge but also to respect his little world. I did not realize it then, but my brother was emerging as one of my greatest teachers. Through him, I learned responsibility, accountability, patience, stamina, self-discipline, and unconditional love.

EARLY SCHOOLING

My brother lived at home and attended a day school. From the beginning, my parents had made a conscious decision to keep him with the family. At that time, the norm was to gravitate toward institutionalization. I was not a party to that decision. I was too young. Their decision, with its long-lasting implications, proved to be the single most significant force that affected my upbringing. I have agreed with the decision for as long as I can recall.

I remember my brother's first preschool. A large backyard, easels out on the playground, bicycles, tricycles, and an enormous sandbox— all within a country setting—made it a child's utopia. I enjoyed visiting and had a hard time leaving. The teachers were patient, gentle souls who spent a lot of quality time with me as well. My playfulness, however, always gave way to a sense of concern and responsibility that, I realized later, was uncharacteristic of a child my age. I observed my brother's school surroundings with a critical eye, constantly trying to ascertain whether this was the right place for him. I was 5 years old.

LANGUAGE ACQUISITION

By the age of 3, my brother had lost what few communication skills he had gained. He began speaking earlier than most children, but soon fell very far behind. His phrases degenerated from "I want water, please" to "Wa." "Open the door" became a message conveyed through a pointing fit and tantrum in front of the door. He wanted to go out but could no longer say so. His singing and recitation of poems, in two languages, remained intact, but when he tried to speak, his mind failed him. Pronouns were reversed, vocabulary was forgotten, words were omitted from sentences. He was categorized as nonverbal by his evaluators.

I could easily recognize my brother's shortcomings in verbal expression. The weaknesses were glaring and needed a great deal of work, but my task was to get around his obstacles and communicate with him, not to solve the enigma of his language disappearance. His physical prompts, short utterances, and fragmented sentences began to have meaning to me. I gradually reached a point where I could decipher most of his messages and needs.

The second half of the puzzle was even trickier. I learned to speak to him in a language that he could understand. I used fragments similar to his, changed my intonations and order of words, and added physical gestures to pronouns and prepositions. In accomplishing my goal of being able to communicate with my brother, however, I fell into a trap that many siblings, parents, and educators have visited. The trap sacrifices any improvement in the child's communication skills for the sake of some mutual understanding. When my brother said "Shoe" as we were leaving the house in a hurry, it was much easier for me to simply help him tie his shoe, rather than coach him in the right way to express a request. Without meaning to, I was harming my brother severely by catering to his inadequacies. An independent speech therapist finally blew the whistle on me (and my family). A therapist sees objectively, listens impartially, and truly has an afflicted child's best interests in mind.

New demands were placed on us. We were to stop accepting my brother's perceived inability to communicate clearly. I say "perceived" because, in retrospect, the improvement that can be drawn from an autistic child, when that child is truly challenged, is striking. Inability and laziness are two very different forces, but they can be easily confused at times. At home, our new job was to turn on my brother by no longer reacting to or acknowledging his one-word prompts. Our goal was to coax more speech from him. "Wa" or "Water" became "Want water, please" as I insisted on more complete sentences. Soon we began to tackle one of his weaknesses: pronouns, and the reversal of "I" and "you." This problem is not rare; Kanner (1946) cited it as one of the most reliably observed behavioral features of autism. We aimed to rid my brother of this confusion. If he wanted a cookie and said, "You want cookie," I would eat the cookie, not giving in to his anger and frustration. I continued to jeopardize our easygoing relationship and our rare understanding of each other—until the day when his learning process came full circle. After passing through the stages of confusion and anger, he finally reached the goal: understanding "*I want cookie*" yielded the result my brother was looking for. There was no reason to make the same mistake again; the success was obvious to him. Self-interest stirs the mind and breeds creativity.

After some resistance to invasion of his routine, my brother started receiving professional speech therapy once a week when he was 12. He worked on completing thoughts and sentences, matching appropriate phrases with pictures, and starting the reading process from scratch. His speech therapist projected the aura of an authority figure—a critical factor in penetrating my brother's mind and undoing many habitual mental processes. Over the years, my brother has had numerous therapists, has been exposed to many teaching philosophies. His language has improved tremendously; he understands commands better and he reads aloud at a first-grade level. Language acquisition has been one of the few areas where I have been able to note tangible and significant progress in my brother's development. He has learned to work with language instead of against it.

TOILET TRAINING

My brother's toilet training was one of the greatest challenges our family had to deal with. He showed absolutely no interest in games that he could win by depositing "pee-pee and BM" in the toilet. Our father would take him into the bathroom and demonstrate how "men" urinate. I joined them in the game of "Let's make an X" or "X marks the spot," to no avail. My mother even thought up songs to coax my brother to use the toilet.

Professionals from the Yale Child Study Center encouraged us to buy a lock box and keep it in the bathroom. We were told to place a favorite food item in the box and produce it as a tangible reward the instant my brother used the toilet. He made no connection between the box contents and the toilet. We were comforted to learn that even the doctors were sometimes at a loss.

One day, my mother heard of a grandmother who used a child's suppository on her autistic grandson when she saw him straining to defecate behind the drapes in her living room. She marched him into the bathroom and sat him down. He went instantly and she praised him instantly. This was repeated for several days until her grandson got the message. He was bowel trained in four days.

We were torn between trying the method, even though it had possible psychological ramifications, and might bring a negative response from our professional advisers (if we decided to tell them), and our exasperation after 12 years of cleaning up my brother's messes. My mother strongly favored the suppository idea and decided to try it. Success took much longer than four days. She used the suppositories only when my brother indicated, by facial expression or bodily movement, that he needed to defecate. He finally reacted while sitting on the toilet, and *voila!* toilet training was underway. Ultimately, my brother was ready for his big step when he chose to be ready; the lapses along the way were definitely linked to a control issue. A few months later, we stripped our family room carpet and replaced it with a plush beige-colored one. How great to have no more stains or odors! We were beginning to resemble a normal family.

SELF-ABUSE

In the early 1970s, I witnessed autistic self-abuse—head banging, biting, and hair pulling—in my brother's special education classes. Shortly after the classroom visit, a slide show at an autism conference in Rhode Island highlighted students whose hands were tied behind their backs to prevent them from hitting themselves, children who were forced to wear helmets to protect them from cranial damage, and a porcelain bathroom sink that an autistic boy had cracked open with his bare forehead. It was not a slide show that a typical preteen would be privy to or would understand.

My brother's self-abuse took the form of wrist biting. A loud, piercing, and prolonged squeal would accompany his bite, triggering a sense of fright and anguish within me. Aside from reacting to my brother's tantrum, I was compelled to deal with curious onlookers and even with police who thought they had spotted some type of abuse. Hearing the squeal, one might think that the noise of the "bark" was worse than the actual bite. A look at his wrist told a different story. The bite was always severe and would usually break the skin. The self-abuse was so concentrated and destructive that a solid callus eventually formed over the majority of his right wrist. It was nature's way of protecting my brother from his most powerful enemy—himself.

I do not recall the first time I saw my brother bite himself. I do recall the first time my mother explained his actions to me. I was 4 years old. I learned that my brother's autism precluded him from communicating effectively. This left him with no conventional outlet for expressing his anger and frustration. King (1990) states, "The consequences of an inability to organize sensory input are devastating to normal function." Wrist biting was his outlet. I can truly say that by the time I was 7, my brother's biting hurt me as much as it hurt him. My anxiety would turn to despair because I could find no means of stopping him. As a normal child, I had been taught that resolution came from going to the root of a conflict. However, I also learned that theory and logic do not always play a role in rearing an autistic individual. Occasionally, a loud noise or an uncomfortable situation would set my brother off. Most of the time, identifying what made him fly off the handle remained one of life's great mysteries. As a child, I cared less about the cause than the effect. My brother was hurting himself right in front of me, and I wanted to stop him. On one occasion, I decided to bite his other arm as he was biting himself. He seemed oblivious. The intensity of his biting fits reminded me of seizures. He did not give me even a moment's notice. On a separate occasion, I imitated him and bit myself. He stopped his biting, looked at me with a startled stare for a moment, and then continued his tantrum. I thought I had broken through to him. I was naive.

I was still intent on making my brother stop his self-abuse. I needed something equally powerful and intense to startle him out of his rage. A day finally came when I addressed him with sheer impulse rather than calculated thought. That day, my brother was headed toward permanent physical damage with an extremely aggressive biting fit. My father and I pulled on his arm with all our might, to save my brother from his own powerful jaws. Unexpectedly, we got his arm free. Knowing that the biting would start again at any moment, I instinctively shot my own wrist into my brother's mouth. Part of me wanted my brother to hurt me rather than himself. Another part of me wanted to learn whether he had enough irrational rage to inflict that kind of damage on another person. He did not bite me. The sweat and redness left his face, his breathing slowed to normal. He maintained eye contact with me the entire time—a rarity. I had done the unthinkable. I had penetrated his defenses and his irrationality with my own irrationality. In his eyes, I saw a newfound unspoken trust between us.

SOCIALIZATION

Very early on, my family realized that contact with neighbors, friends, and relatives was crucial for my brother and for us as a family. In retrospect, I see our social immersion as the best tack ever taken in my brother's upbringing; it outpaced education, training, and speech in its contribution to his overall development. I credit my parents with its early success. Having seen its good effect not only in my family but in many other equally brave families within our special education circle, I urge parents of autistic children to socialize. Avoid social shock, but gently test the bounds of the child's tolerance for social interaction.

We needed a lot of ingenuity and planning to accomplish this task. Before long, we learned which friends tolerated and even accepted my brother in their homes and which ones were concerned about their knickknacks and furnishings and were reluctant to have us over more than once. We felt much more at ease entertaining in our home and having people meet my brother in his own familiar surroundings. He enjoyed these gatherings immensely and always anticipated the meal and the dessert, which were the highlights of a social evening. His curiosity and his hunger outweighed his reclusiveness.

When we visited friends, we made sure that one of us was always on duty. This role involved checking the TV room frequently to make sure my brother was still in that room watching a show. Given the opportunity to venture into the bathroom, he would empty shampoo bottles and any other lotions down the sink. A favorite pastime in someone else's home was to open and close the refrigerator door every few minutes in the hope of finding food that normally was not available at home—such as cheesecake, cold cuts, and soda. He was and still is a junk-food fanatic, as are many autistic individuals whom I have come to know. Food is often one of the few pure satisfactions these individuals experience—hence, it is commonly used in rewarding good behavior.

New Situations

A preview of new environments often helped my brother adjust to them. If we knew we were going to a restaurant on Saturday evening, we would drive by it during the day. Selection of an eating establishment was and still is based on its noise level; my brother is hypersensitive to many sounds. Other considerations included how formal the establishment was and, of course, what type of food it offered.

Attending church services meant sitting in the last pew at the back of the church. This allowed my brother the flexibility of sitting or standing up when he felt like it. After several years, the back pew was informally reserved for our family. I do not recall ever being embarrassed in church by my brother's actions. I was simply happy to be participating in an event as part of an entire family.

Going to the movies was more an adventure in eating than an experience in cinematography. Popcorn was definitely more important than the movie, but we progressed to sitting through an entire film and having a good time. There were moments when his demands for a drink could be heard over the dialogue on the screen, but I grew used to these episodes and learned not to be embarrassed by them.

Shopping was (and still is) a headache. If we went to a mall, my brother had to straighten out every hanger that was askew and rehang clothes that had fallen down. His compulsive behavior always surfaced when we went shopping. My brother also tended to wander. He would spot a water fountain and take off instantly, without any thought about leaving my presence. Grocery shopping is still a challenge. I may tell him, prior to entering the store, "No cookies today." Once in the store, he will carefully push the cart around, picking out items from a list then, like lightning, he will run off—not to the cookie aisle, because he has been told "No," but to the potato chips section. He has figured out that if he tears open the bag, I will be compelled to purchase it. Self-interest tends to provoke creativity within his very active and underestimated mind.

For some mysterious reason, visits to doctors' and dentists' offices posed no problem. In this respect, my brother differed greatly from most other children. He enjoyed the attention he was given during these appointments, not to mention the magical rising chairs. He even requested that his blood pressure be taken! When my brother was younger, we would try to arrange his dental appointments early in the day, when he was fresh and relaxed and so was the periodontist. My parents learned early that professionals who were familiar with autism were, for the most part, caring individuals.

My brother's eventual attendance at my high school soccer and basketball games gave me greater pleasure than all the other experiences we shared. I may have gotten more out of his being there than he did. What better way to involve, entertain, and teach my brother while also educating my friends as to who he was and what he was all about? I always tried to spot him in the bleachers before a game. Even while playing, I worried about how he was behaving and whether he was enjoying himself. He soon got used to the noise level at the games and even learned to clap at the appropriate times. He was my number-one fan.

VACATIONS

Family trips were a vacation from our everyday life at home but never from the responsibilities surrounding the care of my brother. He was a full-time job. By the time I was 9 years old, I could handle my brother mentally, but not physically. He was still bigger than I was and two steps faster. He had curtailed most of his running-away episodes, but keeping up with him was still a chore. I will always remember an incident that happened after a 10-hour flight to Europe. My mother asked me to sit on a suitcase and keep my brother close while she ran to the restroom for a moment. She was a perennial presence in his life, but small absences were unavoidable. Fear washed over me as she left. What if my brother decided to make a run for a snack bar? What about the luggage? How would Mom find us? It was the type of unrelenting worry a child usually feels after being dropped off on the first day of kindergarten. After what seemed like an eternity to me, the knot in my stomach loosened when I saw my mother approaching. I went to the restroom—not to use the toilet, but to look in the mirror for wrinkles on my forehead. I had asked my father once why people get wrinkles. He told me it was from worrying. I was convinced I would find wrinkles after a worrying episode like the one I had just gone through. I was still young.

Walt Disney World was exciting but not fun to me. I remember constantly looking over my shoulder to make sure my brother was following. My concern bordered on obsession at times. I had heard stories about autistic children who got lost in crowds and were recovered by police who had no inkling of how to communicate with them. I firmly believed in being safe rather than sorry. My saddest moments revolved around my brother's disinterest in most activities, and the rest of the family's lack of involvement as a result. My brother would keep on walking when he was not willing to participate as a spectator or wait in line at a ride. We did a lot of walking during that vacation. My happiest times were when we found a ride that my brother would enjoy—a ride we could get on together. Any normal sibling situations we experienced brought me great pride. These minor rewards were signs that my brother had promise, and they brought my parents and me great joy.

Hotel rooms and rented vacation homes were fun. They encouraged close family ties. In smaller living quarters, my brother had no choice but to spend time with us, or at least in our presence. Many times, we were joined by close relatives who offered respite and companionship to us all. Away from home, my brother could not run off to his room to be alone and rock back and forth. I cannot theorize for all autistic individuals, but a smaller home than the one we had might have been beneficial to my brother's overall development.

RECREATION

My brother loved parks, swings, and climbing equipment when he was young. We did our rounds of all the city parks and also discovered out-of-the-way country parks and arboretums. He eventually outgrew these outings, and finding activities that would provide him enjoyment became a challenge.

Our church had a sports center with an Olympic-size pool. We would have family swim times when the pool was not crowded. Mom would dress my brother at home, and I would be responsible for getting him ready in the locker room and for dressing myself. Mom could no longer take him into the ladies' locker rooms, so he became my responsibility. I was 8 years old.

We tried basketball over the years. My brother learned to shoot baskets quite well, but he always wanted to stop after making the first shot. He reasoned that when the ball swished through, his job was done. His thinking was rigid and confined.

We made attempts to go bowling. His school took him on outings of this kind, and we thought it was our responsibility to do the same. The truth is, bowling was not something our family did normally. Like most of the recreational activities, bowling was imposed on my brother; it was not something he truly enjoyed. I have used the term *guardian's guilt* to describe a sibling's or parent's need to involve an autistic child in an activity. It is human nature to try to counter another person's isolation, perceived boredom, or introversion—the typical by-products of autism. For all I know, he may have enjoyed simply sitting in front of the television. Nevertheless, I felt the need to force my brother to be more active.

We had fun washing the cars together. The radio blared "our" music, the sun burned our backs, and the soapsuds covered the windows in well-defined circles that my brother would trace over and over again.

Play

Like many autistic persons, my brother had trouble with interactive play. When he was younger, he focused on puzzles. He liked ball bouncing, slinky toys, and anything else tactile. He also enjoyed playing games, alone, on the computer. He mastered educational games and became quite comfortable with the nuances of the keyboard and the mouse. He was self-taught for the most part. As in the past, his abilities, and most of the activities he enjoyed, such as using the stereo, VCR, and TV, were coaxed along by self-interest. He gathered knowledge and skill through observing others rather than asking them for information. Often, he would surprise me with his minor independent successes, and I would realize that he had been watching me all along. Ultimately, though, he was alone. He was always true to his disorder.

Teaching my brother how to play with others was a difficult task. In retrospect, it would have been easier for my parents and the various educators to teach me how to play with him instead. In nursery school, I learned the basics of playing with other children. I did not learn how to play with an autistic child. No one taught me what to expect—an omission that I regret because my trial-and-error approach at a young age met with such limited success. The happy times that we did discover were momentous, and they remain in my mind today as some of the best experiences I had with my brother over the years.

He never objected to kicking a ball around the yard with me. I placed few demands on him at the time, in the hope of avoiding discouragement and keeping him playing *anything* as long as possible. In the spring of 1987, I was told about a modified Special Olympics event called the ball kick. Without changing our routine too much, I began training my brother for the event. We did our stretches together as he counted to 10. We practiced with a heavier ball than the one that would be used in the event, and I let some of the air out of it so it would be even harder to kick. I also placed my newfound athlete toward the bottom of a hill so he would always be kicking uphill. He smiled appropriately when I applauded his successful kicks. He was getting more out of the activity than he realized. I was ecstatic. The event finally came—a kick for distance on a flat surface with a much lighter ball. We came home with a gold medal that day. It was a perfect day for two brothers to share, in an otherwise imperfect relationship.

ABSTRACT EMOTION

Rarely would my brother show any proper and outright emotion when he was young. Like many autistic individuals, he would giggle and laugh at irrelevant or inappropriate moments. His angry moments were generally excessive, considering the usually minor catalyst that triggered them. He showed signs of agitation and discomfort in settings that most people would find pleasant and soothing. His reactions brought out one of the biggest problems I have had with my brother's autism. I tended to take on his moods. His sour day would become my sour day. At other times, he would smile and giggle for half the day. It brought about my own happiness. Outsiders would wonder why I was the only one in a group who seemed agitated on a particular day. If they had looked in the periphery, they would have seen my brother's mood and its mirror image in me. Few people understood enough to make the connection.

SEPARATION

In 1989, I left for college. When siblings of autistic individuals leave home to pursue higher learning, they generally choose one of two options. Many attend colleges relatively close to home in order to be near the family and continue helping the autistic sibling. Often, an emotional attachment to the autistic person can cause a college student to choose a school on the basis of its geographic location. The second mind-set takes an opposite approach. Some families encourage the nonautistic sibling to withdraw from some of the relentless responsibility and gain a greater sense of freedom by attending school far away. Both approaches are valid and realistic.

I chose the first option. During my college search, I focused on getting into the best school possible within a relatively close distance to home. We lived in Connecticut, and I was fortunate enough to gain admission to Yale University for the 1989 fall term. That August, my plans for maintaining a direct connection with my brother were changed dramatically. My family was transferred halfway across the country because of my father's work. My parents were superior providers and caregivers for my brother. My presence was not a necessity in those respects. The need to stay near my brother was a personal one. I felt a very strong emotional tie to him and wanted the luxury of continuing to participate in his development.

By nature, autistic children do not adjust well to changes in their environment. How would my brother adjust to the major change within our home? No major figure had ever been absent from the mosaic that made up my brother's limited world. During his mid-teen years, he had become more independent and extremely rebellious. Much like a child who is "terrible two," he refused to listen to my parents' directions. By his own choice, he listened to me almost exclusively. When he refused to dress, I dressed him. When no one could get him to join us for a meal or an event, I brought him. When no one could persuade him to stop making his noises, a small prompt from me would put an end to them. I never knew why. My actions were not very different from those of the authority figures surrounding my brother. I was powerful. I was flattered. My brother, now an autistic teenager, showed an undeniable affinity for me. It was a feat in and of itself. I can never confirm it, but I felt that we had an unspoken understanding. Irrespective of any disciplinary action I may have taken, I was always *on his side*. I believe he felt this support wholeheartedly because he never rebelled against me. How would he react to complete and prolonged separation from me? For that matter, how would I react?

My family's move away from Connecticut and my departure to school went surprisingly well. My brother chose a critical time in his life to shine. He was forced to deal with a new home, a new school, unfamiliar faces, a different climate, and not having his brother around for the first time in his 18 years. His initial reactions were frustration and confusion. But he showed no anger. During the first two months,

he displayed signs of sadness. Unfortunately, our new situation was not a controlled experiment. There was little way of knowing which new factor affected him most adversely. After a couple of months had passed, my brother settled into a routine—his routine—and brought equilibrium back into his life. He surprised his family as well as the experts around him. He exhibited tangible progress.

Back on the East Coast, I missed my brother tremendously, but I began to experience something I had never known before. After several months, I no longer looked over my shoulder when I was shopping or walking through large crowds. I was able to walk freely without the pressing fear of losing my brother. I also seemed to have much more time on my hands. There was no constant sense that I needed to occupy my brother with learning or activities. I never mentioned these sensations to any of my friends at school. I assumed that they would not have understood. I was probably right.

My parents would give me news of how my brother was getting along. Speaking with him on the telephone was not an option because he refused to hold the receiver close to his ear for more than a few seconds. I began to feel the direct effects of his limited communication skills. Even though he could never carry on a conversation when we were face-to-face, I could gauge his thinking and ask appropriate questions, which he would answer. Without having my brother in front of me, I was unable to communicate with him. Occasionally, I sent photographs and postcards home. My mother would show them to him and read my messages; she would explain where I was and what I was doing. When I flew home on breaks, I would find the pictures in small frames by his bed. He enjoyed them.

Going home at the first Thanksgiving break, I was worried. I was not sure how—or whether—my brother would welcome me. And if he did, how would he feel about my leaving again? It seemed like a no-win scenario. He came with my father to greet me at the airport. He was armed with a small bag of potato chips and a big grin. I like to think that the grin was a response to my return and not to the chips. We spent a lot of time together that week. I probably got more out of it than he did; I had missed having him around. When it was time for me to leave, we explained to my brother that I was going back to the place he called "campus," and that I would be back for Christmas. This information seemed to have little effect on him. It was difficult to know what he internalized versus what he never felt at all.

CHANGING OF THE GUARD

My stay in the Northeast extended past my college years. I began working in New York after earning my undergraduate degree. My reason for locating there was twofold. Initially, my family had planned, after my father's retirement, to move back to Connecticut, where they could be closer to friends and relatives and I could be in closer proximity to my brother. I gave even deeper thought to my New York stay. When I had contemplated career decisions years before, I always viewed them within the context of my brother's future. How would I be able to help him best in the years to come? Many siblings in similar situations wrestle with this same question. The answer rings of logic. It also rings of burden. For many siblings, becoming the eventual guardian of the autistic person looms as an inescapable life sentence. I had not viewed caring for my brother in this light while I was growing up. Whether because of my upbringing, the moral fiber exhibited by my parents' example, or simply my affinity for my brother, I did not view a future with him as a negative outcome.

In answering the question of how best to help my brother, I considered a wide range of interests, including special education. After a lot of thought and discussion, my family and I concluded that, in a sense, I had already committed my life to special education. A greater contribution would be to provide future security and stability. A successful career in a field that held particular interest would allow me to care for my brother later on in every respect—personally, financially, and as legal guardian. I began a career on Wall Street in 1993.

Dealing with Tragedy

My brother had two strong and capable guardians in my parents, and another guardian was in the making. If only life were so simple. Within two years after I graduated from college, my father was diagnosed with terminal cancer. My mother curtailed her work. I took a leave of absence from my firm in New York. We banded together to form a focused effort that rivaled even our assault on autism. My brother's world was truly turned upside down as he tagged along to clinics and hospitals around the country. He paid notice to the degeneration of the once mentally and physically strong person he knew as his father, but reacted very little. If asked, he would comment, "Daddy's sick." Siegel (1985) cites the difficulty autistic individuals have in expressing appropriate emotion. Opinions vary about how they deal with events after internalizing them. My brother never cried during Dad's illness. He observed the unusual occurrence of many people crying around him. I have yet to see a tangible reaction in him. It may come tomorrow. It may come years from now.

My brother and I lost our father after a seven-month fight with cancer. As the medical staff carried our father's body from the house, my brother observed quietly, then finally spoke. "'Bye, Daddy" was all he said. It was as if he were saying good-bye to someone who was leaving the house for an afternoon of shopping. Years before, I had worried about my brother's reaction to my temporary absence during school terms. That had been a minor concern compared to the more permanent change now taking place in my brother's life. As far as I know, my brother has never understood the concept or finality of death. How could I teach him that someone central to his entire life was never coming back?

My mother and I sat, as true equals, mapping out the benefits and consequences of exposing my brother to the entire reality of my father's death. To others facing a similar situation, I would say that such an issue can be dealt with only on a case-by-case basis. There is no *one* right answer for siblings or parents. I can only offer the decisions that we came to. We felt that sharing the entire experience would be better for my brother than being allowed to see only fragments. Our assumption was that the powers of the imagination are far stronger and more destructive than reality. We also took solace in having him with us. My mother explained, "Daddy is in heaven now." Would he understand the meaning of "heaven" or would he equate it with a geographic place like California or Washington or Chicago? These were places he was accustomed to hearing about over the years, as Dad took off for his various business trips. There had to be clarification; "Daddy is in heaven with Jesus." That would make his departure and his absence permanent. Our family has always found comfort in our religion, and my brother, over the years, learned to recite certain prayers of our faith. We turned to these prayers as a means of having him share in the mourning and grieving. He was a part of this family and he was given the opportunity to be just like us. In looking back, I am amazed that even during the days prior to the burial we continued to plan ahead so that my brother would be somewhat at ease in an environment he was unfamiliar with. We never quit our full-time job of planning and mind reading, of trying to anticipate any emotional stumbling blocks that could get in my brother's way. We took him to the funeral home before visitation hours. He was given the opportunity to find his comfortable chair, to look out into the garden, and to see his peaceful father, long before the crowds would arrive. We had a familiar person accompany him that afternoon so that he would not be our total responsibility. We had a right to mourn without having to look over our shoulders. Regardless, my brother was very well behaved. My father would have been proud of how much his older son had learned. I do not wish many more of these harsh lessons on my brother. Overload tends to breed regression.

The loss of a parent is a devastating event in the life of any young adult. Toward the end of my father's illness, I was faced with the task of parenting my parent. It was a very different role, one that I grew into as circumstances changed. I was assuming a role I had already fallen into with my autistic brother. I could no longer be my father's child. He could no longer be my mentor. I had to become my brother's guardian and my mother's adviser. Inevitably, these duties get in the way of the grieving process, but they must be dealt with. With the loss of my father, I have come to realize fully the love and support my parents gave my brother and me, and how much they sacrificed to achieve these personal goals. We will never be able to recapture what we had as a family of four, but my mother and I will strive to create an environment where my brother will continue to grow. We will always be a part of his life, yet we will encourage as much independence as possible. The course we take may be different from our family's original plans for his future, but not drastically different. Our plans never quite fit the typical scenario of a group home in the suburbs. We have visited some of these group homes and we fully appreciate the dedication of parents and community organizations that are committed to maintaining and staffing these residences. Often, the concept is good in theory, but inadequate staffing, poor compensation, and high staff turnover result in substandard conditions for clients who need stability in their lives. I feel that we can offer my brother far more stability.

I have been fortunate to know that neither of my parents ever assumed that I would be completely responsible for my brother's well-being. That in itself removes an otherwise immense pressure. It has been *my* unspoken desire to oversee my brother's future. Why would I not do that as an adult, when I had already assumed that responsibility when I was 4 years old?

FINAL THOUGHTS

I am 24, my brother is a year older. For the better part of two decades, we have worked together toward a stronger understanding of each other. I have been labeled Sibling of an Autistic Individual. With this label come the highs and lows of a dozen lifetimes. I receive little or no feedback or thanks from the target of my endless efforts—my brother. I speak for a majority of siblings when I say that we are self-motivating. We expect little in return for our efforts. When minor successes do emerge, they take their place as trophies on a shelf—highlights of our lives. We battle to maintain a normal lifestyle for ourselves, all the while bearing a responsibility that few normal siblings could comprehend. We are not martyrs. I have gained infinitely from the relationship I have with my brother. To him, I owe my character. I am a better person, a more complete person—one who achieves the daunting feat of balancing compassion, discipline, and understanding. I have always felt extra pressure to live up to the combined expectations for two sons, but I have raised my own expectations of myself in the process. I carry this benefit, which my brother has fostered within me, to all other aspects of my life. My infinite patience is matched only by my ever-present cynicism. Solving the enigma of autism has proven elusive to the medical profession. Autism is a problem for which no solution is in sight. As siblings, however divergent our means are in managing the disorder, we look toward the same end. We wish for a cure.

Cross-References

Changes in the expression of autism during various stages of development are discussed in Chapters 12 through 14. Work with families and family issues are further described, respectively, in Chapters 27 and 34.

REFERENCES

Harris, S.L. (1994). *Siblings of children of autism: A guide for families.* Bethesda, MD: Woodbine House.

Kanner, L. (1946). Irrelevant and metaphorical language in early infantile autism. *American Journal of Psychiatry, 103,* 242–246.

King, L. (1990). *Methods for reducing hypersensitivity to sensory stimulation in autistic individuals.* Conference: Arizona.

Siegel, L. (1985). *Cognitive development in atypical children.* New York: Springer-Verlag.

CHAPTER 49

A Personal Perspective on Autism

TEMPLE GRANDIN

Many people ask me, "What was the big breakthrough that enabled you to lead a successful life?" There was no single breakthrough. My development was a gradual evolution that had many small but important steps. If I had fallen off any of those steps, I would have ended up in a school for the retarded or at a job that would have been below my abilities. Today, at the age of 49, I am an assistant professor of animal science at Colorado State University. I have designed equipment and stockyards for most of the major U.S. meat companies, and have published a book on livestock handling (Grandin, 1993). During the past 5 years, I have continued to develop and mature. Being autistic is like having a very long childhood. I did not feel like an adult woman until I was 30 years old.

There were 10 major steps in my development, and a good education accounted for 5 of them. My education steps were:

1. I was enrolled, by age 30 months, in a structured nursery school program run by a talented speech therapist. I stayed in the nursery school for 2 years. Five or six other children were in the nursery school class, which lasted for about 3 hours each day. I had about 2½ hours of structured group activities and a half-hour of one-to-one speech therapy on every schoolday. The therapist held my chin, forced eye contact, and made me say different words. I returned home in the middle of the day, and then spent another 3 hours each afternoon playing games with my governess. The games forced me to interact so I would not withdraw into the world of self-stimulation, where I shut off my ears. The governess participated with me during sledding, swinging on the swings, making snowmen, jumping rope, swimming, and catching a ball. I was constantly encouraged to interact with her.

2. I mainstreamed in a normal kindergarten at a school that had small classes (only 12 to 14 students) taught by experienced teachers. I remained in this school through sixth grade

3. My mother taught me how to read when I was in third grade.

4. At the age of 14, I was enrolled in a small country boarding school after I had been expelled from a large junior high school for fighting with another girl, who had teased me. My problems in junior high school started at puberty.

5. Two teachers at the boarding school developed my interest in science and used it to motivate me to study. One of the teachers continued to serve as an important mentor after I enrolled at a small liberal arts college near the boarding school. He was an important source of encouragement and support during my first 2 years in college, which were very difficult.

My educational program was not a heroic magic cure. Steps 1 through 3 above could have easily been achieved in a well-run public education program. I owe my success to my mother, who defied the professionals who told her that I belonged in a school for the retarded. Fortunately, my parents had the financial resources to send me to the boarding school. I speculate, with dread, about what would have happened to me as a teenager if my parents had not had the money to send me to the boarding school. I would have been in big trouble. However, many of the problems in junior high could have been avoided if the kind of mentor teachers I found at the boarding school had been available. Good mentors would have kept me out of trouble and stimulated my interest in science.

The sixth step was Aunt Ann and her ranch in Arizona. I visited her during the summers, in the years I was in high school and college. She tolerated my endless fixations and helped me to understand myself. Other people, and professionals, wanted to normalize my behavior. Ann strove to understand it and direct it toward constructive goals.

High-functioning autistic students in high school and college also need mentors to prepare them for the world of work. At autism conferences, I have met many talented people with autism who have successfully graduated from high school or college and then have been unable to find jobs. Their problem is that they lack the social skills needed to get through the job interviews. The traditional job interview process has to be short-circuited; people with autism must be able to demonstrate their abilities to the people they will actually work for.

The seventh important step was finding mentors in the business community who recognized my abilities and were willing to work with me. Through a freelance writing job for a farm magazine, I found two important mentors who helped me to learn about the meat industry and feedlot construction. Tom Rohrer managed the Swift Meat Packing Plant, and Emil Winnisky worked at a feedlot construction company. Both of these men tolerated my eccentricities and helped to develop my abilities. Emil hired me, and his secretaries gave me lessons in grooming and social niceties. Educators who work with autistic children need to seek out helpful businesspeople who are willing to employ and work with people with autism.

EMPLOYMENT AND INTERESTS

Before describing the eighth step, I would like to outline ways in which people with autism can be helped to gain employment. First, they need a gradual transition from the structured environment of school to the less structured workplace. Autistic students in high school should start working at least one afternoon a week before they graduate. (Sudden transitions were very stressful for me.) Second, people with autism should go into jobs that use their skills and interests. They often become fixated on a favorite subject. Educators should use fixations to motivate schoolwork, instead of trying to stamp them out. My interest in election posters could have been broadened into a way of teaching me arithmetic. My teachers could have had me calculate electoral votes. If an autistic child likes trains, a good teacher can use trains in teaching reading or math. A narrow fixation can, with assistance, be broadened out into a career (Grandin & Scariano, 1986). Leo Kanner (1971) recognized the value of directing fixations into careers and useful activities.

Many high-functioning people with autism have skills in art, computers, mathematics, or mechanics. Talent often shows up early in autistic children. When I was a child, I was encouraged to use my artistic abilities. Young autistic children sometimes draw in three-dimensional perspective. Teachers should work on developing the children's talents. Talents can be turned into a career. The educational system places too much emphasis on children's deficits and not enough emphasis on developing their talents. Among the good jobs for college graduates or high-school-educated, high-functioning autistic people are: computer programming, architectural drawing, computer graphics, auto repair, and electronic equipment repair. These jobs fully utilize the individuals' abilities and shield them from complicated social interactions where they are likely to get into trouble. A person with autism can work at these jobs and have almost no contact with customers. I have heard two sad stories involving an autistic laboratory technician and a draftsman who lost their jobs after having social problems. One was fired after he was promoted to a job with customer contact and the other was fired after he went drinking with his friends. Employers need to recognize the social limitations of people with autism and protect them from situations that are beyond their capacity. An autistic person may be most productive and happy working in an assigned cubicle—fixing cars, drawing, or programming computers. As rewards, these people should be given pay raises or a better computer, instead of being promoted into social situations that they are unable to handle. In my own case, I work for many clients, designing livestock systems on a freelance basis. I go to a client's meat plant, design the system, and leave before I get too involved. My life is my work. At the university, I teach my classes and do my research. I carefully avoid university politics. I always stay at an arm's length from conflicts and fights between faculty members. Even today, my social interactions are limited to work-related activities. I spend most Friday and Saturday nights designing equipment and writing papers. I am happiest when I have my nose to the grindstone doing useful and satisfying work that contributes something of value to society.

To get a good job, people with autism need to develop a portfolio of their work to impress potential employers. I always used to carry photos and drawings of major projects I had done, and would show them to potential clients. Even though they may have thought I was weird, they were impressed with my work. Many people found it hard to believe that I could create such beautiful drawings. People respect talent. Individuals with autism must demonstrate their talents to get hired.

My advice for other high-functioning people with autism is that they should develop a skill in which they can really excel. After the skill is developed, they should make a portfolio of their work. The portfolio can consist of computer disks and printouts of programs, drawings, photographs, or graphic arts samples. People with autism who are good at fixing things can often start by repairing videocassette recorders, automobiles, or small engines for no charge. A person who is really competent at repairs will quickly develop a good reputation. Freelance work is often a good way to get started because it helps to avoid social problems. The worker leaves when the job is finished and avoids social interactions that could cause trouble. Technical writing is another field in which some autistic persons do well. A person can start out doing a column for a local computer magazine. The Internet would

be another useful avenue for making contacts. Written communication is often easier than face-to-face contacts, and it allows social awkwardness to be concealed. For people with autism who have poor social skills, jobs such as tuning pianos and reshelving books at a library make use of inborn talents of memory for numbers and absolute pitch. Both of these jobs can be done in a closely supervised work situation.

VISUALIZATION OF THOUGHTS

Teachers who work with autistic children need to understand visual thinking. I could never handle long strings of verbal directions, I simply could not remember them. Written directions are best. All my thinking is in pictures. When somebody speaks to me, I have to translate the words into a video movie on my imagination's screen. When I search my memory for a piece of information, my brain works like a CD-ROM playing back in a computer. I have to find the right spot on the disk and then play the video in my imagination. Visual thinking is somewhat slower than verbal thought. I have to play an entire videotape segment before I can recall it.

Visual thinking is a great asset for an equipment designer (Grandin, 1992a, 1995). When I design equipment, I can test-run the entire system or a video movie in my imagination. My ability to run the equipment in my imagination far exceeds the best virtual reality computer systems available. If I were 14 years old today, I would be fascinated by virtual reality computer systems that allow organic chemists to walk around inside complex molecules and feel the strength of chemical bonds through a data glove. Virtual reality computer systems would make maximum use of my visualization capabilities and bypass my inability to do algebra. The mathematics of organic chemistry is in the computer program. With these systems, my ability to visualize—which makes designing steel and concrete structures easy for me—could be used to build new organic molecules. Manipulating computer images of organic molecules would make organic chemistry totally concrete and avoid the abstract mathematics that I cannot do. Designing new molecules would be as easy for me as designing a chute system for a meat-packing plant.

Algebra is impossible for me because equations cannot be translated into pictures. For me to understand them, abstract concepts have to be represented by pictures. For example, the word *liberty* is represented in my mind by a picture of the Statue of Liberty, the Declaration of Independence, and images from various movies of people escaping from prisons. The word *over* is represented in my memory as a video of a dog I used to play with as a child. The dog liked to jump over the neighbor's fence.

Basic principles and concepts in my memory are formed from specific examples that are stored as pictures in my imagination. For example, when somebody says the word *boat,* the first memories that are triggered are of specific boats I went on as a child, such as the ferryboat that took the family to our summer house. It was not a general *boat* that took the family to our summer house. There is no general *boat* concept in my memory. My concept of what a boat is comes from images of specific boats I have seen. All my thinking starts with specific examples that are used to form basic principles. During the past few years, I have learned, through interviews, that most people have a generalized concept of *boat* in their memory.

To learn social skills, I had to use the same specific-to-general pattern of thinking. When I had only a few previous experiences in my memory, I often made horrible social blunders. My concept of how to act improved as my knowledge base increased. Asperger (1944) reported that people with autism have to learn social skills through their intellect. I totally agree with Dr. Asperger's assessment. My concepts about many things greatly improved as I was able to fill my memory with more specific examples. If the only boat I had ever seen had been a ferry, I would have had a very limited boat concept. After I had seen many types of specific boats, my boat concept became much broader. However, none of my specific boat images merges into a single generic boat concept. When I think of the concept of boats in general, I see a wall chart or a series of TV screens or Internet webpages displaying specific boats I am familiar with, such as the

ferry boat, my father's boat, the neighbor's boat, and so on. Childhood memories or very recent memories appear first. All the boats are very specific and identifiable. Like Internet webpages my boat images also have associative links. The image of my father's boat is linked to memories of fishing and picnics, but the image of a ferry boat which had a horn that hurt my ears is linked to other memories of loud noises that hurt my ears. All of these associations are in the form of video pictures. My memory system works just like searching the Internet with a web browser. When I find the first memory webpage, I then look at the other pages which it is linked to. Readers who spend time "surfing" the Internet will have a good understanding of how the autistic mind functions.

When I was a child, my ability to do art showed up early, but I had to learn to link the video pictures in my imagination with the symbolic lines on architectural blueprints. One summer, while I was building a house on my aunt's ranch, I struggled with relating the symbolic squares on the house plans to the square concrete foundation columns. When I finally made the connection between the drawing and the real thing, understanding drawings suddenly became really easy. Now I look at an engineering drawing and I almost instantly see the finished piece of equipment in my imagination.

I learned what a blueprint drawing symbolized by taking a drawing of a completed building or piece of equipment and walking around the structure, comparing the drawing with the finished building. A drawing that is an abstract symbol is useless to me. I have to make the blueprint become a real building when I look at it. In college, I learned to read electronic schematics by wiring actual circuits, using a kit I bought from Radio Shack. The kit contained about 20 electronic gadgets that could be assembled on a board with spring clip connectors. I covered up the step-by-step instructions and practiced wiring the board while looking only at the schematics. By studying my mistakes, I was able to decipher the abstract symbols on the electrical diagrams. After doing this for several weeks, I experienced a sudden integration of my knowledge. When I looked at the schematic, I saw the actual wired circuit. When I learned drafting at the cattle feedlot construction company, I studied many drawings until the gates, fences, and feed troughs instantly appeared in my imagination when I looked at drawings of them. Learning drafting was more like turning on a computer plotter than step-by-step learning. The company had a talented draftsman named David. I studied his drawings for hours. When David left the company, I had to do all my own finished drawings. I just bought the same pencils and tools that David used and started drawing. One day, I sat down and said to myself, "Draw like David," and I did. I had input sufficient data in my brain computer that I could do it. My earlier attempts to do architectural drawings had been very crude because I had insufficient images in my memory. My drawings also improved when I slowed down and carefully used a ruler to trace the image in my imagination.

My mind works at and solves problems as though I were putting together a mosaic or a jigsaw puzzle. If only a few pieces of the puzzle are in place, I cannot tell what the picture or the puzzle will be. When half or more of the pieces are assembled, I suddenly see what the picture on the puzzle is. I input data into my memory and read constantly. This is the method I used to learn drafting and circuit wiring. I keep adding data. Suddenly, an entire picture forms and I am able to draw blueprints or wire electronic circuits. My thinking process does not work in a step-by-step linear manner. It jumps around, taking a piece of data here and another piece of data there until enough pieces are assembled for me to see the picture on the puzzle. This method of thinking is very useful when I have to troubleshoot problems in equipment. When a problem arises, I scan my memory and replay previous experiences where similar problems occurred.

Using visual thinking to understand steps in my life is more difficult. When I was in high school, I had very little information in my library of experiences, so I had to use actual objects to provide concrete symbols of life's stages. My first book (Grandin & Scariano, 1986) contains much discussion about the use of doors to symbolize significant changes in

my life, such as graduating from high school and graduating from college. Just thinking about graduation was not enough. I had to actually walk through a door to make the abstract idea of graduation seem real. Graduation was symbolized by a door that led to the roof of the dormitory. Most of the doors that symbolized progress in my life led to high places on campus. Later on in life, after I put much more information into my CD-ROM video memory, I was finally able to discard the door symbols. This process was similar to making the lines on the blueprints turn into real buildings in my imagination. My memory finally held enough facts, information, and knowledge that I no longer needed to physically walk through a door, just as I no longer had to walk through a building to understand a blueprint drawing of that building.

SENSORY PROBLEMS

Touch Sensitivity

After this long digression, I need to get back to the remaining steps that enabled me to succeed. The eighth step was dealing with horrible oversensitivity to sound and touch. Unfortunately, these problems were not handled well when I was a child because nobody knew I had them. When people touched me, I experienced an overwhelming, drowning wave of overstimulation (Grandin, 1984, 1992a, 1992b; Grandin & Scariano, 1986). Wearing scratchy wool hats and party dresses was torture. Scratchy clothes were a major cause of tantrums in church, when I had to wear my Sunday best. They felt like sandpaper on exposed nerve endings. I used to think everybody else was stronger and better than I was because they were able to tolerate the clothes I hated. I did not realize that my senses were different until I started talking to other people with autism and to Lorna King, an occupational therapist in Arizona. Reading about touch sensitivity problems in a book by Jean Ayres (1979) was also very helpful. I was relieved to learn that other people were not better or stronger than I was. One big problem was changing from one type of clothing to another. Switching from pants to a dress or vice versa is difficult because it takes me up to 2 weeks to fully adapt to the feeling of pants against my legs or the absence of pants against my legs. Today, I have solved the clothing problem by wearing soft cotton underwear against my skin. My work clothes and my dress clothes now feel the same.

When people hugged me, I stiffened up and pulled away. It was an approach–avoid situation. I wanted the nice feeling of being hugged, but the sensation was too intense. As a child, I craved deep pressure and often crawled under sofa cushions to attempt to satisfy this craving. Many parents of autistic children report that their autistic child will often pull away when hugged, but he or she will seek pressure by getting under mattresses, rugs, or large pillows. Touch was easier to tolerate if I initiated the touching.

When I was 18, I built a pressure machine that I could use to apply pressure to my body (Grandin, 1984, 1992a, 1992b, 1995; Grandin & Scariano, 1986). Using this machine helped me to relax and to learn how to tolerate touch. It also helped me to learn empathy. Volkmar and Cohen (1985) and Bemporad (1979) report that people with autism often lack empathy. I think this gap may be partially related to the absence of comforting touching. The pressure machine consists of foam-padded panels that press against the sides of the body. The user of the machine can completely control the amount and duration of the pressure by pulling a control lever. I get into the machine in a hands-and-knees position between two padded sides and I place my head through a padded neck opening. When I first started using the machine, I flinched and pulled away, but gradually I relaxed and gave in to the soothing pressure. When I fully relax in the machine, I feel waves of soothing comfort.

I find that using the machine once a week keeps bad thoughts out of my mind and helps me to be a kinder and gentler person. I think that people have to feel the comfort of being held in order to have kind feelings. As a child, my hyper nervous system would not allow me to be touched by people. Some autistic children, myself included, squeeze pets too hard because they have seldom been able to experience comforting touching. After I built the squeeze machine, I learned to pet our cat more

gently, and then he stayed with me. I had to experience a feeling of comfort myself before I could give comfort to the cat.

I became fixated on the squeeze machine. Mr. Carlock, my high school science teacher, wisely used the fixation to motivate me in science and schoolwork. Because many of the other professionals I was in contact with thought the machine was weird, I was highly motivated to search the scientific literature and find evidence that pressure has calming effects on both people and animals (Ayres, 1979; Kumazawa, 1963; Takagi & Kobagasi, 1956). I wanted to prove that pressure's relaxing effect was due to physiological mechanisms. I wanted to show people that the machine was not just a product of my weird psychological fixation. Since then, I have written scientific papers and done research on the calming effects of pressure on people and animals (Grandin, Dodman, & Shuster, 1989; Grandin, 1992b, 1993).

My fixation on figuring out how the squeeze machine worked was a key to the beginning of my career in livestock equipment design. I got the idea for the squeeze machine from a cattle squeeze chute that is used to hold cattle for veterinary work. When I was in graduate school at Arizona State University, I visited many cattle feedlots to study the effect of the squeeze chute on animals. Fixations are great motivators; teachers should help students with autism to channel them into motivations for a career.

Sound Sensitivity

Certain noises affected me like a dentist's drill hitting a nerve. I hated balloons. I often became anxious when balloons were present because I was afraid they would pop. Other noises that hurt my ears were the school bell's ringing and the hum of the big industrial vacuum cleaner that was used to clean the elementary school classrooms. Many people with autism have sound sensitivity problems (Stehli, 1991; White & White, 1987). I know one autistic woman whose sound sensitivity is so severe that she cannot tolerate a baby's crying, even when she is wearing earplugs *and* earmuffs. Autistic children need to be protected from noisy, confusing environments. I often misbehaved in the loud school cafeteria, where noise echoed off the tile floor.

Even today, I have problems screening out background noise. When I am using a telephone in a noisy airport, I am unable to screen out the background sounds. If I screen out the background noise, I am unable to hear the telephone. Recent auditory processing tests indicated that I have below-normal ability in a listening task where I hear a man's voice in one ear and a woman's voice in the other. It is difficult for me to screen out one voice and listen to the other. A magnetic resonance imaging scan of my brain indicated that my cerebellum is 20% smaller than normal. I also have balance problems, and I am unable to walk side-by-side with someone. During the past two years, I have noticed increasing problems with accurate hand movements under certain conditions. When I am alert, I never poke my eyes when I want to scratch my eyebrow. If I become distracted while reaching to scratch my eyebrow, however, I almost poke my eye. I have always had a mild version of these problems, but they are worsening with age.

Cerebellar and brain-stem abnormalities could be involved in the sensory problem in autism. Research by Bauman (1994) and Courchesne, Hesselink, Jernigan, Press, and Yeung-Courchesne (1988) indicates that cerebellar abnormalities accompany autism. Animal research indicates that the cerebellum may be involved in modulating sensory input (Crispino & Bullock, 1984; Chambers, 1947). Bauman's (1994) work on autopsied brains has shown that, in autistic individuals, both the cerebellum and the limbic system have immature development.

ANXIETY AT PUBERTY

The ninth step in my development was finding medication to control panic and anxiety attacks. If I had not been able to take antidepressants in my early 30s, I would have crashed. Stress-related health problems such as colitis and headaches were ripping me apart. These problems worsened as I approached age 30. At puberty, the horrible anxiety attacks started. I was in a constant state of stress. I felt as if a

lion would attack me at any second. My sympathetic nervous system was in full fight-or-flight mode all the time. My brain was running at 150 miles per hour. The anxiety attacks, triggered by hormones at puberty, were one reason my behavior got worse. I was finally expelled from high school.

For 20 years, I tried in vain to psychoanalyze myself. I found that using the squeeze machine provided some relief from the nervous anxiety, but as the attacks worsened, the squeeze machine had less and less effect. I desperately tried to find the deep dark secrets of my mind that would make the anxiety go away.

Then I discovered Tofranil® (imipramine). Fifty milligrams at bedtime made the nervous reaction disappear. I learned about Tofranil® from an article in *Psychology Today* and by searching the *Index Medicus* in the library. I found a paper that explained how antidepressants could control anxiety (Sheehan, Beh, Ballenger, & Jacobsen, 1980). It was a revelation to discover that biochemistry could solve my anxiety problem whereas years of probing my inner psyche had been futile. After being on Tofranil® for 4 years, I switched to Norpramin® (desipramine) because it had fewer side effects.

For the past 13 years, I have been on the same 50-mg dose of Norpramin. After I had been on Tofranil® for 3 months, I had another anxiety attack. I resisted the urge to take more Tofranil® and the attack subsided in a few weeks. I have found that my nerve attacks have cycles. I have stayed on the same dose of medication, and the nerve attack relapses have subsided on their own. Today, more effective drugs are available for autism. Research at Yale University has indicated that Anafranil® (clomipramine) significantly improves the behavior of adults with autism (McDougle et al., 1992).

Discussions with other people with autism who take antidepressant medications indicate that care must be taken to avoid overdosing. Doses that are effective for autistic people are often lower than the usual doses for treating depression (J. Ratey, personal communication, 1993). Too high a dose may result in insomnia, agitation, or aggression. I have talked to high-functioning people with autism who are doing well on Prozac® (fluoxetine), Anafranil®, and Zoloft®. One person who takes two 20-mg Prozac® pills per week is doing very well. Several people with autism told me they felt like they were going to jump out of their skin when the dose was too high. When antidepressants are used in autism, the clinician must find the lowest effective dose and then avoid raising it. The correct dose will vary from person to person. A dose that is too high can result in serious side effects, such as aggression and agitation (J. Ratey, personal communication, 1993).

GRADUAL CHANGE AND MY EMOTIONAL LIFE

The tenth step has been more like a ramp—a continuous, gradual improvement in my ability to get along with people. Many people have told me that, during the past 5 years, my ability to lecture keeps steadily improving. I am often not aware of these positive changes until people tell me about them. My learning is continuous. Each day, I collect more data to place in my library of experience. When I encounter a new social situation, I have to search my memory for a similar experience that I can use as a model for my next action. As I fill my database with more and more information, I become better and better at handling different social situations. I have to rehearse how to deal with a person before I interact with him or her. I have a very difficult time when I am confronted with unexpected social surprises. For common social interactions with clients, I use programmed, prerehearsed responses. Everything is done with logic.

In my business, I have learned how to deal with clients under different conditions. Logic has taught me how to detect a plant engineer's jealousy, when he thinks I am invading his turf. Jealous engineers can ruin a project; I have learned how to detect them and stroke their egos. I use logic, not emotions. In my library of experience, I have videolike memories of previous encounters with jealous engineers. I can spot one a mile away, and I have an arsenal of effective responses.

Dr. Oliver Sacks really figured out my mind in his *New Yorker* article about me (Sacks, 1993). I did not realize how my emotions differed from those of nonautistic people. My emotions are simplified. Anger, fear, and sadness are my primary emotions. If I feel cornered or threatened, anger or fear is triggered. I am like a scared animal when I get into a situation to which I do not know how to respond. I also have a kind of gleeful joy when I figure out how to solve a design problem. Emotionally, I am a small child.

It is important to me that I do work that is of value to society. I want to be appreciated for the work I do. I am happiest when I am doing something for fun, like designing an engineering project, or something that makes a contribution to society. I can understand only tangible results, such as those that come from writing a paper, designing a livestock facility, or stopping abuse of animals.

I have no complex emotions, and my emotions pass quickly. When I become angry, I get over it quickly and I do not hold a grudge. I have replaced emotional intensity with intellectual intensity The medication removed the emotional intensity that was driven by anxiety. Now I spend hours and hours trying intellectually to understand the meaning of life. Intellectual intensity provides me with a motivation to work hard at my job. I want my life to make a difference, just in case there is no afterlife when I die.

Many people with autism become disillusioned and upset because they do not fit in socially and they do not have a girlfriend or boyfriend. I have just accepted that such a relationship will not be part of my life. Learning the complex social interactions that would be expected is too complicated. Recently, I sat on a plane next to a couple who were flirting. I felt like the anthropologist from Mars whom Oliver Sacks wrote about. The natives are very strange. I think I will stick to writing and equipment design.

DIFFERENCES IN AUTISM

My discussions with other high-functioning people with autism, and my reading of first-person accounts have indicated to me that the slightly intrusive type of education program that worked for me as a young child may be confusing and painful to a person who has more severe sensory processing problems. My speech therapist forced me to look at her. Doing so jerked me out of my autistic world. I needed to be pulled back into the real world. Intrusive programs that force interaction with a therapist are often very effective in young children aged 18 months to 4 years. The program developed by Lovaas (1987) is effective in about half of very young children. Intrusive programs that are effective in young children, however, may cause sensory overload in older children and adults.

Donna Williams explained to me that if she had been forced to make eye contact, her mind would have shut down. Her sensory processing problems are more severe than mine. She can attend to only one sensory modality at a time. If Donna is listening to somebody speak, she has difficulty processing visual information. In *Somebody Somewhere,* she describes how she confused the intonation of speech with the words being spoken (Williams, 1994). If she listened to the intonation, she was unable to hear the words. Cesaroni and Garber (1991) interviewed a man with autism who described a mixing of sensory channels. Sometimes he confused sounds with color, or experienced a sensation of sound if he was touched. I have touch and sound sensitivity, but my sensory modalities never get mixed up. My vision is normal.

Donna Williams and Therese Joliffe both describe body boundary problems (Williams, 1994; Joliffe, Lakesdown, & Robinson, 1992). Both women have difficulty determining where their body boundary is. The tapping behavior of many nonverbal persons with autism may be an attempt to determine boundaries in the environment. Therese reports that touch was her most reliable sense and that she could learn most easily through touch. Therese learned to put her shoes on the correct feet after someone guided her hand down her leg and then allowed her to touch both her foot and the correct shoe (Joliffe, Lakesdown, & Robinson, 1992).

A classroom full of bright colors made learning fun for me, but it could totally confuse a child with visual processing problems. Some children need a quiet environment and a teacher who speaks softly to avoid overloading a defective sensory system.

I was attracted to visually stimulating things such as kites and automatic sliding doors. Parents of children with more severe sensory problems have told me that their children run and scream when they see automatic doors. Fluorescent lights cause problems for some people with autism because they see the 60-cycle flicker. These lights created problems for Donna Williams (1994). A sound or sight that is pleasant to one autistic child may terrify another. I loved the sound of splashing water, but another autistic child may be fearful of it (Stehli, 1991). Teachers must be observant because each child is different. I was never echolalic. My speech was stressed, and I said "bah" for ball. My problem was getting words out. I could understand what was being said to me; however, conversations between two adults sounded like gibberish. When I was 2 years old, my mother has told me, I appeared to be deaf. Other autistic children can talk easily and often repeat what has been said.

Donna Williams (1994), Jim Sinclair (1992), and Therese Joliffe (Joliffe et al., 1992) all have sensory processing problems that are more severe than mine. Jim and Therese had difficulty figuring out that speech was used for communication. They were both echolalic. They had to repeat words to figure out what was being said. Therese reports that she often missed the first few words of a sentence. Teachers working with children similar to Donna, Therese, or Jim need to speak slowly and give the children time to respond. When Donna and Jim finally learned to talk, they became very articulate.

I learned how to read with old-fashioned phonics. Because I understood speech before I knew how to read, learning with phonics was easier for me than other methods might have been. Whole words were too abstract to remember. However, children who have difficulty understanding speech may learn to read before they can speak. Jim Sinclair (1992) learned to read at age 3 but did not speak until he was 12.

Foreign languages have always been difficult for me. When I go to a non-English-speaking country, the native language sounds like gibberish. I would have to learn a foreign language by reading. When I visited Mexico, I gradually figured out what a few words meant by looking at billboards and TV commercials. Maybe this is how a nonverbal child learns to read. Because speech sounds like gibberish, the child may be able to learn printed words by relating them to pictures in magazines and books. A lady with autism explained to me that she did not know that words were used for communication. She learned to speak when her teacher used flashcards that had a printed word and the picture of an object on them. The teacher spoke the word while showing her the flashcard. When she spoke a word she was immediately given the object such as a cup. This enabled her to learn that words had meaning and that they could be used for communication.

CONCLUSIONS

A successful adaptation to autism is a slow, steady progression. In my early life, a good education and intervention by age $2\frac{1}{2}$ were crucial. My mother was dedicated to my learning. She located the best schools for me. There was no single, dramatic breakthrough. My parents had the financial resources to provide me with top-notch schooling, but I did not experience a heroic or miraculous cure. The methods used on me worked when sensible amounts of effort were applied. They could easily be implemented in any well-run public school system. Success was made possible for me through the patient efforts of the dedicated people who worked with me.

Cross-References

Developmental and behavioral aspects of autism are discussed in Chapters 8 through 14; vocational and integration issues are dealt with in Chapters 28 and 29, and psychopharmacology is the topic of Chapter 32.

REFERENCES

Asperger, H. (1944). Autistic psychopathy in childhood. In U. Frith (Ed.), *Autism and Asperger's Syndrome* (pp. 37–92). Cambridge, England: Cambridge University Press.

Ayres, J.A. (1979). *Sensory integration and the child.* Los Angeles: Western Psychological Service.

Bauman, M.L. (1994). Neuroanatomic observations of the brain in autism. In M.L. Bauman (Ed.), *Neurobiology of autism* (pp. 119–145). Baltimore: Johns Hopkins University Press.

Bemporad, M.L. (1979). Adult recollections of a formerly autistic child. *Journal of Autism and Developmental Disorders, 9,* 179–197.

Cesaroni, L., & Garber, M. (1991). Exploring the experience of autism through first-person accounts. *Journal of Autism and Developmental Disorders, 21,* 303–312.

Chambers, W.W. (1947). Electrical stimulation of the interior cerebellum of the cat. *American Journal of Anatomy, 80,* 55–93.

Courchesne, E., Hesselink, J.R., Jernigan, T.L., Press, G.A., & Yeung-Courchesne, R. (1988). Hypoplasia of cerebellar vermule lobules VI and VII in autism. *New England Journal of Medicine, 318,* 1349–1354.

Crispino, L., & Bullock, T.M. (1984). Cerebellum mediates modality-specific modulation of sensory responses of midbrain and forebrain of rats. *Proceedings National Academy of Sciences, USA, 81,* 2917–2929.

Grandin, T. (1984). My experiences as an autistic child and review of related literature. *Journal of Orthomolecular Psychiatry, 13,* 144–174.

Grandin, T. (1992a). An inside view of autism. In E. Schopler & G.B. Mesibov (Eds.), *High-functioning individuals with autism* (pp. 105–126). New York: Plenum Press.

Grandin, T. (1992b). Calming effects of deep touch pressure in patients with autistic disorder: College students and animals. *Journal of Child and Adolescent Psychopharmacology, 2,* 63–72.

Grandin, T. (Ed.). (1993). *Livestock handling and transport.* Wallingford, Oxon, UK: CAB International.

Grandin, T. (1995). Thinking in pictures. New York: Doubleday.

Grandin, T., Dodman, T.N., & Shuster, L. (1989). Effect of naltrexone on relaxation induced by lateral flank pressure in pigs. *Pharmacology and Biochemistry of Behavior, 33,* 839–842.

Grandin, T., & Scariano, M. (1986). *Emergence labelled autistic.* Novato, CA: Arena Press.

Joliffe, T., Lakesdown, R., & Robinson, C. (1992). Autism: A personal account. *Communication, (26)3,* 12–19.

Kanner, L. (1971). Follow-up study of eleven autistic children originally reported in 1943. *Journal of Autism and Childhood Schizophrenia, 1,* 112–145.

Kumazawa, T. (1963). Deactivation of the rabbit's brain by pressure application to the rabbit's skin. *Electroencephalography and Clinical Neurophysiology, 15,* 660–671.

Lovaas, I. (1987). Behavioral treatment and normal educational and intellectual functioning in young autistic children. *Journal of Consulting and Clinical Psychology, 55,* 3–9.

McDougle, C.J., Price, L.H., Volkmar, F.R., Goodman, W.K., O'Brien, D.W., Nielson, J., Bregman, J., & Cohen, D.J. (1992). Clomipramine in autism. Preliminary evidence of efficacy. *Journal of the American Academy of Child and Adolescent Psychiatry, 31,* 746–750.

Sacks, O. (1993, December 27). An anthropologist on Mars. *The New Yorker,* 106–125.

Sheehan, D.V., Beh, M.B., Ballenger, J., & Jacobsen, G. (1980). Treatment of endogenous anxiety with phobic, hysterical and hypochondriacal symptoms. *Archives of General Psychiatry, 37,* 51–59.

Sinclair, J. (1992). Bridging the gaps: An inside view of autism (or, do you know what I don't know?). In E. Schopler & G.B. Mesibov (Eds.), *High-functioning individuals with autism* (pp. 294–302). New York: Plenum Press.

Stehli, A. (1991). *The sound of a miracle.* New York: Doubleday.

Takagi, K., & Kobagasi, S. (1956). Skin pressure reflex. *Acta Medica et Biologica, 4,* 31–37.

Volkmar, F.R., & Cohen, D.J. (1985). The experience of infantile autism: A first-person account by Tony W. *Journal of Autism and Developmental Disorders, 15,* 47–54.

White, G.B., & White, M.S. (1987). Autism from the inside. *Medical Hypothesis, 24,* 223–229.

Williams, D. (1994). *Somebody somewhere.* New York: Times Books.

CHAPTER 50

A Teacher's Perspective on Autism

VIRGINIA WALKER SPERRY

From 1966 to 1972, when I was director of the Elizabeth Ives School for Special Children, in New Haven, Connecticut, I often saw the painful frustration of parents of the autistic children at the school as they endured the confusion and emotional turmoil of trying to cope with an autistic child.

Soon after my retirement in 1972, I ran into an 11-year-old former Ives pupil and his mother in the aisle of a local supermarket. I had last seen the child when he was 7 or 8. Sandy-haired, freckle-faced, and rangy in build, he beamed as he recognized me. Compared to the hyperactive, constantly chattering boy I had known, he seemed focused and in control. His mother told me proudly that her son was managing well in the special education program of his public school system. The change in him was really remarkable. She thanked me for the attention he had received at Ives, without which, she felt, he never would have come so far. In a flash of conviction and inspiration, I realized the potential benefit of sharing with others, especially the parents of such children, some of the hard-won knowledge we at Ives had gained from working with autism.

Within a year, I began to collect data on the careers of the 11 children I knew with clear autism. I have included here 9 stories of those originally diagnosed as autistic or autistic-like.

The parents gave me permission to obtain information from the various institutions and programs that had treated their children. The Yale University Child Study Center, in New Haven, which originally tested and diagnosed the 9 children, provided facts on their early toddlerhood; doctors' and social workers' analyses; accounts, interviews, test scores, and final diagnoses. (Doctors at the Center's Child Development Unit, specifically Drs. Sally Provence, Martha Leonard, and Mary McGarry, referred their most puzzling younger children to the Ives School from the school's inception. These doctors became consultants for the school.) Other information came from records at nursery schools, public school special education programs, state-funded programs, and private special schools.

I compiled a full set of testing results for each child, from the earliest examinations through the scores and grade-level achievements that were recorded when each of the nine turned 21 and left high school. To help complete the profiles, 7 of the 9 children were retested as adults at the Yale Child Study Center.

I interviewed the children's teachers, social workers, and parents. As the children got older, I attended their graduations and visited their workshops, group homes, and places of work. I took some of them to lunch several times and continued interviewing them, and their parents, through 1989. By the time my research was complete, the children's ages ranged from 23 to 30 years. Much time has passed since I completed my research, but I still keep in touch with all of them.

This chapter has been adapted from the introduction and Chapter IV of *Fragile Success, Nine Autistic Children— Childhood to Adulthood* by Virginia W. Sperry, with permission of the Shoestring Press.

In the 25 years since these autistic persons were students at Ives, the study and treatment of autism have so broadened and developed that the process they experienced as virtual pioneers—enrollment in programs for special children and attendance at special schools—is largely taken for granted. A description of those early years is a history of how autistic children received the first treatment based on research and identification of their particular disorder. But the children themselves are not history. Although they are now adults and have long experience in coping with their disability, their needs and characteristics have not changed, and the puzzles of their diagnosis have not been solved. There are still many children, worldwide, whose behavior confounds and disturbs their parents, doctors, and teachers. Whether diagnosed as autistic or atypical, or even undiagnosed, these children continue to challenge professionals to become involved in the lives of children like those I have taught and followed.

As my research grew, I questioned who would be the principal audience for my observations. There were the pediatricians, who, in the early years of Ives, seemed largely unaware of childhood autism. Then there were the parents, fumbling, often despairing, and totally bewildered. They were constantly asking for guidance and reassurance, or at least some predictions about the future. Other medical specialists, and social workers, too, were baffled by these strange children. I wanted to address all of these groups. During the 1960s and 1970s, we teachers of autistic youngsters were in a no-man's-land where information, resources, and guidance were largely unavailable and where intuition and innovation were the required daily tools of our trade. I wanted to record what we had learned, so that others—whether doctors, teachers, or parents—could access it and benefit from it. I hoped to broaden the understanding of autism for various audiences, including employers and those in the community who deal with autistic individuals on a day-to-day basis.

The subjects of my study are the young adults themselves, from infancy to the present. I also describe their parents' experience of raising a developmentally disabled person, and the effect their autism had on the lives of their parents and siblings. These individuals are dramatic examples of the wide range of autistic behaviors, and their stories demonstrate the parental interventions and the medical, educational, vocational, and recreational services that played an important part in their growing up.

Early, concentrated intervention has allowed these children to achieve comparative success in adulthood. Early diagnosis and medical and educational intervention saved each child. Without the unceasing dedication of their parents, doctors, teachers, and other professionals, many, as adults, would be vegetating at home or in an institution. Like any other youngster, each of these children had talents that might well have been lost, totally blocked by the child's various handicaps. The effectiveness of our work at the Ives School was due largely to our firm belief that each child has his or her own strengths and that, by discovering and using these individual talents, a child can become really strong. The children described in this chapter found and used their talents and accomplished limited self-sufficiency or, in one and perhaps two cases, total independence.

Permission has been obtained for all material herein. To obscure the identities of the children (and families) in the case histories, all names and birth dates have been changed. These children, mothers, fathers, and siblings stand as archetypes of the developmentally handicapped and their families across the country. The problems and solutions touched upon are universal.

CASE HISTORIES

Larry

Nicknamed "Poll Parrot" because of his incessant chatter, 4-year-old Larry looked like a blond cherub, but his far-from-angelic behavior alternated between appealing obedience and wild, out-of-control tantrums. He had earned exclusion from a nursery school for normal children, and, thereafter, was referred to our special preschool by his doctor at the child development clinic.

He came to us in September 1969, as a 5-year-old. He had been tested five times in early 1969 at the child development clinic, and his pediatric specialist reported that Larry had achieved success in problem solving and language at a 54-month level. He was then almost 4 years old. She described Larry as a child of average intelligence who was impaired by severe emotional problems. This emotional disorganization resulted in an acute personality disturbance. Throughout his early school years, he was seen by four successive psychiatrists because of his bizarre behavior. They all agreed on the *DSM* diagnosis of 301.4 Schizoid Personality and stated that Larry's prognosis was guarded.

At age 13, Larry tested at a level of 8.4 years on the Peabody Picture Vocabulary Test, and 6.0 years on a visual motor integration test. In reading and math, he was on 3.8 and 2.4 grade levels, respectively.

Larry graduated from the special education high school in June 1985. Academically, he was on a third- to fourth-grade level and was considered to be high-functioning. During the summer of 1985, he worked as an aide in a day camp for the handicapped while he was waiting to be evaluated for workshop placement by his local regional center. His most severe physical problem was with his eyes; they did not converge at all. He was still unstable emotionally but had developed some control. He was expected to do well in a group home. He had received, at age 5 years, guarded prognosis. To have arrived at some moderate independence constituted fragile success.

Larry was accepted at a group home, much to his delight and that of his stepfather and mother. Shortly after receiving this good news, he died at the age of 23, in his sleep. Although an autopsy was conducted, the cause of his death was not established.

David

In June 1986, David, who was 21, graduated from the communication disorder program of the special education high school. "He is this school's proudest achievement!" exclaimed his supervisor. She glowed with pride as she described his fluency, his warm friendliness, his sense of responsibility, and his popularity with other students.

At age 3, and subsequently at age 4, David was tested by the pediatrician at the child development clinic. During the first session, he said only "Mama." On the test a year later, he scored at a 2-years, 11-months level. He said "ball," "cookie," "key," "car," and "water." This doctor remarked that his language was more delayed than his other performance scores indicated; for this reason, David was referred to a specialist in aphasia. The pediatrician concluded her summary by saying that both she and the specialist believed he was not aphasic because he understood language; however, the cause of his developmental slowness was unclear. Therefore, his placement at our preschool was to be therapeutic and diagnostic.

At 21, David talked with give-and-take fluency. He was often humorous. Academically, he was at a fourth-grade level in reading and math. Socially, he was limited and tentative, as though looking for signposts to guide his behavior. Nevertheless, at graduation, David could look forward to placement in a supervised workshop for handicapped young adults who were 21 and older. However, based on his past excellent record at school, he might work in the community as either a carpenter or a gardener. His family's consistent, loving support made possible this comparatively independent future.

I spoke with David's father recently. He gave me a brief update on his son's situation. Within the past 3 years, David has worked at the telephone company and at two branches of a discount store, where he unloaded and distributed items to their proper storage spaces. David's father said that the second store had recently reduced its workforce, so David is again working at the West Haven Community House. His father wishes David could get a paying job. We talked about the necessity of educating employers about autism. He agreed with me that this was an urgent need. David's father has a severe speech impediment, and so does David's sister. There is a growing conviction that autism may well be genetic, although I say this as a teacher, not as a clinician.

John

At 3 years of age, John was diagnosed as "a brain impaired child of normal intellectual ability," and was referred to the Ives preschool by his specialist in 1964. He was a handsome, sturdy little boy with a round face, blue eyes, and a thatch of brown hair; his smile was beguiling. One's first impression was of total normalcy. A casual observer might have asked, "Why is this child in a special nursery school?" During his first week in school, John was agreeable and anxiously conforming. His nonstop, apparently friendly chatter captivated the teachers. But this persuasive charm was deceptive. He disintegrated rapidly into hyperactive, angry, often hysterical behavior. With constant teacher attention and praise, he could play with one toy for only 1 or 2 minutes.

John stayed at nursery school for 3 years, until he was almost 7. Still distractible and anxious, John could stay with an activity only briefly; he was reading at mid-first-grade level. He refused to paint or play with trucks or blocks. His printing was illegible. He could not build a block structure after a model, or place three-dimensional shapes on a paper pattern. He could sing on tune and could accurately reproduce a simple, tapped-out rhythmic pattern.

John went from nursery school to a private elementary and high school for handicapped children and adolescents. After 8 years, at the age of 15, he went to a residential school for emotionally disturbed adolescents. When he was 16½ years old, he transferred to a new special education program in his hometown. As a young teenager, he spent summers at a special education camp where he was a boarder. In high school, he was an aide at a similar camp.

John began vocational training and first worked part time as a kitchen assistant in a fast-food restaurant. His verbal skills and superficial ability to relate to people, combined with his cooperativeness, ensured that John, given a sympathetic employer, would do well. He trained at several restaurants, making salads and sandwiches, and enjoyed feeling popular and successful. When he finished his vocational training, he was working in a cafeteria. During his senior year in high school, when he was working in another fast-food café, he began getting an hourly wage; he was also paid for his work at the cafeteria. In the summer after his graduation, the cafeteria job ended. John then worked as a volunteer in the maintenance department of the public school system. His subsequent jobs have been as a volunteer.

Throughout his academic career, John's strengths and weaknesses remained the same. He had a persuasive, highly verbal charm, and an ability to master, comparatively well, such subjects as reading, English, and social studies. At graduation, he read on an eighth-grade level and was a star speller. He had a fine singing voice, and sang in his church choir. At camp and at school, he distinguished himself as a master of ceremonies for assemblies. He ad-libbed funny comments and thoroughly enjoyed entertaining a group. He participated in the Special Olympics, competing in track and broad jump. His worst subjects were always math, penmanship, art, and behavior. He used a typewriter and calculator during his final 4 years of school. He was emotionally unpredictable, subject to sudden, angry flare-ups and unexpected tears. In high school, he went into group therapy with his school social worker. In this group, he could interpret his classmates' feelings, but not his own! He exhibited severe passivity and poor critical judgment; his ability to relate to peers and adults improved, but was still rated as insubstantial.

He had no friends until his senior year, when he developed a group of four peers who phoned constantly. John acquired his own phone, began occasionally to spend a night with one of the four, and went to one or two dances.

Upon graduation, John went to the rehabilitation center for evaluation and placement. The social worker told his family that an appropriate move for John would be admission to a particular supervised apartment group home. He was accepted and lived there until 1993. At that time, he moved to a condominium, which he shares with another young man from the group home. He worked as a volunteer aide in a convalescent home.

I visited John at his condo recently. He greeted me warmly: "Why, hello, Mrs. Sperry, come in, come in." As he smiled and enthusiastically shook my hand, I thought, "Ah, the same John, only more so!" He stood 5 feet, 8 inches tall, and was on the borderline of being plump. His sparkling blue eyes and thick curly hair remain, but the cherubic, good looks of youth have disappeared. He is now in his mid-30s. The persuasive, highly verbal charm remains his hallmark, but is marked by more self-assurance and confidence.

We sat at his dining room table and talked. He still works at the nursing home as an aide. He said, "Mrs. Sperry, they like me so much and are so afraid that I will leave. I told them not to worry; . . . I will always be there." Unmentioned were the jobs he had lost because the pressure of the work produced high anxiety and hysterical tears. I thought particularly of a business cafeteria in which, his father told me, John had fallen apart when faced with a large number of dishes to be washed; as the dishes piled up, his anxiety had increased proportionately. The cafeteria supervisor allowed John's father to become the job coach, but even with his father's understanding and supervision, John found that being an efficient part of a chain of workers created too much pressure. John and his family have accepted this situation. His good looks and appearance of normalcy have always been John's worst enemy. But with his family's acceptance of his disability, and his consequent placement under the control of the Department of Mental Retardation, he now receives SSI checks as well as food stamps and some cash. Most importantly, he is covered by Medicare and by Medicaid.

I risked asking him if he still cried unexpectedly. John stopped in mid-sentence, closed his eyes as if thinking this through, then said decidedly, "No, man, *that's* over with! It was an uphill battle, but I've finally made it!" He said these words with great, justifiable pride. That John had come to understand himself so well and could work to conquer his emotional instability to this degree was a triumph.

In closing, I asked him about social life. He bowls and does many things with his friends from the apartment group home. He said some of his friends were coming to the condominium for dinner on Saturday. He had ordered baked chicken and a vegetable platter from Stop and Shop. As we parted, John thanked me for coming, with jovial good humor. I left saying to myself, "He's made it. How wonderful—almost totally independent!"

Eric

Eric came to the preschool in September 1969. He was referred because of lack of speech. His characteristic behavior was a self-absorbed, compulsive walking in circles with his head cocked to one side, smiling at everyone and yet smiling at nothing. He was $3\frac{1}{2}$ years old and tested at a 21-month level. When he was 12, he scored in the mentally defective range; the psychological examiner described him as a child who had at least a moderate impairment of areas of the central nervous system and thus functioned within the trainable retarded range. His specialist emphasized Eric's air of imperviousness.

Yet, Eric had an area of ability that was unimpaired. He had demonstrated good coordination in fine motor skills as a young child. In high school vocational class, he became skilled at woodworking and simple carpentry. If his impulsivity and emotional instability can be controlled, Eric should do well and achieve moderate independence in the sheltered workshop where he now works.

Eric has been a client at the Association for Adults with Pervasive Developmental Disorder, at the Connecticut Mental Health Center, for several years. He has been part of a research study on Risperidone®, and his mother has reported that since he has been taking the drug, his aggressive tantrums and violent attacks have lessened. Earlier, these behaviors had occurred two or three times a week; now, they happen perhaps once every six weeks. His social worker said Eric had improved dramatically. Previously, she had gotten complaining calls several times a week about Eric's behavior at the workshop, but now these calls are rare. In the previous summer, Eric, without provocation, had attacked a woman (his aggression has always been toward women) while he was out walking. A policeman brought him home. This episode was repeated several times, according to his mother.

At the workshop, run by Shoreline Association for Retarded Adults, Eric packages products and goes along on the truck when the packages are delivered. Fortunately, he now can do this job in a controlled and responsible manner. Thus, Eric, the most impaired of the nine adults with autism in my book, has achieved a fragile success—a testament to all his early and subsequent intervention.

Tom

Tom, inarticulate and painfully shy, was diagnosed in 1960, at age 5 years. The pediatrician at the Child Development Clinic said Tom showed slow development, with indications of an atypical personality. Tom was a tall, big-boned, awkward boy with pale blond hair, white skin, and light blue eyes. His physical appearance reproduced the colorlessness of his disposition. This trait of "nothingness" made him a teaching challenge and was one of the reasons the specialist referred him to our nursery school.

But Tom also exhibited a quiet hostility that evolved into stubbornness and then into determination. This characteristic would eventually enable him to achieve comparative success. At the age of 13 years and 7 months, he had an IQ of 55 and was classified in the range of mental defective. Yet he had already proven his skill in bowling and square dancing, and he was popular with all his junior high classmates from both regular and special education courses.

At the age of 26, Tom worked as a dishwasher for a small restaurant. The staff and his employer admired his reliability and good nature. In the Special Olympics regional contest, he placed second in bowling. He is the square dancing star of his Association for Retarded Adults group. He lived at home, paid rent, and bought his clothes, tapes, and records; by 1986, he had saved $6,000. He said confidently: "I'll be a rich man some day!"

Now, at age 35, Tom no longer lives at home. Thanks to the money he had saved throughout the years (and the many hours his father spent researching possibilities), Tom now has his own condominium. It has a living room, a dining room, a kitchen, a deck (Tom is very proud of the deck, calling it "*my* deck"), two bedrooms, and a bath. It is light, airy, and attractive. Tom chose and ordered the curtains and furniture.

Recently, I had lunch with Tom at the restaurant where he has been a dishwasher since his high school graduation. His boss had to coax Tom to come out of the kitchen and to take off his apron. Tom is 6 feet, 3 inches tall, well muscled, and broad-shouldered. He is still very blond and has a lantern-jawed face, ears that stick out, and large-boned hands. Very shyly, and speaking softly, he shook hands with me, looking pleased. We sat down and ordered. Tom, with the pretty waitress's help, ordered his usual cheeseburger, french fries, coleslaw, and Coke. We talked, with my questions prompting the conversation. Typically, Tom would address the space over his right shoulder, lapsing into his typical repetitive statements. He said his condominium "was nice, very nice." Yes, he had chosen his furniture and "it was nice, very nice—yep, very nice." With prompting, he listed the rooms in the condo, including the two bedrooms. He told me his father was finding someone to share the condo. In response to my remark that a roommate would help pay the rent, Tom looked directly at me and said, emphatically, "*Yes*—I have to pay $700 a month to my dad! That's a lot—that's *too* much!"

Tom square dances and bowls each week with a group from the Association for Retarded Citizens (ARC). He "cooks" (microwaves) his own dinners (frozen foods) and does his own housecleaning.

The great thing that I learned from this interview was the extent of Tom's improvement. When he would mumble and look away, I would say, "Tom, I am deaf in my left ear. Look at me and speak loudly!" He would immediately flush a little pink, look me straight in the eye, and, with his eyes wide and clear and a smile on his face, would repeat succinctly what he had mumbled before. The improvement was astonishing. When the waitress came to take our orders, he pointed to me, saying, "She wrote a book and I'm in it! My picture is very small" (meaning that he was young when the picture was taken).

To me, as his former teacher, his whole air of being in touch and communicating directly with me or with the waitress was exciting and rewarding. The owner and manager of the restaurant told me, "Tom has come full circle. He is so improved!" I asked if she could date the improvement. She replied, "Yes, after he went on his medication fluvoxamine." My final comment, as I left, was that Tom was lucky to have found her restaurant and to have received such understanding and kindness. She shot back at me, "Make no mistake. *We* are lucky to have Tom!"

Polly

Polly came to the preschool in September 1966, shortly before her seventh birthday. She was referred to us by the doctors at the Child Development Clinic. Before coming to the preschool, Polly had first attended a church nursery school, then the nursery school for handicapped youngsters at the clinic. The reasons for her referral to all three schools were the same: multiple fears, temper tantrums, inability to play with others, excessive stereotyped talking with stuttering, and as yet undefined perceptual handicaps. In short, at the age of approximately 6 years, Polly, after 2 years of nursery school and at least a year of therapy at the Child Development Clinic, had made little improvement.

We had observed Polly at the clinic's nursery school, watching her scream, push over furniture, and throw toys and juice cups while a teacher desperately tried to help her regain control. We left, awed and somewhat frightened by the prospect of acquiring this miniature dynamo as our student.

When Polly arrived, she appeared to be a dainty, blonde, exquisitely dressed little lady. She was punctiliously obedient and eager to do everything we suggested; however, her anxiety was apparent in the tenseness of her movements, her excited speech mixed with stuttering, her often repeated motion of smoothing down her hair—left hand, left side; right hand, right side.

But we had no illusions. This petite charmer was a walking time bomb. Within 3 months, Polly fell apart under the explosive pressure of her keen fears and anxiety. She defeated all of us (her teachers) as she bit, screamed, hit, kicked, and often succeeded in throwing over the nursery school table.

We consulted her doctor and social worker; they agreed that Polly felt safe with us; therefore, we could send her home when she exploded. We explained to Polly that we cared for her, but that we didn't like her behavior. After giving her one chance, which she failed, we sent her home with her mother, who was very willing to cooperate.

After a week of this procedure, Polly announced to her classmates, "I will behave." With this announcement came an overall improvement. After a year with us, Polly went back to her school system and entered the class for the perceptually handicapped. She was tested on a Stanford-Binet Intelligence Test, Form L-M. Her IQ score was 67. She was 8 years old, with a mental age of 5 years and 9 months. Thereafter, from September 1968 until she graduated, Polly was in a class for the educationally mentally retarded (EMR).

During Polly's last year in high school, I renewed my friendship with her and her parents. I had seen Polly working as a waitress at the new restaurant owned by the Association for Retarded Adults (ARA). The blonde and pink-cheeked good looks, the flashing hazel eyes, and the competent air could only belong to Polly. I looked at her name plate and tentatively introduced myself. Would she remember me? She did, and enthusiastically invited me to "come and see us." After this meeting, I called Polly's mother. She told me that Polly's transition into the regular high school had been difficult. Her special education class had been mainstreamed for some academic classes. Her mother said it was incredible that highly trained professionals could have expected a 12-year-old with an IQ of 68 and a performance score of 2.8 grade level to be comfortable in the eighth-grade math class. The experience had been a tragic mess, and Polly required 2 years of consulting with a pediatrician and a psychiatrist to straighten herself out. At the end of 1972–1973, when her behavior in the classroom became as intolerable as it was at home, the medical consultants' advice was followed. Polly was removed from academic mainstreaming. The psychiatrist described Polly as a "brain-damaged perfectionist." A normal classroom, where she could not succeed, would naturally be intolerable for her. She joined regular classes only for physical education, choir, home economics, and music.

Polly's parents were constantly burdened by the financial cost of her many consultations and treatments. They were often on the edge of economic disaster. After Polly reached junior high age, her mother, Mrs. Daniels, obtained a degree in special education and took a job in a public school. Her salary eased the financial pinch somewhat, but money remained a constant worry. Polly's parents' social life was disrupted for years because Polly could not tolerate strangers in the house. The situation has changed, but both parents remain marked by that isolation. The physical wear and tear on Mrs. Daniels was particularly severe; her two older boys lived in fear that their mother would have a breakdown. Mr. Daniels was very concerned for his wife, but protected himself from those hectic, lonely times by turning to painting and sailing. He remains, to this day, a loner, marked irreparably by the bewilderment, exhaustion, anger, and sorrow of having a child like Polly. It was, as Mrs. Daniels said, a miracle and a triumph of the human spirit that the family stayed together.

In her last 2 years of high school and after graduation, Polly received vocational training as a waitress and for other jobs, such as gardening. She loved being with people, so she chose to concentrate on waitressing.

Polly astonished many people by her success not only at the tearoom but also in the Special Olympics. But her teacher was not surprised. Polly's will to succeed and a late-developing athletic ability earned her a gold medal in the 100-yard dash at a Northeastern States Special Olympics Competition and a silver medal in a girls' relay race. She was also an excellent swimmer and a good softball pitcher.

Polly graduated in June 1979. She was 20 years old. In her final testing, she was at a third-grade level in reading, spelling, and math. The school's overall goal of teaching her survival-level functional reading and simple, job-related math had been accomplished. But Polly's greatest talents and strengths showed up in the area of vocational training. By graduation, she was working daily as a waitress in a setting sponsored by the Shoreline Association. Her ability to handle responsibility and to remain calm under pressure or in sudden crises was remarkable. She was efficient, proved to be a good organizer, and worked particularly well under pressure. As I read this report from the ARA, I wondered, "Could this be Polly—the 5-year-old destructive tornado

of the preschool years?" Maybe miracles can happen. Polly's charm, her blonde good looks, and her warm personality and adaptability were all emphasized in this vocational training year-end report.

The stated objectives for Polly, after graduation, were twofold: first, to work in a community job, and second, to live in a halfway house for the mildly retarded. These goals have now been achieved.

When I went to visit her recently, Polly was waiting for me at the door of her condo. She came running out and jumped in the car, saying delightedly, "Hi, Mrs. Sperry!" Polly is medium height with a sturdy, somewhat overweight figure. Her blonde hair (short-cropped) is now a chestnut color. The fine hazel eyes and chiseled nose remain, but the lower part of her face—the somewhat protruding teeth, and out-of-proportion jaw—is a giveaway that something is out of sync.

We drove to a seaside restaurant, and we talked. I mostly asked questions. Polly is still very verbal, but she no longer "talks and talks" as she did in her teenage years. She is working in a small biomedical factory and likes it the best of all her jobs (she has been a waitress, a salad chef, and a salesperson).

Her big news was that she had a boyfriend. His name is Peter. He lives in the same complex, and they eat dinner together, walk to the movies, and go with their supervised groups to dances, pizza parlors, and "all kinds of parties." Worriedly, Polly said, "You know, Mrs. Sperry, I never thought I would have a boyfriend, but he loves me! " She added later on, "I told him that I loved him. Mrs. Sperry, did I do wrong?" She later said that she was very concerned about two things: Did Peter's mother mind that her son was Polly's boyfriend, and did Polly's own father mind? She was reassured by Peter's delighted mother, who said that her son was happy for the first time in his life. Polly's father also said that he was pleased to see Polly so happy. Although Polly had always been more aware than her Ives School classmates, I found her concern, her sensitivity to the feelings of others, her intensity, and her fluent ability to communicate astonishing. It made me think back to Dr. Sally Provence's comment that, had Polly been born when the current, improved diagnostic and treatment techniques were in use, she might now be totally independent, fully able to use her many abilities.

Just before I left, she told me, happily, that she was going to cook a Valentine dinner for Peter: his favorite—pot roast or roast beef.

When we parted, I promised to come out and have lunch sometime with Polly and her boyfriend. I had a feeling of lighthearted excitement. Polly's progress is very heartening for her family and for us, her former teachers. Let it also be encouraging for others who read this account.

Bill

Bill, blond and personable, looked like a typical 5-year-old. He was in trouble from his first day in kindergarten, in the fall of 1968, because of his behavior. His language was restricted. He often babbled, ran around the room, and gave loud, meaningless shouts. He seemed emotionally distanced from his classmates, who found him odd. Bill's parents explained his behavior to a teacher and a social worker by saying: "Bill marches to his own tune. He does not join in the other children's playing because he is too grown up." However, they also said that Bill was silly because he was immature.

In the spring of 1969, they accepted the decision that Bill needed a different school, one with small classes and more individual attention. He was referred to our preschool, and he began attending in September 1969. He was then 6 years old.

In public school, he scored within borderline limits (94) on a full-scale IQ test. With his parents' consent, Bill was referred by the preschool for evaluation by a specialist at a child development clinic.

The doctor who saw him said that Bill's inability to think logically was typical of the syndrome of personality disturbance. Put another way, Bill's thinking made inner sense to him, but not to those who heard him talk. For instance, in the Draw-A-Man test, when asked which way the man should go, Bill got very excited and answered, "He's falling into a glass. Somebody is going to drink him!"

After 3 years at the preschool, Bill was reevaluated. On the intelligence test, he scored 99—a minimal estimate of his intelligence, in the opinion of the examiner.

Years later, in June 1985, Bill graduated from college with a major in journalism and a minor in drama. His current self-understanding was a triumph in someone who, at age 6, was described as having autistic tendencies! Realizing that he has difficulty in dealing with people, he decided against newspaper work. He took employment in a fast-food restaurant while he studied library science at night. However, he also sought job counseling to explore whether another career would be more appropriate for his capacities.

After job counseling, Bill decided that his best solution was to become a chef. He had always loved to cook (his mother was a fine cook). He spent 3 years at a culinary institute and then apprenticed at several restaurants in his hometown. When his training was complete, he applied for, and got, a job at a resort in Florida. With his own car and his own apartment, he had achieved his and his family's goal of being independent. However, after a year, he discovered that although he had the skill to become a head chef, he could not take the pressure. The need for rapid production and the tension of working in a highly professional kitchen overwhelmed him. His job was adjusted, at his own suggestion, to management of the ordering of supplies via a computer. He had his own office, which allowed him to screen out the noise and confusion of the restaurant's kitchen.

During these first 3 years of independence, Bill became involved with a church and decided to devote his life to God. He enjoyed the social life that grew out of the church group. He even found a girl whom he seriously considered marrying, but theirs was an off-again–on-again relationship.

During the summer of 1995, I was delighted to receive a phone call from Bill. He was home and invited me to lunch. On that very day, I was to be a luncheon speaker on the topic of *Fragile Success in Nine Autistic Children— Childhood to Adulthood,* at a local club. I invited Bill to attend and assured him that no one would know that he was the "Bill" referred to in my book. His good looks are increasing with maturity. When I observed his increased self-confidence and poise, I remembered the unfocused kindergartner and his babbling, meaningless speech. The changes in him were startling and very rewarding.

At the end of my talk, Bill asked for permission to speak. He proudly told everyone that he was the person I had named "Bill" in my book, and that an essay he had written was included in *Fragile Success*. He was proud of the way he had overcome most of his autistic symptoms. Another young man stood up and said he, too, was an adult with autism. He asked Bill, "How did you get to be in such good shape?" But he asked the question in several forms, repeating each one several times. It was touching—and heartbreaking. Bill tried to explain but could not.

Recently, I talked to Bill, by telephone. He is now working in the gift shop at the resort. He sells, takes orders, and, using the computer, searches for items his gift shop does not currently carry. He is asked to be a greeter (his words). On these occasions, he must dress in a business suit, make the customers "feel at home," answer their questions, and, in general, be part of a public relations effort for the resort. He told me that he loved doing all this; he feels confident he has found a job in which he can grow and develop. Amazing!

He is currently acting in a play put on by his church. (Bill has always been interested in drama, and now he also writes poetry.) He has a new girlfriend. We promised to get together when he next returns to visit his parents. I called his mother later, to tell her how pleased I was with her son's progress, and to inform her that everyone else in the case studies was doing reasonably well. She replied, "They wouldn't be like that if it weren't for you and the other teachers at Ives School. Most of them would have had no future."

I received an invitation to Bill's wedding! I phoned him to say that I was so pleased with his news, but could not come to the wedding. "What would you like for a wedding present?" I asked. Bill's fiancé was there. He asked her what kinds of things they needed, sounding every inch the "married man." "Bath towels; white with burgundy initials," was her suggestion.

They were married recently. What a happy ending! And now, another story begins for Bill.

Karen

Four-year-old Karen was diagnosed as possibly autistic and functionally retarded. The pediatric specialist at the Child Development Clinic said that she had no brain dysfunction or other physical impairment. Her chief difficulty lay in her personality structure, which was, in the language of the 1996 doctor's report, "a constitutional deficit." Karen had simply been born that way. When she entered our preschool, she was a delicate, anxious child who had many fears, particularly of balloon or light-bulb shapes. She spoke only four words: "Mom," "Daddy," "balloon," and "light." By the end of 3 years, when she attempted to interact with her classmates, she talked in two- or three-word sentences.

Subsequently, her education included two day schools and two boarding schools, all for emotionally disturbed and developmentally disabled children and adolescents. At age 21, she graduated, classified as educable mentally retarded; she had an academic level of second grade, two months. In 1983, she was described by the school's psychological examiner as profoundly handicapped in visual, motor, and sensory areas; in his opinion, the handicaps were probably of an organic nature. Her performance was impeded by low self-esteem and a high anxiety level. Yet, Karen had blossomed socially. From using little or no language, she had become a nonstop talker; she had friends at school, and a boyfriend, to whom she would say, teasingly, "You hate me, Joe." She lived in an apartment-type group home and worked in the bakery run by her former school. Her family said of her, "Karen is a joy to herself and gives happiness to all of us."

Karen, at age 37, currently lives in a small seaside town, in a house "on the water"—a brown clapboard house, three stories high, that has been divided into apartments. The date 1858 is inscribed beside the front door. When I visited her, I parked and, being early, sat admiring the blue waters of the sound, sparkling in the brilliant sunshine. Near the time of my appointment, I decided to go in. I wondered whether Karen would be shy; she had not seen me for at least 2 years. Typically, she showed a mixture of shyness and eagerness. I opened the outer door and found Karen standing in the small hall, clearly waiting for me. Her eagerness to see me had brought her to the front door, but she was too handicapped by a social inability to call out, "Mrs. Sperry, come in." (This ambivalence ties in with another incident that occurred later in the interview.)

Karen's small apartment had a bedroom, a living room, a kitchen with a breakfast table, and a bath. Unlike Tom's and Polly's neat and pristinely clean condos, Karen's apartment was somewhat untidy. The bedroom was strewn with clothes and the bed was unmade. The living room was more organized. A bookcase was filled with bird and flower books. A fish tank stood in one corner, and a birdcage containing a parakeet (introduced as "Samantha") was perched on a footstool. On the floor, in neat piles in front of the sofa, were flower books, bird books, a plastic food-bag full of necklaces, and a thick J.C. Penney catalog. On the walls hung two of Karen's paintings—brilliant, incisive pictures of flowers, conveying a style and integrity all their own. Somehow, though, they still had the appearance of being painted by a talented second or third grader. I was fascinated to be surrounded by this visual composite of Karen's interests since early childhood: birds, flowers, fish, pretty clothing, art. It lacked only a view of the ocean to be complete. The kitchen was neat, but the bathroom had the chaotic appearance of belonging to a teenage inhabitant.

Karen, now 5 feet, 6 inches tall, has lost the dark good looks she had when she was in her 20s. The flashing dark-blue eyes and fine dark eyebrows remain, but the aquiline nose and finely drawn mouth and chin I remembered are now blurred with too much weight gain. The appearance of her face, along with her chunky figure, sends a message that something is wrong. Karen shakes slightly and sometimes covers her face with her hands before she speaks. At first, during my visit, Karen did not talk; then, suddenly, out of her smiling silence, came brief, crisp, clearly enunciated sentences.

Her staff person, a warm, pretty, young woman, arrived, and we discussed how they had found the 1858 house. She said that Karen had specific requirements. First, her apartment should be on the water (because, since early childhood, she had spent her summers on an island). Second, it needed to be near her family, but not in the same town. And finally, she did not want a roommate. Throughout this discussion, Karen would nod strong affirmation, occasionally saying "Yes" emphatically. As in the earlier incident at the door, Karen gave the impression of possessing a strong and definite personality that was hidden and handicapped by the deficits associated with autism.

Karen works at a do-it-yourself building-equipment store, putting price labels on tiles. Two days a week, she stuffs clams and packs them, at a seafood factory. She prefers the latter job. Karen goes to church on Sundays. We made a date for lunch after church, at the beginning of March. With compulsive coverings of her face with her hands, she saw me out of the apartment. She leaned over, offering her neck, in an awkwardly diffident manner, for me to kiss.

I left her with a mixture of sadness and hope. She had come so far, achieving a two-thirds independence. And yet, and yet. . . . With her talents, what might she have been? An artist? A biologist? A horticulturist? Karen may still use her ability as an artist or gardener. This depends on the general public's understanding of the process of autistic thought and employers' acceptance of the world as persons with autism see it.

Jimmy

Jimmy, described as "an emotionally disturbed child with conspicuous autistic symptoms," was referred to our preschool by the pediatric specialist. The doctor pointed out that, in spite of his hyperactivity and lack of language, Jimmy was very aware of his surroundings and of people, and should benefit from the educational experience.

During his first 2 months at school, Jimmy's behavior was that of a madman. Head down, eyes covered with one hand, he bit, scratched, and screamed in one panic-stricken tantrum after another. By Christmas, he had improved to the extent of taking walks with other children and following instructions, which he clearly understood, although he still did not talk. His poor eyesight, lack of speech, and awkward motor development remained disturbing problems. Because his behavior regressed during the second preschool year, he was sent to a residential school.

After 5 difficult years there, he returned to enter a public school special education program for children and adolescents with developmental problems. In this special program, he found a way to reach the world—through signing. His motivation and drive to learn showed up in the speed with which he mastered simple signing vocabulary. His delight was evident. It was as though his intelligence had been released from a prison of silence. However, his vision remained poor.

He developed some self-confidence during his 7 years in junior and senior high school. He became a great favorite with his teachers. His aggressive, hyperactive behavior diminished and finally stopped. His teachers described him as having intelligence impaired by lack of speech and such characteristics of autism as a compulsion to rock back and forth on his feet, and a repetitive, stereotyped activity—holding one hand clenched in a fist and constantly looking at it with his better eye. But their assessment also described him as ambitious and quick, with a drive to learn and achieve.

During his last school year as a high school senior, Jimmy was reevaluated by the school psychologist. At an actual age of 21 years, 6 months, his nonverbal cognitive ability was at the level of 7 years, 3 months. His receptive vocabulary was at the level of 2 years, 10 months. He was doing relatively well in his adaptive behavior, where his strengths were most prominent. For example, Jimmy could read simple direction signs, he had good table manners, and he interacted with his peers and participated in group activities. He was very successful in his prevocational program and had good fine-motor skills for assembly work. He was a dependable worker; he attended to instructions and persisted until his job was finished. His social behavior had improved; he displayed less inappropriate teasing and less rocking.

A year after graduation, Jimmy was in the supervised workshop of his local regional center. He lived at home. The plan was to find him work on a loading dock or as a trucker's helper. He was also on a waiting list to move into a group home, pending his family's decision. They were reluctant to let him leave home.

His family decided against the group home. Several years earlier, Jimmy's stepfather had died. His death was a tragedy for Jimmy, doubly so because of his inability to communicate and talk through his emotions. His mother and stepfather had planned to start a church; after her husband's death, his mother proceeded with the plans and, by 1994, had become the pastor. During my visit at that time, she told me that Jimmy had had some behavior (masturbation) problems on the bus. For a month, he had been limited in his hours of work, because he was taken to his job in individual transportation. She had explained to him that masturbation was inappropriate behavior in public, and was to be done only in his own bedroom. With improvement in this respect, Jimmy was able to resume on his old work schedule. At that time, in 1994, he was doing so well that he had been written up in the workshop's newspaper. His picture was headlined: "Worker of the Month!"

At home, Jimmy walked his dog, took care of his parakeets, cooked simple dishes, and looked at the newspaper. His mother was sure he could read simple words. He bought certain magazines at the shopping mall, clearly selecting them by name. I thought sadly of the time Jimmy had been tested by a speech specialist who had identified his primary deficit as communication and had recommended lessons in sign language. With his drive to succeed and his excellent eye–hand control, he could have become skilled in sign language. However, with two working parents, no one was available to transport him to lessons.

Recently, I went to see Jimmy and his mother for a short visit. Jimmy now stands 6 feet, 2 inches tall, is well built, and, as always, well dressed. He is a handsome young man. He began rocking back and forth and, with arms extended, flapping his hands. His mother told him to behave like a gentleman and shake hands. He shook hands with me and said, "Hi (and some sounds that I took for Mrs. Sperry"). He sat quietly through part of our conversation with surprising dignity, self-respect, and poise. At one time, he used a signing gesture (his speech was unintelligible). His mother responded in signing. I asked if they used signing, and I was encouraged to hear that his mother had a signing book and used it. As I looked at him, I thought about how far the terrified wild man of the preschool years had come.

Jimmy's mother has told me that Jimmy's workshop has been closed. He was sent to another area workshop, which was located in a large warehouse space. This change and the unstructured space bothered Jimmy. He became "silly" (his mother's word), and his supervisor could not handle him. He was transferred to an office of the Department of Mental Retardation, where he, along with a group of others "do puzzles and play games." His mother is concerned about the change. "He should be doing something constructive," she said.

We talked of her church. She said that the bishop of the church's world organization was Jimmy's guardian, with her power of attorney, and that he would look after Jimmy should anything happen to her.

Of all the updates, this one must end on a somewhat downward note. However, Jimmy has a very aware air and an appearance of being in touch. He also seems, in spite of the flapping gestures, to have a self-control that he once did not. So, in this sense, Jimmy also has made important gains.

Jimmy is back with his original case worker. He goes to a sheltered workshop five days a week, eight hours a day. So, this "to be continued" story does have a happier ending. He also is starting to attend a clinic for Adults with Pervasive Developmental Disorders (this includes adults with autism). Through this organization, he will have exposure socially with 10 or 12 of his peers and his mother will find help and comfort in the parent support group.

WHERE DOES THIS LEAVE US?: PARENTS, TEACHERS, AND CHILDREN

The original purpose of my study was to present case studies of children with varying autistic behaviors whom I had taught and followed to adulthood. One of these individuals, Larry, died in his sleep at age 23; the eight others varied in age from 30 to 36 at the time of this writing. These nine stories lead to some bittersweet conclusions. The nine children are fairly representative of the general population of autistic people—neither as severely impaired as the most disabled nor as brilliant in astonishing ways as some autistic savants.

If this chapter and the stories in it represented the status quo, the inferences to be drawn about the future of autistic adults would be mixed. In one sense, they would be encouraging: Intensive education and one-on-one care of the autistic child through to adulthood do ameliorate and adjust autistic behaviors. The inferences would be equally discouraging, for no matter what the improvement, the young autistic adult remains basically the same—handicapped by problems in relating to the world.

Fortunately, my follow-up does not present the status quo. Advances in medical research are continuing, and various new methods of treatment for autistic individuals are being developed. Although no cure has been found, the outlook is brighter than it has ever been. In fact, so many promising new treatments are available that some experts encourage families to explore any new therapy they think might have an effect. This optimism is shared by Ruth Sullivan, director of the Autism Services Center in Huntington, West Virginia, and mother of Joseph Sullivan, one of the models for the character of Raymond in the movie *Rain Man.* She has said, "Some very exciting things have been happening; we've never seen progress to this extent."[1] So, where do we stand now? In what way is the current situation better for teachers, for parents, and for autistic children now grown to adulthood?

Teachers

A great deal has been learned about autism and childhood developmental disorders since the 1960s. No longer is the teaching of developmentally disabled children nebulous or a matter of guesswork. The special education field has become better delineated, and its

---

[1] Emily Laber, "Symptoms, Treatments for Autism," *New Haven Advocate,* Jan. 20, 1992.

goals have been clarified. Teaching materials and techniques are constantly improving and expanding. Years of clinical and teaching experience and numerous longitudinal studies of autistic children have led to the acceptance of the concept of an underlying organic, though still enigmatic, etiology of autism.[2]

The variety and degree of the abnormalities of behavior and impairments of function found in autistic children are considerable. For instance, computerized axial tomography (CAT) scans done at Yale University found left-hemisphere deficiencies in the brains of some autistic children. Speaking about Kim, another model for Raymond in *Rain Man,* Daniel Christensen, medical director of the Western Institute of Neuropsychiatry at the University of Utah, said: "[Kim] has a photographic memory, but no way to minimize stimuli. Brain scans show an absence of the bundle of nerve fibers that connect the two halves of the brain."[3] The great variation observed in the syndromes of autism and atypical development underscore the importance of precision in diagnosis. Progress in the diagnosis and definition of autism and its related syndromes has been an important factor in the growth and implementation of theories on teaching autistic children. The specificity of diagnosis directly affects the choice of teaching techniques and materials available to the present-day teacher.

In the 1960s, teachers, however well educated, had to teach autistic children with intuition and often with handmade materials. The teachers at Ives used innovative paper cutouts of red, blue, green, and yellow squares, triangles, and circles; block pattern designs; and so on. None had used such materials before, and all had to learn how, when, and why to use these and other novel teaching tools. Teachers now have textbooks and workbooks especially geared for the developmentally disabled, as well as other teaching aids such as computers, cassettes, television, videocassette recorders, and copying machines. A generation of teachers has developed and refined teaching approaches such as behavior modification, signing, mainstreaming, prevocational and vocational training, special physical education, and special techniques for music, art, and recreation. Special educators have been joined by occupational therapists, physical therapists, speech and language specialists, music and dance therapists, and specialists in other disciplines. They all work together in addressing the difficult tasks of communicating with, enhancing the general learning potential of, and otherwise solving or alleviating developmental problems of autistic children. Even with transdisciplinary, multiple, coordinated teaching methods and improved teaching materials and strategies, teachers and their colleagues must still be able to individualize their materials and approaches to a particular child. Resourcefulness, flexibility, knowing a child well, and having the courage to modify and question existing methods remain crucial for the most effective education and therapy.

Teachers now have some idea of what to expect when dealing with the developmentally handicapped. Since passage of the Education of the Handicapped Act in 1970, instructors in child development at teachers' colleges have paid progressively more attention to the educational problems of the handicapped. There is now an educated stratum of sophisticated and well-trained professionals employed in or serving the programs available to the developmentally handicapped—from the directors of these programs, who are often themselves specialists; to social workers, who support the teachers through liaison with parents; and to psychologists, who perform and score developmental testing. In addition, physicians at child development and mental health clinics and in private practice are now able to identify specific developmental problems that were poorly understood a generation ago.

Many teachers today also have the advantage of a state-regulated, federally funded plan, developed in the 1980s, to educate handicapped infants in "Birth-to-Three" programs, as well as older preschool and school-age children in a continuing regimen. The thrust now is

[2] F.R. Volkmar, "Social Development," in D.J. Cohen and A.M. Donnellan, eds., *Handbook of Autism and Pervasive Developmental Disorders* (New York: John Wiley & Sons, 1987), hereinafter cited as Cohen and Donnellan, 41–60.

[3] Associated Press, "Real Rain Man Thrives with Film," *New Haven (Conn.) Register,* Feb. 19, 1989, A2.

for early intervention, and its intention is to give everyone—child, teacher, and parents—a head start. The earlier the intervention, the better are the chances to improve the autistic child's modification of his or her disabilities, to teach the child more effectively, and to help parents develop strategies of informed coping with autistic behaviors.

The college student who today contemplates teaching autistic children has a good chance of making a realistic decision. A variety of classes and programs for the developmentally handicapped can be observed in private schools—nursery school to high school—public school special education programs, state-sponsored service centers, and early intervention programs. From these observations, the aspiring future teacher can decide whether she or he has the capabilities and personality traits needed to be a successful teacher of autistic individuals.

All the progress made in the past 25 years has still not made this teaching an easy job. Anyone starting off on a career of teaching autistic or other developmentally handicapped children often feels lost, not knowing which way to turn, where to go, or what to do. Physical endurance, emotional stability, flexibility, ability and willingness to improvise, and respect for the value of one's own intuition are all needed to work with children who have developmental disabilities. This kind of teaching is not for everyone.

As noted throughout this volume, various methods of research, intervention, and treatment are becoming available. These methods will ultimately have an impact on teachers and teaching methods. Even now, they are raising questions and beginning to bring about change. The basic necessary approach to teaching, however, has not changed: Each child's strengths must be analyzed and used.

The Parents

The central purpose of this chapter has been to profile a group of autistic children and the problems they and their families have faced. After years of enduring bitter struggles, minor hopes, major disappointments, and a few victories, and of dealing with pressures that can lead to quarrels, disagreement, resentment, and sometimes divorce, families are facing only a

comparatively improved situation. These families long ago accepted the fact of their daughters' or sons' multiple impairments, but in their hearts, they hoped for a release from their children's disabilities. The young people themselves, now in their early to mid-30s, are for the most part only marginally independent, and all but Bill continue to rely on their parents and families in ways that unimpaired people do not.

Although none of the families had the good fortune to be supported by a coordinated treatment approach during the many years when it was needed, these families illustrate—effectively in some instances, less so in others—the practical, day-to-day progress and setbacks experienced in learning to cope with an autistic child.

The parents' stories illustrate the common problems, the limited answers, and the qualified future possibilities for all their children. Each of the families—wife, husband, and their nondisabled children—experienced the pain, embarrassment, and hopelessness of having an autistic child in the family. The following concerns emerge in all the accounts:

- The shock of realizing that an infant or toddler is different from other babies.
- The search for diagnosis and the realization that there is no treatment other than education and, in some cases, medication, and that there is no cure.
- The search for guidance on management of the child's behavior once the diagnosis is given.
- The necessity of locating a school appropriate for the child's needs.
- The day-to-day stress of living with puzzling, difficult, and often violent behavior.
- The social isolation caused by lack of understanding of a handicapped child; the inability or unwillingness to entertain at home, either because of family feelings or because the handicapped child cannot tolerate strangers; the inability of siblings to invite friends home.
- The certainty that the mother is trapped. As Karen's mother said, "The buck stops here."
- The search for competent baby-sitters and the need to train them to care for a developmentally disabled, perplexing child.

- The management of some vacation time, even a long weekend. One family (not in this group of nine) is taking their first vacation in 22 years, because their 22-year-old autistic son is now in a group home.
- The constant pressure to guard the interests of the child. Bureaucratic red tape must be honored to get financing, proper educational placement, and such necessities as medical insurance. Parents must read the fine print of all relevant state and federal requirements. As the child gets older, the rapidly changing field of prevocational and vocational training must be mastered.
- The difficulty of financing the staggering cost of clinics, doctors, therapists, medicine, and home care.
- The need for counseling for all the family, including siblings.
- The problem of making living arrangements for the over-21, developmentally disabled adult; the choice between group homes and more independent situations, or, for some, the need to keep the young adult at home.
- The difficulty of creating a social life for the child. How does one handle the isolation of a child who usually cannot play with his neighborhood peers, and who, when older, is left out of normal teenage social activities?
- The problems of dealing with a sexually maturing disabled adult.
- The ever-present worry about how to make sure that the semi-independent autistic adult is cared for appropriately after the parents can no longer do so. Guardianship? Stand-by guardianship? Proper estate planning and wills? What is the answer?

The dilemma of acceptance is acute. Most developmentally disabled children are deceptively normal in appearance and often handsome as infants and toddlers, as were all nine children in this group. The superficial normality can hinder parents' acceptance of their child as he or she truly is, and can affect their ability to handle pragmatic day-to-day living with autism or autistic behavior.

Everyone with a developmentally disabled child feels bitterness, disbelief, and bewilderment at first. The disabilities often are contradictory, and the autistic component is the most difficult to understand. It is normal to feel lost and not to know where to turn for a solution. Parents experience love mixed with hate, anger, black despair, and rebellion that they should be saddled with such a hopeless problem. And there is guilt: guilt as they wonder whether they might be responsible for the child's condition; guilt over the common conscious wish that the problem, or even the child, would disappear or die. Acceptance of the child and his or her handicap, no matter how agonizing, slow, and partial at first, sets a parent free to act as a fighter and advocate for the child.

The Children Grown Up

The stories presented here demonstrate that many autistic persons can accommodate their behavior sufficiently to become comparatively self-sufficient adults. Bill is completely independent. All autistic and other developmentally handicapped people have talents and abilities that, when encouraged, can help them grow from emotionally distant young children to adults who work in workshops or jobs in the community. As is apparent from the stories I have presented, autistic adults can fill a variety of jobs: They work as janitors and clerks (collating and filing), do simple assembly work, and work in fast-food or other restaurants as dishwashers (Tom) and simple food preparers. Polly has a responsible job in a small biomedical factory. Bill is working at a gift shop in a major resort. They can be aides in nursing homes, as John was (he is now at a Jewish Center) or gardeners in landscaping services, or baggers in grocery stores. Others work in more complicated jobs. Temple Grandin is one of the best-known examples (see Chapter 49). Author of many articles, and of the book *Emergence: Labeled Autistic*,[4] she is now an assistant professor of animal science at Colorado State University. One young male autistic adult who

---

[4] T. Grandin and M. Scariano, *Emergence: Labelled Autistic* (Novato, Calif.: Arena Press, 1986); (T. Grandin, *Needs of High Functioning Teenagers and Adults with Autism (Tips from a Recovered Autistic)* (Dept. of Animal Science, Colorado State University, Fort Collins, Col.) 805, 2–3.

graduated *cum laude* from an Ivy League college is now a computer programmer.

It is a measure of victory over their disability that many individuals with autism can earn salaries, work with normal coworkers, live away from home in groups, and have some social life in the community.

But although there has been improvement in services and a growing emphasis on helping autistic people live and work with normal peers, the ideal is not always the reality. Each of the young adults I have described has had serious difficulties along the way, even when the appropriate services were in place. Jimmy was excluded temporarily from his bus for unacceptable behavior (masturbation) and had to go by special car for 4-hour stints at his job, instead of the usual workday; his mother had nowhere else to turn for help. John came close to failing his tests in fast-food services and being dropped by the Department of Vocational Rehabilitation. Thanks to his mother's fighting an entire governmental bureaucracy for him, he was given a second chance. And so the stories go.

Even with the best services that can be offered generally, society must still deal with these people as individuals. Some manage well enough that they do not appear markedly different from others in their age group, even when some problems of social functioning and intimacy remain. Nevertheless, after all their schooling, autistic adults often read and do math on only a second- to fourth-grade level. And each one who can verbalize his or her feelings is conscious of being different, somehow not normal. John once said that he hated his explosions, his losing control, and wondered why it happened to him. Polly describes herself matter-of-factly as mentally retarded, but she cries about it, and cries when her retarded friends cry. Karen denies feeling different from other people, yet her actions betray her awareness. Her constant reassurances, repeated echolalically to herself when visiting me, that she "was not going home now," revealed her joy at being in a new environment.

None of the handicaps of these people will go away. Jimmy will probably never talk and will always have to express himself through sign language and confused attempts at words.

He also needs much help controlling his sexual drives. Eric hears sounds mostly as meaningless. Bill is working successfully but he will never be rid of his subtle anxiety about personal relationships. His mother recounts that he was made an assistant rather than head chef because he could not handle the pressure; eventually he left the culinary area completely. He is now in the big gift shop and was recently married. John is puzzled by his outbursts of crying, his tantrums, his intense anxiety in dealing with people. However, he is now working, preparing food, and serving in the cafeteria of a Jewish Center. This is considered a better job and he and his family are delighted. Tom is inarticulate and shy and suffers from an inability to contact or cope with people. Although he works with normal people in a restaurant, he must still be watched over by them. As noted in his case study, he is living independently in a condo, much improved through medication and the support and care of family and professionals.

All these people have high anxiety levels that may come partially from their perceptual disabilities, which apparently distort their picture of the environment and interfere with their ability to organize and understand their experiences. Karen's lack of depth perception and visual-motor control showed up in her clumsy attempts to use a push-button telephone. She got the wrong number twice before successfully calling her mother. David had to be walked step by step from his bus to the community house and back. He had to be trained to find his way and take note of landmarks between the bus stop and his job until he proved that he could do it by himself. David did work in a discount store, where he was supervised by a job coach. He now works at McDonalds, is paid a minimum wage, and still has a job coach. His father still drives him to work.

The hardest thing for these autistic adults to manage is *not* their lack of ability to be with or to talk with other people but the fact that they can do it only in a detached manner. Many genuinely cannot use speech for communicative purposes. One authority suggests that "autistic children do not fail to represent word meaning in memory"; that is, they know that the letters "d," "o," and "g" mean the same thing as a picture of a dog, but they "fail to use that meaning in the normal way in retrieval or organizational tasks."[5] Most of them find it impossible to understand the feelings of the people around them, so they often say or do things that are inappropriate. Their behavior can cause bewilderment and sometimes amusement or fear in other people; often, it leads to rejection. Like a pebble thrown into the water, creating ever-widening circles, the behavior of autistic people increases their oddness and isolation, and perhaps their loneliness as well.

I wish to offer a plea for understanding of autism. We have white canes, seeing-eye dogs, and Braille for those who are blind; we have adjusted jobs so that they may work in the community. People who are deaf have sign language, special captions on television programs, enhanced-hearing telephones, and hearing aids. They too find jobs that have been adjusted to their handicap. Most of the general public are handicapped by an inability to deal with ignorance about the condition of autism and autistic or autistic-like thinking and conversation. Isn't it time we made a determined effort to educate the public about autistic people so they are not ruled out of jobs because they don't fit perfectly? Shouldn't we try to better understand their thought processes and establish better communication, no longer considering them odd or calling them crazy? Instead, we can learn to welcome the strength of this hitherto unused human potential to our world.

Autistic and atypical disorders comprise a heterogeneous group rather than defining a unitary disease, and this characteristic makes generalizations about people with autism difficult, even hazardous. Their behavior as young children, especially their problems in establishing relationships and developing skill in social communication, as well as their problems of anxiety and cognitive confusion, have justified the terms *autism* or *autistic syndrome* to distinguish between their disabilities and other developmental disabilities and neuropsychiatric disorders. Variations in the severity of the symptoms have been documented repeatedly, as has the variation in findings that accompany the major syndrome: deafness, inborn errors of metabolism, blindness, identifiable brain damage, sensory processing problems, perceptual handicaps, Fragile X syndrome, and many others. Only continued efforts, through basic and clinical research, are likely to yield information that defines clearly the underlying, and probably multiple, causes of this spectrum of disorders.

Meanwhile, those who live and work with children like the adults represented here may find some comfort in the knowledge that appropriate services, rendered early and sustained over many years, can make a difference in the lives of autistic children and their parents.

Cross-References

Developmental aspects of autism are discussed in Chapters 12 through 14. Vocational issues are addressed in Chapter 28, and psychopharmacology is the topic of Chapter 32.

---

[5] R. Paul, "Communication," in Cohen & Donnellan, 66.

Author Index

Subject Index